New!
The Only One of Its Kind

THE A TO Z CROSSWORD PUZZLE SOLVER

The Perfect Companion to

THE NEW COMPREHENSIVE A TO Z CROSSWORD DICTIONARY

From Avon Books

THE A TO Z

CROSSWORD PUZZLE SOLVER

BRIAN PADOL

A Stonesong Press Book

AVON BOOKS NEW YORK

THE A-Z CROSSWORD PUZZLE SOLVER is an original publication of Avon Books. This work has never before appeared in book form.

AVON BOOKS
A division of
The Hearst Corporation
1350 Avenue of the Americas
New York, New York 10019

Copyright © 1995 by The Stonesong Press, Inc. and Brian Padol
"A Stonesong Press Book"
Published by arrangement with Stonesong Press
Library of Congress Catalog Card Number: 94-96554
ISBN: 0-380-77518-2

First Avon Books Printing: June 1995

AVON TRADEMARK REG. U.S. PAT. OFF. AND IN OTHER COUNTRIES, MARCA REGISTRADA, HECHO EN U.S.A.

Printed in the U.S.A.

RA 10 9 8 7 6 5 4 3 2 1

Contents

Introduction

You're doing a crossword puzzle, just as you do every day. You're almost finished with it except for three or four words, which have you really stumped. Those few remaining words have at least a couple of letters filled in, provided by the cross clues.

You can't find the answers you need in your usual reference books even when you know where to look—because clues in the puzzle are designed to obfuscate the locations of the answers. So a new type of resource book is needed, and you are holding it in your hand.

Now, let's say you seek a five-letter word with a *Y* in the second position and a *T* in the fourth position. The clue, as given, doesn't make much sense. Aha! Open this book to the five-letter section, two-four subsection, and find -Y-T-. You'll find the following list:

******

-Y-T-

******

CYSTI
CYSTO
CYSTS
HYETO
KYATS
KYOTO
LYTTA
NYCTI
NYCTO
RYOTS
WYATT
XYSTS

Using the puzzle clue, the process of elimination, and a little common sense, you'll be able to choose the correct fillers. If you want to clinch the answer, just turn to a dictionary. But the beauty of this book is that it adds another puzzle dimension and helps you along without spoon-feeding you the answer. It still allows you the pleasure of being a puzzle detective—the very thing that led you to pick up the crossword in the first place.

The major divisions of this book are word lengths: three-letter, four-letter, five-letter, and six-letter words. In the example above, you would turn to the five-letter section. Each section contains a list of words that are repeated several times, first according to a primary letter position within each word, and then by a secondary letter position. Each occurrence of the list is sorted alphabetically by the two positions of the already known letters.

3-LETTER	4-LETTER	5-LETTER	6-LETTER

Already known 1 and 2

AA-	AA--	AA---	AA----
AB-	AB--	AB---	AB----
AC-	AC--	AC---	AC----
•	•	•	•
•	•	•	•
BA-	BA--	BA---	BA----
BE-	BE--	BE---	BE----
•	•	•	•
•	•	•	•
ZA-	ZA--	ZA---	ZA----
ZE-	ZE--	ZE---	ZE----
•	•	•	•

Already known 1 and 3

| A-A | A-A- | A-A-- | A-A--- |
| • | • | • | • |

Already known 1 and 4

A--A   A--A-   A--A--

Already known 1 and 5

A---A   A---A-

Already known 1 and 6

A----A

Already known 2 and 3

-AA	-AA-	-AA--	-AA---
•	•	•	•
-ZA	-ZA-	-ZA--	-ZA---

For a complete example, here are the five-letter word divisions. The numbers stand in place of the letters that are known and the dashes indicate the unknowns.

12---	-23--	--34-	---45
1-3--	-2-4-	--3-5	
1--4-	-2--5		
1---5			

This book contains over 27,000 different words of three, four, five, and six letter lengths. There are three arrangements of the three-letter words, six of the four-letter, ten of the five-letter, and 15 of the six-letter words, for a total of over 302,000 words. To give you an idea of how this progression works, if we had decided to include seven-letter words, there would be 21 arrangements of that list: 1-2, 1-3, 1-4, 1-5, 1-6, 1-7, 2-3, 2-4, 2-5, 2-6, 2-7, 3-4, 3-5, 3-6, 3-7, 4-5, 4-6, 4-7, 5-6, 5-7, 6-7. All the seven-letter combinations would take as much room as this entire book.

Obviously, one reason for not having the sevens is the sheer size of the list. With the lists in this book, you should be able to complete just about any puzzle. You may never again need a dictionary to solve crosswords.

We've had a lot of fun putting these lists together and we've certainly learned a lot of new words and gotten reacquainted with some old friends. We culled the more than 27,000 different words from dozens of sources.

We hope that you have just as much fun using this book as we had in making it and that your loved ones will be able to have more quality time with you.

Keep on solvin'!

—BAP

AA-	AFL	AMO	ASH	******	******
	AFR	AMP	ASK	BA-	BI-
AAA	AFT	AMT	ASN	******	******
AAF	******	AMU	ASP	BAA	BIB
AAL	AG-	AMY	ASS	BAB	BIC
AAR	******	******	******	BAD	BID
******	AGA	AN-	AT-	BAE	BIG
AB-	AGE	******	******	BAF	BIN
******	AGO	ANA	ATC	BAG	BIO
ABA	******	ANC	ATE	BAH	BIS
ABC	AH-	AND	ATH	BAN	BIT
ABE	******	ANE	ATT	BAR	******
ABS	AHA	ANI	******	BAS	BL-
ABY	******	ANN	AU-	BAT	******
******	AI-	ANS	******	BAV	BLA
AC-	******	ANT	AUC	BAY	BLL
******	AID	ANU	AUE	******	BLS
ACC	AIL	ANY	AUG	BB-	******
ACE	AIM	******	AUK	******	BM-
ACT	AIN	AO-	AUS	BBA	******
ACU	AIR	******	AUT	BBC	BME
ACY	AIS	AOL	AUX	BBL	BMR
******	AIT	******	******	BBS	******
AD-	******	AP-	AV-	******	BN-
******	AK-	******	******	BC-	******
ADA	******	APA	AVA	******	BNA
ADC	AKA	APE	AVE	BCE	******
ADD	AKC	APH	AVI	BCG	BO-
ADE	******	APO	******	BCL	******
ADJ	AL-	APR	AW-	BCP	BOA
ADM	******	APT	******	BCS	BOB
ADO	ALA	******	AWE	******	BOG
ADS	ALB	AR-	AWL	BE-	BOH
ADV	ALE	******	AWN	******	BOL
ADZ	ALF	ARA	******	BEA	BON
******	ALG	ARC	AX-	BED	BOO
AE-	ALI	ARD	******	BEE	BOP
******	ALL	ARE	AXE	BEG	BOT
AEC	ALP	ARG	******	BEL	BOW
AEF	ALS	ARK	AY-	BEN	BOX
AER	ALT	ARM	******	BES	BOY
AES	******	ARN	AYE	BET	BOZ
AET	AM-	ARS	AYN	BEV	******
******	******	ART	AYR	BEY	BP-
AF-	AMA	ARV	AYS	******	******
******	AME	ARY	******	BF-	BPD
AFB	AMG	AS-	AZ-	******	BPE
AFG	AMI	******	******	BFA	BPH
		ASA	AZO		
		ASE			

******	CAR	CHG	CPO	DAL	DID
BR-	CAS	CHI	CPS	DAM	DIE
******	CAT	CHM	******	DAN	DIF
BRA	CAV	******	**CR-**	DAP	DIG
******	CAW	**CI-**	******	DAR	DIM
BS-	CAY	******	CRS	DAW	DIN
******	******	CIA	CRU	DAY	DIO
BSA	**CB-**	CIC	CRY	******	DIP
BSC	******	CID	******	**DB-**	DIR
BSM	CBC	CIE	**CS-**	******	DIS
BSS	CBD	CIF	******	DBA	DIV
******	CBI	CIO	CSA	DBE	DIX
BT-	CBS	CIR	CSC	DBL	******
******	******	CIS	CST	******	**DK-**
BTH	**CC-**	******	******	**DC-**	******
BTU	******	**CL-**	**CT-**	******	DKG
******	CCA	******	******	DCL	DKL
BU-	CCC	CLE	CTN	DCM	DKM
******	******	******	CTS	DCS	DKS
BUB	**CD-**	**CN-**	******	******	******
BUD	******	******	**CU-**	**DD-**	**DL-**
BUG	CDR	CNO	******	******	******
BUL	******	CNS	CUB	DDS	DLS
BUM	**CE-**	******	CUD	DDT	******
BUN	******	**CO-**	CUE	******	**DM-**
BUR	CEA	******	CUL	**DE-**	******
BUS	CEE	COB	CUM	******	DMD
BUT	CEL	COD	CUN	DEB	DME
BUY	CEN	COG	CUP	DEC	DMZ
******	CER	COL	CUR	DEE	******
BV-	CES	COM	CUT	DEG	**DN-**
******	CEY	CON	******	DEI	******
BVM	******	COO	**CW-**	DEK	DNA
******	**CF-**	COP	******	DEL	DNB
BY-	******	COR	CWO	DEM	******
******	CFI	COS	CWT	DEN	**DO-**
BYE	CFM	COT	******	DES	******
******	CFS	COW	**CY-**	DEV	DOD
CA-	******	COX	******	DEW	DOE
******	**CG-**	COY	CYD	DEY	DOG
CAB	******	COZ	CYT	******	DOL
CAD	CGH	******	******	**DF-**	DOM
CAE	CGM	**CP-**	**DA-**	******	DON
CAF	CGS	******	******	DFC	DOP
CAL	******	CPA	DAB	******	DOR
CAM	**CH-**	CPH	DAD	**DI-**	DOS
CAN	******	CPL	DAG	******	DOT
CAP	CHA	CPM	DAK	DIA	DOW
	CHE			DIB	DOZ

******	******	******	******	******	******
DP-	**EA-**	**EI-**	**ER-**	**EY-**	**FH-**
******	******	******	******	******	******
DPH	EAM	EIB	ERA	EYE	FHA
DPW	EAN	EIN	ERE	******	******
******	EAR	EIR	ERG	**FA-**	**FI-**
DR-	EAT	******	ERI	******	******
******	EAU	**EK-**	ERN	FAA	FIB
DRY	******	******	ERR	FAB	FIC
******	**EB-**	EKE	ERS	FAD	FID
DS-	******	EKG	ERV	FAG	FIE
******	EBB	******	ERY	FAM	FIG
DSC	EBN	**EL-**	******	FAN	FIN
DSM	EBS	******	**ES-**	FAO	FIR
DSO	******	ELA	******	FAR	FIT
DSP	**EC-**	ELB	ESC	FAS	FIX
DST	******	ELF	ESE	FAT	******
******	ECG	ELI	ESK	FAX	**FL-**
DT-	ECT	ELK	ESP	FAY	******
******	ECU	ELL	ESQ	******	FLA
DTH	******	ELM	ESS	**FB-**	FLO
******	**ED-**	ELS	EST	******	FLU
DU-	******	ELY	ESU	FBA	FLY
******	EDB	******	******	FBI	******
DUB	EDD	**EM-**	**ET-**	******	**FO-**
DUC	EDE	******	******	**FC-**	******
DUD	EDH	EMF	ETA	******	FOB
DUE	EDM	EMP	ETC	FCA	FOD
DUG	EDO	EMS	ETE	FCC	FOE
DUI	EDP	EMU	ETH	******	FOG
DUN	EDT	******	ETO	**FD-**	FOP
DUO	******	**EN-**	******	******	FOR
DUP	**EE-**	******	**EU-**	FDA	FOX
DUX	******	ENA	******	******	FOY
******	EEC	ENC	EUR	**FE-**	******
DV-	EEG	END	******	******	**FP-**
******	EEL	ENE	**EV-**	FEB	******
DVM	EEN	ENG	******	FED	FPA
******	EER	ENL	EVA	FEE	FPC
DW-	EES	ENS	EVE	FEM	FPM
******	******	ENT	******	FEN	FPO
DWT	**EF-**	ENV	**EW-**	FEU	FPS
******	******	******	******	FEW	******
DY-	EFF	**EO-**	EWE	FEY	**FR-**
******	EFT	******	******	FEZ	******
DYE	******	EON	**EX-**	******	FRA
DYN	**EG-**	EOS	******	**FF-**	FRB
DYS	******	******	EXE	******	FRI
	EGG	**EP-**	EXO	FFA	
	EGO	******	EXT	FFI	
		EPI		FFV	

FRO	GEL	******	******	HOD	******
FRS	GEM	**GR-**	**HE-**	HOE	**IB-**
FRY	GEN	******	******	HOG	******
******	GEO	GRO	HEA	HOI	IBA
FT-	GER	******	HEB	HOL	IBO
******	GET	**GS-**	HED	HON	IBT
FTC	******	******	HEL	HOP	******
******	**GH-**	GSA	HEM	HOR	**IC-**
FU-	******	GSC	HEN	HOT	******
******	GHQ	******	HEP	HOW	ICA
FUL	******	**GT-**	HER	HOY	ICC
FUN	**GI-**	******	HES	******	ICE
FUR	******	GTC	HEW	**HR-**	ICI
******	GIB	******	HEX	******	ICS
FW-	GID	**GU-**	HEY	HRH	ICW
******	GIE	******	******	HRS	ICY
FWA	GIG	GUI	**HG-**	******	******
******	GIL	GUM	******	**HS-**	**ID-**
GA-	GIN	GUN	HGT	******	******
******	GIP	GUP	******	HSH	IDA
GAB	GIS	GUS	**HH-**	HSM	IDE
GAD	******	GUT	******	******	IDO
GAE	**GM-**	GUY	HHD	**HT-**	IDS
GAG	******	******	******	******	******
GAI	GMC	**GY-**	**HI-**	HTS	**IF-**
GAL	GMT	******	******	******	******
GAM	******	GYM	HIC	**HU-**	IFC
GAO	**GN-**	GYN	HID	******	IFS
GAP	******	GYP	HIE	HUB	******
GAR	GNP	GYR	HIH	HUE	**IG-**
GAS	GNU	******	HIM	HUG	******
GAT	******	**HA-**	HIN	HUH	IGN
GAY	**GO-**	******	HIP	HUK	IGY
GAZ	******	HAD	HIS	HUM	******
******	GOA	HAE	HIT	HUN	**IH-**
GB-	GOB	HAG	******	HUT	******
******	GOD	HAH	**HJ-**	HUY	IHP
GBE	GOG	HAL	******	******	IHS
******	GON	HAM	HJS	**HY-**	******
GC-	GOO	HAN	******	******	**IK-**
******	GOP	HAP	**HM-**	HYL	******
GCA	GOT	HAS	******	HYP	IKE
GCB	GOV	HAT	HMS	******	******
GCD	GOY	HAW	******	**IA-**	**IL-**
GCT	******	HAY	**HO-**	******	******
******	**GP-**	******	******	IAL	ILA
GE-	******	**HB-**	HOB	IAN	ILE
******	GPM	******	HOC	IAS	ILI
GEB	GPO	HBM			
GEE	GPU				

ILK	ISR	JER	******	******	LES
ILL	IST	JET	**KE-**	**KW-**	LET
ILO	******	JEU	******	******	LEU
ILP	**IT-**	JEW	KEA	KWH	LEV
ILS	******	******	KEF	******	LEW
******	ITA	**JI-**	KEG	**LA-**	LEX
IM-	ITE	******	KEN	******	LEY
******	ITO	JIB	KER	LAB	******
IMP	ITS	JIG	KET	LAC	**LG-**
******	ITY	JIM	KEY	LAD	******
IN-	******	******	******	LAE	LGE
******	**IU-**	**JO-**	**KG-**	LAG	******
INA	******	******	******	LAM	**LH-**
INC	IUD	JOB	KGB	LAN	******
IND	IUM	JOE	******	LAO	LHA
INE	******	JOG	**KH-**	LAP	LHB
ING	**IV-**	JON	******	LAR	LHD
INK	******	JOS	KHL	LAS	******
INN	IVA	JOT	******	LAT	**LI-**
INS	IVE	JOY	**KI-**	LAW	******
INT	IVY	******	******	LAX	LIB
******	******	**JU-**	KIA	LAY	LID
IO-	**IW-**	******	KID	******	LIE
******	******	JUG	KIL	**LB-**	LIL
IOD	IWW	JUN	KIM	******	LIM
ION	******	JUS	KIN	LBS	LIN
IOU	**JA-**	JUT	KIP	******	LIP
IOW	******	******	KIT	**LC-**	LIQ
******	JAB	**JW-**	******	******	LIT
IP-	JAG	******	**KK-**	LCD	LIZ
******	JAM	JWV	******	LCM	******
IPA	JAN	******	KKK	LCT	**LL-**
******	JAP	**KA-**	KKT	******	******
IR-	JAR	******	******	**LD-**	LLB
******	JAS	KAB	**KO-**	******	LLD
IRA	JAT	KAI	******	LDS	LLM
IRE	JAW	KAL	KOA	******	******
IRK	JAY	KAN	KOP	**LE-**	**LM-**
IRO	******	KAS	KOR	******	******
IRS	**JC-**	KAW	KOS	LEA	LMT
******	******	KAY	******	LED	******
IS-	JCD	******	**KR-**	LEE	**LO-**
******	JCS	**KB-**	******	LEG	******
ISA	JCT	******	KRA	LEI	LOA
ISE	******	KBP	KRP	LEK	LOB
ISH	**JE-**	******	******	LEM	LOC
ISM	******	**KC-**	**KV-**	LEN	LOF
ISO	JEE	******	******	LEO	LOG
	JEM	KCB	KVA		

LON	MAO	******	******	NAG	NIN
LOO	MAP	**MH-**	**MP-**	NAM	NIO
LOP	MAR	******	******	NAN	NIP
LOQ	MAS	MHG	MPD	NAP	NIS
LOT	MAT	MHO	MPE	NAT	NIT
LOU	MAU	******	MPH	NAV	NIX
LOW	MAW	**MI-**	******	NAY	******
LOX	MAX	******	**MR-**	******	**NN-**
******	MAY	MIA	******	**NB-**	******
LP-	******	MIB	MRS	******	NNE
******	**MB-**	MID	******	NBC	NNW
LPS	******	MIG	**MS-**	NBE	******
******	MBA	MIL	******	NBS	**NO-**
LS-	MBW	MIR	MSC	******	******
******	******	MIS	MSL	**NC-**	NOB
LSD	**MC-**	MIX	MSS	******	NOD
LSS	******	******	MST	NCO	NOG
LST	MCH	**MK-**	******	******	NOM
******	MCL	******	**MT-**	**ND-**	NON
LT-	******	MKS	******	******	NOR
******	**MD-**	MKT	MTS	NDP	NOS
LTD	******	******	******	******	NOT
LTH	MDS	**ML-**	**MU-**	**NE-**	NOV
******	******	******	******	******	NOW
LU-	**ME-**	MLA	MUC	NEA	NOX
******	******	MLG	MUD	NEB	******
LUG	MED	MLS	MUG	NED	**NP-**
LUM	MEG	******	MUM	NEE	******
LUT	MEL	**MM-**	MUR	NEF	NPT
LUX	MEM	******	MUS	NEN	******
******	MEN	MME	MUT	NEO	**NR-**
LY-	MER	******	******	NEP	******
******	MES	**MO-**	**MV-**	NER	NRA
LYE	MET	******	******	NET	******
LYO	MEV	MOA	MVD	NEV	**NS-**
LYS	MEW	MOB	MVP	NEW	******
******	MEX	MOD	******	NEY	NSA
MA-	******	MOE	**MY-**	NEZ	NSC
******	**MF-**	MOI	******	******	NSF
MAA	******	MOM	MYC	**NG-**	NSW
MAB	MFD	MON	MYO	******	******
MAC	MFG	MOO	MYX	NGK	**NT-**
MAD	******	MOP	******	******	******
MAE	**MG-**	MOS	**NA-**	**NH-**	NTH
MAG	******	MOT	******	******	******
MAI	MGM	MOW	NAA	NHL	**NU-**
MAL	MGR		NAB	******	******
MAN			NAE	**NI-**	NUB
				******	NUL
				NIB	
				NIL	

NUN	******	******	******	PEE	******
NUS	**OF-**	**OR-**	**OX-**	PEG	**PM-**
NUT	******	******	******	PEI	******
******	OFF	ORA	OXA	PEN	PMG
NW-	OFT	ORB	OXY	PEP	PMS
******	******	ORC	******	PER	******
NWT	**OH-**	ORE	**OY-**	PES	**PO-**
******	******	ORO	******	PET	
NY-	OHM	ORS	OYL	PEW	POD
******	OHO	ORT	******	******	POE
NYC	OHS	ORY	**OZ-**	**PF-**	POH
NYE	******	******	******	******	POI
NYX	**OI-**	**OS-**	OZS	PFC	POL
******	******	******	******	PFG	POP
OA-	OID	OSA	**PA-**	******	POT
******	OIL	OSB	******	**PG-**	POW
OAF	OIT	OSD	PAC	******	POX
OAK	******	OSE	PAD	PGA	******
OAR	**OK-**	OSF	PAH	******	**PP-**
OAS	******	OSP	PAI	**PH-**	******
OAT	OKA	OSS	PAL	******	PPC
******	OKS	******	PAM	PHA	PPD
OB-	******	**OT-**	PAN	PHB	PPI
******	**OL-**	******	PAP	PHC	PPM
OBB	******	OTC	PAR	PHD	PPS
OBI	OLA	OTO	PAS	PHI	******
OBS	OLD	OTT	PAT	PHS	**PR-**
******	OLE	******	PAW	******	******
OC-	******	**OU-**	PAX	**PI-**	PRE
******	**OM-**	******	PAY	******	PRO
OCA	******	OUI	PAZ	PIA	PRS
OCK	OMA	OUR	******	PIE	PRY
OCS	OME	OUS	**PB-**	PIG	******
OCT	OMO	OUT	******	PIN	**PS-**
******	******	******	PBX	PIP	******
OD-	**ON-**	**OV-**	******	PIS	PSF
******	******	******	**PC-**	PIT	PSI
ODA	ONE	OVA	******	PIU	PSS
ODD	ONI	OVI	PCT	PIX	PST
ODE	ONS	OVO	******	******	******
ODS	ONT	******	**PD-**	**PK-**	**PT-**
******	******	**OW-**	******	******	******
OE-	**OP-**	******	PDB	PKG	PTA
******	******	OWE	PDD	PKU	PTO
OED	OPA	OWI	PDQ	******	******
OER	OPE	OWL	******	**PL-**	**PU-**
OES	OPS	OWN	**PE-**	******	******
	OPT		******	PLY	PUB
	OPY		PEA		PUD
			PED		

PUG	******	REL	ROM	******	SIL
PUN	**QR-**	REM	ROO	**SC-**	SIM
PUP	******	REN	ROT	******	SIN
PUS	QRP	REP	ROW	SCB	SIP
PUT	******	REQ	ROY	SCD	SIR
******	**QT-**	RES	******	SCI	SIS
PV-	******	RET	**RP-**	******	SIT
******	QTO	REU	RPD	**SD-**	SIX
PVT	******	REV	RPM	******	******
******	**QU-**	REX	RPS	SDR	**SK-**
PW-	******	******	******	SDS	******
******	QUA	**RF-**	**RS-**	******	SKI
PWT	******	******	******	**SE-**	SKR
******	**RA-**	RFC	RSA	******	SKT
PX-	******	RFD	RSV	SEA	SKY
******	RAD	******	******	SEB	******
PXT	RAE	**RH-**	**RU-**	SEC	**SL-**
******	RAF	******	RUB	SEE	******
PY-	RAG	RHO	RUE	SEL	SLO
******	RAH	******	RUG	SEN	SLY
PYE	RAI	**RI-**	RUM	SEP	******
PYM	RAJ	******	RUN	SEQ	**SM-**
PYO	RAM	RIA	RUT	SER	******
PYR	RAN	RIB	******	SET	SMC
PYX	RAP	RID	**RY-**	SEW	******
******	RAS	RIG	******	SEX	**SN-**
QB-	RAT	RIM	RYE	******	******
******	RAW	RIO	******	**SF-**	SNA
QBP	RAY	RIP	**SA-**	******	******
******	******	RIT	******	SFC	**SO-**
QE-	**RB-**	******	SAC	******	******
******	******	**RM-**	SAD	**SG-**	SOB
QED	RBI	******	SAE	******	SOC
******	******	RMS	SAG	SGD	SOD
QK-	**RC-**	******	SAL	SGT	SOL
******	******	**RN-**	SAM	******	SOM
QKT	RCN	******	SAN	**SH-**	SON
******	RCT	RNA	SAP	******	SOP
QM-	******	RNR	SAR	SHA	SOS
******	**RE-**	******	SAT	SHE	SOT
QMC	******	**RO-**	SAW	SHF	SOU
QMG	REA	******	SAX	SHY	SOW
******	REB	ROB	SAY	******	SOX
QP-	REC	ROC	******	**SI-**	SOY
******	RED	ROD	**SB-**	******	******
QPL	REE	ROE	******	SIB	**SP-**
******	REF	ROI	SBE	SIC	******
QQ-	REG	ROK	SBW	SID	SPA
QQV					SPP
					SPY

******	-******	THE	******	******	USP
SQ-	**SY-**	THI	**TU-**	**UK-**	USS
******	******	THO	******	******	USU
SQQ	SYL	THY	TUB	UKE	USW
******	SYM	******	TUG	UKR	******
SR-	SYN	**TI-**	TUN	******	**UT-**
******	SYR	******	TUP	**UL-**	******
SRA	SYS	TIA	TUT	******	UTA
SRI	******	TIC	******	ULE	UTE
SRO	**TA-**	TIE	**TV-**	ULM	UTS
******	******	TIL	******	ULT	UTU
SS-	TAA	TIM	TVA	******	******
******	TAB	TIN	TVS	**UM-**	**UV-**
SSE	TAD	TIO	******	******	******
SSM	TAG	TIP	**TW-**	UMA	UVA
SSR	TAJ	TIS	******	UMO	******
SSS	TAM	TIT	TWA	UMP	**VA-**
SST	TAN	******	TWI	UMT	******
SSW	TAO	**TK-**	TWO	UMW	VAC
******	TAP	******	TWP	******	VAI
ST-	TAR	TKO	TWY	**UN-**	VAL
******	TAT	******	******	******	VAN
STA	TAU	**TN-**	**TY-**	UNA	VAS
STB	TAV	******	******	UNE	VAT
STD	TAW	TNT	TYP	UNI	VAV
STE	TAX	******	******	UNO	******
STG	TAY	**TO-**	**UA-**	******	**VE-**
STR	******	******	******	**UP-**	******
STU	**TB-**	TOC	UAR	******	VEE
STY	******	TOD	UAW	UPI	VET
******	TBS	TOE	******	UPS	VEX
SU-	******	TOG	**UC-**	UPU	******
******	**TE-**	TOI	******	******	**VF-**
SUA	******	TOM	UCA	**UR-**	******
SUB	TEA	TON	******	******	VFW
SUD	TEC	TOO	**UD-**	URD	******
SUE	TED	TOP	******	URE	**VH-**
SUG	TEE	TOR	UDO	URI	******
SUI	TEG	TOT	******	URN	VHF
SUM	TEL	TOW	**UF-**	URO	******
SUN	TEN	TOY	******	******	**VI-**
SUP	TER	******	UFA	**US-**	******
SUR	TET	**TR-**	UFO	******	VIA
SUS	TEX	******	******	USA	VIC
******	******	TRA	**UG-**	USE	VIE
SW-	**TH-**	TRI	******	USK	VIL
******	******	TRY	UGH	USN	VIM
SWA	THB	******	******	USO	VIN
SWE	THD	**TS-**	**UH-**		
		******	******		
		TSE	UHF		

VIP	******	******	YEP	******	ARC
VIS	**WE-**	**WS-**	YER	**ZO-**	ATC
VIV	******	******	YES	******	AUC
VIZ	WEB	WSW	YET	ZOA	******
******	WED	******	YEW	ZOE	**A-D**
VL-	WEE	**WV-**	******	ZOO	******
******	WEN	******	**YI-**	******	ADD
VLF	WES	WVA	******	**ZS-**	AID
******	WET	******	YIN	******	AND
VM-	WEY	**WY-**	YIP	ZSA	ARD
******	******	******	******	******	******
VMD	**WH-**	WYE	**YO-**	**ZU-**	**A-E**
******	******	WYO	******	******	******
VO-	WHO		YOD	ZUG	ABE
******	WHR	**XE-**	YOM	******	ACE
VOL	WHY	******	YON	**ZY-**	ADE
VON	******	XEN	YOU	******	AGE
VOR	**WI-**	XER	YOW	ZYG	ALE
VOW	******	******	******	******	AME
VOX	WIG	**XI-**	**YR-**	**A-A**	ANE
******	WIN	******	******	******	APE
VU-	WIS	XIS	YRS	AAA	ARE
******	WIT	******	******	ABA	ASE
VUG	WIZ	**XT-**	**YU-**	ADA	ATE
VUL	******	******	******	AGA	AUE
******	**WM-**	XTY	YUC	AHA	AVE
VY-	******	******	YUK	AKA	AWE
******	WMK	**XY-**	YUL	ALA	AXE
VYE	******	******	******	AMA	AYE
******	**WN-**	XYL	**ZA-**	ANA	******
WA-	******	******	******	APA	**A-F**
******	WNW	**YA-**	ZAG	ARA	******
WAC	******	******	ZAK	ASA	AAF
WAD	**WO-**	YAH	ZAP	AVA	AEF
WAF	******	YAK	ZAX	******	ALF
WAG	WOE	YAM	******	**A-B**	******
WAN	WON	YAO	**ZE-**	******	**A-G**
WAP	WOO	YAP	******	AFB	******
WAR	WOT	YAW	ZEA	ALB	AFG
WAS	WOW	YAY	ZED	******	ALG
WAT	******	******	ZEE	**A-C**	AMG
WAX	**WP-**	**YD-**	ZEL	******	ARG
WAY	******	******	ZEN	ABC	AUG
******	WPA	YDS	ZER	ACC	******
WB-	******	******	******	ADC	**A-H**
******	**WR-**	**YE-**	**ZI-**	AEC	******
WBN	******	******	ZIG	AKC	APH
WBS	WRY	YEA	ZIO	ANC	ASH
		YEN	ZIP		ATH

******	******	******	BID	******	******
A-I	**A-P**	**A-V**	BPD	**B-N**	**B-V**
******	******	******	BUD	******	******
ALI	ALP	ADV	******	BAN	BAV
AMI	AMP	ARV	**B-E**	BEN	BEV
ANI	ASP	******	******	BIN	******
AVI	******	**A-X**	BAE	BON	**B-W**
******	**A-R**	******	BCE	BUN	******
A-J	******	AUX	BEE	******	BOW
******	AAR	******	BME	**B-O**	******
ADJ	AER	**A-Y**	BPE	******	**B-X**
******	AFR	******	BYE	BIO	******
A-K	AIR	ABY	******	BOO	BOX
******	APR	ACY	**B-F**	******	******
ARK	AYR	AMY	******	**B-P**	**B-Y**
ASK	******	ANY	BAF	******	******
AUK	**A-S**	ARY	******	BCP	BAY
******	******	******	**B-G**	BOP	BEY
A-L	ABS	**A-Z**	******	******	BOY
******	ADS	******	BAG	**B-R**	BUY
AAL	AES	ADZ	BCG	******	******
AFL	AIS	******	BEG	BAR	**B-Z**
AIL	ALS	**B-A**	BIG	BMR	******
ALL	ANS	******	BOG	BUR	BOZ
AOL	ARS	BAA	BUG	******	******
AWL	ASS	BBA	******	**B-S**	**C-A**
******	AUS	BEA	******	******	******
A-M	AYS	BFA	**B-H**	BAS	CCA
******	******	BLA	******	BBS	CEA
ADM	**A-T**	BNA	BAH	BCS	CHA
AIM	******	BOA	BOH	BES	CIA
ARM	ACT	BRA	BPH	BIS	CPA
******	AET	BSA	BTH	BLS	CSA
A-N	AFT	******	******	BSS	******
******	AIT	**B-B**	**B-L**	BUS	**C-B**
AIN	ALT	******	******	******	******
ANN	AMT	BAB	BBL	**B-T**	CAB
ARN	ANT	BIB	BCL	******	COB
ASN	APT	BOB	BEL	BAT	CUB
AWN	ART	BUB	BLL	BET	******
AYN	ATT	******	BOL	BIT	**C-C**
******	AUT	**B-C**	BUL	BOT	******
A-O	******	******	******	BUT	CBC
******	**A-U**	BBC	**B-M**	******	CCC
ADO	******	BIC	******	**B-U**	CIC
AGO	ACU	BSC	BSM	******	CSC
AMO	AMU	******	BUM	BTU	******
APO	ANU	**B-D**	BVM		**C-D**
AZO		******			******
		BAD			CAD
		BED			CBD

CID
COD
CUD
CYD
******

C-E
******
CAE
CEE
CHE
CIE
CLE
CUE
******

C-F
******
CAF
CIF
******

C-G
******
CHG
COG
******

C-H
******
CGH
CPH
******

C-I
******
CBI
CFI
CHI
******

C-L
******
CAL
CEL
COL
CPL
CUL
******

C-M
******
CAM
CFM
CGM

CHM
COM
CPM
CUM
******

C-N
******
CAN
CEN
CON
CTN
CUN
******

C-O
******
CIO
CNO
COO
CPO
CWO
******

C-P
******
CAP
COP
CUP
******

C-R
******
CAR
CDR
CER
CIR
COR
CUR
******

C-S
******
CAS
CBS
CES
CFS
CGS
CIS
******
COS
CPS
CRS
CTS

******

C-T
******
CAT
COT
CST
CUT
CWT
CYT
******

C-U
******
CRU
******

C-V
******
CAV
******

C-W
******
CAW
COW
******

C-X
******
COX
******

C-Y
******
CAY
CEY
COY
CRY
******

C-Z
******
COZ
******

D-A
******
DBA
DIA
DNA
******

D-B
******
DAB
DEB

DIB
DNB
DUB
******

D-C
******
DEC
DFC
DSC
DUC
******

D-D
******
DAD
DID
DMD
DOD
DUD
******

D-E
******
DBE
DEE
DIE
DME
DOE
DUE
DYE
******

D-F
******
DIF
******

D-G
******
DAG
DEG
DIG
DKG
DOG
DUG
******

D-H
******
DPH
DTH
******

D-I
******
DEI
DUI

******

D-K
******
DAK
DEK
******

D-L
******
DAL
DBL
DCL
DEL
DKL
DOL
******

D-M
******
DAM
DCM
DEM
DIM
DKM
DOM
DSM
DVM
******

D-N
******
DAN
DEN
DIN
DON
DUN
DYN
******

D-O
******
DIO
DSO
DUO
******

D-P
******
DAP
DIP
DOP
DUP
DSP

******

D-R
******
DAR
DIR
DOR
******

D-S
******
DCS
DDS
DES
DIS
DKS
DLS
DOS
DYS
******

D-T
******
DDT
DOT
DST
DWT
******

D-V
******
DEV
DIV
******

D-W
******
DAW
DEW
DOW
DPW
******

D-X
******
DIX
DUX
******

D-Y
******
DAY
DEY
DRY

******	GPM	GET	HOE	******	******
G-B	GUM	GMT	HUE	**H-P**	**I-A**
******	GYM	GOT	******	******	******
GAB	******	GUT	**H-G**	HAP	IBA
GCB	**G-N**	******	******	HEP	ICA
GEB	******	**G-U**	HAG	HIP	IDA
GIB	GEN	******	HOG	HOP	ILA
GOB	GIN	GNU	HUG	HYP	INA
******	GON	GPU	******	******	IPA
G-C	GUN	******	**H-H**	**H-R**	IRA
******	GYN	**G-V**	******	******	ISA
GMC	******	******	HAH	HER	ITA
GSC	**G-O**	GOV	HIH	HOR	IVA
GTC	******	******	HRH	******	******
******	GAO	**G-Y**	HSH	**H-S**	**I-C**
G-D	GEO	******	HUH	******	******
******	GOO	GAY	******	HAS	ICC
GAD	GPO	GOY	**H-I**	HES	IFC
GCD	GRO	GUY	******	HIS	INC
GID	******	******	HOI	HJS	******
GOD	**G-P**	**G-Z**	******	HMS	**I-D**
******	******	******	**H-K**	HRS	******
G-E	GAP	GAZ	******	HTS	IND
******	GIP	******	HUK	******	IOD
GAE	GOP	**H-A**	******	**H-T**	IUD
GBE	GNP	******	**H-L**	******	******
GEE	GUP	HEA	******	HAT	**I-E**
GIE	GYP	******	HAL	HGT	******
******	******	**H-B**	HEL	HIT	ICE
G-G	**G-Q**	******	HOL	HOT	IDE
******	******	HEB	HYL	HUT	IKE
GAG	GHQ	HOB	******	******	ILE
GIG	******	HUB	**H-M**	**H-W**	INE
GOG	**G-R**	******	******	******	IRE
******	******	**H-C**	HAM	HAW	ISE
G-I	GAR	******	HBM	HEW	ITE
******	GER	HIC	HEM	HOW	******
GAI	GYR	HOC	HIM	******	**I-G**
GUI	******	******	HSM	**H-X**	******
******	**G-S**	**H-D**	HUM	******	ING
G-L	******	******	******	HEX	******
******	GAS	HAD	**H-N**	******	**I-H**
GAL	GIS	HED	******	**H-Y**	******
GEL	GUS	HHD	HAN	******	ISH
GIL	******	HID	HEN	HAY	******
******	**G-T**	HOD	HIN	HEY	**I-I**
G-M	******	******	HON	HOY	******
******	GAT	**H-E**	HUN	HUY	ICI
GAM	GCT	******			ILI
GEM		HAE			
		HIE			

```
******        IFS          JOG          ******        ******        ******
I-K           IHS          JUG          J-Y           K-M           L-B
******        ILS          ******        JAY           KIM           ******
ILK           INS          J-M          JOY           ******        LAB
INK           IRS          ******        ******        K-N           LHB
IRK           ITS          JAM          K-A           KAN           LIB
******        ******        JEM          ******        KEN           LLB
I-L           I-T          JIM          KEA           KIN           LOB
******        ******        ******        KIA           ******        ******
IAL           IBT          J-N          KOA           K-P           L-C
ILL           INT          ******        KRA           ******        ******
******        IST          JAN          KVA           KBP           LAC
I-M           ******        JON          ******        KIP           LOC
******        I-U          JUN          K-B           KOP           ******
ISM           ******        ******        ******        KRP           L-D
IUM           IOU          J-P          KAB           ******        ******
******        ******        ******        KCB           K-R           LAD
I-N           I-W          JAP          KGB           ******        LCD
******        ******        ******        ******        KER           LED
IAN           ICW          J-R          K-D           KOR           LHD
IGN           IOW          ******        ******        ******        LID
INN           IWW          JAR          KID           K-S           LLD
ION           ******        JER          ******        ******        LSD
******        I-Y          ******        K-F           KAS           LTD
I-O           ******        J-S          ******        KOS           ******
******        ICY          ******        KEF           ******        L-E
IBO           IGY          JAS          ******        K-T           ******
IDO           ITY          JCS          K-G           ******        LAE
ILO           IVY          JOS          ******        KET           LEE
IRO           ******        JUS          KEG           KIT           LGE
ISO           J-B          ******        ******        KKT           LIE
ITO           ******        J-T          K-H           ******        LYE
******        JAB          JAT          ******        K-W           ******
I-P           JIB          JCT          KWH           ******        L-F
******        JOB          JET          ******        KAW           ******
IHP           ******        JOT          K-I           ******        LOF
ILP           J-D          JUT          ******        K-Y           ******
IMP           ******        ******        KAI           ******        L-G
******        JCD          J-U          ******        KAY           ******
I-R           ******        ******        K-K          KEY           LAG
******        J-E          JEU          ******        ******        LEG
ISR           ******        ******        KKK           L-A           LOG
******        JEE          J-V          ******        ******        LUG
I-S           JOE          ******        K-L           LEA           ******
******        ******        JWV          ******        LHA           L-H
IAS           J-G          ******        KAL           LOA           ******
ICS           ******        J-W          KHL           ******        LTH
IDS           JAG          ******        KIL           ******        ******
              JIG          JAW                                       L-I
                           JEW                                       ******
                                                                     LEI
```

******	LDS	******	******	MGR	******
L-K	LES	**M-A**	**M-H**	MIR	**M-Y**
******	LPS	******	******	MUR	******
LEK	LSS	MAA	MCH	******	MAY
******	LYS	MBA	MPH	**M-S**	******
L-L	******	MIA	******	******	**N-A**
******	**L-T**	MLA	**M-I**	MAS	******
LIL	******	MOA	******	MDS	NAA
******	LAT	******	MAI	MES	NEA
L-M	LCT	**M-B**	MOI	MIS	NRA
******	LET	******	******	MKS	NSA
LAM	LIT	MAB	**M-L**	MLS	******
LCM	LMT	MIB	******	MOS	**N-B**
LEM	LOT	MOB	MAL	MRS	******
LIM	LST	******	MCL	MSS	NAB
LLM	LUT	**M-C**	MEL	MTS	NEB
LUM	******	******	MIL	MUS	NIB
******	**L-U**	MAC	MSL	******	NOB
L-N	******	MSC	******	**M-T**	NUB
******	LEU	MUC	**M-M**	******	******
LAN	LOU	MYC	******	MAT	**N-C**
LEN	******	******	MEM	MET	******
LIN	**L-V**	**M-D**	MGM	MKT	NBC
LON	******	******	MOM	MOT	NSC
******	LEV	MAD	MUM	MST	NYC
L-O	******	MED	******	MUT	******
******	**L-W**	MFD	**M-N**	******	**N-D**
LAO	******	MID	******	**M-U**	******
LEO	LAW	MOD	MAN	******	NED
LOO	LEW	MPD	MEN	MAU	NOD
LYO	LOW	MUD	MON	******	******
******	******	MVD	******	**M-V**	**N-E**
L-P	**L-X**	******	**M-O**	******	******
******	******	**M-E**	******	MEV	NAE
LAP	LAX	******	MAO	******	NBE
LIP	LEX	MAE	MHO	**M-W**	NEE
LOP	LOX	MME	MOO	******	NNE
******	LUX	MOE	MYO	MAW	NYE
L-Q	******	MPE	******	MBW	******
******	**L-Y**	******	**M-P**	MEW	**N-F**
LIQ	******	**M-G**	******	MOW	******
LOQ	LAY	******	MAP	******	NEF
******	LEY	MAG	MOP	**M-X**	NSF
L-R	******	MEG	MVP	******	******
******	**L-Z**	MFG	******	MAX	**N-G**
LAR	******	MHG	**M-R**	MEX	******
******	LIZ	MIG	******	MIX	NAG
L-S		MLG	MAR	MYX	NOG
******		MUG	MER		
LAS					
LBS					

******	NOS	OPA	******	OPS	PED
N-H	NUS	ORA	**O-K**	ORS	PHD
******	******	OSA	******	OSS	POD
NTH	**N-T**	OVA	OAK	OUS	PPD
******	******	OXA	OCK	OZS	PUD
N-K	NAT	******	******	******	******
******	NET	**O-B**	**O-L**	**O-T**	**P-E**
NGK	NIT	******	******	******	******
******	NOT	OBB	OIL	OAT	PEE
N-L	NPT	ORB	OWL	OCT	PIE
******	NUT	OSB	OYL	OFT	POE
NHL	NWT	******	******	OIT	PRE
NIL	******	**O-C**	**O-M**	ONT	PYE
NUL	**N-V**	******	******	OPT	******
******	******	ORC	OHM	ORT	**P-F**
N-M	NAV	OTC	******	OTT	******
******	NEV	******	**O-N**	OUT	PSF
NAM	NOV	**O-D**	******	******	******
NOM	******	******	OWN	**O-Y**	**P-G**
******	**N-W**	ODD	******	******	******
N-N	******	OED	**O-O**	OPY	PEG
******	NEW	OID	******	ORY	PFG
NAN	NNW	OLD	OHO	OXY	PIG
NEN	NOW	OSD	OMO	******	PKG
NIN	NSW	******	ORO	**P-A**	PMG
NON	******	**O-E**	OTO	******	PUG
NUN	**N-X**	******	OVO	PEA	******
******	******	ODE	******	PGA	**P-H**
N-O	NIX	OLE	**O-P**	PHA	******
******	NOX	OME	******	PIA	PAH
NCO	NYX	ONE	OSP	PTA	POH
NEO	******	OPE	******	******	******
NIO	**N-Y**	ORE	**O-R**	**P-B**	**P-I**
******	******	OSE	******	******	******
N-P	NAY	OWE	OAR	PDB	PAI
******	NEY	******	OER	PHB	PEI
NAP	******	**O-F**	OUR	PUB	PHI
NDP	**N-Z**	******	******	******	POI
NEP	******	OAF	**O-S**	**P-C**	PPI
NIP	NEZ	OFF	******	******	PSI
******	******	OSF	OAS	PAC	******
N-R	**O-A**	******	OBS	PFC	**P-L**
******	******	**O-I**	OCS	PHC	******
NER	OCA	******	ODS	PPC	PAL
NOR	ODA	OBI	OES	******	POL
******	OKA	ONI	OHS	**P-D**	******
N-S	OLA	OUI	OKS	******	**P-M**
******	OMA	OVI	ONS	PAD	******
NBS		OWI		PDD	PAM
NIS					PPM
					PYM

P-N	PET	******	RFD	RIM	******
******	PIT	**Q-G**	RID	ROM	**R-V**
PAN	POT	******	ROD	RPM	******
PEN	PST	QMG	RPD	RUM	REV
PIN	PUT	******	******	******	RSV
PUN	PVT	**Q-L**	**R-E**	**R-N**	******
******	PWT	******	******	******	**R-W**
P-O	PXT	QPL	RAE	RAN	******
******	******	******	REE	RCN	RAW
PRO	**P-U**	**Q-O**	ROE	REN	ROW
PTO	******	******	RUE	RUN	******
PYO	PIU	QTO	RYE	******	**R-X**
******	PKU	******	******	**R-O**	******
P-P	******	**Q-P**	**R-F**	******	REX
******	**P-W**	******	******	RHO	******
PAP	******	QBP	RAF	RIO	**R-Y**
PEP	PAW	QRP	REF	ROO	******
PIP	PEW	******	******	******	RAY
POP	POW	**Q-T**	**R-G**	**R-P**	ROY
PUP	******	******	******	******	******
******	**P-X**	QKT	RAG	RAP	**S-A**
P-Q	******	******	REG	REP	******
******	PAX	**Q-V**	RIG	RIP	SEA
PDQ	PBX	******	RUG	******	SHA
******	PIX	QQV	******	**R-Q**	SNA
P-R	POX	******	**R-H**	******	SPA
******	PYX	**R-A**	******	REQ	SRA
PAR	******	******	RAH	******	STA
PER	**P-Y**	REA	******	**R-R**	SUA
PYR	******	RIA	**R-I**	******	SWA
******	PAY	RNA	******	RNR	******
P-S	PLY	RSA	RAI	******	**S-B**
******	PRY	******	RBI	**R-S**	******
PAS	******	**R-B**	ROI	******	SCB
PES	**P-Z**	******	******	RAS	SEB
PHS	******	REB	**R-J**	RES	SIB
PIS	PAZ	RIB	******	RMS	SOB
PMS	******	ROB	RAJ	RPS	STB
PPS	**Q-A**	RUB	******	******	SUB
PRS	******	******	**R-K**	**R-T**	******
PSS	QUA	**R-C**	******	******	**S-C**
PUS	******	******	ROK	RAT	******
******	**Q-C**	REC	******	RCT	SAC
P-T	******	RFC	**R-L**	RET	SEC
******	QMC	ROC	******	RIT	SFC
PAT	******	******	REL	ROT	SIC
PCT	**Q-D**	**R-D**	******	RUT	SOC
	******	******	**R-M**	******	SMC
	QED	RAD	******	**R-U**	
		RED	RAM	******	
			REM	REU	

******	SOM	SOS	TIA	******	******
S-D	SSM	SSS	TRA	**T-L**	**T-T**
******	SUM	SUS	TVA	******	******
SAD	SYM	SYS	TWA	TEL	TAT
SCD	******	******	******	TIL	TET
SGD	**S-N**	**S-T**	**T-B**	******	TIT
SID	******	******	******	**T-M**	TNT
SOD	SAN	SAT	TAB	******	TOT
STD	SEN	SET	THB	TAM	TUT
SUD	SIN	SGT	TUB	TIM	******
******	SON	SIT	******	TOM	**T-U**
S-E	SUN	SKT	**T-C**	******	******
******	SYN	SOT	******	**T-N**	TAU
SAE	******	SST	TEC	******	******
SBE	**S-O**	******	TIC	TAN	**T-V**
SEE	******	**S-U**	TOC	TEN	******
SHE	SLO	******	******	TIN	TAV
SSE	SRO	SOU	**T-D**	TON	******
STE	******	STU	******	TUN	**T-W**
SUE	**S-P**	******	TAD	******	******
SWE	******	**S-W**	TED	**T-O**	TAW
******	SAP	******	THD	******	TOW
S-F	SEP	SAW	TOD	TAO	******
******	SIP	SBW	******	THO	**T-X**
SHF	SOP	SEW	**T-E**	TIO	******
******	SPP	SOW	******	TKO	TAX
S-G	SUP	SSW	TEE	TOO	TEX
******	******	******	THE	TWO	******
SAG	******	******	TIE	******	**T-Y**
STG	**S-Q**	**S-X**	TOE	**T-P**	******
SUG	******	******	TSE	******	TAY
******	SEQ	SAX	******	TAP	THY
S-I	SQQ	SEX	**T-G**	TIP	TOY
******	******	SIX	******	TOP	TRY
SCI	**S-R**	SOX	TAG	TUP	TWY
SKI	******	******	TEG	TWP	******
SRI	SAR	**S-Y**	TOG	TYP	**U-A**
SUI	SDR	******	TUG	******	******
******	SER	SAY	******	**T-R**	UCA
S-L	SIR	SHY	**T-I**	******	UFA
******	SKR	SKY	******	TAR	UMA
SAL	SSR	SLY	******	TER	UNA
SEL	STR	SOY	THI	TOR	USA
SIL	SUR	SPY	TOI	******	UTA
SOL	SYR	STY	TRI	**T-S**	UVA
SYL	******	******	TWI	******	******
******	**S-S**	**T-A**	******	TBS	**U-D**
S-M	******	******	**T-J**	TIS	******
******	SDS	TAA	******	TVS	URD
SAM	SIS	TEA	TAJ		
SIM					

******	******	******	******	******	******
U-E	**U-R**	**V-F**	**V-V**	**W-G**	**W-W**
******	******	******	******	******	******
UKE	UAR	VHF	VAV	WAG	WNW
ULE	UKR	VLF	VIV	WIG	WOW
UNE	******	******	******	******	WSW
URE	**U-S**	**V-G**	**V-W**	**W-K**	******
USE	******	******	******	******	**W-X**
UTE	UPS	VUG	VFW	WMK	******
******	USS	******	VOW	******	WAX
U-F	UTS	**V-I**	******	**W-N**	******
******	******	******	**V-X**	******	**W-Y**
UHF	**U-T**	VAI	******	WAN	******
******	******	******	VEX	WBN	WAY
U-H	ULT	**V-L**	VOX	WEN	WEY
******	UMT	******	******	WIN	WHY
UGH	******	VAL	**V-Z**	WON	WRY
******	**U-U**	VIL	******	******	******
U-I	******	VOL	VIZ	**W-O**	**W-Z**
******	UPU	VUL	******	******	******
UNI	USU	******	**W-A**	WHO	WIZ
UPI	UTU	**V-M**	******	WOO	******
URI	******	******	WPA	WYO	**X-L**
******	**U-W**	VIM	WVA	******	******
U-K	******	******	******	**W-P**	XYL
******	UAW	**V-N**	**W-B**	******	******
USK	UMW	******	******	WAP	**X-N**
******	USW	VAN	WEB	******	******
U-M	******	VIN	******	**W-R**	XEN
******	**V-A**	VON	**W-C**	******	******
ULM	******	******	******	WAR	**X-R**
******	VIA	**V-P**	WAC	WHR	******
U-N	******	******	******	******	XER
******	**V-C**	VIP	**W-D**	**W-S**	******
URN	******	******	******	******	**X-S**
USN	VAC	**V-R**	WAD	WAS	******
******	VIC	******	WED	WBS	XIS
U-O	******	VOR	******	WES	******
******	**V-D**	******	**W-E**	WIS	**X-Y**
UDO	******	**V-S**	******	******	******
UFO	VMD	******	WEE	**W-T**	XTY
UMO	******	VAS	WOE	******	******
UNO	**V-E**	VIS	WYE	WAT	**Y-A**
URO	******	******	******	WET	******
USO	VEE	**V-T**	**W-F**	WIT	YEA
******	VIE	******	******	WOT	******
U-P	VYE	VAT	WAF		**Y-C**
******		VET			******
UMP					YUC
USP					

******	******	******	PAC	HAG	KAL
Y-D	**Y-T**	**Z-N**	SAC	JAG	MAL
******	******	******	VAC	LAG	PAL
YOD	YET	ZEN	WAC	MAG	SAL
******	******	******	******	NAG	VAL
Y-H	**Y-U**	**Z-O**	**-AD**	RAG	******
******	******	******	******	SAG	**-AM**
YAH	YOU	ZIO	BAD	TAG	******
******	******	ZOO	CAD	WAG	CAM
Y-K	**Y-W**	******	DAD	ZAG	DAM
******	******	**Z-P**	FAD	******	EAM
YAK	YAW		GAD	**-AH**	FAM
YUK	YEW	ZAP	HAD	******	GAM
******	YOW	ZIP	LAD	BAH	HAM
Y-L	******	******	MAD	HAH	JAM
******	**Y-Y**	**Z-R**	PAD	PAH	LAM
YUL	******	******	RAD	RAH	NAM
******	YAY	ZER	SAD	YAH	PAM
Y-M	******	******	TAD	******	RAM
******	**Z-A**	**Z-X**	WAD	**-AI**	SAM
YAM	******	******	******	******	TAM
YOM	ZEA	ZAX	**-AE**	GAI	YAM
******	ZOA	******	******	KAI	******
Y-N	ZSA	**-AA**	BAE	MAI	**-AN**
******	******	******	CAE	PAI	******
YEN	**Z-D**	AAA	GAE	RAI	BAN
YIN	******	BAA	HAE	VAI	CAN
YON	ZED	FAA	LAE	******	DAN
******	******	MAA	MAE	**-AJ**	EAN
Y-O	**Z-E**	NAA	NAE	******	FAN
******	******	TAA	RAE	RAJ	HAN
YAO	ZEE	******	SAE	TAJ	IAN
******	ZOE	**-AB**	******	******	JAN
Y-P	******	******	**-AF**	**-AK**	KAN
******	**Z-G**	BAB	******	******	LAN
YAP	******	CAB	AAF	DAK	MAN
YEP	ZAG	DAB	BAF	OAK	NAN
YIP	ZIG	FAB	CAF	YAK	PAN
******	ZUG	GAB	OAF	ZAK	RAN
Y-R	ZYG	JAB	RAF	******	SAN
******	******	KAB	WAF	**-AL**	TAN
YER	**Z-K**	LAB	******	******	VAN
******	******	MAB	**-AG**	AAL	WAN
Y-S	ZAK	NAB	******	CAL	******
******	******	TAB	BAG	DAL	**-AO**
YDS	**Z-L**	******	DAG	GAL	******
YES	******	**-AC**	FAG	HAL	FAO
YRS	ZEL	******	GAG	IAL	GAO
		LAC			
		MAC			

LAO	HAS	HAW	******	******	GCA
MAO	IAS	JAW	**-BA**	**-BN**	ICA
TAO	JAS	KAW	******	******	OCA
YAO	KAS	LAW	ABA	EBN	UCA
******	LAS	MAW	BBA	WBN	******
-AP	MAS	PAW	DBA	******	**-CB**
******	OAS	RAW	FFA	**-BO**	******
CAP	PAS	SAW	IBA	******	GCB
DAP	RAS	TAW	MBA	IBO	KCB
GAP	VAS	UAW	******	******	SCB
HAP	WAS	YAW	**-BB**	**-BP**	******
JAP	******	******	******	******	**-CC**
LAP	**-AT**	**-AX**	EBB	KBP	******
MAP	******	******	OBB	QBP	ACC
NAP	BAT	FAX	**-BC**	******	CCC
PAP	CAT	LAX	******	**-BS**	FCC
RAP	EAT	MAX	ABC	******	ICC
SAP	FAT	PAX	BBC	ABS	******
TAP	GAT	SAX	CBC	BBS	**-CD**
WAP	HAT	TAX	NBC	CBS	******
YAP	JAT	WAX	******	EBS	GCD
ZAP	LAT	ZAX	**-BD**	LBS	JCD
******	MAT	******	******	NBS	LCD
-AR	NAT	**-AY**	CBD	OBS	SCD
******	OAT	******	******	TBS	******
AAR	PAT	BAY	**-BE**	WBS	**-CE**
BAR	RAT	CAY	******	******	******
CAR	SAT	DAY	ABE	**-BT**	ACE
DAR	TAT	FAY	DBE	******	BCE
EAR	VAT	GAY	GBE	IBT	ICE
FAR	WAT	HAY	NBE	******	******
GAR	******	JAY	SBE	**-BW**	**-CG**
JAR	**-AU**	KAY	******	******	******
LAR	******	LAY	**-BI**	MBW	BCG
MAR	EAU	MAY	******	SBW	ECG
OAR	MAU	NAY	CBI	******	******
PAR	TAU	PAY	FBI	**-BX**	**-CH**
SAR	******	RAY	OBI	******	******
TAR	**-AV**	SAY	RBI	PBX	MCH
UAR	******	TAY	******	******	******
WAR	BAV	WAY	**-BL**	**-BY**	**-CI**
******	CAV	YAY	******	******	******
-AS	NAV	******	BBL	ABY	ICI
******	TAV	**-AZ**	DBL	******	SCI
BAS	VAV	******	******	**-CA**	******
CAS	******	GAZ	**-BM**	******	**-CK**
FAS	**-AW**	PAZ	******	CCA	******
GAS	CAW		HBM	FCA	OCK
	DAW				

******	******	******	HEA	DEE	DEL
-CL	**-CY**	**-DO**	KEA	FEE	EEL
******	******	******	LEA	GEE	GEL
BCL	ACY	ADO	NEA	JEE	HEL
DCL	ICY	EDO	PEA	LEE	MEL
MCL	******	IDO	REA	NEE	REL
******	**-DA**	UDO	SEA	PEE	SEL
-CM	******	******	TEA	REE	TEL
******	ADA	**-DP**	YEA	SEE	ZEL
DCM	FDA	******	ZEA	TEE	******
LCM	IDA	EDP	******	VEE	**-EM**
******	ODA	NDP	**-EB**	WEE	******
-CN	******	******	******	ZEE	DEM
******	**-DB**	**-DQ**	DEB	******	FEM
RCN	******	******	FEB	**-EF**	GEM
******	EDB	PDQ	GEB	******	HEM
-CO	PDB	******	HEB	AEF	JEM
******	******	**-DR**	NEB	KEF	LEM
NCO	**-DC**	******	REB	NEF	MEM
******	******	CDR	SEB	REF	REM
-CP	ADC	SDR	WEB	******	******
******	******	******	******	**-EG**	**-EN**
BCP	**-DD**	**-DS**	**-EC**	******	******
******	******	******	******	BEG	BEN
-CS	ADD	ADS	AEC	DEG	CEN
******	EDD	DDS	DEC	EEG	DEN
BCS	ODD	IDS	EEC	KEG	EEN
DCS	PDD	LDS	REC	LEG	FEN
ICS	******	MDS	SEC	MEG	GEN
JCS	**-DE**	ODS	TEC	PEG	HEN
OCS	******	SDS	******	REG	KEN
******	ADE	YDS	**-ED**	TEG	LEN
-CT	EDE	******	******	******	MEN
******	IDE	**-DT**	BED	**-EI**	NEN
ACT	ODE	******	FED	******	PEN
ECT	******	DDT	HED	DEI	REN
GCT	**-DH**	EDT	LED	LEI	SEN
JCT	******	******	MED	PEI	TEN
LCT	EDH	******	NED	******	WEN
OCT	******	**-DV**	OED	**-EK**	XEN
PCT	**-DJ**	******	PED	******	YEN
RCT	******	ADV	QED	DEK	ZEN
******	ADJ	******	RED	LEK	******
-CU	******	**-DZ**	TED	******	**-EO**
******	**-DM**	******	WED	******	******
ACU	******	ADZ	ZED	**-EL**	GEO
ECU	ADM	******	******	******	LEO
******	EDM	**-EA**	**-EE**	BEL	NEO
-CW		******	******	CEL	
******		BEA	BEE		
ICW		CEA	CEE		

******	******	******	******	******	******
-EP	**-ET**	**-EX**	**-FF**	**-GA**	**-GS**
******	******	******	******	******	******
HEP	AET	HEX	EFF	AGA	CGS
NEP	BET	LEX	OFF	PGA	******
PEP	GET	MEX	******	******	**-GT**
REP	JET	REX	**-FG**	**-GB**	******
SEP	KET	SEX	******	******	HGT
YEP	LET	TEX	AFG	KGB	SGT
******	MET	VEX	MFG	******	******
-EQ	NET	******	PFG	**-GD**	**-GY**
******	PET	**-EY**	******	******	******
REQ	RET	******	**-FI**	SGD	IGY
SEQ	SET	BEY	******	******	******
******	TET	CEY	CFI	**-GE**	**-HA**
-ER	VET	DEY	FFI	******	******
******	WET	FEY	******	AGE	AHA
AER	YET	HEY	**-FL**	LGE	CHA
CER	******	KEY	******	******	FHA
EER	**-EU**	LEY	AFL	**-GG**	LHA
GER	******	NEY	******	******	PHA
HER	FEU	WEY	**-FM**	EGG	SHA
JER	JEU	******	******	******	******
KER	LEU	**-EZ**	CFM	**-GH**	**-HB**
MER	REU	******	******	******	******
NER	******	FEZ	**-FO**	CGH	LHB
OER	**-EV**	NEZ	******	UGH	PHB
PER	******	******	UFO	******	THB
SER	BEV	**-FA**	******	**-GK**	******
TER	DEV	******	**-FR**	******	**-HC**
XER	LEV	BFA	******	NGK	******
YER	MEV	FFA	AFR	******	PHC
ZER	NEV	UFA	******	**-GM**	******
******	REV	******	**-FS**	******	**-HD**
-ES	******	**-FB**	******	CGM	******
******	******	******	CFS	MGM	HHD
AES	**-EW**	AFB	IFS	******	LHD
BES	******	******	******	**-GN**	PHD
CES	DEW	**-FC**	**-FT**	******	THD
DES	FEW	******	******	IGN	******
EES	HEW	DFC	AFT	******	**-HE**
HES	JEW	IFC	EFT	**-GO**	******
LES	LEW	PFC	OFT	******	CHE
MES	MEW	RFC	******	AGO	SHE
OES	NEW	SFC	**-FV**	EGO	THE
PES	PEW	******	******	******	******
RES	SEW	**-FD**	FFV	**-GR**	**-HF**
WES	YEW	******	******	******	******
YES		MFD	**-FW**	MGR	SHF
		RFD	******		UHF
			VFW		VHF

******	******	FID	KIL	TIO	******
-HG	**-HY**	GID	LIL	ZIO	**-IT**
******	******	HID	MIL	******	******
CHG	SHY	KID	NIL	**-IP**	AIT
MHG	THY	LID	OIL	******	BIT
******	WHY	MID	SIL	DIP	FIT
-HI	******	OID	TIL	GIP	HIT
******	**-IA**	RID	VIL	HIP	KIT
CHI	******	SID	******	KIP	LIT
PHI	CIA	******	**-IM**	LIP	NIT
THI	DIA	**-IE**	******	NIP	OIT
******	KIA	******	AIM	PIP	PIT
-HL	MIA	CIE	DIM	RIP	RIT
******	PIA	DIE	HIM	SIP	SIT
KHL	RIA	FIE	JIM	TIP	TIT
NHL	TIA	GIE	KIM	VIP	WIT
******	VIA	HIE	LIM	YIP	******
-HM	******	LIE	RIM	ZIP	**-IU**
******	**-IB**	PIE	SIM	******	******
CHM	******	TIE	TIM	**-IQ**	PIU
OHM	BIB	VIE	VIM	******	******
******	DIB	******	******	LIQ	**-IV**
-HO	EIB	**-IF**	**-IN**	******	******
******	FIB	******	******	**-IR**	DIV
MHO	GIB	CIF	AIN	******	VIV
OHO	JIB	DIF	BIN	AIR	******
RHO	LIB	******	DIN	CIR	**-IX**
THO	MIB	**-IG**	EIN	DIR	******
WHO	NIB	******	FIN	EIR	DIX
******	RIB	BIG	GIN	FIR	FIX
-HP	SIB	DIG	HIN	MIR	MIX
******	******	FIG	KIN	SIR	NIX
IHP	**-IC**	GIG	LIN	******	PIX
******	******	JIG	NIN	**-IS**	SIX
-HQ	BIC	MIG	PIN	******	******
******	CIC	PIG	SIN	AIS	**-IZ**
GHQ	FIC	WIG	TIN	BIS	******
******	HIC	RIG	VIN	CIS	LIZ
-HR	SIC	ZIG	WIN	DIS	VIZ
******	TIC	******	YIN	GIS	WIZ
WHR	VIC	**-IH**	******	HIS	******
******	******	******	**-IO**	MIS	**-JS**
-HS	**-ID**	HIH	******	NIS	******
******	******	******	BIO	PIS	HJS
IHS	AID	**-IL**	CIO	SIS	******
OHS	BID	******	DIO	TIS	**-KA**
PHS	CID	AIL	NIO	VIS	******
	DID	GIL	RIO	WIS	AKA
				XIS	OKA

******	******	******	******	******	******
-KC	**-KT**	**-LG**	**-LT**	**-MI**	**-MY**
******	******	******	******	******	******
AKC	KKT	ALG	ALT	AMI	AMY
******	MKT	MLG	ULT	******	******
-KE	QKT			**-MK**	**-MZ**
******	SKT	**-LI**	**-LU**	******	******
EKE	******	******	******	WMK	DMZ
IKE	**-KU**	ALI	FLU	******	******
UKE	******	ELI	******	**-MO**	**-NA**
******	PKU	ILI	**-LY**	******	******
-KG	******	******	******	AMO	ANA
******	**-KY**	**-LK**	ELY	OMO	BNA
DKG	******	******	FLY	UMO	DNA
EKG	SKY	ELK	PLY	******	ENA
PKG	******	ILK	SLY	**-MP**	INA
******	**-LA**	******	******	******	RNA
-KI	******	**-LL**	**-MA**	AMP	SNA
******	ALA	******	******	EMP	UNA
SKI	BLA	ALL	AMA	IMP	******
******	ELA	BLL	OMA	UMP	**-NB**
-KK	FLA	ELL	UMA	******	******
******	ILA	ILL	******	**-MR**	DNB
KKK	MLA	******	**-MC**	******	******
******	OLA	**-LM**	******	BMR	**-NC**
-KL	******	******	GMC	******	******
******	**-LB**	ELM	QMC	**-MS**	ANC
DKL	******	LLM	SMC	******	ENC
******	ALB	ULM	******	EMS	INC
-KM	ELB	******	**-MD**	HMS	******
******	LLB	**-LO**	******	PMS	**-ND**
DKM	******	******	DMD	RMS	******
******	**-LD**	FLO	VMD	******	AND
-KO	******	ILO	******	**-MT**	END
******	LLD	SLO	**-ME**	******	IND
TKO	OLD	******	******	AMT	******
******	******	**-LP**	AME	GMT	**-NE**
-KR	**-LE**	******	BME	LMT	******
******	******	ALP	DME	UMT	ANE
SKR	ALE	ILP	MME	******	ENE
UKR	CLE	******	OME	**-MU**	INE
******	ILE	**-LS**	******	******	NNE
-KS	OLE	******	**-MF**	AMU	ONE
******	ULE	ALS	******	EMU	UNE
DKS	******	BLS	EMF	******	******
MKS	**-LF**	DLS	******	**-MW**	**-NG**
OKS	******	ELS	**-MG**	******	******
	ALF	ILS	******	**-MW**	ENG
	ELF	MLS	AMG	******	ING
	VLF		PMG	UMW	
			QMG		

******	******	******	******	SON	******
-NI	**-NU**	**-OD**	**-OI**	TON	**-OS**
******	******	******	******	VON	******
ANI	ANU	COD	HOI	WON	COS
ONI	GNU	DOD	MOI	YON	DOS
UNI	******	FOD	POI	******	EOS
******	**-NV**	GOD	ROI	**-OO**	JOS
-NK	******	HOD	TOI	******	KOS
******	ENV	IOD	******	BOO	MOS
INK	******	MOD	**-OK**	COO	NOS
******	**-NW**	NOD	******	GOO	SOS
-NL	******	POD	ROK	LOO	******
******	NNW	ROD	******	MOO	**-OT**
ENL	WNW	SOD	**-OL**	ROO	******
******	******	TOD	******	TOO	BOT
-NN	**-NY**	YOD	AOL	WOO	COT
******	******	******	BOL	ZOO	DOT
ANN	ANY	**-OE**	COL	******	GOT
INN	******	******	DOL	**-OP**	HOT
******	**-OA**	DOE	HOL	******	JOT
-NO	******	FOE	POL	BOP	LOT
******	BOA	HOE	SOL	COP	MOT
CNO	GOA	JOE	VOL	DOP	NOT
UNO	KOA	MOE	******	FOP	POT
******	LOA	POE	**-OM**	GOP	ROT
-NP	MOA	ROE	******	HOP	SOT
******	ZOA	TOE	COM	KOP	TOT
GNP	******	WOE	DOM	LOP	WOT
******	**-OB**	ZOE	MOM	MOP	******
-NR	******	******	NOM	POP	**-OU**
******	BOB	**-OF**	ROM	SOP	******
RNR	COB	******	SOM	TOP	IOU
******	FOB	LOF	TOM	******	LOU
-NS	GOB	******	YOM	**-OQ**	SOU
******	HOB	**-OG**	******	******	YOU
ANS	JOB	******	**-ON**	LOQ	******
CNS	LOB	BOG	******	******	**-OV**
ENS	MOB	COG	BON	**-OR**	******
INS	NOB	DOG	CON	******	GOV
ONS	ROB	FOG	DON	COR	NOV
******	SOB	GOG	EON	DOR	******
-NT	******	HOG	GON	FOR	**-OW**
******	**-OC**	JOG	HON	HOR	******
ANT	******	LOG	ION	KOR	BOW
ENT	HOC	NOG	JON	NOR	COW
INT	LOC	TOG	LON	TOR	DOW
ONT	ROC	******	MON	VOR	HOW
TNT	SOC	**-OH**	NON		IOW
	TOC	******			
		BOH			
		POH			

LOW	******	FPO	******	SRI	PRS
MOW	**-PC**	GPO	**-RA**	TRI	YRS
NOW	******	******	******	URI	******
POW	FPC	**-PP**	ARA	******	**-RT**
ROW	PPC	******	BRA	**-RK**	******
SOW	******	SPP	ERA	******	ART
TOW	**-PD**	******	FRA	ARK	ORT
VOW	******	**-PR**	IRA	IRK	******
WOW	BPD	******	KRA	******	**-RU**
YOW	MPD	APR	NRA	**-RM**	******
******	PPD	******	ORA	******	CRU
-OX	RPD	**-PS**	SRA	ARM	******
******	******	******	TRA	******	**-RV**
BOX	**-PE**	CPS	******	**-RN**	******
COX	******	FPS	**-RB**	******	ARV
FOX	APE	LPS	******	ARN	ERV
LOX	BPE	OPS	FRB	ERN	******
NOX	MPE	PPS	ORB	URN	**-RY**
POX	OPE	RPS	******	******	******
SOX	******	UPS	**-RC**	**-RO**	ARY
VOX	**-PH**	******	******	******	CRY
******	******	**-PT**	ARC	FRO	DRY
-OY	APH	******	ORC	GRO	ERY
******	BPH	APT	******	IRO	FRY
BOY	CPH	NPT	**-RD**	ORO	ORY
COY	DPH	OPT	******	PRO	PRY
FOY	MPH	******	ARD	SRO	TRY
GOY	**-PI**	**-PU**	URD	URO	WRY
HOY	******	******	******	******	******
JOY	EPI	GPU	**-RE**	******	**-SA**
ROY	PPI	UPU	******	**-RP**	******
SOY	UPI	******	ARE	******	ASA
TOY	******	**-PW**	ERE	KRP	BSA
******	**-PL**	******	IRE	QRP	CSA
-OZ	******	DPW	ORE	******	GSA
******	CPL	******	PRE	**-RR**	ISA
BOZ	QPL	**-PY**	URE	******	NSA
COZ	******	******	******	ERR	OSA
DOZ	**-PM**	OPY	**-RG**	******	RSA
******	******	SPY	******	**-RS**	USA
-PA	CPM	******	ARG	******	ZSA
******	FPM	**-QQ**	ERG	ARS	******
APA	GPM	******	******	CRS	**-SB**
CPA	PPM	SQQ	**-RH**	ERS	******
FPA	RPM	******	******	FRS	OSB
IPA	******	**-QV**	HRH	HRS	******
OPA	**-PO**	******	******	IRS	**-SC**
SPA	APO	QQV	**-RI**	MRS	******
WPA	CPO		ERI	ORS	BSC
			FRI		CSC

DSC	HSM	EST	******	******	DUE
ESC	ISM	IST	**-TE**	**-TU**	HUE
GSC	SSM	LST	******	******	RUE
MSC	******	MST	ATE	BTU	SUE
NSC	**-SN**	PST	ETE	STU	******
******	******	SST	ITE	UTU	**-UG**
-SD	ASN	******	STE	******	******
******	USN	**-SU**	UTE	**-TY**	AUG
LSD	******	******	******	******	BUG
OSD	**-SO**	ESU	**-TG**	ITY	DUG
******	******	USU	******	STY	HUG
-SE	DSO	******	STG	XTY	JUG
******	ISO	**-SV**	******	******	LUG
ASE	USO	******	**-TH**	**-UA**	MUG
ESE	******	RSV	******	******	PUG
ISE	**-SP**	******	ATH	QUA	RUG
OSE	******	**-SW**	BTH	SUA	SUG
SSE	ASP	******	DTH	******	TUG
TSE	DSP	NSW	ETH	**-UB**	VUG
USE	ESP	SSW	LTH	******	ZUG
******	OSP	USW	NTH	BUB	******
-SF	USP	WSW	******	CUB	**-UH**
******	******	******	**-TN**	DUB	******
NSF	**-SQ**	**-TA**	******	HUB	HUH
OSF	******	******	CTN	NUB	******
PSF	ESQ	ETA	******	PUB	**-UI**
******	******	ITA	**-TO**	RUB	******
-SH	**-SR**	PTA	******	SUB	DUI
******	******	STA	ETO	TUB	GUI
ASH	ISR	UTA	ITO	******	OUI
HSH	SSR	******	OTO	**-UC**	SUI
ISH	******	**-TB**	PTO	******	******
******	**-SS**	******	QTO	AUC	**-UK**
-SI	******	STB	******	DUC	******
******	ASS	******	**-TR**	MUC	AUK
PSI	BSS	**-TC**	******	YUC	HUK
******	ESS	******	STR	******	YUK
-SK	LSS	******	******	**-UD**	******
******	MSS	ATC	**-TS**	******	**-UL**
ASK	OSS	ETC	******	BUD	******
ESK	PSS	FTC	CTS	CUD	BUL
USK	SSS	GTC	HTS	DUD	CUL
******	USS	OTC	ITS	IUD	FUL
-SL	******	******	MTS	MUD	NUL
******	**-ST**	**-TD**	UTS	PUD	VUL
MSL	******	******	******	SUD	YUL
******	******	******	**-TT**	******	******
-SM	**-ST**	**-TD**	**-TT**	**-UE**	**-UM**
******	******	******	******	******	******
BSM	CST	LTD	ATT	AUE	BUM
DSM	DST	STD	OTT	CUE	CUM

GUM	GUS	******	******	******	SYL
HUM	JUS	**-VE**	**-WH**	**-XE**	XYL
IUM	MUS	******	******	******	******
LUM	NUS	AVE	KWH	AXE	**-YM**
MUM	OUS	EVE	******	EXE	******
RUM	PUS	IVE	**-WI**	******	GYM
SUM	SUS	******	******	**-XO**	PYM
******	******	**-VI**	OWI	******	SYM
-UN	**-UT**	******	TWI	EXO	******
******	******	AVI	******	******	**-YN**
BUN	AUT	OVI	**-WL**	**-XT**	******
CUN	BUT	******	******	******	AYN
DUN	CUT	**-VM**	AWL	EXT	DYN
FUN	GUT	******	OWL	PXT	GYN
GUN	HUT	BVM	******	******	SYN
HUN	JUT	DVM	**-WN**	**-XY**	******
JUN	LUT	******	******	******	**-YO**
NUN	MUT	**-VO**	AWN	OXY	******
PUN	NUT	******	OWN	******	LYO
RUN	OUT	OVO	******	**-YC**	MYO
SUN	PUT	******	**-WO**	******	PYO
TUN	RUT	**-VP**	******	MYC	WYO
******	TUT	******	CWO	NYC	******
-UO	******	MVP	TWO	******	**-YP**
******	**-UX**	******	******	**-YD**	******
DUO	******	**-VS**	**-WP**	******	GYP
******	AUX	******	******	CYD	HYP
-UP	DUX	TVS	TWP	******	TYP
******	LUX	******	******	**-YE**	******
CUP	******	**-VT**	**-WT**	******	**-YR**
DUP	**-UY**	******	CWT	AYE	******
GUP	******	PVT	DWT	BYE	AYR
PUP	BUY	******	NWT	DYE	GYR
SUP	GUY	**-VY**	PWT	EYE	PYR
TUP	HUY	******	******	LYE	SYR
******	******	IVY	**-WV**	NYE	******
-UR	**-VA**	******	******	PYE	**-YS**
******	******	**-WA**	JWV	RYE	******
BUR	AVA	******	******	VYE	AYS
CUR	EVA	FWA	**-WW**	WYE	DYS
EUR	IVA	SWA	******	******	LYS
FUR	KVA	TWA	IWW	**-YG**	SYS
MUR	OVA	******	******	******	******
OUR	TVA	**-WE**	**-WY**	ZYG	**-YT**
SUR	UVA	******	TWY	******	******
******	WVA	AWE	******	**-YL**	CYT
-US	******	EWE	**-XA**	******	
******	**-VD**	OWE	******	HYL	
AUS	******	SWE	OXA	OYL	
BUS	MVD				

******	ACES	AGEE	ALAN	AMEN	******
-YX	ACET	AGES	ALAR	AMER	AO--
******	ACHE	AGHA	ALAS	AMES	******
MYX	ACID	AGIO	ALBA	AMIA	AONE
NYX	ACLU	AGNI	ALBS	AMID	AOUL
PYX	ACME	AGOG	ALDE	AMIE	******
******	ACNE	AGON	ALDO	AMIR	AP--
-ZO	ACOR	AGRA	ALEC	AMIS	******
******	ACOU	AGRI	ALEE	AMMO	APED
AZO	ACRE	AGRO	ALEF	AMOI	APES
******	ACRO	AGUA	ALEN	AMOK	APEX
-ZS	ACTA	AGUE	ALES	AMON	APIA
******	ACTH	******	ALEX	AMOR	APIO
OZS	ACTS	AH--	ALFA	AMOS	APIS
	******	******	ALFS	AMOY	APOC
AA--	AD--	AHAB	ALGA	AMPS	APOD
	******	AHAH	ALGY	AMTS	APSE
AALS	ADAH	AHEM	ALIA	AMUR	APUS
AARE	ADAK	AHOY	ALIF	AMUS	******
******	ADAM	******	ALIN	AMYL	AQ--
AB--	ADAR	AI--	ALIT	AMYS	******
******	ADAS	******	ALIX	******	AQUA
ABAS	ADAY	AIDA	ALLE	AN--	AQUI
ABBA	ADDS	AIDE	ALLI	******	******
ABBE	ADDY	AIDS	ALLO	ANAL	AR--
ABBR	ADEN	AILE	ALLY	ANAM	******
ABBY	ADIT	AILS	ALMA	ANAS	ARAB
ABCS	ADZE	AIMS	ALMS	ANAT	ARAD
ABED	******	AINO	ALOE	ANCE	ARAL
ABEL	AE--	AINS	ALOP	ANCY	ARAM
ABES	******	AINT	ALOW	ANDY	ARAN
ABET	AEON	AINU	ALPH	ANEW	ARAS
ABIB	AERI	AIRE	ALPS	ANIL	ARCH
ABIE	AERO	AIRS	ALSO	ANIM	ARCS
ABLE	AERY	AIRY	ALTA	ANIS	AREA
ABLY	******	******	ALTI	ANKH	AREO
ABOU	AF--	AJ--	ALTO	ANNA	ARES
ABRI	******	******	ALUM	ANNE	ARGO
ABUT	AFAR	AJAR	ALVA	ANNO	ARIA
******	AFGH	AJAX	ALYS	ANNS	ARID
AC--	AFRO	******	******	ANOA	ARIL
******	******	AK--	AM--	ANON	ARIZ
ACAD	AG--	******	******	ANSA	ARKS
ACCT	******	AKIN	AMAH	ANTA	ARMS
ACDC	AGAO	******	AMAS	ANTE	ARMY
ACEA	AGAR	AL--	AMAT	ANTH	ARNE
ACED	AGAS	******	AMBI	ANTI	ARNI
ACER	AGED	ALAE	AMBO	ANTS	ARNO
		ALAI		ANUS	

ARNS	******	******	BALM	BEAS	BIBL
AROW	**AU--**	**AY--**	BALT	BEAT	BIBS
ARTE	******	******	BANC	BEAU	BICE
ARTS	AUBE	AYAH	BAND	BECK	BIDE
ARTY	AUBY	AYER	BANE	BEDA	BIDS
ARUM	AUDE	AYES	BANG	BEDE	BIEL
ARYL	AUKS	AYIN	BANI	BEDS	BIER
******	AULD	AYME	BANK	BEEF	BIFF
AS--	AUNE	******	BANN	BEEK	BIHE
******	AUNT	**AZ--**	BANS	BEEN	BIKE
ASAS	AURA	******	BANT	BEEP	BILE
ASCH	AUST	AZAN	BAPT	BEER	BILK
ASCI	AUTH	AZON	BARB	BEES	BILL
ASEA	AUTO	AZOV	BARD	BEET	BIND
ASHA	******	******	BARE	BEGS	BINE
ASHE	**AV--**	**BA--**	BARI	BEKA	BING
ASHY	******	******	BARK	BELA	BINH
ASIA	AVAL	BAAL	BARM	BELG	BINS
ASIR	AVAS	BAAR	BARN	BELL	BIOL
ASIS	AVEC	BAAS	BARO	BELS	BION
ASKS	AVER	BABA	BARS	BELT	BIRD
ASOF	AVES	BABE	BART	BEMA	BIRL
ASPS	AVID	BABI	BASE	BEND	BIRO
ASSN	AVIS	BABS	BASH	BENE	BIRR
ASST	AVIV	BABU	BASK	BENG	BISE
ASTI	AVON	BABY	BASS	BENI	BITE
ASTR	AVOW	BACH	BAST	BENS	BITS
******	******	BACK	BATE	BENT	BITT
AT--	**AW--**	BADE	BATH	BERA	******
******	******	BAEL	BATS	BERG	**BL--**
ATAR	AWAY	BAER	BATT	BERM	******
ATEN	AWED	BAFF	BATZ	BERN	BLAB
ATES	AWES	BAGA	BAWD	BERT	BLAH
ATIC	AWLS	BAGO	BAWL	BESA	BLAT
ATKA	AWNS	BAGR	BAYA	BESS	BLDG
ATLE	AWNY	BAGS	BAYS	BEST	BLEB
ATLI	AWOL	BAHT	******	BETA	BLED
ATMO	AWRY	BAIA	**BB--**	BETH	BLEM
ATOM	******	BAIL	******	BETS	BLET
ATOP	**AX--**	BAIT	BBLS	BEVS	BLEW
ATOR	******	BAJA	******	BEVY	BLIP
ATRI	AXED	BAKE	**BE--**	BEYS	BLIT
ATTA	AXES	BAKU	******	******	BLOB
ATTN	AXIL	BALD	BEAD	**BH--**	BLOC
ATTO	AXIS	BALE	BEAK	******	BLOT
ATTU	AXLE	BALI	BEAM	BHAR	BLOW
ATTY	AXON	BALK	BEAN	******	BLUB
		BALL	BEAR	**BI--**	BLUE
				******	
				BIAS	
				BIBB	

BLUR	BORA	BROW	BUTE	CARD	******
BLVD	BORE	BROZ	BUTS	CARE	**CH--**
******	BORN	BRUT	BUTT	CARL	******
BM--	BORT	******	BUYS	CARO	CHAD
******	BOSH	**BS--**	BUZZ	CARP	CHAP
BMOC	BOSK	******	******	CARR	CHAR
BMUS	BOSN	BSED	**BY--**	CARS	CHAT
******	BOSS	BSSC	******	CART	CHAW
BO--	BOTA	******	BYEE	CARY	CHAY
******	BOTH	**BU--**	BYES	CASE	CHEE
BOAR	BOTS	******	BYRD	CASH	CHEF
BOAS	BOTT	BUBO	BYRE	CASK	CHEM
BOAT	BOUT	BUBS	******	CASS	CHES
BOAZ	BOUW	BUCK	**CA--**	CAST	CHET
BOBS	BOVI	BUDD	******	CATA	CHEW
BOCK	BOWL	BUDS	CABS	CATE	CHEZ
BODE	BOWS	BUFF	CACO	CATH	CHGD
BODY	BOYD	BUGS	CADE	CATO	CHGS
BOER	BOYS	BUHL	CADI	CATS	CHIA
BOGS	BOZO	BULB	CADS	CAUK	CHIC
BOGY	******	BULE	CAEN	CAUL	CHID
BOHR	**BR--**	BULG	CAFE	CAVA	CHIH
BOIL	******	BULK	CAGE	CAVE	CHIL
BOIS	BRAD	BULL	CAGY	CAVY	CHIN
BOLA	BRAE	BUMP	CAIN	CAWS	CHIP
BOLD	BRAG	BUMS	CAKE	CAYS	CHIR
BOLE	BRAN	BUNA	CALF	CAZI	CHIS
BOLL	BRAS	BUND	CALI	******	CHIT
BOLO	BRAT	BUNG	CALK	**CE--**	CHOL
BOLT	BRAW	BUNK	CALL	******	CHOP
BOMB	BRAY	BUNN	CALM	CEBA	CHOU
BONA	BRAZ	BUNS	CALX	CEBU	CHOW
BOND	BREA	BUNT	CAMB	CECA	CHUB
BONE	BRED	BUOY	CAME	CEDE	CHUD
BONG	BREN	BURD	CAMP	CEES	CHUG
BONI	BRER	BURG	CAMS	CEIL	CHUM
BONK	BRET	BURL	CANA	CELE	CHUR
BONN	BREV	BURN	CANC	CELL	******
BONO	BREW	BURP	CANE	CELT	**CI--**
BONY	BRIE	BURR	CANS	CENE	******
BOOB	BRIG	BURS	CANT	CENO	CIDE
BOOK	BRIM	BURT	CAPA	CENT	CIEL
BOOM	BRIO	BURY	CAPE	CEPA	CINE
BOON	BRIT	BUSH	CAPP	CERE	CION
BOOR	BRNO	BUSK	CAPS	CERO	CIRC
BOOS	BROM	BUSS	CAPT	CERT	CIST
BOOT	BRON	BUST	CARA	CESS	CITE
BOPS	BROO	BUSY	CARB	CEST	CITY

******	COEL	CORE	CUBS	DADS	DEAL
CL--	COGS	CORF	CUDS	DAFF	DEAN
******	COHO	CORK	CUED	DAFT	DEAR
CLAD	COIF	CORM	CUES	DAGO	DEBS
CLAM	COIL	CORN	CUFF	DAGS	DEBT
CLAN	COIN	CORP	CUIR	DAIL	DECA
CLAP	COIR	COSH	CULE	DAIS	DECD
CLAR	COKE	COSM	CULL	DAKS	DECI
CLAW	COLA	COSS	CULM	DALE	DECK
CLAY	COLD	COST	CULT	DALI	DEED
CLEE	COLE	COSY	CUPR	DAME	DEEM
CLEF	COLL	COTE	CUPS	DAMN	DEEP
CLEG	COLO	COTS	CURB	DAMP	DEER
CLEM	COLS	COTY	CURD	DAMS	DEES
CLEO	COLT	COUE	CURE	DANA	DEFI
CLEW	COLY	COUP	CURL	DANE	DEFT
CLIO	COMA	COVE	CURS	DANG	DEFY
CLIP	COMB	COWL	CURT	DANK	DEGO
CLOD	COME	COWS	CUSH	DANS	DEIL
CLOG	COMM	COXA	CUSK	DANU	DEJA
CLON	COMO	COZY	CUSP	DAPA	DEKA
CLOP	COMP	******	CUSS	DAPS	DEKE
CLOT	COMR	**CR--**	CUTE	DARB	DELE
CLOY	CONC	******	CUTS	DARE	DELF
CLUB	COND	CRAB	CUYA	DARK	DELI
CLUE	CONE	CRAG	******	DARN	DELL
CLUJ	CONF	CRAM	**CY--**	DART	DEME
******	CONG	CRAN	******	DASH	DEMI
CM--	CONJ	CRAP	CYAN	DATA	DEMO
******	CONK	CRAT	CYCL	DATE	DEMY
CMDR	CONN	CRAW	CYMA	DAUB	DENE
******	CONS	CREE	CYME	DAVE	DENS
CO--	CONT	CRES	CYMO	DAVY	DENT
******	CONY	CREW	CYST	DAWK	DENY
COAL	COOK	CRIB	CYTE	DAWM	DEPA
COAT	COOL	CRIT	CYTO	DAWN	DEPT
COAX	COON	CROP	******	DAWS	DERM
COBB	COOP	CROW	**CZ--**	DAYS	DESC
COBS	COOS	CRUD	******	DAZA	DESI
COCA	COOT	CRUS	CZAR	DAZE	DESK
COCK	COPA	CRUX	******	******	DESL
COCO	COPE	CRYO	******	**DD--**	DESS
CODA	COPR	******	**DA--**	******	DEUS
CODE	COPS	**CT--**	******	DDAY	DEUT
CODS	COPT	******	DABS	******	DEVA
CODY	COPY	CTEN	DACE	**DE--**	DEVI
COED	CORA	******	DADA	******	ꓱEVS
COEF	CORD	**CU--**	DADE	DEAD	DEWS
		******	DADO	DEAF	
		CUBA			
		CUBE			

DEWY	DIRK	DORM	DUDS	EARS	******
DEYS	DIRT	DORP	DUEL	EASE	EF--
******	DISC	DORR	DUES	EAST	******
DH--	DISH	DORS	DUET	EASY	EFFS
******	DISK	DORY	DUFF	EATS	EFIK
DHAI	DIST	DOSE	DUGS	EAUX	EFTS
DHAK	DITA	DOSS	DUIM	******	******
DHAL	DIVA	DOST	DUIT	EB--	EG--
DHAN	DIVE	DOTE	DUKE	******	******
DHAR	DIVI	DOTH	DULL	EBAN	EGAD
DHOW	******	DOTS	DULY	EBBS	EGAN
******	DM--	DOTY	DUMA	EBEN	EGER
DI--	******	DOUG	DUMB	EBON	EGGS
******	DMUS	DOUR	DUMP	EBRO	EGOS
DIAG	******	DOVE	DUNA	******	******
DIAL	DO--	DOWN	DUNE	EC--	EI--
DIAM	******	DOXY	DUNG	******	******
DIAN	DOBY	DOZE	DUNK	ECCL	EIRE
DIAS	DOCK	DOZY	DUNS	ECHO	******
DIAZ	DODO	******	DUNT	ECHT	EK--
DIBS	DOER	DR--	DUOS	ECOL	******
DICE	DOES	******	DUPE	ECON	EKED
DICH	DOFF	DRAB	DURA	ECRU	EKES
DICK	DOGE	DRAG	DURN	ECTO	******
DIDO	DOGS	DRAH	DURO	ECUA	EL--
DIDY	DOGY	DRAM	DURR	ECUS	******
DIED	DOIT	DRAT	DUSE	******	ELAM
DIES	DOLA	DRAW	DUSK	ED--	ELAN
DIET	DOLE	DRAY	DUST	******	ELBA
DIEU	DOLF	DREW	DUTY	EDAM	ELBE
DIGS	DOLL	DRIB	******	EDDA	ELEC
DIKE	DOLS	DRIN	DY--	EDDY	ELEM
DILI	DOLT	DRIP	******	EDEN	ELEO
DILL	DOMA	DROP	DYAD	EDER	ELEV
DILO	DOME	DRUB	DYAK	EDGE	ELIA
DIME	DOMS	DRUG	DYAN	EDGY	ELIS
DIMS	DONA	DRUM	DYED	EDHS	ELKE
DINA	DONE	******	DYER	EDIE	ELKS
DINE	DONS	DU--	DYES	EDIT	ELLA
DING	DONT	******	DYKE	EDNA	ELLS
DINO	DOOM	DUAD	DYNA	EDOM	ELMA
DINS	DOON	DUAL	DYNE	EDUC	ELMO
DINT	DOOR	DUAR	******	******	ELMS
DION	DOPE	DUBS	EA--	EE--	ELMY
DIOS	DOPP	DUCE	******	******	ELSA
DIPL	DOPY	DUCK	EACH	EELS	ELSE
DIPS	DORA	DUCT	EARL	EELY	ELST
DIRE	DORE	DUDE	EARN	EENS	ELUL
				EERY	ELVA

******	ERDA	EVEN	FADS	FENS	FLAM
EM--	ERGO	EVER	FAGS	FEOD	FLAN
******	ERGS	EVES	FAIL	FERN	FLAP
EMEU	ERIA	EVIL	FAIN	FESS	FLAT
EMIA	ERIC	EVOE	FAIR	FEST	FLAW
EMIL	ERIE	******	FAKE	FETE	FLAX
EMIR	ERIK	**EW--**	FALA	FEUD	FLAY
EMIT	ERIN	******	FALL	FEUS	FLEA
EMMA	ERIS	EWAN	FAME	******	FLED
EMMY	ERLE	EWER	FAMN	**FI--**	FLEE
EMUS	ERMA	EWES	FANE	******	FLEM
******	ERNE	******	FANG	FIAT	FLEW
EN--	ERNS	**EX--**	FANO	FIBR	FLEX
******	EROS	******	FANS	FIBS	FLIP
ENCE	ERRS	EXAM	FARE	FICA	FLIT
ENCL	ERSE	EXCH	FARL	FICE	FLOC
ENCY	ERST	EXCL	FARM	FICO	FLOE
ENDO	******	EXEC	FARO	FIDS	FLOG
ENDS	**ES--**	EXES	FASH	FIEF	FLOP
ENGR	******	EXIT	FASS	FIFE	FLOR
ENID	ESAU	EXOD	FAST	FIGS	FLOT
ENNA	ESCE	EXON	FATA	FIJI	FLOW
ENNS	ESNE	******	FATE	FILA	FLUB
ENOL	ESPY	**EY--**	FATS	FILE	FLUE
ENOS	ESSE	******	FAUN	FILL	FLUO
ENOW	ESTE	EYAS	FAWN	FILM	FLUX
ENTE	ESTH	EYED	FAYE	FILO	******
ENTO	******	EYES	FAYS	FILS	**FM--**
ENVY	**ET--**	EYOT	FAZE	FIND	******
ENYO	******	EYRA	******	FINE	FMCS
******	ETAH	EYRE	**FD--**	FINK	******
EO--	ETAL	EYRY	******	FINN	**FN--**
******	ETAS	******	FDIC	FINS	******
EONS	ETCH	**EZ--**	******	FIRE	FNMA
EOUS	ETHN	******	**FE--**	FIRM	******
******	ETHS	EZBA	******	FIRN	**FO--**
EP--	ETNA	EZEK	FEAR	FIRS	******
******	ETON	EZRA	FEAT	FISC	FOAL
EPEE	ETTA	******	FEBR	FISH	FOAM
EPIC	ETTE	**FA--**	FEED	FIST	FOBS
EPOS	ETUI	******	FEEL	FITS	FOCH
******	******	FAAM	FEES	FITZ	FOCI
EQ--	**EU--**	FACE	FEET	FIVE	FOES
******	******	FACP	FELL	FIZZ	FOGS
EQUI	EURO	FACS	FELS	******	FOGY
******	EURY	FACT	FELT	**FL--**	FOHN
ER--	******	FADE	FEME	******	FOIL
******	**EV--**	FADO	FEND	FLAG	FOLD
ERAL	******			FLAK	
ERAS	EVAN				
	EVAS				

FOLK	FUJI	GAMS	GENT	GLEE	GOOF
FOLL	FULA	GAMY	GENU	GLEN	GOOK
FOND	FULL	GANG	GENY	GLIB	GOON
FONG	FUME	GAOL	GEOL	GLIM	GOOP
FONT	FUMY	GAPE	GEOM	GLOB	GORE
FOOD	FUND	GAPS	GERA	GLOT	GORY
FOOL	FUNG	GAPY	GERD	GLOW	GOSH
FOOT	FUNK	GARA	GERI	GLUE	GOTH
FOPS	FUNS	GARB	GERM	GLUM	GOUT
FORA	FURL	GARD	GEST	GLUT	GOVT
FORB	FURN	GARE	GETS	******	GOWK
FORD	FURS	GARM	******	**GM--**	GOWL
FORE	FURY	GARS	**GH--**	******	GOWN
FORK	FUSE	GARY	******	GMAN	GOYA
FORM	FUSS	GASH	GHAT	GMEN	******
FORT	FUYE	GASP	GHEE	******	**GR--**
FOSS	FUZE	GATA	******	**GN--**	******
FOUL	FUZZ	GATE	**GI--**	******	GRAB
FOUR	******	GATH	******	GNAR	GRAD
FOWL	**FY--**	GATS	GIBE	GNAT	GRAF
FOXY	******	GATT	GIBS	GNAW	GRAM
FOYS	FYKE	GAUD	GIDE	GNUS	GRAO
******	******	GAUL	GIED	******	GRAY
FR--	**GA--**	GAUR	GIFT	**GO--**	GRAZ
******	******	GAVE	GIFU	******	GREG
FRAE	GABE	GAWK	GIGA	GOAD	GREW
FRAN	GABS	GAYA	GIGS	GOAL	GREY
FRAP	GABY	GAYS	GILA	GOAR	GRID
FRAS	GADS	GAZA	GILD	GOAS	GRIG
FRAT	GAEA	GAZE	GILL	GOAT	GRIM
FRAU	GAEL	******	GILS	GOBI	GRIN
FRAY	GAFF	**GE--**	GILT	GOBO	GRIP
FREA	GAGA	******	GIMP	GOBS	GRIS
FRED	GAGE	GEAR	GINA	GOBY	GRIT
FREE	GAGS	GECK	GINK	GODS	GROG
FREQ	GAIA	GEED	GINS	GOER	GROS
FRET	GAIL	GEEK	GIPS	GOES	GROT
FREY	GAIN	GEES	GIRD	GOGH	GROW
FRIO	GAIT	GEEZ	GIRL	GOGO	GRUB
FRIT	GALA	GELD	GIRO	GOLD	GRUM
FROE	GALE	GELS	GIRT	GOLF	******
FROG	GALL	GELT	GIST	GOLO	**GU--**
FROM	GALS	GEMS	GIVE	GOMA	******
FROT	GAMA	GENE	GIZA	GOND	GUAM
FROW	GAMB	GENF	******	GONE	GUAN
******	GAME	GENG	**GL--**	GONG	GUAO
FU--	GAMO	GENL	******	GONO	GUAT
******	GAMP	GENS	GLAD	GOOD	GUCK
FUCI			GLED		
FUEL					

GUFF	HAIK	******	HIED	HOMS	HUME
GUHA	HAIL	**HE--**	HIER	HOMY	HUMP
GUIN	HAIR	******	HIES	HOND	HUMS
GULF	HAKA	HEAD	HIFI	HONE	HUNG
GULL	HAKE	HEAL	HIGH	HONG	HUNK
GULP	HAKU	HEAP	HIKE	HONK	HUNS
GUMI	HALE	HEAR	HILL	HOOD	HUNT
GUMS	HALF	HEAT	HILO	HOOF	HUPA
GUNS	HALL	HEBE	HILT	HOOK	HURL
GURU	HALM	HEBR	HIND	HOON	HURT
GUSH	HALO	HECK	HINO	HOOP	HUSH
GUST	HALS	HECT	HINT	HOOT	HUSK
GUTS	HALT	HEED	HIPE	HOPE	HUSS
GUYS	HAMA	HEEL	HIPP	HOPI	HUTS
******	HAME	HEFT	HIPS	HOPS	******
GW--	HAMS	HEHE	HIRE	HORA	**HW--**
******	HAND	HEIR	HIRO	HORN	******
GWEN	HANG	HELD	HISS	HORT	HWAI
GWIN	HANK	HELI	HIST	HOSE	HWAN
GWYN	HANS	HELL	HITS	HOST	******
******	HAPL	HELM	HIVE	HOTE	**HY--**
GY--	HARD	HELP	******	HOTH	******
******	HARE	HEMA	**HL--**	HOTI	HYAL
GYBE	HARK	HEME	******	HOUR	HYDE
GYMN	HARL	HEMI	HLER	HOVE	HYDR
GYMS	HARM	HEML	******	HOWE	HYET
GYNO	HARP	HEMO	**HO--**	HOWL	HYGR
GYOR	HART	HEMP	******	HOYS	HYLA
GYPS	HARZ	HEMS	HOAR	******	HYLO
GYRE	HASH	HENS	HOAX	**HR--**	HYMN
GYRI	HASP	HEPT	HOBO	******	HYPO
GYRO	HAST	HERA	HOBS	HRIP	******
GYVE	HATE	HERB	HOCK	HRON	**IA--**
******	HATH	HERD	HODS	******	******
HA--	HATS	HERE	HOED	**HU--**	IADB
******	HAUL	HERL	HOEN	******	IAGO
HAAF	HAVE	HERM	HOER	HUBS	IAMB
HABE	HAWK	HERO	HOES	HUCK	IANA
HABU	HAWS	HERR	HOGG	HUED	IANS
HACK	HAYA	HERS	HOGS	HUES	******
HADE	HAYS	HEST	HOLD	HUFF	**IB--**
HADJ	HAZE	HETH	HOLE	HUGE	******
HAFT	HAZY	HEWN	HOLM	HUGH	IBEX
HAGI	******	HEWS	HOLO	HUGO	IBID
HAGS	**HD--**	HEXA	HOLT	HUGS	IBIS
HAHA	******	******	HOLY	HULA	IBLE
HAHN	******	**HI--**	HOME	HULK	**IC--**
HAHS	HDBK	******	HOMO	HULL	******
		HICK			ICAL
		HIDE			ICBM

ICED	******	******	******	JEER	JOBO
ICEL	**IM--**	**IR--**	**IZ--**	JEES	JOBS
ICER	******	******	******	JEFE	JOCK
ICES	IMAM	IRAK	IZAR	JEFF	JODO
ICON	IMAN	IRAN	IZZY	JEHU	JOEL
******	IMID	IRAQ	******	JELL	JOES
ID--	IMIN	IRAS	**JA--**	JEMS	JOEY
******	IMMI	IRBM	******	JENA	JOGS
IDAE	IMMY	IRID	JABS	JERK	JOHN
IDAS	IMPI	IRIS	JACA	JERL	JOIN
IDEA	IMPS	IRKS	JACK	JERM	JOKE
IDEM	******	IRMA	JADE	JESS	JOLA
IDEO	**IN--**	IRON	JAEN	JEST	JOLO
IDES	******	IRRA	JAGA	JESU	JOLT
IDFU	INAS	******	JAGG	JETE	JONS
IDIO	INCA	**IS--**	JAGS	JETH	JOOK
IDLE	INCH	******	JAIL	JETS	JOSE
IDLY	INCL	ISAR	JAIN	JEUX	JOSH
IDOL	INDO	ISBA	JAKE	JEWS	JOSS
IDYL	INEE	ISER	JAKO	******	JOTS
******	INEZ	ISIS	JAMA	**JH--**	JOUG
IF--	INFO	ISLE	JAMB	******	JOUY
******	INGA	ISMS	JAMI	JHOW	JOVE
IFFY	INGE	ISNT	JAMS	******	JOWL
IFIL	INIA	ISSY	JANE	**JI--**	JOYS
IFNI	INIT	******	JANN	******	******
******	INKS	**IT--**	JANS	JIBE	**JU--**
IG--	INKY	******	JAOB	JIBI	******
******	INLY	ITAL	JAPE	JIBS	JUAN
IGLU	INNS	ITCH	JARA	JIFF	JUBA
IGNI	INRE	ITEA	JARL	JIGS	JUBE
******	INRI	ITEM	JARS	JILL	JUCA
IK--	INRO	ITER	JASS	JILT	JUDE
******	INSP	ITOL	JATH	JIMS	JUDO
IKES	INST	ITYS	JATO	JIND	JUDY
IKON	INTO	******	JAVA	JINK	JUGS
IKWE	******	**IV--**	JAVE	JINN	JUJU
******	**IO--**	******	JAWS	JINX	JULE
IL--	******	IVAN	JAYS	JIVE	JULY
******	IOBB	IVES	JAZZ	******	JUMP
ILEA	IODO	IVOR	******	**JO--**	JUNC
ILEO	IOLE	IVYS	**JE--**	******	JUNE
ILEX	IONA	******	******	JOAB	JUNG
ILIA	IONS	**IX--**	JEAN	JOAD	JUNK
ILKA	IOTA	******	JEBU	JOAH	JUNO
ILLS	IOUS	IXIA	JEED	JOAN	JURA
ILLY	IOWA	******	JEEL	JOAR	JURY
ILSE		**IY--**	JEEP	JOAT	JUST
ILUS		******			
		IYAR			

JUTE	******	KILN	KOHL	LAHR	LEAH
JUTS	**KE--**	KILO	KOKO	LAIC	LEAK
******	******	KILT	KOLA	LAID	LEAL
KA--	KEAS	KIND	KOLN	LAIN	LEAN
******	KECK	KINE	KOOK	LAIR	LEAP
KAAS	KEEF	KING	KOPH	LAIT	LEAR
KABS	KEEK	KINK	KOPI	LAKE	LEAS
KADA	KEEL	KINO	KOPS	LAKH	LEDA
KADE	KEEN	KIPE	KORS	LAKY	LEDE
KADI	KEEP	KIPS	KOSS	LALL	LEEK
KAGU	KEFS	KIRI	KOTO	LAMA	LEER
KAHA	KEGS	KIRK	******	LAMB	LEES
KAID	KEIR	KISH	**KR--**	LAME	LEET
KAIF	KELA	KISS	******	LAMP	LEFT
KAIL	KELP	KIST	KRAL	LAMS	LEGS
KAIN	KELT	KITE	KRIS	LANA	LEHR
KAKA	KEMP	KITH	******	LAND	LEIF
KAKI	KENO	KITS	**KU--**	LANE	LEIS
KALA	KENS	KITT	******	LANG	LEKS
KALE	KENT	KIVA	KUDU	LANK	LEMS
KALI	KEOS	KIVU	KUNK	LAON	LENA
KAMA	KEPI	KIWI	KURA	LAOS	LEND
KAME	KEPT	******	KURD	LAPP	LENE
KAMI	KERB	**KL--**	KURE	LAPS	LENO
KANA	KERF	******	KURT	LARA	LENS
KANE	KERN	KLAM	******	LARD	LENT
KANO	KETO	KLEE	**KV--**	LARI	LEON
KANS	KETU	******	******	LARK	LEOS
KANT	KEYS	**KN--**	KVAS	LARP	LEPT
KAON	******	******	******	LARS	LESS
KAPA	**KH--**	KNAG	**KY--**	LASH	LEST
KAPH	******	KNAP	******	LASS	LETI
KARA	KHAN	KNAR	KYAT	LAST	LETO
KARI	KHAT	KNEE	KYLE	LATE	LETS
KARL	KHET	KNEW	******	LATH	LETT
KARN	******	KNIT	**LA--**	LATI	LEUC
KARY	**KI--**	KNOB	******	LAUD	LEUD
KASM	******	KNOP	LABS	LAUN	LEUK
KATE	KIAK	KNOT	LACE	LAVA	LEVA
KATY	KIBE	KNOW	LACK	LAVE	LEVI
KAVA	KICK	KNOX	LACT	LAWN	LEVO
KAWA	KIDD	KNUR	LACY	LAWS	LEVY
KAYE	KIDS	******	LADD	LAYS	LEWD
KAYO	KIEL	**KO--**	LADE	LAZE	LEWS
KAYS	KIER	******	LADS	LAZY	******
KAZI	KIEV	KOAE	LADY	******	**LI--**
******	KIHO	KOBE	LAFE	**LE--**	******
KC--	KILL	KOEL	LAGS	******	LIAO
******				LEAD	LIAR
KCAL				LEAF	

LICE	******	LOST	******	MANE	MEEK
LICH	**LO--**	LOTE	**LY--**	MANI	MEET
LICK	******	LOTH	******	MANN	MEGA
LIDO	LOAD	LOTS	LYES	MANO	MEGS
LIDS	LOAF	LOTT	LYLE	MANS	MEIO
LIED	LOAM	LOUD	LYME	MANX	MEIR
LIEF	LOAN	LOUP	LYNN	MANY	MELD
LIEN	LOBE	LOUR	LYNX	MAPS	MELE
LIES	LOBO	LOUT	LYRA	MARA	MELS
LIEU	LOBS	LOVE	LYRE	MARC	MELT
LIFE	LOCH	LOWS	LYSE	MARE	MEMO
LIFT	LOCI	******	LYSI	MARJ	MEMS
LIGN	LOCK	**LU--**	LYTE	MARK	MEND
LIKE	LOCO	******	LYZE	MARL	MENE
LILA	LODE	LUAU	******	MARS	MENI
LILS	LODI	LUBA	**MA--**	MART	MENO
LILT	LODZ	LUBE	******	MARX	MENT
LILY	LOFT	LUCE	MAAL	MARY	MENU
LIMA	LOGE	LUCK	MAAM	MASC	MEOW
LIMB	LOGO	LUCY	MAAS	MASH	MERE
LIME	LOGS	LUDO	MABS	MASK	MERL
LIMN	LOGY	LUES	MACE	MASS	MERO
LIMP	LOIN	LUFF	MACH	MAST	MERU
LIMU	LOIS	LUGE	MACK	MATE	MERV
LIMY	LOKE	LUGS	MACS	MATH	MESA
LINA	LOKI	LUIS	MADE	MATS	MESH
LIND	LOLA	LUIZ	MADS	MATT	MESO
LINE	LOLL	LUKE	MAES	MAUD	MESS
LING	LOMA	LULL	MAGE	MAUI	META
LINK	LOME	LULU	MAGI	MAUL	METE
LINN	LONE	LUMP	MAHA	MAUN	METH
LINO	LONG	LUNA	MAIA	MAWS	METR
LINT	LOOD	LUNE	MAID	MAXI	METZ
LINY	LOOF	LUNG	MAIL	MAYA	MEWL
LINZ	LOOK	LUNI	MAIM	MAYO	MEWS
LION	LOOM	LUNT	MAIN	MAYS	******
LIPO	LOON	LUPE	MAJO	MAZE	**MH--**
LIPS	LOOP	LURE	MAKA	MAZY	******
LIRA	LOOS	LURI	MAKE	******	MHOS
LIRE	LOOT	LURK	MAKO	**ME--**	******
LISA	LOPE	LUSH	MALE	******	**MI--**
LISP	LOPS	LUST	MALI	MEAD	******
LISS	LORD	LUTA	MALL	MEAH	MIBS
LIST	LORE	LUTE	MALM	MEAL	MICA
LITE	LORN	LUTH	MALO	MEAN	MICE
LITH	LORY	LUXE	MALT	MEAT	MICH
LIVE	LOSE	******	MAMA	MEDE	MICK
LIZA	LOSS	**LW--**	MANA	MEDI	MIDI
		******			
		LWOW			

MIEN	MOAS	MOVE	******	******	NICK
MIFF	MOAT	MOWN	**MZ--**	**NC--**	NIDE
MIGS	MOBS	MOWS	******	******	NIDI
MIKE	MOCK	MOXA	MZAB	NCAA	NIEL
MILD	MODE	******	******	NCAR	NIGH
MILE	MODI	**MS--**	**NA--**	******	NIGR
MILK	MODS	******	******	**ND--**	NIKE
MILL	MOES	MSGR	NABO	******	NILE
MILO	MOHO	MSGT	NABS	NDAK	NIMB
MILS	MOHR	MSTH	NADA	******	NINA
MILT	MOIL	MSTS	NAEL	**NE--**	NINE
MIME	MOIO	******	NAGA	******	NINO
MIMI	MOJO	**MU--**	NAGS	NEAL	NIPA
MINA	MOKE	******	NAHA	NEAP	NIPS
MIND	MOKI	MUCH	NAIF	NEAR	NISI
MINE	MOLD	MUCI	NAIL	NEAT	NITA
MING	MOLE	MUCK	NAIN	NEBO	NITR
MINI	MOLL	MUCO	NAIS	NEBS	NITS
MINK	MOLT	MUDS	NAJA	NECK	NIUE
MINN	MOLY	MUFF	NALU	NECR	******
MINT	MOMO	MUGS	NAMA	NEDS	**NK--**
MINX	MOMS	MUIR	NAME	NEED	******
MIRA	MONA	MULE	NANA	NEER	NKVD
MIRE	MONK	MULL	NANO	NEIL	******
MIRO	MONO	MULT	NANS	NEJD	**NL--**
MIRS	MONS	MUMM	NAOS	NELL	******
MIRV	MONT	MUMS	NAPA	NEMA	NLRB
MIRY	MOOD	MUON	NAPE	NEMO	******
MISC	MOON	MURK	NAPS	NENE	**NO--**
MISE	MOOR	MUSE	NARC	NEON	******
MISO	MOOS	MUSH	NARD	NEPH	NOAH
MISS	MOOT	MUSK	NARY	NERO	NOBS
MIST	MOPE	MUSS	NASA	NESS	NOCK
MITE	MOPS	MUST	NASH	NEST	NOCT
MITT	MORA	MUTE	NASO	NETS	NODE
MIXT	MORE	MUTH	NAST	NEUM	NODS
******	MORN	MUTS	NATE	NEUR	NOEL
ML--	MORO	MUTT	NATL	NEVE	NOES
******	MORS	******	NATO	NEVI	NOGG
MLLE	MORT	**MY--**	NATR	NEWS	NOGO
******	MOSE	******	NATS	NEWT	NOGS
MM--	MOSS	MYCO	NATT	NEXT	NOIL
******	MOST	MYEL	NAUT	******	NOMA
MMES	MOTE	MYNA	NAVE	**NG--**	NOME
******	MOTH	MYRA	NAVY	******	NOMO
MO--	MOTS	MYRI	NAWA	NGAN	NOMY
******	MOTT	MYTH	NAYS	******	NONA
MOAB	MOUE	MYXA	NAZE	**NI--**	NONE
MOAN		MYXO	NAZI	******	
				NIBS	
				NICE	

NOOK	OBIS	OINO	ONON	OSSA	PACA
NOON	OBIT	OISE	ONTO	OSSI	PACE
NOPE	OBOE	******	ONUS	OSTE	PACK
NORA	OBOL	**OK--**	ONYX	******	PACO
NORD	******	******	ONZA	**OT--**	PACT
NORM	**OC--**	OKAS	******	******	PADS
NORN	******	OKAY	**OO--**	OTEA	PAED
NOSE	OCHA	OKED	******	OTIC	PAGE
NOSH	OCRA	OKET	OONA	OTIS	PAHA
NOSO	OCTA	OKIE	OOZE	OTOE	PAID
NOSY	OCTO	OKLA	OOZY	OTTO	PAIL
NOTE	OCUL	OKRA	******	******	PAIN
NOTO	******	******	**OP--**	**OU--**	PAIR
NOTT	**OD--**	**OL--**	******	******	PAIS
NOUN	******	******	OPAH	OUCH	PALA
NOUS	ODAL	OLAF	OPAL	OURS	PALE
NOVA	ODDS	OLAV	OPEN	OUSE	PALI
NOWS	ODEA	OLAY	OPHI	OUST	PALL
NOWT	ODER	OLEO	OPIA	OUTS	PALM
******	ODES	OLGA	OPSY	******	PALP
NU--	ODIC	OLIG	OPTS	**OV--**	PALS
******	ODIN	OLIO	OPUS	******	PALY
NUBS	ODOR	OLLA	******	OVAL	PAMS
NUDE	ODUM	OLLY	**OR--**	OVEN	PANE
NUDI	ODYL	OLOR	******	OVER	PANG
NULL	******	OLPE	ORAL	OVID	PANK
NUMB	**OE--**	OLST	ORAN	OVUM	PANS
NUNS	******	******	ORBS	******	PANT
NUTS	OENO	**OM--**	ORCA	**OW--**	PAPA
******	OEUF	******	ORCS	******	PAPS
NY--	******	OMAN	ORDO	OWED	PARA
******	**OG--**	OMAR	OREL	OWEN	PARD
NYET	******	OMBR	ORES	OWES	PARE
******	OGEE	OMEI	ORGY	OWLS	PARI
OA--	OGLE	OMEN	ORIG	OWNS	PARK
******	OGPU	OMER	ORLE	******	PARR
OAFS	OGRE	OMIT	ORLY	**OX--**	PARS
OAHU	******	OMNI	ORNE	******	PART
OAKS	**OH--**	OMSK	ORTH	OXEN	PASH
OARS	******	******	ORTS	OXON	PASS
OAST	OHIA	**ON--**	ORYX	******	PAST
OATH	OHIO	******	******	**OY--**	PATE
OATS	OHMS	ONCA	**OS--**	******	PATH
******	******	ONCE	******	OYER	PATS
OB--	**OI--**	ONDO	OSAR	OYES	PAUL
******	******	ONER	OSEL	OYEZ	PAVE
OBEY	OILS	ONES	OSIS	******	PAVO
OBIA	OILY	ONLY	OSLO	**PA--**	PAWL
				******	
				PAAL	
				PABA	

PAWN	PETR	PION	PODE	PRAO	PUNT
PAWS	PETS	PIOT	PODS	PRAY	PUNY
PAYE	PEWS	PIPA	POEM	PREP	PUPA
PAYS	******	PIPE	POET	PRES	PUPS
******	**PH--**	PIPS	POGO	PREY	PURE
PE--	******	PIPY	POGY	PRIG	PURI
******	PHAG	PIRN	POKE	PRIM	PURL
PEAG	PHDS	PISA	POKU	PROA	PURR
PEAK	PHEN	PISC	POKY	PROD	PUSH
PEAL	PHEW	PISH	POLE	PROF	PUSS
PEAN	PHIL	PISO	POLK	PROM	PUTS
PEAR	PHIS	PITA	POLL	PRON	PUTT
PEAS	PHON	PITH	POLO	PROP	PUUD
PEAT	PHOT	PITO	POLY	PROS	******
PECK	PHUD	PITS	POME	PROT	**PY--**
PECO	PHUT	PITT	POMP	PROW	******
PEDE	PHYL	PITY	POND	PRUE	PYAT
PEDI	PHYT	PIUS	PONE	******	PYEL
PEDO	******	PIXY	PONG	**PS--**	PYES
PEEK	**PI--**	PIZZ	PONS	******	PYET
PEEL	******	******	PONY	PSHA	PYIC
PEEN	PIAF	**PL--**	POOD	PSIS	PYIN
PEEP	PIAY	******	POOH	******	PYLE
PEER	PICA	PLAN	POOK	**PT--**	PYOT
PEES	PICE	PLAT	POOL	******	PYRE
PEGS	PICK	PLAY	POON	PTAH	PYRO
PELE	PICO	PLEA	POOP	PTER	******
PELF	PICR	PLEB	POOR	******	**QA--**
PELT	PICT	PLED	POPE	**PU--**	******
PELU	PIED	PLEW	POPS	******	QAIS
PEND	PIER	PLOD	PORE	PUBS	******
PENN	PIES	PLOP	PORK	PUCE	**QO--**
PENS	PIGS	PLOT	PORN	PUCK	******
PENT	PIKA	PLOW	PORT,	PUFF	QOPH
PEON	PIKE	PLOY	POSE	PUGH	******
PEPO	PIKI	PLUG	POSH	PUGS	**QU--**
PEPS	PILE	PLUM	POST	PUKA	******
PERA	PILI	PLUS	POSY	PUKE	QUAB
PERE	PILL	******	POTS	PULE	QUAD
PERI	PIMA	**PN--**	POUF	PULL	QUAG
PERK	PIMP	******	POUR	PULP	QUAI
PERM	PINA	PNYX	POUT	PUMA	QUAN
PERN	PINE	******	POWS	PUMP	QUAR
PERT	PING	**PO--**	******	PUNA	QUAT
PERU	PINK	******	**PR--**	PUND	QUAY
PESO	PINS	POCK	******	PUNG	QUEI
PEST	PINT	POCO	PRAE	PUNK	QUID
PETE	PINY	PODA	PRAM	PUNS	QUIP

QUIT	RASA	RENO	RIOT	ROTE	RUTA
QUIZ	RASE	RENT	RIPA	ROTI	RUTE
QUNG	RASH	REPP	RIPE	ROTL	RUTH
QUOD	RASP	REPS	RIPS	ROTS	RUTS
******	RATA	RESH	RISE	ROUE	******
RA--	RATE	REST	RISK	ROUP	**RY--**
******	RATH	RETE	RITA	ROUT	******
RAAB	RATI	RETS	RITE	ROUX	RYAN
RAAD	RATO	REVS	RIVA	ROVE	RYES
RABA	RATS	******	RIVE	ROWS	RYND
RACE	RAVE	**RH--**	RIVO	ROXY	RYOT
RACK	RAYS	******	******	ROYS	******
RACY	RAZE	RHEA	**RO--**	******	**SA--**
RADA	RAZZ	RHEO	******	**RS--**	******
RADS	******	RHIN	ROAD	******	SAAH
RAES	**RC--**	RHIZ	ROAM	RSVP	SAAR
RAFF	******	RHOB	ROAN	******	SABE
RAFT	RCMP	RHOS	ROAR	**RU--**	SABS
RAGA	******	RHUM	ROBE	******	SACK
RAGE	**RE--**	RHUS	ROBS	RUAY	SACS
RAGI	******	RHYL	ROCK	RUBE	SADE
RAGS	READ	RHYS	RODE	RUBS	SADH
RAHU	REAL	******	RODS	RUBY	SADI
RAID	REAM	**RI--**	ROES	RUCK	SAFE
RAIK	REAP	******	ROIL	RUDD	SAGA
RAIL	REAR	RIAL	ROLE	RUDE	SAGE
RAIN	REBA	RIBS	ROLF	RUDY	SAGO
RAJA	REBS	RICE	ROLL	RUED	SAGS
RAKE	RECK	RICH	ROMA	RUER	SAGY
RAKI	RECT	RICK	ROME	RUES	SAHH
RALE	REDE	RIDE	ROMP	RUFE	SAIC
RALL	REDO	RIDS	ROMS	RUFF	SAID
RALO	REDS	RIEN	RONA	RUGA	SAIL
RAMA	REED	RIFE	ROOD	RUGS	SAIS
RAME	REEF	RIFF	ROOF	RUHR	SAKE
RAMI	REEK	RIGA	ROOK	RUIN	SAKI
RAMP	REEL	RIGS	ROOM	RULE	SALE
RAMS	REFT	RIIS	ROOP	RUMP	SALK
RANA	REIN	RIJN	ROOT	RUMS	SALP
RAND	REIS	RILE	ROPE	RUNE	SALT
RANG	RELY	RILL	ROPY	RUNG	SAMA
RANI	REMI	RIME	RORY	RUNS	SAME
RANK	REMO	RIMS	ROSA	RUNT	SAMP
RANT	REMS	RIMY	ROSE	RUSE	SAMS
RAPE	RENA	RIND	ROSS	RUSH	SANA
RAPS	REND	RING	ROSY	RUSK	SAND
RAPT	RENE	RINK	ROTA	RUSS	SANE
RARE	RENI		ROTC	RUST	SANG

SANK	SEAN	SHAH	SING	SLEW	SOAR
SANS	SEAR	SHAM	SINK	SLID	SOBS
SAPE	SEAS	SHAN	SINO	SLIM	SOCK
SAPO	SEAT	SHAW	SINS	SLIP	SODA
SAPS	SEBI	SHAY	SION	SLIT	SODS
SARA	SEBO	SHEA	SIPS	SLOB	SOFA
SARD	SECT	SHED	SIRE	SLOE	SOFT
SARI	SECY	SHEM	SIRI	SLOG	SOHO
SARK	SEED	SHES	SIRS	SLOO	SOIL
SASH	SEEK	SHEW	SITE	SLOP	SOIR
SASK	SEEL	SHIM	SITI	SLOT	SOJA
SASS	SEEM	SHIN	SITO	SLOW	SOKE
SATE	SEEN	SHIP	SITS	SLUB	SOLA
SAUD	SEEP	SHIV	SITU	SLUE	SOLD
SAUK	SEER	SHOD	SIVA	SLUG	SOLE
SAUL	SEES	SHOE	SIZE	SLUM	SOLI
SAUR	SEGO	SHOO	SIZY	SLUR	SOLO
SAVE	SEJM	SHOP	******	SLUT	SOLS
SAWN	SELF	SHOQ	**SK--**	******	SOMA
SAWS	SELL	SHOT	******	**SM--**	SOME
SAXE	SEME	SHOW	SKAG	******	SONE
SAYS	SEMI	SHUL	SKAT	SMEE	SONG
******	SEND	SHUN	SKAW	SMEW	SONS
SC--	SENS	SHUT	SKEE	SMIT	SOON
******	SENT	******	SKEG	SMOG	SOOT
SCAB	SEPT	**SI--**	SKEP	SMUG	SOPS
SCAD	SEQQ	******	SKEW	SMUT	SORA
SCAN	SERA	SIAL	SKID	******	SORB
SCAR	SERB	SIAM	SKIM	**SN--**	SORE
SCAT	SERE	SICE	SKIN	******	SORI
SCOP	SERF	SICK	SKIP	SNAG	SORN
SCOT	SERO	SICS	SKIS	SNAP	SORT
SCOW	SERS	SIDE	SKIT	SNEE	SOSO
SCRY	SESS	SIDS	SKUA	SNIG	SOTS
SCUD	SETA	SIFT	SKYE	SNIP	SOUL
SCUM	SETH	SIGH	******	SNIT	SOUP
SCUP	SETI	SIGN	**SL--**	SNOB	SOUR
SCUT	SETS	SIKH	******	SNOG	SOUS
******	SEWN	SILK	SLAB	SNOT	SOWN
SD--	SEWS	SILL	SLAG	SNOW	SOWS
******	SEXI	SILO	SLAM	SNUB	SOYA
SDAK	SEXT	SILT	SLAP	SNUG	SOYS
******	SEXY	SIMA	SLAT	SNYE	******
SE--	******	SIMP	SLAV	******	**SP--**
******	**SH--**	SIMS	SLAW	**SO--**	******
SEAH	******	SIND	SLAY	******	SPAD
SEAL	SHAD	SINE	SLED	SOAK	SPAM
SEAM	SHAG		SLEE	SOAP	SPAN

SPAR	STUS	SWAP	TARO	TENN	TIFF
SPAS	STYX	SWAT	TARP	TENO	TIKE
SPAT	******	SWAY	TARS	TENS	TIKI
SPAY	**SU--**	SWIG	TART	TENT	TILE
SPCA	******	SWIM	TASK	TERA	TILL
SPCC	SUBJ	SWOP	TASS	TERM	TILT
SPEC	SUBS	SWOT	TATA	TERN	TIME
SPED	SUCH	SWUM	TATE	TESS	TIMS
SPES	SUCK	******	TATS	TEST	TINA
SPET	SUDD	**SY--**	TAUR	TETE	TINE
SPEW	SUDS	******	TAUS	TETH	TING
SPIN	SUED	SYCE	TAUT	TETR	TINS
SPIR	SUER	SYNE	TAVS	TEXT	TINT
SPIT	SUES	******	TAWS	******	TINY
SPIV	SUET	**TA--**	TAXI	**TH--**	TION
SPOR	SUEZ	******	TAXY	******	TIPI
SPOT	SUFI	TAAL	******	THAD	TIPS
SPQR	SUIT	TABS	**TB--**	THAN	TIRE
SPRY	SUKY	TABU	******	THAR	TIRO
SPUD	SULK	TACE	TBAR	THAT	TITI
SPUE	SULU	TACK	******	THAW	TITO
SPUN	SUMO	TACT	**TC--**	THEA	TITS
SPUR	SUMP	TADS	******	THEB	TIVY
******	SUMS	TAEL	TCHI	THEE	******
ST--	SUNG	TAFT	******	THEM	**TO--**
******	SUNK	TAGS	**TE--**	THEN	******
STAB	SUNN	TAIL	******	THEO	TOAD
STAG	SUNS	TAIN	TEAK	THEW	TOBY
STAN	SUPA	TAIT	TEAL	THEY	TOCO
STAR	SUPE	TAKE	TEAM	THIN	TODD
STAT	SUPP	TALC	TEAR	THIO	TODO
STAY	SUPS	TALE	TEAS	THIS	TODS
STEM	SUPT	TALK	TEAT	THOR	TODY
STEN	SURA	TALL	TEDS	THOU	TOED
STEP	SURD	TAME	TEED	THRU	TOES
STER	SURE	TAMP	TEEM	THUD	TOFF
STET	SURF	TAMS	TEEN	THUG	TOFT
STEW	SURG	TANA	TEES	THUS	TOGA
STIR	SUSS	TANG	TEGS	******	TOGO
STLO	SUVA	TANK	TEIL	**TI--**	TOGS
STOA	SUZY	TANS	TELA	******	TOIL
STOL	******	TAOS	TELE	TICK	TOLA
STOP	**SW--**	TAPA	TELL	TICS	TOLD
STOW	******	TAPE	TELO	TIDE	TOLE
STUB	SWAB	TAPS	TEMA	TIDY	TOLL
STUD	SWAG	TARA	TEMP	TIED	TOLU
STUM	SWAM	TARE	TEND	TIER	TOMB
STUN	SWAN	TARN	TENG	TIES	TOME

TOMS	TREY	******	******	URNS	VANG
TOMY	TRIG	**TW--**	**UL--**	URSA	VANS
TONE	TRIM	******	******	URUS	VARA
TONG	TRIN	TWAS	ULAN	******	VARI
TONI	TRIO	TWIG	ULEX	**US--**	VARY
TONO	TRIP	TWIN	ULLA	******	VASA
TONS	TRIS	TWIT	ULNA	USAF	VASE
TONY	TRIX	TWOS	******	USAR	VASO
TOOK	TROD	******	**UM--**	USCG	VAST
TOOL	TRON	**TY--**	******	USED	VATS
TOON	TROP	******	UMBO	USER	VAVS
TOOT	TROT	TYEE	UMTS	USES	VAYU
TOPE	TROW	TYKE	******	USIA	******
TOPH	TROY	TYNE	**UN--**	USMA	**VE--**
TOPI	TRUE	TYPE	******	USMC	******
TOPO	TRUK	TYPO	UNAS	USMS	VEAL
TOPS	******	TYRE	UNAU	USNA	VEDA
******	**TS--**	TYRO	UNCO	USNR	VEER
TORA	******	******	UNDE	USSR	VEES
TORE	TSAR	**TZ--**	UNDO	******	VEGA
TORI	TSHI	******	UNDY	**UT--**	VEIL
TORN	TSUN	TZAR	UNGA	******	VEIN
TORS	******	******	UNIE	UTAH	VELA
TORT	**TU--**	**UA--**	UNIO	UTER	VELD
TORY	******	******	UNIT	UTES	VENA
TOSH	TUBA	UANG	UNTO	******	VEND
TOSS	TUBE	******	UNTZ	**UV--**	VENI
TOTE	TUBS	**UB--**	UNZE	******	VENT
TOTI	TUCK	******	******	UVEA	VERA
TOTS	TUDE	UBER	**UP--**	UVIC	VERB
TOUR	TUES	******	******	******	VERN
TOUT	TUFA	**UC--**	UPAS	**UZ--**	VERS
TOWN	TUFF	******	UPON	******	VERT
TOWS	TUFT	UCMJ	******	UZAN	VERY
TOYO	TUGS	******	**UR--**	******	VEST
TOYS	TULA	**UD--**	******	**VA--**	VETO
******	TULE	******	URAL	******	VETS
TR--	TUMP	UDAD	URAN	VAAL	******
******	TUNA	UDEN	URDE	VACA	**VI--**
TRAD	TUNE	UDOS	URDU	VAGI	******
TRAH	TUNS	******	URDY	VAIL	VIAL
TRAM	TUPI	**UE--**	UREA	VAIN	VICE
TRAP	TUPS	******	UREY	VAIR	VICI
TRAY	TURF	UEBA	URFA	VALE	VICK
TREE	TURK	UELE	URGE	VALI	VIDE
TREF	TURN	******	URIA	VALS	VIDI
TREK	TUSH	**UG--**	URIC	VAMP	VIED
TRES	TUSK	******	URNA	VANE	VIES
TRET	TUTU	UGLY			

VIEW	******	WATE	WHIG	WOKE	******
VILE	**WA--**	WATT	WHIM	WOLD	**XN--**
VILI	******	WAUK	WHIN	WOLF	******
VILL	WAAC	WAUL	WHIP	WOMB	XNTY
VIMY	WAAF	WAVE	WHIR	WONT	******
VINA	WAAL	WAVY	WHIT	WOOD	**XO--**
VINE	WABE	WAWL	WHIZ	WOOF	******
VINI	WACK	WAXY	WHOA	WOOL	XOSA
VINO	WACO	WAYS	WHOM	WOOS	******
VINY	WACS	******	WHOP	WORD	**XR--**
VIOL	WADE	**WE--**	WHYS	WORE	******
VIPS	WADI	******	******	WORK	XRAY
VIRA	WADS	WEAK	**WI--**	WORM	XREF
VIRE	WADY	WEAL	******	WORN	XRTS
VISA	WAFS	WEAN	WICH	WORT	******
VISC	WAFT	WEAR	WICK	WOTE	**XY--**
VISE	WAGE	WEBS	WIDE	WOVE	******
VISO	WAGS	WEDS	WIFE	WOWS	XYLO
VISS	WAIF	WEED	WIGS	******	XYST
VITA	WAIL	WEEK	WILD	**WR--**	******
VITE	WAIN	WEEL	WILE	******	**YA--**
VITI	WAIT	WEEP	WILL	WRAF	******
VITR	WAKE	WEFT	WILT	WRAP	YABA
VIVA	WALD	WEIR	WILY	WREN	YAKA
VIVE	WALE	WEKA	WIND	WRIT	YAKO
VIVO	WALK	WEKI	WINE	******	YAKS
******	WALL	WELD	WING	**WY--**	YALE
VO--	WALT	WELL	WINK	******	YALU
******	WAND	WELT	WINO	WYCH	YAMA
VOCE	WANE	WEND	WINS	WYES	YAMP
VOET	WANG	WENS	WINY	WYNN	YAMS
VOID	WANS	WENT	WIPE	******	YANA
VOLA	WANT	WEPT	WIRE	**XD--**	YANG
VOLE	WANY	WERE	WIRY	******	YANK
VOLS	WAPS	WERT	WISC	XDIV	YAPA
VOLT	WARD	WEST	WISE	******	YAPS
VORA	WARE	WETA	WISH	**XE--**	YARD
VORE	WARF	WETS	WISP	******	YARE
VOTE	WARI	******	WIST	XEMA	YARN
VOWS	WARM	**WH--**	WITH	XENO	YAUP
******	WARN	******	WITS	XERO	YAWL
VT--	WARP	WHAM	WIVE	******	YAWN
******	WARS	WHAP	******	**XI--**	YAWP
VTOL	WART	WHAT	**WK--**	******	YAWS
******	WARY	WHEN	******	XINT	YAYA
VU--	WASH	WHET	WKLY	XION	******
******	WASP	WHEW	******	XIPH	**YE--**
VUGS	WAST	WHEY	**WO--**	******	******
			******	**XM--**	YEAH
			WOAD	******	YEAN
			WOES	XMAS	

YEAR	******	ZEPH	ADAH	AMBI	ALEN
YEAS	YS--	ZERO	ADAK	AMBO	ALES
YEGG	******	ZEST	ADAM	AUBE	ALEX
YELD	YSER	ZETA	ADAR	AUBY	AMEN
YELK	******	ZEUS	ADAS	******	AMER
YELL	YU--	******	ADAY	A-C-	AMES
YELP	******	ZI--	AFAR	******	ANEW
YENS	YUAN	******	AGAO	ABCS	APED
YETI	YUGA	ZINC	AGAR	ACCT	APES
YEWS	YUKS	ZING	AGAS	ANCE	APEX
******	YULE	ZION	AHAB	ANCY	AREA
YH--	YUMA	ZIPS	AHAH	ARCH	AREO
******	******	ZIRA	AJAR	ARCS	ARES
YHWH	YV--	ZIZZ	AJAX	ASCH	ASEA
******	******	******	ALAÆ	ASCI	ATEN
YI--	YVES	ZO--	ALAI	******	ATES
******	******	******	ALAN	A-D-	AVEC
YIPE	YW--	ZOAN	ALAR	******	AVER
YIPS	******	ZOAR	ALAS	ACDC	AVES
******	YWCA	ZOES	AMAH	ADDS	AWED
YL--	YWHA	ZOIC	AMAS	ADDY	AWES
******	******	ZOLA	AMAT	AIDA	AXED
YLEM	ZA--	ZONA	ANAL	AIDE	AXES
******	******	ZONE	ANAM	AIDS	AYER
YM--	ZACH	ZOOL	ANAS	ALDE	AYES
******	ZACK	ZOOM	ANAT	ALDO	******
YMCA	ZANT	ZOON	ARAB	ANDY	A-F-
YMER	ZANY	ZOOS	ARAD	AUDE	******
YMHA	ZARA	ZOUG	ARAL	******	ALFA
YMIR	ZARF	******	ARAM	A-E-	ALFS
******	ZARP	ZU--	ARAN	******	******
YO--	ZASU	******	ARAS	ABED	A-G-
******	ZATI	ZULU	ASAS	ABEL	******
YODH	******	ZUNI	ATAR	ABES	AFGH
YODS	ZB--	ZUZA	AVAL	ABET	ALGA
YOGA	******	******	AVAS	ACEA	ALGY
YOGH	ZBAR	ZW--	AWAY	ACED	ARGO
YOGI	******	******	AYAH	ACER	******
YOKE	ZE--	ZWEI	AZAN	ACES	A-H-
YOLK	******	******	******	ACET	******
YOND	ZEAL	ZY--	A-B-	ADEN	ACHE
YORE	ZEBU	******	******	AGED	AGHA
YORK	ZEDS	ZYGO	ABBA	AGEE	ASHA
YOUD	ZEES	******	ABBE	AGES	ASHE
YOUP	ZEIN	A-A-	ABBR	AHEM	ASHY
YOUR	ZEKE	******	ABBY	ALEC	******
YOWL	ZEND	ABAS	ALBA	ALEE	A-I-
YOWS	ZENO	ACAD	ALBS	ALEF	******
YOYO					ABIB
					ABIE

ACID
ADIT
AGIO
AKIN
ALIA
ALIF
ALIN
ALIT
ALIX
AMIA
AMID
AMIE
AMIR
AMIS
ANIL
ANIM
ANIS
APIA
APIO
APIS
ARIA
ARID
ARIL
ARIZ
ASIA
ASIR
ASIS
ATIC
AVID
AVIS
AVIV
AXIL
AXIS
AYIN
******
A-K-
******
ANKH
ARKS
ASKS
ATKA
AUKS
******
A-L-
******
AALS
ABLE
ABLY

ACLU
AILE
AILS
ALLE
ALLI
ALLO
ALLY
ATLE
ATLI
AULD
AWLS
AXLE
******
A-M-
******
ACME
AIMS
ALMA
ALMS
AMMO
ARMS
ARMY
ATMO
AYME
******
A-N-
******
ACNE
AGNI
AINO
AINS
AINT
AINU
ANNA
ANNE
ANNO
ANNS
AONE
ARNE
ARNI
ARNO
ARNS
AUNE
AUNT
AWNS
AWNY
******
A-O-
******
ABOU
ACOR

ACOU
AEON
AGOG
AGON
AHOY
ALOE
ALOP
ALOW
AMOI
AMOK
AMON
AMOR
AMOS
AMOY
ANOA
ANON
APOC
APOD
AROW
ASOF
ATOM
ATOP
ATOR
AVON
AVOW
AWOL
AXON
AZON
AZOV
******
A-P-
******
ALPH
ALPS
AMPS
ASPS
******
A-R-
******
AARE
ABRI
ACRE
ACRO
AERI
AERO
AERY
AFRO
AGRA

AGRI
AGRO
AIRE
AIRS
AIRY
ATRI
AURA
AWRY
******
A-S-
******
ALSO
ANSA
APSE
ASSN
ASST
AUST
******
A-T-
******
ACTA
ACTH
ACTS
ALTA
ALTI
ALTO
AMTS
ANTA
ANTE
ANTH
ANTI
ANTS
ARTE
ARTS
ARTY
ASTI
ASTR
ATTA
ATTN
ATTO
ATTU
ATTY
AUTH
AUTO
******
A-U-
******
ABUT
AGUA

AGUE
ALUM
AMUR
AMUS
ANUS
AOUL
APUS
AQUA
AQUI
ARUM
******
A-V-
******
ALVA
******
A-Y-
******
ALYS
AMYL
AMYS
ARYL
******
A-Z-
******
ADZE
******
B-A-
******
BAAL
BAAR
BAAS
BEAD
BEAK
BEAM
BEAN
BEAR
BEAS
BEAT
BEAU
BHAR
BIAS
BLAB
BLAH
BLAT
BOAR
BOAS
BOAT
BOAZ

BRAD
BRAE
BRAG
BRAN
BRAS
BRAT
BRAW
BRAY
BRAZ
******
B-B-
******
BABA
BABE
BABI
BABS
BABU
BABY
BIBB
BIBL
BIBS
BOBS
BUBO
BUBS
******
B-C-
******
BACH
BACK
BECK
BICE
BOCK
BUCK
******
B-D-
******
BADE
BEDA
BEDE
BEDS
BIDE
BIDS
BLDG
BODE
BODY
BUDD
BUDS

******	******	BELT	BONG	BARI	BUSH
B-E-	**B-H-**	BILE	BONI	BARK	BUSK
******	******	BILK	BONK	BARM	BUSS
BAEL	BAHT	BILL	BONN	BARN	BUST
BAER	BIHE	BOLA	BONO	BARO	BUSY
BEEF	BOHR	BOLD	BONY	BARS	******
BEEK	BUHL	BOLE	BRNO	BART	**B-T-**
BEEN	******	BOLL	BUNA	BERA	******
BEEP	**B-I-**	BOLO	BUND	BERG	BATE
BEER	******	BOLT	BUNG	BERM	BATH
BEES	BAIA	BULB	BUNK	BERN	BATS
BEET	BAIL	BULE	BUNN	BERT	BATT
BIEL	BAIT	BULG	BUNS	BIRD	BATZ
BIER	BLIP	BULK	BUNT	BIRL	BETA
BLEB	BLIT	BULL	******	BIRO	BETH
BLED	BOIL	******	**B-O-**	BIRR	BETS
BLEM	BOIS	**B-M-**	******	BORA	BITE
BLET	BRIE	******	BIOL	BORE	BITS
BLEW	BRIG	BEMA	BION	BORN	BITT
BOER	BRIM	BOMB	BLOB	BORT	BOTA
BREA	BRIO	BUMP	BLOC	BURD	BOTH
BRED	BRIT	BUMS	BLOT	BURG	BOTS
BREN	******	******	BLOW	BURL	BOTT
BRER	**B-J-**	**B-N-**	BMOC	BURN	BUTE
BRET	******	******	BOOB	BURP	BUTS
BREV	BAJA	BANC	BOOK	BURR	BUTT
BREW	******	BAND	BOOM	BURS	******
BSED	**B-K-**	BANE	BOON	BURT	**B-U-**
BYEE	******	BANG	BOOR	BURY	******
BYES	BAKE	BANI	BOOS	BYRD	BLUB
******	BAKU	BANK	BOOT	BYRE	BLUE
B-F-	BEKA	BANN	BROM	******	BLUR
******	BIKE	BANS	BRON	**B-S-**	BMUS
BAFF	******	BANT	BROO	******	BOUT
BIFF	**B-L-**	BEND	BROW	BASE	BOUW
BUFF	******	BENE	BROZ	BASH	BRUT
******	BALD	BENG	BUOY	BASK	******
B-G-	BALE	BENI	******	BASS	**B-V-**
******	BALI	BENS	**B-P-**	BAST	******
BAGA	BALK	BENT	******	BESA	BEVS
BAGO	BALL	BIND	BAPT	BESS	BEVY
BAGR	BALM	BINE	BOPS	BEST	BLVD
BAGS	BALT	BING	******	BISE	BOVI
BEGS	BBLS	BINH	**B-R-**	BOSH	******
BOGS	BELA	BINS	******	BOSK	**B-W-**
BOGY	BELG	BONA	BARB	BOSN	******
BUGS	BELL	BOND	BARD	BOSS	BAWD
	BELS	BONE	BARE	BSSC	BAWL

BOWL	CEBU	COED	CRIT	******	CAPP
BOWS	COBB	COEF	CUIR	**C-N-**	CAPS
******	COBS	COEL	******	******	CAPT
B-Y-	CUBA	CREE	**C-K-**	CANA	CEPA
******	CUBE	CRES	******	CANC	COPA
BAYA	CUBS	CREW	CAKE	CANE	COPE
BAYS	******	CTEN	COKE	CANS	COPR
BEYS	**C-C-**	CUED	******	CANT	COPS
BOYD	******	CUES	**C-L-**	CENE	COPT
BOYS	CACO	******	******	CENO	COPY
BUYS	CECA	**C-F-**	CALF	CENT	CUPR
******	COCA	******	CALI	CINE	CUPS
B-Z-	COCK	CAFE	CALK	CONC	******
******	COCO	CUFF	CALL	COND	**C-R-**
BOZO	CYCL	******	CALM	CONE	******
BUZZ	******	**C-G-**	CALX	CONF	CARA
******	**C-D-**	******	CELE	CONG	CARB
C-A-	******	CAGE	CELL	CONJ	CARD
******	CADE	CAGY	CELT	CONK	CARE
CHAD	CADI	CHGD	COLA	CONN	CARL
CHAP	CADS	CHGS	COLD	CONS	CARO
CHAR	CEDE	COGS	COLE	CONT	CARP
CHAT	CIDE	******	COLL	CONY	CARR
CHAW	CMDR	**C-H-**	COLO	******	CARS
CHAY	CODA	******	COLS	**C-O-**	CART
CLAD	CODE	COHO	COLT	******	CARY
CLAM	CODS	******	COLY	CHOL	CERE
CLAN	CODY	**C-I-**	CULE	CHOP	CERO
CLAP	CUDS	******	CULL	CHOU	CERT
CLAR	******	CAIN	CULM	CHOW	CIRC
CLAW	**C-E-**	CEIL	CULT	CION	CORA
CLAY	******	CHIA	******	CLOD	CORD
COAL	CAEN	CHIC	**C-M-**	CLOG	CORE
COAT	CEES	CHID	******	CLON	CORF
COAX	CHEE	CHIH	CAMB	CLOP	CORK
CRAB	CHEF	CHIL	CAME	CLOT	CORM
CRAG	CHEM	CHIN	CAMP	CLOY	CORN
CRAM	CHES	CHIP	CAMS	COOK	CORP
CRAN	CHET	CHIR	COMA	COOL	CURB
CRAP	CHEW	CHIS	COMB	COON	CURD
CRAT	CHEZ	CHIT	COME	COOP	CURE
CRAW	CIEL	CLIO	COMM	COOS	CURL
CYAN	CLEE	CLIP	COMO	COOT	CURS
CZAR	CLEF	COIF	COMP	CROP	CURT
******	CLEG	COIL	COMR	CROW	******
C-B-	CLEM	COIN	CYMA	******	**C-S-**
******	CLEO	COIR	CYME	**C-P-**	******
CABS	CLEW	CRIB	CYMO	******	CASE
CEBA				CAPA	CASH
				CAPE	

CASK	CRUD	DIAN	DIDY	DEIL	DEMI
CASS	CRUS	DIAS	DODO	DOIT	DEMO
CAST	CRUX	DIAZ	DUDE	DRIB.	DEMY
CESS	******	DRAB	DUDS	DRIN	DIME
CEST	**C-V-**	DRAG	******	DRIP	DIMS
CIST	******	DRAH	**D-E-**	DUIM	DOMA
COSH	CAVA	DRAM	******	DUIT	DOME
COSM	CAVE	DRAT	DEED	******	DOMS
COSS	CAVY	DRAW	DEEM	**D-J-**	DUMA
COST	COVE	DRAY	DEEP	******	DUMB
COSY	******	DUAD	DEER	DEJA	DUMP
CUSH	**C-W-**	DUAL	DEES	******	******
CUSK	******	DUAR	DIED	**D-K-**	**D-N-**
CUSP	CAWS	DYAD	DIES	******	******
CUSS	COWL	DYAK	DIET	DAKS	DANA
CYST	COWS	DYAN	DIEU	DEKA	DANE
******	******	******	DOER	DEKE	DANG
C-T-	**C-X-**	**D-B-**	DOES	DIKE	DANK
******	******	******	DREW	DUKE	DANS
CATA	COXA	DABS	DUEL	DYKE	DANU
CATE	******	DEBS	DUES	******	DENE
CATH	**C-Y-**	DEBT	DUET	**D-L-**	DENS
CATO	******	DIBS	DYED	******	DENT
CATS	CAYS	DOBY	DYER	DALE	DENY
CITE	CRYO	DUBS	DYES	DALI	DINA
CITY	CUYA	******	******	DELE	DINE
COTE	******	**D-C-**	**D-F-**	DELF	DING
COTS	**C-Z-**	******	******	DELI	DINO
COTY	CAZI	DACE	DAFF	DELL	DINS
CUTE	COZY	DECA	DAFT	DILI	DINT
CUTS	******	DECD	DEFI	DILL	DONA
CYTE	**D-A-**	DECI	DEFT	DILO	DONE
CYTO	******	DECK	DEFY	DOLA	DONS
******	DDAY	DICE	DOFF	DOLE	DONT
C-U-	DEAD	DICH	******	DOLF	DUNA
******	DEAF	DICK	**D-G-**	DOLL	DUNE
CAUK	DEAL	DOCK	******	DOLS	DUNG
CAUL	DEAN	DUCE	DAGO	DOLT	DUNK
CHUB	DEAR	DUCK	DAGS	DULL	DUNS
CHUD	DHAI	DUCT	DEGO	DULY	DUNT
CHUG	DHAK	******	DIGS	******	DYNA
CHUM	DHAL	**D-D-**	DOGE	**D-M-**	DYNE
CHUR	DHAN	******	DOGS	******	******
CLUB	DHAR	DADA	DOGY	DAME	**D-O-**
CLUE	DIAG	DADE	DUGS	DAMN	******
CLUJ	DIAL	DADO	******	DAMP	DHOW
COUE	DIAM	DADS	**D-I-**	DAMS	DION
COUP		DIDO	******	DEME	DIOS
			DAIL		
			DAIS		

DOOM	DESL	******	ELBE	******	ELLA
DOON	DESS	**D-W-**	EZBA	**E-G-**	ELLS
DOOR	DISC	******	******	******	ERLE
DROP	DISH	DAWK	**E-C-**	EDGE	******
DUOS	DISK	DAWM	******	EDGY	**E-M-**
******	DIST	DAWN	EACH	EGGS	******
D-P-	DOSE	DAWS	ECCL	ENGR	ELMA
******	DOSS	DEWS	ENCE	ERGO	ELMO
DAPA	DOST	DEWY	ENCL	ERGS	ELMS
DAPS	DUSE	DOWN	ENCY	******	ELMY
DEPA	DUSK	******	ESCE	**E-H-**	EMMA
DEPT	DUST	**D-X-**	ETCH	******	EMMY
DIPL	******	******	EXCH	ECHO	ERMA
DIPS	**D-T-**	DOXY	EXCL	ECHT	******
DOPE	******	******	******	EDHS	**E-N-**
DOPP	DATA	**D-Y-**	**E-D-**	ETHN	******
DOPY	DATE	******	******	ETHS	EDNA
DUPE	DITA	DAYS	EDDA	******	EENS
******	DOTE	DEYS	EDDY	**E-I-**	ENNA
D-R-	DOTH	******	ENDO	******	ENNS
******	DOTS	**D-Z-**	ENDS	EDIE	EONS
DARB	DOTY	******	ERDA	EDIT	ERNE
DARE	DUTY	DAZA	******	EFIK	ERNS
DARK	******	DAZE	**E-E-**	ELIA	ESNE
DARN	**D-U-**	DOZE	******	ELIS	ETNA
DART	******	DOZY	EBEN	EMIA	******
DERM	DAUB	******	EDEN	EMIL	**E-O-**
DIRE	DEUS	**E-A-**	EDER	EMIR	******
DIRK	DEUT	******	EGER	EMIT	EBON
DIRT	DMUS	EBAN	EKED	ENID	ECOL
DORA	DOUG	EDAM	EKES	EPIC	ECON
DORE	DOUR	EGAD	ELEC	ERIA	EDOM
DORM	DRUB	EGAN	ELEM	ERIC	EGOS
DORP	DRUG	ELAM	ELEO	ERIE	ENOL
DORR	DRUM	ELAN	ELEV	ERIK	ENOS
DORS	******	ERAL	EMEU	ERIN	ENOW
DORY	**D-V-**	ERAS	EPEE	ERIS	EPOS
DURA	******	ESAU	EVEN	EVIL	EROS
DURN	DAVE	ETAH	EVER	EXIT	ETON
DURO	DAVY	ETAL	EVES	******	EVOE
DURR	DEVA	ETAS	EWER	**E-K-**	EXOD
******	DEVI	EVAN	EWES	******	EXON
D-S-	DEVS	EVAS	EXEC	ELKE	EYOT
******	DIVA	EWAN	EXES	ELKS	******
DASH	DIVE	EXAM	EYED	******	**E-P-**
DESC	DIVI	EYAS	EYES	**E-L-**	******
DESI	DOVE	******	EZEK	******	ESPY
DESK		**E-B-**	******	EELS	
		******	**E-F-**	EELY	
		EBBS	******		
		ELBA	EFFS		

******
E-R-
******
EARL
EARN
EARS
EBRO
ECRU
EERY
EIRE
ERRS
EURO
EURY
EYRA
EYRE
EYRY
EZRA
******
E-S-
******
EASE
EAST
EASY
ELSA
ELSE
ELST
ERSE
ERST
ESSE
******
E-T-
******
EATS
ECTO
EFTS
ENTE
ENTO
ESTE
ESTH
ETTA
ETTE
******
E-U-
******
EAUX
ECUA
ECUS
EDUC

ELUL
EMUS
EOUS
EQUI
ETUI
******
E-V-
******
ELVA
ENVY
******
E-Y-
******
ENYO
******
F-A-
******
FAAM
FEAR
FEAT
FIAT
FLAG
FLAK
FLAM
FLAN
FLAP
FLAT
FLAW
FLAX
FLAY
FOAL
FOAM
FRAE
FRAN
FRAP
FRAS
FRAT
FRAU
FRAY
******
F-B-
******
FEBR
FIBR
FIBS
FOBS
******
F-C-
******
FACE
FACP

FACS
FACT
FICA
FICE
FICO
FMCS
FOCH
FOCI
FUCI
******
F-D-
******
FADE
FADO
FADS
FIDS
******
F-E-
******
FEED
FEEL
FEES
FEET
FIEF
FLEA
FLED
FLEE
FLEM
FLEW
FLEX
FOES
FREA
FRED
FREE
FREQ
FRET
FREY
FUEL
******
F-F-
******
FIFE
******
F-G-
******
FAGS
FIGS
FOGS
FOGY

******
F-H-
******
FOHN
******
F-I-
******
FAIL
FAIN
FAIR
FDIC
FLIP
FLIT
FOIL
FRIO
FRIT
******
F-J-
******
FIJI
FUJI
******
F-K-
******
FAKE
FYKE
******
F-L-
******
FALA
FALL
FELL
FELS
FELT
FILA
FILE
FILL
FILM
FILO
FILS
FOLD
FOLK
FOLL
FULA
FULL
******
F-M-
******
FAME
FAMN

FEME
FNMA
FUME
FUMY
******
F-N-
******
FANE
FANG
FANO
FANS
FEND
FENS
FIND
FINE
FINK
FINN
FINS
FOND
FONG
FONT
FUND
FUNG
FUNK
FUNS
******
F-O-
******
FEOD
FLOC
FLOE
FLOG
FLOP
FLOR
FLOT
FLOW
FOOD
FOOL
FOOT
FROE
FROG
FROM
FROT
FROW
******
F-P-
******
FOPS

******
F-R-
******
FARE
FARL
FARM
FARO
FERN
FIRE
FIRM
FIRN
FIRS
FORA
FORB
FORD
FORE
FORK
FORM
FORT
FURL
FURN
FURS
FURY
******
F-S-
******
FASH
FASS
FAST
FESS
FEST
FISC
FISH
FIST
FOSS
FUSE
FUSS
******
F-T-
******
FATA
FATE
FATS
FETE
FITS
FITZ
******
F-U-
******
FAUN
FEUD

FEUS	GOAT	GLEE	**G-L-**	GENU	GERA
FLUB	GRAB	GLEN	******	GENY	GERD
FLUE	GRAD	GMEN	GALA	GINA	GERI
FLUO	GRAF	GOER	GALE	GINK	GERM
FLUX	GRAM	GOES	GALL	GINS	GIRD
FOUL	GRAO	GREG	GALS	GOND	GIRL
FOUR	GRAY	GREW	GELD	GONE	GIRO
******	GRAZ	GREY	GELS	GONG	GIRT
F-V-	GUAM	GWEN	GELT	GONO	GORE
******	GUAN	******	GILA	GUNS	GORY
FIVE	GUAO	**G-F-**	GILD	GYNO	GURU
******	GUAT	******	GILL	******	GYRE
F-W-	******	GAFF	GILS	**G-O-**	GYRI
******	**G-B-**	GIFT	GILT	******	GYRO
FAWN	******	GIFU	GOLD	GAOL	******
FOWL	GABE	GUFF	GOLF	GEOL	**G-S-**
******	GABS	******	GOLO	GEOM	******
F-X-	GABY	**G-G-**	GULF	GLOB	GASH
******	GIBE	******	GULL	GLOT	GASP
FOXY	GIBS	GAGA	GULP	GLOW	GEST
******	GOBI	GAGE	******	GOOD	GIST
F-Y-	GOBO	GAGS	**G-M-**	GOOF	GOSH
******	GOBS	GIGA	******	GOOK	GUSH
FAYE	GOBY	GIGS	GAMA	GOON	GUST
FAYS	GYBE	GOGH	GAMB	GOOP	******
FOYS	******	GOGO	GAME	GROG	**G-T-**
FUYE	**G-C-**	******	GAMO	GROS	******
******	******	**G-H-**	GAMP	GROT	GATA
F-Z-	GECK	******	GAMS	GROW	GATE
******	GUCK	GUHA	GAMY	GYOR	GATH
FAZE	******	******	GEMS	******	GATS
FIZZ	**G-D-**	**G-I-**	GIMP	**G-P-**	GATT
FUZE	******	******	GOMA	******	GETS
FUZZ	GADS	GAIA	GUMI	GAPE	GOTH
******	GIDE	GAIL	GUMS	GAPS	GUTS
G-A-	GODS	GAIN	GYMN	GAPY	******
******	******	GAIT	GYMS	GIPS	**G-U-**
GEAR	**G-E-**	GLIB	******	GYPS	******
GHAT	******	GLIM	**G-N-**	******	GAUD
GLAD	GAEA	GRID	******	**G-R-**	GAUL
GMAN	GAEL	GRIG	GANG	******	GAUR
GNAR	GEED	GRIM	GENE	GARA	GLUE
GNAT	GEEK	GRIN	GENF	GARB	GLUM
GNAW	GEES	GRIP	GENG	GARD	GLUT
GOAD	GEEZ	GRIS	GENL	GARE	GNUS
GOAL	GHEE	GRIT	GENS	GARM	GOUT
GOAR	GIED	GUIN	GENT	GARS	GRUB
GOAS	GLED	GWIN		GARY	GRUM

******	HEBE	HIGH	HOLD	HUNK	HORA
G-V-	HEBR	HOGG	HOLE	HUNS	HORN
******	HOBO	HOGS	HOLM	HUNT	HORT
GAVE	HOBS	HUGE	HOLO	******	HURL
GIVE	HUBS	HUGH	HOLT	**H-O-**	HURT
GOVT	******	HUGO	HOLY	******	******
GYVE	**H-C-**	HUGS	HULA	HOOD	**H-S-**
******	******	HYGR	HULK	HOOF	******
G-W-	HACK	******	HULL	HOOK	HASH
******	HECK	**H-H-**	HYLA	HOON	HASP
GAWK	HECT	******	HYLO	HOOP	HAST
GOWK	HICK	HAHA	******	HOOT	HEST
GOWL	HOCK	HAHN	**H-M-**	HRON	HISS
GOWN	HUCK	HAHS	******	******	HIST
******	******	HEHE	HAMA	**H-P-**	HOSE
G-Y-	**H-D-**	******	HAME	******	HOST
******	******	**H-I-**	HAMS	HAPL	HUSH
GAYA	HADE	******	HEMA	HEPT	HUSK
GAYS	HADJ	HAIK	HEME	HIPE	HUSS
GOYA	HIDE	HAIL	HEMI	HIPP	******
GUYS	HODS	HAIR	HEML	HIPS	**H-T-**
GWYN	HYDE	HEIR	HEMO	HOPE	******
******	HYDR	HRIP	HEMP	HOPI	HATE
G-Z-	******	******	HEMS	HOPS	HATH
******	**H-E-**	**H-K-**	HOME	HUPA	HATS
GAZA	******	******	HOMO	HYPO	HETH
GAZE	HEED	HAKA	HOMS	******	HITS
GIZA	HEEL	HAKE	HOMY	**H-R-**	HOTE
******	HIED	HAKU	HUME	******	HOTH
H-A-	HIER	HIKE	HUMP	HARD	HOTI
******	HIES	******	HUMS	HARE	HUTS
HAAF	HLER	**H-L-**	HYMN	HARK	******
HEAD	HOED	******	******	HARL	**H-U-**
HEAL	HOEN	HALE	**H-N-**	HARM	******
HEAP	HOER	HALF	******	HARP	HAUL
HEAR	HOES	HALL	HAND	HART	HOUR
HEAT	HUED	HALM	HANG	HARZ	******
HOAR	HUES	HALO	HANK	HERA	**H-V-**
HOAX	HYET	HALS	HANS	HERB	******
HWAI	******	HALT	HENS	HERD	HAVE
HWAN	**H-F-**	HELD	HIND	HERE	HIVE
HYAL	******	HELI	HINO	HERL	HOVE
******	HAFT	HELL	HINT	HERM	******
H-B-	HEFT	HELM	HOND	HERO	**H-W-**
******	HIFI	HELP	HONE	HERR	******
HABE	HUFF	HILL	HONG	HERS	HAWK
HABU	******	HILO	HONK	HIRE	HAWS
HDBK	**H-G-**	HILT	HUNG	HIRO	HEWN
	******				
	HAGI				
	HAGS				

HEWS	INCL	IDIO	******	******	JEEP
HOWE	ITCH	IFIL	**I-O-**	**I-Z-**	JEER
HOWL	******	ILIA	******	******	JEES
******	**I-D-**	IMID	ICON	IZZY	JOEL
H-X-	******	IMIN	IDOL	******	JOES
******	IADB	INIA	IKON	**J-A-**	JOEY
HEXA	INDO	INIT	IRON	******	
******	IODO	IRID	ITOL	JEAN	**J-F-**
H-Y-	******	IRIS	IVOR	JOAB	******
******	**I-E-**	ISIS	******	JOAD	JEFE
HAYA	******	IXIA	**I-P-**	JOAH	JEFF
HAYS	IBEX	******	******	JOAN	JIFF
HOYS	ICED	**I-K-**	IMPI	JOAR	******
******	ICEL	******	IMPS	JOAT	**J-G-**
H-Z-	ICER	ILKA	******	JUAN	******
******	ICES	INKS	**I-R-**	******	JAGA
HAZE	IDEA	INKY	******	**J-B-**	JAGG
HAZY	IDEM	IRKS	INRE	******	JAGS
******	IDEO	******	INRI	JABS	JIGS
I-A-	IDES	**I-L-**	INRO	JEBU	JOGS
******	IKES	******	IRRA	JIBE	JUGS
ICAL	ILEA	IBLE	******	JIBI	******
IDAE	ILEO	IDLE	**I-S-**	JIBS	**J-H-**
IDAS	ILEX	IDLY	******	JOBO	******
IMAM	INEE	IGLU	ILSE	JOBS	JEHU
IMAN	INEZ	ILLS	INSP	JUBA	JOHN
INAS	ISER	ILLY	INST	JUBE	******
IRAK	ITEA	INLY	ISSY	******	**J-I-**
IRAN	ITEM	IOLE	******	**J-C-**	******
IRAQ	ITER	ISLE	**I-T-**	******	JAIL
IRAS	IVES	******	******	JACA	JAIN
ISAR	******	**I-M-**	INTO	JACK	JOIN
ITAL	**I-F-**	******	IOTA	JOCK	******
IVAN	******	IAMB	******	JUCA	**J-J-**
IYAR	IDFU	IMMI	**I-U-**	******	******
IZAR	IFFY	IMMY	******	**J-D-**	JUJU
******	INFO	IRMA	ILUS	******	******
I-B-	******	ISMS	IOUS	JADE	**J-K-**
******	**I-G-**	******	******	JODO	******
ICBM	******	**I-N-**	**I-W-**	JUDE	JAKE
IOBB	IAGO	******	******	JUDO	JAKO
IRBM	INGA	IANA	IKWE	JUDY	JOKE
ISBA	INGE	IANS	IOWA	******	******
******	******	IFNI	******	**J-E-**	**J-L-**
I-C-	**I-I-**	IGNI	**I-Y-**	******	******
******	******	INNS	******	JAEN	JELL
INCA	IBID	IONA	IDYL	JEED	JILL
INCH	IBIS	IONS	ITYS	JEEL	JILT
		ISNT	IVYS		

JOLA	JERK	******	KEEP	KELT	KEPI
JOLO	JERL	J-Z-	KHET	KILL	KEPT
JOLT	JERM	******	KIEL	KILN	KIPE
JULE	JURA	JAZZ	KIER	KILO	KIPS
JULY	JURY	******	KIEV	KILT	KOPH
******	******	K-A-	KLEE	KOLA	KOPI
J-M-	J-S-	******	KNEE	KOLN	KOPS
******	******	KAAS	KNEW	KYLE	******
JAMA	JASS	KCAL	KOEL	******	K-R-
JAMB	JESS	KEAS	******	K-M-	******
JAMI	JEST	KHAN	K-F-	******	KARA
JAMS	JESU	KHAT	******	KAMA	KARI
JEMS	JOSE	KIAK	KEFS	KAME	KARL
JIMS	JOSH	KLAM	******	KAMI	KARN
JUMP	JOSS	KNAG	K-G-	KEMP	KARY
******	JUST	KNAP	******	******	KERB
J-N-	******	KNAR	KAGU	K-N-	KERF
******	J-T-	KOAE	KEGS	******	KERN
JANE	******	KRAL	******	KANA	KIRI
JANN	JATH	KVAS	K-H-	KANE	KIRK
JANS	JATO	KYAT	******	KANO	KORS
JENA	JETE	******	KAHA	KANS	KURA
JIND	JETH	K-B-	KIHO	KANT	KURD
JINK	JETS	******	KOHL	KENO	KURE
JINN	JOTS	KABS	******	KENS	KURT
JINX	JUTE	KIBE	K-I-	KENT	******
JONS	JUTS	KOBE	******	KIND	K-S-
JUNC	******	******	KAID	KINE	******
JUNE	J-U-	K-C-	KAIF	KING	KASM
JUNG	JEUX	******	KAIL	KINK	KISH
JUNK	JOUG	KECK	KAIN	KINO	KISS
JUNO	JOUY	KICK	KEIR	KUNK	KIST
******	******	******	KNIT	******	KOSS
J-O-	J-V-	K-D-	KRIS	K-O-	******
******	******	******	******	******	K-T-
JAOB	JAVA	KADA	K-K-	KAON	******
JHOW	JAVE	KADE	******	KEOS	KATE
JOOK	JIVE	KADI	KAKA	KNOB	KATY
******	JOVE	KIDD	KAKI	KNOP	KETO
J-P-	******	KIDS	KOKO	KNOT	KETU
******	J-W-	KUDU	******	KNOW	KITE
JAPE	JAWS	******	K-L-	KNOX	KITH
******	JEWS	K-E-	******	KOOK	KITS
J-R-	JOWL	******	KALA	******	KITT
******	******	KEEF	KALE	K-P-	KOTO
JARA	J-Y-	KEEK	KALI	******	******
JARL	******	KEEL	KELA	KAPA	K-U-
JARS	JAYS	KEEN	KELP	KAPH	******
	JOYS				KNUR

******	LUBA	******	LOKE	LENS	******
K-V-	LUBE	**L-F-**	LOKI	LENT	**L-R-**
******	******	******	LUKE	LINA	******
KAVA	**L-C-**	LAFE	******	LIND	LARA
KIVA	******	LEFT	**L-L-**	LINE	LARD
KIVU	LACE	LIFE	******	LING	LARI
******	LACK	LIFT	LALL	LINK	LARK
K-W-	LACT	LOFT	LILA	LINN	LARP
******	LACY	LUFF	LILS	LINO	LARS
KAWA	LICE	******	LILT	LINT	LIRA
KIWI	LICH	**L-G-**	LILY	LINY	LIRE
******	LICK	******	LOLA	LINZ	LORD
K-Y-	LOCH	LAGS	LOLL	LONE	LORE
******	LOCI	LEGS	LULL	LONG	LORN
KAYE	LOCK	LIGN	LULU	LUNA	LORY
KAYO	LOCO	LOGE	LYLE	LUNE	LURE
KAYS	LUCE	LOGO	******	LUNG	LURI
KEYS	LUCK	LOGS	**L-M-**	LUNI	LURK
******	LUCY	LOGY	******	LUNT	LYRA
K-Z-	******	LUGE	LAMA	LYNN	LYRE
******	**L-D-**	LUGS	LAMB	LYNX	******
KAZI	******	******	LAME	******	**L-S-**
******	LADD	**L-H-**	LAMP	**L-O-**	******
L-A-	LADE	******	LAMS	******	LASH
******	LADS	LAHR	LEMS	LAON	LASS
LEAD	LADY	LEHR	LIMA	LAOS	LAST
LEAF	LEDA	******	LIMB	LEON	LESS
LEAH	LEDE	**L-I-**	LIME	LEOS	LEST
LEAK	LIDO	******	LIMN	LION	LISA
LEAL	LIDS	LAIC	LIMP	LOOD	LISP
LEAN	LODE	LAID	LIMU	LOOF	LISS
LEAP	LODI	LAIN	LIMY	LOOK	LIST
LEAR	LODZ	LAIR	LOMA	LOOM	LOSE
LEAS	LUDO	LAIT	LOME	LOON	LOSS
LIAO	******	LEIF	LUMP	LOOP	LOST
LIAR	**L-E-**	LEIS	LYME	LOOS	LUSH
LOAD	******	LOIN	******	LOOT	LUST
LOAF	LEEK	LOIS	**L-N-**	LWOW	LYSE
LOAM	LEER	LUIS	******	******	LYSI
LOAN	LEES	LUIZ	LANA	**L-P-**	******
LUAU	LEET	******	LAND	******	**L-T-**
******	LIED	**L-K-**	LANE	LAPP	******
L-B-	LIEF	******	LANG	LAPS	LATE
******	LIEN	LAKE	LANK	LEPT	LATH
LABS	LIES	LAKH	LENA	LIPO	LATI
LOBE	LIEU	LAKY	LEND	LIPS	LETI
LOBO	LUES	LEKS	LENE	LOPE	LETO
LOBS	LYES	LIKE	LENO	LOPS	LETS
				LUPE	

LETT	******	MEDE	MEIR	******	MOOD
LITE	L-Z-	MEDI	MOIL	M-M-	MOON
LITH	******	MIDI	MOIO	******	MOOR
LOTE	LAZE	MODE	MUIR	MAMA	MOOS
LOTH	LAZY	MODI	******	MEMO	MOOT
LOTS	LIZA	MODS	M-J-	MEMS	MUON
LOTT	LYZE	MUDS	******	MIME	******
LUTA	******	******	MAJO	MIMI	M-P-
LUTE	M-A-	M-E-	MOJO	MOMO	******
LUTH	******	******	******	MOMS	MAPS
LYTE	MAAL	MAES	M-K-	MUMM	MOPE
******	MAAM	MEEK	******	MUMS	MOPS
L-U-	MAAS	MEET	MAKA	******	******
******	MEAD	MIEN	MAKE	M-N-	M-R-
LAUD	MEAH	MMES	MAKO	******	******
LAUN	MEAL	MOES	MIKE	MANA	MARA
LEUC	MEAN	MYEL	MOKE	MANE	MARC
LEUD	MEAT	******	MOKI	MANI	MARE
LEUK	MOAB	M-F-	******	MANN	MARJ
LOUD	MOAN	******	M-L-	MANO	MARK
LOUP	MOAS	MIFF	******	MANS	MARL
LOUR	MOAT	MUFF	MALE	MANX	MARS
LOUT	MZAB	******	MALI	MANY	MART
******	******	M-G-	MALL	MEND	MARX
L-V-	M-B-	******	MALM	MENE	MARY
******	******	MAGE	MALO	MENI	MERE
LAVA	MABS	MAGI	MALT	MENO	MERL
LAVE	MIBS	MEGA	MELD	MENT	MERO
LEVA	MOBS	MEGS	MELE	MENU	MERU
LEVI	******	MIGS	MELS	MINA	MERV
LEVO	M-C-	MSGR	MELT	MIND	MIRA
LEVY	******	MSGT	MILD	MINE	MIRE
LIVE	MACE	MUGS	MILE	MING	MIRO
LOVE	MACH	******	MILK	MINI	MIRS
******	MACK	M-H-	MILL	MINK	MIRV
L-W-	MACS	******	MILO	MINN	MIRY
******	MICA	MAHA	MILS	MINT	MORA
LAWN	MICE	MOHO	MILT	MINX	MORE
LAWS	MICH	MOHR	MLLE	MONA	MORN
LEWD	MICK	******	MOLD	MONK	MORO
LEWS	MOCK	M-I-	MOLE	MONO	MORS
LOWS	MUCH	******	MOLL	MONS	MORT
******	MUCI	MAIA	MOLT	MONT	MURK
L-X-	MUCK	MAID	MOLY	MYNA	MYRA
******	MUCO	MAIL	MULE	******	MYRI
LUXE	MYCO	MAIM	MULL	M-O-	******
******	******	MAIN	MULT	******	M-S-
L-Y-	M-D-	MEIO		MEOW	******
******	******			MHOS	MASC
LAYS	MADE				MASH
	MADS				

MASK
MASS
MAST
MESA
MESH
MESO
MESS
MISC
MISE
MISO
MISS
MIST
MOSE
MOSS
MOST
MUSE
MUSH
MUSK
MUSS
MUST
******
M-T-
******
MATE
MATH
MATS
MATT
META
METE
METH
METR
METZ
MITE
MITT
MOTE
MOTH
MOTS
MOTT
MSTH
MSTS
MUTE
MUTH
MUTS
MUTT
MYTH
******
M-U-
******
MAUD
MAUI

MAUL
MAUN
MOUE
******
M-V-
******
MOVE
******
M-W-
******
MAWS
MEWL
MEWS
MOWN
MOWS
******
M-X-
******
MAXI
MIXT
MOXA
MYXA
MYXO
******
M-Y-
******
MAYA
MAYO
MAYS
******
M-Z-
******
MAZE
MAZY
******
N-A-
******
NCAA
NCAR
NDAK
NEAL
NEAP
NEAR
NEAT
NGAN
NOAH
******
N-B-
******
NABO
NABS

NEBO
NEBS
NIBS
NOBS
NUBS
******
N-C-
******
NECK
NECR
NICE
NICK
NOCK
NOCT
******
N-D-
******
NADA
NEDS
NIDE
NIDI
NODE
NODS
NUDE
NUDI
******
N-E-
******
NAEL
NEED
NEER
NIEL
NOEL
NOES
NYET
******
N-G-
******
NAGA
NAGS
NIGH
NIGR
NOGG
NOGO
NOGS
******
N-H-
******
NAHA

******
N-I-
******
NAIF
NAIL
NAIN
NAIS
NEIL
NOIL
******
N-J-
******
NAJA
NEJD
******
N-K-
******
NIKE
******
N-L-
******
NALU
NELL
NILE
NULL
******
N-M-
******
NAMA
NAME
NEMA
NEMO
NIMB
NOMA
NOME
NOMO
NOMY
NUMB
******
N-N-
******
NANA
NANO
NANS
NENE
NINA
NINE
NINO

NONA
NONE
NUNS
******
N-O-
******
NAOS
NEON
NOOK
NOON
******
NOTO
******
N-P-
******
NAPA
NAPE
NAPS
NEPH
NIPA
NIPS
NOPE
******
N-R-
******
NARC
NARD
NARY
NERO
NLRB
NORA
NORD
NORM
NORN
******
N-S-
******
NASA
NASH
NASO
NAST
NESS
NEST
NISI
NOSE
NOSH
NOSO
NOSY
******
N-T-
******
NATE
NATL

NATO
NATR
NATS
NATT
NETS
NITA
NITR
NITS
NOTE
NOTO
NOTT
NUTS
******
N-U-
******
NAUT
NEUM
NEUR
NIUE
NOUN
NOUS
******
N-V-
******
NAVE
NAVY
NEVE
NEVI
NKVD
NOVA
******
N-W-
******
NAWA
NEWS
NEWT
NOWS
NOWT
******
N-X-
******
NEXT
******
N-Y-
******
NAYS
******
N-Z-
******
NAZE
NAZI

******	OMEN	ORIG	******	******	PICR
O-A-	OMER	OSIS	**O-R-**	**O-Z-**	PICT
******	ONER	OTIC	******	******	POCK
ODAL	ONES	OTIS	OARS	ONZA	POCO
OKAS	OPEN	OVID	OCRA	OOZE	PUCE
OKAY	OREL	******	OGRE	OOZY	PUCK
OLAF	ORES	**O-K-**	OKRA	******	******
OLAV	OSEL	******	OURS	**P-A-**	**P-D-**
OLAY	OTEA	OAKS	******	******	******
OMAN	OVEN	******	**O-S-**	PAAL	PADS
OMAR	OVER	**O-L-**	******	PEAG	PEDE
OPAH	OWED	******	OAST	PEAK	PEDI
OPAL	OWEN	OGLE	OISE	PEAL	PEDO
ORAL	OWES	OILS	OLST	PEAN	PHDS
ORAN	OXEN	OILY	OMSK	PEAR	PODA
OSAR	OYER	OKLA	OPSY	PEAS	PODE
OVAL	OYES	OLLA	OSSA	PEAT	PODS
******	OYEZ	OLLY	OSSI	PHAG	******
O-B-	******	ONLY	OUSE	PIAF	**P-E-**
******	**O-F-**	ORLE	OUST	PIAY	******
OMBR	******	ORLY	******	PLAN	PAED
ORBS	OAFS	OSLO	**O-T-**	PLAT	PEEK
******	******	OWLS	******	PLAY	PEEL
O-C-	**O-G-**	******	OATH	PRAE	PEEN
******	******	**O-M-**	OATS	PRAM	PEEP
ONCA	OLGA	******	OCTA	PRAO	PEER
ONCE	ORGY	OHMS	OCTO	PRAY	PEES
ORCA	******	******	ONTO	PTAH	PHEN
ORCS	**O-H-**	**O-N-**	OPTS	PYAT	PHEW
OUCH	******	******	ORTH	******	PIED
******	OAHU	OENO	ORTS	**P-B-**	PIER
O-D-	OCHA	OINO	OSTE	******	PIES
******	OPHI	OMNI	OTTO	PABA	PLEA
ODDS	******	OONA	OUTS	PUBS	PLEB
ONDO	**O-I-**	ORNE	******	******	PLED
ORDO	******	OWNS	**O-U-**	**P-C-**	PLEW
******	OBIA	******	******	******	POEM
O-E-	OBIS	**O-O-**	OCUL	PACA	POET
******	OBIT	******	ODUM	PACE	PREP
OBEY	ODIC	OBOE	OEUF	PACK	PRES
ODEA	ODIN	OBOL	ONUS	PACO	PREY
ODER	OHIA	ODOR	OPUS	PACT	PTER
ODES	OHIO	OLOR	OVUM	PECK	PYEL
OGEE	OKIE	ONON	******	PECO	PYES
OKED	OLIG	OTOE	**O-Y-**	PICA	PYET
OKET	OLIO	OXON	******	PICE	******
OLEO	OMIT	******	ODYL	PICK	**P-F-**
OMEI	OPIA	**O-P-**	ONYX	PICO	******
		******	ORYX	PICR	PUFF
		OGPU			
		OLPE			

******	PALM	PINY	PEPO	PISA	******
P-G-	PALP	POND	PEPS	PISC	**P-W-**
******	PALS	PONE	PIPA	PISH	******
PAGE	PALY	PONG	PIPE	PISO	PAWL
PEGS	PELE	PONS	PIPS	POSE	PAWN
PIGS	PELF	PONY	PIPY	POSH	PAWS
POGO	PELT	PUNA	POPE	POST	PEWS
POGY	PELU	PUND	POPS	POSY	POWS
PUGH	PILE	PUNG	PUPA	PUSH	******
PUGS	PILI	PUNK	PUPS	PUSS	**P-X-**
******	PILL	PUNS	******	******	******
P-H-	POLE	PUNT	**P-R-**	**P-T-**	PIXY
******	POLK	PUNY	******	******	******
PAHA	POLL	******	PARA	PATE	**P-Y-**
PSHA	POLO	**P-O-**	PARD	PATH	******
******	POLY	******	PARE	PATS	PAYE
P-I-	PULE	PEON	PARI	PETE	PAYS
******	PULL	PHON	PARK	PETR	PHYL
PAID	PULP	PHOT	PARR	PETS	PHYT
PAIL	PYLE	PION	PARS	PITA	PNYX
PAIN	******	PIOT	PART	PITH	******
PAIR	**P-M-**	PLOD	PERA	PITO	**P-Z-**
PAIS	******	PLOP	PERE	PITS	******
PHIL	PAMS	PLOT	PERI	PITT	PIZZ
PHIS	PIMA	PLOW	PERK	PITY	******
PRIG	PIMP	PLOY	PERM	POTS	**Q-A-**
PRIM	POME	POOD	PERN	PUTS	******
PSIS	POMP	POOH	PERT	PUTT	QUAB
PYIC	PUMA	POOK	PERU	******	QUAD
PYIN	PUMP	POOL	PIRN	**P-U-**	QUAG
******	******	POON	PORE	******	QUAI
P-K-	**P-N-**	POOP	PORK	PAUL	QUAN
******	******	POOR	PORN	PHUD	QUAR
PIKA	PANE	PROA	PORT	PHUT	QUAT
PIKE	PANG	PROD	PURE	PIUS	QUAY
PIKI	PANK	PROF	PURI	PLUG	******
POKE	PANS	PROM	PURL	PLUM	**Q-E-**
POKU	PANT	PRON	PURR	PLUS	******
POKY	PEND	PROP	PYRE	POUF	QUEI
PUKA	PENN	PROS	PYRO	POUR	******
PUKE	PENS	PROT	******	POUT	**Q-I-**
******	PENT	PROW	**P-S-**	PRUE	******
P-L-	PINA	PYOT	******	PUUD	QAIS
******	PINE	******	PASH	******	QUID
PALA	PING	**P-P-**	PASS	**P-V-**	QUIP
PALE	PINK	******	PAST	******	QUIT
PALI	PINS	PAPA	PESO	PAVE	QUIZ
PALL	PINT	PAPS	PEST	PAVO	******
					Q-N-
					******
					QUNG

******	ROCK	RAGI	******	RIOT	RATH
Q-O-	RUCK	RAGS	**R-M-**	ROOD	RATI
******	******	RIGA	******	ROOF	RATO
QUOD	**R-D-**	RIGS	RAMA	ROOK	RATS
******	******	RUGA	RAME	ROOM	RETE
Q-P-	RADA	RUGS	RAMI	ROOP	RETS
******	RADS		RAMP	ROOT	RITA
QOPH	REDE	**R-H-**	RAMS	RYOT	RITE
******	REDO	******	RCMP	******	ROTA
R-A-	REDS	RAHU	REMI	**R-P-**	ROTC
******	RIDE	RUHR	REMO	******	ROTE
RAAB	RIDS	******	REMS	RAPE	ROTI
RAAD	RODE	**R-I-**	RIME	RAPS	ROTL
READ	RODS	******	RIMS	RAPT	ROTS
REAL	RUDD	RAID	RIMY	REPP	RUTA
REAM	RUDE	RAIK	ROMA	REPS	RUTE
REAP	RUDY	RAIL	ROME	RIPA	RUTH
REAR	******	RAIN	ROMP	RIPE	RUTS
RIAL	**R-E-**	REIN	ROMS	RIPS	******
ROAD	******	REIS	RUMP	ROPE	**R-U-**
ROAM	RAES	RHIN	RUMS	ROPY	******
ROAN	REED	RHIZ	******	******	RHUM
ROAR	REEF	RIIS	**R-N-**	**R-R-**	RHUS
RUAY	REEK	ROIL	******	******	ROUE
RYAN	REEL	RUIN	RANA	RARE	ROUP
******	RHEA	******	RAND	RORY	ROUT
R-B-	RHEO	**R-J-**	RANG	******	ROUX
******	RIEN	******	RANI	**R-S-**	******
RABA	ROES	RAJA	RANK	******	**R-V-**
REBA	RUED	RIJN	RANT	RASA	******
REBS	RUER	******	RENA	RASE	RAVE
RIBS	RUES	**R-K-**	REND	RASH	REVS
ROBE	RYES	******	RENE	RASP	RIVA
ROBS	******	RAKE	RENI	RESH	RIVE
RUBE	**R-F-**	RAKI	RENO	REST	RIVO
RUBS	******	******	RENT	RISE	ROVE
RUBY	RAFF	**R-L-**	RIND	RISK	RSVP
******	RAFT	******	RING	ROSA	******
R-C-	REFT	RALE	RINK	ROSE	**R-W-**
******	RIFE	RALL	RONA	ROSS	******
RACE	RIFF	RALO	RUNE	ROSY	ROWS
RACK	RIFT	RELY	RUNG	RUSE	******
RACY	RUFE	RILE	RUNS	RUSH	**R-X-**
RECK	RUFF	RILL	RUNT	RUSK	******
RECT	******	ROLE	RYND	RUSS	ROXY
RICE	**R-G-**	ROLF	******	RUST	******
RICH	******	ROLL	**R-O-**	******	**R-Y-**
RICK	RAGA	RULE	******	**R-T-**	******
	RAGE		RHOB	******	RAYS
			RHOS	RATA	RHYL
				RATE	

RHYS	SOAP	******	STEW	SLIM	SOLS
ROYS	SOAR	**S-D-**	SUED	SLIP	STLO
******	SPAD	******	SUER	SLIT	SULK
R-Z-	SPAM	SADE	SUES	SMIT	SULU
******	SPAN	SADH	SUET	SNIG	******
RAZE	SPAR	SADI	SUEZ	SNIP	**S-M-**
RAZZ	SPAS	SIDE	******	SNIT	******
******	SPAT	SIDS	**S-F-**	SOIL	SAMA
S-A-	SPAY	SODA	******	SOIR	SAME
******	STAB	SODS	SAFE	SPIN	SAMP
SAAH	STAG	SUDD	SIFT	SPIR	SAMS
SAAR	STAN	SUDS	SOFA	SPIT	SEME
SCAB	STAR	******	SOFT	SPIV	SEMI
SCAD	STAT	**S-E-**	SUFI	STIR	SIMA
SCAN	STAY	******	******	SUIT	SIMP
SCAR	SWAB	SEED	**S-G-**	SWIG	SIMS
SCAT	SWAG	SEEK	******	SWIM	SOMA
SDAK	SWAM	SEEL	SAGA	******	SOME
SEAH	SWAN	SEEM	SAGE	**S-J-**	SUMO
SEAL	SWAP	SEEN	SAGO	******	SUMP
SEAM	SWAT	SEEP	SAGS	SEJM	SUMS
SEAN	SWAY	SEER	SAGY	SOJA	******
SEAR	******	SEES	SEGO	******	**S-N-**
SEAS	**S-B-**	SHEA	SIGH	**S-K-**	******
SEAT	******	SHED	SIGN	******	SANA
SHAD	SABE	SHEM	******	SAKE	SAND
SHAG	SABS	SHES	**S-H-**	SAKI	SANE
SHAH	SEBI	SHEW	******	SIKH	SANG
SHAM	SEBO	SKEE	SAHH	SOKE	SANK
SHAN	SIBS	SKEG	SOHO	SUKY	SANS
SHAW	SOBS	SKEP	******	******	SEND
SHAY	SUBJ	SKEW	**S-I-**	**S-L-**	SENS
SIAL	SUBS	SLED	******	******	SENT
SIAM	******	SLEE	SAIC	SALE	SIND
SKAG	**S-C-**	SLEW	SAID	SALK	SINE
SKAT	******	SMEE	SAIL	SALP	SING
SKAW	SACK	SMEW	SAIS	SALT	SINK
SLAB	SACS	SNEE	SHIM	SELF	SINO
SLAG	SECT	SPEC	SHIN	SELL	SINS
SLAM	SECY	SPED	SHIP	SILK	SONE
SLAP	SICE	SPES	SHIV	SILL	SONG
SLAT	SICK	SPET	SKID	SILO	SONS
SLAV	SICS	SPEW	SKIM	SILT	SUNG
SLAW	SOCK	STEM	SKIN	SOLA	SUNK
SLAY	SPCA	STEN	SKIP	SOLD	SUNN
SNAG	SPCC	STEP	SKIS	SOLE	SUNS
SNAP	SUCH	STER	SKIT	SOLI	SYNE
SOAK	SUCK	STET	SLID	SOLO	
	SYCE				

******	SUPS	SETH	******	THAD	TEEM
S-O-	SUPT	SETI	**S-V-**	THAN	TEEN
******	******	SETS	******	THAR	TEES
SCOP	**S-Q-**	SITE	SAVE	THAT	THEA
SCOT	******	SITI	SIVA	THAW	THEB
SCOW	SEQQ	SITO	SUVA	TOAD	THEE
SHOD	SPQR	SITS	******	TRAD	THEM
SHOE	******	SITU	**S-W-**	TRAH	THEN
SHOO	**S-R-**	SOTS	******	TRAM	THEO
SHOP	******	******	SAWN	TRAP	THEW
SHOQ	SARA	**S-U-**	SAWS	TRAY	THEY
SHOT	SARD	******	SEWN	TSAR	TIED
SHOW	SARI	SAUD	SEWS	TWAS	TIER
SION	SARK	SAUK	SOWN	TZAR	TIES
SLOB	SCRY	SAUL	SOWS	******	TOED
SLOE	SERA	SAUR	******	**T-B-**	TOES
SLOG	SERB	SCUD	**S-X-**	******	TREE
SLOO	SERE	SCUM	******	TABS	TREF
SLOP	SERF	SCUP	SAXE	TABU	TREK
SLOT	SERO	SCUT	SEXI	TOBY	TRES
SLOW	SERS	SHUL	SEXT	TUBA	TRET
SMOG	SIRE	SHUN	SEXY	TUBE	TREY
SNOB	SIRI	SHUT	******	TUBS	TUES
SNOG	SIRS	SKUA	**S-Y-**	******	TYEE
SNOT	SORA	SLUB	******	**T-C-**	******
SNOW	SORB	SLUE	SAYS	******	**T-F-**
SOON	SORE	SLUG	SKYE	TACE	******
SOOT	SORI	SLUM	SNYE	TACK	TAFT
SPOR	SORN	SLUR	SOYA	TACT	TIFF
SPOT	SORT	SLUT	SOYS	TICK	TOFF
STOA	SPRY	SMUG	STYX	TICS	TOFT
STOL	SURA	SMUT	******	TOCO	TUFA
STOP	SURD	SNUB	**S-Z-**	TUCK	TUFF
STOW	SURE	SNUG	******	******	TUFT
SWOP	SURF	SOUL	SIZE	**T-D-**	******
SWOT	SURG	SOUP	SIZY	******	**T-G-**
******	******	SOUR	SUZY	TADS	******
S-P-	**S-S-**	SOUS	******	TEDS	TAGS
******	******	SPUD	**T-A-**	TIDE	TEGS
SAPE	SASH	SPUE	******	TIDY	TOGA
SAPO	SASK	SPUN	TAAL	TODD	TOGO
SAPS	SASS	SPUR	TBAR	TODO	TOGS
SEPT	SESS	STUB	TEAK	TODS	TUGS
SIPS	SOSO	STUD	TEAL	TODY	******
SOPS	SUSS	STUM	TEAM	TUDE	**T-H-**
SUPA	**S-T-**	STUN	TEAR	******	******
SUPE	******	STUS	TEAS	**T-E-**	TCHI
SUPP	SATE	SWUM	TEAT	******	TSHI
	SETA			TAEL	
				TEED	

******	******	THOU	TORI	TRUE	******
T-I-	**T-M-**	TION	TORN	TRUK	**U-D-**
******	******	TOOK	TORS	TSUN	******
TAIL	TAME	TOOL	TORT	******	UNDE
TAIN	TAMP	TOON	TORY	**T-V-**	UNDO
TAIT	TAMS	TOOT	TURF	******	UNDY
TEIL	TEMA	TROD	TURK	TAVS	URDE
THIN	TEMP	TRON	TURN	TIVY	URDU
THIO	TIME	TROP	TYRE	******	URDY
THIS	TIMS	TROT	TYRO	**T-W-**	******
TOIL	TOMB	TROW	******	******	**U-E-**
TRIG	TOME	TROY	**T-S-**	TAWS	******
TRIM	TOMS	TWOS	******	TOWN	UBER
TRIN	TOMY	******	TASK	TOWS	UDEN
TRIO	TUMP	**T-P-**	TASS	******	ULEX
TRIP	******	******	TESS	**T-X-**	UREA
TRIS	**T-N-**	TAPA	TEST	******	UREY
TRIX	******	TAPE	TOSH	TAXI	USED
TWIG	TANA	TAPS	TOSS	TAXY	USER
TWIN	TANG	TIPI	TUSH	TEXT	USES
TWIT	TANK	TIPS	TUSK	******	UTER
******	TANS	TOPE	******	**T-Y-**	UTES
T-K-	TEND	TOPH	**T-T-**	******	UVEA
******	TENG	TOPI	******	TOYO	******
TAKE	TENN	TOPO	TATA	TOYS	**U-F-**
TIKE	TENO	TOPS	TATE	******	******
TIKI	TENS	TUPI	TATS	**U-A-**	URFA
TYKE	TENT	TUPS	TETE	******	**U-G-**
******	TINA	TYPE	TETH	UDAD	******
T-L-	TINE	TYPO	TETR	ULAN	UNGA
******	TING	******	TITI	UNAS	URGE
TALC	TINS	**T-R-**	TITO	UNAU	******
TALE	TINT	******	TITS	UPAS	**U-I-**
TALK	TINY	TARA	TOTE	URAL	******
TALL	TONE	TARE	TOTI	URAN	UNIE
TELA	TONG	TARN	TOTS	USAF	UNIO
TELE	TONI	TARO	TUTU	USAR	UNIT
TELL	TONO	TARP	******	UTAH	URIA
TELO	TONS	TARS	**T-U-**	UZAN	URIC
TILE	TONY	TART	******	******	USIA
TILL	TUNA	TERA	TAUR	**U-B-**	UVIC
TILT	TUNE	TERM	TAUS	******	******
TOLA	TUNS	TERN	TAUT	UEBA	**U-L-**
TOLD	TYNE	THRU	THUD	UMBO	******
TOLE	******	TIRE	THUG	******	UELE
TOLL	**T-O-**	TIRO	THUS	**U-C-**	UGLY
TOLU	******	TORA	TOUR	******	ULLA
TULA	TAOS	TORE	TOUT	UNCO	
TULE	THOR			USCG	

******	VICI	******	VASO	WRAF	******
U-M-	VICK	**V-M-**	VAST	WRAP	**W-G-**
******	VOCE	******	VEST	******	******
UCMJ	******	VAMP	VISA	**W-B-**	WAGE
USMA	**V-D-**	VIMY	VISC	******	WAGS
USMC	******	******	VISE	WABE	WIGS
USMS	VEDA	**V-N-**	VISO	WEBS	******
******	VIDE	******	VISS	******	**W-I-**
U-N-	VIDI	VANE	******	******	******
******	******	VANG	**V-T-**	**W-C-**	WAIF
UANG	**V-E-**	VANS	******	******	WAIL
ULNA	******	VENA	VATS	WACK	WAIN
URNA	VEER	VEND	VETO	WACO	WAIT
URNS	VEES	VENI	VETS	WACS	WEIR
USNA	VIED	VENT	VITA	WICH	WHIG
USNR	VIES	VINA	VITE	WICK	WHIM
******	VIEW	VINE	VITI	WYCH	WHIN
U-O-	VOET	VINI	VITR	******	WHIP
******	******	VINO	VOTE	**W-D-**	WHIR
UDOS	**V-G-**	VINY	******	******	WHIT
UPON	******	******	**V-V-**	WADE	WHIZ
******	VAGI	**V-O-**	******	WADI	WRIT
U-S-	VEGA	******	VAVS	WADS	******
******	VUGS	VIOL	VIVA	WADY	**W-K-**
URSA	******	VTOL	VIVE	WEDS	******
USSR	**V-I-**	******	VIVO	WIDE	WAKE
******	******	**V-P-**	******	******	WEKA
U-T-	VAIL	******	**V-W-**	**W-E-**	WEKI
******	VAIN	VIPS	******	******	WOKE
UMTS	VAIR	******	VOWS	WEED	******
UNTO	VEIL	**V-R-**	******	WEEK	**W-L-**
UNTZ	VEIN	******	**V-Y-**	WEEL	******
******	VOID	VARA	******	WEEP	WALD
U-U-	******	VARI	VAYU	WHEN	WALE
******	**V-L-**	VARY	******	WHET	WALK
URUS	******	VERA	**W-A-**	WHEW	WALT
******	VALE	VERB	******	WHEY	WELD
U-Z-	VALI	VERN	WAAC	WOES	WELL
******	VALS	VERS	WAAF	WREN	WELT
UNZE	VELA	VERT	WAAL	WYES	WILD
******	VELD	VERY	WEAK	******	WILE
V-A-	VILE	VIRA	WEAL	**W-F-**	WILL
******	VILI	VIRE	WEAN	******	WILT
VAAL	VILL	VORA	WEAR	WAFS	WILY
VEAL	******	VORE	WHAM	WAFT	WKLY
VIAL	**V-C-**	******	WHAP	WEFT	WOLD
******	******	**V-S-**	WHAT	WIFE	WOLF
VACA	VOLE	******	WOAD		
VICE	VOLS	VASA			
	VOLT	VASE			

******	WARM	WIVE	******	YOGH	YIPE
W-M-	WARN	WOVE	**X-R-**	YOGI	YIPS
******	WARP	******	******	YUGA	******
WOMB	WARS	**W-W-**	XERO	******	**Y-R-**
******	WART	******	******	**Y-H-**	******
W-N-	WARY	WAWL	**X-S-**	******	YARD
******	WERE	WOWS	******	YMHA	YARE
WAND	WERT	******	XOSA	YWHA	YARN
WANE	WIRE	**W-X-**	XYST	******	YORE
WANG	WIRY	******	******	**Y-I-**	YORK
WANS	WORD	WAXY	**X-T-**	******	******
WANT	WORE	******	******	YMIR	**Y-T-**
WANY	WORK	**W-Y-**	XNTY	******	******
WEND	WORM	******	XRTS	**Y-K-**	YETI
WENS	WORN	WAYS	******	******	******
WENT	WORT	WHYS	**Y-A-**	YAKA	**Y-U-**
WIND	******	******	******	YAKO	******
WINE	**W-S-**	**X-A-**	YEAH	YAKS	YAUP
WING	******	******	YEAN	YOKE	YOUD
WINK	WASH	XMAS	YEAR	YUKS	YOUP
WINO	WASP	XRAY	YEAS	******	YOUR
WINS	WAST	******	YUAN	**Y-L-**	******
WINY	WEST	**X-E-**	******	******	**Y-W-**
WONT	WISC	******	**Y-B-**	YALE	******
WYNN	WISE	XREF	******	YALU	YAWL
******	WISH	******	YABA	YELD	YAWN
W-O-	WISP	**X-I-**	******	YELK	YAWP
******	WIST	******	**Y-C-**	YELL	YAWS
WHOA	******	XDIV	******	YELP	YEWS
WHOM	**W-T-**	******	YMCA	YOLK	YHWH
WHOP	******	**X-L-**	YWCA	YULE	YOWL
WOOD	WATE	******	******	******	YOWS
WOOF	WATT	XYLO	**Y-D-**	**Y-M-**	******
WOOL	WETA	******	******	******	**Y-Y-**
WOOS	WETS	**X-M-**	YODH	YAMA	******
******	WITH	******	YODS	YAMP	YAYA
W-P-	WITS	XEMA	******	YAMS	YOYO
******	WOTE	******	**Y-E-**	YUMA	******
WAPS	******	**X-N-**	******	******	**Z-A-**
WEPT	**W-U-**	******	YLEM	**Y-N-**	******
WIPE	******	XENO	YMER	******	ZBAR
******	WAUK	XINT	YSER	YANA	ZEAL
W-R-	WAUL	******	YVES	YANG	ZOAN
******	******	**X-O-**	******	YANK	ZOAR
WARD	**W-V-**	******	**Y-G-**	YENS	******
WARE	******	XION	******	YOND	**Z-B-**
WARF	WAVE	******	YEGG	******	******
WARI	WAVY	**X-P-**	YOGA	**Y-P-**	ZEBU
		******		******	
		XIPH		YAPA	
				YAPS	

******	ZOOM	ALGA	AVID	******	ARIL
Z-C-	ZOON	ALIA	AWED	A--H	ARYL
******	ZOOS	ALMA	AXED	******	AVAL
ZACH	******	ALTA	******	ACTH	AWOL
ZACK	Z-P-	ALVA	A--E	ADAH	AXIL
******	******	AMIA	******	AFGH	******
Z-D-	ZEPH	ANNA	AARE	AHAH	A--M
******	ZIPS	ANOA	ABBE	ALPH	******
ZEDS	******	ANSA	ABIE	AMAH	ADAM
******	Z-R-	ANTA	ABLE	ANKH	AHEM
Z-E-	******	APIA	ACHE	ANTH	ALUM
******	ZARA	AQUA	ACME	ARCH	ANAM
ZEES	ZARF	AREA	ACNE	ASCH	ANIM
ZOES	ZARP	ARIA	ACRE	AUTH	ARAM
ZWEI	ZERO	ASEA	ADZE	AYAH	ARUM
******	ZIRA	ASHA	AGEE	******	ATOM
Z-G-	******	ASIA	AGUE	A--I	******
******	Z-S-	ATKA	AIDE	******	A--N
ZYGO	******	ATTA	AILE	ABRI	******
******	ZASU	AURA	AIRE	AERI	ADEN
Z-I-	ZEST	******	ALAE	AGNI	AEON
******	******	A--B	ALDE	AGRI	AGON
ZEIN	Z-T-	******	ALEE	ALAI	AKIN
ZOIC	******	ABIB	ALLE	ALLI	ALAN
******	ZATI	AHAB	ALOE	ALTI	ALEN
Z-K-	ZETA	ARAB	AMIE	AMBI	ALIN
******	******	******	ANCE	AMOI	AMEN
ZEKE	Z-U-	A--C	ANNE	ANTI	AMON
******	******	******	ANTE	AQUI	ANON
Z-L-	ZEUS	ACDC	AONE	ARNI	ARAN
******	ZOUG	ALEC	APSE	ASCI	ASSN
ZOLA	******	APOC	ARNE	ASTI	ATEN
ZULU	Z-Z-	ATIC	ARTE	ATLI	ATTN
******	******	AVEC	ASHE	ATRI	AVON
Z-N-	ZIZZ	******	ATLE	******	AXON
******	ZUZA	A--D	AUBE	A--K	AYIN
ZANT	******	******	AUDE	******	AZAN
ZANY	A--A	ABED	AUNE	ADAK	AZON
ZEND	******	ACAD	AXLE	AMOK	******
ZENO	ABBA	ACED	AYME	******	A--O
ZINC	ACEA	ACID	******	A--L	******
ZING	ACTA	AGED	A--F	******	ACRO
ZONA	AGHA	AMID	******	ABEL	AERO
ZONE	AGRA	APED	ALEF	AMYL	AFRO
ZUNI	AGUA	APOD	ALIF	ANAL	AGAO
******	AIDA	ARAD	ASOF	ANIL	AGIO
Z-O-	ALBA	ARID	******	AOUL	AGRO
******	ALFA	AULD	A--G	ARAL	AINO
ZION			******		
ZOOL			AGOG		

ALDO	ACTS	AVIS	******	******	BALE
ALLO	ADAS	AWES	**A--Y**	**B--B**	BANE
ALSO	ADDS	AWLS	******	******	BARE
ALTO	AGAS	AWNS	ABBY	BARB	BASE
AMBO	AGES	AXES	ABLY	BIBB	BATE
AMMO	AIDS	AXIS	ADAY	BLAB	BEDE
ANNO	AILS	AYES	ADDY	BLEB	BENE
APIO	AIMS	******	AERY	BLOB	BICE
AREO	AINS	**A--T**	AHOY	BLUB	BIDE
ARGO	AIRS	******	AIRY	BOMB	BIHE
ARNO	ALAS	ABET	ALGY	BOOB	BIKE
ATMO	ALBS	ABUT	ALLY	BULB	BILE
ATTO	ALES	ACCT	AMOY	******	BINE
AUTO	ALFS	ACET	ANCY	**B--C**	BISE
******	ALMS	ADIT	ANDY	******	BITE
A--P	ALPS	AINT	ARMY	BANC	BLUE
******	ALYS	ALIT	ARTY	BLOC	BODE
ALOP	AMAS	AMAT	ASHY	BMOC	BOLE
ATOP	AMES	ANAT	ATTY	BSSC	BONE
******	AMIS	ASST	AUBY	******	BORE
A--R	AMOS	AUNT	AWAY	**B--D**	BRAE
******	AMPS	AUST	AWNY	******	BRIE
ABBR	AMTS	******	AWRY	BALD	BULE
ACER	AMUS	**A--U**	******	BAND	BUTE
ACOR	AMYS	******	**A--Z**	BARD	BYEE
ADAR	ANAS	ABOU	******	BAWD	BYRE
AFAR	ANIS	ACLU	ARIZ	BEAD	******
AGAR	ANNS	ACOU		BEND	**B--F**
AJAR	ANTS	AINU	**B--A**	BIND	******
ALAR	ANUS	ATTU	******	BIRD	BAFF
AMER	APES	******	BABA	BLED	BEEF
AMIR	APIS	**A--V**	BAGA	BLVD	BIFF
AMOR	APUS	******	BAIA	BOLD	BUFF
AMUR	ARAS	AVIV	BAJA	BOND	******
ASIR	ARCS	AZOV	BAYA	BOYD	**B--G**
ASTR	ARES	******	BEDA	BRAD	******
ATAR	ARKS	**A--W**	BEKA	BRED	BANG
ATOR	ARMS	******	BELA	BSED	BELG
AVER	ARNS	ALOW	BEMA	BUDD	BENG
AYER	ARTS	ANEW	BERA	BUND	BERG
******	ASAS	AROW	BESA	BURD	BING
A--S	ASIS	AVOW	BETA	BYRD	BLDG
******	ASKS	******	BOLA	******	BONG
AALS	ASPS	**A--X**	BONA	**B--E**	BRAG
ABAS	ATES	******	BORA	******	BRIG
ABCS	AUKS	AJAX	BOTA	BABE	BULG
ABES	AVAS	ALEX	BREA	BADE	BUNG
ACES	AVES	ALIX	BUNA	BAKE	BURG
		APEX			

******	BALL	BIRO	BEGS	BENT	BONY
B--H	BAWL	BOLO	BELS	BERT	BRAY
******	BELL	BONO	BENS	BEST	BUOY
BACH	BIBL	BOZO	BESS	BITT	BURY
BASH	BIEL	BRIO	BETS	BLAT	BUSY
BATH	BILL	BRNO	BEVS	BLET	******
BETH	BIOL	BROO	BEYS	BLIT	B--Z
BINH	BIRL	BUBO	BIAS	BLOT	******
BLAH	BOIL	******	BIBS	BOAT	BATZ
BOSH	BOLL	B--P	BIDS	BOLT	BOAZ
BOTH	BOWL	******	BINS	BOOT	BRAZ
BUSH	BUHL	BEEP	BITS	BORT	BROZ
******	BULL	BLIP	BMUS	BOTT	BUZZ
B--I	BURL	BUMP	BOAS	BOUT	******
******	******	BURP	BOBS	BRAT	C--A
BABI	B--M	******	BOGS	BRET	******
BALI	******	B--R	BOIS	BRIT	CANA
BANI	BALM	******	BOOS	BRUT	CAPA
BARI	BARM	BAAR	BOPS	BUNT	CARA
BENI	BEAM	BAER	BOSS	BURT	CATA
BONI	BERM	BAGR	BOTS	BUST	CAVA
BOVI	BLEM	BEAR	BOWS	BUTT	CEBA
******	BOOM	BEER	BOYS	******	CECA
B--K	BRIM	BHAR	BRAS	B--U	CEPA
******	BROM	BIER	BUBS	******	CHIA
BACK	******	BIRR	BUDS	BABU	COCA
BALK	B--N	BLUR	BUGS	BAKU	CODA
BANK	******	BOAR	BUMS	BEAU	COLA
BARK	BANN	BOER	BUNS	******	COMA
BASK	BARN	BOHR	BURS	B--V	COPA
BEAK	BEAN	BOOR	BUSS	******	CORA
BECK	BEEN	BRER	BUTS	BREV	COXA
BEEK	BERN	BURR	BUYS	******	CUBA
BILK	BION	******	BYES	B--W	CUYA
BOCK	BONN	B--S	******	******	CYMA
BONK	BOON	******	B--T	BLEW	******
BOOK	BORN	BAAS	******	BLOW	C--B
BOSK	BOSN	BABS	BAHT	BOUW	******
BUCK	BRAN	BAGS	BAIT	BRAW	CAMB
BULK	BREN	BANS	BALT	BREW	CARB
BUNK	BRON	BARS	BANT	BROW	CHUB
BUSK	BUNN	BASS	BAPT	******	CLUB
******	BURN	BATS	BART	B--Y	COBB
B--L	******	BAYS	BAST	******	COMB
******	B--O	BBLS	BATT	BABY	CRAB
BAAL	******	BEAS	BEAT	BEVY	CRIB
BAEL	BAGO	BEDS	BEET	BODY	CURB
BAIL	BARO	BEES	BELT	BOGY	

******	CODE	******	******	COUP	CRUS
C--C	COKE	**C--J**	**C--N**	CRAP	CUBS
******	COLE	******	******	CROP	CUDS
CANC	COME	CLUJ	CAEN	CUSP	CUES
CHIC	CONE	CONJ	CAIN	******	CUPS
CIRC	COPE	******	CHIN	**C--R**	CURS
CONC	CORE	**C--K**	CION	******	CUSS
******	COTE	******	CLAN	CARR	CUTS
C--D	COUE	CALK	CLON	CHAR	******
******	COVE	CASK	COIN	CHIR	**C--T**
CARD	CREE	CAUK	CONN	CHUR	******
CHAD	CUBE	COCK	COON	CLAR	CANT
CHGD	CULE	CONK	CORN	CMDR	CAPT
CHID	CURE	COOK	CRAN	COIR	CART
CHUD	CUTE	CORK	CTEN	COMR	CAST
CLAD	CYME	CUSK	CYAN	COPR	CELT
CLOD	CYTE	******	******	CUIR	CENT
COED	******	**C--L**	**C--O**	CUPR	CERT
COLD	**C--F**	******	******	CZAR	CEST
COND	******	CALL	CACO	******	CHAT
CORD	CALF	CARL	CARO	**C--S**	CHET
CRUD	CHEF	CAUL	CATO	******	CHIT
CUED	CLEF	CEIL	CENO	CABS	CIST
CURD	COEF	CELL	CERO	CADS	CLOT
******	COIF	CHIL	CLEO	CAMS	COAT
C--E	CONF	CHOL	CLIO	CANS	COLT
******	CORF	CIEL	COCO	CAPS	CONT
CADE	CUFF	COAL	COHO	CARS	COOT
CAFE	******	COEL	COLO	CASS	COPT
CAGE	**C--G**	COIL	COMO	CATS	COST
CAKE	******	COLL	CRYO	CAWS	CRAT
CAME	CHUG	COOL	CYMO	CAYS	CRIT
CANE	CLEG	COWL	CYTO	CEES	CULT
CAPE	CLOG	CULL	******	CESS	CURT
CARE	CONG	CURL	**C--P**	CHES	CYST
CASE	CRAG	CYCL	******	CHGS	******
CATE	******	******	CAMP	CHIS	**C--U**
CAVE	**C--H**	**C--M**	CAPP	COBS	******
CEDE	******	******	CARP	CODS	CEBU
CELE	CASH	CALM	CHAP	COGS	CHOU
CENE	CATH	CHEM	CHIP	COLS	******
CERE	CHIH	CHUM	CHOP	CONS	**C--W**
CHEE	COSH	CLAM	CLAP	COOS	******
CIDE	CUSH	CLEM	CLIP	COPS	CHAW
CINE	******	COMM	CLOP	COSS	CHEW
CITE	**C--I**	CORM	COMP	COTS	CHOW
CLEE	******	COSM	COOP	COWS	CLAW
CLUE	CADI	CRAM	CORP	CRES	CLEW
	CALI	CULM			
	CAZI				

CRAW	DONA	DIME	******	DERM	DHAR
CREW	DORA	DINE	**D--I**	DIAM	DOER
CROW	DUMA	DIRE	******	DOOM	DOOR
******	DUNA	DIVE	DALI	DORM	DORR
C--X	DURA	DOGE	DECI	DRAM	DOUR
******	DYNA	DOLE	DEFI	DRUM	DUAR
CALX	******	DOME	DELI	DUIM	DURR
COAX	**D--B**	DONE	DEMI	******	DYER
CRUX	******	DOPE	DESI	**D--N**	******
******	DARB	DORE	DEVI	******	**D--S**
C--Y	DAUB	DOSE	DHAI	DAMN	******
******	DRAB	DOTE	DILI	DARN	DABS
CAGY	DRIB	DOVE	DIVI	DAWN	DADS
CARY	DRUB	DOZE	******	DEAN	DAGS
CAVY	DUMB	DUCE	**D--K**	DHAN	DAIS
CHAY	******	DUDE	******	DIAN	DAKS
CITY	**D--C**	DUKE	DANK	DION	DAMS
CLAY	******	DUNE	DARK	DOON	DANS
CLOY	DESC	DUPE	DAWK	DOWN	DAPS
CODY	DISC	DUSE	DECK	DRIN	DAWS
COLY	******	DYKE	DESK	DURN	DAYS
CONY	**D--D**	DYNE	DHAK	DYAN	DEBS
COPY	******	******	DICK	******	DEES
COSY	DEAD	**D--F**	DIRK	**D--O**	DENS
COTY	DECD	******	DISK	******	DESS
COZY	DEED	DAFF	DOCK	DADO	DEUS
******	DIED	DEAF	DUCK	DAGO	DEVS
C--Z	DUAD	DELF	DUNK	DEGO	DEWS
******	DYAD	DOFF	DUSK	DEMO	DEYS
CHEZ	DYED	DOLF	DYAK	DIDO	DIAS
******	******	DUFF	******	DILO	DIBS
D--A	**D--E**	******	**D--L**	DINO	DIES
******	******	**D--G**	******	DODO	DIGS
DADA	DACE	******	DAIL	DURO	DIMS
DANA	DADE	DANG	DEAL	******	DINS
DAPA	DALE	DIAG	DEIL	**D--P**	DIOS
DATA	DAME	DING	DELL	******	DIPS
DAZA	DANE	DOUG	DESL	DAMP	DMUS
DECA	DARE	DRAG	DHAL	DEEP	DOES
DEJA	DATE	DRUG	DIAL	DOPP	DOGS
DEKA	DAVE	DUNG	DILL	DORP	DOLS
DEPA	DAZE	******	DIPL	DRIP	DOMS
DEVA	DEKE	**D--H**	DOLL	DROP	DONS
DINA	DELE	******	DUAL	DUMP	DORS
DITA	DEME	DASH	DUEL	******	DOSS
DIVA	DENE	DICH	DULL	**D--M**	DOTS
DOLA	DICE	DISH	******	******	DUBS
DOMA	DIKE	DOTH	**D--M**	DAWM	DUDS
		DRAH	******	DEEM	

DUES	DEWY	******	******	ENDO	EVAS
DUGS	DIDY	**E--D**	**E--L**	ENTO	EVES
DUNS	DOBY	******	******	ENYO	EWES
DUOS	DOGY	EGAD	EARL	ERGO	EXES
DYES	DOPY	EKED	ECCL	EURO	EYAS
******	DORY	ENID	ECOL	******	EYES
D--T	DOTY	EXOD	ELUL	**E--R**	******
******	DOXY	EYED	EMIL	******	**E--T**
DAFT	DOZY	******	ENCL	EDER	******
DART	DRAY	**E--E**	ENOL	EGER	EAST
DEBT	DULY	******	ERAL	EMIR	ECHT
DEFT	DUTY	EASE	ETAL	ENGR	EDIT
DENT	******	EDGE	EVIL	EVER	ELST
DEPT	**D--Z**	EDIE	EXCL	EWER	EMIT
DEUT	******	EIRE	******	******	ERST
DIET	DIAZ	ELBE	**E--M**	**E--S**	EXIT
DINT	******	ELKE	******	******	EYOT
DIRT	**E--A**	ELSE	EDAM	EARS	******
DIST	******	ENCE	EDOM	EATS	**E--U**
DOIT	ECUA	ENTE	ELAM	EBBS	******
DOLT	EDDA	EPEE	ELEM	ECUS	ECRU
DONT	EDNA	ERIE	EXAM	EDHS	EMEU
DOST	ELBA	ERLE	******	EELS	ESAU
DRAT	ELIA	ERNE	**E--N**	EENS	******
DUCT	ELLA	ERSE	******	EFFS	**E--V**
DUET	ELMA	ESCE	EARN	EFTS	******
DUIT	ELSA	ESNE	EBAN	EGGS	ELEV
DUNT	ELVA	ESSE	EBEN	EGOS	******
DUST	EMIA	ESTE	EBON	EKES	**E--W**
******	EMMA	ETTE	ECON	ELIS	******
D--U	ENNA	EVOE	EDEN	ELKS	ENOW
******	ERDA	EYRE	EGAN	ELLS	******
DANU	ERIA	******	ELAN	ELMS	**E--X**
DIEU	ERMA	**E--H**	ERIN	EMUS	******
******	ETNA	******	ETHN	ENDS	EAUX
D--W	ETTA	EACH	ETON	ENNS	******
******	EYRA	ESTH	EVAN	ENOS	**E--Y**
DHOW	EZBA	ETAH	EVEN	EONS	******
DRAW	EZRA	ETCH	EWAN	EOUS	EASY
DREW	******	EXCH	EXON	EPOS	EDDY
******	**E--C**	******	******	ERAS	EDGY
D--Y	******	**E--I**	**E--O**	ERGS	EELY
******	******	******	******	ERIS	EERY
DAVY	EDUC	EQUI	EBRO	ERNS	ELMY
DDAY	ELEC	ETUI	ECHO	EROS	EMMY
DEFY	EPIC	******	ECTO	ERRS	ENCY
DEMY	ERIC	**E--K**	ELEO	ETAS	ENVY
DENY	EXEC	******	ELMO	ETHS	ESPY
		EFIK			
		ERIK			
		EZEK			

EURY	FARE	FUCI	FINN	FELS	******
EYRY	FATE	FUJI	FIRN	FENS	**F--W**
******	FAYE	******	FLAN	FESS	******
F--A	FAZE	**F--K**	FOHN	FEUS	FLAW
******	FEME	******	FRAN	FIBS	FLEW
FALA	FETE	FINK	FURN	FIDS	FLOW
FATA	FICE	FLAK	******	FIGS	FROW
FICA	FIFE	FOLK	**F--O**	FILS	******
FILA	FILE	FORK	******	FINS	**F--X**
FLEA	FINE	FUNK	FADO	FIRS	******
FNMA	FIRE	******	FANO	FITS	FLAX
FORA	FIVE	**F--L**	FARO	FMCS	FLEX
FREA	FLEE	******	FICO	FOBS	FLUX
FULA	FLOE	FAIL	FILO	FOES	******
******	FLUE	FALL	FLUO	FOGS	**F--Y**
F--B	FORE	FARL	FRIO	FOPS	******
******	FRAE	FEEL	******	FOSS	FLAY
FLUB	FREE	FELL	**F--P**	FOYS	FOGY
FORB	FROE	FILL	******	FRAS	FOXY
******	FUME	FOAL	FACP	FUNS	FRAY
F--C	FUSE	FOIL	FLAP	FURS	FREY
******	FUYE	FOLL	FLIP	FUSS	FUMY
FDIC	FUZE	FOOL	FLOP	******	FURY
FISC	FYKE	FOUL	FRAP	**F--T**	**F--Z**
FLOC	******	FOWL	******	******	******
******	**F--F**	FUEL	**F--Q**	FACT	FITZ
F--D	******	FULL	******	FAST	FIZZ
******	FIEF	FURL	FREQ	FEAT	FUZZ
FEED	******	******	******	FEET	******
FEND	**F--G**	**F--M**	**F--R**	FELT	**G--A**
FEOD	******	******	******	FEST	******
FEUD	FANG	FAAM	FAIR	FIAT	GAEA
FIND	FLAG	FARM	FEAR	FIST	GAGA
FLED	FLOG	FILM	FEBR	FLAT	GAIA
FOLD	FONG	FIRM	FIBR	FLIT	GALA
FOND	FROG	FLAM	FLOR	FLOT	GAMA
FOOD	FUNG	FLEM	FOUR	FONT	GARA
FORD	******	FOAM	******	FOOT	GATA
FRED	**F--H**	FORM	**F--S**	FORT	GAYA
FUND	******	FROM	******	FRAT	GAZA
******	FASH	******	FACS	FRET	GERA
F--E	FISH	**F--N**	FADS	FRIT	GIGA
******	FOCH	******	FAGS	FROT	GILA
FACE	******	FAIN	FANS	******	GINA
FADE	**F--I**	FAMN	FASS	**F--U**	GIZA
FAKE	******	FAUN	FATS	******	GOMA
FAME	FIJI	FAWN	FAYS	FRAU	GOYA
FANE	FOCI	FERN	FEES		GUHA

******	GORE	******	GOBO	GNUS	******
G--B	GYBE	**G--L**	GOGO	GOAS	**G--Y**
******	GYRE	******	GOLO	GOBS	******
GAMB	GYVE	GAEL	GONO	GODS	GABY
GARB	******	GAIL	GRAO	GOES	GAMY
GLIB	**G--F**	GALL	GUAO	GRIS	GAPY
GLOB	******	GAOL	GYNO	GROS	GARY
GRAB	GAFF	GAUL	GYRO	GUMS	GENY
GRUB	GENF	GENL	******	GUNS	GOBY
******	GOLF	GEOL	**G--P**	GUTS	GORY
G--D	GOOF	GILL	******	GUYS	GRAY
******	GRAF	GIRL	GAMP	GYMS	GREY
GARD	GUFF	GOAL	GASP	GYPS	******
GAUD	GULF	GOWL	GIMP	******	**G--Z**
GEED	******	GULL	GOOP	**G--T**	******
GELD	**G--G**	******	GRIP	******	GEEZ
GERD	******	**G--M**	GULP	GAIT	GRAZ
GIED	GANG	******	******	GATT	******
GILD	GENG	GARM	**G--R**	GELT	**H--A**
GIRD	GONG	GEOM	******	GENT	******
GLAD	GREG	GERM	GAUR	GEST	HAHA
GLED	GRIG	GLIM	GEAR	GHAT	HAKA
GOAD	GROG	GLUM	GNAR	GIFT	HAMA
GOLD	******	GRAM	GOAR	GILT	HAYA
GOND	**G--H**	GRIM	GOER	GIRT	HEMA
GOOD	******	GRUM	GYOR	GIST	HERA
GRAD	GASH	GUAM	******	GLOT	HEXA
GRID	GATH	******	**G--S**	GLUT	HORA
******	GOGH	**G--N**	******	GNAT	HULA
G--E	GOSH	******	GABS	GOAT	HUPA
******	GOTH	GAIN	GADS	GOUT	HYLA
GABE	GUSH	GLEN	GAGS	GOVT	******
GAGE	******	GMAN	GALS	GRIT	**H--B**
GALE	**G--I**	GMEN	GAMS	GROT	******
GAME	******	GOON	GAPS	GUAT	HERB
GAPE	GERI	GOWN	GARS	GUST	******
GARE	GOBI	GRIN	GATS	******	**H--D**
GATE	GUMI	GUAN	GAYS	**G--U**	******
GAVE	GYRI	GUIN	GEES	******	HAND
GAZE	******	GWEN	GELS	GENU	HARD
GENE	**G--K**	GWIN	GEMS	GIFU	HEAD
GHEE	******	GWYN	GENS	GURU	HEED
GIBE	GAWK	GYMN	GETS	******	HELD
GIDE	GECK	******	GIBS	**G--W**	HERD
GIVE	GEEK	**G--O**	GIGS	******	HIED
GLEE	GINK	******	GILS	GLOW	HIND
GLUE	GOOK	GAMO	GINS	GNAW	HOED
GONE	GOWK	GIRO	GIPS	GREW	HOLD
	GUCK			GROW	

HOND	HARL	HEAP	HUBS	******
HOOD	**H--H**	HAUL	HELP	HUES	**I--A**
HUED	******	HEAL	HEMP	HUGS	******
******	HASH	HEEL	HIPP	HUMS	IANA
H--E	HATH	HELL	HOOP	HUNS	IDEA
******	HETH	HEML	HRIP	HUSS	ILEA
HABE	HIGH	HERL	HUMP	HUTS	ILIA
HADE	HOTH	HILL	******	******	ILKA
HAKE	HUGH	HOWL	**H--R**	**H--T**	INCA
HALE	HUSH	HULL	******	******	INGA
HAME	******	HURL	HAIR	HAFT	INIA
HARE	**H--I**	HYAL	HEAR	HALT	IONA
HATE	******	******	HEBR	HART	IOTA
HAVE	HAGI	**H--M**	HEIR	HAST	IOWA
HAZE	HELI	******	HERR	HEAT	IRMA
HEBE	HEMI	HALM	HIER	HECT	IRRA
HEHE	HIFI	HARM	HLER	HEFT	ISBA
HEME	HOPI	HELM	HOAR	HEPT	ITEA
HERE	HOTI	HERM	HOER	HEST	IXIA
HIDE	HWAI	HOLM	HOUR	HILT	******
HIKE	******	******	HYDR	HINT	**I--B**
HIPE	**H--J**	**H--N**	HYGR	HIST	******
HIRE	******	******	******	HOLT	IADB
HIVE	HADJ	HAHN	**H--S**	HOOT	IAMB
HOLE	******	HEWN	******	HORT	IOBB
HOME	**H--K**	HOEN	HAGS	HOST	******
HONE	******	HOON	HAHS	HUNT	**I--D**
HOPE	HACK	HORN	HALS	HURT	******
HOSE	HAIK	HRON	HAMS	HYET	IBID
HOTE	HANK	HWAN	HANS	******	ICED
HOVE	HARK	HYMN	HATS	**H--U**	IMID
HOWE	HAWK	******	HAWS	******	IRID
HUGE	HDBK	**H--O**	HAYS	HABU	******
HUME	HECK	******	HEMS	HAKU	**I--E**
HYDE	HICK	HALO	HENS	******	******
******	HOCK	HEMO	HERS	**H--X**	IBLE
H--F	HONK	HERO	HEWS	******	IDAE
******	HOOK	HILO	HIES	HOAX	IDLE
HAAF	HUCK	HINO	HIPS	******	IKWE
HALF	HULK	HIRO	HISS	**H--Y**	ILSE
HOOF	HUNK	HOBO	HITS	******	INEE
HUFF	HUSK	HOLO	HOBS	HAZY	INGE
******	******	HOMO	HODS	HOLY	INRE
H--G	**H--L**	HUGO	HOES	HOMY	IOLE
******	******	HYLO	HOGS	******	ISLE
HANG	HAIL	HYPO	HOMS	**H--Z**	******
HOGG	HALL	******	HOPS	******	**I--H**
HONG	HAPL	**H--P**	HOYS	HARZ	******
HUNG		******			INCH
		HARP			ITCH
		HASP			

*****	INDO	*****	*****	*****	JOLO
I--I	INFO	I--T	J--C	J--I	JUDO
*****	INRO	*****	*****	*****	JUNO
IFNI	INTO	INIT	JUNC	JAMI	*****
IGNI	IODO	INST	*****	JIBI	J--P
IMMI	*****	ISNT	J--D	*****	*****
IMPI	I--P	*****	*****	J--K	JEEP
INRI	*****	I--U	JEED	*****	JUMP
*****	INSP	*****	JIND	JACK	*****
I--K	*****	IDFU	JOAD	JERK	J--R
*****	I--Q	IGLU	*****	JINK	*****
IRAK	*****	*****	J--E	JOCK	JEER
*****	IRAQ	I--X	*****	JOOK	JOAR
I--L	*****	*****	JADE	JUNK	*****
*****	I--R	IBEX	JAKE	*****	J--S
ICAL	*****	ILEX	JANE	J--L	*****
ICEL	ICER	*****	JAPE	*****	JABS
IDOL	ISAR	I--Y	JAVE	JAIL	JAGS
IDYL	ISER	*****	JEFE	JARL	JAMS
IFIL	ITER	IDLY	JETE	JEEL	JANS
INCL	IVOR	IFFY	JIBE	JELL	JARS
ITAL	IYAR	ILLY	JIVE	JERL	JASS
ITOL	IZAR	IMMY	JOKE	JILL	JAWS
*****	*****	INKY	JOSE	JOEL	JAYS
I--M	I--S	INLY	JOVE	JOWL	JEES
*****	*****	ISSY	JUBE	*****	JEMS
ICBM	IANS	IZZY	JUDE	J--M	JESS
IDEM	IBIS	*****	JULE	*****	JETS
IMAM	ICES	I--Z	JUNE	JERM	JEWS
IRBM	IDAS	*****	JUTE	*****	JIBS
ITEM	IDES	INEZ	*****	J--N	JIGS
*****	IKES	*****	J--F	*****	JIMS
I--N	ILLS	J--A	*****	JAEN	JOBS
*****	ILUS	*****	JEFF	JAIN	JOES
ICON	IMPS	JACA	JIFF	JANN	JOGS
IKON	INAS	JAGA	*****	JEAN	JONS
IMAN	INKS	JAMA	J--G	JINN	JOSS
IMIN	INNS	JARA	*****	JOAN	JOTS
IRAN	IONS	JAVA	JAGG	JOHN	JOYS
IRON	IOUS	JENA	JOUG	JOIN	JUGS
IVAN	IRAS	JOLA	JUNG	JUAN	JUTS
*****	IRIS	JUBA	*****	*****	*****
I--O	IRKS	JUCA	J--H	J--O	J--T
*****	ISIS	JURA	*****	*****	*****
IAGO	ISMS	*****	JATH	JAKO	JEST
IDEO	ITYS	J--B	JETH	JATO	JILT
IDIO	IVES	*****	JOAH	JOBO	JOAT
ILEO	IVYS	JAMB	JOSH	JODO	JOLT
		JAOB			JUST
		JOAB			

******	******	KALI	******	******	LEDA
J--U	**K--D**	KAMI	**K--O**	**K--T**	LENA
******	******	KARI	******	******	LEVA
JEBU	KAID	KAZI	KANO	KANT	LILA
JEHU	KIDD	KEPI	KAYO	KELT	LIMA
JESU	KIND	KIRI	KENO	KENT	LINA
JUJU	KURD	KIWI	KETO	KEPT	LIRA
******	******	KOPI	KIHO	KHAT	LISA
J--W	**K--E**	******	KILO	KHET	LIZA
******	******	**K--K**	KINO	KILT	LOLA
JHOW	KADE	******	KOKO	KIST	LOMA
******	KALE	KECK	KOTO	KITT	LUBA
J--X	KAME	KEEK	******	KNIT	LUNA
******	KANE	KIAK	**K--P**	KNOT	LUTA
JEUX	KATE	KICK	******	KURT	LYRA
JINX	KAYE	KINK	KEEP	KYAT	******
******	KIBE	KIRK	KELP	******	**L--B**
J--Y	KINE	KOOK	KEMP	**K--U**	******
******	KIPE	KUNK	KNAP	******	LAMB
JOEY	KITE	******	KNOP	KAGU	LIMB
JOUY	KLEE	**K--L**	******	KETU	******
JUDY	KNEE	******	**K--R**	KIVU	**L--C**
JULY	KOAE	KAIL	******	KUDU	******
JURY	KOBE	KARL	KEIR	******	LAIC
******	KURE	KCAL	KIER	**K--V**	LEUC
J--Z	KYLE	KEEL	KNAR	******	******
******	******	KIEL	KNUR	KIEV	**L--D**
JAZZ	**K--F**	KILL	******	******	******
******	******	KOEL	**K--S**	**K--W**	LADD
K--A	KAIF	KOHL	******	******	LAID
******	KEEF	KRAL	KAAS	KNEW	LAND
KADA	KERF	******	KABS	KNOW	LARD
KAHA	******	**K--M**	KANS	******	LAUD
KAKA	**K--G**	******	KAYS	**K--X**	LEAD
KALA	******	KASM	KEAS	******	LEND
KAMA	KING	KLAM	KEFS	KNOX	LEUD
KANA	KNAG	******	KEGS	******	LEWD
KAPA	******	**K--N**	KENS	**K--Y**	LIED
KARA	**K--H**	******	KEOS	******	LIND
KAVA	******	KAIN	KEYS	KARY	LOAD
KAWA	KAPH	KAON	KIDS	KATY	LOOD
KELA	KISH	KARN	KIPS	******	LORD
KIVA	KITH	KEEN	KISS	**L--A**	LOUD
KOLA	KOPH	KERN	KITS	******	******
KURA	******	KHAN	KOPS	LAMA	**L--E**
******	**K--I**	KILN	KORS	LANA	******
K--B	******	KOLN	KOSS	LARA	LACE
******	KADI		KRIS	LAVA	LADE
KERB	KAKI		KVAS		
KNOB					

LAFE	LIEF	LOCK	******	LILS	******
LAKE	LOAF	LOOK	**L--P**	LIPS	**L--X**
LAME	LOOF	LUCK	******	LISS	******
LANE	LUFF	LURK	LAMP	LOBS	LYNX
LATE	******	******	LAPP	LOGS	******
LAVE	**L--G**	**L--L**	LARP	LOIS	**L--Y**
LAZE	******	******	LEAP	LOOS	******
LEDE	LANG	LALL	LIMP	LOPS	LACY
LENE	LING	LEAL	LISP	LOSS	LADY
LICE	LONG	LOLL	LOOP	LOTS	LAKY
LIFE	LUNG	LULL	LOUP	LOWS	LAZY
LIKE	******	******	LUMP	LUES	LEVY
LIME	**L--H**	**L--M**	******	LUGS	LILY
LINE	******	******	**L--R**	LUIS	LIMY
LIRE	LAKH	LOAM	******	LYES	LINY
LITE	LASH	LOOM	LAHR	******	LOGY
LIVE	LATH	******	LAIR	**L--T**	LORY
LOBE	LEAH	**L--N**	LEAR	******	LUCY
LODE	LICH	******	LEER	LACT	******
LOGE	LITH	LAIN	LEHR	LAIT	**L--Z**
LOKE	LOCH	LAON	LIAR	LAST	******
LOME	LOTH	LAUN	LOUR	LEET	LINZ
LONE	LUSH	LAWN	******	LEFT	LODZ
LOPE	LUTH	LEAN	**L--S**	LENT	LUIZ
LORE	******	LEON	******	LEPT	******
LOSE	**L--I**	LIEN	LABS	LEST	**M--A**
LOTE	******	LIGN	LADS	LETT	******
LOVE	LARI	LIMN	LAGS	LIFT	MAHA
LUBE	LATI	LINN	LAMS	LILT	MAIA
LUCE	LEVI	LION	LAOS	LINT	MAKA
LUGE	LOCI	LOAN	LAPS	LIST	MAMA
LUKE	LODI	LOIN	LARS	LOFT	MANA
LUNE	LOKI	LOON	LASS	LOOT	MARA
LUPE	LUNI	LORN	LAWS	LOST	MAYA
LURE	LURI	LYNN	LAYS	LOTT	MEGA
LUTE	LYSI	******	LEAS	LOUT	MESA
LUXE	******	**L--O**	LEES	LUNT	META
LYLE	******	******	LEGS	LUST	MICA
LYME	**L--K**	LENO	LEIS	******	MINA
LYRE	******	LETO	LEKS	**L--U**	MIRA
LYSE	LACK	LEVO	LEMS	******	MONA
LYTE	LANK	LIAO	LENS	LIEU	MORA
LYZE	LARK	LIDO	LEOS	LIMU	MOXA
******	LEAK	LINO	LESS	LUAU	MYNA
L--F	LEEK	LIPO	LETS	LULU	MYRA
******	LEUK	LOBO	LEWS	******	MYXA
LEAF	LICK	LOCO	LIDS	**L--W**	******
LEIF	LINK	LOGO	LIES	******	**M--B**
		LUDO		LWOW	******
					MOAB
					MZAB

******	MORE	MUCI	MAUN	MACS	MEET
M--C	MOSE	MYRI	MEAN	MADS	MELT
******	MOTE	******	MIEN	MAES	MENT
MARC	MOUE	**M--J**	MINN	MANS	MILT
MASC	MOVE	******	MOAN	MAPS	MINT
MISC	MULE	MARJ	MOON	MARS	MIST
******	MUSE	******	MORN	MASS	MITT
M--D	MUTE	**M--K**	MOWN	MATS	MIXT
******	******	******	MUON	MAWS	MOAT
MAID	**M--F**	MACK	******	MAYS	MOLT
MAUD	******	MARK	**M--O**	MEGS	MONT
MEAD	MIFF	MASK	******	MELS	MOOT
MELD	MUFF	MEEK	MAJO	MEMS	MORT
MEND	******	MICK	MAKO	MESS	MOST
MILD	**M--G**	MILK	MALO	MEWS	MOTT
MIND	******	MINK	MANO	MHOS	MSGT
MOLD	MING	MOCK	MAYO	MIBS	MULT
MOOD	******	MONK	MEIO	MIGS	MUST
******	**M--H**	MUCK	MEMO	MILS	MUTT
M--E	******	MURK	MENO	MIRS	******
******	MACH	MUSK	MERO	MISS	**M--U**
MACE	MASH	******	MESO	MMES	******
MADE	MATH	**M--L**	MILO	MOAS	MENU
MAGE	MEAH	******	MIRO	MOBS	MERU
MAKE	MESH	MAAL	MISO	MODS	******
MALE	METH	MAIL	MOHO	MOES	**M--V**
MANE	MICH	MALL	MOIO	MOMS	******
MARE	MOTH	MARL	MOJO	MONS	MERV
MATE	MSTH	MAUL	MOMO	MOOS	MIRV
MAZE	MUCH	MEAL	MONO	MOPS	******
MEDE	MUSH	MERL	MORO	MORS	**M--W**
MELE	MUTH	MEWL	MUCO	MOSS	******
MENE	MYTH	MILL	MYCO	MOTS	MEOW
MERE	******	MOIL	MYXO	MOWS	******
METE	**M--I**	MOLL	******	MSTS	**M--X**
MICE	******	MULL	**M--R**	MUDS	******
MIKE	MAGI	MYEL	******	MUGS	MANX
MILE	MALI	******	MEIR	MUMS	MARX
MIME	MANI	**M--M**	METR	MUSS	MINX
MINE	MAUI	******	MOHR	MUTS	******
MIRE	MAXI	MAAM	MOOR	******	**M--Y**
MISE	MEDI	MAIM	MSGR	**M--T**	******
MITE	MENI	MALM	MUIR	******	MANY
MLLE	MIDI	MUMM	******	MALT	MARY
MODE	MIMI	******	**M--S**	MART	MAZY
MOKE	MINI	**M--N**	******	MAST	MIRY
MOLE	MODI	******	MAAS	MATT	MOLY
MOPE	MOKI	MAIN	MABS	MEAT	******
		MANN			**M--Z**
					******
					METZ

```
******        NEVE    NATL    NEER    ******    ONCE
N--A          NICE    NEAL    NEUR    N--Y      OOZE
******        NIDE    NEIL    NIGR    ******    ORLE
NADA          NIKE    NELL    NITR    NARY      ORNE
NAGA          NILE    NIEL    ******  NAVY      OSTE
NAHA          NINE    NOEL    N--S    NOMY      OTOE
NAJA          NIUE    NOIL    ******  NOSY      OUSE
NAMA          NODE    NULL    NABS    ******    ******
NANA          NOME    ******  NAGS    O--A      O--F
NAPA          NONE    N--M    NAIS    ******    ******
NASA          NOPE    ******  NANS    OBIA      OEUF
NAWA          NOSE    NEUM    NAOS    OCHA      OLAF
NCAA          NOTE    NORM    NAPS    OCRA      ******
NEMA          NUDE    ******  NATS    OCTA      O--G
NINA          ******  N--N    NAYS    ODEA      ******
NIPA          N--F    ******  NEBS    OHIA      OLIG
NITA          ******  NAIN    NEDS    OKLA      ORIG
NOMA          NAIF    NEON    NESS    OKRA      ******
NONA          ******  NGAN    NETS    OLGA      O--H
NORA          N--G    NOON    NEWS    OLLA      ******
NOVA          ******  NORN    NIBS    ONCA      OATH
******        NOGG    NOUN    NIPS    ONZA      OPAH
N--B          ******  ******  NITS    OONA      ORTH
******        N--H    N--O    NOBS    OPIA      OUCH
NIMB          ******  ******  NODS    ORCA      ******
NLRB          NASH    NABO    NOES    OSSA      O--I
NUMB          NEPH    NANO    NOGS    OTEA      ******
******        NIGH    NASO    NOUS    ******    OMEI
N--C          NOAH    NATO    NOWS    O--C      OMNI
******        NOSH    NEBO    NUBS    ******    OPHI
NARC          ******  NEMO    NUNS    ODIC      OSSI
******        N--I    NERO    NUTS    OTIC      ******
N--D          ******  NINO    ******  ******    O--K
******        NAZI    NOGO    N--T    O--D      ******
NARD          NEVI    NOMO    ******  ******    OMSK
NEED          NIDI    NOSO    NAST    OKED      ******
NEJD          NISI    NOTO    NATT    OVID      O--L
NKVD          NUDI    ******  NAUT    OWED      ******
NORD          ******  N--P    NEAT    ******    OBOL
******        N--K    ******  NEST    O--E      OCUL
N--E          ******  NEAP    NEWT    ******    ODAL
******        NDAK    ******  NEXT    OBOE      ODYL
NAME          NECK    N--R    NOCT    OGEE      OPAL
NAPE          NICK    ******  NOTT    OGLE      ORAL
NATE          NOCK    NATR    NOWT    OGRE      OREL
NAVE          NOOK    NCAR    NYET    OISE      OSEL
NAZE          ******  NEAR    ******  OKIE      OVAL
NENE          N--L    NECR    N--U    OLPE
              ******                  ******
              NAEL    NALU
              NAIL
```

******	OARS	******	******	PULE	PARK
O--M	OATS	**O--Y**	**P--D**	PURE	PEAK
******	OBIS	******	******	PYLE	PECK
ODUM	ODDS	OBEY	PAED	PYRE	PEEK
OVUM	ODES	OILY	PAID	******	PERK
******	OHMS	OKAY	PARD	**P--F**	PICK
O--N	OILS	OLAY	PEND	******	PINK
******	OKAS	OLLY	PHUD	PELF	POCK
ODIN	ONES	ONLY	PIED	PIAF	POLK
OMAN	ONUS	OOZY	PLED	POUF	POOK
OMEN	OPTS	OPSY	PLOD	PROF	PORK
ONON	OPUS	ORGY	POND	PUFF	PUCK
OPEN	ORBS	ORLY	POOD	******	PUNK
ORAN	ORCS	******	PROD	**P--G**	******
OVEN	ORES	**O--Z**	PUND	******	**P--L**
OWEN	ORTS	******	PUUD	PANG	******
OXEN	OSIS	OYEZ	******	PEAG	PAAL
OXON	OTIS	******	**P--E**	PHAG	PAIL
******	OURS	**P--A**	******	PING	PALL
O--O	OUTS	******	PACE	PLUG	PAUL
******	OWES	PABA	PAGE	PONG	PAWL
OCTO	OWLS	PACA	PALE	PRIG	PEAL
OENO	OWNS	PAHA	PANE	PUNG	PEEL
OHIO	OYES	PALA	PARE	******	PHIL
OINO	******	PAPA	PATE	**P--H**	PHYL
OLEO	**O--T**	PARA	PAVE	******	PILL
OLIO	******	PERA	PAYE	PASH	POLL
ONDO	OAST	PICA	PEDE	PATH	POOL
ONTO	OBIT	PIKA	PELE	PISH	PULL
ORDO	OKET	PIMA	PERE	PITH	PURL
OSLO	OLST	PINA	PETE	POOH	PYEL
OTTO	OMIT	PIPA	PICE	POSH	******
******	OUST	PISA	PIKE	PTAH	**P--M**
O--R	******	PITA	PILE	PUGH	******
******	**O--U**	PLEA	PINE	PUSH	PALM
ODER	******	PODA	PIPE	******	PERM
ODOR	OAHU	PROA	PODE	**P--I**	PLUM
OLOR	OGPU	PSHA	POKE	******	POEM
OMAR	******	PUKA	POLE	PALI	PRAM
OMBR	**O--V**	PUMA	POME	PARI	PRIM
OMER	******	PUNA	PONE	PEDI	PROM
ONER	OLAV	PUPA	POPE	PERI	******
OSAR	******	******	PORE	PIKI	**P--N**
OVER	**O--X**	**P--B**	POSE	PILI	******
OYER	******	******	PRAE	PURI	PAIN
******	ONYX	PLEB	PRUE	******	PAWN
O--S	ORYX	******	PUCE	**P--K**	PEAN
******		**P--C**	PUKE	******	PEEN
OAFS		******		PACK	
OAKS		PISC		PANK	
		PYIC			

PENN	PEER	PUNS	******	******	RONA
PEON	PETR	PUPS	**P--X**	**Q--N**	ROSA
PERN	PICR	PUSS	******	******	ROTA
PHEN	PIER	PUTS	PNYX	QUAN	RUGA
PHON	POOR	PYES	******	******	RUTA
PION	POUR	******	**P--Y**	**Q--P**	******
PIRN	PTER	**P--T**	******	******	**R--B**
PLAN	PURR	******	PALY	QUIP	******
POON	******	PACT	PIAY	******	RAAB
PORN	**P--S**	PANT	PINY	**Q--R**	RHOB
PRON	******	PART	PIPY	******	**R--C**
PYIN	PADS	PAST	PITY	QUAR	******
******	PAIS	PEAT	PIXY	******	ROTC
P--O	PALS	PELT	PLAY	**Q--S**	**R--D**
******	PAMS	PENT	PLOY	******	******
PACO	PANS	PERT	POGY	QAIS	RAAD
PAVO	PAPS	PEST	POKY	******	RAID
PECO	PARS	PHOT	POLY	**Q--T**	RAND
PEDO	PASS	PHUT	PONY	******	READ
PEPO	PATS	PHYT	POSY	QUAT	REED
PESO	PAWS	PICT	PRAY	QUIT	REND
PICO	PAYS	PINT	PREY	******	RIND
PISO	PEAS	PIOT	PUNY	**Q--Y**	ROAD
PITO	PEES	PITT	******	******	ROOD
POCO	PEGS	PLAT	**P--Z**	QUAY	RUDD
POGO	PENS	PLOT	******	******	RUED
POLO	PEPS	POET	PIZZ	**Q--Z**	RYND
PRAO	PETS	PORT	******	******	******
PYRO	PEWS	POST	**Q--B**	QUIZ	**R--E**
******	PHDS	POUT	******	******	******
P--P	PHIS	PROT	QUAB	**R--A**	RACE
******	PIES	PUNT	******	******	RAGE
PALP	PIGS	PUTT	**Q--D**	RABA	RAKE
PEEP	PINS	PYAT	******	RADA	RALE
PIMP	PIPS	PYET	QUAD	RAGA	RAME
PLOP	PITS	PYOT	QUID	RAJA	RAPE
POMP	PIUS	******	QUOD	RAMA	RARE
POOP	PLUS	**P--U**	******	RANA	RASE
PREP	PODS	******	**Q--G**	RASA	RATE
PROP	PONS	PELU	******	RATA	RAVE
PULP	POPS	PERU	QUAG	REBA	RAZE
PUMP	POTS	POKU	QUNG	RENA	REDE
******	POWS	******	******	RHEA	RENE
P--R	PRES	**P--W**	**Q--H**	RIGA	RETE
******	PROS	******	******	RIPA	RICE
PAIR	PSIS	PHEW	QOPH	RITA	RIDE
PARR	PUBS	PLEW	******	RIVA	
PEAR	PUGS	PLOW	**Q--I**	ROMA	
		PROW	******		
			QUAI		
			QUEI		

RIFE	******	RHIN	REIS	******	******
RILE	**R--I**	RIEN	REMS	**R--X**	**S--B**
RIME	******	RIJN	REPS	******	******
RIPE	RAGI	ROAN	RETS	ROUX	SCAB
RISE	RAKI	RUIN	REVS	******	SERB
RITE	RAMI	RYAN	RHOS	**R--Y**	SLAB
RIVE	RANI	******	RHUS	******	SLOB
ROBE	RATI	**R--O**	RHYS	RACY	SLUB
RODE	REMI	******	RIBS	RELY	SNOB
ROLE	RENI	RALO	RIDS	RIMY	SNUB
ROME	ROTI	RATO	RIGS	ROPY	SORB
ROPE	******	REDO	RIIS	RORY	STAB
ROSE	**R--K**	REMO	RIMS	ROSY	STUB
ROTE	******	RENO	RIPS	ROXY	SWAB
ROUE	RACK	RHEO	ROBS	RUAY	******
ROVE	RAIK	RIVO	RODS	RUBY	**S--C**
RUBE	RANK	******	ROES	RUDY	******
RUDE	RECK	**R--P**	ROMS	******	SAIC
RUFE	REEK	******	ROSS	**R--Z**	SPCC
RULE	RICK	RAMP	ROTS	******	SPEC
RUNE	RINK	RASP	ROWS	RAZZ	******
RUSE	RISK	RCMP	ROYS	RHIZ	**S--D**
RUTE	ROCK	REAP	RUBS	******	******
******	ROOK	REPP	RUES	**S--A**	SAID
R--F	RUCK	ROMP	RUGS	******	SAND
******	RUSK	ROOP	RUMS	SAGA	SARD
RAFF	******	ROUP	RUNS	SAMA	SAUD
REEF	**R--L**	RSVP	RUSS	SANA	SCAD
RIFF	******	RUMP	RUTS	SARA	SCUD
ROLF	RAIL	******	RYES	SERA	SEED
ROOF	RALL	**R--R**	******	SETA	SEND
RUFF	REAL	******	**R--T**	SHEA	SHAD
******	REEL	REAR	******	SIMA	SHED
R--G	RHYL	ROAR	RAFT	SIVA	SHOD
******	RIAL	RUER	RANT	SKUA	SIND
RANG	RILL	RUHR	RAPT	SODA	SKID
RING	ROIL	******	RECT	SOFA	SLED
RUNG	ROLL	**R--S**	REFT	SOJA	SLID
******	ROTL	******	RENT	SOLA	SOLD
R--H	******	RADS	REST	SOMA	SPAD
******	**R--M**	RAES	RIFT	SORA	SPED
RASH	******	RAGS	RIOT	SOYA	SPUD
RATH	REAM	RAMS	ROOT	SPCA	STUD
RESH	RHUM	RAPS	ROUT	STOA	SUDD
RICH	ROAM	RATS	RUNT	SUPA	SUED
RUSH	ROOM	RAYS	RUST	SURA	SURD
RUTH	******	REBS	RYOT	SUVA	******
	R--N	REDS	******		**S--E**
	******		**R--U**		******
	RAIN		******		SABE
	REIN		RAHU		SADE

SAFE	SING	******	SPAM	******	STAR
SAGE	SKAG	**S--K**	STEM	**S--P**	STER
SAKE	SKEG	******	STUM	******	STIR
SALE	SLAG	SACK	SWAM	SALP	SUER
SAME	SLOG	SALK	SWIM	SAMP	******
SANE	SLUG	SANK	SWUM	SCOP	**S--S**
SAPE	SMOG	SARK	******	SCUP	******
SATE	SMUG	SASK	**S--N**	SEEP	SABS
SAVE	SNAG	SAUK	******	SHIP	SACS
SAXE	SNIG	SDAK	SAWN	SHOP	SAGS
SEME	SNOG	SEEK	SCAN	SIMP	SAIS
SERE	SNUG	SICK	SEAN	SKEP	SAMS
SHOE	SONG	SILK	SEEN	SKIP	SANS
SICE	STAG	SINK	SEWN	SLAP	SAPS
SIDE	SUNG	SOAK	SHAN	SLIP	SASS
SINE	SURG	SOCK	SHIN	SLOP	SAWS
SIRE	SWAG	SUCK	SHUN	SNAP	SAYS
SITE	SWIG	SULK	SIGN	SNIP	SEAS
SIZE	******	SUNK	SION	SOAP	SEES
SKEE	**S--H**	******	SKIN	SOUP	SENS
SKYE	******	**S--L**	SOON	STEP	SERS
SLEE	SAAH	******	SORN	STOP	SESS
SLOE	SADH	SAIL	SOWN	SUMP	SETS
SLUE	SAHH	SAUL	SPAN	SUPP	SEWS
SMEE	SASH	SEAL	SPIN	SWAP	SHES
SNEE	SEAH	SEEL	SPUN	SWOP	SIBS
SNYE	SETH	SELL	STAN	******	SICS
SOKE	SHAH	SHUL	STEN	**S--Q**	SIDS
SOLE	SIGH	SIAL	STUN	******	SIMS
SOME	SIKH	SILL	SUNN	SEQQ	SINS
SONE	SUCH	SOIL	SWAN	SHOQ	SIPS
SORE	******	SOUL	******	******	SIRS
SPUE	**S--I**	STOL	**S--O**	**S--R**	SITS
SUPE	******	******	******	******	SKIS
SURE	SADI	**S--M**	SAGO	SAAR	SOBS
SYCE	SAKI	******	SAPO	SAUR	SODS
SYNE	SARI	SCUM	SEBO	SCAR	SOLS
******	SEBI	SEAM	SEGO	SEAR	SONS
S--F	SEMI	SEEM	SERO	SEER	SOPS
******	SETI	SEJM	SHOO	SLUR	SOTS
SELF	SEXI	SHAM	SILO	SOAR	SOUS
SERF	SIRI	SHEM	SINO	SOIR	SOWS
SURF	SITI	SHIM	SITO	SOUR	SOYS
******	SOLI	SIAM	SLOO	SPAR	SPAS
S--G	SORI	SKIM	SOHO	SPIR	SPES
******	SUFI	SLAM	SOLO	SPOR	STUS
SANG	******	SLIM	SOSO	SPQR	SUBS
SHAG	**S--J**	SLUM	STLO	SPUR	SUDS
	SUBJ		SUMO		

SUES
SUMS
SUNS
SUPS
SUSS

******

S--T

******

SALT
SCAT
SCOT
SCUT
SEAT
SECT
SENT
SEPT
SEXT
SHOT
SHUT
SIFT
SILT
SKAT
SKIT
SLAT
SLIT
SLOT
SLUT
SMIT
SMUT
SNIT
SNOT
SOFT
SOOT
SORT
SPAT
SPET
SPIT
SPOT
STAT
STET
SUET
SUIT
SUPT
SWAT
SWOT

******

S--U

******

SITU
SULU

******

S--V

******

SHIV
SLAV
SPIV

******

S--W

******

SCOW
SHAW
SHEW
SHOW
SKAW
SKEW
SLAW
SLEW
SLOW
SMEW
SNOW
SPEW
STEW
STOW

******

S--X

******

STYX

******

S--Y

******

SAGY
SCRY
SECY
SEXY
SHAY
SIZY
SLAY
SPAY
SPRY
STAY
SUKY
SUZY
SWAY

******

S-Z

******

SUEZ

T--A

******

TANA
TAPA
TARA
TATA
TELA
TEMA
TERA
THEA
TINA
TOGA
TOLA
TORA
TUBA
TUFA
TULA
TUNA

******

T--B

******

THEB
TOMB

******

T--C

******

TALC

******

T--D

******

TEED
TEND
THAD
THUD
TIED
TOAD
TODD
TOED
TOLD
TRAD
TROD

******

T--E

******

TACE
TAKE
TALE
TAME
TAPE
TARE
TATE
TELE
TETE
THEE
TIDE
TIKE
TILE
TIME
TINE
TIRE
TOLE
TOME
TONE
TOPE
TORE
TOTE
TREE
TRUE
TUBE
TUDE
TULE
TUNE
TYEE
TYKE
TYNE
TYPE
TYRE

******

T--F

******

TIFF
TOFF
TUFF
TURF

******

T--G

******

TANG
TENG
THUG
TING
TONG
TRIG
TWIG

T--H

******

TETH
TOPH
TOSH
TRAH
TUSH

******

T--I

TAXI
TCHI
TIKI
TIPI
TITI
TONI
TOPI
TORI
TOTI
TSHI
TUPI

******

T--K

******

TACK
TALK
TANK
TASK
TEAK
TICK
TOOK
TREK
TRUK
TUCK
TURK
TUSK

******

T--L

******

TAAL
TAEL
TAIL
TALL
TEAL
TEIL
TELL
TILL
TOIL
TOLL
TOOL

******

T--M

******

TEAM
TEEM
TERM
THEM
TRAM
TRIM

******

T--N

******

TAIN
TARN
TEEN
TENN
TERN
THAN
THEN
THIN
TION
TOON
TORN
TOWN
TRIN
TRON
TSUN
TURN
TWIN

******

T--O

******

TARO
TELO
TENO
THEO
THIO
TIRO
TITO
TOCO
TODO
TOGO
TONO
TOPO
TOYO

TRIO	THIS	TROT	URSA	UPON	URDY
TYPO	THUS	TUFT	USIA	URAN	UREY
TYRO	TICS	TWIT	USMA	UZAN	******
******	TIES	******	USNA	******	**U--Z**
T--P	TIMS	**T--U**	UVEA	**U--O**	******
******	TINS	******	******	******	UNTZ
TAMP	TIPS	TABU	**U--C**	UMBO	******
TARP	TITS	THOU	******	UNCO	**V--A**
TEMP	TODS	THRU	URIC	UNDO	******
TRAP	TOES	TOLU	USMC	UNIO	VACA
TRIP	TOGS	TUTU	UVIC	UNTO	VARA
TROP	TOMS	******	******	******	VASA
TUMP	TONS	**T--W**	**U--D**	**U--R**	VEDA
******	TOPS	******	******	******	VEGA
T--R	TORS	THAW	UDAD	UBER	VELA
******	TOSS	THEW	USED	USAR	VENA
TAUR	TOTS	TROW	******	USER	VERA
TBAR	TOWS	******	**U--E**	USNR	VINA
TEAR	TOYS	**T--X**	******	USSR	VIRA
TETR	TRES	******	UELE	UTER	VISA
THAR	TRIS	TRIX	UNDE	******	VITA
THOR	TUBS	******	UNIE	**U--S**	VIVA
TIER	TUES	**T--Y**	UNZE	******	VOLA
TOUR	TUGS	******	URDE	UDOS	VORA
TSAR	TUNS	TAXY	URGE	UMTS	******
TZAR	TUPS	THEY	******	UNAS	**V--B**
******	TWAS	TIDY	**U--F**	UPAS	******
T--S	TWOS	TINY	******	URNS	VERB
******	******	TIVY	USAF	URUS	******
TABS	**T--T**	TOBY	******	USES	**V--C**
TADS	******	TODY	**U--G**	USMS	******
TAGS	TACT	TOMY	******	UTES	VISC
TAMS	TAFT	TONY	UANG	******	******
TANS	TAIT	TORY	USCG	**U--T**	**V--D**
TAOS	TART	TRAY	******	******	******
TAPS	TAUT	TREY	**U--H**	UNIT	VELD
TARS	TEAT	TROY	******	******	VEND
TASS	TENT	******	UTAH	**U--U**	VIED
TATS	TEST	**U--A**	******	******	VOID
TAUS	TEXT	******	**U--J**	UNAU	******
TAVS	THAT	UEBA	******	URDU	**V--E**
TAWS	TILT	ULLA	UCMJ	******	******
TEAS	TINT	ULNA	******	**U--X**	VALE
TEDS	TOFT	UNGA	**U--L**	******	VANE
TEES	TOOT	UREA	******	ULEX	VASE
TEGS	TORT	URFA	URAL	******	VICE
TENS	TOUT	URIA	******	**U--Y**	VIDE
TESS	TRET	URNA	**U--N**	******	VILE
			******	UGLY	
			UDEN	UNDY	
			ULAN		

VINE	VINO	VIMY	WINE	******	******
VIRE	VISO	VINY	WIPE	**W--L**	**W--R**
VISE	VIVO	******	WIRE	******	******
VITE	******	**W--A**	WISE	WAAL	WEAR
VIVE	**V--P**	******	WIVE	WAIL	WEIR
VOCE	******	WEKA	WOKE	WALL	WHIR
VOLE	VAMP	WETA	WORE	WAUL	******
VORE	******	WHOA	WOTE	WAWL	**W--S**
VOTE	**V--R**	******	WOVE	WEAL	******
******	******	**W--B**	******	WEEL	WACS
V--G	VAIR	******	**W--F**	WELL	WADS
******	VEER	WOMB	******	WILL	WAFS
VANG	VITR	******	WAAF	WOOL	WAGS
******	******	**W--C**	WAIF	******	WANS
V--I	**V--S**	******	WARF	**W--M**	WAPS
******	******	WAAC	WOLF	******	WARS
VAGI	VALS	WISC	WOOF	WARM	WAYS
VALI	VANS	******	WRAF	WHAM	WEBS
VARI	VATS	**W--D**	******	WHIM	WEDS
VENI	VAVS	******	**W--G**	WHOM	WENS
VICI	VEES	WALD	******	WORM	WETS
VIDI	VERS	WAND	WANG	******	WHYS
VILI	VETS	WARD	WHIG	**W--N**	WIGS
VINI	VIES	WEED	WING	******	WINS
VITI	VIPS	WELD	******	WAIN	WITS
******	VISS	WEND	**W--H**	WARN	WOES
V--K	VOLS	WILD	******	WEAN	WOOS
******	VOWS	WIND	WASH	WHEN	WOWS
VICK	VUGS	WOAD	WICH	WHIN	WYES
******	******	WOLD	WISH	WORN	******
V--L	**V--T**	WOOD	WITH	WREN	**W--T**
******	******	WORD	WYCH	WYNN	******
VAAL	VAST	******	******	******	WAFT
VAIL	VENT	**W--E**	**W--I**	**W--O**	WAIT
VEAL	VERT	******	******	******	WALT
VEIL	VEST	WABE	WADI	WACO	WANT
VIAL	VOET	WADE	WARI	WINO	WART
VILL	VOLT	WAGE	WEKI	******	WAST
VIOL	******	WAKE	******	**W--P**	WATT
VTOL	**V--U**	WALE	**W--K**	******	WEFT
******	******	WANE	******	WARP	WELT
V--N	VAYU	WARE	WACK	WASP	WENT
******	******	WATE	WALK	WEEP	WEPT
VAIN	**V--W**	WAVE	WAUK	WHAP	WERT
VEIN	******	WERE	WEAK	WHIP	WEST
VERN	VIEW	WIDE	WEEK	WHOP	WHAT
******	******	WIFE	WICK	WISP	WHET
V--O	**V--Y**	WILE	WINK	WRAP	WHIT
******	******		WORK		
VASO	VARY				
VETO	VERY				

WILT	******	YOKE	******	******	******
WIST	X--S	YORE	Y--P	Z--D	Z--O
WONT	******	YULE	******	******	******
WORT	XMAS	******	YAMP	ZEND	ZENO
WRIT	XRTS	Y--G	YAUP	******	ZERO
******	******	******	YAWP	Z--E	ZYGO
W--W	X--T	YANG	YELP	******	******
******	******	YEGG	YOUP	ZEKE	Z--P
WHEW	XINT	******	******	ZONE	******
******	XYST	Y--H	Y--R	******	ZARP
W--Y	******	******	******	Z--F	******
******	X--V	YEAH	YEAR	******	Z--R
WADY	******	YHWH	YMER	ZARF	******
WANY	XDIV	YODH	YMIR	******	ZBAR
WARY	******	YOGH	YOUR	Z--G	ZOAR
WAVY	X--Y	******	YSER	******	******
WAXY	******	Y--I	******	ZING	Z--S
WHEY	XNTY	******	Y--S	ZOUG	******
WILY	XRAY	YETI	******	******	ZEDS
WINY	******	YOGI	YAKS	Z--H	ZEES
WIRY	Y--A	******	YAMS	******	ZEUS
WKLY	******	Y--K	YAPS	ZACH	ZIPS
******	YABA	******	YAWS	ZEPH	ZOES
W--Z	YAKA	YANK	YEAS	******	ZOOS
******	YAMA	YELK	YENS	Z--I	******
WHIZ	YANA	YOLK	YEWS	******	Z--T
******	YAPA	YORK	YIPS	ZATI	******
X--A	YAYA	******	YODS	ZUNI	ZANT
******	YMCA	Y--L	YOWS	ZWEI	ZEST
XEMA	YMHA	******	YUKS	******	******
XOSA	YOGA	YAWL	YVES	Z--K	Z--U
******	YUGA	YELL	******	******	******
X--F	YUMA	YOWL	Y--U	ZACK	ZASU
******	YWCA	******	******	******	ZEBU
XREF	YWHA	Y--M	YALU	Z--L	ZULU
******	******	******	******	******	******
X--H	Y--D	YLEM	Z--A	ZEAL	Z--Y
******	******	******	******	ZOOL	******
XIPH	YARD	Y--N	ZARA	******	ZANY
******	YELD	******	ZETA	Z--M	******
X--N	YOND	YARN	ZIRA	******	Z--Z
******	YOUD	YAWN	ZOLA	ZOOM	******
XION	******	YEAN	ZONA	******	ZIZZ
******	Y--E	YUAN	ZUZA	Z--N	******
X--O	******	******	******	******	-AA-
******	YALE	Y--O	Z--C	ZEIN	******
XENO	YARE	******	******	ZION	BAAL
XERO	YIPE	YAKO	ZINC	ZOAN	BAAR
XYLO		YOYO	ZOIC	ZOON	

BAAS	******	CADS	******	RAGS	KAIL
FAAM	-AC-	DADA	-AF-	SAGA	KAIN
HAAF	******	DADE	******	SAGE	LAIC
KAAS	BACH	DADO	BAFF	SAGO	LAID
MAAL	BACK	DADS	CAFE	SAGS	LAIN
MAAM	CACO	FADE	DAFF	SAGY	LAIR
MAAS	DACE	FADO	DAFT	TAGS	LAIT
PAAL	EACH	FADS	GAFF	VAGI	MAIA
RAAB	FACE	GADS	HAFT	WAGE	MAID
RAAD	FACP	HADE	LAFE	WAGS	MAIL
SAAH	FACS	HADJ	OAFS	******	MAIM
SAAR	FACT	IADB	RAFF	-AH-	MAIN
TAAL	HACK	JADE	RAFT	******	NAIF
VAAL	JACA	KADA	SAFE	BAHT	NAIL
WAAC	JACK	KADE	TAFT	HAHA	NAIN
WAAF	LACE	KADI	WAFS	HAHN	NAIS
WAAL	LACK	LADD	WAFT	HAHS	PAID
******	LACT	LADE	******	KAHA	PAIL
-AB-	LACY	LADS	-AG-	LAHR	PAIN
******	MACE	LADY	******	MAHA	PAIR
BABA	MACH	MADE	BAGA	NAHA	PAIS
BABE	MACK	MADS	BAGO	OAHU	QAIS
BABI	MACS	NADA	BAGR	PAHA	RAID
BABS	PACA	PADS	BAGS	RAHU	RAIK
BABU	PACE	RADA	CAGE	SAHH	RAIL
BABY	PACK	RADS	CAGY	******	RAIN
CABS	PACO	SADE	DAGO	-AI-	SAIC
DABS	PACT	SADH	DAGS	******	SAID
GABE	RACE	SADI	FAGS	BAIA	SAIL
GABS	RACK	TADS	GAGA	BAIL	SAIS
GABY	RACY	WADE	GAGE	BAIT	TAIL
HABE	SACK	WADI	GAGS	CAIN	TAIN
HABU	SACS	WADS	HAGI	DAIL	TAIT
JABS	TACE	WADY	HAGS	DAIS	VAIL
KABS	TACK	******	IAGO	FAIL	VAIN
LABS	TACT	-AE-	JAGA	FAIN	VAIR
MABS	VACA	******	JAGG	FAIR	WAIF
NABO	WACK	BAEL	JAGS	GAIA	WAIL
NABS	WACO	BAER	KAGU	GAIL	WAIN
PABA	WACS	CAEN	LAGS	GAIN	WAIT
RABA	ZACH	GAEA	MAGE	GAIT	******
SABE	ZACK	GAEL	MAGI	HAIK	-AJ-
SABS	******	JAEN	NAGA	HAIL	******
TABS	-AD-	MAES	NAGS	HAIR	BAJA
TABU	******	NAEL	PAGE	JAIL	MAJO
WABE	BADE	PAED	RAGA	JAIN	NAJA
YABA	CADE	RAES	RAGE	KAID	RAJA
	CADI	TAEL	RAGI	KAIF	

******	DALE	WALD	RAME	IANS	VANG
-AK-	DALI	WALE	RAMI	JANE	VANS
******	FALA	WALK	RAMP	JANN	WAND
BAKE	FALL	WALL	RAMS	JANS	WANE
BAKU	GALA	WALT	SAMA	KANA	WANG
CAKE	GALE	YALE	SAME	KANE	WANS
DAKS	GALL	YALU	SAMP	KANO	WANT
FAKE	GALS	******	SAMS	KANS	WANY
HAKA	HALE	-AM-	TAME	KANT	YANA
HAKE	HALF	******	TAMP	LANA	YANG
HAKU	HALL	CAMB	TAMS	LAND	YANK
JAKE	HALM	CAME	VAMP	LANE	ZANT
JAKO	HALO	CAMP	YAMA	LANG	ZANY
KAKA	HALS	CAMS	YAMP	LANK	******
KAKI	HALT	DAME	YAMS	MANA	-AO-
LAKE	KALA	DAMN	******	MANE	******
LAKH	KALE	DAMP	-AN-	MANI	GAOL
LAKY	KALI	DAMS	******	MANN	JAOB
MAKA	LALL	FAME	BANC	MANO	KAON
MAKE	MALE	FAMN	BAND	MANS	LAON
MAKO	MALI	GAMA	BANE	MANX	LAOS
OAKS	MALL	GAMB	BANG	MANY	NAOS
RAKE	MALM	GAME	BANI	NANA	TAOS
RAKI	MALO	GAMO	BANK	NANO	******
SAKE	MALT	GAMP	BANN	NANS	-AP-
SAKI	NALU	GAMS	BANS	PANE	******
TAKE	PALA	GAMY	BANT	PANG	BAPT
WAKE	PALE	HAMA	CANA	PANK	CAPA
YAKA	PALI	HAME	CANC	PANS	CAPE
YAKO	PALL	HAMS	CANE	PANT	CAPP
YAKS	PALM	IAMB	CANS	RANA	CAPS
******	PALP	JAMA	CANT	RAND	CAPT
-AL-	PALS	JAMB	DANA	RANG	DAPA
******	PALY	JAMI	DANE	RANI	DAPS
AALS	RALE	JAMS	DANG	RANK	GAPE
BALD	RALL	KAMA	DANK	RANT	GAPS
BALE	RALO	KAME	DANS	SANA	GAPY
BALI	SALE	KAMI	DANU	SAND	HAPL
BALK	SALK	LAMA	FANE	SANE	JAPE
BALL	SALP	LAMB	FANG	SANG	KAPA
BALM	SALT	LAME	FANO	SANK	KAPH
BALT	TALC	LAMP	FANS	SANS	LAPP
CALF	TALE	LAMS	GANG	TANA	LAPS
CALI	TALK	MAMA	HAND	TANG	MAPS
CALK	TALL	NAMA	HANG	TANK	NAPA
CALL	VALE	NAME	HANK	TANS	NAPE
CALM	VALI	PAMS	HANS	UANG	NAPS
CALX	VALS	RAMA	IANA	VANE	PAPA

PAPS	FARM	PARI	CAST	******	PATS
RAPE	FARO	PARK	DASH	-AT-	RATA
RAPS	GARA	PARR	EASE	******	RATE
RAPT	GARB	PARS	EAST	BATE	RATH
SAPE	GARD	PART	EASY	BATH	RATI
SAPO	GARE	RARE	FASH	BATS	RATO
SAPS	GARM	SARA	FASS	BATT	RATS
TAPA	GARS	SARD	FAST	BATZ	SATE
TAPE	GARY	SARI	GASH	CATA	TATA
TAPS	HARD	SARK	GASP	CATE	TATE
WAPS	HARE	TARA	HASH	CATH	TATS
YAPA	HARK	TARE	HASP	CATO	VATS
YAPS	HARL	TARN	HAST	CATS	WATE
******	HARM	TARO	JASS	DATA	WATT
-AR-	HARP	TARP	KASM	DATE	ZATI
******	HART	TARS	LASH	EATS	******
AARE	HARZ	TART	LASS	FATA	-AU-
BARB	JARA	VARA	LAST	FATE	******
BARD	JARL	VARI	MASC	FATS	CAUK
BARE	JARS	WARD	MASH	GATA	CAUL
BARI	KARA	WARE	MASK	GATE	DAUB
BARK	KARI	WARF	MASS	GATH	EAUX
BARM	KARL	WARI	MAST	GATS	FAUN
BARN	KARN	WARM	NASA	GATT	GAUD
BARO	KARY	WARN	NASH	HATE	GAUL
BARS	LARA	WARP	NASO	HATH	GAUR
BART	LARD	WARS	NAST	HATS	HAUL
CARA	LARI	WART	OAST	JATH	LAUD
CARB	LARK	WARY	PASH	JATO	LAUN
CARD	LARP	YARD	PASS	KATE	MAUD
CARE	LARS	YARE	PAST	KATY	MAUI
CARL	MARA	YARN	RASA	LATE	MAUL
CARO	MARC	ZARA	RASE	LATH	MAUN
CARP	MARE	ZARF	RASH	LATI	NAUT
CARR	MARJ	ZARP	RASP	MATE	PAUL
CARS	MARK	******	SASH	MATH	SAUD
CART	MARL	-AS-	SASK	MATS	SAUK
CARY	MARS	******	SASS	MATT	SAUL
DARB	MART	BASE	TASK	NATE	SAUR
DARE	MARX	BASH	TASS	NATL	TAUR
DARK	MARY	BASK	VASA	NATO	TAUS
DARN	NARC	BASS	VASE	NATR	TAUT
DART	NARD	BAST	VASO	NATS	WAUK
EARL	NARY	CASE	VAST	NATT	WAUL
EARN	OARS	CASH	WASH	OATH	YAUP
EARS	PARA	CASK	WASP	OATS	******
FARE	PARD	CASS	WAST	PATE	-AV-
FARL	PARE		ZASU	PATH	******
					CAVA
					CAVE

CAVY	YAWN	GAZE	IBID	******	ECON
DAVE	YAWP	HAZE	IBIS	-CD-	ICON
DAVY	YAWS	HAZY	OBIA	******	SCOP
GAVE	******	JAZZ	OBIS	ACDC	SCOT
HAVE	-AX-	KAZI	OBIT	******	SCOW
JAVA	******	LAZE	******	-CE-	******
JAVE	MAXI	LAZY	-BL-	******	-CR-
KAVA	SAXE	MAZE	******	ACEA	******
LAVA	TAXI	MAZY	ABLE	ACED	ACRE
LAVE	TAXY	NAZE	ABLY	ACER	ACRO
NAVE	WAXY	NAZI	BBLS	ACES	ECRU
NAVY	******	RAZE	IBLE	ACET	OCRA
PAVE	-AY-	RAZZ	******	ICED	SCRY
PAVO	******	******	-BO-	ICEL	******
RAVE	BAYA	-BA-	******	ICER	-CT-
SAVE	BAYS	******	ABOU	ICES	******
TAVS	CAYS	ABAS	EBON	******	ACTA
VAVS	DAYS	EBAN	OBOE	-CH-	ACTH
WAVE	FAYE	TBAR	OBOL	******	ACTS
WAVY	FAYS	ZBAR	******	ACHE	ECTO
******	GAYA	******	-BR-	ECHO	OCTA
-AW-	GAYS	-BB-	******	ECHT	OCTO
******	HAYA	******	ABRI	OCHA	******
BAWD	HAYS	ABBA	EBRO	TCHI	-CU-
BAWL	JAYS	ABBE	******	******	******
CAWS	KAYE	ABBR	-BU-	-CI-	ECUA
DAWK	KAYO	ABBY	******	******	ECUS
DAWM	KAYS	EBBS	ABUT	ACID	OCUL
DAWN	LAYS	******	******	******	SCUD
DAWS	MAYA	-BC-	-CA-	-CL-	SCUM
FAWN	MAYO	******	******	******	SCUP
GAWK	MAYS	ABCS	ACAD	ACLU	SCUT
HAWK	NAYS	******	ICAL	******	******
HAWS	PAYE	-BE-	KCAL	-CM-	-DA-
JAWS	PAYS	******	NCAA	******	******
KAWA	RAYS	ABED	NCAR	ACME	ADAH
LAWN	SAYS	ABEL	SCAB	RCMP	ADAK
LAWS	VAYU	ABES	SCAD	UCMJ	ADAM
MAWS	WAYS	ABET	SCAN	******	ADAR
NAWA	YAYA	EBEN	SCAR	-CN-	ADAS
PAWL	******	IBEX	SCAT	******	ADAY
PAWN	-AZ-	OBEY	******	ACNE	DDAY
PAWS	******	UBER	-CB-	******	EDAM
SAWN	CAZI	******	ICBM	-CO-	IDAE
SAWS	DAZA	-BI-	******	******	IDAS
TAWS	DAZE	******	-CC-	ACOR	NDAK
WAWL	FAZE	ABIB	ACCT	ACOU	ODAL
YAWL	GAZA	ABIE	ECCL	ECOL	SDAK
					UDAD

******	ODIN	FEAR	TEAL	NECK	FEES
-DB-	XDIV	FEAT	TEAM	NECR	FEET
******	******	GEAR	TEAR	PECK	GEED
HDBK	**-DL-**	HEAD	TEAS	PECO	GEEK
******	******	HEAL	TEAT	RECK	GEES
-DD-	IDLE	HEAP	VEAL	RECT	GEEZ
******	IDLY	HEAR	WEAK	SECT	HEED
ADDS	******	HEAT	WEAL	SECY	HEEL
ADDY	**-DN-**	JEAN	WEAN	******	JEED
EDDA	******	KEAS	WEAR	**-ED-**	JEEL
EDDY	EDNA	LEAD	YEAH	******	JEEP
ODDS	******	LEAF	YEAN	BEDA	JEER
******	**-DO-**	LEAH	YEAR	BEDE	JEES
-DE-	******	LEAK	YEAS	BEDS	KEEF
******	EDOM	LEAL	ZEAL	CEDE	KEEK
ADEN	IDOL	LEAN	******	LEDA	KEEL
EDEN	ODOR	LEAP	**-EB-**	LEDE	KEEN
EDER	UDOS	LEAR	******	MEDE	KEEP
IDEA	******	LEAS	CEBA	MEDI	LEEK
IDEM	**-DU-**	MEAD	CEBU	NEDS	LEER
IDEO	******	MEAH	DEBS	PEDE	LEES
IDES	EDUC	MEAL	DEBT	PEDI	LEET
ODEA	ODUM	MEAN	FEBR	PEDO	MEEK
ODER	******	MEAT	HEBE	REDE	MEET
ODES	**-DY-**	NEAL	HEBR	REDO	NEED
UDEN	******	NEAP	JEBU	REDS	NEER
******	IDYL	NEAR	NEBO	TEDS	PEEK
-DF-	ODYL	NEAT	NEBS	VEDA	PEEL
******	******	PEAG	REBA	WEDS	PEEN
IDFU	**-DZ-**	PEAK	REBS	ZEDS	PEEP
******	******	PEAL	SEBI	******	PEER
-DG-	ADZE	PEAN	SEBO	**-EE-**	PEES
******	******	PEAR	UEBA	******	REED
EDGE	**-EA-**	PEAS	WEBS	BEEF	REEF
EDGY	******	PEAT	ZEBU	BEEK	REEK
******	BEAD	READ	******	BEEN	REEL
-DH-	BEAK	REAL	**-EC-**	BEEP	SEED
******	BEAM	REAM	******	BEER	SEEK
EDHS	BEAN	REAP	BECK	BEES	SEEL
******	BEAR	REAR	CECA	BEET	SEEM
-DI-	BEAS	SEAH	DECA	CEES	SEEN
******	BEAT	SEAL	DECD	DEED	SEEP
ADIT	BEAU	SEAM	DECI	DEEM	SEER
EDIE	DEAD	SEAN	DECK	DEEP	SEES
EDIT	DEAF	SEAR	GECK	DEER	TEED
FDIC	DEAL	SEAS	HECK	DEES	TEEM
IDIO	DEAN	SEAT	HECT	FEED	TEEN
ODIC	DEAR	TEAK	KECK	FEEL	TEES

VEER	LEIS	GELS	HEME	HENS	******
VEES	MEIO	GELT	HEMI	JENA	-EO-
WEED	MEIR	HELD	HEML	KENO	******
WEEK	NEIL	HELI	HEMO	KENS	AEON
WEEL	REIN	HELL	HEMP	KENT	FEOD
WEEP	REIS	HELM	HEMS	LENA	GEOL
ZEES	TEIL	HELP	JEMS	LEND	GEOM
******	VEIL	JELL	KEMP	LENE	KEOS
-EF-	VEIN	KELA	LEMS	LENO	LEON
******	WEIR	KELP	MEMO	LENS	LEOS
DEFI	ZEIN	KELT	MEMS	LENT	MEOW
DEFT	******	MELD	NEMA	MEND	NEON
DEFY	-EJ-	MELE	NEMO	MENE	PEON
HEFT	******	MELS	REMI	MENI	******
JEFE	DEJA	MELT	REMO	MENO	-EP-
JEFF	NEJD	NELL	REMS	MENT	******
KEFS	SEJM	PELE	SEME	MENU	CEPA
LEFT	******	PELF	SEMI	NENE	DEPA
REFT	-EK-	PELT	TEMA	OENO	DEPT
WEFT	******	PELU	TEMP	PEND	HEPT
******	BEKA	RELY	XEMA	PENN	KEPI
-EG-	DEKA	SELF	******	PENS	KEPT
******	DEKE	SELL	-EN-	PENT	LEPT
BEGS	LEKS	TELA	******	RENA	NEPH
DEGO	WEKA	TELE	BEND	REND	PEPO
KEGS	WEKI	TELL	BENE	RENE	PEPS
LEGS	ZEKE	TELO	BENG	RENI	REPP
MEGA	******	UELE	BENI	RENO	REPS
MEGS	-EL-	VELA	BENS	RENT	SEPT
PEGS	******	VELD	BENT	SEND	WEPT
SEGO	BELA	WELD	CENE	SENS	ZEPH
TEGS	BELG	WELL	CENO	SENT	******
VEGA	BELL	WELT	CENT	TEND	-EQ-
YEGG	BELS	YELD	DENE	TENG	******
******	BELT	YELK	DENS	TENN	SEQQ
-EH-	CELE	YELL	DENT	TENO	******
******	CELL	YELP	DENY	TENS	-ER-
HEHE	CELT	******	EENS	TENT	******
JEHU	DELE	-EM-	FEND	VENA	AERI
LEHR	DELF	******	FENS	VEND	AERO
******	DELI	BEMA	GENE	VENI	AERY
-EI-	DELL	DEME	GENF	VENT	BERA
******	EELS	DEMI	GENG	WEND	BERG
CEIL	EELY	DEMO	GENL	WENS	BERM
DEIL	FELL	DEMY	GENS	WENT	BERN
HEIR	FELS	FEME	GENT	XENO	BERT
KEIR	FELT	GEMS	GENU	YENS	CERE
LEIF	GELD	HEMA	GENY	ZEND	CERO

CERT	VERN	BETS	NEUM	******	AGES
DERM	VERS	FETE	NEUR	**-EY-**	EGER
EERY	VERT	GETS	OEUF	******	OGEE
FERN	VERY	HETH	ZEUS	BEYS	******
GERA	WERE	JETE	******	DEYS	**-GG-**
GERD	WERT	JETH	**-EV-**	KEYS	******
GERI	XERO	JETS	******	******	EGGS
GERM	ZERO	KETO	BEVS	**-FA-**	******
HERA	******	KETU	BEVY	******	**-GH-**
HERB	**-ES-**	LETI	DEVA	AFAR	******
HERD	******	LETO	DEVI	******	AGHA
HERE	BESA	LETS	DEVS	**-FF-**	******
HERL	BESS	LETT	LEVA	******	**-GI-**
HERM	BEST	META	LEVI	EFFS	******
HERO	CESS	METE	LEVO	IFFY	AGIO
HERR	CEST	METH	LEVY	******	******
HERS	DESC	METR	NEVE	**-FG-**	**-GL-**
JERK	DESI	METZ	NEVI	******	******
JERL	DESK	NETS	REVS	AFGH	IGLU
JERM	DESL	PETE	******	******	OGLE
KERB	DESS	PETR	**-EW-**	**-FI-**	UGLY
KERF	FESS	PETS	******	******	******
KERN	FEST	RETE	DEWS	EFIK	**-GN-**
MERE	GEST	RETS	DEWY	IFIL	******
MERL	HEST	SETA	HEWN	******	AGNI
MERO	JESS	SETH	HEWS	**-FN-**	IGNI
MERU	JEST	SETI	JEWS	******	******
MERV	JESU	SETS	LEWD	IFNI	**-GO-**
NERO	LESS	TETE	LEWS	******	******
PERA	LEST	TETH	MEWL	**-FR-**	AGOG
PERE	MESA	TETR	MEWS	******	AGON
PERI	MESH	VETO	NEWS	AFRO	EGOS
PERK	MESO	VETS	NEWT	******	******
PERM	MESS	WETA	PEWS	**-FT-**	**-GP-**
PERN	NESS	WETS	SEWN	******	******
PERT	NEST	YETI	SEWS	EFTS	OGPU
PERU	PESO	ZETA	YEWS	******	******
SERA	PEST	******	******	**-GA-**	**-GR-**
SERB	RESH	**-EU-**	******	******	******
SERE	REST	******	**-EX-**	AGAO	AGRA
SERF	SESS	DEUS	******	AGAR	AGRI
SERO	TESS	DEUT	HEXA	AGAS	AGRO
SERS	TEST	FEUD	NEXT	EGAD	OGRE
TERA	VEST	FEUS	SEXI	EGAN	******
TERM	WEST	JEUX	SEXT	NGAN	**-GU-**
TERN	ZEST	LEUC	SEXY	******	******
VERA	******	LEUD	TEXT	**-GE-**	AGUA
VERB	**-ET-**	LEUK		******	AGUE
	******			AGED	
	BETA			AGEE	
	BETH				

******	CHET	RHIN	******	SIAM	RICE
-HA-	CHEW	RHIZ	**-HU-**	VIAL	RICH
******	CHEZ	SHIM	******	******	RICK
AHAB	GHEE	SHIN	CHUB	**-IB-**	SICE
AHAH	KHET	SHIP	CHUD	******	SICK
BHAR	PHEN	SHIV	CHUG	BIBB	SICS
CHAD	PHEW	THIN	CHUM	BIBL	TICK
CHAP	RHEA	THIO	CHUR	BIBS	TICS
CHAR	RHEO	THIS	PHUD	DIBS	VICE
CHAT	SHEA	WHIG	PHUT	FIBR	VICI
CHAW	SHED	WHIM	RHUM	FIBS	VICK
CHAY	SHEM	WHIN	RHUS	GIBE	WICH
DHAI	SHES	WHIP	SHUL	GIBS	WICK
DHAK	SHEW	WHIR	SHUN	JIBE	******
DHAL	THEA	WHIT	SHUT	JIBI	**-ID-**
DHAN	THEB	WHIZ	THUD	JIBS	******
DHAR	THEE	******	THUG	KIBE	AIDA
GHAT	THEM	**-HM-**	THUS	MIBS	AIDE
KHAN	THEN	******	******	NIBS	AIDS
KHAT	THEO	OHMS	**-HW-**	RIBS	BIDE
PHAG	THEW	******	******	SIBS	BIDS
SHAD	THEY	**-HO-**	YHWH	******	CIDE
SHAG	WHEN	******	******	**-IC-**	DIDO
SHAH	WHET	AHOY	**-HY-**	******	DIDY
SHAM	WHEW	CHOL	******	BICE	FIDS
SHAN	WHEY	CHOP	PHYL	DICE	GIDE
SHAW	******	CHOU	PHYT	DICH	HIDE
SHAY	**-HG-**	CHOW	RHYL	DICK	KIDD
THAD	******	DHOW	RHYS	FICA	KIDS
THAN	CHGD	JHOW	WHYS	FICE	LIDO
THAR	CHGS	MHOS	******	FICO	LIDS
THAT	******	PHON	**-IA-**	HICK	MIDI
THAW	**-HI-**	PHOT	******	KICK	NIDE
WHAM	******	RHOB	BIAS	LICE	NIDI
WHAP	CHIA	RHOS	DIAG	LICH	RIDE
WHAT	CHIC	SHOD	DIAL	LICK	RIDS
******	CHID	SHOE	DIAM	MICA	SIDE
-HD-	CHIH	SHOO	DIAN	MICE	SIDS
******	CHIL	SHOP	DIAS	MICH	TIDE
PHDS	CHIN	SHOQ	DIAZ	MICK	TIDY
******	CHIP	SHOT	FIAT	NICE	VIDE
-HE-	CHIR	SHOW	KIAK	NICK	VIDI
******	CHIS	THOR	LIAO	PICA	WIDE
AHEM	CHIT	THOU	LIAR	PICE	******
CHEE	OHIA	WHOA	PIAF	PICK	**-IE-**
CHEF	OHIO	WHOM	PIAY	PICO	******
CHEM	PHIL	WHOP	RIAL	PICR	BIEL
CHES	PHIS	******	SIAL	PICT	BIER
		-HR-			
		******			
		THRU			

CIEL	******	******	RILE	AINT	MINI
DIED	**-IG-**	**-IL-**	RILL	AINU	MINK
DIES	******	******	SILK	BIND	MINN
DIET	DIGS	AILE	SILL	BINE	MINT
DIEU	FIGS	AILS	SILO	BING	MINX
FIEF	GIGA	BILE	SILT	BINH	NINA
GIED	GIGS	BILK	TILE	BINS	NINE
HIED	HIGH	BILL	TILL	CINE	NINO
HIER	JIGS	DILI	TILT	DINA	OINO
HIES	LIGN	DILL	VILE	DINE	PINA
KIEL	MIGS	DILO	VILI	DING	PINE
KIER	NIGH	FILA	VILL	DINO	PING
KIEV	NIGR	FILE	WILD	DINS	PINK
LIED	PIGS	FILL	WILE	DINT	PINS
LIEF	RIGA	FILM	WILL	FIND	PINT
LIEN	RIGS	FILO	WILT	FINE	PINY
LIES	SIGH	FILS	WILY	FINK	RIND
LIEU	SIGN	GILA	******	FINN	RING
MIEN	WIGS	GILD	**-IM-**	FINS	RINK
NIEL	******	GILL	******	GINA	SIND
PIED	**-IH-**	GILS	AIMS	GINK	SINE
PIER	******	GILT	DIME	GINS	SING
PIES	BIHE	HILL	DIMS	HIND	SINK
RIEN	KIHO	HILO	GIMP	HINO	SINO
TIED	******	HILT	JIMS	HINT	SINS
TIER	**-II-**	JILL	LIMA	JIND	TINA
TIES	******	JILT	LIMB	JINK	TINE
VIED	RIIS	KILL	LIME	JINN	TING
VIES	******	KILN	LIMN	JINX	TINS
VIEW	**-IJ-**	KILO	LIMP	KIND	TINT
******	******	KILT	LIMU	KINE	TINY
-IF-	FIJI	LILA	LIMY	KING	VINA
******	RIJN	LILS	MIME	KINK	VINE
BIFF	******	LILT	MIMI	KINO	VINI
FIFE	**-IK-**	LILY	NIMB	LINA	VINO
GIFT	******	MILD	PIMA	LIND	VINY
GIFU	BIKE	MILE	PIMP	LINE	WIND
HIFI	DIKE	MILK	RIME	LING	WINE
JIFF	HIKE	MILL	RIMS	LINK	WING
LIFE	LIKE	MILO	RIMY	LINN	WINK
LIFT	MIKE	MILS	SIMA	LINO	WINO
MIFF	NIKE	MILT	SIMP	LINT	WINS
RIFE	PIKA	NILE	SIMS	LINY	WINY
RIFF	PIKE	OILS	TIME	LINZ	XINT
RIFT	PIKI	OILY	TIMS	MINA	ZINC
SIFT	SIKH	PILE	VIMY	MIND	ZING
TIFF	TIKE	PILI	******	MINE	******
WIFE	TIKI	PILL	**-IN-**	MING	**-IO-**
			******		******
			AINO		BIOL
			AINS		BION

CION	AIRY	DISK	FITZ	HIVE	IKES
DION	BIRD	DIST	HITS	JIVE	OKED
DIOS	BIRL	FISC	KITE	KIVA	OKET
LION	BIRO	FISH	KITH	KIVU	SKEE
PION	BIRR	FIST	KITS	LIVE	SKEG
PIOT	CIRC	GIST	KITT	RIVA	SKEP
RIOT	DIRE	HISS	LITE	RIVE	SKEW
SION	DIRK	HIST	LITH	RIVO	******
TION	DIRT	KISH	MITE	SIVA	-KI-
VIOL	EIRE	KISS	MITT	TIVY	******
XION	FIRE	KIST	NITA	VIVA	AKIN
ZION	FIRM	LISA	NITR	VIVE	OKIE
******	FIRN	LISP	NITS	VIVO	SKID
-IP-	FIRS	LISS	PITA	WIVE	SKIM
******	GIRD	LIST	PITH	******	SKIN
DIPL	GIRL	MISC	PITO	-IW-	SKIP
DIPS	GIRO	MISE	PITS	******	SKIS
GIPS	GIRT	MISO	PITT	KIWI	SKIT
HIPE	HIRE	MISS	PITY	******	******
HIPP	HIRO	MIST	RITA	-IX-	-KL-
HIPS	KIRI	NISI	RITE	******	******
KIPE	KIRK	OISE	SITE	MIXT	OKLA
KIPS	LIRA	PISA	SITI	PIXY	WKLY
LIPO	LIRE	PISC	SITO	******	******
LIPS	MIRA	PISH	SITS	-IZ-	-KO-
NIPA	MIRE	PISO	SITU	******	******
NIPS	MIRO	RISE	TITI	FIZZ	IKON
PIPA	MIRS	RISK	TITO	GIZA	******
PIPE	MIRV	VISA	TITS	LIZA	-KR-
PIPS	MIRY	VISC	VITA	PIZZ	******
PIPY	PIRN	VISE	VITE	SIZE	OKRA
RIPA	SIRE	VISO	VITI	SIZY	******
RIPE	SIRI	VISS	VITR	ZIZZ	-KU-
RIPS	SIRS	WISC	WITH	******	******
SIPS	TIRE	WISE	WITS	-JA-	SKUA
TIPI	TIRO	WISH	******	******	******
TIPS	VIRA	WISP	-IU-	AJAR	-KV-
VIPS	VIRE	WIST	******	AJAX	******
WIPE	WIRE	******	NIUE	******	NKVD
XIPH	WIRY	-IT-	PIUS	-KA-	******
YIPE	ZIRA	******	******	******	-KW-
YIPS	******	BITE	-IV-	OKAS	******
ZIPS	-IS-	BITS		OKAY	IKWE
******	******	BITT	DIVA	SKAG	******
-IR-	BISE	CITE	DIVE	SKAT	-KY-
******	CIST	CITY	DIVI	SKAW	******
AIRE	DISC	DITA	FIVE	-KE-	SKYE
AIRS	DISH	FITS	GIVE	******	
				EKED	
				EKES	

******	ELBA	PLEB	******	FLOR	BLUE
-LA-	ELBE	PLED	**-LL-**	FLOT	BLUR
******	******	PLEW	******	FLOW	CLUB
ALAE	**-LD-**	SLED	ALLE	GLOB	CLUE
ALAI	******	SLEE	ALLI	GLOT	CLUJ
ALAN	ALDE	SLEW	ALLO	GLOW	ELUL
ALAR	ALDO	ULEX	ALLY	OLOR	FLUB
ALAS	BLDG	YLEM	ELLA	PLOD	FLUE
BLAB	******	******	ELLS	PLOP	FLUO
BLAH	**-LE-**	**-LF-**	ILLS	PLOT	FLUX
BLAT	******	******	ILLY	PLOW	GLUE
CLAD	ALEC	ALFA	MLLE	PLOY	GLUM
CLAM	ALEE	ALFS	OLLA	SLOB	GLUT
CLAN	ALEF	******	OLLY	SLOE	ILUS
CLAP	ALEN	**-LG-**	ULLA	SLOG	PLUG
CLAR	ALES	******	******	SLOO	PLUM
CLAW	ALEX	ALGA	**-LM-**	SLOP	PLUS
CLAY	BLEB	ALGY	******	SLOT	SLUB
ELAM	BLED	OLGA	ALMA	SLOW	SLUE
ELAN	BLEM	******	ALMS	******	SLUG
FLAG	BLET	**-LI-**	ELMA	**-LP-**	SLUM
FLAK	BLEW	******	ELMO	******	SLUR
FLAM	CLEE	ALIA	ELMS	ALPH	SLUT
FLAN	CLEF	ALIF	ELMY	ALPS	******
FLAP	CLEG	ALIN	******	OLPE	**-LV-**
FLAT	CLEM	ALIT	**-LN-**	******	******
FLAW	CLEO	ALIX	******	**-LR-**	ALVA
FLAX	CLEW	BLIP	ULNA	******	BLVD
FLAY	ELEC	BLIT	******	NLRB	ELVA
GLAD	ELEM	CLIO	**-LO-**	******	******
KLAM	ELEO	CLIP	******	**-LS-**	**-LY-**
OLAF	ELEV	ELIA	ALOE	******	******
OLAV	FLEA	ELIS	ALOP	ALSO	ALYS
OLAY	FLED	FLIP	ALOW	ELSA	******
PLAN	FLEE	FLIT	BLOB	ELSE	**-MA-**
PLAT	FLEM	GLIB	BLOC	ELST	******
PLAY	FLEW	GLIM	BLOT	ILSE	AMAH
SLAB	FLEX	ILIA	BLOW	OLST	AMAS
SLAG	GLED	OLIG	CLOD	******	AMAT
SLAM	GLEE	OLIO	CLOG	**-LT-**	GMAN
SLAP	GLEN	SLID	CLON	******	IMAM
SLAT	HLER	SLIM	CLOP	ALTA	IMAN
SLAV	ILEA	SLIP	CLOT	ALTI	OMAN
SLAW	ILEO	SLIT	CLOY	ALTO	OMAR
SLAY	ILEX	******	FLOC	******	XMAS
ULAN	KLEE	**-LK-**	FLOE	**-LU-**	******
******	OLEO	******	FLOG	******	**-MB-**
-LB-	PLEA	ELKE	FLOP	ALUM	******
******		ELKS		BLUB	AMBI
ALBA		ILKA			AMBO
ALBS					

OMBR	******	******	******	******	ANTH
UMBO	-MM-	-MY-	-NE-	-NM-	ANTI
******	******	******	******	******	ANTS
-MC-	AMMO	AMYL	ANEW	FNMA	ENTE
******	EMMA	AMYS	INEE	******	ENTO
FMCS	EMMY	******	INEZ	-NN-	INTO
YMCA	IMMI	-NA-	KNEE	******	ONTO
******	IMMY	******	KNEW	ANNA	UNTO
-MD-	******	ANAL	ONER	ANNE	UNTZ
******	-MN-	ANAM	ONES	ANNO	XNTY
CMDR	******	ANAS	SNEE	ANNS	******
******	OMNI	ANAT	******	ENNA	-NU-
-ME-	******	GNAR	-NF-	ENNS	******
******	-MO-	GNAT	******	INNS	ANUS
AMEN	******	GNAW	INFO	******	GNUS
AMER	AMOI	INAS	******	-NO-	KNUR
AMES	AMOK	KNAG	-NG-	******	ONUS
EMEU	AMON	KNAP	******	ANOA	SNUB
GMEN	AMOR	KNAR	ENGR	ANON	SNUG
MMES	AMOS	SNAG	INGA	ENOL	******
OMEI	AMOY	SNAP	INGE	ENOS	-NV-
OMEN	BMOC	UNAS	UNGA	ENOW	******
OMER	SMOG	UNAU	******	KNOB	ENVY
SMEE	******	******	-NI-	KNOP	******
SMEW	-MP-	-NC-	******	KNOT	-NY-
YMER	******	******	ANIL	KNOW	******
******	AMPS	ANCE	ANIM	KNOX	ENYO
-MH-	IMPI	ANCY	ANIS	ONON	ONYX
******	IMPS	ENCE	ENID	SNOB	PNYX
YMHA	******	ENCL	INIA	SNOG	SNYE
******	-MS-	ENCY	INIT	SNOT	******
-MI-	******	INCA	KNIT	SNOW	-NZ-
******	OMSK	INCH	SNIG	******	******
AMIA	******	INCL	SNIP	-NR-	ONZA
AMID	-MT-	ONCA	SNIT	******	UNZE
AMIE	******	ONCE	UNIE	INRE	******
AMIR	AMTS	UNCO	UNIO	INRI	-OA-
AMIS	UMTS	******	UNIT	INRO	******
EMIA	******	-ND-	******	******	BOAR
EMIL	-MU-	******	-NK-	-NS-	BOAS
EMIR	******	ANDY	******	******	BOAT
EMIT	AMUR	ENDO	ANKH	ANSA	BOAZ
IMID	AMUS	ENDS	INKS	INSP	COAL
IMIN	BMUS	INDO	INKY	INST	COAT
OMIT	DMUS	ONDO	******	******	COAX
SMIT	EMUS	UNDE	-NL-	-NT-	FOAL
YMIR	SMUG	UNDO	******	******	FOAM
	SMUT	UNDY	INLY	ANTA	GOAD
			ONLY	ANTE	

GOAL	JOBO	HODS	POET	******	MOKI
GOAR	JOBS	IODO	ROES	-OH-	POKE
GOAS	KOBE	JODO	TOED	******	POKU
GOAT	LOBE	LODE	TOES	BOHR	POKY
HOAR	LOBO	LODI	VOET	COHO	SOKE
HOAX	LOBS	LODZ	WOES	FOHN	WOKE
JOAB	MOBS	MODE	ZOES	JOHN	YOKE
JOAD	NOBS	MODI	******	KOHL	******
JOAH	ROBE	MODS	-OF-	MOHO	-OL-
JOAN	ROBS	NODE	******	MOHR	******
JOAR	SOBS	NODS	DOFF	SOHO	BOLA
JOAT	TOBY	PODA	LOFT	******	BOLD
KOAE	******	PODE	SOFA	-OI-	BOLE
LOAD	-OC-	PODS	SOFT	******	BOLL
LOAF	******	RODE	TOFF	BOIL	BOLO
LOAM	BOCK	RODS	TOFT	BOIS	BOLT
LOAN	COCA	SODA	******	COIF	COLA
MOAB	COCK	SODS	-OG-	COIL	COLD
MOAN	COCO	TODD	******	COIN	COLE
MOAS	DOCK	TODO	BOGS	COIR	COLL
MOAT	FOCH	TODS	BOGY	DOIT	COLO
NOAH	FOCI	TODY	COGS	FOIL	COLS
ROAD	HOCK	YODH	DOGE	JOIN	COLT
ROAM	JOCK	YODS	DOGS	LOIN	COLY
ROAN	LOCH	******	DOGY	LOIS	DOLA
ROAR	LOCI	-OE-	FOGS	MOIL	DOLE
SOAK	LOCK	******	FOGY	MOIO	DOLF
SOAP	LOCO	BOER	GOGH	NOIL	DOLL
SOAR	MOCK	COED	GOGO	ROIL	DOLS
TOAD	NOCK	COEF	HOGG	SOIL	DOLT
WOAD	NOCT	COEL	HOGS	SOIR	FOLD
ZOAN	POCK	DOER	JOGS	TOIL	FOLK
ZOAR	POCO	DOES	LOGE	VOID	FOLL
******	ROCK	FOES	LOGO	ZOIC	GOLD
-OB-	SOCK	GOER	LOGS	******	GOLF
******	TOCO	GOES	LOGY	-OJ-	GOLO
BOBS	VOCE	HOED	NOGG	******	HOLD
COBB	******	HOEN	NOGO	MOJO	HOLE
COBS	-OD-	HOER	NOGS	SOJA	HOLM
DOBY	******	HOES	POGO	******	HOLO
FOBS	BODE	JOEL	POGY	-OK-	HOLT
GOBI	BODY	JOES	TOGA	******	HOLY
GOBO	CODA	JOEY	TOGO	COKE	IOLE
GOBS	CODE	KOEL	TOGS	JOKE	JOLA
GOBY	CODS	MOES	YOGA	KOKO	JOLO
HOBO	CODY	NOEL	YOGH	LOKE	JOLT
HOBS	DODO	NOES	YOGI	LOKI	KOLA
IOBB	GODS	POEM		MOKE	KOLN

LOLA	GOMA	CONT	ZONA	MOOS	KOPH
LOLL	HOME	CONY	ZONE	MOOT	KOPI
MOLD	HOMO	DONA	******	NOOK	KOPS
MOLE	HOMS	DONE	-OO-	NOON	LOPE
MOLL	HOMY	DONS	******	POOD	LOPS
MOLT	LOMA	DON'T	BOOB	POOH	MOPE
MOLY	LOME	EONS	BOOK	POOK	MOPS
POLE	MOMO	FOND	BOOM	POOL	NOPE
POLK	MOMS	FONG	BOON	POON	POPE
POLL	NOMA	FONT	BOOR	POOP	POPS
POLO	NOME	GOND	BOOS	POOR	QOPH
POLY	NOMO	GONE	BOOT	ROOD	ROPE
ROLE	NOMY	GONG	COOK	ROOF	ROPY
ROLF	POME	GONO	COOL	ROOK	SOPS
ROLL	POMP	HOND	COON	ROOM	TOPE
SOLA	ROMA	HONE	COOP	ROOP	TOPH
SOLD	ROME	HONG	COOS	ROOT	TOPI
SOLE	ROMP	HONK	COOT	SOON	TOPO
SOLI	ROMS	IONA	DOOM	SOOT	TOPS
SOLO	SOMA	IONS	DOON	TOOK	******
SOLS	SOME	JONS	DOOR	TOOL	-OR-
TOLA	TOMB	LONE	FOOD	TOON	******
TOLD	TOME	LONG	FOOL	TOOT	BORA
TOLE	TOMS	MONA	FOOT	WOOD	BORE
TOLL	TOMY	MONK	GOOD	WOOF	BORN
TOLU	WOMB	MONO	GOOF	WOOL	BORT
VOLA	******	MONS	GOOK	WOOS	CORA
VOLE	-ON-	MONT	GOON	ZOOL	CORD
VOLS	******	NONA	GOOP	ZOOM	CORE
VOLT	AONE	NONE	HOOD	ZOON	CORF
WOLD	BONA	OONA	HOOF	ZOOS	CORK
WOLF	BOND	POND	HOOK	******	CORM
YOLK	BONE	PONE	HOON	-OP-	CORN
ZOLA	BONG	PONG	HOOP	******	CORP
******	BONI	PONS	HOOT	BOPS	DORA
-OM-	BONK	PONY	JOOK	COPA	DORE
******	BONN	RONA	KOOK	COPE	DORM
BOMB	BONO	SONE	LOOD	COPR	DORP
COMA	BONY	SONG	LOOF	COPS	DORR
COMB	CONC	SONS	LOOK	COPT	DORS
COME	COND	TONE	LOOM	COPY	DORY
COMM	CONE	TONG	LOON	DOPE	FORA
COMO	CONF	TONI	LOOP	DOPP	FORB
COMP	CONG	TONO	LOOS	DOPY	FORD
COMR	CONJ	TONS	LOOT	FOPS	FORE
DOMA	CONK	TONY	MOOD	HOPE	FORK
DOME	CONN	WONT	MOON	HOPI	FORM
DOMS	CONS	YOND	MOOR	HOPS	FORT

GORE	******	BOTS	DOUG	******	ROYS
GORY	-OS-	BOTT	DOUR	-OW-	SOYA
HORA	******	COTE	EOUS	******	SOYS
HORN	BOSH	COTS	FOUL	BOWL	TOYO
HORT	BOSK	COTY	FOUR	BOWS	TOYS
KORS	BOSN	DOTE	GOUT	COWL	YOYO
LORD	BOSS	DOTH	HOUR	COWS	******
LORE	COSH	DOTS	IOUS	DOWN	-OZ-
LORN	COSM	DOTY	JOUG	FOWL	******
LORY	COSS	GOTH	JOUY	GOWK	BOZO
MORA	COST	HOTE	LOUD	GOWL	COZY
MORE	COSY	HOTH	LOUP	GOWN	DOZE
MORN	DOSE	HOTI	LOUR	HOWE	DOZY
MORO	DOSS	IOTA	LOUT	HOWL	OOZE
MORS	DOST	JOTS	MOUE	IOWA	OOZY
MORT	FOSS	KOTO	NOUN	JOWL	******
NORA	GOSH	LOTE	NOUS	LOWS	-PA-
NORD	HOSE	LOTH	POUF	MOWN	******
NORM	HOST	LOTS	POUR	MOWS	OPAH
NORN	JOSE	LOTT	POUT	NOWS	OPAL
PORE	JOSH	MOTE	ROUE	NOWT	SPAD
PORK	JOSS	MOTH	ROUP	POWS	SPAM
PORN	KOSS	MOTS	ROUT	ROWS	SPAN
PORT	LOSE	MOTT	ROUX	SOWN	SPAR
RORY	LOSS	NOTE	SOUL	SOWS	SPAS
SORA	LOST	NOTO	SOUP	TOWN	SPAT
SORB	MOSE	NOTT	SOUR	TOWS	SPAY
SORE	MOSS	POTS	SOUS	VOWS	UPAS
SORI	MOST	ROTA	TOUR	WOWS	******
SORN	NOSE	ROTC	TOUT	YOWL	-PC-
SORT	NOSH	ROTE	YOUD	YOWS	******
TORA	NOSO	ROTI	YOUP	******	SPCA
TORE	NOSY	ROTL	YOUR	-OX-	SPCC
TORI	POSE	ROTS	ZOUG	******	******
TORN	POSH	SOTS	******	COXA	-PE-
TORS	POST	TOTE	-OV-	DOXY	******
TORT	POSY	TOTI	******	FOXY	APED
TORY	ROSA	TOTS	BOVI	MOXA	APES
VORA	ROSE	VOTE	COVE	ROXY	APEX
VORE	ROSS	WOTE	DOVE	******	EPEE
WORD	ROSY	******	GOVT	-OY-	OPEN
WORE	SOSO	-OU-	HOVE	******	SPEC
WORK	TOSH	******	JOVE	BOYD	SPED
WORM	TOSS	AOUL	LOVE	BOYS	SPES
WORN	XOSA	BOUT	MOVE	FOYS	SPET
WORT	******	BOUW	NOVA	GOYA	SPEW
YORE	-OT-	COUE	ROVE	HOYS	******
YORK	BOTA	COUP	WOVE	JOYS	-PH-
	BOTH				******
					OPHI

*****	******	GRAD	******	ERGS	TRIX
PI-	-QU-	GRAF	-RE-	ORGY	URIA
******	******	GRAM	******	URGE	URIC
APIA	AQUA	GRAO	AREA	******	WRIT
APIO	AQUI	GRAY	AREO	-RI-	******
APIS	EQUI	GRAZ	ARES	******	-RK-
EPIC	******	IRAK	BREA	ARIA	******
OPIA	-RA-	IRAN	BRED	ARID	ARKS
SPIN	******	IRAQ	BREN	ARIL	IRKS
SPIR	ARAB	IRAS	BRER	ARIZ	******
SPIT	ARAD	KRAL	BRET	BRIE	-RL-
SPIV	ARAL	ORAL	BREV	BRIG	******
******	ARAM	ORAN	BREW	BRIM	ERLE
-PO-	ARAN	PRAE	CREE	BRIO	ORLE
******	ARAS	PRAM	CRES	BRIT	ORLY
APOC	BRAD	PRAO	CREW	CRIB	******
APOD	BRAE	PRAY	DREW	CRIT	-RM-
EPOS	BRAG	TRAD	FREA	DRIB	******
SPOR	BRAN	TRAH	FRED	DRIN	ARMS
SPOT	BRAS	TRAM	FREE	DRIP	ARMY
UPON	BRAT	TRAP	FREQ	ERIA	ERMA
******	BRAW	TRAY	FRET	ERIC	IRMA
-PQ-	BRAY	URAL	FREY	ERIE	******
******	BRAZ	URAN	GREG	ERIK	-RN-
SPQR	CRAB	WRAF	GREW	ERIN	******
******	CRAG	WRAP	GREY	ERIS	ARNE
-PR-	CRAM	XRAY	OREL	FRIO	ARNI
******	CRAN	******	ORES	FRIT	ARNO
SPRY	CRAP	-RB-	PREP	GRID	ARNS
******	CRAT	******	PRES	GRIG	BRNO
-PS-	CRAW	IRBM	PREY	GRIM	ERNE
******	DRAB	ORBS	TREE	GRIN	ERNS
APSE	DRAG	******	TREF	GRIP	ORNE
OPSY	DRAH	-RC-	TREK	GRIS	URNA
******	DRAM	******	TRES	GRIT	URNS
-PT-	DRAT	ARCH	TRET	HRIP	******
******	DRAW	ARCS	TREY	IRID	-RO-
OPTS	DRAY	ORCA	UREA	IRIS	******
******	ERAL	ORCS	UREY	KRIS	AROW
-PU-	ERAS	******	WREN	ORIG	BROM
******	FRAE	-RD-	XREF	PRIG	BRON
APUS	FRAN	******	******	PRIM	BROO
OPUS	FRAP	ERDA	-RF-	TRIG	BROW
SPUD	FRAS	ORDO	******	TRIM	BROZ
SPUE	FRAT	URDE	URFA	TRIN	CROP
SPUN	FRAU	URDU	******	TRIO	CROW
SPUR	FRAY	URDY	-RG-	TRIP	DROP
	GRAB		******	TRIS	EROS
			ARGO		
			ERGO		

FROE	CRUD	USES	******	STAG	******
FROG	CRUS	YSER	-SO-	STAN	-TL-
FROM	CRUX	******	******	STAR	******
FROT	DRUB	-SG-	ASOF	STAT	ATLE
FROW	DRUG	******	******	STAY	ATLI
GROG	DRUM	MSGR	-SP-	UTAH	STLO
GROS	GRUB	MSGT	******	******	******
GROT	GRUM	******	ASPS	-TC-	-TM-
GROW	PRUE	-SH-	ESPY	******	******
HRON	TRUE	******	******	ETCH	ATMO
IRON	TRUK	ASHA	-SS-	ITCH	******
PROA	URUS	ASHE	******	******	-TN-
PROD		ASHY	ASSN	-TE-	******
PROF	-RY-	PSHA	ASST	******	ETNA
PROM	******	TSHI	BSSC	ATEN	
PRON	ARYL	******	ESSE	ATES	-TO-
PROP	CRYO	-SI-	ISSY	CTEN	******
PROS	ORYX	******	OSSA	ITEA	ATOM
PROT	******	ASIA	OSSI	ITEM	ATOP
PROW	-SA-	ASIR	USSR	ITER	ATOR
TROD	******	ASIS	******	OTEA	ETON
TRON	ASAS	ISIS	-ST-	PTER	ITOL
TROP	ESAU	OSIS	******	STEM	OTOE
TROT	ISAR	PSIS	ASTI	STEN	STOA
TROW	OSAR	USIA	ASTR	STEP	STOL
TROY	TSAR	******	ESTE	STER	STOP
******	USAF	-SK-	ESTH	STET	STOW
-RR-	USAR	******	MSTH	STEW	VTOL
******	******	ASKS	MSTS	UTER	******
ERRS	-SB-	******	OSTE	UTES	-TR-
IRRA	******	-SL-	******	******	******
******	ISBA	******	-SU-	-TH-	ATRI
-RS-	******	ISLE	******	******	******
******	-SC-	OSLO	TSUN	ETHN	-TT-
ERSE	******	******	******	ETHS	******
ERST	ASCH	-SM-	-SV-	******	ATTA
URSA	ASCI	******	******	-TI-	ATTN
******	ESCE	ISMS	RSVP	******	ATTO
-RT-	USCG	USMA	******	ATIC	ATTU
******	******	USMC	-TA-	OTIC	ATTY
ARTE	-SE-	USMS	******	OTIS	ETTA
ARTS	******	******	ATAR	STIR	ETTE
ARTY	ASEA	-SN-	ETAH	******	OTTO
ORTH	BSED	******	ETAL	-TK-	******
ORTS	ISER	ESNE	ETAS	******	-TU-
XRTS	OSEL	ISNT	ITAL	ATKA	******
******	USED	USNA	PTAH		ETUI
-RU-	USER	USNR	STAB		STUB
******					
ARUM					
BRUT					

STUD	PUBS	MUDS	******	******	TULE
STUM	RUBE	NUDE	-UG-	-UK-	YULE
STUN	RUBS	NUDI	******	******	ZULU
STUS	RUBY	RUDD	BUGS	AUKS	******
******	SUBJ	RUDE	DUGS	DUKE	-UM-
-TY-	SUBS	RUDY	HUGE	LUKE	******
******	TUBA	SUDD	HUGH	PUKA	BUMP
ITYS	TUBE	SUDS	HUGO	PUKE	BUMS
STYX	TUBS	TUDE	HUGS	SUKY	DUMA
******	******	******	JUGS	YUKS	DUMB
-UA-	-UC-	-UE-	LUGE	******	DUMP
******	******	******	LUGS	-UL-	FUME
DUAD	BUCK	CUED	MUGS	******	FUMY
DUAL	DUCE	CUES	PUGH	AULD	GUMI
DUAR	DUCK	DUEL	PUGS	BULB	GUMS
GUAM	DUCT	DUES	RUGA	BULE	HUME
GUAN	FUCI	DUET	RUGS	BULG	HUMP
GUAO	GUCK	FUEL	TUGS	BULK	HUMS
GUAT	HUCK	HUED	VUGS	BULL	JUMP
JUAN	JUCA	HUES	YUGA	CULE	LUMP
LUAU	LUCE	LUES	******	CULL	MUMM
QUAB	LUCK	QUEI	-UH-	CULM	MUMS
QUAD	LUCY	RUED	******	CULT	NUMB
QUAG	MUCH	RUER	BUHL	DULL	PUMA
QUAI	MUCI	RUES	GUHA	DULY	PUMP
QUAN	MUCK	SUED	RUHR	FULA	RUMP
QUAR	MUCO	SUER	******	FULL	RUMS
QUAT	OUCH	SUES	-UI-	GULF	SUMO
QUAY	PUCE	SUET	******	GULL	SUMP
RUAY	PUCK	SUEZ	CUIR	GULP	SUMS
YUAN	RUCK	TUES	DUIM	HULA	TUMP
******	SUCH	******	DUIT	HULK	YUMA
-UB-	SUCK	-UF-	GUIN	HULL	******
******	TUCK	******	LUIS	JULE	-UN-
AUBE	******	BUFF	LUIZ	JULY	******
AUBY	-UD-	CUFF	MUIR	LULL	AUNE
BUBO	******	DUFF	QUID	LULU	AUNT
BUBS	AUDE	GUFF	QUIP	MULE	BUNA
CUBA	BUDD	HUFF	QUIT	MULL	BUND
CUBE	BUDS	LUFF	QUIZ	MULT	BUNG
CUBS	CUDS	MUFF	RUIN	NULL	BUNK
DUBS	DUDE	PUFF	SUIT	PULE	BUNN
HUBS	DUDS	RUFE	******	PULL	BUNS
JUBA	JUDE	RUFF	-UJ-	PULP	BUNT
JUBE	JUDO	SUFI	******	RULE	DUNA
LUBA	JUDY	TUFA	FUJI	SULK	DUNE
LUBE	KUDU	TUFF	JUJU	SULU	DUNG
NUBS	LUDO	TUFT		TULA	DUNK

DUNS	MUON	GURU	HUSS	RUTE	EVER
DUNT	QUOD	HURL	JUST	RUTH	EVES
FUND	******	HURT	LUSH	RUTS	IVES
FUNG	**-UP-**	JURA	LUST	TUTU	OVEN
FUNK	******	JURY	MUSE	******	OVER
FUNS	CUPR	KURA	MUSH	**-UU-**	UVEA
GUNS	CUPS	KURD	MUSK	******	YVES
HUNG	DUPE	KURE	MUSS	PUUD	******
HUNK	HUPA	KURT	MUST	******	**-VI-**
HUNS	LUPE	LURE	OUSE	**-UV-**	******
HUNT	PUPA	LURI	OUST	******	AVID
JUNC	PUPS	LURK	PUSH	SUVA	AVIS
JUNE	SUPA	MURK	PUSS	******	AVIV
JUNG	SUPE	OURS	RUSE	**-UX-**	EVIL
JUNK	SUPP	PURE	RUSH	******	OVID
JUNO	SUPS	PURI	RUSK	LUXE	UVIC
KUNK	SUPT	PURL	RUSS	******	******
LUNA	TUPI	PURR	RUST	**-UY-**	**-VO-**
LUNE	TUPS	SURA	SUSS	******	******
LUNG	******	SURD	TUSH	BUYS	AVON
LUNI	**-UR-**	SURE	TUSK	CUYA	AVOW
LUNT	******	SURF	******	FUYE	EVOE
NUNS	AURA	SURG	**-UT-**	GUYS	IVOR
PUNA	BURD	TURF	******	******	******
PUND	BURG	TURK	AUTH	**-UZ-**	**-VU-**
PUNG	BURL	TURN	AUTO	******	******
PUNK	BURN	******	BUTE	BUZZ	OVUM
PUNS	BURP	**-US-**	BUTS	FUZE	******
PUNT	BURR	******	BUTT	FUZZ	**-VY-**
PUNY	BURS	AUST	CUTE	SUZY	******
QUNG	BURT	BUSH	CUTS	ZUZA	IVYS
RUNE	BURY	BUSK	DUTY	******	******
RUNG	CURB	BUSS	GUTS	**-VA-**	**-WA-**
RUNS	CURD	BUST	HUTS	******	******
RUNT	CURE	BUSY	JUTE	AVAL	AWAY
SUNG	CURL	CUSH	JUTS	AVAS	EWAN
SUNK	CURS	CUSK	LUTA	EVAN	HWAI
SUNN	CURT	CUSP	LUTE	EVAS	HWAN
SUNS	DURA	CUSS	LUTH	IVAN	SWAB
TUNA	DURN	DUSE	MUTE	KVAS	SWAG
TUNE	DURO	DUSK	MUTH	OVAL	SWAM
TUNS	DURR	DUST	MUTS	******	SWAN
ZUNI	EURO	FUSE	MUTT	**-VE-**	SWAP
******	EURY	FUSS	NUTS	******	SWAT
-UO-	FURL	GUSH	OUTS	AVEC	SWAY
******	FURN	GUST	PUTS	AVER	TWAS
BUOY	FURS	HUSH	PUTT	AVES	******
DUOS	FURY	HUSK	RUTA	EVEN	**-WC-**
					******
					YWCA

******	******	DYAD	TYEE	RYND	LYTE
-WE-	-WU-	DYAK	WYES	SYNE	MYTH
******	******	DYAN	******	TYNE	******
AWED	SWUM	EYAS	-YG-	WYNN	-YV-
AWES	******	HYAL	******	******	******
EWER	-WY-	IYAR	HYGR	-YO-	GYVE
EWES	******	KYAT	ZYGO	******	******
GWEN	GWYN	PYAT	******	EYOT	-YX-
OWED	******	RYAN	-YI-	GYOR	******
OWEN	-XA-	******	******	PYOT	MYXA
OWES	******	-YB-	AYIN	RYOT	MYXO
ZWEI	EXAM	******	PYIC	******	******
******	******	GYBE	PYIN	-YP-	-YZ-
-WH-	-XC-	******	******	******	******
******	******	-YC-	-YK-	GYPS	LYZE
YWHA	EXCH	******	******	HYPO	******
******	EXCL	CYCL	DYKE	TYPE	-ZA-
-WI-	******	MYCO	FYKE	TYPO	******
******	-XE-	SYCE	TYKE	******	AZAN
GWIN	******	WYCH	******	-YR-	CZAR
SWIG	AXED	******	-YL-	******	IZAR
SWIM	AXES	-YD-	******	BYRD	MZAB
TWIG	EXEC	******	HYLA	BYRE	TZAR
TWIN	EXES	HYDE	HYLO	EYRA	UZAN
TWIT	OXEN	HYDR	KYLE	EYRE	******
******	******	******	LYLE	EYRY	-ZB-
-WL-	-XI-	-YE-	PYLE	GYRE	******
******	******	******	XYLO	GYRI	EZBA
AWLS	AXIL	AYER	******	GYRO	******
OWLS	AXIS	AYES	-YM-	LYRA	-ZE-
******	EXIT	BYEE	******	LYRE	******
-WN-	IXIA	BYES	AYME	MYRA	EZEK
******	******	DYED	CYMA	MYRI	******
AWNS	-XL-	DYER	CYME	PYRE	-ZO-
AWNY	******	DYES	CYMO	PYRO	******
OWNS	AXLE	EYED	GYMN	TYRE	AZON
******	******	EYES	GYMS	TYRO	AZOV
-WO-	-XO-	HYET	HYMN	******	******
******	******	LYES	LYME	-YS-	-ZR-
AWOL	AXON	MYEL	******	******	******
LWOW	EXOD	NYET	-YN-	CYST	EZRA
SWOP	EXON	OYER	******	LYSE	******
SWOT	OXON	OYES	DYNA	LYSI	-ZZ-
TWOS	******	OYEZ	DYNE	XYST	******
******	-YA-	PYEL	GYNO	******	IZZY
-WR-	******	PYES	LYNN	-YT-	******
******	AYAH	PYET	LYNX	******	-A-A
AWRY	CYAN	RYES	MYNA	CYTE	******
				CYTO	BABA
					BAGA

BAIA	MAHA	******	NARD	FACE	MADE
BAJA	MAIA	-A-B	PAED	FADE	MAGE
BAYA	MAKA	******	PAID	FAKE	MAKE
CANA	MAMA	BARB	PARD	FAME	MALE
CAPA	MANA	CAMB	RAAD	FANE	MANE
CARA	MARA	CARB	RAID	FARE	MARE
CATA	MAYA	DARB	RAND	FATE	MATE
CAVA	NADA	DAUB	SAID	FAYE	MAZE
DADA	NAGA	GAMB	SAND	FAZE	NAME
DANA	NAHA	GARB	SARD	GABE	NAPE
DAPA	NAJA	IADB	SAUD	GAGE	NATE
DATA	NAMA	IAMB	WALD	GALE	NAVE
DAZA	NANA	JAMB	WAND	GAME	NAZE
FALA	NAPA	JAOB	WARD	GAPE	PACE
FATA	NASA	LAMB	YARD	GARE	PAGE
GAEA	NAWA	RAAB	******	GATE	PALE
GAGA	PABA	******	-A-E	GAVE	PANE
GAIA	PACA	-A-C	******	GAZE	PARE
GALA	PAHA	******	AARE	HABE	PATE
GAMA	PALA	BANC	BABE	HADE	PAVE
GARA	PAPA	CANC	BADE	HAKE	PAYE
GATA	PARA	LAIC	BAKE	HALE	RACE
GAYA	RABA	MARC	BALE	HAME	RAGE
GAZA	RADA	MASC	BANE	HARE	RAKE
HAHA	RAGA	NARC	BARE	HATE	RALE
HAKA	RAJA	SAIC	BASE	HAVE	RAME
HAMA	RAMA	TALC	BATE	HAZE	RAPE
HAYA	RANA	WAAC	CADE	JADE	RARE
IANA	RASA	******	CAFE	JAKE	RASE
JACA	RATA	-A-D	CAGE	JANE	RATE
JAGA	SAGA	******	CAKE	JAPE	RAVE
JAMA	SAMA	BALD	CAME	JAVE	RAZE
JARA	SANA	BAND	CANE	KADE	SABE
JAVA	SARA	BARD	CAPE	KALE	SADE
KADA	TANA	BAWD	CARE	KAME	SAFE
KAHA	TAPA	CARD	CASE	KANE	SAGE
KAKA	TARA	GARD	CATE	KATE	SAKE
KALA	TATA	GAUD	CAVE	KAYE	SALE
KAMA	VACA	HAND	DACE	LACE	SAME
KANA	VARA	HARD	DADE	LADE	SANE
KAPA	VASA	KAID	DALE	LAFE	SAPE
KARA	YABA	LADD	DAME	LAKE	SATE
KAVA	YAKA	LAID	DANE	LAME	SAVE
KAWA	YAMA	LAND	DARE	LANE	SAXE
LAMA	YANA	LARD	DATE	LATE	TACE
LANA	YAPA	LAUD	DAVE	LAVE	TAKE
LARA	YAYA	MAID	DAZE	LAZE	TALE
LAVA	ZARA	MAUD	EASE	MACE	TAME

TAPE	VANG	DALI	CASK	CARL	WAUL
TARE	WANG	HAGI	CAUK	CAUL	WAWL
TATE	YANG	JAMI	DANK	DAIL	YAWL
VALE	******	KADI	DARK	EARL	******
VANE	-A-H	KAKI	DAWK	FAIL	-A-M
VASE	******	KALI	GAWK	FALL	******
WABE	BACH	KAMI	HACK	FARL	BALM
WADE	BASH	KARI	HAIK	GAEL	BARM
WAGE	BATH	KAZI	HANK	GAIL	CALM
WAKE	CASH	LARI	HARK	GALL	DAWM
WALE	CATH	LATI	HAWK	GAOL	FAAM
WANE	DASH	MAGI	JACK	GAUL	FARM
WARE	EACH	MALI	LACK	HAIL	GARM
WATE	FASH	MANI	LANK	HALL	HALM
WAVE	GASH	MAUI	LARK	HAPL	HARM
YALE	GATH	MAXI	MACK	HARL	KASM
YARE	HASH	NAZI	MARK	HAUL	MAAM
******	HATH	PALI	MASK	JAIL	MAIM
-A-F	JATH	PARI	PACK	JARL	MALM
******	KAPH	RAGI	PANK	KAIL	PALM
BAFF	LAKH	RAKI	PARK	KARL	WARM
CALF	LASH	RAMI	RACK	LALL	******
DAFF	LATH	RANI	RAIK	MAAL	-A-N
GAFF	MACH	RATI	RANK	MAIL	******
HAAF	MASH	SADI	SACK	MALL	BANN
HALF	MATH	SAKI	SALK	MARL	BARN
KAIF	NASH	SARI	SANK	MAUL	CAEN
NAIF	OATH	TAXI	SARK	NAEL	CAIN
RAFF	PASH	VAGI	SASK	NAIL	DAMN
WAAF	PATH	VALI	SAUK	NATL	DARN
WAIF	RASH	VARI	TACK	PAAL	DAWN
WARF	RATH	WADI	TALK	PAIL	EARN
ZARF	SAAH	WARI	TANK	PALL	FAIN
******	SADH	ZATI	TASK	PAUL	FAMN
-A-G	SAHH	******	WACK	PAWL	FAUN
******	SASH	-A-J	WALK	RAIL	FAWN
BANG	WASH	******	WAUK	RALL	GAIN
DANG	ZACH	HADJ	YANK	SAIL	HAHN
FANG	******	MARJ	ZACK	SAUL	JAEN
GANG	-A-I	******	******	TAAL	JAIN
HANG	******	-A-K	-A-L	TAEL	JANN
JAGG	BABI	******	******	TAIL	KAIN
LANG	BALI	BACK	BAAL	TALL	KAON
PANG	BANI	BALK	BAEL	VAAL	KARN
RANG	BARI	BANK	BAIL	VAIL	LAIN
SANG	CADI	BARK	BALL	WAAL	LAON
TANG	CALI	BASK	BAWL	WAIL	LAUN
UANG	CAZI	CALK	CALL	WALL	LAWN

MAIN	SAGO	PAIR	GADS	MATS	TANS
MANN	SAPO	PARR	GAGS	MAWS	TAOS
MAUN	TARO	SAAR	GALS	MAYS	TAPS
NAIN	VASO	SAUR	GAMS	NABS	TARS
PAIN	WACO	TAUR	GAPS	NAGS	TASS
PAWN	YAKO	VAIR	GARS	NAIS	TATS
RAIN	******	******	GATS	NANS	TAUS
SAWN	**-A-P**	**-A-S**	GAYS	NAOS	TAVS
TAIN	******	******	HAGS	NAPS	TAWS
TARN	CAMP	AALS	HALS	NATS	VALS
VAIN	CAPP	BAAS	HAMS	NAYS	VANS
WAIN	CARP	BABS	HANS	OAFS	VATS
WARN	DAMP	BAGS	HATS	OAKS	VAVS
YARN	FACP	BANS	HAWS	OARS	WACS
YAWN	GAMP	BARS	HAYS	OATS	WADS
******	GASP	BASS	IANS	PADS	WAFS
-A-O	HARP	BATS	JABS	PAIS	WAGS
******	HASP	BAYS	JAGS	PALS	WANS
BAGO	LAMP	CABS	JAMS	PAMS	WAPS
BARO	LAPP	CADS	JANS	PANS	WARS
CACO	LARP	CAMS	JARS	PAPS	WAYS
CARO	PALP	CANS	JASS	PARS	YAKS
CATO	RAMP	CAPS	JAWS	PASS	YAMS
DADO	RASP	CARS	JAYS	PATS	YAPS
DAGO	SALP	CASS	KAAS	PAWS	YAWS
FADO	SAMP	CATS	KABS	PAYS	******
FANO	TAMP	CAWS	KANS	QAIS	**-A-T**
FARO	TARP	CAYS	KAYS	RADS	******
GAMO	VAMP	DABS	LABS	RAES	BAHT
HALO	WARP	DADS	LADS	RAGS	BAIT
IAGO	WASP	DAGS	LAGS	RAMS	BALT
JAKO	YAMP	DAIS	LAMS	RAPS	BANT
JATO	YAUP	DAKS	LAOS	RATS	BAPT
KANO	YAWP	DAMS	LAPS	RAYS	BART
KAYO	ZARP	DANS	LARS	SABS	BAST
MAJO	******	DAPS	LASS	SACS	BATT
MAKO	**-A-R**	DAWS	LAWS	SAGS	CANT
MALO	******	DAYS	LAYS	SAIS	CAPT
MANO	BAAR	EARS	MAAS	SAMS	CART
MAYO	BAER	EATS	MABS	SANS	CAST
NABO	BAGR	FACS	MACS	SAPS	DAFT
NANO	CARR	FADS	MADS	SASS	DART
NASO	FAIR	FAGS	MAES	SAWS	EAST
NATO	GAUR	FANS	MANS	SAYS	FACT
PACO	HAIR	FASS	MAPS	TABS	FAST
PAVO	LAHR	FATS	MARS	TADS	GAIT
RALO	LAIR	FAYS	MASS	TAGS	GATT
RATO	NATR	GABS	MASS	TAMS	HAFT

HALT	RAHU	******	******	******	******
HART	TABU	**-A-Z**	**-B-R**	**-C-C**	**-C-N**
HAST	VAYU	******	******	******	******
KANT	YALU	BATZ	ABBR	ACDC	ECON
LACT	ZASU	HARZ	TBAR	******	ICON
LAIT	******	JAZZ	UBER	**-C-D**	SCAN
LAST	**-A-X**	RAZZ	ZBAR	******	******
MALT	******	******	******	ACAD	**-C-O**
MART	CALX	**-B-A**	**-B-S**	ACED	******
MAST	EAUX	******	******	ACID	ACRO
MATT	MANX	ABBA	ABAS	ICED	ECHO
NAST	MARX	OBIA	ABCS	SCAD	ECTO
NATT	******	******	ABES	SCUD	OCTO
NAUT	**-A-Y**	**-B-B**	BBLS	******	******
OAST	******	******	EBBS	**-C-E**	**-C-P**
PACT	BABY	ABIB	IBIS	******	******
PANT	CAGY	******	OBIS	ACHE	RCMP
PART	CARY	**-B-D**	******	ACME	SCOP
PAST	CAVY	******	**-B-T**	ACNE	SCUP
RAFT	DAVY	ABED	******	ACRE	******
RANT	EASY	IBID	ABET	******	**-C-R**
RAPT	GABY	******	ABUT	**-C-H**	******
SALT	GAMY	**-B-E**	OBIT	******	ACER
TACT	GAPY	******	******	ACTH	ACOR
TAFT	GARY	ABBE	**-B-U**	******	ICER
TAIT	HAZY	ABIE	******	**-C-I**	NCAR
TART	KARY	ABLE	ABOU	******	SCAR
TAUT	KATY	IBLE	******	TCHI	******
VAST	LACY	OBOE	**-B-X**	******	**-C-S**
WAFT	LADY	******	******	**-C-J**	******
WAIT	LAKY	**-B-I**	IBEX	******	ACES
WALT	LAZY	******	******	UCMJ	ACTS
WANT	MANY	ABRI	**-B-Y**	******	ECUS
WART	MARY	******	******	**-C-L**	ICES
WAST	MAZY	**-B-L**	ABBY	******	******
WATT	NARY	******	ABLY	ECCL	**-C-T**
ZANT	NAVY	ABEL	OBEY	ECOL	******
******	PALY	OBOL	******	ICAL	ACCT
-A-U	RACY	******	**-C-A**	ICEL	ACET
******	SAGY	**-B-N**	******	KCAL	ECHT
BABU	TAXY	******	ACEA	OCUL	SCAT
BAKU	VARY	EBAN	ACTA	******	SCOT
DANU	WADY	EBEN	ECUA	**-C-M**	SCUT
HABU	WANY	EBON	NCAA	******	******
HAKU	WARY	******	OCHA	ICBM	**-C-U**
KAGU	WAVY	**-B-O**	OCRA	SCUM	******
NALU	WAXY	******	OCTA		ACLU
OAHU	ZANY	EBRO	******	**-C-B**	ACOU
				******	ECRU
				SCAB	

******
-C-W
******
SCOW
******
-C-Y
******
SCRY
******
-D-A
******
EDDA
EDNA
IDEA
ODEA
******
-D-C
******
EDUC
FDIC
ODIC
******
-D-D
******
UDAD
******
-D-E
******
ADZE
EDGE
EDIE
IDAE
IDLE
******
-D-H
******
ADAH
******
-D-K
******
ADAK
HDBK
NDAK
SDAK
******
-D-L
******
IDOL
IDYL

ODAL
ODYL
******
-D-M
******
ADAM
EDAM
EDOM
IDEM
ODUM
******
-D-N
******
ADEN
EDEN
ODIN
UDEN
******
-D-O
******
IDEO
IDIO
******
-D-R
******
ADAR
EDER
ODER
ODOR
******
-D-S
******
ADAS
ADDS
EDHS
IDAS
IDES
ODDS
ODES
UDOS
******
-D-T
******
ADIT
EDIT
******
-D-U
******
IDFU

******
-D-V
******
XDIV
******
-D-Y
******
ADAY
ADDY
DDAY
EDDY
EDGY
IDLY
******
-E-A
******
BEDA
BEKA
BELA
BEMA
BERA
BESA
BETA
CEBA
CECA
CEPA
DECA
DEJA
DEKA
DEPA
DEVA
GERA
HEMA
HERA
HEXA
JENA
KELA
LEDA
LENA
LEVA
MEGA
MESA
META
NEMA
PERA
REBA
RENA
SERA

SETA
TELA
TEMA
TERA
UEBA
VEDA
VEGA
VELA
VENA
VERA
WEKA
WETA
XEMA
ZETA
******
-E-B
******
HERB
KERB
SERB
VERB
******
-E-C
******
DESC
LEUC
******
-E-D
******
BEAD
BEND
DEAD
DECD
DEED
FEED
FEND
FEOD
FEUD
GEED
GELD
GERD
HEAD
HEED
HELD
HERD
JEED
LEAD
LEND

LEUD
LEWD
MEAD
MELD
MEND
NEED
NEJD
PEND
READ
REED
REND
SEED
SEND
TEED
TEND
VELD
VEND
WEED
WELD
WEND
YELD
ZEND
******
-E-E
******
BEDE
BENE
CEDE
CELE
CENE
CERE
DEKE
DELE
DEME
DENE
FEME
FETE
GENE
HEBE
HEHE
HEME
HERE
JEFE
JETE
LEDE
LENE
MEDE
MELE

MENE
MERE
METE
NENE
NEVE
PEDE
PELE
PERE
PETE
REDE
RENE
RETE
SEME
SERE
TELE
TETE
UELE
WERE
ZEKE
******
-E-F
******
BEEF
DEAF
DELF
GENF
JEFF
KEEF
KERF
LEAF
LEIF
OEUF
PELF
REEF
SELF
SERF
******
-E-G
******
BELG
BENG
BERG
GENG
PEAG
TENG
YEGG
******
-E-H
******
BETH
HETH

JETH	BEEK	LEAL	BEEN	MESO	******
LEAH	DECK	MEAL	BERN	NEBO	**-E-R**
MEAH	DESK	MERL	DEAN	NEMO	******
MESH	GECK	MEWL	FERN	NERO	BEAR
METH	GEEK	NEAL	HEWN	OENO	BEER
NEPH	HECK	NEIL	JEAN	PECO	DEAR
RESH	JERK	NELL	KEEN	PEDO	DEER
SEAH	KECK	PEAL	KERN	PEPO	FEAR
SETH	KEEK	PEEL	LEAN	PESO	FEBR
TETH	LEAK	REAL	LEON	REDO	GEAR
YEAH	LEEK	REEL	MEAN	REMO	HEAR
ZEPH	LEUK	SEAL	NEON	RENO	HEBR
******	MEEK	SEEL	PEAN	SEBO	HEIR
-E-I	NECK	SELL	PEEN	SEGO	HERR
******	PEAK	TEAL	PENN	SERO	JEER
AERI	PECK	TEIL	PEON	TELO	KEIR
BENI	PEEK	TELL	PERN	TENO	LEAR
DECI	PERK	VEAL	REIN	VETO	LEER
DEFI	RECK	VEIL	SEAN	XENO	LEHR
DELI	REEK	WEAL	SEEN	XERO	MEIR
DEMI	SEEK	WEEL	SEWN	ZENO	METR
DESI	TEAK	WELL	TEEN	ZERO	NEAR
DEVI	WEAK	YELL	TENN	******	NECR
GERI	WEEK	ZEAL	TERN	**-E-P**	NEER
HELI	YELK	******	VEIN	******	NEUR
HEMI	******	**-E-M**	VERN	BEEP	PEAR
KEPI	**-E-L**	******	WEAN	DEEP	PEER
LETI	******	BEAM	YEAN	HEAP	PETR
LEVI	BELL	BERM	ZEIN	HELP	REAR
MEDI	CEIL	DEEM	******	HEMP	SEAR
MENI	CELL	DERM	**-E-O**	JEEP	SEER
NEVI	DEAL	GEOM	******	KEEP	TEAR
PEDI	DEIL	GERM	AERO	KELP	TETR
PERI	DELL	HELM	CENO	KEMP	VEER
REMI	DESL	HERM	CERO	LEAP	WEAR
RENI	FEEL	JERM	DEGO	NEAP	WEIR
SEBI	FELL	NEUM	DEMO	PEEP	YEAR
SEMI	GENL	PERM	HEMO	REAP	******
SETI	GEOL	REAM	HERO	REPP	**-E-S**
SEXI	HEAL	SEAM	KENO	SEEP	******
VENI	HEEL	SEEM	KETO	TEMP	BEAS
WEKI	HELL	SEJM	LENO	WEEP	BEDS
YETI	HEML	TEAM	LETO	YELP	BEES
******	HERL	TEEM	LEVO	******	BEGS
-E-K	JEEL	TERM	MEIO	**-E-Q**	BELS
******	JELL	******	MEMO	******	BENS
BEAK	JERL	**-E-N**	MENO	SEQQ	BESS
BECK	KEEL	******	MERO		BETS
		AEON			
		BEAN			

BEVS	LETS	YEWS	NEAT	******	******
BEYS	LEWS	ZEDS	NEST	-E-W	-F-R
CEES	MEGS	ZEES	NEWT	******	AFAR
CESS	MELS	ZEUS	NEXT	MEOW	******
DEBS	MEMS	******	PEAT	******	-F-S
DEES	MESS	-E-T	PELT	-E-X	******
DENS	MEWS	******	PENT	******	EFFS
DESS	NEBS	BEAT	PERT	JEUX	EFTS
DEUS	NEDS	BEET	PEST	******	******
DEVS	NESS	BELT	RECT	-E-Y	-F-Y
DEWS	NETS	BENT	REFT	******	******
DEYS	NEWS	BERT	RENT	AERY	IFFY
EELS	PEAS	BEST	REST	BEVY	******
EENS	PEES	CELT	SEAT	DEFY	-G-A
FEES	PEGS	CENT	SECT	DEMY	******
FELS	PENS	CERT	SENT	DENY	AGHA
FENS	PEPS	CEST	SEPT	DEWY	AGRA
FESS	PETS	DEBT	SEXT	EELY	AGUA
FEUS	PEWS	DEFT	TEAT	EERY	******
GEES	REBS	DENT	TENT	GENY	-G-D
GELS	REDS	DEPT	TEST	LEVY	******
GEMS	REIS	DEUT	TEXT	RELY	AGED
GENS	REMS	FEAT	VENT	SECY	EGAD
GETS	REPS	FEET	VERT	SEXY	******
HEMS	RETS	FELT	VEST	VERY	-G-E
HENS	REVS	FEST	WEFT	******	******
HERS	SEAS	GELT	WELT	-E-Z	AGEE
HEWS	SEES	GENT	WENT	******	AGUE
JEES	SENS	GEST	WEPT	GEEZ	OGEE
JEMS	SERS	HEAT	WERT	METZ	OGLE
JESS	SESS	HECT	WEST	******	OGRE
JETS	SETS	HEFT	ZEST	-F-H	******
JEWS	SEWS	HEPT	******	******	-G-G
KEAS	TEAS	HEST	-E-U	AFGH	******
KEFS	TEDS	JEST	******	-F-I	AGOG
KEGS	TEES	KELT	BEAU	******	******
KENS	TEGS	KENT	CEBU	IFNI	-G-I
KEOS	TENS	KEPT	GENU	******	******
KEYS	TESS	LEET	JEBU	-F-K	AGNI
LEAS	VEES	LEFT	JEHU	******	AGRI
LEES	VERS	LENT	JESU	EFIK	IGNI
LEGS	VETS	LEPT	KETU	******	******
LEIS	WEBS	LEST	MENU	-F-L	-G-N
LEKS	WEDS	LETT	MERU	******	******
LEMS	WENS	MEAT	PELU	IFIL	AGON
LENS	WETS	MEET	PERU	******	EGAN
LEOS	YEAS	MELT	ZEBU	-F-O	NGAN
LESS	YENS	MENT	******	******	
			-E-V		
			******		
			MERV		

******	******	******	******	CHIT	******
-G-O	**-H-D**	**-H-L**	**-H-P**	GHAT	**-H-Z**
******	******	******	******	KHAT	******
AGAO	CHAD	CHIL	CHAP	KHET	CHEZ
AGIO	CHGD	CHOL	CHIP	PHOT	RHIZ
AGRO	CHID	DHAL	CHOP	PHUT	WHIZ
******	CHUD	PHIL	SHIP	PHYT	******
-G-R	PHUD	PHYL	SHOP	SHOT	**-I-A**
******	SHAD	RHYL	WHAP	SHUT	******
AGAR	SHED	SHUL	WHIP	THAT	AIDA
EGER	SHOD	******	WHOP	WHAT	DINA
******	THAD	**-H-M**	******	WHET	DITA
-G-S	THUD	******	**-H-Q**	WHIT	DIVA
******	******	AHEM	******	******	FICA
AGAS	**-H-E**	CHEM	SHOQ	**-H-U**	FILA
AGES	******	CHUM	******	******	GIGA
EGGS	CHEE	RHUM	**-H-R**	CHOU	GILA
EGOS	GHEE	SHAM	******	THOU	GINA
******	SHOE	SHEM	BHAR	THRU	GIZA
-G-U	THEE	SHIM	CHAR	******	KIVA
******	******	THEM	CHIR	**-H-V**	LILA
IGLU	**-H-F**	WHAM	CHUR	******	LIMA
OGPU	******	WHIM	DHAR	SHIV	LINA
******	CHEF	WHOM	THAR	******	LIRA
-G-Y	******	******	THOR	**-H-W**	LISA
******	**-H-G**	**-H-N**	WHIR	******	LIZA
UGLY	******	******	******	CHAW	MICA
******	CHUG	CHIN	**-H-S**	CHEW	MINA
-H-A	PHAG	DHAN	******	CHOW	MIRA
******	SHAG	KHAN	CHES	DHOW	NINA
CHIA	THUG	PHEN	CHGS	JHOW	NIPA
OHIA	WHIG	PHON	CHIS	PHEW	NITA
RHEA	******	RHIN	MHOS	SHAW	PICA
SHEA	**-H-H**	SHAN	OHMS	SHEW	PIKA
THEA	******	SHIN	PHDS	SHOW	PIMA
WHOA	AHAH	SHUN	PHIS	THAW	PINA
******	CHIH	THAN	RHOS	THEW	PIPA
-H-B	SHAH	THEN	RHUS	WHEW	PISA
******	YHWH	THIN	RHYS	******	PITA
AHAB	******	WHEN	SHES	**-H-Y**	RIGA
CHUB	**-H-I**	WHIN	THIS	******	RIPA
RHOB	******	******	THUS	AHOY	RITA
THEB	DHAI	**-H-O**	WHYS	CHAY	RIVA
******	******	******	******	SHAY	SIMA
-H-C	**-H-K**	OHIO	**-H-T**	THEY	SIVA
******	******	RHEO	******	WHEY	TINA
CHIC	DHAK	SHOO	CHAT		VINA
		THEO	CHET		VIRA
		THIO			

VISA	******	LINE	VINE	KISH	DISK
VITA	-I-E	LIRE	VIRE	KITH	FINK
VIVA	******	LITE	VISE	LICH	GINK
ZIRA	AIDE	LIVE	VITE	LITH	HICK
******	AILE	MICE	VIVE	MICH	JINK
-I-B	AIRE	MIKE	WIDE	NIGH	KIAK
******	BICE	MILE	WIFE	PISH	KICK
BIBB	BIDE	MIME	WILE	PITH	KINK
LIMB	BIHE	MINE	WINE	RICH	KIRK
NIMB	BIKE	MIRE	WIPE	SIGH	LICK
******	BILE	MISE	WIRE	SIKH	LINK
-I-C	BINE	MITE	WISE	WICH	MICK
******	BISE	NICE	WIVE	WISH	MILK
CIRC	BITE	NIDE	YIPE	WITH	MINK
DISC	CIDE	NIKE	******	XIPH	NICK
FISC	CINE	NILE	-I-F	******	PICK
MISC	CITE	NINE	******	-I-I	PINK
PISC	DICE	NIUE	BIFF	******	RICK
VISC	DIKE	OISE	FIEF	DILI	RINK
WISC	DIME	PICE	JIFF	DIVI	RISK
ZINC	DINE	PIKE	LIEF	FIJI	SICK
******	DIRE	PILE	MIFF	HIFI	SILK
-I-D	DIVE	PINE	PIAF	JIBI	SINK
******	EIRE	PIPE	RIFF	KIRI	TICK
BIND	FICE	RICE	TIFF	KIWI	VICK
BIRD	FIFE	RIDE	******	MIDI	WICK
DIED	FILE	RIFE	-I-G	MIMI	WINK
FIND	FINE	RILE	******	MINI	******
GIED	FIRE	RIME	BING	NIDI	-I-L
GILD	FIVE	RIPE	DIAG	NISI	******
GIRD	GIBE	RISE	DING	PIKI	BIBL
HIED	GIDE	RITE	KING	PILI	BIEL
HIND	GIVE	RIVE	LING	SIRI	BILL
JIND	HIDE	SICE	MING	SITI	BIOL
KIDD	HIKE	SIDE	PING	TIKI	BIRL
KIND	HIPE	SINE	RING	TIPI	CIEL
LIED	HIRE	SIRE	SING	TITI	DIAL
LIND	HIVE	SITE	TING	VICI	DILL
MILD	JIBE	SIZE	WING	VIDI	DIPL
MIND	JIVE	TIDE	ZING	VILI	FILL
PIED	KIBE	TIKE	******	VINI	GILL
RIND	KINE	TILE	-I-H	VITI	GIRL
SIND	KIPE	TIME	******	******	HILL
TIED	KITE	TINE	BINH	-I-K	JILL
VIED	LICE	TIRE	DICH	******	KIEL
WILD	LIFE	VICE	DISH	BILK	KILL
WIND	LIKE	VIDE	FISH	DICK	MILL
	LIME	VILE	HIGH	DIRK	NIEL

PILL	DIDO	FIBR	JIGS	VISS	WILT
RIAL	DILO	HIER	JIMS	WIGS	WIST
RILL	DINO	KIER	KIDS	WINS	XINT
SIAL	FICO	LIAR	KIPS	WITS	******
SILL	FILO	NIGR	KISS	YIPS	**-I-U**
TILL	GIRO	NITR	KITS	ZIPS	******
VIAL	HILO	PICR	LIDS	******	AINU
VILL	HINO	PIER	LIES	**-I-T**	DIEU
VIOL	HIRO	TIER	LILS	******	GIFU
WILL	KIHO	VITR	LIPS	AINT	KIVU
******	KILO	******	LISS	BITT	LIEU
-I-M	KINO	**-I-S**	MIBS	CIST	LIMU
******	LIAO	******	MIGS	DIET	SITU
DIAM	LIDO	AIDS	MILS	DINT	******
FILM	LINO	AILS	MIRS	DIRT	**-I-V**
FIRM	LIPO	AIMS	MISS	DIST	******
SIAM	MILO	AINS	NIBS	FIAT	KIEV
******	MIRO	AIRS	NIPS	FIST	MIRV
-I-N	MISO	BIAS	NITS	GIFT	******
******	NINO	BIBS	OILS	GILT	**-I-W**
BION	OINO	BIDS	PIES	GIRT	******
CION	PICO	BINS	PIGS	GIST	VIEW
DIAN	PISO	BITS	PINS	HILT	******
DION	PITO	DIAS	PIPS	HINT	**-I-X**
FINN	RIVO	DIBS	PITS	HIST	******
FIRN	SILO	DIES	PIUS	JILT	JINX
JINN	SINO	DIGS	RIBS	KILT	MINX
KILN	SITO	DIMS	RIDS	KIST	******
LIEN	TIRO	DINS	RIGS	KITT	**-I-Y**
LIGN	TITO	DIOS	RIIS	LIFT	******
LIMN	VINO	DIPS	RIMS	LILT	AIRY
LINN	VISO	FIBS	RIPS	LINT	CITY
LION	VIVO	FIDS	SIBS	LIST	DIDY
MIEN	WINO	FIGS	SICS	MILT	LILY
MINN	******	FILS	SIDS	MINT	LIMY
PION	**-I-P**	FINS	SIMS	MIST	LINY
PIRN	******	FIRS	SINS	MITT	MIRY
RIEN	GIMP	FITS	SIPS	MIXT	OILY
RIJN	HIPP	GIBS	SIRS	PICT	PIAY
SIGN	LIMP	GIGS	SITS	PINT	PINY
SION	LISP	GILS	TICS	PIOT	PIPY
TION	PIMP	GINS	TIES	PITT	PITY
XION	SIMP	GIPS	TIMS	RIFT	PIXY
ZION	WISP	HIES	TINS	RIOT	RIMY
******	******	HIPS	TIPS	SIFT	SIZY
-I-O	**-I-R**	HISS	TITS	SILT	TIDY
******	******	HITS	VIES	TILT	TINY
AINO	BIER	JIBS	VIPS	TINT	TIVY
BIRO	BIRR				

VIMY	******	ELSA	******	******	PLAN
VINY	-K-N	ELVA	-L-E	-L-I	ULAN
WILY	******	FLEA	******	******	******
WINY	AKIN	ILEA	ALAE	ALAI	-L-O
WIRY	IKON	ILIA	ALDE	ALLI	******
******	SKIN	ILKA	ALEE	ALTI	ALDO
-I-Z	******	OLGA	ALLE	******	ALLO
******	-K-P	OLLA	ALOE	-L-J	ALSO
DIAZ	******	PLEA	BLUE	******	ALTO
FITZ	SKEP	ULLA	CLEE	CLUJ	CLEO
FIZZ	SKIP	ULNA	CLUE	******	CLIO
LINZ	******	******	ELBE	-L-K	ELEO
PIZZ	******	-L-B	ELKE	******	ELMO
ZIZZ	-K-S	******	ELSE	FLAK	FLUO
******	******	BLAB	FLEE	******	ILEO
-J-R	EKES	BLEB	FLOE	-L-L	OLEO
******	IKES	BLOB	FLUE	******	OLIO
AJAR	OKAS	BLUB	GLEE	ELUL	SLOO
******	SKIS	CLUB	GLUE	******	******
-J-X	******	FLUB	ILSE	-L-M	-L-P
******	-K-T	GLIB	KLEE	******	******
AJAX	******	GLOB	MLLE	ALUM	ALOP
******	OKET	NLRB	OLPE	BLEM	BLIP
-K-A	SKAT	PLEB	SLEE	CLAM	CLAP
******	SKIT	SLAB	SLOE	CLEM	CLIP
OKLA	******	SLOB	SLUE	ELAM	CLOP
OKRA	-K-W	SLUB	******	ELEM	FLAP
SKUA	******	******	-L-F	FLAM	FLIP
******	SKAW	-L-C	******	FLEM	FLOP
-K-D	SKEW	******	ALEF	GLIM	PLOP
******	******	ALEC	ALIF	GLUM	SLAP
EKED	-K-Y	BLOC	CLEF	KLAM	SLIP
NKVD	******	ELEC	OLAF	PLUM	SLOP
OKED	OKAY	FLOC	******	SLAM	******
SKID	WKLY	******	-L-G	SLIM	-L-R
******		-L-D	******	SLUM	******
-K-E	-L-A	******	BLDG	YLEM	ALAR
******	******	BLED	CLEG	******	BLUR
IKWE	ALBA	BLVD	CLOG	-L-N	CLAR
OKIE	ALFA	CLAD	FLAG	******	FLOR
SKEE	ALGA	CLOD	FLOG	ALAN	HLER
SKYE	ALIA	FLED	OLIG	ALEN	OLOR
******	ALMA	GLAD	PLUG	ALIN	SLUR
-K-G	ALTA	GLED	SLAG	CLAN	******
******	ALVA	PLED	SLOG	CLON	-L-S
SKAG	ELBA	PLOD	SLUG	ELAN	******
SKEG	ELIA	SLED	******	FLAN	ALAS
******	ELLA	SLID	-L-H	GLEN	ALBS
-K-M	ELMA		******		
******			ALPH		
SKIM			BLAH		

ALES	FLAW	******	******	******	SNEE
ALFS	FLEW	-M-E	-M-O	-M-W	SNYE
ALMS	FLOW	******	******	******	UNDE
ALPS	GLOW	AMIE	AMBO	SMEW	UNIE
ALYS	PLEW	SMEE	AMMO	******	UNZE
ELIS	PLOW	******	UMBO	-M-Y	******
ELKS	SLAW	-M-G	******	******	-N-G
ELLS	SLEW	******	-M-R	AMOY	******
ELMS	SLOW	SMOG	******	EMMY	KNAG
ILLS	******	SMUG	AMER	IMMY	SNAG
ILUS	-L-X	******	AMIR	******	SNIG
PLUS	******	-M-H	AMOR	-N-A	SNOG
******	ALEX	******	AMUR	******	SNUG
-L-T	ALIX	AMAH	CMDR	ANNA	******
******	FLAX	******	EMIR	ANOA	-N-H
ALIT	FLEX	-M-I	OMAR	ANSA	******
BLAT	FLUX	******	OMBR	ANTA	ANKH
BLET	ILEX	AMBI	OMER	ENNA	ANTH
BLIT	ULEX	AMOI	YMER	FNMA	INCH
BLOT	******	IMMI	YMIR	INCA	******
CLOT	-L-Y	IMPI	******	INGA	-N-I
ELST	******	OMEI	-M-S	INIA	******
FLAT	ALGY	OMNI	******	ONCA	ANTI
FLIT	ALLY	******	AMAS	ONZA	INRI
FLOT	CLAY	-M-K	AMES	UNGA	******
GLOT	CLOY	******	AMIS	******	-N-L
GLUT	ELMY	AMOK	AMOS	-N-B	******
OLST	FLAY	OMSK	AMPS	******	ANAL
PLAT	ILLY	******	AMTS	KNOB	ANIL
PLOT	OLAY	-M-L	AMUS	SNOB	ENCL
SLAT	OLLY	******	AMYS	SNUB	ENOL
SLIT	PLAY	AMYL	BMUS	******	INCL
SLOT	PLOY	EMIL	DMUS	-N-D	******
SLUT	SLAY	******	EMUS	******	-N-M
******	-M-A	-M-M	FMCS	ENID	******
-L-V	******	******	IMPS	******	ANAM
******	AMIA	IMAM	MMES	-N-E	ANIM
ELEV	EMIA	******	UMTS	******	******
OLAV	EMMA	-M-N	XMAS	ANCE	-N-N
SLAV	YMCA	******	******	ANNE	******
******	YMHA	AMEN	-M-T	ANTE	ANON
-L-W	******	AMON	******	ENCE	ONON
******	-M-C	GMAN	AMAT	ENTE	******
ALOW	******	GMEN	EMIT	INEE	-N-O
BLEW	BMOC	IMAN	OMIT	INGE	******
BLOW	******	IMIN	SMIT	INRE	ANNO
CLAW	-M-D	OMAN	SMUT	KNEE	ENDO
CLEW	AMID	OMEN	******	ONCE	ENTO
	IMID		-M-U		
			******		
			EMEU		

ENYO	INIT	BORA	VORA	LOAD	DOTE
INDO	INST	BOTA	XOSA	LOOD	DOVE
INFO	KNIT	COCA	YOGA	LORD	DOZE
INRO	KNOT	CODA	ZOLA	LOUD	FORE
INTO	SNIT	COLA	ZONA	MOLD	GONE
ONDO	SNOT	COMA	******	MOOD	GORE
ONTO	UNIT	COPA	**-O-B**	NORD	HOLE
UNCO	******	CORA	******	POND	HOME
UNDO	**-N-U**	COXA	BOMB	POOD	HONE
UNIO	******	DOLA	BOOB	ROAD	HOPE
UNTO	UNAU	DOMA	COBB	ROOD	HOSE
******	******	DONA	COMB	SOLD	HOTE
-N-P	**-N-W**	DORA	FORB	TOAD	HOVE
******	******	FORA	IOBB	TODD	HOWE
INSP	ANEW	GOMA	JOAB	TOED	IOLE
KNAP	ENOW	GOYA	MOAB	TOLD	JOKE
KNOP	GNAW	HORA	SORB	VOID	JOSE
SNAP	KNEW	IONA	TOMB	WOAD	JOVE
SNIP	KNOW	IOTA	WOMB	WOLD	KOAE
******	SNOW	IOWA	******	WOOD	KOBE
-N-R	******	JOLA	**-O-C**	WORD	LOBE
******	**-N-X**	KOLA	******	YOND	LODE
ENGR	******	LOLA	CONC	YOUD	LOGE
GNAR	KNOX	LOMA	ROTC	******	LOKE
KNAR	ONYX	MONA	ZOIC	**-O-E**	LOME
KNUR	PNYX	MORA	******	******	LONE
ONER	******	MOXA	**-O-D**	AONE	LOPE
******	**-N-Y**	NOMA	******	BODE	LORE
-N-S	******	NONA	BOLD	BOLE	LOSE
******	ANCY	NORA	BOND	BONE	LOTE
ANAS	ANDY	NOVA	BOYD	BORE	LOVE
ANIS	ENCY	OONA	COED	CODE	MODE
ANNS	ENVY	PODA	COLD	COKE	MOKE
ANTS	INKY	ROMA	COND	COLE	MOLE
ANUS	INLY	RONA	CORD	COME	MOPE
ENDS	ONLY	ROSA	FOLD	CONE	MORE
ENNS	UNDY	ROTA	FOND	COPE	MOSE
ENOS	XNTY	SODA	FOOD	CORE	MOTE
GNUS	******	SOFA	FORD	COTE	MOUE
INAS	**-N-Z**	SOJA	GOAD	COUE	MOVE
INKS	******	SOLA	GOLD	COVE	NODE
INNS	INEZ	SOMA	GOND	DOGE	NOME
ONES	UNTZ	SORA	GOOD	DOLE	NONE
ONUS	******	SOYA	HOED	DOME	NOPE
UNAS	**-O-A**	TOGA	HOLD	DONE	NOSE
******	******	TOLA	HOND	DOPE	NOTE
-N-T	BOLA	TORA	HOOD	DORE	OOZE
******	BONA	VOLA	JOAD	DOSE	PODE
ANAT					
GNAT					

POKE	GOOF	POSH	GOWK	JOEL	BOSN
POLE	HOOF	QOPH	HOCK	JOWL	COIN
POME	LOAF	TOPH	HONK	KOEL	CONN
PONE	LOOF	TOSH	HOOK	KOHL	COON
POPE	POUF	YODH	JOCK	LOLL	CORN
PORE	ROLF	YOGH	JOOK	MOIL	DOON
POSE	ROOF	******	KOOK	MOLL	DOWN
ROBE	TOFF	**-O-I**	LOCK	NOEL	FOHN
RODE	WOLF	******	LOOK	NOIL	GOON
ROLE	WOOF	BONI	MOCK	POLL	GOWN
ROME	******	BOVI	MONK	POOL	HOEN
ROPE	**-O-G**	FOCI	NOCK	ROIL	HOON
ROSE	******	GOBI	NOOK	ROLL	HORN
ROTE	BONG	HOPI	POCK	ROTL	JOAN
ROUE	CONG	HOTI	POLK	SOIL	JOHN
ROVE	DOUG	KOPI	POOK	SOUL	JOIN
SOKE	FONG	LOCI	PORK	TOIL	KOLN
SOLE	GONG	LODI	ROCK	TOLL	LOAN
SOME	HOGG	LOKI	ROOK	TOOL	LOIN
SONE	HONG	MODI	SOAK	WOOL	LOON
SORE	JOUG	MOKI	SOCK	YOWL	LORN
TOLE	LONG	ROTI	TOOK	ZOOL	MOAN
TOME	NOGG	SOLI	WORK	******	MOON
TONE	PONG	SORI	YOLK	**-O-M**	MORN
TOPE	SONG	TONI	YORK	******	MOWN
TORE	TONG	TOPI	******	BOOM	NOON
TOTE	ZOUG	TORI	**-O-L**	COMM	NORN
VOCE	******	TOTI	******	CORM	NOUN
VOLE	**-O-H**	YOGI	AOUL	COSM	POON
VORE	******	******	BOIL	DOOM	PORN
VOTE	BOSH	**-O-J**	BOLL	DORM	ROAN
WOKE	BOTH	******	BOWL	FOAM	SOON
WORE	COSH	CONJ	COAL	FORM	SORN
WOTE	DOTH	******	COEL	HOLM	SOWN
WOVE	FOCH	**-O-K**	COIL	LOAM	TOON
YOKE	GOGH	******	COLL	LOOM	TORN
YORE	GOSH	BOCK	COOL	NORM	TOWN
ZONE	GOTH	BONK	COWL	POEM	WORN
******	HOTH	BOOK	DOLL	ROAM	ZOAN
-O-F	JOAH	BOSK	FOAL	ROOM	ZOON
******	JOSH	COCK	FOIL	WORM	******
COEF	KOPH	CONK	FOLL	ZOOM	**-O-O**
COIF	LOCH	COOK	FOOL	******	******
CONF	LOTH	CORK	FOUL	**-O-N**	BOLO
CORF	MOTH	DOCK	FOWL	******	BONO
DOFF	NOAH	FOLK	GOAL	BONN	BOZO
DOLF	NOSH	FORK	GOWL	BOON	COCO
GOLF	POOH	GOOK	HOWL	BORN	COHO

COLO	COUP	******	HOPS	ROMS	COST
COMO	DOPP	**-O-S**	HOYS	ROSS	DOIT
DODO	DORP	******	IONS	ROTS	DOLT
GOBO	GOOP	BOAS	IOUS	ROWS	DONT
GOGO	HOOP	BOBS	JOBS	ROYS	DOST
GOLO	LOOP	BOGS	JOES	SOBS	FONT
GONO	LOUP	BOIS	JOGS	SODS	FOOT
HOBO	POMP	BOOS	JONS	SOLS	FORT
HOLO	POOP	BOPS	JOSS	SONS	GOAT
HOMO	ROMP	BOSS	JOTS	SOPS	GOUT
IODO	ROOP	BOTS	JOYS	SOTS	GOVT
JOBO	ROUP	BOWS	KOPS	SOUS	HOLT
JODO	SOAP	BOYS	KORS	SOWS	HOOT
JOLO	SOUP	COBS	KOSS	SOYS	HORT
KOKO	YOUP	CODS	LOBS	TODS	HOST
KOTO	******	COGS	LOGS	TOES	JOAT
LOBO	**-O-R**	COLS	LOIS	TOGS	JOLT
LOCO	******	CONS	LOOS	TOMS	LOFT
LOGO	BOAR	COOS	LOPS	TONS	LOOT
MOHO	BOER	COPS	LOSS	TOPS	LOST
MOIO	BOHR	COSS	LOTS	TORS	LOTT
MOJO	BOOR	COTS	LOWS	TOSS	LOUT
MOMO	COIR	COWS	MOAS	TOTS	MOAT
MONO	COMR	DOES	MOBS	TOWS	MOLT
MORO	COPR	DOGS	MODS	TOYS	MONT
NOGO	DOER	DOLS	MOES	VOLS	MOOT
NOMO	DOOR	DOMS	MOMS	VOWS	MORT
NOSO	DORR	DONS	MONS	WOES	MOST
NOTO	DOUR	DORS	MOOS	WOOS	MOTT
POCO	FOUR	DOSS	MOPS	WOWS	NOCT
POGO	GOAR	DOTS	MORS	YODS	NOTT
POLO	GOER	EONS	MOSS	YOWS	NOWT
SOHO	HOAR	EOUS	MOTS	ZOES	POET
SOLO	HOER	FOBS	MOWS	ZOOS	PORT
SOSO	HOUR	FOES	NOBS	******	POST
TOCO	JOAR	FOGS	NODS	**-O-T**	POUT
TODO	LOUR	FOPS	NOES	******	ROOT
TOGO	MOHR	FOSS	NOGS	BOAT	ROUT
TONO	MOOR	FOYS	NOUS	BOLT	SOFT
TOPO	POOR	GOAS	NOWS	BOOT	SOOT
TOYO	POUR	GOBS	PODS	BORT	SORT
YOYO	ROAR	GODS	PONS	BOTT	TOFT
******	SOAR	GOES	POPS	BOUT	TOOT
-O-P	SOIR	HOBS	POTS	COAT	TORT
******	SOUR	HODS	POWS	COLT	TOUT
COMP	TOUR	HOES	ROBS	CONT	VOET
COOP	YOUR	HOGS	RODS	COOT	VOLT
CORP	ZOAR	HOMS	ROES	COPT	WONT
					WORT

******	OOZY	******	SPIT	******	PRAE
O-U	POGY	-P-I	SPOT	-R-B	PRUE
******	POKY	******	******	******	TREE
POKU	POLY	OPHI	-P-V	ARAB	TRUE
TOLU	PONY	******	******	CRAB	URDE
******	POSY	-P-L	SPIV	CRIB	URGE
O-W	ROPY	******	******	DRAB	******
******	RORY	OPAL	-P-W	DRIB	-R-F
BOUW	RÓSY	******	******	DRUB	******
******	ROXY	-P-M	SPEW	GRAB	GRAF
O-X	TOBY	******	******	GRUB	PROF
******	TODY	SPAM	-P-X	******	TREF
COAX	TOMY	******	******	-R-C	WRAF
HOAX	TONY	-P-N	APEX	******	XREF
ROUX	TORY	******	******	ERIC	******
******	******	OPEN	-P-Y	URIC	-R-G
O-Y	-O-Z	SPAN	******	******	******
******	******	SPIN	OPSY	-R-D	BRAG
BODY	BOAZ	SPUN	SPAY	******	BRIG
BOGY	LODZ	UPON	SPRY	ARAD	CRAG
BONY	******	******	******	ARID	DRAG
CODY	-P-A	-P-O	-Q-A	BRAD	DRUG
COLY	******	******	******	BRED	FROG
CONY	APIA	APIO	AQUA	CRUD	GREG
COPY	OPIA	******	******	FRED	GRIG
COSY	SPCA	-P-R	-Q-I	GRAD	GROG
COTY	******	******	******	GRID	ORIG
COZY	-P-C	SPAR	AQUI	IRID	PRIG
DOBY	******	SPIR	EQUI	PROD	TRIG
DOGY	APOC	SPOR	******	TRAD	******
DOPY	EPIC	SPQR	-R-A	TROD	-R-H
DORY	SPCC	SPUR	******	******	******
DOTY	SPEC	******	AREA	-R-E	ARCH
DOXY	******	-P-S	ARIA	******	DRAH
DOZY	-P-D	******	BREA	ARNE	ORTH
FOGY	******	APES	ERDA	ARTE	TRAH
FOXY	APED	APIS	ERIA	BRAE	******
GOBY	APOD	APUS	ERMA	BRIE	-R-I
GORY	SPAD	EPOS	FREA	CREE	******
HOLY	SPED	OPTS	IRMA	ERIE	ARNI
HOMY	SPUD	OPUS	IRRA	ERLE	******
JOEY	******	SPAS	ORCA	ERNE	-R-K
JOUY	-P-E	SPES	PROA	ERSE	******
LOGY	******	UPAS	UREA	FRAE	ERIK
LORY	APSE	******	URFA	FREE	IRAK
MOLY	EPEE	-P-T	URIA	FROE	TREK
NOMY	SPUE	******	URNA	ORLE	TRUK
NOSY	******	SPAT	URSA	ORNE	
	-P-H	SPET			
	******				
	OPAH				

```
******    TRIN    ARES    GROT    ORGY    ******
-R-L      TRON    ARKS    PROT    ORLY    -S-F
******    URAN    ARMS    TRET    PRAY    ******
ARAL      WREN    ARNS    TROT    PREY    ASOF
ARIL      ******  ARTS    WRIT    TRAY    USAF
ARYL      -R-O    BRAS    ******  TREY    ******
ERAL      ******  CRES    -R-U    TROY    -S-G
KRAL      AREO    CRUS    ******  URDY    ******
ORAL      ARGO    ERAS    FRAU    UREY    USCG
OREL      ARNO    ERGS    URDU    XRAY    ******
URAL      BRIO    ERIS    ******  ******  -S-H
******    BRNO    ERNS    -R-V    -R-Z    ******
-R-M      BROO    EROS    ******  ******  ASCH
******    CRYO    ERRS    BREV    ARIZ    ESTH
ARAM      ERGO    FRAS    ******  BRAZ    MSTH
ARUM      FRIO    GRIS    -R-W    BROZ    ******
BRIM      GRAO    GROS    ******  GRAZ    -S-I
BROM      ORDO    IRAS    AROW    ******  ******
CRAM      PRAO    IRIS    BRAW    -S-A    ASCI
DRAM      TRIO    IRKS    BREW    ******  ASTI
DRUM      ******  KRIS    BROW    ASEA    OSSI
FROM      -R-P    ORBS    CRAW    ASHA    TSHI
GRAM      ******  ORCS    CREW    ASIA    ******
GRIM      CRAP    ORES    CROW    ISBA    -S-L
GRUM      CROP    ORTS    DRAW    OSSA    ******
IRBM      DRIP    PRES    DREW    PSHA    OSEL
PRAM      DROP    PROS    FROW    USIA    ******
PRIM      FRAP    TRES    GREW    USMA    -S-N
PROM      GRIP    TRIS    GROW    USNA    ******
TRAM      HRIP    URNS    PROW    ******  ASSN
TRIM      PREP    URUS    TROW    -S-C    TSUN
******    PROP    XRTS    ******  ******  ******
-R-N      TRAP    ******  -R-X    BSSC    -S-O
******    TRIP    -R-T    ******  USMC    ******
ARAN      TROP    ******  CRUX    ******  OSLO
BRAN      WRAP    BRAT    ORYX    -S-D    ******
BREN      ******  BRET    TRIX    ******  -S-P
BRON      -R-Q    BRIT    ******  BSED    ******
CRAN      ******  BRUT    -R-Y    USED    RSVP
DRIN      FREQ    CRAT    ******  ******  ******
ERIN      IRAQ    CRIT    ARMY    -S-E    -S-R
FRAN      ******  DRAT    ARTY    ******  ******
GRIN      -R-R    ERST    BRAY    ASHE    ASIR
HRON      ******  FRAT    DRAY    ESCE    ASTR
IRAN      BRER    FRET    FRAY    ESNE    ISAR
IRON      ******  FRIT    FREY    ESSE    ISER
ORAN      -R-S    FROT    GRAY    ESTE    MSGR
PRON      ARAS    GRIT    GREY    ISLE    OSAR
          ARCS                    OSTE
```

'SAR	******	******	******	TUBA	BULE
USAR	**-T-C**	**-T-N**	**-T-U**	TUFA	BUTE
USER	******	******	******	TULA	CUBE
USNR	ATIC	ATEN	ATTU	TUNA	CULE
USSR	OTIC	ATTN	******	YUGA	CURE
YSER	******	CTEN	**-T-W**	YUMA	CUTE
******	**-T-D**	ETHN	******	ZUZA	DUCE
-S-S	******	ETON	STEW	******	DUDE
******	STUD	STAN	STOW	**-U-B**	DUKE
ASAS	******	STEN	******	******	DUNE
ASIS	**-T-E**	STUN	**-T-X**	BULB	DUPE
ASKS	******	******	******	CURB	DUSE
ASPS	ATLE	**-T-O**	STYX	DUMB	FUME
SIS	ETTE	******	******	NUMB	FUSE
SMS	OTOE	ATMO	**-T-Y**	QUAB	FUYE
MSTS	******	ATTO	******	******	FUZE
OSIS	**-T-G**	OTTO	ATTY	**-U-C**	HUGE
PSIS	******	STLO	STAY	******	HUME
USES	STAG	******	******	JUNC	JUBE
USMS	******	**-T-P**	**-U-A**	******	JUDE
******	******	******	******	**-U-D**	JULE
-S-T	**-T-H**	ATOP	AURA	******	JUNE
ASST	******	STEP	BUNA	AULD	JUTE
SNT	ETAH	STOP	CUBA	BUDD	KURE
MSGT	ETCH	******	CUYA	BUND	LUBE
******	ITCH	**-T-R**	DUMA	BURD	LUCE
-S-U	PTAH	******	DUNA	CUED	LUGE
******	UTAH	ATAR	DURA	CURD	LUKE
ESAU	******	ATOR	FULA	DUAD	LUNE
******	**-T-I**	ITER	GUHA	FUND	LUPE
-S-Y	******	PTER	HULA	HUED	LURE
******	ATLI	STAR	HUPA	KURD	LUTE
ASHY	ATRI	STER	JUBA	PUND	LUXE
ESPY	ETUI	STIR	JUCA	PUUD	MULE
ISSY	******	UTER	JURA	QUAD	MUSE
******	**-T-L**	******	KURA	QUID	MUTE
-T-A	******	**-T-S**	LUBA	QUOD	NUDE
******	ETAL	******	LUNA	RUDD	OUSE
ATKA	ITAL	ATES	LUTA	RUED	PUCE
ATTA	ITOL	ETAS	PUKA	SUDD	PUKE
ETNA	STOL	ETHS	PUMA	SUED	PULE
ETTA	VTOL	ITYS	PUNA	SURD	PURE
TEA	******	OTIS	PUPA	******	RUBE
OTEA	**-T-M**	STUS	RUGA	**-U-E**	RUDE
STOA	******	UTES	RUTA	******	RUFE
******	ATOM	**-T-T**	SUPA	AUBE	RULE
-T-B	ITEM	******	SURA	AUDE	RUNE
******	STEM	STAT	SUVA	AUNE	RUSE
STAB	STUM	STET			
STUB					

RUTE	HUGH	HULK	******	******	HUES
SUPE	HUSH	HUNK	-U-N	-U-R	HUGS
SURE	LUSH	HUSK	******	******	HUMS
TUBE	LUTH	JUNK	BUNN	BURR	HUNS
TUDE	MUCH	KUNK	BURN	CUIR	HUSS
TULE	MUSH	LUCK	DURN	CUPR	HUTS
TUNE	MUTH	LURK	FURN	DUAR	JUGS
YULE	OUCH	MUCK	GUAN	DURR	JUTS
******	PUGH	MURK	GUIN	MUIR	LUES
-U-F	PUSH	MUSK	JUAN	PURR	LUGS
******	RUSH	PUCK	MUON	QUAR	LUIS
BUFF	RUTH	PUNK	QUAN	RUER	MUDS
CUFF	SUCH	RUCK	RUIN	RUHR	MUGS
DUFF	TUSH	RUSK	SUNN	SUER	MUMS
GUFF	******	SUCK	TURN	******	MUSS
GULF	-U-I	SULK	YUAN	-U-S	MUTS
HUFF	******	SUNK	******	******	NUBS
LUFF	FUCI	TUCK	-U-O	AUKS	NUNS
MUFF	FUJI	TURK	******	BUBS	NUTS
PUFF	GUMI	TUSK	AUTO	BUDS	OURS
RUFF	LUNI	******	BUBO	BUGS	OUTS
SURF	LURI	-U-L	DURO	BUNS	PUBS
TUFF	MUCI	******	EURO	BURS	PUGS
TURF	NUDI	BUHL	GUAO	BUSS	PUNS
******	PURI	BULL	HUGO	BUTS	PUPS
-U-G	QUAI	BURL	JUDO	BUYS	PUSS
******	QUEI	CULL	JUNO	CUBS	PUTS
BULG	SUFI	CURL	LUDO	CUDS	RUBS
BUNG	TUPI	DUAL	MUCO	CUES	RUES
BURG	ZUNI	DUEL	SUMO	CUPS	RUGS
DUNG	******	DULL	******	CURS	RUMS
FUNG	-U-J	FUEL	-U-P	CUSS	RUNS
HUNG	******	FULL	******	CUTS	RUSS
JUNG	SUBJ	FURL	BUMP	DUBS	RUTS
LUNG	******	GULL	BURP	DUDS	SUBS
PUNG	-U-K	HULL	CUSP	DUES	SUDS
QUAG	******	HURL	DUMP	DUGS	SUES
QUNG	BUCK	LULL	GULP	DUNS	SUMS
RUNG	BULK	MULL	HUMP	DUOS	SUNS
SUNG	BUNK	NULL	JUMP	FUNS	SUPS
SURG	BUSK	PULL	LUMP	FURS	SUSS
******	CUSK	PURL	PULP	FUSS	TUBS
-U-H	DUCK	******	PUMP	GUMS	TUES
******	DUNK	-U-M	QUIP	GUNS	TUGS
AUTH	DUSK	******	RUMP	GUTS	TUNS
BUSH	FUNK	CULM	SUMP	GUYS	TUPS
CUSH	GUCK	DUIM	SUPP	HUBS	VUGS
GUSH	HUCK	GUAM	TUMP		YUKS
		MUMM			

```
******        ******        ******        ******        ******        ******
-U-T          -U-Y          -V-L          -W-B          -W-S          -X-L
******        ******        ******        ******        ******        ******
AUNT          AUBY          AVAL          SWAB          AWES          AXIL
AUST          BUOY          EVIL          ******        AWLS          EXCL
BUNT          BURY          OVAL          -W-D          AWNS          ******
BURT          BUSY          ******        ******        EWES          -X-M
BUST          DULY          -V-M          AWED          OWES          ******
BUTT          DUTY          ******        OWED          OWLS          EXAM
CULT          EURY          OVUM          ******        OWNS          ******
CURT          FUMY          ******        -W-G          TWAS          -X-N
DUCT          FURY          -V-N          ******        TWOS          ******
DUET          JUDY          ******        SWAG          ******        AXON
DUIT          JULY          AVON          SWIG          -W-T          EXON
DUNT          JURY          EVAN          TWIG          ******        OXEN
DUST          LUCY          EVEN          ******        SWAT          OXON
GUAT          PUNY          IVAN          -W-I          SWOT          ******
GUST          QUAY          OVEN          ******        TWIT          -X-S
HUNT          RUAY          ******        HWAI          ******        ******
HURT          RUBY          -V-R          ZWEI          -W-W          AXES
JUST          RUDY          ******        ******        ******        AXIS
KURT          SUKY          AVER          -W-L          LWOW          EXES
LUNT          SUZY          EVER          ******        ******        ******
LUST          ******        IVOR          AWOL          -W-Y          -X-T
MULT          -U-Z          OVER          ******        ******        ******
MUST          ******        ******        -W-M          AWAY          EXIT
MUTT          BUZZ          -V-S          ******        AWNY          ******
OUST          FUZZ          ******        SWAM          AWRY          -Y-A
PUNT          LUIZ          AVAS          SWIM          SWAY          ******
PUTT          QUIZ          AVES          SWUM          ******        CYMA
QUAT          SUEZ          AVIS          ******        -X-A          DYNA
QUIT          ******        EVAS          -W-N          ******        EYRA
RUNT          -V-A          EVES          ******        IXIA          HYLA
RUST          ******        IVES          EWAN          ******        LYRA
SUET          UVEA          IVYS          GWEN          -X-C          MYNA
SUIT          ******        KVAS          GWIN          ******        MYRA
SUPT          -V-C          YVES          GWYN          EXEC          MYXA
TUFT          ******        ******        HWAN          ******        ******
******        AVEC          -V-V          OWEN          -X-D          -Y-C
-U-U          UVIC          ******        SWAN          ******        ******
******        ******        AVIV          TWIN          AXED          PYIC
GURU          -V-D          ******        ******        EXOD          ******
JUJU          ******        -V-W          -W-P          ******        -Y-D
KUDU          AVID          ******        ******        -X-E          ******
LUAU          OVID          AVOW          SWAP          ******        BYRD
LULU          ******        ******        SWOP          AXLE          DYAD
******        -V-E          -W-A          ******        ******        DYED
SULU          ******        ******        -W-R          -X-H          EYED
TUTU          EVOE          YWCA          ******        ******        RYND
ZULU                        YWHA          EWER          EXCH
```

******	******	DYES	******	BEAD	WAAF
-Y-E	**-Y-L**	EYAS	**-Z-N**	BRAD	WRAF
******	******	EYES	******	CHAD	******
AYME	CYCL	GYMS	AZAN	CLAD	**--AG**
BYEE	HYAL	GYPS	AZON	DEAD	******
BYRE	MYEL	LYES	UZAN	DUAD	BRAG
CYME	PYEL	OYES	******	DYAD	CRAG
CYTE	******	PYES	**-Z-R**	EGAD	DIAG
DYKE	**-Y-N**	RYES	******	GLAD	DRAG
DYNE	******	WYES	CZAR	GOAD	FLAG
EYRE	AYIN	******	IZAR	GRAD	KNAG
FYKE	CYAN	**-Y-T**	TZAR	HEAD	PEAG
GYBE	DYAN	******	******	JOAD	PHAG
GYRE	GYMN	CYST	**-Z-V**	LEAD	QUAG
GYVE	HYMN	EYOT	******	LOAD	SHAG
HYDE	LYNN	HYET	AZOV	MEAD	SKAG
KYLE	PYIN	KYAT	******	QUAD	SLAG
LYLE	RYAN	NYET	**-Z-Y**	RAAD	SNAG
LYME	WYNN	PYAT	******	READ	STAG
LYRE	******	PYET	IZZY	ROAD	SWAG
LYSE	**-Y-O**	PYOT	******	SCAD	******
LYTE	******	RYOT	**--AA**	SHAD	**--AH**
LYZE	CYMO	XYST	******	SPAD	******
PYLE	CYTO	******	NCAA	THAD	ADAH
PYRE	GYNO	**-Y-X**	******	TOAD	AHAH
SYCE	GYRO	******	**--AB**	TRAD	AMAH
SYNE	HYLO	LYNX	******	UDAD	AYAH
TYEE	HYPO	******	AHAB	WOAD	BLAH
TYKE	MYCO	**-Y-Y**	ARAB	******	DRAH
TYNE	MYXO	******	BLAB	**--AE**	ETAH
TYPE	PYRO	EYRY	CRAB	******	JOAH
TYRE	TYPO	******	DRAB	ALAE	LEAH
******	TYRO	**-Y-Z**	GRAB	BRAE	MEAH
-Y-H	XYLO	******	JOAB	FRAE	NOAH
******	ZYGO	OYEZ	MOAB	IDAE	OPAH
AYAH	******	******	MZAB	KOAE	PTAH
MYTH	**-Y-R**	**-Z-A**	QUAB	PRAE	SAAH
WYCH	******	******	RAAB	******	SEAH
******	AYER	EZBA	SCAB	**--AF**	SHAH
-Y-I	DYER	EZRA	SLAB	******	TRAH
******	GYOR	******	STAB	DEAF	UTAH
GYRI	HYDR	**-Z-B**	SWAB	GRAF	YEAH
LYSI	HYGR	******	******	HAAF	******
MYRI	IYAR	WAAC	**--AC**	LEAF	**--AI**
******	OYER	******	******	LOAF	ALAI
-Y-K	******	MZAB	WAAC	OLAF	DHAI
******	**-Y-S**	******	******	PIAF	HWAI
******	******	**-Z-K**	**--AD**	USAF	QUAI
DYAK	AYES	******	ACAD		
	BYES	EZEK	ARAD		

******	PEAL	******	STAN	AJAR	ZBAR
--AK	REAL	--AN	SWAN	ALAR	ZOAR
******	RIAL	******	THAN	ATAR	******
ADAK	SEAL	ALAN	ULAN	BAAR	--AS
BEAK	SIAL	ARAN	URAN	BEAR	******
DHAK	TAAL	AZAN	UZAN	BHAR	ABAS
DYAK	TEAL	BEAN	WEAN	BOAR	ADAS
FLAK	URAL	BRAN	YEAN	CHAR	AGAS
IRAK	VAAL	CLAN	YUAN	CLAR	ALAS
KIAK	VEAL	CRAN	ZOAN	CZAR	AMAS
LEAK	VIAL	CYAN	******	DEAR	ANAS
NDAK	WAAL	DEAN	--AO	DHAR	ARAS
PEAK	WEAL	DHAN	******	DUAR	ASAS
SDAK	ZEAL	DIAN	AGAO	FEAR	AVAS
SOAK	******	DYAN	GRAO	GEAR	BAAS
TEAK	--AM	EBAN	GUAO	GNAR	BEAS
WEAK	******	EGAN	LIAO	GOAR	BIAS
******	ADAM	ELAN	PRAO	HEAR	BOAS
--AL	ANAM	EVAN	******	HOAR	BRAS
******	ARAM	EWAN	--AP	ISAR	DIAS
ANAL	BEAM	FLAN	******	IYAR	ERAS
ARAL	CLAM	FRAN	CHAP	IZAR	ETAS
AVAL	CRAM	GMAN	CLAP	JOAR	EVAS
BAAL	DIAM	GUAN	CRAP	KNAR	EYAS
COAL	DRAM	HWAN	FLAP	LEAR	FRAS
DEAL	EDAM	IMAN	FRAP	LIAR	GOAS
DHAL	ELAM	IRAN	HEAP	NCAR	IDAS
DIAL	EXAM	IVAN	KNAP	NEAR	INAS
DUAL	FAAM	JEAN	LEAP	OMAR	IRAS
ERAL	FLAM	JOAN	NEAP	OSAR	KAAS
ETAL	FOAM	JUAN	REAP	PEAR	KEAS
FOAL	GRAM	KHAN	SLAP	QUAR	KVAS
GOAL	GUAM	LEAN	SNAP	REAR	LEAS
HEAL	IMAM	LOAN	SOAP	ROAR	MAAS
HYAL	KLAM	MEAN	SWAP	SAAR	MOAS
ICAL	LOAM	MOAN	TRAP	SCAR	OKAS
ITAL	MAAM	NGAN	WHAP	SEAR	PEAS
KCAL	PRAM	OMAN	WRAP	SOAR	SEAS
KRAL	REAM	ORAN	******	SPAR	SPAS
LEAL	ROAM	PEAN	--AQ	STAR	TEAS
MAAL	SEAM	PLAN	******	TBAR	TWAS
MEAL	SHAM	QUAN	IRAQ	TEAR	UNAS
NEAL	SIAM	ROAN	******	THAR	UPAS
ODAL	SLAM	RYAN	--AR	TSAR	XMAS
OPAL	SPAM	SCAN	******	TZAR	YEAS
ORAL	SWAM	SEAN	ADAR	USAR	******
OVAL	TEAM	SHAN	AFAR	WEAR	--AT
PAAL	TRAM	SPAN	AGAR	YEAR	******
	WHAM				AMAT
					ANAT

BEAT	******	******	KOBE	FIBR	SOBS
BLAT	--AW	--AZ	LOBE	HEBR	SUBS
BOAT	******	******	LUBE	OMBR	TABS
BRAT	BRAW	BOAZ	ROBE	******	TUBS
CHAT	CHAW	BRAZ	RUBE	--BS	WEBS
COAT	CLAW	DIAZ	SABE	******	******
CRAT	CRAW	GRAZ	TUBE	ALBS	--BT
DRAT	DRAW	******	WABE	BABS	******
FEAT	FLAW	--BA	******	BIBS	DEBT
FIAT	GNAW	******	--BI	BOBS	******
FLAT	SHAW	ABBA	******	BUBS	--BU
FRAT	SKAW	ALBA	AMBI	CABS	******
GHAT	SLAW	BABA	BABI	COBS	BABU
GNAT	THAW	CEBA	GOBI	CUBS	CEBU
GOAT	******	CUBA	JIBI	DABS	HABU
GUAT	--AX	ELBA	SEBI	DEBS	JEBU
HEAT	******	EZBA	******	DIBS	TABU
JOAT	AJAX	ISBA	--BJ	DUBS	ZEBU
KHAT	COAX	JUBA	******	EBBS	******
KYAT	FLAX	LUBA	SUBJ	FIBS	--BY
MEAT	HOAX	PABA	******	FOBS	******
MOAT	******	RABA	--BK	GABS	ABBY
NEAT	--AY	REBA	******	GIBS	AUBY
PEAT	******	TUBA	HDBK	GOBS	BABY
PLAT	ADAY	UEBA	******	HOBS	DOBY
PYAT	AWAY	YABA	--BL	HUBS	GABY
QUAT	BRAY	******	******	JABS	GOBY
SCAT	CHAY	--BB	BIBL	JIBS	RUBY
SEAT	CLAY	******	******	JOBS	TOBY
SKAT	DDAY	BIBB	--BM	KABS	******
SLAT	DRAY	COBB	******	LABS	--CA
SPAT	FLAY	IOBB	ICBM	LOBS	******
STAT	FRAY	******	IRBM	MABS	CECA
SWAT	GRAY	--BE	******	MIBS	COCA
TEAT	OKAY	******	--BO	MOBS	DECA
THAT	OLAY	ABBE	******	NABS	FICA
WHAT	PIAY	AUBE	AMBO	NEBS	INCA
******	PLAY	BABE	BUBO	NIBS	JACA
--AU	PRAY	CUBE	GOBO	NOBS	JUCA
******	QUAY	ELBE	HOBO	NUBS	MICA
BEAU	RUAY	GABE	JOBO	ORBS	ONCA
ESAU	SHAY	GIBE	LOBO	PUBS	ORCA
FRAU	SLAY	GYBE	NABO	REBS	PACA
LUAU	SPAY	HABE	NEBO	RIBS	PICA
UNAU	STAY	HEBE	SEBO	ROBS	SPCA
******	SWAY	JIBE	UMBO	RUBS	VACA
--AV	TRAY	JUBE	******	SABS	YMCA
******	XRAY	KIBE	--BR	SIBS	YWCA
OLAV			******		
SLAV			ABBR		
			FEBR		

*****	EACH	KECK	LOCO	LACY	CEDE
--CC	ETCH	KICK	MUCO	LUCY	CIDE
*****	EXCH	LACK	MYCO	RACY	CODE
SPCC	FOCH	LICK	PACO	SECY	DADE
*****	INCH	LOCK	PECO	*****	DUDE
--CD	ITCH	LUCK	PICO	--DA	FADE
*****	LICH	MACK	POCO	*****	GIDE
DECD	LOCH	MICK	TOCO	AIDA	HADE
*****	MACH	MOCK	UNCO	BEDA	HIDE
--CE	MICH	MUCK	WACO	CODA	HYDE
*****	MUCH	NECK	*****	DADA	JADE
ANCE	OUCH	NICK	--CP	EDDA	JUDE
BICE	RICH	NOCK	*****	ERDA	KADE
DACE	SUCH	PACK	FACP	KADA	LADE
DICE	WICH	PECK	*****	LEDA	LEDE
DUCE	WYCH	PICK	--CR	NADA	LODE
ENCE	ZACH	POCK	*****	PODA	MADE
ESCE	*****	PUCK	NECR	RADA	MEDE
FACE	--CI	RACK	PICR	SODA	MODE
FICE	*****	RECK	*****	VEDA	NIDE
LACE	ASCI	RICK	--CS	*****	NODE
LICE	DECI	ROCK	*****	--DB	NUDE
LUCE	FOCI	RUCK	ABCS	*****	PEDE
MACE	FUCI	SACK	ARCS	IADB	PODE
MICE	LOCI	SICK	FACS	*****	REDE
NICE	MUCI	SOCK	FMCS	--DC	RIDE
ONCE	VICI	SUCK	MACS	*****	RODE
PACE	*****	TACK	ORCS	ACDC	RUDE
PICE	--CK	TICK	SACS	*****	SADE
PUCE	*****	TUCK	SICS	--DD	SIDE
RACE	BACK	VICK	TICS	*****	TIDE
RICE	BECK	WACK	WACS	BUDD	TUDE
SICE	BOCK	WICK	*****	KIDD	UNDE
SYCE	BUCK	ZACK	--CT	LADD	URDE
TACE	COCK	*****	*****	RUDD	VIDE
VICE	DECK	--CL	ACCT	SUDD	WADE
VOCE	DICK	*****	DUCT	TODD	WIDE
*****	DOCK	CYCL	FACT	*****	*****
--CG	DUCK	ECCL	HECT	--DE	--DG
*****	GECK	ENCL	LACT	*****	*****
USCG	GUCK	EXCL	NOCT	AIDE	BLDG
*****	HACK	INCL	PACT	ALDE	*****
--CH	HECK	*****	PICT	AUDE	--DH
*****	HICK	--CO	RECT	BADE	*****
ARCH	HOCK	*****	SECT	BEDE	SADH
ASCH	HUCK	CACO	TACT	BIDE	YODH
BACH	JACK	COCO	*****	BODE	*****
DICH	JOCK	FICO	--CY	CADE	--DI
			*****	BEDE	*****
			ANCY	BIDE	CADI
			ENCY	CADE	KADI

LODI	CADS	CODY	EXEC	TIED	******
MEDI	CODS	DIDY	SPEC	TOED	--EI
MIDI	CUDS	EDDY	******	USED	******
MODI	DADS	JUDY	--ED	VIED	OMEI
NIDI	DUDS	LADY	******	WEED	QUEI
NUDI	ENDS	RUDY	ABED	******	ZWEI
PEDI	FADS	TIDY	ACED	--EE	******
SADI	FIDS	TODY	AGED	******	--EK
VIDI	GADS	UNDY	APED	AGEE	******
WADI	GODS	URDY	AWED	ALEE	BEEK
******	HODS	WADY	AXED	BYEE	EZEK
--DJ	KIDS	******	BLED	CHEE	GEEK
******	LADS	--DZ	BRED	CLEE	KEEK
HADJ	LIDS	******	BSED	CREE	LEEK
******	MADS	LODZ	COED	EPEE	MEEK
--DO	MODS	******	CUED	FLEE	PEEK
******	MUDS	--EA	DEED	FREE	REEK
ALDO	NEDS	******	DIED	GHEE	SEEK
DADO	NODS	ACEA	DYED	GLEE	TREK
DIDO	ODDS	AREA	EKED	INEE	WEEK
DODO	PADS	ASEA	EYED	KLEE	******
ENDO	PHDS	BREA	FEED	KNEE	--EL
FADO	PODS	FLEA	FLED	OGEE	******
INDO	RADS	FREA	FRED	SKEE	ABEL
IODO	REDS	GAEA	GEED	SLEE	BAEL
JODO	RIDS	IDEA	GIED	SMEE	BIEL
JUDO	RODS	ILEA	GLED	SNEE	CIEL
LIDO	SIDS	ITEA	HEED	THEE	COEL
LUDO	SODS	ODEA	HIED	TREE	DUEL
ONDO	SUDS	OTEA	HOED	TYEE	FEEL
ORDO	TADS	PLEA	HUED	******	FUEL
PEDO	TEDS	RHEA	ICED	--EF	GAEL
REDO	TODS	SHEA	JEED	******	HEEL
TODO	WADS	THEA	LIED	ALEF	ICEL
UNDO	WEDS	UREA	NEED	BEEF	JEEL
******	YODS	UVEA	OKED	CHEF	JOEL
--DR	ZEDS	******	OWED	CLEF	KEEL
******	******	--EB	PAED	COEF	KIEL
CMDR	--DU	******	PIED	FIEF	KOEL
HYDR	******	BLEB	PLED	KEEF	MYEL
******	KUDU	PLEB	REED	LIEF	NAEL
--DS	URDU	THEB	RUED	REEF	NIEL
******	******	******	SEED	TREF	NOEL
ADDS	--DY	--EC	SHED	XREF	******
AIDS	******	******	SLED	******	--EG
BEDS	ADDY	ALEC	SPED	******	OREL
BIDS	ANDY	AVEC	SUED	CLEG	OSEL
BUDS	BODY	ELEC	TEED	GREG	PEEL
				SKEG	PYEL
					REEL

SEEL	OXEN	BIER	APES	OYES	SPET
TAEL	PEEN	BOER	ARES	PEES	STET
WEEL	PHEN	BRER	ATES	PIES	SUET
******	RIEN	DEER	AVES	PRES	TRET
--EM	SEEN	DOER	AWES	PYES	VOET
******	STEN	DYER	AXES	RAES	WHET
AHEM	TEEN	EDER	AYES	ROES	******
BLEM	THEN	EGER	BEES	RUES	**--EU**
CHEM	UDEN	EVER	BYES	RYES	******
CLEM	WHEN	EWER	CEES	SEES	DIEU
DEEM	WREN	GOER	CHES	SHES	EMEU
ELEM	******	HIER	CRES	SPES	LIEU
FLEM	**--EO**	HLER	CUES	SUES	******
IDEM	******	HOER	DEES	TEES	**--EV**
ITEM	AREO	ICER	DIES	TIES	******
POEM	CLEO	ISER	DOES	TOES	BREV
SEEM	ELEO	ITER	DUES	TRES	ELEV
SHEM	IDEO	JEER	DYES	TUES	KIEV
STEM	ILEO	KIER	EKES	USES	******
TEEM	OLEO	LEER	EVES	UTES	**--EW**
THEM	RHEO	NEER	EWES	VEES	******
YLEM	THEO	ODER	EXES	VIES	ANEW
******	******	OMER	EYES	WOES	BLEW
--EN	**--EP**	ONER	FEES	WYES	BREW
******	******	OVER	FOES	YVES	CHEW
ADEN	BEEP	OYER	GEES	ZEES	CLEW
ALEN	DEEP	PEER	GOES	ZOES	CREW
AMEN	JEEP	PIER	HIES	******	DREW
ATEN	KEEP	PTER	HOES	**--ET**	FLEW
BEEN	PEEP	RUER	HUES	******	GREW
BREN	PREP	SEER	ICES	ABET	KNEW
CAEN	SEEP	STER	IDES	ACET	PHEW
CTEN	SKEP	SUER	IKES	BEET	PLEW
EBEN	STEP	TIER	IVES	BLET	SHEW
EDEN	WEEP	UBER	JEES	BRET	SKEW
EVEN	******	USER	JOES	CHET	SLEW
GLEN	**--EQ**	UTER	LEES	DIET	SMEW
GMEN	******	VEER	LIES	DUET	SPEW
GWEN	FREQ	YMER	LUES	FEET	STEW
HOEN	******	YSER	LYES	FRET	THEW
JAEN	**--ER**	******	MAES	HYET	VIEW
KEEN	******	**--ES**	MMES	KHET	WHEW
LIEN	ACER	******	MOES	LEET	******
MIEN	AMER	ABES	NOES	MEET	**--EX**
OMEN	AVER	ACES	ODES	NYET	******
OPEN	AYER	AGES	ONES	OKET	ALEX
OVEN	BAER	ALES	ORES	POET	APEX
OWEN	BEER	AMES	OWES	PYET	FLEX

IBEX	CUFF	RAFT	EDGE	DAGO	KEGS
ILEX	DAFF	REFT	GAGE	DEGO	LAGS
ULEX	DOFF	RIFT	HUGE	ERGO	LEGS
******	DUFF	SIFT	INGE	GOGO	LOGS
--EY	GAFF	SOFT	LOGE	HUGO	LUGS
******	GUFF	TAFT	LUGE	IAGO	MEGS
FREY	HUFF	TOFT	MAGE	LOGO	MIGS
GREY	JEFF	TUFT	PAGE	NOGO	MUGS
JOEY	JIFF	WAFT	RAGE	POGO	NAGS
OBEY	LUFF	WEFT	SAGE	SAGO	NOGS
PREY	MIFF	******	URGE	SEGO	PEGS
THEY	MUFF	**--FU**	WAGE	TOGO	PIGS
TREY	PUFF	******	******	ZYGO	PUGS
UREY	RAFF	GIFU	**--GG**	******	RAGS
WHEY	RIFF	IDFU	******	**--GR**	RIGS
******	RUFF	******	HOGG	******	RUGS
--EZ	TIFF	**--FY**	JAGG	BAGR	SAGS
******	TOFF	******	NOGG	ENGR	TAGS
CHEZ	TUFF	DEFY	YEGG	HYGR	TEGS
GEEZ	******	IFFY	******	MSGR	TOGS
INEZ	**--FI**	******	**--GH**	NIGR	TUGS
OYEZ	******	**--GA**	******	******	VUGS
SUEZ	DEFI	******	AFGH	**--GS**	WAGS
******	HIFI	ALGA	GOGH	******	WIGS
--FA	SUFI	BAGA	HIGH	BAGS	******
******	******	GAGA	HUGH	BEGS	**--GT**
ALFA	**--FO**	GIGA	NIGH	BOGS	******
SOFA	******	INGA	PUGH	BUGS	MSGT
TUFA	INFO	JAGA	SIGH	CHGS	******
URFA	******	MEGA	YOGH	COGS	**--GU**
******	**--FS**	NAGA	******	DAGS	******
--FE	******	OLGA	**--GI**	DIGS	KAGU
******	ALFS	RAGA	******	DOGS	******
CAFE	EFFS	RIGA	HAGI	DUGS	**--GY**
FIFE	KEFS	RUGA	MAGI	EGGS	******
JEFE	OAFS	SAGA	RAGI	ERGS	ALGY
LAFE	WAFS	TOGA	VAGI	FAGS	BOGY
LIFE	******	UNGA	YOGI	FIGS	CAGY
RIFE	**--FT**	VEGA	******	FOGS	DOGY
RUFE	******	YOGA	**--GN**	GAGS	EDGY
SAFE	DAFT	YUGA	******	GIGS	FOGY
WIFE	DEFT	******	LIGN	HAGS	LOGY
******	GIFT	**--GD**	SIGN	HOGS	ORGY
--FF	HAFT	******	******	HUGS	POGY
******	HEFT	CHGD	**--GO**	JAGS	SAGY
BAFF	LEFT	******	******	JIGS	******
BIFF	LIFT	**--GE**	ARGO	JOGS	**--HA**
BUFF	LOFT	CAGE	BAGO	JUGS	******
		DOGE			AGHA
					ASHA

GUHA	******	OHIA	SKID	AXIL	TRIM
HAHA	--HR	OPIA	SLID	BAIL	WHIM
KAHA	******	URIA	VOID	BOIL	******
MAHA	BOHR	USIA	******	CEIL	--IN
NAHA	LAHR	******	--IE	CHIL	******
OCHA	LEHR	--IB	******	COIL	AKIN
PAHA	MOHR	******	ABIE	DAIL	ALIN
PSHA	RUHR	ABIB	AMIE	DEIL	AYIN
YMHA	******	CRIB	BRIE	EMIL	CAIN
YWHA	--HS	DRIB	EDIE	EVIL	CHIN
******	******	GLIB	ERIE	FAIL	COIN
--HE	EDHS	******	OKIE	FOIL	DRIN
******	ETHS	--IC	UNIE	GAIL	ERIN
ACHE	HAHS	******	******	HAIL	FAIN
ASHE	******	ATIC	--IF	IFIL	GAIN
BIHE	--HT	CHIC	******	JAIL	GRIN
HEHE	******	EPIC	ALIF	KAIL	GUIN
******	BAHT	ERIC	COIF	MAIL	GWIN
--HH	ECHT	FDIC	KAIF	MOIL	IMIN
******	******	LAIC	LEIF	NAIL	JAIN
SAHH	--HU	ODIC	NAIF	NEIL	JOIN
******	******	OTIC	WAIF	NOIL	KAIN
--HI	JEHU	PYIC	******	PAIL	LAIN
******	OAHU	SAIC	--IG	PHIL	LOIN
OPHI	RAHU	URIC	******	RAIL	MAIN
TCHI	******	UVIC	BRIG	ROIL	NAIN
TSHI	--HY	ZOIC	GRIG	SAIL	ODIN
******	******	******	OLIG	SOIL	PAIN
--HL	ASHY	--ID	ORIG	TAIL	PYIN
******	******	******	PRIG	TEIL	RAIN
BUHL	--IA	ACID	SNIG	TOIL	REIN
KOHL	******	AMID	SWIG	VAIL	RHIN
******	ALIA	ARID	TRIG	VEIL	RUIN
--HN	AMIA	AVID	TWIG	WAIL	SHIN
******	APIA	CHID	WHIG	******	SKIN
ETHN	ARIA	ENID	******	--IM	SPIN
FOHN	ASIA	GRID	--IH	******	TAIN
HAHN	BAIA	IBID	******	ANIM	THIN
JOHN	CHIA	IMID	CHIH	BRIM	TRIN
******	ELIA	IRID	******	DUIM	TWIN
--HO	EMIA	KAID	--IK	GLIM	VAIN
******	ERIA	LAID	******	GRIM	VEIN
COHO	GAIA	MAID	EFIK	MAIM	WAIN
ECHO	ILIA	OVID	ERIK	PRIM	WHIN
KIHO	INIA	PAID	HAIK	SHIM	ZEIN
MOHO	IXIA	QUID	RAIK	SKIM	******
SOHO	MAIA	RAID	******	SLIM	--IO
	OBIA	SAID	--IL	SWIM	******
			******		AGIO
			ANIL		APIO
			ARIL		

BRIO	VAIR	CHIT	******	******	MOKI
CLIO	WEIR	CRIT	--JA	--KE	PIKI
FRIO	WHIR	DOIT	******	******	RAKI
IDIO	YMIR	DUIT	BAJA	BAKE	SAKI
MEIO	******	EDIT	DEJA	BIKE	TIKI
MOIO	--IS	EMIT	NAJA	CAKE	WEKI
OHIO	******	EXIT	RAJA	COKE	******
OLIO	AMIS	FLIT	SOJA	DEKE	--KO
THIO	ANIS	FRIT	******	DIKE	******
TRIO	APIS	GAIT	--JD	DUKE	JAKO
UNIO	ASIS	GRIT	******	DYKE	KOKO
******	AVIS	INIT	NEJD	ELKE	MAKO
--IP	AXIS	KNIT	******	FAKE	YAKO
******	BOIS	LAIT	--JI	FYKE	******
BLIP	CHIS	OBIT	******	HAKE	--KS
CHIP	DAIS	OMIT	FIJI	HIKE	******
CLIP	ELIS	QUIT	FUJI	JAKE	ARKS
DRIP	ERIS	SKIT	******	JOKE	ASKS
FLIP	GRIS	SLIT	--JM	LAKE	AUKS
GRIP	IBIS	SMIT	******	LIKE	DAKS
HRIP	IRIS	SNIT	SEJM	LOKE	ELKS
QUIP	ISIS	SPIT	******	LUKE	INKS
SHIP	KRIS	SUIT	--JN	MAKE	IRKS
SKIP	LEIS	TAIT	******	MIKE	LEKS
SLIP	LOIS	TWIT	RIJN	MOKE	OAKS
SNIP	LUIS	UNIT	******	NIKE	YAKS
TRIP	NAIS	WAIT	--JO	PIKE	YUKS
WHIP	OBIS	WHIT	******	POKE	******
******	OSIS	WRIT	MAJO	PUKE	--KU
--IR	OTIS	******	MOJO	RAKE	******
******	PAIS	--IV	******	SAKE	BAKU
AMIR	PHIS	******	--JU	SOKE	HAKU
ASIR	PSIS	AVIV	******	TAKE	POKU
CHIR	QAIS	SHIV	JUJU	TIKE	******
COIR	REIS	SPIV	******	TYKE	--KY
CUIR	RIIS	XDIV	--KA	WAKE	******
EMIR	SAIS	******	******	WOKE	INKY
FAIR	SKIS	--IX	ATKA	YOKE	LAKY
HAIR	THIS	******	BEKA	ZEKE	POKY
HEIR	TRIS	ALIX	DEKA	******	SUKY
KEIR	******	TRIX	HAKA	--KH	******
LAIR	--IT	******	ILKA	******	--LA
MEIR	******	--IZ	KAKA	ANKH	******
MUIR	ADIT	******	MAKA	LAKH	BELA
PAIR	ALIT	ARIZ	PIKA	SIKH	BOLA
SOIR	BAIT	LUIZ	PUKA	******	COLA
SPIR	BLIT	QUIZ	WEKA	--KI	DOLA
STIR	BRIT	RHIZ	YAKA	KAKI	ELLA
		WHIZ		LOKI	

FALA	SOLD	PALE	BALI	FELL	HALM
FILA	TOLD	PELE	CALI	FILL	HELM
FULA	VELD	PILE	DALI	FOLL	HOLM
GALA	WALD	POLE	DELI	FULL	MALM
GILA	WELD	PULE	DILI	GALL	PALM
HULA	WILD	PYLE	HELI	GILL	******
HYLA	WOLD	RALE	KALI	GULL	--LN
JOLA	YELD	ROLE	MALI	HALL	******
KALA	******	ROLE	PALI	HELL	KILN
KELA	--LE	RULE	PILI	HILL	KOLN
KOLA	******	SALE	SOLI	HULL	******
LILA	ABLE	SOLE	VALI	JELL	--LO
LOLA	AILE	TALE	VILI	JILL	******
OKLA	ALLE	TELE	******	KILL	ALLO
OLLA	ATLE	TILE	--LK	LALL	BOLO
PALA	AXLE	TOLE	******	LOLL	COLO
SOLA	BALE	TULE	BALK	LULL	DILO
TELA	BILE	UELE	BILK	MALL	FILO
TOLA	BOLE	VALE	BULK	MILL	GOLO
TULA	BULE	VILE	CALK	MOLL	HALO
ULLA	CELE	VOLE	FOLK	MULL	HILO
VELA	COLE	WALE	HULK	NELL	HOLO
VOLA	CULE	WILE	MILK	NULL	HYLO
ZOLA	DALE	YALE	POLK	PALL	JOLO
******	DELE	YULE	SALK	PILL	KILO
--LB	DOLE	******	SILK	POLL	MALO
******	ERLE	--LF	SULK	PULL	MILO
BULB	FILE	******	TALK	RALL	OSLO
******	GALE	CALF	WALK	RILL	POLO
--LC	HALE	DELF	YELK	ROLL	RALO
******	HOLE	DOLF	YOLK	SELL	SILO
TALC	IBLE	GOLF	******	SILL	SOLO
******	IDLE	GULF	--LL	TALL	STLO
--LD	IOLE	HALF	******	TELL	TELO
******	ISLE	PELF	BALL	TILL	XYLO
AULD	JULE	ROLF	BELL	TOLL	******
BALD	KALE	SELF	BILL	VILL	--LP
BOLD	KYLE	WOLF	BOLL	WALL	******
COLD	LYLE	******	BULL	WELL	GULP
FOLD	MALE	--LG	CALL	WILL	HELP
GELD	MELE	******	CELL	YELL	KELP
GILD	MILE	BELG	COLL	******	PALP
GOLD	MLLE	BULG	CULL	--LM	PULP
HELD	MOLE	******	DELL	******	SALP
HOLD	MULE	--LI	DILL	BALM	YELP
MELD	NILE	******	DOLL	CALM	******
MILD	OGLE	ALLI	DULL	CULM	--LS
MOLD	ORLE	ATLI	FALL	FILM	******
					AALS
					AILS

AWLS	MULT	WILY	GAMB	TAME	HOMO
BBLS	PELT	WKLY	IAMB	TIME	MEMO
BELS	SALT	******	JAMB	TOME	MOMO
COLS	SILT	--MA	LAMB	******	NEMO
DOLS	TILT	******	LIMB	--MI	NOMO
EELS	VOLT	ALMA	NIMB	******	REMO
ELLS	WALT	BEMA	NUMB	DEMI	SUMO
FELS	WELT	COMA	TOMB	GUMI	******
FILS	WILT	CYMA	WOMB	HEMI	--MP
GALS	******	DOMA	******	IMMI	******
GELS	--LU	DUMA	--MC	JAMI	BUMP
GILS	******	ELMA	******	KAMI	CAMP
HALS	ACLU	EMMA	USMC	MIMI	COMP
ILLS	IGLU	ERMA	******	RAMI	DAMP
LILS	LULU	FNMA	--ME	REMI	DUMP
MELS	NALU	GAMA	******	SEMI	GAMP
MILS	PELU	GOMA	ACME	******	GIMP
OILS	SULU	HAMA	AYME	--MJ	HEMP
OWLS	TOLU	HEMA	CAME	******	HUMP
PALS	YALU	IRMA	COME	UCMJ	JUMP
SOLS	ZULU	JAMA	CYME	******	KEMP
VALS	******	KAMA	DAME	--ML	LAMP
VOLS	--LX	LAMA	DEME	******	LIMP
******	******	LIMA	DIME	HEML	LUMP
--LT	CALX	LOMA	DOME	******	PIMP
******	******	MAMA	FAME	--MM	POMP
BALT	--LY	NAMA	FEME	******	PUMP
BELT	******	NEMA	FUME	COMM	RAMP
BOLT	ABLY	NOMA	GAME	MUMM	RCMP
CELT	ALLY	PIMA	HAME	******	ROMP
COLT	COLY	PUMA	HEME	--MN	RUMP
CULT	DULY	RAMA	HOME	******	SAMP
DOLT	EELY	ROMA	HUME	DAMN	SIMP
FELT	HOLY	SAMA	KAME	FAMN	SUMP
GELT	IDLY	SIMA	LAME	GYMN	TAMP
GILT	ILLY	SOMA	LIME	HYMN	TEMP
HALT	INLY	TEMA	LOME	LIMN	TUMP
HILT	JULY	USMA	LYME	******	VAMP
HOLT	LILY	XEMA	MIME	--MO	YAMP
JILT	MOLY	YAMA	NAME	******	******
JOLT	OILY	YUMA	NOME	AMMO	--MR
KELT	OLLY	******	POME	ATMO	******
KILT	ONLY	--MB	RAME	COMO	COMR
LILT	ORLY	******	RIME	CYMO	******
MALT	PALY	BOMB	ROME	DEMO	--MS
MELT	POLY	CAMB	SAME	ELMO	******
MILT	RELY	COMB	SEME	GAMO	AIMS
MOLT	UGLY	DUMB	SOME	HEMO	ALMS

ARMS	ELMY	SANA	RIND	LONE	GENG
BUMS	EMMY	TANA	RYND	LUNE	GONG
CAMS	FUMY	TINA	SAND	MANE	HANG
DAMS	GAMY	TUNA	SEND	MENE	HONG
DIMS	HOMY	ULNA	SIND	MINE	HUNG
DOMS	IMMY	URNA	TEND	NENE	JUNG
ELMS	LIMY	USNA	VEND	NINE	KING
GAMS	NOMY	VENA	WAND	NONE	LANG
GEMS	RIMY	VINA	WEND	ORNE	LING
GUMS	TOMY	YANA	WIND	PANE	LONG
GYMS	VIMY	ZONA	YOND	PINE	LUNG
HAMS	******	******	ZEND	PONE	MING
HEMS	--NA	--NC	******	RENE	PANG
HOMS	******	******	--NE	RUNE	PING
HUMS	ANNA	BANC	******	SANE	PONG
ISMS	BONA	CANC	ACNE	SINE	PUNG
JAMS	BUNA	CONC	ANNE	SONE	QUNG
JEMS	CANA	JUNC	AONE	SYNE	RANG
JIMS	DANA	ZINC	ARNE	TINE	RING
LAMS	DINA	******	AUNE	TONE	RUNG
LEMS	DONA	--ND	BANE	TUNE	SANG
MEMS	DUNA	******	BENE	TYNE	SING
MOMS	DYNA	BAND	BINE	VANE	SONG
MUMS	EDNA	BEND	BONE	VINE	SUNG
OHMS	ENNA	BIND	CANE	WANE	TANG
PAMS	ETNA	BOND	CENE	WINE	TENG
RAMS	GINA	BUND	CINE	ZONE	TING
REMS	IANA	COND	CONE	******	TONG
RIMS	IONA	FEND	DANE	--NF	UANG
ROMS	JENA	FIND	DENE	******	VANG
RUMS	KANA	FOND	DINE	CONF	WANG
SAMS	LANA	FUND	DONE	GENF	WING
SIMS	LENA	GOND	DUNE	******	YANG
SUMS	LINA	HAND	DYNE	--NG	ZING
TAMS	LUNA	HIND	ERNE	******	******
TIMS	MANA	HOND	ESNE	BANG	--NH
TOMS	MINA	JIND	FANE	BENG	******
USMS	MONA	KIND	FINE	BING	BINH
YAMS	MYNA	LAND	GENE	BONG	******
******	NANA	LEND	GONE	BUNG	--NI
--MU	NINA	LIND	HONE	CONG	******
******	NONA	MEND	JANE	DANG	AGNI
LIMU	OONA	MIND	JUNE	DING	ARNI
******	PINA	PEND	KANE	DUNG	BANI
--MY	PUNA	POND	KINE	FANG	BENI
******	RANA	PUND	LANE	FONG	BONI
ARMY	RENA	RAND	LENE	FUNG	IFNI
DEMY	RONA	REND	LINE	GANG	IGNI

LUNI	******	OINO	JANS	GENT	DENY
MANI	--NL	RENO	JONS	HINT	GENY
MENI	******	SINO	KANS	HUNT	LINY
MINI	GENL	TENO	KENS	ISNT	MANY
OMNI	******	TONO	LENS	KANT	PINY
RANI	--NN	VINO	MANS	KENT	PONY
RENI	******	WINO	MONS	LENT	PUNY
TONI	BANN	XENO	NANS	LINT	TINY
VENI	BONN	ZENO	NUNS	LUNT	TONY
VINI	BUNN	******	OWNS	MENT	VINY
ZUNI	CONN	--NR	PANS	MINT	WANY
******	FINN	******	PENS	MONT	WINY
--NJ	JANN	USNR	PINS	PANT	ZANY
******	JINN	******	PONS	PENT	******
CONJ	LINN	--NS	PUNS	PINT	--NZ
******	LYNN	******	RUNS	PUNT	******
--NK	MANN	AINS	SANS	RANT	LINZ
******	MINN	ANNS	SENS	RENT	******
BANK	PENN	ARNS	SINS	RUNT	--OA
BONK	SUNN	AWNS	SONS	SENT	******
BUNK	TENN	BANS	SUNS	TENT	ANOA
CONK	WYNN	BENS	TANS	TINT	PROA
DANK	******	BINS	TENS	VENT	STOA
DUNK	--NO	BUNS	TINS	WANT	WHOA
FINK	******	CANS	TONS	WENT	******
FUNK	AINO	CONS	TUNS	WONT	--OB
GINK	ANNO	DANS	URNS	XINT	******
HANK	ARNO	DENS	VANS	ZANT	BLOB
HONK	BONO	DINS	WANS	******	BOOB
HUNK	BRNO	DONS	WENS	--NU	GLOB
JINK	CENO	DUNS	WINS	******	JAOB
JUNK	DINO	EENS	YENS	AINU	KNOB
KINK	FANO	ENNS	******	DANU	RHOB
KUNK	GONO	EONS	--NT	GENU	SLOB
LANK	GYNO	ERNS	******	MENU	SNOB
LINK	HINO	FANS	AINT	******	******
MINK	JUNO	FENS	AUNT	--NX	--OC
MONK	KANO	FINS	BANT	******	******
PANK	KENO	FUNS	BENT	JINX	APOC
PINK	KINO	GENS	BUNT	LYNX	BLOC
PUNK	LENO	GINS	CANT	MANX	BMOC
RANK	LINO	GUNS	CENT	MINX	FLOC
RINK	MANO	HANS	CONT	******	******
SANK	MENO	HENS	DENT	--NY	--OD
SINK	MONO	HUNS	DINT	******	******
SUNK	NANO	IANS	DONT	AWNY	APOD
TANK	NINO	INNS	DUNT	BONY	CLOD
WINK	OENO	IONS	FONT	CONY	EXOD

FEOD	******	EDOM	PHON	******	CLOT
FOOD	--OI	FROM	PION	--OR	COOT
GOOD	******	GEOM	POON	******	EYOT
HOOD	AMOI	LOOM	PRON	ACOR	FLOT
LOOD	******	PROM	SION	AMOR	FOOT
MOOD	--OK	ROOM	SOON	ATOR	FROT
PLOD	******	WHOM	TION	BOOR	GLOT
POOD	AMOK	ZOOM	TOON	DOOR	GROT
PROD	BOOK	******	TRON	FLOR	HOOT
QUOD	COOK	--ON	UPON	GYOR	KNOT
ROOD	GOOK	******	XION	IVOR	LOOT
SHOD	HOOK	AEON	ZION	MOOR	MOOT
TROD	JOOK	AGON	ZOON	ODOR	PHOT
WOOD	KOOK	AMON	******	OLOR	PIOT
******	LOOK	ANON	--OO	POOR	PLOT
--OE	NOOK	AVON	******	SPOR	PROT
******	POOK	AXON	BROO	THOR	PYOT
ALOE	ROOK	AZON	SHOO	******	RIOT
EVOE	TOOK	BION	SLOO	--OS	ROOT
FLOE	******	BOON	******	******	RYOT
FROE	--OL	BRON	--OP	AMOS	SCOT
OBOE	******	CION	******	BOOS	SHOT
OTOE	AWOL	CLON	ALOP	COOS	SLOT
SHOE	BIOL	COON	ATOP	DIOS	SNOT
SLOE	CHOL	DION	CHOP	DUOS	SOOT
******	COOL	DOON	CLOP	EGOS	SPOT
--OF	ECOL	EBON	COOP	ENOS	SWOT
******	ENOL	ECON	CROP	EPOS	TOOT
ASOF	FOOL	ETON	DROP	EROS	TROT
GOOF	GAOL	EXON	FLOP	GROS	******
HOOF	GEOL	GOON	GOOP	KEOS	--OU
LOOF	IDOL	HOON	HOOP	LAOS	******
PROF	ITOL	HRON	KNOP	LEOS	ABOU
ROOF	OBOL	ICON	LOOP	LOOS	ACOU
WOOF	POOL	IKON	PLOP	MHOS	CHOU
******	STOL	IRON	POOP	MOOS	THOU
--OG	TOOL	KAON	PROP	NAOS	******
******	VIOL	LAON	ROOP	PROS	--OV
AGOG	VTOL	LEON	SCOP	RHOS	******
CLOG	WOOL	LION	SHOP	TAOS	AZOV
FLOG	ZOOL	LOON	SLOP	TWOS	******
FROG	******	MOON	STOP	UDOS	--OW
GROG	--OM	MUON	SWOP	WOOS	******
SLOG	******	NEON	TROP	ZOOS	ALOW
SMOG	ATOM	NOON	WHOP	******	AROW
SNOG	BOOM	ONON	******	--OT	AVOW
******	BROM	OXON	--OQ	******	BLOW
--OH	DOOM	PEON	******	BLOT	BROW
******			SHOQ	BOOT	
POOH					

CHOW	NIPA	******	DAPS	LEPT	KURA
CROW	PAPA	--PI	DIPS	RAPT	LARA
DHOW	PIPA	******	FOPS	SEPT	LIRA
ENOW	PUPA	HOPI	GAPS	SUPT	LYRA
FLOW	RIPA	IMPI	GIPS	WEPT	MARA
FROW	SUPA	KEPI	GYPS	******	MIRA
GLOW	TAPA	KOPI	HIPS	--PU	MORA
GROW	YAPA	TIPI	HOPS	******	MYRA
JHOW	******	TOPI	IMPS	OGPU	NORA
KNOW	--PE	TUPI	KIPS	******	OCRA
LWOW	******	******	KOPS	--PY	OKRA
MEOW	CAPE	--PL	LAPS	******	PARA
PLOW	COPE	******	LIPS	COPY	PERA
PROW	DOPE	DIPL	LOPS	DOPY	SARA
SCOW	DUPE	HAPL	MAPS	ESPY	SERA
SHOW	GAPE	******	MOPS	GAPY	SORA
SLOW	HIPE	--PO	NAPS	PIPY	SURA
SNOW	HOPE	******	NIPS	ROPY	TARA
STOW	JAPE	HYPO	PAPS	******	TERA
TROW	KIPE	LIPO	PEPS	--QQ	TORA
******	LOPE	PEPO	PIPS	******	VARA
--OX	LUPE	SAPO	POPS	SEQQ	VERA
******	MOPE	TOPO	PUPS	******	VIRA
KNOX	NAPE	TYPO	RAPS	--QR	VORA
******	NOPE	******	REPS	******	ZARA
--OY	OLPE	--PP	RIPS	SPQR	ZIRA
******	PIPE	******	SAPS	******	******
AHOY	POPE	CAPP	SIPS	--RA	--RB
AMOY	RAPE	DOPP	SOPS	******	******
BUOY	RIPE	HIPP	SUPS	AGRA	BARB
CLOY	ROPE	LAPP	TAPS	AURA	CARB
PLOY	SAPE	REPP	TIPS	BERA	CURB
TROY	SUPE	SUPP	TOPS	BORA	DARB
******	TAPE	******	TUPS	CARA	FORB
--OZ	TOPE	--PR	VIPS	CORA	GARB
******	TYPE	******	WAPS	DORA	HERB
BROZ	WIPE	COPR	YAPS	DURA	KERB
******	YIPE	CUPR	YIPS	EYRA	NLRB
--PA	******	******	ZIPS	EZRA	SERB
******	--PH	--PS	******	FORA	SORB
CAPA	******	******	--PT	GARA	VERB
CEPA	ALPH	ALPS	******	GERA	******
COPA	KAPH	AMPS	BAPT	HERA	--RC
DAPA	KOPH	ASPS	CAPT	HORA	******
DEPA	NEPH	BOPS	COPT	IRRA	CIRC
HUPA	QOPH	CAPS	DEPT	JARA	MARC
KAPA	TOPH	COPS	HEPT	JURA	NARC
NAPA	XIPH	CUPS	KEPT	KARA	
	ZEPH				

******	GARE	******	MARK	WARM	FARO
--RD	GORE	**--RG**	MURK	WORM	GIRO
******	GYRE	******	PARK	******	GYRO
BARD	HARE	BERG	PERK	**--RN**	HERO
BIRD	HERE	BURG	PORK	******	HIRO
BURD	HIRE	SURG	SARK	BARN	INRO
BYRD	INRE	******	TURK	BERN	MERO
CARD	KURE	**--RI**	WORK	BORN	MIRO
CORD	LIRE	******	YORK	BURN	MORO
CURD	LORE	ABRI	******	CORN	NERO
FORD	LURE	AERI	**--RL**	DARN	PYRO
GARD	LYRE	AGRI	******	DURN	SERO
GERD	MARE	ATRI	BIRL	EARN	TARO
GIRD	MERE	BARI	BURL	FERN	TIRO
HARD	MIRE	GERI	CARL	FIRN	TYRO
HERD	MORE	GYRI	CURL	FURN	XERO
KURD	OGRE	INRI	EARL	HORN	ZERO
LARD	PARE	KARI	FARL	KARN	******
LORD	PERE	KIRI	FURL	KERN	**--RP**
NARD	PORE	LARI	GIRL	LORN	******
NORD	PURE	LURI	HARL	MORN	BURP
PARD	PYRE	MYRI	HERL	NORN	CARP
SARD	RARE	PARI	HURL	PERN	CORP
SURD	SERE	PERI	JARL	PIRN	DORP
WARD	SIRE	PURI	JERL	PORN	HARP
WORD	SORE	SARI	KARL	SORN	LARP
YARD	SURE	SIRI	MARL	TARN	TARP
******	TARE	SORI	MERL	TERN	WARP
--RE	TIRE	TORI	PURL	TORN	ZARP
******	TORE	VARI	******	TURN	******
AARE	TYRE	WARI	**--RM**	VERN	**--RR**
ACRE	VIRE	******	******	WARN	******
AIRE	VORE	**--RJ**	BARM	WORN	BIRR
BARE	WARE	******	BERM	YARN	BURR
BORE	WERE	MARJ	CORM	******	CARR
BYRE	WIRE	******	DERM	**--RO**	DORR
CARE	WORE	**--RK**	DORM	******	DURR
CERE	YARE	******	FARM	ACRO	HERR
CORE	YORE	BARK	FIRM	AERO	PARR
CURE	******	CORK	FORM	AFRO	PURR
DARE	**--RF**	DARK	GARM	AGRO	******
DIRE	******	DIRK	GERM	BARO	**--RS**
DORE	CORF	FORK	HARM	BIRO	******
EIRE	KERF	HARK	HERM	CARO	AIRS
EYRE	SERF	JERK	JERM	CERO	BARS
FARE	SURF	KIRK	NORM	DURO	BURS
FIRE	TURF	LARK	PERM	EBRO	CARS
FORE	WARF	LURK	TERM	EURO	CURS
	ZARF				

DORS
EARS
ERRS
FIRS
FURS
GARS
HERS
JARS
KORS
LARS
MARS
MIRS
MORS
OARS
OURS
PARS
SERS
SIRS
TARS
TORS
VERS
WARS
******

--RT
******
BART
BERT
BORT
BURT
CART
CERT
CURT
DART
DIRT
FORT
GIRT
HART
HORT
HURT
KURT
MART
MORT
PART
PERT
PORT
SORT
TART
TORT

VERT
WART
WERT
WORT
******

--RU
******
ECRU
GURU
MERU
PERU
THRU
******

--RV
******
MERV
MIRV
******

--RX
******
MARX
******

--RY
******
AERY
AIRY
AWRY
BURY
CARY
DORY
EERY
EURY
EYRY
FURY
GARY
GORY
JURY
KARY
LORY
MARY
MIRY
NARY
RORY
SCRY
SPRY
TORY
VARY
VERY

WARY
WIRY
******

--RZ
******
HARZ
******

--SA
******
ANSA
BESA
ELSA
LISA
MESA
NASA
OSSA
PISA
RASA
ROSA
URSA
VASA
VISA
XOSA
******
******

--SC
******
BSSC
DESC
DISC
FISC
MASC
MISC
PISC
VISC
WISC
******

--SE
******
APSE
BASE
BISE
CASE
DOSE
DUSE
EASE
ELSE
ERSE
ESSE

FUSE
HOSE
ILSE
JOSE
LOSE
LYSE
MISE
MOSE
MUSE
NOSE
OISE
OUSE
POSE
RASE
RISE
ROSE
RUSE
VASE
VISE
WISE
******

--SH
******
BASH
BOSH
BUSH
CASH
COSH
CUSH
DASH
DISH
FASH
FISH
GASH
GOSH
GUSH
HASH
HUSH
JOSH
KISH
LASH
LUSH
MASH
MESH
MUSH
NASH
NOSH
PASH

PISH
POSH
PUSH
RASH
RESH
RUSH
SASH
TOSH
TUSH
WASH
WISH
******

--SI
******
DESI
LYSI
NISI
OSSI
******

--SK
******
BASK
BOSK
BUSK
CASK
CUSK
DESK
DISK
DUSK
HUSK
MASK
MUSK
OMSK
RISK
RUSK
SASK
TASK
TUSK
******

--SL
******
DESL
******

--SM
******
COSM
KASM

******

--SN
******
ASSN
BOSN
******

--SO
******
ALSO
MESO
MISO
NASO
NOSO
PESO
PISO
SOSO
VASO
VISO
******

--SP
******
CUSP
GASP
HASP
INSP
LISP
RASP
WASP
WISP
******

--SR
******
USSR
******

--SS
******
BASS
BESS
BOSS
BUSS
CASS
CESS
COSS
CUSS
DESS
DOSS
FASS
FESS

FOSS	ERST	******	BATE	VOTE	HOTI
FUSS	FAST	**--SY**	BITE	WATE	LATI
HISS	FEST	******	BUTE	WOTE	LETI
HUSS	FIST	BUSY	CATE	******	RATI
JASS	GEST	COSY	CITE	**--TH**	ROTI
JESS	GIST	EASY	COTE	******	SETI
JOSS	GUST	ISSY	CUTE	ACTH	SITI
KISS	HAST	NOSY	CYTE	ANTH	TITI
KOSS	HEST	OPSY	DATE	AUTH	TOTI
LASS	HIST	POSY	DOTE	BATH	VITI
LESS	HOST	ROSY	ENTE	BETH	YETI
LISS	INST	******	ESTE	BOTH	ZATI
LOSS	JEST	**--TA**	ETTE	CATH	******
MASS	JUST	******	FATE	DOTH	**--TL**
MESS	KIST	ACTA	FETE	ESTH	******
MISS	LAST	ALTA	GATE	GATH	NATL
MOSS	LEST	ANTA	HATE	GOTH	ROTL
MUSS	LIST	ATTA	HOTE	HATH	******
NESS	LOST	BETA	JETE	HETH	**--TN**
PASS	LUST	BOTA	JUTE	HOTH	******
PUSS	MAST	CATA	KATE	JATH	ATTN
ROSS	MIST	DATA	KITE	JETH	******
RUSS	MOST	DITA	LATE	KITH	**--TO**
SASS	MUST	ETTA	LITE	LATH	******
SESS	NAST	FATA	LOTE	LITH	ALTO
SUSS	NEST	GATA	LUTE	LOTH	ATTO
TASS	OAST	IOTA	LYTE	LUTH	AUTO
TESS	OLST	LUTA	MATE	MATH	CATO
TOSS	OUST	META	METE	METH	CYTO
VISS	PAST	NITA	MITE	MOTH	ECTO
******	PEST	OCTA	MOTE	MSTH	ENTO
--ST	POST	PITA	MUTE	MUTH	INTO
******	REST	RATA	NATE	MYTH	JATO
ASST	RUST	RITA	NOTE	OATH	KETO
AUST	TEST	ROTA	OSTE	ORTH	KOTO
BAST	VAST	RUTA	PATE	PATH	LETO
BEST	VEST	SETA	PETE	PITH	NATO
BUST	WAST	TATA	RATE	RATH	NOTO
CAST	WEST	VITA	RETE	RUTH	OCTO
CEST	WIST	WETA	RITE	SETH	ONTO
CIST	XYST	ZETA	ROTE	TETH	OTTO
COST	ZEST	******	RUTE	WITH	PITO
CYST	******	**--TC**	SATE	******	RATO
DIST	**--SU**	******	SITE	**--TI**	SITO
DOST	******	ROTC	TATE	******	TITO
DUST	JESU	******	TETE	ALTI	UNTO
EAST	ZASU	**--TE**	TOTE	ANTI	VETO
ELST		ANTE	VITE	ASTI	
		ARTE			

******	NITS	******	******	SLUG	GRUM
--TR	NUTS	**--TU**	**--UD**	SMUG	NEUM
******	OATS	******	******	SNUG	ODUM
ASTR	OPTS	ATTU	CHUD	THUG	OVUM
METR	ORTS	KETU	CRUD	ZOUG	PLUM
NATR	OUTS	SITU	FEUD	******	RHUM
NITR	PATS	TUTU	GAUD	**--UI**	SCUM
PETR	PETS	******	LAUD	******	SLUM
TETR	PITS	**--TY**	LEUD	AQUI	STUM
VITR	POTS	******	LOUD	EQUI	SWUM
******	PUTS	ARTY	MAUD	ETUI	******
--TS	RATS	ATTY	PHUD	MAUI	**--UN**
******	RETS	CITY	PUUD	******	******
ACTS	ROTS	COTY	SAUD	**--UJ**	FAUN
AMTS	RUTS	DOTY	SCUD	******	LAUN
ANTS	SETS	DUTY	SPUD	CLUJ	MAUN
ARTS	SITS	KATY	STUD	******	NOUN
BATS	SOTS	PITY	THUD	**--UK**	SHUN
BETS	TATS	XNTY	YOUD	******	SPUN
BITS	TITS	******	******	CAUK	STUN
BOTS	TOTS	**--TZ**	**--UE**	LEUK	TSUN
BUTS	UMTS	******	******	SAUK	******
CATS	VATS	BATZ	AGUE	TRUK	**--UO**
COTS	VETS	FITZ	BLUE	WAUK	******
CUTS	WETS	METZ	CLUE	******	FLUO
DOTS	WITS	UNTZ	COUE	**--UL**	******
EATS	XRTS	******	FLUE	******	**--UP**
EFTS	******	**--UA**	GLUE	AOUL	******
FATS		******	MOUE	CAUL	COUP
FITS	**--TT**	AGUA	NIUE	ELUL	LOUP
GATS	******	AQUA	PRUE	FOUL	ROUP
GETS	BATT	ECUA	ROUE	GAUL	SCUP
GUTS	BITT	SKUA	SLUE	HAUL	SOUP
HATS	BOTT	******	SPUE	MAUL	YAUP
HITS	BUTT	**--UB**	TRUE	OCUL	YOUP
HUTS	GATT	******	******	PAUL	******
JETS	KITT	BLUB	**--UF**	SAUL	**--UR**
JOTS	LETT	CHUB	******	SHUL	******
JUTS	LOTT	CLUB	OEUF	SOUL	AMUR
KITS	MATT	DAUB	POUF	WAUL	BLUR
LETS	MITT	DRUB	******	******	CHUR
LOTS	MOTT	FLUB	**--UG**	**--UM**	DOUR
MATS	MUTT	GRUB	******	******	FOUR
MOTS	NATT	SLUB	CHUG	ALUM	GAUR
MSTS	NOTT	SNUB	DOUG	ARUM	HOUR
MUTS	PITT	STUB	DRUG	CHUM	KNUR
NATS	PUTT	******	JOUG	DRUM	LOUR
NETS	WATT	**--UC**	PLUG	GLUM	NEUR
		******			
		EDUC			
		LEUC			

POUR	PHUT	******	******	******	******
SAUR	POUT	--VE	--VP	--WI	--WS
SLUR	ROUT	******	******	******	******
SOUR	SCUT	CAVE	RSVP	KIWI	BOWS
SPUR	SHUT	COVE	******	******	CAWS
TAUR	SLUT	DAVE	--VS	--WK	COWS
TOUR	SMUT	DIVE	******	******	DAWS
YOUR	TAUT	DOVE	BEVS	DAWK	DEWS
******	TOUT	FIVE	DEVS	GAWK	HAWS
--US	******	GAVE	REVS	GOWK	HEWS
******	--UW	GIVE	TAVS	HAWK	JAWS
AMUS	******	GYVE	VAVS	******	JEWS
ANUS	BOUW	HAVE	******	--WL	LAWS
APUS	******	HIVE	--VT	******	LEWS
BMUS	--UX	HOVE	******	BAWL	LOWS
CRUS	******	JAVE	GOVT	BOWL	MAWS
DEUS	CRUX	JIVE	******	COWL	MEWS
DMUS	EAUX	JOVE	--VU	FOWL	MOWS
ECUS	FLUX	LAVE	******	GOWL	NEWS
EMUS	JEUX	LIVE	KIVU	HOWL	NOWS
EOUS	ROUX	LOVE	******	JOWL	PAWS
FEUS	******	MOVE	--VY	MEWL	PEWS
GNUS	--UY	NAVE	******	PAWL	POWS
ILUS	******	NEVE	BEVY	WAWL	ROWS
IOUS	JOUY	PAVE	CAVY	YAWL	SAWS
NOUS	******	RAVE	DAVY	YOWL	SEWS
ONUS	--VA	RIVE	ENVY	******	SOWS
OPUS	******	ROVE	LEVY	--WM	TAWS
PIUS	ALVA	SAVE	NAVY	******	TOWS
PLUS	CAVA	VIVE	TIVY	DAWM	VOWS
RHUS	DEVA	WAVE	WAVY	******	WOWS
SOUS	DIVA	WIVE	******	--WN	YAWS
STUS	ELVA	WOVE	--WA	******	YEWS
TAUS	JAVA	******	******	DAWN	YOWS
THUS	KAVA	--VI	IOWA	DOWN	******
URUS	KIVA	******	KAWA	FAWN	--WT
ZEUS	LAVA	BOVI	NAWA	GOWN	******
******	LEVA	DEVI	******	HEWN	NEWT
--UT	NOVA	DIVI	--WD	LAWN	NOWT
******	RIVA	LEVI	******	MOWN	******
ABUT	SIVA	NEVI	BAWD	PAWN	--WY
BOUT	SUVA	******	LEWD	SAWN	******
BRUT	VIVA	--VO	******	SEWN	DEWY
DEUT	******	******	--WE	SOWN	******
GLUT	--VD	LEVO	******	TOWN	--XA
GOUT	******	PAVO	HOWE	YAWN	******
LOUT	BLVD	RIVO	IKWE	******	COXA
NAUT	NKVD	VIVO	******	--WP	HEXA
			--WH	******	
			******	YAWP	
			YHWH		

MOXA	******	HOYS	DOZE	******	ACERB
MYXA	--YE	ITYS	FAZE	AB---	ACETO
******	******	IVYS	FUZE	******	ACHED
--XE	FAYE	JAYS	GAZE	ABACA	ACHES
******	FUYE	JOYS	HAZE	ABACI	ACIDS
LUXE	KAYE	KAYS	LAZE	ABACK	ACING
SAXE	PAYE	KEYS	LYZE	ABAFT	ACINI
******	SKYE	LAYS	MAZE	ABASE	ACITY
--XI	SNYE	MAYS	NAZE	ABASH	ACOCK
******	******	NAYS	OOZE	ABATE	ACORN
MAXI	--YL	PAYS	RAZE	ABBAS	ACOUO
SEXI	******	RAYS	SIZE	ABBES	ACRED
TAXI	AMYL	RHYS	UNZE	ABBEY	ACRES
******	ARYL	ROYS	******	ABBIE	ACRID
--XO	IDYL	SAYS	--ZI	ABBOT	ACTED
******	ODYL	SOYS	******	ABBYS	ACTIN
MYXO	PHYL	TOYS	CAZI	ABEAM	ACTOR
******	RHYL	WAYS	KAZI	ABELE	ACTUS
--XT	******	WHYS	NAZI	ABELS	ACUTE
******	--YN	******	******	ABETS	******
MIXT	******	--YT	--ZO	ABHOR	AD---
NEXT	GWYN	******	******	ABIBS	******
SEXT	******	PHYT	BOZO	ABIDE	ADAGE
TEXT	--YO	******	******	ABIEL	ADAHS
******	******	--YU	--ZY	ABIES	ADAMS
--XY	CRYO	******	******	ABLER	ADAPT
******	ENYO	VAYU	COZY	ABNER	ADDAX
DOXY	KAYO	******	DOZY	ABODE	ADDED
FOXY	MAYO	--YX	HAZY	ABOHM	ADDER
PIXY	TOYO	******	IZZY	ABOIL	ADDIE
ROXY	YOYO	ONYX	LAZY	ABOMA	ADDLE
SEXY	******	ORYX	MAZY	ABOMB	ADDYS
TAXY	--YS	PNYX	OOZY	ABORT	ADEEM
WAXY	******	STYX	SIZY	ABOUT	ADELA
******	ALYS	******	SUZY	ABOVE	ADELE
--YA	AMYS	--ZA	******	ABRAM	ADENI
******	BAYS	******	--ZZ	ABRIS	ADENO
BAYA	BEYS	DAZA	******	ABUSE	ADEPT
CUYA	BOYS	GAZA	BUZZ	ABUTS	ADIEU
GAYA	BUYS	GIZA	FIZZ	ABYSM	ADIGE
GOYA	CAYS	LIZA	FUZZ	ABYSS	ADIOS
HAYA	DAYS	ONZA	JAZZ	******	ADITS
MAYA	DEYS	ZUZA	PIZZ	AC---	ADLAI
SOYA	FAYS	******	RAZZ	******	ADLER
YAYA	FOYS	--ZE	ZIZZ	ACCEL	ADLIB
******	GAYS	******		ACCRA	ADMAN
--YD	GUYS	ADZE	AA---	ACEAE	ADMEN
******	HAYS	DAZE	AALII	ACEAN	ADMEX
BOYD			AARON		

ADMIN	AGAZE	ALAIN	ALIVE	AMANA	ANDRE
ADMIT	AGENT	ALAMO	ALKYL	AMASS	ANDRO
ADMIX	AGGER	ALAND	ALLAH	AMATE	ANDYS
ADOBE	AGGIE	ALANS	ALLAN	AMATI	ANEAR
ADOLF	AGHAS	ALARM	ALLAY	AMAZE	ANELE
ADOPT	AGILE	ALARY	ALLEN	AMBER	ANEMO
ADORE	AGING	ALATE	ALLEY	AMBIT	ANENT
ADORN	AGIOS	ALBAN	ALLIE	AMBLE	ANGEL
ADOWA	AGIST	ALBAS	ALLIN	AMBOS	ANGER
ADULT	AGLEE	ALBEE	ALLIS	AMBRY	ANGIO
ADUNC	AGLET	ALBIN	ALLOT	AMEBA	ANGLE
ADUST	AGLEY	ALBUM	ALLOW	AMEER	ANGLO
ADUWA	AGLOW	ALCAN	ALLOY	AMEND	ANGRY
ADYTA	AGNES	ALDAN	ALLYL	AMENS	ANGST
ADZES	AGNIS	ALDEN	ALMAH	AMENT	ANGUS
******	AGONY	ALDER	ALMAS	AMIAS	ANILE
	AGORA	ALDIS	ALMUD	AMICE	ANILS
AE---	AGREE	ALDOL	ALMUG	AMIDE	ANIMA
******	AGUES	ALDOS	ALOES	AMIDO	ANIME
AECIA	******	ALDUS	ALOFT	AMIEL	ANION
AEDES		ALECK	ALOHA	AMIES	ANISE
AEGIR	AH---	ALECS	ALOIN	AMIGO	ANISO
AEGIS	AHEAD	ALEFS	ALOIS	AMINE	ANITA
AEMIA	******	ALEPH	ALONE	AMINO	ANJOU
AEONS	AI---	ALERT	ALONG	AMIRS	ANKHS
AERIE	******	ALEUT	ALOOF	AMISH	ANKLE
AESIR	AIDAS	ALEXA	ALOUD	AMISS	ANKUS
AESOP	AIDED	ALFIE	ALPHA	AMITY	ANLAS
AETAT	AIDER	ALGAE	ALPHY	AMMAN	ANNAL
******	AIDES	ALGAL	ALTAI	AMMON	ANNAM
AF---	AIKEN	ALGER	ALTAR	AMNIA	ANNAS
******	AILED	ALGIA	ALTAS	AMOLE	ANNES
AFFIX	AIMED	ALGID	ALTER	AMONG	ANNEX
AFIRE	AIMEE	ALGIE	ALTON	AMOUR	ANNIE
AFOOT	AINOS	ALGIN	ALTOS	AMPHI	ANNOY
AFORE	AINUS	ALGOL	ALUIN	AMPHR	ANNUL
AFOUL	AIRED	ALGOR	ALULA	AMPLE	ANODE
AFROS	AISLE	ALGUM	ALUMS	AMPLY	ANOMY
AFTER	AISNE	ALGYS	ALVAN	AMPUL	ANSAE
AFTRA	AITCH	ALIAS	ALVIN	AMUCK	ANSEL
******	******	ALIBI	ALWAY	AMUSE	ANTAE
AG---	AK---	ALICE	ALWIN	AMYLO	ANTAL
******	******	ALIEN	ALYCE	AMYLS	ANTED
AGAIN	AKENE	ALIFS	******	******	ANTES
AGAMA	AKRON	ALIGN	AM---	AN---	ANTHO
AGANA	******	ALIKE	******	******	ANTIC
AGAPE	AL---	ALINE	AMAHS	ANCON	ANTIS
AGATE	******	ALIST	AMAIN	ANDES	ANTON
AGAVE	ALACK				
	ALADA				

ANTRA	ARDEB	ARTAL	******	AUXIL	******
ANVIL	ARDEN	ARTEL	**AT---**	AUXIN	**AZ---**
ANZAC	ARDOR	ARTER	******	******	******
ANZIO	AREAE	ARTHR	ATAXY	**AV---**	AZANS
******	AREAL	ARTIC	ATHOS	******	AZINE
AO---	AREAS	ARTIE	ATILT	AVAIL	AZOIC
******	ARECA	ARTIS	ATION	AVARS	AZOLE
AORTA	AREIC	ARTUR	ATIVE	AVAST	AZONS
******	ARENA	ARUBA	ATLAS	AVENS	AZOTE
AP---	ARENT	ARUMS	ATMAN	AVERS	AZOTH
******	ARETE	ARVAL	ATOLL	AVERT	AZTEC
APACE	ARGAL	ARYAN	ATOMS	AVERY	AZURE
APART	ARGIL	******	ATONE	AVIAN	******
APEAK	ARGOL	**AS---**	ATONY	AVION	**BA---**
APERY	ARGON	******	ATORY	AVISO	******
APHID	ARGOS	ASCAP	ATPAR	AVOID	BAAED
APHIS	ARGOT	ASCOT	ATRIA	AVOIR	BABAR
APIAN	ARGUE	ASCUS	ATRIP	AVOWS	BABAS
APING	ARGUS	ASHEN	ATTAR	AVRIL	BABEL
APISH	ARIAN	ASHER	ATTIC	******	BABER
APNEA	ARIAS	ASHES	ATTIS	**AW---**	BABES
APORT	ARICA	ASHUR	ATTYS	******	BABOO
APPAL	ARIEL	ASIAN	******	AWAIT	BABUL
APPEL	ARIES	ASIDE	**AU---**	AWAKE	BACCI
APPLE	ARILS	ASKED	******	AWARD	BACHE
APPLY	ARION	ASKER	AUDAD	AWARE	BACKS
APRIL	ARISE	ASKEW	AUDEN	AWASH	BACON
APRON	ARIUM	ASPCA	AUDIE	AWFUL	BACUP
APSES	ARIUS	ASPEN	AUDIO	AWING	BADEN
APSIS	ARLEN	ASPER	AUDIT	AWNED	BADGE
APTER	ARLES	ASPIC	AUGER	AWOKE	BADLY
APTLY	ARMED	ASPIS	AUGHT	******	BAFFS
******	ARMET	ASSAI	AUGUR	**AX---**	BAFFY
AQ---	ARMOR	ASSAM	AULIC	******	BAGEL
******	ARNIE	ASSAY	AULIS	AXIAL	BAGGY
AQABA	AROID	ASSES	AUNTS	AXILE	BAHAI
AQUAE	AROMA	ASSET	AUNTY	AXILS	BAHIA
AQUAS	AROSE	ASSNS	AURAE	AXING	BAHTS
******	ARPAD	ASSOC	AURAL	AXIOM	BAILS
AR---	ARPEN	ASSTS	AURAS	AXLED	BAIRD
******	ARRAN	ASSYR	AUREI	AXLES	BAIRN
ARABS	ARRAS	ASTER	AURES	AXMAN	BAITS
ARABY	ARRAY	ASTIR	AURIC	AXMEN	BAIZE
ARBOR	ARRIS	ASTON	AURIS	AXONE	BAKED
ARCED	ARROW	ASTOR	AURUM	AXONS	BAKER
ARCHI	ARSES	ASTRO	AUSTL	******	BAKES
ARCHY	ARSIS	ASWAN	AUTOS	**AY---**	BALAS
ARCUS	ARSON	ASYLA	AUTRY	******	BALDR
		ASYUT		AYAHS	
				AYDIN	
				AYINS	

BALED	BASIS	BECKS	BEREA	BIFFS	BLAIN
BALER	BASKS	BECKY	BERET	BIFFY	BLAKE
BALES	BASLE	BEDEW	BERGS	BIFID	BLAME
BALKS	BASON	BEDIM	BERIA	BIGHT	BLANC
BALKY	BASRA	BEEBE	BERME	BIGLY	BLAND
BALLS	BASSI	BEECH	BERMS	BIGOT	BLANK
BALMS	BASSO	BEEFS	BERNE	BIHAR	BLARE
BALMY	BASTE	BEEFY	BERRA	BIJOU	BLASE
BALSA	BATAN	BEEPS	BERRY	BIKES	BLAST
BALTS	BATCH	BEERS	BERTA	BIKOL	BLATS
BAMBI	BATED	BEERY	BERTH	BILBO	BLAZE
BANAL	BATEN	BEETS	BERTS	BILES	BLDGS
BANAT	BATES	BEFIT	BERTY	BILGE	BLEAK
BANDA	BATHE	BEFOG	BERYL	BILGY	BLEAR
BANDS	BATHO	BEGAD	BESET	BILKS	BLEAT
BANDY	BATHS	BEGAN	BESOM	BILLS	BLEBS
BANFF	BATHY	BEGAT	BESOT	BILLY	BLEED
BANGS	BATIK	BEGET	BESSY	BINAL	BLEEP
BANJO	BATON	BEGIN	BESTS	BINDS	BLEND
BANKS	BATTY	BEGOT	BETAS	BINES	BLENT
BANNS	BAULK	BEGUM	BETEL	BINET	BLESS
BANTU	BAUME	BEGUN	BETHS	BINGE	BLEST
BARBS	BAWDS	BEHAN	BETON	BINGO	BLIGH
BARCA	BAWDY	BEIGE	BETSO	BINIT	BLIMP
BARDE	BAWLS	BEING	BETSY	BIOTA	BLIND
BARDS	BAYED	BEIRA	BETTE	BIPED	BLINK
BARED	BAYOU	BELAY	BETTY	BIPOD	BLIPS
BARER	******	BELCH	BEULA	BIRCH	BLISS
BARES	**BE---**	BELEM	BEVAN	BIRDS	BLITZ
BARGE	******	BELGA	BEVEL	BIRLE	BLOAT
BARIC	BEACH	BELIE	BEVIN	BIRLS	BLOBS
BARIT	BEADS	BELLA	BEZEL	BIRRS	BLOCK
BARKS	BEADY	BELLE	******	BIRTH	BLOCS
BARKY	BEAKS	BELLS	**BH---**	BISES	BLOIS
BARMY	BEALL	BELLY	******	BISON	BLOKE
BARNS	BEAMS	BELOW	BHANG	BISSE	BLOND
BARON	BEAMY	BELTS	******	BITCH	BLOOD
BARRE	BEANO	BENCH	**BI---**	BITER	BLOOM
BARRY	BEANS	BENDS	******	BITES	BLOTS
BARTH	BEARD	BENDY	BIALY	BITTS	BLOWN
BARYE	BEARS	BENES	BIBBS	BIZET	BLOWS
BASAL	BEAST	BENET	BIBLE	******	BLOWY
BASED	BEATA	BENIN	BICES	**BL---**	BLUED
BASEL	BEATS	BENJY	BIDDY	******	BLUER
BASES	BEAUS	BENNE	BIDED	BLABS	BLUES
BASIC	BEAUT	BENNY	BIDES	BLACK	BLUET
BASIL	BEAUX	BENUE	BIDET	BLADE	BLUFF
BASIN	BEBOP	BERAR	BIERS	BLAHS	BLUNT

BLURB	BONNY	BOWED	BREAK	BRUTE	BURLS
BLURS	BONUS	BOWEL	BREAM	BRYAN	BURLY
BLURT	BONZE	BOWER	BREDA	BRYCE	BURMA
BLUSH	BOOBS	BOWIE	BREED	******	BURNS
BLYTH	BOOBY	BOWLS	BRENT	BU---	BURNT
******	BOOED	BOWSE	BREST	******	BURPS
BM---	BOOKS	BOXED	BREVE	BUBAL	BURRO
******	BOOMS	BOXER	BREVI	BUBER	BURRS
BMEWS	BOONE	BOXES	BREWS	BUCKO	BURRY
******	BOONS	BOYAR	BRIAN	BUCKS	BURSA
BO---	BOORS	BOYDS	BRIAR	BUDDY	BURSE
******	BOOST	BOYLE	BRIBE	BUDGE	BURST
BOARD	BOOTH	BOYNE	BRICE	BUDGY	BUSBY
BOARS	BOOTS	BOZOS	BRICK	BUFFI	BUSED
BOAST	BOOTY	******	BRIDE	BUFFO	BUSES
BOATS	BOOZE	BR---	BRIEF	BUFFS	BUSHY
BOBBY	BOOZY	******	BRIER	BUFFY	BUSKS
BOCHE	BORAX	BRACE	BRIGS	BUGGY	BUSTS
BODED	BORED	BRACT	BRILL	BUGLE	BUTCH
BODES	BORER	BRADS	BRIMS	BUILD	BUTTE
BOERS	BORES	BRADY	BRINE	BUILT	BUTTS
BOGAN	BORIC	BRAES	BRING	BULBS	BUTYL
BOGEY	BORIS	BRAGE	BRINK	BULGE	BUXOM
BOGGY	BORNE	BRAGG	BRINY	BULGY	BUYER
BOGIE	BORNU	BRAGI	BRISK	BULKS	******
BOGLE	BORON	BRAGS	BROAD	BULKY	BW---
BOGOR	BORTS	BRAHE	BROCK	BULLA	******
BOGUS	BORTY	BRAID	BROIL	BULLS	BWANA
BOHEA	BORTZ	BRAIL	BROKE	BULLY	******
BOHOL	BOSCH	BRAIN	BROME	BUMPS	BY---
BOILS	BOSKS	BRAKE	BROMO	BUMPY	******
BOISE	BOSKY	BRAKY	BRONC	BUNCH	BYLAW
BOLAR	BOSOM	BRAND	BRONX	BUNCO	BYRES
BOLAS	BOSON	BRANS	BROOD	BUNDE	BYRON
BOLES	BOSSY	BRANT	BROOK	BUNDS	BYSSI
BOLLS	BOSUN	BRASH	BROOM	BUNGS	BYWAY
BOLOS	BOTCH	BRASS	BROOS	BUNKO	******
BOLTS	BOTHY	BRATS	BROTH	BUNKS	CA---
BOLUS	BOTTS	BRAVA	BROWN	BUNNS	******
BOMBE	BOUGH	BRAVE	BROWS	BUNNY	CABAL
BOMBS	BOULE	BRAVO	BRUCE	BUNTS	CABBY
BONDS	BOUND	BRAWL	BRUIN	BUOYS	CABER
BONED	BOURG	BRAWN	BRUIT	BURAN	CABIN
BONER	BOURN	BRAXY	BRUME	BURDS	CABLE
BONES	BOUSE	BRAYS	BRUNO	BURGH	CABOB
BONGO	BOUSY	BRAZA	BRUNT	BURGS	CABOT
BONGS	BOUTS	BRAZE	BRUSH	BURIN	CACAO
BONIN	BOVID	BREAD	BRUSK	BURKE	CACHE

CACTI	CANNA	CASKS	CERES	CHERT	CHOWS
CADDO	CANNY	CASTE	CERIA	CHESS	CHRIS
CADDY	CANOE	CASTS	CERIC	CHEST	CHROM
CADES	CANON	CASUS	CEROS	CHETH	CHRON
CADET	CANSO	CATCH	CESAR	CHETS	CHRYS
CADGE	CANST	CATER	CESTA	CHEVY	CHUBS
CADIS	CANTO	CATHY	CESTI	CHEWS	CHUCK
CADIZ	CANTS	CATTY	CETIC	CHEWY	CHUFA
CADRE	CAPEK	CAUCA	CETIN	CHIAN	CHUGS
CAFES	CAPER	CAULK	CETUS	CHIAS	CHUMP
CAGED	CAPES	CAULS	CEUTA	CHIBA	CHUMS
CAGES	CAPET	CAUSE	******	CHICK	CHUNK
CAGEY	CAPON	CAVED	CH---	CHICO	CHURL
CAIRD	CAPRI	CAVES	******	CHIDE	CHURN
CAIRN	CAPUA	CAVIE	CHAET	CHIEF	CHURR
CAIRO	CAPUT	CAVIL	CHAFE	CHILD	CHUTE
CAJON	CARAS	CAWED	CHAFF	CHILE	CHYLE
CAJUN	CARAT	******	CHAIN	CHILI	CHYME
CAKED	CARBO	CE---	CHAIR	CHILL	******
CAKES	CARDI	******	CHALK	CHILO	CI---
CALCI	CARDS	CEARA	CHAMP	CHIME	******
CALEB	CARED	CEASE	CHANG	CHIMP	CIBOL
CALIF	CARER	CECAL	CHANT	CHINA	CIDAL
CALIX	CARES	CECIL	CHAOS	CHINE	CIDER
CALKS	CARET	CECUM	CHAPE	CHINK	CIGAR
CALLA	CAREY	CEDAR	CHAPS	CHINO	CILIA
CALLI	CARGO	CEDED	CHAPT	CHINS	CIMEX
CALLS	CARIB	CEDES	CHARD	CHIOS	CINCH
CALMS	CARLA	CEIBA	CHARE	CHIPS	CINDY
CALPE	CARLE	CEILS	CHARM	CHIRM	CIONS
CALVE	CARLO	CELIA	CHARO	CHIRO	CIRCA
CALYX	CARLS	CELIE	CHARS	CHIRP	CIRCE
CAMEL	CAROB	CELLA	CHART	CHIRR	CIRRI
CAMEO	CAROL	CELLO	CHARY	CHITA	CIRRO
CAMES	CAROM	CELLS	CHASE	CHITS	CISCO
CAMPI	CARPI	CELOM	CHASM	CHIVE	CISSY
CAMPO	CARPO	CELTS	CHATS	CHLOE	CISTS
CAMPS	CARPS	CENIS	CHAWS	CHLOR	CITED
CAMPY	CARRY	CENON	CHEAP	CHOCK	CITES
CAMUS	CARTE	CENSE	CHEAT	CHOIR	CITRA
CANAD	CARTS	CENTI	CHECK	CHOKE	CIVET
CANAL	CARVE	CENTO	CHEEK	CHOKY	CIVIC
CANDY	CARYO	CENTR	CHEEP	CHOLE	CIVIL
CANEA	CARYS	CENTS	CHEER	CHOPS	******
CANED	CASCO	CEORL	CHEFS	CHORD	CL---
CANER	CASED	CERAM	CHELA	CHORE	******
CANES	CASES	CERAT	CHEMI	CHORO	CLACK
CANIS	CASEY	CERED	CHEMO	CHOSE	CLAIM

CLAMP	CLOUD	COKER	COOER	COULD	CRAZE
CLAMS	CLOUT	COKES	COOEY	COUNT	CRAZY
CLANG	CLOVE	COKEY	COOKS	COUPE	CREAK
CLANK	CLOWN	COLAS	COOKY	COUPS	CREAM
CLANS	CLOYS	COLDS	COOLS	COURT	CRECY
CLAPS	CLUBS	COLES	COOMB	COUTH	CREDO
CLARA	CLUCK	COLIC	COONS	COVED	CREED
CLARE	CLUED	COLIN	COOPS	COVEN	CREEK
CLARK	CLUES	COLLY	COOPT	COVER	CREEL
CLARO	CLUMP	COLNE	COOTS	COVES	CREEP
CLARY	CLUNG	COLON	COPAL	COVET	CREES
CLASH	CLUNY	COLOR	COPEC	COVEY	CREME
CLASP	CLYDE	COLTS	COPED	COWED	CREON
CLASS	******	COLZA	COPER	COWER	CREPE
CLAWS	CO---	COMAE	COPES	COWES	CREPT
CLAYS	******	COMAL	COPRA	COWLS	CRESC
CLEAN	COACH	COMAS	COPRO	COWRY	CRESS
CLEAR	COALS	COMBO	COPSE	COXAE	CREST
CLEAT	COALY	COMBS	COPTS	COXAL	CRETE
CLEEK	COAST	COMDR	CORAL	COXED	CREWE
CLEFS	COATI	COMDT	CORAS	COXES	CREWS
CLEFT	COATS	COMER	CORBY	COYLY	CRIBS
CLEMS	COBBS	COMES	CORDS	COYPU	CRICK
CLEON	COBIA	COMET	CORED	COZEN	CRIED
CLERK	COBLE	COMFY	CORER	******	CRIER
CLEWS	COBRA	COMIC	CORES	CR---	CRIES
CLICK	COCAS	COMMA	CORFE	******	CRIME
CLIFF	COCCI	COMPO	CORFU	CRAAL	CRIMP
CLIMB	COCKS	COMTE	CORGI	CRABS	CRISP
CLIME	COCKY	COMUS	CORIA	CRACK	CROAK
CLINE	COCOA	CONCH	CORKS	CRACY	CROAT
CLING	COCOS	CONED	CORKY	CRAFT	CROCE
CLINK	CODAS	CONES	CORMS	CRAGS	CROCI
CLINO	CODED	CONEY	CORNS	CRAIG	CROCK
CLINT	CODER	CONGA	CORNU	CRAKE	CROFT
CLIOS	CODES	CONGE	CORNY	CRAMP	CROIX
CLIPS	CODEX	CONGO	COROT	CRAMS	CRONE
CLIVE	COEDS	CONIC	CORPS	CRANE	CRONY
CLOAK	COELE	CONIO	CORSE	CRANI	CROOK
CLOCK	COELO	CONKS	COSEK	CRANK	CROON
CLODS	COENO	CONNY	COSMO	CRAPE	CROPS
CLOGS	COGON	CONTD	COSTA	CRAPS	CRORE
CLONE	COHAN	CONTE	COSTO	CRASH	CROSS
CLONS	COIFS	CONTO	COSTS	CRASS	CROUP
CLOPS	COIGN	CONTR	COTES	CRATE	CROWD
CLOSE	COILS	CONUS	COTTA	CRAVE	CROWN
CLOTH	COINS	COOED	COUCH	CRAWL	CROWS
CLOTS	COKED	COOEE	COUGH	CRAWS	CROZE

CRUCI	CURER	******	DAVES	DEISM	DEWAN
CRUDE	CURES	DA---	DAVEY	DEIST	DEWED
CRUEL	CURIA	******	DAVID	DEITY	DEWEY
CRUET	CURIE	DACCA	DAVIE	DEKED	DEXTR
CRUMB	CURIO	DACES	DAVIS	DEKES	******
CRUMP	CURLS	DACHA	DAVIT	DELAY	DH---
CRUOR	CURLY	DACIA	DAVOS	DELED	******
CRURA	CURRY	DADDY	DAVYS	DELES	DHAKS
CRUSE	CURSE	DAFFY	DAWKS	DELFT	DHOLE
CRUSH	CURST	DAGAN	DAWNS	DELHI	DHOLI
CRUST	CURVE	DAILY	DAZED	DELIA	DHOTI
CRYPT	CURVI	DAIRY	DAZES	DELLA	DHOWS
******	CUSEC	DAISY	******	DELLS	******
CT---	CUSHY	DAKAR	DE---	DELOS	DI---
******	CUSKS	DALAI	******	DELTA	******
CTENO	CUSPS	DALER	DEALS	DELVE	DIALS
******	CUSSO	DALES	DEALT	DEMES	DIANA
CU---	CUTCH	DALLY	DEANE	DEMIT	DIANE
******	CUTER	DAMAN	DEANS	DEMOB	DIARY
CUBAN	CUTEY	DAMES	DEARS	DEMON	DIAZO
CUBBY	CUTIE	DAMNS	DEARY	DEMOS	DICED
CUBEB	CUTIN	DAMON	DEATH	DEMUR	DICER
CUBED	CUTIS	DAMPS	DEBAG	DENDR	DICEY
CUBES	CUTTY	DANAE	DEBAR	DENEB	DICHO
CUBIC	CUTUP	DANCE	DEBBY	DENES	DICKS
CUBIT	******	DANDY	DEBIT	DENIM	DICKY
CUDDY	CY---	DANES	DEBTS	DENIS	DICTA
CUFFS	******	DANGS	DEBUG	DENNY	DIDNT
CUING	CYANO	DANNY	DEBUT	DENSE	DIDOS
CUISH	CYCAD	DANTE	DECAL	DENTI	DIDST
CULCH	CYCLE	DARED	DECAY	DENTO	DIEGO
CULET	CYCLO	DARER	DECIM	DENTS	DIENE
CULEX	CYLIX	DARES	DECKS	DENYS	DIETS
CULLS	CYMAE	DARIC	DECOR	DEOXY	DIGIT
CULMS	CYMAR	DARKY	DECOY	DEPOT	DIJON
CULPA	CYMES	DARNS	DECRY	DEPTH	DIKED
CULTI	CYMRI	DARTS	DEDAL	DERBY	DIKER
CULTS	CYMRY	DASHY	DEEDS	DEREK	DIKES
CUMIN	CYNIC	DATAL	DEEMS	DERMA	DILDO
CUPEL	CYRIL	DATED	DEEPS	DERMO	DILYS
CUPID	CYRUS	DATER	DEFER	DERRY	DIMER
CUPPY	CYSTI	DATES	DEFIS	DESEX	DIMES
CUPRO	CYSTO	DATTO	DEFOE	DESKS	DIMLY
CURBS	CYSTS	DATUM	DEGAS	DETER	DINAH
CURCH	******	DAUBS	DEGUM	DEUCE	DINAR
CZ---	DAUBY	DEICE	DEVAS	DINED
CURDS	******	DAUBY	DEICE	DEVAS	DINED
CURDY	CZARS	DAUNT	DEIFY	DEVIL	DINER
CURED	CZECH	DAVAO	DEIGN	DEVON	DINES

DINGO	DODGY	DOSED	DRAVE	DUANE	******
DINGS	DODOS	DOSER	DRAWL	DUBAI	**DW---**
DINGY	DOERS	DOSES	DRAWN	DUBHE	******
DINKA	DOEST	DOTED	DRAWS	DUCAL	DWARF
DINKY	DOETH	DOTER	DRAYS	DUCAT	DWELL
DINTS	DOFFS	DOTES	DREAD	DUCHY	DWELT
DIODE	DOGES	DOTTY	DREAM	DUCKS	******
DIONE	DOGGY	DOUAI	DREAR	DUCKY	**DY---**
DIPLO	DOGIE	DOUAY	DREGS	DUCTS	******
DIPPY	DOGMA	DOUBT	DRESS	DUDES	DYING
DIRCK	DOILY	DOUGH	DREST	DUELS	DYLAN
DIRER	DOING	DOUGS	DREWS	DUETS	******
DIRGE	DOITS	DOURA	DRIBS	DUFFS	**EA---**
DIRKS	DOLCE	DOURY	DRIED	DUKES	******
DIRTY	DOLED	DOUSE	DRIER	DULCE	EADIE
DISCI	DOLES	DOVAP	DRIES	DULCY	EAGER
DISCO	DOLLS	DOVER	DRIFT	DULIA	EAGLE
DISCS	DOLLY	DOVES	DRILL	DULLS	EAGRE
DISHY	DOLOR	DOWDY	DRILY	DULLY	EAMON
DISKO	DOLPH	DOWEL	DRINK	DULSE	EARED
DISKS	DOLTS	DOWER	DRIPS	DUMAS	EARLE
DITAS	DOMED	DOWNS	DRIPT	DUMMY	EARLS
DITCH	DOMES	DOWNY	DRIVE	DUMPS	EARLY
DITTO	DOMIC	DOWRY	DROIT	DUMPY	EARNS
DITTY	DONAR	DOWSE	DROLL	DUNCE	EARTH
DIVAN	DONAS	DOYEN	DROME	DUNES	EASED
DIVAS	DONEE	DOYLE	DRONE	DUNGS	EASEL
DIVED	DONNA	DOYLY	DROOL	DUNGY	EASES
DIVER	DONNE	DOZED	DROOP	DUNKS	EATEN
DIVES	DONOR	DOZEN	DROPS	DUOMI	EATER
DIVOT	DONTS	DOZER	DROPT	DUOMO	EAVES
DIVVY	DOOLY	DOZES	DROSS	DUPED	******
DIWAN	DOOMS	******	DROVE	DUPER	**EB---**
DIXIE	DOORN	**DR---**	DROWN	DUPES	******
DIXIT	DOORS	******	DRUBS	DUPLE	EBBED
DIZEN	DOPED	DRABS	DRUGS	DURAL	EBOAT
DIZZY	DOPES	DRACO	DRUID	DURER	EBONS
******	DOPEY	DRAFF	DRUMS	DUROS	EBONY
DO---	DORAS	DRAFT	DRUNK	DURRA	******
******	DORIC	DRAGS	DRUPE	DURST	**EC---**
DOALL	DORIS	DRAIL	DRURY	DURUM	******
DOBBY	DORMS	DRAIN	DRUSE	DUSKS	ECHIN
DOBIE	DORMY	DRAKE	DRYAD	DUSKY	ECLAT
DOBLA	DORRS	DRAMA	DRYER	DUSTS	ECOLE
DOBRA	DORSA	DRAMS	DRYLY	DUSTY	******
DOCKS	DORSI	DRANK	******	DUTCH	**ED---**
DODEC	DORSO	DRAPE	**DU---**		******
DODGE	DORUS	DRAVA	******		EDDAS
			DUADS	DUALA	EDDIC

EDDIE	******	EMBOW	******	ERUCT	EVERY
EDEMA	**EL---**	EMBRY	**EO---**	ERUPT	EVICT
EDGAR	******	EMBUS	******	ERWIN	EVILS
EDGED	ELAEO	EMCEE	EOLIC	******	EVITA
EDGES	ELAIN	EMDEN	EOLUS	**ES---**	EVOKE
EDICT	ELAIO	EMEER	EOSIN	******	******
EDIES	ELAND	EMEND	******	ESHER	**EW---**
EDIFY	ELATE	EMERY	**EP---**	ESKER	******
EDILE	ELBOW	EMEUS	******	ESQUE	EWERS
EDINA	ELDER	EMILE	EPACT	ESSAY	EWING
EDITH	ELECT	EMILS	EPEES	ESSEN	******
EDITS	ELEGY	EMILY	EPHAH	ESSES	**EX---**
EDNAS	ELEMI	EMIRS	EPHOD	ESSEX	******
EDRED	ELENA	EMITS	EPHOR	ESSIE	EXACT
EDSEL	ELFIN	EMMAS	EPICS	ESTAR	EXALT
EDUCE	ELGAR	EMMER	EPOCH	ESTER	EXAMS
EDUCT	ELGIN	EMMET	EPODE	ESTES	EXCEL
EDWIN	ELIAS	EMMIE	EPOXY	ESTOP	EXECS
******	ELIDE	EMMYS	EPSOM	******	EXERT
EE---	ELIHU	EMORY	******	**ET---**	EXILE
******	ELIOT	EMOTE	**EQ---**	******	EXIST
EERIE	ELISE	EMPTY	******	ETAPE	EXITS
******	ELITE	******	EQUAL	ETHAN	EXPEL
EF---	ELIZA	**EN---**	EQUIP	ETHEL	EXTOL
******	ELLAS	******	******	ETHER	EXTRA
EFFIE	ELLEN	ENACT	**ER---**	ETHIC	EXUDE
******	ELLIE	ENARE	******	ETHNO	EXULT
EG---	ELLIS	ENATE	ERASE	ETHOS	EXURB
******	ELMAN	ENCYC	ERATO	ETHYL	******
EGEAN	ELMER	ENDED	ERECT	ETNAS	**EY---**
EGEST	ELOIN	ENDOW	ERGOT	ETTAS	******
EGGAR	ELOPE	ENDUE	ERICA	ETTIE	EYDIE
EGGED	ELSAS	ENEAS	ERICH	ETUDE	EYING
EGGER	ELSIE	ENEMA	ERICS	ETUIS	EYRAS
EGRET	ELTON	ENEMY	ERIES	ETYMA	EYRIE
EGYPT	ELUDE	ENIDS	ERIKA	******	EYRIR
******	ELVAN	ENJOY	ERIKS	**EU---**	******
EI---	ELVER	ENNEA	ERLAU	******	**EZ---**
******	ELVES	ENNUI	ERMAS	EULER	******
EIDER	ELVIN	ENOCH	ERNES	EURUS	EZRAS
EIGHT	ELWIN	ENOLA	ERNIE	******	******
EIMER	******	ENOLS	ERNST	**EV---**	**FA---**
******	**EM---**	ENROL	ERODE	******	******
EJ---	******	ENSUE	EROSE	EVADE	FABLE
******	EMBAR	ENTER	ERRED	EVANS	FACED
EJECT	EMBAY	ENTIA	ERROL	EVENS	FACER
******	EMBED	ENTOM	ERROR	EVENT	FACES
EK---	EMBER	ENTRY	ERSES	EVERT	FACET
******		ENVOY			
EKING					

FACIA	FAVOR	FERRI	FILTH	FLAKY	FLOWS
FACTS	FAVUS	FERRO	FILUM	FLAME	FLOYD
FADDY	FAWNS	FERRY	FINAL	FLAMS	FLUBS
FADED	FAXED	FESSE	FINCH	FLAMY	FLUES
FADES	FAXES	FETAL	FINDS	FLANK	FLUFF
FAGOT	FAYAL	FETCH	FINED	FLANS	FLUID
FAILS	FAYED	FETED	FINER	FLAPS	FLUKE
FAINT	FAYES	FETES	FINES	FLARE	FLUKY
FAIRS	FAZED	FETID	FINIS	FLASH	FLUME
FAIRY	FAZES	FETOR	FINKS	FLASK	FLUMP
FAITH	******	FETUS	FINNS	FLATS	FLUNG
FAKED	**FE---**	FEUAR	FINNY	FLAWS	FLUNK
FAKER	******	FEUDS	FIONA	FLAWY	FLUOR
FAKES	FEARS	FEUED	FIORD	FLAXY	FLUSH
FAKIR	FEASE	FEVER	FIQUE	FLAYS	FLUTE
FALLS	FEAST	FEWER	FIRED	FLEAM	FLUTY
FALSE	FEATS	******	FIRER	FLEAS	FLYBY
FAMED	FEBRI	**FI---**	FIRES	FLECK	FLYER
FANCY	FECAL	******	FIRMS	FLEER	******
FANGA	FECES	FIATS	FIRNS	FLEES	**FO---**
FANGS	FECIT	FIBER	FIRRY	FLEET	******
FANNY	FEDOR	FIBRE	FIRST	FLESH	FOALS
FANON	FEEDS	FIBRO	FIRTH	FLEWS	FOAMS
FANOS	FEELS	FICES	FISCS	FLEXI	FOAMY
FANUM	FEEZE	FICHE	FISHY	FLICK	FOCAL
FARAD	FEIGN	FICHU	FISTS	FLIED	FOCUS
FARAH	FEINT	FIDEL	FITCH	FLIER	FOEHN
FARCE	FEIST	FIEFS	FITLY	FLIES	FOGEY
FARCY	FELID	FIELD	FIUME	FLING	FOGGY
FARED	FELIX	FIEND	FIVER	FLINT	FOILS
FARER	FELLS	FIERY	FIVES	FLIPS	FOISM
FARES	FELLY	FIFED	FIXED	FLIRT	FOIST
FARGO	FELON	FIFER	FIXER	FLITE	FOLDS
FARLE	FELTS	FIFES	FIXES	FLITS	FOLIA
FARLS	FEMES	FIFTH	FIZZY	FLOAT	FOLIC
FARMS	FEMME	FIFTY	******	FLOCK	FOLIO
FAROE	FEMTO	FIGHT	**FJ---**	FLOCS	FOLKS
FASTS	FEMUR	FIJIS	******	FLOES	FOLLY
FATAL	FENCE	FILAR	FJELD	FLOGS	FONDA
FATED	FENDS	FILCH	FJORD	FLONG	FONTS
FATES	FENNY	FILED	******	FLOOD	FOODS
FATLY	FEODS	FILER	**FL---**	FLOOR	FOOLS
FATTY	FEOFF	FILES	******	FLOPS	FOOTS
FAUGH	FERAL	FILET	FLACK	FLORA	FOOTY
FAULT	FERIA	FILLS	FLAGS	FLOSS	FORAY
FAUNA	FERMI	FILLY	FLAIL	FLOUR	FORBS
FAUNS	FERNS	FILMS	FLAIR	FLOUT	FORBY
FAUST	FERNY	FILMY	FLAKE	FLOWN	FORCE

FORDS	FREUD	FUNGO	GALAX	GAVLE	GHAUT
FORES	FREYA	FUNKS	GALEA	GAVOT	GHAZI
FORGE	FRIAR	FUNKY	GALEN	GAWKS	GHENT
FORGO	FRIED	FUNNY	GALES	GAWKY	GHOST
FORKS	FRIER	FURAN	GALLS	GAYER	GHOUL
FORLI	FRIES	FURLS	GALOP	GAYLY	******
FORME	FRIGG	FUROR	GAMBS	GAZED	GI---
FORMS	FRILL	FURRY	GAMED	GAZER	******
FORTE	FRIML	FURTH	GAMES	GAZES	GIANT
FORTH	FRISE	FURZE	GAMIC	******	GIBED
FORTS	FRISK	FURZY	GAMIN	GE---	GIBER
FORTY	FRITH	FUSED	GAMMA	******	GIBES
FORUM	FRITS	FUSEE	GAMMY	GEARS	GIBUS
FOSSA	FRITZ	FUSEL	GAMPS	GECKO	GIDDY
FOSSE	FRIZZ	FUSES	GAMUT	GECKS	GIFTS
FOULS	FROCK	FUSIL	GANEF	GEEKS	GIGAS
FOUND	FROES	FUSSY	GANGS	GEESE	GIGOT
FOUNT	FROGS	FUSTY	GAOLS	GEEST	GIGUE
FOURS	FROME	FUZED	GAPED	GELDS	GIING
FOVEA	FROND	FUZEE	GAPER	GELID	GILDA
FOWLS	FRONT	FUZES	GAPES	GEMMA	GILDS
FOXED	FROSH	FUZIL	GAPPY	GEMMY	GILES
FOXES	FROST	FUZZY	GARBO	GEMOT	GILLS
FOYED	FROTH	******	GARBS	GENES	GIMEL
FOYER	FROWN	FY---	GARRY	GENET	GIMPS
******	FROWS	******	GARTH	GENIC	GIMPY
FR---	FROZE	FYKES	GARYS	GENIE	GINKS
******	FRUIT	******	GASES	GENII	GINNY
FRAIL	FRUMP	GA---	GASPE	GENOA	GIPON
FRAME	FRYER	******	GASPS	GENRE	GIPSY
FRANC	******	GABBY	GASSY	GENRO	GIRDS
FRANK	FU---	GABES	GASTR	GENTS	GIRLS
FRANZ	******	GABLE	GATED	GENUA	GIRON
FRAPS	FUCUS	GABON	GATES	GENUS	GIROS
FRATS	FUDGE	GABOR	GATUN	GEODE	GIRSH
FRAUD	FUELS	GABYS	GAUDI	GEOFF	GIRTH
FRAYS	FUGAL	GADID	GAUDS	GEOID	GIRTS
FREAK	FUGIO	GAELS	GAUDY	GERDA	GISMO
FREDA	FUGLE	GAFFE	GAUGE	GERMS	GISTS
FREDS	FUGUE	GAFFS	GAULS	GERRY	GIVEN
FREED	FULLS	GAGED	GAULT	GERTY	GIVER
FREER	FULLY	GAGER	GAUNT	GESSO	GIVES
FREES	FUMED	GAGES	GAURS	GETUP	GIZMO
FRENA	FUMES	GAILS	GAUSS	******	******
FREON	FUNDI	GAILY	GAUZE	GH---	GL---
FRERE	FUNDS	GAINS	GAUZY	******	******
FRESH	FUNGI	GAITS	GAVEL	GHANA	GLACE
FRETS		GALAS	GAVIN	GHATS	GLADE

GLADS	******	GOVYS	GRILL	GULAR	HADJI
GLAIR	**GO---**	GOWAN	GRIME	GULCH	HADNT
GLAND	******	GOWER	GRIMM	GULES	HAFIZ
GLANS	GOADS	GOWNS	GRIMY	GULFS	HAFTS
GLARE	GOALS	GOYIM	GRIND	GULLS	HAGIO
GLARY	GOATS	******	GRINS	GULLY	HAGUE
GLASS	GOBOS	**GR---**	GRIPE	GULPS	HAHAS
GLAUC	GOBYS	******	GRIPS	GUMBO	HAIDA
GLAZE	GODLY	GRAAL	GRIPT	GUMMA	HAIFA
GLAZY	GOERS	GRABS	GRIST	GUMMY	HAIKS
GLEAM	GOFER	GRACE	GRITS	GUNNY	HAIKU
GLEAN	GOGOL	GRADE	GROAN	GUPPY	HAILS
GLEBE	GOING	GRADS	GROAT	GURUS	HAIRS
GLEDE	GOLDA	GRAFT	GROIN	GUSHY	HAIRY
GLEDS	GOLDS	GRAIL	GROOM	GUSTA	HAITI
GLEES	GOLEM	GRAIN	GROPE	GUSTO	HAKES
GLEET	GOLFS	GRAMA	GROSS	GUSTS	HAKIM
GLENN	GOLLY	GRAMS	GROSZ	GUSTY	HALED
GLENS	GONAD	GRAND	GROTS	GUTSY	HALER
GLIDE	GONDI	GRANI	GROUP	GUTTA	HALES
GLIMS	GONER	GRANO	GROUT	GUYED	HALID
GLINT	GONGS	GRANT	GROVE	******	HALLE
GLOAT	GONIA	GRAPE	GROWL	**GW---**	HALLO
GLOBE	GONIO	GRAPH	GROWN	******	HALLS
GLOBS	GOODS	GRAPY	GROWS	GWENN	HALMA
GLOOM	GOODY	GRASP	GRUBS	GWENS	HALOS
GLORY	GOOEY	GRASS	GRUEL	GWYNS	HALTS
GLOSS	GOOFS	GRATE	GRUFF	******	HALVE
GLOST	GOOFY	GRAVE	GRUME	**GY---**	HAMAL
GLOVE	GOOKS	GRAVY	GRUNT	******	HAMER
GLOWS	GOONS	GRAYS	******	GYBED	HAMES
GLOZE	GOOSE	GRAZE	**GU---**	GYMNO	HAMMY
GLUED	GOOSY	GREAT	******	GYNEC	HAMZA
GLUES	GORAL	GREBE	GUACO	GYPSY	HANCE
GLUEY	GORED	GRECO	GUAMA	GYRAL	HANDS
GLUME	GORES	GREED	GUANA	GYRES	HANDY
GLUTS	GORGE	GREEK	GUANO	GYRON	HANGS
GLYCO	GORKI	GREEN	GUANS	GYROS	HANKS
GLYPH	GORKY	GREER	GUARD	GYRUS	HANKY
******	GORME	GREET	GUAVA	GYVED	HANNA
GN---	GORSE	GREGO	GUESS	******	HANOI
******	GORSY	GREGS	GUEST	**HA---**	HANSE
GNARL	GOTHA	GRETA	GUIDE	******	HAPLO
GNASH	GOTHS	GREYS	GUIDO	HABIT	HAPLY
GNATS	GOUDA	GRIDE	GUILD	HABUS	HAPPY
GNAWN	GOUGE	GRIDS	GUILE	HACKS	HARAR
GNAWS	GOURD	GRIEF	GUILT	HADED	HARDS
GNOME	GOUTY	GRIEG	GUISE	HADES	HARDY
GNOMY					

HARED	HEALS	HENRY	HIPPO	HOOCH	HUFFY
HAREM	HEAPS	HEPAT	HIPPY	HOODS	HUGER
HARES	HEARD	HEPTA	HIRAM	HOOEY	HUGHS
HARKS	HEARS	HERAT	HIRED	HOOFS	HUGOS
HARLS	HEART	HERBS	HIRER	HOOKE	HULAS
HARMS	HEATH	HERBY	HIRES	HOOKS	HULDA
HARPS	HEATS	HERDS	HITCH	HOOKY	HULKS
HARPY	HEAVE	HERLS	HIVED	HOOPS	HULKY
HARRY	HEAVY	HERMA	HIVES	HOOTS	HULLS
HARSH	HECTO	HEROD	******	HOOVE	HUMAN
HARTE	HEDDA	HERON	**HO---**	HOPED	HUMIC
HARTS	HEDGE	HERTZ	******	HOPEH	HUMID
HARTZ	HEDGY	HESSE	HOAGY	HOPES	HUMOR
HASNT	HEEDS	HETTY	HOARD	HORAE	HUMPH
HASPS	HEELS	HEWED	HOARY	HORAL	HUMPS
HASTE	HEFTS	HEWER	HOBBS	HORAS	HUMPY
HASTY	HEFTY	HEXAD	HOBBY	HORDE	HUMUS
HATCH	HEGEL	HEXED	HOBOS	HOREB	HUNAN
HATED	HEIGH	HEXES	HOCKS	HORNE	HUNCH
HATER	HEIRS	HEXYL	HOCUS	HORNS	HUNKS
HATES	HEIST	******	HODGE	HORNY	HUNKY
HATTY	HEJAZ	**HH---**	HOERS	HORSE	HUNTS
HAULM	HEKLA	******	HOGAN	HORST	HUPEH
HAULS	HEKTO	HHOUR	HOICK	HORSY	HURDS
HAUNT	HELEN	******	HOIST	HORTA	HURLS
HAVEN	HELGA	**HI---**	HOKAN	HORUS	HURLY
HAVER	HELIC	******	HOKUM	HOSEA	HURON
HAVOC	HELIO	HICKS	HOLDS	HOSED	HURRY
HAWED	HELIX	HIDER	HOLED	HOSES	HURST
HAWKS	HELLE	HIDES	HOLES	HOSTS	HURTS
HAWSE	HELLO	HIDTO	HOLEY	HOTEL	HUSKS
HAYDN	HELLS	HIERO	HOLLY	HOTLY	HUSKY
HAYED	HELMS	HIFIS	HOLMS	HOUGH	HUSSY
HAYES	HELOT	HIGHS	HOLST	HOUND	HUTCH
HAZED	HELPS	HIKED	HOMED	HOURI	******
HAZEL	HELVE	HIKER	HOMEO	HOURS	**HY---**
HAZER	HEMAL	HIKES	HOMER	HOUSE	******
HAZES	HEMAN	HILDA	HOMES	HOVEL	HYALO
******	HEMAT	HILLS	HOMEY	HOVER	HYDRA
HB---	HEMEN	HILLY	HONAN	HOWDY	HYDRO
******	HEMIA	HILTS	HONDO	HOWIE	HYENA
HBEAM	HEMIC	HILUM	HONED	HOWLS	HYETO
HBOMB	HEMIN	HINDI	HONES	HOYLE	HYGRO
******	HEMPS	HINDS	HONEY	******	HYING
HE---	HEMPY	HINDU	HONGS	**HU---**	HYLAS
******	HENCE	HINGE	HONKS	******	HYMEN
HEADS	HENNA	HINNY	HONKY	HUBBY	HYMNS
HEADY	HENRI	HINTS	HONOR	HUFFS	HYOID

HYPER	******	INARM	IRENE	******	JEERS
HYPHA	IG---	INCAN	IRIDO	IZ---	JEFES
HYPNO	******	INCAS	IRISH	******	JEFFS
HYPOS	IGLOO	INCUR	IRKED	IZZYS	JEHUS
HYPSO	IGNAZ	INCUS	IRMAS	******	JELLO
HYRAX	******	INDEX	IRONE	JA---	JELLS
HYSON	IH---	INDIA	IRONS	******	JELLY
******	******	INDIC	IRONY	JABEZ	JEMMY
IA---	IHRAM	INDOW	IRVIN	JABOT	JENNY
******	******	INDRA	IRWIN	JACKS	JEREZ
IAMBI	IK---	INDRI	******	JACKY	JERKS
IAMBS	******	INDUE	IS---	JACOB	JERKY
IASIS	IKONS	INDUS	******	JADED	JERRY
IATRO	******	INEPT	ISAAC	JADES	JESSE
IATRY	IL---	INERT	ISBAS	JAFFA	JESSY
******	******	INFER	ISERE	JAGGS	JESTS
IB---	ILEAC	INFIX	ISLAM	JAGGY	JESUS
******	ILEAL	INFRA	ISLAY	JAILS	JETON
IBEAM	ILEUM	INGLE	ISLED	JAINA	JETTY
IBIZA	ILEUS	INGOT	ISLES	JAINS	JEWEL
IBSEN	ILIAC	INIGO	ISLET	JAKES	JEWRY
******	ILIAD	INION	ISSEI	JAKOB	******
IC---	ILIAN	INKED	ISSUE	JALAP	JI---
******	ILION	INKER	ISTAR	JAMBS	******
ICHOR	ILIUM	INKLE	ISTIC	JAMES	JIBED
ICIAN	ILLUS	INLAW	ISTLE	JAMIE	JIBES
ICIER	ILMEN	INLAY	******	JAMMY	JIDDA
ICILY	ILONA	INLET	IT---	JANES	JIFFS
ICING		INNED	******	JANET	JIFFY
ICONO	IM---	INNER	ITALS	JANIS	JIHAD
ICONS	******	INPUT	ITALY	JANOS	JILLS
ICOSI	IMAGE	INSET	ITCHY	JANUS	JILTS
ICTUS	IMAGO	INTER	ITEMS	JAPAN	JIMMY
******	IMAMS	INTRA	ITION	JAPED	JINGO
ID---	IMBED	INTRO	******	JAPES	JINKS
******	IMBUE	INURE	IV---	JARED	JINNI
IDAHO	IMIDE	INURN	******	JARLS	JINNY
IDEAL	IMIDO	INVAR	IVANS	JASON	JIVED
IDEAS	IMIDS	******	IVIED	JASSY	******
IDEST	IMINE	IO---	IVIES	JATOS	JO---
IDIOM	IMINO	******	IVORY	JAUNT	******
IDIOT	IMMIX	IODIC	IX---	JAWED	JOANS
IDLED	IMPEL	IODOL	******	JAYNE	JOCKO
IDLER	IMPLY	IONIA	IXIAS	JAZZY	JOELS
IDLES	IMPOT	IONIC	IXION	******	JOEYS
IDOLS	******	IOTAS	IXTLE	JE---	JOHNS
IDYLL	IN---	******	******	******	JOINS
IDYLS	INANE	IR---	IY---	JEANS	JOINT
	INAPT	******	******	JEEPS	
		IRAQI	IYYAR		
		IRATE			

JOIST	JUMBO	KATHY	KHMER	KNITS	KUDUS
JOKED	JUMNA	KATIE	KHOND	KNOBS	KUFRA
JOKER	JUMPS	KAUAI	******	KNOCK	KUKRI
JOKES	JUMPY	KAURI	**KI---**	KNOLL	KULAK
JOLES	JUNCO	KAURY	******	KNOPS	KUMIS
JOLLY	JUNES	KAVAS	KIBEI	KNOSP	KURSK
JOLTS	JUNKS	KAYAK	KIBES	KNOTS	KURUS
JOLTY	JUNKY	KAYOS	KICKS	KNOUT	******
JONAH	JUNTA	KAZAN	KIDDY	KNOWN	**KV---**
JONAS	JUNTO	KAZOO	KIERS	KNOWS	******
JONES	JUPON	******	KILAH	KNURL	KVASS
JONNY	JURAL	**KE---**	KILLS	KNURR	******
JORAM	JURAT	******	KILNS	KNURS	**KY---**
JORGE	JUREL	KEATS	KILOS	******	******
JORUM	JUROR	KECKS	KILTS	**KO---**	KYATS
JOSIE	JURUA	KEDAH	KILTY	******	KYLIX
JOSUA	JUSTS	KEDGE	KINDS	KOALA	KYOTO
JOSUE	JUTES	KEEFS	KINGS	KODAK	KYRIE
JOTUN	JUXTA	KEELS	KININ	KOELS	******
JOULE	******	KEENS	KINKS	KOINE	**LA---**
JOUST	**KA---**	KEEPS	KINKY	KOLAS	******
JOWLS	******	KEEVE	KIOSK	KOMOS	LABEL
JOYCE	KAABA	KEITH	KIOWA	KONYA	LABIA
JOYED	KABOB	KELLY	KIRIN	KOOKS	LABIO
******	KABUL	KELPS	KIRKS	KOOKY	LABOR
JU---	KADIS	KELSO	KITED	KOPEC	LABRA
******	KAFIR	KENCH	KITES	KOPEK	LACED
JUANA	KAFKA	KENNY	KITTY	KOPJE	LACES
JUANS	KAGUS	KENTS	KIVAS	KORAN	LACKS
JUBAS	KAKAS	KENYA	KIWIS	KOREA	LACTO
JUBES	KAKIS	KEPIS	******	KORUN	LADDY
JUDAH	KALAT	KERAT	**KL---**	KOTOS	LADED
JUDAS	KAMES	KERBS	******	******	LADEN
JUDEA	KAMET	KERCH	KLARA	**KR---**	LADES
JUDEO	KAMIK	KERES	KLOOF	******	LADIN
JUDES	KANDY	KERFS	******	KRAAL	LADLE
JUDGE	KAPHS	KERNS	**KN---**	KRAFT	LAGAN
JUDYS	KAPOK	KERRY	******	KRAIT	LAGER
JUGAL	KAPPA	KETCH	KNACK	KRAUT	LAGOS
JUICE	KAPUT	KEVEL	KNARS	KRONA	LAIKA
JUICY	KARAT	KEVIN	KNAVE	KRONE	LAINE
JUJUS	KAREN	KEYED	KNEAD	KRUBI	LAIRD
JULEP	KARLS	******	KNEED	KRUPP	LAIRS
JULES	KARMA	**KH---**	KNEEL	******	LAITY
JULIA	KAROL	******	KNEES	**KU---**	LAKED
JULIE	KAROO	KHADI	KNELL	******	LAKER
JULIO	KARYO	KHAKI	KNELT	KUBAN	LAKES
JULYS	KATES	KHANS	KNIFE	KUDOS	LAKEY

LALLS	LAVER	LEHUA	******	LINER	LOAMY
LAMAS	LAVES	LEIFS	**LI---**	LINES	LOANS
LAMBS	LAWED	LEIGH	******	LINEY	LOATH
LAMED	LAWNS	LEILA	LIANA	LINGA	LOBAR
LAMER	LAWNY	LEITH	LIANE	LINGO	LOBBY
LAMES	LAXER	LEMMA	LIANG	LINGS	LOBED
LAMIA	LAXLY	LEMON	LIARS	LININ	LOBES
LAMPS	LAYBY	LEMUR	LIBBY	LINKS	LOBOS
LANAI	LAYER	LENAS	LIBEL	LINTY	LOCAL
LANCE	LAZAR	LENDS	LIBER	LINUS	LOCHS
LANDS	LAZED	LENES	LIBRA	LIONS	LOCKE
LANES	LAZES	LENIN	LIBYA	LIPID	LOCKS
LANKY	******	LENIS	LICHT	LIPPI	LOCOS
LAOAG	**LE---**	LENNY	LICIT	LIPPY	LOCUM
LAPAR	******	LENOS	LICKS	LIRAS	LOCUS
LAPEL	LEACH	LENTO	LIEGE	LISAS	LODEN
LAPIN	LEADS	LENTS	LIEIN	LISLE	LODES
LAPIS	LEADY	LEONA	LIENS	LISPS	LODGE
LAPPS	LEAFS	LEONS	LIEUT	LISTS	LOESS
LAPSE	LEAFY	LEORA	LIFER	LISZT	LOFTS
LARCH	LEAKS	LEPER	LIFTS	LITAI	LOFTY
LARDS	LEAKY	LEPID	LIGAN	LITAS	LOGAN
LARDY	LEANS	LEPSY	LIGHT	LITER	LOGES
LARES	LEANT	LEPTA	LIGNI	LITHE	LOGIA
LARGE	LEAPS	LEPTO	LIGNO	LITHO	LOGIC
LARGO	LEAPT	LEPUS	LIKED	LITRE	LOGOS
LARKS	LEARN	LEROY	LIKEN	LIVED	LOGUE
LARKY	LEARY	LETHE	LIKES	LIVEN	LOINS
LARRY	LEASE	LETTS	LILAC	LIVER	LOIRE
LARVA	LEASH	LETTY	LILAS	LIVES	LOLAS
LASER	LEAST	LETUP	LILLE	LIVIA	LOLLS
LASSA	LEAVE	LEUCO	LILLI	LIVID	LOLLY
LASSO	LEAVY	LEUDS	LILLY	LIVRE	LONER
LASTS	LEDGE	LEUKO	LILTS	LIZAS	LONGI
LATCH	LEECH	LEVEE	LILYS	LIZZY	LONGS
LATER	LEEDS	LEVEL	LIMBI	******	LOOBY
LATEX	LEEKS	LEVEN	LIMBO	**LL---**	LOOED
LATHE	LEERS	LEVER	LIMBS	******	LOOFS
LATHS	LEERY	LEVIS	LIMED	LLAMA	LOOKS
LATHY	LEETS	LEWES	LIMEN	LLANO	LOOMS
LATIN	LEFTS	LEWIE	LIMES	LLOYD	LOONS
LATRO	LEFTY	LEWIS	LIMEY	******	LOONY
LATRY	LEGAL	LEYTE	LIMIT	**LO---**	LOOPS
LAUDS	LEGER	******	LIMNS	******	LOOPY
LAUGH	LEGES	**LH---**	LIMPS	LOACH	LOOSE
LAURA	LEGGY	******	LINDA	LOADS	LOOTS
LAVAS	LEGIT	LHASA	LINED	LOAFS	LOPAT
LAVED	LEHRS		LINEN	LOAMS	LOPED

LOPER	LUISA	LYSES	MALAY	MARLY	******
LOPES	LUISE	LYSIN	MALES	MARNE	ME---
LOPPY	LULLS	LYSIS	MALIC	MARRY	******
LORAN	LULUS	LYSOL	MALLS	MARSH	MEADS
LORCA	LUMEN	LYSSA	MALMO	MARTA	MEALS
LORDS	LUMPS	LYTIC	MALTA	MARTS	MEALY
LORES	LUMPY	LYTTA	MALTS	MARTY	MEANS
LORIS	LUNAR	******	MALTY	MASER	MEANT
LORNA	LUNCH	MA---	MAMAS	MASHY	MEANY
LORRY	LUNES	******	MAMBA	MASKS	MEATS
LOSER	LUNET	MABEL	MAMBO	MASON	MEATY
LOSES	LUNGE	MACAO	MAMEY	MASSE	MECCA
LOTAH	LUNGI	MACAW	MAMIE	MASSY	MEDAL
LOTOS	LUNGS	MACED	MAMMA	MASTO	MEDEA
LOTTA	LUNTS	MACER	MAMMY	MASTS	MEDIA
LOTTE	LUPIN	MACES	MANCY	MATCH	MEDIC
LOTTO	LUPUS	MACHY	MANDY	MATED	MEDIO
LOTTY	LURCH	MACKS	MANED	MATEO	MEDOC
LOTUS	LURED	MACLE	MANES	MATER	MEETS
LOUGH	LURER	MACON	MANET	MATES	MEGAL
LOUIS	LURES	MACRO	MANGE	MATEY	MEGAN
LOUPE	LURID	MADAM	MANGO	MATHS	MELAN
LOUPS	LURKS	MADGE	MANGY	MATIN	MELDS
LOURS	LUSTS	MADLY	MANIA	MATRI	MELEE
LOUSE	LUSTY	MADOC	MANIC	MATSU	MELIC
LOUSY	LUTED	MAFIA	MANLY	MATTE	MELON
LOUTS	LUTES	MAGDA	MANNA	MATTS	MELOS
LOVED	LUTON	MAGES	MANOR	MATTY	MELTS
LOVER	LUXEX	MAGIC	MANSE	MATZO	MEMOS
LOVES	LUXOR	MAGMA	MANTA	MAUDE	MENAI
LOWED	LUZON	MAGNI	MANUS	MAUDS	MENDS
LOWER	******	MAGOG	MAORI	MAULS	MENES
LOWLY	LY---	MAGOT	MAPLE	MAUND	MENSA
LOYAL	******	MAGUS	MAQUI	MAURA	MENUS
******	LYCEA	MAHAN	MARAT	MAUVE	MEOWS
LU---	LYCEE	MAHDI	MARCH	MAVIS	MERCI
******	LYDDA	MAIDS	MARCO	MAXIM	MERCY
LUAUS	LYDIA	MAILS	MARCS	MAYAN	MERGE
LUCCA	LYING	MAIMS	MARES	MAYAS	MERIT
LUCES	LYLES	MAINE	MARGE	MAYBE	MERLE
LUCIA	LYMAN	MAINS	MARGO	MAYNT	MEROE
LUCID	LYMPH	MAINZ	MARIA	MAYOR	MERRY
LUCKY	LYNCH	MAIZE	MARIE	MAYST	MESAS
LUCRE	LYNNS	MAJOR	MARIO	MAZED	MESHY
LUCYS	LYONS	MAKER	MARIS	MAZER	MESIC
LUFFS	LYRES	MAKES	MARKS	MAZES	MESNE
LUGER	LYRIC	MALAC	MARLA	******	MESON
LUIGI	LYSED	MALAR	MARLS	MC---	MESSY
				******	
				MCCOY	

METAL	MILTY	******	MOPES	MOWER	MUTED
METAS	MIMED	**MO---**	MORAE	MOXAS	MUTES
METED	MIMEO	******	MORAL	MOXIE	MUTTS
METER	MIMER	MOANS	MORAS	******	MUZAK
METES	MIMES	MOATS	MORAT	**MU---**	MUZZY
METHO	MIMIC	MOCHA	MORAY	******	******
METIS	MIMIR	MOCKS	MOREL	MUCID	**MY---**
METOL	MIMIS	MODAL	MORES	MUCIN	******
METRE	MINAE	MODEL	MORIN	MUCKS	MYELO
METRO	MINAS	MODES	MORNA	MUCKY	MYLES
METRY	MINCE	MODUS	MORNS	MUCRO	MYNAS
MEUSE	MINDI	MOGUL	MORON	MUCUS	MYOID
MEWED	MINDS	MOHUR	MOROS	MUDDY	MYOMA
MEWLS	MINED	MOILS	MORPH	MUFFS	MYOPE
MEZZO	MINER	MOIRA	MORRO	MUFTI	MYOPY
******	MINES	MOIRE	MORSE	MUGGY	MYRAS
MI---	MINGY	MOIST	MORTA	MUHLY	MYRIA
******	MINIM	MOKES	MORTS	MUJIK	MYRNA
MIAMI	MINKS	MOLAL	MORTY	MULCH	MYRON
MIAOW	MINNA	MOLAR	MOSAN	MULCT	MYRRH
MIAUL	MINOR	MOLDS	MOSEL	MULES	MYTHO
MICAH	MINOS	MOLDY	MOSES	MULEY	MYTHS
MICAS	MINSK	MOLES	MOSEY	MULLS	******
MICKY	MINTS	MOLLS	MOSSO	MULTI	**NA---**
MICRA	MINUS	MOLLY	MOSSY	MUMMS	******
MICRO	MIRED	MOLTO	MOTEL	MUMMY	NAACP
MIDAS	MIRES	MOLTS	MOTES	MUMPS	NABOB
MIDDY	MIRTH	MOMUS	MOTET	MUNCH	NACRE
MIDGE	MIRZA	MONAD	MOTHS	MUNGO	NADAB
MIDST	MISDO	MONAS	MOTHY	MUNRO	NADER
MIENS	MISER	MONDE	MOTIF	MUONS	NADIR
MIFFS	MISES	MONET	MOTOR	MURAL	NAHOR
MIFFY	MISSY	MONEY	MOTTO	MURAT	NAHUA
MIGHT	MISTS	MONKS	MOUCH	MUREX	NAHUM
MIKES	MISTY	MONTE	MOUES	MURKY	NAIAD
MIKEY	MITCH	MONTH	MOULD	MURRA	NAILS
MILAN	MITER	MONTY	MOULT	MURRE	NAIRN
MILCH	MITES	MOOCH	MOUND	MURRY	NAIVE
MILER	MITRE	MOODS	MOUNT	MUSCA	NAKED
MILES	MITTS	MOODY	MOURN	MUSED	NAMED
MILIA	MITZI	MOOED	MOUSE	MUSES	NAMER
MILKS	MITZY	MOONS	MOUSY	MUSHY	NAMES
MILKY	MIXED	MOONY	MOUTH	MUSIC	NAMUR
MILLI	MIXER	MOORE	MOVED	MUSKS	NANAS
MILLS	MIXES	MOORS	MOVER	MUSKY	NANCE
MILLY	MIXUP	MOOSE	MOVES	MUSSY	NANCY
MILNE	MIZEN	MOPED	MOVIE	MUSTS	NANNA
MILTS	******	MOPER	MOWED	MUSTY	NANNY
	ML---				
	******				
	MLLES				

NAOMI	NERVE	NITER	NORIA	OATES	******
NAPES	NERVY	NITON	NORMA	OATHS	**OG---**
NAPPE	NESTS	NITRE	NORMS	OAVES	******
NAPPY	NETER	NITRI	NORNS	******	OGDEN
NARCO	NETTY	NITRO	NORSE	**OB---**	OGEES
NARDS	NEUME	NITTY	NORTH	******	OGHAM
NARES	NEURI	NIVAL	NOSED	OBEAH	OGIVE
NARIS	NEURO	NIXED	NOSES	OBELI	OGLED
NARKY	NEVER	NIXES	NOSEY	OBESE	OGLER
NASAL	NEVIL	NIXIE	NOTCH	OBEYS	OGLES
NASTY	NEVIS	NIXON	NOTED	OBITS	OGMIC
NATAL	NEVUS	NIZAM	NOTER	OBOES	OGRES
NATES	NEWEL	NIZER	NOTES	OBOLE	******
NATTY	NEWER	******	NOUNS	OBOLI	**OH---**
NAURU	NEWLY	**NJ---**	NOVAE	******	******
NAVAL	NEWSY	******	NOVAS	**OC---**	OHMIC
NAVAR	NEWTS	NJORD	NOVEL	******	******
NAVEL	NEXUS	******	NOWAY	OCALA	**OI---**
NAVES	******	**NO---**	NOYES	OCCUR	******
NAVVY	**NI---**	******	******	OCEAN	OIDEA
NAWAB	******	NOAHS	**NU---**	OCHER	OILED
NAZIS	NICER	NOBBY	******	OCHRE	OILER
******	NICHE	NOBEL	NUBBY	OCHRY	******
NE---	NICKS	NOBLE	NUBIA	OCREA	**OK---**
******	NICKY	NOBLY	NUCHA	OCTAD	******
NEALS	NIDED	NOCKS	NUDES	OCTET	OKAPI
NEAPS	NIDES	NOCTI	NUDGE	OCTYL	OKAYS
NEARS	NIDUS	NODAL	NUMBS	OCULO	OKIEH
NEATH	NIECE	NODDY	NUMEN	******	OKIES
NECKS	NIFTY	NODES	NURSE	**OD---**	OKING
NECRO	NIGEL	NODUS	NUTTY	******	OKRAS
NEDDY	NIGER	NOELS	******	ODDER	******
NEEDS	NIGHT	NOGGS	**NY---**	ODDLY	**OL---**
NEEDY	NIGRI	NOISE	******	ODEON	******
NEGEB	NIHIL	NOISY	NYASA	ODETS	OLAFS
NEGEV	NIMBI	NOMAD	NYCTI	ODEUM	OLAVS
NEGRO	NIMES	NOMAS	NYCTO	ODIUM	OLDEN
NEGUS	NINAS	NONAS	NYLON	ODONT	OLDER
NEHRU	NINES	NONCE	NYMPH	ODORS	OLEAN
NEIGH	NINNY	NONES	******	ODOUR	OLEIC
NEILS	NINTH	NONET	**OA---**	ODYLE	OLEIN
NELLS	NINUS	NOOKS	******	******	OLENT
NELLY	NIOBE	NOONS	OAKEN	**OF---**	OLGAS
NEMAT	NIPAS	NOOSE	OAKUM	******	OLIGO
NEPAL	NIPPY	NOPAL	OARED	OFFAL	OLIOS
NEPHO	NISAN	NOPAR	OASES	OFFER	OLIVE
NEPHR	NISEI	NORAH	OASIS	OFTEN	OLLAS
NEROS	NISUS	NORAS	OATEN		OLLIE
					OLOGY

******	ORBED	OUIJA	******	PANES	PATEN
OM---	ORBIT	OUNCE	PA---	PANGS	PATER
******	ORCHI	OURAY	******	PANIC	PATES
OMAHA	ORCIN	OUSEL	PABLO	PANNE	PATHO
OMASA	ORCUS	OUSTS	PACAS	PANSY	PATHS
OMBER	ORCZY	OUTDO	PACED	PANTO	PATHY
OMBRE	ORDER	OUTED	PACER	PANTS	PATIO
OMBRO	OREAD	OUTER	PACES	PANTY	PATNA
OMEGA	ORGAN	OUTGO	PACHY	PAOLO	PATRI
OMENS	ORIBI	OUTRE	PACKS	PAPAL	PATSY
OMERS	ORIEL	OUZEL	PACTS	PAPAS	PATTI
OMITS	ORION	******	PADDY	PAPAW	PATTY
******	ORIYA	OV---	PADRE	PAPEN	PAULA
ON---	ORLES	******	PADUA	PAPER	PAULO
******	ORLON	OVALS	PAEAN	PAPPI	PAULS
ONEGA	ORLOP	OVARY	PAEDO	PAPPY	PAUSE
ONEIR	ORMER	OVATE	PAEON	PAPUA	PAVAN
ONERY	ORNIS	OVENS	PAGAN	PARAS	PAVED
ONION	ORPIN	OVERT	PAGED	PARCA	PAVER
ONIRO	ORRIS	OVINE	PAGER	PARCH	PAVES
ONSET	ORSON	OVOID	PAGES	PARDS	PAVIS
******	ORTHO	OVOLI	PAILS	PARED	PAWED
OO---	******	OVOLO	PAINE	PAREN	PAWER
******	OS---	OVULE	PAINS	PARER	PAWKY
******	******	******	PAINT	PARES	PAWLS
OOMPH	OSAGE	OW---	PAIRS	PAREU	PAWNS
OOZED	OSAKA	******	PAISA	PARGO	PAYED
OOZES	OSCAN	OWENS	PAISE	PARIS	PAYEE
******	OSCAR	OWING	PALAE	PARKA	PAYER
OP---	OSIER	OWLET	PALEA	PARKS	******
******	OSITY	OWNED	PALED	PARMA	PE---
OPAHS	OSLER	OWNER	PALEO	PAROL	******
OPALS	OSMAN	******	PALER	PAROS	PEACE
OPENS	OSMIC	OX---	PALES	PARRS	PEACH
OPERA	OSTED	******	PALEY	PARRY	PEAKS
OPHIO	OSTIA	OXBOW	PALLS	PARSE	PEAKY
OPINE	******	OXEYE	PALLY	PARSI	PEALS
OPIUM	OT---	OXIDE	PALMA	PARTS	PEANS
OPSIA	******	OXIME	PALMI	PARTY	PEARL
OPSIS	OTARU	OXLIP	PALMS	PASCH	PEARS
OPTED	OTERO	******	PALMY	PASHA	PEARY
OPTIC	OTHER	OY---	PALPI	PASSE	PEASE
******	OTOMI	******	PALSY	PASSY	PEATS
OR---	OTTER	OYERS	PANAY	PASTA	PEATY
******	OTTOS	******	PANDA	PASTE	PEAVY
ORACH	******	OZ---	PANDY	PASTS	PECAN
ORALS	OU---	******	PANED	PASTY	PECKS
ORANG	******	OZARK	PANEL	PATCH	PECOS
ORATE	OUGHT	OZONE			
	OUIDA	OZZIE			

PEDAL	PERSE	PHYLL	PINEY	PLASM	POCKY
PEDES	PERTH	PHYLO	PINGO	PLAST	PODGY
PEDRO	PESKY	PHYRE	PINGS	PLASY	PODIA
PEEKS	PESOS	PHYSI	PINKS	PLATA	POEMS
PEELS	PESTS	PHYTE	PINKY	PLATE	POESY
PEENS	PETAL	PHYTO	PINNA	PLATO	POETS
PEEPS	PETER	******	PINNI	PLATS	POGEY
PEERS	PETES	**PI---**	PINNY	PLATY	POILU
PEEVE	PETIT	******	PINON	PLAYA	POIND
PEGGY	PETRO	PIAND	PINTA	PLAYS	POINT
PEKAN	PETRY	PIANO	PINTO	PLAZA	POISE
PEKIN	PETTI	PIAVE	PINTS	PLEAD	POKED
PEKOE	PETTO	PICAL	PINUP	PLEAS	POKER
PELEE	PETTY	PICAS	PIONS	PLEAT	POKES
PELEG	PEWEE	PICKS	PIOUS	PLEBE	POKEY
PELFS	PEWIT	PICOT	PIPAL	PLEBS	POLAR
PELLA	******	PICRO	PIPED	PLEGY	POLED
PELLY	**PH---**	PICTS	PIPER	PLENA	POLES
PELON	******	PICUL	PIPES	PLICA	POLIO
PELTS	PHAGE	PIECE	PIPET	PLIED	POLKA
PELVI	PHAGO	PIERS	PIPIT	PLIER	POLLS
PENAL	PHAGY	PIETA	PIQUE	PLIES	POLLY
PENCE	PHANE	PIETY	PISCI	PLINY	POLYP
PENDS	PHANY	PIEZO	PITAS	PLODS	POMES
PENGO	PHASE	PIGGY	PITCH	PLOID	POMMY
PENIS	PHASY	PIGMY	PITHS	PLONK	PONCE
PENNA	PHEBE	PIKAS	PITHY	PLOPS	PONDS
PENNI	PHENO	PIKED	PITON	PLOTS	PONES
PENNY	PHIAL	PIKER	PITOT	PLOWS	POOCH
PENTA	PHILA	PIKES	PIVOT	PLOYS	POODS
PEONS	PHILE	PILAF	PIXIE	PLUCK	POOLE
PEONY	PHILO	PILAR	PIZZA	PLUGS	POOLS
PEPIN	PHILS	PILEA	*****	PLUMB	POONA
PEPLA	PHILY	PILED	**PL---**	PLUME	POONS
PEPOS	PHIPS	PILEI	******	PLUMP	POOPO
PEPPY	PHLEB	PILES	PLACE	PLUMS	POOPS
PEPYS	PHLOX	PILIS	PLACK	PLUMY	POPES
PERCH	PHOBE	PILLS	PLAGI	PLUNK	POPPY
PERCY	PHONE	PILOT	PLAID	PLURI	POPSY
PERDU	PHONO	PIMAN	PLAIN	PLUSH	PORCH
PERES	PHONY	PIMAS	PLAIT	PLUTO	PORED
PERIL	PHORE	PIMPS	PLANE	PLUVI	PORES
PERIS	PHOTO	PINAS	PLANI	******	PORGE
PERKS	PHOTS	PINCH	PLANK	**PN---**	PORGY
PERKY	PHREN	PINED	PLANO	******	PORKY
PERLE	PHYCO	PINEL	PLANS	PNEUM	PORNO
PERON	PHYLA	PINER	PLANT	******	PORTS
PERRY	PHYLE	PINES	PLASH	**PO---**	POSED
				******	
				POACH	
				POCKS	

POSER	PRINK	PUBIS	PUTTS	QUICK	RAJAH
POSES	PRINT	PUCES	PUTTY	QUIDS	RAKED
POSIT	PRIOR	PUCKA	PUTUP	QUIET	RAKEE
POSSE	PRISE	PUCKS	******	QUIFF	RAKER
POSTS	PRISM	PUDGY	**PY---**	QUILL	RAKES
POTSY	PRIVY	PUDIC	******	QUILT	RALES
POTTO	PRIZE	PUDSY	PYDNA	QUINT	RALLY
POTTY	PROAS	PUFFS	PYELO	QUIPS	RALPH
POUCH	PROBE	PUFFY	PYGMY	QUIPU	RAMIE
POUFS	PROCT	PUGET	PYLON	QUIRE	RAMMY
POULT	PRODS	PUKED	PYOID	QUIRK	RAMPS
POUND	PROEM	PUKES	PYRAN	QUIRT	RAMUS
POURS	PROFS	PUKKA	PYRES	QUITE	RANCE
POUTS	PROLE	PULED	PYREX	QUITO	RANCH
POWER	PROMS	PULER	PYXED	QUITS	RANDS
POWYS	PRONE	PULES	PYXES	QUODS	RANDY
POYOU	PRONG	PULLS	PYXIE	QUOIN	RANEE
******	PROOF	PULMO	PYXIS	QUOIT	RANGE
PR---	PROPS	PULPS	******	QUOTA	RANGY
******	PROSE	PULPY	**QA---**	QUOTE	RANIS
PRAHU	PROSY	PULSE	******	QUOTH	RANKS
PRAMS	PROTO	PUMAS	QATAR	******	RANTS
PRANG	PROUD	PUMPS	******	**RA---**	RAOUL
PRANK	PROVE	PUNAS	**QU---**	******	RAPED
PRASE	PROVO	PUNCH	******	RABAT	RAPES
PRATE	PROWL	PUNGS	QUACK	RABBI	RAPHE
PRAWN	PROWS	PUNIC	QUADS	RABIC	RAPID
PRAYS	PROXY	PUNKA	QUAFF	RABID	RARER
PREEN	PRUDE	PUNKS	QUAGS	RACED	RASPS
PRESA	PRUNE	PUNKY	QUAIL	RACER	RASPY
PRESS	PRYER	PUNTO	QUAKE	RACES	RATAL
PREST	******	PUNTS	QUAKY	RACKS	RATCH
PREXY	**PS---**	PUNTY	QUALM	RADAR	RATED
PREYS	******	PUPAE	QUANT	RADII	RATEL
PRIAM	PSALM	PUPIL	QUARK	RADIO	RATER
PRICE	PSEUD	PUPPY	QUART	RADIX	RATES
PRICK	PSHAW	PUREE	QUASH	RADON	RATIO
PRIDE	PSOAS	PURER	QUASI	RAFTS	RATTY
PRIED	PSYCH	PURGE	QUASS	RAGED	RAVED
PRIER	******	PURIM	QUAYS	RAGEE	RAVEL
PRIES	**PT---**	PURLS	QUEAN	RAGES	RAVEN
PRIGS	******	PURRS	QUEEN	RAGGY	RAVER
PRIMA	PTERO	PURSE	QUEER	RAIDS	RAVES
PRIME	******	PURSY	QUELL	RAILS	RAWER
PRIMI	**PU---**	PUSAN	QUERN	RAINS	RAWLY
PRIMO	******	PUSHY	QUERY	RAINY	RAYAH
PRIMP	PUBES	PUSSY	QUEST	RAISE	RAYED
PRIMS	PUBIC	PUTON	QUEUE	RAJAB	RAYON

RAZED	REIMS	RHOMB	RISKY	ROOFS	RUBYS
RAZEE	REINS	RHONE	RISUS	ROOKS	RUCHE
RAZES	RELAX	RHUMB	RITAS	ROOKY	RUCKS
RAZOR	RELAY	RHYME	RITES	ROOMS	RUDDS
*****	RELIC	*****	RITZY	ROOMY	RUDDY
RE---	REMAN	**RI---**	RIVAL	ROOST	RUDER
*****	REMEX	*****	RIVED	ROOTS	RUDYS
REACH	REMIT	RIALS	RIVEN	ROOTY	RUERS
REACT	REMUS	RIANT	RIVER	ROPED	RUFFS
READS	RENAL	RIATA	RIVES	ROPES	RUFUS
READY	RENAN	RICED	RIVET	ROPEY	RUGAE
REALM	RENDS	RICER	RIYAL	ROQUE	RUGBY
REALS	RENEE	RICES	*****	ROSAS	RUING
REAMS	RENES	RICIN	**RO---**	ROSED	RUINS
REAPS	RENEW	RICKS	*****	ROSES	RULED
REARM	RENIN	RICKY	ROACH	ROSIN	RULER
REARS	RENTE	RIDER	ROADS	ROTAS	RULES
REBEC	RENTS	RIDES	ROALD	ROTCH	RUMBA
REBEL	REPAY	RIDGE	ROAMS	ROTLA	RUMEN
REBID	REPEL	RIDGY	ROANS	ROTOR	RUMLY
REBUS	REPLY	RIFFS	ROARS	ROUEN	RUMMY
REBUT	RERAN	RIFLE	ROAST	ROUES	RUMOR
RECAP	RERUN	RIFTS	ROBED	ROUGE	RUMPS
RECTA	RESET	RIGEL	ROBES	ROUGH	RUNES
RECTI	RESIN	RIGGS	ROBIN	ROUND	RUNGS
RECTO	RESTS	RIGHT	ROBLE	ROUPY	RUNIC
RECUR	RETCH	RIGID	ROBOT	ROUSE	RUNIN
REDAN	RETEM	RIGOR	ROCKS	ROUST	RUNNY
REDID	RETIA	RILED	ROCKY	ROUTE	RUNON
REDLY	RETRO	RILES	RODDY	ROUTS	RUNTS
REEDS	RETRY	RILEY	RODEO	ROVED	RUNTY
REEDY	RETTA	RILLE	RODIN	ROVEN	RUPEE
REEFS	REVEL	RILLS	ROGER	ROVER	RURAL
REEFY	REVET	RIMED	ROGUE	ROVES	RURIK
REEKS	REVUE	RIMER	ROILS	ROWAN	RUSES
REEKY	REZIN	RIMES	ROILY	ROWDY	RUSHY
REELS	*****	RINDS	ROLES	ROWED	RUSKS
REEVE	**RH---**	RINGS	ROLFE	ROWEL	RUSSO
REFER	*****	RINKS	ROLFS	ROWEN	RUSTS
REFIT	RHAGE	RINSE	ROLLO	ROWER	RUSTY
REGAL	RHAGY	RIOTS	ROLLS	ROYAL	RUTHS
REGAN	RHEAS	RIPEN	ROLPH	*****	RUTTY
REGES	RHEUM	RIPER	ROMAN	**RR---**	*****
REGIN	RHINE	RIPON	ROMEO	*****	**RY---**
REGMA	RHINO	RISEN	ROMPS	RRHEA	*****
REICH	RHIZO	RISER	RONDO	*****	RYNDS
REIFY	RHODA	RISES	RONNY	**RU---**	RYOTS
REIGN	RHOEA	RISKS	ROODS	*****	
				RUBES	
				RUBLE	

******	SALTS	SAVES	SCONE	SEATS	SERGE
SA---	SALTY	SAVIN	SCOOP	SEBAT	SERIF
******	SALUS	SAVOR	SCOOT	SEBUM	SERIN
SABAH	SALVE	SAVOY	SCOPE	SECCO	SERON
SABED	SALVO	SAVVY	SCOPS	SECTS	SEROW
SABER	SAMAR	SAWED	SCOPY	SEDAN	SERRA
SABES	SAMBA	SAWER	SCORE	SEDER	SERUM
SABIN	SAMBO	SAXES	SCORN	SEDGE	SERVE
SABLE	SAMEK	SAXON	SCOTO	SEDGY	SERVO
SABOT	SAMMY	SAYER	SCOTS	SEDUM	SETAE
SABRA	SAMOA	SAYID	SCOTT	SEEDS	SETHS
SABRE	SAMOS	SAYSO	SCOUR	SEEDY	SETON
SACKS	SANDS	******	SCOUT	SEEKS	SETTO
SACRA	SANDY	**SC---**	SCOWL	SEEMS	SETUP
SACRO	SANER	******	SCOWS	SEEPS	SEVEN
SADHU	SANTA	SCABS	SCRAG	SEERS	SEVER
SADIE	SAONE	SCADS	SCRAM	SEGNI	SEWED
SADLY	SAPID	SCALD	SCRAP	SEGNO	SEWER
SAFER	SAPOR	SCALE	SCREE	SEGOS	SEXED
SAFES	SAPPY	SCALL	SCREW	SEINE	SEXES
SAGAN	SAPRO	SCALP	SCRIM	SEISE	SEXTO
SAGAS	SARAH	SCALY	SCRIP	SEISM	******
SAGER	SARAN	SCAMP	SCROD	SEIZE	**SH---**
SAGES	SARAS	SCAND	SCRUB	SELAH	******
SAGOS	SARCO	SCANS	SCRUM	SELEN	SHACK
SAGUM	SARIS	SCANT	SCUBA	SELLS	SHADE
SAHEB	SARKS	SCAPA	SCUDI	SELMA	SHADY
SAHIB	SAROS	SCAPE	SCUDO	SEMEN	SHAFT
SAIGA	SARRE	SCAPI	SCUDS	SENDS	SHAGS
SAILS	SARTO	SCARE	SCUFF	SENNA	SHAHS
SAINT	SASIN	SCARF	SCULL	SENNE	SHAKE
SAJOU	SASSY	SCARP	SCULP	SENOR	SHAKO
SAKER	SATAN	SCARS	SCUMS	SENSE	SHAKY
SAKES	SATED	SCARY	SCUPS	SEOUL	SHALE
SALAD	SATES	SCATO	SCURF	SEPAL	SHALL
SALEM	SATIE	SCATS	SCUTA	SEPIA	SHALT
SALEP	SATIN	SCAUP	SCUTE	SEPOY	SHALY
SALES	SATYR	SCENA	SCUTS	SEPTA	SHAME
SALIC	SAUCE	SCEND	SCYPH	SEPTI	SHAMS
SALIX	SAUCY	SCENE	******	SEPTO	SHANK
SALLY	SAULS	SCENT	**SE---**	SEPTS	SHANS
SALMA	SAULT	SCHIZ	******	SERAC	SHANT
SALMI	SAUNA	SCHMO	SEALS	SERAI	SHAPE
SALOL	SAURO	SCHWA	SEAMS	SERAL	SHARD
SALON	SAURY	SCIFI	SEAMY	SERBS	SHARE
SALPA	SAUTE	SCION	SEANS	SERED	SHARI
SALSA	SAVED	SCOFF	SEARS	SERES	SHARK
SALSE	SAVER	SCOLD	SEATO	SERFS	SHARP

SHAUN	SHOOS	SIGNE	******	SLASH	SLUNK
SHAVE	SHOOT	SIGNS	**SK---**	SLATE	SLURP
SHAWL	SHOPS	SIKHS	******	SLATS	SLURS
SHAWM	SHORE	SILAS	SKALD	SLATY	SLUSH
SHAWN	SHORL	SILEX	SKATE	SLAVE	SLUTS
SHAWS	SHORN	SILIC	SKEAN	SLAVO	SLYER
SHAYS	SHORT	SILKS	SKEED	SLAVS	SLYLY
SHEAF	SHOTE	SILKY	SKEES	SLAWS	SLYPE
SHEAR	SHOTS	SILLS	SKEET	SLAYS	******
SHEAS	SHOUT	SILLY	SKEGS	SLEAT	**SM---**
SHEBA	SHOVE	SILOS	SKEIN	SLEDS	******
SHEDS	SHOWN	SILTS	SKEPS	SLEEK	SMACK
SHEEN	SHOWS	SILTY	SKEWS	SLEEP	SMALL
SHEEP	SHOWY	SILVA	SKIDS	SLEET	SMALT
SHEER	SHRED	SIMAR	SKIED	SLEPT	SMART
SHEET	SHREW	SIMON	SKIER	SLEWS	SMASH
SHEIK	SHRUB	SIMPS	SKIES	SLICE	SMAZE
SHELF	SHRUG	SINAI	SKIFF	SLICK	SMEAR
SHELL	SHUCK	SINCE	SKILL	SLIDE	SMELL
SHEOL	SHULS	SINES	SKIMO	SLIER	SMELT
SHERD	SHUNS	SINEW	SKIMP	SLIGO	SMEWS
SHEWN	SHUNT	SINGE	SKIMS	SLILY	SMILE
SHEWS	SHUSH	SINGS	SKINK	SLIME	SMIRK
SHIAH	SHUTE	SINKS	SKINS	SLIMS	SMITE
SHIED	SHUTS	SINON	SKIPS	SLIMY	SMITH
SHIER	SHYER	SINUS	SKIRL	SLING	SMOCK
SHIFT	SHYLY	SIOUX	SKIRR	SLINK	SMOGS
SHILL	******	SIPES	SKIRT	SLIPS	SMOKE
SHILY	**SI---**	SIRED	SKITS	SLIPT	SMOKY
SHIMS	******	SIREN	SKIVE	SLITS	SMOLT
SHINE	SIALO	SIRES	SKOAL	SLOBS	SMOTE
SHINS	SIBYL	SIRUP	SKUAS	SLOES	SMUTS
SHINY	SICES	SISAL	SKULK	SLOGS	******
SHIPS	SICKS	SISSY	SKULL	SLOOP	**SN---**
SHIRE	SIDED	SITAR	SKUNK	SLOPE	******
SHIRK	SIDER	SITED	SKYEY	SLOPS	SNACK
SHIRR	SIDES	SITES	******	SLOSH	SNAFU
SHIRT	SIDLE	SITIN	**SL---**	SLOTH	SNAGS
SHIVE	SIDON	SITKA	******	SLOTS	SNAIL
SHIVS	SIEGE	SITUS	SLABS	SLOWS	SNAKE
SHOAL	SIENA	SIVAN	SLACK	SLOYD	SNAKY
SHOAT	SIEUR	SIXES	SLAGS	SLUBS	SNAPS
SHOCK	SIEVE	SIXTE	SLAIN	SLUED	SNARE
SHOER	SIFTS	SIXTH	SLAKE	SLUES	SNARK
SHOES	SIGHS	SIXTY	SLAMS	SLUGS	SNARL
SHOJI	SIGHT	SIZAR	SLANG	SLUMP	SNATH
SHONE	SIGIL	SIZED	SLANT	SLUMS	SNEAD
SHOOK	SIGMA	SIZES	SLAPS	SLUNG	SNEAK

SNEER	SOLES	SOYAS	SPINI	SQUIB	STERN
SNELL	SOLFA	SOZIN	SPINS	SQUID	STETH
SNICK	SOLID	******	SPINY	******	STETS
SNIDE	SOLON	**SP---**	SPIRE	**ST---**	STEVE
SNIFF	SOLOS	******	SPIRO	******	STEWS
SNIPE	SOLUS	SPACE	SPIRT	STABS	STICH
SNIPS	SOLVE	SPADE	SPIRY	STACK	STICK
SNOBS	SOMAT	SPAHI	SPITE	STACY	STIED
SNOOD	SOMME	SPAIN	SPITS	STAFF	STIES
SNOOK	SOMNI	SPAIT	SPITZ	STAGE	STIFF
SNOOP	SONAR	SPAKE	SPLAT	STAGS	STILE
SNOOT	SONES	SPALL	SPLAY	STAGY	STILL
SNORE	SONGS	SPANG	SPLEN	STAID	STILT
SNORT	SONIA	SPANK	SPLIT	STAIN	STIMY
SNOTS	SONIC	SPANS	SPODE	STAIR	STING
SNOUT	SONJA	SPARE	SPOIL	STAKE	STINK
SNOWS	SONNY	SPARK	SPOKE	STALE	STINT
SNOWY	SONSY	SPARS	SPOOF	STALK	STIPE
SNUBS	SONYA	SPASM	SPOOK	STALL	STIRK
SNUFF	SOOTH	SPATE	SPOOL	STAMP	STIRP
SNUGS	SOOTS	SPATS	SPOON	STAND	STIRS
SNYES	SOOTY	SPAWN	SPOOR	STANK	STOAE
******	SOPHY	SPAYS	SPORE	STANS	STOAS
SO---	SOPOR	SPEAK	SPORO	STAPH	STOAT
******	SOPPY	SPEAR	SPORT	STARE	STOCK
SOAKS	SORAS	SPECK	SPOTS	STARK	STOGY
SOAPS	SORBS	SPECS	SPOUT	STARS	STOIC
SOAPY	SOREL	SPEED	SPRAG	START	STOKE
SOARS	SORER	SPELL	SPRAT	STASH	STOLE
SOBER	SORES	SPELT	SPRAY	STATE	STOMA
SOCIO	SORGO	SPEND	SPREE	STATO	STOME
SOCKS	SORRY	SPENT	SPRIG	STAVE	STOMP
SOCLE	SORTS	SPERM	SPRIT	STAYS	STOMY
SODAS	SORUS	SPEWS	SPRUE	STEAD	STONE
SODOM	SOTOL	SPHEN	SPUDS	STEAK	STONY
SOFAS	SOTTO	SPICA	SPUME	STEAL	STOOD
SOFIA	SOUGH	SPICE	SPUMY	STEAM	STOOK
SOFTA	SOULS	SPICY	SPUNK	STEED	STOOL
SOFTY	SOUND	SPIED	SPURN	STEEL	STOOP
SOGGY	SOUPS	SPIEL	SPURS	STEEN	STOPE
SOILS	SOUPY	SPIER	SPURT	STEEP	STOPS
SOJAS	SOURS	SPIES	******	STEER	STOPT
SOKES	SOUSA	SPIKE	**SQ---**	STEIN	STORE
SOLAN	SOUSE	SPIKY	******	STELE	STORK
SOLAR	SOUTH	SPILE	SQUAB	STEMS	STORM
SOLDI	SOWAR	SPILL	SQUAD	STENO	STORY
SOLDO	SOWED	SPILT	SQUAT	STEPS	STOSS
SOLED	SOWER	SPINE	SQUAW	STERE	STOUP

STOUR	SUFIC	SWAMI	******	TANGY	******
STOUT	SUFIS	SWAMP	TA---	TANIS	TE---
STOVE	SUGAR	SWANK	******	TANKA	******
STOWE	SUING	SWANS	TABAC	TANKS	TEACH
STOWS	SUINT	SWAPS	TABBY	TANSY	TEAKS
STRAD	SUITE	SWARD	TABES	TANTO	TEALS
STRAP	SUITS	SWARM	TABID	TANYA	TEAMS
STRAT	SULCI	SWART	TABLE	TAPAS	TEARS
STRAW	SULFA	SWASH	TABOO	TAPED	TEARY
STRAY	SULFO	SWATH	TABOR	TAPER	TEASE
STREW	SULKS	SWATS	TACET	TAPES	TEATS
STRIA	SULKY	SWAYS	TACHY	TAPIR	TEBET
STRIP	SULLY	SWEAR	TACIT	TAPIS	TEDDY
STROP	SULUS	SWEAT	TACKS	TARDO	TEEMS
STRUM	SUMAC	SWEDE	TACKY	TARDY	TEENS
STRUT	SUMER	SWEEP	TACNA	TARED	TEENY
STUBS	SUMPS	SWEET	TAELS	TARES	TEETH
STUCK	SUNNA	SWELL	TAFFY	TARNS	TEHEE
STUDS	SUNNI	SWEPT	TAFIA	TAROS	TEKEL
STUDY	SUNNS	SWIFT	TAHOE	TAROT	TELAE
STUFF	SUNNY	SWIGS	TAIGA	TARPS	TELEG
STUKA	SUNUP	SWILL	TAILS	TARRY	TELEO
STULL	SUPER	SWIMS	TAINO	TARSI	TELEX
STUMP	SUPES	SWINE	TAINS	TARSO	TELIC
STUMS	SUPRA	SWING	TAINT	TARTS	TELLS
STUNG	SURAH	SWIPE	TAKEN	TARTY	TELLY
STUNK	SURAL	SWIRL	TAKER	TASKS	TEMPE
STUNS	SURAS	SWISH	TAKES	TASSO	TEMPI
STUNT	SURDS	SWISS	TALCS	TASTE	TEMPO
STUPA	SURER	SWOON	TALER	TASTY	TEMPT
STUPE	SURFS	SWOOP	TALES	TATAR	TENCH
STYLE	SURFY	SWORD	TALKS	TATRA	TENDS
STYLI	SURGE	SWORE	TALLY	TATTY	TENET
STYLO	SURGY	SWORN	TALON	TAUNT	TENON
STYMY	SURLY	SWUNG	TALOS	TAUPE	TENOR
******	SUSAN	******	TALUK	TAURO	TENOS
SU---	SUSIE	SY---	TALUS	TAUTO	TENSE
******	SUTRA	******	TAMED	TAWED	TENTH
SUAVE	SUZYS	SYBIL	TAMER	TAWER	TENTS
SUBAH	******	SYCEE	TAMES	TAWNY	TEPEE
SUCKS	SW---	SYCES	TAMIL	TAXED	TEPID
SUCRE	******	SYLPH	TAMIS	TAXER	TERAT
SUDAN	SWABS	SYLVA	TAMMY	TAXES	TERMS
SUDOR	SWAGE	SYNGE	TAMPA	TAXIS	TERNS
SUDSY	SWAGS	SYNOD	TAMPS	TAZZA	TERRA
SUEDE	SWAIL	SYRIA	TANEY	******	TERRI
SUERS	SWAIN	SYROS	TANGO	TB---	TERRY
SUETY	SWALE	SYRUP	TANGS	******	TERSE
				TBONE	

TESLA	THRUM	TINEA	TOLYL	TOUTS	TRICH
TESTA	THUDS	TINED	TOMAN	TOWED	TRICK
TESTS	THUGS	TINES	TOMAS	TOWEL	TRIED
TESTY	THUJA	TINGE	TOMBS	TOWER	TRIER
TETHS	THULE	TINGS	TOMES	TOWNS	TRIES
TETON	THUMB	TINNY	TOMMY	TOXIC	TRIGO
TETRA	THUMP	TINTS	TONAL	TOXIN	TRIGS
TEXAS	THURS	TIOGA	TONED	TOYED	TRILL
TEXTS	THYME	TIPPY	TONER	TOYER	TRIMS
******	THYMY	TIPSY	TONES	TOYON	TRINA
TH---	THYRO	TIRED	TONGA	TOYOS	TRINE
******	******	TIREE	TONGS	******	TRIOL
THADS	**TI---**	TIRES	TONIC	**TR---**	TRIOS
THADY	******	TIROS	TONIS	******	TRIPE
THANE	TIARA	TITAN	TONNE	TRACE	TRIPS
THANK	TIBER	TITER	TONUS	TRACH	TRITE
THAWS	TIBET	TITHE	TONYS	TRACK	TRIXY
THECA	TIBIA	TITIS	TOOLS	TRACT	TROAS
THEDA	TICAL	TITLE	TOOTH	TRACY	TROLL
THEFT	TICKS	TITUS	TOOTS	TRADE	TRONA
THEIR	TIDAL	TIZZY	TOPAZ	TRAGI	TROOP
THEME	TIDED	******	TOPED	TRAIL	TROPE
THERE	TIDES	**TO---**	TOPEE	TRAIN	TROPH
THERM	TIEIN	******	TOPER	TRAIT	TROTH
THESE	TIERS	TOADS	TOPES	TRAMP	TROTS
THETA	TIEUP	TOADY	TOPHI	TRAMS	TROUT
THEWS	TIFFS	TOAST	TOPIC	TRANS	TROVE
THEWY	TIGER	TOBOL	TOPIS	TRAPS	TRUCE
THICK	TIGHT	TOBYS	TOPSY	TRASH	TRUCK
THIEF	TIGRE	TODAY	TOQUE	TRASS	TRUDA
THIGH	TIKIS	TODDS	TORAH	TRAVE	TRUDY
THINE	TILDA	TODDY	TORCH	TRAWL	TRUED
THING	TILDE	TODOS	TORIC	TRAYS	TRUER
THINK	TILED	TOEIN	TORII	TREAD	TRUES
THINS	TILER	TOFTS	TORSI	TREAS	TRULL
THIOL	TILES	TOGAE	TORSK	TREAT	TRULY
THIRD	TILLS	TOGAS	TORSO	TREED	TRUMP
THOLE	TILLY	TOGUE	TORTE	TREES	TRUNK
THONG	TILTH	TOILE	TORTS	TREKS	TRURO
THORN	TILTS	TOILS	TORUS	TREND	TRUSS
THORP	TIMED	TOISE	TOTAL	TRENT	TRUST
THOSE	TIMER	TOKAY	TOTED	TRESS	TRUTH
THOTH	TIMES	TOKEN	TOTEM	TREWS	TRYMA
THREE	TIMID	TOKYO	TOTER	TREYS	TRYON
THREW	TIMMY	TOLAN	TOTES	TRIAD	TRYST
THROB	TIMOR	TOLAS	TOUCH	TRIAL	******
THROE	TINAS	TOLES	TOUGH	TRIBE	**TS---**
THROW	TINCT	TOLLS	TOURS	TRICE	******
					TSADE
					TSANA
					TSARS

*****	TWEAK	*****	UNLAY	USUAL	VARIX
TU---	TWEED	**UK---**	UNLIT	USURP	VARRO
*****	TWEEN	*****	UNMAN	USURY	VARUS
TUBAL	TWEET	UKASE	UNMEW	*****	VARVE
TUBAS	TWERE	*****	UNPEG	**UT---**	VASES
TUBBY	TWERP	**UL---**	UNPEN	*****	VASTY
TUBED	TWICE	*****	UNPIN	UTERI	VATIC
TUBER	TWIGS	ULCER	UNREF	UTERO	VAULT
TUBES	TWILL	ULEMA	UNRIG	UTHER	VAUNT
TUCKS	TWINE	ULENT	UNRIP	UTICA	*****
TUDOR	TWINS	ULNAE	UNSAY	UTILE	**VE---**
TUFTS	TWIRL	ULNAR	UNSEX	UTTER	*****
TUFTY	TWIRP	ULNAS	UNTIE	UTURN	VEDIC
TULES	TWIST	ULOSE	UNTIL	*****	VEERS
TULIP	TWITS	ULOUS	UNWED	**UV---**	VEERY
TULLE	TWIXT	ULTRA	UNZIP	*****	VEILS
TULLY	*****	*****	*****	UVEAL	VEINS
TULSA	**TY---**	**UM---**	**UP---**	UVEAS	VEINY
TUMID	*****	*****	*****	UVULA	VELAR
TUMMY	TYCHE	UMBEL	UPBOW	*****	VELDS
TUMOR	TYEES	UMBER	UPEND	**UX---**	VELDT
TUNAS	TYING	UMBLE	UPPED	*****	VELUM
TUNED	TYKES	UMBOS	UPPER	UXMAL	VENAE
TUNER	TYLER	UMBRA	UPSET	*****	VENAL
TUNES	TYPED	UMIAK	*****	**VA---**	VENDS
TUNIC	TYPES	*****	**UR---**	*****	VENOM
TUNIS	TYPOS	**UN---**	*****	VACUA	VENTS
TUNNY	TYROL	*****	URALS	VADUZ	VENUE
TUPIK	TYROS	UNAPT	URANO	VAGIN	VENUS
TUPIS	*****	UNARM	URATE	VAGUE	VEPSA
TUQUE	**TZ---**	UNAUS	URBAN	VAGUS	VERAS
TURBO	*****	UNBAR	UREAL	VAIRS	VERBS
TURCO	TZARS	UNCAP	UREDO	VALES	VERDI
TURFS	*****	UNCLE	URGED	VALET	VERGE
TURFY	**UB---**	UNCUT	URGES	VALID	VERMI
TURIN	*****	UNDEE	URIAH	VALOR	VERNA
TURKI	UBOAT	UNDER	URICO	VALUE	VERNE
TURKS	UBOLT	UNDID	URIEL	VALVE	VERNS
TURNS	*****	UNDUE	URINE	VAMPS	VERSE
TUSKS	**UD---**	UNFIT	URINO	VANED	VERSO
TUTOR	*****	UNFIX	URSAE	VANES	VERST
TUTTI	UDDER	UNHAT	*****	VANGS	VERTU
TUTTY	UDINE	UNIAT	**US---**	VANIR	VERVE
TUTUS	*****	UNIFY	*****	VAPID	VESIC
*****	**UH---**	UNION	USAGE	VAPOR	VESTA
TW---	*****	UNITE	USERS	VARAS	VESTS
*****	UHLAN	UNITS	USHER	VARIC	VETCH
TWAIN	**UI---**	UNITY	USING	VARIO	VEXED
TWANG	*****				
	UINTA				

VEXER	VISES	******	WARES	WEIGH	WHISH
VEXES	VISIT	**VY---**	WARMS	WEIRD	WHISK
VEXIL	VISOR	******	WARNS	WEIRS	WHIST
******	VISTA	VYING	WARPS	WEKAS	WHITE
VI---	VITAE	******	WARTS	WELCH	WHITS
******	VITAL	**WA---**	WARTY	WELDS	WHOLE
VIALS	VITRI	******	WASHY	WELLS	WHOOP
VIAND	VITTA	WACKE	WASNT	WELSH	WHOPS
VIBES	VIVID	WACKS	WASPS	WELTS	WHORE
VICAR	VIXEN	WACKY	WASPY	WENCH	WHORL
VICES	VIZIR	WADDY	WASTE	WENDS	WHORT
VICHY	VIZOR	WADED	WATAP	WENDY	WHOSE
VICKS	******	WADER	WATCH	WENNY	WHOSO
VICKY	**VN---**	WADES	WATER	WESER	******
VIDAL	******	WAFER	WATTS	WETLY	**WI---**
VIDEO	VNECK	WAFTS	WAUGH	******	******
VIEWS	******	WAGED	WAULS	**WH---**	WICKS
VIEWY	**VO---**	WAGER	WAVED	******	WIDDY
VIGIL	******	WAGES	WAVER	WHACK	WIDEN
VIGOR	VOCAL	WAGON	WAVES	WHALE	WIDER
VILER	VOCES	WAHOO	WAVEY	WHAMS	WIDOW
VILLA	VODKA	WAIFS	WAWLS	WHANG	WIDTH
VILLE	VOGUE	WAILS	WAXED	WHAPS	WIELD
VILLI	VOGUL	WAINS	WAXEN	WHARF	WIGAN
VILLS	VOICE	WAIST	WAXES	WHAUP	WIGHT
VILNA	VOIDS	WAITS	WAYNE	WHEAL	WILDE
VIMEN	VOILA	WAIVE	******	WHEAT	WILDS
VINAS	VOILE	WAKED	**WE---**	WHEEL	WILED
VINCE	VOLAR	WAKEN	******	WHELK	WILES
VINCI	VOLES	WAKES	WEALD	WHELM	WILEY
VINES	VOLGA	WALDO	WEALS	WHELP	WILLA
VINIC	VOLTA	WALED	WEANS	WHENS	WILLS
VINNY	VOLTE	WALER	WEARS	WHERE	WILLY
VINYL	VOLTI	WALES	WEARY	WHETS	WILMA
VIOLA	VOLTS	WALKS	WEAVE	WHEYS	WILTS
VIOLS	VOLVA	WALLA	WEBBY	WHICH	WINCE
VIPER	VOMER	WALLY	WEBER	WHIFF	WINCH
VIRAL	VOMIT	WALTS	WEDGE	WHIGS	WINDS
VIREO	VOTED	WALTZ	WEDGY	WHILE	WINDY
VIRES	VOTER	WAMUS	WEEDS	WHIMS	WINED
VIRGA	VOTES	WANDA	WEEDY	WHINE	WINES
VIRGE	VOUCH	WANDS	WEEKS	WHINS	WINGS
VIRGO	VOWED	WANED	WEEMS	WHINY	WINGY
VIRTU	VOWEL	WANES	WEENY	WHIPS	WINKS
VIRUS	VOWER	WANEY	WEEPS	WHIPT	WINOS
VISAS	******	WANLY	WEEPY	WHIRL	WINZE
VISCT	**VU---**	WANTS	WEEST	WHIRR	WIPED
VISED	******	WARDS	WEFTS	WHIRS	WIPER
	VUGGY				
	VULGO				
	VULVA				

WIPES	WORMY	XENON	YEARS	******	ZONED
WIRED	WORRY	XERIC	YEAST	YS---	ZONES
WIRER	WORSE	XEROX	YEATS	******	ZOOID
WIRES	WORST	XERUS	YEGGS	YSERE	ZOOMS
WIRRA	WORTH	******	YELKS	******	ZOONS
WISED	WORTS	XI---	YELLS	YU---	ZORIL
WISER	WOTAN	******	YELPS	******	******
WISES	WOULD	XIPHI	YEMEN	YUCCA	A-A--
WISPS	WOUND	******	YERBA	YUGAS	******
WISPY	WOVEN	XR---	YESES	YUKON	ABACA
WITAN	WOWED	******	YETIS	YULES	ABACI
WITCH	******	XRAYS	******	YUMMY	ABACK
WITHE	WR---	******	YI---	YUPON	ABAFT
WITHY	******	XT---	******	******	ABASE
WITTE	WRACK	******	YIELD	ZA---	ABASH
WITTY	WRAPS	XTIAN	YIPES	******	ABATE
WIVED	WRAPT	******	******	ZAIRE	ADAGE
WIVER	WRATH	XY---	YO---	ZAMIA	ADAHS
WIVES	WREAK	******	******	ZARFS	ADAMS
WIZEN	WRECK	XYLAN	YODEL	ZAYIN	ADAPT
******	WRENS	XYLEM	YODHS	******	AGAIN
WO---	WREST	XYLOL	YOGEE	ZE---	AGAMA
******	WRICK	XYLYL	YOGHS	******	AGANA
WOADS	WRIED	XYSTS	YOGIC	ZEBEC	AGAPE
WOALD	WRIER	******	YOGIN	ZEBRA	AGATE
WODAN	WRIES	YA---	YOGIS	ZEBUS	AGAVE
WODEN	WRING	******	YOKED	ZEKES	AGAZE
WOKEN	WRIST	YACHT	YOKEL	ZEROS	ALACK
WOLDS	WRITE	YAGER	YOKES	ZESTS	ALADA
WOLFS	WRITS	YAHOO	YOLKS	ZESTY	ALAIN
WOMAN	WRONG	YAHVE	YOLKY	ZETAS	ALAMO
WOMBS	WROTE	YALTA	YOULL	******	ALAND
WOMBY	WROTH	YAMEN	YOUNG	ZI---	ALANS
WOMEN	WRUNG	YAMUN	YOURE	******	ALARM
WOODS	WRYER	YANKS	YOURS	ZIBET	ALARY
WOODY	WRYLY	YAPON	YOUTH	ZIMRI	ALATE
WOOED	******	YARDS	YOUVE	ZINCS	AMAHS
WOOER	WY---	YARNS	YOWED	ZINCY	AMAIN
WOOFS	******	YAUPS	YOWLS	ZINGY	AMANA
WOOLF	WYATT	YAWED	YOYOS	ZINKY	AMASS
WOOLS	******	YAWLS	******	ZIPPY	AMATE
WOOLY	XA---	YAWNS	YP---	ZIRON	AMATI
WOOZY	******	YAWPS	******	******	AMAZE
WORDS	XANTH	YAXES	YPRES	ZL---	APACE
WORDY	XAXES	YAXIS	******	******	APART
WORKS	XAXIS	YAZOO	YQ---	ZLOTY	AQABA
WORLD	XE---	YE---	******	******	ARABS
WORMS	XEBEC	YEANS	YQUEM	ZO---	ARABY
	XENIA	YEARN		******	
				ZOMBI	
				ZONAL	

ATAXY	ADDER	AKENE	ALGID	ACING	ARICA
AVAIL	ADDIE	ALECK	ALGIE	ACINI	ARIEL
AVARS	ADDLE	ALECS	ALGIN	ACITY	ARIES
AVAST	ADDYS	ALEFS	ALGOL	ADIEU	ARILS
AWAIT	AEDES	ALEPH	ALGOR	ADIGE	ARION
AWAKE	AIDAS	ALERT	ALGUM	ADIOS	ARISE
AWARD	AIDED	ALEUT	ALGYS	ADITS	ARIUM
AWARE	AIDER	ALEXA	ANGEL	AFIRE	ARIUS
AWASH	AIDES	AMEBA	ANGER	AGILE	ASIAN
AYAHS	ALDAN	AMEER	ANGIO	AGING	ASIDE
AZANS	ALDEN	AMEND	ANGLE	AGIOS	ATILT
******	ALDER	AMENS	ANGLO	AGIST	ATION
A-B--	ALDIS	AMENT	ANGRY	ALIAS	ATIVE
******	ALDOL	ANEAR	ANGST	ALIBI	AVIAN
ABBAS	ALDOS	ANELE	ANGUS	ALICE	AVION
ABBES	ALDUS	ANEMO	ARGAL	ALIEN	AVISO
ABBEY	ANDES	ANENT	ARGIL	ALIFS	AWING
ABBIE	ANDRE	APEAK	ARGOL	ALIGN	AXIAL
ABBOT	ANDRO	APERY	ARGON	ALIKE	AXILE
ABBYS	ANDYS	AREAE	ARGOS	ALINE	AXILS
ALBAN	ARDEB	AREAL	ARGOT	ALIST	AXING
ALBAS	ARDEN	AREAS	ARGUE	ALIVE	AXIOM
ALBEE	ARDOR	ARECA	ARGUS	AMIAS	AYINS
ALBIN	AUDAD	AREIC	AUGER	AMICE	AZINE
ALBUM	AUDEN	ARENA	AUGHT	AMIDE	******
AMBER	AUDIE	ARENT	AUGUR	AMIDO	A-J--
AMBIT	AUDIO	ARETE	******	AMIEL	******
AMBLE	AUDIT	AVENS	A-H--	AMIES	ANJOU
AMBOS	AYDIN	AVERS	******	AMIGO	******
AMBRY	******	AVERT	ABHOR	AMINE	A-K--
ARBOR	A-E--	AVERY	ACHED	AMINO	******
******	******	A-F--	ACHES	AMIRS	AIKEN
A-C--	ABEAM	******	AGHAS	AMISH	ALKYL
******	ABELE	AFFIX	APHID	AMISS	ANKHS
ACCEL	ABELS	ALFIE	APHIS	AMITY	ANKLE
ACCRA	ABETS	AWFUL	ASHEN	ANILE	ANKUS
AECIA	ACEAE	******	ASHER	ANILS	ASKED
ALCAN	ACEAN	A-G--	ASHES	ANIMA	ASKER
ANCON	ACERB	******	ASHUR	ANIME	ASKEW
ARCED	ACETO	AEGIR	ATHOS	ANION	******
ARCHI	ADEEM	AEGIS	******	ANISE	A-L--
ARCHY	ADELA	AGGER	A-I--	ANISO	******
ARCUS	ADELE	AGGIE	******	ANITA	AALII
ASCAP	ADENI	ALGAE	ABIBS	APIAN	ABLER
ASCOT	ADENO	ALGAL	ABIDE	APING	ADLAI
ASCUS	ADEPT	ALGIA	ABIEL	APISH	ADLER
******	AGENT	ALGER	ABIES	ARIAN	ADLIB
A-D--	AHEAD	ALGIA	ACIDS	ARIAS	AGLEE
******					
ADDAX					
ADDED					

AGLET	******	ALOES	ARPAD	ANSAE	ARTHR
AGLEY	A-N--	ALOFT	ARPEN	ANSEL	ARTIC
AGLOW	******	ALOHA	ASPCA	APSES	ARTIE
AILED	ABNER	ALOIN	ASPEN	APSIS	ARTIS
ALLAH	AGNES	ALOIS	ASPER	ARSES	ARTUR
ALLAN	AGNIS	ALONE	ASPIC	ARSIS	ASTER
ALLAY	AINOS	ALONG	ASPIS	ARSON	ASTIR
ALLEN	AINUS	ALOOF	ATPAR	ASSAI	ASTON
ALLEY	AMNIA	ALOUD	******	ASSAM	ASTOR
ALLIE	ANNAL	AMOLE	A-R--	ASSAY	ASTRO
ALLIN	ANNAM	AMONG	******	ASSES	ATTAR
ALLIS	ANNAS	AMOUR	AARON	ASSET	ATTIC
ALLOT	ANNES	ANODE	ABRAM	ASSNS	ATTIS
ALLOW	ANNEX	ANOMY	ABRIS	ASSOC	ATTYS
ALLOY	ANNIE	APORT	ACRED	ASSTS	AUTOS
ALLYL	ANNOY	AROID	ACRES	ASSYR	AUTRY
ANLAS	ANNUL	AROMA	ACRID	AUSTL	AZTEC
ARLEN	APNEA	AROSE	AERIE	******	******
ARLES	ARNIE	ATOLL	AFROS	A-T--	A-U--
ATLAS	AUNTS	ATOMS	AGREE	******	******
AULIC	AUNTY	ATONE	AIRED	ACTED	ABUSE
AULIS	AWNED	ATONY	AKRON	ACTIN	ABUTS
AXLED	******	ATORY	AORTA	ACTOR	ACUTE
AXLES	A-O--	AVOID	APRIL	ACTUS	ADULT
******	******	AVOIR	APRON	AETAT	ADUNC
A-M--	ABODE	AVOWS	ARRAN	AFTER	ADUST
******	ABOHM	AWOKE	ARRAS	AFTRA	ADUWA
ADMAN	ABOIL	AXONE	ARRAY	AITCH	AGUES
ADMEN	ABOMA	AXONS	ARRIS	ALTAI	ALUIN
ADMEX	ABOMB	AZOIC	ARROW	ALTAR	ALULA
ADMIN	ABORT	AZOLE	ATRIA	ALTAS	ALUMS
ADMIT	ABOUT	AZONS	ATRIP	ALTER	AMUCK
ADMIX	ABOVE	AZOTE	AURAE	ALTON	AMUSE
AEMIA	ACOCK	AZOTH	AURAL	ALTOS	AQUAE
AIMED	ACORN	******	AURAS	ANTAE	AQUAS
AIMEE	ACOUO	A-P--	AUREI	ANTAL	ARUBA
ALMAH	ADOBE	******	AURES	ANTED	ARUMS
ALMAS	ADOLF	ALPHA	AURIC	ANTES	AZURE
ALMUD	ADOPT	ALPHY	AURIS	ANTHO	******
ALMUG	ADORE	AMPHI	AURUM	ANTIC	A-V--
AMMAN	ADORN	AMPHR	AVRIL	ANTIS	******
AMMON	ADOWA	AMPLE	******	ANTON	ALVAN
ARMED	AEONS	AMPLY	A-S--	ANTRA	ALVIN
ARMET	AFOOT	AMPUL	******	APTER	ANVIL
ARMOR	AFORE	APPAL	AESIR	APTLY	ARVAL
ATMAN	AFOUL	APPEL	AESOP	ARTAL	******
AXMAN	AGONY	APPLE	AISLE	ARTEL	A-W--
AXMEN	AGORA	APPLY	AISNE	ARTER	******
					ALWAY
					ALWIN
					ASWAN

******	BLADE	******	******	******	BLIND
A-X--	BLAHS	B-B--	B-E--	B-G--	BLINK
******	BLAIN	******	******	******	BLIPS
AUXIL	BLAKE	BABAR	BEEBE	BAGEL	BLISS
AUXIN	BLAME	BABAS	BEECH	BAGGY	BLITZ
******	BLANC	BABEL	BEEFS	BEGAD	BOILS
A-Y--	BLAND	BABER	BEEFY	BEGAN	BOISE
******	BLANK	BABES	BEEPS	BEGAT	BRIAN
ABYSM	BLARE	BABOO	BEERS	BEGET	BRIAR
ABYSS	BLASE	BABUL	BEERY	BEGIN	BRIBE
ADYTA	BLAST	BEBOP	BEETS	BEGOT	BRICE
ALYCE	BLATS	BIBBS	BIERS	BEGUM	BRICK
AMYLO	BLAZE	BIBLE	BLEAK	BEGUN	BRIDE
AMYLS	BOARD	BOBBY	BLEAR	BIGHT	BRIEF
ARYAN	BOARS	BUBAL	BLEAT	BIGLY	BRIER
ASYLA	BOAST	BUBER	BLEBS	BIGOT	BRIGS
ASYUT	BOATS	******	BLEED	BOGAN	BRILL
******	BRACE	B-C--	BLEEP	BOGEY	BRIMS
A-Z--	BRACT	******	BLEND	BOGGY	BRINE
******	BRADS	BACCI	BLENT	BOGIE	BRING
ADZES	BRADY	BACHE	BLESS	BOGLE	BRINK
ANZAC	BRAES	BACKS	BLEST	BOGOR	BRINY
ANZIO	BRAGE	BACON	BMEWS	BOGUS	BRISK
******	BRAGG	BACUP	BOERS	BUGGY	BUILD
B-A--	BRAGI	BECKS	BREAD	BUGLE	BUILT
******	BRAGS	BECKY	BREAK	******	******
BAAED	BRAHE	BICES	BREAM	B-H--	B-J--
BEACH	BRAID	BOCHE	BREDA	******	******
BEADS	BRAIL	BUCKO	BREED	BAHAI	BIJOU
BEADY	BRAIN	BUCKS	BRENT	BAHIA	******
BEAKS	BRAKE	******	BREST	BAHTS	B-K--
BEALL	BRAKY	B-D--	BREVE	BEHAN	******
BEAMS	BRAND	******	BREVI	BIHAR	BAKED
BEAMY	BRANS	BADEN	BREWS	BOHEA	BAKER
BEANO	BRANT	BADGE	******	BOHOL	BAKES
BEANS	BRASH	BADLY	B-F--	******	BIKES
BEARD	BRASS	BEDEW	******	B-I--	BIKOL
BEARS	BRATS	BEDIM	BAFFS	******	******
BEAST	BRAVA	BIDDY	BAFFY	BAILS	B-L--
BEATA	BRAVE	BIDED	BEFIT	BAIRD	******
BEATS	BRAVO	BIDES	BEFOG	BAIRN	BALAS
BEAUS	BRAWL	BIDET	BIFFS	BAITS	BALDR
BEAUT	BRAWN	BLDGS	BIFFY	BAIZE	BALED
BEAUX	BRAXY	BODED	BIFID	BEIGE	BALER
BHANG	BRAYS	BODES	BUFFI	BEING	BALES
BIALY	BRAZA	BUDDY	BUFFO	BEIRA	BALKS
BLABS	BRAZE	BUDGE	BUFFS	BLIGH	BALKY
BLACK	BWANA	BUDGY	BUFFY	BLIMP	BALLS

BALMS	BANDA	BLOBS	******	BORIS	BESSY
BALMY	BANDS	BLOCK	**B-R--**	BORNE	BESTS
BALSA	BANDY	BLOCS	******	BORNU	BISES
BALTS	BANFF	BLOIS	BARBS	BORON	BISON
BELAY	BANGS	BLOKE	BARCA	BORTS	BISSE
BELCH	BANJO	BLOND	BARDE	BORTY	BOSCH
BELEM	BANKS	BLOOD	BARDS	BORTZ	BOSKS
BELGA	BANNS	BLOOM	BARED	BURAN	BOSKY
BELIE	BANTU	BLOTS	BARER	BURDS	BOSOM
BELLA	BENCH	BLOWN	BARES	BURGH	BOSON
BELLE	BENDS	BLOWS	BARGE	BURGS	BOSSY
BELLS	BENDY	BLOWY	BARIC	BURIN	BOSUN
BELLY	BENES	BOOBS	BARIT	BURKE	BUSBY
BELOW	BENET	BOOBY	BARKS	BURLS	BUSED
BELTS	BENIN	BOOED	BARKY	BURLY	BUSES
BILBO	BENJY	BOOKS	BARMY	BURMA	BUSHY
BILES	BENNE	BOOMS	BARNS	BURNS	BUSKS
BILGE	BENNY	BOONE	BARON	BURNT	BUSTS
BILGY	BENUE	BOONS	BARRE	BURPS	BYSSI
BILKS	BINAL	BOORS	BARRY	BURRO	******
BILLS	BINDS	BOOST	BARTH	BURRS	**B-T--**
BILLY	BINES	BOOTH	BARYE	BURRY	******
BOLAR	BINET	BOOTS	BERAR	BURSA	BATAN
BOLAS	BINGE	BOOTY	BEREA	BURSE	BATCH
BOLES	BINGO	BOOZE	BERET	BURST	BATED
BOLLS	BINIT	BOOZY	BERGS	BYRES	BATEN
BOLOS	BONDS	BROAD	BERIA	BYRON	BATES
BOLTS	BONED	BROCK	BERME	******	BATHE
BOLUS	BONER	BROIL	BERMS	**B-S--**	BATHO
BULBS	BONES	BROKE	BERNE	******	BATHS
BULGE	BONGO	BROME	BERRA	BASAL	BATHY
BULGY	BONGS	BROMO	BERRY	BASED	BATIK
BULKS	BONIN	BRONC	BERTA	BASEL	BATON
BULKY	BONNY	BRONX	BERTH	BASES	BATTY
BULLA	BONUS	BROOD	BERTS	BASIC	BETAS
BULLS	BONZE	BROOK	BERTY	BASIL	BETEL
BULLY	BUNCH	BROOM	BERYL	BASIN	BETHS
BYLAW	BUNCO	BROOS	BIRCH	BASIS	BETON
******	BUNDE	BROTH	BIRDS	BASKS	BETSO
B-M--	BUNDS	BROWN	BIRLE	BASLE	BETSY
******	BUNGS	BROWS	BIRLS	BASON	BETTE
BAMBI	BUNKO	BUOYS	BIRRS	BASRA	BETTY
BOMBE	BUNKS	******	BIRTH	BASSI	BITCH
BOMBS	BUNNS	**B-P--**	BORAX	BASSO	BITER
BUMPS	BUNNY	******	BORED	BASTE	BITES
BUMPY	BUNTS	BIPED	BORER	BESET	BITTS
******	******	BIPOD	BORES	BESOM	BOTCH
B-N--	**B-O--**		BORIC	BESOT	BOTHY
******	******				
BANAL	BIOTA				
BANAT	BLOAT				

BOTTS	BAWLS	CHAOS	CRAMS	COCCI	CHEVY
BUTCH	BOWED	CHAPE	CRANE	COCKS	CHEWS
BUTTE	BOWEL	CHAPS	CRANI	COCKY	CHEWY
BUTTS	BOWER	CHAPT	CRANK	COCOA	CLEAN
BUTYL	BOWIE	CHARD	CRAPE	COCOS	CLEAR
******	BOWLS	CHARE	CRAPS	CYCAD	CLEAT
B-U--	BOWSE	CHARM	CRASH	CYCLE	CLEEK
******	BYWAY	CHARO	CRASS	CYCLO	CLEFS
BAULK		CHARS	CRATE	******	CLEFT
BAUME	**B-X--**	CHART	CRAVE	**C-D--**	CLEMS
BEULA	******	CHARY	CRAWL	******	CLEON
BLUED	BOXED	CHASE	CRAWS	CADDO	CLERK
BLUER	BOXER	CHASM	CRAZE	CADDY	CLEWS
BLUES	BOXES	CHATS	CRAZY	CADES	COEDS
BLUET	BUXOM	CHAWS	CYANO	CADET	COELE
BLUFF	******	CLACK	CZARS	CADGE	COELO
BLUNT		CLAIM	******	CADIS	COENO
BLURB	**B-Y--**	CLAMP	**C-B--**	CADIZ	CREAK
BLURS	******	CLAMS	******	CADRE	CREAM
BLURT	BAYED	CLANG	CABAL	CEDAR	CRECY
BLUSH	BAYOU	CLANK	CABBY	CEDED	CREDO
BOUGH	BLYTH	CLANS	CABER	CEDES	CREED
BOULE	BOYAR	CLAPS	CABIN	CIDAL	CREEK
BOUND	BOYDS	CLARA	CABLE	CIDER	CREEL
BOURG	BOYLE	CLARE	CABOB	CODAS	CREEP
BOURN	BOYNE	CLARK	CABOT	CODED	CREES
BOUSE	BRYAN	CLARO	CIBOL	CODER	CREME
BOUSY	BRYCE	CLARY	COBBS	CODES	CREON
BOUTS	BUYER	CLASH	COBIA	CODEX	CREPE
BRUCE	******	CLASP	COBLE	CUDDY	CREPT
BRUIN	**B-Z--**	CLASS	COBRA	******	CRESC
BRUIT	******	CLAWS	CUBAN	**C-E--**	CRESS
BRUME	BEZEL	CLAYS	CUBBY	******	CREST
BRUNO	BIZET	COACH	CUBEB	CHEAP	CRETE
BRUNT	BOZOS	COALS	CUBED	CHEAT	CREWE
BRUSH	******	COALY	CUBES	CHECK	CREWS
BRUSK	**C-A--**	COAST	CUBIC	CHEEK	CTENO
BRUTE	******	COATI	CUBIT	CHEEP	CZECH
******	CEARA	COATS	******	CHEER	******
B-V--	CEASE	CHAET	**C-C--**	CHEFS	**C-F--**
******	CHAFE	CRABS	******	CHELA	******
BEVAN	CHAFF	CRACK	CACAO	CHEMI	CAFES
BEVEL	CHAIN	CRACY	CACHE	CHEMO	CUFFS
BEVIN	CHAIR	CRAFT	CACTI	CHERT	******
BOVID	CHALK	CRAGS	CECAL	CHESS	**C-G--**
******	CHAMP	CRAIG	CECIL	CHEST	******
B-W--	CHANG	CRAKE	CECUM	CHETH	CAGED
******	CHANT	CRAMP	COCAS	CHETS	CAGES
BAWDS					
BAWDY					

CAGEY	CLING	CALVE	COMBS	CONES	COOER
CIGAR	CLINK	CALYX	COMDR	CONEY	COOEY
COGON	CLINO	CELIA	COMDT	CONGA	COOKS
*****	CLINT	CELIE	COMER	CONGE	COOKY
C-H--	CLIOS	CELLA	COMES	CONGO	COOLS
*****	CLIPS	CELLO	COMET	CONIC	COOMB
COHAN	CLIVE	CELLS	COMFY	CONIO	COONS
*****	COIFS	CELOM	COMIC	CONKS	COOPS
C-I--	COIGN	CELTS	COMMA	CONNY	COOPT
*****	COILS	CHLOE	COMPO	CONTD	COOTS
CAIRD	CRIBS	CHLOR	COMTE	CONTE	CROAK
CAIRN	CRICK	CILIA	COMUS	CONTO	CROAT
CAIRO	CRIED	COLAS	CUMIN	CONTR	CROCE
CEIBA	CRIER	COLDS	CYMAE	CONUS	CROCI
CEILS	CRIES	COLES	CYMAR	CYNIC	CROCK
CHIAN	CRIME	COLIC	CYMES	*****	CROFT
CHIAS	CRIMP	COLIN	CYMRI	C-O--	CROIX
CHIBA	CRISP	COLLY	CYMRY	******	CRONE
CHICK	CUING	COLNE	******	CEORL	CRONY
CHICO	CUISH	COLON	C-N--	CHOCK	CROOK
CHIDE	******	COLOR	******	CHOIR	CROON
CHIEF	C-J--	COLTS	CANAD	CHOKE	CROPS
CHILD	******	COLZA	CANAL	CHOKY	CRORE
CHILE	CAJON	CULCH	CANDY	CHOLE	CROSS
CHILI	CAJUN	CULET	CANEA	CHOPS	CROUP
CHILL	******	CULEX	CANED	CHORD	CROWD
CHILO	C-K--	CULLS	CANER	CHORE	CROWN
CHIME	******	CULMS	CANES	CHORO	CROWS
CHIMP	CAKED	CULPA	CANIS	CHOSE	CROZE
CHINA	CAKES	CULTI	CANNA	CHOWS	******
CHINE	COKED	CULTS	CANNY	CIONS	C-P--
CHINK	COKER	CYLIX	CANOE	CLOAK	******
CHINO	COKES	******	CANON	CLOCK	CAPEK
CHINS	COKEY	C-M--	CANSO	CLODS	CAPER
CHIOS	******	******	CANST	CLOGS	CAPES
CHIPS	C-L--	CAMEL	CANTO	CLONE	CAPET
CHIRM	******	CAMEO	CANTS	CLONS	CAPON
CHIRO	CALCI	CAMES	CENIS	CLOPS	CAPRI
CHIRP	CALEB	CAMPI	CENON	CLOSE	CAPUA
CHIRR	CALIF	CAMPO	CENSE	CLOTH	CAPUT
CHITA	CALIX	CAMPS	CENTI	CLOTS	COPAL
CHITS	CALKS	CAMPY	CENTO	CLOUD	COPEC
CHIVE	CALLA	CAMUS	CENTR	CLOUT	COPED
CLICK	CALLI	CIMEX	CENTS	CLOVE	COPER
CLIFF	CALLS	COMAE	CINCH	CLOWN	COPES
CLIMB	CALMS	COMAL	CINDY	CLOYS	COPRA
CLIME	CALPE	COMAS	CONCH	COOED	COPRO
CLINE		COMBO	CONED	COOEE	COPSE

COPTS	CIRCE	CASEY	******	CAVIE	DEARY
CUPEL	CIRRI	CASKS	**C-U--**	CAVIL	DEATH
CUPID	CIRRO	CASTE	******	CIVET	DHAKS
CUPPY	CORAL	CASTS	CAUCA	CIVIC	DIALS
CUPRO	CORAS	CASUS	CAULK	CIVIL	DIANA
******	CORBY	CESAR	CAULS	COVED	DIANE
C-R--	CORDS	CESTA	CAUSE	COVEN	DIARY
******	CORED	CESTI	CEUTA	COVER	DIAZO
CARAS	CISCO	CISCO	CHUBS	COVES	DOALL
CARAT	CORER	CISSY	CHUCK	COVET	DRABS
CARBO	CORES	CISTS	CHUFA	COVEY	DRACO
CARDI	CORFE	COSEK	CHUGS	******	DRAFF
CARDS	CORFU	COSMO	CHUMP	**C-W--**	DRAFT
CARED	CORGI	COSTA	CHUMS	******	DRAGS
CARER	CORIA	COSTO	CHUNK	CAWED	DRAIL
CARES	CORKS	COSTS	CHURL	COWED	DRAIN
CARET	CORKY	CUSEC	CHURN	COWER	DRAKE
CAREY	CORMS	CUSHY	CHURR	COWES	DRAMA
CARGO	CORNS	CUSKS	CHUTE	COWLS	DRAMS
CARIB	CORNU	CUSPS	CLUBS	COWRY	DRANK
CARLA	CORNY	CUSSO	CLUCK	******	DRAPE
CARLE	COROT	CYSTI	CLUED	**C-X--**	DRAVA
CARLO	CORPS	CYSTO	CLUES	******	DRAVE
CARLS	CORSE	CYSTS	CLUMP	COXAE	DRAWL
CAROB	CURBS	******	CLUNG	COXAL	DRAWN
CAROL	CURCH	**C-T--**	CLUNY	COXED	DRAWS
CAROM	CURDS	******	COUCH	COXES	DRAYS
CARPI	CURDY	CATCH	COUGH	******	DUADS
CARPO	CURED	CATER	COULD	**C-Y--**	DUALA
CARPS	CURER	CATHY	COUNT	******	DUANE
CARRY	CURES	CATTY	COUPE	CHYLE	DWARF
CARTE	CURIA	CETIC	COUPS	CHYME	******
CARTS	CURIE	CETIN	COURT	CLYDE	**D-B--**
CARVE	CURIO	CETUS	COUTH	COYLY	******
CARYO	CURLS	CITED	CRUCI	COYPU	DEBAG
CARYS	CURLY	CITES	CRUDE	CRYPT	DEBAR
CERAM	CURRY	CITRA	CRUEL	******	DEBBY
CERAT	CURSE	COTES	CRUET	**C-Z--**	DEBIT
CERED	CURST	COTTA	CRUMB	******	DEBTS
CERES	CURVE	CUTCH	CRUMP	COZEN	DEBUG
CERIA	CURVI	CUTER	CRUOR	******	DEBUT
CERIC	CYRIL	CUTEY	CRURA	**D-A--**	DOBBY
CEROS	CYRUS	CUTIE	CRUSE	******	DOBIE
CHRIS	******	CUTIN	CRUSH	DEALS	DOBLA
CHROM	**C-S--**	CUTIS	CRUST	DEALT	DOBRA
CHRON	******	CUTTY	******	DEANE	DUBAI
CHRYS	CASCO	CUTUP	**C-V--**	DEANS	DUBHE
CIRCA	CASED		******	DEARS	
	CASES		CAVED		
			CAVES		

*****	DIENE	DOILY	DILYS	DANNY	DOORN
D-C--	DIETS	DOING	DOLCE	DANTE	DOORS
*****	DOERS	DOITS	DOLED	DENDR	DROIT
DACCA	DOEST	DRIBS	DOLES	DENEB	DROLL
DACES	DOETH	DRIED	DOLLS	DENES	DROME
DACHA	DREAD	DRIER	DOLLY	DENIM	DRONE
DACIA	DREAM	DRIES	DOLOR	DENIS	DROOL
DECAL	DREAR	DRIFT	DOLPH	DENNY	DROOP
DECAY	DREGS	DRILL	DOLTS	DENSE	DROPS
DECIM	DRESS	DRILY	DULCE	DENTI	DROPT
DECKS	DREST	DRINK	DULCY	DENTO	DROSS
DECOR	DREWS	DRIPS	DULIA	DENTS	DROVE
DECOY	DUELS	DRIPT	DULLS	DENYS	DROWN
DECRY	DUETS	DRIVE	DULLY	DINAH	DUOMI
DICED	DWELL	DYING	DULSE	DINAR	DUOMO
DICER	DWELT	******	DYLAN	DINED	******
DICEY	******	D-J--	******	DINER	D-P--
DICHO	D-F--	******	D-M--	DINES	******
DICKS	******	DIJON	******	DINGO	DEPOT
DICKY	DAFFY	******	DAMAN	DINGS	DEPTH
DICTA	DEFER	D-K--	DAMES	DINGY	DIPLO
DOCKS	DEFIS	******	DAMNS	DINKA	DIPPY
DUCAL	DEFOE	DAKAR	DAMON	DINKY	DOPED
DUCAT	DOFFS	DEKED	DAMPS	DINTS	DOPES
DUCHY	DUFFS	DEKES	DEMES	DONAR	DOPEY
DUCKS	******	DIKED	DEMIT	DONAS	DUPED
DUCKY	D-G--	DIKER	DEMOB	DONEE	DUPER
DUCTS	******	DIKES	DEMON	DONNA	DUPES
*****	DAGAN	DUKES	DEMOS	DONNE	DUPLE
D-D--	DEGAS	******	DEMUR	DONOR	******
*****	DEGUM	D-L--	DIMER	DONTS	D-R--
DADDY	DIGIT	******	DIMES	DUNCE	******
DEDAL	DOGES	DALAI	DIMLY	DUNES	DARED
DIDNT	DOGGY	DALER	DOMED	DUNGS	DARER
DIDOS	DOGIE	DALES	DOMES	DUNGY	DARES
DIDST	DOGMA	DALLY	DOMIC	DUNKS	DARIC
DODEC	******	DELAY	DUMAS	******	DARKY
DODGE	D-I--	DELED	DUMMY	D-O--	DARNS
DODGY	******	DELES	DUMPS	******	DARTS
DODOS	DAILY	DELFT	DUMPY	DEOXY	DERBY
DUDES	DAIRY	DELHI	******	DHOLE	DEREK
*****	DAISY	DELIA	D-N--	DHOLI	DERMA
D-E--	DEICE	DELLA	******	DHOTI	DERMO
*****	DEIFY	DELLS	DANAE	DHOWS	DERRY
DEEDS	DEIGN	DELOS	DANCE	DIODE	DIRCK
DEEMS	DEISM	DELTA	DANDY	DIONE	DIRER
DEEPS	DEIST	DELVE	DANES	DOOLY	DIRGE
DIEGO	DEITY	DILDO	DANGS	DOOMS	DIRKS

DIRTY
DORAS
DORIC
DORIS
DORMS
DORMY
DORRS
DORSA
DORSI
DORSO
DORUS
DURAL
DURER
DUROS
DURRA
DURST
DURUM
******

D-S--

******
DASHY
DESEX
DESKS
DISCI
DISCO
DISCS
DISHY
DISKO
DISKS
DOSED
DOSER
DOSES
DUSKS
DUSKY
DUSTS
DUSTY
******

D-T--

******
DATAL
DATED
DATER
DATES
DATTO
DATUM
DETER
DITAS
DITCH

DITTO
DITTY
DOTED
DOTER
DOTES
DOTTY
DUTCH
******

D-U--

******
DAUBS
DAUBY
DAUNT
DEUCE
DOUAI
DOUAY
DOUBT
DOUGH
DOUGS
DOURA
DOURY
DOUSE
DRUBS
DRUGS
DRUID
DRUMS
DRUNK
DRUPE
DRURY
DRUSE
******

D-V--

******
DAVAO
DAVES
DAVEY
DAVID
DAVIE
DAVIS
DAVIT
DAVOS
DAVYS
DEVAS
DEVIL
DEVON
DIVAN
DIVAS
DIVED

DIVER
DIVES
DIVOT
DIVVY
DOVAP
DOVER
DOVES
******

D-W--

******
DAWKS
DAWNS
DEWAN
DEWED
DEWEY
DIWAN
DOWDY
DOWEL
DOWER
DOWNS
DOWNY
DOWRY
DOWSE
******

D-X--

******
DEXTR
DIXIE
DIXIT
******

D-Y--

******
DOYEN
DOYLE
DOYLY
DRYAD
DRYER
DRYLY
******

D-Z--

******
DAZED
DAZES
DIZEN
DIZZY
DOZED
DOZEN
DOZER
DOZES

******

E-A--

******
ELAEO
ELAIN
ELAIO
ELAND
ELATE
ENACT
ENARE
ENATE
EPACT
ERASE
ERATO
ETAPE
EVADE
EVANS
EXACT
EXALT
EXAMS
******

E-B--

******
EBBED
ELBOW
EMBAR
EMBAY
EMBED
EMBER
EMBOW
EMBRY
EMBUS
******

E-C--

******
EMCEE
ENCYC
EXCEL
******

E-D--

******
EADIE
EDDAS
EDDIC
EDDIE
EIDER
ELDER
EMDEN

ENDED
ENDOW
ENDUE
EYDIE
******

E-E--

******
EDEMA
EGEAN
EGEST
EJECT
ELECT
ELEGY
ELEMI
ELENA
EMEER
EMEND
EMERY
EMEUS
ENEAS
ENEMA
ENEMY
EPEES
ERECT
EVENS
EVENT
EVERT
EVERY
EWERS
EXECS
EXERT
******

E-F--

******
EFFIE
ELFIN
******

E-G--

******
EAGER
EAGLE
EAGRE
EDGAR
EDGED
EDGES
EGGAR
EGGED
EGGER

EIGHT
ELGAR
ELGIN
ERGOT
******

E-H--

******
ECHIN
EPHAH
EPHOD
EPHOR
ESHER
ETHAN
ETHEL
ETHER
ETHIC
ETHNO
ETHOS
ETHYL
******

E-I--

******
EDICT
EDIES
EDIFY
EDILE
EDINA
EDITH
EDITS
EKING
ELIAS
ELIDE
ELIHU
ELIOT
ELISE
ELITE
ELIZA
EMILE
EMILS
EMILY
EMIRS
EMITS
ENIDS
EPICS
ERICA
ERICH
ERICS
ERIES

ERIKA	ENNUI	ERROL	ELUDE	FLANS	******
ERIKS	ERNES	ERROR	EQUAL	FLAPS	F-D--
EVICT	ERNIE	EURUS	EQUIP	FLARE	******
EVILS	ERNST	EYRAS	ERUCT	FLASH	FADDY
EVITA	ETNAS	EYRIE	ERUPT	FLASK	FADED
EWING	******	EYRIR	ETUDE	FLATS	FADES
EXILE	E-O--	EZRAS	ETUIS	FLAWS	FEDOR
EXIST	******	******	EXUDE	FLAWY	FIDEL
EXITS	EBOAT	E-S--	EXULT	FLAXY	FUDGE
EYING	EBONS	******	EXURB	FLAYS	******
******	EBONY	EASED	******	FOALS	F-E--
E-J--	ECOLE	EASEL	E-V--	FOAMS	******
*****	ELOIN	EASES	******	FOAMY	FEEDS
ENJOY	ELOPE	EDSEL	EAVES	FRAIL	FEELS
*****	EMORY	ELSAS	ELVAN	FRAME	FEEZE
E-K--	EMOTE	ELSIE	ELVER	FRANC	FIEFS
*****	ENOCH	ENSUE	ELVES	FRANK	FIELD
ESKER	ENOLA	EOSIN	ELVIN	FRANZ	FIEND
*****	ENOLS	EPSOM	ENVOY	FRAPS	FIERY
E-L--	EPOCH	ERSES	******	FRATS	FJELD
*****	EPODE	ESSAY	E-W--	FRAUD	FLEAM
ECLAT	EPOXY	ESSEN	******	FRAYS	FLEAS
ELLAS	ERODE	ESSES	EDWIN	******	FLECK
ELLEN	EROSE	ESSEX	ELWIN	F-B--	FLEER
ELLIE	EVOKE	ESSIE	ERWIN	******	FLEES
ELLIS	******	******	******	FABLE	FLEET
EOLIC	E-P--	E-T--	E-Y--	FEBRI	FLESH
EOLUS	******	******	******	FIBER	FLEWS
ERLAU	EMPTY	EATEN	EGYPT	FIBRE	FLEXI
EULER	EXPEL	EATER	ETYMA	FIBRO	FOEHN
*****	******	ELTON		******	FREAK
E-M--	E-Q--	ENTER	F-A--	F-C--	FREDA
*****	******	ENTIA		******	FREDS
EAMON	ESQUE	ENTOM	FEARS	FACED	FREED
EIMER	*****	ENTRY	FEASE	FACER	FREER
ELMAN	E-R--	ESTAR	FEAST	FACES	FREES
ELMER	*****	ESTER	FEATS	FACET	FRENA
EMMAS	EARED	ESTES	FIATS	FACIA	FREON
EMMER	EARLE	ESTOP	FLACK	FACTS	FRERE
EMMET	EARLS	ETTAS	FLAGS	FECAL	FRESH
EMMIE	EARLY	ETTIE	FLAIL	FECES	FRETS
EMMYS	EARNS	EXTOL	FLAIR	FECIT	FREUD
ERMAS	EARTH	EXTRA	FLAKE	FICES	FREYA
*****	EDRED	******	FLAKY	FICHE	FUELS
E-N--	EERIE	E-U--	FLAME	FICHU	******
*****	EGRET	******	FLAMS	FOCAL	F-F--
EDNAS	ENROL	EDUCE	FLAMY	FOCUS	FIFED
ENNEA	ERRED	EDUCT	FLANK	FUCUS	FIFER

FIFES	FRITH	******	FIORD	FARGO	FISCS
FIFTH	FRITS	**F-M--**	FJORD	FARLE	FISHY
FIFTY	FRITZ	******	FLOAT	FARLS	FISTS
******	FRIZZ	FAMED	FLOCK	FARMS	FOSSA
F-G--	******	FEMES	FLOCS	FAROE	FOSSE
******	**F-J--**	FEMME	FLOES	FERAL	FUSED
FAGOT	******	FEMTO	FLOGS	FERIA	FUSEE
FIGHT	FIJIS	FEMUR	FLONG	FERMI	FUSEL
FOGEY	******	FUMED	FLOOD	FERNS	FUSES
FOGGY	**F-K--**	FUMES	FLOOR	FERNY	FUSIL
FUGAL	******	******	FLOPS	FERRI	FUSSY
FUGGY	FAKED	**F-N--**	FLORA	FERRO	FUSTY
FUGIO	FAKER	******	FLOSS	FERRY	******
FUGLE	FAKES	FANCY	FLOUR	FIRED	**F-T--**
FUGUE	FAKIR	FANGA	FLOUT	FIRER	******
******	FYKES	FANGS	FLOWN	FIRES	FATAL
F-I--	******	FANNY	FLOWS	FIRMS	FATED
******	**F-L--**	FANON	FLOYD	FIRNS	FATES
FAILS	******	FANOS	FOODS	FIRRY	FATLY
FAINT	FALLS	FANUM	FOOLS	FIRST	FATTY
FAIRS	FALSE	FENCE	FOOTS	FIRTH	FETAL
FAIRY	FELID	FENDS	FOOTY	FORAY	FETCH
FAITH	FELIX	FENNY	FROCK	FORBS	FETED
FEIGN	FELLS	FINAL	FROES	FORBY	FETES
FEINT	FELLY	FINCH	FROGS	FORCE	FETID
FEIST	FELON	FINDS	FROME	FORDS	FETOR
FLICK	FELTS	FINED	FROND	FORES	FETUS
FLIED	FILAR	FINER	FRONT	FORGE	FITCH
FLIER	FILCH	FINES	FROSH	FORGO	FITLY
FLIES	FILED	FINIS	FROST	FORKS	******
FLING	FILER	FINKS	FROTH	FORLI	**F-U--**
FLINT	FILES	FINNS	FROWN	FORME	******
FLIPS	FILET	FINNY	FROWS	FORMS	FAUGH
FLIRT	FILLS	FONDA	FROZE	FORTE	FAULT
FLITE	FILLY	FONTS	******	FORTH	FAUNA
FLITS	FILMS	FUNDI	**F-Q--**	FORTS	FAUNS
FOILS	FILMY	FUNDS	******	FORTY	FAUST
FOISM	FILTH	FUNGI	FIQUE	FORUM	FEUAR
FOIST	FILUM	FUNGO	******	FURAN	FEUDS
FRIAR	FOLDS	FUNKS	**F-R--**	FURLS	FEUED
FRIED	FOLIA	FUNKY	******	FUROR	FIUME
FRIER	FOLIC	FUNNY	FARAD	FURRY	FLUBS
FRIES	FOLIO	******	FARAH	FURTH	FLUES
FRIGG	FOLKS	**F-O--**	FARCE	FURZE	FLUFF
FRILL	FOLLY	******	FARCY	FURZY	FLUID
FRIML	FULLS	FEODS	FARED	******	FLUKE
FRISE	FULLY	FEOFF	FARER	**F-S--**	FLUKY
FRISK		FIONA	FARES	FASTS	FLUME
				FESSE	

*LUMP	*****	GRAMA	******	GIGOT	GILDA
*LUNG	F-Z--	GRAMS	G-E--	GIGUE	GILDS
*LUNK	*****	GRAND	******	GOGOL	GILES
*LUOR	FAZED	GRANI	GAELS	******	GILLS
*LUSH	FAZES	GRANO	GEEKS	G-I--	GOLDA
*LUTE	FIZZY	GRANT	GEESE	******	GOLDS
*LUTY	FUZED	GRAPE	GEEST	GAILS	GOLEM
*OULS	FUZEE	GRAPH	GHENT	GAILY	GOLFS
*OUND	FUZES	GRAPY	GLEAM	GAINS	GOLLY
*OUNT	FUZIL	GRASP	GLEAN	GAITS	GULAR
*OURS	FUZZY	GRASS	GLEBE	GIING	GULCH
*RUIT	******	GRATE	GLEDE	GLIDE	GULES
*RUMP	G-A--	GRAVE	GLEDS	GLIMS	GULFS
*****	******	GRAVY	GLEES	GLINT	GULLS
*-V--	GEARS	GRAYS	GLEET	GOING	GULLY
*****	GHANA	GRAZE	GLENN	GRIDE	GULPS
*AVOR	GHATS	GUACO	GLENS	GRIDS	******
*AVUS	GHAUT	GUAMA	GOERS	GRIEF	G-M--
*EVER	GHAZI	GUANA	GREAT	GRIEG	******
*IVER	GIANT	GUANO	GREBE	GRILL	GAMBS
*IVES	GLACE	GUANS	GRECO	GRIME	GAMED
*OVEA	GLADE	GUARD	GREED	GRIMM	GAMES
*****	GLADS	GUAVA	GREEK	GRIMY	GAMIC
*-W--	GLAIR	******	GREEN	GRIND	GAMIN
*****	GLAND	G-B--	GREER	GRINS	GAMMA
*AWNS	GLANS	******	GREET	GRIPE	GAMMY
*EWER	GLARE	GABBY	GREGO	GRIPS	GAMPS
*OWLS	GLARY	GABES	GREGS	GRIPT	GAMUT
*****	GLASS	GABLE	GRETA	GRIST	GEMMA
*-X--	GLAUC	GABON	GREYS	GRITS	GEMMY
*****	GLAZE	GABOR	GUESS	GUIDE	GEMOT
*AXED	GLAZY	GABYS	GUEST	GUIDO	GIMEL
*AXES	GNARL	GIBED	GWENN	GUILD	GIMPS
*IXED	GNASH	GIBER	GWENS	GUILE	GIMPY
*IXER	GNATS	GIBES	******	GUILT	GUMBO
*IXES	GNAWN	GIBUS	G-F--	GUISE	GUMMA
*OXED	GNAWS	GOBOS	******	******	GUMMY
*OXES	GOADS	GOBYS	GAFFE	G-L--	GYMNO
*****	GOALS	GYBED	GAFFS	******	******
*-Y--	GOATS	******	GIFTS	GALAS	G-N--
*****	GRAAL	G-C--	GOFER	GALAX	******
*AYAL	GRABS	******	******	GALEA	GANEF
*AYED	GRACE	GECKO	G-G--	GALEN	GANGS
*AYES	GRADE	GECKS	******	GALES	GENES
*LYBY	GRADS	******	GAGED	GALLS	GENET
*LYER	GRAFT	G-D--	GAGER	GALOP	GENIC
*OYED	GRAIL	******	GAGES	GELDS	GENIE
*OYER	GRAIN	GADID	GIGAS	GELID	GENII
*RYER		GIDDY			
		GODLY			

GENOA	GROIN	GORME	GAUZE	GAZES	HIDES
GENRE	GROOM	GORSE	GAUZY	GIZMO	HIDTO
GENRO	GROPE	GORSY	GLUED	******	HODGE
GENTS	GROSS	GURUS	GLUES	H-A--	HYDRA
GENUA	GROSZ	GYRAL	GLUEY	******	HYDRO
GENUS	GROTS	GYRES	GLUME	HEADS	******
GINKS	GROUP	GYRON	GLUTS	HEADY	H-E--
GINNY	GROUT	GYROS	GOUDA	HEALS	******
GONAD	GROVE	GYRUS	GOUGE	HEALS	HBEAM
GONDI	GROWL	******	GOURD	HEAPS	HEEDS
GONER	GROWN	G-S--	GOUTY	HEARD	HEELS
GONGS	GROWS	******	GRUBS	HEARS	HIERO
GONIA	******	GASES	GRUEL	HEART	HOERS
GONIO	G-P--	GASPE	GRUFF	HEATH	HYENA
GUNNY	******	GASPS	GRUME	HEATS	HYETO
GYNEC	GAPED	GASSY	GRUNT	HEAVE	******
******	GAPER	GASTR	******	HEAVY	H-F--
G-O--	GAPES	GESSO	G-V--	HOAGY	******
******	GAPPY	GISMO	******	HOARD	HAFIZ
GAOLS	GIPON	GISTS	GAVEL	HOARY	HAFTS
GEODE	GIPSY	GUSHY	GAVIN	HYALO	HEFTS
GEOFF	GUPPY	GUSTA	GAVLE	******	HEFTY
GEOID	GYPSY	GUSTO	GAVOT	H-B--	HIFIS
GHOST	******	GUSTS	GIVEN	******	HUFFS
GHOUL	G-R--	GUSTY	GIVER	HABIT	HUFFY
GLOAT	******	******	GIVES	HABUS	******
GLOBE	GARBO	G-T--	GOVYS	HOBBS	H-G--
GLOBS	GARBS	******	GYVED	HOBBY	******
GLOOM	GARRY	GATED	******	HOBOS	HAGIO
GLORY	GARTH	GATES	G-W--	HUBBY	HAGUE
GLOSS	GARYS	GATUN	******	******	HEGEL
GLOST	GERDA	GETUP	GAWKS	H-C--	HIGHS
GLOVE	GERMS	GOTHA	GAWKY	******	HOGAN
GLOWS	GERRY	GOTHS	GOWAN	HACKS	HUGER
GLOZE	GERTY	GUTSY	GOWER	HECTO	HUGHS
GNOME	GIRDS	GUTTA	GOWNS	HICKS	HUGOS
GNOMY	GIRLS	******	******	HOCKS	HYGRO
GOODS	GIRON	G-U--	G-Y--	HOCUS	******
GOODY	GIROS	******	******	******	H-H--
GOOEY	GIRSH	GAUDI	GAYER	H-D--	******
GOOFS	GIRTH	GAUDS	GAYLY	******	HAHAS
GOOFY	GIRTS	GAUDY	GLYCO	HADED	******
GOOKS	GORAL	GAUGE	GLYPH	HADES	H-I--
GOONS	GORED	GAULS	GOYIM	HADJI	******
GOOSE	GORES	GAULT	GUYED	HADNT	HAIDA
GOOSY	GORGE	GAUNT	GWYNS	HEDDA	HAIFA
GROAN	GORKI	GAURS	******	HEDGE	HAIKS
GROAT	GORKY	GAUSS	G-Z--	HEDGY	HAIKU
			GAZED	HIDER	
			GAZER		

HAILS	HELMS	HUMPH	HOODS	HERAT	HUSSY
HAIRS	HELOT	HUMPS	HOOEY	HERBS	HYSON
HAIRY	HELPS	HUMPY	HOOFS	HERBY	******
HAITI	HELVE	HUMUS	HOOKE	HERDS	**H-T--**
HEIGH	HILDA	HYMEN	HOOKS	HERLS	******
HEIRS	HILLS	HYMNS	HOOKY	HERMA	HATCH
HEIST	HILLY	******	HOOPS	HEROD	HATED
HOICK	HILTS	**H-N--**	HOOTS	HERON	HATER
HOIST	HILUM	******	HOOVE	HERTZ	HATES
HYING	HOLDS	HANCE	HYOID	HIRAM	HATTY
******	HOLED	HANDS	******	HIRED	HETTY
H-J--	HOLES	HANDY	**H-P--**	HIRER	HITCH
******	HOLEY	HANGS	******	HIRES	HOTEL
HEJAZ	HOLLY	HANKS	HAPLO	HORAE	HOTLY
******	HOLMS	HANKY	HAPLY	HORAL	HUTCH
H-K--	HOLST	HANNA	HAPPY	HORAS	******
******	HULAS	HANOI	HEPAT	HORDE	**H-U--**
HAKES	HULDA	HANSE	HEPTA	HOREB	******
HAKIM	HULKS	HENCE	HIPPO	HORNE	HAULM
HEKLA	HULKY	HENNA	HIPPY	HORNS	HAULS
HEKTO	HULLS	HENRI	HOPED	HORNY	HAUNT
HIKED	HYLAS	HENRY	HOPEH	HORSE	HOUGH
HIKER	******	HINDI	HOPES	HORST	HOUND
HIKES	**H-M--**	HINDS	HUPEH	HORSY	HOURI
HOKAN	******	HINDU	HYPER	HORTA	HOURS
HOKUM	HAMAL	HINGE	HYPHA	HORUS	HOUSE
******	HAMER	HINNY	HYPNO	HURDS	******
H-L--	HAMES	HINTS	HYPOS	HURLS	**H-V--**
******	HAMMY	HONAN	HYPSO	HURLY	******
HALED	HAMZA	HONDO	******	HURON	HAVEN
HALER	HEMAL	HONED	**H-R--**	HURRY	HAVER
HALES	HEMAN	HONES	******	HURST	HAVOC
HALID	HEMAT	HONEY	HARAR	HURTS	HIVED
HALLE	HEMEN	HONGS	HARDS	HYRAX	HIVES
HALLO	HEMIA	HONKS	HARDY	******	HOVEL
HALLS	HEMIC	HONKY	HARED	**H-S--**	HOVER
HALMA	HEMIN	HONOR	HAREM	******	******
HALOS	HEMPS	HUNAN	HARES	HASNT	**H-W--**
HALTS	HEMPY	HUNCH	HARKS	HASPS	******
HALVE	HOMED	HUNKS	HARLS	HASTE	HAWED
HELEN	HOMEO	HUNKY	HARMS	HASTY	HAWKS
HELGA	HOMER	HUNTS	HARPS	HESSE	HAWSE
HELIC	HOMES	******	HARPY	HOSEA	HEWED
HELIO	HOMEY	**H-O--**	HARRY	HOSED	HEWER
HELIX	HUMAN	******	HARSH	HOSES	HOWDY
HELLE	HUMIC	HBOMB	HARTE	HOSTS	HOWIE
HELLO	HUMID	HHOUR	HARTS	HUSKS	HOWLS
HELLS	HUMOR	HOOCH	HARTZ	HUSKY	

*****	INCUR	*****	ISLAY	INSET	*****
H-X--	INCUS	**I-I--**	ISLED	ISSEI	**J-B--**
*****	ITCHY	*****	ISLES	ISSUE	*****
HEXAD	*****	IBIZA	ISLET	*****	JABEZ
HEXED	**I-D--**	ICIAN	*****	**I-T--**	JABOT
HEXES	*****	ICIER	**I-M--**	*****	JIBED
HEXYL	INDEX	ICILY	*****	IATRO	JIBES
*****	INDIA	ICING	IAMBI	IATRY	JUBAS
H-Y--	INDIC	IDIOM	IAMBS	ICTUS	JUBES
*****	INDOW	IDIOT	ILMEN	INTER	
HAYDN	INDRA	ILIAC	IMMIX	INTRA	**J-C--**
HAYED	INDRI	ILIAD	IRMAS	INTRO	*****
HAYES	INDUE	ILIAN	*****	IOTAS	JACKS
HOYLE	INDUS	ILION	**I-N--**	ISTAR	JACKY
*****	IODIC	ILIUM	*****	ISTIC	JACOB
H-Z--	IODOL	IMIDE	IGNAZ	ISTLE	JOCKO
*****	*****	IMIDO	INNED	IXTLE	*****
HAZED	**I-E--**	IMIDS	INNER	*****	**J-D--**
HAZEL	*****	IMINE	IONIA	**I-U--**	*****
HAZER	IBEAM	IMINO	IONIC	*****	JADED
HAZES	IDEAL	INIGO	*****	INURE	JADES
*****	IDEAS	INION	**I-O--**	INURN	JIDDA
I-A--	IDEST	IRIDO	*****	*****	JUDAH
*****	ILEAC	IRISH	ICONO	**I-V--**	JUDAS
IDAHO	ILEAL	ITION	ICONS	*****	JUDEO
IMAGE	ILEUM	IVIED	ICOSI	INVAR	JUDES
IMAGO	ILEUS	IVIES	IDOLS	IRVIN	JUDGE
IMAMS	INEPT	IXIAS	IKONS	*****	JUDYS
INANE	INERT	IXION	ILONA	**I-W--**	*****
INAPT	IRENE	*****	IRONE	*****	**J-E--**
INARM	ISERE	**I-K--**	IRONS	IRWIN	*****
IRAQI	ITEMS	*****	IRONY	*****	JEEPS
IRATE	*****	INKED	IVORY	**I-Y--**	JEERS
ISAAC	**I-F--**	INKER	*****	*****	JOELS
ITALS	*****	INKLE	**I-P--**	IDYLL	JOEYS
ITALY	INFER	IRKED	*****	IDYLS	*****
IVANS	INFIX	*****	IMPEL	IYYAR	**J-F--**
*****	INFRA	**I-L--**	IMPLY	*****	*****
I-B--	*****	*****	IMPOT	**I-Z--**	JAFFA
*****	**I-G--**	IDLED	INPUT	*****	JEFES
IMBED	*****	IDLER	*****	IZZYS	JEFFS
IMBUE	INGLE	IDLES	**I-R--**	*****	JIFFS
ISBAS	INGOT	IGLOO	*****		JIFFY
*****	*****	ILLUS	IHRAM	**J-A--**	*****
I-C--	**I-H--**	INLAW	*****	*****	**J-G--**
*****	*****	INLAY	**I-S--**	JEANS	*****
INCAN	ICHOR	INLET	*****	JOANS	JAGGS
INCAS		ISLAM	IASIS	JUANA	JAGGY
			IBSEN	JUANS	JUGAL

******	******	JEREZ	JEWRY	******	******
J-H--	**J-M--**	JERKS	JOWLS	**K-D--**	**K-L--**
******	******	JERKY	******	******	******
JEHUS	JAMBS	JERRY	**J-X--**	KADIS	KALAT
JIHAD	JAMES	JORAM	******	KEDAH	KELLY
JOHNS	JAMIE	JORGE	JUXTA	KEDGE	KELPS
******	JAMMY	JORUM	******	KIDDY	KELSO
J-I--	JEMMY	JURAL	**J-Y--**	KODAK	KILAH
******	JIMMY	JURAT	******	KUDOS	KILLS
JAILS	JUMBO	JUREL	JAYNE	KUDUS	KILNS
JAINA	JUMNA	JUROR	JOYCE	******	KILOS
JAINS	JUMPS	JURUA	JOYED	**K-E--**	KILTS
JOINS	JUMPY	******	******	******	KILTY
JOINT	******	**J-S--**	**J-Z--**	KEEFS	KOLAS
JOIST	**J-N--**	******	******	KEELS	KULAK
JUICE	******	JASON	JAZZY	KEENS	KYLIX
JUICY	JANES	JASSY	******	KEEPS	******
******	JANET	JESSE	**K-A--**	KEEVE	**K-M--**
J-J--	JANIS	JESSY	******	KIERS	******
******	JANOS	JESTS	KAABA	KNEAD	KAMES
JUJUS	JANUS	JESUS	KEATS	KNEED	KAMET
******	JENNY	JOSIE	KHADI	KNEEL	KAMIK
J-K--	JINGO	JOSUA	KHAKI	KNEES	KHMER
******	JINKS	JOSUE	KHANS	KNELL	KOMOS
JAKES	JINNI	JUSTS	KLARA	KNELT	KUMIS
JAKOB	JINNY	******	KNACK	KOELS	******
JOKED	JONAH	**J-T--**	KNARS	******	**K-N--**
JOKER	JONAS	******	KNAVE	**K-F--**	******
JOKES	JONES	JATOS	KOALA	******	KANDY
******	JONNY	JETON	KRAAL	KAFIR	KENCH
J-L--	JUNCO	JETTY	KRAFT	KAFKA	KENNY
******	JUNES	JOTUN	KRAIT	KUFRA	KENTS
JALAP	JUNKS	JUTES	KRAUT	******	KENYA
JELLO	JUNKY	******	KVASS	**K-G--**	KINDS
JELLS	JUNTA	**J-U--**	KYATS	******	KINGS
JELLY	JUNTO	******	******	KAGUS	KININ
JILLS	******	JAUNT	**K-B--**	******	KINKS
JILTS	**J-P--**	JOULE	******	**K-I--**	KINKY
JOLES	******	JOUST	KABOB	******	KONYA
JOLLY	JAPAN	******	KABUL	KEITH	******
JOLTS	JAPED	**J-V--**	KIBEI	KNIFE	**K-O--**
JOLTY	JAPES	******	KIBES	KNITS	******
JULEP	JUPON	JIVED	KUBAN	KOINE	KHOND
JULES	******	******	******	******	KIOSK
JULIA	**J-R--**	**J-W--**	**K-C--**	**K-K--**	KIOWA
JULIE	******	******	******	******	KLOOF
JULIO	JARED	JAWED	KECKS	KAKAS	KNOBS
JULYS	JARLS	JEWEL	KICKS	KAKIS	KNOCK
				KUKRI	

KNOLL	******	LEADY	******	LEERY	LAIRD
KNOPS	K-T--	LEAFS	L-C--	LEETS	LAIRS
KNOSP	******	LEAFY	******	LIEGE	LAITY
KNOTS	KATES	LEAKS	LACED	LIEIN	LEIFS
KNOUT	KATHY	LEAKY	LACES	LIENS	LEIGH
KNOWN	KATIE	LEANS	LACKS	LIEUT	LEILA
KNOWS	KETCH	LEANT	LACTO	LOESS	LEITH
KOOKS	KITED	LEAPS	LICHT	******	LOINS
KOOKY	KITES	LEAPT	LICIT	L-F--	LOIRE
KRONA	KITTY	LEARN	LICKS	******	LUIGI
KRONE	KOTOS	LEARY	LOCAL	LEFTS	LUISA
KYOTO	******	LEASE	LOCHS	LEFTY	LUISE
******	K-U--	LEASH	LOCKE	LIFER	LYING
K-P--	******	LEAST	LOCKS	LIFTS	******
******	KAUAI	LEAVE	LOCOS	LOFTS	L-K--
KAPHS	KAURI	LEAVY	LOCUM	LOFTY	******
KAPOK	KAURY	LHASA	LOCUS	LUFFS	LAKED
KAPPA	KNURL	LIANA	LUCCA	******	LAKER
KAPUT	KNURR	LIANE	LUCES	L-G--	LAKES
KEPIS	KNURS	LIANG	LUCIA	******	LAKEY
KOPEC	KRUBI	LIARS	LUCID	LAGAN	LIKED
KOPEK	KRUPP	LLAMA	LUCKY	LAGER	LIKEN
KOPJE	******	LLANO	LUCRE	LAGOS	LIKES
******	K-V--	LOACH	LUCYS	LEGAL	******
K-R--	******	LOADS	LYCEA	LEGER	L-L--
******	KAVAS	LOAFS	LYCEE	LEGES	******
KARAT	KEVEL	LOAMS	******	LEGGY	LALLS
KAREN	KEVIN	LOAMY	L-D--	LEGIT	LILAC
KARLS	KIVAS	LOANS	******	LIGAN	LILAS
KARMA	******	LOATH	LADDY	LIGHT	LILLE
KAROL	K-W--	LUAUS	LADED	LIGNI	LILLI
KAROO	******	******	LADEN	LIGNO	LILLY
KARYO	KIWIS	L-B--	LADES	LOGAN	LILTS
KERAT	******	******	LADIN	LOGES	LILYS
KERBS	K-Y--	LABEL	LADLE	LOGIA	LOLAS
KERCH	******	LABIA	LEDGE	LOGIC	LOLLS
KERES	KAYAK	LABIO	LODEN	LOGOS	LOLLY
KERFS	KAYOS	LABOR	LODES	LOGUE	LULLS
KERNS	KEYED	LABRA	LODGE	LUGER	LULUS
KERRY	******	LIBBY	LYDDA	******	LYLES
KIRIN	K-Z--	LIBEL	LYDIA	L-H--	******
KIRKS	******	LIBER	******	******	L-M--
KORAN	KAZAN	LIBRA	L-E--	LEHRS	******
KOREA	KAZOO	LIBYA	******	LEHUA	LAMAS
KORUN	******	LOBAR	LEECH	******	LAMBS
KURSK	L-A--	LOBBY	LEEDS	L-I--	LAMED
KURUS	******	LOBED	LEEKS	******	LAMER
KYRIE	LEACH	LOBES	LEERS	LAIKA	LAMES
	LEADS	LOBOS		LAINE	

LAMIA	LINTY	LEPTA	LASSO	LUTON	LEWES
LAMPS	LINUS	LEPTO	LASTS	LYTIC	LEWIE
LEMMA	LONER	LEPUS	LISAS	LYTTA	LEWIS
LEMON	LONGI	LIPID	LISLE	******	LOWED
LEMUR	LONGS	LIPPI	LISPS	**L-U--**	LOWER
LIMBI	LUNAR	LIPPY	LISTS	******	LOWLY
LIMBO	LUNCH	LOPAT	LISZT	LAUDS	******
LIMBS	LUNES	LOPED	LOSER	LAUGH	**L-X--**
LIMED	LUNET	LOPER	LOSES	LAURA	******
LIMEN	LUNGE	LOPES	LUSTS	LEUCO	LAXER
LIMES	LUNGI	LOPPY	LUSTY	LEUDS	LAXLY
LIMEY	LUNGS	LUPIN	LYSED	LEUKO	LUXEX
LIMIT	LUNTS	LUPUS	LYSES	LOUGH	LUXOR
LIMNS	LYNCH	******	LYSIN	LOUIS	******
LIMPS	LYNNS	**L-R--**	LYSIS	LOUPE	**L-Y--**
LUMEN	******	******	LYSOL	LOUPS	******
LUMPS	**L-O--**	LARCH	LYSSA	LOURS	LAYBY
LUMPY	******	LARDS	******	LOUSE	LAYER
LYMAN	LAOAG	LARDY	**L-T--**	LOUSY	LEYTE
LYMPH	LEONA	LARES	******	LOUTS	LOYAL
******	LEONS	LARGE	LATCH	******	******
L-N--	LEORA	LARGO	LATER	**L-V--**	**L-Z--**
******	LIONS	LARKS	LATEX	******	******
LANAI	LLOYD	LARKY	LATHE	LAVAS	LAZAR
LANCE	LOOBY	LARRY	LATHS	LAVED	LAZED
LANDS	LOOED	LARVA	LATHY	LAVER	LAZES
LANES	LOOFS	LEROY	LATIN	LAVES	LIZAS
LANKY	LOOKS	LIRAS	LATRO	LEVEE	LIZZY
LENAS	LOOMS	LORAN	LATRY	LEVEL	LUZON
LENDS	LOONS	LORCA	LETHE	LEVEN	******
LENES	LOOPS	LORDS	LETTS	LEVER	**M-A--**
LENIN	LOOPY	LORES	LETTY	LEVIS	******
LENIS	LOOSE	LORIS	LETUP	LIVED	MEADS
LENNY	LOOTS	LORNA	LITAI	LIVEN	MEALS
LENOS	LYONS	LORRY	LITAS	LIVER	MEALY
LENTO	******	LURCH	LITER	LIVES	MEANS
LENTS	**L-P--**	LURED	LITHE	LIVIA	MEANT
LINDA	******	LURER	LITHO	LIVID	MEANY
LINED	LAPAR	LURES	LITRE	LIVRE	MEATS
LINEN	LAPEL	LURID	LOTAH	LOVED	MEATY
LINER	LAPIN	LURKS	LOTOS	LOVER	MIAMI
LINES	LAPIS	LYRES	LOTTA	LOVES	MIAOW
LINEY	LAPPS	LYRIC	LOTTE	******	MIAUL
LINGA	LAPSE	******	LOTTO	**L-W--**	MOANS
LINGO	LEPER	**L-S--**	LOTTY	******	MOATS
LINGS	LEPID	******	LOTUS	LAWED	******
LININ	LEPSY	LASER	LUTED	LAWNS	**M-B--**
LINKS	LEPTA	LASSA	LUTES	LAWNY	******
					MABEL

******	MODUS	MAIZE	MILNE	MANES	******
M-C--	MUDDY	MOILS	MILTS	MANET	**M-O--**
******	******	MOIRA	MILTY	MANGE	******
MACAO	**M-E--**	MOIRE	MLLES	MANGO	MAORI
MACAW	******	MOIST	MOLAL	MANGY	MEOWS
MACED	MEETS	******	MOLAR	MANIA	MOOCH
MACER	MIENS	**M-J--**	MOLDS	MANIC	MOODS
MACES	MYELO	******	MOLDY	MANLY	MOODY
MACHY	******	MAJOR	MOLES	MANNA	MOOED
MACKS	**M-F--**	MUJIK	MOLLS	MANOR	MOONS
MACLE	******	******	MOLLY	MANSE	MOONY
MACON	MAFIA	**M-K--**	MOLTO	MANTA	MOORE
MACRO	MIFFS	******	MOLTS	MANUS	MOORS
MCCOY	MIFFY	MAKER	MULCH	MENAI	MOOSE
MECCA	MUFFS	MAKES	MULCT	MENDS	MUONS
MICAH	MUFTI	MIKES	MULES	MENES	MYOID
MICAS	******	MIKEY	MULEY	MENSA	MYOMA
MICKY	**M-G--**	MOKES	MULLS	MENUS	MYOPE
MICRA	******	******	MULTI	MINAE	MYOPY
MICRO	MAGDA	**M-L--**	MYLES	MINAS	******
MOCHA	MAGES	******	******	MINCE	**M-P--**
MOCKS	MAGIC	MALAC	**M-M--**	MINDI	******
MUCID	MAGMA	MALAR	******	MINDS	MAPLE
MUCIN	MAGNI	MALAY	MAMAS	MINED	MOPED
MUCKS	MAGOG	MALES	MAMBA	MINER	MOPER
MUCKY	MAGOT	MALIC	MAMBO	MINES	MOPES
MUCRO	MAGUS	MALLS	MAMEY	MINGY	******
MUCUS	MEGAL	MALMO	MAMIE	MINIM	**M-Q--**
******	MEGAN	MALTA	MAMMA	MINKS	******
M-D--	MIGHT	MALTS	MAMMY	MINNA	MAQUI
******	MOGUL	MALTY	MEMOS	MINOR	******
MADAM	MUGGY	MELAN	MIMED	MINOS	**M-R--**
MADGE	******	MELDS	MIMEO	MINSK	******
MADLY	**M-H--**	MELEE	MIMER	MINTS	MARAT
MADOC	******	MELIC	MIMES	MINUS	MARCH
MEDAL	MAHAN	MELON	MIMIC	MONAD	MARCO
MEDEA	MAHDI	MELOS	MIMIR	MONAS	MARCS
MEDIA	MOHUR	MELTS	MIMIS	MONDE	MARES
MEDIC	MUHLY	MILAN	MOMUS	MONET	MARGE
MEDIO	******	MILCH	MUMMS	MONEY	MARGO
MEDOC	**M-I--**	MILER	MUMMY	MONKS	MARIA
MIDAS	******	MILES	MUMPS	MONTE	MARIE
MIDDY	MAIDS	MILIA	******	MONTH	MARIO
MIDGE	MAILS	MILKS	**M-N--**	MONTY	MARIS
MIDST	MAIMS	MILKY	******	MUNCH	MARKS
MODAL	MAINE	MILLI	MANCY	MUNGO	MARLA
MODEL	MAINS	MILLS	MANDY	MUNRO	MARLS
MODES	MAINZ	MILLY	MANED	MYNAS	MARLY

MARNE	******	MATHS	MEUSE	MAZES	NIDES
MARRY	**M-S--**	MATIN	MOUCH	MEZZO	NIDUS
MARSH	******	MATRI	MOUES	MIZEN	NODAL
MARTA	MASER	MATSU	MOULD	MUZAK	NODDY
MARTS	MASHY	MATTE	MOULT	MUZZY	NODES
MARTY	MASKS	MATTS	MOUND	******	NODUS
MERCI	MASON	MATTY	MOUNT	**N-A--**	NUDES
MERCY	MASSE	MATZO	MOURN	******	NUDGE
MERGE	MASSY	METAL	MOUSE	NAACP	******
MERIT	MASTO	METAS	MOUSY	NEALS	**N-E--**
MERLE	MASTS	METED	MOUTH	NEAPS	******
MEROE	MESAS	METER	******	NEARS	NEEDS
MERRY	MESHY	METES	**M-V--**	NEATH	NEEDY
MIRED	MESIC	METHO	******	NOAHS	NIECE
MIRES	MESNE	METIS	MAVIS	NYASA	NOELS
MIRTH	MESON	METOL	MOVED	******	******
MIRZA	MESSY	METRE	MOVER	**N-B--**	**N-F--**
MORAE	MISDO	METRO	MOVES	******	******
MORAL	MISER	METRY	MOVIE	NABOB	NIFTY
MORAS	MISES	MITCH	******	NOBBY	******
MORAT	MISSY	MITER	**M-W--**	NOBEL	**N-G--**
MORAY	MISTS	MITES	******	NOBLE	******
MOREL	MISTY	MITRE	MEWED	NOBLY	NEGEB
MORES	MOSAN	MITTS	MEWLS	NUBBY	NEGEV
MORIN	MOSEL	MITZI	MOWED	NUBIA	NEGRO
MORNA	MOSES	MITZY	MOWER	******	NEGUS
MORNS	MOSEY	MOTEL	******	**N-C--**	NIGEL
MORON	MOSSO	MOTES	**M-X--**	******	NIGER
MOROS	MOSSY	MOTET	******	NACRE	NIGHT
MORPH	MUSCA	MOTHS	MAXIM	NECKS	NIGRI
MORRO	MUSED	MOTHY	MIXED	NECRO	NOGGS
MORSE	MUSES	MOTIF	MIXER	NICER	******
MORTA	MUSHY	MOTOR	MIXES	NICHE	**N-H--**
MORTS	MUSIC	MOTTO	MIXUP	NICKS	******
MORTY	MUSKS	MUTED	MOXAS	NICKY	NAHOR
MURAL	MUSKY	MUTES	MOXIE	NOCKS	NAHUA
MURAT	MUSSY	MUTTS	******	NOCTI	NAHUM
MUREX	MUSTS	MYTHO	**M-Y--**	NUCHA	NEHRU
MURKY	MUSTY	MYTHS	******	NYCTI	NIHIL
MURRA	******	******	MAYAN	NYCTO	******
MURRE	**M-T--**	**M-U--**	MAYAS	******	**N-I--**
MURRY	******	******	MAYBE	******	******
MYRAS	MATCH	MAUDE	MAYNT	**N-D--**	NAIAD
MYRIA	MATED	MAUDS	MAYOR	******	NAILS
MYRNA	MATEO	MAULS	MAYST	NADAB	NAIRN
MYRON	MATER	MAUND	******	NADER	NAIVE
MYRRH	MATES	MAURA	**M-Z--**	NADIR	NEIGH
	MATEY	MAUVE	******	NEDDY	NEILS
			MAZED	NIDED	
			MAZER		

NOISE	NJORD	******	NEWER	OMBRO	OREAD
NOISY	NOOKS	N-T--	NEWLY	ORBED	OTERO
******	NOONS	******	NEWSY	ORBIT	OVENS
N-K--	NOOSE	NATAL	NEWTS	OXBOW	OVERT
******	******	NATES	NOWAY	******	OWENS
NAKED	N-P--	NATTY	******	O-C--	OXEYE
******	******	NETER	N-X--	******	OYERS
N-L--	NAPES	NETTY	******	OCCUR	******
******	NAPPE	NITER	NEXUS	ORCHI	O-F--
NELLS	NAPPY	NITON	NIXED	ORCIN	******
NELLY	NEPAL	NITRE	NIXES	ORCUS	OFFAL
NYLON	NEPHO	NITRI	NIXIE	ORCZY	OFFER
******	NEPHR	NITRO	NIXON	OSCAN	******
N-M--	NIPAS	NITTY	******	OSCAR	O-G--
******	NIPPY	NOTCH	N-Y--	******	******
NAMED	NOPAL	NOTED	******	O-D--	OLGAS
NAMER	NOPAR	NOTER	NOYES	******	ORGAN
NAMES	******	NOTES	N-Z--	ODDER	OUGHT
NAMUR	N-R--	NUTTY	******	ODDLY	******
NEMAT	******	******	NAZIS	OGDEN	O-H--
NIMBI	NARCO	N-U--	NIZAM	OIDEA	******
NIMES	NARDS	******	NIZER	OLDEN	OCHER
NOMAD	NARES	NAURU	******	OLDER	OCHRE
NOMAS	NARIS	NEUME	O-A--	ORDER	OCHRY
NUMBS	NARKY	NEURI	******	******	OGHAM
NUMEN	NEROS	NEURO	OCALA	O-E--	OPHIO
NYMPH	NERVE	NOUNS	OKAPI	******	OTHER
******	NERVY	******	OKAYS	OBEAH	******
N-N--	NORAH	N-V--	OLAFS	OBELI	O-I--
******	NORAS	******	OLAVS	OBESE	******
NANAS	NORIA	NAVAL	OMAHA	OBEYS	OBITS
NANCE	NORMA	NAVAR	OMASA	OCEAN	ODIUM
NANCY	NORMS	NAVEL	OPAHS	ODEON	OGIVE
NANNA	NORNS	NAVES	ORACH	ODETS	OKIEH
NANNY	NORSE	NAVVY	ORALS	ODEUM	OKIES
NINAS	NORTH	NEVER	ORANG	OGEES	OKING
NINES	NURSE	NEVIL	ORATE	OLEAN	OLIGO
NINNY	******	NEVIS	OSAGE	OLEIC	OLIOS
NINTH	N-S--	NEVUS	OSAKA	OLEIN	OLIVE
NINUS	******	NIVAL	OTARU	OLENT	OMITS
NONAS	NASAL	NOVAE	OVALS	OMEGA	ONION
NONCE	NASTY	NOVAS	OVARY	OMENS	ONIRO
NONES	NESTS	NOVEL	OVATE	OMERS	OPINE
NONET	NISAN	******	OZARK	ONEGA	ORIBI
******	NISEI	N-W--	******	ONEIR	ORIEL
N-O--	NISUS	******	O-B--	ONERY	ORION
******	NOSED	******	******	OPENS	ORIYA
NAOMI	NOSES	NAWAB	OMBER	OPERA	
NIOBE	NOSEY	NEWEL	OMBRE		

OSIER	OBOLI	OSTIA	PHANY	*****	PEENS
OSITY	ODONT	OTTER	PHASE	**P-C--**	PEEPS
OUIDA	ODORS	OTTOS	PHASY	*****	PEERS
OUIJA	ODOUR	OUTDO	PIAND	PACAS	PEEVE
OVINE	OLOGY	OUTED	PIANO	PACED	PHEBE
OWING	OTOMI	OUTER	PIAVE	PACER	PHENO
OXIDE	OVOID	OUTGO	PLACE	PACES	PIECE
OXIME	OVOLI	OUTRE	PLACK	PACHY	PIERS
*****	OVOLO	*****	PLAGI	PACKS	PIETA
O-K--	OZONE	**O-U--**	PLAID	PACTS	PIETY
*****	*****	*****	PLAIN	PECAN	PIEZO
OAKEN	**O-P--**	OCULO	PLAIT	PECKS	PLEAD
OAKUM	*****	OVULE	PLANE	PECOS	PLEAS
*****	ORPIN	*****	PLANI	PICAL	PLEAT
O-L--	*****	**O-V--**	PLANK	PICAS	PLEBE
*****	**O-R--**	*****	PLANO	PICKS	PLEBS
OGLED	*****	OAVES	PLANS	PICOT	PLEGY
OGLER	OARED	*****	PLANT	PICRO	PLENA
OGLES	OCREA	**O-Y--**	PLASH	PICTS	PNEUM
OILED	OGRES	*****	PLASM	PICUL	POEMS
OILER	OKRAS	ODYLE	PLAST	POCKS	POESY
OLLAS	ORRIS	*****	PLASY	POCKY	POETS
OLLIE	OURAY	**O-Z--**	PLATA	PUCES	PREEN
ORLES	*****	*****	PLATE	PUCKA	PRESA
ORLON	**O-S--**	OOZED	PLATO	PUCKS	PRESS
ORLOP	*****	OOZES	PLATS	*****	PREST
OSLER	OASES	OUZEL	PLATY	**P-D--**	PREXY
OWLET	OASIS	OZZIE	PLAYA	*****	PREYS
OXLIP	ONSET	*****	PLAYS	PADDY	PSEUD
*****	OPSIA	**P-A--**	PLAZA	PADRE	PTERO
O-M--	OPSIS	*****	POACH	PADUA	PYELO
*****	ORSON	PEACE	PRAHU	PEDAL	*****
OGMIC	OUSEL	PEACH	PRAMS	PEDES	**P-F--**
OHMIC	OUSTS	PEAKS	PRANG	PEDRO	*****
OOMPH	*****	PEAKY	PRANK	PODGY	PUFFS
ORMER	**O-T--**	PEALS	PRASE	PODIA	PUFFY
OSMAN	*****	PEANS	PRATE	PUDGY	*****
OSMIC	OATEN	PEARL	PRAWN	PUDIC	**P-G--**
*****	OATES	PEARS	PRAYS	PUDSY	*****
O-N--	OATHS	PEARY	PSALM	PYDNA	PAGAN
*****	OCTAD	PEASE	*****	*****	PAGED
ORNIS	OCTET	PEATS	**P-B--**	**P-E--**	PAGER
OUNCE	OCTYL	PEATY	*****	*****	PAGES
OWNED	OFTEN	PEAVY	PABLO	PAEAN	PEGGY
OWNER	OPTED	PHAGE	PUBES	PAEDO	PIGGY
*****	OPTIC	PHAGO	PUBIC	PAEON	PIGMY
O-O--	ORTHO	PHAGY	PUBIS	PEEKS	POGEY
*****	OSTED	PHANE	*****	PEELS	PUGET
OBOES					PYGMY
OBOLE					

******	PRISM	PILAF	PANSY	PEONY	******
P-H--	PRIVY	PILAR	PANTO	PHOBE	**P-P--**
******	PRIZE	PILEA	PANTS	PHONE	******
PSHAW	******	PILED	PANTY	PHONO	PAPAL
******	**P-K--**	PILEI	PENAL	PHONY	PAPAS
P-I--	******	PILES	PENCE	PHORE	PAPAW
******	PEKAN	PILIS	PENDS	PHOTO	PAPEN
PAILS	PEKIN	PILLS	PENGO	PHOTS	PAPER
PAINE	PEKOE	PILOT	PENIS	PIONS	PAPPI
PAINS	PIKAS	POLAR	PENNA	PIOUS	PAPPY
PAINT	PIKED	POLED	PENNI	PLODS	PAPUA
PAIRS	PIKER	POLES	PENNY	PLOID	PEPIN
PAISA	PIKES	POLIO	PENTA	PLONK	PEPLA
PAISE	POKED	POLKA	PINAS	PLOPS	PEPOS
PHIAL	POKER	POLLS	PINCH	PLOTS	PEPPY
PHILA	POKES	POLLY	PINED	PLOWS	PEPYS
PHILE	POKEY	POLYP	PINEL	PLOYS	PIPAL
PHILO	PUKED	PULED	PINER	POOCH	PIPED
PHILS	PUKES	PULER	PINES	POODS	PIPER
PHILY	PUKKA	PULES	PINEY	POOLE	PIPES
PHIPS	******	PULLS	PINGO	POOLS	PIPET
PLICA	**P-L--**	PULMO	PINGS	POONA	PIPIT
PLIED	******	PULPS	PINKS	POONS	POPES
PLIER	PALAE	PULPY	PINKY	POOPO	POPPY
PLIES	PALEA	PULSE	PINNA	POOPS	POPSY
PLINY	PALED	PYLON	PINNI	PROAS	PUPAE
POILU	PALEO	******	PINNY	PROBE	PUPIL
POIND	PALER	**P-M--**	PINON	PROCT	PUPPY
POINT	PALES	******	PINTA	PRODS	******
POISE	PALEY	PIMAN	PINTO	PROEM	**P-Q--**
PRIAM	PALLS	PIMAS	PINTS	PROFS	******
PRICE	PALLY	PIMPS	PINUP	PROLE	PIQUE
PRICK	PALMA	POMES	PONCE	PROMS	******
PRIDE	PALMI	POMMY	PONDS	PRONE	**P-R--**
PRIED	PALMS	PUMAS	PONES	PRONG	******
PRIER	PALMY	PUMPS	PUNAS	PROOF	PARAS
PRIES	PALPI	******	PUNCH	PROPS	PARCA
PRIGS	PALSY	**P-N--**	PUNGS	PROSE	PARCH
PRIMA	PELEE	******	PUNIC	PROSY	PARDS
PRIME	PELEG	PANAY	PUNKA	PROTO	PARED
PRIMI	PELFS	PANDA	PUNKS	PROUD	PAREN
PRIMO	PELLA	PANDY	PUNKY	PROVE	PARER
PRIMP	PELLY	PANED	PUNTO	PROVO	PARES
PRIMS	PELON	PANEL	PUNTS	PROWL	PAREU
PRINK	PELTS	PANES	PUNTY	PROWS	PARGO
PRINT	PELVI	PANGS	******	PROXY	PARIS
PRIOR	PHLEB	PANIC	**P-O--**	PSOAS	PARKA
PRISE	PHLOX	PANNE	******	PYOID	PARKS
			PAOLO		
			PEONS		

PARMA	PASSY	PITOT	PAWKY	QUANT	******
PAROL	PASTA	POTTO	PAWLS	QUARK	R-A--
PAROS	PASTE	POTTO	PAWNS	QUART	******
PARRS	PASTS	POTTY	PEWEE	QUASH	REACH
PARRY	PASTY	PUTON	PEWIT	QUASI	REACT
PARSE	PESKY	PUTTS	POWER	QUASS	READS
PARSI	PESOS	PUTTY	POWYS	QUAYS	READY
PARTS	PESTS	PUTUP	******	******	REALM
PARTY	PISCI	******	P-X--	Q-E--	REALS
PERCH	POSED	P-U--	******	******	REAMS
PERCY	POSER	******	PIXIE	QUEAN	REAPS
PERDU	POSES	PAULA	PYXED	QUEEN	REARM
PERES	POSIT	PAULO	PYXES	QUEER	REARS
PERIL	POSSE	PAULS	PYXIE	QUELL	RHAGE
PERIS	POSTS	PAUSE	PYXIS	QUERN	RHAGY
PERKS	PUSAN	PLUCK	******	QUERY	RIALS
PERKY	PUSHY	PLUGS	P-Y--	QUEST	RIANT
PERLE	PUSSY	PLUMB	******	QUEUE	RIATA
PERON	******	PLUME	PAYED	******	ROACH
PERRY	P-T--	PLUMP	PAYEE	Q-I--	ROADS
PERSE	******	PLUMS	PAYER	******	ROALD
PERTH	PATCH	PLUMY	PHYCO	QUICK	ROAMS
PHREN	PATEN	PLUNK	PHYLA	QUIDS	ROANS
PORCH	PATER	PLURI	PHYLE	QUIET	ROARS
PORED	PATES	PLUSH	PHYLL	QUIFF	ROAST
PORES	PATHO	PLUTO	PHYLO	QUILL	******
PORGE	PATHS	PLUVI	PHYRE	QUILT	R-B--
PORGY	PATHY	POUCH	PHYSI	QUINT	******
PORKY	PATIO	POUFS	PHYTE	QUIPS	RABAT
PORNO	PATNA	POULT	PHYTO	QUIPU	RABBI
PORTS	PATRI	POUND	POYOU	QUIRE	RABIC
PUREE	PATSY	POURS	PRYER	QUIRK	RABID
PURER	PATTI	POUTS	PSYCH	QUIRT	REBEC
PURGE	PATTY	PRUDE	******	QUITE	REBEL
PURIM	PETAL	PRUNE	P-Z--	QUITO	REBID
PURLS	PETER	******	******	QUITS	REBUS
PURRS	PETES	P-V--	PIZZA	******	REBUT
PURSE	PETIT	******		Q-O--	ROBED
PURSY	PETRO	PAVAN	Q-A--	******	ROBES
PYRAN	PETRY	PAVED	******	QUODS	ROBIN
PYRES	PETTI	PAVER	QUACK	QUOIN	ROBLE
PYREX	PETTO	PAVES	QUADS	QUOIT	ROBOT
******	PETTY	PAVIS	QUAFF	QUOTA	RUBES
P-S--	PITAS	PIVOT	QUAGS	QUOTE	RUBLE
******	PITCH	******	QUAIL	QUOTH	RUBYS
PASCH	PITHS	P-W--	QUAKE	******	******
PASHA	PITHY	******	QUAKY	Q-T--	R-C--
PASSE	PITON	PAWED	QUALM	******	******
		PAWER	QATAR		RACED
					RACER

RACES	REELS	RAISE	******	RINSE	******
RACKS	REEVE	REICH	**R-M--**	RONDO	**R-Q--**
RECAP	RHEAS	REIFY	******	RONNY	******
RECTA	RHEUM	REIGN	RAMIE	RUNES	ROQUE
RECTI	RUERS	REIMS	RAMMY	RUNGS	******
RECTO	******	REINS	RAMPS	RUNIC	**R-R--**
RECUR	**R-F--**	RHINE	RAMUS	RUNIN	******
RICED	******	RHINO	REMAN	RUNNY	RARER
RICER	RAFTS	RHIZO	REMEX	RUNON	RERAN
RICES	REFER	ROILS	REMIT	RUNTS	RERUN
RICIN	REFIT	ROILY	REMUS	RUNTY	RURAL
RICKS	RIFFS	RUING	RIMED	RYNDS	RURIK
RICKY	RIFLE	RUINS	RIMER	******	******
ROCKS	RIFTS	******	RIMES	**R-O--**	**R-S--**
ROCKY	RUFFS	**R-J--**	ROMAN	******	******
RUCHE	RUFUS	******	ROMEO	RAOUL	RASPS
RUCKS	******	RAJAB	ROMPS	RHODA	RASPY
******	**R-G--**	RAJAH	RUMBA	RHOEA	RESET
R-D--	******	******	RUMEN	RHOMB	RESIN
******	RAGED	**R-K--**	RUMLY	RHONE	RESTS
RADAR	RAGEE	******	RUMMY	RIOTS	RISEN
RADII	RAGES	RAKED	RUMOR	ROODS	RISER
RADIO	RAGGY	RAKEE	RUMPS	ROOFS	RISES
RADIX	REGAL	RAKER	******	ROOKS	RISKS
RADON	REGAN	RAKES	**R-N--**	ROOKY	RISKY
REDAN	REGES	******	******	ROOMS	RISUS
REDID	REGIN	**R-L--**	RANCE	ROOMY	ROSAS
REDLY	REGMA	******	RANCH	ROOST	ROSED
RIDER	RIGEL	RALES	RANDS	ROOTS	ROSES
RIDES	RIGGS	RALLY	RANDY	ROOTY	ROSIN
RIDGE	RIGHT	RALPH	RANEE	RYOTS	RUSES
RIDGY	RIGID	RELAX	RANGE	******	RUSHY
RODDY	RIGOR	RELAY	RANGY	**R-P--**	RUSKS
RODEO	ROGER	RELIC	RANIS	******	RUSSO
RODIN	ROGUE	RILED	RANKS	RAPED	RUSTS
RUDDS	RUGAE	RILES	RANTS	RAPES	RUSTY
RUDDY	RUGBY	RILEY	RENAL	RAPHE	******
RUDER	******	RILLE	RENAN	RAPID	**R-T--**
RUDYS	**R-H--**	RILLS	RENDS	REPAY	******
******	******	ROLES	RENEE	REPEL	RATAL
R-E--	RRHEA	ROLFE	RENES	REPLY	RATCH
******	******	ROLFS	RENEW	RIPEN	RATED
REEDS	**R-I--**	ROLLO	RENIN	RIPER	RATEL
REEDY	******	ROLLS	RENTE	RIPON	RATER
REEFS	RAIDS	ROLPH	RENTS	ROPED	RATES
REEFY	RAILS	RULED	RINDS	ROPES	RATIO
REEKS	RAINS	RULER	RINGS	ROPEY	RATTY
REEKY	RAINY	RULES	RINKS	RUPEE	RETCH

RETEM	******	SCARS	SLAGS	SPARK	SWARM
RETIA	**R-W--**	SCARY	SLAIN	SPARS	SWART
RETRO	******	SCATO	SLAKE	SPASM	SWASH
RETRY	RAWER	SCATS	SLAMS	SPATE	SWATH
RETTA	RAWLY	SCAUP	SLANG	SPATS	SWATS
RITAS	ROWAN	SEALS	SLANT	SPAWN	SWAYS
RITES	ROWDY	SEAMS	SLAPS	SPAYS	******
RITZY	ROWED	SEAMY	SLASH	STABS	**S-B--**
ROTAS	ROWEL	SEANS	SLATE	STACK	******
ROTCH	ROWEN	SEARS	SLATS	STACY	SABAH
ROTLA	ROWER	SEATO	SLATY	STAFF	SABED
ROTOR	******	SEATS	SLAVE	STAGE	SABER
RUTHS	**R-Y--**	SHACK	SLAVO	STAGS	SABES
RUTTY	******	SHADE	SLAVS	STAGY	SABIN
******	RAYAH	SHADY	SLAWS	STAID	SABLE
R-U--	RAYED	SHAFT	SLAYS	STAIN	SABOT
******	RAYON	SHAGS	SMACK	STAIR	SABRA
RHUMB	RHYME	SHAHS	SMALL	STAKE	SABRE
ROUEN	RIYAL	SHAKE	SMALT	STALE	SEBAT
ROUES	ROYAL	SHAKO	SMART	STALK	SEBUM
ROUGE	******	SHAKY	SMASH	STALL	SIBYL
ROUGH	**R-Z--**	SHALE	SMAZE	STAMP	SOBER
ROUND	******	SHALL	SNACK	STAND	SUBAH
ROUPY	RAZED	SHALT	SNAFU	STANK	SYBIL
ROUSE	RAZEE	SHALY	SNAGS	STANS	******
ROUST	RAZES	SHAME	SNAIL	STAPH	**S-C--**
ROUTE	RAZOR	SHAMS	SNAKE	STARE	******
ROUTS	REZIN	SHANK	SNAKY	STARK	SACKS
******	******	SHANS	SNAPS	STARS	SACRA
R-V--	**S-A--**	SHANT	SNARE	START	SACRO
******	******	SHAPE	SNARK	STASH	SECCO
RAVED	SCABS	SHARD	SNARL	STATE	SECTS
RAVEL	SCADS	SHARE	SNATH	STATO	SICES
RAVEN	SCALD	SHARI	SOAKS	STAVE	SICKS
RAVER	SCALE	SHARK	SOAPS	STAYS	SOCIO
RAVES	SCALL	SHARP	SOAPY	SUAVE	SOCKS
REVEL	SCALP	SHAUN	SOARS	SWABS	SOCLE
REVET	SCALY	SHAVE	SPACE	SWAGE	SUCKS
REVUE	SCAMP	SHAWL	SPADE	SWAGS	SUCRE
RIVAL	SCAND	SHAWM	SPAHI	SWAIL	SYCEE
RIVED	SCANS	SHAWN	SPAIN	SWAIN	SYCES
RIVEN	SCANT	SHAWS	SPAIT	SWALE	******
RIVER	SCAPA	SHAYS	SPAKE	SWAMI	**S-D--**
RIVES	SCAPE	SIALO	SPALL	SWAMP	******
RIVET	SCAPI	SKALD	SPANG	SWANK	SADHU
ROVED	SCARE	SKATE	SPANK	SWANS	SADIE
ROVEN	SCARF	SLABS	SPANS	SWAPS	SADLY
ROVER	SCARP	SLACK	SPARE	SWARD	SEDAN

SEDER	SKEED	STETH	******	SKINS	SPIRO
SEDGE	SKEES	STETH	**S-H--**	SKIPS	SPIRT
SEDGY	SKEET	STETS	******	SKIRL	SPIRY
SEDUM	SKEGS	STEVE	SAHEB	SKIRR	SPITE
SIDED	SKEIN	STEWS	SAHIB	SKIRT	SPITS
SIDER	SKEPS	SUEDE	SCHIZ	SKITS	SPITZ
SIDES	SKEWS	SUERS	SCHMO	SKIVE	STICH
SIDLE	SLEAT	SUETY	SCHWA	SLICE	STICK
SIDON	SLEDS	SWEAR	SPHEN	SLICK	STIED
SODAS	SLEEK	SWEAT	******	SLIDE	STIES
SODOM	SLEEP	SWEDE	**S-I--**	SLIER	STIFF
SUDAN	SLEET	SWEEP	******	SLIGO	STILE
SUDOR	SLEPT	SWEET	SAIGA	SLILY	STILL
SUDSY	SLEWS	SWELL	SAILS	SLIME	STILT
******	SMEAR	SWEPT	SAINT	SLIMS	STIMY
S-E--	SMELL	******	SCIFI	SLIMY	STING
******	SMELT	**S-F--**	SCION	SLING	STINK
SCENA	SMEWS	******	SEINE	SLINK	STINT
SCEND	SNEAD	SAFER	SEISE	SLIPS	STIPE
SCENE	SNEAK	SAFES	SEISM	SLIPT	STIRK
SCENT	SNEER	SIFTS	SEIZE	SLITS	STIRP
SEEDS	SNELL	SOFAS	SHIAH	SMILE	STIRS
SEEDY	SPEAK	SOFIA	SHIED	SMIRK	SUING
SEEKS	SPEAR	SOFTA	SHIER	SMITE	SUINT
SEEMS	SPECK	SOFTY	SHIFT	SMITH	SUITE
SEEPS	SPECS	SUFIC	SHILL	SNICK	SUITS
SEERS	SPEED	SUFIS	SHILY	SNIDE	SWIFT
SHEAF	SPELL	******	SHIMS	SNIFF	SWIGS
SHEAR	SPELT	**S-G--**	SHINE	SNIPE	SWILL
SHEAS	SPEND	******	SHINS	SNIPS	SWIMS
SHEBA	SPENT	SAGAN	SHINY	SOILS	SWINE
SHEDS	SPERM	SAGAS	SHIPS	SPICA	SWING
SHEEN	SPEWS	SAGER	SHIRE	SPICE	SWIPE
SHEEP	STEAD	SAGES	SHIRK	SPICY	SWIRL
SHEER	STEAK	SAGOS	SHIRR	SPIED	SWISH
SHEET	STEAL	SAGUM	SHIRT	SPIEL	SWISS
SHEIK	STEAM	SEGNI	SHIVE	SPIER	******
SHELF	STEED	SEGNO	SHIVS	SPIES	**S-J--**
SHELL	STEEL	SEGOS	SKIDS	SPIKE	******
SHEOL	STEEN	SIGHS	SKIED	SPIKY	SAJOU
SHERD	STEEP	SIGHT	SKIER	SPILE	SOJAS
SHEWN	STEER	SIGIL	SKIES	SPILL	******
SHEWS	STEIN	SIGMA	SKIFF	SPILT	**S-K--**
SIEGE	STELE	SIGNE	SKILL	SPINE	******
SIENA	STEMS	SIGNS	SKIMO	SPINI	SAKER
SIEUR	STENO	SOGGY	SKIMP	SPINS	SAKES
SIEVE	STEPS	SUGAR	SKIMS	SPINY	SIKHS
SKEAN	STERE		SKINK	SPIRE	SOKES

******	SOLVE	SINES	SHOER	SNOWY	STOWS
S-L--	SPLAT	SINEW	SHOES	SOOTH	SWOON
******	SPLAY	SINGE	SHOJI	SOOTS	SWOOP
SALAD	SPLEN	SINGS	SHONE	SOOTY	SWORD
SALEM	SPLIT	SINKS	SHOOK	SPODE	SWORE
SALEP	SULCI	SINON	SHOOS	SPOIL	SWORN
SALES	SULFA	SINUS	SHOOT	SPOKE	******
SALIC	SULFO	SONAR	SHOPS	SPOOF	**S-P--**
SALIX	SULKS	SONES	SHORE	SPOOK	******
SALLY	SULKY	SONGS	SHORL	SPOOL	SAPID
SALMA	SULLY	SONIA	SHORN	SPOON	SAPOR
SALMI	SULUS	SONIC	SHORT	SPOOR	SAPPY
SALOL	SYLPH	SONJA	SHOTE	SPORE	SAPRO
SALON	SYLVA	SONNY	SHOTS	SPORO	SEPAL
SALPA	******	SONSY	SHOUT	SPORT	SEPIA
SALSA	**S-M--**	SONYA	SHOVE	SPOTS	SEPOY
SALSE	******	SUNNA	SHOWN	SPOUT	SEPTA
SALTS	SAMAR	SUNNI	SHOWS	STOAE	SEPTI
SALTY	SAMBA	SUNNS	SHOWY	STOAS	SEPTO
SALUS	SAMBO	SUNNY	SIOUX	STOAT	SEPTS
SALVE	SAMEK	SUNUP	SKOAL	STOCK	SIPES
SALVO	SAMMY	SYNGE	SLOBS	STOGY	SOPHY
SELAH	SAMOA	SYNOD	SLOES	STOIC	SOPOR
SELEN	SAMOS	******	SLOGS	STOKE	SOPPY
SELLS	SEMEN	**S-O--**	SLOOP	STOLE	SUPER
SELMA	SIMAR	******	SLOPE	STOMA	SUPES
SILAS	SIMON	SAONE	SLOPS	STOME	SUPRA
SILEX	SIMPS	SCOFF	SLOSH	STOMP	******
SILIC	SOMAT	SCOLD	SLOTH	STOMY	**S-R--**
SILKS	SOMME	SCONE	SLOTS	STONE	******
SILKY	SOMNI	SCOOP	SLOWS	STONY	SARAH
SILLS	SUMAC	SCOOT	SLOYD	STOOD	SARAN
SILLY	SUMER	SCOPE	SMOCK	STOOK	SARAS
SILOS	SUMPS	SCOPS	SMOGS	STOOL	SARCO
SILTS	******	SCOPY	SMOKE	STOOP	SARIS
SILTY	**S-N--**	SCORE	SMOKY	STOPE	SARKS
SILVA	******	SCORN	SMOLT	STOPS	SAROS
SOLAN	SANDS	SCOTO	SMOTE	STOPT	SARRE
SOLAR	SANDY	SCOTS	SNOBS	STORE	SARTO
SOLDI	SANER	SCOTT	SNOOD	STORK	SCRAG
SOLDO	SANTA	SCOUR	SNOOK	STORM	SCRAM
SOLED	SENDS	SCOUT	SNOOP	STORY	SCRAP
SOLES	SENNA	SCOWL	SNOOT	STOSS	SCREE
SOLFA	SENNE	SCOWS	SNORE	STOUP	SCREW
SOLID	SENOR	SEOUL	SNORT	STOUR	SCRIM
SOLON	SENSE	SHOAL	SNOTS	STOUT	SCRIP
SOLOS	SINAI	SHOAT	SNOUT	STOVE	SCROD
SOLUS	SINCE	SHOCK	SNOWS	STOWE	SCRUB

SCRUM	STRIP	******	SNUBS	SAVOR	******
SERAC	STROP	**S-U--**	SNUFF	SAVOY	**S-Z--**
SERAI	STRUM	******	SNUGS	SAVVY	******
SERAL	STRUT	SAUCE	SOUGH	SEVEN	SIZAR
SERBS	SURAH	SAUCY	SOULS	SEVER	SIZED
SERED	SURAL	SAULS	SOUND	SIVAN	SIZES
SERES	SURAS	SAULT	SOUPS	******	SOZIN
SERFS	SURDS	SAUNA	SOUPY	**S-W--**	SUZYS
SERGE	SURER	SAURO	SOURS	******	******
SERIF	SURFS	SAURY	SOUSA	SAWED	**T-A--**
SERIN	SURFY	SAUTE	SOUSE	SAWER	******
SERON	SURGE	SCUBA	SOUTH	SEWED	TEACH
SEROW	SURGY	SCUDI	SPUDS	SEWER	TEAKS
SERRA	SURLY	SCUDO	SPUME	SOWAR	TEALS
SERUM	SYRIA	SCUDS	SPUMY	SOWED	TEAMS
SERVE	SYROS	SCUFF	SPUNK	SOWER	TEARS
SERVO	SYRUP	SCULL	SPURN	******	TEARY
SHRED	******	SCULP	SPURS	**S-X--**	TEASE
SHREW	**S-S--**	SCUMS	SPURT	******	TEATS
SHRUB	******	SCUPS	SQUAB	SAXES	THADS
SHRUG	SASIN	SCURF	SQUAD	SAXON	THADY
SIRED	SASSY	SCUTA	SQUAT	SEXED	THANE
SIREN	SISAL	SCUTE	SQUAW	SEXES	THANK
SIRES	SISSY	SCUTS	SQUIB	SEXTO	THAWS
SIRUP	SUSAN	SHUCK	SQUID	SIXES	TIARA
SORAS	SUSIE	SHULS	STUBS	SIXTE	TOADS
SORBS	******	SHUNS	STUCK	SIXTH	TOADY
SOREL	**S-T--**	SHUNT	STUDS	SIXTY	TOAST
SORER	******	SHUSH	STUDY	******	TRACE
SORES	SATAN	SHUTE	STUFF	**S-Y--**	TRACH
SORGO	SATED	SHUTS	STUKA	******	TRACK
SORRY	SATES	SKUAS	STULL	SAYER	TRACT
SORTS	SATIE	SKULK	STUMP	SAYID	TRACY
SORUS	SATIN	SKULL	STUMS	SAYSO	TRADE
SPRAG	SATYR	SKUNK	STUNG	SCYPH	TRAGI
SPRAT	SETAE	SLUBS	STUNK	SHYER	TRAIL
SPRAY	SETHS	SLUED	STUNS	SHYLY	TRAIN
SPREE	SETON	SLUES	STUNT	SKYEY	TRAIT
SPRIG	SETTO	SLUGS	STUPA	SLYER	TRAMP
SPRIT	SETUP	SLUMP	STUPE	SLYLY	TRAMS
SPRUE	SITAR	SLUMS	SWUNG	SLYPE	TRANS
STRAD	SITED	SLUNG	******	SNYES	TRAPS
STRAP	SITES	SLUNK	**S-V--**	SOYAS	TRASH
STRAT	SITIN	SLURP	******	STYLE	TRASS
STRAW	SITKA	SLURS	SAVED	STYLI	TRAVE
STRAY	SITUS	SLUSH	SAVER	STYLO	TRAWL
STREW	SOTOL	SLUTS	SAVES	STYMY	TRAYS
STRIA	SUTRA	SMUTS	SAVIN		TSADE

TSANA	TODDS	TIFFS	TRIGS	TELEO	TOMBS
TSARS	TODDY	TOFTS	TRILL	TELEX	TOMES
TWAIN	TODOS	TUFTS	TRIMS	TELIC	TOMMY
TWANG	TUDOR	TUFTY	TRINA	TELLS	TUMID
TZARS	******	******	TRINE	TELLY	TUMMY
******	**T-E--**	**T-G--**	TRIOL	TILDA	TUMOR
T-B--	******	******	TRIOS	TILDE	******
******	TAELS	TIGER	TRIPE	TILED	**T-N--**
TABAC	TEEMS	TIGHT	TRIPS	TILER	******
TABBY	TEENS	TIGRE	TRITE	TILES	TANEY
TABES	TEENY	TOGAE	TRIXY	TILLS	TANGO
TABID	TEETH	TOGAS	TWICE	TILLY	TANGS
TABLE	THECA	TOGUE	TWIGS	TILTH	TANGY
TABOO	THEDA	******	TWILL	TILTS	TANIS
TABOR	THEFT	**T-H--**	TWINE	TOLAN	TANKA
TEBET	THEIR	******	TWINS	TOLAS	TANKS
TIBER	THEME	TAHOE	TWIRL	TOLES	TANSY
TIBET	THERE	TEHEE	TWIRP	TOLLS	TANTO
TIBIA	THERM	******	TWIST	TOLYL	TANYA
TOBOL	THESE	**T-I--**	TWITS	TULES	TENCH
TOBYS	THETA	******	TWIXT	TULIP	TENDS
TUBAL	THEWS	TAIGA	TYING	TULLE	TENET
TUBAS	THEWY	TAILS	******	TULLY	TENON
TUBBY	TIEIN	TAINO	**T-K--**	TULSA	TENOR
TUBED	TIERS	TAINS	******	TYLER	TENOS
TUBER	TIEUP	TAINT	TAKEN	******	TENSE
TUBES	TOEIN	THICK	TAKER	**T-M--**	TENTH
******	TREAD	THIEF	TAKES	******	TENTS
T-C--	TREAS	THIGH	TEKEL	TAMED	TINAS
******	TREAT	THINE	TIKIS	TAMER	TINCT
TACET	TREED	THING	TOKAY	TAMES	TINEA
TACHY	TREES	THINK	TOKEN	TAMIL	TINED
TACIT	TREKS	THINS	TOKYO	TAMIS	TINES
TACKS	TREND	THIOL	TYKES	TAMMY	TINGE
TACKY	TRENT	THIRD	******	TAMPA	TINGS
TACNA	TRESS	TOILE	**T-L--**	TAMPS	TINNY
TICAL	TREWS	TOILS	******	TEMPE	TINTS
TICKS	TREYS	TOISE	TALCS	TEMPI	TONAL
TUCKS	TWEAK	TRIAD	TALER	TEMPO	TONED
TYCHE	TWEED	TRIAL	TALES	TEMPT	TONER
******	TWEEN	TRIBE	TALKS	TIMED	TONES
T-D--	TWEET	TRICE	TALLY	TIMER	TONGA
******	TWERE	TRICH	TALON	TIMES	TONGS
TEDDY	TWERP	TRICK	TALOS	TIMID	TONIC
TIDAL	TYEES	TRIED	TALUK	TIMMY	TONIS
TIDED	******	TRIER	TALUS	TIMOR	TONNE
TIDES	**T-F--**	TRIES	TELAE	TOMAN	TONUS
TODAY	TAFFY	TRIGO	TELEG	TOMAS	TONYS
	TAFIA				

TUNAS	TOPES	TORAH	TOTED	TOWEL	UMBLE
TUNED	TOPHI	TORCH	TOTEM	TOWER	UMBOS
TUNER	TOPIC	TORIC	TOTER	TOWNS	UMBRA
TUNES	TOPIS	TORII	TOTES	******	UNBAR
TUNIC	TOPSY	TORSI	TUTOR	T-X--	UPBOW
TUNIS	TUPIK	TORSK	TUTTI	******	URBAN
TUNNY	TUPIS	TORSO	TUTTY	TAXED	******
******	TYPED	TORTE	TUTUS	TAXER	U-C--
T-O--	TYPES	TORTS	******	TAXES	******
******	TYPOS	TORUS	T-U--	TAXIS	ULCER
TBONE	******	TURBO	******	TEXAS	UNCAP
THOLE	T-Q--	TURCO	TAUNT	TEXTS	UNCLE
THONG	******	TURFS	TAUPE	TOXIC	UNCUT
THORN	TOQUE	TURFY	TAURO	TOXIN	******
THORP	TUQUE	TURIN	TAUTO	******	U-D--
THOSE	******	TURKI	THUDS	T-Y--	******
THOTH	T-R--	TURKS	THUGS	******	UDDER
TIOGA	******	TURNS	THUJA	THYME	UNDEE
TOOLS	TARDO	TYROL	THULE	THYMY	UNDER
TOOTH	TARDY	TYROS	THUMB	THYRO	UNDID
TOOTS	TARED	******	THUMP	TOYED	UNDUE
TROAS	TARES	T-S--	THURS	TOYER	******
TROLL	TARNS	******	TOUCH	TOYON	U-E--
TRONA	TAROS	TASKS	TOUGH	TOYOS	******
TROOP	TAROT	TASSO	TOURS	TRYMA	ULEMA
TROPE	TARPS	TASTE	TOUTS	TRYON	ULENT
TROPH	TARRY	TASTY	TRUCE	TRYST	UPEND
TROTH	TARSI	TESLA	TRUCK	******	UREAL
TROTS	TARSO	TESTA	TRUDA	T-Z--	UREDO
TROUT	TARTS	TESTS	TRUDY	******	USERS
TROVE	TARTY	TESTY	TRUED	TAZZA	UTERI
******	TERAT	TUSKS	TRUER	TIZZY	UTERO
T-P--	TERMS	******	TRUES	******	UVEAL
******	TERNS	T-T--	TRULL	U-A--	UVEAS
TAPAS	TERRA	******	TRULY	******	******
TAPED	TERRI	TATAR	TRUMP	UKASE	U-F--
TAPER	TERRY	TATRA	TRUNK	UNAPT	******
TAPES	TERSE	TATTY	TRURO	UNARM	UNFIT
TAPIR	THREE	TETHS	TRUSS	UNAUS	UNFIX
TAPIS	THREW	TETON	TRUST	URALS	******
TEPEE	THROB	TETRA	TRUTH	URANO	U-G--
TEPID	THROE	TITAN	******	URATE	******
TIPPY	THROW	TITER	T-W--	USAGE	URGED
TIPSY	THRUM	TITHE	******	******	URGES
TOPAZ	TIRED	TITIS	TAWED	U-B--	******
TOPED	TIREE	TITLE	TAWER	******	U-H--
TOPEE	TIRES	TITUS	TAWNY	UMBEL	******
TOPER	TIROS	TOTAL	TOWED	UMBER	UNHAT
					USHER
					UTHER

*****	UNPIN	*****	VOILE	VENOM	VIRES
U-I--	UPPED	**V-C--**	VYING	VENTS	VIRGA
*****	UPPER	*****	*****	VENUE	VIRGE
UDINE	*****	VACUA	**V-L--**	VENUS	VIRGO
UMIAK	**U-R--**	VICAR	*****	VINAS	VIRTU
UNIAT	*****	VICES	VALES	VINCE	VIRUS
UNIFY	UNREF	VICHY	VALET	VINCI	*****
UNION	UNRIG	VICKS	VALID	VINES	**V-S--**
UNITE	UNRIP	VICKY	VALOR	VINIC	*****
UNITS	*****	VOCAL	VALUE	VINNY	VASES
UNITY	**U-S--**	VOCES	VALVE	VINYL	VASTY
URIAH	*****	*****	VELAR	*****	VESIC
URICO	UNSAY	**V-D--**	VELDS	**V-O--**	VESTA
URIEL	UNSEX	*****	VELDT	*****	VESTS
URINE	UPSET	VADUZ	VELUM	VIOLA	VISAS
URINO	URSAE	VEDIC	VILER	VIOLS	VISCT
USING	*****	VIDAL	VILLA	*****	VISED
UTICA	**U-T--**	VIDEO	VILLE	**V-P--**	VISES
UTILE	*****	VODKA	VILLI	*****	VISIT
*****	ULTRA	*****	VILLS	VAPID	VISOR
U-L--	UNTIE	**V-E--**	VILNA	VAPOR	VISTA
*****	UNTIL	*****	VOLAR	VEPSA	*****
UHLAN	UTTER	VEERS	VOLES	VIPER	**V-T--**
UNLAY	*****	VEERY	VOLGA	*****	*****
UNLIT	**U-U--**	VIEWS	VOLTA	**V-R--**	VATIC
*****	*****	VIEWY	VOLTE	*****	VETCH
U-M--	USUAL	VNECK	VOLTI	VARAS	VITAE
*****	USURP	*****	VOLTS	VARIC	VITAL
UNMAN	USURY	**V-G--**	VOLVA	VARIO	VITRI
UNMEW	UTURN	*****	VULVA	VARIX	VITTA
UXMAL	UVULA	VAGIN	*****	VARRO	VOTED
*****	*****	VAGUE	**V-M--**	VARUS	VOTER
U-N--	**U-W--**	VAGUS	*****	VARVE	VOTES
*****	*****	VIGIL	VAMPS	VERAS	*****
UINTA	UNWED	VIGOR	VIMEN	VERBS	**V-U--**
ULNAE	*****	VOGUE	VOMER	VERDI	*****
ULNAR	**U-Z--**	VOGUL	VOMIT	VERGE	VAULT
ULNAS	*****	VUGGY	*****	VERMI	VAUNT
*****	UNZIP	*****	**V-N--**	VERNA	VOUCH
U-O--	*****	**V-I--**	*****	VERNE	*****
*****	*****	*****	*****	VERNS	**V-V--**
UBOAT	**V-A--**	VAIRS	VANED	VERSE	*****
UBOLT	*****	VEILS	VANES	VERSO	VIVID
ULOSE	*****	VEINS	VANGS	VERST	*****
ULOUS	VIALS	VEINY	VANIR	VERTU	**V-W--**
*****	VIAND	VOICE	VENAE	VERVE	*****
U-P--	*****	VOIDS	VENAL	VIRAL	VOWED
*****	**V-B--**	VOILA	VENDS	VIREO	VOWEL
UNPEG	*****				VOWER
UNPEN	VIBES				

*****	*****	*****	WRIST	*****	*****
V-X--	**W-D--**	**W-G--**	WRITE	**W-N--**	**W-P--**
*****	*****	*****	WRITS	*****	*****
VEXED	WADDY	WAGED	*****	WANDA	WIPED
VEXER	WADED	WAGER	**W-K--**	WANDS	WIPER
VEXES	WADER	WAGES	*****	WANED	WIPES
VEXIL	WADES	WAGON	WAKED	WANES	*****
VIXEN	WEDGE	WIGAN	WAKEN	WANEY	**W-R--**
*****	WEDGY	WIGHT	WAKES	WANLY	*****
V-Z--	WIDDY	*****	WEKAS	WANTS	WARDS
*****	WIDEN	**W-H--**	WOKEN	WENCH	WARES
VIZIR	WIDER	*****	*****	WENDS	WARMS
VIZOR	WIDOW	WAHOO	**W-L--**	WENDY	WARNS
*****	WIDTH	*****	*****	WENNY	WARPS
W-A--	WODAN	**W-I--**	WALDO	WINCE	WARTS
*****	WODEN	*****	WALED	WINCH	WARTY
WEALD	*****	WAIFS	WALER	WINDS	WIRED
WEALS	**W-E--**	WAILS	WALES	WINDY	WIRER
WEANS	*****	WAINS	WALKS	WINED	WIRES
WEARS	WEEDS	WAIST	WALLA	WINES	WIRRA
WEARY	WEEDY	WAITS	WALLY	WINGS	WORDS
WEAVE	WEEKS	WAIVE	WALTS	WINGY	WORDY
WHACK	WEEMS	WEIGH	WALTZ	WINKS	WORKS
WHALE	WEENY	WEIRD	WELCH	WINOS	WORLD
WHAMS	WEEPS	WEIRS	WELDS	WINZE	WORMS
WHANG	WEEPY	WHICH	WELLS	*****	WORMY
WHAPS	WEEST	WHIFF	WELSH	**W-O--**	WORRY
WHARF	WHEAL	WHIGS	WELTS	*****	WORSE
WHAUP	WHEAT	WHILE	WILDE	WHOLE	WORST
WOADS	WHEEL	WHIMS	WILDS	WHOOP	WORTH
WOALD	WHELK	WHINE	WILED	WHOPS	WORTS
WRACK	WHELM	WHINS	WILES	WHORE	*****
WRAPS	WHELP	WHINY	WILEY	WHORL	**W-S--**
WRAPT	WHENS	WHIPS	WILLA	WHORT	*****
WRATH	WHERE	WHIPT	WILLS	WHOSE	WASHY
WYATT	WHETS	WHIRL	WILLY	WHOSO	WASNT
*****	WHEYS	WHIRR	WILMA	WOODS	WASPS
W-B--	WIELD	WHIRS	WILTS	WOODY	WASPY
*****	WREAK	WHISH	WOLDS	WOOED	WASTE
WEBBY	WRECK	WHISK	WOLFS	WOOER	WESER
WEBER	WRENS	WHIST	*****	WOOFS	WISED
*****	WREST	WHITE	**W-M--**	WOOLF	WISER
W-C--	*****	WHITS	*****	WOOLS	WISES
*****	**W-F--**	WRICK	WAMUS	WOOLY	WISPS
WACKE	*****	WRIED	WOMAN	WOOZY	WISPY
WACKS	WAFER	WRIER	WOMBS	WRONG	*****
WACKY	WAFTS	WRIES	WOMBY	WROTE	**W-T--**
WICKS	WEFTS	WRING	WOMEN	WROTH	*****
					WATAP
					WATCH

WATER	******	YEARS	YOLKS	YAWNS	******
WATTS	X-A--	YEAST	YOLKY	YAWPS	Z-O--
WETLY	******	YEATS	YULES	YOWED	******
WITAN	XRAYS	******	******	YOWLS	ZLOTY
WITCH	******	Y-C--	Y-M--	******	ZOOID
WITHE	X-B--	******	******	Y-X--	ZOOMS
WITHY	******	YACHT	YAMEN	******	ZOONS
WITTE	XEBEC	YUCCA	YAMUN	YAXES	******
WITTY	******	******	YEMEN	YAXIS	Z-P--
WOTAN	X-I--	Y-D--	YUMMY	******	******
******	******	******	******	Y-Y--	ZIPPY
W-U--	XTIAN	YODEL	Y-N--	******	******
******	******	YODHS	******	YOYOS	Z-R--
WAUGH	X-L--	******	YANKS	******	ZARFS
WAULS	******	Y-E--	******	Y-Z--	ZEROS
WOULD	XYLAN	******	Y-P--	******	ZIRON
WOUND	XYLEM	YIELD	YAPON	YAZOO	ZORIL
WRUNG	XYLOL	YSERE	YIPES	******	******
W-V--	XYLYL	******	YUPON	Z-B--	Z-S--
******	******	Y-G--	******	******	******
WAVED	X-N--	******	Y-R--	ZEBEC	ZESTS
WAVER	******	YAGER	******	ZEBRA	ZESTY
WAVES	XANTH	YEGGS	YARDS	ZEBUS	******
WAVEY	XENIA	YOGEE	YARNS	ZIBET	Z-T--
WIVED	XENON	YOGHS	YERBA	******	******
WIVER	******	YOGIC	YPRES	Z-I--	ZETAS
WIVES	X-P--	YOGIN	******	******	******
WOVEN	******	YOGIS	Y-S--	ZAIRE	Z-Y--
******	XIPHI	YUGAS	******	******	******
W-W--	******	******	YESES	Z-K--	ZAYIN
******	X-R--	Y-H--	******	******	******
WAWLS	******	******	Y-T--	ZEKES	A--A-
WOWED	XERIC	YAHOO	******	******	******
******	XEROX	YAHVE	YETIS	Z-M--	ABBAS
W-X--	XERUS	******	******	******	ABEAM
******	******	Y-K--	Y-U--	ZAMIA	ABRAM
WAXED	X-S--	******	******	ZIMRI	ACEAE
WAXEN	******	YOKED	YAUPS	ZOMBI	ACEAN
WAXES	XYSTS	YOKEL	YOULL	******	ADDAX
******	******	YOKES	YOUNG	Z-N--	ADLAI
W-Y--	X-X--	YUKON	YOURE	******	ADMAN
******	******	******	YOURS	ZINCS	AETAT
WAYNE	XAXES	Y-L--	YOUTH	ZINCY	AGHAS
WRYER	XAXIS	******	YOUVE	ZINGY	AHEAD
WRYLY	******	YALTA	YQUEM	ZINKY	AIDAS
******	Y-A--	YELKS	******	ZONAL	ALBAN
W-Z--	******	YELLS	Y-W--	ZONED	ALBAS
******	YEANS	YELPS	******	ZONES	
WIZEN	YEARN		YAWED		

ALCAN	ASSAY	ACIDS	ALDER	AUGER	ACTIN
ALDAN	ASWAN	ALADA	ALGER	AUREI	ADDIE
ALGAE	ATLAS	AMIDE	ALIEN	AURES	ADLIB
ALGAL	ATMAN	AMIDO	ALLEN	AWNED	ADMIN
ALIAS	ATPAR	ANODE	ALLEY	AXLED	ADMIT
ALLAH	ATTAR	ASIDE	ALOES	AXLES	ADMIX
ALLAN	AUDAD	******	ALTER	AXMEN	AECIA
ALLAY	AURAE	A--E-	AMBER	AZTEC	AEGIR
ALMAH	AURAL	******	AMEER	******	AEGIS
ALMAS	AURAS	ABBES	AMIEL	A--F-	AEMIA
ALTAI	AVIAN	ABBEY	AMIES	******	AERIE
ALTAR	AXIAL	ABIEL	ANDES	ABAFT	AESIR
ALTAS	AXMAN	ABIES	ANGEL	ALEFS	AFFIX
ALVAN	******	ABLER	ANGER	ALIFS	AGAIN
ALWAY	A--B-	ABNER	ANNES	ALOFT	AGGIE
AMIAS	******	ACCEL	ANNEX	******	AGNIS
AMMAN	ABIBS	ACHED	ANSEL	A--G-	ALAIN
ANEAR	ADOBE	ACHES	ANTED	******	ALBIN
ANLAS	ALIBI	ACRED	ANTES	ADAGE	ALDIS
ANNAL	AMEBA	ACRES	APNEA	ADIGE	ALFIE
ANNAM	AQABA	ACTED	APPEL	ALIGN	ALGIA
ANNAS	ARABS	ADDED	APSES	AMIGO	ALGID
ANSAE	ARABY	ADDER	APTER	******	ALGIE
ANTAE	ARUBA	ADEEM	ARCED	A--H-	ALGIN
ANTAL	******	ADIEU	ARDEB	******	ALLIE
ANZAC	A--C-	ADLER	ARDEN	ABOHM	ALLIN
APEAK	******	ADMEN	ARIEL	ADAHS	ALLIS
APIAN	ABACA	ADMEX	ARIES	ALOHA	ALOIN
APPAL	ABACI	ADZES	ARLEN	ALPHA	ALOIS
AQUAE	ABACK	AEDES	ARLES	ALPHY	ALUIN
AQUAS	ACOCK	AFTER	ARMED	AMAHS	ALVIN
AREAE	AITCH	AGGER	ARMET	AMPHI	ALWIN
AREAL	ALACK	AGLEE	ARPEN	AMPHR	AMAIN
AREAS	ALECK	AGLET	ARSES	ANKHS	AMBIT
ARGAL	ALECS	AGLEY	ARTEL	ANTHO	AMNIA
ARIAN	ALICE	AGNES	ARTER	ARCHI	ANGIO
ARIAS	ALYCE	AGREE	ASHEN	ARCHY	ANNIE
ARPAD	AMICE	AGUES	ASHER	ARTHR	ANTIC
ARRAN	AMUCK	AIDED	ASHES	AUGHT	ANTIS
ARRAS	APACE	AIDER	ASKED	AYAHS	ANVIL
ARRAY	ARECA	AIDES	ASKER	******	ANZIO
ARTAL	ARICA	AIKEN	ASKEW	A--I-	APHID
ARVAL	ASPCA	AILED	ASPEN	******	APHIS
ARYAN	******	AIMED	ASPER	AALII	APRIL
ASCAP	A--D-	AIMEE	ASSES	ABBIE	APSIS
ASIAN	******	AIRED	ASSET	ABOIL	AREIC
ASSAI	ABIDE	ALBEE	ASTER	ABRIS	ARGIL
ASSAM	ABODE	ALDEN	AUDEN	ACRID	ARNIE

AROID
ARRIS
ARSIS
ARTIC
ARTIE
ARTIS
ASPIC
ASPIS
ASTIR
ATRIA
ATRIP
ATTIC
ATTIS
AUDIE
AUDIO
AUDIT
AULIC
AULIS
AURIC
AURIS
AUXIL
AUXIN
AVAIL
AVOID
AVOIR
AVRIL
AWAIT
AYDIN
AZOIC
******
A--K-
******
ALIKE
AWAKE
AWOKE
******
A--L-
******
ABELE
ABELS
ADDLE
ADELA
ADELE
ADOLF
ADULT
AGILE
AISLE
ALULA

AMBLE
AMOLE
AMPLE
AMPLY
AMYLO
AMYLS
ANELE
ANGLE
ANGLO
ANILE
ANILS
ANKLE
APPLE
APPLY
APTLY
ARILS
ASYLA
ATILT
ATOLL
AXILE
AXILS
AZOLE
******
A--M-
******
ABOMA
ABOMB
ADAMS
AGAMA
ALAMO
ALUMS
ANEMO
ANIMA
ANIME
ANOMY
AROMA
ARUMS
ATOMS
******
A--N-
******
ACING
ACINI
ADENI
ADENO
ADUNC
AEONS
AGANA

AGENT
AGING
AGONY
AISNE
AKENE
ALAND
ALANS
ALINE
ALONE
ALONG
AMANA
AMEND
AMENS
AMENT
AMINE
AMINO
AMONG
ANENT
APING
ARENA
ARENT
ASSNS
ATONE
ATONY
AVENS
AWING
AXING
AXONE
AXONS
AYINS
AZANS
AZINE
AZONS
******
A--O-
******
AARON
ABBOT
ABHOR
ACTOR
ADIOS
AESOP
AFOOT
AFROS
AGIOS
AGLOW
AINOS
AKRON

ALDOL
ALDOS
ALGOL
ALGOR
ALLOT
ALLOW
ALLOY
ALOOF
ALTON
ALTOS
AMBOS
AMMON
ANCON
ANION
ANJOU
ANNOY
ANTON
APRON
ARBOR
ARDOR
ARGOL
ARGON
ARGOS
ARGOT
ARION
ARMOR
ARROW
ARSON
ASCOT
ASSOC
ASTON
ASTOR
ATHOS
ATION
AUTOS
AVION
AXIOM
******
A--P-
******
A--R-
******
ABORT
ACCRA

ACERB
ACORN
ADORE
ADORN
AFIRE
AFORE
AFTRA
AGORA
ALARM
ALARY
ALERT
AMBRY
AMIRS
ANDRE
ANDRO
ANGRY
ANTRA
APART
APERY
APORT
ASTRO
ATORY
AUTRY
AVARS
AVERS
AVERT
AVERY
AWARD
AWARE
AZURE
******
A--S-
******
ABASE
ABASH
ABUSE
ABYSM
ABYSS
ADUST
AGIST
ALIST
AMASS
AMISH
AMISS
AMUSE
ANGST
ANISE
ANISO

APISH
ARISE
AROSE
AVAST
AVISO
AWASH
******
A--T-
******
ABATE
ABETS
ABUTS
ACETO
ACITY
ACUTE
ADITS
ADYTA
AGATE
ALATE
AMATE
AMATI
AMITY
ANITA
AORTA
ARETE
ASSTS
AUNTS
AUNTY
AUSTL
AZOTE
AZOTH
******
A--U-
******
ABOUT
ACOUO
ACTUS
AFOUL
AINUS
ALBUM
ALDUS
ALEUT
ALGUM
ALMUD
ALMUG
ALOUD
AMOUR
AMPUL

ANGUS	******	BILBO	BAWDS	BENES	BRIER
ANKUS	B--A-	BLABS	BAWDY	BENET	BUBER
ANNUL	******	BLEBS	BEADS	BEREA	BUSED
ARCUS	BABAR	BLOBS	BEADY	BERET	BUSES
ARGUE	BABAS	BOBBY	BENDS	BESET	BUYER
ARGUS	BAHAI	BOMBE	BENDY	BETEL	BYRES
ARIUM	BALAS	BOMBS	BIDDY	BEVEL	******
ARIUS	BANAL	BOOBS	BINDS	BEZEL	B--F-
ARTUR	BANAT	BOOBY	BIRDS	BICES	******
ASCUS	BASAL	BRIBE	BLADE	BIDED	BAFFS
ASHUR	BATAN	BULBS	BONDS	BIDES	BAFFY
ASYUT	BEGAD	BUSBY	BOYDS	BIDET	BANFF
AUGUR	BEGAN	******	BRADS	BIKES	BEEFS
AURUM	BEGAT	B--C-	BRADY	BILES	BEEFY
AWFUL	BEHAN	******	BREDA	BINES	BIFFS
******	BELAY	BACCI	BRIDE	BINET	BIFFY
A--V-	BERAR	BARCA	BUDDY	BIPED	BLUFF
******	BETAS	BATCH	BUNDE	BISES	BUFFI
ABOVE	BEVAN	BEACH	BUNDS	BITER	BUFFO
AGAVE	BIHAR	BEECH	BURDS	BITES	BUFFS
ALIVE	BINAL	BELCH	******	BIZET	BUFFY
ATIVE	BLEAK	BENCH	B--E-	BLEED	******
******	BLEAR	BIRCH	******	BLEEP	B--G-
A--W-	BLEAT	BITCH	BAAED	BLUED	******
******	BLOAT	BLACK	BABEL	BLUER	BADGE
ADOWA	BOGAN	BLOCK	BABER	BLUES	BAGGY
ADUWA	BOLAR	BLOCS	BABES	BLUET	BANGS
AVOWS	BOLAS	BOSCH	BADEN	BODED	BARGE
******	BORAX	BOTCH	BAGEL	BODES	BEIGE
A--X-	BOYAR	BRACE	BAKED	BOGEY	BELGA
******	BREAD	BRACT	BAKER	BOHEA	BERGS
ALEXA	BREAK	BRICE	BAKES	BOLES	BILGE
ATAXY	BREAM	BRICK	BALED	BONED	BILGY
******	BRIAN	BROCK	BALER	BONER	BINGE
A--Y-	BRIAR	BRUCE	BALES	BONES	BINGO
******	BROAD	BRYCE	BARED	BOOED	BLDGS
ABBYS	BRYAN	BUNCH	BARER	BORED	BLIGH
ADDYS	BUBAL	BUNCO	BARES	BORER	BOGGY
ALGYS	BURAN	BUTCH	BASED	BORES	BONGO
ALKYL	BYLAW	******	BASEL	BOWED	BONGS
ALLYL	BYWAY	B--D-	BASES	BOWEL	BOUGH
ANDYS	******	******	BATED	BOWER	BRAGE
ASSYR	B--B-	BALDR	BATEN	BOXED	BRAGG
ATTYS	******	BANDA	BATES	BOXER	BRAGI
******	BAMBI	BANDS	BAYED	BOXES	BRAGS
A--Z-	BARBS	BANDY	BEDEW	BRAES	BRIGS
******	BEEBE	BARDE	BEGET	BREED	BUDGE
AGAZE	BIBBS	BARDS	BELEM	BRIEF	BUDGY
AMAZE					

BUGGY
BULGE
BULGY
BUNGS
BURGH
BURGS
******

B--H-
******
BACHE
BATHE
BATHO
BATHS
BATHY
BETHS
BIGHT
BLAHS
BOCHE
BOTHY
BRAHE
BUSHY
******

B--I-
******
BAHIA
BARIC
BARIT
BASIC
BASIL
BASIN
BASIS
BATIK
BEDIM
BEFIT
BEGIN
BELIE
BENIN
BERIA
BEVIN
BIFID
BINIT
BLAIN
BLOIS
BOGIE
BONIN
BORIC
BORIS
BOVID

BOWIE
BRAID
BRAIL
BRAIN
BROIL
BRUIN
BRUIT
BURIN
******

B--J-
******
BANJO
BENJY
******

B--K-
******
BACKS
BALKS
BALKY
BANKS
BARKS
BARKY
BASKS
BEAKS
BECKS
BECKY
BILKS
BLAKE
BLOKE
BOOKS
BOSKS
BOSKY
BRAKE
BRAKY
BROKE
BUCKO
BUCKS
BULKS
BULKY
BUNKO
BUNKS
BURKE
BUSKS
******

B--L-
******
BADLY
BAILS

BALLS
BASLE
BAULK
BAWLS
BEALL
BELLA
BELLE
BELLS
BELLY
BEULA
BIALY
BIBLE
BIGLY
BILLS
BILLY
BIRLE
BIRLS
BOGLE
BOILS
BOLLS
BOULE
BOWLS
BOYLE
BRILL
BUGLE
BUILD
BUILT
BULLA
BULLS
BULLY
BURLS
BURLY
******

B--M-
******
BALMS
BALMY
BARMY
BAUME
BEAMS
BEAMY
BERME
BERMS
BLAME
BLIMP
BOOMS
BRIMS
BROME

BROMO
BRUME
BURMA
******

B--N-
******
BANNS
BARNS
BEANO
BEANS
BEING
BENNE
BENNY
BERNE
BHANG
BLANC
BLAND
BLANK
BLEND
BLENT
BLIND
BLINK
BLOND
BLUNT
BONNY
BOONE
BOONS
BORNE
BORNU
BOUND
BOYNE
BRAND
BRANS
BRANT
BRENT
BRINE
BRING
BRINK
BRINY
BRONC
BRONX
BRUNO
BRUNT
BUNNS
BUNNY
BURNS
BURNT
BWANA

******

B--O-
******
BABOO
BACON
BARON
BASON
BATON
BAYOU
BEBOP
BEFOG
BEGOT
BELOW
BESOM
BESOT
BETON
BIGOT
BIJOU
BIKOL
BIPOD
BISON
BLOOD
BLOOM
BOGOR
BOHOL
BOLOS
BORON
BOSOM
BOSON
BOZOS
BROOD
BROOK
BROOM
BROOS
BUXOM
BYRON
******

B--P-
******
BEEPS
BLIPS
BUMPS
BUMPY
BURPS
******

B--R-
******
BAIRD
BAIRN

BARRE
BARRY
BASRA
BEARD
BEARS
BEERS
BEERY
BEIRA
BERRA
BERRY
BIERS
BIRRS
BLARE
BLURB
BLURS
BLURT
BOARD
BOARS
BOERS
BOORS
BOURG
BOURN
BURRO
BURRS
BURRY
******

B--S-
******
BALSA
BASSI
BASSO
BEAST
BESSY
BETSO
BETSY
BISSE
BLASE
BLAST
BLESS
BLEST
BLISS
BLUSH
BOAST
BOISE
BOOST
BOSSY
BOUSE
BOUSY

BOWSE	BOUTS	******	COMAS	CLACK	CAFES
BRASH	BRATS	**B--Y-**	COPAL	CLICK	CAGED
BRASS	BROTH	******	CORAL	CLOCK	CAGES
BREST	BRUTE	BARYE	CORAS	CLUCK	CAGEY
BRISK	BUNTS	BERYL	COXAE	COACH	CAKED
BRUSH	BUSTS	BRAYS	COXAL	COCCI	CAKES
BRUSK	BUTTE	BUOYS	CRAAL	CONCH	CALEB
BURSA	BUTTS	BUTYL	CREAK	COUCH	CAMEL
BURSE	******	******	CREAM	CRACK	CAMEO
BURST	**B--U-**	**B--Z-**	CROAK	CRACY	CAMES
BYSSI	******	******	CROAT	CRECY	CANEA
******	BABUL	BAIZE	CUBAN	CRICK	CANED
B--T-	BACUP	BLAZE	CYCAD	CROCE	CANER
******	BEAUS	BONZE	CYMAE	CROCI	CANES
BAHTS	BEAUT	BOOZE	CYMAR	CROCK	CAPEK
BAITS	BEAUX	BOOZY	******	CRUCI	CAPER
BALTS	BEGUM	BRAZA	**C--B-**	CULCH	CAPES
BANTU	BEGUN	BRAZE	******	CURCH	CAPET
BARTH	BENUE	******	CABBY	CUTCH	CARED
BASTE	BOGUS	**C--A-**	CARBO	CZECH	CARER
BATTY	BOLUS	******	CEIBA	******	CARES
BEATA	BONUS	CABAL	CHIBA	**C--D-**	CARET
BEATS	BOSUN	CACAO	CHUBS	******	CAREY
BEETS	******	CANAD	CLUBS	CADDO	CASED
BELTS	**B--V-**	CANAL	COBBS	CADDY	CASES
BERTA	******	CARAS	COMBO	CANDY	CASEY
BERTH	BRAVA	CARAT	COMBS	CARDI	CATER
BERTS	BRAVE	CECAL	CORBY	CARDS	CAVED
BERTY	BRAVO	CEDAR	CRABS	CHIDE	CAVES
BESTS	BREVE	CERAM	CRIBS	CINDY	CAWED
BETTE	BREVI	CERAT	CUBBY	CLODS	CEDED
BETTY	******	CESAR	CURBS	CLYDE	CEDES
BIOTA	**B--W-**	CHEAP	******	COEDS	CERED
BIRTH	******	CHEAT	**C--C-**	COLDS	CERES
BITTS	BLOWN	CHIAN	******	COMDR	CHAET
BLATS	BLOWS	CHIAS	CALCI	COMDT	CHEEK
BLITZ	BLOWY	CIDAL	CASCO	CORDS	CHEEP
BLOTS	BMEWS	CIGAR	CATCH	CREDO	CHEER
BLYTH	BRAWL	CLEAN	CAUCA	CRUDE	CHIEF
BOATS	BRAWN	CLEAR	CHECK	CUDDY	CIDER
BOLTS	BREWS	CLEAT	CHICK	CURDS	CIMEX
BOOTH	BROWN	CLOAK	CHICO	CURDY	CITED
BOOTS	BROWS	COCAS	CHOCK	******	CITES
BOOTY	******	CODAS	CHUCK	**C--E-**	CIVET
BORTS	**B--X-**	COHAN	CINCH	******	CLEEK
BORTY	******	COLAS	CIRCA	CABER	CLUED
BORTZ	BRAXY	COMAE	CIRCE	CADES	CLUES
BOTTS		COMAL	CISCO	CADET	CODED

CODER	CRUET	*****	CYNIC	COELO	CHANT
CODES	CUBEB	C--I-	CYRIL	COILS	CHINA
CODEX	CUBED	*****	*****	COLLY	CHINE
COKED	CUBES	CABIN	C--K-	COOLS	CHINK
COKER	CULET	CADIS	*****	COULD	CHINO
COKES	CULEX	CADIZ	CALKS	COWLS	CHINS
COKEY	CUPEL	CALIF	CASKS	COYLY	CHUNK
COLES	CURED	CALIX	CHOKE	CULLS	CIONS
COMER	CURER	CANIS	CHOKY	CURLS	CLANG
COMES	CURES	CARIB	COCKS	CURLY	CLANK
COMET	CUSEC	CAVIE	COCKY	CYCLE	CLANS
CONED	CUTER	CAVIL	CONKS	CYCLO	CLINE
CONES	CUTEY	CECIL	COOKS	*****	CLING
CONEY	CYMES	CELIA	COOKY	C--M-	CLINK
COOED	*****	CELIE	CORKS	*****	CLINO
COOEE	C--F-	CENIS	CORKY	CALMS	CLINT
COOER	*****	CERIA	CRAKE	CHAMP	CLONE
COOEY	CHAFE	CERIC	CUSKS	CHEMI	CLONS
COPEC	CHAFF	CETIC	*****	CHEMO	CLUNG
COPED	CHUFA	CETIN	C--L-	CHIME	CLUNY
COPER	CLEFS	CHAIN	*****	CHIMP	COENO
COPES	CLEFT	CHAIR	CABLE	CHUMP	COINS
CORED	CLIFF	CHOIR	CALLA	CHUMS	COLNE
CORER	COIFS	CHRIS	CALLI	CHYME	CONNY
CORES	COMFY	CILIA	CALLS	CLAMP	COONS
COSEK	CORFE	CIVIC	CARLA	CLAMS	CORNS
COTES	CORFU	CIVIL	CARLE	CLEMS	CORNU
COVED	CRAFT	CLAIM	CARLO	CLIMB	CORNY
COVEN	CROFT	COBIA	CARLS	CLIME	COUNT
COVER	CUFFS	COLIC	CAULK	CLUMP	CRANE
COVES	*****	COLIN	CAULS	COMMA	CRANI
COVET	C--G-	COMIC	CEILS	COOMB	CRANK
COVEY	*****	CONIC	CELLA	CORMS	CRONE
COWED	CADGE	CONIO	CELLO	COSMO	CRONY
COWER	CARGO	CORIA	CELLS	CRAMP	CTENO
COWES	CHUGS	CRAIG	CHALK	CRAMS	CUING
COXED	CLOGS	CROIX	CHELA	CREME	CYANO
COXES	COIGN	CUBIC	CHILD	CRIME	*****
COZEN	CONGA	CUBIT	CHILE	CRIMP	C--O-
CREED	CONGE	CUMIN	CHILI	CRUMB	*****
CREEK	CONGO	CUPID	CHILL	CRUMP	CABOB
CREEL	CORGI	CURIA	CHILO	CULMS	CABOT
CREEP	COUGH	CURIE	CHOLE	*****	CAJON
CREES	CRAGS	CURIO	CHYLE	C--N-	CANOE
CRIED	*****	CUTIE	COALS	*****	CANON
CRIER	C--H-	CUTIN	COALY	CANNA	CAPON
CRIES	*****	CUTIS	COBLE	CANNY	CAROB
CRUEL	CACHE	CYLIX	COELE	CHANG	CAROL
	CATHY				
	CUSHY				

CAROM	COYPU	COBRA	******	CYSTI	******
CELOM	CRAPE	COPRA	**C--T-**	CYSTO	**C--Y-**
CENON	CRAPS	COPRO	******	CYSTS	******
CEROS	CREPE	COURT	CACTI	******	CALYX
CHAOS	CREPT	COWRY	CANTO	**C--U-**	CARYO
CHIOS	CROPS	CRORE	CANTS	******	CARYS
CHLOE	CRYPT	CRURA	CARTE	CAJUN	CHRYS
CHLOR	CULPA	CUPRO	CARTS	CAMUS	CLAYS
CHROM	CUPPY	CURRY	CASTE	CAPUA	CLOYS
CHRON	CUSPS	CYMRI	CASTS	CAPUT	******
CIBOL	******	CYMRY	CATTY	CASUS	**C--Z-**
CLEON	**C--R-**	CZARS	CELTS	CECUM	******
CLIOS	******	******	CENTI	CETUS	COLZA
COCOA	CADRE	**C--S-**	CENTO	CLOUD	CRAZE
COCOS	CAIRD	******	CENTR	CLOUT	CRAZY
COGON	CAIRN	CANSO	CENTS	COMUS	CROZE
COLON	CAIRO	CANST	CESTA	CONUS	******
COLOR	CAPRI	CAUSE	CESTI	CROUP	**D--A-**
COROT	CARRY	CEASE	CEUTA	CUTUP	******
CREON	CEARA	CENSE	CHATS	CYRUS	DAGAN
CROOK	CEORL	CHASE	CHETH	******	DAKAR
CROON	CHARD	CHASM	CHETS	**C--V-**	DALAI
CRUOR	CHARE	CHESS	CHITA	******	DAMAN
******	CHARM	CHEST	CHITS	CALVE	DANAE
C--P-	CHARO	CHOSE	CHUTE	CARVE	DATAL
******	CHARS	CISSY	CISTS	CHEVY	DAVAO
CALPE	CHART	CLASH	CLOTH	CHIVE	DEBAG
CAMPI	CHARY	CLASP	CLOTS	CLIVE	DEBAR
CAMPO	CHERT	CLASS	COATI	CLOVE	DECAL
CAMPS	CHIRM	CLOSE	COATS	CRAVE	DECAY
CAMPY	CHIRO	COAST	COLTS	CURVE	DEDAL
CARPI	CHIRP	COPSE	COMTE	CURVI	DEGAS
CARPO	CHIRR	CORSE	CONTD	******	DELAY
CARPS	CHORD	CRASH	CONTE	**C--W-**	DEVAS
CHAPE	CHORE	CRASS	CONTO	******	DEWAN
CHAPS	CHORO	CRESC	CONTR	CHAWS	DINAH
CHAPT	CHURL	CRESS	COOTS	CHEWS	DINAR
CHIPS	CHURN	CREST	COPTS	CHEWY	DITAS
CHOPS	CHURR	CRISP	COSTA	CHOWS	DIVAN
CLAPS	CIRRI	CROSS	COSTO	CLAWS	DIVAS
CLIPS	CIRRO	CRUSE	COSTS	CLEWS	DIWAN
CLOPS	CITRA	CRUSH	COTTA	CLOWN	DONAR
COMPO	CLARA	CRUST	COUTH	CRAWL	DONAS
COOPS	CLARE	CUISH	COUTH	CRAWS	DORAS
COOPT	CLARK	CURSE	CRATE	CREWE	DOUAI
CORPS	CLARO	CURST	CRETE	CREWS	DOUAY
COUPE	CLARY	CUSSO	CULTI	CROWD	DOVAP
COUPS	CLERK		CULTS	CROWN	DREAD
			CUTTY	CROWS	

DREAM	DOWDY	DIZEN	*****	DIXIE	DOALL
DREAR	DUADS	DODEC	D--G-	DIXIT	DOBLA
DRYAD	*****	DOGES	*****	DOBIE	DOILY
DUBAI	D--E-	DOLED	DANGS	DOGIE	DOLLS
DUCAL	*****	DOLES	DEIGN	DOMIC	DOLLY
DUCAT	DACES	DOMED	DIEGO	DORIC	DOOLY
DUMAS	DALER	DOMES	DINGO	DORIS	DOYLE
DURAL	DALES	DONEE	DINGS	DRAIL	DOYLY
DYLAN	DAMES	DOPED	DINGY	DRAIN	DRILL
*****	DANES	DOPES	DIRGE	DROIT	DRILY
D--B-	DARED	DOPEY	DODGE	DRUID	DROLL
*****	DARER	DOSED	DODGY	DULIA	DRYLY
DAUBS	DARES	DOSER	DOGGY	*****	DUALA
DAUBY	DATED	DOSES	DOUGH	D--K-	DUELS
DEBBY	DATER	DOTED	DOUGS	*****	DULLS
DERBY	DATES	DOTER	DRAGS	DARKY	DULLY
DOBBY	DAVES	DOTES	DREGS	DAWKS	DUPLE
DOUBT	DAVEY	DOVER	DRUGS	DECKS	DWELL
DRABS	DAZED	DOVES	DUNGS	DESKS	DWELT
DRIBS	DAZES	DOWEL	DUNGY	DHAKS	*****
DRUBS	DEFER	DOWER	*****	DICKS	D--M-
*****	DEKED	DOYEN	D--H-	DICKY	*****
D--C-	DEKES	DOZED	*****	DINKA	DEEMS
*****	DELED	DOZEN	DACHA	DINKY	DERMA
DACCA	DELES	DOZER	DASHY	DIRKS	DERMO
DANCE	DEMES	DOZES	DELHI	DISKO	DOGMA
DEICE	DENEB	DRIED	DICHO	DISKS	DOOMS
DEUCE	DENES	DRIER	DISHY	DOCKS	DORMS
DIRCK	DEREK	DRIES	DUBHE	DRAKE	DORMY
DISCI	DESEX	DRYER	DUCHY	DUCKS	DRAMA
DISCO	DETER	DUDES	*****	DUCKY	DRAMS
DISCS	DEWED	DUKES	D--I-	DUNKS	DROME
DITCH	DEWEY	DUNES	*****	DUSKS	DRUMS
DOLCE	DICED	DUPED	DACIA	DUSKY	DUMMY
DRACO	DICER	DUPER	DARIC	*****	DUOMI
DULCE	DICEY	DUPES	DAVID	D--L-	DUOMO
DULCY	DIKED	DURER	DAVIE	*****	*****
DUNCE	DIKER	*****	DAVIS	DAILY	D--N-
DUTCH	DIKES	D--F-	DAVIT	DALLY	*****
*****	DIMER	*****	DEBIT	DEALS	DAMNS
D--D-	DIMES	DAFFY	DECIM	DEALT	DANNY
*****	DINED	DEIFY	DEFIS	DELLA	DARNS
DADDY	DINER	DELFT	DELIA	DELLS	DAUNT
DANDY	DINES	DOFFS	DEMIT	DHOLE	DAWNS
DEEDS	DIRER	DRAFF	DENIM	DHOLI	DEANE
DENDR	DIVED	DRAFT	DENIS	DIALS	DEANS
DILDO	DIVER	DRIFT	DEVIL	DIMLY	DENNY
DIODE	DIVES	DUFFS	DIGIT	DIPLO	DIANA

DIANE	DROPS	DATTO	DRAWN	ETTAS	EDGES
DIDNT	DROPT	DEATH	DRAWS	EYRAS	EDIES
DIENE	DRUPE	DEBTS	DREWS	EZRAS	EDRED
DIONE	DUMPS	DEITY	DROWN	******	EDSEL
DOING	DUMPY	DELTA	******	E--C-	EGGED
DONNA	******	DENTI	D--X-	******	EGGER
DONNE	D--R-	DENTO	******	EDICT	EGRET
DOWNS	******	DENTS	DEOXY	EDUCE	EIDER
DOWNY	DAIRY	DEPTH	******	EDUCT	EIMER
DRANK	DEARS	DEXTR	D--Y-	EJECT	ELAEO
DRINK	DEARY	DHOTI	******	ELECT	ELDER
DRONE	DECRY	DICTA	DAVYS	ENACT	ELLEN
DRUNK	DERRY	DIETS	DENYS	ENOCH	ELMER
DUANE	DIARY	DINTS	DILYS	EPACT	ELVER
DYING	DOBRA	DIRTY	DRAYS	EPICS	ELVES
******	DOERS	DITTO	******	EPOCH	EMBED
D--O-	DOORN	DITTY	D--Z-	ERECT	EMBER
******	DOORS	DOETH	******	ERICA	EMCEE
DAMON	DORRS	DOITS	DIAZO	ERICH	EMDEN
DAVOS	DOURA	DOLTS	DIZZY	ERICS	EMEER
DECOR	DOURY	DONTS	******	ERUCT	EMMER
DECOY	DOWRY	DOTTY	E--A-	EVICT	EMMET
DEFOE	DRURY	DUCTS	******	EXACT	ENDED
DELOS	DURRA	DUETS	EBOAT	EXECS	ENNEA
DEMOB	DWARF	DUSTS	ECLAT	******	ENTER
DEMON	******	DUSTY	EDDAS	E--D-	EPEES
DEMOS	D--S-	******	EDGAR	******	ERIES
DEPOT	******	D--U-	EDNAS	ELIDE	ERNES
DEVON	DAISY	******	EGEAN	ELUDE	ERRED
DIDOS	DEISM	DATUM	EGGAR	ENIDS	ERSES
DIJON	DEIST	DEBUG	ELGAR	EPODE	ESHER
DIVOT	DENSE	DEBUT	ELIAS	ERODE	ESKER
DODOS	DIDST	DEGUM	ELLAS	ETUDE	ESSEN
DOLOR	DOEST	DEMUR	ELMAN	EVADE	ESSES
DONOR	DORSA	DORUS	ELSAS	EXUDE	ESSEX
DROOL	DORSI	DURUM	ELVAN	******	ESTER
DROOP	DORSO	******	EMBAR	E--E-	ESTES
DUROS	DOUSE	D--V-	EMBAY	******	ETHEL
******	DOWSE	******	EMMAS	EAGER	ETHER
D--P-	DRESS	DELVE	ENEAS	EARED	EULER
******	DREST	DIVVY	EPHAH	EASED	EXCEL
DAMPS	DROSS	DRAVA	EQUAL	EASEL	EXPEL
DEEPS	DRUSE	DRAVE	ERLAU	EASES	******
DIPPY	DULSE	DRIVE	ERMAS	EATEN	E--F-
DOLPH	DURST	DROVE	ESSAY	EATER	******
DRAPE	******	******	ESTAR	EAVES	EDIFY
DRIPS	D--T-	D--W-	ETHAN	EBBED	E--G-
DRIPT	******	******	ETNAS	EDGED	******
	DANTE	DHOWS			ELEGY
	DARTS	DRAWL			

******	EARLS	ENJOY	EDITS	FLEAM	FREDA
E--H-	EARLY	ENROL	ELATE	FLEAS	FREDS
******	ECOLE	ENTOM	ELITE	FLOAT	FUNDI
EIGHT	EDILE	ENVOY	EMITS	FOCAL	FUNDS
ELIHU	EMILE	EPHOD	EMOTE	FORAY	******
******	EMILS	EPHOR	EMPTY	FORBS	F--E-
E--I-	EMILY	EPSOM	ENATE	FREAK	******
******	ENOLA	ERGOT	ERATO	FRIAR	FACED
EADIE	ENOLS	ERROL	EVITA	FUGAL	FACER
ECHIN	EVILS	ERROR	EXITS	FURAN	FACES
EDDIC	EXALT	ESTOP	******	******	FACET
EDDIE	EXILE	ETHOS	F--B-	FADED
EDWIN	EXULT	EXTOL	E--U-	******	FADES
EERIE	******	******	******	FLUBS	FAKED
EFFIE	E--M-	E--P-	EMBUS	FLYBY	FAKER
ELAIN	******	******	EMEUS	FORBS	FAKES
ELAIO	EDEMA	EGYPT	ENDUE	FORBY	FAMED
ELFIN	ELEMI	ELOPE	ENNUI	******	FARED
ELGIN	ENEMA	ERUPT	ENSUE	F--C-	FARER
ELLIE	ENEMY	ETAPE	EOLUS	******	FARES
ELLIS	ETYMA	******	ESQUE	FANCY	FATED
ELOIN	EXAMS	E--R-	EURUS	FARCE	FATES
ELSIE	******	******	******	FARCY	FAXED
ELVIN	******	EAGRE	E--X-	FENCE	FAXES
ELWIN	E--N-	EMBRY	******	FETCH	FAYED
EMMIE	******	EMERY	EPOXY	FILCH	FAYES
ENTIA	EARNS	EMIRS	******	FINCH	FAZED
EOLIC	EBONS	EMORY	E--Y-	FISCS	FAZES
EOSIN	EBONY	ENARE	******	FITCH	FECES
EQUIP	EDINA	ENTRY	EMMYS	FLACK	FEMES
ERNIE	EKING	EVERT	ENCYC	FLECK	FETED
ERWIN	ELAND	EVERY	ETHYL	FLICK	FETES
ESSIE	ELENA	EWERS	******	FLOCK	FEUED
ETHIC	EMEND	EXERT	E--Z-	FLOCS	FEVER
ETTIE	ETHNO	EXTRA	******	FORCE	FEWER
ETUIS	EVANS	EXURB	ELIZA	FROCK	FIBER
EYDIE	EVENS	******	******	******	FICES
EYRIE	EVENT	E--S-	F--A-	F--D-	FIDEL
EYRIR	EWING	******	******	******	FIFED
******	EYING	EGEST	FARAD	FADDY	FIFER
E--K-	******	ELISE	FARAH	FEEDS	FIFES
******	E--O-	ERASE	FATAL	FENDS	FILED
ERIKA	******	ERNST	FAYAL	FEODS	FILER
ERIKS	EAMON	EROSE	FECAL	FEUDS	FILES
EVOKE	ELBOW	EXIST	FERAL	FINDS	FILET
******	ELIOT	******	FETAL	FOLDS	FINED
E--L-	ELTON	E--T-	FEUAR	FONDA	FINER
******	EMBOW	******	FILAR	FOODS	FINES
EAGLE	ENDOW	EARTH	FINAL	FORDS	
EARLE		EDITH			

FIRED	******	FUSIL	FERMI	FROND	******
FIRER	F--G-	FUZIL	FILMS	FRONT	F--S-
FIRES	******	******	FILMY	FUNNY	******
FIVER	FANGA	F--K-	FIRMS	******	FALSE
FIVES	FANGS	******	FIUME	F--O-	FAUST
FIXED	FARGO	FINKS	FLAME	******	FEASE
FIXER	FAUGH	FLAKE	FLAMS	FAGOT	FEAST
FIXES	FEIGN	FLAKY	FLAMY	FANON	FEIST
FLEER	FLAGS	FLUKE	FLUME	FANOS	FESSE
FLEES	FLOGS	FLUKY	FLUMP	FAROE	FIRST
FLEET	FOGGY	FOLKS	FOAMS	FAVOR	FLASH
FLIED	FORGE	FORKS	FOAMY	FEDOR	FLASK
FLIER	FORGO	FUNKS	FORME	FELON	FLESH
FLIES	FRIGG	FUNKY	FORMS	FETOR	FLOSS
FLOES	FROGS	******	FRAME	FLOOD	FLUSH
FLUES	FUDGE	F--L-	FRIML	FLOOR	FOISM
FLYER	FUGGY	******	FROME	FLUOR	FOIST
FOGEY	FUNGI	FABLE	FRUMP	FREON	FOSSA
FORES	FUNGO	FAILS	******	FUROR	FOSSE
FOVEA	******	FALLS	F--N-	******	FRESH
FOXED	F--H-	FARLE	******	F--P-	FRISE
FOXES	******	FARLS	FAINT	******	FRISK
FOYED	FICHE	FATLY	FANNY	FLAPS	FROSH
FOYER	FICHU	FAULT	FAUNA	FLIPS	FROST
FREED	FIGHT	FEELS	FAUNS	FLOPS	FUSSY
FREER	FISHY	FELLS	FAWNS	FRAPS	******
FREES	FOEHN	FELLY	FEINT	******	F--T-
FRIED	******	FIELD	FENNY	F--R-	******
FRIER	F--I-	FILLS	FERNS	******	FACTS
FRIES	******	FILLY	FERNY	FAIRS	FAITH
FROES	FACIA	FITLY	FIEND	FAIRY	FASTS
FRYER	FAKIR	FJELD	FINNS	FEARS	FATTY
FUMED	FECIT	FOALS	FINNY	FEBRI	FEATS
FUMES	FELID	FOILS	FIONA	FERRI	FELTS
FUSED	FELIX	FOLLY	FIRNS	FERRO	FEMTO
FUSEE	FERIA	FOOLS	FLANK	FERRY	FIATS
FUSEL	FETID	FORLI	FLANS	FIBRE	FIFTH
FUSES	FIJIS	FOULS	FLING	FIBRO	FIFTY
FUZED	FINIS	FOWLS	FLINT	FIERY	FILTH
FUZEE	FLAIL	FRILL	FLONG	FIORD	FIRTH
FUZES	FLAIR	FUELS	FLUNG	FIRRY	FISTS
FYKES	FLUID	FUGLE	FLUNK	FJORD	FLATS
******	FOLIA	FULLS	FOUND	FLARE	FLITE
F--F-	FOLIC	FULLY	FOUNT	FLIRT	FLITS
******	FOLIO	FURLS	FRANC	FLORA	FLUTE
FEOFF	FRAIL	******	FRANK	FOURS	FLUTY
FIEFS	FRUIT	F--M-	FRANZ	FRERE	FONTS
FLUFF	FUGIO	******	FRENA	FURRY	FOOTS
		FARMS			
		FEMME			

FOOTY	FRAYS	GRACE	GAPED	******	******
FORTE	FREYA	GRECO	GAPER	**G--F-**	**G--K-**
FORTH	******	GUACO	GAPES	******	******
FORTS	**F--Z-**	GULCH	GASES	GAFFE	GAWKS
FORTY	******	******	GATED	GAFFS	GAWKY
FRATS	FEEZE	**G--D-**	GATES	GEOFF	GECKO
FRETS	FIZZY	******	GAVEL	GOLFS	GECKS
FRITH	FRIZZ	GAUDI	GAYER	GOOFS	GEEKS
FRITS	FROZE	GAUDS	GAZED	GOOFY	GINKS
FRITZ	FURZE	GAUDY	GAZER	GRAFT	GOOKS
FROTH	FURZY	GELDS	GAZES	GRUFF	GORKI
FURTH	FUZZY	GEODE	GENES	GULFS	GORKY
FUSTY	******	GERDA	GENET	******	******
******	**G--A-**	GIDDY	GIBED	**G--G-**	**G--L-**
F--U-	******	GILDA	GIBER	******	******
******	GALAS	GILDS	GIBES	GANGS	GABLE
FANUM	GALAX	GIRDS	GILES	GAUGE	GAELS
FAVUS	GIGAS	GLADE	GIMEL	GONGS	GAILS
FEMUR	GLEAM	GLADS	GIVEN	GORGE	GAILY
FETUS	GLEAN	GLEDE	GIVER	GOUGE	GALLS
FILUM	GLOAT	GLEDS	GIVES	GREGO	GAOLS
FIQUE	GONAD	GLIDE	GLEES	GREGS	GAULS
FLOUR	GORAL	GOADS	GLEET	******	GAULT
FLOUT	GOWAN	GOLDA	GLUED	**G--H-**	GAVLE
FOCUS	GRAAL	GOLDS	GLUES	******	GAYLY
FORUM	GREAT	GONDI	GLUEY	GOTHA	GILLS
FRAUD	GROAN	GOODS	GOFER	GOTHS	GIRLS
FREUD	GROAT	GOODY	GOLEM	GUSHY	GOALS
FUCUS	GULAR	GOUDA	GONER	******	GODLY
FUGUE	GYRAL	GRADE	GOOEY	**G--I-**	GOLLY
******	******	GRADS	GORED	******	GRILL
F--W-	**G--B-**	GRIDE	GORES	GADID	GUILD
******	******	GRIDS	GOWER	GAMIC	GUILE
FLAWS	GABBY	GUIDE	GREED	GAMIN	GUILT
FLAWY	GAMBS	GUIDO	GREEK	GAVIN	GULLS
FLEWS	GARBO	******	GREEN	GELID	GULLY
FLOWN	GARBS	**G--E-**	GREER	GENIC	******
FLOWS	GLEBE	******	GREET	GENIE	**G--M-**
FROWN	GLOBE	GABES	GRIEF	GENII	******
FROWS	GLOBS	GAGED	GRIEG	GEOID	GAMMA
******	GRABS	GAGER	GRUEL	GLAIR	GAMMY
F--X-	GREBE	GAGES	GULES	GONIA	GEMMA
******	GRUBS	GALEA	GUYED	GONIO	GEMMY
FLAXY	GUMBO	GALEN	GYBED	GOYIM	GERMS
FLEXI	******	GALES	GYNEC	GRAIL	GISMO
******	**G--C-**	GAMED	GYRES	GRAIN	GIZMO
F--Y-	******	GAMES	GYVED	GROIN	GLIMS
******	GLACE	GANEF			GLUME
FLAYS	GLYCO				
FLOYD					

GNOME	GALOP	******	GRITS	GRAYS	HENCE
GNOMY	GAVOT	G--S-	GROTS	GREYS	HITCH
GORME	GEMOT	******	GUSTA	******	HOICK
GRAMA	GENOA	GASSY	GUSTO	G--Z-	HOOCH
GRAMS	GIGOT	GAUSS	GUSTS	******	HUNCH
GRIME	GIPON	GEESE	GUSTY	GAUZE	HUTCH
GRIMM	GIRON	GEEST	GUTTA	GAUZY	******
GRIMY	GIROS	GESSO	******	GHAZI	H--D-
GRUME	GLOOM	GHOST	G--U-	GLAZE	******
GUAMA	GOBOS	GIPSY	******	GLAZY	HAIDA
GUMMA	GOGOL	GIRSH	GAMUT	GLOZE	HANDS
GUMMY	GROOM	GLASS	GATUN	GRAZE	HANDY
******	GYRON	GLOSS	GENUA	******	HARDS
G--N-	GYROS	GLOST	GENUS	H--A-	HARDY
******	******	GNASH	GETUP	******	HAYDN
GAINS	G--P-	GOOSE	GHAUT	HAHAS	HEADS
GAUNT	******	GOOSY	GHOUL	HAMAL	HEADY
GHANA	GAMPS	GORSE	GIBUS	HARAR	HEDDA
GHENT	GAPPY	GORSY	GIGUE	HBEAM	HEEDS
GIANT	GASPE	GRASP	GLAUC	HEJAZ	HERDS
GIING	GASPS	GRASS	GROUP	HEMAL	HILDA
GINNY	GIMPS	GRIST	GROUT	HEMAN	HINDI
GLAND	GIMPY	GROSS	GURUS	HEMAT	HINDS
GLANS	GLYPH	GROSZ	GYRUS	HEPAT	HINDU
GLENN	GRAPE	GUESS	******	HERAT	HOLDS
GLENS	GRAPH	GUEST	G--V-	HEXAD	HONDO
GLINT	GRAPY	GUISE	******	HIRAM	HOODS
GOING	GRIPE	GUTSY	GLOVE	HOGAN	HORDE
GOONS	GRIPS	GYPSY	GRAVE	HOKAN	HOWDY
GOWNS	GRIPT	******	GRAVY	HONAN	HULDA
GRAND	GROPE	G--T-	GROVE	HORAE	HURDS
GRANI	GULPS	******	GUAVA	HORAL	H--E-
GRANO	GUPPY	GAITS	******	HORAS	******
GRANT	******	GARTH	G--W-	HULAS	HADED
GRIND	G--R-	GASTR	******	HUMAN	HADES
GRINS	******	GENTS	GLOWS	HUNAN	HAKES
GRUNT	GARRY	GERTY	GNAWN	HYLAS	HALED
GUANA	GAURS	GHATS	GNAWS	HYRAX	HALER
GUANO	GEARS	GIFTS	GROWL	******	HALES
GUANS	GENRE	GIRTH	GROWN	H--B-	HAMER
GUNNY	GENRO	GIRTS	GROWS	******	HAMES
GWENN	GERRY	GISTS	******	HERBS	HARED
GWENS	GLARE	GLUTS	G--Y-	HERBY	HAREM
GWYNS	GLARY	GNATS	******	HOBBS	HARES
GYMNO	GLORY	GOATS	GABYS	HOBBY	HATED
******	GNARL	GOUTY	GARYS	HUBBY	HATER
G--O-	GOERS	GRATE	GOBYS	******	HATES
******	GOURD	GRETA	GOVYS	H--C-	
GABON	GUARD			******	
GABOR				HANCE	
				HATCH	

HAVEN	HUGER	******	HOLLY	HURON	HEIST
HAVER	HUPEH	**H--J-**	HOTLY	HYPOS	HESSE
HAWED	HYMEN	******	HOWLS	HYSON	HOIST
HAYED	HYPER	HADJI	HOYLE	******	HOLST
HAYES	******	******	HULLS	**H--P-**	HORSE
HAZED	**H--F-**	**H--K-**	HURLS	******	HORST
HAZEL	******	******	HURLY	HAPPY	HORSY
HAZER	HAIFA	HACKS	HYALO	HARPS	HOUSE
HAZES	HOOFS	HAIKS	******	HARPY	HURST
HEGEL	HUFFS	HAIKU	**H--M-**	HASPS	HUSSY
HELEN	HUFFY	HANKS	******	HEAPS	HYPSO
HEMEN	******	HANKY	HALMA	HELPS	******
HEWED	**H--G-**	HARKS	HAMMY	HEMPS	**H--T-**
HEWER	******	HAWKS	HARMS	HEMPY	******
HEXED	HANGS	HICKS	HBOMB	HIPPO	HAFTS
HEXES	HEDGE	HOCKS	HELMS	HIPPY	HAITI
HIDER	HEDGY	HONKS	HERMA	HOOPS	HALTS
HIDES	HEIGH	HONKY	HOLMS	HUMPH	HARTE
HIKED	HELGA	HOOKE	******	HUMPS	HARTS
HIKER	HINGE	HOOKS	**H--N-**	HUMPY	HARTZ
HIKES	HOAGY	HOOKY	******	******	HASTE
HIRED	HODGE	HULKS	HADNT	**H--R-**	HASTY
HIRER	HONGS	HULKY	HANNA	******	HATTY
HIRES	HOUGH	HUNKS	HASNT	HAIRS	HEATH
HIVED	******	HUNKY	HAUNT	HAIRY	HEATS
HIVES	**H--H-**	HUSKS	HENNA	HARRY	HECTO
HOLED	******	HUSKY	HINNY	HEARD	HEFTS
HOLES	HIGHS	******	HORNE	HEARS	HEFTY
HOLEY	HUGHS	**H--L-**	HORNS	HEART	HEKTO
HOMED	HYPHA	******	HORNY	HEIRS	HEPTA
HOMEO	******	HAILS	HOUND	HENRI	HERTZ
HOMER	**H--I-**	HALLE	HYENA	HENRY	HETTY
HOMES	******	HALLO	HYING	HIERO	HIDTO
HOMEY	HABIT	HALLS	HYMNS	HOARD	HILTS
HONED	HAFIZ	HAPLO	HYPNO	HOARY	HINTS
HONES	HAGIO	HAPLY	******	HOERS	HOOTS
HONEY	HAKIM	HARLS	**H--O-**	HOURI	HORTA
HOOEY	HALID	HAULM	******	HOURS	HOSTS
HOPED	HELIC	HAULS	HALOS	HURRY	HUNTS
HOPEH	HELIO	HEALS	HANOI	HYDRA	HURTS
HOPES	HELIX	HEELS	HAVOC	HYDRO	HYETO
HOREB	HEMIA	HEKLA	HELOT	HYGRO	******
HOSEA	HEMIC	HELLE	HEROD	******	**H--U-**
HOSED	HEMIN	HELLO	HERON	**H--S-**	******
HOSES	HIFIS	HELLS	HOBOS	******	HABUS
HOTEL	HOWIE	HERLS	HONOR	HANSE	HAGUE
HOVEL	HUMIC	HILLS	HUGOS	HARSH	HHOUR
HOVER	HUMID	HILLY	HUMOR	HAWSE	HILUM

HOCUS	******	******	******	******	JUICY
HOKUM	I--B-	I--I-	I--O-	I--U-	JUNCO
HORUS	******	******	******	******	******
HUMUS	IAMBI	IASIS	ICHOR	ICTUS	J--D-
******	IAMBS	IMMIX	IDIOM	ILEUM	******
H--V-	******	INDIA	IDIOT	ILEUS	JIDDA
******	I--D-	INDIC	IGLOO	ILIUM	******
HALVE	******	INFIX	ILION	ILLUS	J--E-
HEAVE	IMIDE	IODIC	IMPOT	IMBUE	******
HEAVY	IMIDO	IONIA	INDOW	INCUR	JABEZ
HELVE	IMIDS	IONIC	INGOT	INCUS	JADED
HOOVE	IRIDO	IRVIN	INION	INDUE	JADES
******	******	IRWIN	IODOL	INDUS	JAKES
H--Y-	I--E-	ISTIC	ITION	INPUT	JAMES
******	******		IXION	ISSUE	JANES
HEXYL	IBSEN	I--L-	******	******	JANET
******	ICIER	******	I--P-	I--Y-	JAPED
H--Z-	IDLED	ICILY	******	******	JAPES
******	IDLER	IDOLS	INAPT	IZZYS	JARED
HAMZA	IDLES	IDYLL	INEPT	******	JAWED
******	ILMEN	IDYLS	******	I--Z-	JEFES
I--A-	IMBED	IMPLY	I--Q-	******	JEREZ
******	IMPEL	INGLE	******	IBIZA	JEWEL
IBEAM	INDEX	INKLE	IRAQI	******	JIBED
ICIAN	INFER	ISTLE	******	J--A-	JIBES
IDEAL	INKED	ITALS	I--R-	******	JIVED
IDEAS	INKER	ITALY	******	JALAP	JOKED
IGNAZ	INLET	IXTLE	IATRO	JAPAN	JOKER
IHRAM	INNED	******	IATRY	JIHAD	JOKES
ILEAC	INNER	I--M-	INARM	JONAH	JOLES
ILEAL	INSET	******	INDRA	JONAS	JONES
ILIAC	INTER	IMAMS	INDRI	JORAM	JOYED
ILIAD	IRKED	ITEMS	INERT	JUBAS	JUBES
ILIAN	ISLED	******	INFRA	JUDAH	JUDEA
INCAN	ISLES	I--N-	INTRA	JUDAS	JUDEO
INCAS	ISLET	******	INTRO	JUGAL	JUDES
INLAW	ISSEI	ICING	INURE	JURAL	JULEP
INLAY	IVIED	ICONO	INURN	JURAT	JULES
INVAR	IVIES	ICONS	ISERE	******	JUNES
IOTAS	******	IKONS	IVORY	J--B-	JUREL
IRMAS	I--G-	ILONA	******	******	JUTES
ISAAC	******	IMINE	I--S-	JAMBS	******
ISBAS	IMAGE	IMINO	******	JUMBO	J--F-
ISLAM	IMAGO	INANE	ICOSI	******	******
ISLAY	INIGO	IRENE	IDEST	J--C-	JAFFA
ISTAR	******	IRONE	IRISH	******	JEFFS
IXIAS	I--H-	IRONS	******	JOYCE	JIFFS
IYYAR	******	IRONY	I--T-	JUICE	JIFFY
	IDAHO	IVANS	******		
	ITCHY		IRATE		

******
J--G-
******
JAGGS
JAGGY
JINGO
JORGE
JUDGE
******
J--I-
******
JAMIE
JANIS
JOSIE
JULIA
JULIE
JULIO
******
J--K-
******
JACKS
JACKY
JERKS
JERKY
JINKS
JOCKO
JUNKS
JUNKY
******
J--L-
******
JAILS
JARLS
JELLO
JELLS
JELLY
JILLS
JOELS
JOLLY
JOULE
JOWLS
******
J--M-
******
JAMMY
JEMMY
JIMMY

******
J--N-
******
JAINA
JAINS
JAUNT
JAYNE
JEANS
JENNY
JINNI
JINNY
JOANS
JOHNS
JOINS
JOINT
JONNY
JUANA
JUANS
JUMNA
******
J--O-
******
JABOT
JACOB
JAKOB
JANOS
JASON
JATOS
JETON
JUPON
JUROR
******
J--P-
******
JEEPS
JUMPS
JUMPY
******
J--R-
******
JEERS
JERRY
JEWRY
******
J--S-
******
JASSY
JESSE

JESSY
JOIST
JOUST
******
J--T-
******
JESTS
JETTY
JILTS
JOLTS
JOLTY
JUNTA
JUNTO
JUSTS
JUXTA
******
J--U-
******
JANUS
JEHUS
JESUS
JORUM
JOSUA
JOSUE
JOTUN
JUJUS
JURUA
******
J--Y-
******
JOEYS
JUDYS
JULYS
******
J--Z-
******
JAZZY
******
K--A-
******
KAKAS
KALAT
KARAT
KAUAI
KAVAS
KAYAK
KAZAN
KEDAH

KERAT
KILAH
KIVAS
KNEAD
KODAK
KOLAS
KORAN
KRAAL
KUBAN
KULAK
******
K--B-
******
KAABA
KERBS
KNOBS
KRUBI
******
K--C-
******
KENCH
KERCH
KETCH
KNACK
KNOCK
******
K--D-
******
KANDY
KHADI
KIDDY
KINDS
******
K--E-
******
KAMES
KAMET
KAREN
KATES
KERES
KEVEL
KEYED
KHMER
KIBEI
KIBES
KITED
KITES
KNEED

KNEEL
KNEES
KOPEC
KOPEK
KOREA
******
K--F-
******
KEEFS
KERFS
KNIFE
KRAFT
******
K--G-
******
KEDGE
KINGS
******
K--H-
******
KAPHS
KATHY
******
K--I-
******
KADIS
KAFIR
KAKIS
KAMIK
KATIE
KEPIS
KEVIN
KININ
KIRIN
KIWIS
KRAIT
KUMIS
KYLIX
KYRIE
******
K--J-
******
KOPJE
******
K--K-
******
KAFKA
KECKS

KHAKI
KICKS
KINKS
KINKY
KIRKS
KOOKS
KOOKY
******
K--L-
******
KARLS
KEELS
KELLY
KILLS
KNELL
KNELT
KNOLL
KOALA
KOELS
******
K--M-
******
KARMA
******
K--N-
******
KEENS
KENNY
KERNS
KHANS
KHOND
KILNS
KOINE
KRONA
KRONE
******
K--O-
******
KABOB
KAPOK
KAROL
KAROO
KAYOS
KAZOO
KILOS
KLOOF
KOMOS
KOTOS
KUDOS

******	KAPUT	LORAN	******	LIMES	******
K--P-	KNOUT	LOTAH	L--E-	LIMEY	L--F-
******	KORUN	LOYAL	******	LINED	******
KAPPA	KRAUT	LUNAR	LABEL	LINEN	LEAFS
KEEPS	KUDUS	LYMAN	LACED	LINER	LEAFY
KELPS	KURUS	******	LACES	LINES	LEIFS
KNOPS	******	L--B-	LADED	LINEY	LOAFS
KRUPP	K--V-	******	LADEN	LITER	LOOFS
******	******	LAMBS	LADES	LIVED	LUFFS
K--R-	KEEVE	LAYBY	LAGER	LIVEN	******
******	KNAVE	LIBBY	LAKED	LIVER	L--G-
KAURI	******	LIMBI	LAKER	LIVES	******
KAURY	K--W-	LIMBO	LAKES	LOBED	LARGE
KERRY	******	LIMBS	LAKEY	LOBES	LARGO
KIERS	KIOWA	LOBBY	LAMED	LODEN	LAUGH
KLARA	KNOWN	LOOBY	LAMER	LODES	LEDGE
KNARS	KNOWS	******	LAMES	LOGES	LEGGY
KNURL	******	L--C-	LANES	LONER	LEIGH
KNURR	K--Y-	******	LAPEL	LOOED	LIEGE
KNURS	******	LANCE	LARES	LOPED	LINGA
KUFRA	KARYO	LARCH	LASER	LOPER	LINGO
KUKRI	KENYA	LATCH	LATER	LOPES	LINGS
******	KONYA	LEACH	LATEX	LORES	LODGE
K--S-	******	LEECH	LAVED	LOSER	LONGI
******	L--A-	LEUCO	LAVER	LOSES	LONGS
KELSO	******	LOACH	LAVES	LOVED	LOUGH
KIOSK	LAGAN	LORCA	LAWED	LOVER	LUIGI
KNOSP	LAMAS	LUCCA	LAXER	LOVES	LUNGE
KURSK	LANAI	LUNCH	LAYER	LOWED	LUNGI
KVASS	LAOAG	LURCH	LAZED	LOWER	LUNGS
******	LAPAR	LYNCH	LAZES	LUCES	******
K--T-	LAVAS	******	LEGER	LUGER	L--H-
******	LAZAR	L--D-	LEGES	LUMEN	******
KEATS	LEGAL	******	LENES	LUNES	LATHE
KEITH	LENAS	LADDY	LEPER	LUNET	LATHS
KENTS	LIGAN	LANDS	LEVEE	LURED	LATHY
KILTS	LILAC	LARDS	LEVEL	LURER	LETHE
KILTY	LILAS	LARDY	LEVEN	LURES	LICHT
KITTY	LIRAS	LAUDS	LEVER	LUTED	LIGHT
KNITS	LISAS	LEADS	LEWES	LUTES	LITHE
KNOTS	LITAI	LEADY	LIBEL	LUXEX	LITHO
KYATS	LITAS	LEEDS	LIBER	LYCEA	LOCHS
KYOTO	LIZAS	LENDS	LIFER	LYCEE	******
******	LOBAR	LEUDS	LIKED	LYLES	L--I-
K--U-	LOCAL	LINDA	LIKEN	LYRES	******
******	LOGAN	LOADS	LIKES	LYSED	LABIA
KABUL	LOLAS	LORDS	LIMED	LYSES	LABIO
KAGUS	LOPAT	LYDDA	LIMEN		LADIN

LAMIA	LUCKY	LOONY	LATRY	LETTS	******
LAPIN	LURKS	LORNA	LAURA	LETTY	L--Z-
LAPIS	******	LYING	LEARN	LEYTE	******
LATIN	L--L-	LYNNS	LEARY	LIFTS	LISZT
LEGIT	******	LYONS	LEERS	LILTS	LIZZY
LENIN	LADLE	******	LEERY	LINTY	******
LENIS	LALLS	L--O-	LEHRS	LISTS	M--A-
LEPID	LAXLY	******	LEORA	LOATH	******
LEVIS	LEILA	LABOR	LIARS	LOFTS	MACAO
LEWIE	LILLE	LAGOS	LIBRA	LOFTY	MACAW
LEWIS	LILLI	LEMON	LITRE	LOOTS	MADAM
LICIT	LILLY	LENOS	LIVRE	LOTTA	MAHAN
LIEIN	LISLE	LEROY	LOIRE	LOTTE	MALAC
LIMIT	LOLLS	LOBOS	LORRY	LOTTO	MALAR
LININ	LOLLY	LOCOS	LOURS	LOTTY	MALAY
LIPID	LOWLY	LOGOS	LUCRE	LOUTS	MAMAS
LIVIA	LULLS	LOTOS	******	LUNTS	MARAT
LIVID	******	LUTON	L--S-	LUSTS	MAYAN
LOGIA	L--M-	LUXOR	******	LUSTY	MAYAS
LOGIC	******	LUZON	LAPSE	LYTTA	MEDAL
LORIS	LEMMA	LYSOL	LASSA	******	MEGAL
LOUIS	LLAMA	******	LASSO	L--U-	MEGAN
LUCIA	LOAMS	L--P-	LEASE	******	MELAN
LUCID	LOAMY	******	LEASH	LEHUA	MENAI
LUPIN	LOOMS	LAMPS	LEAST	LEMUR	MESAS
LURID	******	LAPPS	LEPSY	LEPUS	METAL
LYDIA	L--N-	LEAPS	LHASA	LETUP	METAS
LYRIC	******	LEAPT	LOESS	LIEUT	MICAH
LYSIN	LAINE	LIMPS	LOOSE	LINUS	MICAS
LYSIS	LAWNS	LIPPI	LOUSE	LOCUM	MIDAS
LYTIC	LAWNY	LIPPY	LOUSY	LOCUS	MILAN
******	LEANS	LISPS	LUISA	LOGUE	MINAE
L--K-	LEANT	LOOPS	LUISE	LOTUS	MINAS
******	LENNY	LOOPY	LYSSA	LUAUS	MODAL
LACKS	LEONA	LOPPY	******	LULUS	MOLAL
LAIKA	LEONS	LOUPE	L--T-	LUPUS	MOLAR
LANKY	LIANA	LOUPS	******	******	MONAD
LARKS	LIANE	LUMPS	LACTO	L--V-	MONAS
LARKY	LIANG	LUMPY	LAITY	******	MORAE
LEAKS	LIENS	LYMPH	LASTS	LARVA	MORAL
LEAKY	LIGNI	******	LEETS	LEAVE	MORAS
LEEKS	LIGNO	L--R-	LEFTS	LEAVY	MORAT
LEUKO	LIMNS	******	LEFTY	******	MORAY
LICKS	LIONS	LABRA	LEITH	L--Y-	MOSAN
LINKS	LLANO	LAIRD	LENTO	******	MOXAS
LOCKE	LOANS	LAIRS	LENTS	LIBYA	MURAL
LOCKS	LOINS	LARRY	LEPTA	LILYS	MURAT
LOOKS	LOONS	LATRO	LEPTO	LLOYD	MUZAK
				LUCYS	

MYNAS	MOODY	MISES	MANGO	MIMIC	MILLI
MYRAS	MUDDY	MITER	MANGY	MIMIR	MILLS
*****	*****	MITES	MARGE	MIMIS	MILLY
M--B-	**M--E-**	MIXED	MARGO	MINIM	MOILS
*****	*****	MIXER	MERGE	MORIN	MOLLS
MAMBA	MABEL	MIXES	MIDGE	MOTIF	MOLLY
MAMBO	MACED	MIZEN	MINGY	MOVIE	MOULD
MAYBE	MACER	MLLES	MUGGY	MOXIE	MOULT
*****	MACES	MODEL	MUNGO	MUCID	MUHLY
M--C-	MAGES	MODES	*****	MUCIN	MULLS
*****	MAKER	MOKES	**M--H-**	MUSIC	MYELO
MANCY	MAKES	MOLES	*****	MYOID	*****
MARCH	MALES	MONET	MACHY	MYRIA	**M--M-**
MARCO	MAMEY	MONEY	MASHY	*****	*****
MARCS	MANED	MOOED	MATHS	**M--K-**	MAGMA
MATCH	MANES	MOPED	MESHY	*****	MAIMS
MECCA	MANET	MOPER	METHO	MACKS	MALMO
MERCI	MARES	MOPES	MIGHT	MARKS	MAMMA
MERCY	MASER	MOREL	MOCHA	MASKS	MAMMY
MILCH	MATED	MORES	MOTHS	MICKY	MIAMI
MINCE	MATEO	MOSEL	MOTHY	MILKS	MUMMS
MITCH	MATER	MOSES	MUSHY	MILKY	MUMMY
MOOCH	MATES	MOSEY	MYTHO	MINKS	MYOMA
MOUCH	MATEY	MOTEL	MYTHS	MOCKS	*****
MULCH	MAZED	MOTES	*****	MONKS	**M--N-**
MULCT	MAZER	MOTET	**M--I-**	MUCKS	*****
MUNCH	MAZES	MOUES	*****	MUCKY	MAGNI
MUSCA	MEDEA	MOVED	MAFIA	MURKY	MAINE
*****	MELEE	MOVER	MAGIC	MUSKS	MAINS
M--D-	MENES	MOVES	MALIC	MUSKY	MAINZ
*****	METED	MOWED	MAMIE	*****	MANNA
MAGDA	METER	MOWER	MANIA	**M--L-**	MARNE
MAHDI	METES	MULES	MANIC	*****	MAUND
MAIDS	MEWED	MULEY	MARIA	MACLE	MAYNT
MANDY	MIKES	MUREX	MARIE	MADLY	MEANS
MAUDE	MIKEY	MUSED	MARIO	MAILS	MEANT
MAUDS	MILER	MUSES	MARIS	MALLS	MEANY
MEADS	MILES	MUTED	MATIN	MANLY	MESNE
MELDS	MIMED	MUTES	MAVIS	MAPLE	MIENS
MENDS	MIMEO	MYLES	MAXIM	MARLA	MILNE
MIDDY	MIMER	*****	MEDIA	MARLS	MINNA
MINDI	MIMES	**M--F-**	MEDIC	MARLY	MOANS
MINDS	MINED	*****	MEDIO	MAULS	MOONS
MISDO	MINER	MIFFS	MELIC	MEALS	MOONY
MOLDS	MINES	MIFFY	MERIT	MEALY	MORNA
MOLDY	MIRED	MUFFS	MESIC	MERLE	MORNS
MONDE	MIRES	*****	METIS	MERLS	MOUND
MOODS	MISER	**M--G-**	MILIA	MEWLS	MOUNT
		*****			
		MADGE			
		MANGE			

MUONS	MICRO	MASTS	******	NOBBY	NITER
MYRNA	MITRE	MATTE	**M--W-**	NUBBY	NIXED
******	MOIRA	MATTS	******	NUMBS	NIXES
M--O-	MOIRE	MATTY	MEOWS	******	NIZER
******	MOORE	MEATS	******	**N--C-**	NOBEL
MACON	MOORS	MEATY	**M--Z-**	******	NODES
MADOC	MORRO	MEETS	******	NAACP	NONES
MAGOG	MOURN	MELTS	MAIZE	NANCE	NONET
MAGOT	MUCRO	MILTS	MATZO	NANCY	NOSED
MAJOR	MUNRO	MILTY	MEZZO	NARCO	NOSES
MANOR	MURRA	MINTS	MIRZA	NIECE	NOSEY
MASON	MURRE	MIRTH	MITZI	NONCE	NOTED
MAYOR	MURRY	MISTS	MITZY	NOTCH	NOTER
MCCOY	MYRRH	MISTY	MUZZY	******	NOTES
MEDOC	******	MITTS	******	**N--D-**	NOVEL
MELON	**M--S-**	MOATS	**N--A-**	******	NOYES
MELOS	******	MOLTO	******	NARDS	NUDES
MEMOS	MANSE	MOLTS	NADAB	NEDDY	NUMEN
MEROE	MARSH	MONTE	NAIAD	NEEDS	******
MESON	MASSE	MONTH	NANAS	NEEDY	**N--G-**
METOL	MASSY	MONTY	NASAL	NODDY	******
MIAOW	MATSU	MORTA	NATAL	******	NEIGH
MINOR	MAYST	MORTS	NAVAL	**N--E-**	NOGGS
MINOS	MENSA	MORTY	NAVAR	******	NUDGE
MORON	MESSY	MOTTO	NAWAB	NADER	******
MOROS	MEUSE	MOUTH	NEMAT	NAKED	**N--H-**
MOTOR	MIDST	MUFTI	NEPAL	NAMED	******
MYRON	MINSK	MULTI	NINAS	NAMER	NEPHO
******	MISSY	MUSTS	NIPAS	NAMES	NEPHR
M--P-	MOIST	MUSTY	NISAN	NAPES	NICHE
******	MOOSE	MUTTS	NIVAL	NARES	NIGHT
MORPH	MORSE	******	NIZAM	NATES	NOAHS
MUMPS	MOSSO	**M--U-**	NODAL	NAVEL	NUCHA
MYOPE	MOSSY	******	NOMAD	NAVES	******
MYOPY	MOUSE	MAGUS	NOMAS	NEGEB	**N--I-**
******	MOUSY	MANUS	NONAS	NEGEV	******
M--R-	MUSSY	MAQUI	NOPAL	NETER	NADIR
******	******	MENUS	NOPAR	NEVER	NARIS
MACRO	**M--T-**	MIAUL	NORAH	NEWEL	NAZIS
MAORI	******	MINUS	NORAS	NEWER	NEVIL
MARRY	MALTA	MIXUP	NOVAE	NICER	NEVIS
MATRI	MALTS	MODUS	NOVAS	NIDED	NIHIL
MAURA	MALTY	MOGUL	NOWAY	NIDES	NIXIE
MERRY	MANTA	MOHUR	******	NIGEL	NORIA
METRE	MARTA	MOMUS	**N--B-**	NIGER	NUBIA
METRO	MARTS	MUCUS	******	NIMES	******
METRY	MARTY	******	NIMBI	NINES	**N--K-**
MICRA	MASTO	**M--V-**	NIOBE	NISEI	******
		******			NARKY
		MAUVE			NECKS

NICKS	******	NAMUR	******	OWLET	******
NICKY	N--R-	NEGUS	O--E-	OWNED	O--J-
NOCKS	******	NEVUS	******	OWNER	OUIJA
NOOKS	NACRE	NEXUS	OAKEN	******	******
******	NAIRN	NIDUS	OARED	O--F-	O--K-
N--L-	NAURU	NINUS	OASES	******	******
******	NEARS	NISUS	OATEN	OLAFS	OSAKA
NAILS	NECRO	NODUS	OATES	******	******
NEALS	NEGRO	******	OAVES	O--G-	O--L-
NEILS	NEHRU	N--V-	OBOES	******	******
NELLS	NEURI	******	OCHER	OLIGO	OBELI
NELLY	NEURO	NAIVE	OCREA	OLOGY	OBOLE
NEWLY	NIGRI	NAVVY	OCTET	OMEGA	OBOLI
NOBLE	NITRE	NERVE	ODDER	ONEGA	OCALA
NOBLY	NITRI	NERVY	OFFER	OSAGE	OCULO
NOELS	NITRO	******	OFTEN	OUTGO	ODDLY
******	NJORD	O--A-	OGDEN	******	ODYLE
N--M-	******	******	OGEES	O--H-	OPALS
******	N--S-	OBEAH	OGLED	******	ORALS
NAOMI	******	OCEAN	OGLER	OATHS	OVALS
NEUME	NEWSY	OCTAD	OGLES	OMAHA	OVOLI
NORMA	NOISE	OFFAL	OGRES	OPAHS	OVOLO
NORMS	NOISY	OGHAM	OIDEA	ORCHI	OVULE
******	NOOSE	OKRAS	OILED	ORTHO	******
N--N-	NORSE	OLEAN	OILER	OUGHT	O--M-
******	NURSE	OLGAS	OKIEH	******	******
NANNA	NYASA	OLLAS	OKIES	O--I-	OTOMI
NANNY	******	OREAD	OLDEN	******	OXIME
NINNY	N--T-	ORGAN	OLDER	OASIS	******
NOONS	******	OSCAN	OMBER	OGMIC	O--N-
NORNS	NASTY	OSCAR	ONSET	OHMIC	******
NOUNS	NATTY	OSMAN	OOZED	OLEIC	ODONT
******	NEATH	OURAY	OOZES	OLEIN	OKING
N--O-	NESTS	******	OPTED	OLLIE	OLENT
******	NETTY	O--B-	ORBED	ONEIR	OMENS
NABOB	NEWTS	******	ORDER	OPHIO	OPENS
NAHOR	NIFTY	ORIBI	ORIEL	OPSIA	OPINE
NEROS	NINTH	******	ORLES	OPSIS	ORANG
NITON	NITTY	O--C-	ORMER	OPTIC	OVENS
NIXON	NOCTI	******	OSIER	ORBIT	OVINE
NYLON	NORTH	ORACH	OSLER	ORCIN	OWENS
******	NUTTY	OUNCE	OSTED	ORNIS	OWING
N--P-	NYCTI	******	OTHER	ORPIN	OZONE
******	NYCTO	O--D-	OTTER	ORRIS	******
NAPPE	******	******	OUSEL	OSMIC	O--O-
NAPPY	N--U-	OUIDA	OUTED	OSTIA	******
NEAPS	******	OUTDO	OUTER	OVOID	ODEON
NIPPY	NAHUA	OXIDE	OUZEL	OXLIP	OLIOS
NYMPH	NAHUM			OZZIE	

ONION	ODEUM	PIMAS	POOCH	PAREU	PONES
ORION	ODIUM	PINAS	PORCH	PATEN	POPES
ORLON	ODOUR	PIPAL	POUCH	PATER	PORED
ORLOP	OPIUM	PITAS	PRICE	PATES	PORES
ORSON	ORCUS	PLEAD	PRICK	PAVED	POSED
OTTOS	******	PLEAS	PROCT	PAVER	POSER
OXBOW		PLEAT	PSYCH	PAVES	POSES
******	**O--V-**	POLAR	PUNCH	PAWED	POWER
	******	PRIAM	******	PAWER	PREEN
O--P-	OGIVE	PROAS	**P--D-**	PAYED	PRIED
******	OLAVS	PSHAW	******	PAYEE	PRIER
OKAPI	OLIVE	PSOAS	PADDY	PAYER	PRIES
OOMPH	******	PUMAS	PAEDO	PEDES	PROEM
******	**O--Y-**	PUNAS	PANDA	PELEE	PRYER
	******	PUPAE	PANDY	PELEG	PUBES
O--R-	OBEYS	PUPAS	PARDS	PERES	PUCES
******	OCTYL	PUSAN	PENDS	PETER	PUGET
OCHRE	OKAYS	PYRAN	PERDU	PETES	PUKED
OCHRY	ORIYA	******	PLODS	PEWEE	PUKES
ODORS	OXEYE		PONDS	PHLEB	PULED
OMBRE	******	**P--B-**	POODS	PHREN	PULER
OMBRO		******	PRIDE	PIKED	PULES
OMERS	**O--Z-**	PHEBE	PRODS	PIKER	PUREE
ONERY	******	PHOBE	PRUDE	PIKES	PURER
ONIRO	ORCZY	PLEBE	******	******	PYRES
OPERA	******	PLEBS	**P--E-**	PILEA	PYREX
OTARU		PROBE	******	PILED	PYXED
OTERO	**P--A-**	******	PACED	PILEI	PYXES
OUTRE	******		PACER	PILES	******
OVARY	PACAS	**P--C-**	PACES	PINED	**P--F-**
OVERT	PAEAN	******	PAGED	PINEL	******
OYERS	PAGAN	PARCA	PAGER	PINER	PELFS
OZARK	PALAE	PARCH	PAGES	PINES	POUFS
******	PANAY	PASCH	PALEA	PINEY	PROFS
	PAPAL	PATCH	PALED	PIPED	PUFFS
O--S-	PAPAS	PEACE	PALEO	PIPER	PUFFY
******	PAPAW	PEACH	PALER	PIPES	******
OBESE	PARAS	PENCE	PALES	PIPET	
OMASA	PAVAN	PERCH	PALEY	PLIED	**P--G-**
******	PECAN	PERCY	PANED	PLIER	******
	PEDAL	PHYCO	PANEL	PLIES	PANGS
O--T-	PEKAN	PIECE	PANES	POGEY	PARGO
******	PENAL	PINCH	PAPEN	POKED	PEGGY
OBITS	PETAL	PISCI	PAPER	POKER	PENGO
ODETS	PHIAL	PITCH	PARED	POKES	PHAGE
OMITS	PICAL	PLACE	PAREN	POKEY	PHAGO
ORATE	PICAS	PLACK	PARER	POLED	PHAGY
OSITY	PIKAS	PLICA	PARES	POLES	PIGGY
OUSTS	PILAF	PLUCK			PINGO
OVATE	PILAR	POACH			
******	PIMAN	PONCE			
O--U-					
******					
OAKUM					
OCCUR					

PINGS	PUBIS	PEELS	PRIMS	PRANG	PULPY
PLAGI	PUDIC	PELLA	PROMS	PRANK	PUMPS
PLEGY	PUNIC	PELLY	PULMO	PRINK	PUPPY
PLUGS	PUPIL	PEPLA	PYGMY	PRINT	******
PODGY	PURIM	PERLE	******	PRONE	**P--R-**
PORGE	PYOID	PHILA	**P--N-**	PRONG	******
PORGY	PYXIE	PHILE	******	PRUNE	PADRE
PRIGS	PYXIS	PHILO	PAINE	PYDNA	PAIRS
PUDGY	******	PHILS	PAINS	******	PARRS
PUNGS	**P--K-**	PHILY	PAINT	**P--O-**	PARRY
PURGE	******	PHYLA	PANNE	******	PATRI
******	PACKS	PHYLE	PATNA	PAEON	PEARL
P--H-	PARKA	PHYLL	PAWNS	PAROL	PEARS
******	PARKS	PHYLO	PEANS	PAROS	PEARY
PACHY	PAWKY	PILLS	PEENS	PECOS	PEDRO
PASHA	PEAKS	POILU	PENNA	PEKOE	PEERS
PATHO	PEAKY	POLLS	PENNI	PELON	PERRY
PATHS	PECKS	POLLY	PENNY	PEPOS	PETRO
PATHY	PEEKS	POOLE	PEONS	PERON	PETRY
PITHS	PERKS	POOLS	PEONY	PESOS	PHORE
PITHY	PERKY	POULT	PHANE	PHLOX	PHYRE
PRAHU	PESKY	PROLE	PHANY	PICOT	PICRO
PUSHY	PICKS	PSALM	PHENO	PILOT	PIERS
******	PINKS	PULLS	PHONE	PINON	PLURI
P--I-	PINKY	PURLS	PHONO	PITON	POURS
******	POCKS	PYELO	PHONY	PITOT	PTERO
PANIC	POCKY	******	PIAND	PIVOT	PURRS
PARIS	POLKA	**P--M-**	PIANO	POYOU	******
PATIO	PORKY	******	PINNA	PRIOR	**P--S-**
PAVIS	PUCKA	PALMA	PINNI	PROOF	******
PEKIN	PUCKS	PALMI	PINNY	PUTON	PAISA
PENIS	PUKKA	PALMS	PIONS	PYLON	PAISE
PEPIN	PUNKA	PALMY	PLANE	******	PALSY
PERIL	PUNKS	PARMA	PLANI	**P--P-**	PANSY
PERIS	PUNKY	PIGMY	PLANK	******	PARSE
PETIT	******	PLUMB	PLANO	PALPI	PARSI
PEWIT	**P--L-**	PLUME	PLANS	PAPPI	PASSE
PILIS	******	PLUMP	PLANT	PAPPY	PASSY
PIPIT	PABLO	PLUMS	PLENA	PEEPS	PATSY
PIXIE	PAILS	PLUMY	PLINY	PEPPY	PAUSE
PLAID	PALLS	POEMS	PLONK	PHIPS	PEASE
PLAIN	PALLY	POMMY	PLUNK	PIMPS	PERSE
PLAIT	PAOLO	PRAMS	POIND	PLOPS	PHASE
PLOID	PAULA	PRIMA	POINT	POOPO	PHASY
PODIA	PAULO	PRIME	POONA	POOPS	PHYSI
POLIO	PAULS	PRIMI	POONS	POPPY	PLASH
POSIT	PAWLS	PRIMO	PORNO	PROPS	PLASM
PUBIC	PEALS	PRIMP	POUND	PULPS	PLAST

PLASY	PICTS	PROVE	******	QUERN	RERAN
PLUSH	PIETA	PROVO	Q--E-	QUERY	RHEAS
POESY	PIETY	******	******	QUIRE	RITAS
POISE	PINTA	P--W-	QUEEN	QUIRK	RIVAL
POPSY	PINTO	******	QUEER	QUIRT	RIYAL
POSSE	PINTS	PLOWS	QUIET	******	ROMAN
POTSY	PLATA	PRAWN	******	Q--S-	ROSAS
PRASE	PLATE	PROWL	Q--F-	******	ROTAS
PRESA	PLATO	PROWS	******	QUASH	ROWAN
PRESS	PLATS	******	QUAFF	QUASI	ROYAL
PREST	PLATY	P--X-	QUIFF	QUASS	RUGAE
PRISE	PLOTS	******	******	QUEST	RURAL
PRISM	PLUTO	PREXY	Q--G-	******	******
PROSE	POETS	PROXY	******	Q--T-	R--B-
PROSY	PORTS	******	QUAGS	******	******
PUDSY	POSTS	P--Y-	******	QUITE	RABBI
PULSE	POTTO	******	Q--I-	QUITO	RUGBY
PURSE	POTTY	PEPYS	******	QUITS	RUMBA
PURSY	POUTS	PLAYA	QUAIL	QUOTA	******
PUSSY	PRATE	PLAYS	QUOIN	QUOTE	R--C-
******	PROTO	PLOYS	QUOIT	QUOTH	******
P--T-	PUNTO	POLYP	******	******	RANCE
******	PUNTS	POWYS	Q--K-	Q--U-	RANCH
PACTS	PUNTY	PRAYS	******	******	RATCH
PANTO	PUTTS	PREYS	QUAKE	QUEUE	REACH
PANTS	PUTTY	******	QUAKY	******	REACT
PANTY	******	P--Z-	******	Q--Y-	REICH
PARTS	P--U-	******	Q--L-	******	RETCH
PARTY	******	PIEZO	******	QUAYS	ROACH
PASTA	PADUA	PIZZA	QUALM	******	ROTCH
PASTE	PAPUA	PLAZA	QUELL	R--A-	R--D-
PASTS	PICUL	PRIZE	QUILL	******	******
PASTY	PINUP	******	QUILT	RABAT	RAIDS
PATTI	PIOUS	Q--A-	******	RADAR	RANDS
PATTY	PIQUE	******	Q--N-	RAJAB	RANDY
PEATS	PNEUM	QATAR	******	RAJAH	READS
PEATY	PROUD	QUEAN	QUANT	RATAL	READY
PELTS	PSEUD	******	QUINT	RAYAH	REEDS
PENTA	PUTUP	Q--C-	******	RECAP	REEDY
PERTH	******	******	Q--P-	REDAN	RENDS
PESTS	P--V-	QUACK	******	REGAL	RHODA
PETTI	******	QUICK	QUIPS	REGAN	RINDS
PETTO	PEAVY	******	QUIPU	RELAX	ROADS
PETTY	PEEVE	Q--D-	******	RELAY	RODDY
PHOTO	PELVI	******	Q--R-	REMAN	RONDO
PHOTS	PIAVE	QUADS	******	RENAL	ROODS
PHYTE	PLUVI	QUIDS	QUARK	RENAN	ROWDY
PHYTO	PRIVY	QUODS	QUART	REPAY	

RUDDS	RHOEA	RULED	RADIO	REALM	******
RUDDY	RICED	RULER	RADIX	REALS	**R--O-**
RYNDS	RICER	RULES	RAMIE	REDLY	******
******	RICES	RUMEN	RANIS	REELS	RADON
R--E-	RIDER	RUNES	RAPID	REPLY	RAYON
******	RIDES	RUPEE	RATIO	RIALS	RAZOR
RACED	RIGEL	RUSES	REBID	RIFLE	RIGOR
RACER	RILED	******	REDID	RILLE	RIPON
RACES	RILES	**R--F-**	REFIT	RILLS	ROBOT
RAGED	RILEY	******	REGIN	ROALD	ROTOR
RAGEE	RIMED	REEFS	RELIC	ROBLE	RUMOR
RAGES	RIMER	REEFY	REMIT	ROILS	RUNON
RAKED	RIMES	REIFY	RENIN	ROILY	******
RAKEE	RIPEN	RIFFS	RESIN	ROLLO	**R--P-**
RAKER	RIPER	ROLFE	RETIA	ROLLS	******
RAKES	RISEN	ROLFS	REZIN	ROTLA	RALPH
RALES	RISER	ROOFS	RICIN	RUBLE	RAMPS
RANEE	RISES	RUFFS	RIGID	RUMLY	RASPS
RAPED	RITES	******	ROBIN	******	RASPY
RAPES	RIVED	**R--G-**	RODIN	**R--M-**	REAPS
RARER	RIVEN	******	ROSIN	******	ROLPH
RATED	RIVER	RAGGY	RUNIC	RAMMY	ROMPS
RATEL	RIVES	RANGE	RUNIN	REAMS	ROUPY
RATER	RIVET	RANGY	RURIK	REGMA	RUMPS
RATES	ROBED	REIGN	******	REIMS	******
RAVED	ROBES	RHAGE	**R--K-**	RHOMB	**R--R-**
RAVEL	RODEO	RHAGY	******	RHUMB	******
RAVEN	ROGER	RIDGE	RACKS	RHYME	REARM
RAVER	ROLES	RIDGY	RANKS	ROAMS	REARS
RAVES	ROMEO	RIGGS	REEKS	ROOMS	RETRO
RAWER	ROPED	RINGS	REEKY	ROOMY	RETRY
RAYED	ROPES	ROUGE	RICKS	RUMMY	ROARS
RAZED	ROPEY	ROUGH	RICKY	******	RUERS
RAZEE	ROSED	RUNGS	RINKS	**R--N-**	******
RAZES	ROSES	******	RISKS	******	**R--S-**
REBEC	ROUEN	**R--H-**	RISKY	RAINS	******
REBEL	ROUES	******	ROCKS	RAINY	RAISE
REFER	ROVED	RAPHE	ROCKY	REINS	RINSE
REGES	ROVEN	RIGHT	ROOKS	RHINE	ROAST
REMEX	ROVER	RUCHE	ROOKY	RHINO	ROOST
RENEE	ROVES	RUSHY	RUCKS	RHONE	ROUSE
RENES	ROWED	RUTHS	RUSKS	RIANT	ROUST
RENEW	ROWEL	******	******	ROANS	RUSSO
REPEL	ROWEN	**R--I-**	**R--L-**	RONNY	******
RESET	ROWER	******	******	ROUND	**R--T-**
RETEM	RRHEA	RABIC	RAILS	RUING	******
REVEL	RUBES	RABID	RALLY	RUINS	RAFTS
REVET	RUDER	RADII	RAWLY	RUNNY	RANTS

RATTY	******	SOMAT	SLOBS	SEEDS	SCREW
RECTA	S--A-	SONAR	SLUBS	SEEDY	SEDER
RECTI	******	SORAS	SNOBS	SENDS	SELEN
RECTO	SABAH	SOWAR	SNUBS	SHADE	SEMEN
RENTE	SAGAN	SOYAS	SORBS	SHADY	SERED
RENTS	SAGAS	SPEAK	STABS	SHEDS	SERES
RESTS	SALAD	SPEAR	STUBS	SKIDS	SEVEN
RETTA	SAMAR	SPLAT	SWABS	SLEDS	SEVER
RIATA	SARAH	SPLAY	******	SLIDE	SEWED
RIFTS	SARAN	SPRAG	S--C-	SNIDE	SEWER
RIOTS	SARAS	SPRAT	******	SOLDI	SEXED
ROOTS	SATAN	SPRAY	SARCO	SOLDO	SEXES
ROOTY	SCRAG	SQUAB	SAUCE	SPADE	SHEEN
ROUTE	SCRAM	SQUAD	SAUCY	SPODE	SHEEP
ROUTS	SCRAP	SQUAT	SECCO	SPUDS	SHEER
RUNTS	SEBAT	SQUAW	SHACK	STUDS	SHEET
RUNTY	SEDAN	STEAD	SHOCK	STUDY	SHIED
RUSTS	SELAH	STEAK	SHUCK	SUEDE	SHIER
RUSTY	SEPAL	STEAL	SINCE	SURDS	SHOER
RUTTY	SERAC	STEAM	SLACK	SWEDE	SHOES
RYOTS	SERAI	STOAE	SLICE	******	SHRED
******	SERAL	STOAS	SLICK	S--E-	SHREW
R--U-	SETAE	STOAT	SMACK	******	SHYER
******	SHEAF	STRAD	SMOCK	SABED	SICES
RAMUS	SHEAR	STRAP	SNACK	SABER	SIDED
RAOUL	SHEAS	STRAT	SNICK	SABES	SIDER
REBUS	SHIAH	STRAW	SPACE	SAFER	SIDES
REBUT	SHOAL	STRAY	SPECK	SAFES	SILEX
RECUR	SHOAT	SUBAH	SPECS	SAGER	SINES
REMUS	SILAS	SUDAN	SPICA	SAGES	SINEW
RERUN	SIMAR	SUGAR	SPICE	SAHEB	SIPES
REVUE	SINAI	SUMAC	SPICY	SAKER	SIRED
RHEUM	SISAL	SURAH	STACK	SAKES	SIREN
RISUS	SITAR	SURAL	STACY	SALEM	SIRES
ROGUE	SIVAN	SURAS	STICH	SALEP	SITED
ROQUE	SIZAR	SUSAN	STICK	SALES	SITES
RUFUS	SKEAN	SWEAR	STOCK	SAMEK	SIXES
******	SKOAL	SWEAT	STUCK	SANER	SIZED
R--V-	SKUAS	******	SULCI	SATED	SIZES
******	SLEAT	S--B-	******	SATES	SKEED
REEVE	SMEAR	******	S--D-	SAVED	SKEES
******	SNEAD	SAMBA	******	SAVER	SKEET
R--Y-	SNEAK	SAMBO	SANDS	SAVES	SKIED
******	SODAS	SCABS	SANDY	SAWED	SKIER
RUBYS	SOFAS	SCUBA	SCADS	SAWER	SKIES
RUDYS	SOJAS	SERBS	SCUDI	SAXES	SKYEY
******	SOLAN	SHEBA	SCUDO	SAYER	SLEEK
R--Z-	SOLAR	SLABS	SCUDS	SCREE	SLEEP
******					
RHIZO					
RITZY					

SLEET	SERFS	******	SPOIL	SPOKE	SMELL
SLIER	SHAFT	S--H-	SPRIG	STAKE	SMELT
SLOES	SHIFT	******	SPRIT	STOKE	SMILE
SLUED	SKIFF	SADHU	SQUIB	STUKA	SMOLT
SLUES	SNAFU	SETHS	SQUID	SUCKS	SNELL
SLYER	SNIFF	SHAHS	STAID	SULKS	SOCLE
SNEER	SNUFF	SIGHS	STAIN	SULKY	SOILS
SNYES	SOLFA	SIGHT	STAIR	******	SOULS
SOBER	STAFF	SIKHS	STEIN	S--L-	SPALL
SOKES	STIFF	SOPHY	STOIC	******	SPELL
SOLED	STUFF	SPAHI	STRIA	SABLE	SPELT
SOLES	SULFA	******	STRIP	SADLY	SPILE
SONES	SULFO	S--I-	SUFIC	SAILS	SPILL
SOREL	SURFS	******	SUFIS	SALLY	SPILT
SORER	SURFY	SABIN	SUSIE	SAULS	STALE
SORES	SWIFT	SADIE	SWAIL	SAULT	STALK
SOWED	******	SAHIB	SWAIN	SCALD	STALL
SOWER	S--G-	SALIC	SYBIL	SCALE	STELE
SPEED	******	SALIX	SYRIA	SCALL	STILE
SPHEN	SAIGA	SAPID	******	SCALP	STILL
SPIED	SEDGE	SARIS	S--J-	SCALY	STILT
SPIEL	SEDGY	SASIN	******	SCOLD	STOLE
SPIER	SERGE	SATIE	SHOJI	SCULL	STULL
SPIES	SHAGS	SATIN	SONJA	SCULP	STYLE
SPLEN	SIEGE	SAVIN	******	SEALS	STYLI
SPREE	SINGE	SAYID	S--K-	SELLS	STYLO
STEED	SINGS	SCHIZ	******	SHALE	SULLY
STEEL	SKEGS	SCRIM	SACKS	SHALL	SURLY
STEEN	SLAGS	SCRIP	SARKS	SHALT	SWALE
STEEP	SLIGO	SEPIA	SEEKS	SHALY	SWELL
STEER	SLOGS	SERIF	SHAKE	SHELF	SWILL
STIED	SLUGS	SERIN	SHAKO	SHELL	******
STIES	SMOGS	SHEIK	SHAKY	SHILL	S--M-
STREW	SNAGS	SIGIL	SICKS	SHILY	******
SUMER	SNUGS	SILIC	SILKS	SHULS	SALMA
SUPER	SOGGY	SITIN	SILKY	SHYLY	SALMI
SUPES	SONGS	SKEIN	SINKS	SIALO	SAMMY
SURER	SORGO	SLAIN	SITKA	SIDLE	SCAMP
SWEEP	SOUGH	SOCIO	SLAKE	SILLS	SCHMO
SWEET	STAGE	SOFIA	SMOKE	SILLY	SCUMS
SYCEE	STAGS	SOLID	SMOKY	SKALD	SEAMS
SYCES	STAGY	SONIA	SNAKE	SKILL	SEAMY
******	STOGY	SONIC	SNAKY	SKULK	SEEMS
S--F-	SURGE	SOZIN	SOAKS	SKULL	SELMA
******	SURGY	SPAIN	SOCKS	SLILY	SHAME
SCIFI	SWAGE	SPAIT	SPAKE	SLYLY	SHAMS
SCOFF	SWAGS	SPLIT	SPIKE	SMALL	SHIMS
SCUFF	SWIGS		SPIKY	SMALT	SIGMA
	SYNGE				

SKIMO	SHINE	SUNNS	SOPOR	SOAPY	SHIRT
SKIMP	SHINS	SUNNY	SOTOL	SOPPY	SHORE
SKIMS	SHINY	SWANK	SPOOF	SOUPS	SHORL
SLAMS	SHONE	SWANS	SPOOK	SOUPY	SHORN
SLIME	SHUNS	SWINE	SPOOL	STAPH	SHORT
SLIMS	SHUNT	SWING	SPOON	STEPS	SKIRL
SLIMY	SIENA	SWUNG	SPOOR	STIPE	SKIRR
SLUMP	SIGNE	******	STOOD	STOPE	SKIRT
SLUMS	SIGNS	**S--O-**	STOOK	STOPS	SLURP
SOMME	SKINK	******	STOOL	STOPT	SLURS
SPUME	SKINS	SABOT	STOOP	STUPA	SMART
SPUMY	SKUNK	SAGOS	STROP	STUPE	SMIRK
STAMP	SLANG	SAJOU	SUDOR	SUMPS	SNARE
STEMS	SLANT	SALOL	SWOON	SWAPS	SNARK
STIMY	SLING	SALON	SWOOP	SWEPT	SNARL
STOMA	SLINK	SAMOA	SYNOD	SWIPE	SNORE
STOME	SLUNG	SAMOS	SYROS	SYLPH	SNORT
STOMP	SLUNK	SAPOR	******	******	SOARS
STOMY	SOMNI	SAROS	**S--P-**	**S--R-**	SORRY
STUMP	SONNY	SAVOR	******	******	SOURS
STUMS	SOUND	SAVOY	SALPA	SABRA	SPARE
STYMY	SPANG	SAXON	SAPPY	SABRE	SPARK
SWAMI	SPANK	SCION	SCAPA	SACRA	SPARS
SWAMP	SPANS	SCOOP	SCAPE	SACRO	SPERM
SWIMS	SPEND	SCOOT	SCAPI	SAPRO	SPIRE
******	SPENT	SCROD	SCOPE	SARRE	SPIRO
S--N-	SPINE	SEGOS	SCOPS	SAURO	SPIRT
******	SPINI	SENOR	SCOPY	SAURY	SPIRY
SAINT	SPINS	SEPOY	SCUPS	SCARE	SPORE
SAONE	SPINY	SERON	SCYPH	SCARF	SPORO
SAUNA	SPUNK	SEROW	SEEPS	SCARP	SPORT
SCAND	STAND	SETON	SHAPE	SCARS	SPURN
SCANS	STANK	SHEOL	SHIPS	SCARY	SPURS
SCANT	STANS	SHOOK	SHOPS	SCORE	SPURT
SCENA	STENO	SHOOS	SIMPS	SCORN	STARE
SCEND	STING	SHOOT	SKEPS	SCURF	STARK
SCENE	STINK	SIDON	SKIPS	SEARS	STARS
SCENT	STINT	SILOS	SLAPS	SEERS	START
SCONE	STONE	SIMON	SLEPT	SERRA	STERE
SEANS	STONY	SINON	SLIPS	SHARD	STERN
SEGNI	STUNG	SLOOP	SLIPT	SHARE	STIRK
SEGNO	STUNK	SNOOD	SLOPE	SHARI	STIRP
SEINE	STUNS	SNOOK	SLOPS	SHARK	STIRS
SENNA	STUNT	SNOOP	SLYPE	SHARP	STORE
SENNE	SUING	SNOOT	SNAPS	SHERD	STORK
SHANK	SUINT	SODOM	SNIPE	SHIRE	STORM
SHANS	SUNNA	SOLON	SNIPS	SHIRK	STORY
SHANT	SUNNI	SOLOS	SOAPS	SHIRR	SUCRE

SUERS	SCOTT	SPITE	SUNUP	SPAWN	TREAD
SUPRA	SCUTA	SPITS	SYRUP	SPEWS	TREAS
SUTRA	SCUTE	SPITZ	******	STEWS	TREAT
SWARD	SCUTS	SPOTS	S--V-	STOWE	TRIAD
SWARM	SEATO	STATE	******	STOWS	TRIAL
SWART	SEATS	STATO	SALVE	******	TROAS
SWIRL	SECTS	STETH	SALVO	S--Y-	TUBAL
SWORD	SEPTA	STETS	SAVVY	******	TUBAS
SWORE	SEPTI	SUETY	SERVE	SATYR	TUNAS
SWORN	SEPTO	SUITE	SERVO	SHAYS	TWEAK
******	SEPTS	SUITS	SHAVE	SIBYL	******
S--S-	SETTO	SWATH	SHIVE	SLAYS	T--B-
******	SEXTO	SWATS	SHIVS	SLOYD	******
SALSA	SHOTE	******	SHOVE	SONYA	TABBY
SALSE	SHOTS	S--U-	SIEVE	SPAYS	TOMBS
SASSY	SHUTE	******	SILVA	STAYS	TRIBE
SAYSO	SHUTS	SAGUM	SKIVE	SUZYS	TUBBY
SEISE	SIFTS	SALUS	SLAVE	SWAYS	TURBO
SEISM	SILTS	SCAUP	SLAVO	******	******
SENSE	SILTY	SCOUR	SOLVE	S--Z-	T--C-
SHUSH	SIXTE	SCOUT	STAVE	******	******
SISSY	SIXTH	SCRUB	STEVE	SEIZE	TALCS
SLASH	SIXTY	SCRUM	STOVE	SMAZE	TEACH
SLOSH	SKATE	SEBUM	SUAVE	******	TENCH
SLUSH	SKITS	SEDUM	SYLVA	T--A-	THECA
SMASH	SLATE	SEOUL	******	******	THICK
SONSY	SLATS	SERUM	S--W-	TABAC	TINCT
SOUSA	SLATY	SETUP	******	TAPAS	TORCH
SOUSE	SLITS	SHAUN	SCHWA	TATAR	TOUCH
SPASM	SLOTH	SHOUT	SCOWL	TELAE	TRACE
STASH	SLOTS	SHRUB	SCOWS	TERAT	TRACH
STOSS	SLUTS	SHRUG	SHAWL	TEXAS	TRACK
SUDSY	SMITE	SIEUR	SHAWM	TICAL	TRACT
SWASH	SMITH	SINUS	SHAWN	TIDAL	TRACY
SWISH	SMOTE	SIOUX	SHAWS	TINAS	TRICE
SWISS	SMUTS	SIRUP	SHEWN	TITAN	TRICH
******	SNATH	SITUS	SHEWS	TODAY	TRICK
S--T-	SNOTS	SNOUT	SHOWN	TOGAE	TRUCE
******	SOFTA	SOLUS	SHOWS	TOGAS	TRUCK
SALTS	SOFTY	SORUS	SHOWY	TOKAY	TURCO
SALTY	SOOTH	SPOUT	SKEWS	TOLAN	TWICE
SANTA	SOOTS	SPRUE	SLAWS	TOLAS	******
SARTO	SOOTY	STOUP	SLEWS	TOMAN	T--D-
SAUTE	SORTS	STOUR	SLOWS	TOMAS	******
SCATO	SOTTO	STOUT	SMEWS	TONAL	TARDO
SCATS	SOUTH	STRUM	SNOWS	TOPAZ	TARDY
SCOTO	SPATE	STRUT	SNOWY	TORAH	TEDDY
SCOTS	SPATS	SULUS		TOTAL	TENDS

THADS	THREW	TUBES	******	TALKS	THYME
THADY	TIBER	TULES	**T--I-**	TANKA	THYMY
THEDA	TIBET	TUNED	******	TANKS	TIMMY
THUDS	TIDED	TUNER	TABID	TASKS	TOMMY
TILDA	TIDES	TUNES	TACIT	TEAKS	TRAMP
TILDE	TIGER	TWEED	TAFIA	TICKS	TRAMS
TOADS	TILED	TWEEN	TAMIL	TREKS	TRIMS
TOADY	TILER	TWEET	TAMIS	TUCKS	TRUMP
TODDS	TILES	TYEES	TANIS	TURKI	TRYMA
TODDY	TIMED	TYKES	TAPIR	TURKS	TUMMY
TRADE	TIMER	TYLER	TAPIS	TUSKS	******
TRUDA	TIMES	TYPED	TAXIS	******	**T--N-**
TRUDY	TINEA	TYPES	TELIC	**T--L-**	******
TSADE	TINED	******	TEPID	******	TACNA
******	TINES	**T--F-**	THEIR	TABLE	TAINO
T--E-	TIRED	******	TIBIA	TAELS	TAINS
******	TIREE	TAFFY	TIEIN	TAILS	TAINT
TABES	TIRES	THEFT	TIKIS	TALLY	TARNS
TACET	TITER	TIFFS	TIMID	TEALS	TAUNT
TAKEN	TOKEN	TURFS	TITIS	TELLS	TAWNY
TAKER	TOLES	TURFY	TOEIN	TELLY	TBONE
TAKES	TOMES	******	TONIC	TESLA	TEENS
TALER	TONED	**T--G-**	TONIS	THOLE	TEENY
TALES	TONER	******	TOPIC	THULE	TERNS
TAMED	TONES	TAIGA	TOPIS	TILLS	THANE
TAMER	TOPED	TANGO	TORIC	TILLY	THANK
TAMES	TOPEE	TANGS	TORII	TITLE	THINE
TANEY	TOPER	TANGY	TOXIC	TOILE	THING
TAPED	TOPES	THIGH	TOXIN	TOILS	THINK
TAPER	TOTED	THUGS	TRAIL	TOLLS	THINS
TAPES	TOTEM	TINGE	TRAIN	TOOLS	THONG
TARED	TOTER	TINGS	TRAIT	TRILL	TINNY
TARES	TOTES	TIOGA	TULIP	TROLL	TONNE
TAWED	TOWED	TONGA	TUMID	TRULL	TOWNS
TAWER	TOWEL	TONGS	TUNIC	TRULY	TRANS
TAXED	TOWER	TOUGH	TUNIS	TULLE	TREND
TAXER	TOYED	TRAGI	TUPIK	TULLY	TRENT
TAXES	TOYER	TRIGO	TUPIS	TWILL	TRINA
TEBET	TREED	TRIGS	TURIN	******	TRINE
TEHEE	TREES	TWIGS	TWAIN	**T--M-**	TRONA
TEKEL	TRIED	******	******	******	TRUNK
TELEG	TRIER	**T--H-**	**T--J-**	TAMMY	TSANA
TELEO	TRIES	******	******	TEAMS	TUNNY
TELEX	TRUED	TACHY	THUJA	TEEMS	TURNS
TENET	TRUER	TETHS	******	TERMS	TWANG
TEPEE	TRUES	TIGHT	**T--K-**	THEME	TWINE
THIEF	TUBED	TITHE	******	THUMB	TWINS
THREE	TUBER	TOPHI	TACKS	THUMP	TYING
		TYCHE	TACKY		

*****	TRIPS	TOPSY	TUTTY	*****	UPPED
T--O-	TROPE	TORSI	TWITS	**U--A-**	UPPER
*****	TROPH	TORSK	*****	*****	UPSET
TABOO	*****	TORSO	**T--U-**	UBOAT	URGED
TABOR	**T--R-**	TRASH	*****	UHLAN	URGES
TAHOE	*****	TRASS	TALUK	ULNAE	URIEL
TALON	TARRY	TRESS	TALUS	ULNAR	USHER
TALOS	TATRA	TRUSS	THRUM	ULNAS	UTHER
TAROS	TAURO	TRUST	TIEUP	UMIAK	UTTER
TAROT	TEARS	TRYST	TITUS	UNBAR	*****
TENON	TEARY	TULSA	TOGUE	UNCAP	**U--F-**
TENOR	TERRA	TWIST	TONUS	UNHAT	*****
TENOS	TERRI	*****	TOQUE	UNIAT	UNIFY
TETON	TERRY	**T--T-**	TORUS	UNLAY	*****
THIOL	TETRA	*****	TROUT	UNMAN	**U--G-**
THROB	THERE	TANTO	TUQUE	UNSAY	*****
THROE	THERM	TARTS	TUTUS	URBAN	USAGE
THROW	THIRD	TARTY	*****	UREAL	*****
TIMOR	THORN	TASTE	**T--V-**	URIAH	**U--I-**
TIROS	THORP	TASTY	*****	URSAE	*****
TOBOL	THURS	TATTY	TRAVE	USUAL	UNDID
TODOS	THYRO	TAUTO	TROVE	UVEAL	UNFIT
TOYON	TIARA	TEATS	*****	UVEAS	UNFIX
TOYOS	TIERS	TEETH	**T--W-**	UXMAL	UNLIT
TRIOL	TOURS	TENTH	*****	*****	UNPIN
TRIOS	TRURO	TENTS	THAWS	**U--C-**	UNRIG
TROOP	TSARS	TESTA	THEWS	*****	UNRIP
TRYON	TWERE	TESTS	THEWY	URICO	UNTIE
TUDOR	TWERP	TESTY	TRAWL	UTICA	UNTIL
TUMOR	TWIRL	TEXTS	TREWS	*****	UNZIP
TUTOR	TWIRP	THETA	*****	**U--D-**	*****
TYPOS	TZARS	THOTH	**T--X-**	*****	**U--L-**
TYROL	*****	TILTH	*****	UREDO	*****
TYROS	**T--S-**	TILTS	TRIXY	*****	UBOLT
*****	*****	TINTS	TWIXT	**U--E-**	UMBLE
T--P-	TANSY	TOFTS	*****	*****	UNCLE
*****	TARSI	TOOTH	**T--Y-**	UDDER	URALS
TAMPA	TARSO	TOOTS	*****	ULCER	UTILE
TAMPS	TASSO	TORTE	TANYA	UMBEL	UVULA
TARPS	TEASE	TORTS	TOBYS	UMBER	*****
TAUPE	TENSE	TORTS	TOKYO	UNDEE	**U--M-**
TEMPE	TERSE	TOUTS	TOLYL	UNDER	*****
TEMPI	THESE	TRITE	TONYS	UNMEW	ULEMA
TEMPO	THOSE	TROTH	TRAYS	UNPEG	*****
TEMPT	TIPSY	TROTS	TREYS	UNPEN	**U--N-**
TIPPY	TOAST	TRUTH	*****	UNREF	*****
TRAPS	TOISE	TUFTS	**T--Z-**	UNSEX	UDINE
TRIPE		TUFTY	TAZZA	UNWED	ULENT
		TUTTI	TIZZY		

UPEND	******	VEXER	VATIC	******	VAGUE
URANO	**V--A-**	VEXES	VEDIC	**V--O-**	VAGUS
URINE	******	VIBES	VESIC	******	VALUE
URINO	VARAS	VICES	VEXIL	VALOR	VARUS
USING	VELAR	VIDEO	VIGIL	VAPOR	VELUM
******	VENAE	VILER	VINIC	VENOM	VENUE
U--O-	VENAL	VIMEN	VISIT	VIGOR	VENUS
******	VERAS	VINES	VIVID	VISOR	VIRUS
UMBOS	VICAR	VIPER	VIZIR	VIZOR	VOGUE
UNION	VIDAL	VIREO	VOMIT	******	VOGUL
UPBOW	VINAS	VIRES	******	**V--P-**	******
******	VIRAL	VISED	**V--K-**	******	**V--V-**
U--P-	VISAS	VISES	******	VAMPS	******
******	VITAE	VIXEN	VICKS	******	VALVE
UNAPT	VITAL	VOCES	VICKY	**V--R-**	VARVE
******	VOCAL	VOLES	VODKA	******	VERVE
U--R-	VOLAR	VOMER	******	VAIRS	VOLVA
******	******	VOTED	**V--L-**	VARRO	VULVA
ULTRA	**V--B-**	VOTER	******	VEERS	******
UMBRA	******	VOTES	VAULT	VEERY	**V--W-**
UNARM	VERBS	VOWED	VEILS	VITRI	******
USERS	******	VOWEL	VIALS	******	VIEWS
USURP	**V--C-**	VOWER	VILLA	**V--S-**	VIEWY
USURY	******	******	VILLE	******	******
UTERI	VETCH	**V--G-**	VILLI	VEPSA	**V--Y-**
UTERO	VINCE	******	VILLS	VERSE	******
UTURN	VINCI	VANGS	VIOLA	VERSO	VINYL
******	VISCT	VERGE	VIOLS	VERST	******
U--S-	VNECK	VIRGA	VOILA	******	**W--A-**
******	VOICE	VIRGE	VOILE	**V--T-**	******
UKASE	VOUCH	VIRGO	******	******	WATAP
ULOSE	******	VOLGA	**V--M-**	VASTY	WEKAS
******	**V--D-**	VUGGY	******	VENTS	WHEAL
U--T-	******	VULGO	VERMI	VERTU	WHEAT
******	VELDS	******	******	VESTA	WIGAN
UINTA	VELDT	**V--H-**	**V--N-**	VESTS	WITAN
UNITE	VENDS	******	******	VIRTU	WODAN
UNITS	VERDI	VICHY	VAUNT	VISTA	WOMAN
UNITY	VOIDS	******	VEINS	VITTA	WOTAN
URATE	******	**V--I-**	VEINY	VOLTA	WREAK
******	**V--E-**	******	VERNA	VOLTE	******
U--U-	******	VAGIN	VERNE	VOLTI	**W--B-**
******	VALES	VALID	VERNS	VOLTS	******
ULOUS	VALET	VANIR	VIAND	******	WEBBY
UNAUS	VANED	VAPID	VILNA	**V--U-**	WOMBS
UNCUT	VANES	VARIC	VINNY	******	WOMBY
UNDUE	VASES	VARIO	VYING	VACUA	******
	VEXED	VARIX		VADUZ	**W--C-**
					******
					WATCH
					WELCH

WENCH	WALES	******	WHALE	******	WHISK
WHACK	WANED	**W--F-**	WHELK	**W--O-**	WHIST
WHICH	WANES	******	WHELM	******	WHOSE
WINCE	WANEY	WAIFS	WHELP	WAGON	WHOSO
WINCH	WARES	WHIFF	WHILE	WAHOO	WORSE
WITCH	WATER	WOLFS	WHOLE	WHOOP	WORST
WRACK	WAVED	WOOFS	WIELD	WIDOW	WREST
WRECK	WAVER	******	WILLA	WINOS	WRIST
WRICK	WAVES	**W--G-**	WILLS	******	******
******	WAVEY	******	WILLY	**W--P-**	**W--T-**
W--D-	WAXED	WAUGH	WOALD	******	******
******	WAXEN	WEDGE	WOOLF	WARPS	WAFTS
WADDY	WAXES	WEDGY	WOOLS	WASPS	WAITS
WALDO	WEBER	WEIGH	WOOLY	WASPY	WALTS
WANDA	WESER	WHIGS	WORLD	WEEPS	WALTZ
WANDS	WHEEL	WINGS	WOULD	WEEPY	WANTS
WARDS	WIDEN	WINGY	WRYLY	WHAPS	WARTS
WEEDS	WIDER	******	******	WHIPS	WARTY
WEEDY	WILED	**W--H-**	**W--M-**	WHIPT	WASTE
WELDS	WILES	******	******	WHOPS	WATTS
WENDS	WILEY	WASHY	WARMS	WISPS	WEFTS
WENDY	WINED	WIGHT	WEEMS	WISPY	WELTS
WIDDY	WINES	WITHE	WHAMS	WRAPS	WHETS
WILDE	WIPED	WITHY	WHIMS	WRAPT	WHITE
WILDS	WIPER	******	WILMA	******	WHITS
WINDS	WIPES	**W--K-**	WORMS	**W--R-**	WIDTH
WINDY	WIRED	******	WORMY	******	WILTS
WOADS	WIRER	WACKE	******	WEARS	WITTE
WOLDS	WIRES	WACKS	**W--N-**	WEARY	WITTY
WOODS	WISED	WACKY	******	WEIRD	WORTH
WOODY	WISER	WALKS	WAINS	WEIRS	WORTS
WORDS	WISES	WEEKS	WARNS	WHARF	WRATH
WORDY	WIVED	WICKS	WASNT	WHERE	WRITE
******	WIVER	WINKS	WAYNE	WHIRL	WRITS
W--E-	WIVES	WORKS	WEANS	WHIRR	WROTE
******	WIZEN	******	WEENY	WHIRS	WROTH
WADED	WODEN	**W--L-**	WENNY	WHORE	WYATT
WADER	WOKEN	******	WHANG	WHORL	******
WADES	WOMEN	WAILS	WHENS	WHORT	**W--U-**
WAFER	WOOED	WALLA	WHINE	WIRRA	******
WAGED	WOOER	WALLY	WHINS	WORRY	WAMUS
WAGER	WOVEN	WANLY	WHINY	******	WHAUP
WAGES	WOWED	WAULS	WOUND	**W--S-**	******
WAKED	WRIED	WAWLS	WRENS	******	**W--V-**
WAKEN	WRIER	WEALD	WRING	WAIST	******
WAKES	WRIES	WEALS	WRONG	WEEST	WAIVE
WALED	WRYER	WELLS	WRUNG	WELSH	WEAVE
WALER		WETLY		WHISH	******
					W--Y-
					******
					WHEYS

******	******	******	******	******	ACCRA
W--Z-	**Y--B-**	**Y--K-**	**Y--S-**	**Z--I-**	ADELA
******	******	******	******	******	ADOWA
WINZE	YERBA	YANKS	YEAST	ZAMIA	ADUWA
WOOZY	******	YELKS	ZAYIN	ADYTA
******	**Y--C-**	YOLKS	**Y--T-**	ZOOID	AECIA
X--A-	******	YOLKY	******	ZORIL	AEMIA
******	YUCCA		YALTA	******	AFTRA
XTIAN	******	**Y--L-**	YEATS	**Z--K-**	AGAMA
XYLAN	**Y--D-**	******	YOUTH	******	AGANA
******	******	YAWLS	******	ZINKY	AGORA
X--E-	YARDS	YELLS	**Y--U-**	******	ALADA
******	******	YIELD	******	**Z--M-**	ALEXA
XAXES	**Y--E-**	YOULL	YAMUN	******	ALGIA
XEBEC	******	YOWLS	******	ZOOMS	ALOHA
XYLEM	YAGER	******	**Y--V-**	******	ALPHA
******	YAMEN	**Y--M-**	******	**Z--N-**	ALULA
X--H-	YAWED	******	YAHVE	******	AMANA
******	YAXES	YUMMY	YOUVE	ZOONS	AMEBA
XIPHI	YEMEN	******	******	******	AMNIA
******	YESES	**Y--N-**	**Z--A-**	**Z--O-**	ANIMA
X--I-	YIPES	******	******	******	ANITA
******	YODEL	YARNS	ZETAS	ZEROS	ANTRA
XAXIS	YOGEE	YAWNS	ZONAL	ZIRON	AORTA
XENIA	YOKED	YEANS	******	******	APNEA
XERIC	YOKEL	YOUNG	**Z--B-**	**Z--P-**	AQABA
******	YOKES	******	ZOMBI	ZIPPY	ARECA
X--O-	YOWED	**Y--O-**	******	******	ARENA
******	YPRES	******	**Z--C-**	**Z--R-**	ARICA
XENON	YQUEM	YAHOO	******	******	AROMA
XEROX	YULES	YAPON	ZINCS	ZAIRE	ARUBA
XYLOL	******	YAZOO	ZINCY	ZEBRA	ASPCA
******	**Y--G-**	YOYOS	******	ZIMRI	ASYLA
X--T-	******	YUKON	**Z--E-**	******	ATRIA
******	YEGGS	YUPON	******	**Z--T-**	******
XANTH.	******	******	ZEBEC	******	**A---B**
XYSTS	**Y--H-**	**Y--P-**	ZEKES	ZESTS	******
******	******	******	ZIBET	ZESTY	ABOMB
X--U-	YACHT	YAUPS	ZONED	ZLOTY	ACERB
******	YODHS	YAWPS	ZONES	******	ADLIB
XERUS	YOGHS	YELPS	******	**Z--U-**	ARDEB
******	******	******	**Z--F-**	******	******
X--Y-	**Y--I-**	**Y--R-**	******	ZEBUS	**A---C**
******	******	******	ZARFS	******	******
XRAYS	YAXIS	YEARN	******	**A---A**	ADUNC
XYLYL	YETIS	YEARS	**Z--G-**	******	ANTIC
******	YOGIC	YOURE	******	ABACA	ANZAC
Y--A-	YOGIN	YOURS	ZINGY	ABOMA	AREIC
******	YOGIS	YSERE			
YUGAS					

ARTIC	ABUSE	ANGLE	******	AMIEL	ACORN
ASPIC	ACEAE	ANILE	A---H	AMPUL	ACTIN
ASSOC	ACUTE	ANIME	******	ANGEL	ADMAN
ATTIC	ADAGE	ANISE	ABASH	ANNAL	ADMEN
AULIC	ADDIE	ANKLE	AITCH	ANNUL	ADMIN
AURIC	ADDLE	ANNIE	ALEPH	ANSEL	ADORN
AZOIC	ADELE	ANODE	ALLAH	ANTAL	AGAIN
AZTEC	ADIGE	ANSAE	ALMAH	ANVIL	AIKEN
******	ADOBE	ANTAE	AMISH	APPAL	AKRON
A---D	ADORE	APACE	APISH	APPEL	ALAIN
******	AERIE	APPLE	AWASH	APRIL	ALBAN
ACHED	AFIRE	AQUAE	AZOTH	AREAL	ALBIN
ACRED	AFORE	AREAE	******	ARGAL	ALCAN
ACRID	AGAPE	ARETE	A---I	ARGIL	ALDAN
ACTED	AGATE	ARGUE	******	ARGOL	ALDEN
ADDED	AGAVE	ARISE	AALII	ARIEL	ALGIN
AHEAD	AGAZE	ARNIE	ABACI	ARTAL	ALIEN
AIDED	AGGIE	AROSE	ACINI	ARTEL	ALIGN
AILED	AGILE	ARTIE	ADENI	ARVAL	ALLAN
AIMED	AGLEE	ASIDE	ADLAI	ATOLL	ALLEN
AIRED	AGREE	ATIVE	ALIBI	AURAL	ALLIN
ALAND	AIMEE	ATONE	ALTAI	AUSTL	ALOIN
ALGID	AISLE	AUDIE	AMATI	AUXIL	ALTON
ALMUD	AISNE	AURAE	AMPHI	AVAIL	ALUIN
ALOUD	AKENE	AWAKE	ARCHI	AVRIL	ALVAN
AMEND	ALATE	AWARE	ASSAI	AWFUL	ALVIN
ANTED	ALBEE	AWOKE	AUREI	AXIAL	ALWIN
APHID	ALFIE	AXILE	******	******	AMAIN
ARCED	ALGAE	AXONE	A---K	A---M	AMMAN
ARMED	ALGIE	AZINE	******	******	AMMON
AROID	ALICE	AZOLE	ABACK	ABEAM	ANCON
ARPAD	ALIKE	AZOTE	ACOCK	ABOHM	ANION
ASKED	ALINE	AZURE	ALACK	ABRAM	ANTON
AUDAD	ALIVE	******	ALECK	ABYSM	APIAN
AVOID	ALLIE	A---F	AMUCK	ADEEM	APRON
AWARD	ALONE	******	APEAK	ALARM	ARDEN
AWNED	ALYCE	ADOLF	******	ALBUM	ARGON
AXLED	AMATE	ALOOF	A---L	ALGUM	ARIAN
******	AMAZE	******	******	ANNAM	ARION
A---E	AMBLE	A---G	ABIEL	ARIUM	ARLEN
******	AMICE	******	ABOIL	ASSAM	ARPEN
ABASE	AMIDE	ACING	ACCEL	AURUM	ARRAN
ABATE	AMINE	AGING	AFOUL	AXIOM	ARSON
ABBIE	AMOLE	ALMUG	ALDOL	******	ARYAN
ABELE	AMPLE	ALONG	ALGAL	A---N	ASHEN
ABIDE	AMUSE	AMONG	ALGOL	******	ASIAN
ABODE	ANDRE	APING	ALKYL	AARON	ASPEN
ABOVE	ANELE	AWING	ALLYL	ACEAN	ASTON
		AXING			

ASWAN	AFTER	ACIDS	ANDES	AVARS	AUGHT
ATION	AGGER	ACRES	ANDYS	AVENS	AVAST
ATMAN	AIDER	ACTUS	ANGUS	AVERS	AVERT
AUDEN	ALDER	ADAHS	ANILS	AVOWS	AWAIT
AUXIN	ALGER	ADAMS	ANKHS	AXILS	******
AVIAN	ALGOR	ADDYS	ANKUS	AXLES	**A---U**
AVION	ALTAR	ADIOS	ANLAS	AXONS	******
AXMAN	ALTER	ADITS	ANNAS	AYAHS	ADIEU
AXMEN	AMBER	ADZES	ANNES	AYINS	ANJOU
AYDIN	AMEER	AEDES	ANTES	AZANS	******
******	AMOUR	AEGIS	ANTIS	AZONS	**A---W**
A---O	AMPHR	AEONS	APHIS	******	******
******	ANEAR	AFROS	APSES	**A---T**	AGLOW
ACETO	ANGER	AGHAS	APSIS	******	ALLOW
ACOUO	APTER	AGIOS	AQUAS	ABAFT	ARROW
ADENO	ARBOR	AGNES	ARABS	ABBOT	ASKEW
ALAMO	ARDOR	AGNIS	ARCUS	ABORT	******
AMIDO	ARMOR	AGUES	AREAS	ABOUT	**A---X**
AMIGO	ARTER	AIDAS	ARGOS	ADAPT	******
AMINO	ARTHR	AIDES	ARGUS	ADEPT	ADDAX
AMYLO	ARTUR	AINOS	ARIAS	ADMIT	ADMEX
ANDRO	ASHER	AINUS	ARIES	ADOPT	ADMIX
ANEMO	ASHUR	ALANS	ARILS	ADULT	AFFIX
ANGIO	ASKER	ALBAS	ARIUS	ADUST	ANNEX
ANGLO	ASPER	ALDIS	ARLES	AETAT	******
ANISO	ASSYR	ALDOS	ARRAS	AFOOT	**A---Y**
ANTHO	ASTER	ALDUS	ARRIS	AGENT	******
ANZIO	ASTIR	ALECS	ARSES	AGIST	ABBEY
ASTRO	ASTOR	ALEFS	ARSIS	AGLET	ACITY
AUDIO	ATPAR	ALGYS	ARTIS	ALERT	AGLEY
AVISO	ATTAR	ALIAS	ARUMS	ALEUT	AGONY
******	AUGER	ALIFS	ASCUS	ALIST	ALARY
A---P	AUGUR	ALLIS	ASHES	ALLOT	ALLAY
******	AVOIR	ALMAS	ASPIS	ALOFT	ALLEY
AESOP	******	ALOES	ASSES	AMBIT	ALLOY
ASCAP	**A---S**	ALOIS	ASSNS	AMENT	ALPHY
ATRIP	******	ALTAS	ASSTS	ANENT	ALWAY
******	ABBAS	ALTOS	ATHOS	ANGST	AMBRY
A---R	ABBES	ALUMS	ATLAS	APART	AMITY
******	ABBYS	AMAHS	ATOMS	APORT	AMPLY
ABHOR	ABELS	AMASS	ATTIS	ARENT	ANGRY
ABLER	ABETS	AMBOS	ATTYS	ARGOT	ANNOY
ABNER	ABIBS	AMENS	AULIS	ARMET	ANOMY
ACTOR	ABIES	AMIAS	AUNTS	ASCOT	APERY
ADDER	ABRIS	AMIES	AURAS	ASSET	APPLY
ADLER	ABUTS	AMIRS	AURES	ASYUT	APTLY
AEGIR	ABYSS	AMISS	AURIS	ATILT	ARABY
AESIR	ACHES	AMYLS	AUTOS	AUDIT	ARCHY

ARRAY
ASSAY
ATAXY
ATONY
ATORY
AUNTY
AUTRY
AVERY
******
B---A
******
BAHIA
BALSA
BANDA
BARCA
BASRA
BEATA
BEIRA
BELGA
BELLA
BEREA
BERIA
BERRA
BERTA
BEULA
BIOTA
BOHEA
BRAVA
BRAZA
BREDA
BULLA
BURMA
BURSA
BWANA
******
B---B
******
BLURB
******
B---C
******
BARIC
BASIC
BLANC
BORIC
BRONC
******
B---D
******
BAAED
BAIRD

BAKED
BALED
BARED
BASED
BATED
BAYED
BEARD
BEGAD
BIDED
BIFID
BIPED
BIPOD
BLAND
BLEED
BLEND
BLIND
BLOND
BLOOD
BLUED
BOARD
BODED
BONED
BOOED
BORED
BOUND
BOVID
BOWED
BOXED
BRAID
BRAND
BREAD
BREED
BROAD
BROOD
BUILD
BUSED
******
B---E
******
BACHE
BADGE
BAIZE
BARDE
BARGE
BARRE
BARYE
BASLE
BASTE

BATHE
BAUME
BEEBE
BEIGE
BELIE
BELLE
BENNE
BENUE
BERME
BERNE
BETTE
BIBLE
BILGE
BINGE
BIRLE
BISSE
BLADE
BLAKE
BLAME
BLARE
BLASE
BLAZE
BLOKE
BOCHE
BOGIE
BOGLE
BOISE
BOMBE
BONZE
BOONE
BOOZE
BORNE
BOULE
BOUSE
BOWIE
BOWSE
BOYLE
BOYNE
BRACE
BRAGE
BRAHE
BRAKE
BRAVE
BRAZE
BREVE
BRIBE
BRICE
BRIDE

BRINE
BROKE
BROME
BRUCE
BRUME
BRUTE
BRYCE
BUDGE
BUGLE
BULGE
BUNDE
BURKE
BURSE
BUTTE
******
B---F
******
BANFF
BLUFF
BRIEF
******
B---G
******
BEFOG
BEING
BHANG
BOURG
BRAGG
BRING
******
B---H
******
BARTH
BATCH
BEACH
BEECH
BELCH
BENCH
BERTH
BIRCH
BIRTH
BITCH
BLIGH
BLUSH
BLYTH
BOOTH
BOSCH
BOTCH

BOUGH
BRASH
BROTH
BRUSH
BUNCH
BURGH
BUTCH
******
B---I
******
BACCI
BAHAI
BAMBI
BASSI
BRAGI
BREVI
BUFFI
BYSSI
******
B---K
******
BATIK
BAULK
BLACK
BLANK
BLEAK
BLINK
BLOCK
BREAK
BRICK
BRINK
BRISK
BROCK
BROOK
BRUSK
******
B---L
******
BABEL
BABUL
BAGEL
BANAL
BASAL
BASEL
BASIL
BEALL
BERYL
BETEL

BEVEL
BEZEL
BIKOL
BINAL
BOHOL
BOWEL
BRAIL
BRAWL
BRILL
BROIL
BUBAL
BUTYL
******
B---M
******
BEDIM
BEGUM
BELEM
BESOM
BLOOM
BOSOM
BREAM
BROOM
BUXOM
******
B---N
******
BACON
BADEN
BAIRN
BARON
BASIN
BASON
BATAN
BATEN
BATON
BEGAN
BEGIN
BEGUN
BEHAN
BENIN
BETON
BEVAN
BEVIN
BISON
BLAIN
BLOWN
BOGAN

BONIN	BALER	BATHS	BLIPS	BRATS	BINET
BORON	BARER	BAWDS	BLISS	BRAYS	BINIT
BOSON	BERAR	BAWLS	BLOBS	BREWS	BIZET
BOSUN	BIHAR	BEADS	BLOCS	BRIGS	BLAST
BOURN	BITER	BEAKS	BLOIS	BRIMS	BLEAT
BRAIN	BLEAR	BEAMS	BLOTS	BROOS	BLENT
BRAWN	BLUER	BEANS	BLOWS	BROWS	BLEST
BRIAN	BOGOR	BEARS	BLUES	BUCKS	BLOAT
BROWN	BOLAR	BEATS	BLURS	BUFFS	BLUET
BRUIN	BONER	BEAUS	BMEWS	BULBS	BLUNT
BRYAN	BORER	BECKS	BOARS	BULKS	BLURT
BURAN	BOWER	BEEFS	BOATS	BULLS	BOAST
BURIN	BOXER	BEEPS	BODES	BUMPS	BOOST
BYRON	BOYAR	BEERS	BOERS	BUNDS	BRACT
******	BRIAR	BEETS	BOGUS	BUNGS	BRANT
B---O	BRIER	BELLS	BOILS	BUNKS	BRENT
******	BUBER	BELTS	BOLAS	BUNNS	BREST
BABOO	BUYER	BENDS	BOLES	BUNTS	BRUIT
BANJO	******	BENES	BOLLS	BUOYS	BRUNT
BASSO	**B---S**	BERGS	BOLOS	BURDS	BUILT
BATHO	******	BERMS	BOLTS	BURGS	BURNT
BEANO	BABAS	BERTS	BOLUS	BURLS	BURST
BETSO	BABES	BESTS	BOMBS	BURNS	******
BILBO	BACKS	BETAS	BONDS	BURPS	**B---U**
BINGO	BAFFS	BETHS	BONES	BURRS	******
BONGO	BAHTS	BIBBS	BONGS	BUSES	BANTU
BRAVO	BAILS	BICES	BONUS	BUSKS	BAYOU
BROMO	BAITS	BIDES	BOOBS	BUSTS	BIJOU
BRUNO	BAKES	BIERS	BOOKS	BUTTS	BORNU
BUCKO	BALAS	BIFFS	BOOMS	BYRES	******
BUFFO	BALES	BIKES	BOONS	******	**B---W**
BUNCO	BALKS	BILES	BOORS	**B---T**	******
BUNKO	BALLS	BILKS	BOOTS	******	BEDEW
BURRO	BALMS	BILLS	BORES	BANAT	BELOW
******	BALTS	BINDS	BORIS	BARIT	BYLAW
B---P	BANDS	BINES	BORTS	BEAST	******
******	BANGS	BIRDS	BOSKS	BEAUT	**B---X**
BACUP	BANKS	BIRLS	BOTTS	BEFIT	******
BEBOP	BANNS	BIRRS	BOUTS	BEGAT	BEAUX
BLEEP	BARBS	BISES	BOWLS	BEGET	BORAX
BLIMP	BARDS	BITES	BOXES	BEGOT	BRONX
******	BARES	BITTS	BOYDS	BENET	******
B---R	BARKS	BLABS	BOZOS	BERET	**B---Y**
******	BARNS	BLAHS	BRADS	BERET	******
BABAR	BASES	BLATS	BRAES	BESET	BADLY
BABER	BASIS	BLDGS	BRAGS	BESOT	BAFFY
BAKER	BASKS	BLEBS	BRANS	BIDET	BAGGY
BALDR	BATES	BLESS	BRASS	BIGOT	BALKY

BALMY	BUFFY	COPRA	CHORD	CHINE	CRUSE
BANDY	BUGGY	CORIA	CITED	CHIVE	CURIE
BARKY	BULGY	COSTA	CLOUD	CHLOE	CURSE
BARMY	BULKY	COTTA	CLUED	CHOKE	CURVE
BARRY	BULLY	CRURA	CODED	CHOLE	CUTIE
BATHY	BUMPY	CULPA	CONED	CHORE	CYCLE
BATTY	BUNNY	CURIA	CONTD	CHOSE	CYMAE
BAWDY	BURLY	******	COOED	CHUTE	******
BEADY	BURRY	**C---B**	COPED	CHYLE	**C---F**
BEAMY	BUSBY	******	CORED	CHYME	******
BECKY	BUSHY	CABOB	COULD	CIRCE	CALIF
BEEFY	BYWAY	CALEB	COVED	CLARE	CHAFF
BEERY	******	CARIB	COWED	CLIME	CHIEF
BELAY	**B---Z**	CAROB	COXED	CLINE	CLIFF
BELLY	******	CLIMB	CREED	CLIVE	******
BENDY	BLITZ	COOMB	CRIED	CLONE	**C---G**
BENJY	BORTZ	CRUMB	CROWD	CLOSE	******
BENNY	******	CUBEB	CUBED	CLOVE	CHANG
BERRY	**C---A**	******	CUPID	CLYDE	CLANG
BERTY	******	**C---C**	CURED	COBLE	CLING
BESSY	CALLA	******	CYCAD	COELE	CLUNG
BETSY	CANEA	CERIC	******	COLNE	CRAIG
BETTY	CANNA	CETIC	**C---E**	COMAE	CUING
BIALY	CAPUA	CIVIC	******	COMTE	******
BIDDY	CARLA	COLIC	CABLE	CONGE	**C---H**
BIFFY	CAUCA	COMIC	CACHE	CONTE	******
BIGLY	CEARA	CONIC	CADGE	COOEE	CATCH
BILGY	CEIBA	COPEC	CADRE	COPSE	CHETH
BILLY	CELIA	CRESC	CALPE	CORFE	CINCH
BLOWY	CELLA	CUBIC	CALVE	CORSE	CLASH
BOBBY	CERIA	CUSEC	CANOE	COUPE	CLOTH
BOGEY	CESTA	CYNIC	CARLE	COXAE	COACH
BOGGY	CEUTA	******	CARTE	CRAKE	CONCH
BONNY	CHELA	**C---D**	CARVE	CRANE	COUCH
BOOBY	CHIBA	******	CASTE	CRAPE	COUGH
BOOTY	CHINA	CAGED	CAUSE	CRATE	COUTH
BOOZY	CHITA	CAIRD	CAVIE	CRAVE	CRASH
BORTY	CHUFA	CAKED	CEASE	CRAZE	CRUSH
BOSKY	CILIA	CANAD	CELIE	CREME	CUISH
BOSSY	CIRCA	CANED	CENSE	CREPE	CULCH
BOTHY	CITRA	CARED	CHAFE	CRETE	CURCH
BOUSY	CLARA	CASED	CHAPE	CREWE	CUTCH
BRADY	COBIA	CAVED	CHARE	CRIME	CZECH
BRAKY	COBRA	CAWED	CHASE	CROCE	******
BRAXY	COCOA	CEDED	CHIDE	CRONE	**C---I**
BRINY	COLZA	CERED	CHILE	CRORE	******
BUDDY	COMMA	CHARD	CHIME	CROZE	CACTI
BUDGY	CONGA	CHILD		CRUDE	CALCI

CALLI	CRICK	CAJON	CHINO	CAPER	CAPES
CAMPI	CROAK	CAJUN	CHIRO	CARER	CARAS
CAPRI	CROCK	CANON	CHORO	CATER	CARDS
CARDI	CROOK	CAPON	CIRRO	CEDAR	CARES
CARPI	******	CENON	CISCO	CENTR	CARLS
CENTI	C---L	CETIN	CLARO	CESAR	CARPS
CESTI	******	CHAIN	CLINO	CHAIR	CARTS
CHEMI	CABAL	CHIAN	COELO	CHEER	CARYS
CHILI	CAMEL	CHRON	COENO	CHIRR	CASES
CIRRI	CANAL	CHURN	COMBO	CHLOR	CASKS
COATI	CAROL	CLEAN	COMPO	CHOIR	CASTS
COCCI	CAVIL	CLEON	CONGO	CHURR	CASUS
CORGI	CECAL	CLOWN	CONIO	CIDER	CAULS
CRANI	CECIL	COGON	CONTO	CIGAR	CAVES
CROCI	CEORL	COHAN	COPRO	CLEAR	CEDES
CRUCI	CHILL	COIGN	COSMO	CODER .	CEILS
CULTI	CHURL	COLIN	COSTO	COKER	CELLS
CURVI	CIBOL	COLON	CREDO	COLOR	CELTS
CYMRI	CIDAL	COVEN	CTENO	COMDR	CENIS
CYSTI	CIVIL	COZEN	CUPRO	COMER	CENTS
******	COMAL	CREON	CURIO	CONTR	CERES
C---K	COPAL	CROON	CUSSO	COOER	CEROS
******	CORAL	CROWN	CYANO	COPER	CETUS
CAPEK	COXAL	CUBAN	CYCLO	CORER	CHAOS
CAULK	CRAAL	CUMIN	CYSTO	COVER	CHAPS
CHALK	CRAWL	CUTIN	******	COWER	CHARS
CHECK	CREEL	******	C---P	CRIER	CHATS
CHEEK	CRUEL	C---O	******	CRUOR	CHAWS
CHICK	CUPEL	******	CHAMP	CURER	CHEFS
CHINK	CYRIL	CACAO	CHEAP	CUTER	CHESS
CHOCK	******	CADDO	CHEEP	CYMAR	CHETS
CHUCK	C---M	CAIRO	CHIMP	******	CHEWS
CHUNK	******	CAMEO	CHIRP	C---S	CHIAS
CLACK	CAROM	CAMPO	CHUMP	******	CHINS
CLANK	CECUM	CANSO	CLAMP	CADES	CHIOS
CLARK	CELOM	CANTO	CLASP	CADIS	CHIPS
CLEEK	CERAM	CARBO	CLUMP	CAFES	CHITS
CLERK	CHARM	CARGO	CRAMP	CAGES	CHOPS
CLICK	CHASM	CARLO	CREEP	CAKES	CHOWS
CLINK	CHIRM	CARPO	CRIMP	CALKS	CHRIS
CLOAK	CHROM	CARYO	CRISP	CALLS	CHRYS
CLOCK	CLAIM	CASCO	CROUP	CALMS	CHUBS
CLUCK	CREAM	CELLO	CRUMP	CAMES	CHUGS
COSEK	******	CENTO	CUTUP	CAMPS	CHUMS
CRACK	C---N	CHARO	******	CAMUS	CIONS
CRANK	******	CHEMO	C---R	CANES	CISTS
CREAK	CABIN	CHICO	******	CANIS	CITES
CREEK	CAIRN	CHILO	CABER	CANTS	CLAMS
			CANER		

CLANS	COPTS	CANST	CIMEX	CUPPY	******
CLAPS	CORAS	CAPET	CODEX	CURDY	D---D
CLASS	CORDS	CAPUT	CROIX	CURLY	******
CLAWS	CORES	CARAT	CULEX	CURRY	DARED
CLAYS	CORKS	CARET	CYLIX	CUSHY	DATED
CLEFS	CORMS	CERAT	******	CUTEY	DAVID
CLEMS	CORNS	CHAET	C---Y	CUTTY	DAZED
CLEWS	CORPS	CHANT	******	CYMRY	DEKED
CLIOS	COSTS	CHAPT	CABBY	******	DELED
CLIPS	COTES	CHART	CADDY	C---Z	DEWED
CLODS	COUPS	CHEAT	CAGEY	******	DICED
CLOGS	COVES	CHERT	CAMPY	CADIZ	DIKED
CLONS	COWES	CHEST	CANDY	******	DINED
CLOPS	COWLS	CIVET	CANNY	D---A	DIVED
CLOTS	COXES	CLEAT	CAREY	******	DOLED
CLOYS	CRABS	CLEFT	CARRY	DACCA	DOMED
CLUBS	CRAGS	CLINT	CASEY	DACHA	DOPED
CLUES	CRAMS	CLOUT	CATHY	DACIA	DOSED
COALS	CRAPS	COAST	CATTY	DELIA	DOTED
COATS	CRASS	COMDT	CHARY	DELLA	DOZED
COBBS	CRAWS	COMET	CHEVY	DELTA	DREAD
COCAS	CREES	COOPT	CHEWY	DERMA	DRIED
COCKS	CRESS	COROT	CHOKY	DIANA	DRUID
COCOS	CREWS	COUNT	CINDY	DICTA	DUPED
CODAS	CRIBS	COURT	CISSY	DINKA	******
CODES	CRIES	COVET	CLARY	DOBLA	D---E
COEDS	CROPS	CRAFT	CLUNY	DOBRA	******
COIFS	CROSS	CREPT	COALY	DOGMA	DANAE
COILS	CROWS	CREST	COCKY	DONNA	DANCE
COINS	CUBES	CROAT	COKEY	DORSA	DANTE
COKES	CUFFS	CROFT	COLLY	DOURA	DAVIE
COLAS	CULLS	CRUET	COMFY	DRAMA	DEANE
COLDS	CULMS	CRUST	CONEY	DRAVA	DEFOE
COLES	CULTS	CRYPT	CONNY	DUALA	DEICE
COLTS	CURBS	CUBIT	COOEY	DULIA	DELVE
COMAS	CURDS	CULET	COOKY	DURRA	DENSE
COMBS	CURES	CURST	CORBY	******	DEUCE
COMES	CURLS	******	CORKY	D---B	DHOLE
COMUS	CUSKS	C---U	CORNY	******	DIANE
CONES	CUSPS	******	COVEY	DEMOB	DIENE
CONKS	CUTIS	CORFU	COWRY	DENEB	DIODE
CONUS	CYMES	CORNU	COYLY	******	DIONE
COOKS	CYRUS	COYPU	CRACY	D---C	DIRGE
COOLS	CYSTS	******	CRAZY	******	DIXIE
COONS	CZARS	C---X	CRECY	DARIC	DOBIE
COOPS	******	******	CRONY	DODEC	DODGE
COOTS	C---T	CALIX	CUBBY	DOMIC	DOGIE
COPES	******	CALYX	CUDDY	DORIC	
	CABOT				
	CADET				

DOLCE	DENTI	DAMON	DECOR	DEALS	DOLTS
DONEE	DHOLI	DEIGN	DEFER	DEANS	DOMES
DONNE	DHOTI	DEMON	DEMUR	DEARS	DONAS
DOUSE	DISCI	DEVON	DENDR	DEBTS	DONTS
DOWSE	DORSI	DEWAN	DETER	DECKS	DOOMS
DOYLE	DOUAI	DIJON	DEXTR	DEEDS	DOORS
DRAKE	DUBAI	DIVAN	DICER	DEEMS	DOPES
DRAPE	DUOMI	DIWAN	DIKER	DEEPS	DORAS
DRAVE	******	DIZEN	DIMER	DEFIS	DORIS
DRIVE	**D---K**	DOORN	DINAR	DEGAS	DORMS
DROME	******	DOYEN	DINER	DEKES	DORRS
DRONE	DEREK	DOZEN	DIRER	DELES	DORUS
DROVE	DIRCK	DRAIN	DIVER	DELLS	DOSES
DRUPE	DRANK	DRAWN	DOLOR	DELOS	DOTES
DRUSE	DRINK	DROWN	DONAR	DEMES	DOUGS
DUANE	DRUNK	DYLAN	DONOR	DEMOS	DOVES
DUBHE	******	******	DOSER	DENES	DOWNS
DULCE	**D---L**	**D---O**	DOTER	DENIS	DOZES
DULSE	******	******	DOVER	DENTS	DRABS
DUNCE	DATAL	DATTO	DOWER	DENYS	DRAGS
DUPLE	DECAL	DAVAO	DOZER	DESKS	DRAMS
******	DEDAL	DENTO	DREAR	DEVAS	DRAWS
D---F	DEVIL	DERMO	DRIER	DHAKS	DRAYS
******	DOALL	DIAZO	DRYER	DHOWS	DREGS
DRAFF	DOWEL	DICHO	DUPER	DIALS	DRESS
DWARF	DRAIL	DIEGO	DURER	DICKS	DREWS
******	DRAWL	DILDO	******	DIDOS	DRIBS
D---G	DRILL	DINGO	**D---S**	DIETS	DRIES
******	DROLL	DIPLO	******	DIKES	DRIPS
DEBAG	DROOL	DISCO	DACES	DILYS	DROPS
DEBUG	DUCAL	DISKO	DALES	DIMES	DROSS
DOING	DURAL	DITTO	DAMES	DINES	DRUBS
DYING	DWELL	DORSO	DAMNS	DINGS	DRUGS
******	******	DRACO	DAMPS	DINTS	DRUMS
D---H	**D---M**	DUOMO	DANES	DIRKS	DUADS
******	******	******	DANGS	DISCS	DUCKS
DEATH	DATUM	**D---P**	DARES	DISKS	DUCTS
DEPTH	DECIM	******	DARNS	DITAS	DUDES
DINAH	DEGUM	DOVAP	DARTS	DIVAS	DUELS
DITCH	DEISM	DROOP	DATES	DIVES	DUETS
DOETH	DENIM	******	DAUBS	DOCKS	DUFFS
DOLPH	DREAM	**D---R**	DAVES	DODOS	DUKES
DOUGH	DURUM	******	DAVIS	DOERS	DULLS
DUTCH	******	DAKAR	DAVOS	DOFFS	DUMAS
******	**D---N**	DALER	DAVYS	DOGES	DUMPS
D---I	******	DARER	DAWKS	DOITS	DUNES
******	DAGAN	DATER	DAWNS	DOLES	DUNGS
DALAI	DAMAN	DEBAR	DAZES	DOLLS	DUNKS
DELHI					

DUPES	DASHY	DULCY	******	******	ELVIN
DUROS	DAUBY	DULLY	**E--E**	**E---H**	ELWIN
DUSKS	DAVEY	DUMMY	******	******	EMDEN
DUSTS	DEARY	DUMPY	EADIE	EARTH	EOSIN
******	DEBBY	DUNGY	EAGLE	EDITH	ERWIN
D---T	DECAY	DUSKY	EAGRE	ENOCH	ESSEN
******	DECOY	DUSTY	EARLE	EPHAH	ETHAN
DAUNT	DECRY	******	ECOLE	EPOCH	******
DAVIT	DEIFY	**E---A**	EDDIE	ERICH	**E---O**
DEALT	DEITY	******	EDILE	******	******
DEBIT	DELAY	EDEMA	EDUCE	**E---I**	ELAEO
DEBUT	DENNY	EDINA	EERIE	******	ELAIO
DEIST	DEOXY	ELENA	EFFIE	ELEMI	ERATO
DELFT	DERBY	ELIZA	ELATE	ENNUI	ETHNO
DEMIT	DERRY	ENEMA	ELIDE	******	******
DEPOT	DEWEY	ENNEA	ELISE	**E---L**	**E---P**
DIDNT	DIARY	ENOLA	ELITE	******	******
DIDST	DICEY	ENTIA	ELLIE	EASEL	EQUIP
DIGIT	DICKY	ERICA	ELOPE	EDSEL	ESTOP
DIVOT	DIMLY	ERIKA	ELSIE	ENROL	******
DIXIT	DINGY	ETYMA	ELUDE	EQUAL	**E---R**
DOEST	DINKY	EVITA	EMCEE	ERROL	******
DOUBT	DIPPY	EXTRA	EMILE	ETHEL	EAGER
DRAFT	DIRTY	******	EMMIE	ETHYL	EATER
DREST	DISHY	**E---B**	EMOTE	EXCEL	EDGAR
DRIFT	DITTY	******	ENARE	EXPEL	EGGAR
DRIPT	DIVVY	EXURB	ENATE	EXTOL	EGGER
DROIT	DIZZY	******	ENDUE	******	EIDER
DROPT	DOBBY	**E---C**	ENSUE	**E---M**	EIMER
DUCAT	DODGY	******	EPODE	******	ELDER
DURST	DOGGY	EDDIC	ERASE	ENTOM	ELGAR
DWELT	DOILY	ENCYC	ERNIE	EPSOM	ELMER
******	DOLLY	EOLIC	ERODE	******	ELVER
D---X	DOOLY	ETHIC	EROSE	**E---N**	EMBAR
******	DOPEY	******	ESQUE	******	EMBER
DESEX	DORMY	**E---D**	ESSIE	ETAPE	EMEER
******	DOTTY	******	ETTIE	EAMON	EMMER
D---Y	DOUAY	EARED	ETUDE	EATEN	ENTER
******	DOURY	EASED	EVADE	ECHIN	EPHOR
DADDY	DOWDY	EBBED	EVOKE	EDWIN	ERROR
DAFFY	DOWNY	EDGED	EXILE	EGEAN	ESHER
DAILY	DOWRY	EDRED	EXUDE	ELAIN	ESKER
DAIRY	DOYLY	EGGED	EYDIE	ELFIN	ESTAR
DAISY	DRILY	ELAND	EYRIE	ELGIN	ESTER
DALLY	DRURY	EMBED	******	ELLEN	ETHER
DANDY	DRYLY	EMEND	**E---G**	ELMAN	EULER
DANNY	DUCHY	ENDED	******	ELOIN	EYRIR
DARKY	DUCKY	EPHOD	EKING	ELTON	
		ERRED	EWING	ELVAN	
			EYING		

******	EXAMS	******	FARAD	FIBRE	FILTH
E---S	EXECS	**E---Y**	FARED	FICHE	FINCH
******	EXITS	******	FATED	FIQUE	FIRTH
EARLS	EYRAS	EARLY	FAXED	FIUME	FITCH
EARNS	EZRAS	EBONY	FAYED	FLAKE	FLASH
EASES	******	EDIFY	FAZED	FLAME	FLESH
EAVES	**E---T**	ELEGY	FELID	FLARE	FLUSH
EBONS	******	EMBAY	FETED	FLITE	FORTH
EDDAS	EBOAT	EMBRY	FETID	FLUKE	FRESH
EDGES	ECLAT	EMERY	FEUED	FLUME	FRITH
EDIES	EDICT	EMILY	FIELD	FLUTE	FROSH
EDITS	EDUCT	EMORY	FIEND	FORCE	FROTH
EDNAS	EGEST	EMPTY	FIFED	FORGE	FURTH
ELIAS	EGRET	ENEMY	FILED	FORME	******
ELLAS	EGYPT	ENJOY	FINED	FORTE	**F---I**
ELLIS	EIGHT	ENTRY	FIORD	FOSSE	******
ELSAS	EJECT	ENVOY	FIRED	FRAME	FEBRI
ELVES	ELECT	EPOXY	FIXED	FRERE	FERMI
EMBUS	ELIOT	ESSAY	FJELD	FRISE	FERRI
EMEUS	EMMET	EVERY	FJORD	FROME	FLEXI
EMILS	ENACT	******	FLIED	FROZE	FORLI
EMIRS	EPACT	**F---A**	FLOOD	FUDGE	FUNDI
EMITS	ERECT	******	FLOYD	FUGLE	FUNGI
EMMAS	ERGOT	FACIA	FLUID	FUGUE	******
EMMYS	ERNST	FANGA	FOUND	FURZE	**F---K**
ENEAS	ERUCT	FAUNA	FOXED	FUSEE	******
ENIDS	ERUPT	FERIA	FOYED	FUZEE	FLACK
ENOLS	EVENT	FIONA	FRAUD	******	FLANK
EOLUS	EVERT	FLORA	FREED	**F---F**	FLASK
EPEES	EVICT	FOLIA	FREUD	******	FLECK
EPICS	EXACT	FONDA	FRIED	FEOFF	FLICK
ERICS	EXALT	FOSSA	FROND	FLUFF	FLOCK
ERIES	EXERT	FOVEA	FUMED	******	FLUNK
ERIKS	EXIST	FREDA	FUSED	**F---G**	FRANK
ERMAS	EXULT	FRENA	FUZED	******	FREAK
ERNES	******	FREYA	******	FLING	FRISK
ERSES	**E---U**	******	**F---E**	FLONG	FROCK
ESSES	******	**F---C**	******	FLUNG	******
ESTES	ELIHU	******	FABLE	FRIGG	**F---L**
ETHOS	ERLAU	FOLIC	FALSE	******	******
ETNAS	******	FRANC	FARCE	**F---H**	FATAL
ETTAS	**E---W**	******	FARLE	******	FAYAL
ETUIS	******	**F---D**	FAROE	FAITH	FECAL
EURUS	ELBOW	******	FEASE	FARAH	FERAL
EVANS	EMBOW	FACED	FEEZE	FAUGH	FETAL
EVENS	ENDOW	FADED	FEMME	FETCH	FIDEL
EVILS	******	FAKED	FENCE	FIFTH	FINAL
EWERS	**E---X**	FAMED	FESSE	FILCH	FLAIL
	******				
	ESSEX				

FOCAL	FAKIR	FAVUS	FLEWS	FUNKS	FELLY
FRAIL	FARER	FAWNS	FLIES	FURLS	FENNY
FRILL	FAVOR	FAXES	FLIPS	FUSES	FERNY
FRIML	FEDOR	FAYES	FLITS	FUZES	FERRY
FUGAL	FEMUR	FAZES	FLOCS	FYKES	FIERY
FUSEL	FETOR	FEARS	FLOES	******	FIFTY
FUSIL	FEUAR	FEATS	FLOGS	**F---T**	FILLY
FUZIL	FEVER	FECES	FLOPS	******	FILMY
******	FEWER	FEEDS	FLOSS	FACET	FINNY
F---M	FIBER	FEELS	FLOWS	FAGOT	FIRRY
******	FIFER	FELLS	FLUBS	FAINT	FISHY
FANUM	FILAR	FELTS	FLUES	FAULT	FITLY
FILUM	FILER	FEMES	FOALS	FAUST	FIZZY
FLEAM	FINER	FENDS	FOAMS	FEAST	FLAKY
FOISM	FIRER	FEODS	FOCUS	FECIT	FLAMY
FORUM	FIVER	FERNS	FOILS	FEINT	FLAWY
******	FIXER	FETES	FOLDS	FEIST	FLAXY
F---N	FLAIR	FETUS	FOLKS	FIGHT	FLUKY
******	FLEER	FEUDS	FONTS	FILET	FLUTY
FANON	FLIER	FIATS	FOODS	FIRST	FLYBY
FEIGN	FLOOR	FICES	FOOLS	FLEET	FOAMY
FELON	FLOUR	FIEFS	FOOTS	FLINT	FOGEY
FLOWN	FLUOR	FIFES	FORBS	FLIRT	FOGGY
FOEHN	FLYER	FIJIS	FORDS	FLOAT	FOLLY
FREON	FOYER	FILES	FORES	FLOUT	FOOTY
FROWN	FREER	FILLS	FORKS	FOIST	FORAY
FURAN	FRIAR	FILMS	FORMS	FOUNT	FORBY
******	FRIER	FINDS	FORTS	FRONT	FORTY
F---O	FRYER	FINES	FOULS	FROST	FUGGY
******	FUROR	FINIS	FOURS	FRUIT	FULLY
FARGO	******	FINKS	FOWLS	******	FUNKY
FEMTO	**F---S**	FINNS	FOXES	**F---U**	FUNNY
FERRO	******	FIRES	FRAPS	******	FURRY
FIBRO	FACES	FIRMS	FRATS	FICHU	FURZY
FOLIO	FACTS	FIRNS	FRAYS	******	FUSSY
FORGO	FADES	FISCS	FREDS	**F---X**	FUSTY
FUGIO	FAILS	FISTS	FREES	******	FUZZY
FUNGO	FAIRS	FIVES	FRETS	FELIX	******
******	FAKES	FIXES	FRIES	******	**F---Z**
F---P	FALLS	FLAGS	FRITS	**F---Y**	******
******	FANGS	FLAMS	FROES	******	FRANZ
FLUMP	FANOS	FLANS	FROGS	FADDY	FRITZ
FRUMP	FARES	FLAPS	FROWS	FAIRY	FRIZZ
******	FARLS	FLATS	FUCUS	FANCY	******
F---R	FARMS	FLAWS	FUELS	FANNY	**G---A**
******	FASTS	FLAYS	FULLS	FARCY	******
FACER	FATES	FLEAS	FUMES	FATLY	GALEA
FAKER	FAUNS	FLEES	FUNDS	FATTY	GAMMA

GEMMA	GYBED	******	GROWL	GUACO	GAOLS
GENOA	GYVED	G---F	GRUEL	GUANO	GAPES
GENUA	******	******	GYRAL	GUIDO	GARBS
GERDA	G---E	GANEF	******	GUMBO	GARYS
GHANA	******	GEOFF	G---M	GUSTO	GASES
GILDA	GABLE	GRIEF	******	GYMNO	GASPS
GOLDA	GAFFE	GRUFF	GLEAM	******	GATES
GONIA	GASPE	******	GLOOM	G---P	GAUDS
GOTHA	GAUGE	G---G	GOLEM	******	GAULS
GOUDA	GAUZE	******	GOYIM	GALOP	GAURS
GRAMA	GAVLE	GIING	GRIMM	GETUP	GAUSS
GRETA	GEESE	GOING	GROOM	GRASP	GAWKS
GUAMA	GENIE	GRIEG	******	GROUP	GAZES
GUANA	GENRE	******	G---N	******	GEARS
GUAVA	GEODE	G---H	******	G---R	GECKS
GUMMA	GIGUE	******	GABON	******	GEEKS
GUSTA	GLACE	GARTH	GALEN	GABOR	GELDS
GUTTA	GLADE	GIRSH	GAMIN	GAGER	GENES
******	GLARE	GIRTH	GATUN	GAPER	GENTS
G---C	GLAZE	GLYPH	GAVIN	GASTR	GENUS
******	GLEBE	GNASH	GIPON	GAYER	GERMS
GAMIC	GLEDE	GRAPH	GIRON	GAZER	GHATS
GENIC	GLIDE	GULCH	GIVEN	GIBER	GIBES
GLAUC	GLOBE	******	GLEAN	GIVER	GIBUS
GYNEC	GLOVE	G---I	GLENN	GLAIR	GIFTS
******	GLOZE	******	GNAWN	GOFER	GIGAS
G---D	GLUME	GAUDI	GOWAN	GONER	GILDS
******	GNOME	GENII	GRAIN	GOWER	GILES
GADID	GOOSE	GHAZI	GREEN	GREER	GILLS
GAGED	GORGE	GONDI	GROAN	GULAR	GIMPS
GAMED	GORME	GORKI	GROIN	******	GINKS
GAPED	GORSE	GRANI	GROWN	G---S	GIRDS
GATED	GOUGE	******	GWENN	******	GIRLS
GAZED	GRACE	G---K	GYRON	GABES	GIROS
GELID	GRADE	******	******	GABYS	GIRTS
GEOID	GRAPE	GREEK	G---O	GAELS	GISTS
GIBED	GRATE	******	******	GAFFS	GIVES
GLAND	GRAVE	G---L	GARBO	GAGES	GLADS
GLUED	GRAZE	******	GECKO	GAILS	GLANS
GONAD	GREBE	GAVEL	GENRO	GAINS	GLASS
GORED	GRIDE	GHOUL	GESSO	GAITS	GLEDS
GOURD	GRIME	GIMEL	GISMO	GALAS	GLEES
GRAND	GRIPE	GNARL	GIZMO	GALES	GLENS
GREED	GROPE	GOGOL	GLYCO	GALLS	GLIMS
GRIND	GROVE	GORAL	GONIO	GAMBS	GLOBS
GUARD	GRUME	GRAAL	GRANO	GAMES	GLOSS
GUILD	GUIDE	GRAIL	GRECO	GAMPS	GLOWS
GUYED	GUISE	GRILL	GREGO	GANGS	GLUES

GLUTS	******	GERRY	HEPTA	******	******
GNATS	G---T	GERTY	HERMA	H---E	H---I
GNAWS	******	GIDDY	HILDA	******	******
GOADS	GAMUT	GIMPY	HORTA	HAGUE	HADJI
GOALS	GAULT	GINNY	HOSEA	HALLE	HAITI
GOATS	GAUNT	GIPSY	HULDA	HALVE	HANOI
GOBOS	GAVOT	GLARY	HYDRA	HANCE	HENRI
GOBYS	GEEST	GLAZY	HYENA	HANSE	HINDI
GOERS	GEMOT	GLORY	HYPHA	HARTE	HOURI
GOLDS	GENET	GLUEY	******	HASTE	******
GOLFS	GHAUT	GNOMY	H---B	HAWSE	H---K
GONGS	GHENT	GODLY	******	HEAVE	******
GOODS	GHOST	GOLLY	HBOMB	HEDGE	HOICK
GOOFS	GIANT	GOODY	HOREB	HELLE	******
GOOKS	GIGOT	GOOEY	******	HELVE	H---L
GOONS	GLEET	GOOFY	H---C	HENCE	******
GORES	GLINT	GOOSY	******	HESSE	HAMAL
GOTHS	GLOAT	GORKY	HAVOC	HINGE	HAZEL
GOVYS	GLOST	GORSY	HELIC	HODGE	HEGEL
GOWNS	GRAFT	GOUTY	HEMIC	HOOKE	HEMAL
GRABS	GRANT	GRAPY	HUMIC	HOOVE	HEXYL
GRADS	GREAT	GRAVY	******	HORAE	HORAL
GRAMS	GREET	GRIMY	H---D	HORDE	HOTEL
GRASS	GRIPT	GULLY	******	HORNE	HOVEL
GRAYS	GRIST	GUMMY	HADED	HORSE	******
GREGS	GROAT	GUNNY	HALED	HOUSE	H---M
GREYS	GROUT	GUPPY	HALID	HOWIE	******
GRIDS	GRUNT	GUSHY	HARED	HOYLE	HAKIM
GRINS	GUEST	GUSTY	HATED	******	HAREM
GRIPS	GUILT	GUTSY	HAWED	H---G	HAULM
GRITS	******	GYPSY	HAYED	******	HBEAM
GROSS	G---X	******	HAZED	HYING	HILUM
GROTS	******	G---Z	HEARD	******	HIRAM
GROWS	GALAX	******	HEROD	******	HOKUM
GRUBS	******	GROSZ	HEWED	H---H	******
GUANS	G---Y	******	HEXAD	******	H---N
GUESS	******	******	HEXED	HARSH	******
GULES	GABBY	H---A	HIKED	HATCH	HAVEN
GULFS	GAILY	******	HIRED	HEATH	HAYDN
GULLS	GAMMY	HAIDA	HIVED	HEIGH	HELEN
GULPS	GAPPY	HAIFA	HOARD	HITCH	HEMAN
GURUS	GARRY	HALMA	HOLED	HOOCH	HEMEN
GUSTS	GASSY	HAMZA	HOMED	HOPEH	HEMIN
GWENS	GAUDY	HANNA	HONED	HOUGH	HERON
GWYNS	GAUZY	HEDDA	HOPED	HUMPH	HOGAN
GYRES	GAWKY	HEKLA	HOSED	HUNCH	HOKAN
GYROS	GAYLY	HELGA	HOUND	HUPEH	HONAN
GYRUS	GEMMY	HEMIA	HUMID	HUTCH	HUMAN
		HENNA	HYOID		

HUNAN	HADES	HIGHS	HYMNS	HENRY	INDIC
HURON	HAFTS	HIKES	HYPOS	HERBY	IODIC
HYMEN	HAHAS	HILLS	******	HETTY	IONIC
HYSON	HAIKS	HILTS	H---T	HILLY	ISAAC
******	HAILS	HINDS	******	HINNY	ISTIC
H---O	HAIRS	HINTS	HABIT	HIPPY	******
******	HAKES	HIRES	HADNT	HOAGY	I---D
HAGIO	HALES	HIVES	HASNT	HOARY	******
HALLO	HALLS	HOBBS	HAUNT	HOBBY	IDLED
HAPLO	HALOS	HOBOS	HEART	HOLEY	ILIAD
HECTO	HALTS	HOCKS	HEIST	HOLLY	IMBED
HEKTO	HAMES	HOCUS	HELOT	HOMEY	INKED
HELIO	HANDS	HOERS	HEMAT	HONEY	INNED
HELLO	HANGS	HOLDS	HEPAT	HONKY	IRKED
HIDTO	HANKS	HOLES	HERAT	HOOEY	ISLED
HIERO	HARDS	HOLMS	HOIST	HOOKY	IVIED
HIPPO	HARES	HOMES	HOLST	HORNY	******
HOMEO	HARKS	HONES	HORST	HORSY	I---E
HONDO	HARLS	HONGS	HURST	HOTLY	******
HYALO	HARMS	HONKS	******	HOWDY	IMAGE
HYDRO	HARPS	HOODS	H---U	HUBBY	IMBUE
HYETO	HARTS	HOOFS	******	HUFFY	IMIDE
HYGRO	HASPS	HOOKS	HAIKU	HULKY	IMINE
HYPNO	HATES	HOOPS	HINDU	HUMPY	INANE
HYPSO	HAULS	HOOTS	******	HUNKY	INDUE
******	HAWKS	HOPES	H---X	HURLY	INGLE
H---R	HAYES	HORAS	******	HURRY	INKLE
******	HAZES	HORNS	HELIX	HUSKY	INURE
HALER	HEADS	HORUS	HYRAX	HUSSY	IRATE
HAMER	HEALS	HOSES	******	******	IRENE
HARAR	HEAPS	HOSTS	H---Y	H---Z	IRONE
HATER	HEARS	HOURS	******	******	ISERE
HAVER	HEATS	HOWLS	HAIRY	HAFIZ	ISSUE
HAZER	HEEDS	HUFFS	HAMMY	HARTZ	ISTLE
HEWER	HEELS	HUGHS	HANDY	HEJAZ	IXTLE
HHOUR	HEFTS	HUGOS	HANKY	HERTZ	******
HIDER	HEIRS	HULAS	HAPLY	******	I---G
HIKER	HELLS	HULKS	HAPPY	I---A	******
HIRER	HELMS	HULLS	HARDY	******	ICING
HOMER	HELPS	HUMPS	HARPY	IBIZA	******
HONOR	HEMPS	HUMUS	HARRY	ILONA	I---H
HOVER	HERBS	HUNKS	HASTY	INDIA	******
HUGER	HERDS	HUNTS	HATTY	INDRA	IRISH
HUMOR	HERLS	HURDS	HEADY	INFRA	******
HYPER	HEXES	HURLS	HEAVY	INTRA	I---I
******	HICKS	HURTS	HEDGY	IONIA	******
H---S	HIDES	HUSKS	HEFTY	******	IAMBI
******	HIFIS	HYLAS	HEMPY	I---C	ICOSI
HABUS				******	
HACKS				ILEAC	
				ILIAC	

INDRI	******	IMPOT	JURUA	******	JANUS
IRAQI	**I---R**	INAPT	JUXTA	**J---M**	JAPES
ISSEI	******	INEPT	******	******	JARLS
******	ICHOR	INERT	**J---B**	JORAM	JATOS
I---L	ICIER	INGOT	******	JORUM	JEANS
******	IDLER	INLET	JACOB	******	JEEPS
IDEAL	INCUR	INPUT	JAKOB	**J---N**	JEERS
IDYLL	INFER	INSET	******	******	JEFES
ILEAL	INKER	ISLET	**J---D**	JAPAN	JEFFS
IMPEL	INNER	******	******	JASON	JEHUS
IODOL	INTER	**I---W**	JADED	JETON	JELLS
******	INVAR	******	JAPED	JOTUN	JERKS
I---M	ISTAR	INDOW	JARED	JUPON	JESTS
******	IYYAR	INLAW	JAWED	******	JESUS
IBEAM	******	******	JIBED	**J---O**	JIBES
IDIOM	**I---S**	**I---X**	JIHAD	******	JIFFS
IHRAM	******	******	JIVED	JELLO	JILLS
ILEUM	IAMBS	IMMIX	JOKED	JINGO	JILTS
ILIUM	IASIS	INDEX	JOYED	JOCKO	JINKS
INARM	ICONS	INFIX	******	JUDEO	JOANS
ISLAM	ICTUS	******	**J---E**	JULIO	JOELS
******	IDEAS	**I---Y**	******	JUMBO	JOEYS
I---N	IDLES	******	JAMIE	JUNCO	JOHNS
******	IDOLS	IATRY	JAYNE	JUNTO	JOINS
IBSEN	IDYLS	ICILY	JESSE	******	JOKES
ICIAN	IKONS	IMPLY	JORGE	**J---P**	JOLES
ILIAN	ILEUS	INLAY	JOSIE	******	JOLTS
ILION	ILLUS	IRONY	JOSUE	JALAP	JONAS
ILMEN	IMAMS	ISLAY	JOULE	JULEP	JONES
INCAN	IMIDS	ITALY	JOYCE	******	JOWLS
INION	INCAS	ITCHY	JUDGE	**J---R**	JUANS
INURN	INCUS	IVORY	JUICE	******	JUBAS
IRVIN	INDUS	******	JULIE	JOKER	JUBES
IRWIN	IOTAS	**I---Z**	******	JUROR	JUDAS
ITION	IRMAS	******	**J---H**	******	JUDES
IXION	IRONS	IGNAZ	******	**J---S**	JUDYS
******	ISBAS	******	JONAH	******	JUJUS
I---O	ISLES	**J---A**	JUDAH	JACKS	JULES
******	ITALS	******	******	JADES	JULYS
IATRO	ITEMS	JAFFA	**J---I**	JAGGS	JUMPS
ICONO	IVANS	JAINA	******	JAILS	JUNES
IDAHO	IVIES	JIDDA	JINNI	JAINS	JUNKS
IGLOO	IXIAS	JOSUA	******	JAKES	JUSTS
IMAGO	IZZYS	JUANA	**J---L**	JAMBS	JUTES
IMIDO	******	JUDEA	******	JAMES	******
IMINO	**I---T**	JULIA	JEWEL	JANES	**J---T**
INIGO	******	JUMNA	JUGAL	JANIS	JABOT
INTRO	IDEST	JUNTA	JURAL	JANOS	JANET
IRIDO	IDIOT		JUREL		

JAUNT	KRONA	KHADI	******	KIRKS	KERRY
JOINT	KUFRA	KHAKI	K---P	KITES	KIDDY
JOIST	******	KIBEI	******	KIVAS	KILTY
JOUST	K---B	KRUBI	KNOSP	KIWIS	KINKY
JURAT		KUKRI	KRUPP	KNARS	KITTY
******	KABOB	******	******	KNEES	KOOKY
J---Y	******	K---K	K---R	KNITS	******
******	K---C	******	******	KNOBS	L---A
JACKY	******	KAMIK	KAFIR	KNOPS	******
JAGGY	KOPEC	KAPOK	KHMER	KNOTS	LABIA
JAMMY	******	KAYAK	KNURR	KNOWS	LABRA
JASSY	K---D	KIOSK	******	KNURS	LAIKA
JAZZY	******	KNACK	K---S	KOELS	LAMIA
JELLY	KEYED	KNOCK	******	KOLAS	LARVA
JEMMY	KHOND	KODAK	KADIS	KOMOS	LASSA
JENNY	KITED	KOPEK	KAGUS	KOOKS	LAURA
JERKY	KNEAD	KULAK	KAKAS	KOTOS	LEHUA
JERRY	KNEED	KURSK	KAKIS	KUDOS	LEILA
JESSY	******	******	KAMES	KUDUS	LEMMA
JETTY	K---E	K---L	KAPHS	KUMIS	LEONA
JEWRY	******	******	KARLS	KURUS	LEORA
JIFFY	KATIE	KABUL	KATES	KVASS	LEPTA
JIMMY	KEDGE	KAROL	KAVAS	KYATS	LHASA
JINNY	KEEVE	KEVEL	KAYOS	******	LIANA
JOLLY	KNAVE	KNEEL	KEATS	K---T	LIBRA
JOLTY	KNIFE	KNELL	KECKS	******	LIBYA
JONNY	KOINE	KNOLL	KEEFS	KALAT	LINDA
JUICY	KOPJE	KNURL	KEELS	KAMET	LINGA
JUMPY	KRONE	KRAAL	KEENS	KAPUT	LIVIA
JUNKY	KYRIE	******	KEEPS	KARAT	LLAMA
******	******	K---N	KELPS	KERAT	LOGIA
J---Z	K---F	******	KENTS	KNELT	LORCA
******	******	KAREN	KEPIS	KNOUT	LORNA
JABEZ	KLOOF	KAZAN	KERBS	KRAFT	LOTTA
JEREZ	******	KEVIN	KERES	KRAIT	LUCCA
******	K---H	KININ	KERFS	KRAUT	LUCIA
K---A	******	KIRIN	KERNS	******	LUISA
******	KEDAH	KNOWN	KHANS	K---X	LYCEA
KAABA	KEITH	KORAN	KIBES	******	LYDDA
KAFKA	KENCH	KORUN	KICKS	KYLIX	LYDIA
KAPPA	KERCH	KUBAN	KIERS	******	LYSSA
KARMA	KETCH	******	KILLS	K---Y	LYTTA
KENYA	KILAH	K---O	KILNS	******	******
KIOWA	******	******	KILOS	KANDY	L---C
KLARA	K---I	KAROO	KILTS	KATHY	******
KOALA	******	KARYO	KINDS	KAURY	LILAC
KONYA	KAUAI	KAZOO	KINGS	KELLY	LOGIC
KOREA	KAURI	KELSO	KINKS	KENNY	LYRIC
		KYOTO			LYTIC

******	LISLE	LIPPI	******	LOSER	LENAS
L---D	LITHE	LITAI	**L---O**	LOVER	LENDS
******	LITRE	LONGI	******	LOWER	LENES
LACED	LIVRE	LUIGI	LABIO	LUGER	LENIS
LADED	LOCKE	LUNGI	LACTO	LURER	LENOS
LAIRD	LODGE	******	LARGO	LUXOR	LENTS
LAKED	LOGUE	**L---L**	LASSO	******	LEONS
LAMED	LOIRE	******	LATRO	**L---S**	LEPUS
LAVED	LOOSE	LABEL	LENTO	******	LETTS
LAWED	LOTTE	LAPEL	LEPTO	LACES	LEUDS
LAZED	LOUPE	LEGAL	LEUCO	LACKS	LEVIS
LEPID	LOUSE	LEVEL	LEUKO	LADES	LEWES
LIKED	LUCRE	LIBEL	LIGNO	LAGOS	LEWIS
LIMED	LUISE	LOCAL	LIMBO	LAIRS	LIARS
LINED	LUNGE	LOYAL	LINGO	LAKES	LICKS
LIPID	LYCEE	LYSOL	LITHO	LALLS	LIENS
LIVED	******	******	LLANO	LAMAS	LIFTS
LIVID	**L---G**	**L---M**	LOTTO	LAMBS	LIKES
LLOYD	******	******	******	LAMES	LILAS
LOBED	LAOAG	LOCUM	**L---P**	LAMPS	LILTS
LOOED	LIANG	******	******	LANDS	LILYS
LOPED	LYING	**L---N**	LETUP	LANES	LIMBS
LOVED	******	******	******	LAPIS	LIMES
LOWED	**L---H**	LADEN	**L---R**	LAPPS	LIMNS
LUCID	******	LADIN	******	LARDS	LIMPS
LURED	LARCH	LAGAN	LABOR	LARES	LINES
LURID	LATCH	LAPIN	LAGER	LARKS	LINGS
LUTED	LAUGH	LATIN	LAKER	LASTS	LINKS
LYSED	LEACH	LEARN	LAMER	LATHS	LINUS
******	LEASH	LEMON	LAPAR	LAUDS	LIONS
L---E	LEECH	LENIN	LASER	LAVAS	LIRAS
******	LEIGH	LEVEN	LATER	LAVES	LISAS
LADLE	LEITH	LIEIN	LAVER	LAWNS	LISPS
LAINE	LOACH	LIGAN	LAXER	LAZES	LISTS
LANCE	LOATH	LIKEN	LAYER	LEADS	LITAS
LAPSE	LOTAH	LIMEN	LAZAR	LEAFS	LIVES
LARGE	LOUGH	LINEN	LEGER	LEAKS	LIZAS
LATHE	LUNCH	LININ	LEMUR	LEANS	LOADS
LEASE	LURCH	LIVEN	LEPER	LEAPS	LOAFS
LEAVE	LYMPH	LODEN	LEVER	LEEDS	LOAMS
LEDGE	LYNCH	LOGAN	LIBER	LEEKS	LOANS
LETHE	******	LORAN	LIFER	LEERS	LOBES
LEVEE	**L---I**	LUMEN	LINER	LEETS	LOBOS
LEWIE	******	LUPIN	LITER	LEFTS	LOCHS
LEYTE	LANAI	LUTON	LIVER	LEGES	LOCKS
LIANE	LIGNI	LUZON	LOBAR	LEHRS	LOCOS
LIEGE	LILLI	LYMAN	LONER	LEIFS	LOCUS
LILLE	LIMBI	LYSIN	LOPER		LODES

LOESS	******	LILLY	MORTA	MAINE	MATCH
LOFTS	L---T	LIMEY	MURRA	MAIZE	MICAH
LOGES	******	LINEY	MUSCA	MAMIE	MILCH
LOGOS	LEANT	LINTY	MYOMA	MANGE	MIRTH
LOINS	LEAPT	LIPPY	MYRIA	MANSE	MITCH
LOLAS	LEAST	LIZZY	MYRNA	MAPLE	MONTH
LOLLS	LEGIT	LOAMY	******	MARGE	MOOCH
LONGS	LICHT	LOBBY	M---C	MARIE	MORPH
LOOFS	LICIT	LOFTY	******	MARNE	MOUCH
LOOKS	LIEUT	LOLLY	MADOC	MASSE	MOUTH
LOOMS	LIGHT	LOOBY	MAGIC	MATTE	MULCH
LOONS	LIMIT	LOONY	MALAC	MAUDE	MUNCH
LOOPS	LISZT	LOOPY	MALIC	MAUVE	MYRRH
LOOTS	LOPAT	LOPPY	MANIC	MAYBE	******
LOPES	LUNET	LORRY	MEDIC	MELEE	M---I
LORDS	******	LOTTY	MEDOC	MERGE	******
LORES	L---X	LOUSY	MELIC	MERLE	MAGNI
LORIS	******	LOWLY	MESIC	MEROE	MAHDI
LOSES	LATEX	LUCKY	MIMIC	MESNE	MAORI
LOTOS	LUXEX	LUMPY	MUSIC	METRE	MAQUI
LOTUS	******	LUSTY	******	MEUSE	MATRI
LOUIS	L---Y	******	M---D	MIDGE	MENAI
LOUPS	******	M---A	******	MILNE	MERCI
LOURS	LADDY	******	MACED	MINAE	MIAMI
LOUTS	LAITY	MAFIA	MANED	MINCE	MILLI
LOVES	LAKEY	MAGDA	MATED	MITRE	MINDI
LUAUS	LANKY	MAGMA	MAUND	MOIRE	MITZI
LUCES	LARDY	MALTA	MAZED	MONDE	MUFTI
LUCYS	LARKY	MAMBA	METED	MONTE	MULTI
LUFFS	LARRY	MAMMA	MEWED	MOORE	******
LULLS	LATHY	MANIA	MIMED	MOOSE	M---K
LULUS	LATRY	MANNA	MINED	MORAE	******
LUMPS	LAWNY	MANTA	MIRED	MORSE	MINSK
LUNES	LAXLY	MARIA	MIXED	MOUSE	MUJIK
LUNGS	LAYBY	MARLA	MONAD	MOVIE	MUZAK
LUNTS	LEADY	MARTA	MOOED	MOXIE	******
LUPUS	LEAFY	MAURA	MOPED	MURRE	M---L
LURES	LEAKY	MECCA	MOULD	MYOPE	******
LURKS	LEARY	MEDEA	MOUND	******	MABEL
LUSTS	LEAVY	MEDIA	MOVED	M---F	MEDAL
LUTES	LEERY	MENSA	MOWED	******	MEGAL
LYLES	LEFTY	MICRA	MUCID	MOTIF	METAL
LYNNS	LEGGY	MILIA	MUSED	******	METOL
LYONS	LENNY	MINNA	MUTED	M---G	MIAUL
LYRES	LEPSY	MIRZA	MYOID	******	MODAL
LYSES	LEROY	MOCHA	******	MAGOG	MODEL
LYSIS	LETTY	MOIRA	M---E	******	MOGUL
	LIBBY	MORNA	******	M---H	MOLAL
			MACLE	******	
			MADGE	MARCH	
				MARSH	

MORAL	MEZZO	MAGES	MIDAS	MOTES	******
MOREL	MICRO	MAGUS	MIENS	MOTHS	**M---X**
MOSEL	MIMEO	MAIDS	MIFFS	MOUES	******
MOTEL	MISDO	MAILS	MIKES	MOVES	MUREX
MURAL	MOLTO	MAIMS	MILES	MOXAS	******
******	MORRO	MAINS	MILKS	MUCKS	**M---Y**
M---M	MOSSO	MAKES	MILLS	MUCUS	******
******	MOTTO	MALES	MILTS	MUFFS	MACHY
MADAM	MUCRO	MALLS	MIMES	MULES	MADLY
MAXIM	MUNGO	MALTS	MIMIS	MULLS	MALAY
MINIM	MUNRO	MAMAS	MINAS	MUMMS	MALTY
******	MYELO	MANES	MINDS	MUMPS	MAMEY
M---N	MYTHO	MANUS	MINES	MUONS	MAMMY
******	******	MARCS	MINKS	MUSES	MANCY
MACON	**M---P**	MARES	MINOS	MUSKS	MANDY
MAHAN	******	MARIS	MINTS	MUSTS	MANGY
MASON	MIXUP	MARKS	MINUS	MUTES	MANLY
MATIN	******	MARLS	MIRES	MUTTS	MARLY
MAYAN	**M---R**	MARTS	MISES	MYLES	MARRY
MEGAN	******	MASKS	MISTS	MYNAS	MARTY
MELAN	MACER	MASTS	MITES	MYRAS	MASHY
MELON	MAJOR	MATES	MITTS	MYTHS	MASSY
MESON	MAKER	MATHS	MIXES	******	MATEY
MILAN	MALAR	MATTS	MLLES	**M---T**	MATTY
MIZEN	MANOR	MAUDS	MOANS	******	MCCOY
MORIN	MASER	MAULS	MOATS	MAGOT	MEALY
MORON	MATER	MAVIS	MOCKS	MANET	MEANY
MOSAN	MAYOR	MAYAS	MODES	MARAT	MEATY
MOURN	MAZER	MAZES	MODUS	MAYNT	MERCY
MUCIN	METER	MEADS	MOILS	MAYST	MERRY
MYRON	MILER	MEALS	MOKES	MEANT	MESHY
******	MIMER	MEANS	MOLDS	MERIT	MESSY
M---O	MIMIR	MEATS	MOLES	MIDST	METRY
******	MINER	MEETS	MOLLS	MIGHT	MICKY
MACAO	MINOR	MELDS	MOLTS	MOIST	MIDDY
MACRO	MISER	MELOS	MOMUS	MONET	MIFFY
MALMO	MITER	MELTS	MONAS	MORAT	MIKEY
MAMBO	MIXER	MEMOS	MONKS	MOTET	MILKY
MANGO	MOHUR	MENDS	MOODS	MOULT	MILLY
MARCO	MOLAR	MENES	MOONS	MOUNT	MILTY
MARGO	MOPER	MENUS	MOORS	MULCT	MINGY
MARIO	MOTOR	MEOWS	MOPES	MURAT	MISSY
MASTO	MOVER	MESAS	MORAS	******	MISTY
MATEO	MOWER	METAS	MORES	**M---U**	MITZY
MATZO	******	METES	MORNS	******	MOLDY
MEDIO	**M---S**	METIS	MOROS	MATSU	MOLLY
METHO	******	MEWLS	MORTS	******	MONEY
METRO	MACES	MICAS	MOSES	**M---W**	MONTY
	MACKS			******	
				MACAW	
				MIAOW	

MOODY
MOONY
MORAY
MORTY
MOSEY
MOSSY
MOTHY
MOUSY
MUCKY
MUDDY
MUGGY
MUHLY
MULEY
MUMMY
MURKY
MURRY
MUSHY
MUSKY
MUSSY
MUSTY
MUZZY
MYOPY
******
M---Z
******
MAINZ
******
N---A
******
NAHUA
NANNA
NORIA
NORMA
NUBIA
NUCHA
NYASA
******
N---B
******
NABOB
NADAB
NAWAB
NEGEB
******
N---D
******
NAIAD
NAKED

NAMED
NIDED
NIXED
NJORD
NOMAD
NOSED
NOTED
******
N---E
******
NACRE
NAIVE
NANCE
NAPPE
NERVE
NEUME
NICHE
NIECE
NIOBE
NITRE
NIXIE
NOBLE
NOISE
NONCE
NOOSE
NORSE
NOVAE
NUDGE
NURSE
******
N---H
******
NEATH
NEIGH
NINTH
NORAH
NORTH
NOTCH
NYMPH
******
N---I
******
NAOMI
NEURI
NIGRI
NIMBI
NISEI
NITRI

NOCTI
NYCTI
******
N---L
******
NASAL
NATAL
NAVAL
NAVEL
NEPAL
NEVIL
NEWEL
NIGEL
NIHIL
NIVAL
NOBEL
NODAL
NOPAL
NOVEL
******
N---M
******
NAHUM
NIZAM
******
N---N
******
NAIRN
NISAN
NITON
NIXON
NUMEN
NYLON
******
N---O
******
NARCO
NECRO
NEGRO
NEPHO
NEURO
NITRO
NYCTO
******
N---P
******
NAACP

******
N---R
******
******
NADER
NADIR
NAHOR
NAMER
NAMUR
NAVAR
NEPHR
NETER
NEVER
NEWER
NICER
NIGER
NITER
NIZER
NOPAR
NOTER
******
N---S
******
NAILS
NAMES
NANAS
NAPES
NARDS
NARES
NARIS
NATES
NAVES
NAZIS
NEALS
NEAPS
NEARS
NECKS
NEEDS
NEGUS
NEILS
NELLS
NEROS
NESTS
NEVIS
NEVUS
NEWTS
NEXUS
NICKS
NIDES

NIDUS
NIMES
NINAS
NINES
NINUS
NIPAS
NISUS
NIXES
NOAHS
NOCKS
NODES
NODUS
NOELS
NOGGS
NOMAS
NONAS
NONES
NOOKS
NOONS
NORAS
NORMS
NORNS
NOSES
NOTES
NOUNS
NOVAS
NOYES
NUDES
NUMBS
******
N---T
******
NEMAT
NIGHT
NONET
******
N---U
******
NAURU
NEHRU
******
N---V
******
NEGEV
******
N---Y
******
NANCY
NANNY

NAPPY
NARKY
NASTY
NATTY
NAVVY
NEDDY
NEEDY
NELLY
NERVY
NETTY
NEWLY
NEWSY
NICKY
NIFTY
NINNY
NIPPY
NITTY
NOBBY
NOBLY
NODDY
NOISY
NOSEY
NOWAY
NUBBY
NUTTY
******
O---A
******
OCALA
OCREA
OIDEA
OMAHA
OMASA
OMEGA
ONEGA
OPERA
OPSIA
ORIYA
OSAKA
OSTIA
OUIDA
OUIJA
******
O---C
******
OGMIC
OHMIC
OLEIC

OPTIC	******	OLEIN	OUTER	OLENT	PILEA
OSMIC	**O---H**	ONION	OWNER	ONSET	PINNA
******	******	ORCIN	******	ORBIT	PINTA
O---D	OBEAH	ORGAN	**O---S**	OUGHT	PIZZA
******	OKIEH	ORION	******	OVERT	PLATA
OARED	OOMPH	ORLON	OASES	OWLET	PLAYA
OCTAD	ORACH	ORPIN	OASIS	******	PLAZA
OGLED	******	ORSON	OATES	**O---U**	PLENA
OILED	**O---I**	OSCAN	OATHS	******	PLICA
OOZED	******	OSMAN	OAVES	OTARU	PODIA
OPTED	OBELI	******	OBEYS	******	POLKA
ORBED	OBOLI	**O---O**	OBITS	**O---W**	POONA
OREAD	OKAPI	******	OBOES	******	PRESA
OSTED	ORCHI	OCULO	ODETS	OXBOW	PRIMA
OUTED	ORIBI	OLIGO	ODORS	******	PUCKA
OVOID	OTOMI	OMBRO	OGEES	**O---Y**	PUKKA
OWNED	OVOLI	ONIRO	OGLES	******	PUNKA
******	******	OPHIO	OGRES	OCHRY	PYDNA
O---E	**O---K**	ORTHO	OKAYS	ODDLY	******
******	******	OTERO	OKIES	OLOGY	**P---B**
OBESE	OZARK	OUTDO	OKRAS	ONERY	******
OBOLE	******	OUTGO	OLAFS	ORCZY	PHLEB
OCHRE	**O---L**	OVOLO	OLAVS	OSITY	PLUMB
ODYLE	******	******	OLGAS	OURAY	******
OGIVE	OCTYL	**O---P**	OLIOS	OVARY	**P---C**
OLIVE	OFFAL	******	OLLAS	******	******
OLLIE	ORIEL	ORLOP	OMENS	**P---A**	PANIC
OMBRE	OUSEL	OXLIP	OMERS	******	PUBIC
OPINE	OUZEL	******	OMITS	PADUA	PUDIC
ORATE	******	**O---R**	OOZES	PAISA	PUNIC
OSAGE	**O---M**	******	OPAHS	PALEA	******
OUNCE	******	OCCUR	OPALS	PALMA	**P---D**
OUTRE	OAKUM	OCHER	OPENS	PANDA	******
OVATE	ODEUM	ODDER	OPSIS	PAPUA	PACED
OVINE	ODIUM	ODOUR	ORALS	PARCA	PAGED
OVULE	OGHAM	OFFER	ORCUS	PARKA	PALED
OXEYE	OPIUM	OGLER	ORLES	PARMA	PANED
OXIDE	******	OILER	ORNIS	PASHA	PARED
OXIME	**O---N**	OLDER	ORRIS	PASTA	PAVED
OZONE	******	OMBER	OTTOS	PATNA	PAWED
OZZIE	OAKEN	ONEIR	OUSTS	PAULA	PAYED
******	OATEN	ORDER	OVALS	PELLA	PIAND
O---G	OCEAN	ORMER	OVENS	PENNA	PIKED
******	ODEON	OSCAR	OWENS	PENTA	PILED
OKING	OFTEN	OSIER	OYERS	PEPLA	PINED
ORANG	OGDEN	OSLER	******	PHILA	PIPED
OWING	OLDEN	OTHER	**O---T**	PHYLA	PLAID
	OLEAN	OTTER	OCTET	PIETA	PLEAD
			ODONT		

PLIED	PIAVE	PATCH	PAROL	PUTON	POLYP
PLOID	PIECE	PEACH	PEARL	PYLON	PRIMP
POIND	PIQUE	PERCH	PEDAL	PYRAN	PUTUP
POKED	PIXIE	PERTH	PENAL	******	******
POLED	PLACE	PINCH	PERIL	**P---O**	**P---R**
PORED	PLANE	PITCH	PETAL	******	******
POSED	PLATE	PLASH	PHIAL	PABLO	PACER
POUND	PLEBE	PLUSH	PHYLL	PAEDO	PAGER
PRIED	PLUME	POACH	PICAL	PALEO	PALER
PROUD	POISE	POOCH	PICUL	PANTO	PAPER
PSEUD	PONCE	PORCH	PINEL	PAOLO	PARER
PUKED	POOLE	POUCH	PIPAL	PARGO	PATER
PULED	PORGE	PSYCH	PROWL	PATHO	PAVER
PYOID	POSSE	PUNCH	PUPIL	PATIO	PAWER
PYXED	PRASE	******	******	PAULO	PAYER
******	PRATE	**P---I**	**P---M**	PEDRO	PAYER
P---E	PRICE	******	******	PENGO	PETER
******	PRIDE	PALMI	PLASM	PETRO	PIKER
PADRE	PRIME	PALPI	PNEUM	PETTO	PILAR
PAINE	PRISE	PAPPI	PRIAM	PHAGO	PINER
PAISE	PRIZE	PARSI	PRISM	PHENO	PIPER
PALAE	PROBE	PATRI	PROEM	PHILO	PLIER
PANNE	PROLE	PATTI	PSALM	PHONO	POKER
PARSE	PRONE	PELVI	PURIM	PHOTO	POLAR
PASSE	PROSE	PENNI	******	PHYCO	POSER
PASTE	PROVE	PETTI	**P---N**	PHYLO	POWER
PAUSE	PRUDE	PHYSI	******	PHYTO	PRIER
PAYEE	PRUNE	PILEI	PAEAN	PIANO	PRIOR
PEACE	PULSE	PINNI	PAEON	PICRO	PRYER
PEASE	PUPAE	PISCI	PAGAN	PIEZO	PULER
PEEVE	PUREE	PLAGI	PAPEN	PINGO	PURER
PEKOE	PURGE	PLANI	PAREN	PINTO	******
PELEE	PURSE	PLURI	PATEN	PLANO	**P---S**
PENCE	PYXIE	PLUVI	PAVAN	PLATO	******
PERLE	******	PRIMI	PECAN	PLUTO	PACAS
PERSE	**P---F**	******	PEKAN	POLIO	PACES
PEWEE	******	**P---K**	PEKIN	POOPO	PACKS
PHAGE	PILAF	******	PELON	PORNO	PACTS
PHANE	PROOF	PLACK	PEPIN	POTTO	PAGES
PHASE	******	PLANK	PERON	PRIMO	PAILS
PHEBE	**P---G**	PLONK	PHREN	PROTO	PAINS
PHILE	******	PLUCK	PIMAN	PROVO	PAIRS
PHOBE	PELEG	PLUNK	PINON	PTERO	PALES
PHONE	PRANG	PRANK	PITON	PULMO	PALLS
PHORE	PRONG	PRICK	PLAIN	PUNTO	PALMS
PHYLE	******	PRINK	PRAWN	PYELO	PANES
PHYRE	**P---H**	******	PREEN	******	PANGS
PHYTE	******	**P---L**	PUSAN	**P---P**	PANTS
	PARCH	******		******	
	PASCH	PANEL	PLAIN	PINUP	
		PAPAL		PLUMP	PAPAS

PHYTE · PARCH · PASCH · PANEL · PAPAL · PUSAN · PLUMP · PAPAS

PARAS	PIERS	POSTS	PIPET	PARTY	PORGY
PARDS	PIKAS	POUFS	PIPIT	PASSY	PORKY
PARES	PIKES	POURS	PITOT	PASTY	POTSY
PARIS	PILES	POUTS	PIVOT	PATHY	POTTY
PARKS	PILIS	POWYS	PLAIT	PATSY	PREXY
PAROS	PILLS	PRAMS	PLANT	PATTY	PRIVY
PARRS	PIMAS	PRAYS	PLAST	PAWKY	PROSY
PARTS	PIMPS	PRESS	PLEAT	PEAKY	PROXY
PASTS	PINAS	PREYS	POINT	PEARY	PUDGY
PATES	PINES	PRIES	POSIT	PEATY	PUDSY
PATHS	PINGS	PRIGS	POULT	PEAVY	PUFFY
PAULS	PINKS	PRIMS	PREST	PEGGY	PULPY
PAVES	PINTS	PROAS	PRINT	PELLY	PUNKY
PAVIS	PIONS	PRODS	PROCT	PENNY	PUNTY
PAWLS	PIOUS	PROFS	PUGET	PEONY	PUPPY
PAWNS	PIPES	PROMS	******	PEPPY	PURSY
PEAKS	PITAS	PROPS	P---U	PERCY	PUSHY
PEALS	PITHS	PROWS	******	PERKY	PUSSY
PEANS	PLANS	PSOAS	PAREU	PERRY	PUTTY
PEARS	PLATS	PUBES	PERDU	PESKY	PYGMY
PEATS	PLAYS	PUBIS	POILU	PETRY	******
PECKS	PLEAS	PUCES	POYOU	PETTY	Q---A
PECOS	PLEBS	PUCKS	PRAHU	PHAGY	******
PEDES	PLIES	PUFFS	******	PHANY	QUOTA
PEEKS	PLODS	PUKES	P---W	PHASY	******
PEELS	PLOPS	PULES	******	PHILY	Q---E
PEENS	PLOTS	PULLS	PAPAW	PHONY	******
PEEPS	PLOWS	PULPS	PSHAW	PIETY	QUAKE
PEERS	PLOYS	PUMAS	******	PIGGY	QUEUE
PELFS	PLUGS	PUMPS	P---X	PIGMY	QUIRE
PELTS	PLUMS	PUNAS	******	PINEY	QUITE
PENDS	POCKS	PUNGS	PHLOX	PINKY	QUOTE
PENIS	POEMS	PUNKS	PYREX	PINNY	******
PEONS	POETS	PUNTS	******	PITHY	Q---F
PEPOS	POKES	PURLS	P---Y	PLASY	******
PEPYS	POLES	PURRS	******	PLATY	QUAFF
PERES	POLLS	PUTTS	PACHY	PLEGY	QUIFF
PERIS	POMES	PYRES	PADDY	PLINY	******
PERKS	PONDS	PYXES	PALEY	PLUMY	Q---H
PESOS	PONES	PYXIS	PALLY	POCKY	******
PESTS	POODS	******	PALMY	PODGY	QUASH
PETES	POOLS	P---T	PALSY	POESY	QUOTH
PHILS	POONS	******	PANAY	POGEY	******
PHIPS	POOPS	PAINT	PANDY	POKEY	Q---I
PHOTS	POPES	PETIT	PANSY	POLLY	******
PICAS	PORES	PEWIT	PANTY	POMMY	QUASI
PICKS	PORTS	PICOT	PAPPY	POPPY	******
PICTS	POSES	PILOT	PARRY	POPSY	Q---K
					******
					QUACK
					QUARK

QUICK	QUIRT	RAYED	RUBLE	ROWEL	RECTO
QUIRK	QUOIT	RAZED	RUCHE	ROYAL	RETRO
******	******	REBID	RUGAE	RURAL	RHINO
Q---L	**Q---U**	REDID	RUPEE	******	RHIZO
******	******	RICED	******	**R---M**	RODEO
QUAIL	QUIPU	RIGID	**R---G**	******	ROLLO
QUELL	******	RILED	******	REALM	ROMEO
QUILL	**Q---Y**	RIMED	RUING	REARM	RONDO
******	QUAKY	RIVED	******	RETEM	RUSSO
Q---M	QUERY	ROALD	**R---H**	RHEUM	******
******	******	ROBED	******	******	**R---P**
QUALM	******	ROPED	RAJAH	**R---N**	******
******	**R---A**	ROSED	RALPH	******	RECAP
Q---N	******	ROUND	RANCH	RADON	******
******	RECTA	ROVED	RATCH	RAVEN	**R---R**
QUEAN	REGMA	ROWED	RAYAH	RAYON	******
QUEEN	RETIA	RULED	REACH	REDAN	RACER
QUERN	RETTA	******	REICH	REGAN	RADAR
QUOIN	RHODA	**R---E**	RETCH	REGIN	RAKER
******	RHOEA	******	ROACH	REIGN	RARER
Q---O	RIATA	RAGEE	ROLPH	REMAN	RATER
******	ROTLA	RAISE	ROTCH	RENAN	RAVER
QUITO	RRHEA	RAKEE	ROUGH	RENIN	RAWER
******	RUMBA	RAMIE	******	RERAN	RAZOR
Q---R	******	RANCE	**R---I**	RERUN	RECUR
******	**R---B**	RANEE	******	RESIN	REFER
QATAR	******	RANGE	RABBI	REZIN	RICER
QUEER	RAJAB	RAPHE	RADII	RICIN	RIDER
******	RHOMB	RAZEE	RECTI	RIPEN	RIGOR
Q---S	RHUMB	REEVE	******	RIPON	RIMER
******	******	RENEE	**R---K**	RISEN	RIPER
QUADS	**R---C**	RENTE	******	RIVEN	RISER
QUAGS	******	REVUE	RURIK	ROBIN	RIVER
QUASS	RABIC	RHAGE	******	RODIN	ROGER
QUAYS	REBEC	RHINE	**R---L**	ROMAN	ROTOR
QUIDS	RELIC	RHONE	******	ROSIN	ROVER
QUIPS	RUNIC	RHYME	RAOUL	ROUEN	ROWER
QUITS	******	RIDGE	RATAL	ROVEN	RUDER
QUODS	**R---D**	RIFLE	RATEL	ROWAN	RULER
******	******	RILLE	RAVEL	ROWEN	RUMOR
Q---T	RABID	RINSE	REBEL	RUMEN	******
******	RACED	ROBLE	REGAL	RUNIN	**R---S**
QUANT	RAGED	ROGUE	RENAL	RUNON	******
QUART	RAKED	ROLFE	REPEL	******	RACES
QUEST	RAPED	ROQUE	REVEL	**R---O**	RACKS
QUIET	RAPID	ROUGE	RIGEL	******	RAFTS
QUILT	RATED	ROUSE	RIVAL	RADIO	RAGES
QUINT	RAVED	ROUTE	RIYAL	RATIO	RAIDS

RAILS	RISES	******	RETRY	SERRA	SAPID
RAINS	RISKS	**R---T**	RHAGY	SHEBA	SATED
RAKES	RISUS	******	RICKY	SIENA	SAVED
RALES	RITAS	RABAT	RIDGY	SIGMA	SAWED
RAMPS	RITES	REACT	RILEY	SILVA	SAYID
RAMUS	RIVES	REBUT	RISKY	SITKA	SCALD
RANDS	ROADS	REFIT	RITZY	SOFIA	SCAND
RANIS	ROAMS	REMIT	ROCKY	SOFTA	SCEND
RANKS	ROANS	RESET	RODDY	SOLFA	SCOLD
RANTS	ROARS	REVET	ROILY	SONIA	SCROD
RAPES	ROBES	RIANT	RONNY	SONJA	SERED
RASPS	ROCKS	RIGHT	ROOKY	SONYA	SEWED
RATES	ROILS	RIVET	ROOMY	SOUSA	SEXED
RAVES	ROLES	ROAST	ROOTY	SPICA	SHARD
RAZES	ROLFS	ROBOT	ROPEY	STOMA	SHERD
READS	ROLLS	ROOST	ROUPY	STRIA	SHIED
REALS	ROMPS	ROUST	ROWDY	STUKA	SHRED
REAMS	ROODS	******	RUDDY	STUPA	SIDED
REAPS	ROOFS	**R---W**	RUGBY	SULFA	SIRED
REARS	ROOKS	******	RUMLY	SUNNA	SITED
REBUS	ROOMS	RENEW	RUMMY	SUPRA	SIZED
REEDS	ROOTS	******	RUNNY	SUTRA	SKALD
REEFS	ROPES	**R---X**	RUNTY	SYLVA	SKEED
REEKS	ROSAS	******	RUSHY	SYRIA	SKIED
REELS	ROSES	RADIX	RUSTY	******	SLOYD
REGES	ROTAS	RELAX	RUTTY	**S---B**	SLUED
REIMS	ROUES	REMEX	******	******	SNEAD
REINS	ROUTS	******	**S---A**	SAHEB	SNOOD
REMUS	ROVES	**R---Y**	******	SAHIB	SOLED
RENDS	RUBES	******	SABRA	SCRUB	SOLID
RENES	RUBYS	RAGGY	SACRA	SHRUB	SOUND
RENTS	RUCKS	RAINY	SAIGA	SQUAB	SOWED
RESTS	RUDDS	RALLY	SALMA	SQUIB	SPEED
RHEAS	RUDYS	RAMMY	SALPA	******	SPEND
RIALS	RUERS	RANDY	SALSA	**S---C**	SPIED
RICES	RUFFS	RANGY	SAMBA	******	SQUAD
RICKS	RUFUS	RASPY	SAMOA	SALIC	SQUID
RIDES	RUINS	RATTY	SANTA	SERAC	STAID
RIFFS	RULES	RAWLY	SAUNA	SILIC	STAND
RIFTS	RUMPS	READY	SCAPA	SONIC	STEAD
RIGGS	RUNES	REDLY	SCENA	STOIC	STEED
RILES	RUNGS	REEDY	SCHWA	SUFIC	STIED
RILLS	RUNTS	REEFY	SCUBA	SUMAC	STOOD
RIMES	RUSES	REEKY	SCUTA	******	STRAD
RINDS	RUSKS	REIFY	SELMA	**S---D**	SWARD
RINGS	RUSTS	RELAY	SENNA	******	SWORD
RINKS	RUTHS	REPAY	SEPIA	SABED	SYNOD
RIOTS	RYNDS	REPLY	SEPTA	SALAD	

******	SIEVE	STALE	STAFF	******	SNOOK
S---E	SIGNE	STARE	STIFF	S---I	SPANK
******	SINCE	STATE	STUFF	******	SPARK
SABLE	SINGE	STAVE	******	SALMI	SPEAK
SABRE	SIXTE	STELE	S---G	SCAPI	SPECK
SADIE	SKATE	STERE	******	SCIFI	SPOOK
SALSE	SKIVE	STEVE	SCRAG	SCUDI	SPUNK
SALVE	SLAKE	STILE	SHRUG	SEGNI	STACK
SAONE	SLATE	STIPE	SLANG	SEPTI	STALK
SARRE	SLAVE	STOAE	SLING	SERAI	STANK
SATIE	SLICE	STOKE	SLUNG	SHARI	STARK
SAUCE	SLIDE	STOLE	SPANG	SHOJI	STEAK
SAUTE	SLIME	STOME	SPRAG	SINAI	STICK
SCALE	SLOPE	STONE	SPRIG	SOLDI	STINK
SCAPE	SLYPE	STOPE	STING	SOMNI	STIRK
SCARE	SMAZE	STORE	STUNG	SPAHI	STOCK
SCENE	SMILE	STOVE	SUING	SPINI	STOOK
SCONE	SMITE	STOWE	SWING	STYLI	STORK
SCOPE	SMOKE	STUPE	SWUNG	SULCI	STUCK
SCORE	SMOTE	STYLE	******	SUNNI	STUNK
SCREE	SNAKE	SUAVE	S---H	SWAMI	SWANK
SCUTE	SNARE	SUCRE	******	******	******
SEDGE	SNIDE	SUEDE	SABAH	S---K	S---L
SEINE	SNIPE	SUITE	SARAH	******	******
SEISE	SNORE	SURGE	SCYPH	SAMEK	SALOL
SEIZE	SOCLE	SUSIE	SELAH	SHACK	SCALL
SENNE	SOLVE	SWAGE	SHIAH	SHANK	SCOWL
SENSE	SOMME	SWALE	SHUSH	SHARK	SCULL
SERGE	SOUSE	SWEDE	SIXTH	SHEIK	SEOUL
SERVE	SPACE	SWINE	SLASH	SHIRK	SEPAL
SETAE	SPADE	SWIPE	SLOSH	SHOCK	SERAL
SHADE	SPAKE	SWORE	SLOTH	SHOOK	SHALL
SHAKE	SPARE	SYCEE	SLUSH	SHUCK	SHAWL
SHALE	SPATE	SYNGE	SMASH	SKINK	SHELL
SHAME	SPICE	******	SMITH	SKULK	SHEOL
SHAPE	SPIKE	S---F	SNATH	SKUNK	SHILL
SHARE	SPILE	******	SOOTH	SLACK	SHOAL
SHAVE	SPINE	SCARF	SOUGH	SLEEK	SHORL
SHINE	SPIRE	SCOFF	SOUTH	SLICK	SIBYL
SHIRE	SPITE	SCUFF	STAPH	SLINK	SIGIL
SHIVE	SPODE	SCURF	STASH	SLUNK	SISAL
SHONE	SPOKE	SERIF	STETH	SMACK	SKILL
SHORE	SPORE	SHEAF	STICH	SMIRK	SKIRL
SHOTE	SPREE	SHELF	SUBAH	SMOCK	SKOAL
SHOVE	SPRUE	SKIFF	SURAH	SNACK	SKULL
SHUTE	SPUME	SNIFF	SWASH	SNARK	SMALL
SIDLE	STAGE	SNUFF	SWATH	SNEAK	SMELL
SIEGE	STAKE	SPOOF	SYLPH	SNICK	SNAIL

SNARL	SARAN	******	SCULP	SHIER	SAMOS
SNELL	SASIN	S---O	SETUP	SHIRR	SANDS
SOREL	SATAN	******	SHARP	SHOER	SARAS
SOTOL	SATIN	SACRO	SHEEP	SHYER	SARIS
SPALL	SAVIN	SALVO	SIRUP	SIDER	SARKS
SPELL	SAXON	SAMBO	SKIMP	SIEUR	SAROS
SPIEL	SCION	SAPRO	SLEEP	SIMAR	SATES
SPILL	SCORN	SARCO	SLOOP	SITAR	SAULS
SPOIL	SEDAN	SARTO	SLUMP	SIZAR	SAVES
SPOOL	SELEN	SAURO	SLURP	SKIER	SAXES
STALL	SEMEN	SAYSO	SNOOP	SKIRR	SCABS
STEAL	SERIN	SCATO	STAMP	SLIER	SCADS
STEEL	SERON	SCHMO	STEEP	SLYER	SCANS
STILL	SETON	SCOTO	STIRP	SMEAR	SCARS
STOOL	SEVEN	SCUDO	STOMP	SNEER	SCATS
STULL	SHAUN	SEATO	STOOP	SOBER	SCOPS
SURAL	SHAWN	SECCO	STOUP	SOLAR	SCOTS
SWAIL	SHEEN	SEGNO	STRAP	SONAR	SCOWS
SWELL	SHEWN	SEPTO	STRIP	SOPOR	SCUDS
SWILL	SHORN	SERVO	STROP	SORER	SCUMS
SWIRL	SHOWN	SETTO	STUMP	SOWAR	SCUPS
SYBIL	SIDON	SEXTO	SUNUP	SOWER	SCUTS
******	SIMON	SHAKO	SWAMP	SPEAR	SEALS
S---M	SINON	SIALO	SWEEP	SPIER	SEAMS
******	SIREN	SKIMO	SWOOP	SPOOR	SEANS
SAGUM	SITIN	SLAVO	SYRUP	STAIR	SEARS
SALEM	SIVAN	SLIGO	******	STEER	SEATS
SCRAM	SKEAN	SOCIO	S---R	STOUR	SECTS
SCRIM	SKEIN	SOLDO	******	SUDOR	SEEDS
SCRUM	SLAIN	SORGO	SABER	SUGAR	SEEKS
SEBUM	SOLAN	SOTTO	SAFER	SUMER	SEEMS
SEDUM	SOLON	SPIRO	SAGER	SUPER	SEEPS
SEISM	SOZIN	SPORO	SAKER	SURER	SEERS
SERUM	SPAIN	STATO	SAMAR	SWEAR	SEGOS
SHAWM	SPAWN	STENO	SANER	******	SELLS
SODOM	SPHEN	STYLO	SAPOR	S---S	SENDS
SPASM	SPLEN	SULFO	SATYR	******	SEPTS
SPERM	SPOON	******	SAVER	SABES	SERBS
STEAM	SPURN	S---P	SAVOR	SACKS	SERES
STORM	STAIN	******	SAWER	SAFES	SERFS
STRUM	STEEN	SALEP	SAYER	SAGAS	SETHS
SWARM	STEIN	SCALP	SCOUR	SAGES	SEXES
******	STERN	SCAMP	SEDER	SAGOS	SHAGS
S---N	SUDAN	SCARP	SENOR	SAILS	SHAHS
******	SUSAN	SCAUP	SEVER	SAKES	SHAMS
SABIN	SWAIN	SCOOP	SEWER	SALES	SHANS
SAGAN	SWOON	SCRAP	SHEAR	SALTS	SHAWS
SALON	SWORN	SCRIP	SHEER	SALUS	SHAYS

SHEAS	SKUAS	SOLOS	SUITS	SLEAT	SHREW
SHEDS	SLABS	SOLUS	SULKS	SLEET	SINEW
SHEWS	SLAGS	SONES	SULUS	SLEPT	SQUAW
SHIMS	SLAMS	SONGS	SUMPS	SLIPT	STRAW
SHINS	SLAPS	SOOTS	SUNNS	SMALT	STREW
SHIPS	SLATS	SORAS	SUPES	SMART	******
SHIVS	SLAVS	SORBS	SURAS	SMELT	
SHOES	SLAWS	SORES	SURDS	SMOLT	**S---X**
SHOOS	SLAYS	SORTS	SURFS	SNOOT	******
SHOPS	SLEDS	SORUS	SUZYS	SNORT	SALIX
SHOTS	SLEWS	SOULS	SWABS	SNOUT	SILEX
SHOWS	SLIMS	SOUPS	SWAGS	SOMAT	SIOUX
SHULS	SLIPS	SOURS	SWANS	SPAIT	******
SHUNS	SLITS	SOYAS	SWAPS	SPELT	**S---Y**
SHUTS	SLOBS	SPANS	SWATS	SPENT	******
SICES	SLOES	SPARS	SWAYS	SPILT	SADLY
SICKS	SLOGS	SPATS	SWIGS	SPIRT	SALLY
SIDES	SLOPS	SPAYS	SWIMS	SPLAT	SALTY
SIFTS	SLOTS	SPECS	SWISS	SPLIT	SAMMY
SIGHS	SLOWS	SPEWS	SYCES	SPORT	SANDY
SIGNS	SLUBS	SPIES	SYROS	SPOUT	SAPPY
SIKHS	SLUES	SPINS	******	SPRAT	SASSY
SILAS	SLUGS	SPITS	**S---T**	SPRIT	SAUCY
SILKS	SLUMS	SPOTS	******	SPURT	SAURY
SILLS	SLURS	SPUDS	SABOT	SQUAT	SAVOY
SILOS	SLUTS	SPURS	SAINT	START	SAVVY
SILTS	SMEWS	STABS	SAULT	STILT	SCALY
SIMPS	SMOGS	STAGS	SCANT	STINT	SCARY
SINES	SMUTS	STANS	SCENT	STOAT	SCOPY
SINGS	SNAGS	STARS	SCOOT	STOPT	SEAMY
SINKS	SNAPS	STAYS	SCOTT	STOUT	SEDGY
SINUS	SNIPS	STEMS	SCOUT	STRAT	SEEDY
SIPES	SNOBS	STEPS	SEBAT	STRUT	SEPOY
SIRES	SNOTS	STETS	SHAFT	STUNT	SHADY
SITES	SNOWS	STEWS	SHALT	SUINT	SHAKY
SITUS	SNUBS	STIES	SHANT	SWART	SHALY
SIXES	SNUGS	STIRS	SHEET	SWEAT	SHILY
SIZES	SNYES	STOAS	SHIFT	SWEET	SHINY
SKEES	SOAKS	STOPS	SHIRT	SWEPT	SHOWY
SKEGS	SOAPS	STOSS	SHOAT	SWIFT	SHYLY
SKEPS	SOARS	STOWS	SHOOT	******	SILKY
SKEWS	SOCKS	STUBS	SHORT	**S---U**	SILLY
SKIDS	SODAS	STUDS	SHOUT	******	SILTY
SKIES	SOFAS	STUMS	SHUNT	SADHU	SISSY
SKIMS	SOILS	STUNS	SIGHT	SAJOU	SIXTY
SKINS	SOJAS	SUCKS	SKEET	SNAFU	SKYEY
SKIPS	SOKES	SUERS	SKIRT	******	SLATY
SKITS	SOLES	SUFIS	SLANT	**S---W**	SLILY
				******	SLIMY
				SCREW	
				SEROW	

SLYLY	TAIGA	TAWED	THREE	******	******
SMOKY	TAMPA	TAXED	THROE	**T---H**	**T---L**
SNAKY	TANKA	TEPID	THULE	******	******
SNOWY	TANYA	THIRD	THYME	TEACH	TAMIL
SOAPY	TATRA	TIDED	TIGRE	TEETH	TEKEL
SOFTY	TAZZA	TILED	TILDE	TENCH	THIOL
SOGGY	TERRA	TIMED	TINGE	TENTH	TICAL
SONNY	TESLA	TIMID	TIREE	THIGH	TIDAL
SONSY	TESTA	TINED	TITHE	THOTH	TOBOL
SOOTY	TETRA	TIRED	TITLE	TILTH	TOLYL
SOPHY	THECA	TONED	TOGAE	TOOTH	TONAL
SOPPY	THEDA	TOPED	TOGUE	TORAH	TOTAL
SORRY	THETA	TOTED	TOILE	TORCH	TOWEL
SOUPY	THUJA	TOWED	TOISE	TOUCH	TRAIL
SPICY	TIARA	TOYED	TONNE	TOUGH	TRAWL
SPIKY	TIBIA	TREAD	TOPEE	TRACH	TRIAL
SPINY	TILDA	TREED	TOQUE	TRASH	TRILL
SPIRY	TINEA	TREND	TORTE	TRICH	TRIOL
SPLAY	TIOGA	TRIAD	TRACE	TROPH	TROLL
SPRAY	TONGA	TRIED	TRADE	TROTH	TRULL
SPUMY	TRINA	TRUED	TRAVE	TRUTH	TUBAL
STACY	TRONA	TUBED	TRIBE	******	TWILL
STAGY	TRUDA	TUMID	TRICE	**T---I**	TWIRL
STIMY	TRYMA	TUNED	TRINE	******	TYROL
STOGY	TSANA	TWEED	TRIPE	TARSI	******
STOMY	TULSA	TYPED	TRITE	TEMPI	**T---M**
STONY	******	******	TROPE	TERRI	******
STORY	**T---B**	**T---E**	TROVE	TOPHI	THERM
STRAY	******	******	TRUCE	TORII	THRUM
STUDY	THROB	TABLE	TSADE	TORSI	TOTEM
STYMY	THUMB	TAHOE	TULLE	TRAGI	******
SUDSY	******	TASTE	TUQUE	TURKI	**T---N**
SUETY	**T---C**	TAUPE	TWERE	TUTTI	******
SULKY	******	TBONE	TWICE	******	TAKEN
SULLY	TABAC	TEASE	TWINE	**T---K**	TALON
SUNNY	TELIC	TEHEE	TYCHE	******	TENON
SURFY	TONIC	TELAE	******	TALUK	TETON
SURGY	TOPIC	TEMPE	**T---F**	THANK	THORN
SURLY	TORIC	TENSE	******	THICK	TIEIN
******	TOXIC	TEPEE	THIEF	THINK	TITAN
S---Z	TUNIC	TERSE	******	TORSK	TOEIN
******	******	THANE	**T---G**	TRACK	TOKEN
SCHIZ	**T---D**	THEME	******	TRICK	TOLAN
SPITZ	******	THERE	TELEG	TRUCK	TOMAN
******	TABID	THESE	THING	TRUNK	TOXIN
T---A	TAMED	THINE	THONG	TUPIK	TOYON
******	TAPED	THOLE	TWANG	TWEAK	TRAIN
TACNA	TARED	THOSE	TYING		TRYON
TAFIA					

TURIN	TENOR	TARTS	TODOS	TUBES	******
TWAIN	THEIR	TASKS	TOFTS	TUCKS	**T---W**
TWEEN	TIBER	TAXES	TOGAS	TUFTS	******
******	TIGER	TAXIS	TOILS	TULES	THREW
T---O	TILER	TEAKS	TOLAS	TUNAS	THROW
******	TIMER	TEALS	TOLES	TUNES	******
TABOO	TIMOR	TEAMS	TOLLS	TUNIS	**T---X**
TAINO	TITER	TEARS	TOMAS	TUPIS	******
TANGO	TONER	TEATS	TOMBS	TURFS	TELEX
TANTO	TOPER	TEEMS	TOMES	TURKS	******
TARDO	TOTER	TEENS	TONES	TURNS	**T---Y**
TARSO	TOWER	TELLS	TONGS	TUSKS	******
TASSO	TOYER	TENDS	TONIS	TUTUS	TABBY
TAURO	TRIER	TENOS	TONUS	TWIGS	TACHY
TAUTO	TRUER	TENTS	TONYS	TWINS	TACKY
TELEO	TUBER	TERMS	TOOLS	TWITS	TAFFY
TEMPO	TUDOR	TERNS	TOOTS	TYEES	TALLY
THYRO	TUMOR	TESTS	TOPES	TYKES	TAMMY
TOKYO	TUNER	TETHS	TOPIS	TYPES	TANEY
TORSO	TUTOR	TEXAS	TORTS	TYPOS	TANGY
TRIGO	TYLER	TEXTS	TORUS	TYROS	TANSY
TRURO	******	THADS	TOTES	TZARS	TARDY
TURBO	**T---S**	THAWS	TOURS	******	TARRY
TURCO	******	THEWS	TOUTS	**T---T**	TARTY
******	TABES	THINS	TOWNS	******	TASTY
T---P	TACKS	THUDS	TOYOS	TACET	TATTY
******	TAELS	THUGS	TRAMS	TACIT	TAWNY
THORP	TAILS	THURS	TRANS	TAINT	TEARY
THUMP	TAINS	TICKS	TRAPS	TAROT	TEDDY
TIEUP	TAKES	TIDES	TRASS	TAUNT	TEENY
TRAMP	TALCS	TIERS	TRAYS	TEBET	TELLY
TROOP	TALES	TIFFS	TREAS	TEMPT	TERRY
TRUMP	TALKS	TIKIS	TREES	TENET	TESTY
TULIP	TALOS	TILES	TREKS	TERAT	THADY
TWERP	TALUS	TILLS	TRESS	THEFT	THEWY
TWIRP	TAMES	TILTS	TREWS	TIBET	THYMY
******	TAMIS	TIMES	TREYS	TIGHT	TILLY
T---R	TAMPS	TINAS	TRIES	TINCT	TIMMY
******	TANGS	TINES	TRIGS	TOAST	TINNY
TABOR	TANIS	TINGS	TRIMS	TRACT	TIPPY
TAKER	TANKS	TINTS	TRIOS	TRAIT	TIPSY
TALER	TAPAS	TIRES	TRIPS	TREAT	TIZZY
TAMER	TAPES	TIROS	TROAS	TRENT	TOADY
TAPER	TAPIS	TITIS	TROTS	TROUT	TODAY
TAPIR	TARES	TITUS	TRUES	TRUST	TODDY
TATAR	TARNS	TOADS	TRUSS	TRYST	TOKAY
TAWER	TAROS	TOBYS	TSARS	TWEET	TOMMY
TAXER	TARPS	TODDS	TUBAS	TWIST	TOPSY
				TWIXT	

TRACY	USAGE	******	UNFIT	VESIC	VILLI
TRIXY	UTILE	**U---O**	UNHAT	VINIC	VINCI
TRUDY	******	******	UNIAT	******	VITRI
TRULY	**U---F**	URANO	UNLIT	**V---D**	VOLTI
TUBBY	******	UREDO	UPSET	******	******
TUFTY	UNREF	URICO	******	VALID	**V---K**
TULLY	******	URINO	**U---W**	VANED	******
TUMMY	**U---G**	UTERO	******	VAPID	VNECK
TUNNY	******	******	UNMEW	VEXED	******
TURFY	UNPEG	**U---P**	UPBOW	VIAND	**V---L**
TUTTY	UNRIG	******	******	VISED	******
******	USING	UNCAP	**U---X**	VIVID	VENAL
T---Z	******	UNRIP	******	VOTED	VEXIL
******	**U---H**	UNZIP	UNFIX	VOWED	VIDAL
TOPAZ	******	USURP	UNSEX	******	VIGIL
******	URIAH	******	******	**V---E**	VINYL
U---A	******	**U---R**	**U---Y**	******	VIRAL
******	**U---I**	******	******	VAGUE	VITAL
UINTA	******	UDDER	UNIFY	VALUE	VOCAL
ULEMA	UTERI	ULCER	UNITY	VALVE	VOGUL
ULTRA	******	ULNAR	UNLAY	VARVE	VOWEL
UMBRA	**U---K**	UMBER	UNSAY	VENAE	******
UTICA	******	UNBAR	USURY	VENUE	**V---M**
UVULA	UMIAK	UNDER	******	VERGE	******
******	******	UPPER	**V---A**	VERNE	VELUM
U---D	**U---L**	USHER	******	VERSE	VENOM
******	******	UTHER	VACUA	VERVE	******
UNDID	UMBEL	UTTER	VEPSA	VILLE	**V---N**
UNWED	UNTIL	******	VERNA	VINCE	******
UPEND	UREAL	**U---S**	VESTA	VIRGE	VAGIN
UPPED	URIEL	******	VILLA	VITAE	VIMEN
URGED	USUAL	ULNAS	VILNA	VOGUE	VIXEN
******	UVEAL	ULOUS	VIOLA	VOICE	******
U---E	UXMAL	UMBOS	VIRGA	VOILE	**V---O**
******	******	UNAUS	VISTA	VOLTE	******
UDINE	**U---M**	UNITS	VITTA	******	VARIO
UKASE	******	URALS	VODKA	**V---G**	VARRO
ULNAE	UNARM	URGES	VOILA	******	VERSO
ULOSE	******	USERS	VOLGA	VYING	VIDEO
UMBLE	**U---N**	UVEAS	VOLTA	******	VIREO
UNCLE	******	******	VOLVA	**V---H**	VIRGO
UNDEE	UHLAN	**U---T**	VULVA	******	VULGO
UNDUE	UNION	******	******	VETCH	******
UNITE	UNMAN	UBOAT	**V---C**	VOUCH	**V---R**
UNTIE	UNPEN	UBOLT	******	******	******
URATE	UNPIN	ULENT	VARIC	**V---I**	VALOR
URINE	URBAN	UNAPT	VATIC	******	VANIR
URSAE	UTURN	UNCUT	VEDIC	VERDI	VAPOR

VELAR	VISAS	WILMA	WITHE	WHIRL	WIDER
VEXER	VISES	WIRRA	WITTE	WHORL	WIPER
VICAR	VOCES	******	WORSE	******	WIRER
VIGOR	VOIDS	**W---D**	WRITE	**W---M**	WISER
VILER	VOLES	******	WROTE	******	WIVER
VIPER	VOLTS	WADED	******	WHELM	WOOER
VISOR	VOTES	WAGED	**W---F**	******	WRIER
VIZIR	******	WAKED	******	**W---N**	WRYER
VIZOR	**V---T**	WALED	WHARF	******	******
VOLAR	******	WANED	WHIFF	WAGON	**W---S**
VOMER	VALET	WAVED	WOOLF	WAKEN	******
VOTER	VAULT	WAXED	******	WAXEN	WACKS
VOWER	VAUNT	WEALD	**W---G**	WIDEN	WADES
******	VELDT	WEIRD	******	WIGAN	WAFTS
V---S	VERST	WIELD	WHANG	WITAN	WAGES
******	VISCT	WILED	WRING	WIZEN	WAIFS
VAGUS	VISIT	WINED	WRONG	WODAN	WAILS
VAIRS	VOMIT	WIPED	WRUNG	WODEN	WAINS
VALES	******	WIRED	******	WOKEN	WAITS
VAMPS	**V---U**	WISED	**W---H**	WOMAN	WAKES
VANES	******	WIVED	******	WOMEN	WALES
VANGS	VERTU	WOALD	WATCH	WOTAN	WALKS
VARAS	VIRTU	WOOED	WAUGH	WOVEN	WALTS
VARUS	******	WORLD	WEIGH	******	WAMUS
VASES	**V---X**	WOULD	WELCH	**W---O**	WANDS
VEERS	******	WOUND	WELSH	******	WANES
VEILS	VARIX	WOWED	WENCH	WAHOO	WANTS
VEINS	******	WRIED	WHICH	WALDO	WARDS
VELDS	**V---Y**	******	WHISH	WHOSO	WARES
VENDS	******	**W---E**	WIDTH	******	WARMS
******	VASTY	******	WINCH	**W---P**	WARNS
VENTS	VEERY	WACKE	WITCH	******	WARPS
VENUS	VEINY	WAIVE	WORTH	WATAP	WARTS
VERAS	VICHY	WASTE	WRATH	WHAUP	WASPS
VERBS	VICKY	WAYNE	WROTH	WHELP	WATTS
VERNS	VIEWY	WEAVE	******	WHOOP	WAULS
VESTS	VINNY	WEDGE	**W---K**	******	WAVES
VEXES	VUGGY	WHALE	******	**W---R**	WAWLS
VIALS	******	WHERE	WHACK	******	WAXES
VIBES	**V---Z**	WHILE	WHELK	WADER	WEALS
VICES	******	WHINE	WHISK	WAFER	WEANS
VICKS	VADUZ	WHITE	WRACK	WAGER	WEARS
VIEWS		WHOLE	WREAK	WALER	WEEDS
VILLS	**W---A**	WHORE	WRECK	WATER	WEEKS
VINAS	******	WHOSE	WRICK	WAVER	WEEMS
VINES	WALLA	WILDE	******	WEBER	WEEPS
VIOLS	WANDA	WINCE	**W---L**	WESER	WEFTS
VIRES	WILLA	WINZE	******	WHIRR	WEIRS
VIRUS			WHEAL		
			WHEEL		

WEKAS	******	WITHY	XERUS	******	YOWLS
WELDS	W---T	WITTY	XRAYS	Y---N	YOYOS
WELLS	******	WOMBY	XYSTS	******	YPRES
WELTS	WAIST	WOODY	******	YAMEN	YUGAS
WENDS	WASNT	WOOLY	X---X	YAMUN	YULES
WHAMS	WEEST	WOOZY	******	YAPON	******
WHAPS	WHEAT	WORDY	XEROX	YEARN	Y---T
WHENS	WHIPT	WORMY	******	YEMEN	******
WHETS	WHIST	WORRY	Y---A	YOGIN	YACHT
WHEYS	WHORT	WRYLY	******	YUKON	YEAST
WHIGS	WIGHT	******	YALTA	YUPON	******
WHIMS	WORST	W---Z	YERBA	******	Y---Y
WHINS	WRAPT	******	YUCCA	Y---O	******
WHIPS	WREST	WALTZ	******	******	YOLKY
WHIRS	WRIST	******	Y---C	YAHOO	YUMMY
WHITS	WYATT	X---A	******	YAZOO	******
WHOPS	******	******	YOGIC	******	Z---A
WICKS	W---W	XENIA	******	Y---R	******
WILDS	******	******	Y---D	******	ZAMIA
WILES	WIDOW	X---C	******	YAGER	ZEBRA
WILLS	******	******	YAWED	******	******
WILTS	W---Y	XEBEC	YIELD	Y---S	Z---C
WINDS	******	XERIC	YOKED	******	******
WINES	WACKY	******	YOWED	YANKS	ZEBEC
WINGS	WADDY	X---H	******	YARDS	******
WINKS	WALLY	******	Y---E	YARNS	Z---D
WINOS	WANEY	XANTH	******	YAUPS	******
WIPES	WANLY	******	YAHVE	YAWLS	ZONED
WIRES	WARTY	X---I	YOGEE	YAWNS	ZOOID
WISES	WASHY	******	YOURE	YAWPS	******
WISPS	WASPY	XIPHI	YOUVE	YAXES	Z---E
WIVES	WAVEY	******	YSERE	YAXIS	******
WOADS	WEARY	X---L	******	YEANS	ZAIRE
WOLDS	WEBBY	******	Y---G	YEARS	******
WOLFS	WEDGY	XYLOL	******	YEATS	Z---I
WOMBS	WEEDY	XYLYL	YOUNG	YEGGS	******
WOODS	WEENY	******	******	YELKS	ZIMRI
WOOFS	WEEPY	X---M	Y---H	YELLS	ZOMBI
WOOLS	WENDY	******	******	YELPS	******
WORDS	WENNY	XYLEM	YOUTH	YESES	Z---L
WORKS	WETLY	******	******	YETIS	******
WORMS	WHINY	X---N	Y---L	YIPES	ZONAL
WORTS	WIDDY	******	******	YODHS	ZORIL
WRAPS	WILEY	XENON	YODEL	YOGHS	******
WRENS	WILLY	XTIAN	YOKEL	YOGIS	Z---N
WRIES	WINDY	XYLAN	YOULL	YOKES	******
WRITS	WINGY	******	Y---M	YOLKS	ZAYIN
	WISPY	XAXES	******	YOURS	ZIRON
		XAXIS	YQUEM		

******	CABOT	BACON	TACET	NADAB	******
Z---S	FABLE	BACUP	TACHY	NADER	-AG--
******	GABBY	CACAO	TACIT	NADIR	******
ZARFS	GABES	CACHE	TACKS	PADDY	BAGEL
ZEBUS	GABLE	CACTI	TACKY	PADRE	BAGGY
ZEKES	GABON	DACCA	TACNA	PADUA	CAGED
ZEROS	GABOR	DACES	VACUA	RADAR	CAGES
ZESTS	GABYS	DACHA	WACKE	RADII	CAGEY
ZETAS	HABIT	DACIA	WACKS	RADIO	DAGAN
ZINCS	HABUS	FACED	WACKY	RADIX	EAGER
ZONES	JABEZ	FACER	YACHT	RADON	EAGLE
ZOOMS	JABOT	FACES	******	SADHU	EAGRE
ZOONS	KABOB	FACET	-AD--	SADIE	FAGOT
******	KABUL	FACIA	******	SADLY	GAGED
Z---T	LABEL	FACTS	BADEN	VADUZ	GAGER
******	LABIA	HACKS	BADGE	WADDY	GAGES
ZIBET	LABIO	JACKS	BADLY	WADED	HAGIO
******	LABOR	JACKY	CADDO	WADER	HAGUE
Z---Y	LABRA	JACOB	CADDY	WADES	JAGGS
******	MABEL	LACED	CADES	******	JAGGY
ZESTY	NABOB	LACES	CADET	-AE--	KAGUS
ZINCY	PABLO	LACKS	CADGE	******	LAGAN
ZINGY	RABAT	LACTO	CADIS	GAELS	LAGER
ZINKY	RABBI	MACAO	CADIZ	PAEAN	LAGOS
ZIPPY	RABIC	MACAW	CADRE	PAEDO	MAGDA
ZLOTY	RABID	MACED	DADDY	PAEON	MAGES
******	SABAH	MACER	EADIE	TAELS	MAGIC
-AA--	SABED	MACES	FADDY	******	MAGMA
******	SABER	MACHY	FADED	-AF--	MAGNI
BAAED	SABES	MACKS	FADES	******	MAGOG
KAABA	SABIN	MACLE	GADID	BAFFS	MAGOT
NAACP	SABLE	MACON	HADED	BAFFY	MAGUS
******	SABOT	MACRO	HADES	CAFES	PAGAN
-AB--	SABRA	NACRE	HADJI	DAFFY	PAGED
******	SABRE	PACAS	HADNT	GAFFE	PAGER
BABAR	TABAC	PACED	JADED	GAFFS	PAGES
BABAS	TABBY	PACER	JADES	HAFIZ	RAGED
BABEL	TABES	PACES	KADIS	HAFTS	RAGEE
BABER	TABID	PACHY	LADDY	JAFFA	RAGES
BABES	TABLE	PACKS	LADED	KAFIR	RAGGY
BABOO	TABOO	PACTS	LADEN	KAFKA	SAGAN
BABUL	TABOR	RACED	LADES	MAFIA	SAGAS
CABAL	******	RACER	LADIN	RAFTS	SAGER
CABBY	-AC--	RACES	LADLE	SAFER	SAGES
CABER	******	RACKS	MADAM	SAFES	SAGOS
CABIN	BACCI	SACKS	MADGE	TAFFY	SAGUM
CABLE	BACHE	SACRA	MADLY	TAFIA	VAGIN
CABOB	BACKS	SACRO	MADOC	WAFER	VAGUE
				WAFTS	

VAGUS	HAIFA	WAILS	SAKES	HALED	SALLY
WAGED	HAIKS	WAINS	TAKEN	HALER	SALMA
WAGER	HAIKU	WAIST	TAKER	HALES	SALMI
WAGES	HAILS	WAITS	TAKES	HALID	SALOL
WAGON	HAIRS	WAIVE	WAKED	HALLE	SALON
YAGER	HAIRY	ZAIRE	WAKEN	HALLO	SALPA
******	HAITI	******	WAKES	HALLS	SALSA
-AH--	JAILS	-AJ--	******	HALMA	SALSE
******	JAINA	******	-AL--	HALOS	SALTS
BAHAI	JAINS	CAJON	******	HALTS	SALTY
BAHIA	LAIKA	CAJUN	AALII	HALVE	SALUS
BAHTS	LAINE	MAJOR	BALAS	JALAP	SALVE
HAHAS	LAIRD	RAJAB	BALDR	KALAT	SALVO
MAHAN	LAIRS	RAJAH	BALED	LALLS	TALCS
MAHDI	LAITY	SAJOU	BALER	MALAC	TALER
NAHOR	MAIDS	******	BALES	MALAR	TALES
NAHUA	MAILS	-AK--	BALKS	MALAY	TALKS
NAHUM	MAIMS	******	BALKY	MALES	TALLY
SAHEB	MAINE	BAKED	BALLS	MALIC	TALON
SAHIB	MAINS	BAKER	BALMS	MALLS	TALOS
TAHOE	MAINZ	BAKES	BALMY	MALMO	TALUK
WAHOO	MAIZE	CAKED	BALSA	MALTA	TALUS
YAHOO	NAIAD	CAKES	BALTS	MALTS	VALES
YAHVE	NAILS	DAKAR	CALCI	MALTY	VALET
******	NAIRN	FAKED	CALEB	PALAE	VALID
-AI--	NAIVE	FAKER	CALIF	PALEA	VALOR
******	PAILS	FAKES	CALIX	PALED	VALUE
BAILS	PAINE	FAKIR	CALKS	PALEO	VALVE
BAIRD	PAINS	HAKES	CALLA	PALER	WALDO
BAIRN	PAINT	HAKIM	CALLI	PALES	WALED
BAITS	PAIRS	JAKES	CALLS	PALEY	WALER
BAIZE	PAISA	JAKOB	CALMS	PALLS	WALES
CAIRD	PAISE	KAKAS	CALPE	PALLY	WALKS
CAIRN	RAIDS	KAKIS	CALVE	PALMA	WALLA
CAIRO	RAILS	LAKED	CALYX	PALMI	WALLY
DAILY	RAINS	LAKER	DALAI	PALMS	WALTS
DAIRY	RAINY	LAKES	DALER	PALMY	WALTZ
DAISY	RAISE	LAKEY	DALES	PALPI	YALTA
FAILS	SAIGA	MAKER	DALLY	PALSY	******
FAINT	SAILS	MAKES	FALLS	RALES	-AM--
FAIRS	SAINT	NAKED	FALSE	RALLY	******
FAIRY	TAIGA	OAKEN	GALAS	RALPH	BAMBI
FAITH	TAILS	OAKUM	GALAX	SALAD	CAMEL
GAILS	TAINO	RAKED	GALEA	SALEM	CAMEO
GAILY	TAINS	RAKEE	GALEN	SALEP	CAMES
GAINS	TAINT	RAKER	GALES	SALES	CAMPI
GAITS	VAIRS	RAKES	GALLS	SALIC	CAMPO
HAIDA	WAIFS	SAKER	GALOP	SALIX	CAMPS

CAMPY	NAMES	CANNA	MANET	TANIS	JAPED
CAMUS	NAMUR	CANNY	MANGE	TANKA	JAPES
DAMAN	RAMIE	CANOE	MANGO	TANKS	KAPHS
DAMES	RAMMY	CANON	MANGY	TANSY	KAPOK
DAMNS	RAMPS	CANSO	MANIA	TANTO	KAPPA
DAMON	RAMUS	CANST	MANIC	TANYA	KAPUT
DAMPS	SAMAR	CANTO	MANLY	VANED	LAPAR
EAMON	SAMBA	CANTS	MANNA	VANES	LAPEL
FAMED	SAMBO	DANAE	MANOR	VANGS	LAPIN
GAMBS	SAMEK	DANCE	MANSE	VANIR	LAPIS
GAMED	SAMMY	DANDY	MANTA	WANDA	LAPPS
GAMES	SAMOA	DANES	MANUS	WANDS	LAPSE
GAMIC	SAMOS	DANGS	NANAS	WANED	MAPLE
GAMIN	TAMED	DANNY	NANCE	WANES	NAPES
GAMMA	TAMER	DANTE	NANCY	WANEY	NAPPE
GAMMY	TAMES	FANCY	NANNA	WANLY	NAPPY
GAMPS	TAMIL	FANGA	NANNY	WANTS	PAPAL
GAMUT	TAMIS	FANGS	PANAY	XANTH	PAPAS
HAMAL	TAMMY	FANNY	PANDA	YANKS	PAPAW
HAMER	TAMPA	FANON	PANDY	******	PAPEN
HAMES	TAMPS	FANOS	PANED	-AO--	PAPER
HAMMY	VAMPS	FANUM	PANEL	******	PAPPI
HAMZA	WAMUS	GANEF	PANES	GAOLS	PAPPY
IAMBI	YAMEN	GANGS	PANGS	LAOAG	PAPUA
IAMBS	YAMUN	HANCE	PANIC	MAORI	RAPED
JAMBS	ZAMIA	HANDS	PANNE	NAOMI	RAPES
JAMES	******	HANDY	PANSY	PAOLO	RAPHE
JAMIE	-AN--	HANGS	PANTO	RAOUL	RAPID
JAMMY	******	HANKS	PANTS	SAONE	SAPID
KAMES	BANAL	HANKY	PANTY	******	SAPOR
KAMET	BANAT	HANNA	RANCE	-AP--	SAPPY
KAMIK	BANDA	HANOI	RANCH	******	SAPRO
LAMAS	BANDS	HANSE	RANDS	CAPEK	TAPAS
LAMBS	BANDY	JANES	RANDY	CAPER	TAPED
LAMED	BANFF	JANET	RANEE	CAPES	TAPER
LAMER	BANGS	JANIS	RANGE	CAPET	TAPES
LAMES	BANJO	JANOS	RANGY	CAPON	TAPIR
LAMIA	BANKS	JANUS	RANIS	CAPRI	TAPIS
LAMPS	BANNS	KANDY	RANKS	CAPUA	VAPID
MAMAS	BANTU	LANAI	RANTS	CAPUT	VAPOR
MAMBA	CANAD	LANCE	SANDS	GAPED	YAPON
MAMBO	CANAL	LANDS	SANDY	GAPER	******
MAMEY	CANDY	LANES	SANER	GAPES	-AQ--
MAMIE	CANEA	LANKY	SANTA	GAPPY	******
MAMMA	CANED	MANCY	TANEY	HAPLO	MAQUI
MAMMY	CANER	MANDY	TANGO	HAPLY	******
NAMED	CANES	MANED	TANGS	HAPPY	-AR--
NAMER	CANIS	MANES	TANGY	JAPAN	******
					AARON
					BARBS

BARCA	DARES	KARLS	PARER	WARMS	IASIS
BARDE	DARIC	KARMA	PARES	WARNS	JASON
BARDS	DARKY	KAROL	PAREU	WARPS	JASSY
BARED	DARNS	KAROO	PARGO	WARTS	LASER
BARER	DARTS	KARYO	PARIS	WARTY	LASSA
BARES	EARED	LARCH	PARKA	YARDS	LASSO
BARGE	EARLE	LARDS	PARKS	YARNS	LASTS
BARIC	EARLS	LARDY	PARMA	ZARFS	MASER
BARIT	EARLY	LARES	PAROL	******	MASHY
BARKS	EARNS	LARGE	PAROS	-AS--	MASKS
BARKY	EARTH	LARGO	PARRS	******	MASON
BARMY	FARAD	LARKS	PARRY	BASAL	MASSE
BARNS	FARAH	LARKY	PARSE	BASED	MASSY
BARON	FARCE	LARRY	PARSI	BASEL	MASTO
BARRE	FARCY	LARVA	PARTS	BASES	MASTS
BARRY	FARED	MARAT	PARTY	BASIC	NASAL
BARTH	FARER	MARCH	RARER	BASIL	NASTY
BARYE	FARES	MARCO	SARAH	BASIN	OASES
CARAS	FARGO	MARCS	SARAN	BASIS	OASIS
CARAT	FARLE	MARES	SARAS	BASKS	PASCH
CARBO	FARLS	MARGE	SARCO	BASLE	PASHA
CARDI	FARMS	MARGO	SARIS	BASON	PASSE
CARDS	FAROE	MARIA	SARKS	BASRA	PASSY
CARED	GARBO	MARIE	SAROS	BASSI	PASTA
CARER	GARBS	MARIO	SARRE	BASSO	PASTE
CARES	GARRY	MARIS	SARTO	BASTE	PASTS
CARET	GARTH	MARKS	TARDO	CASCO	PASTY
CAREY	GARYS	MARLA	TARDY	CASED	RASPS
CARGO	HARAR	MARLS	TARED	CASES	RASPY
CARIB	HARDS	MARLY	TARES	CASEY	SASIN
CARLA	HARDY	MARNE	TARNS	CASKS	SASSY
CARLE	HARED	MARRY	TAROS	CASTE	TASKS
CARLO	HAREM	MARSH	TAROT	CASTS	TASSO
CARLS	HARES	MARTA	TARPS	CASUS	TASTE
CAROB	HARKS	MARTS	TARRY	DASHY	TASTY
CAROL	HARLS	MARTY	TARSI	EASED	VASES
CAROM	HARMS	NARCO	TARSO	EASEL	VASTY
CARPI	HARPS	NARDS	TARTS	EASES	WASHY
CARPO	HARPY	NARES	TARTY	FASTS	WASNT
CARPS	HARRY	NARIS	VARAS	GASES	WASPS
CARRY	HARSH	NARKY	VARIC	GASPE	WASPY
CARTE	HARTE	OARED	VARIO	GASPS	WASTE
CARTS	HARTS	PARAS	VARIX	GASSY	******
CARVE	HARTZ	PARCA	VARRO	GASTR	-AT--
CARYO	JARED	PARCH	VARUS	HASNT	******
CARYS	JARLS	PARDS	VARVE	HASPS	BATAN
DARED	KARAT	PARED	WARDS	HASTE	BATCH
DARER	KAREN	PAREN	WARES	HASTY	BATED

BATEN	LATRY	SATYR	MAUDS	GAVLE	GAWKS
BATES	MATCH	TATAR	MAULS	GAVOT	GAWKY
BATHE	MATED	TATRA	MAUND	HAVEN	HAWED
BATHO	MATEO	TATTY	MAURA	HAVER	HAWKS
BATHS	MATER	VATIC	MAUVE	HAVOC	HAWSE
BATHY	MATES	WATAP	NAURU	KAVAS	JAWED
BATIK	MATEY	WATCH	PAULA	LAVAS	LAWED
BATON	MATHS	WATER	PAULO	LAVED	LAWNS
BATTY	MATIN	WATTS	PAULS	LAVER	LAWNY
CATCH	MATRI	******	PAUSE	LAVES	NAWAB
CATER	MATSU	-AU--	SAUCE	MAVIS	PAWED
CATHY	MATTE	******	SAUCY	NAVAL	PAWER
CATTY	MATTS	BAULK	SAULS	NAVAR	PAWKY
DATAL	MATTY	BAUME	SAULT	NAVEL	PAWLS
DATED	MATZO	CAUCA	SAUNA	NAVES	PAWNS
DATER	NATAL	CAULK	SAURO	NAVVY	RAWER
DATES	NATES	CAULS	SAURY	OAVES	RAWLY
DATTO	NATTY	CAUSE	SAUTE	PAVAN	SAWED
DATUM	OATEN	DAUBS	TAUNT	PAVED	SAWER
EATEN	OATES	DAUBY	TAUPE	PAVER	TAWED
EATER	OATHS	DAUNT	TAURO	PAVES	TAWER
FATAL	PATCH	FAUGH	TAUTO	PAVIS	TAWNY
FATED	PATEN	FAULT	VAULT	RAVED	WAWLS
FATES	PATER	FAUNA	VAUNT	RAVEL	YAWED
FATLY	PATES	FAUNS	WAUGH	RAVEN	YAWLS
FATTY	PATHO	FAUST	WAULS	RAVER	YAWNS
GATED	PATHS	GAUDI	YAUPS	RAVES	YAWPS
GATES	PATHY	GAUDS	******	SAVED	******
GATUN	PATIO	GAUDY	-AV--	SAVER	-AX--
HATCH	PATNA	GAUGE	******	SAVES	******
HATED	PATRI	GAULS	CAVED	SAVIN	FAXED
HATER	PATSY	GAULT	CAVES	SAVOR	FAXES
HATES	PATTI	GAUNT	CAVIE	SAVOY	LAXER
HATTY	PATTY	GAURS	CAVIL	SAVVY	LAXLY
IATRO	QATAR	GAUSS	DAVAO	WAVED	MAXIM
IATRY	RATAL	GAUZE	DAVES	WAVER	SAXES
JATOS	RATCH	GAUZY	DAVEY	WAVES	SAXON
KATES	RATED	HAULM	DAVID	WAVEY	TAXED
KATHY	RATEL	HAULS	DAVIE	******	TAXER
KATIE	RATER	HAUNT	DAVIS	-AW--	TAXES
LATCH	RATES	JAUNT	DAVIT	******	TAXIS
LATER	RATIO	KAUAI	DAVOS	BAWDS	WAXED
LATEX	RATTY	KAURI	DAVYS	BAWDY	WAXEN
LATHE	SATAN	KAURY	EAVES	BAWLS	WAXES
LATHS	SATED	LAUDS	FAVOR	CAWED	XAXES
LATHY	SATES	LAUGH	FAVUS	DAWKS	XAXIS
LATIN	SATIE	LAURA	GAVEL	DAWNS	YAXES
LATRO	SATIN	MAUDE	GAVIN	FAWNS	YAXIS

******	HAZES	OBESE	******	******	ECOLE
-AY--	JAZZY	OBEYS	-BS--	-CE--	ICONO
******	KAZAN	******	******	******	ICONS
BAYED	KAZOO	-BH--	IBSEN	ACEAE	ICOSI
BAYOU	LAZAR	******	******	ACEAN	SCOFF
FAYAL	LAZED	ABHOR	-BU--	ACERB	SCOLD
FAYED	LAZES	******	******	ACETO	SCONE
FAYES	MAZED	-BI--	ABUSE	OCEAN	SCOOP
GAYER	MAZER	******	ABUTS	SCENA	SCOOT
GAYLY	MAZES	ABIBS	******	SCEND	SCOPE
HAYDN	NAZIS	ABIDE	-BY--	SCENE	SCOPS
HAYED	RAZED	ABIEL	******	SCENT	SCOPY
HAYES	RAZEE	ABIES	ABYSM	******	SCORE
JAYNE	RAZES	IBIZA	ABYSS	-CH--	SCORN
KAYAK	RAZOR	OBITS	******	******	SCOTO
KAYOS	TAZZA	******	-CA--	ACHED	SCOTS
LAYBY	YAZOO	-BL--	******	ACHES	SCOTT
LAYER	******	******	OCALA	ECHIN	SCOUR
MAYAN	-BA--	ABLER	SCABS	ICHOR	SCOUT
MAYAS	******	******	SCADS	OCHER	SCOWL
MAYBE	ABACA	-BN--	SCALD	OCHRE	SCOWS
MAYNT	ABACI	******	SCALE	OCHRY	******
MAYOR	ABACK	ABNER	SCALL	SCHIZ	-CR--
MAYST	ABAFT	******	SCALP	SCHMO	******
PAYED	ABASE	-BO--	SCALY	SCHWA	ACRED
PAYEE	ABASH	******	SCAMP	******	ACRES
PAYER	ABATE	ABODE	SCAND	-CI--	ACRID
RAYAH	******	ABOHM	SCANS	******	OCREA
RAYED	-BB--	ABOIL	SCANT	ACIDS	SCRAG
RAYON	******	ABOMA	SCAPA	ACING	SCRAM
SAYER	ABBAS	ABOMB	SCAPE	ACINI	SCRAP
SAYID	ABBES	ABORT	SCAPI	ACITY	SCREE
SAYSO	ABBEY	ABOUT	SCARE	ICIAN	SCREW
WAYNE	ABBIE	ABOVE	SCARF	ICIER	SCRIM
ZAYIN	ABBOT	EBOAT	SCARP	ICILY	SCRIP
******	ABBYS	EBONS	SCARS	ICING	SCROD
-AZ--	EBBED	EBONY	SCARY	SCIFI	SCRUB
******	******	HBOMB	SCATO	SCION	SCRUM
DAZED	-BE--	OBOES	SCATS	******	******
DAZES	******	OBOLE	SCAUP	-CL--	-CT--
FAZED	ABEAM	OBOLI	******	******	******
FAZES	ABELE	TBONE	-CC--	ECLAT	ACTED
GAZED	ABELS	UBOAT	******	******	ACTIN
GAZER	ABETS	UBOLT	ACCEL	-CO--	ACTOR
GAZES	HBEAM	******	ACCRA	******	ACTUS
HAZED	IBEAM	-BR--	MCCOY	ACOCK	ICTUS
HAZEL	OBEAH	******	OCCUR	ACORN	OCTAD
HAZER	OBELI	ABRAM		ACOUO	OCTET
		ABRIS			OCTYL

```
******        ADELE    ADMEX    ******    HEAVY    READS
-CU--         ADENI    ADMIN    -DZ--     JEANS    READY
******        ADENO    ADMIT    ******    KEATS    REALM
ACUTE         ADEPT    ADMIX    ADZES     LEACH    REALS
OCULO         EDEMA    ******   ******    LEADS    REAMS
SCUBA         IDEAL    -DN--    ******    LEADY    REAPS
SCUDI         IDEAS    ******   -EA--     LEAFS    REARM
SCUDO         IDEST    EDNAS    ******    LEAFY    REARS
SCUDS         ODEON    ******   BEACH     LEAKS    SEALS
SCUFF         ODETS    -DO--    BEADS     LEAKY    SEAMS
SCULL         ODEUM    ******   BEADY     LEANS    SEAMY
SCULP         ******   ADOBE    BEAKS     LEANT    SEANS
SCUMS         -DG--    ADOLF    BEALL     LEAPS    SEARS
SCUPS         ******   ADOPT    BEAMS     LEAPT    SEATO
SCURF         EDGAR    ADORE    BEAMY     LEARN    SEATS
SCUTA         EDGED    ADORN    BEANO     LEARY    TEACH
SCUTE         EDGES    ADOWA    BEANS     LEASE    TEAKS
SCUTS         ******   IDOLS    BEARD     LEASH    TEALS
******        -DI--    ODONT    BEARS     LEAST    TEAMS
-CY--         ******   ODORS    BEAST     LEAVE    TEARS
******        ADIEU    ODOUR    BEATA     LEAVY    TEARY
SCYPH         ADIGE    ******   BEATS     MEADS    TEASE
******        ADIOS    -DR--    BEAUS     MEALS    TEATS
-DA--         ADITS    ******   BEAUT     MEALY    WEALD
******        EDICT    EDRED    BEAUX     MEANS    WEALS
ADAGE         EDIES    ******   CEARA     MEANT    WEANS
ADAHS         EDIFY    -DS--    CEASE     MEANY    WEARS
ADAMS         EDILE    ******   DEALS     MEATS    WEARY
ADAPT         EDINA    EDSEL    DEALT     MEATY    WEAVE
IDAHO         EDITH    ******   DEANE     NEALS    YEANS
******        EDITS    -DU--    DEANS     NEAPS    YEARN
-DD--         IDIOM    ******   DEARS     NEARS    YEARS
******        IDIOT    ADULT    DEARY     NEATH    YEAST
ADDAX         ODIUM    ADUNC    DEATH     PEACE    YEATS
ADDED         UDINE    ADUST    FEARS     PEACH    ******
ADDER         ******   ADUWA    FEASE     PEAKS    -EB--
ADDIE         -DL--    EDUCE    FEAST     PEAKY    ******
ADDLE         ******   EDUCT    FEATS     PEALS    BEBOP
ADDYS         ADLAI    ******   GEARS     PEANS    DEBAG
EDDAS         ADLER    -DW--    HEADS     PEARL    DEBAR
EDDIC         ADLIB    ******   HEADY     PEARS    DEBBY
EDDIE         IDLED    EDWIN    HEALS     PEARY    DEBIT
ODDER         IDLER    ******   HEAPS     PEASE    DEBTS
ODDLY         IDLES    -DY--    HEARD     PEATS    DEBUG
UDDER         ******   ******   HEARS     PEATY    DEBUT
******        -DM--    ADYTA    HEART     REACH    FEBRI
-DE--         ******   IDYLL    HEATH     REACT    REBEC
******        ADMAN    IDYLS    HEATS              REBEL
ADEEM         ADMEN    ODYLE    HEAVE
ADELA
```

REBID	******	BEERY	SEERS	LEGAL	HEIRS
REBUS	**-ED--**	BEETS	TEEMS	LEGER	HEIST
REBUT	******	DEEDS	TEENS	LEGES	KEITH
SEBAT	AEDES	DEEMS	TEENY	LEGGY	LEIFS
SEBUM	BEDEW	DEEPS	TEETH	LEGIT	LEIGH
TEBET	BEDIM	FEEDS	VEERS	MEGAL	LEILA
WEBBY	CEDAR	FEELS	VEERY	MEGAN	LEITH
WEBER	CEDED	FEEZE	WEEDS	NEGEB	NEIGH
XEBEC	CEDES	GEEKS	WEEDY	NEGEV	NEILS
ZEBEC	DEDAL	GEESE	WEEKS	NEGRO	REICH
ZEBRA	FEDOR	GEEST	WEEMS	NEGUS	REIFY
ZEBUS	HEDDA	HEEDS	WEENY	PEGGY	REIGN
******	HEDGE	HEELS	WEEPS	REGAL	REIMS
-EC--	HEDGY	JEEPS	WEEPY	REGAN	REINS
******	KEDAH	JEERS	WEEST	REGES	SEINE
AECIA	KEDGE	KEEFS	******	REGIN	SEISE
BECKS	LEDGE	KEELS	**-EF--**	REGMA	SEISM
BECKY	MEDAL	KEENS	******	SEGNI	SEIZE
CECAL	MEDEA	KEEPS	BEFIT	SEGNO	VEILS
CECIL	MEDIA	KEEVE	BEFOG	SEGOS	VEINS
CECUM	MEDIC	LEECH	DEFER	YEGGS	VEINY
DECAL	MEDIO	LEEDS	DEFIS	******	WEIGH
DECAY	MEDOC	LEEKS	DEFOE	**-EH--**	WEIRD
DECIM	NEDDY	LEERS	HEFTS	BEHAN	WEIRS
DECKS	PEDAL	LEERY	HEFTY	JEHUS	******
DECOR	PEDES	LEETS	JEFES	LEHRS	**-EJ--**
DECOY	PEDRO	MEETS	JEFFS	LEHUA	******
DECRY	REDAN	NEEDS	LEFTS	NEHRU	HEJAZ
FECAL	REDID	NEEDY	LEFTY	TEHEE	******
FECES	REDLY	PEEKS	REFER	******	**-EK--**
FECIT	SEDAN	PEELS	REFIT	**-EI--**	DEKED
GECKO	SEDER	PEENS	WEFTS	******	DEKES
GECKS	SEDGE	PEEPS	******	BEIGE	HEKLA
HECTO	SEDGY	PEERS	**-EG--**	BEING	HEKTO
KECKS	SEDUM	PEEVE	******	BEIRA	PEKAN
MECCA	TEDDY	REEDS	AEGIR	CEIBA	PEKIN
NECKS	VEDIC	REEDY	AEGIS	CEILS	PEKOE
NECRO	WEDGE	REEFS	BEGAD	DEICE	TEKEL
PECAN	WEDGY	REEFY	BEGAN	DEIFY	WEKAS
PECKS	******	REEKS	BEGAT	DEIGN	ZEKES
PECOS	**-EE--**	REEKY	BEGET	DEISM	******
RECAP	******	REELS	BEGIN	DEIST	**-EL--**
RECTA	BEEBE	REEVE	BEGOT	DEITY	******
RECTI	BEECH	SEEDS	BEGUM	FEIGN	BELAY
RECTO	BEEFS	SEEDY	BEGUN	FEINT	BELCH
RECUR	BEEFY	SEEKS	DEGAS	FEIST	BELEM
SECCO	BEEPS	SEEMS	DEGUM	HEGEL	BELGA
SECTS	BEERS	SEEPS	HEGEL	HEIGH	

BELIE	KELLY	DEMIT	BENNY	LENNY	WENCH
BELLA	KELPS	DEMOB	BENUE	LENOS	WENDS
BELLE	KELSO	DEMON	CENIS	LENTO	WENDY
BELLS	MELAN	DEMOS	CENON	LENTS	WENNY
BELLY	MELDS	DEMUR	CENSE	MENAI	XENIA
BELOW	MELEE	FEMES	CENTI	MENDS	XENON
BELTS	MELIC	FEMME	CENTO	MENES	******
CELIA	MELON	FEMTO	CENTR	MENSA	-EO--
CELIE	MELOS	FEMUR	CENTS	MENUS	******
CELLA	MELTS	GEMMA	DENDR	PENAL	AEONS
CELLO	NELLS	GEMMY	DENEB	PENCE	CEORL
CELLS	NELLY	GEMOT	DENES	PENDS	DEOXY
CELOM	PELEE	HEMAL	DENIM	PENGO	FEODS
CELTS	PELEG	HEMAN	DENIS	PENIS	FEOFF
DELAY	PELFS	HEMAT	DENNY	PENNA	GEODE
DELED	PELLA	HEMEN	DENSE	PENNI	GEOFF
DELES	PELLY	HEMIA	DENTI	PENNY	GEOID
DELFT	PELON	HEMIC	DENTO	PENTA	LEONA
DELHI	PELTS	HEMIN	DENTS	RENAL	LEONS
DELIA	PELVI	HEMPS	DENYS	RENAN	LEORA
DELLA	RELAX	HEMPY	FENCE	RENDS	MEOWS
DELLS	RELAY	JEMMY	FENDS	RENEE	PEONS
DELOS	RELIC	LEMMA	FENNY	RENES	PEONY
DELTA	SELAH	LEMON	GENES	RENEW	SEOUL
DELVE	SELEN	LEMUR	GENET	RENIN	******
FELID	SELLS	MEMOS	GENIC	RENTE	-EP--
FELIX	SELMA	NEMAT	GENIE	RENTS	******
FELLS	TELAE	REMAN	GENII	SENDS	DEPOT
FELLY	TELEG	REMEX	GENOA	SENNA	DEPTH
FELON	TELEO	REMIT	GENRE	SENNE	HEPAT
FELTS	TELEX	REMUS	GENRO	SENOR	HEPTA
GELDS	TELIC	SEMEN	GENTS	SENSE	KEPIS
GELID	TELLS	TEMPE	GENUA	TENCH	LEPER
HELEN	TELLY	TEMPI	GENUS	TENDS	LEPID
HELGA	VELAR	TEMPO	HENCE	TENET	LEPSY
HELIC	VELDS	TEMPT	HENNA	TENON	LEPTA
HELIO	VELDT	YEMEN	HENRI	TENOR	LEPTO
HELIX	VELUM	******	HENRY	TENOS	LEPUS
HELLE	WELCH	-EN--	JENNY	TENSE	NEPAL
HELLO	WELDS	******	KENCH	TENTH	NEPHO
HELLS	WELLS	BENCH	KENNY	TENTS	NEPHR
HELMS	WELSH	BENDS	KENTS	VENAE	PEPIN
HELOT	WELTS	BENDY	KENYA	VENAL	PEPLA
HELPS	YELKS	BENES	LENAS	VENDS	PEPOS
HELVE	YELLS	BENET	LENDS	VENOM	PEPPY
JELLO	YELPS	BENIN	LENES	VENTS	PEPYS
JELLS	******	BENJY	LENIN	VENUE	REPAY
JELLY	-EM--	BENNE	LENIS	VENUS	REPEL
	******				
	AEMIA				
	DEMES				

REPLY	FERRI	PERRY	BESET	BETON	RETEM
SEPAL	FERRO	PERSE	BESOM	BETSO	RETIA
SEPIA	FERRY	PERTH	BESOT	BETSY	RETRO
SEPOY	GERDA	RERAN	BESSY	BETTE	RETRY
SEPTA	GERMS	RERUN	BESTS	BETTY	RETTA
SEPTI	GERRY	SERAC	CESAR	CETIC	SETAE
SEPTO	GERTY	SERAI	CESTA	CETIN	SETHS
SEPTS	HERAT	SERAL	CESTI	CETUS	SETON
TEPEE	HERBS	SERBS	DESEX	DETER	SETTO
TEPID	HERBY	SERED	DESKS	FETAL	SETUP
VEPSA	HERDS	SERES	FESSE	FETCH	TETHS
******	HERLS	SERFS	GESSO	FETED	TETON
-ER--	HERMA	SERGE	HESSE	FETES	TETRA
******	HEROD	SERIF	JESSE	FETID	VETCH
AERIE	HERON	SERIN	JESSY	FETOR	WETLY
BERAR	HERTZ	SERON	JESTS	FETUS	YETIS
BEREA	JEREZ	SEROW	JESUS	GETUP	ZETAS
BERET	JERKS	SERRA	MESAS	HETTY	******
BERGS	JERKY	SERUM	MESHY	JETON	-EU--
BERIA	JERRY	SERVE	MESIC	JETTY	******
BERME	KERAT	SERVO	MESNE	KETCH	BEULA
BERMS	KERBS	TERAT	MESON	LETHE	CEUTA
BERNE	KERCH	TERMS	MESSY	LETTS	DEUCE
BERRA	KERES	TERNS	NESTS	LETTY	FEUAR
BERRY	KERFS	TERRA	PESKY	LETUP	FEUDS
BERTA	KERNS	TERRI	PESOS	METAL	FEUED
BERTH	KERRY	TERRY	PESTS	METAS	LEUCO
BERTS	LEROY	TERSE	RESET	METED	LEUDS
BERTY	MERCI	VERAS	RESIN	METER	LEUKO
BERYL	MERCY	VERBS	RESTS	METES	MEUSE
CERAM	MERGE	VERDI	TESLA	METHO	NEUME
CERAT	MERIT	VERGE	TESTA	METIS	NEURI
CERED	MERLE	VERMI	TESTS	METOL	NEURO
CERES	MEROE	VERNA	TESTY	METRE	******
CERIA	MERRY	VERNE	VESIC	METRO	-EV--
CERIC	NEROS	VERNS	VESTA	METRY	******
CEROS	NERVE	VERSE	VESTS	NETER	BEVAN
DERBY	NERVY	VERSO	WESER	NETTY	BEVEL
DEREK	PERCH	VERST	YESES	PETAL	BEVIN
DERMA	PERCY	VERTU	ZESTS	PETER	DEVAS
DERMO	PERDU	VERVE	ZESTY	PETES	DEVIL
DERRY	PERES	XERIC	******	PETIT	DEVON
EERIE	PERIL	XEROX	-ET--	PETRO	FEVER
FERAL	PERIS	XERUS	******	PETRY	KEVEL
FERIA	PERKS	YERBA	AETAT	PETTI	KEVIN
FERMI	PERKY	ZEROS	BETAS	PETTO	LEVEE
FERNS	PERLE	******	BETEL	PETTY	LEVEL
FERNY	PERON	-ES--	BETHS	RETCH	LEVEN
		******			
		AESIR			
		AESOP			

LEVER	TEXAS	AGANA	******	CHARM	SHARI
LEVIS	TEXTS	AGAPE	-GM--	CHARO	SHARK
NEVER	VEXED	AGATE	******	CHARS	SHARP
NEVIL	VEXER	AGAVE	OGMIC	CHART	SHAUN
NEVIS	VEXES	AGAZE	******	CHARY	SHAVE
NEVUS	VEXIL	******	-GN--	CHASE	SHAWL
REVEL	******	-GD--	******	CHASM	SHAWM
REVET	-EY--	******	AGNES	CHATS	SHAWN
REVUE	******	OGDEN	AGNIS	CHAWS	SHAWS
SEVEN	KEYED	******	IGNAZ	DHAKS	SHAYS
SEVER	LEYTE	-GE--	******	GHANA	THADS
******	******	******	-GO--	GHATS	THADY
-EW--	-EZ--	AGENT	******	GHAUT	THANE
******	******	EGEAN	AGONY	GHAZI	THANK
DEWAN	BEZEL	EGEST	AGORA	KHADI	THAWS
DEWED	MEZZO	OGEES	******	KHAKI	WHACK
DEWEY	REZIN	******	-GR--	KHANS	WHALE
FEWER	******	-GG--	******	LHASA	WHAMS
HEWED	-FF--	******	AGREE	PHAGE	WHANG
HEWER	******	AGGER	EGRET	PHAGO	WHAPS
JEWEL	AFFIX	AGGIE	OGRES	PHAGY	WHARF
JEWRY	EFFIE	EGGAR	******	PHANE	WHAUP
LEWES	OFFAL	EGGED	-GU--	PHANY	******
LEWIE	OFFER	EGGER	******	PHASE	-HE--
LEWIS	******	******	AGUES	PHASY	******
MEWED	-FI--	-GH--	******	RHAGE	AHEAD
MEWLS	******	******	-GY--	RHAGY	CHEAP
NEWEL	AFIRE	AGHAS	******	SHACK	CHEAT
NEWER	******	OGHAM	EGYPT	SHADE	CHECK
NEWLY	-FO--	******	******	SHADY	CHEEK
NEWSY	******	-GI--	-HA--	SHAFT	CHEEP
NEWTS	AFOOT	******	******	SHAGS	CHEER
PEWEE	AFORE	AGILE	BHANG	SHAHS	CHEFS
PEWIT	AFOUL	AGING	CHAET	SHAKE	CHELA
SEWED	******	AGIOS	CHAFE	SHAKO	CHEMI
SEWER	-FR--	AGIST	CHAFF	SHAKY	CHEMO
******	******	OGIVE	CHAIN	SHALE	CHERT
-EX--	AFROS	******	CHAIR	SHALL	CHESS
******	******	-GL--	CHALK	SHALT	CHEST
DEXTR	-FT--	******	CHAMP	SHALY	CHETH
HEXAD	AFTER	AGLEE	CHANG	SHAME	CHETS
HEXED	AFTRA	AGLET	CHANT	SHAMS	CHEVY
HEXES	OFTEN	AGLEY	CHAOS	SHANK	CHEWS
HEXYL	******	AGLOW	CHAPE	SHANS	CHEWY
NEXUS	-GA--	IGLOO	CHAPS	SHANT	GHENT
SEXED	******	OGLED	CHAPT	SHAPE	PHEBE
SEXES	AGAIN	OGLER	CHARD	SHARD	PHENO
SEXTO	AGAMA	OGLES	CHARE	SHARE	RHEAS

RHEUM	CHILD	THICK	CHOPS	THONG	SHULS
SHEAF	CHILE	THIEF	CHORD	THORN	SHUNS
SHEAR	CHILI	THIGH	CHORE	THORP	SHUNT
SHEAS	CHILL	THINE	CHORO	THOSE	SHUSH
SHEBA	CHILO	THING	CHOSE	THOTH	SHUTE
SHEDS	CHIME	THINK	CHOWS	WHOLE	SHUTS
SHEEN	CHIMP	THINS	DHOLE	WHOOP	THUDS
SHEEP	CHINA	THIOL	DHOLI	WHOPS	THUGS
SHEER	CHINE	THIRD	DHOTI	WHORE	THUJA
SHEET	CHINK	WHICH	DHOWS	WHORL	THULE
SHEIK	CHINO	WHIFF	GHOST	WHORT	THUMB
SHELF	CHINS	WHIGS	GHOUL	WHOSE	THUMP
SHELL	CHIOS	WHILE	HHOUR	WHOSO	THURS
SHEOL	CHIPS	WHIMS	KHOND	******	******
SHERD	CHIRM	WHINE	PHOBE	-HR--	-HY--
SHEWN	CHIRO	WHINS	PHONE	******	******
SHEWS	CHIRP	WHINY	PHONO	CHRIS	CHYLE
THECA	CHIRR	WHIPS	PHONY	CHROM	CHYME
THEDA	CHITA	WHIPT	PHORE	CHRON	PHYCO
THEFT	CHITS	WHIRL	PHOTO	CHRYS	PHYLA
THEIR	CHIVE	WHIRR	PHOTS	IHRAM	PHYLE
THEME	PHIAL	WHIRS	RHODA	PHREN	PHYLL
THERE	PHILA	WHISH	RHOEA	SHRED	PHYLO
THERM	PHILE	WHISK	RHOMB	SHREW	PHYRE
THESE	PHILO	WHIST	RHONE	SHRUB	PHYSI
THETA	PHILS	WHITE	SHOAL	SHRUG	PHYTE
THEWS	PHILY	WHITS	SHOAT	THREE	PHYTO
THEWY	PHIPS	******	SHOCK	THREW	RHYME
WHEAL	RHINE	-HL--	SHOER	THROB	SHYER
WHEAT	RHINO	******	SHOES	THROE	SHYLY
WHEEL	RHIZO	CHLOE	SHOJI	THROW	THYME
WHELK	SHIAH	CHLOR	SHONE	THRUM	THYMY
WHELM	SHIED	PHLEB	SHOOK	******	THYRO
WHELP	SHIER	PHLOX	SHOOS	-HU--	******
WHENS	SHIFT	UHLAN	SHOOT	******	-IA--
WHERE	SHILL	******	SHOPS	CHUBS	******
WHETS	SHILY	-HM--	SHORE	CHUCK	BIALY
WHEYS	SHIMS	******	SHORL	CHUFA	DIALS
******	SHINE	KHMER	SHORN	CHUGS	DIANA
-HI--	SHINS	OHMIC	SHORT	CHUMP	DIANE
******	SHINY	******	SHOTE	CHUMS	DIARY
CHIAN	SHIPS	-HO--	SHOTS	CHUNK	DIAZO
CHIAS	SHIRE	******	SHOUT	CHURL	FIATS
CHIBA	SHIRK	CHOCK	SHOVE	CHURN	GIANT
CHICK	SHIRR	CHOIR	SHOWN	CHURR	LIANA
CHICO	SHIRT	CHOKE	SHOWS	CHUTE	LIANE
CHIDE	SHIVE	CHOKY	SHOWY	RHUMB	LIANG
CHIEF	SHIVS	CHOLE	THOLE	SHUCK	LIARS

MIAMI	DICHO	AIDER	DIENE	MIFFY	WIGAN
MIAOW	DICKS	AIDES	DIETS	NIFTY	WIGHT
MIAUL	DICKY	BIDDY	FIEFS	RIFFS	******
PIAND	DICTA	BIDED	FIELD	RIFLE	-IH--
PIANO	FICES	BIDES	FIEND	RIFTS	******
PIAVE	FICHE	BIDET	FIERY	SIFTS	BIHAR
RIALS	FICHU	CIDAL	HIERO	TIFFS	JIHAD
RIANT	HICKS	CIDER	KIERS	******	NIHIL
RIATA	KICKS	DIDNT	LIEGE	-IG--	******
SIALO	LICHT	DIDOS	LIEIN	******	-II--
TIARA	LICIT	DIDST	LIENS	BIGHT	******
VIALS	LICKS	EIDER	LIEUT	BIGLY	GIING
VIAND	MICAH	FIDEL	MIENS	BIGOT	******
******	MICAS	GIDDY	NIECE	CIGAR	-IJ--
-IB--	MICKY	HIDER	PIECE	DIGIT	******
******	MICRA	HIDES	PIERS	EIGHT	BIJOU
BIBBS	MICRO	HIDTO	PIETA	FIGHT	DIJON
BIBLE	NICER	JIDDA	PIETY	GIGAS	FIJIS
CIBOL	NICHE	KIDDY	PIEZO	GIGOT	******
FIBER	NICKS	MIDAS	SIEGE	GIGUE	-IK--
FIBRE	NICKY	MIDDY	SIENA	HIGHS	******
FIBRO	PICAL	MIDGE	SIEUR	LIGAN	AIKEN
GIBED	PICAS	MIDST	SIEVE	LIGHT	BIKES
GIBER	PICKS	NIDED	TIEIN	LIGNI	BIKOL
GIBES	PICOT	NIDES	TIERS	LIGNO	DIKED
GIBUS	PICRO	NIDUS	TIEUP	MIGHT	DIKER
JIBED	PICTS	OIDEA	VIEWS	NIGEL	DIKES
JIBES	PICUL	RIDER	VIEWY	NIGER	HIKED
KIBEI	RICED	RIDES	WIELD	NIGHT	HIKER
KIBES	RICER	RIDGE	YIELD	NIGRI	HIKES
LIBBY	RICES	RIDGY	******	PIGGY	LIKED
LIBEL	RICIN	SIDED	-IF--	PIGMY	LIKEN
LIBER	RICKS	SIDER	******	RIGEL	LIKES
LIBRA	RICKY	SIDES	BIFFS	RIGGS	MIKES
LIBYA	SICES	SIDLE	BIFFY	RIGHT	MIKEY
SIBYL	SICKS	SIDON	BIFID	RIGID	PIKAS
TIBER	TICAL	TIDAL	FIFED	RIGOR	PIKED
TIBET	TICKS	TIDED	FIFER	SIGHS	PIKER
TIBIA	VICAR	TIDES	FIFES	SIGHT	PIKES
VIBES	VICES	VIDAL	FIFTH	SIGIL	SIKHS
ZIBET	VICHY	VIDEO	FIFTY	SIGMA	TIKIS
******	VICKS	WIDDY	GIFTS	SIGNE	******
-IC--	VICKY	WIDEN	HIFIS	SIGNS	-IL--
******	WICKS	WIDER	JIFFS	TIGER	******
BICES	******	WIDOW	JIFFY	TIGHT	AILED
DICED	-ID--	WIDTH	LIFER	TIGRE	BILBO
DICER	******	******	LIFTS	VIGIL	BILES
DICEY	AIDAS	-IE--	MIFFS	VIGOR	BILGE
	AIDED	******			
		BIERS			
		DIEGO			

BILGY	MILKS	VILLS	RIMED	FINNY	NINAS
BILKS	MILKY	VILNA	RIMER	GINKS	NINES
BILLS	MILLI	WILDE	RIMES	GINNY	NINNY
BILLY	MILLS	WILDS	SIMAR	HINDI	NINTH
CILIA	MILLY	WILED	SIMON	HINDS	NINUS
DILDO	MILNE	WILES	SIMPS	HINDU	PINAS
DILYS	MILTS	WILEY	TIMED	HINGE	PINCH
FILAR	MILTY	WILLA	TIMER	HINNY	PINED
FILCH	OILED	WILLS	TIMES	HINTS	PINEL
FILED	OILER	WILLY	TIMID	JINGO	PINER
FILER	PILAF	WILMA	TIMMY	JINKS	PINES
FILES	PILAR	WILTS	TIMOR	JINNI	PINEY
FILET	PILEA	******	VIMEN	JINNY	PINGO
FILLS	PILED	-IM--	ZIMRI	KINDS	PINGS
FILLY	PILEI	******	******	KINGS	PINKS
FILMS	PILES	AIMED	-IN--	KININ	PINKY
FILMY	PILIS	AIMEE	******	KINKS	PINNA
FILTH	PILLS	CIMEX	AINOS	KINKY	PINNI
FILUM	PILOT	DIMER	AINUS	LINDA	PINNY
GILDA	RILED	DIMES	BINAL	LINED	PINON
GILDS	RILES	DIMLY	BINDS	LINEN	PINTA
GILES	RILEY	EIMER	BINES	LINER	PINTO
GILLS	RILLE	GIMEL	BINET	LINES	PINTS
HILDA	RILLS	GIMPS	BINGE	LINEY	PINUP
HILLS	SILAS	GIMPY	BINGO	LINGA	RINDS
HILLY	SILEX	JIMMY	BINIT	LINGO	RINGS
HILTS	SILIC	LIMBI	CINCH	LINGS	RINKS
HILUM	SILKS	LIMBO	CINDY	LININ	RINSE
JILLS	SILKY	LIMBS	DINAH	LINKS	SINAI
JILTS	SILLS	LIMED	DINAR	LINTY	SINCE
KILAH	SILLY	LIMEN	DINED	LINUS	SINES
KILLS	SILOS	LIMES	DINER	MINAE	SINEW
KILNS	SILTS	LIMEY	DINES	MINAS	SINGE
KILOS	SILTY	LIMIT	DINGO	MINCE	SINGS
KILTS	SILVA	LIMNS	DINGS	MINDI	SINKS
KILTY	TILDA	LIMPS	DINGY	MINDS	SINON
LILAC	TILDE	MIMED	DINKA	MINED	SINUS
LILAS	TILED	MIMEO	DINKY	MINER	TINAS
LILLE	TILER	MIMER	DINTS	MINES	TINCT
LILLI	TILES	MIMES	FINAL	MINGY	TINEA
LILLY	TILLS	MIMIC	FINCH	MINIM	TINED
LILTS	TILLY	MIMIR	FINDS	MINKS	TINES
LILYS	TILTH	MIMIS	FINED	MINNA	TINGE
MILAN	TILTS	NIMBI	FINER	MINOR	TINGS
MILCH	VILER	NIMES	FINES	MINOS	TINNY
MILER	VILLA	PIMAN	FINIS	MINSK	TINTS
MILES	VILLE	PIMAS	FINKS	MINTS	UINTA
MILIA	VILLI	PIMPS	FINNS	MINUS	VINAS

VINCE	GIPON	DIRER	WIRES	VISAS	NITRE
VINCI	GIPSY	DIRGE	WIRRA	VISCT	NITRI
VINES	HIPPO	DIRKS	ZIRON	VISED	NITRO
VINIC	HIPPY	DIRTY	******	VISES	NITTY
VINNY	LIPID	FIRED	-IS--	VISIT	PITAS
VINYL	LIPPI	FIRER	******	VISOR	PITCH
WINCE	LIPPY	FIRES	AISLE	VISTA	PITHS
WINCH	NIPAS	FIRMS	AISNE	WISED	PITHY
WINDS	NIPPY	FIRNS	BISES	WISER	PITON
WINDY	PIPAL	FIRRY	BISON	WISES	PITOT
WINED	PIPED	FIRST	BISSE	WISPS	RITAS
WINES	PIPER	FIRTH	CISCO	WISPY	RITES
WINGS	PIPES	GIRDS	CISSY	******	RITZY
WINGY	PIPET	GIRLS	CISTS	-IT--	SITAR
WINKS	PIPIT	GIRON	DISCI	******	SITED
WINOS	RIPEN	GIROS	DISCO	AITCH	SITES
WINZE	RIPER	GIRSH	DISCS	BITCH	SITIN
ZINCS	RIPON	GIRTH	DISHY	BITER	SITKA
ZINCY	SIPES	GIRTS	DISKO	BITES	SITUS
ZINGY	TIPPY	HIRAM	DISKS	BITTS	TITAN
ZINKY	TIPSY	HIRED	FISCS	CITED	TITER
******	VIPER	HIRER	FISHY	CITES	TITHE
-IO--	WIPED	HIRES	FISTS	CITRA	TITIS
******	WIPER	KIRIN	GISMO	DITAS	TITLE
BIOTA	WIPES	KIRKS	GISTS	DITCH	TITUS
CIONS	XIPHI	LIRAS	LISAS	DITTO	VITAE
DIODE	YIPES	MIRED	LISLE	DITTY	VITAL
DIONE	ZIPPY	MIRES	LISPS	FITCH	VITRI
FIONA	******	MIRTH	LISTS	FITLY	VITTA
FIORD	-IQ--	MIRZA	LISZT	HITCH	WITAN
KIOSK	******	SIRED	MISDO	KITED	WITCH
KIOWA	FIQUE	SIREN	MISER	KITES	WITHE
LIONS	PIQUE	SIRES	MISES	KITTY	WITHY
NIOBE	******	SIRUP	MISSY	LITAI	WITTE
PIONS	-IR--	TIRED	MISTS	LITAS	WITTY
PIOUS	******	TIREE	MISTY	LITER	******
RIOTS	AIRED	TIRES	NISAN	LITHE	-IU--
SIOUX	BIRCH	TIROS	NISEI	LITHO	******
TIOGA	BIRDS	VIRAL	NISUS	LITRE	FIUME
VIOLA	BIRLE	VIREO	PISCI	MITCH	******
VIOLS	BIRLS	VIRES	RISEN	MITER	-IV--
******	BIRRS	VIRGA	RISER	MITES	******
-IP--	BIRTH	VIRGE	RISES	MITRE	CIVET
******	CIRCA	VIRGO	RISKS	MITTS	CIVIC
BIPED	CIRCE	VIRTU	RISKY	MITZI	CIVIL
BIPOD	CIRRI	VIRUS	RISUS	MITZY	DIVAN
DIPLO	CIRRO	WIRED	SISAL	NITER	DIVAS
DIPPY	DIRCK	WIRER	SISSY	NITON	DIVED

DIVER	MIXES	******	******	CLANK	GLAZE
DIVES	MIXUP	-KA--	-KR--	CLANS	GLAZY
DIVOT	NIXED	******	******	CLAPS	KLARA
DIVVY	NIXES	OKAPI	AKRON	CLARA	LLAMA
FIVER	NIXIE	OKAYS	OKRAS	CLARE	LLANO
FIVES	NIXON	SKALD	******	CLARK	OLAFS
GIVEN	PIXIE	SKATE	-KU--	CLARO	OLAVS
GIVER	SIXES	UKASE	******	CLARY	PLACE
GIVES	SIXTE	******	SKUAS	CLASH	PLACK
HIVED	SIXTH	-KE--	SKULK	CLASP	PLAGI
HIVES	SIXTY	******	SKULL	CLASS	PLAID
JIVED	VIXEN	AKENE	SKUNK	CLAWS	PLAIN
KIVAS	******	SKEAN	******	CLAYS	PLAIT
LIVED	-IY--	SKEED	-KY--	******	PLANE
LIVEN	******	SKEES	******	ELAEO	PLANI
LIVER	RIYAL	SKEET	SKYEY	ELAIN	PLANK
LIVES	******	SKEGS	******	ELAIO	PLANO
LIVIA	-IZ--	SKEIN	-LA--	ELAND	PLANS
LIVID	******	SKEPS	******	ELATE	PLANT
LIVRE	BIZET	SKEWS	ALACK	FLACK	PLASH
NIVAL	DIZEN	******	ALADA	FLAGS	PLASM
PIVOT	DIZZY	-KI--	ALAIN	FLAIL	PLAST
RIVAL	FIZZY	******	ALAMO	FLAIR	PLASY
RIVED	GIZMO	EKING	ALAND	FLAKE	PLATA
RIVEN	LIZAS	OKIEH	ALANS	FLAKY	PLATE
RIVER	LIZZY	OKIES	ALARM	FLAME	PLATO
RIVES	MIZEN	OKING	ALARY	FLAMS	PLATS
RIVET	NIZAM	SKIDS	ALATE	FLAMY	PLATY
SIVAN	NIZER	SKIED	BLABS	FLANK	PLAYA
VIVID	PIZZA	SKIER	BLACK	FLANS	PLAYS
WIVED	SIZAR	SKIES	BLADE	FLAPS	PLAZA
WIVER	SIZED	SKIFF	BLAHS	FLARE	SLABS
WIVES	SIZES	SKILL	BLAIN	FLASH	SLACK
******	TIZZY	SKIMO	BLAKE	FLASK	SLAGS
-IW--	VIZIR	SKIMP	BLAME	FLATS	SLAIN
******	VIZOR	SKIMS	BLANC	FLAWS	SLAKE
DIWAN	WIZEN	SKINK	BLAND	FLAWY	SLAMS
KIWIS	******	SKINS	BLANK	FLAXY	SLANG
******	-JE--	SKIPS	BLARE	FLAYS	SLANT
-IX--	******	SKIRL	BLASE	GLACE	SLAPS
******	EJECT	SKIRR	BLAST	GLADE	SLASH
DIXIE	FJELD	SKIRT	BLATS	GLADS	SLATE
DIXIT	******	SKITS	BLAZE	GLAIR	SLATS
FIXED	-JO--	SKIVE	******	GLAND	SLATY
FIXER	******	******	CLACK	GLANS	SLAVE
FIXES	FJORD	-KO--	CLAIM	GLARE	SLAVO
MIXED	NJORD	******	CLAMP	GLARY	SLAVS
MIXER		IKONS	CLAMS	GLASS	SLAWS
		SKOAL	CLANG	GLAUC	SLAYS

******	CLEAN	SLEDS	BLISS	SLICK	ELMER
-LB--	CLEAR	SLEEK	BLITZ	SLIDE	ILMEN
******	CLEAT	SLEEP	CLICK	SLIER	******
ALBAN	CLEEK	SLEET	CLIFF	SLIGO	-LN--
ALBAS	CLEFS	SLEPT	CLIMB	SLILY	******
ALBEE	CLEFT	SLEWS	CLIME	SLIME	ULNAE
ALBIN	CLEMS	ULEMA	CLINE	SLIMS	ULNAR
ALBUM	CLEON	ULENT	CLING	SLIMY	ULNAS
ELBOW	CLERK	******	CLINK	SLING	******
******	CLEWS	-LF--	CLINO	SLINK	-LO--
-LC--	ELECT	******	CLINT	SLIPS	******
******	ELEGY	ALFIE	CLIOS	SLIPT	ALOES
ALCAN	ELEMI	ELFIN	CLIPS	SLITS	ALOFT
ULCER	ELENA	******	CLIVE	******	ALOHA
******	FLEAM	-LG--	ELIAS	-LK--	ALOIN
-LD--	FLEAS	******	ELIDE	******	ALOIS
******	FLECK	ALGAE	ELIHU	ALKYL	ALONE
ALDAN	FLEER	ALGAL	ELIOT	******	ALONG
ALDEN	FLEES	ALGER	ELISE	-LL--	ALOOF
ALDER	FLEET	ALGIA	ELITE	******	ALOUD
ALDIS	FLESH	ALGID	ELIZA	ALLAH	BLOAT
ALDOL	FLEWS	ALGIE	FLICK	ALLAN	BLOBS
ALDOS	FLEXI	ALGIN	FLIED	ALLAY	BLOCK
ALDUS	GLEAM	ALGOL	FLIER	ALLEN	BLOCS
BLDGS	GLEAN	ALGOR	FLIES	ALLEY	BLOIS
ELDER	GLEBE	ALGUM	FLING	ALLIE	BLOKE
OLDEN	GLEDE	ALGYS	FLINT	ALLIN	BLOND
OLDER	GLEDS	ELGAR	FLIPS	ALLIS	BLOOD
******	GLEES	ELGIN	FLIRT	ALLOT	BLOOM
-LE--	GLEET	OLGAS	FLITE	ALLOW	BLOTS
******	GLENN	******	FLITS	ALLOY	BLOWN
ALECK	GLENS	-LI--	GLIDE	ALLYL	BLOWS
ALECS	ILEAC	******	GLIMS	ELLAS	BLOWY
ALEFS	ILEAL	ALIAS	GLINT	ELLEN	CLOAK
ALEPH	ILEUM	ALIBI	ILIAC	ELLIE	CLOCK
ALERT	ILEUS	ALICE	ILIAD	ELLIS	CLODS
ALEUT	OLEAN	ALIEN	ILIAN	ILLUS	CLOGS
ALEXA	OLEIC	ALIFS	ILION	MLLES	CLONE
BLEAK	OLEIN	ALIGN	ILIUM	OLLAS	CLONS
BLEAR	OLENT	ALIKE	OLIGO	OLLIE	CLOPS
BLEAT	PLEAD	ALINE	OLIOS	******	CLOSE
BLEBS	PLEAS	ALIST	OLIVE	-LM--	CLOTH
BLEED	PLEAT	ALIVE	PLICA	******	CLOTS
BLEEP	PLEBE	BLIGH	PLIED	ALMAH	CLOUD
BLEND	PLEBS	BLIMP	PLIER	ALMAS	CLOUT
BLENT	PLEGY	BLIND	PLIES	ALMUD	CLOVE
BLESS	PLENA	BLINK	PLINY	ALMUG	CLOWN
BLEST	SLEAT	BLIPS	SLICE	ELMAN	

CLOYS	SLOTS	CLUNG	ELVAN	AMBLE	******
ELOIN	SLOWS	CLUNY	ELVER	AMBOS	-MI--
ELOPE	SLOYD	ELUDE	ELVES	AMBRY	******
FLOAT	ULOSE	FLUBS	ELVIN	EMBAR	AMIAS
FLOCK	ULOUS	FLUES	******	EMBAY	AMICE
FLOCS	ZLOTY	FLUFF	-LW--	EMBED	AMIDE
FLOES	******	FLUID	******	EMBER	AMIDO
FLOGS	-LP--	FLUKE	ALWAY	EMBOW	AMIEL
FLONG	******	FLUKY	ALWIN	EMBRY	AMIES
FLOOD	ALPHA	FLUME	ELWIN	EMBUS	AMIGO
FLOOR	ALPHY	FLUMP	******	IMBED	AMINE
FLOPS	******	FLUNG	-LY--	IMBUE	AMINO
FLORA	-LS--	FLUNK	******	OMBER	AMIRS
FLOSS	******	FLUOR	ALYCE	OMBRE	AMISH
FLOUR	ELSAS	FLUSH	BLYTH	OMBRO	AMISS
FLOUT	ELSIE	FLUTE	CLYDE	UMBEL	AMITY
FLOWN	******	FLUTY	FLYBY	UMBER	EMILE
FLOWS	-LT--	GLUED	FLYER	UMBLE	EMILS
FLOYD	******	GLUES	GLYCO	UMBOS	EMILY
GLOAT	ALTAI	GLUEY	GLYPH	UMBRA	EMIRS
GLOBE	ALTAR	GLUME	SLYER	******	EMITS
GLOBS	ALTAS	GLUTS	SLYLY	-MC--	IMIDE
GLOOM	ALTER	PLUCK	SLYPE	******	IMIDO
GLORY	ALTON	PLUGS	******	EMCEE	IMIDS
GLOSS	ALTOS	PLUMB	-MA--	******	IMINE
GLOST	ELTON	PLUME	******	-MD--	IMINO
GLOVE	ULTRA	PLUMP	AMAHS	******	OMITS
GLOWS	******	PLUMS	AMAIN	EMDEN	SMILE
GLOZE	-LU--	PLUMY	AMANA	******	SMIRK
ILONA	******	PLUNK	AMASS	-ME--	SMITE
KLOOF	ALUIN	PLURI	AMATE	******	SMITH
LLOYD	ALULA	PLUSH	AMATI	AMEBA	UMIAK
OLOGY	ALUMS	PLUTO	AMAZE	AMEER	******
PLODS	BLUED	PLUVI	IMAGE	AMEND	-MM--
PLOID	BLUER	SLUBS	IMAGO	AMENS	******
PLONK	BLUES	SLUED	IMAMS	AMENT	AMMAN
PLOPS	BLUET	SLUES	OMAHA	BMEWS	AMMON
PLOTS	BLUFF	SLUGS	OMASA	EMEER	EMMAS
PLOWS	BLUNT	SLUMP	SMACK	EMEND	EMMER
PLOYS	BLURB	SLUMS	SMALL	EMERY	EMMET
SLOBS	BLURS	SLUNG	SMALT	EMEUS	EMMIE
SLOES	BLURT	SLUNK	SMART	OMEGA	EMMYS
SLOGS	BLUSH	SLURP	SMASH	OMENS	IMMIX
SLOOP	CLUBS	SLURS	SMAZE	OMERS	******
SLOPE	CLUCK	SLUSH	******	SMEAR	-MN--
SLOPS	CLUED	SLUTS	-MB--	SMELL	******
SLOSH	CLUES	******	******	SMELT	******
SLOTH	CLUMP	-LV--	AMBER	SMEWS	AMNIA
		******	AMBIT		
		ALVAN			
		ALVIN			

******	INANE	INDIC	ANGIO	ANKUS	KNOTS
-MO--	INAPT	INDOW	ANGLE	INKED	KNOUT
******	INARM	INDRA	ANGLO	INKER	KNOWN
AMOLE	KNACK	INDRI	ANGRY	INKLE	KNOWS
AMONG	KNARS	INDUE	ANGST	******	SNOBS
AMOUR	KNAVE	INDUS	ANGUS	-NL--	SNOOD
EMORY	SNACK	UNDEE	INGLE	******	SNOOK
EMOTE	SNAFU	UNDER	INGOT	ANLAS	SNOOP
SMOCK	SNAGS	UNDID	******	INLAW	SNOOT
SMOGS	SNAIL	UNDUE	-NH--	INLAY	SNORE
SMOKE	SNAKE	******	******	INLET	SNORT
SMOKY	SNAKY	-NE--	UNHAT	UNLAY	SNOTS
SMOLT	SNAPS	******	******	UNLIT	SNOUT
SMOTE	SNARE	ANEAR	-NI--	******	SNOWS
******	SNARK	ANELE	******	-NM--	SNOWY
-MP--	SNARL	ANEMO	ANILE	******	******
******	SNATH	ANENT	ANILS	UNMAN	-NP--
AMPHI	UNAPT	ENEAS	ANIMA	UNMEW	******
AMPHR	UNARM	ENEMA	ANIME	******	INPUT
AMPLE	UNAUS	ENEMY	ANION	-NN--	UNPEG
AMPLY	******	INEPT	ANISE	******	UNPEN
AMPUL	-NB--	INERT	ANISO	ANNAL	UNPIN
EMPTY	******	KNEAD	ANITA	ANNAM	******
IMPEL	UNBAR	KNEED	ENIDS	ANNAS	-NR--
IMPLY	******	KNEEL	INIGO	ANNES	
IMPOT	-NC--	KNEES	INION	ANNEX	ENROL
******	******	KNELL	KNIFE	ANNIE	UNREF
-MU--	ANCON	KNELT	KNITS	ANNOY	UNRIG
******	ENCYC	ONEGA	ONION	ANNUL	UNRIP
AMUCK	INCAN	ONEIR	ONIRO	ENNEA	******
AMUSE	INCAS	ONERY	SNICK	ENNUI	-NS--
SMUTS	INCUR	PNEUM	SNIDE	INNED	******
******	INCUS	SNEAD	SNIFF	INNER	ANSAE
-MY--	UNCAP	SNEAK	SNIPE	******	ANSEL
******	UNCLE	SNEER	SNIPS	-NO--	ENSUE
AMYLO	UNCUT	SNELL	UNIAT	******	INSET
AMYLS	******	VNECK	UNIFY	ANODE	ONSET
******	-ND--	******	UNION	ANOMY	UNSAY
-NA--	******	-NF--	UNITE	ENOCH	UNSEX
******	ANDES	******	UNITS	ENOLA	******
ENACT	ANDRE	INFER	UNITY	ENOLS	-NT--
ENARE	ANDRO	INFIX	******	GNOME	******
ENATE	ANDYS	INFRA	-NJ--	GNOMY	ANTAE
GNARL	ENDED	UNFIT	******	KNOBS	ANTAL
GNASH	ENDOW	UNFIX	ANJOU	KNOCK	ANTED
GNATS	ENDUE	******	ENJOY	KNOLL	ANTES
GNAWN	INDEX	-NG--	******	KNOPS	ANTHO
GNAWS	INDIA	******	-NK--	KNOSP	ANTIC
		ANGEL	******		
		ANGER	ANKHS		
			ANKLE		

ANTIS	BOAST	******	HOCUS	NODAL	LOFTS
ANTON	BOATS	-OB--	JOCKO	NODDY	LOFTY
ANTRA	COACH	******	LOCAL	NODES	SOFAS
ENTER	COALS	BOBBY	LOCHS	NODUS	SOFIA
ENTIA	COALY	COBBS	LOCKE	PODGY	SOFTA
ENTOM	COAST	COBIA	LOCKS	PODIA	SOFTY
ENTRY	COATI	COBLE	LOCOS	RODDY	TOFTS
INTER	COATS	COBRA	LOCUM	RODEO	******
INTRA	DOALL	DOBBY	LOCUS	RODIN	-OG--
INTRO	FOALS	DOBIE	MOCHA	SODAS	******
UNTIE	FOAMS	DOBLA	MOCKS	SODOM	BOGAN
UNTIL	FOAMY	DOBRA	NOCKS	TODAY	BOGEY
******	GOADS	GOBOS	NOCTI	TODDS	BOGGY
-NU--	GOALS	GOBYS	POCKS	TODDY	BOGIE
******	GOATS	HOBBS	POCKY	TODOS	BOGLE
INURE	HOAGY	HOBBY	ROCKS	VODKA	BOGOR
INURN	HOARD	HOBOS	ROCKY	WODAN	BOGUS
KNURL	HOARY	LOBAR	SOCIO	WODEN	COGON
KNURR	JOANS	LOBBY	SOCKS	YODEL	DOGES
KNURS	KOALA	LOBED	SOCLE	YODHS	DOGGY
SNUBS	LOACH	LOBES	VOCAL	******	DOGIE
SNUFF	LOADS	LOBOS	VOCES	-OE--	DOGMA
SNUGS	LOAFS	NOBBY	******	******	FOGEY
******	LOAMS	NOBEL	-OD--	BOERS	FOGGY
-NV--	LOAMY	NOBLE	******	COEDS	GOGOL
******	LOANS	NOBLY	BODED	COELE	HOGAN
ANVIL	LOATH	ROBED	BODES	COELO	LOGAN
ENVOY	MOANS	ROBES	CODAS	COENO	LOGES
INVAR	MOATS	ROBIN	CODED	DOERS	LOGIA
******	NOAHS	ROBLE	CODER	DOEST	LOGIC
-NW--	POACH	ROBOT	CODES	DOETH	LOGOS
******	ROACH	SOBER	CODEX	FOEHN	LOGUE
UNWED	ROADS	TOBOL	DODEC	GOERS	MOGUL
******	ROALD	TOBYS	DODGE	HOERS	NOGGS
-NY--	ROAMS	******	DODGY	JOELS	POGEY
******	ROANS	-OC--	DODOS	JOEYS	ROGER
SNYES	ROARS	******	GODLY	KOELS	ROGUE
******	ROAST	BOCHE	HODGE	LOESS	SOGGY
-NZ--	SOAKS	COCAS	IODIC	NOELS	TOGAE
******	SOAPS	COCCI	IODOL	POEMS	TOGAS
ANZAC	SOAPY	COCKS	KODAK	POESY	TOGUE
ANZIO	SOARS	COCKY	LODEN	POETS	VOGUE
UNZIP	TOADS	COCOA	LODES	TOEIN	VOGUL
******	TOADY	COCOS	LODGE	******	YOGEE
-OA--	TOAST	DOCKS	MODAL	-OF--	YOGHS
******	WOADS	FOCAL	MODEL	******	YOGIC
BOARD	WOALD	FOCUS	MODES	DOFFS	YOGIN
BOARS		HOCKS	MODUS	GOFER	YOGIS

******	VOICE	COLLY	MOLLY	COMAE	******
-OH--	VOIDS	COLNE	MOLTO	COMAL	-ON--
******	VOILA	COLON	MOLTS	COMAS	******
BOHEA	VOILE	COLOR	POLAR	COMBO	BONDS
BOHOL	******	COLTS	POLED	COMBS	BONED
COHAN	-OJ--	COLZA	POLES	COMDR	BONER
JOHNS	******	DOLCE	POLIO	COMDT	BONES
MOHUR	SOJAS	DOLED	POLKA	COMER	BONGO
******	******	DOLES	POLLS	COMES	BONGS
-OI--	-OK--	DOLLS	POLLY	COMET	BONIN
******	******	DOLLY	POLYP	COMFY	BONNY
BOILS	COKED	DOLOR	ROLES	COMIC	BONUS
BOISE	COKER	DOLPH	ROLFE	COMMA	BONZE
COIFS	COKES	DOLTS	ROLFS	COMPO	CONCH
COIGN	COKEY	EOLIC	ROLLO	COMTE	CONED
COILS	HOKAN	EOLUS	ROLLS	COMUS	CONES
COINS	HOKUM	FOLDS	ROLPH	DOMED	CONEY
DOILY	JOKED	FOLIA	SOLAN	DOMES	CONGA
DOING	JOKER	FOLIC	SOLAR	DOMIC	CONGE
DOITS	JOKES	FOLIO	SOLDI	HOMED	CONGO
FOILS	MOKES	FOLKS	SOLDO	HOMEO	CONIC
FOISM	POKED	FOLLY	SOLED	HOMER	CONIO
FOIST	POKER	GOLDA	SOLES	HOMES	CONKS
GOING	POKES	GOLDS	SOLFA	HOMEY	CONNY
HOICK	POKEY	GOLEM	SOLID	KOMOS	CONTD
HOIST	SOKES	GOLFS	SOLON	MOMUS	CONTE
JOINS	TOKAY	GOLLY	SOLOS	NOMAD	CONTO
JOINT	TOKEN	HOLDS	SOLUS	NOMAS	CONTR
JOIST	TOKYO	HOLED	SOLVE	OOMPH	CONUS
KOINE	WOKEN	HOLES	TOLAN	POMES	DONAR
LOINS	YOKED	HOLEY	TOLAS	POMMY	DONAS
LOIRE	YOKEL	HOLLY	TOLES	ROMAN	DONEE
MOILS	YOKES	HOLMS	TOLLS	ROMEO	DONNA
MOIRA	******	HOLST	TOLYL	ROMPS	DONNE
MOIRE	-OL--	JOLES	VOLAR	SOMAT	DONOR
MOIST	******	JOLLY	VOLES	SOMME	DONTS
NOISE	BOLAR	JOLTS	VOLGA	SOMNI	FONDA
NOISY	BOLAS	JOLTY	VOLTA	TOMAN	FONTS
POILU	BOLES	KOLAS	VOLTE	TOMAS	GONAD
POIND	BOLLS	LOLAS	VOLTI	TOMBS	GONDI
POINT	BOLOS	LOLLS	VOLTS	TOMES	GONER
POISE	BOLTS	LOLLY	VOLVA	TOMMY	GONGS
ROILS	BOLUS	MOLAL	WOLDS	VOMER	GONIA
ROILY	COLAS	MOLAR	WOLFS	VOMIT	GONIO
SOILS	COLDS	MOLDS	YOLKS	WOMAN	HONAN
TOILE	COLES	MOLDY	YOLKY	WOMBS	HONDO
TOILS	COLIC	MOLES	******	WOMBY	HONED
TOISE	COLIN	MOLLS	-OM--	WOMEN	HONES
			******	ZOMBI	
			BOMBE		
			BOMBS		

HONEY	TONIC	GOOFS	POOPS	KOPJE	BORTY
HONGS	TONIS	GOOFY	ROODS	LOPAT	BORTZ
HONKS	TONNE	GOOKS	ROOFS	LOPED	CORAL
HONKY	TONUS	GOONS	ROOKS	LOPER	CORAS
HONOR	TONYS	GOOSE	ROOKY	LOPES	CORBY
IONIA	ZONAL	GOOSY	ROOMS	LOPPY	CORDS
IONIC	ZONED	HOOCH	ROOMY	MOPED	CORED
JONAH	ZONES	HOODS	ROOST	MOPER	CORER
JONAS	******	HOOEY	ROOTS	MOPES	CORES
JONES	-OO--	HOOFS	ROOTY	NOPAL	CORFE
JONNY	******	HOOKE	SOOTH	NOPAR	CORFU
KONYA	BOOBS	HOOKS	SOOTS	POPES	CORGI
LONER	BOOBY	HOOKY	SOOTY	POPPY	CORIA
LONGI	BOOED	HOOPS	TOOLS	POPSY	CORKS
LONGS	BOOKS	HOOTS	TOOTH	ROPED	CORKY
MONAD	BOOMS	HOOVE	TOOTS	ROPES	CORMS
MONAS	BOONE	KOOKS	WOODS	ROPEY	CORNS
MONDE	BOONS	KOOKY	WOODY	SOPHY	CORNU
MONET	BOORS	LOOBY	WOOED	SOPOR	CORNY
MONEY	BOOST	LOOED	WOOER	SOPPY	COROT
MONKS	BOOTH	LOOFS	WOOFS	TOPAZ	CORPS
MONTE	BOOTS	LOOKS	WOOLF	TOPED	CORSE
MONTH	BOOTY	LOOMS	WOOLS	TOPEE	DORAS
MONTY	BOOZE	LOONS	WOOLY	TOPER	DORIC
NONAS	BOOZY	LOONY	WOOZY	TOPES	DORIS
NONCE	COOED	LOOPS	ZOOID	TOPHI	DORMS
NONES	COOEE	LOOPY	ZOOMS	TOPIC	DORMY
NONET	COOER	LOOSE	ZOONS	TOPIS	DORRS
PONCE	COOEY	LOOTS	******	TOPSY	DORSA
PONDS	COOKS	MOOCH	-OP--	******	DORSI
PONES	COOKY	MOODS	******	-OQ--	DORSO
RONDO	COOLS	MOODY	COPAL	******	DORUS
RONNY	COOMB	MOOED	COPEC	ROQUE	FORAY
SONAR	COONS	MOONS	COPED	TOQUE	FORBS
SONES	COOPS	MOONY	COPER	******	FORBY
SONGS	COOPT	MOORE	COPES	-OR--	FORCE
SONIA	COOTS	MOORS	COPRA	******	FORDS
SONIC	DOOLY	MOOSE	COPRO	AORTA	FORES
SONJA	DOOMS	NOOKS	COPSE	BORAX	FORGE
SONNY	DOORN	NOONS	COPTS	BORED	FORGO
SONSY	DOORS	NOOSE	DOPED	BORER	FORKS
SONYA	FOODS	POOCH	DOPES	BORES	FORLI
TONAL	FOOLS	POODS	DOPEY	BORIC	FORME
TONED	FOOTS	POOLE	HOPED	BORIS	FORMS
TONER	FOOTY	POOLS	HOPEH	BORNE	FORTE
TONES	GOODS	POONA	HOPES	BORNU	FORTH
TONGA	GOODY	POONS	KOPEC	BORON	FORTS
TONGS	GOOEY	POOPO	KOPEK	BORTS	FORTY

FORUM	MORPH	WORSE	POSSE	ROTCH	GOUTY
GORAL	MORRO	WORST	POSTS	ROTLA	HOUGH
GORED	MORSE	WORTH	ROSAS	ROTOR	HOUND
GORES	MORTA	WORTS	ROSED	SOTOL	HOURI
GORGE	MORTS	ZORIL	ROSES	SOTTO	HOURS
GORKI	MORTY	******	ROSIN	TOTAL	HOUSE
GORKY	NORAH	-OS--	******	TOTED	JOULE
GORME	NORAS	******	-OT--	TOTEM	JOUST
GORSE	NORIA	BOSCH	******	TOTER	LOUGH
GORSY	NORMA	BOSKS	BOTCH	TOTES	LOUIS
HORAE	NORMS	BOSKY	BOTHY	VOTED	LOUPE
HORAL	NORNS	BOSOM	BOTTS	VOTER	LOUPS
HORAS	NORSE	BOSON	COTES	VOTES	LOURS
HORDE	NORTH	BOSSY	COTTA	WOTAN	LOUSE
HOREB	PORCH	BOSUN	DOTED	******	LOUSY
HORNE	PORED	COSEK	DOTES	-OU--	LOUTS
HORNS	PORES	COSMO	DOTTY	******	MOUCH
HORNY	PORGE	COSTA	GOTHA	BOUGH	MOUES
HORSE	PORGY	COSTO	GOTHS	BOULE	MOULD
HORST	PORKY	COSTS	HOTEL	BOUND	MOULT
HORSY	PORNO	DOSED	HOTLY	BOURG	MOUND
HORTA	PORTS	DOSER	IOTAS	BOURN	MOUNT
HORUS	SORAS	DOSES	JOTUN	BOUSE	MOURN
JORAM	SORBS	EOSIN	KOTOS	BOUSY	MOUSE
JORGE	SOREL	FOSSA	LOTAH	BOUTS	MOUSY
JORUM	SORER	FOSSE	LOTOS	COUCH	MOUTH
KORAN	SORES	HOSEA	LOTTA	COUGH	NOUNS
KOREA	SORGO	HOSED	LOTTE	COULD	POUCH
KORUN	SORRY	HOSES	LOTTO	COUNT	POUFS
LORAN	SORTS	HOSTS	LOTTY	COUPE	POULT
LORCA	SORUS	JOSIE	LOTUS	COUPS	POUND
LORDS	TORAH	JOSUA	MOTEL	COURT	POURS
LORES	TORCH	JOSUE	MOTES	COUTH	POUTS
LORIS	TORIC	LOSER	MOTET	DOUAI	ROUEN
LORNA	TORII	LOSES	MOTHS	DOUAY	ROUES
LORRY	TORSI	MOSAN	MOTHY	DOUBT	ROUGE
MORAE	TORSK	MOSEL	MOTIF	DOUGH	ROUGH
MORAL	TORSO	MOSES	MOTOR	DOUGS	ROUND
MORAS	TORTE	MOSEY	MOTTO	DOURA	ROUPY
MORAT	TORTS	MOSSO	NOTCH	DOURY	ROUSE
MORAY	TORUS	MOSSY	NOTED	DOUSE	ROUST
MOREL	WORDS	NOSED	NOTER	FOULS	ROUTE
MORES	WORDY	NOSES	NOTES	FOUND	ROUTS
MORIN	WORKS	NOSEY	POTSY	FOUNT	SOUGH
MORNA	WORLD	POSED	POTTO	FOURS	SOULS
MORNS	WORMS	POSER	POTTY	GOUDA	SOUND
MORON	WORMY	POSES	ROTAS	GOUGE	SOUPS
MOROS	WORRY	POSIT	ROTAS	GOURD	SOUPY

SOURS	******	TOWER	TOYER	EPEES	SPINS
SOUSA	-OW--	TOWNS	TOYON	OPENS	SPINY
SOUSE	******	VOWED	TOYOS	OPERA	SPIRE
SOUTH	BOWED	VOWEL	YOYOS	SPEAK	SPIRO
TOUCH	BOWEL	VOWER	******	SPEAR	SPIRT
TOUGH	BOWER	WOWED	-OZ--	SPECK	SPIRY
TOURS	BOWIE	YOWED	******	SPECS	SPITE
TOUTS	BOWLS	YOWLS	BOZOS	SPEED	SPITS
VOUCH	BOWSE	******	COZEN	SPELL	SPITZ
WOULD	COWED	-OX--	DOZED	SPELT	******
WOUND	COWER	******	DOZEN	SPEND	-PL--
YOULL	COWES	BOXED	DOZER	SPENT	******
YOUNG	COWLS	BOXER	DOZES	SPERM	SPLAT
YOURE	COWRY	BOXES	OOZED	SPEWS	SPLAY
YOURS	DOWDY	COXAE	OOZES	UPEND	SPLEN
YOUTH	DOWEL	COXAL	SOZIN	******	SPLIT
YOUVE	DOWER	COXED	-PA--	-PH--	******
******	DOWNS	COXES	******	******	-PN--
-OV--	DOWNY	FOXED	APACE	APHID	******
******	DOWRY	FOXES	APART	APHIS	APNEA
BOVID	DOWSE	MOXAS	EPACT	EPHAH	******
COVED	FOWLS	MOXIE	OPAHS	EPHOD	-PO--
COVEN	GOWAN	TOXIC	OPALS	EPHOR	******
COVER	GOWER	TOXIN	SPACE	OPHIO	APORT
COVES	GOWNS	******	SPADE	SPHEN	EPOCH
COVET	HOWDY	-OY--	SPAHI	******	EPODE
COVEY	HOWIE	******	SPAIN	-PI--	EPOXY
DOVAP	HOWLS	BOYAR	SPAIT	******	SPODE
DOVER	JOWLS	BOYDS	SPAKE	APIAN	SPOIL
DOVES	LOWED	BOYLE	SPALL	APING	SPOKE
FOVEA	LOWER	BOYNE	SPANG	APISH	SPOOF
GOVYS	LOWLY	COYLY	SPANK	EPICS	SPOOK
HOVEL	MOWED	COYPU	SPANS	OPINE	SPOOL
HOVER	MOWER	DOYEN	SPARE	OPIUM	SPOON
LOVED	NOWAY	DOYLE	SPARK	SPICA	SPOOR
LOVER	POWER	DOYLY	SPARS	SPICE	SPORE
LOVES	POWYS	FOYED	SPASM	SPICY	SPORO
MOVED	ROWAN	FOYER	SPATE	SPIED	SPORT
MOVER	ROWDY	GOYIM	SPATS	SPIEL	SPOTS
MOVES	ROWED	HOYLE	SPAWN	SPIER	SPOUT
MOVIE	ROWEL	JOYCE	SPAYS	SPIES	******
NOVAE	ROWEN	JOYED	******	SPIKE	-PP--
NOVAS	ROWER	LOYAL	-PB--	SPIKY	******
NOVEL	SOWAR	NOYES	******	SPILE	APPAL
ROVED	SOWED	POYOU	UPBOW	SPILL	APPEL
ROVEN	SOWER	ROYAL	******	SPILT	APPLE
ROVER	TOWED	SOYAS	-PE--	SPINE	APPLY
ROVES	TOWEL	TOYED	******	SPINI	UPPED
WOVEN			APEAK		UPPER
			APERY		

******	EQUAL	CRAFT	GRAAL	TRAGI	AREAS
-PR--	EQUIP	CRAGS	GRABS	TRAIL	ARECA
******	SQUAB	CRAIG	GRACE	TRAIN	AREIC
APRIL	SQUAD	CRAKE	GRADE	TRAIT	ARENA
APRON	SQUAT	CRAMP	GRADS	TRAMP	ARENT
SPRAG	SQUAW	CRAMS	GRAFT	TRAMS	ARETE
SPRAT	SQUIB	CRANE	GRAIL	TRANS	BREAD
SPRAY	SQUID	CRANI	GRAIN	TRAPS	BREAK
SPREE	YQUEM	CRANK	GRAMA	TRASH	BREAM
SPRIG	******	CRAPE	GRAMS	TRASS	BREDA
SPRIT	**-RA--**	CRAPS	GRAND	TRAVE	BREED
SPRUE	******	CRASH	GRANI	TRAWL	BRENT
YPRES	ARABS	CRASS	GRANO	TRAYS	BREST
******	ARABY	CRATE	GRANT	URALS	BREVE
-PS--	BRACE	CRAVE	GRAPE	URANO	BREVI
******	BRACT	CRAWL	GRAPH	URATE	BREWS
APSES	BRADS	CRAWS	GRAPY	WRACK	CREAK
APSIS	BRADY	CRAZE	GRASP	WRAPS	CREAM
EPSOM	BRAES	CRAZY	GRASS	WRAPT	CRECY
OPSIA	BRAGE	DRABS	GRATE	WRATH	CREDO
OPSIS	BRAGG	DRACO	GRAVE	XRAYS	CREED
UPSET	BRAGI	DRAFF	GRAVY	******	CREEK
******	BRAGS	DRAFT	GRAYS	**-RB--**	CREEL
-PT--	BRAHE	DRAGS	GRAZE	******	CREEP
******	BRAID	DRAIL	IRAQI	ARBOR	CREES
APTER	BRAIL	DRAIN	IRATE	ORBED	CREME
APTLY	BRAIN	DRAKE	KRAAL	ORBIT	CREON
OPTED	BRAKE	DRAMA	KRAFT	URBAN	CREPE
OPTIC	BRAKY	DRAMS	KRAIT	******	CREPT
******	BRAND	DRANK	KRAUT	**-RC--**	CRESC
-PU--	BRANS	DRAPE	ORACH	******	CRESS
******	BRANT	DRAVA	ORALS	ARCED	CREST
SPUDS	BRASH	DRAVE	ORANG	ARCHI	CRETE
SPUME	BRASS	DRAWL	ORATE	ARCHY	CREWE
SPUMY	BRATS	DRAWN	PRAHU	ARCUS	CREWS
SPUNK	BRAVA	DRAWS	PRAMS	ORCHI	DREAD
SPURN	BRAVE	DRAYS	PRANG	ORCIN	DREAM
SPURS	BRAVO	ERASE	PRANK	ORCUS	DREAR
SPURT	BRAWL	ERATO	PRASE	ORCZY	DREGS
******	BRAWN	FRAIL	PRATE	******	DRESS
-QA--	BRAXY	FRAME	PRAWN	**-RD--**	DREST
******	BRAYS	FRANC	PRAYS	******	DREWS
AQABA	BRAZA	FRANK	TRACE	ARDEB	ERECT
******	BRAZE	FRANZ	TRACH	ARDEN	FREAK
-QU--	CRAAL	FRAPS	TRACK	ARDOR	FREDA
******	CRABS	FRATS	TRACT	ORDER	FREDS
AQUAE	CRACK	FRAUD	TRACY	******	FREED
AQUAS	CRACY	FRAYS	TRADE	**-RE--**	FREER
				******	
				AREAE	
				AREAL	

FREES	ARGOL	CRIME	IRIDO	URIAH	AROSE
FRENA	ARGON	CRIMP	IRISH	URICO	BROAD
FREON	ARGOS	CRISP	ORIBI	URIEL	BROCK
FRERE	ARGOT	DRIBS	ORIEL	URINE	BROIL
FRESH	ARGUE	DRIED	ORION	URINO	BROKE
FRETS	ARGUS	DRIER	ORIYA	WRICK	BROME
FREUD	ERGOT	DRIES	PRIAM	WRIED	BROMO
FREYA	ORGAN	DRIFT	PRICE	WRIER	BRONC
GREAT	URGED	DRILL	PRICK	WRIES	BRONX
GREBE	URGES	DRILY	PRIDE	WRING	BROOD
GRECO	******	DRINK	PRIED	WRIST	BROOK
GREED		DRIPS	PRIER	WRITE	BROOM
GREEK	-RH--	DRIPT	PRIES	WRITS	BROOS
GREEN	******	DRIVE	PRIGS	******	BROTH
GREER	RRHEA	ERICA	PRIMA	-RK--	BROWN
GREET	******	ERICH	PRIME	******	BROWS
GREGO	-RI--	ERICS	PRIMI	IRKED	CROAK
GREGS	******	ERIES	PRIMO	******	CROAT
GRETA	ARIAN	ERIKA	PRIMP	-RL--	CROCE
GREYS	ARIAS	ERIKS	PRIMS	******	CROCI
IRENE	ARICA	FRIAR	PRINK	ARLEN	CROCK
OREAD	ARIEL	FRIED	PRINT	ARLES	CROFT
PREEN	ARIES	FRIER	PRIOR	ERLAU	CROIX
PRESA	ARILS	FRIES	PRISE	ORLES	CRONE
PRESS	ARION	FRIGG	PRISM	ORLON	CRONY
PREST	ARISE	FRILL	PRIVY	ORLOP	CROOK
PREXY	ARIUM	FRIML	PRIZE	******	CROON
PREYS	ARIUS	FRISE	TRIAD	-RM--	CROPS
TREAD	BRIAN	FRISK	TRIAL	******	CRORE
TREAS	BRIAR	FRITH	TRIBE	ARMED	CROSS
TREAT	BRIBE	FRITS	TRICE	ARMET	CROUP
TREED	BRICE	FRITZ	TRICH	ARMOR	CROWD
TREES	BRICK	FRIZZ	TRICK	ERMAS	CROWN
TREKS	BRIDE	GRIDE	TRIED	IRMAS	CROWS
TREND	BRIEF	GRIDS	TRIER	ORMER	CROZE
TRENT	BRIER	GRIEF	TRIES	******	DROIT
TRESS	BRIGS	GRIEG	TRIGO	-RN--	DROLL
TREWS	BRILL	GRILL	TRIGS	******	DROME
TREYS	BRIMS	GRIME	TRILL	ARNIE	DRONE
UREAL	BRINE	GRIMM	TRIMS	ERNES	DROOL
UREDO	BRING	GRIMY	TRINA	ERNIE	DROOP
WREAK	BRINK	GRIND	TRINE	ERNST	DROPS
WRECK	BRINY	GRINS	TRIOL	ORNIS	DROPT
WRENS	BRISK	GRIPE	TRIOS	******	DROSS
WREST	CRIBS	GRIPS	TRIPE	-RO--	DROVE
******	CRICK	GRIPT	TRIPS	******	DROWN
-RG--	CRIED	GRIST	TRITE	AROID	ERODE
******	CRIER	GRITS	TRIXY	AROMA	EROSE
ARGAL	CRIES				
ARGIL					

FROCK	PROVO	ARTER	GRUNT	******	******
FROES	PROWL	ARTHR	KRUBI	-SA--	-SK--
FROGS	PROWS	ARTIC	KRUPP	******	******
FROME	PROXY	ARTIE	PRUDE	ISAAC	ASKED
FROND	TROAS	ARTIS	PRUNE	OSAGE	ASKER
FRONT	TROLL	ARTUR	TRUCE	OSAKA	ASKEW
FROSH	TRONA	ORTHO	TRUCK	PSALM	ESKER
FROST	TROOP	******	TRUDA	TSADE	******
FROTH	TROPE	-RU--	TRUDY	TSANA	-SL--
FROWN	TROPH	******	TRUED	TSARS	******
FROWS	TROTH	ARUBA	TRUER	USAGE	ISLAM
FROZE	TROTS	ARUMS	TRUES	******	ISLAY
GROAN	TROUT	BRUCE	TRULL	-SB--	ISLED
GROAT	TROVE	BRUIN	TRULY	******	ISLES
GROIN	WRONG	BRUIT	TRUMP	ISBAS	ISLET
GROOM	WROTE	BRUME	TRUNK	******	OSLER
GROPE	WROTH	BRUNO	TRURO	-SC--	******
GROSS	******	BRUNT	TRUSS	******	-SM--
GROSZ	-RP--	BRUSH	TRUST	ASCAP	******
GROTS	******	BRUSK	TRUTH	ASCOT	OSMAN
GROUP	ARPAD	BRUTE	WRUNG	ASCUS	OSMIC
GROUT	ARPEN	CRUCI	******	OSCAN	******
GROVE	ORPIN	CRUDE	-RV--	OSCAR	-SO--
GROWL	******	CRUEL	******	******	******
GROWN	-RR--	CRUET	ARVAL	-SE--	PSOAS
GROWS	******	CRUMB	IRVIN	******	******
IRONE	ARRAN	CRUMP	******	ISERE	-SP--
IRONS	ARRAS	CRUOR	-RW--	PSEUD	******
IRONY	ARRAY	CRURA	******	USERS	ASPCA
KRONA	ARRIS	CRUSE	ERWIN	YSERE	ASPEN
KRONE	ARROW	CRUSH	IRWIN	******	ASPER
PROAS	ERRED	CRUST	******	-SH--	ASPIC
PROBE	ERROL	DRUBS	-RY--	******	ASPIS
PROCT	ERROR	DRUGS	******	ASHEN	******
PRODS	ORRIS	DRUID	ARYAN	ASHER	-SQ--
PROEM	******	DRUMS	BRYAN	ASHES	******
PROFS	-RS--	DRUNK	BRYCE	ASHUR	ESQUE
PROLE	******	DRUPE	CRYPT	ESHER	******
PROMS	ARSES	DRURY	DRYAD	PSHAW	-SS--
PRONE	ARSIS	DRUSE	DRYER	USHER	******
PRONG	ARSON	ERUCT	DRYLY	******	ASSAI
PROOF	ERSES	ERUPT	FRYER	-SI--	ASSAM
PROPS	ORSON	FRUIT	PRYER	******	ASSAY
PROSE	URSAE	FRUMP	TRYMA	ASIAN	ASSES
PROSY	******	GRUBS	TRYON	ASIDE	ASSET
PROTO	-RT--	GRUEL	TRYST	OSIER	ASSNS
PROUD	******	GRUFF	WRYER	OSITY	ASSOC
PROVE	ARTAL	GRUME	WRYLY	USING	ASSTS

ASSYR	OTARU	STEER	STIRP	STORK	STUCK
ESSAY	STABS	STEIN	STIRS	STORM	STUDS
ESSEN	STACK	STELE	UTICA	STORY	STUDY
ESSES	STACY	STEMS	UTILE	STOSS	STUFF
ESSEX	STAFF	STENO	XTIAN	STOUP	STUKA
ESSIE	STAGE	STEPS	******	STOUR	STULL
ISSEI	STAGS	STERE	**-TL--**	STOUT	STUMP
ISSUE	STAGY	STERN	******	STOVE	STUMS
******	STAID	STETH	ATLAS	STOWE	STUNG
-ST--	STAIN	STETS	******	STOWS	STUNK
******	STAIR	STEVE	**-TM--**	******	STUNS
ASTER	STAKE	STEWS	******	**-TP--**	STUNT
ASTIR	STALE	UTERI	ATMAN	******	STUPA
ASTON	STALK	UTERO	******	ATPAR	STUPE
ASTOR	STALL	******	**-TN--**	******	UTURN
ASTRO	STAMP	**-TH--**	******	**-TR--**	******
ESTAR	STAND	******	ETNAS	******	**-TY--**
ESTER	STANK	ATHOS	******	ATRIA	******
ESTES	STANS	ETHAN	**-TO--**	ATRIP	ETYMA
ESTOP	STAPH	ETHEL	******	STRAD	STYLE
ISTAR	STARE	ETHER	ATOLL	STRAP	STYLI
ISTIC	STARK	ETHIC	ATOMS	STRAT	STYLO
ISTLE	STARS	ETHNO	ATONE	STRAW	STYMY
OSTED	START	ETHOS	ATONY	STRAY	******
OSTIA	STASH	ETHYL	ATORY	STREW	**-UA--**
******	STATE	OTHER	OTOMI	STRIA	******
-SU--	STATO	UTHER	STOAE	STRIP	DUADS
******	STAVE	******	STOAS	STROP	DUALA
USUAL	STAYS	**-TI--**	STOAT	STRUM	DUANE
USURP	******	******	STOCK	STRUT	GUACO
USURY	**-TC--**	ATILT	STOGY	******	GUAMA
******	******	ATION	STOIC	**-TT--**	GUANA
-SW--	ITCHY	ATIVE	STOKE	******	GUANO
******	******	ITION	STOLE	ATTAR	GUANS
ASWAN	**-TE--**	STICH	STOMA	ATTIC	GUARD
******	******	STICK	STOME	ATTIS	GUAVA
-SY--	CTENO	STIED	STOMP	ATTYS	JUANA
******	ITEMS	STIES	STOMY	ETTAS	JUANS
ASYLA	OTERO	STIFF	STONE	ETTIE	LUAUS
ASYUT	PTERO	STILE	STONY	OTTER	QUACK
PSYCH	STEAD	STILL	STOOD	OTTOS	QUADS
******	STEAK	STILT	STOOK	UTTER	QUAFF
-TA--	STEAL	STIMY	STOOL	******	QUAGS
******	STEAM	STING	STOOP	**-TU--**	QUAIL
ATAXY	STEED	STINK	STOPE	******	QUAKE
ETAPE	STEEL	STINT	STOPS	ETUDE	QUAKY
ITALS	STEEN	STIPE	STOPT	ETUIS	QUALM
ITALY	STEEP	STIRK	STORE	STUBS	QUANT

QUARK	DUCKS	KUDOS	LUFFS	GUIDE	******
QUART	DUCKY	KUDUS	MUFFS	GUIDO	-UL--
QUASH	DUCTS	MUDDY	MUFTI	GUILD	******
QUASI	FUCUS	NUDES	PUFFS	GUILE	AULIC
QUASS	LUCCA	NUDGE	PUFFY	GUILT	AULIS
QUAYS	LUCES	PUDGY	RUFFS	GUISE	BULBS
SUAVE	LUCIA	PUDIC	RUFUS	JUICE	BULGE
******	LUCID	PUDSY	SUFIC	JUICY	BULGY
-UB--	LUCKY	RUDDS	SUFIS	LUIGI	BULKS
******	LUCRE	RUDDY	TUFTS	LUISA	BULKY
BUBAL	LUCYS	RUDER	TUFTY	LUISE	BULLA
BUBER	MUCID	RUDYS	******	OUIDA	BULLS
CUBAN	MUCIN	SUDAN	-UG--	OUIJA	BULLY
CUBBY	MUCKS	SUDOR	******	QUICK	CULCH
CUBEB	MUCKY	SUDSY	AUGER	QUIDS	CULET
CUBED	MUCRO	TUDOR	AUGHT	QUIET	CULEX
CUBES	MUCUS	******	AUGUR	QUIFF	CULLS
CUBIC	NUCHA	-UE--	BUGGY	QUILL	CULMS
CUBIT	PUCES	******	BUGLE	QUILT	CULPA
DUBAI	PUCKA	DUELS	FUGAL	QUINT	CULTI
DUBHE	PUCKS	DUETS	FUGGY	QUIPS	CULTS
HUBBY	RUCHE	FUELS	FUGIO	QUIPU	DULCE
JUBAS	RUCKS	GUESS	FUGLE	QUIRE	DULCY
JUBES	SUCKS	GUEST	FUGUE	QUIRK	DULIA
KUBAN	SUCRE	QUEAN	HUGER	QUIRT	DULLS
NUBBY	TUCKS	QUEEN	HUGHS	QUITE	DULLY
NUBIA	YUCCA	QUEER	HUGOS	QUITO	DULSE
PUBES	******	QUELL	JUGAL	QUITS	EULER
PUBIC	-UD--	QUERN	LUGER	RUING	FULLS
PUBIS	******	QUERY	MUGGY	RUINS	FULLY
RUBES	AUDAD	QUEST	OUGHT	SUING	GULAR
RUBLE	AUDEN	QUEUE	PUGET	SUINT	GULCH
RUBYS	AUDIE	RUERS	RUGAE	SUITE	GULES
SUBAH	AUDIO	SUEDE	RUGBY	SUITS	GULFS
TUBAL	AUDIT	SUERS	SUGAR	******	GULLS
TUBAS	BUDDY	SUETY	VUGGY	-UJ--	GULLY
TUBBY	BUDGE	******	YUGAS	******	GULPS
TUBED	BUDGY	-UF--	******	JUJUS	HULAS
TUBER	CUDDY	******	-UH--	MUJIK	HULDA
TUBES	DUDES	BUFFI	******	******	HULKS
******	FUDGE	BUFFO	MUHLY	-UK--	HULKY
-UC--	JUDAH	BUFFS	******	******	HULLS
******	JUDAS	BUFFY	-UI--	DUKES	JULEP
BUCKO	JUDEA	CUFFS	******	KUKRI	JULES
BUCKS	JUDEO	DUFFS	BUILD	PUKED	JULIA
DUCAL	JUDES	HUFFS	BUILT	PUKES	JULIE
DUCAT	JUDGE	HUFFY	CUING	PUKKA	JULIO
DUCHY	JUDYS	KUFRA	CUISH	YUKON	JULYS

KULAK	GUMMA	BUNKO	PUNTO	HUPEH	CURCH
LULLS	GUMMY	BUNKS	PUNTS	JUPON	CURDS
LULUS	HUMAN	BUNNS	PUNTY	LUPIN	CURDY
MULCH	HUMIC	BUNNY	RUNES	LUPUS	CURED
MULCT	HUMID	BUNTS	RUNGS	PUPAE	CURER
MULES	HUMOR	DUNCE	RUNIC	PUPIL	CURES
MULEY	HUMPH	DUNES	RUNIN	PUPPY	CURIA
MULLS	HUMPS	DUNGS	RUNNY	RUPEE	CURIE
MULTI	HUMPY	DUNGY	RUNON	SUPER	CURIO
PULED	HUMUS	DUNKS	RUNTS	SUPES	CURLS
PULER	JUMBO	FUNDI	RUNTY	SUPRA	CURLY
PULES	JUMNA	FUNDS	SUNNA	TUPIK	CURRY
PULLS	JUMPS	FUNGI	SUNNI	TUPIS	CURSE
PULMO	JUMPY	FUNGO	SUNNS	YUPON	CURST
PULPS	KUMIS	FUNKS	SUNNY	******	CURVE
PULPY	LUMEN	FUNKY	SUNUP	-UQ--	CURVI
PULSE	LUMPS	FUNNY	TUNAS	TUQUE	DURAL
RULED	LUMPY	GUNNY	TUNED	******	DURER
RULER	MUMMS	HUNAN	TUNER	-UR--	DUROS
RULES	MUMMY	HUNCH	TUNES	******	DURRA
SULCI	MUMPS	HUNKS	TUNIC	AURAE	DURST
SULFA	NUMBS	HUNKY	TUNIS	AURAL	DURUM
SULFO	NUMEN	HUNTS	TUNNY	AURAS	EURUS
SULKS	PUMAS	JUNCO	******	AUREI	FURAN
SULKY	PUMPS	JUNES	-UO--	AURES	FURLS
SULLY	RUMBA	JUNKS	******	AURIC	FUROR
SULUS	RUMEN	JUNKY	BUOYS	AURIS	FURRY
TULES	RUMLY	JUNTA	DUOMI	AURUM	FURTH
TULIP	RUMMY	JUNTO	DUOMO	BURAN	FURZE
TULLE	RUMOR	LUNAR	MUONS	BURDS	FURZY
TULLY	RUMPS	LUNCH	QUODS	BURGH	GURUS
TULSA	SUMAC	LUNES	QUOIN	BURGS	HURDS
VULGO	SUMER	LUNET	QUOIT	BURIN	HURLS
VULVA	SUMPS	LUNGE	QUOTA	BURKE	HURLY
YULES	TUMID	LUNGI	QUOTE	BURLS	HURON
******	TUMMY	LUNGS	QUOTH	BURLY	HURRY
-UM--	TUMOR	LUNTS	******	BURMA	HURST
******	YUMMY	MUNCH	-UP--	BURNS	HURTS
BUMPS	******	MUNGO	******	BURNT	JURAL
BUMPY	-UN--	MUNRO	CUPEL	BURPS	JURAT
CUMIN	******	OUNCE	CUPID	BURRO	JUREL
DUMAS	AUNTS	PUNAS	CUPPY	BURRS	JUROR
DUMMY	AUNTY	PUNCH	CUPRO	BURRY	JURUA
DUMPS	BUNCH	PUNGS	DUPED	BURSA	KURSK
DUMPY	BUNCO	PUNIC	DUPER	BURSE	KURUS
FUMED	BUNDE	PUNKA	DUPES	BURST	LURCH
FUMES	BUNDS	PUNKS	DUPLE	CURBS	LURED
GUMBO	BUNGS	PUNKY	GUPPY	CURBS	LURER

LURES	BUSKS	RUSTS	TUTTY	AVERY	AWASH
LURID	BUSTS	RUSTY	TUTUS	EVENS	BWANA
LURKS	CUSEC	SUSAN	******	EVENT	DWARF
MURAL	CUSHY	SUSIE	**-UX--**	EVERT	SWABS
MURAT	CUSKS	TUSKS	******	EVERY	SWAGE
MUREX	CUSPS	******	AUXIL	OVENS	SWAGS
MURKY	CUSSO	**-UT--**	AUXIN	OVERT	SWAIL
MURRA	DUSKS	******	BUXOM	UVEAL	SWAIN
MURRE	DUSKY	AUTOS	JUXTA	UVEAS	SWALE
MURRY	DUSTS	AUTRY	LUXEX	******	SWAMI
NURSE	DUSTY	BUTCH	LUXOR	**-VI--**	SWAMP
OURAY	FUSED	BUTTE	******	******	SWANK
PUREE	FUSEE	BUTTS	**-UY--**	AVIAN	SWANS
PURER	FUSEL	BUTYL	******	AVION	SWAPS
PURGE	FUSES	CUTCH	BUYER	AVISO	SWARD
PURIM	FUSIL	CUTER	GUYED	EVICT	SWARM
PURLS	FUSSY	CUTEY	******	EVILS	SWART
PURRS	FUSTY	CUTIE	**-UZ--**	EVITA	SWASH
PURSE	GUSHY	CUTIN	******	IVIED	SWATH
PURSY	GUSTA	CUTIS	FUZED	IVIES	SWATS
RURAL	GUSTO	CUTTY	FUZEE	OVINE	SWAYS
RURIK	GUSTS	CUTUP	FUZES	******	TWAIN
SURAH	GUSTY	DUTCH	FUZIL	**-VO--**	TWANG
SURAL	HUSKS	GUTSY	FUZZY	******	******
SURAS	HUSKY	GUTTA	LUZON	AVOID	**-WE--**
SURDS	HUSSY	HUTCH	MUZAK	AVOIR	******
SURER	JUSTS	JUTES	MUZZY	AVOWS	DWELL
SURFS	LUSTS	LUTED	OUZEL	EVOKE	DWELT
SURFY	LUSTY	LUTES	SUZYS	IVORY	EWERS
SURGE	MUSCA	LUTON	******	OVOID	GWENN
SURGY	MUSED	MUTED	**-VA--**	OVOLI	GWENS
SURLY	MUSES	MUTES	******	OVOLO	OWENS
TURBO	MUSHY	MUTTS	AVAIL	******	SWEAR
TURCO	MUSIC	NUTTY	AVARS	**-VR--**	SWEAT
TURFS	MUSKS	OUTDO	AVAST	******	SWEDE
TURFY	MUSKY	OUTED	EVADE	AVRIL	SWEEP
TURIN	MUSSY	OUTER	EVANS	******	SWEET
TURKI	MUSTS	OUTGO	IVANS	**-VU--**	SWELL
TURKS	MUSTY	OUTRE	KVASS	******	SWEPT
TURNS	OUSEL	PUTON	OVALS	OVULE	TWEAK
******	OUSTS	PUTTS	OVARY	UVULA	TWEED
-US--	PUSAN	PUTTY	OVATE	******	TWEEN
******	PUSHY	PUTUP	******	**-WA--**	TWEET
AUSTL	PUSSY	RUTHS	**-VE--**	******	TWERE
BUSBY	RUSES	RUTTY	******	AWAIT	TWERP
BUSED	RUSHY	SUTRA	AVENS	AWAKE	******
BUSES	RUSKS	TUTOR	AVERS	AWARD	**-WF--**
BUSHY	RUSSO	TUTTI	AVERT	AWARE	******
					AWFUL

******	******	******	******	MYLES	******
-WI--	-WY--	-XO--	-YD--	NYLON	-YP--
******	******	******	******	PYLON	******
AWING	GWYNS	AXONE	AYDIN	SYLPH	GYPSY
EWING	******	AXONS	EYDIE	SYLVA	HYPER
OWING	-XA--	******	HYDRA	TYLER	HYPHA
SWIFT	******	-XP--	HYDRO	XYLAN	HYPNO
SWIGS	EXACT	******	LYDDA	XYLEM	HYPOS
SWILL	EXALT	EXPEL	LYDIA	XYLOL	HYPSO
SWIMS	EXAMS	******	PYDNA	XYLYL	TYPED
SWINE	******	-XT--	******	******	TYPES
SWING	-XB--	******	-YE--	-YM--	TYPOS
SWIPE	******	EXTOL	******	******	******
SWIRL	OXBOW	EXTRA	HYENA	CYMAE	-YR--
SWISH	******	IXTLE	HYETO	CYMAR	******
SWISS	-XC--	******	MYELO	CYMES	BYRES
TWICE	******	-XU--	OYERS	CYMRI	BYRON
TWIGS	EXCEL	******	PYELO	CYMRY	CYRIL
TWILL	******	EXUDE	TYEES	GYMNO	CYRUS
TWINE	-XE--	EXULT	******	HYMEN	EYRAS
TWINS	******	EXURB	-YG--	HYMNS	EYRIE
TWIRL	EXECS	******	******	LYMAN	EYRIR
TWIRP	EXERT	-YA--	HYGRO	LYMPH	GYRAL
TWIST	OXEYE	******	PYGMY	NYMPH	GYRES
TWITS	******	AYAHS	******	******	GYRON
TWIXT	-XI--	CYANO	-YI--	-YN--	GYROS
******	******	HYALO	******	******	GYRUS
-WL--	AXIAL	KYATS	AYINS	CYNIC	HYRAX
******	AXILE	NYASA	DYING	GYNEC	KYRIE
OWLET	AXILS	WYATT	EYING	LYNCH	LYRES
******	AXING	******	HYING	LYNNS	LYRIC
-WN--	AXIOM	-YB--	LYING	MYNAS	MYRAS
******	EXILE	******	TYING	RYNDS	MYRIA
AWNED	EXIST	GYBED	VYING	SYNGE	MYRNA
OWNED	EXITS	SYBIL	******	SYNOD	MYRON
OWNER	IXIAS	******	-YK--	******	MYRRH
******	IXION	-YC--	******	-YO--	PYRAN
-WO--	OXIDE	******	FYKES	******	PYRES
******	OXIME	CYCAD	TYKES	HYOID	PYREX
AWOKE	******	CYCLE	******	KYOTO	SYRIA
SWOON	-XL--	CYCLO	-YL--	LYONS	SYROS
SWOOP	******	LYCEA	******	MYOID	SYRUP
SWORD	AXLED	LYCEE	BYLAW	MYOMA	TYROL
SWORE	AXLES	NYCTI	CYLIX	MYOPE	TYROS
SWORN	OXLIP	NYCTO	DYLAN	MYOPY	******
******	******	SYCEE	HYLAS	PYOID	-YS--
-WU--	-XM--	SYCES	KYLIX	******	******
******	AXMAN	TYCHE	LYLES	RYOTS	BYSSI
SWUNG	AXMEN				CYSTI
	UXMAL				

CYSTO	******	DATAL	PAGAN	MAMBA	******
CYSTS	-ZO--	DAVAO	PALAE	MAMBO	-A-D-
HYSON	******	FARAD	PANAY	MAYBE	******
LYSED	AZOIC	FARAH	PAPAL	RABBI	BALDR
LYSES	AZOLE	FATAL	PAPAS	SAMBA	BANDA
LYSIN	AZONS	FAYAL	PAPAW	SAMBO	BANDS
LYSIS	AZOTE	GALAS	PARAS	TABBY	BANDY
LYSOL	AZOTH	GALAX	PAVAN	******	BARDE
LYSSA	OZONE	HAHAS	QATAR	-A-C-	BARDS
XYSTS	******	HAMAL	RABAT	******	BAWDS
******	-ZR--	HARAR	RADAR	BACCI	BAWDY
-YT--	******	JALAP	RAJAB	BARCA	CADDO
******	EZRAS	JAPAN	RAJAH	BATCH	CADDY
LYTIC	******	KAKAS	RATAL	CALCI	CANDY
LYTTA	-ZT--	KALAT	RAYAH	CASCO	CARDI
MYTHO	******	KARAT	SABAH	CATCH	CARDS
MYTHS	AZTEC	KAUAI	SAGAN	CAUCA	DADDY
******	******	KAVAS	SAGAS	DACCA	DANDY
-YV--	-ZU--	KAYAK	SALAD	DANCE	FADDY
******	******	KAZAN	SAMAR	FANCY	GAUDI
GYVED	AZURE	LAGAN	SARAH	FARCE	GAUDS
******	******	LAMAS	SARAN	FARCY	GAUDY
-YW--	-ZZ--	LANAI	SARAS	HANCE	HAIDA
******	******	LAOAG	SATAN	HATCH	HANDS
BYWAY	IZZYS	LAPAR	TABAC	LANCE	HANDY
******	OZZIE	LAVAS	TAPAS	LARCH	HARDS
-YX--	******	LAZAR	TATAR	LATCH	HARDY
******	-A-A-	MACAO	VARAS	MANCY	HAYDN
PYXED	******	MACAW	WATAP	MARCH	KANDY
PYXES	BABAR	MADAM	******	MARCO	LADDY
PYXIE	BABAS	MAHAN	-A-B-	MARCS	LANDS
PYXIS	BAHAI	MALAC	******	MATCH	LARDS
******	BALAS	MALAR	BAMBI	NAACP	LARDY
-YY--	BANAL	MALAY	BARBS	NANCE	LAUDS
******	BANAT	MAMAS	CABBY	NANCY	MAGDA
IYYAR	BASAL	MARAT	CARBO	NARCO	MAHDI
******	BATAN	MAYAN	DAUBS	PARCA	MAIDS
-ZA--	CABAL	MAYAS	DAUBY	PARCH	MANDY
******	CACAO	NADAB	GABBY	PASCH	MAUDE
AZANS	CANAD	NAIAD	GAMBS	PATCH	MAUDS
CZARS	CANAL	NANAS	GARBO	RANCE	NARDS
OZARK	CARAS	NASAL	GARBS	RANCH	PADDY
TZARS	CARAT	NATAL	IAMBI	RATCH	PAEDO
******	DAGAN	NAVAL	IAMBS	SARCO	PANDA
-ZE--	DAKAR	NAVAR	JAMBS	SAUCE	PANDY
******	DALAI	NAWAB	KAABA	SAUCY	PARDS
CZECH	DAMAN	PACAS	LAMBS	TALCS	RAIDS
******	DANAE	PAEAN	LAYBY	WATCH	RANDS
-ZI--					
******					
AZINE					

RANDY	CAMES	FADED	HARES	LAVED	PACES
SANDS	CANEA	FADES	HATED	LAVER	PAGED
SANDY	CANED	FAKED	HATER	LAVES	PAGER
TARDO	CANER	FAKER	HATES	LAWED	PAGES
TARDY	CANES	FAKES	HAVEN	LAXER	PALEA
WADDY	CAPEK	FAMED	HAVER	LAYER	PALED
WALDO	CAPER	FARED	HAWED	LAZED	PALEO
WANDA	CAPES	FARER	HAYED	LAZES	PALER
WANDS	CAPET	FARES	HAYES	MABEL	PALES
WARDS	CARED	FATED	HAZED	MACED	PALEY
YARDS	CARER	FATES	HAZEL	MACER	PANED
******	CARES	FAXED	HAZER	MACES	PANEL
-A-E-	CARET	FAXES	HAZES	MAGES	PANES
******	CAREY	FAYED	JABEZ	MAKER	PAPEN
BAAED	CASED	FAYES	JADED	MAKES	PAPER
BABEL	CASES	FAZED	JADES	MALES	PARED
BABER	CASEY	FAZES	JAKES	MAMEY	PAREN
BABES	CATER	GABES	JAMES	MANED	PARER
BADEN	CAVED	GAGED	JANES	MANES	PARES
BAGEL	CAVES	GAGER	JANET	MANET	PAREU
BAKED	CAWED	GAGES	JAPED	MARES	PATEN
BAKER	DACES	GALEA	JAPES	MASER	PATER
BAKES	DALER	GALEN	JARED	MATED	PATES
BALED	DALES	GALES	JAWED	MATEO	PAVED
BALER	DAMES	GAMED	KAMES	MATER	PAVER
BALES	DANES	GAMES	KAMET	MATES	PAVES
BARED	DARED	GANEF	KAREN	MATEY	PAWED
BARER	DARER	GAPED	KATES	MAZED	PAWER
BARES	DARES	GAPER	LABEL	MAZER	PAYED
BASED	DATED	GAPES	LACED	MAZES	PAYEE
BASEL	DATER	GASES	LACES	NADER	PAYER
BASES	DATES	GATED	LADED	NAKED	RACED
BATED	DAVES	GATES	LADEN	NAMED	RACER
BATEN	DAVEY	GAVEL	LADES	NAMER	RACES
BATES	DAZED	GAYER	LAGER	NAMES	RAGED
BAYED	DAZES	GAZED	LAKED	NAPES	RAGEE
CABER	EAGER	GAZER	LAKER	NARES	RAGES
CADES	EARED	GAZES	LAKES	NATES	RAKED
CADET	EASED	HADED	LAKEY	NAVEL	RAKEE
CAFES	EASEL	HADES	LAMED	NAVES	RAKER
CAGED	EASES	HAKES	LAMER	OAKEN	RAKES
CAGES	EATEN	HALED	LAMES	OARED	RALES
CAGEY	EATER	HALER	LANES	OASES	RANEE
CAKED	EAVES	HALES	LAPEL	OATEN	RAPED
CAKES	FACED	HAMER	LARES	OATES	RAPES
CALEB	FACER	HAMES	LASER	OAVES	RARER
CAMEL	FACES	HARED	LATER	PACED	RATED
CAMEO	FACET	HAREM	LATEX	PACER	RATEL

RATER	TAPER	BANFF	******	CANIS	MAVIS
RATES	TAPES	DAFFY	-A-H-	CARIB	MAXIM
RAVED	TARED	GAFFE	******	CAVIE	NADIR
RAVEL	TARES	GAFFS	BACHE	CAVIL	NARIS
RAVEN	TAWED	HAIFA	BATHE	DACIA	NAZIS
RAVER	TAWER	JAFFA	BATHO	DARIC	OASIS
RAVES	TAXED	TAFFY	BATHS	DAVID	PANIC
RAWER	TAXER	WAIFS	BATHY	DAVIE	PARIS
RAYED	TAXES	ZARFS	CACHE	DAVIS	PATIO
RAZED	VALES	******	CATHY	DAVIT	PAVIS
RAZEE	VALET	-A-G-	DACHA	EADIE	RABIC
RAZES	VANED	******	DASHY	FACIA	RABID
SABED	VANES	BADGE	KAPHS	FAKIR	RADII
SABER	VASES	BAGGY	KATHY	GADID	RADIO
SABES	WADED	BANGS	LATHE	GAMIC	RADIX
SAFER	WADER	BARGE	LATHS	GAMIN	RAMIE
SAFES	WADES	CADGE	LATHY	GAVIN	RANIS
SAGER	WAFER	CARGO	MACHY	HABIT	RAPID
SAGES	WAGED	DANGS	MASHY	HAFIZ	RATIO
SAHEB	WAGER	FANGA	MATHS	HAGIO	SABIN
SAKER	WAGES	FANGS	OATHS	HAKIM	SADIE
SAKES	WAKED	FARGO	PACHY	HALID	SAHIB
SALEM	WAKEN	FAUGH	PASHA	IASIS	SALIC
SALEP	WAKES	GANGS	PATHO	JAMIE	SALIX
SALES	WALED	GAUGE	PATHS	JANIS	SAPID
SAMEK	WALER	HANGS	PATHY	KADIS	SARIS
SANER	WALES	JAGGS	RAPHE	KAFIR	SASIN
SATED	WANED	JAGGY	SADHU	KAKIS	SATIE
SATES	WANES	LARGE	TACHY	KAMIK	SATIN
SAVED	WANEY	LARGO	WASHY	KATIE	SAVIN
SAVER	WARES	LAUGH	YACHT	LABIA	SAYID
SAVES	WATER	MADGE	******	LABIO	TABID
SAWED	WAVED	MANGE	-A-I-	LADIN	TACIT
SAWER	WAVER	MANGO	******	LAMIA	TAFIA
SAXES	WAVES	MANGY	AALII	LAPIN	TAMIL
SAYER	WAVEY	MARGE	BAHIA	LAPIS	TAMIS
TABES	WAXED	MARGO	BARIC	LATIN	TANIS
TACET	WAXEN	PANGS	BARIT	MAFIA	TAPIR
TAKEN	WAXES	PARGO	BASIC	MAGIC	TAPIS
TAKER	XAXES	RAGGY	BASIL	MALIC	TAXIS
TAKES	YAGER	RANGE	BASIN	MAMIE	VAGIN
TALER	YAMEN	RANGY	BASIS	MANIA	VALID
TALES	YAWED	SAIGA	BATIK	MANIC	VANIR
TAMED	YAXES	TAIGA	CABIN	MARIA	VAPID
TAMER	******	TANGO	CADIS	MARIE	VARIC
TAMES	-A-F-	TANGS	CADIZ	MARIO	VARIO
TANEY	******	TANGY	CALIF	MARIS	VARIX
TAPED	BAFFS	VANGS	CALIX	MATIN	VATIC
	BAFFY	WAUGH			

XAXIS	RACKS	GAELS	SADLY	TAMMY	PAWNS
YAXIS	RANKS	GAILS	SAILS	WARMS	RAINS
ZAMIA	SACKS	GAILY	SALLY	******	RAINY
ZAYIN	SARKS	GALLS	SAULS	-A-N-	SAINT
******	TACKS	GAOLS	SAULT	******	SAONE
-A-J-	TACKY	GAULS	TABLE	BANNS	SAUNA
******	TALKS	GAULT	TAELS	BARNS	TACNA
BANJO	TANKA	GAVLE	TAILS	CANNA	TAINO
HADJI	TANKS	GAYLY	TALLY	CANNY	TAINS
******	TASKS	HAILS	VAULT	DAMNS	TAINT
-A-K-	WACKE	HALLE	WAILS	DANNY	TARNS
******	WACKS	HALLO	WALLA	DARNS	TAUNT
BACKS	WACKY	HALLS	WALLY	DAUNT	TAWNY
BALKS	WALKS	HAPLO	WANLY	DAWNS	VAUNT
BALKY	YANKS	HAPLY	WAULS	EARNS	WAINS
BANKS	******	HARLS	WAWLS	FAINT	WARNS
BARKS	-A-L-	HAULM	YAWLS	FANNY	WASNT
BARKY	******	HAULS	******	FAUNA	WAYNE
BASKS	BADLY	JAILS	-A-M-	FAUNS	YARNS
CALKS	BAILS	JARLS	******	FAWNS	YAWNS
CASKS	BALLS	KARLS	BALMS	GAINS	******
DARKY	BASLE	LADLE	BALMY	GAUNT	-A-O-
DAWKS	BAULK	LALLS	BARMY	HADNT	******
GAWKS	BAWLS	LAXLY	BAUME	HANNA	AARON
GAWKY	CABLE	MACLE	CALMS	HASNT	BABOO
HACKS	CALLA	MADLY	FARMS	HAUNT	BACON
HAIKS	CALLI	MAILS	GAMMA	JAINA	BARON
HAIKU	CALLS	MALLS	GAMMY	JAINS	BASON
HANKS	CARLA	MANLY	HALMA	JAUNT	BATON
HANKY	CARLE	MAPLE	HAMMY	JAYNE	BAYOU
HARKS	CARLO	MARLA	HARMS	LAINE	CABOB
HAWKS	CARLS	MARLS	JAMMY	LAWNS	CABOT
JACKS	CAULK	MARLY	KARMA	LAWNY	CAJON
JACKY	CAULS	MAULS	MAGMA	MAGNI	CANOE
KAFKA	DAILY	NAILS	MAIMS	MAINE	CANON
LACKS	DALLY	PABLO	MALMO	MAINS	CAPON
LAIKA	EAGLE	PAILS	MAMMA	MAINZ	CAROB
LANKY	EARLE	PALLS	MAMMY	MANNA	CAROL
LARKS	EARLS	PALLY	NAOMI	MARNE	CAROM
LARKY	EARLY	PAOLO	PALMA	MAUND	DAMON
MACKS	FABLE	PAULA	PALMI	MAYNT	DAVOS
MARKS	FAILS	PAULO	PALMS	NANNA	EAMON
MASKS	FALLS	PAULS	PALMY	NANNY	FAGOT
NARKY	FARLE	PAWLS	PARMA	PAINE	FANON
PACKS	FARLS	RAILS	RAMMY	PAINS	FANOS
PARKA	FATLY	RALLY	SALMA	PAINT	FAROE
PARKS	FAULT	RAWLY	SALMI	PANNE	FAVOR
PAWKY	GABLE	SABLE	SAMMY	PATNA	GABON

GABOR	TABOO	TAMPA	MAURA	MATSU	GAITS
GALOP	TABOR	TAMPS	NACRE	MAYST	GARTH
GAVOT	TAHOE	TARPS	NAIRN	PAISA	GASTR
HALOS	TALON	TAUPE	NAURU	PAISE	HAFTS
HANOI	TALOS	VAMPS	PADRE	PALSY	HAITI
HAVOC	TAROS	WARPS	PAIRS	PANSY	HALTS
JABOT	TAROT	WASPS	PARRS	PARSE	HARTE
JACOB	VALOR	WASPY	PARRY	PARSI	HARTS
JAKOB	VAPOR	YAUPS	PATRI	PASSE	HARTZ
JANOS	WAGON	YAWPS	SABRA	PASSY	HASTE
JASON	WAHOO	******	SABRE	PATSY	HASTY
JATOS	YAHOO	-A-R-	SACRA	PAUSE	HATTY
KABOB	YAPON	******	SACRO	RAISE	LACTO
KAPOK	YAZOO	BAIRD	SAPRO	SALSA	LAITY
KAROL	******	BAIRN	SARRE	SALSE	LASTS
KAROO	-A-P-	BARRE	SAURO	SASSY	MALTA
KAYOS	******	BARRY	SAURY	SAYSO	MALTS
KAZOO	CALPE	BASRA	TARRY	TANSY	MALTY
LABOR	CAMPI	CADRE	TATRA	TARSI	MANTA
LAGOS	CAMPO	CAIRD	TAURO	TARSO	MARTA
MACON	CAMPS	CAIRN	VAIRS	TASSO	MARTS
MADOC	CAMPY	CAIRO	VARRO	WAIST	MARTY
MAGOG	CARPI	CAPRI	ZAIRE	******	MASTO
MAGOT	CARPO	CARRY	******	-A-T-	MASTS
MAJOR	CARPS	DAIRY	-A-S-	******	MATTE
MANOR	DAMPS	EAGRE	******	BAHTS	MATTS
MASON	GAMPS	FAIRS	BALSA	BAITS	MATTY
MAYOR	GAPPY	FAIRY	BASSI	BALTS	NASTY
NABOB	GASPE	GARRY	BASSO	BANTU	NATTY
NAHOR	GASPS	GAURS	CANSO	BARTH	PACTS
PAEON	HAPPY	HAIRS	CANST	BASTE	PANTO
PAROL	HARPS	HAIRY	CAUSE	BATTY	PANTS
PAROS	HARPY	HARRY	DAISY	CACTI	PANTY
RADON	HASPS	IATRO	FALSE	CANTO	PARTS
RAYON	KAPPA	IATRY	FAUST	CANTS	PARTY
RAZOR	LAMPS	KAURI	GASSY	CARTE	PASTA
SABOT	LAPPS	KAURY	GAUSS	CARTS	PASTE
SAGOS	NAPPE	LABRA	HANSE	CASTE	PASTS
SAJOU	NAPPY	LAIRD	HARSH	CASTS	PASTY
SALOL	PALPI	LAIRS	HAWSE	CATTY	PATTI
SALON	PAPPI	LARRY	JASSY	DANTE	PATTY
SAMOA	PAPPY	LATRO	LAPSE	DARTS	RAFTS
SAMOS	RALPH	LATRY	LASSA	DATTO	RANTS
SAPOR	RAMPS	LAURA	LASSO	EARTH	RATTY
SAROS	RASPS	MACRO	MANSE	FACTS	SALTS
SAVOR	RASPY	MAORI	MARSH	FAITH	SALTY
SAVOY	SALPA	MARRY	MASSE	FASTS	SANTA
SAXON	SAPPY	MATRI	MASSY	FATTY	SARTO

SAUTE	PADUA	GAUZY	******	******	SCUDI
TANTO	PAPUA	HAMZA	-B-H-	-B-T-	SCUDO
TARTS	RAMUS	JAZZY	******	******	SCUDS
TARTY	RAOUL	MAIZE	ABOHM	ABATE	******
TASTE	SAGUM	MATZO	******	ABETS	-C-E-
TASTY	SALUS	TAZZA	-B-I-	ABUTS	******
TATTY	TALUK	******	******	OBITS	ACCEL
TAUTO	TALUS	-B-A-	ABBIE	******	ACHED
VASTY	VACUA	******	ABOIL	-B-U-	ACHES
WAFTS	VADUZ	ABBAS	ABRIS	******	ACRED
WAITS	VAGUE	ABEAM	******	ABOUT	ACRES
WALTS	VAGUS	ABRAM	-B-L-	******	ACTED
WALTZ	VALUE	EBOAT	******	-B-V-	ICIER
WANTS	VARUS	HBEAM	ABELE	******	OCHER
WARTS	WAMUS	IBEAM	ABELS	ABOVE	OCREA
WARTY	YAMUN	OBEAH	OBELI	******	OCTET
WASTE	******	UBOAT	OBOLE	-B-Y-	SCREE
WATTS	-A-V-	******	OBOLI	******	SCREW
XANTH	******	-B-B-	UBOLT	ABBYS	******
YALTA	CALVE	******	******	OBEYS	-C-F-
******	CARVE	ABIBS	-B-M-	******	******
-A-U-	HALVE	******	******	-B-Z-	SCIFI
******	LARVA	-B-C-	ABOMA	******	SCOFF
BABUL	MAUVE	******	ABOMB	IBIZA	SCUFF
BACUP	NAIVE	ABACA	HBOMB	-C-A-	******
CAJUN	NAVVY	ABACI	******	******	-C-I-
CAMUS	SALVE	ABACK	-B-N-	ACEAE	******
CAPUA	SALVO	******	******	ACEAN	ACRID
CAPUT	SAVVY	-B-D-	EBONS	ECLAT	ACTIN
CASUS	VALVE	******	EBONY	ICIAN	ECHIN
DATUM	VARVE	ABIDE	TBONE	OCEAN	SCHIZ
FANUM	WAIVE	ABODE	******	OCTAD	SCRIM
FAVUS	YAHVE	******	-B-O-	SCRAG	SCRIP
GAMUT	******	-B-E-	******	SCRAM	******
GATUN	-A-Y-	******	ABBOT	SCRAP	-C-L-
HABUS	******	ABBES	ABHOR	******	******
HAGUE	BARYE	ABBEY	******	-C-B-	ECOLE
JANUS	CALYX	ABIEL	-B-R-	******	ICILY
KABUL	CARYO	ABIES	******	SCABS	OCALA
KAGUS	CARYS	ABLER	ABORT	SCUBA	OCULO
KAPUT	DAVYS	ABNER	******	******	SCALD
MAGUS	GABYS	EBBED	-B-S-	-C-C-	SCALE
MANUS	GARYS	IBSEN	******	******	SCALL
MAQUI	KARYO	OBOES	ABASE	ACOCK	SCALP
NAHUA	SATYR	******	ABASH	******	SCALY
NAHUM	TANYA	-B-F-	ABUSE	-C-D-	SCOLD
NAMUR	******	******	ABYSM	******	SCULL
OAKUM	-A-Z-	ABAFT	ABYSS	ACIDS	SCULP
	******		OBESE	SCADS	
	BAIZE				
	GAUZE				

******	ACORN	******	******	IDIOT	BEGAT
-C-M-	OCHRE	-D-A-	-D-H-	ODEON	BEHAN
******	OCHRY	******	******	******	BELAY
SCAMP	SCARE	ADDAX	ADAHS	-D-P-	BERAR
SCHMO	SCARF	ADLAI	IDAHO	******	BETAS
SCUMS	SCARP	ADMAN	******	ADAPT	BEVAN
******	SCARS	EDDAS	-D-I-	ADEPT	CECAL
-C-N-	SCARY	EDGAR	******	ADOPT	CEDAR
******	SCORE	EDNAS	ADDIE	******	CERAM
ACING	SCORN	IDEAL	ADLIB	-D-R-	CERAT
ACINI	SCURF	IDEAS	ADMIN	******	CESAR
ICING	******	******	ADMIT	ADORE	DEBAG
ICONO	-C-S-	-D-B-	ADMIX	ADORN	DEBAR
ICONS	******	******	EDDIC	ODORS	DECAL
SCAND	ICOSI	ADOBE	EDDIE	******	DECAY
SCANS	******	******	EDWIN	-D-S-	DEDAL
SCANT	-C-T-	-D-C-	******	******	DEGAS
SCENA	******	******	-D-L-	ADUST	DELAY
SCEND	ACETO	EDICT	******	IDEST	DEVAS
SCENE	ACITY	EDUCE	ADDLE	******	DEWAN
SCENT	ACUTE	EDUCT	ADELA	-D-T-	FECAL
SCONE	SCATO	******	ADELE	******	FERAL
******	SCATS	-D-E-	ADOLF	ADITS	FETAL
-C-O-	SCOTO	******	ADULT	ADYTA	FEUAR
******	SCOTS	ADDED	EDILE	EDITH	HEJAZ
ACTOR	SCOTT	ADDER	IDOLS	EDITS	HEMAL
ICHOR	SCUTA	ADEEM	IDYLL	ODETS	HEMAN
MCCOY	SCUTE	ADIEU	IDYLS	******	HEMAT
SCION	SCUTS	ADLER	ODDLY	-D-U-	HEPAT
SCOOP	******	ADMEN	ODYLE	******	HERAT
SCOOT	-C-U-	ADMEX	******	ODEUM	HEXAD
SCROD	******	ADZES	-D-M-	ODIUM	KEDAH
******	ACOUO	EDGED	******	ODOUR	KERAT
-C-P-	ACTUS	EDGES	ADAMS	******	LEGAL
******	ICTUS	EDIES	EDEMA	-D-W-	LENAS
SCAPA	OCCUR	EDRED	******	******	MEDAL
SCAPE	SCAUP	EDSEL	-D-N-	ADOWA	MEGAL
SCAPI	SCOUR	IDLED	******	ADUWA	MEGAN
SCOPE	SCOUT	IDLER	ADENI	******	MELAN
SCOPS	SCRUB	IDLES	ADENO	-D-Y-	MENAI
SCOPY	SCRUM	ODDER	ADUNC	******	MESAS
SCUPS	******	UDDER	EDINA	ADDYS	METAL
SCYPH	-C-W-	******	ODONT	******	METAS
******	******	-D-F-	UDINE	-E-A-	NEMAT
-C-R-	SCHWA	******	******	******	NEPAL
******	SCOWL	EDIFY	-D-O-	AETAT	PECAN
ACCRA	SCOWS	-D-G-	******	BEGAD	PEDAL
ACERB	OCTYL	ADAGE	ADIOS	BEGAN	PEKAN
		ADIGE	IDIOM		

PENAL	BELCH	HEADY	BETEL	LEVEN	TEHEE
PETAL	BENCH	HEDDA	BEVEL	LEVER	TEKEL
RECAP	DEICE	HEEDS	BEZEL	LEWES	TELEG
REDAN	DEUCE	HERDS	CEDED	MEDEA	TELEO
REGAL	FENCE	LEADS	CEDES	MELEE	TELEX
REGAN	FETCH	LEADY	CERED	MENES	TENET
RELAX	HENCE	LEEDS	CERES	METED	TEPEE
RELAY	KENCH	LEUDS	DEFER	METER	VEXED
REMAN	KERCH	MEADS	DEKED	METES	VEXER
RENAL	KETCH	MELDS	DEKES	MEWED	VEXES
RENAN	LEACH	MENDS	DELED	NEGEB	WEBER
REPAY	LEECH	NEDDY	DELES	NEGEV	WESER
RERAN	LEUCO	NEEDS	DEMES	NETER	XEBEC
SEBAT	MECCA	NEEDY	DENEB	NEVER	YEMEN
SEDAN	MERCI	PENDS	DENES	NEWEL	YESES
SELAH	MERCY	PERDU	DEREK	NEWER	ZEBEC
SEPAL	PEACE	READS	DESEX	PEDES	ZEKES
SERAC	PEACH	READY	DETER	PELEE	******
SERAI	PENCE	REEDS	DEWED	PELEG	-E-F-
SERAL	PERCH	REEDY	DEWEY	PERES	******
SETAE	PERCY	RENDS	FECES	PETER	BEEFS
TELAE	REACH	SEEDS	FEMES	PETES	BEEFY
TERAT	REACT	SEEDY	FETED	PEWEE	DEIFY
TEXAS	REICH	SENDS	FETES	REBEC	DELFT
VELAR	RETCH	TEDDY	FEUED	REBEL	FEOFF
VENAE	SECCO	TENDS	FEVER	REFER	GEOFF
VENAL	TEACH	VELDS	FEWER	REGES	JEFFS
VERAS	TENCH	VELDT	GENES	REMEX	KEEFS
WEKAS	VETCH	VENDS	GENET	RENEE	KERFS
ZETAS	WELCH	VERDI	HEGEL	RENES	LEAFS
******	WENCH	WEEDS	HELEN	RENEW	LEAFY
-E-B-	******	WEEDY	HEMEN	REPEL	LEIFS
******	-E-D-	WELDS	HEWED	RESET	PELFS
BEEBE	******	WENDS	HEWER	RETEM	REEFS
CEIBA	BEADS	WENDY	HEXED	REVEL	REEFY
DEBBY	BEADY	******	HEXES	REVET	REIFY
DERBY	BENDS	-E-E-	JEFES	SEDER	SERFS
HERBS	BENDY	******	JEREZ	SELEN	******
HERBY	DEEDS	AEDES	JEWEL	SEMEN	-E-G-
KERBS	DENDR	BEDEW	KERES	SERED	******
SERBS	FEEDS	BEGET	KEVEL	SERES	BEIGE
VERBS	FENDS	BELEM	KEYED	SEVEN	BELGA
WEBBY	FEODS	BENES	LEGER	SEVER	BERGS
YERBA	FEUDS	BENET	LEGES	SEWED	DEIGN
******	GELDS	BEREA	LENES	SEWER	FEIGN
-E-C-	GEODE	BERET	LEPER	SEXED	HEDGE
******	GERDA	BESET	LEVEE	SEXES	HEDGY
BEACH	HEADS		LEVEL	TEBET	HEIGH
BEECH					

HELGA	CELIE	NEVIS	LEAKY	KELLY	GERMS
KEDGE	CENIS	PEKIN	LEEKS	LEILA	HELMS
LEDGE	CERIA	PENIS	LEUKO	MEALS	HERMA
LEGGY	CERIC	PEPIN	NECKS	MEALY	JEMMY
LEIGH	CETIC	PERIL	PEAKS	MERLE	LEMMA
MERGE	CETIN	PERIS	PEAKY	MEWLS	NEUME
NEIGH	DEBIT	PETIT	PECKS	NEALS	REAMS
PEGGY	DECIM	PEWIT	PEEKS	NEILS	REGMA
PENGO	DEFIS	REBID	PERKS	NELLS	REIMS
REIGN	DELIA	REDID	PERKY	NELLY	SEAMS
SEDGE	DEMIT	REFIT	PESKY	NEWLY	SEAMY
SEDGY	DENIM	REGIN	REEKS	PEALS	SEEMS
SERGE	DENIS	RELIC	REEKY	PEELS	SELMA
VERGE	DEVIL	REMIT	SEEKS	PELLA	TEAMS
WEDGE	EERIE	RENIN	TEAKS	PELLY	TEEMS
WEDGY	FECIT	RESIN	WEEKS	PEPLA	TERMS
WEIGH	FELID	RETIA	YELKS	PERLE	VERMI
YEGGS	FELIX	REZIN	******	REALM	WEEMS
******	FERIA	SEPIA	-E-L-	REALS	******
-E-H-	FETID	SERIF	******	REDLY	-E-N-
******	GELID	SERIN	BEALL	REELS	******
BETHS	GENIC	TELIC	BELLA	REPLY	AEONS
DELHI	GENIE	TEPID	BELLE	SEALS	BEANO
LETHE	GENII	VEDIC	BELLS	SELLS	BEANS
MESHY	GEOID	VESIC	BELLY	TEALS	BEING
METHO	HELIC	VEXIL	BEULA	TELLS	BENNE
NEPHO	HELIO	XENIA	CEILS	TELLY	BENNY
NEPHR	HELIX	XERIC	CELLA	TESLA	BERNE
SETHS	HEMIA	YETIS	CELLO	VEILS	DEANE
TETHS	HEMIC	******	CELLS	WEALD	DEANS
******	HEMIN	-E-J-	DEALS	WEALS	DENNY
-E-I-	KEPIS	******	DEALT	WELLS	FEINT
******	KEVIN	BENJY	DELLA	WETLY	FENNY
AECIA	LEGIT	******	DELLS	YELLS	FERNS
AEGIR	LENIN	-E-K-	FEELS	******	FERNY
AEGIS	LENIS	******	FELLS	-E-M-	HENNA
AEMIA	LEPID	BEAKS	FELLY	******	JEANS
AERIE	LEVIS	BECKS	HEALS	BEAMS	JENNY
AESIR	LEWIE	BECKY	HEELS	BEAMY	KEENS
BEDIM	LEWIS	DECKS	HEKLA	BERME	KENNY
BEFIT	MEDIA	DESKS	HELLE	BERMS	KERNS
BEGIN	MEDIC	GECKO	HELLO	DEEMS	LEANS
BELIE	MEDIO	GECKS	HELLS	DERMA	LEANT
BENIN	MELIC	GEEKS	HERLS	DERMO	LENNY
BERIA	MERIT	JERKS	JELLO	FEMME	LEONA
BEVIN	MESIC	JERKY	JELLS	FERMI	LEONS
CECIL	METIS	KECKS	JELLY	GEMMA	MEANS
CELIA	NEVIL	LEAKS	KEELS	GEMMY	MEANT

MEANY	DEMOS	HEAPS	HEART	WEARY	VERSO
MESNE	DEPOT	HELPS	HEIRS	WEIRD	VERST
PEANS	DEVON	HEMPS	HENRI	WEIRS	WEEST
PEENS	FEDOR	HEMPY	HENRY	YEARN	WELSH
PENNA	FELON	JEEPS	JEERS	YEARS	YEAST
PENNI	FETOR	KEEPS	JERRY	ZEBRA	******
PENNY	GEMOT	KELPS	JEWRY	******	-E-T-
PEONS	GENOA	LEAPS	KERRY	-E-S-	******
PEONY	HELOT	LEAPT	LEARN	******	BEATA
REINS	HEROD	NEAPS	LEARY	BEAST	BEATS
SEANS	HERON	PEEPS	LEERS	BESSY	BEETS
SEGNI	JETON	PEPPY	LEERY	BETSO	BELTS
SEGNO	LEMON	REAPS	LEHRS	BETSY	BERTA
SEINE	LENOS	SEEPS	LEORA	CEASE	BERTH
SENNA	LEROY	TEMPE	MERRY	CENSE	BERTS
SENNE	MEDOC	TEMPI	METRE	DEISM	BERTY
TEENS	MELON	TEMPO	METRO	DEIST	BESTS
TEENY	MELOS	TEMPT	METRY	DENSE	BETTE
TERNS	MEMOS	WEEPS	NEARS	FEASE	BETTY
VEINS	MEROE	WEEPY	NECRO	FEAST	CELTS
VEINY	MESON	YELPS	NEGRO	FEIST	CENTI
VERNA	METOL	******	NEHRU	FESSE	CENTO
VERNE	NEROS	-E-R-	NEURI	GEESE	CENTR
VERNS	PECOS	******	NEURO	GEEST	CENTS
WEANS	PEKOE	BEARD	PEARL	GESSO	CESTA
WEENY	PELON	BEARS	PEARS	HEIST	CESTI
WENNY	PEPOS	BEERS	PEARY	HESSE	CEUTA
YEANS	PERON	BEERY	PEDRO	JESSE	DEATH
******	PESOS	BEIRA	PEERS	JESSY	DEBTS
-E-O-	SEGOS	BERRA	PERRY	KELSO	DEITY
******	SENOR	BERRY	PETRO	LEASE	DELTA
AESOP	SEPOY	CEARA	PETRY	LEASH	DENTI
BEBOP	SERON	CEORL	REARM	LEAST	DENTO
BEFOG	SEROW	DEARS	REARS	LEPSY	DENTS
BEGOT	SETON	DEARY	RETRO	MENSA	DEPTH
BELOW	TENON	DECRY	RETRY	MESSY	DEXTR
BESOM	TENOR	DERRY	SEARS	MEUSE	FEATS
BESOT	TENOS	FEARS	SEERS	NEWSY	FELTS
BETON	TETON	FEBRI	SERRA	PEASE	FEMTO
CELOM	VENOM	FERRI	TEARS	PERSE	GENTS
CENON	XENON	FERRO	TEARY	SEISE	GERTY
CEROS	XEROX	FERRY	TERRA	SEISM	HEATH
DECOR	ZEROS	GEARS	TERRI	SENSE	HEATS
DECOY	******	GENRE	TERRY	TEASE	HECTO
DEFOE	-E-P-	GENRO	TETRA	TENSE	HEFTS
DELOS	******	GERRY	VEERS	TERSE	HEFTY
DEMOB	BEEPS	HEARD	VEERY	VEPSA	HEKTO
DEMON	DEEPS	HEARS	WEARS	VERSE	HEPTA

HERTZ	SEPTS	NEVUS	HEXYL	******	******
HETTY	SETTO	NEXUS	KENYA	-G-E-	-G-P-
JESTS	SEXTO	REBUS	PEPYS	******	******
JETTY	TEATS	REBUT	******	AGGER	AGAPE
KEATS	TEETH	RECUR	-E-Z-	AGLEE	EGYPT
KEITH	TENTH	REMUS	******	AGLET	******
KENTS	TENTS	RERUN	FEEZE	AGLEY	-G-R-
LEETS	TESTA	REVUE	MEZZO	AGNES	******
LEFTS	TESTS	SEBUM	SEIZE	AGREE	AGORA
LEFTY	TESTY	SEDUM	******	AGUES	******
LEITH	TEXTS	SEOUL	-F-A-	EGGED	-G-S-
LENTO	VENTS	SERUM	******	EGGER	******
LENTS	VERTU	SETUP	OFFAL	EGRET	AGIST
LEPTA	VESTA	VELUM	******	OGDEN	EGEST
LEPTO	VESTS	VENUE	-F-E-	OGEES	******
LETTS	WEFTS	VENUS	******	OGLED	-G-T-
LETTY	WELTS	XERUS	AFTER	OGLER	******
LEYTE	YEATS	ZEBUS	OFFER	OGLES	AGATE
MEATS	ZESTS	******	OFTEN	OGRES	******
MEATY	ZESTY	-E-V-	******	******	-G-V-
MEETS	******	******	-F-I-	-G-I-	******
MELTS	-E-U-	DELVE	******	******	AGAVE
NEATH	******	HEAVE	AFFIX	AGAIN	OGIVE
NESTS	BEAUS	HEAVY	EFFIE	AGGIE	******
NETTY	BEAUT	HELVE	******	AGNIS	-G-Z-
NEWTS	BEAUX	KEEVE	-F-O-	OGMIC	******
PEATS	BEGUM	LEAVE	******	******	AGAZE
PEATY	BEGUN	LEAVY	AFOOT	-G-L-	******
PELTS	BENUE	NERVE	AFROS	******	-H-A-
PENTA	CECUM	NERVY	******	AGILE	******
PERTH	CETUS	PEAVY	-F-R-	******	AHEAD
PESTS	DEBUG	PEEVE	******	-G-M-	CHEAP
PETTI	DEBUT	PELVI	AFIRE	******	CHEAT
PETTO	DEGUM	REEVE	AFORE	AGAMA	CHIAN
PETTY	DEMUR	SERVE	AFTRA	******	CHIAS
RECTA	FEMUR	SERVO	WEAVE	-G-N-	IHRAM
RECTI	FETUS	VERVE	******	******	PHIAL
RECTO	GENUA	WEAVE	-E-W-	-F-U-	AGANA	RHEAS
RENTE	GENUS	******	******	AGANA	RHEAS
RENTS	GETUP	MEOWS	AFOUL	AGENT	SHEAF
RESTS	JEHUS	******	******	AGING	SHEAR
RETTA	JESUS	-E-X-	-G-A-	AGONY	SHEAS
SEATO	LEHUA	******	******	******	SHIAH
SEATS	LEMUR	DEOXY	AGHAS	-G-O-	SHOAL
SECTS	LEPUS	-E-Y-	EGEAN	******	SHOAT
SEPTA	LETUP	******	EGGAR	AGIOS	UHLAN
SEPTI	MENUS	BERYL	IGNAZ	AGLOW	WHEAL
SEPTO	NEGUS	DENYS	OGHAM	IGLOO	WHEAT

******	RHOEA	CHOIR	SHELL	CHUNK	SHOOT
-H-B-	SHEEN	CHRIS	SHILL	GHANA	THIOL
******	SHEEP	OHMIC	SHILY	GHENT	THROB
CHIBA	SHEER	SHEIK	SHULS	KHANS	THROE
CHUBS	SHEET	THEIR	SHYLY	KHOND	THROW
PHEBE	SHIED	******	THOLE	PHANE	WHOOP
PHOBE	SHIER	**-H-J-**	THULE	PHANY	******
SHEBA	SHOER	******	WHALE	PHENO	**-H-P-**
******	SHOES	SHOJI	WHELK	PHONE	******
-H-C-	SHRED	THUJA	WHELM	PHONO	CHAPE
******	SHREW	******	WHELP	PHONY	CHAPS
CHECK	SHYER	**-H-K-**	WHILE	RHINE	CHAPT
CHICK	THIEF	******	WHOLE	RHINO	CHIPS
CHICO	THREE	CHOKE	******	RHONE	CHOPS
CHOCK	THREW	CHOKY	**-H-M-**	SHANK	PHIPS
CHUCK	WHEEL	DHAKS	******	SHANS	SHAPE
PHYCO	******	KHAKI	CHAMP	SHANT	SHIPS
SHACK	**-H-F-**	SHAKE	CHEMI	SHINE	SHOPS
SHOCK	******	SHAKO	CHEMO	SHINS	WHAPS
SHUCK	CHAFE	SHAKY	CHIME	SHINY	WHIPS
THECA	CHAFF	******	CHIMP	SHONE	WHIPT
THICK	CHEFS	**-H-L-**	CHUMP	SHUNS	WHOPS
WHACK	CHUFA	******	CHUMS	SHUNT	******
WHICH	SHAFT	CHALK	CHYME	THANE	**-H-R-**
******	SHIFT	CHELA	RHOMB	THANK	******
-H-D-	THEFT	CHILD	RHUMB	THINE	CHARD
******	WHIFF	CHILE	RHYME	THING	CHARE
CHIDE	******	CHILI	SHAME	THINK	CHARM
KHADI	**-H-G-**	CHILL	SHAMS	THINS	CHARO
RHODA	******	CHILO	SHIMS	THONG	CHARS
SHADE	CHUGS	CHOLE	THEME	WHANG	CHART
SHADY	PHAGE	CHYLE	THUMB	WHENS	CHARY
SHEDS	PHAGO	DHOLE	THUMP	WHINE	CHERT
THADS	PHAGY	DHOLI	THYME	WHINS	CHIRM
THADY	RHAGE	PHILA	THYMY	WHINY	CHIRO
THEDA	RHAGY	PHILE	WHAMS	******	CHIRP
THUDS	SHAGS	PHILO	WHIMS	**-H-O-**	CHIRR
******	THIGH	PHILS	******	******	CHORD
-H-E-	THUGS	PHILY	**-H-N-**	CHAOS	CHORE
******	WHIGS	PHYLA	******	CHIOS	CHORO
CHAET	******	PHYLE	BHANG	CHLOE	CHURL
CHEEK	**-H-H-**	PHYLL	CHANG	CHLOR	CHURN
CHEEP	******	PHYLO	CHANT	CHROM	CHURR
CHEER	SHAHS	SHALE	CHINA	CHRON	PHORE
CHIEF	******	SHALL	CHINE	PHLOX	PHYRE
KHMER	**-H-I-**	SHALT	CHINK	SHEOL	SHARD
PHLEB	******	SHALY	CHINO	SHOOK	SHARE
PHREN	CHAIN	SHELF	CHINS	SHOOS	SHARI
	CHAIR				

SHARK	******	CHEWY	LILAC	VITAL	WINCH
SHARP	**-H-T-**	CHOWS	LILAS	WIGAN	WITCH
SHERD	******	DHOWS	LIRAS	WITAN	ZINCS
SHIRE	CHATS	SHAWL	LISAS	******	ZINCY
SHIRK	CHETH	SHAWM	LITAI	**-I-B-**	******
SHIRR	CHETS	SHAWN	LITAS	******	**-I-D-**
SHIRT	CHITA	SHAWS	LIZAS	BIBBS	******
SHORE	CHITS	SHEWN	MICAH	BILBO	BIDDY
SHORL	CHUTE	SHEWS	MICAS	LIBBY	BINDS
SHORN	DHOTI	SHOWN	MIDAS	LIMBI	BIRDS
SHORT	GHATS	SHOWS	MILAN	LIMBO	CINDY
THERE	PHOTO	SHOWY	MINAE	LIMBS	DILDO
THERM	PHOTS	THAWS	MINAS	NIMBI	DIODE
THIRD	PHYTE	THEWS	NINAS	NIOBE	FINDS
THORN	PHYTO	THEWY	NIPAS	******	GIDDY
THORP	SHOTE	******	NISAN	**-I-C-**	GILDA
THURS	SHOTS	**-H-Y-**	NIVAL	******	GILDS
THYRO	SHUTE	******	NIZAM	AITCH	GIRDS
WHARF	SHUTS	CHRYS	PICAL	BIRCH	HILDA
WHERE	THETA	SHAYS	PICAS	BITCH	HINDI
WHIRL	THOTH	WHEYS	PIKAS	CINCH	HINDS
WHIRR	WHETS	******	PILAF	CIRCA	HINDU
WHIRS	WHITE	**-H-Z-**	PILAR	CIRCE	JIDDA
WHORE	WHITS	******	PIMAN	CISCO	KIDDY
WHORL	******	GHAZI	PIMAS	DIRCK	KINDS
WHORT	**-H-U-**	RHIZO	PINAS	DISCI	LINDA
******	******	******	PIPAL	DISCO	MIDDY
-H-S-	GHAUT		PITAS	DISCS	MINDI
******	GHOUL	**-I-A-**	RITAS	DITCH	MINDS
CHASE	HHOUR	******	RIVAL	FILCH	MISDO
CHASM	RHEUM	AIDAS	RIYAL	FINCH	RINDS
CHESS	SHAUN	BIHAR	SILAS	FISCS	TILDA
CHEST	SHOUT	BINAL	SIMAR	FITCH	TILDE
CHOSE	SHRUB	CIDAL	SINAI	HITCH	WIDDY
GHOST	SHRUG	CIGAR	SISAL	MILCH	WILDE
LHASA	THRUM	DINAH	SITAR	MINCE	WILDS
PHASE	WHAUP	DINAR	SIVAN	MITCH	WINDS
PHASY	**-H-V-**	DITAS	SIZAR	NIECE	WINDY
PHYSI	******	DIVAN	TICAL	PIECE	******
SHUSH	CHEVY	DIVAS	TIDAL	PINCH	**-I-E-**
THESE	CHIVE	DIWAN	TIDAS	PISCI	******
THOSE	SHAVE	FILAR	TINAS	PITCH	AIDED
WHISH	SHIVE	FINAL	TITAN	SINCE	AIDER
WHISK	SHIVS	GIGAS	VICAR	TINCT	AIDES
WHIST	SHOVE	HIRAM	VIDAL	VINCE	AIKEN
WHOSE	******	JIHAD	VINAS	VINCI	AILED
WHOSO	**-H-W-**	KILAH	VIRAL	VISCT	AIMED
	******	KIVAS	VISAS	WINCE	AIMEE
	CHAWS	LIGAN	VITAE		
	CHEWS				

AIRED	FINER	LINES	PILEI	SIZED	WIVED
BICES	FINES	LINEY	PILES	SIZES	WIVER
BIDED	FIRED	LITER	PINED	TIBER	WIVES
BIDES	FIRER	LIVED	PINEL	TIBET	WIZEN
BIDET	FIRES	LIVEN	PINER	TIDED	YIPES
BIKES	FIVER	LIVER	PINES	TIDES	ZIBET
BILES	FIVES	LIVES	PINEY	TIGER	******
BINES	FIXED	MIKES	PIPED	TILED	-I-F-
BINET	FIXER	MIKEY	PIPER	TILER	******
BIPED	FIXES	MILER	PIPES	TILES	BIFFS
BISES	GIBED	MILES	PIPET	TIMED	BIFFY
BITER	GIBER	MIMED	RICED	TIMER	FIEFS
BITES	GIBES	MIMEO	RICER	TIMES	JIFFS
BIZET	GILES	MIMER	RICES	TINEA	JIFFY
CIDER	GIMEL	MIMES	RIDER	TINED	MIFFS
CIMEX	GIVEN	MINED	RIDES	TINES	MIFFY
CITED	GIVER	MINER	RIGEL	TIRED	RIFFS
CITES	GIVES	MINES	RILED	TIREE	TIFFS
CIVET	HIDER	MIRED	RILES	TIRES	******
DICED	HIDES	MIRES	RILEY	TITER	-I-G-
DICER	HIKED	MISER	RIMED	VIBES	******
DICEY	HIKER	MISES	RIMER	VICES	BILGE
DIKED	HIKES	MITER	RIMES	VIDEO	BILGY
DIKER	HIRED	MITES	RIPEN	VILER	BINGE
DIKES	HIRER	MIXED	RIPER	VIMEN	BINGO
DIMER	HIRES	MIXER	RISEN	VINES	DIEGO
DIMES	HIVED	MIXES	RISER	VIPER	DINGO
DINED	HIVES	MIZEN	RISES	VIREO	DINGS
DINER	JIBED	NICER	RITES	VIRES	DINGY
DINES	JIBES	NIDED	RIVED	VISED	DIRGE
DIRER	JIVED	NIDES	RIVEN	VISES	HINGE
DIVED	KIBEI	NIGEL	RIVER	VIXEN	JINGO
DIVER	KIBES	NIGER	RIVES	WIDEN	KINGS
DIVES	KITED	NIMES	RIVET	WIDER	LIEGE
DIZEN	KITES	NINES	SICES	WILED	LINGA
EIDER	LIBEL	NISEI	SIDED	WILES	LINGO
EIMER	LIBER	NITER	SIDER	WILEY	LINGS
FIBER	LIFER	NIXED	SIDES	WINED	MIDGE
FICES	LIKED	NIXES	SILEX	WINES	MINGY
FIDEL	LIKEN	NIZER	SINES	WIPED	PIGGY
FIFED	LIKES	OIDEA	SINEW	WIPER	PINGO
FIFER	LIMED	OILED	SIPES	WIPES	PINGS
FIFES	LIMEN	OILER	SIRED	WIRED	RIDGE
FILED	LIMES	PIKED	SIREN	WIRER	RIDGY
FILER	LIMEY	PIKER	SIRES	WIRES	RIGGS
FILES	LINED	PIKES	SITED	WISED	RINGS
FILET	LINEN	PILEA	SITES	WISER	SIEGE
FINED	LINER	PILED	SIXES	WISES	SINGE

SINGS	CIVIC	DICKY	BILLS	******	NINNY
TINGE	CIVIL	DINKA	BILLY	-I-M-	PIAND
TINGS	DIGIT	DINKY	BIRLE	******	PIANO
TIOGA	DIXIE	DIRKS	BIRLS	FILMS	PINNA
VIRGA	DIXIT	DISKO	DIALS	FILMY	PINNI
VIRGE	FIJIS	DISKS	DIMLY	FIRMS	PINNY
VIRGO	FINIS	FINKS	DIPLO	FIUME	PIONS
WINGS	HIFIS	GINKS	FIELD	GISMO	RIANT
WINGY	KININ	HICKS	FILLS	GIZMO	SIENA
ZINGY	KIRIN	JINKS	FILLY	JIMMY	SIGNE
******	KIWIS	KICKS	FITLY	MIAMI	SIGNS
-I-H-	LICIT	KINKS	GILLS	PIGMY	TINNY
******	LIEIN	KINKY	GIRLS	SIGMA	VIAND
BIGHT	LIMIT	KIRKS	HILLS	TIMMY	VILNA
DICHO	LININ	LICKS	HILLY	WILMA	VINNY
DISHY	LIPID	LINKS	JILLS	******	******
EIGHT	LIVIA	MICKY	KILLS	-I-N-	-I-O-
FICHE	LIVID	MILKS	LILLE	******	******
FICHU	MILIA	MILKY	LILLI	AISNE	AINOS
FIGHT	MIMIC	MINKS	LILLY	CIONS	BIGOT
FISHY	MIMIR	NICKS	LISLE	DIANA	BIJOU
HIGHS	MIMIS	NICKY	MILLI	DIANE	BIKOL
LICHT	MINIM	PICKS	MILLS	DIDNT	BIPOD
LIGHT	NIHIL	PINKS	MILLY	DIENE	BISON
LITHE	NIXIE	PINKY	PILLS	DIONE	CIBOL
LITHO	PILIS	RICKS	RIALS	FIEND	DIDOS
MIGHT	PIPIT	RICKY	RIFLE	FINNS	DIJON
NICHE	PIXIE	RINKS	RILLE	FINNY	DIVOT
NIGHT	RICIN	RISKS	RILLS	FIONA	GIGOT
PITHS	RIGID	RISKY	SIALO	FIRNS	GIPON
PITHY	SIGIL	SICKS	SIDLE	GIANT	GIRON
RIGHT	SILIC	SILKS	SILLS	GIING	GIROS
SIGHS	SITIN	SILKY	SILLY	GINNY	KILOS
SIGHT	TIBIA	SINKS	TILLS	HINNY	MIAOW
SIKHS	TIEIN	SITKA	TILLY	JINNI	MINOR
TIGHT	TIKIS	TICKS	TITLE	JINNY	MINOS
TITHE	TIMID	VICKS	VIALS	KILNS	NITON
VICHY	TITIS	VICKY	VILLA	LIANA	NIXON
WIGHT	VIGIL	WICKS	VILLE	LIANE	PICOT
WITHE	VINIC	WINKS	VILLI	LIANG	PILOT
WITHY	VISIT	ZINKY	VILLS	LIENS	PINON
XIPHI	VIVID	******	VIOLA	LIGNI	PITON
******	VIZIR	-I-L-	VIOLS	LIGNO	PITOT
-I-I-	******	******	WIELD	LIMNS	PIVOT
******	-I-K-	AISLE	WILLA	LIONS	RIGOR
BIFID	******	BIALY	WILLS	MIENS	RIPON
BINIT	BILKS	BIBLE	WILLY	MILNE	SIDON
CILIA	DICKS	BIGLY	YIELD	MINNA	SILOS

SIMON	LIVRE	FILTH	VISTA	******	******
SINON	MICRA	FIRTH	VITTA	**-I-Y-**	**-K-E-**
TIMOR	MICRO	FISTS	WIDTH	******	******
TIROS	MITRE	GIFTS	WILTS	DILYS	OKIEH
VIGOR	NIGRI	GIRTH	WITTE	LIBYA	OKIES
VISOR	NITRE	GIRTS	WITTY	LILYS	SKEED
VIZOR	NITRI	GISTS	******	SIBYL	SKEES
WIDOW	NITRO	HIDTO	**-I-U-**	VINYL	SKEET
WINOS	PICRO	HILTS	******		SKIED
ZIRON	PIERS	HINTS	AINUS	**-I-Z-**	SKIER
******	TIARA	JILTS	FILUM	******	SKIES
-I-P-	TIERS	KILTS	FIQUE	DIAZO	SKYEY
******	TIGRE	KILTY	GIBUS	DIZZY	******
DIPPY	VITRI	KITTY	GIGUE	FIZZY	**-K-F-**
GIMPS	WIRRA	LIFTS	HILUM	LISZT	******
GIMPY	ZIMRI	LILTS	LIEUT	LIZZY	SKIFF
HIPPO	******	LINTY	LINUS	MIRZA	******
HIPPY	**-I-S-**	LISTS	MIAUL	MITZI	**-K-G-**
LIMPS	******	MILTS	MINUS	MITZY	******
LIPPI	BISSE	MILTY	MIXUP	PIEZO	SKEGS
LIPPY	CISSY	MINTS	NIDUS	PIZZA	******
LISPS	DIDST	MIRTH	NINUS	RITZY	**-K-I-**
NIPPY	FIRST	MISTS	NISUS	TIZZY	******
PIMPS	GIPSY	MISTY	PICUL	WINZE	SKEIN
SIMPS	GIRSH	MITTS	PINUP	******	******
TIPPY	KIOSK	NIFTY	PIOUS	**-J-C-**	**-K-L-**
WISPS	MIDST	NINTH	PIQUE	******	******
WISPY	MINSK	NITTY	RISUS	EJECT	SKALD
ZIPPY	MISSY	PICTS	SIEUR	******	SKILL
******	RINSE	PIETA	SINUS	**-J-L-**	SKULK
-I-R-	SISSY	PIETY	SIOUX	******	SKULL
******	TIPSY	PINTA	SIRUP	FJELD	******
BIERS	******	PINTO	SITUS	******	**-K-M-**
BIRRS	**-I-T-**	PINTS	TIEUP	**-J-R-**	******
CIRRI	******	RIATA	TITUS	******	SKIMO
CIRRO	BIOTA	RIFTS	VIRUS	FJORD	SKIMP
CITRA	BIRTH	RIOTS	******	NJORD	SKIMS
DIARY	BITTS	SIFTS	**-I-V-**		******
FIBRE	CISTS	SILTS	******	**-K-A-**	**-K-N-**
FIBRO	DICTA	SILTY	DIVVY	******	******
FIERY	DIETS	SIXTE	PIAVE	OKRAS	AKENE
FIORD	DINTS	SIXTH	SIEVE	SKEAN	EKING
FIRRY	DIRTY	SIXTY	SILVA	SKOAL	IKONS
HIERO	DITTO	TILTH	******	SKUAS	OKING
KIERS	DITTY	TILTS	**-I-W-**		SKINK
LIARS	FIATS	TINTS	******	**-K-D-**	SKINS
LIBRA	FIFTH	UINTA	KIOWA	******	SKUNK
LITRE	FIFTY	VIRTU	VIEWS	SKIDS	******
			VIEWY		**-K-O-**
					******
					AKRON

******	ALTAI	FLUBS	ELUDE	GLUES	******
-K-P-	ALTAR	FLYBY	GLADE	GLUEY	-L-H-
******	ALTAS	GLEBE	GLADS	ILMEN	******
OKAPI	ALVAN	GLOBE	GLEDE	MLLES	ALOHA
SKEPS	ALWAY	GLOBS	GLEDS	OLDEN	ALPHA
SKIPS	BLEAK	PLEBE	GLIDE	OLDER	ALPHY
******	BLEAR	PLEBS	PLODS	PLIED	BLAHS
-K-R-	BLEAT	SLABS	SLEDS	PLIER	ELIHU
******	BLOAT	SLOBS	SLIDE	PLIES	******
SKIRL	CLEAN	SLUBS	******	SLEEK	-L-I-
SKIRR	CLEAR	******	-L-E-	SLEEP	******
SKIRT	CLEAT	-L-C-	******	SLEET	ALAIN
******	CLOAK	******	ALBEE	SLIER	ALBIN
-K-S-	ELGAR	ALACK	ALDEN	SLOES	ALDIS
******	ELIAS	ALECK	ALDER	SLUED	ALFIE
UKASE	ELLAS	ALECS	ALGER	SLUES	ALGIA
******	ELMAN	ALICE	ALIEN	SLYER	ALGID
-K-T-	ELSAS	ALYCE	ALLEN	ULCER	ALGIE
******	ELVAN	BLACK	ALLEY	******	ALGIN
SKATE	FLEAM	BLOCK	ALOES	-L-F-	ALLIE
SKITS	FLEAS	BLOCS	ALTER	******	ALLIN
******	FLOAT	CLACK	BLEED	ALEFS	ALLIS
-K-V-	GLEAM	CLICK	BLEEP	ALIFS	ALOIN
******	GLEAN	CLOCK	BLUED	ALOFT	ALOIS
SKIVE	GLOAT	CLUCK	BLUER	BLUFF	ALUIN
******	ILEAC	ELECT	BLUES	CLEFS	ALVIN
-K-W-	ILEAL	FLACK	BLUET	CLEFT	ALWIN
******	ILIAC	FLECK	CLEEK	CLIFF	BLAIN
SKEWS	ILIAD	FLICK	CLUED	FLUFF	BLOIS
******	ILIAN	FLOCK	CLUES	OLAFS	CLAIM
-K-Y-	OLEAN	FLOCS	ELAEO	******	ELAIN
******	OLGAS	GLACE	ELDER	-L-G-	ELAIO
OKAYS	OLLAS	GLYCO	ELLEN	******	ELFIN
******	PLEAD	PLACE	ELMER	ALIGN	ELGIN
-L-A-	PLEAS	PLACK	ELVER	BLDGS	ELLIE
******	PLEAT	PLICA	ELVES	BLIGH	ELLIS
ALBAN	SLEAT	PLUCK	FLEER	CLOGS	ELOIN
ALBAS	ULNAE	SLACK	FLEES	ELEGY	ELSIE
ALCAN	ULNAR	SLICE	FLEET	FLAGS	ELVIN
ALDAN	ULNAS	SLICK	FLIED	FLOGS	ELWIN
ALGAE	******	******	FLIER	OLIGO	FLAIL
ALGAL	-L-B-	-L-D-	FLIES	OLOGY	FLAIR
ALIAS	******	******	FLOES	PLAGI	FLUID
ALLAH	ALIBI	ALADA	FLUES	PLEGY	GLAIR
ALLAN	BLABS	BLADE	FLYER	PLUGS	OLEIC
ALLAY	BLEBS	CLODS	GLEES	SLAGS	OLEIN
ALMAH	BLOBS	CLYDE	GLEET	SLIGO	OLLIE
ALMAS	CLUBS	ELIDE	GLUED	SLOGS	PLAID

PLAIN	SLAMS	GLENS	OLIOS	SLURS	FLITS
PLAIT	SLIME	GLINT	SLOOP	ULTRA	FLUTE
PLOID	SLIMS	ILONA	******	******	FLUTY
SLAIN	SLIMY	LLANO	**-L-P-**	**-L-S-**	GLUTS
******	SLUMP	OLENT	******	******	PLATA
-L-K-	SLUMS	PLANE	ALEPH	ALIST	PLATE
******	ULEMA	PLANI	BLIPS	BLASE	PLATO
ALIKE	******	PLANK	CLAPS	BLAST	PLATS
BLAKE	**-L-N-**	PLANO	CLIPS	BLESS	PLATY
BLOKE	******	PLANS	CLOPS	BLEST	PLOTS
FLAKE	ALAND	PLANT	ELOPE	BLISS	PLUTO
FLAKY	ALANS	PLENA	FLAPS	BLUSH	SLATE
FLUKE	ALINE	PLINY	FLIPS	CLASH	SLATS
FLUKY	ALONE	PLONK	FLOPS	CLASP	SLATY
SLAKE	ALONG	PLUNK	GLYPH	CLASS	SLITS
******	BLANC	SLANG	PLOPS	CLOSE	SLOTH
-L-L-	BLAND	SLANT	SLAPS	ELISE	SLOTS
******	BLANK	SLING	SLEPT	FLASH	SLUTS
ALULA	BLEND	SLINK	SLIPS	FLASK	ZLOTY
SLILY	BLENT	SLUNG	SLIPT	FLESH	******
SLYLY	BLIND	SLUNK	SLOPE	FLOSS	**-L-U-**
******	BLINK	ULENT	SLOPS	FLUSH	******
-L-M-	BLOND	******	SLYPE	GLASS	ALBUM
******	BLUNT	**-L-O-**	******	GLOSS	ALDUS
ALAMO	CLANG	******	**-L-R-**	GLOST	ALEUT
ALUMS	CLANK	ALDOL	******	PLASH	ALGUM
BLAME	CLANS	ALDOS	ALARM	PLASM	ALMUD
BLIMP	CLINE	ALGOL	ALARY	PLAST	ALMUG
CLAMP	CLING	ALGOR	ALERT	PLASY	ALOUD
CLAMS	CLINK	ALLOT	BLARE	PLUSH	CLOUD
CLEMS	CLINO	ALLOW	BLURB	SLASH	CLOUT
CLIMB	CLINT	ALLOY	BLURS	SLOSH	FLOUR
CLIME	CLONE	ALOOF	BLURT	SLUSH	FLOUT
CLUMP	CLONS	ALTON	CLARA	ULOSE	GLAUC
ELEMI	CLUNG	ALTOS	CLARE	******	ILEUM
FLAME	CLUNY	BLOOD	CLARK	**-L-T-**	ILEUS
FLAMS	ELAND	BLOOM	CLARO	******	ILIUM
FLAMY	ELENA	CLEON	CLARY	ALATE	ILLUS
FLUME	FLANK	CLIOS	CLERK	BLATS	ULOUS
FLUMP	FLANS	ELBOW	FLARE	BLITZ	******
GLIMS	FLING	ELIOT	FLIRT	BLOTS	**-L-V-**
GLUME	FLINT	ELTON	FLORA	BLYTH	******
LLAMA	FLONG	FLOOD	GLARE	CLOTH	ALIVE
PLUMB	FLUNG	FLOOR	GLARY	CLOTS	CLIVE
PLUME	FLUNK	FLUOR	GLORY	ELATE	CLOVE
PLUMP	GLAND	GLOOM	KLARA	ELITE	GLOVE
PLUMS	GLANS	ILION	PLURI	FLATS	OLAVS
PLUMY	GLENN	KLOOF	SLURP	FLITE	OLIVE

PLUVI	GLAZE	IMPEL	SMELT	AMISS	ANSAE
SLAVE	GLAZY	OMBER	SMILE	AMUSE	ANTAE
SLAVO	GLOZE	UMBEL	SMOLT	OMASA	ANTAL
SLAVS	PLAZA	UMBER	UMBLE	SMASH	ANZAC
******	******	******	******	******	ENEAS
-L-W-	**-M-A-**	**-M-G-**	**-M-M-**	**-M-T-**	INCAN
******	******	******	******	******	INCAS
BLOWN	AMIAS	AMIGO	IMAMS	AMATE	INLAW
BLOWS	AMMAN	IMAGE	******	AMATI	INLAY
BLOWY	EMBAR	IMAGO	**-M-N-**	AMITY	INVAR
CLAWS	EMBAY	OMEGA	******	EMITS	KNEAD
CLEWS	EMMAS	SMOGS	AMANA	EMOTE	SNEAD
CLOWN	SMEAR	******	AMEND	EMPTY	SNEAK
FLAWS	UMIAK	**-M-H-**	AMENS	OMITS	UNBAR
FLAWY	******	******	AMENT	SMITE	UNCAP
FLEWS	**-M-B-**	AMAHS	AMINE	SMITH	UNHAT
FLOWN	******	AMPHI	AMINO	SMOTE	UNIAT
FLOWS	AMEBA	AMPHR	AMONG	SMUTS	UNLAY
GLOWS	******	OMAHA	EMEND	******	UNMAN
PLOWS	**-M-C-**	******	IMINE	**-M-U-**	UNSAY
SLAWS	******	**-M-I-**	IMINO	******	
SLEWS	AMICE	AMAIN	OMENS	AMOUR	**-N-B-**
SLOWS	AMUCK	AMBIT	******	AMPUL	******
******	SMACK	AMNIA	**-M-O-**	EMBUS	KNOBS
-L-X-	SMOCK	EMMIE	******	EMEUS	SNOBS
******	******	IMMIX	AMBOS	IMBUE	SNUBS
ALEXA	**-M-D-**	******	AMMON	******	******
FLAXY	******	**-M-K-**	EMBOW	**-M-W-**	**-N-C-**
FLEXI	AMIDE	******	IMPOT	******	******
******	AMIDO	SMOKE	UMBOS	BMEWS	ENACT
-L-Y-	IMIDE	SMOKY	******	SMEWS	ENOCH
******	IMIDO	******	**-M-R-**	******	KNACK
ALGYS	IMIDS	**-M-L-**	******	**-M-Y-**	KNOCK
ALKYL	******	******	AMBRY	******	SNACK
ALLYL	**-M-E-**	AMBLE	AMIRS	EMMYS	SNICK
CLAYS	******	AMOLE	EMBRY	******	VNECK
CLOYS	AMBER	AMPLE	EMERY	**-M-Z-**	******
FLAYS	AMEER	AMPLY	EMIRS	******	**-N-D-**
FLOYD	AMIEL	AMYLO	EMORY	AMAZE	******
LLOYD	AMIES	AMYLS	OMBRE	SMAZE	ANODE
PLAYA	EMBED	EMILE	OMBRO	******	ENIDS
PLAYS	EMBER	EMILS	OMERS	**-N-A-**	SNIDE
PLOYS	EMCEE	EMILY	SMART	******	******
SLAYS	EMDEN	IMPLY	SMIRK	ANEAR	**-N-E-**
SLOYD	EMEER	SMALL	UMBRA	ANLAS	******
******	EMMER	SMALT	******	ANNAL	ANDES
-L-Z-	EMMET	SMELL	**-M-S-**	ANNAM	ANGEL
******	IMBED		******	ANNAS	ANGER
BLAZE			AMASS		
ELIZA			AMISH		

ANNES	******	******	******	SNOTS	BORAX
ANNEX	-N-I-	-N-M-	-N-R-	UNITE	BOYAR
ANSEL	******	******	******	UNITS	COCAS
ANTED	ANGIO	ANEMO	ANDRE	UNITY	CODAS
ANTES	ANNIE	ANIMA	ANDRO	******	COHAN
ENDED	ANTIC	ANIME	ANGRY	-N-U-	COLAS
ENNEA	ANTIS	ANOMY	ANTRA	******	COMAE
ENTER	ANVIL	ENEMA	ENARE	ANGUS	COMAL
INDEX	ANZIO	ENEMY	ENTRY	ANKUS	COMAS
INFER	ENTIA	GNOME	GNARL	ANNUL	COPAL
INKED	INDIA	GNOMY	INARM	ENDUE	CORAL
INKER	INDIC	******	INDRA	ENNUI	CORAS
INLET	INFIX	-N-N-	INDRI	ENSUE	COXAE
INNED	ONEIR	******	INERT	INCUR	COXAL
INNER	SNAIL	ANENT	INFRA	INCUS	DONAR
INSET	UNDID	INANE	INTRA	INDUE	DONAS
INTER	UNFIT	******	INTRO	INDUS	DORAS
KNEED	UNFIX	-N-O-	INURE	INPUT	DOUAI
KNEEL	UNLIT	******	INURN	KNOUT	DOUAY
KNEES	UNPIN	ANCON	KNARS	PNEUM	DOVAP
ONSET	UNRIG	ANION	KNURL	SNOUT	FOCAL
SNEER	UNRIP	ANJOU	KNURR	UNAUS	FORAY
SNYES	UNTIE	ANNOY	KNURS	UNCUT	GONAD
UNDEE	UNTIL	ANTON	ONERY	UNDUE	GORAL
UNDER	UNZIP	ENDOW	ONIRO	******	GOWAN
UNMEW	******	ENJOY	SNARE	-N-V-	HOGAN
UNPEG	-N-K-	ENROL	SNARK	******	HOKAN
UNPEN	******	ENTOM	SNARL	KNAVE	HONAN
UNREF	SNAKE	ENVOY	SNORE	******	HORAE
UNSEX	SNAKY	INDOW	SNORT	-N-W-	HORAL
UNWED	******	INGOT	UNARM	******	HORAS
******	-N-L-	INION	******	GNAWN	IOTAS
-N-F-	******	ONION	-N-S-	GNAWS	JONAH
******	ANELE	SNOOD	******	KNOWN	JONAS
KNIFE	ANGLE	SNOOK	ANGST	KNOWS	JORAM
SNAFU	ANGLO	SNOOP	ANISE	SNOWS	KODAK
SNIFF	ANILE	SNOOT	ANISO	SNOWY	KOLAS
SNUFF	ANILS	UNION	GNASH	******	KORAN
UNIFY	ANKLE	******	KNOSP	-N-Y-	LOBAR
******	ENOLA	-N-P-	******	******	LOCAL
-N-G-	ENOLS	******	-N-T-	ANDYS	LOGAN
******	INGLE	INAPT	******	ENCYC	LOLAS
INIGO	INKLE	INEPT	ANITA	******	LOPAT
ONEGA	KNELL	KNOPS	ENATE	-O-A-	LORAN
SNAGS	KNELT	SNAPS	GNATS	******	LOTAH
SNUGS	KNOLL	SNIPE	KNITS	BOGAN	LOYAL
******	SNELL	SNIPS	KNOTS	BOLAR	MODAL
-N-H-	UNCLE	UNAPT	SNATH	BOLAS	MOLAL
******					
ANKHS					
ANTHO					

MOLAR	TOTAL	LORCA	MOODS	COKED	DOSES
MONAD	VOCAL	MOOCH	MOODY	COKER	DOTED
MONAS	VOLAR	MOUCH	NODDY	COKES	DOTER
MORAE	WODAN	NONCE	PONDS	COKEY	DOTES
MORAL	WOMAN	NOTCH	POODS	COLES	DOVER
MORAS	WOTAN	POACH	ROADS	COMER	DOVES
MORAT	ZONAL	PONCE	RODDY	COMES	DOWEL
MORAY	******	POOCH	RONDO	COMET	DOWER
MOSAN	**-O-B-**	PORCH	ROODS	CONED	DOYEN
MOXAS	******	POUCH	ROWDY	CONES	DOZED
NODAL	BOBBY	ROACH	SOLDI	CONEY	DOZEN
NOMAD	BOMBE	ROTCH	SOLDO	COOED	DOZER
NOMAS	BOMBS	TORCH	TOADS	COOEE	DOZES
NONAS	BOOBS	TOUCH	TOADY	COOER	FOGEY
NOPAL	BOOBY	VOICE	TODDS	COOEY	FORES
NOPAR	COBBS	VOUCH	TODDY	COPEC	FOVEA
NORAH	COMBO	******	VOIDS	COPED	FOXED
NORAS	COMBS	**-O-D-**	WOADS	COPER	FOXES
NOVAE	CORBY	******	WOLDS	COPES	FOYED
NOVAS	DOBBY	BONDS	WOODS	CORED	FOYER
NOWAY	DOUBT	BOYDS	WOODY	CORER	GOFER
POLAR	FORBS	COEDS	WORDS	CORES	GOLEM
ROMAN	FORBY	COLDS	WORDY	COSEK	GONER
ROSAS	HOBBS	COMDR	******	COTES	GOOEY
ROTAS	HOBBY	COMDT	**-O-E-**	COVED	GORED
ROWAN	LOBBY	CORDS	******	COVEN	GORES
ROYAL	LOOBY	DOWDY	BODED	COVER	GOWER
SODAS	NOBBY	FOLDS	BODES	COVES	HOLED
SOFAS	SORBS	FONDA	BOGEY	COVET	HOLES
SOJAS	TOMBS	FOODS	BOHEA	COVEY	HOLEY
SOLAN	WOMBS	FORDS	BOLES	COWED	HOMED
SOLAR	WOMBY	GOADS	BONED	COWER	HOMEO
SOMAT	ZOMBI	GOLDA	BONER	COWES	HOMER
SONAR	******	GOLDS	BONES	COXED	HOMES
SORAS	**-O-C-**	GONDI	BOOED	COXES	HOMEY
SOWAR	******	GOODS	BORED	COZEN	HONED
SOYAS	BOSCH	GOODY	BORER	DODEC	HONES
TODAY	BOTCH	GOUDA	BORES	DOGES	HONEY
TOGAE	COACH	HOLDS	BOWED	DOLED	HOOEY
TOGAS	COCCI	HONDO	BOWEL	DOLES	HOPED
TOKAY	CONCH	HOODS	BOWER	DOMED	HOPEH
TOLAN	COUCH	HORDE	BOXED	DOMES	HOPES
TOLAS	DOLCE	HOWDY	BOXER	DONEE	HOREB
TOMAN	FORCE	LOADS	BOXES	DOPED	HOSEA
TOMAS	HOICK	LORDS	CODED	DOPES	HOSED
TONAL	HOOCH	MOLDS	CODER	DOPEY	HOSES
TOPAZ	JOYCE	MOLDY	CODES	DOSED	HOTEL
TORAH	LOACH	MONDE	CODEX	DOSER	HOVEL

HOVER	MOVER	ROVEN	WOOED	DOGGY	******
JOKED	MOVES	ROVER	WOOER	DOUGH	-O-I-
JOKER	MOWED	ROVES	WOVEN	DOUGS	******
JOKES	MOWER	ROWED	WOWED	FOGGY	BOGIE
JOLES	NOBEL	ROWEL	YODEL	FORGE	BONIN
JONES	NODES	ROWEN	YOGEE	FORGO	BORIC
JOYED	NONES	ROWER	YOKED	GONGS	BORIS
KOPEC	NONET	SOBER	YOKEL	GORGE	BOVID
KOPEK	NOSED	SOKES	YOKES	GOUGE	BOWIE
KOREA	NOSES	SOLED	YOWED	HOAGY	COBIA
LOBED	NOSEY	SOLES	ZONED	HODGE	COLIC
LOBES	NOTED	SONES	ZONES	HONGS	COLIN
LODEN	NOTER	SOREL	******	HOUGH	COMIC
LODES	NOTES	SORER	-O-F-	JORGE	CONIC
LOGES	NOVEL	SORES	******	LODGE	CONIO
LONER	NOYES	SOWED	COIFS	LONGI	CORIA
LOOED	OOZED	SOWER	COMFY	LONGS	DOBIE
LOPED	OOZES	TOKEN	CORFE	LOUGH	DOGIE
LOPER	POGEY	TOLES	CORFU	NOGGS	DOMIC
LOPES	POKED	TOMES	DOFFS	PODGY	DORIC
LORES	POKER	TONED	GOLFS	PORGE	DORIS
LOSER	POKES	TONER	GOOFS	PORGY	EOLIC
LOSES	POKEY	TONES	GOOFY	ROUGE	EOSIN
LOVED	POLED	TOPED	HOOFS	ROUGH	FOLIA
LOVER	POLES	TOPEE	LOAFS	SOGGY	FOLIC
LOVES	POMES	TOPER	LOOFS	SONGS	FOLIO
LOWED	PONES	TOPES	POUFS	SORGO	GONIA
LOWER	POPES	TOTED	ROLFE	SOUGH	GONIO
MODEL	PORED	TOTEM	ROLFS	TONGA	GOYIM
MODES	PORES	TOTER	ROOFS	TONGS	HOWIE
MOKES	POSED	TOTES	SOLFA	TOUGH	IODIC
MOLES	POSER	TOWED	WOLFS	VOLGA	IONIA
MONET	POSES	TOWEL	WOOFS	******	IONIC
MONEY	POWER	TOWER	******	-O-H-	JOSIE
MOOED	ROBED	TOYED	-O-G-	******	LOGIA
MOPED	ROBES	TOYER	******	BOCHE	LOGIC
MOPER	RODEO	VOCES	BOGGY	BOTHY	LORIS
MOPES	ROGER	VOLES	BONGO	FOEHN	LOUIS
MOREL	ROLES	VOMER	BONGS	GOTHA	MORIN
MORES	ROMEO	VOTED	BOUGH	GOTHS	MOTIF
MOSEL	ROPED	VOTER	COIGN	LOCHS	MOVIE
MOSES	ROPES	VOTES	CONGA	MOCHA	MOXIE
MOSEY	ROPEY	VOWED	CONGE	MOTHS	NORIA
MOTEL	ROSED	VOWEL	CONGO	MOTHY	PODIA
MOTES	ROSES	VOWER	CORGI	NOAHS	POLIO
MOTET	ROUEN	WODEN	COUGH	SOPHY	POSIT
MOUES	ROUES	WOKEN	DODGE	TOPHI	ROBIN
MOVED	ROVED	WOMEN	DODGY	YODHS	RODIN
				YOGHS	

ROSIN	HONKY	DOALL	ROILY	ROOMY	LOONY
SOCIO	HOOKE	DOBLA	ROLLO	SOMME	LORNA
SOFIA	HOOKS	DOILY	ROLLS	TOMMY	MOANS
SOLID	HOOKY	DOLLS	ROTLA	WORMS	MOONS
SONIA	JOCKO	DOLLY	SOCLE	WORMY	MOONY
SONIC	KOOKS	DOOLY	SOILS	ZOOMS	MORNA
SOZIN	KOOKY	DOYLE	SOULS	******	MORNS
TOEIN	LOCKE	DOYLY	TOILE	-O-N-	MOUND
TONIC	LOCKS	FOALS	TOILS	******	MOUNT
TONIS	LOOKS	FOILS	TOLLS	BONNY	NOONS
TOPIC	MOCKS	FOLLY	TOOLS	BOONE	NORNS
TOPIS	MONKS	FOOLS	VOILA	BOONS	NOUNS
TORIC	NOCKS	FORLI	VOILE	BORNE	POIND
TORII	NOOKS	FOULS	WOALD	BORNU	POINT
TOXIC	POCKS	FOWLS	WOOLF	BOUND	POONA
TOXIN	POCKY	GOALS	WOOLS	BOYNE	POONS
VOMIT	POLKA	GODLY	WOOLY	COENO	PORNO
YOGIC	PORKY	GOLLY	WORLD	COINS	POUND
YOGIN	ROCKS	HOLLY	WOULD	COLNE	ROANS
YOGIS	ROCKY	HOTLY	YOULL	CONNY	RONNY
ZOOID	ROOKS	HOWLS	YOWLS	COONS	ROUND
ZORIL	ROOKY	HOYLE	******	CORNS	SOMNI
******	SOAKS	JOELS	-O-M-	CORNU	SONNY
-O-J-	SOCKS	JOLLY	******	CORNY	SOUND
******	VODKA	JOULE	BOOMS	COUNT	TONNE
KOPJE	WORKS	JOWLS	COMMA	DOING	TOWNS
SONJA	YOLKS	KOALA	COOMB	DONNA	WOUND
******	YOLKY	KOELS	CORMS	DONNE	YOUNG
-O-K-	******	LOLLS	COSMO	DOWNS	ZOONS
******	-O-L-	LOLLY	DOGMA	DOWNY	******
BOOKS	******	LOWLY	DOOMS	FOUND	-O-O-
BOSKS	BOGLE	MOILS	DORMS	FOUNT	******
BOSKY	BOILS	MOLLS	DORMY	GOING	BOGOR
COCKS	BOLLS	MOLLY	FOAMS	GOONS	BOHOL
COCKY	BOULE	MOULD	FOAMY	GOWNS	BOLOS
CONKS	BOWLS	MOULT	FORME	HORNE	BORON
COOKS	BOYLE	NOBLE	FORMS	HORNS	BOSOM
COOKY	COALS	NOBLY	GORME	HORNY	BOSON
CORKS	COALY	NOELS	HOLMS	HOUND	BOZOS
CORKY	COBLE	POILU	LOAMS	JOANS	COCOA
DOCKS	COELE	POLLS	LOAMY	JOHNS	COCOS
FOLKS	COELO	POLLY	LOOMS	JOINS	COGON
FORKS	COILS	POOLE	NORMA	JOINT	COLON
GOOKS	COLLY	POOLS	NORMS	JONNY	COLOR
GORKI	COOLS	POULT	POEMS	KOINE	COROT
GORKY	COULD	ROALD	POMMY	LOANS	DODOS
HOCKS	COWLS	ROBLE	ROAMS	LOINS	DOLOR
HONKS	COYLY	ROILS	ROOMS	LOONS	DONOR

GOBOS	POPPY	POURS	MOIST	COMTE	MORTY
GOGOL	ROLPH	ROARS	MOOSE	CONTD	MOTTO
HOBOS	ROMPS	SOARS	MORSE	CONTE	MOUTH
HONOR	ROUPY	SORRY	MOSSO	CONTO	NOCTI
IODOL	SOAPS	SOURS	MOSSY	CONTR	NORTH
KOMOS	SOAPY	TOURS	MOUSE	COOTS	POETS
KOTOS	SOPPY	WORRY	MOUSY	COPTS	PORTS
LOBOS	SOUPS	YOURE	NOISE	COSTA	POSTS
LOCOS	SOUPY	YOURS	NOISY	COSTO	POTTO
LOGOS	******	******	NOOSE	COSTS	POTTY
LOTOS	-O-R-	-O-S-	NORSE	COTTA	POUTS
MORON	******	******	POESY	COUTH	ROOTS
MOROS	BOARD	BOAST	POISE	DOETH	ROOTY
MOTOR	BOARS	BOISE	POPSY	DOITS	ROUTE
POYOU	BOERS	BOOST	POSSE	DOLTS	ROUTS
ROBOT	BOORS	BOSSY	POTSY	DONTS	SOFTA
ROTOR	BOURG	BOUSE	ROAST	DOTTY	SOFTY
SODOM	BOURN	BOUSY	ROOST	FONTS	SOOTH
SOLON	COBRA	BOWSE	ROUSE	FOOTS	SOOTS
SOLOS	COPRA	COAST	ROUST	FOOTD	SOOTY
SOPOR	COPRO	COPSE	SONSY	FORTE	SORTS
SOTOL	COURT	CORSE	SOUSA	FORTH	SOTTO
TOBOL	COWRY	DOEST	SOUSE	FORTS	SOUTH
TODOS	DOBRA	DORSA	TOAST	FORTY	TOFTS
TOYON	DOERS	DORSI	TOISE	GOATS	TOOTH
TOYOS	DOORN	DORSO	TOPSY	GOUTY	TOOTS
YOYOS	DOORS	DOUSE	TORSI	HOOTS	TORTE
******	DORRS	DOWSE	TORSK	HORTA	TORTS
-O-P-	DOURA	FOISM	TORSO	HOSTS	TOUTS
******	DOURY	FOIST	WORSE	JOLTS	VOLTA
COMPO	DOWRY	FOSSA	WORST	JOLTY	VOLTE
COOPS	FOURS	FOSSE	******	LOATH	VOLTI
COOPT	GOERS	GOOSE	-O-T-	LOFTS	VOLTS
CORPS	GOURD	GOOSY	******	LOFTY	WORTH
COUPE	HOARD	GORSE	AORTA	LOOTS	WORTS
COUPS	HOARY	GORSY	BOATS	LOTTA	YOUTH
COYPU	HOERS	HOIST	BOLTS	LOTTE	******
DOLPH	HOURI	HOLST	BOOTH	LOTTO	-O-U-
HOOPS	HOURS	HORSE	BOOTS	LOTTY	******
LOOPS	LOIRE	HORST	BOOTY	LOUTS	BOGUS
LOOPY	LORRY	HORSY	BORTS	MOATS	BOLUS
LOPPY	LOURS	HOUSE	BORTY	MOLTO	BONUS
LOUPE	MOIRA	JOIST	BORTZ	MOLTS	BOSUN
LOUPS	MOIRE	JOUST	BOTTS	MONTE	COMUS
MORPH	MOORE	LOESS	BOUTS	MONTH	CONUS
OOMPH	MOORS	LOOSE	COATI	MONTY	DORUS
POOPO	MORRO	LOUSE	COATS	MORTA	EOLUS
POOPS	MOURN	LOUSY	COLTS	MORTS	FOCUS

FORUM	******	APTER	APTLY	APORT	******
HOCUS	-O-Z-	EPEES	OPALS	OPERA	-Q-A-
HOKUM	******	OPTED	SPALL	SPARE	******
HORUS	BONZE	SPEED	SPELL	SPARK	AQUAE
JORUM	BOOZE	SPHEN	SPELT	SPARS	AQUAS
JOSUA	BOOZY	SPIED	SPILE	SPERM	EQUAB
JOSUE	COLZA	SPIEL	SPILL	SPIRE	SQUAB
JOTUN	WOOZY	SPIER	SPILT	SPIRO	SQUAD
KORUN	******	SPIES	******	SPIRT	SQUAT
LOCUM	-P-A-	SPLEN	-P-M-	SPIRY	SQUAW
LOCUS	******	SPREE	******	SPORE	******
LOGUE	APEAK	UPPED	SPUME	SPORO	-Q-B-
LOTUS	APIAN	UPPER	SPUMY	SPORT	******
MODUS	APPAL	UPSET	******	SPURN	AQABA
MOGUL	EPHAH	YPRES	-P-N-	SPURS	******
MOHUR	SPEAK	******	******	SPURT	-Q-E-
MOMUS	SPEAR	-P-H-	APING	******	******
NODUS	SPLAT	******	OPENS	-P-S-	YQUEM
ROGUE	SPLAY	OPAHS	OPINE	******	******
ROQUE	SPRAG	SPAHI	SPANG	APISH	-Q-I-
SOLUS	SPRAT	******	SPANK	SPASM	******
SORUS	SPRAY	-P-I-	SPANS	******	EQUIP
TOGUE	******	******	SPEND	-P-T-	SQUIB
TONUS	-P-C-	APHID	SPENT	******	SQUID
TOQUE	******	APHIS	SPINE	SPATE	******
TORUS	APACE	APRIL	SPINI	SPATS	-R-A-
VOGUE	EPACT	APSIS	SPINS	SPITE	******
VOGUL	EPICS	OPHIO	SPINY	SPITS	AREAE
******	EPOCH	OPSIA	SPUNK	SPITZ	AREAL
-O-V-	SPACE	OPSIS	UPEND	SPOTS	AREAS
******	SPECK	OPTIC	******	******	ARGAL
HOOVE	SPECS	SPAIN	-P-O-	-P-U-	ARIAN
SOLVE	SPICA	SPAIT	******	******	ARIAS
VOLVA	SPICE	SPLIT	APRON	OPIUM	ARPAD
YOUVE	SPICY	SPOIL	EPHOD	SPOUT	ARRAN
******	******	SPRIG	EPHOR	SPRUE	ARRAS
-O-Y-	-P-D-	SPRIT	EPSOM	******	ARRAY
******	******	******	SPOOF	-P-W-	ARTAL
GOBYS	EPODE	-P-K-	SPOOK	******	ARVAL
GOVYS	SPADE	******	SPOOL	SPAWN	ARYAN
JOEYS	SPODE	SPAKE	SPOON	SPEWS	BREAD
KONYA	SPUDS	SPIKE	SPOOR	******	BREAK
POLYP	******	SPIKY	UPBOW	-P-X-	BREAM
POWYS	-P-E-	SPOKE	******	******	BRIAN
SONYA	******	******	-P-R-	EPOXY	BRIAR
TOBYS	******	-P-L-	******	******	BROAD
TOKYO	APNEA	******	APART	-P-Y-	BRYAN
TOLYL	APPEL	APPLE	APERY	******	BREAM
TONYS	APSES	APPLY	APERY	SPAYS	CRAAL

CREAK	KRUBI	WRACK	CREEK	TRIED	ARTHR
CREAM	ORIBI	WRECK	CREEL	TRIER	BRAHE
CROAK	PROBE	WRICK	CREEP	TRIES	ORCHI
CROAT	TRIBE	******	CREES	TRUED	ORTHO
DREAD	******	-R-D-	CRIED	TRUER	PRAHU
DREAM	-R-C-	******	CRIER	TRUES	******
DREAR	******	BRADS	CRIES	URGED	-R-I-
DRYAD	ARECA	BRADY	CRUEL	URGES	******
ERLAU	ARICA	BREDA	CRUET	URIEL	AREIC
ERMAS	BRACE	BRIDE	DRIED	WRIED	ARGIL
FREAK	BRACT	CREDO	DRIER	WRIER	ARNIE
FRIAR	BRICE	CRUDE	DRIES	WRIES	AROID
GRAAL	BRICK	ERODE	DRYER	WRYER	ARRIS
GREAT	BROCK	FREDA	ERIES	******	ARSIS
GROAN	BRUCE	FREDS	ERNES	-R-F-	ARTIC
GROAT	BRYCE	GRADE	ERRED	******	ARTIE
IRMAS	CRACK	GRADS	ERSES	CRAFT	ARTIS
KRAAL	CRACY	GRIDE	FREED	CROFT	BRAID
OREAD	CRECY	GRIDS	FREER	DRAFF	BRAIL
ORGAN	CRICK	IRIDO	FREES	DRAFT	BRAIN
PRIAM	CROCE	PRIDE	FRIED	DRIFT	BROIL
PROAS	CROCI	PRODS	FRIER	GRAFT	BRUIN
TREAD	CROCK	PRUDE	FRIES	GRUFF	BRUIT
TREAS	CRUCI	TRADE	FROES	KRAFT	CRAIG
TREAT	DRACO	TRUDA	FRYER	PROFS	CROIX
TRIAD	ERECT	TRUDY	GREED	******	DRAIL
TRIAL	ERICA	UREDO	GREEK	-R-G-	DRAIN
TROAS	ERICH	******	GREEN	******	DROIT
URBAN	ERICS	-R-E-	GREER	BRAGE	DRUID
UREAL	ERUCT	******	GREET	BRAGG	ERNIE
URIAH	FROCK	ARCED	GRIEF	BRAGI	ERWIN
URSAE	GRACE	ARDEB	GRIEG	BRAGS	FRAIL
WREAK	GRECO	ARDEN	GRUEL	BRIGS	FRUIT
******	ORACH	ARIEL	IRKED	CRAGS	GRAIL
-R-B-	PRICE	ARIES	ORBED	DRAGS	GRAIN
******	PRICK	ARLEN	ORDER	DREGS	GROIN
ARABS	PROCT	ARLES	ORIEL	DRUGS	IRVIN
ARABY	TRACE	ARMED	ORLES	FRIGG	IRWIN
ARUBA	TRACH	ARMET	ORMER	FROGS	KRAIT
BRIBE	TRACK	ARPEN	PREEN	GREGO	ORBIT
CRABS	TRACT	ARSES	PRIED	GREGS	ORCIN
CRIBS	TRACY	ARTEL	PRIER	PRIGS	ORNIS
DRABS	TRICE	ARTER	PRIES	TRAGI	ORPIN
DRIBS	TRICH	BRAES	PROEM	TRIGO	ORRIS
DRUBS	TRICK	BREED	PRYER	TRIGS	TRAIL
GRABS	TRUCE	BRIEF	RRHEA	******	TRAIN
GREBE	TRUCK	BRIER	TREED	-R-H-	TRAIT
GRUBS	URICO	CREED	TREES	******	
				ARCHI	
				ARCHY	

******	DROME	DRINK	ARGOL	ERUPT	CRUSE
-R-K-	DRUMS	DRONE	ARGON	FRAPS	CRUSH
******	FRAME	DRUNK	ARGOS	GRAPE	CRUST
BRAKE	FRIML	FRANC	ARGOT	GRAPH	DRESS
BRAKY	FROME	FRANK	ARION	GRAPY	DREST
BROKE	FRUMP	FRANZ	ARMOR	GRIPE	DROSS
CRAKE	GRAMA	FRENA	ARROW	GRIPS	DRUSE
DRAKE	GRAMS	FROND	ARSON	GRIPT	ERASE
ERIKA	GRIME	FRONT	BROOD	GROPE	ERNST
ERIKS	GRIMM	GRAND	BROOK	KRUPP	EROSE
TREKS	GRIMY	GRANI	BROOM	PROPS	FRESH
******	GRUME	GRANO	BROOS	TRAPS	FRISE
-R-L-	PRAMS	GRANT	CREON	TRIPE	FRISK
******	PRIMA	GRIND	CROOK	TRIPS	FROSH
ARILS	PRIME	GRINS	CROON	TROPE	FROST
BRILL	PRIMI	GRUNT	CRUOR	TROPH	GRASP
DRILL	PRIMO	IRENE	DROOL	WRAPS	GRASS
DRILY	PRIMP	IRONE	DROOP	WRAPT	GRIST
DROLL	PRIMS	IRONS	ERGOT	******	GROSS
DRYLY	PROMS	IRONY	ERROL	-R-Q-	GROSZ
FRILL	TRAMP	KRONA	ERROR	******	IRISH
GRILL	TRAMS	KRONE	FREON	IRAQI	PRASE
ORALS	TRIMS	ORANG	GROOM	******	PRESA
PROLE	TRUMP	PRANG	ORION	-R-R-	PRESS
TRILL	TRYMA	PRANK	ORLON	******	PREST
TROLL	******	PRINK	ORLOP	CRORE	PRISE
TRULL	-R-N-	PRINT	ORSON	CRURA	PRISM
TRULY	******	PRONE	PRIOR	DRURY	PROSE
URALS	ARENA	PRONG	PROOF	FRERE	PROSY
WRYLY	ARENT	PRUNE	TRIOL	TRURO	TRASH
******	BRAND	TRANS	TRIOS	******	TRASS
-R-M-	BRANS	TREND	TROOP	-R-S-	TRESS
******	BRANT	TRENT	TRYON	******	TRUSS
AROMA	BRENT	TRINA	******	ARISE	TRUST
ARUMS	BRINE	TRINE	-R-P-	AROSE	TRYST
BRIMS	BRING	TRONA	******	BRASH	WREST
BROME	BRINK	TRUNK	CRAPE	BRASS	WRIST
BROMO	BRINY	URANO	CRAPS	BREST	******
BRUME	BRONC	URINE	CREPE	BRISK	-R-T-
CRAMP	BRONX	URINO	CREPT	BRUSH	******
CRAMS	BRUNO	WRENS	CROPS	BRUSK	ARETE
CREME	BRUNT	WRING	CRYPT	CRASH	BRATS
CRIME	CRANE	WRONG	DRAPE	CRASS	BROTH
CRIMP	CRANI	WRUNG	DRIPS	CRESC	BRUTE
CRUMB	CRONE	******	DRIPT	CRESS	CRATE
CRUMP	CRONY	-R-O-	DROPS	CREST	CRETE
DRAMA	DRANK	******	DROPT	CRISP	ERATO
DRAMS		ARBOR	DRUPE	CROSS	FRATS
		ARDOR			

FRETS	BREVI	PROXY	OSMAN	******	******
FRITH	CRAVE	TRIXY	PSHAW	-S-I-	-S-U-
FRITS	DRAVA	******	PSOAS	******	******
FRITZ	DRAVE	-R-Y-	USUAL	ASPIC	ASCUS
FROTH	DRIVE	******	******	ASPIS	ASHUR
GRATE	DROVE	BRAYS	-S-C-	ASTIR	ASYUT
GRETA	GRAVE	DRAYS	******	ESSIE	ESQUE
GRITS	GRAVY	FRAYS	ASPCA	ISTIC	ISSUE
GROTS	GROVE	FREYA	PSYCH	OSMIC	PSEUD
IRATE	PRIVY	GRAYS	******	OSTIA	
ORATE	PROVE	GREYS	-S-D-	******	-S-Y-
PRATE	PROVO	ORIYA	******	-S-K-	******
PROTO	TRAVE	PRAYS	ASIDE	******	ASSYR
TRITE	TROVE	PREYS	TSADE	OSAKA	******
TROTH	******	TRAYS		******	-T-A-
TROTS	-R-W-	TREYS	-S-E-	-S-L-	******
TRUTH	******	XRAYS	******	******	ATLAS
URATE	BRAWL	******	ASHEN	ASYLA	ATMAN
WRATH	BRAWN	-R-Z-	ASHER	ISTLE	ATPAR
WRITE	BREWS	******	ASHES	PSALM	ATTAR
WRITS	BROWN	BRAZA	ASKED	******	ETHAN
WROTE	BROWS	BRAZE	ASKER	-S-N-	ETNAS
WROTH	CRAWL	CRAZE	ASKEW	******	ETTAS
******	CRAWS	CRAZY	ASPEN	ASSNS	STEAD
-R-U-	CREWE	CROZE	ASPER	TSANA	STEAK
******	CREWS	FRIZZ	ASSES	USING	STEAL
ARCUS	CROWD	FROZE	ASSET	******	STEAM
ARGUE	CROWN	GRAZE	ASTER	-S-O-	STOAE
ARGUS	CROWS	ORCZY	ESHER	******	STOAS
ARIUM	DRAWL	PRIZE	ESKER	ASCOT	STOAT
ARIUS	DRAWN	******	ESSEN	ASSOC	STRAD
ARTUR	DRAWS	-S-A-	ESSES	ASTON	STRAP
CROUP	DREWS	******	ESSEX	ASTOR	STRAT
FRAUD	DROWN	ASCAP	ESTER	ESTOP	STRAW
FREUD	FROWN	ASIAN	ESTES	******	STRAY
GROUP	FROWS	ASSAI	ISLED	-S-R-	XTIAN
GROUT	GROWL	ASSAM	ISLES	******	******
KRAUT	GROWN	ASSAY	ISLET	ASTRO	-T-B-
ORCUS	GROWS	ASWAN	ISSEI	ISERE	******
PROUD	PRAWN	ESSAY	OSIER	TSARS	STABS
TROUT	PROWL	ESTAR	OSLER	USERS	STUBS
******	PROWS	ISAAC	OSTED	USURP	******
-R-V-	TRAWL	ISBAS	USHER	USURY	-T-C-
******	TREWS	ISLAM	******	YSERE	******
BRAVA	******	ISLAY	-S-G-	******	STACK
BRAVE	-R-X-	ISTAR	******	-S-T-	STACY
BRAVO	******	OSCAN	OSAGE	******	STICH
BREVE	BRAXY	OSCAR	USAGE	ASSTS	STICK
	PREXY			OSITY	

STOCK	ATTIC	STOMA	STOPS	******	JURAL
STUCK	ATTIS	STOME	STOPT	-T-V-	JURAT
UTICA	ETHIC	STOMP	STUPA	******	KUBAN
******	ETTIE	STOMY	STUPE	ATIVE	KULAK
-T-D-	ETUIS	STUMP	******	STAVE	LUNAR
******	STAID	STUMS	-T-R-	STEVE	MURAL
ETUDE	STAIN	STYMY	******	STOVE	MURAT
STUDS	STAIR	******	ATORY	******	MUZAK
STUDY	STEIN	-T-N-	OTARU	-T-W-	OURAY
******	STOIC	******	OTERO	******	PUMAS
-T-E-	STRIA	ATONE	PTERO	STEWS	PUNAS
******	STRIP	ATONY	STARE	STOWE	PUPAE
ETHEL	******	CTENO	STARK	STOWS	PUSAN
ETHER	-T-K-	ETHNO	STARS	******	QUEAN
OTHER	******	STAND	START	-T-X-	RUGAE
OTTER	STAKE	STANK	STERE	******	RURAL
STEED	STOKE	STANS	STERN	ATAXY	SUBAH
STEEL	STUKA	STENO	STIRK	******	SUDAN
STEEN	******	STING	STIRP	-T-Y-	SUGAR
STEEP	-T-L-	STINK	STIRS	******	SUMAC
STEER	******	STINT	STORE	ATTYS	SURAH
STIED	ATILT	STONE	STORK	ETHYL	SURAL
STIES	ATOLL	STONY	STORM	STAYS	SURAS
STREW	ITALS	STUNG	STORY	******	SUSAN
UTHER	ITALY	STUNK	UTERI	-U-A-	TUBAL
UTTER	STALE	STUNS	UTERO	******	TUBAS
******	STALK	STUNT	UTURN	AUDAD	TUNAS
-T-F-	STALL	******	******	AURAE	YUGAS
******	STELE	-T-O-	-T-S-	AURAL	******
STAFF	STILE	******	******	AURAS	-U-B-
STIFF	STILL	ATHOS	STASH	BUBAL	******
STUFF	STILT	ATION	STOSS	BURAN	BULBS
******	STOLE	ETHOS	******	CUBAN	BUSBY
-T-G-	STULL	ITION	-T-T-	DUBAI	CUBBY
******	STYLE	OTTOS	******	DUCAL	CURBS
STAGE	STYLI	STOOD	STATE	DUCAT	GUMBO
STAGS	STYLO	STOOK	STATO	DUMAS	HUBBY
STAGY	UTILE	STOOL	STETH	DURAL	JUMBO
STOGY	******	STOOP	STETS	FUGAL	NUBBY
******	-T-M-	STROP	******	FURAN	NUMBS
-T-H-	******	******	-T-U-	GULAR	RUGBY
******	ATOMS	-T-P-	******	HULAS	RUMBA
ITCHY	ETYMA	******	STOUP	HUMAN	TUBBY
-T-I-	ITEMS	ETAPE	STOUR	HUNAN	TURBO
******	OTOMI	STAPH	STOUT	JUBAS	******
ATRIA	STAMP	STEPS	STRUM	JUDAH	-U-C-
ATRIP	STEMS	STIPE	STRUT	JUDAS	******
	STIMY	STOPE		JUGAL	BUNCH
					BUNCO

BUTCH	OUTDO	GULES	QUEER	******	PUSHY
CULCH	QUADS	GUYED	QUIET	**-U-G-**	RUCHE
CURCH	QUIDS	HUGER	RUBES	******	RUSHY
CUTCH	QUODS	HUPEH	RUDER	BUDGE	RUTHS
DULCE	RUDDS	JUBES	RULED	BUDGY	******
DULCY	RUDDY	JUDEA	RULER	BUGGY	**-U-I-**
DUNCE	SUEDE	JUDEO	RULES	BULGE	******
DUTCH	SURDS	JUDES	RUMEN	BULGY	AUDIE
GUACO	******	JULEP	RUNES	BUNGS	AUDIO
GULCH	**-U-E-**	JULES	RUPEE	BURGH	AUDIT
HUNCH	******	JUNES	RUSES	BURGS	AULIC
HUTCH	AUDEN	JUREL	SUMER	DUNGS	AULIS
JUICE	AUGER	JUTES	SUPER	DUNGY	AURIC
JUICY	AUREI	LUCES	SUPES	FUDGE	AURIS
JUNCO	AURES	LUGER	SURER	FUGGY	AUXIL
LUCCA	BUBER	LUMEN	TUBED	FUNGI	AUXIN
LUNCH	BUSED	LUNES	TUBER	FUNGO	BURIN
LURCH	BUSES	LUNET	TUBES	JUDGE	CUBIC
MULCH	BUYER	LURED	TULES	LUIGI	CUBIT
MULCT	CUBEB	LURER	TUNED	LUNGE	CUMIN
MUNCH	CUBED	LURES	TUNER	LUNGI	CUPID
MUSCA	CUBES	LUTED	TUNES	LUNGS	CURIA
OUNCE	CULET	LUTES	YULES	MUGGY	CURIE
PUNCH	CULEX	LUXEX	******	MUNGO	CURIO
QUACK	CUPEL	MULES	**-U-F-**	NUDGE	CUTIE
QUICK	CURED	MULEY	******	OUTGO	CUTIN
SULCI	CURER	MUREX	BUFFI	PUDGY	CUTIS
TURCO	CURES	MUSED	BUFFO	PUNGS	DULIA
YUCCA	CUSEC	MUSES	BUFFS	PURGE	FUGIO
******	CUTER	MUTED	BUFFY	QUAGS	FUSIL
-U-D-	CUTEY	MUTES	CUFFS	RUNGS	FUZIL
******	DUDES	NUDES	DUFFS	SURGE	HUMIC
BUDDY	DUKES	NUMEN	GULFS	SURGY	HUMID
BUNDE	DUNES	OUSEL	HUFFS	VUGGY	JULIA
BUNDS	DUPED	OUTED	HUFFY	VULGO	JULIE
BURDS	DUPER	OUTER	LUFFS	******	JULIO
CUDDY	DUPES	OUZEL	MUFFS	**-U-H-**	KUMIS
CURDS	DURER	PUBES	PUFFS	******	LUCIA
CURDY	EULER	PUCES	PUFFY	AUGHT	LUCID
DUADS	FUMED	PUGET	QUAFF	BUSHY	LUPIN
FUNDI	FUMES	PUKED	QUIFF	CUSHY	LURID
FUNDS	FUSED	PUKES	RUFFS	DUBHE	MUCID
GUIDE	FUSEE	PULED	SULFA	DUCHY	MUCIN
GUIDO	FUSEL	PULER	SULFO	GUSHY	MUJIK
HULDA	FUSES	PULES	SURFS	HUGHS	MUSIC
HURDS	FUZED	PUREE	SURFY	MUSHY	NUBIA
MUDDY	FUZEE	PURER	TURFS	NUCHA	PUBIC
OUIDA	FUZES	QUEEN	TURFY	OUGHT	PUBIS

PUDIC	HUSKY	FULLS	BURNS	TUTOR	MUCRO
PUNIC	JUNKS	FULLY	BURNT	YUKON	MUNRO
PUPIL	JUNKY	FURLS	CUING	YUPON	MURRA
PURIM	LUCKY	GUILD	DUANE	******	MURRE
QUAIL	LURKS	GUILE	FUNNY	**-U-P-**	MURRY
QUOIN	MUCKS	GUILT	GUANA	******	OUTRE
QUOIT	MUCKY	GULLS	GUANO	BUMPS	PURRS
RUNIC	MURKY	GULLY	GUANS	BUMPY	QUARK
RUNIN	MUSKS	HULLS	GUNNY	BURPS	QUART
RURIK	MUSKY	HURLS	JUANA	CULPA	QUERN
SUFIC	PUCKA	HURLY	JUANS	CUPPY	QUERY
SUFIS	PUCKS	LULLS	JUMNA	CUSPS	QUIRE
SUSIE	PUKKA	MUHLY	MUONS	DUMPS	QUIRK
TULIP	PUNKA	MULLS	QUANT	DUMPY	QUIRT
TUMID	PUNKS	PULLS	QUINT	GULPS	RUERS
TUNIC	PUNKY	PURLS	RUING	GUPPY	SUCRE
TUNIS	QUAKE	QUALM	RUINS	HUMPH	SUERS
TUPIK	QUAKY	QUELL	RUNNY	HUMPS	SUPRA
TUPIS	RUCKS	QUILL	SUING	HUMPY	SUTRA
TURIN	RUSKS	QUILT	SUINT	JUMPS	******
******	SUCKS	RUBLE	SUNNA	JUMPY	**-U-S-**
-U-J-	SULKS	RUMLY	SUNNI	LUMPS	******
******	SULKY	SULLY	SUNNS	LUMPY	BURSA
OUIJA	TUCKS	SURLY	SUNNY	MUMPS	BURSE
******	TURKI	TULLE	TUNNY	PULPS	BURST
-U-K-	TURKS	TULLY	TURNS	PULPY	CUISH
******	TUSKS	******	******	PUMPS	CURSE
BUCKO	******	**-U-M-**	**-U-O-**	PUPPY	CURST
BUCKS	**-U-L-**	******	******	QUIPS	CUSSO
BULKS	******	BURMA	AUTOS	QUIPU	DULSE
BULKY	BUGLE	CULMS	BUXOM	RUMPS	DURST
BUNKO	BUILD	DUMMY	DUROS	SUMPS	FUSSY
BUNKS	BUILT	DUOMI	FUROR	******	GUESS
BURKE	BULLA	DUOMO	HUGOS	**-U-R-**	GUEST
BUSKS	BULLS	GUAMA	HUMOR	******	GUISE
CUSKS	BULLY	GUMMA	HURON	AUTRY	GUTSY
DUCKS	BURLS	GUMMY	JUPON	BURRO	HURST
DUCKY	BURLY	MUMMS	JUROR	BURRS	HUSSY
DUNKS	CULLS	MUMMY	KUDOS	BURRY	KURSK
DUSKS	CURLS	PULMO	LUTON	CUPRO	LUISA
DUSKY	CURLY	RUMMY	LUXOR	CURRY	LUISE
FUNKS	DUALA	TUMMY	LUZON	DURRA	MUSSY
FUNKY	DUELS	YUMMY	PUTON	FURRY	NURSE
HULKS	DULLS	******	RUMOR	GUARD	PUDSY
HULKY	DULLY	**-U-N-**	RUNON	HURRY	PULSE
HUNKS	DUPLE	******	SUDOR	KUFRA	PURSE
HUNKY	FUELS	BUNNS	TUDOR	KUKRI	PURSY
HUSKS	FUGLE	BUNNY	TUMOR	LUCRE	PUSSY

QUASH	PUNTS	******	AVOIR	******	SWIGS
QUASI	PUNTY	-U-V-	AVRIL	-V-T-	TWIGS
QUASS	PUTTS	******	OVOID	******	******
QUEST	PUTTY	CURVE	******	EVITA	-W-I-
RUSSO	QUITE	CURVI	-V-K-	OVATE	******
SUDSY	QUITO	GUAVA	******		AWAIT
TULSA	QUITS	SUAVE	EVOKE	-V-W-	SWAIL
******	QUOTA	VULVA	******	******	SWAIN
-U-T-	QUOTE	******	-V-L-	AVOWS	TWAIN
******	QUOTH	-U-Y-	******		******
AUNTS	RUNTS	******	EVILS	-W-A-	-W-K-
AUNTY	RUNTY	BUOYS	OVALS	******	******
AUSTL	RUSTS	BUTYL	OVOLI	SWEAR	AWAKE
BUNTS	RUSTY	JUDYS	OVOLO	SWEAT	AWOKE
BUSTS	RUTTY	JULYS	OVULE	TWEAK	******
BUTTE	SUETY	LUCYS	UVULA	******	-W-L-
BUTTS	SUITE	QUAYS	******	-W-B-	******
CULTI	SUITS	RUBYS	-V-N-	******	DWELL
CULTS	TUFTS	RUDYS	******	SWABS	DWELT
CUTTY	TUFTY	SUZYS	AVENS	******	SWALE
DUCTS	TUTTI	******	EVANS	-W-C-	SWELL
DUETS	TUTTY	-U-Z-	EVENS	******	SWILL
DUSTS	******	******	EVENT	TWICE	TWILL
DUSTY	-U-U-	FURZE	IVANS	******	******
FURTH	******	FURZY	OVENS	-W-D-	-W-M-
FUSTY	AUGUR	FUZZY	OVINE	******	******
GUSTA	AURUM	MUZZY	******	SWEDE	SWAMI
GUSTO	CUTUP	******	-V-O-	******	SWAMP
GUSTS	DURUM	-V-A-	******	-W-E-	SWIMS
GUSTY	EURUS	******	AVION	******	******
GUTTA	FUCUS	AVIAN	******	AWNED	-W-N-
HUNTS	FUGUE	UVEAL	-V-R-	OWLET	******
HURTS	GURUS	UVEAS	******	OWNED	AWING
JUNTA	HUMUS	******	AVARS	OWNER	BWANA
JUNTO	JUJUS	-V-C-	AVERS	SWEEP	EWING
JUSTS	JURUA	EVICT	AVERT	SWEET	GWENN
JUXTA	KUDUS	******	AVERY	TWEED	GWENS
LUNTS	KURUS	-V-D-	EVERT	TWEEN	GWYNS
LUSTS	LUAUS	******	EVERY	TWEET	OWENS
LUSTY	LULUS	EVADE	IVORY	******	OWING
MUFTI	LUPUS	******	OVARY	-W-F-	******
MULTI	MUCUS	-V-E-	OVERT	******	SWANK
MUSTS	PUTUP	******	******	SWIFT	SWANS
MUSTY	QUEUE	IVIED	-V-S-	******	SWINE
MUTTS	RUFUS	IVIES	******	-W-G-	SWING
NUTTY	SULUS	******	AVAST	******	SWUNG
OUSTS	SUNUP	-V-I-	AVISO	SWAGE	TWANG
PUNTO	TUQUE	AVAIL	KVASS	SWAGS	TWINE
	TUTUS	AVOID			TWINS

*****
-W-O-
*****
SWOON
SWOOP
*****
-W-P-
*****
SWAPS
SWEPT
SWIPE
*****
-W-R-
*****
AWARD
AWARE
DWARF
EWERS
SWARD
SWARM
SWART
SWIRL
SWORD
SWORE
SWORN
TWERE
TWERP
TWIRL
TWIRP
*****
-W-S-
*****
AWASH
SWASH
SWISH
SWISS
TWIST
*****
-W-T-
*****
SWATH
SWATS
TWITS
*****
-W-U-
*****
AWFUL
*****
-W-X-
*****
TWIXT

*****
-W-Y-
*****
SWAYS
*****
-X-A-
*****
AXIAL
AXMAN
IXIAS
UXMAL
*****
-X-C-
*****
EXACT
EXECS
*****
-X-D-
*****
EXUDE
OXIDE
*****
-X-E-
*****
AXLED
AXLES
AXMEN
EXCEL
EXPEL
*****
-X-I-
*****
OXLIP
*****
-X-L-
*****
AXILE
AXILS
EXALT
EXILE
EXULT
IXTLE
*****
-X-M-
*****
EXAMS
OXIME

*****
-X-N-
*****
AXING
AXONE
AXONS
*****
-X-O-
*****
AXIOM
EXTOL
IXION
OXBOW
*****
-X-R-
*****
EXERT
EXTRA
EXURB
*****
-X-S-
*****
EXIST
*****
-X-T-
*****
EXITS
*****
-X-Y-
*****
OXEYE
*****
-Y-A-
*****
BYLAW
BYWAY
CYCAD
CYMAE
CYMAR
DYLAN
EYRAS
GYRAL
HYLAS
HYRAX
IYYAR
LYMAN
MYNAS
MYRAS

PYRAN
XYLAN
*****
-Y-C-
*****
LYNCH
*****
-Y-D-
*****
LYDDA
RYNDS
*****
-Y-E-
*****
BYRES
CYMES
FYKES
GYBED
GYNEC
GYRES
GYVED
HYMEN
HYPER
LYCEA
LYCEE
LYLES
LYRES
LYSED
LYSES
MYLES
PYRES
PYREX
PYXED
SYCEE
SYCES
TYEES
TYKES
TYLER
TYPED
TYPES
XYLEM
*****
-Y-G-
*****
SYNGE
*****
-Y-H-
*****
AYAHS
HYPHA

MYTHO
MYTHS
TYCHE
*****
-Y-I-
*****
AYDIN
CYLIX
CYNIC
CYRIL
EYDIE
EYRIE
EYRIR
HYOID
KYLIX
KYRIE
LYDIA
LYRIC
LYSIN
LYSIS
LYTIC
MYOID
MYRIA
PYOID
PYXIE
PYXIS
SYBIL
SYRIA
*****
-Y-L-
*****
CYCLE
CYCLO
HYALO
MYELO
PYELO
*****
-Y-M-
*****
MYOMA
PYGMY
*****
-Y-N-
*****
AYINS
CYANO
DYING
EYING

GYMNO
HYENA
HYING
HYMNS
HYPNO
LYING
LYNNS
LYONS
MYRNA
PYDNA
TYING
VYING
*****
-Y-O-
*****
BYRON
GYRON
GYROS
HYPOS
HYSON
LYSOL
MYRON
NYLON
PYLON
SYNOD
SYROS
TYPOS
TYROL
TYROS
XYLOL
*****
-Y-P-
*****
LYMPH
MYOPE
MYOPY
NYMPH
SYLPH
*****
-Y-R-
*****
CYMRI
CYMRY
HYDRA
HYDRO
HYGRO
MYRRH
OYERS

******	******	DACIA	PASHA	DARIC	FAYED
-Y-S-	-Z-I-	FACIA	PASTA	GAMIC	FAZED
******	******	FANGA	PATNA	HAVOC	GADID
BYSSI	AZOIC	FAUNA	PAULA	MADOC	GAGED
GYPSY	OZZIE	GALEA	SABRA	MAGIC	GAMED
HYPSO	******	GAMMA	SACRA	MALAC	GAPED
LYSSA	-Z-L-	HAIDA	SAIGA	MALIC	GATED
NYASA	******	HAIFA	SALMA	MANIC	GAZED
******	AZOLE	HALMA	SALPA	PANIC	HADED
-Y-T-	******	HAMZA	SALSA	RABIC	HALED
******	-Z-N-	HANNA	SAMBA	SALIC	HALID
CYSTI	******	JAFFA	SAMOA	TABAC	HARED
CYSTO	AZANS	JAINA	SANTA	VARIC	HATED
CYSTS	AZINE	KAABA	SAUNA	VATIC	HAWED
HYETO	AZONS	KAFKA	TACNA	******	HAYED
KYATS	OZONE	KAPPA	TAFIA	-A--D	HAZED
KYOTO	******	KARMA	TAIGA	******	JADED
LYTTA	-Z-R-	LABIA	TAMPA	BAAED	JAPED
NYCTI	******	LABRA	TANKA	BAIRD	JARED
NYCTO	AZURE	LAIKA	TANYA	BAKED	JAWED
RYOTS	CZARS	LAMIA	TATRA	BALED	LACED
WYATT	OZARK	LARVA	TAZZA	BARED	LADED
XYSTS	TZARS	LASSA	VACUA	BASED	LAIRD
******	******	LAURA	WALLA	BATED	LAKED
-Y-U-	-Z-T-	MAFIA	WANDA	BAYED	LAMED
******	******	MAGDA	YALTA	CAGED	LAVED
CYRUS	AZOTE	MAGMA	ZAMIA	CAIRD	LAWED
GYRUS	AZOTH	MALTA	******	CAKED	LAZED
SYRUP	******	MAMBA	-A--B	CANAD	MACED
******	-Z-Y-	MAMMA	******	CANED	MANED
-Y-V-	******	MANIA	CABOB	CARED	MATED
******	IZZYS	MANNA	CALEB	CASED	MAUND
SYLVA	******	MANTA	CARIB	CAVED	MAZED
******	-A--A	MARIA	CAROB	CAWED	NAIAD
-Y-Y-	******	MARLA	JACOB	DARED	NAKED
******	BAHIA	MARTA	JAKOB	DATED	NAMED
XYLYL	BALSA	MAURA	KABOB	DAVID	OARED
******	BANDA	NAHUA	NABOB	DAZED	PACED
-Z-A-	BARCA	NANNA	NADAB	EARED	PAGED
******	BASRA	PADUA	NAWAB	EASED	PALED
EZRAS	CALLA	PAISA	RAJAB	FACED	PANED
******	CANEA	PALEA	SAHEB	FADED	PARED
-Z-C-	CANNA	PALMA	SAHIB	FAKED	PAVED
******	CAPUA	PANDA	******	FAMED	PAWED
CZECH	CARLA	PAPUA	-A--C	FARAD	PAYED
******	CAUCA	PARCA	******	FARED	RABID
-Z-E-	DACCA	PARKA	BARIC	FATED	RACED
******	DACHA	PARMA	BASIC	FAXED	RAGED
AZTEC					

RAKED	CADRE	MAINE	TAHOE	RANCH	******
RAPED	CALPE	MAIZE	TASTE	RATCH	-A--K
RAPID	CALVE	MAMIE	TAUPE	RAYAH	******
RATED	CANOE	MANGE	VAGUE	SABAH	BATIK
RAVED	CARLE	MANSE	VALUE	SARAH	BAULK
RAYED	CARTE	MAPLE	VALVE	WATCH	CAPEK
RAZED	CARVE	MARGE	VARVE	WAUGH	CAULK
SABED	CASTE	MARIE	WACKE	XANTH	KAMIK
SALAD	CAUSE	MARNE	WAIVE	******	KAPOK
SAPID	CAVIE	MASSE	WASTE	-A--I	KAYAK
SATED	DANAE	MATTE	WAYNE	******	SAMEK
SAVED	DANCE	MAUDE	YAHVE	AALII	TALUK
SAWED	DANTE	MAUVE	ZAIRE	BACCI	******
SAYID	DAVIE	MAYBE	******	BAHAI	-A--L
TABID	EADIE	NACRE	-A--F	BAMBI	******
TAMED	EAGLE	NAIVE	******	BASSI	BABEL
TAPED	EAGRE	NANCE	BANFF	CACTI	BABUL
TARED	EARLE	NAPPE	CALIF	CALCI	BAGEL
TAWED	FABLE	PADRE	GANEF	CALLI	BANAL
TAXED	FALSE	PAINE	******	CAMPI	BASAL
VALID	FARCE	PAISE	-A--G	CAPRI	BASEL
VANED	FARLE	PALAE	******	CARDI	BASIL
VAPID	FAROE	PANNE	LAOAG	CARPI	CABAL
WADED	GABLE	PARSE	MAGOG	DALAI	CAMEL
WAGED	GAFFE	PASSE	******	GAUDI	CANAL
WAKED	GASPE	PASTE	-A--H	HADJI	CAROL
WALED	GAUGE	PAUSE	******	HAITI	CAVIL
WANED	GAUZE	PAYEE	BARTH	HANOI	DATAL
WAVED	GAVLE	RAGEE	BATCH	IAMBI	EASEL
WAXED	HAGUE	RAISE	CATCH	KAUAI	FATAL
YAWED	HALLE	RAKEE	EARTH	KAURI	FAYAL
******	HALVE	RAMIE	FAITH	LANAI	GAVEL
-A--E	HANCE	RANCE	FARAH	MAGNI	HAMAL
******	HANSE	RANEE	FAUGH	MAHDI	HAZEL
BACHE	HARTE	RANGE	GARTH	MAORI	KABUL
BADGE	HASTE	RAPHE	HARSH	MAQUI	KAROL
BAIZE	HAWSE	RAZEE	HATCH	MATRI	LABEL
BARDE	JAMIE	SABLE	LARCH	NAOMI	LAPEL
BARGE	JAYNE	SABRE	LATCH	PALMI	MABEL
BARRE	KATIE	SADIE	LAUGH	PALPI	NASAL
BARYE	LADLE	SALSE	MARCH	PAPPI	NATAL
BASLE	LAINE	SALVE	MARSH	PARSI	NAVAL
BASTE	LANCE	SAONE	MATCH	PATRI	NAVEL
BATHE	LAPSE	SARRE	PARCH	PATTI	PANEL
BAUME	LARGE	SATIE	PASCH	RABBI	PAPAL
CABLE	LATHE	SAUCE	PATCH	RADII	PAROL
CACHE	MACLE	SAUTE	RAJAH	SALMI	RAOUL
CADGE	MADGE	TABLE	RALPH	TARSI	RATAL

RAVEL	GAVIN	******	PABLO	BAKER	MANOR
SALOL	HAVEN	-A--O	PAEDO	BALDR	MASER
TAMIL	HAYDN	******	PALEO	BALER	MATER
******	JAPAN	BABOO	PANTO	BARER	MAYOR
-A--M	JASON	BANJO	PAOLO	CABER	MAZER
******	KAREN	BASSO	PARGO	CANER	NADER
CAROM	KAZAN	BATHO	PATHO	CAPER	NADIR
DATUM	LADEN	CACAO	PATIO	CARER	NAHOR
FANUM	LADIN	CADDO	PAULO	CATER	NAMER
HAKIM	LAGAN	CAIRO	RADIO	DAKAR	NAMUR
HAREM	LAPIN	CAMEO	RATIO	DALER	NAVAR
HAULM	LATIN	CAMPO	SACRO	DARER	PACER
MADAM	MACON	CANSO	SALVO	DATER	PAGER
MAXIM	MAHAN	CANTO	SAMBO	EAGER	PALER
NAHUM	MASON	CARBO	SAPRO	EATER	PAPER
OAKUM	MATIN	CARGO	SARCO	FACER	PARER
SAGUM	MAYAN	CARLO	SARTO	FAKER	PATER
SALEM	NAIRN	CARPO	SAURO	FAKIR	PAVER
******	OAKEN	CARYO	SAYSO	FARER	PAWER
-A--N	OATEN	CASCO	TABOO	FAVOR	PAYER
******	PAEAN	DATTO	TAINO	GABOR	QATAR
AARON	PAEON	DAVAO	TANGO	GAGER	RACER
BACON	PAGAN	FARGO	TANTO	GAPER	RADAR
BADEN	PAPEN	GARBO	TARDO	GASTR	RAKER
BAIRN	PAREN	HAGIO	TARSO	GAYER	RARER
BARON	PATEN	HALLO	TASSO	GAZER	RATER
BASIN	PAVAN	HAPLO	TAURO	HALER	RAVER
BASON	RADON	IATRO	TAUTO	HAMER	RAWER
BATAN	RAVEN	KAROO	VARIO	HARAR	RAZOR
BATEN	RAYON	KARYO	VARRO	HATER	SABER
BATON	SABIN	KAZOO	WAHOO	HAVER	SAFER
CABIN	SAGAN	LABIO	WALDO	HAZER	SAGER
CAIRN	SALON	LACTO	YAHOO	KAFIR	SAKER
CAJON	SARAN	LARGO	YAZOO	LABOR	SAMAR
CAJUN	SASIN	LASSO	******	LAGER	SANER
CANON	SATAN	LATRO	-A--P	LAKER	SAPOR
CAPON	SATIN	MACAO	******	LAMER	SATYR
DAGAN	SAVIN	MACRO	BACUP	LAPAR	SAVER
DAMAN	SAXON	MALMO	GALOP	LASER	SAVOR
DAMON	TAKEN	MAMBO	JALAP	LATER	SAWER
EAMON	TALON	MANGO	NAACP	LAVER	SAYER
EATEN	VAGIN	MARCO	SALEP	LAXER	TABOR
FANON	WAGON	MARGO	WATAP	LAYER	TAKER
GABON	WAKEN	MARIO	******	LAZAR	TALER
GALEN	WAXEN	MASTO	-A--R	MACER	TAMER
GAMIN	YAMEN	MATEO	******	MAJOR	TAPER
GATUN	YAMUN	MATZO	BABAR	MAKER	TAPIR
	YAPON	NARCO	BABER	MALAR	TATAR
	ZAYIN				

TAWER	CAGES	FACES	HABUS	KAGUS	MANUS
TAXER	CAKES	FACTS	HACKS	KAKAS	MARCS
VALOR	CALKS	FADES	HADES	KAKIS	MARES
VANIR	CALLS	FAILS	HAFTS	KAMES	MARIS
VAPOR	CALMS	FAIRS	HAHAS	KAPHS	MARKS
WADER	CAMES	FAKES	HAIKS	KARLS	MARLS
WAFER	CAMPS	FALLS	HAILS	KATES	MARTS
WAGER	CAMUS	FANGS	HAIRS	KAVAS	MASKS
WALER	CANES	FANOS	HAKES	KAYOS	MASTS
WATER	CANIS	FARES	HALES	LACES	MATES
WAVER	CANTS	FARLS	HALLS	LACKS	MATHS
YAGER	CAPES	FARMS	HALOS	LADES	MATTS
******	CARAS	FASTS	HALTS	LAGOS	MAUDS
-A--S	CARDS	FATES	HAMES	LAIRS	MAULS
******	CARES	FAUNS	HANDS	LAKES	MAVIS
BABAS	CARLS	FAVUS	HANGS	LALLS	MAYAS
BABES	CARPS	FAWNS	HANKS	LAMAS	MAZES
BACKS	CARTS	FAXES	HARDS	LAMBS	NAILS
BAFFS	CARYS	FAYES	HARES	LAMES	NAMES
BAHTS	CASES	FAZES	HARKS	LAMPS	NANAS
BAILS	CASKS	GABES	HARLS	LANDS	NAPES
BAITS	CASTS	GABYS	HARMS	LANES	NARDS
BAKES	CASUS	GAELS	HARPS	LAPIS	NARES
BALAS	CAULS	GAFFS	HARTS	LAPPS	NARIS
BALES	CAVES	GAGES	HASPS	LARDS	NATES
BALKS	DACES	GAILS	HATES	LARES	NAVES
BALLS	DALES	GAINS	HAULS	LARKS	NAZIS
BALMS	DAMES	GAITS	HAWKS	LASTS	OASES
BALTS	DAMNS	GALAS	HAYES	LATHS	OASIS
BANDS	DAMPS	GALES	HAZES	LAUDS	OATES
BANGS	DANES	GALLS	IAMBS	LAVAS	OATHS
BANKS	DANGS	GAMBS	IASIS	LAVES	OAVES
BANNS	DARES	GAMES	JACKS	LAWNS	PACAS
BARBS	DARNS	GAMPS	JADES	LAZES	PACES
BARDS	DARTS	GANGS	JAGGS	MACES	PACKS
BARES	DATES	GAOLS	JAILS	MACKS	PACTS
BARKS	DAUBS	GAPES	JAINS	MAGES	PAGES
BARNS	DAVES	GARBS	JAKES	MAGUS	PAILS
BASES	DAVIS	GARYS	JAMBS	MAIDS	PAINS
BASIS	DAVOS	GASES	JAMES	MAILS	PAIRS
BASKS	DAVYS	GASPS	JANES	MAIMS	PALES
BATES	DAWKS	GATES	JANIS	MAINS	PALLS
BATHS	DAWNS	GAUDS	JANOS	MAKES	PALMS
BAWDS	DAZES	GAULS	JANUS	MALES	PANES
BAWLS	EARLS	GAURS	JAPES	MALLS	PANGS
CADES	EARNS	GAUSS	JARLS	MALTS	PANTS
CADIS	EASES	GAWKS	JATOS	MAMAS	PAPAS
CAFES	EAVES	GAZES	KADIS	MANES	PARAS

PARDS	SARAS	WAGES	CARET	HAIKU	DAFFY
PARES	SARIS	WAIFS	DAUNT	MATSU	DAILY
PARIS	SARKS	WAILS	DAVIT	NAURU	DAIRY
PARKS	SAROS	WAINS	FACET	PAREU	DAISY
PAROS	SATES	WAITS	FAGOT	SADHU	DALLY
PARRS	SAULS	WAKES	FAINT	SAJOU	DANDY
PARTS	SAVES	WALES	FAULT	******	DANNY
PASTS	SAXES	WALKS	FAUST	-A--W	DARKY
PATES	TABES	WALTS	GAMUT	******	DASHY
PATHS	TACKS	WAMUS	GAULT	MACAW	DAUBY
PAULS	TAELS	WANDS	GAUNT	PAPAW	DAVEY
PAVES	TAILS	WANES	GAVOT	******	EARLY
PAVIS	TAINS	WANTS	HABIT	-A--X	FADDY
PAWLS	TAKES	WARDS	HADNT	******	FAIRY
PAWNS	TALCS	WARES	HASNT	CALIX	FANCY
RACES	TALES	WARMS	HAUNT	CALYX	FANNY
RACKS	TALKS	WARNS	JABOT	GALAX	FARCY
RAFTS	TALOS	WARPS	JANET	LATEX	FATLY
RAGES	TALUS	WARTS	JAUNT	RADIX	FATTY
RAIDS	TAMES	WASPS	KALAT	SALIX	GABBY
RAILS	TAMIS	WATTS	KAMET	VARIX	GAILY
RAINS	TAMPS	WAULS	KAPUT	******	GAMMY
RAKES	TANGS	WAVES	KARAT	-A--Y	GAPPY
RALES	TANKS	WAWLS	MAGOT	******	GARRY
RAMPS	TAPAS	WAXES	MANET	BADLY	GASSY
RAMUS	TAPES	XAXES	MARAT	BAFFY	GAUDY
RANDS	TAPIS	XAXIS	MAYNT	BAGGY	GAUZY
RANIS	TARES	YANKS	MAYST	BALKY	GAWKY
RANKS	TARNS	YARDS	PAINT	BALMY	GAYLY
RANTS	TAROS	YARNS	RABAT	BANDY	HAIRY
RAPES	TARPS	YAUPS	SABOT	BARKY	HAMMY
RASPS	TARTS	YAWLS	SAINT	BARMY	HANDY
RATES	TASKS	YAWNS	SAULT	BARRY	HANKY
RAVES	TAXES	YAWPS	TACET	BATHY	HAPLY
RAZES	TAXIS	YAXES	TACIT	BATTY	HAPPY
SABES	VAGUS	YAXIS	TAINT	BAWDY	HARDY
SACKS	VAIRS	ZARFS	TAROT	CABBY	HARPY
SAFES	VALES	******	TAUNT	CADDY	HARRY
SAGAS	VAMPS	-A--T	VALET	CAGEY	HASTY
SAGES	VANES	******	VAULT	CAMPY	HATTY
SAGOS	VANGS	BANAT	VAUNT	CANDY	IATRY
SAILS	VARAS	BARIT	WAIST	CANNY	JACKY
SAKES	VARUS	CABOT	WASNT	CAREY	JAGGY
SALES	VASES	CADET	YACHT	CARRY	JAMMY
SALTS	WACKS	CANST	******	CASEY	JASSY
SALUS	WADES	CAPET	-A--U	CATHY	JAZZY
SAMOS	WAFTS	CAPUT	******	CATTY	KANDY
SANDS		CARAT	BANTU	DADDY	KATHY
				BAYOU	

KAURY	PARRY	WANLY	******	OBEYS	******
LADDY	PARTY	WARTY	-B--I	OBITS	-C--E
LAITY	PASSY	WASHY	******	OBOES	******
LAKEY	PASTY	WASPY	ABACI	******	ACEAE
LANKY	PATHY	WAVEY	OBELI	-B--T	ACUTE
LARDY	PATSY	******	OBOLI	******	ECOLE
LARKY	PATTY	-A--Z	******	ABAFT	OCHRE
LARRY	PAWKY	******	-B--K	ABBOT	SCALE
LATHY	RAGGY	CADIZ	******	ABORT	SCAPE
LATRY	RAINY	HAFIZ	ABACK	ABOUT	SCARE
LAWNY	RALLY	HARTZ	******	EBOAT	SCENE
LAXLY	RAMMY	JABEZ	-B--L	UBOAT	SCONE
LAYBY	RANDY	MAINZ	******	UBOLT	SCOPE
MACHY	RANGY	VADUZ	ABIEL	******	SCORE
MADLY	RASPY	WALTZ	ABOIL	-B--Y	SCREE
MALAY	RATTY	******	******	******	SCUTE
MALTY	RAWLY	-B--A	-B--M	ABBEY	******
MAMEY	SADLY	******	******	EBONY	-C--F
MAMMY	SALLY	ABACA	ABEAM	******	******
MANCY	SALTY	ABOMA	ABOHM	-C--A	SCARF
MANDY	SAMMY	IBIZA	ABRAM	******	SCOFF
MANGY	SANDY	******	ABYSM	ACCRA	SCUFF
MANLY	SAPPY	-B--B	HBEAM	OCALA	SCURF
MARLY	SASSY	******	IBEAM	OCREA	******
MARRY	SAUCY	ABOMB	******	SCAPA	-C--G
MARTY	SAURY	HBOMB	-B--N	SCENA	******
MASHY	SAVOY	******	******	SCHWA	ACING
MASSY	SAVVY	-B--D	IBSEN	SCUBA	ICING
MATEY	TABBY	******	******	SCUTA	SCRAG
MATTY	TACHY	EBBED	-B--R	******	******
NANCY	TACKY	******	******	-C--B	-C--H
NANNY	TAFFY	-B--E	ABHOR	******	******
NAPPY	TALLY	******	ABLER	ACERB	SCYPH
NARKY	TAMMY	ABASE	ABNER	SCRUB	******
NASTY	TANEY	ABATE	******	******	-C--I
NATTY	TANGY	ABBIE	-B--S	-C--D	******
NAVVY	TANSY	ABELE	******	******	ACINI
PACHY	TARDY	ABIDE	ABBAS	ACHED	ICOSI
PADDY	TARRY	ABODE	ABBES	ACRED	SCAPI
PALEY	TARTY	ABOVE	ABBYS	ACRID	SCIFI
PALLY	TASTY	ABUSE	ABELS	ACTED	SCUDI
PALMY	TATTY	OBESE	ABETS	OCTAD	******
PALSY	TAWNY	OBOLE	ABIBS	SCALD	-C--K
PANAY	VASTY	TBONE	ABIES	SCAND	******
PANDY	WACKY	******	ABRIS	SCEND	ACOCK
PANSY	WADDY	-B--H	ABUTS	SCOLD	******
PANTY	WALLY	******	ABYSS	SCROD	-C--L
PAPPY	WANEY	ABASH	EBONS		******
		OBEAH			ACCEL
					OCTYL

SCALL	OCCUR	******	******	ADDYS	BEATA
SCOWL	OCHER	-C--Z	-D--H	ADIOS	BEIRA
SCULL	SCOUR	******	******	ADITS	BELGA
******	******	SCHIZ	EDITH	ADZES	BELLA
-C--M	-C--S	******	******	EDDAS	BEREA
******	******	-D--A	-D--I	EDGES	BERIA
SCRAM	ACHES	******	******	EDIES	BERRA
SCRIM	ACIDS	ADELA	ADENI	EDITS	BERTA
SCRUM	ACRES	ADOWA	ADLAI	EDNAS	BEULA
******	ACTUS	ADUWA	******	IDEAS	CEARA
-C--N	ICONS	ADYTA	-D--L	IDLES	CEIBA
******	ICTUS	EDEMA	******	IDOLS	CELIA
ACEAN	SCABS	EDINA	EDSEL	IDYLS	CELLA
ACORN	SCADS	******	IDEAL	ODETS	CERIA
ACTIN	SCANS	-D--B	IDYLL	ODORS	CESTA
ECHIN	SCARS	******	******	******	CEUTA
ICIAN	SCATS	ADLIB	-D--M	-D--T	******
OCEAN	SCOPS	******	******	******	DELIA
SCION	SCOTS	-D--C	ADEEM	ADAPT	DELLA
SCORN	SCOWS	******	IDIOM	ADEPT	DELTA
******	SCUDS	ADUNC	ODEUM	ADMIT	DERMA
-C--O	SCUMS	EDDIC	ODIUM	ADOPT	FERIA
******	SCUPS	******	******	ADULT	GEMMA
ACETO	SCUTS	-D--D	-D--N	ADUST	GENOA
ACOUO	******	******	******	EDICT	GENUA
ICONO	-C--T	ADDED	ADMAN	EDUCT	GERDA
OCULO	******	EDGED	ADMEN	IDEST	HEDDA
SCATO	ECLAT	EDRED	ADMIN	IDIOT	HEKLA
SCHMO	OCTET	IDLED	ADORN	ODONT	HELGA
SCOTO	SCANT	******	EDWIN	******	HEMIA
SCUDO	SCENT	-D--E	ODEON	-D--U	HENNA
******	SCOOT	******	******	******	HEPTA
-C--P	SCOTT	ADAGE	-D--O	ADIEU	HERMA
******	SCOUT	ADDIE	******	******	KENYA
SCALP	******	ADDLE	ADENO	-D--X	LEHUA
SCAMP	-C--W	ADELE	IDAHO	******	LEILA
SCARP	******	ADIGE	******	ADDAX	LEMMA
SCAUP	SCREW	ADOBE	-D--R	ADMEX	LEONA
SCOOP	******	ADORE	******	ADMIX	LEORA
SCRAP	-C--Y	EDDIE	ADDER	******	LEPTA
SCRIP	******	EDILE	ADLER	-D--Y	MECCA
SCULP	ACITY	EDUCE	EDGAR	******	MEDEA
******	ICILY	ODYLE	IDLER	EDIFY	MEDIA
-C--R	MCCOY	UDINE	ODDER	ODDLY	MENSA
******	OCHRY	******	ODOUR	******	PELLA
ACTOR	SCALY	-D--F	UDDER	-E--A	PENNA
ICHOR	SCARY	******	******	******	PENTA
ICIER	SCOPY	ADOLF	ADAHS	AECIA	PEPLA
			ADAMS	AEMIA	RECTA

REGMA	CEDED	DELVE	RENEE	BENCH	MERCI
RETIA	CERED	DENSE	RENTE	BERTH	NEURI
RETTA	DEKED	DEUCE	REVUE	DEATH	PELVI
SELMA	DELED	EERIE	SEDGE	DEPTH	PENNI
SENNA	DEWED	FEASE	SEINE	FETCH	PETTI
SEPIA	FELID	FEEZE	SEISE	HEATH	RECTI
SEPTA	FETED	FEMME	SEIZE	HEIGH	SEGNI
SERRA	FETID	FENCE	SENNE	KEDAH	SEPTI
TERRA	FEUED	FESSE	SENSE	KEITH	SERAI
TESLA	GELID	GEESE	SERGE	KENCH	TEMPI
TESTA	GEOID	GENIE	SERVE	KERCH	TERRI
TETRA	HEARD	GENRE	SETAE	KETCH	VERDI
VEPSA	HEROD	GEODE	TEASE	LEACH	VERMI
VERNA	HEWED	HEAVE	TEHEE	LEASH	******
VESTA	HEXAD	HEDGE	TELAE	LEECH	**-E--K**
XENIA	HEXED	HELLE	TEMPE	LEIGH	******
YERBA	KEYED	HELVE	TENSE	LEITH	DEREK
ZEBRA	LEPID	HENCE	TEPEE	NEATH	******
******	METED	HESSE	TERSE	NEIGH	**-E--L**
-E--B	MEWED	JESSE	VENAE	PEACH	******
******	REBID	KEDGE	VENUE	PERCH	BEALL
DEMOB	REDID	KEEVE	VERGE	PERTH	BERYL
DENEB	SERED	LEASE	VERNE	REACH	BETEL
NEGEB	SEWED	LEAVE	VERSE	REICH	BEVEL
******	SEXED	LEDGE	VERVE	RETCH	BEZEL
-E--C	TEPID	LETHE	WEAVE	SELAH	CECAL
******	VEXED	LEVEE	WEDGE	TEACH	CECIL
CERIC	WEALD	LEWIE	******	TEETH	CEORL
CETIC	WEIRD	LEYTE	**-E--F**	TENCH	DECAL
GENIC	******	MELEE	******	TENTH	DEDAL
HELIC		MERGE	FEOFF	VETCH	DEVIL
HEMIC	**-E--E**	MERLE	GEOFF	WEIGH	FECAL
MEDIC	******	MEROE	SERIF	WELCH	FERAL
MEDOC	AERIE	MESNE	******	WELSH	FETAL
MELIC	BEEBE	METRE	**-E--G**	WENCH	HEGEL
MESIC	BEIGE	MEUSE	******	******	HEMAL
REBEC	BELIE	NERVE	BEFOG	**-E--I**	HEXYL
RELIC	BELLE	NEUME	BEING	******	JEWEL
SERAC	BENNE	PEACE	DEBAG	CENTI	KEVEL
TELIC	BENUE	PEASE	DEBUG	CESTI	LEGAL
VEDIC	BERME	PEEVE	PELEG	DELHI	LEVEL
VESIC	BERNE	PEKOE	TELEG	DENTI	MEDAL
XEBEC	BETTE	PELEE	******	FEBRI	MEGAL
XERIC	CEASE	PENCE	**-E--H**	FERMI	METAL
ZEBEC	CELIE	PERLE	******	FERRI	METOL
******	CENSE	PERSE	BEACH	GENII	NEPAL
-E--D	DEANE	PEWEE	BEECH	HENRI	NEVIL
******	DEFOE	REEVE	BELCH	MENAI	NEWEL
BEARD	DEICE				
BEGAD					

PEARL	BEVAN	SEVEN	SERVO	RECUR	DEALS
PEDAL	BEVIN	TENON	SETTO	REFER	DEANS
PENAL	CENON	TETON	SEXTO	SEDER	DEARS
PERIL	CETIN	XENON	TELEO	SENOR	DEBTS
PETAL	DEIGN	YEARN	TEMPO	SEVER	DECKS
REBEL	DEMON	YEMEN	VERSO	SEWER	DEEDS
REGAL	DEVON	******	******	TENOR	DEEMS
RENAL	DEWAN	-E--O	-E--P	VELAR	DEEPS
REPEL	FEIGN	******	******	VEXER	DEFIS
REVEL	FELON	BEANO	AESOP	WEBER	DEGAS
SEOUL	HELEN	BETSO	BEBOP	WESER	DEKES
SEPAL	HEMAN	CELLO	GETUP	******	DELES
SERAL	HEMEN	CENTO	LETUP	-E--S	DELLS
TEKEL	HEMIN	DENTO	RECAP	******	DELOS
VENAL	HERON	DERMO	SETUP	AEDES	DEMES
VEXIL	JETON	FEMTO	******	AEGIS	DEMOS
******	KEVIN	FERRO	-E--R	AEONS	DENES
-E--M	LEARN	GECKO	******	BEADS	DENIS
******	LEMON	GENRO	AEGIR	BEAKS	DENTS
BEDIM	LENIN	GESSO	AESIR	BEAMS	DENYS
BEGUM	LEVEN	HECTO	BERAR	BEANS	DESKS
BELEM	MEGAN	HEKTO	CEDAR	BEARS	DEVAS
BESOM	MELAN	HELIO	CENTR	BEATS	FEARS
CECUM	MELON	HELLO	CESAR	BEAUS	FEATS
CELOM	MESON	JELLO	DEBAR	BECKS	FECES
CERAM	PECAN	KELSO	DECOR	BEEFS	FEEDS
DECIM	PEKAN	LENTO	DEFER	BEEPS	FEELS
DEGUM	PEKIN	LEPTO	DEMUR	BEERS	FELLS
DEISM	PELON	LEUCO	DENDR	BEETS	FELTS
DENIM	PEPIN	LEUKO	DETER	BELLS	FEMES
REALM	PERON	MEDIO	DEXTR	BELTS	FENDS
REARM	REDAN	METHO	FEDOR	BENDS	FEODS
RETEM	REGAN	METRO	FEMUR	BENES	FERNS
SEBUM	REGIN	MEZZO	FETOR	BERGS	FETES
SEDUM	REIGN	NECRO	FEUAR	BERMS	FETUS
SEISM	REMAN	NEGRO	FEVER	BERTS	FEUDS
SERUM	RENAN	NEPHO	FEWER	BESTS	GEARS
VELUM	RENIN	NEURO	HEWER	BETAS	GECKS
VENOM	RERAN	PEDRO	LEGER	BETHS	GEEKS
******	RERUN	PENGO	LEMUR	CEDES	GELDS
-E--N	RESIN	PETRO	LEPER	CEILS	GENES
******	REZIN	PETTO	LEVER	CELLS	GENTS
BEGAN	SEDAN	RECTO	METER	CELTS	GENUS
BEGIN	SELEN	RETRO	NEPHR	CENIS	GERMS
BEGUN	SEMEN	SEATO	NETER	CENTS	HEADS
BEHAN	SERIN	SECCO	NEVER	CERES	HEALS
BENIN	SERON	SEGNO	NEWER	CEROS	HEAPS
BETON	SETON	SEPTO	PETER	CETUS	HEARS

HEATS	LEIFS	PEANS	SEEDS	WEEMS	FEINT
HEEDS	LENAS	PEARS	SEEKS	WEEPS	FEIST
HEELS	LENDS	PEATS	SEEMS	WEFTS	GEEST
HEFTS	LENES	PECKS	SEEPS	WEIRS	GEMOT
HEIRS	LENIS	PECOS	SEERS	WEKAS	GENET
HELLS	LENOS	PEDES	SEGOS	WELDS	HEART
HELMS	LENTS	PEEKS	SELLS	WELLS	HEIST
HELPS	LEONS	PEELS	SENDS	WELTS	HELOT
HEMPS	LEPUS	PEENS	SEPTS	WENDS	HEMAT
HERBS	LETTS	PEEPS	SERBS	XERUS	HEPAT
HERDS	LEUDS	PEERS	SERES	YEANS	HERAT
HERLS	LEVIS	PELFS	SERFS	YEARS	KERAT
HEXES	LEWES	PELTS	SETHS	YEATS	LEANT
JEANS	LEWIS	PENDS	SEXES	YEGGS	LEAPT
JEEPS	MEADS	PENIS	TEAKS	YELKS	LEAST
JEERS	MEALS	PEONS	TEALS	YELLS	LEGIT
JEFES	MEANS	PEPOS	TEAMS	YELPS	MEANT
JEFFS	MEATS	PEPYS	TEARS	YESES	MERIT
JEHUS	MEETS	PERES	TEATS	YETIS	NEMAT
JELLS	MELDS	PERIS	TEEMS	ZEBUS	PETIT
JERKS	MELOS	PERKS	TEENS	ZEKES	PEWIT
JESTS	MELTS	PESOS	TELLS	ZEROS	REACT
JESUS	MEMOS	PESTS	TENDS	ZESTS	REBUT
KEATS	MENDS	PETES	TENOS	ZETAS	REFIT
KECKS	MENES	READS	TENTS	******	REMIT
KEEFS	MENUS	REALS	TERMS	-E--T	RESET
KEELS	MEOWS	REAMS	TERNS	******	REVET
KEENS	MESAS	REAPS	TESTS	AETAT	SEBAT
KEEPS	METAS	REARS	TETHS	BEAST	TEBET
KELPS	METES	REBUS	TEXAS	BEAUT	TEMPT
KENTS	METIS	REEDS	TEXTS	BEFIT	TENET
KEPIS	MEWLS	REEFS	VEERS	BEGAT	TERAT
KERBS	NEALS	REEKS	VEILS	BEGET	VELDT
KERES	NEAPS	REELS	VEINS	BEGOT	VERST
KERFS	NEARS	REGES	VELDS	BENET	WEEST
KERNS	NECKS	REIMS	VENDS	BERET	YEAST
LEADS	NEEDS	REINS	VENTS	BESET	******
LEAFS	NEGUS	REMUS	VENUS	BESOT	-E--U
LEAKS	NEILS	RENDS	VERAS	CERAT	******
LEANS	NELLS	RENES	VERBS	DEALT	NEHRU
LEAPS	NEROS	RENTS	VERNS	DEBIT	PERDU
LEEDS	NESTS	RESTS	VESTS	DEBUT	VERTU
LEEKS	NEVIS	SEALS	VEXES	DEIST	******
LEERS	NEVUS	SEAMS	WEALS	DELFT	-E--V
LEETS	NEWTS	SEANS	WEANS	DEMIT	******
LEFTS	NEXUS	SEARS	WEARS	DEPOT	NEGEV
LEGES	PEAKS	SEATS	WEEDS	FEAST	******
LEHRS	PEALS	SECTS	WEEKS	FECIT	-E--W
					******
					BEDEW
					BELOW

RENEW	GEMMY	NEWSY	******	******	AGNES
SEROW	GERRY	PEAKY	-E--Z	-G--C	AGNIS
******	GERTY	PEARY	******	******	AGUES
-E--X	HEADY	PEATY	HEJAZ	OGMIC	OGEES
******	HEAVY	PEAVY	HERTZ	******	OGLES
BEAUX	HEDGY	PEGGY	JEREZ	-G--D	OGRES
DESEX	HEFTY	PELLY	******	******	******
FELIX	HEMPY	PENNY	-F--A	EGGED	-G--T
HELIX	HENRY	PEONY	******	OGLED	******
RELAX	HERBY	PEPPY	AFTRA	******	AGENT
REMEX	HETTY	PERCY	******	-G--E	AGIST
TELEX	JELLY	PERKY	-F--E	******	AGLET
XEROX	JEMMY	PERRY	******	AGAPE	EGEST
******	JENNY	PESKY	AFIRE	AGATE	EGRET
-E--Y	JERKY	PETRY	AFORE	AGAVE	EGYPT
******	JERRY	PETTY	EFFIE	AGAZE	******
BEADY	JESSY	READY	******	AGGIE	-G--W
BEAMY	JETTY	REDLY	-F--L	AGILE	******
BECKY	JEWRY	REEDY	******	AGLEE	AGLOW
BEEFY	KELLY	REEFY	AFOUL	AGREE	******
BEERY	KENNY	REEKY	OFFAL	OGIVE	-G--Y
BELAY	KERRY	REIFY	******	******	******
BELLY	LEADY	RELAY	-F--N	-G--G	AGLEY
BENDY	LEAFY	REPAY	******	******	AGONY
BENJY	LEAKY	REPLY	OFTEN	AGING	******
BENNY	LEARY	RETRY	******	******	-G--Z
BERRY	LEAVY	SEAMY	-F--R	-G--M	******
BERTY	LEERY	SEDGY	******	******	IGNAZ
BESSY	LEFTY	SEEDY	AFTER	OGHAM	******
BETSY	LEGGY	SEPOY	OFFER	-G--N	-H--A
BETTY	LENNY	TEARY	******	******	******
DEARY	LEPSY	TEDDY	-F--S	AGAIN	CHELA
DEBBY	LEROY	TEENY	******	EGEAN	CHIBA
DECAY	LETTY	TELLY	AFROS	OGDEN	CHINA
DECOY	MEALY	TERRY	******	******	CHITA
DECRY	MEANY	TESTY	-F--T	-G--O	CHUFA
DEIFY	MEATY	VEERY	******	******	GHANA
DEITY	MERCY	VEINY	AFOOT	IGLOO	LHASA
DELAY	MERRY	WEARY	******	-G--R	PHILA
DENNY	MESHY	WEBBY	-F--X	******	PHYLA
DEOXY	MESSY	WEDGY	******	AGGER	RHODA
DERBY	METRY	WEEDY	AFFIX	EGGAR	RHOEA
DERRY	NEDDY	WEENY	******	EGGER	SHEBA
DEWEY	NEEDY	WEEPY	-G--A	OGLER	THECA
FELLY	NELLY	WENDY	******	******	THEDA
FENNY	NERVY	WENNY	AGAMA	-G--S	THETA
FERNY	NETTY	WETLY	AGANA	******	THUJA
FERRY	NEWLY	ZESTY	AGORA	AGHAS	
				AGIOS	

	PHANE	******	CHICK	SHAWM	CHEEP
******	PHASE	**-H--F**	CHINK	THERM	CHIMP
-H--B	PHEBE	******	CHOCK	THRUM	CHIRP
******	PHILE	CHAFF	CHUCK	WHELM	CHUMP
PHLEB	PHOBE	CHIEF	CHUNK	******	SHARP
RHOMB	PHONE	SHEAF	SHACK	**-H--N**	SHEEP
RHUMB	PHORE	SHELF	SHANK	******	THORP
SHRUB	PHYLE	THIEF	SHARK	CHAIN	THUMP
THROB	PHYRE	WHARF	SHEIK	CHIAN	WHAUP
THUMB	PHYTE	WHIFF	SHIRK	CHRON	WHELP
******	RHAGE	******	SHOCK	CHURN	WHOOP
-H--C	RHINE	**-H--G**	SHOOK	PHREN	******
******	RHONE	******	SHUCK	SHAUN	**-H--R**
OHMIC	RHYME	BHANG	THANK	SHAWN	******
******	SHADE	CHANG	THICK	SHEEN	CHAIR
-H--D	SHAKE	SHRUG	THINK	SHEWN	CHEER
******	SHALE	THING	WHACK	SHORN	CHIRR
AHEAD	SHAME	THONG	WHELK	SHOWN	CHLOR
CHARD	SHAPE	WHANG	WHISK	THORN	CHOIR
CHILD	SHARE	******	******	UHLAN	CHURR
CHORD	SHAVE	**-H--H**	**-H--L**	******	HHOUR
KHOND	SHINE	******	******	**-H--O**	KHMER
SHARD	SHIRE	CHETH	CHILL	******	SHEAR
SHERD	SHIVE	SHIAH	CHURL	CHARO	SHEER
SHIED	SHONE	SHUSH	GHOUL	CHEMO	SHIER
SHRED	SHORE	THIGH	PHIAL	CHICO	SHIRR
THIRD	SHOTE	THOTH	PHYLL	CHILO	SHOER
******	SHOVE	WHICH	SHALL	CHINO	SHYER
-H--E	SHUTE	WHISH	SHAWL	CHIRO	THEIR
******	THANE	******	SHELL	CHORO	WHIRR
CHAFE	THEME	**-H--I**	SHEOL	PHAGO	******
CHAPE	THERE	******	SHILL	PHENO	**-H--S**
CHARE	THESE	CHEMI	SHOAL	PHILO	******
CHASE	THINE	CHILI	SHORL	PHONO	CHAOS
CHIDE	THOLE	DHOLI	THIOL	PHOTO	CHAPS
CHILE	THOSE	DHOTI	WHEAL	PHYCO	CHARS
CHIME	THREE	GHAZI	WHEEL	PHYLO	CHATS
CHINE	THROE	KHADI	WHIRL	PHYTO	CHAWS
CHIVE	THULE	KHAKI	WHORL	RHINO	CHEFS
CHLOE	THYME	PHYSI	******	RHIZO	CHESS
CHOKE	WHALE	SHARI	**-H--M**	SHAKO	CHETS
CHOLE	WHERE	SHOJI	******	THYRO	CHEWS
CHORE	WHILE	******	CHARM	WHOSO	CHIAS
CHOSE	WHINE	**-H--K**	CHASM	******	CHINS
CHUTE	WHITE	******	CHIRM	**-H--P**	CHIOS
CHYLE	WHOLE	CHALK	CHROM	******	CHIPS
CHYME	WHORE	CHECK	IHRAM	CHAMP	CHITS
DHOLE	WHOSE	CHEEK	RHEUM	CHEAP	CHOPS
PHAGE					

CHOWS	WHIMS	CHEWY	PINTA	FIFED	VISED
CHRIS	WHINS	CHOKY	PIZZA	FILED	VIVID
CHRYS	WHIPS	PHAGY	RIATA	FINED	WIELD
CHUBS	WHIRS	PHANY	SIENA	FIORD	WILED
CHUGS	WHITS	PHASY	SIGMA	FIRED	WINED
CHUMS	WHOPS	PHILY	SILVA	FIXED	WIPED
DHAKS	******	PHONY	SITKA	GIBED	WIRED
DHOWS	-H--T	RHAGY	TIARA	HIKED	WISED
GHATS	******	SHADY	TIBIA	HIRED	WIVED
KHANS	CHAET	SHAKY	TILDA	HIVED	YIELD
PHILS	CHANT	SHALY	TINEA	JIBED	******
PHIPS	CHAPT	SHILY	TIOGA	JIHAD	-I--E
PHOTS	CHART	SHINY	UINTA	JIVED	******
RHEAS	CHEAT	SHOWY	VILLA	KITED	AIMEE
SHAGS	CHERT	SHYLY	VILNA	LIKED	AISLE
SHAHS	CHEST	THADY	VIOLA	LIMED	AISNE
SHAMS	GHAUT	THEWY	VIRGA	LINED	BIBLE
SHANS	GHENT	THYMY	VISTA	LIPID	BILGE
SHAWS	GHOST	WHINY	VITTA	LIVED	BINGE
SHAYS	SHAFT	******	WILLA	LIVID	BIRLE
SHEAS	SHALT	-I--A	WILMA	MIMED	BISSE
SHEDS	SHANT	******	WIRRA	MINED	CIRCE
SHEWS	SHEET	BIOTA	******	MIRED	DIANE
SHIMS	SHIFT	CILIA	-I--C	MIXED	DIENE
SHINS	SHIRT	CIRCA	******	NIDED	DIODE
SHIPS	SHOAT	CITRA	CIVIC	NIXED	DIONE
SHIVS	SHOOT	DIANA	LILAC	OILED	DIRGE
SHOES	SHORT	DICTA	MIMIC	PIAND	DIXIE
SHOOS	SHOUT	DINKA	SILIC	PIKED	FIBRE
SHOPS	SHUNT	FIONA	VINIC	PILED	FICHE
SHOTS	THEFT	GILDA	******	PINED	FIQUE
SHOWS	WHEAT	HILDA	-I--D	PIPED	FIUME
SHULS	WHIPT	JIDDA	******	RICED	GIGUE
SHUNS	WHIST	KIOWA	AIDED	RIGID	HINGE
SHUTS	WHORT	LIANA	AILED	RILED	LIANE
THADS	******	LIBRA	AIMED	RIMED	LIEGE
THAWS	-H--W	LIBYA	AIRED	RIVED	LILLE
THEWS	******	LINDA	BIDED	SIDED	LISLE
THINS	SHREW	LINGA	BIFID	SIRED	LITHE
THUDS	THREW	LIVIA	BIPED	SITED	LITRE
THUGS	THROW	MICRA	BIPOD	SIZED	LIVRE
THURS	******	MILIA	CITED	TIDED	MIDGE
WHAMS	-H--X	MINNA	DICED	TILED	MILNE
WHAPS	******	MIRZA	DIKED	TIMED	MINAE
WHENS	PHLOX	OIDEA	DINED	TIMID	MINCE
WHETS	******	PIETA	DIVED	TINED	MITRE
WHEYS	-H--Y	PILEA	FIELD	TIRED	NICHE
WHIGS	******	PINNA	FIEND	VIAND	NIECE
	CHARY				
	CHEVY				

NIOBE	BITCH	PINNI	******	TIEIN	******
NITRE	CINCH	PISCI	-I--M	TITAN	-I--P
NIXIE	DINAH	SINAI	******	VIMEN	******
PIAVE	DITCH	VILLI	FILUM	VIXEN	MIXUP
PIECE	FIFTH	VINCI	HILUM	WIDEN	PINUP
PIQUE	FILCH	VITRI	HIRAM	WIGAN	SIRUP
PIXIE	FILTH	XIPHI	MINIM	WITAN	TIEUP
RIDGE	FINCH	ZIMRI	NIZAM	WIZEN	******
RIFLE	FIRTH	******	******	ZIRON	-I--R
RILLE	FITCH	-I--K	-I--N	******	******
RINSE	GIRSH	******	******	-I--O	AIDER
SIDLE	GIRTH	DIRCK	AIKEN	******	BIHAR
SIEGE	HITCH	KIOSK	BISON	BILBO	BITER
SIEVE	KILAH	MINSK	DIJON	BINGO	CIDER
SIGNE	MICAH	******	DIVAN	CIRRO	CIGAR
SINCE	MILCH	-I--L	DIWAN	CISCO	DICER
SINGE	MIRTH	******	DIZEN	DIAZO	DIKER
SIXTE	MITCH	BIKOL	GIPON	DICHO	DIMER
TIGRE	NINTH	BINAL	GIRON	DIEGO	DINAR
TILDE	PINCH	CIBOL	GIVEN	DILDO	DINER
TINGE	PITCH	CIDAL	KININ	DINGO	DIRER
TIREE	SIXTH	CIVIL	KIRIN	DIPLO	DIVER
TITHE	TILTH	FIDEL	LIEIN	DISCO	EIDER
TITLE	WIDTH	FINAL	LIGAN	DISKO	EIMER
VILLE	WINCH	GIMEL	LIKEN	DITTO	FIBER
VINCE	WITCH	LIBEL	LIMEN	FIBRO	FIFER
VIRGE	******	MIAUL	LINEN	GISMO	FILAR
VITAE	-I--I	NIGEL	LININ	GIZMO	FILER
WILDE	******	NIHIL	LIVEN	HIDTO	FINER
WINCE	CIRRI	NIVAL	MILAN	HIERO	FIRER
WINZE	DISCI	PICAL	MIZEN	HIPPO	FIVER
WITHE	HINDI	PICUL	NISAN	JINGO	FIXER
WITTE	JINNI	PINEL	NITON	LIGNO	GIBER
******	KIBEI	PIPAL	NIXON	LIMBO	GIVER
-I--F	LIGNI	RIGEL	PIMAN	LINGO	HIDER
******	LILLI	RIVAL	PINON	LITHO	HIKER
PILAF	LIMBI	RIYAL	PITON	MICRO	HIRER
******	LIPPI	SIBYL	RICIN	MIMEO	LIBER
-I--G	LITAI	SIGIL	RIPEN	MISDO	LIFER
******	MIAMI	SISAL	RIPON	NITRO	LINER
GIING	MILLI	TICAL	RISEN	PIANO	LITER
LIANG	MINDI	TIDAL	RIVEN	PICRO	LIVER
******	MITZI	VIDAL	SIDON	PIEZO	MILER
-I--H	NIGRI	VIGIL	SIMON	PINGO	MIMER
******	NIMBI	VINYL	SINON	PINTO	MIMIR
AITCH	NISEI	VIRAL	SIREN	SIALO	MINER
BIRCH	NITRI	VITAL	SITIN	VIDEO	MINOR
BIRTH	PILEI		SIVAN	VIREO	MISER
				VIRGO	

MITER	BIBBS	FINNS	KINKS	MISES	RINKS
MIXER	BICES	FIRES	KIRKS	MISTS	RIOTS
NICER	BIDES	FIRMS	KITES	MITES	RISES
NIGER	BIERS	FIRNS	KIVAS	MITTS	RISKS
NITER	BIFFS	FISCS	KIWIS	MIXES	RISUS
NIZER	BIKES	FISTS	LIARS	NICKS	RITAS
OILER	BILES	FIVES	LICKS	NIDES	RITES
PIKER	BILKS	FIXES	LIENS	NIDUS	RIVES
PILAR	BILLS	GIBES	LIFTS	NIMES	SICES
PINER	BINDS	GIBUS	LIKES	NINAS	SICKS
PIPER	BINES	GIFTS	LILAS	NINES	SIDES
RICER	BIRDS	GIGAS	LILTS	NINUS	SIFTS
RIDER	BIRLS	GILDS	LILYS	NIPAS	SIGHS
RIGOR	BIRRS	GILES	LIMBS	NISUS	SIGNS
RIMER	BISES	GILLS	LIMES	NIXES	SIKHS
RIPER	BITES	GIMPS	LIMNS	PICAS	SILAS
RISER	BITTS	GINKS	LIMPS	PICKS	SILKS
RIVER	CIONS	GIRDS	LINES	PICTS	SILLS
SIDER	CISTS	GIRLS	LINGS	PIERS	SILOS
SIEUR	CITES	GIROS	LINKS	PIKAS	SILTS
SIMAR	DIALS	GIRTS	LINUS	PIKES	SIMPS
SITAR	DICKS	GISTS	LIONS	PILES	SINES
SIZAR	DIDOS	GIVES	LIRAS	PILIS	SINGS
TIBER	DIETS	HICKS	LISAS	PILLS	SINKS
TIGER	DIKES	HIDES	LISPS	PIMAS	SINUS
TILER	DILYS	HIFIS	LISTS	PIMPS	SIPES
TIMER	DIMES	HIGHS	LITAS	PINAS	SIRES
TIMOR	DINES	HIKES	LIVES	PINES	SITES
TITER	DINGS	HILLS	LIZAS	PINGS	SITUS
VICAR	DINTS	HILTS	MICAS	PINKS	SIXES
VIGOR	DIRKS	HINDS	MIDAS	PINTS	SIZES
VILER	DISCS	HINTS	MIENS	PIONS	TICKS
VIPER	DISKS	HIRES	MIFFS	PIOUS	TIDES
VISOR	DITAS	HIVES	MIKES	PIPES	TIERS
VIZIR	DIVAS	JIBES	MILES	PITAS	TIFFS
VIZOR	DIVES	JIFFS	MILKS	PITHS	TIKIS
WIDER	FIATS	JILLS	MILLS	RIALS	TILES
WIPER	FICES	JILTS	MILTS	RICES	TILLS
WIRER	FIEFS	JINKS	MIMES	RICKS	TILTS
WISER	FIFES	KIBES	MIMIS	RIDES	TIMES
WIVER	FIJIS	KICKS	MINAS	RIFFS	TINAS
******	FILES	KIERS	MINDS	RIFTS	TINES
-I--S	FILLS	KILLS	MINES	RIGGS	TINGS
******	FILMS	KILNS	MINKS	RILES	TINTS
AIDAS	FINDS	KILOS	MINOS	RILLS	TIROS
AIDES	FINES	KILTS	MINTS	RIMES	TITIS
AINOS	FINIS	KINDS	MINUS	RINDS	TITUS
AINUS	FINKS	KINGS	MIRES	RINGS	TITUS

VIALS	FIRST	******	LIMEY	WIDDY	******
VIBES	GIANT	-I--Y	LINEY	WILEY	-K--I
VICES	GIGOT	******	LINTY	WILLY	******
VICKS	LICHT	BIALY	LIPPY	WINDY	OKAPI
VIEWS	LICIT	BIDDY	LIZZY	WINGY	******
VILLS	LIEUT	BIFFY	MICKY	WISPY	-K--K
VINAS	LIGHT	BIGLY	MIDDY	WITHY	******
VINES	LIMIT	BILGY	MIFFY	WITTY	SKINK
VIOLS	LISZT	BILLY	MIKEY	ZINCY	SKULK
VIRES	MIDST	CINDY	MILKY	ZINGY	SKUNK
VIRUS	MIGHT	CISSY	MILLY	ZINKY	******
VISAS	NIGHT	DIARY	MILTY	ZIPPY	-K--L
VISES	PICOT	DICEY	MINGY	******	******
WICKS	PILOT	DICKY	MISSY	-J--D	SKILL
WILDS	PIPET	DIMLY	MISTY	******	SKIRL
WILES	PIPIT	DINGY	MITZY	FJELD	SKOAL
WILLS	PITOT	DINKY	NICKY	FJORD	SKULL
WILTS	PIVOT	DIPPY	NIFTY	NJORD	******
WINDS	RIANT	DIRTY	NINNY	******	-K--N
WINES	RIGHT	DISHY	NIPPY	-J--T	******
WINGS	RIVET	DITTY	NITTY	******	AKRON
WINKS	SIGHT	DIVVY	PIETY	EJECT	SKEAN
WINOS	TIBET	DIZZY	PIGGY	******	SKEIN
WIPES	TIGHT	FIERY	PIGMY	-K--D	******
WIRES	TINCT	FIFTY	PINEY	******	-K--O
WISES	VISCT	FILLY	PINKY	SKALD	******
WISPS	VISIT	FILMY	PINNY	SKEED	SKIMO
WIVES	WIGHT	FINNY	PITHY	SKIED	******
YIPES	ZIBET	FIRRY	RICKY	******	-K--P
ZINCS	******	FISHY	RIDGY	-K--E	******
******	-I--U	FITLY	RILEY	******	SKIMP
-I--T	******	FIZZY	RISKY	AKENE	******
******	BIJOU	GIDDY	RITZY	SKATE	-K--R
BIDET	FICHU	GIMPY	SILKY	SKIVE	******
BIGHT	HINDU	GINNY	SILLY	UKASE	SKIER
BIGOT	VIRTU	GIPSY	SILTY	******	SKIRR
BINET	-I--W	HILLY	SISSY	-K--F	******
BINIT	******	HINNY	SIXTY	******	-K--S
BIZET	MIAOW	HIPPY	TILLY	SKIFF	******
CIVET	SINEW	JIFFY	TIMMY	******	IKONS
DIDNT	WIDOW	JIMMY	TINNY	-K--G	OKAYS
DIDST		JINNY	TIPPY	******	OKIES
DIGIT	******	KIDDY	TIPSY	EKING	OKRAS
DIVOT	-I--X	KILTY	TIZZY	OKING	SKEES
DIXIT	******	KINKY	VICHY	******	SKEGS
EIGHT	CIMEX	KITTY	VICKY	-K--H	SKEPS
FIGHT	SILEX	LIBBY	VIEWY	******	SKEWS
FILET	SIOUX	LILLY	VINNY	OKIEH	SKIDS

SKIES	ILEAC	ALYCE	PLUME	PLASH	PLUNK
SKIMS	ILIAC	BLADE	SLAKE	PLUSH	SLACK
SKINS	OLEIC	BLAKE	SLATE	SLASH	SLEEK
SKIPS	******	BLAME	SLAVE	SLOSH	SLICK
SKITS	**-L--D**	BLARE	SLICE	SLOTH	SLINK
SKUAS	******	BLASE	SLIDE	SLUSH	SLUNK
******	ALAND	BLAZE	SLIME	******	******
-K--T	ALGID	BLOKE	SLOPE	**-L--I**	**-L--L**
******	ALMUD	CLARE	SLYPE	******	******
SKEET	ALOUD	CLIME	ULNAE	ALIBI	ALDOL
SKIRT	BLAND	CLINE	ULOSE	ALTAI	ALGAL
******	BLEED	CLIVE	******	ELEMI	ALGOL
-K--Y	BLEND	CLONE	**-L--F**	FLEXI	ALKYL
******	BLIND	CLOSE	******	PLAGI	ALLYL
SKYEY	BLOND	CLOVE	ALOOF	PLANI	FLAIL
******	BLOOD	CLYDE	BLUFF	PLURI	ILEAL
-L--A	BLUED	ELATE	CLIFF	PLUVI	******
******	CLOUD	ELIDE	FLUFF	******	**-L--M**
ALADA	CLUED	ELISE	KLOOF	**-L--K**	******
ALEXA	ELAND	ELITE	******	******	ALARM
ALGIA	FLIED	ELLIE	**-L--G**	ALACK	ALBUM
ALOHA	FLOOD	ELOPE	******	ALECK	ALGUM
ALPHA	FLOYD	ELSIE	ALMUG	BLACK	BLOOM
ALULA	FLUID	ELUDE	ALONG	BLANK	CLAIM
CLARA	GLAND	FLAKE	CLANG	BLEAK	FLEAM
ELENA	GLUED	FLAME	CLING	BLINK	GLEAM
ELIZA	ILIAD	FLARE	CLUNG	BLOCK	GLOOM
FLORA	LLOYD	FLITE	FLING	CLACK	ILEUM
ILONA	PLAID	FLUKE	FLONG	CLANK	ILIUM
KLARA	PLEAD	FLUME	FLUNG	CLARK	PLASM
LLAMA	PLIED	FLUTE	SLANG	CLEEK	******
PLATA	PLOID	GLACE	SLING	CLERK	**-L--N**
PLAYA	SLOYD	GLADE	SLUNG	CLICK	******
PLAZA	SLUED	GLARE	******	CLINK	ALAIN
PLENA	******	GLAZE	**-L--H**	CLOAK	ALBAN
PLICA	**-L--E**	GLEBE	******	CLOCK	ALBIN
ULEMA	******	GLEDE	ALEPH	CLUCK	ALCAN
ULTRA	ALATE	GLIDE	ALLAH	FLACK	ALDAN
******	ALBEE	GLOBE	ALMAH	FLANK	ALDEN
-L--B	ALFIE	GLOVE	BLIGH	FLASK	ALGIN
******	ALGAE	GLOZE	BLUSH	FLECK	ALIEN
BLURB	ALGIE	GLUME	BLYTH	FLICK	ALIGN
CLIMB	ALICE	OLIVE	CLASH	FLOCK	ALLAN
PLUMB	ALIKE	OLLIE	CLOTH	FLUNK	ALLEN
******	ALIVE	PLACE	FLASH	PLACK	ALLIN
-L--C	ALLIE	PLANE	FLESH	PLANK	ALOIN
******	ALONE	PLATE	FLUSH	PLONK	ALTON
BLANC	ALINE	PLEBE	GLYPH	PLUCK	ALUIN
GLAUC					

ALVAN	CLAMP	ALGYS	ELVES	PLODS	BLUNT
ALVIN	CLASP	ALIAS	FLAGS	PLOPS	BLURT
ALWIN	CLUMP	ALIFS	FLAMS	PLOTS	CLEAT
BLAIN	FLUMP	ALLIS	FLANS	PLOWS	CLEFT
BLOWN	PLUMP	ALMAS	FLAPS	PLOYS	CLINT
CLEAN	SLEEP	ALOES	FLATS	PLUGS	CLOUT
CLEON	SLOOP	ALOIS	FLAWS	PLUMS	ELECT
CLOWN	SLUMP	ALTAS	FLAYS	SLABS	ELIOT
ELAIN	SLURP	ALTOS	FLEAS	SLAGS	FLEET
ELFIN	******	ALUMS	FLEES	SLAMS	FLINT
ELGIN	-L--R	BLABS	FLEWS	SLAPS	FLIRT
ELLEN	******	BLAHS	FLIES	SLATS	FLOAT
ELMAN	ALDER	BLATS	FLIPS	SLAVS	FLOUT
ELOIN	ALGER	BLDGS	FLITS	SLAWS	GLEET
ELTON	ALGOR	BLEBS	FLOCS	SLAYS	GLINT
ELVAN	ALTAR	BLESS	FLOES	SLEDS	GLOAT
ELVIN	ALTER	BLIPS	FLOGS	SLEWS	GLOST
ELWIN	BLEAR	BLISS	FLOPS	SLIMS	OLENT
FLOWN	BLUER	BLOBS	FLOSS	SLIPS	PLAIT
GLEAN	CLEAR	BLOCS	FLOWS	SLITS	PLANT
GLENN	ELDER	BLOIS	FLUBS	SLOBS	PLAST
ILIAN	ELGAR	BLOTS	FLUES	SLOES	PLEAT
ILION	ELMER	BLOWS	GLADS	SLOGS	SLANT
ILMEN	ELVER	BLUES	GLANS	SLOPS	SLEAT
OLDEN	FLAIR	BLURS	GLASS	SLOTS	SLEET
OLEAN	FLEER	CLAMS	GLEDS	SLOWS	SLEPT
OLEIN	FLIER	CLANS	GLEES	SLUBS	SLIPT
PLAIN	FLOOR	CLAPS	GLENS	SLUES	ULENT
SLAIN	FLOUR	CLASS	GLIMS	SLUGS	******
******	FLUOR	CLAWS	GLOBS	SLUMS	-L--U
-L--O	FLYER	CLAYS	GLOSS	SLURS	******
******	GLAIR	CLEFS	GLOWS	SLUTS	ELIHU
ALAMO	OLDER	CLEMS	GLUES	ULNAS	******
CLARO	PLIER	CLEWS	GLUTS	ULOUS	-L--W
CLINO	SLIER	CLIOS	ILEUS	******	******
ELAEO	SLYER	CLIPS	ILLUS	-L--T	ALLOW
ELAIO	ULCER	CLODS	MLLES	******	ELBOW
GLYCO	ULNAR	CLOGS	OLAFS	ALERT	******
LLANO	******	CLONS	OLAVS	ALEUT	-L--Y
OLIGO	-L--S	CLOPS	OLGAS	ALIST	******
PLANO	******	CLOTS	OLIOS	ALLOT	ALARY
PLATO	ALANS	CLOYS	OLLAS	ALOFT	ALLAY
PLUTO	ALBAS	CLUBS	PLANS	BLAST	ALLEY
SLAVO	ALDIS	CLUES	PLATS	BLEAT	ALLOY
SLIGO	ALDOS	ELIAS	PLAYS	BLENT	ALPHY
******	ALDUS	ELLAS	PLEAS	BLEST	ALWAY
-L--P	ALECS	ELLIS	PLEBS	BLOAT	BLOWY
******	ALEFS	ELSAS	PLIES	BLUET	CLARY
BLEEP					
BLIMP					

CLUNY	AMBLE	IMPEL	BMEWS	IMPLY	ANODE
ELEGY	AMICE	SMALL	EMBUS	SMOKY	ANSAE
FLAKY	AMIDE	SMELL	EMEUS	******	ANTAE
FLAMY	AMINE	UMBEL	EMILS	-N--A	ENARE
FLAWY	AMOLE	******	EMIRS	******	ENATE
FLAXY	AMPLE	-M--N	EMITS	ANIMA	ENDUE
FLUKY	AMUSE	******	EMMAS	ANITA	ENSUE
FLUTY	EMCEE	AMAIN	EMMYS	ANTRA	GNOME
FLYBY	EMILE	AMMAN	IMAMS	ENEMA	INANE
GLARY	EMMIE	AMMON	IMIDS	ENNEA	INDUE
GLAZY	EMOTE	EMDEN	OMENS	ENOLA	INGLE
GLORY	IMAGE	******	OMERS	ENTIA	INKLE
GLUEY	IMBUE	-M--O	OMITS	INDIA	INURE
OLOGY	IMIDE	******	SMEWS	INDRA	KNAVE
PLASY	IMINE	AMIDO	SMOGS	INFRA	KNIFE
PLATY	OMBRE	AMIGO	SMUTS	INTRA	SNAKE
PLEGY	SMAZE	AMINO	UMBOS	ONEGA	SNARE
PLINY	SMILE	AMYLO	******	******	SNIDE
PLUMY	SMITE	IMAGO	-M--T	-N--C	SNIPE
SLATY	SMOKE	IMIDO	******	******	SNORE
SLILY	SMOTE	IMINO	AMBIT	ANTIC	UNCLE
SLIMY	UMBLE	OMBRO	AMENT	ANZAC	UNDEE
SLYLY	******	******	EMMET	ENCYC	UNDUE
ZLOTY	-M--G	-M--R	IMPOT	INDIC	UNITE
******	******	AMONG	SMALT	******	UNTIE
-L--Z	AMONG	AMBER	SMART	-N--D	******
******	******	AMEER	SMELT	******	-N--F
BLITZ	-M--H	AMOUR	SMOLT	ANTED	******
******	******	AMPHR	******	ENDED	SNIFF
-M--A	AMISH	EMBAR	-M--W	INKED	SNUFF
******	SMASH	EMBER	******	INNED	UNREF
AMANA	SMITH	EMEER	EMBOW	KNEAD	******
AMEBA	******	EMMER	******	KNEED	-N--G
AMNIA	-M--I	OMBER	-M--X	SNEAD	******
OMAHA	******	SMEAR	******	SNOOD	UNPEG
OMASA	AMATI	UMBER	IMMIX	UNDID	UNRIG
OMEGA	AMPHI	-M--S	******	UNWED	******
UMBRA	******	******	-M--Y	******	-N--H
******	-M--K	AMAHS	******	-N--E	******
-M--D	******	AMASS	AMBRY	******	ENOCH
******	AMUCK	AMBOS	AMITY	ANDRE	GNASH
AMEND	SMACK	AMENS	AMPLY	ANELE	SNATH
EMBED	SMIRK	AMIAS	EMBAY	ANGLE	******
EMEND	SMOCK	AMIES	EMBRY	ANILE	-N--I
IMBED	UMIAK	AMIRS	EMERY	ANIME	******
******	******	AMISS	EMILY	ANISE	ENNUI
-M--E	-M--L	AMYLS	EMORY	ANKLE	INDRI
******	******		EMPTY	ANNIE	
AMATE	AMIEL				
AMAZE	AMPUL				

******	KNOWN	ANGUS	INSET	UNIFY	NORIA
-N--K	ONION	ANILS	KNELT	UNITY	NORMA
******	UNION	ANKHS	KNOUT	UNLAY	PODIA
KNACK	UNMAN	ANKUS	ONSET	UNSAY	POLKA
KNOCK	UNPEN	ANLAS	SNOOT	******	POONA
SNACK	UNPIN	ANNAS	SNORT	**-O--A**	ROTLA
SNARK	******	ANNES	SNOUT	******	SOFIA
SNEAK	**-N--O**	ANTES	UNAPT	AORTA	SOFTA
SNICK	******	ANTIS	UNCUT	BOHEA	SOLFA
SNOOK	ANDRO	ENEAS	UNFIT	COBIA	SONIA
VNECK	ANEMO	ENIDS	UNHAT	COBRA	SONJA
******	ANGIO	ENOLS	UNIAT	COCOA	SONYA
-N--L	ANGLO	GNATS	UNLIT	COLZA	SOUSA
******	ANISO	GNAWS	******	COMMA	TONGA
ANGEL	ANTHO	INCAS	**-N--U**	CONGA	VODKA
ANNAL	ANZIO	INCUS	******	COPRA	VOILA
ANNUL	INIGO	INDUS	ANJOU	CORIA	VOLGA
ANSEL	INTRO	KNARS	SNAFU	COSTA	VOLTA
ANTAL	ONIRO	KNEES	******	COTTA	VOLVA
ANVIL	******	KNITS	**-N--W**	DOBLA	******
ENROL	**-N--P**	KNOBS	******	DOBRA	**-O--B**
GNARL	******	KNOPS	ENDOW	DOGMA	******
KNEEL	KNOSP	KNOTS	INDOW	DONNA	COOMB
KNELL	SNOOP	KNOWS	INLAW	DORSA	HOREB
KNOLL	UNCAP	KNURS	UNMEW	DOURA	******
KNURL	UNRIP	SNAGS	******	FOLIA	**-O--C**
SNAIL	UNZIP	SNAPS	**-N--X**	FONDA	******
SNARL	******	SNIPS	******	FOSSA	BORIC
SNELL	**-N--R**	SNOBS	ANNEX	FOVEA	COLIC
UNTIL	******	SNOTS	INDEX	GOLDA	COMIC
******	ANEAR	SNOWS	INFIX	GONIA	CONIC
-N--M	ANGER	SNUBS	UNFIX	GOTHA	COPEC
******	ENTER	SNUGS	UNSEX	GOUDA	DODEC
ANNAM	INCUR	SNYES	******	HORTA	DOMIC
ENTOM	INFER	UNAUS	**-N--Y**	HOSEA	DORIC
INARM	INKER	UNITS	******	IONIA	EOLIC
PNEUM	INNER	******	ANGRY	JOSUA	FOLIC
UNARM	INTER	**-N--T**	ANNOY	KOALA	IODIC
******	INVAR	******	ANOMY	KONYA	IONIC
-N--N	KNURR	ANENT	ENEMY	KOREA	KOPEC
******	ONEIR	ANGST	ENJOY	LOGIA	LOGIC
ANCON	SNEER	ENACT	ENTRY	LORCA	SONIC
ANION	UNBAR	INAPT	ENVOY	LORNA	TONIC
ANTON	UNDER	INEPT	GNOMY	LOTTA	TOPIC
GNAWN	******	INERT	INLAY	MOCHA	TORIC
INCAN	**-N--S**	INGOT	ONERY	MOIRA	TOXIC
INION	******	INLET	SNAKY	MORNA	YOGIC
INURN	ANDES	INPUT	SNOWY	MORTA	
	ANDYS				

******	LOWED	BOGLE	HORAE	ROUSE	DOUGH
-O--D	MONAD	BOISE	HORDE	ROUTE	FORTH
******	MOOED	BOMBE	HORNE	SOCLE	HOOCH
BOARD	MOPED	BONZE	HORSE	SOLVE	HOPEH
BODED	MOULD	BOONE	HOUSE	SOMME	HOUGH
BONED	MOUND	BOOZE	HOWIE	SOUSE	JONAH
BOOED	MOVED	BORNE	HOYLE	TOGAE	LOACH
BORED	MOWED	BOULE	JORGE	TOGUE	LOATH
BOUND	NOMAD	BOUSE	JOSIE	TOILE	LOTAH
BOVID	NOSED	BOWIE	JOSUE	TOISE	LOUGH
BOWED	NOTED	BOWSE	JOULE	TONNE	MONTH
BOXED	OOZED	BOYLE	JOYCE	TOPEE	MOOCH
CODED	POIND	BOYNE	KOINE	TOQUE	MORPH
COKED	POKED	COBLE	KOPJE	TORTE	MOUCH
CONED	POLED	COELE	LOCKE	VOGUE	MOUTH
CONTD	PORED	COLNE	LODGE	VOICE	NORAH
COOED	POSED	COMAE	LOGUE	VOILE	NORTH
COPED	POUND	COMTE	LOIRE	VOLTE	NOTCH
CORED	ROALD	CONGE	LOOSE	WORSE	OOMPH
COULD	ROBED	CONTE	LOTTE	YOGEE	POACH
COVED	ROPED	COOEE	LOUPE	YOURE	POOCH
COWED	ROSED	COPSE	LOUSE	YOUVE	PORCH
COXED	ROUND	CORFE	MOIRE	******	POUCH
DOLED	ROVED	CORSE	MONDE	-O--F	ROACH
DOMED	ROWED	COUPE	MONTE	******	ROLPH
DOPED	SOLED	COXAE	MOORE	MOTIF	ROTCH
DOSED	SOLID	DOBIE	MOOSE	WOOLF	ROUGH
DOTED	SOUND	DODGE	MORAE	******	SOOTH
DOZED	SOWED	DOGIE	MORSE	-O--G	SOUGH
FOUND	TONED	DOLCE	MOUSE	******	SOUTH
FOXED	TOPED	DONEE	MOVIE	BOURG	TOOTH
FOYED	TOTED	DONNE	MOXIE	DOING	TORAH
GONAD	TOWED	DOUSE	NOBLE	GOING	TORCH
GORED	TOYED	DOWSE	NOISE	YOUNG	TOUCH
GOURD	VOTED	DOYLE	NONCE	******	TOUGH
HOARD	VOWED	FORCE	NOOSE	-O--H	VOUCH
HOLED	WOALD	FORGE	NORSE	******	WORTH
HOMED	WOOED	FORME	NOVAE	BOOTH	YOUTH
HONED	WORLD	FORTE	POISE	BOSCH	******
HOPED	WOULD	FOSSE	PONCE	BOTCH	-O--I
HOSED	WOUND	GOOSE	POOLE	BOUGH	******
HOUND	WOWED	GORGE	PORGE	COACH	COATI
JOKED	YOKED	GORME	POSSE	CONCH	COCCI
JOYED	YOWED	GORSE	ROBLE	COUCH	CORGI
LOBED	ZONED	GOUGE	ROGUE	COUGH	DORSI
LOOED	ZOOID	HODGE	ROLFE	COUTH	DOUAI
LOPED	******	HOOKE	ROQUE	DOETH	FORLI
LOVED	-O--E	HOOVE	ROUGE	DOLPH	GONDI
	******	BOCHE			
	BOGIE				

GORKI	NODAL	COVEN	COENO	BOXER	ROTOR
HOURI	NOPAL	COZEN	COMBO	BOYAR	ROVER
LONGI	NOVEL	DOORN	COMPO	CODER	ROWER
NOCTI	ROWEL	DOYEN	CONGO	COKER	SOBER
SOLDI	ROYAL	DOZEN	CONIO	COLOR	SOLAR
SOMNI	SOREL	EOSIN	CONTO	COMDR	SONAR
TOPHI	SOTOL	FOEHN	COPRO	COMER	SOPOR
TORII	TOBOL	GOWAN	COSMO	CONTR	SORER
TORSI	TOLYL	HOGAN	COSTO	COOER	SOWAR
VOLTI	TONAL	HOKAN	DORSO	COPER	SOWER
ZOMBI	TOTAL	HONAN	FOLIO	CORER	TONER
******	TOWEL	JOTUN	FORGO	COVER	TOPER
-O--K	VOCAL	KORAN	GONIO	COWER	TOTER
******	VOGUL	KORUN	HOMEO	DOLOR	TOWER
COSEK	VOWEL	LODEN	HONDO	DONAR	TOYER
HOICK	YODEL	LOGAN	JOCKO	DONOR	VOLAR
KODAK	YOKEL	LORAN	LOTTO	DOSER	VOMER
KOPEK	YOULL	MORIN	MOLTO	DOTER	VOTER
TORSK	ZONAL	MORON	MORRO	DOVER	VOWER
******	ZORIL	MOSAN	MOSSO	DOWER	WOOER
-O--L	******	MOURN	MOTTO	DOZER	******
******	**-O--M**	ROBIN	POLIO	FOYER	**-O--S**
BOHOL	******	RODIN	POOPO	GOFER	******
BOWEL	BOSOM	ROMAN	PORNO	GONER	BOARS
COMAL	FOISM	ROSIN	POTTO	GOWER	BOATS
COPAL	FORUM	ROUEN	RODEO	HOMER	BODES
CORAL	GOLEM	ROVEN	ROLLO	HONOR	BOERS
COXAL	GOYIM	ROWAN	ROMEO	HOVER	BOGUS
DOALL	HOKUM	ROWEN	RONDO	JOKER	BOILS
DOWEL	JORAM	SOLAN	SOCIO	LOBAR	BOLAS
FOCAL	JORUM	SOLON	SOLDO	LONER	BOLES
GOGOL	LOCUM	SOZIN	SORGO	LOPER	BOLLS
GORAL	SODOM	TOEIN	SOTTO	LOSER	BOLOS
HORAL	TOTEM	TOKEN	TOKYO	LOVER	BOLTS
HOTEL	******	TOLAN	TORSO	LOWER	BOLUS
HOVEL	**-O--N**	TOMAN	******	MOHUR	BOMBS
IODOL	******	TOXIN	**-O--P**	MOLAR	BONDS
LOCAL	BOGAN	TOYON	******	MOPER	BONES
LOYAL	BONIN	WODAN	DOVAP	MOTOR	BONGS
MODAL	BORON	WODEN	POLYP	MOVER	BONUS
MODEL	BOSON	WOKEN	******	MOWER	BOOBS
MOGUL	BOSUN	WOMAN	**-O--R**	NOPAR	BOOKS
MOLAL	BOURN	WOMEN	******	NOTER	BOOMS
MORAL	COGON	WOTAN	BOGOR	POKER	BOONS
MOREL	COHAN	WOVEN	BOLAR	POLAR	BOORS
MOSEL	COIGN	YOGIN	BONER	POSER	BOOTS
MOTEL	COLIN	******	BORER	POWER	BORES
NOBEL	COLON	**-O--O**	BOWER	ROGER	BORIS
		******			
		BONGO			
		COELO			

BORTS	COUPS	FOULS	JOELS	LOUPS	NOTES
BOSKS	COVES	FOURS	JOEYS	LOURS	NOUNS
BOTTS	COWES	FOWLS	JOHNS	LOUTS	NOVAS
BOUTS	COWLS	FOXES	JOINS	LOVES	NOYES
BOWLS	COXES	GOADS	JOKES	MOANS	OOZES
BOXES	DOCKS	GOALS	JOLES	MOATS	POCKS
BOYDS	DODOS	GOATS	JOLTS	MOCKS	POEMS
BOZOS	DOERS	GOBOS	JONAS	MODES	POETS
COALS	DOFFS	GOBYS	JONES	MODUS	POKES
COATS	DOGES	GOERS	JOWLS	MOILS	POLES
COBBS	DOITS	GOLDS	KOELS	MOKES	POLLS
COCAS	DOLES	GOLFS	KOLAS	MOLDS	POMES
COCKS	DOLLS	GONGS	KOMOS	MOLES	PONDS
COCOS	DOLTS	GOODS	KOOKS	MOLLS	PONES
CODAS	DOMES	GOOFS	KOTOS	MOLTS	POODS
CODES	DONAS	GOOKS	LOADS	MOMUS	POOLS
COEDS	DONTS	GOONS	LOAFS	MONAS	POONS
COIFS	DOOMS	GORES	LOAMS	MONKS	POOPS
COILS	DOORS	GOTHS	LOANS	MOODS	POPES
COINS	DOPES	GOVYS	LOBES	MOONS	PORES
COKES	DORAS	GOWNS	LOBOS	MOORS	PORTS
COLAS	DORIS	HOBBS	LOCHS	MOPES	POSES
COLDS	DORMS	HOBOS	LOCKS	MORAS	POSTS
COLES	DORRS	HOCKS	LOCOS	MORES	POUFS
COLTS	DORUS	HOCUS	LOCUS	MORNS	POURS
COMAS	DOSES	HOERS	LODES	MOROS	POUTS
COMBS	DOTES	HOLDS	LOESS	MORTS	POWYS
COMES	DOUGS	HOLES	LOFTS	MOSES	ROADS
COMUS	DOVES	HOLMS	LOGES	MOTES	ROAMS
CONES	DOWNS	HOMES	LOGOS	MOTHS	ROANS
CONKS	DOZES	HONES	LOINS	MOUES	ROARS
CONUS	EOLUS	HONGS	LOLAS	MOVES	ROBES
COOKS	FOALS	HONKS	LOLLS	MOXAS	ROCKS
COOLS	FOAMS	HOODS	LONGS	NOAHS	ROILS
COONS	FOCUS	HOOFS	LOOFS	NOCKS	ROLES
COOPS	FOILS	HOOKS	LOOKS	NODES	ROLFS
COOTS	FOLDS	HOOPS	LOOMS	NODUS	ROLLS
COPES	FOLKS	HOOTS	LOONS	NOELS	ROMPS
COPTS	FONTS	HOPES	LOOPS	NOGGS	ROODS
CORAS	FOODS	HORAS	LOOTS	NOMAS	ROOFS
CORDS	FOOLS	HORNS	LOPES	NONAS	ROOKS
CORES	FOOTS	HORUS	LORDS	NONES	ROOMS
CORKS	FORBS	HOSES	LORES	NOOKS	ROOTS
CORMS	FORDS	HOSTS	LORIS	NOONS	ROPES
CORNS	FORES	HOURS	LOSES	NORAS	ROSAS
CORPS	FORKS	HOWLS	LOTOS	NORMS	ROSES
COSTS	FORMS	IOTAS	LOTUS	NORNS	ROTAS
COTES	FORTS	JOANS	LOUIS	NOSES	ROUES

ROUTS	TORTS	DOUBT	BONNY	GOLLY	MOTHY
ROVES	TORUS	FOIST	BOOBY	GOODY	MOUSY
SOAKS	TOTES	FOUNT	BOOTY	GOOEY	NOBBY
SOAPS	TOURS	HOIST	BOOZY	GOOFY	NOBLY
SOARS	TOUTS	HOLST	BORTY	GOOSY	NODDY
SOCKS	TOWNS	HORST	BOSKY	GORKY	NOISY
SODAS	TOYOS	JOINT	BOSSY	GORSY	NOSEY
SOFAS	VOCES	JOIST	BOTHY	GOUTY	NOWAY
SOILS	VOIDS	JOUST	BOUSY	HOAGY	POCKY
SOJAS	VOLES	LOPAT	COALY	HOARY	PODGY
SOKES	VOLTS	MOIST	COCKY	HOBBY	POESY
SOLES	VOTES	MONET	COKEY	HOLEY	POGEY
SOLOS	WOADS	MORAT	COLLY	HOLLY	POKEY
SOLUS	WOLDS	MOTET	COMFY	HOMEY	POLLY
SONES	WOLFS	MOULT	CONEY	HONEY	POMMY
SONGS	WOMBS	MOUNT	CONNY	HONKY	POPPY
SOOTS	WOODS	NONET	COOEY	HOOEY	POPSY
SORAS	WOOFS	POINT	COOKY	HOOKY	PORGY
SORBS	WOOLS	POSIT	CORBY	HORNY	PORKY
SORES	WORDS	POULT	CORKY	HORSY	POTSY
SORTS	WORKS	ROAST	CORNY	HOTLY	POTTY
SORUS	WORMS	ROBOT	COVEY	HOWDY	ROCKY
SOULS	WORTS	ROOST	COWRY	JOLLY	RODDY
SOUPS	YODHS	ROUST	COYLY	JOLTY	ROILY
SOURS	YOGHS	SOMAT	DOBBY	JONNY	RONNY
SOYAS	YOGIS	TOAST	DODGY	KOOKY	ROOKY
TOADS	YOKES	VOMIT	DOGGY	LOAMY	ROOMY
TOBYS	YOLKS	WORST	DOILY	LOBBY	ROOTY
TODDS	YOURS	******	DOLLY	LOFTY	ROPEY
TODOS	YOWLS	-O--U	DOOLY	LOLLY	ROUPY
TOFTS	YOYOS	******	DOPEY	LOOBY	ROWDY
TOGAS	ZONES	BORNU	DORMY	LOONY	SOAPY
TOILS	ZOOMS	CORFU	DOTTY	LOOPY	SOFTY
TOLAS	ZOONS	CORNU	DOUAY	LOPPY	SOGGY
TOLES	******	COYPU	DOURY	LORRY	SONNY
TOLLS	-O--T	POILU	DOWDY	LOTTY	SONSY
TOMAS	******	POYOU	DOWNY	LOUSY	SOOTY
TOMBS	BOAST	******	DOWRY	LOWLY	SOPHY
TOMES	BOOST	-O--X	DOYLY	MOLDY	SOPPY
TONES	COAST	******	FOAMY	MOLLY	SORRY
TONGS	COMDT	BORAX	FOGEY	MONEY	SOUPY
TONIS	COMET	CODEX	FOGGY	MONTY	TOADY
TONUS	COOPT	******	FOLLY	MOODY	TODAY
TONYS	COROT	-O--Y	FOOTY	MOONY	TODDY
TOOLS	COUNT	******	FORAY	MORAY	TOKAY
TOOTS	COURT	BOBBY	FORBY	MORTY	TOMMY
TOPES	COVET	BOGEY	FORTY	MOSEY	TOPSY
TOPIS	DOEST	BOGGY	GODLY	MOSSY	WOMBY

WOODY	SPILE	SPALL	OPALS	SPINY	******
WOOLY	SPINE	SPELL	OPENS	SPIRY	-R--A
WOOZY	SPIRE	SPIEL	OPSIS	SPLAY	******
WORDY	SPITE	SPILL	SPANS	SPRAY	ARECA
WORMY	SPODE	SPOIL	SPARS	SPUMY	ARENA
WORRY	SPOKE	SPOOL	SPATS	******	ARICA
YOLKY	SPORE	******	SPAYS	-P--Z	AROMA
******	SPREE	-P--M	SPECS	******	ARUBA
-O--Z	SPRUE	******	SPEWS	SPITZ	BRAVA
******	SPUME	EPSOM	SPIES	******	BRAZA
BORTZ	******	OPIUM	SPINS	-Q--A	BREDA
TOPAZ	-P--F	SPASM	SPITS	******	CRURA
******	******	SPERM	SPOTS	AQABA	DRAMA
-P--A	SPOOF	******	SPUDS	-Q--B	DRAVA
******	******	-P--N	SPURS	******	ERICA
APNEA	-P--G	******	YPRES	SQUAB	ERIKA
OPERA	******	APIAN	******	SQUIB	FREDA
OPSIA	APING	APRON	-P--T	******	FRENA
SPICA	SPANG	SPAIN	******	-Q--D	FREYA
******	SPRAG	SPAWN	APART	******	GRAMA
-P--C	SPRIG	SPHEN	APORT	SQUAD	GRETA
******	******	SPLEN	EPACT	SQUID	KRONA
OPTIC	-P--H	SPOON	SPAIT	-Q--E	ORIYA
******	APISH	SPURN	SPELT	******	PRESA
-P--D	EPHAH	******	SPENT	AQUAE	PRIMA
******	EPOCH	-P--O	SPILT	******	RRHEA
APHID	******	******	SPIRT	-Q--L	TRINA
EPHOD	-P--I	OPHIO	SPLAT	******	TRONA
OPTED	******	SPIRO	SPLIT	EQUAL	TRUDA
SPEED	SPAHI	SPORO	SPORT	******	TRYMA
SPEND	SPINI	******	SPOUT	-Q--M	
SPIED	******	-P--R	SPRAT	******	-R--B
UPEND	******	******	SPRIT	YQUEM	******
UPPED	-P--K	APTER	SPURT	******	ARDEB
******	******	EPHOR	UPSET	-Q--P	CRUMB
-P--E	APEAK	SPEAR	******	******	******
******	SPANK	SPIER	-P--W	EQUIP	-R--C
APACE	SPARK	SPOOR	******	******	******
APPLE	SPEAK	UPPER	UPBOW	-Q--S	AREIC
EPODE	SPECK	******	******	******	ARTIC
OPINE	SPOOK	-P--S	-P--Y	AQUAS	BRONC
SPACE	SPUNK	******	******	******	CRESC
SPADE	******	APHIS	APERY	-Q--T	FRANC
SPAKE	-P--L	APSES	APPLY	******	******
SPARE	******	APSIS	APTLY	SQUAT	-R--D
SPATE	APPAL	EPEES	EPOXY	******	******
SPICE	APPEL	EPICS	SPICY	-Q--W	ARCED
SPIKE	APRIL	OPAHS	SPIKY	******	ARMED
				SQUAW	

AROID
ARPAD
BRAID
BRAND
BREAD
BREED
BROAD
BROOD
CREED
CRIED
CROWD
DREAD
DRIED
DRUID
DRYAD
ERRED
FRAUD
FREED
FREUD
FRIED
FROND
GRAND
GREED
GRIND
IRKED
ORBED
OREAD
PRIED
PROUD
TREAD
TREED
TREND
TRIAD
TRIED
TRUED
URGED
WRIED
******

-R--E

******
AREAE
ARETE
ARGUE
ARISE
ARNIE
AROSE
ARTIE
BRACE
BRAGE
BRAHE
BRAKE
BRAVE
BRAZE
BREVE
BRIBE
BRICE
BRIDE
BRINE
BROKE
BROME
BRUCE
BRUME
BRUTE
BRYCE
CRAKE
CRANE
CRAPE
CRATE
CRAVE
CRAZE
CREME
CREPE
CRETE
CREWE
CRIME
CROCE
CRONE
CRORE
CROZE
CRUDE
CRUSE
DRAKE
DRAPE
DRAVE
DRIVE
DROME
DRONE
DROVE
DRUPE
DRUSE
ERASE
ERNIE
ERODE
EROSE
FRAME
FRERE
FRISE
FROME
FROZE
GRACE
GRADE
GRAPE
GRATE
GRAVE
GRAZE
GREBE
GRIDE
GRIME
GRIPE
GROPE
GROVE
GRUME
IRATE
IRENE
IRONE
KRONE
ORATE
PRASE
PRATE
PRICE
PRIDE
PRIME
PRISE
PRIZE
PROBE
PROLE
PRONE
PROSE
PROVE
PRUDE
PRUNE
TRACE
TRADE
TRAVE
TRIBE
TRICE
TRINE
TRIPE
TRITE
TROPE
TROVE
TRUCE
URATE
URINE
URSAE
WRITE
WROTE
******

-R--F

******
BRIEF
DRAFF
GRIEF
GRUFF
PROOF
******

-R--G

******
BRAGG
BRING
CRAIG
FRIGG
GRIEG
ORANG
PRANG
PRONG
WRING
WRONG
WRUNG
******

-R--H

******
BRASH
BROTH
BRUSH
CRASH
CRUSH
ERICH
FRESH
FRITH
FROSH
FROTH
GRAPH
IRISH
ORACH
TRACH
TRASH
TRICH
TROPH
TROTH
TRUTH
URIAH
WRATH
WROTH
******

-R--I

******
ARCHI
BRAGI
BREVI
CRANI
CROCI
CRUCI
GRANI
IRAQI
KRUBI
ORCHI
ORIBI
PRIMI
TRAGI
******

-R--K

******
BREAK
BRICK
BRINK
BRISK
BROCK
BROOK
BRUSK
CRACK
CRANK
CREAK
CREEK
CRICK
CROAK
CROCK
CROOK
DRANK
DRINK
DRUNK
FRANK
FREAK
FRISK
FROCK
GREEK
PRANK
PRICK
PRINK
TRACK
TRICK
TRUCK
TRUNK
WRACK
WREAK
WRECK
WRICK
******

-R--L

******
AREAL
ARGAL
ARGIL
ARGOL
ARIEL
ARTAL
ARTEL
ARVAL
BRAIL
BRAWL
BRILL
BROIL
CRAAL
CRAWL
CREEL
CRUEL
DRAIL
DRAWL
DRILL
DROLL
DROOL
ERROL
FRAIL
FRILL
FRIML
GRAAL
GRAIL
GRILL
GROWL
GRUEL
KRAAL
ORIEL
PROWL
TRAIL
TRAWL
TRIAL
TRILL
TRIOL

TROLL	GROWN	GRASP	ARIES	DROSS	PRIGS
TRULL	IRWIN	GROUP	ARILS	DRUBS	PRIMS
UREAL	IRWIN	KRUPP	ARIUS	DRUGS	PROAS
URIEL	ORCIN	ORLOP	ARLES	DRUMS	PRODS
******	ORGAN	PRIMP	ARRAS	ERICS	PROFS
-R--M	ORION	TRAMP	ARRIS	ERIES	PROMS
******	ORLON	TROOP	ARSES	ERIKS	PROPS
ARIUM	ORPIN	TRUMP	ARSIS	ERMAS	PROWS
BREAM	ORSON	******	ARTIS	ERNES	TRAMS
BROOM	PRAWN	-R--R	ARUMS	ERSES	TRANS
CREAM	PREEN	******	BRADS	FRAPS	TRAPS
DREAM	TRAIN	ARBOR	BRAES	FRATS	TRASS
GRIMM	TRYON	ARDOR	BRAGS	FRAYS	TRAYS
GROOM	URBAN	ARMOR	BRANS	FREDS	TREAS
PRIAM	******	ARTER	BRASS	FREES	TREES
PRISM	-R--O	ARTHR	BRATS	FRETS	TREKS
PROEM	******	ARTUR	BRAYS	FRIES	TRESS
******	BRAVO	BRIAR	BREWS	FRITS	TREWS
-R--N	BROMO	BRIER	BRIGS	FROES	TREYS
******	BRUNO	CRIER	BRIMS	FROGS	TRIES
ARDEN	CREDO	CRUOR	BROOS	FROWS	TRIGS
ARGON	DRACO	DREAR	BROWS	GRABS	TRIMS
ARIAN	ERATO	DRIER	CRABS	GRADS	TRIOS
ARION	GRANO	DRYER	CRAGS	GRAMS	TRIPS
ARLEN	GRECO	ERROR	CRAMS	GRASS	TROAS
ARPEN	GREGO	FREER	CRAPS	GRAYS	TROTS
ARRAN	IRIDO	FRIAR	CRASS	GREGS	TRUES
ARSON	ORTHO	FRIER	CRAWS	GREYS	TRUSS
ARYAN	PRIMO	FRYER	CREES	GRIDS	URALS
BRAIN	PROTO	GREER	CRESS	GRINS	URGES
BRAWN	PROVO	ORDER	CREWS	GRIPS	WRAPS
BRIAN	TRIGO	ORMER	CRIBS	GRITS	WRENS
BROWN	TRURO	PRIER	CRIES	GROSS	WRIES
BRUIN	URANO	PRIOR	CROPS	GROTS	WRITS
BRYAN	UREDO	PRYER	CROSS	GROWS	XRAYS
CREON	URICO	TRIER	CROWS	GRUBS	******
CROON	URINO	TRUER	DRABS	IRMAS	-R--T
CROWN	******	WRIER	DRAGS	IRONS	******
DRAIN	-R--P	WRYER	DRAMS	ORALS	ARENT
DRAWN	******	******	DRAWS	ORCUS	ARGOT
DROWN	CRAMP	-R--S	DRAYS	ORLES	ARMET
ERWIN	CREEP	******	DREGS	ORNIS	BRACT
FREON	CRIMP	ARABS	DRESS	ORRIS	BRANT
FROWN	CRISP	ARCUS	DREWS	PRAMS	BRENT
GRAIN	CROUP	AREAS	DRIBS	PRAYS	BREST
GREEN	CRUMP	ARGOS	DRIES	PRESS	BRUIT
GROAN	DROOP	ARGUS	DRIPS	PREYS	BRUNT
GROIN	FRUMP	ARIAS	DROPS	PRIES	CRAFT

CREPT	*****	FRIZZ	*****	OSIER	STOMA
CREST	-R--U	GROSZ	-S--L	OSLER	STRIA
CROAT	*****	*****	*****	USHER	STUKA
CROFT	ERLAU	-S--A	USUAL	*****	STUPA
CRUET	PRAHU	*****	*****	-S--S	UTICA
CRUST	*****	ASPCA	-S--M	*****	*****
CRYPT	-R--W	ASYLA	*****	ASCUS	-T--C
DRAFT	*****	OSAKA	ASSAM	ASHES	*****
DREST	ARROW	OSTIA	ISLAM	ASPIS	ATTIC
DRIFT	*****	TSANA	PSALM	ASSES	ETHIC
DRIPT	-R--X	*****	*****	ASSNS	STOIC
DROIT	*****	-S--C	-S--N	ASSTS	*****
DROPT	BRONX	*****	*****	ESSES	-T--D
ERECT	CROIX	ASPIC	ASHEN	ESTES	*****
ERGOT	*****	ASSOC	ASIAN	ISBAS	STAID
ERNST	-R--Y	ISAAC	ASPEN	ISLES	STAND
ERUCT	*****	ISTIC	ASTON	PSOAS	STEAD
ERUPT	ARABY	OSMIC	ASWAN	TSARS	STEED
FRONT	ARCHY	*****	ESSEN	USERS	STIED
FROST	ARRAY	-S--D	OSCAN	*****	STOOD
FRUIT	BRADY	*****	OSMAN	-S--T	STRAD
GRAFT	BRAKY	ASKED	*****	*****	*****
GRANT	BRAXY	ISLED	-S--O	ASCOT	-T--E
GREAT	BRINY	OSTED	*****	ASSET	*****
GREET	CRACY	PSEUD	ASTRO	ASYUT	ATIVE
GRIPT	CRAZY	*****	*****	ISLET	ATONE
GRIST	CRECY	-S--E	-S--P	*****	ETAPE
GROAT	CRONY	*****	*****	-S--W	ETTIE
GROUT	DRILY	ASIDE	ASCAP	*****	ETUDE
GRUNT	DRURY	ESQUE	ESTOP	ASKEW	STAGE
KRAFT	DRYLY	ESSIE	USURP	PSHAW	STAKE
KRAIT	GRAPY	ISERE	*****	*****	STALE
KRAUT	GRAVY	ISSUE	-S--R	-S--X	STARE
ORBIT	GRIMY	ISTLE	*****	*****	STATE
PREST	IRONY	OSAGE	ASHER	ESSEX	STAVE
PRINT	ORCZY	TSADE	ASHUR	*****	STELE
PROCT	PREXY	USAGE	ASKER	-S--Y	STERE
TRACT	PRIVY	YSERE	ASPER	*****	STEVE
TRAIT	PROSY	*****	ASSYR	ASSAY	STILE
TREAT	PROXY	-S--G	ASTER	ESSAY	STIPE
TRENT	TRACY	*****	ASTIR	ISLAY	STOAE
TROUT	TRIXY	USING	ASTOR	OSITY	STOKE
TRUST	TRUDY	*****	ESHER	USURY	STOLE
TRYST	TRULY	-S--H	ESKER	*****	STOME
WRAPT	WRYLY	*****	ESTAR	-T--A	STONE
WREST	*****	PSYCH	ESTER	*****	STOPE
WRIST	-R--Z	*****	ISTAR	ATRIA	STORE
	*****	-S--I	OSCAR	ETYMA	STOVE
	FRANZ	*****			
	FRITZ	ASSAI			
		ISSEI			

STOWE	ETHYL	STRIP	STUMS	CULPA	CUBIC
STUPE	STALL	STROP	STUNS	CURIA	CUSEC
STYLE	STEAL	STUMP	******	DUALA	HUMIC
UTILE	STEEL	******	-T--T	DULIA	MUSIC
******	STILL	-T--R	******	DURRA	PUBIC
-T--F	STOOL	******	ATILT	GUAMA	PUDIC
******	STULL	ATPAR	START	GUANA	PUNIC
STAFF	******	ATTAR	STILT	GUAVA	RUNIC
STIFF		ETHER	STINT	GUMMA	SUFIC
STUFF	-T--M	OTHER	STOAT	GUSTA	SUMAC
******	******	OTTER	STOPT	GUTTA	TUNIC
-T--G	STEAM	STAIR	STOUT	HULDA	******
******	STORM	STEER	STRAT	JUANA	-U--D
STING	STRUM	STOUR	STRUT	JUDEA	******
STUNG	******	UTHER	STUNT	JULIA	AUDAD
******	-T--N	UTTER	******	JUMNA	BUILD
-T--H	******	******	-T--U	JUNTA	BUSED
******	ATION	-T--S	******	JURUA	CUBED
STAPH	ATMAN	******	OTARU	JUXTA	CUPID
STASH	ETHAN	ATHOS	******	KUFRA	CURED
STETH	ITION	ATLAS	-T--W	LUCCA	DUPED
STICH	STAIN	ATOMS	******	LUCIA	FUMED
******	STEEN	ATTIS	STRAW	LUISA	FUSED
-T--I	STEIN	ATTYS	STREW	MURRA	FUZED
******	STERN	ETHOS	******	MUSCA	GUARD
OTOMI	UTURN	ETNAS	-T--Y	NUBIA	GUILD
STYLI	XTIAN	ETTAS	ATAXY	NUCHA	GUYED
UTERI	******	ETUIS	ATONY	OUIDA	HUMID
******	-T--O	ITALS	ATORY	OUIJA	LUCID
-T--K	******	ITEMS	ITALY	PUCKA	LURED
******	CTENO	OTTOS	ITCHY	PUKKA	LURID
STACK	ETHNO	STABS	STACY	PUNKA	LUTED
STALK	OTERO	STAGS	STAGY	QUOTA	MUCID
STANK	PTERO	STANS	STIMY	RUMBA	MUSED
STARK	STATO	STARS	STOGY	SULFA	MUTED
STEAK	STENO	STAYS	STOMY	SUNNA	OUTED
STICK	STYLO	STEMS	STONY	SUPRA	PUKED
STINK	UTERO	STEPS	STORY	SUTRA	PULED
STIRK	******	STETS	STRAY	TULSA	PULED
STOCK	-T--P	STEWS	STUDY	VULVA	RULED
STOOK	******	STIES	STYMY	YUCCA	TUBED
STORK	ATRIP	STIRS	******	******	TUMID
STUCK	STAMP	STOAS	-T--U	-U--B	TUNED
STUNK	STEEP	STOPS	******	******	******
******	STIRP	STOSS	-U--A	CUBEB	-U--E
-T--L	STOMP	STOWS	******	******	******
******	STOOP	STUBS	BULLA	-U--C	AUDIE
ATOLL	STOUP	STUDS	BURMA	******	AURAE
ETHEL	STRAP		BURSA	AULIC	BUDGE
				AURIC	

BUGLE	RUGAE	******	FUZIL	QUERN	******
BULGE	RUPEE	-U--I	JUGAL	QUOIN	-U--P
BUNDE	SUAVE	******	JURAL	RUMEN	******
BURKE	SUCRE	AUREI	JUREL	RUNIN	CUTUP
BURSE	SUEDE	BUFFI	MURAL	RUNON	JULEP
BUTTE	SUITE	CULTI	OUSEL	SUDAN	PUTUP
CURIE	SURGE	CURVI	OUZEL	SUSAN	SUNUP
CURSE	SUSIE	DUBAI	PUPIL	TURIN	TULIP
CURVE	TULLE	DUOMI	QUAIL	YUKON	******
CUTIE	TUQUE	FUNDI	QUELL	YUPON	-U--R
DUANE	******	FUNGI	QUILL	******	******
DUBHE	-U--F	KUKRI	RURAL	-U--O	AUGER
DULCE	******	LUIGI	SURAL	******	AUGUR
DULSE	QUAFF	LUNGI	TUBAL	AUDIO	BUBER
DUNCE	QUIFF	MUFTI	******	BUCKO	BUYER
DUPLE	******	MULTI	-U--M	BUFFO	CURER
FUDGE	-U--G	QUASI	******	BUNCO	CUTER
FUGLE	******	SULCI	AURUM	BUNKO	DUPER
FUGUE	CUING	SUNNI	BUXOM	BURRO	DURER
FURZE	RUING	TURKI	DURUM	CUPRO	EULER
FUSEE	SUING	TUTTI	PURIM	CURIO	FUROR
FUZEE	******	******	QUALM	CUSSO	GULAR
GUIDE	-U--H	-U--K	******	DUOMO	HUGER
GUILE	******	******	-U--N	FUGIO	HUMOR
GUISE	BUNCH	KULAK	******	FUNGO	JUROR
JUDGE	BURGH	KURSK	AUDEN	GUACO	LUGER
JUICE	BUTCH	MUJIK	AUXIN	GUANO	LUNAR
JULIE	CUISH	MUZAK	BURAN	GUIDO	LURER
LUCRE	CULCH	QUACK	BURIN	GUMBO	LUXOR
LUISE	CURCH	QUARK	CUBAN	GUSTO	OUTER
LUNGE	CUTCH	QUICK	CUMIN	JUDEO	PULER
MURRE	DUTCH	QUIRK	CUTIN	JULIO	PURER
NUDGE	FURTH	RURIK	FURAN	JUMBO	QUEER
NURSE	GULCH	TUPIK	HUMAN	JUNCO	RUDER
OUNCE	HUMPH	******	HUNAN	JUNTO	RULER
OUTRE	HUPEH	-U--L	HURON	MUCRO	RUMOR
PULSE	HUNCH	******	JUPON	MUNGO	SUDOR
PUPAE	HUTCH	AURAL	KUBAN	MUNRO	SUGAR
PUREE	JUDAH	AUSTL	LUMEN	OUTDO	SUMER
PURGE	LUNCH	AUXIL	LUPIN	OUTGO	SUPER
PURSE	LURCH	BUBAL	LUTON	PULMO	SURER
QUAKE	MULCH	BUTYL	LUZON	PUNTO	TUBER
QUEUE	MUNCH	CUPEL	MUCIN	QUITO	TUDOR
QUIRE	PUNCH	DUCAL	NUMEN	RUSSO	TUMOR
QUITE	QUASH	DURAL	PUSAN	SULFO	TUNER
QUOTE	QUOTH	FUGAL	PUTON	TURBO	TUTOR
RUBLE	SUBAH	FUSEL	QUEAN	TURCO	******
RUCHE	SURAH	FUSIL	QUEEN	VULGO	-U--S
					******
					AULIS
					AUNTS

AURAS	DUMPS	JULYS	PULLS	SURFS	******
AURES	DUNES	JUMPS	PULPS	SUZYS	-U--U
AURIS	DUNGS	JUNES	PUMAS	TUBAS	******
AUTOS	DUNKS	JUNKS	PUMPS	TUBES	QUIPU
BUCKS	DUPES	JUSTS	PUNAS	TUCKS	******
BUFFS	DUROS	JUTES	PUNGS	TUFTS	-U--X
BULBS	DUSKS	KUDOS	PUNKS	TULES	******
BULKS	DUSTS	KUDUS	PUNTS	TUNAS	CULEX
BULLS	EURUS	KUMIS	PURLS	TUNES	LUXEX
BUMPS	FUCUS	KURUS	PURRS	TUNIS	MUREX
BUNDS	FUELS	LUAUS	PUTTS	TUPIS	******
BUNGS	FULLS	LUCES	QUADS	TURFS	-U--Y
BUNKS	FUMES	LUCYS	QUAGS	TURKS	******
BUNNS	FUNDS	LUFFS	QUASS	TURNS	AUNTY
BUNTS	FUNKS	LULLS	QUAYS	TUSKS	AUTRY
BUOYS	FURLS	LULUS	QUIDS	TUTUS	BUDDY
BURDS	FUSES	LUMPS	QUIPS	YUGAS	BUDGY
BURGS	FUZES	LUNES	QUITS	YULES	BUFFY
BURLS	GUANS	LUNGS	QUODS	******	BUGGY
BURNS	GUESS	LUNTS	RUBES	-U--T	BULGY
BURPS	GULES	LUPUS	RUBYS	******	BULKY
BURRS	GULFS	LURES	RUCKS	AUDIT	BULLY
BUSES	GULLS	LURKS	RUDDS	AUGHT	BUMPY
BUSKS	GULPS	LUSTS	RUDYS	BUILT	BUNNY
BUSTS	GURUS	LUTES	RUERS	BURNT	BURLY
BUTTS	GUSTS	MUCKS	RUFFS	BURST	BURRY
CUBES	HUFFS	MUCUS	RUFUS	CUBIT	BUSBY
CUFFS	HUGHS	MUFFS	RUINS	CULET	BUSHY
CULLS	HUGOS	MULES	RULES	CURST	CUBBY
CULMS	HULAS	MULLS	RUMPS	DUCAT	CUDDY
CULTS	HULKS	MUMMS	RUNES	DURST	CUPPY
CURBS	HULLS	MUMPS	RUNGS	GUEST	CURDY
CURDS	HUMPS	MUONS	RUNTS	GUILT	CURLY
CURES	HUMUS	MUSES	RUSES	HURST	CURRY
CURLS	HUNKS	MUSKS	RUSKS	JURAT	CUSHY
CUSKS	HUNTS	MUSTS	RUSTS	LUNET	CUTEY
CUSPS	HURDS	MUTES	RUTHS	MULCT	CUTTY
CUTIS	HURLS	MUTTS	SUCKS	MURAT	DUCHY
DUADS	HURTS	NUDES	SUERS	OUGHT	DUCKY
DUCKS	HUSKS	NUMBS	SUFIS	PUGET	DULCY
DUCTS	JUANS	OUSTS	SUITS	QUANT	DULLY
DUDES	JUBAS	PUBES	SULKS	QUART	DUMMY
DUELS	JUBES	PUBIS	SULUS	QUEST	DUMPY
DUETS	JUDAS	PUCES	SUMPS	QUIET	DUNGY
DUFFS	JUDES	PUCKS	SUNNS	QUILT	DUSKY
DUKES	JUDYS	PUFFS	SUPES	QUINT	DUSTY
DULLS	JUJUS	PUKES	SURAS	QUIRT	FUGGY
DUMAS	JULES	PULES	SURDS	QUOIT	FULLY
				SUINT	

FUNKY	PULPY	******	******	******	******
FUNNY	PUNKY	-V--E	-V--T	-W--G	-W--P
FURRY	PUNTY	******	******	******	******
FURZY	PUPPY	EVADE	AVAST	AWING	SWAMP
FUSSY	PURSY	EVOKE	AVERT	EWING	SWEEP
FUSTY	PUSHY	OVATE	EVENT	OWING	SWOOP
FUZZY	PUSSY	OVINE	EVERT	SWING	TWERP
GULLY	PUTTY	OVULE	EVICT	SWUNG	TWIRP
GUMMY	QUAKY	******	OVERT	TWANG	******
GUNNY	QUERY	-V--I	******	******	-W--R
GUPPY	RUDDY	******	-V--Y	-W--H	******
GUSHY	RUGBY	OVOLI	******	******	OWNER
GUSTY	RUMLY	******	AVERY	AWASH	SWEAR
GUTSY	RUMMY	-V--L	EVERY	SWASH	******
HUBBY	RUNNY	******	IVORY	SWATH	-W--S
HUFFY	RUNTY	AVAIL	OVARY	SWISH	******
HULKY	RUSHY	AVRIL	******	******	EWERS
HUMPY	RUSTY	UVEAL	-W--A	-W--I	GWENS
HUNKY	RUTTY	******	******	******	GWYNS
HURLY	SUDSY	-V--N	BWANA	SWAMI	OWENS
HURRY	SUETY	******	******	******	SWABS
HUSKY	SULKY	AVIAN	-W--D	-W--K	SWAGS
HUSSY	SULLY	AVION	******	******	SWANS
JUICY	SUNNY	******	AWARD	SWANK	SWAPS
JUMPY	SURFY	-V--O	AWNED	TWEAK	SWATS
JUNKY	SURGY	******	OWNED	******	SWAYS
LUCKY	SURLY	AVISO	SWARD	-W--L	SWIGS
LUMPY	TUBBY	OVOLO	SWORD	******	SWIMS
LUSTY	TUFTY	******	TWEED	AWFUL	SWISS
MUCKY	TULLY	-V--R	******	DWELL	TWIGS
MUDDY	TUMMY	******	-W--E	SWELL	TWINS
MUGGY	TUNNY	AVOIR	******	SWILL	TWITS
MUHLY	TURFY	******	AWAKE	SWIRL	******
MULEY	TUTTY	-V--S	AWARE	TWILL	-W--T
MUMMY	VUGGY	******	AWOKE	TWIRL	******
MURKY	YUMMY	AVARS	SWAGE	******	AWAIT
MURRY	******	AVENS	SWALE	-W--M	DWELT
MUSHY	-V--A	AVERS	SWEDE	******	OWLET
MUSKY	******	AVOWS	SWINE	SWARM	SWART
MUSSY	EVITA	EVANS	SWIPE	******	SWEAT
MUSTY	UVULA	EVENS	SWORE	-W--N	SWEET
MUZZY	******	EVILS	TWERE	******	SWEPT
NUBBY	-V--D	IVANS	TWICE	GWENN	SWIFT
NUTTY	******	IVIES	TWINE	SWAIN	TWEET
OURAY	AVOID	KVASS	******	SWOON	TWIST
PUDGY	IVIED	OVALS	-W--F	SWORN	TWIXT
PUDSY	OVOID	OVENS	******	TWAIN	******
PUFFY	******	UVEAS	DWARF	TWEEN	-X--A
					******
					EXTRA

```
******        AXONS    HYOID    LYSOL    ******    TYROS
-X--B         EXAMS    LYSED    SYBIL    -Y--R     XYSTS
******        EXECS    MYOID    TYROL    ******
EXURB         EXITS    PYOID    XYLOL    CYMAR     -Y--T
              IXIAS    PYXED    XYLYL    EYRIR     ******
-X--D         ******   SYNOD             HYPER     WYATT
******        -X--T    TYPED    -Y--M    IYYAR     ******
AXLED         ******             ******  TYLER     -Y--W
              EXACT    -Y--E    XYLEM              ******
******        EXALT    ******            -Y--S     BYLAW
-X--E         EXERT    CYCLE    -Y--N    ******
              EXIST    EYDIE    ******   AYAHS     -Y--X
AXILE         EXULT    EYRIE    AYDIN    AYINS     ******
AXONE         ******   KYRIE    BYRON    BYRES     CYLIX
EXILE         -X--W    LYCEE    DYLAN    CYMES     HYRAX
EXUDE         ******   MYOPE    GYRON    CYRUS     KYLIX
IXTLE         OXBOW    PYXIE    HYMEN    CYSTS     PYREX
OXEYE         ******   SYCEE    HYSON    EYRAS     ******
OXIDE         -Y--A    SYNGE    LYMAN    FYKES     -Y--Y
OXIME         ******   TYCHE    LYSIN    GYRES     ******
******        HYDRA    ******   MYRON    GYROS     BYWAY
-X--G         HYENA    -Y--G    NYLON    GYRUS     CYMRY
******        HYPHA    ******   PYLON    HYLAS     GYPSY
AXING         LYCEA    DYING    PYRAN    HYMNS     MYOPY
              LYDDA    EYING    XYLAN    HYPOS     PYGMY
-X--L         LYDIA    HYING    ******   KYATS     ******
******        LYSSA    LYING    -Y--O    LYLES     -Z--C
AXIAL         LYTTA    TYING    ******   LYNNS     ******
EXCEL         MYOMA    VYING    CYANO    LYONS     AZOIC
EXPEL         MYRIA    ******   CYCLO    LYRES     AZTEC
EXTOL         MYRNA    -Y--H    CYSTO    LYSES
UXMAL         NYASA    ******   GYMNO    LYSIS     -Z--E
******        PYDNA    LYMPH    HYALO    MYLES     ******
-X--M         SYLVA    LYNCH    HYDRO    MYNAS     AZINE
******        SYRIA    MYRRH    HYETO    MYRAS     AZOLE
AXIOM         ******   NYMPH    HYGRO    MYTHS     AZOTE
******        -Y--C    SYLPH    HYPNO    OYERS     AZURE
-X--N         ******   ******   HYPSO    PYRES     OZONE
******        CYNIC    -Y--I    KYOTO    PYXES     OZZIE
AXMAN         GYNEC    ******   MYELO    PYXIS     ******
AXMEN         LYRIC    BYSSI    MYTHO    RYNDS     -Z--H
IXION         LYTIC    CYMRI    NYCTO    RYOTS     ******
******        ******   CYSTI    PYELO    SYCES     AZOTH
-X--P         -Y--D    NYCTI    ******   SYROS     CZECH
******        ******            -Y--P    TYEES     ******
OXLIP         CYCAD    -Y--L    ******   TYKES     -Z--K
******        GYBED    ******   SYRUP    TYPES     ******
-X--S         GYVED    CYRIL             TYPOS     OZARK
******                 GYRAL
AXILS
AXLES
```

******	ENACT	GLADS	QUAFF	PRAHU	******
-Z--S	EPACT	GOADS	SHAFT	SHAHS	--AK-
******	EXACT	GRADE	SNAFU	SPAHI	******
AZANS	FLACK	GRADS	STAFF	******	AWAKE
AZONS	GLACE	HEADS	******	--AI-	BEAKS
CZARS	GRACE	HEADY	--AG-	******	BLAKE
EZRAS	GUACO	KHADI	******	AGAIN	BRAKE
IZZYS	KNACK	LEADS	ADAGE	ALAIN	BRAKY
TZARS	LEACH	LEADY	BRAGE	AMAIN	CRAKE
******	LOACH	LOADS	BRAGG	AVAIL	DHAKS
--AA-	NAACP	MEADS	BRAGI	AWAIT	DRAKE
******	ORACH	QUADS	BRAGS	BLAIN	FLAKE
CRAAL	PEACE	READS	CRAGS	BRAID	FLAKY
GRAAL	PEACH	READY	DRAGS	BRAIL	KHAKI
ISAAC	PLACE	ROADS	FLAGS	BRAIN	LEAKS
KRAAL	PLACK	SCADS	HOAGY	CHAIN	LEAKY
******	POACH	SHADE	IMAGE	CHAIR	OSAKA
--AB-	QUACK	SHADY	IMAGO	CLAIM	PEAKS
******	REACH	SPADE	OSAGE	CRAIG	PEAKY
AQABA	REACT	THADS	PHAGE	DRAIL	QUAKE
ARABS	ROACH	THADY	PHAGO	DRAIN	QUAKY
ARABY	SHACK	TOADS	PHAGY	ELAIN	SHAKE
BLABS	SLACK	TOADY	PLAGI	ELAIO	SHAKO
CRABS	SMACK	TRADE	QUAGS	FLAIL	SHAKY
DRABS	SNACK	TSADE	RHAGE	FLAIR	SLAKE
GRABS	SPACE	WOADS	RHAGY	FRAIL	SNAKE
KAABA	STACK	******	SHAGS	GLAIR	SNAKY
SCABS	STACY	--AE-	SLAGS	GRAIL	SOAKS
SLABS	TEACH	******	SNAGS	GRAIN	SPAKE
STABS	TRACE	BAAED	STAGE	KRAIT	STAKE
SWABS	TRACH	BRAES	STAGS	PLAID	TEAKS
******	TRACK	CHAET	STAGY	PLAIN	******
--AC-	TRACT	ELAEO	SWAGE	PLAIT	--AL-
******	TRACY	******	SWAGS	QUAIL	******
ABACA	WHACK	--AF-	TRAGI	SLAIN	BEALL
ABACI	WRACK	******	USAGE	SNAIL	BIALY
ABACK	******	ABAFT	******	SPAIN	CHALK
ALACK	--AD-	CHAFE	--AH-	SPAIT	COALS
APACE	******	CHAFF	******	STAID	COALY
BEACH	ALADA	CRAFT	ADAHS	STAIN	DEALS
BLACK	BEADS	DRAFF	AMAHS	STAIR	DEALT
BRACE	BEADY	DRAFT	AYAHS	SWAIL	DIALS
BRACT	BLADE	GRAFT	BLAHS	SWAIN	DOALL
CLACK	BRADS	KRAFT	BRAHE	TRAIL	DUALA
COACH	BRADY	LEAFS	IDAHO	TRAIN	EXALT
CRACK	DUADS	LEAFY	NOAHS	TRAIT	FOALS
CRACY	EVADE	LOAFS	OMAHA	TWAIN	GOALS
DRACO	GLADE	OLAFS	OPAHS		HEALS

HYALO	ALAMO	AMANA	JOANS	SWANS	SOAPY
ITALS	BEAMS	AZANS	JUANA	THANE	STAPH
ITALY	BEAMY	BEANO	JUANS	THANK	SWAPS
KOALA	BLAME	BEANS	KHANS	TRANS	TRAPS
MEALS	CHAMP	BHANG	LEANS	TSANA	UNAPT
MEALY	CLAMP	BLANC	LEANT	TWANG	WHAPS
NEALS	CLAMS	BLAND	LIANA	URANO	WRAPS
OCALA	CRAMP	BLANK	LIANE	VIAND	WRAPT
OPALS	CRAMS	BRAND	LIANG	WEANS	******
ORALS	DRAMA	BRANS	LLANO	WHANG	--AQ-
OVALS	DRAMS	BRANT	LOANS	YEANS	******
PEALS	EXAMS	BWANA	MEANS	******	IRAQI
PSALM	FLAME	CHANG	MEANT	--AO-	******
QUALM	FLAMS	CHANT	MEANY	******	--AR-
REALM	FLAMY	CLANG	MOANS	CHAOS	******
REALS	FOAMS	CLANK	ORANG	MIAOW	ALARM
RIALS	FOAMY	CLANS	PEANS	******	ALARY
ROALD	FRAME	CRANE	PHANE	--AP-	APART
SCALD	GRAMA	CRANI	PHANY	******	AVARS
SCALE	GRAMS	CRANK	PIAND	ADAPT	AWARD
SCALL	GUAMA	CYANO	PIANO	AGAPE	AWARE
SCALP	IMAMS	DEANE	PLANE	CHAPE	BEARD
SCALY	LLAMA	DEANS	PLANI	CHAPS	BEARS
SEALS	LOAMS	DIANA	PLANK	CHAPT	BLARE
SHALE	LOAMY	DIANE	PLANO	CLAPS	BOARD
SHALL	MIAMI	DRANK	PLANS	CRAPE	BOARS
SHALT	PRAMS	DUANE	PLANT	CRAPS	CEARA
SHALY	REAMS	ELAND	PRANG	DRAPE	CHARD
SIALO	ROAMS	EVANS	PRANK	ETAPE	CHARE
SKALD	SCAMP	FLANK	QUANT	FLAPS	CHARM
SMALL	SEAMS	FLANS	RIANT	FRAPS	CHARO
SMALT	SEAMY	FRANC	ROANS	GRAPE	CHARS
SPALL	SHAME	FRANK	SCAND	GRAPH	CHART
STALE	SHAMS	FRANZ	SCANS	GRAPY	CHARY
STALK	SLAMS	GHANA	SCANT	HEAPS	CLARA
STALL	STAMP	GIANT	SEANS	INAPT	CLARE
SWALE	SWAMI	GLAND	SHANK	LEAPS	CLARK
TEALS	SWAMP	GLANS	SHANS	LEAPT	CLARO
URALS	TEAMS	GRAND	SHANT	NEAPS	CLARY
VIALS	TRAMP	GRANI	SLANG	OKAPI	CZARS
WEALD	TRAMS	GRANO	SLANT	REAPS	DEARS
WEALS	WHAMS	GRANT	SPANG	SCAPA	DEARY
WHALE	******	GUANA	SPANK	SCAPE	DIARY
WOALD	--AN-	GUANO	SPANS	SCAPI	DWARF
******	******	GUANS	STAND	SHAPE	ENARE
--AM-	AGANA	INANE	STANK	SLAPS	FEARS
******	ALAND	IVANS	STANS	SNAPS	FLARE
ADAMS	ALANS	JEANS	SWANK	SOAPS	GEARS
AGAMA					

GLARE	STARS	KVASS	ELATE	URATE	******
GLARY	START	LEASE	ENATE	WRATH	--AW-
GNARL	SWARD	LEASH	ERATO	WYATT	******
GUARD	SWARM	LEAST	FEATS	YEATS	BRAWL
HEARD	SWART	LHASA	FIATS	******	BRAWN
HEARS	TEARS	NYASA	FLATS	--AU-	CHAWS
HEART	TEARY	OMASA	FRATS	******	CLAWS
HOARD	TIARA	PEASE	GHATS	BEAUS	CRAWL
HOARY	TSARS	PHASE	GNATS	BEAUT	CRAWS
INARM	TZARS	PHASY	GOATS	BEAUX	DRAWL
KLARA	UNARM	PLASH	GRATE	FRAUD	DRAWN
KNARS	WEARS	PLASM	HEATH	GHAUT	DRAWS
LEARN	WEARY	PLAST	HEATS	GLAUC	FLAWS
LEARY	WHARF	PLASY	IRATE	KRAUT	FLAWY
LIARS	YEARN	PRASE	KEATS	LUAUS	GNAWN
NEARS	YEARS	QUASH	KYATS	MIAUL	GNAWS
OTARU	******	QUASI	LOATH	SCAUP	PRAWN
OVARY	--AS-	QUASS	MEATS	SHAUN	SHAWL
OZARK	******	ROAST	MEATY	UNAUS	SHAWM
PEARL	ABASE	SLASH	MOATS	WHAUP	SHAWN
PEARS	ABASH	SMASH	NEATH	******	SHAWS
PEARY	AMASS	SPASM	ORATE	--AV-	SLAWS
QUARK	AVAST	STASH	OVATE	******	SPAWN
QUART	AWASH	SWASH	PEATS	AGAVE	THAWS
REARM	BEAST	TEASE	PEATY	BRAVA	TRAWL
REARS	BLASE	TOAST	PLATA	BRAVE	******
ROARS	BLAST	TRASH	PLATE	BRAVO	--AX-
SCARE	BOAST	TRASS	PLATO	CRAVE	******
SCARF	BRASH	UKASE	PLATS	DRAVA	ATAXY
SCARP	BRASS	YEAST	PLATY	DRAVE	BRAXY
SCARS	CEASE	******	PRATE	GRAVE	FLAXY
SCARY	CHASE	--AT-	RIATA	GRAVY	******
SEARS	CHASM	******	SCATO	GUAVA	--AY-
SHARD	CLASH	ABATE	SCATS	HEAVE	******
SHARE	CLASP	AGATE	SEATO	HEAVY	BRAYS
SHARI	CLASS	ALATE	SEATS	KNAVE	CLAYS
SHARK	COAST	AMATE	SKATE	LEAVE	DRAYS
SHARP	CRASH	AMATI	SLATE	LEAVY	FLAYS
SMART	CRASS	BEATA	SLATS	OLAVS	FRAYS
SNARE	ERASE	BEATS	SLATY	PEAVY	GRAYS
SNARK	FEASE	BLATS	SNATH	PIAVE	OKAYS
SNARL	FEAST	BOATS	SPATE	SHAVE	PLAYA
SOARS	FLASH	BRATS	SPATS	SLAVE	PLAYS
SPARE	FLASK	CHATS	STATE	SLAVO	PRAYS
SPARK	GLASS	COATI	STATO	SLAVS	QUAYS
SPARS	GNASH	COATS	SWATH	STAVE	SHAYS
STARE	GRASP	CRATE	SWATS	SUAVE	SLAYS
STARK	GRASS	DEATH	TEATS	TRAVE	SPAYS
				WEAVE	

STAYS	UNBAR	IMBED	AMBIT	CABOB	DEBUG
SWAYS	URBAN	JABEZ	CABIN	CABOT	DEBUT
TRAYS	******	JIBED	COBIA	CIBOL	EMBUS
XRAYS	--BB-	JIBES	CUBIC	ELBOW	GIBUS
******	******	JUBES	CUBIT	EMBOW	HABUS
--AZ-	BIBBS	KIBEI	DEBIT	GABON	IMBUE
******	BOBBY	KIBES	DOBIE	GABOR	KABUL
AGAZE	CABBY	LABEL	HABIT	GOBOS	REBUS
AMAZE	COBBS	LIBEL	LABIA	HOBOS	REBUT
BLAZE	CUBBY	LIBER	LABIO	JABOT	SEBUM
BRAZA	DEBBY	LOBED	NUBIA	KABOB	ZEBUS
BRAZE	DOBBY	LOBES	ORBIT	LABOR	******
CRAZE	GABBY	MABEL	PUBIC	LOBOS	--BY-
CRAZY	HOBBS	NOBEL	PUBIS	NABOB	******
DIAZO	HOBBY	OMBER	RABIC	OXBOW	ABBYS
GHAZI	HUBBY	ORBED	RABID	ROBOT	GABYS
GLAZE	LIBBY	PUBES	REBID	SABOT	GOBYS
GLAZY	LOBBY	REBEC	ROBIN	TABOO	LIBYA
GRAZE	NOBBY	REBEL	SABIN	TABOR	RUBYS
PLAZA	NUBBY	ROBED	SYBIL	TOBOL	SIBYL
SMAZE	RABBI	ROBES	TABID	UMBOS	TOBYS
******	TABBY	RUBES	TIBIA	UPBOW	******
--BA-	TUBBY	SABED	******	******	--CA-
******	WEBBY	SABER	--BL-	--BR-	******
ABBAS	******	SABES	******	******	ALCAN
ALBAN	--BE-	SOBER	AMBLE	AMBRY	ASCAP
ALBAS	******	TABES	BIBLE	COBRA	CACAO
BABAR	ABBES	TEBET	CABLE	DOBRA	CECAL
BABAS	ABBEY	TIBER	COBLE	EMBRY	COCAS
BUBAL	ALBEE	TIBET	DOBLA	FEBRI	CYCAD
CABAL	AMBER	TUBED	FABLE	FIBRE	DECAL
CUBAN	BABEL	TUBER	GABLE	FIBRO	DECAY
DEBAG	BABER	TUBES	NOBLE	LABRA	DUCAL
DEBAR	BABES	UMBEL	NOBLY	LIBRA	DUCAT
DUBAI	BUBER	UMBER	PABLO	OMBRE	FECAL
EMBAR	CABER	VIBES	ROBLE	OMBRO	FOCAL
EMBAY	CUBEB	WEBER	RUBLE	SABRA	INCAN
ISBAS	CUBED	XEBEC	SABLE	SABRE	INCAS
JUBAS	CUBES	ZEBEC	TABLE	UMBRA	LOCAL
KUBAN	EBBED	ZIBET	UMBLE	ZEBRA	MACAO
LOBAR	EMBED	******	******	******	MACAW
RABAT	EMBER	--BH-	--BO-	--BT-	MICAH
SABAH	FIBER	******	******	******	MICAS
SEBAT	GABES	DUBHE	ABBOT	DEBTS	OSCAN
SUBAH	GIBED	******	AMBOS	******	OSCAR
TABAC	GIBER	--BI-	ARBOR	--BU-	PACAS
TUBAL	GIBES	******	BABOO	******	PECAN
TUBAS	GYBED	ABBIE	BEBOP	ALBUM	PICAL
		ALBIN		BABUL	

PICAS	RACER	LICIT	NOCKS	DECOR	CECUM
RECAP	RACES	LUCIA	PACKS	DECOY	FOCUS
TICAL	RICED	LUCID	PECKS	JACOB	FUCUS
UNCAP	RICER	MUCID	PICKS	LOCOS	HOCUS
VICAR	RICES	MUCIN	POCKS	MACON	INCUR
VOCAL	SICES	ORCIN	POCKY	MCCOY	INCUS
******	SYCEE	RICIN	PUCKA	PECOS	LOCUM
--CC-	SYCES	SOCIO	PUCKS	PICOT	LOCUS
******	TACET	TACIT	RACKS	******	MUCUS
BACCI	ULCER	******	RICKS	--CR-	OCCUR
COCCI	VICES	--CK-	RICKY	******	ORCUS
DACCA	VOCES	******	ROCKS	ACCRA	PICUL
LUCCA	******	BACKS	ROCKY	DECRY	RECUR
MECCA	--CH-	BECKS	RUCKS	LUCRE	UNCUT
SECCO	******	BECKY	SACKS	MACRO	VACUA
YUCCA	ARCHI	BUCKO	SICKS	MICRA	◆******
******	ARCHY	BUCKS	SOCKS	MICRO	--CY-
--CE-	BACHE	COCKS	SUCKS	MUCRO	******
******	BOCHE	COCKY	TACKS	NACRE	ENCYC
ACCEL	CACHE	DECKS	TACKY	NECRO	LUCYS
ARCED	DACHA	DICKS	TICKS	PICRO	******
BICES	DICHO	DICKY	TUCKS	SACRA	--CZ-
DACES	DUCHY	DOCKS	VICKS	SACRO	******
DICED	FICHE	DUCKS	VICKY	SUCRE	ORCZY
DICER	FICHU	DUCKY	WACKE	******	******
DICEY	ITCHY	GECKO	WACKS	--CT-	--DA-
EMCEE	LICHT	GECKS	WACKY	******	******
EXCEL	LOCHS	HACKS	WICKS	CACTI	ADDAX
FACED	MACHY	HICKS	******	DICTA	AIDAS
FACER	MOCHA	HOCKS	--CL-	DUCTS	ALDAN
FACES	NICHE	JACKS	******	FACTS	AUDAD
FACET	NUCHA	JACKY	CYCLE	HECTO	CEDAR
FECES	ORCHI	JOCKO	CYCLO	LACTO	CIDAL
FICES	PACHY	KECKS	MACLE	NOCTI	CODAS
LACED	RUCHE	KICKS	SOCLE	NYCTI	DEDAL
LACES	TACHY	LACKS	UNCLE	NYCTO	EDDAS
LUCES	TYCHE	LICKS	******	PACTS	JUDAH
LYCEA	VICHY	LOCKE	--CN-	PICTS	JUDAS
LYCEE	YACHT	LOCKS	******	RECTA	KEDAH
MACED	******	LUCKY	TACNA	RECTI	KODAK
MACER	--CI-	MACKS	******	RECTO	MADAM
MACES	******	MICKY	--CO-	SECTS	MEDAL
NICER	AECIA	MOCKS	******	******	MIDAS
PACED	CECIL	MUCKS	ANCON	--CU-	MODAL
PACER	DACIA	MUCKY	ASCOT	******	NADAB
PACES	DECIM	NECKS	BACON	ARCUS	NODAL
PUCES	FACIA	NICKS	COCOA	ASCUS	PEDAL
RACED	FECIT	NICKY	COCOS	BACUP	RADAR

REDAN	ANDES	NIDED	LEDGE	RADIO	RADON
SEDAN	ARDEB	NIDES	LODGE	RADIX	SIDON
SODAS	ARDEN	NODES	MADGE	REDID	SODOM
SUDAN	AUDEN	NUDES	MIDGE	RODIN	SUDOR
TIDAL	BADEN	ODDER	NUDGE	SADIE	TODOS
TODAY	BEDEW	OGDEN	PODGY	UNDID	TUDOR
VIDAL	BIDED	OIDEA	PUDGY	VEDIC	WIDOW
WODAN	BIDES	OLDEN	RIDGE	******	******
******	BIDET	OLDER	RIDGY	**--DJ--**	**--DR--**
--DD--	BODED	ORDER	SEDGE	******	******
******	BODES	PEDES	SEDGY	HADJI	ANDRE
BIDDY	CADES	RIDER	WEDGE	******	ANDRO
BUDDY	CADET	RIDES	WEDGY	**--DK--**	CADRE
CADDO	CEDED	RODEO	******	******	HYDRA
CADDY	CEDES	RUDER	**--DH--**	VODKA	HYDRO
CUDDY •	CIDER	SEDER	******	******	INDRA
DADDY	CODED	SIDED	SADHU	**--DL--**	INDRI
FADDY	CODER	SIDER	YODHS	******	PADRE
GIDDY	CODES	SIDES	******	ADDLE	PEDRO
HEDDA	CODEX	TIDED	**--DI--**	BADLY	******
JIDDA	DODEC	TIDES	******	GODLY	**--DS--**
KIDDY	DUDES	UDDER	ADDIE	LADLE	******
LADDY	EIDER	UNDEE	ALDIS	MADLY	DIDST
LYDDA	ELDER	UNDER	AUDIE	ODDLY	MIDST
MIDDY	EMDEN	VIDEO	AUDIO	REDLY	PUDSY
MUDDY	ENDED	WADED	AUDIT	SADLY	SUDSY
NEDDY	FADED	WADER	AYDIN	SIDLE	******
NODDY	FADES	WADES	BEDIM	******	**--DT--**
PADDY	FIDEL	WIDEN	CADIS	**--DN--**	******
RODDY	HADED	WIDER	CADIZ	******	HIDTO
RUDDS	HADES	WODEN	EADIE	DIDNT	WIDTH
RUDDY	HIDER	YODEL	EDDIC	HADNT	******
TEDDY	HIDES	******	EDDIE	PYDNA	**--DU--**
TODDS	INDEX	**--DG--**	EYDIE	******	******
TODDY	JADED	******	GADID	**--DO--**	ALDUS
WADDY	JADES	BADGE	INDIA	******	ENDUE
WIDDY	JUDEA	BLDGS	INDIC	ALDOL	INDUE
******	JUDEO	BUDGE	IODIC	ALDOS	INDUS
--DE--	JUDES	BUDGY	KADIS	ARDOR	KUDUS
******	LADED	CADGE	LADIN	DIDOS	MODUS
ADDED	LADEN	DODGE	LYDIA	DODOS	NIDUS
ADDER	LADES	DODGY	MEDIA	ENDOW	NODUS
AEDES	LODEN	FUDGE	MEDIC	FEDOR	PADUA
AIDED	LODES	HEDGE	MEDIO	INDOW	SEDUM
AIDER	MEDEA	HEDGY	NADIR	IODOL	UNDUE
AIDES	MODEL	HODGE	PODIA	KUDOS	VADUZ
ALDEN	MODES	JUDGE	PUDIC	MADOC	******
ALDER	NADER	KEDGE	RADII	MEDOC	**--DY--**
					******
					ADDYS
					ANDYS

JUDYS	OREAD	ARECA	******	SLEET	******
RUDYS	PAEAN	BEECH	--EE-	SNEER	--EI-
******	PLEAD	CHECK	******	SPEED	******
--EA-	PLEAS	CRECY	ADEEM	STEED	AREIC
******	PLEAT	CZECH	AMEER	STEEL	LIEIN
ABEAM	QUEAN	EJECT	BLEED	STEEN	OLEIC
ACEAE	RHEAS	ELECT	BLEEP	STEEP	OLEIN
ACEAN	SHEAF	ERECT	BREED	STEER	ONEIR
AHEAD	SHEAR	EXECS	CHEEK	SWEEP	SHEIK
ANEAR	SHEAS	FLECK	CHEEP	SWEET	SKEIN
APEAK	SKEAN	GRECO	CHEER	TREED	STEIN
AREAE	SLEAT	LEECH	CLEEK	TREES	THEIR
AREAL	SMEAR	NIECE	CREED	TWEED	TIEIN
AREAS	SNEAD	PIECE	CREEK	TWEEN	TOEIN
BLEAK	SNEAK	SPECK	CREEL	TWEET	******
BLEAR	SPEAK	SPECS	CREEP	TYEES	--EK-
BLEAT	SPEAR	THECA	CREES	WHEEL	******
BREAD	STEAD	VNECK	EMEER	******	GEEKS
BREAK	STEAK	WRECK	EPEES	--EF-	LEEKS
BREAM	STEAL	******	FLEER	******	PEEKS
CHEAP	STEAM	--ED-	FLEES	ALEFS	REEKS
CHEAT	SWEAR	******	FLEET	BEEFS	REEKY
CLEAN	SWEAT	BREDA	FREED	BEEFY	SEEKS
CLEAR	TREAD	COEDS	FREER	CHEFS	TREKS
CLEAT	TREAS	CREDO	FREES	CLEFS	WEEKS
CREAK	TREAT	DEEDS	GLEES	CLEFT	******
CREAM	TWEAK	FEEDS	GLEET	FIEFS	--EL-
DREAD	UREAL	FREDA	GREED	KEEFS	******
DREAM	UVEAL	FREDS	GREEK	REEFS	ABELE
DREAR	UVEAS	GLEDE	GREEN	REEFY	ABELS
EGEAN	WHEAL	GLEDS	GREER	THEFT	ADELA
ENEAS	WHEAT	HEEDS	GREET	******	ADELE
FLEAM	WREAK	LEEDS	KNEED	--EG-	ANELE
FLEAS	******	NEEDS	KNEEL	******	CHELA
FREAK	--EB-	NEEDY	KNEES	DIEGO	COELE
GLEAM	******	PAEDO	OGEES	DREGS	COELO
GLEAN	AMEBA	REEDS	PREEN	ELEGY	DUELS
GREAT	BEEBE	REEDY	QUEEN	GREGO	DWELL
HBEAM	BLEBS	SEEDS	QUEER	GREGS	DWELT
IBEAM	GLEBE	SEEDY	SHEEN	LIEGE	FEELS
IDEAL	GREBE	SHEDS	SHEEP	OMEGA	FIELD
IDEAS	PHEBE	SLEDS	SHEER	ONEGA	FJELD
ILEAC	PLEBE	SUEDE	SHEET	PLEGY	FUELS
ILEAL	PLEBS	SWEDE	SKEED	SIEGE	GAELS
KNEAD	SHEBA	THEDA	SKEES	SKEGS	HEELS
OBEAH	******	UREDO	SKEET	******	JOELS
OCEAN	--EC-	WEEDS	SLEEK	--EH-	KEELS
OLEAN	ALECK	WEEDY	SLEEP	******	KEELS
	ALECS			FOEHN	KNELL

KNELT	AGENT	TEENY	BIERS	VEERY	DUETS
KOELS	AKENE	TREND	BOERS	WHERE	FRETS
MYELO	AMEND	TRENT	CHERT	YSERE	GRETA
NOELS	AMENS	ULENT	CLERK	******	HYETO
OBELI	AMENT	UPEND	DOERS	--ES-	LEETS
PEELS	ANENT	WEENY	EMERY	******	MEETS
PYELO	ARENA	WHENS	EVERT	BLESS	ODETS
QUELL	ARENT	WRENS	EVERY	BLEST	PIETA
REELS	AVENS	******	EWERS	BREST	PIETY
SHELF	BLEND	--EO-	EXERT	CHESS	POETS
SHELL	BLENT	******	FIERY	CHEST	STETH
SMELL	BRENT	CLEON	FRERE	CRESC	STETS
SMELT	COENO	CREON	GOERS	CRESS	SUETY
SNELL	CTENO	FREON	HIERO	CREST	TEETH
SPELL	DIENE	ODEON	HOERS	DOEST	THETA
SPELT	ELENA	PAEON	INERT	DREST	WHETS
STELE	EMEND	SHEOL	ISERE	DRESS	******
SWELL	EVENS	******	JEERS	EGEST	--EU-
TAELS	EVENT	--EP-	KIERS	FLESH	******
WHELK	FIEND	******	LEERS	FRESH	ALEUT
WHELM	FRENA	ADEPT	LEERY	GEESE	EMEUS
WHELP	GHENT	ALEPH	OMERS	GEEST	FREUD
WIELD	GLENN	BEEPS	ONERY	GUESS	ILEUM
YIELD	GLENS	CREPE	OPERA	GUEST	ILEUS
******	GWENN	CREPT	OTERO	IDEST	LIEUT
--EM-	GWENS	DEEPS	OVERT	LOESS	ODEUM
******	HYENA	INEPT	OYERS	OBESE	PNEUM
ANEMO	IRENE	JEEPS	PEERS	POESY	PSEUD
CHEMI	KEENS	KEEPS	PIERS	PRESA	QUEUE
CHEMO	LIENS	PEEPS	PTERO	PRESS	RHEUM
CLEMS	MIENS	SEEPS	QUERN	PREST	SIEUR
CREME	OLENT	SKEPS	QUERY	QUEST	TIEUP
DEEMS	OMENS	SLEPT	RUERS	THESE	******
EDEMA	OPENS	STEPS	SEERS	TRESS	--EV-
ELEMI	OVENS	SWEPT	SHERD	WEEST	******
ENEMA	OWENS	WEEPS	SPERM	WREST	BREVE
ENEMY	PEENS	WEEPY	STERE	******	BREVI
ITEMS	PHENO	******	STERN	--ET-	CHEVY
POEMS	PLENA	--ER-	SUERS	******	KEEVE
SEEMS	SCENA	******	THERE	ABETS	PEEVE
STEMS	SCEND	ACERB	THERM	ACETO	REEVE
TEEMS	SCENE	ALERT	TIERS	ARETE	SIEVE
THEME	SCENT	APERY	TWERE	BEETS	STEVE
ULEMA	SIENA	AVERS	TWERP	CHETH	******
WEEMS	SPEND	AVERT	USERS	CHETS	--EW-
******	SPENT	AVERY	UTERI	CRETE	******
--EN-	STENO	BEERS	UTERO	DIETS	BMEWS
******	TEENS	BEERY	VEERS	DOETH	BREWS
ADENI					
ADENO					

CHEWS	FIFED	BEFIT	LOFTY	REGAN	MAGES
CHEWY	FIFER	BIFID	MUFTI	RUGAE	NEGEB
CLEWS	FIFES	DEFIS	NIFTY	SAGAN	NEGEV
CREWE	GOFER	EFFIE	RAFTS	SAGAS	NIGEL
CREWS	INFER	ELFIN	RIFTS	SUGAR	NIGER
DREWS	JEFES	HAFIZ	SIFTS	TOGAE	PAGED
FLEWS	LIFER	HIFIS	SOFTA	TOGAS	PAGER
SHEWN	OFFER	INFIX	SOFTY	WIGAN	PAGES
SHEWS	REFER	KAFIR	TOFTS	YUGAS	POGEY
SKEWS	SAFER	MAFIA	TUFTS	******	PUGET
SLEWS	SAFES	REFIT	TUFTY	--GB-	RAGED
SMEWS	WAFER	SOFIA	WAFTS	******	RAGEE
SPEWS	******	SUFIC	WEFTS	RUGBY	RAGES
STEWS	--FF-	SUFIS	******	******	REGES
THEWS	******	TAFIA	--FU-	--GD-	RIGEL
THEWY	BAFFS	UNFIT	******	******	ROGER
TREWS	BAFFY	UNFIX	AWFUL	MAGDA	SAGER
VIEWS	BIFFS	******	RUFUS	******	SAGES
VIEWY	BIFFY	--FK-	******	--GE-	TIGER
******	BUFFI	******	--GA-	******	URGED
--EX-	BUFFO	KAFKA	******	AGGER	URGES
******	BUFFS	******	ALGAE	ALGER	WAGED
ALEXA	BUFFY	--FL-	ALGAL	ANGEL	WAGER
FLEXI	CUFFS	******	ARGAL	ANGER	WAGES
PREXY	DAFFY	RIFLE	BEGAD	AUGER	YAGER
******	DOFFS	******	BEGAN	BAGEL	YOGEE
--EY-	DUFFS	--FO-	BEGAT	BEGET	******
******	GAFFE	******	BOGAN	BOGEY	--GG-
FREYA	GAFFS	BEFOG	CIGAR	CAGED	******
GREYS	HUFFS	DEFOE	DAGAN	CAGES	BAGGY
JOEYS	HUFFY	******	DEGAS	CAGEY	BOGGY
OBEYS	JAFFA	--FR-	EDGAR	DOGES	BUGGY
OXEYE	JEFFS	******	EGGAR	EAGER	DOGGY
PREYS	JIFFS	INFRA	ELGAR	EDGED	FOGGY
TREYS	JIFFY	KUFRA	FUGAL	EDGES	FUGGY
WHEYS	LUFFS	******	GIGAS	EGGED	JAGGS
******	MIFFS	--FT-	HOGAN	EGGER	JAGGY
--EZ-	MIFFY	******	JUGAL	FOGEY	LEGGY
******	MUFFS	FIFTH	LAGAN	GAGED	MUGGY
FEEZE	PUFFS	FIFTY	LEGAL	GAGER	NOGGS
PIEZO	PUFFY	GIFTS	LIGAN	GAGES	PEGGY
******	RIFFS	HAFTS	LOGAN	HEGEL	PIGGY
--FA-	RUFFS	HEFTS	MEGAL	HUGER	RAGGY
******	TAFFY	HEFTY	MEGAN	LAGER	RIGGS
OFFAL	TIFFS	LEFTS	OLGAS	LEGER	SOGGY
SOFAS	******	LEFTY	ORGAN	LEGES	VUGGY
******	--FI-	LIFTS	PAGAN	LOGES	YEGGS
--FE-	******	LOFTS	REGAL	LUGER	
******	AFFIX				
CAFES	ALFIE				
DEFER					

******	YOGIN	GOGOL	VAGUE	******	******
--GH-	YOGIS	HUGOS	VAGUS	--HI-	--HU-
******	******	INGOT	VOGUE	******	******
AUGHT	--GL-	LAGOS	VOGUL	APHID	ASHUR
BIGHT	******	LOGOS	******	APHIS	JEHUS
EIGHT	ANGLE	MAGOG	--GY-	BAHIA	LEHUA
FIGHT	ANGLO	MAGOT	******	ECHIN	MOHUR
HIGHS	BIGLY	RIGOR	ALGYS	ETHIC	NAHUA
HUGHS	BOGLE	SAGOS	******	NIHIL	NAHUM
LIGHT	BUGLE	SEGOS	--HA-	OPHIO	******
MIGHT	EAGLE	VIGOR	******	SAHIB	--HV-
NIGHT	FUGLE	WAGON	AGHAS	SCHIZ	******
OUGHT	INGLE	******	BAHAI	******	YAHVE
RIGHT	******	--GR-	BEHAN	--HL-	******
SIGHS	--GM-	******	BIHAR	******	--HW-
SIGHT	******	ANGRY	COHAN	MUHLY	******
TIGHT	DOGMA	EAGRE	EPHAH	******	SCHWA
WIGHT	MAGMA	HYGRO	ETHAN	--HM-	******
YOGHS	PIGMY	NEGRO	HAHAS	******	--HY-
******	PYGMY	NIGRI	JIHAD	SCHMO	******
--GI-	REGMA	TIGRE	MAHAN	******	ETHYL
******	SIGMA	******	OGHAM	--HN-	******
AEGIR	******	--GS-	PSHAW	******	--IA-
AEGIS	--GN-	******	UNHAT	ETHNO	******
AGGIE	******	ANGST	******	JOHNS	ALIAS
ALGIA	LIGNI	******	--HD-	******	AMIAS
ALGID	LIGNO	--GU-	******	--HO-	APIAN
ALGIE	MAGNI	******	MAHDI	******	ARIAN
ALGIN	SEGNI	ALGUM	******	ABHOR	ARIAS
ANGIO	SEGNO	ANGUS	--HE-	ATHOS	ASIAN
ARGIL	SIGNE	ARGUE	******	BOHOL	AVIAN
BEGIN	SIGNS	ARGUS	ACHED	EPHOD	AXIAL
BOGIE	******	AUGUR	ACHES	EPHOR	BRIAN
DIGIT	--GO-	BEGUM	ASHEN	ETHOS	BRIAR
DOGIE	******	BEGUN	ASHER	ICHOR	CHIAN
ELGIN	ALGOL	BOGUS	ASHES	NAHOR	CHIAS
FUGIO	ALGOR	DEGUM	BOHEA	TAHOE	ELIAS
HAGIO	ARGOL	FUGUE	ESHER	WAHOO	FRIAR
LEGIT	ARGON	GIGUE	ETHEL	YAHOO	ICIAN
LOGIA	ARGOS	HAGUE	ETHER	******	ILIAC
LOGIC	ARGOT	KAGUS	OCHER	--HR-	ILIAD
MAGIC	BEGOT	LOGUE	OTHER	******	ILIAN
REGIN	BIGOT	MAGUS	RRHEA	LEHRS	IXIAS
RIGID	BOGOR	MOGUL	SAHEB	NEHRU	NAIAD
SIGIL	COGON	NEGUS	SPHEN	OCHRE	PHIAL
VAGIN	ERGOT	ROGUE	TEHEE	OCHRY	PRIAM
VIGIL	FAGOT	SAGUM	USHER	******	SHIAH
YOGIC	GIGOT	TOGUE	UTHER	--HT-	TRIAD
				******	
				BAHTS	

TRIAL	SPICA	******	SKIES	COIGN	ATILT
UMIAK	SPICE	--IE-	SLIER	DEIGN	AXILE
UNIAT	SPICY	******	SPIED	FEIGN	AXILS
URIAH	STICH	ABIEL	SPIEL	FRIGG	BAILS
XTIAN	STICK	ABIES	SPIER	HEIGH	BOILS
******	THICK	ADIEU	SPIES	INIGO	BRILL
--IB-	TRICE	ALIEN	STIED	LEIGH	BUILD
******	TRICH	AMIEL	STIES	LUIGI	BUILT
ABIBS	TRICK	AMIES	THIEF	NEIGH	CEILS
ALIBI	TWICE	ARIEL	TRIED	OLIGO	CHILD
BRIBE	URICO	ARIES	TRIER	PRIGS	CHILE
CEIBA	UTICA	BRIEF	TRIES	REIGN	CHILI
CHIBA	VOICE	BRIER	URIEL	SAIGA	CHILL
CRIBS	WHICH	CHIEF	WRIED	SLIGO	CHILO
DRIBS	WRICK	CRIED	WRIER	SWIGS	COILS
ORIBI	******	CRIER	WRIES	TAIGA	DAILY
TRIBE	--ID-	CRIES	******	THIGH	DOILY
******	******	DRIED	--IF-	TRIGO	DRILL
--IC-	ABIDE	DRIER	******	TRIGS	DRILY
******	ACIDS	DRIES	ALIFS	TWIGS	EDILE
ALICE	AMIDE	EDIES	CLIFF	WEIGH	EMILE
AMICE	AMIDO	ERIES	COIFS	WHIGS	EMILS
ARICA	ASIDE	FLIED	DEIFY	******	EMILY
BRICE	BRIDE	FLIER	DRIFT	--IH-	EVILS
BRICK	CHIDE	FLIES	EDIFY	******	EXILE
CHICK	ELIDE	FRIED	HAIFA	ELIHU	FAILS
CHICO	ENIDS	FRIER	KNIFE	******	FOILS
CLICK	GLIDE	FRIES	LEIFS	--IJ-	FRILL
CRICK	GRIDE	GRIEF	QUIFF	******	GAILS
DEICE	GRIDS	GRIEG	REIFY	OUIJA	GAILY
EDICT	GUIDE	ICIER	SCIFI	******	GRILL
EPICS	GUIDO	IVIED	SHIFT	--IK-	GUILD
ERICA	HAIDA	IVIES	SKIFF	******	GUILE
ERICH	IMIDE	OKIEH	SNIFF	ALIKE	GUILT
ERICS	IMIDO	OKIES	STIFF	ERIKA	HAILS
EVICT	IMIDS	ORIEL	SWIFT	ERIKS	ICILY
FLICK	IRIDO	OSIER	UNIFY	HAIKS	JAILS
HOICK	MAIDS	PLIED	WAIFS	HAIKU	LEILA
JUICE	OUIDA	PLIER	WHIFF	LAIKA	MAILS
JUICY	OXIDE	PLIES	******	SPIKE	MOILS
PLICA	PRIDE	PRIED	--IG-	SPIKY	NAILS
PRICE	QUIDS	PRIER	******	******	NEILS
PRICK	RAIDS	PRIES	ADIGE	--IL-	PAILS
QUICK	SKIDS	QUIET	ALIGN	******	PHILA
REICH	SLIDE	SHIED	AMIGO	AGILE	PHILE
SLICE	SNIDE	SHIER	BEIGE	ANILE	PHILO
SLICK	VOIDS	SKIED	BLIGH	ANILS	PHILS
SNICK		SKIER	BRIGS	ARILS	PHILY

POILU	GRIMY	CLING	PRINK	VYING	QUIPU
QUILL	MAIMS	CLINK	PRINT	WAINS	SHIPS
QUILT	OXIME	CLINO	QUINT	WHINE	SKIPS
RAILS	PRIMA	CLINT	RAINS	WHINS	SLIPS
ROILS	PRIME	COINS	RAINY	WHINY	SLIPT
ROILY	PRIMI	CUING	REINS	WRING	SNIPE
SAILS	PRIMO	DOING	RHINE	******	SNIPS
SHILL	PRIMP	DRINK	RHINO	--IO-	STIPE
SHILY	PRIMS	DYING	RUING	******	SWIPE
SKILL	REIMS	EDINA	RUINS	ADIOS	TRIPE
SLILY	SHIMS	EKING	SAINT	AGIOS	TRIPS
SMILE	SKIMO	EWING	SEINE	ANION	WHIPS
SOILS	SKIMP	EYING	SHINE	ARION	WHIPT
SPILE	SKIMS	FAINT	SHINS	ATION	******
SPILL	SLIME	FEINT	SHINY	AVION	--IR-
SPILT	SLIMS	FLING	SKINK	AXIOM	******
STILE	SLIMY	FLINT	SKINS	CHIOS	AFIRE
STILL	STIMY	GAINS	SLING	CLIOS	AMIRS
STILT	SWIMS	GIING	SLINK	ELIOT	BAIRD
SWILL	TRIMS	GLINT	SPINE	IDIOM	BAIRN
TAILS	WHIMS	GOING	SPINI	IDIOT	BEIRA
TOILE	******	GRIND	SPINS	ILION	CAIRD
TOILS	--IN-	GRINS	SPINY	INION	CAIRN
TRILL	******	HYING	STING	ITION	CAIRO
TWILL	ACING	ICING	STINK	IXION	CHIRM
UTILE	ACINI	IMINE	STINT	OLIOS	CHIRO
VEILS	AGING	IMINO	SUING	ONION	CHIRP
VOILA	ALINE	JAINA	SUINT	ORION	CHIRR
VOILE	AMINE	JAINS	SWINE	PRIOR	DAIRY
WAILS	AMINO	JOINS	SWING	SCION	EMIRS
WHILE	APING	JOINT	TAINO	THIOL	FAIRS
******	AWING	KOINE	TAINS	TRIOL	FAIRY
--IM-	AXING	LAINE	TAINT	TRIOS	FLIRT
******	AYINS	LOINS	THINE	UNION	HAIRS
ANIMA	AZINE	LYING	THING	******	HAIRY
ANIME	BEING	MAINE	THINK	--IP-	HEIRS
BLIMP	BLIND	MAINS	THINS	******	LAIRD
BRIMS	BLINK	MAINZ	TRINA	BLIPS	LAIRS
CHIME	BRINE	OKING	TRINE	CHIPS	LOIRE
CHIMP	BRING	OPINE	TWINE	CLIPS	MOIRA
CLIMB	BRINK	OVINE	TWINS	DRIPS	MOIRE
CLIME	BRINY	OWING	TYING	DRIPT	NAIRN
CRIME	CHINA	PAINE	UDINE	FLIPS	ONIRO
CRIMP	CHINE	PAINS	URINE	GRIPE	PAIRS
FRIML	CHINK	PAINT	URINO	GRIPS	QUIRE
GLIMS	CHINO	PLINY	USING	GRIPT	QUIRK
GRIME	CHINS	POIND	VEINS	PHIPS	QUIRT
GRIMM	CLINE	POINT	VEINY	QUIPS	SHIRE

SHIRK
SHIRR
SHIRT
SKIRL
SKIRR
SKIRT
SMIRK
SPIRE
SPIRO
SPIRT
SPIRY
STIRK
STIRP
STIRS
SWIRL
THIRD
TWIRL
TWIRP
VAIRS
WEIRD
WEIRS
WHIRL
WHIRR
WHIRS
ZAIRE
******
--IS-
******
AGIST
ALIST
AMISH
AMISS
ANISE
ANISO
APISH
ARISE
AVISO
BLISS
BOISE
BRISK
CRISP
CUISH
DAISY
DEISM
DEIST
ELISE
EXIST
FEIST
FOISM
FOIST
FRISE
FRISK
GRIST
GUISE
HEIST
HOIST
IRISH
JOIST
LUISA
LUISE
MOIST
NOISE
NOISY
PAISA
PAISE
POISE
PRISE
PRISM
RAISE
SEISE
SEISM
SWISH
SWISS
TOISE
TWIST
WAIST
WHISH
WHISK
WHIST
WRIST
******
--IT-
******
ACITY
ADITS
AMITY
ANITA
BAITS
BLITZ
CHITA
CHITS
DEITY
DOITS
EDITH
EDITS
ELITE
EMITS
EVITA
EXITS
FAITH
FLITE
FLITS
FRITH
FRITS
FRITZ
GAITS
GRITS
HAITI
KEITH
KNITS
LAITY
LEITH
OBITS
OMITS
OSITY
QUITE
QUITO
QUITS
SKITS
SLITS
SMITE
SMITH
SPITE
SPITS
SPITZ
SUITE
SUITS
TRITE
TWITS
UNITE
UNITS
UNITY
WAITS
WHITE
WHITS
WRITE
WRITS
******
--IU-
******
ARIUM
ARIUS
ILIUM
ODIUM
OPIUM
******
--IV-
******
ALIVE
ATIVE
CHIVE
CLIVE
DRIVE
NAIVE
OGIVE
OLIVE
PRIVY
SHIVE
SHIVS
SKIVE
WAIVE
******
--IX-
******
TRIXY
TWIXT
******
--IY-
******
ORIYA
******
--IZ-
******
BAIZE
ELIZA
FRIZZ
IBIZA
MAIZE
PRIZE
RHIZO
SEIZE
******
--JA-
******
HEJAZ
RAJAB
RAJAH
SOJAS
******
--JI-
******
FIJIS
MUJIK
******
--JO-
******
ANJOU
BIJOU
CAJON
DIJON
ENJOY
MAJOR
SAJOU
******
--JU-
******
CAJUN
JUJUS
******
--KA-
******
DAKAR
HOKAN
KAKAS
PEKAN
PIKAS
TOKAY
WEKAS
******
--KE-
******
AIKEN
ASKED
ASKER
ASKEW
BAKED
BAKER
BAKES
BIKES
CAKED
CAKES
COKED
COKER
COKES
COKEY
DEKED
DEKES
DIKED
DIKER
DIKES
DUKES
ESKER
FAKED
FAKER
FAKES
FYKES
HAKES
HIKED
HIKER
HIKES
INKED
INKER
IRKED
JAKES
JOKED
JOKER
JOKES
LAKED
LAKER
LAKES
LAKEY
LIKED
LIKEN
LIKES
MAKER
MAKES
MIKES
MIKEY
MOKES
NAKED
OAKEN
PIKED
PIKER
PIKES
POKED
POKER
POKES
POKEY
PUKED
PUKES
RAKED
RAKEE
RAKER
RAKES
SAKER
SAKES
SOKES
TAKEN
TAKER

TAKES	******	LILAS	MULCH	AXLES	MELEE
TEKEL	--KU-	LOLAS	MULCT	BALED	MILER
TOKEN	******	MALAC	SULCI	BALER	MILES
TYKES	ANKUS	MALAR	TALCS	BALES	MLLES
WAKED	HOKUM	MALAY	WELCH	BELEM	MOLES
WAKEN	OAKUM	MELAN	******	BILES	MULES
WAKES	******	MILAN	--LD-	BOLES	MULEY
WOKEN	--KY-	MOLAL	******	CALEB	MYLES
YOKED	******	MOLAR	BALDR	COLES	OGLED
YOKEL	ALKYL	OLLAS	COLDS	CULET	OGLER
YOKES	TOKYO	PALAE	DILDO	CULEX	OGLES
ZEKES	******	PILAF	FOLDS	DALER	OILED
******	--LA-	PILAR	GELDS	DALES	OILER
--KH-	******	POLAR	GILDA	DELED	ORLES
******	ADLAI	RELAX	GILDS	DELES	OSLER
ANKHS	ALLAH	RELAY	GOLDA	DOLED	OWLET
SIKHS	ALLAN	SALAD	GOLDS	DOLES	PALEA
******	ALLAY	SELAH	HILDA	ELLEN	PALED
--KI-	ANLAS	SILAS	HOLDS	EULER	PALEO
******	ATLAS	SOLAN	HULDA	FILED	PALER
FAKIR	BALAS	SOLAR	MELDS	FILER	PALES
HAKIM	BELAY	SPLAT	MOLDS	FILES	PALEY
KAKIS	BOLAR	SPLAY	MOLDY	FILET	PELEE
PEKIN	BOLAS	TELAE	SOLDI	GALEA	PELEG
TIKIS	BYLAW	TOLAN	SOLDO	GALEN	PHLEB
******	COLAS	TOLAS	TILDA	GALES	PILEA
--KK-	DALAI	UHLAN	TILDE	GILES	PILED
******	DELAY	UNLAY	VELDS	GOLEM	PILEI
PUKKA	DYLAN	VELAR	VELDT	GULES	PILES
******	ECLAT	VOLAR	WALDO	HALED	POLED
--KL-	ELLAS	XYLAN	WELDS	HALER	POLES
******	ERLAU	******	WILDE	HALES	PULED
ANKLE	FILAR	--LB-	WILDS	HELEN	PULER
HEKLA	GALAS	******	WOLDS	HOLED	PULES
INKLE	GALAX	BILBO	******	HOLES	RALES
******	GULAR	BULBS	--LE-	HOLEY	RILED
--KO-	HULAS	******	******	IDLED	RILES
******	HYLAS	--LC-	ABLER	IDLER	RILEY
BIKOL	INLAW	******	ADLER	IDLES	ROLES
JAKOB	INLAY	BELCH	AGLEE	INLET	RULED
PEKOE	ISLAM	CALCI	AGLET	ISLED	RULER
YUKON	ISLAY	CULCH	AGLEY	ISLES	RULES
******	JALAP	DOLCE	AILED	ISLET	SALEM
--KR-	KALAT	DULCE	ALLEN	JOLES	SALEP
******	KILAH	DULCY	ALLEY	JULEP	SALES
KUKRI	KOLAS	FILCH	ARLEN	JULES	SELEN
******	KULAK	GULCH	ARLES	LYLES	SILEX
--KT-	LILAC	MILCH	AXLED	MALES	SOLED
******					
HEKTO					

SOLES	******	POLIO	BULLY	LILLI	WILLS
SPLEN	--LH-	RELIC	CALLA	LILLY	WILLY
TALER	******	SALIC	CALLI	LOLLS	YELLS
TALES	DELHI	SALIX	CALLS	LOLLY	******
TELEG	******	SILIC	CELLA	LULLS	--LM-
TELEO	--LI-	SOLID	CELLO	MALLS	******
TELEX	******	SPLIT	CELLS	MILLI	BALMS
TILED	AALII	TELIC	COLLY	MILLS	BALMY
TILER	ADLIB	TULIP	CULLS	MILLY	CALMS
TILES	ALLIE	UNLIT	DALLY	MOLLS	CULMS
TOLES	ALLIN	VALID	DELLA	MOLLY	FILMS
TULES	ALLIS	******	DELLS	MULLS	FILMY
TYLER	AULIC	--LK-	DOLLS	NELLS	HALMA
VALES	AULIS	******	DOLLY	NELLY	HELMS
VALET	BELIE	BALKS	DULLS	PALLS	HOLMS
VILER	CALIF	BALKY	DULLY	PALLY	MALMO
VOLES	CALIX	BILKS	FALLS	PELLA	PALMA
WALED	CELIA	BULKS	FELLS	PELLY	PALMI
WALER	CELIE	BULKY	FELLY	PILLS	PALMS
WALES	CILIA	CALKS	FILLS	POLLS	PALMY
WILED	COLIC	FOLKS	FILLY	POLLY	PULMO
WILES	COLIN	HULKS	FOLLY	PULLS	SALMA
WILEY	CYLIX	HULKY	FULLS	RALLY	SALMI
XYLEM	DELIA	MILKS	FULLY	RILLE	SELMA
YULES	DULIA	MILKY	GALLS	RILLS	WILMA
******	ELLIE	POLKA	GILLS	ROLLO	******
--LF-	ELLIS	SILKS	GOLLY	ROLLS	--LN-
******	EOLIC	SILKY	GULLS	SALLY	******
DELFT	FELID	SULKS	GULLY	SELLS	COLNE
GOLFS	FELIX	SULKY	HALLE	SILLS	KILNS
GULFS	FOLIA	TALKS	HALLO	SILLY	MILNE
PELFS	FOLIC	WALKS	HALLS	SULLY	VILNA
ROLFE	FOLIO	YELKS	HELLE	TALLY	******
ROLFS	GELID	YOLKS	HELLO	TELLS	--LO-
SOLFA	HALID	YOLKY	HELLS	TELLY	******
SULFA	HELIC	******	HILLS	TILLS	AGLOW
SULFO	HELIO	--LL-	HILLY	TILLY	ALLOT
WOLFS	HELIX	******	HOLLY	TOLLS	ALLOW
******	JULIA	BALLS	HULLS	TULLE	ALLOY
--LG-	JULIE	BELLA	JELLO	TULLY	BELOW
******	JULIO	BELLE	JELLS	VILLA	BOLOS
BELGA	KYLIX	BELLS	JELLY	VILLE	CELOM
BILGE	MALIC	BELLY	JILLS	VILLI	CHLOE
BILGY	MELIC	BILLS	JOLLY	VILLS	CHLOR
BULGE	MILIA	BILLY	KELLY	WALLA	COLON
BULGY	OLLIE	BOLLS	KILLS	WALLY	COLOR
HELGA	OXLIP	BULLA	LALLS	WELLS	DELOS
VOLGA	PILIS	BULLS	LILLE	WILLA	DOLOR

FELON	KELSO	VOLTS	******	UXMAL	CAMES
GALOP	PALSY	WALTS	--LZ-	WOMAN	CIMEX
HALOS	PULSE	WALTZ	******	******	COMER
HELOT	SALSA	WELTS	COLZA	--MB-	COMES
IGLOO	SALSE	WILTS	******	******	COMET
KILOS	TULSA	YALTA	--MA-	BAMBI	CYMES
MELON	WELSH	******	******	BOMBE	DAMES
MELOS	******	--LU-	ADMAN	BOMBS	DEMES
NYLON	--LT-	******	ALMAH	COMBO	DIMER
ORLON	******	BOLUS	ALMAS	COMBS	DIMES
ORLOP	BALTS	EOLUS	AMMAN	GAMBS	DOMED
PELON	BELTS	FILUM	ATMAN	GUMBO	DOMES
PHLOX	BOLTS	HILUM	AXMAN	IAMBI	EIMER
PILOT	CELTS	ILLUS	COMAE	IAMBS	ELMER
PYLON	COLTS	LULUS	COMAL	JAMBS	EMMER
SALOL	CULTI	SALUS	COMAS	JUMBO	EMMET
SALON	CULTS	SOLUS	CYMAE	LAMBS	FAMED
SILOS	DELTA	SULUS	CYMAR	LIMBI	FEMES
SOLON	DOLTS	TALUK	DAMAN	LIMBO	FUMED
SOLOS	FELTS	TALUS	DUMAS	LIMBS	FUMES
TALON	FILTH	VALUE	ELMAN	MAMBA	GAMED
TALOS	HALTS	VELUM	EMMAS	MAMBO	GAMES
VALOR	HILTS	******	ERMAS	NIMBI	GIMEL
XYLOL	JILTS	--LV-	HAMAL	NUMBS	HAMER
******	JOLTS	******	HEMAL	RUMBA	HAMES
--LP-	JOLTY	CALVE	HEMAN	SAMBA	HEMEN
******	KILTS	DELVE	HEMAT	SAMBO	HOMED
CALPE	KILTY	HALVE	HUMAN	TOMBS	HOMEO
CULPA	LILTS	HELVE	IRMAS	WOMBS	HOMER
DOLPH	MALTA	PELVI	LAMAS	WOMBY	HOMES
GULPS	MALTS	SALVE	LYMAN	ZOMBI	HOMEY
HELPS	MALTY	SALVO	MAMAS	******	HYMEN
KELPS	MELTS	SILVA	NEMAT	--MD-	ILMEN
PALPI	MILTS	SOLVE	NOMAD	******	JAMES
PULPS	MILTY	SYLVA	NOMAS	COMDR	KAMES
PULPY	MOLTO	VALVE	OSMAN	COMDT	KAMET
RALPH	MOLTS	VOLVA	PIMAN	******	KHMER
ROLPH	MULTI	VULVA	PIMAS	--ME-	LAMED
SALPA	PELTS	******	PUMAS	******	LAMER
SYLPH	SALTS	--LY-	REMAN	ADMEN	LAMES
YELPS	SALTY	******	ROMAN	ADMEX	LIMED
******	SILTS	ALLYL	SAMAR	AIMED	LIMEN
--LS-	SILTY	CALYX	SIMAR	AIMEE	LIMES
******	TILTH	DILYS	SOMAT	ARMED	LIMEY
BALSA	TILTS	JULYS	SUMAC	ARMET	LUMEN
DULSE	VOLTA	LILYS	TOMAN	AXMEN	MAMEY
FALSE	VOLTE	POLYP	TOMAS	CAMEL	MIMED
HOLST	VOLTI	TOLYL	UNMAN	CAMEO	MIMEO

MIMER	GAMIN	LEMMA	CAMPI	******	IGNAZ
MIMES	HEMIA	MAMMA	CAMPO	--MU-	JONAH
NAMED	HEMIC	MAMMY	CAMPS	******	JONAS
NAMER	HEMIN	MUMMS	CAMPY	ALMUD	LANAI
NAMES	HUMIC	MUMMY	COMPO	ALMUG	LENAS
NIMES	HUMID	POMMY	DAMPS	CAMUS	LUNAR
NUMEN	IMMIX	RAMMY	DUMPS	COMUS	MENAI
ORMER	JAMIE	RUMMY	DUMPY	DEMUR	MINAE
POMES	KAMIK	SAMMY	GAMPS	FEMUR	MINAS
REMEX	KUMIS	SOMME	GIMPS	GAMUT	MONAD
RIMED	LAMIA	TAMMY	GIMPY	HUMUS	MONAS
RIMER	LIMIT	TIMMY	HEMPS	LEMUR	MYNAS
RIMES	MAMIE	TOMMY	HEMPY	MOMUS	NANAS
ROMEO	MIMIC	TUMMY	HUMPH	NAMUR	NINAS
RUMEN	MIMIR	YUMMY	HUMPS	RAMUS	NONAS
SAMEK	MIMIS	******	HUMPY	REMUS	PANAY
SEMEN	OGMIC	--MN-	JUMPS	WAMUS	PENAL
SUMER	OHMIC	******	JUMPY	YAMUN	PINAS
TAMED	OSMIC	DAMNS	LAMPS	******	PUNAS
TAMER	RAMIE	GYMNO	LIMPS	--MY-	RENAL
TAMES	REMIT	HYMNS	LUMPS	******	RENAN
TIMED	TAMIL	JUMNA	LUMPY	EMMYS	SINAI
TIMER	TAMIS	LIMNS	LYMPH	******	SONAR
TIMES	TIMID	SOMNI	MUMPS	--MZ-	TINAS
TOMES	TUMID	******	NYMPH	******	TONAL
UNMEW	VOMIT	--MO-	OOMPH	HAMZA	TUNAS
VIMEN	ZAMIA	******	PIMPS	******	ULNAE
VOMER	******	AMMON	PUMPS	--NA-	ULNAR
WOMEN	--ML-	ARMOR	RAMPS	******	ULNAS
YAMEN	******	DAMON	ROMPS	ANNAL	VENAE
YEMEN	DIMLY	DEMOB	RUMPS	ANNAM	VENAL
******	RUMLY	DEMON	SIMPS	ANNAS	VINAS
--MF-	******	DEMOS	SUMPS	BANAL	ZONAL
******	--MM-	EAMON	TAMPA	BANAT	******
COMFY	******	GEMOT	TAMPS	BINAL	--NC-
******	COMMA	HUMOR	TEMPE	CANAD	******
--MI-	DUMMY	KOMOS	TEMPI	CANAL	BENCH
******	FEMME	LEMON	TEMPO	DANAE	BUNCH
ADMIN	GAMMA	MEMOS	TEMPT	DINAH	BUNCO
ADMIT	GAMMY	RUMOR	VAMPS	DINAR	CINCH
ADMIX	GEMMA	SAMOA	******	DONAR	CONCH
AEMIA	GEMMY	SAMOS	--MR-	DONAS	DANCE
COMIC	GUMMA	SIMON	******	EDNAS	DUNCE
CUMIN	GUMMY	TIMOR	CYMRI	ETNAS	FANCY
DEMIT	HAMMY	TUMOR	CYMRY	FINAL	FENCE
DOMIC	JAMMY	******	ZIMRI	GONAD	FINCH
EMMIE	JEMMY	--MP-	******	HONAN	HANCE
GAMIC	JIMMY	******	--MT-	HUNAN	HENCE
		BUMPS	******		
		BUMPY	COMTE		
			FEMTO		

HUNCH	FUNDI	AWNED	LINEY	VANES	LUNGI
JUNCO	FUNDS	BENES	LONER	VINES	LUNGS
KENCH	GONDI	BENET	LUNES	WANED	MANGE
LANCE	HANDS	BINES	LUNET	WANES	MANGO
LUNCH	HANDY	BINET	MANED	WANEY	MANGY
LYNCH	HINDI	BONED	MANES	WINED	MINGY
MANCY	HINDS	BONER	MANET	WINES	MUNGO
MINCE	HINDU	BONES	MENES	ZONED	PANGS
MUNCH	HONDO	CANEA	MINED	ZONES	PENGO
NANCE	KANDY	CANED	MINER	******	PINGO
NANCY	KINDS	CANER	MINES	--NF-	PINGS
NONCE	LANDS	CANES	MONET	******	PUNGS
OUNCE	LENDS	CONED	MONEY	BANFF	RANGE
PENCE	LINDA	CONES	NINES	******	RANGY
PINCH	MANDY	CONEY	NONES	--NG-	RINGS
PONCE	MENDS	DANES	NONET	******	RUNGS
PUNCH	MINDI	DENEB	OWNED	BANGS	SINGE
RANCE	MINDS	DENES	OWNER	BINGE	SINGS
RANCH	MONDE	DINED	PANED	BINGO	SONGS
SINCE	PANDA	DINER	PANEL	BONGO	SYNGE
TENCH	PANDY	DINES	PANES	BONGS	TANGO
TINCT	PENDS	DONEE	PINED	BUNGS	TANGS
VINCE	PONDS	DUNES	PINEL	CONGA	TANGY
VINCI	RANDS	ENNEA	PINER	CONGE	TINGE
WENCH	RANDY	ERNES	PINES	CONGO	TINGS
WINCE	RENDS	FINED	PINEY	DANGS	TONGA
WINCH	RINDS	FINER	PONES	DINGO	TONGS
ZINCS	RONDO	FINES	RANEE	DINGS	VANGS
ZINCY	RYNDS	GANEF	RENEE	DINGY	WINGS
******	SANDS	GENES	RENES	DUNGS	WINGY
--ND-	SANDY	GENET	RENEW	DUNGY	ZINGY
******	SENDS	GONER	RUNES	FANGA	******
BANDA	TENDS	GYNEC	SANER	FANGS	--NI-
BANDS	VENDS	HONED	SINES	FUNGI	******
BANDY	WANDA	HONES	SINEW	FUNGO	AGNIS
BENDS	WANDS	HONEY	SONES	GANGS	AMNIA
BENDY	WENDS	INNED	TANEY	GONGS	ANNIE
BINDS	WENDY	INNER	TENET	HANGS	ARNIE
BONDS	WINDS	JANES	TINEA	HINGE	BENIN
BUNDE	WINDY	JANET	TINED	HONGS	BINIT
BUNDS	******	JONES	TINES	JINGO	BONIN
CANDY	--NE-	JUNES	TONED	KINGS	CANIS
CINDY	******	LANES	TONER	LINGA	CENIS
DANDY	ABNER	LENES	TONES	LINGO	CONIC
DENDR	AGNES	LINED	TUNED	LINGS	CONIO
FENDS	ANNES	LINEN	TUNER	LONGI	CYNIC
FINDS	ANNEX	LINER	TUNES	LONGS	DENIM
FONDA	APNEA	LINES	VANED	LUNGE	DENIS

ERNIE	DINKA	BUNNY	TUNNY	ERNST	MONTH
FINIS	DINKY	CANNA	VINNY	HANSE	MONTY
GENIC	DUNKS	CANNY	WENNY	MANSE	NINTH
GENIE	FINKS	CONNY	******	MENSA	PANTO
GENII	FUNKS	DANNY	--NO-	MINSK	PANTS
GONIA	FUNKY	DENNY	******	PANSY	PANTY
GONIO	GINKS	DONNA	AINOS	RINSE	PENTA
IONIA	HANKS	DONNE	ANNOY	SENSE	PINTA
IONIC	HANKY	FANNY	CANOE	SONSY	PINTO
JANIS	HONKS	FENNY	CANON	TANSY	PINTS
KININ	HONKY	FINNS	CENON	TENSE	PUNTO
LENIN	HUNKS	FINNY	DONOR	******	PUNTS
LENIS	HUNKY	FUNNY	FANON	--NT-	PUNTY
LININ	JINKS	GINNY	FANOS	******	RANTS
MANIA	JUNKS	GUNNY	GENOA	AUNTS	RENTE
MANIC	JUNKY	HANNA	HANOI	AUNTY	RENTS
MINIM	KINKS	HENNA	HONOR	BANTU	RUNTS
ORNIS	KINKY	HINNY	JANOS	BUNTS	RUNTY
PANIC	LANKY	JENNY	LENOS	CANTO	SANTA
PENIS	LINKS	JINNI	MANOR	CANTS	TANTO
PUNIC	MINKS	JINNY	MINOR	CENTI	TENTH
RANIS	MONKS	JONNY	MINOS	CENTO	TENTS
RENIN	PINKS	KENNY	PINON	CENTR	TINTS
RUNIC	PINKY	LENNY	RUNON	CENTS	UINTA
RUNIN	PUNKA	LYNNS	SENOR	CONTD	VENTS
SONIA	PUNKS	MANNA	SINON	CONTE	WANTS
SONIC	PUNKY	MINNA	SYNOD	CONTO	XANTH
TANIS	RANKS	NANNA	TENON	CONTR	******
TONIC	RINKS	NANNY	TENOR	DANTE	--NU-
TONIS	SINKS	NINNY	TENOS	DENTI	******
TUNIC	TANKA	PANNE	VENOM	DENTO	AINUS
TUNIS	TANKS	PENNA	WINOS	DENTS	ANNUL
VANIR	WINKS	PENNI	XENON	DINTS	BENUE
VINIC	YANKS	PENNY	******	DONTS	BONUS
XENIA	ZINKY	PINNA	--NR-	FONTS	CONUS
******	******	PINNI	******	GENTS	ENNUI
--NJ-	--NL-	PINNY	GENRE	HINTS	FANUM
******	******	RONNY	GENRO	HUNTS	GENUA
BANJO	MANLY	RUNNY	HENRI	JUNTA	GENUS
BENJY	WANLY	SENNA	HENRY	JUNTO	JANUS
SONJA	******	SENNE	MUNRO	KENTS	LINUS
******	--NN-	SONNY	******	LENTO	MANUS
--NK-	******	SUNNA	--NS-	LENTS	MENUS
******	BANNS	SUNNI	******	LINTY	MINUS
BANKS	BENNE	SUNNS	CANSO	LUNTS	NINUS
BUNKO	BENNY	SUNNY	CANST	MANTA	PINUP
BUNKS	BONNY	TINNY	CENSE	MINTS	SINUS
CONKS	BUNNS	TONNE	DENSE	MONTE	SUNUP

TONUS	BOOBY	GOODY	ROOFS	******	OVOLI
VENUE	GLOBE	HOODS	SCOFF	--OK-	OVOLO
VENUS	GLOBS	MOODS	WOOFS	******	PAOLO
******	KNOBS	MOODY	******	AWOKE	POOLE
--NY-	LOOBY	PLODS	--OG-	BLOKE	POOLS
******	NIOBE	POODS	******	BOOKS	PROLE
DENYS	PHOBE	PRODS	CLOGS	BROKE	SCOLD
KENYA	PROBE	QUODS	FLOGS	CHOKE	SMOLT
KONYA	SLOBS	RHODA	FROGS	CHOKY	STOLE
SONYA	SNOBS	ROODS	OLOGY	COOKS	THOLE
TANYA	******	SPODE	SLOGS	COOKY	TOOLS
TONYS	--OC-	WOODS	SMOGS	EVOKE	TROLL
VINYL	******	WOODY	STOGY	GOOKS	UBOLT
******	ACOCK	******	TIOGA	HOOKE	VIOLA
--NZ-	BLOCK	--OE-	******	HOOKS	VIOLS
******	BLOCS	******	--OH-	HOOKY	WHOLE
BONZE	BROCK	ALOES	******	KOOKS	WOOLF
WINZE	CHOCK	BOOED	ABOHM	KOOKY	WOOLS
******	CLOCK	COOED	ALOHA	LOOKS	WOOLY
--OA-	CROCE	COOEE	******	NOOKS	******
******	CROCI	COOER	--OI-	ROOKS	--OM-
BLOAT	CROCK	COOEY	******	ROOKY	******
BROAD	ENOCH	FLOES	ABOIL	SMOKE	ABOMA
CLOAK	EPOCH	FROES	ALOIN	SMOKY	ABOMB
CROAK	FLOCK	GOOEY	ALOIS	SPOKE	ANOMY
CROAT	FLOCS	HOOEY	AROID	STOKE	AROMA
EBOAT	FROCK	LOOED	AVOID	******	ATOMS
FLOAT	HOOCH	MOOED	AVOIR	--OL-	BOOMS
GLOAT	KNOCK	OBOES	AZOIC	******	BROME
GROAN	MOOCH	PROEM	BLOIS	ADOLF	BROMO
GROAT	POOCH	RHOEA	BROIL	AMOLE	COOMB
LAOAG	PROCT	SHOER	CHOIR	ATOLL	DOOMS
PROAS	SHOCK	SHOES	CROIX	AZOLE	DROME
PSOAS	SMOCK	SLOES	DROIT	CHOLE	DUOMI
SHOAL	STOCK	WOOED	ELOIN	COOLS	DUOMO
SHOAT	******	WOOER	GEOID	DHOLE	FROME
SKOAL	--OD-	******	GROIN	DHOLI	GNOME
STOAE	******	--OF-	HYOID	DOOLY	GNOMY
STOAS	ABODE	******	MYOID	DROLL	HBOMB
STOAT	ANODE	ALOFT	OVOID	ECOLE	LOOMS
TROAS	CLODS	CROFT	PLOID	ENOLA	MYOMA
UBOAT	DIODE	FEOFF	PYOID	ENOLS	NAOMI
******	EPODE	GEOFF	QUOIN	FOOLS	OTOMI
--OB-	ERODE	GOOFS	QUOIT	GAOLS	PROMS
******	FEODS	GOOFY	SPOIL	IDOLS	RHOMB
ADOBE	FOODS	HOOFS	STOIC	KNOLL	ROOMS
BLOBS	GEODE	LOOFS	ZOOID	OBOLE	ROOMY
BOOBS	GOODS	PROFS	******	OBOLI	STOMA
			--OJ-		
			******		
			SHOJI		

STOME	LEONS	FLOOD	MYOPY	PHORE	MOOSE
STOMP	LIONS	FLOOR	PLOPS	SCORE	NOOSE
STOMY	LOONS	GLOOM	POOPO	SCORN	PROSE
ZOOMS	LOONY	GROOM	POOPS	SHORE	PROSY
******	LYONS	KLOOF	PROPS	SHORL	ROOST
--ON-	MOONS	PROOF	SCOPE	SHORN	SLOSH
******	MOONY	SCOOP	SCOPS	SHORT	STOSS
AEONS	MUONS	SCOOT	SCOPY	SNORE	THOSE
AGONY	NOONS	SHOOK	SHOPS	SNORT	ULOSE
ALONE	ODONT	SHOOS	SLOPE	SPORE	WHOSE
ALONG	OZONE	SHOOT	SLOPS	SPORO	WHOSO
AMONG	PEONS	SLOOP	STOPE	SPORT	******
ATONE	PEONY	SNOOD	STOPS	STORE	--OT-
ATONY	PHONE	SNOOK	STOPT	STORK	******
AXONE	PHONO	SNOOP	TROPE	STORM	AZOTE
AXONS	PHONY	SNOOT	TROPH	STORY	AZOTH
AZONS	PIONS	SPOOF	WHOPS	SWORD	BIOTA
BLOND	PLONK	SPOOK	******	SWORE	BLOTS
BOONE	POONA	SPOOL	--OR-	SWORN	BOOTH
BOONS	POONS	SPOON	******	THORN	BOOTS
BRONC	PRONE	SPOOR	ABORT	THORP	BOOTY
BRONX	PRONG	STOOD	ACORN	WHORE	BROTH
CIONS	RHONE	STOOK	ADORE	WHORL	CLOTH
CLONE	SAONE	STOOL	ADORN	WHORT	CLOTS
CLONS	SCONE	STOOP	AFORE	******	COOTS
COONS	SHONE	SWOON	AGORA	--OS-	DHOTI
CRONE	STONE	SWOOP	APORT	******	EMOTE
CRONY	STONY	TROOP	ATORY	AROSE	FOOTS
DIONE	TBONE	WHOOP	BOORS	BOOST	FOOTY
DRONE	THONG	******	CEORL	CHOSE	FROTH
EBONS	TRONA	--OP-	CHORD	CLOSE	GROTS
EBONY	WRONG	******	CHORE	CROSS	HOOTS
FIONA	ZOONS	ADOPT	CHORO	DROSS	KNOTS
FLONG	******	CHOPS	CRORE	EROSE	KYOTO
FROND	--OO-	CLOPS	DOORN	FLOSS	LOOTS
FRONT	******	COOPS	DOORS	FROSH	PHOTO
GOONS	AFOOT	COOPT	EMORY	FROST	PHOTS
ICONO	ALOOF	CROPS	FIORD	GHOST	PLOTS
ICONS	BLOOD	DROPS	FJORD	GLOSS	PROTO
IKONS	BLOOM	DROPT	FLORA	GLOST	QUOTA
ILONA	BROOD	ELOPE	GLORY	GOOSE	QUOTE
IRONE	BROOK	FLOPS	IVORY	GOOSY	QUOTH
IRONS	BROOM	GROPE	LEORA	GROSS	RIOTS
IRONY	BROOS	HOOPS	MAORI	GROSZ	ROOTS
KHOND	CROOK	KNOPS	MOORE	ICOSI	ROOTY
KRONA	CROON	LOOPS	MOORS	KIOSK	RYOTS
KRONE	DROOL	LOOPY	NJORD	KNOSP	SCOTO
LEONA	DROOP	MYOPE	ODORS	LOOSE	SCOTS

SCOTT	STOUP	PLOWS	NEPAL	HYPER	VIPER
SHOTE	STOUR	PROWL	NIPAS	IMPEL	WIPED
SHOTS	STOUT	PROWS	NOPAL	JAPED	WIPER
SLOTH	TROUT	SCOWL	NOPAR	JAPES	WIPES
SLOTS	ULOUS	SCOWS	PAPAL	KOPEC	YIPES
SMOTE	******	SHOWN	PAPAS	KOPEK	******
SNOTS	**--OV-**	SHOWS	PAPAW	LAPEL	**--PH-**
SOOTH	******	SHOWY	PIPAL	LEPER	******
SOOTS	ABOVE	SLOWS	PUPAE	LOPED	ALPHA
SOOTY	CLOVE	SNOWS	REPAY	LOPER	ALPHY
SPOTS	DROVE	SNOWY	SEPAL	LOPES	AMPHI
THOTH	GLOVE	STOWE	TAPAS	MOPED	AMPHR
TOOTH	GROVE	STOWS	TOPAZ	MOPER	HYPHA
TOOTS	HOOVE	******	******	MOPES	KAPHS
TROTH	PROVE	**--OX-**	**--PC-**	NAPES	NEPHO
TROTS	PROVO	******	******	PAPEN	NEPHR
WROTE	SHOVE	DEOXY	ASPCA	PAPER	RAPHE
WROTH	STOVE	EPOXY	******	PIPED	SOPHY
ZLOTY	TROVE	PROXY	**--PE-**	PIPER	TOPHI
******	******	******	******	PIPES	XIPHI
--OU-	**--OW-**	**--OY-**	APPEL	PIPET	******
******	******	******	ARPEN	POPES	**--PI-**
ABOUT	ADOWA	BUOYS	ASPEN	RAPED	******
ACOUO	AVOWS	CLOYS	ASPER	RAPES	ASPIC
AFOUL	BLOWN	FLOYD	BIPED	REPEL	ASPIS
ALOUD	BLOWS	LLOYD	CAPEK	RIPEN	CUPID
AMOUR	BLOWY	PLOYS	CAPER	RIPER	KEPIS
CLOUD	BROWN	SLOYD	CAPES	ROPED	LAPIN
CLOUT	BROWS	******	CAPET	ROPES	LAPIS
CROUP	CHOWS	**--OZ-**	COPEC	ROPEY	LEPID
FLOUR	CLOWN	******	COPED	RUPEE	LIPID
FLOUT	CROWD	BOOZE	COPER	SIPES	LUPIN
GHOUL	CROWN	BOOZY	COPES	SUPER	ORPIN
GROUP	CROWS	CROZE	CUPEL	SUPES	PEPIN
GROUT	DHOWS	FROZE	DOPED	TAPED	PIPIT
HHOUR	DROWN	GLOZE	DOPES	TAPER	PUPIL
KNOUT	FLOWN	WOOZY	DOPEY	TAPES	RAPID
ODOUR	FLOWS	******	DUPED	TEPEE	SAPID
PIOUS	FROWN	**--PA-**	DUPER	TOPED	SEPIA
PROUD	FROWS	******	DUPES	TOPEE	TAPIR
RAOUL	GLOWS	APPAL	EXPEL	TOPER	TAPIS
SCOUR	GROWL	ARPAD	GAPED	TOPES	TEPID
SCOUT	GROWN	ATPAR	GAPER	TYPED	TOPIC
SEOUL	GROWS	COPAL	GAPES	TYPES	TOPIS
SHOUT	KIOWA	HEPAT	HOPED	UNPEG	TUPIK
SIOUX	KNOWN	JAPAN	HOPEH	UNPEN	TUPIS
SNOUT	KNOWS	LAPAR	HOPES	UPPED	UNPIN
SPOUT	MEOWS	LOPAT	HUPEH	UPPER	VAPID

******	GAPPY	EMPTY	CERAM	SARAH	CIRCA
--PJ-	GUPPY	HEPTA	CERAT	SARAN	CIRCE
******	HAPPY	LEPTA	CORAL	SARAS	CURCH
KOPJE	HIPPO	LEPTO	CORAS	SCRAG	DIRCK
******	HIPPY	SEPTA	DORAS	SCRAM	FARCE
--PL-	KAPPA	SEPTI	DURAL	SCRAP	FARCY
******	LAPPS	SEPTO	EYRAS	SERAC	FORCE
AMPLE	LIPPI	SEPTS	EZRAS	SERAI	KERCH
AMPLY	LIPPY	******	FARAD	SERAL	LARCH
APPLE	LOPPY	--PU-	FARAH	SORAS	LORCA
APPLY	NAPPE	******	FERAL	SPRAG	LURCH
DIPLO	NAPPY	AMPUL	FORAY	SPRAT	MARCH
DUPLE	NIPPY	CAPUA	FURAN	SPRAY	MARCO
HAPLO	PAPPI	CAPUT	GORAL	STRAD	MARCS
HAPLY	PAPPY	INPUT	GYRAL	STRAP	MERCI
IMPLY	PEPPY	KAPUT	HARAR	STRAT	MERCY
MAPLE	POPPY	LEPUS	HERAT	STRAW	NARCO
PEPLA	PUPPY	LUPUS	HIRAM	STRAY	PARCA
REPLY	SAPPY	PAPUA	HORAE	SURAH	PARCH
******	SOPPY	******	HORAL	SURAL	PERCH
--PN-	TIPPY	--PY-	HORAS	SURAS	PERCY
******	ZIPPY	******	HYRAX	TERAT	PORCH
HYPNO	******	PEPYS	IHRAM	TORAH	SARCO
******	--PR-	******	JORAM	VARAS	TORCH
--PO-	******	--QU-	JURAL	VERAS	TURCO
******	CAPRI	******	JURAT	VIRAL	******
BIPOD	COPRA	ESQUE	KARAT	******	--RD-
CAPON	COPRO	FIQUE	KERAT	--RB-	******
DEPOT	CUPRO	MAQUI	KORAN	******	BARDE
GIPON	SAPRO	PIQUE	LIRAS	BARBS	BARDS
HYPOS	SUPRA	ROQUE	LORAN	CARBO	BIRDS
IMPOT	******	TOQUE	MARAT	CORBY	BURDS
JUPON	--PS-	TUQUE	MORAE	CURBS	CARDI
KAPOK	******	******	MORAL	DERBY	CARDS
PEPOS	COPSE	--RA-	MORAS	FORBS	CORDS
RIPON	GIPSY	******	MORAT	FORBY	CURDS
SAPOR	GYPSY	ABRAM	MORAY	GARBO	CURDY
SEPOY	HYPSO	ARRAN	MURAL	GARBS	FORDS
SOPOR	LAPSE	ARRAS	MURAT	HERBS	GERDA
TYPOS	LEPSY	ARRAY	MYRAS	HERBY	GIRDS
VAPOR	POPSY	AURAE	NORAH	KERBS	HARDS
YAPON	TIPSY	AURAL	NORAS	SERBS	HARDY
YUPON	TOPSY	AURAS	OKRAS	SORBS	HERDS
******	VEPSA	BERAR	OURAY	TURBO	HORDE
--PP-	******	BORAX	PARAS	VERBS	HURDS
******	--PT-	BURAN	PYRAN	YERBA	LARDS
CUPPY	******	CARAS	RERAN	******	LARDY
DIPPY	COPTS	CARAT	RURAL	--RC-	LORDS
	DEPTH			******	
				BARCA	
				BIRCH	

NARDS	EARED	PERES	TURFS	BARIC	SPRIT
PARDS	EDRED	PHREN	TURFY	BARIT	STRIA
PERDU	EGRET	PORED	ZARFS	BERIA	STRIP
SURDS	ERRED	PORES	******	BORIC	SYRIA
TARDO	FARED	PUREE	**--RG-**	BORIS	TORIC
TARDY	FARER	PURER	******	BURIN	TORII
VERDI	FARES	PYRES	BARGE	CARIB	TURIN
WARDS	FIRED	RARER	BERGS	CERIA	UNRIG
WORDS	FIRER	SCREE	BURGH	CERIC	UNRIP
WORDY	FIRES	SCREW	BURGS	CHRIS	VARIC
YARDS	FORES	SERED	CARGO	CORIA	VARIO
******	GORED	SERES	CORGI	CURIA	VARIX
--RE-	GORES	SHRED	DIRGE	CURIE	XERIC
******	GYRES	SHREW	FARGO	CURIO	ZORIL
ACRED	HARED	SIRED	FORGE	CYRIL	******
ACRES	HAREM	SIREN	FORGO	DARIC	**--RK-**
AGREE	HARES	SIRES	GORGE	DORIC	******
AIRED	HIRED	SOREL	JORGE	DORIS	BARKS
AUREI	HIRER	SORER	LARGE	EERIE	BARKY
AURES	HIRES	SORES	LARGO	EYRIE	BURKE
BARED	HOREB	SPREE	MARGE	EYRIR	CORKS
BARER	JARED	STREW	MARGO	FERIA	CORKY
BARES	JEREZ	SURER	MERGE	KIRIN	DARKY
BEREA	JUREL	TARED	PARGO	KYRIE	DIRKS
BERET	KAREN	TARES	PORGE	LORIS	FORKS
BORED	KERES	THREE	PORGY	LURID	GORKI
BORER	KOREA	THREW	PURGE	LYRIC	GORKY
BORES	LARES	TIRED	SERGE	MARIA	HARKS
BYRES	LORES	TIRES	SORGO	MARIE	JERKS
CARED	LURED	TIREE	SURGE	MARIO	JERKY
CARER	LURER	UNREF	SURGY	MARIS	KIRKS
CARES	LURES	VIREO	VERGE	MERIT	LARKS
CARET	LYRES	VIRES	VIRGA	MORIN	LARKY
CAREY	MARES	WARES	VIRGE	MYRIA	LURKS
CERED	MIRED	WIRED	VIRGO	NARIS	MARKS
CERES	MIRES	WIRER	******	NORIA	MURKY
CORED	MOREL	WIRES	**--RI-**	ORRIS	NARKY
CORER	MORES	YPRES	******	PARIS	PARKA
CORES	MUREX	******	ABRIS	PERIL	PARKS
CURED	NARES	**--RF-**	ACRID	PERIS	PERKS
CURER	OARED	******	AERIE	PURIM	PERKY
CURES	OCREA	CORFE	APRIL	RURIK	PORKY
DARED	OGRES	CORFU	ARRIS	SARIS	SARKS
DARER	PARED	KERFS	ATRIA	SCRIM	TURKI
DARES	PAREN	SERFS	ATRIP	SCRIP	TURKS
DEREK	PARER	SURFS	AURIC	SERIF	WORKS
DIRER	PARES	SURFY	AURIS	SERIN	******
DURER	PAREU		AVRIL	SPRIG	**--RL-**
					******
					BIRLE
					BIRLS

BURLS	GORME	******	SYROS	GARRY	HORST
BURLY	HARMS	--RO-	TAROS	GERRY	HORSY
CARLA	HERMA	******	TAROT	HARRY	HURST
CARLE	KARMA	AARON	THROB	HURRY	KURSK
CARLO	NORMA	AFROS	THROE	JERRY	MARSH
CARLS	NORMS	AKRON	THROW	KERRY	MORSE
CURLS	PARMA	APRON	TIROS	LARRY	NORSE
CURLY	TERMS	ARROW	TYROL	LORRY	NURSE
EARLE	VERMI	BARON	TYROS	MARRY	PARSE
EARLS	WARMS	BORON	XEROX	MERRY	PARSI
EARLY	WORMS	BYRON	ZEROS	MORRO	PERSE
FARLE	WORMY	CAROB	ZIRON	MURRA	PURSE
FARLS	******	CAROL	******	MURRE	PURSY
FORLI	--RN-	CAROM	--RP-	MURRY	TARSI
FURLS	******	CEROS	******	MYRRH	TARSO
GIRLS	BARNS	CHROM	BURPS	PARRS	TERSE
HARLS	BERNE	CHRON	CARPI	PARRY	TORSI
HERLS	BORNE	COROT	CARPO	PERRY	TORSK
HURLS	BORNU	DUROS	CARPS	PURRS	TORSO
HURLY	BURNS	ENROL	CORPS	SARRE	VERSE
JARLS	BURNT	ERROL	HARPS	SERRA	VERSO
KARLS	CORNS	ERROR	HARPY	SORRY	VERST
MARLA	CORNU	FAROE	MORPH	TARRY	WORSE
MARLS	CORNY	FUROR	TARPS	TERRA	WORST
MARLY	DARNS	GIRON	WARPS	TERRI	******
MERLE	EARNS	GIROS	******	TERRY	--RT-
PERLE	FERNS	GYRON	--RR-	VARRO	******
PURLS	FERNY	GYROS	******	WIRRA	AORTA
SURLY	FIRNS	HEROD	BARRE	WORRY	BARTH
WORLD	HORNE	HERON	BARRY	******	BERTA
******	HORNS	HURON	BERRA	--RS-	BERTH
--RM-	HORNY	JUROR	BERRY	******	BERTS
******	KERNS	KAROL	BIRRS	BURSA	BERTY
BARMY	LORNA	KAROO	BURRO	BURSE	BIRTH
BERME	MARNE	LEROY	BURRS	BURST	BORTS
BERMS	MORNA	MEROE	BURRY	CORSE	BORTY
BURMA	MORNS	MORON	CARRY	CURSE	BORTZ
CORMS	MYRNA	MOROS	CIRRI	CURST	CARTE
DERMA	NORNS	MYRON	CIRRO	DORSA	CARTS
DERMO	PORNO	NEROS	CURRY	DORSI	DARTS
DORMS	TARNS	PAROL	DERRY	DORSO	DIRTY
DORMY	TERNS	PAROS	DORRS	DURST	EARTH
FARMS	TURNS	PERON	DURRA	FIRST	FIRTH
FERMI	VERNA	SAROS	FERRI	GIRSH	FORTE
FIRMS	VERNE	SCROD	FERRO	GORSE	FORTH
FORME	VERNS	SERON	FERRY	GORSY	FORTS
FORMS	WARNS	SEROW	FIRRY	HARSH	FORTY
GERMS	YARNS	STROP	FURRY	HORSE	FURTH

GARTH	KORUN	******	ARSES	MOSEY	ARSIS
GERTY	KURUS	--SA-	ASSES	MUSED	BASIC
GIRTH	RERUN	******	ASSET	MUSES	BASIL
GIRTS	SCRUB	ANSAE	BASED	NISEI	BASIN
HARTE	SCRUM	ASSAI	BASEL	NOSED	BASIS
HARTS	SERUM	ASSAM	BASES	NOSES	BASIS
HARTZ	SHRUB	ASSAY	BESET	NOSEY	ELSIE
HERTZ	SHRUG	BASAL	BISES	OASES	EOSIN
HORTA	SIRUP	CESAR	BUSED	ONSET	ESSIE
HURTS	SORUS	ELSAS	BUSES	OUSEL	FUSIL
MARTA	SPRUE	ESSAY	CASED	POSED	IASIS
MARTS	STRUM	LISAS	CASES	POSER	JOSIE
MARTY	STRUT	MESAS	CASEY	POSES	LYSIN
MIRTH	SYRUP	MOSAN	COSEK	RESET	LYSIS
MORTA	THRUM	NASAL	CUSEC	RISEN	MESIC
MORTS	TORUS	NISAN	DESEX	RISER	MUSIC
MORTY	VARUS	PUSAN	DOSED	RISES	OASIS
NORTH	VIRUS	ROSAS	DOSER	ROSED	OPSIA
PARTS	XERUS	SISAL	DOSES	ROSES	OPSIS
PARTY	******	SUSAN	EASED	RUSES	POSIT
PERTH	--RV-	UNSAY	EASEL	UNSEX	RESIN
PORTS	******	URSAE	EASES	UPSET	ROSIN
SARTO	CARVE	VISAS	EDSEL	VASES	SASIN
SORTS	CURVE	******	ERSES	VISED	SUSIE
TARTS	CURVI	--SB-	ESSEN	VISES	VESIC
TARTY	LARVA	******	ESSES	WESER	VISIT
TORTE	NERVE	BUSBY	ESSEX	WISED	******
TORTS	NERVY	******	FUSED	WISER	--SK-
VERTU	SERVE	--SC-	FUSEE	WISES	******
VIRTU	SERVO	******	FUSEL	YESES	BASKS
WARTS	VARVE	BOSCH	FUSES	******	BOSKS
WARTY	VERVE	CASCO	GASES	--SH-	BOSKY
WORTH	******	CISCO	HOSEA	******	BUSKS
WORTS	--RY-	DISCI	HOSED	BUSHY	CASKS
******	******	DISCO	HOSES	CUSHY	CUSKS
--RU-	BARYE	DISCS	IBSEN	DASHY	DESKS
******	BERYL	FISCS	INSET	DISHY	DISKO
AURUM	CARYO	MUSCA	ISSEI	FISHY	DISKS
CYRUS	CARYS	PASCH	LASER	GUSHY	DUSKS
DORUS	CHRYS	PISCI	LOSER	MASHY	DUSKY
DURUM	GARYS	VISCT	LOSES	MESHY	HUSKS
EURUS	KARYO	******	LYSED	MUSHY	HUSKY
FORUM	******	--SD-	LYSES	PASHA	MASKS
GURUS	--RZ-	******	MASER	PUSHY	MUSKS
GYRUS	******	MISDO	MISER	RUSHY	MUSKY
HORUS	FURZE	******	MISES	WASHY	******
JORUM	FURZY	--SE-	MOSEL	******	PESKY
JURUA	MIRZA	ANSEL	MOSES	--SI-	RISKS
		APSES		******	RISKY
				AESIR	RUSKS
				APSIS	

TASKS	GASPS	PUSSY	MUSTS	******	BITCH
TUSKS	HASPS	RUSSO	MUSTY	--TA-	BOTCH
******	LISPS	SASSY	NASTY	******	BUTCH
--SL-	RASPS	SISSY	NESTS	AETAT	CATCH
******	RASPY	TASSO	OUSTS	ALTAI	CUTCH
AISLE	WASPS	******	PASTA	ALTAR	DITCH
BASLE	WASPY	--ST-	PASTE	ALTAS	DUTCH
LISLE	WISPS	******	PASTS	ANTAE	FETCH
TESLA	WISPY	******	PASTY	ANTAL	FITCH
******	******	ASSTS	PESTS	ARTAL	HATCH
--SM-	--SR-	AUSTL	POSTS	ATTAR	HITCH
******	******	BASTE	RESTS	BATAN	HUTCH
COSMO	BASRA	BESTS	RUSTS	BETAS	KETCH
GISMO	******	BUSTS	RUSTY	DATAL	LATCH
******	--SS-	CASTE	TASTE	DITAS	MATCH
--SN-	******	CASTS	TASTY	ESTAR	MITCH
******	BASSI	CESTA	TESTA	ETTAS	NOTCH
AISNE	BASSO	CESTI	TESTS	FATAL	PATCH
ASSNS	BESSY	CISTS	TESTY	FETAL	PITCH
HASNT	BISSE	COSTA	VASTY	IOTAS	RATCH
MESNE	BOSSY	COSTO	VESTA	ISTAR	RETCH
WASNT	BYSSI	COSTS	VESTS	LITAI	ROTCH
******	CISSY	CYSTI	VISTA	LITAS	VETCH
--SO-	CUSSO	CYSTO	WASTE	LOTAH	WATCH
******	FESSE	CYSTS	XYSTS	METAL	WITCH
AESOP	FOSSA	DUSTS	ZESTS	METAS	******
ARSON	FOSSE	DUSTY	ZESTY	NATAL	--TD-
ASSOC	FUSSY	FASTS	******	OCTAD	******
BASON	GASSY	FISTS	--SU-	PETAL	OUTDO
BESOM	GESSO	FISTY	******	PITAS	******
BESOT	HESSE	GASTR	BOSUN	QATAR	--TE-
BISON	HUSSY	GISTS	CASUS	RATAL	******
BOSOM	JASSY	GUSTA	ENSUE	RITAS	ACTED
BOSON	JESSE	GUSTO	ISSUE	ROTAS	AFTER
EPSOM	JESSY	GUSTS	JESUS	SATAN	ALTER
HYSON	LASSA	GUSTY	JOSUA	SETAE	ANTED
JASON	LASSO	HASTE	JOSUE	SITAR	ANTES
LYSOL	LYSSA	HASTY	NISUS	TATAR	APTER
MASON	MASSE	HOSTS	RISUS	TITAN	ARTEL
MESON	MASSY	JESTS	******	TOTAL	ARTER
ORSON	MESSY	JUSTS	--SY-	VITAE	ASTER
PESOS	MISSY	LASTS	******	VITAL	AZTEC
VISOR	MOSSO	LISTS	ASSYR	WATAP	BATED
******	MOSSY	LUSTS	******	WITAN	BATEN
--SP-	MUSSY	LUSTY	--SZ-	WOTAN	BATES
******	PASSE	MASTO	******	ZETAS	BETEL
CUSPS	PASSY	MASTS	LISZT	******	BITER
GASPE	POSSE	MISTS		--TC-	BITES
		MISTY		******	
				AITCH	
				BATCH	

CATER	MOTEL	******	ARTIS	TITLE	ENTRY
CITED	MOTES	--TH-	ASTIR	WETLY	EXTRA
CITES	MOTET	******	ATTIC	******	IATRO
COTES	MUTED	ANTHO	ATTIS	--TN-	IATRY
CUTER	MUTES	ARTHR	BATIK	******	INTRA
CUTEY	NATES	BATHE	CETIC	PATNA	INTRO
DATED	NETER	BATHO	CETIN	******	LATRO
DATER	NITER	BATHS	CUTIE	--TO-	LATRY
DATES	NOTED	BATHY	CUTIN	******	LITRE
DETER	NOTER	BETHS	CUTIS	ACTOR	MATRI
DOTED	NOTES	BOTHY	ENTIA	ALTON	METRE
DOTER	OATEN	CATHY	ETTIE	ALTOS	METRO
DOTES	OATES	GOTHA	FETID	ANTON	METRY
EATEN	OCTET	GOTHS	ISTIC	ASTON	MITRE
EATER	OFTEN	KATHY	KATIE	ASTOR	NITRE
ENTER	OPTED	LATHE	LATIN	AUTOS	NITRI
ESTER	OSTED	LATHS	LYTIC	BATON	NITRO
ESTES	OTTER	LATHY	MATIN	BETON	OUTRE
FATED	OUTED	LETHE	METIS	ELTON	PATRI
FATES	OUTER	LITHE	MOTIF	ENTOM	PETRO
FETED	PATEN	LITHO	OPTIC	ESTOP	PETRY
FETES	PATER	MATHS	OSTIA	EXTOL	RETRO
GATED	PATES	METHO	PATIO	FETOR	RETRY
GATES	PETER	MOTHS	PETIT	JATOS	SUTRA
HATED	PETES	MOTHY	RATIO	JETON	TATRA
HATER	RATED	MYTHO	RETIA	KOTOS	TETRA
HATES	RATEL	MYTHS	SATIE	LOTOS	ULTRA
HOTEL	RATER	OATHS	SATIN	LUTON	VITRI
INTER	RATES	ORTHO	SITIN	METOL	******
JUTES	RETEM	PATHO	TITIS	MOTOR	--TS-
KATES	RITES	PATHS	UNTIE	NITON	******
KITED	SATED	PATHY	UNTIL	OTTOS ·	BETSO
KITES	SATES	PITHS	VATIC	PITON	BETSY
LATER	SITED	PITHY	YETIS	PITOT	GUTSY
LATEX	SITES	RUTHS	******	PUTON	MATSU
LITER	TITER	SETHS	--TK-	ROTOR	PATSY
LUTED	TOTED	TETHS	******	SETON	POTSY
LUTES	TOTEM	TITHE	SITKA	SOTOL	******
MATED	TOTER	WITHE	******	TETON	--TT-
MATEO	TOTES	WITHY	--TL-	TUTOR	******
MATER	UTTER	******	******	******	BATTY
MATES	VOTED	--TI-	APTLY	--TR-	BETTE
MATEY	VOTER	******	FATLY	******	BETTY
METED	VOTES	ACTIN	FITLY	AFTRA	BITTS
METER	WATER	ANTIC	HOTLY	ANTRA	BOTTS
METES	******	ANTIS	ISTLE	ASTRO	BUTTE
MITER	--TG-	ARTIC	IXTLE	AUTRY	BUTTS
MITES	OUTGO	ARTIE	ROTLA	CITRA	CATTY

COTTA	WITTE	SQUAD	******	SLUES	ETUIS
CUTTY	WITTY	SQUAT	--UD-	TRUED	FLUID
DATTO	******	SQUAW	******	TRUER	FRUIT
DITTO	--TU-	USUAL	CRUDE	TRUES	LOUIS
DITTY	******	******	ELUDE	YQUEM	SQUIB
DOTTY	ACTUS	--UB-	ETUDE	******	SQUID
FATTY	ARTUR	******	EXUDE	--UF-	******
GUTTA	CETUS	ARUBA	FEUDS	******	--UJ-
HATTY	CUTUP	CHUBS	GAUDI	BLUFF	******
HETTY	DATUM	CLUBS	GAUDS	CHUFA	THUJA
JETTY	FETUS	DAUBS	GAUDY	FLUFF	******
KITTY	GATUN	DAUBY	GOUDA	GRUFF	--UK-
LETTS	GETUP	DOUBT	LAUDS	POUFS	******
LETTY	ICTUS	DRUBS	LEUDS	SCUFF	FLUKE
LOTTA	JOTUN	FLUBS	MAUDE	SNUFF	FLUKY
LOTTE	LETUP	GRUBS	MAUDS	STUFF	LEUKO
LOTTO	LOTUS	KRUBI	PRUDE	******	STUKA
LOTTY	PUTUP	SCUBA	SCUDI	--UG-	******
LYTTA	SETUP	SLUBS	SCUDO	******	--UL-
MATTE	SITUS	SNUBS	SCUDS	BOUGH	******
MATTS	TITUS	STUBS	SPUDS	CHUGS	ADULT
MATTY	TUTUS	******	STUDS	COUGH	ALULA
MITTS	******	--UC-	STUDY	DOUGH	BAULK
MOTTO	--TY-	******	THUDS	DOUGS	BEULA
MUTTS	******	AMUCK	TRUDA	DRUGS	BOULE
NATTY	ATTYS	BRUCE	TRUDY	FAUGH	CAULK
NETTY	BUTYL	CAUCA	******	GAUGE	CAULS
NITTY	OCTYL	CHUCK	--UE-	GOUGE	COULD
NUTTY	SATYR	CLUCK	******	HOUGH	EXULT
PATTI	******	COUCH	AGUES	LAUGH	FAULT
PATTY	--TZ-	CRUCI	BLUED	LOUGH	FOULS
PETTI	******	DEUCE	BLUER	PLUGS	GAULS
PETTO	MATZO	EDUCE	BLUES	ROUGE	GAULT
PETTY	MITZI	EDUCT	BLUET	ROUGH	HAULM
POTTO	MITZY	ERUCT	CLUED	SLUGS	HAULS
POTTY	RITZY	LEUCO	CLUES	SNUGS	JOULE
PUTTS	******	MOUCH	CRUEL	SOUGH	MAULS
PUTTY	--UA-	PLUCK	CRUET	THUGS	MOULD
RATTY	******	POUCH	FEUED	TOUGH	MOULT
RETTA	AQUAE	SAUCE	FLUES	WAUGH	OCULO
RUTTY	AQUAS	SAUCY	GLUED	******	OVULE
SETTO	DOUAI	SHUCK	GLUES	--UI-	PAULA
SOTTO	DOUAY	STUCK	GLUEY	******	PAULO
TATTY	EQUAL	TOUCH	GRUEL	ALUIN	PAULS
TUTTI	FEUAR	TRUCE	MOUES	BRUIN	POULT
TUTTY	KAUAI	TRUCK	ROUEN	BRUIT	SAULS
VITTA	SKUAS	VOUCH	ROUES	DRUID	SAULT
WATTS	SQUAB		SLUED	EQUIP	SCULL

SCULP	THUMP	TAUNT	GAURS	BRUSK	SCUTA
SHULS	TRUMP	TRUNK	GOURD	CAUSE	SCUTE
SKULK	******	VAUNT	HOURI	CRUSE	SCUTS
SKULL	--UN-	WOUND	HOURS	CRUSH	SHUTE
SOULS	******	WRUNG	INURE	CRUST	SHUTS
STULL	ADUNC	YOUNG	INURN	DOUSE	SLUTS
THULE	BLUNT	******	KAURI	DRUSE	SMUTS
TRULL	BOUND	--UO-	KAURY	FAUST	SOUTH
TRULY	BRUNO	******	KNURL	FLUSH	TAUTO
UVULA	BRUNT	CRUOR	KNURR	GAUSS	TOUTS
VAULT	CHUNK	FLUOR	KNURS	HOUSE	TRUTH
WAULS	CLUNG	******	LAURA	JOUST	YOUTH
WOULD	CLUNY	--UP-	LOURS	LOUSE	******
YOULL	COUNT	******	MAURA	LOUSY	--UV-
******	DAUNT	COUPE	MOURN	MEUSE	******
--UM-	DRUNK	COUPS	NAURU	MOUSE	MAUVE
******	FAUNA	DRUPE	NEURI	MOUSY	PLUVI
ALUMS	FAUNS	ERUPT	NEURO	PAUSE	YOUVE
ARUMS	FLUNG	KRUPP	PLURI	PLUSH	******
BAUME	FLUNK	LOUPE	POURS	ROUSE	--UW-
BRUME	FOUND	LOUPS	SAURO	ROUST	******
CHUMP	FOUNT	ROUPY	SAURY	SHUSH	ADUWA
CHUMS	GAUNT	SCUPS	SCURF	SLUSH	******
CLUMP	GRUNT	SOUPS	SLURP	SOUSA	--UZ-
CRUMB	HAUNT	SOUPY	SLURS	SOUSE	******
CRUMP	HOUND	STUPA	SOURS	TRUSS	GAUZE
DRUMS	JAUNT	STUPE	SPURN	TRUST	GAUZY
FIUME	MAUND	TAUPE	SPURS	******	******
FLUME	MOUND	YAUPS	SPURT	--UT-	--VA-
FLUMP	MOUNT	******	TAURO	******	******
FRUMP	NOUNS	--UR-	THURS	ABUTS	ALVAN
GLUME	PLUNK	******	TOURS	ACUTE	ARVAL
GRUME	POUND	AZURE	TRURO	BOUTS	BEVAN
NEUME	PRUNE	BLURB	USURP	BRUTE	DAVAO
PLUMB	ROUND	BLURS	USURY	CEUTA	DEVAS
PLUME	SAUNA	BLURT	UTURN	CHUTE	DIVAN
PLUMP	SHUNS	BOURG	YOURE	COUTH	DIVAS
PLUMS	SHUNT	BOURN	YOURS	FLUTE	DOVAP
PLUMY	SKUNK	CHURL	******	FLUTY	ELVAN
RHUMB	SLUNG	CHURN	--US-	GLUTS	INVAR
SCUMS	SLUNK	CHURR	******	GOUTY	KAVAS
SLUMP	SOUND	COURT	ABUSE	LOUTS	KIVAS
SLUMS	SPUNK	CRURA	ADUST	MOUTH	LAVAS
SPUME	STUNG	DOURA	AMUSE	PLUTO	NAVAL
SPUMY	STUNK	DOURY	BLUSH	POUTS	NAVAR
STUMP	STUNS	DRURY	BOUSE	ROUTE	NIVAL
STUMS	STUNT	EXURB	BOUSY	ROUTS	NOVAE
THUMB	SWUNG	FOURS	BRUSH	SAUTE	NOVAS

PAVAN	LEVEN	******	******	DEWED	******
RIVAL	LEVER	--VI-	--VU-	DEWEY	--WI-
SIVAN	LIVED	******	******	DOWEL	******
******	LIVEN	ALVIN	FAVUS	DOWER	ALWIN
--VE-	LIVER	ANVIL	NEVUS	FEWER	BOWIE
******	LIVES	BEVIN	REVUE	GOWER	EDWIN
BEVEL	LOVED	BOVID	******	HAWED	ELWIN
CAVED	LOVER	CAVIE	--VV-	HEWED	ERWIN
CAVES	LOVES	CAVIL	******	HEWER	HOWIE
CIVET	MOVED	CIVIC	DIVVY	JAWED	IRWIN
COVED	MOVER	CIVIL	NAVVY	JEWEL	KIWIS
COVEN	MOVES	DAVID	SAVVY	LAWED	LEWIE
COVER	NAVEL	DAVIE	******	LEWES	LEWIS
COVES	NAVES	DAVIS	--VY-	LOWED	PEWIT
COVET	NEVER	DAVIT	******	LOWER	******
COVEY	NOVEL	DEVIL	DAVYS	MEWED	--WK-
DAVES	OAVES	ELVIN	GOVYS	MOWED	******
DAVEY	PAVED	GAVIN	******	MOWER	DAWKS
DIVED	PAVER	IRVIN	--WA-	NEWEL	GAWKS
DIVER	PAVES	KEVIN	******	NEWER	GAWKY
DIVES	RAVED	LEVIS	ALWAY	PAWED	HAWKS
DOVER	RAVEL	LIVIA	ASWAN	PAWER	PAWKY
DOVES	RAVEN	LIVID	BYWAY	PEWEE	******
EAVES	RAVER	MAVIS	DEWAN	POWER	--WL-
ELVER	RAVES	MOVIE	DIWAN	RAWER	******
ELVES	REVEL	NEVIL	GOWAN	ROWED	BAWLS
FEVER	REVET	NEVIS	NAWAB	ROWEL	BOWLS
FIVER	RIVED	PAVIS	NOWAY	ROWEN	COWLS
FIVES	RIVEN	SAVIN	ROWAN	ROWER	FOWLS
FOVEA	RIVER	VIVID	SOWAR	SAWED	HOWLS
GAVEL	RIVES	******	******	SAWER	JOWLS
GIVEN	RIVET	--VL-	--WD-	SEWED	LOWLY
GIVER	ROVED	******	******	SEWER	MEWLS
GIVES	ROVEN	GAVLE	BAWDS	SOWED	NEWLY
GYVED	ROVER	******	BAWDY	SOWER	PAWLS
HAVEN	ROVES	--VO-	DOWDY	TAWED	RAWLY
HAVER	SAVED	******	HOWDY	TAWER	WAWLS
HIVED	SAVER	DAVOS	ROWDY	TOWED	YAWLS
HIVES	SAVES	DEVON	******	TOWEL	YOWLS
HOVEL	SEVEN	DIVOT	--WE-	TOWER	******
HOVER	SEVER	ENVOY	******	UNWED	--WN-
JIVED	WAVED	FAVOR	BOWED	VOWED	******
KEVEL	WAVER	GAVOT	BOWEL	VOWEL	DAWNS
LAVED	WAVES	HAVOC	BOWER	VOWER	DOWNS
LAVER	WAVEY	PIVOT	CAWED	WOWED	DOWNY
LAVES	WIVED	SAVOR	COWED	YAWED	FAWNS
LEVEE	WIVER	SAVOY	COWER	YOWED	GOWNS
LEVEL	WIVES	******	COWES		LAWNS
	WOVEN	--VR-			
		******			
		LIVRE			

LAWNY	FIXED	VEXIL	ROYAL	RAYED	STYMY
PAWNS	FIXER	XAXIS	SOYAS	SAYER	THYME
TAWNY	FIXES	YAXIS	******	SHYER	THYMY
TOWNS	FOXED	******	--YB-	SKYEY	TRYMA
YAWNS	FOXES	--XL-	******	SLYER	******
******	HEXED	******	FLYBY	SNYES	--YN-
--WP-	HEXES	LAXLY	LAYBY	TOYED	******
******	LAXER	******	MAYBE	TOYER	BOYNE
YAWPS	LUXEX	--XO-	******	WRYER	GWYNS
******	MIXED	******	--YC-	******	JAYNE
--WR-	MIXER	BUXOM	******	--YI-	MAYNT
******	MIXES	LUXOR	ALYCE	******	WAYNE
COWRY	NIXED	NIXON	BRYCE	GOYIM	******
DOWRY	NIXES	SAXON	GLYCO	SAYID	--YO-
JEWRY	PYXED	******	JOYCE	ZAYIN	******
******	PYXES	--XT-	PHYCO	******	BAYOU
--WS-	SAXES	******	PSYCH	--YL-	KAYOS
******	SEXED	DEXTR	******	******	MAYOR
BOWSE	SEXES	JUXTA	--YD-	AMYLO	POYOU
DOWSE	SIXES	SEXTO	******	AMYLS	RAYON
HAWSE	TAXED	SIXTE	BOYDS	ASYLA	TOYON
NEWSY	TAXER	SIXTH	CLYDE	BOYLE	TOYOS
******	TAXES	SIXTY	HAYDN	CHYLE	TRYON
--WT-	VEXED	TEXTS	******	COYLY	YOYOS
******	VEXER	******	--YE-	DOYLE	******
NEWTS	VEXES	--XU-	******	DOYLY	--YP-
******	VIXEN	******	BAYED	DRYLY	******
--WY-	WAXED	MIXUP	BUYER	GAYLY	COYPU
******	WAXEN	NEXUS	DOYEN	HOYLE	CRYPT
POWYS	WAXES	******	DRYER	IDYLL	EGYPT
******	XAXES	--XY-	FAYED	IDYLS	GLYPH
--XA-	YAXES	******	FAYES	ODYLE	SCYPH
******	******	HEXYL	FLYER	PHYLA	SLYPE
COXAE	--XI-	******	FOYED	PHYLE	******
COXAL	******	--YA-	FOYER	PHYLL	--YR-
HEXAD	AUXIL	******	FRYER	PHYLO	******
MOXAS	AUXIN	ARYAN	GAYER	SHYLY	PHYRE
TEXAS	DIXIE	BOYAR	GUYED	SLYLY	THYRO
******	DIXIT	BRYAN	HAYED	STYLE	******
--XE-	MAXIM	DRYAD	HAYES	STYLI	--YS-
******	MOXIE	FAYAL	JOYED	STYLO	******
BOXED	NIXIE	IYYAR	KEYED	WRYLY	ABYSM
BOXER	PIXIE	KAYAK	LAYER	******	ABYSS
BOXES	PYXIE	LOYAL	NOYES	--YM-	MAYST
COXED	PYXIS	MAYAN	PAYED	******	PHYSI
COXES	TAXIS	MAYAS	PAYEE	CHYME	SAYSO
FAXED	TOXIC	RAYAH	PAYER	ETYMA	TRYST
FAXES	TOXIN	RIYAL	PRYER	RHYME	

******	LAZED	FUZZY	SCAPA	AGAPE	FLAME
--YT-	LAZES	JAZZY	TIARA	AGATE	FLARE
******	MAZED	LIZZY	TSANA	AGAVE	FRAME
ADYTA	MAZER	MEZZO	******	AGAZE	GLACE
BLYTH	MAZES	MUZZY	**--A-C**	ALATE	GLADE
LEYTE	MIZEN	PIZZA	******	AMATE	GLARE
PHYTE	NIZER	TAZZA	BLANC	AMAZE	GLAZE
PHYTO	OOZED	TIZZY	FRANC	APACE	GRACE
******	OOZES	******	GLAUC	AWAKE	GRADE
--YU-	OUZEL	**--A-A**	ISAAC	AWARE	GRAPE
******	RAZED	******	******	BLADE	GRATE
ASYUT	RAZEE	ABACA	**--A-D**	BLAKE	GRAVE
******	RAZES	AGAMA	******	BLAME	GRAZE
--ZA-	SIZED	AGANA	ALAND	BLARE	HEAVE
******	SIZES	ALADA	AWARD	BLASE	IMAGE
ANZAC	WIZEN	AMANA	BAAED	BLAZE	INANE
KAZAN	******	AQABA	BEARD	BRACE	IRATE
LAZAR	**--ZI-**	BEATA	BLAND	BRAGE	KNAVE
LIZAS	******	BRAVA	BOARD	BRAHE	LEASE
MUZAK	ANZIO	BRAZA	BRAID	BRAKE	LEAVE
NIZAM	FUZIL	BWANA	BRAND	BRAVE	LIANE
SIZAR	NAZIS	CEARA	CHARD	BRAZE	ORATE
******	OZZIE	CLARA	ELAND	CEASE	OSAGE
--ZE-	REZIN	DIANA	FRAUD	CHAFE	OVATE
******	SOZIN	DRAMA	GLAND	CHAPE	PEACE
ADZES	UNZIP	DRAVA	GRAND	CHARE	PEASE
BEZEL	VIZIR	DUALA	GUARD	CHASE	PHAGE
BIZET	******	GHANA	HEARD	CLARE	PHANE
COZEN	**--ZM-**	GRAMA	HOARD	CRAKE	PHASE
DAZED	******	GUAMA	PIAND	CRANE	PIAVE
DAZES	GIZMO	GUANA	PLAID	CRAPE	PLACE
DIZEN	******	GUAVA	ROALD	CRATE	PLANE
DOZED	**--ZO-**	JUANA	SCALD	CRAVE	PLATE
DOZEN	******	KAABA	SCAND	CRAZE	PRASE
DOZER	BOZOS	KLARA	SHARD	DEANE	PRATE
DOZES	KAZOO	KOALA	SKALD	DIANE	QUAKE
FAZED	LUZON	LHASA	STAID	DRAKE	RHAGE
FAZES	RAZOR	LIANA	STAND	DRAPE	SCALE
FUZED	VIZOR	LLAMA	SWARD	DRAVE	SCAPE
FUZEE	YAZOO	NYASA	VIAND	DUANE	SCARE
FUZES	******	OCALA	WEALD	ELATE	SHADE
GAZED	**--ZY-**	OMAHA	WOALD	ENARE	SHAKE
GAZER	******	OMASA	******	ENATE	SHALE
GAZES	IZZYS	OSAKA	**--A-E**	ERASE	SHAME
HAZED	SUZYS	PLATA	******	ETAPE	SHAPE
HAZEL	******	PLAYA	ABASE	EVADE	SHARE
HAZER	**--ZZ-**	PLAZA	ABATE	FEASE	SHAVE
HAZES	******	RIATA	ADAGE	FLAKE	SKATE
	DIZZY				
	FIZZY				

SLAKE	CRAIG	BRAGI	SNACK	CHASM	CYANO
SLATE	LIANG	COATI	SNARK	CLAIM	DIAZO
SLAVE	ORANG	CRANI	SPANK	INARM	DRACO
SMAZE	PRANG	GHAZI	SPARK	PLASM	ELAEO
SNAKE	SLANG	GRANI	STACK	PSALM	ELAIO
SNARE	SPANG	IRAQI	STALK	QUALM	ERATO
SPACE	TWANG	KHADI	STANK	REALM	GRANO
SPADE	WHANG	KHAKI	STARK	REARM	GUACO
SPAKE	******	MIAMI	SWANK	SHAWM	GUANO
SPARE	--A-H	OKAPI	THANK	SPASM	HYALO
SPATE	******	PLAGI	TRACK	SWARM	IDAHO
STAGE	ABASH	PLANI	WHACK	UNARM	IMAGO
STAKE	AWASH	QUASI	WRACK	******	LLANO
STALE	BEACH	SCAPI	******	--A-N	PHAGO
STARE	BRASH	SHARI	--A-L	******	PIANO
STATE.	CLASH	SPAHI	******	AGAIN	PLANO
STAVE	COACH	SWAMI	AVAIL	ALAIN	PLATO
SUAVE	CRASH	TRAGI	BEALL	AMAIN	SCATO
SWAGE	DEATH	******	BRAIL	BLAIN	SEATO
SWALE	FLASH	--A-K	BRAWL	BRAIN	SHAKO
TEASE	GNASH	******	CRAAL	BRAWN	SIALO
THANE	GRAPH	ABACK	CRAWL	CHAIN	SLAVO
TRACE	HEATH	ALACK	DOALL	DRAIN	STATO
TRADE	LEACH	BLACK	DRAIL	DRAWN	URANO
TRAVE	LEASH	BLANK	DRAWL	ELAIN	******
TSADE	LOACH	CHALK	FLAIL	GNAWN	--A-P
UKASE	LOATH	CLACK	FRAIL	GRAIN	******
URATE	NEATH	CLANK	GNARL	LEARN	CHAMP
USAGE	ORACH	CLARK	GRAAL	PLAIN	CLAMP
WEAVE	PEACH	CRACK	GRAIL	PRAWN	CLASP
WHALE	PLASH	CRANK	KRAAL	SHAUN	CRAMP
******	POACH	DRANK	MIAUL	SHAWN	GRASP
--A-F	QUASH	FLACK	PEARL	SLAIN	NAACP
******	REACH	FLANK	QUAIL	SPAIN	SCALP
CHAFF	ROACH	FLASK	SCALL	SPAWN	SCAMP
DRAFF	SLASH	FRANK	SHALL	STAIN	SCARP
DWARF	SMASH	KNACK	SHAWL	SWAIN	SCAUP
QUAFF	SNATH	OZARK	SMALL	SWAIN	SHARP
SCARF	STAPH	PLACK	SNAIL	TRAIN	STAMP
STAFF	STASH	PLANK	SNARL	TWAIN	SWAMP
WHARF	SWASH	PRANK	SPALL	YEARN	TRAMP
******	SWATH	QUACK	STALL	******	WHAUP
--A-G	TEACH	QUARK	SWAIL	--A-O	******
******	TRACH	SHACK	TRAIL	******	--A-R
BHANG	TRASH	SHANK	TRAWL	ALAMO	******
BRAGG	WRATH	SHARK	******	BEANO	CHAIR
CHANG	******	SLACK	--A-M	BRAVO	FLAIR
CLANG	--A-I	SMACK	******	CHARO	GLAIR
	******		ALARM	CLARO	STAIR
	ABACI		CHARM		
	AMATI				

******	CRASS	HEALS	PLANS	SPANS	APART
--A-S	CRAWS	HEAPS	PLATS	SPARS	AVAST
******	CZARS	HEARS	PLAYS	SPATS	AWAIT
ADAHS	DEALS	HEATS	PRAMS	SPAYS	BEAST
ADAMS	DEANS	IMAMS	PRAYS	STABS	BEAUT
ALANS	DEARS	ITALS	QUADS	STAGS	BLAST
AMAHS	DHAKS	IVANS	QUAGS	STANS	BOAST
AMASS	DIALS	JEANS	QUASS	STARS	BRACT
ARABS	DRABS	JOANS	QUAYS	STAYS	BRANT
AVARS	DRAGS	JUANS	READS	SWABS	CHAET
AYAHS	DRAMS	KEATS	REALS	SWAGS	CHANT
AZANS	DRAWS	KHANS	REAMS	SWANS	CHAPT
BEADS	DRAYS	KNARS	REAPS	SWAPS	CHART
BEAKS	DUADS	KVASS	REARS	SWATS	COAST
BEAMS	EVANS	KYATS	RIALS	SWAYS	CRAFT
BEANS	EXAMS	LEADS	ROADS	TEAKS	DEALT
BEARS	FEARS	LEAFS	ROAMS	TEALS	DRAFT
BEATS	FEATS	LEAKS	ROANS	TEAMS	ENACT
BEAUS	FIATS	LEANS	ROARS	TEARS	EPACT
BLABS	FLAGS	LEAPS	SCABS	TEATS	EXACT
BLAHS	FLAMS	LIARS	SCADS	THADS	EXALT
BLATS	FLANS	LOADS	SCANS	THAWS	FEAST
BOARS	FLAPS	LOAFS	SCARS	TOADS	GHAUT
BOATS	FLATS	LOAMS	SCATS	TRAMS	GIANT
BRADS	FLAWS	LOANS	SEALS	TRANS	GRAFT
BRAES	FLAYS	LUAUS	SEAMS	TRAPS	GRANT
BRAGS	FOALS	MEADS	SEANS	TRASS	HEART
BRANS	FOAMS	MEALS	SEARS	TRAYS	INAPT
BRASS	FRAPS	MEANS	SEATS	TSARS	KRAFT
BRATS	FRATS	MEATS	SHAGS	TZARS	KRAIT
BRAYS	FRAYS	MOANS	SHAHS	UNAUS	KRAUT
CHAOS	GEARS	MOATS	SHAMS	URALS	LEANT
CHAPS	GHATS	NEALS	SHANS	VIALS	LEAPT
CHARS	GLADS	NEAPS	SHAWS	WEALS	LEAST
CHATS	GLANS	NEARS	SHAYS	WEANS	MEANT
CHAWS	GLASS	NOAHS	SLABS	WEARS	PLAIT
CLAMS	GNATS	OKAYS	SLAGS	WHAMS	PLANT
CLANS	GNAWS	OLAFS	SLAMS	WHAPS	PLAST
CLAPS	GOADS	OLAVS	SLAPS	WOADS	QUANT
CLASS	GOALS	OPAHS	SLATS	WRAPS	QUART
CLAWS	GOATS	OPALS	SLAVS	XRAYS	REACT
CLAYS	GRABS	ORALS	SLAWS	YEANS	RIANT
COALS	GRADS	OVALS	SLAYS	YEARS	ROAST
COATS	GRAMS	PEAKS	SNAGS	YEATS	SCANT
CRABS	GRASS	PEALS	SNAPS	******	SHAFT
CRAGS	GRAYS	PEANS	SOAKS	--A-T	SHALT
CRAMS	GUANS	PEARS	SOAPS	******	SHANT
CRAPS	HEADS	PEATS	SOARS	ABAFT	SLANT
				ADAPT	

SMALT	FLAXY	******	ORBED	******	******
SMART	FOAMY	**--A-Z**	RABID	**--B-L**	**--B-R**
SPAIT	GLARY	******	REBID	******	******
START	GLAZY	FRANZ	ROBED	BABEL	AMBER
SWART	GRAPY	******	SABED	BABUL	ARBOR
TOAST	GRAVY	**--B-A**	TABID	BUBAL	BABAR
TRACT	GRAVY	******	TUBED	CABAL	BABER
TRAIT	HEADY	COBIA	******	CIBOL	BUBER
UNAPT	HEAVY	COBRA	**--B-E**	KABUL	CABER
WRAPT	HOAGY	DOBLA	******	LABEL	DEBAR
WYATT	HOARY	DOBRA	ABBIE	LIBEL	EMBAR
YEAST	ITALY	LABIA	ALBEE	MABEL	EMBER
******	LEADY	LABRA	AMBLE	NOBEL	FIBER
--A-U	LEAFY	LIBRA	BIBLE	REBEL	GABOR
******	LEAKY	LIBYA	CABLE	SIBYL	GIBER
OTARU	LEARY	NUBIA	COBLE	SYBIL	LABOR
PRAHU	LEAVY	SABRA	DOBIE	TOBOL	LIBER
SNAFU	LOAMY	TIBIA	DUBHE	TUBAL	LOBAR
******	MEALY	UMBRA	FABLE	UMBEL	OMBER
--A-W	MEANY	ZEBRA	FIBRE	******	SABER
******	MEATY	******	GABLE	**--B-M**	SOBER
MIAOW	OVARY	**--B-B**	IMBUE	******	TABOR
******	PEAKY	******	NOBLE	ALBUM	TIBER
--A-X	PEARY	CABOB	OMBRE	SEBUM	TUBER
******	PEATY	CUBEB	ROBLE	******	UMBER
BEAUX	PEAVY	KABOB	RUBLE	**--B-N**	UNBAR
******	PHAGY	NABOB	SABLE	******	WEBER
--A-Y	PHANY	******	SABRE	ALBAN	******
******	PHASY	**--B-C**	TABLE	ALBIN	**--B-S**
ALARY	PLASY	******	UMBLE	CABIN	******
ARABY	PLATY	CUBIC	******	CUBAN	ABBAS
ATAXY	QUAKY	PUBIC	**--B-G**	GABON	ABBES
BEADY	READY	RABIC	******	KUBAN	ABBYS
BEAMY	RHAGY	REBEC	DEBAG	ROBIN	ALBAS
BIALY	SCALY	TABAC	DEBUG	SABIN	AMBOS
BRADY	SCARY	XEBEC	******	URBAN	BABAS
BRAKY	SEAMY	ZEBEC	**--B-H**	******	BABES
BRAXY	SHADY	******	******	**--B-O**	BIBBS
CHARY	SHAKY	**--B-D**	SABAH	******	COBBS
CLARY	SHALY	******	SUBAH	BABOO	CUBES
COALY	SLATY	CUBED	******	FIBRO	DEBTS
CRACY	SNAKY	EBBED	**--B-I**	LABIO	EMBUS
CRAZY	SOAPY	EMBED	******	OMBRO	GABES
DEARY	STACY	GIBED	DUBAI	PABLO	GABYS
DIARY	STAGY	GYBED	FEBRI	TABOO	GIBES
FLAKY	TEARY	IMBED	KIBEI	******	GIBUS
FLAMY	THADY	JIBED	RABBI	**--B-P**	GOBOS
FLAWY	TOADY	LOBED		******	GOBYS
	TRACY			BEBOP	
	WEARY				

HABUS	OXBOW	RECTA	******	PECAN	******
HOBBS	UPBOW	SACRA	**--C-H**	RICIN	**--C-S**
HOBOS	******	TACNA	******	******	******
ISBAS	**--B-Y**	VACUA	MICAH	**--C-O**	ARCUS
JIBES	******	YUCCA	******	******	ASCUS
JUBAS	ABBEY	******	**--C-I**	BUCKO	BACKS
JUBES	AMBRY	**--C-B**	******	CACAO	BECKS
KIBES	BOBBY	******	ARCHI	CYCLO	BUCKS
LOBES	CABBY	JACOB	BACCI	DICHO	COCAS
LOBOS	CUBBY	******	CACTI	GECKO	COCKS
PUBES	DEBBY	**--C-C**	COCCI	HECTO	COCOS
PUBIS	DOBBY	******	NOCTI	JOCKO	DACES
REBUS	EMBAY	ENCYC	NYCTI	LACTO	DECKS
ROBES	EMBRY	******	ORCHI	MACAO	DICKS
RUBES	GABBY	**--C-D**	RECTI	MACRO	DOCKS
RUBYS	HOBBY	******	******	MICRO	DUCKS
SABES	HUBBY	ARCED	**--C-L**	MUCRO	DUCTS
TABES	LIBBY	CYCAD	******	NECRO	FACES
TOBYS	LOBBY	DICED	ACCEL	NYCTO	FACTS
TUBAS	NOBBY	FACED	CECAL	PICRO	FECES
TUBES	NOBLY	LACED	CECIL	RECTO	FICES
UMBOS	NUBBY	LUCID	DECAL	SACRO	FOCUS
VIBES	TABBY	MACED	DUCAL	SECCO	FUCUS
ZEBUS	TUBBY	MUCID	EXCEL	SOCIO	GECKS
******	WEBBY	PACED	FECAL	******	HACKS
--B-T	******	RACED	FOCAL	**--C-P**	HICKS
******	**--B-Z**	RICED	LOCAL	******	HOCKS
ABBOT	******	******	PICAL	ASCAP	HOCUS
AMBIT	JABEZ	**--C-E**	PICUL	BACUP	INCAS
CABOT	******	******	TICAL	RECAP	INCUS
CUBIT	**--C-A**	BACHE	VOCAL	UNCAP	JACKS
DEBIT	******	BOCHE	******	******	KECKS
DEBUT	ACCRA	CACHE	**--C-M**	**--C-R**	KICKS
HABIT	AECIA	CYCLE	******	******	LACES
JABOT	COCOA	EMCEE	CECUM	DECOR	LACKS
ORBIT	DACCA	FICHE	DECIM	DICER	LICKS
RABAT	DACHA	LOCKE	LOCUM	FACER	LOCHS
REBUT	DACIA	LUCRE	******	INCUR	LOCKS
ROBOT	DICTA	LYCEE	**--C-N**	MACER	LOCOS
SABOT	FACIA	MACLE	******	NICER	LOCUS
SEBAT	LUCCA	NACRE	ALCAN	OCCUR	LUCES
TEBET	LUCIA	NICHE	ANCON	OSCAR	LUCYS
TIBET	LYCEA	RUCHE	BACON	PACER	MACES
ZIBET	MECCA	SOCLE	INCAN	RACER	MACKS
******	MICRA	SUCRE	MACON	RECUR	MICAS
--B-W	MOCHA	SYCEE	MUCIN	RICER	MOCKS
******	NUCHA	TYCHE	ORCIN	ULCER	MUCKS
ELBOW	PUCKA	UNCLE	OSCAN	VICAR	
EMBOW		WACKE			

MUCUS	TACET	INDIA	SIDED	******	RADON
NECKS	TACIT	INDRA	TIDED	--D-I	REDAN
NICKS	UNCUT	JIDDA	UNDID	******	RODIN
NOCKS	YACHT	JUDEA	WADED	HADJI	SEDAN
ORCUS	******	LYDDA	******	INDRI	SIDON
PACAS	--C-U	LYDIA	--D-E	RADII	SUDAN
PACES	******	MEDEA	******	******	WIDEN
PACKS	FICHU	MEDIA	ADDIE	--D-K	WODAN
PACTS	******	OIDEA	ADDLE	******	WODEN
PECKS	--C-W	PADUA	ANDRE	KODAK	******
PECOS	******	PODIA	AUDIE	******	--D-O
PICAS	MACAW	PYDNA	BADGE	--D-L	******
PICKS	******	VODKA	BUDGE	******	ANDRO
PICTS	--C-Y	******	CADGE	ALDOL	AUDIO
POCKS	******	--D-B	CADRE	CIDAL	CADDO
PUCES	ARCHY	******	DODGE	DEDAL	HIDTO
PUCKS	BECKY	ARDEB	EADIE	FIDEL	HYDRO
RACES	COCKY	NADAB	EDDIE	IODOL	JUDEO
RACKS	DECAY	******	ENDUE	MEDAL	MEDIO
RICES	DECOY	--D-C	EYDIE	MODAL	PEDRO
RICKS	DECRY	******	FUDGE	MODEL	RADIO
ROCKS	DICEY	DODEC	HEDGE	NODAL	RODEO
RUCKS	DICKY	EDDIC	HODGE	PEDAL	VIDEO
SACKS	DUCHY	INDIC	INDUE	TIDAL	******
SECTS	DUCKY	IODIC	JUDGE	VIDAL	--D-R
SICES	ITCHY	MADOC	KEDGE	YODEL	******
SICKS	JACKY	MEDIC	LADLE	******	ADDER
SOCKS	LUCKY	MEDOC	LEDGE	--D-M	AIDER
SUCKS	MACHY	PUDIC	LODGE	******	ALDER
SYCES	MCCOY	VEDIC	MADGE	BEDIM	ARDOR
TACKS	MICKY	******	MIDGE	MADAM	CEDAR
TICKS	MUCKY	--D-D	NUDGE	SEDUM	CIDER
TUCKS	NICKY	******	PADRE	SODOM	CODER
VICES	ORCZY	ADDED	RIDGE	******	EIDER
VICKS	PACHY	AIDED	SADIE	--D-N	ELDER
VOCES	POCKY	AUDAD	SEDGE	******	FEDOR
WACKS	RICKY	BIDED	SIDLE	ALDAN	HIDER
WICKS	ROCKY	BODED	UNDEE	ALDEN	NADER
******	TACHY	CEDED	UNDUE	ARDEN	NADIR
--C-T	TACKY	CODED	WEDGE	AUDEN	ODDER
******	VICHY	ENDED	******	AYDIN	OLDER
ASCOT	VICKY	FADED	--D-H	BADEN	ORDER
DUCAT	WACKY	GADID	******	EMDEN	RADAR
FACET	******	HADED	JUDAH	LADEN	RIDER
FECIT	--D-A	JADED	KEDAH	LADIN	RUDER
LICHT	******	LADED	WIDTH	LODEN	SEDER
LICIT	HEDDA	NIDED		OGDEN	SIDER
PICOT	HYDRA	REDID		OLDEN	SUDOR

TUDOR	NODUS	CADDY	EDEMA	FREUD	KEEVE
UDDER	NUDES	CUDDY	ELENA	GREED	LIEGE
UNDER	PEDES	DADDY	ENEMA	KNEAD	NIECE
WADER	RIDES	DODGY	FREDA	KNEED	OBESE
WIDER	RUDDS	FADDY	FRENA	OREAD	OXEYE
******	RUDYS	GIDDY	FREYA	PLEAD	PEEVE
--D-S	SIDES	GODLY	GRETA	PSEUD	PHEBE
******	SODAS	HEDGY	HYENA	SCEND	PIECE
ADDYS	TIDES	KIDDY	OMEGA	SHERD	PLEBE
AEDES	TODDS	LADDY	ONEGA	SKEED	QUEUE
AIDAS	TODOS	MADLY	OPERA	SNEAD	REEVE
AIDES	WADES	MIDDY	PIETA	SPEED	SCENE
ALDIS	YODHS	MUDDY	PLENA	SPEND	SIEGE
ALDOS	******	NEDDY	PRESA	STEAD	SIEVE
ALDUS	**--D-T**	NODDY	SCENA	STEED	STELE
ANDES	******	ODDLY	SHEBA	TREAD	STERE
ANDYS	AUDIT	PADDY	SIENA	TREED	STEVE
BIDES	BIDET	PODGY	THECA	TREND	SUEDE
BLDGS	CADET	PUDGY	THEDA	TWEED	SWEDE
BODES	DIDNT	PUDSY	THETA	UPEND	THEME
CADES	DIDST	REDLY	ULEMA	WIELD	THERE
CADIS	HADNT	RIDGY	******	YIELD	THESE
CEDES	MIDST	RODDY	**--E-B**	******	TWERE
CODAS	******	RUDDY	******	**--E-E**	WHERE
CODES	**--D-U**	SADLY	ACERB	******	YSERE
DIDOS	******	SEDGY	******	ABELE	******
DODOS	SADHU	SUDSY	**--E-C**	ACEAE	**--E-F**
DUDES	******	TEDDY	******	ADELE	******
EDDAS	**--D-W**	TODAY	AREIC	AKENE	SHEAF
FADES	******	TODDY	CRESC	ANELE	SHELF
HADES	BEDEW	WADDY	ILEAC	AREAE	******
HIDES	ENDOW	WEDGY	OLEIC	ARETE	**--E-H**
INDUS	INDOW	WIDDY	******	BEEBE	******
JADES	WIDOW	******	**--E-D**	BREVE	ALEPH
JUDAS	******	**--D-Z**	******	COELE	BEECH
JUDES	**--D-X**	******	AHEAD	CREME	CHETH
JUDYS	******	CADIZ	AMEND	CREPE	CZECH
KADIS	ADDAX	VADUZ	BLEED	CRETE	DOETH
KUDOS	CODEX	******	BLEND	CREWE	FLESH
KUDUS	INDEX	**--E-A**	BREAD	DIENE	FRESH
LADES	RADIX	******	BREED	FEEZE	LEECH
LODES	******	ADELA	CREED	FRERE	OBEAH
MIDAS	**--D-Y**	ALEXA	DREAD	GEESE	STETH
MODES	******	AMEBA	EMEND	GLEBE	TEETH
MODUS	BADLY	ARECA	FIELD	GLEDE	******
NIDES	BIDDY	ARENA	FIEND	GREBE	**--E-I**
NIDUS	BUDDY	BREDA	FJELD	IRENE	******
NODES	BUDGY	CHELA	FREED	ISERE	ADENI
					BREVI

CHEMI	STEAL	PREEN	SLEEP	BMEWS	GUESS
ELEMI	STEEL	QUEAN	STEEP	BOERS	GWENS
FLEXI	SWELL	QUEEN	SWEEP	BREWS	HEEDS
OBELI	UREAL	QUERN	TIEUP	CHEFS	HEELS
UTERI	UVEAL	SHEEN	TWERP	CHESS	HOERS
******	WHEAL	SHEWN	WHELP	CHETS	IDEAS
--E-K	WHEEL	SKEAN	******	CHEWS	ILEUS
******	******	SKEIN	**--E-R**	CLEFS	ITEMS
ALECK	**--E-M**	STEEN	******	CLEMS	JEEPS
APEAK	******	STEIN	AMEER	CLEWS	JEERS
BLEAK	ABEAM	STERN	ANEAR	COEDS	JOELS
BREAK	ADEEM	TIEIN	BLEAR	CREES	JOEYS
CHECK	BREAM	TOEIN	CHEER	CRESS	KEEFS
CHEEK	CREAM	TWEEN	CLEAR	CREWS	KEELS
CLEEK	DREAM	******	DREAR	DEEDS	KEENS
CLERK	FLEAM	**--E-O**	EMEER	DEEMS	KEEPS
CREAK	GLEAM	******	FLEER	DEEPS	KIERS
CREEK	HBEAM	ACETO	FREER	DIETS	KNEES
FLECK	IBEAM	ADENO	GREER	DOERS	KOELS
FREAK	ILEUM	ANEMO	ONEIR	DREGS	LEEDS
GREEK	ODEUM	CHEMO	QUEER	DRESS	LEEKS
SHEIK	PNEUM	COELO	SHEAR	DREWS	LEERS
SLEEK	RHEUM	COENO	SHEER	DUELS	LEETS
SNEAK	SPERM	CREDO	SIEUR	DUETS	LIENS
SPEAK	STEAM	CTENO	SMEAR	EMEUS	LOESS
SPECK	THERM	DIEGO	SNEER	ENEAS	MEETS
STEAK	WHELM	GRECO	SPEAR	EPEES	MIENS
TWEAK	******	GREGO	STEER	EVENS	NEEDS
VNECK	**--E-N**	HIERO	SWEAR	EWERS	NOELS
WHELK	******	HYETO	THEIR	EXECS	OBEYS
WREAK	ACEAN	MYELO	******	FEEDS	ODETS
WRECK	CLEAN	OTERO	**--E-S**	FEELS	OGEES
******	CLEON	PAEDO	******	FIEFS	OMENS
--E-L	CREON	PHENO	ABELS	FLEAS	OMERS
******	EGEAN	PIEZO	ABETS	FLEES	OPENS
AREAL	FOEHN	PTERO	ALECS	FLEWS	OVENS
CREEL	FREON	PYELO	ALEFS	FREDS	OWENS
DWELL	GLEAN	STENO	AMENS	FREES	OYERS
IDEAL	GLENN	UREDO	AREAS	FRETS	PEEKS
ILEAL	GREEN	UTERO	AVENS	FUELS	PEELS
KNEEL	GWENN	******	AVERS	GAELS	PEENS
KNELL	LIEIN	**--E-P**	BEEFS	GEEKS	PEEPS
QUELL	OCEAN	******	BEEPS	GLEDS	PEERS
SHELL	ODEON	BLEEP	BEERS	GLEES	PIERS
SHEOL	OLEAN	CHEAP	BEETS	GLENS	PLEAS
SMELL	OLEIN	CHEEP	BIERS	GOERS	PLEBS
SNELL	PAEAN	CREEP	BLEBS	GREGS	POEMS
SPELL	PAEON	SHEEP	BLESS	GREYS	POETS

PRESS	WEEMS	INERT	POESY	******	HUFFS
PREYS	WEEPS	KNELT	PREXY	--F-I	JEFES
REEDS	WHENS	LIEUT	QUERY	******	JEFFS
REEFS	WHETS	OLENT	REEDY	BUFFI	JIFFS
REEKS	WHEYS	OVERT	REEFY	MUFTI	LEFTS
REELS	WRENS	PLEAT	REEKY	******	LIFTS
RHEAS	******	PREST	SEEDY	--F-L	LOFTS
RUERS	--E-T	QUEST	SUETY	******	LUFFS
SEEDS	******	SCENT	TEENY	AWFUL	MIFFS
SEEKS	ADEPT	SHEET	THEWY	OFFAL	MUFFS
SEEMS	AGENT	SKEET	VEERY	******	PUFFS
SEEPS	ALERT	SLEAT	VIEWY	--F-N	RAFTS
SEERS	ALEUT	SLEET	WEEDY	******	RIFFS
SHEAS	AMENT	SLEPT	WEENY	ELFIN	RIFTS
SHEDS	ANENT	SMELT	WEEPY	******	RUFFS
SHEWS	ARENT	SPELT	******	--F-O	RUFUS
SKEES	AVERT	SPENT	--F-A	******	SAFES
SKEGS	BLEAT	SWEAT	******	BUFFO	SIFTS
SKEPS	BLENT	SWEET	INFRA	******	SOFAS
SKEWS	BLEST	SWEPT	JAFFA	--F-R	SUFIS
SLEDS	BRENT	THEFT	KAFKA	******	TIFFS
SLEWS	BREST	TREAT	KUFRA	DEFER	TOFTS
SMEWS	CHEAT	TRENT	MAFIA	FIFER	TUFTS
SPECS	CHERT	TWEET	SOFIA	GOFER	WAFTS
SPEWS	CHEST	ULENT	SOFTA	INFER	WEFTS
STEMS	CLEAT	WEEST	TAFIA	KAFIR	******
STEPS	CLEFT	WHEAT	******	LIFER	--F-T
STETS	CREPT	WREST	--F-C	OFFER	******
STEWS	CREST	******	******	REFER	BEFIT
SUERS	DOEST	--E-Y	SUFIC	SAFER	REFIT
TAELS	DREST	******	******	WAFER	UNFIT
TEEMS	DWELT	APERY	--F-D	******	******
TEENS	EGEST	AVERY	******	--F-S	--F-X
THEWS	EJECT	BEEFY	BIFID	******	******
TIERS	ELECT	BEERY	FIFED	BAFFS	AFFIX
TREAS	ERECT	CHEVY	******	BIFFS	INFIX
TREES	EVENT	CHEWY	--F-E	BUFFS	UNFIX
TREKS	EVERT	CRECY	******	CAFES	******
TRESS	EXERT	ELEGY	ALFIE	CUFFS	--F-Y
TREWS	FLEET	EMERY	DEFOE	DEFIS	******
TREYS	GEEST	ENEMY	EFFIE	DOFFS	BAFFY
TYEES	GHENT	EVERY	GAFFE	DUFFS	BIFFY
USERS	GLEET	FIERY	RIFLE	FIFES	BUFFY
UVEAS	GREAT	LEERY	******	GAFFS	DAFFY
VEERS	GREET	NEEDY	--F-G	GIFTS	FIFTY
VIEWS	GUEST	ONERY	******	HAFTS	HEFTY
WEEDS	IDEST	PIETY	BEFOG	HEFTS	HUFFY
WEEKS	INEPT	PLEGY	******	HIFIS	JIFFY
			--F-H		
			******		
			FIFTH		

LEFTY	ALGIE	HEGEL	FUGIO	DEGAS	DIGIT
LOFTY	ANGLE	JUGAL	HAGIO	DOGES	EIGHT
MIFFY	ARGUE	LEGAL	HYGRO	EDGES	ERGOT
NIFTY	BOGIE	MEGAL	LIGNO	GAGES	FAGOT
PUFFY	BOGLE	MOGUL	NEGRO	GIGAS	FIGHT
SOFTY	BUGLE	NIGEL	SEGNO	HIGHS	GIGOT
TAFFY	DOGIE	REGAL	******	HUGHS	INGOT
TUFTY	EAGLE	RIGEL	**--G-R**	HUGOS	LEGIT
******	EAGRE	SIGIL	******	JAGGS	LIGHT
--F-Z	FUGLE	VIGIL	AEGIR	KAGUS	MAGOT
******	FUGUE	VOGUL	AGGER	LAGOS	MIGHT
HAFIZ	GIGUE	******	ALGER	LEGES	NIGHT
******	HAGUE	**--G-M**	ALGOR	LOGES	OUGHT
--G-A	INGLE	******	ANGER	LOGOS	PUGET
******	LOGUE	ALGUM	AUGER	MAGES	RIGHT
ALGIA	RAGEE	BEGUM	AUGUR	MAGUS	SIGHT
DOGMA	ROGUE	DEGUM	BOGOR	NEGUS	TIGHT
LOGIA	RUGAE	SAGUM	CIGAR	NOGGS	WIGHT
MAGDA	SIGNE	******	EAGER	OLGAS	******
MAGMA	TIGRE	**--G-N**	EDGAR	PAGES	**--G-V**
REGMA	TOGAE	******	EGGAR	RAGES	******
SIGMA	TOGUE	ALGIN	EGGER	REGES	NEGEV
******	VAGUE	ARGON	ELGAR	RIGGS	******
--G-B	VOGUE	BEGAN	GAGER	SAGAS	**--G-Y**
******	YOGEE	BEGIN	HUGER	SAGES	******
NEGEB	******	BEGUN	LAGER	SAGOS	ANGRY
******	**--G-G**	BOGAN	LEGER	SEGOS	BAGGY
--G-C	******	COGON	LUGER	SIGHS	BIGLY
******	MAGOG	DAGAN	NIGER	SIGNS	BOGEY
LOGIC	******	ELGIN	PAGER	TOGAS	BOGGY
MAGIC	**--G-I**	HOGAN	RIGOR	URGES	BUGGY
YOGIC	******	LAGAN	ROGER	VAGUS	CAGEY
******	LIGNI	LIGAN	SAGER	WAGES	DOGGY
--G-D	MAGNI	LOGAN	SUGAR	YEGGS	FOGEY
******	NIGRI	MEGAN	TIGER	YOGHS	FOGGY
ALGID	SEGNI	ORGAN	VIGOR	YOGIS	FUGGY
BEGAD	******	PAGAN	WAGER	YUGAS	JAGGY
CAGED	**--G-L**	REGAN	YAGER	******	LEGGY
EDGED	******	REGIN	******	**--G-T**	MUGGY
EGGED	ALGAL	SAGAN	**--G-S**	******	PEGGY
GAGED	ALGOL	VAGIN	******	ANGST	PIGGY
PAGED	ANGEL	WAGON	AEGIS	ARGOT	PIGMY
RAGED	ARGAL	WIGAN	ALGYS	AUGHT	POGEY
RIGID	ARGIL	YOGIN	ANGUS	BEGAT	PYGMY
URGED	ARGOL	******	ARGOS	BEGET	RAGGY
WAGED	BAGEL	**--G-O**	ARGUS	BEGOT	RUGBY
******	FUGAL	******	BOGUS	BIGHT	SOGGY
--G-E	GOGOL	ANGIO	CAGES	BIGOT	VUGGY
******		ANGLO			
AGGIE					
ALGAE					

******	******	BAHTS	LEILA	STIED	ELISE
--H-A	--H-M	ETHOS	LUISA	THIRD	ELITE
******	******	HAHAS	MOIRA	TRIAD	EMILE
BAHIA	NAHUM	JEHUS	ORIYA	TRIED	EXILE
BOHEA	OGHAM	JOHNS	OUIDA	WEIRD	FLITE
LEHUA	******	LEHRS	OUIJA	WRIED	FRISE
NAHUA	--H-N	******	PAISA	******	GLIDE
RRHEA	******	--H-T	PHILA	--I-E	GRIDE
SCHWA	ASHEN	******	PLICA	******	GRIME
******	BEHAN	******	PRIMA	ABIDE	GRIPE
--H-B	COHAN	UNHAT	SAIGA	ADIGE	GUIDE
******	ECHIN	******	SPICA	AFIRE	GUILE
SAHEB	ETHAN	--H-U	TAIGA	AGILE	GUISE
SAHIB	MAHAN	******	TRINA	ALICE	IMIDE
******	SPHEN	NEHRU	UTICA	ALIKE	IMINE
--H-C	******	******	VOILA	ALINE	JUICE
******	--H-O	--H-W	******	ALIVE	KNIFE
ETHIC	******	******	--I-B	AMICE	KOINE
******	ETHNO	PSHAW	******	AMIDE	LAINE
--H-D	OPHIO	******	CLIMB	AMINE	LOIRE
******	SCHMO	--H-Y	******	ANILE	LUISE
ACHED	WAHOO	******	--I-C	ANIME	MAINE
APHID	YAHOO	MUHLY	******	ANISE	MAIZE
EPHOD	******	OCHRY	ILIAC	ARISE	MOIRE
JIHAD	--H-R	******	******	ASIDE	NAIVE
--H-E	******	--H-Z	--I-D	ATIVE	NOISE
******	ABHOR	******	******	AXILE	OGIVE
OCHRE	ASHER	SCHIZ	BAIRD	AZINE	OLIVE
TAHOE	ASHUR	--I-A	BLIND	BAIZE	OPINE
TEHEE	BIHAR	******	BUILD	BEIGE	OVINE
YAHVE	EPHOR	ANIMA	CAIRD	BOISE	OXIDE
******	ESHER	ANITA	CHILD	BRIBE	OXIME
--H-H	ETHER	ARICA	CRIED	BRICE	PAINE
******	ICHOR	BEIRA	DRIED	BRIDE	PAISE
EPHAH	MOHUR	CEIBA	FLIED	BRINE	PHILE
******	NAHOR	CHIBA	FRIED	CHIDE	POISE
--H-I	OCHER	CHINA	GRIND	CHILE	PRICE
******	OTHER	CHITA	GUILD	CHIME	PRIDE
BAHAI	USHER	EDINA	ILIAD	CHINE	PRIME
MAHDI	UTHER	ELIZA	IVIED	CHIVE	PRISE
******	******	ERICA	LAIRD	CLIME	PRIZE
--H-L	--H-S	ERIKA	NAIAD	CLINE	QUIRE
******	******	EVITA	PLIED	CLIVE	QUITE
BOHOL	ACHES	HAIDA	POIND	CRIME	RAISE
ETHEL	AGHAS	HAIFA	PRIED	DEICE	RHINE
ETHYL	APHIS	IBIZA	SHIED	DRIVE	SEINE
NIHIL	ASHES	JAINA	SKIED	EDILE	SEISE
	ATHOS	LAIKA	SPIED	ELIDE	SEIZE ·

SHINE	CLIFF	BLIGH	DRINK	TRIAL	IXION
SHIRE	GRIEF	CUISH	FLICK	TRILL	NAIRN
SHIVE	QUIFF	EDITH	FRISK	TRIOL	ONION
SKIVE	SKIFF	ERICH	HOICK	TWILL	ORION
SLICE	SNIFF	FAITH	PRICK	TWIRL	REIGN
SLIDE	STIFF	FRITH	PRINK	URIEL	SCION
SLIME	THIEF	HEIGH	QUICK	WHIRL	UNION
SMILE	WHIFF	IRISH	QUIRK	******	XTIAN
SMITE	******	KEITH	SHIRK	**--I-M**	******
SNIDE	**--I-G**	LEIGH	SKINK	******	**--I-O**
SNIPE	******	LEITH	SLICK	ARIUM	******
SPICE	ACING	NEIGH	SLINK	AXIOM	AMIDO
SPIKE	AGING	OKIEH	SMIRK	CHIRM	AMIGO
SPILE	APING	REICH	SNICK	DEISM	AMINO
SPINE	AWING	SHIAH	STICK	FOISM	ANISO
SPIRE	AXING	SMITH	STINK	GRIMM	AVISO
SPITE	BEING	STICH	STIRK	IDIOM	CAIRO
STILE	BRING	SWISH	THICK	ILIUM	CHICO
STIPE	CLING	THIGH	THINK	ODIUM	CHILO
SUITE	CUING	TRICH	TRICK	OPIUM	CHINO
SWINE	DOING	URIAH	UMIAK	PRIAM	CHIRO
SWIPE	DYING	WEIGH	WHISK	PRISM	CLINO
THINE	EKING	WHICH	WRICK	SEISM	GUIDO
TOILE	EWING	WHISH	******	******	IMIDO
TOISE	EYING	******	**--I-L**	**--I-N**	IMINO
TRIBE	FLING	**--I-I**	******	******	INIGO
TRICE	FRIGG	******	ABIEL	ALIEN	IRIDO
TRINE	GIING	ACINI	AMIEL	ALIGN	OLIGO
TRIPE	GOING	ALIBI	ARIEL	ANION	ONIRO
TRITE	GRIEG	CHILI	AXIAL	APIAN	PHILO
TWICE	HYING	HAITI	BRILL	ARIAN	PRIMO
TWINE	ICING	LUIGI	CHILL	ARION	QUITO
UDINE	LYING	ORIBI	DRILL	ASIAN	RHINO
UNITE	OKING	PRIMI	FRILL	ATION	RHIZO
URINE	OWING	SCIFI	FRIML	AVIAN	SKIMO
UTILE	RUING	SPINI	GRILL	AVION	SLIGO
VOICE	SLING	******	ORIEL	BAIRN	SPIRO
VOILE	STING	**--I-K**	PHIAL	BRIAN	TAINO
WAIVE	SUING	******	QUILL	CAIRN	TRIGO
WHILE	SWING	BLINK	SHILL	CHIAN	URICO
WHINE	THING	BRICK	SKILL	COIGN	URINO
WHITE	TYING	BRINK	SKIRL	DEIGN	******
WRITE	USING	BRISK	SPIEL	FEIGN	**--I-P**
ZAIRE	VYING	CHICK	SPILL	ICIAN	******
******	******	CHINK	STILL	ILIAN	BLIMP
--I-F	**--I-H**	CLICK	SWILL	ILION	CHIMP
******	******	CLINK	SWIRL	INION	CHIRP
BRIEF	AMISH	CRICK	THIOL	ITION	CRIMP
CHIEF	APISH				

CRISP	ARILS	FRITS	RAINS	WAILS	QUINT
PRIMP	ARIUS	GAILS	REIMS	WAINS	QUIRT
SKIMP	AXILS	GAINS	REINS	WAITS	SAINT
STIRP	AYINS	GAITS	ROILS	WEIRS	SHIFT
TWIRP	BAILS	GLIMS	RUINS	WHIGS	SHIRT
******	BAITS	GRIDS	SAILS	WHIMS	SKIRT
--I-R	BLIPS	GRINS	SHIMS	WHINS	SLIPT
******	BLISS	GRIPS	SHINS	WHIPS	SPILT
BRIAR	BOILS	GRITS	SHIPS	WHIRS	SPIRT
BRIER	BRIGS	HAIKS	SHIVS	WHITS	STILT
CHIRR	BRIMS	HAILS	SKIDS	WRIES	STINT
CRIER	CEILS	HAIRS	SKIES	WRITS	SUINT
DRIER	CHIAS	HEIRS	SKIMS	******	SWIFT
FLIER	CHINS	IMIDS	SKINS	**--I-T**	TAINT
FRIAR	CHIOS	IVIES	SKIPS	******	TWIST
FRIER	CHIPS	IXIAS	SKITS	AGIST	TWIXT
ICIER	CHITS	JAILS	SLIMS	ALIST	UNIAT
OSIER	CLIOS	JAINS	SLIPS	ATILT	WAIST
PLIER	CLIPS	JOINS	SLITS	BUILT	WHIPT
PRIER	COIFS	KNITS	SNIPS	CLINT	WHIST
PRIOR	COILS	LAIRS	SOILS	DEIST	WRIST
SHIER	COINS	LEIFS	SPIES	DRIFT	******
SHIRR	CRIBS	LOINS	SPINS	DRIPT	**--I-U**
SKIER	CRIES	MAIDS	SPITS	EDICT	******
SKIRR	DOITS	MAILS	STIES	ELIOT	ADIEU
SLIER	DRIBS	MAIMS	STIRS	EVICT	ELIHU
SPIER	DRIES	MAINS	SUITS	EXIST	HAIKU
TRIER	DRIPS	MOILS	SWIGS	FAINT	POILU
WHIRR	EDIES	NAILS	SWIMS	FEINT	QUIPU
WRIER	EDITS	NEILS	SWISS	FEIST	******
******	ELIAS	OBITS	TAILS	FLINT	**--I-Y**
--I-S	EMILS	OKIES	TAINS	FLIRT	******
******	EMIRS	OLIOS	THINS	FOIST	ACITY
ABIBS	EMITS	OMITS	TOILS	GLINT	AMITY
ABIES	ENIDS	PAILS	TRIES	GRIPT	BRINY
ACIDS	EPICS	PAINS	TRIGS	GRIST	DAILY
ADIOS	ERICS	PAIRS	TRIMS	GUILT	DAIRY
ADITS	ERIES	PHILS	TRIOS	HEIST	DAISY
AGIOS	ERIKS	PHIPS	TRIPS	HOIST	DEIFY
ALIAS	EVILS	PLIES	TWIGS	IDIOT	DEITY
ALIFS	EXITS	PRIES	TWINS	JOINT	DOILY
AMIAS	FAILS	PRIGS	TWITS	JOIST	DRILY
AMIES	FAIRS	PRIMS	UNITS	MOIST	EDIFY
AMIRS	FLIES	QUIDS	VAIRS	PAINT	EMILY
AMISS	FLIPS	QUIPS	VEILS	POINT	FAIRY
ANILS	FLITS	QUITS	VEINS	PRINT	GAILY
ARIAS	FOILS	RAIDS	VOIDS	QUIET	GRIMY
ARIES	FRIES	RAILS	WAIFS	QUILT	HAIRY

ICILY	******	LIKED	******	POKES	HILDA
JUICY	--J-R	NAKED	--K-R	PUKES	HULDA
LAITY	******	PIKED	******	RAKES	JULIA
NOISY	MAJOR	POKED	ASKER	SAKES	MALTA
OSITY	******	PUKED	BAKER	SIKHS	MILIA
PHILY	--J-S	RAKED	COKER	SOKES	PALEA
PLINY	******	WAKED	DAKAR	TAKES	PALMA
PRIVY	FIJIS	YOKED	DIKER	TIKIS	PELLA
RAINY	JUJUS	******	ESKER	TYKES	PILEA
REIFY	SOJAS	--K-E	FAKER	WAKES	POLKA
ROILY	******	******	FAKIR	WEKAS	SALMA
SHILY	--J-U	ANKLE	HIKER	YOKES	SALPA
SHINY	ANJOU	INKLE	INKER	ZEKES	SALSA
SLILY	BIJOU	PEKOE	JOKER	******	SELMA
SLIMY	SAJOU	RAKEE	LAKER	--K-W	SILVA
SPICY	******	******	MAKER	******	SOLFA
SPIKY	--J-Y	--K-I	PIKER	ASKEW	SULFA
SPINY	******	KUKRI	POKER	******	SYLVA
SPIRY	ENJOY	******	RAKER	--K-Y	TILDA
STIMY	******	--K-L	SAKER	******	TULSA
TRIXY	--J-Z	******	TAKER	COKEY	VILLA
UNIFY	******	ALKYL	******	LAKEY	VILNA
UNITY	HEJAZ	BIKOL	--K-S	MIKEY	VOLGA
VEINY	******	TEKEL	******	POKEY	VOLTA
WHINY	--K-A	YOKEL	ANKHS	TOKAY	VOLVA
******	******	******	ANKUS	******	VULVA
--I-Z	HEKLA	--K-M	BAKES	--L-A	WALLA
******	PUKKA	******	BIKES	******	WILLA
BLITZ	******	HAKIM	CAKES	BALSA	WILMA
FRITZ	--K-B	HOKUM	COKES	BELGA	YALTA
FRIZZ	******	OAKUM	DEKES	BELLA	******
MAINZ	JAKOB	--K-N	DIKES	BULLA	--L-B
SPITZ	******	******	DUKES	CALLA	******
******	--K-D	AIKEN	FAKES	CELIA	ADLIB
--J-B	******	HOKAN	FYKES	CELLA	CALEB
******	ASKED	LIKEN	HAKES	CILIA	PHLEB
RAJAB	BAKED	OAKEN	HIKES	COLZA	******
--J-H	CAKED	PEKAN	JAKES	CULPA	--L-C
******	COKED	PEKIN	JOKES	DELIA	******
RAJAH	DEKED	TAKEN	KAKAS	DELLA	AULIC
******	DIKED	TOKEN	KAKIS	DELTA	COLIC
--J-K	FAKED	WAKEN	LAKES	DULIA	EOLIC
******	HIKED	WOKEN	LIKES	FOLIA	FOLIC
MUJIK	INKED	YUKON	MAKES	GALEA	HELIC
******	IRKED	******	MIKES	GILDA	LILAC
--J-N	JOKED	--K-O	MOKES	GOLDA	MALAC
CAJON	LAKED	******	PIKAS	HALMA	MALIC
CAJUN		HEKTO	PIKES	HELGA	MELIC
DIJON		TOKYO			

RELIC	COLNE	DOLPH	XYLOL	DILDO	HALER
SALIC	DELVE	FILCH	XYLYL	FOLIO	IDLER
SILIC	DOLCE	FILTH	******	HALLO	MALAR
TELIC	DULCE	GULCH	**--L-M**	HELIO	MILER
******	DULSE	KILAH	******	HELLO	MOLAR
--L-D	ELLIE	MILCH	BELEM	IGLOO	OGLER
******	FALSE	MULCH	CELOM	JELLO	OILER
AILED	HALLE	RALPH	FILUM	JULIO	OSLER
AXLED	HALVE	ROLPH	GOLEM	KELSO	PALER
BALED	HELLE	SELAH	HILUM	MALMO	PILAR
DELED	HELVE	SYLPH	ISLAM	MOLTO	POLAR
DOLED	JULIE	TILTH	SALEM	PALEO	PULER
FELID	LILLE	WELCH	VELUM	POLIO	RULER
FILED	MELEE	WELSH	XYLEM	PULMO	SOLAR
GELID	MILNE	******	******	ROLLO	TALER
HALED	OLLIE	**--L-I**	**--L-N**	SALVO	TILER
HALID	PALAE	******	******	SOLDO	TYLER
HOLED	PELEE	AALII	ALLAN	SULFO	VALOR
IDLED	PULSE	ADLAI	ALLEN	TELEO	VELAR
ISLED	RILLE	CALCI	ALLIN	VULGO	VILER
OGLED	ROLFE	CALLI	ARLEN	WALDO	VOLAR
OILED	SALSE	CULTI	COLIN	******	WALER
PALED	SALVE	DALAI	COLON	**--L-P**	******
PILED	SOLVE	DELHI	DYLAN	******	**--L-S**
POLED	TELAE	LILLI	ELLEN	GALOP	******
PULED	TILDE	MILLI	FELON	JALAP	ALLIS
RILED	TULLE	MULTI	GALEN	JULEP	ANLAS
RULED	VALUE	PALMI	HELEN	ORLOP	ARLES
SALAD	VALVE	PALPI	MELAN	OXLIP	ATLAS
SOLED	VILLE	PELVI	MELON	POLYP	AULIS
SOLID	VOLTE	PILEI	MILAN	SALEP	AXLES
TILED	WILDE	SALMI	NYLON	TULIP	BALAS
VALID	******	SOLDI	ORLON	******	BALES
WALED	**--L-F**	SULCI	PELON	**--L-R**	BALKS
WILED	******	VILLI	PYLON	******	BALLS
******	CALIF	VOLTI	SALON	ABLER	BALMS
--L-E	PILAF	******	SELEN	ADLER	BALTS
******	******	**--L-K**	SOLAN	BALDR	BELLS
AGLEE	**--L-G**	******	SOLON	BALER	BELTS
ALLIE	******	KULAK	SPLEN	BOLAR	BILES
BELIE	PELEG	TALUK	TALON	CHLOR	BILKS
BELLE	TELEG	******	TOLAN	COLOR	BILLS
BILGE	******	**--L-L**	UHLAN	DALER	BOLAS
BULGE	**--L-H**	******	XYLAN	DOLOR	BOLES
CALPE	******	ALLYL	******	EULER	BOLLS
CALVE	ALLAH	MOLAL	**--L-O**	FILAR	BOLOS
CELIE	BELCH	SALOL	******	FILER	BOLTS
CHLOE	CULCH	TOLYL	BILBO	GULAR	BOLUS
			CELLO		

BULBS	GULPS	MILES	SULKS	INLET	BELAY
BULKS	HALES	MILKS	SULUS	ISLET	BELLY
BULLS	HALLS	MILLS	TALCS	KALAT	BILGY
CALKS	HALOS	MILTS	TALES	MULCT	BILLY
CALLS	HALTS	MLLES	TALKS	OWLET	BULGY
CALMS	HELLS	MOLDS	TALOS	PILOT	BULKY
CELLS	HELMS	MOLES	TALUS	SPLAT	BULLY
CELTS	HELPS	MOLLS	TELLS	SPLIT	COLLY
COLAS	HILLS	MOLTS	TILES	UNLIT	DALLY
COLDS	HILTS	MULES	TILLS	VALET	DELAY
COLES	HOLDS	MULLS	TILTS	VELDT	DOLLY
COLTS	HOLES	MYLES	TOLAS	******	DULCY
CULLS	HOLMS	NELLS	TOLES	--L-U	DULLY
CULMS	HULAS	OGLES	TOLLS	******	FELLY
CULTS	HULKS	OLLAS	TULES	ERLAU	FILLY
DALES	HULLS	ORLES	VALES	******	FILMY
DELES	HYLAS	PALES	VELDS	--L-W	FOLLY
DELLS	IDLES	PALLS	VILLS	******	FULLY
DELOS	ILLUS	PALMS	VOLES	AGLOW	GOLLY
DILYS	ISLES	PELFS	VOLTS	ALLOW	GULLY
DOLES	JELLS	PELTS	WALES	BELOW	HILLY
DOLLS	JILLS	PILES	WALKS	BYLAW	HOLEY
DOLTS	JILTS	PILIS	WALTS	INLAW	HOLLY
DULLS	JOLES	PILLS	WELDS	******	HULKY
ELLAS	JOLTS	POLES	WELLS	--L-X	INLAY
ELLIS	JULES	POLLS	WELTS	******	ISLAY
EOLUS	JULYS	PULES	WILDS	CALIX	JELLY
FALLS	KELPS	PULLS	WILES	CALYX	JOLLY
FELLS	KILLS	PULPS	WILLS	CULEX	JOLTY
FELTS	KILNS	RALES	WILTS	CYLIX	KELLY
FILES	KILOS	RILES	WOLDS	FELIX	KILTY
FILLS	KILTS	RILLS	WOLFS	GALAX	LILLY
FILMS	KOLAS	ROLES	YELKS	HELIX	LOLLY
FOLDS	LALLS	ROLFS	YELLS	KYLIX	MALAY
FOLKS	LILAS	ROLLS	YELPS	PHLOX	MALTY
FULLS	LILTS	RULES	YOLKS	RELAX	MILKY
GALAS	LILYS	SALES	YULES	SALIX	MILLY
GALES	LOLAS	SALTS	******	SILEX	MILTY
GALLS	LOLLS	SALUS	--L-T	TELEX	MOLDY
GELDS	LULLS	SELLS	******	******	MOLLY
GILDS	LULUS	SILAS	AGLET	--L-Y	MULEY
GILES	LYLES	SILKS	ALLOT	******	NELLY
GILLS	MALES	SILLS	CULET	AGLEY	PALEY
GOLDS	MALLS	SILOS	DELFT	ALLAY	PALLY
GOLFS	MALTS	SILTS	ECLAT	ALLEY	PALMY
GULES	MELDS	SOLES	FILET	ALLOY	PALSY
GULFS	MELOS	SOLOS	HELOT	BALKY	PELLY
GULLS	MELTS	SOLUS	HOLST	BALMY	POLLY

PULPY	******	SOMME	AMMAN	HOMEO	CAMES
RALLY	--M-C	TEMPE	AMMON	JUMBO	CAMPS
RELAY	******	******	ATMAN	LIMBO	CAMUS
RILEY	COMIC	--M-G	AXMAN	MAMBO	COMAS
SALLY	DOMIC	******	AXMEN	MIMEO	COMBS
SALTY	GAMIC	ALMUG	CUMIN	ROMEO	COMES
SILKY	HEMIC	******	DAMAN	SAMBO	COMUS
SILLY	HUMIC	--M-H	DAMON	TEMPO	CYMES
SILTY	MIMIC	******	DEMON	******	DAMES
SPLAY	OGMIC	ALMAH	EAMON	--M-R	DAMNS
SULKY	OHMIC	HUMPH	ELMAN	******	DAMPS
SULLY	OSMIC	LYMPH	GAMIN	ARMOR	DEMES
TALLY	SUMAC	NYMPH	HEMAN	COMDR	DEMOS
TELLY	******	OOMPH	HEMEN	COMER	DIMES
TILLY	--M-D	******	HEMIN	CYMAR	DOMES
TULLY	******	--M-I	HUMAN	DEMUR	DUMAS
UNLAY	AIMED	******	HYMEN	DIMER	DUMPS
WALLY	ALMUD	BAMBI	ILMEN	EIMER	EMMAS
WILEY	ARMED	CAMPI	LEMON	ELMER	EMMYS
WILLY	DOMED	CYMRI	LIMEN	EMMER	ERMAS
YOLKY	FAMED	IAMBI	LUMEN	FEMUR	FEMES
******	FUMED	LIMBI	LYMAN	HAMER	FUMES
--L-Z	GAMED	NIMBI	NUMEN	HOMER	GAMBS
******	HOMED	SOMNI	OSMAN	HUMOR	GAMES
WALTZ	HUMID	TEMPI	PIMAN	KHMER	GAMPS
******	LAMED	ZIMRI	REMAN	LAMER	GIMPS
--M-A	LIMED	ZOMBI	ROMAN	LEMUR	HAMES
******	MIMED	******	RUMEN	MIMER	HEMPS
AEMIA	NAMED	--M-K	SEMEN	MIMIR	HOMES
COMMA	NOMAD	******	SIMON	NAMER	HUMPS
GAMMA	RIMED	KAMIK	TOMAN	NAMUR	HUMUS
GEMMA	TAMED	SAMEK	UNMAN	ORMER	HYMNS
GUMMA	TIMED	******	VIMEN	RIMER	IAMBS
HAMZA	TIMID	--M-L	WOMAN	RUMOR	IRMAS
HEMIA	TUMID	******	WOMEN	SAMAR	JAMBS
JUMNA	******	CAMEL	YAMEN	SIMAR	JAMES
LAMIA	******	COMAL	YAMUN	SUMER	JUMPS
LEMMA	--M-E	GIMEL	YEMEN	TAMER	KAMES
MAMBA	******	HAMAL	******	TIMER	KOMOS
MAMMA	AIMEE	HEMAL	--M-O	TIMOR	KUMIS
RUMBA	BOMBE	TAMIL	******	TUMOR	LAMAS
SAMBA	COMAE	UXMAL	CAMEO	VOMER	LAMBS
SAMOA	COMTE	******	CAMPO	******	LAMES
TAMPA	CYMAE	--M-N	COMBO	--M-S	LAMPS
ZAMIA	EMMIE	******	COMPO	******	LIMBS
******	FEMME	ADMAN	FEMTO	ALMAS	LIMES
--M-B	JAMIE	ADMEN	GUMBO	BOMBS	LIMNS
******	MAMIE	ADMIN	GYMNO	BUMPS	LIMPS
DEMOB	RAMIE				

LUMPS	KAMET	RUMLY	SONIA	MONAD	MONTE
MAMAS	LIMIT	RUMMY	SONJA	OWNED	NANCE
MEMOS	NEMAT	SAMMY	SONYA	PANED	NONCE
MIMES	REMIT	TAMMY	SUNNA	PINED	OUNCE
MIMIS	SOMAT	TIMMY	TANKA	SYNOD	PANNE
MOMUS	TEMPT	TOMMY	TANYA	TINED	PENCE
MUMMS	VOMIT	TUMMY	TINEA	TONED	PONCE
MUMPS	******	WOMBY	TONGA	TUNED	RANCE
NAMES	--M-W	YUMMY	UINTA	VANED	RANEE
NIMES	******	******	WANDA	WANED	RANGE
NOMAS	UNMEW	--N-A	XENIA	WINED	RENEE
NUMBS	******	******	******	ZONED	RENTE
PIMAS	--M-X	AMNIA	--N-B	******	RINSE
PIMPS	******	APNEA	******	--N-E	SENNE
POMES	ADMEX	BANDA	DENEB	******	SENSE
PUMAS	ADMIX	CANEA	******	ANNIE	SINCE
PUMPS	CIMEX	CANNA	--N-C	ARNIE	SINGE
RAMPS	IMMIX	CONGA	******	BENNE	SYNGE
RAMUS	REMEX	DINKA	CONIC	BENUE	TENSE
REMUS	******	DONNA	CYNIC	BINGE	TINGE
RIMES	--M-Y	ENNEA	GENIC	BONZE	TONNE
ROMPS	******	FANGA	GYNEC	BUNDE	ULNAE
RUMPS	BUMPY	FONDA	IONIC	CANOE	VENAE
SAMOS	CAMPY	GENOA	MANIC	CENSE	VENUE
SIMPS	COMFY	GENUA	PANIC	CONGE	VINCE
SUMPS	CYMRY	GONIA	PUNIC	CONTE	WINCE
TAMES	DIMLY	HANNA	RUNIC	DANAE	WINZE
TAMIS	DUMMY	HENNA	SONIC	DANCE	******
TAMPS	DUMPY	IONIA	TONIC	DANTE	--N-F
TIMES	GAMMY	JUNTA	TUNIC	DENSE	******
TOMAS	GEMMY	KENYA	VINIC	DONEE	BANFF
TOMBS	GIMPY	KONYA	******	DONNE	GANEF
TOMES	GUMMY	LINDA	--N-D	DUNCE	******
VAMPS	HAMMY	LINGA	******	ERNIE	--N-H
WAMUS	HEMPY	MANIA	AWNED	FENCE	******
WOMBS	HOMEY	MANNA	BONED	GENIE	BENCH
******	HUMPY	MANTA	CANAD	GENRE	BUNCH
--M-T	JAMMY	MENSA	CANED	HANCE	CINCH
******	JEMMY	MINNA	CONED	HANSE	CONCH
ADMIT	JIMMY	NANNA	CONTD	HENCE	DINAH
ARMET	JUMPY	PANDA	DINED	HINGE	FINCH
COMDT	LIMEY	PENNA	FINED	LANCE	HUNCH
COMET	LUMPY	PENTA	GONAD	LUNGE	JONAH
DEMIT	MAMEY	PINNA	HONED	MANGE	KENCH
EMMET	MAMMY	PINTA	INNED	MANSE	LUNCH
GAMUT	MUMMY	PUNKA	LINED	MINAE	LYNCH
GEMOT	POMMY	SANTA	MANED	MINCE	MONTH
HEMAT	RAMMY	SENNA	MINED	MONDE	MUNCH

NINTH	PINEL	CONIO	LUNAR	CONUS	JANUS
PINCH	RENAL	CONTO	MANOR	DANES	JINKS
PUNCH	TONAL	DENTO	MINER	DANGS	JONAS
RANCH	VENAL	DINGO	MINOR	DENES	JONES
TENCH	VINYL	FUNGO	OWNER	DENIS	JUNES
TENTH	ZONAL	GENRO	PINER	DENTS	JUNKS
WENCH	******	GONIO	SANER	DENYS	KENTS
WINCH	**--N-M**	HONDO	SENOR	DINES	KINDS
XANTH	******	JINGO	SONAR	DINGS	KINGS
******	ANNAM	JUNCO	TENOR	DINTS	KINKS
--N-I	DENIM	JUNTO	TONER	DONAS	LANDS
******	FANUM	LENTO	TUNER	DONTS	LANES
CENTI	MINIM	LINGO	ULNAR	DUNES	LENAS
DENTI	VENOM	MANGO	VANIR	DUNGS	LENDS
ENNUI	******	MUNGO	******	DUNKS	LENES
FUNDI	**--N-N**	MUNRO	**--N-S**	EDNAS	LENIS
FUNGI	******	PANTO	******	ERNES	LENOS
GENII	BENIN	PENGO	AGNES	ETNAS	LENTS
GONDI	BONIN	PINGO	AGNIS	FANGS	LINES
HANOI	CANON	PINTO	AINOS	FANOS	LINGS
HENRI	CENON	PUNTO	AINUS	FENDS	LINKS
HINDI	FANON	RONDO	ANNAS	FINDS	LINUS
JINNI	HONAN	TANGO	ANNES	FINES	LONGS
LANAI	HUNAN	TANTO	AUNTS	FINIS	LUNES
LONGI	KININ	******	BANDS	FINKS	LUNGS
LUNGI	LENIN	**--N-P**	BANGS	FINNS	LUNTS
MENAI	LINEN	******	BANKS	FONTS	LYNNS
MINDI	LININ	PINUP	BANNS	FUNDS	MANES
PENNI	PINON	SUNUP	BENDS	FUNKS	MANUS
PINNI	RENAN	******	BENES	GANGS	MENDS
SINAI	RENIN	**--N-R**	BINDS	GENES	MENES
SUNNI	RUNIN	******	BINES	GENTS	MENUS
VINCI	RUNON	ABNER	BONDS	GENUS	MINAS
******	SINON	BONER	BONES	GINKS	MINDS
--N-K	TENON	CANER	BONGS	GONGS	MINES
******	XENON	CENTR	BONUS	HANDS	MINKS
MINSK	******	CONTR	BUNDS	HANGS	MINOS
******	**--N-O**	DENDR	BUNGS	HANKS	MINTS
--N-L	******	DINAR	BUNKS	HINDS	MINUS
******	BANJO	DINER	BUNNS	HINTS	MONAS
ANNAL	BINGO	DONAR	BUNTS	HONES	MONKS
ANNUL	BONGO	DONOR	CANES	HONGS	MYNAS
BANAL	BUNCO	FINER	CANIS	HONKS	NANAS
BINAL	BUNKO	GONER	CANTS	HUNKS	NINAS
CANAL	CANSO	HONOR	CENIS	HUNTS	NINES
FINAL	CANTO	INNER	CENTS	JANES	NINUS
PANEL	CENTO	LINER	CONES	JANIS	NONAS
PENAL	CONGO	LONER	CONKS	JANOS	NONES

ORNIS	TINGS	******	HONEY	VINNY	******
PANES	TINTS	--N-U	HONKY	WANEY	--O-C
PANGS	TONES	******	HUNKY	WANLY	******
PANTS	TONGS	BANTU	JENNY	WENDY	AZOIC
PENDS	TONIS	HINDU	JINNY	WENNY	BRONC
PENIS	TONUS	******	JONNY	WINDY	STOIC
PINAS	TONYS	--N-W	JUNKY	WINGY	******
PINES	TUNAS	******	KANDY	ZINCY	--O-D
PINGS	TUNES	RENEW	KENNY	ZINGY	******
PINKS	TUNIS	SINEW	KINKY	ZINKY	ALOUD
PINTS	ULNAS	******	LANKY	******	AROID
PONDS	VANES	--N-X	LENNY	--N-Z	AVOID
PONES	VANGS	******	LINEY	******	BLOND
PUNAS	VENDS	ANNEX	LINTY	IGNAZ	BLOOD
PUNGS	VENTS	******	MANCY	******	BOOED
PUNKS	VENUS	--N-Y	MANDY	--O-A	BROAD
PUNTS	VINAS	******	MANGY	******	BROOD
RANDS	VINES	ANNOY	MANLY	ABOMA	CHORD
RANIS	WANDS	AUNTY	MINGY	ADOWA	CLOUD
RANKS	WANES	BANDY	MONEY	AGORA	COOED
RANTS	WANTS	BENDY	MONTY	ALOHA	CROWD
RENDS	WENDS	BENJY	NANCY	AROMA	FIORD
RENES	WINDS	BENNY	NANNY	BIOTA	FJORD
RENTS	WINES	BONNY	NINNY	ENOLA	FLOOD
RINDS	WINGS	BUNNY	PANAY	FIONA	FLOYD
RINGS	WINKS	CANDY	PANDY	FLORA	FROND
RINKS	WINOS	CANNY	PANSY	ILONA	GEOID
RUNES	YANKS	CINDY	PANTY	KIOWA	HYOID
RUNGS	ZINCS	CONEY	PENNY	KRONA	KHOND
RUNTS	ZONES	CONNY	PINEY	LEONA	LLOYD
RYNDS	******	DANDY	PINKY	LEORA	LOOED
SANDS	--N-T	DANNY	PINNY	MYOMA	MOOED
SENDS	******	DENNY	PUNKY	POONA	MYOID
SINES	BANAT	DINGY	PUNTY	QUOTA	NJORD
SINGS	BENET	DINKY	RANDY	RHODA	OVOID
SINKS	BINET	DUNGY	RANGY	RHOEA	PLOID
SINUS	BINIT	FANCY	RONNY	STOMA	PROUD
SONES	CANST	FANNY	RUNNY	TIOGA	PYOID
SONGS	ERNST	FENNY	RUNTY	TRONA	SCOLD
SUNNS	GENET	FINNY	SANDY	VIOLA	SLOYD
TANGS	JANET	FUNKY	SONNY	******	SNOOD
TANIS	LUNET	FUNNY	SONSY	--O-B	STOOD
TANKS	MANET	GINNY	SUNNY	******	SWORD
TENDS	MONET	GUNNY	TANEY	ABOMB	WOOED
TENOS	NONET	HANDY	TANGY	******	ZOOID
TENTS	TENET	HANKY	TANSY	ABOMB	******
TINAS	TINCT	HENRY	TINNY	COOMB	--O-E
TINES		HINNY	TUNNY	HBOMB	******
				RHOMB	ABODE
					ABOVE

ADOBE	GNOME	STORE	MOOCH	STOCK	CROWN
ADORE	GOOSE	STOVE	POOCH	STOOK	DOORN
AFORE	GROPE	STOWE	QUOTH	STORK	DROWN
ALONE	GROVE	SWORE	SLOSH	******	ELOIN
AMOLE	HOOKE	TBONE	SLOTH	--O-L	FLOWN
ANODE	HOOVE	THOLE	SOOTH	******	FROWN
AROSE	IRONE	THOSE	THOTH	ABOIL	GROAN
ATONE	KRONE	TROPE	TOOTH	AFOUL	GROIN
AWOKE	LOOSE	TROVE	TROPH	ATOLL	GROWN
AXONE	MOORE	ULOSE	TROTH	BROIL	KNOWN
AZOLE	MOOSE	WHOLE	WROTH	CEORL	QUOIN
AZOTE	MYOPE	WHORE	******	DROLL	SCORN
BLOKE	NIOBE	WHOSE	--O-I	DROOL	SHORN
BOONE	NOOSE	WROTE	******	GHOUL	SHOWN
BOOZE	OBOLE	******	CROCI	GROWL	SPOON
BROKE	OZONE	--O-F	DHOLI	KNOLL	SWOON
BROME	PHOBE	******	DHOTI	PROWL	SWORN
CHOKE	PHONE	ADOLF	DUOMI	RAOUL	THORN
CHOLE	PHORE	ALOOF	ICOSI	SCOWL	******
CHORE	POOLE	FEOFF	MAORI	SEOUL	--O-O
CHOSE	PROBE	GEOFF	NAOMI	SHOAL	******
CLONE	PROLE	KLOOF	OBOLI	SHORL	ACOUO
CLOSE	PRONE	PROOF	OTOMI	SKOAL	BROMO
CLOVE	PROSE	SCOFF	OVOLI	SPOIL	CHORO
COOEE	PROVE	SPOOF	SHOJI	SPOOL	DUOMO
CROCE	QUOTE	WOOLF	******	STOOL	ICONO
CRONE	RHONE	******	--O-K	TROLL	KYOTO
CRORE	SAONE	--O-G	******	WHORL	OVOLO
CROZE	SCONE	******	ACOCK	******	PAOLO
DHOLE	SCOPE	ALONG	BLOCK	--O-M	PHONO
DIODE	SCORE	AMONG	BROCK	******	PHOTO
DIONE	SHONE	FLONG	BROOK	ABOHM	POOPO
DROME	SHORE	LAOAG	CHOCK	BLOOM	PROTO
DRONE	SHOTE	PRONG	CLOAK	BROOM	PROVO
DROVE	SHOVE	THONG	CLOCK	GLOOM	SCOTO
ECOLE	SLOPE	WRONG	CROAK	GROOM	SPORO
ELOPE	SMOKE	******	CROCK	PROEM	WHOSO
EMOTE	SMOTE	--O-H	CROOK	STORM	******
EPODE	SNORE	******	FLOCK	******	--O-P
ERODE	SPODE	AZOTH	FROCK	--O-N	******
EROSE	SPOKE	BOOTH	KIOSK	******	CROUP
EVOKE	SPORE	BROTH	KNOCK	ACORN	DROOP
FROME	STOAE	CLOTH	PLONK	ADORN	GROUP
FROZE	STOKE	ENOCH	SHOCK	ALOIN	KNOSP
GEODE	STOLE	EPOCH	SHOOK	BLOWN	SCOOP
GLOBE	STOME	FROSH	SMOCK	BROWN	SLOOP
GLOVE	STONE	FROTH	SNOOK	CLOWN	SNOOP
GLOZE	STOPE	HOOCH	SPOOK	CROON	STOMP

STOOP	CIONS	HOOKS	PROWS	ADOPT	******
STOUP	CLODS	HOOPS	PSOAS	AFOOT	--O-X
SWOOP	CLOGS	HOOTS	QUODS	ALOFT	******
THORP	CLONS	ICONS	RIOTS	APORT	BRONX
TROOP	CLOPS	IDOLS	ROODS	BLOAT	CROIX
WHOOP	CLOTS	IKONS	ROOFS	BOOST	SIOUX
******	CLOYS	IRONS	ROOKS	CLOUT	******
--O-R	COOKS	KNOBS	ROOMS	COOPT	--O-Y
******	COOLS	KNOPS	ROOTS	CROAT	******
AMOUR	COONS	KNOTS	RYOTS	CROFT	AGONY
AVOIR	COOPS	KNOWS	SCOPS	DROIT	ANOMY
CHOIR	COOTS	KOOKS	SCOTS	DROPT	ATONY
COOER	CROPS	LEONS	SCOWS	EBOAT	ATORY
FLOOR	CROSS	LIONS	SHOES	FLOAT	BLOWY
FLOUR	CROWS	LOOFS	SHOOS	FLOUT	BOOBY
HHOUR	DHOWS	LOOKS	SHOPS	FRONT	BOOTY
ODOUR	DOOMS	LOOMS	SHOTS	FROST	BOOZY
SCOUR	DOORS	LOONS	SHOWS	GHOST	CHOKY
SHOER	DROPS	LOOPS	SLOBS	GLOAT	COOEY
SPOOR	DROSS	LOOTS	SLOES	GLOST	COOKY
STOUR	EBONS	LYONS	SLOGS	GROAT	CRONY
WOOER	ENOLS	MEOWS	SLOPS	GROUT	DEOXY
******	FEODS	MOODS	SLOTS	KNOUT	DOOLY
--O-S	FLOCS	MOONS	SLOWS	ODONT	EBONY
******	FLOES	MOORS	SMOGS	PROCT	EMORY
AEONS	FLOGS	MUONS	SNOBS	QUOIT	EPOXY
ALOES	FLOPS	NOOKS	SNOTS	ROOST	FOOTY
ALOIS	FLOSS	NOONS	SNOWS	SCOOT	GLORY
ATOMS	FLOWS	OBOES	SOOTS	SCOTT	GNOMY
AVOWS	FOODS	ODORS	SPOTS	SCOUT	GOODY
AXONS	FOOLS	PEONS	STOAS	SHOAT	GOOEY
AZONS	FOOTS	PHOTS	STOPS	SHOOT	GOOFY
BLOBS	FROES	PIONS	STOSS	SHORT	GOOSY
BLOCS	FROGS	PIOUS	STOWS	SHOUT	HOOEY
BLOIS	FROWS	PLODS	TOOLS	SMOLT	HOOKY
BLOTS	GAOLS	PLOPS	TOOTS	SNOOT	IRONY
BLOWS	GLOBS	PLOTS	TROAS	SNORT	IVORY
BOOBS	GLOSS	PLOWS	TROTS	SNOUT	KOOKY
BOOKS	GLOWS	PLOYS	ULOUS	SPORT	LOOBY
BOOMS	GOODS	POODS	VIOLS	SPOUT	LOONY
BOONS	GOOFS	POOLS	WHOPS	STOAT	LOOPY
BOORS	GOOKS	POONS	WOODS	STOPT	MOODY
BOOTS	GOONS	POOPS	WOOFS	STOUT	MOONY
BROOS	GROSS	PROAS	WOOLS	******	MYOPY
BROWS	GROTS	PRODS	ZOOMS	--O-T	OLOGY
BUOYS	GROWS	PROFS	ZOONS	******	PEONY
CHOPS	HOODS	PROMS	******	ABORT	PHONY
CHOWS	HOOFS	PROPS	ABOUT	ABOUT	PROSY

PROXY	BIPOD	******	PEPIN	VAPOR	DEPOT
ROOKY	COPED	--P-I	RIPEN	VIPER	HEPAT
ROOMY	CUPID	******	RIPON	WIPER	IMPOT
ROOTY	DOPED	AMPHI	UNPEN	******	INPUT
SCOPY	DUPED	CAPRI	UNPIN	--P-S	KAPUT
SHOWY	GAPED	LIPPI	YAPON	******	LOPAT
SMOKY	HOPED	PAPPI	YUPON	ASPIS	PIPET
SNOWY	JAPED	SEPTI	******	CAPES	PIPIT
SOOTY	LEPID	TOPHI	--P-O	COPES	******
STOGY	LIPID	XIPHI	******	COPTS	--P-W
STOMY	LOPED	******	COPRO	DOPES	******
STONY	MOPED	--P-K	CUPRO	DUPES	PAPAW
STORY	PIPED	******	DIPLO	GAPES	******
WOODY	RAPED	CAPEK	HAPLO	HOPES	--P-Y
WOOLY	RAPID	KAPOK	HIPPO	HYPOS	******
WOOZY	ROPED	KOPEK	HYPNO	JAPES	ALPHY
ZLOTY	SAPID	TUPIK	HYPSO	KAPHS	AMPLY
******	TAPED	******	LEPTO	KEPIS	APPLY
--O-Z	TEPID	--P-L	NEPHO	LAPIS	CUPPY
******	TOPED	******	SAPRO	LAPPS	DIPPY
GROSZ	TYPED	AMPUL	SEPTO	LEPUS	DOPEY
******	UPPED	APPAL	******	LOPES	EMPTY
--P-A	VAPID	APPEL	--P-R	LUPUS	GAPPY
******	WIPED	COPAL	******	MOPES	GIPSY
ALPHA	******	CUPEL	AMPHR	NAPES	GUPPY
ASPCA	--P-E	EXPEL	ASPER	NIPAS	GYPSY
CAPUA	******	IMPEL	ATPAR	PAPAS	HAPLY
COPRA	AMPLE	LAPEL	CAPER	PEPOS	HAPPY
HEPTA	APPLE	NEPAL	COPER	PEPYS	HIPPY
HYPHA	COPSE	NOPAL	DUPER	PIPES	IMPLY
KAPPA	DUPLE	PAPAL	GAPER	POPES	LEPSY
LEPTA	KOPJE	PIPAL	HYPER	RAPES	LIPPY
PAPUA	LAPSE	PUPIL	LAPAR	ROPES	LOPPY
PEPLA	MAPLE	REPEL	LEPER	SEPTS	NAPPY
SEPIA	NAPPAE	SEPAL	LOPER	SIPES	NIPPY
SEPTA	PUPAE	******	MOPER	SUPES	PAPPY
SUPRA	RAPHE	--P-N	NEPHR	TAPAS	PEPPY
VEPSA	RUPEE	******	NOPAR	TAPES	POPPY
******	TEPEE	ARPEN	PAPER	TAPIS	POPSY
--P-C	TOPEE	ASPEN	PIPER	TOPES	PUPPY
******	******	CAPON	RIPER	TOPIS	REPAY
ASPIC	--P-G	GIPON	SAPOR	TUPIS	REPLY
COPEC	******	JAPAN	SOPOR	TYPES	ROPEY
KOPEC	UNPEG	JUPON	SUPER	TYPOS	SAPPY
TOPIC	******	LAPIN	TAPER	WIPES	SEPOY
--P-D	--P-H	LUPIN	TAPIR	YIPES	SOPHY
******	******	ORPIN	TOPER	******	SOPPY
ARPAD	DEPTH	PAPEN	UPPER	--P-T	TIPPY
BIPED	HOPEH			******	
	HUPEH			CAPET	
				CAPUT	

TIPSY	LORCA	******	BARYE	NERVE	BIRTH
TOPSY	LORNA	--R-D	BERME	NORSE	BURGH
ZIPPY	MARIA	******	BERNE	NURSE	CURCH
******	MARLA	ACRED	BIRLE	PARSE	EARTH
--P-Z	MARTA	ACRID	BORNE	PERLE	FARAH
******	MIRZA	AIRED	BURKE	PERSE	FIRTH
TOPAZ	MORNA	BARED	BURSE	PORGE	FORTH
******	MORTA	BORED	CARLE	PUREE	FURTH
--Q-E	MURRA	CARED	CARTE	PURGE	GARTH
******	MYRIA	CERED	CARVE	PURSE	GIRSH
ESQUE	MYRNA	CORED	CIRCE	SARRE	GIRTH
FIQUE	NORIA	CURED	CORFE	SCREE	HARSH
PIQUE	NORMA	DARED	CORSE	SERGE	KERCH
ROQUE	OCREA	EARED	CURIE	SERVE	LARCH
TOQUE	PARCA	EDRED	CURSE	SPREE	LURCH
TUQUE	PARKA	ERRED	CURVE	SPRUE	MARCH
******	PARMA	FARAD	DIRGE	SURGE	MARSH
--Q-I	SERRA	FARED	EARLE	TERSE	MIRTH
******	STRIA	FIRED	EERIE	THREE	MORPH
MAQUI	SYRIA	GORED	EYRIE	THROE	MYRRH
******	TERRA	HARED	FARCE	TIREE	NORAH
--R-A	VERNA	HEROD	FARLE	TORTE	NORTH
******	VIRGA	HIRED	FAROE	VARVE	PARCH
AORTA	WIRRA	JARED	FORCE	VERGE	PERCH
ATRIA	YERBA	LURED	FORGE	VERNE	PERTH
BARCA	******	LURID	FORME	VERSE	PORCH
BEREA	--R-B	MIRED	FORTE	VERVE	SARAH
BERIA	******	OARED	FURZE	VIRGE	SURAH
BERRA	CARIB	PARED	GORGE	WORSE	TORAH
BERTA	CAROB	PORED	GORME	******	TORCH
BURMA	HOREB	SCROD	GORSE	--R-F	WORTH
BURSA	SCRUB	SERED	HARTE	******	******
CARLA	SHRUB	SHRED	HORAE	SERIF	--R-I
CERIA	THROB	SIRED	HORDE	UNREF	******
CIRCA	******	STRAD	HORNE	******	AUREI
CORIA	--R-C	TARED	HORSE	--R-G	CARDI
CURIA	******	TIRED	JORGE	******	CARPI
DERMA	AURIC	WIRED	KYRIE	SCRAG	CIRRI
DORSA	BARIC	WORLD	LARGE	SHRUG	CORGI
DURRA	BORIC	******	MARGE	SPRAG	CURVI
FERIA	CERIC	--R-E	MARIE	SPRIG	DORSI
GERDA	DARIC	******	MARNE	UNRIG	FERMI
HERMA	DORIC	AERIE	MERGE	******	FERRI
HORTA	LYRIC	AGREE	MERLE	--R-H	FORLI
JURUA	SERAC	AURAE	MEROE	******	GORKI
KARMA	TORIC	BARDE	MORAE	BARTH	MERCI
KOREA	VARIC	BARGE	MORSE	BERTH	PARSI
LARVA	XERIC	BARRE	MURRE	BIRCH	SERAI

TARSI	******	PAREN	VARIO	AFROS	CURLS
TERRI	**--R-M**	PERON	VARRO	ARRAS	CYRUS
TORII	******	PHREN	VERSO	ARRIS	DARES
TORSI	ABRAM	PYRAN	VIREO	AURAS	DARNS
TURKI	AURUM	RERAN	VIRGO	AURES	DARTS
VERDI	CAROM	RERUN	******	AURIS	DIRKS
VERMI	CERAM	SARAN	**--R-P**	BARBS	DORAS
******	CHROM	SERIN	******	BARDS	DORIS
--R-K	DURUM	SERON	ATRIP	BARES	DORMS
******	FORUM	SIREN	SCRAP	BARKS	DORRS
DEREK	HAREM	SERON	SCRIP	BARNS	DORUS
DIRCK	HIRAM	TURIN	SIRUP	BERGS	DUROS
KURSK	IHRAM	ZIRON	STRAP	BERMS	EARLS
RURIK	JORAM	******	STRIP	BERTS	EARNS
TORSK	JORUM	**--R-O**	STROP	BIRDS	EURUS
******	PURIM	******	SYRUP	BIRLS	EYRAS
--R-L	SCRAM	BURRO	UNRIP	BIRRS	EZRAS
******	SCRIM	CARBO	******	BORES	FARES
APRIL	SCRUM	CARGO	**--R-R**	BORIS	FARLS
AURAL	SERUM	CARLO	******	BORTS	FARMS
AVRIL	STRUM	CARPO	BARER	BURDS	FERNS
BERYL	THRUM	CARYO	BERAR	BURGS	FIRES
CAROL	******	CIRRO	BORER	BURLS	FIRMS
CORAL	**--R-N**	CURIO	CARER	BURNS	FIRNS
CYRIL	******	DERMO	CORER	BURPS	FORBS
DURAL	AARON	DORSO	CURER	BURRS	FORDS
ENROL	AKRON	FARGO	DARER	BYRES	FORES
ERROL	APRON	FERRO	DIRER	CARAS	FORKS
FERAL	ARRAN	FORGO	DURER	CARDS	FORMS
GORAL	BARON	GARBO	ERROR	CARES	FORTS
GYRAL	BORON	KAROO	EYRIR	CARLS	FURLS
HORAL	BURAN	KARYO	FARER	CARPS	GARBS
JURAL	BURIN	LARGO	FIRER	CARTS	GARYS
JUREL	BYRON	MARCO	FUROR	CARYS	GERMS
KAROL	CHRON	MARGO	HARAR	CERES	GIRDS
MORAL	FURAN	MARIO	HIRER	CEROS	GIRLS
MOREL	GIRON	MORRO	JUROR	CHRIS	GIROS
MURAL	GYRON	NARCO	LURER	CHRYS	GIRTS
PAROL	HERON	PARGO	PARER	CORAS	GORES
PERIL	HURON	PORNO	PURER	CORDS	GURUS
RURAL	KAREN	SARCO	RARER	CORES	GYRES
SERAL	KIRIN	SARTO	SORER	CORKS	GYROS
SOREL	KORAN	SERVO	SURER	CORMS	GYRUS
SURAL	KORUN	SORGO	WIRER	CORNS	HARDS
TYROL	LORAN	TARDO	******	CORPS	HARES
VIRAL	MORIN	TARSO	**--R-S**	CURBS	HARKS
ZORIL	MORON	TORSO	******	CURDS	HARLS
	MYRON	TURBO	ABRIS	CURES	HARMS
		TURCO	ACRES		

HARPS	NORAS	TORTS	JURAT	BARMY	LARRY
HARTS	NORMS	TORUS	KARAT	BARRY	LEROY
HERBS	NORNS	TURFS	KERAT	BERRY	LORRY
HERDS	OGRES	TURKS	MARAT	BERTY	MARLY
HERLS	OKRAS	TURNS	MERIT	BORTY	MARRY
HIRES	ORRIS	TYROS	MORAT	BURLY	MARTY
HORAS	PARAS	VARAS	MURAT	BURRY	MERCY
HORNS	PARDS	VARUS	SPRAT	CAREY	MERRY
HORUS	PARES	VERAS	SPRIT	CARRY	MORAY
HURDS	PARIS	VERBS	STRAT	CORBY	MORTY
HURLS	PARKS	VERNS	STRUT	CORKY	MURKY
HURTS	PAROS	VIRES	TAROT	CORNY	MURRY
JARLS	PARRS	VIRUS	TERAT	CURDY	NARKY
JERKS	PARTS	WARDS	VERST	CURLY	NERVY
KARLS	PERES	WARES	WORST	CURRY	OURAY
KERBS	PERIS	WARMS	******	DARKY	PARRY
KERES	PERKS	WARNS	--R-U	DERBY	PARTY
KERFS	PORES	WARPS	******	DERRY	PERCY
KERNS	PORTS	WARTS	BORNU	DIRTY	PERKY
KIRKS	PURLS	WIRES	CORFU	DORMY	PERRY
KURUS	PURRS	WORDS	CORNU	EARLY	PORGY
LARDS	PYRES	WORKS	PAREU	FARCY	PORKY
LARES	SARAS	WORMS	PERDU	FERNY	PURSY
LARKS	SARIS	WORTS	VERTU	FERRY	SORRY
LIRAS	SARKS	XERUS	VIRTU	FIRRY	SPRAY
LORDS	SAROS	YARDS	******	FORAY	STRAY
LORES	SERBS	YARNS	--R-W	FORBY	SURFY
LORIS	SERES	YPRES	******	FORTY	SURGY
LURES	SERFS	ZARFS	ARROW	FURRY	SURLY
LURKS	SIRES	ZEROS	SCREW	FURZY	TARDY
LYRES	SORAS	******	SEROW	GARRY	TARRY
MARCS	SORBS	--R-T	SHREW	GERRY	TARTY
MARES	SORES	******	STRAW	GERTY	TERRY
MARIS	SORTS	BARIT	STREW	GORKY	TURFY
MARKS	SORUS	BERET	THREW	GORSY	WARTY
MARLS	SURAS	BURNT	THROW	HARDY	WORDY
MARTS	SURDS	BURST	******	HARPY	WORMY
MIRES	SURFS	CARAT	--R-X	HARRY	WORRY
MORAS	SYROS	CARET	******	HERBY	******
MORES	TARES	CERAT	BORAX	HORNY	--R-Z
MORNS	TARNS	COROT	HYRAX	HORSY	******
MOROS	TAROS	CURST	MUREX	HURLY	BORTZ
MORTS	TARPS	DURST	PYREX	HURRY	HARTZ
MYRAS	TARTS	EGRET	VARIX	JERKY	HERTZ
NARDS	TERMS	FIRST	XEROX	JERRY	JEREZ
NARES	TERNS	HERAT	******	JERRY	******
NARIS	TIRES	HORST	--R-Y	KERRY	--S-A
NEROS	TIROS	HURST	******	LARDY	******
			ARRAY	LARKY	BASRA
			BARKY	LARKY	CESTA

COSTA	BASTE	******	SASIN	ARSES	JUSTS
FOSSA	BISSE	**--S-L**	SUSAN	ARSIS	LASTS
GUSTA	CASTE	******	******	ASSES	LISAS
HOSEA	ELSIE	ANSEL	**--S-O**	ASSNS	LISPS
JOSUA	ENSUE	AUSTL	******	ASSTS	LISTS
LASSA	ESSIE	BASAL	BASSO	BASES	LOSES
LYSSA	FESSE	BASEL	CASCO	BASIS	LUSTS
MUSCA	FOSSE	BASIL	CISCO	BASKS	LYSES
OPSIA	FUSEE	EASEL	COSMO	BESTS	LYSIS
PASHA	GASPE	EDSEL	COSTO	BISES	MASKS
PASTA	HASTE	FUSEL	CUSSO	BOSKS	MASTS
TESLA	HESSE	FUSIL	CYSTO	BUSES	MESAS
TESTA	ISSUE	LYSOL	DISCO	BUSKS	MISES
VESTA	JESSE	MOSEL	DISKO	BUSTS	MISTS
VISTA	JOSIE	NASAL	GESSO	CASES	MOSES
******	JOSUE	OUSEL	GISMO	CASKS	MUSES
--S-C	LISLE	SISAL	GUSTO	CASTS	MUSKS
******	MASSE	******	LASSO	CASUS	MUSTS
ASSOC	MESNE	**--S-M**	MASTO	CISTS	NESTS
BASIC	PASSE	******	MISDO	COSTS	NISUS
CUSEC	PASTE	ASSAM	MOSSO	CUSKS	NOSES
MESIC	POSSE	BESOM	RUSSO	CUSPS	OASES
MUSIC	SUSIE	BOSOM	TASSO	CYSTS	OASIS
VESIC	TASTE	EPSOM	******	DESKS	OPSIS
******	URSAE	******	**--S-P**	DISCS	OUSTS
--S-D	WASTE	**--S-N**	******	DISKS	PASTS
******	******	******	AESOP	DOSES	PESOS
BASED	**--S-H**	ARSON	******	DUSKS	PESTS
BUSED	******	BASIN	**--S-R**	DUSTS	POSES
CASED	BOSCH	BASON	******	EASES	POSTS
DOSED	PASCH	BISON	AESIR	ELSAS	RASPS
EASED	******	BOSON	ASSYR	ERSES	RESTS
FUSED	**--S-I**	BOSUN	CESAR	ESSES	RISES
HOSED	******	EOSIN	DOSER	FASTS	RISKS
LYSED	ASSAI	ESSEN	GASTR	FISCS	RISUS
MUSED	BASSI	HYSON	LASER	FISTS	ROSAS
NOSED	BYSSI	IBSEN	LOSER	FUSES	ROSES
POSED	CESTI	JASON	MASER	GASES	RUSES
ROSED	CYSTI	LYSIN	MISER	GASPS	RUSKS
VISED	DISCI	MASON	POSER	GISTS	RUSTS
WISED	ISSEI	MESON	RISER	GUSTS	TASKS
******	NISEI	MOSAN	VISOR	HASPS	TESTS
--S-E	PISCI	NISAN	WESER	HOSES	TUSKS
******	******	ORSON	WISER	HOSTS	VASES
AISLE	**--S-K**	PUSAN	******	HUSKS	VESTS
AISNE	******	RESIN	**--S-S**	IASIS	VISAS
ANSAE	COSEK	RISEN	******	JESTS	VISES
BASLE		ROSIN	APSES	JESUS	WASPS
			APSIS		

WISES	GUSHY	ENTIA	MUTED	BITCH	ARTEL
WISPS	GUSTY	EXTRA	NOTED	BOTCH	BETEL
XYSTS	HASTY	GOTHA	OCTAD	BUTCH	BUTYL
YESES	HUSKY	GUTTA	OPTED	CATCH	DATAL
ZESTS	HUSSY	INTRA	OSTED	CUTCH	EXTOL
******	JASSY	LOTTA	OUTED	DITCH	FATAL
--S-T	JESSY	LYTTA	RATED	DUTCH	FETAL
******	LUSTY	OSTIA	SATED	FETCH	HOTEL
ASSET	MASHY	PATNA	SITED	FITCH	METAL
BESET	MASSY	RETIA	TOTED	HATCH	METOL
BESOT	MESHY	RETTA	VOTED	HITCH	MOTEL
HASNT	MESSY	ROTLA	******	HUTCH	NATAL
INSET	MISSY	SITKA	**--T-E**	KETCH	OCTYL
LISZT	MISTY	SUTRA	******	LATCH	PETAL
ONSET	MOSEY	TATRA	ANTAE	LOTAH	RATAL
POSIT	MOSSY	TETRA	ARTIE	MATCH	RATEL
RESET	MUSHY	ULTRA	BATHE	MITCH	SOTOL
UPSET	MUSKY	VITTA	BETTE	NOTCH	TOTAL
VISCT	MUSSY	******	BUTTE	PATCH	UNTIL
VISIT	MUSTY	**--T-C**	CUTIE	PITCH	VITAL
WASNT	NASTY	******	ETTIE	RATCH	******
******	NOSEY	ANTIC	ISTLE	RETCH	**--T-M**
--S-X	PASSY	ARTIC	IXTLE	ROTCH	******
******	PASTY	ATTIC	KATIE	VETCH	DATUM
DESEX	PESKY	AZTEC	LATHE	WATCH	ENTOM
ESSEX	PUSHY	CETIC	LETHE	WITCH	RETEM
UNSEX	PUSSY	ISTIC	LITHE	******	TOTEM
******	RASPY	LYTIC	LITRE	**--T-I**	******
--S-Y	RISKY	OPTIC	LOTTE	******	**--T-N**
******	RUSHY	VATIC	MATTE	ALTAI	******
ASSAY	RUSTY	******	METRE	LITAI	ACTIN
BESSY	SASSY	**--T-D**	MITRE	MATRI	ALTON
BOSKY	SISSY	******	NITRE	MITZI	ANTON
BOSSY	TASTY	ACTED	OUTRE	NITRI	ASTON
BUSBY	TESTY	ANTED	SATIE	PATRI	BATAN
BUSHY	UNSAY	BATED	SETAE	PATTI	BATEN
CASEY	VASTY	CITED	TITHE	PETTI	BATON
CISSY	WASHY	DATED	TITLE	TUTTI	BETON
CUSHY	WASPY	DOTED	UNTIE	VITRI	CETIN
DASHY	WISPY	FATED	VITAE	******	CUTIN
DISHY	ZESTY	FETED	WITHE	**--T-K**	EATEN
DUSKY	******	FETID	WITTE	******	ELTON
DUSTY	**--T-A**	GATED	******	BATIK	GATUN
ESSAY	******	HATED	**--T-F**	******	JETON
FISHY	AFTRA	KITED	******	**--T-L**	JOTUN
FUSSY	ANTRA	LUTED	MOTIF	******	LATIN
FUSTY	CITRA	MATED	******	ANTAL	LUTON
GASSY	COTTA	METED	**--T-H**	ARTAL	MATIN
			******		
			AITCH		
			BATCH		

NITON	******	OTTER	GATES	SITUS	HETTY
OATEN	--T-P	OUTER	GOTHS	TETHS	HOTLY
OFTEN	******	PATER	HATES	TITIS	IATRY
PATEN	CUTUP	PETER	ICTUS	TITUS	JETTY
PITON	ESTOP	QATAR	IOTAS	TOTES	KATHY
PUTON	GETUP	RATER	JATOS	TUTUS	KITTY
SATAN	LETUP	ROTOR	JUTES	VOTES	LATHY
SATIN	PUTUP	SATYR	KATES	WATTS	LATRY
SETON	SETUP	SITAR	KITES	YETIS	LETTY
SITIN	WATAP	TATAR	KOTOS	ZETAS	LOTTY
TETON	******	TITER	LATHS	******	MATEY
TITAN	--T-R	TOTER	LETTS	--T-T	MATTY
WITAN	******	TUTOR	LITAS	******	METRY
WOTAN	ACTOR	UTTER	LOTOS	AETAT	MITZY
******	AFTER	VOTER	LOTUS	MOTET	MOTHY
--T-O	ALTAR	WATER	LUTES	OCTET	NATTY
******	ALTER	******	MATES	PETIT	NETTY
ANTHO	APTER	--T-S	MATHS	PITOT	NITTY
ASTRO	ARTER	******	MATTS	******	NUTTY
BATHO	ARTHR	ACTUS	METAS	--T-U	PATHY
BETSO	ARTUR	ALTAS	METES	******	PATSY
DATTO	ASTER	ALTOS	METIS	MATSU	PATTY
DITTO	ASTIR	ANTES	MITES	******	PETRY
IATRO	ASTOR	ANTIS	MITTS	--T-X	PETTY
INTRO	ATTAR	ARTIS	MOTES	******	PITHY
LATRO	BITER	ATTIS	MOTHS	LATEX	POTSY
LITHO	CATER	ATTYS	MUTES	******	POTTY
LOTTO	CUTER	AUTOS	MUTTS	--T-Y	PUTTY
MATEO	DATER	BATES	MYTHS	******	RATTY
MATZO	DETER	BATHS	NATES	APTLY	RETRY
METHO	DOTER	BETAS	NOTES	AUTRY	RITZY
METRO	EATER	BETHS	OATES	BATHY	RUTTY
MOTTO	ENTER	BITES	OATHS	BATTY	TATTY
MYTHO	ESTAR	BITTS	OTTOS	BETSY	TUTTY
NITRO	ESTER	BOTTS	PATES	BETTY	WETLY
ORTHO	FETOR	BUTTS	PATHS	BOTHY	WITHY
OUTDO	HATER	CETUS	PETES	CATHY	WITTY
OUTGO	INTER	CITES	PITAS	CATTY	******
PATHO	ISTAR	COTES	PITHS	CUTEY	--U-A
PATIO	LATER	CUTIS	PUTTS	CUTTY	******
PETRO	LITER	DATES	RATES	DITTY	ADUWA
PETTO	MATER	DITAS	RITAS	DOTTY	ALULA
POTTO	METER	DOTES	RITES	ENTRY	ARUBA
RATIO	MITER	ESTES	ROTAS	FATLY	BEULA
RETRO	MOTOR	ETTAS	RUTHS	FATTY	CAUCA
SETTO	NETER	FATES	SATES	FITLY	CEUTA
SOTTO	NITER	FETES	SETHS	GUTSY	CHUFA
	NOTER	FETUS	SITES	HATTY	CRURA

DOURA	ROUND	LOUSE	******	BRUSK	******
FAUNA	SLUED	MAUDE	**--U-H**	CAULK	**--U-O**
GOUDA	SOUND	MAUVE	******	CHUCK	******
LAURA	SQUAD	MEUSE	BLUSH	CHUNK	BRUNO
MAURA	SQUID	MOUSE	BOUGH	CLUCK	LEUCO
PAULA	TRUED	NEUME	BRUSH	DRUNK	LEUKO
SAUNA	WOULD	OVULE	COUCH	FLUNK	NEURO
SCUBA	WOUND	PAUSE	COUGH	PLUCK	OCULO
SCUTA	******	PLUME	COUTH	PLUNK	PAULO
SOUSA	**--U-E**	PRUDE	CRUSH	SHUCK	PLUTO
STUKA	ABUSE	PRUNE	DOUGH	SKULK	SAURO
STUPA	ACUTE	ROUGE	FAUGH	SKUNK	SCUDO
THUJA	AMUSE	ROUSE	FLUSH	SLUNK	TAURO
TRUDA	AQUAE	ROUTE	HOUGH	SPUNK	TAUTO
UVULA	AZURE	SAUCE	LAUGH	STUCK	TRURO
******	BAUME	SAUTE	LOUGH	STUNK	******
--U-B	BOULE	SCUTE	MOUCH	TRUCK	**--U-P**
******	BOUSE	SHUTE	MOUTH	TRUNK	******
BLURB	BRUCE	SOUSE	PLUSH	******	CHUMP
CRUMB	BRUME	SPUME	POUCH	**--U-L**	CLUMP
EXURB	BRUTE	STUPE	ROUGH	******	CRUMP
PLUMB	CAUSE	TAUPE	SHUSH	CHURL	EQUIP
RHUMB	CHUTE	THULE	SLUSH	CRUEL	FLUMP
SQUAB	COUPE	TRUCE	SOUGH	EQUAL	FRUMP
SQUIB	CRUDE	YOURE	SOUTH	GRUEL	KRUPP
THUMB	CRUSE	YOUVE	TOUCH	KNURL	PLUMP
******	DEUCE	******	TOUGH	SCULL	SCULP
--U-C	DOUSE	**--U-F**	TRUTH	SKULL	SLUMP
******	DRUPE	******	VOUCH	STULL	SLURP
ADUNC	DRUSE	BLUFF	WAUGH	TRULL	STUMP
******	EDUCE	FLUFF	YOUTH	USUAL	THUMP
--U-D	ELUDE	GRUFF	******	YOULL	TRUMP
******	ETUDE	SCUFF	**--U-I**	******	USURP
BLUED	EXUDE	SCURF	******	**--U-M**	******
BOUND	FIUME	SNUFF	CRUCI	******	**--U-R**
CLUED	FLUKE	STUFF	DOUAI	HAULM	******
COULD	FLUME	******	GAUDI	YQUEM	BLUER
DRUID	FLUTE	**--U-G**	HOURI	******	CHURR
FEUED	GAUGE	******	KAUAI	**--U-N**	CRUOR
FLUID	GAUZE	BOURG	KAURI	******	FEUAR
FOUND	GLUME	CLUNG	KRUBI	ALUIN	FLUOR
GLUED	GOUGE	FLUNG	NEURI	BOURN	KNURR
GOURD	GRUME	SLUNG	PLURI	BRUIN	TRUER
HOUND	HOUSE	STUNG	PLUVI	CHURN	******
MAUND	INURE	SWUNG	SCUDI	INURN	**--U-S**
MOULD	JOULE	WRUNG	******	MOURN	******
MOUND	LOUPE	YOUNG	**--U-K**	ROUEN	ABUTS
POUND			******	SPURN	AGUES
			AMUCK	UTURN	
			BAULK		

ALUMS	POUFS	BLUNT	DAUBY	MOVED	COVEN
AQUAS	POURS	BLURT	DOUAY	PAVED	DEVON
ARUMS	POUTS	BRUIT	DOURY	RAVED	DIVAN
BLUES	ROUES	BRUNT	DRURY	RIVED	ELVAN
BLURS	ROUTS	COUNT	FLUKY	ROVED	ELVIN
BOUTS	SAULS	COURT	FLUTY	SAVED	GAVIN
CAULS	SCUDS	CRUET	GAUDY	VIVID	GIVEN
CHUBS	SCUMS	CRUST	GAUZY	WAVED	HAVEN
CHUGS	SCUPS	DAUNT	GLUEY	WIVED	IRVIN
CHUMS	SCUTS	DOUBT	GOUTY	******	KEVIN
CLUBS	SHULS	EDUCT	KAURY	--V-E	LEVEN
CLUES	SHUNS	ERUCT	LOUSY	******	LIVEN
COUPS	SHUTS	ERUPT	MOUSY	CAVIE	PAVAN
DAUBS	SKUAS	EXULT	PLUMY	DAVIE	RAVEN
DOUGS	SLUBS	FAULT	ROUPY	GAVLE	RIVEN
DRUBS	SLUES	FAUST	SAUCY	LEVEE	ROVEN
DRUGS	SLUGS	FOUNT	SAURY	LIVRE	SAVIN
DRUMS	SLUMS	FRUIT	SOUPY	MOVIE	SEVEN
ETUIS	SLURS	GAULT	SPUMY	NOVAE	SIVAN
FAUNS	SLUTS	GAUNT	STUDY	REVUE	WOVEN
FEUDS	SMUTS	GRUNT	TRUDY	******	******
FLUBS	SNUBS	HAUNT	TRULY	--V-L	--V-O
FLUES	SNUGS	JAUNT	USURY	ANVIL	******
FOULS	SOULS	JOUST	******	ARVAL	DAVAO
FOURS	SOUPS	MOULT	--V-A	BEVEL	******
GAUDS	SOURS	MOUNT	******	CAVIL	--V-P
GAULS	SPUDS	POULT	FOVEA	CIVIL	******
GAURS	SPURS	ROUST	LIVIA	DEVIL	DOVAP
GAUSS	STUBS	SAULT	******	GAVEL	******
GLUES	STUDS	SHUNT	--V-C	HOVEL	--V-R
GLUTS	STUMS	SPURT	******	KEVEL	******
GRUBS	STUNS	SQUAT	CIVIC	LEVEL	COVER
HAULS	THUDS	STUNT	HAVOC	NAVAL	DIVER
HOURS	THUGS	TAUNT	******	NAVEL	DOVER
KNURS	THURS	TRUST	--V-D	NEVIL	ELVER
LAUDS	TOURS	VAULT	******	NIVAL	FAVOR
LEUDS	TOUTS	VAUNT	BOVID	NOVEL	FEVER
LOUIS	TRUES	******	CAVED	RAVEL	FIVER
LOUPS	TRUSS	--U-U	COVED	REVEL	GIVER
LOURS	WAULS	******	DAVID	RIVAL	HAVER
LOUTS	YAUPS	NAURU	DIVED	******	HOVER
MAUDS	YOURS	******	GYVED	--V-N	INVAR
MAULS	******	--U-W	HIVED	******	LAVER
MOUES	--U-T	******	JIVED	ALVAN	LEVER
NOUNS	******	SQUAW	LAVED	ALVIN	LIVER
******	ADULT	******	LIVED	BEVAN	LOVER
PAULS	ADUST	--U-Y	LIVID	BEVIN	MOVER
PLUGS	BLUET	******	LOVED		NAVAR
PLUMS		BOUSY			
		CLUNY			

NEVER	ROVES	SOWED	FEWER	YAWPS	NIXED
PAVER	SAVES	TAWED	GOWER	YOWLS	PYXED
RAVER	WAVES	TOWED	HEWER	******	SEXED
RIVER	WIVES	UNWED	LOWER	--W-T	TAXED
ROVER	******	VOWED	MOWER	******	VEXED
SAVER	--V-T	WOWED	NEWER	PEWIT	WAXED
SAVOR	******	YAWED	PAWER	******	******
SEVER	CIVET	YOWED	POWER	--W-Y	--X-E
WAVER	COVET	******	RAWER	******	******
WIVER	DAVIT	--W-E	ROWER	ALWAY	COXAE
******	DIVOT	******	SAWER	BAWDY	DIXIE
--V-S	GAVOT	BOWIE	SEWER	BYWAY	MOXIE
******	PIVOT	BOWSE	SOWAR	COWRY	NIXIE
CAVES	REVET	DOWSE	SOWER	DEWEY	PIXIE
COVES	RIVET	HAWSE	TAWER	DOWDY	PYXIE
DAVES	******	HOWIE	TOWER	DOWNY	SIXTE
DAVIS	--V-Y	LEWIE	VOWER	DOWRY	******
DAVOS	******	PEWEE	******	GAWKY	--X-H
DAVYS	COVEY	******	--W-S	HOWDY	******
DEVAS	DAVEY	--W-L	******	JEWRY	SIXTH
DIVAS	DIVVY	******	BAWDS	LAWNY	******
DIVES	ENVOY	BOWEL	BAWLS	LOWLY	--X-L
DOVES	NAVVY	DOWEL	BOWLS	NEWLY	******
EAVES	SAVOY	JEWEL	COWES	NEWSY	AUXIL
ELVES	SAVVY	NEWEL	COWLS	NOWAY	COXAL
FAVUS	WAVEY	ROWEL	DAWKS	PAWKY	HEXYL
FIVES	******	TOWEL	DAWNS	RAWLY	VEXIL
GIVES	--W-B	VOWEL	DOWNS	ROWDY	******
GOVYS	******	******	FAWNS	TAWNY	--X-M
HIVES	NAWAB	--W-N	FOWLS	******	******
KAVAS	******	******	GAWKS	--X-A	BUXOM
KIVAS	--W-D	ALWIN	GOWNS	******	MAXIM
LAVAS	******	ASWAN	HAWKS	JUXTA	******
LAVES	BOWED	DEWAN	HOWLS	******	--X-N
LEVIS	CAWED	DIWAN	JOWLS	--X-C	******
LIVES	COWED	EDWIN	KIWIS	******	AUXIN
LOVES	DEWED	ELWIN	LAWNS	TOXIC	NIXON
MAVIS	HAWED	ERWIN	LEWES	******	SAXON
MOVES	HEWED	GOWAN	LEWIS	--X-D	TOXIN
NAVES	JAWED	IRWIN	MEWLS	******	VIXEN
NEVIS	LAWED	ROWAN	NEWTS	BOXED	WAXEN
NEVUS	LOWED	ROWEN	PAWLS	COXED	******
NOVAS	MEWED	******	PAWNS	FAXED	--X-O
OAVES	MOWED	--W-R	POWYS	FIXED	******
PAVES	PAWED	******	TOWNS	FOXED	SEXTO
PAVIS	ROWED	BOWER	WAWLS	HEXAD	******
RAVES	SAWED	COWER	YAWLS	HEXED	--X-P
RIVES	SEWED	DOWER	YAWNS	MIXED	******
					MIXUP

******	******	PHYTE	******	******	LAZED
--X-R	**--X-Y**	RHYME	**--Y-O**	**--Y-T**	MAZED
******	******	SLYPE	******	******	OOZED
BOXER	LAXLY	STYLE	AMYLO	ASYUT	RAZED
DEXTR	SIXTY	THYME	GLYCO	CRYPT	SIZED
FIXER	******	WAYNE	PHYCO	EGYPT	******
LAXER	**--Y-A**		PHYLO	MAYNT	**--Z-E**
LUXOR	******	**--Y-H**	PHYTO	MAYST	
MIXER	ADYTA	******	SAYSO	TRYST	FUZEE
TAXER	ASYLA	BLYTH	STYLO	******	OZZIE
VEXER	ETYMA	GLYPH	THYRO	**--Y-U**	RAZEE
******	PHYLA	PSYCH	******	******	**--Z-K**
--X-S	TRYMA	RAYAH	**--Y-R**	BAYOU	******
******		SCYPH	******	COYPU	MUZAK
BOXES	**--Y-D**	******	BOYAR	POYOU	******
COXES	******	**--Y-I**	BUYER	******	**--Z-L**
FAXES	BAYED	******	DRYER	**--Y-Y**	******
FIXES	DRYAD	PHYSI	FLYER	******	BEZEL
FOXES	FAYED	STYLI	FOYER	COYLY	FUZIL
HEXES	FOYED	**--Y-K**	FRYER	DOYLY	HAZEL
MIXES	GUYED	******	GAYER	DRYLY	OUZEL
MOXAS	HAYED	KAYAK	IYYAR	FLYBY	******
NEXUS	JOYED	******	LAYER	GAYLY	**--Z-M**
NIXES	KEYED	**--Y-L**	MAYOR	LAYBY	******
PYXES	PAYED	******	PAYER	SHYLY	NIZAM
PYXIS	RAYED	FAYAL	PRYER	SKYEY	******
SAXES	SAYID	IDYLL	SAYER	SLYLY	**--Z-N**
SEXES	TOYED	LOYAL	SHYER	STYMY	******
SIXES	******	PHYLL	SLYER	THYMY	COZEN
TAXES	**--Y-E**	RIYAL	TOYER	WRYLY	DIZEN
TAXIS	******	ROYAL	WRYER	******	DOZEN
TEXAS	ALYCE	******	******	**--Z-A**	KAZAN
TEXTS	BOYLE	**--Y-M**	**--Y-S**	******	LUZON
VEXES	BOYNE	******	******	PIZZA	MIZEN
WAXES	BRYCE	ABYSM	ABYSS	TAZZA	REZIN
XAXES	CHYLE	GOYIM	AMYLS	******	SOZIN
XAXIS	CHYME	**--Y-N**	BOYDS	**--Z-C**	WIZEN
YAXES	CLYDE	******	FAYES	******	******
YAXIS	DOYLE	ARYAN	GWYNS	ANZAC	**--Z-O**
******	HOYLE	BRYAN	HAYES	******	******
--X-T	JAYNE	DOYEN	IDYLS	**--Z-D**	ANZIO
******	JOYCE	HAYDN	KAYOS	******	GIZMO
DIXIT	LEYTE	MAYAN	MAYAS	DAZED	KAZOO
******	MAYBE	RAYON	NOYES	DOZED	MEZZO
--X-X	ODYLE	TOYON	SNYES	FAZED	YAZOO
******	PAYEE	TRYON	SOYAS	FUZED	******
LUXEX	PHYLE	ZAYIN	TOYOS	GAZED	**--Z-P**
	PHYRE		YOYOS	HAZED	******
					UNZIP

******	******	STRAD	DINAH	KODAK	FUGAL
--Z-R	**---AB**	TREAD	EPHAH	KULAK	GORAL
******	******	TRIAD	FARAH	MUZAK	GRAAL
DOZER	NADAB	******	JONAH	SNEAK	GYRAL
GAZER	NAWAB	**---AE**	JUDAH	SPEAK	HAMAL
HAZER	RAJAB	******	KEDAH	STEAK	HEMAL
LAZAR	SQUAB	ACEAE	KILAH	TWEAK	HORAL
MAZER	******	ALGAE	LOTAH	UMIAK	IDEAL
NIZER	**---AC**	ANSAE	MICAH	WREAK	ILEAL
RAZOR	******	ANTAE	NORAH	******	JUGAL
SIZAR	ANZAC	AQUAE	OBEAH	**---AL**	JURAL
VIZIR	ILEAC	AREAE	RAJAH	******	KRAAL
VIZOR	ILIAC	AURAE	RAYAH	ALGAL	LEGAL
******	ISAAC	COMAE	SABAH	ANNAL	LOCAL
--Z-S	LILAC	COXAE	SARAH	ANTAL	LOYAL
******	MALAC	CYMAE	SELAH	APPAL	MEDAL
ADZES	SERAC	DANAE	SHIAH	AREAL	MEGAL
BOZOS	SUMAC	HORAE	SUBAH	ARGAL	METAL
DAZES	TABAC	MINAE	SURAH	ARTAL	MODAL
DOZES	******	MORAE	TORAH	ARVAL	MOLAL
FAZES	**---AD**	NOVAE	URIAH	AURAL	MORAL
FUZES	******	PALAE	******	AXIAL	MURAL
GAZES	AHEAD	PUPAE	**---AI**	BANAL	NASAL
HAZES	ARPAD	RUGAE	******	BASAL	NATAL
IZZYS	AUDAD	SETAE	ADLAI	BINAL	NAVAL
LAZES	BEGAD	STOAE	ALTAI	BUBAL	NEPAL
LIZAS	BREAD	TELAE	ASSAI	CABAL	NIVAL
MAZES	BROAD	TOGAE	BAHAI	CANAL	NODAL
NAZIS	CANAD	ULNAE	DALAI	CECAL	NOPAL
OOZES	CYCAD	URSAE	DOUAI	CIDAL	OFFAL
RAZES	DREAD	VENAE	DUBAI	COMAL	PAPAL
SIZES	DRYAD	VITAE	KAUAI	COPAL	PEDAL
SUZYS	FARAD	******	LANAI	CORAL	PENAL
******	GONAD	**---AF**	LITAI	COXAL	PETAL
--Z-T	HEXAD	******	MENAI	CRAAL	PHIAL
******	ILIAD	PILAF	SERAI	DATAL	PICAL
BIZET	JIHAD	SHEAF	SINAI	DECAL	PIPAL
******	KNEAD	******	******	DEDAL	RATAL
--Z-Y	MONAD	**---AG**	**---AK**	DUCAL	REGAL
******	NAIAD	******	******	DURAL	RENAL
DIZZY	NOMAD	DEBAG	APEAK	EQUAL	RIVAL
FIZZY	OCTAD	LAOAG	BLEAK	FATAL	RIYAL
FUZZY	OREAD	SCRAG	BREAK	FAYAL	ROYAL
JAZZY	PLEAD	SPRAG	CLOAK	FECAL	RURAL
LIZZY	SALAD	******	CREAK	FERAL	SEPAL
MUZZY	SNEAD	**---AH**	CROAK	FETAL	SERAL
TIZZY	SQUAD	******	FREAK	FINAL	SHOAL
	STEAD	ALLAH	KAYAK	FOCAL	SISAL
		ALMAH			

SKOAL	ALBAN	ILIAN	TITAN	CLEAR	VELAR
STEAL	ALCAN	INCAN	TOLAN	CYMAR	VICAR
SURAL	ALDAN	JAPAN	TOMAN	DAKAR	VOLAR
TICAL	ALLAN	KAZAN	UHLAN	DEBAR	******
TIDAL	ALVAN	KORAN	UNMAN	DINAR	---AS
TONAL	AMMAN	KUBAN	URBAN	DONAR	******
TOTAL	APIAN	LAGAN	WIGAN	DREAR	ABBAS
TRIAL	ARIAN	LIGAN	WITAN	EDGAR	AGHAS
TUBAL	ARRAN	LOGAN	WODAN	EGGAR	AIDAS
UREAL	ARYAN	LORAN	WOMAN	ELGAR	ALBAS
USUAL	ASIAN	LYMAN	WOTAN	EMBAR	ALIAS
UVEAL	ASWAN	MAHAN	XTIAN	ESTAR	ALMAS
UXMAL	ATMAN	MAYAN	XYLAN	FEUAR	ALTAS
VENAL	AVIAN	MEGAN	******	FILAR	AMIAS
VIDAL	AXMAN	MELAN	---AO	FRIAR	ANLAS
VIRAL	BATAN	MILAN	******	GULAR	ANNAS
VITAL	BEGAN	MOSAN	CACAO	HARAR	AQUAS
VOCAL	BEHAN	NISAN	DAVAO	INVAR	AREAS
WHEAL	BEVAN	OCEAN	MACAO	ISTAR	ARIAS
ZONAL	BOGAN	OLEAN	******	IYYAR	ARRAS
******	BRIAN	ORGAN	---AP	LAPAR	ATLAS
---AM	BRYAN	OSCAN	******	LAZAR	AURAS
******	BURAN	OSMAN	ASCAP	LOBAR	BABAS
ABEAM	CHIAN	PAEAN	CHEAP	LUNAR	BALAS
ABRAM	CLEAN	PAGAN	DOVAP	MALAR	BETAS
ANNAM	COHAN	PAVAN	JALAP	MOLAR	BOLAS
ASSAM	CUBAN	PECAN	RECAP	NAVAR	CARAS
BREAM	DAGAN	PEKAN	SCRAP	NOPAR	CHIAS
CERAM	DAMAN	PIMAN	STRAP	OSCAR	COCAS
CREAM	DEWAN	PUSAN	UNCAP	PILAR	CODAS
DREAM	DIVAN	PYRAN	WATAP	POLAR	COLAS
FLEAM	DIWAN	QUEAN	******	QATAR	COMAS
GLEAM	DYLAN	REDAN	---AR	RADAR	CORAS
HBEAM	EGEAN	REGAN	******	SAMAR	DEGAS
HIRAM	ELMAN	REMAN	ALTAR	SHEAR	DEVAS
IBEAM	ELVAN	RENAN	ANEAR	SIMAR	DITAS
IHRAM	ETHAN	RERAN	ATPAR	SITAR	DIVAS
ISLAM	FURAN	ROMAN	ATTAR	SIZAR	DONAS
JORAM	GLEAN	ROWAN	BABAR	SMEAR	DORAS
MADAM	GOWAN	SAGAN	BERAR	SOLAR	DUMAS
NIZAM	GROAN	SARAN	BIHAR	SONAR	EDDAS
OGHAM	HEMAN	SATAN	BLEAR	SOWAR	EDNAS
PRIAM	HOGAN	SEDAN	BOLAR	SPEAR	ELIAS
SCRAM	HOKAN	SIVAN	BOYAR	SUGAR	ELLAS
STEAM	HONAN	SKEAN	BRIAR	SWEAR	ELSAS
******	HUMAN	SOLAN	CEDAR	TATAR	EMMAS
---AN	HUNAN	SUDAN	CESAR	ULNAR	ENEAS
******	ICIAN	SUSAN	CIGAR	UNBAR	ERMAS
ACEAN					
ADMAN					

ETNAS	NOMAS	VARAS	STOAT	MALAY	PHOBE
ETTAS	NONAS	VERAS	STRAT	MORAY	PLEBE
EYRAS	NORAS	VINAS	SWEAT	NOWAY	PROBE
EZRAS	NOVAS	VISAS	TERAT	OURAY	TRIBE
FLEAS	OKRAS	WEKAS	TREAT	PANAY	******
GALAS	OLGAS	YUGAS	UBOAT	RELAY	---BI
GIGAS	OLLAS	ZETAS	UNHAT	REPAY	******
HAHAS	PACAS	******	UNIAT	SPLAY	ALIBI
HORAS	PAPAS	---AT	WHEAT	SPRAY	BAMBI
HULAS	PARAS	******	******	STRAY	IAMBI
HYLAS	PICAS	AETAT	---AU	TODAY	KRUBI
IDEAS	PIKAS	BANAT	******	TOKAY	LIMBI
INCAS	PIMAS	BEGAT	ERLAU	UNLAY	NIMBI
IOTAS	PINAS	BLEAT	******	UNSAY	ORIBI
IRMAS	PITAS	BLOAT	---AW	******	RABBI
ISBAS	PLEAS	CARAT	******	---AZ	ZOMBI
IXIAS	PROAS	CERAT	BYLAW	******	******
JONAS	PSOAS	CHEAT	INLAW	HEJAZ	---BO
JUBAS	PUMAS	CLEAT	MACAW	IGNAZ	BILBO
JUDAS	PUNAS	CROAT	PAPAW	TOPAZ	CARBO
KAKAS	RHEAS	DUCAT	PSHAW	******	COMBO
KAVAS	RITAS	EBOAT	SQUAW	---BA	GARBO
KIVAS	ROSAS	ECLAT	STRAW	******	GUMBO
KOLAS	ROTAS	FLOAT	******	AMEBA	JUMBO
LAMAS	SAGAS	GLOAT	---AX	AQABA	LIMBO
LAVAS	SARAS	GREAT	******	ARUBA	MAMBO
LENAS	SHEAS	GROAT	ADDAX	CEIBA	SAMBO
LILAS	SILAS	HEMAT	BORAX	CHIBA	TURBO
LIRAS	SKUAS	HEPAT	GALAX	KAABA	******
LISAS	SODAS	HERAT	HYRAX	MAMBA	---BS
LITAS	SOFAS	JURAT	RELAX	RUMBA	******
LIZAS	SOJAS	KALAT	******	SAMBA	ABIBS
LOLAS	SORAS	KARAT	---AY	SCUBA	ARABS
MAMAS	SOYAS	KERAT	******	SHEBA	BARBS
MAYAS	STOAS	LOPAT	ALLAY	YERBA	BIBBS
MESAS	SURAS	MARAT	ALWAY	******	BLABS
METAS	TAPAS	MORAT	ARRAY	---BE	BLEBS
MICAS	TEXAS	MURAT	ASSAY	******	BLOBS
MIDAS	TINAS	NEMAT	BELAY	ADOBE	BOMBS
MINAS	TOGAS	PLEAT	BYWAY	BEEBE	BOOBS
MONAS	TOLAS	RABAT	DECAY	BOMBE	BULBS
MORAS	TOMAS	SEBAT	DELAY	BRIBE	CHUBS
MOXAS	TREAS	SHOAT	DOUAY	GLEBE	CLUBS
MYNAS	TROAS	SLEAT	EMBAY	GLOBE	COBBS
MYRAS	TUBAS	SOMAT	ESSAY	GREBE	COMBS
NANAS	TUNAS	SPLAT	FORAY	MAYBE	CRABS
NINAS	ULNAS	SPRAT	INLAY	NIOBE	CRIBS
NIPAS	UVEAS	SQUAT	ISLAY	PHEBE	

CURBS	CORBY	AMICE	******	LURCH	******
DAUBS	CUBBY	APACE	---CH	LYNCH	---CI
DRABS	DAUBY	BRACE	******	MARCH	******
DRIBS	DEBBY	BRICE	AITCH	MATCH	ABACI
DRUBS	DERBY	BRUCE	BATCH	MILCH	BACCI
FLUBS	DOBBY	BRYCE	BEACH	MITCH	CALCI
FORBS	FLYBY	CIRCE	BEECH	MOOCH	COCCI
GAMBS	FORBY	CROCE	BELCH	MOUCH	CROCI
GARBS	GABBY	DANCE	BENCH	MULCH	CRUCI
GLOBS	HERBY	DEICE	BIRCH	MUNCH	DISCI
GRABS	HOBBY	DEUCE	BITCH	NOTCH	MERCI
GRUBS	HUBBY	DOLCE	BOSCH	ORACH	PISCI
HERBS	LAYBY	DULCE	BOTCH	PARCH	SULCI
HOBBS	LIBBY	DUNCE	BUNCH	PASCH	VINCI
IAMBS	LOBBY	EDUCE	BUTCH	PATCH	******
JAMBS	LOOBY	FARCE	CATCH	PEACH	---CK
KERBS	NOBBY	FENCE	CINCH	PERCH	******
KNOBS	NUBBY	FORCE	COACH	PINCH	ABACK
LAMBS	RUGBY	GLACE	CONCH	PITCH	ACOCK
LIMBS	TABBY	GRACE	COUCH	POACH	ALACK
NUMBS	TUBBY	HANCE	CULCH	POOCH	ALECK
PLEBS	WEBBY	HENCE	CURCH	PORCH	AMUCK
SCABS	WOMBY	JOYCE	CUTCH	POUCH	BLACK
SERBS	******	JUICE	CZECH	PSYCH	BLOCK
SLABS	---CA	LANCE	DITCH	PUNCH	BRICK
SLOBS	******	MINCE	DUTCH	RANCH	BROCK
SLUBS	ABACA	NANCE	ENOCH	RATCH	CHECK
SNOBS	ARECA	NIECE	EPOCH	REACH	CHICK
SNUBS	ARICA	NONCE	ERICH	REICH	CHOCK
SORBS	ASPCA	OUNCE	FETCH	RETCH	CHUCK
STABS	BARCA	PEACE	FILCH	ROACH	CLACK
STUBS	CAUCA	PENCE	FINCH	ROTCH	CLICK
SWABS	CIRCA	PIECE	FITCH	STICH	CLOCK
TOMBS	DACCA	PLACE	GULCH	TEACH	CLUCK
VERBS	ERICA	PONCE	HATCH	TENCH	CRACK
WOMBS	LORCA	PRICE	HITCH	TORCH	CRICK
******	LUCCA	RANCE	HOOCH	TOUCH	CROCK
---BT	MECCA	SAUCE	HUNCH	TRACH	DIRCK
******	MUSCA	SINCE	HUTCH	TRACH	FLACK
DOUBT	PARCA	SLICE	KENCH	TRICH	FLECK
******	PLICA	SPACE	KERCH	VETCH	FLICK
---BY	SPICA	SPICE	KETCH	VOUCH	FLOCK
******	THECA	TRACE	LARCH	WATCH	FROCK
ARABY	UTICA	TRICE	LATCH	WELCH	HOICK
BOBBY	YUCCA	TRUCE	LEACH	WENCH	KNACK
BOOBY	******	TWICE	LEECH	WHICH	KNOCK
BUSBY	---CE	VINCE	LOACH	WINCH	PLACK
CABBY	******	VOICE	LUNCH	WITCH	PLUCK
	ALICE	WINCE			
	ALYCE				

PRICK	******	SAUCY	ELIDE	******	DEEDS
QUACK	---CS	SPICY	ELUDE	---DO	DUADS
QUICK	******	STACY	EPODE	******	ENIDS
SHACK	ALECS	TRACY	ERODE	AMIDO	FEEDS
SHOCK	BLOCS	ZINCY	ETUDE	CADDO	FENDS
SHUCK	DISCS	******	EVADE	CREDO	FEODS
SLACK	EPICS	---DA	EXUDE	DILDO	FEUDS
SLICK	ERICS	******	GEODE	GUIDO	FINDS
SMACK	EXECS	ALADA	GLADE	HONDO	FOLDS
SMOCK	FISCS	BANDA	GLEDE	IMIDO	FOODS
SNACK	FLOCS	BREDA	GLIDE	IRIDO	FORDS
SNICK	MARCS	FONDA	GRADE	MISDO	FREDS
SPECK	SPECS	FREDA	GRIDE	OUTDO	FUNDS
STACK	TALCS	GERDA	GUIDE	PAEDO	GAUDS
STICK	ZINCS	GILDA	HORDE	RONDO	GELDS
STOCK	******	GOLDA	IMIDE	SCUDO	GILDS
STUCK	---CT	GOUDA	MAUDE	SOLDO	GIRDS
THICK	******	HAIDA	MONDE	TARDO	GLADS
TRACK	BRACT	HEDDA	OXIDE	UREDO	GLEDS
TRICK	EDICT	HILDA	PRIDE	WALDO	GOADS
TRUCK	EDUCT	HULDA	PRUDE	******	GOLDS
VNECK	EJECT	JIDDA	SHADE	---DR	GOODS
WHACK	ELECT	LINDA	SLIDE	******	GRADS
WRACK	ENACT	LYDDA	SNIDE	BALDR	GRIDS
WRECK	EPACT	MAGDA	SPADE	COMDR	HANDS
WRICK	ERECT	OUIDA	SPODE	DENDR	HARDS
******	ERUCT	PANDA	SUEDE	******	HEADS
---CO	EVICT	RHODA	SWEDE	---DS	HEEDS
******	EXACT	THEDA	TILDE	******	HERDS
BUNCO	MULCT	TILDA	TRADE	ACIDS	HINDS
CASCO	PROCT	TRUDA	TSADE	BANDS	HOLDS
CHICO	REACT	WANDA	WILDE	BARDS	HOODS
CISCO	TINCT	******	******	BAWDS	HURDS
DISCO	TRACT	---DE	---DI	BEADS	IMIDS
DRACO	VISCT	******	******	BENDS	KINDS
GLYCO	******	ABIDE	CARDI	BINDS	LANDS
GRECO	---CY	ABODE	FUNDI	BIRDS	LARDS
GUACO	******	AMIDE	GAUDI	BONDS	LAUDS
JUNCO	CRACY	ANODE	GONDI	BOYDS	LEADS
LEUCO	CRECY	ASIDE	HINDI	BRADS	LEEDS
MARCO	DULCY	BARDE	KHADI	BUNDS	LENDS
NARCO	FANCY	BLADE	MAHDI	BURDS	LEUDS
PHYCO	FARCY	BRIDE	MINDI	CARDS	LOADS
SARCO	JUICY	BUNDE	SCUDI	CLODS	LORDS
SECCO	MANCY	CHIDE	SOLDI	COEDS	MAIDS
TURCO	MERCY	CLYDE	VERDI	COLDS	MAUDS
URICO	NANCY	CRUDE	******	CORDS	MEADS
******	PERCY	DIODE	---DN	CURDS	MELDS
---CP					
******			HAYDN		
NAACP					

MENDS	WENDS	LEADY	MEDEA	BAAED	DEWED
MINDS	WILDS	MANDY	OCREA	BAKED	DICED
MOLDS	WINDS	MIDDY	OIDEA	BALED	DIKED
MOODS	WOADS	MOLDY	PALEA	BARED	DINED
NARDS	WOLDS	MOODY	PILEA	BASED	DIVED
NEEDS	WOODS	MUDDY	RHOEA	BATED	DOLED
PARDS	WORDS	NEDDY	RRHEA	BAYED	DOMED
PENDS	YARDS	NEEDY	TINEA	BIDED	DOPED
PLODS	******	NODDY	******	BIPED	DOSED
PONDS	---DT	PADDY	---EB	BLEED	DOTED
POODS	******	PANDY	******	BLUED	DOZED
PRODS	COMDT	RANDY	ARDEB	BODED	DRIED
QUADS	VELDT	READY	CALEB	BONED	DUPED
QUIDS	******	REEDY	CUBEB	BOOED	EARED
QUODS	---DU	RODDY	DENEB	BORED	EASED
RAIDS	******	ROWDY	HOREB	BOWED	EBBED
RANDS	HINDU	RUDDY	NEGEB	BOXED	EDGED
READS	PERDU	SANDY	PHLEB	BREED	EDRED
REEDS	******	SEEDY	SAHEB	BUSED	EGGED
RENDS	---DY	SHADY	******	CAGED	EMBED
RINDS	******	STUDY	---EC	CAKED	ENDED
ROADS	BANDY	TARDY	******	CANED	ERRED
ROODS	BAWDY	TEDDY	AZTEC	CARED	FACED
RUDDS	BEADY	THADY	COPEC	CASED	FADED
RYNDS	BENDY	TOADY	CUSEC	CAVED	FAKED
SANDS	BIDDY	TODDY	DODEC	CAWED	FAMED
SCADS	BRADY	TRUDY	GYNEC	CEDED	FARED
SCUDS	BUDDY	WADDY	KOPEC	CERED	FATED
SEEDS	CADDY	WEEDY	REBEC	CITED	FAXED
SENDS	CANDY	WENDY	XEBEC	CLUED	FAYED
SHEDS	CINDY	WIDDY	ZEBEC	CODED	FAZED
SKIDS	CUDDY	WINDY	******	COKED	FETED
SLEDS	CURDY	WOODY	---ED	CONED	FEUED
SPUDS	DADDY	WORDY	******	COOED	FIFED
STUDS	DANDY	******	ACHED	COPED	FILED
SURDS	DOWDY	---EA	ACRED	CORED	FINED
TENDS	FADDY	******	ACTED	COVED	FIRED
THADS	GAUDY	APNEA	ADDED	COWED	FIXED
THUDS	GIDDY	BEREA	AIDED	COXED	FLIED
TOADS	GOODY	BOHEA	AILED	CREED	FOXED
TODDS	HANDY	CANEA	AIMED	CRIED	FOYED
VELDS	HARDY	ENNEA	AIRED	CUBED	FREED
VENDS	HEADY	FOVEA	ANTED	CURED	FRIED
VOIDS	HOWDY	GALEA	ARCED	DARED	FUMED
WANDS	KANDY	HOSEA	ARMED	DATED	FUSED
WARDS	KIDDY	JUDEA	ASKED	DAZED	FUZED
WEEDS	LADDY	KOREA	AWNED	DEKED	GAGED
WELDS	LARDY	LYCEA	AXLED	DELED	GAMED

GAPED	LAMED	PAGED	SIRED	WAXED	******
GATED	LAVED	PALED	SITED	WILED	---EF
GAZED	LAWED	PANED	SIZED	WINED	******
GIBED	LAZED	PARED	SKEED	WIPED	BRIEF
GLUED	LIKED	PAVED	SKIED	WIRED	CHIEF
GORED	LIMED	PAWED	SLUED	WISED	GANEF
GREED	LINED	PAYED	SOLED	WIVED	GRIEF
GUYED	LIVED	PIKED	SOWED	WOOED	THIEF
GYBED	LOBED	PILED	SPEED	WOWED	UNREF
GYVED	LOOED	PINED	SPIED	WRIED	******
HADED	LOPED	PIPED	STEED	YAWED	---EG
HALED	LOVED	PLIED	STIED	YOKED	******
HARED	LOWED	POKED	TAMED	YOWED	GRIEG
HATED	LURED	POLED	TAPED	ZONED	PELEG
HAWED	LUTED	PORED	TARED	******	TELEG
HAYED	LYSED	POSED	TAWED	---EE	UNPEG
HAZED	MACED	PRIED	TAXED	******	******
HEWED	MANED	PUKED	TIDED	AGLEE	---EH
HEXED	MATED	PULED	TILED	AGREE	******
HIKED	MAZED	PYXED	TIMED	AIMEE	HOPEH
HIRED	METED	RACED	TINED	ALBEE	HUPEH
HIVED	MEWED	RAGED	TIRED	COOEE	OKIEH
HOLED	MIMED	RAKED	TONED	DONEE	******
HOMED	MINED	RAPED	TOPED	EMCEE	---EI
HONED	MIRED	RATED	TOTED	FUSEE	******
HOPED	MIXED	RAVED	TOWED	FUZEE	AUREI
HOSED	MOOED	RAYED	TOYED	LEVEE	ISSEI
IDLED	MOPED	RAZED	TREED	LYCEE	KIBEI
IMBED	MOVED	RICED	TRIED	MELEE	NISEI
INKED	MOWED	RILED	TRUED	PAYEE	PILEI
INNED	MUSED	RIMED	TUBED	PELEE	******
IRKED	MUTED	RIVED	TUNED	PEWEE	---EK
ISLED	NAKED	ROBED	TWEED	PUREE	******
IVIED	NAMED	ROPED	TYPED	RAGEE	CAPEK
JADED	NIDED	ROSED	UNWED	RAKEE	CHEEK
JAPED	NIXED	ROVED	UPPED	RANEE	CLEEK
JARED	NOSED	ROWED	URGED	RAZEE	COSEK
JAWED	NOTED	RULED	VANED	RENEE	CREEK
JIBED	OARED	SABED	VEXED	RUPEE	DEREK
JIVED	OGLED	SATED	VISED	SCREE	GREEK
JOKED	OILED	SAVED	VOTED	SPREE	KOPEK
JOYED	OOZED	SAWED	VOWED	SYCEE	SAMEK
KEYED	OPTED	SERED	WADED	TEHEE	SLEEK
KITED	ORBED	SEWED	WAGED	TEPEE	******
KNEED	OSTED	SEXED	WAKED	THREE	---EL
LACED	OUTED	SHIED	WALED	TIREE	******
LADED	OWNED	SHRED	WANED	TOPEE	ABIEL
LAKED	PACED	SIDED	WAVED	UNDEE	ACCEL
				YOGEE	

AMIEL	NIGEL	ARLEN	RAVEN	******	CABER
ANGEL	NOBEL	ARPEN	RIPEN	---EP	CANER
ANSEL	NOVEL	ASHEN	RISEN	******	CAPER
APPEL	ORIEL	ASPEN	RIVEN	BLEEP	CARER
ARIEL	OUSEL	AUDEN	ROUEN	CHEEP	CATER
ARTEL	OUZEL	AXMEN	ROVEN	CREEP	CHEER
BABEL	PANEL	BADEN	ROWEN	JULEP	CIDER
BAGEL	PINEL	BATEN	RUMEN	SALEP	CODER
BASEL	RATEL	COVEN	SELEN	SHEEP	COKER
BETEL	RAVEL	COZEN	SEMEN	SLEEP	COMER
BEVEL	REBEL	DIZEN	SEVEN	STEEP	COOER
BEZEL	REPEL	DOYEN	SHEEN	SWEEP	COPER
BOWEL	REVEL	DOZEN	SIREN	******	CORER
CAMEL	RIGEL	EATEN	SPHEN	---ER	COVER
CREEL	ROWEL	ELLEN	SPLEN	******	COWER
CRUEL	SOREL	EMDEN	STEEN	ABLER	CRIER
CUPEL	SPIEL	ESSEN	TAKEN	ABNER	CURER
DOWEL	STEEL	GALEN	TOKEN	ADDER	CUTER
EASEL	TEKEL	GIVEN	TWEEN	ADLER	DALER
EDSEL	TOWEL	GREEN	UNPEN	AFTER	DARER
ETHEL	UMBEL	HAVEN	VIMEN	AGGER	DATER
EXCEL	URIEL	HELEN	VIXEN	AIDER	DEFER
EXPEL	VOWEL	HEMEN	WAKEN	ALDER	DETER
FIDEL	WHEEL	HYMEN	WAXEN	ALGER	DICER
FUSEL	YODEL	IBSEN	WIDEN	ALTER	DIKER
GAVEL	YOKEL	ILMEN	WIZEN	AMBER	DIMER
GIMEL	******	KAREN	WODEN	AMEER	DINER
GRUEL	---EM	LADEN	WOKEN	ANGER	DIRER
HAZEL	******	LEVEN	WOMEN	APTER	DIVER
HEGEL	ADEEM	LIKEN	WOVEN	ARTER	DOSER
HOTEL	BELEM	LIMEN	YAMEN	ASHER	DOTER
HOVEL	GOLEM	LINEN	YEMEN	ASKER	DOVER
IMPEL	HAREM	LIVEN	******	ASPER	DOWER
JEWEL	PROEM	LODEN	---EO	ASTER	DOZER
JUREL	RETEM	LUMEN	******	AUGER	DRIER
KEVEL	SALEM	MIZEN	CAMEO	BABER	DRYER
KNEEL	TOTEM	NUMEN	ELAEO	BAKER	DUPER
LABEL	XYLEM	OAKEN	HOMEO	BALER	DURER
LAPEL	YQUEM	OATEN	JUDEO	BARER	EAGER
LEVEL	******	OFTEN	MATEO	BITER	EATER
LIBEL	---EN	OGDEN	MIMEO	BLUER	EGGER
MABEL	******	OLDEN	PALEO	BONER	EIDER
MODEL	ADMEN	PAPEN	RODEO	BORER	EIMER
MOREL	AIKEN	PAREN	ROMEO	BOWER	ELDER
MOSEL	ALDEN	PATEN	TELEO	BOXER	ELMER
MOTEL	ALIEN	PHREN	VIDEO	BRIER	ELVER
NAVEL	ALLEN	PREEN	VIREO	BUBER	EMBER
NEWEL	ARDEN	QUEEN		BUYER	EMEER

EMMER	HYPER	NAMER	RARER	TAWER	******
ENTER	ICIER	NETER	RATER	TAXER	---ES
ESHER	IDLER	NEVER	RAVER	TIBER	******
ESKER	INFER	NEWER	RAWER	TIGER	ABBES
ESTER	INKER	NICER	REFER	TILER	ABIES
ETHER	INNER	NIGER	RICER	TIMER	ACHES
EULER	INTER	NITER	RIDER	TITER	ACRES
FACER	JOKER	NIZER	RIMER	TONER	ADZES
FAKER	KHMER	NOTER	RIPER	TOPER	AEDES
FARER	LAGER	OCHER	RISER	TOTER	AGNES
FEVER	LAKER	ODDER	RIVER	TOWER	AGUES
FEWER	LAMER	OFFER	ROGER	TOYER	AIDES
FIBER	LASER	OGLER	ROVER	TRIER	ALOES
FIFER	LATER	OILER	ROWER	TRUER	AMIES
FILER	LAVER	OLDER	RUDER	TUBER	ANDES
FINER	LAXER	OMBER	RULER	TUNER	ANNES
FIRER	LAYER	ORDER	SABER	TYLER	ANTES
FIVER	LEGER	ORMER	SAFER	UDDER	APSES
FIXER	LEPER	OSIER	SAGER	ULCER	ARIES
FLEER	LEVER	OSLER	SAKER	UMBER	ARLES
FLIER	LIBER	OTHER	SANER	UNDER	ARSES
FLYER	LIFER	OTTER	SAVER	UPPER	ASHES
FOYER	LINER	OUTER	SAWER	USHER	ASSES
FREER	LITER	OWNER	SAYER	UTHER	AURES
FRIER	LIVER	PACER	SEDER	UTTER	AXLES
FRYER	LONER	PAGER	SEVER	VEXER	BABES
GAGER	LOPER	PALER	SEWER	VILER	BAKES
GAPER	LOSER	PAPER	SHEER	VIPER	BALES
GAYER	LOVER	PARER	SHIER	VOMER	BARES
GAZER	LOWER	PATER	SHOER	VOTER	BASES
GIBER	LUGER	PAVER	SHYER	VOWER	BATES
GIVER	LURER	PAWER	SIDER	WADER	BENES
GOFER	MACER	PAYER	SKIER	WAFER	BICES
GONER	MAKER	PETER	SLIER	WAGER	BIDES
GOWER	MASER	PIKER	SLYER	WALER	BIKES
GREER	MATER	PINER	SNEER	WATER	BILES
HALER	MAZER	PIPER	SOBER	WAVER	BINES
HAMER	METER	PLIER	SORER	WEBER	BISES
HATER	MILER	POKER	SOWER	WESER	BITES
HAVER	MIMER	POSER	SPIER	WIDER	BLUES
HAZER	MINER	POWER	STEER	WIPER	BODES
HEWER	MISER	PRIER	SUMER	WIRER	BOLES
HIDER	MITER	PRYER	SUPER	WISER	BONES
HIKER	MIXER	PULER	SURER	WIVER	BORES
HIRER	MOPER	PURER	TAKER	WOOER	BOXES
HOMER	MOVER	QUEER	TALER	WRIER	BRAES
HOVER	MOWER	RACER	TAMER	WRYER	BUSES
HUGER	NADER	RAKER	TAPER	YAGER	BYRES

CADES	DOMES	FROES	JEFES	MALES	OGEES
CAFES	DOPES	FUMES	JIBES	MANES	OGLES
CAGES	DOSES	FUSES	JOKES	MARES	OGRES
CAKES	DOTES	FUZES	JOLES	MATES	OKIES
CAMES	DOVES	FYKES	JONES	MAZES	OOZES
CANES	DOZES	GABES	JUBES	MENES	ORLES
CAPES	DRIES	GAGES	JUDES	METES	PACES
CARES	DUDES	GALES	JULES	MIKES	PAGES
CASES	DUKES	GAMES	JUNES	MILES	PALES
CAVES	DUNES	GAPES	JUTES	MIMES	PANES
CEDES	DUPES	GASES	KAMES	MINES	PARES
CERES	EASES	GATES	KATES	MIRES	PATES
CITES	EAVES	GAZES	KERES	MISES	PAVES
CLUES	EDGES	GENES	KIBES	MITES	PEDES
CODES	EDIES	GIBES	KITES	MIXES	PERES
COKES	ELVES	GILES	KNEES	MLLES	PETES
COLES	EPEES	GIVES	LACES	MODES	PIKES
COMES	ERIES	GLEES	LADES	MOKES	PILES
CONES	ERNES	GLUES	LAKES	MOLES	PINES
COPES	ERSES	GORES	LAMES	MOPES	PIPES
CORES	ESSES	GULES	LANES	MORES	PLIES
COTES	ESTES	GYRES	LARES	MOSES	POKES
COVES	FACES	HADES	LAVES	MOTES	POLES
COWES	FADES	HAKES	LAZES	MOUES	POMES
COXES	FAKES	HALES	LEGES	MOVES	PONES
CREES	FARES	HAMES	LENES	MULES	POPES
CRIES	FATES	HARES	LEWES	MUSES	PORES
CUBES	FAXES	HATES	LIKES	MUTES	POSES
CURES	FAYES	HAYES	LIMES	MYLES	PRIES
CYMES	FAZES	HAZES	LINES	NAMES	PUBES
DACES	FECES	HEXES	LIVES	NAPES	PUCES
DALES	FEMES	HIDES	LOBES	NARES	PUKES
DAMES	FETES	HIKES	LODES	NATES	PULES
DANES	FICES	HIRES	LOGES	NAVES	PYRES
DARES	FIFES	HIVES	LOPES	NIDES	PYXES
DATES	FILES	HOLES	LORES	NIMES	RACES
DAVES	FINES	HOMES	LOSES	NINES	RAGES
DAZES	FIRES	HONES	LOVES	NIXES	RAKES
DEKES	FIVES	HOPES	LUCES	NODES	RALES
DELES	FIXES	HOSES	LUNES	NONES	RAPES
DEMES	FLEES	IDLES	LURES	NOSES	RATES
DENES	FLIES	ISLES	LUTES	NOTES	RAVES
DIKES	FLOES	IVIES	LYLES	NOYES	RAZES
DIMES	FLUES	JADES	LYRES	NUDES	REGES
DINES	FORES	JAKES	LYSES	OASES	RENES
DIVES	FOXES	JAMES	MACES	OATES	RICES
DOGES	FREES	JANES	MAGES	OAVES	RIDES
DOLES	FRIES	JAPES	MAKES	OBOES	RILES

RIMES	TALES	WIRES	KAMET	******	MAMEY
RISES	TAMES	WISES	LUNET	**---EX**	MATEY
RITES	TAPES	WIVES	MANET	******	MIKEY
RIVES	TARES	WRIES	MONET	ADMEX	MONEY
ROBES	TAXES	XAXES	MOTET	ANNEX	MOSEY
ROLES	TIDES	YAXES	NONET	CIMEX	MULEY
ROPES	TILES	YESES	OCTET	CODEX	NOSEY
ROSES	TIMES	YIPES	ONSET	CULEX	PALEY
ROUES	TINES	YOKES	OWLET	DESEX	PINEY
ROVES	TIRES	YPRES	PIPET	ESSEX	POGEY
RUBES	TOLES	YULES	PUGET	INDEX	POKEY
RULES	TOMES	ZEKES	QUIET	LATEX	RILEY
RUNES	TONES	ZONES	RESET	LUXEX	ROPEY
RUSES	TOPES	******	REVET	MUREX	SKYEY
SABES	TOTES	**---ET**	RIVET	PYREX	TANEY
SAFES	TREES	******	SHEET	REMEX	WANEY
SAGES	TRIES	AGLET	SKEET	SILEX	WAVEY
SAKES	TRUES	ARMET	SLEET	TELEX	WILEY
SALES	TUBES	ASSET	SWEET	UNSEX	******
SATES	TULES	BEGET	TACET	******	**---EZ**
SAVES	TUNES	BENET	TEBET	**---EY**	******
SAXES	TYEES	BERET	TENET	******	JABEZ
SERES	TYKES	BESET	TIBET	ABBEY	JEREZ
SEXES	TYPES	BIDET	TWEET	AGLEY	******
SHOES	URGES	BINET	UPSET	ALLEY	**---FA**
SICES	VALES	BIZET	VALET	BOGEY	******
SIDES	VANES	BLUET	ZIBET	CAGEY	CHUFA
SINES	VASES	CADET	******	CAREY	HAIFA
SIPES	VEXES	CAPET	**---EU**	CASEY	JAFFA
SIRES	VIBES	CARET	******	COKEY	SOLFA
SITES	VICES	CHAET	ADIEU	CONEY	SULFA
SIXES	VINES	CIVET	PAREU	COOEY	******
SIZES	VIRES	COMET	******	COVEY	**---FE**
SKEES	VISES	COVET	**---EV**	CUTEY	******
SKIES	VOCES	CRUET	******	DAVEY	CHAFE
SLOES	VOLES	CULET	NEGEV	DEWEY	CORFE
SLUES	VOTES	EGRET	******	DICEY	GAFFE
SNYES	WADES	EMMET	**---EW**	DOPEY	KNIFE
SOKES	WAGES	FACET	******	FOGEY	ROLFE
SOLES	WAKES	FILET	ASKEW	GLUEY	******
SONES	WALES	FLEET	BEDEW	GOOEY	**---FF**
SORES	WANES	GENET	RENEW	HOLEY	******
SPIES	WARES	GLEET	SCREW	HOMEY	BANFF
STIES	WAVES	GREET	SHREW	HONEY	BLUFF
SUPES	WAXES	INLET	SINEW	HOOEY	CHAFF
SYCES	WILES	INSET	STREW	LAKEY	CLIFF
TABES	WINES	ISLET	THREW	LIMEY	DRAFF
TAKES	WIPES	JANET	UNMEW	LINEY	FEOFF

FLUFF	KEEFS	******	BINGE	USAGE	******
GEOFF	KERFS	---FY	BRAGE	VERGE	---GO
GRUFF	LEAFS	******	BUDGE	VIRGE	******
QUAFF	LEIFS	BAFFY	CADGE	WEDGE	AMIGO
QUIFF	LOAFS	BEEFY	CONGE	******	BINGO
SCOFF	LOOFS	BIFFY	DIRGE	---GG	BONGO
SCUFF	LUFFS	BUFFY	DODGE	******	CARGO
SKIFF	MIFFS	COMFY	FORGE	BRAGG	CONGO
SNIFF	MUFFS	DAFFY	FUDGE	FRIGG	DIEGO
SNUFF	OLAFS	DEIFY	GAUGE	******	DINGO
STAFF	PELFS	EDIFY	GORGE	---GH	FARGO
STIFF	POUFS	GOOFY	GOUGE	******	FORGO
STUFF	PROFS	HUFFY	HEDGE	BLIGH	FUNGO
WHIFF	PUFFS	JIFFY	HINGE	BOUGH	GREGO
******	REEFS	LEAFY	HODGE	BURGH	IMAGO
---FI	RIFFS	MIFFY	IMAGE	COUGH	INIGO
******	ROLFS	PUFFY	JORGE	DOUGH	JINGO
BUFFI	ROOFS	REEFY	JUDGE	FAUGH	LARGO
SCIFI	RUFFS	REIFY	KEDGE	HEIGH	LINGO
******	SERFS	SURFY	LARGE	HOUGH	MANGO
---FO	SURFS	TAFFY	LEDGE	LAUGH	MARGO
******	TIFFS	TURFY	LIEGE	LEIGH	MUNGO
BUFFO	TURFS	UNIFY	LODGE	LOUGH	OLIGO
SULFO	WAIFS	******	LUNGE	NEIGH	OUTGO
******	WOLFS	---GA	MADGE	ROUGH	PARGO
---FS	WOOFS	******	MANGE	SOUGH	PENGO
******	ZARFS	BELGA	MARGE	THIGH	PHAGO
ALEFS	******	CONGA	MERGE	TOUGH	PINGO
ALIFS	---FT	FANGA	MIDGE	WAUGH	SLIGO
BAFFS	******	HELGA	NUDGE	WEIGH	SORGO
BEEFS	ABAFT	LINGA	OSAGE	******	TANGO
BIFFS	ALOFT	OMEGA	PHAGE	---GI	TRIGO
BUFFS	CLEFT	ONEGA	PORGE	******	VIRGO
CHEFS	CRAFT	SAIGA	PURGE	BRAGI	VULGO
CLEFS	CROFT	TAIGA	RANGE	CORGI	******
COIFS	DELFT	TIOGA	RHAGE	FUNGI	---GS
CUFFS	DRAFT	TONGA	RIDGE	LONGI	******
DOFFS	DRIFT	VIRGA	ROUGE	LUIGI	BANGS
DUFFS	GRAFT	VOLGA	SEDGE	LUNGI	BERGS
FIEFS	KRAFT	******	SERGE	PLAGI	BLDGS
GAFFS	SHAFT	---GE	SIEGE	TRAGI	BONGS
GOLFS	SHIFT	******	SINGE	******	BRAGS
GOOFS	SWIFT	ADAGE	STAGE	---GN	BRIGS
GULFS	THEFT	ADIGE	SURGE	******	BUNGS
HOOFS	******	BADGE	SWAGE	ALIGN	BURGS
HUFFS	---FU	BARGE	SYNGE	COIGN	CHUGS
JEFFS	******	BEIGE	TINGE	DEIGN	CLOGS
JIFFS	CORFU	BILGE		FEIGN	CRAGS
	SNAFU			REIGN	

DANGS	TRIGS	WEDGY	******	SETHS	LATHY
DINGS	TWIGS	WINGY	---HN	SHAHS	MACHY
DOUGS	VANGS	ZINGY	******	SIGHS	MASHY
DRAGS	WHIGS	******	FOEHN	SIKHS	MESHY
DREGS	WINGS	---HA	******	TETHS	MOTHY
DRUGS	YEGGS	******	---HO	YODHS	MUSHY
DUNGS	******	ALOHA	******	YOGHS	PACHY
FANGS	---GY	ALPHA	ANTHO	******	PATHY
FLAGS	******	DACHA	BATHO	---HT	PITHY
FLOGS	BAGGY	GOTHA	DICHO	******	PUSHY
FROGS	BILGY	HYPHA	IDAHO	AUGHT	RUSHY
GANGS	BOGGY	MOCHA	LITHO	BIGHT	SOPHY
GONGS	BUDGY	NUCHA	METHO	EIGHT	TACHY
GREGS	BUGGY	OMAHA	MYTHO	FIGHT	VICHY
HANGS	BULGY	PASHA	NEPHO	LICHT	WASHY
HONGS	DINGY	******	ORTHO	LIGHT	WITHY
JAGGS	DODGY	---HE	PATHO	MIGHT	******
KINGS	DOGGY	******	******	NIGHT	---IA
LINGS	DUNGY	BACHE	---HR	OUGHT	******
LONGS	ELEGY	BATHE	******	RIGHT	AECIA
LUNGS	FOGGY	BOCHE	AMPHR	SIGHT	AEMIA
NOGGS	FUGGY	BRAHE	ARTHR	TIGHT	ALGIA
PANGS	HEDGY	CACHE	NEPHR	WIGHT	AMNIA
PINGS	HOAGY	DUBHE	******	YACHT	ATRIA
PLUGS	JAGGY	FICHE	---HS	******	BAHIA
PRIGS	LEGGY	LATHE	******	---HU	BERIA
PUNGS	MANGY	LETHE	ADAHS	******	CELIA
QUAGS	MINGY	LITHE	AMAHS	ELIHU	CERIA
RIGGS	MUGGY	NICHE	ANKHS	FICHU	CILIA
RINGS	OLOGY	RAPHE	AYAHS	PRAHU	COBIA
RUNGS	PEGGY	RUCHE	BATHS	SADHU	CORIA
SHAGS	PHAGY	TITHE	BETHS	******	CURIA
SINGS	PIGGY	TYCHE	BLAHS	---HY	DACIA
SKEGS	PLEGY	WITHE	GOTHS	******	DELIA
SLAGS	PODGY	******	HIGHS	ALPHY	DULIA
SLOGS	PORGY	---HI	HUGHS	ARCHY	ENTIA
SLUGS	PUDGY	******	KAPHS	BATHY	FACIA
SMOGS	RAGGY	AMPHI	LATHS	BOTHY	FERIA
SNAGS	RANGY	ARCHI	LOCHS	BUSHY	FOLIA
SNUGS	RHAGY	DELHI	MATHS	CATHY	GONIA
SONGS	RIDGY	ORCHI	MOTHS	CUSHY	HEMIA
STAGS	SEDGY	SPAHI	MYTHS	DASHY	INDIA
SWAGS	SOGGY	TOPHI	NOAHS	DISHY	IONIA
SWIGS	STAGY	XIPHI	OATHS	DUCHY	JULIA
TANGS	STOGY	******	OPAHS	FISHY	LABIA
THUGS	SURGY	---HM	PATHS	GUSHY	LAMIA
TINGS	TANGY	******	PITHS	ITCHY	LIVIA
TONGS	VUGGY	ABOHM	RUTHS	KATHY	LOGIA

LUCIA	COMIC	TELIC	RAPID	ELSIE	******
LYDIA	CONIC	TONIC	REBID	EMMIE	---IK
MAFIA	CUBIC	TOPIC	REDID	ERNIE	******
MANIA	CYNIC	TORIC	RIGID	ESSIE	BATIK
MARIA	DARIC	TOXIC	SAPID	ETTIE	KAMIK
MEDIA	DOMIC	TUNIC	SAYID	EYDIE	MUJIK
MILIA	DORIC	VARIC	SOLID	EYRIE	RURIK
MYRIA	EDDIC	VATIC	SQUID	GENIE	SHEIK
NORIA	EOLIC	VEDIC	STAID	HOWIE	TUPIK
NUBIA	ETHIC	VESIC	TABID	JAMIE	******
OPSIA	FOLIC	VINIC	TEPID	JOSIE	---IL
OSTIA	GAMIC	XERIC	TIMID	JULIE	******
PODIA	GENIC	YOGIC	TUMID	KATIE	ABOIL
RETIA	HELIC	******	UNDID	KYRIE	ANVIL
SEPIA	HEMIC	---ID	VALID	LEWIE	APRIL
SOFIA	HUMIC	******	VAPID	MAMIE	ARGIL
SONIA	INDIC	ACRID	VIVID	MARIE	AUXIL
STRIA	IODIC	ALGID	ZOOID	MOVIE	AVAIL
SYRIA	IONIC	APHID	******	MOXIE	AVRIL
TAFIA	ISTIC	AROID	---IE	NIXIE	BASIL
TIBIA	LOGIC	AVOID	******	OLLIE	BRAIL
XENIA	LYRIC	BIFID	ABBIE	OZZIE	BROIL
ZAMIA	LYTIC	BOVID	ADDIE	PIXIE	CAVIL
******	MAGIC	BRAID	AERIE	PYXIE	CECIL
---IB	MALIC	CUPID	AGGIE	RAMIE	CIVIL
******	MANIC	DAVID	ALFIE	SADIE	CYRIL
ADLIB	MEDIC	DRUID	ALGIE	SATIE	DEVIL
CARIB	MELIC	FELID	ALLIE	SUSIE	DRAIL
SAHIB	MESIC	FETID	ANNIE	UNTIE	FLAIL
SQUIB	MIMIC	FLUID	ARNIE	******	FRAIL
******	MUSIC	GADID	ARTIE	---IF	FUSIL
---IC	OGMIC	GELID	AUDIE	******	FUZIL
******	OHMIC	GEOID	BELIE	CALIF	GRAIL
ANTIC	OLEIC	HALID	BOGIE	MOTIF	NEVIL
AREIC	OPTIC	HUMID	BOWIE	SERIF	NIHIL
ARTIC	OSMIC	HYOID	CAVIE	******	PERIL
ASPIC	PANIC	LEPID	CELIE	---IG	PUPIL
ATTIC	PUBIC	LIPID	CURIE	******	QUAIL
AULIC	PUDIC	LIVID	CUTIE	CRAIG	SIGIL
AURIC	PUNIC	LUCID	DAVIE	SPRIG	SNAIL
AZOIC	RABIC	LURID	DIXIE	UNRIG	SPOIL
BARIC	RELIC	MUCID	DOBIE	******	SWAIL
BASIC	RUNIC	MYOID	DOGIE	---II	SYBIL
BORIC	SALIC	OVOID	EADIE	******	TAMIL
CERIC	SILIC	PLAID	EDDIE	AALII	TRAIL
CETIC	SONIC	PLOID	EERIE	GENII	UNTIL
CIVIC	STOIC	PYOID	EFFIE	RADII	VEXIL
COLIC	SUFIC	RABID	ELLIE	TORII	ZORIL

******	ELAIN	SAVIN	OXLIP	BLOIS	RANIS
---IM	ELFIN	SERIN	SCRIP	BORIS	SARIS
******	ELGIN	SITIN	STRIP	CADIS	SUFIS
BEDIM	ELOIN	SKEIN	TULIP	CANIS	TAMIS
CLAIM	ELVIN	SLAIN	UNRIP	CENIS	TANIS
DECIM	ELWIN	SOZIN	UNZIP	CHRIS	TAPIS
DENIM	EOSIN	SPAIN	******	CUTIS	TAXIS
GOYIM	ERWIN	STAIN	---IR	DAVIS	TIKIS
HAKIM	GAMIN	STEIN	******	DEFIS	TITIS
MAXIM	GAVIN	SWAIN	AEGIR	DENIS	TONIS
MINIM	GRAIN	TIEIN	AESIR	DORIS	TOPIS
PURIM	GROIN	TOEIN	ASTIR	ELLIS	TUNIS
SCRIM	HEMIN	TOXIN	AVOIR	ETUIS	TUPIS
******	IRVIN	TRAIN	CHAIR	FIJIS	XAXIS
---IN	IRWIN	TURIN	CHÒIR	FINIS	YAXIS
******	KEVIN	TWAIN	EYRIR	HIFIS	YETIS
ACTIN	KININ	UNPIN	FAKIR	IASIS	YOGIS
ADMIN	KIRIN	VAGIN	FLAIR	JANIS	******
AGAIN	LADIN	YOGIN	GLAIR	KADIS	---IT
ALAIN	LAPIN	ZAYIN	KAFIR	KAKIS	******
ALBIN	LATIN	******	MIMIR	KEPIS	ADMIT
ALGIN	LENIN	---IO	NADIR	KIWIS	AMBIT
ALLIN	LIEIN	******	ONEIR	KUMIS	AUDIT
ALOIN	LININ	ANGIO	STAIR	LAPIS	AWAIT
ALUIN	LUPIN	ANZIO	TAPIR	LENIS	BARIT
ALVIN	LYSIN	AUDIO	THEIR	LEVIS	BEFIT
ALWIN	MATIN	CONIO	VANIR	LEWIS	BINIT
AMAIN	MORIN	CURIO	VIZIR	LORIS	BRUIT
AUXIN	MUCIN	ELAIO	******	LOUIS	CUBIT
AYDIN	OLEIN	FOLIO	---IS	LYSIS	DAVIT
BASIN	ORCIN	FUGIO	******	MARIS	DEBIT
BEGIN	ORPIN	GONIO	ABRIS	MAVIS	DEMIT
BENIN	PEKIN	HAGIO	AEGIS	METIS	DIGIT
BEVIN	PEPIN	HELIO	AGNIS	MIMIS	DIXIT
BLAIN	PLAIN	JULIO	ALDIS	NARIS	DROIT
BONIN	QUOIN	LABIO	ALLIS	NAZIS	FECIT
BRAIN	REGIN	MARIO	ALOIS	NEVIS	FRUIT
BRUIN	RENIN	MEDIO	ANTIS	OASIS	HABIT
BURIN	RESIN	OPHIO	APHIS	OPSIS	KRAIT
CABIN	REZIN	PATIO	APSIS	ORNIS	LEGIT
CETIN	RICIN	POLIO	ARRIS	ORRIS	LICIT
CHAIN	ROBIN	RADIO	ARSIS	PARIS	LIMIT
COLIN	RODIN	RATIO	ARTIS	PAVIS	MERIT
CUMIN	ROSIN	SOCIO	ASPIS	PENIS	ORBIT
CUTIN	RUNIN	VARIO	ATTIS	PERIS	PETIT
DRAIN	SABIN	******	AULIS	PILIS	PEWIT
ECHIN	SASIN	---IP	AURIS	PUBIS	PIPIT
EDWIN	SATIN	******	BASIS	PYXIS	PLAIT
		ATRIP			
		EQUIP			

POSIT	******	SNAKE	DECKS	LOOKS	TANKS
QUOIT	---JO	SPAKE	DESKS	LURKS	TASKS
REFIT	******	SPIKE	DHAKS	MACKS	TEAKS
REMIT	BANJO	SPOKE	DICKS	MARKS	TICKS
SPAIT	******	STAKE	DIRKS	MASKS	TREKS
SPLIT	---JY	STOKE	DISKS	MILKS	TUCKS
SPRIT	******	WACKE	DOCKS	MINKS	TURKS
TACIT	BENJY	******	DUCKS	MOCKS	TUSKS
TRAIT	******	---KI	DUNKS	MONKS	VICKS
UNFIT	---KA	******	DUSKS	MUCKS	WACKS
UNLIT	******	GORKI	ERIKS	MUSKS	WALKS
VISIT	DINKA	KHAKI	FINKS	NECKS	WEEKS
VOMIT	ERIKA	TURKI	FOLKS	NICKS	WICKS
******	KAFKA	******	FORKS	NOCKS	WINKS
---IX	LAIKA	---KO	FUNKS	NOOKS	WORKS
******	OSAKA	******	GAWKS	PACKS	YANKS
ADMIX	PARKA	BUCKO	GECKS	PARKS	YELKS
AFFIX	POLKA	BUNKO	GEEKS	PEAKS	YOLKS
CALIX	PUCKA	DISKO	GINKS	PECKS	******
CROIX	PUKKA	GECKO	GOOKS	PEEKS	---KU
CYLIX	PUNKA	JOCKO	HACKS	PERKS	******
FELIX	SITKA	LEUKO	HAIKS	PICKS	HAIKU
HELIX	STUKA	SHAKO	HANKS	PINKS	******
IMMIX	TANKA	******	HARKS	POCKS	---KY
INFIX	VODKA	---KS	HAWKS	PUCKS	******
KYLIX	******	******	HICKS	PUNKS	BALKY
RADIX	---KE	BACKS	HOCKS	RACKS	BARKY
SALIX	******	BALKS	HONKS	RANKS	BECKY
UNFIX	ALIKE	BANKS	HOOKS	REEKS	BOSKY
VARIX	AWAKE	BARKS	HULKS	RICKS	BRAKY
******	AWOKE	BASKS	HUNKS	RINKS	BULKY
---IZ	BLAKE	BEAKS	HUSKS	RISKS	CHOKY
******	BLOKE	BECKS	JACKS	ROCKS	COCKY
CADIZ	BRAKE	BILKS	JERKS	ROOKS	COOKY
HAFIZ	BROKE	BOOKS	JINKS	RUCKS	CORKY
SCHIZ	BURKE	BOSKS	JUNKS	RUSKS	DARKY
******	CHOKE	BUCKS	KECKS	SACKS	DICKY
---JA	CRAKE	BULKS	KICKS	SARKS	DINKY
******	DRAKE	BUNKS	KINKS	SEEKS	DUCKY
OUIJA	EVOKE	BUSKS	KIRKS	SICKS	DUSKY
SONJA	FLAKE	CALKS	KOOKS	SILKS	FLAKY
THUJA	FLUKE	CASKS	LACKS	SINKS	FLUKY
******	HOOKE	COCKS	LARKS	SOAKS	FUNKY
---JE	LOCKE	CONKS	LEAKS	SOCKS	GAWKY
******	QUAKE	COOKS	LEEKS	SUCKS	GORKY
KOPJE	SHAKE	CORKS	LICKS	SULKS	HANKY
******	SLAKE	CUSKS	LINKS	TACKS	HONKY
---JI	SMOKE	DAWKS	LOCKS	TALKS	HOOKY
******					
HADJI					
SHOJI					

HULKY	ASYLA	WOULD	GABLE	TULLE	DWELL
HUNKY	BELLA	YIELD	GAVLE	UMBLE	FRILL
HUSKY	BEULA	******	GUILE	UNCLE	GRILL
JACKY	BULLA	---LE	HALLE	UTILE	IDYLL
JERKY	CALLA	******	HELLE	VILLE	KNELL
JUNKY	CARLA	ABELE	HOYLE	VOILE	KNOLL
KINKY	CELLA	ADDLE	INGLE	WHALE	PHYLL
KOOKY	CHELA	ADELE	INKLE	WHILE	QUELL
LANKY	DELLA	AGILE	ISTLE	WHOLE	QUILL
LARKY	DOBLA	AISLE	IXTLE	******	SCALL
LEAKY	DUALA	AMBLE	JOULE	---LF	SCULL
LUCKY	ENOLA	AMOLE	LADLE	******	SHALL
MICKY	HEKLA	AMPLE	LILLE	ADOLF	SHELL
MILKY	KOALA	ANELE	LISLE	SHELF	SHILL
MUCKY	LEILA	ANGLE	MACLE	WOOLF	SKILL
MURKY	MARLA	ANILE	MAPLE	******	SKULL
MUSKY	OCALA	ANKLE	MERLE	---LI	SMALL
NARKY	PAULA	APPLE	NOBLE	******	SMELL
NICKY	PELLA	AXILE	OBOLE	CALLI	SNELL
PAWKY	PEPLA	AZOLE	ODYLE	CHILI	SPALL
PEAKY	PHILA	BASLE	OVULE	DHOLI	SPELL
PERKY	PHYLA	BELLE	PERLE	FORLI	SPILL
PESKY	ROTLA	BIBLE	PHILE	LILLI	STALL
PINKY	TESLA	BIRLE	PHYLE	MILLI	STILL
POCKY	UVULA	BOGLE	POOLE	OBELI	STULL
PORKY	VILLA	BOULE	PROLE	OBOLI	SWELL
PUNKY	VIOLA	BOYLE	RIFLE	OVOLI	SWILL
QUAKY	VOILA	BUGLE	RILLE	STYLI	TRILL
REEKY	WALLA	CABLE	ROBLE	VILLI	TROLL
RICKY	WILLA	CARLE	RUBLE	******	TRULL
RISKY	******	CHILE	SABLE	---LK	TWILL
ROCKY	---LD	CHOLE	SCALE	******	YOULL
ROOKY	******	CHYLE	SHALE	BAULK	******
SHAKY	******	COBLE	SIDLE	CAULK	---LM
SILKY	BUILD	COELE	SMILE	CHALK	******
SMOKY	CHILD	CYCLE	SOCLE	SKULK	HAULM
SNAKY	COULD	DHOLE	SPILE	STALK	PSALM
SPIKY	FIELD	DOYLE	STALE	WHELK	QUALM
SULKY	FJELD	DUPLE	STELE	******	REALM
TACKY	GUILD	EAGLE	STILE	---LL	WHELM
VICKY	MOULD	EARLE	STOLE	******	******
WACKY	ROALD	ECOLE	STYLE	ATOLL	---LO
YOLKY	SCALD	EDILE	SWALE	BEALL	******
ZINKY	SCOLD	EMILE	TABLE	BRILL	AMYLO
******	SKALD	EXILE	THOLE	CHILL	ANGLO
---LA	WEALD	FABLE	THULE	DOALL	CARLO
******	WIELD	FARLE	TITLE	DRILL	CELLO
ADELA	WOALD	FUGLE	TOILE	DROLL	CHILO
ALULA	WORLD				

COELO	CEILS	HERLS	POOLS	DWELT	DRILY
CYCLO	CELLS	HILLS	PULLS	EXALT	DRYLY
DIPLO	COALS	HOWLS	PURLS	EXULT	DULLY
HALLO	COILS	HULLS	RAILS	FAULT	EARLY
HAPLO	COOLS	HURLS	REALS	GAULT	EMILY
HELLO	COWLS	IDOLS	REELS	GUILT	FATLY
HYALO	CULLS	IDYLS	RIALS	KNELT	FELLY
JELLO	CURLS	ITALS	RILLS	MOULT	FILLY
MYELO	DEALS	JAILS	ROILS	POULT	FITLY
OCULO	DELLS	JARLS	ROLLS	QUILT	FOLLY
OVOLO	DIALS	JELLS	SAILS	SAULT	FULLY
PABLO	DOLLS	JILLS	SAULS	SHALT	GAILY
PAOLO	DUELS	JOELS	SEALS	SMALT	GAYLY
PAULO	DULLS	JOWLS	SELLS	SMELT	GODLY
PHILO	EARLS	KARLS	SHULS	SMOLT	GOLLY
PHYLO	EMILS	KEELS	SILLS	SPELT	GULLY
PYELO	ENOLS	KILLS	SOILS	SPILT	HAPLY
ROLLO	EVILS	KOELS	SOULS	STILT	HILLY
SIALO	FAILS	LALLS	TAELS	UBOLT	HOLLY
STYLO	FALLS	LOLLS	TAILS	VAULT	HOTLY
******	FARLS	LULLS	TEALS	******	HURLY
---LP	FEELS	MAILS	TELLS	---LU	ICILY
******	FELLS	MALLS	TILLS	******	IMPLY
SCALP	FILLS	MARLS	TOILS	POILU	ITALY
SCULP	FOALS	MAULS	TOLLS	******	JELLY
WHELP	FOILS	MEALS	TOOLS	---LY	JOLLY
******	FOOLS	MEWLS	URALS	******	KELLY
---LS	FOULS	MILLS	VEILS	AMPLY	LAXLY
******	FOWLS	MOILS	VIALS	APPLY	LILLY
ABELS	FUELS	MOLLS	VILLS	APTLY	LOLLY
AMYLS	FULLS	MULLS	VIOLS	BADLY	LOWLY
ANILS	FURLS	NAILS	WAILS	BELLY	MADLY
ARILS	GAELS	NEALS	WAULS	BIALY	MANLY
AXILS	GAILS	NEILS	WAWLS	BIGLY	MARLY
BAILS	GALLS	NELLS	WEALS	BILLY	MEALY
BALLS	GAOLS	NOELS	WELLS	BULLY	MILLY
BAWLS	GAULS	OPALS	WILLS	BURLY	MOLLY
BELLS	GILLS	ORALS	WOOLS	COALY	MUHLY
BILLS	GIRLS	OVALS	YAWLS	COLLY	NELLY
BIRLS	GOALS	PAILS	YELLS	COYLY	NEWLY
BOILS	GULLS	PALLS	YOWLS	CURLY	NOBLY
BOLLS	HAILS	PAULS	******	DAILY	ODDLY
BOWLS	HALLS	PAWLS	---LT	DALLY	PALLY
BULLS	HARLS	PEALS	******	DIMLY	PELLY
BURLS	HAULS	PEELS	ADULT	DOILY	PHILY
CALLS	HEALS	PHILS	ATILT	DOLLY	POLLY
CARLS	HEELS	PILLS	BUILT	DOOLY	RALLY
CAULS	HELLS	POLLS	DEALT	DOYLY	RAWLY

REDLY	KARMA	FLUME	BROMO	BOOMS	SHIMS
REPLY	LEMMA	FORME	CHEMO	BRIMS	SKIMS
ROILY	LLAMA	FRAME	COSMO	CALMS	SLAMS
RUMLY	MAGMA	FROME	DERMO	CHUMS	SLIMS
SADLY	MAMMA	GLUME	DUOMO	CLAMS	SLUMS
SALLY	MYOMA	GNOME	GISMO	CLEMS	STEMS
SCALY	NORMA	GORME	GIZMO	CORMS	STUMS
SHALY	PALMA	GRIME	MALMO	CRAMS	SWIMS
SHILY	PARMA	GRUME	PRIMO	CULMS	TEAMS
SHYLY	PRIMA	NEUME	PULMO	DEEMS	TEEMS
SILLY	REGMA	OXIME	SCHMO	DOOMS	TERMS
SLILY	SALMA	PLUME	SKIMO	DORMS	TRAMS
SLYLY	SELMA	PRIME	******	DRAMS	TRIMS
SULLY	SIGMA	RHYME	---MP	DRUMS	WARMS
SURLY	STOMA	SHAME	******	EXAMS	WEEMS
TALLY	TRYMA	SLIME	BLIMP	FARMS	WHAMS
TELLY	ULEMA	SOMME	CHAMP	FILMS	WHIMS
TILLY	WILMA	SPUME	CHIMP	FIRMS	WORMS
TRULY	******	STOME	CHUMP	FLAMS	ZOOMS
TULLY	---MB	THEME	CLAMP	FOAMS	******
WALLY	******	THYME	CLUMP	FORMS	---MY
WANLY	ABOMB	******	CRAMP	GERMS	******
WETLY	CLIMB	---MI	CRIMP	GLIMS	ANOMY
WILLY	COOMB	******	CRUMP	GRAMS	BALMY
WOOLY	CRUMB	CHEMI	FLUMP	HARMS	BARMY
WRYLY	HBOMB	DUOMI	FRUMP	HELMS	BEAMY
******	PLUMB	ELEMI	PLUMP	HOLMS	DORMY
---MA	RHOMB	FERMI	PRIMP	IMAMS	DUMMY
******	RHUMB	MIAMI	SCAMP	ITEMS	ENEMY
ABOMA	THUMB	NAOMI	SKIMP	LOAMS	FILMY
AGAMA	******	OTOMI	SLUMP	LOOMS	FLAMY
ANIMA	---ME	PALMI	STAMP	MAIMS	FOAMY
AROMA	******	PRIMI	STOMP	MUMMS	GAMMY
BURMA	ANIME	SALMI	STUMP	NORMS	GEMMY
COMMA	BAUME	SWAMI	SWAMP	PALMS	GNOMY
DERMA	BERME	VERMI	THUMP	PLUMS	GRIMY
DOGMA	BLAME	******	TRAMP	POEMS	GUMMY
DRAMA	BROME	---ML	TRUMP	PRAMS	HAMMY
EDEMA	BRUME	******	******	PRIMS	JAMMY
ENEMA	CHIME	FRIML	---MS	PROMS	JEMMY
ETYMA	CHYME	******	******	REAMS	JIMMY
GAMMA	CLIME	---MM	ADAMS	REIMS	LOAMY
GEMMA	CREME	******	ALUMS	ROAMS	MAMMY
GRAMA	CRIME	GRIMM	ARUMS	ROOMS	MUMMY
GUAMA	DROME	******	ATOMS	SCUMS	PALMY
GUMMA	FEMME	---MO	BALMS	SEAMS	PIGMY
HALMA	FIUME	******	BEAMS	SEEMS	PLUMY
HERMA	FLAME	ALAMO	BERMS	SHAMS	POMMY
		ANEMO			

PYGMY	MINNA	KHOND	INANE	ALONG	WHANG
RAMMY	MORNA	MAUND	IRENE	AMONG	WRING
ROOMY	MYRNA	MOUND	IRONE	APING	WRONG
RUMMY	NANNA	PIAND	JAYNE	AWING	WRUNG
SAMMY	PATNA	POIND	KOINE	AXING	YOUNG
SEAMY	PENNA	POUND	KRONE	BEING	******
SLIMY	PINNA	ROUND	LAINE	BHANG	---NI
SPUMY	PLENA	SCAND	LIANE	BRING	******
STIMY	POONA	SCEND	MAINE	CHANG	ACINI
STOMY	PYDNA	SOUND	MARNE	CLANG	ADENI
STYMY	SAUNA	SPEND	MESNE	CLING	CRANI
TAMMY	SCENA	STAND	MILNE	CLUNG	GRANI
THYMY	SENNA	TREND	OPINE	CUING	JINNI
TIMMY	SIENA	UPEND	OVINE	DOING	LIGNI
TOMMY	SUNNA	VIAND	OZONE	DYING	MAGNI
TUMMY	TACNA	WOUND	PAINE	EKING	PENNI
WORMY	TRINA	******	PANNE	EWING	PINNI
YUMMY	TRONA	---NE	PHANE	EYING	PLANI
******	TSANA	******	PHONE	FLING	SEGNI
---NA	VERNA	AISNE	PLANE	FLONG	SOMNI
******	VILNA	AKENE	PRONE	FLUNG	SPINI
AGANA	******	ALINE	PRUNE	GIING	SUNNI
AMANA	---NC	ALONE	RHINE	GOING	******
ARENA	******	AMINE	RHONE	HYING	---NK
BWANA	ADUNC	ATONE	SAONE	ICING	******
CANNA	BLANC	AXONE	SCENE	LIANG	BLANK
CHINA	BRONC	AZINE	SCONE	LYING	BLINK
DIANA	FRANC	BENNE	SEINE	OKING	BRINK
DONNA	******	BERNE	SENNE	ORANG	CHINK
EDINA	---ND	BOONE	SHINE	OWING	CHUNK
ELENA	******	BORNE	SHONE	PRANG	CLANK
FAUNA	ALAND	BOYNE	SIGNE	PRONG	CLINK
FIONA	AMEND	BRINE	SPINE	RUING	CRANK
FRENA	BLAND	CHINE	STONE	SLANG	DRANK
GHANA	BLEND	CLINE	SWINE	SLING	DRINK
GUANA	BLIND	CLONE	TBONE	SLUNG	DRUNK
HANNA	BLOND	COLNE	THANE	SPANG	FLANK
HENNA	BOUND	CRANE	THINE	STING	FLUNK
HYENA	BRAND	CRONE	TONNE	STUNG	FRANK
ILONA	ELAND	DEANE	TRINE	SUING	PLANK
JAINA	EMEND	DIANE	TWINE	SWING	PLONK
JUANA	FIEND	DIENE	UDINE	SWUNG	PLUNK
JUMNA	FOUND	DIONE	URINE	THING	PRANK
KRONA	FROND	DONNE	VERNE	THONG	PRINK
LEONA	GLAND	DRONE	WAYNE	TWANG	SHANK
LIANA	GRAND	DUANE	WHINE	TYING	SKINK
LORNA	GRIND	HORNE	******	USING	SKUNK
MANNA	HOUND	IMINE	---NG	VYING	SLINK
			******		
			ACING		
			AGING		

SLUNK	******	GWENS	PIONS	BLENT	STINT
SPANK	---NS	GWYNS	PLANS	BLUNT	STUNT
SPUNK	******	HORNS	POONS	BRANT	SUINT
STANK	AEONS	HYMNS	RAINS	BRENT	TAINT
STINK	ALANS	ICONS	REINS	BRUNT	TAUNT
STUNK	AMENS	IKONS	ROANS	BURNT	TRENT
SWANK	ASSNS	IRONS	RUINS	CHANT	ULENT
THANK	AVENS	IVANS	SCANS	CLINT	VAUNT
THINK	AXONS	JAINS	SEANS	COUNT	WASNT
TRUNK	AYINS	JEANS	SHANS	DAUNT	******
******	AZANS	JOANS	SHINS	DIDNT	---NU
---NN	AZONS	JOHNS	SHUNS	EVENT	******
******	BANNS	JOINS	SIGNS	FAINT	BORNU
GLENN	BARNS	JUANS	SKINS	FEINT	CORNU
GWENN	BEANS	KEENS	SPANS	FLINT	******
******	BOONS	KERNS	SPINS	FOUNT	---NX
---NO	BRANS	KHANS	STANS	FRONT	******
******	BUNNS	KILNS	STUNS	GAUNT	BRONX
ADENO	BURNS	LAWNS	SUNNS	GHENT	******
AMINO	CHINS	LEANS	SWANS	GIANT	---NY
BEANO	CIONS	LEONS	TAINS	GLINT	******
BRUNO	CLANS	LIENS	TARNS	GRANT	AGONY
CHINO	CLONS	LIMNS	TEENS	GRUNT	ATONY
CLINO	COINS	LIONS	TERNS	HADNT	BENNY
COENO	COONS	LOANS	THINS	HASNT	BONNY
CTENO	CORNS	LOINS	TOWNS	HAUNT	BRINY
CYANO	DAMNS	LOONS	TRANS	JAUNT	BUNNY
ETHNO	DARNS	LYNNS	TURNS	JOINT	CANNY
GRANO	DAWNS	LYONS	TWINS	LEANT	CLUNY
GUANO	DEANS	MAINS	VEINS	MAYNT	CONNY
GYMNO	DOWNS	MEANS	VERNS	MEANT	CORNY
HYPNO	EARNS	MIENS	WAINS	MOUNT	CRONY
ICONO	EBONS	MOANS	WARNS	ODONT	DANNY
IMINO	EVANS	MOONS	WEANS	OLENT	DENNY
LIGNO	EVENS	MORNS	WHENS	PAINT	DOWNY
LLANO	FAUNS	MUONS	WHINS	PLANT	EBONY
PHENO	FAWNS	NOONS	WRENS	POINT	FANNY
PHONO	FERNS	NORNS	YARNS	PRINT	FENNY
PIANO	FINNS	NOUNS	YAWNS	QUANT	FERNY
PLANO	FIRNS	OMENS	YEANS	QUINT	FINNY
PORNO	FLANS	OPENS	ZOONS	RIANT	FUNNY
RHINO	GAINS	OVENS	******	SAINT	GINNY
SEGNO	GLANS	OWENS	---NT	SCANT	GUNNY
STENO	GLENS	PAINS	******	SCENT	HINNY
TAINO	GOONS	PAWNS	AGENT	SHANT	HORNY
URANO	GOWNS	PEANS	AMENT	SHUNT	IRONY
URINO	GRINS	PEENS	ANENT	SLANT	JENNY
	GUANS	PEONS	ARENT	SPENT	JINNY

JONNY	DEMOB	******	BLOOM	CREON	PYLON
KENNY	JACOB	---OI	BOSOM	CROON	RADON
LAWNY	JAKOB	******	BROOM	DAMON	RAYON
LENNY	KABOB	HANOI	BUXOM	DEMON	RIPON
LOONY	NABOB	******	CAROM	DEVON	RUNON
MEANY	THROB	---OK	CELOM	DIJON	SALON
MOONY	******	******	CHROM	EAMON	SAXON
NANNY	---OC	BROOK	ENTOM	ELTON	SCION
NINNY	******	CROOK	EPSOM	FANON	SERON
PENNY	ASSOC	KAPOK	GLOOM	FELON	SETON
PEONY	HAVOC	SHOOK	GROOM	FREON	SIDON
PHANY	MADOC	SNOOK	IDIOM	GABON	SIMON
PHONY	MEDOC	SPOOK	SODOM	GIPON	SINON
PINNY	******	STOOK	VENOM	GIRON	SOLON
PLINY	---OD	******	******	GYRON	SPOON
RAINY	******	---OL	---ON	HERON	SWOON
RONNY	BIPOD	******	******	HURON	TALON
RUNNY	BLOOD	ALDOL	AARON	HYSON	TENON
SHINY	BROOD	ALGOL	AKRON	ILION	TETON
SONNY	EPHOD	ARGOL	ALTON	INION	TOYON
SPINY	FLOOD	BIKOL	AMMON	ITION	TRYON
STONY	HEROD	BOHOL	ANCON	IXION	UNION
SUNNY	SCROD	CAROL	ANION	JASON	WAGON
TAWNY	SNOOD	CIBOL	ANTON	JETON	XENON
TEENY	STOOD	DROOL	APRON	JUPON	YAPON
TINNY	SYNOD	ENROL	ARGON	LEMON	YUKON
TUNNY	******	ERROL	ARION	LUTON	YUPON
VEINY	---OE	EXTOL	ARSON	LUZON	ZIRON
VINNY	******	GOGOL	ASTON	MACON	******
WEENY	CANOE	IODOL	ATION	MASON	---OO
WENNY	CHLOE	KAROL	AVION	MELON	******
WHINY	DEFOE	LYSOL	BACON	MESON	BABOO
******	FAROE	METOL	BARON	MORON	IGLOO
---NZ	MEROE	PAROL	BASON	MYRON	KAROO
******	PEKOE	SALOL	BATON	NITON	KAZOO
FRANZ	TAHOE	SHEOL	BETON	NIXON	TABOO
MAINZ	THROE	SOTOL	BISON	NYLON	WAHOO
******	******	SPOOL	BORON	ODEON	YAHOO
---OA	---OF	STOOL	BOSON	ONION	YAZOO
******	******	THIOL	BYRON	ORION	******
COCOA	ALOOF	TOBOL	CAJON	ORLON	---OP
GENOA	KLOOF	TRIOL	CANON	ORSON	******
SAMOA	PROOF	TYROL	CAPON	PAEON	AESOP
******	SPOOF	XYLOL	CENON	PELON	BEBOP
---OB	******	******	CHRON	PERON	DROOP
******	---OG	---OM	CLEON	PINON	ESTOP
******	******	******	COGON	PITON	GALOP
CABOB	BEFOG	AXIOM	COLON	PUTON	ORLOP
CAROB	MAGOG	BESOM			

SCOOP	RIGOR	FANOS	TYROS	POYOU	CHAPE
SLOOP	ROTOR	GIROS	UMBOS	SAJOU	COUPE
SNOOP	RUMOR	GOBOS	WINOS	******	CRAPE
STOOP	SAPOR	GYROS	YOYOS	---OW	CREPE
STROP	SAVOR	HALOS	ZEROS	******	DRAPE
SWOOP	SENOR	HOBOS	******	AGLOW	DRUPE
TROOP	SOPOR	HUGOS	---OT	ALLOW	ELOPE
WHOOP	SPOOR	HYPOS	******	ARROW	ETAPE
******	SUDOR	JANOS	ABBOT	BELOW	GASPE
---OR	TABOR	JATOS	AFOOT	ELBOW	GRAPE
******	TENOR	KAYOS	ALLOT	EMBOW	GRIPE
ABHOR	TIMOR	KILOS	ARGOT	ENDOW	GROPE
ACTOR	TUDOR	KOMOS	ASCOT	INDOW	LOUPE
ALGOR	TUMOR	KOTOS	BEGOT	MIAOW	MYOPE
ARBOR	TUTOR	KUDOS	BESOT	OXBOW	NAPPE
ARDOR	VALOR	LAGOS	BIGOT	SEROW	SCAPE
ARMOR	VAPOR	LENOS	CABOT	THROW	SCOPE
ASTOR	VIGOR	LOBOS	COROT	UPBOW	SHAPE
BOGOR	VISOR	LOCOS	DEPOT	WIDOW	SLOPE
CHLOR	VIZOR	LOGOS	DIVOT	******	SLYPE
COLOR	******	LOTOS	ELIOT	---OX	SNIPE
CRUOR	---OS	MELOS	ERGOT	******	STIPE
DECOR	******	MEMOS	FAGOT	PHLOX	STOPE
DOLOR	ADIOS	MINOS	GAVOT	XEROX	STUPE
DONOR	AFROS	MOROS	GEMOT	******	SWIPE
EPHOR	AGIOS	NEROS	GIGOT	---OY	TAUPE
ERROR	AINOS	OLIOS	HELOT	******	TEMPE
FAVOR	ALDOS	OTTOS	IDIOT	ALLOY	TRIPE
FEDOR	ALTOS	PAROS	IMPOT	ANNOY	TROPE
FETOR	AMBOS	PECOS	INGOT	DECOY	******
FLOOR	ARGOS	PEPOS	JABOT	ENJOY	---PH
FLUOR	ATHOS	PESOS	MAGOT	ENVOY	******
FUROR	AUTOS	SAGOS	PICOT	LEROY	ALEPH
GABOR	BOLOS	SAMOS	PILOT	MCCOY	DOLPH
HONOR	BOZOS	SAROS	PITOT	SAVOY	GLYPH
HUMOR	BROOS	SEGOS	PIVOT	SEPOY	GRAPH
ICHOR	CEROS	SHOOS	ROBOT	******	HUMPH
JUROR	CHAOS	SILOS	SABOT	---PA	LYMPH
LABOR	CHIOS	SOLOS	SCOOT	******	MORPH
LUXOR	CLIOS	SYROS	SHOOT	CULPA	NYMPH
MAJOR	COCOS	TALOS	SNOOT	KAPPA	OOMPH
MANOR	DAVOS	TAROS	TAROT	SALPA	RALPH
MAYOR	DELOS	TENOS	******	SCAPA	ROLPH
MINOR	DEMOS	TIROS	---OU	STUPA	******
MOTOR	DIDOS	TODOS	******	TAMPA	---PE
NAHOR	DODOS	TOYOS	ANJOU	******	******
PRIOR	DUROS	TRIOS	BAYOU	---PE	AGAPE
RAZOR	ETHOS	TYPOS	BIJOU	******	CALPE

*****	DROPS	SCUPS	GRIPT	ROUPY	MOIRA
---PI	DUMPS	SEEPS	INAPT	SAPPY	MURRA
*****	FLAPS	SHIPS	INEPT	SCOPY	OPERA
CAMPI	FLIPS	SHOPS	LEAPT	SOAPY	SABRA
CARPI	FLOPS	SIMPS	SLEPT	SOPPY	SACRA
LIPPI	FRAPS	SKEPS	SLIPT	SOUPY	SERRA
OKAPI	GAMPS	SKIPS	STOPT	TIPPY	SUPRA
PALPI	GASPS	SLAPS	SWEPT	WASPY	SUTRA
PAPPI	GIMPS	SLIPS	TEMPT	WEEPY	TATRA
SCAPI	GRIPS	SLOPS	UNAPT	WISPY	TERRA
TEMPI	GULPS	SNAPS	WHIPT	ZIPPY	TETRA
*****	HARPS	SNIPS	WRAPT	*****	TIARA
---PO	HASPS	SOAPS	*****	---QI	ULTRA
*****	HEAPS	SOUPS	---PU	*****	UMBRA
CAMPO	HELPS	STEPS	*****	IRAQI	WIRRA
CARPO	HEMPS	STOPS	COYPU	*****	ZEBRA
COMPO	HOOPS	SUMPS	QUIPU	---RA	*****
HIPPO	HUMPS	SWAPS	*****	ACCRA	---RB
POOPO	JEEPS	TAMPS	---PY	AFTRA	*****
TEMPO	JUMPS	TARPS	*****	AGORA	ACERB
*****	KEEPS	TRAPS	BUMPY	ANTRA	BLURB
---PP	KELPS	TRIPS	CAMPY	BASRA	EXURB
*****	KNOPS	VAMPS	CUPPY	BEIRA	*****
KRUPP	LAMPS	WARPS	DIPPY	BERRA	---RD
*****	LAPPS	WASPS	DUMPY	CEARA	*****
---PS	LEAPS	WEEPS	GAPPY	CITRA	AWARD
*****	LIMPS	WHAPS	GIMPY	CLARA	BAIRD
BEEPS	LISPS	WHIPS	GRAPY	COBRA	BEARD
BLIPS	LOOPS	WHOPS	GUPPY	COPRA	BOARD
BUMPS	LOUPS	WISPS	HAPPY	CRURA	CAIRD
BURPS	LUMPS	WRAPS	HARPY	DOBRA	CHARD
CAMPS	MUMPS	YAUPS	HEMPY	DOURA	CHORD
CARPS	NEAPS	YAWPS	HIPPY	DURRA	FIORD
CHAPS	PEEPS	YELPS	HUMPY	EXTRA	FJORD
CHIPS	PHIPS	*****	JUMPY	FLORA	GOURD
CHOPS	PIMPS	---PT	LIPPY	HYDRA	GUARD
CLAPS	PLOPS	*****	LOOPY	INDRA	HEARD
CLIPS	POOPS	ADAPT	LOPPY	INFRA	HOARD
CLOPS	PROPS	ADEPT	LUMPY	INTRA	LAIRD
COOPS	PULPS	ADOPT	MYOPY	KLARA	NJORD
CORPS	PUMPS	CHAPT	NAPPY	KUFRA	SHARD
COUPS	QUIPS	COOPT	NIPPY	LABRA	SHERD
CRAPS	RAMPS	CREPT	PAPPY	LAURA	SWARD
CROPS	RASPS	CRYPT	PEPPY	LEORA	SWORD
CUSPS	REAPS	DRIPT	POPPY	LIBRA	THIRD
DAMPS	ROMPS	DROPT	PULPY	MAURA	WEIRD
DEEPS	RUMPS	EGYPT	PUPPY	MICRA	*****
DRIPS	SCOPS	ERUPT	RASPY		---RE
					*****
					ADORE
					AFIRE

AFORE	SPIRE	PATRI	SWARM	LATRO	SKIRR
ANDRE	SPORE	PLURI	THERM	MACRO	WHIRR
AWARE	STARE	SHARI	UNARM	METRO	******
AZURE	STERE	TERRI	******	MICRO	---RS
BARRE	STORE	UTERI	---RN	MORRO	******
BLARE	SUCRE	VITRI	******	MUCRO	AMIRS
CADRE	SWORE	ZIMRI	ACORN	MUNRO	AVARS
CHARE	THERE	******	ADORN	NECRO	AVERS
CHORE	TIGRE	---RK	BAIRN	NEGRO	BEARS
CLARE	TWERE	******	BOURN	NEURO	BEERS
CRORE	WHERE	CLARK	CAIRN	NITRO	BIERS
EAGRE	WHORE	CLERK	CHURN	OMBRO	BIRRS
ENARE	YOURE	OZARK	DOORN	ONIRO	BLURS
FIBRE	YSERE	QUARK	INURN	OTERO	BOARS
FLARE	ZAIRE	QUIRK	LEARN	PEDRO	BOERS
FRERE	******	SHARK	MOURN	PETRO	BOORS
GENRE	---RF	SHIRK	NAIRN	PICRO	BURRS
GLARE	******	SMIRK	QUERN	PTERO	CHARS
INURE	DWARF	SNARK	SCORN	RETRO	CZARS
ISERE	SCARF	SPARK	SHORN	SACRO	DEARS
LITRE	SCURF	STARK	SPURN	SAPRO	DOERS
LIVRE	WHARF	STIRK	STERN	SAURO	DOORS
LOIRE	******	STORK	SWORN	SPIRO	DORRS
LUCRE	---RG	******	THORN	SPORO	EMIRS
METRE	******	---RL	UTURN	TAURO	EWERS
MITRE	BOURG	******	YEARN	THYRO	FAIRS
MOIRE	******	CEORL	******	TRURO	FEARS
MOORE	---RH	CHURL	---RO	UTERO	FOURS
MURRE	******	GNARL	******	VARRO	GAURS
NACRE	MYRRH	KNURL	ANDRO	******	GEARS
NITRE	******	PEARL	ASTRO	---RP	GOERS
OCHRE	---RI	SHORL	BURRO	******	HAIRS
OMBRE	******	SKIRL	CAIRO	CHIRP	HEARS
OUTRE	CAPRI	SNARL	CHARO	SCARP	HEIRS
PADRE	CIRRI	SWIRL	CHIRO	SHARP	HOERS
PHORE	CYMRI	TWIRL	CHORO	SLURP	HOURS
PHYRE	FEBRI	WHIRL	CIRRO	STIRP	JEERS
QUIRE	FERRI	WHORL	CLARO	THORP	KIERS
SABRE	HENRI	******	COPRO	TWERP	KNARS
SARRE	HOURI	---RM	CUPRO	TWIRP	KNURS
SCARE	INDRI	******	FERRO	USURP	LAIRS
SCORE	KAURI	ALARM	FIBRO	******	LEERS
SHARE	KUKRI	CHARM	GENRO	---RR	LEHRS
SHIRE	MAORI	CHIRM	HIERO	******	LIARS
SHORE	MATRI	INARM	HYDRO	CHIRR	LOURS
SNARE	NEURI	REARM	HYGRO	CHURR	MOORS
SNORE	NIGRI	SPERM	IATRO	KNURR	NEARS
SPARE	NITRI	STORM	INTRO	SHIRR	ODORS

OMERS	COURT	DECRY	RETRY	BOISE	NOISE
OYERS	EVERT	DERRY	SAURY	BOUSE	NOOSE
PAIRS	EXERT	DIARY	SCARY	BOWSE	NORSE
PARRS	FLIRT	DOURY	SORRY	BURSE	NURSE
PEARS	HEART	DOWRY	SPIRY	CAUSE	OBESE
PEERS	INERT	DRURY	STORY	CEASE	PAISE
PIERS	OVERT	EMBRY	TARRY	CENSE	PARSE
POURS	QUART	EMERY	TEARY	CHASE	PASSE
PURRS	QUIRT	EMORY	TERRY	CHOSE	PAUSE
REARS	SHIRT	ENTRY	USURY	CLOSE	PEASE
ROARS	SHORT	EVERY	VEERY	COPSE	PERSE
RUERS	SKIRT	FAIRY	WEARY	CORSE	PHASE
SCARS	SMART	FERRY	WORRY	CRUSE	POISE
SEARS	SNORT	FIERY	******	CURSE	POSSE
SEERS	SPIRT	FIRRY	---SA	DENSE	PRASE
SLURS	SPORT	FURRY	******	DOUSE	PRISE
SOARS	SPURT	GARRY	BALSA	DOWSE	PROSE
SOURS	START	GERRY	BURSA	DRUSE	PULSE
SPARS	SWART	GLARY	DORSA	DULSE	PURSE
SPURS	WHORT	GLORY	FOSSA	ELISE	RAISE
STARS	******	HAIRY	LASSA	ERASE	RINSE
STIRS	---RU	HARRY	LHASA	EROSE	ROUSE
SUERS	******	HENRY	LUISA	FALSE	SALSE
TEARS	NAURU	HOARY	LYSSA	FEASE	SEISE
THURS	NEHRU	HURRY	MENSA	FESSE	SENSE
TIERS	OTARU	IATRY	NYASA	FOSSE	SOUSE
TOURS	******	IVORY	OMASA	FRISE	TEASE
TSARS	---RY	JERRY	PAISA	GEESE	TENSE
TZARS	******	JEWRY	PRESA	GOOSE	TERSE
USERS	ALARY	KAURY	SALSA	GORSE	THESE
VAIRS	AMBRY	KERRY	SOUSA	GUISE	THOSE
VEERS	ANGRY	LARRY	TULSA	HANSE	TOISE
WEARS	APERY	LATRY	VEPSA	HAWSE	UKASE
WEIRS	ATORY	LEARY	******	HESSE	ULOSE
WHIRS	AUTRY	LEERY	---SC	HORSE	VERSE
YEARS	AVERY	LORRY	******	HOUSE	WHOSE
YOURS	BARRY	MARRY	CRESC	JESSE	WORSE
******	BEERY	MERRY	******	LAPSE	******
---RT	BERRY	METRY	---SE	LEASE	---SH
******	BURRY	MURRY	******	LOOSE	******
ABORT	CARRY	OCHRY	ABASE	LOUSE	ABASH
ALERT	CHARY	ONERY	ABUSE	LUISE	AMISH
APART	CLARY	OVARY	AMUSE	MANSE	APISH
APORT	COWRY	PARRY	ANISE	MASSE	AWASH
AVERT	CURRY	PEARY	ARISE	MEUSE	BLUSH
BLURT	CYMRY	PERRY	AROSE	MOOSE	BRASH
CHART	DAIRY	PETRY	BISSE	MORSE	BRUSH
CHERT	DEARY	QUERY	BLASE	MOUSE	CLASH

CRASH	KURSK	AMISS	DEIST	******	SISSY
CRUSH	MINSK	BLESS	DIDST	---SU	SONSY
CUISH	TORSK	BLISS	DOEST	******	SUDSY
FLASH	WHISK	BRASS	DREST	MATSU	TANSY
FLESH	******	CHESS	DURST	******	TIPSY
FLUSH	---SM	CLASS	EGEST	---SY	TOPSY
FRESH	******	CRASS	ERNST	******	******
FROSH	ABYSM	CRESS	EXIST	BESSY	---SZ
GIRSH	CHASM	CROSS	FAUST	BETSY	******
GNASH	DEISM	DRESS	FEAST	BOSSY	GROSZ
HARSH	FOISM	DROSS	FEIST	BOUSY	******
IRISH	PLASM	FLOSS	FIRST	CISSY	---TA
LEASH	PRISM	GAUSS	FOIST	DAISY	******
MARSH	SEISM	GLASS	FROST	FUSSY	ADYTA
PLASH	SPASM	GLOSS	GEEST	GASSY	ANITA
PLUSH	******	GRASS	GHOST	GIPSY	AORTA
QUASH	---SO	GROSS	GLOST	GOOSY	BEATA
SHUSH	******	GUESS	GRIST	GORSY	BERTA
SLASH	ANISO	KVASS	GUEST	GUTSY	BIOTA
SLOSH	AVISO	LOESS	HEIST	GYPSY	CESTA
SLUSH	BASSO	PRESS	HOIST	HORSY	CEUTA
SMASH	BETSO	QUASS	HOLST	HUSSY	CHITA
STASH	CANSO	STOSS	HORST	JASSY	COSTA
SWASH	CUSSO	SWISS	HURST	JESSY	COTTA
SWISH	DORSO	TRASS	IDEST	LEPSY	DELTA
TRASH	GESSO	TRESS	JOIST	LOUSY	DICTA
WELSH	HYPSO	TRUSS	JOUST	MASSY	EVITA
WHISH	KELSO	******	LEAST	MESSY	GRETA
******	LASSO	---ST	MAYST	MISSY	GUSTA
---SI	MOSSO	******	MIDST	MOSSY	GUTTA
******	RUSSO	ADUST	MOIST	MOUSY	HEPTA
BASSI	SAYSO	AGIST	PLAST	MUSSY	HORTA
BYSSI	TARSO	ALIST	PREST	NEWSY	JUNTA
DORSI	TASSO	ANGST	QUEST	NOISY	JUXTA
ICOSI	TORSO	AVAST	ROAST	PALSY	LEPTA
PARSI	VERSO	BEAST	ROOST	PANSY	LOTTA
PHYSI	WHOSO	BLAST	ROUST	PASSY	LYTTA
QUASI	******	BLEST	TOAST	PATSY	MALTA
TARSI	---SP	BOAST	TRUST	PHASY	MANTA
TORSI	******	BOOST	TRYST	PLASY	MARTA
******	CLASP	BREST	TWIST	POESY	MORTA
---SK	CRISP	BURST	VERST	POPSY	PASTA
******	GRASP	CANST	WAIST	POTSY	PENTA
BRISK	KNOSP	CHEST	WEEST	PROSY	PIETA
BRUSK	******	COAST	WHIST	PUDSY	PINTA
FLASK	---SS	CREST	WORST	PURSY	PLATA
FRISK	******	CRUST	WREST	PUSSY	QUOTA
KIOSK	ABYSS	CURST	WRIST	PUSSY	RECTA
	AMASS		YEAST	SASSY	

RETTA	HARTE	BLYTH	WIDTH	HECTO	ADITS
RIATA	HASTE	BOOTH	WORTH	HEKTO	ASSTS
SANTA	IRATE	BROTH	WRATH	HIDTO	AUNTS
SCUTA	LEYTE	CHETH	WROTH	HYETO	BAHTS
SEPTA	LOTTE	CLOTH	XANTH	JUNTO	BAITS
SOFTA	MATTE	COUTH	YOUTH	KYOTO	BALTS
TESTA	MONTE	DEATH	******	LACTO	BEATS
THETA	ORATE	DEPTH	---TI	LENTO	BEETS
UINTA	OVATE	DOETH	******	LEPTO	BELTS
VESTA	PASTE	EARTH	AMATI	LOTTO	BERTS
VISTA	PHYTE	EDITH	CACTI	MASTO	BESTS
VITTA	PLATE	FAITH	CENTI	MOLTO	BITTS
VOLTA	PRATE	FIFTH	CESTI	MOTTO	BLATS
YALTA	QUITE	FILTH	COATI	NYCTO	BLOTS
******	QUOTE	FIRTH	CULTI	PANTO	BOATS
---TD	RENTE	FORTH	CYSTI	PETTO	BOLTS
******	ROUTE	FRITH	DENTI	PHOTO	BOOTS
CONTD	SAUTE	FROTH	DHOTI	PHYTO	BORTS
******	SCUTE	FURTH	HAITI	PINTO	BOTTS
---TE	SHOTE	GARTH	MUFTI	PLATO	BOUTS
******	SHUTE	GIRTH	MULTI	PLUTO	BRATS
ABATE	SIXTE	HEATH	NOCTI	POTTO	BUNTS
ACUTE	SKATE	KEITH	NYCTI	PROTO	BUSTS
AGATE	SLATE	LEITH	PATTI	PUNTO	BUTTS
ALATE	SMITE	LOATH	PETTI	QUITO	CANTS
AMATE	SMOTE	MIRTH	RECTI	RECTO	CARTS
ARETE	SPATE	MONTH	SEPTI	SARTO	CASTS
AZOTE	SPITE	MOUTH	TUTTI	SCATO	CELTS
BASTE	STATE	NEATH	VOLTI	SCOTO	CENTS
BETTE	SUITE	NINTH	******	SEATO	CHATS
BRUTE	TASTE	NORTH	---TL	SEPTO	CHETS
BUTTE	TORTE	PERTH	******	SETTO	CHITS
CARTE	TRITE	QUOTH	AUSTL	SEXTO	CISTS
CASTE	UNITE	SIXTH	******	SOTTO	CLOTS
CHUTE	URATE	SLOTH	---TO	STATO	COATS
COMTE	VOLTE	SMITH	******	TANTO	COLTS
CONTE	WASTE	SNATH	ACETO	TAUTO	COOTS
CRATE	WHITE	SOOTH	CANTO	******	COPTS
CRETE	WITTE	SOUTH	CENTO	---TR	COSTS
DANTE	WRITE	STETH	CONTO	******	CULTS
ELATE	WROTE	SWATH	COSTO	CENTR	CYSTS
ELITE	******	TEETH	CYSTO	CONTR	DARTS
EMOTE	---TH	TENTH	DATTO	DEXTR	DEBTS
ENATE	******	THOTH	DENTO	GASTR	DENTS
FLITE	AZOTH	TILTH	DITTO	******	DIETS
FLUTE	BARTH	TOOTH	ERATO	---TS	DINTS
FORTE	BERTH	TROTH	FEMTO	******	DOITS
GRATE	BIRTH	TRUTH	GUSTO	ABETS	DOLTS

DONTS	KEATS	PHOTS	SWATS	AUNTY	NATTY
DUCTS	KENTS	PICTS	TARTS	BATTY	NETTY
DUETS	KILTS	PINTS	TEATS	BERTY	NIFTY
DUSTS	KNITS	PLATS	TENTS	BETTY	NITTY
EDITS	KNOTS	PLOTS	TESTS	BOOTY	NUTTY
EMITS	KYATS	POETS	TEXTS	BORTY	OSITY
EXITS	LASTS	PORTS	TILTS	CATTY	PANTY
FACTS	LEETS	POSTS	TINTS	CUTTY	PARTY
FASTS	LEFTS	POUTS	TOFTS	DEITY	PASTY
FEATS	LENTS	PUNTS	TOOTS	DIRTY	PATTY
FELTS	LETTS	PUTTS	TORTS	DITTY	PEATY
FIATS	LIFTS	QUITS	TOUTS	DOTTY	PETTY
FISTS	LILTS	RAFTS	TROTS	DUSTY	PIETY
FLATS	LISTS	RANTS	TUFTS	EMPTY	PLATY
FLITS	LOFTS	RENTS	TWITS	FATTY	POTTY
FONTS	LOOTS	RESTS	UNITS	FIFTY	PUNTY
FOOTS	LOUTS	RIFTS	VENTS	FLUTY	PUTTY
FORTS	LUNTS	RIOTS	VESTS	FOOTY	RATTY
FRATS	LUSTS	ROOTS	VOLTS	FORTY	ROOTY
FRETS	MALTS	ROUTS	WAFTS	FUSTY	RUNTY
FRITS	MARTS	RUNTS	WAITS	GERTY	RUSTY
GAITS	MASTS	RUSTS	WALTS	GOUTY	RUTTY
GENTS	MATTS	RYOTS	WANTS	GUSTY	SALTY
GHATS	MEATS	SALTS	WARTS	HASTY	SILTY
GIFTS	MEETS	SCATS	WATTS	HATTY	SIXTY
GIRTS	MELTS	SCOTS	WEFTS	HEFTY	SLATY
GISTS	MILTS	SCUTS	WELTS	HETTY	SOFTY
GLUTS	MINTS	SEATS	WHETS	JETTY	SOOTY
GNATS	MISTS	SECTS	WHITS	JOLTY	SUETY
GOATS	MITTS	SEPTS	WILTS	KILTY	TARTY
GRITS	MOATS	SHOTS	WORTS	KITTY	TASTY
GROTS	MOLTS	SHUTS	WRITS	LAITY	TATTY
GUSTS	MORTS	SIFTS	XYSTS	LEFTY	TESTY
HAFTS	MUSTS	SILTS	YEATS	LETTY	TUFTY
HALTS	MUTTS	SKITS	ZESTS	LINTY	TUTTY
HARTS	NESTS	SLATS	******	LOFTY	UNITY
HEATS	NEWTS	SLITS	---TT	LOTTY	VASTY
HEFTS	OBITS	SLOTS	******	LUSTY	WARTY
HILTS	ODETS	SLUTS	SCOTT	MALTY	WITTY
HINTS	OMITS	SMUTS	WYATT	MARTY	ZESTY
HOOTS	OUSTS	SNOTS	******	MATTY	ZLOTY
HOSTS	PACTS	SOOTS	---TU	MEATY	******
HUNTS	PANTS	SORTS	******	MILTY	---TZ
HURTS	PARTS	SPATS	BANTU	MISTY	******
JESTS	PASTS	SPITS	VERTU	MONTY	BLITZ
JILTS	PEATS	SPOTS	VIRTU	MORTY	BORTZ
JOLTS	PELTS	STETS	******	MUSTY	FRITZ
JUSTS	PESTS	SUITS	---TY	NASTY	HARTZ
			******		
			ACITY		
			AMITY		

HERTZ	ISSUE	******	******	ALDUS	LOCUS
SPITZ	JOSUE	---UM	---UO	ANGUS	LOTUS
WALTZ	LOGUE	******	******	ANKUS	LUAUS
******	PIQUE	ALBUM	ACOUO	ARCUS	LULUS
---UA	QUEUE	ALGUM	******	ARGUS	LUPUS
******	REVUE	ARIUM	---UP	ARIUS	MAGUS
CAPUA	ROGUE	AURUM	******	ASCUS	MANUS
GENUA	ROQUE	BEGUM	BACUP	BEAUS	MENUS
JOSUA	SPRUE	CECUM	CROUP	BOGUS	MINUS
JURUA	TOGUE	DATUM	CUTUP	BOLUS	MODUS
LEHUA	TOQUE	DEGUM	GETUP	BONUS	MOMUS
NAHUA	TUQUE	DURUM	GROUP	CAMUS	MUCUS
PADUA	UNDUE	FANUM	LETUP	CASUS	NEGUS
PAPUA	VAGUE	FILUM	MIXUP	CETUS	NEVUS
VACUA	VALUE	FORUM	PINUP	COMUS	NEXUS
******	VENUE	HILUM	PUTUP	CONUS	NIDUS
---UB	VOGUE	HOKUM	SCAUP	CYRUS	NINUS
******	******	ILEUM	SETUP	DORUS	NISUS
SCRUB	---UG	ILIUM	SIRUP	EMBUS	NODUS
SHRUB	******	JORUM	STOUP	EMEUS	ORCUS
******	ALMUG	LOCUM	SUNUP	EOLUS	PIOUS
---UC	DEBUG	NAHUM	SYRUP	EURUS	RAMUS
******	SHRUG	OAKUM	TIEUP	FAVUS	REBUS
GLAUC	******	ODEUM	WHAUP	FETUS	REMUS
******	---UI	ODIUM	******	FOCUS	RISUS
---UD	******	OPIUM	---UR	FUCUS	RUFUS
******	ENNUI	PNEUM	******	GENUS	SALUS
ALMUD	MAQUI	RHEUM	AMOUR	GIBUS	SINUS
ALOUD	******	SAGUM	ARTUR	GURUS	SITUS
CLOUD	---UK	SCRUM	ASHUR	GYRUS	SOLUS
FRAUD	******	SEBUM	AUGUR	HABUS	SORUS
FREUD	TALUK	SEDUM	DEMUR	HOCUS	SULUS
PROUD	******	SERUM	FEMUR	HORUS	TALUS
PSEUD	---UL	STRUM	FLOUR	HUMUS	TITUS
******	AFOUL	THRUM	HHOUR	ICTUS	TONUS
---UE	AMPUL	VELUM	INCUR	ILEUS	TORUS
******	ANNUL	******	LEMUR	ILLUS	TUTUS
ARGUE	AWFUL	---UN	MOHUR	INCUS	ULOUS
BENUE	BABUL	******	NAMUR	INDUS	UNAUS
ENDUE	GHOUL	BEGUN	OCCUR	JANUS	VAGUS
ENSUE	KABUL	BOSUN	ODOUR	JEHUS	VARUS
ESQUE	MIAUL	CAJUN	RECUR	JESUS	VENUS
FIQUE	MOGUL	GATUN	SCOUR	JUJUS	VIRUS
FUGUE	PICUL	JOTUN	SIEUR	KAGUS	WAMUS
GIGUE	RAOUL	KORUN	STOUR	KUDUS	XERUS
HAGUE	SEOUL	RERUN	******	KURUS	ZEBUS
IMBUE	VOGUL	SHAUN	---US	LEPUS	******
INDUE		YAMUN	******	LINUS	---UT
			ACTUS		******
			AINUS		ABOUT
					ALEUT

ASYUT	ALIVE	TROVE	******	BMEWS	SHOWY
BEAUT	ATIVE	VALVE	---WD	BREWS	SNOWY
CAPUT	BRAVE	VARVE	******	BROWS	THEWY
CLOUT	BREVE	VERVE	CROWD	CHAWS	VIEWY
DEBUT	CALVE	WAIVE	******	CHEWS	******
FLOUT	CARVE	WEAVE	---WE	CHOWS	---XA
GAMUT	CHIVE	YAHVE	******	CLAWS	******
GHAUT	CLIVE	YOUVE	CREWE	CLEWS	ALEXA
GROUT	CLOVE	******	STOWE	CRAWS	******
INPUT	CRAVE	---VI	******	CREWS	---XI
KAPUT	CURVE	******	---WL	CROWS	******
KNOUT	DELVE	BREVI	******	DHOWS	FLEXI
KRAUT	DRAVE	CURVI	BRAWL	DRAWS	******
LIEUT	DRIVE	PELVI	CRAWL	DREWS	---XT
REBUT	DROVE	PLUVI	DRAWL	FLAWS	******
SCOUT	GLOVE	******	GROWL	FLEWS	TWIXT
SHOUT	GRAVE	---VO	PROWL	FLOWS	******
SNOUT	GROVE	******	SCOWL	FROWS	---XY
SPOUT	HALVE	BRAVO	SHAWL	GLOWS	******
STOUT	HEAVE	PROVO	TRAWL	GNAWS	ATAXY
STRUT	HELVE	SALVO	******	GROWS	BRAXY
TROUT	HOOVE	SERVO	---WM	KNOWS	DEOXY
UNCUT	KEEVE	SLAVO	******	MEOWS	EPOXY
******	KNAVE	******	SHAWM	PLOWS	FLAXY
---UX	LEAVE	---VS	******	PROWS	PREXY
******	MAUVE	******	---WN	SCOWS	PROXY
BEAUX	NAIVE	OLAVS	******	SHAWS	TRIXY
SIOUX	NERVE	SHIVS	BLOWN	SHEWS	******
******	OGIVE	SLAVS	BRAWN	SHOWS	---YA
---UZ	OLIVE	******	BROWN	SKEWS	******
******	PEEVE	---VY	CLOWN	SLAWS	FREYA
VADUZ	PIAVE	******	CROWN	SLEWS	KENYA
******	PROVE	CHEVY	DRAWN	SLOWS	KONYA
---VA	REEVE	DIVVY	DROWN	SMEWS	LIBYA
******	SALVE	GRAVY	FLOWN	SNOWS	ORIYA
BRAVA	SERVE	HEAVY	FROWN	SPEWS	PLAYA
DRAVA	SHAVE	LEAVY	GNAWN	STEWS	SONYA
GUAVA	SHIVE	NAVVY	GROWN	STOWS	TANYA
LARVA	SHOVE	NERVY	KNOWN	THAWS	******
SILVA	SIEVE	PEAVY	PRAWN	THEWS	---YC
SYLVA	SKIVE	PRIVY	SHAWN	TREWS	******
VOLVA	SLAVE	SAVVY	SHEWN	VIEWS	ENCYC
VULVA	SOLVE	******	SHOWN	******	******
******	STAVE	---WA	SPAWN	---WY	---YD
---VE	STEVE	******	******	******	******
******	STOVE	ADOWA	---WS	BLOWY	FLOYD
ABOVE	SUAVE	ADUWA	AVOWS	CHEWY	LLOYD
AGAVE	TRAVE	KIOWA	BLOWS	FLAWY	SLOYD
		SCHWA			

******
---YE
******
BARYE
OXEYE
******
---YL
******
ALKYL
ALLYL
BERYL
BUTYL
ETHYL
HEXYL
OCTYL
SIBYL
TOLYL
VINYL
XYLYL
******
---YO
******
CARYO
KARYO
TOKYO
******
---YP
******
POLYP
******
---YR
******
ASSYR
SATYR
******
---YS
******
ABBYS
ADDYS
ALGYS
ANDYS
ATTYS
BRAYS
BUOYS
CARYS
CHRYS
CLAYS
CLOYS

DAVYS
DENYS
DILYS
DRAYS
EMMYS
FLAYS
FRAYS
GABYS
GARYS
GOBYS
GOVYS
GRAYS
GREYS
IZZYS
JOEYS
JUDYS
JULYS
LILYS
LUCYS
OBEYS
OKAYS
PEPYS
PLAYS
PLOYS
POWYS
PRAYS
PREYS
QUAYS
RUBYS
RUDYS
SHAYS
SLAYS
SPAYS
STAYS
SUZYS
SWAYS
TOBYS
TONYS
TRAYS
TREYS
WHEYS
XRAYS
******
---YX
******
CALYX
******
---ZA
******
BRAZA
COLZA

ELIZA
HAMZA
IBIZA
MIRZA
PIZZA
PLAZA
TAZZA
******
---ZE
******
AGAZE
AMAZE
BAIZE
BLAZE
BONZE
BOOZE
BRAZE
CRAZE
CROZE
FEEZE
FROZE
FURZE
GAUZE
GLAZE
GLOZE
GRAZE
MAIZE
PRIZE
SEIZE
SMAZE
WINZE
******
---ZI
******
GHAZI
MITZI
******
---ZO
******
DIAZO
MATZO
MEZZO
PIEZO
RHIZO
******
---ZT
******
LISZT

******
---ZY
******
BOOZY
CRAZY
DIZZY
FIZZY
FURZY
FUZZY
GAUZY
GLAZY
JAZZY
LIZZY
MITZY
MUZZY
ORCZY
RITZY
TIZZY
WOOZY
******
---ZZ
******
FRIZZ

AA----
AACHEN
AALAND
AALIIS
AARONS
******
AB----
******
ABACAS
ABACUS
ABADAN
ABASED
ABASER
ABASES
ABATED
ABATER
ABATES
ABATIS
ABATOR
ABBACY
ABBESS
ABBEYS
ABBIES

ABBOTS
ABDUCT
ABELES
ABHORS
ABIDED
ABIDER
ABIDES
ABIJAH
ABJECT
ABJURE
ABLAUT
ABLAZE
ABLEST
ABLOOM
ABLUSH
ABNERS
ABOARD
ABODES
ABOHMS
ABOLLA
ABOMAS
ABOMBS
ABORAL
ABORTS
ABOUND
ABRADE
ABRAMS
ABROAD
ABRUPT
ABSENT
ABSORB
ABSURD
ABULIA
ABUSED
ABUSER
ABUSES
ABVOLT
ABWATT
ABYDOS
ABYSMS
******
AC----
******
ACACIA
ACADIA
ACAENA
ACAJOU
ACANTH

ACARID
ACCEDE
ACCENT
ACCEPT
ACCESS
ACCORD
ACCOST
ACCRUE
ACCUSE
ACEDIA
ACEIUM
ACEOUS
ACERIC
ACETAL
ACETIC
ACETUM
ACETYL
ACHAEA
ACHAIA
ACHENE
ACHING
ACIDIC
ACIDLY
ACINUS
ACIOUS
ACKACK
ACNODE
ACORNS
ACQUIT
ACROSS
ACTING
ACTINI
ACTINO
ACTION
ACTIUM
ACTIVE
ACTORS
ACTUAL
ACUATE
ACUITY
ACUMEN
******
AD----
******
ADAGES
ADAGIO
ADAPTS
ADDAMS

ADDEND	******	AGARIC	AIRILY	ALERTS	ALMUDE
ADDERS	AE----	AGATES	AIRING	ALEUTS	ALMUDS
ADDICT	******	AGATHA	AIRMAN	ALEXIA	ALONSO
ADDING	AEACUS	AGAVES	AIRMEN	ALEXIN	ALONZO
ADDLED	AECIAL	AGEDLY	AIRSAC	ALEXIS	ALPACA
ADDLES	AEDILE	AGEING	AIRWAY	ALFAKI	ALPHAS
ADDUCE	AEETES	AGENCY	AISLED	ALFONS	ALPHOS
ADDUCT	AEGEAN	AGENDA	AISLES	ALFRED	ALPHYL
ADEEMS	AEGEUS	AGENTS	******	ALGOID	ALPINE
ADENIS	AENEAS	AGEOLD	AJ----	ALGOUS	ALSACE
ADEPTS	AENEID	AGGERS	******	ALIBIS	ALSIKE
ADHERE	AEOLIA	AGHAST	AJOWAN	ALIBLE	ALTAIC
ADIEUS	AEOLIC	AGISTS	******	ALICES	ALTAIR
ADIEUX	AEOLIS	AGLAIA	AK----	ALICIA	ALTARS
ADIPIC	AEOLUS	AGLEAM	******	ALIDAD	ALTERS
ADJECT	AERATE	AGLETS	AKENES	ALIENS	ALTHEA
ADJOIN	AERIAL	AGNAIL	AKIMBO	ALIGHT	ALUDEL
ADJURE	AERIED	AGNATE	******	ALIGNS	ALUINO
ADJUST	AERIES	AGOGUE	AL----	ALINED	ALUINS
ADLIBS	AERIFY	AGONES	******	ALINES	ALULAE
ADMIRE	AEROBE	AGONIC	ALALIA	ALIPED	ALULAR
ADMITS	AERUGO	AGORAE	ALAMOS	ALISON	ALUMIN
ADMIXT	AETHER	AGORAS	ALARIC	ALKALI	ALUMNA
ADNATE	******	AGOUTI	ALARMS	ALKANE	ALUMNI
ADNOUN	AF----	AGOUTY	ALARUM	ALKENE	ALVANS
ADOBES	******	AGRAFE	ALASKA	ALKYLS	ALVINA
ADOLPH	AFFAIR	AGREED	ALATED	ALKYNE	ALVINE
ADONAI	AFFECT	AGREES	ALBANY	ALLANS	ALWAYS
ADONIC	AFFIRM	AGUISH	ALBATA	ALLAYS	******
ADONIS	AFFLUX	******	ALBEDO	ALLEGE	AM----
ADOPTS	AFFORD	AH----	ALBEIT	ALLELE	******
ADORED	AFFRAY	******	ALBERT	ALLENS	AMADOU
ADORER	AFGHAN	AHIMSA	ALBINO	ALLEYS	AMALIE
ADORES	AFIELD	******	ALBION	ALLIED	AMANDA
ADORNS	AFLAME	AI----	ALBITE	ALLIES	AMANIA
ADRIAN	AFLCIO	******	ALBUMS	ALLIUM	AMATOL
ADRIEN	AFLOAT	AIDERS	ALCAIC	ALLOTS	AMAZED
ADRIFT	AFRAID	AIDING	ALCOTT	ALLOUT	AMAZES
ADROIT	AFRAME	AIDMAN	ALCOVE	ALLOWS	AMAZON
ADSORB	AFRESH	AIDMEN	ALCUIN	ALLOYS	AMBAGE
ADULTS	AFRICA	AIGLET	ALDERS	ALLUDE	AMBARI
ADVENT	AFTOSA	AILEEN	ALDINE	ALLURE	AMBARY
ADVERB	AG----	AILING	ALDOSE	ALLYLS	AMBERS
ADVERT	******	AIMING	ALDOUS	ALMAHS	AMBERY
ADVICE	AGAMAS	AIRBED	ALECTO	ALMIRA	AMBITS
ADVISE	AGAMIC	AIRDRY	ALEGAR	ALMOND	AMBLED
ADYTUM	AGAPAE	AIRGUN	ALEPHS	ALMOST	AMBLER
		AIRIER	ALEPPO	ALMUCE	AMBLES

AMBUSH	ANCONA	ANOINT	APHIDS	ARBUTE	ARISTO
AMEBAE	ANCONE	ANOMIA	APHONY	ARCADE	ARLEEN
AMEBAS	ANDEAN	ANOMIC	APHTHA	ARCANA	ARLENE
AMEBIC	ANDREA	ANOMIE	APIARY	ARCANE	ARLINE
AMECHE	ANDREI	ANONYM	APICAL	ARCHED	ARMADA
AMELIA	ANDRES	ANORAK	APICES	ARCHEO	ARMAGH
AMELIE	ANDREW	ANOXIA	APIECE	ARCHER	ARMAND
AMENDS	ANEMIA	ANOXIC	APLITE	ARCHES	ARMETS
AMENRA	ANEMIC	ANSATE	APLOMB	ARCHIE	ARMFUL
AMENTI	ANERGY	ANSELM	APNEAL	ARCHIL	ARMIES
AMENTS	ANGARY	ANSWER	APNEIC	ARCHLY	ARMING
AMERCE	ANGELA	ANTEED	APNOEA	ARCHON	ARMLET
AMICES	ANGELO	ANTERO	APODAL	ARCHYS	ARMORS
AMIDES	ANGELS	ANTHEA	APOGEE	ARCING	ARMORY
AMIDIC	ANGERS	ANTHEM	APOLLO	ARCKED	ARMOUR
AMIDIN	ANGINA	ANTHER	APOLOG	ARCTIC	ARMPIT
AMIDOL	ANGKOR	ANTIAR	APPALL	ARDEBS	ARMURE
AMIDST	ANGLED	ANTICS	APPALS	ARDENT	ARNAUD
AMIENS	ANGLER	ANTLER	APPEAL	ARDORS	ARNICA
AMIGOS	ANGLES	ANTLIA	APPEAR	ARDOUR	ARNIES
AMNION	ANGLIA	ANTONS	APPELS	ARECAS	ARNOLD
AMOEBA	ANGLIC	ANTONY	APPEND	ARENAS	AROIDS
AMOLES	ANGOLA	ANTRIM	APPIAN	AREOLA	AROMAS
AMORAL	ANGORA	ANTRUM	APPLES	ARERCU	AROUND
AMOUNT	ANILIN	ANUBIS	APPORT	ARETES	AROUSE
AMOURS	ANIMAL	ANURAN	APPOSE	AREZZO	ARPENS
AMPERE	ANIMAS	ANUSES	APRILS	ARGALA	ARPENT
AMPHRS	ANIMUS	ANVILS	APRONS	ARGALI	ARRACK
AMPULE	ANIONS	ANYHOW	APULIA	ARGALS	ARRANT
AMPULS	ANISES	ANYONE	******	ARGENT	ARRAYS
AMRITA	ANITAS	ANYWAY	AQ----	ARGIVE	ARREAR
AMULET	ANITRA	******	******	ARGOSY	ARREST
AMUSED	ANKARA	AO----	AQUILA	ARGOTS	ARRIVE
AMUSER	ANKLES	******	******	ARGUED	ARROBA
AMUSES	ANKLET	AORIST	AR----	ARGUER	ARROWS
AMYLIC	ANKYLO	AORTAE	******	ARGUES	ARROWY
AMYLUM	ANLACE	AORTAL	ARABEL	ARGUFY	ARROYO
AMYTAL	ANLAGE	AORTAS	ARABIA	ARGYLL	ARSINE
******	ANNALS	AORTIC	ARABIC	ARIANS	ARTELS
AN----	ANNEAL	AOUDAD	ARABLE	ARIDLY	ARTERY
******	ANNEXE	******	ARAGON	ARIELS	ARTFUL
ANABAS	ANNIES	AP----	ARANTA	ARIGHT	ARTHRO
ANADEM	ANNONA	******	ARARAT	ARIOSE	ARTHUR
ANALOG	ANNOYS	APACHE	ARAWAK	ARIOSO	ARTIES
ANANAS	ANNUAL	APATHY	ARBELA	ARIOUS	ARTILY
ANANKE	ANNULS	APEMAN	ARBORI	ARISEN	ARTIST
ANATTO	ANODES	APEPSY	ARBORS	ARISES	ARTOIS
ANCHOR	ANODIC	APEXES	ARBOUR	ARISTA	ARTURO

ARUNTA	ASTERO	AUBURN	AVIDLY	AZOLES	BAILEY
ARYANS	ASTERS	AUDADS	AVISOS	AZONIC	BAILIE
******	ASTHMA	AUDILE	AVOCET	AZORES	BAILOR
AS----	ASTRAL	AUDITS	AVOIDS	AZOTIC	BAIRNS
******	ASTRAY	AUDREY	AVOSET	AZRAEL	BAITED
ASARUM	ASTRID	AUGEAN	AVOUCH	AZTECS	BAKERS
ASBURY	ASTUTE	AUGEND	AVOWAL	AZURES	BAKERY
ASCEND	ASYLUM	AUGERS	AVOWED	******	BAKING
ASCENT	******	AUGHTS	AVOWER	BA----	BALAAM
ASCOTS	AT----	AUGITE	******	******	BALATA
ASGARD	******	AUGURS	AW----	BAAING	BALBOA
ASHCAN	ATABAL	AUGURY	******	BAALIM	BALDER
ASHIER	ATAMAN	AUGUST	AWAITS	BABBIE	BALDLY
ASHLAR	ATAVIC	AUKLET	AWAKED	BABBLE	BALEEN
ASHLEY	ATAXIA	AUNTIE	AWAKEN	BABIED	BALERS
ASHMAN	ATAXIC	AURATE	AWAKES	BABIES	BALING
ASHMEN	ATHENA	AUREUS	AWARDS	BABISM	BALKAN
ASHORE	ATHENE	AURIGA	AWEARY	BABIST	BALKED
ASIANS	ATHENS	AURIST	AWEIGH	BABITE	BALLAD
ASIDES	ATHOME	AURORA	AWEING	BABOON	BALLED
ASIMOV	ATOLLS	AUROUS	AWHEEL	BABOOS	BALLET
ASKANT	ATOMIC	AUSPEX	AWHILE	BABULS	BALLOT
ASKERS	ATONAL	AUSTEN	AWHIRL	BACHED	BALSAM
ASKING	ATONED	AUSTER	AWLESS	BACHES	BALSAS
ASLANT	ATONER	AUSTIN	AWNING	BACKED	BALTIC
ASLEEP	ATONES	AUSTRO	AWOKEN	BACKER	BALTIM
ASLOPE	ATONIC	AUTHOR	******	BACONY	BALZAC
ASPECT	ATREUS	AUTISM	AX----	BADGED	BAMAKO
ASPENS	ATRIAL	AUTOED	******	BADGER	BAMBOO
ASPERS	ATRIUM	AUTUMN	AXEMAN	BADGES	BANANA
ASPICS	ATTACH	AUXINS	AXEMEN	BADMAN	BANDED
ASPIRE	ATTACK	******	AXILLA	BADMEN	BANDIT
ASSAIL	ATTAIN	AV----	AXIOMS	BAFFED	BANGED
ASSAIS	ATTARS	******	AXLIKE	BAFFIN	BANGLE
ASSAYS	ATTEND	AVAILS	AXONES	BAFFLE	BANGOR
ASSENT	ATTEST	AVALON	AXSEED	BAGASS	BANGUI
ASSERT	ATTICA	AVATAR	******	BAGDAD	BANGUP
ASSESS	ATTICS	AVAUNT	AY----	BAGELS	BANIAN
ASSETS	ATTILA	AVENGE	******	BAGGED	BANISH
ASSIGN	ATTIRE	AVENUE	AYEAYE	BAGMAN	BANJOS
ASSISI	ATTLEE	AVERNO	AYESHA	BAGMEN	BANKED
ASSIST	ATTORN	AVERSE	AYMARA	BAGNIO	BANKER
ASSIZE	ATTUNE	AVERTS	******	BAHAIS	BANNED
ASSORT	******	AVERYS	AZ----	BAHAMA	BANNER
ASSUME	AU----	AVESTA	******	BAIKAL	BANTAM
ASSURE	******	AVIARY	AZALEA	BAILED	BANTER
ASTERI	AUBADE	AVIATE	AZAZEL	BAILEE	BANTUS
ASTERN	AUBREY	AVIDIN	AZINES	BAILER	BANYAN

BANZAI	BASALT	BAYOUS	BEFALL	BELUGA	BETAKE
BAOBAB	BASELY	BAZAAR	BEFELL	BEMATA	BETELS
BARBED	BASEST	******	BEFITS	BEMEAN	BETHEL
BARBEL	BASHAW	**BE----**	BEFOGS	BEMIRE	BETIDE
BARBER	BASHED	******	BEFOOL	BEMOAN	BETISE
BARBET	BASHES	BEACHY	BEFORE	BEMUSE	BETONY
BARBIE	BASICS	BEACON	BEFOUL	BENDAY	BETOOK
BARBRA	BASIFY	BEADED	BEGETS	BENDED	BETRAY
BARDED	BASILS	BEADLE	BEGGAR	BENDEE	BETSYS
BARDES	BASING	BEAGLE	BEGGED	BENDER	BETTED
BARDIC	BASINS	BEAKED	BEGINS	BENGAL	BETTER
BAREGE	BASION	BEAKER	BEGIRD	BENIGN	BETTES
BARELY	BASKED	BEAMED	BEGIRT	BENITA	BETTOR
BAREST	BASKET	BEANED	BEGONE	BENITO	BETTYS
BARFLY	BASQUE	BEANIE	BEGUIN	BENJYS	BEULAH
BARGED	BASRAH	BEARDS	BEGUMS	BENNES	BEULAS
BARGEE	BASSES	BEARED	BEHALF	BENNET	BEVELS
BARGES	BASSET	BEARER	BEHAVE	BENNYS	BEVIES
BARING	BASSOS	BEASTS	BEHEAD	BENTON	BEWAIL
BARITE	BASTED	BEATEN	BEHELD	BENUMB	BEWARE
BARIUM	BASTES	BEATER	BEHEST	BENZOL	BEYOND
BARKED	BASUTO	BEAUTS	BEHIND	BENZYL	BEZANT
BARKER	BATAAN	BEAUTY	BEHOLD	BERATE	BEZELS
BARLEY	BATEAU	BEAVER	BEHOOF	BERBER	BEZOAR
BARMAN	BATHED	BECALM	BEHOVE	BEREFT	******
BARMEN	BATHER	BECAME	BEIGES	BERETS	**BH----**
BARMIE	BATHOS	BECKED	BEINGS	BERGEN	******
BARNEY	BATIKS	BECKET	BEIRUT	BERING	BHUTAN
BARNUM	BATING	BECKON	BELAYS	BERLIN	******
BARONG	BATMAN	BECKYS	BELDAM	BERMES	**BI----**
BARONS	BATMEN	BECOME	BELFRY	BERNEY	******
BARONY	BATONS	BEDAUB	BELGAS	BERNIE	BIAFRA
BARQUE	BATTED	BEDBUG	BELGIC	BERTHA	BIALYS
BARRED	BATTEN	BEDDED	BELIAL	BERTHE	BIANCA
BARREL	BATTER	BEDDER	BELIED	BERTHS	BIASED
BARREN	BATTIK	BEDECK	BELIEF	BERTIE	BIASES
BARRET	BATTIN	BEDEWS	BELIER	BERYLS	BIAXAL
BARRIE	BATTLE	BEDIMS	BELIES	BESANT	BIBBED
BARRIO	BATTUE	BEDLAM	BELIKE	BESEEM	BIBBER
BARROW	BAUBLE	BEDPAN	BELIZE	BESETS	BIBLES
BARRYS	BAUCIS	BEDRID	BELLAS	BESIDE	BIBLIO
BARTER	BAWDRY	BEDSIT	BELLED	BESOMS	BICARB
BARTOK	BAWLED	BEDUIN	BELLES	BESOTS	BICEPS
BARTON	BAWLER	BEECHY	BELLOC	BESSIE	BICKER
BARUCH	BAXTER	BEEFED	BELLOW	BESSYS	BICORN
BARYES	BAYARD	BEEPED	BELOIT	BESTED	BIDDEN
BARYON	BAYEUX	BEETLE	BELONG	BESTIR	BIDDER
BARYTA	BAYING	BEEVES	BELTED	BESTOW	BIDETS

BIDING	BIRRED	BLINDS	BODIED	BOOBOO	BOUGHS
BIERCE	BIRTHS	BLINKS	BODIES	BOODLE	BOUGHT
BIFFED	BISCAY	BLINTZ	BODILY	BOOGIE	BOUGIE
BIFFIN	BISECT	BLITHE	BODING	BOOHOO	BOULES
BIFLEX	BISHOP	BLOATS	BODKIN	BOOING	BOUNCE
BIFOLD	BISQUE	BLOCKS	BOFFIN	BOOKED	BOUNCY
BIFORM	BISTER	BLOCKY	BOGANS	BOOKIE	BOUNDS
BIGAMY	BISTRO	BLOKES	BOGEYS	BOOMED	BOUNTY
BIGGER	BITCHY	BLONDE	BOGGED	BOOMER	BOURGS
BIGGIN	BITERS	BLONDS	BOGGLE	BOOSTS	BOURNE
BIGHTS	BITING	BLOODS	BOGIES	BOOTED	BOURNS
BIGONE	BITTED	BLOODY	BOGLES	BOOTEE	BOURSE
BIGOTS	BITTEN	BLOOMS	BOGOAK	BOOTHS	BOUSED
BIGWIG	BITTER	BLOOMY	BOGOTA	BOOTIE	BOUSES
BIHARI	******	BLOTCH	BOILED	BOOTLE	BOVATE
BIJOUX	BL----	BLOUSE	BOILER	BOOZED	BOVINE
BIKINI	******	BLOWBY	BOLDER	BOOZER	BOWELS
BIKOLS	BLACKS	BLOWER	BOLDLY	BOOZES	BOWERS
BILBAO	BLADED	BLOWUP	BOLERO	BOPPED	BOWERY
BILGED	BLADES	BLOWZY	BOLEYN	BORAGE	BOWFIN
BILGES	BLAINS	BLUELY	BOLIDE	BORANE	BOWING
BILITY	BLAISE	BLUEST	BOLLED	BORATE	BOWLED
BILKED	BLAMED	BLUETS	BOLLIX	BORDEL	BOWLEG
BILKER	BLAMES	BLUFFS	BOLSON	BORDER	BOWLER
BILLED	BLANCH	BLUING	BOLTED	BOREAL	BOWMAN
BILLET	BLANKS	BLUISH	BOLTER	BOREAS	BOWMEN
BILLIE	BLARED	BLUNGE	BOLTON	BORERS	BOWSAW
BILLON	BLARES	BLUNTS	BOMBAY	BORGIA	BOWSED
BILLOW	BLASTO	BLURBS	BOMBED	BORIDE	BOWSES
BILLYS	BLASTS	BLURRY	BOMBER	BORING	BOWTIE
BILOXI	BLAZED	BLURTS	BOMBES	BORNEO	BOWWOW
BINARY	BLAZER	******	BOMBIC	BORROW	BOWYER
BINATE	BLAZES	BO----	BONACI	BORSCH	BOXCAR
BINDER	BLAZON	******	BONBON	BORZOI	BOXERS
BINGES	BLEACH	BOARDS	BONDED	BOSHES	BOXING
BINITS	BLEAKS	BOASTS	BONDER	BOSKET	BOYARD
BINNED	BLEARS	BOATED	BONERS	BOSOMS	BOYARS
BIOGEN	BLEARY	BOATER	BONGED	BOSSED	BOYISH
BIOPSY	BLEATS	BOBBED	BONGOS	BOSSES	******
BIOSIS	BLEBBY	BOBBER	BONIER	BOSTON	BR----
BIOTIC	BLEEDS	BOBBIE	BONING	BOTANY	******
BIOTIN	BLENCH	BOBBIN	BONITO	BOTCHY	BRACED
BIPEDS	BLENDE	BOBBLE	BONNET	BOTFLY	BRACER
BIPODS	BLENDS	BOBBYS	BONNIE	BOTHER	BRACES
BIRDIE	BLENNY	BOBCAT	BONNYS	BOTTLE	BRACHI
BIREME	BLIGHT	BOCCIE	BONSAI	BOTTOM	BRACHY
BIRLED	BLIMEY	BODEGA	BONZER	BOUCLE	BRACTS
BIRLES	BLIMPS	BODICE	BONZES	BOUFFE	BRAHMA

BRAHMS	BRENTS	BROODY	BUFFED	BURGEE	BUTANE
BRAIDS	BRETON	BROOKE	BUFFER	BURGER	BUTLER
BRAILS	BREVES	BROOKS	BUFFET	BURGHS	BUTTED
BRAINS	BREVET	BROOMS	BUGGED	BURGLE	BUTTER
BRAINY	BREWED	BROOMY	BUGGER	BURGOO	BUTTES
BRAISE	BREWER	BROTHS	BUGLED	BURGOS	BUTTON
BRAIZE	BREWIS	BROWNS	BUGLER	BURIAL	BUXTON
BRAKED	BRIARS	BROWSE	BUGLES	BURIED	BUYERS
BRAKES	BRIBED	BRUCES	BUILDS	BURIES	BUYING
BRANCH	BRIBER	BRUGES	BULBAR	BURINS	BUZZED
BRANDS	BRIBES	BRUINS	BULBED	BURKED	BUZZER
BRANDT	BRICKS	BRUISE	BULBEL	BURKES	BUZZES
BRANDY	BRIDAL	BRUITS	BULBIL	BURLAP	******
BRANNY	BRIDES	BRULOT	BULBUL	BURLED	**BY----**
BRANTS	BRIDGE	BRUMAL	BULGAR	BURLER	******
BRAQUE	BRIDIE	BRUMES	BULGED	BURLEY	BYBLOW
BRASHY	BRIDLE	BRUNCH	BULGER	BURNED	BYEBYE
BRASSY	BRIEFS	BRUNEI	BULGES	BURNER	BYGONE
BRAVED	BRIERS	BRUNEL	BULKED	BURNET	BYLANE
BRAVER	BRIERY	BRUNOS	BULLAE	BURPED	BYLAWS
BRAVES	BRIGHT	BRUSHY	BULLET	BURRED	BYLINE
BRAVOS	BRIGID	BRUTAL	BUMBLE	BURROS	BYNAME
BRAWLS	BRILLS	BRUTES	BUMKIN	BURROW	BYPASS
BRAWNY	BRINED	BRUTUS	BUMMED	BURSAE	BYPAST
BRAYED	BRINES	BRYANT	BUMMER	BURSAL	BYPATH
BRAYER	BRINGS	BRYONY	BUMPED	BURSAR	BYPLAY
BRAZAS	BRINKS	******	BUMPER	BURSAS	BYROAD
BRAZED	BRISKS	**BU----**	BUNCHE	BURSES	BYSSUS
BRAZEN	BRITON	******	BUNCHY	BURSTS	BYTALK
BRAZER	BROACH	BUBALS	BUNCOS	BURTON	BYWAYS
BRAZES	BROADS	BUBBLE	BUNDLE	BUSHED	BYWORD
BRAZIL	BROCHE	BUBBLY	BUNGED	BUSHEL	BYWORK
BRAZOS	BROGAN	BUBOES	BUNGLE	BUSHES	******
BREACH	BROGUE	BUCCAL	BUNION	BUSHEY	**CA----**
BREADS	BROILS	BUCHAN	BUNKED	BUSIED	******
BREAKS	BROKEN	BUCKED	BUNKER	BUSIES	CABALA
BREAMS	BROKER	BUCKER	BUNKUM	BUSILY	CABALS
BREAST	BROLLY	BUCKET	BUNSEN	BUSING	CABANA
BREATH	BROMAL	BUCKLE	BUNTED	BUSKER	CABINS
BRECHT	BROMES	BUCKRA	BUNYAN	BUSKIN	CABLED
BREECH	BROMIC	BUDDED	BUNYIP	BUSMAN	CABLES
BREEDS	BRONCO	BUDDER	BUOYED	BUSMEN	CABLET
BREEKS	BRONCS	BUDDHA	BURANS	BUSSED	CABMAN
BREEZE	BRONTE	BUDDLE	BURBLE	BUSSES	CABMEN
BREEZY	BRONZE	BUDGED	BURBOT	BUSTED	CABOBS
BREGMA	BRONZY	BUDGES	BURDEN	BUSTER	CACAOS
BREMEN	BROOCH	BUDGET	BURDIE	BUSTIC	CACHED
BRENDA	BROODS	BUDGIE	BUREAU	BUSTLE	CACHES

CACHET	CALMED	CANNON	CARGOS	CASHED	CAUSES
CACHOU	CALMER	CANNOT	CARHOP	CASHES	CAUTER
CACKLE	CALMLY	CANOED	CARIBE	CASHEW	CAVEAT
CACTUS	CALORY	CANOES	CARIBS	CASHOO	CAVEIN
CADDIE	CALPAC	CANONS	CARIES	CASING	CAVELL
CADDIS	CALVED	CANOPY	CARINA	CASINO	CAVERN
CADENT	CALVES	CANSOS	CARING	CASKET	CAVIAR
CADETS	CALVIN	CANTAB	CARLAS	CASPAR	CAVIES
CADGED	CALXES	CANTED	CARLOS	CASPER	CAVILS
CADGER	CAMASS	CANTER	CARLOW	CASQUE	CAVING
CADGES	CAMBER	CANTHI	CARMAN	CASSIA	CAVITE
CADMUS	CAMDEN	CANTLE	CARMEL	CASSIE	CAVITY
CADRES	CAMELS	CANTON	CARMEN	CASSIS	CAVORT
CAECUM	CAMEOS	CANTOR	CARNAL	CASTER	CAWING
CAEOMA	CAMERA	CANTOS	CAROBS	CASTES	CAXTON
CAESAR	CAMILA	CANTUS	CAROLE	CASTLE	CAYMAN
CAFTAN	CAMION	CANUCK	CAROLS	CASTOR	CAYUGA
CAGIER	CAMISE	CANULA	CAROMS	CASTRO	CAYUSE
CAGILY	CAMLET	CANUTE	CARPAL	CASUAL	******
CAGING	CAMPED	CANVAS	CARPED	CATALO	CE----
CAHIER	CAMPER	CANYON	CARPEL	CATCHY	******
CAHOOT	CAMPOS	CAPERS	CARPER	CATENA	CEASED
CAIMAN	CAMPUS	CAPIAS	CARPET	CATERS	CEASES
CAIQUE	CANAAN	CAPITA	CARPIC	CATGUT	CEBOID
CAIRNS	CANADA	CAPLIN	CARPUS	CATHAY	CECILE
CAJOLE	CANALS	CAPONE	CARREL	CATHER	CECILS
CAJUNS	CANAPE	CAPONS	CARRIE	CATHYS	CECILY
CAKING	CANARD	CAPOTE	CARROT	CATION	CEDARS
CALAIS	CANARY	CAPPED	CARSON	CATKIN	CEDING
CALASH	CANCAN	CAPPER	CARTED	CATLIN	CEDRIC
CALCAR	CANCEL	CAPRIC	CARTEL	CATNAP	CEDULA
CALCES	CANCER	CAPTOR	CARTER	CATNIP	CEIBAS
CALCIC	CANDIA	CARACK	CARTES	CATSUP	CEILED
CALEBS	CANDID	CARAFE	CARTON	CATTED	CELERY
CALESA	CANDLE	CARATE	CARUSO	CATTIE	CELIAC
CALICO	CANDOR	CARATS	CARVED	CATTLE	CELIAS
CALIFS	CANERS	CARBON	CARVEL	CAUCUS	CELLAE
CALIPH	CANGUE	CARBOY	CARVEN	CAUDAD	CELLAR
CALKED	CANINE	CARCEL	CARVER	CAUDAL	CELLOS
CALKER	CANING	CARDED	CARVES	CAUDEX	CELTIC
CALKIN	CANKER	CARDER	CASABA	CAUDLE	CEMENT
CALLAO	CANNAE	CARDIO	CASALS	CAUGHT	CENSED
CALLAS	CANNAS	CAREEN	CASAVA	CAULES	CENSER
CALLED	CANNED	CAREER	CASBAH	CAULIS	CENSES
CALLER	CANNEL	CARERS	CASEFY	CAULKS	CENSOR
CALLOW	CANNER	CARESS	CASEIN	CAUSAL	CENSUR
CALLUP	CANNES	CARETS	CASERN	CAUSED	CENSUS
CALLUS	CANNIE	CARFAX	CASHAW	CAUSER	CENTAL

CENTER	CHAMPS	CHEVVY	CHOOSE	CINDYS	CLAYEY
CENTOS	CHANCE	CHEWED	CHOOSY	CINEMA	CLEANS
CENTRA	CHANCY	CHEWER	CHOPIN	CINEOL	CLEARS
CENTRE	CHANGE	CHIASM	CHOPPY	CINQUE	CLEATS
CENTRI	CHANGS	CHIAUS	CHORAL	CIPHER	CLEAVE
CENTRO	CHANTS	CHIBUK	CHORDS	CIRCLE	CLEFTS
CEORLS	CHANTY	CHICHI	CHOREA	CIRCUM	CLEIST
CERATE	CHAPEL	CHICKS	CHOREO	CIRCUS	CLENCH
CERATO	CHAPES	CHICLE	CHORES	CIRQUE	CLEOME
CEREAL	CHARDS	CHICOS	CHORIC	CIRRUS	CLERGY
CEREUS	CHARED	CHIDED	CHORUS	CISCOS	CLERIC
CERING	CHARES	CHIDER	CHOSEN	CISSIE	CLERID
CERIPH	CHARGE	CHIDES	CHOUGH	CISSYS	CLERKS
CERISE	CHARMS	CHIEFS	CHRISM	CITHER	CLEVER
CERITE	CHARON	CHIGOE	CHRIST	CITIED	CLEVIS
CERIUM	CHARRY	CHILLI	CHROMA	CITIES	CLEWED
CERMET	CHARTS	CHILLS	CHROME	CITING	CLICHE
CEROUS	CHASED	CHILLY	CHROMO	CITOLA	CLICKS
CERTES	CHASER	CHIMED	CHRONO	CITRAL	CLIENT
CERUSE	CHASES	CHIMER	CHRYSO	CITRIC	CLIFFS
CERVIX	CHASMS	CHIMES	CHUBBY	CITRON	CLIFFY
CESARE	CHASSE	CHINCH	CHUCKS	CITRUS	CLIMAT
CESIUM	CHASTE	CHINES	CHUFAS	CIVETS	CLIMAX
CESTUS	CHATTY	CHINKS	CHUMMY	CIVICS	CLIMBS
CESURA	CHAWED	CHINKY	CHUMPS	CIVIES	CLIMES
CETANE	CHEATS	CHINTZ	CHUNKS	CIVISM	CLINCH
CEYLON	CHEBEC	CHIPPY	CHUNKY	******	CLINES
******	CHECKS	CHIRMS	CHURCH	**CL----**	CLINGS
CH----	CHEEKS	CHIRON	CHURLS	******	CLINGY
******	CHEEKY	CHIRPS	CHURNS	CLACKS	CLINIC
CHABUK	CHEEPS	CHIRPY	CHURRS	CLAIMS	CLINKS
CHACMA	CHEERS	CHIRRS	CHUTES	CLAIRE	CLINTS
CHAETA	CHEERY	CHISEL	CHYMIC	CLAMMY	CLIQUE
CHAETO	CHEESE	CHITIN	******	CLAMOR	CLIQUY
CHAFED	CHEESY	CHITON	**CI----**	CLAMPS	CLIVES
CHAFER	CHEGOE	CHITTY	******	CLANGS	CLOACA
CHAFES	CHEILO	CHIVES	CIBOLS	CLANKS	CLOAKS
CHAFFS	CHEIRO	CHIVVY	CICADA	CLAQUE	CLOCHE
CHAFFY	CHELAE	CHLOES	CICALA	CLARAS	CLOCKS
CHAINS	CHELAS	CHLORO	CICELY	CLARES	CLODDY
CHAIRS	CHEOPS	CHOCKS	CICERO	CLARET	CLOGGY
CHAISE	CHEQUE	CHOICE	CIDERS	CLAROS	CLONES
CHALCO	CHERRY	CHOIRS	CIGARS	CLASPS	CLONIC
CHALEH	CHERUB	CHOKED	CILIAT	CLASSY	CLONUS
CHALET	CHERYL	CHOKER	CILICE	CLAUDE	CLOSED
CHALKS	CHESTS	CHOKES	CILIUM	CLAUSE	CLOSER
CHALKY	CHESTY	CHOLER	CIMBRI	CLAWED	CLOSES
CHAMMY	CHETAH	CHOLLA	CINDER	CLAYED	CLOSET

CLOTHE	COCCID	COLINE	CONFAB	COPECK	CORTIN
CLOTHO	COCCUS	COLINS	CONFER	COPIED	CORVEE
CLOTHS	COCCYX	COLLAR	CONGAS	COPIER	CORVES
CLOTTY	COCHIN	COLLET	CONGER	COPIES	CORVUS
CLOUDS	COCKED	COLLIE	CONGES	COPING	CORYMB
CLOUDY	COCKER	COLLOP	CONGOU	COPLEY	CORYZA
CLOUGH	COCKLE	COLONS	CONICS	COPOUT	COSHED
CLOUTS	COCKUP	COLONY	CONIES	COPPED	COSHER
CLOVEN	COCOAS	COLORS	CONING	COPPER	COSHES
CLOVER	COCOON	COLOUR	CONIUM	COPPRA	COSIGN
CLOVES	CODDER	COLOUS	CONKED	COPRAH	COSILY
CLOVIS	CODDLE	COLTER	CONKER	COPSES	COSINE
CLOWNS	CODEIA	COLUGO	CONMAN	COPTIC	COSMIC
CLOYED	CODEIN	COLUMN	CONNED	COPULA	COSMOS
CLUCKS	CODGER	COLURE	CONNER	COQUET	COSSES
CLUING	CODIFY	COLZAS	CONNIE	CORALS	COSSET
CLUMPS	CODING	COMATE	CONOID	CORBAN	COSTAE
CLUMPY	COELED	COMBAT	CONRAD	CORBEL	COSTAL
CLUMSY	COELOM	COMBED	CONSUL	CORBIE	COSTAR
CLUTCH	COEMPT	COMBER	CONTES	CORDAY	COSTED
CLYDES	COERCE	COMBOS	CONTIN	CORDED	COSTER
CLYPEI	COEVAL	COMEDO	CONTOS	CORDER	COSTLY
******	COFFEE	COMEDY	CONTRA	CORDON	COTEAU
CO----	COFFER	COMELY	CONTRE	CORERS	COTTAE
******	COFFIN	COMEON	CONVEX	CORGIS	COTTAR
COALED	COFFLE	COMERS	CONVEY	CORING	COTTAS
COALER	COGENT	COMETS	CONVOY	CORIUM	COTTER
COARSE	COGGED	COMFIT	CONWAY	CORKED	COTTON
COASTS	COGNAC	COMICS	COODLE	CORKER	COUGAR
COATED	COGWAY	COMING	COOEED	CORNEA	COUGHS
COATEE	COHEIR	COMITY	COOEES	CORNED	COULEE
COATIS	COHERE	COMMAS	COOERS	CORNEL	COUNTS
COAXAL	COHORT	COMMIE	COOEYS	CORNER	COUNTY
COAXED	COHOSH	COMMIT	COOING	CORNET	COUPES
COAXER	COHUNE	COMMIX	COOKED	CORNUA	COUPLE
COAXES	COIFED	COMMON	COOKER	CORNUS	COUPON
COBALT	COIGNS	COMOSE	COOKEY	CORODY	COURSE
COBBER	COILED	COMOUS	COOKIE	CORONA	COURTS
COBBLE	COILER	COMPEL	COOLED	CORPSE	COUSIN
COBBLY	COINED	COMPLY	COOLER	CORPUS	COVERS
COBIAS	COINER	COMPOS	COOLIE	CORRAL	COVERT
COBLES	COITAL	CONCHA	COOLLY	CORRIE	COVETS
COBNUT	COITUS	CONCHS	COOMBS	CORSAC	COVEYS
COBRAS	COKING	CONCHY	COOPED	CORSES	COVING
COBURG	COLDER	CONCUR	COOPER	CORSET	COWAGE
COBWEB	COLDLY	CONDOM	COOPTS	CORTES	COWARD
COCAIN	COLEUS	CONDOR	COOTIE	CORTEX	COWBOY
COCCAL	COLIES	CONEYS	COPALM	CORTEZ	COWERS

COWING	CRAVER	CRISIS	CRYPTO	CURBED	******
COWMAN	CRAVES	CRISPS	CRYPTS	CURDED	CY----
COWMEN	CRAWLS	CRISPY	******	CURDLE	******
COWPEA	CRAWLY	CRITIC	CU----	CURERS	CYANIC
COWPER	CRAYON	CROAKS	******	CURFEW	CYANID
COWPOX	CRAZED	CROAKY	CUBAGE	CURIAE	CYANIN
COWRIE	CRAZES	CROATS	CUBANS	CURIAL	CYBELE
COXING	CREAKS	CROCKS	CUBBED	CURIES	CYCADS
COYISH	CREAKY	CROCKY	CUBEBS	CURING	CYCLED
COYOTE	CREAMS	CROCUS	CUBING	CURIOS	CYCLER
COYPUS	CREAMY	CROFTS	CUBISM	CURIUM	CYCLES
COZENS	CREASE	CROJIK	CUBIST	CURLED	CYCLIC
COZIER	CREASY	CRONES	CUBITS	CURLER	CYGNET
COZIES	CREATE	CRONOS	CUBOID	CURLEW	CYGNUS
COZILY	CRECHE	CRONUS	CUCKOO	CURSED	CYMARS
******	CREDAL	CROOKS	CUDDIE	CURSES	CYMBAL
CR----	CREDIT	CROONS	CUDDLF	CURSOR	CYMENE
******	CREDOS	CRORES	CUDDLY	CURTIS	CYMLIN
CRAALS	CREEDS	CROSSE	CUDGEL	CURTLY	CYMOID
CRABBY	CREEKS	CROTCH	CUESTA	CURTSY	CYMOSE
CRACKS	CREELS	CROTON	CUFFED	CURULE	CYMOUS
CRACKY	CREEPS	CROUCH	CUISSE	CURVED	CYMRIC
CRACOW	CREEPY	CROUPE	CULETS	CURVES	CYNICS
CRADLE	CREESE	CROUPS	CULLAY	CURVET	CYPHER
CRAFTS	CREMES	CROUPY	CULLED	CUSCUS	CYPRIN
CRAFTY	CRENEL	CROWDS	CULLER	CUSHAT	CYPRUS
CRAGGY	CREOLE	CROWED	CULLET	CUSHAW	CYRANO
CRAIGS	CREPED	CROWNS	CULLIS	CUSPED	CYRENE
CRAKES	CREPES	CROZER	CULMED	CUSPID	CYRILS
CRAMBO	CRESOL	CROZES	CULTCH	CUSPIS	CYSTIC
CRAMPS	CRESTS	CRUCES	CULTUS	CUSSED	******
CRANED	CRETAN	CRUDER	CULVER	CUSSES	DA----
CRANES	CRETIC	CRUETS	CUMBER	CUSSOS	******
CRANIA	CRETIN	CRUISE	CUMINS	CUSTER	
CRANIO	CRETON	CRUMBS	CUNEAL	CUSTOM	DABBED
CRANKS	CREUSA	CRUMBY	CUNNER	CUSTOS	DABBER
CRANKY	CREVAS	CRUMMY	CUPELS	CUTELY	DABBLE
CRANNY	CREWEL	CRUMPS	CUPFUL	CUTEST	DACHAS
CRAPED	CRICKS	CRUNCH	CUPOLA	CUTEYS	DACHAU
CRAPES	CRIERS	CRURAL	CUPPED	CUTIES	DACOIT
CRASIS	CRIKEY	CRUSES	CUPPER	CUTINS	DACRON
CRATCH	CRIMEA	CRUSET	CUPRIC	CUTLAS	DACTYL
CRATED	CRIMES	CRUSOE	CUPRUM	CUTLER	DADDLE
CRATER	CRIMPS	CRUSTS	CUPTIE	CUTLET	DADOES
CRATES	CRIMPY	CRUSTY	CUPULE	CUTOFF	DAEDAL
CRAVAT	CRINGE	CRUTCH	CURACY	CUTOUT	DAEMON
CRAVED	CRINUM	CRUXES	CURARE	CUTTER	DAFTLY
CRAVEN	CRISES	CRYING	CURATE	CUTTLE	DAGGER
				CUTUPS	DAGGLE

DAGMAR	DAPHNE	******	DECOYS	DELIAS	DEPEND
DAGOBA	DAPPED	DE----	DECREE	DELICT	DEPICT
DAHLIA	DAPPER	******	DECUMA	DELIUS	DEPLOY
DAHOON	DAPPLE	DEACON	DECURY	DELLAS	DEPONE
DAIMIO	DARDAN	DEADEN	DEDANS	DELPHI	DEPORT
DAIMON	DARERS	DEADLY	DEDUCE	DELTAS	DEPOSE
DAIMYO	DARICS	DEAFEN	DEDUCT	DELUDE	DEPOTS
DAINTY	DARIEN	DEAFLY	DEEDED	DELUGE	DEPTHS
DAISES	DARING	DEALER	DEEMED	DELUXE	DEPUTE
DAISYS	DARIUS	DEARER	DEEPEN	DELVED	DEPUTY
DAKOIT	DARKEN	DEARIE	DEEPER	DELVER	DERAIL
DAKOTA	DARKER	DEARLY	DEEPLY	DELVES	DERAIN
DALETH	DARKLE	DEARTH	DEEWAN	DEMAND	DERATE
DALLAS	DARKLY	DEATHS	DEFACE	DEMEAN	DEREKS
DALLES	DARNED	DEATHY	DEFAME	DEMENT	DERIDE
DALTON	DARNEL	DEBARK	DEFEAT	DEMIES	DERIVE
DAMAGE	DARNER	DEBARS	DEFECT	DEMISE	DERMAL
DAMANS	DARROW	DEBASE	DEFEND	DEMITS	DERMAS
DAMASK	DARTED	DEBATE	DEFERS	DEMOBS	DERMAT
DAMMAR	DARTER	DEBBIE	DEFIED	DEMODE	DERMIC
DAMMED	DARTLE	DEBBYS	DEFIER	DEMONO	DERMIS
DAMMER	DARWIN	DEBITS	DEFIES	DEMONS	DERRIS
DAMNED	DASHED	DEBRIS	DEFILE	DEMOTE	DESALT
DAMPED	DASHER	DEBTOR	DEFINE	DEMURE	DESCRY
DAMPEN	DASHES	DEBUGS	DEFORM	DEMURS	DESERT
DAMPER	DATARY	DEBUNK	DEFRAY	DENARY	DESIGN
DAMPLY	DATERS	DEBUTS	DEFTER	DENDRI	DESIRE
DAMSEL	DATING	DECADE	DEFTLY	DENDRO	DESIST
DAMSON	DATIVE	DECALS	DEFUSE	DENGUE	DESMAN
DANAID	DATTOS	DECAMP	DEGAGE	DENIAL	DESMID
DANAUS	DATURA	DECANE	DEGAME	DENIED	DESOXY
DANCED	DAUBED	DECANT	DEGREE	DENIER	DESPOT
DANCER	DAUBER	DECARE	DEGUMS	DENIES	DESSAU
DANCES	DAUBRY	DECAYS	DEGUST	DENIMS	DETACH
DANDER	DAUDET	DECCAN	DEHORN	DENISE	DETAIL
DANDLE	DAUNTS	DECEIT	DEICED	DENNED	DETAIN
DANGED	DAVEYS	DECENT	DEICER	DENNIS	DETECT
DANGER	DAVIDS	DECERN	DEICES	DENNYS	DETENT
DANGLE	DAVIES	DECIDE	DEIFIC	DENOTE	DETERS
DANIEL	DAVITS	DECILE	DEIGNS	DENSER	DETEST
DANISH	DAWDLE	DECKED	DEISTS	DENTAL	DETOUR
DANITE	DAWNED	DECKEL	DEJECT	DENTED	DEUCED
DANKER	DAWSON	DECKER	DEKARE	DENTIL	DEUCES
DANKLY	DAYBED	DECKLE	DEKING	DENTIN	DEVEIN
DANNYS	DAYBOY	DECOCT	DELATE	DENUDE	DEVEST
DANTON	DAYFLY	DECODE	DELAYS	DENVER	DEVICE
DANUBE	DAYTON	DECOKE	DELETE	DEODAR	DEVILS
DANZIG	DAZING	DECORS	DELIAN	DEPART	DEVISE
	DAZZLE				

DEVOID	DIESIS	DIPSAS	DOBLAS	DONNAS	DOURLY
DEVOIR	DIETAL	DIRECT	DOBLON	DONNED	DOUSED
DEVOTE	DIETED	DIRELY	DOBRAS	DONNIE	DOUSES
DEVOUR	DIETER	DIREST	DOBSON	DONORS	DOVISH
DEVOUT	DIFFER	DIRGES	DOCENT	DOODAD	DOWELS
DEWANS	DIGAMY	DIRHAM	DOCILE	DOODLE	DOWERS
DEWIER	DIGEST	DIRKED	DOCKED	DOOLEE	DOWERY
DEWITT	DIGGED	DIRNDL	DOCKER	DOOLIE	DOWLAS
DEWLAP	DIGGER	DISARM	DOCKET	DOOMED	DOWNED
DEXTER	DIGITI	DISBAR	DOCTOR	DOPING	DOWSED
DEXTRO	DIGITS	DISCAL	DODDER	DOPTER	DOWSER
******	DIGLOT	DISCUS	DODECA	DORADO	DOWSES
DH----	DIKDIK	DISHED	DODGED	DORBUG	DOXIES
******	DIKING	DISHES	DODGER	DOREEN	DOYENS
DHARMA	DILATE	DISMAL	DODGES	DORIAN	DOYLEY
DHARNA	DILUTE	DISMAY	DODOES	DORIES	DOZENS
DHOLES	DIMERS	DISNEY	DOESNT	DORMER	DOZIER
DHOTIS	DIMITY	DISOWN	DOFFED	DORMIE	DOZILY
DHURNA	DIMMED	DISPEL	DOFFER	DORSAD	DOZING
******	DIMMER	DISTAL	DOGAPE	DORSAL	******
DI----	DIMOUT	DISTIL	DOGEAR	DORSET	DR----
******	DIMPLE	DISUSE	DOGFOX	DORSUM	******
DIADEM	DIMPLY	DITHER	DOGGED	DOSAGE	DRABLY
DIALED	DIMWIT	DITONE	DOGGER	DOSERS	DRACHM
DIALER	DINAHS	DITTOS	DOGGIE	DOSING	DRAFFS
DIALOG	DINARS	DIVANS	DOGIES	DOSSAL	DRAFFY
DIANAS	DINDER	DIVERS	DOGMAS	DOSSED	DRAFTS
DIANES	DINERO	DIVERT	DOINGS	DOSSEL	DRAFTY
DIAPER	DINERS	DIVEST	DOITED	DOSSER	DRAGEE
DIATOM	DINGED	DIVIDE	DOLING	DOSSIL	DRAGON
DIAZIN	DINGEY	DIVINE	DOLLAR	DOTAGE	DRAINS
DIBBED	DINGHY	DIVING	DOLLED	DOTARD	DRAKES
DIBBER	DINGLE	DIVOTS	DOLLIE	DOTERS	DRAMAS
DIBBLE	DINGUS	DIWANS	DOLLOP	DOTIER	DRAPED
DICAST	DINING	DIXITS	DOLLYS	DOTING	DRAPER
DICERS	DINKEY	DIZENS	DOLMAN	DOTTED	DRAPES
DICING	DINKUM	******	DOLMEN	DOTTEL	DRAWEE
DICKER	DINNED	DM----	DOLOUR	DOTTER	DRAWER
DICKEY	DINNER	******	DOLPHS	DOTTLE	DRAWLS
DICKIE	DINTED	DMITRI	DOMAIN	DOUBLE	DRAWLY
DICTUM	DIOBOL	******	DOMING	DOUBLY	DRAYED
DIDDLE	DIODES	DO----	DOMINO	DOUBTS	DREADS
DIDERO	DIPLEX	******	DONALD	DOUCHE	DREAMS
DIDIES	DIPLOE	DOABLE	DONATE	DOUGAL	DREAMT
DIDOES	DIPODY	DOALLS	DONEES	DOUGHS	DREAMY
DIEPPE	DIPOLE	DOBBER	DONETS	DOUGHY	DREARY
DIESEL	DIPPED	DOBBIN	DONJON	DOUGIE	DREDGE
DIESES	DIPPER	DOBIES	DONKEY	DOUGIE	DREGGY

DRENCH	******	DUPLET	EASIER	EDMOND	EILEEN
DRESSY	DU----	DUPLEX	EASILY	EDMUND	EITHER
DRIERS	******	DURBAN	EASING	EDSELS	******
DRIEST	DUBBED	DURBAR	EASTER	EDUARD	EJ----
DRIFTS	DUBBIN	DURESS	EASTON	EDUCED	******
DRIFTY	DUBLIN	DURHAM	EATERS	EDUCES	EJECTA
DRILLS	DUCATS	DURIAN	EATERY	EDUCTS	EJECTS
DRINKS	DUCKED	DURING	EATING	EDWARD	******
DRIPPY	DUCKER	DURION	******	EDWINA	EK----
DRIVEL	DUDEEN	DUSKED	EB----	EDWINS	******
DRIVEN	DUDISH	DUSTED	******	******	EKEING
DRIVER	DUDLEY	DUSTER	EBBING	EE----	******
DRIVES	DUELED	DUTIES	******	******	EL----
DROGUE	DUELER	******	EC----	EERILY	******
DROITS	DUELLO	DV----	******	******	ELAINE
DROLLS	DUENNA	******	ECARTE	EF----	ELANDS
DROLLY	DUFFED	DVORAK	ECCLES	******	ELAPSE
DROMON	DUFFEL	******	ECESIS	EFFACE	ELATED
DRONED	DUFFER	DW----	ECHARD	EFFECT	ELATER
DRONES	DUFFLE	******	ECHINI	EFFETE	ELATES
DRONGO	DUGONG	DWARFS	ECHINO	EFFIGY	ELAYNE
DROOLS	DUGOUT	DWELLS	ECHOED	EFFLUX	ELBERT
DROOPS	DUIKER	DWIGHT	ECHOER	EFFORT	ELBOWS
DROOPY	DULCET	******	ECHOES	EFFUSE	ELBRUS
DROPSY	DULCIE	DY----	ECHOIC	******	ELDERS
DROSKY	DULLED	******	ECLAIR	EG----	ELDEST
DROSSY	DULLER	DYADIC	ECOLES	******	ELDRED
DROUTH	DULLES	DYBBUK	ECTOMY	EGBERT	ELECTS
DROVED	DULUTH	DYEING	ECTYPE	EGERIA	ELEGIT
DROVER	DUMBLY	DYNAMO	ECZEMA	EGESTA	ELEMIS
DROVES	DUMDUM	DYNAST	******	EGESTS	ELENAS
DROWNS	DUMPED	******	ED----	EGGARS	ELEVEN
DROWSE	DUMPER	EA----	******	EGGCUP	ELEVON
DROWSY	DUMPTY	******	EDDAIC	EGGERS	ELFINS
DRUDGE	DUNBAR	EAGLES	EDDIED	EGGING	ELFISH
DRUIDS	DUNCAN	EAGLET	EDDIES	EGGNOG	ELICIT
DRUNKS	DUNCES	EALING	EDDISH	EGOISM	ELIDED
DRUPEL	DUNDEE	EARFUL	EDENIC	EGOIST	ELIDES
DRUPES	DUNGED	EARING	EDGARS	EGRESS	ELIJAH
DRUSES	DUNKED	EARLAP	EDGIER	EGRETS	ELINOR
DRYADS	DUNKER	EARLES	EDGING	******	ELIOTS
DRYDEN	DUNLIN	EARNED	EDIBLE	EI----	ELISHA
DRYERS	DUNNED	EARNER	EDICTS	******	ELIXIR
DRYEST	DUODEN	EARTHS	EDILES	EIDOLA	ELIZAS
DRYFLY	DUOLOG	EARTHY	EDISON	EIFFEL	ELLENS
DRYICE	DUPERS	EARWAX	EDITED	EIGHTH	ELLIES
DRYING	DUPERY	EARWIG	EDITHS	EIGHTS	ELLIOT
DRYISH	DUPING	EASELS	EDITOR	EIGHTY	ELMERS

ELMIRA	EMILIO	ENJOIN	EOLITH	ERODED	ETERNA
ELOHIM	EMILYS	ENJOYS	EONIAN	ERODES	ETHANE
ELOIGN	EMMETS	ENLACE	EONISM	EROTIC	ETHANS
ELOINS	EMMETT	ENLIST	EOZOIC	ERRAND	ETHELS
ELOISE	EMMIES	ENMESH	******	ERRANT	ETHERS
ELOPED	EMOTED	ENMITY	EP----	ERRATA	ETHICS
ELOPER	EMOTES	ENNEAD	******	ERRING	ETHNIC
ELOPES	EMPALE	ENOSIS	EPACTS	ERRORS	ETHYLS
ELSIES	EMPERY	ENOUGH	EPARCH	ERSATZ	ETUDES
ELUDED	EMPIRE	ENRAGE	EPHAHS	ERUCTS	ETYMON
ELUDES	EMPLOY	ENRAPT	EPHEBI	ERUPTS	******
ELVERS	******	ENRICH	EPHODS	ERWINS	EU----
ELVIRA	EN----	ENRICO	EPHORI	ERYNGO	******
ELVISH	******	ENROBE	EPHORS	******	EUBOEA
ELYSEE	ENABLE	ENROLL	EPICAL	ES----	EUCHER
ELYTRA	ENACTS	ENROOT	EPILOG	******	EUCHRE
******	ENAMEL	ENSIGN	EPIRUS	ESCAPE	EUCLID
EM----	ENAMOR	ENSILE	EPIZOA	ESCARP	EUDOAR
******	ENATES	ENSOUL	EPOCHS	ESCENT	EUGENE
EMBALM	ENCAGE	ENSUED	EPODES	ESCHAR	EULOGY
EMBANK	ENCAMP	ENSUES	EPONYM	ESCHER	EUNICE
EMBARK	ENCASE	ENSURE	EPOPEE	ESCHEW	EUNUCH
EMBARS	ENCASH	ENTAIL	EPPING	ESCORT	EUPNEA
EMBAYS	ENCINA	ENTERA	******	ESCROW	EUREKA
EMBEDS	ENCODE	ENTERE	EQ----	ESCUDO	EURIPI
EMBERS	ENCORE	ENTERO	******	ESKERS	EUROPA
EMBLEM	ENCYST	ENTERS	EQUALS	ESKIMO	EUROPE
EMBODY	ENDALL	ENTICE	EQUATE	ESPANA	******
EMBOLI	ENDEAR	ENTIRE	EQUINE	ESPIAL	EV----
EMBOSS	ENDING	ENTITY	EQUIPS	ESPIED	******
EMBOWS	ENDIVE	ENTOMB	EQUITY	ESPIES	EVADED
EMBRUE	ENDOWS	ENTOMO	******	ESPRIT	EVADER
EMBRYO	ENDUED	ENTRAP	ER----	ESSAYS	EVADES
EMCEED	ENDUES	ENTREE	******	ESSENE	EVELYN
EMCEES	ENDURE	ENVIED	ERASED	ESTATE	EVENED
EMEERS	ENEMAS	ENVIER	ERASER	ESTEEM	EVENLY
EMENDS	ENERGY	ENVIES	ERASES	ESTERS	EVENTS
EMERGE	ENFACE	ENVOYS	ERBIUM	ESTHER	EVERET
EMERIC	ENFOLD	ENWIND	EREBUS	ESTOPS	EVERTS
EMERIE	ENGAGE	ENWOMB	ERECTS	ESTRAY	EVICTS
EMESIS	ENGELS	ENWRAP	ERFURT	ESTRUS	EVILLY
EMETIC	ENGINE	ENZYME	ERGATE	******	EVINCE
EMETIN	ENGIRD	******	ERICHS	ET----	EVITAS
EMEUTE	ENGIRT	EO----	ERINGO	******	EVOKED
EMIGRE	ENGRAM	******	ERINYS	ETAPES	EVOKES
EMILES	ENGULF	EOCENE	ERMINE	ETCHED	EVOLVE
EMILIA	ENIGMA	EOGENE	ERNEST	ETCHER	******
EMILIE	ENISLE	EOLIAN	ERNIES	ETCHES	EX----
					******
					EXACTA
					EXACTS

EXALTS	EXUDES	FAIRLY	FASTEN	FEIGNS	FETIAL
EXAMEN	EXULTS	FAITHS	FASTER	FEINTS	FETICH
EXARCH	EXURBS	FAKERS	FATHER	FEISTS	FETING
EXCEED	******	FAKERY	FATHOM	FEISTY	FETISH
EXCELS	EY----	FAKING	FATIMA	FELICE	FETORS
EXCEPT	******	FAKIRS	FATING	FELIDS	FETTER
EXCESS	EYASES	FALCON	FATTED	FELINE	FETTLE
EXCIDE	EYECUP	FALLAL	FATTEN	FELIPE	FEUARS
EXCISE	EYEFUL	FALLEN	FATTER	FELLAH	FEUDAL
EXCITE	EYEING	FALLER	FAUCAL	FELLED	FEUDED
EXCUSE	EYELET	FALLOW	FAUCES	FELLER	FEUING
EXEDRA	EYELID	FALSER	FAUCET	FELLOE	FEVERS
EXEMPT	EYEOUT	FALTER	FAULTS	FELLOW	FEWEST
EXEQUY	EYRIES	FAMILY	FAULTY	FELONS	FEZZAN
EXERTS	******	FAMINE	FAUNAE	FELONY	FEZZES
EXETER	FA----	FAMISH	FAUNAL	FELTED	******
EXEUNT	******	FAMOUS	FAUNAS	FEMALE	FI----
EXHALE	FABIAN	FANEGA	FAUNUS	FEMORA	******
EXHORT	FABLED	FANGAS	FAUVES	FEMURS	FIACRE
EXHUME	FABLER	FANGED	FAVORS	FENCED	FIANCE
EXILED	FABLES	FANION	FAVOUR	FENCER	FIASCO
EXILES	FABRIC	FANJET	FAWKES	FENCES	FIBBED
EXILIC	FACADE	FANNED	FAWNED	FENDED	FIBBER
EXISTS	FACERS	FANNER	FAWNER	FENDER	FIBERS
EXITED	FACETS	FANNIE	FAXING	FENIAN	FIBRIL
EXMOOR	FACIAL	FANNYS	FAYING	FENNEC	FIBRIN
EXODUS	FACIES	FANONS	FAZING	FENNEL	FIBULA
EXOGEN	FACILE	FANTAN	******	FENRIR	FICHES
EXOTIC	FACING	FANTOM	FE----	FEODOR	FICHUS
EXPAND	FACTOR	FANUMS	******	FEOFFS	FICKLE
EXPECT	FACTUM	FARADS	FEALTY	FERBER	FIDDLE
EXPELS	FACULA	FARBAD	FEARED	FERIAL	FIDGET
EXPEND	FADEIN	FARCED	FEARER	FERINE	FIELDS
EXPERT	FADING	FARCER	FEASED	FERITY	FIENDS
EXPIRE	FAECAL	FARCES	FEASES	FERMIS	FIERCE
EXPIRY	FAECES	FARERS	FEASTS	FEROUS	FIESTA
EXPORT	FAERIE	FARINA	FECIAL	FERRET	FIFERS
EXPOSE	FAEROE	FARING	FECULA	FERRIC	FIFING
EXSECT	FAFNIR	FARLES	FECUND	FERRIS	FIFTHS
EXSERT	FAGEND	FARLEY	FEDORA	FERRUM	FIGGED
EXTANT	FAGGED	FARMED	FEEBLE	FERULA	FIGHTS
EXTEND	FAGGOT	FARMER	FEEBLY	FERULE	FIGURE
EXTENT	FAGOTS	FAROFF	FEEDER	FERVID	FIJIAN
EXTERN	FAILED	FAROUT	FEEING	FERVOR	FILERS
EXTOLS	FAILLE	FARROW	FEELER	FESCUE	FILETS
EXTORT	FAINTS	FASCES	FEEZED	FESSES	FILIAL
EXTRAS	FAIRED	FASCIA	FEEZES	FESTAL	FILING
EXUDED	FAIRER	FASTED	FEIGNE	FESTER	FILLED

FILLER	FIXERS	FLEECY	FLUFFY	FOLIOS	FOULER
FILLET	FIXING	FLEERS	FLUIDS	FOLIUM	FOULLY
FILLIN	FIXITY	FLEETS	FLUKED	FOLKSY	FOUNDS
FILLIP	FIZGIG	FLENCH	FLUKES	FOLLOW	FOUNTS
FILMED	FIZZED	FLENSE	FLUKEY	FOMENT	FOURTH
FILMIC	FIZZER	FLESHY	FLUMED	FONDER	FOVEAE
FILOSE	FIZZES	FLETCH	FLUMES	FONDLE	FOVEAL
FILTER	FIZZLE	FLEURY	FLUMPS	FONDLY	FOWLED
FILTHY	******	FLEXED	FLUNKS	FONDUE	FOWLER
FIMBLE	**FL----**	FLEXES	FLUNKY	FONTAL	FOXIER
FINALE	******	FLEXOR	FLUORO	FOOLED	FOXILY
FINALS	FLABBY	FLICKS	FLUORS	FOOTED	FOXING
FINDER	FLACKS	FLIERS	FLURRY	FOOTER	FOYERS
FINELY	FLACON	FLIEST	FLUTED	FOOTLE	******
FINERY	FLAGGY	FLIGHT	FLUTER	FOOZLE	**FR----**
FINEST	FLAGON	FLIMSY	FLUTES	FORAGE	******
FINGER	FLAILS	FLINCH	FLUVIO	FORAYS	FRACAS
FINIAL	FLAIRS	FLINGS	FLUXED	FORBID	FRAILS
FINING	FLAKED	FLINTS	FLUXES	FORCED	FRAISE
FINISH	FLAKER	FLINTY	FLYBYS	FORCER	FRAMED
FINITE	FLAKES	FLIRTS	FLYERS	FORCES	FRAMER
FINNAN	FLAMBE	FLIRTY	FLYING	FORDED	FRAMES
FINNED	FLAMED	FLITCH	FLYMAN	FOREGO	FRANCE
FINNER	FLAMEN	FLOATS	******	FOREST	FRANCK
FINNIC	FLAMES	FLOATY	**FO----**	FORGED	FRANCO
FINNOC	FLANGE	FLOCKS	******	FORGER	FRANCS
FIORDS	FLANKS	FLOCKY	FOALED	FORGES	FRANKS
FIPPLE	FLARED	FLONGS	FOAMED	FORGET	FRAPPE
FIQUES	FLARES	FLOODS	FOBBED	FORGOT	FRATER
FIRERS	FLASHY	FLOORS	FOCSLE	FORINT	FRAUDS
FIRING	FLASKS	FLOOZY	FODDER	FORKED	FRAUEN
FIRKIN	FLATLY	FLOPPY	FOEHNS	FORMAL	FRAYED
FIRMAN	FLATUS	FLORAE	FOEMAN	FORMAT	FREAKS
FIRMED	FLAUNT	FLORAL	FOEMEN	FORMED	FREAKY
FIRMER	FLAVIA	FLORAS	FOETAL	FORMER	FREDAS
FIRMLY	FLAVIN	FLORES	FOETID	FORMIC	FREDDY
FIRSTS	FLAVOR	FLORET	FOETOR	FORMYL	FREELY
FIRTHS	FLAWED	FLORID	FOETUS	FORNAX	FREEST
FISCAL	FLAXEN	FLORIN	FOGBOW	FORNIX	FREEZE
FISHER	FLAXES	FLOSSY	FOGDOG	FORTES	FRENCH
FISHES	FLAYED	FLOURS	FOGGED	FORTIS	FRENUM
FISTED	FLAYER	FLOURY	FOGIES	FORUMS	FRENZY
FISTIC	FLEAMS	FLOUTS	FOIBLE	FOSSAE	FREONS
FITFUL	FLECHE	FLOWED	FOILED	FOSSES	FRESCO
FITTED	FLECKS	FLOWER	FOISTS	FOSSIL	FRESNO
FITTER	FLEDGE	FLOYDS	FOLDED	FOSTER	FRETTY
FIVERS	FLEDGY	FLUENT	FOLDER	FOUGHT	FRIARS
FIXATE	FLEECE	FLUFFS	FOLIAR	FOULED	FRIARY

FRIDAY	FUDGED	FUZILS	GALLUP	GARISH	******
FRIDGE	FUDGES	FUZING	GALLUS	GARLIC	GE----
FRIEDA	FUELED	FUZZED	GALOOT	GARNER	******
FRIEND	FUELER	FUZZES	GALOPS	GARNET	GEARED
FRIERS	FUGIOS	******	GALORE	GARRET	GECKOS
FRIEZE	FUGLED	FY----	GALOSH	GARTER	GEEING
FRIGGA	FUGLES	FYLFOT	GALWAY	GASBAG	GEEZER
FRIGHT	FUGUES	******	GALYAK	GASCON	GEIGER
FRIGID	FUHRER	******	GAMBIA	GASHED	GEISHA
FRIJOL	FULCRA	GA----	GAMBIR	GASHES	GELDED
FRILLS	FULFIL	******	GAMBIT	GASIFY	GELLED
FRILLY	FULGID	GABBED	GAMBLE	GASJET	GEMARA
FRINGE	FULLED	GABBER	GAMBOL	GASKET	GEMERT
FRINGY	FULLER	GABBLE	GAMELY	GASKIN	GEMINI
FRISES	FULMAR	GABBRO	GAMETE	GASMAN	GEMMAE
FRISKS	FULTON	GABION	GAMETO	GASMEN	GEMMED
FRISKY	FUMBLE	GABLED	GAMIER	GASPAR	GEMOTS
FRITHS	FUMIER	GABLES	GAMILY	GASPED	GEMSBO
FRIVOL	FUMING	GADDED	GAMING	GASPER	GENDER
FRIZZY	FUMOUS	GADDER	GAMINS	GASSED	GENERA
FROCKS	FUNDED	GADFLY	GAMMAS	GASSES	GENESI
FROGGY	FUNDUS	GADGET	GAMMED	GASTON	GENETS
FROLIC	FUNEST	GADOID	GAMMER	GASTRO	GENEVA
FRONDS	FUNGAL	GAELIC	GAMMON	GATEAU	GENIAL
FRONTO	FUNGUS	GAFFED	GAMOUS	GATHER	GENIES
FRONTS	FUNKED	GAFFER	GAMUTS	GATING	GENITO
FROSTS	FUNNEL	GAFFES	GANDER	GAUCHE	GENIUS
FROSTY	FURFUR	GAGERS	GANDHI	GAUCHO	GENOUS
FROTHS	FURIES	GAGGED	GANEFS	GAUGED	GENRES
FROTHY	FURLED	GAGGER	GANGED	GAUGER	GENROS
FROWNS	FURORE	GAGGLE	GANGER	GAUGES	GENTES
FROWZY	FURORS	GAGING	GANGES	GAULLE	GENTLE
FROZEN	FURRED	GAIETY	GANGLI	GAUZES	GENTLY
FRUGAL	FURROW	GAINED	GANGUE	GAVELS	GENTOO
FRUITS	FURZES	GAINER	GANNET	GAVIAL	GENTRY
FRUITY	FUSAIN	GAINLY	GANOID	GAVOTS	GEODES
FRUMPS	FUSEES	GAITED	GANTRY	GAWAIN	GEODIC
FRUMPY	FUSILE	GAITER	GAOLER	GAWKED	GEORGE
FRUNZE	FUSILS	GALACT	GAPERS	GAYEST	GEORGI
FRUSTA	FUSING	GALAXY	GAPING	GAYETY	GERALD
FRYERS	FUSION	GALEAE	GAPPED	GAZABO	GERARD
FRYING	FUSSED	GALENA	GARAGE	GAZEBO	GERBIL
******	FUSSER	GALIOT	GARBED	GAZERS	GERENT
FU----	FUSSES	GALLED	GARBLE	GAZING	GERMAN
******	FUSTIC	GALLEY	GARCON	******	GERMEN
FUCOID	FUTILE	GALLIC	GARDEN	GD----	GEROUS
FUCOUS	FUTURE	GALLON	GARGET	******	GERRYS
FUDDLE	FUZEES	GALLOP	GARGLE	GDANSK	GERTIE
				GDYNIA	

GERTYS	GILLIE	GLEETS	GNOMON	GOOSEY	GRANNY
GERUND	GIMELS	GLEETY	GNOSIS	GOPHER	GRANTS
GERYON	GIMLET	GLIBLY	******	GORALS	GRAPES
GESELL	GIMPED	GLIDED	GO----	GORDON	GRAPHO
GESSOS	GINGAL	GLIDER	******	GORGED	GRAPHS
GESTIC	GINGER	GLIDES	GOADED	GORGER	GRAPHY
GETTER	GINGKO	GLINTS	GOALIE	GORGES	GRASPS
GETUPS	GINNED	GLIOMA	GOATEE	GORGET	GRASSY
GEWGAW	GINNER	GLOATS	GOBANG	GORGON	GRATED
GEYSER	GIOTTO	GLOBAL	GOBBET	GORHEN	GRATER
******	GIPONS	GLOBED	GOBBLE	GORIER	GRATES
GH----	GIPPED	GLOBES	GOBIES	GORILY	GRATIN
******	GIRDED	GLOBIN	GOBLET	GORING	GRATIS
GHARRI	GIRDER	GLOOMS	GOBLIN	GORSES	GRAVED
GHARRY	GIRDLE	GLOOMY	GOCART	GOSHEN	GRAVEL
GHAUTS	GIRTED	GLORIA	GODDAM	GOSPEL	GRAVEN
GHEBER	GISELE	GLOSSO	GODIVA	GOSSIP	GRAVER
GHETTO	GISMOS	GLOSSY	GODSON	GOTAMA	GRAVES
GHOSTS	GITANO	GLOSTS	GODWIN	GOTHAM	GRAVID
GHOULS	GIULIA	GLOTTO	GODWIT	GOTHIC	GRAYED
******	GIULIO	GLOVED	GOETHE	GOTTEN	GRAYER
GI----	GIVING	GLOVER	GOFFER	GOUGED	GRAYLY
******	GIZMOS	GLOVES	GOGGLE	GOUGER	GRAZED
GIANTS	******	GLOWED	GOGLET	GOUGES	GRAZER
GIAOUR	GL----	GLOWER	GOINGS	GOURDE	GRAZES
GIBBED	******	GLOZED	GOITER	GOURDS	GREASE
GIBBER	GLACES	GLOZES	GOITRE	GOVERN	GREASY
GIBBET	GLACIS	GLUIER	GOKART	GOWNED	GREATS
GIBBON	GLADES	GLUING	GOLDEN	******	GREAVE
GIBERS	GLADLY	GLUMES	GOLFED	GR----	GREBES
GIBING	GLADYS	GLUMLY	GOLFER	******	GREECE
GIBLET	GLAIRS	GLUTEI	GOLOSH	GRABEN	GREEDS
GIBRAN	GLAIRY	GLUTEN	GOMUTI	GRACED	GREEDY
GIBSON	GLAMIS	GLYCOL	GONADS	GRACES	GREEKS
GIDEON	GLANCE	GLYNIS	GONERS	GRACIE	GREENE
GIFTED	GLANDS	GLYPHS	GONION	GRADED	GREENS
GIGANT	GLARED	GLYPTO	GONIUM	GRADER	GREETS
GIGGED	GLARES	******	GOOBER	GRADES	GREGOS
GIGGLE	GLASSY	GN----	GOODBY	GRADIN	GREIFS
GIGGLY	GLAUCO	******	GOODLY	GRADUS	GREIGE
GIGLET	GLAZED	GNARLS	GOOFED	GRAECO	GRETAS
GIGLOT	GLAZER	GNARLY	GOOGLY	GRAFTS	GRETEL
GIGOLO	GLAZES	GNATHO	GOOGOL	GRAHAM	GRETNA
GIGUES	GLEAMS	GNAWED	GOOIER	GRAINS	GRIDED
GILDAS	GLEAMY	GNAWER	GOONEY	GRAINY	GRIDES
GILDED	GLEANS	GNEISS	GOORAL	GRAMME	GRIEVE
GILDER	GLEBES	GNOMES	GOOSED	GRANDE	GRIFFE
GILEAD	GLEDES	GNOMIC	GOOSES	GRANGE	GRIGRI

GRILLE	GRUNDY	GUSHES	HAGGLE	HANSOM	HAULER
GRILLS	GRUNTS	GUSSET	HAILED	HAPPED	HAULMY
GRILSE	******	GUSSIE	HAILER	HAPPEN	HAUNCH
GRIMED	GU----	GUSTAF	HAIRDO	HARASS	HAUNTS
GRIMES	******	GUSTAV	HAIRED	HARBIN	HAUSEN
GRIMLY	GUACOS	GUTTAE	HAKIMS	HARBOR	HAVANA
GRINDS	GUANIN	GUTTAT	HALERS	HARDEN	HAVENS
GRIPED	GUANOS	GUTTED	HALIDE	HARDER	HAVENT
GRIPER	GUARDS	GUTTER	HALIDS	HARDLY	HAVING
GRIPES	GUAVAS	GUTTLE	HALING	HAREMS	HAWAII
GRIPPE	GUENON	GUYANA	HALITE	HARING	HAWHAW
GRIPPY	GUESTS	GUYING	HALLAH	HARKED	HAWING
GRISLY	GUFFAW	GUZZLE	HALLEL	HARKEN	HAWKED
GRITTY	GUIANA	******	HALLEY	HARLAN	HAWKER
GRIVET	GUIDED	GW----	HALLOO	HARLEM	HAWSER
GRIZEL	GUIDER	******	HALLOW	HARLEY	HAWSES
GROANS	GUIDES	GWENNS	HALLUX	HARLOT	HAYBOX
GROATS	GUIDON	GWYNNE	HALOED	HARLOW	HAYING
GROCER	GUILDS	******	HALOES	HARMED	HAYMOW
GROGGY	GUILES	GY----	HALOID	HARMIN	HAZARD
GROINS	GUILTS	******	HALSEY	HAROLD	HAZELS
GROOMS	GUILTY	GYBING	HALTED	HARPED	HAZERS
GROOVE	GUIMPE	GYNECO	HALTER	HARPER	HAZIER
GROOVY	GUINEA	GYNOUS	HALUTZ	HARRIS	HAZILY
GROPED	GUISES	GYPPED	HALVED	HARROW	HAZING
GROPER	GUITAR	GYPSUM	HALVES	HARRYS	HAZZAN
GROPES	GULDEN	GYRATE	HAMALS	HARTAL	******
GROSZY	GULFED	GYRONS	HAMAUL	HARVEY	HE----
GROTTO	GULLAH	GYROSE	HAMDEN	HASHED	******
GROTTY	GULLED	GYVING	HAMITE	HASHES	HEADED
GROUCH	GULLET	******	HAMLET	HASLET	HEADER
GROUND	GULPED	HA----	HAMMAL	HASPED	HEADON
GROUPS	GULPER	******	HAMMED	HASSEL	HEALED
GROUSE	GUMBOS	HABEAS	HAMMER	HASSLE	HEALER
GROUTS	GUMMAS	HABILE	HAMPER	HASTED	HEALTH
GROVEL	GUMMED	HABITS	HAMZAS	HASTEN	HEAPED
GROVER	GUNMAN	HACKED	HANCES	HASTES	HEARER
GROVES	GUNMEN	HACKEE	HANDED	HATBOX	HEARSE
GROWER	GUNNAR	HACKER	HANDEL	HATERS	HEARST
GROWLS	GUNNED	HACKIE	HANDLE	HATFUL	HEARTH
GROWTH	GUNNEL	HACKLE	HANGAR	HATING	HEARTS
GROYNE	GUNNER	HADING	HANGED	HATPIN	HEARTY
GRUBBY	GUNSHY	HAEMAL	HANGER	HATRED	HEATED
GRUDGE	GUNTER	HAFTED	HANGUP	HATTED	HEATER
GRUELS	GURGLE	HAGBUT	HANKER	HATTER	HEATHS
GRUGRU	GURKHA	HAGDON	HANNAH	HATTIE	HEATHY
GRUMES	GUSHED	HAGGED	HANNAS	HATTYS	HEAUME
GRUMPY	GUSHER	HAGGIS	HANSEL	HAULED	HEAVED

HEAVEN	HENBIT	******	HOAXED	HONORS	HOTROD
HEAVER	HENDON	**HI----**	HOAXER	HONOUR	HOTTED
HEAVES	HENLEY	******	HOAXES	HONSHU	HOTTER
HEBREW	HENNAS	HIATUS	HOBART	HOODED	HOUNDS
HEBRON	HENRIS	HICCUP	HOBBES	HOODOO	HOURIS
HECATE	HENRYS	HICKEY	HOBBLE	HOOFED	HOURLY
HECKLE	HEPATO	HICKOK	HOBNOB	HOOFER	HOUSED
HECTIC	HEPTAD	HIDDEN	HOBOES	HOOKAH	HOUSES
HECTOR	HERALD	HIDERS	HOCKED	HOOKED	HOVELS
HECUBA	HERBAL	HIDING	HOCKEY	HOOKER	HOVERS
HEDDLE	HERDED	HIEING	HODDEN	HOOKEY	HOWARD
HEDGED	HERDER	HIEMAL	HODMAN	HOOKUP	HOWDAH
HEDGER	HERDIC	HIGGLE	HOEING	HOOPED	HOWLED
HEDGES	HEREAT	HIGHER	HOGANS	HOOPER	HOWLER
HEDRAL	HEREBY	HIGHLY	HOGGED	HOOPLA	HOYDEN
HEDRON	HEREIN	HIJACK	HOGNUT	HOOPOE	******
HEDWIG	HEREOF	HIKERS	HOGTIE	HOORAY	**HU----**
HEEDED	HEREON	HIKING	HOICKS	HOOTCH	******
HEEDER	HERESY	HILARY	HOIDEN	HOOTED	HUBBUB
HEEHAW	HERETO	HILDAS	HOISTS	HOOTER	HUBCAP
HEELED	HERIOT	HILLED	HOLARD	HOOVED	HUBERT
HEELER	HERMAE	HILLER	HOLDER	HOOVER	HUBRIS
HEFTED	HERMAI	HILTED	HOLDUP	HOOVES	HUCKLE
HEGIRA	HERMAN	HINDER	HOLIER	HOPING	HUDDLE
HEIFER	HERMES	HINDUS	HOLIES	HOPPED	HUDSON
HEIGHT	HERMIT	HINGED	HOLILY	HOPPER	HUELVA
HEISTS	HERNIA	HINGES	HOLING	HOPPLE	HUFFED
HEJIRA	HERNIO	HINTED	HOLISM	HORACE	HUGELY
HELENA	HEROES	HIPPED	HOLLER	HORARY	HUGEST
HELENS	HEROIC	HIPPIE	HOLLOW	HORDED	HUGGED
HELICO	HEROIN	HIPPOS	HOLLYS	HORDES	HUGHES
HELIOS	HERONS	HIPPUS	HOLMES	HORNED	HUGHIE
HELIUM	HERPES	HIRAMS	HOLMIC	HORNET	HULKED
HELLAS	HESIOD	HIRERS	HOMAGE	HORNIE	HULLED
HELLEN	HESTER	HIRING	HOMBRE	HORRID	HUMANE
HELLER	HESTIA	HISPID	HOMELY	HORROR	HUMANS
HELMED	HETERO	HISSED	HOMERS	HORSED	HUMBER
HELMET	HETMAN	HISSER	HOMIER	HORSES	HUMBLE
HELOTS	HETTYS	HISSES	HOMILY	HORSEY	HUMBLY
HELPED	HEWERS	HITHER	HOMING	HORSTE	HUMBUG
HELPER	HEWING	HITLER	HOMINY	HOSIER	HUMIFY
HELTER	HEXADS	HITTER	HONEST	HOSING	HUMMED
HELVES	HEXANE	HIVING	HONEYS	HOSTED	HUMMER
HEMATO	HEXONE	HIVITE	HONIED	HOSTEL	HUMORS
HEMMED	HEXOSE	******	HONING	HOTBED	HUMOUR
HEMMER	HEXYLS	**HO----**	HONKED	HOTBOX	HUMPED
HEMOID	HEYDAY	HOARDS	HONKER	HOTELS	HUMPTY
HEMPEN	HEZION	HOARSE	HONORE	HOTPOT	HUNGER

HUNGRY	******	IGNIFY	IMPISH	INFANT	INSIDE
HUNTED	IA----	IGNITE	IMPORT	INFECT	INSIST
HUNTER	******	IGNORE	IMPOSE	INFERO	INSOLE
HURDLE	IAMBIC	IGOROT	IMPOST	INFERS	INSOUL
HURLED	IAMBUS	IGUANA	IMPUGN	INFEST	INSPAN
HURLER	IATRIC	******	IMPURE	INFIRM	INSTAR
HURLEY	******	IL----	IMPUTE	INFLOW	INSTEP
HURONS	IB----	******	******	INFLUX	INSTIL
HURRAH	******	ILEXES	IN----	INFOLD	INSULT
HURRAY	IBADAN	ILFORD	******	INFORM	INSURE
HURTER	IBEAMS	ILLUME	INARCH	INFUSE	INTACT
HURTLE	IBERIA	ILLUSE	INARMS	INGEST	INTAKE
HUSHED	IBEXES	ILLUST	INBAND	INGOTS	INTEND
HUSHES	IBICES	ILOILO	INBORN	INGRES	INTENT
HUSKED	IBIDEM	******	INBRED	INGRID	INTERN
HUSKER	IBISES	IM----	INCAGE	INGULF	INTERS
HUSSAR	******	******	INCASE	INHALE	INTIMA
HUSTLE	IC----	IMAGED	INCEPT	INHAUL	INTOMB
HUTTED	******	IMAGES	INCEST	INHERE	INTONE
HUXLEY	ICALLY	IMARET	INCHED	INHUME	INTUIT
******	ICARUS	IMBALM	INCHES	INJECT	INTURN
HY----	ICEAXE	IMBARK	INCHON	INJOKE	INULIN
******	ICEBOX	IMBEDS	INCISE	INJURE	INURED
HYADES	ICECAP	IMBIBE	INCITE	INJURY	INURES
HYBRID	ICEMAN	IMBODY	INCOME	INKERS	INURNS
HYBRIS	ICEMEN	IMBRUE	INCORP	INKIER	INVADE
HYDRAE	ICHTHY	IMBUED	INCUBI	INKING	INVENT
HYDRAS	ICICLE	IMBUES	INCURS	INKLES	INVERT
HYDRIC	ICIEST	IMIDES	INCUSE	INKPOT	INVEST
HYDROS	ICINGS	IMINES	INDABA	INLACE	INVITE
HYENAS	ICONIC	IMMESH	INDEED	INLAID	INVOKE
HYETAL	******	IMMIES	INDENE	INLAND	INWALL
HYGEIA	ID----	IMMUNE	INDENT	INLAWS	INWARD
HYMENO	******	IMMUNO	INDIAN	INLAYS	INWIND
HYMENS	IDEALS	IMMURE	INDICT	INLETS	INWOVE
HYMNAL	IDEATE	IMOGEN	INDIES	INLIER	INWRAP
HYMNED	IDIOCY	IMPACT	INDIGO	INMATE	******
HYMNIC	IDIOMS	IMPAIR	INDITE	INMESH	IO----
HYOIDS	IDIOTS	IMPALA	INDIUM	INMOST	******
HYPHAE	IDLERS	IMPALE	INDOOR	INNATE	IODATE
HYPHAL	IDLEST	IMPARK	INDOWS	INNING	IODIDE
HYPHEN	IDLING	IMPART	INDRIS	INPUTS	IODINE
HYPNIC	IDYLLS	IMPASS	INDUCE	INROAD	IODISM
HYPNOS	******	IMPAWN	INDUCT	INRUSH	IODIZE
HYSSOP	IG----	IMPEDE	INDUED	INSANE	IODOUS
HYSTER	******	IMPELS	INDUES	INSECT	IOLCUS
	IGLOOS	IMPEND	INDULT	INSERT	IOLITE
	IGNACE	IMPING	INFAMY	INSETS	IONIAN

IONIUM	ISOMER	JANICE	JESUIT	JOGGED	JUDAEA
IONIZE	ISOPOD	JAPANS	JETHRO	JOGGER	JUDAEO
IONONE	ISRAEL	JAPHET	JETSAM	JOGGLE	JUDAHS
******	ISSEIS	JAPHIA	JETTED	JOHANN	JUDAIC
IP----	ISSUED	JAPING	JETTON	JOHNNY	JUDEAN
******	ISSUER	JARFUL	JEWELS	JOINED	JUDGED
IPECAC	ISSUES	JARGON	JEWESS	JOINER	JUDGER
******	ISTRIA	JARINA	JEWISH	JOINTS	JUDGES
IR----	******	JARRED	JEZAIL	JOISTS	JUDITH
******	**IT----**	JARROW	******	JOKERS	JUGATE
IRANIS	******	JARVEY	**JI----**	JOKING	JUGFUL
IRAQIS	ITALIC	JARVIS	******	JOLIET	JUGGED
IREFUL	ITCHED	JASONS	JIBBED	JOLTED	JUGGLE
IRENES	ITCHES	JASPER	JIBBER	JOLTER	JUICER
IRENIC	ITHACA	JAUNTS	JIBING	JONAHS	JUICES
IRIDES	ITIOUS	JAUNTY	JIGGED	JONNIE	JUJUBE
IRIDIC	ITSELF	JAWING	JIGGER	JONSON	JULEPS
IRISED	******	JAYVEE	JIGGLE	JOPLIN	JULIAN
IRISES	**JA----**	JAZZED	JIGSAW	JORAMS	JULIAS
IRITIC	******	JAZZER	JIHADS	JORDAN	JULIES
IRITIS	JABBED	JAZZES	JILTED	JORGES	JULIET
IRKING	JABBER	******	JILTER	JORUMS	JULIUS
IRONED	JABIRU	**JE----**	JIMINY	JOSEPH	JUMBAL
IRONER	JABOTS	******	JIMMIE	JOSHED	JUMBLE
IRONIC	JACANA	JEANNE	JIMMYS	JOSHER	JUMPED
IRVING	JACKAL	JEEING	JINGAL	JOSHES	JUMPER
IRVINS	JACKED	JEERED	JINGLE	JOSHUA	JUNCOS
IRWINS	JACKET	JEERER	JINGLY	JOSIAH	JUNEAU
******	JACKIE	JEJUNE	JINKED	JOSIAS	JUNGLE
IS----	JACKYS	JEKYLL	JINKER	JOSIEA	JUNGLY
******	JACOBS	JELLED	JINNEE	JOSSES	JUNIOR
ISAACS	JADING	JEMIMA	JINNYS	JOSTLE	JUNIUS
ISABEL	JADISH	JENNET	JINXED	JOTHAM	JUNKED
ISADOR	JAEGER	JENNYS	JINXES	JOTTED	JUNKER
ISAIAH	JAGGED	JERBOA	JITNEY	JOTTER	JUNKET
ISATIN	JAGUAR	JEREED	JITTER	JOULES	JUNKIE
ISCHIA	JAILED	JEREMY	JIVING	JOUNCE	JUNTAS
ISEULT	JAILER	JERKED	******	JOUSTS	JUPONS
ISHTAR	JAILOR	JERKIN	**JO----**	JOVIAL	JURANT
ISIDOR	JAINAS	JEROME	******	JOVIAN	JURATS
ISLAND	JAIPUR	JERRYS	JOANNA	JOYCES	JURELS
ISLETS	JALOPS	JERSEY	JOANNE	JOYFUL	JURIES
ISLING	JALOPY	JERVIS	JOBBED	JOYING	JURIST
ISOBAR	JAMIES	JESSED	JOBBER	JOYOUS	JURORS
ISOBEL	JAMJAR	JESSES	JOCKEY	******	JUSTIN
ISOGON	JAMMED	JESSIE	JOCKOS	**JU----**	JUSTLY
ISOHEL	JANETS	JESTED	JOCOSE	******	JUSTUS
ISOLDE	JANGLE	JESTER	JOCUND	JUAREZ	JUTISH
				JUBBAH	JUTTED

******	KEDDAH	******	KITTLE	******	LACUNA
KA----	KEDGED	**KI----**	KITTYS	**KR----**	LADDER
******	KEDGES	******	******	******	LADDIE
KAASES	KEDRON	KIBBLE	**KL----**	KRAALS	LADIES
KABAKA	KEELED	KIBEIS	******	KRAITS	LADING
KABALA	KEENED	KIBITZ	KLAXON	KRAKEN	LADINO
KABAYA	KEENER	KIBLAH	******	KRISES	LADLED
KABIKI	KEENLY	KIBOSH	**KN----**	KRONEN	LADLER
KABOBS	KEEPER	KICKED	******	KRONER	LADLES
KABUKI	KEEVES	KICKER	KNACKS	KRONOR	LADOGA
KAFFIR	KEGLER	KIDDED	KNARRY	KRONOS	LAGERS
KAFTAN	KEITHS	KIDDER	KNAVES	KRONUR	LAGGED
KAISER	KELLER	KIDDIE	KNEADS	KRUBIS	LAGGER
KAKAPO	KELOID	KIDNAP	KNEELS	KRUBUT	LAGOON
KALIAN	KELPIE	KIDNEY	KNELLS	******	LAGUNE
KALIUM	KELSON	KILLED	KNIFED	**KU----**	LAHORE
KALMIA	KELTIC	KILLER	KNIFES	******	LAIRDS
KALONG	KELVIN	KILMER	KNIGHT	KUCHEN	LAIRED
KALPAK	KENDAL	KILTED	KNIVES	KULAKS	LAKERS
KAMALA	KENITE	KILTER	KNOBBY	KULTUR	LAKIER
KAMIKS	KENNED	KILTIE	KNOCKS	KUMISS	LAKING
KAMSIN	KENNEL	KIMONO	KNOLLS	KUMMEL	LALLED
KANAKA	KENNIE	KINASE	KNOSPS	KUWAIT	LAMBDA
KANSAN	KENNYS	KINDER	KNOTTY	******	LAMBED
KANSAS	KEPLER	KINDLE	KNOUTS	**KY----**	LAMBIE
KAOLIN	KERALA	KINDLY	KNOWER	******	LAMECH
KAPOKS	KERATO	KINESI	KNURLS	KYUSHU	LAMEDS
KAPPAS	KERBED	KINETO	KNURLY	******	LAMELY
KARATE	KERMES	KINGED	******	**LA----**	LAMENT
KARATS	KERMIS	KINGLY	******	******	LAMEST
KARENS	KERMIT	KININS	**KO----**	LAAGER	LAMIAE
KARMAS	KERNED	KINKED	******	LABELS	LAMIAS
KARNAK	KERNEL	KINSEY	KOALAS	LABIAL	LAMINA
KARROO	KERRIE	KIOSKS	KOBOLD	LABILE	LAMING
KASPER	KERSEY	KIPPED	KODAKS	LABIUM	LAMMAS
KATHIE	KETENE	KIPPER	KODIAK	LABORS	LAMMED
KATHYS	KETONE	KIRSCH	KOINES	LABOUR	LAMPAD
KATIES	KETOSE	KIRTLE	KOKOMO	LABRET	LAMPAS
KATION	KETTLE	KISLEW	KONRAD	LABRUM	LAMPED
KAURIS	KEVELS	KISMET	KOODOO	LACHES	LANAIS
KAVASS	KEVINS	KISSED	KOPECK	LACIAL	LANATE
KAYAKS	KEWPIE	KISSER	KOPEKS	LACIER	LANCED
KAYOED	KEYING	KISSES	KOPJES	LACILY	LANCER
KAZOOS	KEYNES	KITBAG	KOREAN	LACING	LANCES
******	KEYWAY	KITING	KORUNA	LACKED	LANCET
KE----	******	KITSCH	KORUNY	LACKEY	LANDAU
******	**KH----**	KITTED	KOSHER	LACTAM	LANDED
KECKED	******	KITTEN	KOWTOW	LACTIC	LANDER
KECKLE	KHAKIS				
	KHYBER				

LANGUR	LATEEN	LEADEN	LENITY	LIBBYS	LIMPET
LANKER	LATELY	LEADER	LENNYS	LIBELS	LIMPID
LANKLY	LATENT	LEADIN	LENORE	LIBIDO	LIMPLY
LANNER	LATERA	LEAFED	LENSES	LIBRAE	LIMULI
LANOSE	LATEST	LEAGUE	LENTEN	LIBRAS	LINAGE
LANUGO	LATHED	LEAKED	LENTIL	LIBYAN	LINDAS
LAOTSE	LATHER	LEANED	LENTOS	LICHEE	LINDEN
LAPARO	LATHES	LEANER	LEONAS	LICHEN	LINEAL
LAPDOG	LATINS	LEANLY	LEONIE	LICKED	LINEAR
LAPELS	LATISH	LEANTO	LEPERS	LICTOR	LINENS
LAPFUL	LATRIA	LEAPED	LEPIDO	LIDDED	LINERS
LAPINS	LATTEN	LEAPER	LEPSIA	LIEBIG	LINEUP
LAPPED	LATTER	LEARNS	LEPTON	LIEDER	LINGAM
LAPPER	LATVIA	LEARNT	LEROYS	LIEGES	LINGAS
LAPPET	LAUDED	LEASED	LESBOS	LIERNE	LINGER
LAPSED	LAUDER	LEASES	LESION	LIFERS	LINGUA
LAPSER	LAUGHS	LEAVED	LESLEY	LIFTED	LINIER
LAPSES	LAUNCE	LEAVEN	LESLIE	LIFTER	LINING
LAPSUS	LAUNCH	LEAVER	LESSEE	LIGAND	LINKED
LARDED	LAURAE	LEAVES	LESSEN	LIGATE	LINNET
LARDER	LAURAS	LECHER	LESSER	LIGHTS	LINTEL
LARDON	LAUREL	LECTOR	LESSON	LIGNIN	LINTER
LAREDO	LAURIE	LEDGER	LESSOR	LIGNUM	LIONEL
LARGER	LAVABO	LEDGES	LESTER	LIGULA	LIPASE
LARGOS	LAVAGE	LEERED	LETHAL	LIGULE	LIPIDS
LARIAT	LAVERS	LEEWAY	LETTER	LIGURE	LIPOID
LARINE	LAVING	LEGACY	LETUPS	LIKELY	LIPOMA
LARKED	LAVISH	LEGATE	LEUDES	LIKENS	LIPPED
LARKER	LAWFUL	LEGATO	LEVANT	LIKING	LIPPER
LARRUP	LAWING	LEGEND	LEVEES	LILACS	LIQUID
LARRYS	LAWYER	LEGERS	LEVELS	LILIAN	LIQUOR
LARVAE	LAXEST	LEGGED	LEVERS	LILIED	LISBOA
LARVAL	LAXITY	LEGION	LEVIED	LILIES	LISBON
LARYNG	LAYDAY	LEGIST	LEVIER	LILTED	LISPED
LARYNX	LAYERS	LEGMAN	LEVIES	LIMBED	LISPER
LASCAR	LAYING	LEGMEN	LEVITE	LIMBER	LISSOM
LASERS	LAYMAN	LEGREE	LEVITY	LIMBIC	LISTED
LASHED	LAYMEN	LEGUME	LEWDER	LIMBUS	LISTEL
LASHER	LAYOFF	LEHUAS	LEWDLY	LIMENS	LISTEN
LASHES	LAYOUT	LEIGHS	LEYDEN	LIMEYS	LISTER
LASSEN	LAZARS	LEMMAS	******	LIMIER	LITANY
LASSES	LAZIER	LEMNOS	LI----	LIMINA	LITCHI
LASSIE	LAZILY	LEMONS	******	LIMING	LITERS
LASSOS	LAZING	LEMUEL	LIABLE	LIMITS	LITHER
LASTED	LAZULI	LEMURS	LIAISE	LIMNED	LITHIA
LASTER	******	LENAPE	LIANAS	LIMNER	LITHIC
LASTEX	LE----	LENDER	LIANES	LIMPED	LITMUS
LASTLY	LEACHY	LENGTH	LIASED	LIMPER	LITTER
	LEADED				

LITTLE
LIVELY
LIVENS
LIVERS
LIVERY
LIVIAS
LIVIER
LIVING
LIVRES
LIVYER
LIZARD
LIZZIE
LIZZYS
******

LL----
******
LLAMAS
LLANOS
LLOYDS
******

LO----
******
LOADED
LOADER
LOAFED
LOAFER
LOAMED
LOANED
LOATHE
LOAVES
LOBATE
LOBBED
LOBBER
LOBULE
LOCALE
LOCALS
LOCATE
LOCHIA
LOCKED
LOCKER
LOCKET
LOCKUP
LOCOED
LOCUST
LODGED
LODGER
LODGES
LOFTED

LOFTER
LOGGED
LOGGER
LOGGIA
LOGIER
LOGION
LOGJAM
LOITER
LOLITA
LOLLED
LOLLER
LOLLOP
LOMENT
LOMOND
LONDON
LONELY
LONERS
LONGAN
LONGED
LONGER
LOOFAH
LOOING
LOOKED
LOOKER
LOOKIN
LOOMED
LOOPED
LOOPER
LOOSED
LOOSEN
LOOSER
LOOSES
LOOTED
LOOTER
LOPERS
LOPING
LOPPED
LOQUAR
LOQUAT
LORAIN
LORDED
LORDLY
LOREEN
LORENE
LORENZ
LORICA
LORIES
LOSERS

LOSING
LOSSES
LOTAHS
LOTION
LOTTIE
LOUDEN
LOUDER
LOUDLY
LOUGHS
LOUISA
LOUISE
LOUNGE
LOUPES
LOURED
LOUSED
LOUSES
LOUVER
LOUVRE
LOVAGE
LOVEIN
LOVELL
LOVELY
LOVERS
LOVING
LOWBOY
LOWELL
LOWERS
LOWERY
LOWEST
LOWING
LOWKEY
******

LU----
******
LUANDA
LUBBER
LUBECK
LUBLIN
LUCENT
LUCIAN
LUCIAS
LUCIEN
LUCILE
LUCITE
LUCIUS
LUDLOW
LUDWIG
LUELLA

LUETIC
LUFFED
LUGERS
LUGGED
LUGGER
LULLED
LUMBAR
LUMBER
LUMENS
LUMINA
LUMINI
LUMINO
LUMMOX
LUMPED
LUMPEN
LUNACY
LUNATE
LUNETS
LUNGED
LUNGEE
LUNGER
LUNGES
LUNGIS
LUNKER
LUNULA
LUNULE
LUPINE
LURERS
LURING
LURKED
LURKER
LUSHED
LUSHER
LUSHES
LUSTED
LUSTER
LUSTRE
LUTEAL
LUTEUM
LUTHER
LUTING
LUTIST
LUXATE
LUXURY
******

LY----
******
LYCEES
LYCEUM

LYDIAS
LYMPHO
LYNXES
LYRICS
LYRISM
LYRIST
LYSINE
LYSING
LYSINS
LYTTAE
******

MA----
******
MABELS
MACACO
MACAWS
MACERS
MACING
MACKLE
MACLES
MACRON
MACULA
MACULE
MADAME
MADAMS
MADCAP
MADDED
MADDEN
MADDER
MADEUP
MADGES
MADMAN
MADMEN
MADRAS
MADRID
MADURA
MADURO
MAENAD
MAGGIE
MAGGOT
MAGNET
MAGNOX
MAGNUM
MAGOTS
MAGPIE
MAGUEY
MAGYAR
MAHBUB

MAHLER
MAHOUT
MAIDEN
MAIGRE
MAILED
MAILER
MAIMED
MAIMER
MAINLY
MAISIE
MAISON
MAITRE
MAIZES
MAJORS
MAKERS
MAKEUP
MAKING
MALACO
MALADY
MALAGA
MALATE
MALAWI
MALAYA
MALAYS
MALGRE
MALICE
MALIGN
MALINE
MALLED
MALLEE
MALLET
MALLOW
MALORY
MALTED
MALTHA
MAMBAS
MAMBOS
MAMEYS
MAMIES
MAMMAE
MAMMAL
MAMMAS
MAMMET
MAMMON
MANAGE
MANANA
MANCHU

MANDAN	MARIAN	MASTED	******	MELVYN	METAGE
MANDYS	MARIAS	MASTER	ME----	MEMBER	METALS
MANEGE	MARIES	MASTIC	******	MEMOIR	METEOR
MANFUL	MARINA	MATEOS	MEADOW	MEMORY	METERS
MANGER	MARINE	MATEYS	MEAGER	MENACE	METHOD
MANGLE	MARION	MATINE	MEAGRE	MENAGE	METHYL
MANGOS	MARIST	MATING	MEALIE	MENDED	METIER
MANIAC	MARKED	MATINS	MEANER	MENDEL	METING
MANIAS	MARKER	MATRIX	MEANIE	MENDER	METOPE
MANILA	MARKET	MATRON	MEANLY	MENDIP	METRIC
MANIOC	MARKKA	MATTED	MEASLY	MENHIR	METROS
MANITO	MARKUP·	MATTEO	MEATUS	MENIAL	METTLE
MANITU	MARLED	MATTER	MECCAN	MENINX	METUMP
MANNED	MARLIN	MATTES	MECCAS	MENSAL	MEWING
MANNER	MARLOW	MATTIE	MEDALS	MENSES	MEWLED
MANORS	MARMOT	MATURE	MEDDLE	MENTAL	MEXICO
MANQUE	MAROON	MATZOS	MEDIAE	MENTOR	MEZUZA
MANSES	MARQUE	MATZOT	MEDIAL	MEOWED	MEZZOS
MANTAS	MARRED	MAUDES	MEDIAN	MERCER	******
MANTEL	MARRER	MAULED	MEDICI	MERCIA	MI----
MANTES	MARROW	MAULER	MEDICO	MERELY	******
MANTIC	MARSHA	MAUMAU	MEDICS	MEREST	MIASMA
MANTIS	MARSHY	MAUNDS	MEDIUM	MERGED	MIAULS
MANTLE	MARTAS	MAUNDY	MEDLAR	MERGER	MICELL
MANTUA	MARTEN	MAUSER	MEDLEY	MERGES	MICHEL
MANUAL	MARTHA	MAUVES	MEDUSA	MERINO	MICKEY
MANUEL	MARTHE	MAXIMA	MEDWAY	MERITS	MICKLE
MANURE	MARTIN	MAXIMS	MEEKER	MERLES	MICKYS
MAOISM	MARTYR	MAXINE	MEEKLY	MERLIN	MICMAC
MAOIST	MARTYS	MAXIXE	MEETER	MERLON	MICRON
MAORIS	MARVEL	MAYBUG	MEETLY	MERMAN	MIDAIR
MAPLES	MARVIN	MAYDAY	MEGALO	MERMEN	MIDDAY
MAPPED	MASCON	MAYEST	MEGASS	MEROUS	MIDDEN
MAQUIS	MASCOT	MAYFLY	MEGILP	MERSEY	MIDDLE
MARACA	MASERS	MAYHAP	MEGRIM	MERVIN	MIDGES
MARAUD	MASHED	MAYHEM	MEJICO	MESCAL	MIDGET
MARBLE	MASHER	MAYING	MEKONG	MESHED	MIDGUT
MARCEL	MASHES	MAYORS	MELANO	MESHER	MIDRIB
MARCIA	MASHIE	MAYPOP	MELDED	MESHES	MIDWAY
MARCOS	MASKED	MAZERS	MELEES	MESIAL	MIFFED
MARCUS	MASKEG	MAZIER	MELLON	MESIAN	MIGGLE
MARDUK	MASKER	MAZILY	MELLOW	MESMER	MIGHTY
MARGAY	MASONS	MAZING	MELODY	MESNES	MIGNON
MARGES	MASORA	MAZUMA	MELONS	MESONS	MIGUEL
MARGIE	MASQUE	******	MELTED	MESSED	MIKADO
MARGIN	MASSED	MC----	MELTER	MESSES	MIKLOS
MARGOS	MASSES	******	MELTON	MESSRS	MILADY
MARGOT	MASSIF	MCCOYS	MELVIN	MESTEE	MILAGE

MILDEN	MIRIAM	MODIFY	MONTHS	MOSTLY	MUFFLE
MILDER	MIRING	MODISH	MONTYS	MOTELS	MUFTIS
MILDEW	MIRROR	MODULE	MOOING	MOTHER	MUGGAR
MILDLY	MISCUE	MOGULS	MOOLAH	MOTIFS	MUGGED
MILERS	MISDID	MOHAIR	MOOLEY	MOTILE	MUGGER
MILIEU	MISERE	MOHAVE	MOONED	MOTION	MUGGUR
MILIUM	MISERS	MOHAWK	MOORED	MOTIVE	MUKLUK
MILKED	MISERY	MOHOCK	MOOTED	MOTLEY	MULCTS
MILKER	MISFIT	MOHOLE	MOOTER	MOTMOT	MULISH
MILLAY	MISHAP	MOHURS	MOPERS	MOTORS	MULLAH
MILLED	MISKAL	MOIETY	MOPING	MOTTLE	MULLED
MILLER	MISLAY	MOILED	MOPISH	MOTTOS	MULLEN
MILLET	MISLED	MOILER	MOPOKE	MOULDS	MULLER
MILLIE	MISSAL	MOIRAS	MOPPED	MOULDY	MULLET
MILLYS	MISSED	MOISHE	MOPPET	MOULIN	MULLEY
MILORD	MISSEL	MOJAVE	MORALE	MOULTS	MUMBLE
MILTED	MISSES	MOLARS	MORALS	MOUNTS	MUMMED
MILTER	MISSIS	MOLDED	MORASS	MOUNTY	MUMMER
MILTON	MISSUS	MOLDER	MORAYS	MOURNS	MUNICH
MIMERS	MISTED	MOLEST	MORBID	MOUSED	MURALS
MIMICS	MISTER	MOLIES	MOREAU	MOUSER	MURDER
MIMING	MISTLE	MOLINE	MOREEN	MOUSES	MURIEL
MIMOSA	MISUSE	MOLLAH	MORELS	MOUSSE	MURINE
MINCED	MITERS	MOLLIE	MORGAN	MOUTHS	MURMUR
MINCER	MITRAL	MOLLYS	MORGEN	MOUTHY	MURRAY
MINCES	MITRED	MOLOCH	MORGUE	MOUTON	MURRES
MINDED	MITTEN	MOLTED	MORION	MOVERS	MURREY
MINDER	MIXERS	MOLTEN	MORLEY	MOVIES	MUSCAE
MINERS	MIXING	MOLTER	MORMON	MOVING	MUSCAT
MINGLE	MIXUPS	MOLTKE	MORONS	MOWERS	MUSCLE
MINIFY	MIZZEN	MOMENT	MOROSE	MOWING	MUSEUM
MINIMA	MIZZLE	MOMISM	MORPHO	MOZART	MUSHED
MINIMS	******	MONACO	MORRIS	******	MUSHER
MINING	MO----	MONADS	MORROS	MU----	MUSHES
MINION	******	MONDAY	MORROW	******	MUSING
MINIUM	MOANED	MONEYS	MORSEL	MUCKED	MUSKEG
MINNIE	MOATED	MONGER	MORTAL	MUCKER	MUSKET
MINNOW	MOBBED	MONGOL	MORTAR	MUCKLE	MUSKIT
MINOAN	MOBBER	MONGST	MORTON	MUCOID	MUSKOX
MINORS	MOBCAP	MONICA	MORTYS	MUCOSA	MUSLIM
MINTED	MOBILE	MONIED	MORULA	MUCOSE	MUSLIN
MINTER	MOBIUS	MONIES	MOSAIC	MUCOUS	MUSSED
MINUET	MOCKED	MONISM	MOSCOW	MUDCAP	MUSSEL
MINUTE	MOCKER	MONIST	MOSEYS	MUDDED	MUSSES
MINXES	MOCKUP	MONKEY	MOSLEM	MUDDER	MUSTEE
MIOSIS	MODELS	MONODY	MOSLEY	MUDDLE	MUSTER
MIOTIC	MODERN	MONROE	MOSQUE	MUFFED	MUSTNT
MIRAGE	MODEST	MONTES	MOSSES	MUFFIN	MUTANT

MUTATE
MUTING
MUTINY
MUTISM
MUTTER
MUTTON
MUTUAL
MUTULE
MUUMUU
MUZHIK
MUZZLE
******

MY----
******

MYCETE
MYELIN
MYOPES
MYOPIA
MYOPIC
MYOSIN
MYOSIS
MYRIAD
MYRICA
MYRMEC
MYRNAS
MYRTLE
MYSELF
MYSTIC
MYTHIC
MYTHOI
MYTHOS
MYXOMA
******

NA----
******

NABBED
NABOBS
NADINE
NADIRS
NAEVUS
NAGANA
NAGGED
NAGGER
NAGOYA
NAHUMS
NAIADS
NAILED
NAMELY

NAMERS
NAMING
NANCYS
NANISM
NANTES
NAOMIS
NAOSES
NAPALM
NAPERY
NAPIER
NAPKIN
NAPLES
NAPPED
NAPPER
NAPPES
NAPPIE
NARIAL
NARINE
NARKED
NARROW
NARWAL
NASALS
NASHUA
NASIAL
NASION
NASSAU
NASSER
NASTIC
NATANT
NATHAN
NATION
NATIVE
NATRON
NATTER
NATURE
NAUGHT
NAUSEA
NAUTCH
NAVAHO
NAVAJO
NAVELS
NAVIES
NAWABS
NAZIFY
NAZISM
******

NE----
******

NEARBY
NEARED

NEARER
NEARLY
NEATEN
NEATER
NEATLY
NEBULA
NECKED
NECTAR
NEEDED
NEEDER
NEEDLE
NEGATE
NEIGHS
NEKTON
NELLIE
NELLYS
NELSON
NEMATO
NEPHEW
NEPHRO
NEREID
NEREIS
NEROLI
NERVED
NERVES
NESSUS
NESTED
NESTLE
NESTOR
NETHER
NETTED
NETTIE
NETTLE
NEUMES
NEURAL
NEURON
NEUTER
NEVADA
NEVILE
NEVILL
NEVOID
NEVSKI
NEWARK
NEWELS
NEWEST
NEWTON
******

NI----
******

NIACIN
NIBBED

NIBBLE
NICELY
NICENE
NICEST
NICETY
NICHED
NICHES
NICKED
NICKEL
NICKER
NICKYS
NICOLE
NIDIFY
NIDING
NIECES
NIELLI
NIELLO
NIGELS
NIGGER
NIGGLE
NIGHER
NIGHTS
NIGHTY
NILGAI
NIMBLE
NIMBLY
NIMBUS
NIMITZ
NIMROD
NINETY
NINTHS
NIOBIC
NIPPED
NIPPER
NIPPLE
NIPPON
NISEIS
NITRIC
NITRID
NITWIT
NIXIES
NIXING
******

NO----
******

NOBALL
NOBBED
NOBBLE

NOBLER
NOBODY
NOCENT
NOCKED
NODDED
NODDER
NODDLE
NODOSE
NODULE
NOELLE
NOESIS
NOETIC
NOGGIN
NOGOOD
NOISED
NOISES
NOMADS
NOMISM
NOMURA
NONAGE
NONARY
NONCOM
NONEGO
NOODLE
NOOSED
NOOSES
NOPALS
NORDIC
NOREEN
NORIAS
NORMAL
NORMAN
NORMAS
NORNIR
NORRIS
NORWAY
NOSHED
NOSHOW
NOSIER
NOSILY
NOSING
NOSTIC
NOTARY
NOTERS
NOTICE
NOTIFY
NOTING
NOTION

NOUGAT
NOUGHT
NOUNAL
NOVELS
NOVENA
NOVICE
NOWAYS
NOWISE
NOZZLE
******

NU----
******

NUANCE
NUBBIN
NUBBLE
NUBBLY
NUBIAN
NUBIAS
NUBILE
NUCHAE
NUCLEI
NUDELY
NUDGED
NUDGES
NUDISM
NUDIST
NUDITY
NUDNIK
NUGGET
NULLAH
NUMBED
NUMBER
NUMBLY
NUMINA
NUNCIO
NURSED
NURSER
NURSES
NUTLET
NUTMEG
NUTRIA
NUTTED
NUTTER
NUZZLE
******

NY----
******

NYLONS
NYMPHA

NYMPHO	OCTAVE	*****	ONIONS	ORANGS	ORWELL
NYMPHS	OCTAVO	OI----	ONIONY	ORATED	ORYXES
*****	OCTETS	*****	ONLINE	ORATES	*****
OA----	OCTOPI	OILCAN	ONRUSH	ORATOR	OS----
*****	OCTROI	OILERS	ONSETS	ORBING	*****
OAFISH	OCULAR	OILIER	ONUSES	ORBITS	OSBERT
OAKLEY	*****	OILILY	ONWARD	ORCEIN	OSBORN
OARING	OD----	OILING	*****	ORCHID	OSCANS
*****	*****	*****	OO----	ORCHIL	OSCARS
OB----	ODDEST	OJ----	*****	ORCHIO	OSCINE
*****	ODDITY	*****	OOCYTE	ORCHIS	OSCULE
OBELUS	ODDJOB	OJIBWA	OODLES	ORDAIN	OSIERS
OBERON	ODESSA	*****	OOLITE	ORDEAL	OSIRIS
OBEYED	ODETTE	OK----	OOLOGY	ORDERS	OSMIUM
OBEYER	ODIOUS	*****	OOLONG	ORDURE	OSMOND
OBIISM	ODONTO	OKAPIS	OOMIAK	OREADS	OSMOSE
OBITER	ODYNIA	OKAYED	OOPHOR	OREGAN	OSMUND
OBJECT	*****	*****	OOZIER	OREGON	OSPREY
OBLAST	OE----	OL----	OOZILY	OREIDE	OSSEIN
OBLATE	*****	*****	OOZING	ORGANA	OSSIAN
OBLIGE	OEDEMA	OLDEST	*****	ORGANO	OSSIFY
OBLONG	OEPEMA	OLDHAM	OP----	ORGANS	OSTEAL
OBOIST	OEUVRE	OLDISH	*****	ORGASM	OSTEND
OBOLUS	*****	OLEATE	OPAQUE	ORGEAT	OSTLER
OBSESS	OF----	OLEFIN	OPENED	ORGIES	OSWALD
OBTAIN	*****	OLIVER	OPENER	ORIBIS	OSWEGO
OBTECT	OFFDAY	OLIVES	OPENLY	ORIELS	*****
OBTEST	OFFEND	OLIVIA	OPERAS	ORIENT	OT----
OBTUND	OFFERS	OLLIES	OPHITE	ORIGAN	*****
OBTUSE	OFFICE	*****	OPIATE	ORIGEN	OTHERS
OBVERT	OFFING	OM----	OPINED	ORIGIN	OTIOSE
*****	OFFISH	*****	OPINES	ORIOLE	OTITIS
OC----	OFFSET	OMASUM	OPORTO	ORISON	OTTAVA
*****	*****	OMEGAS	OPPOSE	ORKNEY	OTTAWA
OCASEY	OG----	OMELET	OPPUGN	ORLOPS	OTTERS
OCCULT	*****	OMENTA	OPTANT	ORMERS	OTTOWA
OCCUPY	OGDOAD	OMNIUM	OPTICS	ORMOLU	*****
OCCURS	OGIVAL	*****	OPTIMA	ORMUZD	OU----
OCEANS	OGIVES	ON----	OPTIME	ORNATE	*****
OCELLI	OGLERS	*****	OPTING	ORNERY	OUNCES
OCELOT	OGLING	ONAGER	OPTION	ORNITH	OUSELS
OCHERS	OGRESS	ONAGRI	*****	OROIDE	OUSTED
OCHERY	OGRISH	ONEIDA	OR----	ORPHAN	OUSTER
OCLOCK	*****	ONEILL	*****	ORPHIC	OUTBID
OCREAE	OH----	ONEIRO	ORACHS	ORPINE	OUTCRY
OCTADS	*****	ONEOFF	ORACLE	ORPINS	OUTDID
OCTANE	OHENRY	ONEWAY	ORALLY	ORRERY	OUTERS
OCTANT	OHIOAN	ONFALL	ORANGE	ORRICE	OUTFIT
	OHMAGE				

PELTER	PERUKE	PHONIA	PIGGIE	PINTER	PLAGIO
PELTRY	PERUSE	PHONIC	PIGGIN	PINTLE	PLAGUE
PELVES	PESACH	PHOOEY	PIGLET	PINTOS	PLAGUY
PELVIC	PESADE	PHOSPH	PIGNUS	PINUPS	PLAICE
PELVIS	PESETA	PHOTIC	PIGNUT	PINXIT	PLAIDS
PENCEL	PESTER	PHOTON	PIGPEN	PIPAGE	PLAINS
PENCIL	PESTLE	PHOTOS	PIGSTY	PIPERS	PLAINT
PENDED	PETALS	PHRASE	PIKERS	PIPETS	PLAITS
PENGOS	PETARD	PHRENO	PIKING	PIPIER	PLANAR
PENIAL	PETERS	PHYLAE	PILAFF	PIPING	PLANCH
PENILE	PETITE	PHYLLO	PILAFS	PIPITS	PLANCK
PENMAN	PETREL	PHYLUM	PILATE	PIPKIN	PLANED
PENMEN	PETRIE	PHYSIC	PILEUM	PIPPED	PLANER
PENNAE	PETROL	PHYSIO	PILEUP	PIPPIN	PLANES
PENNED	PETTED	PHYTIN	PILEUS	PIQUED	PLANET
PENNER	PETULA	******	PILFER	PIQUES	PLANKS
PENNIA	PEWEES	**PI----**	PILING	PIQUET	PLANTS
PENNIS	PEWITS	******	PILLAR	PIRACY	PLAQUE
PENNON	PEWTER	PIAFFE	PILLED	PIRANA	PLASHY
PENNYS	PEYOTE	PIANOS	PILLOW	PIRATE	PLASIA
PENPAL	******	PIAZZA	PILOSE	PISCES	PLASIS
PENTAD	**PH----**	PICKAX	PILOTS	PISGAH	PLASMA
PENTUP	******	PICKED	PILOUS	PISHED	PLASMO
PENULT	PHAGIA	PICKER	PILULE	PISHES	PLASTY
PENURY	PHANON	PICKET	PIMPED	PISTIL	PLATAN
PEOPLE	PHAROS	PICKLE	PIMPLE	PISTOL	PLATED
PEORIA	PHASED	PICKUP	PIMPLY	PISTON	PLATEN
PEPLOS	PHASES	PICNIC	PINANG	PITCHY	PLATER
PEPLUM	PHASIA	PICOTS	PINDAR	PITHED	PLATES
PEPLUS	PHASIC	PICRIC	PINDUS	PITIED	PLATTE
PEPPED	PHASIS	PICTOR	PINEAL	PITIES	PLAYAS
PEPPER	PHENOL	PICULS	PINENE	PITMAN	PLAYED
PEPSIN	PHENYL	PIDDLE	PINERY	PITMEN	PLAYER
PEPTIC	PHIALS	PIDGIN	PINGED	PITONS	PLAZAS
PEQUOD	PHILIA	PIECED	PINGOS	PIVOTS	PLEACH
PEQUOT	PHILIP	PIECER	PINIER	PIXIES	PLEADS
PERCYS	PHILOS	PIECES	PINIES	PIZZAS	PLEASE
PERILS	PHIPPS	PIEMAN	PINING	******	PLEATS
PERIOD	PHLEBO	PIEMEN	PINION	**PL----**	PLEBES
PERISH	PHLEGM	PIENAL	PINITE	******	PLEDGE
PERKED	PHLOEM	PIERCE	PINKED	PLACED	PLEGIA
PERMED	PHOBIA	PIERRE	PINKIE	PLACER	PLEIAD
PERMIT	PHOBIC	PIERUS	PINNAE	PLACES	PLENTY
PERRON	PHOCIS	PIETER	PINNAL	PLACET	PLENUM
PERRYS	PHOEBE	PIETRO	PINNED	PLACID	PLEURA
PERSIA	PHONED	PIFFLE	PINNER	PLACKS	PLEURO
PERSON	PHONES	PIGEON	PINOLE	PLAGAL	PLEXOR
PERTLY	PHONEY	PIGGED	PINONS	PLAGIO	PLEXUS

PLIANT	POINTE	POOLED	POTTER	PREVUE	PROSER
PLICAE	POINTS	POOPED	POTTLE	PREWAR	PROSES
PLIERS	POINTY	POORER	POTTOS	PREYED	PROSIT
PLIGHT	POISED	POORLY	POUCHY	PREYER	PROTON
PLINTH	POISES	POPERY	POULTS	PRICED	PROUST
PLOUGH	POISON	POPGUN	POUNCE	PRICES	PROVED
PLOVER	POKERS	POPISH	POUNDS	PRICKS	PROVEN
PLOWED	POKIER	POPLAR	POURED	PRIDED	PROVER
PLOWER	POKIES	POPLIN	POURER	PRIDES	PROVES
PLUCKS	POKING	POPPED	POUSTO	PRIERS	PROWLS
PLUCKY	POLACK	POPPER	POUTED	PRIEST	PRUDES
PLUGIN	POLAND	POPPET	POUTER	PRIMAL	PRUNED
PLUMBO	POLDER	POPPLE	POWDER	PRIMED	PRUNER
PLUMBS	POLEAX	POPPYS	POWELL	PRIMER	PRUNES
PLUMED	POLICE	PORING	POWERS	PRIMES	PRYERS
PLUMES	POLICY	PORKER	POWTER	PRIMLY	PRYING
PLUMMY	POLING	POROUS	POWWOW	PRIMPS	******
PLUMPS	POLISH	PORTAL	POYOUS	PRIMUS	PS----
PLUNGE	POLITE	PORTED	******	PRINCE	******
PLUNKS	POLITY	PORTER	PR----	PRINKS	PSALMS
PLURAL	POLKAS	PORTIA	******	PRINTS	PSEUDO
PLUSES	POLLED	PORTLY	PRAGUE	PRIORS	PSHAWS
PLUSHY	POLLEE	POSADA	PRAISE	PRIORY	PSYCHE
PLUTUS	POLLEN	POSERS	PRANCE	PRISMS	PSYCHO
PLUVIO	POLLER	POSEUR	PRANKS	PRISON	******
PLYING	POLLEX	POSHLY	PRATED	PRISSY	PT----
******	POLLUX	POSIES	PRATER	PRIVET	******
PN----	POLLYS	POSING	PRATES	PRIZED	PTISAN
******	POLYPS	POSITS	PRAVDA	PRIZER	PTOSIS
PNEUMA	POMACE	POSSES	PRAWNS	PRIZES	******
PNEUMO	POMADE	POSSET	PRAXIS	PROBED	PU----
******	POMELO	POSSUM	PRAYED	PROBER	******
PO----	POMMEL	POSTAL	PRAYER	PROBES	PUBLIC
******	POMONA	POSTED	PREACH	PROCNE	PUCKER
POACHY	POMPEY	POSTER	PRECIS	PROCTO	PUDDLE
POCKET	POMPOM	POTAGE	PREENS	PROEMS	PUDDLY
PODDED	POMPON	POTALE	PREFAB	PROFIT	PUEBLO
PODIUM	PONCHO	POTASH	PREFER	PROJET	PUFFED
PODOUS	PONDER	POTATO	PREFIX	PROLEG	PUFFER
PODSOL	PONENT	POTBOY	PRELIM	PROLIX	PUFFIN
PODUNK	PONGEE	POTEEN	PREMED	PROMPT	PUGGED
PODZOL	PONIED	POTENT	PREPAY	PRONGS	PUGGRY
POETIC	PONIES	POTHER	PRESAS	PRONTO	PUGREE
POETRY	PONTES	POTION	PRESTO	PROOFS	PUISNE
POGIES	PONTIC	POTMAN	PRETER	PROPEL	PUKING
POGROM	PONTIL	POTPIE	PRETOR	PROPER	PULERS
POILUS	PONTON	POTSIE	PRETTY	PROPYL	PULING
POINDS	POODLE	POTTED	PRESAS	PROSED	PULLED

PULLER	PURLIN	******	QUIPUS	RADOME	RANEES
PULLET	PURPLE	QU----	QUIRED	RADULA	RANGED
PULLEY	PURRED	******	QUIRES	RAFFIA	RANGER
PULLIN	PURSED	QUACKS	QUIRKS	RAFFLE	RANGES
PULPED	PURSER	QUADRI	QUIRTS	RAFTED	RANKED
PULPER	PURSES	QUAERE	QUITCH	RAFTER	RANKER
PULPIT	PURSUE	QUAFFS	QUIVER	RAGBAG	RANKLE
PULQUE	PURVEY	QUAGGA	QUOINS	RAGDAY	RANKLY
PULSAR	PUSHED	QUAGGY	QUOITS	RAGGED	RANSOM
PULSED	PUSHER	QUAHOG	QUORUM	RAGING	RANTED
PULSES	PUSHES	QUAILS	QUOTAS	RAGLAN	RANTER
PUMICE	PUSHTU	QUAINT	QUOTED	RAGMAN	RAOULS
PUMMEL	PUSHUP	QUAKED	QUOTER	RAGMEN	RAPHAE
PUMPED	PUSSES	QUAKER	QUOTES	RAGOUT	RAPHIS
PUMPER	PUSSEY	QUAKES	QUOTHA	RAGTAG	RAPIDS
PUNCHY	PUSSLY	QUALMS	******	RAIDED	RAPIER
PUNDIT	PUTLOG	QUALMY	RA----	RAIDER	RAPINE
PUNIER	PUTNAM	QUANTA	******	RAILED	RAPING
PUNILY	PUTOFF	QUANTS	RABBET	RAINED	RAPIST
PUNISH	PUTONS	QUAPAW	RABBIN	RAISED	RAPPED
PUNJAB	PUTOUT	QUARKS	RABBIS	RAISER	RAPPEE
PUNKAS	PUTPUT	QUARRY	RABBIT	RAISES	RAPPEL
PUNNED	PUTRID	QUARTE	RABBLE	RAISIN	RAPPER
PUNNER	PUTSCH	QUARTO	RABIES	RAJABS	RAPTLY
PUNTED	PUTTED	QUARTS	RACEME	RAJAHS	RAPTOR
PUNTER	PUTTEE	QUARTZ	RACERS	RAJPUT	RAREFY
PUNTOS	PUTTER	QUASAR	RACHEL	RAKERS	RARELY
PUPATE	PUZZLE	QUATRE	RACHIS	RAKING	RAREST
PUPILS	******	QUAVER	RACIAL	RAKISH	RARING
PUPPED	PY----	QUEANS	RACIER	RALPHS	RARITY
PUPPET	******	QUEASY	RACILY	RAMBLE	RASCAL
PURANA	PYEMIA	QUEBEC	RACINE	RAMIES	RASHER
PURDAH	PYEMIC	QUEENS	RACING	RAMIFY	RASHES
PUREED	PYJAMA	QUEERS	RACISM	RAMJET	RASHLY
PUREES	PYKNIC	QUELLS	RACIST	RAMMED	RASPED
PURELY	PYLONS	QUENCH	RACKED	RAMMER	RASPER
PUREST	PYOSIS	QUERNS	RACKER	RAMONA	RASTER
PURFLE	PYRANS	QUESTS	RACKET	RAMOSE	RATALS
PURGED	PYRENE	QUEUED	RACOON	RAMOUS	RATELS
PURGER	PYRITE	QUEUES	RADARS	RAMPED	RATERS
PURGES	PYRONE	QUEZON	RADDLE	RAMROD	RATHER
PURIFY	PYROPE	QUILLS	RADIAL	RAMSON	RATIFY
PURINE	PYRRHA	QUILTS	RADIAN	RANCHO	RATINE
PURISM	PYTHIA	QUINCE	RADIOS	RANCID	RATING
PURIST	PYTHIC	QUINCY	RADISH	RANCOR	RATION
PURITY	PYTHON	QUINIC	RADIUM	RANDAL	RATIOS
PURLED	PYURIA	QUINSY	RADIUS	RANDAN	RATITE
PURLER	PYXIES	QUINTS	RADNOR	RANDOM	RATLIN

RATOON	REBILL	REECHO	RELAYS	REPEAT	REUBEN
RATTAN	REBORE	REEDED	RELENT	REPELS	REVAMP
RATTED	REBORN	REEDIT	RELICS	REPENT	REVEAL
RATTEN	REBOZO	REEFED	RELICT	REPINE	REVELS
RATTER	REBUFF	REEFER	RELIED	REPLAY	REVERE
RATTLE	REBUKE	REEKED	RELIEF	REPORT	REVERS
RAVAGE	REBUTS	REEKER	RELIER	REPOSE	REVERT
RAVELS	RECALL	REELED	RELIES	REPUTE	REVEST
RAVENS	RECANT	REELER	RELINE	RERUNS	REVETS
RAVERS	RECAPS	REEVED	RELISH	RESALE	REVIEW
RAVINE	RECAST	REEVES	RELIVE	RESCUE	REVILE
RAVING	RECEDE	REFACE	RELOAD	RESEAT	REVISE
RAVISH	RECENT	REFERS	REMADE	RESEAU	REVIVE
RAWEST	RECEPT	REFILL	REMAIN	RESECT	REVOKE
RAWISH	RECESS	REFINE	REMAKE	RESEDA	REVOLT
RAYAHS	RECIPE	REFITS	REMAND	RESELL	REVUES
RAYING	RECITE	REFLET	REMANS	RESEND	REVVED
RAYONS	RECKON	REFLEX	REMARK	RESENT	REWARD
RAZEED	RECOIL	REFLUX	REMEDY	RESETS	REWIND
RAZEES	RECORD	REFOOT	REMIND	RESIDE	REWORD
RAZING	RECOUP	REFORM	REMISE	RESIGN	******
RAZORS	RECTAL	REFUEL	REMISS	RESILE	RH----
RAZZED	RECTOR	REFUGE	REMITS	RESINS	******
RAZZES	RECTOS	REFUND	REMORA	RESIST	RHEIMS
RAZZIA	RECTUM	REFUSE	REMOTE	RESOLD	RHESUS
******	RECTUS	REFUTE	REMOVE	RESOLE	RHETOR
RE----	RECURS	REGAIN	REMUDA	RESORB	RHEUMY
******	RECUSE	REGALE	RENDED	RESORT	RHINAL
REACTS	REDACT	REGARD	RENDER	RESTED	RHINOS
READER	REDANS	REGENT	RENEES	RESTER	RHIZIC
REALES	REDBAY	REGGIE	RENEGE	RESULT	RHODAS
REALLY	REDBUD	REGIME	RENEWS	RESUME	RHODES
REALMS	REDBUG	REGINA	RENNET	RETAIL	RHODIC
REALTY	REDCAP	REGION	RENNIN	RETAIN	RHOMBI
REAMED	REDDEN	REGIUS	RENOIR	RETAKE	RHUMBA
REAMER	REDDER	REGLET	RENOWN	RETARD	RHUMBS
REAPED	REDDLE	REGNAL	RENTAL	RETELL	RHYMED
REAPER	REDDOG	REGRET	RENTED	RETENE	RHYMER
REARED	REDEEM	REHASH	RENTER	RETINA	RHYMES
REARER	REDEYE	REHEAR	RENTES	RETIRE	RHYTHM
REARMS	REDFIN	REHEAT	REOPEN	RETOLD	******
REASON	REDGUM	REICHS	REPAID	RETOOK	RI----
REAVOW	REDHOT	REIGNS	REPAIR	RETOOL	******
REBATE	REDOES	REINED	REPAND	RETORT	RIALTO
REBATO	REDONE	REJECT	REPASS	RETROD	RIATAS
REBECK	REDOWA	REJOIN	REPAST	RETTED	RIBALD
REBECS	REDTOP	RELAID	REPAYS	RETURN	RIBAND
REBELS	REDUCE	RELATE	REPEAL	RETUSE	RIBBED

RIBBON	RIOTER	ROCHET	ROQUET	******	RUNONS
RIBOSE	RIPELY	ROCKED	ROSARY	**RU----**	RUNOUT
RICERS	RIPENS	ROCKER	ROSCOE	******	RUNWAY
RICHER	RIPEST	ROCKET	ROSEAL	RUBACE	RUNYON
RICHES	RIPLEY	ROCKNE	ROSIER	RUBATO	RUPEES
RICHIE	RIPOFF	ROCOCO	ROSILY	RUBBED	RUPERT
RICHLY	RIPOST	RODDYS	ROSING	RUBBER	RUPIAH
RICING	RIPPED	RODENT	ROSINS	RUBBLE	RUSHED
RICKED	RIPPER	RODEOS	ROSINY	RUBENS	RUSHER
RICKEY	RIPPLE	RODMAN	ROSTER	RUBIES	RUSHES
RICKYS	RIPPLY	RODMEN	ROSTRA	RUBIGO	RUSINE
RICTAL	RIPRAP	RODNEY	ROTARY	RUBLES	RUSKIN
RICTUS	RIPSAW	ROGERS	ROTATE	RUBRIC	RUSSET
RIDDED	RISERS	ROGUED	ROTCHE	RUCHES	RUSSIA
RIDDEN.	RISING	ROGUES	ROTGUT	RUCKED	RUSTED
RIDDLE	RISKED	ROILED	ROTORS	RUCKUS	RUSTIC
RIDENT	RISKER	ROLAND	ROTTED	RUDDER	RUSTLE
RIDERS	RISQUE	ROLLED	ROTTEN	RUDDLE	RUTILE
RIDGED	RITARD	ROLLER	ROTTER	RUDELY	RUTTED
RIDGES	RITTER	ROLLUP	ROTUND	RUDEST	******
RIDING	RITUAL	ROLPHS	ROUBLE	RUEFUL	**RW----**
RIFFLE	RIVALS	ROMAIC	ROUCHE	RUEING	******
RIFLED	RIVERS	ROMANS	ROUGED	RUFFED	RWANDA
RIFLER	RIVETS	ROMANY	ROUGES	RUFFLE	******
RIFLES	RIVING	ROMISH	ROUGHS	RUFOUS	**RY----**
RIFTED	RIYALS	ROMMEL	ROUNDS	RUGATE	******
RIGGED	******	ROMNEY	ROUSED	RUGGED	RYUKYU
RIGGER	**RO----**	ROMOLA	ROUSER	RUGGER	******
RIGHTO	******	ROMPED	ROUSES	RUGOSE	**SA----**
RIGHTS	ROALDS	ROMPER	ROUSTS	RUGOUS	******
RIGORS	ROAMED	ROMULO	ROUTED	RUINED	SABBAT
RIGOUR	ROAMER	RONALD	ROUTER	RUINER	SABEAN
RILING	ROARED	RONDEL	ROUTES	RULERS	SABERS
RILLET	ROARER	RONDOS	ROVERS	RULING	SABINA
RIMERS	ROASTS	RONNIE	ROVING	RUMBAS	SABINE
RIMING	ROBALO	ROOFED	ROWANS	RUMBLE	SABINS
RIMMED	ROBAND	ROOFER	ROWELS	RUMINA	SABLES
RIMMER	ROBBED	ROOKED	ROWENA	RUMMER	SABOTS
RIMOSE	ROBBER	ROOKIE	ROWERS	RUMORS	SABRAS
RIMOUS	ROBBIA	ROOMED	ROWING	RUMOUR	SACHEM
RIMPLE	ROBBIE	ROOMER	ROXANA	RUMPLE	SACHET
RINGED	ROBERT	ROOSTS	ROXANE	RUMPUS	SACKED
RINGER	ROBING	ROOTED	ROYALE	RUNDLE	SACKER
RINKED	ROBINS	ROOTER	ROYALS	RUNINS	SACRAL
RINSED	ROBLES	ROOTLE	******	RUNLET	SACRED
RINSER	ROBOTS	ROPIER	**RR----**	RUNNEL	SACRUM
RINSES	ROBSON	ROPILY	******	RUNNER	SADDEN
RIOTED	ROBUST	ROPING	RRHAGE	RUNOFF	SADDER
			RRHAGY		

SADDLE	SALTER	SARAPE	SAXONY	SCLERO	SCUBAS
SADHUS	SALUKI	SARGON	SAYERS	SCOFFS	SCUFFS
SADIES	SALUTE	SARONG	SAYING	SCOLDS	SCULLS
SADISM	SALVED	SARSAR	******	SCOLEX	SCULPT
SADIST	SALVER	SARTOR	SC----	SCONCE	SCUMMY
SAFARI	SALVES	SARTRE	******	SCONES	SCURFY
SAFELY	SALVIA	SASHAY	SCABBY	SCOOPS	SCURRY
SAFEST	SALVOR	SASHED	SCALAR	SCOOTS	SCURVY
SAFETY	SALVOS	SASHES	SCALDS	SCOPES	SCUTCH
SAGELY	SAMARA	SASINS	SCALED	SCOPUS	SCUTES
SAGEST	SAMBAS	SASSED	SCALER	SCORCH	SCUTUM
SAGGAR	SAMBOS	SASSES	SCALES	SCORED	SCYLLA
SAGGED	SAMBUR	SATANG	SCALPS	SCORER	SCYPHI
SAGGER	SAMIAN	SATARA	SCAMPI	SCORES	SCYPHO
SAGIER	SAMIEL	SATEEN	SCAMPS	SCORIA	SCYTHE
SAHARA	SAMITE	SATING	SCANTY	SCORNS	******
SAHEBS	SAMLET	SATINS	SCAPES	SCOTCH	SE----
SAHIBS	SAMMYS	SATINY	SCARAB	SCOTER	******
SAIGAS	SAMOAN	SATIRE	SCARCE	SCOTIA	SEABEE
SAIGON	SAMPAN	SATORY	SCARED	SCOTTS	SEACOW
SAILED	SAMPLE	SATRAP	SCARER	SCOURS	SEADOG
SAILER	SAMSHU	SATURN	SCARES	SCOUSE	SEALED
SAILOR	SAMSON	SATYRS	SCARFS	SCOUTS	SEALER
SAINTS	SAMUEL	SAUCED	SCARPS	SCOWLS	SEAMAN
SAIPAN	SANDAL	SAUCER	SCATHE	SCRAGS	SEAMED
SAITIC	SANDED	SAUCES	SCATTY	SCRAMS	SEAMEN
SAJOUS	SANDER	SAUGER	SCAUPS	SCRAPE	SEAMER
SAKERS	SANDHI	SAULTS	SCENDS	SCRAPS	SEAMUS
SALAAM	SANDRA	SAUNAS	SCENES	SCRAWL	SEANCE
SALADS	SANDYS	SAUREL	SCENIC	SCREAK	SEAPEN
SALAMI	SANELY	SAURUS	SCENTS	SCREAM	SEARCH
SALARY	SANEST	SAUTES	SCHEMA	SCREED	SEARED
SALIFY	SANGAR	SAVAGE	SCHEME	SCREEN	SEARIN
SALINE	SANGER	SAVANT	SCHICK	SCREWS	SEASON
SALISH	SANGUI	SAVATE	SCHISM	SCREWY	SEATED
SALIVA	SANIES	SAVERS	SCHIST	SCRIBE	SEAWAN
SALLET	SANITY	SAVING	SCHIZO	SCRIED	SEAWAY
SALLOW	SANJAK	SAVINS	SCHMOS	SCRIMP	SEBATS
SALLYS	SANNUP	SAVIOR	SCHOOL	SCRIPS	SECANT
SALMIS	SANSAR	SAVORS	SCHORL	SCRIPT	SECEDE
SALMON	SANSEI	SAVORY	SCHUIT	SCRIVE	SECERN
SALOME	SANTOL	SAVOUR	SCHUSS	SCRODS	SECKEL
SALONS	SAPHAR	SAWERS	SCHWAS	SCROLL	SECOND
SALOON	SAPIEN	SAWFLY	SCILLY	SCROOP	SECPAR
SALOOP	SAPPED	SAWING	SCIONS	SCROTA	SECRET
SALPAS	SAPPER	SAWNEY	SCIPIO	SCRUBS	SECTOR
SALPID	SAPPHO	SAWYER	SCLAFF	SCRUFF	SECUND
SALTED	SARAHS	SAXONS	SCLERA	SCRUMS	SECURE

SEDANS	SENDAL	SESQUI	SHALED	SHERIF	SHOUTS
SEDATE	SENDER	SESTET	SHALES	SHERPA	SHOVED
SEDERS	SENECA	SETOFF	SHAMAN	SHERRY	SHOVEL
SEDGES	SENILE	SETONS	SHAMED	SHEWED	SHOVER
SEDILE	SENIOR	SETOSE	SHAMES	SHEWER	SHOVES
SEDUCE	SENLAC	SETOUS	SHAMMY	SHIELD	SHOWED
SEDUMS	SENNAS	SETOUT	SHAMUS	SHIEST	SHOWER
SEEDED	SENNET	SETTEE	SHANDY	SHIFTS	SHRANK
SEEDER	SENNIT	SETTER	SHANKS	SHIFTY	SHREDS
SEEING	SENORA	SETTLE	SHANTY	SHIISM	SHREWD
SEEKER	SENSED	SETTOS	SHAPED	SHIITE	SHREWS
SEEMED	SENSES	SETUPS	SHAPEN	SHIKAR	SHRIEK
SEEMER	SENSOR	SEURAT	SHAPER	SHILLS	SHRIFT
SEEMLY	SENTRY	SEVENS	SHAPES	SHILOH	SHRIKE
SEEPED	SEPALS	SEVERE	SHARDS	SHIMMY	SHRILL
SEESAW	SEPIAS	SEVERN	SHARED	SHINDY	SHRIMP
SEETHE	SEPOYS	SEVERS	SHARER	SHINED	SHRINE
SEGGAR	SEPSIS	SEWAGE	SHARES	SHINER	SHRINK
SEICHE	SEPTAL	SEWALL	SHARKS	SHINES	SHRIVE
SEINED	SEPTET	SEWARD	SHARON	SHINNY	SHROFF
SEINER	SEPTIC	SEWELL	SHARPS	SHINTO	SHROUD
SEINES	SEPTUM	SEWERS	SHASTA	SHIRES	SHROVE
SEISED	SEQUEL	SEWING	SHAVED	SHIRKS	SHRUBS
SEISIN	SEQUIN	SEXIER	SHAVEN	SHIRRS	SHRUGS
SEISMO	SERACS	SEXILY	SHAVER	SHIRTS	SHRUNK
SEISMS	SERAIS	SEXING	SHAVES	SHIRTY	SHTICK
SEISOR	SERAPE	SEXISM	SHAWLS	SHIVER	SHUCKS
SEIZED	SERAPH	SEXIST	SHAWMS	SHIVES	SHUNTS
SEIZER	SERBIA	SEXPOT	SHEARS	SHOALS	SHUTIN
SEIZES	SERDAB	SEXTAN	SHEATH	SHOALY	SHYEST
SEIZIN	SEREIN	SEXTET	SHEAVE	SHOATS	SHYING
SEIZOR	SERENA	SEXTON	SHEBAT	SHOCKS	******
SEJANT	SERENE	SEXUAL	SHEENS	SHODDY	SI----
SELDOM	SERIAL	******	SHEENY	SHOERS	******
SELECT	SERIES	SH----	SHEEPS	SHOFAR	SIALIC
SELENE	SERIFS	******	SHEERS	SHOGUN	SIBYLS
SELENO	SERINE	SHABBY	SHEETS	SHOJIS	SICILY
SELJUK	SERINS	SHACKO	SHEIKH	SHOOED	SICKED
SELLER	SERMON	SHACKS	SHEIKS	SHOOIN	SICKEN
SELSYN	SEROUS	SHADED	SHEILA	SHOOTS	SICKER
SELVES	SEROWS	SHADES	SHEILD	SHOPPE	SICKLE
SELWYN	SERUMS	SHADOW	SHEKEL	SHORAN	SICKLY
SEMELE	SERVAL	SHAFTS	SHELBY	SHORED	SIDDUR
SEMEME	SERVED	SHAGGY	SHELLS	SHORES	SIDERO
SEMITE	SERVER	SHAKEN	SHELLY	SHORLS	SIDING
SEMPRE	SERVES	SHAKER	SHELTY	SHORTS	SIDLED
SENARY	SERVOS	SHAKES	SHELVE	SHOTES	SIDLER
SENATE	SESAME	SHAKOS	SHERDS	SHOULD	SIDLES

SIDNEY	SIMPLY	SKEINS	SLEAVE	SLUICE	SNAGGY
SIECLE	SINBAD	SKERRY	SLEAZY	SLUING	SNAILS
SIEGED	SINEON	SKETCH	SLEDGE	SLUMMY	SNAKED
SIEGES	SINEWS	SKEWED	SLEEKS	SLUMPS	SNAKES
SIENNA	SINEWY	SKEWER	SLEEKY	SLURPS	SNAPPY
SIERRA	SINFUL	SKIERS	SLEEPS	SLURRY	SNARED
SIESTA	SINGED	SKIFFS	SLEEPY	SLUSHY	SNARER
SIEURS	SINGER	SKIING	SLEETS	SLYEST	SNARES
SIEVED	SINGES	SKILLS	SLEETY	******	SNARLS
SIEVES	SINGLE	SKIMOS	SLEEVE	SM----	SNARLY
SIFTED	SINGLY	SKIMPS	SLEIGH	******	SNATCH
SIFTER	SINKER	SKIMPY	SLEUTH	SMACKS	SNATHE
SIGHED	SINNED	SKINKS	SLEWED	SMALLS	SNATHS
SIGHTS	SINNER	SKINNY	SLICED	SMALTI	SNAZZY
SIGILS	SINTER	SKIRRS	SLICER	SMALTO	SNEAKS
SIGMAS	SIOUAN	SKIRTS	SLICES	SMARMY	SNEAKY
SIGNAL	SIPHON	SKIVED	SLICKS	SMARTS	SNEERS
SIGNED	SIPPED	SKIVER	SLIDER	SMAZES	SNEEZE
SIGNER	SIPPER	SKIVES	SLIDES	SMEARS	SNEEZY
SIGNET	SIPPET	SKIVVY	SLIEST	SMEARY	SNELLS
SIGNOR	SIRDAR	SKOPJE	SLIGHT	SMELLS	SNICKS
SIGRID	SIRENS	SKULKS	SLIMED	SMELLY	SNIFFS
SIKKIM	SIRING	SKULLS	SLIMES	SMELTS	SNIFFY
SILAGE	SIRIUS	SKUNKS	SLIMLY	SMILAX	SNIPED
SILENI	SIRUPS	SKYCAP	SLIMSY	SMILED	SNIPER
SILENT	SIRUPY	SKYING	SLINGS	SMILER	SNIPES
SILICA	SISERA	SKYMAN	SLINKS	SMILES	SNIPPY
SILICO	SISKIN	SKYMEN	SLINKY	SMIRCH	SNITCH
SILKEN	SISTER	SKYWAY	SLIPON	SMIRKS	SNIVEL
SILOED	SITARS	******	SLIPUP	SMITER	SNOBBY
SILTED	SITING	SL----	SLIVER	SMITES	SNOCAT
SILVAE	SITINS	******	SLOGAN	SMITHS	SNOODS
SILVAN	SITTER	SLACKS	SLOOPS	SMITHY	SNOOKS
SILVAS	SIWASH	SLAGGY	SLOPED	SMOCKS	SNOOPS
SILVER	SIXTES	SLAKED	SLOPER	SMOKED	SNOOPY
SILVIA	SIXTHS	SLAKES	SLOPES	SMOKER	SNOOTS
SIMARS	SIZARS	SLALOM	SLOPPY	SMOKES	SNOOTY
SIMIAN	SIZIER	SLANGY	SLOSHY	SMOLTS	SNOOZE
SIMILE	SIZING	SLANTS	SLOTHS	SMOOCH	SNORED
SIMLIN	SIZZLE	SLAPUP	SLOUCH	SMOOTH	SNORER
SIMMER	******	SLATED	SLOUGH	SMUDGE	SNORES
SIMNEL	SK----	SLATER	SLOVAK	SMUDGY	SNORTS
SIMONE	******	SLATES	SLOVEN	SMUGLY	SNOTTY
SIMONS	SKALDS	SLAVED	SLOWED	SMUTCH	SNOUTS
SIMONY	SKATED	SLAVER	SLOWER	SMUTTY	SNOWED
SIMOOM	SKATER	SLAVES	SLOWLY	******	SNUFFS
SIMPER	SKATES	SLAVIC	SLUDGE	SN----	SNUFFY
SIMPLE	SKEANS	SLAYER	SLUDGY	******	SNUGLY
				SNACKS	
				SNAFUS	

******	SOLVES	SOWARS	SPHENO	SPONGY	SQUALL
SO----	SOMALI	SOWERS	SPHERE	SPOOFS	SQUAMA
******	SOMATA	SOWING	SPHERY	SPOOKS	SQUARE
SOAKED	SOMATO	SOZINE	SPHINX	SPOOKY	SQUASH
SOAKER	SOMBER	SOZINS	SPICED	SPOOLS	SQUATS
SOAPED	SOMBRE	******	SPICER	SPOONS	SQUAWK
SOARED	SOMITE	**SP----**	SPICES	SPOONY	SQUAWS
SOARER	SONANT	******	SPIDER	SPOORS	SQUEAK
SOBBED	SONARS	SPACAE	SPIELS	SPORED	SQUEAL
SOBERS	SONATA	SPACED	SPIERS	SPORES	SQUIBS
SOCAGE	SONDER	SPACER	SPIFFY	SPORTS	SQUIDS
SOCCER	SONIAS	SPACES	SPIGOT	SPORTY	SQUILL
SOCIAL	SONNET	SPADED	SPIKED	SPOTTY	SQUINT
SOCKED	SONYAS	SPADER	SPIKES	SPOUSE	SQUIRE
SOCKET	SOONER	SPADES	SPILED	SPOUTS	SQUIRM
SOCLES	SOOTED	SPADIX	SPILES	SPRAGS	SQUIRT
SOCMAN	SOOTHE	SPAHIS	SPILLS	SPRAIN	SQUISH
SOCMEN	SOPHIA	SPAITS	SPILTH	SPRANG	******
SOCRED	SOPHIE	SPALLS	SPINAL	SPRATS	**ST----**
SODDED	SOPPED	SPANKS	SPINEL	SPRAWL	******
SODDEN	SORBET	SPARED	SPINES	SPRAYS	STABLE
SODIUM	SORDID	SPARER	SPINET	SPREAD	STABLY
SODOMY	SORELS	SPARES	SPINNY	SPREES	STACIE
SOEVER	SORELY	SPARGE	SPIRAL	SPRIER	STACKS
SOFFIT	SOREST	SPARKS	SPIREA	SPRIGS	STACTE
SOFTAS	SORGHO	SPARRY	SPIRED	SPRING	STACYS
SOFTEN	SORGOS	SPARSE	SPIRES	SPRINT	STADIA
SOFTER	SORREL	SPARTA	SPIRIT	SPRITE	STAFFS
SOFTLY	SORROW	SPASMS	SPIRTS	SPRITS	STAGED
SOIGNE	SORTED	SPATES	SPITAL	SPROUT	STAGER
SOILED	SORTER	SPATHE	SPITED	SPRUCE	STAGES
SOIREE	SORTIE	SPAVIN	SPITES	SPRUES	STAGEY
SOLACE	SOTHIC	SPAWNS	SPLAKE	SPRUNG	STAGGY
SOLAND	SOTHIS	SPAYED	SPLASH	SPRYER	STAINS
SOLANO	SOTOLS	SPEAKS	SPLATS	SPRYLY	STAIRS
SOLANS	SOUARI	SPEARS	SPLAYS	SPUMED	STAITH
SOLDER	SOUGHS	SPECIE	SPLEEN	SPUMES	STAKED
SOLELY	SOUGHT	SPECKS	SPLENO	SPUNKY	STAKES
SOLEMN	SOULED	SPEECH	SPLICE	SPURGE	STALAG
SOLENT	SOUNDS	SPEEDS	SPLINE	SPURNS	STALED
SOLIDI	SOUPED	SPEEDY	SPLINT	SPURRY	STALER
SOLIDS	SOURCE	SPEISS	SPLITS	SPURTS	STALES
SOLING	SOURED	SPELLS	SPOILS	SPUTUM	STALIN
SOLION	SOURER	SPENDS	SPOILT	SPYING	STALKS
SOLOED	SOURLY	SPERMO	SPOKED	******	STALKY
SOLUTE	SOUSED	SPERRY	SPOKEN	**SQ----**	STALLS
SOLVED	SOUSES	SPEWED	SPOKES	******	STAMEN
SOLVER	SOVIET	SPHENE	SPONGE	SQUABS	STAMIN
				SQUADS	

STAMPS	STELLI	STOKES	STRIAE	STYLUS	SUNBOW
STANCE	STENCH	STOLED	STRICK	STYMIE	SUNDAE
STANCH	STENOG	STOLEN	STRICT	******	SUNDAY
STANDS	STEPAN	STOLES	STRIDE	SU----	SUNDER
STANZA	STEPIN	STOLID	STRIFE	******	SUNDEW
STAPES	STEPPE	STOLON	STRIKE	SUABLE	SUNDOG
STAPLE	STEPUP	STOMAT	STRING	SUBAHS	SUNDRY
STARCH	STEREO	STOMPS	STRIPE	SUBDEB	SUNGOD
STARED	STERES	STONED	STRIPS	SUBDUE	SUNHAT
STARER	STERIC	STONER	STRIPT	SUBITO	SUNKEN
STARES	STERNA	STONES	STRIPY	SUBLET	SUNLIT
STARRY	STERNO	STOOGE	STRIVE	SUBMIT	SUNNAH
STARTS	STERNS	STOOKS	STROBE	SUBORN	SUNNED
STARVE	STEROL	STOOLS	STRODE	SUBTER	SUNSET
STASES	STETHO	STOOPS	STROKE	SUBTLE	SUNTAN
STASIS	STEVEN	STOPED	STROLL	SUBTLY	SUNUPS
STATAL	STEVES	STOPES	STROMA	SUBURB	SUOMIC
STATED	STEVIE	STORAX	STRONG	SUBWAY	SUPERB
STATEN	STEWED	STORED	STROPS	SUCCOR	SUPERS
STATER	STHENO	STORES	STROUD	SUCKED	SUPINE
STATES	STICKS	STOREY	STROVE	SUCKER	SUPPED
STATIC	STICKY	STORKS	STRUCK	SUCKLE	SUPPER
STATOR	STIFLE	STORMS	STRUMA	SUCRES	SUPPLE
STATUE	STIGMA	STORMY	STRUMS	SUDARY	SUPPLY
STATUS	STILES	STOUPS	STRUNG	SUDDEN	SURAHS
STAURO	STILLS	STOUTS	STRUTS	SUEDES	SURELY
STAVED	STILLY	STOVER	STUART	SUFFER	SUREST
STAVES	STILTS	STOVES	STUBBS	SUFFIX	SURETY
STAYED	STINGS	STOWED	STUBBY	SUFISM	SURFED
STAYER	STINGY	STRAFE	STUCCO	SUGARS	SURFER
STEADY	STINKS	STRAIN	STUDIO	SUGARY	SURGED
STEAKS	STINTS	STRAIT	STUFFS	SUITED	SURGER
STEALS	STIPEL	STRAKE	STUFFY	SUITES	SURGES
STEAMS	STIPES	STRAND	STULLS	SUITOR	SURREY
STEAMY	STIRKS	STRAPS	STUMPS	SULCUS	SURTAX
STEEDS	STIRPS	STRASS	STUMPY	SULFUR	SURVEY
STEELS	STITCH	STRATA	STUNTS	SULKED	SUSANS
STEELY	STITHY	STRATH	STUPAS	SULLEN	SUSIES
STEEPS	STIVER	STRATI	STUPES	SULPHA	SUSLIK
STEERS	STOATS	STRAWS	STUPID	SULPHO	SUSSED
STEEVE	STOCKS	STRAWY	STUPOR	SULTAN	SUSSEX
STEFAN	STOCKY	STRAYS	STURDY	SULTRY	SUTLER
STEINS	STODGE	STREAK	STYING	SUMACS	SUTRAS
STELAE	STODGY	STREAM	STYLAR	SUMMED	SUTTEE
STELAR	STOGEY	STREET	STYLED	SUMMER	SUTTON
STELES	STOICS	STRESS	STYLER	SUMMIT	SUTURE
STELIC	STOKED	STREWN	STYLES	SUMMON	******
STELLA	STOKER	STREWS	STYLET	SUMNER	SV----
					******
					SVELTE

******	******	TAILED	TANREC	TAUTOG	TELEGA
SW----	SY----	TAILLE	TAOISM	TAVERN	TELFER
******	******	TAILOR	TAOIST	TAWDRY	TELLER
SWAGED	SYBILS	TAINOS	TAPALO	TAWERS	TELLUS
SWAGES	SYCEES	TAINTS	TAPERS	TAWING	TELSON
SWAILS	SYDNEY	TAIPEI	TAPING	TAXEME	TELUGU
SWAINS	SYLPHS	TAIWAN	TAPIRS	TAXERS	TEMPER
SWALES	SYLPHY	TAKEIN	TAPPED	TAXIED	TEMPLE
SWAMIS	SYLVAE	TAKERS	TAPPER	TAXING	TEMPOS
SWAMPS	SYLVAN	TAKEUP	TAPPET	TAXITE	TEMPTS
SWAMPY	SYLVAS	TAKING	TARGET	TAYLOR	TENACE
SWANEE	SYLVIA	TALARI	TARIFF	TAZZAS	TENANT
SWANKY	SYMBOL	TALCED	TARING	******	TENDED
SWARAJ	SYNDET	TALCUM	TARMAC	TB----	TENDER
SWARDS	SYNDIC	TALENT	TARNAL	******	TENDON
SWARMS	SYNODS	TALERS	TAROTS	TBONES	TENETS
SWARTH	SYNTAX	TALION	TARPAN	******	TENNIS
SWARTY	SYNURA	TALKED	TARRED	TE----	TENONS
SWATCH	SYPHER	TALKER	TARSAL	******	TENORS
SWATHE	SYPHON	TALKIE	TARSIA	TEABAG	TENPIN
SWATHS	SYRIAC	TALLER	TARSUS	TEACUP	TENREC
SWAYED	SYRIAN	TALLOW	TARTAN	TEAMED	TENSED
SWEARS	SYRINX	TALMUD	TARTAR	TEAMOT	TENSER
SWEATS	SYRUPS	TALONS	TARTED	TEAPOT	TENSES
SWEATY	SYRUPY	TAMALE	TARTER	TEAPOY	TENSOR
SWEDEN	SYSTEM	TAMBAC	TARTLY	TEARED	TENTED
SWEDES	SYZYGY	TAMELY	TARZAN	TEASED	TENTER
SWEENY	******	TAMERS	TASKED	TEASEL	TENTHS
SWEEPS	TA----	TAMEST	TASMAN	TEASER	TENUES
SWEEPY	******	TAMING	TASSEL	TEASES	TENUIS
SWEETS	TABARD	TAMPAN	TASSET	TEASET	TENURE
SWELLS	TABBED	TAMPED	TASTED	TEAURN	TENUTO
SWERVE	TABLED	TAMPER	TASTER	TECHNO	TEPEES
SWIFTS	TABLES	TAMPON	TASTES	TEDDED	TEPEFY
SWILLS	TABLET	TAMTAM	TATARS	TEDDER	TERAPH
SWINGE	TABOOS	TANDEM	TATLER	TEDDYS	TERATO
SWINGS	TABORS	TANGED	TATTED	TEDIUM	TERBIA
SWIPED	TACKED	TANGLE	TATTER	TEEING	TERCEL
SWIPES	TACKER	TANGLY	TATTLE	TEEMED	TERCET
SWIPLE	TACKEY	TANGOS	TATTLY	TEEMER	TEREDO
SWIRLS	TACKLE	TANIST	TATTOO	TEENSY	TERESA
SWIRLY	TACOMA	TANKAS	TAUGHT	TEETER	TERETE
SWITCH	TACTIC	TANKED	TAUNTS	TEETHE	TEREUS
SWIVEL	TAENIA	TANKER	TAUPES	TEFLON	TERGAL
SWIVET	TAGGED	TANNED	TAURUS	TEGMEN	TERGUM
SWOONS	TAGGER	TANNER	TAUTEN	TEHEED	TERMED
SWOOPS	TAHITI	TANNIC	TAUTER	TEHEES	TERMER
SWORDS	TAIGAS	TANNIN	TAUTLY	TELARY	TERMLY

TERMOR	THEIST	THRIVE	TIEUPS	TIPTOE	TOMANS
TERNAL	THELMA	THROAT	TIFFED	TIPTOP	TOMATO
TERRET	THEMES	THROBS	TIFFIN	TIRADE	TOMBAC
TERROR	THEMIS	THROES	TIGERS	TIRANA	TOMBED
TERRYS	THENAL	THRONE	TIGHTS	TIRING	TOMBOY
TERSER	THENAR	THRONG	TIGRIS	TISANE	TOMCAT
TESSIE	THENCE	THROVE	TILDES	TISHRI	TOMCOD
TESTAE	THEORY	THROWN	TILERS	TISSUE	TOMMYS
TESTED	THERMO	THROWS	TILING	TITANS	TOMTIT
TESTER	THERMS	THRUMS	TILLED	TITBIT	TOMTOM
TESTES	THESES	THRUSH	TILLER	TITHED	TONERS
TESTIS	THESIS	THRUST	TILLIE	TITHER	TONGED
TESTON	THETAS	THUJAS	TILLYS	TITHES	TONGUE
TETANY	THETIC	THULIA	TILTED	TITIAN	TONICS
TETCHY	THETIS	THUMBS	TILTER	TITLED	TONIER
TETHER	THEWED	THUMPS	TILTHS	TITLES	TONING
TETHYS	THIEVE	THUSLY	TIMBAL	TITTER	TONITE
TETONS	THIGHS	THWACK	TIMBER	TITTLE	TONKIN
TETRAD	THINGS	THWART	TIMBRE	TITTUP	TONSIL
TETRYL	THINLY	THYMES	TIMELY	******	TOOLED
TETTER	THIOLS	THYMIC	TIMERS	TO----	TOOLER
TETZEL	THIRDS	THYMOL	TIMING	******	TOOTED
TEUCER	THIRST	THYMUS	TIMMYS	TOASTS	TOOTER
TEUTON	THIRTY	THYREO	TINCAL	TOBAGO	TOOTHY
TEVERE	THISBE	THYRSE	TINCAN	TOBIAH	TOOTLE
******	THOLES	THYRSI	TINCTS	TOBIAS	TOOTSY
TH----	THOMAS	******	TINDER	TOBIES	TOPEKA
******	THONGS	TI----	TINEID	TOCSIN	TOPERS
THADDY	THORAC	******	TINGED	TODDLE	TOPHAT
THADYS	THORAX	TIARAS	TINGES	TODIES	TOPICS
THALER	THORIA	TIBIAE	TINGLE	TOECAP	TOPING
THALES	THORIC	TIBIAL	TINGLY	TOEING	TOPPED
THALIA	THORNS	TIBIAS	TINIER	TOFFEE	TOPPER
THAMES	THORNY	TICALS	TINILY	TOGAED	TOPPLE
THANAT	THORON	TICKED	TINKER	TOGGED	TOQUES
THANES	THORPE	TICKER	TINKLE	TOGGLE	TORAHS
THANKS	THOUGH	TICKET	TINKLY	TOGUES	TORERO
THATCH	THRALL	TICKLE	TINNED	TOILED	TORIES
THAWED	THRASH	TIDBIT	TINNER	TOILER	TORIIS
THAYER	THREAD	TIDIED	TINPOT	TOILES	TOROID
THEBAE	THREAT	TIDIER	TINSEL	TOILET	TOROSE
THEBES	THREED	TIDIES	TINTED	TOKENS	TOROUS
THECAE	THREES	TIDILY	TIPCAT	TOLEDO	TORPID
THECAL	THRESH	TIDING	TIPOFF	TOLLED	TORPOR
THEDAS	THRICE	TIEINS	TIPPED	TOLLER	TORQUE
THEFTS	THRIFT	TIEPIN	TIPPER	TOLTEC	TORRID
THEIRS	THRILL	TIERCE	TIPPET	TOLUOL	TORSKS
THEISM	THRIPS	TIERED	TIPPLE	TOLUYL	TORSOS

TOSHES	TRAILS	TRIPOS	******	TURBOT	TWINES
TOSSED	TRAINS	TRISTE	**TS----**	TURCOS	TWINGE
TOSSES	TRAITS	TRITER	******	TUREEN	TWIRLS
TOSSUP	TRAMPS	TRITON	TSADES	TURFED	TWIRPS
TOTALS	TRANCE	TRIUNE	TSETSE	TURGID	TWISTS
TOTEMS	TRASHY	TRIVET	TSHIRT	TURKEY	TWISTY
TOTERS	TRAUMA	TRIVIA	******	TURKIC	TWITCH
TOTHER	TRAVEL	TRIXIE	**TU----**	TURKIS	TWOBIT
TOTING	TRAVES	TRIXYS	******	TURNED	TWOFER
TOTTED	TRAWLS	TROCAR	TUBATE	TURNER	TWOPLY
TOTTER	TREADS	TROCHE	TUBBED	TURNIP	TWOULD
TOUCAN	TREATS	TROGON	TUBBER	TURNUP	TWOWAY
TOUCHE	TREATY	TROIKA	TUBERS	TURRET	******
TOUCHY	TREBLE	TROJAN	TUBING	TURTLE	**TY----**
TOUGHS	TREMOR	TROLLS	TUBULE	TURVES	******
TOULON	TRENCH	TROOPS	TUCHUN	TUSCAN	TYBALT
TOUPEE	TRENDS	TROPAL	TUCKED	TUSHED	TYCOON
TOURED	TRENDY	TROPHO	TUCKER	TUSHES	TYMPAN
TOURER	TREPAN	TROPHY	TUCKET	TUSKED	TYPHLO
TOUSLE	TRESSY	TROPIC	TUCSON	TUSKER	TYPHON
TOUTED	TREVOR	TROPPO	TUFFET	TUSSAH	TYPHUS
TOUTER	TRIADS	TROTHS	TUFTED	TUSSAL	TYPIFY
TOWAGE	TRIALS	TROTYL	TUGGED	TUSSAR	TYPING
TOWARD	TRIBAL	TROUGH	TUILLE	TUSSIS	TYPIST
TOWELS	TRIBES	TROUPE	TULADI	TUSSLE	TYRANT
TOWERS	TRICAR	TROUTS	TULIPS	TUTORS	TYRIAN
TOWERY	TRICED	TROVER	TULLES	TUTTED	TYRONE
TOWING	TRICES	TROVES	TUMBLE	TUTTIS	******
TOXINS	TRICHI	TROWEL	TUMEFY	TUXEDO	**UB----**
TOYERS	TRICHO	TRUANT	TUMORS	TUYERE	******
TOYING	TRICKS	TRUCES	TUMOUR	******	UBANGI
TOYISH	TRICKY	TRUCKS	TUMULT	**TW----**	UBIETY
TOYONS	TRICOT	TRUDGE	TUNDRA	******	UBOATS
******	TRIERS	TRUDYS	TUNERS	TWANGS	******
TR----	TRIFID	TRUEST	TUNEUP	TWANGY	**UD----**
******	TRIFLE	TRUING	TUNGUS	TWEAKS	******
TRACED	TRIGLY	TRUISM	TUNICA	TWEAKY	UDDERS
TRACER	TRIGON	TRUMAN	TUNICS	TWEEDS	******
TRACES	TRILBY	TRUMPS	TUNING	TWEETS	**UG----**
TRACHE	TRILLS	TRUNKS	TUNNED	TWELVE	******
TRACHY	TRIMLY	TRUSTS	TUNNEL	TWENTY	UGANDA
TRACKS	TRINAL	TRUSTY	TUPELO	TWERPS	UGLIER
TRACTS	TRINED	TRUTHS	TUPIKS	TWIBIL	UGLIFY
TRADED	TRINES	TRYING	TUPPED	TWIGGY	UGLILY
TRADER	TRIODE	TRYOUT	TUQUES	TWILIT	******
TRADES	TRIOSE	TRYSTS	TURBAN	TWILLS	**UK----**
TRAGIC	TRIPLE		TURBID	TWINED	******
TRAGUS	TRIPOD		TURBIT	TWINER	UKASES

******	UNDINE	UNLESS	UNTROD	******	******
UL----	UNDOER	UNLIKE	UNTRUE	UR----	UZ----
******	UNDOES	UNLIVE	UNUSED	******	******
ULCERS	UNDONE	UNLOAD	UNVEIL	URAEUS	UZZIAH
ULEMAS	UNDRAW	UNLOCK	UNVEXT	URALIC	******
ULENCE	UNDREW	UNMADE	UNWARY	URANIA	VA----
ULLAGE	UNDSET	UNMAKE	UNWELL	URANIC	******
ULSTER	UNDULY	UNMANS	UNWEPT	URANUS	VACANT
ULTIMA	UNEASE	UNMASK	UNWIND	URANYL	VACATE
ULTIMO	UNEASY	UNMEET	UNWISE	URBANE	VACUNA
******	UNESCO	UNMEWS	UNWISH	URCHIN	VACUUM
UM----	UNEVEN	UNMOOR	UNWORN	UREASE	VADOSE
******	UNFAIR	UNPACK	UNWRAP	UREIDE	VAGARY
UMBELS	UNFOLD	UNPEGS	UNYOKE	UREMIA	VAGINA
UMBERS	UNFURL	UNPICK	******	URETER	VAGINO
UMBLES	UNGIRD	UNPILE	UP----	URETIC	VAGUER
UMBRAE	UNGIRT	UNPINS	******	URGENT	VAINER
UMBRAL	UNGUAL	UNPLUG	UPASES	URGING	VAINLY
UMBRAS	UNGUES	UNREAD	UPBEAT	URINAL	VALATE
UMIAKS	UNGUIS	UNREAL	UPBOWS	UROPOD	VALERY
UMLAUT	UNGULA	UNREEL	UPCAST	URSINE	VALETS
UMPIRE	UNHAIR	UNREST	UPDATE	URSULA	VALGUS
******	UNHAND	UNRIGS	UPDIKE	URTEXT	VALISE
UN----	UNHASP	UNRIPE	UPENDS	******	VALKYR
******	UNHATS	UNRIPS	UPHELD	US----	VALLEY
UNABLE	UNHEWN	UNROBE	UPHILL	******	VALLUM
UNAPID	UNHOLY	UNROLL	UPHOLD	USABLE	VALOIS
UNBARS	UNHOOK	UNROOT	UPHROE	USABLY	VALOUR
UNBEAR	UNHURT	UNRULY	UPKEEP	USAGES	VALUED
UNBELT	UNHUSK	UNSAFE	UPLAND	USANCE	VALUER
UNBEND	UNICEF	UNSAID	UPLIFT	USEFUL	VALUES
UNBENT	UNIFIC	UNSAYS	UPMOST	USHERS	VALUTA
UNBIND	UNIONS	UNSEAL	UPPERS	USURER	VALVAL
UNBOLT	UNIPED	UNSEAM	UPPING	USURPS	VALVAR
UNBORN	UNIQUE	UNSEAT	UPPISH	******	VALVED
UNBRED	UNISEX	UNSEEN	UPPITY	UT----	VALVES
UNCAGE	UNISON	UNSHIP	UPRISE	******	VAMOSE
UNCAPS	UNITED	UNSHOD	UPROAR	UTAHAN	VAMPED
UNCASE	UNITES	UNSOLD	UPROOT	UTERUS	VANDAL
UNCIAL	UNJUST	UNSTEP	UPROSE	UTGARD	VANISH
UNCLAD	UNKIND	UNSTOP	UPRUSH	UTMOST	VANITY
UNCLES	UNKNIT	UNSUNG	UPSETS	UTOPIA	VANMAN
UNCOCK	UNLACE	UNSURE	UPSHOT	UTTERS	VANMEN
UNCOIL	UNLADE	UNTACK	UPSIDE	UTURNS	VAPORI
UNCORD	UNLAID	UNTIDY	UPTAKE	******	VAPORS
UNCORK	UNLASH	UNTIED	UPTOWN	UV----	VAPOUR
UNCURL	UNLAYS	UNTIES	UPTURN	******	VARICO
UNDIES	UNLEAD	UNTOLD	UPWARD	UVULAE	VARIED
				UVULAR	
				UVULAS	

VARIER	VENULE	VIANDS	VISHNU	VOTERS	WAIFED
VARIES	VERBAL	VIATIC	VISING	VOTING	WAILED
VARLET	VERDIN	VIATOR	VISION	VOTIVE	WAILER
VARUNA	VERDUN	VIBRIO	VISITS	VOWELS	WAISTS
VARVES	VEREIN	VICARS	VISORS	VOWERS	WAITED
VASARI	VERGED	VICKYS	VISTAS	VOWING	WAITER
VASHTI	VERGER	VICTIM	VISUAL	VOYAGE	WAIVED
VASILI	VERGES	VICTOR	VITALS	VOYEUR	WAIVER
VASSAL	VERGIL	VICUNA	VITRIC	******	WAIVES
VASTER	VERIFY	VIDUAL	VITTAE	VU----	WAKENS
VASTLY	VERILY	VIENNA	VIVACE	******	WAKIKI
VATFUL	VERISM	VIEWED	VIVIAN	VULCAN	WAKING
VATTED	VERIST	VIEWER	VIVIEN	VULGAR	WALDOS
VAULTS	VERITY	VIGILS	VIVIFY	VULVAE	WALERS
VAUNTS	VERMIN	VIGOUR	VIXENS	VULVAL	WALING
******	VERNAL	VIKING	VIZARD	VULVAR	WALKED
VE----	VERNAS	VILELY	VIZIER	******	WALKER
******	VERNIX	VILEST	VIZIRS	VY----	WALKON
VEADAR	VERNON	VILIFY	VIZORS	******	WALKUP
VECTOR	VERONA	VILLAS	******	VYRNWY	WALLAH
VEDIAC	VERSED	VILLON	VO----	******	WALLAS
VEERED	VERSES	VILLUS	******	WA----	WALLED
VEILED	VERSET	VIMINA	VOCALS	******	WALLET
VEILER	VERSOS	VINCES	VODKAS	WABASH	WALLIE
VEINED	VERSTS	VINERY	VOGUES	WABBLE	WALLIS
VELDTS	VERSUS	VINIER	VOGULS	WABBLY	WALLOP
VELLUM	VERTEX	VINNYS	VOICED	WADDED	WALLOW
VELOCE	VERVET	VINOUS	VOICES	WADDLE	WALLYS
VELOUR	VESICA	VINSON	VOIDED	WADDLY	WALNUT
VELURE	VESICO	VINYLS	VOILES	WADERS	WALRUS
VELVET	VESPER	VIOLAS	VOLANT	WADIES	WALTER
VENDED	VESPID	VIOLET	VOLERY	WADING	WALTON
VENDEE	VESSEL	VIOLIN	VOLING	WADSET	WALVIS
VENDER	VESTAL	VIPERS	VOLLEY	WAFERS	WAMBLE
VENDOR	VESTAS	VIRAGO	VOLOST	WAFFLE	WAMBLY
VENDUE	VESTED	VIREOS	VOLTED	WAFTED	WAMMUS
VENEER	VESTEE	VIRGAS	VOLUME	WAFTER	WAMOUS
VENERY	VESTRY	VIRGIE	VOLUTE	WAGERS	WAMPUM
VENIAL	VETOED	VIRGIL	VOLVAS	WAGGED	WANDAS
VENICE	VETOER	VIRGIN	VOLVOX	WAGGLE	WANDER
VENIRE	VETOES	VIRILE	VOMERS	WAGGLY	WANDLE
VENOMS	VETTED	VIRTUE	VOMICA	WAGGON	WANGLE
VENOSE	VEXERS	VISAED	VOMITO	WAGING	WANING
VENOUS	VEXILS	VISAGE	VOMITS	WAGNER	WANION
VENTED	VEXING	VISARD	VOODOO	WAGONS	WANNED
VENTER	******	VISCID	VOROUS	WAHABI	WANNER
VENTRO	VI----	VISCUS	VORTEX	WAHINE	WANTED
VENUES	******	VISEED	VOTARY	WAHOOS	WANTER
	VIABLE				
	VIALED				

WANTON	******	WETTED	WHOOPS	WILLYS	WITNEY
WAPITI	WE----	WETTER	WHOOSH	WILMAS	WITTED
WAPPED	******	******	WHORED	WILSON	WIVERN
WARBLE	WEAKEN	WH----	WHORES	WILTED	WIVERS
WARDED	WEAKER	******	WHORLS	WILTON	WIVING
WARDEN	WEAKLY	WHACKS	WHORTS	WIMBLE	WIZARD
WARDER	WEALDS	WHALED	WHYDAH	WIMPLE	WIZENS
WARHOL	WEALTH	WHALER	******	WINCED	******
WARIER	WEANED	WHALES	WI----	WINCER	WO----
WARILY	WEANER	WHAMMY	******	WINCES	******
WARMED	WEAPON	WHANGS	WICHES	WINCEY	WOADED
WARMER	WEARER	WHARFS	WICKED	WINDED	WOALDS
WARMLY	WEASEL	WHARVE	WICKER	WINDER	WOBBLE
WARMTH	WEAVED	WHEALS	WICKET	WINDOW	WOBBLY
WARMUP	WEAVER	WHEATS	WICOPY	WINDUP	WOEFUL
WARNED	WEAVES	WHEELS	WIDDIE	WINERY	WOLFED
WARNER	WEBBED	WHEEZE	WIDELY	WINGED	WOLSEY
WARPED	WEBERS	WHEEZY	WIDENS	WINIER	WOLVER
WARPER	WEDDED	WHELKS	WIDEST	WINING	WOLVES
WARRED	WEDELN	WHELKY	WIDOWS	WINKED	WOMBAT
WARREN	WEDGED	WHELMS	WIDTHS	WINKER	WOMBED
WARSAW	WEDGES	WHELPS	WIELDS	WINKLE	WOMERA
WASHED	WEDGIE	WHENCE	WIELDY	WINNER	WONDER
WASHER	WEEDED	WHERRY	WIENER	WINNIE	WONTED
WASHES	WEEDER	WHERVE	WIENIE	WINNOW	WOODED
WASTED	WEEKLY	WHEYEY	WIFELY	WINOES	WOODEN
WASTER	WEENIE	WHIDAH	WIGANS	WINTER	WOODSY
WASTES	WEENSY	WHIFFS	WIGEON	WINTRY	WOOERS
WATAPE	WEEPER	WHILED	WIGGED	WINZES	WOOFER
WATAPS	WEEVER	WHILES	WIGGLE	WIPERS	WOOING
WATERS	WEEVIL	WHILOM	WIGGLY	WIPING	WOOLEN
WATERY	WEIGHS	WHILST	WIGWAG	WIRERS	WOOLLY
WATSON	WEIGHT	WHIMSY	WIGWAM	WIRIER	WORDED
WATTLE	WEIMAR	WHINED	WIKIUP	WIRILY	WORKED
WATUSI	WEIRDY	WHINER	WILBER	WIRING	WORKER
WAULED	WELDED	WHINES	WILBUR	WISDOM	WORLDS
WAVERS	WELDER	WHINNY	WILDER	WISELY	WORMED
WAVEYS	WELKIN	WHIPPY	WILDLY	WISEST	WORMER
WAVIER	WELLED	WHIRLS	WILFUL	WISHED	WORSEN
WAVIES	WELTED	WHISKS	WILIER	WISHES	WORSER
WAVILY	WELTER	WHISKY	WILILY	WISING	WORSTS
WAVING	WENDED	WHITBY	WILING	WISPED	WORTHY
WAWLED	WENDYS	WHITED	WILLED	WITHAL	WOUNDS
WAXIER	WERENT	WHITEN	WILLER	WITHED	WOWING
WAXING	WESLEY	WHITER	WILLET	WITHER	WOWSER
WAYLAY	WESSEX	WHITES	WILLIE	WITHES	******
WAYNES	WESTER	WHITEY	WILLIS	WITHIN	WR----
WAYOUT	WETHER	WHOLLY	WILLOW	WITHIT	******
					WRACKS
					WRAITH

WRAPUP	XYLENE	YEASTY	******	ZIGZAG	******
WRASSE	XYLITE	YEHUDI	YU----	ZILLAH	ZY----
WRATHY	XYLOID	YELLED	******	ZINCED	******
WREAKS	XYLOLS	YELLER	YUCCAS	ZINCIC	ZYGOMA
WREATH	XYLOSE	YELLOW	YUKKED	ZINCKY	ZYGOTE
WRECKS	XYSTER	YELPED	YUPONS	ZINGED	******
WRENCH	XYSTOS	YELPER	YUPPIE	ZINNIA	A-A---
WRESTS	******	YEMENI	******	ZIPPED	******
WRETCH	YA----	YENNED	YV----	ZIPPER	ABACAS
WRIEST	******	YEOMAN	******	ZIRCON	ABACUS
WRIGHT	YABBER	YEOMEN	YVONNE	ZIRONS	ABADAN
WRINGS	YACHTS	YERBAS	******	ZITHER	ABASED
WRISTS	YAGERS	YESMAN	ZA----	ZIZITH	ABASER
WRITER	YAHOOS	YESSED	******	ZIZZLE	ABASES
WRITES	YAHVEH	YESSES	ZAFFAR	******	ABATED
WRITHE	YAHWEH	YESTER	ZAFFER	ZL----	ABATER
WRONGS	YAKIMA	******	ZAFFIR	******	ABATES
WRYEST	YAKKED	YI----	ZAFFRE	ZLOTYS	ABATIS
WRYING	YAMENS	******	ZAFTIG	******	ABATOR
******	YAMMER	YIELDS	ZAMBIA	ZO----	ACACIA
WY----	YAMUNS	YIPPED	ZAMIAS	******	ACADIA
******	YANKED	YIPPIE	ZANANA	ZODIAC	ACAENA
WYSTAN	YANKEE	******	ZANIER	ZOMBIE	ACAJOU
WYVERN	YAOURT	YO----	ZANIES	ZOMBIS	ACANTH
******	YAPONS	******	ZARATA	ZONARY	ACARID
XA----	YAPPED	YODELS	ZARIBA	ZONATE	ADAGES
******	YARDED	YOGEES	ZAYINS	ZONING	ADAGIO
XANADU	YARROW	YOGINS	******	ZONULA	ADAPTS
XANTHO	YASMAK	YOGURT	ZE----	ZONULE	AEACUS
XAVIER	YAUPED	YOICKS	******	ZOOIDS	AGAMAS
******	YAUPON	YOKELS	ZEALOT	ZOOMED	AGAMIC
XE----	YAWING	YOKING	ZEBECK	ZOONAL	AGAPAE
******	YAWLED	YONDER	ZEBECS	ZORILS	AGARIC
XEBECS	YAWNED	YONKER	ZEBRAS	ZOSTER	AGATES
XENIAL	YAWNER	YOOHOO	ZECHIN	ZOUAVE	AGATHA
******	YAWPED	YORICK	ZENANA	ZOUNDS	AGAVES
XR----	YAWPER	YORKER	ZENGER	ZOYSIA	ALALIA
******	******	YORUBA	ZENITH	******	ALAMOS
XRAYED	YC----	YOUPON	ZEPHYR	ZS----	ALARIC
******	******	YOUTHS	ZEROED	******	ALARMS
XT----	YCLEPT	YOWING	ZEROES	ZSAZSA	ALARUM
******	******	YOWLED	ZESTED	******	ALASKA
XTSTUS	YE----	******	ZETHOS	ZU----	ALATED
******	******	YT----	ZETHUS	******	AMADOU
XY----	YEANED	******	ZEUGMA	******	AMALIE
******	YEARLY	YTTRIA	******	ZUIDER	AMANDA
XYLANS	YEARNS	YTTRIC	ZI----	ZURICH	AMANIA
XYLEMS	YEASTS		******	ZUYDER	AMATOL
			ZIBETH		
			ZIBETS		

AMAZED	ALBERT	ARCHEO	******	APEXES	ANGINA
AMAZES	ALBINO	ARCHER	A-E---	ARECAS	ANGKOR
AMAZON	ALBION	ARCHES	******	ARENAS	ANGLED
ANABAS	ALBITE	ARCHIE	ABELES	AREOLA	ANGLER
ANADEM	ALBUMS	ARCHIL	ACEDIA	ARERCU	ANGLES
ANALOG	AMBAGE	ARCHLY	ACEIUM	ARETES	ANGLIA
ANANAS	AMBARI	ARCHON	ACEOUS	AREZZO	ANGLIC
ANANKE	AMBARY	ARCHYS	ACERIC	AVENGE	ANGOLA
ANATTO	AMBERS	ARCING	ACETAL	AVENUE	ANGORA
APACHE	AMBERY	ARCKED	ACETIC	AVERNO	ARGALA
APATHY	AMBITS	ARCTIC	ACETUM	AVERSE	ARGALI
ARABEL	AMBLED	ASCEND	ACETYL	AVERTS	ARGALS
ARABIA	AMBLER	ASCENT	ADEEMS	AVERYS	ARGENT
ARABIC	AMBLES	ASCOTS	ADENIS	AVESTA	ARGIVE
ARABLE	AMBUSH	******	ADEPTS	AWEARY	ARGOSY
ARAGON	ARBELA	A-D---	AEETES	AWEIGH	ARGOTS
ARANTA	ARBORI	******	AGEDLY	AWEING	ARGUED
ARARAT	ARBORS	ABDUCT	AGEING	AXEMAN	ARGUER
ARAWAK	ARBOUR	ADDAMS	AGENCY	AXEMEN	ARGUES
ASARUM	ARBUTE	ADDEND	AGENDA	AYEAYE	ARGUFY
ATABAL	ASBURY	ADDERS	AGENTS	AYESHA	ARGYLL
ATAMAN	AUBADE	ADDICT	AGEOLD	******	ASGARD
ATAVIC	AUBREY	ADDING	AKENES	A-F---	AUGEAN
ATAXIA	AUBURN	ADDLED	ALECTO	******	AUGEND
ATAXIC	******	ADDLES	ALEGAR	AFFAIR	AUGERS
AVAILS	A-C---	ADDUCE	ALEPHS	AFFECT	AUGHTS
AVALON	******	ADDUCT	ALEPPO	AFFIRM	AUGITE
AVATAR	AACHEN	AEDILE	ALERTS	AFFLUX	AUGURS
AVAUNT	ACCEDE	AIDERS	ALEUTS	AFFORD	AUGURY
AWAITS	ACCENT	AIDING	ALEXIA	AFFRAY	AUGUST
AWAKED	ACCEPT	AIDMAN	ALEXIN	ALFAKI	******
AWAKEN	ACCESS	AIDMEN	ALEXIS	ALFONS	A-H---
AWAKES	ACCORD	ALDERS	AMEBAE	ALFRED	******
AWARDS	ACCOST	ALDINE	AMEBAS	******	ABHORS
AZALEA	ACCRUE	ALDOSE	AMEBIC	A-G---	ACHAEA
AZAZEL	ACCUSE	ALDOUS	AMECHE	******	ACHAIA
******	AECIAL	ANDEAN	AMELIA	AEGEAN	ACHENE
A-B---	ALCAIC	ANDREA	AMELIE	AEGEUS	ACHING
******	ALCOTT	ANDREI	AMENDS	AFGHAN	ADHERE
ABBACY	ALCOVE	ANDRES	AMENRA	AGGERS	AGHAST
ABBESS	ALCUIN	ANDREW	AMENTI	AIGLET	APHIDS
ABBEYS	ANCHOR	ARDEBS	AMENTS	ALGOID	APHONY
ABBIES	ANCONA	ARDENT	AMERCE	ALGOUS	APHTHA
ABBOTS	ANCONE	ARDORS	ANEMIA	ANGARY	ASHCAN
ALBANY	ARCADE	ARDOUR	ANEMIC	ANGELA	ASHIER
ALBATA	ARCANA	AUDADS	ANERGY	ANGELO	ASHLAR
ALBEDO	ARCANE	AUDILE	APEMAN	ANGELS	ASHLEY
ALBEIT	ARCHED	AUDITS	APEPSY	ANGERS	ASHMAN
		AUDREY			

ASHMEN	ANIMAL	ALKENE	APLITE	AGNATE	AGONIC
ASHORE	ANIMAS	ALKYLS	APLOMB	AMNION	AGORAE
ATHENA	ANIMUS	ALKYNE	ARLEEN	ANNALS	AGORAS
ATHENE	ANIONS	ANKARA	ARLENE	ANNEAL	AGOUTI
ATHENS	ANISES	ANKLES	ARLINE	ANNEXE	AGOUTY
ATHOME	ANITAS	ANKLET	ASLANT	ANNIES	AJOWAN
AWHEEL	ANITRA	ANKYLO	ASLEEP	ANNONA	ALONSO
AWHILE	APIARY	ASKANT	ASLOPE	ANNOYS	ALONZO
AWHIRL	APICAL	ASKERS	AWLESS	ANNUAL	AMOEBA
******	APICES	ASKING	AXLIKE	ANNULS	AMOLES
A-I---	APIECE	AUKLET	******	APNEAL	AMORAL
******	ARIANS	******	A-M---	APNEIC	AMOUNT
ABIDED	ARIDLY	A-L---	******	APNOEA	AMOURS
ABIDER	ARIELS	******	ADMIRE	ARNAUD	ANODES
ABIDES	ARIGHT	AALAND	ADMITS	ARNICA	ANODIC
ABIJAH	ARIOSE	AALIIS	ADMIXT	ARNIES	ANOINT
ACIDIC	ARIOSO	ABLAUT	AIMING	ARNOLD	ANOMIA
ACIDLY	ARIOUS	ABLAZE	ALMAHS	AUNTIE	ANOMIC
ACINUS	ARISEN	ABLEST	ALMIRA	AWNING	ANOMIE
ACIOUS	ARISES	ABLOOM	ALMOND	******	ANONYM
ADIEUS	ARISTA	ABLUSH	ALMOST	A-O---	ANORAK
ADIEUX	ARISTO	ADLIBS	ALMUCE	******	ANOXIA
ADIPIC	ASIANS	AFLAME	ALMUDE	ABOARD	ANOXIC
AFIELD	ASIDES	AFLCIO	ALMUDS	ABODES	APODAL
AGISTS	ASIMOV	AFLOAT	ARMADA	ABOHMS	APOGEE
AHIMSA	AVIARY	AGLAIA	ARMAGH	ABOLLA	APOLLO
AKIMBO	AVIATE	AGLEAM	ARMAND	ABOMAS	APOLOG
ALIBIS	AVIDIN	AGLETS	ARMETS	ABOMBS	AROIDS
ALIBLE	AVIDLY	AILEEN	ARMFUL	ABORAL	AROMAS
ALICES	AVISOS	AILING	ARMIES	ABORTS	AROUND
ALICIA	AXILLA	ALLANS	ARMING	ABOUND	AROUSE
ALIDAD	AXIOMS	ALLAYS	ARMLET	ACORNS	ATOLLS
ALIENS	AZINES	ALLEGE	ARMORS	ADOBES	ATOMIC
ALIGHT	******	ALLELE	ARMORY	ADOLPH	ATONAL
ALIGNS	A-J---	ALLENS	ARMOUR	ADONAI	ATONED
ALINED	******	ALLEYS	ARMPIT	ADONIC	ATONER
ALINES	ABJECT	ALLIED	ARMURE	ADONIS	ATONES
ALIPED	ABJURE	ALLIES	AYMARA	ADOPTS	ATONIC
ALISON	ADJECT	ALLIUM	******	ADORED	AVOCET
AMICES	ADJOIN	ALLOTS	A-N---	ADORER	AVOIDS
AMIDES	ADJURE	ALLOUT	******	ADORES	AVOSET
AMIDIC	ADJUST	ALLOWS	ABNERS	ADORNS	AVOUCH
AMIDIN	******	ALLOYS	ACNODE	AEOLIA	AVOWAL
AMIDOL	A-K---	ALLUDE	ADNATE	AEOLIC	AVOWED
AMIDST	******	ALLURE	ADNOUN	AEOLIS	AVOWER
AMIENS	ACKACK	ALLYLS	AENEAS	AEOLUS	AWOKEN
AMIGOS	ALKALI	ANLACE	AENEID	AGOGUE	AXONES
ANILIN	ALKANE	ANLAGE	AGNAIL	AGONES	AZOLES

AZONIC	ADROIT	AURIGA	ACTIVE	ATTICA	ADVERB
AZORES	AERATE	AURIST	ACTORS	ATTICS	ADVERT
AZOTIC	AERIAL	AURORA	ACTUAL	ATTILA	ADVICE
******	AERIED	AUROUS	AETHER	ATTIRE	ADVISE
A-P---	AERIES	AZRAEL	AFTOSA	ATTLEE	ALVANS
******	AERIFY	******	ALTAIC	ATTORN	ALVINA
ALPACA	AEROBE	A-S---	ALTAIR	ATTUNE	ALVINE
ALPHAS	AERUGO	******	ALTARS	AUTHOR	ANVILS
ALPHOS	AFRAID	ABSENT	ALTERS	AUTISM	******
ALPHYL	AFRAME	ABSORB	ALTHEA	AUTOED	A-W---
ALPINE	AFRESH	ABSURD	ANTEED	AUTUMN	******
AMPERE	AFRICA	ADSORB	ANTERO	AZTECS	ABWATT
AMPHRS	AGRAFE	AISLED	ANTHEA	******	ALWAYS
AMPULE	AGREED	AISLES	ANTHEM	A-U---	******
AMPULS	AGREES	ALSACE	ANTHER	******	A-X---
APPALL	AIRBED	ALSIKE	ANTIAR	ABULIA	******
APPALS	AIRDRY	ANSATE	ANTICS	ABUSED	AUXINS
APPEAL	AIRGUN	ANSELM	ANTLER	ABUSER	******
APPEAR	AIRIER	ANSWER	ANTLIA	ABUSES	A-Y---
APPELS	AIRILY	ARSINE	ANTONS	ACUATE	******
APPEND	AIRING	ASSAIL	ANTONY	ACUITY	ABYDOS
APPIAN	AIRMAN	ASSAIS	ANTRIM	ACUMEN	ABYSMS
APPLES	AIRMEN	ASSAYS	ANTRUM	ADULTS	ADYTUM
APPORT	AIRSAC	ASSENT	ARTELS	AGUISH	AMYLIC
APPOSE	AIRWAY	ASSERT	ARTERY	ALUDEL	AMYLUM
ARPENS	AMRITA	ASSESS	ARTFUL	ALUINO	AMYTAL
ARPENT	AORIST	ASSETS	ARTHRO	ALUINS	ANYHOW
ASPECT	AORTAE	ASSIGN	ARTHUR	ALULAE	ANYONE
ASPENS	AORTAL	ASSISI	ARTIES	ALULAR	ANYWAY
ASPERS	AORTAS	ASSIST	ARTILY	ALUMIN	ARYANS
ASPICS	AORTIC	ASSIZE	ARTIST	ALUMNA	ASYLUM
ASPIRE	APRILS	ASSORT	ARTOIS	ALUMNI	******
******	APRONS	ASSUME	ARTURO	AMULET	B-A---
A-Q---	ARRACK	ASSURE	ASTERI	AMUSED	******
******	ARRANT	AUSPEX	ASTERN	AMUSER	BAAING
ACQUIT	ARRAYS	AUSTEN	ASTERO	AMUSES	BAALIM
******	ARREAR	AUSTER	ASTERS	ANUBIS	BEACHY
A-R---	ARREST	AUSTIN	ASTHMA	ANURAN	BEACON
******	ARRIVE	AUSTRO	ASTRAL	ANUSES	BEADED
AARONS	ARROBA	AXSEED	ASTRAY	AOUDAD	BEADLE
ABRADE	ARROWS	******	ASTRID	APULIA	BEAGLE
ABRAMS	ARROWY	A-T---	ASTUTE	AQUILA	BEAKED
ABROAD	ARROYO	******	ATTACH	ARUNTA	BEAKER
ABRUPT	ATREUS	ACTING	ATTACK	AZURES	BEAMED
ACROSS	ATRIAL	ACTINI	ATTAIN	******	BEANED
ADRIAN	ATRIUM	ACTINO	ATTARS	A-V---	BEANIE
ADRIEN	AURATE	ACTION	ATTEND	******	BEARDS
ADRIFT	AUREUS	ACTIUM	ATTEST	ABVOLT	BEARED
				ADVENT	

BEARER	BRAKED	BOBBYS	BEDIMS	BREAMS	BAGGED
BEASTS	BRAKES	BOBCAT	BEDLAM	BREAST	BAGMAN
BEATEN	BRANCH	BUBALS	BEDPAN	BREATH	BAGMEN
BEATER	BRANDS	BUBBLE	BEDRID	BRECHT	BAGNIO
BEAUTS	BRANDT	BUBBLY	BEDSIT	BREECH	BEGETS
BEAUTY	BRANDY	BUBOES	BEDUIN	BREEDS	BEGGAR
BEAVER	BRANNY	BYBLOW	BIDDEN	BREEKS	BEGGED
BIAFRA	BRANTS	******	BIDDER	BREEZE	BEGINS
BIALYS	BRAQUE	**B-C---**	BIDETS	BREEZY	BEGIRD
BIANCA	BRASHY	******	BIDING	BREGMA	BEGIRT
BIASED	BRASSY	BACHED	BODEGA	BREMEN	BEGONE
BIASES	BRAVED	BACHES	BODICE	BRENDA	BEGUIN
BIAXAL	BRAVER	BACKED	BODIED	BRENTS	BEGUMS
BLACKS	BRAVES	BACKER	BODIES	BRETON	BIGAMY
BLADED	BRAVOS	BACONY	BODILY	BREVES	BIGGER
BLADES	BRAWLS	BECALM	BODING	BREVET	BIGGIN
BLAINS	BRAWNY	BECAME	BODKIN	BREWED	BIGHTS
BLAISE	BRAYED	BECKED	BUDDED	BREWER	BIGONE
BLAMED	BRAYER	BECKET	BUDDER	BREWIS	BIGOTS
BLAMES	BRAZAS	BECKON	BUDDHA	BYEBYE	BIGWIG
BLANCH	BRAZED	BECKYS	BUDDLE	******	BOGANS
BLANKS	BRAZEN	BECOME	BUDGED	**B-F---**	BOGEYS
BLARED	BRAZER	BICARB	BUDGES	******	BOGGED
BLARES	BRAZES	BICEPS	BUDGET	BAFFED	BOGGLE
BLASTO	BRAZIL	BICKER	BUDGIE	BAFFIN	BOGIES
BLASTS	BRAZOS	BICORN	******	BAFFLE	BOGLES
BLAZED	******	BOCCIE	**B-E---**	BEFALL	BOGOAK
BLAZER	**B-B---**	BUCCAL	******	BEFELL	BOGOTA
BLAZES	******	BUCHAN	BEECHY	BEFITS	BUGGED
BLAZON	BABBIE	BUCKED	BEEFED	BEFOGS	BUGGER
BOARDS	BABBLE	BUCKER	BEEPED	BEFOOL	BUGLED
BOASTS	BABIED	BUCKET	BEETLE	BEFORE	BUGLER
BOATED	BABIES	BUCKLE	BEEVES	BEFOUL	BUGLES
BOATER	BABISM	BUCKRA	BIERCE	BIFFED	BYGONE
BRACED	BABIST	******	BLEACH	BIFFIN	******
BRACER	BABITE	**B-D---**	BLEAKS	BIFLEX	**B-H---**
BRACES	BABOON	******	BLEARS	BIFOLD	******
BRACHI	BABOOS	BADGED	BLEARY	BIFORM	BAHAIS
BRACHY	BABULS	BADGER	BLEATS	BOFFIN	BAHAMA
BRACTS	BIBBED	BADGES	BLEBBY	BUFFED	BEHALF
BRAHMA	BIBBER	BADMAN	BLEEDS	BUFFER	BEHAVE
BRAHMS	BIBLES	BADMEN	BLENCH	BUFFET	BEHEAD
BRAIDS	BIBLIO	BEDAUB	BLENDE	******	BEHELD
BRAILS	BOBBED	BEDBUG	BLENDS	**B-G---**	BEHEST
BRAINS	BOBBER	BEDDED	BLENNY	******	BEHIND
BRAINY	BOBBIE	BEDDER	BREACH	BAGASS	BEHOLD
BRAISE	BOBBIN	BEDECK	BREADS	BAGDAD	BEHOOF
BRAIZE	BOBBLE	BEDEWS	BREAKS	BAGELS	BEHOVE
					BIHARI

******	******	BELONG	BEMEAN	BENNET	BIOPSY
B-I---	**B-K---**	BELTED	BEMIRE	BENNYS	BIOSIS
******	******	BELUGA	BEMOAN	BENTON	BIOTIC
BAIKAL	BAKERS	BILBAO	BEMUSE	BENUMB	BIOTIN
BAILED	BAKERY	BILGED	BOMBAY	BENZOL	BLOATS
BAILEE	BAKING	BILGES	BOMBED	BENZYL	BLOCKS
BAILER	BIKINI	BILITY	BOMBER	BINARY	BLOCKY
BAILEY	BIKOLS	BILKED	BOMBES	BINATE	BLOKES
BAILIE	******	BILKER	BOMBIC	BINDER	BLONDE
BAILOR	**B-L---**	BILLED	BUMBLE	BINGES	BLONDS
BAIRNS	******	BILLET	BUMKIN	BINITS	BLOODS
BAITED	BALAAM	BILLIE	BUMMED	BINNED	BLOODY
BEIGES	BALATA	BILLON	BUMMER	BONACI	BLOOMS
BEINGS	BALBOA	BILLOW	BUMPED	BONBON	BLOOMY
BEIRUT	BALDER	BILLYS	BUMPER	BONDED	BLOTCH
BLIGHT	BALDLY	BILOXI	******	BONDER	BLOUSE
BLIMEY	BALEEN	BOLDER	**B-N---**	BONERS	BLOWBY
BLIMPS	BALERS	BOLDLY	******	BONGED	BLOWER
BLINDS	BALING	BOLERO	BANANA	BONGOS	BLOWUP
BLINKS	BALKAN	BOLEYN	BANDED	BONIER	BLOWZY
BLINTZ	BALKED	BOLIDE	BANDIT	BONING	BOOBOO
BLITHE	BALLAD	BOLLED	BANGED	BONITO	BOODLE
BOILED	BALLED	BOLLIX	BANGLE	BONNET	BOOGIE
BOILER	BALLET	BOLSON	BANGOR	BONNIE	BOOHOO
BRIARS	BALLOT	BOLTED	BANGUI	BONNYS	BOOING
BRIBED	BALSAM	BOLTER	BANGUP	BONSAI	BOOKED
BRIBER	BALSAS	BOLTON	BANIAN	BONZER	BOOKIE
BRIBES	BALTIC	BULBAR	BANISH	BONZES	BOOMED
BRICKS	BALTIM	BULBED	BANJOS	BUNCHE	BOOMER
BRIDAL	BALZAC	BULBEL	BANKED	BUNCHY	BOOSTS
BRIDES	BELAYS	BULBIL	BANKER	BUNCOS	BOOTED
BRIDGE	BELDAM	BULBUL	BANNED	BUNDLE	BOOTEE
BRIDIE	BELFRY	BULGAR	BANNER	BUNGED	BOOTHS
BRIDLE	BELGAS	BULGED	BANTAM	BUNGLE	BOOTIE
BRIEFS	BELGIC	BULGER	BANTER	BUNION	BOOTLE
BRIERS	BELIAL	BULGES	BANTUS	BUNKED	BOOZED
BRIERY	BELIED	BULKED	BANYAN	BUNKER	BOOZER
BRIGHT	BELIEF	BULLAE	BANZAI	BUNKUM	BOOZES
BRIGID	BELIER	BULLET	BENDAY	BUNSEN	BROACH
BRILLS	BELIES	BYLANE	BENDED	BUNTED	BROADS
BRINED	BELIKE	BYLAWS	BENDEE	BUNYAN	BROCHE
BRINES	BELIZE	BYLINE	BENDER	BUNYIP	BROGAN
BRINGS	BELLAS	******	BENGAL	BYNAME	BROGUE
BRINKS	BELLED	**B-M---**	BENIGN	******	BROILS
BRISKS	BELLES	******	BENITA	**B-O---**	BROKEN
BRITON	BELLOC	BAMAKO	BENITO	******	BROKER
BUILDS	BELLOW	BAMBOO	BENJYS	BAOBAB	BROLLY
******	BELOIT	BEMATA	BENNES	BIOGEN	BROMAL
B-J---					
******					
BIJOUX					

BROMES	BARITE	BIRRED	BURSAR	BOSHES	BETIDE
BROMIC	BARIUM	BIRTHS	BURSAS	BOSKET	BETISE
BRONCO	BARKED	BORAGE	BURSES	BOSOMS	BETONY
BRONCS	BARKER	BORANE	BURSTS	BOSSED	BETOOK
BRONTE	BARLEY	BORATE	BURTON	BOSSES	BETRAY
BRONZE	BARMAN	BORDEL	BYROAD	BOSTON	BETSYS
BRONZY	BARMEN	BORDER	******	BUSHED	BETTED
BROOCH	BARMIE	BOREAL	B-S---	BUSHEL	BETTER
BROODS	BARNEY	BOREAS	******	BUSHES	BETTES
BROODY	BARNUM	BORERS	BASALT	BUSHEY	BETTOR
BROOKE	BARONG	BORGIA	BASELY	BUSIED	BETTYS
BROOKS	BARONS	BORIDE	BASEST	BUSIES	BITCHY
BROOMS	BARONY	BORING	BASHAW	BUSILY	BITERS
BROOMY	BARQUE	BORNEO	BASHED	BUSING	BITING
BROTHS	BARRED	BORROW	BASHES	BUSKER	BITTED
BROWNS	BARREL	BORSCH	BASICS	BUSKIN	BITTEN
BROWSE	BARREN	BORZOI	BASIFY	BUSMAN	BITTER
BUOYED	BARRET	BURANS	BASILS	BUSMEN	BOTANY
******	BARRIE	BURBLE	BASING	BUSSED	BOTCHY
B-P---	BARRIO	BURBOT	BASINS	BUSSES	BOTFLY
******	BARROW	BURDEN	BASION	BUSTED	BOTHER
BIPEDS	BARRYS	BURDIE	BASKED	BUSTER	BOTTLE
BIPODS	BARTER	BUREAU	BASKET	BUSTIC	BOTTOM
BOPPED	BARTOK	BURGEE	BASQUE	BUSTLE	BUTANE
BYPASS	BARTON	BURGER	BASRAH	BYSSUS	BUTLER
BYPAST	BARUCH	BURGHS	BASSES	******	BUTTED
BYPATH	BARYES	BURGLE	BASSET	B-T---	BUTTER
BYPLAY	BARYON	BURGOO	BASSOS	******	BUTTES
******	BARYTA	BURGOS	BASTED	BATAAN	BUTTON
B-R---	BERATE	BURIAL	BASTES	BATEAU	BYTALK
******	BERBER	BURIED	BASUTO	BATHED	******
BARBED	BEREFT	BURIES	BESANT	BATHER	B-U---
BARBEL	BERETS	BURINS	BESEEM	BATHOS	******
BARBER	BERGEN	BURKED	BESETS	BATIKS	BAUBLE
BARBET	BERING	BURKES	BESIDE	BATING	BAUCIS
BARBIE	BERLIN	BURLAP	BESOMS	BATMAN	BEULAH
BARBRA	BERMES	BURLED	BESOTS	BATMEN	BEULAS
BARDED	BERNEY	BURLER	BESSIE	BATONS	BHUTAN
BARDES	BERNIE	BURLEY	BESSYS	BATTED	BLUELY
BARDIC	BERTHA	BURNED	BESTED	BATTEN	BLUEST
BAREGE	BERTHE	BURNER	BESTIR	BATTER	BLUETS
BARELY	BERTHS	BURNET	BESTOW	BATTIK	BLUFFS
BAREST	BERTIE	BURPED	BISCAY	BATTIN	BLUING
BARFLY	BERYLS	BURRED	BISECT	BATTLE	BLUISH
BARGED	BIRDIE	BURROS	BISHOP	BATTUE	BLUNGE
BARGEE	BIREME	BURROW	BISQUE	BETAKE	BLUNTS
BARGES	BIRLED	BURSAE	BISTER	BETELS	BLURBS
BARING	BIRLES	BURSAL	BISTRO	BETHEL	BLURRY

BLURTS	BOWELS	BEZELS	CHASMS	CRAMPS	COBLES
BOUCLE	BOWERS	BEZOAR	CHASSE	CRANED	COBNUT
BOUFFE	BOWERY	BUZZED	CHASTE	CRANES	COBRAS
BOUGHS	BOWFIN	BUZZER	CHATTY	CRANIA	COBURG
BOUGHT	BOWING	BUZZES	CHAWED	CRANIO	COBWEB
BOUGIE	BOWLED	******	CLACKS	CRANKS	CUBAGE
BOULES	BOWLEG	C-A---	CLAIMS	CRANKY	CUBANS
BOUNCE	BOWLER	******	CLAIRE	CRANNY	CUBBED
BOUNCY	BOWMAN	CEASED	CLAMMY	CRAPED	CUBEBS
BOUNDS	BOWMEN	CEASES	CLAMOR	CRAPES	CUBING
BOUNTY	BOWSAW	CHABUK	CLAMPS	CRASIS	CUBISM
BOURGS	BOWSED	CHACMA	CLANGS	CRATCH	CUBIST
BOURNE	BOWSES	CHAETA	CLANKS	CRATED	CUBITS
BOURNS	BOWTIE	CHAETO	CLAQUE	CRATER	CUBOID
BOURSE	BO-	CHAFED	CLARAS	CRATES	CYBELE
BOUSED	WWOW	CHAFER	CLARES	CRAVAT	******
BOUSES	BOWYER	CHAFES	CLARET	CRAVED	C-C---
BRUCES	BYWAYS	CHAFFS	CLAROS	CRAVEN	******
BRUGES	BYWORD	CHAFFY	CLASPS	CRAVER	CACAOS
BRUINS	BYWORK	CHAINS	CLASSY	CRAVES	CACHED
BRUISE	******	CHAIRS	CLAUDE	CRAWLS	CACHES
BRUITS	B-X---	CHAISE	CLAUSE	CRAWLY	CACHET
BRULOT	******	CHALCO	CLAWED	CRAYON	CACHOU
BRUMAL	BAXTER	CHALEH	CLAYED	CRAZED	CACKLE
BRUMES	BOXCAR	CHALET	CLAYEY	CRAZES	CACTUS
BRUNCH	BOXERS	CHALKS	COALED	CYANIC	CECILE
BRUNEI	BOXING	CHALKY	COALER	CYANID	CECILS
BRUNEL	BUXTON	CHAMMY	COARSE	CYANIN	CECILY
BRUNOS	******	CHAMPS	COASTS	******	CICADA
BRUSHY	B-Y---	CHANCE	COATED	C-B---	CICALA
BRUTAL	******	CHANCY	COATEE	******	CICELY
BRUTES	BAYARD	CHANGE	COATIS	CABALA	CICERO
BRUTUS	BAYEUX	CHANGS	COAXAL	CABALS	COCAIN
******	BAYING	CHANTS	COAXED	CABANA	COCCAL
B-V---	BAYOUS	CHANTY	COAXER	CABINS	COCCID
******	BEYOND	CHAPEL	COAXES	CABLED	COCCUS
BEVELS	BOYARD	CHAPES	CRAALS	CABLES	COCCYX
BEVIES	BOYARS	CHARDS	CRABBY	CABLET	COCHIN
BOVATE	BOYISH	CHARED	CRACKS	CABMAN	COCKED
BOVINE	BRYANT	CHARES	CRACKY	CABMEN	COCKER
******	BRYONY	CHARGE	CRACOW	CABOBS	COCKLE
B-W---	BUYERS	CHARMS	CRADLE	CEBOID	COCKUP
******	BUYING	CHARON	CRAFTS	CIBOLS	COCOAS
BAWDRY	******	CHARRY	CRAFTY	COBALT	COCOON
BAWLED	B-Z---	CHARTS	CRAGGY	COBBER	CUCKOO
BAWLER	******	CHASED	CRAIGS	COBBLE	CYCADS
BEWAIL	BAZAAR	CHASER	CRAKES	COBBLY	CYCLED
BEWARE	BEZANT	CHASES	CRAMBO	COBIAS	CYCLER

CYCLES
CYCLIC
******
******
CADDIE
CADDIS
CADENT
CADETS
CADGED
CADGER
CADGES
CADMUS
CADRES
CEDARS
CEDING
CEDRIC
CEDULA
CIDERS
CODDER
CODDLE
CODEIA
CODEIN
CODGER
CODIFY
CODING
CUDDIE
CUDDLE
CUDDLY
CUDGEL
******
******
CAECUM
CAEOMA
CAESAR
CHEATS
CHEBEC
CHECKS
CHEEKS
CHEEKY
CHEEPS
CHEERS
CHEERY
CHEESE
CHEESY
CHEGOE
CHEILO

CHEIRO
CHELAE
CHELAS
CHEOPS
CHEQUE
CHERRY
CHERUB
CHERYL
CHESTS
CHESTY
CHETAH
CHEVVY
CHEWED
CHEWER
CLEANS
CLEARS
CLEATS
CLEAVE
CLEFTS
CLEIST
CLENCH
CLEOME
CLERGY
CLERIC
CLERID
CLERKS
CLEVER
CLEVIS
CLEWED
COELED
COELOM
COEMPT
COERCE
COEVAL
CREAKS
CREAKY
CREAMS
CREAMY
CREASE
CREASY
CREATE
CRECHE
CREDAL
CREDIT
CREDOS
CREEDS
CREEKS
CREELS

CREEPS
CREEPY
CREESE
CREMES
CRENEL
CREOLE
CREPED
CREPES
CRESOL
CRESTS
CRETAN
CRETIC
CRETIN
CRETON
CREUSA
CREVAS
CREWEL
CUESTA
******
******
CAFTAN
COFFEE
COFFER
COFFIN
COFFLE
CUFFED
******
******
CAGIER
CAGILY
CAGING
CIGARS
COGENT
COGGED
COGNAC
COGWAY
CYGNET
CYGNUS
******
******
CAHIER
CAHOOT
COHEIR
COHERE
COHORT

COHOSH
COHUNE
******
******
CAIMAN
CAIQUE
CAIRNS
CEIBAS
CEILED
CHIASM
CHIAUS
CHIBUK
CHICHI
CHICKS
CHICLE
CHICOS
CHIDED
CHIDER
CHIDES
CHIEFS
CHIGOE
CHILLI
CHILLS
CHILLY
CHIMED
CHIMER
CHIMES
CHINCH
CHINES
CHINKS
CHINKY
CHINTZ
CHIPPY
CHIRMS
CHIRON
CHIRPS
CHIRPY
CHIRRS
CHISEL
CHITIN
CHITON
CHITTY
CHIVES
CHIVVY
CLICHE
CLICKS
CLIENT

CLIFFS
CLIFFY
CLIMAT
CLIMAX
CLIMBS
CLIMES
CLINCH
CLINES
CLINGS
CLINGY
CLINIC
CLINKS
CLINTS
CLIQUE
CLIQUY
CLIVES
COIFED
COIGNS
COILED
COILER
COINED
COINER
COITAL
COITUS
CRICKS
CRIERS
CRIKEY
CRIMEA
CRIMES
CRIMPS
CRIMPY
CRINGE
CRINUM
CRISES
CRISIS
CRISPS
CRISPY
CRITIC
CUISSE
******
******
CAJOLE
CAJUNS
******
******
CAKING
COKING

******
******
CALAIS
CALASH
CALCAR
CALCES
CALCIC
CALEBS
CALESA
CALICO
CALIFS
CALIPH
CALKED
CALKER
CALKIN
CALLAO
CALLAS
CALLED
CALLER
CALLOW
CALLUP
CALLUS
CALMED
CALMER
CALMLY
CALORY
CALPAC
CALVED
CALVES
CALVIN
CALXES
CELERY
CELIAC
CELIAS
CELLAE
CELLAR
CELLOS
CELTIC
CHLOES
CHLORO
CILIAT
CILICE
CILIUM
COLDER
COLDLY
COLEUS
COLIES

COLINE	COMBER	CANERS	CINEMA	CHOKED	COOERS
COLINS	COMBOS	CANGUE	CINEOL	CHOKER	COOEYS
COLLAR	COMEDO	CANINE	CINQUE	CHOKES	COOING
COLLET	COMEDY	CANING	CONCHA	CHOLER	COOKED
COLLIE	COMELY	CANKER	CONCHS	CHOLLA	COOKER
COLLOP	COMEON	CANNAE	CONCHY	CHOOSE	COOKEY
COLONS	COMERS	CANNAS	CONCUR	CHOOSY	COOKIE
COLONY	COMETS	CANNED	CONDOM	CHOPIN	COOLED
COLORS	COMFIT	CANNEL	CONDOR	CHOPPY	COOLER
COLOUR	COMICS	CANNER	CONEYS	CHORAL	COOLIE
COLOUS	COMING	CANNES	CONFAB	CHORDS	COOLLY
COLTER	COMITY	CANNIE	CONFER	CHOREA	COOMBS
COLUGO	COMMAS	CANNON	CONGAS	CHOREO	COOPED
COLUMN	COMMIE	CANNOT	CONGER	CHORES	COOPER
COLURE	COMMIT	CANOED	CONGES	CHORIC	COOPTS
COLZAS	COMMIX	CANOES	CONGOU	CHORUS	COOTIE
CULETS	COMMON	CANONS	CONICS	CHOSEN	CROAKS
CULLAY	COMOSE	CANOPY	CONIES	CHOUGH	CROAKY
CULLED	COMOUS	CANSOS	CONING	CLOACA	CROATS
CULLER	COMPEL	CANTAB	CONIUM	CLOAKS	CROCKS
CULLET	COMPLY	CANTED	CONKED	CLOCHE	CROCKY
CULLIS	COMPOS	CANTER	CONKER	CLOCKS	CROCUS
CULMED	CUMBER	CANTHI	CONMAN	CLODDY	CROFTS
CULTCH	CUMINS	CANTLE	CONNED	CLOGGY	CROJIK
CULTUS	CYMARS	CANTON	CONNER	CLONES	CRONES
CULVER	CYMBAL	CANTOR	CONNIE	CLONIC	CRONOS
******	CYMENE	CANTOS	CONOID	CLONUS	CRONUS
C-M---	CYMLIN	CANTUS	CONRAD	CLOSED	CROOKS
******	CYMOID	CANUCK	CONSUL	CLOSER	CROONS
CAMASS	CYMOSE	CANULA	CONTES	CLOSES	CRORES
CAMBER	CYMOUS	CANUTE	CONTIN	CLOSET	CROSSE
CAMDEN	CYMRIC	CANVAS	CONTOS	CLOTHE	CROTCH
CAMELS	******	CANYON	CONTRA	CLOTHO	CROTON
CAMEOS	C-N---	CENSED	CONTRE	CLOTHS	CROUCH
CAMERA	******	CENSER	CONVEX	CLOTTY	CROUPE
CAMILA	CANAAN	CENSES	CONVEY	CLOUDS	CROUPS
CAMION	CANADA	CENSOR	CONVOY	CLOUDY	CROUPY
CAMISE	CANALS	CENSUR	CONWAY	CLOUGH	CROWDS
CAMLET	CANAPE	CENSUS	CUNEAL	CLOUTS	CROWED
CAMPED	CANARD	CENTAL	CUNNER	CLOVEN	CROWNS
CAMPER	CANARY	CENTER	CYNICS	CLOVER	CROZER
CAMPOS	CANCAN	CENTOS	******	CLOVES	CROZES
CAMPUS	CANCEL	CENTRA	C-O---	CLOVIS	******
CEMENT	CANCER	CENTRE	******	CLOWNS	C-P---
CIMBRI	CANDIA	CENTRI	CEORLS	CLOYED	******
COMATE	CANDID	CENTRO	CHOCKS	COODLE	CAPERS
COMBAT	CANDLE	CINDER	CHOICE	COOEED	CAPIAS
COMBED	CANDOR	CINDYS	CHOIRS	COOEES	CAPITA

CAPLIN	CARBOY	CARVEN	CORNUA	CYRENE	COSSET
CAPONE	CARCEL	CARVER	CORNUS	CYRILS	COSTAE
CAPONS	CARDED	CARVES	CORODY	******	COSTAL
CAPOTE	CARDER	CERATE	CORONA	C-S---	COSTAR
CAPPED	CARDIO	CERATO	CORPSE	******	COSTED
CAPPER	CAREEN	CEREAL	CORPUS	CASABA	COSTER
CAPRIC	CAREER	CEREUS	CORRAL	CASALS	COSTLY
CAPTOR	CARERS	CERING	CORRIE	CASAVA	CUSCUS
CIPHER	CARESS	CERIPH	CORSAC	CASBAH	CUSHAT
COPALM	CARETS	CERISE	CORSES	CASEFY	CUSHAW
COPECK	CARFAX	CERITE	CORSET	CASEIN	CUSPED
COPIED	CARGOS	CERIUM	CORTES	CASERN	CUSPID
COPIER	CARHOP	CERMET	CORTEX	CASHAW	CUSPIS
COPIES	CARIBE	CEROUS	CORTEZ	CASHED	CUSSED
COPING	CARIBS	CERTES	CORTIN	CASHES	CUSSES
COPLEY	CARIES	CERUSE	CORVEE	CASHEW	CUSSOS
COPOUT	CARINA	CERVIX	CORVES	CASHOO	CUSTER
COPPED	CARING	CHRISM	CORVUS	CASING	CUSTOM
COPPER	CARLAS	CHRIST	CORYMB	CASINO	CUSTOS
COPPRA	CARLOS	CHROMA	CORYZA	CASKET	CYSTIC
COPRAH	CARLOW	CHROME	CURACY	CASPAR	******
COPSES	CARMAN	CHROMO	CURARE	CASPER	C-T---
COPTIC	CARMEL	CHRONO	CURATE	CASQUE	******
COPULA	CARMEN	CHRYSO	CURBED	CASSIA	CATALO
CUPELS	CARNAL	CIRCLE	CURDED	CASSIE	CATCHY
CUPFUL	CAROBS	CIRCUM	CURDLE	CASSIS	CATENA
CUPOLA	CAROLE	CIRCUS	CURERS	CASTER	CATERS
CUPPED	CAROLS	CIRQUE	CURFEW	CASTES	CATGUT
CUPPER	CAROMS	CIRRUS	CURIAE	CASTLE	CATHAY
CUPRIC	CARPAL	CORALS	CURIAL	CASTOR	CATHER
CUPRUM	CARPED	CORBAN	CURIES	CASTRO	CATHYS
CUPTIE	CARPEL	CORBEL	CURING	CASUAL	CATION
CUPULE	CARPER	CORBIE	CURIOS	CESARE	CATKIN
CYPHER	CARPET	CORDAY	CURIUM	CESIUM	CATLIN
CYPRIN	CARPIC	CORDED	CURLED	CESTUS	CATNAP
CYPRUS	CARPUS	CORDER	CURLER	CESURA	CATNIP
******	CARREL	CORDON	CURLEW	CISCOS	CATSUP
C-Q---	CARRIE	CORERS	CURSED	CISSIE	CATTED
******	CARROT	CORGIS	CURSES	CISSYS	CATTIE
COQUET	CARSON	CORING	CURSOR	COSHED	CATTLE
******	CARTED	CORIUM	CURTIS	COSHER	CETANE
C-R---	CARTEL	CORKED	CURTLY	COSHES	CITHER
******	CARTER	CORKER	CURTSY	COSIGN	CITIED
CARACK	CARTES	CORNEA	CURULE	COSILY	CITIES
CARAFE	CARTON	CORNED	CURVED	COSINE	CITING
CARATE	CARUSO	CORNEL	CURVES	COSMIC	CITOLA
CARATS	CARVED	CORNER	CURVET	COSMOS	CITRAL
CARBON	CARVEL	CORNET	CYRANO	COSSES	CITRIC

CITRON	CHURRS	CAVITY	******	DRAPES	DECADE
CITRUS	CHUTES	CAVORT	**C-Z---**	DRAWEE	DECALS
COTEAU	CLUCKS	CIVETS	******	DRAWER	DECAMP
COTTAE	CLUING	CIVICS	COZENS	DRAWLS	DECANE
COTTAR	CLUMPS	CIVIES	COZIER	DRAWLY	DECANT
COTTAS	CLUMPY	CIVISM	COZIES	DRAYED	DECARE
COTTER	CLUMSY	COVERS	COZILY	DWARFS	DECAYS
COTTON	CLUTCH	COVERT	******	DYADIC	DECCAN
CUTELY	COUGAR	COVETS	**D-A---**	******	DECEIT
CUTEST	COUGHS	COVEYS	******	**D-B---**	DECENT
CUTEYS	COULEE	COVING	DEACON	******	DECERN
CUTIES	COUNTS	******	DEADEN	DABBED	DECIDE
CUTINS	COUNTY	**C-W---**	DEADLY	DABBER	DECILE
CUTLAS	COUPES	******	DEAFEN	DABBLE	DECKED
CUTLER	COUPLE	CAWING	DEAFLY	DEBARK	DECKEL
CUTLET	COUPON	COWAGE	DEALER	DEBARS	DECKER
CUTOFF	COURSE	COWARD	DEARER	DEBASE	DECKLE
CUTOUT	COURTS	COWBOY	DEARIE	DEBATE	DECOCT
CUTTER	COUSIN	COWERS	DEARLY	DEBBIE	DECODE
CUTTLE	CRUCES	COWING	DEARTH	DEBBYS	DECOKE
CUTUPS	CRUDER	COWMAN	DEATHS	DEBITS	DECORS
******	CRUETS	COWMEN	DEATHY	DEBRIS	DECOYS
C-U---	CRUISE	COWPEA	DHARMA	DEBTOR	DECREE
******	CRUMBS	COWPER	DHARNA	DEBUGS	DECUMA
CAUCUS	CRUMBY	COWPOX	DIADEM	DEBUNK	DECURY
CAUDAD	CRUMMY	COWRIE	DIALED	DEBUTS	DICAST
CAUDAL	CRUMPS	******	DIALER	DIBBED	DICERS
CAUDEX	CRUNCH	**C-X---**	DIANAS	DIBBER	DICING
CAUDLE	CRURAL	******	DIANES	DIBBLE	DICKER
CAUGHT	CRUSES	CAXTON	DIAPER	DOBBER	DICKEY
CAULES	CRUSET	COXING	DIATOM	DOBBIN	DICKIE
CAULIS	CRUSOE	******	DIAZIN	DOBIES	DICTUM
CAULKS	CRUSTS	**C-Y---**	DOABLE	DOBLAS	DOCENT
CAUSAL	CRUSTY	******	DOALLS	DOBLON	DOCILE
CAUSED	CRUTCH	CAYMAN	DRABLY	DOBRAS	DOCKED
CAUSER	CRUXES	CAYUGA	DRACHM	DOBSON	DOCKER
CAUSES	******	CAYUSE	DRAFFS	DUBBED	DOCKET
CAUTER	**C-V---**	CEYLON	DRAFFY	DUBBIN	DOCTOR
CHUBBY	******	CHYMIC	DRAFTS	DUBLIN	DUCATS
CHUCKS	CAVEAT	CLYDES	DRAFTY	DYBBUK	DUCKED
CHUFAS	CAVEIN	CLYPEI	DRAGEE	******	DUCKER
CHUMMY	CAVELL	COYISH	DRAGON	**D-C---**	******
CHUMPS	CAVERN	COYOTE	DRAINS	******	**D-D---**
CHUNKS	CAVIAR	COYPUS	DRAKES	DACHAS	******
CHUNKY	CAVIES	CRYING	DRAMAS	DACHAU	DADDLE
CHURCH	CAVILS	CRYPTO	DRAPED	DACOIT	DADOES
CHURLS	CAVING	CRYPTS	DRAPER	DACRON	DEDANS
CHURNS	CAVITE			DACTYL	DEDUCE

DEDUCT	******	DOGFOX	******	DULLES	******
DIDDLE	**D-F---**	DOGGED	**D-K---**	DULUTH	**D-N---**
DIDERO	******	DOGGER	******	******	******
DIDIES	DAFTLY	DOGGIE	DAKOIT	**D-M---**	DANAID
DIDOES	DEFACE	DOGIES	DAKOTA	******	DANAUS
DODDER	DEFAME	DOGMAS	DEKARE	DAMAGE	DANCED
DODECA	DEFEAT	DUGONG	DEKING	DAMANS	DANCER
DODGED	DEFECT	DUGOUT	DIKDIK	DAMASK	DANCES
DODGER	DEFEND	******	DIKING	DAMMAR	DANDER
DODGES	DEFERS	**D-H---**	******	DAMMED	DANDLE
DODOES	DEFIED	******	**D-L---**	DAMMER	DANGED
DUDEEN	DEFIER	DAHLIA	******	DAMNED	DANGER
DUDISH	DEFIES	DAHOON	DALETH	DAMPED	DANGLE
DUDLEY	DEFILE	DEHORN	DALLAS	DAMPEN	DANIEL
******	DEFINE	******	DALLES	DAMPER	DANISH
D-E---	DEFORM	**D-I---**	DALTON	DAMPLY	DANITE
******	DEFRAY	******	DELATE	DAMSEL	DANKER
DAEDAL	DEFTER	DAIMIO	DELAYS	DAMSON	DANKLY
DAEMON	DEFTLY	DAIMON	DELETE	DEMAND	DANNYS
DEEDED	DEFUSE	DAIMYO	DELIAN	DEMEAN	DANTON
DEEMED	DIFFER	DAINTY	DELIAS	DEMENT	DANUBE
DEEPEN	DOFFED	DAISES	DELICT	DEMIES	DANZIG
DEEPER	DOFFER	DAISYS	DELIUS	DEMISE	DENARY
DEEPLY	DUFFED	DEICED	DELLAS	DEMITS	DENDRI
DEEWAN	DUFFEL	DEICER	DELPHI	DEMOBS	DENDRO
DIEPPE	DUFFER	DEICES	DELTAS	DEMODE	DENGUE
DIESEL	DUFFLE	DEIFIC	DELUDE	DEMONO	DENIAL
DIESES	******	DEIGNS	DELUGE	DEMONS	DENIED
DIESIS	**D-G---**	DEISTS	DELUXE	DEMOTE	DENIER
DIETAL	******	DMITRI	DELVED	DEMURE	DENIES
DIETED	DAGGER	DOINGS	DELVER	DEMURS	DENIMS
DIETER	DAGGLE	DOITED	DELVES	DIMERS	DENISE
DOESNT	DAGMAR	DRIERS	DILATE	DIMITY	DENNED
DREADS	DAGOBA	DRIEST	DILUTE	DIMMED	DENNIS
DREAMS	DEGAGE	DRIFTS	DOLING	DIMMER	DENNYS
DREAMT	DEGAME	DRIFTY	DOLLAR	DIMOUT	DENOTE
DREAMY	DEGREE	DRILLS	DOLLED	DIMPLE	DENSER
DREARY	DEGUMS	DRINKS	DOLLIE	DIMPLY	DENTAL
DREDGE	DEGUST	DRIPPY	DOLLOP	DIMWIT	DENTED
DREGGY	DIGAMY	DRIVEL	DOLLYS	DOMAIN	DENTIL
DRENCH	DIGEST	DRIVEN	DOLMAN	DOMING	DENTIN
DRESSY	DIGGED	DRIVER	DOLMEN	DOMINO	DENUDE
DUELED	DIGGER	DRIVES	DOLOUR	DUMBLY	DENVER
DUELER	DIGITI	DUIKER	DOLPHS	DUMDUM	DINAHS
DUELLO	DIGITS	DWIGHT	DULCET	DUMPED	DINARS
DUENNA	DIGLOT	******	DULCIE	DUMPER	DINDER
DWELLS	DOGAPE	**D-J---**	DULLED	DUMPTY	DINERO
DYEING	DOGEAR	DEJECT	DULLER		DINERS

DINGED	DROLLY	DOPTER	DOREEN	DOSERS	DEUCED
DINGEY	DROMON	DUPERS	DORIAN	DOSING	DEUCES
DINGHY	DRONED	DUPERY	DORIES	DOSSAL	DHURNA
DINGLE	DRONES	DUPING	DORMER	DOSSED	DOUBLE
DINGUS	DRONGO	DUPLET	DORMIE	DOSSEL	DOUBLY
DINING	DROOLS	DUPLEX	DORSAD	DOSSER	DOUBTS
DINKEY	DROOPS	******	DORSAL	DOSSIL	DOUCHE
DINKUM	DROOPY	D-R---	DORSET	DUSKED	DOUGAL
DINNED	DROPSY	******	DORSUM	DUSTED	DOUGHS
DINNER	DROSKY	DARDAN	DURBAN	DUSTER	DOUGHY
DINTED	DROSSY	DARERS	DURBAR	******	DOUGIE
DONALD	DROUTH	DARICS	DURESS	D-T---	DOURLY
DONATE	DROVED	DARIEN	DURHAM	******	DOUSED
DONEES	DROVER	DARING	DURIAN	DATARY	DOUSES
DONETS	DROVES	DARIUS	DURING	DATERS	DRUDGE
DONJON	DROWNS	DARKEN	DURION	DATING	DRUIDS
DONKEY	DROWSE	DARKER	******	DATIVE	DRUNKS
DONNAS	DROWSY	DARKLE	D-S---	DATTOS	DRUPEL
DONNED	DUODEN	DARKLY	******	DATURA	DRUPES
DONNIE	DUOLOG	DARNED	DASHED	DETACH	DRUSES
DONORS	DVORAK	DARNEL	DASHER	DETAIL	******
DUNBAR	******	DARNER	DASHES	DETAIN	D-V---
DUNCAN	D-P---	DARROW	DESALT	DETECT	******
DUNCES	******	DARTED	DESCRY	DETENT	DAVEYS
DUNDEE	DAPHNE	DARTER	DESERT	DETERS	DAVIDS
DUNGED	DAPPED	DARTLE	DESIGN	DETEST	DAVIES
DUNKED	DAPPER	DARWIN	DESIRE	DETOUR	DAVITS
DUNKER	DAPPLE	DERAIL	DESIST	DITHER	DEVEIN
DUNLIN	DEPART	DERAIN	DESMAN	DITONE	DEVEST
DUNNED	DEPEND	DERATE	DESMID	DITTOS	DEVICE
DYNAMO	DEPICT	DEREKS	DESOXY	DOTAGE	DEVILS
DYNAST	DEPLOY	DERIDE	DESPOT	DOTARD	DEVISE
******	DEPONE	DERIVE	DESSAU	DOTERS	DEVOID
D-O---	DEPORT	DERMAL	DISARM	DOTIER	DEVOIR
******	DEPOSE	DERMAS	DISBAR	DOTING	DEVOTE
DEODAR	DEPOTS	DERMAT	DISCAL	DOTTED	DEVOUR
DHOLES	DEPTHS	DERMIC	DISCUS	DOTTEL	DEVOUT
DHOTIS	DEPUTE	DERMIS	DISHED	DOTTER	DIVANS
DIOBOL	DEPUTY	DERRIS	DISHES	DOTTLE	DIVERS
DIODES	DIPLEX	DIRECT	DISMAL	DUTIES	DIVERT
DOODAD	DIPLOE	DIRELY	DISMAY	******	DIVEST
DOODLE	DIPODY	DIREST	DISNEY	D-U---	DIVIDE
DOOLEE	DIPOLE	DIRGES	DISOWN	******	DIVINE
DOOLIE	DIPPED	DIRHAM	DISPEL	DAUBED	DIVING
DOOMED	DIPPER	DIRKED	DISTAL	DAUBER	DIVOTS
DROGUE	DIPSAS	DIRNDL	DISTIL	DAUBRY	DOVISH
DROITS	DOPIER	DORADO	DISUSE	DAUDET	******
DROLLS	DOPING	DORBUG	DOSAGE	DAUNTS	D-W---
					******
					DAWDLE
					DAWNED

DAWSON	******	EMBOLI	EDDIES	EVENLY	ENGAGE
DEWANS	**E-A---**	EMBOSS	EDDISH	EVENTS	ENGELS
DEWIER	******	EMBOWS	EIDOLA	EVERET	ENGINE
DEWITT	ECARTE	EMBRUE	ELDERS	EVERTS	ENGIRD
DEWLAP	ELAINE	EMBRYO	ELDEST	EXEDRA	ENGIRT
DIWANS	ELANDS	ERBIUM	ELDRED	EXEMPT	ENGRAM
DOWELS	ELAPSE	EUBOEA	ENDALL	EXEQUY	ENGULF
DOWERS	ELATED	******	ENDEAR	EXERTS	EOGENE
DOWERY	ELATER	**E-C---**	ENDING	EXETER	ERGATE
DOWLAS	ELATES	******	ENDIVE	EXEUNT	EUGENE
DOWNED	ELAYNE	ECCLES	ENDOWS	EYECUP	
DOWSED	ENABLE	EMCEED	ENDUED	EYEFUL	**E-H---**
DOWSER	ENACTS	EMCEES	ENDUES	EYEING	******
DOWSES	ENAMEL	ENCAGE	ENDURE	EYELET	ECHARD
******	ENAMOR	ENCAMP	EUDOAR	EYELID	ECHINI
D-X---	ENATES	ENCASE	******	EYEOUT	ECHINO
******	EPACTS	ENCASH	**E-E---**	EYELID	ECHOED
DEXTER	EPARCH	ENCINA	******	******	ECHOER
DEXTRO	ERASED	ENCODE	ECESIS	**E-F---**	ECHOES
DIXITS	ERASER	ENCORE	EDENIC	******	ECHOIC
DOXIES	ERASES	ENCYST	EGERIA	EFFACE	EPHAHS
******	ETAPES	EOCENE	EGESTA	EFFECT	EPHEBI
D-Y---	EVADED	ESCAPE	EGESTS	EFFETE	EPHODS
******	EVADER	ESCARP	EJECTA	EFFIGY	EPHORI
DAYBED	EVADES	ESCENT	EJECTS	EFFLUX	EPHORS
DAYBOY	EXACTA	ESCHAR	EKEING	EFFORT	ETHANE
DAYFLY	EXACTS	ESCHER	ELECTS	EFFUSE	ETHANS
DAYTON	EXALTS	ESCHEW	ELEGIT	EIFFEL	ETHELS
DOYENS	EXAMEN	ESCORT	ELEMIS	ELFINS	ETHERS
DOYLEY	EXARCH	ESCROW	ELENAS	ELFISH	ETHICS
DRYADS	EYASES	ESCUDO	ELEVEN	ENFACE	ETHNIC
DRYDEN	******	ETCHED	ELEVON	ENFOLD	ETHYLS
DRYERS	**E-B---**	ETCHER	EMEERS	ERFURT	EXHALE
DRYEST	******	ETCHES	EMENDS	******	EXHORT
DRYFLY	EBBING	EUCHER	EMERGE	**E-G---**	EXHUME
DRYICE	EGBERT	EUCHRE	EMERIC	******	******
DRYING	ELBERT	EUCLID	EMERIE	EAGLES	**E-I---**
DRYISH	ELBOWS	EXCEED	EMESIS	EAGLET	******
DRYROT	ELBRUS	EXCELS	EMETIC	EDGARS	EDIBLE
******	EMBALM	EXCEPT	EMETIN	EDGIER	EDICTS
D-Z---	EMBANK	EXCESS	EMEUTE	EDGING	EDILES
******	EMBARK	EXCIDE	ENEMAS	EGGARS	EDISON
DAZING	EMBARS	EXCISE	ENERGY	EGGCUP	EDITED
DAZZLE	EMBAYS	EXCITE	EREBUS	EGGERS	EDITHS
DIZENS	EMBEDS	EXCUSE	ERECTS	EGGING	EDITOR
DOZENS	EMBERS	******	ETERNA	EGGNOG	ELICIT
DOZIER	EMBLEM	**E-D---**	EVELYN	EIGHTH	ELIDED
DOZILY	EMBODY	EDDAIC	EVENED	EIGHTS	ELIDES
DOZING		EDDIED		EIGHTY	

ELIJAH	ELLIOT	EPODES	EERILY	ECTOMY	EXULTS
ELINOR	ENLACE	EPONYM	EGRESS	ECTYPE	EXURBS
ELIOTS	ENLIST	EPOPEE	EGRETS	EITHER	******
ELISHA	EOLIAN	ERODED	ENRAGE	ENTAIL	E-V---
ELIXIR	EOLITH	ERODES	ENRAPT	ENTERA	******
ELIZAS	EULOGY	EROTIC	ENRICH	ENTERE	ELVERS
EMIGRE	******	EVOKED	ENRICO	ENTERO	ELVIRA
EMILES	E-M---	EVOKES	ENROBE	ENTERS	ELVISH
EMILIA	******	EVOLVE	ENROLL	ENTICE	ENVIED
EMILIE	EDMOND	EXODUS	ENROOT	ENTIRE	ENVIER
EMILIO	EDMUND	EXOGEN	ERRAND	ENTITY	ENVIES
EMILYS	ELMERS	EXOTIC	ERRANT	ENTOMB	ENVOYS
ENIGMA	ELMIRA	******	ERRATA	ENTOMO	******
ENISLE	EMMETS	E-P---	ERRING	ENTRAP	E-W---
EPICAL	EMMETT	******	ERRORS	ENTREE	******
EPILOG	EMMIES	EMPALE	EUREKA	ESTATE	EDWARD
EPIRUS	ENMESH	EMPERY	EURIPI	ESTEEM	EDWINA
EPIZOA	ENMITY	EMPIRE	EUROPA	ESTERS	EDWINS
ERICHS	ERMINE	EMPLOY	EUROPE	ESTHER	ENWIND
ERINGO	EXMOOR	EPPING	EYRIES	ESTOPS	ENWOMB
ERINYS	******	ESPANA	******	ESTRAY	ENWRAP
EVICTS	E-N---	ESPIAL	E-S---	ESTRUS	ERWINS
EVILLY	******	ESPIED	******	EXTANT	******
EVINCE	ENNEAD	ESPIES	EASELS	EXTEND	E-Y---
EVITAS	EONIAN	ESPRIT	EASIER	EXTENT	******
EXILED	EONISM	EUPNEA	EASILY	EXTERN	ELYSEE
EXILES	ERNEST	EXPAND	EASING	EXTOLS	ELYTRA
EXILIC	ERNIES	EXPECT	EASTER	EXTORT	ERYNGO
EXISTS	EUNICE	EXPELS	EASTON	EXTRAS	ETYMON
EXITED	EUNUCH	EXPEND	EDSELS	******	******
******	******	EXPERT	ELSIES	E-U---	E-Z---
E-J---	E-O---	EXPIRE	ENSIGN	******	******
******	******	EXPIRY	ENSILE	EDUARD	ECZEMA
ENJOIN	ECOLES	EXPORT	ENSOUL	EDUCED	ENZYME
ENJOYS	EGOISM	EXPOSE	ENSUED	EDUCES	EOZOIC
******	EGOIST	******	ENSUES	EDUCTS	******
E-K---	ELOHIM	E-R---	ENSURE	ELUDED	F-A---
******	ELOIGN	******	ERSATZ	ELUDES	******
ESKERS	ELOINS	EARFUL	ESSAYS	EQUALS	FEALTY
ESKIMO	ELOISE	EARING	ESSENE	EQUATE	FEARED
******	ELOPED	EARLAP	EXSECT	EQUINE	FEARER
E-L---	ELOPER	EARLES	EXSERT	EQUIPS	FEASED
******	ELOPES	EARNED	******	EQUITY	FEASES
EALING	EMOTED	EARNER	E-T---	ERUCTS	FEASTS
ECLAIR	EMOTES	EARTHS	******	ERUPTS	FIACRE
EILEEN	ENOSIS	EARTHY	EATERS	ETUDES	FIANCE
ELLENS	ENOUGH	EARWAX	EATERY	EXUDED	FIASCO
ELLIES	EPOCHS	EARWIG	EATING	EXUDES	FLABBY

FLACKS	******	******	FREEZE	FAITHS	******
FLACON	**F-B---**	**F-E---**	FRENCH	FEIGNE	**F-K---**
FLAGGY	******	******	FRENUM	FEIGNS	******
FLAGON	FABIAN	FAECAL	FRENZY	FEINTS	FAKERS
FLAILS	FABLED	FAECES	FREONS	FEISTS	FAKERY
FLAIRS	FABLER	FAERIE	FRESCO	FEISTY	FAKING
FLAKED	FABLES	FAEROE	FRESNO	FLICKS	FAKIRS
FLAKER	FABRIC	FEEBLE	FRETTY	FLIERS	******
FLAKES	FIBBED	FEEBLY	FUELED	FLIEST	**F-L---**
FLAMBE	FIBBER	FEEDER	FUELER	FLIGHT	******
FLAMED	FIBERS	FEEING	******	FLIMSY	FALCON
FLAMEN	FIBRIL	FEELER	**F-F---**	FLINCH	FALLAL
FLAMES	FIBRIN	FEEZED	******	FLINGS	FALLEN
FLANGE	FIBULA	FEEZES	FAFNIR	FLINTS	FALLER
FLANKS	FOBBED	FIELDS	FIFERS	FLINTY	FALLOW
FLARED	******	FIENDS	FIFING	FLIRTS	FALSER
FLARES	**F-C---**	FIERCE	FIFTHS	FLIRTY	FALTER
FLASHY	******	FIESTA	******	FLITCH	FELICE
FLASKS	FACADE	FLEAMS	**F-G---**	FOIBLE	FELIDS
FLATLY	FACERS	FLECHE	******	FOILED	FELINE
FLATUS	FACETS	FLECKS	FAGEND	FOISTS	FELIPE
FLAUNT	FACIAL	FLEDGE	FAGGED	FRIARS	FELLAH
FLAVIA	FACIES	FLEDGY	FAGGOT	FRIARY	FELLED
FLAVIN	FACILE	FLEECE	FAGOTS	FRIDAY	FELLER
FLAVOR	FACING	FLEECY	FIGGED	FRIDGE	FELLOE
FLAWED	FACTOR	FLEERS	FIGHTS	FRIEDA	FELLOW
FLAXEN	FACTUM	FLEETS	FIGURE	FRIEND	FELONS
FLAXES	FACULA	FLENCH	FOGBOW	FRIERS	FELONY
FLAYED	FECIAL	FLENSE	FOGDOG	FRIEZE	FELTED
FLAYER	FECULA	FLESHY	FOGGED	FRIGGA	FILERS
FOALED	FECUND	FLETCH	FOGIES	FRIGHT	FILETS
FOAMED	FICHES	FLEURY	FUGIOS	FRIGID	FILIAL
FRACAS	FICHUS	FLEXED	FUGLED	FRIJOL	FILING
FRAILS	FICKLE	FLEXES	FUGLES	FRILLS	FILLED
FRAISE	FOCSLE	FLEXOR	FUGUES	FRILLY	FILLER
FRAMED	FUCOID	FOEHNS	******	FRINGE	FILLET
FRAMER	FUCOUS	FOEMAN	**F-H---**	FRINGY	FILLIN
FRAMES	******	FOEMEN	******	FRISES	FILLIP
FRANCE	**F-D---**	FOETAL	FUHRER	FRISKS	FILMED
FRANCK	******	FOETID	******	FRISKY	FILMIC
FRANCO	FADEIN	FOETOR	**F-I---**	FRITHS	FILOSE
FRANCS	FADING	FOETUS	******	FRIVOL	FILTER
FRANKS	FEDORA	FREAKS	FAILED	FRIZZY	FILTHY
FRAPPE	FIDDLE	FREAKY	FAILLE	******	FOLDED
FRATER	FIDGET	FREDAS	FAINTS	**F-J---**	FOLDER
FRAUDS	FODDER	FREDDY	FAIRED	******	FOLIAR
FRAUEN	FUDDLE	FREELY	FAIRER	FIJIAN	FOLIOS
FRAYED	FUDGES	FREEST	FAIRLY		FOLIUM

FOLKSY	FENNEC	FLORAS	FARING	FORMAT	******
FOLLOW	FENNEL	FLORES	FARLES	FORMED	**F-T---**
FULCRA	FENRIR	FLORET	FARLEY	FORMER	******
FULFIL	FINALE	FLORID	FARMED	FORMIC	FATHER
FULGID	FINALS	FLORIN	FARMER	FORMYL	FATHOM
FULLED	FINDER	FLOSSY	FAROFF	FORNAX	FATIMA
FULLER	FINELY	FLOURS	FAROUT	FORNIX	FATING
FULMAR	FINERY	FLOURY	FARROW	FORTES	FATTED
FULTON	FINEST	FLOUTS	FERBER	FORTIS	FATTEN
FYLFOT	FINGER	FLOWED	FERIAL	FORUMS	FATTER
******	FINIAL	FLOWER	FERINE	FURFUR	FETIAL
F-M---	FINING	FLOYDS	FERITY	FURIES	FETICH
******	FINISH	FOOLED	FERMIS	FURLED	FETING
FAMILY	FINITE	FOOTED	FEROUS	FURORE	FETISH
FAMINE	FINNAN	FOOTER	FERRET	FURORS	FETORS
FAMISH	FINNED	FOOTLE	FERRIC	FURRED	FETTER
FAMOUS	FINNER	FOOZLE	FERRIS	FURROW	FETTLE
FEMALE	FINNIC	FROCKS	FERRUM	FURZES	FITFUL
FEMORA	FINNOC	FROGGY	FERULA	******	FITTED
FEMURS	FONDER	FROLIC	FERULE	**F-S---**	FITTER
FIMBLE	FONDLE	FRONDS	FERVID	******	FUTILE
FOMENT	FONDLY	FRONTO	FERVOR	FASCES	FUTURE
FUMBLE	FONDUE	FRONTS	FIRERS	FASCIA	******
FUMIER	FONTAL	FROSTS	FIRING	FASTED	**F-U---**
FUMING	FUNDED	FROSTY	FIRKIN	FASTEN	******
FUMOUS	FUNDUS	FROTHS	FIRMAN	FASTER	FAUCAL
******	FUNEST	FROTHY	FIRMED	FESCUE	FAUCES
F-N---	FUNGAL	FROWNS	FIRMER	FESSES	FAUCET
******	FUNGUS	FROWZY	FIRMLY	FESTAL	FAULTS
FANEGA	FUNKED	FROZEN	FIRSTS	FESTER	FAULTY
FANGAS	FUNNEL	******	FIRTHS	FISCAL	FAUNAE
FANGED	******	**F-P---**	FORAGE	FISHER	FAUNAL
FANION	**F-O---**	******	FORAYS	FISHES	FAUNAS
FANJET	******	FIPPLE	FORBID	FISTED	FAUNUS
FANNED	FEODOR	******	FORCED	FISTIC	FAUVES
FANNER	FEOFFS	**F-Q---**	FORCER	FOSSAE	FEUARS
FANNIE	FIORDS	******	FORCES	FOSSES	FEUDAL
FANNYS	FLOATS	FIQUES	FORDED	FOSSIL	FEUDED
FANONS	FLOATY	******	FOREGO	FOSTER	FEUING
FANTAN	FLOCKS	**F-R---**	FOREST	FUSAIN	FLUENT
FANTOM	FLOCKY	******	FORGED	FUSEES	FLUFFS
FANUMS	FLONGS	FARADS	FORGER	FUSILE	FLUFFY
FENCED	FLOODS	FARBAD	FORGES	FUSILS	FLUIDS
FENCER	FLOORS	FARCED	FORGET	FUSING	FLUKED
FENCES	FLOOZY	FARCER	FORGOT	FUSION	FLUKES
FENDED	FLOPPY	FARCES	FORINT	FUSSED	FLUKEY
FENDER	FLORAE	FARERS	FORKED	FUSSER	FLUMED
FENIAN	FLORAL	FARINA	FORMAL	FUSTIC	FLUMES

FLUMPS	FIXERS	GLAIRS	GRATIN	******	GRETNA
FLUNKS	FIXING	GLAIRY	GRATIS	**G-D---**	GUENON
FLUNKY	FIXITY	GLAMIS	GRAVED	******	GUESTS
FLUORO	FOXIER	GLANCE	GRAVEL	GADDED	GWENNS
FLUORS	FOXILY	GLANDS	GRAVEN	GADDER	******
FLURRY	FOXING	GLARED	GRAVER	GADFLY	**G-F---**
FLUTED	******	GLARES	GRAVES	GADGET	******
FLUTER	**F-Y---**	GLASSY	GRAVID	GADOID	GAFFED
FLUTES	******	GLAUCO	GRAYED	GIDEON	GAFFER
FLUVIO	FAYING	GLAZED	GRAYER	GODDAM	GAFFES
FLUXED	FLYBYS	GLAZER	GRAYLY	GODIVA	GIFTED
FLUXES	FLYERS	GLAZES	GRAZED	GODSON	GOFFER
FOUGHT	FLYING	GNARLS	GRAZER	GODWIN	GUFFAW
FOULED	FLYMAN	GNARLY	GRAZES	GODWIT	******
FOULER	FOYERS	GNATHO	GUACOS	******	**G-G---**
FOULLY	FRYERS	GNAWED	GUANIN	**G-E---**	******
FOUNDS	FRYING	GNAWER	GUANOS	******	GAGERS
FOUNTS	******	GOADED	GUARDS	GAELIC	GAGGED
FOURTH	**F-Z---**	GOALIE	GUAVAS	GEEING	GAGGER
FRUGAL	******	GOATEE	******	GEEZER	GAGGLE
FRUITS	FAZING	GRABEN	**G-B---**	GHEBER	GAGING
FRUITY	FEZZAN	GRACED	******	GHETTO	GIGANT
FRUMPS	FEZZES	GRACES	GABBED	GLEAMS	GIGGED
FRUMPY	FIZGIG	GRACIE	GABBER	GLEAMY	GIGGLE
FRUNZE	FIZZED	GRADED	GABBLE	GLEANS	GIGGLY
FRUSTA	FIZZER	GRADER	GABBRO	GLEBES	GIGLET
******	FIZZES	GRADES	GABION	GLEDES	GIGLOT
F-V---	FIZZLE	GRADIN	GABLED	GLEETS	GIGOLO
******	FUZEES	GRADUS	GABLES	GLEETY	GIGUES
FAVORS	FUZILS	GRAECO	GIBBED	GNEISS	GOGGLE
FAVOUR	FUZING	GRAFTS	GIBBER	GOETHE	GOGLET
FEVERS	FUZZED	GRAHAM	GIBBET	GREASE	******
FIVERS	FUZZES	GRAINS	GIBBON	GREASY	**G-I---**
FOVEAE	******	GRAINY	GIBERS	GREATS	******
FOVEAL	**G-A---**	GRAMME	GIBING	GREAVE	GAIETY
******	******	GRANDE	GIBLET	GREBES	GAINED
F-W---	GDANSK	GRANGE	GIBRAN	GREECE	GAINER
******	GEARED	GRANNY	GIBSON	GREEDS	GAINLY
FAWKES	GHARRI	GRANTS	GOBANG	GREEDY	GAITED
FAWNED	GHARRY	GRAPES	GOBBET	GREEKS	GAITER
FAWNER	GHAUTS	GRAPHO	GOBBLE	GREENE	GEIGER
FEWEST	GIANTS	GRAPHS	GOBIES	GREENS	GEISHA
FOWLED	GIAOUR	GRAPHY	GOBLET	GREETS	GLIBLY
FOWLER	GLACES	GRASPS	GOBLIN	GREGOS	GLIDED
******	GLACIS	GRASSY	GYBING	GREIFS	GLIDER
F-X---	GLADES	GRATED	******	GREIGE	GLIDES
******	GLADLY	GRATER	**G-C---**	GRETAS	GLINTS
FAXING	GLADYS	GRATES	******	GRETEL	GLIOMA
FIXATE			GECKOS		
			GOCART		

GOINGS	GALIOT	GAMMED	GENTOO	GLOWER	GAPPED
GOITER	GALLED	GAMMER	GENTRY	GLOZED	GIPONS
GOITRE	GALLEY	GAMMON	GINGAL	GLOZES	GIPPED
GRIDED	GALLIC	GAMOUS	GINGER	GNOMES	GOPHER
GRIDES	GALLON	GAMUTS	GINGKO	GNOMIC	GYPPED
GRIEVE	GALLOP	GEMARA	GINNED	GNOMON	GYPSUM
GRIFFE	GALLUP	GEMERT	GINNER	GNOSIS	******
GRIGRI	GALLUS	GEMINI	GONADS	GOOBER	G-R---
GRILLE	GALOOT	GEMMAE	GONERS	GOODBY	******
GRILLS	GALOPS	GEMMED	GONION	GOODLY	GARAGE
GRILSE	GALORE	GEMOTS	GONIUM	GOOFED	GARBED
GRIMED	GALOSH	GEMSBO	GUNMAN	GOOGLY	GARBLE
GRIMES	GALWAY	GIMELS	GUNMEN	GOOGOL	GARCON
GRIMLY	GALYAK	GIMLET	GUNNAR	GOOIER	GARDEN
GRINDS	GELDED	GIMPED	GUNNED	GOONEY	GARGET
GRIPED	GELLED	GOMUTI	GUNNEL	GOORAL	GARGLE
GRIPER	GILDAS	GUMBOS	GUNNER	GOOSED	GARISH
GRIPES	GILDED	GUMMAS	GUNSHY	GOOSES	GARLIC
GRIPPE	GILDER	GUMMED	GUNTER	GOOSEY	GARNER
GRIPPY	GILEAD	******	GYNECO	GROANS	GARNET
GRISLY	GILLIE	G-N---	GYNOUS	GROATS	GARRET
GRITTY	GOLDEN	******	******	GROCER	GARTER
GRIVET	GOLFED	GANDER	G-O---	GROGGY	GERALD
GRIZEL	GOLFER	GANDHI	******	GROINS	GERARD
GUIANA	GOLOSH	GANEFS	GAOLER	GROOMS	GERBIL
GUIDED	GULDEN	GANGED	GEODES	GROOVE	GERENT
GUIDER	GULFED	GANGER	GEODIC	GROOVY	GERMAN
GUIDES	GULLAH	GANGES	GEORGE	GROPED	GERMEN
GUIDON	GULLED	GANGLI	GEORGI	GROPER	GEROUS
GUILDS	GULLET	GANGUE	GHOSTS	GROPES	GERRYS
GUILES	GULPED	GANNET	GHOULS	GROSZY	GERTIE
GUILTS	GULPER	GANOID	GIOTTO	GROTTO	GERTYS
GUILTY	******	GANTRY	GLOATS	GROTTY	GERUND
GUIMPE	G-M---	GENDER	GLOBAL	GROUCH	GERYON
GUINEA	******	GENERA	GLOBED	GROUND	GIRDED
GUISES	GAMBIA	GENESI	GLOBES	GROUPS	GIRDER
GUITAR	GAMBIR	GENETS	GLOBIN	GROUSE	GIRDLE
******	GAMBIT	GENEVA	GLOOMS	GROUTS	GIRTED
G-K---	GAMBLE	GENIAL	GLOOMY	GROVEL	GORALS
******	GAMBOL	GENIES	GLORIA	GROVER	GORDON
GOKART	GAMELY	GENITO	GLOSSO	GROVES	GORGED
******	GAMETE	GENIUS	GLOSSY	GROWER	GORGER
G-L---	GAMETO	GENOUS	GLOSTS	GROWLS	GORGES
******	GAMIER	GENRES	GLOTTO	GROWTH	GORGET
GALACT	GAMILY	GENROS	GLOVED	GROYNE	GORGON
GALAXY	GAMING	GENTES	GLOVER	******	GORHEN
GALEAE	GAMINS	GENTLE	GLOVES	G-P---	GORIER
GALENA	GAMMAS	GENTLY	GLOWED	******	GORILY
				GAPERS	
				GAPING	

GORING	GETTER	GAVOTS	HEARTS	HECTOR	******
GORSES	GETUPS	GIVING	HEARTY	HECUBA	**H-G---**
GURGLE	GITANO	GOVERN	HEATED	HICCUP	******
GURKHA	GOTAMA	GYVING	HEATER	HICKEY	HAGBUT
GYRATE	GOTHAM	******	HEATHS	HICKOK	HAGDON
GYRONS	GOTHIC	**G-W---**	HEATHY	HOCKED	HAGGED
GYROSE	GOTTEN	******	HEAUME	HOCKEY	HAGGIS
******	GUTTAE	GAWAIN	HEAVED	HUCKLE	HAGGLE
G-S---	GUTTAT	GAWKED	HEAVEN	******	HEGIRA
******	GUTTED	GEWGAW	HEAVER	**H-D---**	HIGGLE
GASBAG	GUTTER	GOWNED	HEAVES	******	HIGHER
GASCON	GUTTLE	******	HIATUS	HADING	HIGHLY
GASHED	******	**G-Y---**	HOARDS	HEDDLE	HOGANS
GASHES	**G-U---**	******	HOARSE	HEDGED	HOGGED
GASIFY	******	GAYEST	HOAXED	HEDGER	HOGNUT
GASJET	GAUCHE	GAYETY	HOAXER	HEDGES	HOGTIE
GASKET	GAUCHO	GDYNIA	HOAXES	HEDRAL	HUGELY
GASKIN	GAUGED	GEYSER	HYADES	HEDRON	HUGEST
GASMAN	GAUGER	GLYCOL	******	HEDWIG	HUGGED
GASMEN	GAUGES	GLYNIS	**H-B---**	HIDDEN	HUGHES
GASPAR	GAULLE	GLYPHS	******	HIDERS	HUGHIE
GASPED	GAUZES	GLYPTO	HABEAS	HIDING	HYGEIA
GASPER	GIULIA	GUYANA	HABILE	HODDEN	******
GASSED	GIULIO	GUYING	HABITS	HODMAN	**H-I---**
GASSES	GLUIER	GWYNNE	HEBREW	HUDDLE	******
GASTON	GLUING	******	HEBRON	HUDSON	HAILED
GASTRO	GLUMES	**G-Z---**	HOBART	HYDRAE	HAILER
GESELL	GLUMLY	******	HOBBES	HYDRAS	HAIRDO
GESSOS	GLUTEI	GAZABO	HOBBLE	HYDRIC	HAIRED
GESTIC	GLUTEN	GAZEBO	HOBNOB	HYDROS	HEIFER
GISELE	GOUGED	GAZERS	HOBOES	******	HEIGHT
GISMOS	GOUGER	GAZING	HUBBUB	**H-E---**	HEISTS
GOSHEN	GOUGES	GIZMOS	HUBCAP	******	HOICKS
GOSPEL	GOURDE	GUZZLE	HUBERT	HAEMAL	HOIDEN
GOSSIP	GOURDS	******	HUBRIS	HEEDED	HOISTS
GUSHED	GRUBBY	**H-A---**	HYBRID	HEEDER	******
GUSHER	GRUDGE	******	HYBRIS	HEEHAW	**H-J---**
GUSHES	GRUELS	HEADED	******	HEELED	******
GUSSET	GRUGRU	HEADER	**H-C---**	HEELER	HEJIRA
GUSSIE	GRUMES	HEADON	******	HIEING	HIJACK
GUSTAF	GRUMPY	HEALED	HACKED	HIEMAL	******
GUSTAV	GRUNDY	HEALER	HACKEE	HOEING	**H-K---**
******	GRUNTS	HEALTH	HACKER	HUELVA	******
G-T---	******	HEAPED	HACKIE	HYENAS	HAKIMS
******	**G-V---**	HEARER	HACKLE	HYETAL	HIKERS
GATEAU	******	HEARSE	HECATE	******	HIKING
GATHER	GAVELS	HEARST	HECKLE	**H-F---**	******
GATING	GAVIAL	HEARTH	HECTIC	******	**H-L---**
				HAFTED	******
				HEFTED	HALERS
				HUFFED	HALIDE

HALIDS	HOLLYS	******	HOOKAH	HARKED	HORDES
HALING	HOLMES	**H-N---**	HOOKED	HARKEN	HORNED
HALITE	HOLMIC	******	HOOKER	HARLAN	HORNET
HALLAH	HULKED	HANCES	HOOKEY	HARLEM	HORNIE
HALLEL	HULLED	HANDED	HOOKUP	HARLEY	HORRID
HALLEY	******	HANDEL	HOOPED	HARLOT	HORROR
HALLOO	**H-M---**	HANDLE	HOOPER	HARLOW	HORSED
HALLOW	******	HANGAR	HOOPLA	HARMED	HORSES
HALLUX	HAMALS	HANGED	HOOPOE	HARMIN	HORSEY
HALOED	HAMAUL	HANGER	HOORAY	HAROLD	HORSTE
HALOES	HAMDEN	HANGUP	HOOTCH	HARPED	HURDLE
HALOID	HAMITE	HANKER	HOOTED	HARPER	HURLED
HALSEY	HAMLET	HANNAH	HOOTER	HARRIS	HURLER
HALTED	HAMMAL	HANNAS	HOOVED	HARROW	HURLEY
HALTER	HAMMED	HANSEL	HOOVER	HARRYS	HURONS
HALUTZ	HAMMER	HANSOM	HOOVES	HARTAL	HURRAH
HALVED	HAMPER	HENBIT	HYOIDS	HARVEY	HURRAY
HALVES	HAMZAS	HENDON	******	HERALD	HURTER
HELENA	HEMATO	HENLEY	**H-P---**	HERBAL	HURTLE
HELENS	HEMMED	HENNAS	******	HERDED	******
HELICO	HEMMER	HENRIS	HAPPED	HERDER	**H-S---**
HELIOS	HEMOID	HENRYS	HAPPEN	HERDIC	******
HELIUM	HEMPEN	HINDER	HEPATO	HEREAT	HASHED
HELLAS	HOMAGE	HINDUS	HEPTAD	HEREBY	HASHES
HELLEN	HOMBRE	HINGED	HIPPED	HEREIN	HASLET
HELLER	HOMELY	HINGES	HIPPIE	HEREOF	HASPED
HELMED	HOMERS	HINTED	HIPPOS	HEREON	HASSEL
HELMET	HOMIER	HONEST	HIPPUS	HERESY	HASSLE
HELOTS	HOMILY	HONEYS	HOPING	HERETO	HASTED
HELPED	HOMING	HONIED	HOPPED	HERIOT	HASTEN
HELPER	HOMINY	HONING	HOPPER	HERMAE	HASTES
HELTER	HUMANE	HONKED	HOPPLE	HERMAI	HESOID
HELVES	HUMANS	HONKER	HYPHAE	HERMAN	HESTER
HILARY	HUMBER	HONORE	HYPHAL	HERMES	HESTIA
HILDAS	HUMBLE	HONORS	HYPHEN	HERMIT	HISPID
HILLED	HUMBLY	HONOUR	HYPNIC	HERNIA	HISSED
HILLER	HUMBUG	HONSHU	HYPNOS	HERNIO	HISSER
HILTED	HUMIFY	HUNGER	******	HEROES	HISSES
HOLARD	HUMMED	HUNGRY	**H-R---**	HEROIC	HOSIER
HOLDER	HUMMER	HUNTED	******	HEROIN	HOSING
HOLDUP	HUMORS	HUNTER	HARASS	HERONS	HOSTED
HOLIER	HUMOUR	******	HARBIN	HERPES	HOSTEL
HOLIES	HUMPED	**H-O---**	HARBOR	HIRAMS	HUSHED
HOLILY	HUMPTY	******	HARDEN	HIRERS	HUSHES
HOLING	HYMENO	HOODED	HARDER	HIRING	HUSKED
HOLISM	HYMENS	HOODOO	HARDLY	HORACE	HUSKER
HOLLER	HYMNAL	HOOFED	HAREMS	HORARY	HUSSAR
HOLLOW	HYMNED	HOOFER	HARING	HORDED	HUSTLE

HYSSOP	HAVENT	HAZILY	INCITE	IDEATE	ICIEST
HYSTER	HAVING	HAZING	INCOME	ILEXES	ICINGS
******	HIVING	HAZZAN	INCORP	IPECAC	IDIOCY
H-T---	HIVITE	HEZION	INCUBI	IREFUL	IDIOMS
******	HOVELS	******	INCURS	IRENES	IDIOTS
HATBOX	HOVERS	I-A---	INCUSE	IRENIC	IMIDES
HATERS	******	******	ISCHIA	ISEULT	IMINES
HATFUL	H-W---	IBADAN	ITCHED	******	IRIDES
HATING	******	ICALLY	ITCHES	I-F---	IRIDIC
HATPIN	HAWAII	ICARUS	******	******	IRISED
HATRED	HAWHAW	IMAGED	I-D---	ILFORD	IRISES
HATTED	HAWING	IMAGES	******	INFAMY	IRITIC
HATTER	HAWKED	IMARET	INDABA	INFANT	IRITIS
HATTIE	HAWKER	INARCH	INDEED	INFECT	ISIDOR
HATTYS	HAWSER	INARMS	INDENE	INFERO	ITIOUS
HETERO	HAWSES	IRANIS	INDENT	INFERS	
HETMAN	HEWERS	IRAQIS	INDIAN	INFEST	I-J---
HETTYS	HEWING	ISAACS	INDICT	INFIRM	******
HITHER	HOWARD	ISABEL	INDIES	INFLOW	INJECT
HITLER	HOWDAH	ISADOR	INDIGO	INFLUX	INJOKE
HITTER	HOWLED	ISAIAH	INDITE	INFOLD	INJURE
HOTBED	HOWLER	ISATIN	INDIUM	INFORM	INJURY
HOTBOX	******	ITALIC	INDOOR	INFUSE	******
HOTELS	H-X---	******	INDOWS	******	I-K---
HOTPOT	******	I-B---	INDRIS	I-G---	******
HOTROD	HEXADS	******	INDUCE	******	INKERS
HOTTED	HEXANE	IMBALM	INDUCT	INGEST	INKIER
HOTTER	HEXING	IMBARK	INDUED	INGOTS	INKING
HUTTED	HEXONE	IMBEDS	INDUES	INGRES	INKLES
******	HEXOSE	IMBIBE	INDULT	INGRID	INKPOT
H-U---	HEXYLS	IMBODY	IODATE	INGULF	IRKING
******	HUXLEY	IMBRUE	IODIDE	******	******
HAULED	******	IMBUED	IODINE	I-H---	I-L---
HAULER	H-Y---	IMBUES	IODISM	******	******
HAULMY	******	INBAND	IODIZE	ICHTHY	IDLERS
HAUNCH	HAYBOX	INBORN	IODOUS	INHALE	IDLEST
HAUNTS	HAYING	INBRED	******	INHAUL	IDLING
HAUSEN	HAYMOW	******	I-E---	INHERE	IGLOOS
HOUNDS	HEYDAY	I-C---	******	INHUME	ILLUME
HOURIS	HOYDEN	******	IBEAMS	ISHTAR	ILLUSE
HOURLY	******	INCAGE	IBERIA	ITHACA	ILLUST
HOUSED	H-Z---	INCASE	IBEXES	******	INLACE
HOUSES	******	INCEPT	ICEAXE	I-I---	INLAID
******	HAZARD	INCEST	ICEBOX	******	INLAND
H-V---	HAZELS	INCHED	ICECAP	IBICES	INLAWS
******	HAZERS	INCHES	ICEMAN	IBIDEM	INLAYS
HAVANA	HAZIER	INCHON	ICEMEN	IBISES	INLETS
HAVENS		INCISE	IDEALS	ICICLE	INLIER

IOLCUS	******	ISSUER	******	******	******
IOLITE	I-P---	ISSUES	J-A---	J-E---	J-K---
ISLAND	******	ITSELF	******	******	******
ISLETS	IMPACT	******	JEANNE	JAEGER	JEKYLL
ISLING	IMPAIR	I-T---	JOANNA	JEEING	JOKERS
******	IMPALA	******	JOANNE	JEERED	JOKING
I-M---	IMPALE	IATRIC	JUAREZ	JEERER	******
******	IMPARK	INTACT	******	******	J-L---
IAMBIC	IMPART	INTAKE	J-B---	J-G---	******
IAMBUS	IMPASS	INTEND	******	******	JALOPS
IMMESH	IMPAWN	INTENT	JABBED	JAGGED	JALOPY
IMMIES	IMPEDE	INTERN	JABBER	JAGUAR	JELLED
IMMUNE	IMPELS	INTERS	JABIRU	JIGGED	JILTED
IMMUNO	IMPEND	INTIMA	JABOTS	JIGGER	JILTER
IMMURE	IMPING	INTOMB	JIBBED	JIGGLE	JOLIET
INMATE	IMPISH	INTONE	JIBBER	JIGSAW	JOLTED
INMESH	IMPORT	INTUIT	JIBING	JOGGED	JOLTER
INMOST	IMPOSE	INTURN	JOBBED	JOGGER	JULEPS
******	IMPOST	ISTRIA	JOBBER	JOGGLE	JULIAN
I-N---	IMPUGN	******	JUBBAH	JUGATE	JULIAS
******	IMPURE	I-U---	******	JUGFUL	JULIES
IGNACE	IMPUTE	******	J-C---	JUGGED	JULIET
IGNIFY	INPUTS	IGUANA	******	JUGGLE	JULIUS
IGNITE	******	INULIN	JACANA	******	******
IGNORE	I-R---	INURED	JACKAL	J-H---	J-M---
INNATE	******	INURES	JACKED	******	******
INNING	INROAD	INURNS	JACKET	JIHADS	JAMIES
IONIAN	INRUSH	******	JACKIE	JOHANN	JAMJAR
IONIUM	ISRAEL	I-V---	JACKYS	JOHNNY	JAMMED
IONIZE	******	******	JACOBS	******	JEMIMA
IONONE	I-S---	INVADE	JOCKEY	J-I---	JIMINY
******	******	INVENT	JOCKOS	******	JIMMIE
I-O---	INSANE	INVERT	JOCOSE	JAILED	JIMMYS
******	INSECT	INVEST	JOCUND	JAILER	JUMBAL
ICONIC	INSERT	INVITE	******	JAILOR	JUMBLE
IGOROT	INSETS	INVOKE	J-D---	JAINAS	JUMPED
ILOILO	INSIDE	IRVING	******	JAIPUR	JUMPER
IMOGEN	INSIST	IRVINS	JADING	JOINED	******
IRONED	INSOLE	******	JADISH	JOINER	J-N---
IRONER	INSOUL	I-W---	JUDAEA	JOINTS	******
IRONIC	INSPAN	******	JUDAEO	JOISTS	JANETS
ISOBAR	INSTAR	INWALL	JUDAHS	JUICER	JANGLE
ISOBEL	INSTEP	INWARD	JUDAIC	JUICES	JANICE
ISOGON	INSTIL	INWIND	JUDEAN	******	JENNET
ISOHEL	INSULT	INWOVE	JUDGED	J-J---	JENNYS
ISOLDE	INSURE	INWRAP	JUDGER	******	JINGAL
ISOMER	ISSEIS	IRWINS	JUDGES	JEJUNE	JINGLE
ISOPOD	ISSUED	IDYLLS	JUDITH	JUJUBE	JINGLY

JINKED	JORAMS	******	******	******	******
JINKER	JORDAN	**J-U---**	**K-B---**	**K-F---**	**K-M---**
JINNEE	JORGES	******	******	******	******
JINNYS	JORUMS	JAUNTS	KABAKA	KAFFIR	KAMALA
JINXED	JURANT	JAUNTY	KABALA	KAFTAN	KAMIKS
JINXES	JURATS	JOULES	KABAYA	******	KAMSIN
JONAHS	JURELS	JOUNCE	KABIKI	**K-G---**	KIMONO
JONNIE	JURIES	JOUSTS	KABOBS	******	KUMISS
JONSON	JURIST	******	KABUKI	KEGLER	KUMMEL
JUNCOS	JURORS	**J-V---**	KIBBLE	******	******
JUNEAU	******	******	KIBEIS	**K-I---**	**K-N---**
JUNGLE	**J-S---**	JIVING	KIBITZ	******	******
JUNGLY	******	JOVIAL	KIBLAH	KAISER	KANAKA
JUNIOR	JASONS	JOVIAN	KIBOSH	KEITHS	KANSAN
JUNIUS	JASPER	******	KOBOLD	KNIFED	KANSAS
JUNKED	JESSED	**J-W---**	******	KNIFES	KENDAL
JUNKER	JESSES	******	**K-C---**	KNIGHT	KENITE
JUNKET	JESSIE	JAWING	******	KNIVES	KENNED
JUNKIE	JESTED	JEWELS	KECKED	KOINES	KENNEL
JUNTAS	JESTER	JEWESS	KECKLE	KRISES	KENNIE
******	JESUIT	JEWISH	KICKED	******	KENNYS
J-P---	JOSEPH	******	KICKER	**K-K---**	KINASE
******	JOSHED	**J-Y---**	KUCHEN	******	KINDER
JAPANS	JOSHER	******	******	KAKAPO	KINDLE
JAPHET	JOSHES	JAYVEE	**K-D---**	KOKOMO	KINDLY
JAPHIA	JOSHUA	JOYCES	******	******	KINESI
JAPING	JOSIAH	JOYFUL	KEDDAH	**K-L---**	KINETO
JOPLIN	JOSIAS	JOYING	KEDGED	******	KINGED
JUPONS	JOSIEA	JOYOUS	KEDGES	KALIAN	KINGLY
******	JOSSES	******	KEDRON	KALIUM	KININS
J-R---	JOSTLE	**J-Z---**	KIDDED	KALMIA	KINKED
******	JUSTIN	******	KIDDER	KALONG	KINSEY
JARFUL	JUSTLY	JAZZED	KIDDIE	KALPAK	KONRAD
JARGON	JUSTUS	JAZZER	KIDNAP	KELLER	******
JARINA	******	JAZZES	KIDNEY	KELOID	**K-O---**
JARRED	**J-T---**	JEZAIL	KODAKS	KELPIE	******
JARROW	******	******	KODIAK	KELSON	KAOLIN
JARVEY	JETHRO	**K-A---**	******	KELTIC	KIOSKS
JARVIS	JETSAM	******	**K-E---**	KELVIN	KNOBBY
JERBOA	JETTED	KAASES	******	KILLED	KNOCKS
JEREED	JETTON	KHAKIS	KEELED	KILLER	KNOLLS
JEREMY	JITNEY	KLAXON	KEENED	KILMER	KNOSPS
JERKED	JITTER	KNACKS	KEENER	KILTED	KNOTTY
JERKIN	JOTHAM	KNARRY	KEENLY	KILTER	KNOUTS
JEROME	JOTTED	KNAVES	KEEPER	KILTIE	KNOWER
JERRYS	JOTTER	KOALAS	KEEVES	KULAKS	KOODOO
JERSEY	JUTISH	KRAALS	KNEADS	KULTUR	KRONEN
JERVIS	JUTTED	KRAITS	KNEELS	KULTUR	KRONER
		KRAKEN	KNELLS		

KRONOR ****** ****** LABILE LUCENT LOFTER
KRONOS K-T--- K-Z--- LABIUM LUCIAN LUFFED
KRONUR ****** ****** LABORS LUCIAS ******
****** KATHIE KAZOOS LABOUR LUCIEN L-G---
K-P--- KATHYS ****** LABRET LUCILE ******
****** KATIES L-A--- LABRUM LUCITE LAGERS
KAPOKS KATION ****** LIBBYS LUCIUS LAGGED
KAPPAS KETENE LAAGER LIBELS LYCEES LAGGER
KEPLER KETONE LEACHY LIBIDO LYCEUM LAGOON
KIPPED KETOSE LEADED LIBRAE ****** LAGUNE
KIPPER KETTLE LEADEN LIBRAS L-D--- LEGACY
KOPECK KITBAG LEADER LIBYAN ****** LEGATE
KOPEKS KITING LEADIN LOBATE LADDER LEGATO
KOPJES KITSCH LEAFED LOBBED LADDIE LEGEND
****** KITTED LEAGUE LOBBER LADIES LEGERS
K-R--- KITTEN LEAKED LOBULE LADING LEGGED
****** KITTLE LEANED LUBBER LADINO LEGION
KARATE KITTYS LEANER LUBECK LADLED LEGIST
KARATS ****** LEANLY LUBLIN LADLER LEGMAN
KARENS K-U--- LEANTO ****** LADLES LEGMEN
KARMAS ****** LEAPED L-C--- LADOGA LEGREE
KARNAK KAURIS LEAPER ****** LEDGER LEGUME
KARROO KNURLS LEARNS LACHES LEDGES LIGAND
KERALA KNURLY LEARNT LACIAL LIDDED LIGATE
KERATO KRUBIS LEASED LACIER LODGED LIGHTS
KERBED KRUBUT LEASES LACILY LODGER LIGNIN
KERMES KYUSHU LEAVED LACING LODGES LIGNUM
KERMIS ****** LEAVEN LACKED LUDLOW LIGULA
KERMIT K-V--- LEAVER LACKEY LUDWIG LIGULE
KERNED ****** LEAVES LACTAM LYDIAS LIGURE
KERNEL KAVASS LIABLE LACTIC ****** LOGGED
KERRIE KEVELS LIAISE LACUNA L-E--- LOGGER
KERSEY KEVINS LIANAS LECHER ****** LOGGIA
KIRSCH ****** LIANES LECTOR LEERED LOGIER
KIRTLE K-W--- LIASED LICHEE LEEWAY LOGION
KOREAN ****** LLAMAS LICHEN LIEBIG LOGJAM
KORUNA KEWPIE LLANOS LICKED LIEDER LUGERS
KORUNY KOWTOW LOADED LICTOR LIEGES LUGGED
****** KUWAIT LOADER LOCALE LIERNE LUGGER
K-S--- ****** LOAFED LOCALS LUELLA ******
****** K-Y--- LOAFER LOCATE LUETIC L-H---
KASPER ****** LOAMED LOCHIA ****** ******
KISLEW KAYAKS LOANED LOCKED L-F--- LAHORE
KISMET KAYOED LOATHE LOCKER ****** LEHUAS
KISSED KEYING LOAVES LOCKET LIFERS L-I---
KISSER KEYNES LUANDA LOCKUP LIFTED ******
KISSES KEYWAY ****** LOCOED LIFTER LAIRDS
KOSHER KHYBER L-B--- LOCUST LOFTED LAIRED
 LABELS
 LABIAL

LEIGHS
LOITER
******
L-K---
******
LAKERS
LAKIER
LAKING
LIKELY
LIKENS
LIKING
******
L-L---
******
LALLED
LILACS
LILIAN
LILIED
LILIES
LILTED
LOLITA
LOLLED
LOLLER
LOLLOP
LULLED
******
L-M---
******
LAMBDA
LAMBED
LAMBIE
LAMECH
LAMEDS
LAMELY
LAMENT
LAMEST
LAMIAE
LAMIAS
LAMINA
LAMING
LAMMAS
LAMMED
LAMPAD
LAMPAS
LAMPED
LEMMAS
LEMNOS
LEMONS

LEMUEL
LEMURS
LIMBED
LIMBER
LIMBIC
LIMBUS
LIMENS
LIMEYS
LIMIER
LIMINA
LIMING
LIMITS
LIMNED
LIMNER
LIMPED
LIMPER
LIMPET
LIMPID
LIMPLY
LIMULI
LOMENT
LOMOND
LUMBAR
LUMBER
LUMENS
LUMINA
LUMINI
LUMINO
LUMMOX
LUMPED
LUMPEN
LYMPHO
******
L-N---
******
LANAIS
LANATE
LANCED
LANCER
LANCES
LANCET
LANDAU
LANDED
LANDER
LANGUR
LANKER
LANKLY
LANNER

LANOSE
LANUGO
LENAPE
LENDER
LENGTH
LENITY
LENNYS
LENORE
LENSES
LENTEN
LENTIL
LENTOS
LINAGE
LINDAS
LINDEN
LINEAL
LINEAR
LINENS
LINERS
LINEUP
LINGAM
LINGAS
LINGER
LINGUA
LINIER
LINING
LINKED
LINNET
LINTEL
LINTER
LONDON
LONELY
LONERS
LONGAN
LONGED
LONGER
LUNACY
LUNATE
LUNETS
LUNGED
LUNGEE
LUNGER
LUNGES
LUNGIS
LUNKER
LUNULA
LUNULE
LYNXES

******
L-O---
******
LAOTSE
LEONAS
LEONIE
LIONEL
LLOYDS
LOOFAH
LOOING
LOOKED
LOOKER
LOOKIN
LOOMED
LOOPED
LOOPER
LOOSED
LOOSEN
LOOSER
LOOSES
LOOTED
LOOTER
******
L-P---
******
LAPARO
LAPDOG
LAPELS
LAPFUL
LAPINS
LAPPED
LAPPER
LAPPET
LAPSED
LAPSER
LAPSES
LAPSUS
LEPERS
LEPIDO
LEPSIA
LEPTON
LIPASE
LIPIDS
LIPOID
LIPOMA
LIPPED
LIPPER
LOPERS

LOPING
LOPPED
LUPINE
******
L-Q---
******
LIQUID
LIQUOR
LOQUAR
LOQUAT
******
L-R---
******
LARDED
LARDER
LARDON
LAREDO
LARGER
LARGOS
LARIAT
LARINE
LARKED
LARKER
LARRUP
LARRYS
LARVAE
LARVAL
LARYNG
LARYNX
LEROYS
LORAIN
LORDED
LORDLY
LOREEN
LORENE
LORENZ
LORICA
LORIES
LURERS
LURING
LURKED
LURKER
LYRICS
LYRISM
LYRIST
******
******
L-S---
******
LASCAR
LASERS

LASHED
LASHER
LASHES
LASSEN
LASSES
LASSIE
LASSOS
LASTED
LASTER
LASTEX
LASTLY
LESBOS
LESION
LESLEY
LESLIE
LESSEE
LESSEN
LESSER
LESSON
LESSOR
LESTER
LISBOA
LISBON
LISPED
LISPER
LISSOM
LISTED
LISTEL
LISTEN
LISTER
LOSERS
LOSING
LOSSES
LUSHED
LUSHER
LUSHES
LUSTED
LUSTER
LUSTRE
LYSINE
LYSING
LYSINS
******
L-T---
******
LATEEN
LATELY
LATENT

LATERA	LOUGHS	LEWDER	MEASLY	******	******
LATEST	LOUISA	LEWDLY	MEATUS	**M-D---**	**M-E---**
LATHED	LOUISE	LOWBOY	MIASMA	******	******
LATHER	LOUNGE	LOWELL	MIAULS	MADAME	MAENAD
LATHES	LOUPES	LOWERS	MOANED	MADAMS	MEEKER
LATINS	LOURED	LOWERY	MOATED	MADCAP	MEEKLY
LATISH	LOUSED	LOWEST	******	MADDED	MEETER
LATRIA	LOUSES	LOWING	**M-B---**	MADDEN	MEETLY
LATTEN	LOUVER	LOWKEY	******	MADDER	MYELIN
LATTER	LOUVRE	******	MABELS	MADEUP	******
LATVIA	******	**L-X---**	MOBBED	MADGES	**M-F---**
LETHAL	**L-V---**	******	MOBBER	MADMAN	******
LETTER	******	LAXEST	MOBCAP	MADMEN	MIFFED
LETUPS	LAVABO	LAXITY	MOBILE	MADRAS	MUFFED
LITANY	LAVAGE	LUXATE	MOBIUS	MADRID	MUFFIN
LITCHI	LAVERS	LUXURY	******	MADURA	MUFFLE
LITERS	LAVING	******	**M-C---**	MADURO	MUFTIS
LITHER	LAVISH	**L-Y---**	******	MEDALS	******
LITHIA	LEVANT	******	MACACO	MEDDLE	**M-G---**
LITHIC	LEVEES	LAYDAY	MACAWS	MEDIAE	******
LITMUS	LEVELS	LAYERS	MACERS	MEDIAL	MAGGIE
LITTER	LEVERS	LAYING	MACING	MEDIAN	MAGGOT
LITTLE	LEVIED	LAYMAN	MACKLE	MEDICI	MAGNET
LOTAHS	LEVIER	LAYMEN	MACLES	MEDICO	MAGNOX
LOTION	LEVIES	LAYOFF	MACRON	MEDICS	MAGNUM
LOTTIE	LEVITE	LAYOUT	MACULA	MEDIUM	MAGOTS
LUTEAL	LEVITY	LEYDEN	MACULE	MEDLAR	MAGPIE
LUTEUM	LIVELY	******	MCCOYS	MEDLEY	MAGUEY
LUTHER	LIVENS	**L-Z---**	MECCAN	MEDUSA	MAGYAR
LUTING	LIVERS	******	MECCAS	MEDWAY	MEGALO
LUTIST	LIVERY	LAZARS	MICELL	MIDAIR	MEGASS
LYTTAE	LIVIAS	LAZIER	MICHEL	MIDDAY	MEGILP
******	LIVIER	LAZILY	MICKEY	MIDDEN	MEGRIM
L-U---	LIVING	LAZING	MICKLE	MIDDLE	MIGGLE
******	LIVRES	LAZULI	MICKYS	MIDGES	MIGHTY
LAUDED	LIVYER	LIZARD	MICMAC	MIDGET	MIGNON
LAUDER	LOVAGE	LIZZIE	MICRON	MIDGUT	MIGUEL
LAUGHS	LOVEIN	LIZZYS	MOCKED	MIDRIB	MOGULS
LAUNCE	LOVELL	******	MOCKER	MIDWAY	MUGGAR
LAUNCH	LOVELY	**M-A---**	MOCKUP	MODELS	MUGGED
LAURAE	LOVERS	******	MUCKED	MODERN	MUGGER
LAURAS	LOVING	MEADOW	MUCKER	MODEST	MUGGUR
LAUREL	******	MEAGER	MUCKLE	MODIFY	******
LAURIE	**L-W---**	MEAGRE	MUCOID	MODISH	**M-H---**
LEUDES	******	MEALIE	MUCOSA	MODULE	******
LOUDEN	LAWFUL	MEANER	MUCOSE	MUDCAP	MAHBUB
LOUDER	LAWING	MEANIE	MUCOUS	MUDDED	MAHLER
LOUDLY	LAWYER	MEANLY	MYCETE	MUDDER	

MAHOUT
MOHAIR
MOHAVE
MOHAWK
MOHOCK
MOHOLE
MOHURS
******

M-I---
******
MAIDEN
MAIGRE
MAILED
MAILER
MAIMED
MAIMER
MAINLY
MAISIE
MAISON
MAITRE
MAIZES
MOIETY
MOILED
MOILER
MOIRAS
MOISHE
******

M-J---
******
MAJORS
MEJICO
MOJAVE
******

M-K---
******
MAKERS
MAKEUP
MAKING
MEKONG
MIKADO
MIKLOS
MUKLUK
******

M-L---
******
MALACO
MALADY
MALAGA

MALATE
MALAWI
MALAYA
MALAYS
MALGRE
MALICE
MALIGN
MALINE
MALLED
MALLEE
MALLET
MALLOW
MALORY
MALTED
MALTHA
MELANO
MELDED
MELEES
MELLON
MELLOW
MELODY
MELONS
MELTED
MELTER
MELTON
MELVIN
MELVYN
MILADY
MILAGE
MILDEN
MILDER
MILDEW
MILDLY
MILERS
MILIEU
MILIUM
MILKED
MILKER
MILLAY
MILLED
MILLER
MILLET
MILLIE
MILLYS
MILORD
MILTED
MILTER
MILTON

MOLARS
MOLDED
MOLDER
MOLEST
MOLIES
MOLINE
MOLLAH
MOLLIE
MOLLYS
MOLOCH
MOLTED
MOLTEN
MOLTER
MOLTKE
MULCTS
MULISH
MULLAH
MULLED
MULLEN
MULLER
MULLET
MULLEY
******

M-M---
******
MAMBAS
MAMBOS
MAMEYS
MAMIES
MAMMAE
MAMMAL
MAMMAS
MAMMET
MAMMON
MEMBER
MEMOIR
MEMORY
MIMERS
MIMICS
MIMING
MIMOSA
MOMENT
MOMISM
MUMBLE
MUMMED
MUMMER
******

M-N---
******
MANAGE
MANANA

MANCHU
MANDAN
MANDYS
MANEGE
MANFUL
MANGER
MANGLE
MANGOS
MANIAC
MANIAS
MANILA
MANIOC
MANITO
MANITU
MANNED
MANNER
MANORS
MANQUE
MANSES
MANTAS
MANTEL
MANTES
MANTIC
MANTIS
MANTLE
MANTUA
MANUAL
MANUEL
MANURE
MENACE
MENAGE
MENDED
MENDEL
MENDER
MENDIP
MENHIR
MENIAL
MENINX
MENSAL
MENSES
MENTAL
MENTOR
MINCED
MINCER
MINCES
MINDED
MINDER
MINERS

MINGLE
MINIFY
MINIMA
MINIMS
MINING
MINION
MINIUM
MINNIE
MINNOW
MINOAN
MINORS
MINTED
MINTER
MINUET
MINUTE
MINXES
MONACO
MONADS
MONDAY
MONEYS
MONGER
MONGOL
MONGST
MONICA
MONIED
MONIES
MONISM
MONIST
MONKEY
MONODY
MONROE
MONTES
MONTHS
MONTYS
MUNICH
******

M-O---
******
MAOISM
MAOIST
MAORIS
MEOWED
MIOSIS
MIOTIC
MOOING
MOOLAH
MOOLEY
MOONED

MOORED
MOOTED
MOOTER
MYOPES
MYOPIA
MYOPIC
MYOSIN
MYOSIS
******

M-P---
******
MAPLES
MAPPED
MOPERS
MOPING
MOPISH
MOPOKE
MOPPED
MOPPET
******

M-Q---
******
MAQUIS
******

M-R---
******
MARACA
MARAUD
MARBLE
MARCEL
MARCIA
MARCOS
MARCUS
MARDUK
MARGAY
MARGES
MARGIE
MARGIN
MARGOS
MARGOT
MARIAN
MARIAS
MARIES
MARINA
MARINE
MARION
MARIST
MARKED

MARKER	MORAYS	MASKER	MOSQUE	METHYL	MOULIN
MARKET	MORBID	MASONS	MOSSES	METIER	MOULTS
MARKKA	MOREAU	MASORA	MOSTLY	METING	MOUNTS
MARKUP	MOREEN	MASQUE	MUSCAE	METOPE	MOUNTY
MARLED	MORELS	MASSED	MUSCAT	METRIC	MOURNS
MARLIN	MORGAN	MASSES	MUSCLE	METROS	MOUSED
MARLOW	MORGEN	MASSIF	MUSEUM	METTLE	MOUSER
MARMOT	MORGUE	MASTED	MUSHED	METUMP	MOUSES
MAROON	MORION	MASTER	MUSHER	MITERS	MOUSSE
MARQUE	MORLEY	MASTIC	MUSHES	MITRAL	MOUTHS
MARRED	MORMON	MESCAL	MUSING	MITRED	MOUTHY
MARRER	MORONS	MESHED	MUSKEG	MITTEN	MOUTON
MARROW	MOROSE	MESHER	MUSKET	MOTELS	MUUMUU
MARSHA	MORPHO	MESHES	MUSKIT	MOTHER	******
MARSHY	MORRIS	MESIAL	MUSKOX	MOTIFS	M-V---
MARTAS	MORROS	MESIAN	MUSLIM	MOTILE	******
MARTEN	MORROW	MESMER	MUSLIN	MOTION	MOVERS
MARTHA	MORSEL	MESNES	MUSSED	MOTIVE	MOVIES
MARTHE	MORTAL	MESONS	MUSSEL	MOTLEY	MOVING
MARTIN	MORTAR	MESSED	MUSSES	MOTMOT	******
MARTYR	MORTON	MESSES	MUSTEE	MOTORS	M-W---
MARTYS	MORTYS	MESSRS	MUSTER	MOTTLE	******
MARVEL	MORULA	MESTEE	MUSTNT	MOTTOS	MEWING
MARVIN	MURALS	MISCUE	MYSELF	MUTANT	MEWLED
MERCER	MURDER	MISDID	MYSTIC	MUTATE	MOWERS
MERCIA	MURIEL	MISERE	******	MUTING	MOWING
MERELY	MURINE	MISERS	M-T---	MUTINY	******
MEREST	MURMUR	MISERY	******	MUTISM	M-X---
MERGED	MURRAY	MISFIT	MATEOS	MUTTER	******
MERGER	MURRES	MISHAP	MATEYS	MUTTON	MAXIMA
MERGES	MURREY	MISKAL	MATINE	MUTUAL	MAXIMS
MERINO	MYRIAD	MISLAY	MATING	MUTULE	MAXINE
MERITS	MYRICA	MISLED	MATINS	MYTHIC	MAXIXE
MERLES	MYRMEC	MISSAL	MATRIX	MYTHOI	MEXICO
MERLIN	MYRNAS	MISSED	MATRON	MYTHOS	MIXERS
MERLON	MYRTLE	MISSEL	MATTED	******	MIXING
MERMAN	******	MISSES	MATTEO	M-U---	MIXUPS
MERMEN	M-S---	MISSIS	MATTER	******	MYXOMA
MEROUS	******	MISSUS	MATTES	MAUDES	******
MERSEY	MASCON	MISTED	MATTIE	MAULED	M-Y---
MERVIN	MASCOT	MISTER	MATURE	MAULER	******
MIRAGE	MASERS	MISTLE	MATZOS	MAUMAU	MAYBUG
MIRIAM	MASHED	MISUSE	MATZOT	MAUNDS	MAYDAY
MIRING	MASHER	MOSAIC	METAGE	MAUNDY	MAYEST
MIRROR	MASHES	MOSCOW	METALS	MAUSER	MAYFLY
MORALE	MASHIE	MOSEYS	METEOR	MAUVES	MAYHAP
MORALS	MASKED	MOSLEM	METERS	MOULDS	MAYHEM
MORASS	MASKEG	MOSLEY	METHOD	MOULDY	MAYING

MAYORS	******	NIELLO	NAMING	NAPPER	NESTOR
MAYPOP	N-C---	NOELLE	NEMATO	NAPPES	NISEIS
******	******	NOESIS	NIMBLE	NAPPIE	NOSHED
M-Z---	NECKED	NOETIC	NIMBLY	NEPHEW	NOSHOW
******	NECTAR	******	NIMBUS	NEPHRO	NOSIER
MAZERS	NICELY	N-G---	NIMITZ	NIPPED	NOSILY
MAZIER	NICENE	******	NIMROD	NIPPER	NOSING
MAZILY	NICEST	NAGANA	NOMADS	NIPPLE	NOSTIC
MAZING	NICETY	NAGGED	NOMISM	NIPPON	******
MAZUMA	NICHED·	NAGGER	NOMURA	NOPALS	N-T---
MEZUZA	NICHES	NAGOYA	NUMBED	******	******
MEZZOS	NICKED	NEGATE	NUMBER	N-R---	NATANT
MIZZEN	NICKEL	NIGELS	NUMBLY	******	NATHAN
MIZZLE	NICKER	NIGGER	NUMINA	NARIAL	NATION
MOZART	NICKYS	NIGGLE	NYMPHA	NARINE	NATIVE
MUZHIK	NICOLE	NIGHER	NYMPHO	NARKED	NATRON
MUZZLE	NOCENT	NIGHTS	NYMPHS	NARROW	NATTER
******	NOCKED	NIGHTY	******	NARWAL	NATURE
N-A---	NUCHAE	NOGGIN	N-N---	NEREID	NETHER
******	NUCLEI	NOGOOD	******	NEREIS	NETTED
NEARBY	******	NUGGET	NANCYS	NEROLI	NETTIE
NEARED	N-D---	******	NANISM	NERVED	NETTLE
NEARER	******	N-H---	NANTES	NERVES	NITRIC
NEARLY	NADINE	******	NINETY	NORDIC	NITRID
NEATEN	NADIRS	NAHUMS	NINTHS	NOREEN	NITWIT
NEATER	NIDIFY	******	NONAGE	NORIAS	NOTARY
NEATLY	NIDING	N-I---	NONARY	NORMAL	NOTERS
NIACIN	NODDED	******	NONCOM	NORMAN	NOTICE
NUANCE	NODDER	NAIADS	NONEGO	NORMAS	NOTIFY
******	NODDLE	NAILED	NUNCIO	NORNIR	NOTING
N-B---	NODOSE	NEIGHS	******	NORRIS	NOTION
******	NODULE	NOISED	N-O---	NORWAY	NUTLET
NABBED	NUDELY	NOISES	******	NURSED	NUTMEG
NABOBS	NUDGED	N-K---	NAOMIS	NURSER	NUTRIA
NEBULA	NUDGES	******	NAOSES	NURSES	NUTTED
NIBBED	NUDISM	NEKTON	NIOBIC	******	NUTTER
NIBBLE	NUDIST	******	NOODLE	N-S---	******
NOBALL	NUDITY	N-L---	NOOSED	******	N-U---
NOBBED	NUDNIK	******	NOOSES	NASALS	******
NOBBLE	******	NELLIE	******	NASHUA	NAUGHT
NOBLER	N-E---	NELLYS	N-P---	NASIAL	NAUSEA
NOBODY	******	NELSON	******	NASION	NAUTCH
NUBBIN	NAEVUS	NILGAI	NAPALM	NASSAU	NEUMES
NUBBLE	NEEDED	NULLAH	NAPERY	NASSER	NEURAL
NUBBLY	NEEDER	NYLONS	NAPIER	NASTIC	NEURON
NUBIAN	NEEDLE	******	NAPKIN	NESSUS	NEUTER
NUBIAS	NIECES	N-M---	NAPLES	NESTED	NOUGAT
NUBILE	NIELLI	NAMELY	NAPPED	NESTLE	NOUGHT
		NAMERS			NOUNAL

******	ORACLE	ORDERS	ONFALL	OTITIS	******
N-V---	ORALLY	ORDURE	OXFORD	OVIBOS	**O-N---**
******	ORANGE	******	******	OVISAC	******
NAVAHO	ORANGS	**O-E---**	**O-G---**	OXIDES	OMNIUM
NAVAJO	ORATED	******	******	******	ORNATE
NAVELS	ORATES	OBELUS	ORGANA	**O-J---**	ORNERY
NAVIES	ORATOR	OBERON	ORGANO	******	ORNITH
NEVADA	OVALLY	OBEYED	ORGANS	OBJECT	OUNCES
NEVILE	OXALIC	OBEYER	ORGASM	******	OWNERS
NEVILL	OXALIS	OCEANS	ORGEAT	**O-K---**	OWNING
NEVOID	******	OCELLI	ORGIES	******	******
NEVSKI	**O-B---**	OCELOT	******	OAKLEY	**O-O---**
NOVELS	******	ODESSA	**O-H---**	ORKNEY	******
NOVENA	ORBING	ODETTE	******	******	OBOIST
NOVICE	ORBITS	OHENRY	OCHERS	**O-L---**	OBOLUS
******	OSBERT	OLEATE	OCHERY	******	ODONTO
N-W---	OSBORN	OLEFIN	OPHITE	OBLAST	OPORTO
******	OXBOWS	OMEGAS	OTHERS	OBLATE	OROIDE
NAWABS	******	OMELET	OXHIDE	OBLIGE	OZONIC
NEWARK	**O-C---**	OMENTA	******	OBLONG	******
NEWELS	******	ONEIDA	**O-I---**	OCLOCK	**O-P---**
NEWEST	OCCULT	ONEILL	******	OGLERS	******
NEWTON	OCCUPY	ONEIRO	OBIISM	OGLING	OEPEMA
NOWAYS	OCCURS	ONEOFF	OBITER	OILCAN	OOPHOR
NOWISE	OOCYTE	ONEWAY	ODIOUS	OILERS	OPPOSE
******	ORCEIN	OPENED	OGIVAL	OILIER	OPPUGN
N-X---	ORCHID	OPENER	OGIVES	OILILY	ORPHAN
******	ORCHIL	OPENLY	OHIOAN	OILING	ORPHIC
NIXIES	ORCHIO	OPERAS	OJIBWA	OLLIES	ORPINE
NIXING	ORCHIS	OREADS	OLIVER	ONLINE	ORPINS
******	OSCANS	OREGAN	OLIVES	OOLITE	OSPREY
N-Z---	OSCARS	OREGON	OLIVIA	OOLOGY	******
******	OSCINE	OREIDE	ONIONS	OOLONG	**O-R---**
NAZIFY	OSCULE	OVERDO	ONIONY	ORLOPS	******
NAZISM	******	OVERLY	OPIATE	OWLETS	OARING
NOZZLE	**O-D---**	OXEYED	OPINED	OWLISH	OCREAE
NUZZLE	******	OXEYES	OPINES	OXLIPS	OGRESS
******	ODDEST		ORIBIS	******	OGRISH
O-A---	ODDITY	**O-F---**	ORIELS	**O-M---**	ONRUSH
******	ODDJOB	******	ORIENT	******	ORRERY
OCASEY	OEDEMA	OAFISH	ORIGAN	OHMAGE	ORRICE
OKAPIS	OGDOAD	OFFDAY	ORIGEN	OOMIAK	******
OKAYED	OLDEST	OFFEND	ORIGIN	ORMERS	**O-S---**
OMASUM	OLDHAM	OFFERS	ORIOLE	ORMOLU	******
ONAGER	OLDISH	OFFICE	ORISON	ORMUZD	OBSESS
ONAGRI	OODLES	OFFING	OSIERS	OSMIUM	ONSETS
OPAQUE	ORDAIN	OFFISH	OSIRIS	OSMOND	OSSEIN
ORACHS	ORDEAL	OFFSET	OTIOSE	OSMOSE	OSSIAN

OSSIFY	OUTSAT	PEASES	PLATES	PICOTS	PHENOL
OUSELS	OUTSET	PEAVEY	PLATTE	PICRIC	PHENYL
OUSTED	OUTSIT	PHAGIA	PLAYAS	PICTOR	PIECED
OUSTER	OUTWIT	PHANON	PLAYED	PICULS	PIECER
OYSTER	OXTAIL	PHAROS	PLAYER	POCKET	PIECES
******	******	PHASED	PLAZAS	PUCKER	PIEMAN
O-T---	O-U---	PHASES	POACHY	******	PIEMEN
******	******	PHASIA	PRAGUE	P-D---	PIENAL
OBTAIN	OCULAR	PHASIC	PRAISE	******	PIERCE
OBTECT	OEUVRE	PHASIS	PRANCE	PADDED	PIERRE
OBTEST	ONUSES	PIAFFE	PRANKS	PADDLE	PIERUS
OBTUND	OVULAR	PIANOS	PRATED	PADDYS	PIETER
OBTUSE	OVULES	PIAZZA	PRATER	PADRES	PIETRO
OCTADS	******	PLACED	PRATES	PEDALS	PLEACH
OCTANE	O-V---	PLACER	PRAVDA	PEDANT	PLEADS
OCTANT	******	PLACES	PRAWNS	PEDATE	PLEASE
OCTAVE	OBVERT	PLACET	PRAXIS	PEDATI	PLEATS
OCTAVO	******	PLACID	PRAYED	PEDDLE	PLEBES
OCTETS	O-W---	PLACKS	PRAYER	PEDLAR	PLEDGE
OCTOPI	******	PLAGAL	PSALMS	PEDROS	PLEGIA
OCTROI	ONWARD	PLAGIO	******	PIDDLE	PLEIAD
OPTANT	ORWELL	PLAGUE	P-B---	PIDGIN	PLENTY
OPTICS	OSWALD	PLAGUY	******	PODDED	PLENUM
OPTIMA	OSWEGO	PLAICE	PEBBLE	PODIUM	PLEURA
OPTIME	******	PLAIDS	PEBBLY	PODOUS	PLEURO
OPTING	O-Y---	PLAINS	PUBLIC	PODSOL	PLEXOR
OPTION	******	PLAINT	******	PODUNK	PLEXUS
OSTEAL	ODYNIA	PLAITS	P-C---	PODZOL	PNEUMA
OSTEND	ORYXES	PLANAR	******	PUDDLE	PNEUMO
OSTLER	OXYGEN	PLANCH	PACERS	PUDDLY	POETIC
OTTAVA	******	PLANCK	PACIFY	******	POETRY
OTTAWA	O-Z---	PLANED	PACING	P-E---	PREACH
OTTERS	******	PLANER	PACKED	******	PRECIS
OTTOWA	OOZIER	PLANES	PACKER	PAEANS	PREENS
OUTBID	OOZILY	PLANET	PACKET	PAEONS	PREFAB
OUTCRY	OOZING	PLANKS	PECANS	PAEONY	PREFER
OUTDID	OUZELS	PLANTS	PECKED	PEEKED	PREFIX
OUTERS	******	PLAQUE	PECKER	PEEKER	PRELIM
OUTFIT	P-A---	PLASHY	PECTEN	PEELED	PREMED
OUTFOX	******	PLASIA	PECTIC	PEELER	PREPAY
OUTING	PEACHY	PLASIS	PECTIN	PEENED	PRESAS
OUTLAW	PEAHEN	PLASMA	PICKAX	PEEPED	PRESTO
OUTLAY	PEAKED	PLASMO	PICKED	PEEPER	PRETER
OUTLET	PEALED	PLASTY	PICKER	PEERED	PRETOR
OUTMAN	PEANUT	PLATAN	PICKET	PEEVED	PRETTY
OUTPUT	PEARLS	PLATED	PICKLE	PEEVES	PREVUE
OUTRAN	PEARLY	PLATEN	PICKUP	PEEWEE	PREWAR
OUTRUN	PEASEN	PLATER	PICNIC	PEEWIT	PREYED

PREYER	PEIRCE	******	PELLET	PULLED	PANTIE
PSEUDO	PHIALS	**P-J---**	PELOPS	PULLER	PANTRY
PUEBLO	PHILIA	******	PELOTA	PULLET	PANZER
PYEMIA	PHILIP	PAJAMA	PELTED	PULLEY	PENCEL
PYEMIC	PHILOS	PYJAMA	PELTER	PULLIN	PENCIL
******	PHIPPS	******	PELTRY	PULPED	PENDED
P-F---	PLIANT	**P-K---**	PELVES	PULPER	PENGOS
******	PLICAE	******	PELVIC	PULPIT	PENIAL
PIFFLE	PLIERS	PEKANS	PELVIS	PULQUE	PENILE
PUFFED	PLIGHT	PEKING	PHLEBO	PULSAR	PENMAN
PUFFER	PLINTH	PEKOES	PHLEGM	PULSED	PENMEN
PUFFIN	POILUS	PIKERS	PHLOEM	PULSES	PENNAE
******	POINDS	PIKING	PILAFF	PYLONS	PENNED
P-G---	POINTE	POKERS	PILAFS	******	PENNER
******	POINTS	POKIER	PILATE	**P-M---**	PENNIA
PAGANS	POINTY	POKIES	PILEUM	******	PENNIS
PAGING	POISED	POKING	PILEUP	PAMELA	PENNON
PAGODA	POISES	PUKING	PILEUS	PAMPAS	PENNYS
PEGGED	POISON	PYKNIC	PILFER	PAMPER	PENPAL
PEGGYS	PRICED	******	PILING	PIMPED	PENTAD
PEGLEG	PRICES	**P-L---**	PILLAR	PIMPLE	PENTUP
PEGTOP	PRICKS	******	PILLED	PIMPLY	PENULT
PIGEON	PRIDED	PALACE	PILLOW	POMACE	PENURY
PIGGED	PRIDES	PALAEO	PILOSE	POMADE	PINANG
PIGGIE	PRIERS	PALAIS	PILOTS	POMELO	PINDAR
PIGGIN	PRIEST	PALATE	PILOUS	POMMEL	PINDUS
PIGLET	PRIMAL	PALEAE	PILULE	POMONA	PINEAL
PIGNUS	PRIMED	PALELY	POLACK	POMPEY	PINENE
PIGNUT	PRIMER	PALEST	POLAND	POMPOM	PINERY
PIGPEN	PRIMES	PALING	POLDER	POMPON	PINGED
PIGSTY	PRIMLY	PALISH	POLEAX	PUMICE	PINGOS
POGIES	PRIMPS	PALLAS	POLICE	PUMMEL	PINIER
POGROM	PRIMUS	PALLED	POLICY	PUMPED	PINIES
PUGGED	PRINCE	PALLET	POLING	PUMPER	PINING
PUGGRY	PRINKS	PALLID	POLISH	******	PINION
PUGREE	PRINTS	PALLOR	POLITE	**P-N---**	PINITE
******	PRIORS	PALMAR	POLITY	******	PINKED
P-H---	PRIORY	PALMED	POLKAS	PANADA	PINKIE
******	PRISMS	PALMER	POLLED	PANAMA	PINNAE
PSHAWS	PRISON	PALPED	POLLEE	PANCHO	PINNAL
******	PRISSY	PALPUS	POLLEN	PANDAS	PINNED
P-I---	PRIVET	PALTER	POLLER	PANDER	PINNER
******	PRIZED	PALTRY	POLLEX	PANELS	PINOLE
PAINED	PRIZER	PELAGE	POLLUX	PANICE	PINONS
PAINTS	PRIZES	PELEUS	POLLYS	PANICS	PINTER
PAINTY	PTISAN	PELIAS	POLYPS	PANNED	PINTLE
PAIRED	PUISNE	PELION	PULERS	PANSYS	PINTOS
PAIUTE		PELITE	PULING	PANTED	PINUPS

PINXIT	POOPED	PEPLUM	PARERS	PIRANA	PASSEE
PONCHO	POORER	PEPLUS	PAREUS	PIRATE	PASSER
PONDER	POORLY	PEPPED	PARGET	PORING	PASSES
PONENT	PROBED	PEPPER	PARGOS	PORKER	PASSIM
PONGEE	PROBER	PEPSIN	PARIAH	POROUS	PASSUS
PONIED	PROBES	PEPTIC	PARIAN	PORTAL	PASTAS
PONIES	PROCNE	PIPAGE	PARIES	PORTED	PASTED
PONTES	PROCTO	PIPERS	PARING	PORTER	PASTEL
PONTIC	PROEMS	PIPETS	PARISH	PORTIA	PASTER
PONTIL	PROFIT	PIPIER	PARITY	PORTLY	PASTES
PONTON	PROJET	PIPING	PARKAS	PURANA	PASTIL
PUNCHY	PROLEG	PIPITS	PARKED	PURDAH	PASTOR
PUNDIT	PROLIX	PIPKIN	PARKER	PUREED	PASTRY
PUNIER	PROMPT	PIPPED	PARLAY	PUREES	PESACH
PUNILY	PRONGS	PIPPIN	PARLEY	PURELY	PESADE
PUNISH	PRONTO	POPERY	PARLOR	PUREST	PESETA
PUNJAB	PROOFS	POPGUN	PARODY	PURFLE	PESTER
PUNKAS	PROPEL	POPISH	PAROLE	PURGED	PESTLE
PUNNED	PROPER	POPLAR	PARRAL	PURGER	PISCES
PUNNER	PROPYL	POPLIN	PARREL	PURGES	PISGAH
PUNTED	PROSED	POPPED	PARROT	PURIFY	PISHED
PUNTER	PROSER	POPPER	PARSEC	PURINE	PISHES
PUNTOS	PROSES	POPPET	PARSED	PURISM	PISTIL
******	PROSIT	POPPLE	PARSEE	PURIST	PISTOL
	PROTON	POPPYS	PARSES	PURITY	PISTON
P-O---	PROUST	PUPATE	PARSIS	PURLED	POSADA
******	PROVED	PUPILS	PARSON	PURLER	POSERS
	PROVEN	PUPPED	PARTED	PURLIN	POSEUR
PEOPLE	PROVER	PUPPET	PARTLY	PURPLE	POSHLY
PEORIA	PROVES	******	PARURE	PURRED	POSIES
PHOBIA	PROWLS	**P-Q---**	PARVIS	PURSED	POSING
PHOBIC	PTOSIS	******	PERCYS	PURSER	POSITS
PHOCIS	PYOSIS	PEQUOD	PERILS	PURSES	POSSES
PHOEBE	******	PEQUOT	PERIOD	PURSUE	POSSET
PHONED	**P-P---**	PIQUED	PERISH	PURVEY	POSSUM
PHONES	******	PIQUES	PERKED	PYRANS	POSTAL
PHONEY	PAPACY	PIQUET	PERMED	PYRENE	POSTED
PHONIA	PAPAIN	******	PERMIT	PYRITE	POSTER
PHONIC	PAPAWS	**P-R---**	PERRON	PYRONE	PUSHED
PHOOEY	PAPAYA	******	PERRYS	PYROPE	PUSHER
PHOSPH	PAPERS	PARADE	PERSIA	PYRRHA	PUSHES
PHOTIC	PAPERY	PARANG	PERSON	******	PUSHTU
PHOTON	PAPIST	PARAPH	PERTLY	**P-S---**	PUSHUP
PHOTOS	PAPPUS	PARCAE	PERUKE	******	PUSSES
PLOUGH	PAPUAN	PARCEL	PERUSE	PASCAL	PUSSEY
PLOVER	PAPULA	PARDON	PHRASE	PASHAS	PUSSLY
PLOWED	PAPULE	PARENS	PHRENO	PASHTO	******
PLOWER	PEPLOS	PARENT	PIRACY	PASSED	**P-T---**
POODLE					******
POOLED					PATCHY
					PATENS

PATENT	POTTLE	POURED	PAYERS	QUARTZ	******
PATERS	POTTOS	POURER	PAYING	QUASAR	**R-A---**
PATHAN	PUTLOG	POUSTO	PAYNIM	QUATRE	******
PATHIA	PUTNAM	POUTED	PAYOFF	QUAVER	REACTS
PATHOL	PUTOFF	POUTER	PAYOLA	******	READER
PATHOS	PUTONS	PRUDES	PEYOTE	**Q-E---**	REALES
PATINA	PUTOUT	PRUNED	PHYLAE	******	REALLY
PATINE	PUTPUT	PRUNER	PHYLLO	QUEANS	REALMS
PATIOS	PUTRID	PRUNES	PHYLUM	QUEASY	REALTY
PATOIS	PUTSCH	PYURIA	PHYSIC	QUEBEC	REAMED
PATROL	PUTTED	******	PHYSIO	QUEENS	REAMER
PATRON	PUTTEE	**P-V---**	PHYTIN	QUEERS	REAPED
PATSYS	PUTTER	******	PLYING	QUELLS	REAPER
PATTED	PYTHIA	PAVANE	POYOUS	QUENCH	REARED
PATTEN	PYTHIC	PAVANS	PRYERS	QUERNS	REARER
PATTER	PYTHON	PAVERS	PRYING	QUESTS	REARMS
PATTON	******	PAVING	PSYCHE	QUEUED	REASON
PETALS	**P-U---**	PAVIOR	PSYCHO	QUEUES	REAVOW
PETARD	******	PAVISE	******	QUEZON	RIALTO
PETERS	PAUKER	PAVLOV	**P-Z---**	******	RIATAS
PETITE	PAULAS	PIVOTS	******	**Q-I---**	ROALDS
PETREL	PAULIN	******	PIZZAS	******	ROAMED
PETRIE	PAULUS	**P-W---**	PUZZLE	QUILLS	ROAMER
PETROL	PAUNCH	******	******	QUILTS	ROARED
PETTED	PAUPER	PAWERS	**Q-A---**	QUINCE	ROARER
PETULA	PAUSED	PAWING	******	QUINCY	ROASTS
PITCHY	PAUSER	PAWNED	QUACKS	QUINIC	RWANDA
PITHED	PAUSES	PAWNEE	QUADRI	QUINSY	******
PITIED	PLUCKS	PAWNER	QUAERE	QUINTS	**R-B---**
PITIES	PLUCKY	PAWPAW	QUAFFS	QUIPUS	******
PITMAN	PLUGIN	PEWEES	QUAGGA	QUIRED	RABBET
PITMEN	PLUMBO	PEWITS	QUAGGY	QUIRES	RABBIN
PITONS	PLUMBS	PEWTER	QUAHOG	QUIRKS	RABBIS
PITTED	PLUMED	POWDER	QUAILS	QUIRTS	RABBIT
POTAGE	PLUMES	POWELL	QUAINT	QUITCH	RABBLE
POTALE	PLUMMY	POWERS	QUAKED	QUIVER	RABIES
POTASH	PLUMPS	POWTER	QUAKER	******	REBATE
POTATO	PLUNGE	POWWOW	QUAKES	**Q-O---**	REBATO
POTBOY	PLUNKS	******	QUALMS	******	REBECK
POTEEN	PLURAL	**P-X---**	QUALMY	QUOINS	REBECS
POTENT	PLUSES	******	QUANTA	QUOITS	REBELS
POTHER	PLUSHY	PAXWAX	QUANTS	QUORUM	REBILL
POTION	PLUTUS	PIXIES	QUAPAW	QUOTAS	REBORE
POTMAN	PLUVIO	PYXIES	QUARKS	QUOTED	REBORN
POTPIE	POUCHY	******	QUARRY	QUOTER	REBOZO
POTSIE	POULTS	**P-Y---**	QUARTE	QUOTES	REBUFF
POTTED	POUNCE	PAYDAY	QUARTO	QUOTHA	REBUKE
POTTER	POUNDS	PAYEES	QUARTS	QUOTHA	REBUTS

RIBALD	RECAPS	RADIUM	REEDIT	RAGGED	RAISED
RIBAND	RECAST	RADIUS	REEFED	RAGING	RAISER
RIBBED	RECEDE	RADNOR	REEFER	RAGLAN	RAISES
RIBBON	RECENT	RADOME	REEKED	RAGMAN	RAISIN
RIBOSE	RECEPT	RADULA	REEKER	RAGMEN	REICHS
ROBALO	RECESS	REDACT	REELED	RAGOUT	REIGNS
ROBAND	RECIPE	REDANS	REELER	RAGTAG	REINED
ROBBED	RECITE	REDBAY	REEVED	REGAIN	RHINAL
ROBBER	RECKON	REDBUD	REEVES	REGALE	RHINOS
ROBBIA	RECOIL	REDBUG	RHEIMS	REGARD	RHIZIC
ROBBIE	RECORD	REDCAP	RHESUS	REGENT	ROILED
ROBERT	RECOUP	REDDEN	RHETOR	REGGIE	RUINED
ROBING	RECTAL	REDDER	RHEUMY	REGIME	RUINER
ROBINS	RECTOR	REDDLE	RUEFUL	REGINA	******
ROBLES	RECTOS	REDDOG	RUEING	REGION	**R-J---**
ROBOTS	RECTUM	REDEEM	******	REGIUS	******
ROBSON	RECTUS	REDEYE	**R-F---**	REGLET	RAJABS
ROBUST	RECURS	REDFIN	******	REGNAL	RAJAHS
RUBACE	RECUSE	REDGUM	RAFFIA	REGRET	RAJPUT
RUBATO	RICERS	REDHOT	RAFFLE	RIGGED	REJECT
RUBBED	RICHER	REDOES	RAFTED	RIGGER	REJOIN
RUBBER	RICHES	REDONE	RAFTER	RIGHTO	******
RUBBLE	RICHIE	REDOWA	REFACE	RIGHTS	**R-K---**
RUBENS	RICHLY	REDTOP	REFERS	RIGORS	******
RUBIES	RICING	REDUCE	REFILL	RIGOUR	RAKERS
RUBIGO	RICKED	RIDDED	REFINE	ROGERS	RAKING
RUBLES	RICKEY	RIDDEN	REFITS	ROGUED	RAKISH
RUBRIC	RICKYS	RIDDLE	REFLET	ROGUES	******
******	RICTAL	RIDENT	REFLEX	RUGATE	**R-L---**
R-C---	RICTUS	RIDERS	REFLUX	RUGGED	******
******	ROCHET	RIDGED	REFOOT	RUGGER	RALPHS
RACEME	ROCKED	RIDGES	REFORM	RUGOSE	RELAID
RACERS	ROCKER	RIDING	REFUEL	RUGOUS	RELATE
RACHEL	ROCKET	RODDYS	REFUGE	******	RELAYS
RACHIS	ROCKNE	RODENT	REFUND	**R-H---**	RELENT
RACIAL	ROCOCO	RODEOS	REFUSE	******	RELICS
RACIER	RUCHES	RODMAN	REFUTE	REHASH	RELICT
RACILY	RUCKED	RODMEN	RIFFLE	REHEAR	RELIED
RACINE	RUCKUS	RODNEY	RIFLED	REHEAT	RELIEF
RACING	******	RUDDER	RIFLER	RRHAGE	RELIER
RACISM	**R-D---**	RUDDLE	RIFLES	RRHAGY	RELIES
RACIST	******	RUDELY	RIFTED	******	RELINE
RACKED	RADARS	RUDEST	RUFFED	**R-I---**	RELISH
RACKER	RADDLE	******	RUFFLE	******	RELIVE
RACKET	RADIAL	**R-E---**	RUFOUS	RAIDED	RELOAD
RACOON	RADIAN	******	******	RAIDER	RILING
RECALL	RADIOS	REECHO	**R-G---**	RAILED	RILLET
RECANT	RADISH	REEDED	RAGBAG	RAINED	ROLAND
				RAGDAY	

ROLLED	ROMNEY	RINKED	RAPIST	RAREST	ROSINS
ROLLER	ROMOLA	RINSED	RAPPED	RARING	ROSINY
ROLLUP	ROMPED	RINSER	RAPPEE	RARITY	ROSTER
ROLPHS	ROMPER	RINSES	RAPPEL	RERUNS	ROSTRA
RULERS	ROMULO	RONALD	RAPPER	******	RUSHED
RULING	RUMBAS	RONDEL	RAPTLY	**R-S---**	RUSHER
******	RUMBLE	RONDOS	RAPTOR	******	RUSHES
R-M---	RUMINA	RONNIE	REPAID	RASCAL	RUSINE
******	RUMMER	RUNDLE	REPAIR	RASHER	RUSKIN
RAMBLE	RUMORS	RUNINS	REPAND	RASHES	RUSSET
RAMIES	RUMOUR	RUNLET	REPASS	RASHLY	RUSSIA
RAMIFY	RUMPLE	RUNNEL	REPAST	RASPED	RUSTED
RAMJET	RUMPUS	RUNNER	REPAYS	RASPER	RUSTIC
RAMMED	******	RUNOFF	REPEAL	RASTER	RUSTLE
RAMMER	**R-N---**	RUNONS	REPEAT	RESALE	******
RAMONA	******	RUNOUT	REPELS	RESCUE	**R-T---**
RAMOSE	RANCHO	RUNWAY	REPENT	RESEAT	******
RAMOUS	RANCID	RUNYON	REPINE	RESEAU	RATALS
RAMPED	RANCOR	******	REPLAY	RESECT	RATELS
RAMROD	RANDAL	**R-O---**	REPORT	RESEDA	RATERS
RAMSON	RANDAN	******	REPOSE	RESELL	RATHER
REMADE	RANDOM	RAOULS	REPUTE	RESEND	RATIFY
REMAIN	RANEES	REOPEN	RIPELY	RESENT	RATINE
REMAKE	RANGED	RHODAS	RIPENS	RESETS	RATING
REMAND	RANGER	RHODES	RIPEST	RESIDE	RATION
REMANS	RANGES	RHODIC	RIPLEY	RESIGN	RATIOS
REMARK	RANKED	RHOMBI	RIPOFF	RESILE	RATITE
REMEDY	RANKER	RIOTED	RIPOST	RESINS	RATLIN
REMIND	RANKLE	RIOTER	RIPPED	RESIST	RATOON
REMISE	RANKLY	ROOFED	RIPPER	RESOLD	RATTAN
REMISS	RANSOM	ROOFER	RIPPLE	RESOLE	RATTED
REMITS	RANTED	ROOKED	RIPPLY	RESORB	RATTEN
REMORA	RANTER	ROOKIE	RIPRAP	RESORT	RATTER
REMOTE	RENDED	ROOMED	RIPSAW	RESTED	RATTLE
REMOVE	RENDER	ROOMER	ROPIER	RESTER	RETAIL
REMUDA	RENEES	ROOSTS	ROPILY	RESULT	RETAIN
RIMERS	RENEGE	ROOTED	ROPING	RESUME	RETAKE
RIMING	RENEWS	ROOTER	RUPEES	RISERS	RETARD
RIMMED	RENNET	ROOTLE	RUPERT	RISING	RETELL
RIMMER	RENNIN	******	RUPIAH	RISKED	RETENE
RIMOSE	RENOIR	**R-P---**	******	RISKER	RETINA
RIMOUS	RENOWN	******	**R-Q---**	RISQUE	RETIRE
RIMPLE	RENTAL	RAPHAE	ROQUET	ROSARY	RETOLD
ROMAIC	RENTED	RAPHIS	******	ROSCOE	RETOOK
ROMANS	RENTER	RAPIDS	**R-R---**	ROSEAL	RETOOL
ROMANY	RENTES	RAPIER	******	ROSIER	RETORT
ROMISH	RINGED	RAPINE	RAREFY	ROSILY	RETROD
ROMMEL	RINGER	RAPING	RARELY	ROSING	RETTED

RETURN	REVELS	RIYALS	SEAPEN	SIALIC	SOARER
RETUSE	REVERE	ROYALE	SEARCH	SKALDS	SPACAE
RITARD	REVERS	ROYALS	SEARED	SKATED	SPACED
RITTER	REVERT	******	SEARIN	SKATER	SPACER
RITUAL	REVEST	R-Z---	SEASON	SKATES	SPACES
ROTARY	REVETS	******	SEATED	SLACKS	SPADED
ROTATE	REVIEW	RAZEED	SEAWAN	SLAGGY	SPADER
ROTCHE	REVILE	RAZEES	SEAWAY	SLAKED	SPADES
ROTGUT	REVISE	RAZING	SHABBY	SLAKES	SPADIX
ROTORS	REVIVE	RAZORS	SHACKO	SLALOM	SPAHIS
ROTTED	REVOKE	RAZZED	SHACKS	SLANGY	SPAITS
ROTTEN	REVOLT	RAZZES	SHADED	SLANTS	SPALLS
ROTTER	REVUES	RAZZIA	SHADES	SLAPUP	SPANKS
ROTUND	REVVED	******	SHADOW	SLATED	SPARED
RUTILE	RIVALS	S-A---	SHAFTS	SLATER	SPARER
RUTTED	RIVERS	******	SHAGGY	SLATES	SPARES
******	RIVETS	SCABBY	SHAKEN	SLAVED	SPARGE
R-U---	RIVING	SCALAR	SHAKER	SLAVER	SPARKS
******	ROVERS	SCALDS	SHAKES	SLAVES	SPARRY
REUBEN	ROVING	SCALED	SHAKOS	SLAVIC	SPARSE
RHUMBA	******	SCALER	SHALED	SLAYER	SPARTA
RHUMBS	R-W---	SCALES	SHALES	SMACKS	SPASMS
ROUBLE	RAWEST	SCALPS	SHAMAN	SMALLS	SPATES
ROUCHE	RAWISH	SCAMPI	SHAMED	SMALTI	SPATHE
ROUGED	REWARD	SCAMPS	SHAMES	SMALTO	SPAVIN
ROUGES	REWIND	SCANTY	SHAMMY	SMARMY	SPAWNS
ROUGHS	REWORD	SCAPES	SHAMUS	SMARTS	SPAYED
ROUNDS	ROWANS	SCARAB	SHANDY	SMAZES	STABLE
ROUSED	ROWELS	SCARCE	SHANKS	SNACKS	STABLY
ROUSER	ROWENA	SCARED	SHANTY	SNAFUS	STACIE
ROUSES	ROWERS	SCARER	SHAPED	SNAGGY	STACKS
ROUSTS	ROWING	SCARES	SHAPEN	SNAILS	STACTE
ROUTED	******	SCARFS	SHAPER	SNAKED	STACYS
ROUTER	R-X---	SCARPS	SHAPES	SNAKES	STADIA
ROUTES	******	SCATHE	SHARDS	SNAPPY	STAFFS
RYUKYU	ROXANA	SCATTY	SHARED	SNARED	STAGED
******	ROXANE	SCAUPS	SHARER	SNARER	STAGER
R-V---	******	SEABEE	SHARES	SNARES	STAGES
******	R-Y---	SEACOW	SHARKS	SNARLS	STAGEY
RAVAGE	******	SEADOG	SHARON	SNARLY	STAGGY
RAVELS	RAYAHS	SEALED	SHARPS	SNATCH	STAINS
RAVENS	RAYING	SEALER	SHASTA	SNATHE	STAIRS
RAVERS	RAYONS	SEAMAN	SHAVED	SNATHS	STAITH
RAVINE	RHYMED	SEAMED	SHAVEN	SNAZZY	STAKED
RAVING	RHYMER	SEAMEN	SHAVER	SOAKED	STAKES
RAVISH	RHYMES	SEAMER	SHAVES	SOAKER	STALAG
REVAMP	RHYTHM	SEAMUS	SHAWLS	SOAPED	STALED
REVEAL		SEANCE	SHAWMS	SOARED	STALER

STALES	SWARAJ	SECANT	SIDDUR	SHELTY	SPEAKS
STALIN	SWARDS	SECEDE	SIDERO	SHELVE	SPEARS
STALKS	SWARMS	SECERN	SIDING	SHERDS	SPECIE
STALKY	SWARTH	SECKEL	SIDLED	SHERIF	SPECKS
STALLS	SWARTY	SECOND	SIDLER	SHERPA	SPEECH
STAMEN	SWATCH	SECPAR	SIDLES	SHERRY	SPEEDS
STAMIN	SWATHE	SECRET	SIDNEY	SHEWED	SPEEDY
STAMPS	SWATHS	SECTOR	SODDED	SHEWER	SPEISS
STANCE	SWAYED	SECUND	SODDEN	SIECLE	SPELLS
STANCH	******	SECURE	SODIUM	SIEGED	SPENDS
STANDS	S-B---	SICILY	SODOMY	SIEGES	SPERMO
STANZA	******	SICKED	SUDARY	SIENNA	SPERRY
STAPES	SABBAT	SICKEN	SUDDEN	SIERRA	SPEWED
STAPLE	SABEAN	SICKER	SYDNEY	SIESTA	STEADY
STARCH	SABERS	SICKLE	******	SIEURS	STEAKS
STARED	SABINA	SICKLY	S-E---	SIEVED	STEALS
STARER	SABINE	SOCAGE	******	SIEVES	STEAMS
STARES	SABINS	SOCCER	SCENDS	SKEANS	STEAMY
STARRY	SABLES	SOCIAL	SCENES	SKEINS	STEEDS
STARTS	SABOTS	SOCKED	SCENIC	SKERRY	STEELS
STARVE	SABRAS	SOCKET	SCENTS	SKETCH	STEELY
STASES	SEBATS	SOCLES	SEEDED	SKEWED	STEEPS
STASIS	SIBYLS	SOCMAN	SEEDER	SKEWER	STEERS
STATAL	SOBBED	SOCMEN	SEEING	SLEAVE	STEEVE
STATED	SOBERS	SOCRED	SEEKER	SLEAZY	STEFAN
STATEN	SUBAHS	SUCCOR	SEEMED	SLEDGE	STEINS
STATER	SUBDEB	SUCKED	SEEMER	SLEEKS	STELAE
STATES	SUBDUE	SUCKER	SEEMLY	SLEEKY	STELAR
STATIC	SUBITO	SUCKLE	SEEPED	SLEEPS	STELES
STATOR	SUBLET	SUCRES	SEESAW	SLEEPY	STELIC
STATUE	SUBMIT	SYCEES	SEETHE	SLEETS	STELLA
STATUS	SUBORN	******	SHEARS	SLEETY	STELLI
STAURO	SUBTER	S-D---	SHEATH	SLEEVE	STENCH
STAVED	SUBTLE	******	SHEAVE	SLEIGH	STENOG
STAVES	SUBTLY	SADDEN	SHEBAT	SLEUTH	STEPAN
STAYED	SUBURB	SADDER	SHEENS	SLEWED	STEPIN
STAYER	SUBWAY	SADDLE	SHEENY	SMEARS	STEPPE
SUABLE	SYBILS	SADHUS	SHEEPS	SMEARY	STEPUP
SWAGED	******	SADIES	SHEERS	SMELLS	STEREO
SWAGES	S-C---	SADISM	SHEETS	SMELLY	STERES
SWAILS	******	SADIST	SHEIKH	SMELTS	STERIC
SWAINS	SACHEM	SEDANS	SHEIKS	SNEAKS	STERNA
SWALES	SACHET	SEDATE	SHEILA	SNEAKY	STERNO
SWAMIS	SACKED	SEDERS	SHEILD	SNEERS	STERNS
SWAMPS	SACKER	SEDGES	SHEKEL	SNEEZE	STEROL
SWAMPY	SACRAL	SEDILE	SHELBY	SNEEZY	STETHO
SWANEE	SACRED	SEDUCE	SHELLS	SNELLS	STEVEN
SWANKY	SACRUM	SEDUMS	SHELLY	SOEVER	STEVES

STEVIE	SIGNER	SEISED	SLICED	SPIKED	SWIPLE
STEWED	SIGNET	SEISIN	SLICER	SPIKES	SWIRLS
SUEDES	SIGNOR	SEISMO	SLICES	SPILED	SWIRLY
SVELTE	SIGRID	SEISMS	SLICKS	SPILES	SWITCH
SWEARS	SUGARS	SEISOR	SLIDER	SPILLS	SWIVEL
SWEATS	SUGARY	SEIZED	SLIDES	SPILTH	SWIVET
SWEATY	******	SEIZER	SLIEST	SPINAL	******
SWEDEN	**S-H---**	SEIZES	SLIGHT	SPINEL	**S-J---**
SWEDES	******	SEIZIN	SLIMED	SPINES	******
SWEENY	SAHARA	SEIZOR	SLIMES	SPINET	SAJOUS
SWEEPS	SAHEBS	SHIELD	SLIMLY	SPINNY	SEJANT
SWEEPY	SAHIBS	SHIEST	SLIMSY	SPIRAL	******
SWEETS	SCHEMA	SHIFTS	SLINGS	SPIREA	**S-K---**
SWELLS	SCHEME	SHIFTY	SLINKS	SPIRED	******
SWERVE	SCHICK	SHIISM	SLINKY	SPIRES	SAKERS
******	SCHISM	SHIITE	SLIPON	SPIRIT	SIKKIM
S-F---	SCHIST	SHIKAR	SLIPUP	SPIRTS	******
******	SCHIZO	SHILLS	SLIVER	SPITAL	**S-L---**
SAFARI	SCHMOS	SHILOH	SMILAX	SPITED	SALAAM
SAFELY	SCHOOL	SHIMMY	SMILED	SPITES	SALADS
SAFEST	SCHORL	SHINDY	SMILER	STICKS	SALAMI
SAFETY	SCHUIT	SHINED	SMILES	STICKY	SALARY
SIFTED	SCHUSS	SHINER	SMIRCH	STIFLE	SALIFY
SIFTER	SCHWAS	SHINES	SMIRKS	STIGMA	SALINE
SOFFIT	SPHENE	SHINNY	SMITER	STILES	SALISH
SOFTAS	SPHENO	SHINTO	SMITES	STILLS	SALIVA
SOFTEN	SPHERE	SHIRES	SMITHS	STILLY	SALLET
SOFTER	SPHERY	SHIRKS	SMITHY	STILTS	SALLOW
SOFTLY	SPHINX	SHIRRS	SNICKS	STINGS	SALLYS
SUFFER	STHENO	SHIRTS	SNIFFS	STINGY	SALMIS
SUFFIX	******	SHIRTY	SNIFFY	STINKS	SALMON
SUFISM	**S-I---**	SHIVER	SNIPED	STINTS	SALOME
******	******	SHIVES	SNIPER	STIPEL	SALONS
S-G---	SAIGAS	SKIERS	SNIPES	STIPES	SALOON
******	SAIGON	SKIFFS	SNIPPY	STIRKS	SALOOP
SAGELY	SAILED	SKIING	SNITCH	STIRPS	SALPAS
SAGEST	SAILER	SKILLS	SNIVEL	STITCH	SALPID
SAGGAR	SAILOR	SKIMOS	SOIGNE	STITHY	SALTED
SAGGED	SAINTS	SKIMPS	SOILED	STIVER	SALTER
SAGGER	SAIPAN	SKIMPY	SOIREE	SUITED	SALUKI
SAGIER	SAITIC	SKINKS	SPICED	SUITES	SALUTE
SEGGAR	SCILLY	SKINNY	SPICER	SUITOR	SALVED
SIGHED	SCIONS	SKIRRS	SPICES	SWIFTS	SALVER
SIGHTS	SCIPIO	SKIRTS	SPIDER	SWILLS	SALVES
SIGILS	SEICHE	SKIVED	SPIELS	SWINGE	SALVIA
SIGMAS	SEINED	SKIVER	SPIERS	SWINGS	SALVOR
SIGNAL	SEINER	SKIVES	SPIFFY	SWIPED	SALVOS
SIGNED	SEINES	SKIVVY	SPIGOT	SWIPES	

SCLAFF	SPLICE	SIMONY	SENNET	******	SHOVEL
SCLERA	SPLINE	SIMOOM	SENNIT	S-O---	SHOVER
SCLERO	SPLINT	SIMPER	SENORA	******	SHOVES
SELDOM	SPLITS	SIMPLE	SENSED	SCOFFS	SHOWED
SELECT	SULCUS	SOMALI	SENSES	SCOLDS	SHOWER
SELENE	SULFUR	SOMATA	SENSOR	SCOLEX	SIOUAN
SELENO	SULKED	SOMATO	SENTRY	SCONCE	SKOPJE
SELJUK	SULLEN	SOMBER	SINBAD	SCONES	SLOGAN
SELLER	SULPHA	SOMBRE	SINEON	SCOOPS	SLOOPS
SELSYN	SULPHO	SOMITE	SINEWS	SCOOTS	SLOPED
SELVES	SULTAN	SUMACS	SINEWY	SCOPES	SLOPER
SELWYN	SULTRY	SUMMED	SINFUL	SCOPUS	SLOPES
SILAGE	SYLPHS	SUMMER	SINGED	SCORCH	SLOPPY
SILENI	SYLPHY	SUMMIT	SINGER	SCORED	SLOSHY
SILENT	SYLVAE	SUMMON	SINGES	SCORER	SLOTHS
SILICA	SYLVAN	SUMNER	SINGLE	SCORES	SLOUCH
SILICO	SYLVAS	SYMBOL	SINGLY	SCORIA	SLOUGH
SILKEN	SYLVIA	******	SINKER	SCORNS	SLOVAK
SILOED	******	S-N---	SINNED	SCOTCH	SLOVEN
SILTED	S-M---	******	SINNER	SCOTER	SLOWED
SILVAE	******		SINTER	SCOTIA	SLOWER
SILVAN	SAMARA	SANDAL	SONANT	SCOTTS	SLOWLY
SILVAS	SAMBAS	SANDED	SONARS	SCOURS	SMOCKS
SILVER	SAMBOS	SANDER	SONATA	SCOUSE	SMOKED
SILVIA	SAMBUR	SANDHI	SONDER	SCOUTS	SMOKER
SOLACE	SAMIAN	SANDRA	SONIAS	SCOWLS	SMOKES
SOLAND	SAMIEL	SANDYS	SONNET	SHOALS	SMOLTS
SOLANO	SAMITE	SANELY	SONYAS	SHOALY	SMOOCH
SOLANS	SAMLET	SANEST	SUNBOW	SHOATS	SMOOTH
SOLDER	SAMMYS	SANGAR	SUNDAE	SHOCKS	SNOBBY
SOLELY	SAMOAN	SANGER	SUNDAY	SHODDY	SNOCAT
SOLEMN	SAMPAN	SANGUI	SUNDER	SHOERS	SNOODS
SOLENT	SAMPLE	SANIES	SUNDEW	SHOFAR	SNOOKS
SOLIDI	SAMSHU	SANITY	SUNDOG	SHOGUN	SNOOPS
SOLIDS	SAMSON	SANJAK	SUNDRY	SHOJIS	SNOOPY
SOLING	SAMUEL	SANNUP	SUNGOD	SHOOED	SNOOTS
SOLION	SEMELE	SANSAR	SUNHAT	SHOOIN	SNOOTY
SOLOED	SEMEME	SANSEI	SUNKEN	SHOOTS	SNOOZE
SOLUTE	SEMITE	SANTOL	SUNLIT	SHOPPE	SNORED
SOLVED	SEMPRE	SENARY	SUNNAH	SHORAN	SNORER
SOLVER	SIMARS	SENATE	SUNNED	SHORED	SNORES
SOLVES	SIMIAN	SENDAL	SUNSET	SHORES	SNORTS
SPLAKE	SIMILE	SENDER	SUNTAN	SHORLS	SNOTTY
SPLASH	SIMLIN	SENECA	SUNUPS	SHORTS	SNOUTS
SPLATS	SIMMER	SENILE	SYNDET	SHOTES	SNOWED
SPLAYS	SIMNEL	SENIOR	SYNDIC	SHOULD	SOONER
SPLEEN	SIMONE	SENLAC	SYNODS	SHOUTS	SOOTED
SPLENO	SIMONS	SENNAS	SYNTAX	SHOVED	SOOTHE

SPOILS	STORED	******	SERIAL	SORTER	STRIPE
SPOILT	STORES	**S-Q---**	SERIES	SORTIE	STRIPS
SPOKED	STOREY	******	SERIFS	SPRAGS	STRIPT
SPOKEN	STORKS	SEQUEL	SERINE	SPRAIN	STRIPY
SPOKES	STORMS	SEQUIN	SERINS	SPRANG	STRIVE
SPONGE	STORMY	******	SERMON	SPRATS	STROBE
SPONGY	STOUPS	**S-R---**	SEROUS	SPRAWL	STRODE
SPOOFS	STOUTS	******	SEROWS	SPRAYS	STROKE
SPOOKS	STOVER	SARAHS	SERUMS	SPREAD	STROLL
SPOOKY	STOVES	SARAPE	SERVAL	SPREES	STROMA
SPOOLS	STOWED	SARGON	SERVED	SPRIER	STRONG
SPOONS	SUOMIC	SARONG	SERVER	SPRIGS	STROPS
SPOONY	SWOONS	SARSAR	SERVES	SPRING	STROUD
SPOORS	SWOOPS	SARTOR	SERVOS	SPRINT	STROVE
SPORED	SWORDS	SARTRE	SHRANK	SPRITE	STRUCK
SPORES	******	SCRAGS	SHREDS	SPRITS	STRUMA
SPORTS	**S-P---**	SCRAMS	SHREWD	SPROUT	STRUMS
SPORTY	******	SCRAPE	SHREWS	SPRUCE	STRUNG
SPOTTY	SAPHAR	SCRAPS	SHRIEK	SPRUES	STRUTS
SPOUSE	SAPIEN	SCRAWL	SHRIFT	SPRUNG	SURAHS
SPOUTS	SAPPED	SCREAK	SHRIKE	SPRYER	SURELY
STOATS	SAPPER	SCREAM	SHRILL	SPRYLY	SUREST
STOCKS	SAPPHO	SCREED	SHRIMP	STRAFE	SURETY
STOCKY	SEPALS	SCREEN	SHRINE	STRAIN	SURFED
STODGE	SEPIAS	SCREWS	SHRINK	STRAIT	SURFER
STODGY	SEPOYS	SCREWY	SHRIVE	STRAKE	SURGED
STOGEY	SEPSIS	SCRIBE	SHROFF	STRAND	SURGER
STOICS	SEPTAL	SCRIED	SHROUD	STRAPS	SURGES
STOKED	SEPTET	SCRIMP	SHROVE	STRASS	SURREY
STOKER	SEPTIC	SCRIPS	SHRUBS	STRATA	SURTAX
STOKES	SEPTUM	SCRIPT	SHRUGS	STRATH	SURVEY
STOLED	SIPHON	SCRIVE	SHRUNK	STRATI	SYRIAC
STOLEN	SIPPED	SCRODS	SIRDAR	STRAWS	SYRIAN
STOLES	SIPPER	SCROLL	SIRENS	STRAWY	SYRINX
STOLID	SIPPET	SCROOP	SIRING	STRAYS	SYRUPS
STOLON	SOPHIA	SCROTA	SIRIUS	STREAK	SYRUPY
STOMAT	SOPHIE	SCRUBS	SIRUPS	STREAM	******
STOMPS	SOPPED	SCRUFF	SIRUPY	STREET	**S-S---**
STONED	SUPERB	SCRUMS	SORBET	STRESS	******
STONER	SUPERS	SERACS	SORDID	STREWN	SASHAY
STONES	SUPINE	SERAIS	SORELS	STREWS	SASHED
STOOGE	SUPPED	SERAPE	SORELY	STRIAE	SASHES
STOOKS	SUPPER	SERAPH	SOREST	STRICK	SASINS
STOOLS	SUPPLE	SERBIA	SORGHO	STRICT	SASSED
STOOPS	SUPPLY	SERDAB	SORGOS	STRIDE	SASSES
STOPED	SYPHER	SEREIN	SORREL	STRIFE	SESAME
STOPES	SYPHON	SERENA	SORROW	STRIKE	SESQUI
STORAX		SERENE	SORTED	STRING	SESTET

SISERA	SAUCES	SOURCE	******	SEXTET	TEAPOY
SISKIN	SAUGER	SOURED	**S-V---**	SEXTON	TEARED
SISTER	SAULTS	SOURER	******	SEXUAL	TEASED
SUSANS	SAUNAS	SOURLY	SAVAGE	SIXTES	TEASEL
SUSIES	SAUREL	SOUSED	SAVANT	SIXTHS	TEASER
SUSLIK	SAURUS	SOUSES	SAVATE	******	TEASES
SUSSED	SAUTES	SPUMED	SAVERS	**S-Y---**	TEASET
SUSSEX	SCUBAS	SPUMES	SAVING	******	TEAURN
SYSTEM	SCUFFS	SPUNKY	SAVINS	SAYERS	THADDY
******	SCULLS	SPURGE	SAVIOR	SAYING	THADYS
S-T---	SCULPT	SPURNS	SAVORS	SCYLLA	THALER
******	SCUMMY	SPURRY	SAVORY	SCYPHI	THALES
SATANG	SCURFY	SPURTS	SAVOUR	SCYPHO	THALIA
SATARA	SCURRY	SPUTUM	SEVENS	SCYTHE	THAMES
SATEEN	SCURVY	SQUABS	SEVERE	SHYEST	THANAT
SATING	SCUTCH	SQUADS	SEVERN	SHYING	THANES
SATINS	SCUTES	SQUALL	SEVERS	SKYCAP	THANKS
SATINY	SCUTUM	SQUAMA	SOVIET	SKYING	THATCH
SATIRE	SEURAT	SQUARE	******	SKYMAN	THAWED
SATORY	SHUCKS	SQUASH	**S-W---**	SKYMEN	THAYER
SATRAP	SHUNTS	SQUATS	******	SKYWAY	TIARAS
SATURN	SHUTIN	SQUAWK	SAWERS	SLYEST	TOASTS
SATYRS	SKULKS	SQUAWS	SAWFLY	SPYING	TRACED
SETOFF	SKULLS	SQUEAK	SAWING	STYING	TRACER
SETONS	SKUNKS	SQUEAL	SAWNEY	STYLAR	TRACES
SETOSE	SLUDGE	SQUIBS	SAWYER	STYLED	TRACHE
SETOUS	SLUDGY	SQUIDS	SEWAGE	STYLER	TRACHY
SETTEE	SLUICE	SQUILL	SEWALL	STYLES	TRACKS
SETTER	SLUING	SQUINT	SEWARD	STYLET	TRACTS
SETTLE	SLUMMY	SQUIRE	SEWELL	STYLUS	TRADED
SETTOS	SLUMPS	SQUIRM	SEWERS	STYMIE	TRADER
SETUPS	SLURPS	SQUIRT	SEWING	******	TRADES
SHTICK	SLURRY	SQUISH	SIWASH	**S-Z---**	TRAGIC
SITARS	SLUSHY	STUART	SOWARS	******	TRAGUS
SITING	SMUDGE	STUBBS	SOWERS	SIZARS	TRAILS
SITINS	SMUDGY	STUBBY	SOWING	SIZIER	TRAINS
SITTER	SMUGLY	STUCCO	******	SIZING	TRAITS
SOTHIC	SMUTCH	STUDIO	**S-X---**	SIZZLE	TRAMPS
SOTHIS	SMUTTY	STUFFS	******	SOZINE	TRANCE
SOTOLS	SNUFFS	STUFFY	SAXONS	SOZINS	TRASHY
SUTLER	SNUFFY	STULLS	SAXONY	SYZYGY	TRAUMA
SUTRAS	SNUGLY	STUMPS	SEXIER	******	TRAVEL
SUTTEE	SOUARI	STUMPY	SEXILY	**T-A---**	TRAVES
SUTTON	SOUGHS	STUNTS	SEXING	******	TRAWLS
SUTURE	SOUGHT	STUPAS	SEXISM	TEABAG	TSADES
******	SOULED	STUPES	SEXIST	TEACUP	TWANGS
S-U---	SOUNDS	STUPID	SEXPOT	TEAMED	TWANGY
******	SOUPED	STUPOR	SEXTAN	TEAPOT	
SAUCED		STURDY			
SAUCER					

******	TEDDYS	TIEUPS	TEHEES	TRINES	TALLER
T-B---	TEDIUM	TOECAP	TSHIRT	TRIODE	TALLOW
******	TIDBIT	TOEING	******	TRIOSE	TALMUD
TABARD	TIDIED	TREADS	**T-I---**	TRIPLE	TALONS
TABBED	TIDIER	TREATS	******	TRIPOD	TELARY
TABLED	TIDIES	TREATY	TAIGAS	TRIPOS	TELEDU
TABLES	TIDILY	TREBLE	TAILED	TRISTE	TELEGA
TABLET	TIDING	TREMOR	TAILLE	TRITER	TELFER
TABOOS	TODDLE	TRENCH	TAILOR	TRITON	TELLER
TABORS	TODIES	TRENDS	TAINOS	TRIUNE	TELLUS
TIBIAE	******	TRENDY	TAINTS	TRIVET	TELSON
TIBIAL	**T-E---**	TREPAN	TAIPEI	TRIVIA	TELUGU
TIBIAS	******	TRESSY	TAIWAN	TRIXIE	TILDES
TOBAGO	TAENIA	TREVOR	THIEVE	TRIXYS	TILERS
TOBIAH	TEEING	TSETSE	THIGHS	TUILLE	TILING
TOBIAS	TEEMED	TWEAKS	THINGS	TWIBIL	TILLED
TOBIES	TEEMER	TWEAKY	THINLY	TWIGGY	TILLER
TUBATE	TEENSY	TWEEDS	THIOLS	TWILIT	TILLIE
TUBBED	TEETER	TWEETS	THIRDS	TWILLS	TILLYS
TUBBER	TEETHE	TWELVE	THIRST	TWINED	TILTED
TUBERS	THEBAE	TWENTY	THIRTY	TWINER	TILTER
TUBING	THEBES	TWERPS	THISBE	TWINES	TILTHS
TUBULE	THECAE	******	TOILED	TWINGE	TOLEDO
TYBALT	THECAL	**T-F---**	TOILER	TWIRLS	TOLLED
******	THEDAS	******	TOILES	TWIRPS	TOLLER
T-C---	THEFTS	TEFLON	TOILET	TWISTS	TOLTEC
******	THEIRS	TIFFED	TRIADS	TWISTY	TOLUOL
TACKED	THEISM	TIFFIN	TRIALS	TWITCH	TOLUYL
TACKER	THEIST	TOFFEE	TRIBAL	******	TULADI
TACKEY	THELMA	TUFFET	TRIBES	**T-K---**	TULIPS
TACKLE	THEMES	TUFTED	TRICAR	******	TULLES
TACOMA	THEMIS	******	TRICED	TAKEIN	******
TACTIC	THENAL	**T-G---**	TRICES	TAKERS	**T-M---**
TECHNO	THENAR	******	TRICHI	TAKEUP	******
TICALS	THENCE	TAGGED	TRICHO	TAKING	TAMALE
TICKED	THEORY	TAGGER	TRICKS	TOKENS	TAMBAC
TICKER	THERMO	TEGMEN	TRICKY	******	TAMELY
TICKET	THERMS	TIGERS	TRICOT	**T-L---**	TAMERS
TICKLE	THESES	TIGHTS	TRIERS	******	TAMEST
TOCSIN	THESIS	TIGRIS	TRIFID	TALARI	TAMING
TUCHUN	THETAS	TOGAED	TRIFLE	TALCED	TAMPAN
TUCKED	THETIC	TOGGED	TRIGLY	TALCUM	TAMPED
TUCKER	THETIS	TOGGLE	TRIGON	TALENT	TAMPER
TUCKET	THEWED	TOGUES	TRILBY	TALERS	TAMPON
TUCSON	TIEINS	TUGGED	TRILLS	TALION	TAMTAM
TYCOON	TIEPIN	******	TRIMLY	TALKED	TEMPER
******	TIERCE	**T-H---**	TRINAL	TALKER	TEMPLE
T-D---	TIERED	******	TRINED	TALKIE	TEMPOS
******		TAHITI			
TEDDED		TEHEED			
TEDDER					

TEMPTS	TENONS	TUNICS	TROWEL	******	THRIFT
TIMBAL	TENORS	TUNING	TWOBIT	**T-R---**	THRILL
TIMBER	TENPIN	TUNNED	TWOFER	******	THRIPS
TIMBRE	TENREC	TUNNEL	TWOPLY	TARGET	THRIVE
TIMELY	TENSED	******	TWOULD	TARIFF	THROAT
TIMERS	TENSER	**T-O---**	TWOWAY	TARING	THROBS
TIMING	TENSES	******	******	TARMAC	THROES
TIMMYS	TENSOR	TAOISM	**T-P---**	TARNAL	THRONE
TOMANS	TENTED	TAOIST	******	TAROTS	THRONG
TOMATO	TENTER	TBONES	TAPALO	TARPAN	THROVE
TOMBAC	TENTHS	THOLES	TAPERS	TARRED	THROWN
TOMBED	TENUES	THOMAS	TAPING	TARSAL	THROWS
TOMBOY	TENUIS	THONGS	TAPIRS	TARSIA	THRUMS
TOMCAT	TENURE	THORAC	TAPPED	TARSUS	THRUSH
TOMCOD	TENUTO	THORAX	TAPPER	TARTAN	THRUST
TOMMYS	TINCAL	THORIA	TAPPET	TARTAR	TIRADE
TOMTIT	TINCAN	THORIC	TEPEES	TARTED	TIRANA
TOMTOM	TINCTS	THORNS	TEPEFY	TARTER	TIRING
TUMBLE	TINDER	THORNY	TIPCAT	TARTLY	TORAHS
TUMEFY	TINEID	THORON	TIPOFF	TARZAN	TORERO
TUMORS	TINGED	THORPE	TIPPED	TERAPH	TORIES
TUMOUR	TINGES	THOUGH	TIPPER	TERATO	TORIIS
TUMULT	TINGLE	TOOLED	TIPPET	TERBIA	TOROID
TYMPAN	TINGLY	TOOLER	TIPPLE	TERCEL	TOROSE
******	TINIER	TOOTED	TIPTOE	TERCET	TOROUS
T-N---	TINILY	TOOTER	TIPTOP	TEREDO	TORPID
******	TINKER	TOOTHY	TOPEKA	TERESA	TORPOR
TANDEM	TINKLE	TOOTLE	TOPERS	TERETE	TORQUE
TANGED	TINKLY	TOOTSY	TOPHAT	TEREUS	TORRID
TANGLE	TINNED	TROCAR	TOPICS	TERGAL	TORSKS
TANGLY	TINNER	TROCHE	TOPING	TERGUM	TORSOS
TANGOS	TINPOT	TROGON	TOPPED	TERMED	TURBAN
TANIST	TINSEL	TROIKA	TOPPER	TERMER	TURBID
TANKAS	TINTED	TROJAN	TOPPLE	TERMLY	TURBIT
TANKED	TONERS	TROLLS	TUPELO	TERMOR	TURBOT
TANKER	TONGED	TROOPS	TUPIKS	TERNAL	TURCOS
TANNED	TONGUE	TROPAL	TUPPED	TERRET	TUREEN
TANNER	TONICS	TROPHO	TYPHLO	TERROR	TURFED
TANNIC	TONIER	TROPHY	TYPHON	TERRYS	TURGID
TANNIN	TONING	TROPIC	TYPHUS	TERSER	TURKEY
TANREC	TONITE	TROPPO	TYPIFY	THRALL	TURKIC
TENACE	TONKIN	TROTHS	TYPING	THRASH	TURKIS
TENANT	TONSIL	TROTYL	TYPIST	THREAD	TURNED
TENDED	TUNDRA	TROUGH	******	THREAT	TURNER
TENDER	TUNERS	TROUPE	**T-Q---**	THREED	TURNIP
TENDON	TUNEUP	TROUTS	******	THREES	TURNUP
TENETS	TUNGUS	TROVER	TOQUES	THRESH	TURRET
TENNIS	TUNICA	TROVES	TUQUES	THRICE	TURTLE

TURVES	TETANY	TOUCAN	TAXIED	******	UNDREW
TYRANT	TETCHY	TOUCHE	TAXING	**U-B---**	UNDSET
TYRIAN	TETHER	TOUCHY	TAXITE	******	UNDULY
TYRONE	TETHYS	TOUGHS	TOXINS	UMBELS	UPDATE
******	TETONS	TOULON	TUXEDO	UMBERS	UPDIKE
T-S---	TETRAD	TOUPEE	******	UMBLES	******
******	TETRYL	TOURED	**T-Y---**	UMBRAE	**U-E---**
TASKED	TETTER	TOURER	******	UMBRAL	******
TASMAN	TETZEL	TOUSLE	TAYLOR	UMBRAS	ULEMAS
TASSEL	TITANS	TOUTED	THYMES	UNBARS	ULENCE
TASSET	TITBIT	TOUTER	THYMIC	UNBEAR	UNEASE
TASTED	TITHED	TRUANT	THYMOL	UNBELT	UNEASY
TASTER	TITHER	TRUCES	THYMUS	UNBEND	UNESCO
TASTES	TITHES	TRUCKS	THYREO	UNBENT	UNEVEN
TESSIE	TITIAN	TRUDGE	THYRSE	UNBIND	UPENDS
TESTAE	TITLED	TRUDYS	THYRSI	UNBOLT	UREASE
TESTED	TITLES	TRUEST	TOYERS	UNBORN	UREIDE
TESTER	TITTER	TRUING	TOYING	UNBRED	UREMIA
TESTES	TITTLE	TRUISM	TOYISH	UPBEAT	URETER
TESTIS	TITTUP	TRUMAN	TOYONS	UPBOWS	URETIC
TESTON	TOTALS	TRUMPS	TRYING	URBANE	USEFUL
TISANE	TOTEMS	TRUNKS	TRYOUT	******	UTERUS
TISHRI	TOTERS	TRUSTS	TRYSTS	**U-C---**	******
TISSUE	TOTHER	TRUSTY	TUYERE	******	**U-F---**
TOSHES	TOTING	TRUTHS	******	ULCERS	******
TOSSED	TOTTED	******	******	UNCAGE	UNFAIR
TOSSES	TOTTER	**T-V---**	**T-Z---**	UNCAPS	UNFOLD
TOSSUP	TUTORS	******	TAZZAS	UNCASE	UNFURL
TUSCAN	TUTTED	TAVERN	******	UNCIAL	******
TUSHED	TUTTIS	TEVERE	**U-A---**	UNCLAD	**U-G---**
TUSHES	******	******	******	UNCLES	******
TUSKED	**T-U---**	**T-W---**	UBANGI	UNCOCK	UNGIRD
TUSKER	******	******	UGANDA	UNCOIL	UNGIRT
TUSSAH	TAUGHT	TAWDRY	UKASES	UNCORD	UNGUAL
TUSSAL	TAUNTS	TAWERS	UNABLE	UNCORK	UNGUES
TUSSAR	TAUPES	TAWING	UNAPID	UNCURL	UNGUIS
TUSSIS	TAURUS	THWACK	UPASES	UPCAST	UNGULA
TUSSLE	TAUTEN	THWART	URAEUS	URCHIN	URGENT
******	TAUTER	TOWAGE	URALIC	******	URGING
T-T---	TAUTLY	TOWARD	URANIA	**U-D---**	UTGARD
******	TAUTOG	TOWELS	URANIC	******	******
TATARS	TEUCER	TOWERS	URANUS	UDDERS	**U-H---**
TATLER	TEUTON	TOWERY	URANYL	UNDIES	******
TATTED	THUJAS	TOWING	USABLE	UNDINE	UNHAIR
TATTER	THULIA	******	USABLY	UNDOER	UNHAND
TATTLE	THUMBS	**T-X---**	USAGES	UNDOES	UNHASP
TATTLY	THUMPS	******	USANCE	UNDONE	UNHATS
TATTOO	THUSLY	TAXEME	UTAHAN	UNDRAW	UNHEWN
		TAXERS			

UNHOLY	UNLESS	UNRIPS	URTEXT	******	VOICES
UNHOOK	UNLIKE	UNROBE	UTTERS	**V-C---**	VOIDED
UNHURT	UNLIVE	UNROLL	******	******	VOILES
UNHUSK	UNLOAD	UNROOT	**U-U---**	VACANT	**V-K---**
UPHELD	UNLOCK	UNRULY	******	VACATE	******
UPHILL	UPLAND	UPRISE	UNUSED	VACUNA	VIKING
UPHOLD	UPLIFT	UPROAR	USURER	VACUUM	******
UPHROE	******	UPROOT	USURPS	VECTOR	**V-L---**
USHERS	**U-M---**	UPROSE	UTURNS	VICARS	******
******	******	UPRUSH	UVULAE	VICKYS	VALATE
U-I---	UNMADE	******	UVULAR	VICTIM	VALERY
******	UNMAKE	**U-S---**	UVULAS	VICTOR	VALETS
UBIETY	UNMANS	******	******	VICUNA	VALGUS
UMIAKS	UNMASK	ULSTER	**U-V---**	VOCALS	VALISE
UNICEF	UNMEET	UNSAFE	******	******	VALKYR
UNIFIC	UNMEWS	UNSAID	UNVEIL	**V-D---**	VALLEY
UNIONS	UNMOOR	UNSAYS	UNVEXT	******	VALLUM
UNIPED	UPMOST	UNSEAL	******	VADOSE	VALOIS
UNIQUE	UTMOST	UNSEAM	**U-W---**	VEDIAC	VALOUR
UNISEX	******	UNSEAT	******	VIDUAL	VALUED
UNISON	**U-O---**	UNSEEN	UNWARY	VODKAS	VALUER
UNITED	******	UNSHIP	UNWELL	******	VALUES
UNITES	UBOATS	UNSHOD	UNWEPT	**V-E---**	VALUTA
URINAL	UROPOD	UNSOLD	UNWIND	******	VALVAL
******	UTOPIA	UNSTEP	UNWISE	VEERED	VALVAR
U-J---	******	UNSTOP	UNWISH	VIENNA	VALVED
******	**U-P---**	UNSUNG	UNWORN	VIEWED	VALVES
UNJUST	******	UNSURE	UNWRAP	VIEWER	VELDTS
******	UMPIRE	UPSETS	UPWARD	******	VELLUM
U-K---	UNPACK	UPSHOT	******	**V-G---**	VELOCE
******	UNPEGS	UPSIDE	**U-Y---**	******	VELOUR
UNKIND	UNPICK	URSINE	UNYOKE	VAGARY	VELURE
UNKNIT	UNPILE	URSULA	******	VAGINA	VELVET
UPKEEP	UNPINS	******	**U-Z---**	VAGINO	VILELY
******	UNPLUG	**U-T---**	******	VAGUER	VILEST
U-L---	UPPERS	******	UZZIAH	VIGILS	VILIFY
******	UPPING	ULTIMA	******	VIGOUR	VILLAS
UGLIER	UPPISH	ULTIMO	**V-A---**	VOGUES	VILLON
UGLIFY	UPPITY	UNTACK	******	VOGULS	VILLUS
UGLILY	******	UNTIDY	VEADAR	******	VOLANT
ULLAGE	**U-R---**	UNTIED	VIABLE	**V-I---**	VOLERY
UMLAUT	******	UNTIES	VIALED	******	VOLING
UNLACE	UNREAD	UNTOLD	VIANDS	VAINER	VOLLEY
UNLADE	UNREAL	UNTROD	VIATIC	VAINLY	VOLOST
UNLAID	UNREEL	UNTRUE	VIATOR	VEILED	VOLTED
UNLASH	UNREST	UPTAKE	******	VEILER	VOLUME
UNLAYS	UNRIGS	UPTOWN	**V-B---**	VEINED	VOLUTE
UNLEAD	UNRIPE	UPTURN	VIBRIO	VOICED	

VOLVAS	VINSON	VERSOS	******	VIZIRS	WICKER
VOLVOX	VINYLS	VERSTS	**V-T---**	VIZORS	WICKET
VULCAN	******	VERSUS	******	******	WICOPY
VULGAR	**V-O---**	VERTEX	VATFUL	**W-A---**	******
VULVAE	******	VERVET	VATTED	******	**W-D---**
VULVAL	VIOLAS	VIRAGO	VETOED	WEAKEN	******
VULVAR	VIOLET	VIREOS	VETOER	WEAKER	WADDED
******	VIOLIN	VIRGAS	VETOES	WEAKLY	WADDLE
V-M---	VOODOO	VIRGIE	VETTED	WEALDS	WADDLY
******	******	VIRGIL	VITALS	WEALTH	WADERS
VAMOSE	**V-P---**	VIRGIN	VITRIC	WEANED	WADIES
VAMPED	******	VIRILE	VITTAE	WEANER	WADING
VIMINA	VAPORI	VIRTUE	VOTARY	WEAPON	WADSET
VOMERS	VAPORS	VOROUS	VOTERS	WEARER	WEDDED
VOMICA	VAPOUR	VORTEX	VOTING	WEASEL	WEDELN
VOMITO	VIPERS	VYRNWY	VOTIVE	WEAVED	WEDGED
VOMITS	******	******	******	WEAVER	WEDGES
******	**V-R---**	**V-S---**	**V-U---**	WEAVES	WEDGIE
V-N---	******	******	******	WHACKS	WIDDIE
******	VARICO	VASARI	VAULTS	WHALED	WIDELY
VANDAL	VARIED	VASHTI	VAUNTS	WHALER	WIDENS
VANISH	VARIER	VASILI	******	WHALES	WIDEST
VANITY	VARIES	VASSAL	**V-V---**	WHAMMY	WIDOWS
VANMAN	VARLET	VASTER	******	WHANGS	WIDTHS
VANMEN	VARUNA	VASTLY	VIVACE	WHARFS	******
VENDED	VARVES	VESICA	VIVIAN	WHARVE	**W-E---**
VENDEE	VERBAL	VESICO	VIVIEN	WOADED	******
VENDER	VERDIN	VESPER	VIVIFY	WOALDS	WEEDED
VENDOR	VERDUN	VESPID	******	WRACKS	WEEDER
VENDUE	VEREIN	VESSEL	**V-W---**	WRAITH	WEEKLY
VENEER	VERGED	VESTAL	******	WRAPUP	WEENIE
VENERY	VERGER	VESTAS	VOWELS	WRASSE	WEENSY
VENIAL	VERGES	VESTED	VOWERS	WRATHY	WEEPER
VENICE	VERGIL	VESTEE	VOWING	******	WEEVER
VENIRE	VERIFY	VESTRY	**V-X---**	**W-B---**	WEEVIL
VENOMS	VERILY	VISAED	******	******	WHEALS
VENOSE	VERISM	VISAGE	VEXERS	WABASH	WHEATS
VENOUS	VERIST	VISARD	VEXILS	WABBLE	WHEELS
VENTED	VERITY	VISCID	VEXING	WABBLY	WHEEZE
VENTER	VERMIN	VISCUS	VIXENS	WEBBED	WHEEZY
VENTRO	VERNAL	VISEED	******	WEBERS	WHELKS
VENUES	VERNAS	VISHNU	**V-Y---**	WOBBLE	WHELKY
VENULE	VERNIX	VISING	******	WOBBLY	WHELMS
VINCES	VERNON	VISION	VOYAGE	******	WHELPS
VINERY	VERONA	VISITS	VOYEUR	**W-C---**	WHENCE
VINIER	VERSED	VISORS	******	******	WHERRY
VINNYS	VERSES	VISTAS	**V-Z---**	WICHES	WHERVE
VINOUS	VERSET	VISUAL	VIZARD	WICKED	WHEYEY
			VIZIER		

WIELDS	WAILER	WALING	******	WINTER	WARPED
WIELDY	WAISTS	WALKED	**W-M---**	WINTRY	WARPER
WIENER	WAITED	WALKER	******	WINZES	WARRED
WIENIE	WAITER	WALKON	WAMBLE	WONDER	WARREN
WOEFUL	WAIVED	WALKUP	WAMBLY	WONTED	WARSAW
WREAKS	WAIVER	WALLAH	WAMMUS	******	WERENT
WREATH	WAIVES	WALLAS	WAMOUS	**W-O---**	WIRERS
WRECKS	WEIGHS	WALLED	WAMPUM	******	WIRIER
WRENCH	WEIGHT	WALLET	WIMBLE	WHOLLY	WIRILY
WRESTS	WEIMAR	WALLIE	WIMPLE	WHOOPS	WIRING
WRETCH	WEIRDY	WALLIS	WOMBAT	WHOOSH	WORDED
******	WHIDAH	WALLOP	WOMBED	WHORED	WORKED
W-F---	WHIFFS	WALLOW	WOMERA	WHORES	WORKER
******	WHILED	WALLYS	******	WHORLS	WORLDS
WAFERS	WHILES	WALNUT	**W-N---**	WHORTS	WORMED
WAFFLE	WHILOM	WALRUS	******	WOODED	WORMER
WAFTED	WHILST	WALTER	WANDAS	WOODEN	WORSEN
WAFTER	WHIMSY	WALTON	WANDER	WOODSY	WORSER
WIFELY	WHINED	WALVIS	WANDLE	WOOERS	WORSTS
******	WHINER	WELDED	WANGLE	WOOFER	WORTHY
W-G---	WHINES	WELDER	WANING	WOOING	******
******	WHINNY	WELKIN	WANION	WOOLEN	**W-S---**
WAGERS	WHIPPY	WELLED	WANNED	WOOLLY	******
WAGGED	WHIRLS	WELTED	WANNER	WRONGS	WASHED
WAGGLE	WHISKS	WELTER	WANTED	******	WASHER
WAGGLY	WHISKY	WILBER	WANTER	**W-P---**	WASHES
WAGGON	WHITBY	WILBUR	WANTON	******	WASTED
WAGING	WHITED	WILDER	WENDED	WAPITI	WASTER
WAGNER	WHITEN	WILDLY	WENDYS	WAPPED	WASTES
WAGONS	WHITER	WILFUL	WINCED	WIPERS	WESLEY
WIGANS	WHITES	WILIER	WINCER	WIPING	WESSEX
WIGEON	WHITEY	WILILY	WINCES	******	WESTER
WIGGED	WRIEST	WILING	WINCEY	**W-R---**	WISDOM
WIGGLE	WRIGHT	WILLED	WINDED	******	WISELY
WIGGLY	WRINGS	WILLER	WINDER	WARBLE	WISEST
WIGWAG	WRISTS	WILLET	WINDOW	WARDED	WISHED
WIGWAM	WRITER	WILLIE	WINDUP	WARDEN	WISHES
******	WRITES	WILLIS	WINERY	WARDER	WISING
W-H---	WRITHE	WILLOW	WINGED	WARHOL	WISPED
******	******	WILLYS	WINIER	WARIER	WYSTAN
WAHABI	**W-K---**	WILMAS	WINING	WARILY	******
WAHINE	******	WILSON	WINKED	WARMED	**W-T---**
WAHOOS	WAKENS	WILTED	WINKER	WARMER	******
******	WAKIKI	WILTON	WINKLE	WARMLY	WATAPE
W-I---	WAKING	WOLFED	WINNER	WARMTH	WATAPS
******	WIKIUP	WOLSEY	WINNIE	WARMUP	WATERS
WAIFED	******	WOLVER	WINNOW	WARNED	WATERY
WAILED	**W-L---**	WOLVES	WINOES	WARNER	WATSON
	******				
	WALDOS				
	WALERS				

WATTLE	WHYDAH	YEASTS	YELLER	YESSED	******
WATUSI	WRYEST	YEASTY	YELLOW	YESSES	**Z-F---**
WETHER	WRYING	******	YELPED	YESTER	******
WETTED		**Y-B---**	YELPER	******	ZAFFAR
WETTER	**W-Z---**	******	******	**Y-T---**	ZAFFER
WITHAL	******	YABBER	**Y-M---**	******	ZAFFIR
WITHED	WIZARD	******	******	YTTRIA	ZAFFRE
WITHER	WIZENS	**Y-C---**	YAMENS	YTTRIC	ZAFTIG
WITHES	******	******	YAMMER	******	******
WITHIN	**X-A---**	YACHTS	YAMUNS	**Y-U---**	**Z-G---**
WITHIT		YUCCAS	YEMENI	******	******
WITNEY	XRAYED	******	******	YAUPED	ZIGZAG
WITTED	******	**Y-D---**	**Y-N---**	YAUPON	ZYGOMA
******		******	******	YOUPON	ZYGOTE
W-U---	**X-B---**	YODELS	YANKED	YOUTHS	******
******	******	******	YANKEE	******	**Z-I---**
WAULED	XEBECS	**Y-E---**	YENNED	**Y-W---**	******
WOUNDS	******	******	YONDER	******	ZUIDER
******	**X-L---**	YIELDS	YONKER	YAWING	******
W-V---	XYLANS	******	******	YAWLED	**Z-L---**
******	XYLEMS	**Y-G---**	**Y-O---**	YAWNED	******
WAVERS	XYLENE	******	******	YAWNER	ZILLAH
WAVEYS	XYLITE	YAGERS	YAOURT	YAWPED	******
WAVIER	XYLOID	YOGEES	YEOMAN	YAWPER	**Z-M---**
WAVIES	XYLOLS	YOGINS	YEOMEN	YOWING	******
WAVILY	XYLOSE	YOGURT	YOOHOO	YOWLED	ZAMBIA
WAVING	******	******	YVONNE	******	ZAMIAS
WIVERN	**X-N---**	**Y-H---**	******	**Z-A---**	ZOMBIE
WIVERS	******	******	**Y-P---**	******	ZOMBIS
WIVING	XANADU	YAHOOS	******	ZEALOT	******
WYVERN	XANTHO	YAHVEH	YAPONS	ZSAZSA	**Z-N---**
******	XENIAL	YAHWEH	YAPPED	******	******
W-W---	******	YEHUDI	YIPPED	**Z-B---**	ZANANA
******	**X-S---**	******	YIPPIE	******	ZANIER
WAWLED	******	**Y-I---**	YUPONS	ZEBECK	ZANIES
WOWING	XTSTUS	******	YUPPIE	ZEBECS	ZENANA
WOWSER	XYSTER	YOICKS	******	ZEBRAS	ZENGER
******	XYSTOS	******	**Y-R---**	ZIBETH	ZENITH
W-X---	******	**Y-K---**	******	ZIBETS	ZINCED
******	**X-V---**	******	YARDED	******	ZINCIC
WAXIER	******	YAKIMA	YARROW	**Z-C---**	ZINCKY
WAXING	XAVIER	YAKKED	YERBAS	******	ZINGED
******	******	YOKELS	YORICK	ZECHIN	ZINNIA
W-Y---	**Y-A---**	YOKING	YORKER	******	ZONARY
******	******	YUKKED	YORUBA	**Z-D---**	ZONATE
WAYLAY	YEANED	******	******	******	ZONING
WAYNES	YEARLY	**Y-L---**	**Y-S---**		ZONULA
WAYOUT	YEARNS	YCLEPT	YASMAK	ZODIAC	ZONULE
		YELLED	YESMAN		

******	******	AMBAGE	******	ACIDLY	AENEID
Z-O---	Z-Z---	AMBARI	A--B--	AGEDLY	AFFECT
******	******	AMBARY	******	AIRDRY	AFIELD
ZLOTYS	ZIZITH	ANGARY	ADOBES	ALIDAD	AFRESH
ZOOIDS	ZIZZLE	ANKARA	AIRBED	ALUDEL	AGGERS
ZOOMED	******	ANLACE	ALIBIS	AMADOU	AGLEAM
ZOONAL	A--A--	ANLAGE	ALIBLE	AMIDES	AGLETS
******	******	ANNALS	AMEBAE	AMIDIC	AGREED
Z-P---	AALAND	ANSATE	AMEBAS	AMIDIN	AGREES
******	ABBACY	APIARY	AMEBIC	AMIDOL	AIDERS
ZAPATA	ABLAUT	APPALL	ANABAS	AMIDST	AILEEN
ZEPHYR	ABLAZE	APPALS	ANUBIS	ANADEM	ALBEDO
ZIPPED	ABOARD	ARCADE	ARABEL	ANODES	ALBEIT
ZIPPER	ABRADE	ARCANA	ARABIA	ANODIC	ALBERT
******	ABRAMS	ARCANE	ARABIC	AOUDAD	ALDERS
Z-R---	ABWATT	ARGALA	ARABLE	APODAL	ALIENS
******	ACHAEA	ARGALI	ATABAL	ARIDLY	ALKENE
ZARIBA	ACHAIA	ARGALS	******	ASIDES	ALLEGE
ZEROED	ACKACK	ARIANS	A--C--	AVIDIN	ALLELE
ZEROES	ACUATE	ARMADA	******	AVIDLY	ALLENS
ZIRCON	ADDAMS	ARMAGH	ABACAS	******	ALLEYS
ZIRONS	ADNATE	ARMAND	ABACUS	A--E--	ALTERS
ZORILS	AERATE	ARNAUD	ACACIA	******	AMBERS
ZURICH	AFFAIR	ARRACK	AEACUS	ABBESS	AMBERY
******	AFLAME	ARRANT	AFLCIO	ABBEYS	AMIENS
Z-S---	AFRAID	ARRAYS	ALECTO	ABJECT	AMOEBA
******	AFRAME	ARYANS	ALICES	ABLEST	AMPERE
ZESTED	AGHAST	ASGARD	ALICIA	ABNERS	ANDEAN
ZOSTER	AGLAIA	ASIANS	AMECHE	ABSENT	ANGELA
******	AGNAIL	ASKANT	AMICES	ACAENA	ANGELO
Z-T---	AGNATE	ASLANT	APACHE	ACCEDE	ANGELS
******	AGRAFE	ASSAIL	APICAL	ACCENT	ANGERS
ZETHOS	ALBANY	ASSAIS	APICES	ACCEPT	ANNEAL
ZETHUS	ALBATA	ASSAYS	ARECAS	ACCESS	ANNEXE
ZITHER	ALCAIC	ATTACH	ASHCAN	ACHENE	ANSELM
******	ALFAKI	ATTACK	AVOCET	ADDEND	ANTEED
Z-U---	ALKALI	ATTAIN	******	ADDERS	ANTERO
******	ALKANE	ATTARS	A--D--	ADEEMS	APIECE
ZEUGMA	ALLANS	AUBADE	******	ADHERE	APNEAL
ZOUAVE	ALLAYS	AUDADS	ABADAN	ADIEUS	APNEIC
ZOUNDS	ALMAHS	AURATE	ABIDED	ADIEUX	APPEAL
******	ALPACA	AVIARY	ABIDER	ADJECT	APPEAR
Z-Y---	ALSACE	AVIATE	ABIDES	ADVENT	APPELS
******	ALTAIC	AWEARY	ABODES	ADVERB	APPEND
ZAYINS	ALTAIR	AYEAYE	ABYDOS	ADVERT	ARBELA
ZOYSIA	ALTARS	AYMARA	ACADIA	AEGEAN	ARDEBS
ZUYDER	ALVANS	AZRAEL	ACEDIA	AEGEUS	ARDENT
	ALWAYS		ACIDIC	AENEAS	ARGENT

ARIELS	AGOGUE	ACTINI	AMNION	AVAILS	AMELIA
ARLEEN	AIRGUN	ACTINO	AMRITA	AVOIDS	AMELIE
ARLENE	ALEGAR	ACTION	ANGINA	AWAITS	AMOLES
ARMETS	ALIGHT	ACTIUM	ANNIES	AWEIGH	AMULET
ARPENS	ALIGNS	ACTIVE	ANOINT	AWEING	AMYLIC
ARPENT	AMIGOS	ACUITY	ANTIAR	AWHILE	AMYLUM
ARREAR	APOGEE	ADDICT	ANTICS	AWHIRL	ANALOG
ARREST	ARAGON	ADDING	ANVILS	AWNING	ANGLED
ARTELS	ARIGHT	ADLIBS	AORIST	AXLIKE	ANGLER
ARTERY	******	ADMIRE	APHIDS	******	ANGLES
******	A--H--	ADMITS	APLITE	A--J--	ANGLIA
ASCEND	******	ADMIXT	APPIAN	******	ANGLIC
ASCENT	AACHEN	ADRIAN	APRILS	ABIJAH	ANILIN
ASKERS	ABOHMS	ADRIEN	AQUILA	ACAJOU	ANKLES
ASLEEP	AETHER	ADRIFT	ARCING	******	ANKLET
ASPECT	AFGHAN	ADVICE	ARGIVE	A--K--	ANTLER
ASPENS	ALPHAS	ADVISE	ARLINE	******	ANTLIA
ASPERS	ALPHOS	AECIAL	ARMIES	ANGKOR	APOLLO
ASSENT	ALPHYL	AEDILE	ARMING	ARCKED	APOLOG
ASSERT	ALTHEA	AERIAL	ARNICA	AWAKED	APPLES
ASSESS	AMPHRS	AERIED	ARNIES	AWAKEN	APULIA
ASSETS	ANCHOR	AERIES	AROIDS	AWAKES	ARMLET
ASTERI	ANTHEA	AERIFY	ARRIVE	AWOKEN	ASHLAR
ASTERN	ANTHEM	AFFIRM	ARSINE	******	ASHLEY
ASTERO	ANTHER	AFRICA	ARTIES	A--L--	ASYLUM
ASTERS	ANYHOW	AGEING	ARTILY	******	ATOLLS
ATHENA	ARCHED	AGUISH	ARTIST	ABELES	ATTLEE
ATHENE	ARCHEO	AIDING	ASHIER	ABOLLA	AUKLET
ATHENS	ARCHER	AILING	ASKING	ABULIA	AVALON
ATREUS	ARCHES	AIMING	ASPICS	ADDLED	AXILLA
ATTEND	ARCHIE	AIRIER	ASPIRE	ADDLES	AZALEA
ATTEST	ARCHIL	AIRILY	ASSIGN	ADOLPH	AZOLES
AUGEAN	ARCHLY	AIRING	ASSISI	ADULTS	******
AUGEND	ARCHON	ALBINO	ASSIST	AEOLIA	A--M--
AUGERS	ARCHYS	ALBION	ASSIZE	AEOLIC	******
AUREUS	ARTHRO	ALBITE	ATRIAL	AEOLIS	ABOMAS
AWHEEL	ARTHUR	ALDINE	ATRIUM	AEOLUS	ABOMBS
AWLESS	ASTHMA	ALLIED	ATTICA	AFFLUX	ACUMEN
AXSEED	AUGHTS	ALLIES	ATTICS	AIGLET	AGAMAS
AZTECS	AUTHOR	ALLIUM	ATTILA	AISLED	AGAMIC
******	******	ALMIRA	ATTIRE	AISLES	AHIMSA
A--F--	A--I--	ALPINE	AUDILE	ALALIA	AIDMAN
******	******	ALSIKE	AUDITS	ALULAE	AIDMEN
ARMFUL	AALIIS	ALUINO	AUGITE	ALULAR	AIRMAN
ARTFUL	ABBIES	ALUINS	AURIGA	AMALIE	AIRMEN
******	ACEIUM	ALVINA	AURIST	AMBLED	AKIMBO
A--G--	ACHING	ALVINE	AUTISM	AMBLER	ALAMOS
******	ACTING	AMBITS	AUXINS	AMBLES	ALUMIN
ADAGES					
ADAGIO					

ALUMNA	ARENAS	ALLOYS	******	ARERCU	ABATOR
ALUMNI	ARUNTA	ALMOND	A--P--	ASARUM	ACETAL
ANEMIA	ATONAL	ALMOST	******	ASTRAL	ACETIC
ANEMIC	ATONED	ANCONA	ADAPTS	ASTRAY	ACETUM
ANIMAL	ATONER	ANCONE	ADEPTS	ASTRID	ACETYL
ANIMAS	ATONES	ANGOLA	ADIPIC	AUBREY	ADYTUM
ANIMUS	ATONIC	ANGORA	ADOPTS	AUDREY	AEETES
ANOMIA	AVENGE	ANIONS	AGAPAE	AVERNO	AGATES
ANOMIC	AVENUE	ANNONA	ALEPHS	AVERSE	AGATHA
ANOMIE	AXONES	ANNOYS	ALEPPO	AVERTS	ALATED
APEMAN	AZINES	ANTONS	ALIPED	AVERYS	AMATOL
AROMAS	AZONIC	ANTONY	APEPSY	AWARDS	AMYTAL
ASHMAN	******	ANYONE	ARMPIT	AZORES	ANATTO
ASHMEN	A--O--	APHONY	AUSPEX	AZURES	ANITAS
ASIMOV	******	APLOMB	******	******	ANITRA
ATAMAN	AARONS	APNOEA	A--R--	A--S--	AORTAE
ATOMIC	ABBOTS	APPORT	******	******	AORTAL
AXEMAN	ABHORS	APPOSE	ABORAL	ABASED	AORTAS
AXEMEN	ABLOOM	APRONS	ABORTS	ABASER	AORTIC
******	ABROAD	ARBORI	ACARID	ABASES	APATHY
A--N--	ABSORB	ARBORS	ACCRUE	ABUSED	APHTHA
******	ABVOLT	ARBOUR	ACERIC	ABUSER	ARCTIC
ACANTH	ACCORD	ARDORS	ACORNS	ABUSES	ARETES
ACINUS	ACCOST	ARDOUR	ADORED	ABYSMS	AUNTIE
ADENIS	ACEOUS	AREOLA	ADORER	AGISTS	AUSTEN
ADONAI	ACIOUS	ARGOSY	ADORES	AIRSAC	AUSTER
ADONIC	ACNODE	ARGOTS	ADORNS	ALASKA	AUSTIN
ADONIS	ACROSS	ARIOSE	AFFRAY	ALISON	AUSTRO
AGENCY	ACTORS	ARIOSO	AGARIC	AMUSED	AVATAR
AGENDA	ADJOIN	ARIOUS	AGORAE	AMUSER	AZOTIC
AGENTS	ADNOUN	ARMORS	AGORAS	AMUSES	******
AGONES	ADROIT	ARMORY	ALARIC	ANISES	A--U--
AGONIC	ADSORB	ARMOUR	ALARMS	ANUSES	******
AKENES	AEROBE	ARNOLD	ALARUM	ARISEN	ABDUCT
ALINED	AFFORD	ARROBA	ALERTS	ARISES	ABJURE
ALINES	AFLOAT	ARROWS	ALFRED	ARISTA	ABLUSH
ALONSO	AFTOSA	ARROWY	AMERCE	ARISTO	ABOUND
ALONZO	AGEOLD	ARROYO	AMORAL	AVESTA	ABRUPT
AMANDA	ALCOTT	ARTOIS	ANDREA	AVISOS	ABSURD
AMANIA	ALCOVE	ASCOTS	ANDREI	AVOSET	ACCUSE
AMENDS	ALDOSE	ASHORE	ANDRES	AYESHA	ACQUIT
AMENRA	ALDOUS	ASLOPE	ANDREW	******	ACTUAL
AMENTI	ALFONS	ASSORT	ANERGY	A--T--	ADDUCE
AMENTS	ALGOID	ATHOME	ANORAK	******	ADDUCT
ANANAS	ALGOUS	ATTORN	ANTRIM	ABATED	ADJURE
ANANKE	ALLOTS	AURORA	ANTRUM	ABATER	ADJUST
ANONYM	ALLOUT	AUROUS	ANURAN	ABATES	AERUGO
ARANTA	ALLOWS	AXIOMS	ARARAT	ABATIS	AGOUTI

AGOUTY	ANYWAY	BEDAUB	BYPASS	BULBUL	BEADED
ALBUMS	ARAWAK	BEFALL	BYPAST	BUMBLE	BEADLE
ALCUIN	AVOWAL	BEHALF	BYPATH	BURBLE	BEDDED
ALEUTS	AVOWED	BEHAVE	BYTALK	BURBOT	BEDDER
ALLUDE	AVOWER	BELAYS	BYWAYS	BYEBYE	BELDAM
ALLURE	******	BEMATA	******	******	BENDAY
ALMUCE	A--X--	BERATE	B--B--	B--C--	BENDED
ALMUDE	******	BESANT	******	******	BENDEE
ALMUDS	ALEXIA	BETAKE	BABBIE	BAUCIS	BENDER
AMBUSH	ALEXIN	BEWAIL	BABBLE	BEACHY	BIDDEN
AMOUNT	ALEXIS	BEWARE	BALBOA	BEACON	BIDDER
AMOURS	ANOXIA	BEZANT	BAMBOO	BEECHY	BINDER
AMPULE	ANOXIC	BICARB	BAOBAB	BISCAY	BIRDIE
AMPULS	APEXES	BIGAMY	BARBED	BITCHY	BLADED
ANNUAL	ATAXIA	BIHARI	BARBEL	BLACKS	BLADES
ANNULS	ATAXIC	BINARY	BARBER	BLOCKS	BOLDER
ARBUTE	******	BINATE	BARBET	BLOCKY	BOLDLY
ARGUED	A--Y--	BLEACH	BARBIE	BOBCAT	BONDED
ARGUER	******	BLEAKS	BARBRA	BOCCIE	BONDER
ARGUES	ALKYLS	BLEARS	BAUBLE	BOTCHY	BOODLE
ARGUFY	ALKYNE	BLEARY	BEDBUG	BOUCLE	BORDEL
ARMURE	ALLYLS	BLEATS	BERBER	BOXCAR	BORDER
AROUND	ANKYLO	BLOATS	BIBBED	BRACED	BRIDAL
AROUSE	ARGYLL	BOGANS	BIBBER	BRACER	BRIDES
ARTURO	******	BONACI	BILBAO	BRACES	BRIDGE
ASBURY	A--Z--	BORAGE	BLEBBY	BRACHI	BRIDIE
ASSUME	******	BORANE	BOBBED	BRACHY	BRIDLE
ASSURE	AMAZED	BORATE	BOBBER	BRACTS	BUDDED
ASTUTE	AMAZES	BOTANY	BOBBIE	BRECHT	BUDDER
ATTUNE	AMAZON	BOVATE	BOBBIN	BRICKS	BUDDHA
AUBURN	AREZZO	BOYARD	BOBBLE	BROCHE	BUDDLE
AUGURS	AZAZEL	BOYARS	BOBBYS	BRUCES	BUNDLE
AUGURY	******	BREACH	BOMBAY	BUCCAL	BURDEN
AUGUST	B--A--	BREADS	BOMBED	BUNCHE	BURDIE
AUTUMN	******	BREAKS	BOMBER	BUNCHY	******
AVAUNT	BAGASS	BREAMS	BOMBES	BUNCOS	B--E--
AVOUCH	BAHAIS	BREAST	BOMBIC	******	******
******	BAHAMA	BREATH	BONBON	B--D--	BAGELS
A--V--	BALAAM	BRIARS	BOOBOO	******	BAKERS
******	BALATA	BROACH	BRIBED	BAGDAD	BAKERY
AGAVES	BAMAKO	BROADS	BRIBER	BALDER	BALEEN
ATAVIC	BANANA	BRYANT	BRIBES	BALDLY	BALERS
******	BASALT	BUBALS	BUBBLE	BANDED	BAREGE
A--W--	BATAAN	BURANS	BUBBLY	BANDIT	BARELY
******	BAYARD	BUTANE	BULBAR	BARDED	BAREST
AIRWAY	BAZAAR	BYLANE	BULBED	BARDES	BASELY
AJOWAN	BECALM	BYLAWS	BULBEL	BARDIC	BASEST
ANSWER	BECAME	BYNAME	BULBIL	BAWDRY	BATEAU

BAYEUX	******	BIOGEN	BISHOP	BELIZE	BURIED
BEDECK	B--F--	BLIGHT	BOOHOO	BEMIRE	BURIES
BEDEWS	******	BOGGED	BOSHES	BENIGN	BURINS
BEFELL	BAFFED	BOGGLE	BOTHER	BENITA	BUSIED
BEGETS	BAFFIN	BONGED	BRAHMA	BENITO	BUSIES
BEHEAD	BAFFLE	BONGOS	BRAHMS	BERING	BUSILY
BEHELD	BARFLY	BOOGIE	BUCHAN	BESIDE	BUSING
BEHEST	BEEFED	BORGIA	BUSHED	BETIDE	BUYING
BEMEAN	BELFRY	BOUGHS	BUSHEL	BETISE	BYLINE
BEREFT	BIAFRA	BOUGHT	BUSHES	BEVIES	******
BERETS	BIFFED	BOUGIE	BUSHEY	BIDING	B--J--
BESEEM	BLUFFS	BREGMA	******	BIKINI	******
BESETS	BOFFIN	BRIGHT	B--I--	BILITY	BANJOS
BETELS	BOTFLY	BRIGID	******	BINITS	BENJYS
BEVELS	BOUFFE	BROGAN	BAAING	BITING	******
BEZELS	BOWFIN	BROGUE	BABIED	BLAINS	B--K--
BICEPS	BUFFED	BRUGES	BABIES	BLAISE	******
BIDETS	BUFFER	BUDGED	BABISM	BLUING	BACKED
BIPEDS	BUFFET	BUDGES	BABIST	BLUISH	BACKER
BIREME	******	BUDGET	BABITE	BODICE	BAIKAL
BISECT	B--G--	BUDGIE	BAKING	BODIED	BALKAN
BITERS	******	BUGGED	BALING	BODIES	BALKED
BLEEDS	BADGED	BUGGER	BANIAN	BODILY	BANKED
BLUELY	BADGER	BULGAR	BANISH	BODING	BANKER
BLUEST	BADGES	BULGED	BARING	BOGIES	BARKED
BLUETS	BAGGED	BULGER	BARITE	BOLIDE	BARKER
BODEGA	BANGED	BULGES	BARIUM	BONIER	BASKED
BOGEYS	BANGLE	BUNGED	BASICS	BONING	BASKET
BOLERO	BANGOR	BUNGLE	BASIFY	BONITO	BEAKED
BOLEYN	BANGUI	BURGEE	BASILS	BOOING	BEAKER
BONERS	BANGUP	BURGER	BASING	BORIDE	BECKED
BOREAL	BARGED	BURGHS	BASINS	BORING	BECKET
BOREAS	BARGEE	BURGLE	BASION	BOVINE	BECKON
BORERS	BARGES	BURGOO	BATIKS	BOWING	BECKYS
BOWELS	BEAGLE	BURGOS	BATING	BOXING	BICKER
BOWERS	BEGGAR	******	BAYING	BOYISH	BILKED
BOWERY	BEGGED	B--H--	BEDIMS	BRAIDS	BILKER
BOXERS	BEIGES	******	BEFITS	BRAILS	BLOKES
BREECH	BELGAS	BACHED	BEGINS	BRAINS	BODKIN
BREEDS	BELGIC	BACHES	BEGIRD	BRAINY	BOOKED
BREEKS	BENGAL	BASHAW	BEGIRT	BRAISE	BOOKIE
BREEZE	BERGEN	BASHED	BEHIND	BRAIZE	BOSKET
BREEZY	BIGGER	BASHES	BELIAL	BROILS	BRAKED
BRIEFS	BIGGIN	BATHED	BELIED	BRUINS	BRAKES
BRIERS	BILGED	BATHER	BELIEF	BRUISE	BROKEN
BRIERY	BILGES	BATHOS	BELIER	BRUITS	BROKER
BUREAU	BINGES	BETHEL	BELIES	BUNION	BUCKED
BUYERS		BIGHTS	BELIKE	BURIAL	BUCKER

BUCKET	BIRLED	BOWMEN	BOUNDS	BEMOAN	BISQUE
BUCKLE	BIRLES	BREMEN	BOUNTY	BESOMS	BRAQUE
BUCKRA	BOGLES	BROMAL	BRANCH	BESOTS	******
BULKED	BOILED	BROMES	BRANDS	BETONY	B--R--
BUMKIN	BOILER	BROMIC	BRANDT	BETOOK	******
BUNKED	BOLLED	BRUMAL	BRANDY	BEYOND	BAIRNS
BUNKER	BOLLIX	BRUMES	BRANNY	BEZOAR	BARRED
BUNKUM	BOULES	BUMMED	BRANTS	BICORN	BARREL
BURKED	BOWLED	BUMMER	BRENDA	BIFOLD	BARREN
BURKES	BOWLEG	BUSMAN	BRENTS	BIFORM	BARRET
BUSKER	BRILLS	BUSMEN	BRINED	BIGONE	BARRIE
BUSKIN	BROLLY	******	BRINES	BIGOTS	BARRIO
******	BRULOT	B--N--	BRINGS	BIJOUX	BARROW
B--L--	BUGLED	******	BRINKS	BIKOLS	BARRYS
******	BUGLER	BAGNIO	BRONCO	BILOXI	BASRAH
BAALIM	BUGLES	BANNED	BRONCS	BIPODS	BEARDS
BAILED	BUILDS	BANNER	BRONTE	BLOODS	BEARED
BAILEE	BULLAE	BARNEY	BRONZE	BLOODY	BEARER
BAILER	BULLET	BARNUM	BRONZY	BLOOMS	BEDRID
BAILEY	BURLAP	BEANED	BRUNCH	BLOOMY	BEIRUT
BAILIE	BURLED	BEANIE	BRUNEI	BOGOAK	BETRAY
BAILOR	BURLER	BEINGS	BRUNEL	BOGOTA	BIERCE
BALLAD	BURLEY	BENNES	BRUNOS	BOSOMS	BIRRED
BALLED	BUTLER	BENNET	BRUNCH	BROOCH	BLARED
BALLET	BYBLOW	BENNYS	BURNED	BROODS	BLARES
BALLOT	BYPLAY	BERNEY	BURNER	BROODY	BLURBS
BARLEY	******	BERNIE	BURNET	BROOKE	BLURRY
BAWLED	B--M--	BIANCA	******	BROOKS	BLURTS
BAWLER	******	BINNED	B--O--	BROOMS	BOARDS
BEDLAM	BADMAN	BLANCH	******	BROOMY	BORROW
BELLAS	BADMEN	BLANKS	BABOON	BRYONY	BOURGS
BELLED	BAGMAN	BLENCH	BABOOS	BUBOES	BOURNE
BELLES	BAGMEN	BLENDE	BACONY	BYGONE	BOURNS
BELLOC	BARMAN	BLENDS	BARONG	BYROAD	BOURSE
BELLOW	BARMEN	BLENNY	BARONS	BYWORD	BURRED
BERLIN	BARMIE	BLINDS	BARONY	BYWORK	BURROS
BEULAH	BATMAN	BLINKS	BATONS	******	BURROW
BEULAS	BATMEN	BLINTZ	BAYOUS	B--P--	******
BIALYS	BEAMED	BLONDE	BECOME	******	B--S--
BIBLES	BERMES	BLONDS	BEFOGS	BEDPAN	******
BIBLIO	BLAMED	BLUNGE	BEFOOL	BEEPED	BALSAM
BIFLEX	BLAMES	BLUNTS	BEFORE	BIOPSY	BALSAS
BILLED	BLIMEY	BONNET	BEFOUL	BOPPED	BASSES
BILLET	BLIMPS	BONNIE	BEGONE	BUMPED	BASSET
BILLIE	BOOMED	BONNYS	BEHOLD	BUMPER	BASSOS
BILLON	BOOMER	BORNEO	BEHOOF	BURPED	BEASTS
BILLOW	BOWMAN	BOUNCE	BEHOVE	******	BEDSIT
BILLYS		BOUNCY	BELOIT	B--Q--	BESSIE
			BELONG	******	
				BARQUE	
				BASQUE	

BESSYS	BATTEN	BOWTIE	BLOWER	BRAZED	CLOACA
BETSYS	BATTER	BRETON	BLOWUP	BRAZEN	CLOAKS
BIASED	BATTIK	BRITON	BLOWZY	BRAZER	COBALT
BIASES	BATTIN	BROTHS	BOWWOW	BRAZES	COCAIN
BIOSIS	BATTLE	BRUTAL	BRAWLS	BRAZIL	COMATE
BLASTO	BATTUE	BRUTES	BRAWNY	BRAZOS	COPALM
BLASTS	BAXTER	BRUTUS	BREWED	BUZZED	CORALS
BOASTS	BEATEN	BUNTED	BREWER	BUZZER	COWAGE
BOLSON	BEATER	BURTON	BREWIS	BUZZES	COWARD
BONSAI	BEETLE	BUSTED	BROWNS	******	CRAALS
BOOSTS	BELTED	BUSTER	BROWSE	C--A--	CREAKS
BORSCH	BENTON	BUSTIC	******	******	CREAKY
BOSSED	BERTHA	BUSTLE	B--X--	CABALA	CREAMS
BOSSES	BERTHE	BUTTED	******	CABALS	CREAMY
BOUSED	BERTHS	BUTTER	BIAXAL	CABANA	CREASE
BOUSES	BERTIE	BUTTES	******	CACAOS	CREASY
BOWSAW	BESTED	BUTTON	B--Y--	CALAIS	CREATE
BOWSED	BESTIR	BUXTON	******	CALASH	CROAKS
BOWSES	BESTOW	******	BANYAN	CAMASS	CROAKY
BRASHY	BETTED	B--U--	BARYES	CANAAN	CROATS
BRASSY	BETTER	******	BARYON	CANADA	CUBAGE
BRISKS	BETTES	BABULS	BARYTA	CANALS	CUBANS
BRUSHY	BETTOR	BARUCH	BERYLS	CANAPE	CURACY
BUNSEN	BETTYS	BASUTO	BOWYER	CANARD	CURARE
BURSAE	BHUTAN	BEAUTS	BRAYED	CANARY	CURATE
BURSAL	BIOTIC	BEAUTY	BRAYER	CARACK	CYCADS
BURSAR	BIOTIN	BEDUIN	BUNYAN	CARAFE	CYMARS
BURSAS	BIRTHS	BEGUIN	BUNYIP	CARATE	CYRANO
BURSES	BISTER	BEGUMS	BUOYED	CARATS	******
BURSTS	BISTRO	BELUGA	******	CASABA	C--B--
BUSSED	BITTED	BEMUSE	B--Z--	CASALS	******
BUSSES	BITTEN	BENUMB	******	CASAVA	CAMBER
BYSSUS	BITTER	BLOUSE	BALZAC	CATALO	CARBON
******	BLITHE	******	BANZAI	CEDARS	CARBOY
B--T--	BLOTCH	B--V--	BENZOL	CERATE	CASBAH
******	BOATED	******	BENZYL	CERATO	CEIBAS
BAITED	BOATER	BEAVER	BLAZED	CESARE	CHABUK
BALTIC	BOLTED	BEEVES	BLAZER	CETANE	CHEBEC
BALTIM	BOLTER	BRAVED	BLAZES	CHEATS	CHIBUK
BANTAM	BOLTON	BRAVER	BLAZON	CHIASM	CHUBBY
BANTER	BOOTED	BRAVES	BONZER	CHIAUS	CIMBRI
BANTUS	BOOTEE	BRAVOS	BONZES	CICADA	COBBER
BARTER	BOOTHS	BREVES	BOOZED	CICALA	COBBLE
BARTOK	BOOTIE	BREVET	BOOZER	CIGARS	COBBLY
BARTON	BOOTLE	******	BOOZES	CLEANS	COMBAT
BASTED	BOSTON	B--W--	BORZOI	CLEARS	COMBED
BASTES	BOTTLE	******	BRAZAS	CLEATS	COMBER
BATTED	BOTTOM	BIGWIG	BLOWBY	CLEAVE	COMBOS

CORBAN	CRACKS	CREDOS	CICERO	CYBELE	CONGES
CORBEL	CRACKY	CRUDER	CIDERS	CYMENE	CONGOU
CORBIE	CRACOW	CUDDIE	CINEMA	CYRENE	CORGIS
COWBOY	CRECHE	CUDDLE	CINEOL	******	COUGAR
CRABBY	CRICKS	CUDDLY	CIVETS	C--F--	COUGHS
CUBBED	CROCKS	CURDED	CLIENT	******	CRAGGY
CUMBER	CROCKY	CURDLE	CODEIA	CARFAX	CUDGEL
CURBED	CROCUS	******	CODEIN	CHAFED	******
CYMBAL	CRUCES	C--E--	COGENT	CHAFER	C--H--
******	CUSCUS	******	COHEIR	CHAFES	******
C--C--	******	CADENT	COHERE	CHAFFS	CACHED
******	C--D--	CADETS	COLEUS	CHAFFY	CACHES
CAECUM	******	CALEBS	COMEDO	CHUFAS	CACHET
CALCAR	CADDIE	CALESA	COMEDY	CLEFTS	CACHOU
CALCES	CADDIS	CAMELS	COMELY	CLIFFS	CARHOP
CALCIC	CAMDEN	CAMEOS	COMEON	CLIFFY	CASHAW
CANCAN	CANDIA	CAMERA	COMERS	COFFEE	CASHED
CANCEL	CANDID	CANERS	COMETS	COFFER	CASHES
CANCER	CANDLE	CAPERS	CONEYS	COFFIN	CASHEW
CARCEL	CANDOR	CAREEN	COOEED	COFFLE	CASHOO
CATCHY	CARDED	CAREER	COOEES	COIFED	CATHAY
CAUCUS	CARDER	CARERS	COOERS	COMFIT	CATHER
CHACMA	CARDIO	CARESS	COOEYS	CONFAB	CATHYS
CHECKS	CAUDAD	CARETS	COPECK	CONFER	CIPHER
CHICHI	CAUDAL	CASEFY	CORERS	CRAFTS	CITHER
CHICKS	CAUDEX	CASEIN	COTEAU	CRAFTY	COCHIN
CHICLE	CAUDLE	CASERN	COVERS	CROFTS	COSHED
CHICOS	CHIDED	CATENA	COVERT	CUFFED	COSHER
CHOCKS	CHIDER	CATERS	COVETS	CUPFUL	COSHES
CHUCKS	CHIDES	CAVEAT	COVEYS	CURFEW	CUSHAT
CIRCLE	CINDER	CAVEIN	COWERS	******	CUSHAW
CIRCUM	CINDYS	CAVELL	COZENS	C--G--	CYPHER
CIRCUS	CLODDY	CAVERN	CREEDS	******	******
CISCOS	CLYDES	CELERY	CREEKS	CADGED	C--I--
CLACKS	CODDER	CEMENT	CREELS	CADGER	******
CLICHE	CODDLE	CEREAL	CREEPS	CADGES	CABINS
CLICKS	COLDER	CEREUS	CREEPY	CANGUE	CAGIER
CLOCHE	COLDLY	CHAETA	CREESE	CARGOS	CAGILY
CLOCKS	CONDOM	CHAETO	CRIERS	CATGUT	CAGING
CLUCKS	CONDOR	CHEEKS	CRUETS	CAUGHT	CAHIER
COCCAL	COODLE	CHEEKY	CUBEBS	CHEGOE	CAKING
COCCID	CORDAY	CHEEPS	CULETS	CHIGOE	CALICO
COCCUS	CORDED	CHEERS	CUNEAL	CLOGGY	CALIFS
COCCYX	CORDER	CHEERY	CUPELS	CODGER	CALIPH
CONCHA	CORDON	CHEESE	CURERS	COGGED	CAMILA
CONCHS	CRADLE	CHEESY	CUTELY	COIGNS	CAMION
CONCHY	CREDAL	CHIEFS	CUTEST	CONGAS	CAMISE
CONCUR	CREDIT	CICELY	CUTEYS	CONGER	CANINE

CANING	CLAIMS	CURIUM	CALLUP	CULLET	COMMIE
CAPIAS	CLAIRE	CUTIES	CALLUS	CULLIS	COMMIT
CAPITA	CLEIST	CUTINS	CAMLET	CURLED	COMMIX
CARIBE	CLUING	CYNICS	CAPLIN	CURLER	COMMON
CARIBS	COBIAS	CYRILS	CARLAS	CURLEW	CONMAN
CARIES	CODIFY	******	CARLOS	CUTLAS	COOMBS
CARINA	CODING	C--J--	CARLOW	CUTLER	COSMIC
CARING	COKING	******	CATLIN	CUTLET	COSMOS
CASING	COLIES	CROJIK	CAULES	CYCLED	COWMAN
CASINO	COLINE	******	CAULIS	CYCLER	COWMEN
CATION	COLINS	C--K--	CAULKS	CYCLES	CRAMBO
CAVIAR	COMICS	******	CEILED	CYCLIC	CRAMPS
CAVIES	COMING	CACKLE	CELLAE	CYMLIN	CREMES
CAVILS	COMITY	CALKED	CELLAR	******	CRIMEA
CAVING	CONICS	CALKER	CELLOS	C--M--	CRIMES
CAVITE	CONIES	CALKIN	CEYLON	******	CRIMPS
CAVITY	CONING	CANKER	CHALCO	CABMAN	CRIMPY
CAWING	CONIUM	CASKET	CHALEH	CABMEN	CRUMBS
CECILE	COOING	CATKIN	CHALET	CADMUS	CRUMBY
CECILS	COPIED	CHOKED	CHALKS	CAIMAN	CRUMMY
CECILY	COPIER	CHOKER	CHALKY	CALMED	CRUMPS
CEDING	COPIES	CHOKES	CHELAE	CALMER	CULMED
CELIAC	COPING	COCKED	CHELAS	CALMLY	******
CELIAS	CORING	COCKER	CHILLI	CARMAN	C--N--
CERING	CORIUM	COCKLE	CHILLS	CARMEL	******
CERIPH	COSIGN	COCKUP	CHILLY	CARMEN	CANNAE
CERISE	COSILY	CONKED	CHOLER	CAYMAN	CANNAS
CERITE	COSINE	CONKER	CHOLLA	CERMET	CANNED
CERIUM	COVING	COOKED	COALED	CHAMMY	CANNEL
CESIUM	COWING	COOKER	COALER	CHAMPS	CANNER
CHAINS	COXING	COOKEY	COBLES	CHIMED	CANNES
CHAIRS	COYISH	COOKIE	COELED	CHIMER	CANNIE
CHAISE	COZIER	CORKED	COELOM	CHIMES	CANNON
CHEILO	COZIES	CORKER	COILED	CHUMMY	CANNOT
CHEIRO	COZILY	CRAKES	COILER	CHUMPS	CARNAL
CHOICE	CRAIGS	CRIKEY	COLLAR	CHYMIC	CATNAP
CHOIRS	CRUISE	CUCKOO	COLLET	CLAMMY	CATNIP
CHRISM	CRYING	******	COLLIE	CLAMOR	CHANCE
CHRIST	CUBING	C--L--	COLLOP	CLAMPS	CHANCY
CILIAT	CUBISM	******	COOLED	CLIMAT	CHANGE
CILICE	CUBIST	CABLED	COOLER	CLIMAX	CHANGS
CILIUM	CUBITS	CABLES	COOLIE	CLIMBS	CHANTS
CITIED	CUMINS	CABLET	COOLLY	CLIMES	CHANTY
CITIES	CURIAE	CALLAO	COPLEY	CLUMPS	CHINCH
CITING	CURIAL	CALLAS	COULEE	CLUMPY	CHINES
CIVICS	CURIES	CALLED	CULLAY	CLUMSY	CHINKS
CIVIES	CURING	CALLER	CULLED	COEMPT	CHINKY
CIVISM	CURIOS	CALLOW	CULLER	COMMAS	CHINTZ

CHUNKS	CYANIN	CONOID	COPPRA	CHARON	CUPRUM
CHUNKY	CYGNET	COPOUT	CORPSE	CHARRY	CYMRIC
CLANGS	CYGNUS	CORODY	CORPUS	CHARTS	CYPRIN
CLANKS	******	CORONA	COUPES	CHERRY	CYPRUS
CLENCH	C--O--	COYOTE	COUPLE	CHERUB	******
CLINCH	******	CREOLE	COUPON	CHERYL	C--S--
CLINES	CABOBS	CROOKS	COWPEA	CHIRMS	******
CLINGS	CAEOMA	CROONS	COWPER	CHIRON	CAESAR
CLINGY	CAHOOT	CUBOID	COWPOX	CHIRPS	CANSOS
CLINIC	CAJOLE	CUPOLA	COYPUS	CHIRPY	CARSON
CLINKS	CALORY	CUTOFF	CRAPED	CHIRRS	CASSIA
CLINTS	CANOED	CUTOUT	CRAPES	CHORAL	CASSIE
CLONES	CANOES	CYMOID	CREPED	CHORDS	CASSIS
CLONIC	CANONS	CYMOSE	CREPES	CHOREA	CATSUP
CLONUS	CANOPY	CYMOUS	CRYPTO	CHOREO	CAUSAL
COBNUT	CAPONE	******	CRYPTS	CHORES	CAUSED
COGNAC	CAPONS	C--P--	CUPPED	CHORIC	CAUSER
COINED	CAPOTE	******	CUPPER	CHORUS	CAUSES
COINER	CAROBS	CALPAC	CUSPED	CHURCH	CEASED
CONNED	CAROLE	CAMPED	CUSPID	CHURLS	CEASES
CONNER	CAROLS	CAMPER	CUSPIS	CHURNS	CENSED
CONNIE	CAROMS	CAMPOS	******	CHURRS	CENSER
CORNEA	CAVORT	CAMPUS	C--Q--	CIRRUS	CENSES
CORNED	CEBOID	CAPPED	******	CITRAL	CENSOR
CORNEL	CEROUS	CAPPER	CAIQUE	CITRIC	CENSUR
CORNER	CHEOPS	CARPAL	CASQUE	CITRON	CENSUS
CORNET	CHLOES	CARPED	CHEQUE	CITRUS	CHASED
CORNUA	CHLORO	CARPEL	CINQUE	CLARAS	CHASER
CORNUS	CHOOSE	CARPER	CIRQUE	CLARES	CHASES
COUNTS	CHOOSY	CARPET	CLAQUE	CLARET	CHASMS
COUNTY	CHROMA	CARPIC	CLIQUE	CLAROS	CHASSE
CRANED	CHROME	CARPUS	CLIQUY	CLERGY	CHASTE
CRANES	CHROMO	CASPAR	******	CLERIC	CHESTS
CRANIA	CHRONO	CASPER	C--R--	CLERID	CHESTY
CRANIO	CIBOLS	CHAPEL	******	CLERKS	CHISEL
CRANKS	CITOLA	CHAPES	CADRES	COARSE	CHOSEN
CRANKY	CLEOME	CHIPPY	CAIRNS	COBRAS	CISSIE
CRANNY	COCOAS	CHOPIN	CAPRIC	COERCE	CISSYS
CRENEL	COCOON	CHOPPY	CARREL	CONRAD	CLASPS
CRINGE	COHORT	CLYPEI	CARRIE	COPRAH	CLASSY
CRINUM	COHOSH	COMPEL	CARROT	CORRAL	CLOSED
CRONES	COLONS	COMPLY	CEDRIC	CORRIE	CLOSER
CRONOS	COLONY	COMPOS	CEORLS	COURSE	CLOSES
CRONUS	COLORS	COOPED	CHARDS	COURTS	CLOSET
CRUNCH	COLOUR	COOPER	CHARED	COWRIE	CONSUL
CUNNER	COLOUS	COOPTS	CHARES	CRORES	COPSES
CYANIC	COMOSE	COPPED	CHARGE	CRURAL	CORSAC
CYANID	COMOUS	COPPER	CHARMS	CUPRIC	

CORSES	CASTLE	COSTAR	CLAUDE	CORVEE	CORYMB
CORSET	CASTOR	COSTED	CLAUSE	CORVES	CORYZA
COSSES	CASTRO	COSTER	CLOUDS	CORVUS	CRAYON
COSSET	CATTED	COSTLY	CLOUDY	CRAVAT	******
COUSIN	CATTIE	COTTAE	CLOUGH	CRAVED	C--Z--
CRASIS	CATTLE	COTTAR	CLOUTS	CRAVEN	******
CRESOL	CAUTER	COTTAS	COBURG	CRAVER	COLZAS
CRESTS	CAXTON	COTTER	COHUNE	CRAVES	CRAZED
CRISES	CELTIC	COTTON	COLUGO	CREVAS	CRAZES
CRISIS	CENTAL	CRATCH	COLUMN	CULVER	CROZER
CRISPS	CENTER	CRATED	COLURE	CURVED	CROZES
CRISPY	CENTOS	CRATER	COPULA	CURVES	******
CROSSE	CENTRA	CRATES	COQUET	CURVET	D--A--
CRUSES	CENTRE	CRETAN	CREUSA	******	******
CRUSET	CENTRI	CRETIC	CROUCH	C--W--	DAMAGE
CRUSOE	CENTRO	CRETIN	CROUPE	******	DAMANS
CRUSTS	CERTES	CRETON	CROUPS	CHAWED	DAMASK
CRUSTY	CESTUS	CRITIC	CROUPY	CHEWED	DANAID
CUESTA	CHATTY	CROTCH	CUPULE	CHEWER	DANAUS
CUISSE	CHETAH	CROTON	CURULE	CLAWED	DATARY
CURSED	CHITIN	CRUTCH	CUTUPS	CLEWED	DEBARK
CURSES	CHITON	CULTCH	******	CLOWNS	DEBARS
CURSOR	CHITTY	CULTUS	C--V--	COBWEB	DEBASE
CUSSED	CHUTES	CUPTIE	******	COGWAY	DEBATE
CUSSES	CLOTHE	CURTIS	CALVED	CONWAY	DECADE
CUSSOS	CLOTHO	CURTLY	CALVES	CRAWLS	DECALS
******	CLOTHS	CURTSY	CALVIN	CRAWLY	DECAMP
C--T--	CLOTTY	CUSTER	CANVAS	CREWEL	DECANE
******	CLUTCH	CUSTOM	CARVED	CROWDS	DECANT
CACTUS	COATED	CUSTOS	CARVEL	CROWED	DECARE
CAFTAN	COATEE	CUTTER	CARVEN	CROWNS	DECAYS
CANTAB	COATIS	CUTTLE	CARVER	******	DEDANS
CANTED	COITAL	CYSTIC	CARVES	C--X--	DEFACE
CANTER	COITUS	******	CERVIX	******	DEFAME
CANTHI	COLTER	C--U--	CHEVVY	CALXES	DEGAGE
CANTLE	CONTES	******	CHIVES	COAXAL	DEGAME
CANTON	CONTIN	CAJUNS	CHIVVY	COAXED	DEKARE
CANTOR	CONTOS	CANUCK	CLEVER	COAXER	DELATE
CANTOS	CONTRA	CANULA	CLEVIS	COAXES	DELAYS
CANTUS	CONTRE	CANUTE	CLIVES	CRUXES	DEMAND
CAPTOR	COOTIE	CARUSO	CLOVEN	******	DENARY
CARTED	COPTIC	CASUAL	CLOVER	C--Y--	DEPART
CARTEL	CORTES	CAYUGA	CLOVES	******	DERAIL
CARTER	CORTEX	CAYUSE	CLOVIS	CANYON	DERAIN
CARTES	CORTEZ	CEDULA	COEVAL	CHRYSO	DERATE
CARTON	CORTIN	CERUSE	CONVEX	CLAYED	DESALT
CASTER	COSTAE	CESURA	CONVEY	CLAYEY	DETACH
CASTES	COSTAL	CHOUGH	CONVOY	CLOYED	DETAIL

DETAIN	DORBUG	DENDRO	DINERO	DUFFED	DISHED
DEWANS	DOUBLE	DEODAR	DINERS	DUFFEL	DISHES
DICAST	DOUBLY	DIADEM	DIRECT	DUFFER	DITHER
DIGAMY	DOUBTS	DIDDLE	DIRELY	DUFFLE	DURHAM
DILATE	DRABLY	DIKDIK	DIREST	******	******
DINAHS	DUBBED	DINDER	DIVERS	D--G--	D--I--
DINARS	DUBBIN	DIODES	DIVERT	******	******
DISARM	DUMBLY	DODDER	DIVEST	DAGGER	DANIEL
DIVANS	DUNBAR	DOODAD	DIZENS	DAGGLE	DANISH
DIWANS	DURBAN	DOODLE	DOCENT	DANGED	DANITE
DOGAPE	DURBAR	DREDGE	DODECA	DANGER	DARICS
DOMAIN	DYBBUK	DRUDGE	DOGEAR	DANGLE	DARIEN
DONALD	******	DRYDEN	DONEES	DEIGNS	DARING
DONATE	D--C--	DUMDUM	DONETS	DENGUE	DARIUS
DORADO	******	DUNDEE	DOREEN	DIGGED	DATING
DOSAGE	DANCED	DUODEN	DOSERS	DIGGER	DATIVE
DOTAGE	DANCER	DYADIC	DOTERS	DINGED	DAVIDS
DOTARD	DANCES	******	DOWELS	DINGEY	DAVIES
DREADS	DEACON	D--E--	DOWERS	DINGHY	DAVITS
DREAMS	DECCAN	******	DOWERY	DINGLE	DAZING
DREAMT	DEICED	DALETH	DOYENS	DINGUS	DEBITS
DREAMY	DEICER	DARERS	DOZENS	DIRGES	DECIDE
DREARY	DEICES	DATERS	DRIERS	DODGED	DECILE
DRYADS	DESCRY	DAVEYS	DRIEST	DODGER	DEFIED
DUCATS	DEUCED	DECEIT	DRYERS	DODGES	DEFIER
DYNAMO	DEUCES	DECENT	DRYEST	DOGGED	DEFIES
DYNAST	DISCAL	DECERN	DUDEEN	DOGGER	DEFILE
******	DISCUS	DEFEAT	DUPERS	DOGGIE	DEFINE
D--B--	DOUCHE	DEFECT	DUPERY	DOUGAL	DEKING
******	DRACHM	DEFEND	DURESS	DOUGHS	DELIAN
DABBED	DULCET	DEFERS	******	DOUGHY	DELIAS
DABBER	DULCIE	DEJECT	D--F--	DOUGIE	DELICT
DABBLE	DUNCAN	DELETE	******	DRAGEE	DELIUS
DAUBED	DUNCES	DEMEAN	DAYFLY	DRAGON	DEMIES
DAUBER	******	DEMENT	DEAFEN	DREGGY	DEMISE
DAUBRY	D--D--	DEPEND	DEAFLY	DROGUE	DEMITS
DAYBED	******	DEREKS	DEIFIC	DUNGED	DENIAL
DAYBOY	DADDLE	DESERT	DIFFER	DWIGHT	DENIED
DEBBIE	DAEDAL	DETECT	DOFFED	******	DENIER
DEBBYS	DANDER	DETENT	DOFFER	D--H--	DENIES
DIBBED	DANDLE	DETERS	DOGFOX	******	DENIMS
DIBBER	DARDAN	DETEST	DRAFFS	DACHAS	DENISE
DIBBLE	DAUDET	DEVEIN	DRAFFY	DACHAU	DEPICT
DIOBOL	DAWDLE	DEVEST	DRAFTS	DAPHNE	DERIDE
DISBAR	DEADEN	DICERS	DRAFTY	DASHED	DERIVE
DOABLE	DEADLY	DIDERO	DRIFTS	DASHER	DESIGN
DOBBER	DEEDED	DIGEST	DRIFTY	DASHES	DESIRE
DOBBIN	DENDRI	DIMERS	DRYFLY	DIRHAM	DESIST

DEVICE	******	DOBLAS	DISMAL	DAGOBA	DAMPER
DEVILS	D--K--	DOBLON	DISMAY	DAHOON	DAMPLY
DEVISE	******	DOLLAR	DOGMAS	DAKOIT	DAPPED
DEWIER	DANKER	DOLLED	DOLMAN	DAKOTA	DAPPER
DEWITT	DANKLY	DOLLIE	DOLMEN	DECOCT	DAPPLE
DICING	DARKEN	DOLLOP	DORMER	DECODE	DEEPEN
DIDIES	DARKER	DOLLYS	DORMIE	DECOKE	DEEPER
DIGITI	DARKLE	DOOLEE	DRAMAS	DECORS	DEEPLY
DIGITS	DARKLY	DOOLIE	DROMON	DECOYS	DELPHI
DIKING	DECKED	DOWLAS	******	DEFORM	DESPOT
DIMITY	DECKEL	DOYLEY	D--N--	DEHORN	DIAPER
DINING	DECKER	DRILLS	******	DEMOBS	DIEPPE
DIVIDE	DECKLE	DROLLS	DAINTY	DEMODE	DIMPLE
DIVINE	DICKER	DROLLY	DAMNED	DEMONO	DIMPLY
DIVING	DICKEY	DUBLIN	DANNYS	DEMONS	DIPPED
DIXITS	DICKIE	DUDLEY	DARNED	DEMOTE	DIPPER
DOBIES	DINKEY	DUELED	DARNEL	DENOTE	DISPEL
DOCILE	DINKUM	DUELER	DARNER	DEPONE	DOLPHS
DOGIES	DIRKED	DUELLO	DAUNTS	DEPORT	DRAPED
DOLING	DOCKED	DULLED	DAWNED	DEPOSE	DRAPER
DOMING	DOCKER	DULLER	DENNED	DEPOTS	DRAPES
DOMINO	DOCKET	DULLES	DENNIS	DESOXY	DRIPPY
DOPIER	DONKEY	DUNLIN	DENNYS	DETOUR	DROPSY
DOPING	DRAKES	DUOLOG	DIANAS	DEVOID	DRUPEL
DORIAN	DUCKED	DUPLET	DIANES	DEVOIR	DRUPES
DORIES	DUCKER	DUPLEX	DINNED	DEVOTE	DUMPED
DOSING	DUIKER	DWELLS	DINNER	DEVOUR	DUMPER
DOTIER	DUNKED	******	DIRNDL	DEVOUT	DUMPTY
DOTING	DUNKER	D--M--	DISNEY	DIDOES	******
DOVISH	DUSKED	******	DOINGS	DIMOUT	D--R--
DOXIES	******	DAEMON	DONNAS	DIPODY	******
DOZIER	D--L--	DAGMAR	DONNED	DIPOLE	DACRON
DOZILY	******	DAIMIO	DONNIE	DISOWN	DARROW
DOZING	DAHLIA	DAIMON	DOWNED	DITONE	DEARER
DRAINS	DALLAS	DAIMYO	DRENCH	DIVOTS	DEARIE
DROITS	DALLES	DAMMAR	DRINKS	DODOES	DEARLY
DRUIDS	DEALER	DAMMED	DRONED	DOLOUR	DEARTH
DRYICE	DELLAS	DAMMER	DRONES	DONORS	DEBRIS
DRYING	DEPLOY	DEEMED	DRONGO	DROOLS	DECREE
DRYISH	DEWLAP	DERMAL	DRUNKS	DROOPS	DEFRAY
DUDISH	DHOLES	DERMAS	DUENNA	DROOPY	DEGREE
DUPING	DIALED	DERMAT	DUNNED	DUGONG	DERRIS
DURIAN	DIALER	DERMIC	******	DUGOUT	DHARMA
DURING	DIALOG	DERMIS	D--O--	******	DHARNA
DURION	DIGLOT	DESMAN	******	D--P--	DHURNA
DUTIES	DIPLEX	DESMID	DACOIT	******	DOBRAS
DYEING	DIPLOE	DIMMED	DADOES	DAMPED	DOURLY
******	DOALLS	DIMMER		DAMPEN	DRYROT
D--J--					
******					
DONJON					

DVORAK	DAYTON	DEGUST	******	******	******
DWARFS	DEATHS	DELUDE	E--A--	EDIBLE	EASELS
******	DEATHY	DELUGE	******	ENABLE	EATERS
D--S--	DEBTOR	DELUXE	ECHARD	EREBUS	EATERY
******	DEFTER	DEMURE	ECLAIR	******	ECZEMA
DAISES	DEFTLY	DEMURS	EDDAIC	E--C--	EDSELS
DAISYS	DELTAS	DENUDE	EDGARS	******	EFFECT
DAMSEL	DENTAL	DEPUTE	EDUARD	EDICTS	EFFETE
DAMSON	DENTED	DEPUTY	EDWARD	EDUCED	EGBERT
DAWSON	DENTIL	DILUTE	EFFACE	EDUCES	EGGERS
DEISTS	DENTIN	DISUSE	EGGARS	EDUCTS	EGRESS
DENSER	DEPTHS	DROUTH	EMBALM	EGGCUP	EGRETS
DESSAU	DEXTER	DULUTH	EMBANK	EJECTA	EILEEN
DIESEL	DEXTRO	******	EMBARK	EJECTS	ELBERT
DIESES	DHOTIS	D--V--	EMBARS	ELECTS	ELDERS
DIESIS	DIATOM	******	EMBAYS	ELICIT	ELDEST
DIPSAS	DICTUM	DELVED	EMPALE	ENACTS	ELLENS
DOBSON	DIETAL	DELVER	ENCAGE	EPACTS	ELMERS
DOESNT	DIETED	DELVES	ENCAMP	EPICAL	ELVERS
DORSAD	DIETER	DENVER	ENCASE	EPOCHS	EMBEDS
DORSAL	DINTED	DRIVEL	ENCASH	ERECTS	EMBERS
DORSET	DISTAL	DRIVEN	ENDALL	ERICHS	EMCEED
DORSUM	DISTIL ·	DRIVER	ENFACE	ERUCTS	EMCEES
DOSSAL	DITTOS	DRIVES	ENGAGE	EVICTS	EMEERS
DOSSED	DMITRI	DROVED	ENLACE	EXACTA	EMMETS
DOSSEL	DOCTOR	DROVER	ENRAGE	EXACTS	EMMETT
DOSSER	DOITED	DROVES	ENRAPT	EYECUP	EMPERY
DOSSIL	DOPTER	******	ENTAIL	******	ENDEAR
DOUSED	DOTTED	D--W--	EPHAHS	E--D--	ENGELS
DOUSES	DOTTEL	******	EQUALS	******	ENMESH
DOWSED	DOTTER	DARWIN	EQUATE	ELIDED	ENNEAD
DOWSER	DOTTLE	DEEWAN	ERGATE	ELIDES	ENTERA
DOWSES	DUSTED	DIMWIT	ERRAND	ELUDED	ENTERE
DRESSY	DUSTER	DRAWEE	ERRANT	ELUDES	ENTERO
DROSKY	******	DRAWER	ERRATA	EPODES	ENTERS
DROSSY	D--U--	DRAWLS	ERSATZ	ERODED	EOCENE
DRUSES	******	DRAWLY	ESCAPE	ERODES	EOGENE
******	DANUBE	DROWNS	ESCARP	ETUDES	EPHEBI
D--T--	DATURA	DROWSE	ESPANA	EVADED	ERNEST
******	DEBUGS	DROWSY	ESSAYS	EVADER	ESCENT
DACTYL	DEBUNK	******	ESTATE	EVADES	ESKERS
DAFTLY	DEBUTS	D--Y--	ETHANE	EXEDRA	ESSENE
DALTON	DECUMA	******	ETHANS	EXODUS	ESTEEM
DANTON	DECURY	DRAYED	EXHALE	EXUDED	ESTERS
DARTED	DEDUCE	******	EXPAND	EXUDES	ETHELS
DARTER	DEDUCT	D--Z--	EXTANT		ETHERS
DARTLE	DEFUSE	******			
DATTOS	DEGUMS	DANZIG			
		DAZZLE			
		DIAZIN			

EUGENE	EASIER	ENTITY	ECCLES	ETHNIC	EUROPE
EUREKA	EASILY	ENVIED	ECOLES	EUPNEA	EXHORT
EXCEED	EASING	ENVIER	EDILES	EVENED	EXMOOR
EXCELS	EATING	ENVIES	EFFLUX	EVENLY	EXPORT
EXCEPT	EBBING	ENWIND	EMBLEM	EVENTS	EXPOSE
EXCESS	ECHINI	EOLIAN	EMILES	EVINCE	EXTOLS
EXPECT	ECHINO	EOLITH	EMILIA	******	EXTORT
EXPELS	EDDIED	EONIAN	EMILIE	E--O--	EYEOUT
EXPEND	EDDIES	EONISM	EMILIO	******	******
EXPERT	EDDISH	EPPING	EMILYS	ECHOED	E--P--
EXSECT	EDGIER	EQUINE	EMPLOY	ECHOER	******
EXSERT	EDGING	EQUIPS	EPILOG	ECHOES	ELAPSE
EXTEND	EDWINA	EQUITY	EUCLID	ECHOIC	ELOPED
EXTENT	EDWINS	ERBIUM	EVELYN	ECTOMY	ELOPER
EXTERN	EERILY	ERMINE	EVILLY	EDMOND	ELOPES
******	EFFIGY	ERNIES	EVOLVE	EFFORT	EPOPEE
E--F--	EGGING	ERRING	EXALTS	EIDOLA	ERUPTS
******	EGOISM	ERWINS	EXILED	ELBOWS	ETAPES
EARFUL	EGOIST	ESKIMO	EXILES	ELIOTS	******
EIFFEL	EKEING	ESPIAL	EXILIC	EMBODY	E--Q--
EYEFUL	ELAINE	ESPIED	EXULTS	EMBOLI	******
******	ELFINS	ESPIES	EYELET	EMBOSS	EXEQUY
E--G--	ELFISH	ETHICS	EYELID	EMBOWS	******
******	ELLIES	EUNICE	******	ENCODE	E--R--
ELEGIT	ELLIOT	EURIPI	E--M--	ENCORE	******
EMIGRE	ELMIRA	EXCIDE	******	ENDOWS	ECARTE
ENIGMA	ELOIGN	EXCISE	ELEMIS	ENFOLD	EGERIA
EXOGEN	ELOINS	EXCITE	ENAMEL	ENJOIN	ELBRUS
******	ELOISE	EXPIRE	ENAMOR	ENJOYS	ELDRED
E--H--	ELSIES	EXPIRY	ENEMAS	ENROBE	EMBRUE
******	ELVIRA	EYEING	ETYMON	ENROLL	EMBRYO
EIGHTH	ELVISH	EYRIES	EXAMEN	ENROOT	EMERGE
EIGHTS	EMMIES	******	EXEMPT	ENSOUL	EMERIC
EIGHTY	EMPIRE	E--J--	******	ENTOMB	EMERIE
EITHER	ENCINA	******	E--N--	ENTOMO	ENERGY
ELOHIM	ENDING	ELIJAH	******	ENVOYS	ENGRAM
ESCHAR	ENDIVE	******	EARNED	ENWOMB	ENTRAP
ESCHER	ENGINE	E--K--	EARNER	EOZOIC	ENTREE
ESCHEW	ENGIRD	******	EDENIC	EPHODS	ENWRAP
ESTHER	ENGIRT	EVOKED	EGGNOG	EPHORI	EPARCH
ETCHED	ENLIST	EVOKES	ELANDS	EPHORS	EPIRUS
ETCHER	ENMITY	******	ELENAS	ERRORS	ESCROW
ETCHES	ENRICH	E--L--	ELINOR	ESCORT	ESPRIT
EUCHER	ENRICO	******	EMENDS	ESTOPS	ESTRAY
EUCHRE	ENSIGN	EAGLES	EPONYM	EUBOEA	ESTRUS
******	ENSILE	EAGLET	ERINGO	EUDORA	ETERNA
E--I--	ENTICE	EARLAP	ERINYS	EULOGY	EVERET
******	ENTIRE	EARLES	ERYNGO	EUROPA	EVERTS
EALING					
EARING					

EXARCH	EMEUTE	FEUARS	FESCUE	FADEIN	FLUFFS
EXERTS	ENDUED	FINALE	FIACRE	FAGEND	FLUFFY
EXTRAS	ENDUES	FINALS	FISCAL	FAKERS	FULFIL
EXURBS	ENDURE	FIXATE	FLACKS	FAKERY	FURFUR
******	ENGULF	FLEAMS	FLACON	FANEGA	FYLFOT
E--S--	ENOUGH	FLOATS	FLECHE	FARERS	******
******	ENSUED	FLOATY	FLECKS	FEVERS	F--G--
ECESIS	ENSUES	FORAGE	FLICKS	FEWEST	******
EDISON	ENSURE	FORAYS	FLOCKS	FIBERS	FAGGED
EGESTA	ERFURT	FREAKS	FLOCKY	FIFERS	FAGGOT
EGESTS	ESCUDO	FREAKY	FORCED	FILERS	FANGAS
ELISHA	EUNUCH	FRIARS	FORCER	FILETS	FANGED
ELYSEE	EXCUSE	FRIARY	FORCES	FINELY	FEIGNE
EMESIS	EXEUNT	FUSAIN	FRACAS	FINERY	FEIGNS
ENISLE	EXHUME	******	FROCKS	FINEST	FIDGET
ENOSIS	******	F--B--	FULCRA	FIRERS	FIGGED
ERASED	E--V--	******	******	FIVERS	FINGER
ERASER	******	FARBAD	F--D--	FIXERS	FIZGIG
ERASES	ELEVEN	FEEBLE	******	FLEECE	FLAGGY
EXISTS	ELEVON	FEEBLY	FEEDER	FLEECY	FLAGON
EYASES	******	FERBER	FENDED	FLEERS	FLIGHT
******	E--W--	FIBBED	FENDER	FLEETS	FOGGED
E--T--	******	FIBBER	FEODOR	FLIERS	FORGED
******	EARWAX	FIMBLE	FEUDAL	FLIEST	FORGER
EARTHS	EARWIG	FLABBY	FEUDED	FLUENT	FORGES
EARTHY	******	FLYBYS	FIDDLE	FLYERS	FORGET
EASTER	E--X--	FOBBED	FINDER	FOMENT	FORGOT
EASTON	******	FOGBOW	FLEDGE	FOREGO	FOUGHT
EDITED	ELIXIR	FOIBLE	FLEDGY	FOREST	FRIGGA
EDITHS	******	FORBID	FODDER	FOVEAE	FRIGHT
EDITOR	E--Y--	FUMBLE	FOGDOG	FOVEAL	FRIGID
ELATED	******	******	FOLDED	FOYERS	FROGGY
ELATER	ECTYPE	F--C--	FOLDER	FREELY	FRUGAL
ELATES	ELAYNE	******	FONDER	FREEST	FUDGED
ELYTRA	ENCYST	FAECAL	FONDLE	FREEZE	FUDGES
EMETIC	ENZYME	FAECES	FONDLY	FRIEDA	FULGID
EMETIN	ETHYLS	FALCON	FONDUE	FRIEND	FUNGAL
EMOTED	******	FARCED	FORDED	FRIERS	FUNGUS
EMOTES	E--Z--	FARCER	FREDAS	FRIEZE	******
ENATES	******	FARCES	FREDDY	FRYERS	F--H--
EROTIC	ELIZAS	FASCES	FRIDAY	FUNEST	******
EVITAS	EPIZOA	FASCIA	FRIDGE	FUSEES	FATHER
EXETER	******	FAUCAL	FUDDLE	FUZEES	FATHOM
EXITED	F--A--	FAUCES	FUNDED	******	FICHES
EXOTIC	******	FAUCET	FUNDUS	F--F--	FICHUS
******	FACADE	FENCED	******	******	FIGHTS
E--U--	FARADS	FENCER	F--E--	FEOFFS	FISHER
******	FEMALE	FENCES	******	FITFUL	FISHES
EDMUND			FACERS		FOEHNS
EFFUSE			FACETS		

******	FLAILS	******	******	FAUNUS	FANONS
F--I--	FLAIRS	F--L--	F--M--	FAWNED	FAROFF
******	FLUIDS	******	******	FAWNER	FAROUT
FABIAN	FLYING	FABLED	FARMED	FEINTS	FAVORS
FACIAL	FOGIES	FABLER	FARMER	FENNEC	FAVOUR
FACIES	FOLIAR	FABLES	FERMIS	FENNEL	FEDORA
FACILE	FOLIOS	FAILED	FILMED	FIANCE	FELONS
FACING	FOLIUM	FAILLE	FILMIC	FIENDS	FELONY
FADING	FORINT	FALLAL	FIRMAN	FINNAN	FEMORA
FAKING	FOXIER	FALLEN	FIRMED	FINNED	FEROUS
FAKIRS	FOXILY	FALLER	FIRMER	FINNER	FETORS
FAMILY	FOXING	FALLOW	FIRMLY	FINNIC	FILOSE
FAMINE	FRAILS	FARLES	FLAMBE	FINNOC	FLOODS
FAMISH	FRAISE	FARLEY	FLAMED	FLANGE	FLOORS
FANION	FRUITS	FAULTS	FLAMEN	FLANKS	FLOOZY
FARINA	FRUITY	FAULTY	FLAMES	FLENCH	FLUORO
FARING	FRYING	FEALTY	FLIMSY	FLENSE	FLUORS
FATIMA	FUGIOS	FEELER	FLUMED	FLINCH	FREONS
FATING	FUMIER	FELLAH	FLUMES	FLINGS	FUCOID
FAXING	FUMING	FELLED	FLUMPS	FLINTS	FUCOUS
FAYING	FURIES	FELLER	FLYMAN	FLINTY	FUMOUS
FAZING	FUSILE	FELLOE	FOAMED	FLONGS	FURORE
FECIAL	FUSILS	FELLOW	FOEMAN	FLUNKS	FURORS
FEEING	FUSING	FIELDS	FOEMEN	FLUNKY	******
FELICE	FUSION	FILLED	FORMAL	FORNAX	F--P--
FELIDS	FUTILE	FILLER	FORMAT	FORNIX	******
FELINE	FUZILS	FILLET	FORMED	FOUNDS	FIPPLE
FELIPE	FUZING	FILLIN	FORMER	FOUNTS	FLOPPY
FENIAN	******	FILLIP	FORMIC	FRANCE	FRAPPE
FERIAL	F--J--	FOALED	FORMYL	FRANCK	******
FERINE	******	FOILED	FRAMED	FRANCO	F--R--
FERITY	FANJET	FOLLOW	FRAMER	FRANCS	******
FETIAL	FRIJOL	FOOLED	FRAMES	FRANKS	FABRIC
FETICH	******	FOULED	FRUMPS	FRENCH	FAERIE
FETING	F--K--	FOULER	FRUMPY	FRENUM	FAEROE
FETISH	******	FOULLY	FULMAR	FRENZY	FAIRED
FEUING	FAWKES	FOWLED	******	FRINGE	FAIRER
FIFING	FICKLE	FOWLER	F--N--	FRINGY	FAIRLY
FIJIAN	FIRKIN	FRILLS	******	FRONDS	FARROW
FILIAL	FLAKED	FRILLY	FAFNIR	FRONTO	FEARED
FILING	FLAKER	FROLIC	FAINTS	FRONTS	FEARER
FINIAL	FLAKES	FUELED	FANNED	FRUNZE	FENRIR
FINING	FLUKED	FUELER	FANNER	FUNNEL	FERRET
FINISH	FLUKES	FUGLED	FANNIE	******	FERRIC
FINITE	FLUKEY	FUGLES	FANNYS	F--O--	FERRIS
FIRING	FOLKSY	FULLED	FAUNAE	******	FERRUM
FIXING	FORKED	FULLER	FAUNAL	FAGOTS	FIBRIL
FIXITY	FUNKED	FURLED	FAUNAS	FAMOUS	FIBRIN

FIERCE	FUSSED	FOSTER	FROWNS	GITANO	GOBBLE
FIORDS	FUSSER	FRATER	FROWZY	GLEAMS	GOOBER
FLARED	FUSSES	FRETTY	******	GLEAMY	GRABEN
FLARES	******	FRITHS	F--X--	GLEANS	GREBES
FLIRTS	F--T--	FROTHS	******	GLOATS	GRUBBY
FLIRTY	******	FROTHY	FLAXEN	GOBANG	GUMBOS
FLORAE	FACTOR	FULTON	FLAXES	GOCART	******
FLORAL	FACTUM	FUSTIC	FLEXED	GOKART	G--C--
FLORAS	FAITHS	******	FLEXES	GONADS	******
FLORES	FALTER	F--U--	FLEXOR	GORALS	GARCON
FLORET	FANTAN	******	FLUXED	GOTAMA	GASCON
FLORID	FANTOM	FACULA	FLUXES	GREASE	GAUCHE
FLORIN	FASTED	FANUMS	******	GREASY	GAUCHO
FLURRY	FASTEN	FECULA	F--Y--	GREATS	GLACES
FOURTH	FASTER	FECUND	******	GREAVE	GLACIS
FUHRER	FATTED	FEMURS	FLAYED	GROANS	GLYCOL
FURRED	FATTEN	FERULA	FLAYER	GROATS	GRACED
FURROW	FATTER	FERULE	FLOYDS	GUIANA	GRACES
******	FELTED	FIBULA	FRAYED	GUYANA	GRACIE
F--S--	FESTAL	FIGURE	******	GYRATE	GROCER
******	FESTER	FIQUES	F--Z--	******	GUACOS
FALSER	FETTER	FLAUNT	******	G--B--	******
FEASED	FETTLE	FLEURY	FEEZED	******	G--D--
FEASES	FIFTHS	FLOURS	FEEZES	GABBED	******
FEASTS	FILTER	FLOURY	FEZZAN	GABBER	GADDED
FEISTS	FILTHY	FLOUTS	FEZZES	GABBLE	GADDER
FEISTY	FIRTHS	FORUMS	FIZZED	GABBRO	GANDER
FESSES	FISTED	FRAUDS	FIZZER	GAMBIA	GANDHI
FIASCO	FISTIC	FRAUEN	FIZZES	GAMBIR	GARDEN
FIESTA	FITTED	FUGUES	FIZZLE	GAMBIT	GELDED
FIRSTS	FITTER	FUTURE	FOOZLE	GAMBLE	GENDER
FLASHY	FLATLY	******	FRIZZY	GAMBOL	GEODES
FLASKS	FLATUS	F--V--	FROZEN	GARBED	GEODIC
FLESHY	FLETCH	******	FURZES	GARBLE	GILDAS
FLOSSY	FLITCH	FAUVES	FUZZED	GASBAG	GILDED
FOCSLE	FLUTED	FERVID	FUZZES	GERBIL	GILDER
FOISTS	FLUTER	FERVOR	******	GHEBER	GIRDED
FOSSAE	FLUTES	FLAVIA	G--A--	GIBBED	GIRDER
FOSSES	FOETAL	FLAVIN	******	GIBBER	GIRDLE
FOSSIL	FOETID	FLAVOR	GALACT	GIBBET	GLADES
FRESCO	FOETOR	FLUVIO	GALAXY	GIBBON	GLADLY
FRESNO	FOETUS	FRIVOL	GARAGE	GLEBES	GLADYS
FRISES	FONTAL	******	GAWAIN	GLIBLY	GLEDES
FRISKS	FOOTED	F--W--	GAZABO	GLOBAL	GLIDED
FRISKY	FOOTER	******	GAZEBO	GLOBED	GLIDER
FROSTS	FOOTLE	FLAWED	GEMARA	GLOBES	GLIDES
FROSTY	FORTES	FLOWED	GERALD	GLOBIN	GOADED
FRUSTA	FORTIS	FLOWER	GIGANT	GOBBET	GODDAM

GOLDEN	GLEETY	GIGGED	GARISH	GAELIC	GIZMOS
GOODBY	GONERS	GIGGLE	GASIFY	GALLED	GLAMIS
GOODLY	GOVERN	GIGGLY	GATING	GALLEY	GLUMES
GORDON	GRAECO	GINGAL	GAVIAL	GALLIC	GLUMLY
GRADED	GREECE	GINGER	GAZING	GALLON	GNOMES
GRADER	GREEDS	GINGKO	GEEING	GALLOP	GNOMIC
GRADES	GREEDY	GOGGLE	GEMINI	GALLUP	GNOMON
GRADIN	GREEKS	GOOGLY	GENIAL	GALLUS	GRAMME
GRADUS	GREENE	GOOGOL	GENIES	GAOLER	GRIMED
GRIDED	GREENS	GORGED	GENITO	GARLIC	GRIMES
GRIDES	GREETS	GORGER	GENIUS	GAULLE	GRIMLY
GRUDGE	GRIEVE	GORGES	GIBING	GELLED	GRUMES
GUIDED	GRUELS	GORGET	GIVING	GIBLET	GRUMPY
GUIDER	GYNECO	GORGON	GLAIRS	GIGLET	GUIMPE
GUIDES	******	GOUGED	GLAIRY	GIGLOT	GUMMAS
GUIDON	G--F--	GOUGER	GLUIER	GILLIE	GUMMED
GULDEN	******	GOUGES	GLUING	GIMLET	GUNMAN
******	GADFLY	GREGOS	GNEISS	GIULIA	GUNMEN
G--E--	GAFFED	GRIGRI	GOBIES	GIULIO	******
******	GAFFER	GROGGY	GODIVA	GOALIE	G--N--
GAGERS	GAFFES	GRUGRU	GONION	GOBLET	******
GAIETY	GOFFER	GURGLE	GONIUM	GOBLIN	GAINED
GALEAE	GOLFED	******	GOOIER	GOGLET	GAINER
GALENA	GOLFER	G--H--	GORIER	GRILLE	GAINLY
GAMELY	GOOFED	******	GORILY	GRILLS	GANNET
GAMETE	GRAFTS	GASHED	GORING	GRILSE	GARNER
GAMETO	GRIFFE	GASHES	GRAINS	GUILDS	GARNET
GANEFS	GUFFAW	GATHER	GRAINY	GUILES	GDANSK
GAPERS	GULFED	GOPHER	GREIFS	GUILTS	GDYNIA
GATEAU	******	GORHEN	GREIGE	GUILTY	GIANTS
GAVELS	G--G--	GOSHEN	GROINS	GULLAH	GINNED
GAYEST	******	GOTHAM	GUYING	GULLED	GINNER
GAYETY	GADGET	GOTHIC	GYBING	GULLET	GLANCE
GAZEBO	GAGGED	GRAHAM	GYVING	******	GLANDS
GAZERS	GAGGER	GUSHED	******	G--M--	GLINTS
GEMERT	GAGGLE	GUSHER	G--J--	******	GLYNIS
GENERA	GANGED	GUSHES	******	GAMMAS	GOINGS
GENESI	GANGER	******	GASJET	GAMMED	GOONEY
GENETS	GANGES	G--I--	******	GAMMER	GOWNED
GENEVA	GANGLI	******	G--K--	GAMMON	GRANDE
GERENT	GANGUE	GABION	******	GASMAN	GRANGE
GESELL	GARGET	GAGING	GASKET	GASMEN	GRANNY
GIBERS	GARGLE	GALIOT	GASKIN	GEMMAE	GRANTS
GIDEON	GAUGED	GAMIER	GAWKED	GEMMED	GRINDS
GILEAD	GAUGER	GAMILY	GECKOS	GERMAN	GRUNDY
GIMELS	GAUGES	GAMING	GURKHA	GERMEN	GRUNTS
GISELE	GEIGER	GAMINS	******	GISMOS	GUANIN
GLEETS	GEWGAW	GAPING	G--L--	GISMOS	GUANOS
			GABLED		
			GABLES		

GUENON	GRAPHO	GLOSSO	GOITER	GRAVER	HARASS
GUINEA	GRAPHS	GLOSSY	GOITRE	GRAVES	HAVANA
GUNNAR	GRAPHY	GLOSTS	GOTTEN	GRAVID	HAWAII
GUNNED	GRIPED	GNOSIS	GRATED	GRIVET	HAZARD
GUNNEL	GRIPER	GODSON	GRATER	GROVEL	HECATE
GUNNER	GRIPES	GOOSED	GRATES	GROVER	HEMATO
GWENNS	GRIPPE	GOOSES	GRATIN	GROVES	HEPATO
GWYNNE	GRIPPY	GOOSEY	GRATIS	GUAVAS	HERALD
******	GROPED	GORSES	GRETAS	******	HEXADS
G--O--	GROPER	GOSSIP	GRETEL	**G--W--**	HEXANE
******	GROPES	GRASPS	GRETNA	******	HIJACK
GADOID	GULPED	GRASSY	GRITTY	GALWAY	HILARY
GALOOT	GULPER	GRISLY	GROTTO	GLOWED	HIRAMS
GALOPS	GYPPED	GROSZY	GROTTY	GLOWER	HOBART
GALORE	******	GUESTS	GUITAR	GNAWED	HOGANS
GALOSH	**G--R--**	GUISES	GUNTER	GNAWER	HOLARD
GAMOUS	******	GUNSHY	GUSTAF	GODWIN	HOMAGE
GANOID	GARRET	GUSSET	GUSTAV	GODWIT	HORACE
GAVOTS	GEARED	GUSSIE	GUTTAE	GROWER	HORARY
GEMOTS	GENRES	GYPSUM	GUTTAT	GROWLS	HOWARD
GENOUS	GENROS	******	GUTTED	GROWTH	HUMANE
GEROUS	GEORGE	**G--T--**	GUTTER	******	HUMANS
GIAOUR	GEORGI	******	GUTTLE	**G--Y--**	******
GIGOLO	GERRYS	GAITED	******	******	**H--B--**
GIPONS	GHARRI	GAITER	**G--U--**	GALYAK	******
GLIOMA	GHARRY	GANTRY	******	GERYON	HAGBUT
GLOOMS	GIBRAN	GARTER	GAMUTS	GRAYED	HARBIN
GLOOMY	GLARED	GASTON	GERUND	GRAYER	HARBOR
GOLOSH	GLARES	GASTRO	GETUPS	GRAYLY	HATBOX
GROOMS	GLORIA	GENTES	GHAUTS	GROYNE	HAYBOX
GROOVE	GNARLS	GENTLE	GHOULS	******	HENBIT
GROOVY	GNARLY	GENTLY	GIGUES	**G--Z--**	HERBAL
GYNOUS	GOORAL	GENTOO	GLAUCO	******	HOBBES
GYRONS	GOURDE	GENTRY	GOMUTI	GAUZES	HOBBLE
GYROSE	GOURDS	GERTIE	GROUCH	GEEZER	HOMBRE
******	GUARDS	GERTYS	GROUND	GLAZED	HOTBED
G--P--	******	GESTIC	GROUPS	GLAZER	HOTBOX
******	**G--S--**	GETTER	GROUSE	GLAZES	HUBBUB
GAPPED	******	GHETTO	GROUTS	GLOZED	HUMBER
GASPAR	GASSED	GIFTED	******	GLOZES	HUMBLE
GASPED	GASSES	GIOTTO	**G--V--**	GRAZED	HUMBLY
GASPER	GEISHA	GIRTED	******	GRAZER	HUMBUG
GIMPED	GEMSBO	GLOTTO	GLOVED	GRAZES	******
GIPPED	GESSOS	GLUTEI	GLOVER	GRIZEL	**H--C--**
GLYPHS	GEYSER	GLUTEN	GLOVES	GUZZLE	******
GLYPTO	GHOSTS	GNATHO	GRAVED	******	HANCES
GOSPEL	GIBSON	GOATEE	GRAVEL	**H--A--**	HICCUP
GRAPES	GLASSY	GOETHE	GRAVEN	******	HOICKS
				HAMALS	HUBCAP
				HAMAUL	

*****	HAZELS	HEDGER	HEJIRA	HOCKEY	HOWLED
H--D--	HAZERS	HEDGES	HELICO	HONKED	HOWLER
*****	HELENA	HEIGHT	HELIOS	HONKER	HUELVA
HAGDON	HELENS	HIGGLE	HELIUM	HOOKAH	HULLED
HAMDEN	HEREAT	HINGED	HERIOT	HOOKED	HURLED
HANDED	HEREBY	HINGES	HEWING	HOOKER	HURLER
HANDEL	HEREIN	HOGGED	HEXING	HOOKEY	HURLEY
HANDLE	HEREOF	HUGGED	HEZION	HOOKUP	HUXLEY
HARDEN	HEREON	HUNGER	HIDING	HUCKLE	*****
HARDER	HERESY	HUNGRY	HIEING	HULKED	H--M--
HARDLY	HERETO	*****	HIKING	HUSKED	*****
HEADED	HETERO	H--H--	HIRING	HUSKER	HAEMAL
HEADER	HEWERS	*****	HIVING	*****	HAMMAL
HEADON	HIDERS	HASHED	HIVITE	H--L--	HAMMED
HEDDLE	HIKERS	HASHES	HOEING	*****	HAMMER
HEEDED	HIRERS	HAWHAW	HOLIER	HAILED	HARMED
HEEDER	HOMELY	HEEHAW	HOLIES	HAILER	HARMIN
HENDON	HOMERS	HIGHER	HOLILY	HALLAH	HAYMOW
HERDED	HONEST	HIGHLY	HOLING	HALLEL	HELMED
HERDER	HONEYS	HITHER	HOLISM	HALLEY	HELMET
HERDIC	HOTELS	HUGHES	HOMIER	HALLOO	HEMMED
HEYDAY	HOVELS	HUGHIE	HOMILY	HALLOW	HEMMER
HIDDEN	HOVERS	HUSHED	HOMING	HALLUX	HERMAE
HILDAS	HUBERT	HUSHES	HOMINY	HAMLET	HERMAI
HINDER	HUGELY	HYPHAE	HONIED	HARLAN	HERMAN
HINDUS	HUGEST	HYPHAL	HONING	HARLEM	HERMES
HODDEN	HYGEIA	HYPHEN	HOPING	HARLEY	HERMIT
HOIDEN	HYMENO	*****	HOSIER	HARLOT	HETMAN
HOLDER	HYMENS	H--I--	HOSING	HARLOW	HIEMAL
HOLDUP	*****	*****	HUMIFY	HASLET	HODMAN
HOODED	H--F--	HABILE	HYOIDS	HAULED	HOLMES
HOODOO	*****	HABITS	*****	HAULER	HOLMIC
HORDED	HATFUL	HADING	H--K--	HAULMY	HUMMED
HORDES	HEIFER	HAKIMS	*****	HEALED	HUMMER
HOWDAH	HOOFED	HALIDE	HACKED	HEALER	*****
HOYDEN	HOOFER	HALIDS	HACKEE	HEALTH	H--N--
HUDDLE	HUFFED	HALING	HACKER	HEELED	*****
HURDLE	H--G--	HALITE	HACKIE	HEELER	HANNAH
HYADES	*****	HAMITE	HACKLE	HELLAS	HANNAS
*****	HAGGED	HARING	HANKER	HELLEN	HAUNCH
H--E--	HAGGIS	HATING	HARKED	HELLER	HAUNTS
*****	HAGGLE	HAVING	HARKEN	HENLEY	HENNAS
HABEAS	HANGAR	HAWING	HAWKED	HILLED	HERNIA
HALERS	HANGED	HAYING	HAWKER	HILLER	HERNIO
HAREMS	HANGER	HAZIER	HECKLE	HITLER	HOBNOB
HATERS	HANGUP	HAZILY	HICKEY	HOLLER	HOGNUT
HAVENS	HEDGED	HAZING	HICKOK	HOLLOW	HORNED
HAVENT		HEGIRA	HOCKED	HOLLYS	HORNET

HORNIE	HIPPOS	HYDRAS	HECTOR	******	INNATE
HOUNDS	HIPPUS	HYDRIC	HEFTED	**H--X--**	INSANE
HYENAS	HISPID	HYDROS	HELTER	******	INTACT
HYMNAL	HOOPED	******	HEPTAD	HOAXED	INTAKE
HYMNED	HOOPER	**H--S--**	HESTER	HOAXER	INVADE
HYMNIC	HOOPLA	******	HESTIA	HOAXES	INWALL
HYPNIC	HOOPOE	HALSEY	HETTYS	******	INWARD
HYPNOS	HOPPED	HANSEL	HIATUS	**H--Y--**	IODATE
******	HOPPER	HANSOM	HILTED	******	ISAACS
H--O--	HOPPLE	HASSEL	HINTED	HEXYLS	ISLAND
******	HOTPOT	HASSLE	HITTER	******	ISRAEL
HALOED	HUMPED	HAUSEN	HOGTIE	**H--Z--**	ITHACA
HALOES	HUMPTY	HAWSER	HOOTCH	******	******
HALOID	******	HAWSES	HOOTED	HAMZAS	**I--B--**
HAROLD	**H--R--**	HEISTS	HOOTER	HAZZAN	******
HELOTS	******	HISSED	HOSTED	******	IAMBIC
HEMOID	HAIRDO	HISSER	HOSTEL	**I--A--**	IAMBUS
HEROES	HAIRED	HISSES	HOTTED	******	ICEBOX
HEROIC	HARRIS	HOISTS	HOTTER	IBEAMS	ISABEL
HEROIN	HARROW	HONSHU	HUNTED	ICEAXE	ISOBAR
HERONS	HARRYS	HORSED	HUNTER	IDEALS	ISOBEL
HESOID	HATRED	HORSES	HURTER	IDEATE	******
HEXONE	HEARER	HORSEY	HURTLE	IGNACE	**I--C--**
HEXOSE	HEARSE	HORSTE	HUSTLE	IGUANA	******
HOBOES	HEARST	HOUSED	HUTTED	IMBALM	IBICES
HONORE	HEARTH	HOUSES	HYETAL	IMBARK	ICECAP
HONORS	HEARTS	HUDSON	HYSTER	IMPACT	ICICLE
HONOUR	HEARTY	HUSSAR	******	IMPAIR	IOLCUS
HUMORS	HEBREW	HYSSOP	**H--U--**	IMPALA	IPECAC
HUMOUR	HEBRON	******	******	IMPALE	******
HURONS	HEDRAL	**H--T--**	HALUTZ	IMPARK	**I--D--**
******	HEDRON	******	HEAUME	IMPART	******
H--P--	HENRIS	HAFTED	HECUBA	IMPASS	IBADAN
******	HENRYS	HALTED	******	IMPAWN	IBIDEM
HAMPER	HOARDS	HALTER	**H--V--**	INBAND	IMIDES
HAPPED	HOARSE	HARTAL	HALVED	INCAGE	IRIDES
HAPPEN	HOORAY	HASTED	HALVES	INCASE	IRIDIC
HARPED	HORRID	HASTEN	HARVEY	INDABA	ISADOR
HARPER	HORROR	HASTES	HEAVED	INFAMY	ISIDOR
HASPED	HOTROD	HATTED	HEAVEN	INFANT	******
HATPIN	HOURIS	HATTER	HEAVER	INHALE	**I--E--**
HEAPED	HOURLY	HATTIE	HEAVES	INHAUL	******
HELPED	HUBRIS	HATTYS	HELVES	INLACE	ICIEST
HELPER	HURRAH	HEATED	HOOVED	INLAID	IDLERS
HEMPEN	HURRAY	HEATER	HOOVER	INLAND	IDLEST
HERPES	HYBRID	HEATHS	HOOVES	INLAWS	IMBEDS
HIPPED	HYBRIS	HEATHY	******	INLAYS	IMMESH
HIPPIE	HYDRAE	HECTIC	**H--W--**	INMATE	IMPEDE
			******		
			HEDWIG		

IMPELS	ISOHEL	INFLOW	INSOLE	INSTEP	******
IMPEND	ITCHED	INFLUX	INSOUL	INSTIL	J--A--
INCEPT	ITCHES	INKLES	INTOMB	IRITIC	
INCEST	******	INULIN	INTONE	IRITIS	JACANA
INDEED	I--I--	ISOLDE	INVOKE	ISATIN	JAPANS
INDENE	******	ITALIC	INWOVE	ISHTAR	JEZAIL
INDENT	IDLING	******	IODOUS	******	JIHADS
INFECT	IGNIFY	I--M--	IONONE	I--U--	JOHANN
INFERO	IGNITE	******	ITIOUS	******	JONAHS
INFERS	ILOILO	ICEMAN	******	ILLUME	JORAMS
INFEST	IMBIBE	ICEMEN	I--P--	ILLUSE	JUDAEA
INGEST	IMMIES	ISOMER	******	ILLUST	JUDAEO
INHERE	IMPING	******	INKPOT	IMBUED	JUDAHS
INJECT	IMPISH	I--N--	INSPAN	IMBUES	JUDAIC
INKERS	INCISE	******	ISOPOD	IMMUNE	JUGATE
INLETS	INCITE	ICINGS	******	IMMUNO	JURANT
INMESH	INDIAN	ICONIC	I--Q--	IMMURE	JURATS
INSECT	INDICT	IMINES	******	IMPUGN	******
INSERT	INDIES	IRANIS	IRAQIS	IMPURE	J--B--
INSETS	INDIGO	IRENES		IMPUTE	******
INTEND	INDITE	IRENIC	I--R--	INCUBI	JABBED
INTENT	INDIUM	IRONED	******	INCURS	JABBER
INTERN	INFIRM	IRONER	IATRIC	INCUSE	JERBOA
INTERS	INKIER	IRONIC	IBERIA	INDUCE	JIBBED
INVENT	INKING	******	ICARUS	INDUCT	JIBBER
INVERT	INLIER	I--O--	IGOROT	INDUED	JOBBED
INVEST	INNING	******	IMARET	INDUES	JOBBER
ISLETS	INSIDE	IDIOCY	IMBRUE	INDULT	JUBBAH
ISSEIS	INSIST	IDIOMS	INARCH	INFUSE	JUMBAL
ITSELF	INTIMA	IDIOTS	INARMS	INGULF	JUMBLE
******	INVITE	IGLOOS	INBRED	INHUME	******
I--F--	INWIND	IGNORE	INDRIS	INJURE	J--C--
******	IODIDE	ILFORD	INGRES	INJURY	******
IREFUL	IODINE	IMBODY	INGRID	INPUTS	JOYCES
******	IODISM	IMPORT	INURED	INRUSH	JUICER
I--G--	IODIZE	IMPOSE	INURES	INSULT	JUICES
******	IOLITE	IMPOST	INURNS	INSURE	JUNCOS
IMAGED	IONIAN	INBORN	INWRAP	INTUIT	******
IMAGES	IONIUM	INCOME	ISTRIA	INTURN	J--D--
IMOGEN	IONIZE	INCORP	******	ISEULT	******
ISOGON	IRKING	INDOOR	I--S--	ISSUED	JORDAN
******	IRVING	INDOWS	IBISES	ISSUER	******
I--H--	IRVINS	INFOLD	IRISED	ISSUES	J--E--
******	IRWINS	INFORM	IRISES	******	******
INCHED	ISAIAH	INGOTS	******	I--X--	JANETS
INCHES	ISLING	INJOKE	I--T--	******	JEREED
INCHON	******	INMOST	******	IBEXES	JEREMY
ISCHIA	I--L--	INROAD	ICHTHY	ILEXES	JEWELS
	ICALLY		INSTAR		
	IDYLLS				

JEWESS	******	JERKED	JALOPS	JOLTER	KANAKA
JOKERS	J--I--	JERKIN	JALOPY	JOSTLE	KARATE
JOSEPH	******	JINKED	JASONS	JOTTED	KARATS
JUDEAN	JABIRU	JINKER	JEROME	JOTTER	KAVASS
JULEPS	JADING	JOCKEY	JOCOSE	JUNTAS	KAYAKS
JUNEAU	JADISH	JOCKOS	JOYOUS	JUSTIN	KERALA
JURELS	JAMIES	JUNKED	JUPONS	JUSTLY	KERATO
******	JANICE	JUNKER	JURORS	JUSTUS	KINASE
	JAPING	JUNKET	******	JUTTED	KNEADS
J--F--	JARINA	JUNKIE	J--P--	******	KODAKS
******	JAWING	******	******	J--U--	KRAALS
JARFUL	JEEING	J--L--	JAIPUR	******	KULAKS
JOYFUL	JEMIMA	******	JASPER	JAGUAR	KUWAIT
JUGFUL	JEWISH	JAILED	JUMPED	JEJUNE	******
******	JIBING	JAILER	JUMPER	JESUIT	K--B--
J--G--	JIMINY	JAILOR	******	JOCUND	******
******	JIVING	JELLED	J--R--	JORUMS	KERBED
JAEGER	JOKING	JOPLIN	******	JUJUBE	KHYBER
JAGGED	JOLIET	JOULES	JARRED	******	KIBBLE
JANGLE	JOSIAH	******	JARROW	J--V--	KITBAG
JARGON	JOSIAS	J--M--	JEERED	******	KNOBBY
JIGGED	JOSIEA	******	JEERER	JARVEY	KRUBIS
JIGGER	JOVIAL	JAMMED	JERRYS	JARVIS	KRUBUT
JIGGLE	JOVIAN	JIMMIE	JUAREZ	JAYVEE	******
JINGAL	JOYING	JIMMYS	******	JERVIS	K--C--
JINGLE	JUDITH	******	J--S--	******	******
JINGLY	JULIAN	J--N--	******	J--X--	KNACKS
JOGGED	JULIAS	******	JERSEY	******	KNOCKS
JOGGER	JULIES	JAINAS	JESSED	JINXED	******
JOGGLE	JULIET	JAUNTS	JESSES	JINXES	K--D--
JORGES	JULIUS	JAUNTY	JESSIE	******	******
JUDGED	JUNIOR	JEANNE	JENNET	J--Y--	KEDDAH
JUDGER	JUNIUS	JENNET	JETSAM	******	KENDAL
JUDGES	JURIES	JENNYS	JIGSAW	JEKYLL	KIDDED
JUGGED	JURIST	JINNEE	JOISTS	******	KIDDER
JUGGLE	JUTISH	JINNYS	JONSON	J--Z--	KIDDIE
JUNGLE	******	JITNEY	JOSSES	******	KINDER
JUNGLY	J--J--	JOANNA	JOUSTS	JAZZED	KINDLE
******	******	JOANNE	******	JAZZER	KINDLY
J--H--	JAMJAR	JOHNNY	J--T--	JAZZES	KOODOO
******	******	JOINED	******	******	******
JAPHET	J--K--	JOINER	JESTED	K--A--	K--E--
JAPHIA	******	JOINTS	JESTER	******	******
JETHRO	JACKAL	JONNIE	JETTED	KABAKA	KARENS
JOSHED	JACKED	JOUNCE	JETTON	KABALA	KETENE
JOSHER	JACKET	******	JILTED	KABAYA	KEVELS
JOSHES	JACKIE	J--O--	JILTER	KAKAPO	KIBEIS
JOSHUA	JACKYS	******	JITTER	KAMALA	KINESI
JOTHAM		JABOTS	JOLTED		
		JACOBS			

KINETO	******	KERNEL	******	KNAVES	LESBOS
KNEELS	K--K--	KEYNES	K--S--	KNIVES	LIABLE
KOPECK	******	KIDNAP	******	******	LIBBYS
KOPEKS	KECKED	KIDNEY	KAASES	K--W--	LIEBIG
KOREAN	KECKLE	KOINES	KAISER	******	LIMBED
******	KHAKIS	KRONEN	KAMSIN	KEYWAY	LIMBER
K--F--	KICKED	KRONER	KANSAN	KNOWER	LIMBIC
******	KICKER	KRONOR	KANSAS	******	LIMBUS
KAFFIR	KINKED	KRONOS	KELSON	K--X--	LISBOA
KNIFED	KRAKEN	KRONUR	KERSEY	******	LISBON
KNIFES	******	******	KINSEY	KLAXON	LOBBED
******	K--L--	K--O--	KIOSKS	******	LOBBER
K--G--	******	******	KIRSCH	L--A--	LOWBOY
******	KAOLIN	KABOBS	KISSED	******	LUBBER
KEDGED	KEELED	KALONG	KISSER	LANAIS	LUMBAR
KEDGES	KEGLER	KAPOKS	KISSES	LANATE	LUMBER
KINGED	KELLER	KAYOED	KITSCH	LAPARO	******
KINGLY	KEPLER	KAZOOS	KNOSPS	LAVABO	L--C--
KNIGHT	KIBLAH	KELOID	KRISES	LAVAGE	******
******	KILLED	KETONE	KYUSHU	LAZARS	LANCED
K--H--	KILLER	KETOSE	******	LEGACY	LANCER
******	KISLEW	KIBOSH	K--T--	LEGATE	LANCES
KATHIE	KNELLS	KIMONO	******	LEGATO	LANCET
KATHYS	KNOLLS	KOBOLD	KAFTAN	LENAPE	LASCAR
KOSHER	KOALAS	KOKOMO	KEITHS	LEVANT	LEACHY
KUCHEN	******	******	KELTIC	LIGAND	LITCHI
******	K--M--	K--P--	KETTLE	LIGATE	******
K--I--	******	******	KILTED	LILACS	L--D--
******	KALMIA	KALPAK	KILTER	LINAGE	******
KABIKI	KARMAS	KAPPAS	KILTIE	LIPASE	LADDER
KALIAN	KERMES	KASPER	KIRTLE	LITANY	LADDIE
KALIUM	KERMIS	KEEPER	KITTED	LIZARD	LANDAU
KAMIKS	KERMIT	KELPIE	KITTEN	LOBATE	LANDED
KATIES	KILMER	KEWPIE	KITTLE	LOCALE	LANDER
KATION	KISMET	KIPPED	KITTYS	LOCALS	LAPDOG
KENITE	KUMMEL	KIPPER	KNOTTY	LOCATE	LARDED
KEVINS	******	******	KOWTOW	LORAIN	LARDER
KEYING	K--N--	K--R--	KULTUR	LOTAHS	LARDON
KIBITZ	******	******	******	LOVAGE	LAUDED
KININS	KARNAK	KARROO	K--U--	LUNACY	LAUDER
KITING	KEENED	KAURIS	******	LUNATE	LAYDAY
KODIAK	KEENER	KEDRON	KABUKI	LUXATE	LEADED
KRAITS	KEENLY	KERRIE	KNOUTS	******	LEADEN
KUMISS	KENNED	KNARRY	KORUNA	L--B--	LEADER
******	KENNEL	KNURLS	KORUNY	******	LEADIN
K--J--	KENNIE	KNURLY	******	LAMBDA	LENDER
******	KENNYS	KONRAD	K--V--	LAMBED	LEUDES
KOPJES	KERNED		KEEVES	LAMBIE	LEWDER
			KELVIN		

LEWDLY	LINEAL	LAGGER	LITHER	LEVITE	LYSINE
LEYDEN	LINEAR	LANGUR	LITHIA	LEVITY	LYSING
LIDDED	LINENS	LARGER	LITHIC	LIAISE	LYSINS
LIEDER	LINERS	LARGOS	LOCHIA	LIBIDO	******
LINDAS	LINEUP	LAUGHS	LUSHED	LIKING	**L--J--**
LINDEN	LITERS	LEAGUE	LUSHER	LILIAN	******
LOADED	LIVELY	LEDGER	LUSHES	LILIED	LOGJAM
LOADER	LIVENS	LEDGES	LUTHER	LILIES	******
LONDON	LIVERS	LEGGED	******	LIMIER	**L--K--**
LORDED	LIVERY	LEIGHS	**L--I--**	LIMINA	******
LORDLY	LOMENT	LENGTH	******	LIMING	LACKED
LOUDEN	LONELY	LIEGES	LABIAL	LIMITS	LACKEY
LOUDER	LONERS	LINGAM	LABILE	LINIER	LANKER
LOUDLY	LOPERS	LINGAS	LABIUM	LINING	LANKLY
******	LOREEN	LINGER	LACIAL	LIPIDS	LARKED
L--E--	LORENE	LINGUA	LACIER	LIVIAS	LARKER
******	LORENZ	LODGED	LACILY	LIVIER	LEAKED
LABELS	LOSERS	LODGER	LACING	LIVING	LICKED
LAGERS	LOVEIN	LODGES	LADIES	LOGIER	LINKED
LAKERS	LOVELL	LOGGED	LADING	LOGION	LOCKED
LAMECH	LOVELY	LOGGER	LADINO	LOLITA	LOCKER
LAMEDS	LOVERS	LOGGIA	LAKIER	LOOING	LOCKET
LAMELY	LOWELL	LONGAN	LAKING	LOPING	LOCKUP
LAMENT	LOWERS	LONGED	LAMIAE	LORICA	LOOKED
LAMEST	LOWERY	LONGER	LAMIAS	LORIES	LOOKER
LAPELS	LOWEST	LOUGHS	LAMINA	LOSING	LOOKIN
LAREDO	LUBECK	LUGGED	LAMING	LOTION	LOWKEY
LASERS	LUCENT	LUGGER	LAPINS	LOUISA	LUNKER
LATEEN	LUGERS	LUNGED	LARIAT	LOUISE	LURKED
LATELY	LUMENS	LUNGEE	LARINE	LOVING	LURKER
LATENT	LUNETS	LUNGER	LATINS	LOWING	******
LATERA	LURERS	LUNGES	LATISH	LUCIAN	**L--L--**
LATEST	LUTEAL	LUNGIS	LAVING	LUCIAS	******
LAVERS	LUTEUM	******	LAVISH	LUCIEN	LADLED
LAXEST	LYCEES	**L--H--**	LAWING	LUCILE	LADLER
LAYERS	LYCEUM	******	LAXITY	LUCITE	LADLES
LEGEND	******	LACHES	LAYING	LUCIUS	LALLED
LEGERS	**L--F--**	LASHED	LAZIER	LUMINA	LESLEY
LEPERS	******	LASHER	LAZILY	LUMINI	LESLIE
LEVEES	LAPFUL	LASHES	LAZING	LUMINO	LOLLED
LEVELS	LAWFUL	LATHED	LEGION	LUPINE	LOLLER
LEVERS	LEAFED	LATHER	LEGIST	LURING	LOLLOP
LIBELS	LOAFED	LATHES	LENITY	LUTING	LUBLIN
LIFERS	LOAFER	LECHER	LEPIDO	LUTIST	LUDLOW
LIKELY	LOOFAH	LETHAL	LESION	LYDIAS	LUELLA
LIKENS	LUFFED	LICHEE	LEVIED	LYRICS	LULLED
LIMENS	******	LICHEN	LEVIER	LYRISM	******
LIMEYS	**L--G--**	LIGHTS	LEVIES	LYRIST	**L--M--**
	******				******
	LAAGER				LAMMAS
	LAGGED				LAMMED

LAYMAN	LENORE	LEARNT	LATTER	LIQUID	MADAME
LAYMEN	LEROYS	LEERED	LECTOR	LIQUOR	MADAMS
LEGMAN	LIPOID	LEGREE	LENTEN	LOBULE	MALACO
LEGMEN	LIPOMA	LIBRAE	LENTIL	LOCUST	MALADY
LEMMAS	LOCOED	LIBRAS	LENTOS	LOQUAR	MALAGA
LITMUS	LOMOND	LIERNE	LEPTON	LOQUAT	MALATE
LLAMAS	******	LIVRES	LESTER	LUNULA	MALAWI
LOAMED	L--P--	LOURED	LETTER	LUNULE	MALAYA
LOOMED	******	******	LICTOR	LUXURY	MALAYS
LUMMOX	LAMPAD	L--S--	LIFTED	******	MANAGE
******	LAMPAS	******	LIFTER	L--V--	MANANA
	LAMPED	LAPSED	LILTED	******	MARACA
L--N--	LAPPED	LAPSER	LINTEL	LARVAE	MARAUD
******	LAPPER	LAPSES	LINTER	LARVAL	MEDALS
LANNER	LAPPET	LAPSUS	LISTED	LATVIA	MEGALO
LAUNCE	LEAPED	LASSEN	LISTEL	LEAVED	MEGASS
LAUNCH	LEAPER	LASSES	LISTEN	LEAVEN	MELANO
LEANED	LIMPED	LASSIE	LISTER	LEAVER	MENACE
LEANER	LIMPER	LASSOS	LITTER	LEAVES	MENAGE
LEANLY	LIMPET	LEASED	LITTLE	LOAVES	METAGE
LEANTO	LIMPID	LEASES	LOATHE	LOUVER	METALS
LEMNOS	LIMPLY	LENSES	LOFTED	LOUVRE	MIDAIR
LENNYS	LIPPED	LEPSIA	LOFTER	******	MIKADO
LEONAS	LIPPER	LESSEE	LOITER	L--W--	MILADY
LEONIE	LISPED	LESSEN	LOOTED	******	MILAGE
LIANAS	LISPER	LESSER	LOOTER	LEEWAY	MIRAGE
LIANES	LOOPED	LESSON	LOTTIE	LUDWIG	MOHAIR
LIGNIN	LOOPER	LESSOR	LUETIC	******	MOHAVE
LIGNUM	LOPPED	LIASED	LUSTED	L--X--	MOHAWK
LIMNED	LOUPES	LISSOM	LUSTER	******	MOJAVE
LIMNER	LUMPED	LOOSED	LUSTRE	LYNXES	MOLARS
LINNET	LUMPEN	LOOSEN	LYTTAE	******	MONACO
LIONEL	LYMPHO	LOOSER		L--Y--	MONADS
LLANOS	******	LOOSES	L--U--	******	MORALE
LOANED		LOSSES	******	LARYNG	MORALS
LOUNGE	L--R--	LOUSED	LACUNA	LARYNX	MORASS
LUANDA	******	LOUSES	LAGUNE	LAWYER	MORAYS
******	LABRET	******	LANUGO	LIBYAN	MOSAIC
	LABRUM	L--T--	LAZULI	LIVYER	MOZART
L--O--	LAIRDS	******	LEGUME	LLOYDS	MURALS
******	LAIRED	LACTAM	LEHUAS	******	MUTANT
LABORS	LARRUP	LACTIC	LEMUEL	L--Z--	MUTATE
LABOUR	LARRYS	LAOTSE	LEMURS	******	******
LADOGA	LATRIA	LASTED	LETUPS	LIZZIE	M--B--
LAGOON	LAURAE	LASTER	LIGULA	LIZZYS	******
LAHORE	LAURAS	LASTEX	LIGULE	******	MAHBUB
LANOSE	LAUREL	LASTLY	LIGURE	M--A--	MAMBAS
LAYOFF	LAURIE	LATTEN	LIMULI	******	MAMBOS
LAYOUT	LEARNS			MACACO	
LEMONS				MACAWS	

MARBLE	MELDED	MISERY	MEAGER	MALICE	MEXICO
MAYBUG	MENDED	MITERS	MEAGRE	MALIGN	MILIEU
MEMBER	MENDEL	MIXERS	MERGED	MALINE	MILIUM
MOBBED	MENDER	MODELS	MERGER	MAMIES	MIMICS
MOBBER	MENDIP	MODERN	MERGES	MANIAC	MIMING
MORBID	MIDDAY	MODEST	MIDGES	MANIAS	MINIFY
MUMBLE	MIDDEN	MOIETY	MIDGET	MANILA	MINIMA
******	MIDDLE	MOLEST	MIDGUT	MANIOC	MINIMS
M--C--	MILDEN	MOMENT	MIGGLE	MANITO	MINING
******	MILDER	MONEYS	MINGLE	MANITU	MINION
MADCAP	MILDEW	MOPERS	MONGER	MAOISM	MINIUM
MANCHU	MILDLY	MOREAU	MONGOL	MAOIST	MIRIAM
MARCEL	MINDED	MOREEN	MONGST	MARIAN	MIRING
MARCIA	MINDER	MORELS	MORGAN	MARIAS	MIXING
MARCOS	MISDID	MOSEYS	MORGEN	MARIES	MOBILE
MARCUS	MOLDED	MOTELS	MORGUE	MARINA	MOBIUS
MASCON	MOLDER	MOVERS	MUGGAR	MARINE	MODIFY
MASCOT	MONDAY	MOWERS	MUGGED	MARION	MODISH
MECCAN	MUDDED	MUSEUM	MUGGER	MARIST	MOLIES
MECCAS	MUDDER	MYCETE	MUGGUR	MATINE	MOLINE
MERCER	MUDDLE	MYSELF	******	MATING	MOMISM
MERCIA	MURDER	******	M--H--	MATINS	MONICA
MESCAL	******	M--F--	******	MAXIMA	MONIED
MINCED	M--E--	******	MASHED	MAXIMS	MONIES
MINCER	******	MANFUL	MASHER	MAXINE	MONISM
MINCES	MABELS	MAYFLY	MASHES	MAXIXE	MONIST
MISCUE	MACERS	MIFFED	MASHIE	MAYING	MOOING
MOBCAP	MADEUP	MISFIT	MAYHAP	MAZIER	MOPING
MOSCOW	MAKERS	MUFFED	MAYHEM	MAZILY	MOPISH
MUDCAP	MAKEUP	MUFFIN	MENHIR	MAZING	MORION
MULCTS	MAMEYS	MUFFLE	MESHED	MEDIAE	MOTIFS
MUSCAE	MANEGE	******	MESHER	MEDIAL	MOTILE
MUSCAT	MASERS	M--G--	MESHES	MEDIAN	MOTION
MUSCLE	MATEOS	******	METHOD	MEDICI	MOTIVE
******	MATEYS	MADGES	METHYL	MEDICO	MOVIES
M--D--	MAYEST	MAGGIE	MICHEL	MEDICS	MOVING
******	MAZERS	MAGGOT	MIGHTY	MEDIUM	MOWING
MADDED	MELEES	MAIGRE	MISHAP	MEGILP	MULISH
MADDEN	MERELY	MALGRE	MOTHER	MEJICO	MUNICH
MADDER	MEREST	MANGER	MUSHED	MENIAL	MURIEL
MAIDEN	METEOR	MANGLE	MUSHER	MENINX	MURINE
MANDAN	METERS	MANGOS	MUSHES	MERINO	MUSING
MANDYS	MICELL	MARGAY	MUZHIK	MERITS	MUTING
MARDUK	MILERS	MARGES	MYTHIC	MESIAL	MUTINY
MAUDES	MIMERS	MARGIE	MYTHOI	MESIAN	MUTISM
MAYDAY	MINERS	MARGIN	MYTHOS	METIER	MYRIAD
MEADOW	MISERE	MARGOS	******	METING	MYRICA
MEDDLE	MISERS	MARGOT	M--I--	MEWING	
			******		
			MACING		
			MAKING		

******	MEALIE	MAIMED	MAJORS	MASQUE	MESSED
M--K--	MEDLAR	MAIMER	MALORY	MOSQUE	MESSES
******	MEDLEY	MAMMAE	MANORS	******	MESSRS
MACKLE	MELLON	MAMMAL	MAROON	**M--R--**	MIASMA
MARKED	MELLOW	MAMMAS	MASONS	******	MIOSIS
MARKER	MERLES	MAMMET	MASORA	MACRON	MISSAL
MARKET	MERLIN	MAMMON	MAYORS	MADRAS	MISSED
MARKKA	MERLON	MARMOT	MCCOYS	MADRID	MISSEL
MARKUP	MEWLED	MAUMAU	MEKONG	MAORIS	MISSES
MASKED	MIKLOS	MERMAN	MELODY	MARRED	MISSIS
MASKEG	MILLAY	MERMEN	MELONS	MARRER	MISSUS
MASKER	MILLED	MESMER	MEMOIR	MARROW	MOISHE
MEEKER	MILLER	MICMAC	MEMORY	MATRIX	MORSEL
MEEKLY	MILLET	MORMON	MEROUS	MATRON	MOSSES
MICKEY	MILLIE	MOTMOT	MESONS	MEGRIM	MOUSED
MICKLE	MILLYS	MUMMED	METOPE	METRIC	MOUSER
MICKYS	MISLAY	MUMMER	MILORD	METROS	MOUSES
MILKED	MISLED	MURMUR	MIMOSA	MICRON	MOUSSE
MILKER	MOILED	MUUMUU	MINOAN	MIDRIB	MUSSED
MISKAL	MOILER	MYRMEC	MINORS	MIRROR	MUSSEL
MOCKED	MOLLAH	******	MOHOCK	MITRAL	MUSSES
MOCKER	MOLLIE	**M--N--**	MOHOLE	MITRED	MYOSIN
MOCKUP	MOLLYS	******	MOLOCH	MOIRAS	MYOSIS
MONKEY	MOOLAH	MAENAD	MONODY	MONROE	******
MUCKED	MOOLEY	MAGNET	MOPOKE	MOORED	**M--T--**
MUCKER	MORLEY	MAGNOX	MORONS	MORRIS	******
MUCKLE	MOSLEM	MAGNUM	MOROSE	MORROS	MAITRE
MUSKEG	MOSLEY	MAINLY	MOTORS	MORROW	MALTED
MUSKET	MOTLEY	MANNED	MUCOID	MOURNS	MALTHA
MUSKIT	MOULDS	MANNER	MUCOSA	MURRAY	MANTAS
MUSKOX	MOULDY	MAUNDS	MUCOSE	MURRES	MANTEL
******	MOULIN	MAUNDY	MUCOUS	MURREY	MANTES
M--L--	MOULTS	MEANER	MYXOMA	******	MANTIC
******	MUKLUK	MEANIE	******	**M--S--**	MANTIS
MACLES	MULLAH	MEANLY	**M--P--**	******	MANTLE
MAHLER	MULLED	MESNES	******	MAISIE	MANTUA
MAILED	MULLEN	MIGNON	MAGPIE	MAISON	MARTAS
MAILER	MULLER	MINNIE	MAPPED	MANSES	MARTEN
MALLED	MULLET	MINNOW	MAYPOP	MARSHA	MARTHA
MALLEE	MULLEY	MOANED	MOPPED	MARSHY	MARTHE
MALLET	MUSLIM	MOONED	MOPPET	MASSED	MARTIN
MALLOW	MUSLIN	MOUNTS	MORPHO	MASSES	MARTYR
MAPLES	MYELIN	MOUNTY	MYOPES	MASSIF	MARTYS
MARLED	******	MYRNAS	MYOPIA	MAUSER	MASTED
MARLIN	**M--M--**	******	MYOPIC	MEASLY	MASTER
MARLOW	******	**M--O--**	******	MENSAL	MASTIC
MAULED	MADMAN	******	**M--Q--**	MENSES	MATTED
MAULER	MADMEN	MAGOTS	******	MERSEY	MATTEO
		MAHOUT	MANQUE		
			MARQUE		

MATTER	MUTTON	******	NUBBIN	NOVENA	NAVIES
MATTES	MYRTLE	M--Y--	NUBBLE	NUDELY	NAZIFY
MATTIE	MYSTIC	******	NUBBLY	******	NAZISM
MEATUS	******	MAGYAR	NUMBED	N--G--	NEVILE
MEETER	M--U--	******	NUMBER	******	NEVILL
MEETLY	******	M--Z--	NUMBLY	NAGGED	NIDIFY
MELTED	MACULA	******	******	NAGGER	NIDING
MELTER	MACULE	MAIZES	N--C--	NAUGHT	NIMITZ
MELTON	MADURA	MATZOS	******	NEIGHS	NIXIES
MENTAL	MADURO	MATZOT	NANCYS	NIGGER	NIXING
MENTOR	MAGUEY	MEZZOS	NIACIN	NIGGLE	NOMISM
MESTEE	MANUAL	MIZZEN	NIECES	NILGAI	NORIAS
METTLE	MANUEL	MIZZLE	NONCOM	NOGGIN	NOSIER
MILTED	MANURE	MUZZLE	NUNCIO	NOUGAT	NOSILY
MILTER	MAQUIS	******	******	NOUGHT	NOSING
MILTON	MATURE	N--A--	N--D--	NUDGED	NOTICE
MINTED	MAZUMA	******	******	NUDGES	NOTIFY
MINTER	MEDUSA	NAGANA	NEEDED	NUGGET	NOTING
MIOTIC	METUMP	NAIADS	NEEDER	******	NOTION
MISTED	MEZUZA	NAPALM	NEEDLE	N--H--	NOVICE
MISTER	MIAULS	NASALS	NODDED	******	NOWISE
MISTLE	MIGUEL	NATANT	NODDER	NASHUA	NUBIAN
MITTEN	MINUET	NAVAHO	NODDLE	NATHAN	NUBIAS
MOATED	MINUTE	NAVAJO	NOODLE	NEPHEW	NUBILE
MOLTED	MISUSE	NAWABS	NORDIC	NEPHRO	NUDISM
MOLTEN	MIXUPS	NEGATE	******	NETHER	NUDIST
MOLTER	MODULE	NEMATO	N--E--	NICHED	NUDITY
MOLTKE	MOGULS	NEVADA	******	NICHES	NUMINA
MONTES	MOHURS	NEWARK	NAMELY	NIGHER	******
MONTHS	MORULA	NOBALL	NAMERS	NIGHTS	N--K--
MONTYS	MUTUAL	NOMADS	NAPERY	NIGHTY	******
******	MUTULE	NONAGE	NAVELS	NOSHED	NAPKIN
MOOTED		NONARY	NEREID	NOSHOW	NARKED
MOOTER	M--V--	NOPALS	NEREIS	NUCHAE	NECKED
MORTAL	******	NOTARY	NEWELS	******	NICKED
MORTAR	MARVEL	NOWAYS	NEWEST	N--I--	NICKEL
MORTON	MARVIN	******	NICELY	******	NICKER
MORTYS	MAUVES		NICENE	NADINE	NICKYS
MOSTLY	MELVIN	N--B--	NICEST	NADIRS	NOCKED
MOTTLE	MELVYN	******	NICETY	NAMING	******
MOTTOS	MERVIN	NABBED	NIGELS	NANISM	N--L--
MOUTHS	******	NIBBED	NINETY	NAPIER	******
MOUTHY	M--W--	NIBBLE	NISEIS	NARIAL	NAILED
MOUTON	******	NIMBLE	NOCENT	NARINE	NAPLES
MUFTIS	MEDWAY	NIMBLY	NONEGO	NASIAL	NELLIE
MUSTEE	MEOWED	NIMBUS	NONGO	NASION	NELLYS
MUSTER	MIDWAY	NIOBIC	NOREEN	NATION	NIELLI
MUSTNT	******	NOBBED	NOTERS	NATIVE	NIELLO
MUTTER	M--X--	NOBBLE	NOVELS		
	MINXES				

NOBLER	******	NESTOR	OHMAGE	OCHERS	ONAGRI
NOELLE	N--R--	NETTED	OLEATE	OCHERY	OREGAN
NUCLEI	******	NETTIE	ONFALL	OCREAE	OREGON
NULLAH	NARROW	NETTLE	ONWARD	OCTETS	ORIGAN
NUTLET	NATRON	NEUTER	OPIATE	ODDEST	ORIGEN
******	NEARBY	NEWTON	OPTANT	OEDEMA	ORIGIN
N--M--	NEARED	NINTHS	ORDAIN	OEPEMA	OXYGEN
******	NEARER	NOETIC	OREADS	OFFEND	******
NAOMIS	NEARLY	NOSTIC	ORGANA	OFFERS	O--H--
NEUMES	NEURAL	NUTTED	ORGANO	OGLERS	******
NORMAL	NEURON	NUTTER	ORGANS	OGRESS	OLDHAM
NORMAN	NIMROD	******	ORGASM	OILERS	OOPHOR
NORMAS	NITRIC	N--U--	ORNATE	OLDEST	ORCHID
NUTMEG	NITRID	******	OSCANS	ONSETS	ORCHIL
******	NORRIS	NAHUMS	OSCARS	ORCEIN	ORCHIO
N--N--	NUTRIA	NATURE	OSWALD	ORDEAL	ORCHIS
******	******	NEBULA	OTTAVA	ORDERS	ORPHAN
NORNIR	N--S--	NODULE	OTTAWA	ORGEAT	ORPHIC
NOUNAL	******	NOMURA	OXTAIL	ORIELS	******
NUANCE	NAOSES	******	******	ORIENT	O--I--
NUDNIK	NASSAU	N--V--	O--B--	ORMERS	******
******	NASSER	******	******	ORNERY	OAFISH
N--O--	NAUSEA	NAEVUS	OJIBWA	ORRERY	OARING
******	NELSON	NERVED	ORIBIS	ORWELL	OBIISM
NABOBS	NESSUS	NERVES	OUTBID	OSBERT	OBLIGE
NAGOYA	NEVSKI	******	OVIBOS	OSIERS	OBOIST
NEROLI	NOESIS	N--W--	******	OSSEIN	ODDITY
NEVOID	NOISED	******	O--C--	OSTEAL	OFFICE
NICOLE	NOISES	NARWAL	******	OSTEND	OFFING
NOBODY	NOOSED	NITWIT	OILCAN	OSWEGO	OFFISH
NODOSE	NOOSES	NORWAY	ORACHS	OTHERS	OGLING
NOGOOD	NURSED	******	ORACLE	OTTERS	OGRISH
NYLONS	NURSER	N--Z--	OUNCES	OUSELS	OILIER
******	NURSES	******	OUTCRY	OUTERS	OILILY
N--P--	******	NOZZLE	******	OUZELS	OILING
******	N--T--	NUZZLE	O--D--	OWLETS	OLDISH
******	******	******	******	OWNERS	OLLIES
NAPPED	NANTES	O--A--	OFFDAY	******	OMNIUM
NAPPER	NASTIC	******	OUTDID	O--F--	ONEIDA
NAPPES	NATTER	OBLAST	OXIDES	******	ONEILL
NAPPIE	NAUTCH	OBLATE	******	OLEFIN	ONEIRO
NIPPED	NEATEN	OBTAIN	O--E--	OUTFIT	ONLINE
NIPPER	NEATER	OCEANS	******	OUTFOX	OOLITE
NIPPLE	NEATLY	OCTADS	OBJECT	******	OOMIAK
NIPPON	NECTAR	OCTANE	OBSESS	O--G--	OOZIER
NYMPHA	NEKTON	OCTANT	OBTECT	******	OOZILY
NYMPHO	NESTED	OCTAVE	OBTEST	OMEGAS	OOZING
NYMPHS	NESTLE	OCTAVO	OBVERT	ONAGER	OPHITE

OPTICS	******	******	OCCUPY	PAPAIN	******
OPTIMA	O--M--	O--Q--	OCCURS	PAPAWS	P--B--
OPTIME	******	******	ONRUSH	PAPAYA	******
OPTING	OUTMAN	OPAQUE	OPPUGN	PARADE	PEBBLE
OPTION	******	******	ORDURE	PARANG	PEBBLY
ORBING	O--N--	O--R--	ORMUZD	PARAPH	PHOBIA
ORBITS	******	******	OSCULE	PAVANE	PHOBIC
OREIDE	ODONTO	OBERON	OSMUND	PAVANS	PLEBES
ORGIES	ODYNIA	OCTROI	******	PECANS	POTBOY
ORNITH	OHENRY	OPERAS	O--V--	PEDALS	PROBED
OROIDE	OMENTA	OPORTO	******	PEDANT	PROBER
ORPINE	OPENED	OSIRIS	OEUVRE	PEDATE	PROBES
ORPINS	OPENER	OSPREY	OGIVAL	PEDATI	PUEBLO
ORRICE	OPENLY	OUTRAN	OGIVES	PEKANS	******
OSCINE	OPINED	OUTRUN	OLIVER	PELAGE	P--C--
OSMIUM	OPINES	OVERDO	OLIVES	PESACH	******
OSSIAN	ORANGE	OVERLY	OLIVIA	PESADE	PANCHO
OSSIFY	ORANGS	******	******	PETALS	PARCAE
OUTING	ORKNEY	O--S--	O--W--	PETARD	PARCEL
OWLISH	OZONIC	******	******	PHIALS	PASCAL
OWNING	******	OCASEY	ONEWAY	PHRASE	PATCHY
OXHIDE	O--O--	ODESSA	OUTWIT	PILAFF	PEACHY
OXLIPS	******	OFFSET	******	PILAFS	PENCEL
******	OBLONG	OMASUM	O--X--	PILATE	PENCIL
O--J--	OCLOCK	ONUSES	******	PINANG	PERCYS
******	OCTOPI	ODIOUS	ORISON	ORYXES	PIPAGE	PHOCIS
ODDJOB	OGDOAD	OUTSAT	******	PIRACY	PIECED
******	OHIOAN	OUTSET	O--Y--	PIRANA	PIECER
O--L--	ONEOFF	OUTSIT	******	PIRATE	PIECES
******	ONIONS	OVISAC	OBEYED	PLEACH	PISCES
OAKLEY	ONIONY	******	OBEYER	PLEADS	PITCHY
OBELUS	OOLOGY	O--T--	OKAYED	PLEASE	PLACED
OBOLUS	OOLONG	******	OOCYTE	PLEATS	PLACER
OCELLI	OPPOSE	OBITER	OXEYED	PLIANT	PLACES
OCELOT	ORIOLE	ODETTE	OXEYES	POLACK	PLACET
OCULAR	ORLOPS	ORATED	******	POLAND	PLACID
OMELET	ORMOLU	ORATES	P--A--	POMACE	PLACKS
OODLES	OSBORN	ORATOR	******	POMADE	PLICAE
ORALLY	OSMOND	OTITIS	PAEANS	POSADA	PLUCKS
OSTLER	OSMOSE	OUSTED	PAGANS	POTAGE	PLUCKY
OUTLAW	OTIOSE	OUSTER	PAJAMA	POTALE	POACHY
OUTLAY	OTTOWA	OYSTER	PALACE	POTASH	PONCHO
OUTLET	OXBOWS	******	PALAEO	POTATO	POUCHY
OVALLY	OXFORD	O--U--	PALAIS	PREACH	PRECIS
OVULAR	******	******	PALATE	PSHAWS	PRICED
OVULES	O--P--	OBTUND	PANADA	PUPATE	PRICES
OXALIC	OKAPIS	OBTUSE	PANAMA	PURANA	PRICKS
OXALIS	OUTPUT	OCCULT	PAPACY	PYJAMA	PROCNE
				PYRANS	

PROCTO	PATENT	******	PATHAN	PENILE	PULING
PSYCHE	PATERS	**P--F--**	PATHIA	PERILS	PUMICE
PSYCHO	PAVERS	******	PATHOL	PERIOD	PUNIER
PUNCHY	PAWERS	PIAFFE	PATHOS	PERISH	PUNILY
******	PAYEES	PIFFLE	PEAHEN	PETITE	PUNISH
P--D--	PAYERS	PILFER	PISHED	PEWITS	PUPILS
******	PELEUS	PREFAB	PISHES	PIKING	PURIFY
PADDED	PESETA	PREFER	PITHED	PILING	PURINE
PADDLE	PETERS	PREFIX	POSHLY	PINIER	PURISM
PADDYS	PEWEES	PROFIT	POTHER	PINIES	PURIST
PANDAS	PHLEBO	PUFFED	PUSHED	PINING	PURITY
PANDER	PHLEGM	PUFFER	PUSHER	PINION	PYRITE
PARDON	PHOEBE	PUFFIN	PUSHES	PINITE	PYXIES
PAYDAY	PHRENO	PURFLE	PUSHTU	PIPIER	******
PEDDLE	PIGEON	******	PUSHUP	PIPING	**P--J--**
PENDED	PIKERS	**P--G--**	PYTHIA	PIPITS	******
PIDDLE	PILEUM	******	PYTHIC	PITIED	PROJET
PINDAR	PILEUP	PARGET	PYTHON	PITIES	PUNJAB
PINDUS	PILEUS	PARGOS	******	PIXIES	******
PLEDGE	PINEAL	PEGGED	**P--I--**	PLAICE	**P--K--**
PODDED	PINENE	PEGGYS	******	PLAIDS	******
POLDER	PINERY	PENGOS	PACIFY	PLAINS	PACKED
PONDER	PIPERS	PHAGIA	PACING	PLAINT	PACKER
POODLE	PIPETS	PIDGIN	PAGING	PLAITS	PACKET
POWDER	PLIERS	PIGGED	PALING	PLEIAD	PARKAS
PRIDED	POKERS	PIGGIE	PALISH	PLYING	PARKED
PRIDES	POLEAX	PIGGIN	PANICE	PODIUM	PARKER
PRUDES	POMELO	PINGED	PANICS	POGIES	PAUKER
PUDDLE	PONENT	PINGOS	PAPIST	POKIER	PEAKED
PUDDLY	POPERY	PISGAH	PARIAH	POKIES	PECKED
PUNDIT	POSERS	PLAGAL	PARIAN	POKING	PECKER
PURDAH	POSEUR	PLAGIO	PARIES	POLICE	PEEKED
******	POTEEN	PLAGUE	PARING	POLICY	PEEKER
P--E--	POTENT	PLAGUY	PARISH	POLING	PERKED
******	POWELL	PLEGIA	PARITY	POLISH	PICKAX
PACERS	POWERS	PLIGHT	PATINA	POLITE	PICKED
PALEAE	PREENS	PLUGIN	PATINE	POLITY	PICKER
PALELY	PRIERS	PONGEE	PATIOS	PONIED	PICKET
PALEST	PRIEST	POPGUN	PAVING	PONIES	PICKLE
PAMELA	PROEMS	PRAGUE	PAVIOR	POPISH	PICKUP
PANELS	PRYERS	PUGGED	PAVISE	PORING	PINKED
PAPERS	PULERS	PUGGRY	PAWING	POSIES	PINKIE
PAPERY	PUREED	PURGED	PAYING	POSING	PIPKIN
PARENS	PUREES	PURGER	PEKING	POSITS	POCKET
PARENT	PURELY	PURGES	PELIAS	POTION	POLKAS
PARERS	PUREST	******	PELION	PRAISE	PORKER
PAREUS	PYRENE	**P--H--**	PELITE	PRYING	PUCKER
PATENS		******	PENIAL	PUKING	PUNKAS
		PASHAS			
		PASHTO			

```
******        PROLIX    PAINTY    POINTE    PRIORS    PULPIT
P--L--        PSALMS    PANNED    POINTS    PRIORY    PUMPED
******        PUBLIC    PAUNCH    POINTY    PROOFS    PUMPER
PALLAS        PULLED    PAWNED    POUNCE    PUTOFF    PUPPED
PALLED        PULLER    PAWNEE    POUNDS    PUTONS    PUPPET
PALLET        PULLET    PAWNER    PRANCE    PUTOUT    PURPLE
PALLID        PULLEY    PAYNIM    PRANKS    PYLONS    PUTPUT
PALLOR        PULLIN    PEANUT    PRINCE    PYRONE    ******
PARLAY        PURLED    PEENED    PRINKS    PYROPE    P--Q--
PARLEY        PURLER    PENNAE    PRINTS    ******    ******
PARLOR        PURLIN    PENNED    PRONGS    P--P--    PLAQUE
PAULAS        PUTLOG    PENNER    PRONTO    ******    PULQUE
PAULIN        ******    PENNIA    PRUNED    PALPED    ******
PAULUS        P--M--    PENNIS    PRUNER    PALPUS    P--R--
PAVLOV        ******    PENNON    PRUNES    PAMPAS    ******
PEALED        PALMAR    PENNYS    PUNNED    PAMPER    PADRES
PEDLAR        PALMED    PHANON    PUNNER    PAPPUS    PAIRED
PEELED        PALMER    PHENOL    PUTNAM    PAUPER    PARRAL
PEELER        PENMAN    PHENYL    PYKNIC    PAWPAW    PARREL
PEGLEG        PENMEN    PHONED    ******    PEEPED    PARROT
PELLET        PERMED    PHONES    P--O--    PEEPER    PATROL
PEPLOS        PERMIT    PHONEY    ******    PENPAL    PATRON
PEPLUM        PIEMAN    PHONIA    PAEONS    PEOPLE    PEARLS
PEPLUS        PIEMEN    PHONIC    PAEONY    PEPPED    PEARLY
PHILIA        PITMAN    PIANOS    PAGODA    PEPPER    PEDROS
PHILIP        PITMEN    PICNIC    PARODY    PHIPPS    PEERED
PHILOS        PLUMBO    PIENAL    PAROLE    PIGPEN    PEIRCE
PHYLAE        PLUMBS    PIGNUS    PATOIS    PIMPED    PEORIA
PHYLLO        PLUMED    PIGNUT    PAYOFF    PIMPLE    PERRON
PHYLUM        PLUMES    PINNAE    PAYOLA    PIMPLY    PERRYS
PIGLET        PLUMMY    PINNAL    PEKOES    PIPPED    PETREL
PILLAR        PLUMPS    PINNED    PELOPS    PIPPIN    PETRIE
PILLED        POMMEL    PINNER    PELOTA    POMPEY    PETROL
PILLOW        POTMAN    PLANAR    PEYOTE    POMPOM    PHAROS
POILUS        PREMED    PLANCH    PHLOEM    POMPON    PICRIC
POLLED        PRIMAL    PLANCK    PHOOEY    POOPED    PIERCE
POLLEE        PRIMED    PLANED    PICOTS    POPPED    PIERRE
POLLEN        PRIMER    PLANER    PILOSE    POPPER    PIERUS
POLLER        PRIMES    PLANES    PILOTS    POPPET    PLURAL
POLLEX        PRIMLY    PLANET    PILOUS    POPPLE    POGROM
POLLUX        PRIMPS    PLANKS    PINOLE    POPPYS    POORER
POLLYS        PRIMUS    PLANTS    PINONS    POTPIE    POORLY
POOLED        PROMPT    PLENTY    PITONS    PREPAY    POURED
POPLAR        PUMMEL    PLENUM    PIVOTS    PROPEL    POURER
POPLIN        PYEMIA    PLINTH    PODOUS    PROPER    PUGREE
POULTS        PYEMIC    PLUNGE    POMONA    PROPYL    PURRED
PRELIM        ******    PLUNKS    POROUS    PULPED    PUTRID
PROLEG        P--N--    POINDS    POYOUS    PULPER    PYRRHA
              ******                                  PYURIA
              PAINED
              PAINTS
```

******
P--S--
******
PANSYS
PARSEC
PARSED
PARSEE
PARSES
PARSIS
PARSON
PASSED
PASSEE
PASSER
PASSES
PASSIM
PASSUS
PATSYS
PAUSED
PAUSER
PAUSES
PEASEN
PEASES
PEPSIN
PERSIA
PERSON
PHASED
PHASES
PHASIA
PHASIC
PHASIS
PHOSPH
PHYSIC
PHYSIO
PIGSTY
PLASHY
PLASIA
PLASIS
PLASMA
PLASMO
PLASTY
PLUSES
PLUSHY
PODSOL
POISED
POISES
POISON
POSSES
POSSET
POSSUM
POTSIE
POUSTO
PRESAS
PRESTO
PRISMS
PRISON
PRISSY
PROSED
PROSER
PROSES
PROSIT
PTISAN
PTOSIS
PUISNE
PULSAR
PULSED
PULSES
PURSED
PURSER
PURSES
PURSUE
PUSSES
PUSSEY
PUSSLY
PUTSCH
PYOSIS
******
P--T--
******
PALTER
PALTRY
PANTED
PANTIE
PANTRY
PARTED
PARTLY
PASTAS
PASTED
PASTEL
PASTER
PASTES
PASTIL
PASTOR
PASTRY
PATTED
PATTEN
PATTER
PATTON
PECTEN
PECTIC
PECTIN
PEGTOP
PELTED
PELTER
PELTRY
PENTAD
PENTUP
PEPTIC
PERTLY
PESTER
PESTLE
PETTED
PEWTER
PHOTIC
PHOTON
PHOTOS
PHYTIN
PICTOR
PIETER
PIETRO
PINTER
PINTLE
PINTOS
PISTIL
PISTOL
PISTON
PITTED
PLATAN
PLATED
PLATEN
PLATER
PLATES
PLATTE
PLUTUS
POETIC
POETRY
PONTES
PONTIC
PONTIL
PONTON
PORTAL
PORTED
PORTER
PORTIA
PORTLY
POSTAL
POSTED
POSTER
POTTED
POTTER
POTTLE
POTTOS
POUTED
POUTER
POWTER
PRATED
PRATER
PRATES
PRETER
PRETOR
PRETTY
PROTON
PUNTED
PUNTER
PUNTOS
PUTTED
PUTTEE
PUTTER
******
P--U--
******
PAIUTE
PAPUAN
PAPULA
PAPULE
PARURE
PENULT
PENURY
PEQUOD
PEQUOT
PERUKE
PERUSE
PICULS
PILULE
PINUPS
PIQUED
PIQUES
PIQUET
PLEURA
PLEURO
PLOUGH
PNEUMA
PNEUMO
PODUNK
PROUST
PSEUDO
******
P--V--
******
PARVIS
PEAVEY
PEEVED
PEEVES
PELVES
PELVIC
PELVIS
PLOVER
PLUVIO
PRAVDA
PREVUE
PRIVET
PROVED
PROVEN
PROVER
PROVES
PURVEY
******
P--W--
******
PAXWAX
PEEWEE
PEEWIT
PLOWED
PLOWER
POWWOW
PRAWNS
PREWAR
PROWLS
******
P--X--
******
PINXIT
PLEXOR
PLEXUS
PRAXIS
******
P--Y--
******
PLAYAS
PLAYED
PLAYER
POLYPS
PRAYED
PRAYER
PREYED
PREYER
******
P--Z--
******
PANZER
PIAZZA
PIZZAS
PLAZAS
PODZOL
PRIZED
PRIZER
PRIZES
PUZZLE
******
Q--A--
******
QUEANS
QUEASY
******
Q--B--
******
QUEBEC
******
Q--C--
******
QUACKS
******
Q--D--
******
QUADRI
******
Q--E--
******
QUAERE
QUEENS
QUEERS
******
Q--F--
******
QUAFFS
******
Q--G--
******
QUAGGA
QUAGGY

******	QUARTS	RECALL	ROWANS	ROSCOE	RAVERS
Q--H--	QUARTZ	RECANT	ROXANA	ROTCHE	RAWEST
******	QUERNS	RECAPS	ROXANE	ROUCHE	RAZEED
QUAHOG	QUIRED	RECAST	ROYALE	******	RAZEES
******	QUIRES	REDACT	ROYALS	**R--D--**	REBECK
Q--I--	QUIRKS	REDANS	RRHAGE	******	REBECS
******	QUIRTS	REFACE	RRHAGY	RADDLE	REBELS
QUAILS	QUORUM	REGAIN	RUBACE	RAGDAY	RECEDE
QUAINT	******	REGALE	RUBATO	RAIDED	RECENT
QUOINS	**Q--S--**	REGARD	RUGATE	RAIDER	RECEPT
QUOITS	******	REHASH	******	RANDAL	RECESS
******	QUASAR	RELAID	**R--B--**	RANDAN	REDEEM
Q--K--	QUESTS	RELATE	******	RANDOM	REDEYE
******	******	RELAYS	RABBET	READER	REFERS
QUAKED	**Q--T--**	REMADE	RABBIN	REDDEN	REGENT
QUAKER	******	REMAIN	RABBIS	REDDER	REHEAR
QUAKES	QUATRE	REMAKE	RABBIT	REDDLE	REHEAT
******	QUITCH	REMAND	RABBLE	REDDOG	REJECT
Q--L--	QUOTAS	REMANS	RAGBAG	REEDED	RELENT
******	QUOTED	REMARK	RAMBLE	REEDIT	REMEDY
QUALMS	QUOTER	REPAID	REDBAY	RENDED	RENEES
QUALMY	QUOTES	REPAIR	REDBUD	RENDER	RENEGE
QUELLS	QUOTHA	REPAND	REDBUG	RHODAS	RENEWS
QUILLS	******	REPASS	REUBEN	RHODES	REPEAL
QUILTS	**Q--U--**	REPAST	RIBBED	RHODIC	REPEAT
******	******	REPAYS	RIBBON	RIDDED	REPELS
Q--N--	QUEUED	RESALE	ROBBED	RIDDEN	REPENT
******	QUEUES	RETAIL	ROBBER	RIDDLE	RESEAT
QUANTA	******	RETAIN	ROBBIA	RODDYS	RESEAU
QUANTS	**Q--V--**	RETAKE	ROBBIE	RONDEL	RESECT
QUENCH	******	RETARD	ROUBLE	RONDOS	RESEDA
QUINCE	QUAVER	REVAMP	RUBBED	RUDDER	RESELL
QUINCY	QUIVER	REWARD	RUBBER	RUDDLE	RESEND
QUINIC	******	RIBALD	RUBBLE	RUNDLE	RESENT
QUINSY	**Q--Z--**	RIBAND	RUMBAS	******	RESETS
QUINTS	******	RITARD	RUMBLE	**R--E--**	RETELL
******	QUEZON	RIVALS	******	******	RETENE
Q--P--	******	RIYALS	**R--C--**	RACEME	REVEAL
******	**R--A--**	ROBALO	******	RACERS	REVELS
QUAPAW	******	ROBAND	RANCHO	RAKERS	REVERE
QUIPUS	RADARS	ROLAND	RANCID	RANEES	REVERS
******	RAJABS	ROMAIC	RANCOR	RAREFY	REVERT
Q--R--	RAJAHS	ROMANS	RASCAL	RARELY	REVEST
******	RATALS	ROMANY	REACTS	RAREST	REVETS
QUARKS	RAVAGE	RONALD	REDCAP	RATELS	RICERS
QUARRY	RAYAHS	ROSARY	REECHO	RATERS	RIDENT
QUARTE	REBATE	ROTARY	REICHS	RAVELS	RIDERS
QUARTO	REBATO	ROTATE	RESCUE	RAVENS	RIMERS

RIPELY	RIGGER	RADIUS	REPINE	RACKET	ROBLES
RIPENS	RINGED	RAGING	RESIDE	RANKED	ROILED
RIPEST	RINGER	RAKING	RESIGN	RANKER	ROLLED
RISERS	ROTGUT	RAKISH	RESILE	RANKLE	ROLLER
RIVERS	ROUGED	RAMIES	RESINS	RANKLY	ROLLUP
RIVETS	ROUGES	RAMIFY	RESIST	RECKON	RUBLES
ROBERT	ROUGHS	RAPIDS	RETINA	REEKED	RUNLET
RODENT	RUGGED	RAPIER	RETIRE	REEKER	******
RODEOS	RUGGER	RAPINE	REVIEW	RICKED	R--M--
ROGERS	******	RAPING	REVILE	RICKEY	******
ROSEAL	R--H--	RAPIST	REVISE	RICKYS	RAGMAN
ROVERS	******	RARING	REVIVE	RINKED	RAGMEN
ROWELS	RACHEL	RARITY	REWIND	RISKED	RAMMED
ROWENA	RACHIS	RATIFY	RHEIMS	RISKER	RAMMER
ROWERS	RAPHAE	RATINE	RICING	ROCKED	REAMED
RUBENS	RAPHIS	RATING	RIDING	ROCKER	REAMER
RUDELY	RASHER	RATION	RILING	ROCKET	RHOMBI
RUDEST	RASHES	RATIOS	RIMING	ROCKNE	RHUMBA
RULERS	RASHLY	RATITE	RISING	ROOKED	RHUMBS
RUPEES	RATHER	RAVINE	RIVING	ROOKIE	RHYMED
RUPERT	REDHOT	RAVING	ROBING	RUCKED	RHYMER
******	RICHER	RAVISH	ROBINS	RUCKUS	RHYMES
R--F--	RICHES	RAWISH	ROMISH	RUSKIN	RIMMED
******	RICHIE	RAYING	ROPIER	RYUKYU	RIMMER
RAFFIA	RICHLY	RAZING	ROPILY	******	ROAMED
RAFFLE	RIGHTO	REBILL	ROPING	R--L--	ROAMER
REDFIN	RIGHTS	RECIPE	ROSIER	******	RODMAN
REEFED	ROCHET	RECITE	ROSILY	RAGLAN	RODMEN
REEFER	RUCHES	REFILL	ROSING	RAILED	ROMMEL
RIFFLE	RUSHED	REFINE	ROSINS	RATLIN	ROOMED
ROOFED	RUSHER	REFITS	ROSINY	REALES	ROOMER
ROOFER	RUSHES	REGIME	ROVING	REALLY	RUMMER
RUEFUL	******	REGINA	ROWING	REALMS	******
RUFFED	R--I--	REGION	RUBIES	REALTY	R--N--
RUFFLE	******	REGIUS	RUBIGO	REELED	******
******	RABIES	RELICS	RUEING	REELER	RADNOR
R--G--	RACIAL	RELICT	RULING	REFLET	RAINED
******	RACIER	RELIED	RUMINA	REFLEX	REGNAL
RAGGED	RACILY	RELIEF	RUNINS	REFLUX	REINED
RANGED	RACINE	RELIER	RUPIAH	REGLET	RENNET
RANGER	RACING	RELIES	RUSINE	REPLAY	RENNIN
RANGES	RACISM	RELINE	RUTILE	RIALTO	RHINAL
REDGUM	RACIST	RELISH	******	RIFLED	RHINOS
REGGIE	RADIAL	RELIVE	R--J--	RIFLER	RODNEY
REIGNS	RADIAN	REMIND	******	RIFLES	ROMNEY
RIDGED	RADIOS	REMISE	RAMJET	RILLET	RONNIE
RIDGES	RADISH	REMISS	******	RIPLEY	ROUNDS
RIGGED	RADIUM	REMITS	R--K--	ROALDS	RUINED
			******		
			RACKED		
			RACKER		

RUINER	RIGORS	******	RATTAN	REBUKE	******
RUNNEL	RIGOUR	**R--R--**	RATTED	REBUTS	**S--A--**
RUNNER	RIMOSE	******	RATTEN	RECURS	******
RWANDA	RIMOUS	RAMROD	RATTER	RECUSE	SAFARI
******	RIPOFF	REARED	RATTLE	REDUCE	SAHARA
R--O--	RIPOST	REARER	RECTAL	REFUEL	SALAAM
******	ROBOTS	REARMS	RECTOR	REFUGE	SALADS
RACOON	ROCOCO	REGRET	RECTOS	REFUND	SALAMI
RADOME	ROMOLA	RETROD	RECTUM	REFUSE	SALARY
RAGOUT	ROTORS	RIPRAP	RECTUS	REFUTE	SAMARA
RAMONA	RUFOUS	ROARED	REDTOP	REMUDA	SARAHS
RAMOSE	RUGOSE	ROARER	RENTAL	REPUTE	SARAPE
RAMOUS	RUGOUS	RUBRIC	RENTED	RERUNS	SATANG
RATOON	RUMORS	******	RENTER	RESULT	SATARA
RAYONS	RUMOUR	**R--S--**	RENTES	RESUME	SAVAGE
RAZORS	RUNOFF	******	RESTED	RETURN	SAVANT
REBORE	RUNONS	RAISED	RESTER	RETUSE	SAVATE
REBORN	RUNOUT	RAISER	RETTED	REVUES	SCLAFF
REBOZO	******	RAISES	RHETOR	RHEUMY	SCRAGS
RECOIL	**R--P--**	RAISIN	RHYTHM	RITUAL	SCRAMS
RECORD	******	RAMSON	RIATAS	ROBUST	SCRAPE
RECOUP	RAJPUT	RANSOM	RICTAL	ROGUED	SCRAPS
REDOES	RALPHS	REASON	RICTUS	ROGUES	SCRAWL
REDONE	RAMPED	RHESUS	RIFTED	ROMULO	SEBATS
REDOWA	RAPPED	RINSED	RIOTED	ROQUET	SECANT
REFOOT	RAPPEE	RINSER	RIOTER	ROTUND	SEDANS
REFORM	RAPPEL	RINSES	RITTER	******	SEDATE
REJOIN	RAPPER	RIPSAW	ROOTED	**R--V--**	SEJANT
RELOAD	RASPED	ROASTS	ROOTER	******	SENARY
REMORA	RASPER	ROBSON	ROOTLE	REAVOW	SENATE
REMOTE	REAPED	ROOSTS	ROSTER	REEVED	SEPALS
REMOVE	REAPER	ROSTRA	ROSTRA	REEVES	SERACS
RENOIR	REOPEN	ROUSED	ROTTED	REVVED	SERAIS
RENOWN	RIMPLE	ROUSER	ROTTEN	******	SERAPE
REPORT	RIPPED	ROUSES	ROTTER	**R--W--**	SERAPH
REPOSE	RIPPER	ROUSTS	ROUTED	******	SESAME
RESOLD	RIPPLE	RUSSET	ROUTER	RUNWAY	SEWAGE
RESOLE	RIPPLY	RUSSIA	ROUTES	******	SEWALL
RESORB	ROLPHS	******	RUSTED	**R--Y--**	SEWARD
RESORT	ROMPED	**R--T--**	RUSTIC	******	SHEARS
RETOLD	ROMPER	******	RUSTLE	RUNYON	SHEATH
RETOOK	RUMPLE	RAFTED	RUTTED	******	SHEAVE
RETOOL	RUMPUS	RAFTER	******	**R--Z--**	SHOALS
RETORT	******	RAGTAG	**R--U--**	******	SHOALY
REVOKE	**R--Q--**	RANTED	******	RAZZED	SHOATS
REVOLT	******	RANTER	RADULA	RAZZES	SHRANK
REWORD	RISQUE	RAPTLY	RAOULS	RAZZIA	SILAGE
RIBOSE		RAPTOR	REBUFF	RHIZIC	SIMARS
		RASTER			

SITARS	STEAMY	STUBBY	******	SUDDEN	SENECA
SIWASH	STOATS	SUABLE	**S--D--**	SUEDES	SEREIN
SIZARS	STRAFE	SUNBOW	******	SUNDAE	SERENA
SKEANS	STRAIN	SYMBOL	SADDEN	SUNDAY	SERENE
SLEAVE	STRAIT	******	SADDER	SUNDER	SEVENS
SLEAZY	STRAKE	**S--C--**	SADDLE	SUNDEW	SEVERE
SMEARS	STRAND	******	SANDAL	SUNDOG	SEVERN
SMEARY	STRAPS	SAUCED	SANDED	SUNDRY	SEVERS
SNEAKS	STRASS	SAUCER	SANDER	SWEDEN	SEWELL
SNEAKY	STRATA	SAUCES	SANDHI	SWEDES	SEWERS
SOCAGE	STRATH	SEACOW	SANDRA	SYNDET	SHEENS
SOLACE	STRATI	SEICHE	SANDYS	SYNDIC	SHEENY
SOLAND	STRAWS	SHACKO	SEADOG	******	SHEEPS
SOLANO	STRAWY	SHACKS	SEEDED	**S--E--**	SHEERS
SOLANS	STRAYS	SHOCKS	SEEDER	******	SHEETS
SOMALI	STUART	SHUCKS	SELDOM	SABEAN	SHIELD
SOMATA	SUBAHS	SIECLE	SENDAL	SABERS	SHIEST
SOMATO	SUDARY	SKYCAP	SENDER	SAFELY	SHOERS
SONANT	SUGARS	SLACKS	SERDAB	SAFEST	SHREDS
SONARS	SUGARY	SLICED	SHADED	SAFETY	SHREWD
SONATA	SUMACS	SLICER	SHADES	SAGELY	SHREWS
SOUARI	SURAHS	SLICES	SHADOW	SAGEST	SHYEST
SOWARS	SUSANS	SLICKS	SHODDY	SAHEBS	SIDERO
SPEAKS	SWEARS	SMACKS	SIDDUR	SAKERS	SILENI
SPEARS	SWEATS	SMOCKS	SIRDAR	SANELY	SILENT
SPLAKE	SWEATY	SNACKS	SLEDGE	SANEST	SINEON
SPLASH	******	SNICKS	SLIDER	SATEEN	SINEWS
SPLATS	**S--B--**	SNOCAT	SLIDES	SAVERS	SINEWY
SPLAYS	******	SOCCER	SLUDGE	SAWERS	SIRENS
SPRAGS	SABBAT	SPACAE	SLUDGY	SAYERS	SISERA
SPRAIN	SAMBAS	SPACED	SMUDGE	SCHEMA	SKIERS
SPRANG	SAMBOS	SPACER	SMUDGY	SCHEME	SLEEKS
SPRATS	SAMBUR	SPACES	SODDED	SCLERA	SLEEKY
SPRAWL	SCABBY	SPECIE	SODDEN	SCLERO	SLEEPS
SPRAYS	SCUBAS	SPECKS	SOLDER	SCREAK	SLEEPY
SQUABS	SEABEE	SPICED	SONDER	SCREAM	SLEETS
SQUADS	SERBIA	SPICER	SORDID	SCREED	SLEETY
SQUALL	SHABBY	SPICES	SPADED	SCREEN	SLEEVE
SQUAMA	SHEBAT	STACIE	SPADER	SCREWS	SLIEST
SQUARE	SINBAD	STACKS	SPADES	SCREWY	SLYEST
SQUASH	SNOBBY	STACTE	SPADIX	SECEDE	SNEERS
SQUATS	SOBBED	STACYS	SPIDER	SECERN	SNEEZE
SQUAWK	SOMBER	STICKS	STADIA	SEDERS	SNEEZY
SQUAWS	SOMBRE	STICKY	STODGE	SELECT	SOBERS
STEADY	SORBET	STOCKS	STODGY	SELENE	SOLELY
STEAKS	STABLE	STOCKY	STUDIO	SELENO	SOLEMN
STEALS	STABLY	STUCCO	SUBDEB	SEMELE	SOLENT
STEAMS	STUBBS	SUCCOR	SUBDUE	SEMEME	SORELS

SORELY	SHIFTS	SLIGHT	SABINS	SEXIER	SONIAS
SOREST	SHIFTY	SLOGAN	SADIES	SEXILY	SOVIET
SOWERS	SHOFAR	SMUGLY	SADISM	SEXING	SOWING
SPEECH	SINFUL	SNAGGY	SADIST	SEXISM	SOZINE
SPEEDS	SKIFFS	SNUGLY	SAGIER	SEXIST	SOZINS
SPEEDY	SNAFUS	SOIGNE	SAHIBS	SHEIKH	SPAITS
SPHENE	SNIFFS	SORGHO	SALIFY	SHEIKS	SPEISS
SPHENO	SNIFFY	SORGOS	SALINE	SHEILA	SPHINX
SPHERE	SNUFFS	SOUGHS	SALISH	SHEILD	SPLICE
SPHERY	SNUFFY	SOUGHT	SALIVA	SHIISM	SPLINE
SPIELS	SOFFIT	SPIGOT	SAMIAN	SHIITE	SPLINT
SPIERS	SPIFFY	STAGED	SAMIEL	SHRIEK	SPLITS
SPLEEN	STAFFS	STAGER	SAMITE	SHRIFT	SPOILS
SPLENO	STEFAN	STAGES	SANIES	SHRIKE	SPOILT
SPREAD	STIFLE	STAGEY	SANITY	SHRILL	SPRIER
SPREES	STUFFS	STAGGY	SAPIEN	SHRIMP	SPRIGS
SQUEAK	STUFFY	STIGMA	SASINS	SHRINE	SPRING
SQUEAL	SUFFER	STOGEY	SATING	SHRINK	SPRINT
STEEDS	SUFFIX	SUNGOD	SATINS	SHRIVE	SPRITE
STEELS	SULFUR	SURGED	SATINY	SHTICK	SPRITS
STEELY	SURFED	SURGER	SATIRE	SHYING	SPYING
STEEPS	SURFER	SURGES	SAVING	SICILY	SQUIBS
STEERS	SWIFTS	SWAGED	SAVINS	SIDING	SQUIDS
STEEVE	******	SWAGES	SAVIOR	SIGILS	SQUILL
STHENO	S--G--	******	SAWING	SILICA	SQUINT
STREAK	******	S--H--	SAYING	SILICO	SQUIRE
STREAM	SAGGAR	******	SCHICK	SIMIAN	SQUIRM
STREET	SAGGED	SACHEM	SCHISM	SIMILE	SQUIRT
STRESS	SAGGER	SACHET	SCHIST	SIRING	SQUISH
STREWN	SAIGAS	SADHUS	SCHIZO	SIRIUS	STAINS
STREWS	SAIGON	SAPHAR	SCRIBE	SITING	STAIRS
SUPERB	SANGAR	SASHAY	SCRIED	SITINS	STAITH
SUPERS	SANGER	SASHED	SCRIMP	SIZIER	STEINS
SURELY	SANGUI	SASHES	SCRIPS	SIZING	STOICS
SUREST	SARGON	SIGHED	SCRIPT	SKEINS	STRIAE
SURETY	SAUGER	SIGHTS	SCRIVE	SKIING	STRICK
SWEENY	SEDGES	SIPHON	SEDILE	SKYING	STRICT
SWEEPS	SEGGAR	SOPHIA	SEEING	SLEIGH	STRIDE
SWEEPY	SHAGGY	SOPHIE	SEMITE	SLUICE	STRIFE
SWEETS	SHOGUN	SOTHIC	SENILE	SLUING	STRIKE
SYCEES	SIEGED	SOTHIS	SENIOR	SNAILS	STRING
******	SIEGES	SPAHIS	SEPIAS	SOCIAL	STRIPE
S--F--	SINGED	SUNHAT	SERIAL	SODIUM	STRIPS
******	SINGER	SYPHER	SERIES	SOLIDI	STRIPT
SAWFLY	SINGES	SYPHON	SERIFS	SOLIDS	STRIPY
SCOFFS	SINGLE	******	SERINE	SOLING	STRIVE
SCUFFS	SINGLY	S--I--	SERINS	SOLION	STYING
SHAFTS	SLAGGY	******	SEWING	SOMITE	SUBITO
		SABINA			
		SABINE			

SUFISM	SPIKED	SHELTY	STELLI	SHAMMY	SCENTS
SUPINE	SPIKES	SHELVE	STILES	SHAMUS	SCONCE
SUSIES	SPOKED	SHILLS	STILLS	SHIMMY	SCONES
SWAILS	SPOKEN	SHILOH	STILLY	SIGMAS	SEANCE
SWAINS	SPOKES	SIALIC	STILTS	SIMMER	SEINED
SYBILS	STAKED	SIDLED	STOLED	SKIMOS	SEINER
SYRIAC	STAKES	SIDLER	STOLEN	SKIMPS	SEINES
SYRIAN	STOKED	SIDLES	STOLES	SKIMPY	SENNAS
SYRINX	STOKER	SIMLIN	STOLID	SKYMAN	SENNET
******	STOKES	SKALDS	STOLON	SKYMEN	SENNIT
S--J--	SUCKED	SKILLS	STULLS	SLIMED	SHANDY
******	SUCKER	SKULKS	STYLAR	SLIMES	SHANKS
SANJAK	SUCKLE	SKULLS	STYLED	SLIMLY	SHANTY
SELJUK	SULKED	SLALOM	STYLER	SLIMSY	SHINDY
SHOJIS	SUNKEN	SMALLS	STYLES	SLUMMY	SHINED
******	******	SMALTI	STYLET	SLUMPS	SHINER
S--K--	S--L--	SMALTO	STYLUS	SOCMAN	SHINES
******	******	SMELLS	SUBLET	SOCMEN	SHINNY
SACKED	SABLES	SMELLY	SULLEN	SPUMED	SHINTO
SACKER	SAILED	SMELTS	SUNLIT	SPUMES	SHUNTS
SECKEL	SAILER	SMILAX	SUSLIK	STAMEN	SIDNEY
SEEKER	SAILOR	SMILED	SUTLER	STAMIN	SIENNA
SHAKEN	SALLET	SMILER	SVELTE	STAMPS	SIGNAL
SHAKER	SALLOW	SMILES	SWALES	STOMAT	SIGNED
SHAKES	SALLYS	SMOLTS	SWELLS	STOMPS	SIGNER
SHAKOS	SAMLET	SNELLS	SWILLS	STUMPS	SIGNET
SHEKEL	SAULTS	SOCLES	******	STUMPY	SIGNOR
SHIKAR	SCALAR	SOILED	S--M--	STYMIE	SIMNEL
SICKED	SCALDS	SOULED	******	SUBMIT	SINNED
SICKEN	SCALED	SPALLS	SALMIS	SUMMED	SINNER
SICKER	SCALER	SPELLS	SALMON	SUMMER	SKINKS
SICKLE	SCALES	SPILED	SAMMYS	SUMMIT	SKINNY
SICKLY	SCALPS	SPILES	SCAMPI	SUMMON	SKUNKS
SIKKIM	SCILLY	SPILLS	SCAMPS	SUOMIC	SLANGY
SILKEN	SCOLDS	SPILTH	SCHMOS	SWAMIS	SLANTS
SINKER	SCOLEX	STALAG	SCUMMY	SWAMPS	SLINGS
SISKIN	SCULLS	STALED	SEAMAN	SWAMPY	SLINKS
SLAKED	SCULPT	STALER	SEAMED	******	SLINKY
SLAKES	SCYLLA	STALES	SEAMEN	S--N--	SONNET
SMOKED	SEALED	STALIN	SEAMER	******	SOONER
SMOKER	SEALER	STALKS	SEAMUS	SAINTS	SOUNDS
SMOKES	SELLER	STALKY	SEEMED	SANNUP	SPANKS
SNAKED	SENLAC	STALLS	SEEMER	SAUNAS	SPENDS
SNAKES	SHALED	STELAE	SEEMLY	SAWNEY	SPINAL
SOAKED	SHALES	STELAR	SERMON	SCANTY	SPINEL
SOAKER	SHELBY	STELES	SHAMAN	SCENDS	SPINES
SOCKED	SHELLS	STELIC	SHAMED	SCENES	SPINET
SOCKET	SHELLY	STELLA	SHAMES	SCENIC	SPINNY

SPONGE	SCROLL	STOOPS	SLAPUP	SACRED	SIGRID
SPONGY	SCROOP	STROBE	SLIPON	SACRUM	SKERRY
SPUNKY	SCROTA	STRODE	SLIPUP	SATRAP	SKIRRS
STANCE	SECOND	STROKE	SLOPED	SAUREL	SKIRTS
STANCH	SENORA	STROLL	SLOPER	SAURUS	SLURPS
STANDS	SEPOYS	STROMA	SLOPES	SCARAB	SLURRY
STANZA	SEROUS	STRONG	SLOPPY	SCARCE	SMARMY
STENCH	SEROWS	STROPS	SNAPPY	SCARED	SMARTS
STENOG	SETOFF	STROUD	SNIPED	SCARER	SMIRCH
STINGS	SETONS	STROVE	SNIPER	SCARES	SMIRKS
STINGY	SETOSE	SUBORN	SNIPES	SCARFS	SNARED
STINKS	SETOUS	SWOONS	SNIPPY	SCARPS	SNARER
STINTS	SETOUT	SWOOPS	SOAPED	SCORCH	SNARES
STONED	SHOOED	SYNODS	SOPPED	SCORED	SNARLS
STONER	SHOOIN	******	SOUPED	SCORER	SNARLY
STONES	SHOOTS	S--P--	STAPES	SCORES	SNORED
STUNTS	SHROFF	******	STAPLE	SCORIA	SNORER
SUMNER	SHROUD	SAIPAN	STEPAN	SCORNS	SNORES
SUNNAH	SHROVE	SALPAS	STEPIN	SCURFY	SNORTS
SUNNED	SILOED	SALPID	STEPPE	SCURRY	SOARED
SWANEE	SIMONE	SAMPAN	STEPUP	SCURVY	SOARER
SWANKY	SIMONS	SAMPLE	STIPEL	SEARCH	SOCRED
SWINGE	SIMONY	SAPPED	STIPES	SEARED	SOIREE
SWINGS	SIMOOM	SAPPER	STOPED	SEARIN	SORREL
SYDNEY	SLOOPS	SAPPHO	STOPES	SECRET	SORROW
******	SMOOCH	SCAPES	STUPAS	SEURAT	SOURCE
S--O--	SMOOTH	SCIPIO	STUPES	SHARDS	SOURED
******	SNOODS	SCOPES	STUPID	SHARED	SOURER
SABOTS	SNOOKS	SCOPUS	STUPOR	SHARER	SOURLY
SAJOUS	SNOOPS	SCYPHI	SULPHA	SHARES	SPARED
SALOME	SNOOPY	SCYPHO	SULPHO	SHARKS	SPARER
SALONS	SNOOTS	SEAPEN	SUPPED	SHARON	SPARES
SALOON	SNOOZE	SECPAR	SUPPER	SHARPS	SPARGE
SALOOP	SODOMY	SEEPED	SUPPLE	SHERDS	SPARKS
SAMOAN	SOLOED	SEMPRE	SUPPLY	SHERIF	SPARRY
SARONG	SOTOLS	SEXPOT	SWIPED	SHERPA	SPARSE
SATORY	SPOOFS	SHAPED	SWIPES	SHERRY	SPARTA
SAVORS	SPOOKS	SHAPEN	SWIPLE	SHIRES	SPERMO
SAVORY	SPOOKY	SHAPER	SYLPHS	SHIRKS	SPERRY
SAVOUR	SPOOLS	SHAPES	SYLPHY	SHIRRS	SPIRAL
SAXONS	SPOONS	SHOPPE	******	SHIRTS	SPIREA
SAXONY	SPOONY	SIMPER	S--Q--	SHIRTY	SPIRED
SCHOOL	SPOORS	SIMPLE	******	SHORAN	SPIRES
SCHORL	SPROUT	SIMPLY	SESQUI	SHORED	SPIRIT
SCIONS	STOOGE	SIPPED	******	SHORES	SPIRTS
SCOOPS	STOOKS	SIPPER	S--R--	SHORLS	SPORED
SCOOTS	STOOLS	SIPPET	******	SHORTS	SPORES
SCRODS		SKOPJE	SABRAS	SIERRA	SPORTS
			SACRAL		

SPORTY	SARSAR	SECTOR	SOOTED	SATURN	SUTURE
SPURGE	SASSED	SEETHE	SOOTHE	SCAUPS	SYNURA
SPURNS	SASSES	SENTRY	SORTED	SCHUIT	SYRUPS
SPURRY	SEASON	SEPTAL	SORTER	SCHUSS	SYRUPY
SPURTS	SEESAW	SEPTET	SORTIE	SCOURS	******
STARCH	SEISED	SEPTIC	SPATES	SCOUSE	S--V--
STARED	SEISIN	SEPTUM	SPATHE	SCOUTS	******
STARER	SEISMO	SESTET	SPITAL	SCRUBS	SALVED
STARES	SEISMS	SETTEE	SPITED	SCRUFF	SALVER
STARRY	SEISOR	SETTER	SPITES	SCRUMS	SALVES
STARTS	SELSYN	SETTLE	SPOTTY	SECUND	SALVIA
STARVE	SENSED	SETTOS	SPUTUM	SECURE	SALVOR
STEREO	SENSES	SEXTAN	STATAL	SEDUCE	SALVOS
STERES	SENSOR	SEXTET	STATED	SEDUMS	SELVES
STERIC	SEPSIS	SEXTON	STATEN	SEQUEL	SERVAL
STERNA	SHASTA	SHOTES	STATER	SEQUIN	SERVED
STERNO	SIESTA	SHUTIN	STATES	SERUMS	SERVER
STERNS	SLOSHY	SIFTED	STATIC	SETUPS	SERVES
STEROL	SLUSHY	SIFTER	STATOR	SEXUAL	SERVOS
STIRKS	SOUSED	SILTED	STATUE	SHOULD	SHAVED
STIRPS	SOUSES	SINTER	STATUS	SHOUTS	SHAVEN
STORAX	SPASMS	SISTER	STETHO	SHRUBS	SHAVER
STORED	STASES	SITTER	STITCH	SHRUGS	SHAVES
STORES	STASIS	SIXTES	STITHY	SHRUNK	SHIVER
STOREY	SUNSET	SIXTHS	SUBTER	SIEURS	SHIVES
STORKS	SUSSED	SKATED	SUBTLE	SIOUAN	SHOVED
STORMS	SUSSEX	SKATER	SUBTLY	SIRUPS	SHOVEL
STORMY	******	SKATES	SUITED	SIRUPY	SHOVER
STURDY	S--T--	SKETCH	SUITES	SLEUTH	SHOVES
SUCRES	******	SLATED	SUITOR	SLOUCH	SIEVED
SURREY	SAITIC	SLATER	SULTAN	SLOUGH	SIEVES
SUTRAS	SALTED	SLATES	SULTRY	SNOUTS	SILVAE
SWARAJ	SALTER	SLOTHS	SUNTAN	SOLUTE	SILVAN
SWARDS	SANTOL	SMITER	SURTAX	SPOUSE	SILVAS
SWARMS	SARTOR	SMITES	SUTTEE	SPOUTS	SILVER
SWARTH	SARTRE	SMITHS	SUTTON	SPRUCE	SILVIA
SWARTY	SAUTES	SMITHY	SWATCH	SPRUES	SKIVED
SWERVE	SCATHE	SMUTCH	SWATHE	SPRUNG	SKIVER
SWIRLS	SCATTY	SMUTTY	SWATHS	STAURO	SKIVES
SWIRLY	SCOTCH	SNATCH	SWITCH	STOUPS	SKIVVY
SWORDS	SCOTER	SNATHE	SYNTAX	STOUTS	SLAVED
******	SCOTIA	SNATHS	SYSTEM	STRUCK	SLAVER
S--S--	SCOTTS	SNITCH	******	STRUMA	SLAVES
******	SCUTCH	SNOTTY	S--U--	STRUMS	SLAVIC
SAMSHU	SCUTES	SOFTAS	******	STRUNG	SLIVER
SAMSON	SCUTUM	SOFTEN	SALUKI	STRUTS	SLOVAK
SANSAR	SCYTHE	SOFTER	SALUTE	SUBURB	SLOVEN
SANSEI	SEATED	SOFTLY	SAMUEL	SUNUPS	SNIVEL

SOEVER	******	TITANS	TWIBIL	TEDDED	THREAD
SOLVED	**S--Y--**	TOBAGO	TWOBIT	TEDDER	THREAT
SOLVER	******	TOGAED	******	TEDDYS	THREED
SOLVES	SATYRS	TOMANS	**T--C--**	TENDED	THREES
SPAVIN	SAWYER	TOMATO	******	TENDER	THRESH
STAVED	SIBYLS	TORAHS	TALCED	TENDON	TIGERS
STAVES	SLAYER	TOTALS	TALCUM	THADDY	TILERS
STEVEN	SONYAS	TOWAGE	TEACUP	THADYS	TIMELY
STEVES	SPAYED	TOWARD	TERCEL	THEDAS	TIMERS
STEVIE	SPRYER	TREADS	TERCET	TILDES	TINEID
STIVER	SPRYLY	TREATS	TETCHY	TINDER	TOKENS
STOVER	STAYED	TREATY	TEUCER	TODDLE	TOLEDO
STOVES	STAYER	TRIADS	THECAE	TRADED	TONERS
SURVEY	SWAYED	TRIALS	THECAL	TRADER	TOPEKA
SWIVEL	SYZYGY	TRUANT	TINCAL	TRADES	TOPERS
SWIVET	******	TUBATE	TINCAN	TRUDGE	TORERO
SYLVAE	**S--Z--**	TULADI	TINCTS	TRUDYS	TOTEMS
SYLVAN	******	TWEAKS	TIPCAT	TSADES	TOTERS
SYLVAS	SEIZED	TWEAKY	TOECAP	TUNDRA	TOWELS
SYLVIA	SEIZER	TYBALT	TOMCAT	******	TOWERS
******	SEIZES	TYRANT	TOMCOD	**T--E--**	TOWERY
S--W--	SEIZIN	******	TOUCAN		TOYERS
******	SEIZOR	**T--B--**	TOUCHE	TAKEIN	TRIERS
SCHWAS	SIZZLE	******	TOUCHY	TAKERS	TRUEST
SCOWLS	SMAZES	TABBED	TRACED	TAKEUP	TUBERS
SEAWAN	SNAZZY	TAMBAC	TRACER	TALENT	TUMEFY
SEAWAY	******	TEABAG	TRACES	TALERS	TUNERS
SELWYN	**T--A--**	TERBIA	TRACHE	TAMELY	TUNEUP
SHAWLS	******	THEBAE	TRACHY	TAMERS	TUPELO
SHAWMS	TABARD	THEBES	TRACKS	TAMEST	TUREEN
SHEWED	TALARI	TIDBIT	TRACTS	TAPERS	TUXEDO
SHEWER	TAMALE	TIMBAL	TRICAR	TAVERN	TUYERE
SHOWED	TAPALO	TIMBER	TRICED	TAWERS	TWEEDS
SHOWER	TATARS	TIMBRE	TRICES	TAXEME	TWEETS
SKEWED	TELARY	TITBIT	TRICHI	TAXERS	******
SKEWER	TENACE	TOMBAC	TRICHO	TEHEED	**T--F--**
SKYWAY	TENANT	TOMBED	TRICKS	TEHEES	******
SLEWED	TERAPH	TOMBOY	TRICKY	TELEDU	TELFER
SLOWED	TERATO	TREBLE	TRICOT	TELEGA	THEFTS
SLOWER	TETANY	TRIBAL	TROCAR	TENETS	TIFFED
SLOWLY	THRALL	TRIBES	TROCHE	TEPEES	TIFFIN
SNOWED	THRASH	TUBBED	TRUCES	TEPEFY	TOFFEE
SPAWNS	THWACK	TUBBER	TRUCKS	TEREDO	TRIFID
SPEWED	THWART	TUMBLE	TURCOS	TERESA	TRIFLE
STEWED	TICALS	TURBAN	TUSCAN	TERETE	TUFFET
STOWED	TIRADE	TURBID	******	TEREUS	TURFED
SUBWAY	TIRANA	TURBIT	**T--D--**	TEVERE	TWOFER
	TISANE	TURBOT	******	THIEVE	
			TANDEM		
			TAWDRY		

******	TUSHED	TOBIAH	TALKED	TILLYS	TRIMLY
T--G--	TUSHES	TOBIAS	TALKER	TITLED	TRUMAN
******	TYPHLO	TOBIES	TALKIE	TITLES	TRUMPS
TAGGED	TYPHON	TODIES	TANKAS	TOILED	******
TAGGER	TYPHUS	TOEING	TANKED	TOILER	T--N--
TAIGAS	******	TONICS	TANKER	TOILES	******
TANGED	T--I--	TONIER	TASKED	TOILET	TAENIA
TANGLE	******	TONING	TICKED	TOLLED	TAINOS
TANGLY	TAHITI	TONITE	TICKER	TOLLER	TAINTS
TANGOS	TAKING	TOPICS	TICKET	TOOLED	TANNED
TARGET	TALION	TOPING	TICKLE	TOOLER	TANNER
TAUGHT	TAMING	TORIES	TINKER	TOULON	TANNIC
TERGAL	TANIST	TORIIS	TINKLE	TRILBY	TANNIN
TERGUM	TAOISM	TOTING	TINKLY	TRILLS	TARNAL
THIGHS	TAOIST	TOWING	TONKIN	TROLLS	TAUNTS
TINGED	TAPING	TOXINS	TUCKED	TUILLE	TBONES
TINGES	TAPIRS	TOYING	TUCKER	TULLES	TEENSY
TINGLE	TARIFF	TOYISH	TUCKET	TWELVE	TENNIS
TINGLY	TARING	TRAILS	TURKEY	TWILIT	TERNAL
TOGGED	TAWING	TRAINS	TURKIC	TWILLS	THANAT
TOGGLE	TAXIED	TRAITS	TURKIS	******	THANES
TONGED	TAXING	TROIKA	TUSKED	T--M--	THANKS
TONGUE	TAXITE	TRUING	TUSKER	******	THENAL
TOUGHS	TEDIUM	TRUISM	******	TALMUD	THENAR
TRAGIC	TEEING	TRYING	T--L--	TARMAC	THENCE
TRAGUS	THEIRS	TSHIRT	******	TASMAN	THINGS
TRIGLY	THEISM	TUBING	TABLED	TEAMED	THINLY
TRIGON	THEIST	TULIPS	TABLES	TEEMED	THONGS
TROGON	THRICE	TUNICA	TABLET	TEEMER	TINNED
TUGGED	THRIFT	TUNICS	TAILED	TEGMEN	TINNER
TUNGUS	THRILL	TUNING	TAILLE	TERMED	TRANCE
TURGID	THRIPS	TUPIKS	TAILOR	TERMER	TRENCH
TWIGGY	THRIVE	TYPIFY	TALLER	TERMLY	TRENDS
******	TIBIAE	TYPING	TALLOW	TERMOR	TRENDY
T--H--	TIBIAL	TYPIST	TATLER	THAMES	TRINAL
******	TIBIAS	TYRIAN	TAYLOR	THEMES	TRINED
TECHNO	TIDIED	******	TEFLON	THEMIS	TRINES
TETHER	TIDIER	T--J--	TELLER	THOMAS	TRUNKS
TETHYS	TIDIES	******	TELLUS	THUMBS	TUNNED
TIGHTS	TIDILY	THUJAS	THALER	THUMPS	TUNNEL
TISHRI	TIDING	TROJAN	THALES	THYMES	TURNED
TITHED	TIEINS	******	THALIA	THYMIC	TURNER
TITHER	TILING	T--K--	THELMA	THYMOL	TURNIP
TITHES	TIMING	******	THOLES	THYMUS	TURNUP
TOPHAT	TINIER	TACKED	THULIA	TIMMYS	TWANGS
TOSHES	TINILY	TACKER	TILLED	TOMMYS	TWANGY
TOTHER	TIRING	TACKEY	TILLER	TRAMPS	TWENTY
TUCHUN	TITIAN	TACKLE	TILLIE	TREMOR	TWINED

TWINER	TAPPET	TERRYS	TERSER	TATTOO	TSETSE
TWINES	TARPAN	TETRAD	TESSIE	TAUTEN	TUFTED
TWINGE	TAUPES	TETRYL	THESES	TAUTER	TURTLE
******	TEAPOT	THERMO	THESIS	TAUTLY	TUTTED
T--O--	TEAPOY	THERMS	THISBE	TAUTOG	TUTTIS
******	TEMPER	THIRDS	THUSLY	TEETER	TWITCH
TABOOS	TEMPLE	THIRST	TINSEL	TEETHE	******
TABORS	TEMPOS	THIRTY	TISSUE	TENTED	T--U--
TACOMA	TEMPTS	THORAC	TOASTS	TENTER	******
TALONS	TENPIN	THORAX	TOCSIN	TENTHS	TEAURN
TAROTS	TIEPIN	THORIA	TONSIL	TESTAE	TELUGU
TENONS	TINPOT	THORIC	TORSKS	TESTED	TENUES
TENORS	TIPPED	THORNS	TORSOS	TESTER	TENUIS
TETONS	TIPPER	THORNY	TOSSED	TESTES	TENURE
THEORY	TIPPET	THORON	TOSSES	TESTIS	TENUTO
THIOLS	TIPPLE	THORPE	TOSSUP	TESTON	THOUGH
THROAT	TOPPED	THYREO	TOUSLE	TETTER	THRUMS
THROBS	TOPPER	THYRSE	TRASHY	TEUTON	THRUSH
THROES	TOPPLE	THYRSI	TRESSY	THATCH	THRUST
THRONE	TORPID	TIARAS	TRISTE	THETAS	TIEUPS
THRONG	TORPOR	TIERCE	TRUSTS	THETIC	TOGUES
THROVE	TOUPEE	TIERED	TRUSTY	THETIS	TOLUOL
THROWN	TREPAN	TIGRIS	TRYSTS	TILTED	TOLUYL
THROWS	TRIPLE	TORRID	TUCSON	TILTER	TOQUES
TIPOFF	TRIPOD	TOURED	TUSSAH	TILTHS	TRAUMA
TOROID	TRIPOS	TOURER	TUSSAL	TINTED	TRIUNE
TOROSE	TROPAL	TURRET	TUSSAR	TIPTOE	TROUGH
TOROUS	TROPHO	TWERPS	TUSSIS	TIPTOP	TROUPE
TOYONS	TROPHY	TWIRLS	TUSSLE	TITTER	TROUTS
TRIODE	TROPIC	TWIRPS	TWISTS	TITTLE	TUBULE
TRIOSE	TROPPO	******	TWISTY	TITTUP	TUMULT
TROOPS	TUPPED	T--S--	******	TOLTEC	TUQUES
TRYOUT	TWOPLY	******	T--T--	TOMTIT	TWOULD
TUMORS	TYMPAN	TARSAL	******	TOMTOM	******
TUMOUR	******	TARSIA	TACTIC	TOOTED	T--V--
TUTORS	T--Q--	TARSUS	TAMTAM	TOOTER	******
TYCOON	******	TASSEL	TARTAN	TOOTHY	TRAVEL
TYRONE	TORQUE	TASSET	TARTAR	TOOTLE	TRAVES
******	******	TEASED	TARTED	TOOTSY	TREVOR
T--P--	T--R--	TEASEL	TARTER	TOTTED	TRIVET
******	******	TEASER	TARTLY	TOTTER	TRIVIA
TAIPEI	TANREC	TEASES	TASTED	TOUTED	TROVER
TAMPAN	TARRED	TEASET	TASTER	TOUTER	TROVES
TAMPED	TAURUS	TELSON	TASTES	TRITER	TURVES
TAMPER	TEARED	TENSED	TATTED	TRITON	******
TAMPON	TENREC	TENSER	TATTER	TROTHS	T--W--
TAPPED	TERRET	TENSES	TATTLE	TROTYL	******
TAPPER	TERROR	TENSOR	TATTLY	TRUTHS	TAIWAN
					THAWED

THEWED	UNSAID	UNVEIL	UNLIVE	UPENDS	******
TRAWLS	UNSAYS	UNVEXT	UNPICK	URANIA	U--Q--
TROWEL	UNTACK	UNWELL	UNPILE	URANIC	******
TWOWAY	UNWARY	UNWEPT	UNPINS	URANUS	UNIQUE
******	UPCAST	UPBEAT	UNRIGS	URANYL	******
T--X--	UPDATE	UPHELD	UNRIPE	URINAL	U--R--
******	UPLAND	UPKEEP	UNRIPS	USANCE	******
TRIXIE	UPTAKE	UPPERS	UNTIDY	******	UMBRAE
TRIXYS	UPWARD	UPSETS	UNTIED	U--O--	UMBRAL
******	URBANE	URAEUS	UNTIES	******	UMBRAS
T--Y--	UREASE	URGENT	UNWIND	UNBOLT	UNBRED
******	UTGARD	URTEXT	UNWISE	UNBORN	UNDRAW
THAYER	******	USHERS	UNWISH	UNCOCK	UNDREW
******	U--B--	UTTERS	UPDIKE	UNCOIL	UNTROD
T--Z--	******	******	UPHILL	UNCORD	UNTRUE
******	UNABLE	U--F--	UPLIFT	UNCORK	UNWRAP
TARZAN	USABLE	******	UPPING	UNDOER	UPHROE
TAZZAS	USABLY	UNIFIC	UPPISH	UNDOES	USURER
TETZEL	******	USEFUL	UPPITY	UNDONE	USURPS
******	U--C--	******	UPRISE	UNFOLD	UTERUS
U--A--	******	U--G--	UPSIDE	UNHOLY	UTURNS
******	UNICEF	******	UREIDE	UNHOOK	******
UBOATS	******	USAGES	URGING	UNIONS	U--S--
ULLAGE	U--E--	******	URSINE	UNLOAD	******
UMIAKS	******	U--H--	UZZIAH	UNLOCK	UKASES
UMLAUT	UBIETY	******	******	UNMOOR	UNDSET
UNBARS	UDDERS	UNSHIP	U--L--	UNROBE	UNESCO
UNCAGE	ULCERS	UNSHOD	******	UNROLL	UNISEX
UNCAPS	UMBELS	UPSHOT	UMBLES	UNROOT	UNISON
UNCASE	UMBERS	URCHIN	UNCLAD	UNSOLD	UNUSED
UNEASE	UNBEAR	UTAHAN	UNCLES	UNTOLD	UPASES
UNEASY	UNBELT	******	UNPLUG	UNWORN	
UNFAIR	UNBEND	U--I--	URALIC	UNYOKE	U--T--
UNHAIR	UNBENT	******	UVULAE	UPBOWS	******
UNHAND	UNHEWN	UGLIER	UVULAR	UPHOLD	ULSTER
UNHASP	UNLEAD	UGLIFY	UVULAS	UPMOST	UNITED
UNHATS	UNLESS	UGLILY	******	UPROAR	UNITES
UNLACE	UNMEET	ULTIMA	U--M--	UPROOT	UNSTEP
UNLADE	UNMEWS	ULTIMO	******	UPROSE	UNSTOP
UNLAID	UNPEGS	UMPIRE	ULEMAS	UPTOWN	URETER
UNLASH	UNREAD	UNBIND	UREMIA	UTMOST	URETIC
UNLAYS	UNREAL	UNCIAL	******	******	******
UNMADE	UNREEL	UNDIES	U--N--	U--P--	U--U--
UNMAKE	UNREST	UNDINE	******	******	******
UNMANS	UNSEAL	UNGIRD	UBANGI	UNAPID	UNCURL
UNMASK	UNSEAM	UNGIRT	UGANDA	UNIPED	UNDULY
UNPACK	UNSEAT	UNKIND	ULENCE	UROPOD	UNFURL
UNSAFE	UNSEEN	UNLIKE	UNKNIT	UTOPIA	UNGUAL

UNGUES	VOICES	VERGER	VIVIAN	VAUNTS	******
UNGUIS	VULCAN	VERGES	VIVIEN	VEINED	V--S--
UNGULA	******	VERGIL	VIVIFY	VERNAL	******
UNHURT	V--D--	VIRGAS	VIZIER	VERNAS	VASSAL
UNHUSK	******	VIRGIE	VIZIRS	VERNIX	VERSED
UNJUST	VANDAL	VIRGIL	VOLING	VERNON	VERSES
UNRULY	VEADAR	VIRGIN	VOMICA	VIANDS	VERSET
UNSUNG	VELDTS	VULGAR	VOMITO	VIENNA	VERSOS
UNSURE	VENDED	******	VOMITS	VINNYS	VERSTS
UPRUSH	VENDEE	V--H--	VOTING	VYRNWY	VERSUS
UPTURN	VENDER	******	VOTIVE	******	VESSEL
URSULA	VENDOR	VASHTI	VOWING	V--O--	VINSON
******	VENDUE	VISHNU	******	******	******
U--V--	VERDIN	******	V--K--	VADOSE	V--T--
******	VERDUN	V--I--	******	VALOIS	******
UNEVEN	VOIDED	******	VALKYR	VALOUR	VASTER
******	VOODOO	VAGINA	VICKYS	VAMOSE	VASTLY
V--A--	******	VAGINO	VODKAS	VAPORI	VATTED
******	V--E--	VALISE	******	VAPORS	VECTOR
VACANT	VALERY	VANISH	V--L--	VAPOUR	VENTED
VACATE	VALETS	VANITY	******	VELOCE	VENTER
VAGARY	VENEER	VARICO	VALLEY	VELOUR	VENTRO
VALATE	VENERY	VARIED	VALLUM	VENOMS	VERTEX
VASARI	VEREIN	VARIER	VARLET	VENOSE	VESTAL
VICARS	VEXERS	VARIES	VAULTS	VENOUS	VESTAS
VIRAGO	VILELY	VASILI	VEILED	VERONA	VESTED
VISAED	VILEST	VEDIAC	VEILER	VETOED	VESTEE
VISAGE	VINERY	VENIAL	VELLUM	VETOER	VESTRY
VISARD	VIPERS	VENICE	VIALED	VETOES	VETTED
VITALS	VIREOS	VENIRE	VILLAS	VIGOUR	VIATIC
VIVACE	VISEED	VERIFY	VILLON	VINOUS	VIATOR
VIZARD	VIXENS	VERILY	VILLUS	VISORS	VICTIM
VOCALS	VOLERY	VERISM	VIOLAS	VIZORS	VICTOR
VOLANT	VOMERS	VERIST	VIOLET	VOLOST	VIRTUE
VOTARY	VOTERS	VERITY	VIOLIN	VOROUS	VISTAS
VOYAGE	VOWELS	VESICA	VOILES	******	VITTAE
******	VOWERS	VESICO	VOLLEY	V--P--	VOLTED
V--B--	VOYEUR	VEXILS	******	******	VORTEX
******	******	VEXING	V--M--	VAMPED	******
VERBAL	V--F--	VIGILS	******	VESPER	V--U--
VIABLE	******	VIKING	VANMAN	VESPID	******
******	VATFUL	VILIFY	VANMEN	******	VACUNA
V--C--	V--G--	VIMINA	VERMIN	V--R--	VACUUM
******	******	VINIER	******	******	VAGUER
VINCES	VALGUS	VIRILE	V--N--	VEERED	VALUED
VISCID	******	VISING	******	VIBRIO	VALUER
VISCUS	VALGUS	VISION	VAINER	VITRIC	VALUES
VOICED	VERGED	VISITS	VAINLY		VALUTA

VARUNA	******	WIDDIE	WRYEST	******	WELKIN
VELURE	W--B--	WILDER	WYVERN	W--I--	WICKED
VENUES	******	WILDLY		******	WICKER
VENULE	WABBLE	WINDED	W--F--	WADIES	WICKET
VICUNA	WABBLY	WINDER	******	WADING	WINKED
VIDUAL	WAMBLE	WINDOW	WAFFLE	WAGING	WINKER
VISUAL	WAMBLY	WINDUP	WAIFED	WAHINE	WINKLE
VOGUES	WARBLE	WISDOM	WHIFFS	WAKIKI	WORKED
VOGULS	WEBBED	WOADED	WILFUL	WAKING	WORKER
VOLUME	WILBER	WONDER	WOEFUL	WALING	******
VOLUTE	WILBUR	WOODED	WOLFED	WANING	W--L--
******	WIMBLE	WOODEN	WOOFER	WANION	******
V--V--	WOBBLE	WOODSY	******	WAPITI	WAILED
******	WOBBLY	WORDED	W--G--	WARIER	WAILER
VALVAL	WOMBAT	******	******	WARILY	WALLAH
VALVAR	WOMBED	W--E--	WAGGED	WAVIER	WALLAS
VALVED	******	******	WAGGLE	WAVIES	WALLED
VALVES	W--C--	WADERS	WAGGLY	WAVILY	WALLET
VARVES	******	WAFERS	WAGGON	WAVING	WALLIE
VELVET	WHACKS	WAGERS	WANGLE	WAXIER	WALLIS
VERVET	WINCED	WAKENS	WEDGED	WAXING	WALLOP
VOLVAS	WINCER	WALERS	WEDGES	WIKIUP	WALLOW
VOLVOX	WINCES	WATERS	WEDGIE	WILIER	WALLYS
VULVAE	WINCEY	WATERY	WEIGHS	WILILY	WAULED
VULVAL	WRACKS	WAVERS	WEIGHT	WILING	WAWLED
VULVAR	WRECKS	WAVEYS	WIGGED	WINIER	WAYLAY
******	******	WEBERS	WIGGLE	WINING	WEALDS
V--W--	W--D--	WEDELN	WIGGLY	WIPING	WEALTH
******	******	WERENT	WINGED	WIRIER	WELLED
VIEWED	WADDED	WHEELS	WRIGHT	WIRILY	WESLEY
VIEWER	WADDLE	WHEEZE	******	WIRING	WHALED
******	WADDLY	WHEEZY	W--H--	WISING	WHALER
V--Y--	WALDOS	WIDELY	******	WIVING	WHALES
******	WANDAS	WIDENS	WARHOL	WOOING	WHELKS
VINYLS	WANDER	WIDEST	WASHED	WOWING	WHELKY
******	WANDLE	WIFELY	WASHER	WRAITH	WHELMS
W--A--	WARDED	WIGEON	WASHES	WRYING	WHELPS
******	WARDEN	WINERY	WETHER	******	WHILED
WABASH	WARDER	WIPERS	WICHES	W--K--	WHILES
WAHABI	WEDDED	WIRERS	WISHED	******	WHILOM
WATAPE	WEEDED	WISELY	WISHES	WALKED	WHILST
WATAPS	WEEDER	WISEST	WITHAL	WALKER	WHOLLY
WHEALS	WELDED	WIVERN	WITHED	WALKON	WIELDS
WHEATS	WELDER	WIVERS	WITHER	WALKUP	WIELDY
WIGANS	WENDED	WIZENS	WITHES	WEAKEN	WILLED
WIZARD	WENDYS	WOMERA	WITHIN	WEAKER	WILLER
WREAKS	WHIDAH	WOOERS	WITHIT	WEAKLY	WILLET
WREATH	WHYDAH	WRIEST		WEEKLY	WILLIE

WILLIS	WOUNDS	WARSAW	WONTED	******	******
WILLOW	WRENCH	WATSON	WORTHY	**X--I--**	**Y--H--**
WILLYS	WRINGS	WEASEL	WRATHY	******	******
WOALDS	WRONGS	WESSEX	WRETCH	XAVIER	YACHTS
WOOLEN	******	WHISKS	WRITER	XENIAL	YOOHOO
WOOLLY	**W--O--**	WHISKY	WRITES	XYLITE	
WORLDS	******	WILSON	WRITHE	******	**Y--I--**
******	WAGONS	WOLSEY	WYSTAN	**X--O--**	******
W--M--	WAHOOS	WORSEN	******	******	YAKIMA
******	WAMOUS	WORSER	**W--U--**	XYLOID	YAWING
WAMMUS	WAYOUT	WORSTS		XYLOLS	YOGINS
WARMED	WHOOPS	WOWSER	WATUSI	XYLOSE	YOKING
WARMER	WHOOSH	WRASSE	******	******	YORICK
WARMLY	WICOPY	WRESTS	**W--V--**	**X--T--**	YOWING
WARMTH	WIDOWS	WRISTS	******	******	******
WARMUP	WINOES	******	WAIVED	XANTHO	**Y--K--**
WEIMAR	******	**W--T--**	WAIVER	XTSTUS	******
WHAMMY	**W--P--**	******	WAIVES	XYSTER	YAKKED
WHIMSY	******	WAFTED	WALVIS	XYSTOS	YANKED
WILMAS	WAMPUM	WAFTER	WEAVED	******	YANKEE
WORMED	WAPPED	WAITED	WEAVER	**X--Y--**	YONKER
WORMER	WARPED	WAITER	WEAVES	******	YORKER
******	WARPER	WALTER	WEEVER	XRAYED	YUKKED
W--N--	WEAPON	WALTON	WEEVIL	******	******
******	WEEPER	WANTED	WOLVER	**Y--B--**	**Y--L--**
WAGNER	WHIPPY	WANTER	WOLVES	******	******
WALNUT	WIMPLE	WANTON	**W--W--**	YABBER	YAWLED
WANNED	WISPED	WASTED	******	YERBAS	YELLED
WANNER	WRAPUP	WASTER	WIGWAG	******	YELLER
WARNED	******	WASTES	WIGWAM	**Y--C--**	YELLOW
WARNER	**W--R--**	WATTLE	******	******	YIELDS
WAYNES	******	WELTED	**W--Y--**	YOICKS	YOWLED
WEANED	WALRUS	WELTER	******	YUCCAS	
WEANER	WARRED	WESTER	WHEYEY	******	**Y--M--**
WEENIE	WARREN	WETTED	******	**Y--D--**	******
WEENSY	WEARER	WETTER	**W--Z--**	******	YAMMER
WHANGS	WEIRDY	WHITBY	******	YARDED	YASMAK
WHENCE	WHARFS	WHITED	WINZES	YONDER	YEOMAN
WHINED	WHARVE	WHITEN	******	******	YEOMEN
WHINER	WHERRY	WHITER	**X--A--**	**Y--E--**	YESMAN
WHINES	WHERVE	WHITES	******	******	******
WHINNY	WHIRLS	WHITEY	XANADU	YAGERS	**Y--N--**
WIENER	WHORED	WIDTHS	XYLANS	YAMENS	******
WIENIE	WHORES	WILTED	******	YCLEPT	YAWNED
WINNER	WHORLS	WILTON	**X--E--**	YEMENI	YAWNER
WINNIE	WHORTS	WINTER	******	YODELS	YEANED
WINNOW	******	WINTRY	XEBECS	YOGEES	YENNED
WITNEY	**W--S--**	WITTED	XYLEMS	YOKELS	YVONNE
	******		XYLENE		
	WADSET				
	WAISTS				

*****	*****	*****	ZIRONS	AEGEAN	ARARAT
Y--O--	**Y--V--**	**Z--G--**	ZYGOMA	AENEAS	ARAWAK
*****	*****	*****	ZYGOTE	AERIAL	ARECAS
YAHOOS	YAHVEH	ZENGER	*****	AFFRAY	ARENAS
YAPONS	*****	ZEUGMA	**Z--P--**	AFGHAN	AROMAS
YUPONS	**Y--W--**	ZINGED	*****	AFLOAT	ARREAR
*****	*****	*****	ZIPPED	AGAMAS	ASHCAN
Y--P--	YAHWEH	**Z--H--**	ZIPPER	AGAPAE	ASHLAR
*****	*****	*****	*****	AGLEAM	ASHMAN
YAPPED	**Z--A--**	ZECHIN	**Z--R--**	AGORAE	ASTRAL
YAUPED	*****	ZEPHYR	*****	AGORAS	ASTRAY
YAUPON	ZANANA	ZETHOS	ZEBRAS	AIDMAN	ATABAL
YAWPED	ZAPATA	ZETHUS	*****	AIRMAN	ATAMAN
YAWPER	ZENANA	ZITHER	**Z--S--**	AIRSAC	ATONAL
YELPED	ZONARY	*****	*****	AIRWAY	ATRIAL
YELPER	ZONATE	**Z--I--**	ZOYSIA	AJOWAN	AUGEAN
YIPPED	ZOUAVE	*****	*****	ALEGAR	AVATAR
YIPPIE	*****	ZAMIAS	**Z--T--**	ALIDAD	AVOWAL
YOUPON	**Z--B--**	ZANIER	*****	ALPHAS	AXEMAN
YUPPIE	*****	ZANIES	ZAFTIG	ALULAE	*****
*****	ZAMBIA	ZARIBA	ZESTED	ALULAR	**A---B-**
Y--R--	ZOMBIE	ZAYINS	ZLOTYS	AMEBAE	*****
*****	ZOMBIS	ZENITH	ZOSTER	AMEBAS	ABOMBS
YARROW	*****	ZIZITH	*****	AMORAL	ADLIBS
YEARLY	**Z--C--**	ZODIAC	**Z--U--**	AMYTAL	AEROBE
YEARNS	*****	ZONING	*****	ANABAS	AKIMBO
YTTRIA	ZINCED	ZOOIDS	ZONULA	ANANAS	AMOEBA
YTTRIC	ZINCIC	ZORILS	ZONULE	ANDEAN	ARDEBS
*****	ZINCKY	ZURICH	*****	ANIMAL	ARROBA
Y--S--	ZIRCON	*****	**Z--Z--**	ANIMAS	*****
*****	*****	**Z--L--**	*****	ANITAS	**A---C-**
YEASTS	**Z--D--**	*****	ZIGZAG	ANNEAL	*****
YEASTY	*****	ZEALOT	ZIZZLE	ANNUAL	ABBACY
YESSED	ZUIDER	ZILLAH	ZSAZSA	ANORAK	ABDUCT
YESSES	ZUYDER		*****	ANTIAR	ABJECT
*****	*****	**Z--M--**	**A---A-**	ANURAN	ACKACK
Y--T--	**Z--E--**	*****	*****	ANYWAY	ADDICT
*****	*****	ZOOMED	ABACAS	AORTAE	ADDUCE
YESTER	ZEBECK	*****	ABADAN	AORTAL	ADDUCT
YOUTHS	ZEBECS	**Z--N--**	ABIJAH	AORTAS	ADJECT
*****	ZIBETH	*****	ABOMAS	AOUDAD	ADVICE
Y--U--	ZIBETS	ZINNIA	ABORAL	APEMAN	AFFECT
*****	*****	ZOONAL	ABROAD	APICAL	AFRICA
YAMUNS	**Z--F--**	ZOUNDS	ACETAL	APNEAL	AGENCY
YAOURT	*****	*****	ACTUAL	APODAL	ALMUCE
YEHUDI	ZAFFAR	**Z--O--**	ADONAI	APPEAL	ALPACA
YOGURT	ZAFFER	*****	ADRIAN	APPEAR	ALSACE
YORUBA	ZAFFIR	ZEROED	AECIAL	APPIAN	AMERCE
	ZAFFRE	ZEROES			

ANLACE	ABIDER	AMBLES	ARNIES	AMBAGE	AFLCIO
ANTICS	ABIDES	AMICES	ARTIES	ANERGY	AFRAID
APIECE	ABODES	AMIDES	ASHIER	ANLAGE	AGAMIC
ARERCU	ABUSED	AMOLES	ASHLEY	ARMAGH	AGARIC
ARNICA	ABUSER	AMULET	ASHMEN	ASSIGN	AGLAIA
ARRACK	ABUSES	AMUSED	ASIDES	AURIGA	AGNAIL
ASPECT	ACHAEA	AMUSER	ASLEEP	AVENGE	AGONIC
ASPICS	ACUMEN	AMUSES	ATONED	AWEIGH	ALALIA
ATTACH	ADAGES	ANADEM	ATONER	******	ALARIC
ATTACK	ADDLED	ANDREA	ATONES	A---H-	ALBEIT
ATTICA	ADDLES	ANDREI	ATTLEE	******	ALCAIC
ATTICS	ADOBES	ANDRES	AUBREY	AGATHA	ALCUIN
AVOUCH	ADORED	ANDREW	AUDREY	ALEPHS	ALEXIA
AZTECS	ADORER	ANGLED	AUKLET	ALIGHT	ALEXIN
******	ADORES	ANGLER	AUSPEX	ALMAHS	ALEXIS
A---D-	ADRIEN	ANGLES	AUSTEN	AMECHE	ALGOID
******	AEETES	ANISES	AUSTER	APACHE	ALIBIS
ABRADE	AERIED	ANKLES	AUTOED	APATHY	ALICIA
ACCEDE	AERIES	ANKLET	AVOCET	APHTHA	ALTAIC
ACNODE	AETHER	ANNIES	AVOSET	ARIGHT	ALTAIR
AGENDA	AGATES	ANODES	AVOWED	AYESHA	ALUMIN
ALBEDO	AGAVES	ANSWER	AVOWER	******	AMALIE
ALLUDE	AGONES	ANTEED	AWAKED	A---I-	AMANIA
ALMUDE	AGREED	ANTHEA	AWAKEN	******	AMEBIC
ALMUDS	AGREES	ANTHEM	AWAKES	AALIIS	AMELIA
AMANDA	AIDMEN	ANTHER	AWHEEL	ABATIS	AMELIE
AMENDS	AIGLET	ANTLER	AWOKEN	ABULIA	AMIDIC
APHIDS	AILEEN	ANUSES	AXEMEN	ACACIA	AMIDIN
ARCADE	AIRBED	APEXES	AXONES	ACADIA	AMYLIC
ARMADA	AIRIER	APICES	AXSEED	ACARID	ANEMIA
AROIDS	AIRMEN	APNOEA	AZALEA	ACEDIA	ANEMIC
AUBADE	AISLED	APOGEE	AZAZEL	ACERIC	ANGLIA
AUDADS	AISLES	APPLES	AZINES	ACETIC	ANGLIC
AVOIDS	AKENES	ARABEL	AZOLES	ACHAIA	ANILIN
AWARDS	ALATED	ARCHED	AZORES	ACIDIC	ANODIC
******	ALFRED	ARCHEO	AZRAEL	ACQUIT	ANOMIA
A---E-	ALICES	ARCHER	AZURES	ADAGIO	ANOMIC
******	ALINED	ARCHES	******	ADENIS	ANOMIE
AACHEN	ALINES	ARCKED	A---F-	ADIPIC	ANOXIA
ABASED	ALIPED	ARETES	******	ADJOIN	ANOXIC
ABASER	ALLIED	ARGUED	ADRIFT	ADONIC	ANTLIA
ABASES	ALLIES	ARGUER	AERIFY	ADONIS	ANTRIM
ABATED	ALTHEA	ARGUES	AGRAFE	ADROIT	ANUBIS
ABATER	ALUDEL	ARISEN	ARGUFY	AENEID	AORTIC
ABATES	AMAZED	ARISES	******	AEOLIA	APNEIC
ABBIES	AMAZES	ARLEEN	A---G-	AEOLIC	APULIA
ABELES	AMBLED	ARMIES	******	AEOLIS	ARABIA
ABIDED	AMBLER	ARMLET	AERUGO	AFFAIR	ARABIC
			ALLEGE		

ARCHIE	ANGOLA	AUTUMN	ANCONA	******	ADDERS
ARCHIL	ANKYLO	AXIOMS	ANCONE	A---O-	ADHERE
ARCTIC	ANNALS	******	ANGINA	******	ADJURE
ARMPIT	ANNULS	A---N-	ANIONS	ABATOR	ADMIRE
ARTOIS	ANSELM	******	ANNONA	ABLOOM	ADSORB
ASSAIL	ANVILS	AALAND	ANOINT	ABYDOS	ADVERB
ASSAIS	APOLLO	AARONS	ANTONS	ACAJOU	ADVERT
ASTRID	APPALL	ABOUND	ANTONY	ACTION	AFFIRM
ATAVIC	APPALS	ABSENT	ANYONE	ALAMOS	AFFORD
ATAXIA	APPELS	ACAENA	APHONY	ALBION	AGGERS
ATAXIC	APRILS	ACCENT	APPEND	ALISON	AIDERS
ATOMIC	AQUILA	ACHENE	APRONS	ALPHOS	AIRDRY
ATONIC	ARABLE	ACHING	ARCANA	AMADOU	ALBERT
ATTAIN	ARBELA	ACORNS	ARCANE	AMATOL	ALDERS
AUNTIE	ARCHLY	ACTING	ARCING	AMAZON	ALLURE
AUSTIN	AREOLA	ACTINI	ARDENT	AMIDOL	ALMIRA
AVIDIN	ARGALA	ACTINO	ARGENT	AMIGOS	ALTARS
AZONIC	ARGALI	ADDEND	ARIANS	AMNION	ALTERS
AZOTIC	ARGALS	ADDING	ARLENE	ANALOG	AMBARI
******	ARGYLL	ADORNS	ARLINE	ANCHOR	AMBARY
A---K-	ARIDLY	ADVENT	ARMAND	ANGKOR	AMBERS
******	ARIELS	AGEING	ARMING	ANYHOW	AMBERY
ALASKA	ARNOLD	AIDING	AROUND	APOLOG	AMENRA
ALFAKI	ARTELS	AILING	ARPENS	ARAGON	AMOURS
ALSIKE	ARTILY	AIMING	ARPENT	ARCHON	AMPERE
ANANKE	ATOLLS	AIRING	ARRANT	ASIMOV	AMPHRS
AXLIKE	ATTILA	ALBANY	ARSINE	AUTHOR	ANGARY
******	AUDILE	ALBINO	ARYANS	AVALON	ANGERS
A---L-	AVAILS	ALDINE	ASCEND	AVISOS	ANGORA
******	AVIDLY	ALFONS	ASCENT	******	ANITRA
ABOLLA	AWHILE	ALIENS	ASIANS	A---P-	ANKARA
ABVOLT	AXILLA	ALIGNS	ASKANT	******	ANTERO
ACIDLY	******	ALKANE	ASKING	ABRUPT	APIARY
AEDILE	A---M-	ALKENE	ASLANT	ACCEPT	APPORT
AFIELD	******	ALKYNE	ASPENS	ADOLPH	ARBORI
AGEDLY	ABOHMS	ALLANS	ASSENT	ALEPPO	ARBORS
AGEOLD	ABRAMS	ALLENS	ATHENA	ASLOPE	ARDORS
AIRILY	ABYSMS	ALMOND	ATHENE	******	ARMORS
ALIBLE	ADDAMS	ALPINE	ATHENS	A---R-	ARMORY
ALKALI	ADEEMS	ALUINO	ATTEND	******	ARMURE
ALKYLS	AFLAME	ALUINS	ATTUNE	ABHORS	ARTERY
ALLELE	AFRAME	ALUMNA	AUGEND	ABJURE	ARTHRO
ALLYLS	ALARMS	ALUMNI	AUXINS	ABNERS	ARTURO
AMPULE	ALBUMS	ALVANS	AVAUNT	ABOARD	ASBURY
AMPULS	APLOMB	ALVINA	AVERNO	ABSORB	ASGARD
ANGELA	ASSUME	ALVINE	AWEING	ABSURD	ASHORE
ANGELO	ASTHMA	AMIENS	AWNING	ACCORD	ASKERS
ANGELS	ATHOME	AMOUNT		ACTORS	ASPERS

ASPIRE	ARIOSO	APLITE	ANTRUM	ARROYO	BETRAY
ASSERT	AROUSE	ARANTA	ARBOUR	ASSAYS	BEULAH
ASSORT	ARREST	ARBUTE	ARDOUR	AVERYS	BEULAS
ASSURE	ARTIST	ARGOTS	ARIOUS	AYEAYE	BEZOAR
ASTERI	ASSESS	ARISTA	ARMFUL	******	BHUTAN
ASTERN	ASSISI	ARISTO	ARMOUR	A---Z-	BIAXAL
ASTERO	ASSIST	ARMETS	ARNAUD	******	BILBAO
ASTERS	ATTEST	ARUNTA	ARTFUL	ABLAZE	BISCAY
ATTARS	AUGUST	ASCOTS	ARTHUR	ALONZO	BOBCAT
ATTIRE	AURIST	ASSETS	ASARUM	AREZZO	BOGOAK
ATTORN	AUTISM	ASTUTE	ASYLUM	ASSIZE	BOMBAY
AUBURN	AVERSE	AUDITS	ATREUS	******	BONSAI
AUGERS	AWLESS	AUGHTS	ATRIUM	B---A-	BOREAL
AUGURS	A---T-	AUGITE	AUREUS	******	BOREAS
AUGURY	******	AURATE	AUROUS	BADMAN	BOWMAN
AURORA	ABBOTS	AVERTS	AVENUE	BAGDAD	BOWSAW
AUSTRO	ABORTS	AVESTA	******	BAGMAN	BOXCAR
AVIARY	ABWATT	AVIATE	A---V-	BAIKAL	BRAZAS
AWEARY	ACANTH	AWAITS	******	BALAAM	BRIDAL
AWHIRL	ACUATE	******	ACTIVE	BALKAN	BROGAN
AYMARA	ACUITY	A---U-	ALCOVE	BALLAD	BROMAL
******	ADAPTS	ABACUS	ARGIVE	BALSAM	BRUMAL
A---S-	ADEPTS	ABLAUT	ARRIVE	BALSAS	BRUTAL
******	ADMITS	ACCRUE	******	BALZAC	BUCCAL
ABBESS	ADNATE	ACEIUM	A---W-	BANIAN	BUCHAN
ABLEST	ADOPTS	ACEOUS	******	BANTAM	BULBAR
ABLUSH	ADULTS	ACETUM	ALLOWS	BANYAN	BULGAR
ACCESS	AERATE	ACINUS	ARROWS	BANZAI	BULLAE
ACCOST	AGENTS	ACIOUS	ARROWY	BAOBAB	BUNYAN
ACCUSE	AGISTS	ACTIUM	******	BARMAN	BUREAU
ACROSS	AGLETS	ADIEUS	A---X-	BASHAW	BURIAL
ADJUST	AGNATE	ADIEUX	******	BASRAH	BURLAP
ADVISE	AGOUTI	ADNOUN	ADMIXT	BATAAN	BURSAE
AFRESH	AGOUTY	ADYTUM	ANNEXE	BATEAU	BURSAL
AFTOSA	ALBATA	AEACUS	******	BATMAN	BURSAR
AGHAST	ALBITE	AEGEUS	A---Y-	BAZAAR	BURSAS
AGUISH	ALCOTT	AEOLUS	******	BEDLAM	BUSMAN
AHIMSA	ALECTO	AFFLUX	ABBEYS	BEDPAN	BYPLAY
ALDOSE	ALERTS	AGOGUE	ACETYL	BEGGAR	BYROAD
ALMOST	ALEUTS	AIRGUN	ALLAYS	BEHEAD	******
ALONSO	ALLOTS	ALARUM	ALLEYS	BELDAM	B---B-
AMBUSH	AMBITS	ALDOUS	ALLOYS	BELGAS	******
AMIDST	AMENTI	ALGOUS	ALPHYL	BELIAL	BLEBBY
AORIST	AMENTS	ALLIUM	ALWAYS	BELLAS	BLOWBY
APEPSY	AMRITA	ALLOUT	ANNOYS	BEMEAN	BLURBS
APPOSE	ANATTO	AMYLUM	ANONYM	BEMOAN	******
ARGOSY	ANSATE	ANIMUS	ARCHYS	BENDAY	B---C-
ARIOSE			ARRAYS	BENGAL	******
					BARUCH
					BASICS

BEDECK	BROADS	BARLEY	BELIES	BLADED	BORNEO
BIANCA	BROODS	BARMEN	BELLED	BLADES	BOSHES
BIERCE	BROODY	BARNEY	BELLES	BLAMED	BOSKET
BISECT	BUILDS	BARRED	BELTED	BLAMES	BOSSED
BLANCH	******	BARREL	BENDED	BLARED	BOSSES
BLEACH	B---E-	BARREN	BENDEE	BLARES	BOTHER
BLENCH	******	BARRET	BENDER	BLAZED	BOULES
BLOTCH	BABIED	BARTER	BENNES	BLAZER	BOUSED
BODICE	BABIES	BARYES	BENNET	BLAZES	BOUSES
BONACI	BACHED	BASHED	BERBER	BLIMEY	BOWLED
BORSCH	BACHES	BASHES	BERGEN	BLOKES	BOWLEG
BOUNCE	BACKED	BASKED	BERMES	BLOWER	BOWLER
BOUNCY	BACKER	BASKET	BERNEY	BOATED	BOWMEN
BRANCH	BADGED	BASSES	BESEEM	BOATER	BOWSED
BREACH	BADGER	BASSET	BESTED	BOBBED	BOWSES
BREECH	BADGES	BASTED	BETHEL	BOBBER	BOWYER
BROACH	BADMEN	BASTES	BETTED	BODIED	BRACED
BRONCO	BAFFED	BATHED	BETTER	BODIES	BRACER
BRONCS	BAGGED	BATHER	BETTES	BOGGED	BRACES
BROOCH	BAGMEN	BATMEN	BEVIES	BOGIES	BRAKED
BRUNCH	BAILED	BATTED	BIASED	BOGLES	BRAKES
******	BAILEE	BATTEN	BIASES	BOILED	BRAVED
B---D-	BAILER	BATTER	BIBBED	BOILER	BRAVER
******	BAILEY	BAWLED	BIBBER	BOLDER	BRAVES
BEARDS	BAITED	BAWLER	BIBLES	BOLLED	BRAYED
BESIDE	BALDER	BAXTER	BICKER	BOLTED	BRAYER
BETIDE	BALEEN	BEADED	BIDDEN	BOLTER	BRAZED
BIPEDS	BALKED	BEAKED	BIDDER	BOMBED	BRAZEN
BIPODS	BALLED	BEAKER	BIFFED	BOMBER	BRAZER
BLEEDS	BALLET	BEAMED	BIFLEX	BOMBES	BRAZES
BLENDE	BANDED	BEANED	BIGGER	BONDED	BREMEN
BLENDS	BANGED	BEARED	BILGED	BONDER	BREVES
BLINDS	BANKED	BEARER	BILGES	BONGED	BREVET
BLONDE	BANKER	BEATEN	BILKED	BONIER	BREWED
BLONDS	BANNED	BEATER	BILKER	BONNET	BREWER
BLOODS	BANNER	BEAVER	BILLED	BONZER	BRIBED
BLOODY	BANTER	BECKED	BILLET	BONZES	BRIBER
BOARDS	BARBED	BECKET	BINDER	BOOKED	BRIBES
BOLIDE	BARBEL	BEDDED	BINGES	BOOMED	BRIDES
BORIDE	BARBER	BEDDER	BINNED	BOOMER	BRINED
BOUNDS	BARBET	BEEFED	BIOGEN	BOOTED	BRINES
BRAIDS	BARDED	BEEPED	BIRLED	BOOTEE	BROKEN
BRANDS	BARDES	BEEVES	BIRLES	BOOZED	BROKER
BRANDT	BARGED	BEGGED	BIRRED	BOOZER	BROMES
BRANDY	BARGEE	BEIGES	BISTER	BOOZES	BRUCES
BREADS	BARGES	BELIED	BITTED	BOPPED	BRUGES
BREEDS	BARKED	BELIEF	BITTEN	BORDEL	BRUMES
BRENDA	BARKER	BELIER	BITTER	BORDER	BRUNEI

BRUNEL	BURNET	BERTHA	BELGIC	BELIKE	BODILY
BRUTES	BURPED	BERTHE	BELOIT	BETAKE	BOGGLE
BUBOES	BURRED	BERTHS	BERLIN	BLACKS	BOLDLY
BUCKED	BURSES	BIRTHS	BERNIE	BLANKS	BOODLE
BUCKER	BUSHED	BITCHY	BERTIE	BLEAKS	BOOTLE
BUCKET	BUSHEL	BLIGHT	BESSIE	BLINKS	BOTFLY
BUDDED	BUSHES	BLITHE	BESTIR	BLOCKS	BOTTLE
BUDDER	BUSHEY	BOOTHS	BEWAIL	BLOCKY	BOUCLE
BUDGED	BUSIED	BOTCHY	BIBLIO	BREAKS	BOWELS
BUDGES	BUSIES	BOUGHS	BIFFIN	BREEKS	BRAILS
BUDGET	BUSKER	BOUGHT	BIGGIN	BRICKS	BRAWLS
BUFFED	BUSMEN	BRACHI	BIGWIG	BRINKS	BRIDLE
BUFFER	BUSSED	BRACHY	BILLIE	BRISKS	BRILLS
BUFFET	BUSSES	BRASHY	BIOSIS	BROOKE	BROILS
BUGGED	BUSTED	BRECHT	BIOTIC	BROOKS	BROLLY
BUGGER	BUSTER	BRIGHT	BIOTIN	******	BUBALS
BUGLED	BUTLER	BROCHE	BIRDIE	**B---L-**	BUBBLE
BUGLER	BUTTED	BROTHS	BOBBIE	******	BUBBLY
BUGLES	BUTTER	BRUSHY	BOBBIN	BABBLE	BUCKLE
BULBED	BUTTES	BUDDHA	BOCCIE	BABULS	BUDDLE
BULBEL	BUZZED	BUNCHE	BODKIN	BAFFLE	BUMBLE
BULGED	BUZZER	BUNCHY	BOFFIN	BAGELS	BUNDLE
BULGER	BUZZES	BURGHS	BOLLIX	BALDLY	BUNGLE
BULGES	******	******	BOMBIC	BANGLE	BURBLE
BULKED	**B---F-**	**B---I-**	BONNIE	BARELY	BURGLE
BULLET	******	******	BOOGIE	BARFLY	BUSILY
BUMMED	BASIFY	BAALIM	BOOKIE	BASALT	BUSTLE
BUMMER	BEREFT	BABBIE	BOOTIE	BASELY	BYTALK
BUMPED	BLUFFS	BAFFIN	BORGIA	BASILS	******
BUMPER	BOUFFE	BAGNIO	BOUGIE	BATTLE	**B---M-**
BUNGED	BRIEFS	BAHAIS	BOWFIN	BAUBLE	******
BUNKED	******	BAILIE	BOWTIE	BEADLE	BAHAMA
BUNKER	**B---G-**	BALTIC	BRAZIL	BEAGLE	BECAME
BUNSEN	******	BALTIM	BREWIS	BECALM	BECOME
BUNTED	BAREGE	BANDIT	BRIDIE	BEETLE	BEDIMS
BUOYED	BEFOGS	BARBIE	BRIGID	BEFALL	BEGUMS
BURDEN	BEINGS	BARDIC	BROMIC	BEFELL	BENUMB
BURGEE	BELUGA	BARMIE	BUDGIE	BEHALF	BESOMS
BURGER	BENIGN	BARRIE	BULBIL	BEHELD	BIGAMY
BURIED	BLUNGE	BARRIO	BUMKIN	BEHOLD	BIREME
BURIES	BODEGA	BATTIK	BUNYIP	BERYLS	BLOOMS
BURKED	BORAGE	BATTIN	BURDIE	BETELS	BLOOMY
BURKES	BOURGS	BAUCIS	BUSKIN	BEVELS	BOSOMS
BURLED	BRIDGE	BEANIE	BUSTIC	BEZELS	BRAHMA
BURLER	BRINGS	BEDRID	******	BIFOLD	BRAHMS
BURLEY	******	BEDSIT	**B---K-**	BIKOLS	BREAMS
BURNED	**B---H-**	BEDUIN	******	BLUELY	BREGMA
BURNER	******	BEGUIN	BAMAKO	BOBBLE	BROOMS
	BEACHY		BATIKS		
	BEECHY				

BROOMY	BRAINS	BLAZON	BEMIRE	BRASSY	BRANTS
BYNAME	BRAINY	BOLSON	BEWARE	BREAST	BREATH
******	BRANNY	BOLTON	BIAFRA	BROWSE	BRENTS
B---N-	BRAWNY	BONBON	BICARB	BRUISE	BRONTE
******	BROWNS	BONGOS	BICORN	BYPASS	BRUITS
BAAING	BRUINS	BOOBOO	BIFORM	BYPAST	BURSTS
BACONY	BRYANT	BOOHOO	BIHARI	******	BYPATH
BAIRNS	BRYONY	BORROW	BINARY	B---T-	******
BAKING	BURANS	BORZOI	BISTRO	******	B---U-
BALING	BURINS	BOSTON	BITERS	******	******
BANANA	BUSING	BOTTOM	BLEARS	BABITE	BANGUI
BARING	BUTANE	BOWWOW	BLEARY	BALATA	BANGUP
BARONG	BUYING	BRAVOS	BLURRY	BARITE	BANTUS
BARONS	BYGONE	BRAZOS	BOLERO	BARYTA	BARIUM
BARONY	BYLANE	BRETON	BONERS	BASUTO	BARNUM
BASING	BYLINE	BRITON	BORERS	BEASTS	BARQUE
BASINS	******	BRULOT	BOWERS	BEAUTS	BASQUE
BATING	B---O-	BRUNOS	BOWERY	BEAUTY	BATTUE
BATONS	******	BUNCOS	BOXERS	BEFITS	BAYEUX
BAYING	BABOON	BUNION	BOYARD	BEGETS	BAYOUS
BEGINS	BABOOS	BURBOT	BOYARS	BEMATA	BEDAUB
BEGONE	BAILOR	BURGOO	BRIARS	BENITA	BEDBUG
BEHIND	BALBOA	BURGOS	BRIERS	BENITO	BEFOUL
BELONG	BALLOT	BURROS	BRIERY	BERATE	BEIRUT
BERING	BAMBOO	BURROW	BUCKRA	BERETS	BIJOUX
BESANT	BANGOR	BURTON	BUYERS	BESETS	BISQUE
BETONY	BANJOS	BUTTON	BYWORD	BESOTS	BLOWUP
BEYOND	BARROW	BUXTON	BYWORK	BIDETS	BRAQUE
BEZANT	BARTOK	BYBLOW	******	BIGHTS	BROGUE
BIDING	BARTON	******	B---S-	BILITY	BRUTUS
BIGONE	BARYON.	B---P-	******	BINATE	BULBUL
BIKINI	BASION	******	BABISM	BINITS	BUNKUM
BITING	BASSOS	BICEPS	BABIST	BLASTO	BYSSUS
BLAINS	BATHOS	BLIMPS	BAGASS	BLASTS	******
BLENNY	BEACON	******	BANISH	BLEATS	B---V-
BLUING	BECKON	B---R-	BAREST	BLINTZ	******
BODING	BEFOOL	******	BASEST	BLOATS	BEHAVE
BOGANS	BEHOOF	BAKERS	BEHEST	BLUETS	BEHOVE
BONING	BELLOC	BAKERY	BEMUSE	BLUNTS	******
BOOING	BELLOW	BALERS	BETISE	BLURTS	B---W-
BORANE	BENTON	BARBRA	BIOPSY	BOASTS	******
BORING	BENZOL	BAWDRY	BLAISE	BOGOTA	BEDEWS
BOTANY	BESTOW	BAYARD	BLOUSE	BONITO	BYLAWS
BOURNE	BETOOK	BEFORE	BLUEST	BOOSTS	
BOURNS	BETTOR	BEGIRD	BLUISH	BORATE	B---X-
BOVINE	BILLON	BEGIRT	BOURSE	BOUNTY	******
BOWING	BILLOW	BELFRY	BOYISH	BOVATE	BILOXI
BOXING	BISHOP		BRAISE	BRACTS	

******	CARFAX	CONGAS	******	******	CAREER
B---Y-	CARLAS	CONMAN	C---C-	C---E-	CARIES
******	CARMAN	CONRAD	******	******	CARMEL
BARRYS	CARNAL	CONWAY	CALICO	CABLED	CARMEN
BECKYS	CARPAL	COPRAH	CANUCK	CABLES	CARPED
BELAYS	CASBAH	CORBAN	CARACK	CABLET	CARPEL
BENJYS	CASHAW	CORDAY	CHALCO	CABMEN	CARPER
BENNYS	CASPAR	CORRAL	CHANCE	CACHED	CARPET
BENZYL	CASUAL	CORSAC	CHANCY	CACHES	CARREL
BESSYS	CATHAY	COSTAE	CHINCH	CACHET	CARTED
BETSYS	CATNAP	COSTAL	CHOICE	CADGED	CARTEL
BETTYS	CAUDAD	COSTAR	CHURCH	CADGER	CARTER
BIALYS	CAUDAL	COTEAU	CILICE	CADGES	CARTES
BILLYS	CAUSAL	COTTAE	CIVICS	CADRES	CARVED
BOBBYS	CAVEAT	COTTAR	CLENCH	CAGIER	CARVEL
BOGEYS	CAVIAR	COTTAS	CLINCH	CAHIER	CARVEN
BOLEYN	CAYMAN	COUGAR	CLOACA	CALCES	CARVER
BONNYS	CEIBAS	COWMAN	CLUTCH	CALKED	CARVES
BYEBYE	CELIAC	CRAVAT	COERCE	CALKER	CASHED
BYWAYS	CELIAS	CREDAL	COMICS	CALLED	CASHES
******	CELLAE	CRETAN	CONICS	CALLER	CASHEW
B---Z-	CELLAR	CREVAS	COPECK	CALMED	CASKET
******	CENTAL	CRURAL	CRATCH	CALMER	CASPER
BELIZE	CEREAL	CULLAY	CROTCH	CALVED	CASTER
BLOWZY	CHELAE	CUNEAL	CROUCH	CALVES	CASTES
BRAIZE	CHELAS	CURIAE	CRUNCH	CALXES	CATHER
BREEZE	CHETAH	CURIAL	CRUTCH	CAMBER	CATTED
BREEZY	CHORAL	CUSHAT	CULTCH	CAMDEN	CAUDEX
BRONZE	CHUFAS	CUSHAW	CURACY	CAMLET	CAULES
BRONZY	CILIAT	CUTLAS	CYNICS	CAMPED	CAUSED
******	CITRAL	CYMBAL	******	CAMPER	CAUSER
C---A-	CLARAS	******	C---D-	CANCEL	CAUSES
******	CLIMAT	C---B-	******	CANCER	CAVIES
CABMAN	CLIMAX	******	CANADA	CANKER	CEASED
CAESAR	COAXAL	CABOBS	CHARDS	CANNED	CEASES
CAFTAN	COBIAS	CALEBS	CHORDS	CANNEL	CEILED
CAIMAN	COBRAS	CARIBE	CICADA	CANNER	CENSED
CALCAR	COCCAL	CARIBS	CLAUDE	CANNES	CENSER
CALLAO	COCOAS	CAROBS	CLODDY	CANOED	CENSES
CALLAS	COEVAL	CASABA	CLOUDS	CANOES	CENTER
CALPAC	COITAL	CHUBBY	CLOUDY	CANTED	CERMET
CANAAN	COLLAR	CLIMBS	COMEDO	CANTER	CERTES
CANCAN	COLZAS	COOMBS	COMEDY	CAPPED	CHAFED
CANNAE	COMBAT	CRABBY	CORODY	CAPPER	CHAFER
CANNAS	COMMAS	CRAMBO	CREEDS	CARCEL	CHAFES
CANTAB	CONFAB	CRUMBS	CROWDS	CARDED	CHALEH
CANVAS		CRUMBY	CYCADS	CARDER	CHALET
CAPIAS		CUBEBS		CAREEN	

CHAPEL	CLOSER	CONVEX	COWPER	CURBED	CLINGS
CHAPES	CLOSES	CONVEY	COZIER	CURDED	CLINGY
CHARED	CLOSET	COOEED	COZIES	CURFEW	CLOGGY
CHARES	CLOVEN	COOEES	CRAKES	CURIES	CLOUGH
CHASED	CLOVER	COOKED	CRANED	CURLED	COLUGO
CHASER	CLOVES	COOKER	CRANES	CURLER	COSIGN
CHASES	CLOYED	COOKEY	CRAPED	CURLEW	COWAGE
CHAWED	CLYDES	COOLED	CRAPES	CURSED	CRAGGY
CHEBEC	CLYPEI	COOLER	CRATED	CURSES	CRAIGS
CHEWED	COALED	COOPED	CRATER	CURVED	CRINGE
CHEWER	COALER	COOPER	CRATES	CURVES	CUBAGE
CHIDED	COATED	COPIED	CRAVED	CURVET	******
CHIDER	COATEE	COPIER	CRAVEN	CUSPED	C---H-
CHIDES	COAXED	COPIES	CRAVER	CUSSED	******
CHIMED	COAXER	COPLEY	CRAVES	CUSSES	CANTHI
CHIMER	COAXES	COPPED	CRAZED	CUSTER	CATCHY
CHIMES	COBBER	COPPER	CRAZES	CUTIES	CAUGHT
CHINES	COBLES	COPSES	CREMES	CUTLER	CHICHI
CHISEL	COBWEB	COQUET	CRENEL	CUTLET	CLICHE
CHIVES	COCKED	CORBEL	CREPED	CUTTER	CLOCHE
CHLOES	COCKER	CORDED	CREPES	CYCLED	CLOTHE
CHOKED	CODDER	CORDER	CREWEL	CYCLER	CLOTHO
CHOKER	CODGER	CORKED	CRIKEY	CYCLES	CLOTHS
CHOKES	COELED	CORKER	CRIMEA	CYGNET	CONCHA
CHOLER	COFFEE	CORNEA	CRIMES	CYPHER	CONCHS
CHOREA	COFFER	CORNED	CRISES	******	CONCHY
CHOREO	COGGED	CORNEL	CRONES	C---F-	COUGHS
CHORES	COIFED	CORNER	CRORES	******	CRECHE
CHOSEN	COILED	CORNET	CROWED	CALIFS	******
CHUTES	COILER	CORSES	CROZER	CARAFE	C---I-
CINDER	COINED	CORSET	CROZES	CASEFY	******
CIPHER	COINER	CORTES	CRUCES	CHAFFS	CADDIE
CITHER	COLDER	CORTEX	CRUDER	CHAFFY	CADDIS
CITIED	COLIES	CORTEZ	CRUSES	CHIEFS	CALAIS
CITIES	COLLET	CORVEE	CRUSET	CLIFFS	CALCIC
CIVIES	COLTER	CORVES	CRUXES	CLIFFY	CALKIN
CLARES	COMBED	COSHED	CUBBED	CODIFY	CALVIN
CLARET	COMBER	COSHER	CUDGEL	CUTOFF	CANDIA
CLAWED	COMPEL	COSHES	CUFFED	******	CANDID
CLAYED	CONFER	COSSES	CULLED	C---G-	CANNIE
CLAYEY	CONGER	COSSET	CULLER	******	CAPLIN
CLEVER	CONGES	COSTED	CULLET	CAYUGA	CAPRIC
CLEWED	CONIES	COSTER	CULMED	CHANGE	CARDIO
CLIMES	CONKED	COTTER	CULVER	CHANGS	CARPIC
CLINES	CONKER	COULEE	CUMBER	CHARGE	CARRIE
CLIVES	CONNED	COUPES	CUNNER	CHOUGH	CASEIN
CLONES	CONNER	COWMEN	CUPPED	CLANGS	CASSIA
CLOSED	CONTES	COWPEA	CUPPER	CLERGY	CASSIE

CASSIS	COUSIN	CLINKS	CHILLI	CHACMA	CLEANS
CATKIN	COWRIE	CLOAKS	CHILLS	CHAMMY	CLIENT
CATLIN	CRANIA	CLOCKS	CHILLY	CHARMS	CLOWNS
CATNIP	CRANIO	CLUCKS	CHOLLA	CHASMS	CLUING
CATTIE	CRASIS	CRACKS	CHURLS	CHIRMS	CODING
CAULIS	CREDIT	CRACKY	CIBOLS	CHROMA	COGENT
CAVEIN	CRETIC	CRANKS	CICALA	CHROME	COHUNE
CEBOID	CRETIN	CRANKY	CICELY	CHROMO	COIGNS
CEDRIC	CRISIS	CREAKS	CIRCLE	CHUMMY	COKING
CELTIC	CRITIC	CREAKY	CITOLA	CINEMA	COLINE
CERVIX	CROJIK	CREEKS	COBALT	CLAIMS	COLINS
CHITIN	CUBOID	CRICKS	COBBLE	CLAMMY	COLONS
CHOPIN	CUDDIE	CROAKS	COBBLY	CLEOME	COLONY
CHORIC	CULLIS	CROAKY	COCKLE	COLUMN	COMING
CHYMIC	CUPRIC	CROCKS	CODDLE	CORYMB	CONING
CISSIE	CUPTIE	CROCKY	COFFLE	CREAMS	COOING
CITRIC	CURTIS	CROOKS	COLDLY	CREAMY	COPING
CLERIC	CUSPID	******	COMELY	CRUMMY	CORING
CLERID	CUSPIS	C---L-	COMPLY	******	CORONA
CLEVIS	CYANIC	******	COODLE	C---N-	COSINE
CLINIC	CYANID	CABALA	COOLLY	******	COVING
CLONIC	CYANIN	CABALS	COPALM	CABANA	COWING
CLOVIS	CYCLIC	CACKLE	COPULA	CABINS	COXING
COATIS	CYMLIN	CAGILY	CORALS	CADENT	COZENS
COCAIN	CYMOID	CAJOLE	COSILY	CAGING	CRANNY
COCCID	CYMRIC	CALMLY	COSTLY	CAIRNS	CROONS
COCHIN	CYPRIN	CAMELS	COUPLE	CAJUNS	CROWNS
CODEIA	CYSTIC	CAMILA	COZILY	CAKING	CRYING
CODEIN	******	CANALS	CRAALS	CANINE	CUBANS
COFFIN	C---K-	CANDLE	CRADLE	CANING	CUBING
COHEIR	******	CANTLE	CRAWLS	CANONS	CUMINS
COLLIE	CAULKS	CANULA	CRAWLY	CAPONE	CURING
COMFIT	CHALKS	CAROLE	CREELS	CAPONS	CUTINS
COMMIE	CHALKY	CAROLS	CREOLE	CARINA	CYMENE
COMMIT	CHECKS	CASALS	CUDDLE	CARING	CYRANO
COMMIX	CHEEKS	CASTLE	CUDDLY	CASING	CYRENE
CONNIE	CHEEKY	CATALO	CUPELS	CASINO	******
CONOID	CHICKS	CATTLE	CUPOLA	CATENA	C---O-
CONTIN	CHINKS	CAUDLE	CUPULE	CAVING	******
COOKIE	CHINKY	CAVELL	CURDLE	CAWING	CACAOS
COOLIE	CHOCKS	CAVILS	CURTLY	CEDING	CACHOU
COOTIE	CHUCKS	CECILE	CURULE	CEMENT	CAHOOT
COPTIC	CHUNKS	CECILS	CUTELY	CERING	CALLOW
CORBIE	CHUNKY	CECILY	CUTTLE	CETANE	CAMEOS
CORGIS	CLACKS	CEDULA	CYBELE	CHAINS	CAMION
CORRIE	CLANKS	CEORLS	CYRILS	CHRONO	CAMPOS
CORTIN	CLERKS	CHEILO	******	CHURNS	CANDOR
COSMIC	CLICKS	CHICLE	C---M-	CITING	CANNON
			******		
			CAEOMA		
			CAROMS		

CANNOT	COSMOS	CROUPY	CONTRA	CREESE	COUNTS
CANSOS	COTTON	CRUMPS	CONTRE	CREUSA	COUNTY
CANTON	COUPON	CUTUPS	COOERS	CROSSE	COURTS
CANTOR	COWBOY	******	COPPRA	CRUISE	COVETS
CANTOS	COWPOX	**C---R-**	CORERS	CUBISM	COYOTE
CANYON	CRACOW	******	COVERS	CUBIST	CRAFTS
CAPTOR	CRAYON	CALORY	COVERT	CUISSE	CRAFTY
CARBON	CREDOS	CAMERA	COWARD	CURTSY	CREATE
CARBOY	CRESOL	CANARD	COWERS	CUTEST	CRESTS
CARGOS	CRETON	CANARY	CRIERS	CYMOSE	CROATS
CARHOP	CRONOS	CANERS	CURARE	******	CROFTS
CARLOS	CROTON	CAPERS	CURERS	**C---T-**	CRUETS
CARLOW	CRUSOE	CARERS	CYMARS	******	CRUSTS
CARROT	CUCKOO	CASERN	******	CADETS	CRUSTY
CARSON	CURIOS	CASTRO	**C---S-**	CANUTE	CRYPTO
CARTON	CURSOR	CATERS	******	CAPITA	CRYPTS
CASHOO	CUSSOS	CAVERN	CALASH	CAPOTE	CUBITS
CASTOR	CUSTOM	CAVORT	CALESA	CARATE	CUESTA
CATION	CUSTOS	CEDARS	CAMASS	CARATS	CULETS
CAXTON	******	CELERY	CAMISE	CARETS	CURATE
CELLOS	**C---P-**	CENTRA	CARESS	CAVITE	******
CENSOR	******	CENTRE	CARUSO	CAVITY	**C---U-**
CENTOS	CALIPH	CENTRI	CAYUSE	CERATE	******
CEYLON	CANAPE	CENTRO	CERISE	CERATO	CACTUS
CHARON	CANOPY	CESARE	CERUSE	CERITE	CADMUS
CHEGOE	CERIPH	CESURA	CHAISE	CHAETA	CAECUM
CHICOS	CHAMPS	CHAIRS	CHASSE	CHAETO	CAIQUE
CHIGOE	CHEEPS	CHARRY	CHEESE	CHANTS	CALLUP
CHIRON	CHEOPS	CHEERS	CHEESY	CHANTY	CALLUS
CHITON	CHIPPY	CHEERY	CHIASM	CHARTS	CAMPUS
CINEOL	CHIRPS	CHEIRO	CHOOSE	CHASTE	CANGUE
CISCOS	CHIRPY	CHERRY	CHOOSY	CHATTY	CANTUS
CITRON	CHOPPY	CHIRRS	CHRISM	CHEATS	CARPUS
CLAMOR	CHUMPS	CHLORO	CHRIST	CHESTS	CASQUE
CLAROS	CLAMPS	CHOIRS	CHRYSO	CHESTY	CATGUT
COCOON	CLASPS	CHURRS	CIVISM	CHINTZ	CATSUP
COELOM	CLUMPS	CICERO	CLASSY	CHITTY	CAUCUS
COLLOP	CLUMPY	CIDERS	CLAUSE	CIVETS	CENSUR
COMBOS	COEMPT	CIGARS	CLEIST	CLEATS	CENSUS
COMEON	CRAMPS	CIMBRI	CLUMSY	CLEFTS	CEREUS
COMMON	CREEPS	CLAIRE	COARSE	CLINTS	CERIUM
COMPOS	CREEPY	CLEARS	COHOSH	CLOTTY	CEROUS
CONDOM	CRIMPS	COBURG	COMOSE	CLOUTS	CESIUM
CONDOR	CRIMPY	COHERE	CORPSE	COASTS	CESTUS
CONGOU	CRISPS	COHORT	COURSE	COMATE	CHABUK
CONTOS	CRISPY	COLORS	COYISH	COMETS	CHEQUE
CONVOY	CROUPE	COLURE	CREASE	COMITY	CHERUB
CORDON	CROUPS	COMERS	CREASY	COOPTS	CHIAUS

CHIBUK	CHIVVY	DIPSAS	DETECT	DAPPED	DENTED
CHORUS	CLEAVE	DIRHAM	DEVICE	DAPPER	DENVER
CILIUM	******	DISBAR	DIRECT	DARIEN	DEUCED
CINQUE	C---Y-	DISCAL	DODECA	DARKEN	DEUCES
CIRCUM	******	DISMAL	DRENCH	DARKER	DEWIER
CIRCUS	CATHYS	DISMAY	DRYICE	DARNED	DEXTER
CIRQUE	CHERYL	DISTAL	******	DARNEL	DHOLES
CIRRUS	CINDYS	DOBLAS	D---D-	DARNER	DIADEM
CITRUS	CISSYS	DOBRAS	******	DARTED	DIALED
CLAQUE	COCCYX	DOGEAR	DAVIDS	DARTER	DIALER
CLIQUE	CONEYS	DOGMAS	DECADE	DASHED	DIANES
CLIQUY	COOEYS	DOLLAR	DECIDE	DASHER	DIAPER
CLONUS	COVEYS	DOLMAN	DECODE	DASHES	DIBBED
COBNUT	CUTEYS	DONNAS	DELUDE	DAUBED	DIBBER
COCCUS	******	DOODAD	DEMODE	DAUBER	DICKER
COCKUP	C---Z-	DORIAN	DENUDE	DAUDET	DICKEY
COITUS	******	DORSAD	DERIDE	DAVIES	DIDIES
COLEUS	CORYZA	DORSAL	DIPODY	DAWNED	DIDOES
COLOUR	******	DOSSAL	DIRNDL	DAYBED	DIESEL
COLOUS	D---A-	DOUGAL	DIVIDE	DEADEN	DIESES
COMOUS	******	DOWLAS	DORADO	DEAFEN	DIETED
CONCUR	DACHAS	DRAMAS	DREADS	DEALER	DIETER
CONIUM	DACHAU	DUNBAR	DRUIDS	DEARER	DIFFER
CONSUL	DAEDAL	DUNCAN	DRYADS	DECKED	DIGGED
COPOUT	DAGMAR	DURBAN	******	DECKEL	DIGGER
CORIUM	DALLAS	DURBAR	D---E-	DECKER	DIMMED
CORNUA	DAMMAR	DURHAM	******	DECREE	DIMMER
CORNUS	DARDAN	DURIAN	DABBED	DEEDED	DINDER
CORPUS	DECCAN	DVORAK	DABBER	DEEMED	DINGED
CORVUS	DEEWAN	******	DADOES	DEEPEN	DINGEY
COYPUS	DEFEAT	D---B-	DAGGER	DEEPER	DINKEY
CRINUM	DEFRAY	******	DAISES	DEFIED	DINNED
CROCUS	DELIAN	DAGOBA	DALLES	DEFIER	DINNER
CRONUS	DELIAS	DANUBE	DAMMED	DEFIES	DINTED
CULTUS	DELLAS	DEMOBS	DAMMER	DEFTER	DIODES
CUPFUL	DELTAS	******	DAMNED	DEGREE	DIPLEX
CUPRUM	DEMEAN	D---C-	DAMPED	DEICED	DIPPED
CURIUM	DENIAL	******	DAMPEN	DEICER	DIPPER
CUSCUS	DENTAL	DARICS	DAMPER	DEICES	DIRGES
CUTOUT	DEODAR	DECOCT	DAMSEL	DELVED	DIRKED
CYGNUS	DERMAL	DEDUCE	DANCED	DELVER	DISHED
CYMOUS	DERMAS	DEDUCT	DANCER	DELVES	DISHES
CYPRUS	DERMAT	DEFACE	DANCES	DEMIES	DISNEY
******	DESMAN	DEFECT	DANDER	DENIED	DISPEL
C---V-	DESSAU	DEJECT	DANGED	DENIER	DITHER
******	DEWLAP	DELICT	DANGER	DENIES	DOBBER
CASAVA	DIANAS	DEPICT	DANIEL	DENNED	DOBIES
CHEVVY	DIETAL	DETACH	DANKER	DENSER	DOCKED

DOCKER	DRAWER	******	DERAIL	DANDLE	DUFFLE
DOCKET	DRAYED	D---G-	DERAIN	DANGLE	DUMBLY
DODDER	DRIVEL	******	DERMIC	DANKLY	DWELLS
DODGED	DRIVEN	DAMAGE	DERMIS	DAPPLE	******
DODGER	DRIVER	DEBUGS	DERRIS	DARKLE	D---M-
DODGES	DRIVES	DEGAGE	DESMID	DARKLY	******
DODOES	DRONED	DELUGE	DETAIL	DARTLE	DECAMP
DOFFED	DRONES	DESIGN	DETAIN	DAWDLE	DECUMA
DOFFER	DROVED	DOINGS	DEVEIN	DAYFLY	DEFAME
DOGGED	DROVER	DOSAGE	DEVOID	DAZZLE	DEGAME
DOGGER	DROVES	DOTAGE	DEVOIR	DEADLY	DEGUMS
DOGIES	DRUPEL	DREDGE	DHOTIS	DEAFLY	DENIMS
DOITED	DRUPES	DREGGY	DIAZIN	DEARLY	DHARMA
DOLLED	DRUSES	DRONGO	DICKIE	DECALS	DIGAMY
DOLMEN	DRYDEN	DRUDGE	DIESIS	DECILE	DREAMS
DONEES	DUBBED	******	DIKDIK	DECKLE	DREAMT
DONKEY	DUCKED	D---H-	DIMWIT	DEEPLY	DREAMY
DONNED	DUCKER	******	DISTIL	DEFILE	DYNAMO
DOOLEE	DUDEEN	DEATHS	DOBBIN	DEFTLY	******
DOOMED	DUDLEY	DEATHY	DOGGIE	DESALT	D---N-
DOPIER	DUELED	DELPHI	DOLLIE	DEVILS	******
DOPTER	DUELER	DEPTHS	DOMAIN	DIBBLE	DAMANS
DOREEN	DUFFED	DINAHS	DONNIE	DIDDLE	DAPHNE
DORIES	DUFFEL	DINGHY	DOOLIE	DIMPLE	DARING
DORMER	DUFFER	DOLPHS	DORMIE	DIMPLY	DATING
DORSET	DUIKER	DOUCHE	DOSSIL	DINGLE	DAZING
DOSSED	DULCET	DOUGHS	DOUGIE	DIPOLE	DEBUNK
DOSSEL	DULLED	DOUGHY	DUBBIN	DIRELY	DECANE
DOSSER	DULLER	DRACHM	DUBLIN	DOABLE	DECANT
DOTIER	DULLES	DWIGHT	DULCIE	DOALLS	DECENT
DOTTED	DUMPED	******	DUNLIN	DOCILE	DEDANS
DOTTEL	DUMPER	D---I-	DYADIC	DONALD	DEFEND
DOTTER	DUNCES	******	******	DOODLE	DEFINE
DOUSED	DUNDEE	DACOIT	D---K-	DOTTLE	DEIGNS
DOUSES	DUNGED	DAHLIA	******	DOUBLE	DEKING
DOWNED	DUNKED	DAIMIO	DECOKE	DOUBLY	DEMAND
DOWSED	DUNKER	DAKOIT	DEREKS	DOURLY	DEMENT
DOWSER	DUNNED	DANAID	DRINKS	DOWELS	DEMONO
DOWSES	DUODEN	DANZIG	DROSKY	DOZILY	DEMONS
DOXIES	DUPLET	DARWIN	DRUNKS	DRABLY	DEPEND
DOYLEY	DUPLEX	DEARIE	******	DRAWLS	DEPONE
DOZIER	DUSKED	DEBBIE	D---L-	DRAWLY	DETENT
DRAGEE	DUSTED	DEBRIS	******	DRILLS	DEWANS
DRAKES	DUSTER	DECEIT	DABBLE	DROLLS	DHARNA
DRAPED	DUTIES	DEIFIC	DADDLE	DROLLY	DHURNA
DRAPER	******	DENNIS	DAFTLY	DROOLS	DICING
DRAPES	D---F-	DENTIL	DAGGLE	DRYFLY	DIKING
DRAWEE	******	DENTIN	DAMPLY	DUELLO	DINING
	DRAFFS				
	DRAFFY				
	DWARFS				

DITONE	DIPLOE	DESIRE	DROSSY	DROUTH	DEBBYS
DIVANS	DITTOS	DETERS	DROWSE	DUCATS	DECAYS
DIVINE	DOBLON	DEXTRO	DROWSY	DULUTH	DECOYS
DIVING	DOBSON	DICERS	DRYEST	DUMPTY	DELAYS
DIWANS	DOCTOR	DIDERO	DRYISH	******	DENNYS
DIZENS	DOGFOX	DIMERS	DUDISH	**D---U-**	DOLLYS
DOCENT	DOLLOP	DINARS	DURESS	******	******
DOESNT	DONJON	DINERO	DYNAST	DANAUS	**E---A-**
DOLING	DRAGON	DINERS	******	DARIUS	******
DOMING	DROMON	DISARM	**D---T-**	DELIUS	EARLAP
DOMINO	DRYROT	DIVERS	******	DENGUE	EARWAX
DOPING	DUOLOG	DIVERT	DAINTY	DETOUR	ELENAS
DOSING	DURION	DMITRI	DAKOTA	DEVOUR	ELIJAH
DOTING	******	DONORS	DALETH	DEVOUT	ELIZAS
DOYENS	**D---P-**	DOSERS	DANITE	DICTUM	ENDEAR
DOZENS	******	DOTARD	DAUNTS	DIMOUT	ENEMAS
DOZING	DIEPPE	DOTERS	DAVITS	DINGUS	ENGRAM
DRAINS	DOGAPE	DOWERS	DEARTH	DISCUS	ENNEAD
DROWNS	DRIPPY	DOWERY	DEBATE	DOLOUR	ENTRAP
DRYING	DROOPS	DREARY	DEBITS	DORBUG	ENWRAP
DUENNA	DROOPY	DRIERS	DEBUTS	DORSUM	EOLIAN
DUGONG	******	DRYERS	DEISTS	DROGUE	EONIAN
DUPING	**D---R-**	DUPERS	DELATE	DUGOUT	EPICAL
DURING	******	DUPERY	DELETE	DUMDUM	ESCHAR
DYEING	DARERS	******	DEMITS	DYBBUK	ESPIAL
******	DATARY	**D---S-**	DEMOTE	******	ESTRAY
D---O-	DATERS	******	DENOTE	**D---V-**	EUDOAR
******	DATURA	DAMASK	DEPOTS	******	EVITAS
DACRON	DAUBRY	DANISH	DEPUTE	DATIVE	EXTRAS
DAEMON	DEBARK	DEBASE	DEPUTY	DERIVE	******
DAHOON	DEBARS	DEFUSE	DERATE	******	**E---B-**
DAIMON	DECARE	DEGUST	DEVOTE	**D---W-**	ENROBE
DALTON	DECERN	DEMISE	DEWITT	******	EPHEBI
DAMSON	DECORS	DENISE	DIGITI	DISOWN	EXURBS
DANTON	DECURY	DEPOSE	DIGITS	******	******
DARROW	DEFERS	DESIST	DILATE	**D---X-**	**E---C-**
DATTOS	DEFORM	DETEST	DILUTE	******	******
DAWSON	DEHORN	DEVEST	DIMITY	DELUXE	EFFACE
DAYBOY	DEKARE	DEVISE	DIVOTS	DESOXY	EFFECT
DAYTON	DEMURE	DICAST	DIXITS	******	ENFACE
DEACON	DEMURS	DIGEST	DONATE	**D---Y-**	ENLACE
DEBTOR	DENARY	DIREST	DONETS	******	ENRICH
DEPLOY	DENDRI	DISUSE	DOUBTS	DACTYL	ENRICO
DESPOT	DENDRO	DIVEST	DRAFTS	DAIMYO	ENTICE
DIALOG	DEPART	DOVISH	DRAFTY	DAISYS	EPARCH
DIATOM	DEPORT	DRESSY	DRIFTS	DANNYS	ETHICS
DIGLOT	DESCRY	DRIEST	DRIFTY	DAVEYS	EUNICE
DIOBOL	DESERT	DROPSY	DROITS		

EUNUCH	ELLIES	EVADER	ECHOIC	ENGELS	ELOINS
EVINCE	ELOPED	EVADES	ECLAIR	ENGULF	EMBANK
EXARCH	ELOPER	EVENED	EDDAIC	ENISLE	ENCINA
EXPECT	ELOPES	EVERET	EDENIC	ENROLL	ENDING
EXSECT	ELSIES	EVOKED	EGERIA	ENSILE	ENGINE
******	ELUDED	EVOKES	ELEGIT	EQUALS	ENWIND
E---D-	ELUDES	EXAMEN	ELEMIS	ETHELS	EOCENE
******	ELYSEE	EXCEED	ELICIT	ETHYLS	EOGENE
ELANDS	EMBLEM	EXETER	ELIXIR	EVENLY	EPPING
EMBEDS	EMCEED	EXILED	ELOHIM	EVILLY	EQUINE
EMBODY	EMCEES	EXILES	EMERIC	EXCELS	ERMINE
EMENDS	EMILES	EXITED	EMERIE	EXHALE	ERRAND
ENCODE	EMMIES	EXOGEN	EMESIS	EXPELS	ERRANT
EPHODS	EMOTED	EXUDED	EMETIC	EXTOLS	ERRING
ESCUDO	EMOTES	EXUDES	EMETIN	******	ERWINS
EXCIDE	ENAMEL	EYASES	EMILIA	**E---M-**	ESCENT
******	ENATES	EYELET	EMILIE	******	ESPANA
E---E-	ENDUED	EYRIES	EMILIO	ECTOMY	ESSENE
******	ENDUES	******	ENJOIN	ECZEMA	ETERNA
EAGLES	ENSUED	**E---G-**	ENOSIS	ENCAMP	ETHANE
EAGLET	ENSUES	******	ENTAIL	ENIGMA	ETHANS
EARLES	ENTREE	EFFIGY	EOZOIC	ENTOMB	EUGENE
EARNED	ENVIED	ELOIGN	EROTIC	ENTOMO	EXEUNT
EARNER	ENVIER	EMERGE	ESPRIT	ENWOMB	EXPAND
EASIER	ENVIES	ENCAGE	ETHNIC	ENZYME	EXPEND
EASTER	EPODES	ENERGY	EUCLID	ESKIMO	EXTANT
ECCLES	EPOPEE	ENGAGE	EXILIC	EXHUME	EXTEND
ECHOED	ERASED	ENOUGH	EXOTIC	******	EXTENT
ECHOER	ERASER	ENRAGE	EYELID	**E---N-**	EYEING
ECHOES	ERASES	ENSIGN	******	******	******
ECOLES	ERNIES	ERINGO	**E---K-**	EALING	**E---O-**
EDDIED	ERODED	ERYNGO	******	EARING	******
EDDIES	ERODES	EULOGY	EUREKA	EASING	EASTON
EDGIER	ESCHER	******	******	EATING	EDISON
EDILES	ESCHEW	**E---H-**	**E---L-**	EBBING	EDITOR
EDITED	ESPIED	******	******	ECHINI	EGGNOG
EDUCED	ESPIES	EARTHS	EASELS	ECHINO	ELEVON
EDUCES	ESTEEM	EARTHY	EASILY	EDGING	ELINOR
EIFFEL	ESTHER	EDITHS	EDIBLE	EDMOND	ELLIOT
EILEEN	ETAPES	ELISHA	EDSELS	EDMUND	EMPLOY
EITHER	ETCHED	EPHAHS	EERILY	EDWINA	ENAMOR
ELATED	ETCHER	EPOCHS	EIDOLA	EDWINS	ENROOT
ELATER	ETCHES	ERICHS	EMBALM	EGGING	EPILOG
ELATES	ETUDES	******	EMBOLI	EKEING	EPIZOA
ELDRED	EUBOEA	**E---I-**	EMPALE	ELAINE	ESCROW
ELEVEN	EUCHER	******	ENABLE	ELAYNE	ETYMON
ELIDED	EUPNEA	EARWIG	ENDALL	ELFINS	EXMOOR
ELIDES	EVADED	ECESIS	ENFOLD	ELLENS	

```
*****        ENTERS    EDUCTS    EPIRUS    FENIAN    FLETCH
E---P-       ENTIRE    EFFETE    ERBIUM    FERIAL    FLINCH
*****        EPHORI    EGESTA    EREBUS    FESTAL    FLITCH
ECTYPE       EPHORS    EGESTS    ESTRUS    FETIAL    FRANCE
ENRAPT       ERFURT    EGRETS    EXEQUY    FEUDAL    FRANCK
EQUIPS       ERRORS    EIGHTH    EXODUS    FEZZAN    FRANCO
ESCAPE       ESCARP    EIGHTS    EYECUP    FIJIAN    FRANCS
ESTOPS       ESCORT    EIGHTY    EYEFUL    FILIAL    FRENCH
EURIPI       ESKERS    EJECTA    EYEOUT    FINIAL    FRESCO
EUROPA       ESTERS    EJECTS    *****     FINNAN    *****
EUROPE       ETHERS    ELECTS    E---V-    FIRMAN    F---D-
EXCEPT       EUCHRE    ELIOTS    *****     FISCAL    *****
EXEMPT       EXEDRA    EMEUTE    ENDIVE    FLORAE    FACADE
*****        EXHORT    EMMETS    EVOLVE    FLORAL    FARADS
E---R-       EXPERT    EMMETT    *****     FLORAS    FELIDS
*****        EXPIRE    ENACTS    E---W-    FLYMAN    FIELDS
EATERS       EXPIRY    ENMITY    *****     FOEMAN    FIENDS
EATERY       EXPORT    ENTITY    ELBOWS    FOETAL    FIORDS
ECHARD       EXSERT    EOLITH    EMBOWS    FOLIAR    FLOODS
EDGARS       EXTERN    EPACTS    ENDOWS    FONTAL    FLOYDS
EDUARD       EXTORT    EQUATE    *****     FORMAL    FLUIDS
EDWARD       *****     EQUITY    E---Y-    FORMAT    FOUNDS
EFFORT       E---S-    ERECTS    *****     FORNAX    FRAUDS
EGBERT       *****     ERGATE    EMBAYS    FOSSAE    FREDDY
EGGARS       EDDISH    ERRATA    EMBRYO    FOVEAE    FRIEDA
EGGERS       EFFUSE    ERSATZ    EMILYS    FOVEAL    FRONDS
ELBERT       EGOISM    ERUCTS    ENJOYS    FRACAS    *****
ELDERS       EGOIST    ERUPTS    ENVOYS    FREDAS    F---E-
ELMERS       EGRESS    ESTATE    EPONYM    FRIDAY    *****
ELMIRA       ELAPSE    EVENTS    ERINYS    FRUGAL    FABLED
ELVERS       ELDEST    EVERTS    ESSAYS    FULMAR    FABLER
ELVIRA       ELFISH    EVICTS    EVELYN    FUNGAL    FABLES
ELYTRA       ELOISE    EXACTA    *****     *****     FACIES
EMBARK       ELVISH    EXACTS    F---A-    F---B-    FAECES
EMBARS       EMBOSS    EXALTS    *****     *****     FAGGED
EMBERS       ENCASE    EXCITE    FABIAN    FLABBY    FAILED
EMEERS       ENCASH    EXERTS    FACIAL    FLAMBE    FAIRED
EMIGRE       ENCYST    EXISTS    FAECAL    *****     FAIRER
EMPERY       ENLIST    EXULTS    FALLAL    F---C-    FALLEN
EMPIRE       ENMESH    *****     FANGAS    *****     FALLER
ENCORE       EONISM    E---U-    FANTAN    FELICE    FALSER
ENDURE       ERNEST    *****     FARBAD    FETICH    FALTER
ENGIRD       EXCESS    EARFUL    FAUCAL    FIANCE    FANGED
ENGIRT       EXCISE    EFFLUX    FAUNAE    FIASCO    FANJET
ENSURE       EXCUSE    EGGCUP    FAUNAL    FIERCE    FANNED
ENTERA       EXPOSE    ELBRUS    FAUNAS    FLEECE    FANNER
ENTERE       *****     EMBRUE    FECIAL    FLEECY    FARCED
ENTERO       E---T-    ENSOUL    FELLAH    FLENCH    FARCER
             *****
             ECARTE
             EDICTS
```

FARCES	FIGGED	FLUXED	FUGLES	FILTHY	FULFIL
FARLES	FILLED	FLUXES	FUGUES	FIRTHS	FULGID
FARLEY	FILLER	FOALED	FUHRER	FLASHY	FUSAIN
FARMED	FILLET	FOAMED	FULLED	FLECHE	FUSTIC
FARMER	FILMED	FOBBED	FULLER	FLESHY	******
FASCES	FILTER	FODDER	FUMIER	FLIGHT	**F---K-**
FASTED	FINDER	FOEMEN	FUNDED	FOUGHT	******
FASTEN	FINGER	FOGGED	FUNKED	FRIGHT	FLACKS
FASTER	FINNED	FOGIES	FUNNEL	FRITHS	FLANKS
FATHER	FINNER	FOILED	FURIES	FROTHS	FLASKS
FATTED	FIQUES	FOLDED	FURLED	FROTHY	FLECKS
FATTEN	FIRMED	FOLDER	FURRED	******	FLICKS
FATTER	FIRMER	FONDER	FURZES	**F---I-**	FLOCKS
FAUCES	FISHER	FOOLED	FUSEES	******	FLOCKY
FAUCET	FISHES	FOOTED	FUSSED	FABRIC	FLUNKS
FAUVES	FISTED	FOOTER	FUSSER	FADEIN	FLUNKY
FAWKES	FITTED	FORCED	FUSSES	FAERIE	FRANKS
FAWNED	FITTER	FORCER	FUZEES	FAFNIR	FREAKS
FAWNER	FIZZED	FORCES	FUZZED	FANNIE	FREAKY
FEARED	FIZZER	FORDED	FUZZES	FASCIA	FRISKS
FEARER	FIZZES	FORGED	******	FENRIR	FRISKY
FEASED	FLAKED	FORGER	**F---F-**	FERMIS	FROCKS
FEASES	FLAKER	FORGES	******	FERRIC	******
FEEDER	FLAKES	FORGET	FAROFF	FERRIS	**F---L-**
FEELER	FLAMED	FORKED	FEOFFS	FERVID	******
FEEZED	FLAMEN	FORMED	FLUFFS	FIBRIL	FACILE
FEEZES	FLAMES	FORMER	FLUFFY	FIBRIN	FACULA
FELLED	FLARED	FORTES	******	FILLIN	FAILLE
FELLER	FLARES	FOSSES	**F---G-**	FILLIP	FAIRLY
FELTED	FLAWED	FOSTER	******	FILMIC	FAMILY
FENCED	FLAXEN	FOULED	FANEGA	FINNIC	FECULA
FENCER	FLAXES	FOULER	FLAGGY	FIRKIN	FEEBLE
FENCES	FLAYED	FOWLED	FLANGE	FISTIC	FEEBLY
FENDED	FLAYER	FOWLER	FLEDGE	FIZGIG	FEMALE
FENDER	FLEXED	FOXIER	FLEDGY	FLAVIA	FERULA
FENNEC	FLEXES	FRAMED	FLINGS	FLAVIN	FERULE
FENNEL	FLORES	FRAMER	FLONGS	FLORID	FETTLE
FERBER	FLORET	FRAMES	FORAGE	FLORIN	FIBULA
FERRET	FLOWED	FRATER	FOREGO	FLUVIO	FICKLE
FESSES	FLOWER	FRAUEN	FRIDGE	FOETID	FIDDLE
FESTER	FLUKED	FRAYED	FRIGGA	FORBID	FIMBLE
FETTER	FLUKES	FRISES	FRINGE	FORMIC	FINALE
FEUDED	FLUKEY	FROZEN	FRINGY	FORNIX	FINALS
FEZZES	FLUMED	FUDGED	FROGGY	FORTIS	FINELY
FIBBED	FLUMES	FUDGES	******	FOSSIL	FIPPLE
FIBBER	FLUTED	FUELED	**F---H-**	FRIGID	FIRMLY
FICHES	FLUTER	FUELER	******	FROLIC	FIZZLE
FIDGET	FLUTES	FUGLED	FAITHS	FUCOID	FLAILS
				FIFTHS	

FLATLY	FERINE	FOLLOW	FLOURY	FILETS	******
FOCSLE	FETING	FORGOT	FLUORO	FINITE	**F---Y-**
FOIBLE	FEUING	FRIJOL	FLUORS	FIRSTS	******
FONDLE	FIFING	FRIVOL	FLURRY	FIXATE	FANNYS
FONDLY	FILING	FUGIOS	FLYERS	FIXITY	FLYBYS
FOOTLE	FINING	FULTON	FOYERS	FLEETS	FORAYS
FOOZLE	FIRING	FURROW	FRIARS	FLINTS	FORMYL
FOULLY	FIXING	FUSION	FRIARY	FLINTY	******
FOXILY	FLAUNT	FYLFOT	FRIERS	FLIRTS	**F---Z-**
FRAILS	FLUENT	******	FRYERS	FLIRTY	******
FREELY	FLYING	**F---P-**	FULCRA	FLOATS	FLOOZY
FRILLS	FOEHNS	******	FURORE	FLOATY	FREEZE
FRILLY	FOMENT	FELIPE	FURORS	FLOUTS	FRENZY
FUDDLE	FORINT	FLOPPY	FUTURE	FOISTS	FRIEZE
FUMBLE	FOXING	FLUMPS	******	FOUNTS	FRIZZY
FUSILE	FREONS	FRAPPE	**F---S-**	FOURTH	FROWZY
FUSILS	FRESNO	FRUMPS	******	FRETTY	FRUNZE
FUTILE	FRIEND	FRUMPY	FAMISH	FRONTO	******
FUZILS	FROWNS	******	FETISH	FRONTS	**G---A-**
******	FRYING	**F---R-**	FEWEST	FROSTS	******
F---M-	FUMING	******	FILOSE	FROSTY	GALEAE
******	FUSING	FACERS	FINEST	FRUITS	GALWAY
FANUMS	FUZING	FAKERS	FINISH	FRUITY	GALYAK
FATIMA	******	FAKERY	FLENSE	FRUSTA	GAMMAS
FLEAMS	**F---O-**	FAKIRS	FLIEST	******	GASBAG
FORUMS	******	FARERS	FLIMSY	**F---U-**	GASMAN
******	FACTOR	FAVORS	FLOSSY	******	GASPAR
F---N-	FAEROE	FEDORA	FOLKSY	FACTUM	GATEAU
******	FAGGOT	FEMORA	FOREST	FAMOUS	GAVIAL
FACING	FALCON	FEMURS	FRAISE	FAROUT	GEMMAE
FADING	FALLOW	FETORS	FREEST	FAUNUS	GENIAL
FAGEND	FANION	FEUARS	FUNEST	FAVOUR	GERMAN
FAKING	FANTOM	FEVERS	******	FEROUS	GEWGAW
FAMINE	FARROW	FIACRE	**F---T-**	FERRUM	GIBRAN
FANONS	FATHOM	FIBERS	******	FESCUE	GILDAS
FARINA	FELLOE	FIFERS	FACETS	FICHUS	GILEAD
FARING	FELLOW	FIGURE	FAGOTS	FITFUL	GINGAL
FATING	FEODOR	FILERS	FAINTS	FLATUS	GLOBAL
FAXING	FERVOR	FINERY	FAULTS	FOETUS	GODDAM
FAYING	FINNOC	FIRERS	FAULTY	FOLIUM	GOORAL
FAZING	FLACON	FIVERS	FEALTY	FONDUE	GOTHAM
FECUND	FLAGON	FIXERS	FEASTS	FRENUM	GRAHAM
FEEING	FLAVOR	FLAIRS	FEINTS	FUCOUS	GRETAS
FEIGNE	FLEXOR	FLEERS	FEISTS	FUMOUS	GUAVAS
FEIGNS	FOETOR	FLEURY	FEISTY	FUNDUS	GUFFAW
FELINE	FOGBOW	FLIERS	FERITY	FUNGUS	GUITAR
FELONS	FOGDOG	FLOORS	FIESTA	FURFUR	GULLAH
FELONY	FOLIOS	FLOURS	FIGHTS		GUMMAS

GUNMAN	GAFFED	GEMMED	GLOZED	GRAPES	GUNNED
GUNNAR	GAFFER	GENDER	GLOZES	GRATED	GUNNEL
GUSTAF	GAFFES	GENIES	GLUIER	GRATER	GUNNER
GUSTAV	GAGGED	GENRES	GLUMES	GRATES	GUNTER
GUTTAE	GAGGER	GENTES	GLUTEI	GRAVED	GUSHED
GUTTAT	GAINED	GEODES	GLUTEN	GRAVEL	GUSHER
******	GAINER	GERMEN	GNAWED	GRAVEN	GUSHES
G---B-	GAITED	GETTER	GNAWER	GRAVER	GUSSET
******	GAITER	GEYSER	GNOMES	GRAVES	GUTTED
GAZABO	GALLED	GHEBER	GOADED	GRAYED	GUTTER
GAZEBO	GALLEY	GIBBED	GOATEE	GRAYER	GYPPED
GEMSBO	GAMIER	GIBBER	GOBBET	GRAZED	******
GOODBY	GAMMED	GIBBET	GOBIES	GRAZER	**G---F-**
GRUBBY	GAMMER	GIBLET	GOBLET	GRAZES	******
******	GANDER	GIFTED	GOFFER	GREBES	GANEFS
G---C-	GANGED	GIGGED	GOGLET	GRETEL	GASIFY
******	GANGER	GIGLET	GOITER	GRIDED	GREIFS
GALACT	GANGES	GIGUES	GOLDEN	GRIDES	GRIFFE
GLANCE	GANNET	GILDED	GOLFED	GRIMED	******
GLAUCO	GAOLER	GILDER	GOLFER	GRIMES	**G---G-**
GRAECO	GAPPED	GIMLET	GOOBER	GRIPED	******
GREECE	GARBED	GIMPED	GOOFED	GRIPER	GARAGE
GROUCH	GARDEN	GINGER	GOOIER	GRIPES	GEORGE
GYNECO	GARGET	GINNED	GOONEY	GRIVET	GEORGI
******	GARNER	GINNER	GOOSED	GRIZEL	GOINGS
G---D-	GARNET	GIPPED	GOOSES	GROCER	GRANGE
******	GARRET	GIRDED	GOOSEY	GROPED	GREIGE
GLANDS	GARTER	GIRDER	GOPHER	GROPER	GROGGY
GONADS	GASHED	GIRTED	GORGED	GROPES	GRUDGE
GOURDE	GASHES	GLACES	GORGER	GROVEL	******
GOURDS	GASJET	GLADES	GORGES	GROVER	**G---H-**
GRANDE	GASKET	GLARED	GORGET	GROVES	******
GREEDS	GASMEN	GLARES	GORHEN	GROWER	GANDHI
GREEDY	GASPED	GLAZED	GORIER	GRUMES	GAUCHE
GRINDS	GASPER	GLAZER	GORSES	GUIDED	GAUCHO
GRUNDY	GASSED	GLAZES	GOSHEN	GUIDER	GEISHA
GUARDS	GASSES	GLEBES	GOSPEL	GUIDES	GLYPHS
GUILDS	GATHER	GLEDES	GOTTEN	GUILES	GNATHO
******	GAUGED	GLIDED	GOUGED	GUINEA	GOETHE
G---E-	GAUGER	GLIDER	GOUGER	GUISES	GRAPHO
******	GAUGES	GLIDES	GOUGES	GULDEN	GRAPHS
GABBED	GAUZES	GLOBED	GOWNED	GULFED	GRAPHY
GABBER	GAWKED	GLOBES	GRABEN	GULLED	GUNSHY
GABLED	GEARED	GLOVED	GRACED	GULLET	GURKHA
GABLES	GEEZER	GLOVER	GRACES	GULPED	******
GADDED	GEIGER	GLOVES	GRADED	GULPER	**G---I-**
GADDER	GELDED	GLOWED	GRADER	GUMMED	******
GADGET	GELLED	GLOWER	GRADES	GUNMEN	GADOID
					GAELIC

GALLIC	GAMBLE	GOTAMA	GALLON	GALORE	GAVOTS
GAMBIA	GAMELY	GRAMME	GALLOP	GANTRY	GAYETY
GAMBIR	GAMILY	GROOMS	GALOOT	GAPERS	GEMOTS
GAMBIT	GANGLI	******	GAMBOL	GASTRO	GENETS
GANOID	GARBLE	G---N-	GAMMON	GAZERS	GENITO
GARLIC	GARGLE	******	GARCON	GEMARA	GHAUTS
GASKIN	GAULLE	GAGING	GASCON	GEMERT	GHETTO
GAWAIN	GAVELS	GALENA	GASTON	GENERA	GHOSTS
GDYNIA	GENTLE	GAMING	GECKOS	GENTRY	GIANTS
GEODIC	GENTLY	GAMINS	GENROS	GERARD	GIOTTO
GERBIL	GERALD	GAPING	GENTOO	GHARRI	GLEETS
GERTIE	GESELL	GATING	GERYON	GHARRY	GLEETY
GESTIC	GHOULS	GAZING	GESSOS	GIBERS	GLINTS
GILLIE	GIGGLE	GEEING	GIBBON	GLAIRS	GLOATS
GIULIA	GIGGLY	GEMINI	GIBSON	GLAIRY	GLOSTS
GIULIO	GIGOLO	GERENT	GIDEON	GOCART	GLOTTO
GLACIS	GIMELS	GERUND	GIGLOT	GOITRE	GLYPTO
GLAMIS	GIRDLE	GIBING	GISMOS	GOKART	GOMUTI
GLOBIN	GISELE	GIGANT	GIZMOS	GONERS	GRAFTS
GLORIA	GLADLY	GIPONS	GLYCOL	GOVERN	GRANTS
GLYNIS	GLIBLY	GITANO	GNOMON	GRIGRI	GREATS
GNOMIC	GLUMLY	GIVING	GODSON	GRUGRU	GREETS
GNOSIS	GNARLS	GLEANS	GONION	******	GRITTY
GOALIE	GNARLY	GLUING	GOOGOL	G---S-	GROATS
GOBLIN	GOBBLE	GOBANG	GORDON	******	GROTTO
GODWIN	GOGGLE	GORING	GORGON	GALOSH	GROTTY
GODWIT	GOODLY	GRAINS	GREGOS	GARISH	GROUTS
GOSSIP	GOOGLY	GRAINY	GUACOS	GAYEST	GROWTH
GOTHIC	GORALS	GRANNY	GUANOS	GDANSK	GRUNTS
GRACIE	GORILY	GREENE	GUENON	GENESI	GUESTS
GRADIN	GRAYLY	GREENS	GUIDON	GLASSY	GUILTS
GRATIN	GRILLE	GRETNA	GUMBOS	GLOSSO	GUILTY
GRATIS	GRILLS	GROANS	******	GLOSSY	GYRATE
GRAVID	GRIMLY	GROINS	G---P-	GNEISS	******
GUANIN	GRISLY	GROUND	******	GOLOSH	G---U-
GUSSIE	GROWLS	GROYNE	GALOPS	GRASSY	******
******	GRUELS	GUIANA	GETUPS	GREASE	GALLUP
G---K-	GURGLE	GUYANA	GRASPS	GREASY	GALLUS
******	GUTTLE	GUYING	GRIPPE	GRILSE	GAMOUS
GINGKO	GUZZLE	GWENNS	GRIPPY	GROUSE	GANGUE
GREEKS	******	GWYNNE	GROUPS	GYROSE	GENIUS
******	G---M-	GYBING	GRUMPY	******	GENOUS
G---L-	******	GYRONS	GUIMPE	G---T-	GEROUS
******	GLEAMS	GYVING	******	******	GIAOUR
GABBLE	GLEAMY	******	G---R-	GAIETY	GONIUM
GADFLY	GLIOMA	G---O-	******	GAMETE	GRADUS
GAGGLE	GLOOMS	******	GABBRO	GAMETO	GYNOUS
GAINLY	GLOOMY	GABION	GAGERS	GAMUTS	GYPSUM
		GALIOT			

******	HETMAN	HAFTED	HATTER	HESTER	HOOVER
G---V-	HEYDAY	HAGGED	HAULED	HICKEY	HOOVES
******	HIEMAL	HAILED	HAULER	HIDDEN	HOPPED
GENEVA	HILDAS	HAILER	HAUSEN	HIGHER	HOPPER
GODIVA	HODMAN	HAIRED	HAWKED	HILLED	HORDED
GREAVE	HOOKAH	HALLEL	HAWKER	HILLER	HORDES
GRIEVE	HOORAY	HALLEY	HAWSER	HILTED	HORNED
GROOVE	HOWDAH	HALOED	HAWSES	HINDER	HORNET
GROOVY	HUBCAP	HALOES	HAZIER	HINGED	HORSED
******	HURRAH	HALSEY	HEADED	HINGES	HORSES
G---X-	HURRAY	HALTED	HEADER	HINTED	HORSEY
******	HUSSAR	HALTER	HEALED	HIPPED	HOSIER
GALAXY	HYDRAE	HALVED	HEALER	HISSED	HOSTED
******	HYDRAS	HALVES	HEAPED	HISSER	HOSTEL
G---Y-	HYENAS	HAMDEN	HEARER	HISSES	HOTBED
******	HYETAL	HAMLET	HEATED	HITHER	HOTTED
GERRYS	HYMNAL	HAMMED	HEATER	HITLER	HOTTER
GERTYS	HYPHAE	HAMMER	HEAVED	HITTER	HOUSED
GLADYS	HYPHAL	HAMPER	HEAVEN	HOAXED	HOUSES
******	******	HANCES	HEAVER	HOAXER	HOWLED
G---Z-	H---B-	HANDED	HEAVES	HOAXES	HOWLER
******	******	HANDEL	HEBREW	HOBBES	HOYDEN
GROSZY	HECUBA	HANGED	HEDGED	HOBOES	HUFFED
******	HEREBY	HANGER	HEDGER	HOCKED	HUGGED
H---A-	******	HANKER	HEDGES	HOCKEY	HUGHES
******	H---C-	HANSEL	HEEDED	HODDEN	HULKED
HABEAS	******	HAPPED	HEEDER	HOGGED	HULLED
HAEMAL	HAUNCH	HAPPEN	HEELED	HOIDEN	HUMBER
HALLAH	HELICO	HARDEN	HEELER	HOLDER	HUMMED
HAMMAL	HIJACK	HARDER	HEFTED	HOLIER	HUMMER
HAMZAS	HOOTCH	HARKED	HEIFER	HOLIES	HUMPED
HANGAR	HORACE	HARKEN	HELLEN	HOLLER	HUNGER
HANNAH	******	HARLEM	HELLER	HOLMES	HUNTED
HANNAS	H---D-	HARLEY	HELMED	HOMIER	HUNTER
HARLAN	******	HARMED	HELMET	HONIED	HURLED
HARTAL	HAIRDO	HARPED	HELPED	HONKED	HURLER
HAWHAW	HALIDE	HARPER	HELPER	HONKER	HURLEY
HAZZAN	HALIDS	HARVEY	HELTER	HOODED	HURTER
HEDRAL	HEXADS	HASHED	HELVES	HOOFED	HUSHED
HEEHAW	HOARDS	HASHES	HEMMED	HOOFER	HUSHES
HELLAS	HOUNDS	HASLET	HEMMER	HOOKED	HUSKED
HENNAS	HYOIDS	HASPED	HEMPEN	HOOKER	HUSKER
HEPTAD	******	HASSEL	HENLEY	HOOKEY	HUTTED
HERBAL	H---E-	HASTED	HERDED	HOOPED	HUXLEY
HEREAT	******	HASTEN	HERDER	HOOPER	HYADES
HERMAE	HACKED	HASTES	HERMES	HOOTED	HYMNED
HERMAI	HACKEE	HATRED	HEROES	HOOTER	HYPHEN
HERMAN	HACKER	HATTED	HERPES	HOOVED	HYSTER

```
******      HUBRIS      ******      ******      HEWERS      HOISTS
H---F-      HUGHIE      H---M-      H---O-      HIDERS      HORSTE
******      HYBRID      ******      ******      HIKERS      HUMPTY
HUMIFY      HYBRIS      HAKIMS      HAGDON      HILARY      ******
******      HYDRIC      HAREMS      HALLOO      HIRERS      H---U-
H---G-      HYGEIA      HAULMY      HALLOW      HOBART      ******
******      HYMNIC      HEAUME      HANSOM      HOLARD      HAGBUT
HOMAGE      HYPNIC      HIRAMS      HARBOR      HOMBRE      HALLUX
******      ******      ******      HARLOT      HOMERS      HAMAUL
H---H-      H---K-      H---N-      HARLOW      HONORE      HANGUP
******      ******      ******      HARROW      HONORS      HATFUL
HEATHS      HOICKS      HADING      HATBOX      HORARY      HELIUM
HEATHY      ******      HALING      HAYBOX      HOVERS      HIATUS
HEIGHT      H---L-      HARING      HAYMOW      HOWARD      HICCUP
HONSHU      ******      HATING      HEADON      HUBERT      HINDUS
******      HABILE      HAVANA      HEBRON      HUMORS      HIPPUS
H---I-      HACKLE      HAVENS      HECTOR      HUNGRY      HOGNUT
******      HAGGLE      HAVENT      HEDRON      ******      HOLDUP
HACKIE      HAMALS      HAVING      HELIOS      H---S-      HONOUR
HAGGIS      HANDLE      HAWING      HENDON      ******      HOOKUP
HALOID      HARDLY      HAYING      HEREOF      HARASS      HUBBUB
HARBIN      HAROLD      HAZING      HEREON      HEARSE      HUMBUG
HARMIN      HASSLE      HELENA      HERIOT      HEARST      HUMOUR
HARRIS      HAZELS      HELENS      HEZION      HERESY      ******
HATPIN      HAZILY      HERONS      HICKOK      HEXOSE      H---V-
HATTIE      HECKLE      HEWING      HIPPOS      HOARSE      ******
HAWAII      HEDDLE      HEXANE      HOBNOB      HOLISM      HUELVA
HECTIC      HERALD      HEXING      HOLLOW      HONEST      ******
HEDWIG      HEXYLS      HEXONE      HOODOO      HUGEST      H---Y-
HEMOID      HIGGLE      HIDING      HOOPOE      ******      ******
HENBIT      HIGHLY      HIEING      HORROR      H---T-      HARRYS
HENRIS      HOBBLE      HIKING      HOTBOX      ******      HATTYS
HERDIC      HOLILY      HIRING      HOTPOT      HABITS      HENRYS
HEREIN      HOMELY      HIVING      HOTROD      HALITE      HETTYS
HERMIT      HOMILY      HOEING      HUDSON      HALUTZ      HOLLYS
HERNIA      HOOPLA      HOGANS      HYDROS      HAMITE      HONEYS
HERNIO      HOPPLE      HOLING      HYPNOS      HAUNTS      ******
HEROIC      HOTELS      HOMING      HYSSOP      HEALTH      I---A-
HEROIN      HOURLY      HOMINY      ******      HEARTH      ******
HESIOD      HOVELS      HONING      H---R-      HEARTS      IBADAN
HESTIA      HUCKLE      HOPING      ******      HEARTY      ICECAP
HIPPIE      HUDDLE      HOSING      HALERS      HECATE      ICEMAN
HISPID      HUGELY      HUMANE      HATERS      HEISTS      INDIAN
HOGTIE      HUMBLE      HUMANS      HAZARD      HELOTS      INROAD
HOLMIC      HUMBLY      HURONS      HAZERS      HEMATO      INSPAN
HORNIE      HURDLE      HYMENO      HEGIRA      HEPATO      INSTAR
HORRID      HURTLE      HYMENS      HEJIRA      HERETO      INWRAP
HOURIS      HUSTLE      HYMENS      HETERO      HIVITE      IONIAN
```

IPECAC	IMARET	******	INDULT	IRVINS	INTERS
ISAIAH	IMBUED	**I---H-**	INFOLD	IRWINS	INTURN
ISHTAR	IMBUES	******	INGULF	ISLAND	INVERT
ISOBAR	IMIDES	ICHTHY	INHALE	ISLING	INWARD
******	IMINES	******	INSOLE	******	******
I---B-	IMMIES	**I---I-**	INSULT	**I---O-**	**I---S-**
******	IMOGEN	******	INWALL	******	******
IMBIBE	INBRED	IAMBIC	ISEULT	ICEBOX	ICIEST
INCUBI	INCHED	IATRIC	ITSELF	IGLOOS	IDLEST
INDABA	INCHES	IBERIA	******	IGOROT	ILLUSE
******	INDEED	ICONIC	**I---M-**	INCHON	ILLUST
I---C-	INDIES	IMPAIR	******	INDOOR	IMMESH
******	INDUED	INDRIS	IBEAMS	INFLOW	IMPASS
IDIOCY	INDUES	INGRID	IDIOMS	INKPOT	IMPISH
IGNACE	INGRES	INLAID	ILLUME	ISADOR	IMPOSE
IMPACT	INKIER	INSTIL	INARMS	ISIDOR	IMPOST
INARCH	INKLES	INTUIT	INCOME	ISOGON	INCASE
INDICT	INLIER	INULIN	INFAMY	ISOPOD	INCEST
INDUCE	INSTEP	IRANIS	INHUME	******	INCISE
INDUCT	INURED	IRAQIS	INTIMA	**I---P-**	INCUSE
INFECT	INURES	IRENIC	INTOMB	******	INFEST
INJECT	IRENES	IRIDIC	******	INCEPT	INFUSE
INLACE	IRIDES	IRITIC	**I---N-**	******	INGEST
INSECT	IRISED	IRITIS	******	**I---R-**	INMESH
INTACT	IRISES	IRONIC	IDLING	******	INMOST
ISAACS	IRONED	ISATIN	IGUANA	IDLERS	INRUSH
ITHACA	IRONER	ISCHIA	IMMUNE	IGNORE	INSIST
******	ISABEL	ISSEIS	IMMUNO	ILFORD	INVEST
I---D-	ISOBEL	ISTRIA	IMPEND	IMBARK	IODISM
******	ISOHEL	ITALIC	IMPING	IMMURE	******
IMBEDS	ISOMER	******	INBAND	IMPARK	**I---T-**
IMBODY	ISRAEL	**I---K-**	INDENE	IMPART	******
IMPEDE	ISSUED	******	INDENT	IMPORT	IDEATE
INSIDE	ISSUER	INJOKE	INFANT	IMPURE	IDIOTS
INVADE	ISSUES	INTAKE	INKING	INBORN	IGNITE
IODIDE	ITCHED	INVOKE	INLAND	INCORP	IMPUTE
ISOLDE	ITCHES	******	INNING	INCURS	INCITE
******	******	**I---L-**	INSANE	INFERO	INDITE
I---E-	**I---F-**	******	INTEND	INFERS	INGOTS
******	******	ICALLY	INTENT	INFIRM	INLETS
IBEXES	IGNIFY	ICICLE	INTONE	INFORM	INMATE
IBICES	******	IDEALS	INURNS	INHERE	INNATE
IBIDEM	**I---G-**	IDYLLS	INVENT	INJURE	INPUTS
IBISES	******	ILOILO	INWIND	INJURY	INSETS
ICEMEN	ICINGS	IMBALM	IODINE	INKERS	INVITE
ILEXES	IMPUGN	IMPALA	IONONE	INSERT	IODATE
IMAGED	INCAGE	IMPALE	IRKING	INSURE	IOLITE
IMAGES	INDIGO	IMPELS	IRVING	INTERN	ISLETS

******	JORDAN	JEERED	JUDGED	JUGGLE	JONSON
I---U-	JOSIAH	JEERER	JUDGER	JUMBLE	JUNCOS
******	JOSIAS	JELLED	JUDGES	JUNGLE	JUNIOR
IAMBUS	JOTHAM	JENNET	JUGGED	JUNGLY	******
ICARUS	JOVIAL	JEREED	JUICER	JURELS	J---P-
IMBRUE	JOVIAN	JERKED	JUICES	JUSTLY	******
INDIUM	JUBBAH	JERSEY	JULIES	******	JALOPS
INFLUX	JUDEAN	JESSED	JULIET	J---M-	JALOPY
INHAUL	JULIAN	JESSES	JUMPED	******	JOSEPH
INSOUL	JULIAS	JESTED	JUMPER	JEMIMA	JULEPS
IODOUS	JUMBAL	JESTER	JUNKED	JEREMY	******
IOLCUS	JUNEAU	JETTED	JUNKER	JEROME	J---R-
IONIUM	JUNTAS	JIBBED	JUNKET	JORAMS	******
IREFUL	******	JIBBER	JURIES	JORUMS	JABIRU
ITIOUS	J---B-	JIGGED	JUTTED	******	JETHRO
******	******	JIGGER	******	J---N-	JOKERS
I---V-	JACOBS	JILTED	J---H-	******	JURORS
******	JUJUBE	JILTER	******	JACANA	******
INWOVE		JINKED	JONAHS	JADING	J---S-
******	J---C-	JINKER	JUDAHS	JAPANS	******
I---W-	******	JINNEE	******	JAPING	JADISH
******	JANICE	JINXED	J---I-	JARINA	JEWESS
IMPAWN	JOUNCE	JINXES	******	JASONS	JEWISH
INDOWS	******	JITNEY	JACKIE	JAWING	JOCOSE
INLAWS	J---D-	JITTER	JAPHIA	JEANNE	JURIST
******	******	JOBBED	JARVIS	JEEING	JUTISH
I--X-	JIHADS	JOBBER	JERKIN	JEJUNE	******
******	******	JOCKEY	JERVIS	JIBING	J---T-
ICEAXE	J---E-	JOGGED	JESSIE	JIMINY	******
******	******	JOGGER	JESUIT	JIVING	JABOTS
I---Y-	JABBED	JOINED	JEZAIL	JOANNA	JANETS
******	JABBER	JOINER	JIMMIE	JOANNE	JAUNTS
INLAYS	JACKED	JOLIET	JONNIE	JOCUND	JAUNTY
******	JACKET	JOLTED	JOPLIN	JOHANN	JOINTS
I---Z-	JAEGER	JOLTER	JUDAIC	JOHNNY	JOISTS
******	JAGGED	JORGES	JUNKIE	JOKING	JOUSTS
IODIZE	JAILED	JOSHED	JUSTIN	JOYING	JUDITH
IONIZE	JAILER	JOSHER	******	JUPONS	JUGATE
******	JAMIES	JOSHES	J---L-	JURANT	JURATS
J---A-	JAMMED	JOSIEA	******	******	******
******	JAPHET	JOSSES	JANGLE	J---O-	J---U-
JACKAL	JARRED	JOTTED	JEKYLL	******	******
JAGUAR	JARVEY	JOTTER	JEWELS	JAILOR	JAIPUR
JAINAS	JASPER	JOULES	JIGGLE	JARGON	JARFUL
JAMJAR	JAYVEE	JOYCES	JINGLE	JARROW	JOSHUA
JETSAM	JAZZED	JUAREZ	JINGLY	JERBOA	JOYFUL
JIGSAW	JAZZER	JUDAEA	JOGGLE	JETTON	JOYOUS
JINGAL	JAZZES	JUDAEO	JOSTLE	JOCKOS	JUGFUL

JULIUS
JUNIUS
JUSTUS
******
J---Y-
******
JACKYS
JENNYS
JERRYS
JIMMYS
JINNYS
******
K---A-
******
KAFTAN
KALIAN
KALPAK
KANSAN
KANSAS
KAPPAS
KARMAS
KARNAK
KEDDAH
KENDAL
KEYWAY
KIBLAH
KIDNAP
KITBAG
KOALAS
KODIAK
KONRAD
KOREAN
******
K---B-
******
KABOBS
KNOBBY
******
K---C-
******
KIRSCH
KITSCH
KOPECK
K---D-
******
KNEADS

******
K---E-
******
KAASES
KAISER
KASPER
KATIES
KAYOED
KECKED
KEDGED
KEDGES
KEELED
KEENED
KEENER
KEEPER
KEEVES
KEGLER
KELLER
KENNED
KENNEL
KEPLER
KERBED
KERMES
KERNED
KERNEL
KERSEY
KEYNES
KHYBER
KICKED
KICKER
KIDDED
KIDDER
KIDNEY
KILLED
KILLER
KILMER
KILTED
KILTER
KINDER
KINGED
KINKED
KINSEY
KIPPED
KIPPER
KISLEW
KISMET
KISSED
KISSER

KISSES
KITTED
KITTEN
KNAVES
KNIFED
KNIFES
KNIVES
KNOWER
KOINES
KOPJES
KOSHER
KRAKEN
KRISES
KRONEN
KRONER
KUCHEN
KUMMEL
******
K---H-
******
KEITHS
KNIGHT
KYUSHU
******
K---I-
******
KAFFIR
KALMIA
KAMSIN
KAOLIN
KATHIE
KAURIS
KELOID
KELPIE
KELTIC
KELVIN
KENNIE
KERMIS
KERMIT
KERRIE
KEWPIE
KHAKIS
KIBEIS
KIDDIE
KILTIE
KRUBIS
KUWAIT

******
K---K-
******
KABAKA
KABIKI
KABUKI
KAMIKS
KANAKA
KAPOKS
KAYAKS
KIOSKS
KNACKS
KNOCKS
KODAKS
KOPEKS
KULAKS
K---L-
******
KABALA
KAMALA
KECKLE
KEENLY
KERALA
KETTLE
KEVELS
KIBBLE
KINDLE
KINDLY
KINGLY
KIRTLE
KITTLE
KNEELS
KNELLS
KNOLLS
KNURLS
KNURLY
KOBOLD
KRAALS
******
K---M-
******
KOKOMO
******
K---N-
******
KALONG
KARENS

KETENE
KETONE
KEVINS
KEYING
KIMONO
KININS
KITING
KORUNA
KORUNY
******
K---O-
******
KARROO
KATION
KAZOOS
KEDRON
KELSON
KLAXON
KOODOO
KOWTOW
KRONOR
KRONOS
******
K---P-
******
KAKAPO
KNOSPS
******
K---R-
******
KNARRY
K---S-
******
KAVASS
KETOSE
KIBOSH
KINASE
KINESI
KUMISS
******
K---T-
******
KARATE
KARATS
KENITE
KERATO
KIBITZ

KINETO
KNOTTY
KNOUTS
KRAITS
******
K---U-
******
KALIUM
KRONUR
KRUBUT
KULTUR
******
K---Y-
******
KABAYA
KATHYS
KENNYS
KITTYS
******
L---A-
******
LABIAL
LACIAL
LACTAM
LAMIAE
LAMIAS
LAMMAS
LAMPAD
LAMPAS
LANDAU
LARIAT
LARVAE
LARVAL
LASCAR
LAURAE
LAURAS
LAYDAY
LAYMAN
LEEWAY
LEGMAN
LEHUAS
LEMMAS
LEONAS
LETHAL
LIANAS
LIBRAE
LIBRAS
LIBYAN

LILIAN	******	LASTEX	LEVIER	LOAFED	LUBBER
LINDAS	L---E-	LATEEN	LEVIES	LOAFER	LUCIEN
LINEAL	******	LATHED	LEWDER	LOAMED	LUFFED
LINEAR	LAAGER	LATHER	LEYDEN	LOANED	LUGGED
LINGAM	LABRET	LATHES	LIANES	LOAVES	LUGGER
LINGAS	LACHES	LATTEN	LIASED	LOBBED	LULLED
LIVIAS	LACIER	LATTER	LICHEE	LOBBER	LUMBER
LLAMAS	LACKED	LAUDED	LICHEN	LOCKED	LUMPED
LOGJAM	LACKEY	LAUDER	LICKED	LOCKER	LUMPEN
LONGAN	LADDER	LAUREL	LIDDED	LOCKET	LUNGED
LOOFAH	LADIES	LAWYER	LIEDER	LOCOED	LUNGEE
LOQUAR	LADLED	LAYMEN	LIEGES	LODGED	LUNGER
LOQUAT	LADLER	LAZIER	LIFTED	LODGER	LUNGES
LUCIAN	LADLES	LEADED	LIFTER	LODGES	LUNKER
LUCIAS	LAGGED	LEADEN	LILIED	LOFTED	LURKED
LUMBAR	LAGGER	LEADER	LILIES	LOFTER	LURKER
LUTEAL	LAIRED	LEAFED	LILTED	LOGGED	LUSHED
LYDIAS	LAKIER	LEAKED	LIMBED	LOGGER	LUSHER
LYTTAE	LALLED	LEANED	LIMBER	LOGIER	LUSHES
******	LAMBED	LEANER	LIMIER	LOITER	LUSTED
L---B-	LAMMED	LEAPED	LIMNED	LOLLED	LUSTER
******	LAMPED	LEAPER	LIMNER	LOLLER	LUTHER
LAVABO	LANCED	LEASED	LIMPED	LONGED	LYCEES
******	LANCER	LEASES	LIMPER	LONGER	LYNXES
L---C-	LANCES	LEAVED	LIMPET	LOOKED	******
******	LANCET	LEAVEN	LINDEN	LOOKER	L---F-
LAMECH	LANDED	LEAVER	LINGER	LOOMED	******
LAUNCE	LANDER	LEAVES	LINIER	LOOPED	LAYOFF
LAUNCH	LANKER	LECHER	LINKED	LOOPER	******
LEGACY	LANNER	LEDGER	LINNET	LOOSED	L---G-
LILACS	LAPPED	LEDGES	LINTEL	LOOSEN	******
LORICA	LAPPER	LEERED	LINTER	LOOSER	LADOGA
LUBECK	LAPPET	LEGGED	LIONEL	LOOSES	LANUGO
LUNACY	LAPSED	LEGMEN	LIPPED	LOOTED	LAVAGE
LYRICS	LAPSER	LEGREE	LIPPER	LOOTER	LINAGE
******	LAPSES	LEMUEL	LISPED	LOPPED	LOUNGE
L---D-	LARDED	LENDER	LISPER	LORDED	LOVAGE
******	LARDER	LENSES	LISTED	LOREEN	******
LAIRDS	LARGER	LENTEN	LISTEL	LORIES	L---H-
LAMBDA	LARKED	LESLEY	LISTEN	LOSSES	******
LAMEDS	LARKER	LESSEE	LISTER	LOUDEN	LAUGHS
LAREDO	LASHED	LESSEN	LITHER	LOUDER	LEACHY
LEPIDO	LASHER	LESSER	LITTER	LOUPES	LEIGHS
LIBIDO	LASHES	LESTER	LIVIER	LOURED	LITCHI
LIPIDS	LASSEN	LETTER	LIVRES	LOUSED	LOATHE
LLOYDS	LASSES	LEUDES	LIVYER	LOUSES	LOTAHS
LUANDA	LASTED	LEVEES	LOADED	LOUVER	LOUGHS
	LASTER	LEVIED	LOADER	LOWKEY	LYMPHO

******	LEANLY	LAVING	LASSOS	LINERS	LIGATE
L---I-	LEVELS	LAWING	LECTOR	LITERS	LIGHTS
******	LEWDLY	LAYING	LEGION	LIVERS	LIMITS
LACTIC	LIABLE	LAZING	LEMNOS	LIVERY	LOBATE
LADDIE	LIBELS	LEARNS	LENTOS	LIZARD	LOCATE
LAMBIE	LIGULA	LEARNT	LEPTON	LONERS	LOLITA
LANAIS	LIGULE	LEGEND	LESBOS	LOPERS	LUCITE
LASSIE	LIKELY	LEMONS	LESION	LOSERS	LUNATE
LATRIA	LIMPLY	LEVANT	LESSON	LOUVRE	LUNETS
LATVIA	LIMULI	LIERNE	LESSOR	LOVERS	LUXATE
LAURIE	LITTLE	LIGAND	LICTOR	LOWERS	******
LEADIN	LIVELY	LIKENS	LIQUOR	LOWERY	**L---U-**
LENTIL	LOBULE	LIKING	LISBOA	LUGERS	******
LEONIE	LOCALE	LIMENS	LISBON	LURERS	LABIUM
LEPSIA	LOCALS	LIMINA	LISSOM	LUSTRE	LABOUR
LESLIE	LONELY	LIMING	LLANOS	LUXURY	LABRUM
LIEBIG	LORDLY	LINENS	LOGION	******	LANGUR
LIGNIN	LOUDLY	LINING	LOLLOP	**L---S-**	LAPFUL
LIMBIC	LOVELL	LITANY	LONDON	******	LAPSUS
LIMPID	LOVELY	LIVENS	LOTION	LAMEST	LARRUP
LIPOID	LOWELL	LIVING	LOWBOY	LANOSE	LAWFUL
LIQUID	LUCILE	LOMENT	LUDLOW	LAOTSE	LAYOUT
LITHIA	LUELLA	LOMOND	LUMMOX	LATEST	LEAGUE
LITHIC	LUNULA	LOOING	******	LATISH	LIGNUM
LIZZIE	LUNULE	LOPING	**L---P-**	LAVISH	LIMBUS
LOCHIA	******	LORENE	******	LAXEST	LINEUP
LOGGIA	**L---M-**	LORENZ	LENAPE	LEGIST	LINGUA
LOOKIN	******	LOSING	LETUPS	LIAISE	LITMUS
LORAIN	LEGUME	LOVING	******	LIPASE	LOCKUP
LOTTIE	LIPOMA	LOWING	**L---R-**	LOCUST	LUCIUS
LOVEIN	******	LUCENT	******	LOUISA	LUTEUM
LUBLIN	**L---N-**	LUMENS	LABORS	LOUISE	LYCEUM
LUDWIG	******	LUMINA	LAGERS	LOWEST	******
LUETIC	LACING	LUMINI	LAHORE	LUTIST	**L---Y-**
LUNGIS	LACUNA	LUMINO	LAKERS	LYRISM	******
******	LADING	LUPINE	LAPARO	LYRIST	LARRYS
L---L-	LADINO	LURING	LASERS	******	LENNYS
******	LAGUNE	LUTING	LATERA	**L---T-**	LEROYS
LABELS	LAKING	LYSINE	LAVERS	******	LIBBYS
LABILE	LAMENT	LYSING	LAYERS	LANATE	LIMEYS
LACILY	LAMINA	LYSINS	LAZARS	LAXITY	LIZZYS
LAMELY	LAMING	******	LEGERS	LEANTO	******
LANKLY	LAPINS	**L---O-**	LEMURS	LEGATE	**M---A-**
LAPELS	LARINE	******	LENORE	LEGATO	******
LASTLY	LARYNG	LAGOON	LEPERS	LENGTH	MADCAP
LATELY	LARYNX	LAPDOG	LEVERS	LENITY	MADMAN
LAZILY	LATENT	LARDON	LIFERS	LEVITE	MADRAS
LAZULI	LATINS	LARGOS	LIGURE	LEVITY	MAENAD

MAGYAR	MORGAN	MADDEN	MASTER	MIDGET	MONIES
MAMBAS	MORTAL	MADDER	MATTED	MIFFED	MONKEY
MAMMAE	MORTAR	MADGES	MATTEO	MIGUEL	MONTES
MAMMAL	MUDCAP	MADMEN	MATTER	MILDEN	MOOLEY
MAMMAS	MUGGAR	MAGNET	MATTES	MILDER	MOONED
MANDAN	MULLAH	MAGUEY	MAUDES	MILDEW	MOORED
MANIAC	MURRAY	MAHLER	MAULED	MILIEU	MOOTED
MANIAS	MUSCAE	MAIDEN	MAULER	MILKED	MOOTER
MANTAS	MUSCAT	MAILED	MAUSER	MILKER	MOPPED
MANUAL	MUTUAL	MAILER	MAUVES	MILLED	MOPPET
MARGAY	MYRIAD	MAIMED	MAYHEM	MILLER	MOREEN
MARIAN	MYRNAS	MAIMER	MAZIER	MILLET	MORGEN
MARIAS	******	MAIZES	MEAGER	MILTED	MORLEY
MARTAS	M---C-	MALLED	MEANER	MILTER	MORSEL
MAUMAU	******	MALLEE	MEDLEY	MINCED	MOSLEM
MAYDAY	MACACO	MALLET	MEEKER	MINCER	MOSLEY
MAYHAP	MALACO	MALTED	MEETER	MINCES	MOSSES
MECCAN	MALICE	MAMIES	MELDED	MINDED	MOTHER
MECCAS	MARACA	MAMMET	MELEES	MINDER	MOTLEY
MEDIAE	MEDICI	MANGER	MELTED	MINTED	MOUSED
MEDIAL	MEDICO	MANNED	MELTER	MINTER	MOUSER
MEDIAN	MEDICS	MANNER	MEMBER	MINUET	MOUSES
MEDLAR	MEJICO	MANSES	MENDED	MINXES	MOVIES
MEDWAY	MENACE	MANTEL	MENDEL	MISLED	MUCKED
MENIAL	MEXICO	MANTES	MENDER	MISSED	MUCKER
MENSAL	MIMICS	MANUEL	MENSES	MISSEL	MUDDED
MENTAL	MOHOCK	MAPLES	MEOWED	MISSES	MUDDER
MERMAN	MOLOCH	MAPPED	MERCER	MISTED	MUFFED
MESCAL	MONACO	MARCEL	MERGED	MISTER	MUGGED
MESIAL	MONICA	MARGES	MERGER	MITRED	MUGGER
MESIAN	MUNICH	MARIES	MERGES	MITTEN	MULLED
MICMAC	MYRICA	MARKED	MERLES	MIZZEN	MULLEN
MIDDAY	******	MARKER	MERMEN	MOANED	MULLER
MIDWAY	M---D-	MARKET	MERSEY	MOATED	MULLET
MILLAY	******	MARLED	MESHED	MOBBED	MULLEY
MINOAN	MALADY	MARRED	MESHER	MOBBER	MUMMED
MIRIAM	MAUNDS	MARRER	MESHES	MOCKED	MUMMER
MISHAP	MAUNDY	MARTEN	MESMER	MOCKER	MURDER
MISKAL	MELODY	MARVEL	MESNES	MOILED	MURIEL
MISLAY	MIKADO	MASHED	MESSED	MOILER	MURRES
MISSAL	MILADY	MASHER	MESSES	MOLDED	MURREY
MITRAL	MONADS	MASHES	MESTEE	MOLDER	MUSHED
MOBCAP	MONODY	MASKED	METIER	MOLIES	MUSHER
MOIRAS	MOULDS	MASKEG	MEWLED	MOLTED	MUSHES
MOLLAH	MOULDY	MASKER	MICHEL	MOLTEN	MUSKEG
MONDAY	******	MASSED	MICKEY	MOLTER	MUSKET
MOOLAH	M---E-	MASSES	MIDDEN	MONGER	MUSSED
MOREAU	******	MASTED	MIDGES	MONIED	MUSSEL
	MACLES				
	MADDED				

MUSSES	MARCIA	MYOSIS	MORALE	MELANO	MATRON
MUSTEE	MARGIE	MYSTIC	MORALS	MELONS	MATZOS
MUSTER	MARGIN	MYTHIC	MORELS	MENINX	MATZOT
MUTTER	MARLIN	******	MORULA	MERINO	MAYPOP
MYOPES	MARTIN	M---K-	MOSTLY	MESONS	MEADOW
MYRMEC	MARVIN	******	MOTELS	METING	MELLON
******	MASHIE	MARKKA	MOTILE	MEWING	MELLOW
M---F-	MASSIF	MOLTKE	MOTTLE	MIMING	MELTON
******	MASTIC	MOPOKE	MUCKLE	MINING	MENTOR
MINIFY	MATRIX	******	MUDDLE	MIRING	MERLON
MODIFY	MATTIE	M---L-	MUFFLE	MIXING	METEOR
MOTIFS	MEALIE	******	MUMBLE	MOLINE	METHOD
******	MEANIE	MABELS	MURALS	MOMENT	METROS
M---G-	MEGRIM	MACKLE	MUSCLE	MOOING	MEZZOS
******	MELVIN	MACULA	MUTULE	MOPING	MICRON
MALAGA	MEMOIR	MACULE	MUZZLE	MORONS	MIGNON
MALIGN	MENDIP	MAINLY	MYRTLE	MOURNS	MIKLOS
MANAGE	MENHIR	MANGLE	MYSELF	MOVING	MILTON
MANEGE	MERCIA	MANILA	******	MOWING	MINION
MENAGE	MERLIN	MANTLE	M---M-	MURINE	MINNOW
METAGE	MERVIN	MARBLE	******	MUSING	MIRROR
MILAGE	METRIC	MAYFLY	MADAME	MUSTNT	MONGOL
MIRAGE	MIDAIR	MAZILY	MADAMS	MUTANT	MONROE
******	MIDRIB	MEANLY	MAXIMA	MUTING	MORION
M---H-	MILLIE	MEASLY	MAXIMS	MUTINY	MORMON
******	MINNIE	MEDALS	MAZUMA	******	MORROS
MALTHA	MIOSIS	MEDDLE	METUMP	M---O-	MORROW
MANCHU	MIOTIC	MEEKLY	MIASMA	******	MORTON
MARSHA	MISDID	MEETLY	MINIMA	MACRON	MOSCOW
MARSHY	MISFIT	MEGALO	MINIMS	MAGGOT	MOTION
MARTHA	MISSIS	MEGILP	MYXOMA	MAGNOX	MOTMOT
MARTHE	MOHAIR	MERELY	******	MAISON	MOTTOS
MOISHE	MOLLIE	METALS	M---N-	MALLOW	MOUTON
MONTHS	MORBID	METTLE	******	MAMBOS	MUSKOX
MORPHO	MORRIS	MIAULS	MACING	MAMMON	MUTTON
MOUTHS	MOSAIC	MICELL	MAKING	MANGOS	MYTHOI
MOUTHY	MOULIN	MICKLE	MALINE	MANIOC	MYTHOS
******	MUCOID	MIDDLE	MANANA	MARCOS	******
M---I-	MUFFIN	MIGGLE	MARINA	MARGOS	M---P-
******	MUFTIS	MILDLY	MARINE	MARGOT	METOPE
MADRID	MUSKIT	MINGLE	MASONS	MARION	MIXUPS
MAGGIE	MUSLIM	MISTLE	MATINE	MARLOW	******
MAGPIE	MUSLIN	MIZZLE	MATING	MARMOT	M---R-
MAISIE	MUZHIK	MOBILE	MATINS	MAROON	******
MANTIC	MYELIN	MODELS	MAXINE	MARROW	MACERS
MANTIS	MYOPIA	MODULE	MAYING	MASCON	MADURA
MAORIS	MYOPIC	MOGULS	MAZING	MASCOT	MADURO
MAQUIS	MYOSIN	MOHOLE	MEKONG	MATEOS	

MAIGRE	MODISH	MAYBUG	MICKYS	******	NIGGER
MAITRE	MOLEST	MEATUS	MILLYS	**N---D-**	NIGHER
MAJORS	MOMISM	MEDIUM	MOLLYS	******	NIPPED
MAKERS	MONGST	MEROUS	MONEYS	NAIADS	NIPPER
MALGRE	MONISM	MIDGUT	MONTYS	NEVADA	NIXIES
MALORY	MONIST	MILIUM	MORAYS	NOBODY	NOBBED
MANORS	MOPISH	MINIUM	MORTYS	NOMADS	NOBLER
MANURE	MORASS	MISCUE	MOSEYS	******	NOCKED
MASERS	MOROSE	MISSUS	******	**N---E-**	NODDED
MASORA	MOUSSE	MOBIUS	**M---Z-**	******	NODDER
MATURE	MUCOSA	MOCKUP	******	NABBED	NOISED
MAYORS	MUCOSE	MORGUE	MEZUZA	NAGGED	NOISES
MAZERS	MULISH	MOSQUE	******	NAGGER	NOOSED
MEAGRE	MUTISM	MUCOUS	**N---A-**	NAILED	NOOSES
MEMORY	******	MUGGUR		NANTES	NOREEN
MESSRS	**M---T-**	MUKLUK	NARIAL	NAOSES	NOSHED
METERS	******	MURMUR	NARWAL	NAPIER	NOSIER
MILERS	MAGOTS	MUSEUM	NASIAL	NAPLES	NUCLEI
MILORD	MALATE	MUUMUU	NASSAU	NAPPED	NUDGED
MIMERS	MANITO	******	NATHAN	NAPPER	NUDGES
MINERS	MANITU	**M---V-**	NECTAR	NAPPES	NUGGET
MINORS	MERITS	******	NEURAL	NARKED	NUMBED
MISERE	MIGHTY	MOHAVE	NILGAI	NASSER	NUMBER
MISERS	MINUTE	MOJAVE	NORIAS	NATTER	NURSED
MISERY	MOIETY	MOTIVE	NORMAL	NAUSEA	NURSER
MITERS	MOULTS	******	NORMAN	NAVIES	NURSES
MIXERS	MOUNTS	**M---W-**	NORMAS	NEARED	NUTLET
MODERN	MOUNTY	******	NORWAY	NEARER	NUTMEG
MOHURS	MULCTS	MACAWS	NOUGAT	NEATEN	NUTTED
MOLARS	MUTATE	MALAWI	NOUNAL	NEATER	NUTTER
MOPERS	MYCETE	MOHAWK	NUBIAN	NECKED	******
MOTORS	******	******	NUBIAS	NEEDED	**N---F-**
MOVERS	**M---U-**	**M---X-**	NUCHAE	NEEDER	
MOWERS	******	******	NULLAH	NEPHEW	NAZIFY
MOZART	MADEUP	MAXIXE	******	NERVED	NIDIFY
******	MAGNUM	******	**N---B-**	NERVES	NOTIFY
M---S-	MAHBUB	**M---Y-**	******	NESTED	******
******	MAHOUT	******	NABOBS	NETHER	**N---G-**
MAOISM	MAKEUP	MALAYA	NAWABS	NETTED	******
MAOIST	MANFUL	MALAYS	NEARBY	NEUMES	NONAGE
MARIST	MANQUE	MAMEYS	******	NEUTER	NONEGO
MAYEST	MANTUA	MANDYS	**N---C-**	NIBBED	******
MEDUSA	MARAUD	MARTYR	******	NICHED	**N---H-**
MEGASS	MARCUS	MARTYS	NAUTCH	NICHES	******
MEREST	MARDUK	MATEYS	NOTICE	NICKED	NAUGHT
MIMOSA	MARKUP	MCCOYS	NOVICE	NICKEL	NAVAHO
MISUSE	MARQUE	MELVYN	NUANCE	NICKER	NEIGHS
MODEST	MASQUE	METHYL		NIECES	NINTHS

NOUGHT	NEARLY	NICENE	NOMISM	OPERAS	OLLIES
NYMPHA	NEATLY	NIDING	NOWISE	ORDEAL	OMELET
NYMPHO	NEBULA	NIXING	NUDISM	OREGAN	ONAGER
NYMPHS	NEEDLE	NOCENT	NUDIST	ORGEAT	ONUSES
******	NEROLI	NOSING	******	ORIGAN	OODLES
N---I-	NESTLE	NOTING	N---T-	ORPHAN	OOZIER
******	NETTLE	NOVENA	******	OSSIAN	OPENED
NAOMIS	NEVILE	NUMINA	NEGATE	OSTEAL	OPENER
NAPKIN	NEVILL	NYLONS	NEMATO	OUTLAW	OPINED
NAPPIE	NEWELS	******	NICETY	OUTLAY	OPINES
NASTIC	NIBBLE.	N---O-	NIGHTS	OUTMAN	ORATED
NELLIE	NICELY	******	NIGHTY	OUTRAN	ORATES
NEREID	NICOLE	NARROW	NIMITZ	OUTSAT	ORGIES
NEREIS	NIELLI	NASION	NINETY	OVISAC	ORIGEN
NETTIE	NIELLO	NATION	NUDITY	OVULAR	ORKNEY
NEVOID	NIGELS	NATRON	******	******	ORYXES
NIACIN	NIGGLE	NEKTON	N---U-	O---C-	OSPREY
NIOBIC	NIMBLE	NELSON	******	******	OSTLER
NISEIS	NIMBLY	NESTOR	NAEVUS	OBJECT	OUNCES
NITRIC	NIPPLE	NEURON	NASHUA	OBTECT	OUSTED
NITRID	NOBALL	NEWTON	NESSUS	OCLOCK	OUSTER
NITWIT	NOBBLE	NIMROD	NIMBUS	OFFICE	OUTLET
NOESIS	NODDLE	NIPPON	******	OPTICS	OUTSET
NOETIC	NODULE	NOGOOD	N---V-	ORRICE	OVULES
NOGGIN	NOELLE	NONCOM	******	******	OXEYED
NORDIC	NOODLE	NOSHOW	NATIVE	O---D-	OXEYES
NORNIR	NOPALS	NOTION	******	******	OXIDES
NORRIS	NOSILY	******	N---Y-	OCTADS	OXYGEN
NOSTIC	NOVELS	N---R-	******	ONEIDA	OYSTER
NUBBIN	NOZZLE	******	NAGOYA	OREADS	******
NUDNIK	NUBBLE	NADIRS	NANCYS	OREIDE	O---F-
NUNCIO	NUBBLY	NAMERS	NELLYS	OROIDE	******
NUTRIA	NUBILE	NAPERY	NICKYS	OVERDO	ONEOFF
******	NUDELY	NATURE	NOWAYS	OXHIDE	OSSIFY
N---J-	NUMBLY	NEPHRO	******	******	******
******	NUZZLE	NEWARK	O---A-	O---E-	O---G-
NAVAJO		NOMURA	******	******	******
******	N---M-	NONARY	OCREAE	OAKLEY	OBLIGE
N---K-	******	NOTARY	OCULAR	OBEYED	OHMAGE
******	NAHUMS	NOTERS	OFFDAY	OBEYER	OOLOGY
NEVSKI	******	******	OGDOAD	OBITER	OPPUGN
******	N---N-	N---S-	OGIVAL	OCASEY	ORANGE
N---L-	******	******	OHIOAN	OFFSET	ORANGS
******	NADINE	NANISM	OILCAN	OGIVES	OSWEGO
NAMELY	NAGANA	NAZISM	OLDHAM	OILIER	******
NAPALM	NAMING	NEWEST	OMEGAS	OKAYED	O---H-
NASALS	NARINE	NICEST	ONEWAY	OLIVER	******
NAVELS	NATANT	NODOSE	OOMIAK	OLIVES	ORACHS

```
******        OUZELS    OCTROI    OBLAST    OUTPUT    PENTAD
O---I-        OVALLY    ODDJOB    OBOIST    OUTRUN    PHYLAE
******        OVERLY    OOPHOR    OBSESS    ******    PICKAX
OBTAIN        ******    OPTION    OBTEST    O---V-    PIEMAN
ODYNIA        O---M-    ORATOR    OBTUSE    ******    PIENAL
OKAPIS        ******    OREGON    ODDEST    OCTAVE    PILLAR
OLEFIN        OEDEMA    ORISON    ODESSA    OCTAVO    PINDAR
OLIVIA        OEPEMA    OUTFOX    OFFISH    OTTAVA    PINEAL
ORCEIN        OPTIMA    OVIBOS    OGRESS    ******    PINNAE
ORCHID        OPTIME    ******    OGRISH    O---W-    PINNAL
ORCHIL        ******    O---P-    OLDEST    ******    PISGAH
ORCHIO        O---N-    ******    OLDISH    OJIBWA    PITMAN
ORCHIS        ******    OCCUPY    ONRUSH    OTTAWA    PIZZAS
ORDAIN        OARING    OCTOPI    OPPOSE    OTTOWA    PLAGAL
ORIBIS        OBLONG    ORLOPS    ORGASM    OXBOWS    PLANAR
ORIGIN        OBTUND    OXLIPS    OSMOSE    ******    PLATAN
ORPHIC        OCEANS    ******    OTIOSE    O---Z-    PLAYAS
OSIRIS        OCTANE    O---R-    OWLISH    ******    PLAZAS
OSSEIN        OCTANT    ******    ******    ORMUZD    PLEIAD
OTITIS        OFFEND    OBVERT    O---T-    ******    PLICAE
OUTBID        OFFING    OCCURS    ******    P---A-    PLURAL
OUTDID        OGLING    OCHERS    ******    ******    POLEAX
OUTFIT        OILING    OCHERY    OBLATE    PALEAE    POLKAS
OUTSIT        ONIONS    OEUVRE    OCTETS    PALLAS    POPLAR
OUTWIT        ONIONY    OFFERS    ODDITY    PALMAR    PORTAL
OXALIC        ONLINE    OGLERS    ODETTE    PAMPAS    POSTAL
OXALIS        OOLONG    OHENRY    ODONTO    PANDAS    POTMAN
OXTAIL        OOZING    OILERS    OLEATE    PAPUAN    PREFAB
OZONIC        OPTANT    ONAGRI    OMENTA    PARCAE    PREPAY
******        OPTING    ONEIRO    ONSETS    PARIAH    PRESAS
O---L-        ORBING    ONWARD    OOCYTE    PARIAN    PREWAR
******        ORGANA    ORDERS    OOLITE    PARKAS    PRIMAL
OCCULT        ORGANO    ORDURE    OPHITE    PARLAY    PTISAN
OCELLI        ORGANS    ORMERS    OPIATE    PARRAL    PULSAR
OILILY        ORIENT    ORNERY    OPORTO    PARRAL    PUNJAB
ONEILL        ORPINE    ORRERY    ORBITS    PASCAL    PUNKAS
ONFALL        ORPINS    OSBERT    ORNATE    PASHAS    PURDAH
OOZILY        OSCANS    OSBORN    ORNITH    PASTAS    PUTNAM
OPENLY        OSCINE    OSCARS    OWLETS    PATHAN    ******
ORACLE        OSMOND    OSIERS    ******    PAULAS    P---B-
ORALLY        OSMUND    OTHERS    O---U-    PAWPAW    ******
ORIELS        OSTEND    OTTERS    ******    PAXWAX    PHLEBO
ORIOLE        OUTING    OUTCRY    OBELUS    PAYDAY    PHOEBE
ORMOLU        OWNING    OUTERS    OBOLUS    PEDLAR    PLUMBO
ORWELL        ******    OWNERS    ODIOUS    PELIAS    PLUMBS
OSCULE        O---O-    OXFORD    OMASUM    PENIAL    ******
OSWALD        ******    ******    OMNIUM    PENMAN    P---C-
OUSELS        OBERON    O---S-    OPAQUE    PENNAE    ******
              OCELOT    OAFISH    OSMIUM    PENPAL    PALACE
                        OBIISM                       PANICE
```

PANICS	PALLED	PEAVEY	PIECES	PLUMED	PRATER
PAPACY	PALLET	PECKED	PIEMEN	PLUMES	PRATES
PAUNCH	PALMED	PECKER	PIETER	PLUSES	PRAYED
PEIRCE	PALMER	PECTEN	PIGGED	POCKET	PRAYER
PESACH	PALPED	PEEKED	PIGLET	PODDED	PREFER
PIERCE	PALTER	PEEKER	PIGPEN	POGIES	PREMED
PIRACY	PAMPER	PEELED	PILFER	POISED	PRETER
PLAICE	PANDER	PEELER	PILLED	POISES	PREYED
PLANCH	PANNED	PEENED	PIMPED	POKIER	PREYER
PLANCK	PANTED	PEEPED	PINGED	POKIES	PRICED
PLEACH	PANZER	PEEPER	PINIER	POLDER	PRICES
POLACK	PARCEL	PEERED	PINIES	POLLED	PRIDED
POLICE	PARGET	PEEVED	PINKED	POLLEE	PRIDES
POLICY	PARIES	PEEVES	PINNED	POLLEN	PRIMED
POMACE	PARKED	PEEWEE	PINNER	POLLER	PRIMER
POUNCE	PARKER	PEGGED	PINTER	POLLEX	PRIMES
PRANCE	PARLEY	PEGLEG	PIPIER	POMMEL	PRIVET
PREACH	PARREL	PEKOES	PIPPED	POMPEY	PRIZED
PRINCE	PARSEC	PELLET	PIQUED	PONDER	PRIZER
PUMICE	PARSED	PELTED	PIQUES	PONGEE	PRIZES
PUTSCH	PARSEE	PELTER	PIQUET	PONIED	PROBED
******	PARSES	PELVES	PISCES	PONIES	PROBER
P---D-	PARTED	PENCEL	PISHED	PONTES	PROBES
******	PASSED	PENDED	PISHES	POOLED	PROJET
PAGODA	PASSEE	PENMEN	PITHED	POOPED	PROLEG
PANADA	PASSER	PENNED	PITIED	POORER	PROPEL
PARADE	PASSES	PENNER	PITIES	POPPED	PROPER
PARODY	PASTED	PEPPED	PITMEN	POPPER	PROSED
PESADE	PASTEL	PEPPER	PITTED	POPPET	PROSER
PLAIDS	PASTER	PERKED	PIXIES	PORKER	PROSES
PLEADS	PASTES	PERMED	PLACED	PORTED	PROVED
POINDS	PATTED	PESTER	PLACER	PORTER	PROVEN
POMADE	PATTEN	PETREL	PLACES	POSIES	PROVER
POSADA	PATTER	PETTED	PLACET	POSSES	PROVES
POUNDS	PAUKER	PEWEES	PLANED	POSSET	PRUDES
PRAVDA	PAUPER	PEWTER	PLANER	POSTED	PRUNED
PSEUDO	PAUSED	PHASED	PLANES	POSTER	PRUNER
******	PAUSER	PHASES	PLANET	POTEEN	PRUNES
P---E-	PAUSES	PHLOEM	PLATED	POTHER	PUCKER
******	PAWNED	PHONED	PLATEN	POTTED	PUFFED
PACKED	PAWNEE	PHONES	PLATER	POTTER	PUFFER
PACKER	PAWNER	PHONEY	PLATES	POURED	PUGGED
PACKET	PAYEES	PHOOEY	PLAYED	POURER	PUGREE
PADDED	PEAHEN	PICKED	PLAYER	POUTED	PULLED
PADRES	PEAKED	PICKER	PLEBES	POUTER	PULLER
PAINED	PEALED	PICKET	PLOVER	POWDER	PULLET
PAIRED	PEASEN	PIECED	PLOWED	POWTER	PULLEY
PALAEO	PEASES	PIECER	PLOWER	PRATED	PULPED

PULPER	PIPAGE	PEPTIC	PROLIX	PENULT	PNEUMO
PULSED	PLEDGE	PERMIT	PROSIT	PEOPLE	PRISMS
PULSES	PLOUGH	PERSIA	PTOSIS	PERILS	PROEMS
PUMMEL	PLUNGE	PETRIE	PUBLIC	PERTLY	PSALMS
PUMPED	POTAGE	PHAGIA	PUFFIN	PESTLE	PYJAMA
PUMPER	PRONGS	PHASIA	PULLIN	PETALS	******
PUNIER	******	PHASIC	PULPIT	PETULA	**P---N-**
PUNNED	**P---H-**	PHASIS	PUNDIT	PHIALS	******
PUNNER	******	PHILIA	PURLIN	PHYLLO	PACING
PUNTED	PANCHO	PHILIP	PUTRID	PICKLE	PAEANS
PUNTER	PATCHY	PHOBIA	PYEMIA	PICULS	PAEONS
PUPPED	PEACHY	PHOBIC	PYEMIC	PIDDLE	PAEONY
PUPPET	PITCHY	PHOCIS	PYKNIC	PIFFLE	PAGANS
PUREED	PLASHY	PHONIA	PYOSIS	PILULE	PAGING
PUREES	PLIGHT	PHONIC	PYTHIA	PIMPLE	PALING
PURGED	PLUSHY	PHOTIC	PYTHIC	PIMPLY	PARANG
PURGER	POACHY	PHYSIC	PYURIA	PINOLE	PARENS
PURGES	PONCHO	PHYSIO	******	PINTLE	PARENT
PURLED	POUCHY	PHYTIN	**P---K-**	POMELO	PARING
PURLER	PSYCHE	PICNIC	******	POODLE	PATENS
PURRED	PSYCHO	PICRIC	PERUKE	POORLY	PATENT
PURSED	PUNCHY	PIDGIN	PLACKS	POPPLE	PATINA
PURSER	PYRRHA	PIGGIE	PLANKS	PORTLY	PATINE
PURSES	******	PIGGIN	PLUCKS	POSHLY	PAVANE
PURVEY	**P---I-**	PINKIE	PLUCKY	POTALE	PAVANS
PUSHED	******	PINXIT	PLUNKS	POTTLE	PAVING
PUSHER	PALAIS	PIPKIN	PRANKS	POWELL	PAWING
PUSHES	PALLID	PIPPIN	PRICKS	PRIMLY	PAYING
PUSSES	PANTIE	PISTIL	PRINKS	PROWLS	PECANS
PUSSEY	PAPAIN	PLACID	******	PUDDLE	PEDANT
PUTTED	PARSIS	PLAGIO	**P---L-**	PUDDLY	PEKANS
PUTTEE	PARVIS	PLASIA	******	PUEBLO	PEKING
PUTTER	PASSIM	PLASIS	PADDLE	PUNILY	PHRENO
PYXIES	PASTIL	PLEGIA	PALELY	PUPILS	PIKING
******	PATHIA	PLUGIN	PAMELA	PURELY	PILING
P---F-	PATOIS	PLUVIO	PANELS	PURFLE	PINANG
******	PAULIN	POETIC	PAPULA	PURPLE	PINENE
PACIFY	PAYNIM	PONTIC	PAPULE	PUSSLY	PINING
PAYOFF	PECTIC	PONTIL	PAROLE	PUZZLE	PINONS
PIAFFE	PECTIN	POPLIN	PARTLY	******	PIPING
PILAFF	PEEWIT	PORTIA	PAYOLA	**P---M-**	PIRANA
PILAFS	PELVIC	POTPIE	PEARLS	******	PITONS
PROOFS	PELVIS	POTSIE	PEARLY	PAJAMA	PLAINS
PURIFY	PENCIL	PRAXIS	PEBBLE	PANAMA	PLAINT
PUTOFF	PENNIA	PRECIS	PEBBLY	PLASMA	PLIANT
******	PENNIS	PREFIX	PEDALS	PLASMO	PLYING
P---G-	PEORIA	PRELIM	PEDDLE	PLUMMY	PODUNK
******	PEPSIN	PROFIT	PENILE	PNEUMA	POKING
PELAGE					
PHLEGM					

POLAND	PERRON	PROMPT	PERISH	PLINTH	PODIUM
POLING	PERSON	PYROPE	PERUSE	POINTE	PODOUS
POMONA	PETROL	******	PHRASE	POINTS	POILUS
PONENT	PHANON		PILOSE	POINTY	POLLUX
PORING	PHAROS	**P---R-**	PLEASE	POLITE	POPGUN
POSING	PHENOL	******	POLISH	POLITY	POROUS
POTENT	PHILOS	PACERS	POPISH	POSITS	POSEUR
PRAWNS	PHOTON	PALTRY	POTASH	POTATO	POSSUM
PREENS	PHOTOS	PANTRY	PRAISE	POULTS	POYOUS
PROCNE	PIANOS	PAPERS	PRIEST	POUSTO	PRAGUE
PRYING	PICTOR	PAPERY	PRISSY	PRESTO	PREVUE
PUISNE	PIGEON	PARERS	PROUST	PRETTY	PRIMUS
PUKING	PILLOW	PARURE	PUNISH	PRINTS	PULQUE
PULING	PINGOS	PASTRY	PUREST	PROCTO	PURSUE
PURANA	PINION	PATERS	PURISM	PRONTO	PUSHUP
PURINE	PINTOS	PAVERS	PURIST	PUPATE	PUTOUT
PUTONS	PISTOL	PAWERS	******	PURITY	PUTPUT
PYLONS	PISTON	PAYERS		PUSHTU	******
PYRANS	PLEXOR	PELTRY	**P---T-**	PYRITE	
PYRENE	PODSOL	PENURY	******	******	**P---W-**
PYRONE	PODZOL	PETARD	PAINTS		******
******	POGROM	PETERS	PAINTY	**P---U-**	PAPAWS
	POISON	PIERRE	PAIUTE	******	PSHAWS
P---O-	POMPOM	PIETRO	PALATE	PALPUS	******
******	POMPON	PIKERS	PARITY	PAPPUS	
PALLOR	PONTON	PINERY	PASHTO	PAREUS	**P---Y-**
PARDON	POTBOY	PIPERS	PEDATE	PASSUS	******
PARGOS	POTION	PLEURA	PEDATI	PAULUS	PADDYS
PARLOR	POTTOS	PLEURO	PELITE	PELEUS	PANSYS
PARROT	POWWOW	PLIERS	PELOTA	PENTUP	PAPAYA
PARSON	PRETOR	POETRY	PESETA	PEPLUM	PATSYS
PASTOR	PRISON	POKERS	PETITE	PEPLUS	PEGGYS
PATHOL	PROTON	POPERY	PEWITS	PHYLUM	PENNYS
PATHOS	PUNTOS	POSERS	PEYOTE	PICKUP	PERCYS
PATIOS	PUTLOG	POWERS	PICOTS	PIERUS	PERRYS
PATROL	PYTHON	PRIERS	PIGSTY	PIGNUS	PHENYL
PATRON	******	PRIORS	PILATE	PIGNUT	POLLYS
PATTON	**P---P-**	PRIORY	PILOTS	PILEUM	POPPYS
PAVIOR	******	PRYERS	PINITE	PILEUP	PROPYL
PAVLOV	PARAPH	PUGGRY	PIPETS	PILEUS	******
PEDROS	PELOPS	PULERS	PIPITS	PILOUS	**P---Z-**
PEGTOP	PHIPPS	******	PIRATE	PINDUS	******
PELION	PHOSPH		PIVOTS	PLAGUE	PIAZZA
PENGOS	PINUPS	**P---S-**	PLAITS	PLAGUY	******
PENNON	PLUMPS	******	PLANTS	PLAQUE	**Q---A-**
PEPLOS	POLYPS	PALEST	PLASTY	PLENUM	******
PEQUOD	PRIMPS	PAPIST	PLATTE	PLEXUS	QUAPAW
PEQUOT		PARISH	PLEATS	PLUTUS	QUASAR
PERIOD		PAVISE	PLENTY		QUOTAS

******	******	QUINTS	RUNWAY	RAGGED	REDDEN
Q---C-	**Q---L-**	QUIRTS	RUPIAH	RAGMEN	REDDER
******	******	QUOITS	******	RAIDED	REDEEM
QUENCH	QUAILS	******	**R---B-**	RAIDER	REDOES
QUINCE	QUELLS	**Q---U-**	******	RAILED	REEDED
QUINCY	QUILLS	******	RAJABS	RAINED	REEFED
QUITCH	******	QUIPUS	RHOMBI	RAISED	REEFER
******	**Q---M-**	QUORUM	RHUMBA	RAISER	REEKED
Q---E-	******	******	RHUMBS	RAISES	REEKER
******	QUALMS	**R---A-**	******	RAMIES	REELED
QUAKED	QUALMY	******	**R---C-**	RAMJET	REELER
QUAKER	******	RACIAL	******	RAMMED	REEVED
QUAKES	**Q---N-**	RADIAL	REBECK	RAMMER	REEVES
QUAVER	******	RADIAN	REBECS	RAMPED	REFLET
QUEBEC	QUAINT	RAGBAG	REDACT	RANEES	REFLEX
QUEUED	QUEANS	RAGDAY	REDUCE	RANGED	REFUEL
QUEUES	QUEENS	RAGLAN	REFACE	RANGER	REGLET
QUIRED	QUERNS	RAGMAN	REJECT	RANGES	REGRET
QUIRES	QUOINS	RAGTAG	RELICS	RANKED	REINED
QUIVER	******	RANDAL	RELICT	RANKER	RELIED
QUOTED	**Q---O-**	RANDAN	RESECT	RANTED	RELIEF
QUOTER	******	RAPHAE	ROCOCO	RANTER	RELIER
QUOTES	QUAHOG	RASCAL	RUBACE	RAPIER	RELIES
******	QUEZON	RATTAN	******	RAPPED	RENDED
Q---F-	******	RECTAL	**R---D-**	RAPPEE	RENDER
******	**Q---R-**	REDBAY	******	RAPPEL	RENEES
QUAFFS	QUADRI	REDCAP	RAPIDS	RAPPER	RENNET
******	QUAERE	REGNAL	RECEDE	RASHER	RENTED
Q---G-	QUARRY	REHEAR	REMADE	RASHES	RENTER
******	QUATRE	REHEAT	REMEDY	RASPED	RENTES
QUAGGA	QUEERS	RELOAD	REMUDA	RASPER	REOPEN
QUAGGY	******	RENTAL	RESEDA	RASTER	RESTED
******	**Q---S-**	REPEAL	RESIDE	RATHER	RESTER
Q---H-	******	REPEAT	ROALDS	RATTED	RETTED
******	QUEASY	REPLAY	ROUNDS	RATTEN	REUBEN
QUOTHA	QUINSY	RESEAT	RWANDA	RATTER	REVIEW
******	******	RESEAU	******	RAZEED	REVUES
Q---I-	**Q---T-**	REVEAL	**R---E-**	RAZEES	REVVED
******	******	RHINAL	******	RAZZED	RHODES
QUINIC	QUANTA	RHODAS	RABBET	RAZZES	RHYMED
******	QUANTS	RIATAS	RABIES	READER	RHYMER
Q---K-	QUARTE	RICTAL	RACHEL	REALES	RHYMES
******	QUARTO	RIPRAP	RACIER	REAMED	RIBBED
QUACKS	QUARTS	RIPSAW	RACKED	REAMER	RICHER
QUARKS	QUARTZ	RITUAL	RACKER	REAPED	RICHES
QUIRKS	QUESTS	RODMAN	RACKET	REAPER	RICKED
QUIRKS	QUILTS	ROSEAL	RAFTED	REARED	RICKEY
		RUMBAS	RAFTER	REARER	RIDDED

RIDDEN	RONDEL	RATIFY	REMAIN	RECALL	REALMS
RIDGED	ROOFED	REBUFF	RENNIN	REDDLE	REARMS
RIDGES	ROOFER	RIPOFF	RENOIR	REFILL	REGIME
RIFLED	ROOKED	RUNOFF	REPAID	REGALE	RESUME
RIFLER	ROOMED	******	REPAIR	REPELS	REVAMP
RIFLES	ROOMER		RETAIL	RESALE	RHEIMS
RIFTED	ROOTED	**R---G-**	RETAIN	RESELL	RHEUMY
RIGGED	ROOTER	******	RHIZIC	RESILE	******
RIGGER	ROPIER	RAVAGE	RHODIC	RESOLD	
RILLET	ROQUET	REFUGE	RICHIE	RESOLE	**R---N-**
RIMMED	ROSIER	RENEGE	ROBBIA	RESULT	******
RIMMER	ROSTER	RESIGN	ROBBIE	RETELL	RACINE
RINGED	ROTTED	RRHAGE	ROMAIC	RETOLD	RACING
RINGER	ROTTEN	RRHAGY	RONNIE	REVELS	RAGING
RINKED	ROTTER	RUBIGO	ROOKIE	REVILE	RAKING
RINSED	ROUGED	******	RUBRIC	REVOLT	RAMONA
RINSER	ROUGES		RUSKIN	RIBALD	RAPINE
RINSES	ROUSED	**R---H-**	RUSSIA	RICHLY	RAPING
RIOTED	ROUSER	******	RUSTIC	RIDDLE	RARING
RIOTER	ROUSES	RAJAHS	******	RIFFLE	RATINE
RIPLEY	ROUTED	RALPHS		RIMPLE	RATING
RIPPED	ROUTER	RANCHO	**R---K-**	RIPELY	RAVENS
RIPPER	ROUTES	RAYAHS	******	RIPPLE	RAVINE
RISKED	RUBBED	REECHO	REBUKE	RIPPLY	RAVING
RISKER	RUBBER	REICHS	REMAKE	RIVALS	RAYING
RITTER	RUBIES	RHYTHM	RETAKE	RIYALS	RAYONS
ROAMED	RUBLES	ROLPHS	REVOKE	ROBALO	RAZING
ROAMER	RUCHES	ROTCHE	******	ROMOLA	RECANT
ROARED	RUCKED	ROUCHE		ROMULO	RECENT
ROARER	RUDDER	ROUGHS	**R---L-**	RONALD	REDANS
ROBBED	RUFFED	******	******	ROOTLE	REDONE
ROBBER	RUGGED	**R---I-**	RABBLE	ROPILY	REFINE
ROBLES	RUGGER	******	RACILY	ROSILY	REFUND
ROCHET	RUINED	RABBIN	RADDLE	ROUBLE	REGENT
ROCKED	RUINER	RABBIS	RADULA	ROWELS	REGINA
ROCKER	RUMMER	RABBIT	RAFFLE	ROYALE	REIGNS
ROCKET	RUNLET	RACHIS	RAMBLE	ROYALS	RELENT
RODMEN	RUNNEL	RAFFIA	RANKLE	RUBBLE	RELINE
RODNEY	RUNNER	RAISIN	RANKLY	RUDDLE	REMAND
ROGUED	RUPEES	RANCID	RAOULS	RUDELY	REMANS
ROGUES	RUSHED	RAPHIS	RAPTLY	RUFFLE	REMIND
ROILED	RUSHER	RATLIN	RARELY	RUMBLE	REPAND
ROLLED	RUSHES	RAZZIA	RASHLY	RUMPLE	REPENT
ROLLER	RUSSET	RECOIL	RATALS	RUNDLE	REPINE
ROMMEL	RUSTED	REDFIN	RATELS	RUSTLE	RERUNS
ROMNEY	RUTTED	REEDIT	RATTLE	RUTILE	RESEND
ROMNEY	******	REGAIN	RAVELS	******	RESENT
ROMPED	**R---F-**	REGGIE	REALLY	**R---M-**	RESINS
ROMPER	******	REJOIN	REBELS	******	RETENE
	RAMIFY	RELAID	REBILL	RACEME	
	RAREFY			RADOME	

RETINA	RAPTOR	REMORA	REHASH	******	REPAYS
REWIND	RATION	REPORT	RELISH	**R---U-**	RICKYS
RIBAND	RATIOS	RESORB	REMISE	******	RODDYS
RICING	RATOON	RESORT	REMISS	RADIUM	RYUKYU
RIDENT	REASON	RETARD	REPASS	RADIUS	******
RIDING	REAVOW	RETIRE	REPAST	RAGOUT	**R---Z-**
RILING	RECKON	RETORT	REPOSE	RAJPUT	******
RIMING	RECTOR	RETURN	RESIST	RAMOUS	REBOZO
RIPENS	RECTOS	REVERE	RETUSE	RECOUP	******
RISING	REDDOG	REVERS	REVEST	RECTUM	**S---A-**
RIVING	REDHOT	REVERT	REVISE	RECTUS	******
ROBAND	REDTOP	REWARD	RIBOSE	REDBUD	SABBAT
ROBING	REFOOT	REWORD	RIMOSE	REDBUG	SABEAN
ROBINS	REGION	RICERS	RIPEST	REDGUM	SABRAS
ROCKNE	RETOOK	RIDERS	RIPOST	REFLUX	SACRAL
RODENT	RETOOL	RIGORS	ROBUST	REGIUS	SAGGAR
ROLAND	RETROD	RIMERS	ROMISH	RESCUE	SAIGAS
ROMANS	RHETOR	RISERS	RUDEST	RHESUS	SAIPAN
ROMANY	RHINOS	RITARD	RUGOSE	RICTUS	SALAAM
ROPING	RIBBON	RIVERS	******	RIGOUR	SALPAS
ROSING	ROBSON	ROBERT	**R---T-**	RIMOUS	SAMBAS
ROSINS	RODEOS	ROGERS	******	RISQUE	SAMIAN
ROSINY	RONDOS	ROSARY	RARITY	ROLLUP	SAMOAN
ROTUND	ROSCOE	ROSTRA	RATITE	ROTGUT	SAMPAN
ROVING	RUNYON	ROTARY	REACTS	RUCKUS	SANDAL
ROWANS	******	ROTORS	REALTY	RUEFUL	SANGAR
ROWENA	**R---P-**	ROVERS	REBATE	RUFOUS	SANJAK
ROWING	******	ROWERS	REBATO	RUGOUS	SANSAR
ROXANA	RECAPS	RULERS	REBUTS	RUMOUR	SAPHAR
ROXANE	RECEPT	RUMORS	RECITE	RUMPUS	SARSAR
RUBENS	RECIPE	RUPERT	REFITS	RUNOUT	SASHAY
RUEING	******	******	REFUTE	******	SATRAP
RULING	**R---R-**	**R---S-**	RELATE	**R---V-**	SAUNAS
RUMINA	******	******	REMITS	******	SCALAR
RUNINS	RACERS	RACISM	REMOTE	RELIVE	SCARAB
RUNONS	RADARS	RACIST	REPUTE	REMOVE	SCHWAS
RUSINE	RAKERS	RADISH	RESETS	REVIVE	SCREAK
******	RATERS	RAKISH	REVETS	******	SCREAM
R---O-	RAVERS	RAMOSE	RIALTO	**R---W-**	SCUBAS
******	RAZORS	RAPIST	RIGHTO	******	SEAMAN
RACOON	REBORE	RAREST	RIGHTS	REDOWA	SEAWAN
RADIOS	REBORN	RAVISH	RIVETS	RENEWS	SEAWAY
RADNOR	RECORD	RAWEST	ROASTS	RENOWN	SECPAR
RAMROD	RECURS	RAWISH	ROBOTS	******	SEESAW
RAMSON	REFERS	RECAST	ROOSTS	**R---Y-**	SEGGAR
RANCOR	REFORM	RECESS	ROTATE	******	SENDAL
RANDOM	REGARD	RECUSE	ROUSTS	REDEYE	SENLAC
RANSOM	REMARK	REFUSE	RUBATO	RELAYS	SENNAS
			RUGATE		

SEPIAS	STORAX	SEANCE	SHODDY	SANDER	SECKEL
SEPTAL	STREAK	SEARCH	SHREDS	SANGER	SECRET
SERDAB	STREAM	SEDUCE	SKALDS	SANIES	SEDGES
SERIAL	STRIAE	SELECT	SNOODS	SANSEI	SEEDED
SERVAL	STUPAS	SENECA	SOLIDI	SAPIEN	SEEDER
SEURAT	STYLAR	SERACS	SOLIDS	SAPPED	SEEKER
SEXTAN	SUBWAY	SHTICK	SOUNDS	SAPPER	SEEMED
SEXUAL	SULTAN	SILICA	SPEEDS	SASHED	SEEMER
SHAMAN	SUNDAE	SILICO	SPEEDY	SASHES	SEEPED
SHEBAT	SUNDAY	SKETCH	SPENDS	SASSED	SEINED
SHIKAR	SUNHAT	SLOUCH	SQUADS	SASSES	SEINER
SHOFAR	SUNNAH	SLUICE	SQUIDS	SATEEN	SEINES
SHORAN	SUNTAN	SMIRCH	STANDS	SAUCED	SEISED
SIGMAS	SURTAX	SMOOCH	STEADY	SAUCER	SEIZED
SIGNAL	SUTRAS	SMUTCH	STEEDS	SAUCES	SEIZER
SILVAE	SWARAJ	SNATCH	STRIDE	SAUGER	SEIZES
SILVAN	SYLVAE	SNITCH	STRODE	SAUREL	SELLER
SILVAS	SYLVAN	SOLACE	STURDY	SAUTES	SELVES
SIMIAN	SYLVAS	SOURCE	SWARDS	SAWNEY	SENDER
SINBAD	SYNTAX	SPEECH	SWORDS	SAWYER	SENNET
SIOUAN	SYRIAC	SPLICE	SYNODS	SCALED	SENSED
SIRDAR	SYRIAN	SPRUCE	******	SCALER	SENSES
SKYCAP	******	STANCE	S---E-	SCALES	SEPTET
SKYMAN	S---B-	STANCH	******	SCAPES	SEQUEL
SKYWAY	******	STARCH	SABLES	SCARED	SERIES
SLOGAN	SAHEBS	STENCH	SACHEM	SCARER	SERVED
SLOVAK	SAHIBS	STITCH	SACHET	SCARES	SERVER
SMILAX	SCABBY	STOICS	SACKED	SCENES	SERVES
SNOCAT	SCRIBE	STRICK	SACKER	SCOLEX	SESTET
SOCIAL	SCRUBS	STRICT	SACRED	SCONES	SETTEE
SOCMAN	SHABBY	STRUCK	SADDEN	SCOPES	SETTER
SOFTAS	SHELBY	STUCCO	SADDER	SCORED	SEXIER
SONIAS	SHRUBS	SUMACS	SADIES	SCORER	SEXTET
SONYAS	SNOBBY	SWATCH	SAGGED	SCORES	SHADED
SPACAE	SQUABS	SWITCH	SAGGER	SCOTER	SHADES
SPINAL	SQUIBS	******	SAGIER	SCREED	SHAKEN
SPIRAL	STROBE	S---D-	SAILED	SCREEN	SHAKER
SPITAL	STUBBS	******	SAILER	SCRIED	SHAKES
SPREAD	STUBBY	SALADS	SALLET	SCUTES	SHALED
SQUEAK	******	SCALDS	SALTED	SEABEE	SHALES
SQUEAL	S---C-	SCENDS	SALTER	SEALED	SHAMED
STALAG	******	SCOLDS	SALVED	SEALER	SHAMES
STATAL	SCARCE	SCRODS	SALVER	SEAMED	SHAPED
STEFAN	SCHICK	SECEDE	SALVES	SEAMEN	SHAPEN
STELAE	SCONCE	SHANDY	SAMIEL	SEAMER	SHAPER
STELAR	SCORCH	SHARDS	SAMLET	SEAPEN	SHAPES
STEPAN	SCOTCH	SHERDS	SAMUEL	SEARED	SHARED
STOMAT	SCUTCH	SHINDY	SANDED	SEATED	SHARER

SHARES	SIMPER	SMAZES	SONNET	SPORES	STONER
SHAVED	SINGED	SMILED	SOONER	SPREES	STONES
SHAVEN	SINGER	SMILER	SOOTED	SPRIER	STOPED
SHAVER	SINGES	SMILES	SOPPED	SPRUES	STOPES
SHAVES	SINKER	SMITER	SORBET	SPRYER	STORED
SHEKEL	SINNED	SMITES	SORREL	SPUMED	STORES
SHEWED	SINNER	SMOKED	SORTED	SPUMES	STOREY
SHEWER	SINTER	SMOKER	SORTER	STAGED	STOVER
SHINED	SIPPED	SMOKES	SOULED	STAGER	STOVES
SHINER	SIPPER	SNAKED	SOUPED	STAGES	STOWED
SHINES	SIPPET	SNAKES	SOURED	STAGEY	STOWED
SHIRES	SISTER	SNARED	SOURER	STAKED	STREET
SHIVER	SITTER	SNARER	SOUSED	STAKES	STUPES
SHIVES	SIXTES	SNARES	SOUSES	STALED	STYLED
SHOOED	SIZIER	SNIPED	SOVIET	STALER	STYLER
SHORED	SKATED	SNIPER	SPACED	STALES	STYLES
SHORES	SKATER	SNIPES	SPACER	STAMEN	STYLET
SHOTES	SKATES	SNIVEL	SPACES	STAPES	SUBDEB
SHOVED	SKEWED	SNORED	SPADED	STARED	SUBLET
SHOVEL	SKEWER	SNORER	SPADER	STARER	SUBTER
SHOVER	SKIVED	SNORES	SPADES	STARES	SUCKED
SHOVES	SKIVER	SNOWED	SPARED	STASES	SUCKER
SHOWED	SKIVES	SOAKED	SPARER	STATED	SUCRES
SHOWER	SKYMEN	SOAKER	SPARES	STATEN	SUDDEN
SHRIEK	SLAKED	SOAPED	SPATES	STATER	SUEDES
SICKED	SLAKES	SOARED	SPAYED	STATES	SUFFER
SICKEN	SLATED	SOARER	SPEWED	STAVED	SUITED
SICKER	SLATER	SOBBED	SPICED	STAVES	SUITES
SIDLED	SLATES	SOCCER	SPICER	STAYED	SULKED
SIDLER	SLAVED	SOCKED	SPICES	STAYER	SULLEN
SIDLES	SLAVER	SOCKET	SPIDER	STELES	SUMMED
SIDNEY	SLAVES	SOCLES	SPIKED	STEREO	SUMMER
SIEGED	SLAYER	SOCMEN	SPIKES	STERES	SUMNER
SIEGES	SLEWED	SOCRED	SPILED	STEVEN	SUNDER
SIEVED	SLICED	SODDED	SPILES	STEVES	SUNDEW
SIEVES	SLICER	SODDEN	SPINEL	STEWED	SUNKEN
SIFTED	SLICES	SOEVER	SPINES	STILES	SUNNED
SIFTER	SLIDER	SOFTEN	SPINET	STIPEL	SUNSET
SIGHED	SLIDES	SOFTER	SPIREA	STIPES	SUPPED
SIGNED	SLIMED	SOILED	SPIRED	STIVER	SUPPER
SIGNER	SLIMES	SOIREE	SPIRES	STOGEY	SURFED
SIGNET	SLIVER	SOLDER	SPITED	STOKED	SURFER
SILKEN	SLOPED	SOLOED	SPITES	STOKER	SURGED
SILOED	SLOPER	SOLVED	SPLEEN	STOKES	SURGER
SILTED	SLOPES	SOLVER	SPOKED	STOLED	SURGES
SILVER	SLOVEN	SOLVES	SPOKEN	STOLEN	SURREY
SIMMER	SLOWED	SOMBER	SPOKES	STOLES	SURVEY
SIMNEL	SLOWER	SONDER	SPORED	STONED	SUSIES
					SUSSED

SUSSEX	SEWAGE	SLUSHY	SIKKIM	******	STOCKY
SUTLER	SHAGGY	SMITHS	SILVIA	**S---K-**	STOOKS
SUTTEE	SHRUGS	SMITHY	SIMLIN	******	STORKS
SWAGED	SILAGE	SNATHE	SISKIN	SALUKI	STRAKE
SWAGES	SLAGGY	SNATHS	SLAVIC	SHACKO	STRIKE
SWALES	SLANGY	SOOTHE	SOFFIT	SHACKS	STROKE
SWANEE	SLEDGE	SORGHO	SOPHIA	SHANKS	SWANKY
SWAYED	SLEIGH	SOUGHS	SOPHIE	SHARKS	******
SWEDEN	SLINGS	SOUGHT	SORDID	SHEIKH	**S---L-**
SWEDES	SLOUGH	SPATHE	SORTIE	SHEIKS	******
SWIPED	SLUDGE	STETHO	SOTHIC	SHIRKS	SADDLE
SWIPES	SLUDGY	STITHY	SOTHIS	SHOCKS	SAFELY
SWIVEL	SMUDGE	SUBAHS	SPADIX	SHRIKE	SAGELY
SWIVET	SMUDGY	SULPHA	SPAHIS	SHUCKS	SAMPLE
SYCEES	SNAGGY	SULPHO	SPAVIN	SKINKS	SANELY
SYDNEY	SOCAGE	SURAHS	SPECIE	SKULKS	SAWFLY
SYNDET	SPARGE	SWATHE	SPIRIT	SKUNKS	SCILLY
SYPHER	SPONGE	SWATHS	SPRAIN	SLACKS	SCOWLS
SYSTEM	SPONGY	SYLPHS	STACIE	SLEEKS	SCROLL
******	SPRAGS	SYLPHY	STADIA	SLEEKY	SCULLS
S---F-	SPRIGS	******	STALIN	SLICKS	SCYLLA
******	SPURGE	**S---I-**	STAMIN	SLINKS	SEDILE
SALIFY	STAGGY	******	STASIS	SLINKY	SEEMLY
SCARFS	STINGS	SAITIC	STATIC	SMACKS	SEMELE
SCLAFF	STINGY	SALMIS	STELIC	SMIRKS	SENILE
SCOFFS	STODGE	SALPID	STEPIN	SMOCKS	SEPALS
SCRUFF	STODGY	SALVIA	STERIC	SNACKS	SETTLE
SCUFFS	STOOGE	SCENIC	STEVIE	SNEAKS	SEWALL
SCURFY	SWINGE	SCHUIT	STOLID	SNEAKY	SEWELL
SERIFS	SWINGS	SCIPIO	STRAIN	SNICKS	SEXILY
SETOFF	SYZYGY	SCORIA	STRAIT	SNOOKS	SHAWLS
SHRIFT	******	SCOTIA	STUDIO	SPANKS	SHEILA
SHROFF	**S---H-**	SEARIN	STUPID	SPARKS	SHEILD
SKIFFS	******	SEISIN	STYMIE	SPEAKS	SHELLS
SNIFFS	SAMSHU	SEIZIN	SUBMIT	SPECKS	SHELLY
SNIFFY	SANDHI	SENNIT	SUFFIX	SPLAKE	SHIELD
SNUFFS	SAPPHO	SEPSIS	SUMMIT	SPOOKS	SHILLS
SNUFFY	SARAHS	SEPTIC	SUNLIT	SPOOKY	SHOALS
SPIFFY	SCATHE	SEQUIN	SUOMIC	SPUNKY	SHOALY
SPOOFS	SCYPHI	SERAIS	SUSLIK	STACKS	SHORLS
STAFFS	SCYPHO	SERBIA	SWAMIS	STALKS	SHOULD
STRAFE	SCYTHE	SEREIN	SYLVIA	STALKY	SHRILL
STRIFE	SEETHE	SHERIF	SYNDIC	STEAKS	SIBYLS
STUFFS	SEICHE	SHOJIS	******	STICKS	SICILY
STUFFY	SIXTHS	SHOOIN	**S---J-**	STICKY	SICKLE
******	SLIGHT	SHUTIN	******	STINKS	SICKLY
S---G-	SLOSHY	SIALIC	SKOPJE	STIRKS	SIECLE
******	SLOTHS	SIGRID		STOCKS	SIGILS
SAVAGE					
SCRAGS					

SIMILE	STOOLS	STORMS	SHRANK	SPYING	SERMON
SIMPLE	STROLL	STORMY	SHRINE	SQUINT	SERVOS
SIMPLY	STULLS	STROMA	SHRINK	STAINS	SETTOS
SINGLE	SUABLE	STRUMA	SHRUNK	STEINS	SEXPOT
SINGLY	SUBTLE	STRUMS	SHYING	STERNA	SEXTON
SIZZLE	SUBTLY	SWARMS	SIDING	STERNO	SHADOW
SKILLS	SUCKLE	******	SIENNA	STERNS	SHAKOS
SKULLS	SUPPLE	S---N-	SILENI	STHENO	SHARON
SLIMLY	SUPPLY	******	SILENT	STRAND	SHILOH
SLOWLY	SURELY	SABINA	SIMONE	STRING	SIGNOR
SMALLS	SWAILS	SABINE	SIMONS	STRONG	SIMOOM
SMELLS	SWELLS	SABINS	SIMONY	STRUNG	SINEON
SMELLY	SWILLS	SALINE	SIRENS	STYING	SIPHON
SMUGLY	SWIPLE	SALONS	SIRING	SUPINE	SKIMOS
SNAILS	SWIRLS	SARONG	SITING	SUSANS	SLALOM
SNARLS	SWIRLY	SASINS	SITINS	SWAINS	SLIPON
SNARLY	SYBILS	SATANG	SIZING	SWEENY	SOLION
SNELLS	******	SATING	SKEANS	SWOONS	SORGOS
SNUGLY	S---M-	SATINS	SKEINS	SYRINX	SORROW
SOFTLY	******	SATINY	SKIING	******	SPIGOT
SOLELY	SALAMI	SAVANT	SKINNY	S---O-	STATOR
SOMALI	SALOME	SAVING	SKYING	******	STENOG
SORELS	SCHEMA	SAVINS	SLUING	SAIGON	STEROL
SORELY	SCHEME	SAWING	SOIGNE	SAILOR	STOLON
SOTOLS	SCRAMS	SAXONS	SOLAND	SALLOW	STUPOR
SOURLY	SCRIMP	SAXONY	SOLANO	SALMON	SUCCOR
SPALLS	SCRUMS	SAYING	SOLANS	SALOON	SUITOR
SPELLS	SCUMMY	SCIONS	SOLENT	SALOOP	SUMMON
SPIELS	SEDUMS	SCORNS	SOLING	SALVOR	SUNBOW
SPILLS	SEISMO	SECANT	SONANT	SALVOS	SUNDOG
SPOILS	SEISMS	SECOND	SOWING	SAMBOS	SUNGOD
SPOILT	SEMEME	SECUND	SOZINE	SAMSON	SUTTON
SPOOLS	SERUMS	SEDANS	SOZINS	SANTOL	SYMBOL
SPRYLY	SESAME	SEEING	SPAWNS	SARGON	SYPHON
SQUALL	SHAMMY	SEJANT	SPHENE	SARTOR	******
SQUILL	SHAWMS	SELENE	SPHENO	SAVIOR	S---P-
STABLE	SHIMMY	SELENO	SPHINX	SCHMOS	******
STABLY	SHRIMP	SERENA	SPINNY	SCHOOL	SARAPE
STALLS	SLUMMY	SERENE	SPLENO	SCROOP	SCALPS
STAPLE	SMARMY	SERINE	SPLINE	SEACOW	SCAMPI
STEALS	SODOMY	SERINS	SPLINT	SEADOG	SCAMPS
STEELS	SOLEMN	SETONS	SPOONS	SEASON	SCARPS
STEELY	SPASMS	SEVENS	SPOONY	SECTOR	SCAUPS
STELLA	SPERMO	SEWING	SPRANG	SEISOR	SCOOPS
STELLI	SQUAMA	SEXING	SPRING	SEIZOR	SCRAPE
STIFLE	STEAMS	SHEENS	SPRINT	SELDOM	SCRAPS
STILLS	STEAMY	SHEENY	SPRUNG	SENIOR	SCRIPS
STILLY	STIGMA	SHINNY	SPURNS	SENSOR	SCRIPT

SCULPT	SAHARA	SLURRY	SCHISM	SHANTY	SPOTTY
SERAPE	SAKERS	SMEARS	SCHIST	SHASTA	SPOUTS
SERAPH	SALARY	SMEARY	SCHUSS	SHEATH	SPRATS
SETUPS	SAMARA	SNEERS	SCOUSE	SHEETS	SPRITE
SHARPS	SANDRA	SOBERS	SETOSE	SHELTY	SPRITS
SHEEPS	SARTRE	SOMBRE	SEXISM	SHIFTS	SPURTS
SHERPA	SATARA	SONARS	SEXIST	SHIFTY	SQUATS
SHOPPE	SATIRE	SOUARI	SHIEST	SHIITE	STACTE
SIRUPS	SATORY	SOWARS	SHIISM	SHINTO	STAITH
SIRUPY	SATURN	SOWERS	SHYEST	SHIRTS	STARTS
SKIMPS	SATYRS	SPARRY	SIWASH	SHIRTY	STILTS
SKIMPY	SAVERS	SPEARS	SLIEST	SHOATS	STINTS
SLEEPS	SAVORS	SPERRY	SLIMSY	SHOOTS	STOATS
SLEEPY	SAVORY	SPHERE	SLYEST	SHORTS	STOUTS
SLOOPS	SAWERS	SPHERY	SOREST	SHOUTS	STRATA
SLOPPY	SAYERS	SPIERS	SPARSE	SHUNTS	STRATH
SLUMPS	SCHORL	SPOORS	SPEISS	SIESTA	STRATI
SLURPS	SCLERA	SPURRY	SPLASH	SIGHTS	STRUTS
SNAPPY	SCLERO	SQUARE	SPOUSE	SKIRTS	STUNTS
SNIPPY	SCOURS	SQUIRE	SQUASH	SLANTS	SUBITO
SNOOPS	SCURRY	SQUIRM	SQUISH	SLEETS	SURETY
SNOOPY	SECERN	SQUIRT	STRASS	SLEETY	SVELTE
STAMPS	SECURE	STAIRS	STRESS	SLEUTH	SWARTH
STEEPS	SEDERS	STARRY	SUFISM	SMALTI	SWARTY
STEPPE	SEMPRE	STAURO	SUREST	SMALTO	SWEATS
STIRPS	SENARY	STEERS	******	SMARTS	SWEATY
STOMPS	SENORA	STUART	S---T-	SMELTS	SWEETS
STOOPS	SENTRY	SUBORN	******	SMOLTS	SWIFTS
STOUPS	SEVERE	SUBURB	SABOTS	SMOOTH	******
STRAPS	SEVERN	SUDARY	SAFETY	SMUTTY	S---U-
STRIPE	SEVERS	SUGARS	SAINTS	SNOOTS	******
STRIPS	SEWARD	SUGARY	SALUTE	SNOOTY	SACRUM
STRIPT	SEWERS	SULTRY	SAMITE	SNORTS	SADHUS
STRIPY	SHEARS	SUNDRY	SANITY	SNOTTY	SAJOUS
STROPS	SHEERS	SUPERB	SAULTS	SNOUTS	SAMBUR
STUMPS	SHERRY	SUPERS	SAVATE	SOLUTE	SANGUI
STUMPY	SHIRRS	SUTURE	SCANTY	SOMATA	SANNUP
SUNUPS	SHOERS	SWEARS	SCATTY	SOMATO	SAURUS
SWAMPS	SIDERO	SYNURA	SCENTS	SOMITE	SAVOUR
SWAMPY	SIERRA	******	SCOOTS	SONATA	SCOPUS
SWEEPS	SIEURS	S---S-	SCOTTS	SPAITS	SCUTUM
SWEEPY	SIMARS	******	SCOUTS	SPARTA	SEAMUS
SWOOPS	SISERA	SADISM	SCROTA	SPILTH	SELJUK
SYRUPS	SITARS	SADIST	SEBATS	SPIRTS	SEPTUM
SYRUPY	SIZARS	SAFEST	SEDATE	SPLATS	SEROUS
******	SKERRY	SAGEST	SEMITE	SPLITS	SESQUI
S---R-	SKIERS	SALISH	SENATE	SPORTS	SETOUS
******	SKIRRS	SANEST	SHAFTS	SPORTY	SETOUT
SABERS					
SAFARI					

SHAMUS	SINEWY	TAZZAS	TUSSAL	TABLES	TEASES
SHOGUN	SPRAWL	TEABAG	TUSSAR	TABLET	TEASET
SHROUD	SQUAWK	TERGAL	TWOWAY	TACKED	TEDDED
SIDDUR	SQUAWS	TERNAL	TYMPAN	TACKER	TEDDER
SINFUL	STRAWS	TESTAE	TYRIAN	TACKEY	TEEMED
SIRIUS	STRAWY	TETRAD	******	TAGGED	TEEMER
SLAPUP	STREWN	THANAT	**T---B-**	TAGGER	TEETER
SLIPUP	STREWS	THEBAE	******	TAILED	TEGMEN
SNAFUS	******	THECAE	THISBE	TAIPEI	TEHEED
SODIUM	**S---Y-**	THECAL	THROBS	TALCED	TEHEES
SPROUT	******	THEDAS	THUMBS	TALKED	TELFER
SPUTUM	SALLYS	THENAL	TRILBY	TALKER	TELLER
STATUE	SAMMYS	THENAR	******	TALLER	TEMPER
STATUS	SANDYS	THETAS	**T---C-**	TAMPED	TENDED
STEPUP	SELSYN	THOMAS	******	TAMPER	TENDER
STROUD	SELWYN	THORAC	TENACE	TANDEM	TENREC
STYLUS	SEPOYS	THORAX	THATCH	TANGED	TENSED
SUBDUE	SPLAYS	THREAD	THENCE	TANKED	TENSER
SULCUS	SPRAYS	THREAT	THRICE	TANKER	TENSES
SULFUR	STACYS	THROAT	THWACK	TANNED	TENTED
******	STRAYS	THUJAS	TIERCE	TANNER	TENTER
S---V-	******	TIARAS	TONICS	TANREC	TENUES
******	**S---Z-**	TIBIAE	TOPICS	TAPPED	TEPEES
SALIVA	******	TIBIAL	TRANCE	TAPPER	TERCEL
SCRIVE	SCHIZO	TIBIAS	TRENCH	TAPPET	TERCET
SCURVY	SLEAZY	TIMBAL	TUNICA	TARGET	TERMED
SHEAVE	SNAZZY	TINCAL	TUNICS	TARRED	TERMER
SHELVE	SNEEZE	TINCAN	TWITCH	TARTED	TERRET
SHRIVE	SNEEZY	TIPCAT	******	TARTER	TERSER
SHROVE	SNOOZE	TITIAN	**T---D-**	TASKED	TESTED
SKIVVY	STANZA	TOBIAH	******	TASSEL	TESTER
SLEAVE	******	TOBIAS	TELEDU	TASSET	TESTES
SLEEVE	**T---A-**	TOECAP	TEREDO	TASTED	TETHER
STARVE	******	TOMBAC	THADDY	TASTER	TETTER
STEEVE	TAIGAS	TOMCAT	THIRDS	TASTES	TETZEL
STRIVE	TAIWAN	TOPHAT	TIRADE	TATLER	TEUCER
STROVE	TAMBAC	TOUCAN	TOLEDO	TATTED	THALER
SWERVE	TAMPAN	TREPAN	TREADS	TATTER	THALES
******	TAMTAM	TRIBAL	TRENDS	TAUPES	THAMES
S---W-	TANKAS	TRICAR	TRENDY	TAUTEN	THANES
******	TARMAC	TRINAL	TRIADS	TAUTER	THAWED
SCRAWL	TARNAL	TROCAR	TRIODE	TAXIED	THAYER
SCREWS	TARPAN	TROJAN	TULADI	TBONES	THEBES
SCREWY	TARSAL	TROPAL	TUXEDO	TEAMED	THEMES
SEROWS	TARTAN	TRUMAN	TWEEDS	TEARED	THESES
SHREWD	TARTAR	TURBAN	******	TEASED	THEWED
SHREWS	TARZAN	TUSCAN	**T---E-**	TEASEL	THOLES
SINEWS	TASMAN	TUSSAH	******	TEASER	THREED
			TABBED		
			TABLED		

THREES	TOLTEC	TUFFET	******	THYMIC	******
THROES	TOMBED	TUFTED	**T---H-**	TIDBIT	**T---L-**
THYMES	TONGED	TUGGED	******	TIEPIN	******
THYREO	TONIER	TULLES	TAUGHT	TIFFIN	TACKLE
TICKED	TOOLED	TUNNED	TEETHE	TIGRIS	TAILLE
TICKER	TOOLER	TUNNEL	TENTHS	TILLIE	TAMALE
TICKET	TOOTED	TUPPED	TETCHY	TINEID	TAMELY
TIDIED	TOOTER	TUQUES	THIGHS	TITBIT	TANGLE
TIDIER	TOPPED	TUREEN	TILTHS	TOCSIN	TANGLY
TIDIES	TOPPER	TURFED	TOOTHY	TOMTIT	TAPALO
TIERED	TOQUES	TURKEY	TORAHS	TONKIN	TARTLY
TIFFED	TORIES	TURNED	TOUCHE	TONSIL	TATTLE
TILDES	TOSHES	TURNER	TOUCHY	TORIIS	TATTLY
TILLED	TOSSED	TURRET	TOUGHS	TOROID	TAUTLY
TILLER	TOSSES	TURVES	TRACHE	TORPID	TEMPLE
TILTED	TOTHER	TUSHED	TRACHY	TORRID	TERMLY
TILTER	TOTTED	TUSHES	TRASHY	TRAGIC	THINLY
TIMBER	TOTTER	TUSKED	TRICHI	TRIFID	THIOLS
TINDER	TOUPEE	TUSKER	TRICHO	TRIVIA	THRALL
TINGED	TOURED	TUTTED	TROCHE	TRIXIE	THRILL
TINGES	TOURER	TWINED	TROPHO	TROPIC	THUSLY
TINIER	TOUTED	TWINER	TROPHY	TURBID	TICALS
TINKER	TOUTER	TWINES	TROTHS	TURBIT	TICKLE
TINNED	TRACED	TWOFER	TRUTHS	TURGID	TIDILY
TINNER	TRACER	******	******	TURKIC	TIMELY
TINSEL	TRACES	**T---F-**	**T---I-**	TURKIS	TINGLE
TINTED	TRADED	******	******	TURNIP	TINGLY
TIPPED	TRADER	TARIFF	TACTIC	TUSSIS	TINILY
TIPPER	TRADES	TEPEFY	TAENIA	TUTTIS	TINKLE
TIPPET	TRAVEL	THRIFT	TAKEIN	TWIBIL	TINKLY
TITHED	TRAVES	TIPOFF	TALKIE	TWILIT	TIPPLE
TITHER	TRIBES	TUMEFY	TANNIC	TWOBIT	TITTLE
TITHES	TRICED	TYPIFY	TANNIN	******	TODDLE
TITLED	TRICES	******	TARSIA	**T---K-**	TOGGLE
TITLES	TRINED	**T---G-**	TENNIS	******	TOOTLE
TITTER	TRINES	******	TENPIN	THANKS	TOPPLE
TOBIES	TRITER	TELEGA	TENUIS	TOPEKA	TOTALS
TODIES	TRIVET	TELUGU	TERBIA	TORSKS	TOUSLE
TOFFEE	TROVER	THINGS	TESSIE	TRACKS	TOWELS
TOGAED	TROVES	THONGS	TESTIS	TRICKS	TRAILS
TOGGED	TROWEL	THOUGH	THALIA	TRICKY	TRAWLS
TOGUES	TRUCES	TOBAGO	THEMIS	TROIKA	TREBLE
TOILED	TSADES	TOWAGE	THESIS	TRUCKS	TRIALS
TOILER	TUBBED	TROUGH	THETIC	TRUNKS	TRIFLE
TOILES	TUBBER	TRUDGE	THETIS	TUPIKS	TRIGLY
TOILET	TUCKED	TWANGS	THORIA	TWEAKS	TRILLS
TOLLED	TUCKER	TWANGY	THORIC	TWEAKY	TRIMLY
TOLLER	TUCKET	TWIGGY	THULIA		TRIPLE
		TWINGE			

TROLLS	TILING	TESTON	TAKERS	TERESA	TUBATE
TUBULE	TIMING	TEUTON	TALARI	THEISM	TWEETS
TUILLE	TIRANA	THORON	TALERS	THEIST	TWENTY
TUMBLE	TIRING	THYMOL	TAMERS	THIRST	TWISTS
TUMULT	TISANE	TINPOT	TAPERS	THRASH	TWISTY
TUPELO	TITANS	TIPTOE	TAPIRS	THRESH	******
TURTLE	TOEING	TIPTOP	TATARS	THRUSH	T---U-
TUSSLE	TOKENS	TOLUOL	TAVERN	THRUST	******
TWILLS	TOMANS	TOMBOY	TAWDRY	THYRSE	TAKEUP
TWIRLS	TONING	TOMCOD	TAWERS	THYRSI	TALCUM
TWOPLY	TOPING	TOMTOM	TAXERS	TOOTSY	TALMUD
TWOULD	TOTING	TORPOR	TEAURN	TOROSE	TARSUS
TYBALT	TOWING	TORSOS	TELARY	TOYISH	TAURUS
TYPHLO	TOXINS	TOULON	TENORS	TRESSY	TEACUP
******	TOYING	TREMOR	TENURE	TRIOSE	TEDIUM
T---M-	TOYONS	TREVOR	TEVERE	TRUEST	TELLUS
******	TRAINS	TRICOT	THEIRS	TRUISM	TEREUS
TACOMA	TRIUNE	TRIGON	THEORY	TSETSE	TERGUM
TAXEME	TRUANT	TRIPOD	THWART	TYPIST	THYMUS
THELMA	TRUING	TRIPOS	TIGERS	******	TISSUE
THERMO	TRYING	TRITON	TILERS	T---T-	TITTUP
THERMS	TUBING	TROGON	TIMBRE	******	TONGUE
THRUMS	TUNING	TUCSON	TIMERS	TAHITI	TOROUS
TOTEMS	TYPING	TURBOT	TISHRI	TAINTS	TORQUE
TRAUMA	TYRANT	TURCOS	TONERS	TAROTS	TOSSUP
******	TYRONE	TYCOON	TOPERS	TAUNTS	TRAGUS
T---N-	******	TYPHON	TORERO	TAXITE	TRYOUT
******	T---O-	******	TOTERS	TEMPTS	TUCHUN
TAKING	******	T---P-	TOWARD	TENETS	TUMOUR
TALENT	TABOOS	******	TOWERS	TENUTO	TUNEUP
TALONS	TAILOR	TERAPH	TOWERY	TERATO	TUNGUS
TAMING	TAINOS	THORPE	TOYERS	TERETE	TURNUP
TAPING	TALION	THRIPS	TRIERS	THEFTS	TYPHUS
TARING	TALLOW	THUMPS	TSHIRT	THIRTY	******
TAWING	TAMPON	TIEUPS	TUBERS	TIGHTS	T---V-
TAXING	TANGOS	TRAMPS	TUMORS	TINCTS	******
TECHNO	TATTOO	TROOPS	TUNDRA	TOASTS	THIEVE
TEEING	TAUTOG	TROPPO	TUNERS	TOMATO	THRIVE
TENANT	TAYLOR	TROUPE	TUTORS	TONITE	THROVE
TENONS	TEAPOT	TRUMPS	TUYERE	TRACTS	TWELVE
TETANY	TEAPOY	TULIPS	******	TRAITS	******
TETONS	TEFLON	TWERPS	T---S-	TREATS	T---W-
THORNS	TELSON	TWIRPS	******	TREATY	******
THORNY	TEMPOS	******	TAMEST	TRISTE	THROWN
THRONE	TENDON	T---R-	TANIST	TROUTS	THROWS
THRONG	TENSOR	******	TAOISM	TRUSTS	******
TIDING	TERMOR	TABARD	TAOIST	TRUSTY	T---Y-
TIEINS	TERROR	TABORS	TEENSY	TRYSTS	******
					TEDDYS
					TERRYS

TETHYS	UNLACE	******	UNABLE	UNMOOR	UNHASP
TETRYL	UNLOCK	U---F-	UNBELT	UNROOT	UNHUSK
THADYS	UNPACK		UNBOLT	UNSHOD	UNJUST
TILLYS	UNPICK	UGLIFY	UNDULY	UNSTOP	UNLASH
TIMMYS	UNTACK	UNSAFE	UNFOLD	UNTROD	UNLESS
TOLUYL	USANCE	UPLIFT	UNGULA	UPHROE	UNMASK
TOMMYS	******	******	UNHOLY	UPROOT	UNREST
TRIXYS	U---D-	U---G-	UNPILE	UPSHOT	UNWISE
TROTYL	******		UNROLL	UROPOD	UNWISH
TRUDYS	UGANDA	UBANGI	UNRULY	******	UPCAST
******	UNLADE	ULLAGE	UNSOLD	U---P-	UPMOST
U---A-	UNMADE	UNCAGE	UNTOLD	******	UPPISH
******	UNTIDY	UNPEGS	UNWELL	UNCAPS	UPRISE
ULEMAS	UPENDS	UNRIGS	UPHELD	UNRIPE	UPROSE
UMBRAE	UPSIDE	******	UPHILL	UNRIPS	UPRUSH
UMBRAL	UREIDE	U---I-	UPHOLD	UNWEPT	UREASE
UMBRAS	******	******	URSULA	USURPS	UTMOST
UNBEAR	U---E-	UNAPID	USABLE	******	******
UNCIAL	******	UNCOIL	USABLY	U---R-	U---T-
UNCLAD	UGLIER	UNFAIR	******	******	******
UNDRAW	UKASES	UNGUIS	U---M-	UDDERS	UBIETY
UNGUAL	ULSTER	UNHAIR	******	ULCERS	UBOATS
UNLEAD	UMBLES	UNIFIC	ULTIMA	UMBERS	UNHATS
UNLOAD	UNBRED	UNKNIT	ULTIMO	UMPIRE	UPDATE
UNREAD	UNCLES	UNLAID	******	UNBARS	UPPITY
UNREAL	UNDIES	UNSAID	U---N-	UNBORN	UPSETS
UNSEAL	UNDOER	UNSHIP	******	UNCORD	******
UNSEAM	UNDOES	UNVEIL	UNBEND	UNCORK	U---U-
UNSEAT	UNDREW	URALIC	UNBENT	UNCURL	******
UNWRAP	UNDSET	URANIA	UNBIND	UNFURL	UMLAUT
UPBEAT	UNEVEN	URANIC	UNDINE	UNGIRD	UNIQUE
UPROAR	UNGUES	URCHIN	UNDONE	UNGIRT	UNPLUG
URINAL	UNICEF	UREMIA	UNHAND	UNHURT	UNTRUE
UTAHAN	UNIPED	URETIC	UNIONS	UNSURE	URAEUS
UVULAE	UNISEX	UTOPIA	UNKIND	UNWARY	URANUS
UVULAR	UNITED	******	UNMANS	UNWORN	USEFUL
UVULAS	UNITES	U---K-	UNPINS	UPPERS	UTERUS
UZZIAH	UNMEET	******	UNSUNG	UPTURN	******
******	UNREEL	UMIAKS	UNWIND	UPWARD	U---V-
U---B-	UNSEEN	UNLIKE	UPLAND	USHERS	******
******	UNSTEP	UNMAKE	UPPING	UTGARD	UNLIVE
UNROBE	UNTIED	UNYOKE	URBANE	UTTERS	******
******	UNTIES	UPDIKE	URGENT	******	U---W-
U---C-	UNUSED	UPTAKE	URGING	U---S-	******
******	UPASES	******	URSINE	******	UNHEWN
ULENCE	UPKEEP	U---L-	UTURNS	UNCASE	UNMEWS
UNCOCK	URETER	******	******	UNEASE	UPBOWS
UNESCO	USAGES	UGLILY	UNHOOK	UNEASY	UPTOWN
	USURER	UMBELS	UNISON		

******	VESICA	VESPER	VIATIC	VIXENS	******
U---X-	VESICO	VESSEL	VIBRIO	VOLANT	**V---S-**
******	VIVACE	VESTED	VICTIM	VOLING	******
UNVEXT	VOMICA	VESTEE	VIOLIN	VOTING	VADOSE
URTEXT	******	VETOED	VIRGIE	VOWING	VALISE
******	**V---D-**	VETOER	VIRGIL	******	VAMOSE
U---Y-	******	VETOES	VIRGIN	**V---O-**	VANISH
******	VIANDS	VETTED	VISCID	******	VENOSE
UNLAYS	******	VIALED	VITRIC	VECTOR	VERISM
UNSAYS	**V---E-**	VIEWED	******	VENDOR	VERIST
URANYL	******	VIEWER	**V---L-**	VERNON	VILEST
******	VAGUER	VINCES	******	VERSOS	VOLOST
V---A-	VAINER	VINIER	VAINLY	VIATOR	******
******	VALLEY	VIOLET	VASILI	VICTOR	**V---T-**
VALVAL	VALUED	VISAED	VASTLY	VILLON	******
VALVAR	VALUER	VISEED	VENULE	VINSON	VACATE
VANDAL	VALUES	VIVIEN	VERILY	VIREOS	VALATE
VANMAN	VALVED	VIZIER	VEXILS	VISION	VALETS
VASSAL	VALVES	VOGUES	VIABLE	VOLVOX	VALUTA
VEADAR	VAMPED	VOICED	VIGILS	VOODOO	VANITY
VEDIAC	VANMEN	VOICES	VILELY	******	VASHTI
VENIAL	VARIED	VOIDED	VINYLS	**V---R-**	VAULTS
VERBAL	VARIER	VOILES	VIRILE	******	VAUNTS
VERNAL	VARIES	VOLLEY	VITALS	VAGARY	VELDTS
VERNAS	VARLET	VOLTED	VOCALS	VALERY	VERITY
VESTAL	VARVES	VORTEX	VOGULS	VAPORI	VERSTS
VESTAS	VASTER	******	VOWELS	VAPORS	VISITS
VIDUAL	VATTED	**V---F-**	******	VASARI	VOLUTE
VILLAS	VEERED	******	**V---M-**	VELURE	VOMITO
VIOLAS	VEILED	VERIFY	******	VENERY	VOMITS
VIRGAS	VEILER	VILIFY	VENOMS	VENIRE	******
VISTAS	VEINED	VIVIFY	VOLUME	VENTRO	**V---U-**
VISUAL	VELVET	******	******	VESTRY	VACUUM
VITTAE	VENDED	**V---G-**	**V---N-**	VEXERS	VALGUS
VIVIAN	VENDEE	******	******	VICARS	VALLUM
VODKAS	VENDER	VIRAGO	VACANT	VINERY	VALOUR
VOLVAS	VENEER	VISAGE	VACUNA	VIPERS	VAPOUR
VULCAN	VENTED	VOYAGE	VAGINA	VISARD	VATFUL
VULGAR	VENTER	******	VAGINO	VISORS	VELLUM
VULVAE	VENUES	**V---I-**	VARUNA	VIZARD	VELOUR
VULVAL	VERGED	******	VERONA	VIZIRS	VENDUE
VULVAR	VERGER	VALOIS	VEXING	VIZORS	VENOUS
******	VERGES	VERDIN	VICUNA	VOLERY	VERDUN
V---C-	VERSED	VEREIN	VIENNA	VOMERS	VERSUS
******	VERSES	VERGIL	VIKING	VOTARY	VIGOUR
VARICO	VERSET	VERMIN	VIMINA	VOTERS	VILLUS
VELOCE	VERTEX	VERNIX	VISHNU	VOWERS	VINOUS
VENICE	VERVET	VESPID	VISING		

VIRTUE	WIELDS	WASHES	WHITED	WOMBED	WIDDIE
VISCUS	WIELDY	WASTED	WHITEN	WONDER	WIENIE
VOROUS	WOALDS	WASTER	WHITER	WONTED	WILLIE
VOYEUR	WORLDS	WASTES	WHITES	WOODED	WILLIS
******	WOUNDS	WAULED	WHITEY	WOODEN	WINNIE
V---V-	******	WAVIER	WHORED	WOOFER	WITHIN
******	W---E-	WAVIES	WHORES	WOOLEN	WITHIT
VOTIVE	******	WAWLED	WICHES	WORDED	******
******	WADDED	WAXIER	WICKED	WORKED	W---K-
V---W-	WADIES	WAYNES	WICKER	WORKER	******
******	WADSET	WEAKEN	WICKET	WORMED	WAKIKI
VYRNWY	WAFTED	WEAKER	WIENER	WORMER	WHACKS
******	WAFTER	WEANED	WIGGED	WORSEN	WHELKS
V---Y-	WAGGED	WEANER	WILBER	WORSER	WHELKY
******	WAGNER	WEARER	WILDER	WOWSER	WHISKS
VALKYR	WAIFED	WEASEL	WILIER	WRITER	WHISKY
VICKYS	WAILED	WEAVED	WILLED	WRITES	WRACKS
VINNYS	WAILER	WEAVER	WILLER	******	WREAKS
******	WAITED	WEAVES	WILLET	W---F-	WRECKS
W---A-	WAITER	WEBBED	WILTED	******	******
******	WAIVED	WEDDED	WINCED	WHARFS	W---L-
WALLAH	WAIVER	WEDGED	WINCER	WHIFFS	******
WALLAS	WAIVES	WEDGES	WINCES	******	WABBLE
WANDAS	WALKED	WEEDED	WINCEY	W---G-	WABBLY
WARSAW	WALKER	WEEDER	WINDED	******	WADDLE
WAYLAY	WALLED	WEEPER	WINDER	WHANGS	WADDLY
WEIMAR	WALLET	WEEVER	WINGED	WRINGS	WAFFLE
WHIDAH	WALTER	WELDED	WINIER	WRONGS	WAGGLE
WHYDAH	WANDER	WELDER	WINKED	******	WAGGLY
WIGWAG	WANNED	WELLED	WINKER	W---H-	WAMBLE
WIGWAM	WANNER	WELTED	WINNER	******	WAMBLY
WILMAS	WANTED	WELTER	WINOES	WEIGHS	WANDLE
WITHAL	WANTER	WENDED	WINTER	WEIGHT	WANGLE
WOMBAT	WAPPED	WESLEY	WINZES	WIDTHS	WARBLE
WYSTAN	WARDED	WESSEX	WIRIER	WORTHY	WARILY
******	WARDEN	WESTER	WISHED	WRATHY	WARMLY
W---B-	WARDER	WETHER	WISHES	WRIGHT	WATTLE
******	WARIER	WETTED	WISPED	WRITHE	WAVILY
WAHABI	WARMED	WETTER	WITHED	******	WEAKLY
WHITBY	WARMER	WHALED	WITHER	W---I-	WEDELN
******	WARNED	WHALER	WITHES	******	WEEKLY
W---C-	WARNER	WHALES	WITNEY	WALLIE	WHEALS
******	WARPED	WHEYEY	WITTED	WALLIS	WHEELS
WHENCE	WARPER	WHILED	WOADED	WALVIS	WHIRLS
WRENCH	WARRED	WHILES	WOLFED	WEDGIE	WHOLLY
WRETCH	WARREN	WHINED	WOLSEY	WEENIE	WHORLS
******	WASHED	WHINER	WOLVER	WEEVIL	WIDELY
W---D-	WASHER	WHINES	WOLVES	WELKIN	WIFELY
******					
WEALDS					
WEIRDY					

WIGGLE	WALDOS	******	******	******	YAKKED
WIGGLY	WALKON	**W---S-**	**W---W-**	**X---N-**	YAMMER
WILDLY	WALLOP	******	******	******	YANKED
WILILY	WALLOW	WABASH	WIDOWS	XYLANS	YANKEE
WIMBLE	WALTON	WATUSI		XYLENE	YAPPED
WIMPLE	WANION	WEENSY	**W---Y-**	******	YARDED
WINKLE	WANTON	WHILST	******	**X---O-**	YAUPED
WIRILY	WARHOL	WHIMSY	WALLYS	******	YAWLED
WISELY	WATSON	WHOOSH	WAVEYS	XYSTOS	YAWNED
WOBBLE	WEAPON	WIDEST	WENDYS	******	YAWNER
WOBBLY	WHILOM	WISEST	WILLYS	**X---S-**	YAWPED
WOOLLY	WIGEON	WOODSY	******	******	YAWPER
******	WILLOW	WRASSE	**W---Z-**	XYLOSE	YEANED
W---M-	WILSON	WRIEST	******	******	YELLED
******	WILTON	WRYEST	WHEEZE	**X---T-**	YELLER
WHAMMY	WINDOW	******	WHEEZY	******	YELPED
WHELMS	WINNOW	**W---T-**	******	XYLITE	YELPER
******	WISDOM	******	**X---A-**	******	YENNED
W---N-	******	WAISTS	******	**X---U-**	YEOMEN
******	**W---P-**	WAPITI	XENIAL	******	YESSED
WADING	******	WARMTH	**X---C-**	XTSTUS	YESSES
WAGING	WATAPE	WEALTH	******	**Y---A-**	YESTER
WAGONS	WATAPS	WHEATS	XEBECS	******	YIPPED
WAHINE	WHELPS	WHORTS	******	YASMAK	YOGEES
WAKENS	WHIPPY	WORSTS	**X---D-**	YEOMAN	YONDER
WAKING	WHOOPS	WRAITH	******	YERBAS	YONKER
WALING	WICOPY	WREATH	XANADU	YESMAN	YORKER
WANING	******	WRESTS	******	YUCCAS	YOWLED
WAVING	**W---R-**	WRISTS	**X---E-**	******	YUKKED
WAXING	******	******	******	**Y---B-**	******
WERENT	WADERS	**W---U-**	XAVIER	******	**Y---H-**
WHINNY	WAFERS	******	XRAYED	YORUBA	******
WIDENS	WAGERS	WALKUP	XYSTER	******	YOUTHS
WIGANS	WALERS	WALNUT	******	**Y---C-**	******
WILING	WATERS	WALRUS	**X---H-**	******	**Y---I-**
WINING	WATERY	WAMMUS	******	YORICK	******
WIPING	WAVERS	WAMOUS	XANTHO	******	YIPPIE
WIRING	WEBERS	WAMPUM	******	**Y---D-**	YTTRIA
WISING	WHERRY	WARMUP	**X---I-**	******	YTTRIC
WIVING	WINERY	WAYOUT	******	YEHUDI	YUPPIE
WIZENS	WINTRY	WIKIUP	XYLOID	YIELDS	******
WOOING	WIPERS	WILBUR	******	******	**Y---K-**
WOWING	WIRERS	WILFUL	**X---L-**	**Y---E-**	******
WRYING	WIVERN	WINDUP	******	******	YOICKS
******	WIVERS	WOEFUL	XYLOLS	YABBER	******
W---O-	WIZARD	WRAPUP	******	YAHVEH	**Y---L-**
******	WOMERA	******	**X---M-**	YAHWEH	******
WAGGON	WOOERS	**W---V-**	******		YEARLY
WAHOOS	WYVERN	******	XYLEMS		YODELS
		WHARVE			YOKELS
		WHERVE			

*****	ZEBRAS	ZOMBIE	ZIBETS	AMENRA	ADVERB
Y---M-	ZIGZAG	ZOMBIS	ZIZITH	AMOEBA	APLOMB
*****	ZILLAH	ZOYSIA	ZONATE	AMRITA	*****
YAKIMA	ZODIAC	*****	ZYGOTE	ANCONA	A----C
*****	ZOONAL	Z---K-	*****	ANDREA	*****
Y---N-	*****	ZINCKY	Z---U-	ANEMIA	ACERIC
*****	Z---B-	*****	*****	ANGELA	ACETIC
YAMENS	*****	Z---L-	ZETHUS	ANGINA	ACIDIC
YAMUNS	ZARIBA	*****	*****	ANGLIA	ADIPIC
YAPONS	Z---C-	ZIZZLE	Z---V-	ANGOLA	ADONIC
YAWING	*****	ZONULA	*****	ANGORA	AEOLIC
YEARNS	ZEBECK	ZONULE	ZOUAVE	ANITRA	AGAMIC
YEMENI	ZEBECS	ZORILS	*****	ANKARA	AGARIC
YOGINS	ZURICH	*****	Z---Y-	ANNONA	AGONIC
YOKING	*****	Z---M-	*****	ANOMIA	AIRSAC
YOWING	Z---D-	*****	ZEPHYR	ANOXIA	ALARIC
YUPONS	*****	ZEUGMA	ZLOTYS	ANTHEA	ALCAIC
YVONNE	ZOOIDS	ZYGOMA	*****	ANTLIA	ALTAIC
*****	ZOUNDS	*****	A----A	APHTHA	AMEBIC
Y---O-		Z---N-	*****	APNOEA	AMIDIC
*****	Z---E-	*****	ABOLLA	APULIA	AMYLIC
YAHOOS	*****	ZANANA	ABULIA	AQUILA	ANEMIC
YARROW	ZAFFER	ZAYINS	ACACIA	ARABIA	ANGLIC
YAUPON	ZANIER	ZENANA	ACADIA	ARANTA	ANODIC
YELLOW	ZANIES	ZIRONS	ACAENA	ARBELA	ANOMIC
YOOHOO	ZENGER	ZONING	ACEDIA	ARCANA	ANOXIC
YOUPON	ZEROED	*****	ACHAEA	AREOLA	AORTIC
*****	ZEROES	Z---O-	ACHAIA	ARGALA	APNEIC
Y---P-	ZESTED	*****	AEOLIA	ARISTA	ARABIC
*****	ZINCED	ZEALOT	AFRICA	ARMADA	ARCTIC
YCLEPT	ZINGED	ZETHOS	AFTOSA	ARNICA	ATAVIC
*****	ZIPPED	ZIRCON	AGATHA	ARROBA	ATAXIC
Y---R-	ZIPPER	*****	AGENDA	ARUNTA	ATOMIC
YAGERS	ZITHER	Z---R-	AGLAIA	ASTHMA	ATONIC
YAOURT	ZOOMED	*****	AHIMSA	ATAXIA	AZONIC
YOGURT	ZOSTER	ZAFFRE	ALALIA	ATHENA	AZOTIC
*****	ZUIDER	ZONARY	ALASKA	ATTICA	*****
Y---T-	ZUYDER	*****	ALBATA	ATTILA	A----D
*****	*****	Z---S-	ALEXIA	AURIGA	*****
YACHTS	Z---I-	*****	ALICIA	AURORA	AALAND
YEASTS	*****	ZSAZSA	ALMIRA	AVESTA	ABASED
YEASTY	ZAFFIR	*****	ALPACA	AXILLA	ABATED
*****	ZAFTIG	Z---T-	ALTHEA	AYESHA	ABIDED
Z---A-	ZAMBIA	*****	ALUMNA	AYMARA	ABOARD
*****	ZECHIN	ZAPATA	ALVINA	AZALEA	ABOUND
ZAFFAR	ZINCIC	ZENITH	AMANDA	*****	ABROAD
ZAMIAS	ZINNIA	ZIBETH	AMANIA	A----B	ABSURD
			AMELIA	*****	ABUSED
				ABSORB	
				ADSORB	

ACARID	ABRADE	AMELIE	AVENGE	AMBARI	ATONAL
ACCORD	ACCEDE	AMERCE	AVENUE	AMENTI	ATRIAL
ADDEND	ACCRUE	AMPERE	AVERSE	ANDREI	AVOWAL
ADDLED	ACCUSE	AMPULE	AVIATE	ARBORI	AWHEEL
ADORED	ACHENE	ANANKE	AWHILE	ARGALI	AWHIRL
AENEID	ACNODE	ANCONE	AXLIKE	ASSISI	AZAZEL
AERIED	ACTIVE	ANLACE	AYEAYE	ASTERI	AZRAEL
AFFORD	ACUATE	ANLAGE	******	******	******
AFIELD	ADDUCE	ANNEXE	**A----G**	**A----K**	**A----M**
AFRAID	ADHERE	ANOMIE	******	******	******
AGEOLD	ADJURE	ANSATE	ACHING	ACKACK	ABLOOM
AGREED	ADMIRE	ANYONE	ACTING	ANORAK	ACEIUM
AIRBED	ADNATE	AORTAE	ADDING	ARAWAK	ACETUM
AISLED	ADVICE	APACHE	AGEING	ARRACK	ACTIUM
ALATED	ADVISE	APIECE	AIDING	ATTACK	ADYTUM
ALFRED	AEDILE	APLITE	AILING	******	AFFIRM
ALGOID	AERATE	APOGEE	AIMING	**A----L**	AGLEAM
ALIDAD	AEROBE	APPOSE	AIRING	******	ALARUM
ALINED	AFLAME	ARABLE	ANALOG	ABORAL	ALLIUM
ALIPED	AFRAME	ARBUTE	APOLOG	ACETAL	AMYLUM
ALLIED	AGAPAE	ARCADE	ARCING	ACETYL	ANADEM
ALMOND	AGNATE	ARCANE	ARMING	ACTUAL	ANONYM
AMAZED	AGOGUE	ARCHIE	ASKING	AECIAL	ANSELM
AMBLED	AGORAE	ARGIVE	AWEING	AERIAL	ANTHEM
AMUSED	AGRAFE	ARIOSE	AWNING	AGNAIL	ANTRIM
ANGLED	ALBITE	ARLENE	******	ALPHYL	ANTRUM
ANTEED	ALCOVE	ARLINE	**A----H**	ALUDEL	ASARUM
AOUDAD	ALDINE	ARMURE	******	AMATOL	ASYLUM
APPEND	ALDOSE	AROUSE	ABIJAH	AMIDOL	ATRIUM
ARCHED	ALIBLE	ARRIVE	ABLUSH	AMORAL	AUTISM
ARCKED	ALKANE	ARSINE	ACANTH	AMYTAL	******
ARGUED	ALKENE	ASHORE	ADOLPH	ANIMAL	**A----N**
ARMAND	ALKYNE	ASLOPE	AFRESH	ANNEAL	******
ARNAUD	ALLEGE	ASPIRE	AGUISH	ANNUAL	AACHEN
ARNOLD	ALLELE	ASSIZE	AMBUSH	AORTAL	ABADAN
AROUND	ALLUDE	ASSUME	ARMAGH	APICAL	ACTION
ASCEND	ALLURE	ASSURE	ATTACH	APNEAL	ACUMEN
ASGARD	ALMUCE	ASTUTE	AVOUCH	APODAL	ADJOIN
ASTRID	ALMUDE	ATHENE	AWEIGH	APPALL	ADNOUN
ATONED	ALPINE	ATHOME	******	APPEAL	ADRIAN
ATTEND	ALSACE	ATTIRE	**A----I**	ARABEL	ADRIEN
AUGEND	ALSIKE	ATTLEE	******	ARCHIL	AEGEAN
AUTOED	ALULAE	ATTUNE	ACTINI	ARGYLL	AFGHAN
AVOWED	ALVINE	AUBADE	ADONAI	ARMFUL	AIDMAN
AWAKED	AMALIE	AUDILE	AGOUTI	ARTFUL	AIDMEN
AXSEED	AMBAGE	AUGITE	ALFAKI	ASSAIL	AILEEN
******	AMEBAE	AUNTIE	ALKALI	ASTRAL	AIRGUN
A----E	AMECHE	AURATE	ALUMNI	ATABAL	AIRMAN
******					
ABJURE					
ABLAZE					

AIRMEN	ALECTO	APPEAR	ACTORS	ALGOUS	ANIMUS
AJOWAN	ALEPPO	ARBOUR	ADAGES	ALIBIS	ANIONS
ALBION	ALONSO	ARCHER	ADAPTS	ALICES	ANISES
ALCUIN	ALONZO	ARDOUR	ADDAMS	ALIENS	ANITAS
ALEXIN	ALUINO	ARGUER	ADDERS	ALIGNS	ANKLES
ALISON	ANATTO	ARMOUR	ADDLES	ALINES	ANNALS
ALUMIN	ANGELO	ARREAR	ADEEMS	ALKYLS	ANNIES
AMAZON	ANKYLO	ARTHUR	ADENIS	ALLANS	ANNOYS
AMIDIN	ANTERO	ASHIER	ADEPTS	ALLAYS	ANNULS
AMNION	APOLLO	ASHLAR	ADIEUS	ALLENS	ANODES
ANDEAN	ARCHEO	ATONER	ADLIBS	ALLEYS	ANTICS
ANILIN	AREZZO	AUSTER	ADMITS	ALLIES	ANTONS
ANURAN	ARIOSO	AUTHOR	ADOBES	ALLOTS	ANUBIS
APEMAN	ARISTO	AVATAR	ADONIS	ALLOWS	ANUSES
APPIAN	ARROYO	AVOWER	ADOPTS	ALLOYS	ANVILS
ARAGON	ARTHRO	******	ADORES	ALLYLS	AORTAS
ARCHON	ARTURO	A----S	ADORNS	ALMAHS	APEXES
ARISEN	ASTERO	******	ADULTS	ALMUDS	APHIDS
ARLEEN	AUSTRO	AALIIS	AEACUS	ALPHAS	APICES
ASHCAN	AVERNO	AARONS	AEETES	ALPHOS	APPALS
ASHMAN	******	ABACAS	AEGEUS	ALTARS	APPELS
ASHMEN	A----P	ABACUS	AENEAS	ALTERS	APPLES
ASSIGN	******	ABASES	AEOLIS	ALUINS	APRILS
ASTERN	ASLEEP	ABATES	AEOLUS	ALVANS	APRONS
ATAMAN	******	ABATIS	AERIES	ALWAYS	ARBORS
ATTAIN	A----R	ABBESS	AGAMAS	AMAZES	ARCHES
ATTORN	******	ABBEYS	AGATES	AMBERS	ARCHYS
AUBURN	ABASER	ABBIES	AGAVES	AMBITS	ARDEBS
AUGEAN	ABATER	ABBOTS	AGENTS	AMBLES	ARDORS
AUSTEN	ABATOR	ABELES	AGGERS	AMEBAS	ARECAS
AUSTIN	ABIDER	ABHORS	AGISTS	AMENDS	ARENAS
AUTUMN	ABUSER	ABIDES	AGLETS	AMENTS	ARETES
AVALON	ADORER	ABNERS	AGONES	AMICES	ARGALS
AVIDIN	AETHER	ABODES	AGORAS	AMIDES	ARGOTS
AWAKEN	AFFAIR	ABOHMS	AGREES	AMIENS	ARGUES
AWOKEN	AIRIER	ABOMAS	AIDERS	AMIGOS	ARIANS
AXEMAN	ALEGAR	ABOMBS	AISLES	AMOLES	ARIELS
AXEMEN	ALTAIR	ABORTS	AKENES	AMOURS	ARIOUS
******	ALULAR	ABRAMS	ALAMOS	AMPHRS	ARISES
A----O	AMBLER	ABUSES	ALARMS	AMPULS	ARMETS
******	AMUSER	ABYDOS	ALBUMS	AMUSES	ARMIES
ACTINO	ANCHOR	ABYSMS	ALDERS	ANABAS	ARMORS
ADAGIO	ANGKOR	ACCESS	ALDOUS	ANANAS	ARNIES
AERUGO	ANGLER	ACEOUS	ALEPHS	ANDRES	AROIDS
AFLCIO	ANSWER	ACINUS	ALERTS	ANGELS	AROMAS
AKIMBO	ANTHER	ACIOUS	ALEUTS	ANGERS	ARPENS
ALBEDO	ANTIAR	ACORNS	ALEXIS	ANGLES	ARRAYS
ALBINO	ANTLER	ACROSS	ALFONS	ANIMAS	ARROWS

ARTELS	ABLAUT	ASLANT	ALBANY	BRENDA	BASTED
ARTIES	ABLEST	ASPECT	AMBARY	BUCKRA	BATHED
ARTOIS	ABRUPT	ASSENT	AMBERY	BUDDHA	BATTED
ARYANS	ABSENT	ASSERT	ANERGY	******	BAWLED
ASCOTS	ABVOLT	ASSIST	ANGARY	B----B	BAYARD
ASIANS	ABWATT	ASSORT	ANTONY	******	BEADED
ASIDES	ACCENT	ATTEST	ANYWAY	BAOBAB	BEAKED
ASKERS	ACCEPT	AUGUST	APATHY	BEDAUB	BEÁMED
ASPENS	ACCOST	AUKLET	APEPSY	BENUMB	BEANED
ASPERS	ACQUIT	AURIST	APHONY	BICARB	BEARED
ASPICS	ADDICT	AVAUNT	APIARY	******	BECKED
ASSAIS	ADDUCT	AVOCET	ARCHLY	B----C	BEDDED
ASSAYS	ADJECT	AVOSET	ARGOSY	******	BEDRID
ASSESS	ADJUST	******	ARGUFY	BALTIC	BEEFED
ASSETS	ADMIXT	A----U	ARIDLY	BALZAC	BEEPED
ASTERS	ADRIFT	******	ARMORY	BARDIC	BEGGED
ATHENS	ADROIT	ACAJOU	ARROWY	BELGIC	BEGIRD
ATOLLS	ADVENT	AMADOU	ARTERY	BELLOC	BEHEAD
ATONES	ADVERT	ARERCU	ARTILY	BIOTIC	BEHELD
ATREUS	AFFECT	******	ASBURY	BOMBIC	BEHIND
ATTARS	AFLOAT	A----V	ASHLEY	BROMIC	BEHOLD
ATTICS	AGHAST	******	ASTRAY	BUSTIC	BELIED
AUDADS	AIGLET	ASIMOV	AUBREY	******	BELLED
AUDITS	ALBEIT	******	AUDREY	B----D	BELTED
AUGERS	ALBERT	A----W	AUGURY	******	BENDED
AUGHTS	ALCOTT	******	AVIARY	BABIED	BESTED
AUGURS	ALIGHT	ANDREW	AVIDLY	BACHED	BETTED
AUREUS	ALLOUT	ANYHOW	AWEARY	BACKED	BEYOND
AUROUS	ALMOST	******	******	BADGED	BIASED
AUXINS	AMIDST	A----X	B----A	BAFFED	BIBBED
AVAILS	AMOUNT	******	******	BAGDAD	BIFFED
AVERTS	AMULET	ADIEUX	BAHAMA	BAGGED	BIFOLD
AVERYS	ANKLET	AFFLUX	BALATA	BAILED	BILGED
AVISOS	ANOINT	AUSPEX	BALBOA	BAITED	BILKED
AVOIDS	AORIST	******	BANANA	BALKED	BILLED
AWAITS	APPORT	A----Y	BARBRA	BALLAD	BINNED
AWAKES	ARARAT	******	BARYTA	BALLED	BIRLED
AWARDS	ARDENT	ABBACY	BELUGA	BANDED	BIRRED
AWLESS	ARGENT	ACIDLY	BEMATA	BANGED	BITTED
AXIOMS	ARIGHT	ACUITY	BENITA	BANKED	BLADED
AXONES	ARMLET	AERIFY	BERTHA	BANNED	BLAMED
AZINES	ARMPIT	AFFRAY	BIAFRA	BARBED	BLARED
AZOLES	ARPENT	AGEDLY	BIANCA	BARDED	BLAZED
AZORES	ARRANT	AGENCY	BODEGA	BARGED	BOATED
AZTECS	ARREST	AGOUTY	BOGOTA	BARKED	BOBBED
AZURES	ARTIST	AIRDRY	BORGIA	BARRED	BODIED
******	ASCENT	AIRILY	BRAHMA	BASHED	BOGGED
A----T	ASKANT	AIRWAY	BREGMA	BASKED	BOILED
******					
ABDUCT					
ABJECT					

BOLLED	BUSTED	BETIDE	BRIDIE	BELONG	BRACHI
BOLTED	BUTTED	BETISE	BRIDLE	BERING	BRUNEI
BOMBED	BUZZED	BEWARE	BROCHE	BIDING	******
BONDED	BYROAD	BIERCE	BROGUE	BIGWIG	**B----K**
BONGED	BYWORD	BIGONE	BRONTE	BITING	******
BOOKED	******	BILLIE	BRONZE	BLUING	BARTOK
BOOMED	**B----E**	BINATE	BROOKE	BODING	BATTIK
BOOTED	******	BIRDIE	BROWSE	BONING	BEDECK
BOOZED	BABBIE	BIREME	BRUISE	BOOING	BETOOK
BOPPED	BABBLE	BISQUE	BUBBLE	BORING	BOGOAK
BOSSED	BABITE	BLAISE	BUCKLE	BOWING	BYTALK
BOUSED	BAFFLE	BLENDE	BUDDLE	BOWLEG	BYWORK
BOWLED	BAILEE	BLITHE	BUDGIE	BOXING	******
BOWSED	BAILIE	BLONDE	BULLAE	BUSING	**B----L**
BOYARD	BANGLE	BLOUSE	BUMBLE	BUYING	******
BRACED	BARBIE	BLUNGE	BUNCHE	******	BAIKAL
BRAKED	BAREGE	BOBBIE	BUNDLE	**B----H**	BARBEL
BRAVED	BARGEE	BOBBLE	BUNGLE	******	BARREL
BRAYED	BARITE	BOCCIE	BURBLE	BANISH	BEFALL
BRAZED	BARMIE	BODICE	BURDIE	BARUCH	BEFELL
BREWED	BARQUE	BOGGLE	BURGEE	BASRAH	BEFOOL
BRIBED	BARRIE	BOLIDE	BURGLE	BEULAH	BEFOUL
BRIGID	BASQUE	BONNIE	BURSAE	BLANCH	BELIAL
BRINED	BATTLE	BOODLE	BUSTLE	BLEACH	BENGAL
BUCKED	BATTUE	BOOGIE	BUTANE	BLENCH	BENZOL
BUDDED	BAUBLE	BOOKIE	BYEBYE	BLOTCH	BENZYL
BUDGED	BEADLE	BOOTEE	BYGONE	BLUISH	BETHEL
BUFFED	BEAGLE	BOOTIE	BYLANE	BORSCH	BEWAIL
BUGGED	BEANIE	BOOTLE	BYLINE	BOYISH	BIAXAL
BUGLED	BECAME	BORAGE	BYNAME	BRANCH	BORDEL
BULBED	BECOME	BORANE	******	BREACH	BOREAL
BULGED	BEETLE	BORATE	**B----F**	BREATH	BRAZIL
BULKED	BEFORE	BORIDE	******	BREECH	BRIDAL
BUMMED	BEGONE	BOTTLE	BEHALF	BROACH	BROMAL
BUMPED	BEHAVE	BOUCLE	BEHOOF	BROOCH	BRUMAL
BUNGED	BEHOVE	BOUFFE	BELIEF	BRUNCH	BRUNEL
BUNKED	BELIKE	BOUGIE	******	BYPATH	BRUTAL
BUNTED	BELIZE	BOUNCE	**B----G**	******	BUCCAL
BUOYED	BEMIRE	BOURNE	******	**B----I**	BULBEL
BURIED	BEMUSE	BOURSE	BAAING	******	BULBIL
BURKED	BENDEE	BOVATE	BAKING	BANGUI	BULBUL
BURLED	BERATE	BOVINE	BALING	BANZAI	BURIAL
BURNED	BERNIE	BOWTIE	BARING	BIHARI	BURSAL
BURPED	BERTHE	BRAISE	BARONG	BIKINI	BUSHEL
BURRED	BERTIE	BRAIZE	BASING	BILOXI	******
BUSHED	BESIDE	BRAQUE	BATING	BONACI	**B----M**
BUSIED	BESSIE	BREEZE	BAYING	BONSAI	******
BUSSED	BETAKE	BRIDGE	BEDBUG	BORZOI	BAALIM
					BABISM

BALAAM	BERLIN	BENITO	BERBER	BUNKER	BEDEWS
BALSAM	BHUTAN	BIBLIO	BESTIR	BURGER	BEDIMS
BALTIM	BICORN	BILBAO	BETTER	BURLER	BEEVES
BANTAM	BIDDEN	BISTRO	BETTOR	BURNER	BEFITS
BARIUM	BIFFIN	BLASTO	BEZOAR	BURSAR	BEFOGS
BARNUM	BIGGIN	BOLERO	BIBBER	BUSKER	BEGETS
BECALM	BILLON	BONITO	BICKER	BUSTER	BEGINS
BEDLAM	BIOGEN	BOOBOO	BIDDER	BUTLER	BEGUMS
BELDAM	BIOTIN	BOOHOO	BIGGER	BUTTER	BEIGES
BESEEM	BITTEN	BORNEO	BILKER	BUZZER	BEINGS
BIFORM	BLAZON	BRONCO	BINDER	******	BELAYS
BOTTOM	BOBBIN	BURGOO	BISTER	**B----S**	BELGAS
BUNKUM	BODKIN	******	BITTER	******	BELIES
******	BOFFIN	**B----P**	BLAZER	BABIES	BELLAS
B----N	BOLEYN	******	BLOWER	BABOOS	BELLES
******	BOLSON	BANGUP	BOATER	BABULS	BENJYS
BABOON	BOLTON	BISHOP	BOBBER	BACHES	BENNES
BADMAN	BONBON	BLOWUP	BOILER	BADGES	BENNYS
BADMEN	BOSTON	BUNYIP	BOLDER	BAGASS	BERETS
BAFFIN	BOWFIN	BURLAP	BOLTER	BAGELS	BERMES
BAGMAN	BOWMAN	******	BOMBER	BAHAIS	BERTHS
BAGMEN	BOWMEN	**B----R**	BONDER	BAIRNS	BERYLS
BALEEN	BRAZEN	******	BONIER	BAKERS	BESETS
BALKAN	BREMEN	BACKER	BONZER	BALERS	BESOMS
BANIAN	BRETON	BADGER	BOOMER	BALSAS	BESOTS
BANYAN	BRITON	BAILER	BOOZER	BANJOS	BESSYS
BARMAN	BROGAN	BAILOR	BORDER	BANTUS	BETELS
BARMEN	BROKEN	BALDER	BOTHER	BARDES	BETSYS
BARREN	BUCHAN	BANGOR	BOWLER	BARGES	BETTES
BARTON	BUMKIN	BANKER	BOWYER	BARONS	BETTYS
BARYON	BUNION	BANNER	BOXCAR	BARRYS	BEULAS
BASION	BUNSEN	BANTER	BRACER	BARYES	BEVELS
BATAAN	BUNYAN	BARBER	BRAVER	BASHES	BEVIES
BATMAN	BURDEN	BARKER	BRAYER	BASICS	BEZELS
BATMEN	BURTON	BARTER	BRAZER	BASILS	BIALYS
BATTEN	BUSKIN	BATHER	BREWER	BASINS	BIASES
BATTIN	BUSMAN	BATTER	BRIBER	BASSES	BIBLES
BEACON	BUSMEN	BAWLER	BROKER	BASSOS	BICEPS
BEATEN	BUTTON	BAXTER	BUCKER	BASTES	BIDETS
BECKON	BUXTON	BAZAAR	BUDDER	BATHOS	BIGHTS
BEDPAN	******	BEAKER	BUFFER	BATIKS	BIGOTS
BEDUIN	**B----O**	BEARER	BUGGER	BATONS	BIKOLS
BEGUIN	******	BEATER	BUGLER	BAUCIS	BILGES
BEMEAN	BAGNIO	BEAVER	BULBAR	BAYOUS	BILLYS
BEMOAN	BAMAKO	BEDDER	BULGAR	BEARDS	BINGES
BENIGN	BAMBOO	BEGGAR	BULGER	BEASTS	BINITS
BENTON	BARRIO	BELIER	BUMMER	BEAUTS	BIOSIS
BERGEN	BASUTO	BENDER	BUMPER	BECKYS	BIPEDS

BIPODS	BORERS	BRISKS	BALLOT	BELLOW	BLIMEY
BIRLES	BOSHES	BROADS	BANDIT	BESTOW	BLOCKY
BIRTHS	BOSOMS	BROILS	BARBET	BILLOW	BLOODY
BITERS	BOSSES	BROMES	BAREST	BORROW	BLOOMY
BLACKS	BOUGHS	BRONCS	BARRET	BOWSAW	BLOWBY
BLADES	BOULES	BROODS	BASALT	BOWWOW	BLOWZY
BLAINS	BOUNDS	BROOKS	BASEST	BURROW	BLUELY
BLAMES	BOURGS	BROOMS	BASKET	BYBLOW	BLURRY
BLANKS	BOURNS	BROTHS	BASSET	******	BODILY
BLARES	BOUSES	BROWNS	BECKET	B----X	BOLDLY
BLASTS	BOWELS	BRUCES	BEDSIT	******	BOMBAY
BLAZES	BOWERS	BRUGES	BEGIRT	BAYEUX	BOTANY
BLEAKS	BOWSES	BRUINS	BEHEST	BIFLEX	BOTCHY
BLEARS	BOXERS	BRUITS	BEIRUT	BIJOUX	BOTFLY
BLEATS	BOYARS	BRUMES	BELOIT	BOLLIX	BOUNCY
BLEEDS	BRACES	BRUNOS	BENNET	******	BOUNTY
BLENDS	BRACTS	BRUTES	BEREFT	B----Y	BOWERY
BLIMPS	BRAHMS	BRUTUS	BESANT	******	BRACHY
BLINDS	BRAIDS	BUBALS	BEZANT	BACONY	BRAINY
BLINKS	BRAILS	BUBOES	BILLET	BAILEY	BRANDY
BLOATS	BRAINS	BUDGES	BISECT	BAKERY	BRANNY
BLOCKS	BRAKES	BUGLES	BLIGHT	BALDLY	BRASHY
BLOKES	BRANDS	BUILDS	BLUEST	BARELY	BRASSY
BLONDS	BRANTS	BULGES	BOBCAT	BARFLY	BRAWNY
BLOODS	BRAVES	BUNCOS	BONNET	BARLEY	BREEZY
BLOOMS	BRAVOS	BURANS	BOSKET	BARNEY	BRIERY
BLUETS	BRAWLS	BURGHS	BOUGHT	BARONY	BROLLY
BLUFFS	BRAZAS	BURGOS	BRANDT	BASELY	BRONZY
BLUNTS	BRAZES	BURIES	BREAST	BASIFY	BROODY
BLURBS	BRAZOS	BURINS	BRECHT	BAWDRY	BROOMY
BLURTS	BREADS	BURKES	BREVET	BEACHY	BRUSHY
BOARDS	BREAKS	BURROS	BRIGHT	BEAUTY	BRYONY
BOASTS	BREAMS	BURSAS	BRULOT	BEECHY	BUBBLY
BOBBYS	BREEDS	BURSES	BRYANT	BELFRY	BUNCHY
BODIES	BREEKS	BURSTS	BUCKET	BENDAY	BURLEY
BOGANS	BRENTS	BUSHES	BUDGET	BERNEY	BUSHEY
BOGEYS	BREVES	BUSIES	BUFFET	BETONY	BUSILY
BOGIES	BREWIS	BUSSES	BULLET	BETRAY	BYPLAY
BOGLES	BRIARS	BUTTES	BURBOT	BIGAMY	******
BOMBES	BRIBES	BUYERS	BURNET	BILITY	B----Z
BONERS	BRICKS	BUZZES	BYPAST	BINARY	******
BONGOS	BRIDES	BYLAWS	******	BIOPSY	BLINTZ
BONNYS	BRIEFS	BYPASS	B----U	BISCAY	******
BONZES	BRIERS	BYSSUS	******	BITCHY	C----A
BOOSTS	BRILLS	BYWAYS	BATEAU	BLEARY	******
BOOTHS	BRINES	******	BUREAU	BLEBBY	CABALA
BOOZES	BRINGS	B----T	******	BLENNY	CABANA
BOREAS	BRINKS	******	B----W		CAEOMA
		BABIST	******		
		BALLET	BARROW		
			BASHAW		

CALESA	******	CARVED	COSHED	CAROLE	CLOTHE
CAMERA	C----C	CASHED	COSTED	CARRIE	COARSE
CAMILA	******	CATTED	COWARD	CASQUE	COATEE
CANADA	CALCIC	CAUDAD	CRANED	CASSIE	COBBLE
CANDIA	CALPAC	CAUSED	CRAPED	CASTLE	COCKLE
CANULA	CAPRIC	CEASED	CRATED	CATTIE	CODDLE
CAPITA	CARPIC	CEBOID	CRAVED	CATTLE	COERCE
CARINA	CEDRIC	CEILED	CRAZED	CAUDLE	COFFEE
CASABA	CELIAC	CENSED	CREPED	CAVITE	COFFLE
CASAVA	CELTIC	CHAFED	CROWED	CAYUSE	COHERE
CASSIA	CHEBEC	CHARED	CUBBED	CECILE	COHUNE
CATENA	CHORIC	CHASED	CUBOID	CELLAE	COLINE
CAYUGA	CHYMIC	CHAWED	CUFFED	CENTRE	COLLIE
CEDULA	CITRIC	CHEWED	CULLED	CERATE	COLURE
CENTRA	CLERIC	CHIDED	CULMED	CERISE	COMATE
CESURA	CLINIC	CHIMED	CUPPED	CERITE	COMMIE
CHACMA	CLONIC	CHOKED	CURBED	CERUSE	COMOSE
CHAETA	COGNAC	CITIED	CURDED	CESARE	CONNIE
CHOLLA	COPTIC	CLAWED	CURLED	CETANE	CONTRE
CHOREA	CORSAC	CLAYED	CURSED	CHAISE	COODLE
CHROMA	COSMIC	CLERID	CURVED	CHANCE	COOKIE
CICADA	CRETIC	CLEWED	CUSPED	CHANGE	COOLIE
CICALA	CRITIC	CLOSED	CUSPID	CHARGE	COOTIE
CINEMA	CUPRIC	CLOYED	CUSSED	CHASSE	CORBIE
CITOLA	CYANIC	COALED	CYANID	CHASTE	CORPSE
CLOACA	CYCLIC	COATED	CYCLED	CHEESE	CORRIE
CODEIA	CYMRIC	COAXED	CYMOID	CHEGOE	CORVEE
CONCHA	CYSTIC	COCCID	******	CHELAE	COSINE
CONTRA	******	COCKED	C----E	CHEQUE	COSTAE
COPPRA	C----D	COELED	******	CHICLE	COTTAE
COPULA	******	COGGED	CACKLE	CHIGOE	COULEE
CORNEA	CABLED	COIFED	CADDIE	CHOICE	COUPLE
CORNUA	CACHED	COILED	CAIQUE	CHOOSE	COURSE
CORONA	CADGED	COINED	CAJOLE	CHROME	COWAGE
CORYZA	CALKED	COMBED	CAMISE	CILICE	COWRIE
COWPEA	CALLED	CONKED	CANAPE	CINQUE	COYOTE
CRANIA	CALMED	CONNED	CANDLE	CIRCLE	CRADLE
CREUSA	CALVED	CONOID	CANGUE	CIRQUE	CREASE
CRIMEA	CAMPED	CONRAD	CANINE	CISSIE	CREATE
CUESTA	CANARD	COOEED	CANNAE	CLAIRE	CRECHE
CUPOLA	CANDID	COOKED	CANNIE	CLAQUE	CREESE
******	CANNED	COOLED	CANTLE	CLAUDE	CREOLE
C----B	CANOED	COOPED	CANUTE	CLAUSE	CRINGE
******	CANTED	COPIED	CAPONE	CLEAVE	CROSSE
CANTAB	CAPPED	COPPED	CAPOTE	CLEOME	CROUPE
CHERUB	CARDED	CORDED	CARAFE	CLICHE	CRUISE
COBWEB	CARPED	CORKED	CARATE	CLIQUE	CRUSOE
CONFAB	CARTED	CORNED	CARIBE	CLOCHE	CUBAGE
CORYMB					

CUDDIE	******	CARCEL	CILIUM	CHIRON	CHAETO
CUDDLE	C----H	CARMEL	CIRCUM	CHITIN	CHALCO
CUISSE	******	CARNAL	CIVISM	CHITON	CHEILO
CUPTIE	CALASH	CARPAL	COELOM	CHOPIN	CHEIRO
CUPULE	CALIPH	CARPEL	CONDOM	CHOSEN	CHLORO
CURARE	CASBAH	CARREL	CONIUM	CITRON	CHOREO
CURATE	CERIPH	CARTEL	COPALM	CLOVEN	CHROMO
CURDLE	CHALEH	CARVEL	CORIUM	COCAIN	CHRONO
CURIAE	CHETAH	CASUAL	CRINUM	COCHIN	CHRYSO
CURULE	CHINCH	CAUDAL	CUBISM	COCOON	CICERO
CUTTLE	CHOUGH	CAUSAL	CUPRUM	CODEIN	CLOTHO
CYBELE	CHURCH	CAVELL	CURIUM	COFFIN	COLUGO
CYMENE	CLENCH	CENTAL	CUSTOM	COLUMN	COMEDO
CYMOSE	CLINCH	CEREAL	******	COMEON	CRAMBO
CYRENE	CLOUGH	CHAPEL	C----N	COMMON	CRANIO
******	CLUTCH	CHERYL	******	CONMAN	CRYPTO
C----F	COHOSH	CHISEL	CABMAN	CONTIN	CUCKOO
******	COPRAH	CHORAL	CABMEN	CORBAN	CYRANO
CUTOFF	COYISH	CINEOL	CAFTAN	CORDON	******
******	CRATCH	CITRAL	CAIMAN	CORTIN	C----P
C----G	CROTCH	COAXAL	CALKIN	COSIGN	******
******	CROUCH	COCCAL	CALVIN	COTTON	CALLUP
CAGING	CRUNCH	COEVAL	CAMDEN	COUPON	CARHOP
CAKING	CRUTCH	COITAL	CAMION	COUSIN	CATNAP
CANING	CULTCH	COMPEL	CANAAN	COWMAN	CATNIP
CARING	******	CONSUL	CANCAN	COWMEN	CATSUP
CASING	C----I	CORBEL	CANNON	CRAVEN	COCKUP
CAVING	******	CORNEL	CANTON	CRAYON	COLLOP
CAWING	CANTHI	CORRAL	CANYON	CRETAN	******
CEDING	CENTRI	COSTAL	CAPLIN	CRETIN	C----R
CERING	CHICHI	CREDAL	CARBON	CRETON	******
CITING	CHILLI	CRENEL	CAREEN	CROTON	CADGER
CLUING	CIMBRI	CRESOL	CARMAN	CYANIN	CAESAR
COBURG	CLYPEI	CREWEL	CARMEN	CYMLIN	CAGIER
CODING	******	CRURAL	CARSON	CYPRIN	CAHIER
COKING	C----K	CUDGEL	CARTON	******	CALCAR
COMING	******	CUNEAL	CARVEN	C----O	CALKER
CONING	CANUCK	CUPFUL	CASEIN	******	CALLER
COOING	CARACK	CURIAL	CASERN	CALICO	CALMER
COPING	CHABUK	CYMBAL	CATION	CALLAO	CAMBER
CORING	CHIBUK	******	CATKIN	CARDIO	CAMPER
COVING	COPECK	C----M	CATLIN	CARUSO	CANCER
COWING	CROJIK	******	CAVEIN	CASHOO	CANDOR
COXING	******	CAECUM	CAVERN	CASINO	CANKER
CRYING	C----L	CERIUM	CAXTON	CASTRO	CANNER
CUBING	CANCEL	CESIUM	CAYMAN	CATALO	CANTER
CURING	CANNEL	CHIASM	CEYLON	CENTRO	CANTOR
		CHRISM	CHARON	CERATO	CAPPER

CAPTOR	CONCUR	CADDIS	CASALS	CHEOPS	CLARAS
CARDER	CONDOR	CADETS	CASHES	CHESTS	CLARES
CAREER	CONFER	CADGES	CASSIS	CHIAUS	CLAROS
CARPER	CONGER	CADMUS	CASTES	CHICKS	CLASPS
CARTER	CONKER	CADRES	CATERS	CHICOS	CLEANS
CARVER	CONNER	CAIRNS	CATHYS	CHIDES	CLEARS
CASPAR	COOKER	CAJUNS	CAUCUS	CHIEFS	CLEATS
CASPER	COOLER	CALAIS	CAULES	CHILLS	CLEFTS
CASTER	COOPER	CALCES	CAULIS	CHIMES	CLERKS
CASTOR	COPIER	CALEBS	CAULKS	CHINES	CLEVIS
CATHER	COPPER	CALIFS	CAUSES	CHINKS	CLICKS
CAUSER	CORDER	CALLAS	CAVIES	CHIRMS	CLIFFS
CAUTER	CORKER	CALLUS	CAVILS	CHIRPS	CLIMBS
CAVIAR	CORNER	CALVES	CEASES	CHIRRS	CLIMES
CELLAR	COSHER	CALXES	CECILS	CHIVES	CLINES
CENSER	COSTAR	CAMASS	CEDARS	CHLOES	CLINGS
CENSOR	COSTER	CAMELS	CEIBAS	CHOCKS	CLINKS
CENSUR	COTTAR	CAMEOS	CELIAS	CHOIRS	CLINTS
CENTER	COTTER	CAMPOS	CELLOS	CHOKES	CLIVES
CHAFER	COUGAR	CAMPUS	CENSES	CHORDS	CLOAKS
CHASER	COWPER	CANALS	CENSUS	CHORES	CLOCKS
CHEWER	COZIER	CANERS	CENTOS	CHORUS	CLONES
CHIDER	CRATER	CANNAS	CEORLS	CHUCKS	CLONUS
CHIMER	CRAVER	CANNES	CEREUS	CHUFAS	CLOSES
CHOKER	CROZER	CANOES	CEROUS	CHUMPS	CLOTHS
CHOLER	CRUDER	CANONS	CERTES	CHUNKS	CLOUDS
CINDER	CULLER	CANSOS	CESTUS	CHURLS	CLOUTS
CIPHER	CULVER	CANTOS	CHAFES	CHURNS	CLOVES
CITHER	CUMBER	CANTUS	CHAFFS	CHURRS	CLOVIS
CLAMOR	CUNNER	CANVAS	CHAINS	CHUTES	CLOWNS
CLEVER	CUPPER	CAPERS	CHAIRS	CIBOLS	CLUCKS
CLOSER	CURLER	CAPIAS	CHALKS	CIDERS	CLUMPS
CLOVER	CURSOR	CAPONS	CHAMPS	CIGARS	CLYDES
COALER	CUSTER	CARATS	CHANGS	CINDYS	COASTS
COAXER	CUTLER	CARERS	CHANTS	CIRCUS	COATIS
COBBER	CUTTER	CARESS	CHAPES	CIRRUS	COAXES
COCKER	CYCLER	CARETS	CHARDS	CISCOS	COBIAS
CODDER	CYPHER	CARGOS	CHARES	CISSYS	COBLES
CODGER	******	CARIBS	CHARMS	CITIES	COBRAS
COFFER	C----S	CARIES	CHARTS	CITRUS	COCCUS
COHEIR	******	CARLAS	CHASES	CIVETS	COCOAS
COILER	CABALS	CARLOS	CHASMS	CIVICS	COIGNS
COINER	CABINS	CAROBS	CHEATS	CIVIES	COITUS
COLDER	CABLES	CAROLS	CHECKS	CLACKS	COLEUS
COLLAR	CABOBS	CAROMS	CHEEKS	CLAIMS	COLIES
COLOUR	CACAOS	CARPUS	CHEEPS	CLAMPS	COLINS
COLTER	CACHES	CARTES	CHEERS	CLANGS	COLONS
COMBER	CACTUS	CARVES	CHELAS	CLANKS	COLORS

COLOUS CRAALS CRUETS CARPET ****** CHERRY
COLZAS CRACKS CRUMBS CARROT C----W CHESTY
COMBOS CRAFTS CRUMPS CASKET ****** CHEVVY
COMERS CRAIGS CRUSES CATGUT CALLOW CHILLY
COMETS CRAKES CRUSTS CAUGHT CARLOW CHINKY
COMICS CRAMPS CRUXES CAVEAT CASHAW CHIPPY
COMMAS CRANES CRYPTS CAVORT CASHEW CHIRPY
COMOUS CRANKS CUBANS CEMENT CRACOW CHITTY
COMPOS CRAPES CUBEBS CERMET CURFEW CHIVVY
CONCHS CRASIS CUBITS CHALET CURLEW CHOOSY
CONEYS CRATES CULETS CHRIST CUSHAW CHOPPY
CONGAS CRAVES CULLIS CILIAT ****** CHUBBY
CONGES CRAWLS CULTUS CLARET C----X CHUMMY
CONICS CRAZES CUMINS CLEIST ****** CHUNKY
CONIES CREAKS CUPELS CLIENT CARFAX CICELY
CONTES CREAMS CURERS CLIMAT CAUDEX CLAMMY
CONTOS CREDOS CURIES CLOSET CERVIX CLASSY
COOEES CREEDS CURIOS COBALT CLIMAX CLAYEY
COOERS CREEKS CURSES COBNUT COCCYX CLERGY
COOEYS CREELS CURTIS COEMPT COMMIX CLIFFY
COOMBS CREEPS CURVES COGENT CONVEX CLINGY
COOPTS CREMES CUSCUS COHORT CORTEX CLIQUY
COPIES CREPES CUSPIS COLLET COWPOX CLODDY
COPSES CRESTS CUSSES COMBAT ****** CLOGGY
CORALS CREVAS CUSSOS COMFIT C----Y CLOTTY
CORERS CRICKS CUSTOS COMMIT ****** CLOUDY
CORGIS CRIERS CUTEYS COPOUT CAGILY CLUMPY
CORNUS CRIMES CUTIES COQUET CALMLY CLUMSY
CORPUS CRIMPS CUTINS CORNET CALORY COBBLY
CORSES CRISES CUTLAS CORSET CANARY CODIFY
CORTES CRISIS CUTUPS COSSET CANOPY COGWAY
CORVES CRISPS CYCADS COVERT CARBOY COLDLY
CORVUS CROAKS CYCLES CRAVAT CASEFY COLONY
COSHES CROATS CYGNUS CREDIT CATCHY COMEDY
COSMOS CROCKS CYMARS CRUSET CATHAY COMELY
COSSES CROCUS CYMOUS CUBIST CAVITY COMITY
COTTAS CROFTS CYNICS CULLET CECILY COMPLY
COUGHS CRONES CYPRUS CURVET CELERY CONCHY
COUNTS CRONOS CYRILS CUSHAT CHAFFY CONVEY
COUPES CRONUS ****** CUTEST CHALKY CONVOY
COURTS CROOKS C----T CUTLET CHAMMY CONWAY
COVERS CROONS ****** CUTOUT CHANCY COOKEY
COVETS CRORES CABLET CYGNET CHANTY COOLLY
COVEYS CROUPS CACHET ****** CHARRY COPLEY
COWERS CROWDS CADENT C----U CHATTY CORDAY
COYPUS CROWNS CAHOOT ****** CHEEKY CORODY
COZENS CROZES CAMLET CACHOU CHEERY COSILY
COZIES CRUCES CANNOT CONGOU CHEESY COSTLY
                            COTEAU

COUNTY
COWBOY
COZILY
CRABBY
CRACKY
CRAFTY
CRAGGY
CRANKY
CRANNY
CRAWLY
CREAKY
CREAMY
CREASY
CREEPY
CRIKEY
CRIMPY
CRISPY
CROAKY
CROCKY
CROUPY
CRUMBY
CRUMMY
CRUSTY
CUDDLY
CULLAY
CURACY
CURTLY
CURTSY
CUTELY
******

C----Z
******
CHINTZ
CORTEZ
******

D----A
******
DAGOBA
DAHLIA
DAKOTA
DATURA
DECUMA
DHARMA
DHARNA
DHURNA
DODECA
DUENNA

******

D----C
DEIFIC
DERMIC
DYADIC
******

D----D
******
DABBED
DAMMED
DAMNED
DAMPED
DANAID
DANCED
DANGED
DAPPED
DARNED
DARTED
DASHED
DAUBED
DAWNED
DAYBED
DECKED
DEEDED
DEEMED
DEFEND
DEFIED
DEICED
DELVED
DEMAND
DENIED
DENNED
DENTED
DEPEND
DESMID
DEUCED
DEVOID
DIALED
DIBBED
DIETED
DIGGED
DIMMED
DINGED
DINNED
DINTED
DIPPED
DIRKED

DISHED
DOCKED
DODGED
DOFFED
DOGGED
DOITED
DOLLED
DONALD
DONNED
DOODAD
DOOMED
DORSAD
DOSSED
DOTARD
DOTTED
DOUSED
DOWNED
DOWSED
DRAPED
DRAYED
DRONED
DROVED
DUBBED
DUCKED
DUELED
DUFFED
DULLED
DUMPED
DUNGED
DUNKED
DUNNED
DUSKED
DUSTED
******

D----E
******
DABBLE
DADDLE
DAGGLE
DAMAGE
DANDLE
DANGLE
DANITE
DANUBE
DAPHNE
DAPPLE
DARKLE
DARTLE

DATIVE
DAWDLE
DAZZLE
DEARIE
DEBASE
DEBATE
DEBBIE
DECADE
DECANE
DECARE
DECIDE
DECILE
DECKLE
DECODE
DECOKE
DECREE
DEDUCE
DEFACE
DEFAME
DEFILE
DEFINE
DEFUSE
DEGAGE
DEGAME
DEGREE
DEKARE
DELATE
DELETE
DELUDE
DELUGE
DELUXE
DEMISE
DEMODE
DEMOTE
DEMURE
DENGUE
DENISE
DENOTE
DENUDE
DEPONE
DEPOSE
DEPUTE
DERATE
DERIDE
DERIVE
DESIRE
DEVICE
DEVISE

DEVOTE
DIBBLE
DICKIE
DIDDLE
DIEPPE
DILATE
DILUTE
DIMPLE
DINGLE
DIPLOE
DIPOLE
DISUSE
DITONE
DIVIDE
DIVINE
DOABLE
DOCILE
DOGAPE
DOGGIE
DOLLIE
DONATE
DONNIE
DOODLE
DOOLEE
DOOLIE
DORMIE
DOSAGE
DOTAGE
DOTTLE
DOUBLE
DOUCHE
DOUGIE
DRAGEE
DRAWEE
DREDGE
DROGUE
DROWSE
DRUDGE
DRYICE
DUFFLE
DULCIE
DUNDEE
******

D----G
******
DANZIG
DARING
DATING

DAZING
DEKING
DIALOG
DICING
DIKING
DINING
DIVING
DOLING
DOMING
DOPING
DORBUG
DOSING
DOTING
DOZING
DRYING
DUGONG
DUOLOG
DUPING
DURING
DYEING
******

D----H
******
DALETH
DANISH
DEARTH
DETACH
DOVISH
DRENCH
DROUTH
DRYISH
DUDISH
DULUTH
******

D----I
******
DELPHI
DENDRI
DIGITI
DMITRI
******

D----K
******
DAMASK
DEBARK
DEBUNK
DIKDIK
DVORAK
DYBBUK

		DUBBIN	DAUBER	DOWSER	DECAYS
******	******	DUBLIN	DEALER	DOZIER	DECORS
D----L	**D----N**	DUDEEN	DEARER	DRAPER	DECOYS
******	******	DUNCAN	DEBTOR	DRAWER	DEDANS
DACTYL	DACRON	DUNLIN	DECKER	DRIVER	DEFERS
DAEDAL	DAEMON	DUODEN	DEEPER	DROVER	DEFIES
DAMSEL	DAHOON	DURBAN	DEFIER	DUCKER	DEGUMS
DANIEL	DAIMON	DURIAN	DEFTER	DUELER	DEICES
DARNEL	DALTON	DURION	DEICER	DUFFER	DEIGNS
DECKEL	DAMPEN	******	DELVER	DUIKER	DEISTS
DENIAL	DAMSON	**D----O**	DENIER	DULLER	DELAYS
DENTAL	DANTON	******	DENSER	DUMPER	DELIAS
DENTIL	DARDAN	DAIMIO	DENVER	DUNBAR	DELIUS
DERAIL	DARIEN	DAIMYO	DEODAR	DUNKER	DELLAS
DERMAL	DARKEN	DEMONO	DETOUR	DURBAR	DELTAS
DETAIL	DARWIN	DENDRO	DEVOIR	DUSTER	DELVES
DIESEL	DAWSON	DEXTRO	DEVOUR	******	DEMIES
DIETAL	DAYTON	DIDERO	DEWIER	**D----S**	DEMITS
DIOBOL	DEACON	DINERO	DEXTER	******	DEMOBS
DIRNDL	DEADEN	DOMINO	DIALER	DACHAS	DEMONS
DISCAL	DEAFEN	DORADO	DIAPER	DADOES	DEMURS
DISMAL	DECCAN	DRONGO	DIBBER	DAISES	DENIES
DISPEL	DECERN	DUELLO	DICKER	DAISYS	DENIMS
DISTAL	DEEPEN	DYNAMO	DIETER	DALLAS	DENNIS
DISTIL	DEEWAN	******	DIFFER	DALLES	DENNYS
DORSAL	DEHORN	**D----P**	DIGGER	DAMANS	DEPOTS
DOSSAL	DELIAN	******	DIMMER	DANAUS	DEPTHS
DOSSEL	DEMEAN	DECAMP	DINDER	DANCES	DEREKS
DOSSIL	DENTIN	DEWLAP	DINNER	DANNYS	DERMAS
DOTTEL	DERAIN	DOLLOP	DIPPER	DARERS	DERMIS
DOUGAL	DESIGN	******	DISBAR	DARICS	DERRIS
DRIVEL	DESMAN	**D----R**	DITHER	DARIUS	DETERS
DRUPEL	DETAIN	******	DOBBER	DASHES	DEUCES
DUFFEL	DEVEIN	DABBER	DOCKER	DATERS	DEVILS
******	DIAZIN	DAGGER	DOCTOR	DATTOS	DEWANS
D----M	DISOWN	DAGMAR	DODDER	DAUNTS	DHOLES
******	DOBBIN	DAMMAR	DODGER	DAVEYS	DHOTIS
DEFORM	DOBLON	DAMMER	DOFFER	DAVIDS	DIANAS
DIADEM	DOBSON	DAMPER	DOGEAR	DAVIES	DIANES
DIATOM	DOLMAN	DANCER	DOGGER	DAVITS	DICERS
DICTUM	DOLMEN	DANDER	DOLLAR	DEATHS	DIDIES
DINKUM	DOMAIN	DANGER	DOLOUR	DEBARS	DIDOES
DIRHAM	DONJON	DANKER	DOPIER	DEBBYS	DIESES
DISARM	DOREEN	DAPPER	DOPTER	DEBITS	DIESIS
DORSUM	DORIAN	DARKER	DORMER	DEBRIS	DIGITS
DRACHM	DRAGON	DARNER	DOSSER	DEBUGS	DIMERS
DUMDUM	DROMON	DARTER	DOTIER	DEBUTS	DINAHS
DURHAM	DRYDEN	DASHER	DOTTER	DECALS	DINARS

DINERS	DRAWLS	DEPORT	******	DREARY	******
DINGUS	DREADS	DERMAT	**D----Y**	DREGGY	**E----C**
DIODES	DREAMS	DESALT	******	DRESSY	******
DIPSAS	DRIERS	DESERT	DAFTLY	DRIFTY	ECHOIC
DIRGES	DRIFTS	DESIST	DAINTY	DRIPPY	EDDAIC
DISCUS	DRILLS	DESPOT	DAMPLY	DROLLY	EDENIC
DISHES	DRINKS	DETECT	DANKLY	DROOPY	EMERIC
DITTOS	DRIVES	DETENT	DARKLY	DROPSY	EMETIC
DIVANS	DROITS	DETEST	DATARY	DROSKY	EOZOIC
DIVERS	DROLLS	DEVEST	DAUBRY	DROSSY	EROTIC
DIVOTS	DRONES	DEVOUT	DAYBOY	DROWSY	ETHNIC
DIWANS	DROOLS	DEWITT	DAYFLY	DRYFLY	EXILIC
DIXITS	DROOPS	DICAST	DEADLY	DUDLEY	EXOTIC
DIZENS	DROVES	DIGEST	DEAFLY	DUMBLY	******
DOALLS	DROWNS	DIGLOT	DEARLY	DUMPTY	**E----D**
DOBIES	DRUIDS	DIMOUT	DEATHY	DUPERY	******
DOBLAS	DRUPES	DIMWIT	DECURY	******	EARNED
DOBRAS	DRUSES	DIRECT	DEEPLY	**E----A**	ECHARD
DODGES	DRYADS	DIREST	DEFRAY	******	ECHOED
DODOES	DRYERS	DIVERT	DEFTLY	ECZEMA	EDDIED
DOGIES	DUCATS	DIVEST	DENARY	EDWINA	EDITED
DOGMAS	DULLES	DOCENT	DEPLOY	EGERIA	EDMOND
DOINGS	DUNCES	DOCKET	DEPUTY	EGESTA	EDMUND
DOLLYS	DUPERS	DOESNT	DESCRY	EIDOLA	EDUARD
DOLPHS	DURESS	DORSET	DESOXY	EJECTA	EDUCED
DONEES	DUTIES	DREAMT	DICKEY	ELISHA	EDWARD
DONETS	DWARFS	DRIEST	DIGAMY	ELMIRA	ELATED
DONNAS	DWELLS	DRYEST	DIMITY	ELVIRA	ELDRED
DONORS	******	DRYROT	DIMPLY	ELYTRA	ELIDED
DORIES	******	DUGOUT	DINGEY	EMILIA	ELOPED
DOSERS	**D----T**	DULCET	DINGHY	ENCINA	ELUDED
DOTERS	******	DUPLET	DINKEY	ENIGMA	EMCEED
DOUBTS	DACOIT	DWIGHT	DIPODY	ENTERA	EMOTED
DOUGHS	DAKOIT	DYNAST	DIRELY	EPIZOA	ENDUED
DOUSES	DAUDET	******	DISMAY	ERRATA	ENFOLD
DOWELS	DECANT	**D----U**	DISNEY	ESPANA	ENGIRD
DOWERS	DECEIT	******	DONKEY	ETERNA	ENNEAD
DOWLAS	DECENT	DACHAU	DOUBLY	EUBOEA	ENSUED
DOWSES	DECOCT	DESSAU	DOUGHY	EUPNEA	ENVIED
DOXIES	DEDUCT	******	DOURLY	EUREKA	ENWIND
DOYENS	DEFEAT	**D----W**	DOWERY	EUROPA	ERASED
DOZENS	DEFECT	******	DOYLEY	EXACTA	ERODED
DRAFFS	DEFENT	DARROW	DOZILY	EXEDRA	ERRAND
DRAFTS	DEGUST	******	DRABLY	******	ESPIED
DRAINS	DEJECT	**D----X**	DRAFFY	**E---B**	ETCHED
DRAKES	DELICT	******	DRAFTY	******	EUCLID
DRAMAS	DEMENT	DIPLEX	DRAWLY	ENTOMB	EVADED
DRAPES	DEPICT	DOGFOX	DREAMY	ENWOMB	EVENED

EVOKED ENTICE EPPING EMBALM ****** EDWINS
EXCEED ENTIRE ERRING EMBLEM **E----R** EGESTS
EXILED ENTREE EYEING ENGRAM ****** EGGARS
EXITED ENZYME ****** EONISM EARNER EGGERS
EXPAND EOCENE **E----H** EPONYM EASIER EGRESS
EXPEND EOGENE ****** ERBIUM EASTER EGRETS
EXTEND EPOPEE EDDISH ESTEEM ECHOER EIGHTS
EXUDED EQUATE EIGHTH ****** ECLAIR EJECTS
EYELID EQUINE ELFISH **E----N** EDGIER ELANDS
****** ERGATE ELIJAH ****** EDITOR ELATES
E----E ERMINE ELVISH EASTON EITHER ELBOWS
****** ESCAPE ENCASH EDISON ELATER ELBRUS
ECARTE ESSENE ENMESH EILEEN ELINOR ELDERS
ECTYPE ESTATE ENOUGH ELEVEN ELIXIR ELECTS
EDIBLE ETHANE ENRICH ELEVON ELOPER ELEMIS
EFFACE EUCHRE EOLITH ELOIGN ENAMOR ELENAS
EFFETE EUGENE EPARCH EMETIN ENDEAR ELFINS
EFFUSE EUNICE EUNUCH ENJOIN ENVIER ELIDES
ELAINE EUROPE EXARCH ENSIGN ERASER ELIOTS
ELAPSE EVINCE ****** EOLIAN ESCHAR ELIZAS
ELAYNE EVOLVE **E----I** EONIAN ESCHER ELLENS
ELOISE EXCIDE ****** ETYMON ESTHER ELLIES
ELYSEE EXCISE ECHINI EVELYN ETCHER ELMERS
EMBRUE EXCITE EMBOLI EXAMEN EUCHER ELOINS
EMERGE EXCUSE EPHEBI EXOGEN EUDOAR ELOPES
EMERIE EXHALE EPHORI EXTERN EVADER ELSIES
EMEUTE EXHUME EURIPI ****** EXETER ELUDES
EMIGRE EXPIRE ****** **E----O** EXMOOR ELVERS
EMILIE EXPOSE **E----K** ****** ****** ******
EMPALE ****** ****** ECHINO **E----S** EMBARS
EMPIRE **E----F** EMBANK EMBRYO ****** EMBAYS
ENABLE ****** EMBARK EMILIO ****** EMBEDS
ENCAGE ENGULF ****** ENRICO EAGLES EMBERS
ENCASE ****** **E----L** ENTERO EARLES EMBOSS
ENCODE **E----G** ****** ENTOMO EARTHS EMBOWS
ENCORE ****** EARFUL ERINGO EASELS EMCEES
ENDIVE EALING EIFFEL ERYNGO EATERS EMEERS
ENDURE EARING ENAMEL ESCUDO ECCLES EMENDS
ENFACE EARWIG ENDALL ESKIMO ECESIS EMESIS
ENGAGE EASING ENROLL ****** ECHOES EMILES
ENGINE EATING ENSOUL **E----P** ECOLES EMILYS
ENISLE EBBING ENTAIL ****** EDDIES EMMETS
ENLACE EDGING EPICAL EARLAP EDGARS EMMIES
ENRAGE EGGING ESPIAL EGGCUP EDICTS EMOTES
ENROBE EGGNOG EYEFUL ENCAMP EDILES ENACTS
ENSILE EKEING ****** ENTRAP EDITHS ENATES
ENSURE ENDING **E----M** ENWRAP EDSELS ENDOWS
ENTERE EPILOG ****** ESCARP EDUCES ENDUES
           EGOISM ESCARP EYECUP EDUCTS ENEMAS
           ELOHIM

ENGELS	EXALTS	EXSECT	FARINA	FELTED	FUDGED
ENJOYS	EXCELS	EXSERT	FASCIA	FENCED	FUELED
ENOSIS	EXCESS	EXTANT	FATIMA	FENDED	FUGLED
ENSUES	EXERTS	EXTENT	FECULA	FERVID	FULGID
ENTERS	EXILES	EXTORT	FEDORA	FEUDED	FULLED
ENVIES	EXISTS	EYELET	FEMORA	FIBBED	FUNDED
ENVOYS	EXODUS	EYEOUT	FERULA	FIGGED	FUNKED
EPACTS	EXPELS	******	FIBULA	FILLED	FURLED
EPHAHS	EXTOLS	**E----W**	FIESTA	FILMED	FURRED
EPHODS	EXTRAS	******	FLAVIA	FINNED	FUSSED
EPHORS	EXUDES	ESCHEW	FRIEDA	FIRMED	FUZZED
EPIRUS	EXULTS	ESCROW	FRIGGA	FISTED	******
EPOCHS	EXURBS	******	FRUSTA	FITTED	**F----E**
EPODES	EYASES	**E----X**	FULCRA	FIZZED	******
EQUALS	EYRIES	******	******	FLAKED	FACADE
EQUIPS	******	EARWAX	**F----C**	FLAMED	FACILE
ERASES	**E----T**	EFFLUX	******	FLARED	FAERIE
EREBUS	******	******	FABRIC	FLAWED	FAEROE
ERECTS	EAGLET	**E----Y**	FENNEC	FLAYED	FAILLE
ERICHS	EFFECT	******	FERRIC	FLEXED	FAMINE
ERINYS	EFFORT	EARTHY	FILMIC	FLORID	FANNIE
ERNIES	EGBERT	EASILY	FINNIC	FLOWED	FAUNAE
ERODES	EGOIST	EATERY	FINNOC	FLUKED	FEEBLE
ERRORS	ELBERT	ECTOMY	FISTIC	FLUMED	FEIGNE
ERUCTS	ELDEST	EERILY	FORMIC	FLUTED	FELICE
ERUPTS	ELEGIT	EFFIGY	FROLIC	FLUXED	FELINE
ERWINS	ELICIT	EIGHTY	FUSTIC	FOALED	FELIPE
ESKERS	ELLIOT	EMBODY	******	FOAMED	FELLOE
ESPIES	EMMETT	EMPERY	**F----D**	FOBBED	FEMALE
ESSAYS	ENCYST	EMPLOY	******	FOETID	FERINE
ESTERS	ENGIRT	ENERGY	FABLED	FOGGED	FERULE
ESTOPS	ENLIST	ENMITY	FAGEND	FOILED	FESCUE
ESTRUS	ENRAPT	ENTITY	FAGGED	FOLDED	FETTLE
ETAPES	ENROOT	EQUITY	FAILED	FOOLED	FIACRE
ETCHES	ERFURT	ESTRAY	FAIRED	FOOTED	FIANCE
ETHANS	ERNEST	EULOGY	FANGED	FORBID	FICKLE
ETHELS	ERRANT	EVENLY	FANNED	FORCED	FIDDLE
ETHERS	ESCENT	EVILLY	FARBAD	FORDED	FIERCE
ETHICS	ESCORT	EXEQUY	FARCED	FORGED	FIGURE
ETHYLS	ESPRIT	EXPIRY	FARMED	FORKED	FILOSE
ETUDES	EVERET	******	FASTED	FORMED	FIMBLE
EVADES	EXCEPT	**E----Z**	FATTED	FOULED	FINALE
EVENTS	EXEMPT	******	FAWNED	FOWLED	FINITE
EVERTS	EXEUNT	ERSATZ	FEARED	FRAMED	FIPPLE
EVICTS	EXHORT	******	FEASED	FRAYED	FIXATE
EVITAS	EXPECT	**F----A**	FECUND	FRIEND	FIZZLE
EVOKES	EXPERT	******	FEEZED	FRIGID	FLAMBE
EXACTS	EXPORT	FACULA	FELLED	FUCOID	FLANGE
		FANEGA			

FLECHE	FINING	FLORAL	FOEMAN	FERBER	FACIES
FLEDGE	FIRING	FOETAL	FOEMEN	FERVOR	FAECES
FLEECE	FIXING	FONTAL	FRAUEN	FESTER	FAGOTS
FLENSE	FIZGIG	FORMAL	FROZEN	FETTER	FAINTS
FLORAE	FLYING	FORMYL	FULTON	FIBBER	FAITHS
FOCSLE	FOGDOG	FOSSIL	FUSAIN	FILLER	FAKERS
FOIBLE	FOXING	FOVEAL	FUSION	FILTER	FAKIRS
FONDLE	FRYING	FRIJOL	******	FINDER	FAMOUS
FONDUE	FUMING	FRIVOL	**F----O**	FINGER	FANGAS
FOOTLE	FUSING	FRUGAL	******	FINNER	FANNYS
FOOZLE	FUZING	FULFIL	FIASCO	FIRMER	FANONS
FORAGE	******	FUNGAL	FLUORO	FISHER	FANUMS
FOSSAE	**F----H**	FUNNEL	FLUVIO	FITTER	FARADS
FOVEAE	******	******	FOREGO	FIZZER	FARCES
FRAISE	FAMISH	**F----M**	FRANCO	FLAKER	FARERS
FRANCE	FELLAH	******	FRESCO	FLAVOR	FARLES
FRAPPE	FETICH	FACTUM	FRESNO	FLAYER	FASCES
FREEZE	FETISH	FANTOM	FRONTO	FLEXOR	FAUCES
FRIDGE	FINISH	FATHOM	******	FLOWER	FAULTS
FRIEZE	FLENCH	FERRUM	**F----P**	FLUTER	FAUNAS
FRINGE	FLETCH	FOLIUM	******	FODDER	FAUNUS
FRUNZE	FLINCH	FRENUM	FILLIP	FOETOR	FAUVES
FUDDLE	FLITCH	******	******	FOLDER	FAVORS
FUMBLE	FOURTH	**F----N**	**F----R**	FOLIAR	FAWKES
FURORE	FRENCH	******	******	FONDER	FEASES
FUSILE	******	FABIAN	FABLER	FOOTER	FEASTS
FUTILE	**F----K**	FADEIN	FACTOR	FORCER	FEEZES
FUTURE	******	FALCON	FAFNIR	FORGER	FEIGNS
******	FRANCK	FALLEN	FAIRER	FORMER	FEINTS
F----F	******	FANION	FALLER	FOSTER	FEISTS
******	**F----L**	FANTAN	FALSER	FOULER	FELIDS
FAROFF	******	FASTEN	FALTER	FOWLER	FELONS
******	FACIAL	FATTEN	FANNER	FOXIER	FEMURS
F----G	FAECAL	FENIAN	FARCER	FRAMER	FENCES
******	FALLAL	FEZZAN	FARMER	FRATER	FEOFFS
FACING	FAUCAL	FIBRIN	FASTER	FUELER	FERMIS
FADING	FAUNAL	FIJIAN	FATHER	FUHRER	FEROUS
FAKING	FECIAL	FILLIN	FATTER	FULLER	FERRIS
FARING	FENNEL	FINNAN	FAVOUR	FULMAR	FESSES
FATING	FERIAL	FIRKIN	FAWNER	FUMIER	FETORS
FAXING	FESTAL	FIRMAN	FEARER	FURFUR	FEUARS
FAYING	FETIAL	FLACON	FEEDER	FUSSER	FEVERS
FAZING	FEUDAL	FLAGON	FEELER	******	FEZZES
FEEING	FIBRIL	FLAMEN	FELLER	**F----S**	FIBERS
FETING	FILIAL	FLAVIN	FENCER	******	FICHES
FEUING	FINIAL	FLAXEN	FENDER	FABLES	FICHUS
FIFING	FISCAL	FLORIN	FENRIR	FACERS	FIELDS
FILING	FITFUL	FLYMAN	FEODOR	FACETS	FIENDS

FIFERS	FLUMES	FUDGES	FELLOW	FOLKSY	GESTIC
FIFTHS	FLUMPS	FUGIOS	FOGBOW	FONDLY	GNOMIC
FIGHTS	FLUNKS	FUGLES	FOLLOW	FOULLY	GOTHIC
FILERS	FLUORS	FUGUES	FURROW	FOXILY	******
FILETS	FLUTES	FUMOUS	******	FREAKY	**G----D**
FINALS	FLUXES	FUNDUS	**F----X**	FREDDY	******
FIORDS	FLYBYS	FUNGUS	******	FREELY	GABBED
FIQUES	FLYERS	FURIES	FORNAX	FRENZY	GABLED
FIRERS	FOEHNS	FURORS	FORNIX	FRETTY	GADDED
FIRSTS	FOETUS	FURZES	******	FRIARY	GADOID
FIRTHS	FOGIES	FUSEES	**F----Y**	FRIDAY	GAFFED
FISHES	FOISTS	FUSILS	******	FRILLY	GAGGED
FIVERS	FOLIOS	FUSSES	FAIRLY	FRINGY	GAINED
FIXERS	FORAYS	FUZEES	FAKERY	FRISKY	GAITED
FIZZES	FORCES	FUZILS	FAMILY	FRIZZY	GALLED
FLACKS	FORGES	FUZZES	FARLEY	FROGGY	GAMMED
FLAILS	FORTES	******	FAULTY	FROSTY	GANGED
FLAIRS	FORTIS	**F----T**	FEALTY	FROTHY	GANOID
FLAKES	FORUMS	******	FEEBLY	FROWZY	GAPPED
FLAMES	FOSSES	FAGGOT	FEISTY	FRUITY	GARBED
FLANKS	FOUNDS	FANJET	FELONY	FRUMPY	GASHED
FLARES	FOUNTS	FAROUT	FERITY	******	GASPED
FLASKS	FOYERS	FAUCET	FILTHY	**G----A**	GASSED
FLATUS	FRACAS	FERRET	FINELY	******	GAUGED
FLAXES	FRAILS	FEWEST	FINERY	GALENA	GAWKED
FLEAMS	FRAMES	FIDGET	FIRMLY	GAMBIA	GEARED
FLECKS	FRANCS	FILLET	FIXITY	GDYNIA	GELDED
FLEERS	FRANKS	FINEST	FLABBY	GEISHA	GELLED
FLEETS	FRAUDS	FLAUNT	FLAGGY	GEMARA	GEMMED
FLEXES	FREAKS	FLIEST	FLASHY	GENERA	GERALD
FLICKS	FREDAS	FLIGHT	FLATLY	GENEVA	GERARD
FLIERS	FREONS	FLORET	FLEDGY	GIULIA	GERUND
FLINGS	FRIARS	FLUENT	FLEECY	GLIOMA	GIBBED
FLINTS	FRIERS	FOMENT	FLESHY	GLORIA	GIFTED
FLIRTS	FRILLS	FOREST	FLEURY	GODIVA	GIGGED
FLOATS	FRISES	FORGET	FLIMSY	GOTAMA	GILDED
FLOCKS	FRISKS	FORGOT	FLINTY	GRETNA	GILEAD
FLONGS	FRITHS	FORINT	FLIRTY	GUIANA	GIMPED
FLOODS	FROCKS	FORMAT	FLOATY	GUINEA	GINNED
FLOORS	FRONDS	FOUGHT	FLOCKY	GURKHA	GIPPED
FLORAS	FRONTS	FREEST	FLOOZY	GUYANA	GIRDED
FLORES	FROSTS	FRIGHT	FLOPPY	******	GIRTED
FLOURS	FROTHS	FUNEST	FLOSSY	**G----C**	GLARED
FLOUTS	FROWNS	FYLFOT	FLOURY	******	GLAZED
FLOYDS	FRUITS	******	FLUFFY	GAELIC	GLIDED
FLUFFS	FRUMPS	**F----W**	FLUKEY	GALLIC	GLOBED
FLUIDS	FRYERS	******	FLUNKY	GARLIC	GLOVED
FLUKES	FUCOUS	FARROW	FLURRY	GEODIC	GLOWED

GLOZED	GERTIE	GAPING	GLOBAL	GORGON	******
GNAWED	GIGGLE	GASBAG	GLYCOL	GORHEN	**G----R**
GOADED	GILLIE	GATING	GOOGOL	GOSHEN	******
GOLFED	GIRDLE	GAZING	GOORAL	GOTTEN	GABBER
GOOFED	GISELE	GEEING	GOSPEL	GOVERN	GADDER
GOOSED	GLANCE	GIBING	GRAVEL	GRABEN	GAFFER
GORGED	GOALIE	GIVING	GRETEL	GRADIN	GAGGER
GOUGED	GOATEE	GLUING	GRIZEL	GRATIN	GAINER
GOWNED	GOBBLE	GOBANG	GROVEL	GRAVEN	GAITER
GRACED	GOETHE	GORING	GUNNEL	GUANIN	GAMBIR
GRADED	GOGGLE	GUYING	******	GUENON	GAMIER
GRATED	GOITRE	GYBING	**G----M**	GUIDON	GAMMER
GRAVED	GOURDE	GYVING	******	GULDEN	GANDER
GRAVID	GRACIE	******	GODDAM	GUNMAN	GANGER
GRAYED	GRAMME	**G----H**	GONIUM	GUNMEN	GAOLER
GRAZED	GRANDE	******	GOTHAM	******	GARNER
GRIDED	GRANGE	GALOSH	GRAHAM	**G----O**	GARTER
GRIMED	GREASE	GARISH	GYPSUM		GASPAR
GRIPED	GREAVE	GOLOSH	******	GABBRO	GASPER
GROPED	GREECE	GROUCH	**G----N**	GAMETO	GATHER
GROUND	GREENE	GROWTH	******	GASTRO	GAUGER
GUIDED	GREIGE	GULLAH	GABION	GAUCHO	GEEZER
GULFED	GRIEVE	******	GALLON	GAZABO	GEIGER
GULLED	GRIFFE	**G----I**	GAMMON	GAZEBO	GENDER
GULPED	GRILLE	******	GARCON	GEMSBO	GETTER
GUMMED	GRILSE	GANDHI	GARDEN	GENITO	GEYSER
GUNNED	GRIPPE	GANGLI	GASCON	GENTOO	GHEBER
GUSHED	GROOVE	GEMINI	GASKIN	GHETTO	GIAOUR
GUTTED	GROUSE	GENESI	GASMAN	GIGOLO	GIBBER
GYPPED	GROYNE	GEORGI	GASMEN	GINGKO	GILDER
******	GRUDGE	GHARRI	GASTON	GIOTTO	GINGER
G----E	GUIMPE	GLUTEI	GAWAIN	GITANO	GINNER
******	GURGLE	GOMUTI	GERMAN	GIULIO	GIRDER
GABBLE	GUSSIE	GRIGRI	GERMEN	GLAUCO	GLAZER
GAGGLE	GUTTAE	******	GERYON	GLOSSO	GLIDER
GALEAE	GUTTLE	**G----K**	GIBBON	GLOTTO	GLOVER
GALORE	GUZZLE	******	GIBRAN	GLYPTO	GLOWER
GAMBLE	GWYNNE	GALYAK	GIBSON	GNATHO	GLUIER
GAMETE	GYRATE	GDANSK	GIDEON	GRAECO	GNAWER
GANGUE	GYROSE	******	GLOBIN	GRAPHO	GOFFER
GARAGE	******	**G----L**	GLUTEN	GROTTO	GOITER
GARBLE	**G----F**	******	GNOMON	GYNECO	GOLFER
GARGLE	******	GAMBOL	GOBLIN	******	GOOBER
GAUCHE	GUSTAF	GAVIAL	GODSON	**G----P**	GOOIER
GAULLE	******	GENIAL	GODWIN	******	GOPHER
GEMMAE	**G----G**	GERBIL	GOLDEN	GALLOP	GORGER
GENTLE	******	GESELL	GONION	GALLUP	GORIER
GEORGE	GAGING	GINGAL	GORDON	GOSSIP	GOUGER

GRADER	GENTES	GOINGS	GUACOS	GUSSET	GOOSEY
GRATER	GEODES	GONADS	GUANOS	GUTTAT	GORILY
GRAVER	GEROUS	GONERS	GUARDS	******	GRAINY
GRAYER	GERRYS	GOOSES	GUAVAS	**G----U**	GRANNY
GRAZER	GERTYS	GORALS	GUESTS	******	GRAPHY
GRIPER	GESSOS	GORGES	GUIDES	GATEAU	GRASSY
GROCER	GETUPS	GORSES	GUILDS	GRUGRU	GRAYLY
GROPER	GHAUTS	GOUGES	GUILES	******	GREASY
GROVER	GHOSTS	GOURDS	GUILTS	**G----V**	GREEDY
GROWER	GHOULS	GRACES	GUISES	******	GRIMLY
GUIDER	GIANTS	GRADES	GUMBOS	GUSTAV	GRIPPY
GUITAR	GIBERS	GRADUS	GUMMAS	******	GRISLY
GULPER	GIGUES	GRAFTS	GUSHES	**G----W**	GRITTY
GUNNAR	GILDAS	GRAINS	GWENNS	******	GROGGY
GUNNER	GIMELS	GRANTS	GYNOUS	GEWGAW	GROOVY
GUNTER	GIPONS	GRAPES	GYRONS	GUFFAW	GROSZY
GUSHER	GISMOS	GRAPHS	******	******	GROTTY
GUTTER	GIZMOS	GRASPS	**G----T**	**G----Y**	GRUBBY
******	GLACES	GRATES	******	******	GRUMPY
G----S	GLACIS	GRATIS	GADGET	GADFLY	GRUNDY
******	GLADES	GRAVES	GALACT	GAIETY	GUILTY
GABLES	GLADYS	GRAZES	GALIOT	GAINLY	GUNSHY
GAFFES	GLAIRS	GREATS	GALOOT	GALAXY	******
GAGERS	GLAMIS	GREBES	GAMBIT	GALLEY	**H----A**
GALLUS	GLANDS	GREEDS	GANNET	GALWAY	******
GALOPS	GLARES	GREEKS·	GARGET	GAMELY	HAVANA
GAMINS	GLAZES	GREENS	GARNET	GAMILY	HECUBA
GAMMAS	GLEAMS	GREETS	GARRET	GANTRY	HEGIRA
GAMOUS	GLEANS	GREGOS	GASJET	GASIFY	HEJIRA
GAMUTS	GLEBES	GREIFS	GASKET	GAYETY	HELENA
GANEFS	GLEDES	GRETAS	GAYEST	GENTLY	HERNIA
GANGES	GLEETS	GRIDES	GEMERT	GENTRY	HESTIA
GAPERS	GLIDES	GRILLS	GERENT	GHARRY	HOOPLA
GASHES	GLINTS	GRIMES	GIBBET	GIGGLY	HUELVA
GASSES	GLOATS	GRINDS	GIBLET	GLADLY	HYGEIA
GAUGES	GLOBES	GRIPES	GIGANT	GLAIRY	******
GAUZES	GLOOMS	GROANS	GIGLET	GLASSY	**H----B**
GAVELS	GLOSTS	GROATS	GIGLOT	GLEAMY	******
GAVOTS	GLOVES	GROINS	GIMLET	GLEETY	HOBNOB
GAZERS	GLOZES	GROOMS	GOBBET	GLIBLY	HUBBUB
GECKOS	GLUMES	GROPES	GOBLET	GLOOMY	******
GEMOTS	GLYNIS	GROUPS	GOCART	GLOSSY	**H----C**
GENETS	GLYPHS	GROUTS	GODWIT	GLUMLY	******
GENIES	GNARLS	GROVES	GOGLET	GNARLY	HECTIC
GENIUS	GNEISS	GROWLS	GOKART	GOODBY	HERDIC
GENOUS	GNOMES	GRUELS	GORGET	GOODLY	HEROIC
GENRES	GNOSIS	GRUMES	GRIVET	GOOGLY	HOLMIC
GENROS	GOBIES	GRUNTS	GULLET	GOONEY	HYDRIC

HYMNIC	HILTED	HACKIE	HARING	HAMAUL	HEZION
HYPNIC	HINGED	HACKLE	HATING	HAMMAL	HIDDEN
******	HINTED	HAGGLE	HAVING	HANDEL	HODDEN
H----D	HIPPED	HALIDE	HAWING	HANSEL	HODMAN
******	HISPID	HALITE	HAYING	HARTAL	HOIDEN
HACKED	HISSED	HAMITE	HAZING	HASSEL	HOYDEN
HAFTED	HOAXED	HANDLE	HEDWIG	HATFUL	HUDSON
HAGGED	HOCKED	HASSLE	HEWING	HEDRAL	HYPHEN
HAILED	HOGGED	HATTIE	HEXING	HERBAL	******
HAIRED	HOLARD	HEARSE	HIDING	HIEMAL	**H----O**
HALOED	HONIED	HEAUME	HIEING	HOSTEL	******
HALOID	HONKED	HECATE	HIKING	HYETAL	HAIRDO
HALTED	HOODED	HECKLE	HIRING	HYMNAL	HALLOO
HALVED	HOOFED	HEDDLE	HIVING	HYPHAL	HELICO
HAMMED	HOOKED	HERMAE	HOEING	******	HEMATO
HANDED	HOOPED	HEXANE	HOLING	**H----M**	HEPATO
HANGED	HOOTED	HEXONE	HOMING	******	HERETO
HAPPED	HOOVED	HEXOSE	HONING	HANSOM	HERNIO
HARKED	HOPPED	HIGGLE	HOPING	HARLEM	HETERO
HARMED	HORDED	HIPPIE	HOSING	HELIUM	HOODOO
HAROLD	HORNED	HIVITE	HUMBUG	HOLISM	HYMENO
HARPED	HORRID	HOARSE	******	******	******
HASHED	HORSED	HOBBLE	**H----H**	**H----N**	**H----P**
HASPED	HOSTED	HOGTIE	******	******	******
HASTED	HOTBED	HOMAGE	HALLAH	HAGDON	HANGUP
HATRED	HOTROD	HOMBRE	HANNAH	HAMDEN	HICCUP
HATTED	HOTTED	HONORE	HAUNCH	HAPPEN	HOLDUP
HAULED	HOUSED	HOOPOE	HEALTH	HARBIN	HOOKUP
HAWKED	HOWARD	HOPPLE	HEARTH	HARDEN	HUBCAP
HAZARD	HOWLED	HORACE	HOOKAH	HARKEN	HYSSOP
HEADED	HUFFED	HORNIE	HOOTCH	HARLAN	******
HEALED	HUGGED	HORSTE	HOWDAH	HARMIN	**H----R**
HEAPED	HULKED	HUCKLE	HURRAH	HASTEN	******
HEATED	HULLED	HUDDLE	******	HATPIN	HACKER
HEAVED	HUMMED	HUGHIE	**H----I**	HAUSEN	HAILER
HEDGED	HUMPED	HUMANE	******	HAZZAN	HALTER
HEEDED	HUNTED	HUMBLE	HAWAII	HEADON	HAMMER
HEELED	HURLED	HURDLE	HERMAI	HEAVEN	HAMPER
HEFTED	HUSHED	HURTLE	******	HEBRON	HANGAR
HELMED	HUSKED	HUSTLE	**H----K**	HEDRON	HANGER
HELPED	HUTTED	HYDRAE	******	HELLEN	HANKER
HEMMED	HYBRID	HYPHAE	HICKOK	HEMPEN	HARBOR
HEMOID	HYMNED	******	HIJACK	HENDON	HARDER
HEPTAD	******	**H----F**	******	HEREIN	HARPER
HERALD	**H----E**	******	**H----L**	HEREON	HATTER
HERDED	******	HEREOF	******	HERMAN	HAULER
HESOID	HABILE	******	HAEMAL	HEROIN	HAWKER
HILLED	HACKEE	**H----G**	HALLEL	HETMAN	HAWSER
		HADING	HALING		
		HALING			

HAZIER	HUSKER	HETTYS	HYMENS	******	INTIMA
HEADER	HUSSAR	HEWERS	HYOIDS	**H----Y**	ISCHIA
HEALER	HYSTER	HEXADS	HYPNOS	******	ISTRIA
HEARER	******	HEXYLS	******	HALLEY	ITHACA
HEATER	**H----S**	HIATUS	**H----T**	HALSEY	******
HEAVER	******	HIDERS	******	HARDLY	**I----B**
HECTOR	HABEAS	HIKERS	HAGBUT	HARLEY	******
HEDGER	HABITS	HILDAS	HAMLET	HARVEY	INTOMB
HEEDER	HAGGIS	HINDUS	HARLOT	HAULMY	******
HEELER	HAKIMS	HINGES	HASLET	HAZILY	**I----C**
HEIFER	HALERS	HIPPOS	HAVENT	HEARTY	******
HELLER	HALIDS	HIPPUS	HEARST	HEATHY	IAMBIC
HELPER	HALOES	HIRAMS	HEIGHT	HENLEY	IATRIC
HELTER	HALVES	HIRERS	HELMET	HEREBY	ICONIC
HEMMER	HAMALS	HISSES	HENBIT	HERESY	IPECAC
HERDER	HAMZAS	HOARDS	HEREAT	HEYDAY	IRENIC
HESTER	HANCES	HOAXES	HERIOT	HICKEY	IRIDIC
HIGHER	HANNAS	HOBBES	HERMIT	HIGHLY	IRITIC
HILLER	HARASS	HOBOES	HOBART	HILARY	IRONIC
HINDER	HAREMS	HOGANS	HOGNUT	HOCKEY	ITALIC
HISSER	HARRIS	HOICKS	HONEST	HOLILY	******
HITHER	HARRYS	HOISTS	HORNET	HOMELY	**I----D**
HITLER	HASHES	HOLIES	HOTPOT	HOMILY	******
HITTER	HASTES	HOLLYS	HUBERT	HOMINY	ILFORD
HOAXER	HATERS	HOLMES	HUGEST	HOOKEY	IMAGED
HOLDER	HATTYS	HOMERS	******	HOORAY	IMBUED
HOLIER	HAUNTS	HONEYS	**H----U**	HORARY	IMPEND
HOLLER	HAVENS	HONORS	******	HORSEY	INBAND
HOMIER	HAWSES	HOOVES	HONSHU	HOURLY	INBRED
HONKER	HAZELS	HORDES	******	HUGELY	INCHED
HONOUR	HAZERS	HORSES	**H----W**	HUMBLY	INDEED
HOOFER	HEARTS	HOTELS	******	HUMIFY	INDUED
HOOKER	HEATHS	HOUNDS	HALLOW	HUMPTY	INFOLD
HOOPER	HEAVES	HOURIS	HARLOW	HUNGRY	INGRID
HOOTER	HEDGES	HOUSES	HARROW	HURLEY	INLAID
HOOVER	HEISTS	HOVELS	HAWHAW	HURRAY	INLAND
HOPPER	HELENS	HOVERS	HAYMOW	HUXLEY	INROAD
HORROR	HELIOS	HUBRIS	HEBREW	******	INTEND
HOSIER	HELLAS	HUGHES	HEEHAW	**H----Z**	INURED
HOTTER	HELOTS	HUMANS	HOLLOW	******	INWARD
HOWLER	HELVES	HUMORS	******	HALUTZ	INWIND
HUMBER	HENNAS	HURONS	**H----X**	******	IRISED
HUMMER	HENRIS	HUSHES	******	**I----A**	IRONED
HUMOUR	HENRYS	HYADES	HALLUX	******	ISLAND
HUNGER	HERMES	HYBRIS	HATBOX	IBERIA	ISOPOD
HUNTER	HEROES	HYDRAS	HAYBOX	IGUANA	ISSUED
HURLER	HERONS	HYDROS	HOTBOX	IMPALA	ITCHED
HURTER	HERPES	HYENAS		INDABA	

******	IODATE	IREFUL	******	INGOTS	INFEST
I----E	IODIDE	ISABEL	**I----R**	INGRES	INGEST
******	IODINE	ISOBEL	******	INKERS	INJECT
ICEAXE	IODIZE	ISOHEL	IMPAIR	INKLES	INKPOT
ICICLE	IOLITE	ISRAEL	INDOOR	INLAWS	INMOST
IDEATE	IONIZE	******	INKIER	INLAYS	INSECT
IGNACE	IONONE	**I----M**	INLIER	INLETS	INSERT
IGNITE	ISOLDE	******	INSTAR	INPUTS	INSIST
IGNORE	******	IBIDEM	IRONER	INSETS	INSULT
ILLUME	**I----F**	IMBALM	ISADOR	INTERS	INTACT
ILLUSE		INDIUM	ISHTAR	INURES	INTENT
IMBIBE	INGULF	INFIRM	ISIDOR	INURNS	INTUIT
IMBRUE	ITSELF	INFORM	ISOBAR	IODOUS	INVENT
IMMUNE	******	IODISM	ISOMER	IOLCUS	INVERT
IMMURE	**I----G**	IONIUM	ISSUER	IRANIS	INVEST
IMPALE	******	******	******	IRAQIS	ISEULT
IMPEDE	IDLING	**I----N**	**I----S**	IRENES	******
IMPOSE	IMPING	******	******	IRIDES	**I----W**
IMPURE	INKING	IBADAN	IAMBUS	IRISES	******
IMPUTE	INNING	ICEMAN	IBEAMS	IRITIS	INFLOW
INCAGE	IRKING	ICEMEN	IBEXES	IRVINS	******
INCASE	IRVING	IMOGEN	IBICES	IRWINS	**I----X**
INCISE	ISLING	IMPAWN	IBISES	ISAACS	******
INCITE	******	IMPUGN	ICARUS	ISLETS	ICEBOX
INCOME	**I----H**	INBORN	ICINGS	ISSEIS	INFLUX
INCUSE	******	INCHON	IDEALS	ISSUES	******
INDENE	IMMESH	INDIAN	IDIOMS	ITCHES	**I----Y**
INDITE	IMPISH	INSPAN	IDIOTS	ITIOUS	******
INDUCE	INARCH	INTERN	IDLERS	******	ICALLY
INFUSE	INMESH	INTURN	IDYLLS	**I----T**	ICHTHY
INHALE	INRUSH	INULIN	IGLOOS	******	IDIOCY
INHERE	ISAIAH	IONIAN	ILEXES	ICIEST	IGNIFY
INHUME	******	ISATIN	IMAGES	IDLEST	IMBODY
INJOKE	**I----I**	ISOGON	IMBEDS	IGOROT	INFAMY
INJURE	******	******	IMBUES	ILLUST	INJURY
INLACE	INCUBI	**I----O**	IMIDES	IMARET	******
INMATE	******	******	IMINES	IMPACT	**J----A**
INNATE	**I----K**	ILOILO	IMMIES	IMPART	******
INSANE	******	IMMUNO	IMPASS	IMPORT	JACANA
INSIDE	IMBARK	INDIGO	IMPELS	IMPOST	JAPHIA
INSOLE	IMPARK	INFERO	INARMS	INCEPT	JARINA
INSURE	******	******	INCHES	INCEST	JEMIMA
INTAKE	**I----L**	**I----P**	INCURS	INDENT	JERBOA
INTONE	******	******	INDIES	INDICT	JOANNA
INVADE	INHAUL	ICECAP	INDOWS	INDUCT	JOSHUA
INVITE	INSOUL	INCORP	INDRIS	INDULT	JOSIEA
INVOKE	INSTIL	INSTEP	INDUES	INFANT	JUDAEA
INWOVE	INWALL	INWRAP	INFERS	INFECT	******
					J----C
					******
					JUDAIC

******	JINNEE	******	******	JUNIUS	******
J----D	JOANNE	**J----N**	**J----S**	JUNTAS	**K----A**
******	JOCOSE	******	******	JUPONS	******
JABBED	JOGGLE	JARGON	JABOTS	JURATS	KABAKA
JACKED	JONNIE	JERKIN	JACKYS	JURELS	KABALA
JAGGED	JOSTLE	JETTON	JACOBS	JURIES	KABAYA
JAILED	JOUNCE	JOHANN	JAINAS	JURORS	KALMIA
JAMMED	JUGATE	JONSON	JALOPS	JUSTUS	KAMALA
JARRED	JUGGLE	JOPLIN	JAMIES	******	KANAKA
JAZZED	JUJUBE	JORDAN	JANETS	**J----T**	KERALA
JEERED	JUMBLE	JOVIAN	JAPANS	******	KORUNA
JELLED	JUNGLE	JUDEAN	JARVIS	JACKET	******
JEREED	JUNKIE	JULIAN	JASONS	JAPHET	**K----C**
JERKED	******	JUSTIN	JAUNTS	JENNET	******
JESSED	**J----G**	******	JAZZES	JESUIT	KELTIC
JESTED	******	**J----O**	JENNYS	JOLIET	******
JETTED	JADING	******	JERRYS	JULIET	**K----D**
JIBBED	JAPING	JETHRO	JERVIS	JUNKET	******
JIGGED	JAWING	JUDAEO	JESSES	JURANT	KAYOED
JILTED	JEEING	******	JEWELS	JURIST	KECKED
JINKED	JIBING	**J----R**	JEWESS	******	KEDGED
JINXED	JIVING	******	JIHADS	**J----U**	KEELED
JOBBED	JOKING	JABBER	JIMMYS	******	KEENED
JOCUND	JOYING	JAEGER	JINNYS	JABIRU	KELOID
JOGGED	******	JAGUAR	JINXES	JUNEAU	KENNED
JOINED	**J----H**	JAILER	JOCKOS	******	KERBED
JOLTED	******	JAILOR	JOINTS	**J----W**	KERNED
JOSHED	JADISH	JAIPUR	JOISTS	******	KICKED
JOTTED	JEWISH	JAMJAR	JOKERS	JARROW	KIDDED
JUDGED	JOSEPH	JASPER	JONAHS	JIGSAW	KILLED
JUGGED	JOSIAH	JAZZER	JORAMS	******	KILTED
JUMPED	JUBBAH	JEERER	JORGES	**J----Y**	KINGED
JUNKED	JUDITH	JESTER	JORUMS	******	KINKED
JUTTED	JUTISH	JIBBER	JOSHES	JALOPY	KIPPED
******	******	JIGGER	JOSIAS	JARVEY	KISSED
J----E	**J----L**	JILTER	JOSSES	JAUNTY	KITTED
******	******	JINKER	JOULES	JEREMY	KNIFED
JACKIE	JACKAL	JITTER	JOUSTS	JERSEY	KOBOLD
JANGLE	JARFUL	JOBBER	JOYCES	JIMINY	KONRAD
JANICE	JEKYLL	JOGGER	JOYOUS	JINGLY	******
JAYVEE	JEZAIL	JOINER	JUDAHS	JITNEY	**K----E**
JEANNE	JINGAL	JOLTER	JUDGES	JOCKEY	******
JEJUNE	JOVIAL	JOSHER	JUICES	JOHNNY	KARATE
JEROME	JOYFUL	JOTTER	JULEPS	JUNGLY	KATHIE
JESSIE	JUGFUL	JUDGER	JULIAS	JUSTLY	KECKLE
JIGGLE	JUMBAL	JUICER	JULIES	******	KELPIE
JIMMIE	******	JUMPER	JULIUS	**J----Z**	KENITE
JINGLE	**J----M**	JUNIOR	JUNCOS	******	KENNIE
	******	JUNKER		JUAREZ	
	JETSAM				
	JOTHAM				

KERRIE	******	KICKER	KNAVES	KINGLY	LAGGED
KETENE	K----M	KIDDER	KNEADS	KINSEY	LAIRED
KETONE	******	KILLER	KNEELS	KNARRY	LALLED
KETOSE	KALIUM	KILMER	KNELLS	KNOBBY	LAMBED
KETTLE	******	KILTER	KNIFES	KNOTTY	LAMMED
KEWPIE	K----N	KINDER	KNIVES	KNURLY	LAMPAD
KIBBLE	******	KIPPER	KNOCKS	KORUNY	LAMPED
KIDDIE	KAFTAN	KISSER	KNOLLS	******	LANCED
KILTIE	KALIAN	KNOWER	KNOSPS	K----Z	LANDED
KINASE	KAMSIN	KOSHER	KNOUTS	******	LAPPED
KINDLE	KANSAN	KRONER	KNURLS	KIBITZ	LAPSED
KIRTLE	KAOLIN	KRONOR	KOALAS	******	LARDED
KITTLE	KATION	KRONUR	KODAKS	L----A	LARKED
******	KEDRON	KULTUR	KOINES	******	LASHED
K----G	KELSON	******	KOPEKS	LACUNA	LASTED
******	KELVIN	K----S	KOPJES	LADOGA	LATHED
KALONG	KITTEN	******	KRAALS	LAMBDA	LAUDED
KEYING	KLAXON	KAASES	KRAITS	LAMINA	LEADED
KITBAG	KOREAN	KABOBS	KRISES	LATERA	LEAFED
KITING	KRAKEN	KAMIKS	KRONOS	LATRIA	LEAKED
******	KRONEN	KANSAS	KRUBIS	LATVIA	LEANED
K----H	KUCHEN	KAPOKS	KULAKS	LEPSIA	LEAPED
******	******	KAPPAS	KUMISS	LIGULA	LEASED
KEDDAH	K----O	KARATS	******	LIMINA	LEAVED
KIBLAH	******	KARENS	K----T	LINGUA	LEERED
KIBOSH	KAKAPO	KARMAS	******	LIPOMA	LEGEND
KIRSCH	KARROO	KATHYS	KERMIT	LISBOA	LEGGED
KITSCH	KERATO	KATIES	KISMET	LITHIA	LEVIED
******	KIMONO	KAURIS	KNIGHT	LOCHIA	LIASED
K----I	KINETO	KAVASS	KRUBUT	LOGGIA	LICKED
******	KOKOMO	KAYAKS	KUWAIT	LOLITA	LIDDED
KABIKI	KOODOO	KAZOOS	******	LORICA	LIFTED
KABUKI	******	KEDGES	K----U	LOUISA	LIGAND
KINESI	K----P	KEEVES	******	LUANDA	LILIED
******	******	KEITHS	KYUSHU	LUELLA	LILTED
K----K	KIDNAP	KENNYS	******	LUMINA	LIMBED
******	******	KERMES	K----W	LUNULA	LIMNED
KALPAK	K----R	KERMIS	******	******	LIMPED
KARNAK	******	KEVELS	KISLEW	L----C	LIMPID
KODIAK	KAFFIR	KEVINS	KOWTOW	******	LINKED
KOPECK	KAISER	KEYNES	******	LACTIC	LIPOID
******	KASPER	KHAKIS	K----Y	LIMBIC	LIPPED
K----L	KEENER	KIBEIS	******	LITHIC	LIQUID
******	KEEPER	KININS	KEENLY	LUETIC	LISPED
KENDAL	KEGLER	KIOSKS	KERSEY	******	LISTED
KENNEL	KELLER	KISSES	KEYWAY	L----D	LIZARD
KERNEL	KEPLER	KITTYS	KIDNEY	******	LOADED
KUMMEL	KHYBER	KNACKS	KINDLY	LACKED	LOAFED
				LADLED	

LOAMED	LEGATE	LAKING	LARVAL	LIBYAN	LADDER
LOANED	LEGREE	LAMING	LAUREL	LICHEN	LADLER
LOBBED	LEGUME	LAPDOG	LAWFUL	LIGNIN	LAGGER
LOCKED	LENAPE	LARYNG	LEMUEL	LILIAN	LAKIER
LOCOED	LENORE	LAVING	LENTIL	LINDEN	LANCER
LODGED	LEONIE	LAWING	LETHAL	LISBON	LANDER
LOFTED	LESLIE	LAYING	LINEAL	LISTEN	LANGUR
LOGGED	LESSEE	LAZING	LINTEL	LOGION	LANKER
LOLLED	LEVITE	LIEBIG	LIONEL	LONDON	LANNER
LOMOND	LIABLE	LIKING	LISTEL	LONGAN	LAPPER
LONGED	LIAISE	LIMING	LOVELL	LOOKIN	LAPSER
LOOKED	LIBRAE	LINING	LOWELL	LOOSEN	LARDER
LOOMED	LICHEE	LIVING	LUTEAL	LORAIN	LARGER
LOOPED	LIERNE	LOOING	******	LOREEN	LARKER
LOOSED	LIGATE	LOPING	L----M	LOTION	LASCAR
LOOTED	LIGULE	LOSING	******	LOUDEN	LASHER
LOPPED	LIGURE	LOVING	LABIUM	LOVEIN	LASTER
LORDED	LINAGE	LOWING	LABRUM	LUBLIN	LATHER
LOURED	LIPASE	LUDWIG	LACTAM	LUCIAN	LATTER
LOUSED	LITTLE	LURING	LIGNUM	LUCIEN	LAUDER
LUFFED	LIZZIE	LUTING	LINGAM	LUMPEN	LAWYER
LUGGED	LOATHE	LYSING	LISSOM	******	LAZIER
LULLED	LOBATE	******	LOGJAM	L----O	LEADER
LUMPED	LOBULE	L----H	LUTEUM	******	LEANER
LUNGED	LOCALE	******	LYCEUM	LADINO	LEAPER
LURKED	LOCATE	LAMECH	LYRISM	LANUGO	LEAVER
LUSHED	LORENE	LATISH	******	LAPARO	LECHER
LUSTED	LOTTIE	LAUNCH	L----N	LAREDO	LECTOR
******	LOUISE	LAVISH	******	LAVABO	LEDGER
L----E	LOUNGE	LENGTH	LAGOON	LEANTO	LENDER
******	LOUVRE	LOOFAH	LARDON	LEGATO	LESSER
LABILE	LOVAGE	******	LASSEN	LEPIDO	LESSOR
LADDIE	LUCILE	L----I	LATEEN	LIBIDO	LESTER
LAGUNE	LUCITE	******	LATTEN	LUMINO	LETTER
LAHORE	LUNATE	LAZULI	LAYMAN	LYMPHO	LEVIER
LAMBIE	LUNGEE	LIMULI	LAYMEN	******	LEWDER
LAMIAE	LUNULE	LITCHI	LEADEN	L----P	LICTOR
LANATE	LUPINE	LUMINI	LEADIN	******	LIEDER
LANOSE	LUSTRE	******	LEAVEN	LARRUP	LIFTER
LAOTSE	LUXATE	L----K	LEGION	LINEUP	LIMBER
LARINE	LYSINE	******	LEGMAN	LOCKUP	LIMIER
LARVAE	LYTTAE	LUBECK	LEGMEN	LOLLOP	LIMNER
LASSIE	******	******	LENTEN	******	LIMPER
LAUNCE	L---F	L----L	LEPTON	L----R	LINEAR
LAURAE	******	******	LESION	******	LINGER
LAURIE	LAYOFF	LABIAL	LESSEN	LAAGER	LINIER
LAVAGE	******	LACIAL	LESSON	LABOUR	LINTER
LEAGUE	L----G	LAPFUL	LEYDEN	LACIER	LIPPER
	******				
	LACING				
	LADING				

LIQUOR	LAMMAS	LIBELS	LUNGIS	******	MANTUA
LISPER	LAMPAS	LIBRAS	LURERS	**L----Y**	MARACA
LISTER	LANAIS	LIEGES	LUSHES	******	MARCIA
LITHER	LANCES	LIFERS	LYCEES	LACILY	MARINA
LITTER	LAPELS	LIGHTS	LYDIAS	LACKEY	MARKKA
LIVIER	LAPINS	LIKENS	LYNXES	LAMELY	MARSHA
LIVYER	LAPSES	LILACS	LYRICS	LANKLY	MARTHA
LOADER	LAPSUS	LILIES	LYSINS	LASTLY	MASORA
LOAFER	LARGOS	LIMBUS	******	LATELY	MAXIMA
LOBBER	LARRYS	LIMENS	**L----T**	LAXITY	MAZUMA
LOCKER	LASERS	LIMEYS	******	LAYDAY	MEDUSA
LODGER	LASHES	LIMITS	LABRET	LAZILY	MERCIA
LOFTER	LASSES	LINDAS	LAMENT	LEACHY	MEZUZA
LOGGER	LASSOS	LINENS	LAMEST	LEANLY	MIASMA
LOGIER	LATHES	LINERS	LANCET	LEEWAY	MIMOSA
LOITER	LATINS	LINGAS	LAPPET	LEGACY	MINIMA
LOLLER	LAUGHS	LIPIDS	LARIAT	LENITY	MONICA
LONGER	LAURAS	LITERS	LATENT	LESLEY	MORULA
LOOKER	LAVERS	LITMUS	LATEST	LEVITY	MUCOSA
LOOPER	LAYERS	LIVENS	LAXEST	LEWDLY	MYOPIA
LOOSER	LAZARS	LIVERS	LAYOUT	LIKELY	MYRICA
LOOTER	LEARNS	LIVIAS	LEARNT	LIMPLY	MYXOMA
LOQUAR	LEASES	LIVRES	LEGIST	LITANY	******
LOUDER	LEAVES	LIZZYS	LEVANT	LIVELY	**M----B**
LOUVER	LEDGES	LLAMAS	LIMPET	LIVERY	******
LUBBER	LEGERS	LLANOS	LINNET	LONELY	MAHBUB
LUGGER	LEHUAS	LLOYDS	LOCKET	LORDLY	MIDRIB
LUMBAR	LEIGHS	LOAVES	LOCUST	LOUDLY	******
LUMBER	LEMMAS	LOCALS	LOMENT	LOVELY	**M----C**
LUNGER	LEMNOS	LODGES	LOQUAT	LOWBOY	******
LUNKER	LEMONS	LONERS	LOWEST	LOWERY	MANIAC
LURKER	LEMURS	LOOSES	LUCENT	LOWKEY	MANIOC
LUSHER	LENNYS	LOPERS	LUTIST	LUNACY	MANTIC
LUSTER	LENSES	LORIES	LYRIST	LUXURY	MASTIC
LUTHER	LENTOS	LOSERS	******	******	METRIC
******	LEONAS	LOSSES	**L----U**	**L----Z**	MICMAC
L----S	LEPERS	LOTAHS	******	******	MIOTIC
******	LEROYS	LOUGHS	LANDAU	LORENZ	MOSAIC
LABELS	LESBOS	LOUPES	******	******	MYOPIC
LABORS	LETUPS	LOUSES	**L----W**	**M----A**	MYRMEC
LACHES	LEUDES	LOVERS	******	******	MYSTIC
LADIES	LEVEES	LOWERS	LUDLOW	MACULA	MYTHIC
LADLES	LEVELS	LUCIAS	******	MADURA	******
LAGERS	LEVERS	LUCIUS	**L----X**	MALAGA	**M----D**
LAIRDS	LEVIES	LUGERS	******	MALAYA	******
LAKERS	LIANAS	LUMENS	LARYNX	MALTHA	MADDED
LAMEDS	LIANES	LUNETS	LASTEX	MANANA	MADRID
LAMIAS	LIBBYS	LUNGES	LUMMOX	MANILA	MAENAD

MAILED	MOOTED	MAXIXE	MUFFLE	MULISH	******
MAIMED	MOPPED	MEAGRE	MUMBLE	MULLAH	**M----M**
MALLED	MORBID	MEALIE	MURINE	MUNICH	******
MALTED	MOUSED	MEANIE	MUSCAE	******	MAGNUM
MANNED	MUCKED	MEDDLE	MUSCLE	**M----I**	MAOISM
MAPPED	MUCOID	MEDIAE	MUSTEE	******	MAYHEM
MARAUD	MUDDED	MENACE	MUTATE	MALAWI	MEDIUM
MARKED	MUFFED	MENAGE	MUTULE	MEDICI	MEGRIM
MARLED	MUGGED	MESTEE	MUZZLE	MYTHOI	MILIUM
MARRED	MULLED	METAGE	MYCETE	******	MINIUM
MASHED	MUMMED	METOPE	MYRTLE	**M----K**	MIRIAM
MASKED	MUSHED	METTLE	******	******	MOMISM
MASSED	MUSSED	MICKLE	**M----F**	MARDUK	MONISM
MASTED	MYRIAD	MIDDLE	******	MOHAWK	MOSLEM
MATTED	******	MIGGLE	MASSIF	MOHOCK	MUSEUM
MAULED	**M----E**	MILAGE	MYSELF	MUKLUK	MUSLIM
MELDED	******	MILLIE	******	MUZHIK	MUTISM
MELTED	MACKLE	MINGLE	**M----G**	******	******
MENDED	MACULE	MINNIE	******	**M----L**	**M----N**
MEOWED	MADAME	MINUTE	MACING	******	******
MERGED	MAGGIE	MIRAGE	MAKING	MAMMAL	MACRON
MESHED	MAGPIE	MISCUE	MASKEG	MANFUL	MADDEN
MESSED	MAIGRE	MISERE	MATING	MANTEL	MADMAN
METHOD	MAISIE	MISTLE	MAYBUG	MANUAL	MADMEN
MEWLED	MAITRE	MISUSE	MAYING	MANUEL	MAIDEN
MIFFED	MALATE	MIZZLE	MAZING	MARCEL	MAISON
MILKED	MALGRE	MOBILE	MEKONG	MARVEL	MALIGN
MILLED	MALICE	MODULE	METING	MEDIAL	MAMMON
MILORD	MALINE	MOHAVE	MEWING	MENDEL	MANDAN
MILTED	MALLEE	MOHOLE	MIMING	MENIAL	MARGIN
MINCED	MAMMAE	MOISHE	MINING	MENSAL	MARIAN
MINDED	MANAGE	MOJAVE	MIRING	MENTAL	MARION
MINTED	MANEGE	MOLINE	MIXING	MESCAL	MARLIN
MISDID	MANGLE	MOLLIE	MOOING	MESIAL	MAROON
MISLED	MANQUE	MOLTKE	MOPING	METHYL	MARTEN
MISSED	MANTLE	MONROE	MOVING	MICELL	MARTIN
MISTED	MANURE	MOPOKE	MOWING	MICHEL	MARVIN
MITRED	MARBLE	MORALE	MUSING	MIGUEL	MASCON
MOANED	MARGIE	MORGUE	MUSKEG	MISKAL	MATRON
MOATED	MARINE	MOROSE	MUTING	MISSAL	MECCAN
MOBBED	MARQUE	MOSQUE	******	MISSEL	MEDIAN
MOCKED	MARTHE	MOTILE	**M----H**	MITRAL	MELLON
MOILED	MASHIE	MOTIVE	******	MONGOL	MELTON
MOLDED	MASQUE	MOTTLE	MODISH	MORSEL	MELVIN
MOLTED	MATINE	MOUSSE	MOLLAH	MORTAL	MELVYN
MONIED	MATTIE	MUCKLE	MOLOCH	MURIEL	MERLIN
MOONED	MATURE	MUCOSE	MOOLAH	MUSSEL	MERLON
MOORED	MAXINE	MUDDLE	MOPISH	MUTUAL	MERMAN

MERMEN	MAKEUP	MIDAIR	MAMBAS	MERGES	MOPERS
MERVIN	MARKUP	MILDER	MAMBOS	MERITS	MORALS
MESIAN	MAYHAP	MILKER	MAMEYS	MERLES	MORASS
MICRON	MAYPOP	MILLER	MAMIES	MEROUS	MORAYS
MIDDEN	MEGILP	MILTER	MAMMAS	MESHES	MORELS
MIGNON	MENDIP	MINCER	MANDYS	MESNES	MORONS
MILDEN	METUMP	MINDER	MANGOS	MESONS	MORRIS
MILTON	MISHAP	MINTER	MANIAS	MESSES	MORROS
MINION	MOBCAP	MIRROR	MANORS	MESSRS	MORTYS
MINOAN	MOCKUP	MISTER	MANSES	METALS	MOSEYS
MITTEN	MUDCAP	MOBBER	MANTAS	METERS	MOSSES
MIZZEN	******	MOCKER	MANTES	METROS	MOTELS
MODERN		MOHAIR	MANTIS	MEZZOS	MOTIFS
MOLTEN	M----R	MOILER	MAORIS	MIAULS	MOTORS
MOREEN	******	MOLDER	MAPLES	MICKYS	MOTTOS
MORGAN	MADDER	MOLTER	MAQUIS	MIDGES	MOULDS
MORGEN	MAGYAR	MONGER	MARCOS	MIKLOS	MOULTS
MORION	MAHLER	MOOTER	MARCUS	MILERS	MOUNTS
MORMON	MAILER	MORTAR	MARGES	MILLYS	MOURNS
MORTON	MAIMER	MOTHER	MARGOS	MIMERS	MOUSES
MOTION	MANGER	MOUSER	MARIAS	MIMICS	MOUTHS
MOULIN	MANNER	MUCKER	MARIES	MINCES	MOVERS
MOUTON	MARKER	MUDDER	MARTAS	MINERS	MOVIES
MUFFIN	MARRER	MUGGAR	MARTYS	MINIMS	MOWERS
MULLEN	MARTYR	MUGGER	MASERS	MINORS	MUCOUS
MUSLIN	MASHER	MUGGUR	MASHES	MINXES	MUFTIS
MUTTON	MASKER	MULLER	MASONS	MIOSIS	MULCTS
MYELIN	MASTER	MUMMER	MASSES	MISERS	MURALS
MYOSIN	MATTER	MURDER	MATEOS	MISSES	MURRES
******	MAULER	MURMUR	MATEYS	MISSIS	MUSHES
M----O	MAUSER	MUSHER	MATINS	MISSUS	MUSSES
******	MAZIER	MUSTER	MATTES	MITERS	MYOPES
MACACO	MEAGER	MUTTER	MATZOS	MIXERS	MYOSIS
MADURO	MEANER	******	MAUDES	MIXUPS	MYRNAS
MALACO	MEDLAR	M----S	MAUNDS	MOBIUS	MYTHOS
MANITO	MEEKER	******	MAUVES	MODELS	******
MATTEO	MEETER	MABELS	MAXIMS	MOGULS	M----T
MEDICO	MELTER	MACAWS	MAYORS	MOHURS	******
MEGALO	MEMBER	MACERS	MAZERS	MOIRAS	MAGGOT
MEJICO	MEMOIR	MACLES	MCCOYS	MOLARS	MAGNET
MELANO	MENDER	MADAMS	MEATUS	MOLIES	MAHOUT
MERINO	MENHIR	MADGES	MECCAS	MOLLYS	MALLET
MEXICO	MENTOR	MADRAS	MEDALS	MONADS	MAMMET
MIKADO	MERCER	MAGOTS	MEDICS	MONEYS	MAOIST
MONACO	MERGER	MAIZES	MEGASS	MONIES	MARGOT
MORPHO	MESHER	MAJORS	MELEES	MONTES	MARIST
******	MESMER	MAKERS	MELONS	MONTHS	MARKET
M----P	METEOR	MALAYS	MENSES	MONTYS	MARMOT
******	METIER				
MADCAP					
MADEUP					

MASCOT	MENINX	MULLEY	NITRID	******	******
MATZOT	MUSKOX	MURRAY	NOBBED	**N----G**	**N----N**
MAYEST	******	MURREY	NOCKED	******	******
MEREST	**M----Y**	MUTINY	NODDED	NAMING	NAPKIN
MIDGET	******	******	NOGOOD	NIDING	NASION
MIDGUT	MAGUEY	**N----A**	NOISED	NIXING	NATHAN
MILLET	MAINLY	******	NOOSED	NOSING	NATION
MINUET	MALADY	NAGANA	NOSHED	NOTING	NATRON
MISFIT	MALORY	NAGOYA	NUDGED	NUTMEG	NEATEN
MODEST	MARGAY	NASHUA	NUMBED	******	NEKTON
MOLEST	MARSHY	NAUSEA	NURSED	**N----H**	NELSON
MOMENT	MAUNDY	NEBULA	NUTTED	******	NEURON
MONGST	MAYDAY	NEVADA	******	NAUTCH	NEWTON
MONIST	MAYFLY	NOMURA	**N----E**	NULLAH	NIACIN
MOPPET	MAZILY	NOVENA	******	******	NIPPON
MOTMOT	MEANLY	NUMINA	NADINE	**N----I**	NOGGIN
MOZART	MEASLY	NUTRIA	NAPPIE	******	NOREEN
MULLET	MEDLEY	NYMPHA	NARINE	NEROLI	NORMAN
MUSCAT	MEDWAY	******	NATIVE	NEVSKI	NOTION
MUSKET	MEEKLY	**N----C**	NATURE	NIELLI	NUBBIN
MUSKIT	MEETLY	******	NEEDLE	NILGAI	NUBIAN
MUSTNT	MELODY	NASTIC	NEGATE	NUCLEI	******
MUTANT	MEMORY	NIOBIC	NELLIE	******	**N----O**
******	MERELY	NITRIC	NESTLE	**N----K**	******
M----U	MERSEY	NOETIC	NETTIE	******	NAVAHO
******	MICKEY	NORDIC	NETTLE	NEWARK	NAVAJO
MANCHU	MIDDAY	NOSTIC	NEVILE	NUDNIK	NEMATO
MANITU	MIDWAY	******	NIBBLE	******	NEPHRO
MAUMAU	MIGHTY	**N----D**	NICENE	**N----L**	NIELLO
MILIEU	MILADY	******	NICOLE	******	NONEGO
MOREAU	MILDLY	NABBED	NIGGLE	NARIAL	NUNCIO
MUUMUU	MILLAY	NAGGED	NIMBLE	NARWAL	NYMPHO
******	MINIFY	NAILED	NIPPLE	NASIAL	******
M----W	MISERY	NAPPED	NOBBLE	NEURAL	**N----R**
******	MISLAY	NARKED	NODDLE	NEVILL	******
MALLOW	MODIFY	NEARED	NODOSE	NICKEL	NAGGER
MARLOW	MOIETY	NECKED	NODULE	NOBALL	NAPIER
MARROW	MONDAY	NEEDED	NOELLE	NORMAL	NAPPER
MEADOW	MONKEY	NEREID	NONAGE	NOUNAL	NASSER
MELLOW	MONODY	NERVED	NOODLE	******	NATTER
MILDEW	MOOLEY	NESTED	NOTICE	**N----M**	NEARER
MINNOW	MORLEY	NETTED	NOVICE	******	NEATER
MORROW	MOSLEY	NEVOID	NOWISE	NANISM	NECTAR
MOSCOW	MOSTLY	NIBBED	NOZZLE	NAPALM	NEEDER
******	MOTLEY	NICHED	NUANCE	NAZISM	NESTOR
M----X	MOULDY	NICKED	NUBBLE	NOMISM	NETHER
******	MOUNTY	NIMROD	NUBILE	NONCOM	NEUTER
MAGNOX	MOUTHY	NIPPED	NUCHAE	NONCOM	NEUTER
MATRIX			NUZZLE	NUDISM	NICKER

NIGGER	NOOSES	NIDIFY	OFFEND	ORRICE	ONFALL
NIGHER	NOPALS	NIGHTY	OGDOAD	OSCINE	ORCHIL
NIPPER	NORIAS	NIMBLY	OKAYED	OSCULE	ORDEAL
NOBLER	NORMAS	NINETY	ONWARD	OSMOSE	ORWELL
NODDER	NORRIS	NOBODY	OPENED	OTIOSE	OSTEAL
NORNIR	NOTERS	NONARY	OPINED	OXHIDE	OXTAIL
NOSIER	NOVELS	NORWAY	ORATED	******	******
NUMBER	NOWAYS	NOSILY	ORCHID	**O----F**	**O----M**
NURSER	NUBIAS	NOTARY	ORMUZD	******	******
NUTTER	NUDGES	NOTIFY	OSMOND	ONEOFF	OBIISM
******	NURSES	NUBBLY	OSMUND	******	OLDHAM
N----S	NYLONS	NUDELY	OSTEND	**O----G**	OMASUM
******	NYMPHS	NUDITY	OSWALD	******	OMNIUM
NABOBS	******	NUMBLY	OUSTED	OARING	ORGASM
NADIRS	**N----T**	******	OUTBID	OBLONG	OSMIUM
NAEVUS	******	**N----Z**	OUTDID	OFFING	******
NAHUMS	NATANT	******	OXEYED	OGLING	**O----N**
NAIADS	NAUGHT	NIMITZ	OXFORD	OILING	******
NAMERS	NEWEST	******	******	OOLONG	OBERON
NANCYS	NICEST	**O----A**	**O----E**	OOZING	OBTAIN
NANTES	NITWIT	******	******	OPTING	OHIOAN
NAOMIS	NOCENT	ODESSA	OBLATE	ORBING	OILCAN
NAOSES	NOUGAT	ODYNIA	OBLIGE	OUTING	OLEFIN
NAPLES	NOUGHT	OEDEMA	OBTUSE	OWNING	OPPUGN
NAPPES	NUDIST	OEPEMA	OCREAE	******	OPTION
NASALS	NUGGET	OJIBWA	OCTANE	**O----H**	ORCEIN
NAVELS	NUTLET	OLIVIA	OCTAVE	******	ORDAIN
NAVIES	******	OMENTA	ODETTE	OAFISH	OREGAN
NAWABS	**N----U**	ONEIDA	OEUVRE	OFFISH	OREGON
NEIGHS	******	OPTIMA	OFFICE	OGRISH	ORIGAN
NELLYS	NASSAU	ORGANA	OHMAGE	OLDISH	ORIGEN
NEREIS	******	OTTAVA	OLEATE	ONRUSH	ORIGIN
NERVES	**N----W**	OTTAWA	ONLINE	ORNITH	ORISON
NESSUS	******	OTTOWA	OOCYTE	OWLISH	ORPHAN
NEUMES	NARROW	******	OOLITE	******	OSBORN
NEWELS	NEPHEW	**O----B**	OPAQUE	**O----I**	OSSEIN
NICHES	NOSHOW	******	OPHITE	******	OSSIAN
NICKYS	******	ODDJOB	OPIATE	OCELLI	OUTMAN
NIECES	**N----Y**	******	OPPOSE	OCTOPI	OUTRAN
NIGELS	******	**O----C**	OPTIME	OCTROI	OUTRUN
NIGHTS	NAMELY	******	ORACLE	ONAGRI	OXYGEN
NIMBUS	NAPERY	ORPHIC	ORANGE	******	******
NINTHS	NAZIFY	OVISAC	ORDURE	**O----K**	**O----O**
NISEIS	NEARBY	OXALIC	OREIDE	******	******
NIXIES	NEARLY	OZONIC	ORIOLE	OCLOCK	OCTAVO
NOESIS	NEATLY	******	ORNATE	OOMIAK	ODONTO
NOISES	NICELY	**O----D**	OROIDE	******	ONEIRO
NOMADS	NICETY	OBEYED	ORPINE	**O----L**	OPORTO
		OBTUND		OGIVAL	
				ONEILL	

ORCHIO	OPTICS	ODDEST	OSSIFY	******	PEERED
ORGANO	ORACHS	OFFSET	OUTCRY	**P----C**	PEEVED
OSWEGO	ORANGS	OLDEST	OUTLAY	******	PEGGED
OVERDO	ORATES	OMELET	OVALLY	PARSEC	PELTED
******	ORBITS	OPTANT	OVERLY	PECTIC	PENDED
O----R	ORCHIS	ORGEAT	******	PELVIC	PENNED
******	ORDERS	ORIENT	**P----A**	PEPTIC	PENTAD
OBEYER	OREADS	OSBERT	******	PHASIC	PEPPED
OBITER	ORGANS	OUTFIT	PAGODA	PHOBIC	PEQUOD
OCULAR	ORGIES	OUTLET	PAJAMA	PHONIC	PERIOD
OILIER	ORIBIS	OUTPUT	PAMELA	PHOTIC	PERKED
OLIVER	ORIELS	OUTSAT	PANADA	PHYSIC	PERMED
ONAGER	ORLOPS	OUTSET	PANAMA	PICNIC	PETARD
OOPHOR	ORMERS	OUTSIT	PAPAYA	PICRIC	PETTED
OOZIER	ORPINS	OUTWIT	PAPULA	POETIC	PHASED
OPENER	ORYXES	******	PATHIA	PONTIC	PHONED
ORATOR	OSCANS	**O----U**	PATINA	PUBLIC	PICKED
OSTLER	OSCARS	******	PAYOLA	PYEMIC	PIECED
OUSTER	OSIERS	ORMOLU	PELOTA	PYKNIC	PIGGED
OVULAR	OSIRIS	******	PENNIA	PYTHIC	PILLED
OYSTER	OTHERS	**O----W**	PEORIA	******	PIMPED
******	OTITIS	******	PERSIA	**P----D**	PINGED
O----S	OTTERS	OUTLAW	PESETA	******	PINKED
******	OUNCES	******	PETULA	PACKED	PINNED
OBELUS	OUSELS	**O----X**	PHAGIA	PADDED	PIPPED
OBOLUS	OUTERS	******	PHASIA	PAINED	PIQUED
OBSESS	OUZELS	OUTFOX	PHILIA	PAIRED	PISHED
OCCURS	OVIBOS	******	PHOBIA	PALLED	PITHED
OCEANS	OVULES	**O----Y**	PHONIA	PALLID	PITIED
OCHERS	OWLETS	******	PIAZZA	PALMED	PITTED
OCTADS	OWNERS	OAKLEY	PIRANA	PALPED	PLACED
OCTETS	OXALIS	OCASEY	PLASIA	PANNED	PLACID
ODIOUS	OXBOWS	OCCUPY	PLASMA	PANTED	PLANED
OFFERS	OXEYES	OCHERY	PLEGIA	PARKED	PLATED
OGIVES	OXIDES	ODDITY	PLEURA	PARSED	PLAYED
OGLERS	OXLIPS	OFFDAY	PNEUMA	PARTED	PLEIAD
OGRESS	******	OHENRY	POMONA	PASSED	PLOWED
OILERS	**O----T**	OILILY	PORTIA	PASTED	PLUMED
OKAPIS	******	ONEWAY	POSADA	PATTED	PODDED
OLIVES	OBJECT	ONIONY	PRAVDA	PAUSED	POISED
OLLIES	OBLAST	OOLOGY	PURANA	PAWNED	POLAND
OMEGAS	OBOIST	OOZILY	PYEMIA	PEAKED	POLLED
ONIONS	OBTECT	OPENLY	PYJAMA	PEALED	PONIED
ONSETS	OBTEST	ORALLY	PYRRHA	PECKED	POOLED
ONUSES	OBVERT	ORKNEY	PYTHIA	PEEKED	POOPED
OODLES	OCCULT	ORNERY	PYURIA	PEELED	POPPED
OPERAS	OCELOT	ORRERY	******	PEENED	PORTED
OPINES	OCTANT	OSPREY	**P----B**	PEEPED	POSTED
			******		
			PREFAB		
			PUNJAB		

POTTED	PASSEE	PLEASE	******	PUNISH	PROPYL
POURED	PATINE	PLEDGE	**P----G**	PURDAH	PUMMEL
POUTED	PAVANE	PLICAE	******	PUTSCH	******
PRATED	PAVISE	PLUNGE	PACING	******	**P----M**
PRAYED	PAWNEE	POINTE	PAGING	**P----I**	******
PREMED	PEBBLE	POLICE	PALING	******	PASSIM
PREYED	PEDATE	POLITE	PARANG	PEDATI	PAYNIM
PRICED	PEDDLE	POLLEE	PARING	******	PEPLUM
PRIDED	PEEWEE	POMACE	PAVING	**P----K**	PHLEGM
PRIMED	PEIRCE	POMADE	PAWING	******	PHLOEM
PRIZED	PELAGE	PONGEE	PAYING	PLANCK	PHYLUM
PROBED	PELITE	POODLE	PEGLEG	PODUNK	PILEUM
PROSED	PENILE	POPPLE	PEKING	POLACK	PLENUM
PROVED	PENNAE	POTAGE	PIKING	******	PODIUM
PRUNED	PEOPLE	POTALE	PILING	**P----L**	POGROM
PUFFED	PERUKE	POTPIE	PINANG	******	POMPOM
PUGGED	PERUSE	POTSIE	PINING	PARCEL	POSSUM
PULLED	PESADE	POTTLE	PIPING	PARRAL	PRELIM
PULPED	PESTLE	POUNCE	PLYING	PARREL	PURISM
PULSED	PETITE	PRAGUE	POKING	PASCAL	PUTNAM
PUMPED	PETRIE	PRAISE	POLING	PASTEL	******
PUNNED	PEYOTE	PRANCE	PORING	PASTIL	**P----N**
PUNTED	PHOEBE	PREVUE	POSING	PATHOL	******
PUPPED	PHRASE	PRINCE	PROLEG	PATROL	PAPAIN
PUREED	PHYLAE	PROCNE	PRYING	PENCEL	PAPUAN
PURGED	PIAFFE	PSYCHE	PUKING	PENCIL	PARDON
PURLED	PICKLE	PUDDLE	PULING	PENIAL	PARIAN
PURRED	PIDDLE	PUGREE	PUTLOG	PENPAL	PARSON
PURSED	PIERCE	PUISNE	******	PETREL	PATHAN
PUSHED	PIERRE	PULQUE	**P----H**	PETROL	PATRON
PUTRID	PIFFLE	PUMICE	******	PHENOL	PATTEN
PUTTED	PIGGIE	PUPATE	PALISH	PHENYL	PATTON
******	PILATE	PURFLE	PARAPH	PIENAL	PAULIN
P----E	PILOSE	PURINE	PARIAH	PINEAL	PEAHEN
******	PILULE	PURPLE	PARISH	PINNAL	PEASEN
PADDLE	PIMPLE	PURSUE	PAUNCH	PISTIL	PECTEN
PAIUTE	PINENE	PUTTEE	PERISH	PISTOL	PECTIN
PALACE	PINITE	PUZZLE	PESACH	PLAGAL	PELION
PALATE	PINKIE	PYRENE	PHOSPH	PLURAL	PENMAN
PALEAE	PINNAE	PYRITE	PISGAH	PODSOL	PENMEN
PANICE	PINOLE	PYRONE	PLANCH	PODZOL	PENNON
PANTIE	PINTLE	PYROPE	PLEACH	POMMEL	PEPSIN
PAPULE	PIPAGE	******	PLINTH	PONTIL	PERRON
PARADE	PIRATE	**P----F**	PLOUGH	PORTAL	PERSON
PARCAE	PLAGUE	******	POLISH	POSTAL	PHANON
PAROLE	PLAICE	PAYOFF	POPISH	POWELL	PHOTON
PARSEE	PLAQUE	PILAFF	POTASH	PRIMAL	PHYTIN
PARURE	PLATTE	PUTOFF	PREACH	PROPEL	PIDGIN

PIEMAN	POMELO	PEPPER	PROBER	PARVIS	PHASIS
PIEMEN	PONCHO	PESTER	PROPER	PASHAS	PHIALS
PIGEON	POTATO	PEWTER	PROSER	PASSES	PHILOS
PIGGIN	POUSTO	PICKER	PROVER	PASSUS	PHIPPS
PIGPEN	PRESTO	PICTOR	PRUNER	PASTAS	PHOCIS
PINION	PROCTO	PIECER	PUCKER	PASTES	PHONES
PIPKIN	PRONTO	PIETER	PUFFER	PATENS	PHOTOS
PIPPIN	PSEUDO	PILFER	PULLER	PATERS	PIANOS
PISTON	PSYCHO	PILLAR	PULPER	PATHOS	PICOTS
PITMAN	PUEBLO	PINDAR	PULSAR	PATIOS	PICULS
PITMEN	******	PINIER	PUMPER	PATOIS	PIECES
PLATAN	**P----P**	PINNER	PUNIER	PATSYS	PIERUS
PLATEN	******	PINTER	PUNNER	PAULAS	PIGNUS
PLUGIN	PEGTOP	PIPIER	PUNTER	PAULUS	PIKERS
POISON	PENTUP	PLACER	PURGER	PAUSES	PILAFS
POLLEN	PHILIP	PLANAR	PURLER	PAVANS	PILEUS
POMPON	PICKUP	PLANER	PURSER	PAVERS	PILOTS
PONTON	PILEUP	PLATER	PUSHER	PAWERS	PILOUS
POPGUN	PUSHUP	PLAYER	PUTTER	PAYEES	PINDUS
POPLIN	******	PLEXOR	******	PAYERS	PINGOS
POTEEN	**P----R**	PLOVER	**P----S**	PEARLS	PINIES
POTION	******	PLOWER	******	PEASES	PINONS
POTMAN	PACKER	POKIER	PACERS	PECANS	PINTOS
PRISON	PALLOR	POLDER	PADDYS	PEDALS	PINUPS
PROTON	PALMAR	POLLER	PADRES	PEDROS	PIPERS
PROVEN	PALMER	PONDER	PAEANS	PEEVES	PIPETS
PTISAN	PALTER	POORER	PAEONS	PEGGYS	PIPITS
PUFFIN	PAMPER	POPLAR	PAGANS	PEKANS	PIQUES
PULLIN	PANDER	POPPER	PAINTS	PEKOES	PISCES
PURLIN	PANZER	PORKER	PALAIS	PELEUS	PISHES
PYTHON	PARKER	PORTER	PALLAS	PELIAS	PITIES
******	PARLOR	POSEUR	PALPUS	PELOPS	PITONS
P----O	PASSER	POSTER	PAMPAS	PELVES	PIVOTS
******	PASTER	POTHER	PANDAS	PELVIS	PIXIES
PALAEO	PASTOR	POTTER	PANELS	PENGOS	PIZZAS
PANCHO	PATTER	POURER	PANICS	PENNIS	PLACES
PASHTO	PAUKER	POUTER	PANSYS	PENNYS	PLACKS
PHLEBO	PAUPER	POWDER	PAPAWS	PEPLOS	PLAIDS
PHRENO	PAUSER	POWTER	PAPERS	PEPLUS	PLAINS
PHYLLO	PAVIOR	PRATER	PAPPUS	PERCYS	PLAITS
PHYSIO	PAWNER	PRAYER	PARENS	PERILS	PLANES
PIETRO	PECKER	PREFER	PARERS	PERRYS	PLANKS
PLAGIO	PEDLAR	PRETER	PAREUS	PETALS	PLANTS
PLASMO	PEEKER	PRETOR	PARGOS	PETERS	PLASIS
PLEURO	PEELER	PREWAR	PARIES	PEWEES	PLATES
PLUMBO	PEEPER	PREYER	PARKAS	PEWITS	PLAYAS
PLUVIO	PELTER	PRIMER	PARSES	PHAROS	PLAZAS
PNEUMO	PENNER	PRIZER	PARSIS	PHASES	PLEADS

PLEATS	PRIMUS	PELLET	******	PLUMMY	******
PLEBES	PRINKS	PENULT	P----X	PLUSHY	Q----E
PLEXUS	PRINTS	PEQUOT	******	POACHY	******
PLIERS	PRIORS	PERMIT	PAXWAX	POETRY	QUAERE
PLUCKS	PRISMS	PICKET	PICKAX	POINTY	QUARTE
PLUMBS	PRIZES	PIGLET	POLEAX	POLICY	QUATRE
PLUMES	PROBES	PIGNUT	POLLEX	POLITY	QUINCE
PLUMPS	PROEMS	PINXIT	POLLUX	POMPEY	******
PLUNKS	PRONGS	PIQUET	PREFIX	POORLY	Q----G
PLUSES	PROOFS	PLACET	PROLIX	POPERY	******
PLUTUS	PROSES	PLAINT	******	PORTLY	QUAHOG
PODOUS	PROVES	PLANET	P----Y	POSHLY	******
POGIES	PROWLS	PLIANT	******	POTBOY	Q----H
POILUS	PRUDES	PLIGHT	PACIFY	POUCHY	******
POINDS	PRUNES	POCKET	PAEONY	PREPAY	QUENCH
POINTS	PRYERS	PONENT	PAINTY	PRETTY	QUITCH
POISES	PSALMS	POPPET	PALELY	PRIMLY	******
POKERS	PSHAWS	POSSET	PALTRY	PRIORY	Q----I
POKIES	PTOSIS	POTENT	PANTRY	PRISSY	******
POLKAS	PULERS	PRIEST	PAPACY	PUDDLY	QUADRI
POLLYS	PULSES	PRIVET	PAPERY	PUGGRY	******
POLYPS	PUNKAS	PROFIT	PARITY	PULLEY	Q----M
PONIES	PUNTOS	PROJET	PARLAY	PUNCHY	******
PONTES	PUPILS	PROMPT	PARLEY	PUNILY	QUORUM
POPPYS	PUREES	PROSIT	PARODY	PURELY	******
POROUS	PURGES	PROUST	PARTLY	PURIFY	Q----N
POSERS	PURSES	PULLET	PASTRY	PURITY	******
POSIES	PUSHES	PULPIT	PATCHY	PURVEY	QUEZON
POSITS	PUSSES	PUNDIT	PAYDAY	PUSSEY	******
POSSES	PUTONS	PUPPET	PEACHY	PUSSLY	Q----O
POTTOS	PYLONS	PUREST	PEARLY	******	******
POULTS	PYOSIS	PURIST	PEAVEY	Q----A	QUARTO
POUNDS	PYRANS	PUTOUT	PEBBLY	******	******
POWERS	PYXIES	PUTPUT	PELTRY	QUAGGA	Q----R
POYOUS	******	******	PENURY	QUANTA	******
PRANKS	P----T	P----U	PERTLY	QUOTHA	QUAKER
PRATES	******	******	PHONEY	******	QUASAR
PRAWNS	PACKET	PUSHTU	PHOOEY	Q----C	QUAVER
PRAXIS	PALEST	******	PIGSTY	******	QUIVER
PRECIS	PALLET	P----V	PIMPLY	QUEBEC	QUOTER
PREENS	PAPIST	******	PINERY	QUINIC	******
PRESAS	PARENT	PAVLOV	PIRACY	******	Q----S
PRICES	PARGET	******	PITCHY	Q----D	******
PRICKS	PARROT	P----W	PLAGUY	******	QUACKS
PRIDES	PATENT	******	PLASHY	QUAKED	QUAFFS
PRIERS	PEANUT	PAWPAW	PLASTY	QUEUED	QUAILS
PRIMES	PEDANT	PILLOW	PLENTY	QUIRED	QUAKES
PRIMPS	PEEWIT	POWWOW	PLUCKY	QUOTED	QUALMS

QUANTS	RAZZIA	RAZEED	RINSED	RATINE	REVISE
QUARKS	REDOWA	RAZZED	RIOTED	RATITE	REVIVE
QUARTS	REGINA	REAMED	RIPPED	RATTLE	REVOKE
QUEANS	REMORA	REAPED	RISKED	RAVAGE	RIBOSE
QUEENS	REMUDA	REARED	RITARD	RAVINE	RICHIE
QUEERS	RESEDA	RECORD	ROAMED	REBATE	RIDDLE
QUELLS	RETINA	REDBUD	ROARED	REBORE	RIFFLE
QUERNS	RHUMBA	REEDED	ROBAND	REBUKE	RIMOSE
QUESTS	ROBBIA	REEFED	ROBBED	RECEDE	RIMPLE
QUEUES	ROMOLA	REEKED	ROCKED	RECIPE	RIPPLE
QUILLS	ROSTRA	REELED	ROGUED	RECITE	RISQUE
QUILTS	ROWENA	REEVED	ROILED	RECUSE	ROBBIE
QUINTS	ROXANA	REFUND	ROLAND	REDDLE	ROCKNE
QUIPUS	RUMINA	REGARD	ROLLED	REDEYE	RONNIE
QUIRES	RUSSIA	REINED	ROMPED	REDONE	ROOKIE
QUIRKS	RWANDA	RELAID	RONALD	REDUCE	ROOTLE
QUIRTS	******	RELIED	ROOFED	REFACE	ROSCOE
QUOINS	R----B	RELOAD	ROOKED	REFINE	ROTATE
QUOITS	******	REMAND	ROOMED	REFUGE	ROTCHE
QUOTAS	RESORB	REMIND	ROOTED	REFUSE	ROUBLE
QUOTES	******	RENDED	ROTTED	REFUTE	ROUCHE
******	R----C	RENTED	ROTUND	REGALE	ROXANE
Q----T	******	REPAID	ROUGED	REGGIE	ROYALE
******	RHIZIC	REPAND	ROUSED	REGIME	RRHAGE
QUAINT	RHODIC	RESEND	ROUTED	RELATE	RUBACE
******	ROMAIC	RESOLD	RUBBED	RELINE	RUBBLE
Q----W	RUBRIC	RESTED	RUCKED	RELIVE	RUDDLE
******	RUSTIC	RETARD	RUFFED	REMADE	RUFFLE
QUAPAW	******	RETOLD	RUGGED	REMAKE	RUGATE
******	R----D	RETROD	RUINED	REMISE	RUGOSE
Q----Y	******	RETTED	RUSHED	REMOTE	RUMBLE
******	RACKED	REVVED	RUSTED	REMOVE	RUMPLE
QUAGGY	RAFTED	REWARD	RUTTED	RENEGE	RUNDLE
QUALMY	RAGGED	REWIND	******	REPINE	RUSINE
QUARRY	RAIDED	REWORD	R----E	REPOSE	RUSTLE
QUEASY	RAILED	RHYMED	******	REPUTE	RUTILE
QUINCY	RAINED	RIBALD	RABBLE	RESALE	******
QUINSY	RAISED	RIBAND	RACEME	RESCUE	R----F
******	RAMMED	RIBBED	RACINE	RESIDE	******
Q----Z	RAMPED	RICKED	RADDLE	RESILE	REBUFF
******	RAMROD	RIDDED	RADOME	RESOLE	RELIEF
QUARTZ	RANCID	RIDGED	RAFFLE	RESUME	RIPOFF
******	RANGED	RIFLED	RAMBLE	RETAKE	RUNOFF
R----A	RANKED	RIFTED	RAMOSE	RETENE	******
******	RANTED	RIGGED	RANKLE	RETIRE	R----G
RADULA	RAPPED	RIMMED	RAPHAE	RETUSE	******
RAFFIA	RASPED	RINGED	RAPINE	REVERE	RACING
RAMONA	RATTED	RINKED	RAPPEE	REVILE	RAGBAG

RAGING	RADIAL	RAMSON	REDTOP	RIMMER	RANGES
RAGTAG	RANDAL	RANDAN	REVAMP	RINGER	RAOULS
RAKING	RAPPEL	RATION	RIPRAP	RINSER	RAPHIS
RAPING	RASCAL	RATLIN	ROLLUP	RIOTER	RAPIDS
RARING	REBILL	RATOON	******	RIPPER	RASHES
RATING	RECALL	RATTAN	**R----R**	RISKER	RATALS
RAVING	RECOIL	RATTEN	******	RITTER	RATELS
RAYING	RECTAL	REASON	RACIER	ROAMER	RATERS
RAZING	REFILL	REBORN	RACKER	ROARER	RATIOS
REDBUG	REFUEL	RECKON	RADNOR	ROBBER	RAVELS
REDDOG	REGNAL	REDDEN	RAFTER	ROCKER	RAVENS
RICING	RENTAL	REDFIN	RAIDER	ROLLER	RAVERS
RIDING	REPEAL	REGAIN	RAISER	ROMPER	RAYAHS
RILING	RESELL	REGION	RAMMER	ROOFER	RAYONS
RIMING	RETAIL	REJOIN	RANCOR	ROOMER	RAZEES
RISING	RETELL	REMAIN	RANGER	ROOTER	RAZORS
RIVING	RETOOL	RENNIN	RANKER	ROPIER	RAZZES
ROBING	REVEAL	RENOWN	RANTER	ROSIER	REACTS
ROPING	RHINAL	REOPEN	RAPIER	ROSTER	REALES
ROSING	RICTAL	RESIGN	RAPPER	ROTTER	REALMS
ROVING	RITUAL	RETAIN	RAPTOR	ROUSER	REARMS
ROWING	ROMMEL	RETURN	RASHER	ROUTER	REBECS
RUEING	RONDEL	REUBEN	RASPER	RUBBER	REBELS
RULING	ROSEAL	RIBBON	RASTER	RUDDER	REBUTS
******	RUEFUL	RIDDEN	RATHER	RUGGER	RECAPS
R----H	RUNNEL	ROBSON	RATTER	RUINER	RECESS
******	******	RODMAN	READER	RUMMER	RECTOS
RADISH	**R----M**	RODMEN	REAMER	RUMOUR	RECTUS
RAKISH	******	ROTTEN	REAPER	RUNNER	RECURS
RAVISH	RACISM	RUNYON	REARER	RUSHER	REDANS
RAWISH	RADIUM	RUSKIN	RECTOR	******	REDOES
REHASH	RANDOM	******	REDDER	**R----S**	REEVES
RELISH	RANSOM	**R----O**	REEFER	******	REFERS
ROMISH	RECTUM	******	REEKER	RABBIS	REFITS
RUPIAH	REDEEM	RANCHO	REELER	RABIES	REGIUS
******	REDGUM	REBATO	REHEAR	RACERS	REICHS
R----I	REBOZO	RELIER	RACHIS	REIGNS
******	REFORM	REECHO	RENDER	RADARS	RELAYS
RHOMBI	RHYTHM	RIALTO	RENOIR	RADIOS	RELICS
******	******	RIGHTO	RENTER	RADIUS	RELIES
R----K	**R----N**	ROBALO	REPAIR	RAISES	REMANS
******	******	ROCOCO	RESTER	RAJABS	REMISS
REBECK	RABBIN	ROMULO	RHETOR	RAJAHS	REMITS
REMARK	RACOON	RUBATO	RHYMER	RAKERS	RENEES
RETOOK	RADIAN	RUBIGO	RICHER	RALPHS	RENEWS
******	RAGLAN	******	RIFLER	RAMIES	RENTES
R----L	RAGMAN	**R----P**	RIGGER	RAMOUS	REPASS
******	RAGMEN	******	RIGOUR	RANEES	REPAYS
RACHEL	RAISIN	RECOUP	REDCAP		
RACIAL					

REPELS	ROTORS	REFOOT	*****	SANDRA	SENLAC
RERUNS	ROUGES	REGENT	**R----X**	SATARA	SEPTIC
RESETS	ROUGHS	REGLET	*****	SCHEMA	SIALIC
RESINS	ROUNDS	REGRET	REFLEX	SCLERA	SLAVIC
REVELS	ROUSES	REHEAT	REFLUX	SCORIA	SOTHIC
REVERS	ROUSTS	REJECT	*****	SCOTIA	STATIC
REVETS	ROUTES	RELENT	**R----Y**	SCROTA	STELIC
REVUES	ROVERS	RELICT	*****	SCYLLA	STERIC
RHEIMS	ROWANS	RENNET	RACILY	SENECA	SUOMIC
RHESUS	ROWELS	REPAST	RAGDAY	SENORA	SYNDIC
RHINOS	ROWERS	REPEAT	RAMIFY	SERBIA	SYRIAC
RHODAS	ROYALS	REPENT	RANKLY	SERENA	*****
RHODES	RUBENS	REPORT	RAPTLY	SHASTA	**S----D**
RHUMBS	RUBIES	RESEAT	RAREFY	SHEILA	*****
RHYMES	RUBLES	RESECT	RARELY	SHERPA	SACKED
RIATAS	RUCHES	RESENT	RARITY	SIENNA	SACRED
RICERS	RUCKUS	RESIST	RASHLY	SIERRA	SAGGED
RICHES	RUFOUS	RESORT	RATIFY	SIESTA	SAILED
RICKYS	RUGOUS	RESULT	REALLY	SILICA	SALPID
RICTUS	RULERS	RETORT	REALTY	SILVIA	SALTED
RIDERS	RUMBAS	REVERT	REDBAY	SISERA	SALVED
RIDGES	RUMORS	REVEST	REMEDY	SOMATA	SANDED
RIFLES	RUMPUS	REVOLT	REPLAY	SONATA	SAPPED
RIGHTS	RUNINS	RIDENT	RHEUMY	SOPHIA	SASHED
RIGORS	RUNONS	RILLET	RICHLY	SPARTA	SASSED
RIMERS	RUPEES	RIPEST	RICKEY	SPIREA	SAUCED
RIMOUS	RUSHES	RIPOST	RIPELY	SQUAMA	SCALED
RINSES	*****	ROBERT	RIPLEY	STADIA	SCARED
RIPENS	**R----T**	ROBUST	RIPPLY	STANZA	SCORED
RISERS	*****	ROCHET	RODNEY	STELLA	SCREED
RIVALS	RABBET	ROCKET	ROMANY	STERNA	SCRIED
RIVERS	RABBIT	RODENT	ROMNEY	STIGMA	SEALED
RIVETS	RACIST	ROQUET	ROPILY	STRATA	SEAMED
RIYALS	RACKET	ROTGUT	ROSARY	STROMA	SEARED
ROALDS	RAGOUT	RUDEST	ROSILY	STRUMA	SEATED
ROASTS	RAJPUT	RUNLET	ROSINY	SULPHA	SECOND
ROBINS	RAMJET	RUNOUT	ROTARY	SYLVIA	SECUND
ROBLES	RAPIST	RUPERT	*****	SYNURA	SEEDED
ROBOTS	RAREST	RUSSET	**S----B**	*****	SEEMED
RODDYS	RAWEST	*****	*****	SCARAB	SEEPED
RODEOS	RECANT	**R----U**	RUDELY	SERDAB	SEINED
ROGERS	RECAST	*****	RUNWAY	SUBDEB	SEISED
ROGUES	RECENT	RESEAU		SUBURB	SEIZED
ROLPHS	RECEPT	RYUKYU	**S----A**	SUPERB	*****
ROMANS	REDACT	*****	*****	*****	SENSED
RONDOS	REDHOT	**R----W**	SABINA	**S----C**	SERVED
ROOSTS	REEDIT	*****	SAHARA	*****	SEWARD
ROSINS	REFLET	REAVOW	SALIVA	SAITIC	SHADED
		REVIEW	SALVIA	SCENIC	SHALED
		RIPSAW	SAMARA		

SHAMED	SOAPED	STROUD	SEICHE	SOLUTE	STRODE
SHAPED	SOARED	STUPID	SELENE	SOMBRE	STROKE
SHARED	SOBBED	STYLED	SEMELE	SOMITE	STROVE
SHAVED	SOCKED	SUCKED	SEMEME	SOOTHE	STYMIE
SHEILD	SOCRED	SUITED	SEMITE	SOPHIE	SUABLE
SHEWED	SODDED	SULKED	SEMPRE	SORTIE	SUBDUE
SHIELD	SOILED	SUMMED	SENATE	SOURCE	SUBTLE
SHINED	SOLAND	SUNGOD	SENILE	SOZINE	SUCKLE
SHOOED	SOLOED	SUNNED	SERAPE	SPACAE	SUNDAE
SHORED	SOLVED	SUPPED	SERENE	SPARGE	SUPINE
SHOULD	SOOTED	SURFED	SERINE	SPARSE	SUPPLE
SHOVED	SOPPED	SURGED	SESAME	SPATHE	SUTTEE
SHOWED	SORDID	SUSSED	SETOSE	SPECIE	SUTURE
SHREWD	SORTED	SWAGED	SETTEE	SPHENE	SVELTE
SHROUD	SOULED	SWAYED	SETTLE	SPHERE	SWANEE
SICKED	SOUPED	SWIPED	SEVERE	SPLAKE	SWATHE
SIDLED	SOURED	******	SEWAGE	SPLICE	SWERVE
SIEGED	SOUSED	**S----E**	SHEAVE	SPLINE	SWINGE
SIEVED	SPACED	******	SHELVE	SPONGE	SWIPLE
SIFTED	SPADED	SABINE	SHIITE	SPOUSE	SYLVAE
SIGHED	SPARED	SADDLE	SHOPPE	SPRITE	******
SIGNED	SPAYED	SALINE	SHRIKE	SPRUCE	**S----F**
SIGRID	SPEWED	SALOME	SHRINE	SPURGE	******
SILOED	SPICED	SALUTE	SHRIVE	SQUARE	SCLAFF
SILTED	SPIKED	SAMITE	SHROVE	SQUIRE	SCRUFF
SINBAD	SPILED	SAMPLE	SICKLE	STABLE	SETOFF
SINGED	SPIRED	SARAPE	SIECLE	STACIE	SHERIF
SINNED	SPITED	SARTRE	SILAGE	STACTE	SHROFF
SIPPED	SPOKED	SATIRE	SILVAE	STANCE	******
SKATED	SPORED	SAVAGE	SIMILE	STAPLE	**S----G**
SKEWED	SPREAD	SAVATE	SIMONE	STARVE	******
SKIVED	SPUMED	SCARCE	SIMPLE	STATUE	SARONG
SLAKED	STAGED	SCATHE	SINGLE	STEEVE	SATANG
SLATED	STAKED	SCHEME	SIZZLE	STELAE	SATING
SLAVED	STALED	SCONCE	SKOPJE	STEPPE	SAVING
SLEWED	STARED	SCOUSE	SLEAVE	STEVIE	SAWING
SLICED	STATED	SCRAPE	SLEDGE	STIFLE	SAYING
SLIMED	STAVED	SCRIBE	SLEEVE	STODGE	SEADOG
SLOPED	STAYED	SCRIVE	SLUDGE	STOOGE	SEEING
SLOWED	STEWED	SCYTHE	SLUICE	STRAFE	SEWING
SMILED	STOKED	SEABEE	SMUDGE	STRAKE	SEXING
SMOKED	STOLED	SEANCE	SNATHE	STRIAE	SHYING
SNAKED	STOLID	SECEDE	SNEEZE	STRIDE	SIDING
SNARED	STONED	SECURE	SNOOZE	STRIFE	SIRING
SNIPED	STOPED	SEDATE	SOCAGE	STRIKE	SITING
SNORED	STORED	SEDILE	SOIGNE	STRIPE	SIZING
SNOWED	STOWED	SEDUCE	SOIREE	STRIVE	SKIING
SOAKED	STRAND	SEETHE	SOLACE	STROBE	SKYING

SLUING	STRATH	******	SADISM	SEREIN	STRAIN
SOLING	SUNNAH	S----L	SALAAM	SERMON	STREWN
SOWING	SWARTH	******	SCHISM	SEVERN	SUBORN
SPRANG	SWATCH	SACRAL	SCREAM	SEXTAN	SUDDEN
SPRING	SWITCH	SAMIEL	SCUTUM	SEXTON	SULLEN
SPRUNG	******	SAMUEL	SELDOM	SHAKEN	SULTAN
SPYING	S----I	SANDAL	SEPTUM	SHAMAN	SUMMON
STALAG	******	SANTOL	SEXISM	SHAPEN	SUNKEN
STENOG	SAFARI	SAUREL	SHIISM	SHARON	SUNTAN
STRING	SALAMI	SCHOOL	SIKKIM	SHAVEN	SUTTON
STRONG	SALUKI	SCHORL	SIMOOM	SHOGUN	SWEDEN
STRUNG	SANDHI	SCRAWL	SLALOM	SHOOIN	SYLVAN
STYING	SANGUI	SCROLL	SODIUM	SHORAN	SYPHON
SUNDOG	SANSEI	SECKEL	SPUTUM	SHUTIN	SYRIAN
******	SCAMPI	SENDAL	SQUIRM	SICKEN	******
S----H	SCYPHI	SEPTAL	STREAM	SILKEN	S----O
******	SESQUI	SEQUEL	SUFISM	SILVAN	******
SALISH	SILENI	SERIAL	SYSTEM	SIMIAN	SAPPHO
SCORCH	SMALTI	SERVAL	******	SIMLIN	SCHIZO
SCOTCH	SOLIDI	SEWALL	S----N	SINEON	SCIPIO
SCUTCH	SOMALI	SEWELL	******	SIOUAN	SCLERO
SEARCH	SOUARI	SEXUAL	SABEAN	SIPHON	SCYPHO
SERAPH	STELLI	SHEKEL	SADDEN	SISKIN	SEISMO
SHEATH	STRATI	SHOVEL	SAIGON	SKYMAN	SELENO
SHEIKH	******	SHRILL	SAIPAN	SKYMEN	SHACKO
SHILOH	S----J	SIGNAL	SALMON	SLIPON	SHINTO
SIWASH	******	SIMNEL	SALOON	SLOGAN	SIDERO
SKETCH	SWARAJ	SINFUL	SAMIAN	SLOVEN	SILICO
SLEIGH	******	SNIVEL	SAMOAN	SOCMAN	SMALTO
SLEUTH	S----K	SOCIAL	SAMPAN	SOCMEN	SOLANO
SLOUCH	******	SORREL	SAMSON	SODDEN	SOMATO
SLOUGH	SANJAK	SPINAL	SAPIEN	SOFTEN	SORGHO
SMIRCH	SCHICK	SPINEL	SARGON	SOLEMN	SPERMO
SMOOCH	SCREAK	SPIRAL	SATEEN	SOLION	SPHENO
SMOOTH	SELJUK	SPITAL	SATURN	SPAVIN	SPLENO
SMUTCH	SHRANK	SPRAWL	SCREEN	SPLEEN	STAURO
SNATCH	SHRIEK	SQUALL	SEAMAN	SPOKEN	STEREO
SNITCH	SHRINK	SQUEAL	SEAMEN	SPRAIN	STERNO
SPEECH	SHRUNK	SQUILL	SEAPEN	STALIN	STETHO
SPILTH	SHTICK	STATAL	SEARIN	STAMEN	STHENO
SPLASH	SLOVAK	STEROL	SEASON	STAMIN	STUCCO
SQUASH	SQUAWK	STIPEL	SEAWAN	STATEN	STUDIO
SQUISH	SQUEAK	STROLL	SECERN	STEFAN	SUBITO
STAITH	STREAK	SWIVEL	SEISIN	STEPAN	SULPHO
STANCH	STRICK	SYMBOL	SEIZIN	STEPIN	******
STARCH	STRUCK	******	SELSYN	STEVEN	S----P
STENCH	SUSLIK	S----M	SELWYN	STOLEN	******
STITCH		******	SEQUIN	STOLON	SALOOP
		SACHEM			SANNUP
		SACRUM			

SATRAP	SEINER	SLIVER	SUMMER	SAVINS	SEDANS
SCRIMP	SEISOR	SLOPER	SUMNER	SAVORS	SEDERS
SCROOP	SEIZER	SLOWER	SUNDER	SAWERS	SEDGES
SHRIMP	SEIZOR	SMILER	SUPPER	SAXONS	SEDUMS
SKYCAP	SELLER	SMITER	SURFER	SAYERS	SEINES
SLAPUP	SENDER	SMOKER	SURGER	SCALDS	SEISMS
SLIPUP	SENIOR	SNARER	SUTLER	SCALES	SEIZES
STEPUP	SENSOR	SNIPER	SYPHER	SCALPS	SELVES
******	SERVER	SNORER	******	SCAMPS	SENNAS
S----R	SETTER	SOAKER	**S----S**	SCAPES	SENSES
******	SEXIER	SOARER	******	SCARES	SEPALS
SACKER	SHAKER	SOCCER	SABERS	SCARFS	SEPIAS
SADDER	SHAPER	SOEVER	SABINS	SCARPS	SEPOYS
SAGGAR	SHARER	SOFTER	SABLES	SCAUPS	SEPSIS
SAGGER	SHAVER	SOLDER	SABOTS	SCENDS	SERACS
SAGIER	SHEWER	SOLVER	SABRAS	SCENES	SERAIS
SAILER	SHIKAR	SOMBER	SADHUS	SCENTS	SERIES
SAILOR	SHINER	SONDER	SADIES	SCHMOS	SERIFS
SALTER	SHIVER	SOONER	SAHEBS	SCHUSS	SERINS
SALVER	SHOFAR	SORTER	SAHIBS	SCHWAS	SEROUS
SALVOR	SHOVER	SOURER	SAIGAS	SCIONS	SEROWS
SAMBUR	SHOWER	SPACER	SAINTS	SCOFFS	SERUMS
SANDER	SICKER	SPADER	SAJOUS	SCOLDS	SERVES
SANGAR	SIDDUR	SPARER	SAKERS	SCONES	SERVOS
SANGER	SIDLER	SPICER	SALADS	SCOOPS	SETONS
SANSAR	SIFTER	SPIDER	SALLYS	SCOOTS	SETOUS
SAPHAR	SIGNER	SPRIER	SALMIS	SCOPES	SETTOS
SAPPER	SIGNOR	SPRYER	SALONS	SCOPUS	SETUPS
SARSAR	SILVER	STAGER	SALPAS	SCORES	SEVENS
SARTOR	SIMMER	STALER	SALVES	SCORNS	SEVERS
SAUCER	SIMPER	STARER	SALVOS	SCOTTS	SEWERS
SAUGER	SINGER	STATER	SAMBAS	SCOURS	SHACKS
SAVIOR	SINKER	STATOR	SAMBOS	SCOUTS	SHADES
SAVOUR	SINNER	STAYER	SAMMYS	SCOWLS	SHAFTS
SAWYER	SINTER	STELAR	SANDYS	SCRAGS	SHAKES
SCALAR	SIPPER	STIVER	SANIES	SCRAMS	SHAKOS
SCALER	SIRDAR	STOKER	SARAHS	SCRAPS	SHALES
SCARER	SISTER	STONER	SASHES	SCREWS	SHAMES
SCORER	SITTER	STOVER	SASINS	SCRIPS	SHAMUS
SCOTER	SIZIER	STUPOR	SASSES	SCRODS	SHANKS
SEALER	SKATER	STYLAR	SATINS	SCRUBS	SHAPES
SEAMER	SKEWER	STYLER	SATYRS	SCRUMS	SHARDS
SECPAR	SKIVER	SUBTER	SAUCES	SCUBAS	SHARES
SECTOR	SLATER	SUCCOR	SAULTS	SCUFFS	SHARKS
SEEDER	SLAVER	SUCKER	SAUNAS	SCULLS	SHARPS
SEEKER	SLAYER	SUFFER	SAURUS	SCUTES	SHAVES
SEEMER	SLICER	SUITOR	SAUTES	SEAMUS	SHAWLS
SEGGAR	SLIDER	SULFUR	SAVERS	SEBATS	SHAWMS

SHEARS	SIRIUS	SMELTS	SPACES	SPUMES	STIPES
SHEENS	SIRUPS	SMILES	SPADES	SPURNS	STIRKS
SHEEPS	SITARS	SMIRKS	SPAHIS	SPURTS	STIRPS
SHEERS	SITINS	SMITES	SPAITS	SQUABS	STOATS
SHEETS	SIXTES	SMITHS	SPALLS	SQUADS	STOCKS
SHEIKS	SIXTHS	SMOCKS	SPANKS	SQUATS	STOICS
SHELLS	SIZARS	SMOKES	SPARES	SQUAWS	STOKES
SHERDS	SKALDS	SMOLTS	SPARKS	SQUIBS	STOLES
SHIFTS	SKATES	SNACKS	SPASMS	SQUIDS	STOMPS
SHILLS	SKEANS	SNAFUS	SPATES	STACKS	STONES
SHINES	SKEINS	SNAILS	SPAWNS	STACYS	STOOKS
SHIRES	SKIERS	SNAKES	SPEAKS	STAFFS	STOOLS
SHIRKS	SKIFFS	SNARES	SPEARS	STAGES	STOOPS
SHIRRS	SKILLS	SNARLS	SPECKS	STAINS	STOPES
SHIRTS	SKIMOS	SNATHS	SPEEDS	STAIRS	STORES
SHIVES	SKIMPS	SNEAKS	SPEISS	STAKES	STORKS
SHOALS	SKINKS	SNEERS	SPELLS	STALES	STORMS
SHOATS	SKIRRS	SNELLS	SPENDS	STALKS	STOUPS
SHOCKS	SKIRTS	SNICKS	SPICES	STALLS	STOUTS
SHOERS	SKIVES	SNIFFS	SPIELS	STAMPS	STOVES
SHOJIS	SKULKS	SNIPES	SPIERS	STANDS	STRAPS
SHOOTS	SKULLS	SNOODS	SPIKES	STAPES	STRASS
SHORES	SKUNKS	SNOOKS	SPILES	STARES	STRAWS
SHORLS	SLACKS	SNOOPS	SPILLS	STARTS	STRAYS
SHORTS	SLAKES	SNOOTS	SPINES	STASES	STRESS
SHOTES	SLANTS	SNORES	SPIRES	STASIS	STREWS
SHOUTS	SLATES	SNORTS	SPIRTS	STATES	STRIPS
SHOVES	SLAVES	SNOUTS	SPITES	STATUS	STROPS
SHREDS	SLEEKS	SNUFFS	SPLATS	STAVES	STRUMS
SHREWS	SLEEPS	SOBERS	SPLAYS	STEAKS	STRUTS
SHRUBS	SLEETS	SOCLES	SPLITS	STEALS	STUBBS
SHRUGS	SLICES	SOFTAS	SPOILS	STEAMS	STUFFS
SHUCKS	SLICKS	SOLANS	SPOKES	STEEDS	STULLS
SHUNTS	SLIDES	SOLIDS	SPOOFS	STEELS	STUMPS
SIBYLS	SLIMES	SOLVES	SPOOKS	STEEPS	STUNTS
SIDLES	SLINGS	SONARS	SPOOLS	STEERS	STUPAS
SIEGES	SLINKS	SONIAS	SPOONS	STEINS	STUPES
SIEURS	SLOOPS	SONYAS	SPOORS	STELES	STYLES
SIEVES	SLOPES	SORELS	SPORES	STERES	STYLUS
SIGHTS	SLOTHS	SORGOS	SPORTS	STERNS	SUBAHS
SIGILS	SLUMPS	SOTHIS	SPOUTS	STEVES	SUCRES
SIGMAS	SLURPS	SOTOLS	SPRAGS	STICKS	SUEDES
SILVAS	SMACKS	SOUGHS	SPRATS	STILES	SUGARS
SIMARS	SMALLS	SOUNDS	SPRAYS	STILLS	SUITES
SIMONS	SMARTS	SOUSES	SPREES	STILTS	SULCUS
SINEWS	SMAZES	SOWARS	SPRIGS	STINGS	SUMACS
SINGES	SMEARS	SOWERS	SPRITS	STINKS	SUNUPS
SIRENS	SMELLS	SOZINS	SPRUES	STINTS	SUPERS

SURAHS	SCRIPT	STRIPT	SANITY	SKIMPY	SPERRY
SURGES	SCULPT	STUART	SASHAY	SKINNY	SPHERY
SUSANS	SECANT	STYLET	SATINY	SKIVVY	SPIFFY
SUSIES	SECRET	SUBLET	SATORY	SKYWAY	SPINNY
SUTRAS	SEJANT	SUBMIT	SAVORY	SLAGGY	SPONGY
SWAGES	SELECT	SUMMIT	SAWFLY	SLANGY	SPOOKY
SWAILS	SENNET	SUNHAT	SAWNEY	SLEAZY	SPOONY
SWAINS	SENNIT	SUNLIT	SAXONY	SLEEKY	SPORTY
SWALES	SEPTET	SUNSET	SCABBY	SLEEPY	SPOTTY
SWAMIS	SESTET	SUREST	SCANTY	SLEETY	SPRYLY
SWAMPS	SETOUT	SWIVET	SCATTY	SLIMLY	SPUNKY
SWARDS	SEURAT	SYNDET	SCILLY	SLIMSY	SPURRY
SWARMS	SEXIST	******	SCREWY	SLINKY	STABLY
SWATHS	SEXPOT	S----U	SCUMMY	SLOPPY	STAGEY
SWEARS	SEXTET	******	SCURFY	SLOSHY	STAGGY
SWEATS	SHEBAT	SAMSHU	SCURRY	SLOWLY	STALKY
SWEDES	SHIEST	******	SCURVY	SLUDGY	STARRY
SWEEPS	SHRIFT	S----W	SEAWAY	SLUMMY	STEADY
SWEETS	SHYEST	******	SEEMLY	SLURRY	STEAMY
SWELLS	SIGNET	SALLOW	SENARY	SLUSHY	STEELY
SWIFTS	SILENT	SEACOW	SENTRY	SMARMY	STICKY
SWILLS	SIPPET	SEESAW	SEXILY	SMEARY	STILLY
SWINGS	SLIEST	SHADOW	SHABBY	SMELLY	STINGY
SWIPES	SLIGHT	SORROW	SHAGGY	SMITHY	STITHY
SWIRLS	SLYEST	SUNBOW	SHAMMY	SMUDGY	STOCKY
SWOONS	SNOCAT	SUNDEW	SHANDY	SMUGLY	STODGY
SWOOPS	SOCKET	******	SHANTY	SMUTTY	STOGEY
SWORDS	SOFFIT	S----X	SHEENY	SNAGGY	STOREY
SYBILS	SOLENT	******	SHELBY	SNAPPY	STORMY
SYCEES	SONANT	SCOLEX	SHELLY	SNARLY	STRAWY
SYLPHS	SONNET	SMILAX	SHELTY	SNAZZY	STRIPY
SYLVAS	SORBET	SPADIX	SHERRY	SNEAKY	STUBBY
SYNODS	SOREST	SPHINX	SHIFTY	SNEEZY	STUFFY
SYRUPS	SOUGHT	STORAX	SHIMMY	SNIFFY	STUMPY
******	SOVIET	SUFFIX	SHINDY	SNIPPY	STURDY
S----T	SPIGOT	SURTAX	SHINNY	SNOBBY	SUBTLY
******	SPINET	SUSSEX	SHIRTY	SNOOPY	SUBWAY
SABBAT	SPIRIT	SYNTAX	SHOALY	SNOOTY	SUDARY
SACHET	SPLINT	SYRINX	SHODDY	SNOTTY	SUGARY
SADIST	SPOILT	******	SICILY	SNUFFY	SULTRY
SAFEST	SPRINT	S----Y	SICKLY	SNUGLY	SUNDAY
SAGEST	SPROUT	******	SIDNEY	SODOMY	SUNDRY
SALLET	SQUINT	SAFELY	SIMONY	SOFTLY	SUPPLY
SAMLET	SQUIRT	SAFETY	SIMPLY	SOLELY	SURELY
SANEST	STOMAT	SAGELY	SINEWY	SORELY	SURETY
SAVANT	STRAIT	SALARY	SINGLY	SOURLY	SURREY
SCHIST	STREET	SALIFY	SIRUPY	SPARRY	SURVEY
SCHUIT	STRICT	SANELY	SKERRY	SPEEDY	SWAMPY

SWANKY	******	TINTED	TALKIE	TOUPEE	TIRING
SWARTY	**T----D**	TIPPED	TAMALE	TOUSLE	TOEING
SWEATY	******	TITHED	TANGLE	TOWAGE	TONING
SWEENY	TABARD	TITLED	TATTLE	TRACHE	TOPING
SWEEPY	TABBED	TOGAED	TAXEME	TRANCE	TOTING
SWIRLY	TABLED	TOGGED	TAXITE	TREBLE	TOWING
SYDNEY	TACKED	TOILED	TEETHE	TRIFLE	TOYING
SYLPHY	TAGGED	TOLLED	TEMPLE	TRIODE	TRUING
SYRUPY	TAILED	TOMBED	TENACE	TRIOSE	TRYING
SYZYGY	TALCED	TOMCOD	TENURE	TRIPLE	TUBING
******	TALKED	TONGED	TERETE	TRISTE	TUNING
T----A	TALMUD	TOOLED	TESSIE	TRIUNE	TYPING
******	TAMPED	TOOTED	TESTAE	TRIXIE	******
TACOMA	TANGED	TOPPED	TEVERE	TROCHE	**T----H**
TAENIA	TANKED	TOROID	THEBAE	TROUPE	******
TARSIA	TANNED	TORPID	THECAE	TRUDGE	TERAPH
TELEGA	TAPPED	TORRID	THENCE	TSETSE	THATCH
TERBIA	TARRED	TOSSED	THIEVE	TUBATE	THOUGH
TERESA	TARTED	TOTTED	THISBE	TUBULE	THRASH
THALIA	TASKED	TOURED	THORPE	TUILLE	THRESH
THELMA	TASTED	TOUTED	THRICE	TUMBLE	THRUSH
THORIA	TATTED	TOWARD	THRIVE	TURTLE	TOBIAH
THULIA	TAXIED	TRACED	THRONE	TUSSLE	TOYISH
TIRANA	TEAMED	TRADED	THROVE	TUYERE	TRENCH
TOPEKA	TEARED	TRICED	THYRSE	TWELVE	TROUGH
TRAUMA	TEASED	TRIFID	TIBIAE	TWINGE	TUSSAH
TRIVIA	TEDDED	TRINED	TICKLE	TWINGE	TWITCH
TROIKA	TEEMED	TRIPOD	TIERCE	******	******
TUNDRA	TEHEED	TUBBED	TILLIE	**T----F**	**T----I**
TUNICA	TENDED	TUCKED	TIMBRE	******	******
******	TENSED	TUFTED	TINGLE	TARIFF	TAHITI
T----C	TENTED	TUGGED	TINKLE	TIPOFF	TAIPEI
******	TERMED	TUNNED	TIPPLE	******	TALARI
TACTIC	TESTED	TUPPED	TIPTOE	**T----G**	THYRSI
TAMBAC	TETRAD	TURBID	TIRADE	******	TISHRI
TANNIC	THAWED	TURFED	TISANE	TAKING	TRICHI
TANREC	THEWED	TURGID	TISSUE	TAMING	TULADI
TARMAC	THREAD	TURNED	TITTLE	TAPING	******
TENREC	THREED	TUSHED	TODDLE	TARING	**T----K**
THETIC	TICKED	TUSKED	TOFFEE	TAUTOG	******
THORAC	TIDIED	TUTTED	TOGGLE	TAWING	THWACK
THORIC	TIERED	TWINED	TONGUE	TAXING	******
THYMIC	TIFFED	TWOULD	TONITE	TEABAG	**T----L**
TOLTEC	TILLED	******	TOOTLE	TEEING	******
TOMBAC	TILTED	**T----E**	TOPPLE	THRONG	TARNAL
TRAGIC	TINEID	******	TOROSE	TIDING	TARSAL
TROPIC	TINGED	TACKLE	TORQUE	TILING	TASSEL
TURKIC	TINNED	TAILLE	TOUCHE	TIMING	TEASEL

TERCEL	TARTAN	THYREO	TEMPER	TUCKER	TENUIS
TERGAL	TARZAN	TOBAGO	TENDER	TUMOUR	TEPEES
TERNAL	TASMAN	TOLEDO	TENSER	TURNER	TEREUS
TETRYL	TAUTEN	TOMATO	TENSOR	TUSKER	TERRYS
TETZEL	TAVERN	TORERO	TENTER	TUSSAR	TESTES
THECAL	TEAURN	TRICHO	TERMER	TWINER	TESTIS
THENAL	TEFLON	TROPHO	TERMOR	TWOFER	TETHYS
THRALL	TEGMEN	TROPPO	TERROR	******	TETONS
THRILL	TELSON	TUPELO	TERSER	**T----S**	THADYS
THYMOL	TENDON	TUXEDO	TESTER	******	THALES
TIBIAL	TENPIN	TYPHLO	TETHER	TABLES	THAMES
TIMBAL	TESTON	******	TETTER	TABOOS	THANES
TINCAL	TEUTON	**T----P**	TEUCER	TABORS	THANKS
TINSEL	THORON	******	THALER	TAIGAS	THEBES
TOLUOL	THROWN	TAKEUP	THAYER	TAINOS	THEDAS
TOLUYL	TIEPIN	TEACUP	THENAR	TAINTS	THEFTS
TONSIL	TIFFIN	TIPTOP	TICKER	TAKERS	THEIRS
TRAVEL	TINCAN	TITTUP	TIDIER	TALERS	THEMES
TRIBAL	TITIAN	TOECAP	TILLER	TALONS	THEMIS
TRINAL	TOCSIN	TOSSUP	TILTER	TAMERS	THERMS
TROPAL	TONKIN	TUNEUP	TIMBER	TANGOS	THESES
TROTYL	TOUCAN	TURNIP	TINDER	TANKAS	THESIS
TROWEL	TOULON	TURNUP	TINIER	TAPERS	THETAS
TUNNEL	TREPAN	******	TINKER	TAPIRS	THETIS
TUSSAL	TRIGON	**T----R**	TINNER	TAROTS	THIGHS
TWIBIL	TRITON	******	TIPPER	TARSUS	THINGS
******	TROGON	TACKER	TITHER	TASTES	THIOLS
T----M	TROJAN	TAGGER	TITTER	TATARS	THIRDS
******	TRUMAN	TAILOR	TOILER	TAUNTS	THOLES
TALCUM	TUCHUN	TALKER	TOLLER	TAUPES	THOMAS
TAMTAM	TUCSON	TALLER	TONIER	TAURUS	THONGS
TANDEM	TURBAN	TAMPER	TOOLER	TAWERS	THORNS
TAOISM	TUREEN	TANKER	TOOTER	TAXERS	THREES
TEDIUM	TUSCAN	TANNER	TOPPER	TAZZAS	THRIPS
TERGUM	TYCOON	TAPPER	TORPOR	TBONES	THROBS
THEISM	TYMPAN	TARTAR	TOTHER	TEASES	THROES
TOMTOM	TYPHON	TARTER	TOTTER	TEDDYS	THROWS
TRUISM	TYRIAN	TASTER	TOURER	TEHEES	THRUMS
******	******	TATLER	TOUTER	TELLUS	THUJAS
T----N	**T----O**	TATTER	TRACER	TEMPOS	THUMBS
******	******	TAUTER	TRADER	TEMPTS	THUMPS
TAIWAN	TAPALO	TAYLOR	TREMOR	TENETS	THYMES
TAKEIN	TATTOO	TEASER	TREVOR	TENNIS	THYMUS
TALION	TECHNO	TEDDER	TRICAR	TENONS	TIARAS
TAMPAN	TENUTO	TEEMER	TRITER	TENORS	TIBIAS
TAMPON	TERATO	TEETER	TROCAR	TENSES	TICALS
TANNIN	TEREDO	TELFER	TROVER	TENTHS	TIDIES
TARPAN	THERMO	TELLER	TUBBER	TENUES	TIEINS

TIEUPS	TRACTS	TUSHES	TOMTIT	TETCHY	******
TIGERS	TRADES	TUSSIS	TOPHAT	THADDY	U----C
TIGHTS	TRAGUS	TUTORS	TRICOT	THEORY	******
TIGRIS	TRAILS	TUTTIS	TRIVET	THINLY	UNIFIC
TILDES	TRAINS	TWANGS	TRUANT	THIRTY	URALIC
TILERS	TRAITS	TWEAKS	TRUEST	THORNY	URANIC
TILLYS	TRAMPS	TWEEDS	TRYOUT	THUSLY	URETIC
TILTHS	TRAVES	TWEETS	TSHIRT	TIDILY	******
TIMERS	TRAWLS	TWERPS	TUCKET	TIMELY	U----D
TIMMYS	TREADS	TWILLS	TUFFET	TINGLY	******
TINCTS	TREATS	TWINES	TUMULT	TINILY	UNAPID
TINGES	TRENDS	TWIRLS	TURBIT	TINKLY	UNBEND
TITANS	TRIADS	TWIRPS	TURBOT	TOMBOY	UNBIND
TITHES	TRIALS	TWISTS	TURRET	TOOTHY	UNBRED
TITLES	TRIBES	TYPHUS	TWILIT	TOOTSY	UNCLAD
TOASTS	TRICES	******	TWOBIT	TOUCHY	UNCORD
TOBIAS	TRICKS	T----T	TYBALT	TOWERY	UNFOLD
TOBIES	TRIERS	******	TYPIST	TRACHY	UNGIRD
TODIES	TRILLS	TABLET	TYRANT	TRASHY	UNHAND
TOGUES	TRINES	TALENT	******	TREATY	UNIPED
TOILES	TRIPOS	TAMEST	T----U	TRENDY	UNITED
TOKENS	TRIXYS	TANIST	******	TRESSY	UNKIND
TOMANS	TROLLS	TAOIST	TELEDU	TRICKY	UNLAID
TOMMYS	TROOPS	TAPPET	TELUGU	TRIGLY	UNLEAD
TONERS	TROTHS	TARGET	******	TRILBY	UNLOAD
TONICS	TROUTS	TASSET	T----W	TRIMLY	UNREAD
TOPERS	TROVES	TAUGHT	******	TROPHY	UNSAID
TOPICS	TRUCES	TEAPOT	TALLOW	TRUSTY	UNSHOD
TOQUES	TRUCKS	TEASET	******	TUMEFY	UNSOLD
TORAHS	TRUDYS	TENANT	T----X	TURKEY	UNTIED
TORIES	TRUMPS	TERCET	******	TWANGY	UNTOLD
TORIIS	TRUNKS	TERRET	THORAX	TWEAKY	UNTROD
TOROUS	TRUSTS	THANAT	******	TWENTY	UNUSED
TORSKS	TRUTHS	THEIST	T----Y	TWIGGY	UNWIND
TORSOS	TRYSTS	THIRST	******	TWISTY	UPHELD
TOSHES	TSADES	THREAT	TACKEY	TWOPLY	UPHOLD
TOSSES	TUBERS	THRIFT	TAMELY	TWOWAY	UPLAND
TOTALS	TULIPS	THROAT	TANGLY	TYPIFY	UPWARD
TOTEMS	TULLES	THRUST	TARTLY	******	UROPOD
TOTERS	TUMORS	THWART	TATTLY	U----A	UTGARD
TOUGHS	TUNERS	TICKET	TAUTLY	******	******
TOWELS	TUNGUS	TIDBIT	TAWDRY	UGANDA	U----E
TOWERS	TUNICS	TINPOT	TEAPOY	ULTIMA	******
TOXINS	TUPIKS	TIPCAT	TEENSY	UNGULA	ULENCE
TOYERS	TUQUES	TIPPET	TELARY	URANIA	ULLAGE
TOYONS	TURCOS	TITBIT	TEPEFY	UREMIA	UMBRAE
TRACES	TURKIS	TOILET	TERMLY	URSULA	UMPIRE
TRACKS	TURVES	TOMCAT	TETANY	UTOPIA	UNABLE

UNCAGE	UPPISH	UNISON	UNBARS	UNROOT	******
UNCASE	UPRUSH	UNSEEN	UNCAPS	UNSEAT	**V----C**
UNDINE	UZZIAH	UNWORN	UNCLES	UNVEXT	******
UNDONE	******	UPTOWN	UNDIES	UNWEPT	VEDIAC
UNEASE	**U----I**	UPTURN	UNDOES	UPBEAT	VIATIC
UNIQUE	******	URCHIN	UNGUES	UPCAST	VITRIC
UNLACE	UBANGI	UTAHAN	UNGUIS	UPLIFT	******
UNLADE	******	******	UNHATS	UPMOST	**V----D**
UNLIKE	**U----K**	**U----O**	UNIONS	UPROOT	******
UNLIVE	******	******	UNITES	UPSHOT	VALUED
UNMADE	UNCOCK	ULTIMO	UNLAYS	URGENT	VALVED
UNMAKE	UNCORK	UNESCO	UNLESS	URTEXT	VAMPED
UNPILE	UNHOOK	******	UNMANS	UTMOST	VARIED
UNRIPE	UNHUSK	**U----P**	UNMEWS	******	VATTED
UNROBE	UNLOCK	******	UNPEGS	**U----W**	VEERED
UNSAFE	UNMASK	UNHASP	UNPINS	******	VEILED
UNSURE	UNPACK	UNSHIP	UNRIGS	UNDRAW	VEINED
UNTRUE	UNPICK	UNSTEP	UNRIPS	UNDREW	VENDED
UNWISE	UNTACK	UNSTOP	UNSAYS	******	VENTED
UNYOKE	******	UNWRAP	UNTIES	**U----X**	VERGED
UPDATE	**U----L**	UPKEEP	UPASES	******	VERSED
UPDIKE	******	******	UPBOWS	UNISEX	VESPID
UPHROE	UMBRAL	**U----R**	UPENDS	******	VESTED
UPRISE	UNCIAL	******	UPPERS	**U----Y**	VETOED
UPROSE	UNCOIL	UGLIER	UPSETS		VETTED
UPSIDE	UNCURL	ULSTER	URAEUS	UBIETY	VIALED
UPTAKE	UNFURL	UNBEAR	URANUS	UGLIFY	VIEWED
URBANE	UNGUAL	UNDOER	USAGES	UGLILY	VISAED
UREASE	UNREAL	UNFAIR	USHERS	UNDULY	VISARD
UREIDE	UNREEL	UNHAIR	USURPS	UNEASY	VISCID
URSINE	UNROLL	UNMOOR	UTERUS	UNHOLY	VISEED
USABLE	UNSEAL	UPROAR	UTTERS	UNRULY	VIZARD
USANCE	UNVEIL	URETER	UTURNS	UNTIDY	VOICED
UVULAE	UNWELL	USURER	UVULAS	UNWARY	VOIDED
******	UPHILL	UVULAR	******	UPPITY	VOLTED
U----F	URANYL	******	**U----T**	USABLY	******
******	URINAL	**U----S**	******	******	**V----E**
UNICEF	USEFUL	******	UMLAUT	**V----A**	******
******	******	UBOATS	UNBELT	******	VACATE
U----G	**U----M**	UDDERS	UNBENT	VACUNA	VADOSE
******	******	UKASES	UNBOLT	VAGINA	VALATE
UNPLUG	UNSEAM	ULCERS	UNDSET	VALUTA	VALISE
UNSUNG	******	ULEMAS	UNGIRT	VARUNA	VAMOSE
UPPING	**U----N**	UMBELS	UNHURT	VERONA	VELOCE
URGING	******	UMBERS	UNJUST	VESICA	VELURE
******	UNBORN	UMBLES	UNKNIT	VICUNA	VENDEE
U----H	UNEVEN	UMBRAS	UNMEET	VIENNA	VENDUE
******	UNHEWN	UMIAKS	UNREST	VIMINA	VENICE
UNLASH				VOMICA	
UNWISH					

VENIRE	VESTAL	VALOUR	VERSUS	VERVET	WAIFED
VENOSE	VIDUAL	VALUER	VESTAS	VILEST	WAILED
VENULE	VIRGIL	VALVAR	VETOES	VIOLET	WAITED
VESTEE	VISUAL	VAPOUR	VEXERS	VOLANT	WAIVED
VIABLE	VULVAL	VARIER	VEXILS	VOLOST	WALKED
VIRGIE	******	VASTER	VIANDS	******	WALLED
VIRILE	V----M	VEADAR	VICARS	V----U	WANNED
VIRTUE	******	VECTOR	VICKYS	******	WANTED
VISAGE	VACUUM	VEILER	VIGILS	VISHNU	WAPPED
VITTAE	VALLUM	VELOUR	VILLAS	******	WARDED
VIVACE	VELLUM	VENDER	VILLUS	V----X	WARMED
VOLUME	VERISM	VENDOR	VINCES	******	WARNED
VOLUTE	VICTIM	VENEER	VINNYS	VERNIX	WARPED
VOTIVE	******	VENTER	VINOUS	VERTEX	WARRED
VOYAGE	V----N	VERGER	VINYLS	VORTEX	WASHED
VULVAE	******	VESPER	VIOLAS	******	WASTED
******	VANMAN	VETOER	VIPERS	V----Y	WAULED
V----G	VANMEN	VIATOR	VIREOS	******	WAWLED
******	VERDIN	VICTOR	VIRGAS	VAGARY	WEANED
VEXING	VERDUN	VIEWER	VISCUS	VAINLY	WEAVED
VIKING	VEREIN	VIGOUR	VISITS	VALERY	WEBBED
VISING	VERMIN	VINIER	VISORS	VALLEY	WEDDED
VOLING	VERNON	VIZIER	VISTAS	VANITY	WEDGED
VOTING	VILLON	VOYEUR	VITALS	VASTLY	WEEDED
VOWING	VINSON	VULGAR	VIXENS	VENERY	WELDED
******	VIOLIN	VULVAR	VIZIRS	VERIFY	WELLED
V----H	VIRGIN	******	VIZORS	VERILY	WELTED
******	VISION	V----S	VOCALS	VERITY	WENDED
VANISH	VIVIAN	******	VODKAS	VESTRY	WETTED
******	VIVIEN	VALETS	VOGUES	VILELY	WHALED
V----I	VULCAN	VALGUS	VOGULS	VILIFY	WHILED
******	******	VALOIS	VOICES	VINERY	WHINED
VAPORI	V----O	VALUES	VOILES	VIVIFY	WHITED
VASARI	VAGINO	VALVES	VOLVAS	VOLERY	WHORED
VASHTI	VARICO	VAPORS	VOMERS	VOLLEY	WICKED
VASILI	VENTRO	VARIES	VOMITS	VOTARY	WIGGED
******	VESICO	VARVES	VOROUS	VYRNWY	WILLED
V----L	VIBRIO	VAULTS	VOTERS	******	WILTED
******	VIRAGO	VAUNTS	VOWELS	W----A	WINCED
VALVAL	VOMITO	VELDTS	VOWERS	******	WINDED
VANDAL	VOODOO	VENOMS	******	WOMERA	WINGED
VASSAL	******	VENOUS	V----T	******	WINKED
VATFUL	V----R	VENUES	******	W----D	WISHED
VENIAL	******	VERGES	VACANT	******	WISPED
VERBAL	VAGUER	VERNAS	VARLET	******	WITHED
VERGIL	VAINER	VERSES	VELVET	WADDED	WITTED
VERNAL	VALKYR	VERSOS	VERIST	WAFTED	WIZARD
VESSEL		VERSTS	VERSET	WAGGED	WOADED

WOLFED
WOMBED
WONTED
WOODED
WORDED
WORKED
WORMED
******
W----E
******
WABBLE
WADDLE
WAFFLE
WAGGLE
WAHINE
WALLIE
WAMBLE
WANDLE
WANGLE
WARBLE
WATAPE
WATTLE
WEDGIE
WEENIE
WHARVE
WHEEZE
WHENCE
WHERVE
WIDDIE
WIENIE
WIGGLE
WILLIE
WIMBLE
WIMPLE
WINKLE
WINNIE
WOBBLE
WRASSE
WRITHE
******
W----G
******
WADING
WAGING
WAKING
WALING
WANING
WAVING

WAXING
WIGWAG
WILING
WINING
WIPING
WIRING
WISING
WIVING
WOOING
WOWING
WRYING
******
W----H
******
WABASH
WALLAH
WARMTH
WEALTH
WHIDAH
WHOOSH
WHYDAH
WRAITH
WREATH
WRENCH
WRETCH
******
W----I
******
WAHABI
WAKIKI
WAPITI
WATUSI
******
W----L
******
WARHOL
WEASEL
WEEVIL
WILFUL
WITHAL
WOEFUL
******
W----M
******
WAMPUM
WHILOM
WIGWAM
WISDOM

******
W----N
******
WAGGON
WALKON
WALTON
WANION
WANTON
WARDEN
WARREN
WATSON
WEAKEN
WEAPON
WEDELN
WELKIN
WHITEN
WIGEON
WILSON
WILTON
WITHIN
WIVERN
WOODEN
WOOLEN
WORSEN
WYSTAN
WYVERN
******
W----P
******
WALKUP
WALLOP
WARMUP
WIKIUP
WINDUP
WRAPUP
******
W----R
******
WAFTER
WAGNER
WAILER
WAITER
WAIVER
WALKER
WALTER
WANDER
WANNER
WANTER

WARDER
WARIER
WARMER
WARNER
WARPER
WASHER
WASTER
WAVIER
WAXIER
WEAKER
WEANER
WEARER
WEAVER
WEEDER
WEEPER
WEEVER
WEIMAR
WELDER
WELTER
WESTER
WETHER
WHALER
WHINER
WHITER
WICKER
WIENER
WILBER
WILBUR
WILDER
WILIER
WILLER
WINCER
WINDER
WINIER
WINKER
WINNER
WINTER
WIRIER
WITHER
WOLVER
WONDER
WOOFER
WORKER
WORMER
WORSER
WOWSER
WRITER

******
W----S
******
WADERS
WADIES
WAFERS
WAGERS
WAGONS
WAHOOS
WAISTS
WAIVES
WAKENS
WALDOS
WALERS
WALLAS
WALLIS
WALLYS
WALRUS
WALVIS
WAMMUS
WAMOUS
WANDAS
WASHES
WASTES
WATAPS
WATERS
WAVERS
WAVEYS
WAVIES
WAYNES
WEALDS
WEAVES
WEBERS
WEDGES
WEIGHS
WENDYS
WHACKS
WHALES
WHANGS
WHARFS
WHEALS
WHEATS
WHEELS
WHELKS
WHELMS
WHELPS
WHIFFS
WHILES

WHINES
WHIRLS
WHISKS
WHITES
WHOOPS
WHORES
WHORLS
WHORTS
WICHES
WIDENS
WIDOWS
WIDTHS
WIELDS
WIGANS
WILLIS
WILLYS
WILMAS
WINCES
WINOES
WINZES
WIPERS
WIRERS
WISHES
WITHES
WIVERS
WIZENS
WOALDS
WOLVES
WOOERS
WORLDS
WORSTS
WOUNDS
WRACKS
WREAKS
WRECKS
WRESTS
WRINGS
WRISTS
WRITES
WRONGS
******
W----T
******
WADSET
WALLET
WALNUT
WAYOUT
WEIGHT

WERENT	WHISKY	******	******	YAHOOS	******
WHILST	WHITBY	**X----S**	**Y----G**	YAMENS	**Z----C**
WICKET	WHITEY	******	******	YAMUNS	******
WIDEST	WHOLLY	XEBECS	YAWING	YAPONS	ZINCIC
WILLET	WICOPY	XTSTUS	YOKING	YEARNS	ZODIAC
WISEST	WIDELY	XYLANS	YOWING	YEASTS	******
WITHIT	WIELDY	XYLEMS	******	YERBAS	**Z----D**
WOMBAT	WIFELY	XYLOLS	**Y----H**	YESSES	******
WRIEST	WIGGLY	XYSTOS	******	YIELDS	ZEROED
WRIGHT	WILDLY	******	YAHVEH	YODELS	ZESTED
WRYEST	WILILY	**X----U**	YAHWEH	YOGEES	ZINCED
******	WINCEY	******	******	YOGINS	ZINGED
W----W	WINERY	XANADU	**Y----I**	YOICKS	ZIPPED
******	WINTRY	******	******	YOKELS	ZOOMED
WALLOW	WIRILY	**Y----A**	YEHUDI	YOUTHS	******
WARSAW	WISELY	******	YEMENI	YUCCAS	**Z----E**
WILLOW	WITNEY	YAKIMA	******	YUPONS	******
WINDOW	WOBBLY	YORUBA	**Y----K**	******	ZAFFRE
WINNOW	WOLSEY	YTTRIA	******	**Y----T**	ZIZZLE
******	WOODSY	******	YASMAK	******	ZOMBIE
W----X	WOOLLY	**Y----C**	YORICK	YAOURT	ZONATE
******	WORTHY	******	******	YCLEPT	ZONULE
WESSEX	WRATHY	YTTRIC	**Y----N**	YOGURT	ZOUAVE
******	******	******	******	******	ZYGOTE
W----Y	**X----D**	**Y----D**	YAUPON	**Z---G**	******
******	******	******	YEOMAN		**Z---G**
WABBLY	XRAYED	YAKKED	YEOMEN	**Y----W**	ZAFTIG
WADDLY	XYLOID	YANKED	YESMAN	******	ZIGZAG
WAGGLY	******	YAPPED	YOUPON	YARROW	ZONING
WAMBLY	**X----E**	YARDED	******	YELLOW	******
WARILY	******	YAUPED	**Y---O**	******	**Z----H**
WARMLY	XYLENE	YAWLED	******	**Y----Y**	******
WATERY	XYLITE	YAWNED	YOOHOO	******	ZENITH
WAVILY	XYLOSE	YAWPED	******	YEARLY	ZIBETH
WAYLAY	******	YEANED	**Y----R**	YEASTY	ZILLAH
WEAKLY	**X----L**	YELLED	******	******	ZIZITH
WEEKLY	******	YELPED	YABBER	**Z----A**	ZURICH
WEENSY	XENIAL	YENNED	YAMMER	******	******
WEIRDY	******	YESSED	YAWNER	ZAMBIA	**Z----K**
WESLEY	**X----O**	YIPPED	YAWPER	ZANANA	******
WHAMMY	******	YOWLED	YELLER	ZAPATA	ZEBECK
WHEEZY	XANTHO	YUKKED	YELPER	ZARIBA	******
WHELKY	******	******	YESTER	ZENANA	**Z----L**
WHERRY	**X----R**	**Y---E**	YONDER	ZEUGMA	******
WHEYEY	******	******	YONKER	ZINNIA	ZOONAL
WHIMSY	XAVIER	YANKEE	YORKER	ZONULA	******
WHINNY	XYSTER	YIPPIE	**Y----S**	ZOYSIA	**Z----N**
WHIPPY		YUPPIE	******	ZSAZSA	******
		YVONNE	YACHTS	ZYGOMA	ZECHIN
			YAGERS		ZIRCON

******	******	KABIKI	BACONY	MACING	BADGES
Z----R	-AB---	KABOBS	CACAOS	MACKLE	BADMAN
******	******	KABUKI	CACHED	MACLES	BADMEN
ZAFFAR	BABBIE	LABELS	CACHES	MACRON	CADDIE
ZAFFER	BABBLE	LABIAL	CACHET	MACULA	CADDIS
ZAFFIR	BABIED	LABILE	CACHOU	MACULE	CADENT
ZANIER	BABIES	LABIUM	CACKLE	PACERS	CADETS
ZENGER	BABISM	LABORS	CACTUS	PACIFY	CADGED
ZEPHYR	BABIST	LABOUR	DACHAS	PACING	CADGER
ZIPPER	BABITE	LABRET	DACHAU	PACKED	CADGES
ZITHER	BABOON	LABRUM	DACOIT	PACKER	CADMUS
ZOSTER	BABOOS	MABELS	DACRON	PACKET	CADRES
ZUIDER	BABULS	NABBED	DACTYL	RACEME	DADDLE
ZUYDER	CABALA	NABOBS	FACADE	RACERS	DADOES
******	CABALS	RABBET	FACERS	RACHEL	FADEIN
Z----S	CABANA	RABBIN	FACETS	RACHIS	FADING
******	CABINS	RABBIS	FACIAL	RACIAL	GADDED
ZAMIAS	CABLED	RABBIT	FACIES	RACIER	GADDER
ZANIES	CABLES	RABBLE	FACILE	RACILY	GADFLY
ZAYINS	CABLET	RABIES	FACING	RACINE	GADGET
ZEBECS	CABMAN	SABBAT	FACTOR	RACING	GADOID
ZEBRAS	CABMEN	SABEAN	FACTUM	RACISM	HADING
ZEROES	CABOBS	SABERS	FACULA	RACIST	JADING
ZETHOS	DABBED	SABINA	HACKED	RACKED	JADISH
ZETHUS	DABBER	SABINE	HACKEE	RACKER	LADDER
ZIBETS	DABBLE	SABINS	HACKER	RACKET	LADDIE
ZIRONS	FABIAN	SABLES	HACKIE	RACOON	LADIES
ZLOTYS	FABLED	SABOTS	HACKLE	SACHEM	LADING
ZOMBIS	FABLER	SABRAS	JACANA	SACHET	LADINO
ZOOIDS	FABLES	TABARD	JACKAL	SACKED	LADLED
ZORILS	FABRIC	TABBED	JACKED	SACKER	LADLER
ZOUNDS	GABBED	TABLED	JACKET	SACRAL	LADLES
******	GABBER	TABLES	JACKIE	SACRED	LADOGA
Z----T	GABBLE	TABLET	JACKYS	SACRUM	MADAME
******	GABBRO	TABOOS	JACOBS	TACKED	MADAMS
ZEALOT	GABION	TABORS	LACHES	TACKER	MADCAP
******	GABLED	WABASH	LACIAL	TACKEY	MADDED
Z----Y	GABLES	WABBLE	LACIER	TACKLE	MADDEN
******	HABEAS	WABBLY	LACILY	TACOMA	MADDER
ZINCKY	HABILE	YABBER	LACING	TACTIC	MADEUP
ZONARY	HABITS	******	LACKED	VACANT	MADGES
******	JABBED	-AC---	LACKEY	VACATE	MADMAN
-AA---	JABBER	******	LACTAM	VACUNA	MADMEN
******	JABIRU	AACHEN	LACTIC	VACUUM	MADRAS
BAAING	JABOTS	BACHED	LACUNA	YACHTS	MADRID
BAALIM	KABAKA	BACHES	MACACO	******	MADURA
KAASES	KABALA	BACKED	MACAWS	-AD---	MADURO
LAAGER	KABAYA	BACKER	MACERS	******	NADINE
				BADGED	
				BADGER	

NADIRS	PAEANS	CAGILY	RAGING	YAHOOS	LAIRED
PADDED	PAEONS	CAGING	RAGLAN	YAHVEH	MAIDEN
PADDLE	PAEONY	DAGGER	RAGMAN	YAHWEH	MAIGRE
PADDYS	TAENIA	DAGGLE	RAGMEN	******	MAILED
PADRES	******	DAGMAR	RAGOUT	-AI---	MAILER
RADARS	-AF---	DAGOBA	RAGTAG	******	MAIMED
RADDLE	******	EAGLES	SAGELY	BAIKAL	MAIMER
RADIAL	BAFFED	EAGLET	SAGEST	BAILED	MAINLY
RADIAN	BAFFIN	FAGEND	SAGGAR	BAILEE	MAISIE
RADIOS	BAFFLE	FAGGED	SAGGED	BAILER	MAISON
RADISH	CAFTAN	FAGGOT	SAGGER	BAILEY	MAITRE
RADIUM	DAFTLY	FAGOTS	SAGIER	BAILIE	MAIZES
RADIUS	FAFNIR	GAGERS	TAGGED	BAILOR	NAIADS
RADNOR	GAFFED	GAGGED	TAGGER	BAIRNS	NAILED
RADOME	GAFFER	GAGGER	VAGARY	BAITED	PAINED
RADULA	GAFFES	GAGGLE	VAGINA	CAIMAN	PAINTS
SADDEN	HAFTED	GAGING	VAGINO	CAIQUE	PAINTY
SADDER	KAFFIR	HAGBUT	VAGUER	CAIRNS	PAIRED
SADDLE	KAFTAN	HAGDON	WAGERS	DAIMIO	PAIUTE
SADHUS	OAFISH	HAGGED	WAGGED	DAIMON	RAIDED
SADIES	RAFFIA	HAGGIS	WAGGLE	DAIMYO	RAIDER
SADISM	RAFFLE	HAGGLE	WAGGLY	DAINTY	RAILED
SADIST	RAFTED	JAGGED	WAGGON	DAISES	RAINED
VADOSE	RAFTER	JAGUAR	WAGING	DAISYS	RAISED
WADDED	SAFARI	LAGERS	WAGNER	FAILED	RAISER
WADDLE	SAFELY	LAGGED	WAGONS	FAILLE	RAISES
WADDLY	SAFEST	LAGGER	YAGERS	FAINTS	RAISIN
WADERS	SAFETY	LAGOON	******	FAIRED	SAIGAS
WADIES	WAFERS	LAGUNE	-AH---	FAIRER	SAIGON
WADING	WAFFLE	MAGGIE	******	FAIRLY	SAILED
WADSET	WAFTED	MAGGOT	BAHAIS	FAITHS	SAILER
******	WAFTER	MAGNET	BAHAMA	GAIETY	SAILOR
-AE---	ZAFFAR	MAGNOX	CAHIER	GAINED	SAINTS
******	ZAFFER	MAGNUM	CAHOOT	GAINER	SAIPAN
CAECUM	ZAFFIR	MAGOTS	DAHLIA	GAINLY	SAITIC
CAEOMA	ZAFFRE	MAGPIE	DAHOON	GAITED	TAIGAS
CAESAR	ZAFTIG	MAGUEY	LAHORE	GAITER	TAILED
DAEDAL	******	MAGYAR	MAHBUB	HAILED	TAILLE
DAEMON	-AG---	NAGANA	MAHLER	HAILER	TAILOR
FAECAL	******	NAGGED	MAHOUT	HAIRDO	TAINOS
FAECES	BAGASS	NAGGER	NAHUMS	HAIRED	TAINTS
FAERIE	BAGDAD	NAGOYA	SAHARA	JAILED	TAIPEI
FAEROE	BAGELS	PAGANS	SAHEBS	JAILER	TAIWAN
GAELIC	BAGGED	PAGING	SAHIBS	JAILOR	VAINER
HAEMAL	BAGMAN	PAGODA	TAHITI	JAINAS	VAINLY
JAEGER	BAGMEN	RAGBAG	WAHABI	JAIPUR	WAIFED
MAENAD	BAGNIO	RAGDAY	WAHINE	KAISER	WAILED
NAEVUS	CAGIER	RAGGED	WAHOOS	LAIRDS	WAILER

WAISTS	WAKIKI	CALMED	HALLOW	PALLET	TALKIE
WAITED	WAKING	CALMER	HALLUX	PALLID	TALLER
WAITER	YAKIMA	CALMLY	HALOED	PALLOR	TALLOW
WAIVED	YAKKED	CALORY	HALOES	PALMAR	TALMUD
WAIVER	******	CALPAC	HALOID	PALMED	TALONS
WAIVES	-AL---	CALVED	HALSEY	PALMER	VALATE
******	******	CALVES	HALTED	PALPED	VALERY
-AJ---	AALAND	CALVIN	HALTER	PALPUS	VALETS
******	AALIIS	CALXES	HALUTZ	PALTER	VALGUS
CAJOLE	BALAAM	DALETH	HALVED	PALTRY	VALISE
CAJUNS	BALATA	DALLAS	HALVES	RALPHS	VALKYR
MAJORS	BALBOA	DALLES	JALOPS	SALAAM	VALLEY
PAJAMA	BALDER	DALTON	JALOPY	SALADS	VALLUM
RAJABS	BALDLY	EALING	KALIAN	SALAMI	VALOIS
RAJAHS	BALEEN	FALCON	KALIUM	SALARY	VALOUR
RAJPUT	BALERS	FALLAL	KALMIA	SALIFY	VALUED
SAJOUS	BALING	FALLEN	KALONG	SALINE	VALUER
******	BALKAN	FALLER	KALPAK	SALISH	VALUES
-AK---	BALKED	FALLOW	LALLED	SALIVA	VALUTA
******	BALLAD	FALSER	MALACO	SALLET	VALVAL
BAKERS	BALLED	FALTER	MALADY	SALLOW	VALVAR
BAKERY	BALLET	GALACT	MALAGA	SALLYS	VALVED
BAKING	BALLOT	GALAXY	MALATE	SALMIS	VALVES
CAKING	BALSAM	GALEAE	MALAWI	SALMON	WALDOS
DAKOIT	BALSAS	GALENA	MALAYA	SALOME	WALERS
DAKOTA	BALTIC	GALIOT	MALAYS	SALONS	WALING
FAKERS	BALTIM	GALLED	MALGRE	SALOON	WALKED
FAKERY	BALZAC	GALLEY	MALICE	SALOOP	WALKER
FAKING	CALAIS	GALLIC	MALIGN	SALPAS	WALKON
FAKIRS	CALASH	GALLON	MALINE	SALPID	WALKUP
HAKIMS	CALCAR	GALLOP	MALLED	SALTED	WALLAH
KAKAPO	CALCES	GALLUP	MALLEE	SALTER	WALLAS
LAKERS	CALCIC	GALLUS	MALLET	SALUKI	WALLED
LAKIER	CALEBS	GALOOT	MALLOW	SALUTE	WALLET
LAKING	CALESA	GALOPS	MALORY	SALVED	WALLIE
MAKERS	CALICO	GALORE	MALTED	SALVER	WALLIS
MAKEUP	CALIFS	GALOSH	MALTHA	SALVES	WALLOP
MAKING	CALIPH	GALWAY	PALACE	SALVIA	WALLOW
OAKLEY	CALKED	GALYAK	PALAEO	SALVOR	WALLYS
RAKERS	CALKER	HALERS	PALAIS	SALVOS	WALNUT
RAKING	CALKIN	HALIDE	PALATE	TALARI	WALRUS
RAKISH	CALLAO	HALIDS	PALEAE	TALCED	WALTER
SAKERS	CALLAS	HALING	PALELY	TALCUM	WALTON
TAKEIN	CALLED	HALITE	PALEST	TALENT	WALVIS
TAKERS	CALLER	HALLAH	PALING	TALERS	******
TAKEUP	CALLOW	HALLEL	PALISH	TALION	-AM---
TAKING	CALLUP	HALLEY	PALLAS	TALKED	******
WAKENS	CALLUS	HALLOO	PALLED	TALKER	BAMAKO
					BAMBOO

CAMASS	GAMUTS	PAMELA	WAMPUM	CANNAE	FANGAS
CAMBER	HAMALS	PAMPAS	YAMENS	CANNAS	FANGED
CAMDEN	HAMAUL	PAMPER	YAMMER	CANNED	FANION
CAMELS	HAMDEN	RAMBLE	YAMUNS	CANNEL	FANJET
CAMEOS	HAMITE	RAMIES	ZAMBIA	CANNER	FANNED
CAMERA	HAMLET	RAMIFY	ZAMIAS	CANNES	FANNER
CAMILA	HAMMAL	RAMJET	******	CANNIE	FANNIE
CAMION	HAMMED	RAMMED	-AN---	CANNON	FANNYS
CAMISE	HAMMER	RAMMER	******	CANNOT	FANONS
CAMLET	HAMPER	RAMONA	BANANA	CANOED	FANTAN
CAMPED	HAMZAS	RAMOSE	BANDED	CANOES	FANTOM
CAMPER	IAMBIC	RAMOUS	BANDIT	CANONS	FANUMS
CAMPOS	IAMBUS	RAMPED	BANGED	CANOPY	GANDER
CAMPUS	JAMIES	RAMROD	BANGLE	CANSOS	GANDHI
DAMAGE	JAMJAR	RAMSON	BANGOR	CANTAB	GANEFS
DAMANS	JAMMED	SAMARA	BANGUI	CANTED	GANGED
DAMASK	KAMALA	SAMBAS	BANGUP	CANTER	GANGER
DAMMAR	KAMIKS	SAMBOS	BANIAN	CANTHI	GANGES
DAMMED	KAMSIN	SAMBUR	BANISH	CANTLE	GANGLI
DAMMER	LAMBDA	SAMIAN	BANJOS	CANTON	GANGUE
DAMNED	LAMBED	SAMIEL	BANKED	CANTOR	GANNET
DAMPED	LAMBIE	SAMITE	BANKER	CANTOS	GANOID
DAMPEN	LAMECH	SAMLET	BANNED	CANTUS	GANTRY
DAMPER	LAMEDS	SAMMYS	BANNER	CANUCK	HANCES
DAMPLY	LAMELY	SAMOAN	BANTAM	CANULA	HANDED
DAMSEL	LAMENT	SAMPAN	BANTER	CANUTE	HANDEL
DAMSON	LAMEST	SAMPLE	BANTUS	CANVAS	HANDLE
FAMILY	LAMIAE	SAMSHU	BANYAN	CANYON	HANGAR
FAMINE	LAMIAS	SAMSON	BANZAI	DANAID	HANGED
FAMISH	LAMINA	SAMUEL	CANAAN	DANAUS	HANGER
FAMOUS	LAMING	TAMALE	CANADA	DANCED	HANGUP
GAMBIA	LAMMAS	TAMBAC	CANALS	DANCER	HANKER
GAMBIR	LAMMED	TAMELY	CANAPE	DANCES	HANNAH
GAMBIT	LAMPAD	TAMERS	CANARD	DANDER	HANNAS
GAMBLE	LAMPAS	TAMEST	CANARY	DANDLE	HANSEL
GAMBOL	LAMPED	TAMING	CANCAN	DANGED	HANSOM
GAMELY	MAMBAS	TAMPAN	CANCEL	DANGER	JANETS
GAMETE	MAMBOS	TAMPED	CANCER	DANGLE	JANGLE
GAMETO	MAMEYS	TAMPER	CANDIA	DANIEL	JANICE
GAMIER	MAMIES	TAMPON	CANDID	DANISH	KANAKA
GAMILY	MAMMAE	TAMTAM	CANDLE	DANITE	KANSAN
GAMING	MAMMAL	VAMOSE	CANDOR	DANKER	KANSAS
GAMINS	MAMMAS	VAMPED	CANERS	DANKLY	LANAIS
GAMMAS	MAMMET	WAMBLE	CANGUE	DANNYS	LANATE
GAMMED	MAMMON	WAMBLY	CANINE	DANTON	LANCED
GAMMER	NAMELY	WAMMUS	CANING	DANUBE	LANCER
GAMMON	NAMERS	WAMOUS	CANKER	DANZIG	LANCES
GAMOUS	NAMING			FANEGA	LANCET

LANDAU	PANELS	TANGOS	******	NAPPED	******
LANDED	PANICE	TANIST	-AP---	NAPPER	-AQ---
LANDER	PANICS	TANKAS	******	NAPPES	******
LANGUR	PANNED	TANKED	CAPERS	NAPPIE	MAQUIS
LANKER	PANSYS	TANKER	CAPIAS	PAPACY	******
LANKLY	PANTED	TANNED	CAPITA	PAPAIN	-AR---
LANNER	PANTIE	TANNER	CAPLIN	PAPAWS	******
LANOSE	PANTRY	TANNIC	CAPONE	PAPAYA	AARONS
LANUGO	PANZER	TANNIN	CAPONS	PAPERS	BARBED
MANAGE	RANCHO	TANREC	CAPOTE	PAPERY	BARBEL
MANANA	RANCID	VANDAL	CAPPED	PAPIST	BARBER
MANCHU	RANCOR	VANISH	CAPPER	PAPPUS	BARBET
MANDAN	RANDAL	VANITY	CAPRIC	PAPUAN	BARBIE
MANDYS	RANDAN	VANMAN	CAPTOR	PAPULA	BARBRA
MANEGE	RANDOM	VANMEN	DAPHNE	PAPULE	BARDED
MANFUL	RANEES	WANDAS	DAPPED	RAPHAE	BARDES
MANGER	RANGED	WANDER	DAPPER	RAPHIS	BARDIC
MANGLE	RANGER	WANDLE	DAPPLE	RAPIDS	BAREGE
MANGOS	RANGES	WANGLE	GAPERS	RAPIER	BARELY
MANIAC	RANKED	WANING	GAPING	RAPINE	BAREST
MANIAS	RANKER	WANION	GAPPED	RAPING	BARFLY
MANILA	RANKLE	WANNED	HAPPED	RAPIST	BARGED
MANIOC	RANKLY	WANNER	HAPPEN	RAPPED	BARGEE
MANITO	RANSOM	WANTED	JAPANS	RAPPEE	BARGES
MANITU	RANTED	WANTER	JAPHET	RAPPEL	BARING
MANNED	RANTER	WANTON	JAPHIA	RAPPER	BARITE
MANNER	SANDAL	XANADU	JAPING	RAPTLY	BARIUM
MANORS	SANDED	XANTHO	KAPOKS	RAPTOR	BARKED
MANQUE	SANDER	YANKED	KAPPAS	SAPHAR	BARKER
MANSES	SANDHI	YANKEE	LAPARO	SAPIEN	BARLEY
MANTAS	SANDRA	ZANANA	LAPDOG	SAPPED	BARMAN
MANTEL	SANDYS	ZANIER	LAPELS	SAPPER	BARMEN
MANTES	SANELY	ZANIES	LAPFUL	SAPPHO	BARMIE
MANTIC	SANEST	******	LAPINS	TAPALO	BARNEY
MANTIS	SANGAR	-AO---	LAPPED	TAPERS	BARNUM
MANTLE	SANGER	******	LAPPER	TAPING	BARONG
MANTUA	SANGUI	BAOBAB	LAPPET	TAPIRS	BARONS
MANUAL	SANIES	GAOLER	LAPSED	TAPPED	BARONY
MANUEL	SANITY	KAOLIN	LAPSER	TAPPER	BARQUE
MANURE	SANJAK	LAOTSE	LAPSES	TAPPET	BARRED
NANCYS	SANNUP	MAOISM	LAPSUS	VAPORI	BARREL
NANISM	SANSAR	MAOIST	MAPLES	VAPORS	BARREN
NANTES	SANSEI	MAORIS	MAPPED	VAPOUR	BARRET
PANADA	SANTOL	NAOMIS	NAPALM	WAPITI	BARRIE
PANAMA	TANDEM	NAOSES	NAPERY	WAPPED	BARRIO
PANCHO	TANGED	RAOULS	NAPIER	YAPONS	BARROW
PANDAS	TANGLE	TAOISM	NAPKIN	YAPPED	BARRYS
PANDER	TANGLY	YAOURT	NAPLES	ZAPATA	BARTER

BARTOK	CARRIE	FARINA	JARGON	MARIST	PARISH
BARTON	CARROT	FARING	JARINA	MARKED	PARITY
BARUCH	CARSON	FARLES	JARRED	MARKER	PARKAS
BARYES	CARTED	FARLEY	JARROW	MARKET	PARKED
BARYON	CARTEL	FARMED	JARVEY	MARKKA	PARKER
BARYTA	CARTER	FARMER	JARVIS	MARKUP	PARLAY
CARACK	CARTES	FAROFF	KARATE	MARLED	PARLEY
CARAFE	CARTON	FAROUT	KARATS	MARLIN	PARLOR
CARATE	CARUSO	FARROW	KARENS	MARLOW	PARODY
CARATS	CARVED	GARAGE	KARMAS	MARMOT	PAROLE
CARBON	CARVEL	GARBED	KARNAK	MAROON	PARRAL
CARBOY	CARVEN	GARBLE	KARROO	MARQUE	PARREL
CARCEL	CARVER	GARCON	LARDED	MARRED	PARROT
CARDED	CARVES	GARDEN	LARDER	MARRER	PARSEC
CARDER	DARDAN	GARGET	LARDON	MARROW	PARSED
CARDIO	DARERS	GARGLE	LAREDO	MARSHA	PARSEE
CAREEN	DARICS	GARISH	LARGER	MARSHY	PARSES
CAREER	DARIEN	GARLIC	LARGOS	MARTAS	PARSIS
CARERS	DARING	GARNER	LARIAT	MARTEN	PARSON
CARESS	DARIUS	GARNET	LARINE	MARTHA	PARTED
CARETS	DARKEN	GARRET	LARKED	MARTHE	PARTLY
CARFAX	DARKER	GARTER	LARKER	MARTIN	PARURE
CARGOS	DARKLE	HARASS	LARRUP	MARTYR	PARVIS
CARHOP	DARKLY	HARBIN	LARRYS	MARTYS	RAREFY
CARIBE	DARNED	HARBOR	LARVAE	MARVEL	RARELY
CARIBS	DARNEL	HARDEN	LARVAL	MARVIN	RAREST
CARIES	DARNER	HARDER	LARYNG	NARIAL	RARING
CARINA	DARROW	HARDLY	LARYNX	NARINE	RARITY
CARING	DARTED	HAREMS	MARACA	NARKED	SARAHS
CARLAS	DARTER	HARING	MARAUD	NARROW	SARAPE
CARLOS	DARTLE	HARKED	MARBLE	NARWAL	SARGON
CARLOW	DARWIN	HARKEN	MARCEL	OARING	SARONG
CARMAN	EARFUL	HARLAN	MARCIA	PARADE	SARSAR
CARMEL	EARING	HARLEM	MARCOS	PARANG	SARTOR
CARMEN	EARLAP	HARLEY	MARCUS	PARAPH	SARTRE
CARNAL	EARLES	HARLOT	MARDUK	PARCAE	TARGET
CAROBS	EARNED	HARLOW	MARGAY	PARCEL	TARIFF
CAROLE	EARNER	HARMED	MARGES	PARDON	TARING
CAROLS	EARTHS	HARMIN	MARGIE	PARENS	TARMAC
CAROMS	EARTHY	HAROLD	MARGIN	PARENT	TARNAL
CARPAL	EARWAX	HARPED	MARGOS	PARERS	TAROTS
CARPED	EARWIG	HARPER	MARGOT	PAREUS	TARPAN
CARPEL	FARADS	HARRIS	MARIAN	PARGET	TARRED
CARPER	FARBAD	HARROW	MARIAS	PARGOS	TARSAL
CARPET	FARCED	HARRYS	MARIES	PARIAH	TARSIA
CARPIC	FARCER	HARTAL	MARINA	PARIAN	TARSUS
CARPUS	FARCES	HARVEY	MARINE	PARIES	TARTAN
CARREL	FARERS	JARFUL	MARION	PARING	TARTAR

TARTED	BASKED	FASTED	MASHED	SASHED	CATERS
TARTER	BASKET	FASTEN	MASHER	SASHES	CATGUT
TARTLY	BASQUE	FASTER	MASHES	SASINS	CATHAY
TARZAN	BASRAH	GASBAG	MASHIE	SASSED	CATHER
VARICO	BASSES	GASCON	MASKED	SASSES	CATHYS
VARIED	BASSET	GASHED	MASKEG	TASKED	CATION
VARIER	BASSOS	GASHES	MASKER	TASMAN	CATKIN
VARIES	BASTED	GASIFY	MASONS	TASSEL	CATLIN
VARLET	BASTES	GASJET	MASORA	TASSET	CATNAP
VARUNA	BASUTO	GASKET	MASQUE	TASTED	CATNIP
VARVES	CASABA	GASKIN	MASSED	TASTER	CATSUP
WARBLE	CASALS	GASMAN	MASSES	TASTES	CATTED
WARDED	CASAVA	GASMEN	MASSIF	VASARI	CATTIE
WARDEN	CASBAH	GASPAR	MASTED	VASHTI	CATTLE
WARDER	CASEFY	GASPED	MASTER	VASILI	DATARY
WARHOL	CASEIN	GASPER	MASTIC	VASSAL	DATERS
WARIER	CASERN	GASSED	NASALS	VASTER	DATING
WARILY	CASHAW	GASSES	NASHUA	VASTLY	DATIVE
WARMED	CASHED	GASTON	NASIAL	WASHED	DATTOS
WARMER	CASHES	GASTRO	NASION	WASHER	DATURA
WARMLY	CASHEW	HASHED	NASSAU	WASHES	EATERS
WARMTH	CASHOO	HASHES	NASSER	WASTED	EATERY
WARMUP	CASING	HASLET	NASTIC	WASTER	EATING
WARNED	CASINO	HASPED	PASCAL	WASTES	FATHER
WARNER	CASKET	HASSEL	PASHAS	YASMAK	FATHOM
WARPED	CASPAR	HASSLE	PASHTO	******	FATIMA
WARPER	CASPER	HASTED	PASSED	-AT---	FATING
WARRED	CASQUE	HASTEN	PASSEE	******	FATTED
WARREN	CASSIA	HASTES	PASSER	BATAAN	FATTEN
WARSAW	CASSIE	JASONS	PASSES	BATEAU	FATTER
YARDED	CASSIS	JASPER	PASSIM	BATHED	GATEAU
YARROW	CASTER	KASPER	PASSUS	BATHER	GATHER
ZARIBA	CASTES	LASCAR	PASTAS	BATHOS	GATING
******	CASTLE	LASERS	PASTED	BATIKS	HATBOX
-AS---	CASTOR	LASHED	PASTEL	BATING	HATERS
******	CASTRO	LASHER	PASTER	BATMAN	HATFUL
BASALT	CASUAL	LASHES	PASTES	BATMEN	HATING
BASELY	DASHED	LASSEN	PASTIL	BATONS	HATPIN
BASEST	DASHER	LASSES	PASTOR	BATTED	HATRED
BASHAW	DASHES	LASSIE	PASTRY	BATTEN	HATTED
BASHED	EASELS	LASSOS	RASCAL	BATTER	HATTER
BASHES	EASIER	LASTED	RASHER	BATTIK	HATTIE
BASICS	EASILY	LASTER	RASHES	BATTIN	HATTYS
BASIFY	EASING	LASTEX	RASHLY	BATTLE	IATRIC
BASILS	EASTER	LASTLY	RASPED	BATTUE	KATHIE
BASING	EASTON	MASCON	RASPER	CATALO	KATHYS
BASINS	FASCES	MASCOT	RASTER	CATCHY	KATIES
BASION	FASCIA	MASERS	SASHAY	CATENA	KATION

LATEEN	PATROL	WATSON	HAUNTS	TAUTER	PAVING
LATELY	PATRON	WATTLE	HAUSEN	TAUTLY	PAVIOR
LATENT	PATSYS	WATUSI	JAUNTS	TAUTOG	PAVISE
LATERA	PATTED	******	JAUNTY	VAULTS	PAVLOV
LATEST	PATTEN	-AU---	KAURIS	VAUNTS	RAVAGE
LATHED	PATTER	******	LAUDED	WAULED	RAVELS
LATHER	PATTON	BAUBLE	LAUDER	YAUPED	RAVENS
LATHES	RATALS	BAUCIS	LAUGHS	YAUPON	RAVERS
LATINS	RATELS	CAUCUS	LAUNCE	******	RAVINE
LATISH	RATERS	CAUDAD	LAUNCH	-AV---	RAVING
LATRIA	RATHER	CAUDAL	LAURAE	******	RAVISH
LATTEN	RATIFY	CAUDEX	LAURAS	CAVEAT	SAVAGE
LATTER	RATINE	CAUDLE	LAUREL	CAVEIN	SAVANT
LATVIA	RATING	CAUGHT	LAURIE	CAVELL	SAVATE
MATEOS	RATION	CAULES	MAUDES	CAVERN	SAVERS
MATEYS	RATIOS	CAULIS	MAULED	CAVIAR	SAVING
MATINE	RATITE	CAULKS	MAULER	CAVIES	SAVINS
MATING	RATLIN	CAUSAL	MAUMAU	CAVILS	SAVIOR
MATINS	RATOON	CAUSED	MAUNDS	CAVING	SAVORS
MATRIX	RATTAN	CAUSER	MAUNDY	CAVITE	SAVORY
MATRON	RATTED	CAUSES	MAUSER	CAVITY	SAVOUR
MATTED	RATTEN	CAUTER	MAUVES	CAVORT	TAVERN
MATTEO	RATTER	DAUBED	NAUGHT	DAVEYS	WAVERS
MATTER	RATTLE	DAUBER	NAUSEA	DAVIDS	WAVEYS
MATTES	SATANG	DAUBRY	NAUTCH	DAVIES	WAVIER
MATTIE	SATARA	DAUDET	PAUKER	DAVITS	WAVIES
MATURE	SATEEN	DAUNTS	PAULAS	FAVORS	WAVILY
MATZOS	SATING	FAUCAL	PAULIN	FAVOUR	WAVING
MATZOT	SATINS	FAUCES	PAULUS	GAVELS	XAVIER
NATANT	SATINY	FAUCET	PAUNCH	GAVIAL	******
NATHAN	SATIRE	FAULTS	PAUPER	GAVOTS	-AW---
NATION	SATORY	FAULTY	PAUSED	HAVANA	******
NATIVE	SATRAP	FAUNAE	PAUSER	HAVENS	BAWDRY
NATRON	SATURN	FAUNAL	PAUSES	HAVENT	BAWLED
NATTER	SATYRS	FAUNAS	SAUCED	HAVING	BAWLER
NATURE	TATARS	FAUNUS	SAUCER	KAVASS	CAWING
PATCHY	TATLER	FAUVES	SAUCES	LAVABO	DAWDLE
PATENS	TATTED	GAUCHE	SAUGER	LAVAGE	DAWNED
PATENT	TATTER	GAUCHO	SAULTS	LAVERS	DAWSON
PATERS	TATTLE	GAUGED	SAUNAS	LAVING	FAWKES
PATHAN	TATTLY	GAUGER	SAUREL	LAVISH	FAWNED
PATHIA	TATTOO	GAUGES	SAURUS	NAVAHO	FAWNER
PATHOL	VATFUL	GAULLE	SAUTES	NAVAJO	GAWAIN
PATHOS	VATTED	GAUZES	TAUGHT	NAVELS	GAWKED
PATINA	WATAPE	HAULED	TAUNTS	NAVIES	HAWAII
PATINE	WATAPS	HAULER	TAUPES	PAVANE	HAWHAW
PATIOS	WATERS	HAULMY	TAURUS	PAVANS	HAWING
PATOIS	WATERY	HAUNCH	TAUTEN	PAVERS	HAWKED

HAWKER
HAWSER
HAWSES
JAWING
LAWFUL
LAWING
LAWYER
NAWABS
PAWERS
PAWING
PAWNED
PAWNEE
PAWNER
PAWPAW
RAWEST
RAWISH
SAWERS
SAWFLY
SAWING
SAWNEY
SAWYER
TAWDRY
TAWERS
TAWING
WAWLED
YAWING
YAWLED
YAWNED
YAWNER
YAWPED
YAWPER
******
-AX---
******
BAXTER
CAXTON
FAXING
LAXEST
LAXITY
MAXIMA
MAXIMS
MAXINE
MAXIXE
PAXWAX
SAXONS
SAXONY
TAXEME
TAXERS

TAXIED
TAXING
TAXITE
WAXIER
WAXING
******
-AY---
******
BAYARD
BAYEUX
BAYING
BAYOUS
CAYMAN
CAYUGA
CAYUSE
DAYBED
DAYBOY
DAYFLY
DAYTON
FAYING
GAYEST
GAYETY
HAYBOX
HAYING
HAYMOW
JAYVEE
KAYAKS
KAYOED
LAYDAY
LAYERS
LAYING
LAYMAN
LAYMEN
LAYOFF
LAYOUT
MAYBUG
MAYDAY
MAYEST
MAYFLY
MAYHAP
MAYHEM
MAYING
MAYORS
MAYPOP
PAYDAY
PAYEES
PAYERS
PAYING

PAYNIM
PAYOFF
PAYOLA
RAYAHS
RAYING
RAYONS
SAYERS
SAYING
TAYLOR
WAYLAY
WAYNES
WAYOUT
ZAYINS
******
-AZ---
******
BAZAAR
DAZING
DAZZLE
FAZING
GAZABO
GAZEBO
GAZERS
GAZING
HAZARD
HAZELS
HAZERS
HAZIER
HAZILY
HAZING
HAZZAN
JAZZED
JAZZER
JAZZES
KAZOOS
LAZARS
LAZIER
LAZILY
LAZING
LAZULI
MAZERS
MAZIER
MAZILY
MAZING
MAZUMA
NAZIFY
NAZISM
RAZEED

RAZEES
RAZING
RAZORS
RAZZED
RAZZES
RAZZIA
TAZZAS
******
-BA---
******
ABACAS
ABACUS
ABADAN
ABASED
ABASER
ABASES
ABATED
ABATER
ABATES
ABATIS
ABATOR
IBADAN
UBANGI
******
-BB---
******
ABBACY
ABBESS
ABBEYS
ABBIES
ABBOTS
EBBING
******
-BD---
******
ABDUCT
******
-BE---
******
ABELES
IBEAMS
IBERIA
IBEXES
OBELUS
OBERON
OBEYED
OBEYER
******
-BH---
******
ABHORS

******
-BI---
******
ABIDED
ABIDER
ABIDES
ABIJAH
IBICES
IBIDEM
IBISES
OBIISM
OBITER
UBIETY
******
-BJ---
******
ABJECT
ABJURE
OBJECT
******
-BL---
******
ABLAUT
ABLAZE
ABLEST
ABLOOM
ABLUSH
OBLAST
OBLATE
OBLIGE
OBLONG
******
-BN---
******
ABNERS
******
-BO---
******
ABOARD
ABODES
ABOHMS
ABOLLA
ABOMAS
ABOMBS
ABORAL
ABORTS
ABOUND
OBOIST

OBOLUS
TBONES
UBOATS
******
-BR---
******
ABRADE
ABRAMS
ABROAD
ABRUPT
******
-BS---
******
ABSENT
ABSORB
ABSURD
OBSESS
******
-BT---
******
OBTAIN
OBTECT
OBTEST
OBTUND
OBTUSE
******
-BU---
******
ABULIA
ABUSED
ABUSER
ABUSES
******
-BV---
******
ABVOLT
OBVERT
******
-BW---
******
ABWATT
******
-BY---
******
ABYDOS
ABYSMS
******
-CA---
******
ACACIA
ACADIA

ACAENA	ACEOUS	******	SCORES	ACTINO	ADAPTS
ACAJOU	ACERIC	-CI---	SCORIA	ACTION	GDANSK
ACANTH	ACETAL	******	SCORNS	ACTIUM	******
ACARID	ACETIC	ACIDIC	SCOTCH	ACTIVE	-DD---
ECARTE	ACETUM	ACIDLY	SCOTER	ACTORS	******
ICALLY	ACETYL	ACINUS	SCOTIA	ACTUAL	ADDAMS
ICARUS	ECESIS	ACIOUS	SCOTTS	ECTOMY	ADDEND
OCASEY	ICEAXE	ICICLE	SCOURS	ECTYPE	ADDERS
SCABBY	ICEBOX	ICIEST	SCOUSE	OCTADS	ADDICT
SCALAR	ICECAP	ICINGS	SCOUTS	OCTANE	ADDING
SCALDS	ICEMAN	SCILLY	SCOWLS	OCTANT	ADDLED
SCALED	ICEMEN	SCIONS	******	OCTAVE	ADDLES
SCALER	OCEANS	SCIPIO	-CQ---	OCTAVO	ADDUCE
SCALES	OCELLI	******	******	OCTETS	ADDUCT
SCALPS	OCELOT	-CK---	ACQUIT	OCTOPI	EDDAIC
SCAMPI	SCENDS	******	******	OCTROI	EDDIED
SCAMPS	SCENES	ACKACK	-CR---	******	EDDIES
SCANTY	SCENIC	******	ACROSS	-CU---	EDDISH
SCAPES	SCENTS	-CL---	OCREAE	******	ODDEST
SCARAB	******	******	SCRAGS	ACUATE	ODDITY
SCARCE	-CH---	ECLAIR	SCRAMS	ACUITY	ODDJOB
SCARED	******	OCLOCK	SCRAPE	ACUMEN	UDDERS
SCARER	ACHAEA	SCLAFF	SCRAPS	OCULAR	******
SCARES	ACHAIA	SCLERA	SCRAWL	SCUBAS	-DE---
SCARFS	ACHENE	SCLERO	SCREAK	SCUFFS	******
SCARPS	ACHING	YCLEPT	SCREAM	SCULLS	ADEEMS
SCATHE	ECHARD	******	SCREED	SCULPT	ADENIS
SCATTY	ECHINI	-CN---	SCREEN	SCUMMY	ADEPTS
SCAUPS	ECHINO	******	SCREWS	SCURFY	EDENIC
******	ECHOED	ACNODE	SCREWY	SCURRY	IDEALS
-CC---	ECHOER	******	SCRIBE	SCURVY	IDEATE
******	ECHOES	-CO---	SCRIED	SCUTCH	ODESSA
ACCEDE	ECHOIC	ACORNS	SCRIMP	SCUTES	ODETTE
ACCENT	ICHTHY	ECOLES	SCRIPS	SCUTUM	******
ACCEPT	OCHERS	ICONIC	SCRIPT	******	-DG---
ACCESS	OCHERY	SCOFFS	SCRIVE	-CY---	******
ACCORD	SCHEMA	SCOLDS	SCRODS	******	EDGARS
ACCOST	SCHEME	SCOLEX	SCROLL	SCYLLA	EDGIER
ACCRUE	SCHICK	SCONCE	SCROOP	SCYPHI	EDGING
ACCUSE	SCHISM	SCONES	SCROTA	SCYPHO	******
ECCLES	SCHIZO	SCOOPS	SCRUBS	SCYTHE	-DH---
MCCOYS	SCHMOS	SCOOTS	SCRUFF	******	******
OCCULT	SCHOOL	SCOPES	SCRUMS	-CZ---	ADHERE
OCCUPY	SCHORL	SCOPUS	******		******
OCCURS	SCHUIT	SCORCH	-CT---	ECZEMA	-DI---
******	SCHUSS	SCORED	******	******	******
-CE---	SCHWAS	SCORER	ACTING	-DA---	ADIEUS
******			ACTINI	ADAGES	ADIEUX
ACEDIA				ADAGIO	
ACEIUM					

ADIPIC	ADORED	BEACON	HEARST	NEARLY	TEABAG
EDIBLE	ADORER	BEADED	HEARTH	NEATEN	TEACUP
EDICTS	ADORES	BEADLE	HEARTS	NEATER	TEAMED
EDILES	ADORNS	BEAGLE	HEARTY	NEATLY	TEAPOT
EDISON	ODONTO	BEAKED	HEATED	PEACHY	TEAPOY
EDITED	******	BEAKER	HEATER	PEAHEN	TEARED
EDITHS	-DR---	BEAMED	HEATHS	PEAKED	TEASED
EDITOR	******	BEANED	HEATHY	PEALED	TEASEL
IDIOCY	ADRIAN	BEANIE	HEAUME	PEANUT	TEASER
IDIOMS	ADRIEN	BEARDS	HEAVED	PEARLS	TEASES
IDIOTS	ADRIFT	BEARED	HEAVEN	PEARLY	TEASET
ODIOUS	ADROIT	BEARER	HEAVER	PEASEN	TEAURN
******	******	BEASTS	HEAVES	PEASES	VEADAR
-DJ---	-DS---	BEATEN	JEANNE	PEAVEY	WEAKEN
******	******	BEATER	LEACHY	REACTS	WEAKER
ADJECT	ADSORB	BEAUTS	LEADED	READER	WEAKLY
ADJOIN	EDSELS	BEAUTY	LEADEN	REALES	WEALDS
ADJURE	******	BEAVER	LEADER	REALLY	WEALTH
ADJUST	-DU---	CEASED	LEADIN	REALMS	WEANED
******	******	CEASES	LEAFED	REALTY	WEANER
-DL---	ADULTS	DEACON	LEAGUE	REAMED	WEAPON
******	EDUARD	DEADEN	LEAKED	REAMER	WEARER
ADLIBS	EDUCED	DEADLY	LEANED	REAPED	WEASEL
IDLERS	EDUCES	DEAFEN	LEANER	REAPER	WEAVED
IDLEST	EDUCTS	DEAFLY	LEANLY	REARED	WEAVER
IDLING	******	DEALER	LEANTO	REARER	WEAVES
******	-DV---	DEARER	LEAPED	REARMS	YEANED
-DM---	******	DEARIE	LEAPER	REASON	YEARLY
******	ADVENT	DEARLY	LEARNS	REAVOW	YEARNS
ADMIRE	ADVERB	DEARTH	LEARNT	SEABEE	YEASTS
ADMITS	ADVERT	DEATHS	LEASED	SEACOW	YEASTY
ADMIXT	ADVICE	DEATHY	LEASES	SEADOG	ZEALOT
EDMOND	ADVISE	FEALTY	LEAVED	SEALED	******
EDMUND	******	FEARED	LEAVEN	SEALER	-EB---
******	-DW---	FEARER	LEAVER	SEAMAN	******
-DN---	******	FEASED	LEAVES	SEAMED	CEBOID
******	EDWARD	FEASES	MEADOW	SEAMEN	DEBARK
ADNATE	EDWINA	FEASTS	MEAGER	SEAMER	DEBARS
ADNOUN	EDWINS	GEARED	MEAGRE	SEAMUS	DEBASE
******	******	HEADED	MEALIE	SEANCE	DEBATE
-DO---	-DY---	HEADER	MEANER	SEAPEN	DEBBIE
******	******	HEADON	MEANIE	SEAPEN	DEBBYS
ADOBES	ADYTUM	HEALED	MEANLY	SEARCH	DEBITS
ADOLPH	GDYNIA	HEALER	MEASLY	SEARED	DEBRIS
ADONAI	IDYLLS	HEALTH	MEATUS	SEARIN	DEBTOR
ADONIC	ODYNIA	HEAPED	NEARBY	SEASON	DEBUGS
ADONIS	******	HEARER	NEARED	SEATED	DEBUNK
ADOPTS	-EA---	HEARSE	NEARER	SEAWAN	DEBUTS
	******				
	AEACUS				
	BEACHY				

HEBREW	DECERN	RECKON	HEDDLE	REDHOT	HEEDER
HEBRON	DECIDE	RECOIL	HEDGED	REDOES	HEEHAW
NEBULA	DECILE	RECORD	HEDGER	REDONE	HEELED
PEBBLE	DECKED	RECOUP	HEDGES	REDOWA	HEELER
PEBBLY	DECKEL	RECTAL	HEDRAL	REDTOP	JEEING
REBATE	DECKER	RECTOR	HEDRON	REDUCE	JEERED
REBATO	DECKLE	RECTOS	HEDWIG	SEDANS	JEERER
REBECK	DECOCT	RECTUM	KEDDAH	SEDATE	KEELED
REBECS	DECODE	RECTUS	KEDGED	SEDERS	KEENED
REBELS	DECOKE	RECURS	KEDGES	SEDGES	KEENER
REBILL	DECORS	RECUSE	KEDRON	SEDILE	KEENLY
REBORE	DECOYS	SECANT	LEDGER	SEDUCE	KEEPER
REBORN	DECREE	SECEDE	LEDGES	SEDUMS	KEEVES
REBOZO	DECUMA	SECERN	MEDALS	TEDDED	LEERED
REBUFF	DECURY	SECKEL	MEDDLE	TEDDER	LEEWAY
REBUKE	FECIAL	SECOND	MEDIAE	TEDDYS	MEEKER
REBUTS	FECULA	SECPAR	MEDIAL	TEDIUM	MEEKLY
SEBATS	FECUND	SECRET	MEDIAN	VEDIAC	MEETER
WEBBED	GECKOS	SECTOR	MEDICI	WEDDED	MEETLY
WEBERS	HECATE	SECUND	MEDICO	WEDELN	NEEDED
XEBECS	HECKLE	SECURE	MEDICS	WEDGED	NEEDER
ZEBECK	HECTIC	TECHNO	MEDIUM	WEDGES	NEEDLE
ZEBECS	HECTOR	VECTOR	MEDLAR	WEDGIE	PEEKED
ZEBRAS	HECUBA	ZECHIN	MEDLEY	******	PEEKER
******	KECKED	******	MEDUSA	-EE---	PEELED
-EC---	KECKLE	-ED---	MEDWAY	******	PEELER
******	LECHER	******	OEDEMA	AEETES	PEENED
AECIAL	LECTOR	AEDILE	PEDALS	BEECHY	PEEPED
BECALM	MECCAN	BEDAUB	PEDANT	BEEFED	PEEPER
BECAME	MECCAS	BEDBUG	PEDATE	BEEPED	PEERED
BECKED	NECKED	BEDDED	PEDATI	BEETLE	PEEVED
BECKET	NECTAR	BEDDER	PEDDLE	BEEVES	PEEVES
BECKON	PECANS	BEDECK	PEDLAR	DEEDED	PEEWEE
BECKYS	PECKED	BEDEWS	PEDROS	DEEMED	PEEWIT
BECOME	PECKER	BEDIMS	REDACT	DEEPEN	REECHO
CECILE	PECTEN	BEDLAM	REDANS	DEEPER	REEDED
CECILS	PECTIC	BEDPAN	REDBAY	DEEPLY	REEDIT
CECILY	PECTIN	BEDRID	REDBUD	DEEWAN	REEFED
DECADE	RECALL	BEDSIT	REDBUG	FEEBLE	REEFER
DECALS	RECANT	BEDUIN	REDCAP	FEEBLY	REEKED
DECAMP	RECAPS	CEDARS	REDDEN	FEEDER	REEKER
DECANE	RECAST	CEDING	REDDER	FEEING	REELED
DECANT	RECEDE	CEDRIC	REDDLE	FEELER	REELER
DECARE	RECENT	CEDULA	REDDOG	FEEZED	REEVED
DECAYS	RECEPT	DEDANS	REDEEM	FEEZES	REEVES
DECCAN	RECESS	DEDUCE	REDEYE	GEEING	SEEDED
DECEIT	RECIPE	DEDUCT	REDFIN	GEEZER	SEEDER
DECENT	RECITE	FEDORA	REDGUM	HEEDED	SEEING

SEEKER	HEFTED	LEGREE	BEIRUT	******	CELLAE
SEEMED	REFACE	LEGUME	CEIBAS	-EJ---	CELLAR
SEEMER	REFERS	MEGALO	CEILED	******	CELLOS
SEEMLY	REFILL	MEGASS	DEICED	DEJECT	CELTIC
SEEPED	REFINE	MEGILP	DEICER	HEJIRA	DELATE
SEESAW	REFITS	MEGRIM	DEICES	JEJUNE	DELAYS
SEETHE	REFLET	NEGATE	DEIFIC	MEJICO	DELETE
TEEING	REFLEX	PEGGED	DEIGNS	REJECT	DELIAN
TEEMED	REFLUX	PEGGYS	DEISTS	REJOIN	DELIAS
TEEMER	REFOOT	PEGLEG	FEIGNE	SEJANT	DELICT
TEENSY	REFORM	PEGTOP	FEIGNS	******	DELIUS
TEETER	REFUEL	REGAIN	FEINTS	-EK---	DELLAS
TEETHE	REFUGE	REGALE	FEISTS	******	DELPHI
VEERED	REFUND	REGARD	FEISTY	DEKARE	DELTAS
WEEDED	REFUSE	REGENT	GEIGER	DEKING	DELUDE
WEEDER	REFUTE	REGGIE	GEISHA	JEKYLL	DELUGE
WEEKLY	TEFLON	REGIME	HEIFER	MEKONG	DELUXE
WEENIE	******	REGINA	HEIGHT	NEKTON	DELVED
WEENSY	-EG---	REGION	HEISTS	PEKANS	DELVER
WEEPER	******	REGIUS	KEITHS	PEKING	DELVES
WEEVER	AEGEAN	REGLET	LEIGHS	PEKOES	FELICE
WEEVIL	AEGEUS	REGNAL	NEIGHS	******	FELIDS
******	BEGETS	REGRET	PEIRCE	-EL---	FELINE
-EF---	BEGGAR	SEGGAR	REICHS	******	FELIPE
******	BEGGED	TEGMEN	REIGNS	BELAYS	FELLAH
BEFALL	BEGINS	******	REINED	BELDAM	FELLED
BEFELL	BEGIRD	-EH---	SEICHE	BELFRY	FELLER
BEFITS	BEGIRT	******	SEINED	BELGAS	FELLOE
BEFOGS	BEGONE	BEHALF	SEINER	BELGIC	FELLOW
BEFOOL	BEGUIN	BEHAVE	SEINES	BELIAL	FELONS
BEFORE	BEGUMS	BEHEAD	SEISED	BELIED	FELONY
BEFOUL	DEGAGE	BEHELD	SEISIN	BELIEF	FELTED
DEFACE	DEGAME	BEHEST	SEISMO	BELIER	GELDED
DEFAME	DEGREE	BEHIND	SEISMS	BELIES	GELLED
DEFEAT	DEGUMS	BEHOLD	SEISOR	BELIKE	HELENA
DEFECT	DEGUST	BEHOOF	SEIZED	BELIZE	HELENS
DEFEND	HEGIRA	BEHOVE	SEIZER	BELLAS	HELICO
DEFERS	KEGLER	DEHORN	SEIZES	BELLED	HELIOS
DEFIED	LEGACY	LEHUAS	SEIZIN	BELLES	HELIUM
DEFIER	LEGATE	REHASH	SEIZOR	BELLOC	HELLAS
DEFIES	LEGATO	REHEAR	VEILED	BELLOW	HELLEN
DEFILE	LEGEND	REHEAT	VEILER	BELOIT	HELLER
DEFINE	LEGERS	TEHEED	VEINED	BELONG	HELMED
DEFORM	LEGGED	TEHEES	WEIGHS	BELTED	HELMET
DEFRAY	LEGION	YEHUDI	WEIGHT	BELUGA	HELOTS
DEFTER	LEGIST	******	WEIMAR	CELERY	HELPED
DEFTLY	LEGMAN	-EI---	WEIRDY	CELIAC	HELPER
DEFUSE	LEGMEN	******		CELIAS	HELTER
		BEIGES			
		BEINGS			

HELVES	RELISH	DEMENT	REMOTE	DENDRO	HENNAS
JELLED	RELIVE	DEMIES	REMOVE	DENGUE	HENRIS
KELLER	RELOAD	DEMISE	REMUDA	DENIAL	HENRYS
KELOID	SELDOM	DEMITS	SEMELE	DENIED	JENNET
KELPIE	SELECT	DEMOBS	SEMEME	DENIER	JENNYS
KELSON	SELENE	DEMODE	SEMITE	DENIES	KENDAL
KELTIC	SELENO	DEMONO	SEMPRE	DENIMS	KENITE
KELVIN	SELJUK	DEMONS	TEMPER	DENISE	KENNED
MELANO	SELLER	DEMOTE	TEMPLE	DENNED	KENNEL
MELDED	SELSYN	DEMURE	TEMPOS	DENNIS	KENNIE
MELEES	SELVES	DEMURS	TEMPTS	DENNYS	KENNYS
MELLON	SELWYN	FEMALE	YEMENI	DENOTE	LENAPE
MELLOW	TELARY	FEMORA	******	DENSER	LENDER
MELODY	TELEDU	FEMURS	-EN---	DENTAL	LENGTH
MELONS	TELEGA	GEMARA	******	DENTED	LENITY
MELTED	TELFER	GEMERT	AENEAS	DENTIL	LENNYS
MELTER	TELLER	GEMINI	AENEID	DENTIN	LENORE
MELTON	TELLUS	GEMMAE	BENDAY	DENUDE	LENSES
MELVIN	TELSON	GEMMED	BENDED	DENVER	LENTEN
MELVYN	TELUGU	GEMOTS	BENDEE	FENCED	LENTIL
NELLIE	VELDTS	GEMSBO	BENDER	FENCER	LENTOS
NELLYS	VELLUM	HEMATO	BENGAL	FENCES	MENACE
NELSON	VELOCE	HEMMED	BENIGN	FENDED	MENAGE
PELAGE	VELOUR	HEMMER	BENITA	FENDER	MENDED
PELEUS	VELURE	HEMOID	BENITO	FENIAN	MENDEL
PELIAS	VELVET	HEMPEN	BENJYS	FENNEC	MENDER
PELION	WELDED	JEMIMA	BENNES	FENNEL	MENDIP
PELITE	WELDER	LEMMAS	BENNET	FENRIR	MENHIR
PELLET	WELKIN	LEMNOS	BENNYS	GENDER	MENIAL
PELOPS	WELLED	LEMONS	BENTON	GENERA	MENINX
PELOTA	WELTED	LEMUEL	BENUMB	GENESI	MENSAL
PELTED	WELTER	LEMURS	BENZOL	GENETS	MENSES
PELTER	YELLED	MEMBER	BENZYL	GENEVA	MENTAL
PELTRY	YELLER	MEMOIR	CENSED	GENIAL	MENTOR
PELVES	YELLOW	MEMORY	CENSER	GENIES	PENCEL
PELVIC	YELPED	NEMATO	CENSES	GENITO	PENCIL
PELVIS	YELPER	REMADE	CENSOR	GENIUS	PENDED
RELAID	******	REMAIN	CENSUR	GENOUS	PENGOS
RELATE	-EM---	REMAKE	CENSUS	GENRES	PENIAL
RELAYS	******	REMAND	CENTAL	GENROS	PENILE
RELENT	BEMATA	REMANS	CENTER	GENTES	PENMAN
RELICS	BEMEAN	REMARK	CENTOS	GENTLE	PENMEN
RELICT	BEMIRE	REMEDY	CENTRA	GENTLY	PENNAE
RELIED	BEMOAN	REMIND	CENTRE	GENTOO	PENNED
RELIEF	BEMUSE	REMISE	CENTRI	GENTRY	PENNER
RELIER	CEMENT	REMISS	CENTRO	HENBIT	PENNIA
RELIES	DEMAND	REMITS	DENARY	HENDON	PENNIS
RELINE	DEMEAN	REMORA	DENDRI	HENLEY	PENNON

PENNYS	TENSES	GEORGI	REPELS	BERTIE	GERMEN
PENPAL	TENSOR	LEONAS	REPENT	BERYLS	GEROUS
PENTAD	TENTED	LEONIE	REPINE	CERATE	GERRYS
PENTUP	TENTER	MEOWED	REPLAY	CERATO	GERTIE
PENULT	TENTHS	PEOPLE	REPORT	CEREAL	GERTYS
PENURY	TENUES	PEORIA	REPOSE	CEREUS	GERUND
RENDED	TENUIS	REOPEN	REPUTE	CERING	GERYON
RENDER	TENURE	YEOMAN	SEPALS	CERIPH	HERALD
RENEES	TENUTO	YEOMEN	SEPIAS	CERISE	HERBAL
RENEGE	VENDED	******	SEPOYS	CERITE	HERDED
RENEWS	VENDEE	-EP---	SEPSIS	CERIUM	HERDER
RENNET	VENDER	******	SEPTAL	CERMET	HERDIC
RENNIN	VENDOR	DEPART	SEPTET	CEROUS	HEREAT
RENOIR	VENDUE	DEPEND	SEPTIC	CERTES	HEREBY
RENOWN	VENEER	DEPICT	SEPTUM	CERUSE	HEREIN
RENTAL	VENERY	DEPLOY	TEPEES	CERVIX	HEREOF
RENTED	VENIAL	DEPONE	TEPEFY	DERAIL	HEREON
RENTER	VENICE	DEPORT	ZEPHYR	DERAIN	HERESY
RENTES	VENIRE	DEPOSE	******	DERATE	HERETO
SENARY	VENOMS	DEPOTS	-EQ---	DEREKS	HERIOT
SENATE	VENOSE	DEPTHS	******	DERIDE	HERMAE
SENDAL	VENOUS	DEPUTE	PEQUOD	DERIVE	HERMAI
SENDER	VENTED	DEPUTY	PEQUOT	DERMAL	HERMAN
SENECA	VENTER	HEPATO	SEQUEL	DERMAS	HERMES
SENILE	VENTRO	HEPTAD	SEQUIN	DERMAT	HERMIT
SENIOR	VENUES	KEPLER	******	DERMIC	HERNIA
SENLAC	VENULE	LEPERS	-ER---	DERMIS	HERNIO
SENNAS	WENDED	LEPIDO	******	DERRIS	HEROES
SENNET	WENDYS	LEPSIA	AERATE	EERILY	HEROIC
SENNIT	XENIAL	LEPTON	AERIAL	FERBER	HEROIN
SENORA	YENNED	NEPHEW	AERIED	FERIAL	HERONS
SENSED	ZENANA	NEPHRO	AERIES	FERINE	HERPES
SENSES	ZENGER	OEPEMA	AERIFY	FERITY	JERBOA
SENSOR	ZENITH	PEPLOS	AEROBE	FERMIS	JEREED
SENTRY	******	PEPLUM	AERUGO	FEROUS	JEREMY
TENACE	-EO---	PEPLUS	BERATE	FERRET	JERKED
TENANT	******	PEPPED	BERBER	FERRIC	JERKIN
TENDED	AEOLIA	PEPPER	BEREFT	FERRIS	JEROME
TENDER	AEOLIC	PEPSIN	BERETS	FERRUM	JERRYS
TENDON	AEOLIS	PEPTIC	BERGEN	FERULA	JERSEY
TENETS	AEOLUS	REPAID	BERING	FERULE	JERVIS
TENNIS	CEORLS	REPAIR	BERLIN	FERVID	KERALA
TENONS	DEODAR	REPAND	BERMES	FERVOR	KERATO
TENORS	FEODOR	REPASS	BERNEY	GERALD	KERBED
TENPIN	FEOFFS	REPAST	BERNIE	GERARD	KERMES
TENREC	GEODES	REPAYS	BERTHA	GERBIL	KERMIS
TENSED	GEODIC	REPEAL	BERTHE	GERENT	KERMIT
TENSER	GEORGE	REPEAT	BERTHS	GERMAN	KERNED

KERNEL	SERENA	VERITY	FESCUE	RESALE	YESSES
KERRIE	SERENE	VERMIN	FESSES	RESCUE	YESTER
KERSEY	SERIAL	VERNAL	FESTAL	RESEAT	ZESTED
LEROYS	SERIES	VERNAS	FESTER	RESEAU	******
MERCER	SERIFS	VERNIX	GESELL	RESECT	-ET---
MERCIA	SERINE	VERNON	GESSOS	RESEDA	******
MERELY	SERINS	VERONA	GESTIC	RESELL	AETHER
MEREST	SERMON	VERSED	HESIOD	RESEND	BETAKE
MERGED	SEROUS	VERSES	HESTER	RESENT	BETELS
MERGER	SEROWS	VERSET	HESTIA	RESETS	BETHEL
MERGES	SERUMS	VERSOS	JESSED	RESIDE	BETIDE
MERINO	SERVAL	VERSTS	JESSES	RESIGN	BETISE
MERITS	SERVED	VERSUS	JESSIE	RESILE	BETONY
MERLES	SERVER	VERTEX	JESTED	RESINS	BETOOK
MERLIN	SERVES	VERVET	JESTER	RESIST	BETRAY
MERLON	SERVOS	WERENT	JESUIT	RESOLD	BETSYS
MERMAN	TERAPH	YERBAS	LESBOS	RESOLE	BETTED
MERMEN	TERATO	ZEROED	LESION	RESORB	BETTER
MEROUS	TERBIA	ZEROES	LESLEY	RESORT	BETTES
MERSEY	TERCEL	******	LESLIE	RESTED	BETTOR
MERVIN	TERCET	-ES---	LESSEE	RESTER	BETTYS
NEREID	TEREDO	******	LESSEN	RESULT	CETANE
NEREIS	TERESA	BESANT	LESSER	RESUME	DETACH
NEROLI	TERETE	BESEEM	LESSON	SESAME	DETAIL
NERVED	TEREUS	BESETS	LESSOR	SESQUI	DETAIN
NERVES	TERGAL	BESIDE	LESTER	SESTET	DETECT
PERCYS	TERGUM	BESOMS	MESCAL	TESSIE	DETENT
PERILS	TERMED	BESOTS	MESHED	TESTAE	DETERS
PERIOD	TERMER	BESSIE	MESHER	TESTED	DETEST
PERISH	TERMLY	BESSYS	MESHES	TESTER	DETOUR
PERKED	TERMOR	BESTED	MESIAL	TESTES	FETIAL
PERMED	TERNAL	BESTIR	MESIAN	TESTIS	FETICH
PERMIT	TERRET	BESTOW	MESMER	TESTON	FETING
PERRON	TERROR	CESARE	MESNES	VESICA	FETISH
PERRYS	TERRYS	CESIUM	MESONS	VESICO	FETORS
PERSIA	TERSER	CESTUS	MESSED	VESPER	FETTER
PERSON	VERBAL	CESURA	MESSES	VESPID	FETTLE
PERTLY	VERDIN	DESALT	MESSRS	VESSEL	GETTER
PERUKE	VERDUN	DESCRY	MESTEE	VESTAL	GETUPS
PERUSE	VEREIN	DESERT	NESSUS	VESTAS	HETERO
RERUNS	VERGED	DESIGN	NESTED	VESTED	HETMAN
SERACS	VERGER	DESIRE	NESTLE	VESTEE	HETTYS
SERAIS	VERGES	DESIST	NESTOR	VESTRY	JETHRO
SERAPE	VERGIL	DESMAN	PESACH	WESLEY	JETSAM
SERAPH	VERIFY	DESMID	PESADE	WESSEX	JETTED
SERBIA	VERILY	DESOXY	PESETA	WESTER	JETTON
SERDAB	VERISM	DESPOT	PESTER	YESMAN	KETENE
SEREIN	VERIST	DESSAU	PESTLE	YESSED	KETONE

KETOSE	SETONS	******	SEVENS	HEXANE	AFFIRM
KETTLE	SETOSE	-EV---	SEVERE	HEXING	AFFLUX
LETHAL	SETOUS	******	SEVERN	HEXONE	AFFORD
LETTER	SETOUT	BEVELS	SEVERS	HEXOSE	AFFRAY
LETUPS	SETTEE	BEVIES	TEVERE	HEXYLS	EFFACE
METAGE	SETTER	DEVEIN	******	MEXICO	EFFECT
METALS	SETTLE	DEVEST	-EW---	SEXIER	EFFETE
METEOR	SETTOS	DEVICE	******	SEXILY	EFFIGY
METERS	SETUPS	DEVILS	BEWAIL	SEXING	EFFLUX
METHOD	TETANY	DEVISE	BEWARE	SEXISM	EFFORT
METHYL	TETCHY	DEVOID	DEWANS	SEXIST	EFFUSE
METIER	TETHER	DEVOIR	DEWIER	SEXPOT	OFFDAY
METING	TETHYS	DEVOTE	DEWITT	SEXTAN	OFFEND
METOPE	TETONS	DEVOUR	DEWLAP	SEXTET	OFFERS
METRIC	TETRAD	DEVOUT	FEWEST	SEXTON	OFFICE
METROS	TETRYL	FEVERS	GEWGAW	SEXUAL	OFFING
METTLE	TETTER	KEVELS	HEWERS	VEXERS	OFFISH
METUMP	TETZEL	KEVINS	HEWING	VEXILS	OFFSET
NETHER	VETOED	LEVANT	JEWELS	VEXING	******
NETTED	VETOER	LEVEES	JEWESS	******	-FG---
NETTIE	VETOES	LEVELS	JEWISH	-EY---	******
NETTLE	VETTED	LEVERS	KEWPIE	******	AFGHAN
PETALS	WETHER	LEVIED	LEWDER	BEYOND	******
PETARD	WETTED	LEVIER	LEWDLY	CEYLON	-FI---
PETERS	WETTER	LEVIES	MEWING	GEYSER	******
PETITE	ZETHOS	LEVITE	MEWLED	HEYDAY	AFIELD
PETREL	ZETHUS	LEVITY	NEWARK	KEYING	******
PETRIE	******	NEVADA	NEWELS	KEYNES	-FL---
PETROL	-EU---	NEVILE	NEWEST	KEYWAY	******
PETTED	******	NEVILL	NEWTON	LEYDEN	AFLAME
PETULA	BEULAH	NEVOID	PEWEES	PEYOTE	AFLCIO
RETAIL	BEULAS	NEVSKI	PEWITS	******	AFLOAT
RETAIN	DEUCED	REVAMP	PEWTER	-EZ---	******
RETAKE	DEUCES	REVEAL	REWARD	******	-FR---
RETARD	FEUARS	REVELS	REWIND	BEZANT	******
RETELL	FEUDAL	REVERE	REWORD	BEZELS	AFRAID
RETENE	FEUDED	REVERS	SEWAGE	BEZOAR	AFRAME
RETINA	FEUING	REVERT	SEWALL	FEZZAN	AFRESH
RETIRE	LEUDES	REVEST	SEWARD	FEZZES	AFRICA
RETOLD	NEUMES	REVETS	SEWELL	HEZION	******
RETOOK	NEURAL	REVIEW	SEWERS	JEZAIL	-FT---
RETOOL	NEURON	REVILE	SEWING	MEZUZA	******
RETORT	NEUTER	REVISE	******	MEZZOS	AFTOSA
RETROD	OEUVRE	REVIVE	-EX---	******	******
RETTED	REUBEN	REVOKE	******	-FF---	-GA---
RETURN	SEURAT	REVOLT	DEXTER	******	******
RETUSE	TEUCER	REVUES	DEXTRO	AFFAIR	AGAMAS
SETOFF	ZEUGMA	REVVED	HEXADS	AFFECT	AGAMIC

AGAPAE	AGLETS	CHAETA	PHANON	THADYS	GHEBER
AGARIC	IGLOOS	CHAETO	PHAROS	THALER	GHETTO
AGATES	OGLERS	CHAFED	PHASED	THALES	OHENRY
AGATHA	OGLING	CHAFER	PHASES	THALIA	PHENOL
AGAVES	UGLIER	CHAFES	PHASIA	THAMES	PHENYL
UGANDA	UGLIFY	CHAFFS	PHASIC	THANAT	RHEIMS
******	UGLILY	CHAFFY	PHASIS	THANES	RHESUS
-GB---	******	CHAINS	SHABBY	THANKS	RHETOR
******	-GN---	CHAIRS	SHACKO	THATCH	RHEUMY
EGBERT	******	CHAISE	SHACKS	THAWED	SHEARS
******	AGNAIL	CHALCO	SHADED	THAYER	SHEATH
-GD---	AGNATE	CHALEH	SHADES	WHACKS	SHEAVE
******	IGNACE	CHALET	SHADOW	WHALED	SHEBAT
OGDOAD	IGNIFY	CHALKS	SHAFTS	WHALER	SHEENS
******	IGNITE	CHALKY	SHAGGY	WHALES	SHEENY
-GE---	IGNORE	CHAMMY	SHAKEN	WHAMMY	SHEEPS
******	******	CHAMPS	SHAKER	WHANGS	SHEERS
AGEDLY	-GO---	CHANCE	SHAKES	WHARFS	SHEETS
AGEING	******	CHANCY	SHAKOS	WHARVE	SHEIKH
AGENCY	AGOGUE	CHANGE	SHALED	******	SHEIKS
AGENDA	AGONES	CHANGS	SHALES	-HE---	SHEILA
AGENTS	AGONIC	CHANTS	SHAMAN	******	SHEILD
AGEOLD	AGORAE	CHANTY	SHAMED	CHEATS	SHEKEL
EGERIA	AGORAS	CHAPEL	SHAMES	CHEBEC	SHELBY
EGESTA	AGOUTI	CHAPES	SHAMMY	CHECKS	SHELLS
EGESTS	AGOUTY	CHARDS	SHAMUS	CHEEKS	SHELLY
******	EGOISM	CHARED	SHANDY	CHEEKY	SHELTY
-GG---	EGOIST	CHARES	SHANKS	CHEEPS	SHELVE
******	IGOROT	CHARGE	SHANTY	CHEERS	SHERDS
AGGERS	******	CHARMS	SHAPED	CHEERY	SHERIF
EGGARS	-GR---	CHARON	SHAPEN	CHEESE	SHERPA
EGGCUP	******	CHARRY	SHAPER	CHEESY	SHERRY
EGGERS	AGRAFE	CHARTS	SHAPES	CHEGOE	SHEWED
EGGING	AGREED	CHASED	SHARDS	CHEILO	SHEWER
EGGNOG	AGREES	CHASER	SHARED	CHEIRO	THEBAE
******	EGRESS	CHASES	SHARER	CHELAE	THEBES
-GH---	EGRETS	CHASMS	SHARES	CHELAS	THECAE
******	OGRESS	CHASSE	SHARKS	CHEOPS	THECAL
AGHAST	OGRISH	CHASTE	SHARON	CHEQUE	THEDAS
******	******	CHATTY	SHARPS	CHERRY	THEFTS
-GI---	-GU---	CHAWED	SHASTA	CHERUB	THEIRS
******	******	DHARMA	SHAVED	CHERYL	THEISM
AGISTS	AGUISH	DHARNA	SHAVEN	CHESTS	THEIST
OGIVAL	IGUANA	GHARRI	SHAVER	CHESTY	THELMA
OGIVES	******	GHARRY	SHAVES	CHETAH	THEMES
******	-HA---	GHAUTS	SHAWLS	CHEVVY	THEMIS
-GL---	******	KHAKIS	SHAWMS	CHEWED	THENAL
******	CHABUK	PHAGIA	THADDY	CHEWER	THENAR
AGLAIA	CHACMA				
AGLEAM					

THENCE	CHINKY	THINGS	CHOKES	SHOOIN	SHRANK
THEORY	CHINTZ	THINLY	CHOLER	SHOOTS	SHREDS
THERMO	CHIPPY	THIOLS	CHOLLA	SHOPPE	SHREWD
THERMS	CHIRMS	THIRDS	CHOOSE	SHORAN	SHREWS
THESES	CHIRON	THIRST	CHOOSY	SHORED	SHRIEK
THESIS	CHIRPS	THIRTY	CHOPIN	SHORES	SHRIFT
THETAS	CHIRPY	THISBE	CHOPPY	SHORLS	SHRIKE
THETIC	CHIRRS	WHIDAH	CHORAL	SHORTS	SHRILL
THETIS	CHISEL	WHIFFS	CHORDS	SHOTES	SHRIMP
THEWED	CHITIN	WHILED	CHOREA	SHOULD	SHRINE
WHEALS	CHITON	WHILES	CHOREO	SHOUTS	SHRINK
WHEATS	CHITTY	WHILOM	CHORES	SHOVED	SHRIVE
WHEELS	CHIVES	WHILST	CHORIC	SHOVEL	SHROFF
WHEEZE	CHIVVY	WHIMSY	CHORUS	SHOVER	SHROUD
WHEEZY	OHIOAN	WHINED	CHOSEN	SHOVES	SHROVE
WHELKS	PHIALS	WHINER	CHOUGH	SHOWED	SHRUBS
WHELKY	PHILIA	WHINES	DHOLES	SHOWER	SHRUGS
WHELMS	PHILIP	WHINNY	DHOTIS	THOLES	SHRUNK
WHELPS	PHILOS	WHIPPY	GHOSTS	THOMAS	THRALL
WHENCE	PHIPPS	WHIRLS	GHOULS	THONGS	THRASH
WHERRY	RHINAL	WHISKS	PHOBIA	THORAC	THREAD
WHERVE	RHINOS	WHISKY	PHOBIC	THORAX	THREAT
WHEYEY	RHIZIC	WHITBY	PHOCIS	THORIA	THREED
******	SHIELD	WHITED	PHOEBE	THORIC	THREES
-HI---	SHIEST	WHITEN	PHONED	THORNS	THRESH
******	SHIFTS	WHITER	PHONES	THORNY	THRICE
AHIMSA	SHIFTY	WHITES	PHONEY	THORON	THRIFT
CHIASM	SHIISM	WHITEY	PHONIA	THORPE	THRILL
CHIAUS	SHIITE	******	PHONIC	THOUGH	THRIPS
CHIBUK	SHIKAR	-HL---	PHOOEY	WHOLLY	THRIVE
CHICHI	SHILLS	******	PHOSPH	WHOOPS	THROAT
CHICKS	SHILOH	CHLOES	PHOTIC	WHOOSH	THROBS
CHICLE	SHIMMY	CHLORO	PHOTON	WHORED	THROES
CHICOS	SHINDY	PHLEBO	PHOTOS	WHORES	THRONE
CHIDED	SHINED	PHLEGM	RHODAS	WHORLS	THRONG
CHIDER	SHINER	PHLOEM	RHODES	WHORTS	THROVE
CHIDES	SHINES	******	RHODIC	******	THROWN
CHIEFS	SHINNY	-HM---	RHOMBI	-HR---	THROWS
CHIGOE	SHINTO	******	RHOMBS	******	THRUMS
CHILLI	SHIRES	OHMAGE	SHOALS	CHRISM	THRUSH
CHILLS	SHIRKS	******	SHOALY	CHRIST	THRUST
CHILLY	SHIRRS	-HO---	SHOATS	CHROMA	******
CHIMED	SHIRTS	******	SHOCKS	CHROME	-HT---
CHIMER	SHIRTY	CHOCKS	SHODDY	CHROMO	******
CHIMES	SHIVER	CHOICE	SHOERS	CHRONO	SHTICK
CHINCH	SHIVES	CHOIRS	SHOFAR	CHRYSO	******
CHINES	THIEVE	CHOKED	SHOGUN	PHRASE	-HU---
CHINKS	THIGHS	CHOKER	SHOOED	PHRENO	******
					BHUTAN
					CHUBBY

CHUCKS	THYREO	******	TIBIAE	NICHES	******
CHUFAS	THYRSE	-IB---	TIBIAL	NICKED	-ID---
CHUMMY	THYRSI	******	TIBIAS	NICKEL	******
CHUMPS	WHYDAH	BIBBED	VIBRIO	NICKER	AIDERS
CHUNKS	******	BIBBER	ZIBETH	NICKYS	AIDING
CHUNKY	-IA---	BIBLES	ZIBETS	NICOLE	AIDMAN
CHURCH	BIAFRA	BIBLIO	******	PICKAX	AIDMEN
CHURLS	BIALYS	CIBOLS	-IC---	PICKED	BIDDEN
CHURNS	BIANCA	DIBBED	******	PICKER	BIDDER
CHURRS	BIASED	DIBBER	BICARB	PICKET	BIDETS
CHUTES	BIASES	DIBBLE	BICEPS	PICKLE	BIDING
DHURNA	BIAXAL	FIBBED	BICKER	PICKUP	CIDERS
RHUMBA	DIADEM	FIBBER	BICORN	PICNIC	DIDDLE
RHUMBS	DIALED	FIBERS	CICADA	PICOTS	DIDERO
SHUCKS	DIALER	FIBRIL	CICALA	PICRIC	DIDIES
SHUNTS	DIALOG	FIBRIN	CICELY	PICTOR	DIDOES
SHUTIN	DIANAS	FIBULA	CICERO	PICULS	EIDOLA
THUJAS	DIANES	GIBBED	DICAST	RICERS	FIDDLE
THULIA	DIAPER	GIBBER	DICERS	RICHER	FIDGET
THUMBS	DIATOM	GIBBET	DICING	RICHES	GIDEON
THUMPS	DIAZIN	GIBBON	DICKER	RICHIE	HIDDEN
THUSLY	FIACRE	GIBERS	DICKEY	RICHLY	HIDERS
******	FIANCE	GIBING	DICKIE	RICING	HIDING
-HW---	FIASCO	GIBLET	DICTUM	RICKED	KIDDED
******	GIANTS	GIBRAN	FICHES	RICKEY	KIDDER
THWACK	GIAOUR	GIBSON	FICHUS	RICKYS	KIDDIE
THWART	HIATUS	JIBBED	FICKLE	RICTAL	KIDNAP
******	LIABLE	JIBBER	HICCUP	RICTUS	KIDNEY
-HY---	LIAISE	JIBING	HICKEY	SICILY	LIDDED
******	LIANAS	KIBBLE	HICKOK	SICKED	MIDAIR
CHYMIC	LIANES	KIBEIS	KICKED	SICKEN	MIDDAY
KHYBER	LIASED	KIBITZ	KICKER	SICKER	MIDDEN
PHYLAE	MIASMA	KIBLAH	LICHEE	SICKLE	MIDDLE
PHYLLO	MIAULS	KIBOSH	LICHEN	SICKLY	MIDGES
PHYLUM	NIACIN	LIBBYS	LICKED	TICALS	MIDGET
PHYSIC	PIAFFE	LIBELS	LICTOR	TICKED	MIDGUT
PHYSIO	PIANOS	LIBIDO	MICELL	TICKER	MIDRIB
PHYTIN	PIAZZA	LIBRAE	MICHEL	TICKET	MIDWAY
RHYMED	RIALTO	LIBRAS	MICKEY	TICKLE	NIDIFY
RHYMER	RIATAS	LIBYAN	MICKLE	VICARS	NIDING
RHYMES	SIALIC	NIBBED	MICKYS	VICKYS	PIDDLE
RHYTHM	TIARAS	NIBBLE	MICMAC	VICTIM	PIDGIN
SHYEST	VIABLE	RIBALD	MICRON	VICTOR	RIDDED
SHYING	VIALED	RIBAND	NICELY	VICUNA	RIDDEN
THYMES	VIANDS	RIBBED	NICENE	WICHES	RIDDLE
THYMIC	VIATIC	RIBBON	NICEST	WICKED	RIDENT
THYMOL	VIATOR	RIBOSE	NICETY	WICKER	RIDERS
THYMUS		SIBYLS	NICHED	WICKET	RIDGED
				WICOPY	

RIDGES	PIECES	MIFFED	JIGGED	TIGHTS	BILGED
RIDING	PIEMAN	PIFFLE	JIGGER	TIGRIS	BILGES
SIDDUR	PIEMEN	RIFFLE	JIGGLE	VIGILS	BILITY
SIDERO	PIENAL	RIFLED	JIGSAW	VIGOUR	BILKED
SIDING	PIERCE	RIFLER	LIGAND	WIGANS	BILKER
SIDLED	PIERRE	RIFLES	LIGATE	WIGEON	BILLED
SIDLER	PIERUS	RIFTED	LIGHTS	WIGGED	BILLET
SIDLES	PIETER	SIFTED	LIGNIN	WIGGLE	BILLIE
SIDNEY	PIETRO	SIFTER	LIGNUM	WIGGLY	BILLON
TIDBIT	SIECLE	TIFFED	LIGULA	WIGWAG	BILLOW
TIDIED	SIEGED	TIFFIN	LIGULE	WIGWAM	BILLYS
TIDIER	SIEGES	WIFELY	LIGURE	ZIGZAG	BILOXI
TIDIES	SIENNA	******	MIGGLE	******	CILIAT
TIDILY	SIERRA	-IG---	MIGHTY	-IH---	CILICE
TIDING	SIESTA	******	MIGNON	******	CILIUM
VIDUAL	SIEURS	AIGLET	MIGUEL	BIHARI	DILATE
WIDDIE	SIEVED	BIGAMY	NIGELS	JIHADS	DILUTE
WIDELY	SIEVES	BIGGER	NIGGER	******	EILEEN
WIDENS	TIEINS	BIGGIN	NIGGLE	-IJ---	FILERS
WIDEST	TIEPIN	BIGHTS	NIGHER	******	FILETS
WIDOWS	TIERCE	BIGONE	NIGHTS	BIJOUX	FILIAL
WIDTHS	TIERED	BIGOTS	NIGHTY	FIJIAN	FILING
******	TIEUPS	BIGWIG	PIGEON	HIJACK	FILLED
-IE---	VIENNA	CIGARS	PIGGED	******	FILLER
******	VIEWED	DIGAMY	PIGGIE	-IK---	FILLET
BIERCE	VIEWER	DIGEST	PIGGIN	******	FILLIN
DIEPPE	WIELDS	DIGGED	PIGLET	BIKINI	FILLIP
DIESEL	WIELDY	DIGGER	PIGNUS	BIKOLS	FILMED
DIESES	WIENER	DIGITI	PIGNUT	DIKDIK	FILMIC
DIESIS	WIENIE	DIGITS	PIGPEN	DIKING	FILOSE
DIETAL	YIELDS	DIGLOT	PIGSTY	HIKERS	FILTER
DIETED	******	EIGHTH	RIGGED	HIKING	FILTHY
DIETER	-IF---	EIGHTS	RIGGER	LIKELY	GILDAS
FIELDS	******	EIGHTY	RIGHTO	LIKENS	GILDED
FIENDS	BIFFED	FIGGED	RIGHTS	LIKING	GILDER
FIERCE	BIFFIN	FIGHTS	RIGORS	MIKADO	GILEAD
FIESTA	BIFLEX	FIGURE	RIGOUR	MIKLOS	GILLIE
HIEING	BIFOLD	GIGANT	SIGHED	PIKERS	HILARY
HIEMAL	BIFORM	GIGGED	SIGHTS	PIKING	HILDAS
LIEBIG	DIFFER	GIGGLE	SIGILS	SIKKIM	HILLED
LIEDER	EIFFEL	GIGGLY	SIGMAS	VIKING	HILLER
LIEGES	FIFERS	GIGLET	SIGNAL	WIKIUP	HILTED
LIERNE	FIFING	GIGLOT	SIGNED	******	JILTED
NIECES	FIFTHS	GIGOLO	SIGNER	-IL---	JILTER
NIELLI	GIFTED	GIGUES	SIGNET	******	KILLED
NIELLO	LIFERS	HIGGLE	SIGNOR	AILEEN	KILLER
PIECED	LIFTED	HIGHER	SIGRID	AILING	KILMER
PIECER	LIFTER	HIGHLY	TIGERS	BILBAO	KILTED

KILTER	PILULE	WILSON	NIMBLY	CINEMA	JINKED
KILTIE	RILING	WILTED	NIMBUS	CINEOL	JINKER
LILACS	RILLET	WILTON	NIMITZ	CINQUE	JINNEE
LILIAN	SILAGE	ZILLAH	NIMROD	DINAHS	JINNYS
LILIED	SILENI	******	PIMPED	DINARS	JINXED
LILIES	SILENT	-IM---	PIMPLE	DINDER	JINXES
LILTED	SILICA	******	PIMPLY	DINERO	KINASE
MILADY	SILICO	AIMING	RIMERS	DINERS	KINDER
MILAGE	SILKEN	CIMBRI	RIMING	DINGED	KINDLE
MILDEN	SILOED	DIMERS	RIMMED	DINGEY	KINDLY
MILDER	SILTED	DIMITY	RIMMER	DINGHY	KINESI
MILDEW	SILVAE	DIMMED	RIMOSE	DINGLE	KINETO
MILDLY	SILVAN	DIMMER	RIMOUS	DINGUS	KINGED
MILERS	SILVAS	DIMOUT	RIMPLE	DINING	KINGLY
MILIEU	SILVER	DIMPLE	SIMARS	DINKEY	KININS
MILIUM	SILVIA	DIMPLY	SIMIAN	DINKUM	KINKED
MILKED	TILDES	DIMWIT	SIMILE	DINNED	KINSEY
MILKER	TILERS	FIMBLE	SIMLIN	DINNER	LINAGE
MILLAY	TILING	GIMELS	SIMMER	DINTED	LINDAS
MILLED	TILLED	GIMLET	SIMNEL	FINALE	LINDEN
MILLER	TILLER	GIMPED	SIMONE	FINALS	LINEAL
MILLET	TILLIE	JIMINY	SIMONS	FINDER	LINEAR
MILLIE	TILLYS	JIMMIE	SIMONY	FINELY	LINENS
MILLYS	TILTED	JIMMYS	SIMOOM	FINERY	LINERS
MILORD	TILTER	KIMONO	SIMPER	FINEST	LINEUP
MILTED	TILTHS	LIMBED	SIMPLE	FINGER	LINGAM
MILTER	VILELY	LIMBER	SIMPLY	FINIAL	LINGAS
MILTON	VILEST	LIMBIC	TIMBAL	FINING	LINGER
NILGAI	VILIFY	LIMBUS	TIMBER	FINISH	LINGUA
OILCAN	VILLAS	LIMENS	TIMBRE	FINITE	LINIER
OILERS	VILLON	LIMEYS	TIMELY	FINNAN	LINING
OILIER	VILLUS	LIMIER	TIMERS	FINNED	LINKED
OILILY	WILBER	LIMINA	TIMING	FINNER	LINNET
OILING	WILBUR	LIMING	TIMMYS	FINNIC	LINTEL
PILAFF	WILDER	LIMITS	VIMINA	FINNOC	LINTER
PILAFS	WILDLY	LIMNED	WIMBLE	GINGAL	MINCED
PILATE	WILFUL	LIMNER	WIMPLE	GINGER	MINCER
PILEUM	WILIER	LIMPED	******	GINGKO	MINCES
PILEUP	WILILY	LIMPER	-IN---	GINNED	MINDED
PILEUS	WILING	LIMPET	******	GINNER	MINDER
PILFER	WILLED	LIMPID	BINARY	HINDER	MINERS
PILING	WILLER	LIMPLY	BINATE	HINDUS	MINGLE
PILLAR	WILLET	LIMULI	BINDER	HINGED	MINIFY
PILLED	WILLIE	MIMERS	BINGES	HINGES	MINIMA
PILLOW	WILLIS	MIMICS	BINITS	HINTED	MINIMS
PILOSE	WILLOW	MIMING	BINNED	JINGAL	MINING
PILOTS	WILLYS	MIMOSA	CINDER	JINGLE	MINION
PILOUS	WILMAS	NIMBLE	CINDYS	JINGLY	MINIUM

MINNIE	SINGED	WINKER	DIPPER	TIPPED	DIREST
MINNOW	SINGER	WINKLE	DIPSAS	TIPPER	DIRGES
MINOAN	SINGES	WINNER	FIPPLE	TIPPET	DIRHAM
MINORS	SINGLE	WINNIE	GIPONS	TIPPLE	DIRKED
MINTED	SINGLY	WINNOW	GIPPED	TIPTOE	DIRNDL
MINTER	SINKER	WINOES	HIPPED	TIPTOP	FIRERS
MINUET	SINNED	WINTER	HIPPIE	VIPERS	FIRING
MINUTE	SINNER	WINTRY	HIPPOS	WIPERS	FIRKIN
MINXES	SINTER	WINZES	HIPPUS	WIPING	FIRMAN
NINETY	TINCAL	ZINCED	KIPPED	YIPPED	FIRMED
NINTHS	TINCAN	ZINCIC	KIPPER	YIPPIE	FIRMER
PINANG	TINCTS	ZINCKY	LIPASE	ZIPPED	FIRMLY
PINDAR	TINDER	ZINGED	LIPIDS	ZIPPER	FIRSTS
PINDUS	TINEID	ZINNIA	LIPOID	******	FIRTHS
PINEAL	TINGED	******	LIPOMA	-IQ---	GIRDED
PINENE	TINGES	-IO---	LIPPED	******	GIRDER
PINERY	TINGLE	******	LIPPER	FIQUES	GIRDLE
PINGED	TINGLY	BIOGEN	NIPPED	LIQUID	GIRTED
PINGOS	TINIER	BIOPSY	NIPPER	LIQUOR	HIRAMS
PINIER	TINILY	BIOSIS	NIPPLE	PIQUED	HIRERS
PINIES	TINKER	BIOTIC	NIPPON	PIQUES	HIRING
PINING	TINKLE	BIOTIN	PIPAGE	PIQUET	KIRSCH
PINION	TINKLY	DIOBOL	PIPERS	******	KIRTLE
PINITE	TINNED	DIODES	PIPETS	-IR---	MIRAGE
PINKED	TINNER	FIORDS	PIPIER	******	MIRIAM
PINKIE	TINPOT	GIOTTO	PIPING	AIRBED	MIRING
PINNAE	TINSEL	KIOSKS	PIPITS	AIRDRY	MIRROR
PINNAL	TINTED	LIONEL	PIPKIN	AIRGUN	PIRACY
PINNED	VINCES	MIOSIS	PIPPED	AIRIER	PIRANA
PINNER	VINERY	MIOTIC	PIPPIN	AIRILY	PIRATE
PINOLE	VINIER	NIOBIC	RIPELY	AIRING	SIRDAR
PINONS	VINNYS	RIOTED	RIPENS	AIRMAN	SIRENS
PINTER	VINOUS	RIOTER	RIPEST	AIRMEN	SIRING
PINTLE	VINSON	SIOUAN	RIPLEY	AIRSAC	SIRIUS
PINTOS	VINYLS	VIOLAS	RIPOFF	AIRWAY	SIRUPS
PINUPS	WINCED	VIOLET	RIPOST	BIRDIE	SIRUPY
PINXIT	WINCER	VIOLIN	RIPPED	BIREME	TIRADE
RINGED	WINCES	******	RIPPER	BIRLED	TIRANA
RINGER	WINCEY	-IP---	RIPPLE	BIRLES	TIRING
RINKED	WINDED	******	RIPPLY	BIRRED	VIRAGO
RINSED	WINDER	BIPEDS	RIPRAP	BIRTHS	VIREOS
RINSER	WINDOW	BIPODS	RIPSAW	CIRCLE	VIRGAS
RINSES	WINDUP	CIPHER	SIPHON	CIRCUM	VIRGIE
SINBAD	WINERY	DIPLEX	SIPPED	CIRCUS	VIRGIL
SINEON	WINGED	DIPLOE	SIPPER	CIRQUE	VIRGIN
SINEWS	WINIER	DIPODY	SIPPET	CIRRUS	VIRILE
SINEWY	WINING	DIPOLE	TIPCAT	DIRECT	VIRTUE
SINFUL	WINKED	DIPPED	TIPOFF	DIRELY	WIRERS

WIRIER	KISSES	TISSUE	HITLER	TITLED	LIVING
WIRILY	LISBOA	VISAED	HITTER	TITLES	LIVRES
WIRING	LISBON	VISAGE	JITNEY	TITTER	LIVYER
ZIRCON	LISPED	VISARD	JITTER	TITTLE	PIVOTS
ZIRONS	LISPER	VISCID	KITBAG	TITTUP	RIVALS
******	LISSOM	VISCUS	KITING	VITALS	RIVERS
-IS---	LISTED	VISEED	KITSCH	VITRIC	RIVETS
******	LISTEL	VISHNU	KITTED	VITTAE	RIVING
AISLED	LISTEN	VISING	KITTEN	WITHAL	VIVACE
AISLES	LISTER	VISION	KITTLE	WITHED	VIVIAN
BISCAY	MISCUE	VISITS	KITTYS	WITHER	VIVIEN
BISECT	MISDID	VISORS	LITANY	WITHES	VIVIFY
BISHOP	MISERE	VISTAS	LITCHI	WITHIN	WIVERN
BISQUE	MISERS	VISUAL	LITERS	WITHIT	WIVERS
BISTER	MISERY	WISDOM	LITHER	WITNEY	WIVING
BISTRO	MISFIT	WISELY	LITHIA	WITTED	******
CISCOS	MISHAP	WISEST	LITHIC	ZITHER	**-IW---**
CISSIE	MISKAL	WISHED	LITMUS	******	******
CISSYS	MISLAY	WISHES	LITTER	**-IU---**	DIWANS
DISARM	MISLED	WISING	LITTLE	******	SIWASH
DISBAR	MISSAL	WISPED	MITERS	GIULIA	******
DISCAL	MISSED	******	MITRAL	GIULIO	**-IX---**
DISCUS	MISSEL	**-IT---**	MITRED	******	******
DISHED	MISSES	******	MITTEN	**-IV---**	DIXITS
DISHES	MISSIS	BITCHY	NITRIC	******	FIXATE
DISMAL	MISSUS	BITERS	NITRID	CIVETS	FIXERS
DISMAY	MISTED	BITING	NITWIT	CIVICS	FIXING
DISNEY	MISTER	BITTED	PITCHY	CIVIES	FIXITY
DISOWN	MISTLE	BITTEN	PITHED	CIVISM	MIXERS
DISPEL	MISUSE	BITTER	PITIED	DIVANS	MIXING
DISTAL	NISEIS	CITHER	PITIES	DIVERS	MIXUPS
DISTIL	PISCES	CITIED	PITMAN	DIVERT	NIXIES
DISUSE	PISGAH	CITIES	PITMEN	DIVEST	NIXING
FISCAL	PISHED	CITING	PITONS	DIVIDE	PIXIES
FISHER	PISHES	CITOLA	PITTED	DIVINE	SIXTES
FISHES	PISTIL	CITRAL	RITARD	DIVING	SIXTHS
FISTED	PISTOL	CITRIC	RITTER	DIVOTS	VIXENS
FISTIC	PISTON	CITRON	RITUAL	FIVERS	******
GISELE	RISERS	CITRUS	SITARS	GIVING	**-IY---**
GISMOS	RISING	DITHER	SITING	HIVING	******
HISPID	RISKED	DITONE	SITINS	HIVITE	RIYALS
HISSED	RISKER	DITTOS	SITTER	JIVING	******
HISSER	RISQUE	EITHER	TITANS	LIVELY	**-IZ---**
HISSES	SISERA	FITFUL	TITBIT	LIVENS	******
KISLEW	SISKIN	FITTED	TITHED	LIVERS	DIZENS
KISMET	SISTER	FITTER	TITHER	LIVERY	FIZGIG
KISSED	TISANE	GITANO	TITHES	LIVIAS	FIZZED
KISSER	TISHRI	HITHER	TITIAN	LIVIER	FIZZER

FIZZES	SKEANS	ALARIC	ELAYNE	GLAZES	SLAKES
FIZZLE	SKEINS	ALARMS	FLABBY	KLAXON	SLALOM
GIZMOS	SKERRY	ALARUM	FLACKS	LLAMAS	SLANGY
LIZARD	SKETCH	ALASKA	FLACON	LLANOS	SLANTS
LIZZIE	SKEWED	ALATED	FLAGGY	PLACED	SLAPUP
LIZZYS	SKEWER	BLACKS	FLAGON	PLACER	SLATED
MIZZEN	******	BLADED	FLAILS	PLACES	SLATER
MIZZLE	-KI---	BLADES	FLAIRS	PLACET	SLATES
PIZZAS	******	BLAINS	FLAKED	PLACID	SLAVED
SIZARS	AKIMBO	BLAISE	FLAKER	PLACKS	SLAVER
SIZIER	SKIERS	BLAMED	FLAKES	PLAGAL	SLAVES
SIZING	SKIFFS	BLAMES	FLAMBE	PLAGIO	SLAVIC
SIZZLE	SKIING	BLANCH	FLAMED	PLAGUE	SLAYER
VIZARD	SKILLS	BLANKS	FLAMEN	PLAGUY	******
VIZIER	SKIMOS	BLARED	FLAMES	PLAICE	-LB---
VIZIRS	SKIMPS	BLARES	FLANGE	PLAIDS	******
VIZORS	SKIMPY	BLASTO	FLANKS	PLAINS	ALBANY
WIZARD	SKINKS	BLASTS	FLARED	PLAINT	ALBATA
WIZENS	SKINNY	BLAZED	FLARES	PLAITS	ALBEDO
ZIZITH	SKIRRS	BLAZER	FLASHY	PLANAR	ALBEIT
ZIZZLE	SKIRTS	BLAZES	FLASKS	PLANCH	ALBERT
******	SKIVED	BLAZON	FLATLY	PLANCK	ALBINO
-JE---	SKIVER	CLACKS	FLATUS	PLANED	ALBION
******	SKIVES	CLAIMS	FLAUNT	PLANER	ALBITE
EJECTA	SKIVVY	CLAIRE	FLAVIA	PLANES	ALBUMS
EJECTS	******	CLAMMY	FLAVIN	PLANET	ELBERT
******	-KO---	CLAMOR	FLAVOR	PLANKS	ELBOWS
-JI---	******	CLAMPS	FLAWED	PLANTS	ELBRUS
******	SKOPJE	CLANGS	FLAXEN	PLAQUE	******
OJIBWA	******	CLANKS	FLAXES	PLASHY	-LC---
******	-KU---	CLAQUE	FLAYED	PLASIA	******
-JO---	******	CLARAS	FLAYER	PLASIS	ALCAIC
******	SKULKS	CLARES	GLACES	PLASMA	ALCOTT
AJOWAN	SKULLS	CLARET	GLACIS	PLASMO	ALCOVE
******	SKUNKS	CLAROS	GLADES	PLASTY	ALCUIN
-KA---	******	CLASPS	GLADLY	PLATAN	ULCERS
******	-KY---	CLASSY	GLADYS	PLATED	******
OKAPIS	******	CLAUDE	GLAIRS	PLATEN	-LD---
OKAYED	SKYCAP	CLAUSE	GLAIRY	PLATER	******
SKALDS	SKYING	CLAWED	GLAMIS	PLATES	ALDERS
SKATED	SKYMAN	CLAYED	GLANCE	PLATTE	ALDINE
SKATER	SKYMEN	CLAYEY	GLANDS	PLAYAS	ALDOSE
SKATES	SKYWAY	ELAINE	GLARED	PLAYED	ALDOUS
UKASES	******	ELANDS	GLARES	PLAYER	ELDERS
******	-LA---	ELAPSE	GLASSY	PLAZAS	ELDEST
-KE---	******	ELATED	GLAUCO	SLACKS	ELDRED
******	ALALIA	ELATER	GLAZED	SLAGGY	OLDEST
AKENES	ALAMOS	ELATES	GLAZER	SLAKED	OLDHAM
EKEING					OLDISH

******	FLEDGY	SLEUTH	CLIMES	SLICES	ILLUST
-LE---	FLEECE	SLEWED	CLINCH	SLICKS	OLLIES
******	FLEECY	ULEMAS	CLINES	SLIDER	ULLAGE
ALECTO	FLEERS	ULENCE	CLINGS	SLIDES	******
ALEGAR	FLEETS	******	CLINGY	SLIEST	-LM---
ALEPHS	FLENCH	-LF---	CLINIC	SLIGHT	******
ALEPPO	FLENSE	******	CLINKS	SLIMED	ALMAHS
ALERTS	FLESHY	ALFAKI	CLINTS	SLIMES	ALMIRA
ALEUTS	FLETCH	ALFONS	CLIQUE	SLIMLY	ALMOND
ALEXIA	FLEURY	ALFRED	CLIQUY	SLIMSY	ALMOST
ALEXIN	FLEXED	ELFINS	CLIVES	SLINGS	ALMUCE
ALEXIS	FLEXES	ELFISH	ELICIT	SLINKS	ALMUDE
BLEACH	FLEXOR	ILFORD	ELIDED	SLINKY	ALMUDS
BLEAKS	GLEAMS	******	ELIDES	SLIPON	ELMERS
BLEARS	GLEAMY	-LG---	ELIJAH	SLIPUP	ELMIRA
BLEARY	GLEANS	******	ELINOR	SLIVER	******
BLEATS	GLEBES	ALGOID	ELIOTS	******	-LO---
BLEBBY	GLEDES	ALGOUS	ELISHA	-LK---	******
BLEEDS	GLEETS	******	ELIXIR	******	ALONSO
BLENCH	GLEETY	-LI---	ELIZAS	ALKALI	ALONZO
BLENDE	ILEXES	******	FLICKS	ALKANE	BLOATS
BLENDS	OLEATE	ALIBIS	FLIERS	ALKENE	BLOCKS
BLENNY	OLEFIN	ALIBLE	FLIEST	ALKYLS	BLOCKY
CLEANS	PLEACH	ALICES	FLIGHT	ALKYNE	BLOKES
CLEARS	PLEADS	ALICIA	FLIMSY	******	BLONDE
CLEATS	PLEASE	ALIDAD	FLINCH	-LL---	BLONDS
CLEAVE	PLEATS	ALIENS	FLINGS	******	BLOODS
CLEFTS	PLEBES	ALIGHT	FLINTS	ALLANS	BLOODY
CLEIST	PLEDGE	ALIGNS	FLINTY	ALLAYS	BLOOMS
CLENCH	PLEGIA	ALINED	FLIRTS	ALLEGE	BLOOMY
CLEOME	PLEIAD	ALINES	FLIRTY	ALLELE	BLOTCH
CLERGY	PLENTY	ALIPED	FLITCH	ALLENS	BLOUSE
CLERIC	PLENUM	ALISON	GLIBLY	ALLEYS	BLOWBY
CLERID	PLEURA	BLIGHT	GLIDED	ALLIED	BLOWER
CLERKS	PLEURO	BLIMEY	GLIDER	ALLIES	BLOWUP
CLEVER	PLEXOR	BLIMPS	GLIDES	ALLIUM	BLOWZY
CLEVIS	PLEXUS	BLINDS	GLINTS	ALLOTS	CLOACA
CLEWED	SLEAVE	BLINKS	GLIOMA	ALLOUT	CLOAKS
ELECTS	SLEAZY	BLINTZ	OLIVER	ALLOWS	CLOCHE
ELEGIT	SLEDGE	BLITHE	OLIVES	ALLOYS	CLOCKS
ELEMIS	SLEEKS	CLICHE	OLIVIA	ALLUDE	CLODDY
ELENAS	SLEEKY	CLICKS	PLIANT	ALLURE	CLOGGY
ELEVEN	SLEEPS	CLIENT	PLICAE	ALLYLS	CLONES
ELEVON	SLEEPY	CLIFFS	PLIERS	ELLENS	CLONIC
FLEAMS	SLEETS	CLIFFY	PLIGHT	ELLIES	CLONUS
FLECHE	SLEETY	CLIMAT	PLINTH	ELLIOT	CLOSED
FLECKS	SLEEVE	CLIMAX	SLICED	ILLUME	CLOSER
FLEDGE	SLEIGH	CLIMBS	SLICER	ILLUSE	CLOSES

CLOSET	GLOBES	ELSIES	FLUKEY	ALVINE	******
CLOTHE	GLOBIN	ULSTER	FLUMED	ELVERS	-MB---
CLOTHO	GLOOMS	******	FLUMES	ELVIRA	******
CLOTHS	GLOOMY	-LT---	FLUMPS	ELVISH	AMBAGE
CLOTTY	GLORIA	******	FLUNKS	******	AMBARI
CLOUDS	GLOSSO	ALTAIC	FLUNKY	-LW---	AMBARY
CLOUDY	GLOSSY	ALTAIR	FLUORO	******	AMBERS
CLOUGH	GLOSTS	ALTARS	FLUORS	ALWAYS	AMBERY
CLOUTS	GLOTTO	ALTERS	FLURRY	******	AMBITS
CLOVEN	GLOVED	ALTHEA	FLUTED	-LY---	AMBLED
CLOVER	GLOVER	ULTIMA	FLUTER	******	AMBLER
CLOVES	GLOVES	ULTIMO	FLUTES	CLYDES	AMBLES
CLOVIS	GLOWED	******	FLUVIO	CLYPEI	AMBUSH
CLOWNS	GLOWER	-LU---	FLUXED	ELYSEE	EMBALM
CLOYED	GLOZED	******	FLUXES	ELYTRA	EMBANK
ELOHIM	GLOZES	ALUDEL	GLUIER	FLYBYS	EMBARK
ELOIGN	ILOILO	ALUINO	GLUING	FLYERS	EMBARS
ELOINS	LLOYDS	ALUINS	GLUMES	FLYING	EMBAYS
ELOISE	PLOUGH	ALULAE	GLUMLY	FLYMAN	EMBEDS
ELOPED	PLOVER	ALULAR	GLUTEI	GLYCOL	EMBERS
ELOPER	PLOWED	ALUMIN	GLUTEN	GLYNIS	EMBLEM
ELOPES	PLOWER	ALUMNA	PLUCKS	GLYPHS	EMBODY
FLOATS	SLOGAN	ALUMNI	PLUCKY	GLYPTO	EMBOLI
FLOATY	SLOOPS	BLUELY	PLUGIN	PLYING	EMBOSS
FLOCKS	SLOPED	BLUEST	PLUMBO	SLYEST	EMBOWS
FLOCKY	SLOPER	BLUETS	PLUMBS	******	EMBRUE
FLONGS	SLOPES	BLUFFS	PLUMED	-MA---	EMBRYO
FLOODS	SLOPPY	BLUING	PLUMES	******	IMBALM
FLOORS	SLOSHY	BLUISH	PLUMMY	AMADOU	IMBARK
FLOOZY	SLOTHS	BLUNGE	PLUMPS	AMALIE	IMBEDS
FLOPPY	SLOUCH	BLUNTS	PLUNGE	AMANDA	IMBIBE
FLORAE	SLOUGH	BLURBS	PLUNKS	AMANIA	IMBODY
FLORAL	SLOVAK	BLURRY	PLURAL	AMATOL	IMBRUE
FLORAS	SLOVEN	BLURTS	PLUSES	AMAZED	IMBUED
FLORES	SLOWED	CLUCKS	PLUSHY	AMAZES	IMBUES
FLORET	SLOWER	CLUING	PLUTUS	AMAZON	UMBELS
FLORID	SLOWLY	CLUMPS	PLUVIO	IMAGED	UMBERS
FLORIN	ZLOTYS	CLUMPY	SLUDGE	IMAGES	UMBLES
FLOSSY	******	CLUMSY	SLUDGY	IMARET	UMBRAE
FLOURS	-LP---	CLUTCH	SLUICE	OMASUM	UMBRAL
FLOURY	******	ELUDED	SLUING	SMACKS	UMBRAS
FLOUTS	ALPACA	ELUDES	SLUMMY	SMALLS	******
FLOWED	ALPHAS	FLUENT	SLUMPS	SMALTI	-MC---
FLOWER	ALPHOS	FLUFFS	SLURPS	SMALTO	******
	ALPHYL	FLUFFY	SLURRY	SMARMY	EMCEED
FLOYDS	ALPINE	FLUIDS	SLUSHY	SMARTS	EMCEES
	******	FLUKED	******	SMAZES	******
GLOATS	-LS---	FLUKES	-LV---		-ME---
GLOBAL	******		******		******
GLOBED	ALSACE		ALVANS		AMEBAE
	ALSIKE		ALVINA		AMEBAS

AMEBIC	SMILER	******	******	UNABLE	UNCIAL
AMECHE	SMILES	**-MP---**	**-MY---**	UNAPID	UNCLAD
AMELIA	SMIRCH	******	******	******	UNCLES
AMELIE	SMIRKS	AMPERE	AMYLIC	**-NB---**	UNCOCK
AMENDS	SMITER	AMPHRS	AMYLUM	******	UNCOIL
AMENRA	SMITES	AMPULE	AMYTAL	INBAND	UNCORD
AMENTI	SMITHS	AMPULS	******	INBORN	UNCORK
AMENTS	SMITHY	EMPALE	**-NA---**	INBRED	UNCURL
AMERCE	UMIAKS	EMPERY	******	UNBARS	******
EMEERS	******	EMPIRE	ANABAS	UNBEAR	**-ND---**
EMENDS	**-ML---**	EMPERY	ANADEM	UNBELT	******
EMERGE	******	EMPLOY	ANALOG	UNBEND	ANDEAN
EMERIC	UMLAUT	IMPACT	ANANAS	UNBENT	ANDREA
EMERIE	******	IMPAIR	ANANKE	UNBIND	ANDREI
EMESIS	**-MM---**	IMPALA	ANATTO	UNBOLT	ANDRES
EMETIC	******	IMPALE	ENABLE	UNBORN	ANDREW
EMETIN	EMMETS	IMPARK	ENACTS	UNBRED	ENDALL
EMEUTE	EMMETT	IMPART	ENAMEL	******	ENDEAR
OMEGAS	EMMIES	IMPASS	ENAMOR	**-NC---**	ENDING
OMELET	IMMESH	IMPAWN	ENATES	******	ENDIVE
OMENTA	IMMIES	IMPEDE	GNARLS	ANCHOR	ENDOWS
SMEARS	IMMUNE	IMPELS	GNARLY	ANCONA	ENDUED
SMEARY	IMMUNO	IMPEND	GNATHO	ANCONE	ENDUES
SMELLS	IMMURE	IMPING	GNAWED	ENCAGE	ENDURE
SMELLY	******	IMPISH	GNAWER	ENCAMP	INDABA
SMELTS	**-MN---**	IMPORT	INARCH	ENCASE	INDEED
******	******	IMPOSE	INARMS	ENCASH	INDENE
-MI---	AMNION	IMPOST	KNACKS	ENCINA	INDENT
******	OMNIUM	IMPUGN	KNARRY	ENCODE	INDIAN
AMICES	******	IMPURE	KNAVES	ENCORE	INDICT
AMIDES	**-MO---**	IMPUTE	ONAGER	ENCYST	INDIES
AMIDIC	******	UMPIRE	ONAGRI	INCAGE	INDIGO
AMIDIN	AMOEBA	******	SNACKS	INCASE	INDITE
AMIDOL	AMOLES	**-MR---**	SNAFUS	INCEPT	INDIUM
AMIDST	AMORAL	AMRITA	SNAGGY	INCEST	INDOOR
AMIENS	AMOUNT	******	SNAILS	INCHED	INDOWS
AMIGOS	AMOURS	**-MU---**	SNAKED	INCHES	INDRIS
DMITRI	EMOTED	******	SNAKES	INCHON	INDUCE
EMIGRE	EMOTES	AMULET	SNAPPY	INCISE	INDUCT
EMILES	IMOGEN	AMUSED	SNARED	INCITE	INDUED
EMILIA	SMOCKS	AMUSER	SNARER	INCOME	INDUES
EMILIE	SMOKED	AMUSES	SNARES	INCORP	INDULT
EMILIO	SMOKER	SMUDGE	SNARLS	INCUBI	UNDIES
EMILYS	SMOKES	SMUDGY	SNARLY	INCURS	UNDINE
IMIDES	SMOLTS	SMUGLY	SNATCH	INCUSE	UNDOER
IMINES	SMOOCH	SMUTCH	SNATHE	UNCAGE	UNDOES
SMILAX	SMOOTH	SMUTTY	SNATHS	UNCAPS	UNDONE
SMILED			SNAZZY	UNCASE	UNDRAW

UNDREW	INFUSE	UNHAND	INJECT	INMATE	KNOUTS
UNDSET	ONFALL	UNHASP	INJOKE	INMESH	KNOWER
UNDULY	UNFAIR	UNHATS	INJURE	INMOST	SNOBBY
******	UNFOLD	UNHEWN	INJURY	UNMADE	SNOCAT
-NE---	UNFURL	UNHOLY	UNJUST	UNMAKE	SNOODS
******	******	UNHOOK	******	UNMANS	SNOOKS
ANEMIA	-NG---	UNHURT	-NK---	UNMASK	SNOOPS
ANEMIC	******	UNHUSK	******	UNMEET	SNOOPY
ANERGY	ANGARY	******	ANKARA	UNMEWS	SNOOTS
ENEMAS	ANGELA	-NI---	ANKLES	UNMOOR	SNOOTY
ENERGY	ANGELO	******	ANKLET	******	SNOOZE
GNEISS	ANGELS	ANILIN	ANKYLO	-NN---	SNORED
KNEADS	ANGERS	ANIMAL	INKERS	******	SNORER
KNEELS	ANGINA	ANIMAS	INKIER	ANNALS	SNORES
KNELLS	ANGKOR	ANIMUS	INKING	ANNEAL	SNORTS
ONEIDA	ANGLED	ANIONS	INKLES	ANNEXE	SNOTTY
ONEILL	ANGLER	ANISES	INKPOT	ANNIES	SNOUTS
ONEIRO	ANGLES	ANITAS	UNKIND	ANNONA	SNOWED
ONEOFF	ANGLIA	ANITRA	UNKNIT	ANNOYS	******
ONEWAY	ANGLIC	ENIGMA	******	ANNUAL	-NP---
PNEUMA	ANGOLA	ENISLE	-NL---	ANNULS	******
PNEUMO	ANGORA	KNIFED	******	ENNEAD	INPUTS
SNEAKS	ENGAGE	KNIFES	ANLACE	INNATE	UNPACK
SNEAKY	ENGELS	KNIGHT	ANLAGE	INNING	UNPEGS
SNEERS	ENGINE	KNIVES	ENLACE	******	UNPICK
SNEEZE	ENGIRD	ONIONS	ENLIST	-NO---	UNPILE
SNEEZY	ENGIRT	ONIONY	INLACE	******	UNPINS
SNELLS	ENGRAM	SNICKS	INLAID	ANODES	UNPLUG
UNEASE	ENGULF	SNIFFS	INLAND	ANODIC	******
UNEASY	INGEST	SNIFFY	INLAWS	ANOINT	-NR---
UNESCO	INGOTS	SNIPED	INLAYS	ANOMIA	******
UNEVEN	INGRES	SNIPER	INLETS	ANOMIC	ENRAGE
******	INGRID	SNIPES	INLIER	ANOMIE	ENRAPT
-NF---	INGULF	SNIPPY	ONLINE	ANONYM	ENRICH
******	UNGIRD	SNITCH	UNLACE	ANORAK	ENRICO
ENFACE	UNGIRT	SNIVEL	UNLADE	ANOXIA	ENROBE
ENFOLD	UNGUAL	UNICEF	UNLAID	ANOXIC	ENROLL
INFAMY	UNGUES	UNIFIC	UNLASH	ENOSIS	ENROOT
INFANT	UNGUIS	UNIONS	UNLAYS	ENOUGH	INROAD
INFECT	UNGULA	UNIPED	UNLEAD	GNOMES	INRUSH
INFERO	******	UNIQUE	UNLESS	GNOMIC	ONRUSH
INFERS	-NH---	UNISEX	UNLIKE	GNOMON	UNREAD
INFEST	******	UNISON	UNLIVE	GNOSIS	UNREAL
INFIRM	INHALE	UNITED	UNLOAD	KNOBBY	UNREEL
INFLOW	INHAUL	UNITES	UNLOCK	KNOCKS	UNREST
INFLUX	INHERE	******	******	KNOLLS	UNRIGS
INFOLD	INHUME	-NJ---	-NM---	KNOSPS	UNRIPE
INFORM	UNHAIR	******	******	KNOTTY	UNRIPS
		ENJOIN	ENMESH		
		ENJOYS	ENMITY		

UNROBE	ANTHEA	INURED	ANYWAY	MOATED	GOBLET
UNROLL	ANTHEM	INURES	UNYOKE	POACHY	GOBLIN
UNROOT	ANTHER	INURNS	******	ROALDS	HOBART
UNRULY	ANTIAR	KNURLS	**-NZ---**	ROAMED	HOBBES
******	ANTICS	KNURLY	******	ROAMER	HOBBLE
-NS---	ANTLER	ONUSES	ENZYME	ROARED	HOBNOB
******	ANTLIA	SNUFFS	******	ROARER	HOBOES
ANSATE	ANTONS	SNUFFY	**-OA---**	ROASTS	JOBBED
ANSELM	ANTONY	SNUGLY	******	SOAKED	JOBBER
ANSWER	ANTRIM	UNUSED	BOARDS	SOAKER	KOBOLD
ENSIGN	ANTRUM	******	BOASTS	SOAPED	LOBATE
ENSILE	ENTAIL	**-NV---**	BOATED	SOARED	LOBBED
ENSOUL	ENTERA	******	BOATER	SOARER	LOBBER
ENSUED	ENTERE	ANVILS	COALED	TOASTS	LOBULE
ENSUES	ENTERO	ENVIED	COALER	WOADED	MOBBED
ENSURE	ENTERS	ENVIER	COARSE	WOALDS	MOBBER
INSANE	ENTICE	ENVIES	COASTS	******	MOBCAP
INSECT	ENTIRE	ENVOYS	COATED	**-OB---**	MOBILE
INSERT	ENTITY	INVADE	COATEE	******	MOBIUS
INSETS	ENTOMB	INVENT	COATIS	BOBBED	NOBALL
INSIDE	ENTOMO	INVERT	COAXAL	BOBBER	NOBBED
INSIST	ENTRAP	INVEST	COAXED	BOBBIE	NOBBLE
INSOLE	ENTREE	INVITE	COAXER	BOBBIN	NOBLER
INSOUL	INTACT	INVOKE	COAXES	BOBBLE	NOBODY
INSPAN	INTAKE	UNVEIL	DOABLE	BOBBYS	ROBALO
INSTAR	INTEND	UNVEXT	DOALLS	BOBCAT	ROBAND
INSTEP	INTENT	******	FOALED	COBALT	ROBBED
INSTIL	INTERN	**-NW---**	FOAMED	COBBER	ROBBER
INSULT	INTERS	ENWIND	GOADED	COBBLE	ROBBIA
INSURE	INTIMA	ENWOMB	GOALIE	COBBLY	ROBBIE
ONSETS	INTOMB	ENWRAP	GOATEE	COBIAS	ROBERT
UNSAFE	INTONE	INWALL	GOATED	COBLES	ROBING
UNSAID	INTUIT	INWARD	HOARDS	COBNUT	ROBINS
UNSAYS	INTURN	INWIND	HOARSE	COBRAS	ROBLES
UNSEAL	UNTACK	INWOVE	HOAXED	COBURG	ROBOTS
UNSEAM	UNTIDY	INWRAP	HOAXER	COBWEB	ROBSON
UNSEAT	UNTIED	ONWARD	HOAXES	DOBBER	ROBUST
UNSEEN	UNTIES	UNWARY	JOANNA	DOBBIN	SOBBED
UNSHIP	UNTOLD	UNWELL	JOANNE	DOBIES	SOBERS
UNSHOD	UNTROD	UNWEPT	KOALAS	DOBLAS	TOBAGO
UNSOLD	UNTRUE	UNWIND	LOADED	DOBLON	TOBIAH
UNSTEP	******	UNWISE	LOADER	DOBRAS	TOBIAS
UNSTOP	**-NU---**	UNWISH	LOAFED	DOBSON	TOBIES
UNSUNG	******	UNWORN	LOAFER	FOBBED	WOBBLE
UNSURE	**-NU---**	UNWRAP	LOAMED	GOBANG	WOBBLY
******	ANUBIS	******	LOANED	GOBBET	******
-NT---	ANURAN	**-NY---**	LOATHE	GOBBLE	**-OC---**
******	ANUSES	******	LOAVES	GOBIES	******
ANTEED	INULIN	ANYHOW	MOANED	GOBLET	BOCCIE
ANTERO		ANYONE			COCAIN

COCCAL
COCCID
COCCUS
COCCYX
COCHIN
COCKED
COCKER
COCKLE
COCKUP
COCOAS
COCOON
DOCENT
DOCILE
DOCKED
DOCKER
DOCKET
DOCTOR
EOCENE
FOCSLE
GOCART
HOCKED
HOCKEY
JOCKEY
JOCKOS
JOCOSE
JOCUND
LOCALE
LOCALS
LOCATE
LOCHIA
LOCKED
LOCKER
LOCKET
LOCKUP
LOCOED
LOCUST
MOCKED
MOCKER
MOCKUP
NOCENT
NOCKED
OOCYTE
POCKET
ROCHET
ROCKED
ROCKER
ROCKET
ROCKNE

ROCOCO
SOCAGE
SOCCER
SOCIAL
SOCKED
SOCKET
SOCLES
SOCMAN
SOCMEN
SOCRED
TOCSIN
VOCALS
******
-OD---
******
BODEGA
BODICE
BODIED
BODIES
BODILY
BODING
BODKIN
CODDER
CODDLE
CODEIA
CODEIN
CODGER
CODIFY
CODING
DODDER
DODECA
DODGED
DODGER
DODGES
DODOES
FODDER
GODDAM
GODIVA
GODSON
GODWIN
GODWIT
HODDEN
HODMAN
IODATE
IODIDE
IODINE
IODISM
IODIZE

IODOUS
KODAKS
KODIAK
LODGED
LODGER
LODGES
MODELS
MODERN
MODEST
MODIFY
MODISH
MODULE
NODDED
NODDER
NODDLE
NODOSE
NODULE
OODLES
PODDED
PODIUM
PODOUS
PODSOL
PODUNK
PODZOL
RODDYS
RODENT
RODEOS
RODMAN
RODMEN
RODNEY
SODDED
SODDEN
SODIUM
SODOMY
TODDLE
TODIES
VODKAS
YODELS
ZODIAC
******
-OE---
******
COELED
COELOM
COEMPT
COERCE
COEVAL
DOESNT

FOEHNS
FOEMAN
FOEMEN
FOETAL
FOETID
FOETOR
FOETUS
GOETHE
HOEING
NOELLE
NOESIS
NOETIC
POETIC
POETRY
SOEVER
TOECAP
TOEING
WOEFUL
******
-OF---
******
BOFFIN
COFFEE
COFFER
COFFIN
COFFLE
DOFFED
DOFFER
GOFFER
LOFTED
LOFTER
SOFFIT
SOFTAS
SOFTEN
SOFTER
SOFTLY
TOFFEE
******
-OG---
******
BOGANS
BOGEYS
BOGGED
BOGGLE
BOGIES
BOGLES
BOGOAK
BOGOTA

COGENT
COGGED
COGNAC
COGWAY
DOGAPE
DOGEAR
DOGFOX
DOGGED
DOGGER
DOGGIE
DOGIES
DOGMAS
EOGENE
FOGBOW
FOGDOG
FOGGED
FOGIES
GOGGLE
GOGLET
HOGANS
HOGGED
HOGNUT
HOGTIE
JOGGED
JOGGER
JOGGLE
LOGGED
LOGGER
LOGGIA
LOGIER
LOGION
LOGJAM
MOGULS
NOGGIN
NOGOOD
POGIES
POGROM
ROGERS
ROGUED
ROGUES
TOGAED
TOGGED
TOGGLE
TOGUES
VOGUES
VOGULS
YOGEES
YOGINS
YOGURT

******
-OH---
******
COHEIR
COHERE
COHORT
COHOSH
COHUNE
JOHANN
JOHNNY
MOHAIR
MOHAVE
MOHAWK
MOHOCK
MOHOLE
MOHURS
******
-OI---
******
BOILED
BOILER
COIFED
COIGNS
COILED
COILER
COINED
COINER
COITAL
COITUS
DOINGS
DOITED
FOIBLE
FOILED
FOISTS
GOINGS
GOITER
GOITRE
HOICKS
HOIDEN
HOISTS
JOINED
JOINER
JOINTS
JOISTS
KOINES
LOITER
MOIETY

MOILED	BOLERO	GOLDEN	POLICY	VOLUME	HOMELY
MOILER	BOLEYN	GOLFED	POLING	VOLUTE	HOMERS
MOIRAS	BOLIDE	GOLFER	POLISH	VOLVAS	HOMIER
MOISHE	BOLLED	GOLOSH	POLITE	VOLVOX	HOMILY
NOISED	BOLLIX	HOLARD	POLITY	WOLFED	HOMING
NOISES	BOLSON	HOLDER	POLKAS	WOLSEY	HOMINY
POILUS	BOLTED	HOLDUP	POLLED	WOLVER	LOMENT
POINDS	BOLTER	HOLIER	POLLEE	WOLVES	LOMOND
POINTE	BOLTON	HOLIES	POLLEN	******	MOMENT
POINTS	COLDER	HOLILY	POLLER	-OM---	MOMISM
POINTY	COLDLY	HOLING	POLLEX	******	NOMADS
POISED	COLEUS	HOLISM	POLLUX	BOMBAY	NOMISM
POISES	COLIES	HOLLER	POLLYS	BOMBED	NOMURA
POISON	COLINE	HOLLOW	POLYPS	BOMBER	OOMIAK
ROILED	COLINS	HOLLYS	ROLAND	BOMBES	POMACE
SOIGNE	COLLAR	HOLMES	ROLLED	BOMBIC	POMADE
SOILED	COLLET	HOLMIC	ROLLER	COMATE	POMELO
SOIREE	COLLIE	IOLCUS	ROLLUP	COMBAT	POMMEL
TOILED	COLLOP	IOLITE	ROLPHS	COMBED	POMONA
TOILER	COLONS	JOLIET	SOLACE	COMBER	POMPEY
TOILES	COLONY	JOLTED	SOLAND	COMBOS	POMPOM
TOILET	COLORS	JOLTER	SOLANO	COMEDO	POMPON
VOICED	COLOUR	LOLITA	SOLANS	COMEDY	ROMAIC
VOICES	COLOUS	LOLLED	SOLDER	COMELY	ROMANS
VOIDED	COLTER	LOLLER	SOLELY	COMEON	ROMANY
VOILES	COLUGO	LOLLOP	SOLEMN	COMERS	ROMISH
YOICKS	COLUMN	MOLARS	SOLENT	COMETS	ROMMEL
******	COLURE	MOLDED	SOLIDI	COMFIT	ROMNEY
-OJ---	COLZAS	MOLDER	SOLIDS	COMICS	ROMOLA
******	DOLING	MOLEST	SOLING	COMING	ROMPED
MOJAVE	DOLLAR	MOLIES	SOLION	COMITY	ROMPER
******	DOLLED	MOLINE	SOLOED	COMMAS	ROMULO
-OK---	DOLLIE	MOLLAH	SOLUTE	COMMIE	SOMALI
******	DOLLOP	MOLLIE	SOLVED	COMMIT	SOMATA
COKING	DOLLYS	MOLLYS	SOLVER	COMMIX	SOMATO
GOKART	DOLMAN	MOLOCH	SOLVES	COMMON	SOMBER
JOKERS	DOLMEN	MOLTED	TOLEDO	COMOSE	SOMBRE
JOKING	DOLOUR	MOLTEN	TOLLED	COMOUS	SOMITE
KOKOMO	DOLPHS	MOLTER	TOLLER	COMPEL	TOMANS
POKERS	EOLIAN	MOLTKE	TOLTEC	COMPLY	TOMATO
POKIER	EOLITH	OOLITE	TOLUOL	COMPOS	TOMBAC
POKIES	FOLDED	OOLOGY	TOLUYL	DOMAIN	TOMBED
POKING	FOLDER	OOLONG	VOLANT	DOMING	TOMBOY
TOKENS	FOLIAR	POLACK	VOLERY	DOMINO	TOMCAT
YOKELS	FOLIOS	POLAND	VOLING	FOMENT	TOMCOD
YOKING	FOLIUM	POLDER	VOLLEY	GOMUTI	TOMMYS
******	FOLKSY	POLEAX	VOLOST	HOMAGE	TOMTIT
-OL---	FOLLOW	POLICE	VOLTED	HOMBRE	TOMTOM
******					
BOLDER					
BOLDLY					

VOMERS	CONNED	IONIZE	SONANT	COOEES	HOOPED
VOMICA	CONNER	IONONE	SONARS	COOERS	HOOPER
VOMITO	CONNIE	JONAHS	SONATA	COOEYS	HOOPLA
VOMITS	CONOID	JONNIE	SONDER	COOING	HOOPOE
WOMBAT	CONRAD	JONSON	SONIAS	COOKED	HOORAY
WOMBED	CONSUL	KONRAD	SONNET	COOKER	HOOTCH
WOMERA	CONTES	LONDON	SONYAS	COOKEY	HOOTED
ZOMBIE	CONTIN	LONELY	TONERS	COOKIE	HOOTER
ZOMBIS	CONTOS	LONERS	TONGED	COOLED	HOOVED
******	CONTRA	LONGAN	TONGUE	COOLER	HOOVER
-ON---	CONTRE	LONGED	TONICS	COOLIE	HOOVES
******	CONVEX	LONGER	TONIER	COOLLY	KOODOO
BONACI	CONVEY	MONACO	TONING	COOMBS	LOOFAH
BONBON	CONVOY	MONADS	TONITE	COOPED	LOOING
BONDED	CONWAY	MONDAY	TONKIN	COOPER	LOOKED
BONDER	DONALD	MONEYS	TONSIL	COOPTS	LOOKER
BONERS	DONATE	MONGER	WONDER	COOTIE	LOOKIN
BONGED	DONEES	MONGOL	WONTED	DOODAD	LOOMED
BONGOS	DONETS	MONGST	YONDER	DOODLE	LOOPED
BONIER	DONJON	MONICA	YONKER	DOOLEE	LOOPER
BONING	DONKEY	MONIED	ZONARY	DOOLIE	LOOSED
BONITO	DONNAS	MONIES	ZONATE	DOOMED	LOOSEN
BONNET	DONNED	MONISM	ZONING	FOOLED	LOOSER
BONNIE	DONNIE	MONIST	ZONULA	FOOTED	LOOSES
BONNYS	DONORS	MONKEY	ZONULE	FOOTER	LOOTED
BONSAI	EONIAN	MONODY	******	FOOTLE	LOOTER
BONZER	EONISM	MONROE	-OO---	FOOZLE	MOOING
BONZES	FONDER	MONTES	******	GOOBER	MOOLAH
CONCHA	FONDLE	MONTHS	BOOBOO	GOODBY	MOOLEY
CONCHS	FONDLY	MONTYS	BOODLE	GOODLY	MOONED
CONCHY	FONDUE	NONAGE	BOOGIE	GOOFED	MOORED
CONCUR	FONTAL	NONARY	BOOHOO	GOOGLY	MOOTED
CONDOM	GONADS	NONCOM	BOOING	GOOGOL	MOOTER
CONDOR	GONERS	NONEGO	BOOKED	GOOIER	NOODLE
CONEYS	GONION	PONCHO	BOOKIE	GOONEY	NOOSED
CONFAB	GONIUM	PONDER	BOOMED	GOORAL	NOOSES
CONFER	HONEST	PONENT	BOOMER	GOOSED	POODLE
CONGAS	HONEYS	PONGEE	BOOSTS	GOOSES	POOLED
CONGER	HONIED	PONIED	BOOTED	GOOSEY	POOPED
CONGES	HONING	PONIES	BOOTEE	HOODED	POORER
CONGOU	HONKED	PONTES	BOOTHS	HOODOO	POORLY
CONICS	HONKER	PONTIC	BOOTIE	HOOFED	ROOFED
CONIES	HONORE	PONTIL	BOOTLE	HOOFER	ROOFER
CONING	HONORS	PONTON	BOOZED	HOOKAH	ROOKED
CONIUM	HONOUR	RONALD	BOOZER	HOOKED	ROOKIE
CONKED	HONSHU	RONDEL	BOOZES	HOOKER	ROOMED
CONKER	IONIAN	RONDOS	COODLE	HOOKEY	ROOMER
CONMAN	IONIUM	RONNIE	COOEED	HOOKUP	ROOSTS

ROOTED	GOPHER	LOQUAT	CORONA	FORMIC	MORALS
ROOTER	HOPING	ROQUET	CORPSE	FORMYL	MORASS
ROOTLE	HOPPED	TOQUES	CORPUS	FORNAX	MORAYS
SOONER	HOPPER	******	CORRAL	FORNIX	MORBID
SOOTED	HOPPLE	**-OR---**	CORRIE	FORTES	MOREAU
SOOTHE	JOPLIN	******	CORSAC	FORTIS	MOREEN
TOOLED	KOPECK	AORIST	CORSES	FORUMS	MORELS
TOOLER	KOPEKS	AORTAE	CORSET	GORALS	MORGAN
TOOTED	KOPJES	AORTAL	CORTES	GORDON	MORGEN
TOOTER	LOPERS	AORTAS	CORTEX	GORGED	MORGUE
TOOTHY	LOPING	AORTIC	CORTEZ	GORGER	MORION
TOOTLE	LOPPED	BORAGE	CORTIN	GORGES	MORLEY
TOOTSY	MOPERS	BORANE	CORVEE	GORGET	MORMON
VOODOO	MOPING	BORATE	CORVES	GORGON	MORONS
WOODED	MOPISH	BORDEL	CORVUS	GORHEN	MOROSE
WOODEN	MOPOKE	BORDER	CORYMB	GORIER	MORPHO
WOODSY	MOPPED	BOREAL	CORYZA	GORILY	MORRIS
WOOERS	MOPPET	BOREAS	DORADO	GORING	MORROS
WOOFER	NOPALS	BORERS	DORBUG	GORSES	MORROW
WOOING	OOPHOR	BORGIA	DOREEN	HORACE	MORSEL
WOOLEN	POPERY	BORIDE	DORIAN	HORARY	MORTAL
WOOLLY	POPGUN	BORING	DORIES	HORDED	MORTAR
YOOHOO	POPISH	BORNEO	DORMER	HORDES	MORTON
ZOOIDS	POPLAR	BORROW	DORMIE	HORNED	MORTYS
ZOOMED	POPLIN	BORSCH	DORSAD	HORNET	MORULA
ZOONAL	POPPED	BORZOI	DORSAL	HORNIE	NORDIC
******	POPPER	CORALS	DORSET	HORRID	NOREEN
-OP---	POPPET	CORBAN	DORSUM	HORROR	NORIAS
******	POPPLE	CORBEL	FORAGE	HORSED	NORMAL
BOPPED	POPPYS	CORBIE	FORAYS	HORSES	NORMAN
COPALM	ROPIER	CORDAY	FORBID	HORSEY	NORMAS
COPECK	ROPILY	CORDED	FORCED	HORSTE	NORNIR
COPIED	ROPING	CORDER	FORCER	JORAMS	NORRIS
COPIER	SOPHIA	CORDON	FORCES	JORDAN	NORWAY
COPIES	SOPHIE	CORERS	FORDED	JORGES	PORING
COPING	SOPPED	CORGIS	FOREGO	JORUMS	PORKER
COPLEY	TOPEKA	CORING	FOREST	KOREAN	POROUS
COPOUT	TOPERS	CORIUM	FORGED	KORUNA	PORTAL
COPPED	TOPHAT	CORKED	FORGER	KORUNY	PORTED
COPPER	TOPICS	CORKER	FORGES	LORAIN	PORTER
COPPRA	TOPING	CORNEA	FORGET	LORDED	PORTIA
COPRAH	TOPPED	CORNED	FORGOT	LORDLY	PORTLY
COPSES	TOPPER	CORNEL	FORINT	LOREEN	SORBET
COPTIC	TOPPLE	CORNER	FORKED	LORENE	SORDID
COPULA	******	CORNET	FORMAL	LORENZ	SORELS
DOPIER	**-OQ---**	CORNUA	FORMAT	LORICA	SORELY
DOPING	******	CORNUS	FORMED	LORIES	SOREST
DOPTER	COQUET	CORODY	FORMER	MORALE	SORGHO
	LOQUAR				

SORGOS	COSILY	MOSLEM	COTEAU	NOTION	BOUGIE
SORREL	COSINE	MOSLEY	COTTAE	POTAGE	BOULES
SORROW	COSMIC	MOSQUE	COTTAR	POTALE	BOUNCE
SORTED	COSMOS	MOSSES	COTTAS	POTASH	BOUNCY
SORTER	COSSES	MOSTLY	COTTER	POTATO	BOUNDS
SORTIE	COSSET	NOSHED	COTTON	POTBOY	BOUNTY
TORAHS	COSTAE	NOSHOW	DOTAGE	POTEEN	BOURGS
TORERO	COSTAL	NOSIER	DOTARD	POTENT	BOURNE
TORIES	COSTAR	NOSILY	DOTERS	POTHER	BOURNS
TORIIS	COSTED	NOSING	DOTIER	POTION	BOURSE
TOROID	COSTER	NOSTIC	DOTING	POTMAN	BOUSED
TOROSE	COSTLY	POSADA	DOTTED	POTPIE	BOUSES
TOROUS	DOSAGE	POSERS	DOTTEL	POTSIE	COUGAR
TORPID	DOSERS	POSEUR	DOTTER	POTTED	COUGHS
TORPOR	DOSING	POSHLY	DOTTLE	POTTER	COULEE
TORQUE	DOSSAL	POSIES	GOTAMA	POTTLE	COUNTS
TORRID	DOSSED	POSING	GOTHAM	POTTOS	COUNTY
TORSKS	DOSSEL	POSITS	GOTHIC	ROTARY	COUPES
TORSOS	DOSSER	POSSES	GOTTEN	ROTATE	COUPLE
VOROUS	DOSSIL	POSSET	HOTBED	ROTCHE	COUPON
VORTEX	FOSSAE	POSSUM	HOTBOX	ROTGUT	COURSE
WORDED	FOSSES	POSTAL	HOTELS	ROTORS	COURTS
WORKED	FOSSIL	POSTED	HOTPOT	ROTTED	COUSIN
WORKER	FOSTER	POSTER	HOTROD	ROTTEN	DOUBLE
WORLDS	GOSHEN	ROSARY	HOTTED	ROTTER	DOUBLY
WORMED	GOSPEL	ROSCOE	HOTTER	ROTUND	DOUBTS
WORMER	GOSSIP	ROSEAL	JOTHAM	SOTHIC	DOUCHE
WORSEN	HOSIER	ROSIER	JOTTED	SOTHIS	DOUGAL
WORSER	HOSING	ROSILY	JOTTER	SOTOLS	DOUGHS
WORSTS	HOSTED	ROSING	LOTAHS	TOTALS	DOUGHY
WORTHY	HOSTEL	ROSINS	LOTION	TOTEMS	DOUGIE
YORICK	JOSEPH	ROSINY	LOTTIE	TOTERS	DOURLY
YORKER	JOSHED	ROSTER	MOTELS	TOTHER	DOUSED
YORUBA	JOSHER	ROSTRA	MOTHER	TOTING	DOUSES
ZORILS	JOSHES	TOSHES	MOTIFS	TOTTED	FOUGHT
******	JOSHUA	TOSSED	MOTILE	TOTTER	FOULED
-OS---	JOSIAH	TOSSES	MOTION	VOTARY	FOULER
******	JOSIAS	TOSSUP	MOTIVE	VOTERS	FOULLY
BOSHES	JOSIEA	ZOSTER	MOTLEY	VOTING	FOUNDS
BOSKET	JOSSES	******	MOTMOT	VOTIVE	FOUNTS
BOSOMS	JOSTLE	**-OT---**	MOTORS	******	FOURTH
BOSSED	KOSHER	******	MOTTLE	**-OU---**	GOUGED
BOSSES	LOSERS	BOTANY	MOTTOS	******	GOUGER
BOSTON	LOSING	BOTCHY	NOTARY	AOUDAD	GOUGES
COSHED	LOSSES	BOTFLY	NOTERS	BOUCLE	GOURDE
COSHER	MOSAIC	BOTHER	NOTICE	BOUFFE	GOURDS
COSHES	MOSCOW	BOTTLE	NOTIFY	BOUGHS	HOUNDS
COSIGN	MOSEYS	BOTTOM	NOTING	BOUGHT	HOURIS

HOURLY	ROUGES	DOWISH	COWMAN	TOWELS	TOYONS
HOUSED	ROUGHS	FOVEAE	COWMEN	TOWERS	VOYAGE
HOUSES	ROUNDS	FOVEAL	COWPEA	TOWERY	VOYEUR
JOULES	ROUSED	GOVERN	COWPER	TOWING	ZOYSIA
JOUNCE	ROUSER	HOVELS	COWPOX	VOWELS	******
JOUSTS	ROUSES	HOVERS	COWRIE	VOWERS	-OZ---
LOUDEN	ROUSTS	JOVIAL	DOWELS	VOWING	******
LOUDER	ROUTED	JOVIAN	DOWERS	WOWING	COZENS
LOUDLY	ROUTER	LOVAGE	DOWERY	WOWSER	COZIER
LOUGHS	ROUTES	LOVEIN	DOWLAS	YOWING	COZIES
LOUISA	SOUARI	LOVELL	DOWNED	YOWLED	COZILY
LOUISE	SOUGHS	LOVELY	DOWSED	******	DOZENS
LOUNGE	SOUGHT	LOVERS	DOWSER	-OX---	DOZIER
LOUPES	SOULED	LOVING	DOWSES	******	DOZILY
LOURED	SOUNDS	MOVERS	FOWLED	BOXCAR	DOZING
LOUSED	SOUPED	MOVIES	FOWLER	BOXERS	EOZOIC
LOUSES	SOURCE	MOVING	GOWNED	BOXING	MOZART
LOUVER	SOURED	NOVELS	HOWARD	COXING	NOZZLE
LOUVRE	SOURER	NOVENA	HOWDAH	DOXIES	OOZIER
MOULDS	SOURLY	NOVICE	HOWLED	FOXIER	OOZILY
MOULDY	SOUSED	ROVERS	HOWLER	FOXILY	OOZING
MOULIN	SOUSES	ROVING	KOWTOW	FOXING	SOZINE
MOULTS	TOUCAN	SOVIET	LOWBOY	ROXANA	SOZINS
MOUNTS	TOUCHE	******	LOWELL	ROXANE	******
MOUNTY	TOUCHY	-OW---	LOWERS	TOXINS	-PA---
MOURNS	TOUGHS	******	LOWERY	******	******
MOUSED	TOULON	BOWELS	LOWEST	-OY---	APACHE
MOUSER	TOUPEE	BOWERS	LOWING	******	APATHY
MOUSES	TOURED	BOWERY	LOWKEY	BOYARD	EPACTS
MOUSSE	TOURER	BOWFIN	MOWERS	BOYARS	EPARCH
MOUTHS	TOUSLE	BOWING	MOWING	BOYISH	OPAQUE
MOUTHY	TOUTED	BOWLED	NOWAYS	COYISH	SPACAE
MOUTON	TOUTER	BOWLEG	NOWISE	COYOTE	SPACED
NOUGAT	WOUNDS	BOWLER	POWDER	COYPUS	SPACER
NOUGHT	YOUPON	BOWMAN	POWELL	DOYENS	SPACES
NOUNAL	YOUTHS	BOWMEN	POWERS	DOYLEY	SPADED
POUCHY	ZOUAVE	BOWSAW	POWTER	FOYERS	SPADER
POULTS	ZOUNDS	BOWSED	POWWOW	HOYDEN	SPADES
POUNCE	******	BOWSES	ROWANS	JOYCES	SPADIX
POUNDS	-OV---	BOWTIE	ROWELS	JOYFUL	SPAHIS
POURED	******	BOWWOW	ROWENA	JOYING	SPAITS
POURER	BOVATE	BOWYER	ROWERS	JOYOUS	SPALLS
POUSTO	BOVINE	COWAGE	ROWING	POYOUS	SPANKS
POUTED	COVERS	COWARD	SOWARS	ROYALE	SPARED
POUTER	COVERT	COWBOY	SOWERS	ROYALS	SPARER
ROUBLE	COVETS	COWERS	SOWING	TOYERS	SPARES
ROUCHE	COVEYS	COWING	TOWAGE	TOYING	SPARGE
ROUGED	COVING	COWISH	TOWARD	TOYISH	SPARKS

SPARRY	******	SPILTH	APOLLO	******	******
SPARSE	**-PH---**	SPINAL	APOLOG	**-PR---**	**-PU---**
SPARTA	******	SPINEL	EPOCHS	******	******
SPASMS	APHIDS	SPINES	EPODES	APRILS	APULIA
SPATES	APHONY	SPINET	EPONYM	APRONS	SPUMED
SPATHE	APHTHA	SPINNY	EPOPEE	SPRAGS	SPUMES
SPAVIN	EPHAHS	SPIRAL	OPORTO	SPRAIN	SPUNKY
SPAWNS	EPHEBI	SPIREA	SPOILS	SPRANG	SPURGE
SPAYED	EPHODS	SPIRED	SPOILT	SPRATS	SPURNS
UPASES	EPHORI	SPIRES	SPOKED	SPRAWL	SPURRY
******	EPHORS	SPIRIT	SPOKEN	SPRAYS	SPURTS
-PB---	OPHITE	SPIRTS	SPOKES	SPREAD	SPUTUM
******	SPHENE	SPITAL	SPONGE	SPREES	******
UPBEAT	SPHENO	SPITED	SPONGY	SPRIER	**-PW---**
UPBOWS	SPHERE	SPITES	SPOOFS	SPRIGS	******
******	SPHERY	******	SPOOKS	SPRING	UPWARD
-PC---	SPHINX	**-PK---**	SPOOKY	SPRINT	
******	UPHELD	******	SPOOLS	SPRITE	**-PY---**
UPCAST	UPHILL	UPKEEP	SPOONS	SPRITS	******
******	UPHOLD	******	SPOONY	SPROUT	SPYING
-PD---	UPHROE	**-PL---**	SPOORS	SPRUCE	******
******	******	******	SPORED	SPRUES	**-QU---**
UPDATE	**-PI---**	APLITE	SPORES	SPRUNG	******
UPDIKE	******	APLOMB	SPORTS	SPRYER	AQUILA
******	APIARY	SPLAKE	SPORTY	SPRYLY	EQUALS
-PE---	APICAL	SPLASH	SPOTTY	UPRISE	EQUATE
******	APICES	SPLATS	SPOUSE	UPROAR	EQUINE
APEMAN	APIECE	SPLAYS	SPOUTS	UPROOT	EQUIPS
APEPSY	EPICAL	SPLEEN	******	UPROSE	EQUITY
APEXES	EPILOG	SPLENO	**-PP---**	UPRUSH	SQUABS
IPECAC	EPIRUS	SPLICE	******	******	SQUADS
OPENED	EPIZOA	SPLINE	APPALL	**-PS---**	SQUALL
OPENER	OPIATE	SPLINT	APPALS	******	SQUAMA
OPENLY	OPINED	SPLITS	APPEAL	UPSETS	SQUARE
OPERAS	OPINES	UPLAND	APPEAR	UPSHOT	SQUASH
SPEAKS	SPICED	UPLIFT	APPELS	UPSIDE	SQUATS
SPEARS	SPICER	******	APPEND	******	SQUAWK
SPECIE	SPICES	**-PM---**	APPIAN	**-PT---**	SQUAWS
SPECKS	SPIDER	******	APPLES	******	SQUEAK
SPEECH	SPIELS	UPMOST	APPORT	OPTANT	SQUEAL
SPEEDS	SPIERS	******	APPOSE	OPTICS	SQUIBS
SPEEDY	SPIFFY	**-PN---**	EPPING	OPTIMA	SQUIDS
SPEISS	SPIGOT	******	OPPOSE	OPTIME	SQUILL
SPELLS	SPIKED	APNEAL	OPPUGN	OPTING	SQUINT
SPENDS	SPIKES	APNEIC	UPPERS	OPTION	SQUIRE
SPERMO	SPILED	APNOEA	UPPING	UPTAKE	SQUIRM
SPERRY	SPILES	******	UPPISH	UPTOWN	SQUIRT
SPEWED	SPILLS	**-PO---**	UPPITY	UPTURN	SQUISH
UPENDS		******			
		APODAL			
		APOGEE			

******	BRAZES	DRAINS	GRANTS	PRAYER	******
-RA---	BRAZIL	DRAKES	GRAPES	TRACED	-RC---
******	BRAZOS	DRAMAS	GRAPHO	TRACER	******
ARABEL	CRAALS	DRAPED	GRAPHS	TRACES	ARCADE
ARABIA	CRABBY	DRAPER	GRAPHY	TRACHE	ARCANA
ARABIC	CRACKS	DRAPES	GRASPS	TRACHY	ARCANE
ARABLE	CRACKY	DRAWEE	GRASSY	TRACKS	ARCHED
ARAGON	CRACOW	DRAWER	GRATED	TRACTS	ARCHEO
ARANTA	CRADLE	DRAWLS	GRATER	TRADED	ARCHER
ARARAT	CRAFTS	DRAWLY	GRATES	TRADER	ARCHES
ARAWAK	CRAFTY	DRAYED	GRATIN	TRADES	ARCHIE
BRACED	CRAGGY	ERASED	GRATIS	TRAGIC	ARCHIL
BRACER	CRAIGS	ERASER	GRAVED	TRAGUS	ARCHLY
BRACES	CRAKES	ERASES	GRAVEL	TRAILS	ARCHON
BRACHI	CRAMBO	FRACAS	GRAVEN	TRAINS	ARCHYS
BRACHY	CRAMPS	FRAILS	GRAVER	TRAITS	ARCING
BRACTS	CRANED	FRAISE	GRAVES	TRAMPS	ARCKED
BRAHMA	CRANES	FRAMED	GRAVID	TRANCE	ARCTIC
BRAHMS	CRANIA	FRAMER	GRAYED	TRASHY	ORCEIN
BRAIDS	CRANIO	FRAMES	GRAYER	TRAUMA	ORCHID
BRAILS	CRANKS	FRANCE	GRAYLY	TRAVEL	ORCHIL
BRAINS	CRANKY	FRANCK	GRAZED	TRAVES	ORCHIO
BRAINY	CRANNY	FRANCO	GRAZER	TRAWLS	ORCHIS
BRAISE	CRAPED	FRANCS	GRAZES	URAEUS	URCHIN
BRAIZE	CRAPES	FRANKS	IRANIS	URALIC	******
BRAKED	CRASIS	FRAPPE	IRAQIS	URANIA	-RD---
BRAKES	CRATCH	FRATER	KRAALS	URANIC	******
BRANCH	CRATED	FRAUDS	KRAITS	URANUS	ARDEBS
BRANDS	CRATER	FRAUEN	KRAKEN	URANYL	ARDENT
BRANDT	CRATES	FRAYED	ORACHS	WRACKS	ARDORS
BRANDY	CRAVAT	GRABEN	ORACLE	WRAITH	ARDOUR
BRANNY	CRAVED	GRACED	ORALLY	WRAPUP	ORDAIN
BRANTS	CRAVEN	GRACES	ORANGE	WRASSE	ORDEAL
BRAQUE	CRAVER	GRACIE	ORANGS	WRATHY	ORDERS
BRASHY	CRAVES	GRADED	ORATED	XRAYED	ORDURE
BRASSY	CRAWLS	GRADER	ORATES	******	******
BRAVED	CRAWLY	GRADES	ORATOR	-RB---	-RE---
BRAVER	CRAYON	GRADIN	PRAGUE	******	******
BRAVES	CRAZED	GRADUS	PRAISE	ARBELA	ARECAS
BRAVOS	CRAZES	GRAECO	PRANCE	ARBORI	ARENAS
BRAWLS	DRABLY	GRAFTS	PRANKS	ARBORS	AREOLA
BRAWNY	DRACHM	GRAHAM	PRATED	ARBOUR	ARERCU
BRAYED	DRAFFS	GRAINS	PRATER	ARBUTE	ARETES
BRAYER	DRAFFY	GRAINY	PRATES	ERBIUM	AREZZO
BRAZAS	DRAFTS	GRAMME	PRAVDA	ORBING	BREACH
BRAZED	DRAFTY	GRANDE	PRAWNS	ORBITS	BREADS
BRAZEN	DRAGEE	GRANGE	PRAXIS	URBANE	BREAKS
BRAZER	DRAGON	GRANNY	PRAYED		BREAMS

BREAST	CREWEL	OREGAN	******	BRIDAL	FRIDGE
BREATH	DREADS	OREGON	-RG---	BRIDES	FRIEDA
BRECHT	DREAMS	OREIDE	******	BRIDGE	FRIEND
BREECH	DREAMT	PREACH	ARGALA	BRIDIE	FRIERS
BREEDS	DREAMY	PRECIS	ARGALI	BRIDLE	FRIEZE
BREEKS	DREARY	PREENS	ARGALS	BRIEFS	FRIGGA
BREEZE	DREDGE	PREFAB	ARGENT	BRIERS	FRIGHT
BREEZY	DREGGY	PREFER	ARGIVE	BRIERY	FRIGID
BREGMA	DRENCH	PREFIX	ARGOSY	BRIGHT	FRIJOL
BREMEN	DRESSY	PRELIM	ARGOTS	BRIGID	FRILLS
BRENDA	EREBUS	PREMED	ARGUED	BRILLS	FRILLY
BRENTS	ERECTS	PREPAY	ARGUER	BRINED	FRINGE
BRETON	FREAKS	PRESAS	ARGUES	BRINES	FRINGY
BREVES	FREAKY	PRESTO	ARGUFY	BRINGS	FRISES
BREVET	FREDAS	PRETER	ARGYLL	BRINKS	FRISKS
BREWED	FREDDY	PRETOR	ERGATE	BRISKS	FRISKY
BREWER	FREELY	PRETTY	ORGANA	BRITON	FRITHS
BREWIS	FREEST	PREVUE	ORGANO	CRICKS	FRIVOL
CREAKS	FREEZE	PREWAR	ORGANS	CRIERS	FRIZZY
CREAKY	FRENCH	PREYED	ORGASM	CRIKEY	GRIDED
CREAMS	FRENUM	PREYER	ORGEAT	CRIMEA	GRIDES
CREAMY	FRENZY	TREADS	ORGIES	CRIMES	GRIEVE
CREASE	FREONS	TREATS	URGENT	CRIMPS	GRIFFE
CREASY	FRESCO	TREATY	URGING	CRIMPY	GRIGRI
CREATE	FRESNO	TREBLE	******	CRINGE	GRILLE
CRECHE	FRETTY	TREMOR	-RH---	CRINUM	GRILLS
CREDAL	GREASE	TRENCH	******	CRISES	GRILSE
CREDIT	GREASY	TRENDS	RRHAGE	CRISIS	GRIMED
CREDOS	GREATS	TRENDY	RRHAGY	CRISPS	GRIMES
CREEDS	GREAVE	TREPAN	******	CRISPY	GRIMLY
CREEKS	GREBES	TRESSY	-RI---	CRITIC	GRINDS
CREELS	GREECE	TREVOR	******	DRIERS	GRIPED
CREEPS	GREEDS	UREASE	ARIANS	DRIEST	GRIPER
CREEPY	GREEDY	UREIDE	ARIDLY	DRIFTS	GRIPES
CREESE	GREEKS	UREMIA	ARIELS	DRIFTY	GRIPPE
CREMES	GREENE	URETER	ARIGHT	DRILLS	GRIPPY
CRENEL	GREENS	URETIC	ARIOSE	DRINKS	GRISLY
CREOLE	GREETS	WREAKS	ARIOSO	DRIPPY	GRITTY
CREPED	GREGOS	WREATH	ARIOUS	DRIVEL	GRIVET
CREPES	GREIFS	WRECKS	ARISEN	DRIVEN	GRIZEL
CRESOL	GREIGE	WRENCH	ARISES	DRIVER	IRIDES
CRESTS	GRETAS	WRESTS	ARISTA	DRIVES	IRIDIC
CRETAN	GRETEL	WRETCH	ARISTO	ERICHS	IRISED
CRETIC	GRETNA	******	BRIARS	ERINGO	IRISES
CRETIN	IREFUL	-RF---	BRIBED	ERINYS	IRITIC
CRETON	IRENES	******	BRIBER	FRIARS	IRITIS
CREUSA	IRENIC	ERFURT	BRIBES	FRIARY	KRISES
CREVAS	OREADS		BRICKS	FRIDAY	ORIBIS

ORIELS	TRIGLY	ARMFUL	BRONZY	DROPSY	GROWER
ORIENT	TRIGON	ARMIES	BROOCH	DROSKY	GROWLS
ORIGAN	TRILBY	ARMING	BROODS	DROSSY	GROWTH
ORIGEN	TRILLS	ARMLET	BROODY	DROUTH	GROYNE
ORIGIN	TRIMLY	ARMORS	BROOKE	DROVED	IRONED
ORIOLE	TRINAL	ARMORY	BROOKS	DROVER	IRONER
ORISON	TRINED	ARMOUR	BROOMS	DROVES	IRONIC
PRICED	TRINES	ARMPIT	BROOMY	DROWNS	KRONEN
PRICES	TRIODE	ARMURE	BROTHS	DROWSE	KRONER
PRICKS	TRIOSE	ERMINE	BROWNS	DROWSY	KRONOR
PRIDED	TRIPLE	ORMERS	BROWSE	ERODED	KRONOS
PRIDES	TRIPOD	ORMOLU	CROAKS	ERODES	KRONUR
PRIERS	TRIPOS	ORMUZD	CROAKY	EROTIC	OROIDE
PRIEST	TRISTE	******	CROATS	FROCKS	PROBED
PRIMAL	TRITER	**-RN---**	CROCKS	FROGGY	PROBER
PRIMED	TRITON	******	CROCKY	FROLIC	PROBES
PRIMER	TRIUNE	ARNAUD	CROCUS	FRONDS	PROCNE
PRIMES	TRIVET	ARNICA	CROFTS	FRONTO	PROCTO
PRIMLY	TRIVIA	ARNIES	CROJIK	FRONTS	PROEMS
PRIMPS	TRIXIE	ARNOLD	CRONES	FROSTS	PROFIT
PRIMUS	TRIXYS	ERNEST	CRONOS	FROSTY	PROJET
PRINCE	URINAL	ERNIES	CRONUS	FROTHS	PROLEG
PRINKS	WRIEST	ORNATE	CROOKS	FROTHY	PROLIX
PRINTS	WRIGHT	ORNERY	CROONS	FROWNS	PROMPT
PRIORS	WRINGS	ORNITH	CRORES	FROWZY	PRONGS
PRIORY	WRISTS	******	CROSSE	FROZEN	PRONTO
PRISMS	WRITER	**-RO---**	CROTCH	GROANS	PROOFS
PRISON	WRITES	******	CROTON	GROATS	PROPEL
PRISSY	WRITHE	AROIDS	CROUCH	GROCER	PROPER
PRIVET	******	AROMAS	CROUPE	GROGGY	PROPYL
PRIZED	**-RK---**	AROUND	CROUPS	GROINS	PROSED
PRIZER	******	AROUSE	CROUPY	GROOMS	PROSER
PRIZES	IRKING	BROACH	CROWDS	GROOVE	PROSES
TRIADS	ORKNEY	BROADS	CROWED	GROOVY	PROSIT
TRIALS	******	BROCHE	CROWNS	GROPED	PROTON
TRIBAL	**-RL---**	BROGAN	CROZER	GROPER	PROUST
TRIBES	******	BROGUE	CROZES	GROPES	PROVED
TRICAR	ARLEEN	BROILS	DROGUE	GROSZY	PROVEN
TRICED	ARLENE	BROKEN	DROITS	GROTTO	PROVER
TRICES	ARLINE	BROKER	DROLLS	GROTTY	PROVES
TRICHI	ORLOPS	BROLLY	DROLLY	GROUCH	PROWLS
TRICHO	******	BROMAL	DROMON	GROUND	TROCAR
TRICKS	**-RM---**	BROMES	DRONED	GROUPS	TROCHE
TRICKY	******	BROMIC	DRONES	GROUSE	TROGON
TRICOT	ARMADA	BRONCO	DRONGO	GROUTS	TROIKA
TRIERS	ARMAGH	BRONCS	DROOLS	GROVEL	TROJAN
TRIFID	ARMAND	BRONTE	DROOPS	GROVER	TROLLS
TRIFLE	ARMETS	BRONZE	DROOPY	GROVES	TROOPS

TROPAL	URSINE	CRUSOE	******	ISATIN	ASHLAR
TROPHO	URSULA	CRUSTS	**-RV---**	PSALMS	ASHLEY
TROPHY	******	CRUSTY	******	TSADES	ASHMAN
TROPIC	**-RT---**	CRUTCH	IRVING	USABLE	ASHMEN
TROPPO	******	CRUXES	IRVINS	USABLY	ASHORE
TROTHS	ARTELS	DRUDGE	******	USAGES	ISHTAR
TROTYL	ARTERY	DRUIDS	**-RW---**	USANCE	PSHAWS
TROUGH	ARTFUL	DRUNKS	******	ZSAZSA	TSHIRT
TROUPE	ARTHRO	DRUPEL	ERWINS	******	USHERS
TROUTS	ARTHUR	DRUPES	IRWINS	**-SB---**	******
TROVER	ARTIES	DRUSES	ORWELL	******	**-SI---**
TROVES	ARTILY	ERUCTS	******	ASBURY	******
TROWEL	ARTIST	ERUPTS	**-RY---**	OSBERT	ASIANS
UROPOD	ARTOIS	FRUGAL	******	OSBORN	ASIDES
WRONGS	ARTURO	FRUITS	ARYANS	******	ASIMOV
******	URTEXT	FRUITY	BRYANT	**-SC---**	ISIDOR
-RP---	******	FRUMPS	BRYONY	******	OSIERS
******	**-RU---**	FRUMPY	CRYING	ASCEND	OSIRIS
ARPENS	******	FRUNZE	CRYPTO	ASCENT	******
ARPENT	ARUNTA	FRUSTA	CRYPTS	ASCOTS	**-SK---**
ORPHAN	BRUCES	GRUBBY	DRYADS	ESCAPE	******
ORPHIC	BRUGES	GRUDGE	DRYDEN	ESCARP	ASKANT
ORPINE	BRUINS	GRUELS	DRYERS	ESCENT	ASKERS
ORPINS	BRUISE	GRUGRU	DRYEST	ESCHAR	ASKING
******	BRUITS	GRUMES	DRYFLY	ESCHER	ESKERS
-RR---	BRULOT	GRUMPY	DRYICE	ESCHEW	ESKIMO
******	BRUMAL	GRUNDY	DRYING	ESCORT	******
ARRACK	BRUMES	GRUNTS	DRYISH	ESCROW	**-SL---**
ARRANT	BRUNCH	KRUBIS	DRYROT	ESCUDO	******
ARRAYS	BRUNEI	KRUBUT	ERYNGO	ISCHIA	ASLANT
ARREAR	BRUNEL	PRUDES	FRYERS	OSCANS	ASLEEP
ARREST	BRUNOS	PRUNED	FRYING	OSCARS	ASLOPE
ARRIVE	BRUSHY	PRUNER	ORYXES	OSCINE	ISLAND
ARROBA	BRUTAL	PRUNES	PRYERS	OSCULE	ISLETS
ARROWS	BRUTES	TRUANT	PRYING	******	ISLING
ARROWY	BRUTUS	TRUCES	TRYING	**-SE---**	******
ARROYO	CRUCES	TRUCKS	TRYOUT	******	**-SM---**
ERRAND	CRUDER	TRUDGE	TRYSTS	ISEULT	******
ERRANT	CRUETS	TRUDYS	WRYEST	PSEUDO	OSMIUM
ERRATA	CRUISE	TRUEST	WRYING	TSETSE	OSMOND
ERRING	CRUMBS	TRUING	******	USEFUL	OSMOSE
ERRORS	CRUMBY	TRUISM	**-SA---**	******	OSMUND
ORRERY	CRUMMY	TRUMAN	******	**-SG---**	******
ORRICE	CRUMPS	TRUMPS	ASARUM	******	**-SO---**
******	CRUNCH	TRUNKS	ISAACS	ASGARD	******
-RS---	CRURAL	TRUSTS	ISABEL	******	ISOBAR
******	CRUSES	TRUSTY	ISADOR	**-SH---**	ISOBEL
ARSINE	CRUSET	TRUTHS	ISAIAH	******	ISOGON
ERSATZ				ASHCAN	
				ASHIER	

ISOHEL	******	ITALIC	STATER	STEPUP	STILLY
ISOLDE	-ST---	STABLE	STATES	STEREO	STILTS
ISOMER	******	STABLY	STATIC	STERES	STINGS
ISOPOD	ASTERI	STACIE	STATOR	STERIC	STINGY
******	ASTERN	STACKS	STATUE	STERNA	STINKS
-SP---	ASTERO	STACTE	STATUS	STERNO	STINTS
******	ASTERS	STACYS	STAURO	STERNS	STIPEL
ASPECT	ASTHMA	STADIA	STAVED	STEROL	STIPES
ASPENS	ASTRAL	STAFFS	STAVES	STETHO	STIRKS
ASPERS	ASTRAY	STAGED	STAYED	STEVEN	STIRPS
ASPICS	ASTRID	STAGER	STAYER	STEVES	STITCH
ASPIRE	ASTUTE	STAGES	UTAHAN	STEVIE	STITHY
ESPANA	ESTATE	STAGEY	******	STEWED	STIVER
ESPIAL	ESTEEM	STAGGY	-TC---	UTERUS	******
ESPIED	ESTERS	STAINS	******	******	-TM---
ESPIES	ESTHER	STAIRS	ETCHED	-TG---	******
ESPRIT	ESTOPS	STAITH	ETCHER	******	UTMOST
OSPREY	ESTRAY	STAKED	ETCHES	UTGARD	******
******	ESTRUS	STAKES	ITCHED	******	-TO---
-SR---	ISTRIA	STALAG	ITCHES	-TH---	******
******	OSTEAL	STALED	******	******	ATOLLS
ISRAEL	OSTEND	STALER	-TE---	ATHENA	ATOMIC
******	OSTLER	STALES	******	ATHENE	ATONAL
-SS---	******	STALIN	ETERNA	ATHENS	ATONED
******	-SU---	STALKS	STEADY	ATHOME	ATONER
ASSAIL	******	STALKY	STEAKS	ETHANE	ATONES
ASSAIS	USURER	STALLS	STEALS	ETHANS	ATONIC
ASSAYS	USURPS	STAMEN	STEAMS	ETHELS	PTOSIS
ASSENT	******	STAMIN	STEAMY	ETHERS	STOATS
ASSERT	-SW---	STAMPS	STEEDS	ETHICS	STOCKS
ASSESS	******	STANCE	STEELS	ETHNIC	STOCKY
ASSETS	OSWALD	STANCH	STEELY	ETHYLS	STODGE
ASSIGN	OSWEGO	STANDS	STEEPS	ITHACA	STODGY
ASSISI	******	STANZA	STEERS	OTHERS	STOGEY
ASSIST	-SY---	STAPES	STEEVE	STHENO	STOICS
ASSIZE	******	STAPLE	STEFAN	******	STOKED
ASSORT	ASYLUM	STARCH	STEINS	-TI---	STOKER
ASSUME	PSYCHE	STARED	STELAE	******	STOKES
ASSURE	PSYCHO	STARER	STELAR	ITIOUS	STOLED
ESSAYS	******	STARES	STELES	OTIOSE	STOLEN
ESSENE	-TA---	STARRY	STELIC	OTITIS	STOLES
ISSEIS	******	STARTS	STELLA	PTISAN	STOLID
ISSUED	ATABAL	STARVE	STELLI	STICKS	STOLON
ISSUER	ATAMAN	STASES	STENCH	STICKY	STOMAT
ISSUES	ATAVIC	STASIS	STENOG	STIFLE	STOMPS
OSSEIN	ATAXIA	STATAL	STEPAN	STIGMA	STONED
OSSIAN	ATAXIC	STATED	STEPIN	STILES	STONER
OSSIFY	ETAPES	STATEN	STEPPE	STILLS	STONES

STOOGE	STRIFE	YTTRIA	QUAERE	HUBBUB	BUCKED
STOOKS	STRIKE	YTTRIC	QUAFFS	HUBCAP	BUCKER
STOOLS	STRING	******	QUAGGA	HUBERT	BUCKET
STOOPS	STRIPE	-TU---	QUAGGY	HUBRIS	BUCKLE
STOPED	STRIPS	******	QUAHOG	JUBBAH	BUCKRA
STOPES	STRIPT	ETUDES	QUAILS	LUBBER	CUCKOO
STORAX	STRIPY	STUART	QUAINT	LUBECK	DUCATS
STORED	STRIVE	STUBBS	QUAKED	LUBLIN	DUCKED
STORES	STROBE	STUBBY	QUAKER	NUBBIN	DUCKER
STOREY	STRODE	STUCCO	QUAKES	NUBBLE	EUCHER
STORKS	STROKE	STUDIO	QUALMS	NUBBLY	EUCHRE
STORMS	STROLL	STUFFS	QUALMY	NUBIAN	EUCLID
STORMY	STROMA	STUFFY	QUANTA	NUBIAS	FUCOID
STOUPS	STRONG	STULLS	QUANTS	NUBILE	FUCOUS
STOUTS	STROPS	STUMPS	QUAPAW	PUBLIC	HUCKLE
STOVER	STROUD	STUMPY	QUARKS	RUBACE	KUCHEN
STOVES	STROVE	STUNTS	QUARRY	RUBATO	LUCENT
STOWED	STRUCK	STUPAS	QUARTE	RUBBED	LUCIAN
UTOPIA	STRUMA	STUPES	QUARTO	RUBBER	LUCIAS
******	STRUMS	STUPID	QUARTS	RUBBLE	LUCIEN
-TR---	STRUNG	STUPOR	QUARTZ	RUBENS	LUCILE
******	STRUTS	STURDY	QUASAR	RUBIES	LUCITE
ATREUS	******	UTURNS	QUATRE	RUBIGO	LUCIUS
ATRIAL	-TS---	******	QUAVER	RUBLES	MUCKED
ATRIUM	******	-TY---	SUABLE	RUBRIC	MUCKER
STRAFE	ITSELF	******	******	SUBAHS	MUCKLE
STRAIN	XTSTUS	ETYMON	-UB---	SUBDEB	MUCOID
STRAIT	******	STYING	******	SUBDUE	MUCOSA
STRAKE	-TT---	STYLAR	AUBADE	SUBITO	MUCOSE
STRAND	******	STYLED	AUBREY	SUBLET	MUCOUS
STRAPS	ATTACH	STYLER	AUBURN	SUBMIT	NUCHAE
STRASS	ATTACK	STYLES	BUBALS	SUBORN	NUCLEI
STRATA	ATTAIN	STYLET	BUBBLE	SUBTER	PUCKER
STRATH	ATTARS	STYLUS	BUBBLY	SUBTLE	RUCHES
STRATI	ATTEND	STYMIE	BUBOES	SUBTLY	RUCKED
STRAWS	ATTEST	******	CUBAGE	SUBURB	RUCKUS
STRAWY	ATTICA	-UA---	CUBANS	SUBWAY	SUCCOR
STRAYS	ATTICS	******	CUBBED	TUBATE	SUCKED
STREAK	ATTILA	GUACOS	CUBEBS	TUBBED	SUCKER
STREAM	ATTIRE	GUANIN	CUBING	TUBBER	SUCKLE
STREET	ATTLEE	GUANOS	CUBISM	TUBERS	SUCRES
STRESS	ATTORN	GUARDS	CUBIST	TUBING	TUCHUN
STREWN	ATTUNE	GUAVAS	CUBITS	TUBULE	TUCKED
STREWS	OTTAVA	JUAREZ	CUBOID	******	TUCKER
STRIAE	OTTAWA	LUANDA	DUBBED	-UC---	TUCKET
STRICK	OTTERS	NUANCE	DUBBIN	******	TUCSON
STRICT	OTTOWA	QUACKS	DUBLIN	BUCCAL	TUCSON
STRIDE	UTTERS	QUADRI	EUBOEA	BUCHAN	YUCCAS

******	NUDITY	DUFFED	HUGHES	JUICER	BULLAE
-UD---	NUDNIK	DUFFEL	HUGHIE	JUICES	BULLET
******	PUDDLE	DUFFER	JUGATE	PUISNE	CULETS
AUDADS	PUDDLY	DUFFLE	JUGFUL	QUILLS	CULLAY
AUDILE	RUDDER	GUFFAW	JUGGED	QUILTS	CULLED
AUDITS	RUDDLE	HUFFED	JUGGLE	QUINCE	CULLER
AUDREY	RUDELY	LUFFED	LUGERS	QUINCY	CULLET
BUDDED	RUDEST	MUFFED	LUGGED	QUINIC	CULLIS
BUDDER	SUDARY	MUFFIN	LUGGER	QUINSY	CULMED
BUDDHA	SUDDEN	MUFFLE	MUGGAR	QUINTS	CULTCH
BUDDLE	******	MUFTIS	MUGGED	QUIPUS	CULTUS
BUDGED	**-UE---**	PUFFED	MUGGER	QUIRED	CULVER
BUDGES	******	PUFFER	MUGGUR	QUIRES	DULCET
BUDGET	CUESTA	PUFFIN	NUGGET	QUIRKS	DULCIE
BUDGIE	DUELED	RUFFED	PUGGED	QUIRTS	DULLED
CUDDIE	DUELER	RUFFLE	PUGGRY	QUITCH	DULLER
CUDDLE	DUELLO	RUFOUS	PUGREE	QUIVER	DULLES
CUDDLY	DUENNA	SUFFER	RUGATE	RUINED	DULUTH
CUDGEL	FUELED	SUFFIX	RUGGED	RUINER	EULOGY
DUDEEN	FUELER	SUFISM	RUGGER	SUITED	FULCRA
DUDISH	GUENON	TUFFET	RUGOSE	SUITES	FULFIL
DUDLEY	GUESTS	TUFTED	RUGOUS	SUITOR	FULGID
EUDOAR	HUELVA	******	SUGARS	TUILLE	FULLED
FUDDLE	LUELLA	**-UG---**	SUGARY	ZUIDER	FULLER
FUDGED	LUETIC	******	TUGGED	******	FULMAR
FUDGES	PUEBLO	AUGEAN	******	**-UJ---**	FULTON
HUDDLE	QUEANS	AUGEND	**-UH---**	******	GULDEN
HUDSON	QUEASY	AUGERS	******	JUJUBE	GULFED
JUDAEA	QUEBEC	AUGHTS	FUHRER	******	GULLAH
JUDAEO	QUEENS	AUGITE	******	**-UK---**	GULLED
JUDAHS	QUEERS	AUGURS	**-UI---**	******	GULLET
JUDAIC	QUELLS	AUGURY	******	AUKLET	GULPED
JUDEAN	QUENCH	AUGUST	BUILDS	MUKLUK	GULPER
JUDGED	QUERNS	BUGGED	CUISSE	PUKING	HULKED
JUDGER	QUESTS	BUGGER	DUIKER	YUKKED	HULLED
JUDGES	QUEUED	BUGLED	GUIANA	******	JULEPS
JUDITH	QUEUES	BUGLER	GUIDED	**-UL---**	JULIAN
LUDLOW	QUEZON	BUGLES	GUIDER	******	JULIAS
LUDWIG	RUEFUL	DUGONG	GUIDES	BULBAR	JULIES
MUDCAP	RUEING	DUGOUT	GUIDON	BULBED	JULIET
MUDDED	SUEDES	EUGENE	GUILDS	BULBEL	JULIUS
MUDDER	******	FUGIOS	GUILES	BULBIL	KULAKS
MUDDLE	**-UF---**	FUGLED	GUILTS	BULBUL	KULTUR
NUDELY	******	FUGLES	GUILTY	BULGAR	LULLED
NUDGED	BUFFED	FUGUES	GUIMPE	BULGED	MULCTS
NUDGES	BUFFER	HUGELY	GUINEA	BULGER	MULISH
NUDISM	BUFFET	HUGEST	GUISES	BULGES	MULLAH
NUDIST	CUFFED	HUGGED	GUITAR	BULKED	MULLED

MULLEN	DUMBLY	PUMICE	DUNKED	NUNCIO	******
MULLER	DUMDUM	PUMMEL	DUNKER	OUNCES	-UO---
MULLET	DUMPED	PUMPED	DUNLIN	PUNCHY	******
MULLEY	DUMPER	PUMPER	DUNNED	PUNDIT	BUOYED
NULLAH	DUMPTY	RUMBAS	EUNICE	PUNIER	DUODEN
PULERS	FUMBLE	RUMBLE	EUNUCH	PUNILY	DUOLOG
PULING	FUMIER	RUMINA	FUNDED	PUNISH	QUOINS
PULLED	FUMING	RUMMER	FUNDUS	PUNJAB	QUOITS
PULLER	FUMOUS	RUMORS	FUNEST	PUNKAS	QUORUM
PULLET	GUMBOS	RUMOUR	FUNGAL	PUNNED	QUOTAS
PULLEY	GUMMAS	RUMPLE	FUNGUS	PUNNER	QUOTED
PULLIN	GUMMED	RUMPUS	FUNKED	PUNTED	QUOTER
PULPED	HUMANE	SUMACS	FUNNEL	PUNTER	QUOTES
PULPER	HUMANS	SUMMED	GUNMAN	PUNTOS	QUOTHA
PULPIT	HUMBER	SUMMER	GUNMEN	RUNDLE	SUOMIC
PULQUE	HUMBLE	SUMMIT	GUNNAR	RUNINS	******
PULSAR	HUMBLY	SUMMON	GUNNED	RUNLET	-UP---
PULSED	HUMBUG	SUMNER	GUNNEL	RUNNEL	******
PULSES	HUMIFY	TUMBLE	GUNNER	RUNNER	CUPELS
RULERS	HUMMED	TUMEFY	GUNSHY	RUNOFF	CUPFUL
RULING	HUMMER	TUMORS	GUNTER	RUNONS	CUPOLA
SULCUS	HUMORS	TUMOUR	HUNGER	RUNOUT	CUPPED
SULFUR	HUMOUR	TUMULT	HUNGRY	RUNWAY	CUPPER
SULKED	HUMPED	******	HUNTED	RUNYON	CUPRIC
SULLEN	HUMPTY	-UN---	HUNTER	SUNBOW	CUPRUM
SULPHA	JUMBAL	******	JUNCOS	SUNDAE	CUPTIE
SULPHO	JUMBLE	AUNTIE	JUNEAU	SUNDAY	CUPULE
SULTAN	JUMPED	BUNCHE	JUNGLE	SUNDER	DUPERS
SULTRY	JUMPER	BUNCHY	JUNGLY	SUNDEW	DUPERY
TULADI	KUMISS	BUNCOS	JUNIOR	SUNDOG	DUPING
TULIPS	KUMMEL	BUNDLE	JUNIUS	SUNDRY	DUPLET
TULLES	LUMBAR	BUNGED	JUNKED	SUNGOD	DUPLEX
VULCAN	LUMBER	BUNGLE	JUNKER	SUNHAT	EUPNEA
VULGAR	LUMENS	BUNION	JUNKET	SUNKEN	JUPONS
VULVAE	LUMINA	BUNKED	JUNKIE	SUNLIT	LUPINE
VULVAL	LUMINI	BUNKER	JUNTAS	SUNNAH	PUPATE
VULVAR	LUMINO	BUNKUM	LUNACY	SUNNED	PUPILS
******	LUMMOX	BUNSEN	LUNATE	SUNSET	PUPPED
-UM---	LUMPED	BUNTED	LUNETS	SUNTAN	PUPPET
******	LUMPEN	BUNYAN	LUNGED	SUNUPS	RUPEES
BUMBLE	MUMBLE	BUNYIP	LUNGEE	TUNDRA	RUPERT
BUMKIN	MUMMED	CUNEAL	LUNGER	TUNERS	RUPIAH
BUMMED	MUMMER	CUNNER	LUNGES	TUNEUP	SUPERB
BUMMER	NUMBED	DUNBAR	LUNGIS	TUNGUS	SUPERS
BUMPED	NUMBER	DUNCAN	LUNKER	TUNICA	SUPINE
BUMPER	NUMBLY	DUNCES	LUNULA	TUNICS	SUPPED
CUMBER	NUMINA	DUNDEE	LUNULE	TUNING	SUPPER
CUMINS		DUNGED	MUNICH	TUNNED	SUPPLE

SUPPLY	BURSAE	FURORE	PURINE	AUSTER	GUSHES
TUPELO	BURSAL	FURORS	PURISM	AUSTIN	GUSSET
TUPIKS	BURSAR	FURRED	PURIST	AUSTRO	GUSSIE
TUPPED	BURSAS	FURROW	PURITY	BUSHED	GUSTAF
YUPONS	BURSES	FURZES	PURLED	BUSHEL	GUSTAV
YUPPIE	BURSTS	GURGLE	PURLER	BUSHES	HUSHED
******	BURTON	GURKHA	PURLIN	BUSHEY	HUSHES
-UQ---	CURACY	HURDLE	PURPLE	BUSIED	HUSKED
******	CURARE	HURLED	PURRED	BUSIES	HUSKER
TUQUES	CURATE	HURLER	PURSED	BUSILY	HUSSAR
******	CURBED	HURLEY	PURSER	BUSING	HUSTLE
-UR---	CURDED	HURONS	PURSES	BUSKER	JUSTIN
******	CURDLE	HURRAH	PURSUE	BUSKIN	JUSTLY
AURATE	CURERS	HURRAY	PURVEY	BUSMAN	JUSTUS
AUREUS	CURFEW	HURTER	SURAHS	BUSMEN	LUSHED
AURIGA	CURIAE	HURTLE	SURELY	BUSSED	LUSHER
AURIST	CURIAL	JURANT	SUREST	BUSSES	LUSHES
AURORA	CURIES	JURATS	SURETY	BUSTED	LUSTED
AUROUS	CURING	JURELS	SURFED	BUSTER	LUSTER
BURANS	CURIOS	JURIES	SURFER	BUSTIC	LUSTRE
BURBLE	CURIUM	JURIST	SURGED	BUSTLE	MUSCAE
BURBOT	CURLED	JURORS	SURGER	CUSCUS	MUSCAT
BURDEN	CURLER	LURERS	SURGES	CUSHAT	MUSCLE
BURDIE	CURLEW	LURING	SURREY	CUSHAW	MUSEUM
BUREAU	CURSED	LURKED	SURTAX	CUSPED	MUSHED
BURGEE	CURSES	LURKER	SURVEY	CUSPID	MUSHER
BURGER	CURSOR	MURALS	TURBAN	CUSPIS	MUSHES
BURGHS	CURTIS	MURDER	TURBID	CUSSED	MUSING
BURGLE	CURTLY	MURIEL	TURBIT	CUSSES	MUSKEG
BURGOO	CURTSY	MURINE	TURBOT	CUSSOS	MUSKET
BURGOS	CURULE	MURMUR	TURCOS	CUSTER	MUSKIT
BURIAL	CURVED	MURRAY	TUREEN	CUSTOM	MUSKOX
BURIED	CURVES	MURRES	TURFED	CUSTOS	MUSLIM
BURIES	CURVET	MURREY	TURGID	DUSKED	MUSLIN
BURINS	DURBAN	NURSED	TURKEY	DUSTED	MUSSED
BURKED	DURBAR	NURSER	TURKIC	DUSTER	MUSSEL
BURKES	DURESS	NURSES	TURKIS	FUSAIN	MUSSES
BURLAP	DURHAM	PURANA	TURNED	FUSEES	MUSTEE
BURLED	DURIAN	PURDAH	TURNER	FUSILE	MUSTER
BURLER	DURING	PUREED	TURNIP	FUSILS	MUSTNT
BURLEY	DURION	PUREES	TURNUP	FUSING	OUSELS
BURNED	EUREKA	PURELY	TURRET	FUSION	OUSTED
BURNER	EURIPI	PUREST	TURTLE	FUSSED	OUSTER
BURNET	EUROPA	PURFLE	TURVES	FUSSER	PUSHED
BURPED	EUROPE	PURGED	ZURICH	FUSSES	PUSHER
BURRED	FURFUR	PURGER	******	FUSTIC	PUSHES
BURROS	FURIES	PURGES	-US---	GUSHED	PUSHTU
BURROW	FURLED	PURIFY	******	GUSHER	PUSHUP
			AUSPEX		
			AUSTEN		

PUSSES	CUTLET	OUTRAN	GUYANA	OVERDO	DWARFS
PUSSEY	CUTOFF	OUTRUN	GUYING	OVERLY	RWANDA
PUSSLY	CUTOUT	OUTSAT	TUYERE	SVELTE	SWAGED
RUSHED	CUTTER	OUTSET	ZUYDER	******	SWAGES
RUSHER	CUTTLE	OUTSIT	******	-VI---	SWAILS
RUSHES	CUTUPS	OUTWIT	-UZ---	******	SWAINS
RUSINE	DUTIES	PUTLOG	******	AVIARY	SWALES
RUSKIN	FUTILE	PUTNAM	BUZZED	AVIATE	SWAMIS
RUSSET	FUTURE	PUTOFF	BUZZER	AVIDIN	SWAMPS
RUSSIA	GUTTAE	PUTONS	BUZZES	AVIDLY	SWAMPY
RUSTED	GUTTAT	PUTOUT	FUZEES	AVISOS	SWANEE
RUSTIC	GUTTED	PUTPUT	FUZILS	EVICTS	SWANKY
RUSTLE	GUTTER	PUTRID	FUZING	EVILLY	SWARAJ
SUSANS	GUTTLE	PUTSCH	FUZZED	EVINCE	SWARDS
SUSIES	HUTTED	PUTTED	FUZZES	EVITAS	SWARMS
SUSLIK	JUTISH	PUTTEE	GUZZLE	OVIBOS	SWARTH
SUSSED	JUTTED	PUTTER	MUZHIK	OVISAC	SWARTY
SUSSEX	LUTEAL	RUTILE	MUZZLE	******	SWATCH
TUSCAN	LUTEUM	RUTTED	NUZZLE	-VO---	SWATHE
TUSHED	LUTHER	SUTLER	OUZELS	******	SWATHS
TUSHES	LUTING	SUTRAS	PUZZLE	AVOCET	SWAYED
TUSKED	LUTIST	SUTTEE	******	AVOIDS	TWANGS
TUSKER	MUTANT	SUTTON	-VA---	AVOSET	TWANGY
TUSSAH	MUTATE	SUTURE	******	AVOUCH	******
TUSSAL	MUTING	TUTORS	AVAILS	AVOWAL	-WE---
TUSSAR	MUTINY	TUTTED	AVALON	AVOWED	******
TUSSIS	MUTISM	TUTTIS	AVATAR	AVOWER	AWEARY
TUSSLE	MUTTER	******	AVAUNT	DVORAK	AWEIGH
******	MUTTON	-UU---	EVADED	EVOKED	AWEING
-UT---	MUTUAL	******	EVADER	EVOKES	DWELLS
******	MUTULE	MUUMUU	EVADES	EVOLVE	GWENNS
AUTHOR	NUTLET	******	OVALLY	YVONNE	SWEARS
AUTISM	NUTMEG	-UW---	******	******	SWEATS
AUTOED	NUTRIA	******	-VE---	-VU---	SWEATY
AUTUMN	NUTTED	KUWAIT	******	******	SWEDEN
BUTANE	NUTTER	******	AVENGE	OVULAR	SWEDES
BUTLER	OUTBID	-UX---	AVENUE	OVULES	SWEENY
BUTTED	OUTCRY	******	AVERNO	UVULAE	SWEEPS
BUTTER	OUTDID	AUXINS	AVERSE	UVULAR	SWEEPY
BUTTES	OUTERS	BUXTON	AVERTS	UVULAS	SWEETS
BUTTON	OUTFIT	HUXLEY	AVERYS	******	SWELLS
CUTELY	OUTFOX	LUXATE	AVESTA	-WA---	SWERVE
CUTEST	OUTING	LUXURY	EVELYN	******	TWEAKS
CUTEYS	OUTLAW	TUXEDO	EVENED	AWAITS	TWEAKY
CUTIES	OUTLAY	******	EVENLY	AWAKED	TWEEDS
CUTINS	OUTLET	-UY---	EVENTS	AWAKEN	TWEETS
CUTLAS	OUTMAN	******	EVERET	AWAKES	TWELVE
CUTLER	OUTPUT	BUYERS	EVERTS	AWARDS	TWENTY
		BUYING			TWERPS

******	******	EXEQUY	EXPELS	DYBBUK	******
-WH---	**-WO---**	EXERTS	EXPEND	GYBING	**-YG---**
******	******	EXETER	EXPERT	HYBRID	******
AWHEEL	AWOKEN	EXEUNT	EXPIRE	HYBRIS	BYGONE
AWHILE	SWOONS	OXEYED	EXPIRY	SYBILS	CYGNET
AWHIRL	SWOOPS	OXEYES	EXPORT	TYBALT	CYGNUS
******	SWORDS	******	EXPOSE	******	HYGEIA
-WI---	TWOBIT	**-XF---**	******	**-YC---**	ZYGOMA
******	TWOFER	******	**-XS---**	******	ZYGOTE
DWIGHT	TWOPLY	OXFORD	******	CYCADS	******
SWIFTS	TWOULD	******	AXSEED	CYCLED	**-YJ---**
SWILLS	TWOWAY	**-XH---**	EXSECT	CYCLER	******
SWINGE	******	******	EXSERT	CYCLES	PYJAMA
SWINGS	**-WY---**	EXHALE	******	CYCLIC	
SWIPED	******	EXHORT	**-XT---**	LYCEES	**-YK---**
SWIPES	GWYNNE	EXHUME	******	LYCEUM	******
SWIPLE	******	OXHIDE	EXTANT	MYCETE	PYKNIC
SWIRLS	**-XA---**	******	EXTEND	SYCEES	******
SWIRLY	******	**-XI---**	EXTENT	TYCOON	**-YL---**
SWITCH	EXACTA	******	EXTERN	******	******
SWIVEL	EXACTS	AXILLA	EXTOLS	******	BYLANE
SWIVET	EXALTS	AXIOMS	EXTORT	**-YD---**	BYLAWS
TWIBIL	EXAMEN	EXILED	EXTRAS	******	BYLINE
TWIGGY	EXARCH	EXILES	OXTAIL	HYDRAE	FYLFOT
TWILIT	OXALIC	EXILIC	******	HYDRAS	NYLONS
TWILLS	OXALIS	EXISTS	**-XU---**	HYDRIC	PYLONS
TWINED	******	EXITED	******	HYDROS	SYLPHS
TWINER	**-XB---**	OXIDES	EXUDED	LYDIAS	SYLPHY
TWINES	******	******	EXUDES	SYDNEY	SYLVAE
TWINGE	OXBOWS	**-XL---**	EXULTS	******	SYLVAN
TWIRLS	******	AXLIKE	EXURBS	**-YE---**	SYLVAS
TWIRPS	**-XC---**	OXLIPS	******	******	SYLVIA
TWISTS	******	******	**-XY---**	AYEAYE	XYLANS
TWISTY	EXCEED	**-XM---**	******	AYESHA	XYLEMS
TWITCH	EXCELS	******	OXYGEN	BYEBYE	XYLENE
******	EXCEPT	EXMOOR	******	DYEING	XYLITE
-WL---	EXCESS	******	**-YA---**	EYECUP	XYLOID
******	EXCIDE	**-XO---**	******	EYEFUL	XYLOLS
AWLESS	EXCISE	******	CYANIC	EYEING	XYLOSE
OWLETS	EXCITE	AXONES	CYANID	EYELET	******
OWLISH	EXCUSE	EXODUS	CYANIN	EYELID	**-YM---**
******	******	EXOGEN	DYADIC	EYEOUT	******
-WN---	**-XE---**	EXOTIC	EYASES	HYADES	AYMARA
******	******	******	HYADES	HYENAS	CYMARS
AWNING	AXEMAN	**-XP---**	**-YB---**	HYETAL	CYMBAL
OWNERS	AXEMEN	******	******	MYELIN	CYMENE
OWNING	EXEDRA	EXPAND	BYBLOW	PYEMIA	CYMLIN
	EXEMPT	EXPECT	CYBELE	PYEMIC	CYMOID

CYMOSE
CYMOUS
CYMRIC
HYMENO
HYMENS
HYMNAL
HYMNED
HYMNIC
LYMPHO
NYMPHA
NYMPHO
NYMPHS
SYMBOL
TYMPAN
******

-YN---
******
BYNAME
CYNICS
DYNAMO
DYNAST
GYNECO
GYNOUS
LYNXES
SYNDET
SYNDIC
SYNODS
SYNTAX
SYNURA
******

-YO---
******
HYOIDS
MYOPES
MYOPIA
MYOPIC
MYOSIN
MYOSIS
PYOSIS
******

-YP---
******
BYPASS
BYPAST
BYPATH
BYPLAY
CYPHER
CYPRIN

CYPRUS
GYPPED
GYPSUM
HYPHAE
HYPHAL
HYPHEN
HYPNIC
HYPNOS
SYPHER
SYPHON
TYPHLO
TYPHON
TYPHUS
TYPIFY
TYPING
TYPIST
******

-YR---
******
BYROAD
CYRANO
CYRENE
CYRILS
EYRIES
GYRATE
GYRONS
GYROSE
LYRICS
LYRISM
LYRIST
MYRIAD
MYRICA
MYRMEC
MYRNAS
MYRTLE
PYRANS
PYRENE
PYRITE
PYRONE
PYROPE
PYRRHA
SYRIAC
SYRIAN
SYRINX
SYRUPS
SYRUPY
TYRANT
TYRIAN

TYRONE
VYRNWY
******

-YS---
******
BYSSUS
CYSTIC
HYSSOP
HYSTER
LYSINE
LYSING
LYSINS
MYSELF
MYSTIC
OYSTER
SYSTEM
WYSTAN
XYSTER
XYSTOS
******

-YT---
******
BYTALK
LYTTAE
MYTHIC
MYTHOI
MYTHOS
PYTHIA
PYTHIC
PYTHON
******

-YU---
******
KYUSHU
PYURIA
RYUKYU
******

-YV---
******
GYVING
WYVERN
******

-YW---
******
BYWAYS
BYWORD
BYWORK

******

-YX---
******
MYXOMA
PYXIES
******

-YZ---
******
SYZYGY
******

-ZA---
******
AZALEA
AZAZEL
******

-ZI---
******
AZINES
******

-ZO---
******
AZOLES
AZONIC
AZORES
AZOTIC
OZONIC
******

-ZR---
******
AZRAEL
******

-ZT---
******
AZTECS
******

-ZU---
******
AZURES
******

-ZZ---
******
UZZIAH
******

-A-A--
AALAND
BAGASS
BAHAIS

BAHAMA
BALAAM
BALATA
BAMAKO
BANANA
BASALT
BATAAN
BAYARD
BAZAAR
CABALA
CABALS
CABANA
CACAOS
CALAIS
CALASH
CAMASS
CANAAN
CANADA
CANALS
CANAPE
CANARD
CANARY
CARACK
CARAFE
CARATE
CARATS
CASABA
CASALS
CASAVA
CATALO
DAMAGE
DAMANS
DAMASK
DANAID
DANAUS
DATARY
FACADE
FARADS
GALACT
GALAXY
GARAGE
GAWAIN
GAZABO
HAMALS
HAMAUL
HARASS
HAVANA
HAWAII

HAZARD
JACANA
JAPANS
KABAKA
KABALA
KABAYA
KAKAPO
KAMALA
KANAKA
KARATE
KARATS
KAVASS
KAYAKS
LANAIS
LANATE
LAPARO
LAVABO
LAVAGE
LAZARS
MACACO
MACAWS
MADAME
MADAMS
MALACO
MALADY
MALAGA
MALATE
MALAWI
MALAYA
MALAYS
MANAGE
MANANA
MARACA
MARAUD
NAGANA
NAIADS
NAPALM
NASALS
NATANT
NAVAHO
NAVAJO
NAWABS
PAEANS
PAGANS
PAJAMA
PALACE
PALAEO
PALAIS

PALATE	******	JABBER	FAECES	BALDLY	LARDER
PANADA	-A-B--	LAMBDA	FALCON	BANDED	LARDON
PANAMA	******	LAMBED	FARCED	BANDIT	LAUDED
PAPACY	BABBIE	LAMBIE	FARCER	BARDED	LAUDER
PAPAIN	BABBLE	MAHBUB	FARCES	BARDES	LAYDAY
PAPAWS	BALBOA	MAMBAS	FASCES	BARDIC	MADDED
PAPAYA	BAMBOO	MAMBOS	FASCIA	BAWDRY	MADDEN
PARADE	BAOBAB	MARBLE	FAUCAL	CADDIE	MADDER
PARANG	BARBED	MAYBUG	FAUCES	CADDIS	MAIDEN
PARAPH	BARBEL	NABBED	FAUCET	CAMDEN	MANDAN
PAVANE	BARBER	RABBET	GARCON	CANDIA	MANDYS
PAVANS	BARBET	RABBIN	GASCON	CANDID	MARDUK
RADARS	BARBIE	RABBIS	GAUCHE	CANDLE	MAUDES
RAJABS	BARBRA	RABBIT	GAUCHO	CANDOR	MAYDAY
RAJAHS	BAUBLE	RABBLE	HANCES	CARDED	PADDED
RATALS	CAMBER	RAGBAG	LANCED	CARDER	PADDLE
RAVAGE	CARBON	RAMBLE	LANCER	CARDIO	PADDYS
RAYAHS	CARBOY	SABBAT	LANCES	CAUDAD	PANDAS
SAFARI	CASBAH	SAMBAS	LANCET	CAUDAL	PANDER
SAHARA	DABBED	SAMBOS	LASCAR	CAUDEX	PARDON
SALAAM	DABBER	SAMBUR	MADCAP	CAUDLE	PAYDAY
SALADS	DABBLE	TABBED	MANCHU	DADDLE	RADDLE
SALAMI	DAUBED	TAMBAC	MARCEL	DAEDAL	RAGDAY
SALARY	DAUBER	WABBLE	MARCIA	DANDER	RAIDED
SAMARA	DAUBRY	WABBLY	MARCOS	DANDLE	RAIDER
SARAHS	DAYBED	WAMBLE	MARCUS	DARDAN	RANDAL
SARAPE	DAYBOY	WAMBLY	MASCON	DAUDET	RANDAN
SATANG	FARBAD	WARBLE	MASCOT	DAWDLE	RANDOM
SATARA	GABBED	YABBER	NANCYS	GADDED	SADDEN
SAVAGE	GABBER	ZAMBIA	PANCHO	GADDER	SADDER
SAVANT	GABBLE	******	PARCAE	GANDER	SADDLE
SAVATE	GABBRO	-A-C--	PARCEL	GANDHI	SANDAL
TABARD	GAMBIA	******	PASCAL	GARDEN	SANDED
TALARI	GAMBIR	BAUCIS	PATCHY	HAGDON	SANDER
TAMALE	GAMBIT	CAECUM	RANCHO	HAMDEN	SANDHI
TAPALO	GAMBLE	CALCAR	RANCID	HANDED	SANDRA
TATARS	GAMBOL	CALCES	RANCOR	HANDEL	SANDYS
VACANT	GARBED	CALCIC	RASCAL	HANDLE	TANDEM
VACATE	GARBLE	CANCAN	SAUCED	HARDEN	TAWDRY
VAGARY	GASBAG	CANCEL	SAUCER	HARDER	VANDAL
VALATE	HAGBUT	CANCER	SAUCES	HARDLY	WADDED
VASARI	HARBIN	CARCEL	TALCED	LADDER	WADDLE
WABASH	HARBOR	CATCHY	TALCUM	LADDIE	WADDLY
WAHABI	HATBOX	CAUCUS	******	LANDAU	WALDOS
WATAPE	HAYBOX	DANCED	-A-D--	LANDED	WANDAS
WATAPS	IAMBIC	DANCER	******	LANDER	WANDER
XANADU	IAMBUS	DANCES	BAGDAD	LAPDOG	WANDLE
ZANANA	JABBED	FAECAL	BALDER	LARDED	WARDED

WARDEN	FACERS	LATEST	RAVELS	******	CADGES
WARDER	FACETS	LAVERS	RAVENS	-A-F--	CANGUE
YARDED	FADEIN	LAXEST	RAVERS	******	CARGOS
******	FAGEND	LAYERS	RAWEST	BAFFED	CATGUT
-A-E-->	FAKERS	MABELS	RAZEED	BAFFIN	CAUGHT
******	FAKERY	MACERS	RAZEES	BAFFLE	DAGGER
BAGELS	FANEGA	MADEUP	SABEAN	BARFLY	DAGGLE
BAKERS	FARERS	MAKERS	SABERS	CARFAX	DANGED
BAKERY	GAGERS	MAKEUP	SAFELY	DAYFLY	DANGER
BALEEN	GAIETY	MAMEYS	SAFEST	EARFUL	DANGLE
BALERS	GALEAE	MANEGE	SAFETY	GADFLY	FAGGED
BAREGE	GALENA	MASERS	SAGELY	GAFFED	FAGGOT
BARELY	GAMELY	MATEOS	SAGEST	GAFFER	FANGAS
BAREST	GAMETE	MATEYS	SAHEBS	GAFFES	FANGED
BASELY	GAMETO	MAYEST	SAKERS	HATFUL	GADGET
BASEST	GANEFS	MAZERS	SANELY	JARFUL	GAGGED
BATEAU	GAPERS	NAMELY	SANEST	KAFFIR	GAGGER
BAYEUX	GATEAU	NAMERS	SATEEN	LAPFUL	GAGGLE
CADENT	GAVELS	NAPERY	SAVERS	LAWFUL	GANGED
CADETS	GAYEST	NAVELS	SAWERS	MANFUL	GANGER
CALEBS	GAYETY	PACERS	SAYERS	MAYFLY	GANGES
CALESA	GAZEBO	PALEAE	TAKEIN	RAFFIA	GANGLI
CAMELS	GAZERS	PALELY	TAKERS	RAFFLE	GANGUE
CAMEOS	HABEAS	PALEST	TAKEUP	SAWFLY	GARGET
CAMERA	HALERS	PAMELA	TALENT	VATFUL	GARGLE
CANERS	HAREMS	PANELS	TALERS	WAFFLE	GAUGED
CAPERS	HATERS	PAPERS	TAMELY	WAIFED	GAUGER
CAREEN	HAVENS	PAPERY	TAMERS	ZAFFAR	GAUGES
CAREER	HAVENT	PARENS	TAMEST	ZAFFER	HAGGED
CARERS	HAZELS	PARENT	TAPERS	ZAFFIR	HAGGIS
CARESS	HAZERS	PARERS	TAVERN	ZAFFRE	HAGGLE
CARETS	JANETS	PAREUS	TAWERS	******	HANGAR
CASEFY	KARENS	PATENS	TAXEME	-A-G--	HANGED
CASEIN	LABELS	PATENT	TAXERS	******	HANGER
CASERN	LAGERS	PATERS	VALERY	BADGED	HANGUP
CATENA	LAKERS	PAVERS	VALETS	BADGER	JAEGER
CATERS	LAMECH	PAWERS	WADERS	BADGES	JAGGED
CAVEAT	LAMEDS	PAYEES	WAFERS	BAGGED	JANGLE
CAVEIN	LAMELY	PAYERS	WAGERS	BANGED	JARGON
CAVELL	LAMENT	RACEME	WAKENS	BANGLE	LAAGER
CAVERN	LAMEST	RACERS	WALERS	BANGOR	LAGGED
DALETH	LAPELS	RAKERS	WATERS	BANGUI	LAGGER
DARERS	LAREDO	RANEES	WATERY	BANGUP	LANGUR
DATERS	LASERS	RAREFY	WAVERS	BARGED	LARGER
DAVEYS	LATEEN	RARELY	WAVEYS	BARGEE	LARGOS
EASELS	LATELY	RAREST	YAGERS	BARGES	LAUGHS
EATERS	LATENT	RATELS	YAMENS	CADGED	MADGES
EATERY	LATERA	RATERS		CADGER	MAGGIE

MAGGOT	******	LATHER	BALING	DANITE	GAZING
MAIGRE	-A-H--	LATHES	BANIAN	DARICS	HABILE
MALGRE	******	MASHED	BANISH	DARIEN	HABITS
MANGER	AACHEN	MASHER	BARING	DARING	HADING
MANGLE	BACHED	MASHES	BARITE	DARIUS	HAKIMS
MANGOS	BACHES	MASHIE	BARIUM	DATING	HALIDE
MARGAY	BASHAW	MAYHAP	BASICS	DATIVE	HALIDS
MARGES	BASHED	MAYHEM	BASIFY	DAVIDS	HALING
MARGIE	BASHES	NASHUA	BASILS	DAVIES	HALITE
MARGIN	BATHED	NATHAN	BASING	DAVITS	HAMITE
MARGOS	BATHER	PASHAS	BASINS	DAZING	HARING
MARGOT	BATHOS	PASHTO	BASION	EALING	HATING
NAGGED	CACHED	PATHAN	BATIKS	EARING	HAVING
NAGGER	CACHES	PATHIA	BATING	EASIER	HAWING
NAUGHT	CACHET	PATHOL	BAYING	EASILY	HAYING
PARGET	CACHOU	PATHOS	CABINS	EASING	HAZIER
PARGOS	CARHOP	RACHEL	CAGIER	EATING	HAZILY
RAGGED	CASHAW	RACHIS	CAGILY	FABIAN	HAZING
RANGED	CASHED	RAPHAE	CAGING	FACIAL	JABIRU
RANGER	CASHES	RAPHIS	CAHIER	FACIES	JADING
RANGES	CASHEW	RASHER	CAKING	FACILE	JADISH
SAGGAR	CASHOO	RASHES	CALICO	FACING	JAMIES
SAGGED	CATHAY	RASHLY	CALIFS	FADING	JANICE
SAGGER	CATHER	RATHER	CALIPH	FAKING	JAPING
SAIGAS	CATHYS	SACHEM	CAMILA	FAKIRS	JARINA
SAIGON	DACHAS	SACHET	CAMION	FAMILY	JAWING
SANGAR	DACHAU	SADHUS	CAMISE	FAMINE	KABIKI
SANGER	DAPHNE	SAPHAR	CANINE	FAMISH	KALIAN
SANGUI	DASHED	SASHAY	CANING	FANION	KALIUM
SARGON	DASHER	SASHED	CAPIAS	FARINA	KAMIKS
SAUGER	DASHES	SASHES	CAPITA	FARING	KATIES
TAGGED	FATHER	VASHTI	CARIBE	FATIMA	KATION
TAGGER	FATHOM	WARHOL	CARIBS	FATING	LABIAL
TAIGAS	GASHED	WASHED	CARIES	FAXING	LABILE
TANGED	GASHES	WASHER	CARINA	FAYING	LABIUM
TANGLE	GATHER	WASHES	CARING	FAZING	LACIAL
TANGLY	HASHED	YACHTS	CASING	GABION	LACIER
TANGOS	HASHES	******	CASINO	GAGING	LACILY
TARGET	HAWHAW	-A-I--	CATION	GALIOT	LACING
TAUGHT	JAPHET	******	CAVIAR	GAMIER	LADIES
VALGUS	JAPHIA	AALIIS	CAVIES	GAMILY	LADING
WAGGED	KATHIE	BAAING	CAVILS	GAMING	LADINO
WAGGLE	KATHYS	BABIED	CAVING	GAMINS	LAKIER
WAGGLY	LACHES	BABIES	CAVITE	GAPING	LAKING
WAGGON	LASHED	BABISM	CAVITY	GARISH	LAMIAE
WANGLE	LASHER	BABIST	CAWING	GASIFY	LAMIAS
	LASHES	BABITE	DANIEL	GATING	LAMINA
	LATHED	BAKING	DANISH	GAVIAL	LAMING

LAPINS	NANISM	RADIUS	SAVING	XAVIER	HACKED
LARIAT	NAPIER	RAGING	SAVINS	YAKIMA	HACKEE
LARINE	NARIAL	RAKING	SAVIOR	YAWING	HACKER
LATINS	NARINE	RAKISH	SAWING	ZAMIAS	HACKIE
LATISH	NASIAL	RAMIES	SAYING	ZANIER	HACKLE
LAVING	NASION	RAMIFY	TAHITI	ZANIES	HANKER
LAVISH	NATION	RAPIDS	TAKING	ZARIBA	HARKED
LAWING	NATIVE	RAPIER	TALION	ZAYINS	HARKEN
LAXITY	NAVIES	RAPINE	TAMING	******	HAWKED
LAYING	NAZIFY	RAPING	TANIST	-A-J--	HAWKER
LAZIER	NAZISM	RAPIST	TAOISM	******	JACKAL
LAZILY	OAFISH	RARING	TAOIST	BANJOS	JACKED
LAZING	OARING	RARITY	TAPING	FANJET	JACKET
MACING	PACIFY	RATIFY	TAPIRS	GASJET	JACKIE
MAKING	PACING	RATINE	TARIFF	JAMJAR	JACKYS
MALICE	PAGING	RATING	TARING	RAMJET	LACKED
MALIGN	PALING	RATION	TAWING	SANJAK	LACKEY
MALINE	PALISH	RATIOS	TAXIED	******	LANKER
MAMIES	PANICE	RATITE	TAXING	-A-K--	LANKLY
MANIAC	PANICS	RAVINE	TAXITE	******	LARKED
MANIAS	PAPIST	RAVING	VAGINA	BACKED	LARKER
MANILA	PARIAH	RAVISH	VAGINO	BACKER	MACKLE
MANIOC	PARIAN	RAWISH	VALISE	BAIKAL	MARKED
MANITO	PARIES	RAYING	VANISH	BALKAN	MARKER
MANITU	PARING	RAZING	VANITY	BALKED	MARKET
MAOISM	PARISH	SABINA	VARICO	BANKED	MARKKA
MAOIST	PARITY	SABINE	VARIED	BANKER	MARKUP
MARIAN	PATINA	SABINS	VARIER	BARKED	MASKED
MARIAS	PATINE	SADIES	VARIES	BARKER	MASKEG
MARIES	PATIOS	SADISM	VASILI	BASKED	MASKER
MARINA	PAVING	SADIST	WADIES	BASKET	NAPKIN
MARINE	PAVIOR	SAGIER	WADING	CACKLE	NARKED
MARION	PAVISE	SAHIBS	WAGING	CALKED	PACKED
MARIST	PAWING	SALIFY	WAHINE	CALKER	PACKER
MATINE	PAYING	SALINE	WAKIKI	CALKIN	PACKET
MATING	RABIES	SALISH	WAKING	CANKER	PARKAS
MATINS	RACIAL	SALIVA	WALING	CASKET	PARKED
MAXIMA	RACIER	SAMIAN	WANING	CATKIN	PARKER
MAXIMS	RACILY	SAMIEL	WANION	DANKER	PAUKER
MAXINE	RACINE	SAMITE	WAPITI	DANKLY	RACKED
MAXIXE	RACING	SANIES	WARIER	DARKEN	RACKER
MAYING	RACISM	SANITY	WARILY	DARKER	RACKET
MAZIER	RACIST	SAPIEN	WAVIER	DARKLE	RANKED
MAZILY	RADIAL	SASINS	WAVIES	DARKLY	RANKER
MAZING	RADIAN	SATING	WAVILY	FAWKES	RANKLE
NADINE	RADIOS	SATINS	WAVING	GASKET	RANKLY
NADIRS	RADISH	SATINY	WAXIER	GASKIN	SACKED
NAMING	RADIUM	SATIRE	WAXING	GAWKED	SACKER

TACKED	CARLAS	HAMLET	RAILED	BARMEN	MAIMER
TACKER	CARLOS	HARLAN	RATLIN	BARMIE	MAMMAE
TACKEY	CARLOW	HARLEM	SABLES	BATMAN	MAMMAL
TACKLE	CATLIN	HARLEY	SAILED	BATMEN	MAMMAS
TALKED	CAULES	HARLOT	SAILER	CABMAN	MAMMET
TALKER	CAULIS	HARLOW	SAILOR	CABMEN	MAMMON
TALKIE	CAULKS	HASLET	SALLET	CADMUS	MARMOT
TANKAS	DAHLIA	HAULED	SALLOW	CAIMAN	MAUMAU
TANKED	DALLAS	HAULER	SALLYS	CALMED	NAOMIS
TANKER	DALLES	HAULMY	SAMLET	CALMER	PALMAR
TASKED	EAGLES	JAILED	SAULTS	CALMLY	PALMED
VALKYR	EAGLET	JAILER	TABLED	CARMAN	PALMER
WALKED	EARLAP	JAILOR	TABLES	CARMEL	RAGMAN
WALKER	EARLES	KAOLIN	TABLET	CARMEN	RAGMEN
WALKON	FABLED	LADLED	TAILED	CAYMAN	RAMMED
WALKUP	FABLER	LADLER	TAILLE	DAEMON	RAMMER
YAKKED	FABLES	LADLES	TAILOR	DAGMAR	SALMIS
YANKED	FAILED	LALLED	TALLER	DAIMIO	SALMON
YANKEE	FAILLE	MACLES	TALLOW	DAIMON	SAMMYS
******	FALLAL	MAHLER	TATLER	DAIMYO	TALMUD
-A-L--	FALLEN	MAILED	TAYLOR	DAMMAR	TARMAC
******	FALLER	MAILER	VALLEY	DAMMED	TASMAN
BAALIM	FALLOW	MALLED	VALLUM	DAMMER	VANMAN
BAILED	FARLES	MALLEE	VARLET	FARMED	VANMEN
BAILEE	FARLEY	MALLET	VAULTS	FARMER	WAMMUS
BAILER	FAULTS	MALLOW	WAILED	GAMMAS	WARMED
BAILEY	FAULTY	MAPLES	WAILER	GAMMED	WARMER
BAILIE	GABLED	MARLED	WALLAH	GAMMER	WARMLY
BAILOR	GABLES	MARLIN	WALLAS	GAMMON	WARMTH
BALLAD	GAELIC	MARLOW	WALLED	GASMAN	WARMUP
BALLED	GALLED	MAULED	WALLET	GASMEN	YAMMER
BALLET	GALLEY	MAULER	WALLIE	HAEMAL	YASMAK
BALLOT	GALLIC	NAILED	WALLIS	HAMMAL	******
BARLEY	GALLON	NAPLES	WALLOP	HAMMED	-A-N--
BAWLED	GALLOP	OAKLEY	WALLOW	HAMMER	******
BAWLER	GALLUP	PALLAS	WALLYS	HARMED	BAGNIO
CABLED	GALLUS	PALLED	WAULED	HARMIN	BANNED
CABLES	GAOLER	PALLET	WAWLED	HAYMOW	BANNER
CABLET	GARLIC	PALLID	WAYLAY	JAMMED	BARNEY
CALLAO	GAULLE	PALLOR	YAWLED	KALMIA	BARNUM
CALLAS	HAILED	PARLAY	******	KARMAS	CANNAE
CALLED	HAILER	PARLEY	-A-M--	LAMMAS	CANNAS
CALLER	HALLAH	PARLOR	******	LAMMED	CANNED
CALLOW	HALLEL	PAULAS	BADMAN	LAYMAN	CANNEL
CALLUP	HALLEY	PAULIN	BADMEN	LAYMEN	CANNER
CALLUS	HALLOO	PAULUS	BAGMAN	MADMAN	CANNES
CAMLET	HALLOW	PAVLOV	BAGMEN	MADMEN	CANNIE
CAPLIN	HALLUX	RAGLAN	BARMAN	MAIMED	

CANNON	MAINLY	BARONG	JACOBS	SALONS	DAMPED
CANNOT	MANNED	BARONS	JALOPS	SALOON	DAMPEN
CARNAL	MANNER	BARONY	JALOPY	SALOOP	DAMPER
CATNAP	MAUNDS	BATONS	JASONS	SAMOAN	DAMPLY
CATNIP	MAUNDY	BAYOUS	KABOBS	SARONG	DAPPED
DAINTY	PAINED	CABOBS	KALONG	SATORY	DAPPER
DAMNED	PAINTS	CAEOMA	KAPOKS	SAVORS	DAPPLE
DANNYS	PAINTY	CAHOOT	KAYOED	SAVORY	GAPPED
DARNED	PANNED	CAJOLE	KAZOOS	SAVOUR	GASPAR
DARNEL	PAUNCH	CALORY	LABORS	SAXONS	GASPED
DARNER	PAWNED	CANOED	LABOUR	SAXONY	GASPER
DAUNTS	PAWNEE	CANOES	LADOGA	TABOOS	HAMPER
DAWNED	PAWNER	CANONS	LAGOON	TABORS	HAPPED
EARNED	PAYNIM	CANOPY	LAHORE	TACOMA	HAPPEN
EARNER	RADNOR	CAPONE	LANOSE	TALONS	HARPED
FAFNIR	RAINED	CAPONS	LAYOFF	TAROTS	HARPER
FAINTS	SAINTS	CAPOTE	LAYOUT	VADOSE	HASPED
FANNED	SANNUP	CAROBS	MAGOTS	VALOIS	HATPIN
FANNER	SAUNAS	CAROLE	MAHOUT	VALOUR	JAIPUR
FANNIE	SAWNEY	CAROLS	MAJORS	VAMOSE	JASPER
FANNYS	TAENIA	CAROMS	MALORY	VAPORI	KALPAK
FAUNAE	TAINOS	CAVORT	MANORS	VAPORS	KAPPAS
FAUNAL	TAINTS	DACOIT	MAROON	VAPOUR	KASPER
FAUNAS	TANNED	DADOES	MASONS	WAGONS	LAMPAD
FAUNUS	TANNER	DAGOBA	MASORA	WAHOOS	LAMPAS
FAWNED	TANNIC	DAHOON	MAYORS	WAMOUS	LAMPED
FAWNER	TANNIN	DAKOIT	NABOBS	WAYOUT	LAPPED
GAINED	TARNAL	DAKOTA	NAGOYA	YAHOOS	LAPPER
GAINER	TAUNTS	FAGOTS	PAEONS	YAPONS	LAPPET
GAINLY	VAINER	FAMOUS	PAEONY	******	MAGPIE
GANNET	VAINLY	FANONS	PAGODA	-A-P--	MAPPED
GARNER	VAUNTS	FAROFF	PARODY	******	MAYPOP
GARNET	WAGNER	FAROUT	PAROLE	CALPAC	NAPPED
HANNAH	WALNUT	FAVORS	PATOIS	CAMPED	NAPPER
HANNAS	WANNED	FAVOUR	PAYOFF	CAMPER	NAPPES
HAUNCH	WANNER	GADOID	PAYOLA	CAMPOS	NAPPIE
HAUNTS	WARNED	GALOOT	RACOON	CAMPUS	PALPED
JAINAS	WARNER	GALOPS	RADOME	CAPPED	PALPUS
JAUNTS	WAYNES	GALORE	RAGOUT	CAPPER	PAMPAS
JAUNTY	YAWNED	GALOSH	RAMONA	CARPAL	PAMPER
KARNAK	YAWNER	GAMOUS	RAMOSE	CARPED	PAPPUS
LANNER	******	GANOID	RAMOUS	CARPEL	PAUPER
LAUNCE	-A-O--	GAVOTS	RATOON	CARPER	PAWPAW
LAUNCH	******	HALOED	RAYONS	CARPET	RAJPUT
MAENAD	AARONS	HALOES	RAZORS	CARPIC	RALPHS
MAGNET	BABOON	HALOID	SABOTS	CARPUS	RAMPED
MAGNOX	BABOOS	HAROLD	SAJOUS	CASPAR	RAPPED
MAGNUM	BACONY	JABOTS	SALOME	CASPER	RAPPEE

RAPPEL	BARREL	MADRID	CAUSER	PARSES	BASTED
RAPPER	BARREN	MAORIS	CAUSES	PARSIS	BASTES
RASPED	BARRET	MARRED	DAISES	PARSON	BATTED
RASPER	BARRIE	MARRER	DAISYS	PASSED	BATTEN
SAIPAN	BARRIO	MARROW	DAMSEL	PASSEE	BATTER
SALPAS	BARROW	MATRIX	DAMSON	PASSER	BATTIK
SALPID	BARRYS	MATRON	DAWSON	PASSES	BATTIN
SAMPAN	BASRAH	NARROW	FALSER	PASSIM	BATTLE
SAMPLE	CADRES	NATRON	GASSED	PASSUS	BATTUE
SAPPED	CAIRNS	PADRES	GASSES	PATSYS	BAXTER
SAPPER	CAPRIC	PAIRED	HALSEY	PAUSED	CACTUS
SAPPHO	CARREL	PARRAL	HANSEL	PAUSER	CAFTAN
TAIPEI	CARRIE	PARREL	HANSOM	PAUSES	CANTAB
TAMPAN	CARROT	PARROT	HASSEL	RAISED	CANTED
TAMPED	DACRON	PATROL	HASSLE	RAISER	CANTER
TAMPER	DARROW	PATRON	HAUSEN	RAISES	CANTHI
TAMPON	FABRIC	RAMROD	HAWSER	RAISIN	CANTLE
TAPPED	FAERIE	SABRAS	HAWSES	RAMSON	CANTON
TAPPER	FAEROE	SACRAL	KAASES	RANSOM	CANTOR
TAPPET	FAIRED	SACRED	KAISER	SAMSHU	CANTOS
TARPAN	FAIRER	SACRUM	KAMSIN	SAMSON	CANTUS
TAUPES	FAIRLY	SATRAP	KANSAN	SANSAR	CAPTOR
VAMPED	FARROW	SAUREL	KANSAS	SANSEI	CARTED
WAMPUM	GARRET	SAURUS	LAPSED	SARSAR	CARTEL
WAPPED	HAIRDO	TANREC	LAPSER	SASSED	CARTER
WARPED	HAIRED	TARRED	LAPSES	SASSES	CARTES
WARPER	HARRIS	TAURUS	LAPSUS	TARSAL	CARTON
YAPPED	HARROW	WALRUS	LASSEN	TARSIA	CASTER
YAUPED	HARRYS	WARRED	LASSES	TARSUS	CASTES
YAUPON	HATRED	WARREN	LASSIE	TASSEL	CASTLE
YAWPED	IATRIC	YARROW	LASSOS	TASSET	CASTOR
YAWPER	JARRED	******	MAISIE	VASSAL	CASTRO
******	JARROW	-A-S--	MAISON	WADSET	CATTED
-A-Q--	KARROO	******	MANSES	WAISTS	CATTIE
******	KAURIS	BALSAM	MARSHA	WARSAW	CATTLE
BARQUE	LABRET	BALSAS	MARSHY	WATSON	CAUTER
BASQUE	LABRUM	BASSES	MASSED	******	CAXTON
CAIQUE	LAIRDS	BASSET	MASSES	-A-T--	DACTYL
CASQUE	LAIRED	BASSOS	MASSIF	******	DAFTLY
MANQUE	LARRUP	CAESAR	MAUSER	BAITED	DALTON
MARQUE	LARRYS	CANSOS	NAOSES	BALTIC	DANTON
MASQUE	LATRIA	CARSON	NASSAU	BALTIM	DARTED
******	LAURAE	CASSIA	NASSER	BANTAM	DARTER
-A-R--	LAURAS	CASSIE	NAUSEA	BANTER	DARTLE
******	LAUREL	CASSIS	PANSYS	BANTUS	DATTOS
BAIRNS	LAURIE	CATSUP	PARSEC	BARTER	DAYTON
BARRED	MACRON	CAUSAL	PARSED	BARTOK	EARTHS
	MADRAS	CAUSED	PARSEE	BARTON	EARTHY

EASTER	MANTIS	RASTER	XANTHO	SALUKI	VALV..
EASTON	MANTLE	RATTAN	ZAFTIG	SALUTE	VALVAR
FACTOR	MANTUA	RATTED	******	SAMUEL	VALVED
FACTUM	MARTAS	RATTEN	-A-U--	SATURN	VALVES
FAITHS	MARTEN	RATTER	******	VACUNA	VARVES
FALTER	MARTHA	RATTLE	BABULS	VACUUM	WAIVED
FANTAN	MARTHE	SAITIC	BARUCH	VAGUER	WAIVER
FANTOM	MARTIN	SALTED	BASUTO	VALUED	WAIVES
FASTED	MARTYR	SALTER	CAJUNS	VALUER	WALVIS
FASTEN	MARTYS	SANTOL	CANUCK	VALUES	YAHVEH
FASTER	MASTED	SARTOR	CANULA	VALUTA	******
FATTED	MASTER	SARTRE	CANUTE	VARUNA	-A-W--
FATTEN	MASTIC	SAUTES	CARUSO	WATUSI	******
FATTER	MATTED	TACTIC	CASUAL	YAMUNS	DARWIN
GAITED	MATTEO	TAMTAM	CAYUGA	YAOURT	EARWAX
GAITER	MATTER	TARTAN	CAYUSE	******	EARWIG
GANTRY	MATTES	TARTAR	DANUBE	-A-V--	GALWAY
GARTER	MATTIE	TARTED	DATURA	******	NARWAL
GASTON	NANTES	TARTER	FACULA	CALVED	PAXWAX
GASTRO	NASTIC	TARTLY	FANUMS	CALVES	TAIWAN
HAFTED	NATTER	TASTED	GAMUTS	CALVIN	YAHWEH
HALTED	NAUTCH	TASTER	HALUTZ	CANVAS	******
HALTER	PALTER	TASTES	JAGUAR	CARVED	-A-X--
HARTAL	PALTRY	TATTED	KABUKI	CARVEL	******
HASTED	PANTED	TATTER	LACUNA	CARVEN	CALXES
HASTEN	PANTIE	TATTLE	LAGUNE	CARVER	******
HASTES	PANTRY	TATTLY	LANUGO	CARVES	-A-Y--
HATTED	PARTED	TATTOO	LAZULI	FAUVES	******
HATTER	PARTLY	TAUTEN	MACULA	HALVED	BANYAN
HATTIE	PASTAS	TAUTER	MACULE	HALVES	BARYES
HATTYS	PASTED	TAUTLY	MADURA	HARVEY	BARYON
KAFTAN	PASTEL	TAUTOG	MADURO	JARVEY	BARYTA
LACTAM	PASTER	VASTER	MAGUEY	JARVIS	CANYON
LACTIC	PASTES	VASTLY	MANUAL	JAYVEE	GALYAK
LAOTSE	PASTIL	VATTED	MANUEL	LARVAE	LARYNG
LASTED	PASTOR	WAFTED	MANURE	LARVAL	LARYNX
LASTER	PASTRY	WAFTER	MAQUIS	LATVIA	LAWYER
LASTEX	PATTED	WAITED	MATURE	MARVEL	MAGYAR
LASTLY	PATTEN	WAITER	MAZUMA	MARVIN	SATYRS
LATTEN	PATTER	WALTER	NAHUMS	MAUVES	SAWYER
LATTER	PATTON	WALTON	NATURE	NAEVUS	******
MAITRE	RAFTED	WANTED	PAIUTE	PARVIS	-A-Z--
MALTED	RAFTER	WANTER	PAPUAN	SALVED	******
MALTHA	RAGTAG	WANTON	PAPULA	SALVER	BALZAC
MANTAS	RANTED	WASTED	PAPULE	SALVES	BANZAI
MANTEL	RANTER	WASTER	PARURE	SALVIA	DANZIG
MANTES	RAPTLY	WASTES	RADULA	SALVOR	DAZZLE
MANTIC	RAPTOR	WATTLE	RAOULS	SALVOS	GAUZES

HAMZAS
HAZZAN
JAZZED
JAZZER
JAZZES
MAIZES
MATZOS
MATZOT
PANZER
RAZZED
RAZZES
RAZZIA
TARZAN
TAZZAS
******

-B-A--
******
ABBACY
ABLAUT
ABLAZE
ABOARD
ABRADE
ABRAMS
ABWATT
IBEAMS
OBLAST
OBLATE
OBTAIN
UBOATS
******

-B-C--
******
ABACAS
ABACUS
IBICES
******

-B-D--
******
ABADAN
ABIDED
ABIDER
ABIDES
ABODES
ABYDOS
IBADAN
IBIDEM

******
-B-E--
******
ABBESS
ABBEYS
ABJECT
ABLEST
ABNERS
ABSENT
OBJECT
OBSESS
OBTECT
OBTEST
OBVERT
UBIETY
******

-B-H--
******
ABOHMS
******

-B-I--
******
ABBIES
EBBING
OBIISM
OBLIGE
OBOIST
******

-B-J--
******
ABIJAH

-B-L--
******
ABELES
ABOLLA
ABULIA
OBELUS
OBOLUS
******

-B-M--
******
ABOMAS
ABOMBS
******

-B-N--
******
TBONES
UBANGI

******
-B-O--
******
ABBOTS
ABHORS
ABLOOM
ABROAD
ABSORB
ABVOLT
OBLONG
******

-B-R--
******
ABORAL
ABORTS
IBERIA
OBERON
******

-B-S--
******
ABASED
ABASER
ABASES
ABUSED
ABUSER
ABUSES
ABYSMS
IBISES
******

-B-T--
******
ABATED
ABATER
ABATES
ABATIS
ABATOR
OBITER
******

-B-U--
******
ABDUCT
ABJURE
ABLUSH
ABOUND
ABRUPT
ABSURD
OBTUND
OBTUSE

******
-B-X--
******
IBEXES
******

-B-Y--
******
OBEYED
OBEYER
******

-C-A--
******
ACHAEA
ACHAIA
ACKACK
ACUATE
ECHARD
ECLAIR
ICEAXE
OCEANS
OCTADS
OCTANE
OCTANT
OCTAVE
OCTAVO
SCLAFF
SCRAGS
SCRAMS
SCRAPE
SCRAPS
SCRAWL
******

-C-B--
******
ICEBOX
SCABBY
SCUBAS
******

-C-C--
******
ACACIA
ICECAP
ICICLE
******

-C-D--
******
ACADIA
ACEDIA

ACIDIC
ACIDLY
******

-C-E--
******
ACAENA
ACCEDE
ACCENT
ACCEPT
ACCESS
ACHENE
ECZEMA
ICIEST
OCHERS
OCHERY
OCREAE
OCTETS
SCHEMA
SCHEME
SCLERA
SCLERO
SCREAK
SCREAM
SCREED
SCREEN
SCREWS
SCREWY
YCLEPT
******

-C-F--
******
SCOFFS
SCUFFS
******

-C-I--
******
ACEIUM
ACHING
ACTING
ACTINI
ACTINO
ACTION
ACTIUM
ACTIVE
ACUITY
ECHINI
ECHINO
SCHICK

SCHISM
SCHIST
SCHIZO
SCRIBE
SCRIED
SCRIMP
SCRIPS
SCRIPT
SCRIVE
******

-C-J--
******
ACAJOU
******

-C-L--
******
ECCLES
ECOLES
ICALLY
OCELLI
OCELOT
OCULAR
SCALAR
SCALDS
SCALED
SCALER
SCALES
SCALPS
SCILLY
SCOLDS
SCOLEX
SCULLS
SCULPT
SCYLLA
******

-C-M--
******
ACUMEN
ICEMAN
ICEMEN
SCAMPI
SCAMPS
SCHMOS
SCUMMY
******

-C-N--
******
ACANTH
ACINUS

ICINGS	ACERIC	ACTUAL	ADEEMS	ADOLPH	******
ICONIC	ACORNS	OCCULT	ADHERE	ADULTS	-D-T--
SCANTY	ECARTE	OCCUPY	ADIEUS	EDILES	******
SCENDS	ICARUS	OCCURS	ADIEUX	IDYLLS	ADYTUM
SCENES	OCTROI	SCAUPS	ADJECT	******	EDITED
SCENIC	SCARAB	SCHUIT	ADVENT	-D-N--	EDITHS
SCENTS	SCARCE	SCHUSS	ADVERB	******	EDITOR
SCONCE	SCARED	SCOURS	ADVERT	ADENIS	ODETTE
SCONES	SCARER	SCOUSE	EDSELS	ADONAI	******
******	SCARES	SCOUTS	IDLERS	ADONIC	-D-U--
-C-O--	SCARFS	SCRUBS	IDLEST	ADONIS	******
******	SCARPS	SCRUFF	ODDEST	EDENIC	ADDUCE
ACCORD	SCORCH	SCRUMS	UDDERS	GDANSK	ADDUCT
ACCOST	SCORED	******	******	GDYNIA	ADJURE
ACEOUS	SCORER	-C-W--	-D-G--	ODONTO	ADJUST
ACIOUS	SCORES	******	******	ODYNIA	EDMUND
ACNODE	SCORIA	SCHWAS	ADAGES	******	******
ACROSS	SCORNS	SCOWLS	ADAGIO	-D-O--	-E-A--
ACTORS	SCURFY	******	-D-I--	******	******
ECHOED	SCURRY	-C-Y--	******	ADJOIN	AERATE
ECHOER	SCURVY	******	ADDICT	ADNOUN	BECALM
ECHOES	******	ECTYPE	ADDING	ADROIT	BECAME
ECHOIC	-C-S--	******	ADLIBS	ADSORB	BEDAUB
ECTOMY	******	-D-A--	ADMIRE	EDMOND	BEFALL
MCCOYS	ECESIS	******	ADMITS	IDIOCY	BEHALF
OCLOCK	OCASEY	ADDAMS	ADMIXT	IDIOMS	BEHAVE
OCTOPI	******	ADNATE	ADRIAN	IDIOTS	BELAYS
SCHOOL	-C-T--	EDDAIC	ADRIEN	ODIOUS	BEMATA
SCHORL	******	EDGARS	ADRIFT	******	BERATE
SCIONS	ACETAL	EDUARD	ADVICE	-D-P--	BESANT
SCOOPS	ACETIC	EDWARD	ADVISE	******	BETAKE
SCOOTS	ACETUM	IDEALS	EDDIED	ADAPTS	BEWAIL
SCRODS	ACETYL	IDEATE	EDDIES	ADEPTS	BEWARE
SCROLL	ICHTHY	******	EDDISH	ADIPIC	BEZANT
SCROOP	SCATHE	-D-B--	EDGIER	ADOPTS	CEDARS
SCROTA	SCATTY	******	EDGING	******	CERATE
******	SCOTCH	ADOBES	EDWINA	-D-R--	CERATO
-C-P--	SCOTER	EDIBLE	EDWINS	******	CESARE
******	SCOTIA	******	IDLING	ADORED	CETANE
SCAPES	SCOTTS	-D-C--	ODDITY	ADORER	DEBARK
SCIPIO	SCUTCH	******	******	ADORES	DEBARS
SCOPES	SCUTES	EDICTS	-D-J--	ADORNS	DEBASE
SCOPUS	SCUTUM	EDUCED	******	******	DEBATE
SCYPHI	SCYTHE	EDUCES	ODDJOB	-D-S--	DECADE
SCYPHO	******	EDUCTS	******	******	DECALS
******	-C-U--	******	-D-L--	EDISON	DECAMP
-C-R--	******	-D-E--	******	ODESSA	DECANE
******	ACCUSE	******	ADDLED		DECANT
ACARID	ACQUIT	ADDEND	ADDLES		
ACCRUE		ADDERS			

DECARE	NEGATE	REVAMP	REUBEN	******	LEWDLY
DECAYS	NEMATO	REWARD	SEABEE	-E-D--	LEYDEN
DEDANS	NEVADA	SEBATS	SERBIA	******	MEADOW
DEFACE	NEWARK	SECANT	TEABAG	BEADED	MEDDLE
DEFAME	PECANS	SEDANS	TERBIA	BEADLE	MELDED
DEGAGE	PEDALS	SEDATE	VERBAL	BEDDED	MENDED
DEGAME	PEDANT	SEJANT	WEBBED	BEDDER	MENDEL
DEKARE	PEDATE	SENARY	YERBAS	BELDAM	MENDER
DELATE	PEDATI	SENATE	******	BENDAY	MENDIP
DELAYS	PEKANS	SEPALS	-E-C--	BENDED	NEEDED
DEMAND	PELAGE	SERACS	******	BENDEE	NEEDER
DENARY	PESACH	SERAIS	AEACUS	BENDER	NEEDLE
DEPART	PESADE	SERAPE	BEACHY	DEADEN	PEDDLE
DERAIL	PETALS	SERAPH	BEACON	DEADLY	PENDED
DERAIN	PETARD	SESAME	BEECHY	DEEDED	READER
DERATE	REBATE	SEWAGE	DEACON	DENDRI	REDDEN
DESALT	REBATO	SEWALL	DECCAN	DENDRO	REDDER
DETACH	RECALL	SEWARD	DEICED	DEODAR	REDDLE
DETAIL	RECANT	TELARY	DEICER	FEEDER	REDDOG
DETAIN	RECAPS	TENACE	DEICES	FENDED	REEDED
DEWANS	RECAST	TENANT	DESCRY	FENDER	REEDIT
FEMALE	REDACT	TERAPH	DEUCED	FEODOR	RENDED
FEUARS	REDANS	TERATO	DEUCES	FEUDAL	RENDER
GEMARA	REFACE	TETANY	FENCED	FEUDED	SEADOG
GERALD	REGAIN	ZENANA	FENCER	GELDED	SEEDED
GERARD	REGALE	******	FENCES	GENDER	SEEDER
HECATE	REGARD	-E-B--	FESCUE	GEODES	SELDOM
HEMATO	REHASH	******	LEACHY	GEODIC	SENDAL
HEPATO	RELAID	BEDBUG	MECCAN	HEADED	SENDER
HERALD	RELATE	BERBER	MECCAS	HEADER	SERDAB
HEXADS	RELAYS	CEIBAS	MERCER	HEADON	TEDDED
HEXANE	REMADE	DEBBIE	MERCIA	HEDDLE	TEDDER
JEZAIL	REMAIN	DEBBYS	MESCAL	HEEDED	TEDDYS
KERALA	REMAKE	FEEBLE	PEACHY	HEEDER	TENDED
KERATO	REMAND	FEEBLY	PENCEL	HENDON	TENDER
LEGACY	REMANS	FERBER	PENCIL	HERDED	TENDON
LEGATE	REMARK	GERBIL	PERCYS	HERDER	VEADAR
LEGATO	REPAID	HENBIT	REACTS	HERDIC	VELDTS
LENAPE	REPAIR	HERBAL	REDCAP	HEYDAY	VENDED
LEVANT	REPAND	JERBOA	REECHO	KEDDAH	VENDEE
MEDALS	REPASS	KERBED	REICHS	KENDAL	VENDER
MEGALO	REPAST	LESBOS	RESCUE	LEADED	VENDOR
MEGASS	REPAYS	MEMBER	SEACOW	LEADEN	VENDUE
MELANO	RESALE	PEBBLE	SEICHE	LEADER	VERDIN
MENACE	RETAIL	PEBBLY	TEACUP	LEADIN	VERDUN
MENAGE	RETAIN	REDBAY	TERCEL	LENDER	WEDDED
METAGE	RETAKE	REDBUD	TERCET	LEUDES	WEEDED
METALS	RETARD	REDBUG	TETCHY	LEWDER	WEEDER
			TEUCER		

WELDED
WELDER
WENDED
WENDYS
******

-E-E--
******

AEGEAN
AEGEUS
AENEAS
AENEID
BEDECK
BEDEWS
BEFELL
BEGETS
BEHEAD
BEHELD
BEHEST
BEMEAN
BEREFT
BERETS
BESEEM
BESETS
BETELS
BEVELS
BEZELS
CELERY
CEMENT
CEREAL
CEREUS
DECEIT
DECENT
DECERN
DEFEAT
DEFECT
DEFEND
DEFERS
DEJECT
DELETE
DEMEAN
DEMENT
DEPEND
DEREKS
DESERT
DETECT
DETENT
DETERS
DETEST

DEVEIN
DEVEST
FEVERS
FEWEST
GEMERT
GENERA
GENESI
GENETS
GENEVA
GERENT
GESELL
HELENA
HELENS
HEREAT
HEREBY
HEREIN
HEREOF
HEREON
HERESY
HERETO
HETERO
HEWERS
JEREED
JEREMY
JEWELS
JEWESS
KETENE
KEVELS
LEGEND
LEGERS
LEPERS
LEVEES
LEVELS
LEVERS
MELEES
MERELY
MEREST
METEOR
METERS
NEREID
NEREIS
NEWELS
NEWEST
OEDEMA
OEPEMA
PELEUS
PESETA
PETERS

PEWEES
REBECK
REBECS
REBELS
RECEDE
RECENT
RECEPT
RECESS
REDEEM
REDEYE
REFERS
REGENT
REHEAR
REHEAT
REJECT
RELENT
REMEDY
RENEES
RENEGE
RENEWS
REPEAL
REPEAT
REPELS
REPENT
RESEAT
RESEAU
RESECT
RESEDA
RESELL
RESEND
RESENT
RESETS
RETELL
RETENE
REVEAL
REVELS
REVERE
REVERS
REVERT
REVEST
REVETS
SECEDE
SECERN
SEDERS
SELECT
SELENE
SELENO
SEMELE

SEMEME
SENECA
SEREIN
SERENA
SERENE
SEVENS
SEVERE
SEVERN
SEVERS
SEWELL
SEWERS
TEHEED
TEHEES
TELEDU
TELEGA
TENETS
TEPEES
TEPEFY
TEREDO
TERESA
TERETE
TEREUS
TEVERE
VENEER
VENERY
VEREIN
VEXERS
WEBERS
WEDELN
WERENT
XEBECS
YEMENI
ZEBECK
ZEBECS
******

-E-F--
******

BEEFED
BELFRY
DEAFEN
DEAFLY
DEIFIC
FEOFFS
HEIFER
LEAFED
REDFIN
REEFED
REEFER
TELFER

******

-E-G--
******

BEAGLE
BEGGAR
BEGGED
BEIGES
BELGAS
BELGIC
BENGAL
BERGEN
DEIGNS
DENGUE
FEIGNE
FEIGNS
GEIGER
GEWGAW
HEDGED
HEDGER
HEDGES
HEIGHT
KEDGED
KEDGES
LEAGUE
LEDGER
LEDGES
LEGGED
LEIGHS
LENGTH
MEAGER
MEAGRE
MERGED
MERGER
MERGES
NEIGHS
PEGGED
PEGGYS
PENGOS
REDGUM
REGGIE
REIGNS
SEDGES
SEGGAR
TERGAL
TERGUM
VERGED
VERGER
VERGES

VERGIL
WEDGED
WEDGES
WEDGIE
WEIGHS
WEIGHT
ZENGER
ZEUGMA
******

-E-H--
******

AETHER
BETHEL
HEEHAW
JETHRO
LECHER
LETHAL
MENHIR
MESHED
MESHER
MESHES
METHOD
METHYL
NEPHEW
NEPHRO
NETHER
PEAHEN
REDHOT
TECHNO
TETHER
TETHYS
WETHER
ZECHIN
ZEPHYR
ZETHOS
ZETHUS
******

-E-I--
******

AECIAL
AEDILE
AERIAL
AERIED
AERIES
AERIFY
BEDIMS
BEFITS
BEGINS

BEGIRD	DENIED	JEMIMA	RECIPE	SEXILY	NECKED
BEGIRT	DENIER	JEWISH	RECITE	SEXING	PEAKED
BEHIND	DENIES	KENITE	REFILL	SEXISM	PECKED
BELIAL	DENIMS	KEVINS	REFINE	SEXIST	PECKER
BELIED	DENISE	KEYING	REFITS	TEDIUM	PEEKED
BELIEF	DEPICT	LEGION	REGIME	TEEING	PEEKER
BELIER	DERIDE	LEGIST	REGINA	VEDIAC	PERKED
BELIES	DERIVE	LENITY	REGION	VENIAL	RECKON
BELIKE	DESIGN	LEPIDO	REGIUS	VENICE	REEKED
BELIZE	DESIRE	LESION	RELICS	VENIRE	REEKER
BEMIRE	DESIST	LEVIED	RELICT	VERIFY	SECKEL
BENIGN	DEVICE	LEVIER	RELIED	VERILY	SEEKER
BENITA	DEVILS	LEVIES	RELIEF	VERISM	WEAKEN
BENITO	DEVISE	LEVITE	RELIER	VERIST	WEAKER
BERING	DEWIER	LEVITY	RELIES	VERITY	WEAKLY
BESIDE	DEWITT	MEDIAE	RELINE	VESICA	WEEKLY
BETIDE	EERILY	MEDIAL	RELISH	VESICO	WELKIN
BETISE	FECIAL	MEDIAN	RELIVE	VEXILS	******
BEVIES	FEEING	MEDICI	REMIND	VEXING	-E-L--
CECILE	FELICE	MEDICO	REMISE	XENIAL	******
CECILS	FELIDS	MEDICS	REMISS	ZENITH	AEOLIA
CECILY	FELINE	MEDIUM	REMITS	******	AEOLIC
CEDING	FELIPE	MEGILP	REPINE	-E-J--	AEOLIS
CELIAC	FENIAN	MEJICO	RESIDE	******	AEOLUS
CELIAS	FERIAL	MENIAL	RESIGN	BENJYS	BEDLAM
CERING	FERINE	MENINX	RESILE	SELJUK	BELLAS
CERIPH	FERITY	MERINO	RESINS	******	BELLED
CERISE	FETIAL	MERITS	RESIST	-E-K--	BELLES
CERITE	FETICH	MESIAL	RETINA	******	BELLOC
CERIUM	FETING	MESIAN	RETIRE	BEAKED	BELLOW
CESIUM	FETISH	METIER	REVIEW	BEAKER	BERLIN
DEBITS	FEUING	METING	REVILE	BECKED	BEULAH
DECIDE	GEEING	MEWING	REVISE	BECKET	BEULAS
DECILE	GEMINI	MEXICO	REVIVE	BECKON	CEILED
DEFIED	GENIAL	NEVILE	REWIND	BECKYS	CELLAE
DEFIER	GENIES	NEVILL	SEDILE	DECKED	CELLAR
DEFIES	GENITO	PEKING	SEEING	DECKEL	CELLOS
DEFILE	GENIUS	PELIAS	SEMITE	DECKER	CEYLON
DEFINE	HEGIRA	PELION	SENILE	DECKLE	DEALER
DEKING	HEJIRA	PELITE	SENIOR	GECKOS	DELLAS
DELIAN	HELICO	PENIAL	SEPIAS	HECKLE	DEPLOY
DELIAS	HELIOS	PENILE	SERIAL	HELICO	DEWLAP
DELICT	HELIUM	PERILS	SERIES	JERKED	FEALTY
DELIUS	HERIOT	PERIOD	SERIFS	JERKIN	FEELER
DEMIES	HEWING	PERISH	SERINE	KECKED	FELLAH
DEMISE	HEXING	PETITE	SERINS	KECKLE	FELLED
DEMITS	HEZION	PEWITS	SEWING	LEAKED	FELLER
DENIAL	JEEING	REBILL	SEXIER	MEEKER	FELLOE
					MEEKLY

FELLOW
GELLED
HEALED
HEALER
HEALTH
HEELED
HEELER
HELLAS
HELLEN
HELLER
HENLEY
JELLED
KEELED
KEGLER
KELLER
KEPLER
LESLEY
LESLIE
MEALIE
MEDLAR
MEDLEY
MELLON
MELLOW
MERLES
MERLIN
MERLON
MEWLED
NELLIE
NELLYS
PEALED
PEDLAR
PEELED
PEELER
PEGLEG
PELLET
PEPLOS
PEPLUM
PEPLUS
REALES
REALLY
REALMS
REALTY
REELED
REELER
REFLET
REFLEX
REFLUX
REGLET

REPLAY
SEALED
SEALER
SELLER
SENLAC
TEFLON
TELLER
TELLUS
VEILED
VEILER
VELLUM
WEALDS
WEALTH
WELLED
WESLEY
YELLED
YELLER
YELLOW
ZEALOT
******

-E-M--
******
BEAMED
BERMES
CERMET
DEEMED
DERMAL
DERMAS
DERMAT
DERMIC
DERMIS
DESMAN
DESMID
FERMIS
GEMMAE
GEMMED
GERMAN
GERMEN
HELMED
HELMET
HEMMED
HEMMER
HERMAE
HERMAI
HERMAN
HERMES
HERMIT
HETMAN

KERMES
KERMIS
KERMIT
LEGMAN
LEGMEN
LEMMAS
MERMAN
MERMEN
MESMER
NEUMES
PENMAN
PENMEN
PERMED
PERMIT
REAMED
REAMER
SEAMAN
SEAMED
SEAMEN
SEAMER
SEAMUS
SEEMED
SEEMER
SEEMLY
SERMON
TEAMED
TEEMED
TEEMER
TEGMEN
TERMED
TERMER
TERMLY
TERMOR
VERMIN
WEIMAR
YEOMAN
YEOMEN
YESMAN
******

-E-N--
******
BEANED
BEANIE
BEINGS
BENNES
BENNET
BENNYS
BERNEY

BERNIE
DENNED
DENNIS
DENNYS
FEINTS
FENNEC
FENNEL
HENNAS
HERNIA
HERNIO
JEANNE ,
JENNET
JENNYS
KEENED
KEENER
KEENLY
KENNED
KENNEL
KENNIE
KENNYS
KERNED
KERNEL
KEYNES
LEANED
LEANER
LEANLY
LEANTO
LEMNOS
LENNYS
LEONAS
LEONIE
MEANER
MEANIE
MEANLY
MESNES
PEANUT
PEENED
PENNAE
PENNED
PENNER
PENNIA
PENNIS
PENNON
PENNYS
REGNAL
REINED
RENNET
RENNIN

SEANCE
SEINED
SEINER
SEINES
SENNAS
SENNET
SENNIT
TEENSY
TENNIS
TERNAL
VEINED
VERNAL
VERNAS
VERNIX
VERNON
WEANED
WEANER
WEENIE
WEENSY
YEANED
YENNED
******

-E-O--
******
AEROBE
BECOME
BEFOGS
BEFOOL
BEFORE
BEFOUL
BEGONE
BEHOLD
BEHOOF
BEHOVE
BELOIT
BELONG
BEMOAN
BESOMS
BESOTS
BETONY
BETOOK
BEYOND
BEZOAR
CEBOID
CEROUS
DECOCT
DECODE
DECOKE

DECORS
DECOYS
DEFORM
DEHORN
DEMOBS
DEMODE
DEMONO
DEMONS
DEMOTE
DENOTE
DEPONE
DEPORT
DEPOSE
DEPOTS
DESOXY
DETOUR
DEVOID
DEVOIR
DEVOTE
DEVOUR
DEVOUT
FEDORA
FELONS
FELONY
FEMORA
FEROUS
FETORS
GEMOTS
GENOUS
GEROUS
HELOTS
HEMOID
HEROES
HEROIC
HEROIN
HERONS
HESOID
HEXONE
HEXOSE
JEROME
KELOID
KETONE
KETOSE
LEMONS
LENORE
LEROYS
MEKONG
MELODY

MELONS	SETOFF	SEAPEN	FERRUM	REARED	GEISHA
MEMOIR	SETONS	SECPAR	GEARED	REARER	GEMSBO
MEMORY	SETOSE	SEEPED	GENRES	REARMS	GESSOS
MEROUS	SETOUS	SEMPRE	GENROS	REGRET	GEYSER
MESONS	SETOUT	SEXPOT	GEORGE	RETROD	HEISTS
METOPE	TENONS	TEAPOT	GEORGI	SEARCH	JERSEY
NEROLI	TENORS	TEAPOY	GERRYS	SEARED	JESSED
NEVOID	TETONS	TEMPER	HEARER	SEARIN	JESSES
PEKOES	VELOCE	TEMPLE	HEARSE	SECRET	JESSIE
PELOPS	VELOUR	TEMPOS	HEARST	SEURAT	JETSAM
PELOTA	VENOMS	TEMPTS	HEARTH	TEARED	KELSON
PEYOTE	VENOSE	TENPIN	HEARTS	TENREC	KERSEY
REBORE	VENOUS	VESPER	HEARTY	TERRET	LEASED
REBORN	VERONA	VESPID	HEBREW	TERROR	LEASES
REBOZO	VETOED	WEAPON	HEBRON	TERRYS	LENSES
RECOIL	VETOER	WEEPER	HEDRAL	TETRAD	LEPSIA
RECORD	VETOES	YELPED	HEDRON	TETRYL	LESSEE
RECOUP	ZEROED	YELPER	HENRIS	VEERED	LESSEN
REDOES	ZEROES	******	HENRYS	WEARER	LESSER
REDONE	******	-E-Q--	JEERED	WEIRDY	LESSON
REDOWA	-E-P--	******	JEERER	YEARLY	LESSOR
REFOOT	******	SESQUI	JERRYS	YEARNS	MEASLY
REFORM	BEDPAN	******	KEDRON	ZEBRAS	MENSAL
REJOIN	BEEPED	-E-R--	KERRIE	******	MENSES
RELOAD	DEEPEN	******	LEARNS	-E-S--	MERSEY
REMORA	DEEPER	BEARDS	LEARNT	******	MESSED
REMOTE	DEEPLY	BEARED	LEERED	BEASTS	MESSES
REMOVE	DELPHI	BEARER	LEGREE	BEDSIT	MESSRS
RENOIR	DESPOT	BEDRID	MEGRIM	BESSIE	NELSON
RENOWN	HEAPED	BEIRUT	METRIC	BESSYS	NESSUS
REPORT	HELPED	BETRAY	METROS	BETSYS	NEVSKI
REPOSE	HELPER	CEDRIC	NEARBY	CEASED	PEASEN
RESOLD	HEMPEN	CEORLS	NEARED	CEASES	PEASES
RESOLE	HERPES	DEARER	NEARER	CENSED	PEPSIN
RESORB	KEEPER	DEARIE	NEARLY	CENSER	PERSIA
RESORT	KELPIE	DEARLY	NEURAL	CENSES	PERSON
RETOLD	KEWPIE	DEARTH	NEURON	CENSOR	REASON
RETOOK	LEAPED	DEBRIS	PEARLS	CENSUR	SEASON
RETOOL	LEAPER	DECREE	PEARLY	CENSUS	SEESAW
RETORT	PEEPED	DEFRAY	PEDROS	DEISTS	SEISED
REVOKE	PEEPER	DEGREE	PEERED	DENSER	SEISIN
REVOLT	PENPAL	DERRIS	PEIRCE	DESSAU	SEISMO
REWORD	PEOPLE	FEARED	PEORIA	FEASED	SEISMS
SECOND	PEPPED	FEARER	PERRON	FEASES	SEISOR
SENORA	PEPPER	FENRIR	PERRYS	FEASTS	SELSYN
SEPOYS	REAPED	FERRET	PETREL	FEISTS	SENSED
SEROUS	REAPER	FERRIC	PETRIE	FEISTY	SENSES
SEROWS	REOPEN	FERRIS	PETROL	FESSES	SENSOR

SEPSIS	CENTAL	JESTED	PESTER	VENTER	DEPUTY
TEASED	CENTER	JESTER	PESTLE	VENTRO	FECULA
TEASEL	CENTOS	JETTED	PETTED	VERTEX	FECUND
TEASER	CENTRA	JETTON	PEWTER	VESTAL	FEMURS
TEASES	CENTRE	KEITHS	RECTAL	VESTAS	FERULA
TEASET	CENTRI	KELTIC	RECTOR	VESTED	FERULE
TELSON	CENTRO	KETTLE	RECTOS	VESTEE	GERUND
TENSED	CERTES	LECTOR	RECTUM	VESTRY	GETUPS
TENSER	CESTUS	LENTEN	RECTUS	VETTED	HEAUME
TENSES	DEATHS	LENTIL	REDTOP	WELTED	HECUBA
TENSOR	DEATHY	LENTOS	RENTAL	WELTER	JEJUNE
TERSER	DEBTOR	LEPTON	RENTED	WESTER	JESUIT
TESSIE	DEFTER	LESTER	RENTER	WESTED	LEGUME
VERSED	DEFTLY	LETTER	RENTES	WETTED	LEHUAS
VERSES	DELTAS	MEATUS	RESTED	WETTER	LEMUEL
VERSET	DENTAL	MEETER	RESTER	YESTER	LEMURS
VERSOS	DENTED	MEETLY	RETTED	ZESTED	LETUPS
VERSTS	DENTIL	MELTED	SEATED	******	MEDUSA
VERSUS	DENTIN	MELTER	SECTOR	-E-U--	METUMP
VESSEL	DEPTHS	MELTON	SEETHE	******	MEZUZA
WEASEL	DEXTER	MENTAL	SENTRY	AERUGO	NEBULA
WESSEX	DEXTRO	MENTOR	SEPTAL	BEAUTS	PENULT
YEASTS	FELTED	MESTEE	SEPTET	BEAUTY	PENURY
YEASTY	FESTAL	METTLE	SEPTIC	BEDUIN	PEQUOD
YESSED	FESTER	NEATEN	SEPTUM	BEGUIN	PEQUOT
YESSES	FETTER	NEATER	SESTET	BEGUMS	PERUKE
******	FETTLE	NEATLY	SETTEE	BELUGA	PERUSE
-E-T--	GENTES	NECTAR	SETTER	BEMUSE	PETULA
******	GENTLE	NEKTON	SETTLE	BENUMB	REBUFF
AEETES	GENTLY	NESTED	SETTOS	CEDULA	REBUKE
BEATEN	GENTOO	NESTLE	SEXTAN	CERUSE	REBUTS
BEATER	GENTRY	NESTOR	SEXTET	CESURA	RECURS
BEETLE	GERTIE	NETTED	SEXTON	DEBUGS	RECUSE
BELTED	GERTYS	NETTIE	TEETER	DEBUNK	REDUCE
BENTON	GESTIC	NETTLE	TEETHE	DEBUTS	REFUEL
BERTHA	GETTER	NEUTER	TENTED	DECUMA	REFUGE
BERTHE	HEATED	NEWTON	TENTER	DECURY	REFUND
BERTHS	HEATER	PECTEN	TENTHS	DEDUCE	REFUSE
BERTIE	HEATHS	PECTIC	TESTAE	DEDUCT	REFUTE
BESTED	HEATHY	PECTIN	TESTED	DEFUSE	REMUDA
BESTIR	HECTIC	PEGTOP	TESTER	DEGUMS	REPUTE
BESTOW	HECTOR	PELTED	TESTES	DEGUST	RERUNS
BETTED	HEFTED	PELTER	TESTIS	DELUDE	RESULT
BETTER	HELTER	PELTRY	TESTON	DELUGE	RESUME
BETTES	HEPTAD	PENTAD	TETTER	DELUXE	RETURN
BETTOR	HESTER	PENTUP	TEUTON	DEMURE	RETUSE
BETTYS	HESTIA	PEPTIC	VECTOR	DEMURS	REVUES
CELTIC	HETTYS	PERTLY	VENTED	DENUDE	SECUND

SECURE	PEAVEY	FEEZED	OFFICE	******	******
SEDUCE	PEEVED	FEEZES	OFFING	-G-E--	-G-O--
SEDUMS	PEEVES	FEZZAN	OFFISH	******	******
SEQUEL	PELVES	FEZZES	******	AGGERS	AGEOLD
SEQUIN	PELVIC	GEEZER	-F-L--	AGLEAM	IGLOOS
SERUMS	PELVIS	MEZZOS	******	AGLETS	IGNORE
SETUPS	REAVOW	SEIZED	AFFLUX	AGREED	OGDOAD
SEXUAL	REEVED	SEIZER	EFFLUX	AGREES	******
TEAURN	REEVES	SEIZES	******	EGBERT	-G-P--
TELUGU	REVVED	SEIZIN	-F-O--	EGGERS	******
TENUES	SELVES	SEIZOR	******	EGRESS	AGAPAE
TENUIS	SERVAL	TETZEL	AFFORD	EGRETS	******
TENURE	SERVED	******	AFLOAT	OGLERS	-G-R--
TENUTO	SERVER	-F-A--	AFTOSA	OGRESS	******
VELURE	SERVES	******	EFFORT	******	AGARIC
VENUES	SERVOS	AFFAIR	******	-G-G--	AGORAE
VENULE	VELVET	AFLAME	-F-R--	******	AGORAS
YEHUDI	VERVET	AFRAID	AFFRAY	AGOGUE	EGERIA
******	WEAVED	AFRAME	******	******	IGOROT
-E-V--	WEAVER	EFFACE	-F-S--	-G-I--	******
******	WEAVES	******	******	******	-G-S--
BEAVER	WEEVER	-F-C--	OFFSET	AGEING	******
BEEVES	WEEVIL	******	******	AGUISH	AGISTS
CERVIX	******	AFLCIO	-F-U--	EGGING	EGESTA
DELVED	-E-W--	******	******	EGOISM	EGESTS
DELVER	******	-F-D--	EFFUSE	EGOIST	******
DELVES	DEEWAN	******	******	IGNIFY	-G-T--
DENVER	HEDWIG	OFFDAY	-G-A--	IGNITE	******
FERVID	KEYWAY	******	******	OGLING	AGATES
FERVOR	LEEWAY	-F-E--	AGHAST	OGRISH	AGATHA
HEAVED	MEDWAY	******	AGLAIA	UGLIER	******
HEAVEN	MEOWED	AFFECT	AGNAIL	UGLILY	-G-U--
HEAVER	PEEWEE	AFIELD	AGNATE	******	******
HEAVES	PEEWIT	AFRESH	AGRAFE	-G-M--	AGOUTI
HELVES	SEAWAN	EFFECT	EGGARS	******	AGOUTY
JERVIS	SEAWAY	EFFETE	IGNACE	AGAMAS	******
KEEVES	SELWYN	OFFEND	IGUANA	AGAMIC	-G-V--
KELVIN	******	OFFERS	******	******	******
LEAVED	-E-Y--	******	-G-C--	-G-N--	AGAVES
LEAVEN	******	-F-H--	******	******	OGIVAL
LEAVER	BERYLS	******	EGGCUP	AGENCY	OGIVES
LEAVES	GERYON	AFGHAN	******	AGENDA	******
MELVIN	HEXYLS	******	-G-D--	AGENTS	-H-A--
MELVYN	JEKYLL	-F-I--	******	AGONES	******
MERVIN	******	******	AGEDLY	AGONIC	CHEATS
NERVED	-E-Z--	AFFIRM		EGGNOG	CHIASM
NERVES	******	AFRICA		UGANDA	CHIAUS
OEUVRE	BENZOL	EFFIGY			OHMAGE
	BENZYL				

PHIALS	******	THREAD	SHEILD	CHELAS	CHIMES
PHRASE	**-H-D--**	THREAT	SHIISM	CHILLI	CHUMMY
SHEARS	******	THREED	SHIITE	CHILLS	CHUMPS
SHEATH	CHIDED	THREES	SHRIEK	CHILLY	CHYMIC
SHEAVE	CHIDER	THRESH	SHRIFT	CHOLER	RHOMBI
SHOALS	CHIDES	WHEELS	SHRIKE	CHOLLA	RHUMBA
SHOALY	RHODAS	WHEEZE	SHRILL	DHOLES	RHUMBS
SHOATS	RHODES	WHEEZY	SHRIMP	PHILIA	RHYMED
SHRANK	RHODIC	******	SHRINE	PHILIP	RHYMER
THRALL	SHADED	**-H-F--**	SHRINK	PHILOS	RHYMES
THRASH	SHADES	******	SHRIVE	PHYLAE	SHAMAN
THWACK	SHADOW	CHAFED	SHTICK	PHYLLO	SHAMED
THWART	SHODDY	CHAFER	SHYING	PHYLUM	SHAMES
WHEALS	THADDY	CHAFES	THEIRS	SHALED	SHAMMY
WHEATS	THADYS	CHAFFS	THEISM	SHALES	SHAMUS
******	THEDAS	CHAFFY	THEIST	SHELBY	SHIMMY
-H-B--	WHIDAH	CHUFAS	THRICE	SHELLS	THAMES
******	WHYDAH	SHAFTS	THRIFT	SHELLY	THEMES
CHABUK	******	SHIFTS	THRILL	SHELTY	THEMIS
CHEBEC	**-H-E--**	SHIFTY	THRIPS	SHELVE	THOMAS
CHIBUK	******	SHOFAR	THRIVE	SHILLS	THUMBS
CHUBBY	CHAETA	THEFTS	******	SHILOH	THUMPS
GHEBER	CHAETO	WHIFFS	**-H-J--**	THALER	THYMES
KHYBER	CHEEKS	******	******	THALES	THYMIC
PHOBIA	CHEEKY	**-H-G--**	SHOJIS	THALIA	THYMOL
PHOBIC	CHEEPS	******	THUJAS	THELMA	THYMUS
SHABBY	CHEERS	CHEGOE	******	THOLES	WHAMMY
SHEBAT	CHEERY	CHIGOE	**-H-K--**	THULIA	WHIMSY
THEBAE	CHEESE	PHAGIA	******	WHALED	
THEBES	CHEESY	SHAGGY	CHOKED	WHALER	**-H-N--**
******	CHIEFS	SHOGUN	CHOKER	WHALES	******
-H-C--	PHLEBO	THIGHS	CHOKES	WHELKS	CHANCE
******	PHLEGM	******	KHAKIS	WHELKY	CHANCY
CHACMA	PHOEBE	**-H-I--**	SHAKEN	WHELMS	CHANGE
CHECKS	PHRENO	******	SHAKER	WHELPS	CHANGS
CHICHI	SHEENS	CHAINS	SHAKES	WHILED	CHANTS
CHICKS	SHEENY	CHAIRS	SHAKOS	WHILES	CHANTY
CHICLE	SHEEPS	CHAISE	SHEKEL	WHILOM	CHINCH
CHICOS	SHEERS	CHEILO	SHIKAR	WHILST	CHINES
CHOCKS	SHEETS	CHEIRO	******	WHOLLY	CHINKS
CHUCKS	SHIELD	CHOICE	**-H-L--**	******	CHINKY
PHOCIS	SHIEST	CHOIRS	******	**-H-M--**	CHINTZ
SHACKO	SHOERS	CHRISM	CHALCO	******	CHUNKS
SHACKS	SHREDS	CHRIST	CHALEH	AHIMSA	CHUNKY
SHOCKS	SHREWD	RHEIMS	CHALET	CHAMMY	OHENRY
SHUCKS	SHREWS	SHEIKH	CHALKS	CHAMPS	PHANON
THECAE	SHYEST	SHEIKS	CHALKY	CHIMED	PHENOL
THECAL	THIEVE	SHEILA	CHELAE	CHIMER	PHENYL
WHACKS					

PHONED	SHOOIN	CHERUB	THIRST	THISBE	THRUSH
PHONES	SHOOTS	CHERYL	THIRTY	THUSLY	THRUST
PHONEY	SHROFF	CHIRMS	THORAC	WHISKS	******
PHONIA	SHROUD	CHIRON	THORAX	WHISKY	-H-V--
PHONIC	SHROVE	CHIRPS	THORIA	******	******
RHINAL	THEORY	CHIRPY	THORIC	-H-T--	CHEVVY
RHINOS	THIOLS	CHIRRS	THORNS	******	CHIVES
SHANDY	THROAT	CHORAL	THORNY	BHUTAN	CHIVVY
SHANKS	THROBS	CHORDS	THORON	CHATTY	SHAVED
SHANTY	THROES	CHOREA	THORPE	CHETAH	SHAVEN
SHINDY	THRONE	CHOREO	THYREO	CHITIN	SHAVER
SHINED	THRONG	CHORES	THYRSE	CHITON	SHAVES
SHINER	THROVE	CHORIC	THYRSI	CHITTY	SHIVER
SHINES	THROWN	CHORUS	WHARFS	CHUTES	SHIVES
SHINNY	THROWS	CHURCH	WHARVE	DHOTIS	SHOVED
SHINTO	WHOOPS	CHURLS	WHERRY	GHETTO	SHOVEL
SHUNTS	WHOOSH	CHURNS	WHERVE	PHOTIC	SHOVER
THANAT	******	CHURRS	WHIRLS	PHOTON	SHOVES
THANES	-H-P--	DHARMA	WHORED	PHOTOS	******
THANKS	******	DHARNA	WHORES	PHYTIN	-H-W--
THENAL	CHAPEL	DHURNA	WHORLS	RHETOR	******
THENAR	CHAPES	GHARRI	WHORTS	RHYTHM	CHAWED
THENCE	CHIPPY	GHARRY	******	SHOTES	CHEWED
THINGS	CHOPIN	PHAROS	-H-S--	SHUTIN	CHEWER
THINLY	CHOPPY	SHARDS	******	THATCH	SHAWLS
THONGS	PHIPPS	SHARED	CHASED	THETAS	SHAWMS
WHANGS	SHAPED	SHARER	CHASER	THETIC	SHEWED
WHENCE	SHAPEN	SHARES	CHASES	THETIS	SHEWER
WHINED	SHAPER	SHARKS	CHASMS	WHITBY	SHOWED
WHINER	SHAPES	SHARON	CHASSE	WHITED	SHOWER
WHINES	SHOPPE	SHARPS	CHASTE	WHITEN	THAWED
WHINNY	WHIPPY	SHERDS	CHESTS	WHITER	THEWED
******	******	SHERIF	CHESTY	WHITES	******
-H-O--	-H-Q--	SHERPA	CHISEL	WHITEY	-H-Y--
******	******	SHERRY	CHOSEN	******	******
CHEOPS	CHEQUE	SHIRES	GHOSTS	-H-U--	CHRYSO
CHLOES	******	SHIRKS	PHASED	******	THAYER
CHLORO	-H-R--	SHIRRS	PHASES	CHOUGH	WHEYEY
CHOOSE	******	SHIRTS	PHASIA	GHAUTS	******
CHOOSY	CHARDS	SHIRTY	PHASIC	GHOULS	-H-Z--
CHROMA	CHARED	SHORAN	PHASIS	RHEUMY	******
CHROME	CHARES	SHORED	PHOSPH	SHOULD	RHIZIC
CHROMO	CHARGE	SHORES	PHYSIC	SHOUTS	-I-A--
CHRONO	CHARMS	SHORLS	PHYSIO	SHRUBS	******
OHIOAN	CHARON	SHORTS	RHESUS	SHRUGS	BICARB
PHLOEM	CHARRY	THERMO	SHASTA	SHRUNK	BIGAMY
PHOOEY	CHARTS	THERMS	THESES	THOUGH	BIHARI
SHOOED	CHERRY	THIRDS	THESIS	THRUMS	

BINARY	SILAGE	LIMBER	PISCES	KINDER	CIDERS
BINATE	SIMARS	LIMBIC	PITCHY	KINDLE	CINEMA
CICADA	SITARS	LIMBUS	SIECLE	KINDLY	CINEOL
CICALA	SIWASH	LISBOA	TINCAL	LIDDED	CIVETS
CIGARS	SIZARS	LISBON	TINCAN	LIEDER	DICERS
DICAST	TICALS	NIBBED	TINCTS	LINDAS	DIDERO
DIGAMY	TIRADE	NIBBLE	TIPCAT	LINDEN	DIGEST
DILATE	TIRANA	NIMBLE	VINCES	MIDDAY	DIMERS
DINAHS	TISANE	NIMBLY	VISCID	MIDDEN	DINERO
DINARS	TITANS	NIMBUS	VISCUS	MIDDLE	DINERS
DISARM	VICARS	NIOBIC	WINCED	MILDEN	DIRECT
DIVANS	VIRAGO	RIBBED	WINCER	MILDER	DIRELY
DIWANS	VISAED	RIBBON	WINCES	MILDEW	DIREST
FINALE	VISAGE	SINBAD	WINCEY	MILDLY	DIVERS
FINALS	VISARD	TIDBIT	ZINCED	MINDED	DIVERT
FIXATE	VITALS	TIMBAL	ZINCIC	MINDER	DIVEST
GIGANT	VIVACE	TIMBER	ZINCKY	MISDID	DIZENS
GITANO	VIZARD	TIMBRE	ZIRCON	PIDDLE	EILEEN
HIJACK	WIGANS	TITBIT	******	PINDAR	FIBERS
HILARY	WIZARD	VIABLE	**-I-D--**	PINDUS	FIFERS
HIRAMS	******	WILBER	******	RIDDED	FILERS
JIHADS	**-I-B--**	WILBUR	AIRDRY	RIDDEN	FILETS
KINASE	******	WIMBLE	BIDDEN	RIDDLE	FINELY
LIGAND	AIRBED	******	BIDDER	SIDDUR	FINERY
LIGATE	BIBBED	**-I-C--**	BINDER	SIRDAR	FINEST
LILACS	BIBBER	******	BIRDIE	TILDES	FIRERS
LINAGE	BILBAO	BISCAY	CINDER	TINDER	FIVERS
LIPASE	CIMBRI	BITCHY	CINDYS	WIDDIE	FIXERS
LITANY	DIBBED	CIRCLE	DIADEM	WILDER	GIBERS
LIZARD	DIBBER	CIRCUM	DIDDLE	WILDLY	GIDEON
MIDAIR	DIBBLE	CIRCUS	DIKDIK	WINDED	GILEAD
MIKADO	DIOBOL	CISCOS	DINDER	WINDER	GIMELS
MILADY	DISBAR	DISCAL	DIODES	WINDOW	GISELE
MILAGE	FIBBED	DISCUS	FIDDLE	WINDUP	HIDERS
MIRAGE	FIBBER	FIACRE	FINDER	WISDOM	HIKERS
PILAFF	FIMBLE	FISCAL	GILDAS	******	HIRERS
PILAFS	GIBBED	HICCUP	GILDED	**-I-E--**	KIBEIS
PILATE	GIBBER	LITCHI	GILDER	******	KINESI
PINANG	GIBBET	MINCED	GIRDED	AIDERS	KINETO
PIPAGE	GIBBON	MINCER	GIRDER	AILEEN	LIBELS
PIRACY	JIBBED	MINCES	GIRDLE	BICEPS	LIFERS
PIRANA	JIBBER	MISCUE	HIDDEN	BIDETS	LIKELY
PIRATE	KIBBLE	NIACIN	HILDAS	BIPEDS	LIKENS
RIBALD	KITBAG	NIECES	HINDER	BIREME	LIMENS
RIBAND	LIABLE	OILCAN	HINDUS	BISECT	LIMEYS
RITARD	LIBBYS	PIECED	KIDDED	BITERS	LINEAL
RIVALS	LIEBIG	PIECER	KIDDER	CICELY	LINEAR
RIYALS	LIMBED	PIECES	KIDDIE	CICERO	LINENS

LINERS	SINEWS	TIFFIN	MIDGUT	DISHES	WISHES
LINEUP	SINEWY	WILFUL	MIGGLE	DITHER	WITHAL
LITERS	SIRENS	******	MINGLE	EIGHTH	WITHED
LIVELY	SISERA	**-I-G--**	NIGGER	EIGHTS	WITHER
LIVENS	TIGERS	******	NIGGLE	EIGHTY	WITHES
LIVERS	TILERS	AIRGUN	NILGAI	EITHER	WITHIN
LIVERY	TIMELY	BIGGER	PIDGIN	FICHES	WITHIT
MICELL	TIMERS	BIGGIN	PIGGED	FICHUS	ZITHER
MILERS	TINEID	BILGED	PIGGIE	FIGHTS	******
MIMERS	VILELY	BILGES	PIGGIN	FISHER	**-I-I--**
MINERS	VILEST	BINGES	PINGED	FISHES	******
MISERE	VINERY	BIOGEN	PINGOS	HIGHER	AIDING
MISERS	VIPERS	DIGGED	PISGAH	HIGHLY	AILING
MISERY	VIREOS	DIGGER	RIDGED	HITHER	AIMING
MITERS	VISEED	DINGED	RIDGES	LICHEE	AIRIER
MIXERS	VIXENS	DINGEY	RIGGED	LICHEN	AIRILY
NICELY	WIDELY	DINGHY	RIGGER	LIGHTS	AIRING
NICENE	WIDENS	DINGLE	RINGED	LITHER	BIDING
NICEST	WIDEST	DINGUS	RINGER	LITHIA	BIKINI
NICETY	WIFELY	DIRGES	SIEGED	LITHIC	BILITY
NIGELS	WIGEON	FIDGET	SIEGES	MICHEL	BINITS
NINETY	WINERY	FIGGED	SINGED	MIGHTY	BITING
NISEIS	WIPERS	FINGER	SINGER	MISHAP	CILIAT
OILERS	WIRERS	FIZGIG	SINGES	NICHED	CILICE
PIGEON	WISELY	GIGGED	SINGLE	NICHES	CILIUM
PIKERS	WISEST	GIGGLE	SINGLY	NIGHER	CITIED
PILEUM	WIVERN	GIGGLY	TINGED	NIGHTS	CITIES
PILEUP	WIVERS	GINGAL	TINGES	NIGHTY	CITING
PILEUS	WIZENS	GINGER	TINGLE	PISHED	CIVICS
PINEAL	ZIBETH	GINGKO	TINGLY	PISHES	CIVIES
PINENE	ZIBETS	HIGGLE	VIRGAS	PITHED	CIVISM
PINERY	******	HINGED	VIRGIE	RICHER	DICING
PIPERS	**-I-F--**	HINGES	VIRGIL	RICHES	DIDIES
PIPETS	******	JIGGED	VIRGIN	RICHIE	DIGITI
RICERS	BIAFRA	JIGGER	WIGGED	RICHLY	DIGITS
RIDENT	BIFFED	JIGGLE	WIGGLE	RIGHTO	DIKING
RIDERS	BIFFIN	JINGAL	WIGGLY	RIGHTS	DIMITY
RIMERS	DIFFER	JINGLE	WINGED	SIGHED	DINING
RIPELY	EIFFEL	JINGLY	ZINGED	SIGHTS	DIVIDE
RIPENS	FITFUL	KINGED	******	SIPHON	DIVINE
RIPEST	MIFFED	KINGLY	**-I-H--**	TIGHTS	DIVING
RISERS	MISFIT	LIEGES	******	TISHRI	DIXITS
RIVERS	PIAFFE	LINGAM	BIGHTS	TITHED	FIFING
RIVETS	PIFFLE	LINGAS	BISHOP	TITHER	FIJIAN
SIDERO	PILFER	LINGER	CIPHER	TITHES	FILIAL
SILENI	RIFFLE	LINGUA	CITHER	VISHNU	FILING
SILENT	SINFUL	MIDGES	DIRHAM	WICHES	FINIAL
SINEON	TIFFED	MIDGET	DISHED	WISHED	FINING

FINISH	NIDIFY	TIEINS	HICKEY	TINKLE	HITLER
FINITE	NIDING	TILING	HICKOK	TINKLY	KIBLAH
FIRING	NIMITZ	TIMING	JINKED	VICKYS	KILLED
FIXING	NIXIES	TINIER	JINKER	WICKED	KILLER
FIXITY	NIXING	TINILY	KICKED	WICKER	KISLEW
GIBING	OILIER	TIRING	KICKER	WICKET	MIKLOS
GIVING	OILILY	TITIAN	KINKED	WINKED	MILLAY
HIDING	OILING	VIGILS	LICKED	WINKER	MILLED
HIEING	PIKING	VIKING	LINKED	WINKLE	MILLER
HIKING	PILING	VILIFY	MICKEY	******	MILLET
HIRING	PINIER	VIMINA	MICKLE	-I-L--	MILLIE
HIVING	PINIES	VINIER	MICKYS	******	MILLYS
HIVITE	PINING	VIRILE	MILKED	AIGLET	MISLAY
JIBING	PINION	VISING	MILKER	AISLED	MISLED
JIMINY	PINITE	VISION	MISKAL	AISLES	NIELLI
JIVING	PIPIER	VISITS	NICKED	BIALYS	NIELLO
KIBITZ	PIPING	VIVIAN	NICKEL	BIBLES	PIGLET
KININS	PIPITS	VIVIEN	NICKER	BIBLIO	PILLAR
KITING	PITIED	VIVIFY	NICKYS	BIFLEX	PILLED
LIAISE	PITIES	VIZIER	PICKAX	BILLED	PILLOW
LIBIDO	PIXIES	VIZIRS	PICKED	BILLET	RIALTO
LIKING	RICING	WIKIUP	PICKER	BILLIE	RIFLED
LILIAN	RIDING	WILIER	PICKET	BILLON	RIFLER
LILIED	RILING	WILILY	PICKLE	BILLOW	RIFLES
LILIES	RIMING	WILING	PICKUP	BILLYS	RILLET
LIMIER	RISING	WINIER	PINKED	BIRLED	RIPLEY
LIMINA	RIVING	WINING	PINKIE	BIRLES	SIALIC
LIMING	SICILY	WIPING	PIPKIN	DIALED	SIDLED
LIMITS	SIDING	WIRIER	RICKED	DIALER	SIDLER
LINIER	SIGILS	WIRILY	RICKEY	DIALOG	SIDLES
LINING	SILICA	WIRING	RICKYS	DIGLOT	SIMLIN
LIPIDS	SILICO	WISING	RINKED	DIPLEX	TILLED
LIVIAS	SIMIAN	WIVING	RISKED	DIPLOE	TILLER
LIVIER	SIMILE	ZIZITH	RISKER	FIELDS	TILLIE
LIVING	SIRING	******	SICKED	FILLED	TILLYS
MILIEU	SIRIUS	-I-K--	SICKEN	FILLER	TITLED
MILIUM	SITING	******	SICKER	FILLET	TITLES
MIMICS	SITINS	BICKER	SICKLE	FILLIN	VIALED
MIMING	SIZIER	BILKED	SICKLY	FILLIP	VILLAS
MINIFY	SIZING	BILKER	SIKKIM	GIBLET	VILLON
MINIMA	TIBIAE	DICKER	SILKEN	GIGLET	VILLUS
MINIMS	TIBIAL	DICKEY	SINKER	GIGLOT	VIOLAS
MINING	TIBIAS	DICKIE	SISKIN	GILLIE	VIOLET
MINION	TIDIED	DINKEY	TICKED	GIMLET	VIOLIN
MINIUM	TIDIER	DINKUM	TICKER	GIULIA	WIELDS
MIRIAM	TIDIES	DIRKED	TICKET	GIULIO	WIELDY
MIRING	TIDILY	FICKLE	TICKLE	HILLED	WILLED
MIXING	TIDING	FIRKIN	TINKER	HILLER	WILLER

WILLET	DIANAS	SIMNEL	MINORS	HIPPUS	******
WILLIE	DIANES	SINNED	NICOLE	HISPID	**-I-Q--**
WILLIS	DINNED	SINNER	PICOTS	KIPPED	******
WILLOW	DINNER	TINNED	PILOSE	KIPPER	BISQUE
WILLYS	DIRNDL	TINNER	PILOTS	LIMPED	CINQUE
YIELDS	DISNEY	VIANDS	PILOUS	LIMPER	CIRQUE
ZILLAH	FIANCE	VIENNA	PINOLE	LIMPET	RISQUE
******	FIENDS	VINNYS	PINONS	LIMPID	******
-I-M--	FINNAN	WIENER	PITONS	LIMPLY	**-I-R--**
******	FINNED	WIENIE	PIVOTS	LIPPED	******
AIDMAN	FINNER	WINNER	RIBOSE	LIPPER	BIERCE
AIDMEN	FINNIC	WINNIE	RIGORS	LISPED	BIRRED
AIRMAN	FINNOC	WINNOW	RIGOUR	LISPER	CIRRUS
AIRMEN	GIANTS	WITNEY	RIMOSE	NIPPED	CITRAL
DIMMED	GINNED	ZINNIA	RIMOUS	NIPPER	CITRIC
DIMMER	GINNER	******	RIPOFF	NIPPLE	CITRON
DISMAL	JINNEE	**-I-O--**	RIPOST	NIPPON	CITRUS
DISMAY	JINNYS	******	SILOED	PIGPEN	FIBRIL
FILMED	JITNEY	BICORN	SIMONE	PIMPED	FIBRIN
FILMIC	KIDNAP	BIFOLD	SIMONS	PIMPLE	FIERCE
FIRMAN	KIDNEY	BIFORM	SIMONY	PIMPLY	FIORDS
FIRMED	LIANAS	BIGONE	SIMOOM	PIPPED	GIBRAN
FIRMER	LIANES	BIGOTS	TIPOFF	PIPPIN	LIBRAE
FIRMLY	LIGNIN	BIJOUX	VIGOUR	RIMPLE	LIBRAS
GISMOS	LIGNUM	BIKOLS	VINOUS	RIPPED	LIERNE
GIZMOS	LIMNED	BILOXI	VISORS	RIPPER	LIVRES
HIEMAL	LIMNER	BIPODS	VIZORS	RIPPLE	MICRON
JIMMIE	LINNET	CIBOLS	WICOPY	RIPPLY	MIDRIB
JIMMYS	LIONEL	CITOLA	WIDOWS	SIMPER	MIRROR
KILMER	MIGNON	DIDOES	WINOES	SIMPLE	MITRAL
KISMET	MINNIE	DIMOUT	ZIRONS	SIMPLY	MITRED
LITMUS	MINNOW	DIPODY	******	SIPPED	NIMROD
MICMAC	PIANOS	DIPOLE	**-I-P--**	SIPPER	NITRIC
PIEMAN	PICNIC	DISOWN	******	SIPPET	NITRID
PIEMEN	PIENAL	DITONE	BIOPSY	TIEPIN	PICRIC
PITMAN	PIGNUS	DIVOTS	DIAPER	TINPOT	PIERCE
PITMEN	PIGNUT	EIDOLA	DIEPPE	TIPPED	PIERRE
RIMMED	PINNAE	FILOSE	DIMPLE	TIPPER	PIERUS
RIMMER	PINNAL	GIAOUR	DIMPLY	TIPPET	RIPRAP
SIGMAS	PINNED	GIGOLO	DIPPED	TIPPLE	SIERRA
SIMMER	PINNER	GIPONS	DIPPER	WIMPLE	SIGRID
TIMMYS	SIDNEY	KIBOSH	DISPEL	WISPED	TIARAS
WILMAS	SIENNA	KIMONO	FIPPLE	YIPPED	TIERCE
******	SIGNAL	LIPOID	GIMPED	YIPPIE	TIERED
-I-N--	SIGNED	LIPOMA	GIPPED	ZIPPED	TIGRIS
******	SIGNER	MILORD	HIPPED	ZIPPER	VIBRIO
BIANCA	SIGNET	MIMOSA	HIPPIE		VITRIC
BINNED	SIGNOR	MINOAN	HIPPOS		

******	******	LIFTER	TILTHS	SIEURS	FIZZER
-I-S--	**-I-T--**	LILTED	TINTED	SIOUAN	FIZZES
******	******	LINTEL	TIPTOE	SIRUPS	FIZZLE
AIRSAC	BIOTIC	LINTER	TIPTOP	SIRUPY	LIZZIE
BIASED	BIOTIN	LISTED	TITTER	TIEUPS	LIZZYS
BIASES	BIRTHS	LISTEL	TITTLE	VICUNA	MIZZEN
BIOSIS	BISTER	LISTEN	TITTUP	VIDUAL	MIZZLE
CISSIE	BISTRO	LISTER	VIATIC	VISUAL	PIAZZA
CISSYS	BITTED	LITTER	VIATOR	******	PIZZAS
DIESEL	BITTEN	LITTLE	VICTIM	**-I-V--**	SIZZLE
DIESES	BITTER	MILTED	VICTOR	******	WINZES
DIESIS	DIATOM	MILTER	VIRTUE	SIEVED	ZIGZAG
DIPSAS	DICTUM	MILTON	VISTAS	SIEVES	ZIZZLE
FIASCO	DIETAL	MINTED	VITTAE	SILVAE	******
FIESTA	DIETED	MINTER	WIDTHS	SILVAN	**-J-B--**
FIRSTS	DIETER	MIOTIC	WILTED	SILVAS	******
GIBSON	DINTED	MISTED	WILTON	SILVER	OJIBWA
HISSED	DISTAL	MISTER	WINTER	SILVIA	******
HISSER	DISTIL	MISTLE	WINTRY	******	**-J-C--**
HISSES	DITTOS	MITTEN	WITTED	**-I-W--**	******
JIGSAW	FIFTHS	NINTHS	******	******	EJECTA
KINSEY	FILTER	PICTOR	**-I-U--**	AIRWAY	EJECTS
KIOSKS	FILTHY	PIETER	******	BIGWIG	******
KIRSCH	FIRTHS	PIETRO	DILUTE	DIMWIT	**-J-W--**
KISSED	FISTED	PINTER	DISUSE	MIDWAY	******
KISSER	FISTIC	PINTLE	FIBULA	NITWIT	AJOWAN
KISSES	FITTED	PINTOS	FIGURE	VIEWED	******
KITSCH	FITTER	PISTIL	FIQUES	VIEWER	**-K-A--**
LIASED	GIFTED	PISTOL	GIGUES	WIGWAG	******
LISSOM	GIOTTO	PISTON	LIGULA	WIGWAM	SKEANS
MIASMA	GIRTED	PITTED	LIGULE	******	******
MIOSIS	HIATUS	RIATAS	LIGURE	**-I-X--**	**-K-C--**
MISSAL	HILTED	RICTAL	LIMULI	******	******
MISSED	HINTED	RICTUS	LIQUID	BIAXAL	SKYCAP
MISSEL	HITTER	RIFTED	LIQUOR	JINXED	******
MISSES	JILTED	RIOTED	MIAULS	JINXES	**-K-E--**
MISSIS	JILTER	RIOTER	MIGUEL	MINXES	******
MISSUS	JITTER	RITTER	MINUET	PINXIT	SKIERS
PIGSTY	KILTED	SIFTED	MINUTE	******	******
RINSED	KILTER	SIFTER	MISUSE	**-I-Y--**	**-K-F--**
RINSER	KILTIE	SILTED	MIXUPS	******	******
RINSES	KIRTLE	SINTER	PICULS	LIBYAN	SKIFFS
RIPSAW	KITTED	SISTER	PILULE	LIVYER	******
SIESTA	KITTEN	SITTER	PINUPS	SIBYLS	**-K-I--**
TINSEL	KITTLE	SIXTES	PIQUED	VINYLS	******
TISSUE	KITTYS	SIXTHS	PIQUES	******	EKEING
VINSON	LICTOR	TILTED	PIQUET	**-J-Z--**	SKEINS
WILSON	LIFTED	TILTER	RITUAL	******	SKIING
				DIAZIN	SKYING
				FIZZED	

	SKIVES	GLEANS	FLOCKS	******	******
******	SKIVVY	GLOATS	FLOCKY	-L-E--	-L-F--
-K-L--	******	OLEATE	GLACES	******	******
******	-K-W--	PLEACH	GLACIS	ALBEDO	BLUFFS
SKALDS	******	PLEADS	GLYCOL	ALBEIT	CLEFTS
SKILLS	SKEWED	PLEASE	PLACED	ALBERT	CLIFFS
SKULKS	SKEWER	PLEATS	PLACER	ALDERS	CLIFFY
SKULLS	SKYWAY	PLIANT	PLACES	ALIENS	FLUFFS
******	******	SLEAVE	PLACET	ALKENE	FLUFFY
-K-M--	-K-Y--	SLEAZY	PLACID	ALLEGE	OLEFIN
******	******	ULLAGE	PLACKS	ALLELE	******
AKIMBO	OKAYED	******	PLICAE	ALLENS	-L-G--
SKIMOS	******	-L-B--	PLUCKS	ALLEYS	******
SKIMPS	-L-A--	******	PLUCKY	ALTERS	ALEGAR
SKIMPY	******	ALIBIS	SLACKS	BLEEDS	ALIGHT
SKYMAN	ALBANY	ALIBLE	SLICED	BLUELY	ALIGNS
SKYMEN	ALBATA	BLEBBY	SLICER	BLUEST	BLIGHT
******	ALCAIC	FLABBY	SLICES	BLUETS	CLOGGY
-K-N--	ALFAKI	FLYBYS	SLICKS	CLIENT	ELEGIT
******	ALKALI	GLEBES	******	ELBERT	FLAGGY
AKENES	ALKANE	GLIBLY	-L-D--	ELDERS	FLAGON
SKINKS	ALLANS	GLOBAL	******	ELDEST	FLIGHT
SKINNY	ALLAYS	GLOBED	ALIDAD	ELLENS	PLAGAL
SKUNKS	ALMAHS	GLOBES	ALUDEL	ELMERS	PLAGIO
******	ALPACA	GLOBIN	BLADED	ELVERS	PLAGUE
-K-P--	ALSACE	PLEBES	BLADES	FLEECE	PLAGUY
******	ALTAIC	******	CLODDY	FLEECY	PLEGIA
OKAPIS	ALTAIR	-L-C--	CLYDES	FLEERS	PLIGHT
SKOPJE	ALTARS	******	ELIDED	FLEETS	PLUGIN
******	ALVANS	ALECTO	ELIDES	FLIERS	SLAGGY
-K-R--	ALWAYS	ALICES	ELUDED	FLIEST	SLIGHT
******	BLEACH	ALICIA	ELUDES	FLUENT	SLOGAN
SKERRY	BLEAKS	BLACKS	FLEDGE	FLYERS	******
SKIRRS	BLEARS	BLOCKS	FLEDGY	GLEETS	-L-H--
SKIRTS	BLEARY	BLOCKY	GLADES	GLEETY	******
******	BLEATS	CLACKS	GLADLY	OLDEST	ALPHAS
-K-S--	BLOATS	CLICHE	GLADYS	PLIERS	ALPHOS
******	CLEANS	CLICKS	GLEDES	SLEEKS	ALPHYL
UKASES	CLEARS	CLOCHE	GLIDED	SLEEKY	ALTHEA
******	CLEATS	CLOCKS	GLIDER	SLEEPS	ELOHIM
-K-T--	CLEAVE	CLUCKS	GLIDES	SLEEPY	OLDHAM
******	CLOACA	ELECTS	PLEDGE	SLEETS	******
SKATED	CLOAKS	ELICIT	SLEDGE	SLEETY	-L-I--
SKATER	FLEAMS	FLACKS	SLIDER	SLEEVE	******
SKATES	FLOATS	FLACON	SLIDES	SLIEST	ALBINO
SKETCH	FLOATY	FLECHE	SLUDGE	SLYEST	ALBION
******	GLEAMS	FLECKS	SLUDGY	ULCERS	ALBITE
-K-V--	GLEAMY	FLICKS			ALDINE
******					
SKIVED					
SKIVER					

ALLIED	SLEIGH	CLUMSY	CLANGS	SLINGS	FLOPPY
ALLIES	SLUICE	ELEMIS	CLANKS	SLINKS	GLYPHS
ALLIUM	SLUING	FLAMBE	CLENCH	SLINKY	GLYPTO
ALMIRA	ULTIMA	FLAMED	CLINCH	ULENCE	SLAPUP
ALPINE	ULTIMO	FLAMEN	CLINES	******	SLIPON
ALSIKE	******	FLAMES	CLINGS	-L-O--	SLIPUP
ALUINO	-L-J--	FLIMSY	CLINGY	******	SLOPED
ALUINS	******	FLUMED	CLINIC	ALCOTT	SLOPER
ALVINA	ELIJAH	FLUMES	CLINKS	ALCOVE	SLOPES
ALVINE	******	FLUMPS	CLINTS	ALDOSE	SLOPPY
BLAINS	-L-K--	FLYMAN	CLONES	ALDOUS	******
BLAISE	******	GLAMIS	CLONIC	ALFONS	-L-Q--
BLUING	BLOKES	GLUMES	CLONUS	ALGOID	******
BLUISH	FLAKED	GLUMLY	ELANDS	ALGOUS	CLAQUE
CLAIMS	FLAKER	LLAMAS	ELENAS	ALLOTS	CLIQUE
CLAIRE	FLAKES	PLUMBO	ELINOR	ALLOUT	CLIQUY
CLEIST	FLUKED	PLUMBS	FLANGE	ALLOWS	PLAQUE
CLUING	FLUKES	PLUMED	FLANKS	ALLOYS	******
ELAINE	FLUKEY	PLUMES	FLENCH	ALMOND	-L-R--
ELFINS	SLAKED	PLUMMY	FLENSE	ALMOST	******
ELFISH	SLAKES	PLUMPS	FLINCH	BLOODS	ALARIC
ELLIES	******	SLIMED	FLINGS	BLOODY	ALARMS
ELLIOT	-L-L--	SLIMES	FLINTS	BLOOMS	ALARUM
ELMIRA	******	SLIMLY	FLINTY	BLOOMY	ALERTS
ELOIGN	ALALIA	SLIMSY	FLONGS	CLEOME	ALFRED
ELOINS	ALULAE	SLUMMY	FLUNKS	ELBOWS	BLARED
ELOISE	ALULAR	SLUMPS	FLUNKY	ELIOTS	BLARES
ELSIES	SLALOM	ULEMAS	GLANCE	FLOODS	BLURBS
ELVIRA	******	******	GLANDS	FLOORS	BLURRY
ELVISH	-L-M--	-L-N--	GLINTS	FLOOZY	BLURTS
FLAILS	******	******	GLYNIS	FLUORO	CLARAS
FLAIRS	ALAMOS	ALINED	LLANOS	FLUORS	CLARES
FLUIDS	ALUMIN	ALINES	PLANAR	GLIOMA	CLARET
FLYING	ALUMNA	ALONSO	PLANCH	GLOOMS	CLAROS
GLAIRS	ALUMNI	ALONZO	PLANCK	GLOOMY	CLERGY
GLAIRY	BLAMED	BLANCH	PLANED	ILFORD	CLERIC
GLUIER	BLAMES	BLANKS	PLANER	SLOOPS	CLERID
GLUING	BLIMEY	BLENCH	PLANES	******	CLERKS
ILOILO	BLIMPS	BLENDE	PLANET	-L-P--	ELBRUS
OLDISH	CLAMMY	BLENDS	PLANKS	******	ELDRED
OLLIES	CLAMOR	BLENNY	PLANTS	ALEPHS	FLARED
PLAICE	CLAMPS	BLINDS	PLENTY	ALEPPO	FLARES
PLAIDS	CLIMAT	BLINKS	PLENUM	ALIPED	FLIRTS
PLAINS	CLIMAX	BLINTZ	PLINTH	CLYPEI	FLIRTY
PLAINT	CLIMBS	BLONDE	PLUNGE	ELAPSE	FLORAE
PLAITS	CLIMES	BLONDS	PLUNKS	ELOPED	FLORAL
PLEIAD	CLUMPS	BLUNGE	SLANGY	ELOPER	FLORAS
PLYING	CLUMPY	BLUNTS	SLANTS	ELOPES	FLORES

FLORET	BLOTCH	CLOUDY	******	ELAYNE	******
FLORID	CLOTHE	CLOUGH	-L-W--	FLAYED	-M-B--
FLORIN	CLOTHO	CLOUTS	******	FLAYER	******
FLURRY	CLOTHS	FLAUNT	BLOWBY	FLOYDS	AMEBAE
GLARED	CLOTTY	FLEURY	BLOWER	LLOYDS	AMEBAS
GLARES	CLUTCH	FLOURS	BLOWUP	PLAYAS	AMEBIC
GLORIA	ELATED	FLOURY	BLOWZY	PLAYED	******
PLURAL	ELATER	FLOUTS	CLAWED	PLAYER	-M-C--
SLURPS	ELATES	GLAUCO	CLEWED	SLAYER	******
SLURRY	ELYTRA	ILLUME	CLOWNS	******	AMECHE
******	FLATLY	ILLUSE	FLAWED	-L-Z--	AMICES
-L-S--	FLATUS	ILLUST	FLOWED	******	SMACKS
******	FLETCH	PLEURA	FLOWER	BLAZED	SMOCKS
ALASKA	FLITCH	PLEURO	GLOWED	BLAZER	******
ALISON	FLUTED	PLOUGH	GLOWER	BLAZES	-M-D--
BLASTO	FLUTER	SLEUTH	PLOWED	BLAZON	******
BLASTS	FLUTES	SLOUCH	PLOWER	ELIZAS	AMADOU
CLASPS	GLOTTO	SLOUGH	SLEWED	GLAZED	AMIDES
CLASSY	GLUTEI	******	SLOWED	GLAZER	AMIDIC
CLOSED	GLUTEN	-L-V--	SLOWER	GLAZES	AMIDIN
CLOSER	PLATAN	******	SLOWLY	GLOZED	AMIDOL
CLOSES	PLATED	CLEVER	******	GLOZES	AMIDST
CLOSET	PLATEN	CLEVIS	-L-X--	PLAZAS	IMIDES
ELISHA	PLATER	CLIVES	******	******	SMUDGE
ELYSEE	PLATES	CLOVEN	ALEXIA	-M-A--	SMUDGY
FLASHY	PLATTE	CLOVER	ALEXIN	******	******
FLASKS	PLUTUS	CLOVES	ALEXIS	AMBAGE	-M-E--
FLESHY	SLATED	CLOVIS	ELIXIR	AMBARI	******
FLOSSY	SLATER	ELEVEN	FLAXEN	AMBARY	AMBERS
GLASSY	SLATES	ELEVON	FLAXES	EMBALM	AMBERY
GLOSSO	SLOTHS	FLAVIA	FLEXED	EMBANK	AMIENS
GLOSSY	ULSTER	FLAVIN	FLEXES	EMBARK	AMOEBA
GLOSTS	ZLOTYS	FLAVOR	FLEXOR	EMBARS	AMPERE
PLASHY	******	FLUVIO	FLUXED	EMBAYS	EMBEDS
PLASIA	-L-U--	GLOVED	FLUXES	EMPALE	EMBERS
PLASIS	******	GLOVER	ILEXES	IMBALM	EMCEED
PLASMA	ALBUMS	GLOVES	KLAXON	IMBARK	EMCEES
PLASMO	ALCUIN	OLIVER	PLEXOR	IMPACT	EMEERS
PLASTY	ALEUTS	OLIVES	PLEXUS	IMPAIR	EMMETS
PLUSES	ALLUDE	OLIVIA	******	IMPALA	EMMETT
PLUSHY	ALLURE	PLOVER	-L-Y--	IMPALE	EMPERY
SLOSHY	ALMUCE	PLUVIO	******	IMPARK	IMBEDS
SLUSHY	ALMUDE	SLAVED	ALKYLS	IMPART	IMMESH
******	ALMUDS	SLAVER	ALKYNE	IMPASS	IMPEDE
-L-T--	BLOUSE	SLAVES	ALLYLS	IMPAWN	IMPELS
******	CLAUDE	SLAVIC	CLAYED	SMEARS	IMPEND
ALATED	CLAUSE	SLIVER	CLAYEY	SMEARY	UMBELS
BLITHE	CLOUDS	SLOVAK	CLOYED	UMIAKS	UMBERS
		SLOVEN		UMLAUT	

******	EMILES	EMBRUE	IMBUES	INNATE	******
-M-G--	EMILIA	EMBRYO	IMMUNE	INSANE	**-N-C--**
******	EMILIE	EMERGE	IMMUNO	INTACT	******
AMIGOS	EMILIO	EMERIC	IMMURE	INTAKE	ENACTS
EMIGRE	EMILYS	EMERIE	IMPUGN	INVADE	KNACKS
IMAGED	EMPLOY	IMARET	IMPURE	INWALL	KNOCKS
IMAGES	OMELET	IMBRUE	IMPUTE	INWARD	SNACKS
IMOGEN	SMALLS	SMARMY	******	KNEADS	SNICKS
OMEGAS	SMALTI	SMARTS	**-M-Z--**	ONFALL	SNOCAT
SMUGLY	SMALTO	SMIRCH	******	ONWARD	UNICEF
******	SMELLS	SMIRKS	AMAZED	SNEAKS	******
-M-H--	SMELLY	UMBRAE	AMAZES	SNEAKY	**-N-D--**
******	SMELTS	UMBRAL	AMAZON	UNBARS	******
AMPHRS	SMILAX	UMBRAS	SMAZES	UNCAGE	ANADEM
******	SMILED	******	******	UNCAPS	ANODES
-M-I--	SMILER	**-M-S--**	**-N-A--**	UNCASE	ANODIC
******	SMILES	******	******	UNEASE	******
AMBITS	SMOLTS	AMUSED	ANGARY	UNEASY	**-N-E--**
AMNION	UMBLES	AMUSER	ANKARA	UNFAIR	******
AMRITA	******	AMUSES	ANLACE	UNHAIR	ANDEAN
EMMIES	**-M-N--**	EMESIS	ANLAGE	UNHAND	ANGELA
EMPIRE	******	OMASUM	ANNALS	UNHASP	ANGELO
IMBIBE	AMANDA	******	ANSATE	UNHATS	ANGELS
IMMIES	AMANIA	**-M-T--**	ENCAGE	UNLACE	ANGERS
IMPING	AMENDS	******	ENCAMP	UNLADE	ANNEAL
IMPISH	AMENRA	AMATOL	ENCASE	UNLAID	ANNEXE
OMNIUM	AMENTI	AMYTAL	ENCASH	UNLASH	ANSELM
UMPIRE	AMENTS	DMITRI	ENDALL	UNLAYS	ANTEED
******	EMENDS	EMETIC	ENFACE	UNMADE	ANTERO
-M-K--	IMINES	EMETIN	ENGAGE	UNMAKE	ENDEAR
******	OMENTA	EMOTED	ENLACE	UNMANS	ENGELS
SMOKED	******	EMOTES	ENRAGE	UNMASK	ENMESH
SMOKER	**-M-O--**	SMITER	ENRAPT	UNPACK	ENNEAD
SMOKES	******	SMITES	ENTAIL	UNSAFE	ENTERA
******	EMBODY	SMITHS	INBAND	UNSAID	ENTERE
-M-L--	EMBOLI	SMITHY	INCAGE	UNSAYS	ENTERO
******	EMBOSS	SMUTCH	INCASE	UNTACK	ENTERS
AMALIE	EMBOWS	SMUTTY	INDABA	UNWARY	INCEPT
AMBLED	IMBODY	******	INFAMY	******	INCEST
AMBLER	IMPORT	**-M-U--**	INFANT	**-N-B--**	INDEED
AMBLES	IMPOSE	******	INHALE	******	INDENE
AMELIA	IMPOST	AMBUSH	INHAUL	ANABAS	INDENT
AMELIE	SMOOCH	AMOUNT	INLACE	ANUBIS	INFECT
AMOLES	SMOOTH	AMOURS	INLAID	ENABLE	INFERO
AMULET	******	AMPULE	INLAND	KNOBBY	INFERS
AMYLIC	**-M-R--**	AMPULS	INLAWS	SNOBBY	INFEST
AMYLUM	******	EMEUTE	INLAYS	UNABLE	INGEST
EMBLEM	AMERCE	IMBUED	INMATE		INHERE

INJECT	SNIFFY	ENTIRE	UNWIND	GNOMIC	INSOUL
INKERS	SNUFFS	ENTITY	UNWISE	GNOMON	INTOMB
INLETS	SNUFFY	ENVIED	UNWISH	******	INTONE
INMESH	UNIFIC	ENVIER	******	**-N-N--**	INVOKE
INSECT	******	ENVIES	**-N-K--**	******	INWOVE
INSERT	**-N-G--**	ENWIND	******	ANANAS	ONEOFF
INSETS	******	GNEISS	ANGKOR	ANANKE	ONIONS
INTEND	ENIGMA	INCISE	SNAKED	ANONYM	ONIONY
INTENT	KNIGHT	INCITE	SNAKES	UNKNIT	SNOODS
INTERN	ONAGER	INDIAN	******	******	SNOOKS
INTERS	ONAGRI	INDICT	**-N-L--**	**-N-O--**	SNOOPS
INVENT	SNAGGY	INDIES	******	******	SNOOPY
INVERT	SNUGLY	INDIGO	ANALOG	ANCONA	SNOOTS
INVEST	******	INDITE	ANGLED	ANCONE	SNOOTY
KNEELS	**-N-H--**	INDIUM	ANGLER	ANGOLA	SNOOZE
ONSETS	******	INFIRM	ANGLES	ANGORA	UNBOLT
SNEERS	ANCHOR	INKIER	ANGLIA	ANIONS	UNBORN
SNEEZE	ANTHEA	INKING	ANGLIC	ANNONA	UNCOCK
SNEEZY	ANTHEM	INLIER	ANILIN	ANNOYS	UNCOIL
UNBEAR	ANTHER	INNING	ANKLES	ANTONS	UNCORD
UNBELT	ANYHOW	INSIDE	ANKLET	ANTONY	UNCORK
UNBEND	INCHED	INSIST	ANTLER	ANYONE	UNDOER
UNBENT	INCHES	INTIMA	ANTLIA	ENCODE	UNDOES
UNHEWN	INCHON	INVITE	INFLOW	ENCORE	UNDONE
UNLEAD	UNSHIP	INWIND	INFLUX	ENDOWS	UNFOLD
UNLESS	UNSHOD	ONEIDA	INKLES	ENFOLD	UNHOLY
UNMEET	******	ONEILL	INULIN	ENJOIN	UNHOOK
UNMEWS	**-N-I--**	ONEIRO	KNELLS	ENJOYS	UNIONS
UNPEGS	******	ONLINE	KNOLLS	ENROBE	UNLOAD
UNREAD	ANGINA	SNAILS	SNELLS	ENROLL	UNLOCK
UNREAL	ANNIES	UNBIND	UNCLAD	ENROOT	UNMOOR
UNREEL	ANOINT	UNCIAL	UNCLES	ENSOUL	UNROBE
UNREST	ANTIAR	UNDIES	UNPLUG	ENTOMB	UNROLL
UNSEAL	ANTICS	UNDINE	******	ENTOMO	UNROOT
UNSEAM	ANVILS	UNGIRD	**-N-M--**	ENVOYS	UNSOLD
UNSEAT	ENCINA	UNGIRT	******	ENWOMB	UNTOLD
UNSEEN	ENDING	UNKIND	ANEMIA	INBORN	UNWORN
UNVEIL	ENDIVE	UNLIKE	ANEMIC	INCOME	UNYOKE
UNVEXT	ENGINE	UNLIVE	ANIMAL	INCORP	******
UNWELL	ENGIRD	UNPICK	ANIMAS	INDOOR	**-N-P--**
UNWEPT	ENGIRT	UNPILE	ANIMUS	INDOWS	******
******	ENLIST	UNPINS	ANOMIA	INFOLD	INKPOT
-N-F--	ENMITY	UNRIGS	ANOMIC	INFORM	INSPAN
******	ENRICH	UNRIPE	ANOMIE	INGOTS	SNAPPY
KNIFED	ENRICO	UNRIPS	ENAMEL	INJOKE	SNIPED
KNIFES	ENSIGN	UNTIDY	ENAMOR	INMOST	SNIPER
SNAFUS	ENSILE	UNTIED	ENEMAS	INROAD	SNIPES
SNIFFS	ENTICE	UNTIES	GNOMES	INSOLE	SNIPPY

UNAPID	UNDRAW	ENDURE	SNIVEL	DONALD	NONAGE
UNIPED	UNDREW	ENGULF	UNEVEN	DONATE	NONARY
******	UNTROD	ENOUGH	******	DORADO	NOPALS
-N-Q--	UNTRUE	ENSUED	-N-W--	DOSAGE	NOTARY
******	UNWRAP	ENSUES	******	DOTAGE	NOWAYS
UNIQUE	******	ENSURE	ANSWER	DOTARD	POLACK
******	-N-S--	INCUBI	ANYWAY	FORAGE	POLAND
-N-R--	******	INCURS	GNAWED	FORAYS	POMACE
******	ANISES	INCUSE	GNAWER	GOBANG	POMADE
ANDREA	ANUSES	INDUCE	KNOWER	GOCART	POSADA
ANDREI	ENISLE	INDUCT	ONEWAY	GOKART	POTAGE
ANDRES	ENOSIS	INDUED	SNOWED	GONADS	POTALE
ANDREW	GNOSIS	INDUES	******	GORALS	POTASH
ANERGY	KNOSPS	INDULT	-N-X--	GOTAMA	POTATO
ANORAK	ONUSES	INFUSE	******	HOBART	ROBALO
ANTRIM	UNDSET	INGULF	ANOXIA	HOGANS	ROBAND
ANTRUM	UNESCO	INHUME	ANOXIC	HOLARD	ROLAND
ANURAN	UNISEX	INJURE	******	HOMAGE	ROMAIC
ENERGY	UNISON	INJURY	-N-Y--	HORACE	ROMANS
ENGRAM	UNUSED	INPUTS	******	HORARY	ROMANY
ENTRAP	******	INRUSH	ANKYLO	HOWARD	RONALD
ENTREE	-N-T--	INSULT	ENCYST	IODATE	ROSARY
ENWRAP	******	INSURE	ENZYME	JOHANN	ROTARY
GNARLS	ANATTO	INTUIT	******	JONAHS	ROTATE
GNARLY	ANITAS	INTURN	-N-Z--	JORAMS	ROWANS
INARCH	ANITRA	KNOUTS	******	KODAKS	ROXANA
INARMS	ENATES	ONRUSH	SNAZZY	LOBATE	ROXANE
INBRED	GNATHO	PNEUMA	******	LOCALE	ROYALE
INDRIS	INSTAR	PNEUMO	-O-A--	LOCALS	ROYALS
INGRES	INSTEP	SNOUTS	******	LOCATE	SOCAGE
INGRID	INSTIL	UNCURL	BOGANS	LORAIN	SOLACE
INURED	KNOTTY	UNDULY	BONACI	LOTAHS	SOLAND
INURES	SNATCH	UNFURL	BORAGE	LOVAGE	SOLANO
INURNS	SNATHE	UNGUAL	BORANE	MOHAIR	SOLANS
INWRAP	SNATHS	UNGUES	BORATE	MOHAVE	SOMALI
KNARRY	SNITCH	UNGUIS	BOTANY	MOHAWK	SOMATA
KNURLS	SNOTTY	UNGULA	BOVATE	MOJAVE	SOMATO
KNURLY	UNITED	UNHURT	BOYARD	MOLARS	SONANT
SNARED	UNITES	UNHUSK	BOYARS	MONACO	SONARS
SNARER	UNSTEP	UNJUST	COBALT	MONADS	SONATA
SNARES	UNSTOP	UNRULY	COCAIN	MORALE	SOUARI
SNARLS	******	UNSUNG	COMATE	MORALS	SOWARS
SNARLY	-N-U--	UNSURE	COPALM	MORASS	TOBAGO
SNORED	******	******	CORALS	MORAYS	TOGAED
SNORER	ANNUAL	-N-V--	COWAGE	MOSAIC	TOMANS
SNORES	ANNULS	******	COWARD	MOZART	TOMATO
SNORTS	ENDUED	KNAVES	DOGAPE	NOBALL	TORAHS
UNBRED	ENDUES	KNIVES	DOMAIN	NOMADS	TOTALS

TOWAGE	GOBBLE	CONCHA	CORDAY	NOODLE	COMELY
TOWARD	GOOBER	CONCHS	CORDED	NORDIC	COMEON
VOCALS	HOBBES	CONCHY	CORDER	PODDED	COMERS
VOLANT	HOBBLE	CONCUR	CORDON	POLDER	COMETS
VOTARY	HOMBRE	DOUCHE	DODDER	PONDER	CONEYS
VOYAGE	HOTBED	FORCED	DOODAD	POODLE	COOEED
ZONARY	HOTBOX	FORCER	DOODLE	POWDER	COOEES
ZONATE	JOBBED	FORCES	FODDER	RODDYS	COOERS
ZOUAVE	JOBBER	HOICKS	FOGDOG	RONDEL	COOEYS
******	LOBBED	IOLCUS	FOLDED	RONDOS	COPECK
-O-B--	LOBBER	JOYCES	FOLDER	SODDED	COTEAU
******	LOWBOY	MOBCAP	FONDER	SODDEN	COVERS
BOBBED	MOBBED	MOSCOW	FONDLE	SOLDER	COVERT
BOBBER	MOBBER	NONCOM	FONDLY	SONDER	COVETS
BOBBIE	MORBID	POACHY	FONDUE	SORDID	COVEYS
BOBBIN	NOBBED	PONCHO	FORDED	TODDLE	COWERS
BOBBLE	NOBBLE	POUCHY	GOADED	VOIDED	COZENS
BOBBYS	POTBOY	ROSCOE	GODDAM	VOODOO	DOCENT
BOMBAY	ROBBED	ROTCHE	GOLDEN	WOADED	DODECA
BOMBED	ROBBER	ROUCHE	GOODBY	WONDER	DOGEAR
BOMBER	ROBBIA	SOCCER	GOODLY	WOODED	DONEES
BOMBES	ROBBIE	TOECAP	GORDON	WOODEN	DONETS
BOMBIC	ROUBLE	TOMCAT	HODDEN	WOODSY	DOREEN
BONBON	SOBBED	TOMCOD	HOIDEN	WORDED	DOSERS
BOOBOO	SOMBER	TOUCAN	HOLDER	YONDER	DOTERS
COBBER	SOMBRE	TOUCHE	HOLDUP	******	DOWELS
COBBLE	SORBET	TOUCHY	HOODED	-O-E--	DOWERS
COBBLY	TOMBAC	VOICED	HOODOO	******	DOWERY
COMBAT	TOMBED	VOICES	HORDED	BODEGA	DOYENS
COMBED	TOMBOY	YOICKS	HORDES	BOGEYS	DOZENS
COMBER	WOBBLE	******	HOWDAH	BOLERO	EOCENE
COMBOS	WOBBLY	-O-D--	HOYDEN	BOLEYN	EOGENE
CORBAN	WOMBAT	******	JORDAN	BONERS	FOMENT
CORBEL	WOMBED	AOUDAD	KOODOO	BOREAL	FOREGO
CORBIE	ZOMBIE	BOLDER	LOADED	BOREAS	FOREST
COWBOY	ZOMBIS	BOLDLY	LOADER	BORERS	FOVEAE
DOABLE	******	BONDED	LONDON	BOWELS	FOVEAL
DOBBER	-O-C--	BONDER	LORDED	BOWERS	FOYERS
DOBBIN	******	BOODLE	LORDLY	BOWERY	GONERS
DORBUG	BOBCAT	BORDEL	LOUDEN	BOXERS	GOVERN
DOUBLE	BOCCIE	BORDER	LOUDER	CODEIA	HOMELY
DOUBLY	BOTCHY	CODDER	LOUDLY	CODEIN	HOMERS
DOUBTS	BOUCLE	CODDLE	MOLDED	COGENT	HONEST
FOBBED	BOXCAR	COLDER	MOLDER	COHEIR	HONEYS
FOGBOW	COCCAL	COLDLY	MONDAY	COHERE	HOTELS
FOIBLE	COCCID	CONDOM	NODDED	COLEUS	HOVELS
FORBID	COCCUS	CONDOR	NODDER	COMEDO	HOVERS
GOBBET	COCCYX	COODLE	NODDLE	COMEDY	HOVERS

JOKERS	POSEUR	BOUFFE	CONGOU	MONGOL	NOSHED
JOSEPH	POTEEN	BOWFIN	CORGIS	MONGST	NOSHOW
KOPECK	POTENT	COFFEE	COUGAR	MORGAN	OOPHOR
KOPEKS	POWELL	COFFER	COUGHS	MORGEN	POSHLY
KOREAN	POWERS	COFFIN	DODGED	MORGUE	POTHER
LOMENT	ROBERT	COFFLE	DODGER	NOGGIN	ROCHET
LONELY	RODENT	COIFED	DODGES	NOUGAT	SOPHIA
LONERS	RODEOS	COMFIT	DOGGED	NOUGHT	SOPHIE
LOPERS	ROGERS	CONFAB	DOGGER	PONGEE	SOTHIC
LOREEN	ROSEAL	CONFER	DOGGIE	POPGUN	SOTHIS
LORENE	ROVERS	DOFFED	DOUGAL	ROTGUT	TOPHAT
LORENZ	ROWELS	DOFFER	DOUGHS	ROUGED	TOSHES
LOSERS	ROWENA	DOGFOX	DOUGHY	ROUGES	TOTHER
LOVEIN	ROWERS	GOFFER	DOUGIE	ROUGHS	YOOHOO
LOVELL	SOBERS	GOLFED	FOGGED	SOIGNE	******
LOVELY	SOLELY	GOLFER	FORGED	SORGHO	-O-I--
LOVERS	SOLEMN	GOOFED	FORGER	SORGOS	******
LOWELL	SOLENT	HOOFED	FORGES	SOUGHS	AORIST
LOWERS	SORELS	HOOFER	FORGET	SOUGHT	BODICE
LOWERY	SORELY	JOYFUL	FORGOT	TOGGED	BODIED
LOWEST	SOREST	LOAFED	FOUGHT	TOGGLE	BODIES
MODELS	SOWERS	LOAFER	GOGGLE	TONGED	BODILY
MODERN	TOKENS	LOOFAH	GOOGLY	TONGUE	BODING
MODEST	TOLEDO	ROOFED	GOOGOL	TOUGHS	BOGIES
MOIETY	TONERS	ROOFER	GORGED	******	BOLIDE
MOLEST	TOPEKA	SOFFIT	GORGER	-O-H--	BONIER
MOMENT	TOPERS	TOFFEE	GORGES	******	BONING
MONEYS	TORERO	WOEFUL	GORGET	BOOHOO	BONITO
MOPERS	TOTEMS	WOLFED	GORGON	BOSHES	BOOING
MOREAU	TOTERS	WOOFER	GOUGED	BOTHER	BORIDE
MOREEN	TOWELS	******	GOUGER	COCHIN	BORING
MORELS	TOWERS	-O-G--	GOUGES	COSHED	BOVINE
MOSEYS	TOWERY	******	HOGGED	COSHER	BOWING
MOTELS	TOYERS	BOGGED	JOGGED	COSHES	BOXING
MOVERS	VOLERY	BOGGLE	JOGGER	FOEHNS	BOYISH
MOWERS	VOMERS	BONGED	JOGGLE	GOPHER	COBIAS
NOCENT	VOTERS	BONGOS	JORGES	GORHEN	CODIFY
NONEGO	VOWELS	BOOGIE	LODGED	GOSHEN	CODING
NOREEN	VOWERS	BORGIA	LODGER	GOTHAM	COKING
NOTERS	VOYEUR	BOUGHS	LODGES	GOTHIC	COLIES
NOVELS	WOMERA	BOUGHT	LOGGED	JOSHED	COLINE
NOVENA	WOOERS	BOUGIE	LOGGER	JOSHER	COLINS
POKERS	YODELS	CODGER	LOGGIA	JOSHES	COMICS
POLEAX	YOGEES	COGGED	LONGAN	JOSHUA	COMING
POMELO	YOKELS	COIGNS	LONGED	JOTHAM	COMITY
PONENT	******	CONGAS	LONGER	KOSHER	CONICS
POPERY	-O-F--	CONGER	LOUGHS	LOCHIA	CONIES
POSERS	******	CONGES	MONGER	MOTHER	CONING
	BOFFIN				
	BOTFLY				

CONIUM	GOBIES	LOTION	POKING	TONITE	COOKEY
COOING	GODIVA	LOUISA	POLICE	TOPICS	COOKIE
COPIED	GONION	LOUISE	POLICY	TOPING	CORKED
COPIER	GONIUM	LOVING	POLING	TORIES	CORKER
COPIES	GOOIER	LOWING	POLISH	TORIIS	DOCKED
COPING	GORIER	MOBILE	POLITE	TOTING	DOCKER
CORING	GORILY	MOBIUS	POLITY	TOWING	DOCKET
CORIUM	GORING	MODIFY	PONIED	TOXINS	DONKEY
COSIGN	HOEING	MODISH	PONIES	TOYING	FOLKSY
COSILY	HOLIER	MOLIES	POPISH	TOYISH	FORKED
COSINE	HOLIES	MOLINE	PORING	VOLING	HOCKED
COVING	HOLILY	MOMISM	POSIES	VOMICA	HOCKEY
COWING	HOLING	MONICA	POSING	VOMITO	HONKED
COXING	HOLISM	MONIED	POSITS	VOMITS	HONKER
COYISH	HOMIER	MONIES	POTION	VOTING	HOOKAH
COZIER	HOMILY	MONISM	ROBING	VOTIVE	HOOKED
COZIES	HOMING	MONIST	ROBINS	VOWING	HOOKER
COZILY	HOMINY	MOOING	ROMISH	WOOING	HOOKEY
DOBIES	HONIED	MOPING	ROPIER	WOWING	HOOKUP
DOCILE	HONING	MOPISH	ROPILY	YOGINS	JOCKEY
DOGIES	HOPING	MORION	ROPING	YOKING	JOCKOS
DOLING	HOSIER	MOTIFS	ROSIER	YORICK	LOCKED
DOMING	HOSING	MOTILE	ROSILY	YOWING	LOCKER
DOMINO	IODIDE	MOTION	ROSING	ZODIAC	LOCKET
DOPIER	IODINE	MOTIVE	ROSINS	ZONING	LOCKUP
DOPING	IODISM	MOVIES	ROSINY	ZOOIDS	LOOKED
DORIAN	IODIZE	MOVING	ROVING	ZORILS	LOOKER
DORIES	IOLITE	MOWING	ROWING	******	LOOKIN
DOSING	IONIAN	NOMISM	SOCIAL	-O-J--	LOWKEY
DOTIER	IONIUM	NORIAS	SODIUM	******	MOCKED
DOTING	IONIZE	NOSIER	SOLIDI	DONJON	MOCKER
DOVISH	JOKING	NOSILY	SOLIDS	KOPJES	MOCKUP
DOXIES	JOLIET	NOSING	SOLING	LOGJAM	MONKEY
DOZIER	JOSIAH	NOTICE	SOLION	******	NOCKED
DOZILY	JOSIAS	NOTIFY	SOMITE	-O-K--	POCKET
DOZING	JOSIEA	NOTING	SONIAS	******	POLKAS
EOLIAN	JOVIAL	NOTION	SOVIET	BODKIN	PORKER
EOLITH	JOVIAN	NOWISE	SOWING	BOOKED	ROCKED
EONIAN	JOYING	OOLITE	SOZINE	BOOKIE	ROCKER
EONISM	KODIAK	OOMIAK	SOZINS	BOSKET	ROCKET
FOGIES	LOGIER	OOZIER	TOBIAH	COCKED	ROCKNE
FOLIAR	LOGION	OOZILY	TOBIAS	COCKER	ROOKED
FOLIOS	LOLITA	OOZING	TOBIES	COCKLE	ROOKIE
FOLIUM	LOOING	PODIUM	TODIES	COCKUP	SOAKED
FORINT	LOPING	POGIES	TOEING	CONKED	SOAKER
FOXIER	LORICA	POKIER	TONICS	CONKER	SOCKED
FOXILY	LORIES	POKIES	TONIER	COOKED	SOCKET
FOXING	LOSING		TONING	COOKER	TONKIN

VODKAS	FOLLOW	POOLED	DOGMAS	BOUNCY	MOANED
WORKED	FOOLED	POPLAR	DOLMAN	BOUNDS	MOONED
WORKER	FOULED	POPLIN	DOLMEN	BOUNTY	MOUNTS
YONKER	FOULER	POULTS	DOOMED	COBNUT	MOUNTY
YORKER	FOULLY	ROALDS	DORMER	COGNAC	NORNIR
******	FOWLED	ROBLES	DORMIE	COINED	NOUNAL
-O-L--	FOWLER	ROILED	FOAMED	COINER	POINDS
******	GOALIE	ROLLED	FOEMAN	CONNED	POINTE
BOGLES	GOBLET	ROLLER	FOEMEN	CONNER	POINTS
BOILED	GOBLIN	ROLLUP	FORMAL	CONNIE	POINTY
BOILER	GOGLET	SOCLES	FORMAT	CORNEA	POUNCE
BOLLED	HOLLER	SOILED	FORMED	CORNED	POUNDS
BOLLIX	HOLLOW	SOULED	FORMER	CORNEL	RODNEY
BOULES	HOLLYS	TOILED	FORMIC	CORNER	ROMNEY
BOWLED	HOWLED	TOILER	FORMYL	CORNET	RONNIE
BOWLEG	HOWLER	TOILES	HODMAN	CORNUA	ROUNDS
BOWLER	JOPLIN	TOILET	HOLMES	CORNUS	SONNET
COALED	JOULES	TOLLED	HOLMIC	COUNTS	SOONER
COALER	KOALAS	TOLLER	LOAMED	COUNTY	SOUNDS
COBLES	LOLLED	TOOLED	LOOMED	DOINGS	WOUNDS
COELED	LOLLER	TOOLER	MORMON	DONNAS	ZOONAL
COELOM	LOLLOP	TOULON	MOTMOT	DONNED	ZOUNDS
COILED	MOILED	VOILES	NORMAL	DONNIE	******
COILER	MOILER	VOLLEY	NORMAN	DOWNED	**-O-O--**
COLLAR	MOLLAH	WOALDS	NORMAS	FORNAX	******
COLLET	MOLLIE	WOOLEN	POMMEL	FORNIX	BOGOAK
COLLIE	MOLLYS	WOOLLY	POTMAN	FOUNDS	BOGOTA
COLLOP	MOOLAH	WORLDS	ROAMED	FOUNTS	BOSOMS
COOLED	MOOLEY	YOWLED	ROAMER	GOINGS	COCOAS
COOLER	MORLEY	******	RODMAN	GOONEY	COCOON
COOLIE	MOSLEM	**-O-M--**	RODMEN	GOWNED	COHORT
COOLLY	MOSLEY	******	ROMMEL	HOBNOB	COHOSH
COPLEY	MOTLEY	BOOMED	ROOMED	HOGNUT	COLONS
COULEE	MOULDS	BOOMER	ROOMER	HORNED	COLONY
DOALLS	MOULDY	BOWMAN	SOCMAN	HORNET	COLORS
DOBLAS	MOULIN	BOWMEN	SOCMEN	HORNIE	COLOUR
DOBLON	MOULTS	COEMPT	TOMMYS	HOUNDS	COLOUS
DOLLAR	NOBLER	COMMAS	WORMED	JOANNA	COMOSE
DOLLED	NOELLE	COMMIE	WORMER	JOANNE	COMOUS
DOLLIE	OODLES	COMMIT	ZOOMED	JOHNNY	CONOID
DOLLOP	POILUS	COMMIX	******	JOINED	COPOUT
DOLLYS	POLLED	COMMON	**-O-N--**	JOINER	CORODY
DOOLEE	POLLEE	CONMAN	******	JOINTS	CORONA
DOOLIE	POLLEN	COOMBS	BONNET	JONNIE	COYOTE
DOWLAS	POLLER	COSMIC	BONNIE	JOUNCE	DODOES
DOYLEY	POLLEX	COSMOS	BONNYS	KOINES	DOLOUR
FOALED	POLLUX	COWMAN	BORNEO	LOANED	DONORS
FOILED	POLLYS	COWMEN	BOUNCE	LOUNGE	EOZOIC

GOLOSH	COMPLY	SOPPED	LOURED	CORSES	LOSSES
HOBOES	COMPOS	SOUPED	MOIRAS	CORSET	LOUSED
HONORE	COOPED	TOPPED	MONROE	COSSES	LOUSES
HONORS	COOPER	TOPPER	MOORED	COSSET	MOISHE
HONOUR	COOPTS	TOPPLE	MORRIS	COUSIN	MORSEL
IODOUS	COPPED	TORPID	MORROS	DOBSON	MOSSES
IONONE	COPPER	TORPOR	MORROW	DOESNT	MOUSED
JOCOSE	COPPRA	TOUPEE	MOURNS	DORSAD	MOUSER
JOYOUS	CORPSE	YOUPON	NORRIS	DORSAL	MOUSES
KOBOLD	CORPUS	******	POGROM	DORSET	MOUSSE
KOKOMO	COUPES	**-O-Q--**	POORER	DORSUM	NOESIS
LOCOED	COUPLE	******	POORLY	DOSSAL	NOISED
LOMOND	COUPON	MOSQUE	POURED	DOSSED	NOISES
MOHOCK	COWPEA	TORQUE	POURER	DOSSEL	NOOSED
MOHOLE	COWPER	******	ROARED	DOSSER	NOOSES
MOLOCH	COWPOX	**-O-R--**	ROARER	DOSSIL	PODSOL
MONODY	COYPUS	******	SOARED	DOUSED	POISED
MOPOKE	DOLPHS	BOARDS	SOARER	DOUSES	POISES
MORONS	GOSPEL	BORROW	SOCRED	DOWSED	POISON
MOROSE	HOOPED	BOURGS	SOIREE	DOWSER	POSSES
MOTORS	HOOPER	BOURNE	SORREL	DOWSES	POSSET
NOBODY	HOOPLA	BOURNS	SORROW	FOCSLE	POSSUM
NODOSE	HOOPOE	BOURSE	SOURCE	FOISTS	POTSIE
NOGOOD	HOPPED	COARSE	SOURED	FOSSAE	POUSTO
OOLOGY	HOPPER	COBRAS	SOURER	FOSSES	ROASTS
OOLONG	HOPPLE	COERCE	SOURLY	FOSSIL	ROBSON
PODOUS	HOTPOT	CONRAD	TORRID	GODSON	ROOSTS
POMONA	LOOPED	COPRAH	TOURED	GOOSED	ROUSED
POROUS	LOOPER	CORRAL	TOURER	GOOSES	ROUSER
POYOUS	LOPPED	CORRIE	******	GOOSEY	ROUSES
ROBOTS	LOUPES	COURSE	**-O-S--**	GORSES	ROUSTS
ROCOCO	MOPPED	COURTS	******	GOSSIP	SOUSED
ROMOLA	MOPPET	COWRIE	BOASTS	HOISTS	SOUSES
ROTORS	MORPHO	DOBRAS	BOLSON	HONSHU	TOASTS
SODOMY	POMPEY	DOURLY	BONSAI	HORSED	TOCSIN
SOLOED	POMPOM	FOURTH	BOOSTS	HORSES	TONSIL
SOTOLS	POMPON	GOORAL	BORSCH	HORSEY	TORSKS
TOROID	POOPED	GOURDE	BOSSED	HORSTE	TORSOS
TOROSE	POPPED	GOURDS	BOSSES	HOUSED	TOSSED
TOROUS	POPPER	HOARDS	BOUSED	HOUSES	TOSSES
TOYONS	POPPET	HOARSE	BOUSES	JOISTS	TOSSUP
VOLOST	POPPLE	HOORAY	BOWSAW	JONSON	TOUSLE
VOROUS	POPPYS	HORRID	BOWSED	JOSSES	WOLSEY
******	POTPIE	HORROR	BOWSES	JOUSTS	WORSEN
-O-P--	ROLPHS	HOTROD	COASTS	LOOSED	WORSER
******	ROMPED	HOURIS	CONSUL	LOOSEN	WORSTS
BOPPED	ROMPER	HOURLY	COPSES	LOOSER	WOWSER
COMPEL	SOAPED	KONRAD	CORSAC	LOOSES	ZOYSIA

******	COTTON	MOLTER	ROUTED	LOQUAR	VOLVAS
-O-T--	DOCTOR	MOLTKE	ROUTER	LOQUAT	VOLVOX
******	DOITED	MONTES	ROUTES	MODULE	WOLVER
AORTAE	DOPTER	MONTHS	SOFTAS	MOGULS	WOLVES
AORTAL	DOTTED	MONTYS	SOFTEN	MOHURS	******
AORTAS	DOTTEL	MOOTED	SOFTER	MORULA	-O-W--
AORTIC	DOTTER	MOOTER	SOFTLY	NODULE	******
BOATED	DOTTLE	MORTAL	SOOTED	NOMURA	BOWWOW
BOATER	FOETAL	MORTAR	SOOTHE	PODUNK	COBWEB
BOLTED	FOETID	MORTON	SORTED	ROBUST	COGWAY
BOLTER	FOETOR	MORTYS	SORTER	ROGUED	CONWAY
BOLTON	FOETUS	MOSTLY	SORTIE	ROGUES	GODWIN
BOOTED	FONTAL	MOTTLE	TOLTEC	ROMULO	GODWIT
BOOTEE	FOOTED	MOTTOS	TOMTIT	ROQUET	NORWAY
BOOTHS	FOOTER	MOUTHS	TOMTOM	ROTUND	POWWOW
BOOTIE	FOOTLE	MOUTHY	TOOTED	SOLUTE	******
BOOTLE	FORTES	MOUTON	TOOTER	TOGUES	-O-X--
BOSTON	FORTIS	NOETIC	TOOTHY	TOLUOL	******
BOTTLE	FOSTER	NOSTIC	TOOTLE	TOLUYL	COAXAL
BOTTOM	GOATEE	POETIC	TOOTSY	TOQUES	COAXED
BOWTIE	GOETHE	POETRY	TOTTED	VOGUES	COAXER
COATED	GOITER	PONTES	TOTTER	VOGULS	COAXES
COATEE	GOITRE	PONTIC	TOUTED	VOLUME	HOAXED
COATIS	GOTTEN	PONTIL	TOUTER	VOLUTE	HOAXER
COITAL	HOGTIE	PONTON	VOLTED	YOGURT	HOAXES
COITUS	HOOTCH	PORTAL	VORTEX	YORUBA	******
COLTER	HOOTED	PORTED	WONTED	ZONULA	-O-Y--
CONTES	HOOTER	PORTER	WORTHY	ZONULE	******
CONTIN	HOSTED	PORTIA	YOUTHS	******	BOWYER
CONTOS	HOSTEL	PORTLY	ZOSTER	-O-V--	CORYMB
CONTRA	HOTTED	POSTAL	******	******	CORYZA
CONTRE	HOTTER	POSTED	-O-U--	COEVAL	OOCYTE
COOTIE	JOLTED	POSTER	******	CONVEX	POLYPS
COPTIC	JOLTER	POTTED	COBURG	CONVEY	SONYAS
CORTES	JOSTLE	POTTER	COHUNE	CONVOY	******
CORTEX	JOTTED	POTTLE	COLUGO	CORVEE	-O-Z--
CORTEZ	JOTTER	POTTOS	COLUMN	CORVES	******
CORTIN	KOWTOW	POUTED	COLURE	CORVUS	BONZER
COSTAE	LOATHE	POUTER	COPULA	HOOVED	BONZES
COSTAL	LOFTED	POWTER	COQUET	HOOVER	BOOZED
COSTAR	LOFTER	ROOTED	FORUMS	HOOVES	BOOZER
COSTED	LOITER	ROOTER	GOMUTI	LOAVES	BOOZES
COSTER	LOOTED	ROOTLE	JOCUND	LOUVER	BORZOI
COSTLY	LOOTER	ROSTER	JORUMS	LOUVRE	COLZAS
COTTAE	LOTTIE	ROSTRA	KORUNA	SOEVER	FOOZLE
COTTAR	MOATED	ROTTED	KORUNY	SOLVED	NOZZLE
COTTAS	MOLTED	ROTTEN	LOBULE	SOLVER	PODZOL
COTTER	MOLTEN	ROTTER	LOCUST	SOLVES	

******	SPADED	******	******	APRONS	SPIRED
-P-A--	SPADER	-P-I--	-P-L--	EPHODS	SPIRES
******	SPADES	******	******	EPHORI	SPIRIT
APIARY	SPADIX	APHIDS	APOLLO	EPHORS	SPIRTS
APPALL	SPIDER	APLITE	APOLOG	OPPOSE	SPORED
APPALS	******	APPIAN	APPLES	SPOOFS	SPORES
EPHAHS	-P-E--	APRILS	APULIA	SPOOKS	SPORTS
OPIATE	******	EPPING	EPILOG	SPOOKY	SPORTY
OPTANT	APIECE	OPHITE	SPALLS	SPOOLS	SPURGE
SPEAKS	APNEAL	OPTICS	SPELLS	SPOONS	SPURNS
SPEARS	APNEIC	OPTIMA	SPILED	SPOONY	SPURRY
SPLAKE	APPEAL	OPTIME	SPILES	SPOORS	SPURTS
SPLASH	APPEAR	OPTING	SPILLS	SPROUT	UPHROE
SPLATS	APPELS	OPTION	SPILTH	UPBOWS	******
SPLAYS	APPEND	SPAITS	******	UPHOLD	-P-S--
SPRAGS	EPHEBI	SPEISS	-P-M--	UPMOST	******
SPRAIN	SPEECH	SPHINX	******	UPROAR	SPASMS
SPRANG	SPEEDS	SPLICE	APEMAN	UPROOT	UPASES
SPRATS	SPEEDY	SPLINE	SPUMED	UPROSE	******
SPRAWL	SPHENE	SPLINT	SPUMES	UPTOWN	-P-T--
SPRAYS	SPHENO	SPLITS	******	******	******
UPCAST	SPHERE	SPOILS	-P-N--	-P-P--	APATHY
UPDATE	SPHERY	SPOILT	******	******	APHTHA
UPLAND	SPIELS	SPRIER	EPONYM	APEPSY	SPATES
UPTAKE	SPIERS	SPRIGS	OPENED	EPOPEE	SPATHE
UPWARD	SPLEEN	SPRING	OPENER	******	SPITAL
******	SPLENO	SPRINT	OPENLY	-P-Q--	SPITED
-P-C--	SPREAD	SPRITE	OPINED	******	SPITES
******	SPREES	SPRITS	OPINES	OPAQUE	SPOTTY
APACHE	UPBEAT	SPYING	SPANKS	******	SPUTUM
APICAL	UPHELD	UPDIKE	SPENDS	-P-R--	******
APICES	UPKEEP	UPHILL	SPINAL	******	-P-U--
EPACTS	UPPERS	UPLIFT	SPINEL	EPARCH	******
EPICAL	UPSETS	UPPING	SPINES	EPIRUS	OPPUGN
EPOCHS	******	UPPISH	SPINET	OPERAS	SPOUSE
IPECAC	-P-F--	UPPITY	SPINNY	OPORTO	SPOUTS
SPACAE	******	UPRISE	SPONGE	SPARED	SPRUCE
SPACED	SPIFFY	UPSIDE	SPONGY	SPARER	SPRUES
SPACER	******	******	SPUNKY	SPARES	SPRUNG
SPACES	-P-G--	-P-K--	UPENDS	SPARGE	UPRUSH
SPECIE	******	******	******	SPARKS	UPTURN
SPECKS	APOGEE	SPIKED	-P-O--	SPARRY	******
SPICED	SPIGOT	SPIKES	******	SPARSE	-P-V--
SPICER	******	SPOKED	APHONY	SPARTA	******
SPICES	-P-H--	SPOKEN	APLOMB	SPERMO	SPAVIN
******	******	SPOKES	APNOEA	SPERRY	******
-P-D--	SPAHIS		APPORT	SPIRAL	-P-W--
******	UPSHOT		APPOSE	SPIREA	******
APODAL					SPAWNS
EPODES					SPEWED

******	******	ERRATA	GRUBBY	PRICKS	GRADER
-P-X--	-R-A--	ERSATZ	KRUBIS	PROCNE	GRADES
******	******	FREAKS	KRUBUT	PROCTO	GRADIN
APEXES	ARCADE	FREAKY	ORIBIS	TRACED	GRADUS
******	ARCANA	FRIARS	PROBED	TRACER	GRIDED
-P-Y--	ARCANE	FRIARY	PROBER	TRACES	GRIDES
******	ARGALA	GREASE	PROBES	TRACHE	GRUDGE
SPAYED	ARGALI	GREASY	TREBLE	TRACHY	IRIDES
SPRYER	ARGALS	GREATS	TRIBAL	TRACKS	IRIDIC
SPRYLY	ARIANS	GREAVE	TRIBES	TRACTS	PRIDED
******	ARMADA	GROANS	******	TRICAR	PRIDES
-P-Z--	ARMAGH	GROATS	-R-C--	TRICED	PRUDES
******	ARMAND	KRAALS	******	TRICES	TRADED
EPIZOA	ARNAUD	ORDAIN	ARECAS	TRICHI	TRADER
******	ARRACK	OREADS	BRACED	TRICHO	TRADES
-Q-A--	ARRANT	ORGANA	BRACER	TRICKS	TRUDGE
******	ARRAYS	ORGANO	BRACES	TRICKY	TRUDYS
EQUALS	ARYANS	ORGANS	BRACHI	TRICOT	******
EQUATE	BREACH	ORGASM	BRACHY	TROCAR	-R-E--
SQUABS	BREADS	ORNATE	BRACTS	TROCHE	******
SQUADS	BREAKS	PREACH	BRECHT	TRUCES	ARBELA
SQUALL	BREAMS	RRHAGE	BRICKS	TRUCKS	ARDEBS
SQUAMA	BREAST	RRHAGY	BROCHE	WRACKS	ARDENT
SQUARE	BREATH	TREADS	BRUCES	WRECKS	ARGENT
SQUASH	BRIARS	TREATS	CRACKS	******	ARIELS
SQUATS	BROACH	TREATY	CRACKY	-R-D--	ARLEEN
SQUAWK	BROADS	TRIADS	CRACOW	******	ARLENE
SQUAWS	BRYANT	TRIALS	CRECHE	ARIDLY	ARMETS
******	CRAALS	TRUANT	CRICKS	BRIDAL	ARPENS
-Q-E--	CREAKS	URBANE	CROCKS	BRIDES	ARPENT
******	CREAKY	UREASE	CROCKY	BRIDGE	ARREAR
SQUEAK	CREAMS	WREAKS	CROCUS	BRIDIE	ARREST
SQUEAL	CREAMY	WREATH	CRUCES	BRIDLE	ARTELS
******	CREASE	******	DRACHM	CRADLE	ARTERY
-Q-I--	CREASY	-R-B--	ERECTS	CREDAL	BREECH
******	CREATE	******	ERICHS	CREDIT	BREEDS
AQUILA	CROAKS	ARABEL	ERUCTS	CREDOS	BREEKS
EQUINE	CROAKY	ARABIA	FRACAS	CRUDER	BREEZE
EQUIPS	CROATS	ARABIC	FROCKS	DREDGE	BREEZY
EQUITY	DREADS	ARABLE	GRACED	DRUDGE	BRIEFS
SQUIBS	DREAMS	BRIBED	GRACES	DRYDEN	BRIERS
SQUIDS	DREAMT	BRIBER	GRACIE	ERODED	BRIERY
SQUILL	DREAMY	BRIBES	GROCER	ERODES	CREEDS
SQUINT	DREARY	CRABBY	ORACHS	FREDAS	CREEKS
SQUIRE	DRYADS	DRABLY	ORACLE	FREDDY	CREELS
SQUIRM	ERGATE	EREBUS	PRECIS	FRIDAY	CREEPS
SQUIRT	ERRAND	GRABEN	PRICED	FRIDGE	CREEPY
SQUISH	ERRANT	GREBES	PRICES	GRADED	CREESE

CRIERS	******	GRUGRU	ARRIVE	ORNITH	FRILLS
CRUETS	**-R-F--**	OREGAN	ARSINE	OROIDE	FRILLY
DRIERS	******	OREGON	ARTIES	ORPINE	FROLIC
DRIEST	ARMFUL	ORIGAN	ARTILY	ORPINS	GRILLE
DRYERS	ARTFUL	ORIGEN	ARTIST	ORRICE	GRILLS
DRYEST	CRAFTS	ORIGIN	BRAIDS	PRAISE	GRILSE
ERNEST	CRAFTY	PRAGUE	BRAILS	PRYING	ORALLY
FREELY	CROFTS	TRAGIC	BRAINS	TRAILS	PRELIM
FREEST	DRAFFS	TRAGUS	BRAINY	TRAINS	PROLEG
FREEZE	DRAFFY	TRIGLY	BRAISE	TRAITS	PROLIX
FRIEDA	DRAFTS	TRIGON	BRAIZE	TROIKA	TRILBY
FRIEND	DRAFTY	TROGON	BROILS	TRUING	TRILLS
FRIERS	DRIFTS	WRIGHT	BRUINS	TRUISM	TROLLS
FRIEZE	DRIFTY	******	BRUISE	TRYING	URALIC
FRYERS	DRYFLY	**-R-H--**	BRUITS	UREIDE	******
GRAECO	GRAFTS	******	CRAIGS	URGING	**-R-M--**
GREECE	GRIFFE	ARCHED	CRUISE	URSINE	******
GREEDS	IREFUL	ARCHEO	CRYING	WRAITH	AROMAS
GREEDY	PREFAB	ARCHER	DRAINS	WRYING	BREMEN
GREEKS	PREFER	ARCHES	DROITS	******	BROMAL
GREENE	PREFIX	ARCHIE	DRUIDS	**-R-J--**	BROMES
GREENS	PROFIT	ARCHIL	DRYICE	******	BROMIC
GREETS	TRIFID	ARCHLY	DRYING	CROJIK	BRUMAL
GRIEVE	TRIFLE	ARCHON	DRYISH	FRIJOL	BRUMES
GRUELS	******	ARCHYS	ERBIUM	PROJET	CRAMBO
ORCEIN	**-R-G--**	ARTHRO	ERMINE	TROJAN	CRAMPS
ORDEAL	******	ARTHUR	ERNIES	******	CREMES
ORDERS	ARAGON	BRAHMA	ERRING	**-R-K--**	CRIMEA
ORGEAT	ARIGHT	BRAHMS	ERWINS	******	CRIMES
ORIELS	BREGMA	GRAHAM	FRAILS	ARCKED	CRIMPS
ORIENT	BRIGHT	ORCHID	FRAISE	BRAKED	CRIMPY
ORMERS	BRIGID	ORCHIL	FRUITS	BRAKES	CRUMBS
ORNERY	BROGAN	ORCHIO	FRUITY	BROKEN	CRUMBY
ORRERY	BROGUE	ORCHIS	FRYING	BROKER	CRUMMY
ORWELL	BRUGES	ORPHAN	GRAINS	CRAKES	CRUMPS
PREENS	CRAGGY	ORPHIC	GRAINY	CRIKEY	DRAMAS
PRIERS	DRAGEE	URCHIN	GREIFS	DRAKES	DROMON
PRIEST	DRAGON	******	GREIGE	KRAKEN	FRAMED
PROEMS	DREGGY	**-R-I--**	GROINS	******	FRAMER
PRYERS	DROGUE	******	IRKING	**-R-L--**	FRAMES
TRIERS	FRIGGA	ARCING	IRVING	******	FRUMPS
TRUEST	FRIGHT	ARGIVE	IRVINS	ARMLET	FRUMPY
URAEUS	FRIGID	ARLINE	IRWINS	BRILLS	GRAMME
URGENT	FROGGY	ARMIES	KRAITS	BROLLY	GRIMED
URTEXT	FRUGAL	ARMING	ORBING	BRULOT	GRIMES
WRIEST	GREGOS	ARNICA	ORBITS	DRILLS	GRIMLY
WRYEST	GRIGRI	ARNIES	OREIDE	DROLLS	GRUMES
	GROGGY	AROIDS	ORGIES	DROLLY	GRUMPY

PREMED	CRANNY	KRONUR	ARROBA	DROPSY	ARISTA
PRIMAL	CRENEL	ORANGE	ARROWS	DRUPEL	ARISTO
PRIMED	CRINGE	ORANGS	ARROWY	DRUPES	BRASHY
PRIMER	CRINUM	ORKNEY	ARROYO	ERUPTS	BRASSY
PRIMES	CRONES	PRANCE	ARTOIS	FRAPPE	BRISKS
PRIMLY	CRONOS	PRANKS	BROOCH	GRAPES	BRUSHY
PRIMPS	CRONUS	PRINCE	BROODS	GRAPHO	CRASIS
PRIMUS	CRUNCH	PRINKS	BROODY	GRAPHS	CRESOL
PROMPT	DRENCH	PRINTS	BROOKE	GRAPHY	CRESTS
TRAMPS	DRINKS	PRONGS	BROOKS	GRIPED	CRISES
TREMOR	DRONED	PRONTO	BROOMS	GRIPER	CRISIS
TRIMLY	DRONES	PRUNED	BROOMY	GRIPES	CRISPS
TRUMAN	DRONGO	PRUNER	BRYONY	GRIPPE	CRISPY
TRUMPS	DRUNKS	PRUNES	CREOLE	GRIPPY	CROSSE
UREMIA	ERINGO	TRANCE	CROOKS	GROPED	CRUSES
******	ERINYS	TRENCH	CROONS	GROPER	CRUSET
-R-N--	ERYNGO	TRENDS	DROOLS	GROPES	CRUSOE
******	FRANCE	TRENDY	DROOPS	PREPAY	CRUSTS
ARANTA	FRANCK	TRINAL	DROOPY	PROPEL	CRUSTY
ARENAS	FRANCO	TRINED	ERRORS	PROPER	DRESSY
ARUNTA	FRANCS	TRINES	FREONS	PROPYL	DROSKY
BRANCH	FRANKS	TRUNKS	GROOMS	TREPAN	DROSSY
BRANDS	FRENCH	URANIA	GROOVE	TRIPLE	DRUSES
BRANÐT	FRENUM	URANIC	GROOVY	TRIPOD	ERASED
BRANDY	FRENZY	URANUS	ORIOLE	TRIPOS	ERASER
BRANNY	FRINGE	URANYL	ORLOPS	TROPAL	ERASES
BRANTS	FRINGY	URINAL	ORMOLU	TROPHO	FRESCO
BRENDA	FRONDS	WRENCH	PRIORS	TROPHY	FRESNO
BRENTS	FRONTO	WRINGS	PRIORY	TROPIC	FRISES
BRINED	FRONTS	WRONGS	PROOFS	TROPPO	FRISKS
BRINES	FRUNZE	******	TRIODE	UROPOD	FRISKY
BRINGS	GRANDE	-R-O--	TRIOSE	WRAPUP	FROSTS
BRINKS	GRANGE	******	TROOPS	******	FROSTY
BRONCO	GRANNY	ARBORI	TRYOUT	-R-Q--	FRUSTA
BRONCS	GRANTS	ARBORS	******	******	GRASPS
BRONTE	GRINDS	ARBOUR	-R-P--	BRAQUE	GRASSY
BRONZE	GRUNDY	ARDORS	******	IRAQIS	GRISLY
BRONZY	GRUNTS	ARDOUR	ARMPIT	******	GROSZY
BRUNCH	IRANIS	AREOLA	CRAPED	-R-R--	IRISED
BRUNEI	IRENES	ARGOSY	CRAPES	******	IRISES
BRUNEL	IRENIC	ARGOTS	CREPED	ARARAT	KRISES
BRUNOS	IRONED	ARIOSE	CREPES	ARERCU	ORISON
CRANED	IRONER	ARIOSO	CRYPTO	CRORES	PRESAS
CRANES	IRONIC	ARIOUS	CRYPTS	CRURAL	PRESTO
CRANIA	KRONEN	ARMORS	DRAPED	DRYROT	PRISMS
CRANIO	KRONER	ARMORY	DRAPER	******	PRISON
CRANKS	KRONOR	ARMOUR	DRAPES	-R-S--	PRISSY
CRANKY	KRONOS	ARNOLD	DRIPPY	ARISEN	PROSED
				ARISES	

PROSER	GRETNA	FRAUEN	PRAVDA	******	PRIZER
PROSES	GRITTY	GROUCH	PREVUE	-R-X--	PRIZES
PROSIT	GROTTO	GROUND	PRIVET	******	******
TRASHY	GROTTY	GROUPS	PROVED	CRUXES	-S-A--
TRESSY	IRITIC	GROUSE	PROVEN	ORYXES	******
TRISTE	IRITIS	GROUTS	PROVER	PRAXIS	ASGARD
TRUSTS	ORATED	ORDURE	PROVES	TRIXIE	ASIANS
TRUSTY	ORATES	ORMUZD	TRAVEL	TRIXYS	ASKANT
TRYSTS	ORATOR	PROUST	TRAVES	******	ASLANT
WRASSE	PRATED	TRAUMA	TREVOR	-R-Y--	ASSAIL
WRESTS	PRATER	TRIUNE	TRIVET	******	ASSAIS
WRISTS	PRATES	TROUGH	TRIVIA	ARGYLL	ASSAYS
******	PRETER	TROUPE	TROVER	BRAYED	ESCAPE
-R-T--	PRETOR	TROUTS	TROVES	BRAYER	ESCARP
******	PRETTY	URSULA	******	CRAYON	ESPANA
ARCTIC	PROTON	******	-R-W--	DRAYED	ESSAYS
ARETES	TRITER	-R-V--	******	FRAYED	ESTATE
BRETON	TRITON	******	ARAWAK	GRAYED	ISAACS
BRITON	TROTHS	BRAVED	BRAWLS	GRAYER	ISLAND
BROTHS	TROTYL	BRAVER	BRAWNY	GRAYLY	ISRAEL
BRUTAL	TRUTHS	BRAVES	BREWED	GROYNE	OSCANS
BRUTES	URETER	BRAVOS	BREWER	PRAYED	OSCARS
BRUTUS	URETIC	BREVES	BREWIS	PRAYER	OSWALD
CRATCH	WRATHY	BREVET	BROWNS	PREYED	PSHAWS
CRATED	WRETCH	CRAVAT	BROWSE	PREYER	******
CRATER	WRITER	CRAVED	CRAWLS	XRAYED	-S-B--
CRATES	WRITES	CRAVEN	CRAWLY	******	******
CRETAN	WRITHE	CRAVER	CREWEL	-R-Z--	ISABEL
CRETIC	******	CRAVES	CROWDS	******	ISOBAR
CRETIN	-R-U--	CREVAS	CROWED	AREZZO	ISOBEL
CRETON	******	DRIVEL	CROWNS	BRAZAS	USABLE
CRITIC	ARBUTE	DRIVEN	DRAWEE	BRAZED	USABLY
CROTCH	ARGUED	DRIVER	DRAWER	BRAZEN	******
CROTON	ARGUER	DRIVES	DRAWLS	BRAZER	-S-C--
CRUTCH	ARGUES	DROVED	DRAWLY	BRAZES	******
EROTIC	ARGUFY	DROVER	DROWNS	BRAZIL	ASHCAN
FRATER	ARMURE	DROVES	DROWSE	BRAZOS	PSYCHE
FRETTY	AROUND	FRIVOL	DROWSY	CRAZED	PSYCHO
FRITHS	AROUSE	GRAVED	FROWNS	CRAZES	******
FROTHS	ARTURO	GRAVEL	FROWZY	CROZER	-S-D--
FROTHY	CREUSA	GRAVEN	GROWER	CROZES	******
GRATED	CROUCH	GRAVER	GROWLS	FRIZZY	ASIDES
GRATER	CROUPE	GRAVES	GROWTH	FROZEN	ISADOR
GRATES	CROUPS	GRAVID	PRAWNS	GRAZED	ISIDOR
GRATIN	CROUPY	GRIVET	PREWAR	GRAZER	TSADES
GRATIS	DROUTH	GROVEL	PROWLS	GRAZES	******
GRETAS	ERFURT	GROVER	TRAWLS	GRIZEL	-S-E--
GRETEL	FRAUDS	GROVES	TROWEL	PRIZED	******
					ASCEND
					ASCENT

ASKERS	******	ASSORT	******	STACTE	STIFLE
ASLEEP	**-S-I--**	ESCORT	**-S-Z--**	STACYS	STUFFS
ASPECT	******	ESTOPS	******	STICKS	STUFFY
ASPENS	ASHIER	OSBORN	ZSAZSA	STICKY	******
ASPERS	ASKING	OSMOND	******	STOCKS	**-T-G--**
ASSENT	ASPICS	OSMOSE	**-T-A--**	STOCKY	******
ASSERT	ASPIRE	******	******	STUCCO	STAGED
ASSESS	ASSIGN	**-S-P--**	ATTACH	******	STAGER
ASSETS	ASSISI	******	ATTACK	**-T-D--**	STAGES
ASTERI	ASSIST	ISOPOD	ATTAIN	******	STAGEY
ASTERN	ASSIZE	******	ATTARS	ETUDES	STAGGY
ASTERO	ESKIMO	**-S-R--**	ETHANE	STADIA	STIGMA
ASTERS	ESPIAL	******	ETHANS	STODGE	STOGEY
ESCENT	ESPIED	ASARUM	ITHACA	STODGY	******
ESKERS	ESPIES	ASTRAL	OTTAVA	STUDIO	**-T-H--**
ESSENE	ISAIAH	ASTRAY	OTTAWA	******	******
ESTEEM	ISLING	ASTRID	STEADY	**-T-E--**	ETCHED
ESTERS	OSCINE	ESCROW	STEAKS	******	ETCHER
ISLETS	OSMIUM	ESPRIT	STEALS	ATHENA	ETCHES
ISSEIS	OSSIAN	ESTRAY	STEAMS	ATHENE	ITCHED
OSBERT	OSSIFY	ESTRUS	STEAMY	ATHENS	ITCHES
OSIERS	TSHIRT	ISTRIA	STOATS	ATREUS	UTAHAN
OSSEIN	******	OSIRIS	STRAFE	ATTEND	******
OSTEAL	**-S-L--**	OSPREY	STRAIN	ATTEST	**-T-I--**
OSTEND	******	USURER	STRAIT	ETHELS	******
OSWEGO	ASHLAR	USURPS	STRAKE	ETHERS	ATRIAL
USHERS	ASHLEY	******	STRAND	ITSELF	ATRIUM
******	ASYLUM	**-S-T--**	STRAPS	OTHERS	ATTICA
-S-F--	ISOLDE	******	STRASS	OTTERS	ATTICS
******	OSTLER	ISATIN	STRATA	STEEDS	ATTILA
USEFUL	PSALMS	ISHTAR	STRATH	STEELS	ATTIRE
******	******	TSETSE	STRATI	STEELY	ETHICS
-S-G--	**-S-M--**	******	STRAWS	STEEPS	STAINS
******	******	**-S-U--**	STRAWY	STEERS	STAIRS
ISOGON	ASHMAN	******	STRAYS	STEEVE	STAITH
USAGES	ASHMEN	ASBURY	STUART	STHENO	STEINS
******	ASIMOV	ASSUME	UTGARD	STREAK	STOICS
-S-H--	ISOMER	ASSURE	******	STREAM	STRIAE
******	******	ASTUTE	**-T-B--**	STREET	STRICK
ASTHMA	**-S-N--**	ESCUDO	******	STRESS	STRICT
ESCHAR	******	ISEULT	ATABAL	STREWN	STRIDE
ESCHER	USANCE	ISSUED	STABLE	STREWS	STRIFE
ESCHEW	******	ISSUER	STABLY	UTTERS	STRIKE
ESTHER	**-S-O--**	ISSUES	STUBBS	******	STRING
ISCHIA	ASCOTS	OSCULE	STUBBY	**-T-F--**	STRIPE
ISOHEL	ASHORE	OSMUND	******	******	STRIPS
	ASLOPE	PSEUDO	**-T-C--**	STAFFS	STRIPT
			STACIE	STEFAN	STRIPY
			STACKS		

STRIVE	******	STOOPS	STIRKS	STRUNG	HUMANE
STYING	-T-M--	STROBE	STIRPS	STRUTS	HUMANS
******	******	STRODE	STORAX	******	JUDAEA
-T-K--	ATAMAN	STROKE	STORED	-T-V--	JUDAEO
******	ATOMIC	STROLL	STORES	******	JUDAHS
STAKED	ETYMON	STROMA	STOREY	ATAVIC	JUDAIC
STAKES	STAMEN	STRONG	STORKS	STAVED	JUGATE
STOKED	STAMIN	STROPS	STORMS	STAVES	JURANT
STOKER	STAMPS	STROUD	STORMY	STEVEN	JURATS
STOKES	STOMAT	STROVE	STURDY	STEVES	KULAKS
******	STOMPS	UTMOST	UTERUS	STEVIE	KUWAIT
-T-L--	STUMPS	******	UTURNS	STIVER	LUNACY
******	STUMPY	-T-P--	YTTRIA	STOVER	LUNATE
ATOLLS	STYMIE	******	YTTRIC	STOVES	LUXATE
ATTLEE	******	ETAPES	******	******	MURALS
ITALIC	-T-N--	STAPES	-T-S--	-T-W--	MUTANT
STALAG	******	STAPLE	******	******	MUTATE
STALED	ATONAL	STEPAN	PTISAN	STEWED	PUPATE
STALER	ATONED	STEPIN	PTOSIS	STOWED	PURANA
STALES	ATONER	STEPPE	STASES	******	QUEANS
STALIN	ATONES	STEPUP	STASIS	-T-X--	QUEASY
STALKS	ATONIC	STIPEL	******	******	RUBACE
STALKY	ETHNIC	STIPES	-T-T--	ATAXIA	RUBATO
STALLS	STANCE	STOPED	******	ATAXIC	RUGATE
STELAE	STANCH	STOPES	OTITIS	******	SUBAHS
STELAR	STANDS	STUPAS	STATAL	-T-Y--	SUDARY
STELES	STANZA	STUPES	STATED	******	SUGARS
STELIC	STENCH	STUPID	STATEN	ETHYLS	SUGARY
STELLA	STENOG	STUPOR	STATER	STAYED	SUMACS
STELLI	STINGS	UTOPIA	STATES	STAYER	SURAHS
STILES	STINGY	******	STATIC	******	SUSANS
STILLS	STINKS	-T-R--	STATOR	-U-A--	TUBATE
STILLY	STINTS	******	STATUE	******	TULADI
STILTS	STONED	ETERNA	STATUS	AUBADE	******
STOLED	STONER	STARCH	STETHO	AUDADS	-U-B--
STOLEN	STONES	STARED	STITCH	AURATE	******
STOLES	STUNTS	STARER	STITHY	BUBALS	BUBBLE
STOLID	******	STARES	XTSTUS	BURANS	BUBBLY
STOLON	-T-O--	STARRY	******	BUTANE	BULBAR
STULLS	******	STARTS	-T-U--	CUBAGE	BULBED
STYLAR	ATHOME	STARVE	******	CUBANS	BULBEL
STYLED	ATTORN	STEREO	ATTUNE	CURACY	BULBIL
STYLER	ITIOUS	STERES	STAURO	CURARE	BULBUL
STYLES	OTIOSE	STERIC	STOUPS	CURATE	BUMBLE
STYLET	OTTOWA	STERNA	STOUTS	DUCATS	BURBLE
STYLUS	STOOGE	STERNO	STRUCK	FUSAIN	BURBOT
	STOOKS	STEROL	STRUMA	GUIANA	CUBBED
	STOOLS		STRUMS	GUYANA	CUMBER

CURBED	BUNCHY	FUDDLE	CUPELS	SUPERB	SULFUR
DUBBED	BUNCOS	FUNDED	CURERS	SUPERS	SURFED
DUBBIN	CUSCUS	FUNDUS	CUTELY	SURELY	SURFER
DUMBLY	DULCET	GUIDED	CUTEST	SUREST	TUFFET
DUNBAR	DULCIE	GUIDER	CUTEYS	SURETY	TURFED
DURBAN	DUNCAN	GUIDES	DUDEEN	TUBERS	******
DURBAR	DUNCES	GUIDON	DUPERS	TUMEFY	-U-G--
FUMBLE	FULCRA	GULDEN	DUPERY	TUNERS	******
GUMBOS	GUACOS	HUDDLE	DURESS	TUNEUP	BUDGED
HUBBUB	HUBCAP	HURDLE	EUGENE	TUPELO	BUDGES
HUMBER	JUICER	MUDDED	EUREKA	TUREEN	BUDGET
HUMBLE	JUICES	MUDDER	FUNEST	TUXEDO	BUDGIE
HUMBLY	JUNCOS	MUDDLE	FUSEES	TUYERE	BUGGED
HUMBUG	MUDCAP	MURDER	FUZEES	******	BUGGER
JUBBAH	MULCTS	OUTDID	HUBERT	-U-F--	BULGAR
JUMBAL	MUSCAE	PUDDLE	HUGELY	******	BULGED
JUMBLE	MUSCAT	PUDDLY	HUGEST	BUFFED	BULGER
LUBBER	MUSCLE	PUNDIT	JUDEAN	BUFFER	BULGES
LUMBAR	NUNCIO	PURDAH	JULEPS	BUFFET	BUNGED
LUMBER	OUNCES	QUADRI	JUNEAU	CUFFED	BUNGLE
MUMBLE	OUTCRY	RUDDER	JURELS	CUPFUL	BURGEE
NUBBIN	PUNCHY	RUDDLE	LUBECK	CURFEW	BURGER
NUBBLE	QUACKS	RUNDLE	LUCENT	DUFFED	BURGHS
NUBBLY	SUCCOR	SUBDEB	LUGERS	DUFFEL	BURGLE
NUMBED	SULCUS	SUBDUE	LUMENS	DUFFER	BURGOO
NUMBER	TURCOS	SUDDEN	LUNETS	DUFFLE	BURGOS
NUMBLY	TUSCAN	SUEDES	LURERS	FULFIL	CUDGEL
OUTBID	VULCAN	SUNDAE	LUTEAL	FURFUR	DUNGED
PUEBLO	YUCCAS	SUNDAY	LUTEUM	GUFFAW	FUDGED
QUEBEC	******	SUNDER	MUSEUM	GULFED	FUDGES
RUBBED	-U-D--	SUNDEW	NUDELY	HUFFED	FULGID
RUBBER	******	SUNDOG	OUSELS	JUGFUL	FUNGAL
RUBBLE		SUNDRY	OUTERS	LUFFED	FUNGUS
RUMBAS	BUDDED	TUNDRA	OUZELS	MUFFED	GURGLE
RUMBLE	BUDDER	ZUIDER	PULERS	MUFFIN	HUGGED
SUABLE	BUDDHA	ZUYDER	PUREED	MUFFLE	HUNGER
SUNBOW	BUDDLE	******	PUREES	OUTFIT	HUNGRY
TUBBED	BUNDLE	-U-E--	PURELY	OUTFOX	JUDGED
TUBBER	BURDEN	******	PUREST	PUFFED	JUDGER
TUMBLE	BURDIE	AUGEAN	QUAERE	PUFFER	JUDGES
TURBAN	CUDDIE	AUGEND	QUEENS	PUFFIN	JUGGED
TURBID	CUDDLE	AUGERS	QUEERS	PURFLE	JUGGLE
TURBIT	CUDDLY	AUREUS	RUBENS	QUAFFS	JUNGLE
TURBOT	CURDED	BUREAU	RUDELY	RUEFUL	JUNGLY
******	CURDLE	BUYERS	RUDEST	RUFFED	LUGGED
-U-C--	DUMDUM	CUBEBS	RULERS	RUFFLE	LUGGER
******	DUNDEE	CULETS	RUPEES	SUFFER	LUNGED
BUCCAL	DUODEN	CUNEAL	RUPERT	SUFFIX	LUNGEE
BUNCHE					

LUNGER	HUSHES	CUBITS	LUCIUS	RUTILE	JUNKET
LUNGES	KUCHEN	CUMINS	LUMINA	SUBITO	JUNKIE
LUNGIS	LUSHED	CURIAE	LUMINI	SUFISM	LUNKER
MUGGAR	LUSHER	CURIAL	LUMINO	SUPINE	LURKED
MUGGED	LUSHES	CURIES	LUPINE	SUSIES	LURKER
MUGGER	LUTHER	CURING	LURING	TUBING	MUCKED
MUGGUR	MUSHED	CURIOS	LUTING	TULIPS	MUCKER
NUDGED	MUSHER	CURIUM	LUTIST	TUNICA	MUCKLE
NUDGES	MUSHES	CUTIES	MULISH	TUNICS	MUSKEG
NUGGET	MUZHIK	CUTINS	MUNICH	TUNING	MUSKET
PUGGED	NUCHAE	DUDISH	MURIEL	TUPIKS	MUSKIT
PUGGRY	PUSHED	DUPING	MURINE	ZURICH	MUSKOX
PURGED	PUSHER	DURIAN	MUSING	******	PUCKER
PURGER	PUSHES	DURING	MUTING	-U-J--	PUNKAS
PURGES	PUSHTU	DURION	MUTINY	******	QUAKED
QUAGGA	PUSHUP	DUTIES	MUTISM	PUNJAB	QUAKER
QUAGGY	QUAHOG	EUNICE	NUBIAN	******	QUAKES
RUGGED	RUCHES	EURIPI	NUBIAS	-U-K--	RUCKED
RUGGER	RUSHED	FUGIOS	NUBILE	******	RUCKUS
SUNGOD	RUSHER	FUMIER	NUDISM	BUCKED	RUSKIN
SURGED	RUSHES	FUMING	NUDIST	BUCKER	SUCKED
SURGER	SUNHAT	FURIES	NUDITY	BUCKET	SUCKER
SURGES	TUCHUN	FUSILE	NUMINA	BUCKLE	SUCKLE
TUGGED	TUSHED	FUSILS	OUTING	BUCKRA	SULKED
TUNGUS	TUSHES	FUSING	PUKING	BULKED	SUNKEN
TURGID	******	FUSION	PULING	BUMKIN	TUCKED
VULGAR	-U-I--	FUTILE	PUMICE	BUNKED	TUCKER
******	******	FUZILS	PUNIER	BUNKER	TUCKET
-U-H--	AUDILE	FUZING	PUNILY	BUNKUM	TURKEY
******	AUDITS	GUYING	PUNISH	BURKED	TURKIC
AUGHTS	AUGITE	HUMIFY	PUPILS	BURKES	TURKIS
AUTHOR	AURIGA	JUDITH	PURIFY	BUSKER	TUSKED
BUCHAN	AURIST	JULIAN	PURINE	BUSKIN	TUSKER
BUSHED	AUTISM	JULIAS	PURISM	CUCKOO	YUKKED
BUSHEL	AUXINS	JULIES	PURIST	DUCKED	******
BUSHES	BUNION	JULIET	PURITY	DUCKER	-U-L--
BUSHEY	BURIAL	JULIUS	QUAILS	DUIKER	******
CUSHAT	BURIED	JUNIOR	QUAINT	DUNKED	AUKLET
CUSHAW	BURIES	JUNIUS	QUOINS	DUNKER	BUGLED
DURHAM	BURINS	JURIES	QUOITS	DUSKED	BUGLER
EUCHER	BUSIED	JURIST	RUBIES	FUNKED	BUGLES
EUCHRE	BUSIES	JUTISH	RUBIGO	GURKHA	BUILDS
GUSHED	BUSILY	KUMISS	RUEING	HUCKLE	BULLAE
GUSHER	BUSING	LUCIAN	RULING	HULKED	BULLET
GUSHES	BUYING	LUCIAS	RUMINA	HUSKED	BURLAP
HUGHES	CUBING	LUCIEN	RUNINS	HUSKER	BURLED
HUGHIE	CUBISM	LUCILE	RUPIAH	JUNKED	BURLER
HUSHED	CUBIST	LUCITE	RUSINE	JUNKER	BURLEY

BUTLER	LULLED	FULMAR	PUTNAM	JUPONS	PULPIT
CULLAY	MUKLUK	GUIMPE	QUANTA	JURORS	PUMPED
CULLED	MULLAH	GUMMAS	QUANTS	MUCOID	PUMPER
CULLER	MULLED	GUMMED	QUENCH	MUCOSA	PUPPED
CULLET	MULLEN	GUNMAN	QUINCE	MUCOSE	PUPPET
CULLIS	MULLER	GUNMEN	QUINCY	MUCOUS	PURPLE
CURLED	MULLET	HUMMED	QUINIC	PUTOFF	PUTPUT
CURLER	MULLEY	HUMMER	QUINSY	PUTONS	QUAPAW
CURLEW	MUSLIM	KUMMEL	QUINTS	PUTOUT	QUIPUS
CUTLAS	MUSLIN	LUMMOX	RUINED	RUFOUS	RUMPLE
CUTLER	NUCLEI	MUMMED	RUINER	RUGOSE	RUMPUS
CUTLET	NULLAH	MUMMER	RUNNEL	RUGOUS	SULPHA
DUBLIN	NUTLET	MURMUR	RUNNER	RUMORS	SULPHO
DUDLEY	OUTLAW	MUUMUU	SUMNER	RUMOUR	SUPPED
DUELED	OUTLAY	NUTMEG	SUNNAH	RUNOFF	SUPPER
DUELER	OUTLET	OUTMAN	SUNNED	RUNONS	SUPPLE
DUELLO	PUBLIC	PUMMEL	TUNNED	RUNOUT	SUPPLY
DULLED	PULLED	RUMMER	TUNNEL	SUBORN	TUPPED
DULLER	PULLER	SUBMIT	TURNED	TUMORS	YUPPIE
DULLES	PULLET	SUMMED	TURNER	TUMOUR	******
DUNLIN	PULLEY	SUMMER	TURNIP	TUTORS	-U-Q--
DUOLOG	PULLIN	SUMMIT	TURNUP	YUPONS	******
DUPLET	PURLED	SUMMON	******	******	PULQUE
DUPLEX	PURLER	SUOMIC	-U-O--	-U-P--	******
EUCLID	PURLIN	******	******	******	******
FUELED	PUTLOG	-U-N--	AURORA	AUSPEX	-U-R--
FUELER	QUALMS	******	AUROUS	BUMPED	******
FUGLED	QUALMY	BURNED	AUTOED	BUMPER	AUBREY
FUGLES	QUELLS	BURNER	BUBOES	BURPED	AUDREY
FULLED	QUILLS	BURNET	CUBOID	CUPPED	BURRED
FULLER	QUILTS	CUNNER	CUPOLA	CUPPER	BURROS
FURLED	RUBLES	DUENNA	CUTOFF	CUSPED	BURROW
GUILDS	RUNLET	DUNNED	CUTOUT	CUSPID	CUPRIC
GUILES	SUBLET	EUPNEA	DUGONG	CUSPIS	CUPRUM
GUILTS	SULLEN	FUNNEL	DUGOUT	DUMPED	FUHRER
GUILTY	SUNLIT	GUANIN	EUBOEA	DUMPER	FURRED
GULLAH	SUSLIK	GUANOS	EUDOAR	DUMPTY	FURROW
GULLED	SUTLER	GUENON	EULOGY	GULPED	GUARDS
GULLET	TUILLE	GUINEA	EUROPA	GULPER	HUBRIS
HUELVA	TULLES	GUNNAR	EUROPE	HUMPED	HURRAH
HULLED	******	GUNNED	FUCOID	HUMPTY	HURRAY
HURLED	-U-M--	GUNNEL	FUCOUS	JUMPED	JUAREZ
HURLER	******	GUNNER	FUMOUS	JUMPER	MURRAY
HURLEY	BUMMED	LUANDA	FURORE	LUMPED	MURRES
HUXLEY	BUMMER	NUANCE	FURORS	LUMPEN	MURREY
LUBLIN	BUSMAN	NUDNIK	HUMORS	OUTPUT	NUTRIA
LUDLOW	BUSMEN	PUNNED	HUMOUR	PULPED	OUTRAN
LUELLA	CULMED	PUNNER	HURONS	PULPER	PUGREE

PURRED	HUSSAR	BUSTLE	MUSTER	AUTUMN	BUOYED
PUTRID	MUSSED	BUTTED	MUSTNT	CUPULE	RUNYON
QUARKS	MUSSEL	BUTTER	MUTTER	CURULE	******
QUARRY	MUSSES	BUTTES	MUTTON	CUTUPS	-U-Z--
QUARTE	NURSED	BUTTON	NUTTED	DULUTH	******
QUARTO	NURSER	BUXTON	NUTTER	EUNUCH	BUZZED
QUARTS	NURSES	CULTCH	OUSTED	FUGUES	BUZZER
QUARTZ	OUTSAT	CULTUS	OUSTER	FUTURE	BUZZES
QUERNS	OUTSET	CUPTIE	PUNTED	JUJUBE	FURZES
QUIRED	OUTSIT	CURTIS	PUNTER	LUNULA	FUZZED
QUIRES	PUISNE	CURTLY	PUNTOS	LUNULE	FUZZES
QUIRKS	PULSAR	CURTSY	PUTTED	LUXURY	GUZZLE
QUIRTS	PULSED	CUSTER	PUTTEE	MUTUAL	MUZZLE
QUORUM	PULSES	CUSTOM	PUTTER	MUTULE	NUZZLE
RUBRIC	PURSED	CUSTOS	QUATRE	QUEUED	PUZZLE
SUCRES	PURSER	CUTTER	QUITCH	QUEUES	QUEZON
SURREY	PURSES	CUTTLE	QUOTAS	SUBURB	******
SUTRAS	PURSUE	DUSTED	QUOTED	SUNUPS	-V-A--
TURRET	PUSSES	DUSTER	QUOTER	SUTURE	******
******	PUSSEY	FULTON	QUOTES	TUBULE	AVIARY
-U-S--	PUSSLY	FUSTIC	QUOTHA	TUMULT	AVIATE
******	PUTSCH	GUITAR	RUSTED	TUQUES	******
BUNSEN	QUASAR	GUNTER	RUSTIC	******	-V-B--
BURSAE	QUESTS	GUSTAF	RUSTLE	-U-V--	******
BURSAL	RUSSET	GUSTAV	RUTTED	******	OVIBOS
BURSAR	RUSSIA	GUTTAE	SUBTER	CULVER	******
BURSAS	SUNSET	GUTTAT	SUBTLE	CURVED	-V-C--
BURSES	SUSSED	GUTTED	SUBTLY	CURVES	******
BURSTS	SUSSEX	GUTTER	SUITED	CURVET	AVOCET
BUSSED	TUCSON	GUTTLE	SUITES	GUAVAS	EVICTS
BUSSES	TUSSAH	HUNTED	SUITOR	PURVEY	******
CUESTA	TUSSAL	HUNTER	SULTAN	QUAVER	-V-D--
CUISSE	TUSSAR	HURTER	SULTRY	QUIVER	******
CURSED	TUSSIS	HURTLE	SUNTAN	SURVEY	AVIDIN
CURSES	TUSSLE	HUSTLE	SURTAX	TURVES	AVIDLY
CURSOR	******	HUTTED	SUTTEE	VULVAE	EVADED
CUSSED	-U-T--	JUNTAS	SUTTON	VULVAL	EVADER
CUSSES	******	JUSTIN	TUFTED	VULVAR	EVADES
CUSSOS	AUNTIE	JUSTLY	TURTLE	******	******
FUSSED	AUSTEN	JUSTUS	TUTTED	-U-W--	-V-I--
FUSSER	AUSTER	JUTTED	TUTTIS	******	******
FUSSES	AUSTIN	KULTUR	******	LUDWIG	AVAILS
GUESTS	AUSTRO	LUETIC	-U-U--	OUTWIT	AVOIDS
GUISES	BUNTED	LUSTED	******	RUNWAY	******
GUNSHY	BURTON	LUSTER	AUBURN	SUBWAY	-V-K--
GUSSET	BUSTED	LUSTRE	AUGURS	******	******
GUSSIE	BUSTER	MUFTIS	AUGURY	-U-Y--	EVOKED
HUDSON	BUSTIC	MUSTEE	AUGUST	******	EVOKES
				BUNYAN	
				BUNYIP	

*****	*****	*****	RWANDA	*****	EXCELS
-V-L--	**-V-U--**	**-W-G--**	SWANEE	**-W-T--**	EXCEPT
*****	*****	*****	SWANKY	*****	EXCESS
AVALON	AVAUNT	DWIGHT	SWINGE	SWATCH	EXPECT
EVELYN	AVOUCH	SWAGED	SWINGS	SWATHE	EXPELS
EVILLY	*****	SWAGES	TWANGS	SWATHS	EXPEND
EVOLVE	**-V-W--**	TWIGGY	TWANGY	SWITCH	EXPERT
OVALLY	*****	*****	TWENTY	TWITCH	EXSECT
OVULAR	AVOWAL	**-W-I--**	TWINED	*****	EXSERT
OVULES	AVOWED	*****	TWINER	**-W-U--**	EXTEND
SVELTE	AVOWER	AWAITS	TWINES	*****	EXTENT
UVULAE	*****	AWEIGH	TWINGE	TWOULD	EXTERN
UVULAR	**-W-A--**	AWEING	*****	*****	*****
UVULAS	*****	AWHILE	**-W-O--**	**-W-V--**	**-X-G--**
*****	AWEARY	AWHIRL	*****	*****	*****
-V-N--	SWEARS	AWNING	SWOONS	SWIVEL	EXOGEN
*****	SWEATS	OWLISH	SWOOPS	SWIVET	OXYGEN
AVENGE	SWEATY	OWNING	*****	*****	*****
AVENUE	TWEAKS	SWAILS	**-W-P--**	**-W-W--**	**-X-I--**
EVENED	TWEAKY	SWAINS	*****	TWOWAY	AXLIKE
EVENLY	*****	*****	SWIPED	*****	EXCIDE
EVENTS	**-W-B--**	**-W-K--**	SWIPES	**-W-Y--**	EXCISE
EVINCE	*****	*****	SWIPLE	*****	EXCITE
YVONNE	TWIBIL	AWAKED	TWOPLY	SWAYED	EXPIRE
*****	TWOBIT	AWAKEN	*****	*****	EXPIRY
-V-R--	*****	AWAKES	**-X-A--**	*****	OXHIDE
*****	**-W-D--**	AWOKEN	*****	EXHALE	OXLIPS
AVERNO	*****	*****	**-W-R--**	EXPAND	*****
AVERSE	SWEDEN	**-W-L--**	*****	EXTANT	**-X-L--**
AVERTS	SWEDES	*****	AWARDS	OXTAIL	*****
AVERYS	*****	DWELLS	DWARFS	*****	AXILLA
DVORAK	**-W-E--**	SWALES	SWARAJ	**-X-C--**	EXALTS
EVERET	*****	SWELLS	SWARDS	*****	EXILED
EVERTS	AWHEEL	SWILLS	SWARMS	EXACTA	EXILES
OVERDO	AWLESS	TWELVE	SWARTH	EXACTS	EXILIC
OVERLY	OWLETS	TWILIT	SWARTY	*****	EXULTS
*****	OWNERS	TWILLS	SWERVE	**-X-D--**	OXALIC
-V-S--	SWEENY	*****	SWIRLS	*****	OXALIS
*****	SWEEPS	**-W-M--**	SWIRLY	EXEDRA	*****
AVESTA	SWEEPY	*****	SWORDS	EXODUS	**-X-M--**
AVISOS	SWEETS	SWAMIS	TWERPS	EXUDED	*****
AVOSET	TWEEDS	SWAMPS	TWIRLS	EXUDES	AXEMAN
OVISAC	TWEETS	SWAMPY	TWIRPS	OXIDES	AXEMEN
*****	*****	*****	*****	*****	EXAMEN
-V-T--	**-W-F--**	**-W-N--**	**-W-S--**	**-X-E--**	EXEMPT
*****	*****	*****	*****	*****	*****
AVATAR	SWIFTS	GWENNS	TWISTS	AXSEED	**-X-N--**
EVITAS	TWOFER	GWYNNE	TWISTY	EXCEED	AXONES

******
-X-O--
******
AXIOMS
EXHORT
EXMOOR
EXPORT
EXPOSE
EXTOLS
EXTORT
OXBOWS
OXFORD
******
-X-Q--
******
EXEQUY
******
-X-R--
******
EXARCH
EXERTS
EXTRAS
EXURBS
******
-X-S--
******
EXISTS
******
-X-T--
******
EXETER
EXITED
EXOTIC
******
-X-U--
******
EXCUSE
EXEUNT
EXHUME
******
-X-Y--
******
OXEYED
OXEYES
******
-Y-A--
******
AYEAYE
AYMARA

BYLANE
BYLAWS
BYNAME
BYPASS
BYPAST
BYPATH
BYTALK
BYWAYS
CYCADS
CYMARS
CYRANO
DYNAMO
DYNAST
GYRATE
PYJAMA
PYRANS
TYBALT
TYRANT
XYLANS
******
-Y-B--
******
BYEBYE
CYMBAL
DYBBUK
SYMBOL
******
-Y-C--
******
EYECUP
******
-Y-D--
******
DYADIC
HYADES
SYNDET
SYNDIC
******
-Y-E--
******
CYBELE
CYMENE
CYRENE
GYNECO
HYGEIA
HYMENO
HYMENS
LYCEES

LYCEUM
MYCETE
MYSELF
PYRENE
SYCEES
WYVERN
XYLEMS
XYLENE
******
-Y-F--
******
EYEFUL
FYLFOT
******
-Y-H--
******
CYPHER
HYPHAE
HYPHAL
HYPHEN
MYTHIC
MYTHOI
MYTHOS
PYTHIA
PYTHIC
PYTHON
SYPHER
SYPHON
TYPHLO
TYPHON
TYPHUS
******
-Y-I--
******
BYLINE
CYNICS
CYRILS
DYEING
EYEING
EYRIES
GYBING
GYVING
HYOIDS
LYDIAS
LYRICS
LYRISM
LYRIST
LYSINE

LYSING
LYSINS
MYRIAD
MYRICA
PYRITE
PYXIES
SYBILS
SYRIAC
SYRIAN
SYRINX
TYPIFY
TYPING
TYPIST
TYRIAN
XYLITE
******
-Y-K--
******
RYUKYU
-Y-L--
******
BYBLOW
BYPLAY
CYCLED
CYCLER
CYCLES
CYCLIC
CYMLIN
EYELET
EYELID
MYELIN
******
-Y-M--
******
MYRMEC
PYEMIA
PYEMIC
******
-Y-N--
******
CYANIC
CYANID
CYANIN
CYGNET
CYGNUS
HYENAS
HYMNAL

HYMNED
HYMNIC
HYPNIC
HYPNOS
MYRNAS
PYKNIC
SYDNEY
VYRNWY
******
-Y-O--
******
BYGONE
BYROAD
BYWORD
BYWORK
CYMOID
CYMOSE
CYMOUS
EYEOUT
GYNOUS
GYRONS
GYROSE
MYXOMA
NYLONS
PYLONS
PYRONE
PYROPE
SYNODS
TYCOON
TYRONE
XYLOID
XYLOLS
XYLOSE
ZYGOMA
ZYGOTE
******
-Y-P--
******
GYPPED
LYMPHO
MYOPES
MYOPIA
MYOPIC
NYMPHA
NYMPHO
NYMPHS
SYLPHS

SYLPHY
TYMPAN
******
-Y-R--
******
CYMRIC
CYPRIN
CYPRUS
HYBRID
HYBRIS
HYDRAE
HYDRAS
HYDRIC
HYDROS
PYRRHA
PYURIA
******
-Y-S--
******
AYESHA
BYSSUS
EYASES
GYPSUM
HYSSOP
KYUSHU
MYOSIN
MYOSIS
PYOSIS
******
-Y-T--
******
CYSTIC
HYETAL
HYSTER
LYTTAE
MYRTLE
MYSTIC
OYSTER
SYNTAX
SYSTEM
WYSTAN
XYSTER
XYSTOS
******
-Y-U--
******
SYNURA
SYRUPS
SYRUPY

******	******	CARPAL	HANNAH	MANUAL	SABRAS
-Y-V--	-Z-Z--	CASBAH	HANNAS	MARGAY	SACRAL
******	******	CASHAW	HARLAN	MARIAN	SAGGAR
SYLVAE	AZAZEL	CASPAR	HARTAL	MARIAS	SAIGAS
SYLVAN	******	CASUAL	HAWHAW	MARTAS	SAIPAN
SYLVAS	-A--A-	CATHAY	HAZZAN	MAUMAU	SALAAM
SYLVIA	******	CATNAP	JACKAL	MAYDAY	SALPAS
******	BADMAN	CAUDAD	JAGUAR	MAYHAP	SAMBAS
-Y-X--	BAGDAD	CAUDAL	JAINAS	NARIAL	SAMIAN
******	BAGMAN	CAUSAL	JAMJAR	NARWAL	SAMOAN
LYNXES	BAIKAL	CAVEAT	KAFTAN	NASIAL	SAMPAN
******	BALAAM	CAVIAR	KALIAN	NASSAU	SANDAL
-Y-Y--	BALKAN	CAYMAN	KALPAK	NATHAN	SANGAR
******	BALLAD	DACHAS	KANSAN	PALEAE	SANJAK
SYZYGY	BALSAM	DACHAU	KANSAS	PALLAS	SANSAR
******	BALSAS	DAEDAL	KAPPAS	PALMAR	SAPHAR
-Z-A--	BALZAC	DAGMAR	KARMAS	PAMPAS	SARSAR
******	BANIAN	DALLAS	KARNAK	PANDAS	SASHAY
AZRAEL	BANTAM	DAMMAR	LABIAL	PAPUAN	SATRAP
******	BANYAN	DARDAN	LACIAL	PARCAE	SAUNAS
-Z-E--	BANZAI	EARLAP	LACTAM	PARIAH	TAIGAS
******	BAOBAB	EARWAX	LAMIAE	PARIAN	TAIWAN
AZTECS	BARMAN	FABIAN	LAMIAS	PARKAS	TAMBAC
******	BASHAW	FACIAL	LAMMAS	PARLAY	TAMPAN
-Z-I--	BASRAH	FAECAL	LAMPAD	PARRAL	TAMTAM
******	BATAAN	FALLAL	LAMPAS	PASCAL	TANKAS
UZZIAH	BATEAU	FANGAS	LANDAU	PASHAS	TARMAC
******	BATMAN	FANTAN	LARIAT	PASTAS	TARNAL
-Z-L--	BAZAAR	FARBAD	LARVAE	PATHAN	TARPAN
******	CABMAN	FAUCAL	LARVAL	PAULAS	TARSAL
AZALEA	CAESAR	FAUNAE	LASCAR	PAWPAW	TARTAN
AZOLES	CAFTAN	FAUNAL	LAURAE	PAXWAX	TARTAR
******	CAIMAN	FAUNAS	LAURAS	PAYDAY	TARZAN
-Z-N--	CALCAR	GALEAE	LAYDAY	RACIAL	TASMAN
******	CALLAO	GALWAY	LAYMAN	RADIAL	TAZZAS
AZINES	CALLAS	GALYAK	MADCAP	RADIAN	VALVAL
AZONIC	CALPAC	GAMMAS	MADMAN	RAGBAG	VALVAR
OZONIC	CANAAN	GASBAG	MADRAS	RAGDAY	VANDAL
******	CANCAN	GASMAN	MAENAD	RAGLAN	VANMAN
-Z-R--	CANNAE	GASPAR	MAGYAR	RAGMAN	VASSAL
******	CANNAS	GATEAU	MAMBAS	RAGTAG	WALLAH
AZORES	CANTAB	GAVIAL	MAMMAE	RANDAL	WALLAS
AZURES	CANVAS	HABEAS	MAMMAL	RANDAN	WANDAS
******	CAPIAS	HAEMAL	MAMMAS	RAPHAE	WARSAW
-Z-T--	CARFAX	HALLAH	MANDAN	RASCAL	WAYLAY
******	CARLAS	HAMMAL	MANIAC	RATTAN	YASMAK
AZOTIC	CARMAN	HAMZAS	MANIAS	SABBAT	ZAFFAR
	CARNAL	HANGAR	MANTAS	SABEAN	ZAMIAS

******	******	BALEEN	CABLED	CARMEN	DANGED
-A--B-	-A--D-	BALKED	CABLES	CARPED	DANGER
******	******	BALLED	CABLET	CARPEL	DANIEL
CABOBS	CANADA	BALLET	CABMEN	CARPER	DANKER
CALEBS	DAVIDS	BANDED	CACHED	CARPET	DAPPED
CARIBE	FACADE	BANGED	CACHES	CARREL	DAPPER
CARIBS	FARADS	BANKED	CACHET	CARTED	DARIEN
CAROBS	HAIRDO	BANKER	CADGED	CARTEL	DARKEN
CASABA	HALIDE	BANNED	CADGER	CARTER	DARKER
DAGOBA	HALIDS	BANNER	CADGES	CARTES	DARNED
DANUBE	LAIRDS	BANTER	CADRES	CARVED	DARNEL
GAZABO	LAMBDA	BARBED	CAGIER	CARVEL	DARNER
GAZEBO	LAMEDS	BARBEL	CAHIER	CARVEN	DARTED
JACOBS	LAREDO	BARBER	CALCES	CARVER	DARTER
KABOBS	MALADY	BARBET	CALKED	CARVES	DASHED
LAVABO	MAUNDS	BARDED	CALKER	CASHED	DASHER
NABOBS	MAUNDY	BARDES	CALLED	CASHES	DASHES
NAWABS	NAIADS	BARGED	CALLER	CASHEW	DAUBED
RAJABS	PAGODA	BARGEE	CALMED	CASKET	DAUBER
SAHEBS	PANADA	BARGES	CALMER	CASPER	DAUDET
SAHIBS	PARADE	BARKED	CALVED	CASTER	DAVIES
WAHABI	PARODY	BARKER	CALVES	CASTES	DAWNED
ZARIBA	RAPIDS	BARLEY	CALXES	CATHER	DAYBED
******	SALADS	BARMEN	CAMBER	CATTED	EAGLES
-A--C-	XANADU	BARNEY	CAMDEN	CAUDEX	EAGLET
******	******	BARRED	CAMLET	CAULES	EARLES
BARUCH	-A--E-	BARREL	CAMPED	CAUSED	EARNED
BASICS	******	BARREN	CAMPER	CAUSER	EARNER
CALICO	AACHEN	BARRET	CANCEL	CAUSES	EASIER
CANUCK	BABIED	BARTER	CANCER	CAUTER	EASTER
CARACK	BABIES	BARYES	CANKER	CAVIES	FABLED
DARICS	BACHED	BASHED	CANNED	DABBED	FABLER
GALACT	BACHES	BASHES	CANNEL	DABBER	FABLES
HAUNCH	BACKED	BASKED	CANNER	DADOES	FACIES
JANICE	BACKER	BASKET	CANNES	DAGGER	FAECES
LAMECH	BADGED	BASSES	CANOED	DAISES	FAGGED
LAUNCE	BADGER	BASSET	CANOES	DALLES	FAILED
LAUNCH	BADGES	BASTED	CANTED	DAMMED	FAIRED
MACACO	BADMEN	BASTES	CANTER	DAMMER	FAIRER
MALACO	BAFFED	BATHED	CAPPED	DAMNED	FALLEN
MALICE	BAGGED	BATHER	CAPPER	DAMPED	FALLER
MARACA	BAGMEN	BATMEN	CARCEL	DAMPEN	FALSER
NAUTCH	BAILED	BATTED	CARDED	DAMPER	FALTER
PALACE	BAILEE	BATTEN	CARDER	DAMSEL	FANGED
PANICE	BAILER	BATTER	CAREEN	DANCED	FANJET
PANICS	BAILEY	BAWLED	CAREER	DANCER	FANNED
PAPACY	BAITED	BAWLER	CARIES	DANCES	FANNER
PAUNCH	BALDER	BAXTER	CARMEL	DANDER	FARCED

FARCER	GARBED	HANGER	JAYVEE	LASHER	MAPPED
FARCES	GARDEN	HANKER	JAZZED	LASHES	MARCEL
FARLES	GARGET	HANSEL	JAZZER	LASSEN	MARGES
FARLEY	GARNER	HAPPED	JAZZES	LASSES	MARIES
FARMED	GARNET	HAPPEN	KAASES	LASTED	MARKED
FARMER	GARRET	HARDEN	KAISER	LASTER	MARKER
FASCES	GARTER	HARDER	KASPER	LASTEX	MARKET
FASTED	GASHED	HARKED	KATIES	LATEEN	MARLED
FASTEN	GASHES	HARKEN	KAYOED	LATHED	MARRED
FASTER	GASJET	HARLEM	LAAGER	LATHER	MARRER
FATHER	GASKET	HARLEY	LABRET	LATHES	MARTEN
FATTED	GASMEN	HARMED	LACHES	LATTEN	MARVEL
FATTEN	GASPED	HARPED	LACIER	LATTER	MASHED
FATTER	GASPER	HARPER	LACKED	LAUDED	MASHER
FAUCES	GASSED	HARVEY	LACKEY	LAUDER	MASHES
FAUCET	GASSES	HASHED	LADDER	LAUREL	MASKED
FAUVES	GATHER	HASHES	LADIES	LAWYER	MASKEG
FAWKES	GAUGED	HASLET	LADLED	LAYMEN	MASKER
FAWNED	GAUGER	HASPED	LADLER	LAZIER	MASSED
FAWNER	GAUGES	HASSEL	LADLES	MACLES	MASSES
GABBED	GAUZES	HASTED	LAGGED	MADDED	MASTED
GABBER	GAWKED	HASTEN	LAGGER	MADDEN	MASTER
GABLED	HACKED	HASTES	LAIRED	MADDER	MATTED
GABLES	HACKEE	HATRED	LAKIER	MADGES	MATTEO
GADDED	HACKER	HATTED	LALLED	MADMEN	MATTER
GADDER	HAFTED	HATTER	LAMBED	MAGNET	MATTES
GADGET	HAGGED	HAULED	LAMMED	MAGUEY	MAUDES
GAFFED	HAILED	HAULER	LAMPED	MAHLER	MAULED
GAFFER	HAILER	HAUSEN	LANCED	MAIDEN	MAULER
GAFFES	HAIRED	HAWKED	LANCER	MAILED	MAUSER
GAGGED	HALLEL	HAWKER	LANCES	MAILER	MAUVES
GAGGER	HALLEY	HAWSER	LANCET	MAIMED	MAYHEM
GAINED	HALOED	HAWSES	LANDED	MAIMER	MAZIER
GAINER	HALOES	HAZIER	LANDER	MAIZES	NABBED
GAITED	HALSEY	JABBED	LANKER	MALLED	NAGGED
GAITER	HALTED	JABBER	LANNER	MALLEE	NAGGER
GALLED	HALTER	JACKED	LAPPED	MALLET	NAILED
GALLEY	HALVED	JACKET	LAPPER	MALTED	NANTES
GAMIER	HALVES	JAEGER	LAPPET	MAMIES	NAOSES
GAMMED	HAMDEN	JAGGED	LAPSED	MAMMET	NAPIER
GAMMER	HAMLET	JAILED	LAPSER	MANGER	NAPLES
GANDER	HAMMED	JAILER	LAPSES	MANNED	NAPPED
GANGED	HAMMER	JAMIES	LARDED	MANNER	NAPPER
GANGER	HAMPER	JAMMED	LARDER	MANSES	NAPPES
GANGES	HANCES	JAPHET	LARGER	MANTEL	NARKED
GANNET	HANDED	JARRED	LARKED	MANTES	NASSER
GAOLER	HANDEL	JARVEY	LARKER	MANUEL	NATTER
GAPPED	HANGED	JASPER	LASHED	MAPLES	NAUSEA

NAVIES	PAUSES	RATTEN	SAWNEY	VALLEY	WARNER
OAKLEY	PAWNED	RATTER	SAWYER	VALUED	WARPED
PACKED	PAWNEE	RAZEED	TABBED	VALUER	WARPER
PACKER	PAWNER	RAZEES	TABLED	VALUES	WARRED
PACKET	PAYEES	RAZZED	TABLES	VALVED	WARREN
PADDED	RABBET	RAZZES	TABLET	VALVES	WASHED
PADRES	RABIES	SABLES	TACKED	VAMPED	WASHER
PAINED	RACHEL	SACHEM	TACKER	VANMEN	WASHES
PAIRED	RACIER	SACHET	TACKEY	VARIED	WASTED
PALAEO	RACKED	SACKED	TAGGED	VARIER	WASTER
PALLED	RACKER	SACKER	TAGGER	VARIES	WASTES
PALLET	RACKET	SACRED	TAILED	VARLET	WAULED
PALMED	RAFTED	SADDEN	TAIPEI	VARVES	WAVIER
PALMER	RAFTER	SADDER	TALCED	VASTER	WAVIES
PALPED	RAGGED	SADIES	TALKED	VATTED	WAWLED
PALTER	RAGMEN	SAGGED	TALKER	WADDED	WAXIER
PAMPER	RAIDED	SAGGER	TALLER	WADIES	WAYNES
PANDER	RAIDER	SAGIER	TAMPED	WADSET	XAVIER
PANNED	RAILED	SAILED	TAMPER	WAFTED	YABBER
PANTED	RAINED	SAILER	TANDEM	WAFTER	YAHVEH
PANZER	RAISED	SALLET	TANGED	WAGGED	YAHWEH
PARCEL	RAISER	SALTED	TANKED	WAGNER	YAKKED
PARGET	RAISES	SALTER	TANKER	WAIFED	YAMMER
PARIES	RAMIES	SALVED	TANNED	WAILED	YANKED
PARKED	RAMJET	SALVER	TANNER	WAILER	YANKEE
PARKER	RAMMED	SALVES	TANREC	WAITED	YAPPED
PARLEY	RAMMER	SAMIEL	TAPPED	WAITER	YARDED
PARREL	RAMPED	SAMLET	TAPPER	WAIVED	YAUPED
PARSEC	RANEES	SAMUEL	TAPPET	WAIVER	YAWLED
PARSED	RANGED	SANDED	TARGET	WAIVES	YAWNED
PARSEE	RANGER	SANDER	TARRED	WALKED	YAWNER
PARSES	RANGES	SANGER	TARTED	WALKER	YAWPED
PARTED	RANKED	SANIES	TARTER	WALLED	YAWPER
PASSED	RANKER	SANSEI	TASKED	WALLET	ZAFFER
PASSEE	RANTED	SAPIEN	TASSEL	WALTER	ZANIER
PASSER	RANTER	SAPPED	TASSET	WANDER	ZANIES
PASSES	RAPIER	SAPPER	TASTED	WANNED	******
PASTED	RAPPED	SASHED	TASTER	WANNER	-A--F-
PASTEL	RAPPEE	SASHES	TASTES	WANTED	******
PASTER	RAPPEL	SASSED	TATLER	WANTER	BASIFY
PASTES	RAPPER	SASSES	TATTED	WAPPED	CALIFS
PATTED	RASHER	SATEEN	TATTER	WARDED	CARAFE
PATTEN	RASHES	SAUCED	TAUPES	WARDEN	CASEFY
PATTER	RASPED	SAUCER	TAUTEN	WARDER	FAROFF
PAUKER	RASPER	SAUCES	TAUTER	WARIER	GANEFS
PAUPER	RASTER	SAUGER	TAXIED	WARMED	GASIFY
PAUSED	RATHER	SAUREL	VAGUER	WARMER	LAYOFF
PAUSER	RATTED	SAUTES	VAINER	WARNED	NAZIFY

PACIFY	RALPHS	CATKIN	KATHIE	RACHIS	BAFFLE
PAYOFF	RANCHO	CATLIN	KAURIS	RAFFIA	BAGELS
RAMIFY	RAYAHS	CATNIP	LACTIC	RAISIN	BALDLY
RAREFY	SAMSHU	CATTIE	LADDIE	RANCID	BANGLE
RATIFY	SANDHI	CAULIS	LAMBIE	RAPHIS	BARELY
SALIFY	SAPPHO	CAVEIN	LANAIS	RATLIN	BARFLY
TARIFF	SARAHS	DACOIT	LASSIE	RAZZIA	BASALT
******	TAUGHT	DAHLIA	LATRIA	SAITIC	BASELY
-A--G-	XANTHO	DAIMIO	LATVIA	SALMIS	BASILS
******	******	DAKOIT	LAURIE	SALPID	BATTLE
BAREGE	-A--I-	DANAID	MADRID	SALVIA	BAUBLE
CAYUGA	******	DANZIG	MAGGIE	TACTIC	CABALA
DAMAGE	AALIIS	DARWIN	MAGPIE	TAENIA	CABALS
FANEGA	BAALIM	EARWIG	MAISIE	TAKEIN	CACKLE
GARAGE	BABBIE	FABRIC	MANTIC	TALKIE	CAGILY
LADOGA	BAFFIN	FADEIN	MANTIS	TANNIC	CAJOLE
LANUGO	BAGNIO	FAERIE	MAORIS	TANNIN	CALMLY
LAVAGE	BAHAIS	FAFNIR	MAQUIS	TARSIA	CAMELS
MALAGA	BAILIE	FANNIE	MARCIA	VALOIS	CAMILA
MALIGN	BALTIC	FASCIA	MARGIE	WALLIE	CANALS
MANAGE	BALTIM	GADOID	MARGIN	WALLIS	CANDLE
MANEGE	BANDIT	GAELIC	MARLIN	WALVIS	CANTLE
RAVAGE	BARBIE	GALLIC	MARTIN	ZAFFIR	CANULA
SAVAGE	BARDIC	GAMBIA	MARVIN	ZAFTIG	CAROLE
******	BARMIE	GAMBIR	MASHIE	ZAMBIA	CAROLS
-A--H-	BARRIE	GAMBIT	MASSIF	******	CASALS
******	BARRIO	GANOID	MASTIC	-A--J-	CASTLE
CANTHI	BATTIK	GARLIC	MATRIX	******	CATALO
CATCHY	BATTIN	GASKIN	MATTIE	NAVAJO	CATTLE
CAUGHT	BAUCIS	GAWAIN	NAOMIS	******	CAUDLE
EARTHS	CADDIE	HACKIE	NAPKIN	-A--K-	CAVELL
EARTHY	CADDIS	HAGGIS	NAPPIE	******	CAVILS
FAITHS	CALAIS	HALOID	NASTIC	BAMAKO	DABBLE
GANDHI	CALCIC	HARBIN	PALAIS	BATIKS	DADDLE
GAUCHE	CALKIN	HARMIN	PALLID	CAULKS	DAFTLY
GAUCHO	CALVIN	HARRIS	PANTIE	KABAKA	DAGGLE
LAUGHS	CANDIA	HATPIN	PAPAIN	KABIKI	DAMPLY
MALTHA	CANDID	HATTIE	PARSIS	KABUKI	DANDLE
MANCHU	CANNIE	HAWAII	PARVIS	KAMIKS	DANGLE
MARSHA	CAPLIN	IAMBIC	PASSIM	KANAKA	DANKLY
MARSHY	CAPRIC	IATRIC	PASTIL	KAPOKS	DAPPLE
MARTHA	CARDIO	JACKIE	PATHIA	KAYAKS	DARKLE
MARTHE	CARPIC	JAPHIA	PATOIS	MARKKA	DARKLY
NAUGHT	CARRIE	JARVIS	PAULIN	SALUKI	DARTLE
NAVAHO	CASEIN	KAFFIR	PAYNIM	WAKIKI	DAWDLE
PANCHO	CASSIA	KALMIA	RABBIN	******	DAYFLY
PATCHY	CASSIE	KAMSIN	RABBIS	-A--L-	DAZZLE
RAJAHS	CASSIS	KAOLIN	RABBIT	******	EASELS
				BABBLE	
				BABULS	

EASILY	MANTLE	TATTLY	******	FACING	LAPINS
FACILE	MARBLE	TAUTLY	-A--N-	FADING	LARINE
FACULA	MAYFLY	VAINLY	******	FAGEND	LARYNG
FAILLE	MAZILY	VASILI	AALAND	FAKING	LARYNX
FAIRLY	NAMELY	VASTLY	AARONS	FAMINE	LATENT
FAMILY	NAPALM	WABBLE	BAAING	FANONS	LATINS
GABBLE	NASALS	WABBLY	BACONY	FARINA	LAVING
GADFLY	NAVELS	WADDLE	BAIRNS	FARING	LAWING
GAGGLE	PADDLE	WADDLY	BAKING	FATING	LAYING
GAINLY	PALELY	WAFFLE	BALING	FAXING	LAZING
GAMBLE	PAMELA	WAGGLE	BANANA	FAYING	MACING
GAMELY	PANELS	WAGGLY	BARING	FAZING	MAKING
GAMILY	PAPULA	WAMBLE	BARONG	GAGING	MALINE
GANGLI	PAPULE	WAMBLY	BARONS	GALENA	MANANA
GARBLE	PAROLE	WANDLE	BARONY	GAMING	MARINA
GARGLE	PARTLY	WANGLE	BASING	GAMINS	MARINE
GAULLE	PAYOLA	WARBLE	BASINS	GAPING	MASONS
GAVELS	RABBLE	WARILY	BATING	GATING	MATINE
HABILE	RACILY	WARMLY	BATONS	GAZING	MATING
HACKLE	RADDLE	WATTLE	BAYING	HADING	MATING
HAGGLE	RADULA	WAVILY	CABANA	HALING	MATINS
HAMALS	RAFFLE	******	CABINS	HARING	MAXINE
HANDLE	RAMBLE	-A--M-	CADENT	HATING	MAYING
HARDLY	RANKLE	******	CAGING	HAVANA	MAZING
HAROLD	RANKLY	BAHAMA	CAIRNS	HAVENS	NADINE
HASSLE	RAOULS	CAEOMA	CAJUNS	HAVENT	NAGANA
HAZELS	RAPTLY	CAROMS	CAKING	HAVING	NAMING
HAZILY	RARELY	FANUMS	CANINE	HAWING	NARINE
JANGLE	RASHLY	FATIMA	CANING	HAYING	NATANT
KABALA	RATALS	HAKIMS	CANONS	HAZING	OARING
KAMALA	RATELS	HAREMS	CAPONE	JACANA	PACING
LABELS	RATTLE	HAULMY	CAPONS	JADING	PAEANS
LABILE	RAVELS	MADAME	CARINA	JAPANS	PAEONS
LACILY	SADDLE	MADAMS	CARING	JAPING	PAEONY
LAMELY	SAFELY	MAXIMA	CASING	JARINA	PAGANS
LANKLY	SAGELY	MAXIMS	CASINO	JASONS	PAGING
LAPELS	SAMPLE	MAZUMA	CATENA	JAWING	PALING
LASTLY	SANELY	NAHUMS	CAVING	KALONG	PARANG
LATELY	SAWFLY	PAJAMA	CAWING	KARENS	PARENS
LAZILY	TACKLE	PANAMA	DAMANS	LACING	PARENT
LAZULI	TAILLE	RACEME	DAPHNE	LACUNA	PARING
MABELS	TAMALE	RADOME	DARING	LADING	PATENS
MACKLE	TAMELY	SALAMI	DATING	LADINO	PATENT
MACULA	TANGLE	SALOME	DAZING	LAGUNE	PATINA
MACULE	TANGLY	TACOMA	EALING	LAKING	PATINE
MAINLY	TAPALO	TAXEME	EARING	LAMENT	PAVANE
MANGLE	TARTLY	YAKIMA	EASING	LAMINA	PAVANS
MANILA	TATTLE		EATING	LAMING	PAVING
					PAWING

PAYING	WADING	CANYON	HAGDON	NARROW	TALION
RACINE	WAGING	CAPTOR	HALLOO	NASION	TALLOW
RACING	WAGONS	CARBON	HALLOW	NATION	TAMPON
RAGING	WAHINE	CARBOY	HANSOM	NATRON	TANGOS
RAKING	WAKENS	CARGOS	HARBOR	PALLOR	TATTOO
RAMONA	WAKING	CARHOP	HARLOT	PARDON	TAUTOG
RAPINE	WALING	CARLOS	HARLOW	PARGOS	TAYLOR
RAPING	WANING	CARLOW	HARROW	PARLOR	WAGGON
RARING	WAVING	CARROT	HATBOX	PARROT	WAHOOS
RATINE	WAXING	CARSON	HAYBOX	PARSON	WALDOS
RATING	YAMENS	CARTON	HAYMOW	PASTOR	WALKON
RAVENS	YAMUNS	CASHOO	JAILOR	PATHOL	WALLOP
RAVINE	YAPONS	CASTOR	JARGON	PATHOS	WALLOW
RAVING	YAWING	CATION	JARROW	PATIOS	WALTON
RAYING	ZANANA	CAXTON	KARROO	PATROL	WANION
RAYONS	ZAYINS	DACRON	KATION	PATRON	WANTON
RAZING	******	DAEMON	KAZOOS	PATTON	WARHOL
SABINA	-A--O-	DAHOON	LAGOON	PAVIOR	WATSON
SABINE	******	DAIMON	LAPDOG	PAVLOV	YAHOOS
SABINS	BABOON	DALTON	LARDON	RACOON	YARROW
SALINE	BABOOS	DAMSON	LARGOS	RADIOS	YAUPON
SALONS	BAILOR	DANTON	LASSOS	RADNOR	******
SARONG	BALBOA	DARROW	MACRON	RAMROD	-A-P-
SASINS	BALLOT	DATTOS	MAGGOT	RAMSON	******
SATANG	BAMBOO	DAWSON	MAGNOX	RANCOR	CALIPH
SATING	BANGOR	DAYBOY	MAISON	RANDOM	CANAPE
SATINS	BANJOS	DAYTON	MALLOW	RANSOM	CANOPY
SATINY	BARROW	EASTON	MAMBOS	RAPTOR	GALOPS
SAVANT	BARTOK	FACTOR	MAMMON	RATION	JALOPS
SAVING	BARTON	FAEROE	MANGOS	RATIOS	JALOPY
SAVINS	BARYON	FAGGOT	MANIOC	RATOON	KAKAPO
SAWING	BASION	FALCON	MARCOS	SAIGON	PARAPH
SAXONS	BASSOS	FALLOW	MARGOS	SAILOR	SARAPE
SAXONY	BATHOS	FANION	MARGOT	SALLOW	WATAPE
SAYING	CACAOS	FANTOM	MARION	SALMON	WATAPS
TAKING	CACHOU	FARROW	MARLOW	SALOON	******
TALENT	CAHOOT	FATHOM	MARMOT	SALOOP	-A-R-
TALONS	CALLOW	GABION	MAROON	SALVOR	******
TAMING	CAMEOS	GALIOT	MARROW	SALVOS	BAKERS
TAPING	CAMION	GALLON	MASCON	SAMBOS	BAKERY
TARING	CAMPOS	GALLOP	MASCOT	SAMSON	BALERS
TAWING	CANDOR	GALOOT	MATEOS	SANTOL	BARBRA
TAXING	CANNON	GAMBOL	MATRON	SARGON	BAWDRY
VACANT	CANNOT	GAMMON	MATZOS	SARTOR	BAYARD
VACUNA	CANSOS	GARCON	MATZOT	SAVIOR	CALORY
VAGINA	CANTON	GASCON	MAYPOP	TABOOS	CAMERA
VAGINO	CANTOR	GASTON		TAILOR	CANARD
VARUNA	CANTOS			TAINOS	CANARY

CANERS	MAJORS	SAVORY	DANISH	VALISE	KARATE
CAPERS	MAKERS	SAWERS	FAMISH	VAMOSE	KARATS
CARERS	MALGRE	SAYERS	GALOSH	VANISH	LANATE
CASERN	MALORY	TABARD	GARISH	WABASH	LAXITY
CASTRO	MANORS	TABORS	GAYEST	WATUSI	MAGOTS
CATERS	MANURE	TAKERS	HARASS	******	MALATE
CAVERN	MASERS	TALARI	JADISH	-A--T-	MANITO
CAVORT	MASORA	TALERS	KAVASS	******	MANITU
DARERS	MATURE	TAMERS	LAMEST	BABITE	PAINTS
DATARY	MAYORS	TAPERS	LANOSE	BALATA	PAINTY
DATERS	MAZERS	TAPIRS	LAOTSE	BARITE	PAIUTE
DATURA	NADIRS	TATARS	LATEST	BARYTA	PALATE
DAUBRY	NAMERS	TAVERN	LATISH	BASUTO	PARITY
EATERS	NAPERY	TAWDRY	LAVISH	CADETS	PASHTO
EATERY	NATURE	TAWERS	LAXEST	CANUTE	RARITY
FACERS	PACERS	TAXERS	MAOISM	CAPITA	RATITE
FAKERS	PALTRY	VAGARY	MAOIST	CAPOTE	SABOTS
FAKERY	PANTRY	VALERY	MARIST	CARATE	SAFETY
FAKIRS	PAPERS	VAPORI	MAYEST	CARATS	SAINTS
FARERS	PAPERY	VAPORS	NANISM	CARETS	SALUTE
FAVORS	PARERS	VASARI	NAZISM	CAVITE	SAMITE
GABBRO	PARURE	WADERS	OAFISH	CAVITY	SANITY
GAGERS	PASTRY	WAFERS	PALEST	DAINTY	SAULTS
GALORE	PATERS	WAGERS	PALISH	DAKOTA	SAVATE
GANTRY	PAVERS	WALERS	PAPIST	DALETH	TAHITI
GAPERS	PAWERS	WATERS	PARISH	DANITE	TAINTS
GASTRO	PAYERS	WATERY	PAVISE	DAUNTS	TAROTS
GAZERS	RACERS	WAVERS	RACISM	DAVITS	TAUNTS
HALERS	RADARS	YAGERS	RACIST	FACETS	TAXITE
HATERS	RAKERS	YAOURT	RADISH	FAGOTS	VACATE
HAZARD	RATERS	ZAFFRE	RAKISH	FAINTS	VALATE
HAZERS	RAVERS	******	RAMOSE	FAULTS	VALETS
JABIRU	RAZORS	-A--S-	RAPIST	FAULTY	VALUTA
LABORS	SABERS	******	RAREST	GAIETY	VANITY
LAGERS	SAFARI	BABISM	RAVISH	GAMETE	VASHTI
LAHORE	SAHARA	BABIST	RAWEST	GAMETO	VAULTS
LAKERS	SAKERS	BAGASS	RAWISH	GAMUTS	VAUNTS
LAPARO	SALARY	BANISH	SADISM	GAVOTS	WAISTS
LASERS	SAMARA	BAREST	SADIST	GAYETY	WAPITI
LATERA	SANDRA	BASEST	SAFEST	HABITS	WARMTH
LAVERS	SARTRE	CALASH	SAGEST	HALITE	YACHTS
LAYERS	SATARA	CALESA	SALISH	HALUTZ	ZAPATA
LAZARS	SATIRE	CAMASS	SANEST	HAMITE	******
MACERS	SATORY	CAMISE	TAMEST	HAUNTS	-A--U-
MADURA	SATURN	CARESS	TANIST	JABOTS	******
MADURO	SATYRS	CARUSO	TAOISM	JANETS	BANGUI
MAIGRE	SAVERS	CAYUSE	TAOIST	JAUNTS	BANGUP
MAITRE	SAVORS	DAMASK	VADOSE	JAUNTY	BANTUS

BARIUM
BARNUM
BARQUE
BASQUE
BATTUE
BAYEUX
BAYOUS
CACTUS
CADMUS
CAECUM
CAIQUE
CALLUP
CALLUS
CAMPUS
CANGUE
CANTUS
CARPUS
CASQUE
CATGUT
CATSUP
CAUCUS
DANAUS
DARIUS
EARFUL
FACTUM
FAMOUS
FAROUT
FAUNUS
FAVOUR
GALLUP
GALLUS
GAMOUS
GANGUE
HAGBUT
HALLUX
HAMAUL
HANGUP
HATFUL
IAMBUS
JAIPUR
JARFUL
KALIUM
LABIUM
LABOUR
LABRUM
LANGUR
LAPFUL
LAPSUS

LARRUP
LAWFUL
LAYOUT
MADEUP
MAGNUM
MAHBUB
MAHOUT
MAKEUP
MANFUL
MANQUE
MANTUA
MARAUD
MARCUS
MARDUK
MARKUP
MARQUE
MASQUE
MAYBUG
NAEVUS
NASHUA
PALPUS
PAPPUS
PAREUS
PASSUS
PAULUS
RADIUM
RADIUS
RAGOUT
RAJPUT
RAMOUS
SACRUM
SADHUS
SAJOUS
SAMBUR
SANGUI
SANNUP
SAURUS
SAVOUR
TAKEUP
TALCUM
TALMUD
TARSUS
TAURUS
VACUUM
VALGUS
VALLUM
VALOUR

VAPOUR
VATFUL
WALKUP
WALNUT
WALRUS
WAMMUS
WAMOUS
WAMPUM
WARMUP
WAYOUT
******
-A--V-
******
CASAVA
DATIVE
NATIVE
SALIVA
******
-A--W-
******
MACAWS
MALAWI
PAPAWS
******
-A--X-
******
GALAXY
MAXIXE
******
-A--Y-
******
BARRYS
CATHYS
DACTYL
DAIMYO
DAISYS
DANNYS
DAVEYS
FANNYS
HARRYS
HATTYS
JACKYS
KABAYA
KATHYS
LARRYS
MALAYA

MALAYS
MAMEYS
MANDYS
MARTYR
MARTYS
MATEYS
NAGOYA
NANCYS
PADDYS
PANSYS
PAPAYA
PATSYS
SALLYS
SAMMYS
SANDYS
VALKYR
WALLYS
WAVEYS
******
-B--A-
******
ABACAS
ABADAN
ABIJAH
ABOMAS
ABORAL
ABROAD
IBADAN
******
-B--B-
******
ABOMBS
******
-B--C-
******
ABBACY
ABDUCT
ABJECT
OBJECT
OBTECT
******
-B--D-
******
ABRADE
******
-B--E-
******
ABASED
ABASER

ABASES
ABATED
ABATER
ABATES
ABBIES
ABELES
ABIDED
ABIDER
ABIDES
ABODES
ABUSED
ABUSER
ABUSES
IBEXES
IBICES
IBIDEM
IBISES
OBEYED
OBEYER
OBITER
TBONES
******
-B--G-
******
OBLIGE
UBANGI
-B--I-
******
ABATIS
ABULIA
IBERIA
OBTAIN
******
-B--L-
******
ABOLLA
ABVOLT
******
-B--M-
******
ABOHMS
ABRAMS
ABYSMS
IBEAMS
******
-B--N-
******
ABOUND
ABSENT

EBBING
OBLONG
OBTUND
******
-B--O-
******
ABATOR
ABLOOM
ABYDOS
OBERON
******
-B--P-
******
ABRUPT
******
-B--R-
******
ABHORS
ABJURE
ABNERS
ABOARD
ABSORB
ABSURD
OBVERT
******
-B--S-
******
ABBESS
ABLEST
ABLUSH
OBIISM
OBLAST
OBOIST
OBSESS
OBTEST
OBTUSE
******
-B--T-
******
ABBOTS
ABORTS
ABWATT
OBLATE
UBIETY
UBOATS
******
-B--U-
******
ABACUS
ABLAUT

OBELUS	SCALDS	******	SCHEME	SCRAPS	******
OBOLUS	SCENDS	-C--H-	SCRAMS	SCRIPS	-C--U-
******	SCOLDS	******	SCRIMP	SCRIPT	******
-B--Y-	SCRODS	ICHTHY	SCRUMS	SCULPT	ACCRUE
******	******	SCATHE	SCUMMY	YCLEPT	ACEIUM
ABBEYS	-C--E-	SCYPHI		******	ACEOUS
******	******	SCYPHO	-C--N-	-C--R-	ACETUM
-B--Z-	ACHAEA	SCYTHE	******	******	ACINUS
******	ACUMEN	******	ACAENA	ACCORD	ACIOUS
ABLAZE	ECCLES	-C--I-	ACCENT	ACTORS	ACTIUM
******	ECHOED	******	ACHENE	ECHARD	ICARUS
-C--A-	ECHOER	ACACIA	ACHING	OCCURS	SCOPUS
******	ECHOES	ACADIA	ACORNS	OCHERS	SCUTUM
ACETAL	ECOLES	ACARID	ACTING	OCHERY	******
ACTUAL	ICEMEN	ACEDIA	ACTINI	SCHORL	-C--V-
ICECAP	OCASEY	ACERIC	ACTINO	SCLERA	******
ICEMAN	SCALED	ACETIC	ECHINI	SCLERO	ACTIVE
OCREAE	SCALER	ACHAIA	ECHINO	SCOURS	OCTAVE
OCULAR	SCALES	ACIDIC	OCEANS	SCURRY	OCTAVO
SCALAR	SCAPES	ACQUIT	OCTANE	******	SCRIVE
SCARAB	SCARED	ECESIS	OCTANT	-C--S-	SCURVY
SCHWAS	SCARER	ECHOIC	SCIONS	******	******
SCREAK	SCARES	ECLAIR	SCORNS	ACCESS	-C--W-
SCREAM	SCENES	ICONIC	******	ACCOST	******
SCUBAS	SCOLEX	SCENIC	-C--O-	ACCUSE	SCRAWL
******	SCONES	SCHUIT	******	ACROSS	SCREWS
-C--B-	SCOPES	SCIPIO	ACAJOU	ICIEST	SCREWY
******	SCORED	SCORIA	ACTION	SCHISM	******
SCABBY	SCORER	SCOTIA	ICEBOX	SCHIST	-C--X-
SCRIBE	SCORES	******	OCELOT	SCHUSS	******
SCRUBS	SCOTER	-C--L-	OCTROI	SCOUSE	ICEAXE
******	SCREED	******	SCHMOS	******	******
-C--C-	SCREEN	ACIDLY	SCHOOL	-C--T-	-C--Y-
******	SCRIED	ICALLY	SCROOP	******	******
ACKACK	SCUTES	ICICLE	******	ACANTH	ACETYL
OCLOCK	******	OCCULT	-C--P-	ACUATE	MCCOYS
SCARCE	-C--F-	OCELLI	******	ACUITY	******
SCHICK	******	SCILLY	ACCEPT	ECARTE	-C--Z-
SCONCE	SCARFS	SCOWLS	ECTYPE	OCTETS	******
SCORCH	SCLAFF	SCROLL	OCCUPY	SCANTY	SCHIZO
SCOTCH	SCOFFS	SCULLS	OCTOPI	SCATTY	******
SCUTCH	SCRUFF	SCYLLA	SCALPS	SCENTS	-D--A-
******	SCUFFS	******	SCAMPI	SCOOTS	******
-C--D-	SCURFY	-C--M-	SCAMPS	SCOTTS	ADONAI
******	******	******	SCARPS	SCOUTS	ADRIAN
ACCEDE	-C--G-	ECTOMY	SCAUPS	SCOUTS	******
ACNODE	******	ECZEMA	SCOOPS	SCROTA	-D--B-
OCTADS	ICINGS	SCHEMA	SCRAPE	SCROTA	******
	SCRAGS				ADLIBS

******	******	EDWARD	BEDLAM	FEZZAN	PENPAL
-D--C-	-D--L-	IDLERS	BEDPAN	GEMMAE	PENTAD
******	******	UDDERS	BEGGAR	GENIAL	RECTAL
ADDICT	EDIBLE	******	BEHEAD	GERMAN	REDBAY
ADDUCE	EDSELS	-D--S-	BELDAM	GEWGAW	REDCAP
ADDUCT	IDEALS	******	BELGAS	HEDRAL	REGNAL
ADJECT	IDYLLS	ADJUST	BELIAL	HEEHAW	REHEAR
ADVICE	******	ADVISE	BELLAS	HELLAS	REHEAT
IDIOCY	-D--M-	EDDISH	BEMEAN	HENNAS	RELOAD
******	******	GDANSK	BEMOAN	HEPTAD	RENTAL
-D--E-	ADDAMS	IDLEST	BENDAY	HERBAL	REPEAL
******	ADEEMS	ODDEST	BENGAL	HEREAT	REPEAT
ADAGES	IDIOMS	ODESSA	BETRAY	HERMAE	REPLAY
ADDLED	******	******	BEULAH	HERMAI	RESEAT
ADDLES	-D--N-	-D--T-	BEULAS	HERMAN	RESEAU
ADOBES	******	******	BEZOAR	HETMAN	REVEAL
ADORED	ADDEND	ADAPTS	CEIBAS	HEYDAY	SEAMAN
ADORER	ADDING	ADEPTS	CELIAC	JETSAM	SEAWAN
ADORES	ADORNS	ADMITS	CELIAS	KEDDAH	SEAWAY
ADRIEN	ADVENT	ADNATE	CELLAE	KENDAL	SECPAR
EDDIED	EDGING	ADOPTS	CELLAR	KEYWAY	SEESAW
EDDIES	EDMOND	ADULTS	CENTAL	LEEWAY	SEGGAR
EDGIER	EDMUND	EDICTS	CEREAL	LEGMAN	SENDAL
EDILES	EDWINA	EDUCTS	DECCAN	LEHUAS	SENLAC
EDITED	EDWINS	IDEATE	DEEWAN	LEMMAS	SENNAS
EDUCED	IDLING	IDIOTS	DEFEAT	LEONAS	SEPIAS
EDUCES	******	ODDITY	DEFRAY	LETHAL	SEPTAL
******	-D--O-	ODETTE	DELIAN	MECCAN	SERDAB
-D--F-	******	ODONTO	DELIAS	MECCAS	SERIAL
******	EDISON	******	DELLAS	MEDIAE	SERVAL
ADRIFT	EDITOR	-D--U-	DELTAS	MEDIAL	SEURAT
******	ODDJOB	******	DEMEAN	MEDIAN	SEXTAN
-D--H-	******	ADIEUS	DENIAL	MEDLAR	SEXUAL
******	-D--P-	ADIEUX	DENTAL	MENIAL	TEABAG
EDITHS	******	ADNOUN	DEODAR	MENSAL	TERGAL
******	ADOLPH	ADYTUM	DERMAL	MENTAL	TERNAL
-D--I-	******	ODIOUS	DERMAS	MERMAN	TESTAE
******	-D--R-	******	DERMAT	MESCAL	TETRAD
ADAGIO	******	-D--X-	DESMAN	MESIAL	VEADAR
ADENIS	ADDERS	******	DESSAU	MESIAN	VEDIAC
ADIPIC	ADHERE	ADMIXT	DEWLAP	NECTAR	VENIAL
ADJOIN	ADJURE	******	FECIAL	NEURAL	VERBAL
ADONIC	ADMIRE	-E--A-	FELLAH	PEDLAR	VERNAL
ADONIS	ADSORB	******	FENIAN	PELIAS	VERNAS
ADROIT	ADVERB	AECIAL	FERIAL	PENIAL	VESTAL
EDDAIC	ADVERT	AEGEAN	FESTAL	PENMAN	VESTAS
EDENIC	EDGARS	AENEAS	FETIAL	PENNAE	WEIMAR
GDYNIA	EDUARD	AERIAL	FEUDAL	PENNAE	XENIAL
ODYNIA					

YEOMAN	RESECT	******	BEVIES	FEASES	HEBREW
YERBAS	SEANCE	-E--E-	CEASED	FEEDER	HEDGED
YESMAN	SEARCH	******	CEASES	FEELER	HEDGER
ZEBRAS	SEDUCE	AEETES	CEILED	FEEZED	HEDGES
******	SELECT	AERIED	CENSED	FEEZES	HEEDED
-E--B-	SENECA	AERIES	CENSER	FELLED	HEEDER
******	SERACS	AETHER	CENSES	FELLER	HEELED
AEROBE	TENACE	BEADED	CENTER	FELTED	HEELER
DEMOBS	VELOCE	BEAKED	CERMET	FENCED	HEFTED
GEMSBO	VENICE	BEAKER	CERTES	FENCER	HEIFER
HECUBA	VESICA	BEAMED	DEADEN	FENCES	HELLEN
HEREBY	VESICO	BEANED	DEAFEN	FENDED	HELLER
NEARBY	XEBECS	BEARED	DEALER	FENDER	HELMED
******	ZEBECK	BEARER	DEARER	FENNEC	HELMET
-E--C-	ZEBECS	BEATEN	DECKED	FENNEL	HELPED
******	******	BEATER	DECKEL	FERBER	HELPER
BEDECK	-E--D-	BEAVER	DECKER	FERRET	HELTER
DECOCT	******	BECKED	DECREE	FESSES	HELVES
DEDUCE	BEARDS	BECKET	DEEDED	FESTER	HEMMED
DEDUCT	BESIDE	BEDDED	DEEMED	FETTER	HEMMER
DEFACE	BETIDE	BEDDER	DEEPEN	FEUDED	HEMPEN
DEFECT	DECADE	BEEFED	DEEPER	FEZZES	HENLEY
DEJECT	DECIDE	BEEPED	DEFIED	GEARED	HERDED
DELICT	DECODE	BEEVES	DEFIER	GEEZER	HERDER
DEPICT	DELUDE	BEGGED	DEFIES	GEIGER	HERMES
DETACH	DEMODE	BEIGES	DEFTER	GELDED	HEROES
DETECT	DENUDE	BELIED	DEGREE	GELLED	HERPES
DEVICE	DERIDE	BELIER	DEICED	GEMMED	HESTER
FELICE	FELIDS	BELIES	DEICER	GENDER	JEERED
FETICH	HEXADS	BELLED	DEICES	GENIES	JEERER
HELICO	LEPIDO	BELLES	DELVED	GENRES	JELLED
LEGACY	MELODY	BELTED	DELVER	GENTES	JENNET
MEDICI	NEVADA	BENDED	DELVES	GEODES	JEREED
MEDICO	PESADE	BENDEE	DEMIES	GERMEN	JERKED
MEDICS	RECEDE	BENDER	DENIED	GETTER	JERSEY
MEJICO	REMADE	BENNES	DENIER	GEYSER	JESSED
MENACE	REMEDY	BENNET	DENIES	HEADED	JESSES
MEXICO	REMUDA	BERBER	DENNED	HEADER	JESTED
PEIRCE	RESEDA	BERGEN	DENSER	HEALED	JESTER
PESACH	RESIDE	BERMES	DENTED	HEALER	JETTED
REBECK	SECEDE	BERNEY	DENVER	HEAPED	KECKED
REBECS	TELEDU	BESEEM	DEUCED	HEARER	KEDGED
REDACT	TEREDO	BESTED	DEUCES	HEATED	KEDGES
REDUCE	WEALDS	BETHEL	DEWIER	HEATER	KEELED
REFACE	WEIRDY	BETTED	DEXTER	HEAVED	KEENED
REJECT	YEHUDI	BETTER	FEARED	HEAVEN	KEENER
RELICS		BETTES	FEARER	HEAVER	KEEPER
RELICT			FEASED	HEAVES	KEEVES

KEGLER	LEWDER	NEUTER	REARED	SEATED	TEHEES
KELLER	LEYDEN	PEAHEN	REARER	SECKEL	TELFER
KENNED	MEAGER	PEAKED	REDDEN	SECRET	TELLER
KENNEL	MEANER	PEALED	REDDER	SEDGES	TEMPER
KEPLER	MEDLEY	PEASEN	REDEEM	SEEDED	TENDED
KERBED	MEEKER	PEASES	REDOES	SEEDER	TENDER
KERMES	MEETER	PEAVEY	REEDED	SEEKER	TENREC
KERNED	MELDED	PECKED	REEFED	SEEMED	TENSED
KERNEL	MELEES	PECKER	REEFER	SEEMER	TENSER
KERSEY	MELTED	PECTEN	REEKED	SEEPED	TENSES
KEYNES	MELTER	PEEKED	REEKER	SEINED	TENTED
LEADED	MEMBER	PEEKER	REELED	SEINER	TENTER
LEADEN	MENDED	PEELED	REELER	SEINES	TENUES
LEADER	MENDEL	PEELER	REEVED	SEISED	TEPEES
LEAFED	MENDER	PEENED	REEVES	SEIZED	TERCEL
LEAKED	MENSES	PEEPED	REFLET	SEIZER	TERCET
LEANED	MEOWED	PEEPER	REFLEX	SEIZES	TERMED
LEANER	MERCER	PEERED	REFUEL	SELLER	TERMER
LEAPED	MERGED	PEEVED	REGLET	SELVES	TERRET
LEAPER	MERGER	PEEVES	REGRET	SENDER	TERSER
LEASED	MERGES	PEEWEE	REINED	SENNET	TESTED
LEASES	MERLES	PEGGED	RELIED	SENSED	TESTER
LEAVED	MERMEN	PEGLEG	RELIEF	SENSES	TESTES
LEAVEN	MERSEY	PEKOES	RELIER	SEPTET	TETHER
LEAVER	MESHED	PELLET	RELIES	SEQUEL	TETTER
LEAVES	MESHER	PELTED	RENDED	SERIES	TETZEL
LECHER	MESHES	PELTER	RENDER	SERVED	TEUCER
LEDGER	MESMER	PELVES	RENEES	SERVER	VEERED
LEDGES	MESNES	PENCEL	RENNET	SERVES	VEILED
LEERED	MESSED	PENDED	RENTED	SESTET	VEILER
LEGGED	MESSES	PENMEN	RENTER	SETTEE	VEINED
LEGMEN	MESTEE	PENNED	RENTES	SETTER	VELVET
LEGREE	METIER	PENNER	REOPEN	SEXIER	VENDED
LEMUEL	MEWLED	PEPPED	RESTED	SEXTET	VENDEE
LENDER	NEARED	PEPPER	RESTER	TEAMED	VENDER
LENSES	NEARER	PERKED	RETTED	TEARED	VENEER
LENTEN	NEATEN	PERMED	REUBEN	TEASED	VENTED
LESLEY	NEATER	PESTER	REVIEW	TEASEL	VENTER
LESSEE	NECKED	PETREL	REVUES	TEASER	VENUES
LESSEN	NEEDED	PETTED	REVVED	TEASES	VERGED
LESSER	NEEDER	PEWEES	SEABEE	TEASET	VERGER
LESTER	NEPHEW	PEWTER	SEALED	TEDDED	VERGES
LETTER	NERVED	READER	SEALER	TEDDER	VERSED
LEUDES	NERVES	REALES	SEAMED	TEEMED	VERSES
LEVEES	NESTED	REAMED	SEAMEN	TEEMER	VERSET
LEVIED	NETHER	REAMER	SEAMER	TEETER	VERTEX
LEVIER	NETTED	REAPED	SEAPEN	TEGMEN	VERVET
LEVIES	NEUMES	REAPER	SEARED	TEHEED	VESPER

VESSEL	ZEROES	GEISHA	DENTIL	KERRIE	REPAIR
VESTED	ZESTED	HEATHS	DENTIN	KEWPIE	RETAIL
VESTEE	******	HEATHY	DERAIL	LEADIN	RETAIN
VETOED	-E--F-	HEIGHT	DERAIN	LENTIL	SEARIN
VETOER	******	KEITHS	DERMIC	LEONIE	SEISIN
VETOES	AERIFY	LEACHY	DERMIS	LEPSIA	SEIZIN
VETTED	BEREFT	LEIGHS	DERRIS	LESLIE	SENNIT
WEAKEN	FEOFFS	NEIGHS	DESMID	MEALIE	SEPSIS
WEAKER	REBUFF	PEACHY	DETAIL	MEANIE	SEPTIC
WEANED	SERIFS	REECHO	DETAIN	MEGRIM	SEQUIN
WEANER	SETOFF	REICHS	DEVEIN	MELVIN	SERAIS
WEARER	TEPEFY	SEETHE	DEVOID	MEMOIR	SERBIA
WEASEL	VERIFY	SEICHE	DEVOIR	MENDIP	SEREIN
WEAVED	******	TEETHE	FENRIR	MENHIR	TENNIS
WEAVER	-E--G-	TENTHS	FERMIS	MERCIA	TENPIN
WEAVES	******	TETCHY	FERRIC	MERLIN	TENUIS
WEBBED	AERUGO	WEIGHS	FERRIS	MERVIN	TERBIA
WEDDED	BEFOGS	WEIGHT	FERVID	METRIC	TESSIE
WEDGED	BEINGS	******	GEODIC	NELLIE	TESTIS
WEDGES	BELUGA	-E--I-	GERBIL	NEREID	VERDIN
WEEDED	BENIGN	******	GERTIE	NEREIS	VEREIN
WEEDER	DEBUGS	AENEID	GESTIC	NETTIE	VERGIL
WEEPER	DEGAGE	AEOLIA	HECTIC	NEVOID	VERMIN
WEEVER	DELUGE	AEOLIC	HEDWIG	PECTIC	VERNIX
WELDED	DESIGN	AEOLIS	HEMOID	PECTIN	VESPID
WELDER	GEORGE	BEANIE	HENBIT	PEEWIT	WEDGIE
WELLED	GEORGI	BEDRID	HENRIS	PELVIC	WEENIE
WELTED	MENAGE	BEDSIT	HERDIC	PELVIS	WEEVIL
WELTER	METAGE	BEDUIN	HEREIN	PENCIL	WELKIN
WENDED	PELAGE	BEGUIN	HERMIT	PENNIA	ZECHIN
WESLEY	REFUGE	BELGIC	HERNIA	PENNIS	******
WESSEX	RENEGE	BELOIT	HERNIO	PEORIA	-E--K-
WESTER	RESIGN	BERLIN	HEROIC	PEPSIN	******
WETHER	SEWAGE	BERNIE	HEROIN	PEPTIC	BELIKE
WETTED	TELEGA	BERTIE	HESOID	PERMIT	BETAKE
WETTER	TELUGU	BESSIE	HESTIA	PERSIA	DECOKE
YEANED	******	BESTIR	JERKIN	PETRIE	DEREKS
YELLED	-E--H-	BEWAIL	JERVIS	RECOIL	NEVSKI
YELLER	******	CEBOID	JESSIE	REDFIN	PERUKE
YELPED	BEACHY	CEDRIC	JESUIT	REEDIT	REBUKE
YELPER	BEECHY	CELTIC	JEZAIL	REGAIN	REMAKE
YENNED	BERTHA	CERVIX	KELOID	REGGIE	RETAKE
YEOMEN	BERTHE	DEARIE	KELPIE	REJOIN	REVOKE
YESSED	BERTHS	DEBBIE	KELTIC	RELAID	******
YESSES	DEATHS	DEBRIS	KELVIN	REMAIN	-E--L-
YESTER	DEATHY	DECEIT	KENNIE	RENNIN	******
ZENGER	DELPHI	DEIFIC	KERMIS	RENOIR	AEDILE
ZEROED	DEPTHS	DENNIS	KERMIT	REPAID	BEADLE

BEAGLE	KERALA	REPELS	JEROME	DEPONE	RECANT
BECALM	KETTLE	RESALE	LEGUME	DETENT	RECENT
BEETLE	KEVELS	RESELL	METUMP	DEWANS	REDANS
BEFALL	LEANLY	RESILE	OEDEMA	FECUND	REDONE
BEFELL	LEVELS	RESOLD	OEPEMA	FEEING	REFINE
BEHALF	LEWDLY	RESOLE	REALMS	FEIGNE	REFUND
BEHELD	MEANLY	RESULT	REARMS	FEIGNS	REGENT
BEHOLD	MEASLY	RETELL	REGIME	FELINE	REGINA
BERYLS	MEDALS	RETOLD	RESUME	FELONS	REIGNS
BETELS	MEDDLE	REVELS	REVAMP	FELONY	RELENT
BEVELS	MEEKLY	REVILE	SEDUMS	FERINE	RELINE
BEZELS	MEETLY	REVOLT	SEISMO	FETING	REMAND
CECILE	MEGALO	SEDILE	SEISMS	FEUING	REMANS
CECILS	MEGILP	SEEMLY	SEMEME	GEEING	REMIND
CECILY	MERELY	SEMELE	SERUMS	GEMINI	REPAND
CEDULA	METALS	SENILE	SESAME	GERENT	REPENT
CEORLS	METTLE	SEPALS	VENOMS	GERUND	REPINE
DEADLY	NEARLY	SETTLE	ZEUGMA	HELENA	RERUNS
DEAFLY	NEATLY	SEWALL	******	HELENS	RESEND
DEARLY	NEBULA	SEWELL	-E--N-	HERONS	RESENT
DECALS	NEEDLE	SEXILY	******	HEWING	RESINS
DECILE	NEROLI	TEMPLE	BEGINS	HEXANE	RETENE
DECKLE	NESTLE	TERMLY	BEGONE	HEXING	RETINA
DEEPLY	NETTLE	VENULE	BEHIND	HEXONE	REWIND
DEFILE	NEVILE	VERILY	BELONG	JEANNE	SECANT
DEFTLY	NEVILL	VEXILS	BERING	JEEING	SECOND
DESALT	NEWELS	WEAKLY	BESANT	JEJUNE	SECUND
DEVILS	PEARLS	WEDELN	BETONY	KETENE	SEDANS
EERILY	PEARLY	WEEKLY	BEYOND	KETONE	SEEING
FECULA	PEBBLE	YEARLY	BEZANT	KEVINS	SEJANT
FEEBLE	PEBBLY	******	CEDING	KEYING	SELENE
FEEBLY	PEDALS	-E--M-	CEMENT	LEARNS	SELENO
FEMALE	PEDDLE	******	CERING	LEARNT	SERENA
FERULA	PENILE	BECAME	CETANE	LEGEND	SERENE
FERULE	PENULT	BECOME	DEBUNK	LEMONS	SERINE
FETTLE	PEOPLE	BEDIMS	DECANE	LEVANT	SERINS
GENTLE	PERILS	BEGUMS	DECANT	MEKONG	SETONS
GENTLY	PERTLY	BENUMB	DECENT	MELANO	SEVENS
GERALD	PESTLE	BESOMS	DEDANS	MELONS	SEWING
GESELL	PETALS	DECAMP	DEFEND	MENINX	SEXING
HECKLE	PETULA	DECUMA	DEFINE	MERINO	TECHNO
HEDDLE	REALLY	DEFAME	DEIGNS	MESONS	TEEING
HERALD	REBELS	DEGAME	DEKING	METING	TENANT
HEXYLS	REBILL	DEGUMS	DEMAND	MEWING	TENONS
JEKYLL	RECALL	DENIMS	DEMENT	PECANS	TETANY
JEWELS	REDDLE	HEAUME	DEMONO	PEDANT	TETONS
KECKLE	REFILL	JEMIMA	DEMONS	PEKANS	VERONA
KEENLY	REGALE	JEREMY	DEPEND	PEKING	VEXING

WERENT	KELSON	RETOOL	SERAPE	FEVERS	SECERN
YEARNS	LECTOR	RETROD	SERAPH	GEMARA	SECURE
YEMENI	LEGION	SEACOW	SETUPS	GEMERT	SEDERS
ZENANA	LEMNOS	SEADOG	TERAPH	GENERA	SEMPRE
******	LENTOS	SEASON	******	GENTRY	SENARY
-E--O-	LEPTON	SECTOR	**-E--R-**	GERARD	SENORA
******	LESBOS	SEISOR	******	HEGIRA	SENTRY
BEACON	LESION	SEIZOR	BEFORE	HEJIRA	SEVERE
BECKON	LESSON	SELDOM	BEGIRD	HETERO	SEVERN
BEFOOL	LESSOR	SENIOR	BEGIRT	HEWERS	SEVERS
BEHOOF	MEADOW	SENSOR	BELFRY	JETHRO	SEWARD
BELLOC	MELLON	SERMON	BEMIRE	LEGERS	SEWERS
BELLOW	MELLOW	SERVOS	BEWARE	LEMURS	TEAURN
BENTON	MELTON	SETTOS	CEDARS	LENORE	TELARY
BENZOL	MENTOR	SEXPOT	CELERY	LEPERS	TENORS
BESTOW	MERLON	SEXTON	CENTRA	LEVERS	TENURE
BETOOK	METEOR	TEAPOT	CENTRE	MEAGRE	TEVERE
BETTOR	METHOD	TEAPOY	CENTRI	MEMORY	VELURE
CELLOS	METROS	TEFLON	CENTRO	MESSRS	VENERY
CENSOR	MEZZOS	TELSON	CESARE	METERS	VENIRE
CENTOS	NEKTON	TEMPOS	CESURA	NEPHRO	VENTRO
CEYLON	NELSON	TENDON	DEBARK	NEWARK	VESTRY
DEACON	NESTOR	TENSOR	DEBARS	OEUVRE	VEXERS
DEBTOR	NEURON	TERMOR	DECARE	PELTRY	WEBERS
DEPLOY	NEWTON	TERROR	DECERN	PENURY	******
DESPOT	PEDROS	TESTON	DECORS	PETARD	**-E-S-**
FELLOE	PEGTOP	TEUTON	DECURY	PETERS	******
FELLOW	PELION	VECTOR	DEFERS	REBORE	BEHEST
FEODOR	PENGOS	VENDOR	DEFORM	REBORN	BEMUSE
FERVOR	PENNON	VERNON	DEHORN	RECORD	BETISE
GECKOS	PEPLOS	VERSOS	DEKARE	RECURS	CERISE
GENROS	PEQUOD	WEAPON	DEMURE	REFERS	CERUSE
GENTOO	PEQUOT	YELLOW	DEMURS	REFORM	DEBASE
GERYON	PERIOD	ZEALOT	DENARY	REGARD	DEFUSE
GESSOS	PERRON	ZETHOS	DENDRI	REMARK	DEGUST
HEADON	PERSON	******	DENDRO	REMORA	DEMISE
HEBRON	PETROL	**-E--P-**	DEPART	REPORT	DENISE
HECTOR	REASON	******	DEPORT	RESORB	DEPOSE
HEDRON	REAVOW	CERIPH	DESCRY	RESORT	DESIST
HELIOS	RECKON	FELIPE	DESERT	RETARD	DETEST
HENDON	RECTOR	GETUPS	DESIRE	RETIRE	DEVEST
HEREOF	RECTOS	LENAPE	DETERS	RETORT	DEVISE
HEREON	REDDOG	LETUPS	DEXTRO	RETURN	FETISH
HERIOT	REDHOT	METOPE	FEDORA	REVERE	FEWEST
HEZION	REDTOP	PELOPS	FEMORA	REVERS	GENESI
JERBOA	REFOOT	RECAPS	FEMURS	REVERT	HEARSE
JETTON	REGION	RECEPT	FETORS	REWARD	HEARST
KEDRON	RETOOK	RECIPE	FEUARS	REWORD	HERESY

HEXOSE	BERETS	LEVITE	AEOLUS	SETOUS	DEBBYS
JEWESS	BESETS	LEVITY	BEDAUB	SETOUT	DECAYS
JEWISH	BESOTS	MERITS	BEDBUG	TEACUP	DECOYS
KETOSE	CERATE	NEGATE	BEFOUL	TEDIUM	DELAYS
LEGIST	CERATO	NEMATO	BEIRUT	TELLUS	DENNYS
MEDUSA	CERITE	PEDATE	CENSUR	TEREUS	GERRYS
MEGASS	DEARTH	PEDATI	CENSUS	TERGUM	GERTYS
MEREST	DEBATE	PELITE	CEREUS	VELLUM	HENRYS
NEWEST	DEBITS	PELOTA	CERIUM	VELOUR	HETTYS
PERISH	DEBUTS	PESETA	CEROUS	VENDUE	JENNYS
PERUSE	DEISTS	PETITE	CESIUM	VENOUS	JERRYS
RECAST	DELATE	PEWITS	CESTUS	VERDUN	KENNYS
RECESS	DELETE	PEYOTE	DELIUS	VERSUS	LENNYS
RECUSE	DEMITS	REACTS	DENGUE	ZETHUS	LEROYS
REFUSE	DEMOTE	REALTY	DETOUR	******	MELVYN
REHASH	DENOTE	REBATE	DEVOUR	-E--V-	METHYL
RELISH	DEPOTS	REBATO	DEVOUT	******	NELLYS
REMISE	DEPUTE	REBUTS	FEROUS	BEHAVE	PEGGYS
REMISS	DEPUTY	RECITE	FERRUM	BEHOVE	PENNYS
REPASS	DERATE	REFITS	FESCUE	DERIVE	PERCYS
REPAST	DEVOTE	REFUTE	GENIUS	GENEVA	PERRYS
REPOSE	DEWITT	RELATE	GENOUS	RELIVE	REDEYE
RESIST	FEALTY	REMITS	GEROUS	REMOVE	RELAYS
RETUSE	FEASTS	REMOTE	HELIUM	REVIVE	REPAYS
REVEST	FEINTS	REPUTE	LEAGUE	******	SELSYN
REVISE	FEISTS	RESETS	MEATUS	-E--W-	SELWYN
SETOSE	FEISTY	REVETS	MEDIUM	******	SEPOYS
SEXISM	FERITY	SEBATS	MEROUS	BEDEWS	TEDDYS
SEXIST	GEMOTS	SEDATE	NESSUS	REDOWA	TERRYS
TEENSY	GENETS	SEMITE	PEANUT	RENEWS	TETHYS
TERESA	GENITO	SENATE	PELEUS	RENOWN	TETRYL
VENOSE	HEALTH	TEMPTS	PENTUP	SEROWS	WENDYS
VERISM	HEARTH	TENETS	PEPLUM	******	ZEPHYR
VERIST	HEARTS	TENUTO	PEPLUS	-E--X-	******
WEENSY	HEARTY	TERATO	RECOUP	******	-E-Z-
******	HECATE	TERETE	RECTUM	DELUXE	******
-E--T-	HEISTS	VELDTS	RECTUS	DESOXY	BELIZE
******	HELOTS	VERITY	REDBUD	******	MEZUZA
AERATE	HEMATO	VERSTS	REDBUG	-E--Y-	REBOZO
BEASTS	HEPATO	WEALTH	REDGUM	******	******
BEAUTS	HERETO	YEASTS	REFLUX	BECKYS	-F--A-
BEAUTY	KENITE	YEASTY	REGIUS	BELAYS	******
BEFITS	KERATO	ZENITH	RESCUE	BENJYS	AFFRAY
BEGETS	LEANTO	******	SEAMUS	BENNYS	AFGHAN
BEMATA	LEGATE	-E--U-	SELJUK	BENZYL	AFLOAT
BENITA	LEGATO	******	SEPTUM	BESSYS	OFFDAY
BENITO	LENGTH	AEACUS	SEROUS	BETSYS	
BERATE	LENITY	AEGEUS	SESQUI	BETTYS	

******	EFFUSE	******	EGRESS	THORAC	SHODDY
-F--C-	OFFISH	-G--H-	OGRESS	THORAX	SHREDS
******	******	******	OGRISH	THREAD	THADDY
AFFECT	-F--T-	AGATHA	******	THREAT	THIRDS
AFRICA	******	******	-G--T-	THROAT	******
EFFACE	EFFETE	-G--I-	******	THUJAS	-H--E-
EFFECT	******	******	AGENTS	WHIDAH	******
OFFICE	-F--U-	AGAMIC	AGISTS	WHYDAH	CHAFED
******	******	AGARIC	AGLETS	******	CHAFER
-F--E-	AFFLUX	AGLAIA	AGNATE	-H--B-	CHAFES
******	EFFLUX	AGNAIL	AGOUTI	******	CHALEH
OFFSET	******	AGONIC	AGOUTY	CHUBBY	CHALET
******	-G--A-	EGERIA	EGESTA	PHLEBO	CHAPEL
-F--G-	******	******	EGESTS	PHOEBE	CHAPES
******	AGAMAS	-G--L-	EGRETS	RHOMBI	CHARED
EFFIGY	AGAPAE	******	IGNITE	RHUMBA	CHARES
******	AGLEAM	AGEDLY	******	RHUMBS	CHASED
-F--I-	AGORAE	AGEOLD	-G--U-	SHABBY	CHASER
******	AGORAS	UGLILY	******	SHELBY	CHASES
AFFAIR	OGDOAD	******	AGOGUE	SHRUBS	CHAWED
AFLCIO	OGIVAL	-G--N-	EGGCUP	THISBE	CHEBEC
AFRAID	******	******	******	THROBS	CHEWED
******	-G--C-	AGEING	-H--A-	THUMBS	CHEWER
-F--L-	******	EGGING	******	WHITBY	CHIDED
******	AGENCY	IGUANA	BHUTAN	******	CHIDER
AFIELD	IGNACE	OGLING	CHELAE	-H--C-	CHIDES
******	******	******	CHELAS	******	CHIMED
-F--M-	-G--D-	-G--O-	CHETAH	CHALCO	CHIMER
******	******	******	CHORAL	CHANCE	CHIMES
AFLAME	AGENDA	EGGNOG	CHUFAS	CHANCY	CHINES
AFRAME	UGANDA	IGLOOS	OHIOAN	CHINCH	CHISEL
******	******	IGOROT	PHYLAE	CHOICE	CHIVES
-F--N-	-G--E-	******	RHINAL	CHURCH	CHLOES
******	******	-G--R-	RHODAS	SHTICK	CHOKED
OFFEND	AGATES	******	SHAMAN	THATCH	CHOKER
OFFING	AGAVES	AGGERS	SHEBAT	THENCE	CHOKES
******	AGONES	EGBERT	SHIKAR	THRICE	CHOLER
-F--R-	AGREED	EGGARS	SHOFAR	THWACK	CHOREA
******	AGREES	EGGERS	SHORAN	WHENCE	CHOREO
AFFIRM	OGIVES	IGNORE	THANAT	******	CHORES
AFFORD	UGLIER	OGLERS	THEBAE	-H--D-	CHOSEN
EFFORT	******	******	THECAE	******	CHUTES
OFFERS	-G--F-	-G--S-	THECAL	CHARDS	DHOLES
******	******	******	THEDAS	CHORDS	GHEBER
-F--S-	AGRAFE	AGHAST	THENAL	SHANDY	KHYBER
******	IGNIFY	AGUISH	THENAR	SHARDS	PHASED
AFRESH	UGLIFY	EGOISM	THETAS	SHERDS	PHASES
AFTOSA		EGOIST	THOMAS	SHINDY	PHLOEM

PHONED	THALER	CHARGE	THESIS	GHOULS	WHAMMY
PHONES	THALES	CHOUGH	THETIC	PHIALS	WHELMS
PHONEY	THAMES	OHMAGE	THETIS	PHYLLO	******
PHOOEY	THANES	PHLEGM	THORIA	SHAWLS	-H--N-
RHODES	THAWED	SHAGGY	THORIC	SHEILA	******
RHYMED	THAYER	SHRUGS	THULIA	SHEILD	CHAINS
RHYMER	THEBES	THINGS	THYMIC	SHELLS	CHRONO
RHYMES	THEMES	THONGS	******	SHELLY	CHURNS
SHADED	THESES	THOUGH	-H--K-	SHIELD	DHARNA
SHADES	THEWED	WHANGS	******	SHILLS	DHURNA
SHAKEN	THOLES	******	CHALKS	SHOALS	PHRENO
SHAKER	THREED	-H--H-	CHALKY	SHOALY	SHEENS
SHAKES	THREES	******	CHECKS	SHORLS	SHEENY
SHALED	THROES	CHICHI	CHEEKS	SHOULD	SHINNY
SHALES	THYMES	RHYTHM	CHEEKY	SHRILL	SHRANK
SHAMED	THYREO	THIGHS	CHICKS	THINLY	SHRINE
SHAMES	WHALED	******	CHINKS	THIOLS	SHRINK
SHAPED	WHALER	-H--I-	CHINKY	THRALL	SHRUNK
SHAPEN	WHALES	******	CHOCKS	THRILL	SHYING
SHAPER	WHEYEY	CHITIN	CHUCKS	THUSLY	THORNS
SHAPES	WHILED	CHOPIN	CHUNKS	WHEALS	THORNY
SHARED	WHILES	CHORIC	CHUNKY	WHEELS	THRONE
SHARER	WHINED	CHYMIC	SHACKO	WHIRLS	THRONG
SHARES	WHINER	DHOTIS	SHACKS	WHOLLY	WHINNY
SHAVED	WHINES	KHAKIS	SHANKS	WHORLS	******
SHAVEN	WHITED	PHAGIA	SHARKS	******	-H--O-
SHAVER	WHITEN	PHASIA	SHEIKH	-H--M-	******
SHAVES	WHITER	PHASIC	SHEIKS	******	CHARON
SHEKEL	WHITES	PHASIS	SHIRKS	CHACMA	CHEGOE
SHEWED	WHITEY	PHILIA	SHOCKS	CHAMMY	CHICOS
SHEWER	WHORED	PHILIP	SHRIKE	CHARMS	CHIGOE
SHINED	WHORES	PHOBIA	SHUCKS	CHASMS	CHIRON
SHINER	******	PHOBIC	THANKS	CHIRMS	CHITON
SHINES	-H--F-	PHOCIS	WHACKS	CHROMA	PHANON
SHIRES	******	PHONIA	WHELKS	CHROME	PHAROS
SHIVER	CHAFFS	PHONIC	WHELKY	CHROMO	PHENOL
SHIVES	CHAFFY	PHOTIC	WHISKS	CHUMMY	PHILOS
SHOOED	CHIEFS	PHYSIC	WHISKY	DHARMA	PHOTON
SHORED	SHRIFT	PHYSIO	******	RHEIMS	PHOTOS
SHORES	SHROFF	PHYTIN	-H--L-	RHEUMY	RHETOR
SHOTES	THRIFT	RHIZIC	******	SHAMMY	RHINOS
SHOVED	WHARFS	RHODIC	CHEILO	SHAWMS	SHADOW
SHOVEL	WHIFFS	SHERIF	CHICLE	SHIMMY	SHAKOS
SHOVER	******	SHOJIS	CHILLI	SHRIMP	SHARON
SHOVES	-H--G-	SHOOIN	CHILLS	THELMA	SHILOH
SHOWED	******	SHUTIN	CHILLY	THERMO	THORON
SHOWER	CHANGE	THALIA	CHOLLA	THERMS	THYMOL
SHRIEK	CHANGS	THEMIS	CHURLS	THRUMS	WHILOM

******	******	SHAFTS	WHARVE	GILDAS	RIPSAW
-H--P-	-H--S-	SHANTY	WHERVE	GILEAD	RITUAL
******	******	SHASTA	******	GINGAL	SIGMAS
CHAMPS	AHIMSA	SHEATH	-H--W-	HIEMAL	SIGNAL
CHEEPS	CHAISE	SHEETS	******	HILDAS	SILVAE
CHEOPS	CHASSE	SHELTY	SHREWD	JIGSAW	SILVAN
CHIPPY	CHEESE	SHIFTS	SHREWS	JINGAL	SILVAS
CHIRPS	CHEESY	SHIFTY	THROWN	KIBLAH	SIMIAN
CHIRPY	CHIASM	SHIITE	THROWS	KIDNAP	SINBAD
CHOPPY	CHOOSE	SHINTO	******	KITBAG	SIOUAN
CHUMPS	CHOOSY	SHIRTS	-H--Y-	LIANAS	SIRDAR
PHIPPS	CHRISM	SHIRTY	******	LIBRAE	TIARAS
PHOSPH	CHRIST	SHOATS	CHERYL	LIBRAS	TIBIAE
SHARPS	CHRYSO	SHOOTS	PHENYL	LIBYAN	TIBIAL
SHEEPS	PHRASE	SHORTS	THADYS	LILIAN	TIBIAS
SHERPA	SHIEST	SHOUTS	******	LINDAS	TIMBAL
SHOPPE	SHIISM	SHUNTS	-H--Z-	LINEAL	TINCAL
THORPE	SHYEST	THEFTS	******	LINEAR	TINCAN
THRIPS	THEISM	THIRTY	WHEEZE	LINGAM	TIPCAT
THUMPS	THEIST	WHEATS	WHEEZY	LINGAS	TITIAN
WHELPS	THIRST	WHORTS	******	LIVIAS	VIDUAL
WHIPPY	THRASH	******	-I--A-	MICMAC	VILLAS
WHOOPS	THRESH	-H--U-	******	MIDDAY	VIOLAS
******	THRUSH	******	AIDMAN	MIDWAY	VIRGAS
-H--R-	THYRSE	CHABUK	AIRMAN	MILLAY	VISTAS
******	THYRSI	CHEQUE	AIRSAC	MINOAN	VISUAL
CHAIRS	WHILST	CHERUB	AIRWAY	MIRIAM	VITTAE
CHARRY	WHIMSY	CHIAUS	BIAXAL	MISHAP	VIVIAN
CHEERS	WHOOSH	CHIBUK	BILBAO	MISKAL	WIGWAG
CHEERY	******	CHORUS	BISCAY	MISLAY	WIGWAM
CHEIRO	-H--T-	PHYLUM	CILIAT	MISSAL	WILMAS
CHERRY	******	RHESUS	CITRAL	MITRAL	WITHAL
CHIRRS	CHAETA	SHAMUS	DIANAS	NILGAI	ZIGZAG
CHLORO	CHAETO	SHOGUN	DIETAL	OILCAN	ZILLAH
CHOIRS	CHANTS	SHROUD	DIPSAS	PICKAX	******
CHURRS	CHANTY	THYMUS	DIRHAM	PIEMAN	-I--C-
GHARRI	CHARTS	******	DISBAR	PIENAL	******
GHARRY	CHASTE	-H--V-	DISCAL	PILLAR	BIANCA
OHENRY	CHATTY	******	DISMAL	PINDAR	BIERCE
SHEARS	CHEATS	CHEVVY	DISMAY	PINEAL	BISECT
SHEERS	CHESTS	CHIVVY	DISTAL	PINNAE	CILICE
SHERRY	CHESTY	SHEAVE	FIJIAN	PINNAL	CIVICS
SHIRRS	CHINTZ	SHELVE	FILIAL	PISGAH	DIRECT
SHOERS	CHITTY	SHRIVE	FINIAL	PITMAN	FIANCE
THEIRS	GHAUTS	SHROVE	FINNAN	PIZZAS	FIASCO
THEORY	GHETTO	THIEVE	FIRMAN	RIATAS	FIERCE
THWART	GHOSTS	THRIVE	FISCAL	RICTAL	HIJACK
WHERRY		THROVE	GIBRAN	RIPRAP	KIRSCH

KITSCH	BIDDEN	DINDER	GIBBET	KICKER	LINTEL
LILACS	BIDDER	DINGED	GIBLET	KIDDED	LINTER
MIMICS	BIFFED	DINGEY	GIFTED	KIDDER	LIONEL
PIERCE	BIFLEX	DINKEY	GIGGED	KIDNEY	LIPPED
PIRACY	BIGGER	DINNED	GIGLET	KILLED	LIPPER
SILICA	BILGED	DINNER	GIGUES	KILLER	LISPED
SILICO	BILGES	DINTED	GILDED	KILMER	LISPER
TIERCE	BILKED	DIODES	GILDER	KILTED	LISTED
VIVACE	BILKER	DIPLEX	GIMLET	KILTER	LISTEL
******	BILLED	DIPPED	GIMPED	KINDER	LISTEN
-I--D-	BILLET	DIPPER	GINGER	KINGED	LISTER
******	BINDER	DIRGES	GINNED	KINKED	LITHER
BIPEDS	BINGES	DIRKED	GINNER	KINSEY	LITTER
BIPODS	BINNED	DISHED	GIPPED	KIPPED	LIVIER
CICADA	BIOGEN	DISHES	GIRDED	KIPPER	LIVRES
DIPODY	BIRLED	DISNEY	GIRDER	KISLEW	LIVYER
DIRNDL	BIRLES	DISPEL	GIRTED	KISMET	MICHEL
DIVIDE	BIRRED	DITHER	HICKEY	KISSED	MICKEY
FIELDS	BISTER	EIFFEL	HIDDEN	KISSER	MIDDEN
FIENDS	BITTED	EILEEN	HIGHER	KISSES	MIDGES
FIORDS	BITTEN	EITHER	HILLED	KITTED	MIDGET
JIHADS	BITTER	FIBBED	HILLER	KITTEN	MIFFED
LIBIDO	CINDER	FIBBER	HILTED	LIANES	MIGUEL
LIPIDS	CIPHER	FICHES	HINDER	LIASED	MILDEN
MIKADO	CITHER	FIDGET	HINGED	LICHEE	MILDER
MILADY	CITIED	FIGGED	HINGES	LICHEN	MILDEW
TIRADE	CITIES	FILLED	HINTED	LICKED	MILIEU
VIANDS	CIVIES	FILLER	HIPPED	LIDDED	MILKED
WIELDS	DIADEM	FILLET	HISSED	LIEDER	MILKER
WIELDY	DIALED	FILMED	HISSER	LIEGES	MILLED
YIELDS	DIALER	FILTER	HISSES	LIFTED	MILLER
******	DIANES	FINDER	HITHER	LIFTER	MILLET
-I--E-	DIAPER	FINGER	HITLER	LILIED	MILTED
******	DIBBED	FINNED	HITTER	LILIES	MILTER
AIDMEN	DIBBER	FINNER	JIBBED	LILTED	MINCED
AIGLET	DICKER	FIQUES	JIBBER	LIMBED	MINCER
AILEEN	DICKEY	FIRMED	JIGGED	LIMBER	MINCES
AIRBED	DIDIES	FIRMER	JIGGER	LIMIER	MINDED
AIRIER	DIDOES	FISHER	JILTED	LIMNED	MINDER
AIRMEN	DIESEL	FISHES	JILTER	LIMNER	MINTED
AISLED	DIESES	FISTED	JINKED	LIMPED	MINTER
AISLES	DIETED	FITTED	JINKER	LIMPER	MINUET
BIASED	DIETER	FITTER	JINNEE	LIMPET	MINXES
BIASES	DIFFER	FIZZED	JINNEE	LINDEN	MISLED
BIBBED	DIGGED	FIZZER	JINXED	LINGER	MISSED
BIBBER	DIGGER	FIZZES	JINXES	LINIER	MISSEL
BIBLES	DIMMED	GIBBED	JITNEY	LINKED	MISSES
BICKER	DIMMER	GIBBER	JITTER	LINNET	MISTED

MISTER	PITIES	SIFTER	TINTED	WISHED	PITCHY
MITRED	PITMEN	SIGHED	TIPPED	WISHES	SIXTHS
MITTEN	PITTED	SIGNED	TIPPER	WISPED	TILTHS
MIZZEN	PIXIES	SIGNER	TIPPET	WITHED	WIDTHS
NIBBED	RIBBED	SIGNET	TITHED	WITHER	******
NICHED	RICHER	SILKEN	TITHER	WITHES	-I--I-
NICHES	RICHES	SILOED	TITHES	WITNEY	******
NICKED	RICKED	SILTED	TITLED	WITTED	BIBLIO
NICKEL	RICKEY	SILVER	TITLES	YIPPED	BIFFIN
NICKER	RIDDED	SIMMER	TITTER	ZINCED	BIGGIN
NIECES	RIDDEN	SIMNEL	VIALED	ZINGED	BIGWIG
NIGGER	RIDGED	SIMPER	VIEWED	ZIPPED	BILLIE
NIGHER	RIDGES	SINGED	VIEWER	ZIPPER	BIOSIS
NIPPED	RIFLED	SINGER	VINCES	ZITHER	BIOTIC
NIPPER	RIFLER	SINGES	VINIER	******	BIOTIN
NIXIES	RIFLES	SINKER	VIOLET	-I--F-	BIRDIE
OILIER	RIFTED	SINNED	VISAED	******	CISSIE
PICKED	RIGGED	SINNER	VISEED	MINIFY	CITRIC
PICKER	RIGGER	SINTER	VIVIEN	NIDIFY	DIAZIN
PICKET	RILLET	SIPPED	VIZIER	PIAFFE	DICKIE
PIECED	RIMMED	SIPPER	WICHES	PILAFF	DIESIS
PIECER	RIMMER	SIPPET	WICKED	PILAFS	DIKDIK
PIECES	RINGED	SISTER	WICKER	RIPOFF	DIMWIT
PIEMEN	RINGER	SITTER	WICKET	TIPOFF	DISTIL
PIETER	RINKED	SIXTES	WIENER	VILIFY	FIBRIL
PIGGED	RINSED	SIZIER	WIGGED	VIVIFY	FIBRIN
PIGLET	RINSER	TICKED	WILBER	******	FILLIN
PIGPEN	RINSES	TICKER	WILDER	-I--G-	FILLIP
PILFER	RIOTED	TICKET	WILIER	******	FILMIC
PILLED	RIOTER	TIDIED	WILLED	LINAGE	FINNIC
PIMPED	RIPLEY	TIDIER	WILLER	MILAGE	FIRKIN
PINGED	RIPPED	TIDIES	WILLET	MIRAGE	FISTIC
PINIER	RIPPER	TIERED	WILTED	PIPAGE	FIZGIG
PINIES	RISKED	TIFFED	WINCED	SILAGE	GILLIE
PINKED	RISKER	TILDES	WINCER	VIRAGO	GIULIA
PINNED	RITTER	TILLED	WINCES	VISAGE	GIULIO
PINNER	SICKED	TILLER	WINCEY	******	HIPPIE
PINTER	SICKEN	TILTED	WINDED	-I--H-	HISPID
PIPIER	SICKER	TILTER	WINDER	******	JIMMIE
PIPPED	SIDLED	TIMBER	WINGED	BIRTHS	KIBEIS
PIQUED	SIDLER	TINDER	WINIER	BITCHY	KIDDIE
PIQUES	SIDLES	TINGED	WINKED	DINAHS	KILTIE
PIQUET	SIDNEY	TINGES	WINKER	DINGHY	LIEBIG
PISCES	SIEGED	TINIER	WINNER	FIFTHS	LIGNIN
PISHED	SIEGES	TINKER	WINOES	FILTHY	LIMBIC
PISHES	SIEVED	TINNED	WINTER	FIRTHS	LIMPID
PITHED	SIEVES	TINNER	WINZES	LITCHI	LIPOID
PITIED	SIFTED	TINSEL	WIRIER	NINTHS	LIQUID

LITHIA	VIRGIN	GIGGLE	PIDDLE	WIGGLE	GIBING
LITHIC	VISCID	GIGGLY	PIFFLE	WIGGLY	GIGANT
LIZZIE	VITRIC	GIGOLO	PILULE	WILDLY	GIPONS
MIDAIR	WIDDIE	GIMELS	PIMPLE	WILILY	GITANO
MIDRIB	WIENIE	GIRDLE	PIMPLY	WIMBLE	GIVING
MILLIE	WILLIE	GISELE	PINOLE	WIMPLE	HIDING
MINNIE	WILLIS	HIGGLE	PINTLE	WINKLE	HIEING
MIOSIS	WINNIE	HIGHLY	RIBALD	WIRILY	HIKING
MIOTIC	WITHIN	JIGGLE	RICHLY,	WISELY	HIRING
MISDID	WITHIT	JINGLE	RIDDLE	ZIZZLE	HIVING
MISFIT	YIPPIE	JINGLY	RIFFLE	******	JIBING
MISSIS	ZINCIC	KIBBLE	RIMPLE	-I--M-	JIMINY
NIACIN	ZINNIA	KINDLE	RIPELY	******	JIVING
NIOBIC	******	KINDLY	RIPPLE	BIGAMY	KIMONO
NISEIS	-I--K-	KINGLY	RIPPLY	BIREME	KININS
NITRIC	******	KIRTLE	RIVALS	CINEMA	KITING
NITRID	GINGKO	KITTLE	RIYALS	DIGAMY	LIERNE
NITWIT	KIOSKS	LIABLE	SIBYLS	HIRAMS	LIGAND
PICNIC	ZINCKY	LIBELS	SICILY	LIPOMA	LIKENS
PICRIC	******	LIGULA	SICKLE	MIASMA	LIKING
PIDGIN	-I--L-	LIGULE	SICKLY	MINIMA	LIMENS
PIGGIE	******	LIKELY	SIECLE	MINIMS	LIMINA
PIGGIN	AIRILY	LIMPLY	SIGILS	******	LIMING
PINKIE	BIFOLD	LIMULI	SIMILE	-I--N-	LINENS
PINXIT	BIKOLS	LITTLE	SIMPLE	******	LINING
PIPKIN	CIBOLS	LIVELY	SIMPLY	AIDING	LITANY
PIPPIN	CICALA	MIAULS	SINGLE	AILING	LIVENS
PISTIL	CICELY	MICELL	SINGLY	AIMING	LIVING
RICHIE	CIRCLE	MICKLE	SIZZLE	AIRING	MIMING
SIALIC	CITOLA	MIDDLE	TICALS	BIDING	MINING
SIGRID	DIBBLE	MIGGLE	TICKLE	BIGONE	MIRING
SIKKIM	DIDDLE	MILDLY	TIDILY	BIKINI	MIXING
SILVIA	DIMPLE	MINGLE	TIMELY	BITING	NICENE
SIMLIN	DIMPLY	MISTLE	TINGLE	CITING	NIDING
SISKIN	DINGLE	MIZZLE	TINGLY	DICING	NIXING
TIDBIT	DIPOLE	NIBBLE	TINILY	DIKING	OILING
TIEPIN	DIRELY	NICELY	TINKLE	DINING	PIKING
TIFFIN	EIDOLA	NICOLE	TINKLY	DITONE	PILING
TIGRIS	FIBULA	NIELLI	TIPPLE	DIVANS	PINANG
TILLIE	FICKLE	NIELLO	TITTLE	DIVINE	PINENE
TINEID	FIDDLE	NIGELS	VIABLE	DIVING	PINING
TITBIT	FIMBLE	NIGGLE	VIGILS	DIWANS	PINONS
VIATIC	FINALE	NIMBLE	VILELY	DIZENS	PIPING
VIBRIO	FINALS	NIMBLY	VINYLS	FIFING	PIRANA
VICTIM	FINELY	NIPPLE	VIRILE	FILING	PITONS
VIOLIN	FIPPLE	OILILY	VITALS	FINING	RIBAND
VIRGIE	FIRMLY	PICKLE	WIDELY	FIRING	RICING
VIRGIL	FIZZLE	PICULS	WIFELY	FIXING	RIDENT

RIDING	BISHOP	TIPTOE	DINERO	RIVERS	NICEST
RILING	CINEOL	TIPTOP	DINERS	SIDERO	PILOSE
RIMING	CISCOS	VIATOR	DISARM	SIERRA	RIBOSE
RIPENS	CITRON	VICTOR	DIVERS	SIEURS	RIMOSE
RISING	DIALOG	VILLON	DIVERT	SIMARS	RIPEST
RIVING	DIATOM	VINSON	FIACRE	SISERA	RIPOST
SIDING	DIGLOT	VIREOS	FIBERS	SITARS	SIWASH
SIENNA	DIOBOL	VISION	FIFERS	SIZARS	VILEST
SILENI	DIPLOE	WIGEON	FIGURE	TIGERS	WIDEST
SILENT	DITTOS	WILLOW	FILERS	TILERS	WISEST
SIMONE	FINNOC	WILSON	FINERY	TIMBRE	******
SIMONS	GIBBON	WILTON	FIRERS	TIMERS	-I--T-
SIMONY	GIBSON	WINDOW	FIVERS	TISHRI	******
SIRENS	GIDEON	WINNOW	FIXERS	VICARS	BIDETS
SIRING	GIGLOT	WISDOM	GIBERS	VINERY	BIGHTS
SITING	GISMOS	ZIRCON	HIDERS	VIPERS	BIGOTS
SITINS	GIZMOS	******	HIKERS	VISARD	BILITY
SIZING	HICKOK	-I--P-	HILARY	VISORS	BINATE
TIDING	HIPPOS	******	HIRERS	VIZARD	BINITS
TIEINS	LICTOR	BICEPS	LIFERS	VIZIRS	CIVETS
TILING	LIQUOR	DIEPPE	LIGURE	VIZORS	DIGITI
TIMING	LISBOA	MIXUPS	LINERS	WINERY	DIGITS
TIRANA	LISBON	PINUPS	LITERS	WINTRY	DILATE
TIRING	LISSOM	SIRUPS	LIVERS	WIPERS	DILUTE
TISANE	MICRON	SIRUPY	LIVERY	WIRERS	DIMITY
TITANS	MIGNON	TIEUPS	LIZARD	WIVERN	DIVOTS
VICUNA	MIKLOS	WICOPY	MILERS	WIVERS	DIXITS
VIENNA	MILTON	******	MILORD	WIZARD	EIGHTH
VIKING	MINION	-I--R-	MIMERS	******	EIGHTS
VIMINA	MINNOW	******	MINERS	-I--S-	EIGHTY
VISHNU	MIRROR	AIDERS	MINORS	******	FIESTA
VISING	NIMROD	AIRDRY	MISERE	BIOPSY	FIGHTS
VIXENS	NIPPON	BIAFRA	MISERS	CIVISM	FILETS
WIDENS	PIANOS	BICARB	MISERY	DICAST	FINITE
WIGANS	PICTOR	BICORN	MITERS	DIGEST	FIRSTS
WILING	PIGEON	BIFORM	MIXERS	DIREST	FIXATE
WINING	PILLOW	BIHARI	OILERS	DISUSE	FIXITY
WIPING	PINGOS	BINARY	PIERRE	DIVEST	GIANTS
WIRING	PINION	BISTRO	PIETRO	FILOSE	GIOTTO
WISING	PINTOS	BITERS	PIKERS	FINEST	HIVITE
WIVING	PISTOL	CICERO	PINERY	FINISH	KIBITZ
WIZENS	PISTON	CIDERS	PIPERS	KIBOSH	KINETO
ZIRONS	RIBBON	CIGARS	RICERS	KINASE	LIGATE
******	SIGNOR	CIMBRI	RIDERS	KINESI	LIGHTS
-I--O-	SIMOOM	DICERS	RIGORS	LIAISE	LIMITS
******	SINEON	DIDERO	RIMERS	LIPASE	MIGHTY
BILLON	SIPHON	DIMERS	RISERS	MIMOSA	MINUTE
BILLOW	TINPOT	DINARS	RITARD	MISUSE	NICETY

NIGHTS	HINDUS	******	******	******	FLORAS
NIGHTY	HIPPUS	-I--X-	-K--B-	-K--N-	FLYMAN
NIMITZ	LIGNUM	******	******	******	GLOBAL
NINETY	LIMBUS	BILOXI	AKIMBO	EKEING	LLAMAS
PICOTS	LINEUP	******	******	SKEANS	OLDHAM
PIGSTY	LINGUA	-I--Y-	-K--C-	SKEINS	PLAGAL
PILATE	LITMUS	******	******	SKIING	PLANAR
PILOTS	MIDGUT	BIALYS	SKETCH	SKINNY	PLATAN
PINITE	MILIUM	BILLYS		SKYING	PLAYAS
PIPETS	MINIUM	CINDYS	-K--D-	******	PLAZAS
PIPITS	MISCUE	CISSYS	******	-K--O-	PLEIAD
PIRATE	MISSUS	JIMMYS	SKALDS	******	PLICAE
PIVOTS	NIMBUS	JINNYS	******	SKIMOS	PLURAL
RIALTO	PICKUP	KITTYS	-K--E-	******	SLOGAN
RIGHTO	PIERUS	LIBBYS	******	-K--P-	SLOVAK
RIGHTS	PIGNUS	LIMEYS	AKENES	******	ULEMAS
RIVETS	PIGNUT	LIZZYS	OKAYED	SKIMPS	******
SIESTA	PILEUM	MICKYS	SKATED	SKIMPY	-L--B-
SIGHTS	PILEUP	MILLYS	SKATER	******	******
TIGHTS	PILEUS	NICKYS	SKATES	-K--R-	BLEBBY
TINCTS	PILOUS	RICKYS	SKEWED	******	BLOWBY
VISITS	PINDUS	TILLYS	SKEWER	SKERRY	BLURBS
ZIBETH	RICTUS	TIMMYS	SKIVED	SKIERS	CLIMBS
ZIBETS	RIGOUR	VICKYS	SKIVER	SKIRRS	FLABBY
ZIZITH	RIMOUS	VINNYS	SKIVES	******	FLAMBE
******	RIMOUS	WILLYS	SKYMEN	-K--T-	PLUMBO
-I--U-	RISQUE	******	UKASES	******	PLUMBS
******	SIDDUR	-I--Z-	******	SKIRTS	******
AIRGUN	SINFUL	******	-K--F-	******	-L--C-
BIJOUX	SIRIUS	PIAZZA	******	-K--V-	******
BISQUE	TISSUE	******	SKIFFS	******	ALMUCE
CILIUM	TITTUP	-J--A-	******	SKIVVY	ALPACA
CINQUE	VIGOUR	******	-K--I-	******	ALSACE
CIRCUM	VILLUS	AJOWAN	******	-L--A-	BLANCH
CIRCUS	VINOUS	******	OKAPIS	******	BLEACH
CIRQUE	VIRTUE	-J--T-	******	ALEGAR	BLENCH
CIRRUS	VISCUS	******	-K--J-	ALIDAD	BLOTCH
CITRUS	WIKIUP	EJECTA	******	ALPHAS	CLENCH
DICTUM	WILBUR	EJECTS	SKOPJE	ALULAE	CLINCH
DIMOUT	WILFUL	******	******	ALULAR	CLOACA
DINGUS	WINDUP	-J--W-	-K--K-	CLARAS	CLUTCH
DINKUM	******	******	******	CLIMAT	FLEECE
DISCUS	-I--W-	OJIBWA	SKINKS	CLIMAX	FLEECY
FICHUS	******	******	SKULKS	ELENAS	FLENCH
FITFUL	DISOWN	-K--A-	SKUNKS	ELIJAH	FLETCH
GIAOUR	SINEWS	******	******	ELIZAS	FLINCH
HIATUS	SINEWY	SKYCAP	-K--L-	FLORAE	FLITCH
HICCUP	WIDOWS	SKYMAN	SKILLS	FLORAL	GLANCE
		SKYWAY	SKULLS		

GLAUCO	BLADED	FLAKED	GLOZED	SLIVER	******
PLAICE	BLADES	FLAKER	GLOZES	SLOPED	-L--H-
PLANCH	BLAMED	FLAKES	GLUIER	SLOPER	******
PLANCK	BLAMES	FLAMED	GLUMES	SLOPES	ALEPHS
PLEACH	BLARED	FLAMEN	GLUTEI	SLOVEN	ALIGHT
SLOUCH	BLARES	FLAMES	GLUTEN	SLOWED	ALMAHS
SLUICE	BLAZED	FLARED	ILEXES	SLOWER	BLIGHT
ULENCE	BLAZER	FLARES	OLIVER	ULSTER	BLITHE
******	BLAZES	FLAWED	OLIVES	******	CLICHE
-L--D-	BLIMEY	FLAXEN	OLLIES	-L--F-	CLOCHE
******	BLOKES	FLAXES	PLACED	******	CLOTHE
ALBEDO	BLOWER	FLAYED	PLACER	BLUFFS	CLOTHO
ALLUDE	CLARES	FLAYER	PLACES	CLIFFS	CLOTHS
ALMUDE	CLARET	FLEXED	PLACET	CLIFFY	ELISHA
ALMUDS	CLAWED	FLEXES	PLANED	FLUFFS	FLASHY
BLEEDS	CLAYED	FLORES	PLANER	FLUFFY	FLECHE
BLENDE	CLAYEY	FLORET	PLANES	******	FLESHY
BLENDS	CLEVER	FLOWED	PLANET	-L--G-	FLIGHT
BLINDS	CLEWED	FLOWER	PLATED	******	GLYPHS
BLONDE	CLIMES	FLUKED	PLATEN	ALLEGE	PLASHY
BLONDS	CLINES	FLUKES	PLATER	BLUNGE	PLIGHT
BLOODS	CLIVES	FLUKEY	PLATES	CLANGS	PLUSHY
BLOODY	CLONES	FLUMED	PLAYED	CLERGY	SLIGHT
CLAUDE	CLOSED	FLUMES	PLAYER	CLINGS	SLOSHY
CLODDY	CLOSER	FLUTED	PLEBES	CLINGY	SLOTHS
CLOUDS	CLOSES	FLUTER	PLOVER	CLOGGY	SLUSHY
CLOUDY	CLOSET	FLUTES	PLOWED	CLOUGH	******
ELANDS	CLOVEN	FLUXED	PLOWER	ELOIGN	-L--I-
FLOODS	CLOVER	FLUXES	PLUMED	FLAGGY	******
FLOYDS	CLOVES	GLACES	PLUMES	FLANGE	ALALIA
FLUIDS	CLOYED	GLADES	PLUSES	FLEDGE	ALARIC
GLANDS	CLYDES	GLARED	SLAKED	FLEDGY	ALBEIT
LLOYDS	CLYPEI	GLARES	SLAKES	FLINGS	ALCAIC
PLAIDS	ELATED	GLAZED	SLATED	FLONGS	ALCUIN
PLEADS	ELATER	GLAZER	SLATER	PLEDGE	ALEXIA
******	ELATES	GLAZES	SLATES	PLOUGH	ALEXIN
-L--E-	ELDRED	GLEBES	SLAVED	PLUNGE	ALEXIS
******	ELEVEN	GLEDES	SLAVER	SLAGGY	ALGOID
ALATED	ELIDED	GLIDED	SLAVES	SLANGY	ALIBIS
ALFRED	ELIDES	GLIDER	SLAYER	SLEDGE	ALICIA
ALICES	ELLIES	GLIDES	SLEWED	SLEIGH	ALTAIC
ALINED	ELOPED	GLOBED	SLICED	SLINGS	ALTAIR
ALINES	ELOPER	GLOBES	SLICER	SLOUGH	ALUMIN
ALIPED	ELOPES	GLOVED	SLICES	SLUDGE	CLERIC
ALLIED	ELSIES	GLOVER	SLIDER	SLUDGY	CLERID
ALLIES	ELUDED	GLOVES	SLIDES	ULLAGE	CLEVIS
ALTHEA	ELUDES	GLOWED	SLIMED		CLINIC
ALUDEL	ELYSEE	GLOWER	SLIMES		CLONIC

CLOVIS	FLASKS	GLIOMA	GLEANS	******	BLUEST
ELEGIT	FLECKS	GLOOMS	GLUING	**-L--R-**	BLUISH
ELEMIS	FLICKS	GLOOMY	PLAINS	******	CLASSY
ELICIT	FLOCKS	ILLUME	PLAINT	ALBERT	CLAUSE
ELIXIR	FLOCKY	PLASMA	PLIANT	ALDERS	CLEIST
ELOHIM	FLUNKS	PLASMO	PLYING	ALLURE	CLUMSY
FLAVIA	FLUNKY	PLUMMY	SLUING	ALMIRA	ELAPSE
FLAVIN	PLACKS	SLUMMY	******	ALTARS	ELDEST
FLORID	PLANKS	ULTIMA	**-L--O-**	ALTERS	ELFISH
FLORIN	PLUCKS	ULTIMO	******	BLEARS	ELOISE
FLUVIO	PLUCKY	******	ALAMOS	BLEARY	ELVISH
GLACIS	PLUNKS	**-L--N-**	ALBION	BLURRY	FLENSE
GLAMIS	SLACKS	******	ALISON	CLAIRE	FLIEST
GLOBIN	SLEEKS	ALBANY	ALPHOS	CLEARS	FLIMSY
GLORIA	SLEEKY	ALBINO	BLAZON	ELBERT	FLOSSY
GLYNIS	SLICKS	ALDINE	CLAMOR	ELDERS	GLASSY
OLEFIN	SLINKS	ALFONS	CLAROS	ELMERS	GLOSSO
OLIVIA	SLINKY	ALIENS	ELEVON	ELMIRA	GLOSSY
PLACID	******	ALIGNS	ELINOR	ELVERS	ILLUSE
PLAGIO	**-L--L-**	ALKANE	ELLIOT	ELVIRA	ILLUST
PLASIA	******	ALKENE	FLACON	ELYTRA	OLDEST
PLASIS	ALIBLE	ALKYNE	FLAGON	FLAIRS	OLDISH
PLEGIA	ALKALI	ALLANS	FLAVOR	FLEERS	PLEASE
PLUGIN	ALKYLS	ALLENS	FLEXOR	FLEURY	SLIEST
PLUVIO	ALLELE	ALMOND	GLYCOL	FLIERS	SLIMSY
SLAVIC	ALLYLS	ALPINE	KLAXON	FLOORS	SLYEST
******	BLUELY	ALUINO	LLANOS	FLOURS	******
-L--K-	FLAILS	ALUINS	PLEXOR	FLOURY	**-L--T-**
******	FLATLY	ALUMNA	SLALOM	FLUORO	******
ALASKA	GLADLY	ALUMNI	SLIPON	FLUORS	ALBATA
ALFAKI	GLIBLY	ALVANS	******	FLURRY	ALBITE
ALSIKE	GLUMLY	ALVINA	**-L--P-**	FLYERS	ALCOTT
BLACKS	ILOILO	ALVINE	******	GLAIRS	ALECTO
BLANKS	SLIMLY	BLAINS	ALEPPO	GLAIRY	ALERTS
BLEAKS	SLOWLY	BLENNY	BLIMPS	ILFORD	ALEUTS
BLINKS	******	BLUING	CLAMPS	PLEURA	ALLOTS
BLOCKS	**-L--M-**	CLEANS	CLASPS	PLEURO	BLASTO
BLOCKY	******	CLIENT	CLUMPS	PLIERS	BLASTS
CLACKS	ALARMS	CLOWNS	CLUMPY	SLURRY	BLEATS
CLANKS	ALBUMS	CLUING	FLOPPY	ULCERS	BLINTZ
CLERKS	BLOOMS	ELAINE	FLUMPS	******	BLOATS
CLICKS	BLOOMY	ELAYNE	PLUMPS	**-L--S-**	BLUETS
CLINKS	CLAIMS	ELFINS	SLEEPS	******	BLUNTS
CLOAKS	CLAMMY	ELLENS	SLEEPY	ALDOSE	BLURTS
CLOCKS	CLEOME	ELOINS	SLOOPS	ALMOST	CLEATS
CLUCKS	FLEAMS	ELAUNT	SLOPPY	ALONSO	CLEFTS
FLACKS	GLEAMS	FLUENT	SLUMPS	BLAISE	CLINTS
FLANKS	GLEAMY	FLYING	SLURPS	BLOUSE	CLOTTY

CLOUTS	PLENUM	******	IMARET	EMILIA	AMIDOL
ELECTS	PLEXUS	-M--B-	IMBUED	EMILIE	AMIGOS
ELIOTS	PLUTUS	******	IMBUES	EMILIO	AMNION
FLEETS	SLAPUP	AMOEBA	IMIDES	IMPAIR	EMPLOY
FLINTS	SLIPUP	IMBIBE	IMINES	******	******
FLINTY	******	******	IMMIES	-M--K-	-M--R-
FLIRTS	-L--V-	-M--C-	IMOGEN	******	******
FLIRTY	******	******	OMELET	SMACKS	AMBARI
FLOATS	ALCOVE	AMERCE	SMAZES	SMIRKS	AMBARY
FLOATY	CLEAVE	IMPACT	SMILED	SMOCKS	AMBERS
FLOUTS	SLEAVE	SMIRCH	SMILER	UMIAKS	AMBERY
GLEETS	SLEEVE	SMOOCH	SMILES	******	AMENRA
GLEETY	******	SMUTCH	SMITER	-M--L-	AMOURS
GLINTS	-L--W-	******	SMITES	******	AMPERE
GLOATS	******	-M--D-	SMOKED	AMPULE	AMPHRS
GLOSTS	ALLOWS	******	SMOKER	AMPULS	DMITRI
GLOTTO	ELBOWS	AMANDA	SMOKES	EMBALM	EMBARK
GLYPTO	******	AMENDS	UMBLES	EMBOLI	EMBARS
OLEATE	-L--Y-	EMBEDS	******	EMPALE	EMBERS
PLAITS	******	EMBODY	-M--G-	IMBALM	EMEERS
PLANTS	ALLAYS	EMENDS	******	IMPALA	EMIGRE
PLASTY	ALLEYS	IMBEDS	AMBAGE	IMPALE	EMPERY
PLATTE	ALLOYS	IMBODY	EMERGE	IMPELS	EMPIRE
PLEATS	ALPHYL	IMPEDE	IMPUGN	SMALLS	IMBARK
PLENTY	ALWAYS	******	SMUDGE	SMELLS	IMMURE
PLINTH	FLYBYS	-M--E-	SMUDGY	SMELLY	IMPARK
SLANTS	GLADYS	******	******	SMUGLY	IMPART
SLEETS	ZLOTYS	AMAZED	-M--H-	UMBELS	IMPORT
SLEETY	******	AMAZES	******	******	IMPURE
SLEUTH	-L--Z-	AMBLED	AMECHE	-M--M-	SMEARS
******		AMBLER	SMITHS	******	SMEARY
-L--U-	ALONZO	AMBLES	SMITHY	SMARMY	UMBERS
******	BLOWZY	AMICES	******	-M--N-	UMPIRE
ALARUM	FLOOZY	AMIDES	-M--I-	******	******
ALDOUS	SLEAZY	AMOLES	******	AMIENS	-M--S-
ALGOUS	******	AMULET	AMALIE	AMOUNT	******
ALLIUM	-M--A-	AMUSED	AMANIA	EMBANK	AMBUSH
ALLOUT	******	AMUSER	AMEBIC	IMMUNE	AMIDST
BLOWUP	AMEBAE	AMUSES	AMELIA	IMMUNO	EMBOSS
CLAQUE	AMEBAS	EMBLEM	AMELIE	IMPEND	IMMESH
CLIQUE	AMORAL	EMCEED	AMIDIC	IMPING	IMPASS
CLIQUY	AMYTAL	EMCEES	AMIDIN	******	IMPISH
CLONUS	OMEGAS	EMILES	AMYLIC	-M--O-	IMPOSE
ELBRUS	SMILAX	EMMIES	EMERIC	******	IMPOST
FLATUS	UMBRAE	EMOTED	EMERIE	AMADOU	******
PLAGUE	UMBRAL	EMOTES	EMESIS	AMATOL	-M--T-
PLAGUY	UMBRAS	IMAGED	EMETIC	AMAZON	******
PLAQUE		IMAGES	EMETIN		AMBITS
					AMENTI

AMENTS	ANYWAY	INDUCE	ANTHER	SNORES	******
AMRITA	ENDEAR	INDUCT	ANTLER	SNOWED	**-N--H-**
EMEUTE	ENEMAS	INFECT	ANUSES	UNBRED	******
EMMETS	ENGRAM	INJECT	ENAMEL	UNCLES	GNATHO
EMMETT	ENNEAD	INLACE	ENATES	UNDIES	KNIGHT
IMPUTE	ENTRAP	INSECT	ENDUED	UNDOER	SNATHE
OMENTA	ENWRAP	INTACT	ENDUES	UNDOES	SNATHS
SMALTI	INDIAN	SNATCH	ENSUED	UNDREW	******
SMALTO	INROAD	SNITCH	ENSUES	UNDSET	**-N--I-**
SMARTS	INSPAN	UNCOCK	ENTREE	UNEVEN	******
SMELTS	INSTAR	UNESCO	ENVIED	UNGUES	ANEMIA
SMOLTS	INWRAP	UNLACE	ENVIER	UNICEF	ANEMIC
SMOOTH	ONEWAY	UNLOCK	ENVIES	UNIPED	ANGLIA
SMUTTY	SNOCAT	UNPACK	GNAWED	UNISEX	ANGLIC
******	UNBEAR	UNPICK	GNAWER	UNITED	ANILIN
-M--U-	UNCIAL	UNTACK	GNOMES	UNITES	ANODIC
******	UNCLAD	******	INBRED	UNMEET	ANOMIA
AMYLUM	UNDRAW	**-N--D-**	INCHED	UNREEL	ANOMIC
EMBRUE	UNGUAL	******	INCHES	UNSEEN	ANOMIE
IMBRUE	UNLEAD	ENCODE	INDEED	UNSTEP	ANOXIA
OMASUM	UNLOAD	INSIDE	INDIES	UNTIED	ANOXIC
OMNIUM	UNREAD	INVADE	INDUED	UNTIES	ANTLIA
UMLAUT	UNREAL	KNEADS	INDUES	UNUSED	ANTRIM
******	UNSEAL	ONEIDA	INGRES	******	ANUBIS
-M--W-	UNSEAM	SNOODS	INKIER	**-N--F-**	ENJOIN
******	UNSEAT	UNLADE	INKLES	******	ENOSIS
EMBOWS	UNWRAP	UNMADE	INLIER	ONEOFF	ENTAIL
IMPAWN	******	UNTIDY	INSTEP	SNIFFS	GNOMIC
******	**-N--B-**	******	INURED	SNIFFY	GNOSIS
-M--Y-	******	**-N--E-**	INURES	SNUFFS	INDRIS
******	ENROBE	******	KNAVES	SNUFFY	INGRID
EMBAYS	INCUBI	ANADEM	KNIFED	UNSAFE	INLAID
EMBRYO	INDABA	ANDREA	KNIFES	******	INSTIL
EMILYS	KNOBBY	ANDREI	KNIVES	**-N--G-**	INTUIT
******	SNOBBY	ANDRES	KNOWER	******	INULIN
-N--A-	UNROBE	ANDREW	ONAGER	ANERGY	UNAPID
******	******	ANGLED	ONUSES	ANLAGE	UNCOIL
ANABAS	**-N--C-**	ANGLER	SNAKED	ENCAGE	UNFAIR
ANANAS	******	ANGLES	SNAKES	ENERGY	UNGUIS
ANDEAN	ANLACE	ANISES	SNARED	ENGAGE	UNHAIR
ANIMAL	ANTICS	ANKLES	SNARER	ENOUGH	UNIFIC
ANIMAS	ENFACE	ANKLET	SNARES	ENRAGE	UNKNIT
ANITAS	ENLACE	ANNIES	SNIPED	ENSIGN	UNLAID
ANNEAL	ENRICH	ANODES	SNIPER	INCAGE	UNSAID
ANNUAL	ENRICO	ANSWER	SNIPES	INDIGO	UNSHIP
ANORAK	ENTICE	ANTEED	SNIVEL	SNAGGY	UNVEIL
ANTIAR	INARCH	ANTHEA	SNORED	UNCAGE	
ANURAN	INDICT	ANTHEM	SNORER	UNPEGS	
				UNRIGS	

******	KNOLLS	ANOINT	INDOOR	INFIRM	INRUSH
-N--K-	KNURLS	ANTONS	INFLOW	INFORM	INSIST
******	KNURLY	ANTONY	INKPOT	INHERE	INVEST
ANANKE	ONEILL	ANYONE	UNHOOK	INJURE	ONRUSH
INJOKE	ONFALL	ENCINA	UNISON	INJURY	UNCASE
INTAKE	SNAILS	ENDING	UNMOOR	INKERS	UNEASE
INVOKE	SNARLS	ENGINE	UNROOT	INSERT	UNEASY
KNACKS	SNARLY	ENWIND	UNSHOD	INSURE	UNHASP
KNOCKS	SNELLS	INBAND	UNSTOP	INTERN	UNHUSK
SNACKS	SNUGLY	INDENE	UNTROD	INTERS	UNJUST
SNEAKS	UNABLE	INDENT	******	INTURN	UNLASH
SNEAKY	UNBELT	INFANT	**-N--P-**	INVERT	UNLESS
SNICKS	UNBOLT	INKING	******	INWARD	UNMASK
SNOOKS	UNDULY	INLAND	ENRAPT	KNARRY	UNREST
UNLIKE	UNFOLD	INNING	INCEPT	ONAGRI	UNWISE
UNMAKE	UNGULA	INSANE	KNOSPS	ONEIRO	UNWISH
UNYOKE	UNHOLY	INTEND	SNAPPY	ONWARD	******
******	UNPILE	INTENT	SNIPPY	SNEERS	**-N--T-**
-N--L-	UNROLL	INTONE	SNOOPS	UNBARS	******
******	UNRULY	INURNS	SNOOPY	UNBORN	ANATTO
ANGELA	UNSOLD	INVENT	UNCAPS	UNCORD	ANSATE
ANGELO	UNTOLD	INWIND	UNRIPE	UNCORK	ENACTS
ANGELS	UNWELL	ONIONS	UNRIPS	UNCURL	ENMITY
ANGOLA	******	ONIONY	UNWEPT	UNFURL	ENTITY
ANKYLO	**-N--M-**	ONLINE	******	UNGIRD	INCITE
ANNALS	******	UNBEND	**-N--R-**	UNGIRT	INDITE
ANNULS	ENCAMP	UNBENT	******	UNHURT	INGOTS
ANSELM	ENIGMA	UNBIND	ANGARY	UNSURE	INLETS
ANVILS	ENTOMB	UNDINE	ANGERS	UNWARY	INMATE
ENABLE	ENTOMO	UNDONE	ANGORA	UNWORN	INNATE
ENDALL	ENWOMB	UNHAND	ANITRA	******	INPUTS
ENFOLD	ENZYME	UNIONS	ANKARA	**-N--S-**	INSETS
ENGELS	INARMS	UNKIND	ANTERO	******	INVITE
ENGULF	INCOME	UNMANS	ENCORE	ENCASE	KNOTTY
ENISLE	INFAMY	UNPINS	ENDURE	ENCASH	KNOUTS
ENROLL	INHUME	UNSUNG	ENGIRD	ENCYST	ONSETS
ENSILE	INTIMA	UNWIND	ENGIRT	ENLIST	SNOOTS
GNARLS	INTOMB	******	ENSURE	ENMESH	SNOOTY
GNARLY	PNEUMA	**-N--O-**	ENTERA	GNEISS	SNORTS
INDULT	PNEUMO	******	ENTERE	INCASE	SNOTTY
INFOLD	******	ANALOG	ENTERO	INCEST	SNOUTS
INGULF	**-N--N-**	ANCHOR	ENTERS	INCISE	UNHATS
INHALE	******	ANGKOR	ENTIRE	INCUSE	******
INSOLE	ANCONA	ANYHOW	INBORN	INFEST	**-N--U-**
INSULT	ANCONE	ENAMOR	INCORP	INFUSE	******
INWALL	ANGINA	ENROOT	INCURS	INGEST	ANIMUS
KNEELS	ANIONS	GNOMON	INFERO	INMESH	ANTRUM
KNELLS	ANNONA	INCHON	INFERS	INMOST	ENSOUL

INDIUM	AORTAS	DOGMAS	MOLLAH	******	GONADS
INFLUX	AOUDAD	DOLLAR	MONDAY	-O--C-	GOURDE
INHAUL	BOBCAT	DOLMAN	MOOLAH	******	GOURDS
INSOUL	BOGOAK	DONNAS	MOREAU	BODICE	HOARDS
SNAFUS	BOMBAY	DOODAD	MORGAN	BONACI	HOUNDS
UNIQUE	BONSAI	DORIAN	MORTAL	BORSCH	IODIDE
UNPLUG	BOREAL	DORSAD	MORTAR	BOUNCE	MONADS
UNTRUE	BOREAS	DORSAL	NORIAS	BOUNCY	MONODY
******	BOWMAN	DOSSAL	NORMAL	COERCE	NOBODY
-N--V-	BOWSAW	DOUGAL	NORMAN	COMICS	NOMADS
******	BOXCAR	DOWLAS	NORMAS	CONICS	POINDS
ENDIVE	COAXAL	EOLIAN	NORWAY	COPECK	POMADE
INWOVE	COBIAS	EONIAN	NOUGAT	DODECA	POSADA
UNLIVE	COBRAS	FOEMAN	NOUNAL	HOOTCH	POUNDS
******	COCCAL	FOETAL	OOMIAK	HORACE	ROALDS
-N--W-	COCOAS	FOLIAR	POLEAX	JOUNCE	ROUNDS
******	COEVAL	FONTAL	POLKAS	KOPECK	SOLIDI
ENDOWS	COGNAC	FORMAL	POPLAR	LORICA	SOLIDS
INDOWS	COGWAY	FORMAT	PORTAL	MOHOCK	SOUNDS
INLAWS	COITAL	FORNAX	POSTAL	MOLOCH	TOLEDO
UNHEWN	COLLAR	FOSSAE	POTMAN	MONACO	WOALDS
UNMEWS	COLZAS	FOVEAE	RODMAN	MONICA	WORLDS
******	COMBAT	FOVEAL	ROSEAL	NOTICE	WOUNDS
-N--X-	COMMAS	GODDAM	SOCIAL	NOVICE	ZOOIDS
******	CONFAB	GOORAL	SOCMAN	POLACK	ZOUNDS
ANNEXE	CONGAS	GOTHAM	SOFTAS	POLICE	******
UNVEXT	CONMAN	HODMAN	SONIAS	POLICY	-O--E-
******	CONRAD	HOOKAH	SONYAS	POMACE	******
-N--Y-	CONWAY	HOORAY	TOBIAH	POUNCE	BOATED
******	COPRAH	HOWDAH	TOBIAS	ROCOCO	BOATER
ANNOYS	CORBAN	IONIAN	TOECAP	SOLACE	BOBBED
ANONYM	CORDAY	JORDAN	TOMBAC	SOURCE	BOBBER
ENJOYS	CORRAL	JOSIAH	TOMCAT	TONICS	BODIED
ENVOYS	CORSAC	JOSIAS	TOPHAT	TOPICS	BODIES
INLAYS	COSTAE	JOTHAM	TOUCAN	VOMICA	BOGGED
UNLAYS	COSTAL	JOVIAL	VODKAS	YORICK	BOGIES
UNSAYS	COSTAR	JOVIAN	VOLVAS	******	BOGLES
******	COTEAU	KOALAS	WOMBAT	-O--D-	BOILED
-N--Z-	COTTAE	KODIAK	ZODIAC	******	BOILER
******	COTTAR	KONRAD	ZOONAL	BOARDS	BOLDER
SNAZZY	COTTAS	KOREAN	******	BOLIDE	BOLLED
SNEEZE	COUGAR	LOGJAM	-O--B-	BORIDE	BOLTED
SNEEZY	COWMAN	LONGAN	******	BOUNDS	BOLTER
SNOOZE	DOBLAS	LOOFAH	COOMBS	COMEDO	BOMBED
******	DOBRAS	LOQUAR	GOODBY	COMEDY	BOMBER
-O--A-	DOGEAR	LOQUAT	YORUBA	CORODY	BOMBES
******		MOBCAP		DORADO	
AORTAE		MOIRAS		FOUNDS	
AORTAL					

BONDED	COELED	CORKER	DONNED	FORMED	HOCKED
BONDER	COFFEE	CORNEA	DOOLEE	FORMER	HOCKEY
BONGED	COFFER	CORNED	DOOMED	FORTES	HODDEN
BONIER	COGGED	CORNEL	DOPIER	FOSSES	HOGGED
BONNET	COIFED	CORNER	DOPTER	FOSTER	HOIDEN
BONZER	COILED	CORNET	DOREEN	FOULED	HOLDER
BONZES	COILER	CORSES	DORIES	FOULER	HOLIER
BOOKED	COINED	CORSET	DORMER	FOWLED	HOLIES
BOOMED	COINER	CORTES	DORSET	FOWLER	HOLLER
BOOMER	COLDER	CORTEX	DOSSED	FOXIER	HOLMES
BOOTED	COLIES	CORTEZ	DOSSEL	GOADED	HOMIER
BOOTEE	COLLET	CORVEE	DOSSER	GOATEE	HONIED
BOOZED	COLTER	CORVES	DOTIER	GOBBET	HONKED
BOOZER	COMBED	COSHED	DOTTED	GOBIES	HONKER
BOOZES	COMBER	COSHER	DOTTEL	GOBLET	HOODED
BOPPED	COMPEL	COSHES	DOTTER	GOFFER	HOOFED
BORDEL	CONFER	COSSES	DOUSED	GOGLET	HOOFER
BORDER	CONGER	COSSET	DOUSES	GOITER	HOOKED
BORNEO	CONGES	COSTED	DOWNED	GOLDEN	HOOKER
BOSHES	CONIES	COSTER	DOWSED	GOLFED	HOOKEY
BOSKET	CONKED	COTTER	DOWSER	GOLFER	HOOPED
BOSSED	CONKER	COULEE	DOWSES	GOOBER	HOOPER
BOSSES	CONNED	COUPES	DOXIES	GOOFED	HOOTED
BOTHER	CONNER	COWMEN	DOYLEY	GOOIER	HOOTER
BOULES	CONTES	COWPEA	DOZIER	GOONEY	HOOVED
BOUSED	CONVEX	COWPER	FOALED	GOOSED	HOOVER
BOUSES	CONVEY	COZIER	FOAMED	GOOSES	HOOVES
BOWLED	COOEED	COZIES	FOBBED	GOOSEY	HOPPED
BOWLEG	COOEES	DOBBER	FODDER	GOPHER	HOPPER
BOWLER	COOKED	DOBIES	FOEMEN	GORGED	HORDED
BOWMEN	COOKER	DOCKED	FOGGED	GORGER	HORDES
BOWSED	COOKEY	DOCKER	FOGIES	GORGES	HORNED
BOWSES	COOLED	DOCKET	FOILED	GORGET	HORNET
BOWYER	COOLER	DODDER	FOLDED	GORHEN	HORSED
COALED	COOPED	DODGED	FOLDER	GORIER	HORSES
COALER	COOPER	DODGER	FONDER	GORSES	HORSEY
COATED	COPIED	DODGES	FOOLED	GOSHEN	HOSIER
COATEE	COPIER	DODOES	FOOTED	GOSPEL	HOSTED
COAXED	COPIES	DOFFED	FOOTER	GOTTEN	HOSTEL
COAXER	COPLEY	DOFFER	FORCED	GOUGED	HOTBED
COAXES	COPPED	DOGGED	FORCER	GOUGER	HOTTED
COBBER	COPPER	DOGGER	FORCES	GOUGES	HOTTER
COBLES	COPSES	DOGIES	FORDED	GOWNED	HOUSED
COBWEB	COQUET	DOITED	FORGED	HOAXED	HOUSES
COCKED	CORBEL	DOLLED	FORGER	HOAXER	HOWLED
COCKER	CORDED	DOLMEN	FORGES	HOAXES	HOWLER
CODDER	CORDER	DONEES	FORGET	HOBBES	HOYDEN
CODGER	CORKED	DONKEY	FORKED	HOBOES	JOBBED

JOBBER	LOOKED	MOPPED	PONTES	ROOFED	SONNET
JOCKEY	LOOKER	MOPPET	POOLED	ROOFER	SOONER
JOGGED	LOOMED	MOREEN	POOPED	ROOKED	SOOTED
JOGGER	LOOPED	MORGEN	POORER	ROOMED	SOPPED
JOINED	LOOPER	MORLEY	POPPED	ROOMER	SORBET
JOINER	LOOSED	MORSEL	POPPER	ROOTED	SORREL
JOLIET	LOOSEN	MOSLEM	POPPET	ROOTER	SORTED
JOLTED	LOOSER	MOSLEY	PORKER	ROPIER	SORTER
JOLTER	LOOSES	MOSSES	PORTED	ROQUET	SOULED
JORGES	LOOTED	MOTHER	PORTER	ROSIER	SOUPED
JOSHED	LOOTER	MOTLEY	POSIES	ROSTER	SOURED
JOSHER	LOPPED	MOUSED	POSSES	ROTTED	SOURER
JOSHES	LORDED	MOUSER	POSSET	ROTTEN	SOUSED
JOSIEA	LOREEN	MOUSES	POSTED	ROTTER	SOUSES
JOSSES	LORIES	MOVIES	POSTER	ROUGED	SOVIET
JOTTED	LOSSES	NOBBED	POTEEN	ROUGES	TOBIES
JOTTER	LOUDEN	NOBLER	POTHER	ROUSED	TODIES
JOULES	LOUDER	NOCKED	POTTED	ROUSER	TOFFEE
JOYCES	LOUPES	NODDED	POTTER	ROUSES	TOGAED
KOINES	LOURED	NODDER	POURED	ROUTED	TOGGED
KOPJES	LOUSED	NOISED	POURER	ROUTER	TOGUES
KOSHER	LOUSES	NOISES	POUTED	ROUTES	TOILED
LOADED	LOUVER	NOOSED	POUTER	SOAKED	TOILER
LOADER	LOWKEY	NOOSES	POWDER	SOAKER	TOILES
LOAFED	MOANED	NOREEN	POWTER	SOAPED	TOILET
LOAFER	MOATED	NOSHED	ROAMED	SOARED	TOLLED
LOAMED	MOBBED	NOSIER	ROAMER	SOARER	TOLLER
LOANED	MOBBER	OODLES	ROARED	SOBBED	TOLTEC
LOAVES	MOCKED	OOZIER	ROARER	SOCCER	TOMBED
LOBBED	MOCKER	POCKET	ROBBED	SOCKED	TONGED
LOBBER	MOILED	PODDED	ROBBER	SOCKET	TONIER
LOCKED	MOILER	POGIES	ROBLES	SOCLES	TOOLED
LOCKER	MOLDED	POISED	ROCHET	SOCMEN	TOOLER
LOCKET	MOLDER	POISES	ROCKED	SOCRED	TOOTED
LOCOED	MOLIES	POKIER	ROCKER	SODDED	TOOTER
LODGED	MOLTED	POKIES	ROCKET	SODDEN	TOPPED
LODGER	MOLTEN	POLDER	RODMEN	SOEVER	TOPPER
LODGES	MOLTER	POLLED	RODNEY	SOFTEN	TOQUES
LOFTED	MONGER	POLLEE	ROGUED	SOFTER	TORIES
LOFTER	MONIED	POLLEN	ROGUES	SOILED	TOSHES
LOGGED	MONIES	POLLER	ROILED	SOIREE	TOSSED
LOGGER	MONKEY	POLLEX	ROLLED	SOLDER	TOSSES
LOGIER	MONTES	POMMEL	ROLLER	SOLOED	TOTHER
LOITER	MOOLEY	POMPEY	ROMMEL	SOLVED	TOTTED
LOLLED	MOONED	PONDER	ROMNEY	SOLVER	TOTTER
LOLLER	MOORED	PONGEE	ROMPED	SOLVES	TOUPEE
LONGED	MOOTED	PONIED	ROMPER	SOMBER	TOURED
LONGER	MOOTER	PONIES	RONDEL	SONDER	TOURER

TOUTED	BOURGS	NOUGHT	COMMIE	LOOKIN	******
TOUTER	COLUGO	POACHY	COMMIT	LORAIN	-O--K-
VOGUES	COSIGN	PONCHO	COMMIX	LOTTIE	******
VOICED	COWAGE	POUCHY	CONNIE	LOVEIN	HOICKS
VOICES	DOINGS	ROLPHS	CONOID	MOHAIR	KODAKS
VOIDED	DOSAGE	ROTCHE	CONTIN	MOLLIE	KOPEKS
VOILES	DOTAGE	ROUCHE	COOKIE	MORBID	MOLTKE
VOLLEY	FORAGE	ROUGHS	COOLIE	MORRIS	MOPOKE
VOLTED	FOREGO	SOOTHE	COOTIE	MOSAIC	TOPEKA
VORTEX	GOINGS	SORGHO	COPTIC	MOULIN	TORSKS
WOADED	HOMAGE	SOUGHS	CORBIE	NOESIS	YOICKS
WOLFED	LOUNGE	SOUGHT	CORGIS	NOETIC	******
WOLSEY	LOVAGE	TOOTHY	CORRIE	NOGGIN	-O--L-
WOLVER	NONAGE	TORAHS	CORTIN	NORDIC	******
WOLVES	NONEGO	TOUCHE	COSMIC	NORNIR	BOBBLE
WOMBED	OOLOGY	TOUCHY	COUSIN	NORRIS	BODILY
WONDER	POTAGE	TOUGHS	COWRIE	NOSTIC	BOGGLE
WONTED	SOCAGE	WORTHY	DOBBIN	POETIC	BOLDLY
WOODED	TOBAGO	YOUTHS	DOGGIE	PONTIC	BOODLE
WOODEN	TOWAGE	******	DOLLIE	PONTIL	BOOTLE
WOOFER	VOYAGE	-O--I-	DOMAIN	POPLIN	BOTFLY
WOOLEN	******	******	DONNIE	PORTIA	BOTTLE
WORDED	******	AORTIC	DOOLIE	POTPIE	BOUCLE
WORKED	-O--H-	BOBBIE	DORMIE	POTSIE	BOWELS
WORKER	******	BOBBIN	DOSSIL	ROBBIA	COBALT
WORMED	BOOTHS	BOCCIE	DOUGIE	ROBBIE	COBBLE
WORMER	BOTCHY	BODKIN	EOZOIC	ROMAIC	COBBLY
WORSEN	BOUGHS	BOFFIN	FOETID	RONNIE	COCKLE
WORSER	BOUGHT	BOLLIX	FORBID	ROOKIE	CODDLE
WOWSER	CONCHA	BOMBIC	FORMIC	SOFFIT	COFFLE
YOGEES	CONCHS	BONNIE	FORNIX	SOPHIA	COLDLY
YONDER	CONCHY	BOOGIE	FORTIS	SOPHIE	COMELY
YONKER	COUGHS	BOOKIE	FOSSIL	SORDID	COMPLY
YORKER	DOLPHS	BOOTIE	GOALIE	SORTIE	COODLE
YOWLED	DOUCHE	BORGIA	GOBLIN	SOTHIC	COOLLY
ZOOMED	DOUGHS	BOUGIE	GODWIN	SOTHIS	COPALM
ZOSTER	DOUGHY	BOWFIN	GODWIT	TOCSIN	COPULA
******	FOUGHT	BOWTIE	GOSSIP	TOMTIT	CORALS
-O--F-	GOETHE	COATIS	GOTHIC	TONKIN	COSILY
******	HONSHU	COCAIN	HOGTIE	TONSIL	COSTLY
BOUFFE	JONAHS	COCCID	HOLMIC	TORIIS	COUPLE
CODIFY	LOATHE	COCHIN	HORNIE	TOROID	COZILY
MODIFY	LOTAHS	CODEIA	HORRID	TORPID	DOABLE
MOTIFS	LOUGHS	CODEIN	HOURIS	TORRID	DOALLS
NOTIFY	MOISHE	COFFIN	JONNIE	ZOMBIE	DOCILE
******	MONTHS	COHEIR	JOPLIN	ZOMBIS	DONALD
-O--G-	MORPHO	COLLIE	LOCHIA	ZOYSIA	DOODLE
******	MOUTHS	COMFIT	LOGGIA		DOTTLE
BODEGA	MOUTHY				
BORAGE					

DOUBLE	MORULA	TOUSLE	COLINE	JOHNNY	ROSINY
DOUBLY	MOSTLY	TOWELS	COLINS	JOKING	ROTUND
DOURLY	MOTELS	VOCALS	COLONS	JOYING	ROVING
DOWELS	MOTILE	VOGULS	COLONY	KORUNA	ROWANS
DOZILY	MOTTLE	VOWELS	COMING	KORUNY	ROWENA
FOCSLE	NOBALL	WOBBLE	CONING	LOMENT	ROWING
FOIBLE	NOBBLE	WOBBLY	COOING	LOMOND	ROXANA
FONDLE	NODDLE	WOOLLY	COPING	LOOING	ROXANE
FONDLY	NODULE	YODELS	CORING	LOPING	SOIGNE
FOOTLE	NOELLE	YOKELS	CORONA	LORENE	SOLAND
FOOZLE	NOODLE	ZONULA	COSINE	LORENZ	SOLANO
FOULLY	NOPALS	ZONULE	COVING	LOSING ·	SOLANS
FOXILY	NOSILY	ZORILS	COWING	LOVING	SOLENT
GOBBLE	NOVELS	******	COXING	LOWING	SOLING
GOGGLE	NOZZLE	-O--M-	COZENS	MOLINE	SONANT
GOODLY	OOZILY	******	DOCENT	MOMENT	SOWING
GOOGLY	POMELO	BOSOMS	DOESNT	MOOING	SOZINE
GORALS	POODLE	COLUMN	DOLING	MOPING	SOZINS
GORILY	POORLY	CORYMB	DOMING	MORONS	TOEING
HOBBLE	POPPLE	FORUMS	DOMINO	MOURNS	TOKENS
HOLILY	PORTLY	GOTAMA	DOPING	MOVING	TOMANS
HOMELY	POSHLY	JORAMS	DOSING	MOWING	TONING
HOMILY	POTALE	JORUMS	DOTING	NOCENT	TOPING
HOOPLA	POTTLE	KOKOMO	DOYENS	NOSING	TOTING
HOPPLE	POWELL	SODOMY	DOZENS	NOTING	TOWING
HOTELS	ROBALO	SOLEMN	DOZING	NOVENA	TOXINS
HOURLY	ROMOLA	TOTEMS	EOCENE	OOLONG	TOYING
HOVELS	ROMULO	VOLUME	EOGENE	OOZING	TOYONS
JOGGLE	RONALD	******	FOEHNS	PODUNK	VOLANT
JOSTLE	ROOTLE	-O--N-	FOMENT	POKING	VOLING
KOBOLD	ROPILY	******	FORINT	POLAND	VOTING
LOBULE	ROSILY	BODING	FOXING	POLING	VOWING
LOCALE	ROUBLE	BOGANS	GOBANG	POMONA	WOOING
LOCALS	ROWELS	BONING	GORING	PONENT	WOWING
LONELY	ROYALE	BOOING	HOEING	PORING	YOGINS
LORDLY	ROYALS	BORANE	HOGANS	POSING	YOKING
LOUDLY	SOFTLY	BORING	HOLING	POTENT	YOWING
LOVELL	SOLELY	BOTANY	HOMING	ROBAND	ZONING
LOVELY	SOMALI	BOURNE	HOMINY	ROBING	******
LOWELL	SORELS	BOURNS	HONING	ROBINS	-O--O-
MOBILE	SORELY	BOVINE	HOPING	ROCKNE	******
MODELS	SOTOLS	BOWING	HOSING	RODENT	BOLSON
MODULE	SOURLY	BOXING	IODINE	ROLAND	BOLTON
MOGULS	TODDLE	CODING	IONONE	ROMANS	BONBON
MOHOLE	TOGGLE	COGENT	JOANNA	ROMANY	BONGOS
MORALE	TOOTLE	COHUNE	JOANNE	ROPING	BOOBOO
MORALS	TOPPLE	COIGNS	JOCUND	ROSING	BOOHOO
MORELS	TOTALS	COKING	JOHANN	ROSINS	BORROW

BORZOI	JOCKOS	TORPOR	GOITRE	SONARS	MODISH
BOSTON	JONSON	TORSOS	GOKART	SOUARI	MOLEST
BOTTOM	KOODOO	TOULON	GONERS	SOWARS	MOMISM
BOWWOW	KOWTOW	VOLVOX	GOVERN	SOWERS	MONGST
COCOON	LOGION	VOODOO	HOBART	TONERS	MONISM
COELOM	LOLLOP	YOOHOO	HOLARD	TOPERS	MONIST
COLLOP	LONDON	YOUPON	HOMBRE	TORERO	MOPISH
COMBOS	LOTION	******	HOMERS	TOTERS	MORASS
COMEON	LOWBOY	-O--P-	HONORE	TOWARD	MOROSE
COMMON	MONGOL	******	HONORS	TOWERS	MOUSSE
COMPOS	MONROE	COEMPT	HORARY	TOWERY	NODOSE
CONDOM	MORION	DOGAPE	HOVERS	TOYERS	NOMISM
CONDOR	MORMON	JOSEPH	HOWARD	VOLERY	NOWISE
CONGOU	MORROS	POLYPS	JOKERS	VOMERS	POLISH
CONTOS	MORROW	******	LONERS	VOTARY	POPISH
CONVOY	MORTON	-O--R-	LOPERS	VOTERS	POTASH
CORDON	MOSCOW	******	LOSERS	VOWERS	ROBUST
COSMOS	MOTION	BOLERO	LOUVRE	WOMERA	ROMISH
COTTON	MOTMOT	BONERS	LOVERS	WOOERS	SOREST
COUPON	MOTTOS	BORERS	LOWERS	YOGURT	TOOTSY
COWBOY	MOUTON	BOWERS	LOWERY	ZONARY	TOROSE
COWPOX	NOGOOD	BOWERY	MODERN	******	TOYISH
DOBLON	NONCOM	BOXERS	MOHURS	-O--S-	VOLOST
DOBSON	NOSHOW	BOYARD	MOLARS	******	WOODSY
DOCTOR	NOTION	BOYARS	MOPERS	AORIST	******
DOGFOX	OOPHOR	COBURG	MOTORS	BOURSE	-O--T-
DOLLOP	PODSOL	COHERE	MOVERS	BOYISH	******
DONJON	PODZOL	COHORT	MOWERS	COARSE	BOASTS
FOETOR	POGROM	COLORS	MOZART	COHOSH	BOGOTA
FOGBOW	POISON	COLURE	NOMURA	COMOSE	BONITO
FOGDOG	POMPOM	COMERS	NONARY	CORPSE	BOOSTS
FOLIOS	POMPON	CONTRA	NOTARY	COURSE	BORATE
FOLLOW	PONTON	CONTRE	NOTERS	COYISH	BOUNTY
FORGOT	POTBOY	COOERS	POETRY	DOVISH	BOVATE
GODSON	POTION	COPPRA	POKERS	EONISM	COASTS
GONION	POTTOS	CORERS	POPERY	FOLKSY	COMATE
GOOGOL	POWWOW	COVERS	POSERS	FOREST	COMETS
GORDON	ROBSON	COVERT	POWERS	GOLOSH	COMITY
GORGON	RODEOS	COWARD	ROBERT	HOARSE	COOPTS
HOBNOB	RONDOS	COWERS	ROGERS	HOLISM	COUNTS
HOLLOW	ROSCOE	DONORS	ROSARY	HONEST	COUNTY
HOODOO	SOLION	DOSERS	ROSTRA	IODISM	COURTS
HOOPOE	SORGOS	DOTARD	ROTARY	JOCOSE	COVETS
HORROR	SORROW	DOTERS	ROTORS	LOCUST	COYOTE
HOTBOX	TOLUOL	DOWERS	ROVERS	LOUISA	DONATE
HOTPOT	TOMBOY	DOWERY	ROWERS	LOUISE	DONETS
HOTROD	TOMCOD	FOYERS	SOBERS	LOWEST	DOUBTS
	TOMTOM	GOCART	SOMBRE	MODEST	EOLITH

FOISTS	******	POROUS	MOSEYS	******	SPIRED
FOUNTS	-O--U-	POSEUR	NOWAYS	-P--D-	SPIRES
FOURTH	******	POSSUM	POLLYS	******	SPITED
GOMUTI	COBNUT	POYOUS	POPPYS	APHIDS	SPITES
HOISTS	COCCUS	ROLLUP	RODDYS	EPHODS	SPLEEN
HORSTE	COCKUP	ROTGUT	TOLUYL	SPEEDS	SPOKED
IODATE	COITUS	SODIUM	TOMMYS	SPEEDY	SPOKEN
IOLITE	COLEUS	TONGUE	******	SPENDS	SPOKES
JOINTS	COLOUR	TOROUS	-O--Z-	UPENDS	SPORED
JOISTS	COLOUS	TORQUE	******	UPSIDE	SPORES
JOUSTS	COMOUS	TOSSUP	CORYZA	******	SPREES
LOBATE	CONCUR	VOROUS	IODIZE	-P--E-	SPRIER
LOCATE	CONIUM	VOYEUR	IONIZE	******	SPRUES
LOLITA	CONSUL	WOEFUL	******	APEXES	SPRYER
MOIETY	COPOUT	******	-P--A-	APICES	SPUMED
MOULTS	CORIUM	-O--V-	******	APNOEA	SPUMES
MOUNTS	CORNUA	******	APEMAN	APOGEE	UPASES
MOUNTY	CORNUS	GODIVA	APICAL	APPLES	UPKEEP
OOCYTE	CORPUS	MOHAVE	APNEAL	EPODES	******
OOLITE	CORVUS	MOJAVE	APODAL	EPOPEE	-P--F-
POINTE	COYPUS	MOTIVE	APPEAL	OPENED	******
POINTS	DOLOUR	VOTIVE	APPEAR	OPENER	SPIFFY
POINTY	DORBUG	ZOUAVE	APPIAN	OPINED	SPOOFS
POLITE	DORSUM	******	EPICAL	OPINES	UPLIFT
POLITY	FOETUS	-O--W-	IPECAC	SPACED	******
POSITS	FOLIUM	******	OPERAS	SPACER	-P--G-
POTATO	FONDUE	MOHAWK	SPACAE	SPACES	******
POULTS	GONIUM	******	SPINAL	SPADED	OPPUGN
POUSTO	HOGNUT	-O--Y-	SPIRAL	SPADER	SPARGE
ROASTS	HOLDUP	******	SPITAL	SPADES	SPONGE
ROBOTS	HONOUR	BOBBYS	SPREAD	SPARED	SPONGY
ROOSTS	HOOKUP	BOGEYS	UPBEAT	SPARER	SPRAGS
ROTATE	IODOUS	BOLEYN	UPROAR	SPARES	SPRIGS
ROUSTS	IOLCUS	BONNYS	******	SPATES	SPURGE
SOLUTE	IONIUM	COCCYX	-P--B-	SPAYED	******
SOMATA	JOSHUA	CONEYS	******	SPEWED	-P--H-
SOMATO	JOYFUL	COOEYS	EPHEBI	SPICED	******
SOMITE	JOYOUS	COVEYS	******	SPICER	APACHE
SONATA	LOCKUP	DOLLYS	-P--C-	SPICES	APATHY
TOASTS	MOBIUS	FORAYS	******	SPIDER	APHTHA
TOMATO	MOCKUP	FORMYL	APIECE	SPIKED	EPHAHS
TONITE	MORGUE	HOLLYS	EPARCH	SPIKES	EPOCHS
VOLUTE	MOSQUE	HONEYS	OPTICS	SPILED	SPATHE
VOMITO	PODIUM	MOLLYS	SPEECH	SPILES	******
VOMITS	PODOUS	MONEYS	SPLICE	SPINEL	-P--I-
WORSTS	POILUS	MONTYS	SPRUCE	SPINES	******
ZONATE	POLLUX	MORAYS	SPRUCE	SPINET	APNEIC
	POPGUN	MORTYS		SPIREA	APULIA

SPADIX	******	SPHERE	******	******	FRACAS
SPAHIS	-P--N-	SPHERY	-P--U-	-Q--P-	FREDAS
SPAVIN	******	SPIERS	******	******	FRIDAY
SPECIE	APHONY	SPOORS	EPIRUS	EQUIPS	FRUGAL
SPIRIT	APPEND	SPURRY	OPAQUE	******	GRAHAM
SPRAIN	APRONS	UPPERS	SPROUT	-Q--R-	GRETAS
******	EPPING	UPTURN	SPUTUM	******	ORDEAL
-P--K-	OPTANT	UPWARD	******	SQUARE	OREGAN
******	OPTING	******	-P--W-	SQUIRE	ORGEAT
SPANKS	SPAWNS	-P--S-	******	SQUIRM	ORIGAN
SPARKS	SPHENE	******	SPRAWL	SQUIRT	ORPHAN
SPEAKS	SPHENO	APEPSY	UPBOWS	******	PREFAB
SPECKS	SPHINX	APPOSE	UPTOWN	-Q--S-	PREPAY
SPLAKE	SPINNY	OPPOSE	******	******	PRESAS
SPOOKS	SPLENO	SPARSE	-P--Y-	SQUASH	PREWAR
SPOOKY	SPLINE	SPEISS	******	SQUISH	PRIMAL
SPUNKY	SPLINT	SPLASH	EPONYM	******	TREPAN
UPDIKE	SPOONS	SPOUSE	SPLAYS	-Q--T-	TRIBAL
UPTAKE	SPOONY	UPCAST	SPRAYS	******	TRICAR
******	SPRANG	UPMOST	******	EQUATE	TRINAL
-P--L-	SPRING	UPPISH	-Q--A-	EQUITY	TROCAR
******	SPRINT	UPRISE	******	SQUATS	TROJAN
APOLLO	SPRUNG	UPROSE	SQUEAK	******	TROPAL
APPALL	SPURNS	UPRUSH	SQUEAL	-Q--W-	TRUMAN
APPALS	SPYING	******	******	******	URINAL
APPELS	UPLAND	-P--T-	-Q--B-	SQUAWK	******
APRILS	UPPING	******	******	SQUAWS	-R--B-
OPENLY	******	APLITE	SQUABS	******	******
SPALLS	-P--O-	EPACTS	SQUIBS	-R--A-	ARDEBS
SPELLS	******	OPHITE	******	******	ARROBA
SPIELS	APOLOG	OPIATE	-Q--D-	ARARAT	CRABBY
SPILLS	EPILOG	OPORTO	******	ARAWAK	CRAMBO
SPOILS	EPIZOA	SPAITS	SQUADS	ARECAS	CRUMBS
SPOILT	OPTION	SPARTA	SQUIDS	ARENAS	CRUMBY
SPOOLS	SPIGOT	SPILTH	******	AROMAS	GRUBBY
SPRYLY	UPHROE	SPIRTS	-Q--L-	ARREAR	TRILBY
UPHELD	UPROOT	SPLATS	******	BRAZAS	******
UPHILL	UPSHOT	SPLITS	AQUILA	BRIDAL	-R--C-
UPHOLD	******	SPORTS	EQUALS	BROGAN	******
******	-P--R-	SPORTY	SQUALL	BROMAL	ARERCU
-P--M-	******	SPOTTY	SQUILL	BRUMAL	ARNICA
******	APIARY	SPOUTS	******	BRUTAL	ARRACK
APLOMB	APPORT	SPRATS	-Q--M-	CRAVAT	BRANCH
OPTIMA	EPHORI	SPRITE	******	CREDAL	BREACH
OPTIME	EPHORS	SPRITS	SQUAMA	CRETAN	BREECH
SPASMS	SPARRY	SPURTS	******	CREVAS	BROACH
SPERMO	SPEARS	UPDATE	-Q--N-	CRURAL	BRONCO
	SPERRY	UPPITY	******	DRAMAS	BRONCS
		UPSETS	EQUINE		
			SQUINT		

BROOCH	FREDDY	BRAZED	CRORES	GRADER	ORGIES
BRUNCH	FRIEDA	BRAZEN	CROWED	GRADES	ORIGEN
CRATCH	FRONDS	BRAZER	CROZER	GRAPES	ORKNEY
CROTCH	GRANDE	BRAZES	CROZES	GRATED	ORYXES
CROUCH	GREEDS	BREMEN	CRUCES	GRATER	PRATED
CRUNCH	GREEDY	BREVES	CRUDER	GRATES	PRATER
CRUTCH	GRINDS	BREVET	CRUSES	GRAVED	PRATES
DRENCH	GRUNDY	BREWED	CRUSET	GRAVEL	PRAYED
DRYICE	OREADS	BREWER	CRUXES	GRAVEN	PRAYER
FRANCE	OREIDE	BRIBED	DRAGEE	GRAVER	PREFER
FRANCK	OROIDE	BRIBER	DRAKES	GRAVES	PREMED
FRANCO	PRAVDA	BRIBES	DRAPED	GRAYED	PRETER
FRANCS	TREADS	BRIDES	DRAPER	GRAYER	PREYED
FRENCH	TRENDS	BRINED	DRAPES	GRAZED	PREYER
FRESCO	TRENDY	BRINES	DRAWEE	GRAZER	PRICED
GRAECO	TRIADS	BROKEN	DRAWER	GRAZES	PRICES
GREECE	TRIODE	BROKER	DRAYED	GREBES	PRIDED
GROUCH	UREIDE	BROMES	DRIVEL	GRETEL	PRIDES
ORRICE	******	BRUCES	DRIVEN	GRIDED	PRIMED
PRANCE	-R--E-	BRUGES	DRIVER	GRIDES	PRIMER
PREACH	******	BRUMES	DRIVES	GRIMED	PRIMES
PRINCE	ARABEL	BRUNEI	DRONED	GRIMES	PRIVET
TRANCE	ARCHED	BRUNEL	DRONES	GRIPED	PRIZED
TRENCH	ARCHEO	BRUTES	DROVED	GRIPER	PRIZER
WRENCH	ARCHER	CRAKES	DROVER	GRIPES	PRIZES
WRETCH	ARCHES	CRANED	DROVES	GRIVET	PROBED
******	ARCKED	CRANES	DRUPEL	GRIZEL	PROBER
-R--D-	ARETES	CRAPED	DRUPES	GROCER	PROBES
******	ARGUED	CRAPES	DRUSES	GROPED	PROJET
ARCADE	ARGUER	CRATED	DRYDEN	GROPER	PROLEG
ARMADA	ARGUES	CRATER	ERASED	GROPES	PROPEL
AROIDS	ARISEN	CRATES	ERASER	GROVEL	PROPER
BRAIDS	ARISES	CRAVED	ERASES	GROVER	PROSED
BRANDS	ARLEEN	CRAVEN	ERNIES	GROVES	PROSER
BRANDT	ARMIES	CRAVER	ERODED	GROWER	PROSES
BRANDY	ARMLET	CRAVES	ERODES	GRUMES	PROVED
BREADS	ARNIES	CRAZED	FRAMED	IRENES	PROVEN
BREEDS	ARTIES	CRAZES	FRAMER	IRIDES	PROVER
BRENDA	BRACED	CREMES	FRAMES	IRISED	PROVES
BROADS	BRACER	CRENEL	FRATER	IRISES	PRUDES
BROODS	BRACES	CREPED	FRAUEN	IRONED	PRUNED
BROODY	BRAKED	CREPES	FRAYED	IRONER	PRUNER
CREEDS	BRAKES	CREWEL	FRISES	KRAKEN	PRUNES
CROWDS	BRAVED	CRIKEY	FROZEN	KRISES	TRACED
DREADS	BRAVER	CRIMEA	GRABEN	KRONEN	TRACER
DRUIDS	BRAVES	CRIMES	GRACED	KRONER	TRACES
DRYADS	BRAYED	CRISES	GRACES	ORATED	TRADED
FRAUDS	BRAYER	CRONES	GRADED	ORATES	TRADER

TRADES	GRANGE	******	ORPHIC	FRISKS	DROLLS
TRAVEL	GREIGE	**-R--I-**	PRAXIS	FRISKY	DROLLY
TRAVES	GROGGY	******	PRECIS	FROCKS	DROOLS
TRIBES	GRUDGE	ARABIA	PREFIX	GREEKS	DRYFLY
TRICED	ORANGE	ARABIC	PRELIM	PRANKS	FRAILS
TRICES	ORANGS	ARCHIE	PROFIT	PRICKS	FREELY
TRINED	PRONGS	ARCHIL	PROLIX	PRINKS	FRILLS
TRINES	RRHAGE	ARCTIC	PROSIT	TRACKS	FRILLY
TRITER	RRHAGY	ARMPIT	TRAGIC	TRICKS	GRAYLY
TRIVET	TROUGH	ARTOIS	TRIFID	TRICKY	GRILLE
TROVER	TRUDGE	BRAZIL	TRIVIA	TROIKA	GRILLS
TROVES	WRINGS	BREWIS	TRIXIE	TRUCKS	GRIMLY
TROWEL	WRONGS	BRIDIE	TROPIC	TRUNKS	GRISLY
TRUCES	******	BRIGID	URALIC	WRACKS	GROWLS
URETER	**-R--H-**	BROMIC	URANIA	WREAKS	GRUELS
WRITER	******	CRANIA	URANIC	WRECKS	KRAALS
WRITES	ARIGHT	CRANIO	URCHIN	******	ORACLE
XRAYED	BRACHI	CRASIS	UREMIA	**-R--L-**	ORALLY
******	BRACHY	CREDIT	URETIC	******	ORIELS
-R--F-	BRASHY	CRETIC	******	ARABLE	ORIOLE
******	BRECHT	CRETIN	**-R--K-**	ARBELA	ORMOLU
ARGUFY	BRIGHT	CRISIS	******	ARCHLY	ORWELL
BRIEFS	BROCHE	CRITIC	BREAKS	AREOLA	PRIMLY
DRAFFS	BROTHS	CROJIK	BREEKS	ARGALA	PROWLS
DRAFFY	BRUSHY	EROTIC	BRICKS	ARGALI	TRAILS
GREIFS	CRECHE	FRIGID	BRINKS	ARGALS	TRAWLS
GRIFFE	DRACHM	FROLIC	BRISKS	ARGYLL	TREBLE
PROOFS	ERICHS	GRACIE	BROOKE	ARIDLY	TRIALS
******	FRIGHT	GRADIN	BROOKS	ARIELS	TRIFLE
-R--G-	FRITHS	GRATIN	CRACKS	ARNOLD	TRIGLY
******	FROTHS	GRATIS	CRACKY	ARTELS	TRILLS
ARMAGH	FROTHY	GRAVID	CRANKS	ARTILY	TRIMLY
BRIDGE	GRAPHO	IRANIS	CRANKY	BRAILS	TRIPLE
BRINGS	GRAPHS	IRAQIS	CREAKS	BRAWLS	TROLLS
CRAGGY	GRAPHY	IRENIC	CREAKY	BRIDLE	URSULA
CRAIGS	ORACHS	IRIDIC	CREEKS	BRILLS	******
CRINGE	TRACHE	IRITIC	CRICKS	BROILS	**-R--M-**
DREDGE	TRACHY	IRITIS	CROAKS	BROLLY	******
DREGGY	TRASHY	IRONIC	CROAKY	CRAALS	BRAHMA
DRONGO	TRICHI	KRUBIS	CROCKS	CRADLE	BRAHMS
DRUDGE	TRICHO	ORCEIN	CROCKY	CRAWLS	BREAMS
ERINGO	TROCHE	ORCHID	CROOKS	CRAWLY	BREGMA
ERYNGO	TROPHO	ORCHIL	DRINKS	CREELS	BROOMS
FRIDGE	TROPHY	ORCHIO	DROSKY	CREOLE	BROOMY
FRIGGA	TROTHS	ORCHIS	DRUNKS	DRABLY	CREAMS
FRINGE	TRUTHS	ORDAIN	FRANKS	DRAWLS	CREAMY
FRINGY	WRATHY	ORIBIS	FREAKS	DRAWLY	CRUMMY
FROGGY	WRIGHT	ORIGIN	FREAKY	DRILLS	DREAMS
	WRITHE				

DREAMT	FRIEND	BRUNOS	DROOPY	ORRERY	TRIOSE
DREAMY	FROWNS	CRACOW	FRAPPE	PRIERS	TRUEST
GRAMME	FRYING	CRAYON	FRUMPS	PRIORS	TRUISM
GROOMS	GRAINS	CREDOS	FRUMPY	PRIORY	UREASE
PRISMS	GRAINY	CRESOL	GRASPS	PRYERS	WRASSE
PROEMS	GRANNY	CRETON	GRIPPE	TRIERS	WRIEST
TRAUMA	GREENE	CRONOS	GRIPPY	******	WRYEST
******	GREENS	CROTON	GROUPS	**-R--S-**	******
-R--N-	GRETNA	CRUSOE	GRUMPY	******	**-R--T-**
******	GROANS	DRAGON	ORLOPS	ARGOSY	******
ARCANA	GROINS	DROMON	PRIMPS	ARIOSE	ARANTA
ARCANE	GROUND	DRYROT	PROMPT	ARIOSO	ARBUTE
ARCING	GROYNE	FRIJOL	TRAMPS	AROUSE	ARGOTS
ARDENT	IRKING	FRIVOL	TROOPS	ARREST	ARISTA
ARGENT	IRVING	GREGOS	TROPPO	ARTIST	ARISTO
ARIANS	IRVINS	KRONOR	TROUPE	BRAISE	ARMETS
ARLENE	IRWINS	KRONOS	TRUMPS	BRASSY	ARUNTA
ARLINE	ORBING	ORATOR	******	BREAST	BRACTS
ARMAND	ORGANA	ORISON	**-R--R-**	BROWSE	BRANTS
ARMING	ORGANO	PRETOR	******	BRUISE	BREATH
AROUND	ORGANS	PRISON	ARBORI	CREASE	BRENTS
ARPENS	ORIENT	PROTON	ARBORS	CREASY	BRONTE
ARPENT	ORPINE	TREMOR	ARDORS	CREESE	BRUITS
ARRANT	ORPINS	TREVOR	ARMORS	CREUSA	CRAFTS
ARSINE	PRAWNS	TRICOT	ARMORY	CROSSE	CRAFTY
ARYANS	PREENS	TRIGON	ARMURE	CRUISE	CREATE
BRAINS	PROCNE	TRIPOD	ARTERY	DRESSY	CRESTS
BRAINY	PRYING	TRIPOS	ARTHRO	DRIEST	CROATS
BRANNY	TRAINS	TRITON	ARTURO	DROPSY	CROFTS
BRAWNY	TRIUNE	TROGON	BRIARS	DROSSY	CRUETS
BROWNS	TRUANT	UROPOD	BRIERS	DROWSE	CRUSTS
BRUINS	TRUING	******	BRIERY	DROWSY	CRUSTY
BRYANT	TRYING	**-R--P-**	CRIERS	DRYEST	CRYPTO
BRYONY	URBANE	******	DREARY	DRYISH	CRYPTS
CRANNY	URGENT	CRAMPS	DRIERS	ERNEST	DRAFTS
CROONS	URGING	CREEPS	DRYERS	FRAISE	DRAFTY
CROWNS	URSINE	CREEPY	ERFURT	FREEST	DRIFTS
CRYING	WRYING	CRIMPS	ERRORS	GRASSY	DRIFTY
DRAINS	******	CRIMPY	FRIARS	GREASE	DROITS
DROWNS	**-R--O-**	CRISPS	FRIARY	GREASY	DROUTH
DRYING	******	CRISPY	FRIERS	GRILSE	ERECTS
ERMINE	ARAGON	CROUPE	FRYERS	GROUSE	ERGATE
ERRAND	ARCHON	CROUPS	GRIGRI	ORGASM	ERRATA
ERRANT	BRAVOS	CROUPY	GRUGRU	PRAISE	ERSATZ
ERRING	BRAZOS	CRUMPS	ORDERS	PRIEST	ERUCTS
ERWINS	BRETON	DRIPPY	ORDURE	PRISSY	ERUPTS
FREONS	BRITON	DROOPS	ORMERS	PROUST	FRETTY
FRESNO	BRULOT	DROOPS	ORNERY	TRESSY	FRONTO

FRONTS	ARTFUL	ERINYS	******	******	******
FROSTS	ARTHUR	PROPYL	-S--D-	-S--I-	-S--O-
FROSTY	BRAQUE	TRIXYS	******	******	******
FRUITS	BROGUE	TROTYL	ESCUDO	ASSAIL	ASIMOV
FRUITY	BRUTUS	TRUDYS	ISOLDE	ASSAIS	ESCROW
FRUSTA	CRINUM	URANYL	PSEUDO	ASTRID	ISADOR
GRAFTS	CROCUS	******	******	ESPRIT	ISIDOR
GRANTS	CRONUS	-R--Z-	-S--E-	ISATIN	ISOGON
GREATS	DROGUE	******	******	ISCHIA	ISOPOD
GREETS	ERBIUM	AREZZO	ASHIER	ISSEIS	******
GRITTY	EREBUS	BRAIZE	ASHLEY	ISTRIA	-S--P-
GROATS	FRENUM	BREEZE	ASHMEN	OSIRIS	******
GROTTO	GRADUS	BREEZY	ASIDES	OSSEIN	ASLOPE
GROTTY	IREFUL	BRONZE	ASLEEP	******	ESCAPE
GROUTS	KRONUR	BRONZY	ESCHER	-S--L-	ESTOPS
GROWTH	KRUBUT	FREEZE	ESCHEW	ISEULT	USURPS
GRUNTS	PRAGUE	FRENZY	ESPIED	OSCULE	******
KRAITS	PREVUE	FRIEZE	ESPIES	OSWALD	-S--R-
ORBITS	PRIMUS	FRIZZY	ESTEEM	USABLE	******
ORNATE	TRAGUS	FROWZY	ESTHER	USABLY	ASBURY
ORNITH	TRYOUT	FRUNZE	ISABEL	******	ASGARD
PRESTO	URAEUS	GROSZY	ISOBEL	-S--M-	ASHORE
PRETTY	URANUS	ORMUZD	ISOHEL	******	ASKERS
PRINTS	WRAPUP	******	ISOMER	ASSUME	ASPERS
PROCTO	******	-S--A-	ISRAEL	ASTHMA	ASPIRE
PRONTO	-R--V-	******	ISSUED	ESKIMO	ASSERT
TRACTS	******		ISSUER	PSALMS	ASSORT
TRAITS	ARGIVE	ASHCAN	ISSUES	******	ASSURE
TREATS	ARRIVE	ASHLAR	OSPREY	-S--N-	ASTERI
TREATY	GREAVE	ASHMAN	OSTLER	******	ASTERN
TRISTE	GRIEVE	ASTRAL	TSADES	ASCEND	ASTERO
TROUTS	GROOVE	ASTRAY	USAGES	ASCENT	ASTERS
TRUSTS	GROOVY	ESCHAR	USURER	ASIANS	ESCARP
TRUSTY	******	ESPIAL	******	ASKANT	ESCORT
TRYSTS	-R--W-	ESTRAY	-S--F-	ASKING	ESKERS
WRAITH	******	ISAIAH	******	ASLANT	ESTERS
WREATH	ARROWS	ISHTAR	OSSIFY	ASPENS	OSBERT
WRESTS	ARROWY	ISOBAR	******	ASSENT	OSBORN
WRISTS	******	OSSIAN	-S--G-	ESCENT	OSCARS
******	-R--X-	OSTEAL	******	ESPANA	OSIERS
-R--U-	******	******	ASSIGN	ESSENE	TSHIRT
******	URTEXT	-S--C-	OSWEGO	ISLAND	USHERS
ARBOUR	******	******		ISLING	******
ARDOUR	-R--Y-	ASPECT	-S--H-	OSCANS	-S--S-
ARIOUS	******	ASPICS	******	OSCINE	ASSESS
ARMFUL	ARCHYS	ISAACS	PSYCHE	OSMOND	ASSISI
ARMOUR	ARRAYS	USANCE	PSYCHO	OSMUND	ASSIST
ARNAUD	ARROYO			OSTEND	

OSMOSE	STREAK	ETCHED	STONES	OTITIS	STABLY
TSETSE	STREAM	ETCHER	STOPED	PTOSIS	STALLS
ZSAZSA	STRIAE	ETCHES	STOPES	STACIE	STAPLE
******	STUPAS	ETUDES	STORED	STADIA	STEALS
-S--T-	STYLAR	ITCHED	STORES	STALIN	STEELS
******	UTAHAN	ITCHES	STOREY	STAMIN	STEELY
ASCOTS	******	STAGED	STOVER	STASIS	STELLA
ASSETS	-T--B-	STAGER	STOVES	STATIC	STELLI
ASTUTE	******	STAGES	STOWED	STELIC	STIFLE
ESTATE	STROBE	STAGEY	STREET	STEPIN	STILLS
ISLETS	STUBBS	STAKED	STUPES	STERIC	STILLY
******	STUBBY	STAKES	STYLED	STEVIE	STOOLS
-S--U-	******	STALED	STYLER	STOLID	STROLL
******	-T--C-	STALER	STYLES	STRAIN	STULLS
ASARUM	******	STALES	STYLET	STRAIT	******
ASYLUM	ATTACH	STAMEN	******	STUDIO	-T--M-
ESTRUS	ATTACK	STAPES	-T--F-	STUPID	******
OSMIUM	ATTICA	STARED	******	STYMIE	ATHOME
USEFUL	ATTICS	STARER	STAFFS	UTOPIA	STEAMS
******	ETHICS	STARES	STRAFE	YTTRIA	STEAMY
-S--W-	ITHACA	STASES	STRIFE	YTTRIC	STIGMA
******	STANCE	STATED	STUFFS	******	STORMS
PSHAWS	STANCH	STATEN	STUFFY	-T--K-	STORMY
******	STARCH	STATER	******	******	STROMA
-S--Y-	STENCH	STATES	-T--G-	STACKS	STRUMA
******	STITCH	STAVED	******	STALKS	STRUMS
ASSAYS	STOICS	STAVES	STAGGY	STALKY	******
ESSAYS	STRICK	STAYED	STINGS	STEAKS	-T--N-
******	STRICT	STAYER	STINGY	STICKS	******
-S--Z-	STRUCK	STELES	STODGE	STICKY	ATHENA
******	STUCCO	STEREO	STODGY	STINKS	ATHENE
ASSIZE	******	STERES	STOOGE	STIRKS	ATHENS
******	-T--D-	STEVEN	******	STOCKS	ATTEND
-T--A-	******	STEVES	-T--H-	STOCKY	ATTUNE
******	STANDS	STEWED	******	STOOKS	ETERNA
ATABAL	STEADY	STILES	STETHO	STORKS	ETHANE
ATAMAN	STEEDS	STIPEL	STITHY	STRAKE	ETHANS
ATONAL	STRIDE	STIPES	******	STRIKE	STAINS
ATRIAL	STRODE	STIVER	-T--I-	STROKE	STEINS
PTISAN	STURDY	STOGEY	******	******	STERNA
STALAG	******	STOKED	ATAVIC	-T--L-	STERNO
STATAL	-T--E-	STOKER	ATAXIA	******	STERNS
STEFAN	******	STOKES	ATAXIC	ATOLLS	STHENO
STELAE	ATONED	STOLED	ATOMIC	ATTILA	STRAND
STELAR	ATONER	STOLEN	ATONIC	ETHELS	STRING
STEPAN	ATONES	STOLES	ATTAIN	ETHYLS	STRONG
STOMAT	ATTLEE	STONED	ETHNIC	ITSELF	STRUNG
STORAX	ETAPES	STONER	ITALIC	STABLE	STYING
					UTURNS

******	STRASS	******	GUNMAN	SUBWAY	******
-T--O-	STRESS	-T--Y-	GUNNAR	SULTAN	-U--D-
******	UTMOST	******	GUSTAF	SUNDAE	******
ETYMON	******	STACYS	GUSTAV	SUNDAY	AUBADE
STATOR	-T--T-	STRAYS	GUTTAE	SUNHAT	AUDADS
STENOG	******		GUTTAT	SUNNAH	BUILDS
STEROL	STACTE	-T--Z-	HUBCAP	SUNTAN	GUARDS
STOLON	STAITH	******	HURRAH	SURTAX	GUILDS
STUPOR	STARTS	STANZA	HURRAY	SUTRAS	LUANDA
******	STILTS	******	HUSSAR	TURBAN	TULADI
-T--P-	STINTS	-U--A-	JUBBAH	TUSCAN	TUXEDO
******	STOATS	******	JUDEAN	TUSSAH	******
STAMPS	STOUTS	AUGEAN	JULIAN	TUSSAL	-U--E-
STEEPS	STRATA	BUCCAL	JULIAS	TUSSAR	******
STEPPE	STRATH	BUCHAN	JUMBAL	VULCAN	AUBREY
STIRPS	STRATI	BULBAR	JUNEAU	VULGAR	AUDREY
STOMPS	STRUTS	BULGAR	JUNTAS	VULVAE	AUKLET
STOOPS	STUNTS	BULLAE	LUCIAN	VULVAL	AUSPEX
STOUPS	******	BUNYAN	LUCIAS	VULVAR	AUSTEN
STRAPS	-T--U-	BUREAU	LUMBAR	YUCCAS	AUSTER
STRIPE	******	BURIAL	LUTEAL	******	AUTOED
STRIPS	ATREUS	BURLAP	MUDCAP	-U--B-	BUBOES
STRIPT	ATRIUM	BURSAE	MUGGAR	******	BUCKED
STRIPY	ITIOUS	BURSAL	MULLAH	CUBEBS	BUCKER
STROPS	STATUE	BURSAR	MURRAY	JUJUBE	BUCKET
STUMPS	STATUS	BURSAS	MUSCAE	******	BUDDED
STUMPY	STEPUP	BUSMAN	MUSCAT	-U--C-	BUDDER
******	STROUD	CULLAY	MUTUAL	******	BUDGED
-T--R-	STYLUS	CUNEAL	NUBIAN	CULTCH	BUDGES
******	UTERUS	CURIAE	NUBIAS	CURACY	BUDGET
ATTARS	XTSTUS	CURIAL	NUCHAE	EUNICE	BUFFED
ATTIRE	******	CUSHAT	NULLAH	EUNUCH	BUFFER
ATTORN	-T--V-	CUSHAW	OUTLAW	LUBECK	BUFFET
ETHERS	******	CUTLAS	OUTLAY	LUNACY	BUGGED
OTHERS	OTTAVA	DUNBAR	OUTMAN	MUNICH	BUGGER
OTTERS	STARVE	DUNCAN	OUTRAN	NUANCE	BUGLED
STAIRS	STEEVE	DURBAN	OUTSAT	PUMICE	BUGLER
STARRY	STRIVE	DURBAR	PULSAR	PUTSCH	BUGLES
STAURO	STROVE	DURHAM	PUNJAB	QUENCH	BULBED
STEERS	******	DURIAN	PUNKAS	QUINCE	BULBEL
STUART	-T--W-	EUDOAR	PURDAH	QUINCY	BULGED
UTGARD	******	FULMAR	PUTNAM	QUITCH	BULGER
UTTERS	OTTAWA	FUNGAL	QUAPAW	RUBACE	BULGES
******	OTTOWA	GUAVAS	QUASAR	SUMACS	BULKED
-T--S-	STRAWS	GUFFAW	QUOTAS	TUNICA	BULLET
******	STRAWY	GUITAR	RUMBAS	TUNICS	BUMMED
ATTEST	STREWN	GULLAH	RUNWAY	ZURICH	BUMMER
OTIOSE	STREWS	GUMMAS	RUPIAH		BUMPED

BUMPER	CULMED	DUNNED	GUMMED	JUNKER	MUSHES
BUNGED	CULVER	DUODEN	GUNMEN	JUNKET	MUSKEG
BUNKED	CUMBER	DUPLET	GUNNED	JURIES	MUSKET
BUNKER	CUNNER	DUPLEX	GUNNEL	JUTTED	MUSSED
BUNSEN	CUPPED	DUSKED	GUNNER	KUCHEN	MUSSEL
BUNTED	CUPPER	DUSTED	GUNTER	KUMMEL	MUSSES
BUOYED	CURBED	DUSTER	GUSHED	LUBBER	MUSTEE
BURDEN	CURDED	DUTIES	GUSHER	LUCIEN	MUSTER
BURGEE	CURFEW	EUBOEA	GUSHES	LUFFED	MUTTER
BURGER	CURIES	EUCHER	GUSSET	LUGGED	NUCLEI
BURIED	CURLED	EUPNEA	GUTTED	LUGGER	NUDGED
BURIES	CURLER	FUDGED	GUTTER	LULLED	NUDGES
BURKED	CURLEW	FUDGES	HUFFED	LUMBER	NUGGET
BURKES	CURSED	FUELED	HUGGED	LUMPED	NUMBED
BURLED	CURSES	FUELER	HUGHES	LUMPEN	NUMBER
BURLER	CURVED	FUGLED	HULKED	LUNGED	NURSED
BURLEY	CURVES	FUGLES	HULLED	LUNGEE	NURSER
BURNED	CURVET	FUGUES	HUMBER	LUNGER	NURSES
BURNER	CUSPED	FUHRER	HUMMED	LUNGES	NUTLET
BURNET	CUSSED	FULLED	HUMMER	LUNKER	NUTMEG
BURPED	CUSSES	FULLER	HUMPED	LURKED	NUTTED
BURRED	CUSTER	FUMIER	HUNGER	LURKER	NUTTER
BURSES	CUTIES	FUNDED	HUNTED	LUSHED	OUNCES
BUSHED	CUTLER	FUNKED	HUNTER	LUSHER	OUSTED
BUSHEL	CUTLET	FUNNEL	HURLED	LUSHES	OUSTER
BUSHES	CUTTER	FURIES	HURLER	LUSTED	OUTLET
BUSHEY	DUBBED	FURLED	HURLEY	LUSTER	OUTSET
BUSIED	DUCKED	FURRED	HURTER	LUTHER	PUCKER
BUSIES	DUCKER	FURZES	HUSHED	MUCKED	PUFFED
BUSKER	DUDEEN	FUSEES	HUSHES	MUCKER	PUFFER
BUSMEN	DUDLEY	FUSSED	HUSKED	MUDDED	PUGGED
BUSSED	DUELED	FUSSER	HUSKER	MUDDER	PUGREE
BUSSES	DUELER	FUSSES	HUTTED	MUFFED	PULLED
BUSTED	DUFFED	FUZEES	HUXLEY	MUGGED	PULLER
BUSTER	DUFFEL	FUZZED	JUAREZ	MUGGER	PULLET
BUTLER	DUFFER	FUZZES	JUDAEA	MULLED	PULLEY
BUTTED	DUIKER	GUIDED	JUDAEO	MULLEN	PULPED
BUTTER	DULCET	GUIDER	JUDGED	MULLER	PULPER
BUTTES	DULLED	GUIDES	JUDGER	MULLET	PULSED
BUZZED	DULLER	GUILES	JUDGES	MULLEY	PULSES
BUZZER	DULLES	GUINEA	JUGGED	MUMMED	PUMMEL
BUZZES	DUMPED	GUISES	JUICER	MUMMER	PUMPED
CUBBED	DUMPER	GULDEN	JUICES	MURDER	PUMPER
CUDGEL	DUNCES	GULFED	JULIES	MURIEL	PUNIER
CUFFED	DUNDEE	GULLED	JULIET	MURRES	PUNNED
CULLED	DUNGED	GULLET	JUMPED	MURREY	PUNNER
CULLER	DUNKED	GULPED	JUMPER	MUSHED	PUNTED
CULLET	DUNKER	GULPER	JUNKED	MUSHER	PUNTER

PUPPED	RUNLET	TUCKER	BUNCHY	KUWAIT	******
PUPPET	RUNNEL	TUCKET	BURGHS	LUBLIN	-U--K-
PUREED	RUNNER	TUFFET	GUNSHY	LUDWIG	******
PUREES	RUPEES	TUFTED	GURKHA	LUETIC	EUREKA
PURGED	RUSHED	TUGGED	JUDAHS	LUNGIS	KULAKS
PURGER	RUSHER	TULLES	PUNCHY	MUCOID	QUACKS
PURGES	RUSHES	TUNNED	QUOTHA	MUFFIN	QUARKS
PURLED	RUSSET	TUNNEL	SUBAHS	MUFTIS	QUIRKS
PURLER	RUSTED	TUPPED	SULPHA	MUSKIT	TUPIKS
PURRED	RUTTED	TUQUES	SULPHO	MUSLIM	******
PURSED	SUBDEB	TUREEN	SURAHS	MUSLIN	-U--L-
PURSER	SUBLET	TURFED	******	MUZHIK	******
PURSES	SUBTER	TURKEY	-U--I-	NUBBIN	AUDILE
PURVEY	SUCKED	TURNED	******	NUDNIK	BUBALS
PUSHED	SUCKER	TURNER	AUNTIE	NUNCIO	BUBBLE
PUSHER	SUCRES	TURRET	AUSTIN	NUTRIA	BUBBLY
PUSHES	SUDDEN	TURVES	BUDGIE	OUTBID	BUCKLE
PUSSES	SUEDES	TUSHED	BULBIL	OUTDID	BUDDLE
PUSSEY	SUFFER	TUSHES	BUMKIN	OUTFIT	BUMBLE
PUTTED	SUITED	TUSKED	BUNYIP	OUTSIT	BUNDLE
PUTTEE	SUITES	TUSKER	BURDIE	OUTWIT	BUNGLE
PUTTER	SULKED	TUTTED	BUSKIN	PUBLIC	BURBLE
QUAKED	SULLEN	YUKKED	BUSTIC	PUFFIN	BURGLE
QUAKER	SUMMED	ZUIDER	CUBOID	PULLIN	BUSILY
QUAKES	SUMMER	ZUYDER	CUDDIE	PULPIT	BUSTLE
QUAVER	SUMNER	******	CULLIS	PUNDIT	CUDDLE
QUEBEC	SUNDER	-U--F-	CUPRIC	PURLIN	CUDDLY
QUEUED	SUNDEW	******	CUPTIE	PUTRID	CUPELS
QUEUES	SUNKEN	CUTOFF	CURTIS	QUINIC	CUPOLA
QUIRED	SUNNED	HUMIFY	CUSPID	RUBRIC	CUPULE
QUIRES	SUNSET	PURIFY	CUSPIS	RUSKIN	CURDLE
QUIVER	SUPPED	PUTOFF	DUBBIN	RUSSIA	CURTLY
QUOTED	SUPPER	QUAFFS	DUBLIN	RUSTIC	CURULE
QUOTER	SURFED	RUNOFF	DULCIE	SUBMIT	CUTELY
QUOTES	SURFER	TUMEFY	DUNLIN	SUFFIX	CUTTLE
RUBBED	SURGED	******	EUCLID	SUMMIT	DUELLO
RUBBER	SURGER	-U--G-	FUCOID	SUNLIT	DUFFLE
RUBIES	SURGES	******	FULFIL	SUOMIC	DUMBLY
RUBLES	SURREY	AURIGA	FULGID	SUSLIK	FUDDLE
RUCHES	SURVEY	CUBAGE	FUSAIN	TURBID	FUMBLE
RUCKED	SUSIES	EULOGY	FUSTIC	TURBIT	FUSILE
RUDDER	SUSSED	QUAGGA	GUANIN	TURGID	FUSILS
RUFFED	SUSSEX	QUAGGY	GUSSIE	TURKIC	FUTILE
RUGGED	SUTLER	RUBIGO	HUBRIS	TURKIS	FUZILS
RUGGER	SUTTEE	******	HUGHIE	TURNIP	GURGLE
RUINED	TUBBED	-U--H-	JUDAIC	TUSSIS	GUTTLE
RUINER	TUBBER	******	JUNKIE	TUTTIS	GUZZLE
RUMMER	TUCKED	BUDDHA	JUSTIN	YUPPIE	HUCKLE
		BUNCHE			

HUDDLE	RUDELY	FUSING	******	SUNDOG	PULERS
HUGELY	RUFFLE	FUZING	-U--O-	SUNGOD	QUADRI
HUMBLE	RUMBLE	GUIANA	******	SUTTON	QUAERE
HUMBLY	RUMPLE	GUYANA	AUTHOR	TUCSON	QUARRY
HURDLE	RUNDLE	GUYING	BUNCOS	TURBOT	QUATRE
HURTLE	RUSTLE	HUMANE	BUNION	TURCOS	QUEERS
HUSTLE	RUTILE	HUMANS	BURBOT	******	RULERS
JUGGLE	SUABLE	HURONS	BURGOO	-U--P-	RUMORS
JUMBLE	SUBTLE	JUPONS	BURGOS	******	RUPERT
JUNGLE	SUBTLY	JURANT	BURROS	CUTUPS	SUBORN
JUNGLY	SUCKLE	LUCENT	BURROW	EURIPI	SUBURB
JURELS	SUPPLE	LUMENS	BURTON	EUROPA	SUDARY
JUSTLY	SUPPLY	LUMINA	BUTTON	EUROPE	SUGARS
LUCILE	SURELY	LUMINI	BUXTON	GUIMPE	SUGARY
LUELLA	TUBULE	LUMINO	CUCKOO	JULEPS	SULTRY
LUNULA	TUILLE	LUPINE	CURIOS	SUNUPS	SUNDRY
LUNULE	TUMBLE	LURING	CURSOR	TULIPS	SUPERB
MUCKLE	TUMULT	LUTING	CUSSOS	******	SUPERS
MUDDLE	TUPELO	MURINE	CUSTOM	-U--R-	SUTURE
MUFFLE	TURTLE	MUSING	CUSTOS	******	TUBERS
MUMBLE	TUSSLE	MUSTNT	DUOLOG	AUBURN	TUMORS
MURALS	******	MUTANT	DURION	AUGERS	TUNDRA
MUSCLE	-U--M-	MUTING	FUGIOS	AUGURS	TUNERS
MUTULE	******	MUTINY	FULTON	AUGURY	TUTORS
MUZZLE	AUTUMN	NUMINA	FURROW	AURORA	TUYERE
NUBBLE	QUALMS	OUTING	FUSION	AUSTRO	******
NUBBLY	QUALMY	PUISNE	GUACOS	BUCKRA	-U--S-
NUBILE	******	PUKING	GUANOS	BUYERS	******
NUDELY	-U--N-	PULING	GUENON	CURARE	AUGUST
NUMBLY	******	PURANA	GUIDON	CURERS	AURIST
NUZZLE	AUGEND	PURINE	GUMBOS	DUPERS	AUTISM
OUSELS	AUXINS	PUTONS	HUDSON	DUPERY	CUBISM
OUZELS	BURANS	QUAINT	JUNCOS	EUCHRE	CUBIST
PUDDLE	BURINS	QUEANS	JUNIOR	FULCRA	CUISSE
PUDDLY	BUSING	QUEENS	LUDLOW	FURORE	CURTSY
PUEBLO	BUTANE	QUERNS	LUMMOX	FURORS	CUTEST
PUNILY	BUYING	QUOINS	MUSKOX	FUTURE	DUDISH
PUPILS	CUBANS	RUBENS	MUTTON	HUBERT	DURESS
PURELY	CUBING	RUEING	OUTFOX	HUMORS	FUNEST
PURFLE	CUMINS	RULING	PUNTOS	HUNGRY	HUGEST
PURPLE	CURING	RUMINA	PUTLOG	JURORS	JURIST
PUSSLY	CUTINS	RUNINS	QUAHOG	LUGERS	JUTISH
PUZZLE	DUENNA	RUNONS	QUEZON	LURERS	KUMISS
QUAILS	DUGONG	RUSINE	RUNYON	LUSTRE	LUTIST
QUELLS	DUPING	SUPINE	SUCCOR	LUXURY	MUCOSA
QUILLS	DURING	SUSANS	SUITOR	OUTCRY	MUCOSE
RUBBLE	EUGENE	TUBING	SUMMON	OUTERS	MULISH
RUDDLE	FUMING	TUNING	SUNBOW	PUGGRY	MUTISM
		YUPONS			

NUDISM	QUARTS	OUTPUT	******	******	SWORDS
NUDIST	QUARTZ	OUTRUN	-V--D-	-V--R-	TWEEDS
PUNISH	QUESTS	PULQUE	******	******	******
PUREST	QUILTS	PURSUE	AVOIDS	AVIARY	-W--E-
PURISM	QUINTS	PUSHUP	OVERDO	******	******
PURIST	QUIRTS	PUTOUT	******	-V--S-	AWAKED
QUEASY	QUOITS	PUTPUT	-V--E-	******	AWAKEN
QUINSY	RUBATO	QUIPUS	******	AVERSE	AWAKES
RUDEST	RUGATE	QUORUM	AVOCET	******	AWHEEL
RUGOSE	SUBITO	RUCKUS	AVOSET	-V--T-	AWOKEN
SUFISM	SURETY	RUEFUL	AVOWED	******	SWAGED
SUREST	TUBATE	RUFOUS	AVOWER	AVERTS	SWAGES
******	******	RUGOUS	EVADED	AVESTA	SWALES
-U--T-	-U--U-	RUMOUR	EVADER	AVIATE	SWANEE
******	******	RUMPUS	EVADES	EVENTS	SWAYED
AUDITS	AUREUS	RUNOUT	EVENED	EVERTS	SWEDEN
AUGHTS	AUROUS	SUBDUE	EVERET	EVICTS	SWEDES
AUGITE	BULBUL	SULCUS	EVOKED	SVELTE	SWIPED
AURATE	BUNKUM	SULFUR	EVOKES	******	SWIPES
BURSTS	CULTUS	TUCHUN	OVULES	-V--U-	SWIVEL
CUBITS	CUPFUL	TUMOUR	******	******	SWIVET
CUESTA	CUPRUM	TUNEUP	-V--G-	AVENUE	TWINED
CULETS	CURIUM	TUNGUS	******	******	TWINER
CURATE	CUSCUS	TURNUP	AVENGE	-V--V-	TWINES
DUCATS	CUTOUT	******	******	******	TWOFER
DULUTH	DUGOUT	-U--V-	-V--I-	EVOLVE	******
DUMPTY	DUMDUM	******	******	******	-W--F-
GUESTS	FUCOUS	HUELVA	AVIDIN	-V--Y-	******
GUILTS	FUMOUS	******	******	******	DWARFS
GUILTY	FUNDUS	-U--Y-	-V--L-	AVERYS	******
HUMPTY	FUNGUS	******	******	EVELYN	-W--G-
JUDITH	FURFUR	CUTEYS	AVAILS	******	******
JUGATE	HUBBUB	******	AVIDLY	-W--A-	AWEIGH
JURATS	HUMBUG	-V--A-.	EVENLY	******	SWINGE
LUCITE	HUMOUR	******	EVILLY	SWARAJ	SWINGS
LUNATE	JUGFUL	AVATAR	OVALLY	TWOWAY	TWANGS
LUNETS	JULIUS	AVOWAL	OVERLY	******	TWANGY
LUXATE	JUNIUS	DVORAK	******	-W--C-	TWIGGY
MULCTS	JUSTUS	EVITAS	-V--N-	******	TWINGE
MUTATE	KULTUR	OVISAC	******	SWATCH	******
NUDITY	LUCIUS	OVULAR	AVAUNT	SWITCH	-W--H-
PUPATE	LUTEUM	UVULAE	AVERNO	TWITCH	******
PURITY	MUCOUS	UVULAR	YVONNE	******	DWIGHT
PUSHTU	MUGGUR	UVULAS	******	-W--D-	SWATHE
QUANTA	MUKLUK	******	-V--O-	******	SWATHS
QUANTS	MURMUR	-V--C-	******	AWARDS	******
QUARTE	MUSEUM	******	AVALON	RWANDA	-W--I-
QUARTO	MUUMUU	AVOUCH	AVISOS	SWARDS	SWAMIS
		EVINCE	OVIBOS	SWORDS	TWIBIL

TWILIT	******	******	******	******	******
TWOBIT	-W--R-	-X--D-	-X--N-	-X--U-	-Y--E-
******	******	******	******	******	******
-W--K-	AWEARY	EXCIDE	EXEUNT	EXEQUY	CYCLED
******	AWHIRL	OXHIDE	EXPAND	EXODUS	CYCLER
SWANKY	OWNERS	******	EXPEND	******	CYCLES
TWEAKS	SWEARS	-X--E-	EXTANT	-X--W-	CYGNET
TWEAKY	******	******	EXTEND	******	CYPHER
******	-W--S-	AXEMEN	EXTENT	OXBOWS	EYASES
-W--L-	******	AXONES	******	******	EYELET
******	AWLESS	AXSEED	-X--O-	-Y--A-	EYRIES
AWHILE	OWLISH	EXAMEN	******	******	GYPPED
DWELLS	******	EXCEED	EXMOOR	BYPLAY	HYADES
SWAILS	-W--T-	EXETER	******	BYROAD	HYMNED
SWELLS	******	EXILED	-X--P-	CYMBAL	HYPHEN
SWILLS	AWAITS	EXILES	******	HYDRAE	HYSTER
SWIPLE	OWLETS	EXITED	EXCEPT	HYDRAS	LYCEES
SWIRLS	SWARTH	EXOGEN	EXEMPT	HYENAS	LYNXES
SWIRLY	SWARTY	EXUDED	OXLIPS	HYETAL	MYOPES
TWILLS	SWEATS	EXUDES	******	HYMNAL	MYRMEC
TWIRLS	SWEATY	OXEYED	-X--R-	HYPHAE	OYSTER
TWOPLY	SWEETS	OXEYES	******	HYPHAL	PYXIES
TWOULD	SWIFTS	OXIDES	EXEDRA	LYDIAS	SYCEES
******	TWEETS	OXYGEN	EXHORT	LYTTAE	SYDNEY
-W--M-	TWENTY	******	EXPERT	MYRIAD	SYNDET
******	TWISTS	-X--I-	EXPIRE	MYRNAS	SYPHER
SWARMS	TWISTY	******	EXPIRY	SYLVAE	SYSTEM
******	******	EXILIC	EXPORT	SYLVAN	XYSTER
-W--N-	-W--V-	EXOTIC	EXSERT	SYLVAS	******
******	******	OXALIC	EXTERN	SYNTAX	-Y--F-
AWEING	SWERVE	OXALIS	EXTORT	SYRIAC	******
AWNING	TWELVE	OXTAIL	OXFORD	SYRIAN	TYPIFY
GWENNS	******	******	******	TYMPAN	******
GWYNNE	-X--A-	-X--K-	-X--S-	TYRIAN	-Y--G-
OWNING	******	******	******	WYSTAN	******
SWAINS	AXEMAN	AXLIKE	EXCESS	******	SYZYGY
SWEENY	EXTRAS	******	EXCISE	-Y--C-	******
SWOONS	******	-X--L-	EXCUSE	******	-Y--H-
******	-X--B-	******	EXPOSE	CYNICS	******
-W--P-	******	AXILLA	******	GYNECO	AYESHA
******	EXURBS	EXCELS	-X--T-	LYRICS	KYUSHU
SWAMPS	******	EXHALE	******	MYRICA	LYMPHO
SWAMPY	-X--C-	EXPELS	EXACTA	******	NYMPHA
SWEEPS	******	EXTOLS	EXACTS	-Y--D-	NYMPHO
SWEEPY	EXARCH	******	EXALTS	******	NYMPHS
SWOOPS	EXPECT	-X--M-	EXCITE	CYCADS	PYRRHA
TWERPS	EXSECT	AXIOMS	EXERTS	HYOIDS	SYLPHS
TWIRPS		EXHUME	EXISTS	SYNODS	SYLPHY

******	******	MYTHOS	CYMOUS	******	LAMBDA
-Y--I-	-Y--M-	PYTHON	CYPRUS	-A---A	LAMINA
******	******	SYMBOL	DYBBUK	******	LATERA
CYANIC	BYNAME	SYPHON	EYECUP	BAHAMA	LATRIA
CYANID	DYNAMO	TYCOON	EYEFUL	BALATA	LATVIA
CYANIN	MYXOMA	TYPHON	EYEOUT	BALBOA	MACULA
CYCLIC	PYJAMA	XYSTOS	GYNOUS	BANANA	MADURA
CYMLIN	XYLEMS	******	GYPSUM	BARBRA	MALAGA
CYMOID	ZYGOMA	-Y--P-	LYCEUM	BARYTA	MALAYA
CYMRIC	******	******	TYPHUS	CABALA	MALTHA
CYPRIN	-Y--N-	PYROPE	******	CABANA	MANANA
CYSTIC	******	SYRUPS	-Y--W-	CAEOMA	MANILA
DYADIC	BYGONE	SYRUPY	******	CALESA	MANTUA
EYELID	BYLANE	******	BYLAWS	CAMERA	MARACA
HYBRID	BYLINE	-Y--R-	VYRNWY	CAMILA	MARCIA
HYBRIS	CYMENE	******	******	CANADA	MARINA
HYDRIC	CYRANO	AYMARA	-Y--Y-	CANDIA	MARKKA
HYGEIA	CYRENE	BYWORD	******	CANULA	MARSHA
HYMNIC	DYEING	BYWORK	AYEAYE	CAPITA	MARTHA
HYPNIC	EYEING	CYMARS	BYEBYE	CARINA	MASORA
MYELIN	GYBING	SYNURA	BYWAYS	CASABA	MAXIMA
MYOPIA	GYRONS	WYVERN	RYUKYU	CASAVA	MAZUMA
MYOPIC	GYVING	******	******	CASSIA	NAGANA
MYOSIN	HYMENO	-Y--S-	-Z--A-	CATENA	NAGOYA
MYOSIS	HYMENS	******	******	CAYUGA	NASHUA
MYSTIC	LYSINE	BYPASS	UZZIAH	DAGOBA	NAUSEA
MYTHIC	LYSING	BYPAST	******	DAHLIA	PAGODA
PYEMIA	LYSINS	CYMOSE	-Z--C-	DAKOTA	PAJAMA
PYEMIC	NYLONS	DYNAST	******	DATURA	PAMELA
PYKNIC	PYLONS	GYROSE	AZTECS	FACULA	PANADA
PYOSIS	PYRANS	LYRISM	******	FANEGA	PANAMA
PYTHIA	PYRENE	LYRIST	-Z--E-	FARINA	PAPAYA
PYTHIC	PYRONE	TYPIST	******	FASCIA	PAPULA
PYURIA	SYRINX	XYLOSE	AZALEA	FATIMA	PATHIA
SYLVIA	TYPING	******	AZAZEL	GALENA	PATINA
SYNDIC	TYRANT	-Y--T-	AZINES	GAMBIA	PAYOLA
XYLOID	TYRONE	******	AZOLES	HAVANA	RADULA
******	XYLANS	BYPATH	AZORES	JACANA	RAFFIA
-Y--L-	XYLENE	GYRATE	AZRAEL	JAPHIA	RAMONA
******	******	MYCETE	AZURES	JARINA	RAZZIA
BYTALK	-Y--O-	PYRITE	******	KABAKA	SABINA
CYBELE	******	XYLITE	-Z--I-	KABALA	SAHARA
CYRILS	BYBLOW	ZYGOTE	******	KABAYA	SALIVA
MYRTLE	FYLFOT	******	AZONIC	KALMIA	SALVIA
MYSELF	HYDROS	-Y--U-	AZOTIC	KAMALA	SAMARA
SYBILS	HYPNOS	******	OZONIC	KANAKA	SANDRA
TYBALT	HYSSOP	BYSSUS		LACUNA	SATARA
TYPHLO	MYTHOI	CYGNUS		LADOGA	TACOMA

TAENIA	******	CARTED	GASHED	LANDED	PATTED
TARSIA	-A---D	CARVED	GASPED	LAPPED	PAUSED
VACUNA	******	CASHED	GASSED	LAPSED	PAWNED
VAGINA	AALAND	CATTED	GAUGED	LARDED	RACKED
VALUTA	BABIED	CAUDAD	GAWKED	LARKED	RAFTED
VARUNA	BACHED	CAUSED	HACKED	LASHED	RAGGED
YAKIMA	BACKED	DABBED	HAFTED	LASTED	RAIDED
ZAMBIA	BADGED	DAMMED	HAGGED	LATHED	RAILED
ZANANA	BAFFED	DAMNED	HAILED	LAUDED	RAINED
ZAPATA	BAGDAD	DAMPED	HAIRED	MADDED	RAISED
ZARIBA	BAGGED	DANAID	HALOED	MADRID	RAMMED
******	BAILED	DANCED	HALOID	MAENAD	RAMPED
-A---B	BAITED	DANGED	HALTED	MAILED	RAMROD
******	BALKED	DAPPED	HALVED	MAIMED	RANCID
BAOBAB	BALLAD	DARNED	HAMMED	MALLED	RANGED
CANTAB	BALLED	DARTED	HANDED	MALTED	RANKED
MAHBUB	BANDED	DASHED	HANGED	MANNED	RANTED
******	BANGED	DAUBED	HAPPED	MAPPED	RAPPED
-A---C	BANKED	DAWNED	HARKED	MARAUD	RASPED
******	BARBED	DAYBED	HARMED	MARKED	RATTED
BALTIC	BARDED	EARNED	HAROLD	MARLED	RAZEED
BALZAC	BARGED	FABLED	HARPED	MARRED	RAZZED
BARDIC	BARKED	FAGEND	HASHED	MASHED	SACKED
CALCIC	BARRED	FAGGED	HASPED	MASKED	SACRED
CALPAC	BASHED	FAILED	HASTED	MASSED	SAGGED
CAPRIC	BASKED	FAIRED	HATRED	MASTED	SAILED
CARPIC	BASTED	FANGED	HATTED	MATTED	SALPID
FABRIC	BATHED	FANNED	HAULED	MAULED	SALTED
GAELIC	BATTED	FARBAD	HAWKED	NABBED	SALVED
GALLIC	BAWLED	FARCED	HAZARD	NAGGED	SANDED
GARLIC	BAYARD	FARMED	JABBED	NAILED	SAPPED
IAMBIC	CABLED	FASTED	JACKED	NAPPED	SASHED
IATRIC	CACHED	FATTED	JAGGED	NARKED	SASSED
LACTIC	CADGED	FAWNED	JAILED	PACKED	SAUCED
MANIAC	CALKED	GABBED	JAMMED	PADDED	TABARD
MANIOC	CALLED	GABLED	JARRED	PAINED	TABBED
MANTIC	CALMED	GADDED	JAZZED	PAIRED	TABLED
MASTIC	CALVED	GADOID	KAYOED	PALLED	TACKED
NASTIC	CAMPED	GAFFED	LACKED	PALLID	TAGGED
PARSEC	CANARD	GAGGED	LADLED	PALMED	TAILED
SAITIC	CANDID	GAINED	LAGGED	PALPED	TALCED
TACTIC	CANNED	GAITED	LAIRED	PANNED	TALKED
TAMBAC	CANOED	GALLED	LALLED	PANTED	TALMUD
TANNIC	CANTED	GAMMED	LAMBED	PARKED	TAMPED
TANREC	CAPPED	GANGED	LAMMED	PARSED	TANGED
TARMAC	CARDED	GANOID	LAMPAD	PARTED	TANKED
	CARPED	GAPPED	LAMPED	PASSED	TANNED
		GARBED	LANCED	PASTED	TAPPED

TARRED	BAILIE	DANUBE	LAHORE	NATIVE	SAVATE
TARTED	BANGLE	DAPHNE	LAMBIE	NATURE	TACKLE
TASKED	BARBIE	DAPPLE	LAMIAE	PADDLE	TAILLE
TASTED	BAREGE	DARKLE	LANATE	PAIUTE	TALKIE
TATTED	BARGEE	DARTLE	LANOSE	PALACE	TAMALE
TAXIED	BARITE	DATIVE	LAOTSE	PALATE	TANGLE
VALUED	BARMIE	DAWDLE	LARINE	PALEAE	TATTLE
VALVED	BARQUE	DAZZLE	LARVAE	PANICE	TAXEME
VAMPED	BARRIE	FACADE	LASSIE	PANTIE	TAXITE
VARIED	BASQUE	FACILE	LAUNCE	PAPULE	VACATE
VATTED	BATTLE	FAERIE	LAURAE	PARADE	VADOSE
WADDED	BATTUE	FAEROE	LAURIE	PARCAE	VALATE
WAFTED	BAUBLE	FAILLE	LAVAGE	PAROLE	VALISE
WAGGED	CACKLE	FAMINE	MACKLE	PARSEE	VAMOSE
WAIFED	CADDIE	FANNIE	MACULE	PARURE	WABBLE
WAILED	CAIQUE	FAUNAE	MADAME	PASSEE	WADDLE
WAITED	CAJOLE	GABBLE	MAGGIE	PATINE	WAFFLE
WAIVED	CAMISE	GAGGLE	MAGPIE	PAVANE	WAGGLE
WALKED	CANAPE	GALEAE	MAIGRE	PAVISE	WAHINE
WALLED	CANDLE	GALORE	MAISIE	PAWNEE	WALLIE
WANNED	CANGUE	GAMBLE	MAITRE	RABBLE	WAMBLE
WANTED	CANINE	GAMETE	MALATE	RACEME	WANDLE
WAPPED	CANNAE	GANGUE	MALGRE	RACINE	WANGLE
WARDED	CANNIE	GARAGE	MALICE	RADDLE	WARBLE
WARMED	CANTLE	GARBLE	MALINE	RADOME	WATAPE
WARNED	CANUTE	GARGLE	MALLEE	RAFFLE	WATTLE
WARPED	CAPONE	GAUCHE	MAMMAE	RAMBLE	YANKEE
WARRED	CAPOTE	GAULLE	MANAGE	RAMOSE	ZAFFRE
WASHED	CARAFE	HABILE	MANEGE	RANKLE	******
WASTED	CARATE	HACKEE	MANGLE	RAPHAE	-A---F
WAULED	CARIBE	HACKIE	MANQUE	RAPINE	******
WAWLED	CAROLE	HACKLE	MANTLE	RAPPEE	FAROFF
YAKKED	CARRIE	HAGGLE	MANURE	RATINE	LAYOFF
YANKED	CASQUE	HALIDE	MARBLE	RATITE	MASSIF
YAPPED	CASSIE	HALITE	MARGIE	RATTLE	PAYOFF
YARDED	CASTLE	HAMITE	MARINE	RAVAGE	TARIFF
YAUPED	CATTIE	HANDLE	MARQUE	RAVINE	******
YAWLED	CATTLE	HASSLE	MARTHE	SABINE	-A---G
YAWNED	CAUDLE	HATTIE	MASHIE	SADDLE	******
YAWPED	CAVITE	JACKIE	MASQUE	SALINE	BAAING
******	CAYUSE	JANGLE	MATINE	SALOME	BAKING
-A---E	DABBLE	JANICE	MATTIE	SALUTE	BALING
******	DADDLE	JAYVEE	MATURE	SAMITE	BARING
BABBIE	DAGGLE	KARATE	MAXINE	SAMPLE	BARONG
BABBLE	DAMAGE	KATHIE	MAXIXE	SARAPE	BASING
BABITE	DANDLE	LABILE	NADINE	SARTRE	BATING
BAFFLE	DANGLE	LADDIE	NAPPIE	SATIRE	BAYING
BAILEE	DANITE	LAGUNE	NARINE	SAVAGE	CAGING

CAKING	LAWING	WANING	CANTHI	CARMEL	MARVEL
CANING	LAYING	WAVING	GANDHI	CARNAL	NARIAL
CARING	LAZING	WAXING	GANGLI	CARPAL	NARWAL
CASING	MACING	YAWING	HAWAII	CARPEL	NASIAL
CAVING	MAKING	ZAFTIG	KABIKI	CARREL	PARCEL
CAWING	MASKEG	******	KABUKI	CARTEL	PARRAL
DANZIG	MATING	-A---H	LAZULI	CARVEL	PARREL
DARING	MAYBUG	******	MALAWI	CASUAL	PASCAL
DATING	MAYING	BANISH	SAFARI	CAUDAL	PASTEL
DAZING	MAZING	BARUCH	SALAMI	CAUSAL	PASTIL
EALING	NAMING	BASRAH	SALUKI	CAVELL	PATHOL
EARING	OARING	CALASH	SANDHI	DACTYL	PATROL
EARWIG	PACING	CALIPH	SANGUI	DAEDAL	RACHEL
EASING	PAGING	CASBAH	SANSEI	DAMSEL	RACIAL
EATING	PALING	DALETH	TAHITI	DANIEL	RADIAL
FACING	PARANG	DANISH	TAIPEI	DARNEL	RANDAL
FADING	PARING	FAMISH	TALARI	EARFUL	RAPPEL
FAKING	PAVING	GALOSH	VAPORI	FACIAL	RASCAL
FARING	PAWING	GARISH	VASARI	FAECAL	SACRAL
FATING	PAYING	HALLAH	VASHTI	FALLAL	SAMIEL
FAXING	RACING	HANNAH	VASILI	FAUCAL	SAMUEL
FAYING	RAGBAG	HAUNCH	WAHABI	FAUNAL	SANDAL
FAZING	RAGING	JADISH	WAKIKI	GAMBOL	SANTOL
GAGING	RAGTAG	LAMECH	WAPITI	GAVIAL	SAUREL
GAMING	RAKING	LATISH	WATUSI	HAEMAL	TARNAL
GAPING	RAPING	LAUNCH	******	HALLEL	TARSAL
GASBAG	RARING	LAVISH	-A---K	HAMAUL	TASSEL
GATING	RATING	NAUTCH	******	HAMMAL	VALVAL
GAZING	RAVING	OAFISH	BARTOK	HANDEL	VANDAL
HADING	RAYING	PALISH	BATTIK	HANSEL	VASSAL
HALING	RAZING	PARAPH	CANUCK	HARTAL	VATFUL
HARING	SARONG	PARIAH	CARACK	HASSEL	WARHOL
HATING	SATANG	PARISH	DAMASK	HATFUL	******
HAVING	SATING	PAUNCH	GALYAK	JACKAL	-A---M
HAWING	SAVING	RADISH	KALPAK	JARFUL	******
HAYING	SAWING	RAKISH	KARNAK	LABIAL	BAALIM
HAZING	SAYING	RAVISH	MARDUK	LACIAL	BABISM
JADING	TAKING	RAWISH	SANJAK	LAPFUL	BALAAM
JAPING	TAMING	SALISH	YASMAK	LARVAL	BALSAM
JAWING	TAPING	VANISH	******	LAUREL	BALTIM
KALONG	TARING	WABASH	-A---L	LAWFUL	BANTAM
LACING	TAUTOG	WALLAH	******	MAMMAL	BARIUM
LADING	TAWING	WARMTH	BAIKAL	MANFUL	BARNUM
LAKING	TAXING	YAHVEH	BARBEL	MANTEL	CAECUM
LAMING	WADING	YAHWEH	BARREL	MANUAL	FACTUM
LAPDOG	WAGING	******	CANCEL	MANUEL	FANTOM
LARYNG	WAKING	-A---I	CANNEL	MARCEL	FATHOM
LAVING	WALING	******	CARCEL		HANSOM
		BANGUI			
		BANZAI			

HARLEM	BATAAN	DAYTON	MADDEN	SADDEN	CASHOO
KALIUM	BATMAN	EASTON	MADMAN	SAIGON	CASINO
LABIUM	BATMEN	FABIAN	MADMEN	SAIPAN	CASTRO
LABRUM	BATTEN	FADEIN	MAIDEN	SALMON	CATALO
LACTAM	BATTIN	FALCON	MAISON	SALOON	DAIMIO
MAGNUM	CABMAN	FALLEN	MALIGN	SAMIAN	DAIMYO
MAOISM	CABMEN	FANION	MAMMON	SAMOAN	GABBRO
MAYHEM	CAFTAN	FANTAN	MANDAN	SAMPAN	GAMETO
NANISM	CAIMAN	FASTEN	MARGIN	SAMSON	GASTRO
NAPALM	CALKIN	FATTEN	MARIAN	SAPIEN	GAUCHO
NAZISM	CALVIN	GABION	MARION	SARGON	GAZABO
PASSIM	CAMDEN	GALLON	MARLIN	SATEEN	GAZEBO
PAYNIM	CAMION	GAMMON	MAROON	SATURN	HAIRDO
RACISM	CANAAN	GARCON	MARTEN	TAIWAN	HALLOO
RADIUM	CANCAN	GARDEN	MARTIN	TAKEIN	KAKAPO
RANDOM	CANNON	GASCON	MARVIN	TALION	KARROO
RANSOM	CANTON	GASKIN	MASCON	TAMPAN	LADINO
SACHEM	CANYON	GASMAN	MATRON	TAMPON	LANUGO
SACRUM	CAPLIN	GASMEN	NAPKIN	TANNIN	LAPARO
SADISM	CARBON	GASTON	NASION	TARPAN	LAREDO
SALAAM	CAREEN	GAWAIN	NATHAN	TARTAN	LAVABO
TALCUM	CARMAN	HAGDON	NATION	TARZAN	MACACO
TAMTAM	CARMEN	HAMDEN	NATRON	TASMAN	MADURO
TANDEM	CARSON	HAPPEN	PAPAIN	TAUTEN	MALACO
TAOISM	CARTON	HARBIN	PAPUAN	TAVERN	MANITO
VACUUM	CARVEN	HARDEN	PARDON	VANMAN	MATTEO
VALLUM	CASEIN	HARKEN	PARIAN	VANMEN	NAVAHO
WAMPUM	CASERN	HARLAN	PARSON	WAGGON	NAVAJO
******	CATION	HARMIN	PATHAN	WALKON	PALAEO
-A---N	CATKIN	HASTEN	PATRON	WALTON	PANCHO
******	CATLIN	HATPIN	PATTEN	WANION	PASHTO
AACHEN	CAVEIN	HAUSEN	PATTON	WANTON	RANCHO
BABOON	CAVERN	HAZZAN	PAULIN	WARDEN	SAPPHO
BADMAN	CAXTON	JARGON	RABBIN	WARREN	TAPALO
BADMEN	CAYMAN	KAFTAN	RACOON	WATSON	TATTOO
BAFFIN	DACRON	KALIAN	RADIAN	YAUPON	VAGINO
BAGMAN	DAEMON	KAMSIN	RAGLAN	******	VARICO
BAGMEN	DAHOON	KANSAN	RAGMAN	-A---O	XANTHO
BALEEN	DAIMON	KAOLIN	RAGMEN	******	******
BALKAN	DALTON	KATION	RAISIN	BAGNIO	-A---P
BANIAN	DAMPEN	LAGOON	RAMSON	BAMAKO	******
BANYAN	DAMSON	LARDON	RANDAN	BAMBOO	BANGUP
BARMAN	DANTON	LASSEN	RATION	BARRIO	CALLUP
BARMEN	DARDAN	LATEEN	RATLIN	BASUTO	CARHOP
BARREN	DARIEN	LATTEN	RATOON	CALICO	CATNAP
BARTON	DARKEN	LAYMAN	RATTAN	CALLAO	CATNIP
BARYON	DARWIN	LAYMEN	RATTEN	CARDIO	CATSUP
BASION	DAWSON	MACRON	SABEAN	CARUSO	EARLAP

GALLOP	CANDOR	FARMER	JAZZER	NAPPER	SALTER
GALLUP	CANKER	FASTER	KAFFIR	NASSER	SALVER
HANGUP	CANNER	FATHER	KAISER	NATTER	SALVOR
LARRUP	CANTER	FATTER	KASPER	PACKER	SAMBUR
MADCAP	CANTOR	FAVOUR	LAAGER	PALLOR	SANDER
MADEUP	CAPPER	FAWNER	LABOUR	PALMAR	SANGAR
MAKEUP	CAPTOR	GABBER	LACIER	PALMER	SANGER
MARKUP	CARDER	GADDER	LADDER	PALTER	SANSAR
MAYHAP	CAREER	GAFFER	LADLER	PAMPER	SAPHAR
MAYPOP	CARPER	GAGGER	LAGGER	PANDER	SAPPER
SALOOP	CARTER	GAINER	LAKIER	PANZER	SARSAR
SANNUP	CARVER	GAITER	LANCER	PARKER	SARTOR
SATRAP	CASPAR	GAMBIR	LANDER	PARLOR	SAUCER
TAKEUP	CASPER	GAMIER	LANGUR	PASSER	SAUGER
WALKUP	CASTER	GAMMER	LANKER	PASTER	SAVIOR
WALLOP	CASTOR	GANDER	LANNER	PASTOR	SAVOUR
WARMUP	CATHER	GANGER	LAPPER	PATTER	SAWYER
******	CAUSER	GAOLER	LAPSER	PAUKER	TACKER
-A---R	CAUTER	GARNER	LARDER	PAUPER	TAGGER
******	CAVIAR	GARTER	LARGER	PAUSER	TAILOR
BACKER	DABBER	GASPAR	LARKER	PAVIOR	TALKER
BADGER	DAGGER	GASPER	LASCAR	PAWNER	TALLER
BAILER	DAGMAR	GATHER	LASHER	RACIER	TAMPER
BAILOR	DAMMAR	GAUGER	LASTER	RACKER	TANKER
BALDER	DAMMER	HACKER	LATHER	RADNOR	TANNER
BANGOR	DAMPER	HAILER	LATTER	RAFTER	TAPPER
BANKER	DANCER	HALTER	LAUDER	RAIDER	TARTAR
BANNER	DANDER	HAMMER	LAWYER	RAISER	TARTER
BANTER	DANGER	HAMPER	LAZIER	RAMMER	TASTER
BARBER	DANKER	HANGAR	MADDER	RANCOR	TATLER
BARKER	DAPPER	HANGER	MAGYAR	RANGER	TATTER
BARTER	DARKER	HANKER	MAHLER	RANKER	TAUTER
BATHER	DARNER	HARBOR	MAILER	RANTER	TAYLOR
BATTER	DARTER	HARDER	MAIMER	RAPIER	VAGUER
BAWLER	DASHER	HARPER	MANGER	RAPPER	VAINER
BAXTER	DAUBER	HATTER	MANNER	RAPTOR	VALKYR
BAZAAR	EARNER	HAULER	MARKER	RASHER	VALOUR
CADGER	EASIER	HAWKER	MARRER	RASPER	VALUER
CAESAR	EASTER	HAWSER	MARTYR	RASTER	VALVAR
CAGIER	FABLER	HAZIER	MASHER	RATHER	VAPOUR
CAHIER	FACTOR	JABBER	MASKER	RATTER	VARIER
CALCAR	FAFNIR	JAEGER	MASTER	SACKER	VASTER
CALKER	FAIRER	JAGUAR	MATTER	SADDER	WAFTER
CALLER	FALLER	JAILER	MAULER	SAGGAR	WAGNER
CALMER	FALSER	JAILOR	MAUSER	SAGGER	WAILER
CAMBER	FALTER	JAIPUR	MAZIER	SAGIER	WAITER
CAMPER	FANNER	JAMJAR	NAGGER	SAILER	WAIVER
CANCER	FARCER	JASPER	NAPIER	SAILOR	WALKER

WALTER	BASILS	CAPIAS	DAVIDS	GASSES	KAPOKS
WANDER	BASINS	CAPONS	DAVIES	GAUGES	KAPPAS
WANNER	BASSES	CARATS	DAVITS	GAUZES	KARATS
WANTER	BASSOS	CARERS	EAGLES	GAVELS	KARENS
WARDER	BASTES	CARESS	EARLES	GAVOTS	KARMAS
WARIER	BATHOS	CARETS	EARTHS	GAZERS	KATHYS
WARMER	BATIKS	CARGOS	EASELS	HABEAS	KATIES
WARNER	BATONS	CARIBS	EATERS	HABITS	KAURIS
WARPER	BAUCIS	CARIES	FABLES	HAGGIS	KAVASS
WASHER	BAYOUS	CARLAS	FACERS	HAKIMS	KAYAKS
WASTER	CABALS	CARLOS	FACETS	HALERS	KAZOOS
WAVIER	CABINS	CAROBS	FACIES	HALIDS	LABELS
WAXIER	CABLES	CAROLS	FAECES	HALOES	LABORS
XAVIER	CABOBS	CAROMS	FAGOTS	HALVES	LACHES
YABBER	CACAOS	CARPUS	FAINTS	HAMALS	LADIES
YAMMER	CACHES	CARTES	FAITHS	HAMZAS	LADLES
YAWNER	CACTUS	CARVES	FAKERS	HANCES	LAGERS
YAWPER	CADDIS	CASALS	FAKIRS	HANNAS	LAIRDS
ZAFFAR	CADETS	CASHES	FAMOUS	HARASS	LAKERS
ZAFFER	CADGES	CASSIS	FANGAS	HAREMS	LAMEDS
ZAFFIR	CADMUS	CASTES	FANNYS	HARRIS	LAMIAS
ZANIER	CADRES	CATERS	FANONS	HARRYS	LAMMAS
******	CAIRNS	CATHYS	FANUMS	HASHES	LAMPAS
-A---S	CAJUNS	CAUCUS	FARADS	HASTES	LANAIS
******	CALAIS	CAULES	FARCES	HATERS	LANCES
AALIIS	CALCES	CAULIS	FARERS	HATTYS	LAPELS
AARONS	CALEBS	CAULKS	FARLES	HAUNTS	LAPINS
BABIES	CALIFS	CAUSES	FASCES	HAVENS	LAPSES
BABOOS	CALLAS	CAVIES	FAUCES	HAWSES	LAPSUS
BABULS	CALLUS	CAVILS	FAULTS	HAZELS	LARGOS
BACHES	CALVES	DACHAS	FAUNAS	HAZERS	LARRYS
BADGES	CALXES	DADOES	FAUNUS	IAMBUS	LASERS
BAGASS	CAMASS	DAISES	FAUVES	JABOTS	LASHES
BAGELS	CAMELS	DAISYS	FAVORS	JACKYS	LASSES
BAHAIS	CAMEOS	DALLAS	FAWKES	JACOBS	LASSOS
BAIRNS	CAMPOS	DALLES	GABLES	JAINAS	LATHES
BAKERS	CAMPUS	DAMANS	GAFFES	JALOPS	LATINS
BALERS	CANALS	DANAUS	GAGERS	JAMIES	LAUGHS
BALSAS	CANERS	DANCES	GALLUS	JANETS	LAURAS
BANJOS	CANNAS	DANNYS	GALOPS	JAPANS	LAVERS
BANTUS	CANNES	DARERS	GAMINS	JARVIS	LAYERS
BARDES	CANOES	DARICS	GAMMAS	JASONS	LAZARS
BARGES	CANONS	DARIUS	GAMOUS	JAUNTS	MABELS
BARONS	CANSOS	DASHES	GAMUTS	JAZZES	MACAWS
BARRYS	CANTOS	DATERS	GANEFS	KAASES	MACERS
BARYES	CANTUS	DATTOS	GANGES	KABOBS	MACLES
BASHES	CANVAS	DAUNTS	GAPERS	KAMIKS	MADAMS
BASICS	CAPERS	DAVEYS	GASHES	KANSAS	MADGES

MADRAS	NAHUMS	PATIOS	SADHUS	TANKAS	WAVIES
MAGOTS	NAIADS	PATOIS	SADIES	TAPERS	WAYNES
MAIZES	NAMERS	PATSYS	SAHEBS	TAPIRS	YACHTS
MAJORS	NANCYS	PAULAS	SAHIBS	TAROTS	YAGERS
MAKERS	NANTES	PAULUS	SAIGAS	TARSUS	YAHOOS
MALAYS	NAOMIS	PAUSES	SAINTS	TASTES	YAMENS
MAMBAS	NAOSES	PAVANS	SAJOUS	TATARS	YAMUNS
MAMBOS	NAPLES	PAVERS	SAKERS	TAUNTS	YAPONS
MAMEYS	NAPPES	PAWERS	SALADS	TAUPES	ZAMIAS
MAMIES	NASALS	PAYEES	SALLYS	TAURUS	ZANIES
MAMMAS	NAVELS	PAYERS	SALMIS	TAWERS	ZAYINS
MANDYS	NAVIES	RABBIS	SALONS	TAXERS	******
MANGOS	NAWABS	RABIES	SALPAS	TAZZAS	-A---T
MANIAS	PACERS	RACERS	SALVES	VALETS	******
MANORS	PADDYS	RACHIS	SALVOS	VALGUS	BABIST
MANSES	PADRES	RADARS	SAMBAS	VALOIS	BALLET
MANTAS	PAEANS	RADIOS	SAMBOS	VALUES	BALLOT
MANTES	PAEONS	RADIUS	SAMMYS	VALVES	BANDIT
MANTIS	PAGANS	RAISES	SANDYS	VAPORS	BARBET
MAORIS	PAINTS	RAJABS	SANIES	VARIES	BAREST
MAPLES	PALAIS	RAJAHS	SARAHS	VARVES	BARRET
MAQUIS	PALLAS	RAKERS	SASHES	VAULTS	BASALT
MARCOS	PALPUS	RALPHS	SASINS	VAUNTS	BASEST
MARCUS	PAMPAS	RAMIES	SASSES	WADERS	BASKET
MARGES	PANDAS	RAMOUS	SATINS	WADIES	BASSET
MARGOS	PANELS	RANEES	SATYRS	WAFERS	CABLET
MARIAS	PANICS	RANGES	SAUCES	WAGERS	CACHET
MARIES	PANSYS	RAOULS	SAULTS	WAGONS	CADENT
MARTAS	PAPAWS	RAPHIS	SAUNAS	WAHOOS	CAHOOT
MARTYS	PAPERS	RAPIDS	SAURUS	WAISTS	CAMLET
MASERS	PAPPUS	RASHES	SAUTES	WAIVES	CANNOT
MASHES	PARENS	RATALS	SAVERS	WAKENS	CARPET
MASONS	PARERS	RATELS	SAVINS	WALDOS	CARROT
MASSES	PAREUS	RATERS	SAVORS	WALERS	CASKET
MATEOS	PARGOS	RATIOS	SAWERS	WALLAS	CATGUT
MATEYS	PARIES	RAVELS	SAXONS	WALLIS	CAUGHT
MATINS	PARKAS	RAVENS	SAYERS	WALLYS	CAVEAT
MATTES	PARSES	RAVERS	TABLES	WALRUS	CAVORT
MATZOS	PARSIS	RAYAHS	TABOOS	WALVIS	DACOIT
MAUDES	PARVIS	RAYONS	TABORS	WAMMUS	DAKOIT
MAUNDS	PASHAS	RAZEES	TAIGAS	WAMOUS	DAUDET
MAUVES	PASSES	RAZORS	TAINOS	WANDAS	EAGLET
MAXIMS	PASSUS	RAZZES	TAINTS	WASHES	FAGGOT
MAYORS	PASTAS	SABERS	TAKERS	WASTES	FANJET
MAZERS	PASTES	SABINS	TALERS	WATAPS	FAROUT
NABOBS	PATENS	SABLES	TALONS	WATERS	FAUCET
NADIRS	PATERS	SABOTS	TAMERS	WAVERS	GADGET
NAEVUS	PATHOS	SABRAS	TANGOS	WAVEYS	GALACT

GALIOT	PARROT	MAUMAU	MAGNOX	GALAXY	PAPERY
GALOOT	PATENT	NASSAU	MATRIX	GALLEY	PARITY
GAMBIT	RABBET	SAMSHU	PAXWAX	GALWAY	PARLAY
GANNET	RABBIT	XANADU	******	GAMELY	PARLEY
GARGET	RACIST	******	-A---Y	GAMILY	PARODY
GARNET	RACKET	-A---V	******	GANTRY	PARTLY
GARRET	RAGOUT	******	BACONY	GASIFY	PASTRY
GASJET	RAJPUT	PAVLOV	BAILEY	GAYETY	PATCHY
GASKET	RAMJET	******	BAKERY	HALLEY	PAYDAY
GAYEST	RAPIST	-A---W	BALDLY	HALSEY	RACILY
HAGBUT	RAREST	******	BARELY	HARDLY	RAGDAY
HAMLET	RAWEST	BARROW	BARFLY	HARLEY	RAMIFY
HARLOT	SABBAT	BASHAW	BARLEY	HARVEY	RANKLY
HASLET	SACHET	CALLOW	BARNEY	HAULMY	RAPTLY
HAVENT	SADIST	CARLOW	BARONY	HAZILY	RAREFY
JACKET	SAFEST	CASHAW	BASELY	JALOPY	RARELY
JAPHET	SAGEST	CASHEW	BASIFY	JARVEY	RARITY
LABRET	SALLET	DARROW	BAWDRY	JAUNTY	RASHLY
LAMENT	SAMLET	FALLOW	CAGILY	LACILY	RATIFY
LAMEST	SANEST	FARROW	CALMLY	LACKEY	SAFELY
LANCET	SAVANT	HALLOW	CALORY	LAMELY	SAFETY
LAPPET	TABLET	HARLOW	CANARY	LANKLY	SAGELY
LARIAT	TALENT	HARROW	CANOPY	LASTLY	SALARY
LATENT	TAMEST	HAWHAW	CARBOY	LATELY	SALIFY
LATEST	TANIST	HAYMOW	CASEFY	LAXITY	SANELY
LAXEST	TAOIST	JARROW	CATCHY	LAYDAY	SANITY
LAYOUT	TAPPET	MALLOW	CATHAY	LAZILY	SASHAY
MAGGOT	TARGET	MARLOW	CAVITY	MAGUEY	SATINY
MAGNET	TASSET	MARROW	DAFTLY	MAINLY	SATORY
MAHOUT	TAUGHT	NARROW	DAINTY	MALADY	SAVORY
MALLET	VACANT	PAWPAW	DAMPLY	MALORY	SAWFLY
MAMMET	VARLET	SALLOW	DANKLY	MARGAY	SAWNEY
MAOIST	WADSET	TALLOW	DARKLY	MARSHY	SAXONY
MARGOT	WALLET	WALLOW	DATARY	MAUNDY	TACKEY
MARIST	WALNUT	WARSAW	DAUBRY	MAYDAY	TAMELY
MARKET	WAYOUT	YARROW	DAYBOY	MAYFLY	TANGLY
MARMOT	YAOURT	******	DAYFLY	MAZILY	TARTLY
MASCOT	******	-A---X	EARTHY	NAMELY	TATTLY
MATZOT	-A---U	******	EASILY	NAPERY	TAUTLY
MAYEST	******	BAYEUX	EATERY	NAZIFY	TAWDRY
NATANT	BATEAU	CARFAX	FAIRLY	OAKLEY	VAGARY
NAUGHT	CACHOU	CAUDEX	FAKERY	PACIFY	VAINLY
PACKET	DACHAU	EARWAX	FAMILY	PAEONY	VALERY
PALEST	GATEAU	HALLUX	FARLEY	PAINTY	VALLEY
PALLET	JABIRU	HATBOX	FAULTY	PALELY	VANITY
PAPIST	LANDAU	HAYBOX	GADFLY	PALTRY	VASTLY
PARENT	MANCHU	LARYNX	GAIETY	PANTRY	WABBLY
PARGET	MANITU	LASTEX	GAINLY	PAPACY	WADDLY

WAGGLY	******	ABELES	ACAENA	ICEAXE	******
WAMBLY	-B---H	ABHORS	ACEDIA	ICICLE	-C---L
WARILY	******	ABIDES	ACHAEA	OCREAE	******
WARMLY	ABIJAH	ABNERS	ACHAIA	OCTANE	ACETAL
WATERY	ABLUSH	ABODES	ECZEMA	OCTAVE	ACETYL
WAVILY	******	ABOHMS	SCHEMA	SCARCE	ACTUAL
WAYLAY	-B---I	ABOMAS	SCLERA	SCATHE	SCHOOL
******	******	ABOMBS	SCORIA	SCHEME	SCHORL
-A---Z	UBANGI	ABORTS	SCOTIA	SCONCE	SCRAWL
******	******	ABRAMS	SCROTA	SCOUSE	SCROLL
HALUTZ	-B---L	ABUSES	SCYLLA	SCRAPE	******
******	******	ABYDOS	******	SCRIBE	-C---M
-B---A	ABORAL	ABYSMS	-C---B	SCRIVE	******
******	******	IBEAMS	******	SCYTHE	ACEIUM
ABOLLA	-B---M	IBEXES	SCARAB	******	ACETUM
ABULIA	******	IBICES	******	******	ACTIUM
IBERIA	ABLOOM	IBISES	******	-C---F	SCHISM
******	IBIDEM	OBELUS	-C---C	******	SCREAM
-B---B	OBIISM	OBOLUS	******	SCLAFF	SCUTUM
******	******	OBSESS	ACERIC	SCRUFF	******
ABSORB	-B---N	TBONES	ACETIC	******	-C---N
******	******	UBOATS	ACIDIC	-C---G	******
-B---D	ABADAN	******	ECHOIC	******	ACTION
******	IBADAN	-B---T	ICONIC	ACHING	ACUMEN
ABASED	OBERON	******	SCENIC	ACTING	ICEMAN
ABATED	OBTAIN	ABDUCT	******	******	ICEMEN
ABIDED	******	ABJECT	-C---D	-C---H	SCREEN
ABOARD	-B---R	ABLAUT	******	******	******
ABOUND	******	ABLEST	ACARID	ACANTH	-C---O
ABROAD	ABASER	ABRUPT	ACCORD	SCORCH	******
ABSURD	ABATER	ABSENT	ECHARD	SCOTCH	ACTINO
ABUSED	ABATOR	ABVOLT	ECHOED	SCUTCH	ECHINO
OBEYED	ABIDER	ABWATT	SCALED	******	OCTAVO
OBTUND	ABUSER	OBJECT	SCARED	-C---I	SCHIZO
******	OBEYER	OBLAST	SCORED	******	SCIPIO
-B---E	OBITER	OBOIST	SCREED	ACTINI	SCLERO
******	******	OBTECT	SCRIED	ECHINI	SCYPHO
ABJURE	-B---S	OBTEST	******	OCELLI	******
ABLAZE	******	OBVERT	-C---E	OCTOPI	-C---P
ABRADE	ABACAS	******	******	OCTROI	******
OBLATE	ABACUS	-B---Y	ACCEDE	SCAMPI	ICECAP
OBLIGE	ABASES	******	ACCRUE	SCYPHI	SCRIMP
OBTUSE	ABATES	ABBACY	ACCUSE	******	SCROOP
******	ABATIS	UBIETY	ACHENE	-C---K	******
-B---G	ABBESS	******	ACNODE	******	-C---R
******	ABBEYS	-C---A	ACTIVE	ACKACK	******
EBBING	ABBIES	******	ACUATE	OCLOCK	ECHOER
OBLONG	ABBOTS	ACACIA	ECARTE	SCHICK	ECLAIR
		ACADIA	ECTYPE	SCREAK	

OCULAR	SCOOTS	******	EDMOND	******	******
SCALAR	SCOPES	-C---Y	EDMUND	-D---O	-D---T
SCALER	SCOPUS	******	EDUARD	******	******
SCARER	SCORES	ACIDLY	EDUCED	ADAGIO	ADDICT
SCORER	SCORNS	ACUITY	EDWARD	ODONTO	ADDUCT
SCOTER	SCOTTS	ECTOMY	******	******	ADJECT
******	SCOURS	ICALLY	-D---E	-D---R	ADJUST
-C---S	SCOUTS	ICHTHY	******	******	ADMIXT
******	SCOWLS	OCASEY	ADDUCE	ADORER	ADRIFT
ACCESS	SCRAGS	OCCUPY	ADHERE	EDGIER	ADROIT
ACEOUS	SCRAMS	OCHERY	ADJURE	EDITOR	ADVENT
ACINUS	SCRAPS	SCABBY	ADMIRE	******	ADVERT
ACIOUS	SCREWS	SCANTY	ADNATE	-D---S	IDLEST
ACORNS	SCRIPS	SCATTY	ADVICE	******	ODDEST
ACROSS	SCRODS	SCILLY	ADVISE	ADAGES	******
ACTORS	SCRUBS	SCREWY	EDIBLE	ADAPTS	-D---X
ECCLES	SCRUMS	SCUMMY	IDEATE	ADDAMS	******
ECESIS	SCUBAS	SCURFY	ODETTE	ADDERS	ADIEUX
ECHOES	SCUFFS	SCURRY	******	ADDLES	******
ECOLES	SCULLS	SCURVY	-D---G	ADEEMS	-D---Y
ICARUS	SCUTES	******	******	ADENIS	******
ICINGS	******	-D---A	ADDING	ADEPTS	IDIOCY
MCCOYS	-C---T	******	EDGING	ADIEUS	ODDITY
OCCURS	******	EDWINA	IDLING	ADLIBS	******
OCEANS	ACCENT	GDYNIA	******	ADMITS	-E---A
OCHERS	ACCEPT	ODESSA	-D---H	ADOBES	******
OCTADS	ACCOST	ODYNIA	******	ADONIS	AEOLIA
OCTETS	ACQUIT	******	ADOLPH	ADOPTS	BELUGA
SCALDS	ICIEST	-D---B	EDDISH	ADORES	BEMATA
SCALES	OCCULT	******	******	ADORNS	BENITA
SCALPS	OCELOT	ADSORB	-D---I	ADULTS	BERTHA
SCAMPS	OCTANT	ADVERB	******	EDDIES	CEDULA
SCAPES	SCHIST	ODDJOB	ADONAI	EDGARS	CENTRA
SCARES	SCHUIT	******	******	EDICTS	CESURA
SCARFS	SCRIPT	-D---C	-D---K	EDILES	DECUMA
SCARPS	SCULPT	******	******	EDITHS	FECULA
SCAUPS	YCLEPT	ADIPIC	GDANSK	EDSELS	FEDORA
SCENDS	******	ADONIC	******	EDUCES	FEMORA
SCENES	-C---U	EDDAIC	-D---M	EDUCTS	FERULA
SCENTS	******	EDENIC	******	EDWINS	GEISHA
SCHMOS	ACAJOU	******	ADYTUM	IDEALS	GEMARA
SCHUSS	******	-D---D	******	IDIOMS	GENERA
SCHWAS	-C---X	******	-D---N	IDIOTS	GENEVA
SCIONS	******	ADDEND	******	IDLERS	HECUBA
SCOFFS	ICEBOX	ADDLED	ADJOIN	IDYLLS	HEGIRA
SCOLDS	******	ADORED	ADNOUN	ODIOUS	HEJIRA
SCONES	ICEBOX	EDDIED	ADRIAN	UDDERS	HELENA
SCOOPS	SCOLEX	EDITED	ADRIEN		HERNIA
			EDISON		

HESTIA	CEDRIC	BEYOND	HEMMED	NEVOID	RETOLD
JEMIMA	CELIAC	CEASED	HEMOID	PEAKED	RETROD
JERBOA	CELTIC	CEBOID	HEPTAD	PEALED	RETTED
KERALA	DEIFIC	CEILED	HERALD	PECKED	REVVED
LEPSIA	DERMIC	CENSED	HERDED	PEEKED	REWARD
MEDUSA	FENNEC	DECKED	HESOID	PEELED	REWIND
MERCIA	FERRIC	DEEDED	JEERED	PEENED	REWORD
MEZUZA	GEODIC	DEEMED	JELLED	PEEPED	SEALED
NEBULA	GESTIC	DEFEND	JEREED	PEERED	SEAMED
NEVADA	HECTIC	DEFIED	JERKED	PEEVED	SEARED
OEDEMA	HERDIC	DEICED	JESSED	PEGGED	SEATED
OEPEMA	HEROIC	DELVED	JESTED	PELTED	SECOND
PELOTA	KELTIC	DEMAND	JETTED	PENDED	SECUND
PENNIA	METRIC	DENIED	KECKED	PENNED	SEEDED
PEORIA	PECTIC	DENNED	KEDGED	PENTAD	SEEMED
PERSIA	PELVIC	DENTED	KEELED	PEPPED	SEEPED
PESETA	PEPTIC	DEPEND	KEENED	PEQUOD	SEINED
PETULA	SENLAC	DESMID	KELOID	PERIOD	SEISED
REDOWA	SEPTIC	DEUCED	KENNED	PERKED	SEIZED
REGINA	TENREC	DEVOID	KERBED	PERMED	SENSED
REMORA	VEDIAC	FEARED	KERNED	PETARD	SERVED
REMUDA	******	FEASED	LEADED	PETTED	SEWARD
RESEDA	-E---D	FECUND	LEAFED	REAMED	TEAMED
RETINA	******	FEEZED	LEAKED	REAPED	TEARED
SENECA	AENEID	FELLED	LEANED	REARED	TEASED
SENORA	AERIED	FELTED	LEAPED	RECORD	TEDDED
SERBIA	BEADED	FENCED	LEASED	REDBUD	TEEMED
SERENA	BEAKED	FENDED	LEAVED	REEDED	TEHEED
TELEGA	BEAMED	FERVID	LEERED	REEFED	TENDED
TERBIA	BEANED	FEUDED	LEGEND	REEKED	TENSED
TERESA	BEARED	GEARED	LEGGED	REELED	TENTED
VERONA	BECKED	GELDED	LEVIED	REEVED	TERMED
VESICA	BEDDED	GELLED	MELDED	REFUND	TESTED
ZENANA	BEDRID	GEMMED	MELTED	REGARD	TETRAD
ZEUGMA	BEEFED	GERALD	MENDED	REINED	VEERED
******	BEEPED	GERARD	MEOWED	RELAID	VEILED
-E---B	BEGGED	GERUND	MERGED	RELIED	VEINED
******	BEGIRD	HEADED	MESHED	RELOAD	VENDED
BEDAUB	BEHEAD	HEALED	MESSED	REMAND	VENTED
BENUMB	BEHELD	HEAPED	METHOD	REMIND	VERGED
RESORB	BEHIND	HEATED	MEWLED	RENDED	VERSED
SERDAB	BEHOLD	HEAVED	NEARED	RENTED	VESPID
******	BELIED	HEDGED	NECKED	REPAID	VESTED
-E---C	BELLED	HEEDED	NEEDED	REPAND	VETOED
******	BELTED	HEELED	NEREID	RESEND	VETTED
AEOLIC	BENDED	HEFTED	NERVED	RESOLD	WEANED
BELGIC	BESTED	HELMED	NESTED	RESTED	WEAVED
BELLOC	BETTED	HELPED	NETTED	RETARD	WEBBED

WEDDED	CENTRE	DERIVE	LENORE	REDDLE	SELENE
WEDGED	CERATE	DESIRE	LEONIE	REDEYE	SEMELE
WEEDED	CERISE	DEVICE	LESLIE	REDONE	SEMEME
WELDED	CERITE	DEVISE	LESSEE	REDUCE	SEMITE
WELLED	CERUSE	DEVOTE	LEVITE	REFACE	SEMPRE
WELTED	CESARE	FEEBLE	MEAGRE	REFINE	SENATE
WENDED	CETANE	FEIGNE	MEALIE	REFUGE	SENILE
WETTED	DEARIE	FELICE	MEANIE	REFUSE	SERAPE
YEANED	DEBASE	FELINE	MEDDLE	REFUTE	SERENE
YELLED	DEBATE	FELIPE	MEDIAE	REGALE	SERINE
YELPED	DEBBIE	FELLOE	MENACE	REGGIE	SESAME
YENNED	DECADE	FEMALE	MENAGE	REGIME	SETOSE
YESSED	DECANE	FERINE	MESTEE	RELATE	SETTEE
ZEROED	DECARE	FERULE	METAGE	RELINE	SETTLE
ZESTED	DECIDE	FESCUE	METOPE	RELIVE	SEVERE
******	DECILE	FETTLE	METTLE	REMADE	SEWAGE
-E---E	DECKLE	GEMMAE	NEEDLE	REMAKE	TEETHE
******	DECODE	GENTLE	NEGATE	REMISE	TEMPLE
AEDILE	DECOKE	GEORGE	NELLIE	REMOTE	TENACE
AERATE	DECREE	GERTIE	NESTLE	REMOVE	TENURE
AEROBE	DEDUCE	HEARSE	NETTIE	RENEGE	TERETE
BEADLE	DEFACE	HEAUME	NETTLE	REPINE	TESSIE
BEAGLE	DEFAME	HECATE	NEVILE	REPOSE	TESTAE
BEANIE	DEFILE	HECKLE	OEUVRE	REPUTE	TEVERE
BECAME	DEFINE	HEDDLE	PEBBLE	RESALE	VELOCE
BECOME	DEFUSE	HERMAE	PEDATE	RESCUE	VELURE
BEETLE	DEGAGE	HEXANE	PEDDLE	RESIDE	VENDEE
BEFORE	DEGAME	HEXONE	PEEWEE	RESILE	VENDUE
BEGONE	DEGREE	HEXOSE	PEIRCE	RESOLE	VENICE
BEHAVE	DEKARE	JEANNE	PELAGE	RESUME	VENIRE
BEHOVE	DELATE	JEJUNE	PELITE	RETAKE	VENOSE
BELIKE	DELETE	JEROME	PENILE	RETENE	VENULE
BELIZE	DELUDE	JESSIE	PENNAE	RETIRE	VESTEE
BEMIRE	DELUGE	KECKLE	PEOPLE	RETUSE	WEDGIE
BEMUSE	DELUXE	KELPIE	PERUKE	REVERE	WEENIE
BENDEE	DEMISE	KENITE	PERUSE	REVILE	******
BERATE	DEMODE	KENNIE	PESADE	REVISE	-E---F
BERNIE	DEMOTE	KERRIE	PESTLE	REVIVE	******
BERTHE	DEMURE	KETENE	PETITE	REVOKE	BEHALF
BERTIE	DENGUE	KETONE	PETRIE	SEABEE	BEHOOF
BESIDE	DENISE	KETOSE	PEYOTE	SEANCE	BELIEF
BESSIE	DENOTE	KETTLE	REBATE	SECEDE	HEREOF
BETAKE	DENUDE	KEWPIE	REBORE	SECURE	REBUFF
BETIDE	DEPONE	LEAGUE	REBUKE	SEDATE	RELIEF
BETISE	DEPOSE	LEGATE	RECEDE	SEDILE	SETOFF
BEWARE	DEPUTE	LEGREE	RECIPE	SEDUCE	******
CECILE	DERATE	LEGUME	RECITE	SEETHE	-E---G
CELLAE	DERIDE	LENAPE	RECUSE	SEICHE	******
					BEDBUG
					BELONG

BERING	TERAPH	CENTAL	REFILL	MEGRIM	GERMAN
CEDING	WEALTH	CEREAL	REFUEL	PEPLUM	GERMEN
CERING	ZENITH	DECKEL	REGNAL	RECTUM	GERYON
DEKING	******	DENIAL	RENTAL	REDEEM	HEADON
FEEING	-E---I	DENTAL	REPEAL	REDGUM	HEAVEN
FETING	******	DENTIL	RESELL	REFORM	HEBRON
FEUING	CENTRI	DERAIL	RETAIL	SELDOM	HEDRON
GEEING	DELPHI	DERMAL	RETELL	SEPTUM	HELLEN
HEDWIG	DENDRI	DETAIL	RETOOL	SEXISM	HEMPEN
HEWING	GEMINI	FECIAL	REVEAL	TEDIUM	HENDON
HEXING	GENESI	FENNEL	SECKEL	TERGUM	HEREIN
JEEING	GEORGI	FERIAL	SENDAL	VELLUM	HEREON
KEYING	HERMAI	FESTAL	SEPTAL	VERISM	HERMAN
MEKONG	MEDICI	FETIAL	SEQUEL	******	HEROIN
METING	NEROLI	FEUDAL	SERIAL	-E---N	HETMAN
MEWING	NEVSKI	GENIAL	SERVAL	******	HEZION
PEGLEG	PEDATI	GERBIL	SEWALL	AEGEAN	JERKIN
PEKING	SESQUI	GESELL	SEWELL	BEACON	JETTON
REDBUG	YEHUDI	HEDRAL	SEXUAL	BEATEN	KEDRON
REDDOG	YEMENI	HERBAL	TEASEL	BECKON	KELSON
SEADOG	******	JEKYLL	TERCEL	BEDPAN	KELVIN
SEEING	-E---K	JEZAIL	TERGAL	BEDUIN	LEADEN
SEWING	******	KENDAL	TERNAL	BEGUIN	LEADIN
SEXING	BEDECK	KENNEL	TETRYL	BEMEAN	LEAVEN
TEABAG	BETOOK	KERNEL	TETZEL	BEMOAN	LEGION
TEEING	DEBARK	LEMUEL	VENIAL	BENIGN	LEGMAN
VEXING	DEBUNK	LENTIL	VERBAL	BENTON	LEGMEN
******	NEWARK	LETHAL	VERGIL	BERGEN	LENTEN
-E---H	REBECK	MEDIAL	VERNAL	BERLIN	LEPTON
******	REMARK	MENDEL	VESSEL	CEYLON	LESION
BEULAH	RETOOK	MENIAL	VESTAL	DEACON	LESSEN
CERIPH	SELJUK	MENSAL	WEASEL	DEADEN	LESSON
DEARTH	ZEBECK	MENTAL	WEEVIL	DEAFEN	LEYDEN
DETACH	******	MESCAL	XENIAL	DECCAN	MECCAN
******	-E---L	MESIAL	******	DECERN	MEDIAN
FELLAH	******	METHYL	-E---M	DEEPEN	MELLON
FETICH	AECIAL	NEURAL	******	DEEWAN	MELTON
FETISH	AERIAL	NEVILL	BECALM	DEHORN	MELVIN
HEALTH	BEFALL	PENCEL	BEDLAM	DELIAN	MELVYN
HEARTH	BEFELL	PENCIL	BELDAM	DEMEAN	MERLIN
JEWISH	BEFOOL	PENIAL	BESEEM	DENTIN	MERLON
KEDDAH	BEFOUL	PENPAL	CERIUM	DERAIN	MERMAN
LENGTH	BELIAL	PETREL	CESIUM	DESIGN	MERMEN
PERISH	BENGAL	PETROL	DEFORM	DESMAN	MERVIN
PESACH	BENZOL	REBILL	FERRUM	DETAIN	MESIAN
REHASH	BENZYL	RECALL	HELIUM	DEVEIN	NEATEN
RELISH	BETHEL	RECOIL	JETSAM	FENIAN	NEKTON
SEARCH	BEWAIL	RECTAL	MEDIUM	FEZZAN	NELSON
SERAPH					

NEURON	TEGMEN	MEXICO	CENSOR	HELLER	NESTOR
NEWTON	TELSON	NEMATO	CENSUR	HELPER	NETHER
PEAHEN	TENDON	NEPHRO	CENTER	HELTER	NEUTER
PEASEN	TENPIN	REBATO	DEALER	HEMMER	PECKER
PECTEN	TESTON	REBOZO	DEARER	HERDER	PEDLAR
PECTIN	TEUTON	REECHO	DEBTOR	HESTER	PEEKER
PELION	VERDIN	SEISMO	DECKER	JEERER	PEELER
PENMAN	VERDUN	SELENO	DEEPER	JESTER	PEEPER
PENMEN	VEREIN	TECHNO	DEFIER	KEENER	PELTER
PENNON	VERMIN	TENUTO	DEFTER	KEEPER	PENNER
PEPSIN	VERNON	TERATO	DEICER	KEGLER	PEPPER
PERRON	WEAKEN	TEREDO	DELVER	KELLER	PESTER
PERSON	WEAPON	VENTRO	DENIER	KEPLER	PEWTER
REASON	WEDELN	VESICO	DENSER	LEADER	READER
REBORN	WELKIN	******	DENVER	LEANER	REAMER
RECKON	YEOMAN	**-E---P**	DEODAR	LEAPER	REAPER
REDDEN	YEOMEN	******	DETOUR	LEAVER	REARER
REDFIN	YESMAN	DECAMP	DEVOIR	LECHER	RECTOR
REGAIN	ZECHIN	DEWLAP	DEVOUR	LECTOR	REDDER
REGION	******	MEGILP	DEWIER	LEDGER	REEFER
REJOIN	**-E---O**	MENDIP	DEXTER	LENDER	REEKER
REMAIN	******	METUMP	FEARER	LESSER	REELER
RENNIN	AERUGO	PEGTOP	FEEDER	LESSOR	REHEAR
RENOWN	BENITO	PENTUP	FEELER	LESTER	RELIER
REOPEN	CENTRO	RECOUP	FELLER	LETTER	RENDER
RESIGN	CERATO	REDCAP	FENCER	LEVIER	RENOIR
RETAIN	DEMONO	REDTOP	FENDER	LEWDER	RENTER
RETURN	DENDRO	REVAMP	FENRIR	MEAGER	REPAIR
REUBEN	DEXTRO	TEACUP	FEODOR	MEANER	RESTER
SEAMAN	GEMSBO	******	FERBER	MEDLAR	SEALER
SEAMEN	GENITO	**-E---R**	FERVOR	MEEKER	SEAMER
SEAPEN	GENTOO	******	FESTER	MEETER	SECPAR
SEARIN	HELICO	AETHER	FETTER	MELTER	SECTOR
SEASON	HEMATO	BEAKER	GEEZER	MEMBER	SEEDER
SEAWAN	HEPATO	BEARER	GEIGER	MEMOIR	SEEKER
SECERN	HERETO	BEATER	GENDER	MENDER	SEEMER
SEISIN	HERNIO	BEAVER	GETTER	MENHIR	SEGGAR
SEIZIN	HETERO	BEDDER	GEYSER	MENTOR	SEINER
SELSYN	JETHRO	BEGGAR	HEADER	MERCER	SEISOR
SELWYN	KERATO	BELIER	HEALER	MERGER	SEIZER
SEQUIN	LEANTO	BENDER	HEARER	MESHER	SEIZOR
SEREIN	LEGATO	BERBER	HEATER	MESMER	SELLER
SERMON	LEPIDO	BESTIR	HEAVER	METEOR	SENDER
SEVERN	MEDICO	BETTER	HECTOR	METIER	SENIOR
SEXTAN	MEGALO	BETTOR	HEDGER	NEARER	SENSOR
SEXTON	MEJICO	BEZOAR	HEEDER	NEATER	SERVER
TEAURN	MELANO	CELLAR	HEELER	NECTAR	SETTER
TEFLON	MERINO	CENSER	HEIFER	NEEDER	SEXIER

TEASER	******	CEASES	DEPTHS	HELENS	LESBOS
TEDDER	-E---S	CECILS	DEREKS	HELIOS	LETUPS
TEEMER	******	CEDARS	DERMAS	HELLAS	LEUDES
TEETER	AEACUS	CEIBAS	DERMIS	HELOTS	LEVEES
TELFER	AEETES	CELIAS	DERRIS	HELVES	LEVELS
TELLER	AEGEUS	CELLOS	DETERS	HENNAS	LEVERS
TEMPER	AENEAS	CENSES	DEUCES	HENRIS	LEVIES
TENDER	AEOLIS	CENSUS	DEVILS	HENRYS	MEATUS
TENSER	AEOLUS	CENTOS	DEWANS	HERMES	MECCAS
TENSOR	AERIES	CEORLS	FEASES	HEROES	MEDALS
TENTER	BEARDS	CEREUS	FEASTS	HERONS	MEDICS
TERMER	BEASTS	CEROUS	FEEZES	HERPES	MEGASS
TERMOR	BEAUTS	CERTES	FEIGNS	HETTYS	MELEES
TERROR	BECKYS	CESTUS	FEINTS	HEWERS	MELONS
TERSER	BEDEWS	DEATHS	FEISTS	HEXADS	MENSES
TESTER	BEDIMS	DEBARS	FELIDS	HEXYLS	MERGES
TETHER	BEEVES	DEBBYS	FELONS	JENNYS	MERITS
TETTER	BEFITS	DEBITS	FEMURS	JERRYS	MERLES
TEUCER	BEFOGS	DEBRIS	FENCES	JERVIS	MEROUS
VEADAR	BEGETS	DEBUGS	FEOFFS	JESSES	MESHES
VECTOR	BEGINS	DEBUTS	FERMIS	JEWELS	MESNES
VEILER	BEGUMS	DECALS	FEROUS	JEWESS	MESONS
VELOUR	BEIGES	DECAYS	FERRIS	KEDGES	MESSES
VENDER	BEINGS	DECORS	FESSES	KEEVES	MESSRS
VENDOR	BELAYS	DECOYS	FETORS	KEITHS	METALS
VENEER	BELGAS	DEDANS	FEUARS	KENNYS	METERS
VENTER	BELIES	DEFERS	FEVERS	KERMES	METROS
VERGER	BELLAS	DEFIES	FEZZES	KERMIS	MEZZOS
VESPER	BELLES	DEGUMS	GECKOS	KEVELS	NEIGHS
VETOER	BENJYS	DEICES	GEMOTS	KEVINS	NELLYS
WEAKER	BENNES	DEIGNS	GENETS	KEYNES	NEREIS
WEANER	BENNYS	DEISTS	GENIES	LEARNS	NERVES
WEARER	BERETS	DELAYS	GENIUS	LEASES	NESSUS
WEAVER	BERMES	DELIAS	GENOUS	LEAVES	NEUMES
WEEDER	BERTHS	DELIUS	GENRES	LEDGES	NEWELS
WEEPER	BERYLS	DELLAS	GENROS	LEGERS	PEARLS
WEEVER	BESETS	DELTAS	GENTES	LEHUAS	PEASES
WEIMAR	BESOMS	DELVES	GEODES	LEIGHS	PECANS
WELDER	BESOTS	DEMIES	GEROUS	LEMMAS	PEDALS
WELTER	BESSYS	DEMITS	GERRYS	LEMNOS	PEDROS
WESTER	BETELS	DEMOBS	GERTYS	LEMONS	PEEVES
WETHER	BETSYS	DEMONS	GESSOS	LEMURS	PEGGYS
WETTER	BETTES	DEMURS	GETUPS	LENNYS	PEKANS
YELLER	BETTYS	DENIES	HEARTS	LENSES	PEKOES
YELPER	BEULAS	DENIMS	HEATHS	LENTOS	PELEUS
YESTER	BEVELS	DENNIS	HEAVES	LEONAS	PELIAS
ZENGER	BEVIES	DENNYS	HEDGES	LEPERS	PELOPS
ZEPHYR	BEZELS	DEPOTS	HEISTS	LEROYS	PELVES

PELVIS	REVELS	TENTHS	BELOIT	LEVANT	SESTET
PENGOS	REVERS	TENUES	BENNET	MEREST	SETOUT
PENNIS	REVETS	TENUIS	BEREFT	NEWEST	SEURAT
PENNYS	REVUES	TEPEES	BESANT	PEANUT	SEXIST
PEPLOS	SEAMUS	TEREUS	BEZANT	PEDANT	SEXPOT
PEPLUS	SEBATS	TERRYS	CEMENT	PEEWIT	SEXTET
PERCYS	SEDANS	TESTES	CERMET	PELLET	TEAPOT
PERILS	SEDERS	TESTIS	DECANT	PENULT	TEASET
PERRYS	SEDGES	TETHYS	DECEIT	PEQUOT	TENANT
PETALS	SEDUMS	TETONS	DECENT	PERMIT	TERCET
PETERS	SEINES	VELDTS	DECOCT	RECANT	TERRET
PEWEES	SEISMS	VENOMS	DEDUCT	RECAST	VELVET
PEWITS	SEIZES	VENOUS	DEFEAT	RECENT	VERIST
REACTS	SELVES	VENUES	DEFECT	RECEPT	VERSET
REALES	SENNAS	VERGES	DEGUST	REDACT	VERVET
REALMS	SENSES	VERNAS	DEJECT	REDHOT	WEIGHT
REARMS	SEPALS	VERSES	DELICT	REEDIT	WERENT
REBECS	SEPIAS	VERSOS	DEMENT	REFLET	ZEALOT
REBELS	SEPOYS	VERSTS	DEPART	REFOOT	******
REBUTS	SEPSIS	VERSUS	DEPICT	REGENT	-E---U
RECAPS	SERACS	VESTAS	DEPORT	REGLET	******
RECESS	SERAIS	VETOES	DERMAT	REGRET	DESSAU
RECTOS	SERIES	VEXERS	DESALT	REHEAT	RESEAU
RECTUS	SERIFS	VEXILS	DESERT	REJECT	TELEDU
RECURS	SERINS	WEALDS	DESIST	RELENT	TELUGU
REDANS	SEROUS	WEAVES	DESPOT	RELICT	******
REDOES	SEROWS	WEBERS	DETECT	RENNET	-E---W
REEVES	SERUMS	WEDGES	DETENT	REPAST	******
REFERS	SERVES	WEIGHS	DETEST	REPEAT	BELLOW
REFITS	SERVOS	WENDYS	DEVEST	REPENT	BESTOW
REGIUS	SETONS	XEBECS	DEVOUT	REPORT	FELLOW
REICHS	SETOUS	YEARNS	DEWITT	RESEAT	GEWGAW
REIGNS	SETTOS	YEASTS	FERRET	RESECT	HEBREW
RELAYS	SETUPS	YERBAS	FEWEST	RESENT	HEEHAW
RELICS	SEVENS	YESSES	GEMERT	RESIST	MEADOW
RELIES	SEVERS	ZEBECS	GERENT	RESORT	MELLOW
REMANS	SEWERS	ZEBRAS	HEARST	RESULT	NEPHEW
REMISS	TEASES	ZEROES	HEIGHT	RETORT	REAVOW
REMITS	TEDDYS	ZETHOS	HELMET	REVERT	REVIEW
RENEES	TEHEES	ZETHUS	HENBIT	REVEST	SEACOW
RENEWS	TELLUS	******	HEREAT	REVOLT	SEESAW
RENTES	TEMPOS	-E---T	HERIOT	SECANT	YELLOW
REPASS	TEMPTS	******	HERMIT	SECRET	******
REPAYS	TENETS	BECKET	JENNET	SEJANT	-E---X
REPELS	TENNIS	BEDSIT	JESUIT	SELECT	******
RERUNS	TENONS	BEGIRT	KERMIT	SENNET	CERVIX
RESETS	TENORS	BEHEST	LEARNT	SENNIT	MENINX
RESINS	TENSES	BEIRUT	LEGIST	SEPTET	REFLEX

REFLUX	KERSEY	VERIFY	******	******	******
VERNIX	KEYWAY	VERILY	-F---O	-G---D	-G---R
VERTEX	LEACHY	VERITY	******	AGEOLD	UGLIER
WESSEX	LEANLY	VESTRY	AFLCIO	AGREED	******
******	LEEWAY	WEAKLY	******	OGDOAD	-G---S
-E---Y	LEGACY	WEEKLY	-F---R	******	******
******	LENITY	WEENSY	******	-G---E	AGAMAS
AERIFY	LESLEY	WEIRDY	AFFAIR	******	AGATES
BEACHY	LEVITY	WESLEY	******	AGAPAE	AGAVES
BEAUTY	LEWDLY	YEARLY	-F---S	AGNATE	AGENTS
BEECHY	MEANLY	YEASTY	******	AGOGUE	AGGERS
BELFRY	MEASLY	******	OFFERS	AGORAE	AGISTS
BENDAY	MEDLEY	-F---A	******	AGRAFE	AGLETS
BERNEY	MEDWAY	******	-F---T	IGNACE	AGONES
BETONY	MEEKLY	AFRICA	******	IGNITE	AGORAS
BETRAY	MEETLY	AFTOSA	AFFECT	IGNORE	AGREES
CECILY	MELODY	******	AFLOAT	******	EGESTS
CELERY	MEMORY	-F---D	EFFECT	-G---G	EGGARS
DEADLY	MERELY	******	EFFORT	******	EGGERS
DEAFLY	MERSEY	AFFORD	OFFSET	AGEING	EGRESS
DEARLY	NEARBY	AFIELD	******	EGGING	EGRETS
DEATHY	NEARLY	AFRAID	-F---X	EGGNOG	IGLOOS
DECURY	NEATLY	OFFEND	******	OGLING	OGIVES
DEEPLY	PEACHY	******	AFFLUX	******	OGLERS
DEFRAY	PEARLY	-F---E	EFFLUX	-G---H	OGRESS
DEFTLY	PEAVEY	******	******	******	******
DENARY	PEBBLY	AFLAME	-F---Y	AGUISH	-G---T
DEPLOY	PELTRY	AFRAME	******	OGRISH	******
DEPUTY	PENURY	EFFACE	AFFRAY	******	AGHAST
DESCRY	PERTLY	EFFETE	EFFIGY	-G---I	EGBERT
DESOXY	REALLY	EFFUSE	OFFDAY	******	EGOIST
EERILY	REALTY	OFFICE	******	AGOUTI	IGOROT
FEALTY	REDBAY	******	-G---A	******	******
FEEBLY	REMEDY	-F---G	******	-G---L	-G---Y
FEISTY	REPLAY	******	AGATHA	******	******
FELONY	SEAWAY	OFFING	AGENDA	AGNAIL	AGEDLY
FERITY	SEEMLY	******	AGLAIA	OGIVAL	AGENCY
GENTLY	SENARY	-F---H	EGERIA	******	AGOUTY
GENTRY	SENTRY	******	EGESTA	-G---M	IGNIFY
HEARTY	SEXILY	AFRESH	IGUANA	******	UGLIFY
HEATHY	TEAPOY	OFFISH	UGANDA	AGLEAM	UGLILY
HENLEY	TEENSY	******	******	EGOISM	******
HEREBY	TELARY	-F---M	-G---C	******	-H---A
HERESY	TEPEFY	******	******	-G---P	******
HEYDAY	TERMLY	AFFIRM	AGAMIC	******	AHIMSA
JEREMY	TETANY	******	AGARIC	******	CHACMA
JERSEY	TETCHY	-F---N	AGONIC	EGGCUP	CHAETA
KEENLY	VENERY	AFGHAN			

CHOLLA	CHIDED	CHOOSE	SHEATH	******	CHRONO
CHOREA	CHIMED	CHROME	SHEIKH	-H---M	CHRYSO
CHROMA	CHOKED	OHMAGE	SHILOH	******	GHETTO
DHARMA	PHASED	PHOEBE	THATCH	CHIASM	PHLEBO
DHARNA	PHONED	PHRASE	THOUGH	CHRISM	PHRENO
DHURNA	RHYMED	PHYLAE	THRASH	PHLEGM	PHYLLO
PHAGIA	SHADED	SHEAVE	THRESH	PHLOEM	PHYSIO
PHASIA	SHALED	SHELVE	THRUSH	PHYLUM	SHACKO
PHILIA	SHAMED	SHIITE	WHIDAH	RHYTHM	SHINTO
PHOBIA	SHAPED	SHOPPE	WHOOSH	SHIISM	THERMO
PHONIA	SHARED	SHRIKE	WHYDAH	THEISM	THYREO
RHUMBA	SHAVED	SHRINE	******	WHILOM	******
SHASTA	SHEILD	SHRIVE	-H---I	******	-H---P
SHEILA	SHEWED	SHROVE	******	-H--N	******
SHERPA	SHIELD	THEBAE	CHICHI	******	PHILIP
THALIA	SHINED	THECAE	CHILLI	******	SHRIMP
THELMA	SHOOED	THENCE	GHARRI	BHUTAN	******
THORIA	SHORED	THIEVE	RHOMBI	CHARON	-H---R
THULIA	SHOULD	THISBE	THYRSI	CHIRON	******
******	SHOVED	THORPE	******	CHITIN	CHAFER
-H---B	SHOWED	THRICE	-H---K	CHITON	CHASER
******	SHREWD	THRIVE	******	CHOPIN	CHEWER
CHERUB	SHROUD	THRONE	CHABUK	CHOSEN	CHIDER
******	THAWED	THROVE	CHIBUK	OHIOAN	CHIMER
-H---C	THEWED	THYRSE	SHRANK	PHANON	CHOKER
******	THREAD	WHARVE	SHRIEK	PHOTON	CHOLER
CHEBEC	THREED	WHEEZE	SHRINK	PHYTIN	GHEBER
CHORIC	WHALED	WHENCE	SHRUNK	SHAKEN	KHYBER
CHYMIC	WHILED	WHERVE	SHTICK	SHAMAN	RHETOR
PHASIC	WHINED	******	THWACK	SHAPEN	RHYMER
PHOBIC	WHITED	-H---F	******	SHARON	SHAKER
PHONIC	WHORED	******	-H---L	SHAVEN	SHAPER
PHOTIC	******	SHERIF	******	SHOGUN	SHARER
PHYSIC	-H---E	SHROFF	CHAPEL	SHOOIN	SHAVER
RHIZIC	******	******	CHERYL	SHORAN	SHEWER
RHODIC	CHAISE	-H---G	CHISEL	SHUTIN	SHIKAR
THETIC	CHANCE	******	CHORAL	THORON	SHINER
THORAC	CHANGE	SHYING	PHENOL	THROWN	SHIVER
THORIC	CHARGE	THRONG	PHENYL	WHITEN	SHOFAR
THYMIC	CHASSE	******	RHINAL	******	SHOVER
******	CHASTE	-H--H	SHEKEL	-H---O	SHOWER
-H---D	CHEESE	******	SHOVEL	******	THALER
******	CHEGOE	CHALEH	SHRILL	CHAETO	THAYER
CHAFED	CHELAE	CHETAH	THECAL	CHALCO	THENAR
CHARED	CHEQUE	CHINCH	THENAL	CHEILO	WHALER
CHASED	CHICLE	CHOUGH	THRALL	CHEIRO	WHINER
CHAWED	CHIGOE	CHURCH	THRILL	CHLORO	WHITER
CHEWED	CHOICE	PHOSPH	THYMOL	CHOREO	

******	CHUMPS	SHEERS	THINGS	THEIST	SHABBY
-H---S	CHUNKS	SHEETS	THIOLS	THIRST	SHAGGY
******	CHURLS	SHEIKS	THIRDS	THREAT	SHAMMY
CHAFES	CHURNS	SHELLS	THOLES	THRIFT	SHANDY
CHAFFS	CHURRS	SHERDS	THOMAS	THROAT	SHANTY
CHAINS	CHUTES	SHIFTS	THONGS	THRUST	SHEENY
CHAIRS	DHOLES	SHILLS	THORNS	THWART	SHELBY
CHALKS	DHOTIS	SHINES	THREES	WHILST	SHELLY
CHAMPS	GHAUTS	SHIRES	THRIPS	******	SHELTY
CHANGS	GHOSTS	SHIRKS	THROBS	-H---W	SHERRY
CHANTS	GHOULS	SHIRRS	THROES	******	SHIFTY
CHAPES	KHAKIS	SHIRTS	THROWS	SHADOW	SHIMMY
CHARDS	PHAROS	SHIVES	THRUMS	******	SHINDY
CHARES	PHASES	SHOALS	THUJAS	-H---X	SHINNY
CHARMS	PHASIS	SHOATS	THUMBS	******	SHIRTY
CHARTS	PHIALS	SHOCKS	THUMPS	THORAX	SHOALY
CHASES	PHILOS	SHOERS	THYMES	******	SHODDY
CHASMS	PHIPPS	SHOJIS	THYMUS	-H---Y	THADDY
CHEATS	PHOCIS	SHOOTS	WHACKS	******	THEORY
CHECKS	PHONES	SHORES	WHALES	CHAFFY	THINLY
CHEEKS	PHOTOS	SHORLS	WHANGS	CHALKY	THIRTY
CHEEPS	RHEIMS	SHORTS	WHARFS	CHAMMY	THORNY
CHEERS	RHESUS	SHOTES	WHEALS	CHANCY	THUSLY
CHELAS	RHINOS	SHOUTS	WHEATS	CHANTY	WHAMMY
CHEOPS	RHODAS	SHOVES	WHEELS	CHARRY	WHEEZY
CHESTS	RHODES	SHREDS	WHELKS	CHATTY	WHELKY
CHIAUS	RHUMBS	SHREWS	WHELMS	CHEEKY	WHERRY
CHICKS	RHYMES	SHRUBS	WHELPS	CHEERY	WHEYEY
CHICOS	SHACKS	SHRUGS	WHIFFS	CHEESY	WHIMSY
CHIDES	SHADES	SHUCKS	WHILES	CHERRY	WHINNY
CHIEFS	SHAFTS	SHUNTS	WHINES	CHESTY	WHIPPY
CHILLS	SHAKES	THADYS	WHIRLS	CHEVVY	WHISKY
CHIMES	SHAKOS	THALES	WHISKS	CHILLY	WHITBY
CHINES	SHALES	THAMES	WHITES	CHINKY	WHITEY
CHINKS	SHAMES	THANES	WHOOPS	CHIPPY	WHOLLY
CHIRMS	SHAMUS	THANKS	WHORES	CHIRPY	******
CHIRPS	SHANKS	THEBES	WHORLS	CHITTY	-H---Z
CHIRRS	SHAPES	THEDAS	WHORTS	CHIVVY	******
CHIVES	SHARDS	THEFTS	******	CHOOSY	CHINTZ
CHLOES	SHARES	THEIRS	-H---T	CHOPPY	******
CHOCKS	SHARKS	THEMES	******	CHUBBY	-I---A
CHOIRS	SHARPS	THEMIS	CHALET	CHUMMY	******
CHOKES	SHAVES	THERMS	CHRIST	CHUNKY	BIAFRA
CHORDS	SHAWLS	THESES	SHEBAT	GHARRY	BIANCA
CHORES	SHAWMS	THESIS	SHIEST	OHENRY	CICADA
CHORUS	SHEARS	THETAS	SHRIFT	PHONEY	CICALA
CHUCKS	SHEENS	THETIS	SHYEST	PHOOEY	CINEMA
CHUFAS	SHEEPS	THIGHS	THANAT	RHEUMY	CITOLA

EIDOLA	PICRIC	GINNED	MINCED	SIEVED	******
FIBULA	SIALIC	GIPPED	MINDED	SIFTED	-I---E
FIESTA	VIATIC	GIRDED	MINTED	SIGHED	******
GIULIA	VITRIC	GIRTED	MISDID	SIGNED	BIERCE
LIGULA	ZINCIC	HILLED	MISLED	SIGRID	BIGONE
LIMINA	******	HILTED	MISSED	SILOED	BILLIE
LINGUA	-I---D	HINGED	MISTED	SILTED	BINATE
LIPOMA	******	HINTED	MITRED	SINBAD	BIRDIE
LISBOA	AIRBED	HIPPED	NIBBED	SINGED	BIREME
LITHIA	AISLED	HISPID	NICHED	SINNED	BISQUE
MIASMA	BIASED	HISSED	NICKED	SIPPED	CILICE
MIMOSA	BIBBED	JIBBED	NIMROD	TICKED	CINQUE
MINIMA	BIFFED	JIGGED	NIPPED	TIDIED	CIRCLE
PIAZZA	BIFOLD	JILTED	NITRID	TIERED	CIRQUE
PIRANA	BILGED	JINKED	PICKED	TIFFED	CISSIE
SIENNA	BILKED	JINXED	PIECED	TILLED	DIBBLE
SIERRA	BILLED	KICKED	PIGGED	TILTED	DICKIE
SIESTA	BINNED	KIDDED	PILLED	TINEID	DIDDLE
SILICA	BIRLED	KILLED	PIMPED	TINGED	DIEPPE
SILVIA	BIRRED	KILTED	PINGED	TINNED	DILATE
SISERA	BITTED	KINGED	PINKED	TINTED	DILUTE
TIRANA	CITIED	KINKED	PINNED	TIPPED	DIMPLE
VICUNA	DIALED	KIPPED	PIPPED	TITHED	DINGLE
VIENNA	DIBBED	KISSED	PIQUED	TITLED	DIPLOE
VIMINA	DIETED	KITTED	PISHED	VIALED	DIPOLE
ZINNIA	DIGGED	LIASED	PITHED	VIEWED	DISUSE
******	DIMMED	LICKED	PITIED	VISAED	DITONE
-I---B	DINGED	LIDDED	PITTED	VISARD	DIVIDE
******	DINNED	LIFTED	RIBALD	VISCID	DIVINE
BICARB	DINTED	LIGAND	RIBAND	VISEED	FIACRE
MIDRIB	DIPPED	LILIED	RIBBED	VIZARD	FIANCE
******	DIRKED	LILTED	RICKED	WICKED	FICKLE
-I---C	DISHED	LIMBED	RIDDED	WIGGED	FIDDLE
******	FIBBED	LIMNED	RIDGED	WILLED	FIERCE
AIRSAC	FIGGED	LIMPED	RIFLED	WILTED	FIGURE
BIOTIC	FILLED	LIMPID	RIFTED	WINCED	FILOSE
CITRIC	FILMED	LINKED	RIGGED	WINDED	FIMBLE
FILMIC	FINNED	LIPOID	RIMMED	WINGED	FINALE
FINNIC	FIRMED	LIPPED	RINGED	WINKED	FINITE
FINNOC	FISTED	LIQUID	RINKED	WISHED	FIPPLE
FISTIC	FITTED	LISPED	RINSED	WISPED	FIXATE
LIMBIC	FIZZED	LISTED	RIOTED	WITHED	FIZZLE
LITHIC	GIBBED	LIZARD	RIPPED	WITTED	GIGGLE
MICMAC	GIFTED	MIFFED	RISKED	WIZARD	GILLIE
MIOTIC	GIGGED	MILKED	RITARD	YIPPED	GIRDLE
NIOBIC	GILDED	MILLED	SICKED	ZINCED	GISELE
NITRIC	GILEAD	MILORD	SIDLED	ZINGED	HIGGLE
PICNIC	GIMPED	MILTED	SIEGED	ZIPPED	HIPPIE

HIVITE	PIERRE	VIRTUE	HIVING	******	DISTAL
JIGGLE	PIFFLE	VISAGE	JIBING	-I---H	DISTIL
JIMMIE	PIGGIE	VITTAE	JIVING	******	EIFFEL
JINGLE	PILATE	VIVACE	KITBAG	EIGHTH	FIBRIL
JINNEE	PILOSE	WIDDIE	KITING	FINISH	FILIAL
KIBBLE	PILULE	WIENIE	LIEBIG	KIBLAH	FINIAL
KIDDIE	PIMPLE	WIGGLE	LIKING	KIBOSH	FISCAL
KILTIE	PINENE	WILLIE	LIMING	KIRSCH	FITFUL
KINASE	PINITE	WIMBLE	LINING	KITSCH	GINGAL
KINDLE	PINKIE	WIMPLE	LIVING	PISGAH	HIEMAL
KIRTLE	PINNAE	WINKLE	MIMING	SIWASH	JINGAL
KITTLE	PINOLE	WINNIE	MINING	ZIBETH	LINEAL
LIABLE	PINTLE	YIPPIE	MIRING	ZILLAH	LINTEL
LIAISE	PIPAGE	ZIZZLE	MIXING	ZIZITH	LIONEL
LIBRAE	PIRATE	******	NIDING	******	LISTEL
LICHEE	RIBOSE	-I---F	NIXING	-I---I	MICELL
LIERNE	RICHIE	******	OILING	******	MICHEL
LIGATE	RIDDLE	PILAFF	PIKING	BIHARI	MIGUEL
LIGULE	RIFFLE	RIPOFF	PILING	BIKINI	MISKAL
LIGURE	RIMOSE	TIPOFF	PINANG	BILOXI	MISSAL
LINAGE	RIMPLE	******	PINING	CIMBRI	MISSEL
LIPASE	RIPPLE	-I---G	PIPING	DIGITI	MITRAL
LITTLE	RISQUE	******	RICING	KINESI	NICKEL
LIZZIE	SICKLE	AIDING	RIDING	LIMULI	PIENAL
MICKLE	SIECLE	AILING	RILING	LITCHI	PINEAL
MIDDLE	SILAGE	AIMING	RIMING	NIELLI	PINNAL
MIGGLE	SILVAE	AIRING	RISING	NILGAI	PISTIL
MILAGE	SIMILE	BIDING	RIVING	SILENI	PISTOL
MILLIE	SIMONE	BIGWIG	SIDING	TISHRI	RICTAL
MINGLE	SIMPLE	BITING	SIRING	******	RITUAL
MINNIE	SINGLE	CITING	SITING	-I---K	SIGNAL
MINUTE	SIZZLE	DIALOG	SIZING	******	SIMNEL
MIRAGE	TIBIAE	DICING	TIDING	DIKDIK	SINFUL
MISCUE	TICKLE	DIKING	TILING	HICKOK	TIBIAL
MISERE	TIERCE	DINING	TIMING	HIJACK	TIMBAL
MISTLE	TILLIE	DIVING	TIRING	******	TINCAL
MISUSE	TIMBRE	FIFING	VIKING	-I---L	TINSEL
MIZZLE	TINGLE	FILING	VISING	******	VIDUAL
NIBBLE	TINKLE	FINING	WIGWAG	BIAXAL	VIRGIL
NICENE	TIPPLE	FIRING	WILING	CINEOL	VISUAL
NICOLE	TIPTOE	FIXING	WINING	CITRAL	WILFUL
NIGGLE	TIRADE	FIZGIG	WIPING	DIESEL	WITHAL
NIMBLE	TISANE	GIBING	WIRING	DIETAL	******
NIPPLE	TISSUE	GIVING	WISING	DIOBOL	-I---M
PIAFFE	TITTLE	HIDING	WIVING	DIRNDL	******
PICKLE	VIABLE	HIEING	ZIGZAG	DISCAL	BIFORM
PIDDLE	VIRGIE	HIKING		DISMAL	CILIUM
PIERCE	VIRILE	HIRING		DISPEL	CIRCUM

CIVISM	GIBSON	TINCAN	KIDNAP	FIZZER	MILKER
DIADEM	GIDEON	TITIAN	LINEUP	GIAOUR	MILLER
DIATOM	HIDDEN	VILLON	MISHAP	GIBBER	MILTER
DICTUM	KITTEN	VINSON	PICKUP	GILDER	MINCER
DINKUM	LIBYAN	VIOLIN	PILEUP	GINGER	MINDER
DIRHAM	LICHEN	VIRGIN	RIPRAP	GINNER	MINTER
DISARM	LIGNIN	VISION	TIPTOP	GIRDER	MIRROR
LIGNUM	LILIAN	VIVIAN	TITTUP	HIGHER	MISTER
LINGAM	LINDEN	VIVIEN	WIKIUP	HILLER	NICKER
LISSOM	LISBON	WIGEON	WINDUP	HINDER	NIGGER
MILIUM	LISTEN	WILSON	******	HISSER	NIGHER
MINIUM	MICRON	WILTON	-I---R	HITHER	NIPPER
MIRIAM	MIDDEN	WITHIN	******	HITLER	OILIER
PILEUM	MIGNON	WIVERN	AIRIER	HITTER	PICKER
SIKKIM	MILDEN	ZIRCON	BIBBER	JIBBER	PICTOR
SIMOOM	MILTON	******	BICKER	JIGGER	PIECER
VICTIM	MINION	-I---O	BIDDER	JILTER	PIETER
WIGWAM	MINOAN	******	BIGGER	JINKER	PILFER
WISDOM	MITTEN	BIBLIO	BILKER	JITTER	PILLAR
******	MIZZEN	BILBAO	BINDER	KICKER	PINDAR
-I---N	NIACIN	BISTRO	BISTER	KIDDER	PINIER
******	NIPPON	CICERO	BITTER	KILLER	PINNER
AIDMAN	OILCAN	DIDERO	CINDER	KILMER	PINTER
AIDMEN	PIDGIN	DINERO	CIPHER	KILTER	PIPIER
AILEEN	PIEMAN	FIASCO	CITHER	KINDER	RICHER
AIRGUN	PIEMEN	GIGOLO	DIALER	KIPPER	RIFLER
AIRMAN	PIGEON	GINGKO	DIAPER	KISSER	RIGGER
AIRMEN	PIGGIN	GIOTTO	DIBBER	LICTOR	RIGOUR
BICORN	PIGPEN	GITANO	DICKER	LIEDER	RIMMER
BIDDEN	PINION	GIULIO	DIETER	LIFTER	RINGER
BIFFIN	PIPKIN	KIMONO	DIFFER	LIMBER	RINSER
BIGGIN	PIPPIN	KINETO	DIGGER	LIMIER	RIOTER
BILLON	PISTON	LIBIDO	DIMMER	LIMNER	RIPPER
BIOGEN	PITMAN	MIKADO	DINDER	LIMPER	RISKER
BIOTIN	PITMEN	NIELLO	DINNER	LINEAR	RITTER
BITTEN	RIBBON	PIETRO	DIPPER	LINGER	SICKER
CITRON	RIDDEN	RIALTO	DISBAR	LINIER	SIDDUR
DIAZIN	SICKEN	RIGHTO	DITHER	LINTER	SIDLER
DISOWN	SILKEN	SIDERO	EITHER	LIPPER	SIFTER
EILEEN	SILVAN	SILICO	FIBBER	LIQUOR	SIGNER
FIBRIN	SIMIAN	VIBRIO	FILLER	LISPER	SIGNOR
FIJIAN	SIMLIN	VIRAGO	FILTER	LISTER	SILVER
FILLIN	SINEON	******	FINDER	LITHER	SIMMER
FINNAN	SIOUAN	-I---P	FINGER	LITTER	SIMPER
FIRKIN	SIPHON	******	FINNER	LIVIER	SINGER
FIRMAN	SISKIN	BISHOP	FIRMER	LIVYER	SINKER
GIBBON	TIEPIN	FILLIP	FISHER	MIDAIR	SINNER
GIBRAN	TIFFIN	HICCUP	FITTER	MILDER	SINTER

SIPPER	BICEPS	DIVERS	JINXES	MISSES	RICTUS
SIRDAR	BIDETS	DIVOTS	KIBEIS	MISSIS	RIDERS
SISTER	BIGHTS	DIWANS	KININS	MISSUS	RIDGES
SITTER	BIGOTS	DIXITS	KIOSKS	MITERS	RIFLES
SIZIER	BIKOLS	DIZENS	KISSES	MIXERS	RIGHTS
TICKER	BILGES	EIGHTS	KITTYS	MIXUPS	RIGORS
TIDIER	BILLYS	FIBERS	LIANAS	NICHES	RIMERS
TILLER	BINGES	FICHES	LIANES	NICKYS	RIMOUS
TILTER	BINITS	FICHUS	LIBBYS	NIECES	RINSES
TIMBER	BIOSIS	FIELDS	LIBELS	NIGELS	RIPENS
TINDER	BIPEDS	FIENDS	LIBRAS	NIGHTS	RISERS
TINIER	BIPODS	FIFERS	LIEGES	NIMBUS	RIVALS
TINKER	BIRLES	FIFTHS	LIFERS	NINTHS	RIVERS
TINNER	BIRTHS	FIGHTS	LIGHTS	NISEIS	RIVETS
TIPPER	BITERS	FILERS	LIKENS	NIXIES	RIYALS
TITHER	CIBOLS	FILETS	LILACS	OILERS	SIBYLS
TITTER	CIDERS	FINALS	LILIES	PIANOS	SIDLES
VIATOR	CIGARS	FIORDS	LIMBUS	PICOTS	SIEGES
VICTOR	CINDYS	FIQUES	LIMENS	PICULS	SIEURS
VIEWER	CIRCUS	FIRERS	LIMEYS	PIECES	SIEVES
VIGOUR	CIRRUS	FIRSTS	LIMITS	PIERUS	SIGHTS
VINIER	CISCOS	FIRTHS	LINDAS	PIGNUS	SIGILS
VIZIER	CISSYS	FISHES	LINENS	PIKERS	SIGMAS
WICKER	CITIES	FIVERS	LINERS	PILAFS	SILVAS
WIENER	CITRUS	FIXERS	LINGAS	PILEUS	SIMARS
WILBER	CIVETS	FIZZES	LIPIDS	PILOTS	SIMONS
WILBUR	CIVICS	GIANTS	LITERS	PILOUS	SINEWS
WILDER	CIVIES	GIBERS	LITMUS	PINDUS	SINGES
WILIER	DIANAS	GIGUES	LIVENS	PINGOS	SIRENS
WILLER	DIANES	GILDAS	LIVERS	PINIES	SIRIUS
WINCER	DICERS	GIMELS	LIVIAS	PINONS	SIRUPS
WINDER	DIDIES	GIPONS	LIVRES	PINTOS	SITARS
WINIER	DIDOES	GISMOS	LIZZYS	PINUPS	SITINS
WINKER	DIESES	GIZMOS	MIAULS	PIPERS	SIXTES
WINNER	DIESIS	HIATUS	MICKYS	PIPETS	SIXTHS
WINTER	DIGITS	HIDERS	MIDGES	PIPITS	SIZARS
WIRIER	DIMERS	HIKERS	MIKLOS	PIQUES	TIARAS
WITHER	DINAHS	HILDAS	MILERS	PISCES	TIBIAS
ZIPPER	DINARS	HINDUS	MILLYS	PISHES	TICALS
ZITHER	DINERS	HINGES	MIMERS	PITIES	TIDIES
******	DINGUS	HIPPOS	MIMICS	PITONS	TIEINS
-I---S	DIODES	HIPPUS	MINCES	PIVOTS	TIEUPS
******	DIPSAS	HIRAMS	MINERS	PIXIES	TIGERS
AIDERS	DIRGES	HIRERS	MINIMS	PIZZAS	TIGHTS
AISLES	DISCUS	HISSES	MINORS	RIATAS	TIGRIS
BIALYS	DISHES	JIHADS	MINXES	RICERS	TILDES
BIASES	DITTOS	JIMMYS	MIOSIS	RICHES	TILERS
BIBLES	DIVANS	JINNYS	MISERS	RICKYS	TILLYS

TILTHS	YIELDS	SILENT	BINARY	NICELY	******
TIMERS	ZIBETS	SIPPET	BIOPSY	NICETY	-I---Z
TIMMYS	ZIRONS	TICKET	BISCAY	NIDIFY	******
TINCTS	******	TIDBIT	BITCHY	NIGHTY	KIBITZ
TINGES	-I---T	TINPOT	CICELY	NIMBLY	NIMITZ
TITANS	******	TIPCAT	DICKEY	NINETY	******
TITHES	AIGLET	TIPPET	DIGAMY	OILILY	-J---A
TITLES	BILLET	TITBIT	DIMITY	PIGSTY	******
VIANDS	BISECT	VILEST	DIMPLY	PIMPLY	EJECTA
VICARS	CILIAT	VIOLET	DINGEY	PINERY	OJIBWA
VICKYS	DICAST	WICKET	DINGHY	PIRACY	******
VIGILS	DIGEST	WIDEST	DINKEY	PITCHY	-J---N
VILLAS	DIGLOT	WILLET	DIPODY	RICHLY	******
VILLUS	DIMOUT	WISEST	DIRELY	RICKEY	AJOWAN
VINCES	DIMWIT	WITHIT	DISMAY	RIPELY	******
VINNYS	DIRECT	******	DISNEY	RIPLEY	-J---S
VINOUS	DIREST	-I---U	EIGHTY	RIPPLY	******
VINYLS	DIVERT	******	FILTHY	SICILY	EJECTS
VIOLAS	DIVEST	MILIEU	FINELY	SICKLY	******
VIPERS	FIDGET	VISHNU	FINERY	SIDNEY	-K---D
VIREOS	FILLET	******	FIRMLY	SIMONY	******
VIRGAS	FINEST	-I---W	FIXITY	SIMPLY	OKAYED
VISCUS	GIBBET	******	GIGGLY	SINEWY	SKATED
VISITS	GIBLET	BILLOW	HICKEY	SINGLY	SKEWED
VISORS	GIGANT	JIGSAW	HIGHLY	SIRUPY	SKIVED
VISTAS	GIGLET	KISLEW	HILARY	TIDILY	******
VITALS	GIGLOT	MILDEW	JIMINY	TIMELY	-K---E
VIXENS	GIMLET	MINNOW	JINGLY	TINGLY	******
VIZIRS	KISMET	PILLOW	JITNEY	TINILY	SKOPJE
VIZORS	LIMPET	RIPSAW	KIDNEY	TINKLY	******
WICHES	LINNET	WILLOW	KINDLY	VILELY	-K---G
WIDENS	MIDGET	WINDOW	KINGLY	VILIFY	******
WIDOWS	MIDGUT	WINNOW	KINSEY	VINERY	EKEING
WIDTHS	MILLET	******	LIKELY	VIVIFY	SKIING
WIELDS	MINUET	-I---X	LIMPLY	WICOPY	SKYING
WIGANS	MISFIT	******	LITANY	WIDELY	******
WILLIS	NICEST	BIFLEX	LIVELY	WIELDY	-K---H
WILLYS	NITWIT	BIJOUX	LIVERY	WIFELY	******
WILMAS	PICKET	DIPLEX	MICKEY	WIGGLY	SKETCH
WINCES	PIGLET	PICKAX	MIDDAY	WILDLY	******
WINOES	PIGNUT	******	MIDWAY	WILILY	-K---N
WINZES	PINXIT	-I---Y	MIGHTY	WINCEY	******
WIPERS	PIQUET	******	MILADY	WINERY	SKYMAN
WIRERS	RIDENT	AIRDRY	MILDLY	WINTRY	SKYMEN
WISHES	RILLET	AIRILY	MILLAY	WIRILY	******
WITHES	RIPEST	AIRWAY	MINIFY	WISELY	-K---O
WIVERS	RIPOST	BIGAMY	MISERY	WITNEY	******
WIZENS	SIGNET	BILITY	MISLAY	ZINCKY	AKIMBO

******	ALMIRA	CLOSED	ALDINE	OLEATE	PLOUGH
-K---P	ALPACA	CLOYED	ALDOSE	PLAGUE	SLEIGH
******	ALTHEA	ELATED	ALIBLE	PLAICE	SLEUTH
SKYCAP	ALUMNA	ELDRED	ALKANE	PLAQUE	SLOUCH
******	ALVINA	ELIDED	ALKENE	PLATTE	SLOUGH
-K---R	CLOACA	ELOPED	ALKYNE	PLEASE	******
******	ELISHA	ELUDED	ALLEGE	PLEDGE	-L---I
SKATER	ELMIRA	FLAKED	ALLELE	PLICAE	******
SKEWER	ELVIRA	FLAMED	ALLUDE	PLUNGE	ALFAKI
SKIVER	ELYTRA	FLARED	ALLURE	SLEAVE	ALKALI
******	FLAVIA	FLAWED	ALMUCE	SLEDGE	ALUMNI
-K---S	GLIOMA	FLAYED	ALMUDE	SLEEVE	CLYPEI
******	GLORIA	FLEXED	ALPINE	SLUDGE	GLUTEI
AKENES	OLIVIA	FLORID	ALSACE	SLUICE	******
OKAPIS	PLASIA	FLOWED	ALSIKE	ULENCE	-L---K
SKALDS	PLASMA	FLUKED	ALULAE	ULLAGE	******
SKATES	PLEGIA	FLUMED	ALVINE	******	PLANCK
SKEANS	PLEURA	FLUTED	BLAISE	-L---G	SLOVAK
SKEINS	ULTIMA	FLUXED	BLENDE	******	******
SKIERS	******	GLARED	BLITHE	BLUING	-L---L
SKIFFS	-L---C	GLAZED	BLONDE	CLUING	******
SKILLS	******	GLIDED	BLOUSE	FLYING	ALPHYL
SKIMOS	ALARIC	GLOBED	BLUNGE	GLUING	ALUDEL
SKIMPS	ALCAIC	GLOVED	CLAIRE	PLYING	FLORAL
SKINKS	ALTAIC	GLOWED	CLAQUE	SLUING	GLOBAL
SKIRRS	CLERIC	GLOZED	CLAUDE	******	GLYCOL
SKIRTS	CLINIC	ILFORD	CLAUSE	-L---H	PLAGAL
SKIVES	CLONIC	PLACED	CLEAVE	******	PLURAL
SKULKS	SLAVIC	PLACID	CLEOME	BLANCH	******
SKULLS	******	PLANED	CLICHE	BLEACH	-L---M
SKUNKS	-L---D	PLATED	CLIQUE	BLENCH	******
UKASES	******	PLAYED	CLOCHE	BLOTCH	ALARUM
******	ALATED	PLEIAD	CLOTHE	BLUISH	ALLIUM
-K---Y	ALFRED	PLOWED	ELAINE	CLENCH	ELOHIM
******	ALGOID	PLUMED	ELAPSE	CLINCH	OLDHAM
SKERRY	ALIDAD	SLAKED	ELAYNE	CLOUGH	PLENUM
SKIMPY	ALINED	SLATED	ELOISE	CLUTCH	SLALOM
SKINNY	ALIPED	SLAVED	ELYSEE	ELFISH	******
SKIVVY	ALLIED	SLEWED	FLAMBE	ELIJAH	-L---N
SKYWAY	ALMOND	SLICED	FLANGE	ELVISH	******
******	BLADED	SLIMED	FLECHE	FLENCH	ALBION
-L---A	BLAMED	SLOPED	FLEDGE	FLETCH	ALCUIN
******	BLARED	SLOWED	FLEECE	FLINCH	ALEXIN
ALALIA	BLAZED	******	FLENSE	FLITCH	ALISON
ALASKA	CLAWED	-L---E	FLORAE	OLDISH	ALUMIN
ALBATA	CLAYED	******	GLANCE	PLANCH	BLAZON
ALEXIA	CLERID	ALBITE	ILLUME	PLEACH	CLOVEN
ALICIA	CLEWED	ALCOVE	ILLUSE	PLINTH	ELEVEN

ELEVON	******	ALBUMS	BLINKS	CLUMPS	FLORES
ELOIGN	-L---R	ALDERS	BLOATS	CLYDES	FLOURS
FLACON	******	ALDOUS	BLOCKS	ELANDS	FLOUTS
FLAGON	ALEGAR	ALEPHS	BLOKES	ELATES	FLOYDS
FLAMEN	ALTAIR	ALERTS	BLONDS	ELBOWS	FLUFFS
FLAVIN	ALULAR	ALEUTS	BLOODS	ELBRUS	FLUIDS
FLAXEN	BLAZER	ALEXIS	BLOOMS	ELDERS	FLUKES
FLORIN	BLOWER	ALFONS	BLUETS	ELECTS	FLUMES
FLYMAN	CLAMOR	ALGOUS	BLUFFS	ELEMIS	FLUMPS
GLOBIN	CLEVER	ALIBIS	BLUNTS	ELENAS	FLUNKS
GLUTEN	CLOSER	ALICES	BLURBS	ELFINS	FLUORS
KLAXON	CLOVER	ALIENS	BLURTS	ELIDES	FLUTES
OLEFIN	ELATER	ALIGNS	CLACKS	ELIOTS	FLUXES
PLATAN	ELINOR	ALINES	CLAIMS	ELIZAS	FLYBYS
PLATEN	ELIXIR	ALKYLS	CLAMPS	ELLENS	FLYERS
PLUGIN	ELOPER	ALLANS	CLANGS	ELLIES	GLACES
SLIPON	FLAKER	ALLAYS	CLANKS	ELMERS	GLACIS
SLOGAN	FLAVOR	ALLENS	CLARAS	ELOINS	GLADES
SLOVEN	FLAYER	ALLEYS	CLARES	ELOPES	GLADYS
******	FLEXOR	ALLIES	CLAROS	ELSIES	GLAIRS
-L---O	FLOWER	ALLOTS	CLASPS	ELUDES	GLAMIS
******	FLUTER	ALLOWS	CLEANS	ELVERS	GLANDS
ALBEDO	GLAZER	ALLOYS	CLEARS	FLACKS	GLARES
ALBINO	GLIDER	ALLYLS	CLEATS	FLAILS	GLAZES
ALECTO	GLOVER	ALMAHS	CLEFTS	FLAIRS	GLEAMS
ALEPPO	GLOWER	ALMUDS	CLERKS	FLAKES	GLEANS
ALONSO	GLUIER	ALPHAS	CLEVIS	FLAMES	GLEBES
ALONZO	OLIVER	ALPHOS	CLICKS	FLANKS	GLEDES
ALUINO	PLACER	ALTARS	CLIFFS	FLARES	GLEETS
BLASTO	PLANAR	ALTERS	CLIMBS	FLASKS	GLIDES
CLOTHO	PLANER	ALUINS	CLIMES	FLATUS	GLINTS
FLUORO	PLATER	ALVANS	CLINES	FLAXES	GLOATS
FLUVIO	PLAYER	ALWAYS	CLINGS	FLEAMS	GLOBES
GLAUCO	PLEXOR	BLACKS	CLINKS	FLECKS	GLOOMS
GLOSSO	PLOVER	BLADES	CLINTS	FLEERS	GLOSTS
GLOTTO	PLOWER	BLAINS	CLIVES	FLEETS	GLOVES
GLYPTO	SLATER	BLAMES	CLOAKS	FLEXES	GLOZES
ILOILO	SLAVER	BLANKS	CLOCKS	FLICKS	GLUMES
PLAGIO	SLAYER	BLARES	CLONES	FLIERS	GLYNIS
PLASMO	SLICER	BLASTS	CLONUS	FLINGS	GLYPHS
PLEURO	SLIDER	BLAZES	CLOSES	FLINTS	ILEXES
PLUMBO	SLIVER	BLEAKS	CLOTHS	FLIRTS	LLAMAS
PLUVIO	SLOPER	BLEARS	CLOUDS	FLOATS	LLANOS
ULTIMO	SLOWER	BLEATS	CLOUTS	FLOCKS	LLOYDS
******	ULSTER	BLEEDS	CLOVES	FLONGS	OLIVES
-L---P	******	BLENDS	CLOVIS	FLOODS	OLLIES
******	-L---S	BLIMPS	CLOWNS	FLOORS	PLACES
BLOWUP	******	BLINDS	CLUCKS	FLORAS	PLACKS
SLAPUP	ALAMOS				
SLIPUP	ALARMS				

PLAIDS	ALCOTT	BLUELY	PLENTY	AMUSED	IMPISH
PLAINS	ALIGHT	BLURRY	PLUCKY	EMCEED	SMIRCH
PLAITS	ALLOUT	CLAMMY	PLUMMY	EMOTED	SMOOCH
PLANES	ALMOST	CLASSY	PLUSHY	IMAGED	SMOOTH
PLANKS	BLIGHT	CLAYEY	SLAGGY	IMBUED	SMUTCH
PLANTS	BLUEST	CLERGY	SLANGY	IMPEND	******
PLASIS	CLARET	CLIFFY	SLEAZY	SMILED	-M---I
PLATES	CLEIST	CLINGY	SLEEKY	SMOKED	******
PLAYAS	CLIENT	CLIQUY	SLEEPY	******	AMBARI
PLAZAS	CLIMAT	CLODDY	SLEETY	-M---E	AMENTI
PLEADS	CLOSET	CLOGGY	SLIMLY	******	DMITRI
PLEATS	ELBERT	CLOTTY	SLIMSY	AMALIE	EMBOLI
PLEBES	ELDEST	CLOUDY	SLINKY	AMBAGE	SMALTI
PLEXUS	ELEGIT	CLUMPY	SLOPPY	AMEBAE	******
PLIERS	ELICIT	CLUMSY	SLOSHY	AMECHE	-M---K
PLUCKS	ELLIOT	FLABBY	SLOWLY	AMELIE	******
PLUMBS	FLAUNT	FLAGGY	SLUDGY	AMERCE	EMBANK
PLUMES	FLIEST	FLASHY	SLUMMY	AMPERE	EMBARK
PLUMPS	FLIGHT	FLATLY	SLURRY	AMPULE	IMBARK
PLUNKS	FLORET	FLEDGY	SLUSHY	EMBRUE	IMPARK
PLUSES	FLUENT	FLEECY	******	EMERGE	******
PLUTUS	ILLUST	FLESHY	-L---Z	EMERIE	-M---L
SLACKS	OLDEST	FLEURY	******	EMEUTE	******
SLAKES	PLACET	FLIMSY	BLINTZ	EMIGRE	AMATOL
SLANTS	PLAINT	FLINTY	******	EMILIE	AMIDOL
SLATES	PLANET	FLIRTY	-M---A	EMPALE	AMORAL
SLAVES	PLIANT	FLOATY	******	EMPIRE	AMYTAL
SLEEKS	PLIGHT	FLOCKY	AMANDA	IMBIBE	UMBRAL
SLEEPS	SLIEST	FLOOZY	AMANIA	IMBRUE	******
SLEETS	SLIGHT	FLOPPY	AMELIA	IMMUNE	-M---M
SLICES	SLYEST	FLOSSY	AMENRA	IMMURE	******
SLICKS	******	FLOURY	AMOEBA	IMPALE	AMYLUM
SLIDES	-L---X	FLUFFY	AMRITA	IMPEDE	EMBALM
SLIMES	******	FLUKEY	EMILIA	IMPOSE	EMBLEM
SLINGS	CLIMAX	FLUNKY	IMPALA	IMPURE	IMBALM
SLINKS	******	FLURRY	OMENTA	IMPUTE	OMASUM
SLOOPS	-L---Y	GLADLY	******	SMUDGE	OMNIUM
SLOPES	******	GLAIRY	-M---C	UMBRAE	******
SLOTHS	ALBANY	GLASSY	******	UMPIRE	-M---N
SLUMPS	BLEARY	GLEAMY	AMEBIC	******	******
SLURPS	BLEBBY	GLEETY	AMIDIC	-M---G	AMAZON
ULCERS	BLENNY	GLIBLY	AMYLIC	******	AMIDIN
ULEMAS	BLIMEY	GLOOMY	EMERIC	IMPING	AMNION
ZLOTYS	BLOCKY	GLOSSY	EMETIC	******	EMETIN
******	BLOODY	GLUMLY	******	-M---H	IMOGEN
-L---T	BLOOMY	PLAGUY	-M---D	******	IMPAWN
******	BLOWBY	PLASHY	******	AMBUSH	IMPUGN
ALBEIT	BLOWZY	PLASTY	AMAZED	IMMESH	
ALBERT			AMBLED		

******	EMMIES	******	******	SNORED	ENLACE
-M---O	EMOTES	**-M---X**	**-N---B**	SNOWED	ENRAGE
******	IMAGES	******	******	UNAPID	ENROBE
EMBRYO	IMBEDS	SMILAX	ENTOMB	UNBEND	ENSILE
EMILIO	IMBUES	******	ENWOMB	UNBIND	ENSURE
IMMUNO	IMIDES	**-M---Y**	INTOMB	UNBRED	ENTERE
SMALTO	IMINES	******	******	UNCLAD	ENTICE
******	IMMIES	AMBARY	**-N---C**	UNCORD	ENTIRE
-M---R	IMPASS	AMBERY	******	UNFOLD	ENTREE
******	IMPELS	EMBODY	ANEMIC	UNGIRD	ENZYME
AMBLER	OMEGAS	EMPERY	ANGLIC	UNHAND	INCAGE
AMUSER	SMACKS	EMPLOY	ANODIC	UNIPED	INCASE
IMPAIR	SMALLS	IMBODY	ANOMIC	UNITED	INCISE
SMILER	SMARTS	SMARMY	ANOXIC	UNKIND	INCITE
SMITER	SMAZES	SMEARY	GNOMIC	UNLAID	INCOME
SMOKER	SMEARS	SMELLY	UNIFIC	UNLEAD	INCUSE
******	SMELLS	SMITHY	******	UNLOAD	INDENE
-M---S	SMELTS	SMUDGY	**-N---D**	UNREAD	INDITE
******	SMILES	SMUGLY	******	UNSAID	INDUCE
AMAZES	SMIRKS	SMUTTY	ANGLED	UNSHOD	INFUSE
AMBERS	SMITES	******	ANTEED	UNSOLD	INHALE
AMBITS	SMITHS	**-N---A**	ENDUED	UNTIED	INHERE
AMBLES	SMOCKS	******	ENFOLD	UNTOLD	INHUME
AMEBAS	SMOKES	ANCONA	ENGIRD	UNTROD	INJOKE
AMENDS	SMOLTS	ANDREA	ENNEAD	UNUSED	INJURE
AMENTS	UMBELS	ANEMIA	ENSUED	UNWIND	INLACE
AMICES	UMBERS	ANGELA	ENVIED	******	INMATE
AMIDES	UMBLES	ANGINA	ENWIND	**-N---E**	INNATE
AMIENS	UMBRAS	ANGLIA	GNAWED	******	INSANE
AMIGOS	UMIAKS	ANGOLA	INBAND	ANANKE	INSIDE
AMOLES	******	ANGORA	INBRED	ANCONE	INSOLE
AMOURS	**-M---T**	ANITRA	INCHED	ANLACE	INSURE
AMPHRS	******	ANKARA	INDEED	ANLAGE	INTAKE
AMPULS	AMIDST	ANNONA	INDUED	ANNEXE	INTONE
AMUSES	AMOUNT	ANOMIA	INFOLD	ANOMIE	INVADE
EMBARS	AMULET	ANOXIA	INGRID	ANSATE	INVITE
EMBAYS	EMMETT	ANTHEA	INLAID	ANYONE	INVOKE
EMBEDS	IMARET	ANTLIA	INLAND	ENABLE	INWOVE
EMBERS	IMPACT	ENCINA	INROAD	ENCAGE	ONLINE
EMBOSS	IMPART	ENIGMA	INTEND	ENCASE	SNATHE
EMBOWS	IMPORT	ENTERA	INURED	ENCODE	SNEEZE
EMCEES	IMPOST	INDABA	INWARD	ENCORE	SNOOZE
EMEERS	OMELET	INTIMA	INWIND	ENDIVE	UNABLE
EMENDS	UMLAUT	ONEIDA	KNIFED	ENDURE	UNCAGE
EMESIS	******	PNEUMA	ONWARD	ENFACE	UNCASE
EMILES	**-M---U**	UNGULA	SNAKED	ENGAGE	UNDINE
EMILYS	******		SNARED	ENGINE	UNDONE
EMMETS	AMADOU		SNIPED	ENISLE	UNEASE

UNIQUE	******	******	INFERO	******	INFERS
UNLACE	-N---I	-N---M	ONEIRO	-N---S	INGOTS
UNLADE	******	******	PNEUMO	******	INGRES
UNLIKE	ANDREI	ANADEM	UNESCO	ANABAS	INKERS
UNLIVE	INCUBI	ANONYM	******	ANANAS	INKLES
UNMADE	ONAGRI	ANSELM	-N---P	ANDRES	INLAWS
UNMAKE	******	ANTHEM	******	ANGELS	INLAYS
UNPILE	-N---K	ANTRIM	ENCAMP	ANGERS	INLETS
UNRIPE	******	ANTRUM	ENTRAP	ANGLES	INPUTS
UNROBE	ANORAK	ENGRAM	ENWRAP	ANIMAS	INSETS
UNSAFE	UNCOCK	INDIUM	INCORP	ANIMUS	INTERS
UNSURE	UNCORK	INFIRM	INSTEP	ANIONS	INURES
UNTRUE	UNHOOK	INFORM	INWRAP	ANISES	INURNS
UNWISE	UNHUSK	UNSEAM	UNHASP	ANITAS	KNACKS
UNYOKE	UNLOCK	******	UNSHIP	ANKLES	KNAVES
******	UNMASK	-N---N	UNSTEP	ANNALS	KNEADS
-N---F	UNPACK	******	UNSTOP	ANNIES	KNEELS
******	UNPICK	ANDEAN	UNWRAP	ANNOYS	KNELLS
ENGULF	UNTACK	ANILIN	******	ANNULS	KNIFES
INGULF	******	ANURAN	-N---R	ANODES	KNIVES
ONEOFF	-N---L	ENJOIN	******	ANTICS	KNOCKS
UNICEF	******	ENSIGN	ANCHOR	ANTONS	KNOLLS
******	ANIMAL	GNOMON	ANGKOR	ANUBIS	KNOSPS
-N---G	ANNEAL	INBORN	ANGLER	ANUSES	KNOUTS
******	ANNUAL	INCHON	ANSWER	ANVILS	KNURLS
ANALOG	ENAMEL	INDIAN	ANTHER	ENACTS	ONIONS
ENDING	ENDALL	INSPAN	ANTIAR	ENATES	ONSETS
INKING	ENROLL	INTERN	ANTLER	ENDOWS	ONUSES
INNING	ENSOUL	INTURN	ENAMOR	ENDUES	SNACKS
UNPLUG	ENTAIL	INULIN	ENDEAR	ENEMAS	SNAFUS
UNSUNG	INHAUL	UNBORN	ENVIER	ENGELS	SNAILS
******	INSOUL	UNEVEN	GNAWER	ENJOYS	SNAKES
-N---H	INSTIL	UNHEWN	INDOOR	ENOSIS	SNARES
******	INWALL	UNISON	INKIER	ENSUES	SNARLS
ENCASH	ONEILL	UNSEEN	INLIER	ENTERS	SNATHS
ENMESH	ONFALL	UNWORN	INSTAR	ENVIES	SNEAKS
ENOUGH	SNIVEL	******	KNOWER	ENVOYS	SNEERS
ENRICH	UNCIAL	-N---O	ONAGER	GNARLS	SNELLS
INARCH	UNCOIL	******	SNARER	GNEISS	SNICKS
INMESH	UNCURL	ANATTO	SNIPER	GNOMES	SNIFFS
INRUSH	UNFURL	ANGELO	SNORER	GNOSIS	SNIPES
ONRUSH	UNGUAL	ANKYLO	UNBEAR	INARMS	SNOODS
SNATCH	UNREAL	ANTERO	UNDOER	INCHES	SNOOKS
SNITCH	UNREEL	ENRICO	UNFAIR	INCURS	SNOOPS
UNLASH	UNROLL	ENTERO	UNHAIR	INDIES	SNOOTS
UNWISH	UNSEAL	ENTOMO	UNMOOR	INDOWS	SNORES
	UNVEIL	GNATHO		INDRIS	SNORTS
	UNWELL	INDIGO		INDUES	SNOUTS

SNUFFS	INTACT	KNARRY	JOSIEA	MOSAIC	CONOID
UNBARS	INTENT	KNOBBY	KORUNA	NOETIC	CONRAD
UNCAPS	INTUIT	KNOTTY	LOCHIA	NORDIC	COOEED
UNCLES	INVENT	KNURLY	LOGGIA	NOSTIC	COOKED
UNDIES	INVERT	ONEWAY	LOLITA	POETIC	COOLED
UNDOES	INVEST	ONIONY	LORICA	PONTIC	COOPED
UNGUES	KNIGHT	SNAGGY	LOUISA	ROMAIC	COPIED
UNGUIS	SNOCAT	SNAPPY	MONICA	SOTHIC	COPPED
UNHATS	UNBELT	SNARLY	MORULA	TOLTEC	CORDED
UNIONS	UNBENT	SNAZZY	NOMURA	TOMBAC	CORKED
UNITES	UNBOLT	SNEAKY	NOVENA	ZODIAC	CORNED
UNLAYS	UNDSET	SNEEZY	POMONA	******	COSHED
UNLESS	UNGIRT	SNIFFY	PORTIA	-O---D	COSTED
UNMANS	UNHURT	SNIPPY	POSADA	******	COWARD
UNMEWS	UNJUST	SNOBBY	ROBBIA	AOUDAD	DOCKED
UNPEGS	UNKNIT	SNOOPY	ROMOLA	BOATED	DODGED
UNPINS	UNMEET	SNOOTY	ROSTRA	BOBBED	DOFFED
UNRIGS	UNREST	SNOTTY	ROWENA	BODIED	DOGGED
UNRIPS	UNROOT	SNUFFY	ROXANA	BOGGED	DOITED
UNSAYS	UNSEAT	SNUGLY	SOMATA	BOILED	DOLLED
UNTIES	UNVEXT	UNDULY	SONATA	BOLLED	DONALD
******	UNWEPT	UNEASY	SOPHIA	BOLTED	DONNED
-N---T	******	UNHOLY	TOPEKA	BOMBED	DOODAD
******	-N---W	UNRULY	VOMICA	BONDED	DOOMED
ANKLET	******	UNTIDY	WOMERA	BONGED	DORSAD
ANOINT	ANDREW	UNWARY	YORUBA	BOOKED	DOSSED
ENCYST	ANYHOW	******	ZONULA	BOOMED	DOTARD
ENGIRT	INFLOW	-O---A	ZOYSIA	BOOTED	DOTTED
ENLIST	UNDRAW	******	******	BOOZED	DOUSED
ENRAPT	UNDREW	BODEGA	-O---B	BOPPED	DOWNED
ENROOT	UNDREW	BOGOTA	******	BOSSED	DOWSED
INCEPT	-N---X	BORGIA	COBWEB	BOUSED	FOALED
INCEST	******	CODEIA	CONFAB	BOWLED	FOAMED
INDENT	INFLUX	CONCHA	CORYMB	BOWSED	FOBBED
INDICT	UNISEX	CONTRA	HOBNOB	BOYARD	FOETID
INDUCT	******	COPPRA	******	COALED	FOGGED
INDULT	-N---Y	COPULA	-O---C	COATED	FOILED
INFANT	******	CORNEA	******	COAXED	FOLDED
INFECT	ANERGY	CORNUA	AORTIC	COCCID	FOOLED
INFEST	ANGARY	CORONA	BOMBIC	COCKED	FOOTED
INGEST	ANTONY	CORYZA	COGNAC	COELED	FORBID
INJECT	ANYWAY	COWPEA	COPTIC	COGGED	FORCED
INKPOT	ENERGY	DODECA	CORSAC	COIFED	FORDED
INMOST	ENMITY	GODIVA	COSMIC	COILED	FORGED
INSECT	ENTITY	GOTAMA	EOZOIC	COINED	FORKED
INSERT	GNARLY	HOOPLA	FORMIC	COMBED	FORMED
INSIST	INFAMY	JOANNA	GOTHIC	CONKED	FOULED
INSULT	INJURY	JOSHUA	HOLMIC	CONNED	FOWLED

GOADED	LOFTED	ROAMED	TOPPED	BOURNE	DOOLEE
GOLFED	LOGGED	ROARED	TOROID	BOURSE	DOOLIE
GOOFED	LOLLED	ROBAND	TORPID	BOVATE	DORMIE
GOOSED	LOMOND	ROBBED	TORRID	BOVINE	DOSAGE
GORGED	LONGED	ROCKED	TOSSED	BOWTIE	DOTAGE
GOUGED	LOOKED	ROGUED	TOTTED	COARSE	DOTTLE
GOWNED	LOOMED	ROILED	TOURED	COATEE	DOUBLE
HOAXED	LOOPED	ROLAND	TOUTED	COBBLE	DOUCHE
HOCKED	LOOSED	ROLLED	TOWARD	COCKLE	DOUGIE
HOGGED	LOOTED	ROMPED	VOICED	CODDLE	EOCENE
HOLARD	LOPPED	RONALD	VOIDED	COERCE	EOGENE
HONIED	LORDED	ROOFED	VOLTED	COFFEE	FOCSLE
HONKED	LOURED	ROOKED	WOADED	COFFLE	FOIBLE
HOODED	LOUSED	ROOMED	WOLFED	COHERE	FONDLE
HOOFED	MOANED	ROOTED	WOMBED	COHUNE	FONDUE
HOOKED	MOATED	ROTTED	WONTED	COLINE	FOOTLE
HOOPED	MOBBED	ROTUND	WOODED	COLLIE	FOOZLE
HOOTED	MOCKED	ROUGED	WORDED	COLURE	FORAGE
HOOVED	MOILED	ROUSED	WORKED	COMATE	FOSSAE
HOPPED	MOLDED	ROUTED	WORMED	COMMIE	FOVEAE
HORDED	MOLTED	SOAKED	YOWLED	COMOSE	GOALIE
HORNED	MONIED	SOAPED	ZOOMED	CONNIE	GOATEE
HORRID	MOONED	SOARED	******	CONTRE	GOBBLE
HORSED	MOORED	SOBBED	-O---E	COODLE	GOETHE
HOSTED	MOOTED	SOCKED	******	COOKIE	GOGGLE
HOTBED	MOPPED	SOCRED	AORTAE	COOLIE	GOITRE
HOTROD	MORBID	SODDED	BOBBIE	COOTIE	GOURDE
HOTTED	MOUSED	SOILED	BOBBLE	CORBIE	HOARSE
HOUSED	NOBBED	SOLAND	BOCCIE	CORPSE	HOBBLE
HOWARD	NOCKED	SOLOED	BODICE	CORRIE	HOGTIE
HOWLED	NODDED	SOLVED	BOGGLE	CORVEE	HOMAGE
JOBBED	NOGOOD	SOOTED	BOLIDE	COSINE	HOMBRE
JOCUND	NOISED	SOPPED	BONNIE	COSTAE	HONORE
JOGGED	NOOSED	SORDID	BOODLE	COTTAE	HOOPOE
JOINED	NOSHED	SORTED	BOOGIE	COULEE	HOPPLE
JOLTED	PODDED	SOULED	BOOKIE	COUPLE	HORACE
JOSHED	POISED	SOUPED	BOOTEE	COURSE	HORNIE
JOTTED	POLAND	SOURED	BOOTIE	COWAGE	HORSTE
KOBOLD	POLLED	SOUSED	BOOTLE	COWRIE	IODATE
KONRAD	PONIED	TOGAED	BORAGE	COYOTE	IODIDE
LOADED	POOLED	TOGGED	BORANE	DOABLE	IODINE
LOAFED	POOPED	TOILED	BORATE	DOCILE	IODIZE
LOAMED	POPPED	TOLLED	BORIDE	DOGAPE	IOLITE
LOANED	PORTED	TOMBED	BOTTLE	DOGGIE	IONIZE
LOBBED	POSTED	TOMCOD	BOUCLE	DOLLIE	IONONE
LOCKED	POTTED	TONGED	BOUFFE	DONATE	JOANNE
LOCOED	POURED	TOOLED	BOUGIE	DONNIE	JOCOSE
LODGED	POUTED	TOOTED	BOUNCE	DOODLE	JOGGLE

JONNIE	POLITE	TOUSLE	HOSING	COYISH	BOREAL
JOSTLE	POLLEE	TOWAGE	JOKING	DOVISH	COAXAL
JOUNCE	POMACE	VOLUME	JOYING	EOLITH	COCCAL
LOATHE	POMADE	VOLUTE	LOOING	FOURTH	COEVAL
LOBATE	PONGEE	VOTIVE	LOPING	GOLOSH	COITAL
LOBULE	POODLE	VOYAGE	LOSING	HOOKAH	COMPEL
LOCALE	POPPLE	WOBBLE	LOVING	HOOTCH	CONSUL
LOCATE	POTAGE	ZOMBIE	LOWING	HOWDAH	CORBEL
LORENE	POTALE	ZONATE	MOOING	JOSEPH	CORNEL
LOTTIE	POTPIE	ZONULE	MOPING	JOSIAH	CORRAL
LOUISE	POTSIE	ZOUAVE	MOVING	LOOFAH	COSTAL
LOUNGE	POTTLE	******	MOWING	MODISH	DORSAL
LOUVRE	POUNCE	-O---G	NOSING	MOLLAH	DOSSAL
LOVAGE	ROBBIE	******	NOTING	MOLOCH	DOSSEL
MOBILE	ROCKNE	BODING	OOLONG	MOOLAH	DOSSIL
MODULE	RONNIE	BONING	OOZING	MOPISH	DOTTEL
MOHAVE	ROOKIE	BOOING	POKING	POLISH	DOUGAL
MOHOLE	ROOTLE	BORING	POLING	POPISH	FOETAL
MOISHE	ROSCOE	BOWING	PORING	POTASH	FONTAL
MOJAVE	ROTATE	BOWLEG	POSING	ROMISH	FORMAL
MOLINE	ROTCHE	BOXING	ROBING	TOBIAH	FORMYL
MOLLIE	ROUBLE	COBURG	ROPING	TOYISH	FOSSIL
MOLTKE	ROUCHE	CODING	ROSING	******	FOVEAL
MONROE	ROXANE	COKING	ROVING	-O---I	GOOGOL
MOPOKE	ROYALE	COMING	ROWING	******	GOORAL
MORALE	SOCAGE	CONING	SOLING	BONACI	GOSPEL
MORGUE	SOIGNE	COOING	SOWING	BONSAI	HOSTEL
MOROSE	SOIREE	COPING	TOEING	BORZOI	JOVIAL
MOSQUE	SOLACE	CORING	TONING	GOMUTI	JOYFUL
MOTILE	SOLUTE	COVING	TOPING	SOLIDI	LOVELL
MOTIVE	SOMBRE	COWING	TOTING	SOMALI	LOWELL
MOTTLE	SOMITE	COXING	TOWING	SOUARI	MONGOL
MOUSSE	SOOTHE	DOLING	TOYING	******	MORSEL
NOBBLE	SOPHIE	DOMING	VOLING	-O---K	MORTAL
NODDLE	SORTIE	DOPING	VOTING	******	NOBALL
NODOSE	SOURCE	DORBUG	VOWING	BOGOAK	NORMAL
NODULE	SOZINE	DOSING	WOOING	COPECK	NOUNAL
NOELLE	TODDLE	DOTING	WOWING	KODIAK	PODSOL
NONAGE	TOFFEE	DOZING	YOKING	KOPECK	PODZOL
NOODLE	TOGGLE	FOGDOG	YOWING	MOHAWK	POMMEL
NOTICE	TONGUE	FOXING	ZONING	MOHOCK	PONTIL
NOVICE	TONITE	GOBANG	******	OOMIAK	PORTAL
NOWISE	TOOTLE	GORING	-O---H	PODUNK	POSTAL
NOZZLE	TOPPLE	-O---H	******	POLACK	POWELL
OOCYTE	TOROSE	******	BORSCH	YORICK	ROMMEL
OOLITE	TORQUE	HOEING	BOYISH	******	RONDEL
POINTE	TOUCHE	HOLING	COHOSH	-O---L	ROSEAL
POLICE	TOUPEE	HOMING	COPRAH	******	SOCIAL
		HONING		AORTAL	
		HOPING		BORDEL	

SORREL	BOWFIN	HOIDEN	SOCMEN	******	COLTER
TOLUOL	BOWMAN	HOYDEN	SODDEN	-O---P	COMBER
TOLUYL	BOWMEN	IONIAN	SOFTEN	******	CONCUR
TONSIL	COCAIN	JOHANN	SOLEMN	COCKUP	CONDOR
WOEFUL	COCHIN	JONSON	SOLION	COLLOP	CONFER
ZOONAL	COCOON	JOPLIN	TOCSIN	DOLLOP	CONGER
******	CODEIN	JORDAN	TONKIN	GOSSIP	CONKER
-O---M	COFFIN	JOVIAN	TOUCAN	HOLDUP	CONNER
******	COLUMN	KOREAN	TOULON	HOOKUP	COOKER
BOTTOM	COMEON	LOGION	WOODEN	LOCKUP	COOLER
COELOM	COMMON	LONDON	WOOLEN	LOLLOP	COOPER
CONDOM	CONMAN	LONGAN	WORSEN	MOBCAP	COPIER
CONIUM	CONTIN	LOOKIN	YOUPON	MOCKUP	COPPER
COPALM	CORBAN	LOOSEN	******	ROLLUP	CORDER
CORIUM	CORDON	LORAIN	-O---O	TOECAP	CORKER
DORSUM	CORTIN	LOREEN	******	TOSSUP	CORNER
EONISM	COSIGN	LOTION	BOLERO	******	COSHER
FOLIUM	COTTON	LOUDEN	BONITO	-O---R	COSTAR
GODDAM	COUPON	LOVEIN	BOOBOO	******	COSTER
GONIUM	COUSIN	MODERN	BOOHOO	BOATER	COTTAR
GOTHAM	COWMAN	MOLTEN	BORNEO	BOBBER	COTTER
HOLISM	COWMEN	MOREEN	COLUGO	BOILER	COUGAR
IODISM	DOBBIN	MORGAN	COMEDO	BOLDER	COWPER
IONIUM	DOBLON	MORGEN	DOMINO	BOLTER	COZIER
JOTHAM	DOBSON	MORION	DORADO	BOMBER	DOBBER
LOGJAM	DOLMAN	MORMON	FOREGO	BONDER	DOCKER
MOMISM	DOLMEN	MORTON	HOODOO	BONIER	DOCTOR
MONISM	DOMAIN	MOTION	KOKOMO	BONZER	DODDER
MOSLEM	DONJON	MOULIN	KOODOO	BOOMER	DODGER
NOMISM	DOREEN	MOUTON	MONACO	BOOZER	DOFFER
NONCOM	DORIAN	NOGGIN	MORPHO	BORDER	DOGEAR
PODIUM	EOLIAN	NOREEN	NONEGO	BOTHER	DOGGER
POGROM	EONIAN	NORMAN	POMELO	BOWLER	DOLLAR
POMPOM	FOEMAN	NOTION	PONCHO	BOWYER	DOLOUR
POSSUM	FOEMEN	POISON	POTATO	BOXCAR	DOPIER
SODIUM	GOBLIN	POLLEN	POUSTO	COALER	DOPTER
TOMTOM	GODSON	POMPON	ROBALO	COAXER	DORMER
******	GODWIN	PONTON	ROCOCO	COBBER	DOSSER
-O---N	GOLDEN	POPGUN	ROMULO	COCKER	DOTIER
******	GONION	POPLIN	SOLANO	CODDER	DOTTER
BOBBIN	GORDON	POTEEN	SOMATO	CODGER	DOWSER
BODKIN	GORGON	POTION	SORGHO	COFFER	DOZIER
BOFFIN	GORHEN	POTMAN	TOBAGO	COHEIR	FODDER
BOLEYN	GOSHEN	ROBSON	TOLEDO	COILER	FOETOR
BOLSON	GOTTEN	RODMAN	TOMATO	COINER	FOLDER
BOLTON	GOVERN	RODMEN	TORERO	COLDER	FOLIAR
BONBON	HODDEN	ROTTEN	VOMITO	COLLAR	FONDER
BOSTON	HODMAN	SOCMAN	VOODOO	COLOUR	FOOTER

FORCER	LOITER	ROLLER	******	COLINS	COYPUS
FORGER	LOLLER	ROMPER	-O---S	COLONS	COZENS
FORMER	LONGER	ROOFER	******	COLORS	COZIES
FOSTER	LOOKER	ROOMER	AORTAS	COLOUS	DOALLS
FOULER	LOOPER	ROOTER	BOARDS	COLZAS	DOBIES
FOWLER	LOOSER	ROPIER	BOASTS	COMBOS	DOBLAS
FOXIER	LOOTER	ROSIER	BOBBYS	COMERS	DOBRAS
GOFFER	LOQUAR	ROSTER	BODIES	COMETS	DODGES
GOITER	LOUDER	ROTTER	BOGANS	COMICS	DODOES
GOLFER	LOUVER	ROUSER	BOGEYS	COMMAS	DOGIES
GOOBER	MOBBER	ROUTER	BOGIES	COMOUS	DOGMAS
GOOIER	MOCKER	SOAKER	BOGLES	COMPOS	DOINGS
GOPHER	MOHAIR	SOARER	BOMBES	CONCHS	DOLLYS
GORGER	MOILER	SOCCER	BONERS	CONEYS	DOLPHS
GORIER	MOLDER	SOEVER	BONGOS	CONGAS	DONEES
GOUGER	MOLTER	SOFTER	BONNYS	CONGES	DONETS
HOAXER	MONGER	SOLDER	BONZES	CONICS	DONNAS
HOLDER	MOOTER	SOLVER	BOOSTS	CONIES	DONORS
HOLIER	MORTAR	SOMBER	BOOTHS	CONTES	DORIES
HOLLER	MOTHER	SONDER	BOOZES	CONTOS	DOSERS
HOMIER	MOUSER	SOONER	BOREAS	COOEES	DOTERS
HONKER	NOBLER	SORTER	BORERS	COOERS	DOUBTS
HONOUR	NODDER	SOURER	BOSHES	COOEYS	DOUGHS
HOOFER	NORNIR	TOILER	BOSOMS	COOMBS	DOUSES
HOOKER	NOSIER	TOLLER	BOSSES	COOPTS	DOWELS
HOOPER	OOPHOR	TONIER	BOUGHS	COPIES	DOWERS
HOOTER	OOZIER	TOOLER	BOULES	COPSES	DOWLAS
HOOVER	POKIER	TOOTER	BOUNDS	CORALS	DOWSES
HOPPER	POLDER	TOPPER	BOURGS	CORERS	DOXIES
HORROR	POLLER	TORPOR	BOURNS	CORGIS	DOYENS
HOSIER	PONDER	TOTHER	BOUSES	CORNUS	DOZENS
HOTTER	POORER	TOTTER	BOWELS	CORPUS	FOEHNS
HOWLER	POPLAR	TOURER	BOWERS	CORSES	FOETUS
JOBBER	POPPER	TOUTER	BOWSES	CORTES	FOGIES
JOGGER	PORKER	VOYEUR	BOXERS	CORVES	FOISTS
JOINER	PORTER	WOLVER	BOYARS	CORVUS	FOLIOS
JOLTER	POSEUR	WONDER	COASTS	COSHES	FORAYS
JOSHER	POSTER	WOOFER	COATIS	COSMOS	FORCES
JOTTER	POTHER	WORKER	COAXES	COSSES	FORGES
KOSHER	POTTER	WORMER	COBIAS	COTTAS	FORTES
LOADER	POURER	WORSER	COBLES	COUGHS	FORTIS
LOAFER	POUTER	WOWSER	COBRAS	COUNTS	FORUMS
LOBBER	POWDER	YONDER	COCCUS	COUPES	FOSSES
LOCKER	POWTER	YONKER	COCOAS	COURTS	FOUNDS
LODGER	ROAMER	YORKER	COIGNS	COVERS	FOUNTS
LOFTER	ROARER	ZOSTER	COITUS	COVETS	FOYERS
LOGGER	ROBBER		COLEUS	COVEYS	GOBIES
LOGIER	ROCKER		COLIES	COWERS	GOINGS

GONADS	KODAKS	MOULDS	ROBLES	TOKENS	YOKELS
GONERS	KOINES	MOULTS	ROBOTS	TOMANS	YOUTHS
GOOSES	KOPEKS	MOUNTS	RODDYS	TOMMYS	ZOMBIS
GORALS	KOPJES	MOURNS	RODEOS	TONERS	ZOOIDS
GORGES	LOAVES	MOUSES	ROGERS	TONICS	ZORILS
GORSES	LOCALS	MOUTHS	ROGUES	TOPERS	ZOUNDS
GOUGES	LODGES	MOVERS	ROLPHS	TOPICS	******
GOURDS	LONERS	MOVIES	ROMANS	TOQUES	-O---T
HOARDS	LOOSES	MOWERS	RONDOS	TORAHS	******
HOAXES	LOPERS	NOESIS	ROOSTS	TORIES	AORIST
HOBBES	LORIES	NOISES	ROSINS	TORIIS	BOBCAT
HOBOES	LOSERS	NOMADS	ROTORS	TOROUS	BONNET
HOGANS	LOSSES	NOOSES	ROUGES	TORSKS	BOSKET
HOICKS	LOTAHS	NOPALS	ROUGHS	TORSOS	BOUGHT
HOISTS	LOUGHS	NORIAS	ROUNDS	TOSHES	COBALT
HOLIES	LOUPES	NORMAS	ROUSES	TOSSES	COBNUT
HOLLYS	LOUSES	NORRIS	ROUSTS	TOTALS	COEMPT
HOLMES	LOVERS	NOTERS	ROUTES	TOTEMS	COGENT
HOMERS	LOWERS	NOVELS	ROVERS	TOTERS	COHORT
HONEYS	MOBIUS	NOWAYS	ROWANS	TOUGHS	COLLET
HONORS	MODELS	OODLES	ROWELS	TOWELS	COMBAT
HOOVES	MOGULS	PODOUS	ROWERS	TOWERS	COMFIT
HORDES	MOHURS	POGIES	ROYALS	TOXINS	COMMIT
HORSES	MOIRAS	POILUS	SOBERS	TOYERS	COPOUT
HOTELS	MOLARS	POINDS	SOCLES	TOYONS	COQUET
HOUNDS	MOLIES	POINTS	SOFTAS	VOCALS	CORNET
HOURIS	MOLLYS	POISES	SOLANS	VODKAS	CORSET
HOUSES	MONADS	POKERS	SOLIDS	VOGUES	COSSET
HOVELS	MONEYS	POKIES	SOLVES	VOGULS	COVERT
HOVERS	MONIES	POLKAS	SONARS	VOICES	DOCENT
IODOUS	MONTES	POLLYS	SONIAS	VOILES	DOCKET
IOLCUS	MONTHS	POLYPS	SONYAS	VOLVAS	DOESNT
JOCKOS	MONTYS	PONIES	SORELS	VOMERS	DORSET
JOINTS	MOPERS	PONTES	SORGOS	VOMITS	FOMENT
JOISTS	MORALS	POPPYS	SOTHIS	VOROUS	FOREST
JOKERS	MORASS	POROUS	SOTOLS	VOTERS	FORGET
JONAHS	MORAYS	POSERS	SOUGHS	VOWELS	FORGOT
JORAMS	MORELS	POSIES	SOUNDS	VOWERS	FORINT
JORGES	MORONS	POSITS	SOUSES	WOALDS	FORMAT
JORUMS	MORRIS	POSSES	SOWARS	WOLVES	FOUGHT
JOSHES	MORROS	POTTOS	SOWERS	WOOERS	GOBBET
JOSIAS	MORTYS	POULTS	SOZINS	WORLDS	GOBLET
JOSSES	MOSEYS	POUNDS	TOASTS	WORSTS	GOCART
JOULES	MOSSES	POWERS	TOBIAS	WOUNDS	GODWIT
JOUSTS	MOTELS	POYOUS	TOBIES	YODELS	GOGLET
JOYCES	MOTIFS	ROALDS	TODIES	YOGEES	GOKART
JOYOUS	MOTORS	ROASTS	TOGUES	YOGINS	GORGET
KOALAS	MOTTOS	ROBINS	TOILES	YOICKS	HOBART

HOGNUT	WOMBAT	BOMBAY	HOLILY	PORTLY	******
HONEST	YOGURT	BOTANY	HOMELY	POSHLY	-P---C
HORNET	******	BOTCHY	HOMILY	POTBOY	******
HOTPOT	-O---U	BOTFLY	HOMINY	POUCHY	APNEIC
JOLIET	******	BOUNCY	HOOKEY	RODNEY	IPECAC
LOCKET	CONGOU	BOUNTY	HOORAY	ROMANY	******
LOCUST	COTEAU	BOWERY	HORARY	ROMNEY	-P---D
LOMENT	HONSHU	COBBLY	HORSEY	ROPILY	******
LOQUAT	MOREAU	CODIFY	HOURLY	ROSARY	APPEND
LOWEST	******	COGWAY	JOCKEY	ROSILY	OPENED
MODEST	-O---W	COLDLY	JOHNNY	ROSINY	OPINED
MOLEST	******	COLONY	KORUNY	ROTARY	SPACED
MOMENT	BORROW	COMEDY	LONELY	SODOMY	SPADED
MONGST	BOWSAW	COMELY	LORDLY	SOFTLY	SPARED
MONIST	BOWWOW	COMITY	LOUDLY	SOLELY	SPAYED
MOPPET	FOGBOW	COMPLY	LOVELY	SORELY	SPEWED
MOTMOT	FOLLOW	CONCHY	LOWBOY	SOURLY	SPICED
MOZART	HOLLOW	CONVEY	LOWERY	TOMBOY	SPIKED
NOCENT	KOWTOW	CONVOY	LOWKEY	TOOTHY	SPILED
NOUGAT	MORROW	CONWAY	MODIFY	TOOTSY	SPIRED
NOUGHT	MOSCOW	COOKEY	MOIETY	TOUCHY	SPITED
POCKET	NOSHOW	COOLLY	MONDAY	TOWERY	SPOKED
PONENT	POWWOW	COPLEY	MONKEY	VOLERY	SPORED
POPPET	SORROW	CORDAY	MONODY	VOLLEY	SPREAD
POSSET	******	CORODY	MOOLEY	VOTARY	SPUMED
POTENT	-O---X	COSILY	MORLEY	WOBBLY	UPHELD
ROBERT	******	COSTLY	MOSLEY	WOLSEY	UPHOLD
ROBUST	BOLLIX	COUNTY	MOSTLY	WOODSY	UPLAND
ROCHET	COCCYX	COWBOY	MOTLEY	WOOLLY	UPWARD
ROCKET	COMMIX	COZILY	MOULDY	WORTHY	******
RODENT	CONVEX	DONKEY	MOUNTY	ZONARY	-P---E
ROQUET	CORTEX	DOUBLY	MOUTHY	******	******
ROTGUT	COWPOX	DOUGHY	NOBODY	-O---Z	APACHE
SOCKET	DOGFOX	DOURLY	NONARY	******	APIECE
SOFFIT	FORNAX	DOWERY	NORWAY	CORTEZ	APLITE
SOLENT	FORNIX	DOYLEY	NOSILY	LORENZ	APOGEE
SONANT	HOTBOX	DOZILY	NOTARY	******	APPOSE
SONNET	POLEAX	FOLKSY	NOTIFY	-P---A	EPOPEE
SORBET	POLLEX	FONDLY	OOLOGY	******	OPAQUE
SOREST	POLLUX	FOULLY	OOZILY	APHTHA	OPHITE
SOUGHT	VOLVOX	FOXILY	POACHY	APNOEA	OPIATE
SOVIET	VORTEX	GOODBY	POETRY	APULIA	OPPOSE
TOILET	******	GOODLY	POINTY	EPIZOA	OPTIME
TOMCAT	-O---Y	GOOGLY	POLICY	OPTIMA	SPACAE
TOMTIT	******	GOONEY	POLITY	SPARTA	SPARGE
TOPHAT	******	GOOSEY	POMPEY	SPIREA	SPARSE
VOLANT	BODILY	GORILY	POORLY	******	SPATHE
VOLOST	BOLDLY	HOCKEY	POPERY	-P---B	SPECIE
				******	
				APLOMB	

SPHENE	APODAL	SPICER	SPILES	UPLIFT	******
SPHERE	APPALL	SPIDER	SPILLS	UPMOST	-Q---K
SPLAKE	APPEAL	SPRIER	SPINES	UPROOT	******
SPLICE	EPICAL	SPRYER	SPIRES	UPSHOT	SQUAWK
SPLINE	SPINAL	UPROAR	SPIRTS	******	SQUEAK
SPONGE	SPINEL	******	SPITES	-P---X	******
SPOUSE	SPIRAL	-P---S	SPLATS	******	-Q---L
SPRITE	SPITAL	******	SPLAYS	SPADIX	******
SPRUCE	SPRAWL	APEXES	SPLITS	SPHINX	SQUALL
SPURGE	UPHILL	APHIDS	SPOILS	******	SQUEAL
UPDATE	******	APICES	SPOKES	-P---Y	SQUILL
UPDIKE	-P---M	APPALS	SPOOFS	******	******
UPHROE	******	APPELS	SPOOKS	APATHY	-Q---M
UPRISE	EPONYM	APPLES	SPOOLS	APEPSY	******
UPROSE	SPUTUM	APRILS	SPOONS	APHONY	SQUIRM
UPSIDE	******	APRONS	SPOORS	APIARY	******
UPTAKE	-P---N	EPACTS	SPORES	OPENLY	-Q---S
******		EPHAHS	SPORTS	SPARRY	
-P---G	APEMAN	EPHODS	SPOUTS	SPEEDY	EQUALS
******	APPIAN	EPHORS	SPRAGS	SPERRY	EQUIPS
APOLOG	OPPUGN	EPIRUS	SPRATS	SPHERY	SQUABS
EPILOG	OPTION	EPOCHS	SPRAYS	SPIFFY	SQUADS
EPPING	SPAVIN	EPODES	SPREES	SPINNY	SQUATS
OPTING	SPLEEN	OPERAS	SPRIGS	SPONGY	SQUAWS
SPRANG	SPOKEN	OPINES	SPRITS	SPOOKY	SQUIBS
SPRING	SPRAIN	OPTICS	SPRUES	SPOONY	SQUIDS
SPRUNG	UPTOWN	SPACES	SPUMES	SPORTY	******
SPYING	UPTURN	SPADES	SPURNS	SPOTTY	-Q---T
UPPING	******	SPAHIS	SPURTS	SPRYLY	******
******	-P---O	SPAITS	UPASES	SPUNKY	SQUINT
-P---H	******	SPALLS	UPBOWS	SPURRY	SQUIRT
******	APOLLO	SPANKS	UPENDS	UPPITY	
EPARCH	OPORTO	SPARES	UPPERS	******	-Q---Y
SPEECH	SPERMO	SPARKS	UPSETS	-Q---A	******
SPILTH	SPHENO	SPASMS	******	******	EQUITY
SPLASH	SPLENO	SPATES	-P---T	AQUILA	******
UPPISH	******	SPAWNS	******	SQUAMA	-R---A
UPRUSH	-P---P	SPEAKS	APPORT	******	******
******	******	SPEARS	OPTANT	-Q---E	ARABIA
-P---I	UPKEEP	SPECKS	SPIGOT	******	ARANTA
******	******	SPEEDS	SPINET	EQUATE	ARBELA
EPHEBI	-P---R	SPEISS	SPIRIT	EQUINE	ARCANA
EPHORI	******	SPELLS	SPLINT	SQUARE	AREOLA
******	APPEAR	SPENDS	SPOILT	SQUIRE	ARGALA
-P---L	OPENER	SPICES	SPRINT	******	ARISTA
******	SPACER	SPIELS	SPROUT	-Q---H	ARMADA
APICAL	SPADER	SPIERS	UPBEAT	******	ARNICA
APNEAL	SPARER	SPIKES	UPCAST	SQUISH	ARROBA

ARUNTA	ARGUED	ORMUZD	BROOKE	GRUDGE	PROLEG
BRAHMA	ARMAND	PRATED	BROWSE	ORACLE	PRYING
BREGMA	ARNAUD	PRAYED	BRUISE	ORANGE	TRUING
BRENDA	ARNOLD	PREMED	CRADLE	ORDURE	TRYING
CRANIA	AROUND	PREYED	CREASE	OREIDE	URGING
CREUSA	BRACED	PRICED	CREATE	ORIOLE	WRYING
CRIMEA	BRAKED	PRIDED	CRECHE	ORNATE	******
ERRATA	BRAVED	PRIMED	CREESE	OROIDE	-R---H
FRIEDA	BRAYED	PRIZED	CREOLE	ORPINE	******
FRIGGA	BRAZED	PROBED	CRINGE	ORRICE	ARMAGH
FRUSTA	BREWED	PROSED	CROSSE	PRAGUE	BRANCH
GRETNA	BRIBED	PROVED	CROUPE	PRAISE	BREACH
ORGANA	BRIGID	PRUNED	CRUISE	PRANCE	BREATH
PRAVDA	BRINED	TRACED	CRUSOE	PREVUE	BREECH
TRAUMA	CRANED	TRADED	DRAGEE	PRINCE	BROACH
TRIVIA	CRAPED	TRICED	DRAWEE	PROCNE	BROOCH
TROIKA	CRATED	TRIFID	DREDGE	RRHAGE	BRUNCH
URANIA	CRAVED	TRINED	DROGUE	TRACHE	CRATCH
UREMIA	CRAZED	TRIPOD	DROWSE	TRANCE	CROTCH
URSULA	CREPED	UROPOD	DRUDGE	TREBLE	CROUCH
******	CROWED	XRAYED	DRYICE	TRIFLE	CRUNCH
-R---B	DRAPED	******	ERGATE	TRIODE	CRUTCH
******	DRAYED	-R---E	ERMINE	TRIOSE	DRENCH
PREFAB	DRONED	******	FRAISE	TRIPLE	DROUTH
******	DROVED	ARABLE	FRANCE	TRISTE	DRYISH
-R---C	ERASED	ARBUTE	FRAPPE	TRIUNE	FRENCH
******	ERODED	ARCADE	FREEZE	TRIXIE	GROUCH
ARABIC	ERRAND	ARCANE	FRIDGE	TROCHE	GROWTH
ARCTIC	FRAMED	ARCHIE	FRIEZE	TROUPE	ORNITH
BROMIC	FRAYED	ARGIVE	FRINGE	TRUDGE	PREACH
CRETIC	FRIEND	ARIOSE	FRUNZE	URBANE	TRENCH
CRITIC	FRIGID	ARLENE	GRACIE	UREASE	TROUGH
EROTIC	GRACED	ARLINE	GRAMME	UREIDE	WRAITH
FROLIC	GRADED	ARMURE	GRANDE	URSINE	WREATH
IRENIC	GRATED	AROUSE	GRANGE	WRASSE	WRENCH
IRIDIC	GRAVED	ARRIVE	GREASE	WRITHE	WRETCH
IRITIC	GRAVID	ARSINE	GREAVE	******	******
IRONIC	GRAYED	BRAISE	GREECE	-R---G	-R---I
ORPHIC	GRAZED	BRAIZE	GREENE	******	******
TRAGIC	GRIDED	BRAQUE	GREIGE	ARCING	ARBORI
TROPIC	GRIMED	BREEZE	GRIEVE	ARMING	ARGALI
URALIC	GRIPED	BRIDGE	GRIFFE	CRYING	BRACHI
URANIC	GROPED	BRIDIE	GRILLE	DRYING	BRUNEI
URETIC	GROUND	BRIDLE	GRILSE	ERRING	GRIGRI
******	IRISED	BROCHE	GRIPPE	FRYING	TRICHI
-R---D	IRONED	BROGUE	GROOVE	IRKING	******
******	ORATED	BRONTE	GROUSE	IRVING	-R---K
ARCHED	ORCHID	BRONZE	GROYNE	ORBING	******
ARCKED					ARAWAK
					ARRACK

CROJIK	ERBIUM	PROVEN	ARDOUR	PROPER	BRAIDS
FRANCK	FRENUM	TREPAN	ARGUER	PROSER	BRAILS
******	GRAHAM	TRIGON	ARMOUR	PROVER	BRAINS
-R---L	ORGASM	TRITON	ARREAR	PRUNER	BRAKES
******	PRELIM	TROGON	ARTHUR	TRACER	BRANDS
ARABEL	TRUISM	TROJAN	BRACER	TRADER	BRANTS
ARCHIL	******	TRUMAN	BRAVER	TREMOR	BRAVES
ARGYLL	**-R---N**	URCHIN	BRAYER	TREVOR	BRAVOS
ARMFUL	******	******	BRAZER	TRICAR	BRAWLS
ARTFUL	ARAGON	**-R---O**	BREWER	TRITER	BRAZAS
BRAZIL	ARCHON	******	BRIBER	TROCAR	BRAZES
BRIDAL	ARISEN	ARCHEO	BROKER	TROVER	BRAZOS
BROMAL	ARLEEN	AREZZO	CRATER	URETER	BREADS
BRUMAL	BRAZEN	ARIOSO	CRAVER	WRITER	BREAKS
BRUNEL	BREMEN	ARISTO	CROZER	******	BREAMS
BRUTAL	BRETON	ARROYO	CRUDER	**-R---S**	BREEDS
CREDAL	BRITON	ARTHRO	DRAPER	******	BREEKS
CRENEL	BROGAN	ARTURO	DRAWER	ARBORS	BRENTS
CRESOL	BROKEN	BRONCO	DRIVER	ARCHES	BREVES
CREWEL	CRAVEN	CRAMBO	DROVER	ARCHYS	BREWIS
CRURAL	CRAYON	CRANIO	ERASER	ARDEBS	BRIARS
DRIVEL	CRETAN	CRYPTO	FRAMER	ARDORS	BRIBES
DRUPEL	CRETIN	DRONGO	FRATER	ARECAS	BRICKS
FRIJOL	CRETON	ERINGO	GRADER	ARENAS	BRIDES
FRIVOL	CROTON	ERYNGO	GRATER	ARETES	BRIEFS
FRUGAL	DRAGON	FRANCO	GRAVER	ARGALS	BRIERS
GRAVEL	DRIVEN	FRESCO	GRAYER	ARGOTS	BRILLS
GRETEL	DROMON	FRESNO	GRAZER	ARGUES	BRINES
GRIZEL	DRYDEN	FRONTO	GRIPER	ARIANS	BRINGS
GROVEL	FRAUEN	GRAECO	GROCER	ARIELS	BRINKS
IREFUL	FROZEN	GRAPHO	GROPER	ARIOUS	BRISKS
ORCHIL	GRABEN	GROTTO	GROVER	ARISES	BROADS
ORDEAL	GRADIN	ORCHIO	GROWER	ARMETS	BROILS
ORWELL	GRATIN	ORGANO	IRONER	ARMIES	BROMES
PRIMAL	GRAVEN	PRESTO	KRONER	ARMORS	BRONCS
PROPEL	KRAKEN	PROCTO	KRONOR	ARNIES	BROODS
PROPYL	KRONEN	PRONTO	KRONUR	AROIDS	BROOKS
TRAVEL	ORCEIN	TRICHO	ORATOR	AROMAS	BROOMS
TRIBAL	ORDAIN	TROPHO	PRATER	ARPENS	BROTHS
TRINAL	OREGAN	TROPPO	PRAYER	ARRAYS	BROWNS
TROPAL	OREGON	******	PREFER	ARROWS	BRUCES
TROTYL	ORIGAN	**-R---P**	PRETER	ARTELS	BRUGES
TROWEL	ORIGEN	******	PRETOR	ARTIES	BRUINS
URANYL	ORIGIN	WRAPUP	PREWAR	ARTOIS	BRUITS
URINAL	ORISON	******	PREYER	ARYANS	BRUMES
******	ORPHAN	**-R---R**	PRIMER	BRACES	BRUNOS
-R---M	PRISON	******	PRIZER	BRACTS	BRUTES
******	PROTON	ARBOUR	PROBER	BRAHMS	BRUTUS
CRINUM		ARCHER			
DRACHM					

CRAALS	CRUETS	FRANCS	GROANS	PRICKS	TROUTS
CRACKS	CRUMBS	FRANKS	GROATS	PRIDES	TROVES
CRAFTS	CRUMPS	FRAUDS	GROINS	PRIERS	TRUCES
CRAIGS	CRUSES	FREAKS	GROOMS	PRIMES	TRUCKS
CRAKES	CRUSTS	FREDAS	GROPES	PRIMPS	TRUDYS
CRAMPS	CRUXES	FREONS	GROUPS	PRIMUS	TRUMPS
CRANES	CRYPTS	FRIARS	GROUTS	PRINKS	TRUNKS
CRANKS	DRAFFS	FRIERS	GROVES	PRINTS	TRUSTS
CRAPES	DRAFTS	FRILLS	GROWLS	PRIORS	TRUTHS
CRASIS	DRAINS	FRISES	GRUELS	PRISMS	TRYSTS
CRATES	DRAKES	FRISKS	GRUMES	PRIZES	URAEUS
CRAVES	DRAMAS	FRITHS	GRUNTS	PROBES	URANUS
CRAWLS	DRAPES	FROCKS	IRANIS	PROEMS	WRACKS
CRAZES	DRAWLS	FRONDS	IRAQIS	PRONGS	WREAKS
CREAKS	DREADS	FRONTS	IRENES	PROOFS	WRECKS
CREAMS	DREAMS	FROSTS	IRIDES	PROSES	WRESTS
CREDOS	DRIERS	FROTHS	IRISES	PROVES	WRINGS
CREEDS	DRIFTS	FROWNS	IRITIS	PROWLS	WRISTS
CREEKS	DRILLS	FRUITS	IRVINS	PRUDES	WRITES
CREELS	DRINKS	FRUMPS	IRWINS	PRUNES	WRONGS
CREEPS	DRIVES	FRYERS	KRAALS	PRYERS	******
CREMES	DROITS	GRACES	KRAITS	TRACES	-R---T
CREPES	DROLLS	GRADES	KRISES	TRACKS	******
CRESTS	DRONES	GRADUS	KRONOS	TRACTS	ARARAT
CREVAS	DROOLS	GRAFTS	KRUBIS	TRADES	ARDENT
CRICKS	DROOPS	GRAINS	ORACHS	TRAGUS	ARGENT
CRIERS	DROVES	GRANTS	ORANGS	TRAILS	ARIGHT
CRIMES	DROWNS	GRAPES	ORATES	TRAINS	ARMLET
CRIMPS	DRUIDS	GRAPHS	ORBITS	TRAITS	ARMPIT
CRISES	DRUNKS	GRASPS	ORCHIS	TRAMPS	ARPENT
CRISIS	DRUPES	GRATES	ORDERS	TRAVES	ARRANT
CRISPS	DRUSES	GRATIS	OREADS	TRAWLS	ARREST
CROAKS	DRYADS	GRAVES	ORGANS	TREADS	ARTIST
CROATS	DRYERS	GRAZES	ORGIES	TREATS	BRANDT
CROCKS	ERASES	GREATS	ORIBIS	TRENDS	BREAST
CROCUS	EREBUS	GREBES	ORIELS	TRIADS	BRECHT
CROFTS	ERECTS	GREEDS	ORLOPS	TRIALS	BREVET
CRONES	ERICHS	GREEKS	ORMERS	TRIBES	BRIGHT
CRONOS	ERINYS	GREENS	ORPINS	TRICES	BRULOT
CRONUS	ERNIES	GREETS	ORYXES	TRICKS	BRYANT
CROOKS	ERODES	GREGOS	PRANKS	TRIERS	CRAVAT
CROONS	ERRORS	GREIFS	PRATES	TRILLS	CREDIT
CRORES	ERUCTS	GRETAS	PRAWNS	TRINES	CRUSET
CROUPS	ERUPTS	GRIDES	PRAXIS	TRIPOS	DREAMT
CROWDS	ERWINS	GRILLS	PRECIS	TRIXYS	DRIEST
CROWNS	FRACAS	GRIMES	PREENS	TROLLS	DRYEST
CROZES	FRAILS	GRINDS	PRESAS	TROOPS	DRYROT
CRUCES	FRAMES	GRIPES	PRICES	TROTHS	ERFURT

ERNEST	ARROWY	DROLLY	PRIMLY	ASSIZE	******
ERRANT	ARTERY	DROOPY	PRIORY	ASSUME	-S---N
FREEST	ARTILY	DROPSY	PRISSY	ASSURE	******
FRIGHT	BRACHY	DROSKY	RRHAGY	ASTUTE	ASHCAN
GRIVET	BRAINY	DROSSY	TRACHY	ESCAPE	ASHMAN
KRUBUT	BRANDY	DROWSY	TRASHY	ESSENE	ASHMEN
ORGEAT	BRANNY	DRYFLY	TREATY	ESTATE	ASSIGN
ORIENT	BRASHY	FREAKY	TRENDY	ISOLDE	ASTERN
PRIEST	BRASSY	FREDDY	TRESSY	OSCINE	ISATIN
PRIVET	BRAWNY	FREELY	TRICKY	OSCULE	ISOGON
PROFIT	BREEZY	FRENZY	TRIGLY	OSMOSE	OSBORN
PROJET	BRIERY	FRETTY	TRILBY	PSYCHE	OSSEIN
PROMPT	BROLLY	FRIARY	TRIMLY	TSETSE	OSSIAN
PROSIT	BRONZY	FRIDAY	TROPHY	USABLE	******
PROUST	BROODY	FRILLY	TRUSTY	USANCE	-S---O
TRICOT	BROOMY	FRINGY	WRATHY	******	******
TRIVET	BRUSHY	FRISKY	******	-S---G	ASTERO
TRUANT	BRYONY	FRIZZY	-R---Z	******	ESCUDO
TRUEST	CRABBY	FROGGY	******	ASKING	ESKIMO
TRYOUT	CRACKY	FROSTY	ERSATZ	ISLING	OSWEGO
URGENT	CRAFTY	FROTHY	******	******	PSEUDO
URTEXT	CRAGGY	FROWZY	-S---A	-S---H	PSYCHO
WRIEST	CRANKY	FRUITY	******	******	******
WRIGHT	CRANNY	FRUMPY	ASTHMA	ISAIAH	-S---P
WRYEST	CRAWLY	GRAINY	ESPANA	******	******
******	CREAKY	GRANNY	ISCHIA	-S---I	ASLEEP
-R---U	CREAMY	GRAPHY	ISTRIA	******	ESCARP
******	CREASY	GRASSY	ZSAZSA	ASSISI	******
ARERCU	CREEPY	GRAYLY	******	ASTERI	-S---R
GRUGRU	CRIKEY	GREASY	-S---D	******	******
ORMOLU	CRIMPY	GREEDY	******	-S---L	ASHIER
******	CRISPY	GRIMLY	ASCEND	******	ASHLAR
-R---W	CROAKY	GRIPPY	ASGARD	ASSAIL	ESCHAR
******	CROCKY	GRISLY	ASTRID	ASTRAL	ESCHER
CRACOW	CROUPY	GRITTY	ESPIED	ESPIAL	ESTHER
******	CRUMBY	GROGGY	ISLAND	ISABEL	ISADOR
-R---X	CRUMMY	GROOVY	ISOPOD	ISOBEL	ISHTAR
******	CRUSTY	GROSZY	ISSUED	ISOHEL	ISIDOR
PREFIX	DRABLY	GROTTY	OSMOND	ISRAEL	ISOBAR
PROLIX	DRAFFY	GRUBBY	OSMUND	OSTEAL	ISOMER
******	DRAFTY	GRUMPY	OSTEND	USEFUL	ISSUER
-R---Y	DRAWLY	GRUNDY	OSWALD	******	OSTLER
******	DREAMY	ORALLY	******	-S---M	USURER
ARCHLY	DREARY	ORKNEY	-S---E	******	******
ARGOSY	DREGGY	ORNERY	******	ASARUM	-S---S
ARGUFY	DRESSY	ORRERY	ASHORE	ASYLUM	******
ARIDLY	DRIFTY	PREPAY	ASLOPE	ESTEEM	ASCOTS
ARMORY	DRIPPY	PRETTY	ASPIRE	OSMIUM	ASIANS

ASIDES	******	ETHNIC	STARVE	******	STERNO
ASKERS	-S---V	ITALIC	STATUE	-T---K	STETHO
ASPENS	******	STATIC	STEEVE	******	STHENO
ASPERS	ASIMOV	STELIC	STELAE	ATTACK	STUCCO
ASPICS	******	STERIC	STEPPE	STREAK	STUDIO
ASSAIS	-S---W	YTTRIC	STEVIE	STRICK	******
ASSAYS	******	******	STIFLE	STRUCK	-T---P
ASSESS	ESCHEW	-T---D	STODGE	******	******
ASSETS	ESCROW	******	STOOGE	-T---L	STEPUP
ASTERS	******	ATONED	STRAFE	******	******
ESKERS	-S---Y	ATTEND	STRAKE	ATABAL	-T---R
ESPIES	******	ETCHED	STRIAE	ATONAL	******
ESSAYS	ASBURY	ITCHED	STRIDE	ATRIAL	ATONER
ESTERS	ASHLEY	STAGED	STRIFE	STATAL	ETCHER
ESTOPS	ASTRAY	STAKED	STRIKE	STEROL	STAGER
ESTRUS	ESTRAY	STALED	STRIPE	STIPEL	STALER
ISAACS	OSPREY	STARED	STRIVE	STROLL	STARER
ISLETS	OSSIFY	STATED	STROBE	******	STATER
ISSEIS	USABLY	STAVED	STRODE	-T---M	STATOR
ISSUES	******	STAYED	STROKE	******	STAYER
OSCANS	-T---A	STEWED	STROVE	ATRIUM	STELAR
OSCARS	******	STOKED	STYMIE	STREAM	STIVER
OSIERS	ATAXIA	STOLED	******	******	STOKER
OSIRIS	ATHENA	STOLID	-T---F	-T---N	STONER
PSALMS	ATTICA	STONED	******	******	STOVER
PSHAWS	ATTILA	STOPED	ITSELF	ATAMAN	STUPOR
TSADES	ETERNA	STORED	******	ATTAIN	STYLAR
USAGES	ITHACA	STOWED	-T---G	ATTORN	STYLER
USHERS	OTTAVA	STRAND	******	ETYMON	******
USURPS	OTTAWA	STROUD	STALAG	PTISAN	-T---S
******	OTTOWA	STUPID	STENOG	STALIN	******
-S---T	STADIA	STYLED	STRING	STAMEN	ATHENS
******	STANZA	UTGARD	STRONG	STAMIN	ATOLLS
ASCENT	STELLA	******	STRUNG	STATEN	ATONES
ASKANT	STERNA	-T---E	STYING	STEFAN	ATREUS
ASLANT	STIGMA	******	******	STEPAN	ATTARS
ASPECT	STRATA	ATHENE	-T---H	STEPIN	ATTICS
ASSENT	STROMA	ATHOME	******	STEVEN	ETAPES
ASSERT	STRUMA	ATTIRE	ATTACH	STOLEN	ETCHES
ASSIST	UTOPIA	ATTLEE	STAITH	STOLON	ETHANS
ASSORT	YTTRIA	ATTUNE	STANCH	STRAIN	ETHELS
ESCENT	******	ETHANE	STARCH	STREWN	ETHERS
ESCORT	-T---C	OTIOSE	STENCH	UTAHAN	ETHICS
ESPRIT	******	STABLE	STITCH	******	ETHYLS
ISEULT	ATAVIC	STACIE	STRATH	-T---O	ETUDES
OSBERT	ATAXIC	STACTE	******	******	ITCHES
TSHIRT	ATOMIC	STANCE	-T---I	STAURO	ITIOUS
	ATONIC	STAPLE	STELLI	STEREO	OTHERS
			STRATI		

OTITIS	STOKES	******	GUYANA	BUDDED	DUNNED
OTTERS	STOLES	-T---X	HUELVA	BUDGED	DUSKED
PTOSIS	STOMPS	******	JUDAEA	BUFFED	DUSTED
STACKS	STONES	STORAX	LUANDA	BUGGED	EUCLID
STACYS	STOOKS	******	LUELLA	BUGLED	FUCOID
STAFFS	STOOLS	-T---Y	LUMINA	BULBED	FUDGED
STAGES	STOOPS	******	LUNULA	BULGED	FUELED
STAINS	STOPES	STABLY	MUCOSA	BULKED	FUGLED
STAIRS	STORES	STAGEY	NUMINA	BUMMED	FULGID
STAKES	STORKS	STAGGY	NUTRIA	BUMPED	FULLED
STALES	STORMS	STALKY	PURANA	BUNGED	FUNDED
STALKS	STOUPS	STARRY	QUAGGA	BUNKED	FUNKED
STALLS	STOUTS	STEADY	QUANTA	BUNTED	FURLED
STAMPS	STOVES	STEAMY	QUOTHA	BUOYED	FURRED
STANDS	STRAPS	STEELY	RUMINA	BURIED	FUSSED
STAPES	STRASS	STICKY	RUSSIA	BURKED	FUZZED
STARES	STRAWS	STILLY	SULPHA	BURLED	GUIDED
STARTS	STRAYS	STINGY	TUNDRA	BURNED	GULFED
STASES	STRESS	STITHY	TUNICA	BURPED	GULLED
STASIS	STREWS	STOCKY	******	BURRED	GULPED
STATES	STRIPS	STODGY	-U---B	BUSHED	GUMMED
STATUS	STROPS	STOGEY	******	BUSIED	GUNNED
STAVES	STRUMS	STOREY	HUBBUB	BUSSED	GUSHED
STEAKS	STRUTS	STORMY	PUNJAB	BUSTED	GUTTED
STEALS	STUBBS	STRAWY	SUBDEB	BUTTED	HUFFED
STEAMS	STUFFS	STRIPY	SUBURB	BUZZED	HUGGED
STEEDS	STULLS	STUBBY	SUPERB	CUBBED	HULKED
STEELS	STUMPS	STUFFY	******	CUBOID	HULLED
STEEPS	STUNTS	STUMPY	-U---C	CUFFED	HUMMED
STEERS	STUPAS	STURDY	******	CULLED	HUMPED
STEINS	STUPES	******	BUSTIC	CULMED	HUNTED
STELES	STYLES	-U---A	CUPRIC	CUPPED	HURLED
STERES	STYLUS	******	FUSTIC	CURBED	HUSHED
STERNS	UTERUS	AURIGA	JUDAIC	CURDED	HUSKED
STEVES	UTTERS	AURORA	LUETIC	CURLED	HUTTED
STICKS	UTURNS	BUCKRA	PUBLIC	CURSED	JUDGED
STILES	XTSTUS	BUDDHA	QUEBEC	CURVED	JUGGED
STILLS	******	CUESTA	QUINIC	CUSPED	JUMPED
STILTS	-T---T	CUPOLA	RUSTIC	CUSPID	JUNKED
STINGS	******	DUENNA	SUOMIC	CUSSED	JUTTED
STINKS	ATTEST	EUBOEA	TURKIC	DUBBED	LUFFED
STINTS	STOMAT	EUPNEA	******	DUCKED	LUGGED
STIPES	STRAIT	EUREKA	-U---D	DUELED	LULLED
STIRKS	STREET	EUROPA	******	DUFFED	LUMPED
STIRPS	STRICT	FULCRA	AUGEND	DULLED	LUNGED
STOATS	STRIPT	GUIANA	AUTOED	DUMPED	LURKED
STOCKS	STUART	GUINEA	BUCKED	DUNGED	LUSHED
STOICS	UTMOST	GURKHA	BUCKED	DUNKED	LUSTED

MUCKED	SUMMED	CUISSE	LUSTRE	SUBDUE	PUKING
MUCOID	SUNGOD	CUPTIE	LUXATE	SUBTLE	PULING
MUDDED	SUNNED	CUPULE	MUCKLE	SUCKLE	PUTLOG
MUFFED	SUPPED	CURARE	MUCOSE	SUNDAE	QUAHOG
MUGGED	SURFED	CURATE	MUDDLE	SUPINE	RUEING
MULLED	SURGED	CURDLE	MUFFLE	SUPPLE	RULING
MUMMED	SUSSED	CURIAE	MUMBLE	SUTTEE	SUNDOG
MUSHED	TUBBED	CURULE	MURINE	SUTURE	TUBING
MUSSED	TUCKED	CUTTLE	MUSCAE	TUBATE	TUNING
NUDGED	TUFTED	DUFFLE	MUSCLE	TUBULE	******
NUMBED	TUGGED	DULCIE	MUSTEE	TUILLE	-U---H
NURSED	TUNNED	DUNDEE	MUTATE	TUMBLE	******
NUTTED	TUPPED	EUCHRE	MUTULE	TURTLE	CULTCH
OUSTED	TURBID	EUGENE	MUZZLE	TUSSLE	DUDISH
OUTBID	TURFED	EUNICE	NUANCE	TUYERE	DULUTH
OUTDID	TURGID	EUROPE	NUBBLE	VULVAE	EUNUCH
PUFFED	TURNED	FUDDLE	NUBILE	YUPPIE	GULLAH
PUGGED	TUSHED	FUMBLE	NUCHAE	******	HURRAH
PULLED	TUSKED	FURORE	NUZZLE	-U---F	JUBBAH
PULPED	TUTTED	FUSILE	PUDDLE	******	JUDITH
PULSED	YUKKED	FUTILE	PUGREE	CUTOFF	JUTISH
PUMPED	******	FUTURE	PUISNE	GUSTAF	MULISH
PUNNED	-U---E	GUIMPE	PULQUE	PUTOFF	MULLAH
PUNTED	******	GURGLE	PUMICE	RUNOFF	MUNICH
PUPPED	AUBADE	GUSSIE	PUPATE	******	NULLAH
PUREED	AUDILE	GUTTAE	PURFLE	-U---G	PUNISH
PURGED	AUGITE	GUTTLE	PURINE	******	PURDAH
PURLED	AUNTIE	GUZZLE	PURPLE	BUSING	PUTSCH
PURRED	AURATE	HUCKLE	PURSUE	BUYING	QUENCH
PURSED	BUBBLE	HUDDLE	PUTTEE	CUBING	QUITCH
PUSHED	BUCKLE	HUGHIE	PUZZLE	CURING	RUPIAH
PUTRID	BUDDLE	HUMANE	QUAERE	DUGONG	SUNNAH
PUTTED	BUDGIE	HUMBLE	QUARTE	DUOLOG	TUSSAH
QUAKED	BULLAE	HURDLE	QUATRE	DUPING	ZURICH
QUEUED	BUMBLE	HURTLE	QUINCE	DURING	******
QUIRED	BUNCHE	HUSTLE	RUBACE	FUMING	-U---I
QUOTED	BUNDLE	JUGATE	RUBBLE	FUSING	******
RUBBED	BUNGLE	JUGGLE	RUDDLE	FUZING	EURIPI
RUCKED	BURBLE	JUJUBE	RUFFLE	GUYING	LUMINI
RUFFED	BURDIE	JUMBLE	RUGATE	HUMBUG	NUCLEI
RUGGED	BURGEE	JUNGLE	RUGOSE	LUDWIG	QUADRI
RUINED	BURGLE	JUNKIE	RUMBLE	LURING	TULADI
RUSHED	BURSAE	LUCILE	RUMPLE	LUTING	******
RUSTED	BUSTLE	LUCITE	RUNDLE	MUSING	-U---K
RUTTED	BUTANE	LUNATE	RUSINE	MUSKEG	******
SUCKED	CUBAGE	LUNGEE	RUSTLE	MUTING	LUBECK
SUITED	CUDDIE	LUNULE	RUTILE	NUTMEG	MUKLUK
SULKED	CUDDLE	LUPINE	SUABLE	OUTING	MUZHIK

NUDNIK	MUTISM	KUCHEN	SUBITO	CUTLER	LUNGER
SUSLIK	NUDISM	LUBLIN	SULPHO	CUTTER	LUNKER
******	PURISM	LUCIAN	TUPELO	DUCKER	LURKER
-U---L	PUTNAM	LUCIEN	TUXEDO	DUELER	LUSHER
******	QUORUM	LUMPEN	******	DUFFER	LUSTER
BUCCAL	SUFISM	MUFFIN	-U---P	DUIKER	LUTHER
BULBEL	******	MULLEN	******	DULLER	MUCKER
BULBIL	-U---N	MUSLIN	BUNYIP	DUMPER	MUDDER
BULBUL	******	MUTTON	BURLAP	DUNBAR	MUGGAR
BURIAL	AUBURN	NUBBIN	HUBCAP	DUNKER	MUGGER
BURSAL	AUGEAN	NUBIAN	MUDCAP	DURBAR	MUGGUR
BUSHEL	AUSTEN	OUTMAN	PUSHUP	DUSTER	MULLER
CUDGEL	AUSTIN	OUTRAN	TUNEUP	EUCHER	MUMMER
CUNEAL	AUTUMN	OUTRUN	TURNIP	EUDOAR	MURDER
CUPFUL	BUCHAN	PUFFIN	TURNUP	FUELER	MURMUR
CURIAL	BUMKIN	PULLIN	******	FUHRER	MUSHER
DUFFEL	BUNION	PURLIN	-U---R	FULLER	MUSTER
FULFIL	BUNSEN	QUEZON	******	FULMAR	MUTTER
FUNGAL	BUNYAN	RUNYON	AUSTER	FUMIER	NUMBER
FUNNEL	BURDEN	RUSKIN	AUTHOR	FURFUR	NURSER
GUNNEL	BURTON	SUBORN	BUCKER	FUSSER	NUTTER
JUGFUL	BUSKIN	SUDDEN	BUDDER	GUIDER	OUSTER
JUMBAL	BUSMAN	SULLEN	BUFFER	GUITAR	PUCKER
KUMMEL	BUSMEN	SULTAN	BUGGER	GULPER	PUFFER
LUTEAL	BUTTON	SUMMON	BUGLER	GUNNAR	PULLER
MURIEL	BUXTON	SUNKEN	BULBAR	GUNNER	PULPER
MUSSEL	DUBBIN	SUNTAN	BULGAR	GUNTER	PULSAR
MUTUAL	DUBLIN	SUTTON	BULGER	GUSHER	PUMPER
PUMMEL	DUDEEN	TUCHUN	BUMMER	GUTTER	PUNIER
RUEFUL	DUNCAN	TUCSON	BUMPER	HUMBER	PUNNER
RUNNEL	DUNLIN	TURBAN	BUNKER	HUMMER	PUNTER
TUNNEL	DUODEN	TUREEN	BURGER	HUMOUR	PURGER
TUSSAL	DURBAN	TUSCAN	BURLER	HUNGER	PURLER
VULVAL	DURIAN	VULCAN	BURNER	HUNTER	PURSER
******	DURION	******	BURSAR	HURLER	PUSHER
-U---M	FULTON	-U---O	BUSKER	HURTER	PUTTER
******	FUSAIN	******	BUSTER	HUSKER	QUAKER
AUTISM	FUSION	AUSTRO	BUTLER	HUSSAR	QUASAR
BUNKUM	GUANIN	BURGOO	BUTTER	JUDGER	QUAVER
CUBISM	GUENON	CUCKOO	BUZZER	JUICER	QUIVER
CUPRUM	GUIDON	DUELLO	CULLER	JUMPER	QUOTER
CURIUM	GULDEN	JUDAEO	CULVER	JUNIOR	RUBBER
CUSTOM	GUNMAN	LUMINO	CUMBER	JUNKER	RUDDER
DUMDUM	GUNMEN	NUNCIO	CUNNER	KULTUR	RUGGER
DURHAM	HUDSON	PUEBLO	CUPPER	LUBBER	RUINER
LUTEUM	JUDEAN	QUARTO	CURLER	LUGGER	RUMMER
MUSEUM	JULIAN	RUBATO	CURSOR	LUMBAR	RUMOUR
MUSLIM	JUSTIN	RUBIGO	CUSTER	LUMBER	RUNNER

RUSHER	BURROS	FURIES	LUGERS	QUILTS	TURCOS
SUBTER	BURSAS	FURORS	LUMENS	QUINTS	TURKIS
SUCCOR	BURSES	FURZES	LUNETS	QUIPUS	TURVES
SUCKER	BURSTS	FUSEES	LUNGES	QUIRES	TUSHES
SUFFER	BUSHES	FUSILS	LUNGIS	QUIRKS	TUSSIS
SUITOR	BUSIES	FUSSES	LURERS	QUIRTS	TUTORS
SULFUR	BUSSES	FUZEES	LUSHES	QUOINS	TUTTIS
SUMMER	BUTTES	FUZILS	MUCOUS	QUOITS	YUCCAS
SUMNER	BUYERS	FUZZES	MUFTIS	QUOTAS	YUPONS
SUNDER	BUZZES	GUACOS	MULCTS	QUOTES	******
SUPPER	CUBANS	GUANOS	MURALS	RUBENS	-U---T
SURFER	CUBEBS	GUARDS	MURRES	RUBIES	******
SURGER	CUBITS	GUAVAS	MUSHES	RUBLES	AUGUST
SUTLER	CULETS	GUESTS	MUSSES	RUCHES	AUKLET
TUBBER	CULLIS	GUIDES	NUBIAS	RUCKUS	AURIST
TUCKER	CULTUS	GUILDS	NUDGES	RUFOUS	BUCKET
TUMOUR	CUMINS	GUILES	NURSES	RUGOUS	BUDGET
TURNER	CUPELS	GUILTS	OUNCES	RULERS	BUFFET
TUSKER	CURERS	GUISES	OUSELS	RUMBAS	BULLET
TUSSAR	CURIES	GUMBOS	OUTERS	RUMORS	BURBOT
VULGAR	CURIOS	GUMMAS	OUZELS	RUMPUS	BURNET
VULVAR	CURSES	GUSHES	PULERS	RUNINS	CUBIST
ZUIDER	CURTIS	HUBRIS	PULSES	RUNONS	CULLET
ZUYDER	CURVES	HUGHES	PUNKAS	RUPEES	CURVET
******	CUSCUS	HUMANS	PUNTOS	RUSHES	CUSHAT
-U---S	CUSPIS	HUMORS	PUPILS	SUBAHS	CUTEST
******	CUSSES	HURONS	PUREES	SUCRES	CUTLET
AUDADS	CUSSOS	HUSHES	PURGES	SUEDES	CUTOUT
AUDITS	CUSTOS	JUDAHS	PURSES	SUGARS	DUGOUT
AUGERS	CUTEYS	JUDGES	PUSHES	SUITES	DULCET
AUGHTS	CUTIES	JUICES	PUSSES	SULCUS	DUPLET
AUGURS	CUTINS	JULEPS	PUTONS	SUMACS	FUNEST
AUREUS	CUTLAS	JULIAS	QUACKS	SUNUPS	GULLET
AUROUS	CUTUPS	JULIES	QUAFFS	SUPERS	GUSSET
AUXINS	DUCATS	JULIUS	QUAILS	SURAHS	GUTTAT
BUBALS	DULLES	JUNCOS	QUAKES	SURGES	HUBERT
BUBOES	DUNCES	JUNIUS	QUALMS	SUSANS	HUGEST
BUDGES	DUPERS	JUNTAS	QUANTS	SUSIES	JULIET
BUGLES	DURESS	JUPONS	QUARKS	SUTRAS	JUNKET
BUILDS	DUTIES	JURATS	QUARTS	TUBERS	JURANT
BULGES	FUCOUS	JURELS	QUEANS	TULIPS	JURIST
BUNCOS	FUDGES	JURIES	QUEENS	TULLES	KUWAIT
BURANS	FUGIOS	JURORS	QUEERS	TUMORS	LUCENT
BURGHS	FUGLES	JUSTUS	QUELLS	TUNERS	LUTIST
BURGOS	FUGUES	KULAKS	QUERNS	TUNGUS	MULLET
BURIES	FUMOUS	KUMISS	QUESTS	TUNICS	MUSCAT
BURINS	FUNDUS	LUCIAS	QUEUES	TUPIKS	MUSKET
BURKES	FUNGUS	LUCIUS	QUILLS	TUQUES	MUSKIT

MUSTNT	*****	GUNSHY	SUNDRY	*****	*****
MUTANT	-U---W	HUGELY	SUPPLY	-V---L	-V---Y
NUDIST	*****	HUMBLY	SURELY	*****	*****
NUGGET	BURROW	HUMIFY	SURETY	AVOWAL	AVIARY
NUTLET	CURFEW	HUMPTY	SURREY	*****	AVIDLY
OUTFIT	CURLEW	HUNGRY	SURVEY	-V---N	EVENLY
OUTLET	CUSHAW	HURLEY	TUMEFY	*****	EVILLY
OUTPUT	FURROW	HURRAY	TURKEY	AVALON	OVALLY
OUTSAT	GUFFAW	HUXLEY	*****	AVIDIN	OVERLY
OUTSET	LUDLOW	JUNGLY	-U---Z	EVELYN	*****
OUTSIT	OUTLAW	JUSTLY	*****	*****	-W---A
OUTWIT	QUAPAW	LUNACY	JUAREZ	-V---O	*****
PULLET	SUNBOW	LUXURY	QUARTZ	*****	RWANDA
PULPIT	SUNDEW	MULLEY	*****	AVERNO	*****
PUNDIT	*****	MURRAY	-V---A	OVERDO	-W---D
PUPPET	-U---X	MURREY	*****	*****	*****
PUREST	*****	MUTINY	AVESTA	-V---R	AWAKED
PURIST	AUSPEX	NUBBLY	*****	*****	SWAGED
PUTOUT	DUPLEX	NUDELY	-V---C	AVATAR	SWAYED
PUTPUT	LUMMOX	NUDITY	*****	AVOWER	SWIPED
QUAINT	MUSKOX	NUMBLY	OVISAC	EVADER	TWINED
RUDEST	OUTFOX	OUTCRY	*****	OVULAR	TWOULD
RUNLET	SUFFIX	OUTLAY	-V---D	UVULAR	*****
RUNOUT	SURTAX	PUDDLY	*****	*****	-W---E
RUPERT	SUSSEX	PUGGRY	AVOWED	-V---S	*****
RUSSET	*****	PULLEY	EVADED	*****	AWHILE
SUBLET	-U---Y	PUNCHY	EVENED	AVAILS	GWYNNE
SUBMIT	*****	PUNILY	EVOKED	AVERTS	SWANEE
SUMMIT	AUBREY	PURELY	*****	AVERYS	SWATHE
SUNHAT	AUDREY	PURIFY	-V---E	AVISOS	SWERVE
SUNLIT	AUGURY	PURITY	*****	AVOIDS	SWINGE
SUNSET	BUBBLY	PURVEY	AVENGE	EVADES	SWIPLE
SUREST	BUNCHY	PUSSEY	AVENUE	EVENTS	TWELVE
TUCKET	BURLEY	PUSSLY	AVERSE	EVERTS	TWINGE
TUFFET	BUSHEY	QUAGGY	AVIATE	EVICTS	*****
TUMULT	BUSILY	QUALMY	EVINCE	EVITAS	-W---G
TURBIT	CUDDLY	QUARRY	EVOLVE	EVOKES	*****
TURBOT	CULLAY	QUEASY	SVELTE	OVIBOS	AWEING
TURRET	CURACY	QUINCY	UVULAE	OVULES	AWNING
*****	CURTLY	QUINSY	YVONNE	UVULAS	OWNING
-U---U	CURTSY	RUDELY	*****	*****	*****
*****	CUTELY	RUNWAY	-V---H	-V---T	-W--H
BUREAU	DUDLEY	SUBTLY	*****	*****	*****
JUNEAU	DUMBLY	SUBWAY	AVOUCH	AVAUNT	AWEIGH
MUUMUU	DUMPTY	SUDARY	-V---K	AVOCET	OWLISH
PUSHTU	DUPERY	SUGARY	*****	AVOSET	SWARTH
*****	EULOGY	SULTRY	*****	EVERET	SWATCH
-U---V	GUILTY	SUNDAY	DVORAK		SWITCH
*****					TWITCH
GUSTAV					

******	SWEETS	******	******	EXSECT	******
-W---J	SWELLS	-X---A	-X---N	EXSERT	-Y---D
******	SWIFTS	******	******	EXTANT	******
SWARAJ	SWILLS	AXILLA	AXEMAN	EXTENT	BYROAD
	SWINGS	EXACTA	AXEMEN	EXTORT	BYWORD
-W---L	SWIPES	EXEDRA	EXAMEN	******	CYANID
******	SWIRLS	******	EXOGEN	-X---Y	CYCLED
AWHEEL	SWOONS	-X---C	EXTERN	******	CYMOID
AWHIRL	SWOOPS	******	OXYGEN	EXEQUY	EYELID
SWIVEL	SWORDS	EXILIC	******	EXPIRY	GYPPED
TWIBIL	TWANGS	EXOTIC	-X---R	******	HYBRID
******	TWEAKS	OXALIC	******	-Y---A	HYMNED
-W---N	TWEEDS	******	EXETER	******	MYRIAD
******	TWEETS	-X---D	EXMOOR	AYESHA	XYLOID
AWAKEN	TWERPS	******	******	AYMARA	******
AWOKEN	TWILLS	AXSEED	-X---S	HYGEIA	-Y---E
SWEDEN	TWINES	EXCEED	******	MYOPIA	******
******	TWIRLS	EXILED	AXIOMS	MYRICA	AYEAYE
-W---R	TWIRPS	EXITED	AXONES	MYXOMA	BYEBYE
******	TWISTS	EXPAND	EXACTS	NYMPHA	BYGONE
TWINER	******	EXPEND	EXALTS	PYEMIA	BYLANE
TWOFER	-W---T	EXTEND	EXCELS	PYJAMA	BYLINE
******	******	EXUDED	EXCESS	PYRRHA	BYNAME
-W---S	DWIGHT	OXEYED	EXERTS	PYTHIA	CYBELE
******	SWIVET	OXFORD	EXILES	PYURIA	CYMENE
AWAITS	TWILIT	******	EXISTS	SYLVIA	CYMOSE
AWAKES	TWOBIT	-X---E	EXODUS	SYNURA	CYRENE
AWARDS	******	******	EXPELS	ZYGOMA	GYRATE
AWLESS	-W---Y	AXLIKE	EXTOLS	******	GYROSE
DWARFS	******	EXCIDE	EXTRAS	-Y---C	HYDRAE
DWELLS	AWEARY	EXCISE	EXUDES	******	HYPHAE
GWENNS	SWAMPY	EXCITE	EXULTS	CYANIC	LYSINE
OWLETS	SWANKY	EXCUSE	EXURBS	CYCLIC	LYTTAE
OWNERS	SWARTY	EXHALE	OXALIS	CYMRIC	MYCETE
SWAGES	SWEATY	EXHUME	OXBOWS	CYSTIC	MYRTLE
SWAILS	SWEENY	EXPIRE	OXEYES	DYADIC	PYRENE
SWAINS	SWEEPY	EXPOSE	OXIDES	HYDRIC	PYRITE
SWALES	SWIRLY	OXHIDE	OXLIPS	HYMNIC	PYRONE
SWAMIS	TWANGY	******	******	HYPNIC	PYROPE
SWAMPS	TWEAKY	-X---H	-X---T	MYOPIC	SYLVAE
SWARDS	TWENTY	******	******	MYRMEC	TYRONE
SWARMS	TWIGGY	EXARCH	EXCEPT	MYSTIC	XYLENE
SWATHS	TWISTY	******	EXEMPT	MYTHIC	XYLITE
SWEARS	TWOPLY	-X---L	EXEUNT	PYEMIC	XYLOSE
SWEATS	TWOWAY	******	EXHORT	PYKNIC	ZYGOTE
SWEDES		OXTAIL	EXPECT	PYTHIC	******
SWEEPS			EXPERT	SYNDIC	-Y---F
			EXPORT	SYRIAC	******
					MYSELF

******	PYTHON	CYRILS	LYRIST	******	ACACIA
-Y---G	SYLVAN	EYASES	SYNDET	-Z---S	AEACUS
******	SYPHON	EYRIES	TYBALT	******	APACHE
DYEING	SYRIAN	GYNOUS	TYPIST	AZINES	BEACHY
EYEING	TYCOON	GYRONS	TYRANT	AZOLES	BEACON
GYBING	TYMPAN	HYADES	******	AZORES	BLACKS
GYVING	TYPHON	HYBRIS	-Y---U	AZTECS	BRACED
LYSING	TYRIAN	HYDRAS	******	AZURES	BRACER
TYPING	WYSTAN	HYDROS	KYUSHU	******	BRACES
******	WYVERN	HYENAS	RYUKYU	--AA--	BRACHI
-Y---H	******	HYMENS	******	******	BRACHY
******	-Y---O	HYOIDS	-Y---W	CRAALS	BRACTS
BYPATH	******	HYPNOS	******	ISAACS	CHACMA
******	CYRANO	LYCEES	BYBLOW	KRAALS	CLACKS
-Y---I	DYNAMO	LYDIAS	******	******	CRACKS
******	GYNECO	LYNXES	-Y---X	--AB--	CRACKY
MYTHOI	HYMENO	LYRICS	******	******	CRACOW
******	LYMPHO	LYSINS	SYNTAX	ANABAS	DEACON
-Y---K	NYMPHO	MYOPES	SYRINX	ARABEL	DRACHM
******	TYPHLO	MYOSIS	******	ARABIA	ENACTS
BYTALK	******	MYRNAS	-Y---Y	ARABIC	EPACTS
BYWORK	-Y---P	MYTHOS	******	ARABLE	EXACTA
DYBBUK	******	NYLONS	BYPLAY	ATABAL	EXACTS
******	EYECUP	NYMPHS	SYDNEY	CHABUK	FIACRE
-Y---L	HYSSOP	PYLONS	SYLPHY	CRABBY	FLACKS
******	******	PYOSIS	SYRUPY	DOABLE	FLACON
CYMBAL	-Y---R	PYRANS	SYZYGY	DRABLY	FRACAS
EYEFUL	******	PYXIES	TYPIFY	ENABLE	GLACES
HYETAL	CYCLER	SYBILS	VYRNWY	FLABBY	GLACIS
HYMNAL	CYPHER	SYCEES	******	GRABEN	GRACED
HYPHAL	HYSTER	SYLPHS	-Z---A	ISABEL	GRACES
SYMBOL	OYSTER	SYLVAS	******	LIABLE	GRACIE
******	SYPHER	SYNODS	AZALEA	SCABBY	GUACOS
-Y---M	XYSTER	SYRUPS	******	SEABEE	KNACKS
******	******	TYPHUS	-Z---C	SHABBY	LEACHY
GYPSUM	-Y---S	XYLANS	******	STABLE	NIACIN
LYCEUM	******	XYLEMS	AZONIC	STABLY	ORACHS
LYRISM	BYLAWS	XYLOLS	AZOTIC	SUABLE	ORACLE
SYSTEM	BYPASS	XYSTOS	OZONIC	TEABAG	PEACHY
-Y---N	BYSSUS	-Y---T	******	UNABLE	PLACED
******	BYWAYS	******	-Z---H	USABLE	PLACER
CYANIN	CYCADS	BYPAST	UZZIAH	USABLY	PLACES
CYMLIN	CYCLES	CYGNET	******	VIABLE	PLACET
CYPRIN	CYGNUS	DYNAST	-Z---L	******	PLACID
HYPHEN	CYMARS	EYELET	******	--AC--	PLACKS
MYELIN	CYMOUS	EYEOUT	AZAZEL	******	POACHY
MYOSIN	CYNICS	FYLFOT	AZRAEL	ABACAS	QUACKS
	CYPRUS			ABACUS	REACTS

SEACOW	GRADER	CHAFER	QUAGGY	FRAILS	KRAKEN
SHACKO	GRADES	CHAFES	SHAGGY	FRAISE	LEAKED
SHACKS	GRADIN	CHAFFS	SLAGGY	GLAIRS	PEAKED
SLACKS	GRADUS	CHAFFY	SNAGGY	GLAIRY	QUAKED
SMACKS	HEADED	CRAFTS	STAGED	GRAINS	QUAKER
SNACKS	HEADER	CRAFTY	STAGER	GRAINY	QUAKES
SPACAE	HEADON	DEAFEN	STAGES	ISAIAH	SHAKEN
SPACED	HYADES	DEAFLY	STAGEY	KRAITS	SHAKER
SPACER	IBADAN	DRAFFS	STAGGY	LIAISE	SHAKES
SPACES	ISADOR	DRAFFY	SWAGED	PLAICE	SHAKOS
STACIE	LEADED	DRAFTS	SWAGES	PLAIDS	SLAKED
STACKS	LEADEN	DRAFTY	TRAGIC	PLAINS	SLAKES
STACTE	LEADER	GRAFTS	TRAGUS	PLAINT	SNAKED
STACYS	LEADIN	LEAFED	USAGES	PLAITS	SNAKES
TEACUP	LOADED	LOAFED	******	PRAISE	SOAKED
TRACED	LOADER	LOAFER	--AH--	QUAILS	SOAKER
TRACER	MEADOW	PIAFFE	******	QUAINT	STAKED
TRACES	QUADRI	QUAFFS	BRAHMA	SNAILS	STAKES
TRACHE	READER	SHAFTS	BRAHMS	SPAITS	WEAKEN
TRACHY	SEADOG	SNAFUS	GRAHAM	STAINS	WEAKER
TRACKS	SHADED	STAFFS	PEAHEN	STAIRS	WEAKLY
TRACTS	SHADES	******	QUAHOG	STAITH	******
WHACKS	SHADOW	--AG--	SPAHIS	SWAILS	--AL--
WRACKS	SPADED	******	UTAHAN	SWAINS	******
******	SPADER	ADAGES	******	TRAILS	ALALIA
--AD--	SPADES	ADAGIO	--AI--	TRAINS	AMALIE
******	SPADIX	ARAGON	******	TRAITS	ANALOG
ABADAN	STADIA	BEAGLE	AVAILS	WRAITH	AVALON
ACADIA	THADDY	CRAGGY	AWAITS	******	AZALEA
AMADOU	THADYS	DRAGEE	BAAING	--AJ--	BAALIM
ANADEM	TRADED	DRAGON	BLAINS	******	BIALYS
BEADED	TRADER	FLAGGY	BLAISE	ACAJOU	CHALCO
BEADLE	TRADES	FLAGON	BRAIDS	******	CHALEH
BLADED	TSADES	IMAGED	BRAILS	--AK--	CHALET
BLADES	VEADAR	IMAGES	BRAINS	******	CHALKS
CRADLE	WOADED	LAAGER	BRAINY	AWAKED	CHALKY
DEADEN	******	LEAGUE	BRAISE	AWAKEN	COALED
DEADLY	--AE--	MEAGER	BRAIZE	AWAKES	COALER
DIADEM	******	MEAGRE	CHAINS	BEAKED	DEALER
DYADIC	ACAENA	ONAGER	CHAIRS	BEAKER	DIALED
EVADED	CHAETA	ONAGRI	CHAISE	BRAKED	DIALER
EVADER	CHAETO	PHAGIA	CLAIMS	BRAKES	DIALOG
EVADES	GRAECO	PLAGAL	CLAIRE	CRAKES	DOALLS
GLADES	QUAERE	PLAGIO	CRAIGS	DRAKES	EXALTS
GLADLY	URAEUS	PLAGUE	DRAINS	FLAKED	FEALTY
GLADYS	******	PLAGUY	ELAINE	FLAKER	FOALED
GOADED	--AF--	PRAGUE	FLAILS	FLAKES	GOALIE
GRADED	******	QUAGGA	FLAIRS	KHAKIS	HEALED
	BIAFRA				
	CHAFED				

HEALER	THALIA	SCAMPS	CLANKS	MOANED	VIANDS
HEALTH	URALIC	SEAMAN	CRANED	NUANCE	WEANED
ICALLY	VIALED	SEAMED	CRANES	ORANGE	WEANER
ITALIC	WEALDS	SEAMEN	CRANIA	ORANGS	WHANGS
KOALAS	WEALTH	SEAMER	CRANIO	PEANUT	YEANED
MEALIE	WHALED	SEAMUS	CRANKS	PHANON	******
ORALLY	WHALER	SHAMAN	CRANKY	PIANOS	--AO--
OVALLY	WHALES	SHAMED	CRANNY	PLANAR	******
OXALIC	WOALDS	SHAMES	CYANIC	PLANCH	GIAOUR
OXALIS	ZEALOT	SHAMMY	CYANID	PLANCK	******
PEALED	******	SHAMUS	CYANIN	PLANED	--AP--
PSALMS	--AM--	STAMEN	DIANAS	PLANER	******
QUALMS	******	STAMIN	DIANES	PLANES	ADAPTS
QUALMY	AGAMAS	STAMPS	ELANDS	PLANET	AGAPAE
REALES	AGAMIC	SWAMIS	FIANCE	PLANKS	CHAPEL
REALLY	ALAMOS	SWAMPS	FLANGE	PLANTS	CHAPES
REALMS	ATAMAN	SWAMPY	FLANKS	PRANCE	CRAPED
REALTY	BEAMED	TEAMED	FRANCE	PRANKS	CRAPES
RIALTO	BLAMED	THAMES	FRANCK	QUANTA	DIAPER
ROALDS	BLAMES	TRAMPS	FRANCO	QUANTS	DRAPED
SCALAR	CHAMMY	WHAMMY	FRANCS	RWANDA	DRAPER
SCALDS	CHAMPS	******	FRANKS	SCANTY	DRAPES
SCALED	CLAMMY	--AN--	GDANSK	SEANCE	ELAPSE
SCALER	CLAMOR	******	GIANTS	SHANDY	ETAPES
SCALES	CLAMPS	ACANTH	GLANCE	SHANKS	FRAPPE
SCALPS	CRAMBO	AMANDA	GLANDS	SHANTY	GRAPES
SEALED	CRAMPS	AMANIA	GRANDE	SLANGY	GRAPHO
SEALER	DRAMAS	ANANAS	GRANGE	SLANTS	GRAPHS
SHALED	ENAMEL	ANANKE	GRANNY	SPANKS	GRAPHY
SHALES	ENAMOR	ARANTA	GRANTS	STANCE	HEAPED
SIALIC	EXAMEN	BEANED	GUANIN	STANCH	LEAPED
SKALDS	FLAMBE	BEANIE	GUANOS	STANDS	LEAPER
SLALOM	FLAMED	BIANCA	IRANIS	STANZA	OKAPIS
SMALLS	FLAMEN	BLANCH	JEANNE	SWANEE	QUAPAW
SMALTI	FLAMES	BLANKS	JOANNA	SWANKY	REAPED
SMALTO	FOAMED	BRANCH	JOANNE	THANAT	REAPER
SPALLS	FRAMED	BRANDS	LEANED	THANES	SCAPES
STALAG	FRAMER	BRANDT	LEANER	THANKS	SEAPEN
STALED	FRAMES	BRANDY	LEANLY	TRANCE	SHAPED
STALER	GLAMIS	BRANNY	LEANTO	TWANGS	SHAPEN
STALES	GRAMME	BRANTS	LIANAS	TWANGY	SHAPER
STALIN	LLAMAS	CHANCE	LIANES	UBANGI	SHAPES
STALKS	LOAMED	CHANCY	LLANOS	UGANDA	SLAPUP
STALKY	REAMED	CHANGE	LOANED	URANIA	SNAPPY
STALLS	REAMER	CHANGS	LUANDA	URANIC	SOAPED
SWALES	ROAMED	CHANTS	MEANER	URANUS	STAPES
THALER	ROAMER	CHANTY	MEANIE	URANYL	STAPLE
THALES	SCAMPI	CLANGS	MEANLY	USANCE	TEAPOT

TEAPOY	DWARFS	ROARED	TEARED	LEASED	ABATOR
UNAPID	ECARTE	ROARER	TIARAS	LEASES	AGATES
WEAPON	EPARCH	SCARAB	WEARER	LIASED	AGATHA
WRAPUP	EXARCH	SCARCE	WHARFS	MEASLY	ALATED
******	FEARED	SCARED	WHARVE	MIASMA	AMATOL
--AQ--	FEARER	SCARER	YEARLY	OCASEY	ANATTO
******	FLARED	SCARES	YEARNS	OMASUM	APATHY
BRAQUE	FLARES	SCARFS	******	PEASEN	AVATAR
CLAQUE	GEARED	SCARPS	--AS--	PEASES	BEATEN
IRAQIS	GHARRI	SEARCH	******	PHASED	BEATER
OPAQUE	GHARRY	SEARED	ABASED	PHASES	BOATED
PLAQUE	GLARED	SEARIN	ABASER	PHASIA	BOATER
******	GLARES	SHARDS	ABASES	PHASIC	CHATTY
--AR--	GNARLS	SHARED	ALASKA	PHASIS	COATED
******	GNARLY	SHARER	BEASTS	PLASHY	COATEE
ACARID	GUARDS	SHARES	BIASED	PLASIA	COATIS
AGARIC	HEARER	SHARKS	BIASES	PLASIS	CRATCH
ALARIC	HEARSE	SHARON	BLASTO	PLASMA	CRATED
ALARMS	HEARST	SHARPS	BLASTS	PLASMO	CRATER
ALARUM	HEARTH	SMARMY	BOASTS	PLASTY	CRATES
ARARAT	HEARTS	SMARTS	BRASHY	QUASAR	DEATHS
ASARUM	HEARTY	SNARED	BRASSY	REASON	DEATHY
AWARDS	HOARDS	SNARER	CEASED	ROASTS	DIATOM
BEARDS	HOARSE	SNARES	CEASES	SEASON	ELATED
BEARED	ICARUS	SNARLS	CHASED	SHASTA	ELATER
BEARER	IMARET	SNARLY	CHASER	SPASMS	ELATES
BLARED	INARCH	SOARED	CHASES	STASES	ENATES
BLARES	INARMS	SOARER	CHASMS	STASIS	FLATLY
BOARDS	JUAREZ	SPARED	CHASSE	TEASED	FLATUS
CHARDS	KNARRY	SPARER	CHASTE	TEASEL	FRATER
CHARED	LEARNS	SPARES	CLASPS	TEASER	GNATHO
CHARES	LEARNT	SPARGE	CLASSY	TEASES	GOATEE
CHARGE	NEARBY	SPARKS	COASTS	TEASET	GRATED
CHARMS	NEARED	SPARRY	CRASIS	TOASTS	GRATER
CHARON	NEARER	SPARSE	ERASED	TRASHY	GRATES
CHARRY	NEARLY	SPARTA	ERASER	UKASES	GRATIN
CHARTS	PEARLS	STARCH	ERASES	UPASES	GRATIS
CLARAS	PEARLY	STARED	EYASES	WEASEL	HEATED
CLARES	PHAROS	STARER	FEASED	WRASSE	HEATER
CLARET	QUARKS	STARES	FEASES	YEASTS	HEATHS
CLAROS	QUARRY	STARRY	FEASTS	YEASTY	HEATHY
COARSE	QUARTE	STARTS	FIASCO	******	HIATUS
DEARER	QUARTO	STARVE	FLASHY	--AT--	ISATIN
DEARIE	QUARTS	SWARAJ	FLASKS	******	LOATHE
DEARLY	QUARTZ	SWARDS	GLASSY	ABATED	MEATUS
DEARTH	REARED	SWARMS	GRASPS	ABATER	MOATED
DHARMA	REARER	SWARTH	GRASSY	ABATES	NEATEN
DHARNA	REARMS	SWARTY	KAASES	ABATIS	NEATER

NEATLY	BEAUTY	LOAVES	BIAXAL	BLAZED	EMBARK
ORATED	CLAUDE	PEAVEY	COAXAL	BLAZER	EMBARS
ORATES	CLAUSE	PRAVDA	COAXED	BLAZES	EMBAYS
ORATOR	FLAUNT	QUAVER	COAXER	BLAZON	GOBANG
PLATAN	FRAUDS	REAVOW	COAXES	BRAZAS	HOBART
PLATED	FRAUEN	SHAVED	FLAXEN	BRAZED	IMBALM
PLATEN	GHAUTS	SHAVEN	FLAXES	BRAZEN	IMBARK
PLATER	GLAUCO	SHAVER	HOAXED	BRAZER	INBAND
PLATES	HEAUME	SHAVES	HOAXER	BRAZES	KABAKA
PLATTE	MIAULS	SLAVED	HOAXES	BRAZIL	KABALA
PRATED	SCAUPS	SLAVER	KLAXON	BRAZOS	KABAYA
PRATER	STAURO	SLAVES	PRAXIS	CRAZED	LOBATE
PRATES	TEAURN	SLAVIC	******	CRAZES	NOBALL
QUATRE	TRAUMA	SPAVIN	--AY--	DIAZIN	REBATE
RIATAS	******	STAVED	******	GLAZED	REBATO
SCATHE	--AV--	STAVES	BRAYED	GLAZER	RIBALD
SCATTY	******	TRAVEL	BRAYER	GLAZES	RIBAND
SEATED	AGAVES	TRAVES	CLAYED	GRAZED	ROBALO
SKATED	ATAVIC	WEAVED	CLAYEY	GRAZER	ROBAND
SKATER	BEAVER	WEAVER	CRAYON	GRAZES	RUBACE
SKATES	BRAVED	WEAVES	DRAYED	PIAZZA	RUBATO
SLATED	BRAVER	******	ELAYNE	PLAZAS	SEBATS
SLATER	BRAVES	--AW--	FLAYED	SMAZES	SUBAHS
SLATES	BRAVOS	******	FLAYER	SNAZZY	TABARD
SNATCH	CRAVAT	ARAWAK	FRAYED	ZSAZSA	TOBAGO
SNATHE	CRAVED	BRAWLS	GRAYED	******	TUBATE
SNATHS	CRAVEN	BRAWNY	GRAYER	--BA--	TYBALT
SPATES	CRAVER	CHAWED	GRAYLY	******	UNBARS
SPATHE	CRAVES	CLAWED	OKAYED	ABBACY	URBANE
STATAL	FLAVIA	CRAWLS	PLAYAS	ALBANY	WABASH
STATED	FLAVIN	CRAWLY	PLAYED	ALBATA	******
STATEN	FLAVOR	DRAWEE	PLAYER	AMBAGE	--BB--
STATER	GRAVED	DRAWER	PRAYED	AMBARI	******
STATES	GRAVEL	DRAWLS	PRAYER	AMBARY	BABBIE
STATIC	GRAVEN	DRAWLY	SLAYER	AUBADE	BABBLE
STATOR	GRAVER	FLAWED	SPAYED	BUBALS	BIBBED
STATUE	GRAVES	GNAWED	STAYED	CABALA	BIBBER
STATUS	GRAVID	GNAWER	STAYER	CABALS	BOBBED
SWATCH	GUAVAS	PRAWNS	SWAYED	CABANA	BOBBER
SWATHE	HEAVED	SEAWAN	THAYER	COBALT	BOBBIE
SWATHS	HEAVEN	SEAWAY	XRAYED	CUBAGE	BOBBIN
THATCH	HEAVER	SHAWLS	******	CUBANS	BOBBLE
VIATIC	HEAVES	SHAWMS	--AZ--	******	BOBBYS
VIATOR	KNAVES	SPAWNS	******	DEBARK	BUBBLE
WRATHY	LEAVED	THAWED	AMAZED	DEBARS	BUBBLY
******	LEAVEN	TRAWLS	AMAZES	DEBASE	COBBER
--AU--	LEAVER	******	AMAZON	DEBATE	COBBLE
******	LEAVES	--AX--	AZAZEL	EMBALM	COBBLY
AVAUNT		******		EMBALM	
BEAUTS		ATAXIA		EMBANK	
		ATAXIC			

CUBBED	NOBBLE	ALBEIT	ALBION	SABINE	******
DABBED	NUBBIN	ALBERT	ALBITE	SABINS	--BM--
DABBER	NUBBLE	AMBERS	AMBITS	SUBITO	******
DABBLE	NUBBLY	AMBERY	BABIED	SYBILS	CABMAN
DEBBIE	PEBBLE	ARBELA	BABIES	TIBIAE	CABMEN
DEBBYS	PEBBLY	CUBEBS	BABISM	TIBIAL	SUBMIT
DIBBED	RABBET	CYBELE	BABIST	TIBIAS	******
DIBBER	RABBIN	EGBERT	BABITE	TOBIAH	--BN--
DIBBLE	RABBIS	ELBERT	CABINS	TOBIAS	******
DOBBER	RABBIT	EMBEDS	COBIAS	TOBIES	COBNUT
DOBBIN	RABBLE	EMBERS	CUBING	TUBING	HOBNOB
DUBBED	RIBBED	FIBERS	CUBISM	UNBIND	******
DUBBIN	RIBBON	GIBERS	CUBIST	******	--BO--
DYBBUK	ROBBED	HABEAS	CUBITS	--BL--	******
FIBBED	ROBBER	HUBERT	DEBITS	******	ABBOTS
FIBBER	ROBBIA	IMBEDS	DOBIES	AMBLED	ARBORI
FOBBED	ROBBIE	KIBEIS	EBBING	AMBLER	ARBORS
GABBED	RUBBED	LABELS	ERBIUM	AMBLES	ARBOUR
GABBER	RUBBER	LIBELS	FABIAN	BIBLES	BABOON
GABBLE	RUBBLE	LUBECK	GABION	BIBLIO	BABOOS
GABBRO	SABBAT	MABELS	GIBING	BYBLOW	BUBOES
GIBBED	SOBBED	OSBERT	GOBIES	CABLED	CABOBS
GIBBER	TABBED	REBECK	GYBING	CABLES	CEBOID
GIBBET	TUBBED	REBECS	HABILE	CABLET	CIBOLS
GIBBON	TUBBER	REBELS	HABITS	COBLES	CUBOID
GOBBET	WABBLE	ROBERT	IMBIBE	DOBLAS	ELBOWS
GOBBLE	WABBLY	RUBENS	JABIRU	DOBLON	EMBODY
HOBBES	WEBBED	SABEAN	JIBING	DUBLIN	EMBOLI
HOBBLE	WOBBLE	SABERS	KABIKI	EMBLEM	EMBOSS
HUBBUB	WOBBLY	SOBERS	KIBITZ	FABLED	EMBOWS
JABBED	YABBER	TUBERS	LABIAL	FABLER	EUBOEA
JABBER	******	UMBELS	LABILE	FABLES	HOBOES
JIBBED	--BC--	UMBERS	LABIUM	GABLED	IMBODY
JIBBER	******	UNBEAR	LIBIDO	GABLES	INBORN
JOBBED	BOBCAT	UNBELT	MOBILE	GIBLET	JABOTS
JOBBER	HUBCAP	UNBEND	MOBIUS	GOBLET	KABOBS
JUBBAH	MOBCAP	UNBENT	NUBIAN	GOBLIN	KIBOSH
KIBBLE	******	UPBEAT	NUBIAS	KIBLAH	KOBOLD
LIBBYS	--BD--	WEBERS	NUBILE	LUBLIN	LABORS
LOBBED	******	XEBECS	ORBING	NOBLER	LABOUR
LOBBER	SUBDEB	ZEBECK	ORBITS	PUBLIC	NABOBS
LUBBER	SUBDUE	ZEBECS	RABIES	ROBLES	NOBODY
MOBBED	******	ZIBETH	REBILL	RUBLES	OSBORN
MOBBER	--BE--	ZIBETS	ROBING	SABLES	OXBOWS
NABBED	******	******	ROBINS	SUBLET	REBORE
NIBBED	ABBESS	--BI--	RUBIES	TABLED	REBORN
NIBBLE	ABBEYS	******	RUBIGO	TABLES	REBOZO
NOBBED	ALBEDO	ABBIES	SABINA	TABLET	RIBOSE
		ALBINO		UMBLES	

ROBOTS	******	ARCANE	UPCAST	INCEPT	DACHAS
SABOTS	--BT--	BECALM	VACANT	INCEST	DACHAU
SUBORN	******	BECAME	VACATE	LUCENT	ESCHAR
TABOOS	DEBTOR	BICARB	VICARS	LYCEES	ESCHER
TABORS	SUBTER	CACAOS	VOCALS	LYCEUM	ESCHEW
UNBOLT	SUBTLE	CICADA	******	MACERS	ETCHED
UNBORN	SUBTLY	CICALA	--CC--	MICELL	ETCHER
UPBOWS	******	COCAIN	******	MYCETE	ETCHES
******	--BU--	CYCADS	BOCCIE	NICELY	EUCHER
--BR--	******	DECADE	BUCCAL	NICENE	EUCHRE
******	ALBUMS	DECALS	COCCAL	NICEST	FICHES
AUBREY	AMBUSH	DECAMP	COCCID	NICETY	FICHUS
COBRAS	ARBUTE	DECANE	COCCUS	NOCENT	INCHED
DEBRIS	ASBURY	DECANT	COCCYX	ORCEIN	INCHES
DOBRAS	AUBURN	DECARE	DECCAN	PACERS	INCHON
ELBRUS	BABULS	DECAYS	HICCUP	RACEME	ISCHIA
EMBRUE	COBURG	DICAST	MECCAN	RACERS	ITCHED
EMBRYO	DEBUGS	DUCATS	MECCAS	RECEDE	ITCHES
FABRIC	DEBUNK	ENCAGE	SOCCER	RECENT	KUCHEN
FIBRIL	DEBUTS	ENCAMP	SUCCOR	RECEPT	LACHES
FIBRIN	FIBULA	ENCASE	YUCCAS	RECESS	LECHER
GIBRAN	IMBUED	ENCASH	******	RICERS	LICHEE
HEBREW	IMBUES	ESCAPE	--CE--	SECEDE	LICHEN
HEBRON	KABUKI	ESCARP	******	SECERN	LOCHIA
HUBRIS	LOBULE	FACADE	ACCEDE	SYCEES	MICHEL
HYBRID	NEBULA	GOCART	ACCENT	ULCERS	NICHED
HYBRIS	REBUFF	HECATE	ACCEPT	******	NICHES
IMBRUE	REBUKE	INCAGE	ACCESS	--CH--	NUCHAE
INBRED	REBUTS	INCASE	ASCEND	******	ORCHID
LABRET	ROBUST	JACANA	ASCENT	AACHEN	ORCHIL
LABRUM	SUBURB	LOCALE	BICEPS	ANCHOR	ORCHIO
LIBRAE	TUBULE	LOCALS	CICELY	ARCHED	ORCHIS
LIBRAS	******	LOCATE	CICERO	ARCHEO	RACHEL
RUBRIC	--BW--	MACACO	DECEIT	ARCHER	RACHIS
SABRAS	******	MACAWS	DECENT	ARCHES	RICHER
UMBRAE	COBWEB	OSCANS	DECERN	ARCHIE	RICHES
UMBRAL	SUBWAY	OSCARS	DICERS	ARCHIL	RICHIE
UMBRAS	******	PECANS	DOCENT	ARCHLY	RICHLY
UNBRED	--BY--	RECALL	EMCEED	ARCHON	ROCHET
VIBRIO	******	RECANT	EMCEES	ARCHYS	RUCHES
ZEBRAS	LIBYAN	RECAPS	EOCENE	BACHED	SACHEM
******	SIBYLS	RECAST	ESCENT	BACHES	SACHET
--BS--	******	SECANT	EXCEED	BUCHAN	TECHNO
******	--CA--	SOCAGE	EXCELS	CACHED	TUCHUN
DOBSON	******	TICALS	EXCEPT	CACHES	URCHIN
GIBSON	ALCAIC	UNCAGE	EXCESS	CACHET	WICHES
ROBSON	ARCADE	UNCAPS	FACERS	CACHOU	YACHTS
	ARCANA	UNCASE	FACETS	COCHIN	ZECHIN

******	SOCIAL	HUCKLE	RACKED	ECCLES	MCCOYS
--CI--	UNCIAL	JACKAL	RACKER	EUCLID	MUCOID
******	******	JACKED	RACKET	MACLES	MUCOSA
AECIAL	--CK--	JACKET	RECKON	NUCLEI	MUCOSE
ARCING	******	JACKIE	RICKED	SOCLES	MUCOUS
CECILE	ARCKED	JACKYS	RICKEY	UNCLAD	NICOLE
CECILS	BACKED	JOCKEY	RICKYS	UNCLES	PICOTS
CECILY	BACKER	JOCKOS	ROCKED	******	RACOON
DECIDE	BECKED	KECKED	ROCKER	--CM--	RECOIL
DECILE	BECKET	KECKLE	ROCKET	******	RECORD
DICING	BECKON	KICKED	ROCKNE	MICMAC	RECOUP
DOCILE	BECKYS	KICKER	RUCKED	SOCMAN	ROCOCO
ENCINA	BICKER	LACKED	RUCKUS	SOCMEN	SECOND
EXCIDE	BUCKED	LACKEY	SACKED	******	TACOMA
EXCISE	BUCKER	LICKED	SACKER	--CN--	TYCOON
EXCITE	BUCKET	LOCKED	SECKEL	******	UNCOCK
FACIAL	BUCKLE	LOCKER	SICKED	PICNIC	UNCOIL
FACIES	BUCKRA	LOCKET	SICKEN	******	UNCORD
FACILE	CACKLE	LOCKUP	SICKER	--CO--	UNCORK
FACING	COCKED	MACKLE	SICKLE	******	WICOPY
FECIAL	COCKER	MICKEY	SICKLY	ACCORD	******
INCISE	COCKLE	MICKLE	SOCKED	ACCOST	--CP--
INCITE	COCKUP	MICKYS	SOCKET	ALCOTT	******
LACIAL	CUCKOO	MOCKED	SUCKED	ALCOVE	SECPAR
LACIER	DECKED	MOCKER	SUCKER	ANCONA	******
LACILY	DECKEL	MOCKUP	SUCKLE	ANCONE	--CR--
LACING	DECKER	MUCKED	TACKED	ASCOTS	******
LUCIAN	DECKLE	MUCKER	TACKER	BACONY	ACCRUE
LUCIAS	DICKER	MUCKLE	TACKEY	BECOME	DACRON
LUCIEN	DICKEY	NECKED	TACKLE	BICORN	DECREE
LUCILE	DICKIE	NICKED	TICKED	COCOAS	ESCROW
LUCITE	DOCKED	NICKEL	TICKER	COCOON	MACRON
LUCIUS	DOCKER	NICKER	TICKET	DACOIT	MICRON
MACING	DOCKET	NICKYS	TICKLE	DECOCT	PICRIC
OSCINE	DUCKED	NOCKED	TUCKED	DECODE	SACRAL
PACIFY	DUCKER	PACKED	TUCKER	DECOKE	SACRED
PACING	FICKLE	PACKER	TUCKET	DECORS	SACRUM
RACIAL	GECKOS	PACKET	VICKYS	DECOYS	SECRET
RACIER	HACKED	PECKED	WICKED	ENCODE	SOCRED
RACILY	HACKEE	PECKER	WICKER	ENCORE	SUCRES
RACINE	HACKER	PICKAX	WICKET	ESCORT	******
RACING	HACKIE	PICKED	******	FUCOID	--CS--
RACISM	HACKLE	PICKER	--CL--	FUCOUS	******
RACIST	HECKLE	PICKET	******	INCOME	FOCSLE
RECIPE	HICKEY	PICKLE	CYCLED	INCORP	TOCSIN
RECITE	HICKOK	PICKUP	CYCLER	JACOBS	TUCSON
RICING	HOCKED	POCKET	CYCLES	JOCOSE	******
SICILY	HOCKEY	PUCKER	CYCLIC	LOCOED	--CT--
					******
					ARCTIC
					CACTUS

DACTYL	MACULE	SEDANS	HUDDLE	TEDDER	ORDEAL
DICTUM	OCCULT	SEDATE	KEDDAH	TEDDYS	ORDERS
DOCTOR	OCCUPY	SUDARY	KIDDED	TODDLE	REDEEM
FACTOR	OCCURS	UPDATE	KIDDER	WADDED	REDEYE
FACTUM	OSCULE	******	KIDDIE	WADDLE	RIDENT
HECTIC	PICULS	--DB--	LADDER	WADDLY	RIDERS
HECTOR	RECURS	******	LADDIE	WEDDED	RODENT
LACTAM	RECUSE	BEDBUG	LIDDED	WIDDIE	RODEOS
LACTIC	SECUND	REDBAY	MADDED	******	RUDELY
LECTOR	SECURE	REDBUD	MADDEN	--DE--	RUDEST
LICTOR	UNCURL	REDBUG	MADDER	******	SEDERS
NECTAR	VACUNA	TIDBIT	MEDDLE	ADDEND	SIDERO
PECTEN	VACUUM	******	MIDDAY	ADDERS	UDDERS
PECTIC	VICUNA	--DC--	MIDDEN	AIDERS	WADERS
PECTIN	******	******	MIDDLE	ALDERS	WEDELN
PICTOR	--CY--	MADCAP	MUDDED	ANDEAN	WIDELY
RECTAL	******	MUDCAP	MUDDER	ARDEBS	WIDENS
RECTOR	ENCYST	REDCAP	MUDDLE	ARDENT	WIDEST
RECTOS	OOCYTE	******	NODDED	BEDECK	YODELS
RECTUM	******	--DD--	NODDER	BEDEWS	******
RECTUS	--DA--	******	NODDLE	BIDETS	--DF--
RICTAL	******	BEDDED	PADDED	BODEGA	******
RICTUS	ADDAMS	BEDDER	PADDLE	CADENT	GADFLY
SECTOR	AUDADS	BIDDEN	PADDYS	CADETS	REDFIN
TACTIC	BEDAUB	BIDDER	PEDDLE	CIDERS	******
VECTOR	CEDARS	BUDDED	PIDDLE	CODEIA	--DG--
VICTIM	DEDANS	BUDDER	PODDED	CODEIN	BADGED
VICTOR	EDDAIC	BUDDHA	PUDDLE	DIDERO	BADGER
******	ENDALL	BUDDLE	PUDDLY	DODECA	BADGES
--CU--	INDABA	CADDIE	RADDLE	DUDEEN	BUDGED
******	IODATE	CADDIS	REDDEN	ELDERS	BUDGES
ACCUSE	JUDAEA	CODDER	REDDER	ELDEST	BUDGET
ALCUIN	JUDAEO	CODDLE	REDDLE	ENDEAR	BUDGIE
DECUMA	JUDAHS	CUDDIE	REDDOG	FADEIN	CADGED
DECURY	JUDAIC	CUDDLE	RIDDED	GIDEON	CADGER
ESCUDO	KODAKS	CUDDLY	RIDDEN	HIDERS	CADGES
EXCUSE	MADAME	DADDLE	RIDDLE	INDEED	CODGER
FACULA	MADAMS	DIDDLE	RODDYS	INDENE	CUDGEL
FECULA	MEDALS	DODDER	RUDDER	INDENT	DODGED
FECUND	MIDAIR	FIDDLE	RUDDLE	JUDEAN	DODGER
HECUBA	ORDAIN	FODDER	SADDEN	MADEUP	DODGES
INCUBI	PEDALS	FUDDLE	SADDER	MODELS	FIDGET
INCURS	PEDANT	GADDED	SADDLE	MODERN	FUDGED
INCUSE	PEDATE	GADDER	SIDDUR	MODEST	FUDGES
JOCUND	PEDATI	GODDAM	SODDED	NUDELY	GADGET
LACUNA	RADARS	HEDDLE	SODDEN	ODDEST	HEDGED
LOCUST	REDACT	HIDDEN	SUDDEN	OEDEMA	HEDGER
MACULA	REDANS	HODDEN	TEDDED	OLDEST	

HEDGES	CEDING	ODDITY	LADLES	INDOWS	******
JUDGED	CODIFY	OLDISH	LUDLOW	IODOUS	--DS--
JUDGER	CODING	PODIUM	MEDLAR	LADOGA	******
JUDGES	DIDIES	RADIAL	MEDLEY	NODOSE	BEDSIT
KEDGED	DUDISH	RADIAN	OODLES	OGDOAD	GODSON
KEDGES	EDDIED	RADIOS	PEDLAR	PODOUS	HUDSON
LEDGER	EDDIES	RADISH	SIDLED	RADOME	PODSOL
LEDGES	EDDISH	RADIUM	SIDLER	REDOES	UNDSET
LODGED	ENDING	RADIUS	SIDLES	REDONE	WADSET
LODGER	ENDIVE	RIDING	******	REDOWA	******
LODGES	FADING	SADIES	--DM--	SODOMY	--DT--
MADGES	GODIVA	SADISM	******	UNDOER	******
MIDGES	HADING	SADIST	AIDMAN	UNDOES	REDTOP
MIDGET	HIDING	SEDILE	AIDMEN	UNDONE	WIDTHS
MIDGUT	INDIAN	SIDING	BADMAN	VADOSE	******
NUDGED	INDICT	SODIUM	BADMEN	WIDOWS	--DU--
NUDGES	INDIES	TEDIUM	CADMUS	******	******
PIDGIN	INDIGO	TIDIED	HODMAN	--DP--	ABDUCT
REDGUM	INDITE	TIDIER	MADMAN	******	ADDUCE
RIDGED	INDIUM	TIDIES	MADMEN	BEDPAN	ADDUCT
RIDGES	IODIDE	TIDILY	RODMAN	******	BEDUIN
SEDGES	IODINE	TIDING	RODMEN	--DR--	CEDULA
WEDGED	IODISM	TODIES	******	******	DEDUCE
WEDGES	IODIZE	UNDIES	--DN--	ANDREA	DEDUCT
WEDGIE	JADING	UNDINE	******	ANDREI	ENDUED
******	JADISH	UPDIKE	KIDNAP	ANDRES	ENDUES
--DH--	JUDITH	VEDIAC	KIDNEY	ANDREW	ENDURE
******	KODIAK	WADIES	NUDNIK	AUDREY	INDUCE
OLDHAM	LADIES	WADING	RADNOR	BEDRID	INDUCT
REDHOT	LADING	ZODIAC	RODNEY	CADRES	INDUED
SADHUS	LADINO	******	SIDNEY	CEDRIC	INDUES
******	LYDIAS	--DJ--	SYDNEY	ELDRED	INDULT
--DI--	MEDIAE	******	******	HEDRAL	MADURA
******	MEDIAL	ODDJOB	--DO--	HEDRON	MADURO
ADDICT	MEDIAN	******	******	HYDRAE	MEDUSA
ADDING	MEDICI	--DK--	ALDOSE	HYDRAS	MODULE
AEDILE	MEDICO	******	ALDOUS	HYDRIC	NODULE
AIDING	MEDICS	BODKIN	ARDORS	HYDROS	ORDURE
ALDINE	MEDIUM	VODKAS	ARDOUR	INDRIS	PODUNK
AUDILE	MODIFY	******	DADOES	KEDRON	RADULA
AUDITS	MODISH	--DL--	DIDOES	MADRAS	REDUCE
BEDIMS	NADINE	******	DODOES	MADRID	SEDUCE
BIDING	NADIRS	ADDLED	EIDOLA	MIDRIB	SEDUMS
BODICE	NIDIFY	ADDLES	ENDOWS	PADRES	UNDULY
BODIED	NIDING	BEDLAM	EUDOAR	PEDROS	VIDUAL
BODIES	NUDISM	DUDLEY	FEDORA	UNDRAW	******
BODILY	NUDIST	LADLED	GADOID		--DW--
BODING	NUDITY	LADLER	INDOOR	UNDREW	******
					GODWIN
					GODWIT

HEDWIG	GREASY	WHEATS	IPECAC	WEEDED	SHEEPS
LUDWIG	GREATS	WREAKS	NIECES	WEEDER	SHEERS
MEDWAY	GREAVE	WREATH	PIECED	******	SHEETS
MIDWAY	IBEAMS	******	PIECER	--EE--	SLEEKS
******	ICEAXE	--EB--	PIECES	******	SLEEKY
--DZ--	IDEALS	******	PRECIS	ADEEMS	SLEEPS
******	IDEATE	AMEBAE	REECHO	BLEEDS	SLEEPY
PODZOL	KNEADS	AMEBAS	SIECLE	BREECH	SLEETS
******	OCEANS	AMEBIC	SPECIE	BREEDS	SLEETY
--EA--	OLEATE	BLEBBY	SPECKS	BREEKS	SLEEVE
******	OREADS	BYEBYE	THECAE	BREEZE	SNEERS
AWEARY	PAEANS	CHEBEC	THECAL	BREEZY	SNEEZE
AYEAYE	PLEACH	EREBUS	TOECAP	CHEEKS	SNEEZY
BLEACH	PLEADS	FEEBLE	WRECKS	CHEEKY	SPEECH
BLEAKS	PLEASE	FEEBLY	******	CHEEPS	SPEEDS
BLEARS	PLEATS	GHEBER	--ED--	CHEERS	SPEEDY
BLEARY	PREACH	GLEBES	******	CHEERY	STEEDS
BLEATS	QUEANS	GREBES	ACEDIA	CHEESE	STEELS
BREACH	QUEASY	ICEBOX	AGEDLY	CHEESY	STEELY
BREADS	SHEARS	LIEBIG	CREDAL	CREEDS	STEEPS
BREAKS	SHEATH	PLEBES	CREDIT	CREEKS	STEERS
BREAMS	SHEAVE	PUEBLO	CREDOS	CREELS	STEEVE
BREAST	SKEANS	QUEBEC	DAEDAL	CREEPS	SWEENY
BREATH	SLEAVE	SHEBAT	DEEDED	CREEPY	SWEEPS
CHEATS	SLEAZY	THEBAE	DREDGE	CREESE	SWEEPY
CLEANS	SMEARS	THEBES	EXEDRA	EMEERS	SWEETS
CLEARS	SMEARY	TREBLE	FEEDER	FLEECE	TWEEDS
CLEATS	SNEAKS	******	FLEDGE	FLEECY	TWEETS
CLEAVE	SNEAKY	--EC--	FLEDGY	FLEERS	WHEELS
CREAKS	SPEAKS	******	FREDAS	FLEETS	WHEEZE
CREAKY	SPEARS	ALECTO	FREDDY	FREELY	WHEEZY
CREAMS	STEADY	AMECHE	GLEDES	FREEST	******
CREAMY	STEAKS	ARECAS	HEEDED	FREEZE	--EF--
CREASE	STEALS	BEECHY	HEEDER	GLEETS	******
CREASY	STEAMS	BRECHT	LIEDER	GLEETY	BEEFED
CREATE	STEAMY	CAECUM	NEEDED	GREECE	CLEFTS
DREADS	SWEARS	CHECKS	NEEDER	GREEDS	EYEFUL
DREAMS	SWEATS	CRECHE	NEEDLE	GREEDY	IREFUL
DREAMT	SWEATY	EJECTA	PLEDGE	GREEKS	OLEFIN
DREAMY	TREADS	EJECTS	REEDED	GREENE	PREFAB
DREARY	TREATS	ELECTS	REEDIT	GREENS	PREFER
FLEAMS	TREATY	ERECTS	SEEDED	GREETS	PREFIX
FREAKS	TWEAKS	EYECUP	SEEDER	KNEELS	REEFED
FREAKY	TWEAKY	FAECAL	SLEDGE	PREENS	REEFER
GLEAMS	UNEASE	FAECES	SUEDES	QUEENS	RUEFUL
GLEAMY	UNEASY	FLECHE	SWEDEN	QUEERS	STEFAN
GLEANS	UREASE	FLECKS	SWEDES	SHEENS	THEFTS
GREASE	WHEALS	ICECAP	THEDAS	SHEENY	USEFUL
					WOEFUL

******	RHEIMS	FIELDS	WIELDS	AMENDS	PLENUM
--EG--	RUEING	FUELED	WIELDY	AMENRA	QUENCH
******	SEEING	FUELER	YIELDS	AMENTI	SCENDS
ALEGAR	SHEIKH	GAELIC	******	AMENTS	SCENES
BREGMA	SHEIKS	HEELED	--EM--	AVENGE	SCENIC
CHEGOE	SHEILA	HEELER	******	AVENUE	SCENTS
DREGGY	SHEILD	HUELVA	ANEMIA	BLENCH	SIENNA
ELEGIT	SKEINS	KEELED	ANEMIC	BLENDE	SPENDS
GREGOS	SLEIGH	KNELLS	APEMAN	BLENDS	STENCH
JAEGER	SPEISS	LUELLA	AXEMAN	BLENNY	STENOG
LIEGES	STEINS	MYELIN	AXEMEN	BRENDA	TAENIA
OMEGAS	TEEING	NIELLI	BREMEN	BRENTS	TEENSY
OREGAN	THEIRS	NIELLO	COEMPT	CLENCH	THENAL
OREGON	THEISM	NOELLE	CREMES	CRENEL	THENAR
PLEGIA	THEIST	OBELUS	DAEMON	DRENCH	THENCE
SIEGED	TIEINS	OCELLI	DEEMED	DUENNA	TRENCH
SIEGES	TOEING	OCELOT	ELEMIS	EDENIC	TRENDS
******	UREIDE	OMELET	ENEMAS	ELENAS	TRENDY
--EH--	******	PEELED	EXEMPT	EMENDS	TWENTY
******	--EK--	PEELER	FOEMAN	EVENED	ULENCE
FOEHNS	******	PRELIM	FOEMEN	EVENLY	UPENDS
HEEHAW	MEEKER	QUELLS	HAEMAL	EVENTS	VIENNA
******	MEEKLY	REELED	HIEMAL	FIENDS	WEENIE
--EI--	PEEKED	REELER	ICEMAN	FLENCH	WEENSY
******	PEEKER	SHELBY	ICEMEN	FLENSE	WHENCE
ACEIUM	REEKED	SHELLS	PIEMAN	FRENCH	WIENER
AGEING	REEKER	SHELLY	PIEMEN	FRENUM	WIENIE
AWEIGH	SEEKER	SHELTY	PREMED	FRENZY	WRENCH
AWEING	SHEKEL	SHELVE	PYEMIA	GUENON	******
CHEILO	WEEKLY	SMELLS	PYEMIC	GWENNS	--EO--
CHEIRO	******	SMELLY	SEEMED	HYENAS	******
CLEIST	--EL--	SMELTS	SEEMER	IRENES	ACEOUS
DYEING	******	SNELLS	SEEMLY	IRENIC	AGEOLD
EKEING	ABELES	SPELLS	TEEMED	KEENED	AREOLA
EYEING	AMELIA	STELAE	TEEMER	KEENER	CAEOMA
FEEING	AMELIE	STELAR	THEMES	KEENLY	CHEOPS
GEEING	CHELAE	STELES	THEMIS	MAENAD	CLEOME
GNEISS	CHELAS	STELIC	TREMOR	OHENRY	CREOLE
GREIFS	COELED	STELLA	ULEMAS	OMENTA	EYEOUT
GREIGE	COELOM	STELLI	UREMIA	OPENED	FREONS
HIEING	DUELED	SVELTE	******	OPENER	ONEOFF
HOEING	DUELER	SWELLS	--EN--	OPENLY	PAEONS
JEEING	DUELLO	THELMA	******	PEENED	PAEONY
ONEIDA	DWELLS	TWELVE	ADENIS	PHENOL	THEORY
ONEILL	EVELYN	WHELKS	AGENCY	PHENYL	******
ONEIRO	EYELET	WHELKY	AGENDA	PIENAL	--EP--
OREIDE	EYELID	WHELMS	AGENTS	PLENTY	******
PLEIAD	FEELER	WHELPS	AKENES		ADEPTS
					ALEPHS

ALEPPO	EMERGE	WHERRY	ARETES	URETER	STEVIE
APEPSY	EMERIC	WHERVE	BEETLE	URETIC	TREVOR
BEEPED	EMERIE	******	BRETON	WRETCH	UNEVEN
CREPED	ENERGY	--ES--	CHETAH	******	WEEVER
CREPES	ETERNA	******	CRETAN	--EU--	WEEVIL
DEEPEN	EVERET	AVESTA	CRETIC	******	******
DEEPER	EVERTS	AYESHA	CRETIN	ALEUTS	--EW--
DEEPLY	EXERTS	CAESAR	CRETON	CREUSA	******
DIEPPE	FAERIE	CHESTS	DIETAL	EMEUTE	BREWED
KEEPER	FAEROE	CHESTY	DIETED	EXEUNT	BREWER
PEEPED	FIERCE	CRESOL	DIETER	FLEURY	BREWIS
PEEPER	IBERIA	CRESTS	EMETIC	ISEULT	CHEWED
PREPAY	JEERED	CUESTA	EMETIN	PLEURA	CHEWER
SEEPED	JEERER	DIESEL	EXETER	PLEURO	CLEWED
STEPAN	LEERED	DIESES	FLETCH	PNEUMA	CREWEL
STEPIN	LIERNE	DIESIS	FOETAL	PNEUMO	DEEWAN
STEPPE	OBERON	DOESNT	FOETID	PSEUDO	LEEWAY
STEPUP	OPERAS	DRESSY	FOETOR	QUEUED	ONEWAY
TIEPIN	OVERDO	ECESIS	FOETUS	QUEUES	PEEWEE
TREPAN	OVERLY	EGESTA	FRETTY	RHEUMY	PEEWIT
WEEPER	PEERED	EGESTS	GHETTO	SIEURS	PREWAR
******	PIERCE	EMESIS	GOETHE	SLEUTH	SHEWED
--EQ--	PIERRE	FIESTA	GRETAS	TIEUPS	SHEWER
******	PIERUS	FLESHY	GRETEL	******	SKEWED
CHEQUE	QUERNS	FRESCO	GRETNA	--EV--	SKEWER
EXEQUY	SHERDS	FRESNO	HYETAL	******	SLEWED
******	SHERIF	GUESTS	LUETIC	BEEVES	SPEWED
--ER--	SHERPA	NOESIS	MEETER	BREVES	STEWED
******	SHERRY	ODESSA	MEETLY	BREVET	THEWED
ACERIC	SIERRA	PRESAS	NOETIC	CHEVVY	VIEWED
ALERTS	SKERRY	PRESTO	ODETTE	CLEVER	VIEWER
AMERCE	SPERMO	QUESTS	PIETER	CLEVIS	******
ANERGY	SPERRY	RHESUS	PIETRO	COEVAL	--EX--
ARERCU	STEREO	SEESAW	POETIC	CREVAS	******
AVERNO	STERES	SIESTA	POETRY	ELEVEN	ALEXIA
AVERSE	STERIC	THESES	PRETER	ELEVON	ALEXIN
AVERTS	STERNA	THESIS	PRETOR	KEEVES	ALEXIS
AVERYS	STERNO	TRESSY	PRETTY	NAEVUS	APEXES
BIERCE	STERNS	UNESCO	RHETOR	PEEVED	FLEXED
CHERRY	STEROL	WRESTS	SEETHE	PEEVES	FLEXES
CHERUB	SWERVE	******	SKETCH	PREVUE	FLEXOR
CHERYL	THERMO	--ET--	STETHO	REEVED	IBEXES
CLERGY	THERMS	******	TEETER	REEVES	ILEXES
CLERIC	TIERCE	ACETAL	TEETHE	SIEVED	PLEXOR
CLERID	TIERED	ACETIC	THETAS	SIEVES	PLEXUS
CLERKS	TWERPS	ACETUM	THETIC	SOEVER	******
COERCE	UTERUS	ACETYL	THETIS	STEVEN	--EY--
EGERIA	VEERED	AEETES	TSETSE	STEVES	******
					OBEYED
					OBEYER

OXEYED	INFEST	PUFFED	EFFLUX	DEFTER	BOGANS
OXEYES	LIFERS	PUFFER	INFLOW	DEFTLY	CIGARS
PREYED	OFFEND	PUFFIN	INFLUX	FIFTHS	DEGAGE
PREYER	OFFERS	RAFFIA	REFLET	GIFTED	DEGAME
WHEYEY	REFERS	RAFFLE	REFLEX	HAFTED	DIGAMY
******	SAFELY	RIFFLE	REFLUX	HEFTED	DOGAPE
--EZ--	SAFEST	RUFFED	RIFLED	KAFTAN	EDGARS
******	SAFETY	RUFFLE	RIFLER	LIFTED	EGGARS
AREZZO	WAFERS	SOFFIT	RIFLES	LIFTER	ENGAGE
FEEZED	WIFELY	SUFFER	TEFLON	LOFTED	ERGATE
FEEZES	******	SUFFIX	******	LOFTER	GIGANT
GEEZER	**--FF--**	TIFFED	**--FN--**	MUFTIS	HOGANS
QUEZON	******	TIFFIN	******	RAFTED	JUGATE
******	BAFFED	TOFFEE	FAFNIR	RAFTER	LEGACY
--FA--	BAFFIN	TUFFET	******	RIFTED	LEGATE
******	BAFFLE	WAFFLE	**--FO--**	SIFTED	LEGATO
AFFAIR	BIFFED	ZAFFAR	******	SIFTER	LIGAND
ALFAKI	BIFFIN	ZAFFER	AFFORD	SOFTAS	LIGATE
BEFALL	BOFFIN	ZAFFIR	ALFONS	SOFTEN	MEGALO
DEFACE	BUFFED	ZAFFRE	BEFOGS	SOFTER	MEGASS
DEFAME	BUFFER	******	BEFOOL	SOFTLY	NAGANA
EFFACE	BUFFET	**--FI--**	BEFORE	TUFTED	NEGATE
ENFACE	COFFEE	******	BEFOUL	WAFTED	ORGANA
INFAMY	COFFER	AFFIRM	BIFOLD	WAFTER	ORGANO
INFANT	COFFIN	BEFITS	BIFORM	ZAFTIG	ORGANS
ONFALL	COFFLE	DEFIED	DEFORM	******	ORGASM
REFACE	CUFFED	DEFIER	EFFORT	**--FU--**	PAGANS
SAFARI	DIFFER	DEFIES	ENFOLD	******	REGAIN
UNFAIR	DOFFED	DEFILE	ILFORD	DEFUSE	REGALE
******	DOFFER	DEFINE	INFOLD	EFFUSE	REGARD
--FD--	DUFFED	EFFIGY	INFORM	ERFURT	RUGATE
******	DUFFEL	ELFINS	OXFORD	INFUSE	SUGARS
OFFDAY	DUFFER	ELFISH	REFOOT	REFUEL	SUGARY
******	DUFFLE	FIFING	REFORM	REFUGE	TOGAED
--FE--	EIFFEL	INFIRM	RUFOUS	******	UTGARD
******	GAFFED	OAFISH	UNFOLD	REFUND	VAGARY
AFFECT	GAFFER	OFFICE	******	REFUSE	WIGANS
BEFELL	GAFFES	OFFING	**--FR--**	REFUTE	******
DEFEAT	GOFFER	OFFISH	******	UNFURL	**--GB--**
DEFECT	GUFFAW	REFILL	AFFRAY	******	FOGBOW
DEFEND	HUFFED	REFINE	ALFRED	**--GA--**	HAGBUT
DEFERS	KAFFIR	REFITS	DEFRAY	******	RAGBAG
EFFECT	LUFFED	SUFISM	******	ANGARY	******
EFFETE	MIFFED	******	**--FS--**	ARGALA	**--GC--**
FIFERS	MUFFED	**--FL--**	OFFSET	ARGALI	******
INFECT	MUFFIN	******	******	ARGALS	EGGCUP
INFERO	MUFFLE	AFFLUX	**--FT--**	ASGARD	
INFERS	PIFFLE	BIFLEX	CAFTAN	BAGASS	
			DAFTLY	BIGAMY	

******	TIGERS	JAGGED	TAGGER	DIGITI	ANGLER
--GD--	URGENT	JIGGED	TOGGED	DIGITS	ANGLES
******	WAGERS	JIGGER	TOGGLE	DOGIES	ANGLIA
BAGDAD	WIGEON	JIGGLE	TUGGED	EDGIER	ANGLIC
FOGDOG	YAGERS	JOGGED	WAGGED	EDGING	BOGLES
HAGDON	YOGEES	JOGGER	WAGGLE	EGGING	BUGLED
RAGDAY	******	JOGGLE	WAGGLY	ENGINE	BUGLER
******	--GF--	JUGGED	WAGGON	ENGIRD	BUGLES
--GE--	******	JUGGLE	WIGGED	ENGIRT	DIGLOT
******	DOGFOX	LAGGED	WIGGLE	FOGIES	EAGLES
AEGEAN	JUGFUL	LAGGER	WIGGLY	FUGIOS	EAGLET
AEGEUS	******	LEGGED	******	GAGING	FUGLED
AGGERS	--GG--	LOGGED	--GH--	HEGIRA	FUGLES
ANGELA	******	LOGGER	******	LEGION	GIGLET
ANGELO	BAGGED	LOGGIA	AFGHAN	LEGIST	GIGLOT
ANGELS	BEGGAR	LUGGED	AUGHTS	LOGIER	GOGLET
ANGERS	BEGGED	LUGGER	BIGHTS	LOGION	KEGLER
ARGENT	BIGGER	MAGGIE	EIGHTH	MEGILP	PEGLEG
AUGEAN	BIGGIN	MAGGOT	EIGHTS	ORGIES	PIGLET
AUGEND	BOGGED	MIGGLE	EIGHTY	PAGING	RAGLAN
AUGERS	BOGGLE	MUGGAR	FIGHTS	POGIES	REGLET
BAGELS	BUGGED	MUGGED	HIGHER	RAGING	******
BEGETS	BUGGER	MUGGER	HIGHLY	REGIME	--GM--
BOGEYS	COGGED	MUGGUR	HUGHES	REGINA	******
COGENT	DAGGER	NAGGED	HUGHIE	REGION	BAGMAN
DIGEST	DAGGLE	NAGGER	LIGHTS	REGIUS	BAGMEN
DOGEAR	DIGGED	NIGGER	MIGHTY	SAGIER	DAGMAR
EGGERS	DIGGER	NIGGLE	NIGHER	SIGILS	DOGMAS
ENGELS	DOGGED	NOGGIN	NIGHTS	UNGIRD	LEGMAN
EOGENE	DOGGER	NUGGET	NIGHTY	UNGIRT	LEGMEN
EUGENE	DOGGIE	PEGGED	RIGHTO	URGING	RAGMAN
FAGEND	FAGGED	PEGGYS	RIGHTS	VAGINA	RAGMEN
GAGERS	FAGGOT	PIGGED	SIGHED	VAGINO	SIGMAS
HUGELY	FIGGED	PIGGIE	SIGHTS	VIGILS	TEGMEN
HUGEST	FOGGED	PIGGIN	TIGHTS	WAGING	******
HYGEIA	GAGGED	PUGGED	******	YOGINS	--GN--
INGEST	GAGGER	PUGGRY	--GI--	******	******
LAGERS	GAGGLE	RAGGED	******	--GJ--	BAGNIO
LEGEND	GIGGED	REGGIE	ANGINA	******	COGNAC
LEGERS	GIGGLE	RIGGED	ARGIVE	LOGJAM	CYGNET
LUGERS	GIGGLY	RIGGER	AUGITE	******	CYGNUS
NIGELS	GOGGLE	RUGGED	BEGINS	--GK--	EGGNOG
ORGEAT	HAGGED	RUGGER	BEGIRD	******	HOGNUT
PIGEON	HAGGIS	SAGGAR	BEGIRT	ANGKOR	LIGNIN
REGENT	HAGGLE	SAGGED	BOGIES	******	LIGNUM
ROGERS	HIGGLE	SAGGER	CAGIER	--GL--	MAGNET
SAGELY	HOGGED	SEGGAR	CAGILY	******	MAGNOX
SAGEST	HUGGED	TAGGED	CAGING	AIGLET	MAGNUM
				ANGLED	

MIGNON	******	LIGULE	INHALE	REHEAR	******
PIGNUS	--GR--	LIGURE	INHAUL	REHEAT	--HM--
PIGNUT	******	MAGUEY	ITHACA	SAHEBS	******
REGNAL	DEGREE	MIGUEL	JIHADS	SCHEMA	ASHMAN
SIGNAL	ENGRAM	MOGULS	JOHANN	SCHEME	ASHMEN
SIGNED	INGRES	ROGUED	MOHAIR	SPHENE	SCHMOS
SIGNER	INGRID	ROGUES	MOHAVE	SPHENO	******
SIGNET	LEGREE	TOGUES	MOHAWK	SPHERE	--HN--
SIGNOR	MEGRIM	UNGUAL	PSHAWS	SPHERY	******
WAGNER	POGROM	UNGUES	REHASH	STHENO	ETHNIC
******	PUGREE	UNGUIS	RRHAGE	TEHEED	JOHNNY
--GO--	REGRET	UNGULA	RRHAGY	TEHEES	******
******	SIGRID	VAGUER	SAHARA	UNHEWN	--HO--
ALGOID	TIGRIS	VOGUES	UNHAIR	UPHELD	******
ALGOUS	******	VOGULS	UNHAND	USHERS	ABHORS
ANGOLA	--GS--	YOGURT	UNHASP	******	APHONY
ANGORA	******	******	UNHATS	--HI--	ASHORE
ARGOSY	JIGSAW	--GW--	WAHABI	******	ATHOME
ARGOTS	PIGSTY		******	ACHING	BEHOLD
BEGONE	******	BIGWIG	--HB--	APHIDS	BEHOOF
BIGONE	--GT--	COGWAY	******	ASHIER	BEHOVE
BIGOTS	******	WIGWAG	MAHBUB	AWHILE	CAHOOT
BOGOAK	HOGTIE	WIGWAM	******	AWHIRL	COHORT
BOGOTA	PEGTOP	******	--HC--	BEHIND	COHOSH
BYGONE	RAGTAG	--GY--	******	CAHIER	DAHOON
DAGOBA	******	ARGYLL	ASHCAN	ECHINI	DEHORN
DUGONG	--GU--	MAGYAR	******	ECHINO	ECHOED
DUGOUT	******	******	--HE--	ETHICS	ECHOER
FAGOTS	ARGUED	--GZ--	******	OPHITE	ECHOES
GIGOLO	ARGUER	******	ACHENE	OXHIDE	ECHOIC
INGOTS	ARGUES	ZIGZAG	ADHERE	SAHIBS	EPHODS
LAGOON	ARGUFY	******	ATHENA	SCHICK	EPHORI
MAGOTS	AUGURS	--HA--	ATHENE	SCHISM	EPHORS
NAGOYA	AUGURY	******	ATHENS	SCHIST	EXHORT
NOGOOD	AUGUST	ACHAEA	AWHEEL	SCHIZO	LAHORE
PAGODA	BEGUIN	ACHAIA	BEHEAD	SPHINX	MAHOUT
RAGOUT	BEGUMS	ACHAIA	BEHELD	TAHITI	MOHOCK
RIGORS	DEGUMS	AGHAST	BEHEST	TSHIRT	MOHOLE
RIGOUR	DEGUST	BAHAIS	COHEIR	UPHILL	SCHOOL
RUGOSE	ENGULF	BAHAMA	COHERE	WAHINE	SCHORL
RUGOUS	FIGURE	BEHALF	EPHEBI	******	UNHOLY
VIGOUR	FUGUES	BEHAVE	ETHELS	--HL--	UNHOOK
WAGONS	GIGUES	BIHARI	ETHERS	******	UPHOLD
ZYGOMA	INGULF	ECHARD	INHERE	ASHLAR	WAHOOS
ZYGOTE	JAGUAR	EPHAHS	OCHERS	ASHLEY	YAHOOS
******	LAGUNE	ETHANE	OCHERY	DAHLIA	******
--GP--	LEGUME	ETHANS	OTHERS	MAHLER	--HR--
******	LIGULA	EXHALE			******
MAGPIE					FUHRER
PIGPEN					UPHROE

	OPIATE	EVICTS	AMIDST	AFIELD	GRIFFE
--HT--	PHIALS	FLICKS	ARIDLY	ALIENS	HEIFER
******	PLIANT	HOICKS	ASIDES	AMIENS	KNIFED
APHTHA	TRIADS	IBICES	AVIDIN	APIECE	KNIFES
ICHTHY	TRIALS	ICICLE	AVIDLY	ARIELS	SHIFTS
ISHTAR	UMIAKS	JUICER	BRIDAL	BRIEFS	SHIFTY
******	******	JUICES	BRIDES	BRIERS	SKIFFS
--HU--	**--IB--**	PLICAE	BRIDGE	BRIERY	SNIFFS
******	******	PRICED	BRIDIE	CHIEFS	SNIFFY
COHUNE	ALIBIS	PRICES	BRIDLE	CLIENT	SPIFFY
EXHUME	ALIBLE	PRICKS	CHIDED	CRIERS	STIFLE
INHUME	BRIBED	REICHS	CHIDER	DRIERS	SWIFTS
LEHUAS	BRIBER	SEICHE	CHIDES	DRIEST	TRIFID
MOHURS	BRIBES	SLICED	ELIDED	FLIERS	TRIFLE
NAHUMS	CEIBAS	SLICER	ELIDES	FLIEST	UNIFIC
SCHUIT	CHIBUK	SLICES	FRIDAY	FRIEDA	WAIFED
SCHUSS	EDIBLE	SLICKS	FRIDGE	FRIEND	WHIFFS
UNHURT	FOIBLE	SNICKS	GLIDED	FRIERS	******
UNHUSK	GLIBLY	SPICED	GLIDER	FRIEZE	**--IG--**
YEHUDI	OJIBWA	SPICER	GLIDES	GAIETY	******
******	ORIBIS	SPICES	GRIDED	GRIEVE	ALIGHT
--HV--	OVIBOS	STICKS	GRIDES	ICIEST	ALIGNS
******	TRIBAL	STICKY	GUIDED	MOIETY	AMIGOS
YAHVEH	TRIBES	TRICAR	GUIDER	ORIELS	ARIGHT
******	TWIBIL	TRICED	GUIDES	ORIENT	BEIGES
--HW--	******	TRICES	GUIDON	OSIERS	BLIGHT
******	**--IC--**	TRICHI	HOIDEN	PLIERS	BRIGHT
SCHWAS	******	TRICHO	IBIDEM	PRIERS	BRIGID
YAHWEH	ALICES	TRICKS	IMIDES	PRIEST	CHIGOE
******	ALICIA	TRICKY	IRIDES	SHIELD	COIGNS
--HY--	AMICES	TRICOT	IRIDIC	SHIEST	DEIGNS
******	APICAL	UNICEF	ISIDOR	SKIERS	DWIGHT
ETHYLS	APICES	VOICED	MAIDEN	SLIEST	EMIGRE
******	BRICKS	VOICES	OXIDES	SPIELS	ENIGMA
--IA--	CHICHI	YOICKS	PRIDED	SPIERS	FEIGNE
******	CHICKS	******	PRIDES	THIEVE	FEIGNS
APIARY	CHICLE	**--ID--**	RAIDED	TRIERS	FLIGHT
ARIANS	CHICOS	******	RAIDER	UBIETY	FRIGGA
ASIANS	CLICHE	ABIDED	SLIDER	WRIEST	FRIGHT
AVIARY	CLICKS	ABIDER	SLIDES	******	FRIGID
AVIATE	CRICKS	ABIDES	SPIDER	**--IF--**	GEIGER
BRIARS	DEICED	ACIDIC	VOIDED	******	GRIGRI
CHIASM	DEICER	ACIDLY	WHIDAH	CLIFFS	HEIGHT
CHIAUS	DEICES	ALIDAD	ZUIDER	CLIFFY	KNIGHT
FRIARS	EDICTS	AMIDES	******	COIFED	LEIGHS
FRIARY	ELICIT	AMIDIC	**--IE--**	DEIFIC	MAIGRE
GUIANA	EPICAL	AMIDIN	******	DRIFTS	NEIGHS
NAIADS	ERICHS	AMIDOL	ADIEUS	DRIFTY	ORIGAN
			ADIEUX		

ORIGEN	BAILEY	PHILIP	******	TRIMLY	FRINGY
ORIGIN	BAILIE	PHILOS	--IM--	WEIMAR	GAINED
PLIGHT	BAILOR	POILUS	******	WHIMSY	GAINER
REIGNS	BOILED	QUILLS	AHIMSA	******	GAINLY
SAIGAS	BOILER	QUILTS	AKIMBO	--IN--	GLINTS
SAIGON	BRILLS	RAILED	ANIMAL	ACINUS	GOINGS
SLIGHT	BUILDS	ROILED	ANIMAS	ALINED	GRINDS
SOIGNE	CEILED	SAILED	ANIMUS	ALINES	GUINEA
SPIGOT	CHILLI	SAILER	ASIMOV	AZINES	ICINGS
STIGMA	CHILLS	SAILOR	BLIMEY	BEINGS	IMINES
TAIGAS	CHILLY	SCILLY	BLIMPS	BLINDS	JAINAS
THIGHS	COILED	SHILLS	CAIMAN	BLINKS	JOINED
TRIGLY	COILER	SHILOH	CHIMED	BLINTZ	JOINER
TRIGON	DRILLS	SKILLS	CHIMER	BRINED	JOINTS
TWIGGY	EDILES	SMILAX	CHIMES	BRINES	KOINES
WEIGHS	EMILES	SMILED	CLIMAT	BRINGS	MAINLY
WEIGHT	EMILIA	SMILER	CLIMAX	BRINKS	OPINED
WRIGHT	EMILIE	SMILES	CLIMBS	CHINCH	OPINES
******	EMILIO	SOILED	CLIMES	CHINES	PAINED
--II--	EMILYS	SPILED	CRIMEA	CHINKS	PAINTS
******	EPILOG	SPILES	CRIMES	CHINKY	PAINTY
OBIISM	EVILLY	SPILLS	CRIMPS	CHINTZ	PLINTH
SHIISM	EXILED	SPILTH	CRIMPY	CLINCH	POINDS
SHIITE	EXILES	STILES	DAIMIO	CLINES	POINTE
SKIING	EXILIC	STILLS	DAIMON	CLINGS	POINTS
******	FAILED	STILLY	DAIMYO	CLINGY	POINTY
--IJ--	FAILLE	STILTS	FLIMSY	CLINIC	PRINCE
******	FOILED	SWILLS	GRIMED	CLINKS	PRINKS
ABIJAH	FRILLS	TAILED	GRIMES	CLINTS	PRINTS
ELIJAH	FRILLY	TAILLE	GRIMLY	COINED	QUINCE
FRIJOL	GRILLE	TAILOR	GUIMPE	COINER	QUINCY
******	GRILLS	TOILED	MAIMED	CRINGE	QUINIC
--IK--	GRILSE	TOILER	MAIMER	CRINUM	QUINSY
******	GUILDS	TOILES	PRIMAL	DAINTY	QUINTS
BAIKAL	GUILES	TOILET	PRIMED	DOINGS	RAINED
CRIKEY	GUILTS	TRILBY	PRIMER	DRINKS	REINED
DUIKER	GUILTY	TRILLS	PRIMES	ELINOR	RHINAL
SHIKAR	HAILED	TUILLE	PRIMLY	ERINGO	RHINOS
SPIKED	HAILER	TWILIT	PRIMPS	ERINYS	RUINED
SPIKES	JAILED	TWILLS	PRIMUS	EVINCE	RUINER
******	JAILER	VEILED	SHIMMY	FAINTS	SAINTS
--IL--	JAILOR	VEILER	SKIMOS	FEINTS	SEINED
******	MAILED	VOILES	SKIMPS	FLINCH	SEINER
ANILIN	MAILER	WAILED	SKIMPY	FLINGS	SEINES
AXILLA	MOILED	WAILER	SLIMED	FLINTS	SHINDY
BAILED	MOILER	WHILED	SLIMES	FLINTY	SHINED
BAILEE	NAILED	WHILES	SLIMLY	FRINGE	SHINER
BAILER	PHILIA	WHILOM	SLIMSY	FRINGE	SHINES

SHINNY	GLIOMA	TRIPOD	SMIRKS	FRISKS	******
SHINTO	IDIOCY	TRIPOS	SOIREE	FRISKY	--IT--
SKINKS	IDIOMS	UNIPED	SPIRAL	GEISHA	******
SKINNY	IDIOTS	WHIPPY	SPIREA	GRISLY	ANITAS
SLINGS	ITIOUS	******	SPIRED	GUISES	ANITRA
SLINKS	ODIOUS	--IQ--	SPIRES	HEISTS	BAITED
SLINKY	OHIOAN	******	SPIRIT	HOISTS	BLITHE
SPINAL	ONIONS	CAIQUE	SPIRTS	IBISES	BRITON
SPINEL	ONIONY	CLIQUE	STIRKS	IRISED	CHITIN
SPINES	ORIOLE	CLIQUY	STIRPS	IRISES	CHITON
SPINET	OTIOSE	UNIQUE	SWIRLS	JOISTS	CHITTY
SPINNY	PRIORS	******	SWIRLY	KAISER	COITAL
STINGS	PRIORY	--IR--	THIRDS	KRISES	COITUS
STINGY	SCIONS	******	THIRST	MAISIE	CRITIC
STINKS	THIOLS	BAIRNS	THIRTY	MAISON	DMITRI
STINTS	TRIODE	BEIRUT	TWIRLS	MOISHE	DOITED
SWINGE	TRIOSE	CAIRNS	TWIRPS	NOISED	EDITED
SWINGS	UNIONS	CHIRMS	WEIRDY	NOISES	EDITHS
TAINOS	******	CHIRON	WHIRLS	ORISON	EDITOR
TAINTS	--IP--	CHIRPS	******	OVISAC	EVITAS
THINGS	******	CHIRPY	--IS--	POISED	EXITED
THINLY	ADIPIC	CHIRRS	******	POISES	FAITHS
TRINAL	ALIPED	EPIRUS	AGISTS	POISON	FLITCH
TRINED	CHIPPY	FAIRED	ALISON	PRISMS	FRITHS
TRINES	DRIPPY	FAIRER	ANISES	PRISON	GAITED
TWINED	GRIPED	FAIRLY	ARISEN	PRISSY	GAITER
TWINER	GRIPER	FLIRTS	ARISES	PTISAN	GOITER
TWINES	GRIPES	FLIRTY	ARISTA	PUISNE	GOITRE
TWINGE	GRIPPE	HAIRDO	ARISTO	RAISED	GRITTY
URINAL	GRIPPY	HAIRED	AVISOS	RAISER	GUITAR
VAINER	JAIPUR	LAIRDS	BRISKS	RAISES	IRITIC
VAINLY	PHIPPS	LAIRED	CHISEL	RAISIN	IRITIS
VEINED	QUIPUS	MOIRAS	CRISES	SEISED	KEITHS
WHINED	SAIPAN	OSIRIS	CRISIS	SEISIN	LOITER
WHINER	SCIPIO	PAIRED	CRISPS	SEISMO	MAITRE
WHINES	SLIPON	PEIRCE	CRISPY	SEISMS	OBITER
WHINNY	SLIPUP	QUIRED	CUISSE	SEISOR	OTITIS
WRINGS	SNIPED	QUIRES	DAISES	THISBE	QUITCH
******	SNIPER	QUIRKS	DAISYS	TRISTE	SAITIC
--IO--	SNIPES	QUIRTS	DEISTS	TWISTS	SMITER
******	SNIPPY	SHIRES	EDISON	TWISTY	SMITES
ACIOUS	STIPEL	SHIRKS	ELISHA	UNISEX	SMITHS
ANIONS	STIPES	SHIRRS	ENISLE	UNISON	SMITHY
ARIOSE	SWIPED	SHIRTS	EXISTS	WAISTS	SNITCH
ARIOSO	SWIPES	SHIRTY	FEISTS	WHISKS	SPITAL
ARIOUS	SWIPLE	SKIRRS	FEISTY	WHISKY	SPITED
AXIOMS	TAIPEI	SKIRTS	FOISTS	WRISTS	SPITES
ELIOTS	TRIPLE	SMIRCH	FRISES		STITCH

STITHY	SKIVED	RAJABS	ALKANE	COKING	******
SUITED	SKIVER	RAJAHS	ANKARA	DEKING	--KN--
SUITES	SKIVES	SEJANT	ASKANT	DIKING	******
SUITOR	SKIVVY	******	DEKARE	ESKIMO	ORKNEY
SWITCH	SLIVER	--JE--	GOKART	FAKING	PYKNIC
TRITER	SNIVEL	******	KAKAPO	FAKIRS	UNKNIT
TRITON	STIVER	ABJECT	MIKADO	HAKIMS	******
TWITCH	SWIVEL	ADJECT	PEKANS	HIKING	--KO--
UNITED	SWIVET	DEJECT	******	INKIER	******
UNITES	TRIVET	INJECT	--KD--	INKING	BIKOLS
WAITED	TRIVIA	OBJECT	******	IRKING	DAKOIT
WAITER	WAIVED	REJECT	DIKDIK	JOKING	DAKOTA
WHITBY	WAIVER	******	******	LAKIER	KOKOMO
WHITED	WAIVES	--JI--	--KE--	LAKING	MEKONG
WHITEN	******	******	******	LIKING	PEKOES
WHITER	--IW--	FIJIAN	ALKENE	MAKING	******
WHITES	******	HEJIRA	ASKERS	PEKING	--KP--
WHITEY	TAIWAN	MEJICO	BAKERS	PIKING	******
WRITER	******	******	BAKERY	POKIER	INKPOT
WRITES	--IX--	--JO--	ESKERS	POKIES	******
WRITHE	******	******	FAKERS	POKING	--KT--
******	ELIXIR	ADJOIN	FAKERY	PUKING	******
--IU--	TRIXIE	BIJOUX	HIKERS	RAKING	NEKTON
******	TRIXYS	CAJOLE	INKERS	RAKISH	******
PAIUTE	******	ENJOIN	JOKERS	TAKING	--KY--
TRIUNE	--IZ--	ENJOYS	LAKERS	UNKIND	******
******	******	INJOKE	LIKELY	VIKING	ALKYLS
--IV--	ELIZAS	MAJORS	LIKENS	WAKIKI	ALKYNE
******	EPIZOA	REJOIN	MAKERS	WAKING	ANKYLO
CHIVES	FRIZZY	SAJOUS	MAKEUP	WIKIUP	JEKYLL
CHIVVY	GRIZEL	******	PIKERS	YAKIMA	******
CLIVES	MAIZES	--JP--	POKERS	YOKING	--LA--
DRIVEL	PRIZED	******	RAKERS	******	******
DRIVEN	PRIZER	RAJPUT	SAKERS	--KK--	AALAND
DRIVER	PRIZES	******	TAKEIN	******	ABLAUT
DRIVES	RHIZIC	--JU--	TAKERS	SIKKIM	ABLAZE
FRIVOL	SEIZED	******	TAKEUP	YAKKED	AFLAME
GRIVET	SEIZER	ABJURE	TOKENS	YUKKED	AGLAIA
KNIVES	SEIZES	ADJURE	UPKEEP	******	ALLANS
OGIVAL	SEIZIN	ADJUST	WAKENS	--KL--	ALLAYS
OGIVES	SEIZOR	CAJUNS	YOKELS	******	ANLACE
OLIVER	******	INJURE	******	ANKLES	ANLAGE
OLIVES	--JA--	INJURY	--KI--	ANKLET	ASLANT
OLIVIA	******	JEJUNE	******	AUKLET	BALAAM
PRIVET	HIJACK	JUJUBE	ASKING	INKLES	BALATA
QUIVER	MOJAVE	UNJUST	BAKING	MIKLOS	BELAYS
SHIVER	PAJAMA	******	BIKINI	MUKLUK	BYLANE
SHIVES	PYJAMA	--KA--	CAKING	OAKLEY	BYLAWS

CALAIS	SALAMI	FULCRA	AGLETS	PILEUM	WILFUL
CALASH	SALARY	IOLCUS	AILEEN	PILEUP	WOLFED
DELATE	SCLAFF	MULCTS	ALLEGE	PILEUS	******
DELAYS	SILAGE	OILCAN	ALLELE	POLEAX	--LG--
DILATE	SOLACE	SULCUS	ALLENS	PULERS	******
ECLAIR	SOLAND	TALCED	ALLEYS	RELENT	BELGAS
ENLACE	SOLANO	TALCUM	ARLEEN	RULERS	BELGIC
GALACT	SOLANS	VULCAN	ARLENE	SCLERA	BILGED
GALAXY	SPLAKE	******	ASLEEP	SCLERO	BILGES
HILARY	SPLASH	--LD--	AWLESS	SELECT	BULGAR
HOLARD	SPLATS	******	BALEEN	SELENE	BULGED
INLACE	SPLAYS	BALDER	BALERS	SELENO	BULGER
INLAID	TALARI	BALDLY	BOLERO	SILENI	BULGES
INLAND	TELARY	BELDAM	BOLEYN	SILENT	FULGID
INLAWS	TULADI	BOLDER	CALEBS	SOLELY	MALGRE
INLAYS	ULLAGE	BOLDLY	CALESA	SOLEMN	NILGAI
ISLAND	UMLAUT	COLDER	CELERY	SOLENT	VALGUS
KULAKS	UNLACE	COLDLY	COLEUS	SPLEEN	VULGAR
LILACS	UNLADE	FOLDED	CULETS	SPLENO	******
MALACO	UNLAID	FOLDER	DALETH	TALENT	--LI--
MALADY	UNLASH	GELDED	DELETE	TALERS	******
MALAGA	UNLAYS	GILDAS	EILEEN	TELEDU	AALIIS
MALATE	UPLAND	GILDED	ELLENS	TELEGA	ADLIBS
MALAWI	VALATE	GILDER	FILERS	TILERS	AILING
MALAYA	VOLANT	GOLDEN	FILETS	TOLEDO	ALLIED
MALAYS	XYLANS	GULDEN	GALEAE	UNLEAD	ALLIES
MELANO	******	HILDAS	GALENA	UNLESS	ALLIUM
MILADY	--LB--	HOLDER	GILEAD	VALERY	APLITE
MILAGE	******	HOLDUP	HALERS	VALETS	ARLINE
MOLARS	BALBOA	MELDED	HELENA	VILELY	AXLIKE
OBLAST	BILBAO	MILDEN	HELENS	VILEST	BALING
OBLATE	BULBAR	MILDER	IDLERS	VOLERY	BELIAL
PALACE	BULBED	MILDEW	IDLEST	WALERS	BELIED
PALAEO	BULBEL	MILDLY	INLETS	XYLEMS	BELIEF
PALAIS	BULBIL	MOLDED	ISLETS	XYLENE	BELIER
PALATE	BULBUL	MOLDER	JULEPS	YCLEPT	BELIES
PELAGE	WILBER	POLDER	MELEES	******	BELIKE
PILAFF	WILBUR	SELDOM	MILERS	--LF--	BELIZE
PILAFS	******	SOLDER	MOLEST	******	BILITY
PILATE	--LC--	TILDES	OGLERS	BELFRY	BOLIDE
POLACK	******	VELDTS	OILERS	FULFIL	BYLINE
POLAND	AFLCIO	WALDOS	OWLETS	FYLFOT	CALICO
RELAID	CALCAR	WELDED	PALEAE	GOLFED	CALIFS
RELATE	CALCES	WELDER	PALELY	GOLFER	CALIPH
RELAYS	CALCIC	WILDER	PALEST	GULFED	CELIAC
ROLAND	DULCET	WILDLY	PELEUS	PILFER	CELIAS
SALAAM	DULCIE	******	PHLEBO	SULFUR	CILIAT
SALADS	FALCON	--LE--	PHLEGM	TELFER	CILICE
		******			
		ABLEST			
		AGLEAM			

CILIUM	KALIUM	SALINE	MILKER	COLLOP	HALLEY
COLIES	LILIAN	SALISH	POLKAS	CULLAY	HALLOO
COLINE	LILIED	SALIVA	SILKEN	CULLED	HALLOW
COLINS	LILIES	SILICA	SULKED	CULLER	HALLUX
DELIAN	LOLITA	SILICO	TALKED	CULLET	HELLAS
DELIAS	MALICE	SOLIDI	TALKER	CULLIS	HELLEN
DELICT	MALIGN	SOLIDS	TALKIE	DALLAS	HELLER
DELIUS	MALINE	SOLING	VALKYR	DALLES	HILLED
DOLING	MILIEU	SOLION	WALKED	DELLAS	HILLER
EALING	MILIUM	SPLICE	WALKER	DOLLAR	HOLLER
ELLIES	MOLIES	SPLINE	WALKON	DOLLED	HOLLOW
ELLIOT	MOLINE	SPLINT	WALKUP	DOLLIE	HOLLYS
ENLIST	MULISH	SPLITS	WELKIN	DOLLOP	HULLED
EOLIAN	OBLIGE	TALION	******	DOLLYS	JELLED
EOLITH	OGLING	TILING	--LL--	DULLED	KELLER
FELICE	OILIER	TULIPS	******	DULLER	KILLED
FELIDS	OILILY	UGLIER	BALLAD	DULLES	KILLER
FELINE	OILING	UGLIFY	BALLED	FALLAL	LALLED
FELIPE	OLLIES	UGLILY	BALLET	FALLEN	LOLLED
FILIAL	ONLINE	UNLIKE	BALLOT	FALLER	LOLLER
FILING	OOLITE	UNLIVE	BELLAS	FALLOW	LOLLOP
FOLIAR	OWLISH	UPLIFT	BELLED	FELLAH	LULLED
FOLIOS	OXLIPS	VALISE	BELLES	FELLED	MALLED
FOLIUM	PALING	VILIFY	BELLOC	FELLER	MALLEE
GALIOT	PALISH	VOLING	BELLOW	FELLOE	MALLET
HALIDE	PELIAS	WALING	BILLED	FELLOW	MALLOW
HALIDS	PELION	WILIER	BILLET	FILLED	MELLON
HALING	PELITE	WILILY	BILLIE	FILLER	MELLOW
HALITE	PILING	WILING	BILLON	FILLET	MILLAY
HELICO	POLICE	XYLITE	BILLOW	FILLIN	MILLED
HELIOS	POLICY	******	BILLYS	FILLIP	MILLER
HELIUM	POLING	--LJ--	BOLLED	FOLLOW	MILLET
HOLIER	POLISH	******	BOLLIX	FULLED	MILLIE
HOLIES	POLITE	SELJUK	BULLAE	FULLER	MILLYS
HOLILY	POLITY	******	BULLET	GALLED	MOLLAH
HOLING	PULING	--LK--	CALLAO	GALLEY	MOLLIE
HOLISM	RELICS	******	CALLAS	GALLIC	MOLLYS
IDLING	RELICT	BALKAN	CALLED	GALLON	MULLAH
INLIER	RELIED	BALKED	CALLER	GALLOP	MULLED
IOLITE	RELIEF	BILKED	CALLOW	GALLUP	MULLEN
ISLING	RELIER	BILKER	CALLUP	GALLUS	MULLER
JOLIET	RELIES	BULKED	CALLUS	GELLED	MULLET
JULIAN	RELINE	CALKED	CELLAE	GILLIE	MULLEY
JULIAS	RELISH	CALKER	CELLAR	GULLAH	NELLIE
JULIES	RELIVE	CALKIN	CELLOS	GULLED	NELLYS
JULIET	RILING	FOLKSY	COLLAR	GULLET	NULLAH
JULIUS	RULING	HULKED	COLLET	HALLAH	PALLAS
KALIAN	SALIFY	MILKED	COLLIE	HALLEL	PALLED

PALLET	WALLED	******	OCLOCK	SALPAS	FALTER
PALLID	WALLET	--LO--	OOLOGY	SALPID	FELTED
PALLOR	WALLIE	******	OOLONG	SULPHA	FILTER
PELLET	WALLIS	ABLOOM	ORLOPS	SULPHO	FILTHY
PILLAR	WALLOP	AFLOAT	PELOPS	SYLPHS	FULTON
PILLED	WALLOW	ALLOTS	PELOTA	SYLPHY	HALTED
PILLOW	WALLYS	ALLOUT	PHLOEM	YELPED	HALTER
POLLED	WELLED	ALLOWS	PILOSE	YELPER	HELTER
POLLEE	WILLED	ALLOYS	PILOTS	******	HILTED
POLLEN	WILLER	APLOMB	PILOUS	--LQ--	JILTED
POLLER	WILLET	ASLOPE	PYLONS	******	JILTER
POLLEX	WILLIE	BELOIT	RELOAD	PULQUE	JOLTED
POLLUX	WILLIS	BELONG	SALOME	******	JOLTER
POLLYS	WILLOW	BILOXI	SALONS	--LR--	KELTIC
PULLED	WILLYS	CALORY	SALOON	******	KILTED
PULLER	YELLED	CHLOES	SALOOP	WALRUS	KILTER
PULLET	YELLER	CHLORO	SILOED	******	KILTIE
PULLEY	YELLOW	COLONS	SOLOED	--LS--	KULTUR
PULLIN	ZILLAH	COLONY	TALONS	******	LILTED
RILLET	******	COLORS	UNLOAD	BALSAM	MALTED
ROLLED	--LM--	COLOUR	UNLOCK	BALSAS	MALTHA
ROLLER	******	COLOUS	VALOIS	BOLSON	MELTED
ROLLUP	CALMED	DOLOUR	VALOUR	FALSER	MELTER
SALLET	CALMER	EULOGY	VELOCE	HALSEY	MELTON
SALLOW	CALMLY	FELONS	VELOUR	KELSON	MILTED
SALLYS	CULMED	FELONY	VOLOST	NELSON	MILTER
SELLER	DOLMAN	FILOSE	XYLOID	PULSAR	MILTON
SULLEN	DOLMEN	GALOOT	XYLOLS	PULSED	MOLTED
TALLER	FILMED	GALOPS	XYLOSE	PULSES	MOLTEN
TALLOW	FILMIC	GALORE	******	SELSYN	MOLTER
TELLER	FULMAR	GALOSH	--LP--	TELSON	MOLTKE
TELLUS	HELMED	GOLOSH	******	WILSON	PALTER
TILLED	HELMET	HALOED	CALPAC	WOLSEY	PALTRY
TILLER	HOLMES	HALOES	DELPHI	******	PELTED
TILLIE	HOLMIC	HALOID	DOLPHS	--LT--	PELTER
TILLYS	KALMIA	HELOTS	GULPED	******	PELTRY
TOLLED	KILMER	IGLOOS	GULPER	BALTIC	SALTED
TOLLER	PALMAR	JALOPS	HELPED	BALTIM	SALTER
TULLES	PALMED	JALOPY	HELPER	BELTED	SILTED
VALLEY	PALMER	KALONG	KALPAK	BOLTED	SULTAN
VALLUM	SALMIS	KELOID	KELPIE	BOLTER	SULTRY
VELLUM	SALMON	MALORY	PALPED	BOLTON	TILTED
VILLAS	TALMUD	MELODY	PALPUS	CELTIC	TILTER
VILLON	WILMAS	MELONS	PULPED	COLTER	TILTHS
VILLUS	******	MILORD	PULPER	CULTCH	TOLTEC
VOLLEY	--LN--	MOLOCH	PULPIT	CULTUS	VOLTED
WALLAH	******	NYLONS	RALPHS	DALTON	WALTER
WALLAS	WALNUT	OBLONG	ROLPHS	DELTAS	WALTON

WELTED	HALVES	******	REMANS	HUMBLY	ZOMBIE
WELTER	HELVES	--LY--	REMARK	HUMBUG	ZOMBIS
WILTED	KELVIN	******	ROMAIC	IAMBIC	******
WILTON	MELVIN	ALLYLS	ROMANS	IAMBUS	--MC--
******	MELVYN	GALYAK	ROMANY	JUMBAL	******
--LU--	PELVES	POLYPS	SAMARA	JUMBLE	TOMCAT
******	PELVIC	******	SIMARS	LAMBDA	TOMCOD
ABLUSH	PELVIS	--LZ--	SOMALI	LAMBED	******
ALLUDE	SALVED	******	SOMATA	LAMBIE	--MD--
ALLURE	SALVER	BALZAC	SOMATO	LIMBED	******
BELUGA	SALVES	COLZAS	SUMACS	LIMBER	CAMDEN
COLUGO	SALVIA	******	TAMALE	LIMBIC	DUMDUM
COLUMN	SALVOR	--MA--	TOMANS	LIMBUS	HAMDEN
COLURE	SALVOS	******	TOMATO	LUMBAR	******
DELUDE	SELVES	ALMAHS	UNMADE	LUMBER	--ME--
DELUGE	SILVAE	ARMADA	UNMAKE	MAMBAS	******
DELUXE	SILVAN	ARMAGH	UNMANS	MAMBOS	ARMETS
DILUTE	SILVAS	ARMAND	UNMASK	MEMBER	BEMEAN
DULUTH	SILVER	AYMARA	******	MUMBLE	CAMELS
HALUTZ	SILVIA	BAMAKO	--MB--	NIMBLE	CAMEOS
ILLUME	SOLVED	BEMATA	******	NIMBLY	CAMERA
ILLUSE	SOLVER	CAMASS	BAMBOO	NIMBUS	CEMENT
ILLUST	SOLVES	COMATE	BOMBAY	NUMBED	COMEDO
PILULE	SYLVAE	CYMARS	BOMBED	NUMBER	COMEDY
SALUKI	SYLVAN	DAMAGE	BOMBER	NUMBLY	COMELY
SALUTE	SYLVAS	DAMANS	BOMBES	RAMBLE	COMEON
SOLUTE	SYLVIA	DAMASK	BOMBIC	RUMBAS	COMERS
TELUGU	VALVAL	DEMAND	BUMBLE	RUMBLE	COMETS
TOLUOL	VALVAR	DOMAIN	CAMBER	SAMBAS	CYMENE
TOLUYL	VALVED	FEMALE	CIMBRI	SAMBOS	DEMEAN
VALUED	VALVES	GEMARA	COMBAT	SAMBUR	DEMENT
VALUER	VELVET	HAMALS	COMBED	SOMBER	DIMERS
VALUES	VOLVAS	HAMAUL	COMBER	SOMBRE	ELMERS
VALUTA	VOLVOX	HEMATO	COMBOS	SYMBOL	EMMETS
VELURE	VULVAE	HOMAGE	CUMBER	TAMBAC	EMMETT
VOLUME	VULVAL	HUMANE	CYMBAL	TIMBAL	ENMESH
VOLUTE	VULVAR	HUMANS	DUMBLY	TIMBER	FOMENT
******	WALVIS	INMATE	FIMBLE	TIMBRE	GAMELY
--LV--	WOLVER	KAMALA	FUMBLE	TOMBAC	GAMETE
******	WOLVES	NEMATO	GAMBIA	TOMBED	GAMETO
CALVED	******	NOMADS	GAMBIR	TOMBOY	GEMERT
CALVES	--LW--	OHMAGE	GAMBIT	TUMBLE	GIMELS
CALVIN	******	POMACE	GAMBLE	WAMBLE	HOMELY
CULVER	GALWAY	POMADE	GAMBOL	WAMBLY	HOMERS
DELVED	SELWYN	REMADE	GUMBOS	WIMBLE	HYMENO
DELVER	******	REMAIN	HOMBRE	WOMBAT	HYMENS
DELVES	--LX--	REMAKE	HUMBER	WOMBED	IMMESH
HALVED	CALXES	REMAND	HUMBLE	ZAMBIA	INMESH

LAMECH	BEMIRE	LUMINA	CYMLIN	MUMMED	DEMODE
LAMEDS	CAMILA	LUMINI	GIMLET	MUMMER	DEMONO
LAMELY	CAMION	LUMINO	HAMLET	POMMEL	DEMONS
LAMENT	CAMISE	MAMIES	SAMLET	PUMMEL	DEMOTE
LAMEST	COMICS	MIMICS	SIMLIN	RAMMED	DIMOUT
LIMENS	COMING	MIMING	******	RAMMER	EDMOND
LIMEYS	COMITY	MOMISM	--MM--	RIMMED	EXMOOR
LOMENT	CUMINS	NAMING	******	RIMMER	FAMOUS
LUMENS	DEMIES	NIMITZ	BUMMED	ROMMEL	FEMORA
MAMEYS	DEMISE	NOMISM	BUMMER	RUMMER	FUMOUS
MIMERS	DEMITS	NUMINA	COMMAS	SAMMYS	GAMOUS
MOMENT	DIMITY	OOMIAK	COMMIE	SIMMER	GEMOTS
NAMELY	DOMING	OSMIUM	COMMIT	SUMMED	HEMOID
NAMERS	DOMINO	PUMICE	COMMIX	SUMMER	HUMORS
ORMERS	ELMIRA	RAMIES	COMMON	SUMMIT	HUMOUR
PAMELA	EMMIES	RAMIFY	DAMMAR	SUMMON	INMOST
POMELO	ENMITY	REMIND	DAMMED	TIMMYS	KIMONO
REMEDY	ERMINE	REMISE	DAMMER	TOMMYS	LEMONS
RIMERS	FAMILY	REMISS	DIMMED	WAMMUS	LOMOND
SEMELE	FAMINE	REMITS	DIMMER	YAMMER	MEMOIR
SEMEME	FAMISH	RIMING	GAMMAS	******	MEMORY
TAMELY	FUMIER	ROMISH	GAMMED	--MN--	MIMOSA
TAMERS	FUMING	RUMINA	GAMMER	******	ORMOLU
TAMEST	GAMIER	SAMIAN	GAMMON	DAMNED	OSMOND
TIMELY	GAMILY	SAMIEL	GEMMAE	HYMNAL	OSMOSE
TIMERS	GAMING	SAMITE	GEMMED	HYMNED	POMONA
TUMEFY	GAMINS	SEMITE	GUMMAS	HYMNIC	RAMONA
UNMEET	GEMINI	SIMIAN	GUMMED	LEMNOS	RAMOSE
UNMEWS	HAMITE	SIMILE	HAMMAL	LIMNED	RAMOUS
VOMERS	HOMIER	SOMITE	HAMMED	LIMNER	REMORA
WOMERA	HOMILY	TAMING	HAMMER	ROMNEY	REMOTE
YAMENS	HOMING	TIMING	HEMMED	SIMNEL	REMOVE
YEMENI	HOMINY	VIMINA	HEMMER	SUMNER	RIMOSE
******	HUMIFY	VOMICA	HUMMED	******	RIMOUS
--MF--	IMMIES	VOMITO	HUMMER	--MO--	ROMOLA
******	JAMIES	VOMITS	JAMMED	******	RUMORS
ARMFUL	JEMIMA	ZAMIAS	JIMMIE	ALMOND	RUMOUR
COMFIT	JIMINY	******	JIMMYS	ALMOST	SAMOAN
******	KAMIKS	--MJ--	KUMMEL	ARMORS	SIMONE
--MI--	KUMISS	******	LAMMAS	ARMORY	SIMONS
******	LAMIAE	JAMJAR	LAMMED	ARMOUR	SIMONY
ADMIRE	LAMIAS	RAMJET	LEMMAS	BEMOAN	SIMOOM
ADMITS	LAMINA	******	LUMMOX	COMOSE	TUMORS
ADMIXT	LAMING	--MK--	MAMMAE	COMOUS	TUMOUR
AIMING	LIMIER	******	MAMMAL	CYMOID	UNMOOR
ALMIRA	LIMINA	BUMKIN	MAMMAS	CYMOSE	UPMOST
ARMIES	LIMING	******	MAMMET	CYMOUS	UTMOST
ARMING	LIMITS	--ML--	MAMMON	DEMBS	VAMOSE
		******			WAMOUS
		ARMLET			
		CAMLET			

******	POMPEY	******	ANNALS	RONALD	MANCHU
--MP--	POMPOM	**--MT--**	ARNAUD	SENARY	MINCED
******	POMPON	******	BANANA	SENATE	MINCER
ARMPIT	PUMPED	TAMTAM	BINARY	SONANT	MINCES
BUMPED	PUMPER	TOMTIT	BINATE	SONARS	NANCYS
BUMPER	RAMPED	TOMTOM	BONACI	SONATA	NONCOM
CAMPED	RIMPLE	******	BYNAME	TENACE	NUNCIO
CAMPER	ROMPED	**--MU--**	CANAAN	TENANT	OUNCES
CAMPOS	ROMPER	******	CANADA	XANADU	PANCHO
CAMPUS	RUMPLE	ALMUCE	CANALS	ZANANA	PENCEL
COMPEL	RUMPUS	ALMUDE	CANAPE	ZENANA	PENCIL
COMPLY	SAMPAN	ALMUDS	CANARD	ZONARY	PONCHO
COMPOS	SAMPLE	ARMURE	CANARY	ZONATE	PUNCHY
DAMPED	SEMPRE	BEMUSE	DANAID	******	RANCHO
DAMPEN	SIMPER	DEMURE	DANAUS	**--NB--**	RANCID
DAMPER	SIMPLE	DEMURS	DENARY	******	RANCOR
DAMPLY	SIMPLY	EDMUND	DINAHS	BONBON	TINCAL
DIMPLE	TAMPAN	FEMURS	DINARS	DUNBAR	TINCAN
DIMPLY	TAMPED	GAMUTS	DONALD	HENBIT	TINCTS
DUMPED	TAMPER	GOMUTI	DONATE	SINBAD	VINCES
DUMPER	TAMPON	IMMUNE	DYNAMO	SUNBOW	WINCED
DUMPTY	TEMPER	IMMUNO	DYNAST	******	WINCER
GIMPED	TEMPLE	IMMURE	FINALE	**--NC--**	WINCES
HAMPER	TEMPOS	LEMUEL	FINALS	******	WINCEY
HEMPEN	TEMPTS	LEMURS	GONADS	BUNCHE	ZINCED
HUMPED	TYMPAN	LIMULI	IGNACE	BUNCHY	ZINCIC
HUMPTY	VAMPED	NOMURA	INNATE	BUNCOS	ZINCKY
JUMPED	WAMPUM	ORMUZD	JONAHS	CANCAN	******
JUMPER	WIMPLE	OSMUND	KANAKA	CANCEL	**--ND--**
LAMPAD	******	REMUDA	KINASE	CANCER	******
LAMPAS	**--MR--**	ROMULO	LANAIS	CONCHA	BANDED
LAMPED	******	SAMUEL	LANATE	CONCHS	BANDIT
LIMPED	CYMRIC	TUMULT	LENAPE	CONCHY	BENDAY
LIMPER	NIMROD	YAMUNS	LINAGE	CONCUR	BENDED
LIMPET	RAMROD	******	LUNACY	DANCED	BENDEE
LIMPID	******	**--MW--**	LUNATE	DANCER	BENDER
LIMPLY	**--MS--**	******	MANAGE	DANCES	BINDER
LUMPED	******	DIMWIT	MANANA	DUNCAN	BONDED
LUMPEN	DAMSEL	******	MENACE	DUNCES	BONDER
LYMPHO	DAMSON	**--MZ--**	MENAGE	FENCED	BUNDLE
NYMPHA	GEMSBO	******	MONACO	FENCER	CANDIA
NYMPHO	KAMSIN	HAMZAS	MONADS	FENCES	CANDID
NYMPHS	RAMSON	******	NONAGE	HANCES	CANDLE
PAMPAS	SAMSHU	**--NA--**	NONARY	JUNCOS	CANDOR
PAMPER	SAMSON	******	ORNATE	LANCED	CINDER
PIMPED		ADNATE	PANADA	LANCER	CINDYS
PIMPLE		AGNAIL	PANAMA	LANCES	CONDOM
PIMPLY		AGNATE	PINANG	LANCET	CONDOR

DANDER	PINDUS	WINDUP	LONELY	BANGUP	JUNGLY
DANDLE	PONDER	WONDER	LONERS	BENGAL	KINGED
DENDRI	PUNDIT	YONDER	LUNETS	BINGES	KINGLY
DENDRO	RANDAL	******	MANEGE	BONGED	LANGUR
DINDER	RANDAN	--NE--	MINERS	BONGOS	LENGTH
DUNDEE	RANDOM	******	MONEYS	BUNGED	LINGAM
FENDED	RENDED	ABNERS	NINETY	BUNGLE	LINGAS
FENDER	RENDER	AENEAS	NONEGO	CANGUE	LINGER
FINDER	RONDEL	AENEID	ORNERY	CONGAS	LINGUA
FONDER	RONDOS	ANNEAL	OWNERS	CONGER	LONGAN
FONDLE	RUNDLE	ANNEXE	PANELS	CONGES	LONGED
FONDLY	SANDAL	APNEAL	PINEAL	CONGOU	LONGER
FONDUE	SANDED	APNEIC	PINENE	DANGED	LUNGED
FUNDED	SANDER	BONERS	PINERY	DANGER	LUNGEE
FUNDUS	SANDHI	CANERS	PONENT	DANGLE	LUNGER
GANDER	SANDRA	CINEMA	RANEES	DENGUE	LUNGES
GANDHI	SANDYS	CINEOL	RENEES	DINGED	LUNGIS
GENDER	SENDAL	CONEYS	RENEGE	DINGEY	MANGER
HANDED	SENDER	CUNEAL	RENEWS	DINGHY	MANGLE
HANDEL	SONDER	DINERO	SANELY	DINGLE	MANGOS
HANDLE	SUNDAE	DINERS	SANEST	DINGUS	MINGLE
HENDON	SUNDAY	DONEES	SENECA	DUNGED	MONGER
HINDER	SUNDER	DONETS	SINEON	FANGAS	MONGOL
HINDUS	SUNDEW	ENNEAD	SINEWS	FANGED	MONGST
KENDAL	SUNDOG	ERNEST	SINEWY	FINGER	PENGOS
KINDER	SUNDRY	FANEGA	TENETS	FUNGAL	PINGED
KINDLE	SYNDET	FINELY	TINEID	FUNGUS	PINGOS
KINDLY	SYNDIC	FINERY	TONERS	GANGED	PONGEE
LANDAU	TANDEM	FINEST	TUNERS	GANGER	RANGED
LANDED	TENDED	FUNEST	TUNEUP	GANGES	RANGER
LANDER	TENDER	GANEFS	VENEER	GANGLI	RANGES
LENDER	TENDON	GENERA	VENERY	GANGUE	RINGED
LINDAS	TINDER	GENESI	VINERY	GINGAL	RINGER
LINDEN	TUNDRA	GENETS	WINERY	GINGER	SANGAR
LONDON	VANDAL	GENEVA	******	GINGKO	SANGER
MANDAN	VENDED	GONERS	--NF--	HANGAR	SANGUI
MANDYS	VENDEE	GYNECO	******	HANGED	SINGED
MENDED	VENDER	HONEST	CONFAB	HANGER	SINGER
MENDEL	VENDOR	HONEYS	CONFER	HANGUP	SINGES
MENDER	VENDUE	JANETS	MANFUL	HINGED	SINGLE
MENDIP	WANDAS	JUNEAU	SINFUL	HINGES	SINGLY
MINDED	WANDER	KINESI	******	HUNGER	SUNGOD
MINDER	WANDLE	KINETO	--NG--	HUNGRY	TANGED
MONDAY	WENDED	LINEAL	******	JANGLE	TANGLE
PANDAS	WENDYS	LINEAR	BANGED	JINGAL	TANGLY
PANDER	WINDED	LINENS	BANGLE	JINGLE	TANGOS
PENDED	WINDER	LINERS	BANGOR	JINGLY	TINGED
PINDAR	WINDOW	LINEUP	BANGUI	JUNGLE	TINGES

TINGLE	DINING	MONIED	WINING	MONKEY	BENNET
TINGLY	EONIAN	MONIES	XENIAL	PINKED	BENNYS
TONGED	EONISM	MONISM	ZANIER	PINKIE	BINNED
TONGUE	ERNIES	MONIST	ZANIES	PUNKAS	BONNET
TUNGUS	EUNICE	MUNICH	ZENITH	RANKED	BONNIE
WANGLE	FANION	NANISM	ZONING	RANKER	BONNYS
WINGED	FENIAN	OMNIUM	******	RANKLE	CANNAE
ZENGER	FINIAL	ORNITH	--NJ--	RANKLY	CANNAS
ZINGED	FINING	OWNING	******	RINKED	CANNED
******	FINISH	PANICE	BANJOS	SINKER	CANNEL
--NH--	FINITE	PANICS	BENJYS	SUNKEN	CANNER
******	GENIAL	PENIAL	DONJON	TANKAS	CANNES
MENHIR	GENIES	PENILE	FANJET	TANKED	CANNIE
SUNHAT	GENITO	PINIER	PUNJAB	TANKER	CANNON
******	GENIUS	PINIES	SANJAK	TINKER	CANNOT
--NI--	GONION	PINING	******	TINKLE	CONNED
******	GONIUM	PINION	--NK--	TINKLY	CONNER
AMNION	HONIED	PINITE	******	TONKIN	CONNIE
ANNIES	HONING	PONIED	BANKED	WINKED	CUNNER
ARNICA	IGNIFY	PONIES	BANKER	WINKER	DANNYS
ARNIES	IGNITE	PUNIER	BUNKED	WINKLE	DENNED
AWNING	INNING	PUNILY	BUNKER	YANKED	DENNIS
BANIAN	IONIAN	PUNISH	BUNKUM	YANKEE	DENNYS
BANISH	IONIUM	RUNINS	CANKER	YONKER	DINNED
BENIGN	IONIZE	SANIES	CONKED	******	DINNER
BENITA	JANICE	SANITY	CONKER	--NL--	DONNAS
BENITO	JUNIOR	SENILE	DANKER	******	DONNED
BINITS	JUNIUS	SENIOR	DANKLY	DUNLIN	DONNIE
BONIER	KENITE	SONIAS	DINKEY	HENLEY	DUNNED
BONING	KININS	TANIST	DINKUM	RUNLET	FANNED
BONITO	LENITY	TINIER	DONKEY	SENLAC	FANNER
BUNION	LINIER	TINILY	DUNKED	SUNLIT	FANNIE
CANINE	LINING	TONICS	DUNKER	******	FANNYS
CANING	MANIAC	TONIER	FUNKED	--NM--	FENNEC
CONICS	MANIAS	TONING	HANKER	******	FENNEL
CONIES	MANILA	TONITE	HONKED	CONMAN	FINNAN
CONING	MANIOC	TUNICA	HONKER	GUNMAN	FINNED
CONIUM	MANITO	TUNICS	JINKED	GUNMEN	FINNER
CYNICS	MANITU	TUNING	JINKER	PENMAN	FINNIC
DANIEL	MENIAL	VANISH	JUNKED	PENMEN	FINNOC
DANISH	MENINX	VANITY	JUNKER	VANMAN	FUNNEL
DANITE	MINIFY	VENIAL	JUNKET	VANMEN	GANNET
DENIAL	MINIMA	VENICE	JUNKIE	******	GINNED
DENIED	MINIMS	VENIRE	KINKED	--NN--	GINNER
DENIER	MINING	VINIER	LANKER	******	GUNNAR
DENIES	MINION	WANING	LANKLY	BANNED	GUNNED
DENIMS	MINIUM	WANION	LINKED	BANNER	GUNNEL
DENISE	MONICA	WINIER	LUNKER	BENNES	GUNNER

HANNAH	TANNER	PINONS	CENSOR	CANTLE	MANTUA
HANNAS	TANNIC	RENOIR	CENSUR	CANTON	MENTAL
HENNAS	TANNIN	RENOWN	CENSUS	CANTOR	MENTOR
JENNET	TENNIS	RUNOFF	CONSUL	CANTOS	MINTED
JENNYS	TINNED	RUNONS	DENSER	CANTUS	MINTER
JINNEE	TINNER	RUNOUT	GUNSHY	CENTAL	MONTES
JINNYS	TUNNED	SENORA	HANSEL	CENTER	MONTHS
JONNIE	TUNNEL	SYNODS	HANSOM	CENTOS	MONTYS
KENNED	VINNYS	TENONS	HONSHU	CENTRA	NANTES
KENNEL	WANNED	TENORS	JONSON	CENTRE	NINTHS
KENNIE	WANNER	VENOMS	KANSAN	CENTRI	PANTED
KENNYS	WINNER	VENOSE	KANSAS	CENTRO	PANTIE
LANNER	WINNIE	VENOUS	KINSEY	CONTES	PANTRY
LENNYS	WINNOW	VINOUS	LENSES	CONTIN	PENTAD
LINNET	YENNED	WINOES	MANSES	CONTOS	PENTUP
MANNED	ZINNIA	******	MENSAL	CONTRA	PINTER
MANNER	******	--NP--	MENSES	CONTRE	PINTLE
MINNIE	--NO--	******	PANSYS	DANTON	PINTOS
MINNOW	******	PENPAL	RANSOM	DENTAL	PONTES
PANNED	ACNODE	TENPIN	RINSED	DENTED	PONTIC
PENNAE	ADNOUN	TINPOT	RINSER	DENTIL	PONTIL
PENNED	ANNONA	******	RINSES	DENTIN	PONTON
PENNER	ANNOYS	--NQ--	SANSAR	DINTED	PUNTED
PENNIA	APNOEA	******	SANSEI	FANTAN	PUNTER
PENNIS	ARNOLD	CINQUE	SENSED	FANTOM	PUNTOS
PENNON	CANOED	MANQUE	SENSES	FONTAL	RANTED
PENNYS	CANOES	******	SENSOR	GANTRY	RANTER
PINNAE	CANONS	--NR--	SUNSET	GENTES	RENTAL
PINNAL	CANOPY	******	TENSED	GENTLE	RENTED
PINNED	CONOID	CONRAD	TENSER	GENTLY	RENTER
PINNER	DENOTE	FENRIR	TENSES	GENTOO	RENTES
PUNNED	DONORS	GENRES	TENSOR	GENTRY	SANTOL
PUNNER	FANONS	GENROS	TINSEL	GUNTER	SENTRY
RENNET	GANOID	HENRIS	TONSIL	HINTED	SINTER
RENNIN	GENOUS	HENRYS	VINSON	HUNTED	SUNTAN
RONNIE	GYNOUS	KONRAD	******	HUNTER	SYNTAX
RUNNEL	HONORE	MONROE	--NT--	JUNTAS	TENTED
RUNNER	HONORS	TANREC	******	LENTEN	TENTER
SANNUP	HONOUR	TENREC	AUNTIE	LENTIL	TENTHS
SENNAS	IGNORE	******	BANTAM	LENTOS	TINTED
SENNET	IONONE	--NS--	BANTER	LINTEL	VENTED
SENNIT	LANOSE	******	BANTUS	LINTER	VENTER
SINNED	LENORE	BONSAI	BENTON	MANTAS	VENTRO
SINNER	MANORS	BUNSEN	BUNTED	MANTEL	WANTED
SONNET	MINOAN	CANSOS	CANTAB	MANTES	WANTER
SUNNAH	MINORS	CENSED	CANTED	MANTIC	WANTON
SUNNED	MONODY	CENSER	CANTER	MANTIS	WINTER
TANNED	PINOLE	CENSES	CANTHI	MANTLE	WINTRY

WONTED	******	SHOATS	SHOCKS	COOEES	ELOHIM
XANTHO	--NX--	STOATS	SMOCKS	COOERS	ISOHEL
******	******	UBOATS	SNOCAT	COOEYS	YOOHOO
--NU--	JINXED	******	STOCKS	PHOEBE	******
******	JINXES	--OB--	STOCKY	PROEMS	--OI--
ANNUAL	LYNXES	******	TROCAR	SHOERS	******
ANNULS	MINXES	ADOBES	TROCHE	WOOERS	ANOINT
BENUMB	PINXIT	BAOBAB	******	******	AROIDS
CANUCK	******	BOOBOO	--OD--	--OF--	AVOIDS
CANULA	--NY--	DIOBOL	******	******	BOOING
CANUTE	BANYAN	GLOBAL	ABODES	CROFTS	BROILS
DANUBE	BUNYAN	GLOBED	ANODES	FEOFFS	CHOICE
DENUDE	BUNYIP	GLOBES	ANODIC	GOOFED	CHOIRS
EUNUCH	CANYON	GLOBIN	APODAL	HOOFED	COOING
FANUMS	RUNYON	GOOBER	BOODLE	HOOFER	DROITS
LANUGO	SONYAS	ISOBAR	CLODDY	LOOFAH	EGOISM
LUNULA	VINYLS	ISOBEL	COODLE	PROFIT	EGOIST
LUNULE	******	KNOBBY	DEODAR	ROOFED	ELOIGN
MANUAL	--NZ--	NIOBIC	DIODES	ROOFER	ELOINS
MANUEL	******	PHOBIA	DOODAD	SCOFFS	ELOISE
MANURE	BANZAI	PHOBIC	DOODLE	SHOFAR	GOOIER
MINUET	BENZOL	PROBED	DUODEN	TWOFER	GROINS
MINUTE	BENZYL	PROBER	EPODES	WOOFER	HYOIDS
PENULT	BONZER	PROBES	ERODED	******	ILOILO
PENURY	BONZES	SNOBBY	ERODES	--OG--	LOOING
PINUPS	DANZIG	TWOBIT	EXODUS	******	MAOISM
SUNUPS	PANZER	******	FEODOR	AGOGUE	MAOIST
SYNURA	WINZES	--OC--	GEODES	APOGEE	MOOING
TENUES	******	******	GEODIC	BIOGEN	OBOIST
TENUIS	--OA--	AVOCET	GOODBY	BOOGIE	OROIDE
TENURE	******	BLOCKS	GOODLY	BROGAN	QUOINS
TENUTO	ABOARD	BLOCKY	HOODED	BROGUE	QUOITS
VENUES	BLOATS	BROCHE	HOODOO	CLOGGY	SPOILS
VENULE	BROACH	CHOCKS	KOODOO	DROGUE	SPOILT
ZONULA	BROADS	CLOCHE	NOODLE	EXOGEN	STOICS
ZONULE	CLOACA	CLOCKS	POODLE	FROGGY	TAOISM
******	CLOAKS	CROCKS	RHODAS	GOOGLY	TAOIST
--NV--	CROAKS	CROCKY	RHODES	GOOGOL	TROIKA
******	CROAKY	CROCUS	RHODIC	GROGGY	WOOING
CANVAS	CROATS	EPOCHS	SHODDY	IMOGEN	ZOOIDS
CONVEX	FLOATS	FLOCKS	STODGE	ISOGON	******
CONVEY	FLOATY	FLOCKY	STODGY	SHOGUN	--OJ--
CONVOY	GLOATS	FROCKS	VOODOO	SLOGAN	******
DENVER	GROANS	GROCER	WOODED	STOGEY	CROJIK
******	GROATS	KNOCKS	WOODEN	TROGON	PROJET
--NW--	SHOALS	PHOCIS	WOODSY	******	SHOJIS
******	SHOALY	PROCNE	******	--OH--	TROJAN
CONWAY		PROCTO	--OE--	******	
RUNWAY			******	ABOHMS	
			AMOEBA	BOOHOO	
			COOEED		

******	APOLOG	******	ATONER	PRONTO	SHOOIN
--OK--	ATOLLS	--OM--	ATONES	SCONCE	SHOOTS
******	AZOLES	******	ATONIC	SCONES	SLOOPS
AWOKEN	BROLLY	ABOMAS	AXONES	SOONER	SMOOCH
BLOKES	CHOLER	ABOMBS	AZONIC	SPONGE	SMOOTH
BOOKED	CHOLLA	ANOMIA	BLONDE	SPONGY	SNOODS
BOOKIE	COOLED	ANOMIC	BLONDS	STONED	SNOOKS
BROKEN	COOLER	ANOMIE	BRONCO	STONER	SNOOPS
BROKER	COOLIE	AROMAS	BRONCS	STONES	SNOOPY
CHOKED	COOLLY	ATOMIC	BRONTE	TBONES	SNOOTS
CHOKER	DHOLES	BOOMED	BRONZE	THONGS	SNOOTY
CHOKES	DOOLEE	BOOMER	BRONZY	WRONGS	SNOOZE
COOKED	DOOLIE	BROMAL	CLONES	YVONNE	SPOOFS
COOKER	DROLLS	BROMES	CLONIC	ZOONAL	SPOOKS
COOKEY	DROLLY	BROMIC	CLONUS	******	SPOOKY
COOKIE	DUOLOG	COOMBS	CRONES	--OO--	SPOOLS
EVOKED	ECOLES	DOOMED	CRONOS	******	SPOONS
EVOKES	EVOLVE	DROMON	CRONUS	BLOODS	SPOONY
HOOKAH	FOOLED	GNOMES	DRONED	BLOODY	SPOORS
HOOKED	FROLIC	GNOMIC	DRONES	BLOOMS	STOOGE
HOOKER	GAOLER	GNOMON	DRONGO	BLOOMY	STOOKS
HOOKEY	ISOLDE	ISOMER	EPONYM	BROOCH	STOOLS
HOOKUP	KAOLIN	LOOMED	FLONGS	BROODS	STOOPS
LOOKED	KNOLLS	NAOMIS	FRONDS	BROODY	SWOONS
LOOKER	MOOLAH	PROMPT	FRONTO	BROOKE	SWOOPS
LOOKIN	MOOLEY	RHOMBI	FRONTS	BROOKS	TROOPS
ROOKED	OBOLUS	ROOMED	GOONEY	BROOMS	WHOOPS
ROOKIE	POOLED	ROOMER	ICONIC	BROOMY	WHOOSH
SMOKED	PROLEG	STOMAT	IRONED	CHOOSE	******
SMOKER	PROLIX	STOMPS	IRONER	CHOOSY	--OP--
SMOKES	SCOLDS	SUOMIC	IRONIC	CROOKS	******
SPOKED	SCOLEX	THOMAS	KRONEN	CROONS	ADOPTS
SPOKEN	SMOLTS	YEOMAN	KRONER	DROOLS	BIOPSY
SPOKES	STOLED	YEOMEN	KRONOR	DROOPS	CHOPIN
STOKED	STOLEN	ZOOMED	KRONOS	DROOPY	CHOPPY
STOKER	STOLES	******	KRONUR	FLOODS	COOPED
STOKES	STOLID	--ON--	LEONAS	FLOORS	COOPER
******	STOLON	******	LEONIE	FLOOZY	COOPTS
--OL--	THOLES	ADONAI	LIONEL	GLOOMS	DROPSY
******	TOOLED	ADONIC	MOONED	GLOOMY	ELOPED
ABOLLA	TOOLER	ADONIS	ODONTO	GROOMS	ELOPER
ADOLPH	TROLLS	AGONES	OZONIC	GROOVE	ELOPES
AEOLIA	VIOLAS	AGONIC	PHONED	GROOVY	EPOPEE
AEOLIC	VIOLET	ALONSO	PHONES	PHOOEY	FLOPPY
AEOLIS	VIOLIN	ALONZO	PHONEY	PROOFS	GROPED
AEOLUS	WHOLLY	ANONYM	PHONIA	SCOOPS	GROPER
AMOLES	WOOLEN	ATONAL	PHONIC	SCOOTS	GROPES
APOLLO	WOOLLY	ATONED	PRONGS	SHOOED	HOOPED

HOOPER	CEORLS	SPORTS	GROSZY	FOOTER	TROTYL
HOOPLA	CHORAL	SPORTY	KIOSKS	FOOTLE	ZLOTYS
HOOPOE	CHORDS	STORAX	KNOSPS	FROTHS	******
ISOPOD	CHOREA	STORED	LOOSED	FROTHY	--OU--
LOOPED	CHOREO	STORES	LOOSEN	GIOTTO	******
LOOPER	CHORES	STOREY	LOOSER	GLOTTO	ABOUND
MYOPES	CHORIC	STORKS	LOOSES	GROTTO	AGOUTI
MYOPIA	CHORUS	STORMS	MIOSIS	GROTTY	AGOUTY
MYOPIC	CRORES	STORMY	MYOSIN	HOOTCH	AMOUNT
PEOPLE	DVORAK	SWORDS	MYOSIS	HOOTED	AMOURS
POOPED	FIORDS	THORAC	NAOSES	HOOTER	AROUND
PROPEL	FLORAE	THORAX	NOOSED	KNOTTY	AROUSE
PROPER	FLORAL	THORIA	NOOSES	LAOTSE	AVOUCH
PROPYL	FLORAS	THORIC	PHOSPH	LOOTED	BLOUSE
REOPEN	FLORES	THORNS	PROSED	LOOTER	CHOUGH
SCOPES	FLORET	THORNY	PROSER	MIOTIC	CLOUDS
SCOPUS	FLORID	THORON	PROSES	MOOTED	CLOUDY
SHOPPE	FLORIN	THORPE	PROSIT	MOOTER	CLOUGH
SKOPJE	GEORGE	WHORED	PTOSIS	PHOTIC	CLOUTS
SLOPED	GEORGI	WHORES	PYOSIS	PHOTON	CROUCH
SLOPER	GLORIA	WHORLS	ROOSTS	PHOTOS	CROUPE
SLOPES	GOORAL	WHORTS	SLOSHY	PROTON	CROUPS
SLOPPY	HOORAY	******	******	QUOTAS	CROUPY
STOPED	IGOROT	--OS--	--OT--	QUOTED	DROUTH
STOPES	MAORIS	******	******	QUOTER	ENOUGH
TROPAL	MOORED	AVOSET	AZOTIC	QUOTES	FLOURS
TROPHO	OPORTO	BIOSIS	BIOTIC	QUOTHA	FLOURY
TROPHY	PEORIA	BOOSTS	BIOTIN	RIOTED	FLOUTS
TROPIC	POORER	CHOSEN	BLOTCH	RIOTER	GHOULS
TROPPO	POORLY	CLOSED	BOOTED	ROOTED	GROUCH
TWOPLY	QUORUM	CLOSER	BOOTEE	ROOTER	GROUND
UROPOD	SCORCH	CLOSES	BOOTHS	ROOTLE	GROUPS
UTOPIA	SCORED	CLOSET	BOOTIE	SCOTCH	GROUSE
******	SCORER	CROSSE	BOOTLE	SCOTER	GROUTS
--OR--	SCORES	DROSKY	BROTHS	SCOTIA	KNOUTS
******	SCORIA	DROSSY	CLOTHE	SCOTTS	PLOUGH
ABORAL	SCORNS	ENOSIS	CLOTHO	SHOTES	PROUST
ABORTS	SHORAN	FLOSSY	CLOTHS	SLOTHS	RAOULS
ACORNS	SHORED	FROSTS	CLOTTY	SNOTTY	SCOURS
ADORED	SHORES	FROSTY	COOTIE	SOOTED	SCOUSE
ADORER	SHORLS	GHOSTS	CROTCH	SOOTHE	SCOUTS
ADORES	SHORTS	GLOSSO	CROTON	SPOTTY	SHOULD
ADORNS	SNORED	GLOSSY	DHOTIS	TOOTED	SHOUTS
AGORAE	SNORER	GLOSTS	EMOTED	TOOTER	SIOUAN
AGORAS	SNORES	GNOSIS	EMOTES	TOOTHY	SLOUCH
AMORAL	SNORTS	GOOSED	EROTIC	TOOTLE	SLOUGH
ANORAK	SPORED	GOOSES	EXOTIC	TOOTSY	SNOUTS
AZORES	SPORES	GOOSEY	FOOTED	TROTHS	SPOUSE

SPOUTS	AVOWED	FLOYDS	PUPATE	KOPECK	ALPHYL
STOUPS	AVOWER	GROYNE	REPAID	KOPEKS	AMPHRS
STOUTS	BLOWBY	LLOYDS	REPAIR	LAPELS	CIPHER
THOUGH	BLOWER	******	REPAND	LEPERS	CYPHER
TROUGH	BLOWUP	--OZ--	REPASS	LOPERS	DAPHNE
TROUPE	BLOWZY	******	REPAST	MOPERS	GOPHER
TROUTS	BROWNS	BOOZED	REPAYS	NAPERY	HYPHAE
TWOULD	BROWSE	BOOZER	SEPALS	OEPEMA	HYPHAL
YAOURT	CLOWNS	BOOZES	TAPALO	PAPERS	HYPHEN
******	CROWDS	CROZER	UNPACK	PAPERY	JAPHET
--OV--	CROWED	CROZES	ZAPATA	PIPERS	JAPHIA
******	CROWNS	FOOZLE	******	PIPETS	NEPHEW
CLOVEN	DROWNS	FROZEN	--PC--	POPERY	NEPHRO
CLOVER	DROWSE	GLOZED	******	REPEAL	OOPHOR
CLOVES	DROWSY	GLOZES	TIPCAT	REPEAT	ORPHAN
CLOVIS	FLOWED	******	******	REPELS	ORPHIC
DROVED	FLOWER	--PA--	--PD--	REPENT	RAPHAE
DROVER	FROWNS	******	******	RIPELY	RAPHIS
DROVES	FROWZY	ALPACA	LAPDOG	RIPENS	SAPHAR
GLOVED	GLOWED	APPALL	******	RIPEST	SIPHON
GLOVER	GLOWER	APPALS	--PE--	RUPEES	SOPHIA
GLOVES	GROWER	BYPASS	******	RUPERT	SOPHIE
GROVEL	GROWLS	BYPAST	AMPERE	SUPERB	SYPHER
GROVER	GROWTH	BYPATH	APPEAL	SUPERS	SYPHON
GROVES	KNOWER	COPALM	APPEAR	TAPERS	TOPHAT
HOOVED	MEOWED	DEPART	APPELS	TEPEES	TYPHLO
HOOVER	PLOWED	EMPALE	APPEND	TEPEFY	TYPHON
HOOVES	PLOWER	ESPANA	ARPENS	TOPEKA	TYPHUS
PLOVER	PROWLS	EXPAND	ARPENT	TOPERS	ZEPHYR
PROVED	SCOWLS	HEPATO	ASPECT	TUPELO	******
PROVEN	SHOWED	IMPACT	ASPENS	UNPEGS	--PI--
PROVER	SHOWER	IMPAIR	ASPERS	UPPERS	******
PROVES	SLOWED	IMPALA	BIPEDS	VIPERS	ALPINE
SHOVED	SLOWER	IMPALE	CAPERS	WIPERS	APPIAN
SHOVEL	SLOWLY	IMPARK	COPECK	******	ASPICS
SHOVER	SNOWED	IMPART	CUPELS	--PF--	ASPIRE
SHOVES	STOWED	IMPASS	DEPEND	******	CAPIAS
SLOVAK	TROWEL	IMPAWN	DUPERS	CUPFUL	CAPITA
SLOVEN	TWOWAY	JAPANS	DUPERY	LAPFUL	COPIED
STOVER	******	LAPARO	EMPERY	******	COPIER
STOVES	--OX--	LIPASE	EXPECT	--PG--	COPIES
TROVER	ANOXIA	NAPALM	EXPELS	******	COPING
TROVES	ANOXIC	NOPALS	EXPEND	POPGUN	DEPICT
******	******	PAPACY	EXPERT	******	DOPIER
--OW--	--OY--	PAPAIN	GAPERS	--PH--	DOPING
******	******	PAPAWS	IMPEDE	******	DUPING
AJOWAN	BUOYED	PAPAYA	IMPELS	ALPHAS	EMPIRE
AVOWAL	CLOYED	PIPAGE	IMPEND	ALPHOS	EPPING

ESPIAL	UNPICK	******	COPPRA	POPPET	CUPRUM
ESPIED	UNPILE	--PO--	CUPPED	POPPLE	CYPRIN
ESPIES	UNPINS	******	CUPPER	POPPYS	CYPRUS
EXPIRE	UPPING	APPORT	DAPPED	PUPPED	ESPRIT
EXPIRY	UPPISH	APPOSE	DAPPER	PUPPET	OSPREY
GAPING	UPPITY	BIPODS	DAPPLE	PUPPET	RIPRAP
HOPING	WAPITI	CAPONE	DIPPED	RAPPED	******
IMPING	WIPING	CAPONS	DIPPER	RAPPEE	--PS--
IMPISH	******	CAPOTE	FIPPLE	RAPPEL	******
JAPING	--PJ--	COPOUT	GAPPED	RAPPER	COPSES
LAPINS	******	CUPOLA	GIPPED	RIPPED	DIPSAS
LEPIDO	KOPJES	DEPONE	GYPPED	RIPPER	GYPSUM
LIPIDS	******	DEPORT	HAPPED	RIPPLE	LAPSED
LOPING	--PK--	DEPOSE	HAPPEN	RIPPLY	LAPSER
LUPINE	******	DEPOTS	HIPPED	SAPPED	LAPSES
MOPING	NAPKIN	DIPODY	HIPPIE	SAPPER	LAPSUS
MOPISH	PIPKIN	DIPOLE	HIPPOS	SAPPHO	LEPSIA
NAPIER	******	EXPORT	HIPPUS	SIPPED	PEPSIN
ORPINE	--PL--	EXPOSE	HOPPED	SIPPER	RIPSAW
ORPINS	******	GIPONS	HOPPER	SIPPET	SEPSIS
PAPIST	APPLES	IMPORT	HOPPLE	SOPPED	******
PIPIER	BYPLAY	IMPOSE	KAPPAS	SUPPED	--PT--
PIPING	CAPLIN	IMPOST	KIPPED	SUPPER	******
PIPITS	COPLEY.	JUPONS	KIPPER	SUPPLE	CAPTOR
POPISH	DEPLOY	KAPOKS	LAPPED	SUPPLY	COPTIC
PUPILS	DIPLEX	LIPOID	LAPPER	TAPPED	CUPTIE
RAPIDS	DIPLOE	LIPOMA	LAPPET	TAPPER	DEPTHS
RAPIER	DUPLET	MOPOKE	LIPPED	TAPPET	DOPTER
RAPINE	DUPLEX	OPPOSE	LIPPER	TIPPED	HEPTAD
RAPING	EMPLOY	REPORT	LOPPED	TIPPER	LEPTON
RAPIST	JOPLIN	REPOSE	MAPPED	TIPPET	PEPTIC
REPINE	KEPLER	RIPOFF	MOPPED	TIPPLE	RAPTLY
ROPIER	MAPLES	RIPOST	MOPPET	TOPPED	RAPTOR
ROPILY	NAPLES	SEPOYS	NAPPED	TOPPER	SEPTAL
ROPING	PEPLOS	TIPOFF	NAPPER	TOPPLE	SEPTET
RUPIAH	PEPLUM	VAPORI	NAPPES	TUPPED	SEPTIC
SAPIEN	PEPLUS	VAPORS	NAPPIE	WAPPED	SEPTUM
SEPIAS	POPLAR	VAPOUR	NIPPED	YAPPED	TIPTOE
SUPINE	POPLIN	YAPONS	NIPPER	YIPPED	TIPTOP
TAPING	REPLAY	YUPONS	NIPPLE	YIPPIE	******
TAPIRS	RIPLEY	******	NIPPON	YUPPIE	--PU--
TOPICS	UNPLUG	--PP--	PAPPUS	ZIPPED	******
TOPING	******	******	PEPPED	ZIPPER	AMPULE
TUPIKS	--PN--	BOPPED	PEPPER	******	AMPULS
TYPIFY	******	CAPPED	PIPPED	--PR--	COPULA
TYPING	EUPNEA	CAPPER	PIPPIN	******	CUPULE
TYPIST	HYPNIC	COPPED	POPPED	CAPRIC	DEPUTE
UMPIRE	HYPNOS	COPPER	POPPER	COPRAH	DEPUTY
				CUPRIC	

IMPUGN	BURANS	MORASS	TIRADE	WARBLE.	CURDED
IMPURE	CARACK	MORAYS	TIRANA	YERBAS	CURDLE
IMPUTE	CARAFE	MURALS	TORAHS	******	DARDAN
INPUTS	CARATE	PARADE	TYRANT	--RC--	FORDED
OPPUGN	CARATS	PARANG	VIRAGO	******	GARDEN
PAPUAN	CERATE	PARAPH	******	CARCEL	GIRDED
PAPULA	CERATO	PHRASE	--RB--	CIRCLE	GIRDER
PAPULE	CORALS	PIRACY	******	CIRCUM	GIRDLE
REPUTE	CURACY	PIRANA	AIRBED	CIRCUS	GORDON
******	CURARE	PIRATE	BARBED	FARCED	HARDEN
--QU--	CURATE	PURANA	BARBEL	FARCER	HARDER
******	CYRANO	PYRANS	BARBER	FARCES	HARDLY
ACQUIT	DERAIL	SARAHS	BARBET	FORCED	HERDED
COQUET	DERAIN	SARAPE	BARBIE	FORCER	HERDER
FIQUES	DERATE	SCRAGS	BARBRA	FORCES	HERDIC
LIQUID	DORADO	SCRAMS	BERBER	GARCON	HORDED
LIQUOR	ENRAGE	SCRAPE	BURBLE	MARCEL	HORDES
LOQUAR	ENRAPT	SCRAPS	BURBOT	MARCIA	HURDLE
LOQUAT	ERRAND	SCRAWL	CARBON	MARCOS	JORDAN
MAQUIS	ERRANT	SERACS	CARBOY	MARCUS	LARDED
PEQUOD	ERRATA	SERAIS	CORBAN	MERCER	LARDER
PEQUOT	FARADS	SERAPE	CORBEL	MERCIA	LARDON
PIQUED	FORAGE	SERAPH	CORBIE	PARCAE	LORDED
PIQUES	FORAYS	SHRANK	CURBED	PARCEL	LORDLY
PIQUET	GARAGE	SPRAGS	DORBUG	PERCYS	MARDUK
ROQUET	GERALD	SPRAIN	DURBAN	TERCEL	MURDER
SEQUEL	GERARD	SPRANG	DURBAR	TERCET	NORDIC
SEQUIN	GORALS	SPRATS	FARBAD	TURCOS	PARDON
TOQUES	GYRATE	SPRAWL	FERBER	ZIRCON	PURDAH
TUQUES	HARASS	SPRAYS	FORBID	******	SERDAB
******	HERALD	STRAFE	GARBED	--RD--	SIRDAR
--RA--	HIRAMS	STRAIN	GARBLE	******	SORDID
******	HORACE	STRAIT	GERBIL	AIRDRY	VERDIN
ABRADE	HORARY	STRAKE	HARBIN	BARDED	VERDUN
ABRAMS	ISRAEL	STRAND	HARBOR	BARDES	WARDED
AERATE	JORAMS	STRAPS	HERBAL	BARDIC	WARDEN
AFRAID	JURANT	STRASS	JERBOA	BIRDIE	WARDER
AFRAME	JURATS	STRATA	KERBED	BORDEL	WORDED
AGRAFE	KARATE	STRATH	MARBLE	BORDER	YARDED
ARRACK	KARATS	STRATI	MORBID	BURDEN	******
ARRANT	KERALA	STRAWS	SERBIA	BURDIE	--RE--
ARRAYS	KERATO	STRAWY	SORBET	CARDED	******
AURATE	LORAIN	STRAYS	TERBIA	CARDER	AFRESH
AZRAEL	MARACA	SURAHS	TURBAN	CARDIO	AGREED
BERATE	MARAUD	TERAPH	TURBID	CORDAY	AGREES
BORAGE	MIRAGE	TERATO	TURBIT	CORDED	ARREAR
BORANE	MORALE	THRALL	TURBOT	CORDER	ARREST
BORATE	MORALS	THRASH	VERBAL	CORDON	ATREUS

AUREUS	KARENS	SPREES	BARGES	SORGOS	BARIUM
BAREGE	KOREAN	STREAK	BERGEN	SURGED	BERING
BARELY	LAREDO	STREAM	BORGIA	SURGER	BORIDE
BAREST	LOREEN	STREET	BURGEE	SURGES	BORING
BEREFT	LORENE	STRESS	BURGER	TARGET	BURIAL
BERETS	LORENZ	STREWN	BURGHS	TERGAL	BURIED
BIREME	LURERS	STREWS	BURGLE	TERGUM	BURIES
BOREAL	MERELY	SURELY	BURGOO	TURGID	BURINS
BOREAS	MEREST	SUREST	BURGOS	VERGED	CARIBE
BORERS	MOREAU	SURETY	CARGOS	VERGER	CARIBS
BUREAU	MOREEN	TEREDO	CORGIS	VERGES	CARIES
CAREEN	MORELS	TERESA	DIRGES	VERGIL	CARINA
CAREER	NEREID	TERETE	FORGED	VIRGAS	CARING
CARERS	NEREIS	TEREUS	FORGER	VIRGIE	CERING
CARESS	NOREEN	THREAD	FORGES	VIRGIL	CERIPH
CARETS	OCREAE	THREAT	FORGET	VIRGIN	CERISE
CEREAL	OGRESS	THREED	FORGOT	******	CERITE
CEREUS	ORRERY	THREES	GARGET	--RH--	CERIUM
CORERS	PARENS	THRESH	GARGLE	******	CHRISM
CURERS	PARENT	TORERO	GORGED	CARHOP	CHRIST
CYRENE	PARERS	TUREEN	GORGER	DIRHAM	CORING
DARERS	PAREUS	UNREAD	GORGES	DURHAM	CORIUM
DEREKS	PHRENO	UNREAL	GORGET	GORHEN	CURIAE
DIRECT	PUREED	UNREEL	GORGON	WARHOL	CURIAL
DIRELY	PUREES	UNREST	GURGLE	******	CURIES
DIREST	PURELY	VEREIN	JARGON	--RI--	CURING
DOREEN	PUREST	VIREOS	JORGES	******	CURIOS
DURESS	PYRENE	WERENT	LARGER	ADRIAN	CURIUM
EGRESS	RAREFY	WIRERS	LARGOS	ADRIEN	CYRILS
EGRETS	RARELY	******	MARGAY	ADRIFT	DARICS
EUREKA	RAREST	--RF--	MARGES	AERIAL	DARIEN
FARERS	SCREAK	******	MARGIE	AERIED	DARING
FIRERS	SCREAM	BARFLY	MARGIN	AERIES	DARIUS
FOREGO	SCREED	CARFAX	MARGOS	AERIFY	DERIDE
FOREST	SCREEN	CURFEW	MARGOT	AFRICA	DERIVE
GERENT	SCREWS	EARFUL	MERGED	AIRIER	DORIAN
HAREMS	SCREWY	FURFUR	MERGER	AIRILY	DORIES
HEREAT	SEREIN	JARFUL	MERGES	AIRING	DURIAN
HEREBY	SERENA	PURFLE	MORGAN	AMRITA	DURING
HEREIN	SERENE	SURFED	MORGEN	AORIST	DURION
HEREOF	SHREDS	SURFER	MORGUE	APRILS	EARING
HEREON	SHREWD	TURFED	PARGET	ARRIVE	EERILY
HERESY	SHREWS	******	PARGOS	ATRIAL	ENRICH
HERETO	SIRENS	--RG--	PURGED	ATRIUM	ENRICO
HIRERS	SORELS	******	PURGER	AURIGA	ERRING
JEREED	SORELY	AIRGUN	PURGES	AURIST	EURIPI
JEREMY	SOREST	BARGED	SARGON	BARING	EYRIES
JURELS	SPREAD	BARGEE	SORGHO	BARITE	FARINA

FARING	PARIAN	STRIFE	BURKED	CARLAS	DERMAL
FERIAL	PARIES	STRIKE	BURKES	CARLOS	DERMAS
FERINE	PARING	STRING	CORKED	CARLOW	DERMAT
FERITY	PARISH	STRIPE	CORKER	CURLED	DERMIC
FIRING	PARITY	STRIPS	DARKEN	CURLER	DERMIS
FORINT	PERILS	STRIPT	DARKER	CURLEW	DORMER
FURIES	PERIOD	STRIPY	DARKLE	EARLAP	DORMIE
GARISH	PERISH	STRIVE	DARKLY	EARLES	FARMED
GORIER	PORING	SYRIAC	DIRKED	FARLES	FARMER
GORILY	PURIFY	SYRIAN	FIRKIN	FARLEY	FERMIS
GORING	PURINE	SYRINX	FORKED	FURLED	FIRMAN
HARING	PURISM	TARIFF	GURKHA	GARLIC	FIRMED
HERIOT	PURIST	TARING	HARKED	HARLAN	FIRMER
HIRING	PURITY	THRICE	HARKEN	HARLEM	FIRMLY
JARINA	PYRITE	THRIFT	JERKED	HARLEY	FORMAL
JURIES	RARING	THRILL	JERKIN	HARLOT	FORMAT
JURIST	RARITY	THRIPS	LARKED	HARLOW	FORMED
LARIAT	SCRIBE	THRIVE	LARKER	HURLED	FORMER
LARINE	SCRIED	TIRING	LURKED	HURLER	FORMIC
LORICA	SCRIMP	TORIES	LURKER	HURLEY	FORMYL
LORIES	SCRIPS	TORIIS	MARKED	MARLED	GERMAN
LURING	SCRIPT	TYRIAN	MARKER	MARLIN	GERMEN
LYRICS	SCRIVE	UNRIGS	MARKET	MARLOW	HARMED
LYRISM	SERIAL	UNRIPE	MARKKA	MERLES	HARMIN
LYRIST	SERIES	UNRIPS	MARKUP	MERLIN	HERMAE
MARIAN	SERIFS	UPRISE	NARKED	MERLON	HERMAI
MARIAS	SERINE	VARICO	PARKAS	MORLEY	HERMAN
MARIES	SERINS	VARIED	PARKED	PARLAY	HERMES
MARINA	SHRIEK	VARIER	PARKER	PARLEY	HERMIT
MARINE	SHRIFT	VARIES	PERKED	PARLOR	KARMAS
MARION	SHRIKE	VERIFY	PORKER	PURLED	KERMES
MARIST	SHRILL	VERILY	TURKEY	PURLER	KERMIS
MERINO	SHRIMP	VERISM	TURKIC	PURLIN	KERMIT
MERITS	SHRINE	VERIST	TURKIS	VARLET	MARMOT
MIRIAM	SHRINK	VERITY	WORKED	WORLDS	MERMAN
MIRING	SHRIVE	VIRILE	WORKER	******	MERMEN
MORION	SIRING	WARIER	YORKER	--RM--	MORMON
MURIEL	SIRIUS	WARILY	******	******	MURMUR
MURINE	SPRIER	WIRIER	--RL--	AIRMAN	MYRMEC
MYRIAD	SPRIGS	WIRILY	******	AIRMEN	NORMAL
MYRICA	SPRING	WIRING	BARLEY	BARMAN	NORMAN
NARIAL	SPRINT	YORICK	BERLIN	BARMEN	NORMAS
NARINE	SPRITE	ZARIBA	BIRLED	BARMIE	PERMED
NORIAS	SPRITS	ZORILS	BIRLES	BERMES	PERMIT
OARING	STRIAE	ZURICH	BURLAP	CARMAN	SERMON
OGRISH	STRICK	******	BURLED	CARMEL	TARMAC
ORRICE	STRICT	--RK--	BURLER	CARMEN	TERMED
PARIAH	STRIDE	******	BURLEY	CERMET	TERMER
		BARKED			
		BARKER			

TERMLY	NORNIR	EUROPA	STROUD	******	JARROW
TERMOR	TARNAL	EUROPE	STROVE	--RQ--	JERRYS
VERMIN	TERNAL	FAROFF	TAROTS	******	KARROO
WARMED	TURNED	FAROUT	THROAT	BARQUE	KERRIE
WARMER	TURNER	FEROUS	THROBS	CIRQUE	LARRUP
WARMLY	TURNIP	FURORE	THROES	MARQUE	LARRYS
WARMTH	TURNUP	FURORS	THRONE	TORQUE	MARRED
WARMUP	VERNAL	GEROUS	THRONG	******	MARRER
WORMED	VERNAS	GYRONS	THROVE	--RR--	MARROW
WORMER	VERNIX	GYROSE	THROWN	******	MIRROR
******	VERNON	HAROLD	THROWS	BARRED	MORRIS
--RN--	VYRNWY	HEROES	TOROID	BARREL	MORROS
******	WARNED	HEROIC	TOROSE	BARREN	MORROW
BARNEY	WARNER	HEROIN	TOROUS	BARRET	MURRAY
BARNUM	******	HERONS	TYRONE	BARRIE	MURRES
BERNEY	--RO--	HURONS	UNROBE	BARRIO	MURREY
BERNIE	******	INROAD	UNROLL	BARROW	NARROW
BORNEO	AARONS	JEROME	UNROOT	BARRYS	NORRIS
BURNED	ABROAD	JURORS	UPROAR	BIRRED	PARRAL
BURNER	ACROSS	LEROYS	UPROOT	BORROW	PARREL
BURNET	ADROIT	MAROON	UPROSE	BURRED	PARROT
CARNAL	AEROBE	MEROUS	VERONA	BURROS	PERRON
CORNEA	APRONS	MORONS	VOROUS	BURROW	PERRYS
CORNED	ARROBA	MOROSE	ZEROED	CARREL	PURRED
CORNEL	ARROWS	NEROLI	ZEROES	CARRIE	PYRRHA
CORNER	ARROWY	PARODY	ZIRONS	CARROT	SORREL
CORNET	ARROYO	PAROLE	******	CIRRUS	SORROW
CORNUA	AURORA	POROUS	--RP--	CORRAL	SURREY
CORNUS	AUROUS	PYRONE	******	CORRIE	TARRED
DARNED	BARONG	PYROPE	BURPED	DARROW	TERRET
DARNEL	BARONS	SARONG	CARPAL	DERRIS	TERROR
DARNER	BARONY	SCRODS	CARPED	FARROW	TERRYS
DIRNDL	BYROAD	SCROLL	CARPEL	FERRET	TORRID
EARNED	CAROBS	SCROOP	CARPER	FERRIC	TURRET
EARNER	CAROLE	SCROTA	CARPET	FERRIS	WARRED
FORNAX	CAROLS	SEROUS	CARPIC	FERRUM	WARREN
FORNIX	CAROMS	SEROWS	CARPUS	FURRED	YARROW
GARNER	CEROUS	SHROFF	CORPSE	FURROW	******
GARNET	CHROMA	SHROUD	CORPUS	GARRET	--RS--
HERNIA	CHROME	SHROVE	HARPED	GERRYS	******
HERNIO	CHROMO	SPROUT	HARPER	HARRIS	AIRSAC
HORNED	CHRONO	STROBE	HERPES	HARROW	BORSCH
HORNET	CORODY	STRODE	MORPHO	HARRYS	BURSAE
HORNIE	CORONA	STROKE	PURPLE	HORRID	BURSAL
KARNAK	ENROBE	STROLL	TARPAN	HORROR	BURSAR
KERNED	ENROLL	STROMA	TORPID	HURRAH	BURSAS
KERNEL	ENROOT	STRONG	TORPOR	HURRAY	BURSES
MYRNAS	ERRORS	STROPS	WARPED	JARRED	BURSTS

CARSON	VERSET	GIRTED	CERUSE	CARVER	BERYLS
CORSAC	VERSOS	HARTAL	CURULE	CARVES	CHRYSO
CORSES	VERSTS	HURTER	FERULA	CERVIX	CORYMB
CORSET	VERSUS	HURTLE	FERULE	CORVEE	CORYZA
CURSED	WARSAW	KIRTLE	FORUMS	CORVES	GERYON
CURSES	WORSEN	MARTAS	GERUND	CORVUS	LARYNG
CURSOR	WORSER	MARTEN	INRUSH	CURVED	LARYNX
DORSAD	WORSTS	MARTHA	JORUMS	CURVES	SPRYER
DORSAL	******	MARTHE	KORUNA	CURVET	SPRYLY
DORSET	--RT--	MARTIN	KORUNY	FERVID	******
DORSUM	******	MARTYR	MORULA	FERVOR	--RZ--
FIRSTS	AORTAE	MARTYS	ONRUSH	HARVEY	******
GORSES	AORTAL	MORTAL	PARURE	JARVEY	BORZOI
HORSED	AORTAS	MORTAR	PERUKE	JARVIS	FURZES
HORSES	AORTIC	MORTON	PERUSE	JERVIS	TARZAN
HORSEY	BARTER	MORTYS	RERUNS	LARVAE	******
HORSTE	BARTOK	MYRTLE	SCRUBS	LARVAL	--SA--
JERSEY	BARTON	PARTED	SCRUFF	MARVEL	******
KERSEY	BERTHA	PARTLY	SCRUMS	MARVIN	ALSACE
KIRSCH	BERTHE	PERTLY	SERUMS	MERVIN	ANSATE
MARSHA	BERTHS	PORTAL	SHRUBS	NERVED	ASSAIL
MARSHY	BERTIE	PORTED	SHRUGS	NERVES	ASSAIS
MERSEY	BIRTHS	PORTER	SHRUNK	PARVIS	ASSAYS
MORSEL	BURTON	PORTIA	SIRUPS	PURVEY	BASALT
NURSED	CARTED	PORTLY	SIRUPY	SERVAL	BESANT
NURSER	CARTEL	SARTOR	SPRUCE	SERVED	CASABA
NURSES	CARTER	SARTRE	SPRUES	SERVER	CASALS
PARSEC	CARTES	SORTED	SPRUNG	SERVES	CASAVA
PARSED	CARTON	SORTER	STRUCK	SERVOS	CESARE
PARSEE	CERTES	SORTIE	STRUMA	SURVEY	DESALT
PARSES	CORTES	SURTAX	STRUMS	TURVES	DISARM
PARSIS	CORTEX	TARTAN	STRUNG	VARVES	DOSAGE
PARSON	CORTEZ	TARTAR	STRUTS	VERVET	ERSATZ
PERSIA	CORTIN	TARTED	SYRUPS	******	ESSAYS
PERSON	CURTIS	TARTER	SYRUPY	--RW--	FUSAIN
PURSED	CURTLY	TARTLY	THRUMS	******	INSANE
PURSER	CURTSY	TURTLE	THRUSH	AIRWAY	MOSAIC
PURSES	DARTED	VERTEX	THRUST	DARWIN	NASALS
PURSUE	DARTER	VIRTUE	UNRULY	EARWAX	PESACH
SARSAR	DARTLE	VORTEX	UPRUSH	EARWIG	PESADE
TARSAL	EARTHS	WORTHY	VARUNA	NARWAL	POSADA
TARSIA	EARTHY	******	YORUBA	NORWAY	RESALE
TARSUS	FIRTHS	--RU--	******	******	ROSARY
TERSER	FORTES	******	--RV--	--RY--	SESAME
TORSKS	FORTIS	ABRUPT	******	******	SUSANS
TORSOS	GARTER	AERUGO	CARVED	BARYES	TISANE
VERSED	GERTIE	BARUCH	CARVEL	BARYON	UNSAFE
VERSES	GERTYS	CARUSO	CARVEN	BARYTA	UNSAID

UNSAYS	******	PESETA	COSHER	PISHED	BUSIES
VASARI	--SE--	POSERS	COSHES	PISHES	BUSILY
VISAED	******	POSEUR	CUSHAT	POSHLY	BUSING
VISAGE	ABSENT	RESEAT	CUSHAW	PUSHED	CASING
VISARD	ANSELM	RESEAU	DASHED	PUSHER	CASINO
******	ASSENT	RESECT	DASHER	PUSHES	CESIUM
--SB--	ASSERT	RESEDA	DASHES	PUSHTU	COSIGN
******	ASSESS	RESELL	DISHED	PUSHUP	COSILY
CASBAH	ASSETS	RESEND	DISHES	RASHER	COSINE
DISBAR	AXSEED	RESENT	FISHER	RASHES	DESIGN
GASBAG	BASELY	RESETS	FISHES	RASHLY	DESIRE
LESBOS	BASEST	RISERS	GASHED	RUSHED	DESIST
LISBOA	BESEEM	ROSEAL	GASHES	RUSHER	DOSING
LISBON	BESETS	SISERA	GOSHEN	RUSHES	EASIER
******	BISECT	UNSEAL	GUSHED	SASHAY	EASILY
--SC--	CASEFY	UNSEAM	GUSHER	SASHED	EASING
******	CASEIN	UNSEAT	GUSHES	SASHES	ELSIES
BISCAY	CASERN	UNSEEN	HASHED	TISHRI	ENSIGN
CISCOS	DESERT	UPSETS	HASHES	TOSHES	ENSILE
CUSCUS	DOSERS	VISEED	HUSHED	TUSHED	FUSILE
DESCRY	EASELS	WISELY	HUSHES	TUSHES	FUSILS
DISCAL	EDSELS	WISEST	JOSHED	UNSHIP	FUSING
DISCUS	ESSENE	******	JOSHER	UNSHOD	FUSION
FASCES	EXSECT	--SF--	JOSHES	UPSHOT	GASIFY
FASCIA	EXSERT	******	JOSHUA	VASHTI	HOSIER
FESCUE	FUSEES	MISFIT	KOSHER	VISHNU	HOSING
FISCAL	GESELL	******	LASHED	WASHED	INSIDE
GASCON	GISELE	--SG--	LASHER	WASHER	INSIST
LASCAR	INSECT	******	LASHES	WASHES	JOSIAH
MASCON	INSERT	PISGAH	LUSHED	WISHED	JOSIAS
MASCOT	INSETS	******	LUSHER	WISHES	JOSIEA
MESCAL	ISSEIS	--SH--	LUSHES	******	LESION
MISCUE	ITSELF	******	MASHED	--SI--	LOSING
MOSCOW	JOSEPH	BASHAW	MASHER	******	LYSINE
MUSCAE	LASERS	BASHED	MASHES	ALSIKE	LYSING
MUSCAT	LOSERS	BASHES	MASHIE	ARSINE	LYSINS
MUSCLE	MASERS	BISHOP	MESHED	ASSIGN	MESIAL
PASCAL	MISERE	BOSHES	MESHER	ASSISI	MESIAN
PISCES	MISERS	BUSHED	MESHES	ASSIST	MUSING
RASCAL	MISERY	BUSHEL	MISHAP	ASSIZE	NASIAL
RESCUE	MOSEYS	BUSHES	MUSHED	BASICS	NASION
ROSCOE	MUSEUM	BUSHEY	MUSHER	BASIFY	NOSIER
TUSCAN	MYSELF	CASHAW	MUSHES	BASILS	NOSILY
VISCID	NISEIS	CASHED	NASHUA	BASING	NOSING
VISCUS	OBSESS	CASHES	NOSHED	BASINS	OSSIAN
******	ONSETS	CASHEW	NOSHOW	BASION	OSSIFY
--SD--	OSSEIN	CASHOO	PASHAS	BESIDE	POSIES
******	OUSELS	COSHED	PASHTO	BUSIED	POSING
MISDID					
WISDOM					

POSITS	MUSKIT	******	RASPER	FOSSAE	MISSUS
RESIDE	MUSKOX	--SO--	VESPER	FOSSES	MOSSES
RESIGN	RISKED	******	VESPID	FOSSIL	MUSSED
RESILE	RISKER	ABSORB	WISPED	FUSSED	MUSSEL
RESINS	RUSKIN	ADSORB	******	FUSSER	MUSSES
RESIST	SISKIN	ASSORT	--SQ--	FUSSES	NASSAU
RISING	TASKED	BESOMS	******	GASSED	NASSER
ROSIER	TUSKED	BESOTS	BASQUE	GASSES	NESSUS
ROSILY	TUSKER	BOSOMS	BISQUE	GESSOS	PASSED
ROSING	******	DESOXY	CASQUE	GOSSIP	PASSEE
ROSINS	--SL--	DISOWN	MASQUE	GUSSET	PASSER
ROSINY	******	ENSOUL	MOSQUE	GUSSIE	PASSES
RUSINE	AISLED	HESOID	RISQUE	HASSEL	PASSIM
SASINS	AISLES	INSOLE	SESQUI	HASSLE	PASSUS
SUSIES	HASLET	INSOUL	******	HISSED	POSSES
UPSIDE	KISLEW	JASONS	--SR--	HISSER	POSSET
URSINE	LESLEY	MASONS	******	HISSES	POSSUM
VASILI	LESLIE	MASORA	BASRAH	HUSSAR	PUSSES
VESICA	MISLAY	MESONS	******	HYSSOP	PUSSEY
VESICO	MISLED	RESOLD	--SS--	JESSED	PUSSLY
VISING	MOSLEM	RESOLE	******	JESSES	RUSSET
VISION	MOSLEY	RESORB	BASSES	JESSIE	RUSSIA
VISITS	MUSLIM	RESORT	BASSET	JOSSES	SASSED
WISING	MUSLIN	UNSOLD	BASSOS	KISSED	SASSES
******	SUSLIK	VISORS	BESSIE	KISSER	SUSSED
--SJ--	WESLEY	******	BESSYS	KISSES	SUSSEX
******	******	--SP--	BOSSED	LASSEN	TASSEL
GASJET	--SM--	******	BOSSES	LASSES	TASSET
******	******	AUSPEX	BUSSED	LASSIE	TESSIE
--SK--	BUSMAN	CASPAR	BUSSES	LASSOS	TISSUE
******	BUSMEN	CASPER	BYSSUS	LESSEE	TOSSED
BASKED	COSMIC	CUSPED	CASSIA	LESSEN	TOSSES
BASKET	COSMOS	CUSPID	CASSIE	LESSER	TOSSUP
BOSKET	DESMAN	CUSPIS	CASSIS	LESSON	TUSSAH
BUSKER	DESMID	DESPOT	CISSIE	LESSOR	TUSSAL
BUSKIN	DISMAL	DISPEL	CISSYS	LISSOM	TUSSAR
CASKET	DISMAY	GASPAR	COSSES	LOSSES	TUSSIS
DUSKED	GASMAN	GASPED	COSSET	MASSED	TUSSLE
GASKET	GASMEN	GASPER	CUSSED	MASSES	VASSAL
GASKIN	GISMOS	GOSPEL	CUSSES	MASSIF	VESSEL
HUSKED	KISMET	HASPED	CUSSOS	MESSED	WESSEX
HUSKER	MESMER	HISPID	DESSAU	MESSES	YESSED
MASKED	TASMAN	INSPAN	DOSSAL	MESSRS	YESSES
MASKEG	YASMAK	JASPER	DOSSED	MISSAL	******
MASKER	YESMAN	KASPER	DOSSEL	MISSED	--ST--
MISKAL	******	LISPED	DOSSER	MISSEL	******
MUSKEG	--SN--	LISPER	DOSSIL	MISSES	AUSTEN
MUSKET	DISNEY	RASPED	FESSES	MISSIS	AUSTER
	MESNES				

AUSTIN	GUSTAF	NOSTIC	VESTEE	ALTARS	POTATO
AUSTRO	GUSTAV	OUSTED	VESTRY	ATTACH	RATALS
BASTED	HASTED	OUSTER	VISTAS	ATTACK	RETAIL
BASTES	HASTEN	OYSTER	WASTED	ATTAIN	RETAIN
BESTED	HASTES	PASTAS	WASTER	ATTARS	RETAKE
BESTIR	HESTER	PASTED	WASTES	BATAAN	RETARD
BESTOW	HESTIA	PASTEL	WESTER	BETAKE	RITARD
BISTER	HOSTED	PASTER	WYSTAN	BOTANY	ROTARY
BISTRO	HOSTEL	PASTES	XTSTUS	BUTANE	ROTATE
BOSTON	HUSTLE	PASTIL	XYSTER	BYTALK	SATANG
BUSTED	HYSTER	PASTOR	XYSTOS	CATALO	SATARA
BUSTER	INSTAR	PASTRY	YESTER	CETANE	SITARS
BUSTIC	INSTEP	PESTER	ZESTED	DATARY	TATARS
BUSTLE	INSTIL	PESTLE	ZOSTER	DETACH	TETANY
CASTER	JESTED	PISTIL	******	DETAIL	TITANS
CASTES	JESTER	PISTOL	--SU--	DETAIN	TOTALS
CASTLE	JOSTLE	PISTON	******	DOTAGE	UNTACK
CASTOR	JUSTIN	POSTAL	ABSURD	DOTARD	UPTAKE
CASTRO	JUSTLY	POSTED	ASSUME	ENTAIL	VITALS
CESTUS	JUSTUS	POSTER	ASSURE	ESTATE	VOTARY
COSTAE	LASTED	RASTER	BASUTO	EXTANT	WATAPE
COSTAL	LASTER	RESTED	CASUAL	GITANO	WATAPS
COSTAR	LASTEX	RESTER	CESURA	GOTAMA	******
COSTED	LASTLY	ROSTER	DISUSE	INTACT	--TB--
COSTER	LESTER	ROSTRA	ENSUED	INTAKE	******
COSTLY	LISTED	RUSTED	ENSUES	LITANY	HATBOX
CUSTER	LISTEL	RUSTIC	ENSURE	LOTAHS	HOTBED
CUSTOM	LISTEN	RUSTLE	INSULT	METAGE	HOTBOX
CUSTOS	LISTER	SESTET	INSURE	METALS	KITBAG
CYSTIC	LUSTED	SISTER	ISSUED	MUTANT	OUTBID
DISTAL	LUSTER	SYSTEM	ISSUER	MUTATE	POTBOY
DISTIL	LUSTRE	TASTED	ISSUES	NATANT	TITBIT
DUSTED	MASTED	TASTER	JESUIT	NOTARY	******
DUSTER	MASTER	TASTES	MISUSE	OBTAIN	--TC--
EASTER	MASTIC	TESTAE	RESULT	OCTADS	******
EASTON	MESTEE	TESTED	RESUME	OCTANE	BITCHY
FASTED	MISTED	TESTER	UNSUNG	OCTANT	BOTCHY
FASTEN	MISTER	TESTES	UNSURE	OCTAVE	CATCHY
FASTER	MISTLE	TESTIS	URSULA	OCTAVO	LITCHI
FESTAL	MOSTLY	TESTON	VISUAL	OPTANT	OUTCRY
FESTER	MUSTEE	ULSTER	******	OTTAVA	PATCHY
FISTED	MUSTER	UNSTEP	--SW--	OTTAWA	PITCHY
FISTIC	MUSTNT	UNSTOP	******	OXTAIL	ROTCHE
FOSTER	MYSTIC	VASTER	ANSWER	PETALS	TETCHY
FUSTIC	NASTIC	VASTLY	******	PETARD	******
GASTON	NESTED	VESTAL	--TA--	POTAGE	--TD--
GASTRO	NESTLE	VESTAS	******	POTALE	******
GESTIC	NESTOR	VESTED	ALTAIC	POTASH	OUTDID
				ALTAIR	

******	INTERS	HATFUL	LITHIA	ANTIAR	LUTIST
--TE--	KETENE	OUTFIT	LITHIC	ANTICS	MATINE
******	LATEEN	OUTFOX	LUTHER	ARTIES	MATING
ALTERS	LATELY	VATFUL	METHOD	ARTILY	MATINS
ANTEED	LATENT	******	METHYL	ARTIST	METIER
ANTERO	LATERA	--TG--	MOTHER	ATTICA	METING
ARTELS	LATEST	******	MYTHIC	ATTICS	MOTIFS
ARTERY	LITERS	CATGUT	MYTHOI	ATTILA	MOTILE
ASTERI	LUTEAL	ROTGUT	MYTHOS	ATTIRE	MOTION
ASTERN	LUTEUM	******	NATHAN	AUTISM	MOTIVE
ASTERO	MATEOS	--TH--	NETHER	BATIKS	MUTING
ASTERS	MATEYS	******	PATHAN	BATING	MUTINY
ATTEND	METEOR	AETHER	PATHIA	BETIDE	MUTISM
ATTEST	METERS	ALTHEA	PATHOL	BETISE	NATION
AZTECS	MITERS	ANTHEA	PATHOS	BITING	NATIVE
BATEAU	MOTELS	ANTHEM	PITHED	CATION	NOTICE
BETELS	NOTERS	ANTHER	POTHER	CITIED	NOTIFY
BITERS	OBTECT	ARTHRO	PYTHIA	CITIES	NOTING
CATENA	OBTEST	ARTHUR	PYTHIC	CITING	NOTION
CATERS	OCTETS	ASTHMA	PYTHON	CUTIES	OPTICS
COTEAU	OSTEAL	AUTHOR	RATHER	CUTINS	OPTIMA
CUTELY	OSTEND	BATHED	SOTHIC	DATING	OPTIME
CUTEST	OTTERS	BATHER	SOTHIS	DATIVE	OPTING
CUTEYS	OUTERS	BATHOS	TETHER	DOTIER	OPTION
DATERS	PATENS	BETHEL	TETHYS	DOTING	OUTING
DETECT	PATENT	BOTHER	TITHED	DUTIES	PATINA
DETENT	PATERS	CATHAY	TITHER	EATING	PATINE
DETERS	PETERS	CATHER	TITHES	ENTICE	PATIOS
DETEST	POTEEN	CATHYS	TOTHER	ENTIRE	PETITE
DOTERS	POTENT	CITHER	WETHER	ENTITY	PITIED
EATERS	RATELS	DITHER	WITHAL	FATIMA	PITIES
EATERY	RATERS	EITHER	WITHED	FATING	POTION
ENTERA	RETELL	ESTHER	WITHER	FETIAL	RATIFY
ENTERE	RETENE	FATHER	WITHES	FETICH	RATINE
ENTERO	SATEEN	FATHOM	WITHIN	FETING	RATING
ENTERS	TOTEMS	GATHER	WITHIT	FETISH	RATION
ESTEEM	TOTERS	GOTHAM	ZETHOS	FUTILE	RATIOS
ESTERS	URTEXT	GOTHIC	ZETHUS	GATING	RATITE
EXTEND	UTTERS	HITHER	ZITHER	HATING	RETINA
EXTENT	VOTERS	JETHRO	******	INTIMA	RETIRE
EXTERN	WATERS	JOTHAM	--TI--	JUTISH	RUTILE
GATEAU	WATERY	KATHIE	******	KATIES	SATING
HATERS	******	KATHYS	ACTING	KATION	SATINS
HETERO	--TF--	LATHED	ACTINI	KITING	SATINY
HOTELS	******	LATHER	ACTINO	LATINS	SATIRE
INTEND	ARTFUL	LATHES	ACTION	LATISH	SHTICK
INTENT	BOTFLY	LETHAL	ACTIUM	LOTION	SITING
INTERN	FITFUL	LITHER	ACTIVE	LUTING	SITINS

TITIAN	PITMEN	RATOON	IATRIC	BATTER	GUTTLE
TOTING	POTMAN	RETOLD	ISTRIA	BATTIK	HATTED
ULTIMA	******	RETOOK	LATRIA	BATTIN	HATTER
ULTIMO	--TN--	RETOOL	MATRIX	BATTLE	HATTIE
UNTIDY	******	RETORT	MATRON	BATTUE	HATTYS
UNTIED	CATNAP	ROTORS	METRIC	BETTED	HETTYS
UNTIES	CATNIP	SATORY	METROS	BETTER	HITTER
VOTING	JITNEY	SETOFF	MITRAL	BETTES	HOTTED
VOTIVE	PUTNAM	SETONS	MITRED	BETTOR	HOTTER
******	WITNEY	SETOSE	NATRON	BETTYS	HUTTED
--TK--	******	SETOUS	NITRIC	BITTED	JETTED
******	--TO--	SETOUT	NITRID	BITTEN	JETTON
CATKIN	******	SOTOLS	NUTRIA	BITTER	JITTER
******	ACTORS	TETONS	OCTROI	BOTTLE	JOTTED
--TL--	AFTOSA	TUTORS	OUTRAN	BOTTOM	JOTTER
******	ANTONS	UNTOLD	OUTRUN	BUTTED	JUTTED
ANTLER	ANTONY	UPTOWN	PATROL	BUTTER	KETTLE
ANTLIA	ARTOIS	VETOED	PATRON	BUTTES	KITTED
ATTLEE	ATTORN	VETOER	PETREL	BUTTON	KITTEN
BUTLER	AUTOED	VETOES	PETRIE	CATTED	KITTLE
CATLIN	BATONS	******	PETROL	CATTIE	KITTYS
CUTLAS	BETONY	--TP--	PUTRID	CATTLE	LATTEN
CUTLER	BETOOK	******	RETROD	COTTAE	LATTER
CUTLET	CITOLA	HATPIN	SATRAP	COTTAR	LETTER
HITLER	CUTOFF	HOTPOT	SUTRAS	COTTAS	LITTER
MOTLEY	CUTOUT	OUTPUT	TETRAD	COTTER	LITTLE
NUTLET	DETOUR	POTPIE	TETRYL	COTTON	LOTTIE
OSTLER	DITONE	PUTPUT	UNTROD	CUTTER	LYTTAE
OUTLAW	ECTOMY	******	UNTRUE	CUTTLE	MATTED
OUTLAY	ENTOMB	--TR--	VITRIC	DATTOS	MATTEO
OUTLET	ENTOMO	******	YTTRIA	DITTOS	MATTER
PUTLOG	ESTOPS	ANTRIM	YTTRIC	DOTTED	MATTES
RATLIN	EXTOLS	ANTRUM	******	DOTTEL	MATTIE
SUTLER	EXTORT	ASTRAL	--TS--	DOTTER	METTLE
TATLER	FETORS	ASTRAY	******	DOTTLE	MITTEN
TITLED	INTOMB	ASTRID	BETSYS	FATTED	MOTTLE
TITLES	INTONE	BETRAY	CATSUP	FATTEN	MOTTOS
******	KETONE	CITRAL	JETSAM	FATTER	MUTTER
--TM--	KETOSE	CITRIC	KITSCH	FETTER	MUTTON
******	METOPE	CITRON	OUTSAT	FETTLE	NATTER
BATMAN	MOTORS	CITRUS	OUTSET	FITTED	NETTED
BATMEN	OCTOPI	ENTRAP	OUTSIT	FITTER	NETTIE
HETMAN	OTTOWA	ENTREE	PATSYS	GETTER	NETTLE
LITMUS	PATOIS	ESTRAY	POTSIE	GOTTEN	NUTTED
MOTMOT	PITONS	ESTRUS	PUTSCH	GUTTAE	NUTTER
NUTMEG	PUTOFF	EXTRAS	WATSON	GUTTAT	PATTED
OUTMAN	PUTONS	HATRED	******	GUTTED	PATTEN
PITMAN	PUTOUT	HOTROD	BATTED	GUTTER	PATTER
				BATTEN	

	--TU--	--TZ--	--UC--	DRUDGE	
PATTON	******	******	******	DRUDGE	******
PETTED	--TU--	--TZ--	--UC--	ELUDED	--UG--
PITTED	******	******	******	ELUDES	******
POTTED	ACTUAL	MATZOS	BAUCIS	ETUDES	BOUGHS
POTTER	ARTURO	MATZOT	BOUCLE	EXUDED	BOUGHT
POTTLE	ASTUTE	TETZEL	BRUCES	EXUDES	BOUGIE
POTTOS	ATTUNE	******	CAUCUS	FEUDAL	BRUGES
PUTTED	AUTUMN	--UA--	CHUCKS	FEUDED	CAUGHT
PUTTEE	CUTUPS	******	CLUCKS	GRUDGE	COUGAR
PUTTER	DATURA	ACUATE	CRUCES	LAUDED	COUGHS
RATTAN	FUTURE	EDUARD	DEUCED	LAUDER	DOUGAL
RATTED	GETUPS	EQUALS	DEUCES	LEUDES	DOUGHS
RATTEN	INTUIT	EQUATE	DOUCHE	LOUDEN	DOUGHY
RATTER	INTURN	FEUARS	EDUCED	LOUDER	DOUGIE
RATTLE	LETUPS	IGUANA	EDUCES	LOUDLY	FOUGHT
RETTED	MATURE	SOUARI	EDUCTS	MAUDES	FRUGAL
RITTER	METUMP	SQUABS	ERUCTS	PRUDES	GAUGED
ROTTED	MUTUAL	SQUADS	FAUCAL	SLUDGE	GAUGER
ROTTEN	MUTULE	SQUALL	FAUCES	SLUDGY	GAUGES
ROTTER	NATURE	SQUAMA	FAUCET	SMUDGE	GOUGED
RUTTED	OBTUND	SQUARE	GAUCHE	SMUDGY	GOUGER
SETTEE	OBTUSE	SQUASH	GAUCHO	STUDIO	GOUGES
SETTER	PETULA	SQUATS	PLUCKS	TRUDGE	GRUGRU
SETTLE	RETURN	SQUAWK	PLUCKY	TRUDYS	LAUGHS
SETTOS	RETUSE	SQUAWS	POUCHY	******	LOUGHS
SITTER	RITUAL	STUART	ROUCHE	--UE--	NAUGHT
SUTTEE	ROTUND	TRUANT	SAUCED	******	NOUGAT
SUTTON	SATURN	ZOUAVE	SAUCER	BLUELY	NOUGHT
TATTED	SETUPS	******	SAUCES	BLUEST	PLUGIN
TATTER	SUTURE	--UB--	SHUCKS	BLUETS	ROUGED
TATTLE	UPTURN	******	STUCCO	CRUETS	ROUGES
TATTLY	WATUSI	ANUBIS	TEUCER	FLUENT	ROUGHS
TATTOO	******	BAUBLE	TOUCAN	GRUELS	SAUGER
TETTER	--TV--	CHUBBY	TOUCHE	SQUEAK	SMUGLY
TITTER	******	DAUBED	TOUCHY	SQUEAL	SNUGLY
TITTLE	LATVIA	DAUBER	TRUCES	TRUEST	SOUGHS
TITTUP	******	DAUBRY	TRUCKS	******	SOUGHT
TOTTED	--TW--	DOUBLE	******	--UF--	TAUGHT
TOTTER	******	DOUBLY	--UD--	******	TOUGHS
TUTTED	NITWIT	DOUBTS	******	BLUFFS	ZEUGMA
TUTTIS	OUTWIT	GRUBBY	ALUDEL	BOUFFE	******
VATTED	******	KRUBIS	AOUDAD	CHUFAS	--UI--
VETTED	--TY--	KRUBUT	CAUDAD	FLUFFS	******
VITTAE	******	REUBEN	CAUDAL	FLUFFY	ACUITY
WATTLE	ECTYPE	ROUBLE	CAUDEX	SCUFFS	AGUISH
WETTED	SATYRS	SCUBAS	CAUDLE	SNUFFS	ALUINO
WETTER		STUBBS	CRUDER	SNUFFY	ALUINS
WITTED		STUBBY	DAUDET	STUFFS	AQUILA

BLUING	ALULAE	UVULAE	STUMPS	MAUNDY	YAUPON
BLUISH	ALULAR	UVULAR	STUMPY	MOUNTS	YOUPON
BRUINS	AMULET	UVULAS	THUMBS	MOUNTY	******
BRUISE	APULIA	VAULTS	THUMPS	NOUNAL	--UR--
BRUITS	BEULAH	WAULED	TRUMAN	PAUNCH	******
CLUING	BEULAS	******	TRUMPS	PLUNGE	ANURAN
CRUISE	BOULES	--UM--	******	PLUNKS	AZURES
DRUIDS	BRULOT	******	--UN--	POUNCE	BLURBS
EQUINE	CAULES	ACUMEN	******	POUNDS	BLURRY
EQUIPS	CAULIS	ALUMIN	ARUNTA	PRUNED	BLURTS
EQUITY	CAULKS	ALUMNA	BLUNGE	PRUNER	BOURGS
FEUING	COULEE	ALUMNI	BLUNTS	PRUNES	BOURNE
FLUIDS	EXULTS	BRUMAL	BOUNCE	ROUNDS	BOURNS
FRUITS	FAULTS	BRUMES	BOUNCY	SAUNAS	BOURSE
FRUITY	FAULTY	CHUMMY	BOUNDS	SHUNTS	CHURCH
GLUIER	FOULED	CHUMPS	BOUNTY	SKUNKS	CHURLS
GLUING	FOULER	CLUMPS	BRUNCH	SOUNDS	CHURNS
LOUISA	FOULLY	CLUMPY	BRUNEI	SPUNKY	CHURRS
LOUISE	GAULLE	CLUMSY	BRUNEL	STUNTS	COURSE
SLUICE	GIULIA	CRUMBS	BRUNOS	TAUNTS	COURTS
SLUING	GIULIO	CRUMBY	CHUNKS	TRUNKS	CRURAL
SQUIBS	HAULED	CRUMMY	CHUNKY	VAUNTS	DHURNA
SQUIDS	HAULER	CRUMPS	COUNTS	WOUNDS	DOURLY
SQUILL	HAULMY	FLUMED	COUNTY	ZOUNDS	EXURBS
SQUINT	INULIN	FLUMES	CRUNCH	******	FLURRY
SQUIRE	JOULES	FLUMPS	DAUNTS	--UO--	FOURTH
SQUIRM	MAULED	FRUMPS	DRUNKS	******	GOURDE
SQUIRT	MAULER	FRUMPY	FAUNAE	FLUORO	GOURDS
SQUISH	MOULDS	GLUMES	FAUNAL	FLUORS	HOURIS
TRUING	MOULDY	GLUMLY	FAUNAS	******	HOURLY
TRUISM	MOULIN	GRUMES	FAUNUS	--UP--	INURED
******	MOULTS	GRUMPY	FLUNKS	******	INURES
--UJ--	OCULAR	MAUMAU	FLUNKY	COUPES	INURNS
******	OVULAR	MUUMUU	FOUNDS	COUPLE	KAURIS
THUJAS	OVULES	NEUMES	FOUNTS	COUPON	KNURLS
******	PAULAS	PLUMBO	FRUNZE	DRUPEL	KNURLY
--UK--	PAULIN	PLUMBS	GRUNDY	DRUPES	LAURAE
******	PAULUS	PLUMED	GRUNTS	ERUPTS	LAURAS
FLUKED	POULTS	PLUMES	HAUNCH	LOUPES	LAUREL
FLUKES	SAULTS	PLUMMY	HAUNTS	PAUPER	LAURIE
FLUKEY	SCULLS	PLUMPS	HOUNDS	SOUPED	LOURED
PAUKER	SCULPT	RHUMBA	JAUNTS	STUPAS	MOURNS
RYUKYU	SKULKS	RHUMBS	JAUNTY	STUPES	NEURAL
******	SKULLS	SCUMMY	JOUNCE	STUPID	NEURON
--UL--	SOULED	SLUMMY	LAUNCE	STUPOR	PLURAL
******	STULLS	SLUMPS	LAUNCH	TAUPES	POURED
ABULIA	THULIA	SPUMED	LOUNGE	TOUPEE	POURER
ADULTS	TOULON	SPUMES	MAUNDS	YAUPED	PYURIA

SAUREL	DRUSES	GLUTEI	*****	FEVERS	SEVERN
SAURUS	FRUSTA	GLUTEN	--VA--	FIVERS	SEVERS
SCURFY	HAUSEN	MOUTHS	*****	FOVEAE	TAVERN
SCURRY	HOUSED	MOUTHY	ALVANS	FOVEAL	TEVERE
SCURVY	HOUSES	MOUTON	BOVATE	GAVELS	UNVEIL
SEURAT	JOUSTS	NAUTCH	DIVANS	GOVERN	UNVEXT
SLURPS	KYUSHU	NEUTER	HAVANA	HAVENS	WAVERS
SLURRY	LOUSED	PLUTUS	INVADE	HAVENT	WAVEYS
SOURCE	LOUSES	POUTED	KAVASS	HOVELS	WIVERN
SOURED	MAUSER	POUTER	LAVABO	HOVERS	WIVERS
SOURER	MOUSED	ROUTED	LAVAGE	INVENT	WYVERN
SOURLY	MOUSER	ROUTER	LEVANT	INVERT	*****
SPURGE	MOUSES	ROUTES	LOVAGE	INVEST	--VI--
SPURNS	MOUSSE	SAUTES	NAVAHO	KEVELS	*****
SPURRY	NAUSEA	SCUTCH	NAVAJO	LAVERS	ADVICE
SPURTS	ONUSES	SCUTES	NEVADA	LEVEES	ADVISE
STURDY	PAUSED	SCUTUM	PAVANE	LEVELS	ALVINA
TAURUS	PAUSER	SHUTIN	PAVANS	LEVERS	ALVINE
TOURED	PAUSES	SMUTCH	RAVAGE	LIVELY	ANVILS
TOURER	PLUSES	SMUTTY	REVAMP	LIVENS	BEVIES
USURER	PLUSHY	SPUTUM	RIVALS	LIVERS	BOVINE
USURPS	POUSTO	TAUTEN	SAVAGE	LIVERY	CAVIAR
UTURNS	ROUSED	TAUTER	SAVANT	LOVEIN	CAVIES
*****	ROUSER	TAUTLY	SAVATE	LOVELL	CAVILS
--US--	ROUSES	TAUTOG	VIVACE	LOVELY	CAVING
*****	ROUSTS	TEUTON	*****	LOVERS	CAVITE
ABUSED	SLUSHY	TOUTED	--VE--	MOVERS	CAVITY
ABUSER	SOUSED	TOUTER	*****	NAVELS	CIVICS
ABUSES	SOUSES	TRUTHS	ADVENT	NOVELS	CIVIES
AMUSED	THUSLY	YOUTHS	ADVERB	NOVENA	CIVISM
AMUSER	TOUSLE	*****	ADVERT	OBVERT	COVING
AMUSES	TRUSTS	--UV--	BEVELS	PAVERS	DAVIDS
ANUSES	TRUSTY	*****	CAVEAT	RAVELS	DAVIES
BOUSED	UNUSED	FAUVES	CAVEIN	RAVENS	DAVITS
BOUSES	*****	FLUVIO	CAVELL	RAVERS	DEVICE
BRUSHY	--UT--	LOUVER	CAVERN	REVEAL	DEVILS
CAUSAL	*****	LOUVRE	CIVETS	REVELS	DEVISE
CAUSED	BHUTAN	MAUVES	COVERS	REVERE	DIVIDE
CAUSER	BRUTAL	OEUVRE	COVERT	REVERS	DIVINE
CAUSES	BRUTES	PLUVIO	COVETS	REVERT	DIVING
COUSIN	BRUTUS	*****	COVEYS	REVEST	DOVISH
CRUSES	CAUTER	--UX--	DAVEYS	REVETS	ELVIRA
CRUSET	CHUTES	*****	DEVEIN	RIVERS	ELVISH
CRUSOE	CLUTCH	CRUXES	DEVEST	RIVETS	ENVIED
CRUSTS	CRUTCH	FLUXED	DIVERS	ROVERS	ENVIER
CRUSTY	FLUTED	FLUXES	DIVERT	SAVERS	ENVIES
DOUSED	FLUTER	*****	DIVEST	SEVENS	GAVIAL
DOUSES	FLUTES	GAUZES	ELVERS	SEVERE	GIVING

GYVING	WAVIES	******	HOWDAH	******	UNWISE
HAVING	WAVILY	--VY--	LEWDER	--WF--	UNWISH
HIVING	WAVING	******	LEWDLY	******	VOWING
HIVITE	WIVING	LIVYER	POWDER	BOWFIN	WOWING
INVITE	XAVIER	******	TAWDRY	LAWFUL	YAWING
IRVING	******	--WA--	******	SAWFLY	YOWING
IRVINS	--VL--	******	--WE--	******	******
JIVING	******	ABWATT	******	--WG--	--WK--
JOVIAL	PAVLOV	ALWAYS	BOWELS	******	******
JOVIAN	******	BEWAIL	BOWERS	GEWGAW	FAWKES
KEVINS	--VO--	BEWARE	BOWERY	******	GAWKED
LAVING	******	BYWAYS	COWERS	--WH--	HAWKED
LAVISH	ABVOLT	COWAGE	DOWELS	******	HAWKER
LEVIED	CAVORT	COWARD	DOWERS	HAWHAW	LOWKEY
LEVIER	DEVOID	DEWANS	DOWERY	******	******
LEVIES	DEVOIR	DIWANS	FEWEST	--WI--	--WL--
LEVITE	DEVOTE	EDWARD	HEWERS	******	******
LEVITY	DEVOUR	GAWAIN	JEWELS	BOWING	BAWLED
LIVIAS	DEVOUT	HAWAII	JEWESS	CAWING	BAWLER
LIVIER	DIVOTS	HOWARD	LOWELL	COWING	BOWLED
LIVING	ENVOYS	INWALL	LOWERS	DEWIER	BOWLEG
LOVING	FAVORS	INWARD	LOWERY	DEWITT	BOWLER
MOVIES	FAVOUR	KUWAIT	LOWEST	EDWINA	DEWLAP
MOVING	GAVOTS	NAWABS	MOWERS	EDWINS	DOWLAS
NAVIES	INVOKE	NEWARK	NEWELS	ENWIND	FOWLED
NEVILE	NEVOID	NOWAYS	NEWEST	ERWINS	FOWLER
NEVILL	PIVOTS	ONWARD	ORWELL	HAWING	HOWLED
NOVICE	REVOKE	OSWALD	OSWEGO	HEWING	HOWLER
PAVING	REVOLT	REWARD	PAWERS	INWIND	MEWLED
PAVIOR	SAVORS	ROWANS	PEWEES	IRWINS	WAWLED
PAVISE	SAVORY	SEWAGE	POWELL	JAWING	YAWLED
RAVINE	SAVOUR	SEWALL	POWERS	JEWISH	YOWLED
RAVING	******	SEWARD	RAWEST	LAWING	******
RAVISH	--VR--	SIWASH	ROWELS	LOWING	--WM--
REVIEW	******	SOWARS	ROWENA	MEWING	******
REVILE	LIVRES	THWACK	ROWERS	MOWING	BOWMAN
REVISE	******	THWART	SAWERS	NOWISE	BOWMEN
REVIVE	--VS--	TOWAGE	SEWELL	PAWING	COWMAN
RIVING	******	TOWARD	SEWERS	PEWITS	COWMEN
ROVING	NEVSKI	UNWARY	SOWERS	RAWISH	******
SAVING	******	UPWARD	TAWERS	REWIND	--WN--
SAVINS	--VU--	******	TOWELS	ROWING	******
SAVIOR	******	--WB--	TOWERS	SAWING	DAWNED
SOVIET	REVUES	******	TOWERY	SEWING	DOWNED
VIVIAN	******	COWBOY	UNWELL	SOWING	FAWNED
VIVIEN	--VV--	LOWBOY	UNWEPT	TAWING	FAWNER
VIVIFY	******	******	VOWELS	TOWING	GOWNED
WAVIER	REVVED	--WD--	VOWERS	UNWIND	PAWNED
		******			
		BAWDRY			
		DAWDLE			

PAWNEE	NEWTON	FAXING	******	FLYBYS	TUYERE
PAWNER	PEWTER	FIXING	--XT--	HAYBOX	VOYEUR
SAWNEY	POWTER	FIXITY	******	KHYBER	WRYEST
YAWNED	******	FOXIER	BAXTER	MAYBUG	******
YAWNER	--WW--	FOXILY	BUXTON	******	--YF--
******	******	FOXING	CAXTON	--YC--	******
--WO--	BOWWOW	HEXING	DEXTER	******	DAYFLY
******	POWWOW	LAXITY	DEXTRO	GLYCOL	DRYFLY
BYWORD	******	MAXIMA	SEXTAN	JOYCES	JOYFUL
BYWORK	--WY--	MAXIMS	SEXTET	PSYCHE	MAYFLY
ENWOMB	******	MAXINE	SEXTON	PSYCHO	******
INWOVE	BOWYER	MAXIXE	SIXTES	SKYCAP	--YG--
REWORD	LAWYER	MEXICO	SIXTHS	******	******
UNWORN	SAWYER	MIXING	******	--YD--	OXYGEN
******	******	NIXIES	--XU--	******	******
--WP--	--XA--	NIXING	******	ABYDOS	--YH--
******	******	PIXIES	LUXURY	CLYDES	******
COWPEA	FIXATE	PYXIES	MIXUPS	DRYDEN	ANYHOW
COWPER	HEXADS	SEXIER	SEXUAL	HEYDAY	MAYHAP
COWPOX	HEXANE	SEXILY	******	HOYDEN	MAYHEM
KEWPIE	LUXATE	SEXING	--XW--	LAYDAY	******
PAWPAW	ROXANA	SEXISM	******	LEYDEN	--YI--
YAWPED	ROXANE	SEXIST	PAXWAX	MAYDAY	******
YAWPER	******	TAXIED	******	PAYDAY	BAYING
******	--XC--	TAXING	--XY--	WHYDAH	BOYISH
--WR--	******	TAXITE	******	ZUYDER	BUYING
******	BOXCAR	TOXINS	HEXYLS	******	COYISH
COWRIE	******	VEXILS	******	--YE--	CRYING
ENWRAP	--XE--	VEXING	--YA--	******	DRYICE
INWRAP	******	WAXIER	******	BAYEUX	DRYING
UNWRAP	******	WAXING	ARYANS	BUYERS	DRYISH
******	BOXERS	******	BAYARD	DOYENS	FAYING
--WS--	FIXERS	--XL--	BOYARD	DRYERS	FLYING
******	LAXEST	******	BOYARS	DRYEST	FRYING
BOWSAW	MIXERS	HUXLEY	BRYANT	FLYERS	GUYING
BOWSED	TAXEME	******	DRYADS	FOYERS	HAYING
BOWSES	TAXERS	--XO--	GUYANA	FRYERS	JOYING
DAWSON	TUXEDO	******	KAYAKS	GAYEST	KEYING
DOWSED	VEXERS	HEXONE	RAYAHS	GAYETY	LAYING
DOWSER	VIXENS	HEXOSE	RIYALS	LAYERS	MAYING
DOWSES	******	MYXOMA	ROYALE	MAYEST	PAYING
HAWSER	--XI--	SAXONS	ROYALS	PAYEES	PLYING
HAWSES	******	SAXONY	VOYAGE	PAYERS	PRYING
WOWSER	AUXINS	******	******	PRYERS	RAYING
******	BOXING	--XP--	--YB--	SAYERS	SAYING
--WT--	COXING	******	******	SHYEST	SHYING
******	DIXITS	******	DAYBED	SLYEST	SKYING
BOWTIE	DOXIES	SEXPOT	DAYBOY	TOYERS	SPYING
KOWTOW					

STYING	******	THYRSE	JEZAIL	HAZILY	BUZZES
TOYING	--YN--	THYRSI	LAZARS	HAZING	DAZZLE
TOYISH	******	******	LIZARD	HEZION	FEZZAN
TRYING	ERYNGO	--YS--	MOZART	LAZIER	FEZZES
WRYING	GDYNIA	******	SIZARS	LAZILY	FIZZED
ZAYINS	GLYNIS	ABYSMS	VIZARD	LAZING	FIZZER
******	GWYNNE	ELYSEE	WIZARD	MAZIER	FIZZES
--YL--	KEYNES	GEYSER	******	MAZILY	FIZZLE
******	ODYNIA	PHYSIC	--ZE--	MAZING	FUZZED
AMYLIC	PAYNIM	PHYSIO	******	NAZIFY	FUZZES
AMYLUM	WAYNES	TRYSTS	BEZELS	NAZISM	GUZZLE
ASYLUM	******	ZOYSIA	COZENS	OOZIER	HAZZAN
CEYLON	--YO--	******	DIZENS	OOZILY	JAZZED
DOYLEY	******	--YT--	DOZENS	OOZING	JAZZER
IDYLLS	ANYONE	******	ECZEMA	RAZING	JAZZES
PHYLAE	BAYOUS	ADYTUM	FUZEES	SIZIER	LIZZIE
PHYLLO	BEYOND	AMYTAL	GAZEBO	SIZING	LIZZYS
PHYLUM	BRYONY	DAYTON	GAZERS	SOZINE	MEZZOS
SCYLLA	COYOTE	ELYTRA	HAZELS	SOZINS	MIZZEN
STYLAR	JOYOUS	PHYTIN	HAZERS	UZZIAH	MIZZLE
STYLED	KAYOED	RHYTHM	MAZERS	VIZIER	MUZZLE
STYLER	LAYOFF	SCYTHE	OUZELS	VIZIRS	NOZZLE
STYLES	LAYOUT	******	RAZEED	ZIZITH	NUZZLE
STYLET	MAYORS	--YU--	RAZEES	******	PIZZAS
STYLUS	PAYOFF	******	WIZENS	--ZM--	PUZZLE
TAYLOR	PAYOLA	CAYUGA	******	******	RAZZED
WAYLAY	PEYOTE	CAYUSE	--ZG--	GIZMOS	RAZZES
******	POYOUS	******	******	******	RAZZIA
--YM--	RAYONS	--YV--	FIZGIG	--ZO--	SIZZLE
******	TOYONS	******	******	BEZOAR	TAZZAS
CAYMAN	TRYOUT	JAYVEE	--ZH--	EOZOIC	ZIZZLE
CHYMIC	UNYOKE	******	******	KAZOOS	******
ETYMON	WAYOUT	--YW--	MUZHIK	RAZORS	--A-A--
FLYMAN	******	******	******	VIZORS	******
HAYMOW	--YP--	ANYWAY	--ZI--	******	ABACAS
LAYMAN	******	KEYWAY	******	--ZU--	ABADAN
LAYMEN	CLYPEI	SKYWAY	COZIER	******	AGAMAS
RHYMED	COYPUS	******	COZIES	LAZULI	AGAPAE
RHYMER	CRYPTO	--YX--	COZILY	MAZUMA	ANABAS
RHYMES	CRYPTS	******	DAZING	MEZUZA	ANANAS
SKYMAN	GLYPHS	ORYXES	DOZIER	******	ARARAT
SKYMEN	GLYPTO	******	DOZILY	--ZY--	ARAWAK
STYMIE	MAYPOP	--ZA--	DOZING	******	ATABAL
THYMES	SCYPHI	******	FAZING	ENZYME	ATAMAN
THYMIC	SCYPHO	BAZAAR	FUZILS	SYZYGY	AVATAR
THYMOL	******	BEZANT	FUZING	******	BIAXAL
THYMUS	--YR--	GAZABO	GAZING	--ZZ--	BRAZAS
	******	HAZARD	HAZIER	******	CLARAS
	DRYROT			BUZZED	
	THYREO			BUZZER	

COAXAL	BRANCH	FRAUDS	BEARED	CLARET	ERASER
CRAVAT	CHALCO	GLANDS	BEARER	CLAWED	ERASES
DIANAS	CHANCE	GRANDE	BEATEN	CLAYED	ETAPES
DRAMAS	CHANCY	GUARDS	BEATER	CLAYEY	EVADED
FRACAS	CRATCH	HOARDS	BEAVER	COALED	EVADER
GRAHAM	EPARCH	LUANDA	BIASED	COALER	EVADES
GUAVAS	EXARCH	PLAIDS	BIASES	COATED	EXAMEN
IBADAN	FIANCE	PRAVDA	BLADED	COATEE	EYASES
ISAIAH	FIASCO	ROALDS	BLADES	COAXED	FEARED
KOALAS	FRANCE	RWANDA	BLAMED	COAXER	FEARER
LIANAS	FRANCK	SCALDS	BLAMES	COAXES	FEASED
LLAMAS	FRANCO	SHANDY	BLARED	CRAKES	FEASES
PLAGAL	FRANCS	SHARDS	BLARES	CRANED	FLAKED
PLANAR	GLANCE	SKALDS	BLAZED	CRANES	FLAKER
PLATAN	GLAUCO	STANDS	BLAZER	CRAPED	FLAKES
PLAYAS	GRAECO	SWARDS	BLAZES	CRAPES	FLAMED
PLAZAS	INARCH	THADDY	BOATED	CRATED	FLAMEN
QUAPAW	ISAACS	UGANDA	BOATER	CRATER	FLAMES
QUASAR	NUANCE	VIANDS	BRACED	CRATES	FLARED
RIATAS	PLAICE	WEALDS	BRACER	CRAVED	FLARES
SCALAR	PLANCH	WOALDS	BRACES	CRAVEN	FLAWED
SCARAB	PLANCK	******	BRAKED	CRAVER	FLAXEN
SEAMAN	PRANCE	--A-E-	BRAKES	CRAVES	FLAXES
SEAWAN	SCARCE	******	BRAVED	CRAZED	FLAYED
SEAWAY	SEANCE	ABASED	BRAVER	CRAZES	FLAYER
SHAMAN	SEARCH	ABASER	BRAVES	DEADEN	FOALED
SPACAE	SNATCH	ABASES	BRAYED	DEAFEN	FOAMED
STALAG	STANCE	ABATED	BRAYER	DEALER	FRAMED
STATAL	STANCH	ABATER	BRAZED	DEARER	FRAMER
SWARAJ	STARCH	ABATES	BRAZEN	DIADEM	FRAMES
TEABAG	SWATCH	ADAGES	BRAZER	DIALED	FRATER
THANAT	THATCH	AGATES	BRAZES	DIALER	FRAUEN
TIARAS	TRANCE	AGAVES	CEASED	DIANES	FRAYED
UTAHAN	USANCE	ALATED	CEASES	DIAPER	GEARED
VEADAR	******	AMAZED	CHAFED	DRAGEE	GLACES
******	--A-D-	AMAZES	CHAFER	DRAKES	GLADES
--A-B-	******	ANADEM	CHAFES	DRAPED	GLARED
******	AMANDA	ARABEL	CHALEH	DRAPER	GLARES
CRABBY	AWARDS	AWAKED	CHALET	DRAPES	GLAZED
CRAMBO	BEARDS	AWAKEN	CHAPEL	DRAWEE	GLAZER
FLABBY	BOARDS	AWAKES	CHAPES	DRAWER	GLAZES
FLAMBE	BRAIDS	AZALEA	CHARED	DRAYED	GNAWED
NEARBY	BRANDS	AZAZEL	CHARES	ELATED	GNAWER
SCABBY	BRANDT	BEADED	CHASED	ELATER	GOADED
SHABBY	BRANDY	BEAKED	CHASER	ELATES	GOATEE
******	CHARDS	BEAKER	CHASES	ENAMEL	GRABEN
--A-C-	CLAUDE	BEAMED	CHAWED	ENATES	GRACED
******	ELANDS	BEANED	CLARES	ERASED	GRACES
BIANCA					
BLANCH					

GRADED	LEANER	PLATEN	SHALES	STAGED	TRAVES
GRADER	LEAPED	PLATER	SHAMED	STAGER	TSADES
GRADES	LEAPER	PLATES	SHAMES	STAGES	UKASES
GRAPES	LEASED	PLAYED	SHAPED	STAGEY	UPASES
GRATED	LEASES	PLAYER	SHAPEN	STAKED	USAGES
GRATER	LEAVED	PRATED	SHAPER	STAKES	VIALED
GRATES	LEAVEN	PRATER	SHAPES	STALED	WEAKEN
GRAVED	LEAVER	PRATES	SHARED	STALER	WEAKER
GRAVEL	LEAVES	PRAYED	SHARER	STALES	WEANED
GRAVEN	LIANES	PRAYER	SHARES	STAMEN	WEANER
GRAVER	LIASED	QUAKED	SHAVED	STAPES	WEARER
GRAVES	LOADED	QUAKER	SHAVEN	STARED	WEASEL
GRAYED	LOADER	QUAKES	SHAVER	STARER	WEAVED
GRAYER	LOAFED	QUAVER	SHAVES	STARES	WEAVER
GRAZED	LOAFER	READER	SKATED	STASES	WEAVES
GRAZER	LOAMED	REALES	SKATER	STATED	WHALED
GRAZES	LOANED	REAMED	SKATES	STATEN	WHALER
HEADED	LOAVES	REAMER	SLAKED	STATER	WHALES
HEADER	MEAGER	REAPED	SLAKES	STATES	WOADED
HEALED	MEANER	REAPER	SLATED	STAVED	XRAYED
HEALER	MOANED	REARED	SLATER	STAVES	YEANED
HEAPED	MOATED	REARER	SLATES	STAYED	******
HEARER	NEARED	ROAMED	SLAVED	STAYER	--A-F-
HEATED	NEARER	ROAMER	SLAVER	SWAGED	******
HEATER	NEATEN	ROARED	SLAVES	SWAGES	CHAFFS
HEAVED	NEATER	ROARER	SLAYER	SWALES	CHAFFY
HEAVEN	OCASEY	SCALED	SMAZES	SWANEE	DRAFFS
HEAVER	OKAYED	SCALER	SNAKED	SWAYED	DRAFFY
HEAVES	ONAGER	SCALES	SNAKES	TEAMED	DWARFS
HOAXED	ORATED	SCAPES	SNARED	TEARED	PIAFFE
HOAXER	ORATES	SCARED	SNARER	TEASED	QUAFFS
HOAXES	PEAHEN	SCARER	SNARES	TEASEL	SCARFS
HYADES	PEAKED	SCARES	SOAKED	TEASER	STAFFS
IMAGED	PEALED	SEABEE	SOAKER	TEASES	WHARFS
IMAGES	PEASEN	SEALED	SOAPED	TEASET	******
IMARET	PEASES	SEALER	SOARED	THALER	--A-G-
ISABEL	PEAVEY	SEAMED	SOARER	THALES	******
JUAREZ	PHASED	SEAMEN	SPACED	THAMES	CHANGE
KAASES	PHASES	SEAMER	SPACER	THANES	CHANGS
KNAVES	PLACED	SEAPEN	SPACES	THAWED	CHARGE
KRAKEN	PLACER	SEARED	SPADED	THAYER	CLANGS
LAAGER	PLACES	SEATED	SPADER	TRACED	CRAGGY
LEADED	PLACET	SHADED	SPADES	TRACER	CRAIGS
LEADEN	PLANED	SHADES	SPARED	TRACES	FLAGGY
LEADER	PLANER	SHAKEN	SPARER	TRADED	FLANGE
LEAFED	PLANES	SHAKER	SPARES	TRADER	GRANGE
LEAKED	PLANET	SHAKES	SPATES	TRADES	ORANGE
LEANED	PLATED	SHALED	SPAYED	TRAVEL	ORANGS

QUAGGA	******	LEADIN	CRACKY	DRABLY	******
QUAGGY	--A-I-	MEALIE	CRANKS	DRAWLS	--A-M-
SHAGGY	******	MEANIE	CRANKY	DRAWLY	******
SLAGGY	ABATIS	NIACIN	FLACKS	ENABLE	ALARMS
SLANGY	ACACIA	OKAPIS	FLANKS	FLAILS	BRAHMA
SNAGGY	ACADIA	OXALIC	FLASKS	FLATLY	BRAHMS
SPARGE	ACARID	OXALIS	FRANKS	FRAILS	CHACMA
STAGGY	ADAGIO	PHAGIA	KNACKS	GLADLY	CHAMMY
TWANGS	AGAMIC	PHASIA	PLACKS	GNARLS	CHARMS
TWANGY	AGARIC	PHASIC	PLANKS	GNARLY	CHASMS
UBANGI	ALALIA	PHASIS	PRANKS	GRAYLY	CLAIMS
WHANGS	ALARIC	PLACID	QUACKS	ICALLY	CLAMMY
******	AMALIE	PLAGIO	QUARKS	KRAALS	DHARMA
--A-H-	AMANIA	PLASIA	SHACKO	LEANLY	GRAMME
******	ARABIA	PLASIS	SHACKS	LIABLE	HEAUME
AGATHA	ARABIC	PRAXIS	SHANKS	MEANLY	INARMS
APACHE	ATAVIC	SEARIN	SHARKS	MEASLY	MIASMA
APATHY	ATAXIA	SIALIC	SLACKS	MIAULS	PLASMA
BEACHY	ATAXIC	SLAVIC	SMACKS	NEARLY	PLASMO
BRACHI	BAALIM	SPADIX	SNACKS	NEATLY	PSALMS
BRACHY	BEANIE	SPAHIS	SPANKS	ORACLE	QUALMS
BRASHY	BRAZIL	SPAVIN	SPARKS	ORALLY	QUALMY
DEATHS	COATIS	STACIE	STACKS	OVALLY	REALMS
DEATHY	CRANIA	STADIA	STALKS	PEARLS	REARMS
DRACHM	CRANIO	STALIN	STALKY	PEARLY	SHAMMY
FLASHY	CRASIS	STAMIN	SWANKY	QUAILS	SHAWMS
GNATHO	CYANIC	STASIS	THANKS	REALLY	SMARMY
GRAPHO	CYANID	STATIC	TRACKS	SHAWLS	SPASMS
GRAPHS	CYANIN	SWAMIS	WHACKS	SMALLS	SWARMS
GRAPHY	DEARIE	THALIA	WRACKS	SNAILS	TRAUMA
HEATHS	DIAZIN	TRAGIC	******	SNARLS	WHAMMY
HEATHY	DYADIC	UNAPID	--A-L-	SNARLY	******
LEACHY	FLAVIA	URALIC	******	SPALLS	--A-N-
LOATHE	FLAVIN	URANIA	ARABLE	STABLE	******
ORACHS	GLACIS	URANIC	AVAILS	STABLY	ACAENA
PEACHY	GLAMIS	VIATIC	BEADLE	STALLS	AVAUNT
PLASHY	GOALIE	******	BEAGLE	STAPLE	BAAING
POACHY	GRACIE	--A-K-	BRAILS	SUABLE	BLAINS
SCATHE	GRADIN	******	BRAWLS	SWAILS	BRAINS
SNATHE	GRATIN	ALASKA	CRAALS	SWAILS	BRAINY
SNATHS	GRATIS	ANANKE	CRADLE	TRAILS	BRANNY
SPATHE	GRAVID	BLACKS	CRAWLS	TRAWLS	BRAWNY
SWATHE	GUANIN	BLANKS	CRAWLY	UNABLE	CHAINS
SWATHS	IRANIS	CHALKS	DEADLY	USABLE	CRANNY
TRACHE	IRAQIS	CHALKY	DEAFLY	USABLY	DHARNA
TRACHY	ISATIN	CLACKS	DEARLY	VIABLE	DRAINS
TRASHY	ITALIC	CLANKS	DOABLE	WEAKLY	ELAINE
WRATHY	KHAKIS	CRACKS	DOALLS	YEARLY	ELAYNE

FLAUNT	GUANOS	CHARRY	ANATTO	QUARTE	OMASUM
GRAINS	HEADON	CLAIRE	ARANTA	QUARTO	OPAQUE
GRAINY	ISADOR	FIACRE	AWAITS	QUARTS	PEANUT
GRANNY	KLAXON	FLAIRS	BEASTS	QUARTZ	PLAGUE
JEANNE	LLANOS	GHARRI	BEAUTS	REACTS	PLAGUY
JOANNA	MEADOW	GHARRY	BEAUTY	REALTY	PLAQUE
JOANNE	ORATOR	GLAIRS	BLASTO	RIALTO	PRAGUE
LEARNS	PHANON	GLAIRY	BLASTS	ROASTS	SEAMUS
LEARNT	PHAROS	KNARRY	BOASTS	SCANTY	SHAMUS
PLAINS	PIANOS	MEAGRE	BRACTS	SCATTY	SLAPUP
PLAINT	QUAHOG	ONAGRI	BRANTS	SHAFTS	SNAFUS
PRAWNS	REASON	QUADRI	CHAETA	SHANTY	STATUE
QUAINT	REAVOW	QUAERE	CHAETO	SHASTA	STATUS
SPAWNS	SEACOW	QUARRY	CHANTS	SLANTS	TEACUP
STAINS	SEADOG	QUATRE	CHANTY	SMALTI	TRAGUS
SWAINS	SEASON	SPARRY	CHARTS	SMALTO	URAEUS
TRAINS	SHADOW	STAIRS	CHASTE	SMARTS	URANUS
YEARNS	SHAKOS	STARRY	CHATTY	SPAITS	WRAPUP
******	SHARON	STAURO	COASTS	SPARTA	******
--A-O-	SLALOM	TEAURN	CRAFTS	STACTE	--A-V-
******	STATOR	******	CRAFTY	STAITH	******
ABATOR	TEAPOT	--A-S-	DEARTH	STARTS	STARVE
ACAJOU	TEAPOY	******	DRAFTS	SWARTH	WHARVE
ALAMOS	VIATOR	BLAISE	DRAFTY	SWARTY	******
AMADOU	WEAPON	BRAISE	ECARTE	TOASTS	--A-Y-
AMATOL	ZEALOT	BRASSY	ENACTS	TRACTS	******
AMAZON	******	CHAISE	EPACTS	TRAITS	BIALYS
ANALOG	--A-P-	CHASSE	EXACTA	WEALTH	GLADYS
ARAGON	******	CLASSY	EXACTS	WRAITH	STACYS
AVALON	CHAMPS	CLAUSE	EXALTS	YEASTS	THADYS
BEACON	CLAMPS	COARSE	FEALTY	YEASTY	URANYL
BLAZON	CLASPS	ELAPSE	FEASTS	******	******
BRAVOS	CRAMPS	FRAISE	GHAUTS	--A-U-	--A-Z-
BRAZOS	FRAPPE	GDANSK	GIANTS	******	******
CHARON	GRASPS	GLASSY	GRAFTS	ABACUS	BRAIZE
CLAMOR	SCALPS	GRASSY	GRANTS	AEACUS	PIAZZA
CLAROS	SCAMPI	HEARSE	HEALTH	ALARUM	SNAZZY
CRACOW	SCAMPS	HEARST	HEARTH	ASARUM	STANZA
CRAYON	SCARPS	HOARSE	HEARTS	BRAQUE	******
DEACON	SCAUPS	LIAISE	HEARTY	CHABUK	--B-A-
DIALOG	SHARPS	PRAISE	KRAITS	CLAQUE	******
DIATOM	SNAPPY	SPARSE	LEANTO	FLATUS	BOBCAT
DRAGON	STAMPS	WRASSE	PLAITS	GIAOUR	CABMAN
ENAMOR	SWAMPS	ZSAZSA	PLANTS	GRADUS	COBIAS
FLACON	SWAMPY	******	PLASTY	HIATUS	COBRAS
FLAGON	TRAMPS	--A-T-	PLATTE	ICARUS	DOBLAS
FLAVOR	******	******	QUANTA	LEAGUE	DOBRAS
GUACOS	--A-R-	ACANTH	QUANTS	MEATUS	FABIAN
	******	ADAPTS			
	BIAFRA				
	CHAIRS				

GIBRAN	EMBEDS	GABLES	TABLET	NUBBIN	LABILE
HABEAS	EMBODY	GIBBED	TOBIES	PUBLIC	LIBELS
HUBCAP	IMBEDS	GIBBER	TUBBED	RABBIN	LOBULE
JUBBAH	IMBODY	GIBBET	TUBBER	RABBIS	MABELS
KIBLAH	LIBIDO	GIBLET	UMBLES	RABBIT	MOBILE
LABIAL	NOBODY	GOBBET	UNBRED	ROBBIA	NEBULA
LIBRAE	******	GOBIES	WEBBED	ROBBIE	NIBBLE
LIBRAS	--B-E-	GOBLET	YABBER	RUBRIC	NOBALL
LIBYAN	******	HEBREW	******	SUBMIT	NOBBLE
MOBCAP	ABBIES	HOBBES	--B-F-	VIBRIO	NUBBLE
NUBIAN	AMBLED	HOBOES	******		NUBBLY
NUBIAS	AMBLER	IMBUED	REBUFF	--B-K-	NUBILE
SABBAT	AMBLES	IMBUES	******	******	PEBBLE
SABEAN	AUBREY	INBRED	--B-G-	KABAKA	PEBBLY
SABRAS	BABIED	JABBED	******	KABIKI	RABBLE
SUBWAY	BABIES	JABBER	AMBAGE	KABUKI	REBELS
TIBIAE	BIBBED	JIBBED	CUBAGE	REBUKE	REBILL
TIBIAL	BIBBER	JIBBER	DEBUGS	******	RIBALD
TIBIAS	BIBLES	JOBBED	RUBIGO	--B-L-	ROBALO
TOBIAH	BOBBED	JOBBER	TOBAGO	******	RUBBLE
TOBIAS	BOBBER	LABRET	******	ARBELA	SIBYLS
UMBRAE	BUBOES	LOBBED	--B-H-	BABBLE	SUBTLE
UMBRAL	CABLED	LOBBER	******	BABULS	SUBTLY
UMBRAS	CABLES	LUBBER	SUBAHS	BOBBLE	SYBILS
UNBEAR	CABLET	MOBBED	******	BUBALS	TUBULE
UPBEAT	CABMEN	MOBBER	--B-I-	BUBBLE	TYBALT
ZEBRAS	COBBER	NABBED	******	BUBBLY	UMBELS
******	COBLES	NIBBED	ALBEIT	CABALA	UNBELT
--B-B-	COBWEB	NOBBED	BABBIE	CABALS	UNBOLT
******	CUBBED	NOBLER	BIBLIO	CIBOLS	WABBLE
CABOBS	DABBED	RABBET	BOBBIE	COBALT	WABBLY
CUBEBS	DABBER	RABIES	BOBBIN	COBBLE	WOBBLE
IMBIBE	DIBBED	RIBBED	CEBOID	COBBLY	WOBBLY
KABOBS	DIBBER	ROBBED	CUBOID	CYBELE	******
NABOBS	DOBBER	ROBBER	DEBBIE	DABBLE	--B-M-
******	DOBIES	ROBLES	DEBRIS	DIBBLE	******
--B-C-	DUBBED	RUBBED	DOBBIN	EMBALM	ALBUMS
******	EMBLEM	RUBBER	DUBBIN	EMBOLI	
ABBACY	EUBOEA	RUBIES	DUBLIN	FIBULA	--B-N-
LUBECK	FABLED	RUBLES	FABRIC	GABBLE	******
REBECK	FABLER	SABLES	FIBRIL	GOBBLE	ALBANY
REBECS	FABLES	SOBBED	FIBRIN	HABILE	ALBINO
RUBACE	FIBBED	SUBDEB	GOBLIN	HOBBLE	CABANA
XEBECS	FIBBER	SUBLET	HUBRIS	IMBALM	CABINS
ZEBECK	FOBBED	SUBTER	HYBRID	KABALA	CUBANS
ZEBECS	GABBED	TABBED	HYBRIS	KIBBLE	CUBING
******	GABBER	TABLED	KIBEIS	KOBOLD	DEBUNK
--B-D-	GABLED	TABLES	LUBLIN	LABELS	EBBING
******					
ALBEDO					
AUBADE					

EMBANK	ASBURY	ROBUST	******	RICTAL	BACKED
GIBING	AUBURN	WABASH	**--B-W-**	SACRAL	BACKER
GOBANG	COBURG	******	******	SECPAR	BECKED
GYBING	DEBARK	**--B-T-**	ELBOWS	SOCIAL	BECKET
INBAND	DEBARS	******	EMBOWS	SOCMAN	BICKER
JIBING	EGBERT	ABBOTS	OXBOWS	UNCIAL	BUCKED
ORBING	ELBERT	ALBATA	UPBOWS	UNCLAD	BUCKER
RIBAND	EMBARK	ALBITE	******	YUCCAS	BUCKET
ROBAND	EMBARS	AMBITS	**--B-Y-**	******	CACHED
ROBING	EMBERS	ARBUTE	******	**--C-B-**	CACHES
ROBINS	FIBERS	BABITE	ABBEYS	******	CACHET
RUBENS	GABBRO	CUBITS	BOBBYS	HECUBA	COCKED
SABINA	GIBERS	DEBATE	DEBBYS	INCUBI	COCKER
SABINE	HOBART	DEBITS	EMBAYS	JACOBS	CYCLED
SABINS	HUBERT	DEBUTS	EMBRYO	******	CYCLER
TUBING	IMBARK	HABITS	KABAYA	**--C-C-**	CYCLES
UNBEND	INBORN	JABOTS	LIBBYS	******	DECKED
UNBENT	JABIRU	KIBITZ	******	DECOCT	DECKEL
UNBIND	LABORS	LOBATE	**--B-Z-**	MACACO	DECKER
URBANE	OSBERT	ORBITS	******	ROCOCO	DECREE
******	OSBORN	REBATE	REBOZO	UNCOCK	DICKER
--B-O-	REBORE	REBATO	******	******	DICKEY
******	REBORN	REBUTS	**--C-A-**	**--C-D-**	DOCKED
ALBION	ROBERT	ROBOTS	******	******	DOCKER
BABOON	SABERS	RUBATO	AECIAL	ACCEDE	DOCKET
BABOOS	SOBERS	SABOTS	BUCCAL	ARCADE	DUCKED
BYBLOW	SUBORN	SEBATS	BUCHAN	CICADA	DUCKER
DEBTOR	SUBURB	SUBITO	COCCAL	CYCADS	ECCLES
DOBLON	TABARD	TUBATE	COCOAS	DECADE	EMCEED
DOBSON	TABORS	ZIBETH	DACHAS	DECIDE	EMCEES
GABION	TUBERS	ZIBETS	DACHAU	DECODE	ESCHER
GIBBON	UMBERS	******	DECCAN	ENCODE	ESCHEW
GIBSON	UNBARS	**--B-U-**	ESCHAR	ESCUDO	ETCHED
HEBRON	UNBORN	******	FACIAL	EXCIDE	ETCHER
HOBNOB	WEBERS	ARBOUR	FECIAL	FACADE	ETCHES
RIBBON	******	COBNUT	JACKAL	RECEDE	EUCHER
ROBSON	**--B-S-**	DYBBUK	LACIAL	SECEDE	EXCEED
TABOOS	******	ELBRUS	LACTAM	******	FACIES
******	ABBESS	EMBRUE	LUCIAN	**--C-E-**	FICHES
--B-R-	AMBUSH	ERBIUM	LUCIAS	******	HACKED
******	BABISM	HUBBUB	MECCAN	AACHEN	HACKEE
ALBERT	BABIST	IMBRUE	MECCAS	ARCHED	HACKER
AMBARI	CUBISM	LABIUM	MICMAC	ARCHEO	HICKEY
AMBARY	CUBIST	LABOUR	NECTAR	ARCHER	HOCKED
AMBERS	DEBASE	LABRUM	NUCHAE	ARCHES	HOCKEY
AMBERY	EMBOSS	MOBIUS	PICKAX	ARCKED	INCHED
ARBORI	KIBOSH	SUBDUE	RACIAL	BACHED	INCHES
ARBORS	RIBOSE		RECTAL	BACHES	ITCHED

ITCHES	RACHEL	******	TACTIC	NICOLE	FECUND
JACKED	RACIER	--C-F-	TOCSIN	OCCULT	JACANA
JACKET	RACKED	******	UNCOIL	OSCULE	JOCUND
JOCKEY	RACKER	PACIFY	URCHIN	PICKLE	LACING
KECKED	RACKET	******	VICTIM	PICULS	LACUNA
KICKED	RICHER	--C-G-	ZECHIN	RACILY	LUCENT
KICKER	RICHES	******	******	RECALL	MACING
KUCHEN	RICKED	ENCAGE	--C-K-	RICHLY	NICENE
LACHES	RICKEY	INCAGE	******	SICILY	NOCENT
LACIER	ROCHET	SOCAGE	DECOKE	SICKLE	OSCANS
LACKED	ROCKED	UNCAGE	******	SICKLY	OSCINE
LACKEY	ROCKER	******	--C-L-	SUCKLE	PACING
LECHER	ROCKET	--C-I-	******	TACKLE	PECANS
LICHEE	RUCHES	******	ARCHLY	TICALS	RACINE
LICHEN	RUCKED	ALCAIC	BECALM	TICKLE	RACING
LICKED	SACHEM	ALCUIN	BUCKLE	VOCALS	RECANT
LOCKED	SACHET	ARCHIE	CACKLE	******	RECENT
LOCKER	SACKED	ARCHIL	CECILE	--C-M-	RICING
LOCKET	SACKER	ARCTIC	CECILS	******	ROCKNE
LOCOED	SACRED	BOCCIE	CECILY	BECAME	SECANT
LUCIEN	SECKEL	COCAIN	CICALA	BECOME	SECOND
LYCEES	SECRET	COCCID	CICELY	DECAMP	SECUND
MACLES	SICKED	COCHIN	COCKLE	DECUMA	TECHNO
MICHEL	SICKEN	CYCLIC	DECALS	ENCAMP	VACANT
MICKEY	SICKER	DACOIT	DECILE	INCOME	VACUNA
MOCKED	SOCCER	DECEIT	DECKLE	RACEME	VICUNA
MOCKER	SOCKED	DICKIE	DOCILE	TACOMA	******
MUCKED	SOCKET	EUCLID	EXCELS	******	--C-O-
MUCKER	SOCLES	FUCOID	FACILE	--C-N-	******
NECKED	SOCMEN	HACKIE	FACULA	******	ANCHOR
NICHED	SOCRED	HECTIC	FECULA	ACCENT	ARCHON
NICHES	SUCKED	ISCHIA	FICKLE	ANCONA	BECKON
NICKED	SUCKER	JACKIE	FOCSLE	ANCONE	CACAOS
NICKEL	SUCRES	LACTIC	HACKLE	ARCANA	CACHOU
NICKER	SYCEES	LOCHIA	HECKLE	ARCANE	COCOON
NOCKED	TACKED	MUCOID	HUCKLE	ARCING	CUCKOO
NUCLEI	TACKER	ORCEIN	KECKLE	ASCEND	DACRON
PACKED	TACKEY	ORCHID	LACILY	ASCENT	DOCTOR
PACKER	TICKED	ORCHIL	LOCALE	BACONY	ESCROW
PACKET	TICKER	ORCHIO	LOCALS	DECANE	FACTOR
PECKED	TICKET	ORCHIS	LUCILE	DECANT	GECKOS
PECKER	TUCKED	PECTIC	MACKLE	DECENT	HECTOR
PECTEN	TUCKER	PECTIN	MACULA	DICING	HICKOK
PICKED	TUCKET	PICNIC	MACULE	DOCENT	INCHON
PICKER	UNCLES	PICRIC	MICELL	ENCINA	JOCKOS
PICKET	WICHES	RACHIS	MICKLE	EOCENE	LECTOR
POCKET	WICKED	RECOIL	MUCKLE	ESCENT	LICTOR
PUCKER	WICKER	RICHIE	NICELY	FACING	MACRON

MICRON	OCCURS	DUCATS	******	OLDHAM	AIDMEN
PICTOR	OSCARS	EXCITE	--C-Y-	ORDEAL	ANDREA
RACOON	PACERS	FACETS	******	PEDLAR	ANDREI
RECKON	RACERS	HECATE	ARCHYS	RADIAL	ANDRES
RECTOR	RECORD	INCITE	BECKYS	RADIAN	ANDREW
RECTOS	RECURS	LOCATE	COCCYX	REDBAY	AUDREY
SECTOR	RICERS	LUCITE	DACTYL	REDCAP	BADGED
SUCCOR	SECERN	MYCETE	DECAYS	RODMAN	BADGER
TUCSON	SECURE	NICETY	DECOYS	UNDRAW	BADGES
TYCOON	ULCERS	OOCYTE	JACKYS	VEDIAC	BADMEN
VECTOR	UNCORD	PICOTS	MCCOYS	VIDUAL	BEDDED
VICTOR	UNCORK	RECITE	MICKYS	VODKAS	BEDDER
******	UNCURL	VACATE	NICKYS	ZODIAC	BIDDEN
--C-P-	VICARS	YACHTS	RICKYS	******	BIDDER
******	******	******	VICKYS	--D-B-	BODIED
ACCEPT	--C-S-	--C-U-	******	******	BODIES
BICEPS	******	******	--D-A-	ARDEBS	BUDDED
ESCAPE	ACCESS	ACCRUE	******	INDABA	BUDDER
EXCEPT	ACCOST	CACTUS	AIDMAN	******	BUDGED
INCEPT	ACCUSE	COCCUS	ANDEAN	--D-C-	BUDGES
OCCUPY	DICAST	COCKUP	BADMAN	******	BUDGET
RECAPS	ENCASE	DICTUM	BEDLAM	ABDUCT	CADGED
RECEPT	ENCASH	FACTUM	BEDPAN	ADDICT	CADGER
RECIPE	ENCYST	FICHUS	ENDEAR	ADDUCE	CADGES
UNCAPS	EXCESS	FUCOUS	EUDOAR	ADDUCT	CADRES
WICOPY	EXCISE	HICCUP	GODDAM	BEDECK	CODDER
******	EXCUSE	LOCKUP	HEDRAL	BODICE	CODGER
--C-R-	INCASE	LUCIUS	HODMAN	DEDUCE	CUDGEL
******	INCEST	LYCEUM	HYDRAE	DEDUCT	DADOES
ACCORD	INCISE	MOCKUP	HYDRAS	DODECA	DIDIES
BICARB	INCUSE	MUCOUS	INDIAN	INDICT	DIDOES
BICORN	JOCOSE	PICKUP	JUDEAN	INDUCE	DODDER
BUCKRA	LOCUST	RECOUP	KEDDAH	INDUCT	DODGED
CICERO	MUCOSA	RECTUM	KIDNAP	MEDICL	DODGER
DECARE	MUCOSE	RECTUS	KODIAK	MEDICO	DODGES
DECERN	NICEST	RICTUS	LYDIAS	MEDICS	DODOES
DECORS	RACISM	RUCKUS	MADCAP	REDACT	DUDEEN
DECURY	RACIST	SACRUM	MADMAN	REDUCE	DUDLEY
DICERS	RECAST	TUCHUN	MADRAS	SEDUCE	EDDIED
ENCORE	RECESS	VACUUM	MEDIAE	******	EDDIES
ESCARP	RECUSE	******	MEDIAL	--D-D-	ELDRED
ESCORT	UNCASE	--C-V-	MEDIAN	******	ENDUED
EUCHRE	UPCAST	******	MEDLAR	AUDADS	ENDUES
FACERS	******	ALCOVE	MEDWAY	IODIDE	FIDGET
GOCART	--C-T-	******	MIDDAY	******	FODDER
INCORP	******	--C-W-	MIDWAY	--D-E-	FUDGED
INCURS	ALCOTT	******	MUDCAP	ADDLED	FUDGES
MACERS	ASCOTS	MACAWS	OGDOAD	ADDLES	GADDED

GADDER	PADDED	******	******	SEDILE	REDANS
GADGET	PADRES	--D-G-	--D-K-	TIDILY	REDONE
HEDGED	PODDED	******	******	TODDLE	RIDENT
HEDGER	REDDEN	BODEGA	KODAKS	UNDULY	RIDING
HEDGES	REDDER	INDIGO	UPDIKE	WADDLE	RODENT
HIDDEN	REDEEM	LADOGA	******	WADDLY	SEDANS
HODDEN	REDOES	******	--D-L-	WEDELN	SIDING
INDEED	RIDDED	--D-H-	******	WIDELY	TIDING
INDIES	RIDDEN	******	AEDILE	YODELS	UNDINE
INDUED	RIDGED	BUDDHA	AUDILE	******	UNDONE
INDUES	RIDGES	JUDAHS	BODILY	--D-M-	WADING
JUDAEA	RODMEN	WIDTHS	BUDDLE	******	WIDENS
JUDAEO	RODNEY	******	CEDULA	ADDAMS	******
JUDGED	RUDDER	--D-I-	CODDLE	BEDIMS	--D-O-
JUDGER	SADDEN	******	CUDDLE	MADAME	******
JUDGES	SADDER	BEDRID	CUDDLY	MADAMS	GIDEON
KEDGED	SADIES	BEDSIT	DADDLE	OEDEMA	GODSON
KEDGES	SEDGES	BEDUIN	DIDDLE	RADOME	HEDRON
KIDDED	SIDLED	BODKIN	EIDOLA	SEDUMS	HUDSON
KIDDER	SIDLER	BUDGIE	ENDALL	SODOMY	HYDROS
KIDNEY	SIDLES	CADDIE	FIDDLE	******	INDOOR
LADDER	SIDNEY	CADDIS	FUDDLE	--D-N-	KEDRON
LADIES	SODDED	CEDRIC	GADFLY	******	LUDLOW
LADLED	SODDEN	CODEIA	HEDDLE	ADDEND	ODDJOB
LADLER	SUDDEN	CODEIN	HUDDLE	ADDING	PEDROS
LADLES	SYDNEY	CUDDIE	INDULT	AIDING	PODSOL
LEDGER	TEDDED	EDDAIC	MEDALS	ALDINE	PODZOL
LEDGES	TEDDER	FADEIN	MEDDLE	ARDENT	RADIOS
LIDDED	TIDIED	GADOID	MIDDLE	BIDING	RADNOR
LODGED	TIDIER	GODWIN	MODELS	BODING	REDDOG
LODGER	TIDIES	GODWIT	MODULE	CADENT	REDHOT
LODGES	TODIES	HEDWIG	MUDDLE	CEDING	REDTOP
MADDED	UNDIES	HYDRIC	NODDLE	CODING	RODEOS
MADDEN	UNDOER	INDRIS	NODULE	DEDANS	******
MADDER	UNDOES	JUDAIC	NUDELY	ENDING	--D-R-
MADGES	UNDREW	KIDDIE	PADDLE	FADING	******
MADMEN	UNDSET	LADDIE	PEDALS	HADING	ADDERS
MEDLEY	WADDED	LUDWIG	PEDDLE	HIDING	AIDERS
MIDDEN	WADIES	MADRID	PIDDLE	INDENE	ALDERS
MIDGES	WADSET	MIDAIR	PUDDLE	INDENT	ARDORS
MIDGET	WEDDED	MIDRIB	PUDDLY	IODINE	CEDARS
MUDDED	WEDGED	NUDNIK	RADDLE	JADING	CIDERS
MUDDER	WEDGES	ORDAIN	RADULA	LADING	DIDERO
NODDED	******	PIDGIN	REDDLE	LADINO	ELDERS
NODDER	--D-F-	REDFIN	RIDDLE	NADINE	ENDURE
NUDGED	******	TIDBIT	RUDDLE	NIDING	FEDORA
NUDGES	CODIFY	WEDGIE	RUDELY	PEDANT	HIDERS
OODLES	MODIFY	WIDDIE	SADDLE	PODUNK	MADURA
	NIDIFY				

MADURO	PEDATI	******	PRESAS	QUENCH	TWEEDS
MODERN	SEDATE	--E-A-	PREWAR	SKETCH	UPENDS
NADIRS	UPDATE	******	SEESAW	SPEECH	UREIDE
ORDERS	******	ACETAL	SHEBAT	STENCH	WIELDS
ORDURE	--D-U-	ALEGAR	STEFAN	TIERCE	WIELDY
RADARS	******	AMEBAE	STELAE	TRENCH	YIELDS
RIDERS	ALDOUS	AMEBAS	STELAR	ULENCE	******
SEDERS	ARDOUR	APEMAN	STEPAN	UNESCO	--E-E-
SIDERO	BEDAUB	ARECAS	THEBAE	WHENCE	******
SUDARY	BEDBUG	ARENAS	THECAE	WRENCH	ABELES
UDDERS	CADMUS	AXEMAN	THECAL	WRETCH	AEETES
WADERS	INDIUM	CAESAR	THEDAS	******	AKENES
******	IODOUS	CHELAE	THENAL	--E-D-	APEXES
--D-S-	MADEUP	CHELAS	THENAR	******	ARETES
******	MEDIUM	CHETAH	THETAS	AGENDA	AXEMEN
ALDOSE	MIDGUT	COEVAL	TOECAP	AMENDS	BEEFED
DUDISH	PODIUM	CREDAL	TREPAN	BLEEDS	BEEPED
EDDISH	PODOUS	CRETAN	ULEMAS	BLENDE	BEEVES
ELDEST	RADIUM	CREVAS	******	BLENDS	BREMEN
IODISM	RADIUS	DAEDAL	--E-B-	BREADS	BREVES
JADISH	REDBUD	DEEWAN	******	BREEDS	BREVET
MEDUSA	REDBUG	DIETAL	BLEBBY	BRENDA	BREWED
MODEST	REDGUM	ELENAS	SHELBY	CREEDS	BREWER
MODISH	SADHUS	ENEMAS	******	DREADS	CHEBEC
NODOSE	SIDDUR	FAECAL	--E-C-	EMENDS	CHEWED
NUDISM	SODIUM	FOEMAN	******	FIELDS	CHEWER
NUDIST	TEDIUM	FOETAL	AGENCY	FIENDS	CLEVER
ODDEST	******	FREDAS	AMERCE	FREDDY	CLEWED
OLDEST	--D-V-	GRETAS	ARERCU	GREEDS	COELED
OLDISH	******	HAEMAL	BIERCE	GREEDY	CREMES
RADISH	ENDIVE	HEEHAW	BLEACH	KNEADS	CRENEL
RUDEST	GODIVA	HIEMAL	BLENCH	ONEIDA	CREPED
SADISM	******	HYENAS	BREACH	OREADS	CREPES
SADIST	--D-W-	HYETAL	BREECH	OREIDE	CREWEL
VADOSE	******	ICECAP	CLENCH	OVERDO	DEEDED
WIDEST	BEDEWS	ICEMAN	COERCE	PLEADS	DEEMED
******	ENDOWS	IPECAC	DRENCH	PSEUDO	DEEPEN
--D-T-	INDOWS	LEEWAY	FIERCE	SCENDS	DEEPER
******	REDOWA	MAENAD	FLEECE	SHERDS	DIESEL
AUDITS	WIDOWS	OMEGAS	FLEECY	SPEEDS	DIESES
BIDETS	******	ONEWAY	FLENCH	SPEEDY	DIETED
CADETS	--D-Y-	OPERAS	FLETCH	SPENDS	DIETER
INDITE	******	OREGAN	FRENCH	STEADY	DUELED
IODATE	PADDYS	PIEMAN	FRESCO	STEEDS	DUELER
JUDITH	REDEYE	PIENAL	GREECE	TREADS	ELEVEN
NUDITY	RODDYS	PLEIAD	PIERCE	TRENDS	EVENED
ODDITY	TEDDYS	PREFAB	PLEACH	TRENDY	EVERET
PEDATE	--D-Z-	PREPAY	PREACH		EXETER
	IODIZE				

EYELET	PEEKED	SKEWED	ENERGY	EGERIA	******
FAECES	PEEKER	SKEWER	FLEDGE	ELEGIT	--E-K-
FEEDER	PEELED	SLEWED	FLEDGY	ELEMIS	******
FEELER	PEELER	SOEVER	GREIGE	EMERIC	BLEAKS
FEEZED	PEENED	SPEWED	PLEDGE	EMERIE	BREAKS
FEEZES	PEEPED	STELES	SLEDGE	EMESIS	BREEKS
FLEXED	PEEPER	STEREO	SLEIGH	EMETIC	CHECKS
FLEXES	PEERED	STERES	******	EMETIN	CHEEKS
FOEMEN	PEEVED	STEVEN	--E-H-	EYELID	CHEEKY
FUELED	PEEVES	STEVES	******	FAERIE	CLERKS
FUELER	PEEWEE	STEWED	ALEPHS	FOETID	CREAKS
GEEZER	PIECED	SUEDES	AMECHE	GAELIC	CREAKY
GHEBER	PIECER	SWEDEN	AYESHA	IBERIA	CREEKS
GLEBES	PIECES	SWEDES	BEECHY	IRENIC	FLECKS
GLEDES	PIEMEN	TEEMED	BRECHT	LIEBIG	FREAKS
GREBES	PIETER	TEEMER	CRECHE	LUETIC	FREAKY
GRETEL	PLEBES	TEETER	FLECHE	MYELIN	GREEKS
HEEDED	PREFER	THEBES	FLESHY	NOESIS	SHEIKH
HEEDER	PREMED	THEMES	GOETHE	NOETIC	SHEIKS
HEELED	PRETER	THESES	REECHO	OLEFIN	SLEEKS
HEELER	PREYED	THEWED	SEETHE	PEEWIT	SLEEKY
IBEXES	PREYER	TIERED	STETHO	PLEGIA	SNEAKS
ICEMEN	QUEBEC	UNEVEN	TEETHE	POETIC	SNEAKY
ILEXES	QUEUED	URETER	******	PRECIS	SPEAKS
IRENES	QUEUES	VEERED	--E-I-	PREFIX	SPECKS
JAEGER	REEDED	VIEWED	******	PRELIM	STEAKS
JEERED	REEFED	VIEWER	ACEDIA	PYEMIA	TWEAKS
JEERER	REEFER	WEEDED	ACERIC	PYEMIC	TWEAKY
KEELED	REEKED	WEEDER	ACETIC	REEDIT	WHELKS
KEENED	REEKER	WEEPER	ADENIS	SCENIC	WHELKY
KEENER	REELED	WEEVER	ALEXIA	SHERIF	WREAKS
KEEPER	REELER	WHEYEY	ALEXIN	SPECIE	WRECKS
KEEVES	REEVED	WIENER	ALEXIS	STELIC	******
LEERED	REEVES	******	AMEBIC	STEPIN	--E-L-
LIEDER	SCENES	--E-F-	AMELIA	STERIC	******
LIEGES	SEEDED	******	AMELIE	STEVIE	AGEDLY
MEEKER	SEEDER	GREIFS	ANEMIA	TAENIA	AGEOLD
MEETER	SEEKER	ONEOFF	ANEMIC	THEMIS	AREOLA
NEEDED	SEEMED	******	BREWIS	THESIS	BEETLE
NEEDER	SEEMER	--E-G-	CLERIC	THETIC	CHEILO
NIECES	SEEPED	******	CLERID	THETIS	CREELS
OBEYED	SHEKEL	ANERGY	CLEVIS	TIEPIN	CREOLE
OBEYER	SHEWED	AVENGE	CREDIT	UREMIA	DEEPLY
OMELET	SHEWER	AWEIGH	CRETIC	URETIC	DUELLO
OPENED	SIEGED	CLERGY	CRETIN	WEENIE	DWELLS
OPENER	SIEGES	DREDGE	DIESIS	WEEVIL	EVENLY
OXEYED	SIEVED	DREGGY	ECESIS	WIENIE	FEEBLE
OXEYES	SIEVES	EMERGE	EDENIC		FEEBLY

FREELY	CREAMY	OCEANS	RHETOR	PLEURA	UNEASE
IDEALS	DREAMS	PAEANS	STENOG	PLEURO	UNEASY
ISEULT	DREAMT	PAEONS	STEROL	POETRY	UREASE
KEENLY	DREAMY	PAEONY	TREMOR	QUEERS	WEENSY
KNEELS	FLEAMS	PREENS	TREVOR	SHEARS	******
KNELLS	GLEAMS	QUEANS	******	SHEERS	--E-T-
LUELLA	GLEAMY	QUEENS	--E-P-	SHERRY	******
MEEKLY	IBEAMS	QUERNS	******	SIERRA	ADEPTS
MEETLY	PNEUMA	RUEING	ALEPPO	SIEURS	AGENTS
NEEDLE	PNEUMO	SEEING	CHEEPS	SKERRY	ALECTO
NIELLI	RHEIMS	SHEENS	CHEOPS	SMEARS	ALERTS
NIELLO	RHEUMY	SHEENY	COEMPT	SMEARY	ALEUTS
NOELLE	SPERMO	SIENNA	CREEPS	SNEERS	AMENTI
OCELLI	STEAMS	SKEANS	CREEPY	SPEARS	AMENTS
ONEILL	STEAMY	SKEINS	DIEPPE	SPERRY	AVERTS
OPENLY	THELMA	STEINS	EXEMPT	STEERS	AVESTA
OVERLY	THERMO	STERNA	SHEEPS	SWEARS	BLEATS
PUEBLO	THERMS	STERNO	SHERPA	THEIRS	BREATH
QUELLS	WHELMS	STERNS	SLEEPS	THEORY	BRENTS
SEEMLY	******	SWEENY	SLEEPY	WHERRY	CHEATS
SHEILA	--E-N-	TEEING	STEEPS	******	CHESTS
SHEILD	******	TIEINS	STEPPE	--E-S-	CHESTY
SHELLS	AGEING	TOEING	SWEEPS	******	CLEATS
SHELLY	AVERNO	VIENNA	SWEEPY	APEPSY	CLEFTS
SIECLE	AWEING	******	TIEUPS	AVERSE	CREATE
SMELLS	BLENNY	--E-O-	TWERPS	BREAST	CRESTS
SMELLY	CLEANS	******	WHELPS	CHEESE	CUESTA
SNELLS	DOESNT	BRETON	******	CHEESY	EGESTA
SPELLS	DUENNA	CHEGOE	--E-R-	CLEIST	EGESTS
STEALS	DYEING	COELOM	******	CREASE	EJECTA
STEELS	EKEING	CREDOS	AMENRA	CREASY	EJECTS
STEELY	ETERNA	CRESOL	AWEARY	CREESE	ELECTS
STELLA	EXEUNT	CRETON	BLEARS	CREUSA	EMEUTE
STELLI	EYEING	DAEMON	BLEARY	DRESSY	ERECTS
SWELLS	FEEING	ELEVON	CHEERS	FLENSE	EVENTS
TREBLE	FOEHNS	FAEROE	CHEERY	FREEST	EVERTS
WEEKLY	FREONS	FLEXOR	CHEIRO	GNEISS	EXERTS
WHEALS	FRESNO	FOETOR	CHERRY	GREASE	FIESTA
WHEELS	GEEING	GREGOS	CLEARS	GREASY	FLEETS
******	GLEANS	GUENON	DREARY	ODESSA	FRETTY
--E-M-	GREENE	ICEBOX	EMEERS	PLEASE	GHETTO
******	GREENS	OBERON	EXEDRA	QUEASY	GLEETS
ADEEMS	GRETNA	OCELOT	FLEERS	SPEISS	GLEETY
BREAMS	GWENNS	OREGON	FLEURY	TEENSY	GREATS
BREGMA	HIEING	PHENOL	OHENRY	THEISM	GREETS
CAEOMA	HOEING	PLEXOR	ONEIRO	THEIST	GUESTS
CLEOME	JEEING	PRETOR	PIERRE	TRESSY	IDEATE
CREAMS	LIERNE	QUEZON	PIETRO	TSETSE	ODETTE

OLEATE	PIERUS	SNEEZE	DUFFED	******	RUFFLE
OMENTA	PLENUM	SNEEZY	DUFFEL	--F-H-	SAFELY
PLEATS	PLEXUS	WHEEZE	DUFFER	******	SOFTLY
PLENTY	PREVUE	WHEEZY	EIFFEL	FIFTHS	UNFOLD
PRESTO	RHESUS	******	GAFFED	******	WAFFLE
PRETTY	RUEFUL	--F-A-	GAFFER	--F-I-	WIFELY
QUESTS	STEPUP	******	GAFFES	******	******
SCENTS	USEFUL	AFFRAY	GIFTED	AFFAIR	--F-M-
SHEATH	UTERUS	CAFTAN	GOFFER	BAFFIN	******
SHEETS	WOEFUL	DEFEAT	HAFTED	BIFFIN	DEFAME
SHELTY	******	DEFRAY	HEFTED	BOFFIN	INFAMY
SIESTA	--E-V-	GUFFAW	HUFFED	COFFIN	******
SLEETS	******	KAFTAN	LIFTED	FAFNIR	--F-N-
SLEETY	CHEVVY	OFFDAY	LIFTER	KAFFIR	******
SLEUTH	CLEAVE	SOFTAS	LOFTED	MUFFIN	ALFONS
SMELTS	GREAVE	ZAFFAR	LOFTER	MUFTIS	DEFEND
SVELTE	HUELVA	******	LUFFED	PUFFIN	DEFINE
SWEATS	SHEAVE	--F-C-	MIFFED	RAFFIA	ELFINS
SWEATY	SHELVE	******	MUFFED	SOFFIT	FIFING
SWEETS	SLEAVE	AFFECT	OFFSET	SUFFIX	INFANT
THEFTS	SLEEVE	DEFACE	PUFFED	TIFFIN	OFFEND
TREATS	STEEVE	DEFECT	PUFFER	UNFAIR	OFFING
TREATY	SWERVE	EFFACE	RAFTED	ZAFFIR	REFINE
TWEETS	TWELVE	EFFECT	RAFTER	ZAFTIG	REFUND
TWENTY	WHERVE	ENFACE	REFLET	******	******
WHEATS	******	INFECT	REFLEX	--F-K-	--F-O-
WREATH	--E-X-	OFFICE	REFUEL	******	BEFOOL
WRESTS	******	REFACE	RIFLED	ALFAKI	INFLOW
******	ICEAXE	******	RIFLER	******	REFOOT
--E-U-	******	--F-E-	RIFLES	--F-L-	TEFLON
******	--E-Y-	******	RIFTED	******	******
ACEIUM	******	ALFRED	RUFFED	BAFFLE	******
ACEOUS	ACETYL	BAFFED	SIFTED	BEFALL	--F-R-
ACETUM	AVERYS	BIFFED	SIFTER	BEFELL	******
AVENUE	AYEAYE	BIFLEX	SOFTEN	BIFOLD	AFFIRM
CAECUM	BYEBYE	BUFFED	SOFTER	COFFLE	AFFORD
CHEQUE	CHERYL	BUFFER	SUFFER	DAFTLY	BEFORE
CHERUB	EVELYN	BUFFET	TIFFED	DEFILE	BIFORM
EREBUS	PHENYL	COFFEE	TOFFEE	DEFTLY	DEFERS
EXEQUY	******	COFFER	TUFFET	DUFFLE	DEFORM
EYECUP	--E-Z-	CUFFED	TUFTED	ENFOLD	EFFORT
EYEFUL	******	DEFIED	WAFTED	INFOLD	ERFURT
EYEOUT	AREZZO	DEFIER	WAFTER	MUFFLE	FIFERS
FOETUS	BREEZE	DEFIES	ZAFFER	ONFALL	ILFORD
FRENUM	BREEZY	DEFTER	******	PIFFLE	INFERO
IREFUL	FREEZE	DIFFER	--F-G-	RAFFLE	INFERS
NAEVUS	FRENZY	DOFFED	******	REFILL	INFIRM
OBELUS	SLEAZY	DOFFER	BEFOGS	RIFFLE	INFORM
			EFFIGY		
			REFUGE		

LIFERS	BOGOAK	ARGUER	JIGGER	SIGNED	PIGGIE
OFFERS	COGNAC	ARGUES	JOGGED	SIGNER	PIGGIN
OXFORD	COGWAY	BAGGED	JOGGER	SIGNET	REGAIN
REFERS	DAGMAR	BAGMEN	JUGGED	TAGGED	REGGIE
REFORM	DOGEAR	BEGGED	KEGLER	TAGGER	SIGRID
SAFARI	DOGMAS	BIGGER	LAGGED	TEGMEN	TIGRIS
UNFURL	ENGRAM	BOGGED	LAGGER	TOGAED	UNGUIS
WAFERS	JAGUAR	BOGIES	LEGGED	TOGGED	******
ZAFFRE	JIGSAW	BOGLES	LEGMEN	TOGUES	--G-L-
******	LEGMAN	BUGGED	LEGREE	TUGGED	******
--F-S-	LOGJAM	BUGGER	LOGGED	UNGUES	ANGELA
******	MAGYAR	BUGLED	LOGGER	VAGUER	ANGELO
DEFUSE	MUGGAR	BUGLER	LOGIER	VOGUES	ANGELS
EFFUSE	ORGEAT	BUGLES	LUGGED	WAGGED	ANGOLA
ELFISH	RAGBAG	CAGIER	LUGGER	WAGNER	ARGALA
INFEST	RAGDAY	COGGED	MAGNET	WIGGED	ARGALI
INFUSE	RAGLAN	CYGNET	MAGUEY	YOGEES	ARGALS
OAFISH	RAGMAN	DAGGER	MIGUEL	******	ARGYLL
OFFISH	RAGTAG	DEGREE	MUGGED	--G-F-	BAGELS
REFUSE	REGNAL	DIGGED	MUGGER	******	BOGGLE
SAFEST	SAGGAR	DIGGER	NAGGED	ARGUFY	CAGILY
SUFISM	SEGGAR	DOGGED	NAGGER	******	DAGGLE
******	SIGMAS	DOGGER	NIGGER	--G-G-	ENGELS
--F-T-	SIGNAL	DOGIES	NIGHER	******	ENGULF
******	UNGUAL	EAGLES	NUGGET	DEGAGE	GAGGLE
BEFITS	WIGWAG	EAGLET	ORGIES	ENGAGE	GIGGLE
EFFETE	WIGWAM	EDGIER	PEGGED	******	GIGGLY
REFITS	ZIGZAG	FAGGED	PEGLEG	--G-I-	GIGOLO
REFUTE	******	FIGGED	PIGGED	******	GOGGLE
SAFETY	--G-B-	FOGGED	PIGLET	ALGOID	HAGGLE
******	******	FOGIES	PIGPEN	ANGLIA	HIGGLE
--F-U-	DAGOBA	FUGLED	POGIES	ANGLIC	HIGHLY
******	******	FUGLES	PUGGED	BAGNIO	HUGELY
AFFLUX	--G-C-	FUGUES	PUGREE	BEGUIN	INGULF
BEFOUL	******	GAGGED	RAGGED	BIGGIN	JIGGLE
EFFLUX	LEGACY	GAGGER	RAGMEN	BIGWIG	JOGGLE
INFLUX	******	GIGGED	REGLET	DOGGIE	JUGGLE
REFLUX	--G-D-	GIGLET	REGRET	HAGGIS	LIGULA
RUFOUS	******	GIGUES	RIGGED	HOGTIE	LIGULE
******	PAGODA	GOGLET	RIGGER	HUGHIE	MEGALO
--G-A-	******	HAGGED	ROGUED	HYGEIA	MEGILP
******	--G-E-	HIGHER	ROGUES	INGRID	MIGGLE
AEGEAN	******	HOGGED	RUGGED	LIGNIN	MOGULS
AFGHAN	AIGLET	HUGGED	RUGGER	LOGGIA	NIGELS
AUGEAN	ANGLED	HUGHES	SAGGED	MAGGIE	NIGGLE
BAGDAD	ANGLER	INGRES	SAGGER	MAGPIE	REGALE
BAGMAN	ANGLES	JAGGED	SAGIER	MEGRIM	SAGELY
BEGGAR	ARGUED	JIGGED	SIGHED	NOGGIN	SIGILS

TOGGLE	ORGANS	ANGERS	RUGOSE	JUGFUL	******
UNGULA	PAGANS	ANGORA	SAGEST	LIGNUM	--H-D-
VIGILS	PAGING	ASGARD	******	MAGNUM	******
VOGULS	RAGING	AUGERS	--G-T-	MUGGUR	APHIDS
WAGGLE	REGENT	AUGURS	******	PIGNUS	EPHODS
WAGGLY	REGINA	AUGURY	ARGOTS	PIGNUT	JIHADS
WIGGLE	URGENT	BEGIRD	AUGHTS	RAGOUT	OXHIDE
WIGGLY	URGING	BEGIRT	AUGITE	REGIUS	YEHUDI
******	VAGINA	CIGARS	BEGETS	RIGOUR	******
--G-M-	VAGINO	EDGARS	BIGHTS	RUGOUS	--H-E-
******	WAGING	EGGARS	BIGOTS	VIGOUR	******
BEGUMS	WAGONS	EGGERS	BOGOTA	******	ACHAEA
BIGAMY	WIGANS	ENGIRD	DIGITI	--G-V-	ASHIER
DEGAME	YOGINS	ENGIRT	DIGITS	******	ASHLEY
DEGUMS	******	FIGURE	EIGHTH	ARGIVE	ASHMEN
DIGAMY	--G-O-	GAGERS	EIGHTS	******	AWHEEL
LEGUME	******	HEGIRA	EIGHTY	--G-Y-	CAHIER
REGIME	ANGKOR	LAGERS	ERGATE	******	ECHOED
ZYGOMA	DIGLOT	LEGERS	FAGOTS	BOGEYS	ECHOER
******	DOGFOX	LIGURE	FIGHTS	NAGOYA	ECHOES
--G-N-	EGGNOG	LUGERS	INGOTS	PEGGYS	FUHRER
******	FAGGOT	PUGGRY	JUGATE	******	MAHLER
ANGINA	FOGBOW	REGARD	LEGATE	--H-A-	TEHEED
ARGENT	FOGDOG	RIGORS	LEGATO	******	TEHEES
AUGEND	FUGIOS	ROGERS	LIGATE	ASHCAN	YAHVEH
BEGINS	GIGLOT	SUGARS	LIGHTS	ASHLAR	YAHWEH
BEGONE	HAGDON	SUGARY	MAGOTS	ASHMAN	******
BIGONE	LAGOON	TIGERS	MIGHTY	BEHEAD	--H-G-
BOGANS	LEGION	UNGIRD	NEGATE	ISHTAR	******
BYGONE	LOGION	UNGIRT	NIGHTS	LEHUAS	RRHAGE
CAGING	MAGGOT	UTGARD	NIGHTY	REHEAR	RRHAGY
COGENT	MAGNOX	VAGARY	PIGSTY	REHEAT	******
DUGONG	MIGNON	WAGERS	RIGHTO	SCHWAS	--H-H-
EDGING	NOGOOD	YAGERS	RIGHTS	******	******
EGGING	PEGTOP	YOGURT	RUGATE	--H-B-	APHTHA
ENGINE	PIGEON	******	SIGHTS	******	EPHAHS
EOGENE	POGROM	--G-S-	TIGHTS	EPHEBI	ICHTHY
EUGENE	REGION	******	ZYGOTE	SAHEBS	******
FAGEND	SIGNOR	ARGOSY		SAHIBS	--H-I-
GAGING	WAGGON	AUGUST	--G-U-	WAHABI	******
GIGANT	WIGEON	BAGASS	******	******	ACHAIA
HOGANS	******	DEGUST	AEGEUS	--H-C-	BAHAIS
LAGUNE	--G-P-	DIGEST	ALGOUS	******	COHEIR
LEGEND	******	HUGEST	CYGNUS	ETHICS	DAHLIA
LIGAND	DOGAPE	INGEST	DUGOUT	ITHACA	ECHOIC
NAGANA	******	LEGIST	EGGCUP	MOHOCK	ETHNIC
ORGANA	--G-R-	MEGASS	HAGBUT	SCHUIT	MOHAIR
ORGANO	AGGERS	ORGASM	HOGNUT	SCHICK	SCHUIT
	ANGARY				UNHAIR

******	******	SCHISM	CLIMAX	FLINCH	BAILED
--H-L-	--H-O-	SCHIST	COITAL	FLITCH	BAILEE
******	******	SCHUSS	ELIJAH	IDIOCY	BAILER
AWHILE	BEHOOF	UNHASP	ELIZAS	PEIRCE	BAILEY
BEHALF	CAHOOT	UNHUSK	EPICAL	PRINCE	BAITED
BEHELD	DAHOON	******	EVITAS	QUINCE	BEIGES
BEHOLD	SCHMOS	--H-T-	FRIDAY	QUINCY	BLIMEY
ETHELS	SCHOOL	******	GUITAR	QUITCH	BOILED
ETHYLS	UNHOOK	OPHITE	JAINAS	SMIRCH	BOILER
EXHALE	UPHROE	TAHITI	MOIRAS	SNITCH	BRIBED
INHALE	WAHOOS	UNHATS	OGIVAL	STITCH	BRIBER
MOHOLE	YAHOOS	******	OHIOAN	SWITCH	BRIBES
UNHOLY	******	--H-U-	ORIGAN	TWITCH	BRIDES
UPHELD	--H-R-	******	OVISAC	******	BRINED
UPHILL	******	INHAUL	PLICAE	--I-D-	BRINES
UPHOLD	ABHORS	MAHBUB	PRIMAL	******	CEILED
******	ADHERE	MAHOUT	PTISAN	BLINDS	CHIDED
--H-M-	ASHORE	******	RHINAL	BUILDS	CHIDER
******	AWHIRL	--H-V-	SAIGAS	FRIEDA	CHIDES
ATHOME	BIHARI	******	SAIPAN	GRINDS	CHIMED
BAHAMA	COHERE	BEHAVE	SHIKAR	GUILDS	CHIMER
EXHUME	COHORT	BEHOVE	SMILAX	HAIRDO	CHIMES
INHUME	DEHORN	MOHAVE	SPINAL	LAIRDS	CHINES
NAHUMS	ECHARD	******	SPIRAL	NAIADS	CHISEL
SCHEMA	EPHORI	--H-W-	SPITAL	POINDS	CHIVES
SCHEME	EPHORS	******	TAIGAS	SHINDY	CLIMES
******	ETHERS	MO-	TAIWAN	THIRDS	CLINES
--H-N-	EXHORT	HAWK	TRIBAL	TRIADS	CLIVES
******	INHERE	PSHAWS	TRICAR	TRIODE	COIFED
ACHENE	LAHORE	UNHEWN	TRINAL	WEIRDY	COILED
ACHING	MOHURS	******	URINAL	******	COILER
APHONY	OCHERS	--H-Z-	WEIMAR	--I-E-	COINED
ATHENA	OCHERY	******	WHIDAH	******	COINER
ATHENE	OTHERS	SCHIZO	******	ABIDED	CRIKEY
ATHENS	SAHARA	******	--I-B-	ABIDER	CRIMEA
BEHIND	SCHORL	--I-A-	******	ABIDES	CRIMES
COHUNE	SPHERE	******	AKIMBO	ALICES	CRISES
ECHINI	SPHERY	ABIJAH	CLIMBS	ALINED	DAISES
ECHINO	TSHIRT	ALIDAD	THISBE	ALINES	DEICED
ETHANE	UNHURT	ANIMAL	TRILBY	ALIPED	DEICER
ETHANS	USHERS	ANIMAS	WHITBY	AMICES	DEICES
JOHANN	******	ANITAS	******	AMIDES	DOITED
JOHNNY	--H-S-	APICAL	--I-C-	ANISES	DRIVEL
SPHENE	******	BAIKAL	******	APICES	DRIVEN
SPHENO	AGHAST	BRIDAL	APIECE	ARISEN	DRIVER
SPHINX	BEHEST	CAIMAN	CHINCH	ARISES	DRIVES
STHENO	COHOSH	CEIBAS	CLINCH	ASIDES	DUIKER
UNHAND	REHASH	CLIMAT	EVINCE	AZINES	EDILES

EDITED
ELIDED
ELIDES
EMILES
EXILED
EXILES
EXITED
FAILED
FAIRED
FAIRER
FOILED
FRISES
GAINED
GAINER
GAITED
GAITER
GEIGER
GLIDED
GLIDER
GLIDES
GOITER
GRIDED
GRIDES
GRIMED
GRIMES
GRIPED
GRIPER
GRIPES
GRIVET
GRIZEL
GUIDED
GUIDER
GUIDES
GUILES
GUINEA
GUISES
HAILED
HAILER
HAIRED
HEIFER
HOIDEN
IBICES
IBIDEM
IBISES
IMIDES
IMINES
IRIDES
IRISED

IRISES
JAILED
JAILER
JOINED
JOINER
JUICER
JUICES
KAISER
KNIFED
KNIFES
KNIVES
KOINES
KRISES
LAIRED
LOITER
MAIDEN
MAILED
MAILER
MAIMED
MAIMER
MAIZES
MOILED
MOILER
NAILED
NOISED
NOISES
OBITER
OGIVES
OLIVER
OLIVES
OPINED
OPINES
ORIGEN
OXIDES
PAINED
PAIRED
POISED
POISES
PRICED
PRICES
PRIDED
PRIDES
PRIMED
PRIMER
PRIMES
PRIVET
PRIZED
PRIZER

PRIZES
QUIRED
QUIRES
QUIVER
RAIDED
RAIDER
RAILED
RAINED
RAISED
RAISER
RAISES
REINED
ROILED
RUINED
RUINER
SAILED
SAILER
SEINED
SEINER
SEINES
SEISED
SEIZED
SEIZER
SEIZES
SHINED
SHINER
SHINES
SHIRES
SHIVER
SHIVES
SKIVED
SKIVER
SKIVES
SLICED
SLICER
SLICES
SLIDER
SLIDES
SLIMED
SLIMES
SLIVER
SMILED
SMILER
SMILES
SMITER
SMITES
SNIPED
SNIPER

SNIPES
SNIVEL
SOILED
SOIREE
SPICED
SPICER
SPICES
SPIDER
SPIKED
SPIKES
SPILED
SPILES
SPINEL
SPINES
SPINET
SPIREA
SPIRED
SPIRES
SPITED
SPITES
STILES
STIPEL
STIPES
STIVER
SUITED
SUITES
SWIPED
SWIPES
SWIVEL
SWIVET
TAILED
TAIPEI
TOILED
TOILER
TOILES
TOILET
TRIBES
TRICED
TRICES
TRINED
TRINES
TRITER
TRIVET
TWINED
TWINER
TWINES
UNICEF
UNIPED

UNISEX
UNITED
UNITES
VAINER
VEILED
VEILER
VEINED
VOICED
VOICES
VOIDED
VOILES
WAIFED
WAILED
WAILER
WAITED
WAITER
WAIVED
WAIVER
WAIVES
WHILED
WHILES
WHINED
WHINER
WHINES
WHITED
WHITEN
WHITER
WHITES
WHITEY
WRITER
WRITES
ZUIDER
******
--I-F-
******
BRIEFS
CHIEFS
CLIFFS
CLIFFY
GRIFFE
SKIFFS
SNIFFS
SNIFFY
SPIFFY
WHIFFS
******
--I-G-
******
BEINGS
BRIDGE

BRINGS
CLINGS
CLINGY
CRINGE
DOINGS
ERINGO
FLINGS
FRIDGE
FRIGGA
FRINGE
FRINGY
GOINGS
ICINGS
SLINGS
STINGS
STINGY
SWINGE
SWINGS
THINGS
TWIGGY
TWINGE
WRINGS
******
--I-H-
******
ALIGHT
ARIGHT
BLIGHT
BLITHE
BRIGHT
CHICHI
CLICHE
DWIGHT
EDITHS
ELISHA
ERICHS
FAITHS
FLIGHT
FRIGHT
FRITHS
GEISHA
HEIGHT
KEITHS
KNIGHT
LEIGHS
MOISHE
NEIGHS
PLIGHT

REICHS	OTITIS	STIRKS	SKILLS	CAIRNS	MAISON
SEICHE	PHILIA	TRICKS	SLIMLY	CLIENT	ORISON
SLIGHT	PHILIP	TRICKY	SPIELS	COIGNS	OVIBOS
SMITHS	QUINIC	UMIAKS	SPILLS	DEIGNS	PHILOS
SMITHY	RAISIN	WHISKS	STIFLE	FEIGNE	POISON
STITHY	RHIZIC	WHISKY	STILLS	FEIGNS	PRISON
THIGHS	SAITIC	YOICKS	STILLY	FRIEND	RHINOS
TRICHI	SCIPIO	******	SWILLS	GUIANA	SAIGON
TRICHO	SEISIN	--I-L-	SWIPLE	ONIONS	SAILOR
WEIGHS	SEIZIN	******	SWIRLS	ONIONY	SEISOR
WEIGHT	SPIRIT	ACIDLY	SWIRLY	ORIENT	SEIZOR
WRIGHT	TRIFID	AFIELD	TAILLE	PLIANT	SHILOH
WRITHE	TRIVIA	ALIBLE	THINLY	PUISNE	SKIMOS
******	TRIXIE	ARIDLY	THIOLS	REIGNS	SLIPON
--I-I-	TWIBIL	ARIELS	TRIALS	SCIONS	SPIGOT
******	TWILIT	AVIDLY	TRIFLE	SHINNY	SUITOR
ACIDIC	UNIFIC	AXILLA	TRIGLY	SKIING	TAILOR
ADIPIC	******	BRIDLE	TRILLS	SKINNY	TAINOS
ALIBIS	--I-K-	BRILLS	TRIMLY	SOIGNE	TRICOT
ALICIA	******	CHICLE	TRIPLE	SPINNY	TRIGON
AMIDIC	BLINKS	CHILLI	TUILLE	TRIUNE	TRIPOD
AMIDIN	BRICKS	CHILLS	TWILLS	UNIONS	TRIPOS
ANILIN	BRINKS	CHILLY	TWIRLS	WHINNY	TRITON
AVIDIN	BRISKS	DRILLS	VAINLY	******	UNISON
BAILIE	CHICKS	EDIBLE	WHIRLS	--I-O-	WHILOM
BRIDIE	CHINKS	ENISLE	******	******	******
BRIGID	CHINKY	EVILLY	--I-M-	ALISON	--I-P-
CHITIN	CLICKS	FAILLE	******	AMIDOL	******
CLINIC	CLINKS	FAIRLY	AXIOMS	AMIGOS	BLIMPS
CRISIS	CRICKS	FOIBLE	CHIRMS	ASIMOV	CHIPPY
CRITIC	DRINKS	FRILLS	ENIGMA	AVISOS	CHIRPS
DAIMIO	FLICKS	FRILLY	GLIOMA	BAILOR	CHIRPY
DEIFIC	FRISKS	GAINLY	IDIOMS	BRITON	CRIMPS
ELICIT	FRISKY	GLIBLY	PRISMS	CHICOS	CRIMPY
ELIXIR	HOICKS	GRILLE	SEISMO	CHIGOE	CRISPS
EMILIA	PRICKS	GRILLS	SEISMS	CHIRON	CRISPY
EMILIE	PRINKS	GRIMLY	SHIMMY	CHITON	DRIPPY
EMILIO	QUIRKS	GRISLY	STIGMA	DAIMON	GRIPPE
EXILIC	SHIRKS	ICICLE	******	EDISON	GRIPPY
FRIGID	SKINKS	MAINLY	--I-N-	EDITOR	GUIMPE
IRIDIC	SLICKS	ORIELS	******	ELINOR	PHIPPS
IRITIC	SLINKS	ORIOLE	ALIENS	EPILOG	PRIMPS
IRITIS	SLINKY	PHIALS	ALIGNS	EPIZOA	SKIMPS
MAISIE	SMIRKS	PRIMLY	AMIENS	FRIJOL	SKIMPY
OLIVIA	SNICKS	QUILLS	ANIONS	FRIVOL	SNIPPY
ORIBIS	STICKS	SCILLY	ARIANS	GUIDON	STIRPS
ORIGIN	STICKY	SHIELD	ASIANS	ISIDOR	TWIRPS
OSIRIS	STINKS	SHILLS	BAIRNS	JAILOR	WHIPPY

******	PRIEST	JOINTS	CHIBUK	******	******
--I-R-	PRISSY	JOISTS	CLIQUE	--J-C-	--J-S-
******	QUINSY	MOIETY	CLIQUY	******	******
ANITRA	SHIEST	OPIATE	COITUS	ABJECT	ADJUST
APIARY	SHIISM	PAINTS	CRINUM	ADJECT	UNJUST
AVIARY	SLIEST	PAINTY	EPIRUS	DEJECT	******
BRIARS	SLIMSY	PAIUTE	ITIOUS	HIJACK	--J-U-
BRIERS	THIRST	PLINTH	JAIPUR	INJECT	******
BRIERY	TRIOSE	POINTE	ODIOUS	MEJICO	BIJOUX
CHIRRS	WHILST	POINTS	POILUS	OBJECT	RAJPUT
CRIERS	WHIMSY	POINTY	PRIMUS	REJECT	SAJOUS
DMITRI	WRIEST	PRINTS	QUIPUS	******	******
DRIERS	******	QUILTS	SLIPUP	--J-H-	--J-V-
EMIGRE	--I-T-	QUINTS	UNIQUE	******	******
FLIERS	******	QUIRTS	******	RAJAHS	MOJAVE
FRIARS	AGISTS	SAINTS	--I-V-	******	******
FRIARY	ARISTA	SHIFTS	******	--J-I-	--J-Y-
FRIERS	ARISTO	SHIFTY	CHIVVY	******	******
GOITRE	AVIATE	SHIITE	GRIEVE	ADJOIN	ENJOYS
GRIGRI	BLINTZ	SHINTO	SKIVVY	ENJOIN	******
MAIGRE	CHINTZ	SHIRTS	THIEVE	REJOIN	--K-C-
MAITRE	CHITTY	SHIRTY	******	******	******
OSIERS	CLINTS	SKIRTS	--J-K-	--J-K-	ACKACK
PLIERS	DAINTY	SPILTH	--I-W-	******	******
PRIERS	DEISTS	SPIRTS	******	INJOKE	--K-D-
PRIORS	DRIFTS	STILTS	OJIBWA	******	******
PRIORY	DRIFTY	STINTS	******	--J-L-	MIKADO
SHIRRS	EDICTS	SWIFTS	--I-Y-	******	--K-E-
SKIERS	ELIOTS	TAINTS	******	CAJOLE	******
SKIRRS	EVICTS	THIRTY	DAIMYO	******	ANKLES
SPIERS	EXISTS	TRISTE	DAISYS	--J-M-	ANKLET
TRIERS	FAINTS	TWISTS	EMILYS	******	AUKLET
******	FEINTS	TWISTY	ERINYS	PAJAMA	INKIER
--I-S-	FEISTS	UBIETY	TRIXYS	PYJAMA	INKLES
******	FEISTY	WAISTS	******	******	LAKIER
AHIMSA	FLINTS	WRISTS	--I-Z-	--J-N-	OAKLEY
AMIDST	FLINTY	******	******	******	ORKNEY
ARIOSE	FLIRTS	--I-U-	FRIEZE	CAJUNS	PEKOES
ARIOSO	FLIRTY	******	FRIZZY	JEJUNE	POKIER
CHIASM	FOISTS	ACINUS	******	SEJANT	POKIES
CUISSE	GAIETY	ACIOUS	--J-A-	******	UPKEEP
DRIEST	GLINTS	ADIEUS	******	--J-R-	YAKKED
FLIEST	GRITTY	ADIEUX	FIJIAN	******	YUKKED
FLIMSY	GUILTS	ANIMUS	******	ABJURE	******
GRILSE	GUILTY	ARIOUS	--J-B-	ADJURE	--K-I-
ICIEST	HEISTS	BEIRUT	******	HEJIRA	******
OBIISM	HOISTS	CAIQUE	JUJUBE	INJURE	DAKOIT
OTIOSE	IDIOTS	CHIAUS	RAJABS	INJURY	DIKDIK
				MAJORS	

PYKNIC	MEKONG	******	DOLMAN	VALVAR	UNLOCK
SIKKIM	PEKANS	--K-T-	EOLIAN	VILLAS	VELOCE
TAKEIN	PEKING	******	FALLAL	VOLVAS	******
UNKNIT	PIKING	DAKOTA	FELLAH	VULCAN	--L-D-
******	POKING	******	FILIAL	VULGAR	******
--K-K-	PUKING	--K-U-	FOLIAR	VULVAE	ALLUDE
******	RAKING	******	FULMAR	VULVAL	BOLIDE
WAKIKI	TAKING	MAKEUP	GALEAE	VULVAR	DELUDE
******	TOKENS	MUKLUK	GALWAY	WALLAH	FELIDS
--K-L-	UNKIND	TAKEUP	GALYAK	WALLAS	HALIDE
******	VIKING	WIKIUP	GILDAS	WILMAS	HALIDS
ALKALI	WAKENS	******	GILEAD	ZILLAH	MALADY
ALKYLS	WAKING	--L-A-	GULLAH	******	MELODY
ANKYLO	YOKING	******	HALLAH	--L-B-	MILADY
BIKOLS	******	AFLOAT	HELLAS	******	SALADS
JEKYLL	--K-O-	AGLEAM	HILDAS	ADLIBS	SOLIDI
LIKELY	******	BALAAM	JULIAN	CALEBS	SOLIDS
YOKELS	INKPOT	BALKAN	JULIAS	PHLEBO	TELEDU
******	MIKLOS	BALLAD	KALIAN	******	TOLEDO
--K-M-	NEKTON	BALSAM	KALPAK	--L-C-	TULADI
******	******	BALSAS	LILIAN	******	UNLADE
ESKIMO	--K-P-	BALZAC	MILLAY	ANLACE	******
HAKIMS	******	BELDAM	MOLLAH	CALICO	--L-E-
KOKOMO	KAKAPO	BELGAS	MULLAH	CILICE	******
YAKIMA	******	BELIAL	NILGAI	CULTCH	AILEEN
******	--K-R-	BELLAS	NULLAH	DELICT	ALLIED
--K-N-	******	BILBAO	OILCAN	ENLACE	ALLIES
******	ANKARA	BULBAR	PALEAE	FELICE	ARLEEN
ALKANE	ASKERS	BULGAR	PALLAS	GALACT	ASLEEP
ALKENE	BAKERS	BULLAE	PALMAR	HELICO	BALDER
ALKYNE	BAKERY	CALCAR	PELIAS	INLACE	BALEEN
ASKANT	DEKARE	CALLAO	PILLAR	LILACS	BALKED
ASKING	ESKERS	CALLAS	POLEAX	MALACO	BALLED
BAKING	FAKERS	CALPAC	POLKAS	MALICE	BALLET
BIKINI	FAKERY	CELIAC	PULSAR	MOLOCH	BELIED
CAKING	FAKIRS	CELIAS	RELOAD	OCLOCK	BELIEF
COKING	GOKART	CELLAE	SALAAM	PALACE	BELIER
DEKING	HIKERS	CELLAR	SALPAS	POLACK	BELIES
DIKING	INKERS	CILIAT	SILVAE	POLICE	BELLED
FAKING	JOKERS	COLLAR	SILVAN	POLICY	BELLES
HIKING	LAKERS	COLZAS	SILVAS	RELICS	BELTED
INKING	MAKERS	CULLAY	SULTAN	RELICT	BILGED
IRKING	PIKERS	DALLAS	SYLVAE	SELECT	BILGES
JOKING	POKERS	DELIAN	SYLVAN	SILICA	BILKED
LAKING	RAKERS	DELIAS	SYLVAS	SILICO	BILKER
LIKENS	SAKERS	DELLAS	UNLEAD	SOLACE	BILLED
LIKING	TAKERS	DELTAS	UNLOAD	SPLICE	BILLET
MAKING	******	DOLLAR	VALVAL	UNLACE	BOLDER
	--K-S-				
	******				
	RAKISH				

BOLLED	FELTED	HOLLER	MOLTED	SALVED	WELDER
BOLTED	FILLED	HOLMES	MOLTEN	SALVER	WELLED
BOLTER	FILLER	HULKED	MOLTER	SALVES	WELTED
BULBED	FILLET	HULLED	MULLED	SELLER	WELTER
BULBEL	FILMED	INLIER	MULLEN	SELVES	WILBER
BULGED	FILTER	JELLED	MULLER	SILKEN	WILDER
BULGER	FOLDED	JILTED	MULLET	SILOED	WILIER
BULGES	FOLDER	JILTER	MULLEY	SILTED	WILLED
BULKED	FULLED	JOLIET	OILIER	SILVER	WILLER
BULLET	FULLER	JOLTED	OLLIES	SOLDER	WILLET
CALCES	GALLED	JOLTER	PALAEO	SOLOED	WILTED
CALKED	GALLEY	JULIES	PALLED	SOLVED	WOLFED
CALKER	GELDED	JULIET	PALLET	SOLVER	WOLSEY
CALLED	GELLED	KELLER	PALMED	SOLVES	WOLVER
CALLER	GILDED	KILLED	PALMER	SPLEEN	WOLVES
CALMED	GILDER	KILLER	PALPED	SULKED	YELLED
CALMER	GOLDEN	KILMER	PALTER	SULLEN	YELLER
CALVED	GOLFED	KILTED	PELLET	TALCED	YELPED
CALVES	GOLFER	KILTER	PELTED	TALKED	YELPER
CALXES	GULDEN	LALLED	PELTER	TALKER	******
CHLOES	GULFED	LILIED	PELVES	TALLER	--L-F-
COLDER	GULLED	LILIES	PHLOEM	TELFER	******
COLIES	GULLET	LILTED	PILFER	TELLER	CALIFS
COLLET	GULPED	LOLLED	PILLED	TILDES	PILAFF
COLTER	GULPER	LOLLER	POLDER	TILLED	PILAFS
CULLED	HALLEL	LULLED	POLLED	TILLER	SALIFY
CULLER	HALLEY	MALLED	POLLEE	TILTED	SCLAFF
CULLET	HALOED	MALLEE	POLLEN	TILTER	UGLIFY
CULMED	HALOES	MALLET	POLLER	TOLLED	UPLIFT
CULVER	HALSEY	MALTED	POLLEX	TOLLER	VILIFY
DALLES	HALTED	MELDED	PULLED	TOLTEC	******
DELVED	HALTER	MELEES	PULLER	TULLES	--L-G-
DELVER	HALVED	MELTED	PULLET	UGLIER	******
DELVES	HALVES	MELTER	PULLEY	VALLEY	ALLEGE
DOLLED	HELLEN	MILDEN	PULPED	VALUED	ANLAGE
DOLMEN	HELLER	MILDER	PULPER	VALUER	BELUGA
DULCET	HELMED	MILDEW	PULSED	VALUES	COLUGO
DULLED	HELMET	MILIEU	PULSES	VALVED	DELUGE
DULLER	HELPED	MILKED	RELIED	VALVES	EULOGY
DULLES	HELPER	MILKER	RELIEF	VELVET	MALAGA
EILEEN	HELTER	MILLED	RELIER	VOLLEY	MALIGN
ELLIES	HELVES	MILLER	RELIES	VOLTED	MILAGE
FALLEN	HILLED	MILLET	RILLET	WALKED	OBLIGE
FALLER	HILLER	MILTED	ROLLED	WALKER	OOLOGY
FALSER	HILTED	MILTER	ROLLER	WALLED	PELAGE
FALTER	HOLDER	MOLDED	SALLET	WALLET	PHLEGM
FELLED	HOLIER	MOLDER	SALTED	WALTER	SILAGE
FELLER	HOLIES	MOLIES	SALTER	WELDED	TELEGA

TELUGU	INLAID	BALDLY	FELINE	SPLINT	MALLOW
ULLAGE	KALMIA	BOLDLY	FELONS	TALENT	MELLON
******	KELOID	CALMLY	FELONY	TALONS	MELLOW
--L-H-	KELPIE	COLDLY	FILING	TILING	MELTON
******	KELTIC	HOLILY	GALENA	UPLAND	MILTON
DELPHI	KELVIN	MILDLY	HALING	VOLANT	NELSON
DOLPHS	KILTIE	OILILY	HELENA	VOLING	PALLOR
FILTHY	MELVIN	PALELY	HELENS	WALING	PELION
MALTHA	MILLIE	PILULE	HOLING	WILING	PILLOW
RALPHS	MOLLIE	SOLELY	IDLING	XYLANS	SALLOW
ROLPHS	NELLIE	UGLILY	INLAND	XYLENE	SALMON
SULPHA	PALAIS	VILELY	ISLAND	******	SALOON
SULPHO	PALLID	WILDLY	ISLING	--L-O-	SALOOP
SYLPHS	PELVIC	WILILY	KALONG	******	SALVOR
SYLPHY	PELVIS	XYLOLS	MALINE	ABLOOM	SALVOS
TILTHS	PULLIN	******	MELANO	BALBOA	SELDOM
******	PULPIT	--L-M-	MELONS	BALLOT	SOLION
--L-I-	RELAID	******	MOLINE	BELLOC	TALION
******	SALMIS	AFLAME	NYLONS	BELLOW	TALLOW
AALIIS	SALPID	APLOMB	OBLONG	BILLON	TELSON
AFLCIO	SALVIA	COLUMN	OGLING	BILLOW	TOLUOL
AGLAIA	SILVIA	ILLUME	OILING	BOLSON	VILLON
BALTIC	SYLVIA	SALAMI	ONLINE	BOLTON	VOLVOX
BALTIM	TALKIE	SALOME	OOLONG	CALLOW	WALDOS
BELGIC	TILLIE	SOLEMN	PALING	CELLOS	WALKON
BELOIT	UNLAID	VOLUME	PILING	COLLOP	WALLOP
BILLIE	VALOIS	XYLEMS	POLAND	DALTON	WALLOW
BOLLIX	WALLIE	******	POLING	DOLLOP	WALTON
BULBIL	WALLIS	--L-N-	******	ELLIOT	WILLOW
CALAIS	WALVIS	******	--L-N-	FALCON	WILSON
CALCIC	WELKIN	AALAND	******	FALLOW	WILTON
CALKIN	WILLIE	AILING	PYLONS	FELLOE	YELLOW
CALVIN	WILLIS	ALLANS	RELENT	FELLOW	******
CELTIC	XYLOID	ALLENS	RELINE	FOLIOS	--L-P-
COLLIE	******	ARLENE	RILING	FOLLOW	******
CULLIS	--L-K-	ARLINE	ROLAND	FULTON	ASLOPE
DOLLIE	******	ASLANT	RULING	FYLFOT	CALIPH
DULCIE	AXLIKE	BALING	SALINE	GALIOT	FELIPE
ECLAIR	BELIKE	BELONG	SALONS	GALLON	GALOPS
FILLIN	KULAKS	BYLANE	SELENE	GALLOP	JALOPS
FILLIP	MOLTKE	BYLINE	SELENO	GALOOT	JALOPY
FILMIC	SALUKI	COLINE	SILENI	HALLOO	JULEPS
FULFIL	SPLAKE	COLINS	SILENT	HALLOW	ORLOPS
FULGID	UNLIKE	COLONS	SOLAND	HELIOS	OXLIPS
GALLIC	******	COLONY	SOLANO	HOLLOW	PELOPS
GILLIE	--L-L-	DOLING	SOLANS	IGLOOS	POLYPS
HALOID	******	EALING	SOLENT	KELSON	TULIPS
HOLMIC	ALLELE	ELLENS	SOLING	LOLLOP	YCLEPT
	ALLYLS		SPLENO		
			SPLINE		

*****	CALASH	INLETS	HOLDUP	*****	COMBAT
--L-R-	CALESA	IOLITE	IOLCUS	--L-X-	COMMAS
*****	ENLIST	ISLETS	JULIUS	*****	CYMBAL
ALLURE	FILOSE	LOLITA	KALIUM	BILOXI	DAMMAR
BALERS	FOLKSY	MALATE	KULTUR	DELUXE	DEMEAN
BELFRY	GALOSH	MULCTS	MILIUM	GALAXY	GAMMAS
BOLERO	GOLOSH	OBLATE	PALPUS	*****	GEMMAE
CALORY	HOLISM	OOLITE	PELEUS	--L-Y-	GUMMAS
CELERY	IDLEST	OWLETS	PILEUM	*****	HAMMAL
CHLORO	ILLUSE	PALATE	PILEUP	ALLAYS	HAMZAS
COLORS	ILLUST	PELITE	PILEUS	ALLEYS	HYMNAL
COLURE	MOLEST	PELOTA	PILOUS	ALLOYS	JAMJAR
FILERS	MULISH	PILATE	POLLUX	BELAYS	JUMBAL
FULCRA	OBLAST	PILOTS	PULQUE	BILLYS	LAMIAE
GALORE	OWLISH	POLITE	ROLLUP	BOLEYN	LAMIAS
HALERS	PALEST	POLITY	SELJUK	DELAYS	LAMMAS
HILARY	PALISH	RELATE	SULCUS	DOLLYS	LAMPAD
HOLARD	PILOSE	SALUTE	SULFUR	HOLLYS	LAMPAS
IDLERS	POLISH	SOLUTE	TALCUM	INLAYS	LEMMAS
MALGRE	RELISH	SPLATS	TALMUD	MALAYA	LUMBAR
MALORY	SALISH	SPLITS	TELLUS	MALAYS	MAMBAS
MILERS	SPLASH	VALATE	UMLAUT	MELVYN	MAMMAE
MILORD	UNLASH	VALETS	VALGUS	MILLYS	MAMMAL
MOLARS	UNLESS	VALUTA	VALLUM	MOLLYS	MAMMAS
OGLERS	VALISE	VELDTS	VALOUR	NELLYS	OOMIAK
OILERS	VILEST	VOLUTE	VELLUM	POLLYS	PAMPAS
PALTRY	VOLOST	XYLITE	VELOUR	RELAYS	RUMBAS
PELTRY	XYLOSE	*****	VILLUS	SALLYS	SAMBAS
PULERS	*****	--L-U-	WALKUP	SELSYN	SAMIAN
RULERS	--L-T-	*****	WALNUT	SELWYN	SAMOAN
SALARY	*****	ABLAUT	WALRUS	SPLAYS	SAMPAN
SCLERA	AGLETS	ALLIUM	WILBUR	TILLYS	SIMIAN
SCLERO	ALLOTS	ALLOUT	WILFUL	TOLUYL	TAMBAC
SULTRY	APLITE	BULBUL	*****	UNLAYS	TAMPAN
TALARI	BALATA	CALLUP	--L-V-	VALKYR	TAMTAM
TALERS	BILITY	CALLUS	*****	WALLYS	TIMBAL
TELARY	CULETS	CILIUM	RELIVE	WILLYS	TOMBAC
TILERS	DALETH	COLEUS	SALIVA	*****	TOMCAT
VALERY	DELATE	COLOUR	UNLIVE	--L-Z-	TYMPAN
VELURE	DELETE	COLOUS	*****	*****	WOMBAT
VOLERY	DILATE	CULTUS	--L-W-	ABLAZE	ZAMIAS
WALERS	DILUTE	DELIUS	*****	BELIZE	*****
*****	DULUTH	DOLOUR	ALLOWS	*****	--M-B-
--L-S-	EOLITH	FOLIUM	BYLAWS	--M-A-	*****
*****	FILETS	GALLUP	INLAWS	*****	DEMOBS
ABLEST	HALITE	GALLUS	MALAWI	BEMEAN	GEMSBO
ABLUSH	HALUTZ	HALLUX		BEMOAN	*****
AWLESS	HELOTS	HELIUM		BOMBAY	--M-C-
					*****
					ALMUCE
					COMICS

LAMECH	DAMPEN	LIMPET	******	MEMOIR	NIMBLE
MIMICS	DAMPER	LUMBER	--M-F-	REMAIN	NIMBLY
POMACE	DAMSEL	LUMPED	******	ROMAIC	NUMBLY
PUMICE	DEMIES	LUMPEN	HUMIFY	SIMLIN	ORMOLU
SUMACS	DIMMED	MAMIES	RAMIFY	SUMMIT	PAMELA
VOMICA	DIMMER	MAMMET	TUMEFY	TOMTIT	PIMPLE
******	DUMPED	MEMBER	******	ZAMBIA	PIMPLY
--M-D-	DUMPER	MUMMED	--M-G-	ZOMBIE	POMELO
******	EMMIES	MUMMER	******	ZOMBIS	RAMBLE
ALMUDE	FUMIER	NUMBED	ARMAGH	******	RIMPLE
ALMUDS	GAMIER	NUMBER	DAMAGE	--M-K-	ROMOLA
ARMADA	GAMMED	PAMPER	HOMAGE	******	ROMULO
COMEDO	GAMMER	PIMPED	OHMAGE	BAMAKO	RUMBLE
COMEDY	GEMMED	POMMEL	******	KAMIKS	RUMPLE
DEMODE	GIMLET	POMPEY	--M-H-	REMAKE	SAMPLE
LAMBDA	GIMPED	PUMMEL	******	UNMAKE	SEMELE
LAMEDS	GUMMED	PUMPED	ALMAHS	******	SIMILE
NOMADS	HAMDEN	PUMPER	LYMPHO	--M-L-	SIMPLE
POMADE	HAMLET	RAMIES	NYMPHA	******	SIMPLY
REMADE	HAMMED	RAMJET	NYMPHO	BUMBLE	SOMALI
REMEDY	HAMMER	RAMMED	NYMPHS	CAMELS	TAMALE
REMUDA	HAMPER	RAMMER	SAMSHU	CAMILA	TAMELY
UNMADE	HEMMED	RAMPED	******	COMELY	TEMPLE
******	HEMMER	RIMMED	--M-I-	COMPLY	TIMELY
--M-E-	HEMPEN	RIMMER	******	DAMPLY	TUMBLE
******	HOMIER	ROMMEL	ARMPIT	DIMPLE	TUMULT
ARMIES	HUMBER	ROMNEY	BOMBIC	DIMPLY	WAMBLE
ARMLET	HUMMED	ROMPED	BUMKIN	DUMBLY	WAMBLY
BOMBED	HUMMER	ROMPER	COMFIT	FAMILY	WIMBLE
BOMBER	HUMPED	RUMMER	COMMIE	FEMALE	WIMPLE
BOMBES	HYMNED	SAMIEL	COMMIT	FIMBLE	******
BUMMED	IMMIES	SAMLET	COMMIX	FUMBLE	--M-M-
BUMMER	JAMIES	SAMUEL	CYMLIN	GAMBLE	******
BUMPED	JAMMED	SIMMER	CYMOID	GAMELY	JEMIMA
BUMPER	JUMPED	SIMNEL	CYMRIC	GAMILY	SEMEME
CAMBER	JUMPER	SIMPER	DIMWIT	GIMELS	******
CAMDEN	KUMMEL	SOMBER	DOMAIN	HAMALS	--M-N-
CAMLET	LAMBED	SUMMED	GAMBIA	HOMELY	******
CAMPED	LAMMED	SUMMER	GAMBIR	HOMILY	AIMING
CAMPER	LAMPED	SUMNER	GAMBIT	HUMBLE	ALMOND
COMBED	LEMUEL	TAMPED	HEMOID	HUMBLY	ARMAND
COMBER	LIMBED	TAMPER	HYMNIC	JUMBLE	ARMING
COMPEL	LIMBER	TEMPER	IAMBIC	KAMALA	CEMENT
CUMBER	LIMIER	TIMBER	JIMMIE	LAMELY	COMING
DAMMED	LIMNED	TOMBED	KAMSIN	LIMPLY	CUMINS
DAMMER	LIMNER	UNMEET	LAMBIE	LIMULI	CYMENE
DAMNED	LIMPED	VAMPED	LIMBIC	MUMBLE	DAMANS
DAMPED	LIMPER	WOMBED	LIMPID	NAMELY	DEMAND
		YAMMER			

DEMENT	RIMING	TOMCOD	VOMERS	EMMETT	RUMOUR
DEMONO	ROMANS	TOMTOM	WOMERA	ENMITY	RUMPUS
DEMONS	ROMANY	UNMOOR	******	GAMETE	SAMBUR
DOMING	RUMINA	******	--M-S-	GAMETO	TUMOUR
DOMINO	SIMONE	--M-R-	******	GAMUTS	WAMMUS
EDMOND	SIMONS	******	ALMOST	GEMOTS	WAMOUS
EDMUND	SIMONY	ADMIRE	BEMUSE	GOMUTI	WAMPUM
ERMINE	TAMING	ALMIRA	CAMASS	HAMITE	******
FAMINE	TIMING	ARMORS	CAMISE	HEMATO	--M-V-
FOMENT	TOMANS	ARMORY	COMOSE	HUMPTY	******
FUMING	UNMANS	ARMURE	CYMOSE	INMATE	REMOVE
GAMING	VIMINA	AYMARA	DAMASK	LIMITS	******
GAMINS	YAMENS	BEMIRE	DEMISE	NEMATO	--M-W-
GEMINI	YAMUNS	CAMERA	ENMESH	NIMITZ	******
HOMING	YEMENI	CIMBRI	FAMISH	REMITS	UNMEWS
HOMINY	******	COMERS	IMMESH	REMOTE	******
HUMANE	--M-O-	CYMARS	INMESH	SAMITE	--M-X-
HUMANS	******	DEMURE	INMOST	SEMITE	******
HYMENO	BAMBOO	DEMURS	KUMISS	SOMATA	ADMIXT
HYMENS	CAMEOS	DIMERS	LAMEST	SOMATO	******
IMMUNE	CAMION	ELMERS	MIMOSA	SOMITE	--M-Y-
IMMUNO	CAMPOS	ELMIRA	MOMISM	TEMPTS	******
JIMINY	COMBOS	FEMORA	NOMISM	TOMATO	JIMMYS
KIMONO	COMEON	FEMURS	OSMOSE	VOMITO	LIMEYS
LAMENT	COMMON	GEMARA	RAMOSE	VOMITS	MAMEYS
LAMINA	COMPOS	GEMERT	REMISE	******	SAMMYS
LAMING	DAMSON	HOMBRE	REMISS	--M-U-	TIMMYS
LEMONS	EXMOOR	HOMERS	RIMOSE	******	TOMMYS
LIMENS	GAMBOL	HUMORS	ROMISH	ARMFUL	******
LIMINA	GAMMON	IMMURE	TAMEST	ARMOUR	--M-Z-
LIMING	GUMBOS	LEMURS	UNMASK	CAMPUS	******
LOMENT	LEMNOS	MEMORY	UPMOST	COMOUS	ORMUZD
LOMOND	LUMMOX	MIMERS	UTMOST	CYMOUS	******
LUMENS	MAMBOS	NAMERS	VAMOSE	DIMOUT	--N-A-
LUMINA	MAMMON	NOMURA	******	DUMDUM	******
LUMINI	NIMROD	ORMERS	--M-T-	FAMOUS	AENEAS
LUMINO	POMPOM	REMARK	******	FUMOUS	ANNEAL
MIMING	POMPON	REMORA	ADMITS	GAMOUS	ANNUAL
MOMENT	RAMROD	RIMERS	ARMETS	HAMAUL	APNEAL
NAMING	RAMSON	RUMORS	BEMATA	HUMBUG	BANIAN
NUMINA	SAMBOS	SAMARA	COMATE	HUMOUR	BANTAM
OSMOND	SAMSON	SEMPRE	COMETS	IAMBUS	BANYAN
OSMUND	SIMOOM	SIMARS	COMITY	LIMBUS	BANZAI
POMONA	SUMMON	SOMBRE	DEMITS	NIMBUS	BENDAY
RAMONA	SYMBOL	TAMERS	DEMOTE	OSMIUM	BENGAL
REMAND	TAMPON	TIMBRE	DIMITY	RAMOUS	BONSAI
REMANS	TEMPOS	TIMERS	DUMPTY	RIMOUS	BUNYAN
REMIND	TOMBOY	TUMORS	EMMETS		CANAAN

CANCAN	LONGAN	VENIAL	ARNIES	CONKED	FENDER
CANNAE	MANDAN	WANDAS	BANDED	CONKER	FENNEC
CANNAS	MANIAC	XENIAL	BANGED	CONNED	FENNEL
CANTAB	MANIAS	******	BANKED	CONNER	FINDER
CANVAS	MANTAS	--N-B-	BANKER	CONTES	FINGER
CENTAL	MANUAL	******	BANNED	CONVEX	FINNED
CONFAB	MENIAL	DANUBE	BANNER	CONVEY	FINNER
CONGAS	MENSAL	******	BANTER	CUNNER	FONDER
CONMAN	MENTAL	--N-C-	BENDED	DANCED	FUNDED
CONRAD	MINOAN	******	BENDEE	DANCER	FUNKED
CONWAY	MONDAY	ARNICA	BENDER	DANCES	FUNNEL
CUNEAL	PANDAS	BONACI	BENNES	DANDER	GANDER
DENIAL	PENIAL	CANUCK	BENNET	DANGED	GANGED
DENTAL	PENMAN	CONICS	BINDER	DANGER	GANGER
DONNAS	PENNAE	CYNICS	BINGES	DANIEL	GANGES
DUNBAR	PENPAL	EUNICE	BINNED	DANKER	GANNET
DUNCAN	PENTAD	EUNUCH	BONDED	DENIED	GENDER
ENNEAD	PINDAR	GYNECO	BONDER	DENIER	GENIES
EONIAN	PINEAL	IGNACE	BONGED	DENIES	GENRES
FANGAS	PINNAE	JANICE	BONIER	DENNED	GENTES
FANTAN	PINNAL	LUNACY	BONNET	DENSER	GINGER
FENIAN	PUNJAB	MENACE	BONZER	DENTED	GINNED
FINIAL	PUNKAS	MONACO	BONZES	DENVER	GINNER
FINNAN	RANDAL	MONICA	BUNGED	DINDER	GUNMEN
FONTAL	RANDAN	MUNICH	BUNKED	DINGED	GUNNED
FUNGAL	RENTAL	PANICE	BUNKER	DINGEY	GUNNEL
GENIAL	RUNWAY	PANICS	BUNSEN	DINKEY	GUNNER
GINGAL	SANDAL	SENECA	BUNTED	DINNED	GUNTER
GUNMAN	SANGAR	TENACE	CANCEL	DINNER	HANCES
GUNNAR	SANJAK	TONICS	CANCER	DINTED	HANDED
HANGAR	SANSAR	TUNICA	CANKER	DONEES	HANDEL
HANNAH	SENDAL	TUNICS	CANNED	DONKEY	HANGED
HANNAS	SENLAC	VENICE	CANNEL	DONNED	HANGER
HENNAS	SENNAS	******	CANNER	DUNCES	HANKER
IONIAN	SINBAD	--N-D-	CANNES	DUNDEE	HANSEL
JINGAL	SONIAS	******	CANOED	DUNGED	HENLEY
JUNEAU	SONYAS	ACNODE	CANOES	DUNKED	HINDER
JUNTAS	SUNDAE	CANADA	CANTED	DUNKER	HINGED
KANSAN	SUNDAY	DENUDE	CANTER	DUNNED	HINGES
KANSAS	SUNHAT	GONADS	CENSED	DUNNER	HINTED
KENDAL	SUNNAH	MONADS	CENSER	ERNIES	HONIED
KONRAD	SUNTAN	MONODY	CENSES	FANGED	HONKED
LANDAU	SYNTAX	PANADA	CENTER	FANJET	HONKER
LINDAS	TANKAS	SYNODS	CINDER	FANNED	HUNGER
LINEAL	TINCAL	XANADU	CONFER	FANNER	HUNTED
LINEAR	TINCAN	******	CONGER	FENCED	HUNTER
LINGAM	VANDAL	--N-E-	CONGES	FENCER	JENNET
LINGAS	VANMAN	******	CONIES	FENCES	JINKED
		ANNIES		FENDED	
		APNOEA			

JINKER	MENDER	RANKED	TANKER	WINGED	CONCHY
JINNEE	MENSES	RANKER	TANNED	WINIER	DINAHS
JINXED	MINCED	RANTED	TANNER	WINKED	DINGHY
JINXES	MINCER	RANTER	TANREC	WINKER	GANDHI
JUNKED	MINCES	RENDED	TENDED	WINNER	GUNSHY
JUNKER	MINDED	RENDER	TENDER	WINOES	HONSHU
JUNKET	MINDER	RENEES	TENREC	WINTER	JONAHS
KENNED	MINTED	RENNET	TENSED	WINZES	MANCHU
KENNEL	MINTER	RENTED	TENSER	WONDER	MONTHS
KINDER	MINUET	RENTER	TENSES	WONTED	NINTHS
KINGED	MINXES	RENTES	TENTED	YANKED	PANCHO
KINKED	MONGER	RINGED	TENTER	YANKEE	PONCHO
KINSEY	MONIED	RINGER	TENUES	YENNED	PUNCHY
LANCED	MONIES	RINKED	TINDER	YONDER	RANCHO
LANCER	MONKEY	RINSED	TINGED	YONKER	SANDHI
LANCES	MONTES	RINSER	TINGES	ZANIER	TENTHS
LANCET	NANTES	RINSES	TINIER	ZANIES	XANTHO
LANDED	OUNCES	RONDEL	TINKER	ZENGER	******
LANDER	PANDER	RUNLET	TINNED	ZINCED	--N-I-
LANKER	PANNED	RUNNEL	TINNER	ZINGED	******
LANNER	PANTED	RUNNER	TINSEL	******	AENEID
LENDER	PANZER	SANDED	TINTED	--N-F-	AGNAIL
LENSES	PENCEL	SANDER	TONGED	******	APNEIC
LENTEN	PENDED	SANGER	TONIER	GANEFS	AUNTIE
LINDEN	PENMEN	SANIES	TUNNED	IGNIFY	BANDIT
LINGER	PENNED	SANSEI	TUNNEL	MINIFY	BONNIE
LINIER	PENNER	SENDER	VANMEN	RUNOFF	BUNYIP
LINKED	PINGED	SENNET	VENDED	******	CANDIA
LINNET	PINIER	SENSED	VENDEE	--N-G-	CANDID
LINTEL	PINIES	SENSES	VENDER	******	CANNIE
LINTER	PINKED	SINGED	VENEER	BENIGN	CONNIE
LONGED	PINNED	SINGER	VENTED	FANEGA	CONOID
LONGER	PINNER	SINGES	VENTER	LANUGO	CONTIN
LUNGED	PINTER	SINKER	VENUES	LINAGE	DANAID
LUNGEE	PONDER	SINNED	VINCES	MANAGE	DANZIG
LUNGER	PONGEE	SINNER	VINIER	MANEGE	DENNIS
LUNGES	PONIED	SINTER	WANDER	MENAGE	DENTIL
LUNKER	PONIES	SONDER	WANNED	NONAGE	DENTIN
LYNXES	PONTES	SONNET	WANNER	NONEGO	DONNIE
MANGER	PUNIER	SUNDER	WANTED	RENEGE	DUNLIN
MANNED	PUNNED	SUNDEW	WANTER	******	FANNIE
MANNER	PUNNER	SUNKEN	WENDED	--N-H-	FENRIR
MANSES	PUNTED	SUNNED	WINCED	******	FINNIC
MANTEL	PUNTER	SUNSET	WINCER	BUNCHE	GANOID
MANTES	RANEES	SYNDET	WINCES	BUNCHY	HENBIT
MANUEL	RANGED	TANDEM	WINCEY	CANTHI	HENRIS
MENDED	RANGER	TANGED	WINDED	CONCHA	JONNIE
MENDEL	RANGES	TANKED	WINDER	CONCHS	JUNKIE

KENNIE	ARNOLD	SANELY	KININS	CONDOR	TENSOR
LANAIS	BANGLE	SENILE	LINENS	CONGOU	TINPOT
LENTIL	BUNDLE	SINGLE	LINING	CONTOS	VENDOR
LUNGIS	BUNGLE	SINGLY	MANANA	CONVOY	VINSON
MANTIC	CANALS	TANGLE	MENINX	DANTON	WANION
MANTIS	CANDLE	TANGLY	MINING	DONJON	WANTON
MENDIP	CANTLE	TINGLE	OWNING	FANION	WINDOW
MENHIR	CANULA	TINGLY	PINANG	FANTOM	WINNOW
MINNIE	DANDLE	TINILY	PINENE	FINNOC	******
NUNCIO	DANGLE	TINKLE	PINING	GENROS	--N-P-
PANTIE	DANKLY	TINKLY	PINONS	GENTOO	******
PENCIL	DINGLE	VENULE	PONENT	GONION	CANAPE
PENNIA	DONALD	VINYLS	RUNINS	HANSOM	CANOPY
PENNIS	FINALE	WANDLE	RUNONS	HENDON	LENAPE
PINKIE	FINALS	WANGLE	SONANT	JONSON	PINUPS
PINXIT	FINELY	WINKLE	TENANT	JUNCOS	SUNUPS
PONTIC	FONDLE	ZONULA	TENONS	JUNIOR	******
PONTIL	FONDLY	ZONULE	TONING	LENTOS	--N-R-
PUNDIT	GANGLI	******	TUNING	LONDON	******
RANCID	GENTLE	--N-M-	WANING	MANGOS	ABNERS
RENNIN	GENTLY	******	WINING	MANIOC	BINARY
RENOIR	HANDLE	BENUMB	ZANANA	MENTOR	BONERS
RONNIE	JANGLE	BYNAME	ZENANA	MINION	CANARD
SENNIT	JINGLE	CINEMA	ZONING	MINNOW	CANARY
SUNLIT	JINGLY	DENIMS	******	MONGOL	CANERS
SYNDIC	JUNGLE	DYNAMO	--N-O-	MONROE	CENTRA
TANNIC	JUNGLY	FANUMS	******	NONCOM	CENTRE
TANNIN	KINDLE	MINIMA	AMNION	PENGOS	CENTRI
TENNIS	KINDLY	MINIMS	BANGOR	PENNON	CENTRO
TENPIN	KINGLY	PANAMA	BANJOS	PINGOS	CONTRA
TENUIS	LANKLY	VENOMS	BENTON	PINION	CONTRE
TINEID	LONELY	******	BENZOL	PINTOS	DENARY
TONKIN	LUNULA	--N-N-	BONBON	PONTON	DENDRI
TONSIL	LUNULE	******	BONGOS	PUNTOS	DENDRO
WINNIE	MANGLE	ANNONA	BUNCOS	RANCOR	DINARS
ZINCIC	MANILA	AWNING	BUNION	RANDOM	DINERO
ZINNIA	MANTLE	BANANA	CANDOR	RANSOM	DINERS
******	MINGLE	BONING	CANNON	RONDOS	DONORS
--N-K-	PANELS	CANINE	CANNOT	RUNYON	FINERY
******	PENILE	CANING	CANSOS	SANTOL	GANTRY
GINGKO	PENULT	CANONS	CANTON	SENIOR	GENERA
KANAKA	PINOLE	CONING	CANTOR	SENSOR	GENTRY
ZINCKY	PINTLE	DINING	CANTOS	SINEON	GONERS
******	PUNILY	FANONS	CANYON	SUNBOW	HONORE
--N-L-	RANKLE	FINING	CENSOR	SUNDOG	HONORS
******	RANKLY	HONING	CENTOS	SUNGOD	HUNGRY
ANNALS	RONALD	INNING	CINEOL	TANGOS	IGNORE
ANNULS	RUNDLE	IONONE	CONDOM	TENDON	LENORE

LINERS	MONGST	TENUTO	PENTUP	MONEYS	SHORAN
LONERS	MONISM	TINCTS	PINDUS	MONTYS	SIOUAN
MANORS	MONIST	TONITE	RUNOUT	NANCYS	SLOGAN
MANURE	NANISM	VANITY	SANGUI	PANSYS	SLOVAK
MINERS	PUNISH	ZENITH	SANNUP	PENNYS	SNOCAT
MINORS	SANEST	ZONATE	SINFUL	SANDYS	STOMAT
NONARY	TANIST	******	TONGUE	VINNYS	STORAX
ORNERY	VANISH	--N-U-	TUNEUP	WENDYS	THOMAS
OWNERS	VENOSE	******	TUNGUS	******	THORAC
PANTRY	******	ADNOUN	VENDUE	--N-Z-	THORAX
PENURY	--N-T-	ARNAUD	VENOUS	******	TROCAR
PINERY	******	BANGUI	VINOUS	IONIZE	TROJAN
SANDRA	ADNATE	BANGUP	WINDUP	******	TROPAL
SENARY	AGNATE	BANTUS	******	--O-A-	TWOWAY
SENORA	BENITA	BUNKUM	--N-V-	******	VIOLAS
SENTRY	BENITO	CANGUE	******	ABOMAS	YEOMAN
SONARS	BINATE	CANTUS	GENEVA	ABORAL	ZOONAL
SUNDRY	BINITS	CENSUR	******	ADONAI	******
SYNURA	BONITO	CENSUS	--N-W-	AGORAE	--O-B-
TENORS	CANUTE	CINQUE	******	AGORAS	******
TENURE	DANITE	CONCUR	RENEWS	AJOWAN	ABOMBS
TONERS	DENOTE	CONIUM	RENOWN	AMORAL	AMOEBA
TUNDRA	DONATE	CONSUL	SINEWS	ANORAK	BLOWBY
TUNERS	DONETS	DANAUS	SINEWY	APODAL	COOMBS
VENERY	FINITE	DENGUE	******	AROMAS	GOODBY
VENIRE	GENETS	DINGUS	--N-X-	ATONAL	KNOBBY
VENTRO	GENITO	DINKUM	******	AVOWAL	PHOEBE
VINERY	IGNITE	FONDUE	ANNEXE	BAOBAB	RHOMBI
WINERY	INNATE	FUNDUS	******	BROGAN	SNOBBY
WINTRY	JANETS	FUNGUS	--N-Y-	BROMAL	******
ZONARY	KENITE	GANGUE	******	CHORAL	--O-C-
******	KINETO	GENIUS	ANNOYS	DEODAR	******
--N-S-	LANATE	GENOUS	BENJYS	DOODAD	AVOUCH
******	LENGTH	GONIUM	BENNYS	DVORAK	BLOTCH
BANISH	LENITY	GYNOUS	BENZYL	FLORAE	BROACH
DANISH	LUNATE	HANGUP	BONNYS	FLORAL	BRONCO
DENISE	LUNETS	HINDUS	CINDYS	FLORAS	BRONCS
DYNAST	MANITO	HONOUR	CONEYS	GLOBAL	BROOCH
EONISM	MANITU	IONIUM	DANNYS	GOORAL	CHOICE
ERNEST	MINUTE	JUNIUS	DENNYS	HOOKAH	CLOACA
FINEST	NINETY	LANGUR	FANNYS	HOORAY	CROTCH
FINISH	ORNATE	LINEUP	HENRYS	ISOBAR	CROUCH
FUNEST	ORNITH	LINGUA	HONEYS	LEONAS	GROUCH
GENESI	PINITE	MANFUL	JENNYS	LOOFAH	HOOTCH
HONEST	SANITY	MANQUE	JINNYS	MOOLAH	SCONCE
KINASE	SENATE	MANTUA	KENNYS	QUOTAS	SCORCH
KINESI	SONATA	MINIUM	LENNYS	RHODAS	SCOTCH
LANOSE	TENETS	OMNIUM	MANDYS	SHOFAR	

SLOUCH	AVOCET	COOPER	GNOMES	LOOTED	ROOTED
SMOOCH	AVOSET	CRONES	GOOBER	LOOTER	ROOTER
STOICS	AVOWED	CRORES	GOOFED	MEOWED	SCOLEX
******	AVOWER	CROWED	GOOIER	MOOLEY	SCONES
--O-D-	AWOKEN	CROZER	GOONEY	MOONED	SCOPES
******	AXONES	CROZES	GOOSED	MOORED	SCORED
AROIDS	AZOLES	DHOLES	GOOSES	MOOTED	SCORER
AVOIDS	AZORES	DIODES	GOOSEY	MOOTER	SCORES
BLONDE	BIOGEN	DOOLEE	GROCER	MYOPES	SCOTER
BLONDS	BLOKES	DOOMED	GROPED	NAOSES	SHOOED
BLOODS	BLOWER	DRONED	GROPER	NOOSED	SHORED
BLOODY	BOOKED	DRONES	GROPES	NOOSES	SHORES
BROADS	BOOMED	DROVED	GROVEL	PHONED	SHOTES
BROODS	BOOMER	DROVER	GROVER	PHONES	SHOVED
BROODY	BOOTED	DROVES	GROVES	PHONEY	SHOVEL
CHORDS	BOOTEE	DUODEN	GROWER	PHOOEY	SHOVER
CLODDY	BOOZED	ECOLES	HOODED	PLOVER	SHOVES
CLOUDS	BOOZER	ELOPED	HOOFED	PLOWED	SHOWED
CLOUDY	BOOZES	ELOPER	HOOFER	PLOWER	SHOWER
CROWDS	BROKEN	ELOPES	HOOKED	POOLED	SLOPED
FIORDS	BROKER	EMOTED	HOOKER	POOPED	SLOPER
FLOODS	BROMES	EMOTES	HOOKEY	POORER	SLOPES
FLOYDS	BUOYED	EPODES	HOOPED	PROBED	SLOVEN
FRONDS	CHOKED	EPOPEE	HOOPER	PROBER	SLOWED
HYOIDS	CHOKER	ERODED	HOOTED	PROBES	SLOWER
ISOLDE	CHOKES	ERODES	HOOTER	PROJET	SMOKED
LLOYDS	CHOLER	EVOKED	HOOVED	PROLEG	SMOKER
OROIDE	CHOREA	EVOKES	HOOVER	PROPEL	SMOKES
SCOLDS	CHOREO	EXOGEN	HOOVES	PROPER	SNORED
SHODDY	CHORES	FLORES	IMOGEN	PROSED	SNORER
SNOODS	CHOSEN	FLORET	IRONED	PROSER	SNORES
SWORDS	CLONES	FLOWED	IRONER	PROSES	SNOWED
ZOOIDS	CLOSED	FLOWER	ISOBEL	PROVED	SOONER
******	CLOSER	FOOLED	ISOHEL	PROVEN	SOOTED
--O-E-	CLOSES	FOOTED	ISOMER	PROVER	SPOKED
******	CLOSET	FOOTER	KNOWER	PROVES	SPOKEN
ABODES	CLOVEN	FROZEN	KRONEN	QUOTED	SPOKES
ADOBES	CLOVER	GAOLER	KRONER	QUOTER	SPORED
ADORED	CLOVES	GEODES	LIONEL	QUOTES	SPORES
ADORER	CLOYED	GLOBED	LOOKED	REOPEN	STOGEY
ADORES	COOEED	GLOBES	LOOKER	RHODES	STOKED
AGONES	COOEES	GLOVED	LOOMED	RIOTED	STOKER
AMOLES	COOKED	GLOVER	LOOPED	RIOTER	STOKES
ANODES	COOKER	GLOVES	LOOPER	ROOFED	STOLED
APOGEE	COOKEY	GLOWED	LOOSED	ROOFER	STOLEN
ATONED	COOLED	GLOWER	LOOSEN	ROOKED	STOLES
ATONER	COOLER	GLOZED	LOOSER	ROOMED	STONED
ATONES	COOPED	GLOZES	LOOSES	ROOMER	STONER

STONES	GROGGY	ANOXIA	NIOBIC	FLOCKS	ROOTLE
STOPED	PLOUGH	ANOXIC	OZONIC	FLOCKY	SCOWLS
STOPES	PRONGS	ATOMIC	PEORIA	FROCKS	SHOALS
STORED	SLOUGH	ATONIC	PHOBIA	KIOSKS	SHOALY
STORES	SPONGE	AZONIC	PHOBIC	KNOCKS	SHORLS
STOREY	SPONGY	AZOTIC	PHOCIS	SHOCKS	SHOULD
STOVER	STODGE	BIOSIS	PHONIA	SMOCKS	SLOWLY
STOVES	STODGY	BIOTIC	PHONIC	SNOOKS	SPOILS
STOWED	STOOGE	BIOTIN	PHOTIC	SPOOKS	SPOILT
TBONES	THONGS	BOOGIE	PROFIT	SPOOKY	SPOOLS
THOLES	THOUGH	BOOKIE	PROLIX	STOCKS	STOOLS
TOOLED	TROUGH	BOOTIE	PROSIT	STOCKY	TOOTLE
TOOLER	WRONGS	BROMIC	PTOSIS	STOOKS	TROLLS
TOOTED	******	CHOPIN	PYOSIS	STORKS	TWOPLY
TOOTER	--O-H-	CHORIC	RHODIC	TROIKA	TWOULD
TROVER	******	CLONIC	ROOKIE	******	WHOLLY
TROVES	BOOTHS	CLOVIS	SCORIA	--O-L-	WHORLS
TROWEL	BROCHE	COOKIE	SCOTIA	******	WOOLLY
TWOFER	BROTHS	COOTIE	SHOJIS	ABOLLA	******
VIOLET	CLOCHE	CROJIK	SHOOIN	APOLLO	--O-M-
WHORED	CLOTHE	DHOTIS	STOLID	ATOLLS	******
WHORES	CLOTHO	DOOLIE	SUOMIC	BOODLE	ABOHMS
WOODED	CLOTHS	ELOHIM	THORIA	BOOTLE	BLOOMS
WOODEN	EPOCHS	ENOSIS	THORIC	BROILS	BLOOMY
WOOFER	FROTHS	EROTIC	TROPIC	BROLLY	BROOMS
WOOLEN	FROTHY	EXOTIC	TWOBIT	CEORLS	BROOMY
YEOMEN	QUOTHA	FLORID	UTOPIA	CHOLLA	GLOOMS
ZOOMED	SLOSHY	FLORIN	VIOLIN	COODLE	GLOOMY
******	SLOTHS	FROLIC	******	COOLLY	GROOMS
--O-F-	SOOTHE	GEODIC	--O-J-	DOODLE	PROEMS
******	TOOTHY	GLOBIN	******	DROLLS	STORMS
FEOFFS	TROCHE	GLORIA	SKOPJE	DROLLY	STORMY
PROOFS	TROPHO	GNOMIC	******	DROOLS	******
SCOFFS	TROPHY	GNOSIS	--O-K-	FOOTLE	--O-N-
SPOOFS	TROTHS	ICONIC	******	FOOZLE	******
******	******	IRONIC	BLOCKS	GHOULS	ABOUND
--O-G-	--O-I-	KAOLIN	BLOCKY	GOODLY	ACORNS
******	******	LEONIE	BROOKE	GOOGLY	ADORNS
CHOUGH	ADONIC	LOOKIN	BROOKS	GROWLS	AMOUNT
CLOGGY	ADONIS	MAORIS	CHOCKS	HOOPLA	ANOINT
CLOUGH	AEOLIA	MIOSIS	CLOAKS	ILOILO	AROUND
DRONGO	AEOLIC	MIOTIC	CLOCKS	KNOLLS	BOOING
ELOIGN	AEOLIS	MYOPIA	CROAKS	NOODLE	BROWNS
ENOUGH	AGONIC	MYOPIC	CROAKY	PEOPLE	CLOWNS
FLONGS	ANODIC	MYOSIN	CROCKS	POODLE	COOING
FROGGY	ANOMIA	MYOSIS	CROCKY	POORLY	CROONS
GEORGE	ANOMIC	NAOMIS	CROOKS	PROWLS	CROWNS
GEORGI	ANOMIE		DROSKY	RAOULS	DROWNS

ELOINS	******	BIOPSY	FLOUTS	BLOWUP	CAPIAS
FROWNS	--O-P-	BLOUSE	FRONTO	BROGUE	COPRAH
GROANS	******	BROWSE	FRONTS	CHORUS	DIPSAS
GROINS	ADOLPH	CHOOSE	FROSTS	CLONUS	ESPIAL
GROUND	CHOPPY	CHOOSY	FROSTY	CROCUS	HEPTAD
GROYNE	CROUPE	CROSSE	GHOSTS	CRONUS	HYPHAE
LOOING	CROUPS	DROPSY	GIOTTO	DROGUE	HYPHAL
MOOING	CROUPY	DROSSY	GLOATS	EXODUS	KAPPAS
PROCNE	DROOPS	DROWSE	GLOSTS	HOOKUP	ORPHAN
QUOINS	DROOPY	DROWSY	GLOTTO	KRONUR	PAPUAN
SCORNS	FLOPPY	EGOISM	GROATS	OBOLUS	POPLAR
SPOONS	GROUPS	EGOIST	GROTTO	QUORUM	RAPHAE
SPOONY	KNOSPS	ELOISE	GROTTY	SCOPUS	REPEAL
SWOONS	PHOSPH	FLOSSY	GROUTS	SHOGUN	REPEAT
THORNS	PROMPT	GLOSSO	GROWTH	******	REPLAY
THORNY	SCOOPS	GLOSSY	KNOTTY	--O-V-	RIPRAP
WOOING	SHOPPE	GROUSE	KNOUTS	******	RIPSAW
YVONNE	SLOOPS	LAOTSE	ODONTO	EVOLVE	RUPIAH
******	SLOPPY	MAOISM	OPORTO	GROOVE	SAPHAR
--O-O-	SNOOPS	MAOIST	PROCTO	GROOVY	SEPIAS
******	SNOOPY	OBOIST	PRONTO	******	SEPTAL
APOLOG	STOMPS	PROUST	QUOITS	--O-Y-	TIPCAT
BOOBOO	STOOPS	SCOUSE	ROOSTS	******	TOPHAT
BOOHOO	STOUPS	SPOUSE	SCOOTS	ANONYM	******
CRONOS	SWOOPS	TAOISM	SCOTTS	COOEYS	--P-C-
CROTON	THORPE	TAOIST	SCOUTS	EPONYM	******
DIOBOL	TROOPS	TOOTSY	SHOATS	PROPYL	ALPACA
DROMON	TROPPO	WHOOSH	SHOOTS	TROTYL	ASPECT
DUOLOG	TROUPE	WOODSY	SHORTS	ZLOTYS	ASPICS
FEODOR	WHOOPS	******	SHOUTS	******	COPECK
GNOMON	******	--O-T-	SMOLTS	--O-Z-	DEPICT
GOOGOL	--O-R-	******	SMOOTH	******	EXPECT
HOODOO	******	ABORTS	SNOOTS	ALONZO	IMPACT
HOOPOE	ABOARD	ADOPTS	SNOOTY	BLOWZY	KOPECK
IGOROT	AMOURS	AGOUTI	SNORTS	BRONZE	PAPACY
ISOGON	CHOIRS	AGOUTY	SNOTTY	BRONZY	TOPICS
ISOPOD	COOERS	BLOATS	SNOUTS	FLOOZY	UNPACK
KOODOO	FLOORS	BOOSTS	SPORTS	FROWZY	UNPICK
KRONOR	FLOURS	BRONTE	SPORTY	GROSZY	******
KRONOS	FLOURY	CLOTTY	SPOTTY	SNOOZE	--P-D-
PHOTON	SCOURS	CLOUTS	SPOUTS	******	******
PHOTOS	SHOERS	COOPTS	STOATS	--P-A-	BIPEDS
PROTON	SPOORS	CROATS	STOUTS	******	BIPODS
STOLON	WOOERS	CROFTS	TROUTS	ALPHAS	DIPODY
THORON	YAOURT	DROITS	UBOATS	APPEAL	IMPEDE
TROGON	******	DROUTH	WHORTS	APPEAR	LEPIDO
UROPOD	--O-S-	FLOATS	******	APPIAN	LIPIDS
VOODOO	******	FLOATY	--O-U-	BYPLAY	RAPIDS
YOOHOO	ALONSO		******		
	AROUSE		AEOLUS		
			AGOGUE		

******	LAPSED	SYPHER	JAPHIA	HOPPLE	EPPING
--P-E-	LAPSER	TAPPED	JOPLIN	IMPALA	ESPANA
******	LAPSES	TAPPER	LEPSIA	IMPALE	EXPAND
APPLES	LIPPED	TAPPET	LIPOID	IMPELS	EXPEND
BOPPED	LIPPER	TEPEES	NAPKIN	LAPELS	GAPING
CAPPED	LOPPED	TIPPED	NAPPIE	NAPALM	GIPONS
CAPPER	MAPLES	TIPPER	ORPHIC	NIPPLE	HOPING
CIPHER	MAPPED	TIPPET	PAPAIN	NOPALS	IMPEND
COPIED	MOPPED	TOPPED	PEPSIN	PAPULA	IMPING
COPIER	MOPPET	TOPPER	PEPTIC	PAPULE	JAPANS
COPIES	NAPIER	TUPPED	PIPKIN	POPPLE	JAPING
COPLEY	NAPLES	WAPPED	PIPPIN	PUPILS	JUPONS
COPPED	NAPPED	YAPPED	POPLIN	RAPTLY	LAPINS
COPPER	NAPPER	YIPPED	RAPHIS	REPELS	LOPING
COPSES	NAPPES	ZIPPED	REPAID	RIPELY	LUPINE
CUPPED	NEPHEW	ZIPPER	REPAIR	RIPPLE	MOPING
CUPPER	NIPPED	******	SEPSIS	RIPPLY	ORPINE
CYPHER	NIPPER	--P-F-	SEPTIC	ROPILY	ORPINS
DAPPED	OSPREY	******	SOPHIA	SEPALS	PIPING
DAPPER	PEPPED	RIPOFF	SOPHIE	SUPPLE	RAPINE
DIPLEX	PEPPER	TEPEFY	YIPPIE	SUPPLY	RAPING
DIPPED	PIPIER	TIPOFF	YUPPIE	TAPALO	REPAND
DIPPER	PIPPED	TYPIFY	******	TIPPLE	REPENT
DOPIER	POPPED	******	--P-K-	TOPPLE	REPINE
DOPTER	POPPER	--P-G-	******	TUPELO	RIPENS
DUPLET	POPPET	******	KAPOKS	TYPHLO	ROPING
DUPLEX	PUPPED	IMPUGN	KOPEKS	UNPILE	SUPINE
ESPIED	PUPPET	OPPUGN	MOPOKE	******	TAPING
ESPIES	RAPIER	PIPAGE	TOPEKA	--P-M-	TOPING
EUPNEA	RAPPED	UNPEGS	TUPIKS	******	TYPING
GAPPED	RAPPEE	******	******	LIPOMA	UNPINS
GIPPED	RAPPEL	--P-H-	--P-L-	OEPEMA	UPPING
GOPHER	RAPPER	******	******	******	WIPING
GYPPED	RIPLEY	DEPTHS	AMPULE	--P-N-	YAPONS
HAPPED	RIPPED	SAPPHO	AMPULS	******	YUPONS
HAPPEN	RIPPER	******	APPALL	ALPINE	******
HIPPED	ROPIER	--P-I-	APPALS	APPEND	--P-O-
HOPPED	RUPEES	******	APPELS	ARPENS	******
HOPPER	SAPIEN	CAPLIN	COPALM	ARPENT	ALPHOS
HYPHEN	SAPPED	CAPRIC	COPULA	ASPENS	CAPTOR
JAPHET	SAPPER	COPTIC	CUPELS	CAPONE	DEPLOY
KEPLER	SEPTET	CUPRIC	CUPOLA	CAPONS	DIPLOE
KIPPED	SIPPED	CUPTIE	CUPULE	COPING	EMPLOY
KIPPER	SIPPER	CYPRIN	DAPPLE	DAPHNE	HIPPOS
KOPJES	SIPPET	ESPRIT	DIPOLE	DEPEND	HYPNOS
LAPPED	SOPPED	HIPPIE	EMPALE	DEPONE	LAPDOG
LAPPER	SUPPED	HYPNIC	EXPELS	DOPING	LEPTON
LAPPET	SUPPER	IMPAIR	FIPPLE	DUPING	NIPPON

OOPHOR	TAPIRS	REPUTE	PIQUES	CARPAL	MARIAS
PEPLOS	TOPERS	UPPITY	PIQUET	CEREAL	MARTAS
RAPTOR	UMPIRE	WAPITI	ROQUET	CORBAN	MERMAN
SIPHON	UPPERS	ZAPATA	SEQUEL	CORDAY	MIRIAM
SYPHON	VAPORI	******	TOQUES	CORRAL	MOREAU
TIPTOE	VAPORS	--P-U-	TUQUES	CORSAC	MORGAN
TIPTOP	VIPERS	******	******	CURIAE	MORTAL
TYPHON	WIPERS	COPOUT	--Q-I-	CURIAL	MORTAR
******	******	CUPFUL	******	DARDAN	MURRAY
--P-R-	--P-S-	CUPRUM	ACQUIT	DERMAL	MYRIAD
******	******	CYPRUS	LIQUID	DERMAS	MYRNAS
AMPERE	APPOSE	GYPSUM	MAQUIS	DERMAT	NARIAL
AMPHRS	BYPASS	HIPPUS	SEQUIN	DIRHAM	NARWAL
APPORT	BYPAST	LAPFUL	******	DORIAN	NORIAS
ASPERS	DEPOSE	LAPSUS	--Q-O-	DORSAD	NORMAL
ASPIRE	EXPOSE	PAPPUS	******	DORSAL	NORMAN
CAPERS	IMPASS	PEPLUM	LIQUOR	DURBAN	NORMAS
COPPRA	IMPISH	PEPLUS	PEQUOD	DURBAR	NORWAY
DEPART	IMPOSE	POPGUN	PEQUOT	DURHAM	OCREAE
DEPORT	IMPOST	SEPTUM	******	DURIAN	PARCAE
DUPERS	LIPASE	TYPHUS	--R-A-	EARLAP	PARIAH
DUPERY	MOPISH	UNPLUG	******	EARWAX	PARIAN
EMPERY	OPPOSE	VAPOUR	ABROAD	FARBAD	PARKAS
EMPIRE	PAPIST	******	ADRIAN	FERIAL	PARLAY
EXPERT	POPISH	--P-W-	AERIAL	FIRMAN	PARRAL
EXPIRE	RAPIST	******	AIRMAN	FORMAL	PORTAL
EXPIRY	REPASS	IMPAWN	AIRSAC	FORMAT	PURDAH
EXPORT	REPAST	PAPAWS	AIRWAY	FORNAX	SARSAR
GAPERS	REPOSE	******	AORTAE	GERMAN	SCREAK
IMPARK	RIPEST	--P-Y-	AORTAL	HARLAN	SCREAM
IMPART	RIPOST	******	AORTAS	HARTAL	SERDAB
IMPORT	TYPIST	ALPHYL	ARREAR	HERBAL	SERIAL
IMPURE	UPPISH	PAPAYA	ATRIAL	HEREAT	SERVAL
LAPARO	******	POPPYS	BARMAN	HERMAE	SIRDAR
LEPERS	--P-T-	REPAYS	BOREAL	HERMAI	SPREAD
LOPERS	******	SEPOYS	BOREAS	HERMAN	STREAK
MOPERS	BYPATH	ZEPHYR	BUREAU	HURRAH	STREAM
NAPERY	CAPITA	******	BURIAL	HURRAY	STRIAE
NEPHRO	CAPOTE	--Q-A-	BURLAP	INROAD	SURTAX
PAPERS	DEPOTS	******	BURSAE	JORDAN	SYRIAC
PAPERY	DEPUTE	LOQUAR	BURSAL	KARMAS	SYRIAN
PIPERS	DEPUTY	LOQUAT	BURSAR	KARNAK	TARMAC
POPERY	HEPATO	******	BURSAS	KOREAN	TARNAL
REPORT	IMPUTE	--Q-E-	BYROAD	LARIAT	TARPAN
RUPERT	INPUTS	******	CARFAX	LARVAE	TARSAL
SUPERB	PIPETS	COQUET	CARLAS	LARVAL	TARTAN
SUPERS	PIPITS	FIQUES	CARMAN	MARGAY	TARTAR
TAPERS	PUPATE	PIQUED	CARNAL	MARIAN	TARZAN

TERGAL	KIRSCH	BARBED	CARDER	CURVED	GARBED
TERNAL	LORICA	BARBEL	CAREEN	CURVES	GARDEN
THREAD	LYRICS	BARBER	CAREER	CURVET	GARGET
THREAT	MARACA	BARBET	CARIES	DARIEN	GARNER
THROAT	MYRICA	BARDED	CARMEL	DARKEN	GARNET
TURBAN	ORRICE	BARDES	CARMEN	DARKER	GARRET
TYRIAN	PIRACY	BARGED	CARPED	DARNED	GARTER
UNREAD	SERACS	BARGEE	CARPEL	DARNEL	GERMEN
UNREAL	SPRUCE	BARGES	CARPER	DARNER	GIRDED
UPROAR	STRICK	BARKED	CARPET	DARTED	GIRDER
VERBAL	STRICT	BARKER	CARREL	DARTER	GIRTED
VERNAL	STRUCK	BARLEY	CARTED	DIRGES	GORGED
VERNAS	THRICE	BARMEN	CARTEL	DIRKED	GORGER
VIRGAS	VARICO	BARNEY	CARTER	DOREEN	GORGES
WARSAW	YORICK	BARRED	CARTES	DORIES	GORGET
YERBAS	ZURICH	BARREL	CARVED	DORMER	GORHEN
******		BARREN	CARVEL	DORSET	GORIER
--R-B-	**--R-D-**	BARRET	CARVEN	EARLES	GORSES
******	******	BARTER	CARVER	EARNED	HARDEN
AEROBE	ABRADE	BARYES	CARVES	EARNER	HARDER
ARROBA	BORIDE	BERBER	CERMET	EYRIES	HARKED
CARIBE	CORODY	BERGEN	CERTES	FARCED	HARKEN
CARIBS	DERIDE	BERMES	CORBEL	FARCER	HARLEM
CAROBS	DIRNDL	BERNEY	CORDED	FARCES	HARLEY
ENROBE	DORADO	BIRLED	CORDER	FARLES	HARMED
HEREBY	FARADS	BIRLES	CORKED	FARLEY	HARPED
SCRIBE	LAREDO	BIRRED	CORKER	FARMED	HARPER
SCRUBS	PARADE	BORDEL	CORNEA	FARMER	HARVEY
SHRUBS	PARODY	BORDER	CORNED	FERBER	HERDED
STROBE	SCRODS	BORNEO	CORNEL	FERRET	HERDER
THROBS	SHREDS	BURDEN	CORNER	FIRMED	HERMES
UNROBE	STRIDE	BURGEE	CORNET	FIRMER	HEROES
YORUBA	STRODE	BURGER	CORSES	FORCED	HERPES
ZARIBA	TEREDO	BURIED	CORSET	FORCER	HORDED
******	TIRADE	BURIES	CORTES	FORCES	HORDES
--R-C-	WORLDS	BURKED	CORTEX	FORDED	HORNED
******	******	BURKES	CORTEZ	FORGED	HORNET
AFRICA	**--R-E-**	BURLED	CORVEE	FORGER	HORSED
ARRACK	******	BURLER	CORVES	FORGES	HORSES
BARUCH	ADRIEN	BURLEY	CURBED	FORGET	HORSEY
BORSCH	AERIED	BURNED	CURDED	FORKED	HURLED
CARACK	AERIES	BURNER	CURFEW	FORMED	HURLER
CURACY	AGREED	BURNET	CURIES	FORMER	HURLEY
DARICS	AGREES	BURPED	CURLED	FORTES	HURTER
DIRECT	AIRBED	BURRED	CURLER	FURIES	ISRAEL
ENRICH	AIRIER	BURSES	CURLEW	FURLED	JARRED
ENRICO	AIRMEN	CARCEL	CURSED	FURRED	JARVEY
HORACE	AZRAEL	CARDED	CURSES	FURZES	JEREED

JERKED	NERVES	SPRUES	WARDER	BORAGE	BERTIE
JERSEY	NOREEN	SPRYER	WARIER	ENRAGE	BIRDIE
JORGES	NURSED	STREET	WARMED	FORAGE	BORGIA
JURIES	NURSER	SURFED	WARMER	FOREGO	BURDIE
KERBED	NURSES	SURFER	WARNED	GARAGE	CARDIO
KERMES	PARCEL	SURGED	WARNER	MIRAGE	CARPIC
KERNED	PARGET	SURGER	WARPED	SCRAGS	CARRIE
KERNEL	PARIES	SURGES	WARPER	SHRUGS	CERVIX
KERSEY	PARKED	SURREY	WARRED	SPRAGS	CORBIE
LARDED	PARKER	SURVEY	WARREN	SPRIGS	CORGIS
LARDER	PARLEY	TARGET	WIRIER	UNRIGS	CORRIE
LARGER	PARREL	TARRED	WORDED	VIRAGO	CORTIN
LARKED	PARSEC	TARTED	WORKED	******	CURTIS
LARKER	PARSED	TARTER	WORKER	--R-H-	DARWIN
LORDED	PARSEE	TERCEL	WORMED	******	DERAIL
LOREEN	PARSES	TERCET	WORMER	BERTHA	DERAIN
LORIES	PARTED	TERMED	WORSEN	BERTHE	DERMIC
LURKED	PERKED	TERMER	WORSER	BERTHS	DERMIS
LURKER	PERMED	TERRET	YARDED	BIRTHS	DERRIS
MARCEL	PORKER	TERSER	YORKER	BURGHS	DORMIE
MARGES	PORTED	THREED	ZEROED	EARTHS	EARWIG
MARIES	PORTER	THREES	ZEROES	EARTHY	FERMIS
MARKED	PUREED	THROES	******	FIRTHS	FERRIC
MARKER	PUREES	TORIES	--R-F-	GURKHA	FERRIS
MARKET	PURGED	TUREEN	******	MARSHA	FERVID
MARLED	PURGER	TURFED	ADRIFT	MARSHY	FIRKIN
MARRED	PURGES	TURKEY	AERIFY	MARTHA	FORBID
MARRER	PURLED	TURNED	AGRAFE	MARTHE	FORMIC
MARTEN	PURLER	TURNER	BEREFT	MORPHO	FORNIX
MARVEL	PURRED	TURRET	CARAFE	PYRRHA	FORTIS
MERCER	PURSED	TURVES	FAROFF	SARAHS	GARLIC
MERGED	PURSER	UNREEL	PURIFY	SORGHO	GERBIL
MERGER	PURSES	VARIED	RAREFY	SURAHS	GERTIE
MERGES	PURVEY	VARIER	SCRUFF	TORAHS	HARBIN
MERLES	SCREED	VARIES	SERIFS	WORTHY	HARMIN
MERMEN	SCREEN	VARLET	SHRIFT	******	HARRIS
MERSEY	SCRIED	VARVES	SHROFF	--R-I-	HERDIC
MOREEN	SERIES	VERGED	STRAFE	******	HEREIN
MORGEN	SERVED	VERGER	STRIFE	ADROIT	HERMIT
MORLEY	SERVER	VERGES	TARIFF	AFRAID	HERNIA
MORSEL	SERVES	VERSED	THRIFT	AORTIC	HERNIO
MURDER	SHRIEK	VERSES	VERIFY	BARBIE	HEROIC
MURIEL	SORBET	VERSET	******	BARDIC	HEROIN
MURRES	SORREL	VERTEX	--R-G-	BARMIE	HORNIE
MURREY	SORTED	VERVET	******	BARRIE	HORRID
MYRMEC	SORTER	VORTEX	AERUGO	BARRIO	JARVIS
NARKED	SPREES	WARDED	AURIGA	BERLIN	JERKIN
NERVED	SPRIER	WARDEN	BAREGE	BERNIE	JERVIS

KERMIS	VERGIL	GIRDLE	WARILY	CARING	PARENT
KERMIT	VERMIN	GORALS	WARMLY	CERING	PARING
KERRIE	VERNIX	GORILY	WIRILY	CHRONO	PHRENO
LORAIN	VIRGIE	GURGLE	ZORILS	CORING	PIRANA
MARCIA	VIRGIL	HARDLY	******	CORONA	PORING
MARGIE	VIRGIN	HAROLD	--R-M-	CURING	PURANA
MARGIN	******	HERALD	******	CYRANO	PURINE
MARLIN	--R-K-	HURDLE	ABRAMS	CYRENE	PYRANS
MARTIN	******	HURTLE	AFRAME	DARING	PYRENE
MARVIN	DEREKS	JURELS	BIREME	DURING	PYRONE
MERCIA	EUREKA	KERALA	CAROMS	EARING	RARING
MERLIN	MARKKA	KIRTLE	CHROMA	ERRAND	RERUNS
MERVIN	PERUKE	LORDLY	CHROME	ERRANT	SARONG
MORBID	SHRIKE	MARBLE	CHROMO	ERRING	SERENA
MORRIS	STRAKE	MERELY	CORYMB	FARINA	SERENE
NEREID	STRIKE	MORALE	FORUMS	FARING	SERINE
NEREIS	STROKE	MORALS	HAREMS	FERINE	SERINS
NORDIC	TORSKS	MORELS	HIRAMS	FIRING	SHRANK
NORNIR	******	MORULA	JEREMY	FORINT	SHRINE
NORRIS	--R-L-	MURALS	JEROME	GERENT	SHRINK
PARSIS	******	MYRTLE	JORAMS	GERUND	SHRUNK
PARVIS	AIRILY	NEROLI	JORUMS	GORING	SIRENS
PERMIT	APRILS	PAROLE	SCRAMS	GYRONS	SIRING
PERSIA	BARELY	PARTLY	SCRIMP	HARING	SPRANG
PORTIA	BARFLY	PERILS	SCRUMS	HERONS	SPRING
PURLIN	BERYLS	PERTLY	SERUMS	HIRING	SPRINT
SERAIS	BURBLE	PORTLY	SHRIMP	HURONS	SPRUNG
SERBIA	BURGLE	PURELY	STROMA	JARINA	STRAND
SEREIN	CAROLE	PURFLE	STRUMA	JURANT	STRING
SORDID	CAROLS	PURPLE	STRUMS	KARENS	STRONG
SORTIE	CIRCLE	RARELY	THRUMS	KORUNA	STRUNG
SPRAIN	CORALS	SCROLL	******	KORUNY	SYRINX
STRAIN	CURDLE	SHRILL	--R-N-	LARINE	TARING
STRAIT	CURTLY	SORELS	******	LARYNG	THRONE
TARSIA	CURULE	SORELY	AARONS	LARYNX	THRONG
TERBIA	CYRILS	SPRYLY	AIRING	LORENE	TIRANA
TORIIS	DARKLE	STROLL	APRONS	LORENZ	TIRING
TOROID	DARKLY	SURELY	ARRANT	LURING	TYRANT
TORPID	DARTLE	TARTLY	BARING	MARINA	TYRONE
TORRID	DIRELY	TERMLY	BARONG	MARINE	VARUNA
TURBID	EERILY	THRALL	BARONS	MERINO	VERONA
TURBIT	ENROLL	THRILL	BARONY	MIRING	WERENT
TURGID	FERULA	TURTLE	BERING	MORONS	WIRING
TURKIC	FERULE	UNROLL	BORANE	MURINE	ZIRONS
TURKIS	FIRMLY	UNRULY	BORING	NARINE	******
TURNIP	GARBLE	VERILY	BURANS	OARING	--R-O-
VERDIN	GARGLE	VIRILE	BURINS	PARANG	******
VEREIN	GERALD	WARBLE	CARINA	PARENS	BARROW
					BARTOK

BARTON	MARGOS	ENRAPT	LURERS	PUREST	KARATE
BARYON	MARGOT	EURIPI	ORRERY	PURISM	KARATS
BORROW	MARION	EUROPA	PARERS	PURIST	KERATO
BORZOI	MARLOW	EUROPE	PARURE	RAREST	MERITS
BURBOT	MARMOT	PARAPH	SARTRE	SOREST	PARITY
BURGOO	MAROON	PYROPE	TORERO	STRASS	PIRATE
BURGOS	MARROW	SARAPE	WIRERS	STRESS	PURITY
BURROS	MERLON	SCRAPE	******	SUREST	PYRITE
BURROW	MIRROR	SCRAPS	--R-S-	TERESA	RARITY
BURTON	MORION	SCRIPS	******	THRASH	SCROTA
CARBON	MORMON	SCRIPT	ACROSS	THRESH	SPRATS
CARBOY	MORROS	SERAPE	AFRESH	THRUSH	SPRITE
CARGOS	MORROW	SERAPH	AORIST	THRUST	SPRITS
CARHOP	MORTON	SIRUPS	ARREST	TOROSE	STRATA
CARLOS	NARROW	SIRUPY	AURIST	UNREST	STRATH
CARLOW	PARDON	STRAPS	BAREST	UPRISE	STRATI
CARROT	PARGOS	STRIPE	CARESS	UPROSE	STRUTS
CARSON	PARLOR	STRIPS	CARUSO	UPRUSH	SURETY
CARTON	PARROT	STRIPT	CERISE	VERISM	TAROTS
CORDON	PARSON	STRIPY	CERUSE	VERIST	TERATO
CURIOS	PERIOD	STROPS	CHRISM	******	TERETE
CURSOR	PERRON	SYRUPS	CHRIST	--R-T-	VERITY
DARROW	PERSON	SYRUPY	CHRYSO	******	VERSTS
DURION	SARGON	TERAPH	CORPSE	AERATE	WARMTH
ENROOT	SARTOR	THRIPS	CURTSY	AMRITA	WORSTS
FARROW	SCROOP	UNRIPE	DIREST	AURATE	******
FERVOR	SERMON	UNRIPS	DURESS	BARITE	--R-U-
FORGOT	SERVOS	******	EGRESS	BARYTA	******
FURROW	SORGOS	--R-R-	FOREST	BERATE	AIRGUN
GARCON	SORROW	******	GARISH	BERETS	ATREUS
GERYON	TERMOR	AIRDRY	GYROSE	BORATE	ATRIUM
GORDON	TERROR	AURORA	HARASS	BURSTS	AUREUS
GORGON	TORPOR	BARBRA	HERESY	CARATE	AUROUS
HARBOR	TORSOS	BORERS	INRUSH	CARATS	BARIUM
HARLOT	TURBOT	CARERS	JURIST	CARETS	BARNUM
HARLOW	TURCOS	CORERS	LYRISM	CERATE	BARQUE
HARROW	UNROOT	CURARE	LYRIST	CERATO	CARPUS
HEREOF	UPROOT	CURERS	MARIST	CERITE	CEREUS
HEREON	VERNON	DARERS	MEREST	CURATE	CERIUM
HERIOT	VERSOS	ERRORS	MORASS	DERATE	CEROUS
HORROR	VIREOS	FARERS	MOROSE	EGRETS	CIRCUM
JARGON	WARHOL	FIRERS	OGRESS	ERRATA	CIRCUS
JARROW	YARROW	FURORE	OGRISH	FERITY	CIRQUE
JERBOA	ZIRCON	FURORS	ONRUSH	FIRSTS	CIRRUS
KARROO	******	GERARD	PARISH	GYRATE	CORIUM
LARDON	--R-P-	HIRERS	PERISH	HERETO	CORNUA
LARGOS	******	HORARY	PERUSE	HORSTE	CORNUS
MARCOS	ABRUPT	JURORS	PHRASE	JURATS	CORPUS
	CERIPH				

CORVUS	STRIVE	******	NASSAU	PESADE	CASTES
CURIUM	STROVE	--S-A-	OSSIAN	POSADA	COSHED
DARIUS	THRIVE	******	PASCAL	RESEDA	COSHER
DORBUG	THROVE	BASHAW	PASHAS	RESIDE	COSHES
DORSUM	******	BASRAH	PASTAS	UPSIDE	COSSES
EARFUL	--R-W-	BISCAY	PISGAH	******	COSSET
FAROUT	******	BUSMAN	POSTAL	--S-E-	COSTED
FEROUS	ARROWS	CASBAH	RASCAL	******	COSTER
FERRUM	ARROWY	CASHAW	RESEAT	AISLED	CUSPED
FURFUR	SCRAWL	CASPAR	RESEAU	AISLES	CUSSED
GEROUS	SCREWS	CASUAL	ROSEAL	ANSWER	CUSSES
JARFUL	SCREWY	COSTAE	SASHAY	AUSPEX	CUSTER
LARRUP	SEROWS	COSTAL	TASMAN	AUSTEN	DASHED
MARAUD	SHREWD	COSTAR	TESTAE	AUSTER	DASHER
MARCUS	SHREWS	CUSHAT	TUSCAN	AXSEED	DASHES
MARDUK	SPRAWL	CUSHAW	TUSSAH	BASHED	DISHED
MARKUP	STRAWS	DESMAN	TUSSAL	BASHES	DISHES
MARQUE	STRAWY	DESSAU	TUSSAR	BASKED	DISNEY
MEROUS	STREWN	DISBAR	UNSEAL	BASKET	DISPEL
MORGUE	STREWS	DISCAL	UNSEAM	BASSES	DOSSED
MURMUR	THROWN	DISMAL	UNSEAT	BASSET	DOSSEL
PAREUS	THROWS	DISMAY	VASSAL	BASTED	DOSSER
POROUS	VYRNWY	DISTAL	VESTAL	BASTES	DUSKED
PURSUE	--R-Y-	DOSSAL	VESTAS	BESEEM	DUSTED
SEROUS	******	FESTAL	VISTAS	BESTED	DUSTER
SHROUD	ARRAYS	FISCAL	VISUAL	BISTER	EASIER
SIRIUS	ARROYO	FOSSAE	WYSTAN	BOSHES	EASTER
SPROUT	BARRYS	GASBAG	YASMAK	BOSKET	ELSIES
STROUD	FORAYS	GASMAN	YESMAN	BOSSED	ENSUED
TARSUS	FORMYL	GASPAR	******	BOSSES	ENSUES
TEREUS	GERRYS	GUSTAF	--S-B-	BUSHED	FASCES
TERGUM	GERTYS	GUSTAV	******	BUSHEL	FASTED
TOROUS	HARRYS	HUSSAR	CASABA	BUSHES	FASTEN
TORQUE	JERRYS	INSPAN	******	BUSHEY	FASTER
TURNUP	LARRYS	INSTAR	--S-C-	BUSIED	FESSES
VERDUN	LEROYS	JOSIAH	ALSACE	BUSIES	FESTER
VERSUS	MARTYR	JOSIAS	BASICS	BUSKER	FISHER
VIRTUE	MARTYS	LASCAR	BISECT	BUSMEN	FISHES
VOROUS	MORAYS	MESCAL	EXSECT	BUSSED	FISTED
WARMUP	MORTYS	MESIAL	INSECT	BUSSES	FOSSES
******	PERCYS	MESIAN	PESACH	BUSTED	FOSTER
--R-V-	PERRYS	MISHAP	RESECT	BUSTER	FUSEES
******	SPRAYS	MISKAL	VESICA	CASHED	FUSSED
ARRIVE	STRAYS	MISLAY	VESICO	CASHES	FUSSER
DERIVE	TERRYS	MISSAL	--S-D-	CASHEW	FUSSES
SCRIVE	******	MUSCAE	******	CASKET	GASHED
SHRIVE	--R-Z-	MUSCAT	BESIDE	CASPER	GASHES
SHROVE	CORYZA	NASIAL	INSIDE	CASTER	GASJET

GASKET	KISMET	MISLED	RASHER	VESTED	BUSKIN
GASMEN	KISSED	MISSED	RASHES	VESTEE	BUSTIC
GASPED	KISSER	MISSEL	RASPED	VISAED	CASEIN
GASPER	KISSES	MISSES	RASPER	VISEED	CASSIA
GASSED	KOSHER	MISTED	RASTER	WASHED	CASSIE
GASSES	LASHED	MISTER	RESTED	WASHER	CASSIS
GOSHEN	LASHER	MOSLEM	RESTER	WASHES	CISSIE
GOSPEL	LASHES	MOSLEY	RISKED	WASTED	COSMIC
GUSHED	LASSEN	MOSSES	RISKER	WASTER	CUSPID
GUSHER	LASSES	MUSHED	ROSIER	WASTES	CUSPIS
GUSHES	LASTED	MUSHER	ROSTER	WESLEY	CYSTIC
GUSSET	LASTER	MUSHES	RUSHED	WESSEX	DESMID
HASHED	LASTEX	MUSKEG	RUSHER	WESTER	DISTIL
HASHES	LESLEY	MUSKET	RUSHES	WISHED	DOSSIL
HASLET	LESSEE	MUSSED	RUSSET	WISHES	FASCIA
HASPED	LESSEN	MUSSEL	RUSTED	WISPED	FISTIC
HASSEL	LESSER	MUSSES	SASHED	XYSTER	FOSSIL
HASTED	LESTER	MUSTEE	SASHES	YESSED	FUSAIN
HASTEN	LISPED	MUSTER	SASSED	YESSES	FUSTIC
HASTES	LISPER	NASSER	SASSES	YESTER	GASKIN
HESTER	LISTED	NESTED	SESTET	ZESTED	GESTIC
HISSED	LISTEL	NOSHED	SISTER	ZOSTER	GOSSIP
HISSER	LISTEN	NOSIER	SUSIES	******	GUSSIE
HISSES	LISTER	OUSTED	SUSSED	--S-F-	HESOID
HOSIER	LOSSES	OUSTER	SUSSEX	******	HESTIA
HOSTED	LUSHED	OYSTER	SYSTEM	BASIFY	HISPID
HOSTEL	LUSHER	PASSED	TASKED	CASEFY	INSTIL
HUSHED	LUSHES	PASSEE	TASSEL	GASIFY	ISSEIS
HUSHES	LUSTED	PASSER	TASSET	OSSIFY	JESSIE
HUSKED	LUSTER	PASSES	TASTED	UNSAFE	JESUIT
HUSKER	MASHED	PASTED	TASTER	******	JUSTIN
HYSTER	MASHER	PASTEL	TASTES	--S-G-	LASSIE
INSTEP	MASHES	PASTER	TESTED	******	LESLIE
ISSUED	MASKED	PASTES	TESTER	ASSIGN	MASHIE
ISSUER	MASKEG	PESTER	TESTES	COSIGN	MASSIF
ISSUES	MASKER	PISCES	TOSHES	DESIGN	MASTIC
JASPER	MASSED	PISHED	TOSSED	DOSAGE	MISDID
JESSED	MASSES	PISHES	TOSSES	ENSIGN	MISFIT
JESSES	MASTED	POSIES	TUSHED	RESIGN	MISSIS
JESTED	MASTER	POSSES	TUSHES	VISAGE	MOSAIC
JESTER	MESHED	POSSET	TUSKED	******	MUSKIT
JOSHED	MESHER	POSTED	TUSKER	--S-I-	MUSLIM
JOSHER	MESHES	POSTER	ULSTER	******	MUSLIN
JOSHES	MESMER	PUSHED	UNSEEN	ASSAIL	MYSTIC
JOSIEA	MESNES	PUSHER	UNSTEP	ASSAIS	NASTIC
JOSSES	MESSED	PUSHES	VASTER	AUSTIN	NISEIS
KASPER	MESSES	PUSSES	VESPER	BESSIE	NOSTIC
KISLEW	MESTEE	PUSSEY	VESSEL	BESTIR	OSSEIN

PASSIM	LASTLY	DOSING	DESPOT	BISTRO	MISUSE
PASTIL	MISTLE	EASING	EASTON	CASERN	OBSESS
PISTIL	MOSTLY	ESSENE	FUSION	CASTRO	RESIST
RUSKIN	MUSCLE	FUSING	GASCON	CESARE	WISEST
RUSSIA	MYSELF	HOSING	GASTON	CESURA	******
RUSTIC	NASALS	INSANE	GESSOS	DESCRY	--S-T-
SISKIN	NESTLE	JASONS	GISMOS	DESERT	******
SUSLIK	NOSILY	LOSING	HYSSOP	DESIRE	ANSATE
TESSIE	OUSELS	LYSINE	LASSOS	DISARM	ASSETS
TESTIS	PESTLE	LYSING	LESBOS	DOSERS	BASUTO
TUSSIS	POSHLY	LYSINS	LESION	ENSURE	BESETS
UNSAID	PUSSLY	MASONS	LESSON	EXSERT	BESOTS
UNSHIP	RASHLY	MESONS	LESSOR	GASTRO	ERSATZ
VESPID	RESALE	MUSING	LISBOA	INSERT	INSETS
VISCID	RESELL	MUSTNT	LISBON	INSURE	ONSETS
******	RESILE	NOSING	LISSOM	LASERS	PASHTO
--S-K-	RESOLD	POSING	MASCON	LOSERS	PESETA
******	RESOLE	RESEND	MASCOT	LUSTRE	POSITS
ALSIKE	RESULT	RESENT	MOSCOW	MASERS	PUSHTU
******	ROSILY	RESINS	MUSKOX	MASORA	RESETS
--S-L-	RUSTLE	RISING	NASION	MESSRS	UPSETS
******	TUSSLE	ROSING	NESTOR	MISERE	VASHTI
ANSELM	UNSOLD	ROSINS	NOSHOW	MISERS	VISITS
BASALT	URSULA	ROSINY	PASTOR	MISERY	******
BASELY	VASILI	RUSINE	PISTOL	PASTRY	--S-U-
BASILS	VASTLY	SASINS	PISTON	POSERS	******
BUSILY	WISELY	SUSANS	ROSCOE	RESORB	BASQUE
BUSTLE	******	TISANE	TESTON	RESORT	BISQUE
CASALS	--S-M-	UNSUNG	UNSHOD	RISERS	BYSSUS
CASTLE	******	URSINE	UNSTOP	ROSARY	CASQUE
COSILY	ASSUME	VISHNU	UPSHOT	ROSTRA	CESIUM
COSTLY	BESOMS	VISING	VISION	SISERA	CESTUS
DESALT	BOSOMS	WISING	WISDOM	TISHRI	CUSCUS
EASELS	RESUME	******	XYSTOS	UNSURE	DISCUS
EASILY	SESAME	--S-O-	******	VASARI	ENSOUL
EDSELS	******	******	--S-P-	VESTRY	FESCUE
ENSILE	--S-N-	BASION	******	VISARD	INSOUL
FUSILE	******	BASSOS	JOSEPH	VISORS	JOSHUA
FUSILS	ABSENT	BESTOW	******	******	JUSTUS
GESELL	ARSINE	BISHOP	--S-R-	--S-S-	MASQUE
GISELE	ASSENT	BOSTON	******	******	MISCUE
HASSLE	BASING	CASHOO	ABSORB	ASSESS	MISSUS
HUSTLE	BASINS	CASTOR	ABSURD	ASSISI	MOSQUE
INSOLE	BESANT	CISCOS	ADSORB	ASSIST	MUSEUM
INSULT	BUSING	COSMOS	ASSERT	BASEST	NASHUA
ITSELF	CASING	CUSSOS	ASSORT	DESIST	NESSUS
JOSTLE	CASINO	CUSTOM	ASSURE	DISUSE	PASSUS
JUSTLY	COSINE	CUSTOS	AUSTRO	INSIST	POSEUR

POSSUM	COTEAU	ATTICS	BUTTED	JOTTED	POTTED
PUSHUP	COTTAE	AZTECS	BUTTER	JOTTER	POTTER
RESCUE	COTTAR	DETACH	BUTTES	JUTTED	PUTTED
RISQUE	COTTAS	DETECT	CATHER	KATIES	PUTTEE
SESQUI	CUTLAS	ENTICE	CATTED	KITTED	PUTTER
TISSUE	ENTRAP	FETICH	CITHER	KITTEN	RATHER
TOSSUP	ESTRAY	INTACT	CITIED	LATEEN	RATTED
VISCUS	EXTRAS	KITSCH	CITIES	LATHED	RATTEN
XTSTUS	FETIAL	NOTICE	COTTER	LATHER	RATTER
******	GATEAU	OBTECT	CUTIES	LATHES	RETTED
--S-V-	GOTHAM	OPTICS	CUTLER	LATTEN	RITTER
******	GUTTAE	PUTSCH	CUTLET	LATTER	ROTTED
CASAVA	GUTTAT	SHTICK	CUTTER	LETTER	ROTTEN
******	HETMAN	UNTACK	DITHER	LITHER	ROTTER
--S-W-	JETSAM	******	DOTIER	LITTER	RUTTED
******	JOTHAM	--T-D-	DOTTED	LUTHER	SATEEN
DISOWN	KITBAG	******	DOTTEL	MATTED	SETTEE
******	LETHAL	BETIDE	DOTTER	MATTEO	SETTER
--S-X-	LUTEAL	OCTADS	DUTIES	MATTER	SITTER
******	LYTTAE	UNTIDY	EITHER	MATTES	SUTLER
DESOXY	MITRAL	******	ENTREE	METIER	SUTTEE
******	MUTUAL	--T-E-	ESTEEM	MITRED	TATLER
--S-Y-	NATHAN	******	ESTHER	MITTEN	TATTED
******	OSTEAL	AETHER	FATHER	MOTHER	TATTER
ASSAYS	OUTLAW	ALTHEA	FATTED	MOTLEY	TETHER
BESSYS	OUTLAY	ANTEED	FATTEN	MUTTER	TETTER
CISSYS	OUTMAN	ANTHEA	FATTER	NATTER	TETZEL
ESSAYS	OUTRAN	ANTHEM	FETTER	NETHER	TITHED
MOSEYS	OUTSAT	ANTHER	FITTED	NETTED	TITHER
UNSAYS	PATHAN	ANTLER	FITTER	NUTLET	TITHES
******	PITMAN	ARTIES	GATHER	NUTMEG	TITLED
--S-Z-	POTMAN	ATTLEE	GETTER	NUTTED	TITLES
******	PUTNAM	AUTOED	GOTTEN	NUTTER	TITTER
ASSIZE	RATTAN	BATHED	GUTTED	OSTLER	TOTHER
******	RITUAL	BATHER	GUTTER	OUTLET	TOTTED
--T-A-	SATRAP	BATMEN	HATRED	OUTSET	TOTTER
******	SUTRAS	BATTED	HATTED	PATTED	TUTTED
ACTUAL	TETRAD	BATTEN	HATTER	PATTEN	UNTIED
ANTIAR	TITIAN	BATTER	HITHER	PATTER	UNTIES
ASTRAL	VITTAE	BETHEL	HITLER	PETREL	VATTED
ASTRAY	WITHAL	BETTED	HITTER	PETTED	VETOED
BATAAN	******	BETTER	HOTBED	PITHED	VETOER
BATEAU	--T-C-	BETTES	HOTTED	PITIED	VETOES
BATMAN	******	BITTED	HOTTER	PITIES	VETTED
BETRAY	ANTICS	BITTEN	HUTTED	PITMEN	WETHER
CATHAY	ATTACH	BITTER	JETTED	PITTED	WETTED
CATNAP	ATTACK	BOTHER	JITNEY	POTEEN	WETTER
CITRAL	ATTICA	BUTLER	JITTER	POTHER	WITHED

WITHER	CITRIC	WITHIN	POTTLE	BOTANY	PATINE
WITHES	DETAIL	WITHIT	RATALS	BUTANE	PITONS
WITNEY	DETAIN	YTTRIA	RATELS	CATENA	POTENT
WITTED	ENTAIL	YTTRIC	RATTLE	CETANE	PUTONS
ZITHER	GOTHIC	******	RETELL	CITING	RATINE
******	HATPIN	--T-K-	RETOLD	CUTINS	RATING
--T-F-	HATTIE	******	RUTILE	DATING	RETENE
******	IATRIC	BATIKS	SETTLE	DETENT	RETINA
CUTOFF	INTUIT	BETAKE	SOTOLS	DITONE	ROTUND
MOTIFS	ISTRIA	INTAKE	TATTLE	DOTING	SATANG
NOTIFY	KATHIE	RETAKE	TATTLY	EATING	SATING
PUTOFF	LATRIA	UPTAKE	TITTLE	EXTANT	SATINS
RATIFY	LATVIA	******	TOTALS	EXTEND	SATINY
SETOFF	LITHIA	--T-L-	UNTOLD	EXTENT	SETONS
******	LITHIC	******	VITALS	FATING	SITING
--T-G-	LOTTIE	ARTELS	WATTLE	FETING	SITINS
******	MATRIX	ARTILY	******	GATING	TETANY
DOTAGE	MATTIE	ATTILA	--T-M-	HATING	TETONS
METAGE	METRIC	BATTLE	******	INTEND	TITANS
POTAGE	MYTHIC	BETELS	ASTHMA	INTENT	TOTING
******	NETTIE	BOTFLY	AUTUMN	INTONE	VOTING
--T-H-	NITRIC	BOTTLE	ECTOMY	KETENE	******
******	NITRID	BYTALK	ENTOMB	KETONE	--T-O-
BITCHY	NITWIT	CATALO	ENTOMO	KITING	******
BOTCHY	NUTRIA	CATTLE	FATIMA	LATENT	ACTION
CATCHY	OBTAIN	CITOLA	GOTAMA	LATINS	AUTHOR
LITCHI	OUTBID	CUTELY	INTIMA	LITANY	BATHOS
LOTAHS	OUTDID	CUTTLE	INTOMB	LUTING	BETOOK
PATCHY	OUTFIT	DOTTLE	METUMP	MATINE	BETTOR
PITCHY	OUTSIT	EXTOLS	OPTIMA	MATING	BOTTOM
ROTCHE	OUTWIT	FETTLE	OPTIME	MATINS	BUTTON
TETCHY	OXTAIL	FUTILE	TOTEMS	METING	CATION
******	PATHIA	GUTTLE	ULTIMA	MUTANT	CITRON
--T-I-	PATOIS	HOTELS	ULTIMO	MUTING	COTTON
******	PETRIE	KETTLE	******	MUTINY	DATTOS
ALTAIC	POTPIE	KITTLE	--T-N-	NATANT	DITTOS
ALTAIR	POTSIE	LATELY	******	NOTING	FATHOM
ANTLIA	PUTRID	LITTLE	ACTING	OBTUND	HATBOX
ANTRIM	PYTHIA	METALS	ACTINI	OCTANE	HOTBOX
ARTOIS	PYTHIC	METTLE	ACTINO	OCTANT	HOTPOT
ASTRID	RATLIN	MOTELS	ANTONS	OPTANT	HOTROD
ATTAIN	RETAIL	MOTILE	ANTONY	OPTING	JETTON
BATTIK	RETAIN	MOTTLE	ATTEND	OSTEND	KATION
BATTIN	SOTHIC	MUTULE	ATTUNE	OUTING	LOTION
CATKIN	SOTHIS	NETTLE	BATING	PATENS	MATEOS
CATLIN	TITBIT	PETALS	BATONS	PATENT	MATRON
CATNIP	TUTTIS	PETULA	BETONY	PATINA	MATZOS
CATTIE	VITRIC	POTALE	BITING	PATINA	MATZOT

METEOR	OCTOPI	LITERS	FETISH	SETOUS	ANURAN
METHOD	SETUPS	MATURE	JUTISH	SETOUT	AOUDAD
METROS	WATAPE	METERS	KETOSE	TITTUP	BEULAH
MOTION	WATAPS	MITERS	LATEST	UNTRUE	BEULAS
MOTMOT	******	MOTORS	LATISH	VATFUL	BHUTAN
MOTTOS	--T-R-	NATURE	LUTIST	ZETHUS	BRUMAL
MUTTON	******	NOTARY	MUTISM	******	BRUTAL
MYTHOI	ACTORS	NOTERS	OBTEST	--T-V-	CAUDAD
MYTHOS	ALTARS	OTTERS	OBTUSE	******	CAUDAL
NATION	ALTERS	OUTCRY	POTASH	ACTIVE	CAUSAL
NATRON	ANTERO	OUTERS	RETUSE	DATIVE	CHUFAS
NOTION	ARTERY	PATERS	SETOSE	MOTIVE	COUGAR
OCTROI	ARTHRO	PETARD	WATUSI	NATIVE	CRURAL
OPTION	ARTURO	PETERS	******	OCTAVE	DOUGAL
OUTFOX	ASTERI	RATERS	--T-T-	OCTAVO	FAUCAL
PATHOL	ASTERN	RETARD	******	OTTAVA	FAUNAE
PATHOS	ASTERO	RETIRE	ASTUTE	VOTIVE	FAUNAL
PATIOS	ASTERS	RETORT	ENTITY	******	FAUNAS
PATROL	ATTARS	RETURN	ESTATE	--T-W-	FEUDAL
PATRON	ATTIRE	RITARD	MUTATE	******	FRUGAL
PATTON	ATTORN	ROTARY	OCTETS	OTTAWA	LAURAE
PETROL	BITERS	ROTORS	PETITE	OTTOWA	LAURAS
POTBOY	CATERS	SATARA	POTATO	UPTOWN	MAUMAU
POTION	DATARY	SATIRE	RATITE	******	NEURAL
POTTOS	DATERS	SATORY	ROTATE	--T-X-	NOUGAT
PUTLOG	DATURA	SATURN	******	******	NOUNAL
PYTHON	DETERS	SATYRS	--T-U-	URTEXT	OCULAR
RATION	DOTARD	SITARS	******	******	OVULAR
RATIOS	DOTERS	SUTURE	ACTIUM	--T-Y-	PAULAS
RATOON	EATERS	TATARS	ANTRUM	******	PLURAL
RETOOK	EATERY	TOTERS	ARTFUL	BETSYS	SAUNAS
RETOOL	ENTERA	TUTORS	ARTHUR	BETTYS	SCUBAS
RETROD	ENTERE	UPTURN	BATTUE	CATHYS	SEURAT
SETTOS	ENTERO	UTTERS	CATGUT	CUTEYS	SQUEAK
SUTTON	ENTERS	VOTARY	CATSUP	HATTYS	SQUEAL
TATTOO	ENTIRE	VOTERS	CITRUS	HETTYS	STUPAS
UNTROD	ESTERS	WATERS	CUTOUT	KATHYS	THUJAS
WATSON	EXTERN	WATERY	DETOUR	KITTYS	TOUCAN
ZETHOS	EXTORT	******	ESTRUS	MATEYS	TRUMAN
******	FETORS	--T-S-	FITFUL	METHYL	UVULAE
--T-P-	FUTURE	******	HATFUL	PATSYS	UVULAR
******	HATERS	AFTOSA	LITMUS	TETHYS	UVULAS
CUTUPS	HETERO	ARTIST	LUTEUM	TETRYL	******
ECTYPE	INTERN	ATTEST	OUTPUT	******	--U-B-
ESTOPS	INTERS	AUTISM	OUTRUN	--U-A-	******
GETUPS	INTURN	BETISE	PUTOUT	******	BLURBS
LETUPS	JETHRO	CUTEST	PUTPUT	ALULAE	CHUBBY
METOPE	LATERA	DETEST	ROTGUT	ALULAR	CRUMBS

CRUMBY	MOULDY	DAUDET	INURED	ROUSES	******
EXURBS	POUNDS	DEUCED	INURES	ROUTED	--U-G-
GRUBBY	ROUNDS	DEUCES	JOULES	ROUTER	******
PLUMBO	SOUNDS	DOUSED	LAUDED	ROUTES	BLUNGE
PLUMBS	SQUADS	DOUSES	LAUDER	SAUCED	BOURGS
RHUMBA	SQUIDS	DRUPEL	LAUREL	SAUCER	DRUDGE
RHUMBS	STURDY	DRUPES	LEUDES	SAUCES	GRUDGE
SQUABS	WOUNDS	DRUSES	LOUDEN	SAUGER	LOUNGE
SQUIBS	ZOUNDS	EDUCED	LOUDER	SAUREL	PLUNGE
STUBBS	******	EDUCES	LOUPES	SAUTES	SLUDGE
STUBBY	--U-E-	ELUDED	LOURED	SCUTES	SLUDGY
THUMBS	******	ELUDES	LOUSED	SOULED	SMUDGE
******	ABUSED	ETUDES	LOUSES	SOUPED	SMUDGY
--U-C-	ABUSER	EXUDED	LOUVER	SOURED	SPURGE
******	ABUSES	EXUDES	MAUDES	SOURER	TRUDGE
BOUNCE	ACUMEN	FAUCES	MAULED	SOUSED	******
BOUNCY	ALUDEL	FAUCET	MAULER	SOUSES	--U-H-
BRUNCH	AMULET	FAUVES	MAUSER	SPUMED	******
CHURCH	AMUSED	FEUDED	MAUVES	SPUMES	BOUGHS
CLUTCH	AMUSER	FLUKED	MOUSED	STUPES	BOUGHT
CRUNCH	AMUSES	FLUKES	MOUSER	TAUPES	BRUSHY
CRUTCH	ANUSES	FLUKEY	MOUSES	TAUTEN	CAUGHT
HAUNCH	AZURES	FLUMED	NAUSEA	TAUTER	COUGHS
JOUNCE	BOULES	FLUMES	NEUMES	TEUCER	DOUCHE
LAUNCE	BOUSED	FLUTED	NEUTER	TOUPEE	DOUGHS
LAUNCH	BOUSES	FLUTER	ONUSES	TOURED	DOUGHY
NAUTCH	BRUCES	FLUTES	OVULES	TOURER	FOUGHT
PAUNCH	BRUGES	FLUXED	PAUKER	TOUTED	GAUCHE
POUNCE	BRUMES	FLUXES	PAUPER	TOUTER	GAUCHO
SCUTCH	BRUNEI	FOULED	PAUSED	TRUCES	KYUSHU
SLUICE	BRUNEL	FOULER	PAUSER	UNUSED	LAUGHS
SMUTCH	BRUTES	GAUGED	PAUSES	USURER	LOUGHS
SOURCE	CAUDEX	GAUGER	PLUMED	WAULED	MOUTHS
STUCCO	CAULES	GAUGES	PLUMES	YAUPED	MOUTHY
******	CAUSED	GAUZES	PLUSES	******	NAUGHT
--U-D-	CAUSER	GLUIER	POURED	--U-F-	NOUGHT
******	CAUSES	GLUMES	POURER	******	PLUSHY
BOUNDS	CAUTER	GLUTEI	POUTED	BLUFFS	POUCHY
DRUIDS	CHUTES	GLUTEN	POUTER	BOUFFE	ROUCHE
FLUIDS	COULEE	GOUGED	PRUDES	FLUFFS	ROUGHS
FOUNDS	COUPES	GOUGER	PRUNED	FLUFFY	SLUSHY
GOURDE	CRUCES	GOUGES	PRUNER	SCUFFS	SOUGHS
GOURDS	CRUDER	GRUMES	PRUNES	SCURFY	SOUGHT
GRUNDY	CRUSES	HAULED	REUBEN	SNUFFS	TAUGHT
HOUNDS	CRUSET	HAULER	ROUGED	SNUFFY	TOUCHE
MAUNDS	CRUXES	HAUSEN	ROUGES	STUFFS	TOUCHY
MAUNDY	DAUBED	HOUSED	ROUSED	STUFFY	TOUGHS
MOULDS	DAUBER	HOUSES	ROUSER		TRUTHS
					YOUTHS

******	******	ALUMNA	GRUMPY	SQUISH	SHUNTS
--U-I-	**--U-L-**	ALUMNI	PLUMPS	TRUEST	SMUTTY
******	******	BLUING	SCULPT	TRUISM	SPURTS
ABULIA	AQUILA	BOURNE	SLUMPS	******	SQUATS
ALUMIN	BAUBLE	BOURNS	SLURPS	**--U-T-**	STUNTS
ANUBIS	BLUELY	BRUINS	STUMPS	******	TAUNTS
APULIA	BOUCLE	CHURNS	STUMPY	ACUATE	TRUSTS
BAUCIS	CAUDLE	CLUING	THUMPS	ACUITY	TRUSTY
BOUGIE	CHURLS	DHURNA	TRUMPS	ADULTS	VAULTS
CAULIS	COUPLE	EQUINE	USURPS	ARUNTA	VAUNTS
COUSIN	DOUBLE	FEUING	******	BLUETS	******
DOUGIE	DOUBLY	FLUENT	**--U-R-**	BLUNTS	**--U-U-**
FLUVIO	DOURLY	GLUING	******	BLURTS	******
GIULIA	EQUALS	IGUANA	BLURRY	BOUNTY	BRUTUS
GIULIO	FOULLY	INURNS	CHURRS	BRUITS	CAUCUS
HOURIS	GAULLE	MOURNS	DAUBRY	COUNTS	FAUNUS
INULIN	GLUMLY	SLUING	EDUARD	COUNTY	KRUBUT
KAURIS	GRUELS	SPURNS	FEUARS	COURTS	MUUMUU
KRUBIS	HOURLY	SQUINT	FLUORO	CRUETS	PAULUS
LAURIE	KNURLS	TRUANT	FLUORS	CRUSTS	PLUTUS
MOULIN	KNURLY	TRUING	FLURRY	CRUSTY	SAURUS
PAULIN	LOUDLY	UTURNS	GRUGRU	DAUNTS	SCUTUM
PLUGIN	ROUBLE	******	LOUVRE	DOUBTS	SPUTUM
PLUVIO	SCULLS	**--U-O-**	OEUVRE	EDUCTS	TAURUS
PYURIA	SKULLS	******	SCURRY	EQUATE	******
SHUTIN	SMUGLY	BRULOT	SLURRY	EQUITY	**--U-V-**
STUDIO	SNUGLY	BRUNOS	SOUARI	ERUCTS	******
STUPID	SOURLY	COUPON	SPURRY	ERUPTS	SCURVY
THULIA	SQUALL	CRUSOE	SQUARE	EXULTS	ZOUAVE
******	SQUILL	MOUTON	SQUIRE	FAULTS	******
--U-K-	STULLS	NEURON	SQUIRM	FAULTY	**--U-W-**
******	TAUTLY	STUPOR	SQUIRT	FOUNTS	******
CAULKS	THUSLY	TAUTOG	STUART	FOURTH	SQUAWK
CHUCKS	TOUSLE	TEUTON	******	FRUITS	SQUAWS
CHUNKS	******	TOULON	**--U-S-**	FRUITY	******
CHUNKY	**--U-M-**	YAUPON	******	FRUSTA	**--U-Y-**
CLUCKS	******	YOUPON	AGUISH	GRUNTS	******
DRUNKS	CHUMMY	******	BLUEST	HAUNTS	RYUKYU
FLUNKS	CRUMMY	**--U-P-**	BLUISH	JAUNTS	TRUDYS
FLUNKY	HAULMY	******	BOURSE	JAUNTY	******
PLUCKS	PLUMMY	CHUMPS	BRUISE	JOUSTS	**--U-Z-**
PLUCKY	SCUMMY	CLUMPS	CLUMSY	MOULTS	******
PLUNKS	SLUMMY	CLUMPY	COURSE	MOUNTS	FRUNZE
SHUCKS	SQUAMA	CRUMPS	CRUISE	MOUNTY	******
SKULKS	ZEUGMA	EQUIPS	LOUISA	POULTS	**--V-A-**
SKUNKS	******	FLUMPS	LOUISE	POUSTO	******
SPUNKY	**--U-N-**	FRUMPS	MOUSSE	ROUSTS	CAVEAT
TRUCKS	ALUINO	FRUMPY	SQUASH	SAULTS	CAVIAR
TRUNKS	ALUINS				

FOVEAE	REVVED	CAVILS	LAVING	LIVERS	COVETS
FOVEAL	SOVIET	DEVILS	LEVANT	LIVERY	DAVITS
GAVIAL	VIVIEN	GAVELS	LIVENS	LOVERS	DEVOTE
JOVIAL	WAVIER	HOVELS	LIVING	MOVERS	DIVOTS
JOVIAN	WAVIES	KEVELS	LOVING	OBVERT	GAVOTS
LIVIAS	XAVIER	LEVELS	MOVING	PAVERS	HIVITE
REVEAL	******	LIVELY	NOVENA	RAVERS	INVITE
VIVIAN	--V-F-	LOVELL	PAVANE	REVERE	LEVITE
******	******	LOVELY	PAVANS	REVERS	LEVITY
--V-B-	VIVIFY	NAVELS	PAVING	REVERT	PIVOTS
******	--V-G-	NEVILE	RAVENS	RIVERS	REVETS
LAVABO	******	NEVILL	RAVINE	ROVERS	RIVETS
******	LAVAGE	NOVELS	RAVING	SAVERS	SAVATE
--V-C-	LOVAGE	RAVELS	RIVING	SAVORS	******
******	RAVAGE	REVELS	ROVING	SAVORY	--V-U-
ADVICE	SAVAGE	REVILE	SAVANT	SEVERE	******
CIVICS	******	REVOLT	SAVING	SEVERN	DEVOUR
DEVICE	RIVALS	RIVALS	SAVINS	SEVERS	DEVOUT
NOVICE	--V-H-	WAVILY	SEVENS	TAVERN	FAVOUR
VIVACE	******	******	WAVING	TEVERE	SAVOUR
******	NAVAHO	--V-M-	WIVING	WAVERS	******
--V-D-	******	******	******	WIVERN	--V-V-
******	--V-I-	REVAMP	--V-O-	WIVERS	******
DAVIDS	******	******	******	WYVERN	REVIVE
DIVIDE	CAVEIN	--V-N-	PAVIOR		******
INVADE	DEVEIN	******	PAVLOV	--V-S-	--V-X-
NEVADA	DEVOID	ADVENT	SAVIOR	******	******
******	DEVOIR	ALVANS	******	ADVISE	UNVEXT
--V-E-	LOVEIN	ALVINA	--V-R-	CIVISM	******
******	NEVOID	ALVINE	******	DEVEST	--V-Y-
BEVIES	UNVEIL	BOVINE	ADVERB	DEVISE	******
CAVIES	******	CAVING	ADVERT	DIVEST	COVEYS
CIVIES	--V-J-	COVING	CAVERN	DOVISH	DAVEYS
DAVIES	******	DIVANS	CAVORT	ELVISH	ENVOYS
ENVIED	NAVAJO	DIVINE	COVERS	INVEST	WAVEYS
ENVIER	******	DIVING	COVERT	KAVASS	******
ENVIES	--V-K-	GIVING	DIVERS	LAVISH	--W-A-
LEVEES	******	GYVING	DIVERT	PAVISE	******
LEVIED	INVOKE	HAVANA	ELVERS	RAVISH	BOWMAN
LEVIER	NEVSKI	HAVENS	ELVIRA	REVEST	BOWSAW
LEVIES	REVOKE	HAVENT	FAVORS	REVISE	COWMAN
LIVIER	******	HAVING	FEVERS	******	DEWLAP
LIVRES	--V-L-	HIVING	FIVERS	--V-T-	DOWLAS
LIVYER	******	INVENT	GOVERN	******	ENWRAP
MOVIES	ABVOLT	IRVING	HOVERS	BOVATE	GEWGAW
NAVIES	ANVILS	IRVINS	INVERT	CAVITE	HAWHAW
REVIEW	BEVELS	JIVING	LAVERS	CAVITY	HOWDAH
REVUES	CAVELL	KEVINS	LEVERS	CIVETS	INWRAP

PAWPAW	PAWNED	POWELL	******	SOWERS	SEXTAN
UNWRAP	PAWNEE	ROWELS	--W-O-	TAWDRY	SEXUAL
******	PAWNER	SAWFLY	******	TAWERS	******
--W-B-	PEWEES	SEWALL	BOWWOW	THWART	--X-C-
******	PEWTER	SEWELL	COWBOY	TOWARD	******
NAWABS	POWDER	TOWELS	COWPOX	TOWERS	MEXICO
******	POWTER	UNWELL	DAWSON	TOWERY	******
--W-C-	SAWNEY	VOWELS	KOWTOW	UNWARY	--X-D-
******	SAWYER	******	LOWBOY	UNWORN	******
THWACK	WAWLED	--W-M-	NEWTON	UPWARD	HEXADS
******	WOWSER	******	POWWOW	VOWERS	TUXEDO
--W-E-	YAWLED	ENWOMB	******	******	******
******	YAWNED	******	--W-P-	--W-S-	--X-E-
BAWLED	YAWNER	--W-N-	******	******	******
BAWLER	YAWPED	******	UNWEPT	FEWEST	BAXTER
BOWLED	YAWPER	BOWING	******	JEWESS	DEXTER
BOWLEG	YOWLED	CAWING	--W-R-	JEWISH	DOXIES
BOWLER	******	COWING	******	LOWEST	FOXIER
BOWMEN	--W-G-	DEWANS	BAWDRY	NEWEST	HUXLEY
BOWSED	******	DIWANS	BEWARE	NOWISE	NIXIES
BOWSES	COWAGE	EDWINA	BOWERS	RAWEST	PIXIES
BOWYER	OSWEGO	EDWINS	BOWERY	RAWISH	PYXIES
COWMEN	SEWAGE	ENWIND	BYWORD	SIWASH	SEXIER
COWPEA	TOWAGE	ERWINS	BYWORK	UNWISE	SEXTET
COWPER	******	HAWING	COWARD	UNWISH	SIXTES
DAWNED	--W-I-	HEWING	COWERS	******	TAXIED
DEWIER	******	INWIND	DOWERS	--W-T-	WAXIER
DOWNED	BEWAIL	IRWINS	DOWERY	******	******
DOWSED	BOWFIN	JAWING	EDWARD	ABWATT	--X-H-
DOWSER	BOWTIE	LAWING	HEWERS	DEWITT	******
DOWSES	COWRIE	LOWING	HOWARD	PEWITS	SIXTHS
FAWKES	GAWAIN	MEWING	INWARD	******	******
FAWNED	HAWAII	MOWING	LOWERS	--W-U-	--X-L-
FAWNER	KEWPIE	PAWING	LOWERY	******	******
FOWLED	KUWAIT	REWIND	MOWERS	LAWFUL	FOXILY
FOWLER	******	ROWANS	NEWARK	******	HEXYLS
GAWKED	--W-L-	ROWENA	ONWARD	--W-V-	SEXILY
GOWNED	******	ROWING	PAWERS	******	VEXILS
HAWKED	BOWELS	SAWING	POWERS	INWOVE	******
HAWKER	DAWDLE	SEWING	REWARD	******	--X-M-
HAWSER	DOWELS	SOWING	REWORD	--W-Y-	******
HAWSES	INWALL	TAWING	ROWERS	******	MAXIMA
HOWLED	JEWELS	TOWING	SAWERS	ALWAYS	MAXIMS
HOWLER	LEWDLY	UNWIND	SEWARD	BYWAYS	MYXOMA
LAWYER	LOWELL	VOWING	SEWERS	NOWAYS	TAXEME
LEWDER	NEWELS	WOWING	SOWARS	******	******
LOWKEY	ORWELL	YAWING	SOWERS	--X-A-	--X-N-
MEWLED	OSWALD	YOWING	BOXCAR	BOXCAR	AUXINS
				PAXWAX	BOXING

COXING	******	DOYLEY	SCYPHO	BUYING	BOYARS
FAXING	--X-T-	DRYDEN	SCYTHE	CRYING	BUYERS
FIXING	******	ELYSEE	******	DOYENS	DRYERS
FOXING	DIXITS	GEYSER	--Y-I-	DRYING	ELYTRA
HEXANE	FIXATE	HOYDEN	******	FAYING	FLYERS
HEXING	FIXITY	JAYVEE	AMYLIC	FLYING	FOYERS
HEXONE	LAXITY	JOYCES	CHYMIC	FRYING	FRYERS
MAXINE	LUXATE	KAYOED	GDYNIA	GUYANA	LAYERS
MIXING	TAXITE	KEYNES	GLYNIS	GUYING	MAYORS
NIXING	******	KHYBER	ODYNIA	GWYNNE	PAYERS
ROXANA	--X-X-	LAYMEN	PAYNIM	HAYING	PRYERS
ROXANE	******	LEYDEN	PHYSIC	JOYING	SAYERS
SAXONS	MAXIXE	MAYHEM	PHYSIO	KEYING	TOYERS
SAXONY	******	ORYXES	PHYTIN	LAYING	TUYERE
SEXING	--Y-A-	OXYGEN	STYMIE	MAYING	******
TAXING	******	PAYEES	THYMIC	PAYING	--Y-S-
TOXINS	AMYTAL	RHYMED	ZOYSIA	PLYING	******
VEXING	ANYWAY	RHYMER		PRYING	BOYISH
VIXENS	CAYMAN	RHYMES	--Y-K-	RAYING	CAYUSE
WAXING	FLYMAN	SKYMEN	******	RAYONS	COYISH
******	HEYDAY	STYLED	KAYAKS	SAYING	DRYEST
--X-O-	KEYWAY	STYLER	UNYOKE	SHYING	DRYISH
******	LAYDAY	STYLES	******	SKYING	GAYEST
BUXTON	LAYMAN	STYLET	--Y-L-	SPYING	MAYEST
CAXTON	MAYDAY	THYMES	******	STYING	SHYEST
SEXPOT	MAYHAP	THYREO	DAYFLY	TOYING	SLYEST
SEXTON	PAYDAY	WAYNES	DRYFLY	TOYONS	THYRSE
******	PHYLAE	ZUYDER	IDYLLS	TRYING	THYRSI
--X-P-	SKYCAP	******	MAYFLY	WRYING	TOYISH
******	SKYMAN	--Y-F-	PAYOLA	ZAYINS	WRYEST
MIXUPS	SKYWAY	******	PHYLLO	******	******
******	STYLAR	LAYOFF	RIYALS	--Y-O-	--Y-T-
--X-R-	WAYLAY	PAYOFF	ROYALE	******	******
******	WHYDAH	******	ROYALS	ABYDOS	COYOTE
BOXERS	******	--Y-G-	SCYLLA	ANYHOW	CRYPTO
DEXTRO	--Y-C-	******	******	CEYLON	CRYPTS
FIXERS	******	CAYUGA	--Y-M-	DAYBOY	GAYETY
LUXURY	DRYICE	ERYNGO	******	DAYTON	GLYPTO
MIXERS	******	VOYAGE	ABYSMS	DRYROT	PEYOTE
TAXERS	--Y-D-	******		ETYMON	TRYSTS
VEXERS	******	--Y-H-	--Y-N-	GLYCOL	******
******	DRYADS	******	******	HAYBOX	--Y-U-
--X-S-	******	GLYPHS	ANYONE	HAYMOW	******
******	--Y-E-	PSYCHE	ARYANS	MAYPOP	ADYTUM
HEXOSE	******	PSYCHO	BAYING	TAYLOR	AMYLUM
LAXEST	CLYDES	RAYAHS	BEYOND	THYMOL	ASYLUM
SEXISM	CLYPEI	RHYTHM	BRYANT	******	BAYEUX
SEXIST	DAYBED	SCYPHI	BRYONY	--Y-R-	BAYOUS
				******	
				BAYARD	
				BOYARD	

COYPUS	JAZZED	NUZZLE	MAZERS	FLAVIA	******
JOYFUL	JAZZER	OOZILY	MOZART	JOANNA	--A--D
JOYOUS	JAZZES	OUZELS	RAZORS	LUANDA	******
LAYOUT	LAZIER	PUZZLE	SIZARS	MIASMA	ABASED
MAYBUG	MAZIER	SIZZLE	VIZARD	PHAGIA	ABATED
PHYLUM	MIZZEN	ZIZZLE	VIZIRS	PHASIA	ACARID
POYOUS	OOZIER	******	VIZORS	PIAZZA	ALATED
STYLUS	RAZEED	--Z-M-	WIZARD	PLASIA	AMAZED
THYMUS	RAZEES	******	******	PLASMA	AWAKED
TRYOUT	RAZZED	ECZEMA	--Z-S-	PRAVDA	BEADED
VOYEUR	RAZZES	ENZYME	******	QUAGGA	BEAKED
WAYOUT	SIZIER	MAZUMA	NAZISM	QUANTA	BEAMED
******	VIZIER		******	RWANDA	BEANED
--Y-Y-	******	--Z-N-	--Z-T-	SHASTA	BEARED
******	--Z-F-	******	******	SPARTA	BIASED
FLYBYS	******	BEZANT	ZIZITH	STADIA	BLADED
******	NAZIFY	COZENS	******	STANZA	BLAMED
--Z-A-	******	DAZING	--Z-Y-	THALIA	BLARED
******	--Z-G-	DIZENS	******	TRAUMA	BLAZED
BAZAAR	******	DOZENS	LIZZYS	UGANDA	BOATED
BEZOAR	SYZYGY	DOZING	******	URANIA	BRACED
FEZZAN	******	FAZING	--Z-Z-	ZSAZSA	BRAKED
HAZZAN	--Z-I-	FUZING	******	******	BRAVED
PIZZAS	******	GAZING	MEZUZA	--A--B	BRAYED
TAZZAS	EOZOIC	HAZING	******	******	BRAZED
UZZIAH	FIZGIG	LAZING	--A--A	SCARAB	CEASED
******	JEZAIL	MAZING	******	******	CHAFED
--Z-B-	LIZZIE	OOZING	ACACIA	--A--C	CHARED
******	MUZHIK	RAZING	ACADIA	******	CHASED
GAZABO	RAZZIA	SIZING	ACAENA	AGAMIC	CHAWED
GAZEBO	******	SOZINE	AGATHA	AGARIC	CLAWED
******	--Z-L-	SOZINS	ALALIA	ALARIC	CLAYED
--Z-E-	******	WIZENS	ALASKA	ARABIC	COALED
******	BEZELS	******	AMANDA	ATAVIC	COATED
BUZZED	COZILY	--Z-O-	AMANIA	ATAXIC	COAXED
BUZZER	DAZZLE	******	ARABIA	CYANIC	CRANED
BUZZES	DOZILY	GIZMOS	ARANTA	DYADIC	CRAPED
COZIER	FIZZLE	HEZION	ATAXIA	ITALIC	CRATED
COZIES	FUZILS	KAZOOS	AZALEA	OXALIC	CRAVED
DOZIER	GUZZLE	MEZZOS	BIAFRA	PHASIC	CRAZED
FEZZES	HAZELS	******	BIANCA	SIALIC	CYANID
FIZZED	HAZILY	--Z-R-	BRAHMA	SLAVIC	DIALED
FIZZER	LAZILY	******	CHACMA	STATIC	DRAPED
FIZZES	LAZULI	GAZERS	CHAETA	TRAGIC	DRAYED
FUZEES	MAZILY	HAZARD	CRANIA	URALIC	ELATED
FUZZED	MIZZLE	HAZERS	DHARMA	URANIC	ERASED
FUZZES	MUZZLE	LAZARS	DHARNA	VIATIC	EVADED
HAZIER	NOZZLE	LIZARD	EXACTA		FEARED

FEASED	PHASED	TEAMED	ELAPSE	SNATHE	PLANCH
FLAKED	PLACED	TEARED	ELAYNE	SPACAE	SEARCH
FLAMED	PLACID	TEASED	ENABLE	SPARGE	SNATCH
FLARED	PLANED	THAWED	FIACRE	SPARSE	STAITH
FLAWED	PLATED	TRACED	FIANCE	SPATHE	STANCH
FLAYED	PLAYED	TRADED	FLAMBE	STABLE	STARCH
FOALED	PRATED	UNAPID	FLANGE	STACIE	SWARTH
FOAMED	PRAYED	VIALED	FRAISE	STACTE	SWATCH
FRAMED	QUAKED	WEANED	FRANCE	STANCE	THATCH
FRAYED	REAMED	WEAVED	FRAPPE	STAPLE	WEALTH
GEARED	REAPED	WHALED	GLANCE	STARVE	WRAITH
GLARED	REARED	WOADED	GOALIE	STATUE	******
GLAZED	ROAMED	XRAYED	GOATEE	SUABLE	--A--I
GNAWED	ROARED	YEANED	GRACIE	SWANEE	******
GOADED	SCALED	******	GRAMME	SWATHE	BRACHI
GRACED	SCARED	--A--E	GRANDE	TRACHE	GHARRI
GRADED	SEALED	******	GRANGE	TRANCE	ONAGRI
GRATED	SEAMED	AGAPAE	HEARSE	UNABLE	QUADRI
GRAVED	SEARED	AMALIE	HEAUME	USABLE	SCAMPI
GRAVID	SEATED	ANANKE	HOARSE	USANCE	SMALTI
GRAYED	SHADED	APACHE	JEANNE	VIABLE	UBANGI
GRAZED	SHALED	ARABLE	JOANNE	WHARVE	******
HEADED	SHAMED	BEADLE	LEAGUE	WRASSE	--A--J
HEALED	SHAPED	BEAGLE	LIABLE	******	******
HEAPED	SHARED	BEANIE	LIAISE	--A--G	SWARAJ
HEATED	SHAVED	BLAISE	LOATHE	******	******
HEAVED	SKATED	BRAISE	MEAGRE	ANALOG	--A--K
HOAXED	SLAKED	BRAIZE	MEALIE	BAAING	******
IMAGED	SLATED	BRAQUE	MEANIE	DIALOG	ARAWAK
LEADED	SLAVED	CHAISE	NUANCE	QUAHOG	CHABUK
LEAFED	SNAKED	CHANCE	OPAQUE	SEADOG	FRANCK
LEAKED	SNARED	CHANGE	ORACLE	STALAG	GDANSK
LEANED	SOAKED	CHARGE	ORANGE	TEABAG	PLANCK
LEAPED	SOAPED	CHASSE	PIAFFE	******	******
LEASED	SOARED	CHASTE	PLAGUE	--A--H	--A--L
LEAVED	SPACED	CLAIRE	PLAICE	******	******
LIASED	SPADED	CLAQUE	PLAQUE	ACANTH	AMATOL
LOADED	SPARED	CLAUDE	PLATTE	BLANCH	ARABEL
LOAFED	SPAYED	CLAUSE	PRAGUE	BRANCH	ATABAL
LOAMED	STAGED	COARSE	PRAISE	CHALEH	AZAZEL
LOANED	STAKED	COATEE	PRANCE	CRATCH	BIAXAL
MOANED	STALED	CRADLE	QUAERE	DEARTH	BRAZIL
MOATED	STARED	DEARIE	QUARTE	EPARCH	CHAPEL
NEARED	STATED	DOABLE	QUATRE	EXARCH	COAXAL
OKAYED	STAVED	DRAGEE	SCARCE	HEALTH	ENAMEL
ORATED	STAYED	DRAWEE	SCATHE	HEARTH	GRAVEL
PEAKED	SWAGED	ECARTE	SEABEE	INARCH	ISABEL
PEALED	SWAYED	ELAINE	SEANCE	ISAIAH	PLAGAL

STATAL	GRADIN	CHALCO	DEARER	PRATER	******
TEASEL	GRATIN	CRAMBO	DIALER	PRAYER	--A--S
TRAVEL	GRAVEN	CRANIO	DIAPER	QUAKER	******
URANYL	GUANIN	FIASCO	DRAPER	QUASAR	ABACAS
WEASEL	HEADON	FRANCO	DRAWER	QUAVER	ABACUS
******	HEAVEN	GLAUCO	ELATER	READER	ABASES
--A--M	IBADAN	GNATHO	ENAMOR	REAMER	ABATES
******	ISATIN	GRAECO	ERASER	REAPER	ABATIS
ALARUM	KLAXON	GRAPHO	EVADER	REARER	ADAGES
ANADEM	KRAKEN	LEANTO	FEARER	ROAMER	ADAPTS
ASARUM	LEADEN	PLAGIO	FLAKER	ROARER	AEACUS
BAALIM	LEADIN	PLASMO	FLAVOR	SCALAR	AGAMAS
DIADEM	LEAVEN	QUARTO	FLAYER	SCALER	AGATES
DIATOM	NEATEN	RIALTO	FRAMER	SCARER	AGAVES
DRACHM	NIACIN	SHACKO	FRATER	SEALER	ALAMOS
GRAHAM	PEAHEN	SMALTO	GIAOUR	SEAMER	ALARMS
OMASUM	PEASEN	STAURO	GLAZER	SHAKER	AMAZES
SLALOM	PHANON	******	GNAWER	SHAPER	ANABAS
******	PLATAN	--A--P	GRADER	SHARER	ANANAS
--A--N	PLATEN	******	GRATER	SHAVER	AVAILS
******	REASON	SLAPUP	GRAVER	SKATER	AWAITS
ABADAN	SEAMAN	TEACUP	GRAYER	SLATER	AWAKES
AMAZON	SEAMEN	WRAPUP	GRAZER	SLAVER	AWARDS
ARAGON	SEAPEN	******	HEADER	SLAYER	BEARDS
ATAMAN	SEARIN	--A--R	HEALER	SNARER	BEASTS
AVALON	SEASON	******	HEARER	SOAKER	BEAUTS
AWAKEN	SEAWAN	ABASER	HEATER	SOARER	BIALYS
BEACON	SHAKEN	ABATER	HEAVER	SPACER	BIASES
BEATEN	SHAMAN	ABATOR	HOAXER	SPADER	BLACKS
BLAZON	SHAPEN	AVATAR	ISADOR	SPARER	BLADES
BRAZEN	SHARON	BEAKER	LAAGER	STAGER	BLAINS
CHARON	SHAVEN	BEARER	LEADER	STALER	BLAMES
CRAVEN	SPAVIN	BEATER	LEANER	STARER	BLANKS
CRAYON	STALIN	BEAVER	LEAPER	STATER	BLARES
CYANIN	STAMEN	BLAZER	LEAVER	STATOR	BLASTS
DEACON	STAMIN	BOATER	LOADER	STAYER	BLAZES
DEADEN	STATEN	BRACER	LOAFER	TEASER	BOARDS
DEAFEN	TEAURN	BRAVER	MEAGER	THALER	BOASTS
DIAZIN	UTAHAN	BRAYER	MEANER	THAYER	BRACES
DRAGON	WEAKEN	BRAZER	NEARER	TRACER	BRACTS
EXAMEN	WEAPON	CHAFER	NEATER	TRADER	BRAHMS
FLACON	******	CHASER	ONAGER	VEADAR	BRAIDS
FLAGON	--A--O	CLAMOR	ORATOR	VIATOR	BRAILS
FLAMEN	******	COALER	PLACER	WEAKER	BRAINS
FLAVIN	ADAGIO	COAXER	PLANAR	WEANER	BRAKES
FLAXEN	ANATTO	CRATER	PLANER	WEARER	BRANDS
FRAUEN	BLASTO	CRAVER	PLATER	WEAVER	BRANTS
GRABEN	CHAETO	DEALER	PLAYER	WHALER	BRAVES

BRAVOS	DIANAS	GLANDS	LOAVES	SCALPS	SPANKS
BRAWLS	DIANES	GLARES	MEATUS	SCAMPS	SPARES
BRAZAS	DOALLS	GLAZES	MIAULS	SCAPES	SPARKS
BRAZES	DRAFFS	GNARLS	OKAPIS	SCARES	SPASMS
BRAZOS	DRAFTS	GRACES	ORACHS	SCARFS	SPATES
CEASES	DRAINS	GRADES	ORANGS	SCARPS	SPAWNS
CHAFES	DRAKES	GRADUS	ORATES	SCAUPS	STACKS
CHAFFS	DRAMAS	GRAFTS	OXALIS	SEAMUS	STACYS
CHAINS	DRAPES	GRAINS	PEARLS	SHACKS	STAFFS
CHAIRS	DRAWLS	GRANTS	PEASES	SHADES	STAGES
CHALKS	DWARFS	GRAPES	PHAROS	SHAFTS	STAINS
CHAMPS	ELANDS	GRAPHS	PHASES	SHAKES	STAIRS
CHANGS	ELATES	GRASPS	PHASIS	SHAKOS	STAKES
CHANTS	ENACTS	GRATES	PIANOS	SHALES	STALES
CHAPES	ENATES	GRATIS	PLACES	SHAMES	STALKS
CHARDS	EPACTS	GRAVES	PLACKS	SHAMUS	STALLS
CHARES	ERASES	GRAZES	PLAIDS	SHANKS	STAMPS
CHARMS	ETAPES	GUACOS	PLAINS	SHAPES	STANDS
CHARTS	EVADES	GUANOS	PLAITS	SHARDS	STAPES
CHASES	EXACTS	GUARDS	PLANES	SHARES	STARES
CHASMS	EXALTS	GUAVAS	PLANKS	SHARKS	STARTS
CLACKS	EYASES	HEARTS	PLANTS	SHARPS	STASES
CLAIMS	FEASES	HEATHS	PLASIS	SHAVES	STASIS
CLAMPS	FEASTS	HEAVES	PLATES	SHAWLS	STATES
CLANGS	FLACKS	HIATUS	PLAYAS	SHAWMS	STATUS
CLANKS	FLAILS	HOARDS	PLAZAS	SKALDS	STAVES
CLARAS	FLAIRS	HOAXES	PRANKS	SKATES	SWAGES
CLARES	FLAKES	HYADES	PRATES	SLACKS	SWAILS
CLAROS	FLAMES	ICARUS	PRAWNS	SLAKES	SWAINS
CLASPS	FLANKS	IMAGES	PRAXIS	SLANTS	SWALES
COASTS	FLARES	INARMS	PSALMS	SLATES	SWAMIS
COATIS	FLASKS	IRANIS	QUACKS	SLAVES	SWAMPS
COAXES	FLATUS	IRAQIS	QUAFFS	SMACKS	SWARDS
CRAALS	FLAXES	ISAACS	QUAILS	SMALLS	SWARMS
CRACKS	FRACAS	KAASES	QUAKES	SMARTS	SWATHS
CRAFTS	FRAILS	KHAKIS	QUALMS	SMAZES	TEASES
CRAIGS	FRAMES	KNACKS	QUANTS	SNACKS	THADYS
CRAKES	FRANCS	KNAVES	QUARKS	SNAFUS	THALES
CRAMPS	FRANKS	KOALAS	QUARTS	SNAILS	THAMES
CRANES	FRAUDS	KRAALS	REACTS	SNAKES	THANES
CRANKS	GHAUTS	KRAITS	REALES	SNARES	THANKS
CRAPES	GIANTS	LEARNS	REALMS	SNARLS	TIARAS
CRASIS	GLACES	LEASES	REARMS	SNATHS	TOASTS
CRATES	GLACIS	LEAVES	RIATAS	SPACES	TRACES
CRAVES	GLADES	LIANAS	ROALDS	SPADES	TRACKS
CRAWLS	GLADYS	LIANES	ROASTS	SPAHIS	TRACTS
CRAZES	GLAIRS	LLAMAS	SCALDS	SPAITS	TRADES
DEATHS	GLAMIS	LLANOS	SCALES	SPALLS	TRAGUS

TRAILS	******	DRAFFY	SHABBY	KABAYA	NABBED
TRAINS	--A--W	DRAFTY	SHAGGY	NEBULA	NIBBED
TRAITS	******	DRAWLY	SHAMMY	ROBBIA	NOBBED
TRAMPS	CRACOW	FEALTY	SHANDY	SABINA	RIBALD
TRAVES	MEADOW	FLABBY	SHANTY	******	RIBAND
TRAWLS	QUAPAW	FLAGGY	SLAGGY	--B--B	RIBBED
TSADES	REAVOW	FLASHY	SLANGY	******	ROBAND
TWANGS	SEACOW	FLATLY	SMARMY	COBWEB	ROBBED
UKASES	SHADOW	GHARRY	SNAGGY	HOBNOB	RUBBED
UPASES	******	GLADLY	SNAPPY	HUBBUB	SOBBED
URAEUS	--A--X	GLAIRY	SNARLY	SUBDEB	TABARD
URANUS		GLASSY	SNAZZY	SUBURB	TABBED
USAGES	SPADIX	GNARLY	SPARRY	******	TABLED
VIANDS	******	GRAINY	STABLY	--B--C	TUBBED
WEALDS	--A--Y	GRANNY	STAGEY	******	UNBEND
WEAVES		GRAPHY	STAGGY	FABRIC	UNBIND
WHACKS	******	GRASSY	STALKY	PUBLIC	UNBRED
WHALES	APATHY	GRAYLY	STARRY	RUBRIC	WEBBED
WHANGS	BEACHY	HEARTY	SWAMPY	******	
WHARFS	BEAUTY	HEATHY	SWANKY	--B--D	--B--E
WOALDS	BRACHY	ICALLY	SWARTY	******	******
WRACKS	BRAINY	KNARRY	TEAPOY	AMBLED	ALBITE
YEARNS	BRANDY	LEACHY	THADDY	BABIED	AMBAGE
YEASTS	BRANNY	LEANLY	TRACHY	BIBBED	ARBUTE
******	BRASHY	MEANLY	TRASHY	BOBBED	AUBADE
--A--T	BRASSY	MEASLY	TWANGY	CABLED	BABBIE
******	BRAWNY	NEARBY	USABLY	CEBOID	BABBLE
ARARAT	CHAFFY	NEARLY	WEAKLY	CUBBED	BABITE
AVAUNT	CHALKY	NEATLY	WHAMMY	CUBOID	BOBBIE
BRANDT	CHAMMY	OCASEY	WRATHY	DABBED	BOBBLE
CHALET	CHANCY	ORALLY	YEARLY	DIBBED	BUBBLE
CLARET	CHANTY	OVALLY	YEASTY	DUBBED	COBBLE
CRAVAT	CHARRY	PEACHY	******	FABLED	CUBAGE
FLAUNT	CHATTY	PEARLY	--A--Z	FIBBED	CYBELE
HEARST	CLAMMY	PEAVEY	******	FOBBED	DABBLE
IMARET	CLASSY	PLAGUY	JUAREZ	GABBED	DEBASE
LEARNT	CLAYEY	PLASHY	QUARTZ	GABLED	DEBATE
PEANUT	CRABBY	PLASTY	******	GIBBED	DEBBIE
PLACET	CRACKY	POACHY	--B--A	HYBRID	DIBBLE
PLAINT	CRAFTY	QUAGGY	******	IMBUED	EMBRUE
PLANET	CRAGGY	QUALMY	ALBATA	INBAND	GABBLE
QUAINT	CRANKY	QUARRY	ARBELA	INBRED	GOBBLE
TEAPOT	CRANNY	REALLY	CABALA	JABBED	HABILE
TEASET	CRAWLY	REALTY	CABANA	JIBBED	HOBBLE
THANAT	DEADLY	SCABBY	EUBOEA	JOBBED	IMBIBE
ZEALOT	DEAFLY	SCANTY	FIBULA	KOBOLD	IMBRUE
******	DEARLY	SCATTY	KABAKA	LOBBED	KIBBLE
--A--U	DEATHY	SEAWAY	KABALA	MOBBED	LABILE
******	DRABLY				
ACAJOU					
AMADOU					

LIBRAE	KIBLAH	BABOON	******	BABOOS	KABOBS
LOBATE	KIBOSH	BOBBIN	--B--P	BABULS	KIBEIS
LOBULE	TOBIAH	CABMAN	******	BIBLES	LABELS
MOBILE	WABASH	CABMEN	HUBCAP	BOBBYS	LABORS
NIBBLE	ZIBETH	DOBBIN	MOBCAP	BUBALS	LIBBYS
NOBBLE	******	DOBLON	******	BUBOES	LIBELS
NUBBLE	--B--I	DOBSON	--B--R	CABALS	LIBRAS
NUBILE	******	DUBBIN	******	CABINS	MABELS
PEBBLE	AMBARI	DUBLIN	AMBLER	CABLES	MOBIUS
RABBLE	ARBORI	FABIAN	ARBOUR	CABOBS	NABOBS
REBATE	EMBOLI	FIBRIN	BIBBER	CIBOLS	NUBIAS
REBORE	KABIKI	GABION	BOBBER	COBIAS	ORBITS
REBUKE	KABUKI	GIBBON	COBBER	COBLES	OXBOWS
RIBOSE	******	GIBRAN	DABBER	COBRAS	RABBIS
ROBBIE	--B--K	GIBSON	DEBTOR	CUBANS	RABIES
RUBACE	******	GOBLIN	DIBBER	CUBEBS	REBECS
RUBBLE	DEBARK	HEBRON	DOBBER	CUBITS	REBELS
SABINE	DEBUNK	INBORN	FABLER	DEBARS	REBUTS
SUBDUE	DYBBUK	LIBYAN	FIBBER	DEBBYS	ROBINS
SUBTLE	EMBANK	LUBLIN	GABBER	DEBITS	ROBLES
TIBIAE	EMBARK	NUBBIN	GIBBER	DEBRIS	ROBOTS
TUBATE	IMBARK	NUBIAN	JABBER	DEBUGS	RUBENS
TUBULE	LUBECK	OSBORN	JIBBER	DEBUTS	RUBIES
UMBRAE	REBECK	RABBIN	JOBBER	DOBIES	RUBLES
URBANE	ZEBECK	REBORN	LABOUR	DOBLAS	SABERS
WABBLE	******	RIBBON	LOBBER	DOBRAS	SABINS
WOBBLE	--B--L	ROBSON	LUBBER	ELBOWS	SABLES
******	******	SABEAN	MOBBER	ELBRUS	SABOTS
--B--F	FIBRIL	SUBORN	NOBLER	EMBARS	SABRAS
******	LABIAL	UNBORN	ROBBER	EMBAYS	SEBATS
REBUFF	NOBALL	******	RUBBER	EMBEDS	SIBYLS
******	REBILL	--B--O	SUBTER	EMBERS	SOBERS
--B--G	TIBIAL	******	TUBBER	EMBOSS	SUBAHS
******	UMBRAL	ALBEDO	UNBEAR	EMBOWS	SYBILS
COBURG	******	ALBINO	YABBER	FABLES	TABLES
CUBING	--B--M	BIBLIO	******	FIBERS	TABOOS
EBBING	******	EMBRYO	--B--S	GABLES	TABORS
GIBING	BABISM	GABBRO	******	GIBERS	TIBIAS
GOBANG	CUBISM	LIBIDO	ABBESS	GOBIES	TOBIAS
GYBING	EMBALM	REBATO	ABBEYS	HABEAS	TOBIES
JIBING	EMBLEM	REBOZO	ABBIES	HABITS	TUBERS
ORBING	ERBIUM	ROBALO	ABBOTS	HOBBES	UMBELS
ROBING	IMBALM	RUBATO	ALBUMS	HOBOES	UMBERS
TUBING	LABIUM	RUBIGO	AMBERS	HUBRIS	UMBLES
******	LABRUM	SUBITO	AMBITS	HYBRIS	UMBRAS
--B--H	******	TOBAGO	AMBLES	IMBEDS	UNBARS
******	--B--N	VIBRIO	ARBORS	IMBUES	UPBOWS
AMBUSH	ALBION		BABIES	JABOTS	WEBERS
JUBBAH	AUBURN				

XEBECS	******	******	LOCOED	COCKLE	MACULE
ZEBECS	--B--Y	--C--C	MOCKED	DECADE	MICKLE
ZEBRAS	******	******	MUCKED	DECANE	MUCKLE
ZIBETS	ABBACY	ALCAIC	MUCOID	DECARE	MUCOSE
******	ALBANY	ARCTIC	NECKED	DECIDE	MYCETE
--B--T	AMBARY	CYCLIC	NICHED	DECILE	NICENE
******	AMBERY	HECTIC	NICKED	DECKLE	NICOLE
ALBEIT	ASBURY	LACTIC	NOCKED	DECODE	NUCHAE
ALBERT	AUBREY	MICMAC	ORCHID	DECOKE	OOCYTE
BABIST	BUBBLY	PECTIC	PACKED	DECREE	OSCINE
BOBCAT	COBBLY	PICNIC	PECKED	DICKIE	OSCULE
CABLET	EMBODY	PICRIC	PICKED	DOCILE	PICKLE
COBALT	IMBODY	TACTIC	RACKED	ENCAGE	RACEME
COBNUT	NOBODY	******	RECORD	ENCASE	RACINE
CUBIST	NUBBLY	--C--D	RICKED	ENCODE	RECEDE
EGBERT	PEBBLY	******	ROCKED	ENCORE	RECIPE
ELBERT	SUBTLY	ACCORD	RUCKED	EOCENE	RECITE
GIBBET	SUBWAY	ARCHED	SACKED	ESCAPE	RECUSE
GIBLET	WABBLY	ARCKED	SACRED	EUCHRE	RICHIE
GOBBET	WOBBLY	ASCEND	SECOND	EXCIDE	ROCKNE
GOBLET	******	BACHED	SECUND	EXCISE	SECEDE
HOBART	--B--Z	BACKED	SICKED	EXCITE	SECURE
HUBERT	******	BECKED	SOCKED	EXCUSE	SICKLE
LABRET	KIBITZ	BUCKED	SOCRED	FACADE	SOCAGE
OSBERT	******	CACHED	SUCKED	FACILE	SUCKLE
RABBET	--C--A	COCCID	TACKED	FICKLE	TACKLE
RABBIT	******	COCKED	TICKED	FOCSLE	TICKLE
ROBERT	ANCONA	CYCLED	TUCKED	HACKEE	UNCAGE
ROBUST	ARCANA	DECKED	UNCLAD	HACKIE	UNCASE
SABBAT	BUCKRA	DOCKED	UNCORD	HACKLE	VACATE
SUBLET	CICADA	DUCKED	WICKED	HECATE	******
SUBMIT	CICALA	EMCEED	******	HECKLE	--C--G
TABLET	DECUMA	ETCHED	--C--E	HECKLE	******
TYBALT	ENCINA	EUCLID	******	HUCKLE	ARCING
UNBELT	FACULA	EXCEED	ACCEDE	INCAGE	DICING
UNBENT	FECULA	FECUND	ACCRUE	INCASE	FACING
UNBOLT	HECUBA	FUCOID	ACCUSE	INCISE	LACING
UPBEAT	ISCHIA	HACKED	ALCOVE	INCITE	MACING
******	JACANA	HOCKED	ANCONE	INCOME	PACING
--B--U	LACUNA	INCHED	ARCADE	INCUSE	RACING
******	LOCHIA	ITCHED	ARCANE	JACKIE	RICING
JABIRU	MACULA	JACKED	ARCHIE	JOCOSE	******
******	MUCOSA	JOCUND	BECAME	KECKLE	--C--H
--B--W	TACOMA	KECKED	BECOME	LICHEE	******
******	VACUNA	KICKED	BOCCIE	LOCALE	ENCASH
BYBLOW	VICUNA	LACKED	BUCKLE	LOCATE	******
HEBREW	******	LICKED	CACKLE	LUCILE	--C--I
	--C--B	LOCKED	CECILE	LUCITE	******
	******			MACKLE	INCUBI
	BICARB				NUCLEI

******	******	******	PICTOR	EXCELS	RUCHES
--C--K	**--C--N**	**--C--P**	PUCKER	EXCESS	RUCKUS
******	******	******	RACIER	FACERS	SOCLES
HICKOK	AACHEN	COCKUP	RACKER	FACETS	SUCRES
UNCOCK	ALCUIN	DECAMP	RECTOR	FACIES	SYCEES
UNCORK	ARCHON	ENCAMP	RICHER	FICHES	TICALS
******	BECKON	ESCARP	ROCKER	FICHUS	ULCERS
--C--L	BICORN	HICCUP	SACKER	FUCOUS	UNCAPS
******	BUCHAN	INCORP	SECPAR	GECKOS	UNCLES
AECIAL	COCAIN	LOCKUP	SECTOR	INCHES	VICARS
ARCHIL	COCHIN	MOCKUP	SICKER	INCURS	VICKYS
BUCCAL	COCOON	PICKUP	SOCCER	ITCHES	VOCALS
COCCAL	DACRON	RECOUP	SUCCOR	JACKYS	WICHES
DACTYL	DECCAN	******	SUCKER	JACOBS	YACHTS
DECKEL	DECERN	**--C--R**	TACKER	JOCKOS	YUCCAS
FACIAL	INCHON	******	TICKER	LACHES	******
FECIAL	KUCHEN	ANCHOR	TUCKER	LOCALS	**--C--T**
JACKAL	LICHEN	ARCHER	VECTOR	LUCIAS	******
LACIAL	LUCIAN	BACKER	VICTOR	LUCIUS	ACCENT
MICELL	LUCIEN	BICKER	WICKER	LYCEES	ACCEPT
MICHEL	MACRON	BUCKER	******	MACAWS	ACCOST
NICKEL	MECCAN	COCKER	**--C--S**	MACERS	ALCOTT
ORCHIL	MICRON	CYCLER	******	MACLES	ASCENT
RACHEL	ORCEIN	DECKER	ACCESS	MCCOYS	BECKET
RACIAL	PECTEN	DICKER	ARCHES	MECCAS	BUCKET
RECALL	PECTIN	DOCKER	ARCHYS	MICKYS	CACHET
RECOIL	RACOON	DOCTOR	ASCOTS	MICKYS	DACOIT
RECTAL	RECKON	DUCKER	BACHES	MUCOUS	DECANT
RICTAL	SECERN	ESCHAR	BECKYS	NICHES	DECEIT
SACRAL	SICKEN	ESCHER	BICEPS	NICKYS	DECENT
SECKEL	SOCMAN	ETCHER	CACAOS	OCCURS	DECOCT
SOCIAL	SOCMEN	EUCHER	CACHES	ORCHIS	DICAST
UNCIAL	TOCSIN	FACTOR	CACTUS	OSCANS	DOCENT
UNCOIL	TUCHUN	HACKER	CECILS	OSCARS	DOCKET
UNCURL	TUCSON	HECTOR	COCCUS	PACERS	ENCYST
******	TYCOON	KICKER	COCOAS	PECANS	ESCENT
--C--M	URCHIN	LACIER	CYCADS	PICOTS	ESCORT
******	ZECHIN	LECHER	CYCLES	PICULS	EXCEPT
BECALM	******	LECTOR	DACHAS	RACERS	GOCART
DICTUM	**--C--O**	LICTOR	DECALS	RACHIS	INCEPT
FACTUM	******	LOCKER	DECAYS	RECAPS	INCEST
LACTAM	ARCHEO	MOCKER	DECORS	RECESS	JACKET
LYCEUM	CICERO	MUCKER	DECOYS	RECTOS	LOCKET
RACISM	CUCKOO	NECTAR	DICERS	RECTUS	LOCUST
RECTUM	ESCUDO	NICKER	DUCATS	RECURS	LUCENT
SACHEM	MACACO	PACKER	ECCLES	RICERS	NICEST
SACRUM	ORCHIO	PECKER	EMCEES	RICHES	NOCENT
VACUUM	ROCOCO	PICKER	ETCHES	RICKYS	OCCULT
VICTIM	TECHNO			RICTUS	

PACKET	LACKEY	******	ALDINE	REDEYE	JADISH
PICKET	MICKEY	--D--D	ALDOSE	REDONE	JUDITH
POCKET	NICELY	******	AUDILE	REDUCE	KEDDAH
RACIST	NICETY	ADDEND	BODICE	RIDDLE	MODISH
RACKET	OCCUPY	ADDLED	BUDDLE	RUDDLE	OLDISH
RECANT	PACIFY	BADGED	BUDGIE	SADDLE	RADISH
RECAST	RACILY	BEDDED	CADDIE	SEDATE	******
RECENT	RICHLY	BEDRID	CODDLE	SEDILE	--D--I
RECEPT	RICKEY	BODIED	CUDDIE	SEDUCE	******
ROCHET	SICILY	BUDDED	CUDDLE	TODDLE	ANDREI
ROCKET	SICKLY	BUDGED	DADDLE	UNDINE	MEDICI
SACHET	TACKEY	CADGED	DEDUCE	UNDONE	PEDATI
SECANT	WICOPY	DODGED	DIDDLE	UPDATE	******
SECRET	******	EDDIED	ENDIVE	UPDIKE	--D--K
SOCKET	--D--A	ELDRED	ENDURE	VADOSE	******
TICKET	******	ENDUED	FIDDLE	WADDLE	BEDECK
TUCKET	ANDREA	FUDGED	FUDDLE	WEDGIE	KODIAK
UPCAST	BODEGA	GADDED	HEDDLE	WIDDIE	NUDNIK
VACANT	BUDDHA	GADOID	HUDDLE	******	PODUNK
WICKET	CEDULA	HEDGED	******	--D--G	******
******	CODEIA	INDEED	--D--G	******	--D--L
--C--U	DODECA	INDUED	INDENE	ADDING	******
******	EIDOLA	JUDGED	INDITE	AIDING	CUDGEL
CACHOU	FEDORA	KEDGED	INDUCE	BEDBUG	ENDALL
DACHAU	GODIVA	KIDDED	IODATE	BIDING	HEDRAL
******	INDABA	LADLED	IODIDE	BODING	MEDIAL
--C--W	JUDAEA	LIDDED	IODINE	CEDING	ORDEAL
******	LADOGA	LODGED	IODIZE	CODING	PODSOL
ESCHEW	MADURA	MADDED	KIDDIE	ENDING	PODZOL
ESCROW	MEDUSA	MADRID	LADDIE	FADING	RADIAL
******	OEDEMA	MUDDED	MADAME	HADING	VIDUAL
--C--X	RADULA	NODDED	MEDDLE	HEDWIG	******
******	REDOWA	NUDGED	MEDIAE	HIDING	--D--M
COCCYX	******	OGDOAD	MIDDLE	JADING	******
PICKAX	--D--B	PADDED	MODULE	LADING	BEDLAM
******	******	PODDED	MUDDLE	LUDWIG	GODDAM
--C--Y	BEDAUB	REDBUD	NADINE	NIDING	INDIUM
******	MIDRIB	RIDDED	NODDLE	REDBUG	IODISM
ARCHLY	ODDJOB	RIDGED	NODOSE	REDDOG	MEDIUM
BACONY	******	SIDLED	NODULE	RIDING	NUDISM
CECILY	--D--C	SODDED	ORDURE	SIDING	OLDHAM
CICELY	******	TEDDED	PADDLE	TIDING	PODIUM
DECURY	CEDRIC	TIDIED	PEDATE	WADING	RADIUM
DICKEY	EDDAIC	WADDED	PEDDLE	******	REDEEM
HICKEY	HYDRIC	WEDDED	PIDDLE	--D--H	REDGUM
HOCKEY	JUDAIC	WEDGED	PUDDLE	******	SADISM
JOCKEY	VEDIAC	******	RADDLE	DUDISH	SODIUM
LACILY	ZODIAC	--D--E	RADOME	EDDISH	TEDIUM
		******	REDDLE		
		ADDUCE			
		AEDILE			

******	JUDAEO	SADDER	INDIES	TODIES	******
--D--N	LADINO	SIDDUR	INDOWS	UDDERS	--D--W
******	MADURO	SIDLER	INDRIS	UNDIES	******
AIDMAN	MEDICO	TEDDER	INDUES	UNDOES	ANDREW
AIDMEN	SIDERO	TIDIER	IODOUS	VODKAS	LUDLOW
ANDEAN	******	UNDOER	JUDAHS	WADERS	UNDRAW
BADMAN	--D--P	******	JUDGES	WADIES	UNDREW
BADMEN	******	--D--S	KEDGES	WEDGES	******
BEDPAN	KIDNAP	******	KODAKS	WIDENS	--D--Y
BEDUIN	MADCAP	ADDAMS	LADIES	WIDOWS	******
BIDDEN	MADEUP	ADDERS	LADLES	WIDTHS	AUDREY
BODKIN	MUDCAP	ADDLES	LEDGES	YODELS	BODILY
CODEIN	REDCAP	AIDERS	LODGES	******	CODIFY
DUDEEN	REDTOP	ALDERS	LYDIAS	--D--T	CUDDLY
FADEIN	******	ALDOUS	MADAMS	******	DUDLEY
GIDEON	--D--R	ANDRES	MADGES	ABDUCT	GADFLY
GODSON	******	ARDEBS	MADRAS	ADDICT	KIDNEY
GODWIN	ARDOUR	ARDORS	MEDALS	ADDUCT	MEDLEY
HEDRON	BADGER	AUDADS	MEDICS	ARDENT	MEDWAY
HIDDEN	BEDDER	AUDITS	MIDGES	BEDSIT	MIDDAY
HODDEN	BIDDER	BADGES	MODELS	BUDGET	MIDWAY
HODMAN	BUDDER	BEDEWS	NADIRS	CADENT	MODIFY
HUDSON	CADGER	BEDIMS	NUDGES	DEDUCT	NIDIFY
INDIAN	CODDER	BIDETS	OODLES	ELDEST	NUDELY
JUDEAN	CODGER	BODIES	ORDERS	FIDGET	NUDITY
KEDRON	DODDER	BUDGES	PADDYS	GADGET	ODDITY
MADDEN	DODGER	CADDIS	PADRES	GODWIT	PUDDLY
MADMAN	ENDEAR	CADETS	PEDALS	INDENT	REDBAY
MADMEN	EUDOAR	CADGES	PEDROS	INDICT	RODNEY
MEDIAN	FODDER	CADMUS	PODOUS	INDUCT	RUDELY
MIDDEN	GADDER	CADRES	RADARS	INDULT	SIDNEY
MODERN	HEDGER	CEDARS	RADIOS	MIDGET	SODOMY
ORDAIN	INDOOR	CIDERS	RADIUS	MIDGUT	SUDARY
PIDGIN	JUDGER	DADOES	REDANS	MODEST	SYDNEY
RADIAN	KIDDER	DEDANS	REDOES	NUDIST	TIDILY
REDDEN	LADDER	DIDIES	RIDERS	ODDEST	UNDULY
REDFIN	LADLER	DIDOES	RIDGES	OLDEST	WADDLY
RIDDEN	LEDGER	DODGES	RODDYS	PEDANT	WIDELY
RODMAN	LODGER	DODOES	RODEOS	REDACT	******
RODMEN	MADDER	EDDIES	SADHUS	REDHOT	--E--A
SADDEN	MEDLAR	ELDERS	SADIES	RIDENT	******
SODDEN	MIDAIR	ENDOWS	SEDANS	RODENT	ACEDIA
SUDDEN	MUDDER	ENDUES	SEDERS	RUDEST	AGENDA
WEDELN	NODDER	FUDGES	SEDGES	SADIST	ALEXIA
******	PEDLAR	HEDGES	SEDUMS	TIDBIT	AMELIA
--D--O	RADNOR	HIDERS	SIDLES	UNDSET	AMENRA
******	REDDER	HYDRAS	TEDDYS	WADSET	ANEMIA
DIDERO	RUDDER	HYDROS	TIDIES	WIDEST	AREOLA
INDIGO					

AVESTA	CHEBEC	NEEDED	BEETLE	PLEASE	FEEING
AYESHA	CLERIC	OBEYED	BIERCE	PLEDGE	GEEING
BREGMA	CRETIC	OPENED	BLENDE	PREVUE	HIEING
BRENDA	EDENIC	OXEYED	BREEZE	SEETHE	HOEING
CAEOMA	EMERIC	PEEKED	BYEBYE	SHEAVE	JEEING
CREUSA	EMETIC	PEELED	CHEESE	SHELVE	LIEBIG
CUESTA	GAELIC	PEENED	CHEGOE	SIECLE	RUEING
DUENNA	IPECAC	PEEPED	CHELAE	SLEAVE	SEEING
EGERIA	IRENIC	PEERED	CHEQUE	SLEDGE	STENOG
EGESTA	LUETIC	PEEVED	CLEAVE	SLEEVE	TEEING
EJECTA	NOETIC	PIECED	CLEOME	SNEEZE	TOEING
ETERNA	POETIC	PLEIAD	COERCE	SPECIE	******
EXEDRA	PYEMIC	PREMED	CREASE	STEEVE	--E--H
FIESTA	QUEBEC	PREYED	CREATE	STELAE	******
GRETNA	SCENIC	QUEUED	CRECHE	STEPPE	AWEIGH
HUELVA	STELIC	REEDED	CREESE	STEVIE	BLEACH
IBERIA	STERIC	REEFED	CREOLE	SVELTE	BLENCH
LUELLA	THETIC	REEKED	DIEPPE	SWERVE	BREACH
ODESSA	URETIC	REELED	DREDGE	TEETHE	BREATH
OMENTA	******	REEVED	EMERGE	THEBAE	BREECH
ONEIDA	--E--D	SEEDED	EMERIE	THECAE	CHETAH
PLEGIA	******	SEEMED	EMEUTE	THENCE	CLENCH
PLEURA	AGEOLD	SEEPED	FAERIE	TIERCE	DRENCH
PNEUMA	BEEFED	SHEILD	FAEROE	TREBLE	FLENCH
PYEMIA	BEEPED	SHEWED	FEEBLE	TSETSE	FLETCH
SHEILA	BREWED	SIEGED	FIERCE	TWELVE	FRENCH
SHERPA	CHEWED	SIEVED	FLECHE	ULENCE	PLEACH
SIENNA	CLERID	SKEWED	FLEDGE	UNEASE	PREACH
SIERRA	CLEWED	SLEWED	FLEECE	UREASE	QUENCH
SIESTA	COELED	SPEWED	FLENSE	UREIDE	SHEATH
STELLA	CREPED	STEWED	FREEZE	WEENIE	SHEIKH
STERNA	DEEDED	TEEMED	GOETHE	WHEEZE	SKETCH
TAENIA	DEEMED	THEWED	GREASE	WHENCE	SLEIGH
THELMA	DIETED	TIERED	GREAVE	WHERVE	SLEUTH
UREMIA	DUELED	VEERED	GREECE	WIENIE	SPEECH
VIENNA	EVENED	VIEWED	GREENE	******	STENCH
******	EYELID	WEEDED	GREIGE	--E--F	TRENCH
--E--B	FEEZED	******	ICEAXE	******	WREATH
******	FLEXED	--E--E	IDEATE	ONEOFF	WRENCH
CHERUB	FOETID	******	LIERNE	SHERIF	WRETCH
PREFAB	FUELED	AMEBAE	NEEDLE	--E--G	******
******	HEEDED	AMECHE	NOELLE	******	--E--I
--E--C	HEELED	AMELIE	ODETTE	******	******
******	JEERED	AMERCE	OLEATE	AGEING	AMENTI
ACERIC	KEELED	AVENGE	OREIDE	AWEING	NIELLI
ACETIC	KEENED	AVENUE	PEEWEE	DYEING	OCELLI
AMEBIC	LEERED	AVERSE	PIERCE	EKEING	STELLI
ANEMIC	MAENAD	AYEAYE	PIERRE	EYEING	

******	AXEMAN	NIELLO	LIEDER	AGENTS	CREELS
--E--L	AXEMEN	ONEIRO	MEEKER	AKENES	CREEPS
******	BREMEN	OVERDO	MEETER	ALEPHS	CREMES
ACETAL	BRETON	PIETRO	NEEDER	ALERTS	CREPES
ACETYL	CRETAN	PLEURO	OBEYER	ALEUTS	CRESTS
CHERYL	CRETIN	PNEUMO	OPENER	ALEXIS	CREVAS
COEVAL	CRETON	PRESTO	PEEKER	AMEBAS	DIESES
CREDAL	DAEMON	PSEUDO	PEELER	AMENDS	DIESIS
CRENEL	DEEPEN	PUEBLO	PEEPER	AMENTS	DREADS
CRESOL	DEEWAN	REECHO	PIECER	APEXES	DREAMS
CREWEL	ELEVEN	SPERMO	PIETER	ARECAS	DWELLS
DAEDAL	ELEVON	STEREO	PLEXOR	ARENAS	ECESIS
DIESEL	EMETIN	STERNO	PREFER	ARETES	EGESTS
DIETAL	EVELYN	STETHO	PRETER	AVERTS	EJECTS
EYEFUL	FOEMAN	THERMO	PRETOR	AVERYS	ELECTS
FAECAL	FOEMEN	UNESCO	PREWAR	BEEVES	ELEMIS
FOETAL	GUENON	******	PREYER	BLEAKS	ELENAS
GRETEL	ICEMAN	**--E--P**	REEFER	BLEARS	EMEERS
HAEMAL	ICEMEN	******	REEKER	BLEATS	EMENDS
HIEMAL	MYELIN	EYECUP	REELER	BLEEDS	EMESIS
HYETAL	OBERON	ICECAP	RHETOR	BLENDS	ENEMAS
IREFUL	OLEFIN	STEPUP	SEEDER	BREADS	EREBUS
ONEILL	OREGAN	TOECAP	SEEKER	BREAKS	ERECTS
PHENOL	OREGON	******	SEEMER	BREAMS	EVENTS
PHENYL	PIEMAN	**--E--R**	SHEWER	BREEDS	EVERTS
PIENAL	PIEMEN	******	SKEWER	BREEKS	EXERTS
RUEFUL	QUEZON	ALEGAR	SOEVER	BRENTS	FAECES
SHEKEL	STEFAN	BREWER	STELAR	BREVES	FEEZES
STEROL	STEPAN	CAESAR	TEEMER	BREWIS	FIELDS
THECAL	STEPIN	CHEWER	TEETER	CHEATS	FIENDS
THENAL	STEVEN	CLEVER	THENAR	CHECKS	FLEAMS
USEFUL	SWEDEN	DEEPER	TREMOR	CHEEKS	FLECKS
WEEVIL	TIEPIN	DIETER	TREVOR	CHEEPS	FLEERS
WOEFUL	TREPAN	DUELER	URETER	CHEERS	FLEETS
******	UNEVEN	EXETER	VIEWER	CHELAS	FLEXES
--E--M	******	FEEDER	WEEDER	CHEOPS	FOEHNS
******	**--E--O**	FEELER	WEEPER	CHESTS	FOETUS
ACEIUM	******	FLEXOR	WEEVER	CLEANS	FREAKS
ACETUM	ALECTO	FOETOR	WIENER	CLEARS	FREDAS
CAECUM	ALEPPO	FUELER	******	CLEATS	FREONS
COELOM	AREZZO	GEEZER	**--E--S**	CLEFTS	GLEAMS
FRENUM	AVERNO	GHEBER	******	CLERKS	GLEANS
PLENUM	CHEILO	HEEDER	ABELES	CLEVIS	GLEBES
PRELIM	CHEIRO	HEELER	ACEOUS	CREAKS	GLEDES
THEISM	DUELLO	JAEGER	ADEEMS	CREAMS	GLEETS
******	FRESCO	JEERER	ADENIS	CREDOS	GNEISS
--E--N	FRESNO	KEENER	ADEPTS	CREEDS	GREATS
******	GHETTO	KEEPER	AEETES	CREEKS	GREBES
ALEXIN					
APEMAN					

GREEDS	REEVES	SWEARS	CREDIT	CHESTY	SHELTY
GREEKS	RHEIMS	SWEATS	DOESNT	CHEVVY	SHERRY
GREENS	RHESUS	SWEDES	DREAMT	CLERGY	SKERRY
GREETS	SCENDS	SWEEPS	ELEGIT	CREAKY	SLEAZY
GREGOS	SCENES	SWEETS	EVERET	CREAMY	SLEEKY
GREIFS	SCENTS	SWELLS	EXEMPT	CREASY	SLEEPY
GRETAS	SHEÁRS	THEBES	EXEUNT	CREEPY	SLEETY
GUESTS	SHEENS	THEDAS	EYELET	DEEPLY	SMEARY
GWENNS	SHEEPS	THEFTS	EYEOUT	DREAMY	SMELLY
HYENAS	SHEERS	THEIRS	FREEST	DREARY	SNEAKY
IBEAMS	SHEETS	THEMES	ISEULT	DREGGY	SNEEZY
IBEXES	SHEIKS	THEMIS	OCELOT	DRESSY	SPEEDY
IDEALS	SHELLS	THERMS	OMELET	ENERGY	SPERRY
ILEXES	SHERDS	THESES	PEEWIT	EVENLY	STEADY
IRENES	SIEGES	THESIS	REEDIT	EXEQUY	STEAMY
KEEVES	SIEURS	THETAS	SHEBAT	FEEBLY	STEELY
KNEADS	SIEVES	THETIS	THEIST	FLEDGY	SWEATY
KNEELS	SKEANS	TIEINS	******	FLEECY	SWEENY
KNELLS	SKEINS	TIEUPS	--E--U	FLESHY	SWEEPY
LIEGES	SLEEKS	TREADS	******	FLEURY	TEENSY
NAEVUS	SLEEPS	TREATS	ARERCU	FREAKY	THEORY
NIECES	SLEETS	TRENDS	******	FREDDY	TREATY
NOESIS	SMEARS	TWEAKS	--E--W	FREELY	TRENDY
OBELUS	SMELLS	TWEEDS	******	FRENZY	TRESSY
OCEANS	SMELTS	TWEETS	HEEHAW	FRETTY	TWEAKY
OMEGAS	SNEAKS	TWERPS	SEESAW	GLEAMY	TWENTY
OPERAS	SNEERS	ULEMAS	******	GLEETY	UNEASY
OREADS	SNELLS	UPENDS	--E--X	GREASY	WEEKLY
OXEYES	SPEAKS	UTERUS	******	GREEDY	WEENSY
PAEANS	SPEARS	WHEALS	ICEBOX	KEENLY	WHEEZY
PAEONS	SPECKS	WHEATS	PREFIX	LEEWAY	WHELKY
PEEVES	SPEEDS	WHEELS	******	MEEKLY	WHERRY
PIECES	SPEISS	WHELKS	--E--Y	MEETLY	WHEYEY
PIERUS	SPELLS	WHELMS	******	OHENRY	WIELDY
PLEADS	SPENDS	WHELPS	AGEDLY	ONEWAY	******
PLEATS	STEAKS	WIELDS	AGENCY	OPENLY	--F--A
PLEBES	STEALS	WREAKS	ANERGY	OVERLY	******
PLEXUS	STEAMS	WRECKS	APEPSY	PAEONY	RAFFIA
PRECIS	STEEDS	WRESTS	AWEARY	PLENTY	******
PREENS	STEELS	YIELDS	BEECHY	POETRY	--F--D
PRESAS	STEEPS	******	BLEARY	PREPAY	******
QUEANS	STEERS	--E--T	BLEBBY	PRETTY	AFFORD
QUEENS	STEINS	******	BLENNY	QUEASY	ALFRED
QUEERS	STELES	BREAST	BREEZY	RHEUMY	BAFFED
QUELLS	STERES	BRECHT	CHEEKY	SEEMLY	BIFFED
QUERNS	STERNS	BREVET	CHEERY	SHEENY	BIFOLD
QUESTS	STEVES	CLEIST	CHEESY	SHELBY	BUFFED
QUEUES	SUEDES	COEMPT	CHERRY	SHELLY	CUFFED

DEFEND	MUFFLE	DEFORM	ZAFFAR	******	******
DEFIED	OFFICE	INFIRM	ZAFFER	--F--X	--G--C
DOFFED	PIFFLE	INFORM	ZAFFIR	******	******
DUFFED	RAFFLE	REFORM	******	AFFLUX	ANGLIC
ENFOLD	REFACE	SUFISM	--F--S	BIFLEX	COGNAC
GAFFED	REFINE	******	******	EFFLUX	******
GIFTED	REFUGE	--F--N	ALFONS	INFLUX	--G--D
HAFTED	REFUSE	******	BEFITS	REFLEX	ALGOID
HEFTED	REFUTE	BAFFIN	BEFOGS	REFLUX	ANGLED
HUFFED	RIFFLE	BIFFIN	DEFERS	SUFFIX	ARGUED
ILFORD	RUFFLE	BOFFIN	DEFIES	******	ASGARD
INFOLD	TOFFEE	CAFTAN	ELFINS	--F--Y	AUGEND
LIFTED	WAFFLE	COFFIN	FIFERS	******	BAGDAD
LOFTED	ZAFFRE	KAFTAN	FIFTHS	AFFRAY	BAGGED
LUFFED	******	MUFFIN	GAFFES	DAFTLY	BEGGED
MIFFED	--F-G	PUFFIN	INFERS	DEFRAY	BEGIRD
MUFFED	******	SOFTEN	LIFERS	DEFTLY	BOGGED
OFFEND	FIFING	TEFLON	MUFTIS	EFFIGY	BUGGED
OXFORD	OFFING	TIFFIN	OFFERS	INFAMY	BUGLED
PUFFED	ZAFTIG	******	REFERS	OFFDAY	COGGED
RAFTED	******	--F--O	REFITS	SAFELY	DIGGED
REFUND	--F--H	******	RIFLES	SAFETY	DOGGED
RIFLED	******	INFERO	RUFOUS	SOFTLY	ENGIRD
RIFTED	ELFISH	******	SOFTAS	WIFELY	FAGEND
RUFFED	OAFISH	--F--R	WAFERS	******	FAGGED
SIFTED	OFFISH	******	******	--G--A	FIGGED
TIFFED	******	AFFAIR	--F--T	******	FOGGED
TUFTED	--F--I	BUFFER	******	ANGELA	FUGLED
UNFOLD	******	COFFER	AFFECT	ANGINA	GAGGED
WAFTED	ALFAKI	DEFIER	BUFFET	ANGLIA	GIGGED
******	SAFARI	DEFTER	DEFEAT	ANGOLA	HAGGED
--F--E	******	DIFFER	DEFECT	ANGORA	HOGGED
******	--F--L	DOFFER	EFFECT	ARGALA	HUGGED
BAFFLE	******	DUFFER	EFFORT	BOGOTA	INGRID
BEFORE	BEFALL	FAFNIR	ERFURT	DAGOBA	JAGGED
COFFEE	BEFELL	GAFFER	INFANT	HEGIRA	JIGGED
COFFLE	BEFOOL	GOFFER	INFECT	HYGEIA	JOGGED
DEFACE	BEFOUL	KAFFIR	INFEST	LIGULA	JUGGED
DEFAME	DUFFEL	LIFTER	OFFSET	LOGGIA	LAGGED
DEFILE	EIFFEL	LOFTER	REFLET	NAGANA	LEGEND
DEFINE	ONFALL	PUFFER	REFOOT	NAGOYA	LEGGED
DEFUSE	REFILL	RAFTER	SAFEST	ORGANA	LIGAND
DUFFLE	REFUEL	RIFLER	SOFFIT	PAGODA	LOGGED
EFFACE	UNFURL	SIFTER	TUFFET	REGINA	LUGGED
EFFETE	******	SOFTER	******	UNGULA	MUGGED
EFFUSE	--F--M	SUFFER	--F--W	VAGINA	NAGGED
ENFACE	AFFIRM	UNFAIR	******	ZYGOMA	NOGOOD
INFUSE	BIFORM	WAFTER	GUFFAW		
			INFLOW		

PEGGED	JIGGLE	URGING	LAGOON	DAGMAR	AUGHTS
PIGGED	JOGGLE	WAGING	LEGION	DIGGER	AUGURS
PUGGED	JUGATE	WIGWAG	LEGMAN	DOGEAR	BAGASS
RAGGED	JUGGLE	ZIGZAG	LEGMEN	DOGGER	BAGELS
REGARD	LAGUNE	******	LIGNIN	EDGIER	BEGETS
RIGGED	LEGATE	--G--H	LOGION	GAGGER	BEGINS
ROGUED	LEGREE	******	MIGNON	HIGHER	BEGUMS
RUGGED	LEGUME	EIGHTH	NOGGIN	JAGUAR	BIGHTS
SAGGED	LIGATE	******	PIGEON	JIGGER	BIGOTS
SIGHED	LIGULE	--G--I	PIGGIN	JOGGER	BOGANS
SIGNED	LIGURE	******	PIGPEN	KEGLER	BOGEYS
SIGRID	MAGGIE	ARGALI	RAGLAN	LAGGER	BOGIES
TAGGED	MAGPIE	DIGITI	RAGMAN	LOGGER	BOGLES
TOGAED	MIGGLE	******	RAGMEN	LOGIER	BUGLES
TOGGED	NEGATE	--G--K	REGAIN	LUGGER	CIGARS
TUGGED	NIGGLE	******	REGION	MAGYAR	CYGNUS
UNGIRD	PIGGIE	BOGOAK	TEGMEN	MUGGAR	DEGUMS
UTGARD	PUGREE	******	WAGGON	MUGGER	DIGITS
WAGGED	REGALE	--G--L	WIGEON	MUGGUR	DOGIES
WIGGED	REGGIE	******	******	NAGGER	DOGMAS
******	REGIME	ARGYLL	--G--O	NIGGER	EAGLES
--G--E	RUGATE	JUGFUL		NIGHER	EDGARS
******	RUGOSE	MIGUEL	ANGELO	RIGGER	EGGARS
ARGIVE	TOGGLE	REGNAL	BAGNIO	RIGOUR	EGGERS
AUGITE	WAGGLE	SIGNAL	GIGOLO	RUGGER	EIGHTS
BEGONE	WIGGLE	UNGUAL	LEGATO	SAGGAR	ENGELS
BIGONE	ZYGOTE	******	MEGALO	SAGGER	FAGOTS
BOGGLE	******	--G--M	ORGANO	SAGIER	FIGHTS
BYGONE	--G--F	******	RIGHTO	SEGGAR	FOGIES
DAGGLE	******	ENGRAM	VAGINO	SIGNER	FUGIOS
DEGAGE	ENGULF	LIGNUM	******	SIGNOR	FUGLES
DEGAME	INGULF	LOGJAM	--G--P	TAGGER	FUGUES
DEGREE	******	MAGNUM	******	VAGUER	GAGERS
DOGAPE	--G--G	MEGRIM	EGGCUP	VIGOUR	GIGUES
DOGGIE	******	ORGASM	MEGILP	WAGNER	HAGGIS
ENGAGE	BIGWIG	POGROM	PEGTOP	******	HOGANS
ENGINE	CAGING	WIGWAM	******	--G--S	HUGHES
EOGENE	DUGONG	******	--G--R	******	INGOTS
ERGATE	EDGING	--G--N	******	AEGEUS	INGRES
EUGENE	EGGING	******	ANGKOR	AGGERS	LAGERS
FIGURE	EGGNOG	AEGEAN	ANGLER	ALGOUS	LEGERS
GAGGLE	FOGDOG	AFGHAN	ARGUER	ANGELS	LIGHTS
GIGGLE	GAGING	AUGEAN	BEGGAR	ANGERS	LUGERS
GOGGLE	PAGING	BAGMAN	BIGGER	ANGLES	MAGOTS
HAGGLE	PEGLEG	BAGMEN	BUGGER	ARGALS	MEGASS
HIGGLE	RAGBAG	BEGUIN	BUGLER	ARGOTS	MOGULS
HOGTIE	RAGING	BIGGIN	CAGIER	ARGUES	NIGELS
HUGHIE	RAGTAG	HAGDON	DAGGER	AUGERS	NIGHTS

ORGANS	GIGLET	LEGACY	ASHORE	TAHITI	CAHIER
ORGIES	GIGLOT	MAGUEY	ATHENE	WAHABI	COHEIR
PAGANS	GOGLET	MIGHTY	ATHOME	YEHUDI	ECHOER
PEGGYS	HAGBUT	NIGHTY	AWHILE	******	FUHRER
PIGNUS	HOGNUT	PIGSTY	BEHAVE	--H--K	ISHTAR
POGIES	HUGEST	PUGGRY	BEHOVE	******	MAHLER
REGIUS	INGEST	RAGDAY	COHERE	MOHAWK	MOHAIR
RIGHTS	LEGIST	SAGELY	COHUNE	MOHOCK	REHEAR
RIGORS	MAGGOT	SUGARY	ETHANE	SCHICK	UNHAIR
ROGERS	MAGNET	VAGARY	EXHALE	UNHOOK	******
ROGUES	NUGGET	WAGGLY	EXHUME	UNHUSK	--H--S
RUGOUS	ORGEAT	WIGGLY	INHALE	******	******
SIGHTS	PIGLET	******	INHERE	--H--L	ABHORS
SIGILS	PIGNUT	--H--A	INHUME	******	APHIDS
SIGMAS	RAGOUT	******	LAHORE	AWHEEL	ATHENS
SUGARS	REGENT	ACHAEA	MOHAVE	AWHIRL	BAHAIS
TIGERS	REGLET	ACHAIA	MOHOLE	INHAUL	ECHOES
TIGHTS	REGRET	APHTHA	OPHITE	SCHOOL	EPHAHS
TIGRIS	SAGEST	ATHENA	OXHIDE	SCHORL	EPHODS
TOGUES	SIGNET	BAHAMA	RRHAGE	UPHILL	EPHORS
UNGUES	UNGIRT	DAHLIA	SCHEME	******	ETHANS
UNGUIS	URGENT	ITHACA	SPHENE	--H--M	ETHELS
VIGILS	YOGURT	SAHARA	SPHERE	******	ETHERS
VOGUES	******	SCHEMA	UPHROE	SCHISM	ETHICS
VOGULS	--G--W	******	WAHINE	******	ETHYLS
WAGERS	******	--H--B	******	--H--N	JIHADS
WAGONS	FOGBOW	******	--H--F	******	LEHUAS
WIGANS	JIGSAW	MAHBUB	******	ASHCAN	MOHURS
YAGERS	******	******	******	ASHMAN	NAHUMS
YOGEES	--G--X	--H--C	BEHALF	ASHMEN	OCHERS
YOGINS	******	******	BEHOOF	DAHOON	OTHERS
******	DOGFOX	ECHOIC	******	DEHORN	PSHAWS
--G--T	MAGNOX	ETHNIC	--H--G	JOHANN	SAHEBS
******	******	******	******	UNHEWN	SAHIBS
AIGLET	--G--Y	--H--D	ACHING	******	SCHMOS
ARGENT	******	******	******	--H--O	SCHUSS
AUGUST	ANGARY	BEHEAD	--H--H	******	SCHWAS
BEGIRT	ARGOSY	BEHELD	******	ECHINO	TEHEES
COGENT	ARGUFY	BEHIND	COHOSH	SCHIZO	UNHATS
CYGNET	AUGURY	BEHOLD	REHASH	SPHENO	USHERS
DEGUST	BIGAMY	ECHARD	YAHVEH	STHENO	WAHOOS
DIGEST	CAGILY	ECHOED	YAHWEH	******	YAHOOS
DIGLOT	COGWAY	TEHEED	******	--H--P	******
DUGOUT	DIGAMY	UNHAND	--H--I	UNHASP	--H--T
EAGLET	EIGHTY	UPHELD	******	******	******
ENGIRT	GIGGLY	UPHOLD	BIHARI	--H--R	AGHAST
FAGGOT	HIGHLY	******	ECHINI	******	BEHEST
GIGANT	HUGELY	--H--E	EPHEBI	ASHIER	CAHOOT
		******	EPHORI	ASHLAR	
		ACHENE			
		ADHERE			

COHORT	******	GAINED	SPIKED	EMILIE	TUILLE
EXHORT	--I--C	GAITED	SPILED	ENISLE	TWINGE
MAHOUT	******	GLIDED	SPIRED	EVINCE	UNIQUE
REHEAT	ACIDIC	GRIDED	SPITED	FAILLE	WRITHE
SCHIST	ADIPIC	GRIMED	SUITED	FEIGNE	******
SCHUIT	AMIDIC	GRIPED	SWIPED	FOIBLE	--I--F
TSHIRT	CLINIC	GUIDED	TAILED	FRIDGE	******
UNHURT	CRITIC	HAILED	TOILED	FRIEZE	UNICEF
******	DEIFIC	HAIRED	TRICED	FRINGE	******
--H--X	EXILIC	IRISED	TRIFID	GOITRE	--I--G
******	IRIDIC	JAILED	TRINED	GRIEVE	******
SPHINX	IRITIC	JOINED	TRIPOD	GRIFFE	EPILOG
******	OVISAC	KNIFED	TWINED	GRILLE	SKIING
--H--Y	QUINIC	LAIRED	UNIPED	GRILSE	******
******	RHIZIC	MAILED	UNITED	GRIPPE	--I--H
APHONY	SAITIC	MAIMED	VEILED	GUIMPE	******
ASHLEY	UNIFIC	MOILED	VEINED	ICICLE	ABIJAH
ICHTHY	******	NAILED	VOICED	MAIGRE	CHINCH
JOHNNY	--I--D	NOISED	VOIDED	MAISIE	CLINCH
OCHERY	******	OPINED	WAIFED	MAITRE	ELIJAH
RRHAGY	ABIDED	PAINED	WAILED	MOISHE	FLINCH
SPHERY	AFIELD	PAIRED	WAITED	OPIATE	FLITCH
UNHOLY	ALIDAD	POISED	WAIVED	ORIOLE	PLINTH
******	ALINED	PRICED	WHILED	OTIOSE	QUITCH
--I--A	ALIPED	PRIDED	WHINED	PAIUTE	SHILOH
******	BAILED	PRIMED	WHITED	PEIRCE	SMIRCH
AHIMSA	BAITED	PRIZED	******	PLICAE	SNITCH
ALICIA	BOILED	QUIRED	--I--E	POINTE	SPILTH
ANITRA	BRIBED	RAIDED	******	PRINCE	STITCH
ARISTA	BRIGID	RAILED	ALIBLE	PUISNE	SWITCH
AXILLA	BRINED	RAINED	APIECE	QUINCE	TWITCH
CRIMEA	CEILED	RAISED	ARIOSE	SEICHE	WHIDAH
ELISHA	CHIDED	REINED	AVIATE	SHIITE	******
EMILIA	CHIMED	ROILED	BAILEE	SOIGNE	--I--I
ENIGMA	COIFED	RUINED	BAILIE	SOIREE	******
EPIZOA	COILED	SAILED	BLITHE	STIFLE	CHICHI
FRIEDA	COINED	SEINED	BRIDGE	SWINGE	CHILLI
FRIGGA	DEICED	SEISED	BRIDIE	SWIPLE	DMITRI
GEISHA	DOITED	SEIZED	BRIDLE	TAILLE	GRIGRI
GLIOMA	EDITED	SHIELD	CAIQUE	THIEVE	TAIPEI
GUIANA	ELIDED	SHINED	CHICLE	THISBE	TRICHI
GUINEA	EXILED	SKIVED	CHIGOE	TRIFLE	******
OJIBWA	EXITED	SLICED	CLICHE	TRIODE	--I--K
OLIVIA	FAILED	SLIMED	CLIQUE	TRIOSE	******
PHILIA	FAIRED	SMILED	CRINGE	TRIPLE	CHIBUK
SPIREA	FOILED	SNIPED	CUISSE	TRISTE	******
STIGMA	FRIEND	SOILED	EDIBLE	TRIUNE	--I--L
TRIVIA	FRIGID	SPICED	EMIGRE	TRIXIE	******
					AMIDOL
					ANIMAL

APICAL	EDISON	BAILOR	SEIZOR	ANIMUS	CLIFFS
BAIKAL	GUIDON	BOILER	SHIKAR	ANIONS	CLIMBS
BRIDAL	HOIDEN	BRIBER	SHINER	ANISES	CLIMES
CHISEL	MAIDEN	CHIDER	SHIVER	ANITAS	CLINES
COITAL	MAISON	CHIMER	SKIVER	APICES	CLINGS
DRIVEL	OHIOAN	COILER	SLICER	ARIANS	CLINKS
EPICAL	ORIGAN	COINER	SLIDER	ARIELS	CLINTS
FRIJOL	ORIGEN	DEICER	SLIVER	ARIOUS	CLIVES
FRIVOL	ORIGIN	DRIVER	SMILER	ARISES	COIGNS
GRIZEL	ORISON	DUIKER	SMITER	ASIANS	COITUS
OGIVAL	POISON	EDITOR	SNIPER	ASIDES	CRICKS
PRIMAL	PRISON	ELINOR	SPICER	AVISOS	CRIERS
RHINAL	PTISAN	ELIXIR	SPIDER	AXIOMS	CRIMES
SNIVEL	RAISIN	FAIRER	STIVER	AZINES	CRIMPS
SPINAL	SAIGON	GAINER	SUITOR	BAIRNS	CRISES
SPINEL	SAIPAN	GAITER	TAILOR	BEIGES	CRISIS
SPIRAL	SEISIN	GEIGER	TOILER	BEINGS	CRISPS
SPITAL	SEIZIN	GLIDER	TRICAR	BLIMPS	DAISES
STIPEL	SLIPON	GOITER	TRITER	BLINDS	DAISYS
SWIVEL	TAIWAN	GRIPER	TWINER	BLINKS	DEICES
TRIBAL	TRIGON	GUIDER	VAINER	BRIARS	DEIGNS
TRINAL	TRITON	GUITAR	VEILER	BRIBES	DEISTS
TWIBIL	UNISON	HAILER	WAILER	BRICKS	DOINGS
URINAL	WHITEN	HEIFER	WAITER	BRIDES	DRIERS
******	******	ISIDOR	WAIVER	BRIEFS	DRIFTS
--I--M	--I--O	JAILER	WEIMAR	BRIERS	DRILLS
******	******	JAILOR	WHINER	BRILLS	DRINKS
CHIASM	AKIMBO	JAIPUR	WHITER	BRINES	DRIVES
CRINUM	ARIOSO	JOINER	WRITER	BRINGS	EDICTS
IBIDEM	ARISTO	JUICER	ZUIDER	BRINKS	EDILES
OBIISM	DAIMIO	KAISER	******	BRISKS	EDITHS
SHIISM	DAIMYO	LOITER	--I--S	BUILDS	ELIDES
WHILOM	EMILIO	MAILER	******	CAIRNS	ELIOTS
******	ERINGO	MAIMER	ABIDES	CEIBAS	ELIZAS
--I--N	HAIRDO	MOILER	ACINUS	CHIAUS	EMILES
******	SCIPIO	OBITER	ACIOUS	CHICKS	EMILYS
ALISON	SEISMO	OLIVER	ADIEUS	CHICOS	EPIRUS
AMIDIN	SHINTO	PRIMER	AGISTS	CHIDES	ERICHS
ANILIN	TRICHO	PRIZER	ALIBIS	CHIEFS	ERINYS
ARISEN	******	QUIVER	ALICES	CHILLS	EVICTS
AVIDIN	--I--P	RAIDER	ALIENS	CHIMES	EVITAS
BRITON	******	RAISER	ALIGNS	CHINES	EXILES
CAIMAN	PHILIP	RUINER	ALINES	CHINKS	EXISTS
CHIRON	SLIPUP	SAILER	AMICES	CHIRMS	FAINTS
CHITIN	******	SAILOR	AMIDES	CHIRPS	FAITHS
CHITON	--I--R	SEINER	AMIENS	CHIRRS	FEIGNS
DAIMON	******	SEISOR	AMIGOS	CHIVES	FEINTS
DRIVEN	ABIDER	SEIZER	ANIMAS	CLICKS	FEISTS
	BAILER				

FLICKS	LAIRDS	REICHS	SPITES	WHIFFS	WEIGHT
FLIERS	LEIGHS	REIGNS	STICKS	WHILES	WHILST
FLINGS	MAIZES	RHINOS	STILES	WHINES	WRIEST
FLINTS	MOIRAS	SAIGAS	STILLS	WHIRLS	WRIGHT
FLIRTS	NAIADS	SAINTS	STILTS	WHISKS	******
FOISTS	NEIGHS	SCIONS	STINGS	WHITES	--I--V
FRIARS	NOISES	SEINES	STINKS	WRINGS	******
FRIERS	ODIOUS	SEISMS	STINTS	WRISTS	ASIMOV
FRILLS	OGIVES	SEIZES	STIPES	WRITES	******
FRISES	OLIVES	SHIFTS	STIRKS	YOICKS	--I--X
FRISKS	ONIONS	SHILLS	STIRPS	******	******
FRITHS	OPINES	SHINES	SUITES	--I--T	ADIEUX
GLIDES	ORIBIS	SHIRES	SWIFTS	******	CLIMAX
GLINTS	ORIELS	SHIRKS	SWILLS	ALIGHT	SMILAX
GOINGS	OSIERS	SHIRRS	SWINGS	AMIDST	UNISEX
GRIDES	OSIRIS	SHIRTS	SWIPES	ARIGHT	******
GRILLS	OTITIS	SHIVES	SWIRLS	BEIRUT	--I--Y
GRIMES	OVIBOS	SKIERS	TAIGAS	BLIGHT	******
GRINDS	OXIDES	SKIFFS	TAINOS	BRIGHT	ACIDLY
GRIPES	PAINTS	SKILLS	TAINTS	CLIENT	APIARY
GUIDES	PHIALS	SKIMOS	THIGHS	CLIMAT	ARIDLY
GUILDS	PHILOS	SKIMPS	THINGS	DRIEST	AVIARY
GUILES	PHIPPS	SKINKS	THIOLS	DWIGHT	AVIDLY
GUILTS	PLIERS	SKIRRS	THIRDS	ELICIT	BAILEY
GUISES	POILUS	SKIRTS	TOILES	FLIEST	BLIMEY
HEISTS	POINDS	SKIVES	TRIADS	FLIGHT	BRIERY
HOICKS	POINTS	SLICES	TRIALS	FRIGHT	CHILLY
HOISTS	POISES	SLICKS	TRIBES	GRIVET	CHINKY
IBICES	PRICES	SLIDES	TRICES	HEIGHT	CHIPPY
IBISES	PRICKS	SLIMES	TRICKS	ICIEST	CHIRPY
ICINGS	PRIDES	SLINGS	TRIERS	KNIGHT	CHITTY
IDIOMS	PRIERS	SLINKS	TRILLS	ORIENT	CHIVVY
IDIOTS	PRIMES	SMILES	TRINES	PLIANT	CLIFFY
IMIDES	PRIMPS	SMIRKS	TRIPOS	PLIGHT	CLINGY
IMINES	PRIMUS	SMITES	TRIXYS	PRIEST	CLIQUY
IRIDES	PRINKS	SMITHS	TWILLS	PRIVET	CRIKEY
IRISES	PRINTS	SNICKS	TWINES	SHIEST	CRIMPY
IRITIS	PRIORS	SNIFFS	TWIRLS	SLIEST	CRISPY
ITIOUS	PRISMS	SNIPES	TWIRPS	SLIGHT	DAINTY
JAINAS	PRIZES	SPICES	TWISTS	SPIGOT	DRIFTY
JOINTS	QUILLS	SPIELS	UMIAKS	SPINET	DRIPPY
JOISTS	QUILTS	SPIERS	UNIONS	SPIRIT	EVILLY
JUICES	QUINTS	SPIKES	UNITES	SWIVET	FAIRLY
KEITHS	QUIPUS	SPILES	VOICES	THIRST	FEISTY
KNIFES	QUIRES	SPILLS	VOILES	TOILET	FLIMSY
KNIVES	QUIRKS	SPINES	WAISTS	TRICOT	FLINTY
KOINES	QUIRTS	SPIRES	WAIVES	TRIVET	FLIRTY
KRISES	RAISES	SPIRTS	WEIGHS	TWILIT	FRIARY

FRIDAY	TRICKY	******	******	******	INKLES
FRILLY	TRIGLY	--J--O	--K--E	--K--L	JOKERS
FRINGY	TRILBY	******	******	******	LAKERS
FRISKY	TRIMLY	MEJICO	ALKANE	JEKYLL	LIKENS
FRIZZY	TWIGGY	******	ALKENE	******	MAKERS
GAIETY	TWISTY	--J--S	ALKYNE	--K--M	MIKLOS
GAINLY	UBIETY	******	DEKARE	******	PEKANS
GLIBLY	VAINLY	CAJUNS	******	SIKKIM	PEKOES
GRIMLY	WEIRDY	ENJOYS	--K--G	******	PIKERS
GRIPPY	WHIMSY	MAJORS	******	--K--N	POKERS
GRISLY	WHINNY	RAJABS	ASKING	******	POKIES
GRITTY	WHIPPY	RAJAHS	BAKING	NEKTON	RAKERS
GUILTY	WHISKY	SAJOUS	CAKING	TAKEIN	SAKERS
IDIOCY	WHITBY	******	COKING	******	TAKERS
MAINLY	WHITEY	--J--T	DEKING	--K--O	TOKENS
MOIETY	******	******	DIKING	******	WAKENS
ONIONY	--I--Z	ABJECT	FAKING	ANKYLO	YOKELS
PAINTY	******	ADJECT	HIKING	ESKIMO	******
POINTY	BLINTZ	ADJUST	INKING	KAKAPO	--K--T
PRIMLY	CHINTZ	DEJECT	IRKING	KOKOMO	ANKLET
PRIORY	******	INJECT	JOKING	MIKADO	ASKANT
PRISSY	--J--A	OBJECT	LAKING	******	AUKLET
QUINCY	******	RAJPUT	LIKING	--K--P	DAKOIT
QUINSY	HEJIRA	REJECT	MAKING	******	GOKART
SCILLY	PAJAMA	SEJANT	MEKONG	MAKEUP	INKPOT
SHIFTY	PYJAMA	UNJUST	PEKING	TAKEUP	UNKNIT
SHIMMY	******	******	PIKING	UPKEEP	******
SHINDY	--J--E	--J--X	POKING	WIKIUP	--K--Y
SHINNY	******	******	PUKING	******	******
SHIRTY	ABJURE	BIJOUX	RAKING	--K--R	BAKERY
SKIMPY	ADJURE	******	TAKING	******	FAKERY
SKINNY	CAJOLE	--J--Y	VIKING	INKIER	LIKELY
SKIVVY	INJOKE	******	WAKING	LAKIER	OAKLEY
SLIMLY	INJURE	INJURY	YOKING	POKIER	ORKNEY
SLIMSY	JEJUNE	******	******	******	******
SLINKY	JUJUBE	--K--A	--K--H	--K--S	--L--A
SMITHY	MOJAVE	******	******	******	******
SNIFFY	******	ANKARA	RAKISH	ALKYLS	AGLAIA
SNIPPY	--J--K	DAKOTA	******	ANKLES	BALATA
SPIFFY	******	YAKIMA	--K--I	ASKERS	BALBOA
SPINNY	HIJACK	******	******	BAKERS	BELUGA
STICKY	******	--K--C	ALKALI	BIKOLS	CALESA
STILLY	--J--N	******	BIKINI	ESKERS	FULCRA
STINGY	******	PYKNIC	WAKIKI	FAKERS	GALENA
STITHY	ADJOIN	******	******	FAKIRS	HELENA
SWIRLY	ENJOIN	--K--D	--K--K	HAKIMS	KALMIA
THINLY	FIJIAN	UNKIND	ACKACK	HIKERS	LOLITA
THIRTY	REJOIN	YAKKED	DIKDIK	INKERS	

YUKKED   MUKLUK

MALAGA	BOLLED	KILLED	TOLLED	DELETE	POLICE
MALAYA	BOLTED	KILTED	UNLAID	DELUDE	POLITE
MALTHA	BULBED	LALLED	UNLEAD	DELUGE	POLLEE
PELOTA	BULGED	LILIED	UNLOAD	DELUXE	PULQUE
SALIVA	BULKED	LILTED	UPLAND	DILATE	RELATE
SALVIA	CALKED	LOLLED	VALUED	DILUTE	RELINE
SCLERA	CALLED	LULLED	VALVED	DOLLIE	RELIVE
SILICA	CALMED	MALLED	VOLTED	DULCIE	SALINE
SILVIA	CALVED	MALTED	WALKED	ENLACE	SALOME
SULPHA	CULLED	MELDED	WALLED	FELICE	SALUTE
SYLVIA	CULMED	MELTED	WELDED	FELINE	SELENE
TELEGA	DELVED	MILKED	WELLED	FELIPE	SILAGE
VALUTA	DOLLED	MILLED	WELTED	FELLOE	SILVAE
******	DULLED	MILORD	WILLED	FILOSE	SOLACE
--L--B	FELLED	MILTED	WILTED	GALEAE	SOLUTE
******	FELTED	MOLDED	WOLFED	GALORE	SPLAKE
APLOMB	FILLED	MOLTED	XYLOID	GILLIE	SPLICE
******	FILMED	MULLED	YELLED	HALIDE	SPLINE
--L--C	FOLDED	PALLED	YELPED	HALITE	SYLVAE
******	FULGID	PALLID	******	ILLUME	TALKIE
BALTIC	FULLED	PALMED	--L--E	ILLUSE	TILLIE
BALZAC	GALLED	PALPED	******	INLACE	ULLAGE
BELGIC	GELDED	PELTED	ABLAZE	IOLITE	UNLACE
BELLOC	GELLED	PILLED	AFLAME	KELPIE	UNLADE
CALCIC	GILDED	POLAND	ALLEGE	KILTIE	UNLIKE
CALPAC	GILEAD	POLLED	ALLELE	MALATE	UNLIVE
CELIAC	GOLFED	PULLED	ALLUDE	MALGRE	VALATE
CELTIC	GULFED	PULPED	ALLURE	MALICE	VALISE
FILMIC	GULLED	PULSED	ANLACE	MALINE	VELOCE
GALLIC	GULPED	RELAID	ANLAGE	MALLEE	VELURE
HOLMIC	HALOED	RELIED	APLITE	MILAGE	VOLUME
KELTIC	HALOID	RELOAD	ARLENE	MILLIE	VOLUTE
PELVIC	HALTED	ROLAND	ARLINE	MOLINE	VULVAE
TOLTEC	HALVED	ROLLED	ASLOPE	MOLLIE	WALLIE
******	HELMED	SALPID	AXLIKE	MOLTKE	WILLIE
--L--D	HELPED	SALTED	BELIKE	NELLIE	XYLENE
******	HILLED	SALVED	BELIZE	OBLATE	XYLITE
AALAND	HILTED	SILOED	BILLIE	OBLIGE	XYLOSE
ALLIED	HOLARD	SILTED	BOLIDE	ONLINE	******
BALKED	HULKED	SOLAND	BULLAE	OOLITE	--L--F
BALLAD	HULLED	SOLOED	BYLANE	PALACE	******
BALLED	INLAID	SOLVED	BYLINE	PALATE	BELIEF
BELIED	INLAND	SULKED	CELLAE	PALEAE	PILAFF
BELLED	ISLAND	TALCED	CILICE	PELAGE	RELIEF
BELTED	JELLED	TALKED	COLINE	PELITE	SCLAFF
BILGED	JILTED	TALMUD	COLLIE	PILATE	******
BILKED	JOLTED	TILLED	COLURE	PILOSE	--L--G
BILLED	KELOID	TILTED	DELATE	PILULE	******
					AILING
					BALING

BELONG	SALISH	ALLIUM	KALIAN	COLUGO	COLLAR
DOLING	SPLASH	BALAAM	KELSON	HALLOO	COLOUR
EALING	UNLASH	BALSAM	KELVIN	HELICO	COLTER
FILING	WALLAH	BALTIM	LILIAN	MALACO	CULLER
HALING	ZILLAH	BELDAM	MALIGN	MELANO	CULVER
HOLING	******	CILIUM	MELLON	PALAEO	DELVER
IDLING	--L--I	FOLIUM	MELTON	PHLEBO	DOLLAR
ISLING	******	HELIUM	MELVIN	SCLERO	DOLOUR
KALONG	BILOXI	HOLISM	MELVYN	SELENO	DULLER
OBLONG	DELPHI	KALIUM	MILDEN	SILICO	ECLAIR
OGLING	MALAWI	MILIUM	MILTON	SOLANO	FALLER
OILING	NILGAI	PHLEGM	MOLTEN	SPLENO	FALSER
OOLONG	SALAMI	PHLOEM	MULLEN	SULPHO	FALTER
PALING	SALUKI	PILEUM	NELSON	TOLEDO	FELLER
PILING	SILENI	SALAAM	OILCAN	******	FILLER
POLING	SOLIDI	SELDOM	PELION	--L--P	FILTER
PULING	TALARI	TALCUM	POLLEN	******	FOLDER
RILING	TULADI	VALLUM	PULLIN	ASLEEP	FOLIAR
RULING	******	VELLUM	SALMON	CALLUP	FULLER
SOLING	--L--K	******	SALOON	COLLOP	FULMAR
TILING	******	--L--N	SELSYN	DOLLOP	GILDER
VOLING	GALYAK	******	SELWYN	FILLIP	GOLFER
WALING	KALPAK	AILEEN	SILKEN	GALLOP	GULPER
WILING	OCLOCK	ARLEEN	SILVAN	GALLUP	HALTER
******	POLACK	BALEEN	SOLEMN	HOLDUP	HELLER
--L--H	SELJUK	BALKAN	SOLION	LOLLOP	HELPER
******	UNLOCK	BILLON	SPLEEN	PILEUP	HELTER
ABLUSH	******	BOLEYN	SULLEN	ROLLUP	HILLER
CALASH	--L--L	BOLSON	SULTAN	SALOOP	HOLDER
CALIPH	******	BOLTON	SYLVAN	WALKUP	HOLIER
CULTCH	BELIAL	CALKIN	TALION	WALLOP	HOLLER
DALETH	BULBEL	CALVIN	TELSON	******	INLIER
DULUTH	BULBIL	COLUMN	VILLON	--L--R	JILTER
EOLITH	BULBUL	DALTON	VULCAN	******	JOLTER
FELLAH	FALLAL	DELIAN	WALKON	BALDER	KELLER
GALOSH	FILIAL	DOLMAN	WALTON	BELIER	KILLER
GOLOSH	FULFIL	DOLMEN	WELKIN	BILKER	KILMER
GULLAH	HALLEL	EILEEN	WILSON	BOLDER	KILTER
HALLAH	TOLUOL	EOLIAN	WILTON	BOLTER	KULTUR
MOLLAH	TOLUYL	FALCON	******	BULBAR	LOLLER
MOLOCH	VALVAL	FALLEN	--L--O	BULGAR	MELTER
MULISH	VULVAL	FILLIN	******	BULGER	MILDER
MULLAH	WILFUL	FULTON	AFLCIO	CALCAR	MILKER
NULLAH	******	GALLON	BILBAO	CALKER	MILLER
OWLISH	--L--M	GOLDEN	BOLERO	CALLER	MILTER
PALISH	******	GULDEN	CALICO	CALMER	MOLDER
POLISH	ABLOOM	HELLEN	CALLAO	CELLAR	MOLTER
RELISH	AGLEAM	JULIAN	CHLORO	COLDER	MULLER

OILIER	YELLER	CULLIS	KULAKS	SALPAS	******	
PALLOR	YELPER	CULTUS	LILACS	SALVES	--L--T	
PALMAR	******	DALLAS	LILIES	SALVOS	******	
PALMER	--L--S	DALLES	MALAYS	SELVES	ABLAUT	
PALTER	******	DELAYS	MELEES	SILVAS	ABLEST	
PELTER	AALIIS	DELIAS	MELONS	SOLANS	AFLOAT	
PILFER	ADLIBS	DELIUS	MILERS	SOLIDS	ALLOUT	
PILLAR	AGLETS	DELLAS	MILLYS	SOLVES	ASLANT	
POLDER	ALLANS	DELTAS	MOLARS	SPLATS	BALLET	
POLLER	ALLAYS	DELVES	MOLIES	SPLAYS	BALLOT	
PULLER	ALLENS	DOLLYS	MOLLYS	SPLITS	BELOIT	
PULPER	ALLEYS	DOLPHS	MULCTS	SULCUS	BILLET	
PULSAR	ALLIES	DULLES	NELLYS	SYLPHS	BULLET	
RELIER	ALLOTS	ELLENS	NYLONS	SYLVAS	CILIAT	
ROLLER	ALLOWS	ELLIES	OGLERS	TALERS	COLLET	
SALTER	ALLOYS	FELIDS	OILERS	TALONS	CULLET	
SALVER	ALLYLS	FELONS	OLLIES	TELLUS	DELICT	
SALVOR	AWLESS	FILERS	ORLOPS	TILDES	DULCET	
SELLER	BALERS	FILETS	OWLETS	TILERS	ELLIOT	
SILVER	BALSAS	FOLIOS	OXLIPS	TILLYS	ENLIST	
SOLDER	BELAYS	GALLUS	PALAIS	TILTHS	FILLET	
SOLVER	BELGAS	GALOPS	PALLAS	TULIPS	FYLFOT	
SULFUR	BELIES	GILDAS	PALPUS	TULLES	GALACT	
TALKER	BELLAS	HALERS	PELEUS	UNLAYS	GALIOT	
TALLER	BELLES	HALIDS	PELIAS	UNLESS	GALOOT	
TELFER	BILGES	HALOES	PELOPS	VALETS	GULLET	
TELLER	BILLYS	HALVES	PELVES	VALGUS	HELMET	
TILLER	BULGES	HELENS	PELVIS	VALOIS	IDLEST	
TILTER	BYLAWS	HELIOS	PILAFS	VALUES	ILLUST	
TOLLER	CALAIS	HELLAS	PILEUS	VALVES	JOLIET	
UGLIER	CALCES	HELOTS	PILOTS	VELDTS	JULIET	
VALKYR	CALEBS	HELVES	PILOUS	VILLAS	MALLET	
VALOUR	CALIFS	HILDAS	POLKAS	VILLUS	MILLET	
VALUER	CALLAS	HOLIES	POLLYS	VOLVAS	MOLEST	
VALVAR	CALLUS	HOLLYS	POLYPS	WALDOS	MULLET	
VELOUR	CALVES	HOLMES	PULERS	WALERS	OBLAST	
VULGAR	CALXES	IDLERS	PULSES	WALLAS	PALEST	
VULVAR	CELIAS	IGLOOS	PYLONS	WALLIS	PALLET	
WALKER	CELLOS	INLAWS	RALPHS	WALLYS	PELLET	
WALTER	CHLOES	INLAYS	RELAYS	WALRUS	PULLET	
WELDER	COLEUS	INLETS	RELICS	WALVIS	PULPIT	
WELTER	COLIES	IOLCUS	RELIES	WILLIS	RELENT	
WILBER	COLINS	ISLETS	ROLPHS	WILLYS	RELICT	
WILBUR	COLONS	JALOPS	RULERS	WILMAS	RILLET	
WILDER	COLORS	JULEPS	SALADS	WOLVES	SALLET	
WILIER	COLOUS	JULIAS	SALLYS	XYLANS	SELECT	
WILLER	COLZAS	JULIES	SALMIS	XYLEMS	SILENT	
WOLVER	CULETS	JULIUS	SALONS	XYLOLS	SOLENT	

SPLINT	******	VALERY	******	LIMPED	FAMINE
TALENT	--L--Y	VALLEY	--M--C	LIMPID	FEMALE
UMLAUT	******	VILELY	******	LOMOND	FIMBLE
UPLIFT	BALDLY	VILIFY	BOMBIC	LUMPED	FUMBLE
VELVET	BELFRY	VOLERY	CYMRIC	MUMMED	GAMBLE
VILEST	BILITY	VOLLEY	HYMNIC	NIMROD	GAMETE
VOLANT	BOLDLY	WILDLY	IAMBIC	NUMBED	GEMMAE
VOLOST	CALMLY	WILILY	LIMBIC	ORMUZD	HAMITE
WALLET	CALORY	WOLSEY	ROMAIC	OSMOND	HOMAGE
WALNUT	CELERY	******	TAMBAC	OSMUND	HOMBRE
WILLET	COLDLY	--L--Z	TOMBAC	PIMPED	HUMANE
YCLEPT	COLONY	******	******	PUMPED	HUMBLE
******	CULLAY	HALUTZ	--M--D	RAMMED	IMMUNE
--L--U	EULOGY	******	******	RAMPED	IMMURE
******	FELONY	--M--A	ALMOND	RAMROD	INMATE
MILIEU	FILTHY	******	ARMAND	REMAND	JIMMIE
TELEDU	FOLKSY	ALMIRA	BOMBED	REMIND	JUMBLE
TELUGU	GALAXY	ARMADA	BUMMED	RIMMED	LAMBIE
******	GALLEY	AYMARA	BUMPED	ROMPED	LAMIAE
--L--W	GALWAY	BEMATA	CAMPED	SUMMED	MAMMAE
******	HALLEY	CAMERA	COMBED	TAMPED	MUMBLE
BELLOW	HALSEY	CAMILA	CYMOID	TOMBED	NIMBLE
BILLOW	HILARY	ELMIRA	DAMMED	TOMCOD	OHMAGE
CALLOW	HOLILY	FEMORA	DAMNED	VAMPED	OSMOSE
FALLOW	JALOPY	GAMBIA	DAMPED	WOMBED	PIMPLE
FELLOW	MALADY	GEMARA	DEMAND	******	POMACE
FOLLOW	MALORY	JEMIMA	DIMMED	--M--E	POMADE
HALLOW	MELODY	KAMALA	DUMPED	******	PUMICE
HOLLOW	MILADY	LAMBDA	EDMOND	ADMIRE	RAMBLE
MALLOW	MILDLY	LAMINA	EDMUND	ALMUCE	RAMOSE
MELLOW	MILLAY	LIMINA	GAMMED	ALMUDE	REMADE
MILDEW	MULLEY	LUMINA	GEMMED	ARMURE	REMAKE
PILLOW	OILILY	MIMOSA	GIMPED	BEMIRE	REMISE
SALLOW	OOLOGY	NOMURA	GUMMED	BEMUSE	REMOTE
TALLOW	PALELY	NUMINA	HAMMED	BUMBLE	REMOVE
WALLOW	PALTRY	NYMPHA	HEMMED	CAMISE	RIMOSE
WILLOW	PELTRY	PAMELA	HEMOID	COMATE	RIMPLE
YELLOW	POLICY	POMONA	HUMMED	COMMIE	RUMBLE
******	POLITY	RAMONA	HUMPED	COMOSE	RUMPLE
--L--X	PULLEY	REMORA	HYMNED	CYMENE	SAMITE
******	SALARY	REMUDA	JAMMED	CYMOSE	SAMPLE
BOLLIX	SALIFY	ROMOLA	JUMPED	DAMAGE	SEMELE
HALLUX	SOLELY	RUMINA	LAMBED	DEMISE	SEMEME
POLEAX	SULTRY	SAMARA	LAMMED	DEMODE	SEMITE
POLLEX	SYLPHY	SOMATA	LAMPAD	DEMOTE	SEMPRE
POLLUX	TELARY	VIMINA	LAMPED	DEMURE	SIMILE
VOLVOX	UGLIFY	VOMICA	LIMBED	DIMPLE	SIMONE
	UGLILY	WOMERA	LIMNED	ERMINE	SIMPLE
		ZAMBIA			

SOMBRE	LUMINI	BUMKIN	ROMULO	ROMPER	EMMETS
SOMITE	SOMALI	CAMDEN	SOMATO	RUMMER	EMMIES
TAMALE	YEMENI	CAMION	TOMATO	RUMOUR	FAMOUS
TEMPLE	******	COMEON	VOMITO	SAMBUR	FEMURS
TIMBRE	--M--K	COMMON	******	SIMMER	FUMOUS
TUMBLE	******	CYMLIN	--M--R	SIMPER	GAMINS
UNMADE	DAMASK	DAMPEN	******	SOMBER	GAMMAS
UNMAKE	OOMIAK	DAMSON	ARMOUR	SUMMER	GAMOUS
VAMOSE	REMARK	DEMEAN	BOMBER	SUMNER	GAMUTS
WAMBLE	UNMASK	DOMAIN	BUMMER	TAMPER	GEMOTS
WIMBLE	******	GAMMON	BUMPER	TEMPER	GIMELS
WIMPLE	--M--L	HAMDEN	CAMBER	TIMBER	GUMBOS
ZOMBIE	******	HEMPEN	CAMPER	TUMOUR	GUMMAS
******	ARMFUL	KAMSIN	COMBER	UNMOOR	HAMALS
--M--G	COMPEL	LUMPEN	CUMBER	YAMMER	HAMZAS
******	CYMBAL	MAMMON	DAMMAR	******	HOMERS
AIMING	DAMSEL	POMPON	DAMMER	--M--S	HUMANS
ARMING	GAMBOL	RAMSON	DAMPER	******	HUMORS
COMING	HAMAUL	REMAIN	DIMMER	ADMITS	HYMENS
DOMING	HAMMAL	SAMIAN	DUMPER	ALMAHS	IAMBUS
FUMING	HYMNAL	SAMOAN	EXMOOR	ALMUDS	IMMIES
GAMING	JUMBAL	SAMPAN	FUMIER	ARMETS	JAMIES
HOMING	KUMMEL	SAMSON	GAMBIR	ARMIES	JIMMYS
HUMBUG	LEMUEL	SIMIAN	GAMIER	ARMORS	KAMIKS
LAMING	MAMMAL	SIMLIN	GAMMER	BOMBES	KUMISS
LIMING	POMMEL	SUMMON	HAMMER	CAMASS	LAMEDS
MIMING	PUMMEL	TAMPAN	HAMPER	CAMELS	LAMIAS
NAMING	ROMMEL	TAMPON	HEMMER	CAMEOS	LAMMAS
RIMING	SAMIEL	TYMPAN	HOMIER	CAMPOS	LAMPAS
TAMING	SAMUEL	******	HUMBER	CAMPUS	LEMMAS
TIMING	SIMNEL	--M--O	HUMMER	COMBOS	LEMNOS
******	SYMBOL	******	HUMOUR	COMERS	LEMONS
--M--H	TIMBAL	BAMAKO	JAMJAR	COMETS	LEMURS
******	******	BAMBOO	JUMPER	COMICS	LIMBUS
ARMAGH	--M--M	COMEDO	LIMBER	COMMAS	LIMENS
ENMESH	******	DEMONO	LIMIER	COMOUS	LIMEYS
FAMISH	DUMDUM	DOMINO	LIMNER	COMPOS	LIMITS
IMMESH	MOMISM	GAMETO	LIMPER	CUMINS	LUMENS
INMESH	NOMISM	GEMSBO	LUMBAR	CYMARS	MAMBAS
LAMECH	OSMIUM	HEMATO	LUMBER	CYMOUS	MAMBOS
ROMISH	POMPOM	HYMENO	MEMBER	DAMANS	MAMEYS
******	SIMOOM	IMMUNO	MEMOIR	DEMIES	MAMIES
--M--I	TAMTAM	KIMONO	MUMMER	DEMITS	MAMMAS
******	TOMTOM	LUMINO	NUMBER	DEMOBS	MIMERS
CIMBRI	WAMPUM	LYMPHO	PAMPER	DEMONS	MIMICS
GEMINI	******	NEMATO	PUMPER	DEMURS	NAMERS
GOMUTI	--M--N	NYMPHO	RAMMER	DIMERS	NIMBUS
LIMULI	BEMEAN	POMELO	RIMMER	ELMERS	NOMADS
	BEMOAN				

NYMPHS	COMFIT	DAMPLY	CANDIA	PONTIC	ENNEAD
ORMERS	COMMIT	DIMITY	CANULA	SENLAC	FANGED
PAMPAS	DEMENT	DIMPLY	CENTRA	SYNDIC	FANNED
RAMIES	DIMOUT	DUMBLY	CINEMA	TANNIC	FENCED
RAMOUS	DIMWIT	DUMPTY	CONCHA	TANREC	FENDED
REMANS	EMMETT	ENMITY	CONTRA	TENREC	FINNED
REMISS	FOMENT	FAMILY	FANEGA	ZINCIC	FUNDED
REMITS	GAMBIT	GAMELY	GENERA	******	FUNKED
RIMERS	GEMERT	GAMILY	GENEVA	--N--D	GANGED
RIMOUS	GIMLET	HOMELY	KANAKA	******	GANOID
ROMANS	HAMLET	HOMILY	LINGUA	AENEID	GINNED
RUMBAS	INMOST	HOMINY	LUNULA	ARNAUD	GUNNED
RUMORS	LAMENT	HUMBLY	MANANA	ARNOLD	HANDED
RUMPUS	LAMEST	HUMIFY	MANILA	BANDED	HANGED
SAMBAS	LIMPET	HUMPTY	MANTUA	BANGED	HINGED
SAMBOS	LOMENT	JIMINY	MINIMA	BANKED	HINTED
SAMMYS	MAMMET	LAMELY	MONICA	BANNED	HONIED
SIMARS	MOMENT	LIMPLY	PANADA	BENDED	HONKED
SIMONS	RAMJET	MEMORY	PANAMA	BINNED	HUNTED
SUMACS	SAMLET	NAMELY	PENNIA	BONDED	JINKED
TAMERS	SUMMIT	NIMBLY	SANDRA	BONGED	JINXED
TEMPOS	TAMEST	NUMBLY	SENECA	BUNGED	JUNKED
TEMPTS	TOMCAT	PIMPLY	SENORA	BUNKED	KENNED
TIMERS	TOMTIT	POMPEY	SONATA	BUNTED	KINGED
TIMMYS	TUMULT	RAMIFY	SYNURA	CANARD	KINKED
TOMANS	UNMEET	REMEDY	TUNDRA	CANDID	KONRAD
TOMMYS	UPMOST	ROMANY	TUNICA	CANNED	LANCED
TUMORS	UTMOST	ROMNEY	ZANANA	CANOED	LANDED
UNMANS	WOMBAT	SIMONY	ZENANA	CANTED	LINKED
UNMEWS	******	SIMPLY	ZINNIA	CENSED	LONGED
VOMERS	--M--U	TAMELY	ZONULA	CONKED	LUNGED
VOMITS	******	TIMELY	******	CONNED	MANNED
WAMMUS	ORMOLU	TOMBOY	--N--B	CONOID	MENDED
WAMOUS	SAMSHU	TUMEFY	******	CONRAD	MINCED
YAMENS	******	WAMBLY	BENUMB	DANAID	MINDED
YAMUNS	--M--X	******	CANTAB	DANCED	MINTED
ZAMIAS	******	--M--Z	CONFAB	DANGED	MONIED
ZOMBIS	COMMIX	******	PUNJAB	DENIED	PANNED
******	LUMMOX	NIMITZ	******	DENNED	PANTED
--M--T	******	--N--A	--N--C	DENTED	PENDED
******	--M--Y	******	******	DINGED	PENNED
ADMIXT	******	ANNONA	APNEIC	DINNED	PENTAD
ALMOST	ARMORY	APNOEA	FENNEC	DINTED	PINGED
ARMLET	BOMBAY	ARNICA	FINNIC	DONALD	PINKED
ARMPIT	COMEDY	BANANA	FINNOC	DONNED	PINNED
CAMLET	COMELY	BENITA	MANIAC	DUNGED	PONIED
CEMENT	COMITY	CANADA	MANIOC	DUNKED	PUNNED
COMBAT	COMPLY	CANDIA	MANTIC	DUNNED	PUNTED

RANCID	AGNATE	INNATE	RENEGE	SUNDOG	ANNUAL
RANGED	ANNEXE	IONIZE	RONNIE	TONING	APNEAL
RANKED	AUNTIE	IONONE	RUNDLE	TUNING	BENGAL
RANTED	BANGLE	JANGLE	SENATE	WANING	BENZOL
RENDED	BENDEE	JANICE	SENILE	WINING	BENZYL
RENTED	BINATE	JINGLE	SINGLE	ZONING	CANCEL
RINGED	BONNIE	JINNEE	SUNDAE	******	CANNEL
RINKED	BUNCHE	JONNIE	TANGLE	--N--H	CENTAL
RINSED	BUNDLE	JUNGLE	TENACE	******	CINEOL
RONALD	BUNGLE	JUNKIE	TENURE	BANISH	CONSUL
SANDED	BYNAME	KENITE	TINGLE	DANISH	CUNEAL
SENSED	CANAPE	KENNIE	TINKLE	EUNUCH	DANIEL
SINBAD	CANDLE	KINASE	TONGUE	FINISH	DENIAL
SINGED	CANGUE	KINDLE	TONITE	HANNAH	DENTAL
SINNED	CANINE	LANATE	VENDEE	LENGTH	DENTIL
SUNGOD	CANNAE	LANOSE	VENDUE	MUNICH	FENNEL
SUNNED	CANNIE	LENAPE	VENICE	ORNITH	FINIAL
TANGED	CANTLE	LENORE	VENIRE	PUNISH	FONTAL
TANKED	CANUTE	LINAGE	VENOSE	SUNNAH	FUNGAL
TANNED	CENTRE	LUNATE	VENULE	VANISH	FUNNEL
TENDED	CINQUE	LUNGEE	WANDLE	ZENITH	GENIAL
TENSED	CONNIE	LUNULE	WANGLE	******	GINGAL
TENTED	CONTRE	MANAGE	WINKLE	--N--I	GUNNEL
TINEID	DANDLE	MANEGE	WINNIE	******	HANDEL
TINGED	DANGLE	MANGLE	YANKEE	BANGUI	HANSEL
TINNED	DANITE	MANQUE	ZONATE	BANZAI	JINGAL
TINTED	DANUBE	MANTLE	ZONULE	BONACI	KENDAL
TONGED	DENGUE	MANURE	******	BONSAI	KENNEL
TUNNED	DENISE	MENACE	--N--F	CANTHI	LENTIL
VENDED	DENOTE	MENAGE	******	CENTRI	LINEAL
VENTED	DENUDE	MINGLE	RUNOFF	DENDRI	LINTEL
WANNED	DINGLE	MINNIE	******	GANDHI	MANFUL
WANTED	DONATE	MINUTE	--N--G	GANGLI	MANTEL
WENDED	DONNIE	MONROE	******	GENESI	MANUAL
WINCED	DUNDEE	NONAGE	AWNING	KINESI	MANUEL
WINDED	EUNICE	ORNATE	BONING	SANDHI	MENDEL
WINGED	FANNIE	PANICE	CANING	SANGUI	MENIAL
WINKED	FINALE	PANTIE	CONING	SANSEI	MENSAL
WONTED	FINITE	PENILE	DANZIG	******	MENTAL
YANKED	FONDLE	PENNAE	DINING	--N--K	MONGOL
YENNED	FONDUE	PINENE	FINING	******	PENCEL
ZINCED	GANGUE	PINITE	HONING	CANUCK	PENCIL
ZINGED	GENTLE	PINKIE	INNING	SANJAK	PENIAL
******	HANDLE	PINNAE	LINING	******	PENPAL
--N--E	HONORE	PINOLE	MINING	--N--L	PINEAL
******	IGNACE	PINTLE	OWNING	******	PINNAL
ACNODE	IGNITE	PONGEE	PINANG	AGNAIL	PONTIL
ADNATE	IGNORE	RANKLE	PINING	ANNEAL	RANDAL

RENTAL	BUNYAN	TONKIN	BANNER	GINGER	PUNNER
RONDEL	CANAAN	VANMAN	BANTER	GINNER	PUNTER
RUNNEL	CANCAN	VANMEN	BENDER	GUNNAR	RANCOR
SANDAL	CANNON	VINSON	BINDER	GUNNER	RANGER
SANTOL	CANTON	WANION	BONDER	GUNTER	RANKER
SENDAL	CANYON	WANTON	BONIER	HANGAR	RANTER
SINFUL	CONMAN	******	BONZER	HANGER	RENDER
TINCAL	CONTIN	--N--O	BUNKER	HANKER	RENOIR
TINSEL	DANTON	******	CANCER	HINDER	RENTER
TONSIL	DENTIN	BENITO	CANDOR	HONKER	RINGER
TUNNEL	DONJON	BONITO	CANKER	HONOUR	RINSER
VANDAL	DUNCAN	CENTRO	CANNER	HUNGER	RUNNER
VENIAL	DUNLIN	DENDRO	CANTER	HUNTER	SANDER
XENIAL	EONIAN	DINERO	CANTOR	JINKER	SANGAR
******	FANION	DYNAMO	CENSER	JUNIOR	SANGER
--N--M	FANTAN	GENITO	CENSOR	JUNKER	SANSAR
******	FENIAN	GENTOO	CENSUR	KINDER	SENDER
BANTAM	FINNAN	GINGKO	CENTER	LANCER	SENIOR
BUNKUM	GONION	GYNECO	CINDER	LANDER	SENSOR
CONDOM	GUNMAN	KINETO	CONCUR	LANGUR	SINGER
CONIUM	GUNMEN	LANUGO	CONDOR	LANKER	SINKER
DINKUM	HENDON	MANITO	CONFER	LANNER	SINNER
EONISM	IONIAN	MONACO	CONGER	LENDER	SINTER
FANTOM	JONSON	NONEGO	CONKER	LINEAR	SONDER
GONIUM	KANSAN	NUNCIO	CONNER	LINGER	SUNDER
HANSOM	LENTEN	PANCHO	CUNNER	LINIER	TANKER
IONIUM	LINDEN	PONCHO	DANCER	LINTER	TANNER
LINGAM	LONDON	RANCHO	DANDER	LONGER	TENDER
MINIUM	LONGAN	TENUTO	DANGER	LUNGER	TENSER
MONISM	MANDAN	VENTRO	DANKER	LUNKER	TENSOR
NANISM	MINION	XANTHO	DENIER	MANGER	TENTER
NONCOM	MINOAN	******	DENSER	MANNER	TINDER
OMNIUM	PENMAN	--N--P	DENVER	MENDER	TINIER
RANDOM	PENMEN	******	DINDER	MENHIR	TINKER
RANSOM	PENNON	BANGUP	DINNER	MENTOR	TINNER
TANDEM	PINION	BUNYIP	DUNBAR	MINCER	TONIER
******	PONTON	HANGUP	DUNKER	MINDER	VENDER
--N--N	RANDAN	LINEUP	FANNER	MINTER	VENDOR
******	RENNIN	MENDIP	FENCER	MONGER	VENEER
ADNOUN	RENOWN	PENTUP	FENDER	PANDER	VENTER
AMNION	RUNYON	SANNUP	FENRIR	PANZER	VINIER
BANIAN	SINEON	TUNEUP	FINDER	PENNER	WANDER
BANYAN	SUNKEN	WINDUP	FINGER	PINDAR	WANNER
BENIGN	SUNTAN	******	FINNER	PINIER	WANTER
BENTON	TANNIN	--N--R	FONDER	PINNER	WINCER
BONBON	TENDON	******	GANDER	PINTER	WINDER
BUNION	TENPIN	BANGOR	GANGER	PONDER	WINIER
BUNSEN	TINCAN	BANKER	GENDER	PUNIER	WINKER

WINNER	CONIES	HONEYS	NANTES	TENTHS	PUNDIT
WINTER	CONTES	HONORS	NINTHS	TENUES	RENNET
WONDER	CONTOS	JANETS	OUNCES	TENUIS	RUNLET
YONDER	CYNICS	JENNYS	OWNERS	TINCTS	RUNOUT
YONKER	DANAUS	JINNYS	PANDAS	TINGES	SANEST
ZANIER	DANCES	JINXES	PANELS	TONERS	SENNET
ZENGER	DANNYS	JONAHS	PANICS	TONICS	SENNIT
******	DENIES	JUNCOS	PANSYS	TUNERS	SONANT
--N--S	DENIMS	JUNIUS	PENGOS	TUNGUS	SONNET
******	DENNIS	JUNTAS	PENNIS	TUNICS	SUNHAT
ABNERS	DENNYS	KANSAS	PENNYS	VENOMS	SUNLIT
AENEAS	DINAHS	KENNYS	PINDUS	VENOUS	SUNSET
ANNALS	DINARS	KININS	PINGOS	VENUES	SYNDET
ANNIES	DINERS	LANAIS	PINIES	VINCES	TANIST
ANNOYS	DINGUS	LANCES	PINONS	VINNYS	TENANT
ANNULS	DONEES	LENNYS	PINTOS	VINOUS	TINPOT
ARNIES	DONETS	LENSES	PINUPS	VINYLS	******
BANJOS	DONNAS	LENTOS	PONIES	WANDAS	--N--U
BANTUS	DONORS	LINDAS	PONTES	WENDYS	******
BENJYS	DUNCES	LINENS	PUNKAS	WINCES	CONGOU
BENNES	ERNIES	LINERS	PUNTOS	WINOES	HONSHU
BENNYS	FANGAS	LINGAS	RANEES	WINZES	JUNEAU
BINGES	FANNYS	LONERS	RANGES	ZANIES	LANDAU
BINITS	FANONS	LUNETS	RENEES	******	MANCHU
BONERS	FANUMS	LUNGES	RENEWS	--N--T	MANITU
BONGOS	FENCES	LUNGIS	RENTES	******	XANADU
BONNYS	FINALS	LYNXES	RINSES	BANDIT	******
BONZES	FUNDUS	MANDYS	RONDOS	BENNET	--N--W
BUNCOS	FUNGUS	MANGOS	RUNINS	BONNET	******
CANALS	GANEFS	MANIAS	RUNONS	CANNOT	MINNOW
CANERS	GANGES	MANORS	SANDYS	DYNAST	SUNBOW
CANNAS	GENETS	MANSES	SANIES	ERNEST	SUNDEW
CANNES	GENIES	MANTAS	SENNAS	FANJET	WINDOW
CANOES	GENIUS	MANTES	SENSES	FINEST	WINNOW
CANONS	GENOUS	MANTIS	SINEWS	FUNEST	******
CANSOS	GENRES	MENSES	SINGES	GANNET	--N--X
CANTOS	GENROS	MINCES	SONARS	HENBIT	******
CANTUS	GENTES	MINERS	SONIAS	HONEST	CONVEX
CANVAS	GONADS	MINIMS	SONYAS	JENNET	MENINX
CENSES	GONERS	MINORS	SUNUPS	JUNKET	SYNTAX
CENSUS	GYNOUS	MINXES	SYNODS	LANCET	******
CENTOS	HANCES	MONADS	TANGOS	LINNET	--N--Y
CINDYS	HANNAS	MONEYS	TANKAS	MINUET	******
CONCHS	HENNAS	MONIES	TENETS	MONGST	BENDAY
CONEYS	HENRIS	MONTES	TENNIS	MONIST	BINARY
CONGAS	HENRYS	MONTHS	TENONS	PENULT	BUNCHY
CONGES	HINDUS	MONTYS	TENORS	PINXIT	CANARY
CONICS	HINGES	NANCYS	TENSES	PONENT	CANOPY

CONCHY	SINGLY	ANODIC	COOKED	PROVED	BOOTEE
CONVEY	SUNDAY	ANOMIC	COOLED	QUOTED	BOOTIE
CONVOY	SUNDRY	ANOXIC	COOPED	RIOTED	BOOTLE
CONWAY	TANGLY	ATOMIC	CROWED	ROOFED	BROCHE
DANKLY	TINGLY	ATONIC	DOODAD	ROOKED	BROGUE
DENARY	TINILY	AZONIC	DOOMED	ROOMED	BRONTE
DINGEY	TINKLY	AZOTIC	DRONED	ROOTED	BRONZE
DINGHY	VANITY	BIOTIC	DROVED	SCORED	BROOKE
DINKEY	VENERY	BROMIC	ELOPED	SHOOED	BROWSE
DONKEY	VINERY	CHORIC	EMOTED	SHORED	CHOICE
FINELY	WINCEY	CLONIC	ERODED	SHOULD	CHOOSE
FINERY	WINERY	EROTIC	EVOKED	SHOVED	CLOCHE
FONDLY	WINTRY	EXOTIC	FLORID	SHOWED	CLOTHE
GANTRY	ZINCKY	FROLIC	FLOWED	SLOPED	COODLE
GENTLY	ZONARY	GEODIC	FOOLED	SLOWED	COOKIE
GENTRY	******	GNOMIC	FOOTED	SMOKED	COOLIE
GUNSHY	--O--A	ICONIC	GLOBED	SNORED	COOTIE
HENLEY	******	IRONIC	GLOVED	SNOWED	CROSSE
HUNGRY	ABOLLA	MIOTIC	GLOWED	SOOTED	CROUPE
IGNIFY	AEOLIA	MYOPIC	GLOZED	SPOKED	DOODLE
JINGLY	AMOEBA	NIOBIC	GOOFED	SPORED	DOOLEE
JUNGLY	ANOMIA	OZONIC	GOOSED	STOKED	DOOLIE
KINDLY	ANOXIA	PHOBIC	GROPED	STOLED	DROGUE
KINGLY	CHOLLA	PHONIC	GROUND	STOLID	DROWSE
KINSEY	CHOREA	PHOTIC	HOODED	STONED	ELOISE
LANKLY	CLOACA	RHODIC	HOOFED	STOPED	EPOPEE
LENITY	GLORIA	SUOMIC	HOOKED	STORED	EVOLVE
LONELY	HOOPLA	THORAC	HOOPED	STOWED	FLORAE
LUNACY	MYOPIA	THORIC	HOOTED	TOOLED	FOOTLE
MINIFY	PEORIA	TROPIC	HOOVED	TOOTED	FOOZLE
MONDAY	PHOBIA	******	IRONED	TWOULD	GEORGE
MONKEY	PHONIA	--O--D	ISOPOD	UROPOD	GROOVE
MONODY	QUOTHA	******	LOOKED	WHORED	GROUSE
NINETY	SCORIA	ABOARD	LOOMED	WOODED	GROYNE
NONARY	SCOTIA	ABOUND	LOOPED	ZOOMED	HOOPOE
ORNERY	THORIA	ADORED	LOOSED	******	ISOLDE
PANTRY	TROIKA	AROUND	LOOTED	--O--E	LAOTSE
PENURY	UTOPIA	ATONED	MEOWED	******	LEONIE
PINERY	******	AVOWED	MOONED	AGOGUE	NOODLE
PUNCHY	--O--B	BOOKED	MOORED	AGORAE	OROIDE
PUNILY	******	BOOMED	MOOTED	ANOMIE	PEOPLE
RANKLY	BAOBAB	BOOTED	NOOSED	APOGEE	PHOEBE
RUNWAY	******	BOOZED	PHONED	AROUSE	POODLE
SANELY	--O--C	BUOYED	PLOWED	BLONDE	PROCNE
SANITY	******	CHOKED	POOLED	BLOUSE	ROOKIE
SENARY	ADONIC	CLOSED	POOPED	BOODLE	ROOTLE
SENTRY	AEOLIC	CLOYED	PROBED	BOOGIE	SCONCE
SINEWY	AGONIC	COOEED	PROSED	BOOKIE	SCOUSE

SHOPPE	SLOUCH	******	SPOKEN	AVOWER	PROBER
SKOPJE	SLOUGH	--O--M	STOLEN	BLOWER	PROPER
SNOOZE	SMOOCH	******	STOLON	BOOMER	PROSER
SOOTHE	SMOOTH	ANONYM	THORON	BOOZER	PROVER
SPONGE	THOUGH	EGOISM	TROGON	BROKER	QUOTER
SPOUSE	TROUGH	ELOHIM	TROJAN	CHOKER	RIOTER
STODGE	WHOOSH	EPONYM	VIOLIN	CHOLER	ROOFER
STOOGE	******	MAOISM	WOODEN	CLOSER	ROOMER
THORPE	--O--I	QUORUM	WOOLEN	CLOVER	ROOTER
TOOTLE	******	TAOISM	YEOMAN	COOKER	SCORER
TROCHE	ADONAI	******	YEOMEN	COOLER	SCOTER
TROUPE	AGOUTI	--O--N	******	COOPER	SHOFAR
YVONNE	GEORGI	******	--O--O	CROZER	SHOVER
******	RHOMBI	AJOWAN	******	DEODAR	SHOWER
--O--G	******	AWOKEN	ALONSO	DROVER	SLOPER
******	--O--K	BIOGEN	ALONZO	ELOPER	SLOWER
APOLOG	******	BIOTIN	APOLLO	FEODOR	SMOKER
BOOING	ANORAK	BROGAN	BOOBOO	FLOWER	SNORER
COOING	CROJIK	BROKEN	BOOHOO	FOOTER	SOONER
DUOLOG	DVORAK	CHOPIN	BRONCO	GAOLER	STOKER
LOOING	SLOVAK	CHOSEN	CHOREO	GLOVER	STONER
MOOING	******	CLOVEN	CLOTHO	GLOWER	STOVER
PROLEG	--O--L	CROTON	DRONGO	GOOBER	TOOLER
WOOING	******	DROMON	FRONTO	GOOIER	TOOTER
******	ABORAL	DUODEN	GIOTTO	GROCER	TROCAR
--O--H	AMORAL	ELOIGN	GLOSSO	GROPER	TROVER
******	APODAL	EXOGEN	GLOTTO	GROVER	TWOFER
ADOLPH	ATONAL	FLORIN	GROTTO	GROWER	WOOFER
AVOUCH	AVOWAL	FROZEN	HOODOO	HOOFER	******
BLOTCH	BROMAL	GLOBIN	ILOILO	HOOKER	--O--S
BROACH	CHORAL	GNOMON	KOODOO	HOOPER	******
BROOCH	DIOBOL	IMOGEN	ODONTO	HOOTER	ABODES
CHOUGH	FLORAL	ISOGON	OPORTO	HOOVER	ABOHMS
CLOUGH	GLOBAL	KAOLIN	PROCTO	IRONER	ABOMAS
CROTCH	GOOGOL	KRONEN	PRONTO	ISOBAR	ABOMBS
CROUCH	GOORAL	LOOKIN	TROPHO	ISOMER	ABORTS
DROUTH	GROVEL	LOOSEN	TROPPO	KNOWER	ACORNS
ENOUGH	ISOBEL	MYOSIN	VOODOO	KRONER	ADOBES
GROUCH	ISOHEL	PHOTON	YOOHOO	KRONOR	ADONIS
GROWTH	LIONEL	PROTON	******	KRONUR	ADOPTS
HOOKAH	PROPEL	PROVEN	--O--P	LOOKER	ADORES
HOOTCH	PROPYL	REOPEN	******	LOOPER	ADORNS
LOOFAH	SHOVEL	SHOGUN	BLOWUP	LOOSER	AEOLIS
MOOLAH	TROPAL	SHOOIN	HOOKUP	LOOTER	AEOLUS
PHOSPH	TROTYL	SHORAN	******	MOOTER	AGONES
PLOUGH	TROWEL	SIOUAN	--O--R	PLOVER	AGORAS
SCORCH	ZOONAL	SLOGAN	******	PLOWER	AMOLES
SCOTCH		SLOVEN	ADORER	POORER	AMOURS
			ATONER		

ANODES	COOEYS	FLOUTS	PHOCIS	SMOCKS	TROUTS
AROIDS	COOMBS	FLOYDS	PHONES	SMOKES	TROVES
AROMAS	COOPTS	FROCKS	PHOTOS	SMOLTS	UBOATS
ATOLLS	CROAKS	FRONDS	PROBES	SNOODS	VIOLAS
ATONES	CROATS	FRONTS	PROEMS	SNOOKS	WHOOPS
AVOIDS	CROCKS	FROSTS	PRONGS	SNOOPS	WHORES
AXONES	CROCUS	FROTHS	PROOFS	SNOOTS	WHORLS
AZOLES	CROFTS	FROWNS	PROSES	SNORES	WHORTS
AZORES	CRONES	GEODES	PROVES	SNORTS	WOOERS
BIOSIS	CRONOS	GHOSTS	PROWLS	SNOUTS	WRONGS
BLOATS	CRONUS	GHOULS	PTOSIS	SPOILS	ZLOTYS
BLOCKS	CROOKS	GLOATS	PYOSIS	SPOKES	ZOOIDS
BLOKES	CROONS	GLOBES	QUOINS	SPOOFS	******
BLONDS	CRORES	GLOOMS	QUOITS	SPOOKS	--O--T
BLOODS	CROUPS	GLOSTS	QUOTAS	SPOOLS	******
BLOOMS	CROWDS	GLOVES	QUOTES	SPOONS	AMOUNT
BOOSTS	CROWNS	GLOZES	RAOULS	SPOORS	ANOINT
BOOTHS	CROZES	GNOMES	RHODAS	SPORES	AVOCET
BOOZES	DHOLES	GNOSIS	RHODES	SPORTS	AVOSET
BROADS	DHOTIS	GOOSES	ROOSTS	SPOUTS	CLOSET
BROILS	DIODES	GROANS	SCOFFS	STOATS	EGOIST
BROMES	DROITS	GROATS	SCOLDS	STOCKS	FLORET
BRONCS	DROLLS	GROINS	SCONES	STOICS	IGOROT
BROODS	DRONES	GROOMS	SCOOPS	STOKES	MAOIST
BROOKS	DROOLS	GROPES	SCOOTS	STOLES	OBOIST
BROOMS	DROOPS	GROUPS	SCOPES	STOMPS	PROFIT
BROTHS	DROVES	GROUTS	SCOPUS	STONES	PROJET
BROWNS	DROWNS	GROVES	SCORES	STOOKS	PROMPT
CEORLS	ECOLES	GROWLS	SCORNS	STOOLS	PROSIT
CHOCKS	ELOINS	HOOVES	SCOTTS	STOOPS	PROUST
CHOIRS	ELOPES	HYOIDS	SCOURS	STOPES	SNOCAT
CHOKES	EMOTES	KIOSKS	SCOUTS	STORES	SPOILT
CHORDS	ENOSIS	KNOCKS	SCOWLS	STORKS	STOMAT
CHORES	EPOCHS	KNOLLS	SHOALS	STORMS	TAOIST
CHORUS	EPODES	KNOSPS	SHOATS	STOUPS	TWOBIT
CLOAKS	ERODES	KNOUTS	SHOCKS	STOUTS	VIOLET
CLOCKS	EVOKES	KRONOS	SHOERS	STOVES	YAOURT
CLONES	EXODUS	LEONAS	SHOJIS	SWOONS	******
CLONUS	FEOFFS	LLOYDS	SHOOTS	SWOOPS	--O--X
CLOSES	FIORDS	LOOSES	SHORES	SWORDS	******
CLOTHS	FLOATS	MAORIS	SHORLS	TBONES	PROLIX
CLOUDS	FLOCKS	MIOSIS	SHORTS	THOLES	SCOLEX
CLOUTS	FLONGS	MYOPES	SHOTES	THOMAS	STORAX
CLOVES	FLOODS	MYOSIS	SHOUTS	THONGS	THORAX
CLOVIS	FLOORS	NAOMIS	SHOVES	THORNS	******
CLOWNS	FLORAS	NAOSES	SLOOPS	TROLLS	--O--Y
COOEES	FLORES	NOOSES	SLOPES	TROOPS	******
COOERS	FLOURS	OBOLUS	SLOTHS	TROTHS	AGOUTY
					BIOPSY

BLOCKY	HOORAY	LIPOMA	LIPPED	EXPOSE	DUPING
BLOODY	KNOBBY	OEPEMA	LOPPED	FIPPLE	EPPING
BLOOMY	KNOTTY	PAPAYA	MAPPED	HIPPIE	GAPING
BLOWBY	MOOLEY	PAPULA	MOPPED	HOPPLE	HOPING
BLOWZY	PHONEY	SOPHIA	NAPPED	HYPHAE	IMPING
BROLLY	PHOOEY	TOPEKA	NIPPED	IMPALE	JAPING
BRONZY	POORLY	ZAPATA	PEPPED	IMPEDE	LAPDOG
BROODY	SHOALY	******	PIPPED	IMPOSE	LOPING
BROOMY	SHODDY	--P--B	POPPED	IMPURE	MOPING
CHOOSY	SLOPPY	******	PUPPED	IMPUTE	PIPING
CHOPPY	SLOSHY	SUPERB	RAPPED	LIPASE	RAPING
CLODDY	SLOWLY	******	REPAID	LUPINE	ROPING
CLOGGY	SNOBBY	--P--C	REPAND	MOPOKE	TAPING
CLOTTY	SNOOPY	******	RIPPED	NAPPIE	TOPING
CLOUDY	SNOOTY	CAPRIC	SAPPED	NIPPLE	TYPING
COOKEY	SNOTTY	COPTIC	SIPPED	OPPOSE	UNPLUG
COOLLY	SPONGY	CUPRIC	SOPPED	ORPINE	UPPING
CROAKY	SPOOKY	HYPNIC	SUPPED	PAPULE	WIPING
CROCKY	SPOONY	ORPHIC	TAPPED	PIPAGE	******
CROUPY	SPORTY	PEPTIC	TIPPED	POPPLE	--P--H
DROLLY	SPOTTY	SEPTIC	TOPPED	PUPATE	******
DROOPY	STOCKY	******	TUPPED	RAPHAE	BYPATH
DROPSY	STODGY	--P--D	WAPPED	RAPINE	COPRAH
DROSKY	STOGEY	******	YAPPED	RAPPEE	IMPISH
DROSSY	STOREY	APPEND	YIPPED	REPINE	MOPISH
DROWSY	STORMY	BOPPED	ZIPPED	REPOSE	POPISH
FLOATY	THORNY	CAPPED	******	REPUTE	RUPIAH
FLOCKY	TOOTHY	COPIED	--P--E	RIPPLE	UPPISH
FLOOZY	TOOTSY	COPPED	******	SOPHIE	******
FLOPPY	TROPHY	CUPPED	ALPINE	SUPINE	--P--I
FLOSSY	TWOPLY	DAPPED	AMPERE	SUPPLE	******
FLOURY	TWOWAY	DEPEND	AMPULE	TIPPLE	VAPORI
FROGGY	WHOLLY	DIPPED	APPOSE	TIPTOE	WAPITI
FROSTY	WOODSY	ESPIED	ASPIRE	TOPPLE	******
FROTHY	WOOLLY	EXPAND	CAPONE	UMPIRE	--P--K
FROWZY	******	EXPEND	CAPOTE	UNPILE	******
GLOOMY	--P--A	GAPPED	CUPTIE	YIPPIE	COPECK
GLOSSY	******	GIPPED	CUPULE	YUPPIE	IMPARK
GOODBY	ALPACA	GYPPED	DAPHNE	******	KOPECK
GOODLY	CAPITA	HAPPED	DAPPLE	--P--F	UNPACK
GOOGLY	COPPRA	HEPTAD	DEPONE	******	UNPICK
GOONEY	COPULA	HIPPED	DEPOSE	RIPOFF	******
GOOSEY	CUPOLA	HOPPED	DEPUTE	TIPOFF	--P--L
GROGGY	ESPANA	IMPEND	DIPLOE	******	******
GROOVY	EUPNEA	KIPPED	DIPOLE	--P--G	ALPHYL
GROSZY	IMPALA	LAPPED	EMPALE	******	APPALL
GROTTY	JAPHIA	LAPSED	EMPIRE	COPING	APPEAL
HOOKEY	LEPSIA	LIPOID	EXPIRE	DOPING	CUPFUL

ESPIAL	NEPHRO	SAPPER	JAPANS	UNPEGS	******
HYPHAL	SAPPHO	SIPPER	JUPONS	UNPINS	--P--W
LAPFUL	TAPALO	SUPPER	KAPOKS	UPPERS	******
RAPPEL	TUPELO	SYPHER	KAPPAS	VAPORS	NEPHEW
REPEAL	TYPHLO	TAPPER	KOPEKS	VIPERS	RIPSAW
SEPTAL	******	TIPPER	KOPJES	WIPERS	******
******	--P--P	TOPPER	LAPELS	YAPONS	--P--X
--P--M	******	VAPOUR	LAPINS	YUPONS	******
******	RIPRAP	ZEPHYR	LAPSES	******	DIPLEX
COPALM	TIPTOP	ZIPPER	LAPSUS	--P--T	DUPLEX
CUPRUM	******	******	LEPERS	******	******
GYPSUM	--P--R	--P--S	LIPIDS	APPORT	--P--Y
NAPALM	******	******	LOPERS	ARPENT	******
PEPLUM	APPEAR	ALPHAS	MAPLES	ASPECT	BYPLAY
SEPTUM	CAPPER	ALPHOS	MOPERS	BYPAST	COPLEY
******	CAPTOR	AMPHRS	NAPLES	COPOUT	DEPLOY
--P--N	CIPHER	AMPULS	NAPPES	DEPART	DEPUTY
******	COPIER	APPALS	NOPALS	DEPICT	DIPODY
APPIAN	COPPER	APPELS	ORPINS	DEPORT	DUPERY
CAPLIN	CUPPER	APPLES	PAPAWS	DUPLET	EMPERY
CYPRIN	CYPHER	ARPENS	PAPERS	ESPRIT	EMPLOY
HAPPEN	DAPPER	ASPENS	PAPPUS	EXPECT	EXPIRY
HYPHEN	DIPPER	ASPERS	PEPLOS	EXPERT	NAPERY
IMPAWN	DOPIER	ASPICS	PEPLUS	EXPORT	OSPREY
IMPUGN	DOPTER	BIPEDS	PIPERS	IMPACT	PAPACY
JOPLIN	GOPHER	BIPODS	PIPETS	IMPART	PAPERY
LEPTON	HOPPER	BYPASS	PIPITS	IMPORT	POPERY
NAPKIN	IMPAIR	CAPERS	POPPYS	IMPOST	RAPTLY
NIPPON	KEPLER	CAPIAS	PUPILS	JAPHET	REPLAY
OPPUGN	KIPPER	CAPONS	RAPHIS	LAPPET	RIPELY
ORPHAN	LAPPER	COPIES	RAPIDS	MOPPET	RIPLEY
PAPAIN	LAPSER	COPSES	REPASS	PAPIST	RIPPLY
PAPUAN	LIPPER	CUPELS	REPAYS	POPPET	ROPILY
PEPSIN	NAPIER	CYPRUS	REPELS	PUPPET	SUPPLY
PIPKIN	NAPPER	DEPOTS	RIPENS	RAPIST	TEPEFY
PIPPIN	NIPPER	DEPTHS	RUPEES	REPAST	TYPIFY
POPGUN	OOPHOR	DIPSAS	SEPALS	REPEAT	UPPITY
POPLIN	PEPPER	DUPERS	SEPIAS	REPENT	******
SAPIEN	PIPIER	ESPIES	SEPOYS	REPORT	--Q--D
SIPHON	POPLAR	EXPELS	SEPSIS	RIPEST	******
SYPHON	POPPER	GAPERS	SUPERS	RIPOST	LIQUID
TYPHON	RAPIER	GIPONS	TAPERS	RUPERT	PEQUOD
******	RAPPER	HIPPOS	TAPIRS	SEPTET	PIQUED
--P--O	RAPTOR	HIPPUS	TEPEES	SIPPET	******
******	REPAIR	HYPNOS	TOPERS	TAPPET	--Q--L
HEPATO	RIPPER	IMPASS	TOPICS	TIPCAT	******
LAPARO	ROPIER	IMPELS	TUPIKS	TIPPET	SEQUEL
LEPIDO	SAPHAR	INPUTS	TYPHUS	TOPHAT	******
				TYPIST	--Q--N
					******
					SEQUIN

******	JERBOA	GARLIC	ERRAND	MYRIAD	WARPED
--Q--R	KERALA	HERDIC	FARBAD	NARKED	WARRED
******	KORUNA	HEROIC	FARCED	NEREID	WORDED
LIQUOR	LORICA	MYRMEC	FARMED	NERVED	WORKED
LOQUAR	MARACA	NORDIC	FERVID	NURSED	WORMED
******	MARCIA	PARSEC	FIRMED	PARKED	YARDED
--Q--S	MARINA	SYRIAC	FORBID	PARSED	ZEROED
******	MARKKA	TARMAC	FORCED	PARTED	******
FIQUES	MARSHA	TURKIC	FORDED	PERIOD	--R--E
MAQUIS	MARTHA	******	FORGED	PERKED	******
PIQUES	MERCIA	--R--D	FORKED	PERMED	ABRADE
TOQUES	MORULA	******	FORMED	PORTED	AERATE
TUQUES	MYRICA	ABROAD	FURLED	PUREED	AEROBE
******	PERSIA	AERIED	FURRED	PURGED	AFRAME
--Q--T	PIRANA	AFRAID	GARBED	PURLED	AGRAFE
******	PORTIA	AGREED	GERALD	PURRED	AORTAE
ACQUIT	PURANA	AIRBED	GERARD	PURSED	ARRIVE
COQUET	PYRRHA	BARBED	GERUND	SCREED	AURATE
LOQUAT	SCROTA	BARDED	GIRDED	SCRIED	BARBIE
PEQUOT	SERBIA	BARGED	GIRTED	SERVED	BAREGE
PIQUET	SERENA	BARKED	GORGED	SHREWD	BARGEE
ROQUET	STRATA	BARRED	HARKED	SHROUD	BARITE
******	STROMA	BIRLED	HARMED	SORDID	BARMIE
--R--A	STRUMA	BIRRED	HAROLD	SORTED	BARQUE
******	TARSIA	BURIED	HARPED	SPREAD	BARRIE
AFRICA	TERBIA	BURKED	HERALD	STRAND	BERATE
AMRITA	TERESA	BURLED	HERDED	STROUD	BERNIE
ARROBA	TIRANA	BURNED	HORDED	SURFED	BERTHE
AURIGA	VARUNA	BURPED	HORNED	SURGED	BERTIE
AURORA	VERONA	BURRED	HORRID	TARRED	BIRDIE
BARBRA	YORUBA	BYROAD	HORSED	TARTED	BIREME
BARYTA	ZARIBA	CARDED	HURLED	TERMED	BORAGE
BERTHA	******	CARPED	INROAD	THREAD	BORANE
BORGIA	--R--B	CARTED	JARRED	THREED	BORATE
CARINA	******	CARVED	JEREED	TOROID	BORIDE
CHROMA	CORYMB	CORDED	JERKED	TORPID	BURBLE
CORNEA	SERDAB	CORKED	KERBED	TORRID	BURDIE
CORNUA	******	CORNED	KERNED	TURBID	BURGEE
CORONA	--R--C	CURBED	LARDED	TURFED	BURGLE
CORYZA	******	CURDED	LARKED	TURGID	BURSAE
ERRATA	AIRSAC	CURLED	LORDED	TURNED	CARAFE
EUREKA	AORTIC	CURSED	LURKED	UNREAD	CARATE
EUROPA	BARDIC	CURVED	MARAUD	VARIED	CARIBE
FARINA	CARPIC	DARNED	MARKED	VERGED	CAROLE
FERULA	CORSAC	DARTED	MARLED	VERSED	CARRIE
GURKHA	DERMIC	DIRKED	MARRED	WARDED	CERATE
HERNIA	FERRIC	DORSAD	MERGED	WARMED	CERISE
JARINA	FORMIC	EARNED	MORBID	WARNED	CERITE

CERUSE	MARBLE	STRIAE	DARING	PERISH	BURSAL
CHROME	MARGIE	STRIDE	DORBUG	PURDAH	CARCEL
CIRCLE	MARINE	STRIFE	DURING	SERAPH	CARMEL
CIRQUE	MARQUE	STRIKE	EARING	STRATH	CARNAL
CORBIE	MARTHE	STRIPE	EARWIG	TERAPH	CARPAL
CORPSE	MIRAGE	STRIVE	ERRING	THRASH	CARPEL
CORRIE	MORALE	STROBE	FARING	THRESH	CARREL
CORVEE	MORGUE	STRODE	FIRING	THRUSH	CARTEL
CURARE	MOROSE	STROKE	GORING	UPRUSH	CARVEL
CURATE	MURINE	STROVE	HARING	WARMTH	CEREAL
CURDLE	MYRTLE	TERETE	HIRING	ZURICH	CORBEL
CURIAE	NARINE	THRICE	LARYNG	******	CORNEL
CURULE	OCREAE	THRIVE	LURING	--R--I	CORRAL
CYRENE	ORRICE	THRONE	MIRING	******	CURIAL
DARKLE	PARADE	THROVE	OARING	BORZOI	DARNEL
DARTLE	PARCAE	TIRADE	PARANG	EURIPI	DERAIL
DERATE	PAROLE	TOROSE	PARING	HERMAI	DERMAL
DERIDE	PARSEE	TORQUE	PORING	NEROLI	DIRNDL
DERIVE	PARURE	TURTLE	RARING	STRATI	DORSAL
DORMIE	PERUKE	TYRONE	SARONG	******	EARFUL
ENRAGE	PERUSE	UNRIPE	SIRING	--R--K	ENROLL
ENROBE	PHRASE	UNROBE	SPRANG	ARRACK	FERIAL
EUROPE	PIRATE	UPRISE	SPRING	BARTOK	FORMAL
FERINE	PURFLE	UPROSE	SPRUNG	CARACK	FORMYL
FERULE	PURINE	VIRGIE	STRING	KARNAK	GERBIL
FORAGE	PURPLE	VIRILE	STRONG	MARDUK	HARTAL
FURORE	PURSUE	VIRTUE	STRUNG	SCREAK	HERBAL
GARAGE	PYRENE	WARBLE	TARING	SHRANK	ISRAEL
GARBLE	PYRITE	******	THRONG	SHRIEK	JARFUL
GARGLE	PYRONE	--R--F	TIRING	SHRINK	KERNEL
GERTIE	PYROPE	******	WIRING	SHRUNK	LARVAL
GIRDLE	SARAPE	FAROFF	******	STREAK	MARCEL
GURGLE	SARTRE	HEREOF	--R--H	STRICK	MARVEL
GYRATE	SCRAPE	SCRUFF	******	STRUCK	MORSEL
GYROSE	SCRIBE	SHROFF	AFRESH	YORICK	MORTAL
HERMAE	SCRIVE	TARIFF	BARUCH	******	MURIEL
HORACE	SERAPE	******	BORSCH	--R--L	NARIAL
HORNIE	SERENE	--R--G	CERIPH	******	NARWAL
HORSTE	SERINE	******	ENRICH	******	NORMAL
HURDLE	SHRIKE	AIRING	GARISH	AERIAL	PARCEL
HURTLE	SHRINE	BARING	HURRAH	AORTAL	PARRAL
JEROME	SHRIVE	BARONG	INRUSH	ATRIAL	PARREL
KARATE	SHROVE	BERING	KIRSCH	AZRAEL	PORTAL
KERRIE	SORTIE	BORING	OGRISH	BARBEL	SCRAWL
KIRTLE	SPRITE	CARING	ONRUSH	BARREL	SCROLL
LARINE	SPRUCE	CERING	PARAPH	BORDEL	SERIAL
LARVAE	STRAFE	CORING	PARIAH	BOREAL	SERVAL
LORENE	STRAKE	CURING	PARISH	BURIAL	SHRILL

SORREL
SPRAWL
STROLL
TARNAL
TARSAL
TERCEL
TERGAL
TERNAL
THRALL
THRILL
UNREAL
UNREEL
UNROLL
VERBAL
VERGIL
VERNAL
VIRGIL
WARHOL
******

--R--M

******
ATRIUM
BARIUM
BARNUM
CERIUM
CHRISM
CIRCUM
CORIUM
CURIUM
DIRHAM
DORSUM
DURHAM
FERRUM
HARLEM
LYRISM
MIRIAM
PURISM
SCREAM
STREAM
TERGUM
VERISM
******

--R--N

******
ADRIAN
ADRIEN
AIRGUN
AIRMAN

AIRMEN
BARMAN
BARMEN
BARREN
BARTON
BARYON
BERGEN
BERLIN
BURDEN
BURTON
CARBON
CAREEN
CARMAN
CARMEN
CARSON
CARTON
CARVEN
CORBAN
CORDON
CORTIN
DARDAN
DARIEN
DARKEN
DARWIN
DERAIN
DOREEN
DORIAN
DURBAN
DURIAN
DURION
FIRKIN
FIRMAN
GARCON
GARDEN
GERMAN
GERMEN
GERYON
GORDON
GORGON
GORHEN
HARBIN
HARDEN
HARKEN
HARLAN
HARMIN
HEREIN
HEREON
HERMAN

HEROIN
JARGON
JERKIN
JORDAN
KOREAN
LARDON
LORAIN
LOREEN
MARGIN
MARIAN
MARION
MARLIN
MAROON
MARTEN
MARTIN
MARVIN
MERLIN
MERLON
MERMAN
MERMEN
MERVIN
MOREEN
MORGAN
MORGEN
MORION
MORMON
MORTON
NOREEN
NORMAN
PARDON
PARIAN
PARSON
PERRON
PERSON
PURLIN
SARGON
SCREEN
SEREIN
SERMON
SPRAIN
STRAIN
STREWN
SYRIAN
TARPAN
TARTAN
TARZAN
THROWN
TURBAN

TUREEN
TYRIAN
VERDIN
VERDUN
VEREIN
VERMIN
VERNON
VIRGIN
WARDEN
WARREN
WORSEN
ZIRCON
******

--R--O

******
AERUGO
ARROYO
BARRIO
BORNEO
BURGOO
CARDIO
CARUSO
CERATO
CHROMO
CHRONO
CHRYSO
CYRANO
DORADO
ENRICO
FOREGO
HERETO
HERNIO
KARROO
KERATO
LAREDO
MERINO
MORPHO
PHRENO
SORGHO
TERATO
TEREDO
TORERO
VARICO
VIRAGO
******

--R--P

******
BURLAP
CARHOP

EARLAP
LARRUP
MARKUP
SCRIMP
SCROOP
SHRIMP
TURNIP
TURNUP
WARMUP
******

--R--R

******
AIRIER
ARREAR
BARBER
BARKER
BARTER
BERBER
BORDER
BURGER
BURLER
BURNER
BURSAR
CARDER
CAREER
CARPER
CARTER
CARVER
CORDER
CORKER
CORNER
CURLER
CURSOR
DARKER
DARNER
DARTER
DORMER
DURBAR
EARNER
FARCER
FARMER
FERBER
FERVOR
FIRMER
FORCER
FORGER
FORMER
FURFUR

GARNER
GARTER
GIRDER
GORGER
GORIER
HARBOR
HARDER
HARPER
HERDER
HORROR
HURLER
HURTER
LARDER
LARGER
LARKER
LURKER
MARKER
MARRER
MARTYR
MERCER
MERGER
MIRROR
MORTAR
MURDER
MURMUR
NORNIR
NURSER
PARKER
PARLOR
PORKER
PORTER
PURGER
PURLER
PURSER
SARSAR
SARTOR
SERVER
SIRDAR
SORTER
SPRIER
SPRYER
SURFER
SURGER
TARTAR
TARTER
TERMER
TERMOR
TERROR

TERSER	BURIES	DERMIS	HORSES	NORIAS	SIRUPS
TORPOR	BURINS	DERRIS	HURONS	NORMAS	SORELS
TURNER	BURKES	DIRGES	JARVIS	NORRIS	SORGOS
UPROAR	BURROS	DORIES	JERRYS	NURSES	SPRAGS
VARIER	BURSAS	DURESS	JERVIS	OGRESS	SPRATS
VERGER	BURSES	EARLES	JORAMS	PARENS	SPRAYS
WARDER	BURSTS	EARTHS	JORGES	PARERS	SPREES
WARIER	CARATS	EGRESS	JORUMS	PAREUS	SPRIGS
WARMER	CARERS	EGRETS	JURATS	PARGOS	SPRITS
WARNER	CARESS	ERRORS	JURELS	PARIES	SPRUES
WARPER	CARETS	EYRIES	JURIES	PARKAS	STRAPS
WIRIER	CARGOS	FARADS	JURORS	PARSES	STRASS
WORKER	CARIBS	FARCES	KARATS	PARSIS	STRAWS
WORMER	CARIES	FARERS	KARENS	PARVIS	STRAYS
WORSER	CARLAS	FARLES	KARMAS	PERCYS	STRESS
YORKER	CARLOS	FERMIS	KERMES	PERILS	STREWS
******	CAROBS	FEROUS	KERMIS	PERRYS	STRIPS
--R--S	CAROLS	FERRIS	LARGOS	POROUS	STROPS
******	CAROMS	FIRERS	LARRYS	PUREES	STRUMS
AARONS	CARPUS	FIRSTS	LEROYS	PURGES	STRUTS
ABRAMS	CARTES	FIRTHS	LORIES	PURSES	SURAHS
ACROSS	CARVES	FORAYS	LURERS	PYRANS	SURGES
AERIES	CEREUS	FORCES	LYRICS	RERUNS	SYRUPS
AGREES	CEROUS	FORGES	MARCOS	SARAHS	TAROTS
AORTAS	CERTES	FORTES	MARCUS	SCRAGS	TARSUS
APRILS	CIRCUS	FORTIS	MARGES	SCRAMS	TEREUS
APRONS	CIRRUS	FORUMS	MARGOS	SCRAPS	TERRYS
ARRAYS	CORALS	FURIES	MARIAS	SCREWS	THREES
ARROWS	CORERS	FURORS	MARIES	SCRIPS	THRIPS
ATREUS	CORGIS	FURZES	MARTAS	SCRODS	THROBS
AUREUS	CORNUS	GEROUS	MARTYS	SCRUBS	THROES
AUROUS	CORPUS	GERRYS	MERGES	SCRUMS	THROWS
BARDES	CORSES	GERTYS	MERITS	SERACS	THRUMS
BARGES	CORTES	GORALS	MERLES	SERAIS	TORAHS
BARONS	CORVES	GORGES	MEROUS	SERIES	TORIES
BARRYS	CORVUS	GORSES	MORALS	SERIFS	TORIIS
BARYES	CURERS	GYRONS	MORASS	SERINS	TOROUS
BERETS	CURIES	HARASS	MORAYS	SEROUS	TORSKS
BERMES	CURIOS	HAREMS	MORELS	SEROWS	TORSOS
BERTHS	CURSES	HARRIS	MORONS	SERUMS	TURCOS
BERYLS	CURTIS	HARRYS	MORRIS	SERVES	TURKIS
BIRLES	CURVES	HERMES	MORROS	SERVOS	TURVES
BIRTHS	CYRILS	HEROES	MORTYS	SHREDS	UNRIGS
BOREAS	DARERS	HERONS	MURALS	SHREWS	UNRIPS
BORERS	DARICS	HERPES	MURRES	SHRUBS	VARIES
BURANS	DARIUS	HIRAMS	MYRNAS	SHRUGS	VARVES
BURGHS	DEREKS	HIRERS	NEREIS	SIRENS	VERGES
BURGOS	DERMAS	HORDES	NERVES	SIRIUS	VERNAS

VERSES	FORGOT	TURBIT	LARYNX	KORUNY	******
VERSOS	FORINT	TURBOT	SURTAX	LORDLY	--R--Z
VERSTS	FORMAT	TURRET	SYRINX	MARGAY	******
VERSUS	GARGET	TYRANT	VERNIX	MARSHY	CORTEZ
VIREOS	GARNET	UNREST	VERTEX	MERELY	LORENZ
VIRGAS	GARRET	UNROOT	VORTEX	MERSEY	******
VOROUS	GERENT	UPROOT	******	MORLEY	--S--A
WIRERS	GORGET	VARLET	--R--Y	MURRAY	******
WORLDS	HARLOT	VERIST	******	MURREY	CASABA
WORSTS	HEREAT	VERSET	AERIFY	NORWAY	CASAVA
YERBAS	HERIOT	VERVET	AIRDRY	ORRERY	CASSIA
ZEROES	HERMIT	WERENT	AIRILY	PARITY	CESURA
ZIRONS	HORNET	******	AIRWAY	PARLAY	FASCIA
ZORILS	JURANT	--R--U	ARROWY	PARLEY	HESTIA
******	JURIST	******	BARELY	PARODY	JOSHUA
--R--T	KERMIT	BUREAU	BARFLY	PARTLY	JOSIEA
******	LARIAT	MOREAU	BARLEY	PERTLY	LISBOA
ABRUPT	LYRIST	******	BARNEY	PIRACY	MASORA
ADRIFT	MARGOT	--R--W	BARONY	PORTLY	NASHUA
ADROIT	MARIST	******	BERNEY	PURELY	PESETA
AORIST	MARKET	BARROW	BURLEY	PURIFY	POSADA
ARRANT	MARMOT	BORROW	CARBOY	PURITY	RESEDA
ARREST	MEREST	BURROW	CORDAY	PURVEY	ROSTRA
AURIST	PARENT	CARLOW	CORODY	RAREFY	RUSSIA
BARBET	PARGET	CURFEW	CURACY	RARELY	SISERA
BAREST	PARROT	CURLEW	CURTLY	RARITY	URSULA
BARRET	PERMIT	DARROW	CURTSY	SCREWY	VESICA
BEREFT	PUREST	FARROW	DARKLY	SIRUPY	******
BURBOT	PURIST	FURROW	DIRELY	SORELY	--S--B
BURNET	RAREST	HARLOW	EARTHY	SPRYLY	******
CARPET	SCRIPT	HARROW	EERILY	STRAWY	ABSORB
CARROT	SHRIFT	JARROW	FARLEY	STRIPY	ADSORB
CERMET	SORBET	MARLOW	FERITY	SURELY	RESORB
CHRIST	SOREST	MARROW	FIRMLY	SURETY	******
CORNET	SPRINT	MORROW	GORILY	SURREY	--S--C
CORSET	SPROUT	NARROW	HARDLY	SURVEY	******
CURVET	STRAIT	SORROW	HARLEY	SYRUPY	BUSTIC
DERMAT	STREET	WARSAW	HARVEY	TARTLY	COSMIC
DIRECT	STRICT	YARROW	HEREBY	TERMLY	CYSTIC
DIREST	STRIPT	******	HERESY	TURKEY	FISTIC
DORSET	SUREST	--R--X	HORARY	UNRULY	FUSTIC
ENRAPT	TARGET	******	HORSEY	VERIFY	GESTIC
ENROOT	TERCET	CARFAX	HURLEY	VERILY	MASTIC
ERRANT	TERRET	CERVIX	HURRAY	VERITY	MOSAIC
FAROUT	THREAT	CORTEX	JARVEY	VYRNWY	MYSTIC
FERRET	THRIFT	EARWAX	JEREMY	WARILY	NASTIC
FOREST	THROAT	FORNAX	JERSEY	WARMLY	NOSTIC
FORGET	THRUST	FORNIX	KERSEY	WIRILY	RUSTIC
				WORTHY	

******	KISSED	VISAED	INSURE	MASSIF	******
--S--D	LASHED	VISARD	JESSIE	MYSELF	**--S--L**
******	LASTED	VISCID	JOSTLE	******	******
ABSURD	LISPED	VISEED	LASSIE	**--S--G**	ASSAIL
AISLED	LISTED	WASHED	LESLIE	******	BUSHEL
AXSEED	LUSHED	WASTED	LESSEE	BASING	CASUAL
BASHED	LUSTED	WISHED	LUSTRE	BUSING	COSTAL
BASKED	MASHED	WISPED	LYSINE	CASING	DISCAL
BASTED	MASKED	YESSED	MASHIE	DOSING	DISMAL
BESTED	MASSED	ZESTED	MASQUE	EASING	DISPEL
BOSSED	MASTED	******	MESTEE	FUSING	DISTAL
BUSHED	MESHED	**--S--E**	MISCUE	GASBAG	DISTIL
BUSIED	MESSED	******	MISERE	HOSING	DOSSAL
BUSSED	MISDID	ALSACE	MISTLE	LOSING	DOSSEL
BUSTED	MISLED	ALSIKE	MISUSE	LYSING	DOSSIL
CASHED	MISSED	ANSATE	MOSQUE	MASKEG	ENSOUL
COSHED	MISTED	ARSINE	MUSCAE	MUSING	FESTAL
COSTED	MUSHED	ASSIZE	MUSCLE	MUSKEG	FISCAL
CUSPED	MUSSED	ASSUME	MUSTEE	NOSING	FOSSIL
CUSPID	NESTED	ASSURE	NESTLE	POSING	GESELL
CUSSED	NOSHED	BASQUE	PASSEE	RISING	GOSPEL
DASHED	OUSTED	BESIDE	PESADE	ROSING	HASSEL
DESMID	PASSED	BESSIE	PESTLE	UNSUNG	HOSTEL
DISHED	PASTED	BISQUE	RESALE	VISING	INSOUL
DOSSED	PISHED	BUSTLE	RESCUE	WISING	INSTIL
DUSKED	POSTED	CASQUE	RESIDE	******	LISTEL
DUSTED	PUSHED	CASSIE	RESILE	**--S--H**	MESCAL
ENSUED	RASPED	CASTLE	RESOLE	******	MESIAL
FASTED	RESEND	CESARE	RESUME	BASRAH	MISKAL
FISTED	RESOLD	CISSIE	RISQUE	CASBAH	MISSAL
FUSSED	RESTED	COSINE	ROSCOE	JOSEPH	MISSEL
GASHED	RISKED	COSTAE	RUSINE	JOSIAH	MUSSEL
GASPED	RUSHED	DESIRE	RUSTLE	PESACH	NASIAL
GASSED	RUSTED	DISUSE	SESAME	PISGAH	PASCAL
GUSHED	SASHED	DOSAGE	TESSIE	TUSSAH	PASTEL
HASHED	SASSED	ENSILE	TESTAE	******	PASTIL
HASPED	SUSSED	ENSURE	TISANE	**--S--I**	PISTIL
HASTED	TASKED	ESSENE	TISSUE	******	PISTOL
HESOID	TASTED	FESCUE	TUSSLE	ASSISI	POSTAL
HISPID	TESTED	FOSSAE	UNSAFE	SESQUI	RASCAL
HISSED	TOSSED	FUSILE	UNSURE	TISHRI	RESELL
HOSTED	TUSHED	GISELE	UPSIDE	VASARI	ROSEAL
HUSHED	TUSKED	GUSSIE	URSINE	VASHTI	TASSEL
HUSKED	UNSAID	HASSLE	VESTEE	VASILI	TUSSAL
ISSUED	UNSHOD	HUSTLE	VISAGE	******	UNSEAL
JESSED	UNSOLD	INSANE	******	******	VASSAL
JESTED	VESPID	INSIDE	**--S--F**	**--S--K**	VESSEL
JOSHED	VESTED	INSOLE	******	******	VESTAL
			GUSTAF	SUSLIK	VISUAL
			ITSELF	YASMAK	

******	LASSEN	******	LESSER	******	ENSUES
--S--M	LESION	--S--R	LESSOR	--S--S	ESSAYS
******	LESSEN	******	LESTER	******	FASCES
ANSELM	LESSON	ANSWER	LISPER	AISLES	FESSES
BESEEM	LISBON	AUSTER	LISTER	ASSAIS	FISHES
CESIUM	LISTEN	BESTIR	LUSHER	ASSAYS	FOSSES
CUSTOM	MASCON	BISTER	LUSTER	ASSESS	FUSEES
DISARM	MESIAN	BUSKER	MASHER	ASSETS	FUSILS
LISSOM	MUSLIN	BUSTER	MASKER	BASHES	FUSSES
MOSLEM	NASION	CASPAR	MASTER	BASICS	GASHES
MUSEUM	OSSEIN	CASPER	MESHER	BASILS	GASSES
MUSLIM	OSSIAN	CASTER	MESMER	BASINS	GESSOS
PASSIM	PISTON	CASTOR	MISTER	BASSES	GISMOS
POSSUM	RESIGN	COSHER	MUSHER	BASSOS	GUSHES
SYSTEM	RUSKIN	COSTAR	MUSTER	BASTES	HASHES
UNSEAM	SISKIN	COSTER	NASSER	BESETS	HASTES
WISDOM	TASMAN	CUSTER	NESTOR	BESOMS	HISSES
******	TESTON	DASHER	NOSIER	BESOTS	HUSHES
--S--N	TUSCAN	DISBAR	OUSTER	BESSYS	INSETS
******	UNSEEN	DOSSER	OYSTER	BOSHES	ISSEIS
ASSIGN	VISION	DUSTER	PASSER	BOSOMS	ISSUES
AUSTEN	WYSTAN	EASIER	PASTER	BOSSES	JASONS
AUSTIN	YESMAN	EASTER	PASTOR	BUSHES	JESSES
BASION	******	FASTER	PESTER	BUSIES	JOSHES
BOSTON	--S--O	FESTER	POSEUR	BUSSES	JOSIAS
BUSKIN	******	FISHER	POSTER	BYSSUS	JOSSES
BUSMAN	AUSTRO	FOSTER	PUSHER	CASALS	JUSTUS
BUSMEN	BASUTO	FUSSER	RASHER	CASHES	KISSES
CASEIN	BISTRO	GASPAR	RASPER	CASSIS	LASERS
CASERN	CASHOO	GASPER	RASTER	CASTES	LASHES
COSIGN	CASINO	GUSHER	RESTER	CESTUS	LASSES
DESIGN	CASTRO	HESTER	RISKER	CISCOS	LASSOS
DESMAN	GASTRO	HISSER	ROSIER	CISSYS	LESBOS
DISOWN	PASHTO	HOSIER	ROSTER	COSHES	LOSERS
EASTON	VESICO	HUSKER	RUSHER	COSMOS	LOSSES
ENSIGN	******	HUSSAR	SISTER	COSSES	LUSHES
FASTEN	--S--P	HYSTER	TASTER	CUSCUS	LYSINS
FUSAIN	******	INSTAR	TESTER	CUSPIS	MASERS
FUSION	BISHOP	ISSUER	TUSKER	CUSSES	MASHES
GASCON	GOSSIP	JASPER	TUSSAR	CUSSOS	MASONS
GASKIN	HYSSOP	JESTER	ULSTER	CUSTOS	MASSES
GASMAN	INSTEP	JOSHER	VASTER	DASHES	MESHES
GASMEN	MISHAP	KASPER	VESPER	DISCUS	MESNES
GASTON	PUSHUP	KISSER	WASHER	DISHES	MESONS
GOSHEN	TOSSUP	KOSHER	WASTER	DOSERS	MESSES
HASTEN	UNSHIP	LASCAR	WESTER	EASELS	MESSRS
INSPAN	UNSTEP	LASHER	XYSTER	EDSELS	MISERS
JUSTIN	UNSTOP	LASTER	YESTER	ELSIES	MISSES

MISSIS	VISORS	POSSET	BISCAY	CATENA	ATTEND
MISSUS	VISTAS	RESEAT	BUSHEY	CITOLA	AUTOED
MOSEYS	WASHES	RESECT	BUSILY	DATURA	BATHED
MOSSES	WASTES	RESENT	CASEFY	ENTERA	BATTED
MUSHES	WISHES	RESIST	COSILY	FATIMA	BETTED
MUSSES	XTSTUS	RESORT	COSTLY	GOTAMA	BITTED
NASALS	XYSTOS	RESULT	DESCRY	INTIMA	BUTTED
NESSUS	YESSES	RUSSET	DESOXY	ISTRIA	CATTED
NISEIS	******	SESTET	DISMAY	LATERA	CITIED
OBSESS	--S--T	TASSET	DISNEY	LATRIA	DOTARD
ONSETS	******	UNSEAT	EASILY	LATVIA	DOTTED
OUSELS	ABSENT	UPSHOT	GASIFY	LITHIA	EXTEND
PASHAS	ASSENT	WISEST	JUSTLY	NUTRIA	FATTED
PASSES	ASSERT	******	LASTLY	OPTIMA	FITTED
PASSUS	ASSIST	--S--U	LESLEY	OTTAVA	GUTTED
PASTAS	ASSORT	******	MISERY	OTTAWA	HATRED
PASTES	BASALT	DESSAU	MISLAY	OTTOWA	HATTED
PISCES	BASEST	NASSAU	MOSLEY	PATHIA	HOTBED
PISHES	BASKET	PUSHTU	MOSTLY	PATINA	HOTROD
POSERS	BASSET	RESEAU	NOSILY	PETULA	HOTTED
POSIES	BESANT	VISHNU	OSSIFY	PYTHIA	HUTTED
POSITS	BISECT	******	PASTRY	RETINA	INTEND
POSSES	BOSKET	--S--V	POSHLY	SATARA	JETTED
PUSHES	CASKET	******	PUSSEY	ULTIMA	JOTTED
PUSSES	COSSET	GUSTAV	PUSSLY	YTTRIA	JUTTED
RASHES	CUSHAT	******	RASHLY	******	KITTED
RESETS	DESALT	--S--W	ROSARY	--T--B	LATHED
RESINS	DESERT	******	ROSILY	******	MATTED
RISERS	DESIST	BASHAW	ROSINY	ENTOMB	METHOD
ROSINS	DESPOT	BESTOW	SASHAY	INTOMB	MITRED
RUSHES	EXSECT	CASHAW	VASTLY	******	NETTED
SASHES	EXSERT	CASHEW	VESTRY	--T--C	NITRID
SASINS	GASJET	CUSHAW	WESLEY	******	NUTTED
SASSES	GASKET	KISLEW	WISELY	ALTAIC	OBTUND
SUSANS	GUSSET	MOSCOW	******	CITRIC	OSTEND
SUSIES	HASLET	NOSHOW	--S--Z	GOTHIC	OUTBID
TASTES	INSECT	******	******	IATRIC	OUTDID
TESTES	INSERT	--S--X	ERSATZ	LITHIC	OUTDID
TESTIS	INSIST	******	******	METRIC	PATTED
TOSHES	INSULT	AUSPEX	--T--A	MYTHIC	PETARD
TOSSES	JESUIT	LASTEX	******	NITRIC	PETTED
TUSHES	KISMET	MUSKOX	AFTOSA	PYTHIC	PITHED
TUSSIS	MASCOT	SUSSEX	ALTHEA	SOTHIC	PITIED
UNSAYS	MISFIT	WESSEX	ANTHEA	VITRIC	PITTED
UPSETS	MUSCAT	******	ANTLIA	YTTRIC	POTTED
VESTAS	MUSKET	--S--Y	ASTHMA	******	PUTRID
VISCUS	MUSKIT	******	ATTICA	--T--D	PUTTED
VISITS	MUSTNT	BASELY	ATTILA	******	RATTED
		BASIFY		ANTEED	RETARD
				ASTRID	

RETOLD	ENTICE	POTTLE	LUTING	******	MUTISM
RETROD	ENTIRE	PUTTEE	MATING	--T--L	PUTNAM
RETTED	ENTREE	RATINE	METING	******	******
RITARD	ESTATE	RATITE	MUTING	ACTUAL	--T--N
ROTTED	FETTLE	RATTLE	NOTING	ARTFUL	******
ROTUND	FUTILE	RETAKE	NUTMEG	ASTRAL	ACTION
RUTTED	FUTURE	RETENE	OPTING	BETHEL	ASTERN
TATTED	GUTTAE	RETIRE	OUTING	CITRAL	ATTAIN
TETRAD	GUTTLE	RETUSE	PUTLOG	DETAIL	ATTORN
TITHED	HATTIE	ROTATE	RATING	DOTTEL	AUTUMN
TITLED	INTAKE	ROTCHE	SATANG	ENTAIL	BATAAN
TOTTED	INTONE	RUTILE	SATING	FETIAL	BATMAN
TUTTED	KATHIE	SATIRE	SITING	FITFUL	BATMEN
UNTIED	KETENE	SETOSE	TOTING	HATFUL	BATTEN
UNTOLD	KETONE	SETTEE	VOTING	LETHAL	BATTIN
UNTROD	KETOSE	SETTLE	******	LUTEAL	BITTEN
VATTED	KETTLE	SUTTEE	--T--H	METHYL	BUTTON
VETOED	KITTLE	SUTURE	******	MITRAL	CATION
VETTED	LITTLE	TATTLE	ATTACH	MUTUAL	CATKIN
WETTED	LOTTIE	TITTLE	DETACH	OSTEAL	CATLIN
WITHED	LYTTAE	UNTRUE	FETICH	OXTAIL	CITRON
WITTED	MATINE	UPTAKE	FETISH	PATHOL	COTTON
******	MATTIE	VITTAE	JUTISH	PATROL	DETAIN
--T--E	MATURE	VOTIVE	KITSCH	PETREL	EXTERN
******	METAGE	WATAPE	LATISH	PETROL	FATTEN
ACTIVE	METOPE	WATTLE	POTASH	RETAIL	GOTTEN
ASTUTE	METTLE	******	PUTSCH	RETELL	HATPIN
ATTIRE	MOTILE	--T--F	******	RETOOL	HETMAN
ATTLEE	MOTIVE	******	--T--I	RITUAL	INTERN
ATTUNE	MOTTLE	CUTOFF	******	TETRYL	INTURN
BATTLE	MUTATE	PUTOFF	ACTINI	TETZEL	JETTON
BATTUE	MUTULE	SETOFF	ASTERI	VATFUL	KATION
BETAKE	NATIVE	******	LITCHI	WITHAL	KITTEN
BETIDE	NATURE	--T--G	MYTHOI	******	LATEEN
BETISE	NETTIE	******	OCTOPI	--T--M	LATTEN
BOTTLE	NETTLE	ACTING	OCTROI	******	LOTION
BUTANE	NOTICE	BATING	WATUSI	ACTIUM	MATRON
CATTIE	OBTUSE	BITING	******	ANTHEM	MITTEN
CATTLE	OCTANE	CITING	--T--K	ANTRIM	MOTION
CETANE	OCTAVE	DATING	******	ANTRUM	MUTTON
COTTAE	OPTIME	DOTING	ATTACK	AUTISM	NATHAN
CUTTLE	PATINE	EATING	BATTIK	BOTTOM	NATION
DATIVE	PETITE	FATING	BETOOK	ESTEEM	NATRON
DITONE	PETRIE	FETING	BYTALK	FATHOM	NOTION
DOTAGE	POTAGE	GATING	RETOOK	GOTHAM	OBTAIN
DOTTLE	POTALE	HATING	SHTICK	JETSAM	OPTION
ECTYPE	POTPIE	KITBAG	UNTACK	JOTHAM	OUTMAN
ENTERE	POTSIE	KITING		LUTEUM	OUTRAN

OUTRUN	CATSUP	JOTTER	ARTELS	KITTYS	SETTOS
PATHAN	ENTRAP	LATHER	ARTIES	LATHES	SETUPS
PATRON	METUMP	LATTER	ARTOIS	LATINS	SITARS
PATTEN	SATRAP	LETTER	ASTERS	LETUPS	SITINS
PATTON	TITTUP	LITHER	ATTARS	LITERS	SOTHIS
PITMAN	******	LITTER	ATTICS	LITMUS	SOTOLS
PITMEN	--T--R	LUTHER	AZTECS	LOTAHS	SUTRAS
POTEEN	******	MATTER	BATHOS	MATEOS	TATARS
POTION	AETHER	METEOR	BATIKS	MATEYS	TETHYS
POTMAN	ALTAIR	METIER	BATONS	MATINS	TETONS
PYTHON	ANTHER	MOTHER	BETELS	MATTES	TITANS
RATION	ANTIAR	MUTTER	BETSYS	MATZOS	TITHES
RATLIN	ANTLER	NATTER	BETTES	METALS	TITLES
RATOON	ARTHUR	NETHER	BETTYS	METERS	TOTALS
RATTAN	AUTHOR	NUTTER	BITERS	METROS	TOTEMS
RATTEN	BATHER	OSTLER	BUTTES	MITERS	TOTERS
RETAIN	BATTER	PATTER	CATERS	MOTELS	TUTORS
RETURN	BETTER	POTHER	CATHYS	MOTIFS	TUTTIS
ROTTEN	BETTOR	POTTER	CITIES	MOTORS	UNTIES
SATEEN	BITTER	PUTTER	CITRUS	MOTTOS	UTTERS
SATURN	BOTHER	RATHER	COTTAS	MYTHOS	VETOES
SUTTON	BUTLER	RATTER	CUTEYS	NOTERS	VITALS
TITIAN	BUTTER	RITTER	CUTIES	OCTADS	VOTERS
UPTOWN	CATHER	ROTTER	CUTINS	OCTETS	WATAPS
UPTURN	CITHER	SETTER	CUTLAS	OPTICS	WATERS
WATSON	COTTAR	SITTER	CUTUPS	OTTERS	WITHES
WITHIN	COTTER	SUTLER	DATERS	OUTERS	ZETHOS
******	CUTLER	TATLER	DATTOS	PATENS	ZETHUS
--T--O	CUTTER	TATTER	DETERS	PATERS	******
******	DETOUR	TETHER	DITTOS	PATHOS	--T--T
ACTINO	DITHER	TETTER	DOTERS	PATIOS	******
ANTERO	DOTIER	TITHER	DUTIES	PATOIS	ARTIST
ARTHRO	DOTTER	TITTER	EATERS	PATSYS	ATTEST
ARTURO	EITHER	TOTHER	ENTERS	PETALS	CATGUT
ASTERO	ESTHER	TOTTER	ESTERS	PETERS	CUTEST
CATALO	FATHER	VETOER	ESTOPS	PITIES	CUTLET
ENTERO	FATTER	WETHER	ESTRUS	PITONS	CUTOUT
ENTOMO	FETTER	WETTER	EXTOLS	POTTOS	DETECT
GITANO	FITTER	WITHER	EXTRAS	PUTONS	DETENT
HETERO	GATHER	ZITHER	FETORS	RATALS	DETEST
JETHRO	GETTER	******	GETUPS	RATELS	EXTANT
MATTEO	GUTTER	--T--S	HATERS	RATERS	EXTENT
OCTAVO	HATTER	******	HATTYS	RATIOS	EXTORT
POTATO	HITHER	ACTORS	HETTYS	ROTORS	GUTTAT
TATTOO	HITLER	ALTARS	HOTELS	SATINS	HOTPOT
ULTIMO	HITTER	ALTERS	INTERS	SATYRS	INTACT
******	HOTTER	ANTICS	KATHYS	SETONS	INTENT
--T--P	JITTER	ANTONS	KATIES	SETOUS	INTUIT
******					
CATNAP					
CATNIP					

LATENT	******	APULIA	POURED	GOURDE	CRUTCH
LATEST	--T--Y	AQUILA	POUTED	GRUDGE	FOURTH
LUTIST	******	ARUNTA	PRUNED	JOUNCE	HAUNCH
MATZOT	ANTONY	DHURNA	ROUGED	LAUNCE	LAUNCH
MOTMOT	ARTERY	FRUSTA	ROUSED	LAURAE	NAUTCH
MUTANT	ARTILY	GIULIA	ROUTED	LAURIE	PAUNCH
NATANT	ASTRAY	IGUANA	SAUCED	LOUISE	SCUTCH
NITWIT	BETONY	LOUISA	SOULED	LOUNGE	SMUTCH
NUTLET	BETRAY	NAUSEA	SOUPED	LOUVRE	SQUASH
OBTECT	BITCHY	PYURIA	SOURED	MOUSSE	SQUISH
OBTEST	BOTANY	RHUMBA	SOUSED	OEUVRE	******
OCTANT	BOTCHY	SQUAMA	SPUMED	PLUNGE	--U--I
OPTANT	BOTFLY	THULIA	STUPID	POUNCE	******
OUTFIT	CATCHY	ZEUGMA	TOURED	ROUBLE	ALUMNI
OUTLET	CATHAY	******	TOUTED	ROUCHE	BRUNEI
OUTPUT	CUTELY	--U--D	UNUSED	SLUDGE	GLUTEI
OUTSAT	DATARY	******	WAULED	SLUICE	SOUARI
OUTSET	EATERY	ABUSED	YAUPED	SMUDGE	******
OUTSIT	ECTOMY	AMUSED	******	SOURCE	--U--K
OUTWIT	ENTITY	AOUDAD	--U--E	SPURGE	******
PATENT	ESTRAY	BOUSED	******	SQUARE	SQUAWK
POTENT	JITNEY	CAUDAD	ACUATE	SQUIRE	SQUEAK
PUTOUT	LATELY	CAUSED	ALULAE	TOUCHE	******
PUTPUT	LITANY	DAUBED	BAUBLE	TOUPEE	--U--L
RETORT	MOTLEY	DEUCED	BLUNGE	TOUSLE	******
ROTGUT	MUTINY	DOUSED	BOUCLE	TRUDGE	ALUDEL
SETOUT	NOTARY	EDUARD	BOUFFE	UVULAE	BRUMAL
TITBIT	NOTIFY	EDUCED	BOUGIE	ZOUAVE	BRUNEL
URTEXT	OUTCRY	ELUDED	BOUNCE	******	BRUTAL
WITHIT	OUTLAY	EXUDED	BOURNE	--U--G	CAUDAL
******	PATCHY	FEUDED	BOURSE	******	CAUSAL
--T--U	PITCHY	FLUKED	BRUISE	BLUING	CRURAL
******	POTBOY	FLUMED	CAUDLE	CLUING	DOUGAL
BATEAU	RATIFY	FLUTED	COULEE	FEUING	DRUPEL
COTEAU	ROTARY	FLUXED	COUPLE	GLUING	FAUCAL
GATEAU	SATINY	FOULED	COURSE	SLUING	FAUNAL
******	SATORY	GAUGED	CRUISE	TAUTOG	FEUDAL
--T--W	TATTLY	GOUGED	CRUSOE	TRUING	FRUGAL
******	TETANY	HAULED	DOUBLE	******	LAUREL
OUTLAW	TETCHY	HOUSED	DOUCHE	--U--H	NEURAL
******	UNTIDY	INURED	DOUGIE	******	NOUNAL
--T--X	VOTARY	LAUDED	DRUDGE	AGUISH	PLURAL
******	WATERY	LOURED	EQUATE	BEULAH	SAUREL
******	WITNEY	LOUSED	EQUINE	BLUISH	SQUALL
HATBOX	******	MAULED	FAUNAE	BRUNCH	SQUEAL
HOTBOX	--U--A	MOUSED	FRUNZE	CHURCH	SQUILL
MATRIX	******	PAUSED	GAUCHE	CLUTCH	******
OUTFOX	ABULIA	PLUMED	GAULLE	CRUNCH	--U--M
	ALUMNA				******
					SCUTUM
					SPUTUM

SQUIRM	CAUSER	BAUCIS	DEUCES	HOURIS	ROUTES
TRUISM	CAUTER	BEULAS	DOUBTS	HOUSES	SAUCES
******	COUGAR	BLUETS	DOUGHS	INURES	SAULTS
--U--N	CRUDER	BLUFFS	DOUSES	INURNS	SAUNAS
******	DAUBER	BLUNTS	DRUIDS	JAUNTS	SAURUS
ACUMEN	FLUTER	BLURBS	DRUNKS	JOULES	SAUTES
ALUMIN	FOULER	BLURTS	DRUPES	JOUSTS	SCUBAS
ANURAN	GAUGER	BOUGHS	DRUSES	KAURIS	SCUFFS
BHUTAN	GLUIER	BOULES	EDUCES	KNURLS	SCULLS
COUPON	GOUGER	BOUNDS	EDUCTS	KRUBIS	SCUTES
COUSIN	HAULER	BOURGS	ELUDES	LAUGHS	SHUCKS
GLUTEN	LAUDER	BOURNS	EQUALS	LAURAS	SHUNTS
HAUSEN	LOUDER	BOUSES	EQUIPS	LEUDES	SKULKS
INULIN	LOUVER	BRUCES	ERUCTS	LOUGHS	SKULLS
LOUDEN	MAULER	BRUGES	ERUPTS	LOUPES	SKUNKS
MOULIN	MAUSER	BRUINS	ETUDES	LOUSES	SLUMPS
MOUTON	MOUSER	BRUITS	EXUDES	MAUDES	SLURPS
NEURON	NEUTER	BRUMES	EXULTS	MAUNDS	SNUFFS
PAULIN	OCULAR	BRUNOS	EXURBS	MAUVES	SOUGHS
PLUGIN	OVULAR	BRUTES	FAUCES	MOULDS	SOUNDS
REUBEN	PAUKER	BRUTUS	FAULTS	MOULTS	SOUSES
SHUTIN	PAUPER	CAUCUS	FAUNAS	MOUNTS	SPUMES
TAUTEN	PAUSER	CAULES	FAUNUS	MOURNS	SPURNS
TEUTON	POURER	CAULIS	FAUVES	MOUSES	SPURTS
TOUCAN	POUTER	CAULKS	FEUARS	MOUTHS	SQUABS
TOULON	PRUNER	CAUSES	FLUFFS	NEUMES	SQUADS
TRUMAN	ROUSER	CHUCKS	FLUIDS	ONUSES	SQUATS
YAUPON	ROUTER	CHUFAS	FLUKES	OVULES	SQUAWS
YOUPON	SAUCER	CHUMPS	FLUMES	PAULAS	SQUIBS
******	SAUGER	CHUNKS	FLUMPS	PAULUS	SQUIDS
--U--O	SOURER	CHURLS	FLUNKS	PAUSES	STUBBS
******	STUPOR	CHURNS	FLUORS	PLUCKS	STUFFS
ALUINO	TAUTER	CHURRS	FLUTES	PLUMBS	STULLS
FLUORO	TEUCER	CHUTES	FLUXES	PLUMES	STUMPS
FLUVIO	TOURER	CLUCKS	FOUNDS	PLUMPS	STUNTS
GAUCHO	TOUTER	CLUMPS	FOUNTS	PLUNKS	STUPAS
GIULIO	USURER	COUGHS	FRUITS	PLUSES	STUPES
PLUMBO	UVULAR	COUNTS	FRUMPS	PLUTUS	TAUNTS
PLUVIO	******	COUPES	GAUGES	POULTS	TAUPES
POUSTO	--U--S	COURTS	GAUZES	POUNDS	TAURUS
STUCCO	******	CRUCES	GLUMES	PRUDES	THUJAS
STUDIO	ABUSES	CRUETS	GOUGES	PRUNES	THUMBS
******	ADULTS	CRUMBS	GOURDS	RHUMBS	THUMPS
--U--R	ALUINS	CRUMPS	GRUELS	ROUGES	TOUGHS
******	AMUSES	CRUSES	GRUMES	ROUGHS	TRUCES
ABUSER	ANUBIS	CRUSTS	GRUNTS	ROUNDS	TRUCKS
ALULAR	ANUSES	CRUXES	HAUNTS	ROUSES	TRUDYS
AMUSER	AZURES	DAUNTS	HOUNDS	ROUSTS	TRUMPS

TRUNKS	******	SCUMMY	ALVINE	MOVING	******
TRUSTS	--U--Y	SCURFY	BOVATE	PAVING	--V--O
TRUTHS	******	SCURRY	BOVINE	RAVING	******
USURPS	ACUITY	SCURVY	CAVITE	RIVING	LAVABO
UTURNS	BLUELY	SLUDGY	DEVICE	ROVING	NAVAHO
UVULAS	BLURRY	SLUMMY	DEVISE	SAVING	NAVAJO
VAULTS	BOUNCY	SLURRY	DEVOTE	WAVING	******
VAUNTS	BOUNTY	SLUSHY	DIVIDE	WIVING	--V--P
WOUNDS	BRUSHY	SMUDGY	DIVINE	******	******
YOUTHS	CHUBBY	SMUGLY	FOVEAE	--V--H	REVAMP
ZOUNDS	CHUMMY	SMUTTY	HIVITE	******	******
******	CHUNKY	SNUFFY	INVADE	DOVISH	--V--R
--U--T	CLUMPY	SNUGLY	INVITE	ELVISH	
******	CLUMSY	SOURLY	INVOKE	LAVISH	CAVIAR
AMULET	COUNTY	SPUNKY	LAVAGE	RAVISH	DEVOIR
BLUEST	CRUMBY	SPURRY	LEVITE	******	DEVOUR
BOUGHT	CRUMMY	STUBBY	LOVAGE	--V--I	ENVIER
BRULOT	CRUSTY	STUFFY	NEVILE	******	FAVOUR
CAUGHT	DAUBRY	STUMPY	NOVICE	NEVSKI	LEVIER
CRUSET	DOUBLY	STURDY	PAVANE	******	LIVIER
DAUDET	DOUGHY	TAUTLY	PAVISE	--V--L	LIVYER
FAUCET	DOURLY	THUSLY	RAVAGE	******	PAVIOR
FLUENT	EQUITY	TOUCHY	RAVINE	CAVELL	SAVIOR
FOUGHT	FAULTY	TRUSTY	REVERE	FOVEAL	SAVOUR
KRUBUT	FLUFFY	******	REVILE	GAVIAL	WAVIER
NAUGHT	FLUKEY	--V--A	REVISE	JOVIAL	XAVIER
NOUGAT	FLUNKY	******	REVIVE	LOVELL	******
NOUGHT	FLURRY	ALVINA	REVOKE	NEVILL	--V--S
SCULPT	FOULLY	ELVIRA	REVEAL	REVEAL	******
SEURAT	FRUITY	HAVANA	SAVAGE	UNVEIL	ALVANS
SOUGHT	FRUMPY	NEVADA	SAVATE	******	ANVILS
SQUINT	GLUMLY	NOVENA	SEVERE	--V--M	BEVELS
SQUIRT	GRUBBY	******	TEVERE	******	BEVIES
STUART	GRUMPY	--V--B	VIVACE	CIVISM	CAVIES
TAUGHT	GRUNDY	******	******	******	CAVILS
TRUANT	HAULMY	ADVERB	--V--G	--V--N	CIVETS
TRUEST	HOURLY	******		******	CIVICS
******	JAUNTY	--V--D	CAVING	CAVEIN	CIVIES
--U--U	KNURLY	******	COVING	CAVERN	COVERS
******	LOUDLY	DEVOID	DIVING	DEVEIN	COVETS
GRUGRU	MAUNDY	ENVIED	GIVING	GOVERN	COVEYS
KYUSHU	MOULDY	LEVIED	GYVING	JOVIAN	DAVEYS
MAUMAU	MOUNTY	NEVOID	HAVING	LOVEIN	DAVIDS
MUUMUU	MOUTHY	REVVED	HIVING	SEVERN	DAVIES
RYUKYU	PLUCKY	******	IRVING	TAVERN	DAVITS
******	PLUMMY	--V--E	JIVING	VIVIAN	DEVILS
--U--X	PLUSHY	******	LAVING	VIVIEN	DIVANS
******	POUCHY	ADVICE	LIVING	WIVERN	DIVERS
CAUDEX		ADVISE	LOVING	WYVERN	DIVERS

DIVOTS	SEVENS	VIVIFY	YAWPED	SIWASH	******
ELVERS	SEVERS	WAVILY	YOWLED	UNWISH	--W--R
ENVIES	WAVERS	******	******	******	******
ENVOYS	WAVEYS	--W--A	--W--E	--W--I	BAWLER
FAVORS	WAVIES	******	******	******	BOWLER
FEVERS	WIVERS	COWPEA	BEWARE	HAWAII	BOWYER
FIVERS	******	EDWINA	BOWTIE	******	COWPER
GAVELS	--V--T	ROWENA	COWAGE	--W--K	DEWIER
GAVOTS	******	******	COWRIE	******	DOWSER
HAVENS	ABVOLT	--W--B	DAWDLE	BYWORK	FAWNER
HOVELS	ADVENT	******	INWOVE	NEWARK	FOWLER
HOVERS	ADVERT	ENWOMB	KEWPIE	THWACK	HAWKER
IRVINS	CAVEAT	******	NOWISE	******	HAWSER
KAVASS	CAVORT	--W--D	PAWNEE	--W--L	HOWLER
KEVELS	COVERT	******	SEWAGE	******	LAWYER
KEVINS	DEVEST	BAWLED	TOWAGE	BEWAIL	LEWDER
LAVERS	DEVOUT	BOWLED	UNWISE	INWALL	PAWNER
LEVEES	DIVERT	BOWSED	******	LAWFUL	PEWTER
LEVELS	DIVEST	BYWORD	--W--G	LOWELL	POWDER
LEVERS	HAVENT	COWARD	******	ORWELL	POWTER
LEVIES	INVENT	DAWNED	BOWING	POWELL	SAWYER
LIVENS	INVERT	DOWNED	BOWLEG	SEWALL	WOWSER
LIVERS	INVEST	DOWSED	CAWING	SEWELL	YAWNER
LIVIAS	LEVANT	EDWARD	COWING	UNWELL	YAWPER
LIVRES	OBVERT	ENWIND	HAWING	******	******
LOVERS	REVERT	FAWNED	HEWING	--W--N	--W--S
MOVERS	REVEST	FOWLED	JAWING	******	******
MOVIES	REVOLT	GAWKED	LAWING	BOWFIN	ALWAYS
NAVELS	SAVANT	GOWNED	LOWING	BOWMAN	BOWELS
NAVIES	SOVIET	HAWKED	MEWING	BOWMEN	BOWERS
NOVELS	UNVEXT	HOWARD	MOWING	COWMAN	BOWSES
PAVANS	******	HOWLED	PAWING	COWMEN	BYWAYS
PAVERS	--V--V	INWARD	ROWING	DAWSON	COWERS
PIVOTS	******	INWIND	SAWING	GAWAIN	DEWANS
RAVELS	PAVLOV	MEWLED	SEWING	NEWTON	DIWANS
RAVENS	******	ONWARD	SOWING	UNWORN	DOWELS
RAVERS	--V--W	OSWALD	TAWING	******	DOWERS
REVELS	******	PAWNED	TOWING	--W--O	DOWLAS
REVERS	REVIEW	REWARD	VOWING	******	DOWSES
REVETS	******	REWIND	WOWING	OSWEGO	EDWINS
REVUES	--V--Y	REWORD	YAWING	******	ERWINS
RIVALS	******	SEWARD	YOWING	--W--P	FAWKES
RIVERS	CAVITY	TOWARD	******	******	HAWSES
RIVETS	LEVITY	UNWIND	--W--H	DEWLAP	HEWERS
ROVERS	LIVELY	UPWARD	******	ENWRAP	IRWINS
SAVERS	LIVERY	WAWLED	HOWDAH	INWRAP	JEWELS
SAVINS	LOVELY	YAWLED	JEWISH	UNWRAP	JEWESS
SAVORS	SAVORY	YAWNED	RAWISH		LOWERS

MOWERS	******	MIXING	MIXUPS	PHYSIC	HAYING
NAWABS	--W--Y	NIXING	NIXIES	THYMIC	JOYING
NEWELS	******	SEXING	PIXIES	******	KEYING
NOWAYS	BAWDRY	TAXING	PYXIES	--Y--D	LAYING
PAWERS	BOWERY	VEXING	SAXONS	******	MAYBUG
PEWEES	COWBOY	WAXING	SIXTES	BAYARD	MAYING
PEWITS	DOWERY	******	SIXTHS	BEYOND	PAYING
POWERS	LEWDLY	--X--L	TAXERS	BOYARD	PLYING
ROWANS	LOWBOY	******	TOXINS	DAYBED	PRYING
ROWELS	LOWERY	SEXUAL	VEXERS	KAYOED	RAYING
ROWERS	LOWKEY	******	VEXILS	RHYMED	SAYING
SAWERS	SAWFLY	--X--M	VIXENS	STYLED	SHYING
SEWERS	SAWNEY	******	******	******	SKYING
SOWARS	TAWDRY	SEXISM	--X--T	--Y--E	SPYING
SOWERS	TOWERY	******	******	ANYONE	STYING
TAWERS	UNWARY	--X--N	LAXEST	CAYUSE	TOYING
TOWELS	******	******	SEXIST	COYOTE	TRYING
TOWERS	--X--A	BUXTON	SEXPOT	DRYICE	WRYING
VOWELS	******	CAXTON	SEXTET	ELYSEE	******
VOWERS	MAXIMA	SEXTAN	******	GWYNNE	--Y--H
******	MYXOMA	SEXTON	--X--X	JAYVEE	******
--W--T	ROXANA	******	******	PEYOTE	BOYISH
******	******	--X--O	PAXWAX	PHYLAE	COYISH
ABWATT	--X--D	******	******	PSYCHE	DRYISH
DEWITT	******	DEXTRO	--X--Y	ROYALE	TOYISH
FEWEST	TAXIED	MEXICO	******	SCYTHE	WHYDAH
KUWAIT	******	TUXEDO	FIXITY	STYMIE	******
LOWEST	--X--E	******	FOXILY	THYRSE	--Y--I
NEWEST	******	--X--R	HUXLEY	TUYERE	******
RAWEST	FIXATE	******	LAXITY	UNYOKE	CLYPEI
THWART	HEXANE	BAXTER	LUXURY	VOYAGE	SCYPHI
UNWEPT	HEXONE	BOXCAR	SAXONY	******	THYRSI
******	HEXOSE	DEXTER	SEXILY	--Y--F	******
--W--W	LUXATE	FOXIER	******	******	--Y--L
******	MAXINE	SEXIER	--Y--A	LAYOFF	******
BOWSAW	MAXIXE	WAXIER	******	PAYOFF	AMYTAL
BOWWOW	ROXANE	******	CAYUGA	******	GLYCOL
GEWGAW	TAXEME	--X--S	ELYTRA	--Y--G	JOYFUL
HAWHAW	TAXITE	******	GDYNIA	******	THYMOL
KOWTOW	******	AUXINS	GUYANA	******	******
PAWPAW	--X--G	BOXERS	ODYNIA	BAYING	--Y--M
POWWOW	******	DIXITS	PAYOLA	BUYING	******
******	BOXING	DOXIES	SCYLLA	CRYING	ADYTUM
--W--X	COXING	FIXERS	ZOYSIA	DRYING	AMYLUM
******	FAXING	HEXADS	******	FAYING	ASYLUM
COWPOX	FIXING	HEXYLS	--Y--C	FLYING	MAYHEM
	FOXING	MAXIMS	******	FRYING	PAYNIM
	HEXING	MIXERS	AMYLIC	GUYING	PHYLUM
			CHYMIC		RHYTHM

******
--Y--N
******
CAYMAN
CEYLON
DAYTON
DRYDEN
ETYMON
FLYMAN
HOYDEN
LAYMAN
LAYMEN
LEYDEN
OXYGEN
PHYTIN
SKYMAN
SKYMEN
******
--Y--O
******
CRYPTO
ERYNGO
GLYPTO
PHYLLO
PHYSIO
PSYCHO
SCYPHO
THYREO
******
--Y--P
******
MAYHAP
MAYPOP
SKYCAP
******
--Y--R
******
GEYSER
KHYBER
RHYMER
STYLAR
STYLER
TAYLOR
VOYEUR
ZUYDER
******
--Y--S
******
ABYDOS
ABYSMS

ARYANS
BAYOUS
BOYARS
BUYERS
CLYDES
COYPUS
CRYPTS
DOYENS
DRYADS
DRYERS
FLYBYS
FLYERS
FOYERS
FRYERS
GLYNIS
GLYPHS
IDYLLS
JOYCES
JOYOUS
KAYAKS
KEYNES
LAYERS
MAYORS
ORYXES
PAYEES
PAYERS
POYOUS
PRYERS
RAYAHS
RAYONS
RHYMES
RIYALS
ROYALS
SAYERS
STYLES
STYLUS
THYMES
THYMUS
TOYERS
TOYONS
TRYSTS
WAYNES
ZAYINS
******
--Y--T
******
BRYANT
DRYEST

DRYROT
GAYEST
LAYOUT
MAYEST
SHYEST
SLYEST
STYLET
TRYOUT
WAYOUT
WRYEST
******
--Y--W
******
ANYHOW
HAYMOW
******
--Y--X
******
BAYEUX
HAYBOX
******
--Y--Y
******
ANYWAY
BRYONY
DAYBOY
DAYFLY
DOYLEY
DRYFLY
GAYETY
HEYDAY
KEYWAY
LAYDAY
MAYDAY
MAYFLY
PAYDAY
SKYWAY
WAYLAY
******
--Z--A
******
ECZEMA
MAZUMA
MEZUZA
RAZZIA
******
--Z--C
******
EOZOIC

******
--Z--D
******
BUZZED
FIZZED
FUZZED
HAZARD
JAZZED
LIZARD
RAZEED
RAZZED
VIZARD
WIZARD
******
--Z--E
******
DAZZLE
ENZYME
FIZZLE
GUZZLE
LIZZIE
MIZZLE
MUZZLE
NOZZLE
NUZZLE
PUZZLE
SIZZLE
SOZINE
ZIZZLE
******
--Z--G
******
DAZING
DOZING
FAZING
FIZGIG
FUZING
GAZING
HAZING
LAZING
MAZING
OOZING
RAZING
SIZING
******
--Z--H
******
UZZIAH
ZIZITH

******
--Z--I
******
LAZULI
******
--Z--K
******
MUZHIK
******
--Z--L
******
JEZAIL
******
--Z--M
******
NAZISM
******
--Z--N
******
FEZZAN
HAZZAN
HEZION
MIZZEN
******
--Z--O
******
GAZABO
GAZEBO
******
--Z--R
******
BAZAAR
BEZOAR
BUZZER
COZIER
DOZIER
FIZZER
HAZIER
JAZZER
LAZIER
MAZIER
OOZIER
SIZIER
VIZIER
******
--Z--S
******
BEZELS
BUZZES

COZENS
COZIES
DIZENS
DOZENS
FEZZES
FIZZES
FUZEES
FUZILS
FUZZES
GAZERS
GIZMOS
HAZELS
HAZERS
JAZZES
KAZOOS
LAZARS
LIZZYS
MAZERS
MEZZOS
OUZELS
PIZZAS
RAZEES
RAZORS
RAZZES
SIZARS
SOZINS
TAZZAS
VIZIRS
VIZORS
WIZENS
******
--Z--T
******
BEZANT
MOZART
******
--Z--Y
******
COZILY
DOZILY
HAZILY
LAZILY
MAZILY
NAZIFY
OOZILY
SYZYGY

******	INTACT	FACADE	PILAFF	TOBAGO	EDDAIC
---AA-	ISAACS	FARADS	PILAFS	TOWAGE	ENTAIL
******	ITHACA	GONADS	SCLAFF	ULLAGE	FUSAIN
BALAAM	LEGACY	HEXADS	STRAFE	UNCAGE	GAWAIN
BATAAN	LILACS	INVADE	UNSAFE	VIRAGO	HAWAII
BAZAAR	LUNACY	JIHADS	******	VISAGE	IMPAIR
CANAAN	MACACO	KNEADS	---AG-	VOYAGE	INLAID
SALAAM	MALACO	MALADY	******	******	JEZAIL
******	MARACA	MILADY	AMBAGE	---AH-	JUDAIC
---AB-	MENACE	MONADS	ANLAGE	******	KUWAIT
******	MONACO	NAIADS	ARMAGH	ALMAHS	LANAIS
CASABA	PALACE	NEVADA	BORAGE	DINAHS	LORAIN
GAZABO	PAPACY	NOMADS	COWAGE	EPHAHS	MIDAIR
INDABA	PESACH	OCTADS	CUBAGE	JONAHS	MOHAIR
LAVABO	PIRACY	OREADS	DAMAGE	JUDAHS	MOSAIC
NAWABS	PLEACH	PANADA	DEGAGE	LOTAHS	OBTAIN
RAJABS	POLACK	PARADE	DOSAGE	NAVAHO	ORDAIN
SQUABS	POMACE	PESADE	DOTAGE	RAJAHS	OXTAIL
WAHABI	PREACH	PLEADS	ENCAGE	RAYAHS	PALAIS
******	REDACT	POMADE	ENGAGE	SARAHS	PAPAIN
---AC-	REFACE	POSADA	ENRAGE	SUBAHS	REGAIN
******	RUBACE	REMADE	FORAGE	SURAHS	RELAID
ABBACY	SERACS	SALADS	GARAGE	TORAHS	REMAIN
ACKACK	SOLACE	SQUADS	HOMAGE	******	REPAID
ALPACA	SUMACS	STEADY	INCAGE	---AI-	REPAIR
ALSACE	TENACE	TIRADE	LAVAGE	******	RETAIL
ANLACE	THWACK	TREADS	LINAGE	ACHAIA	RETAIN
ARRACK	UNLACE	TRIADS	LOVAGE	AFFAIR	ROMAIC
ATTACH	UNPACK	TULADI	MALAGA	AFRAID	SERAIS
ATTACK	UNTACK	UNLADE	MANAGE	AGLAIA	SPRAIN
BLEACH	VIVACE	UNMADE	MENAGE	AGNAIL	STRAIN
BONACI	******	XANADU	METAGE	ALCAIC	STRAIT
BREACH	---AD-	******	MILAGE	ALTAIC	UNFAIR
BROACH	******	---AE-	MIRAGE	ALTAIR	UNHAIR
CARACK	ABRADE	******	NONAGE	ASSAIL	UNLAID
CLOACA	ARCADE	ACHAEA	OHMAGE	ASSAIS	UNSAID
CURACY	ARMADA	AZRAEL	PELAGE	ATTAIN	******
DEFACE	AUBADE	ISRAEL	PIPAGE	BAHAIS	---AJ-
DETACH	AUDADS	JUDAEA	POTAGE	BEWAIL	******
EFFACE	BREADS	JUDAEO	RAVAGE	CALAIS	NAVAJO
ENFACE	BROADS	PALAEO	RRHAGE	COCAIN	******
ENLACE	CANADA	TOGAED	RRHAGY	DANAID	---AK-
GALACT	CICADA	VISAED	SAVAGE	DERAIL	******
HIJACK	CYCADS	******	SCRAGS	DERAIN	ALFAKI
HORACE	DECADE	---AF-	SEWAGE	DETAIL	BAMAKO
IGNACE	DORADO	******	SILAGE	DETAIN	BETAKE
IMPACT	DREADS	AGRAFE	SOCAGE	DOMAIN	BLEAKS
INLACE	DRYADS	CARAFE	SPRAGS	ECLAIR	BREAKS

CLOAKS	CICALA	RATALS	DREAMY	BUTANE	MANANA
CREAKS	COBALT	RECALL	DYNAMO	BYLANE	MELANO
CREAKY	COPALM	REGALE	ENCAMP	CABANA	MUTANT
CROAKS	CORALS	RESALE	FLEAMS	CETANE	NAGANA
CROAKY	CRAALS	RIBALD	GLEAMS	CLEANS	NATANT
FREAKS	DECALS	RIVALS	GLEAMY	CUBANS	OCEANS
FREAKY	DESALT	RIYALS	GOTAMA	CYRANO	OCTANE
INTAKE	DONALD	ROBALO	HIRAMS	DAMANS	OCTANT
KABAKA	EMBALM	RONALD	IBEAMS	DECANE	OPTANT
KANAKA	EMPALE	ROYALE	INFAMY	DECANT	ORGANA
KAYAKS	ENDALL	ROYALS	JORAMS	DEDANS	ORGANO
KODAKS	EQUALS	SEPALS	MADAME	DEMAND	ORGANS
KULAKS	EXHALE	SEWALL	MADAMS	DEWANS	OSCANS
REMAKE	FEMALE	SHOALS	PAJAMA	DIVANS	PAEANS
RETAKE	FINALE	SHOALY	PANAMA	DIWANS	PAGANS
SNEAKS	FINALS	SOMALI	PYJAMA	EMBANK	PARANG
SNEAKY	GERALD	SQUALL	REVAMP	ERRAND	PAVANE
SPEAKS	GORALS	STEALS	SALAMI	ERRANT	PAVANS
SPLAKE	HAMALS	TAMALE	SCRAMS	ESPANA	PECANS
STEAKS	HERALD	TAPALO	SESAME	ETHANE	PEDANT
STRAKE	IDEALS	THRALL	SQUAMA	ETHANS	PEKANS
TWEAKS	IMBALM	TICALS	STEAMS	EXPAND	PINANG
TWEAKY	IMPALA	TOTALS	STEAMY	EXTANT	PIRANA
UMIAKS	IMPALE	TRIALS	******	GIGANT	PLIANT
UNMAKE	INHALE	TYBALT	---AN-	GITANO	POLAND
UPTAKE	INWALL	VITALS	******	GLEANS	PURANA
WREAKS	KABALA	VOCALS	AALAND	GOBANG	PYRANS
******	KAMALA	WHEALS	ALBANY	GROANS	QUEANS
---AL-	KERALA	******	ALKANE	GUIANA	RECANT
******	KRAALS	---AM-	ALLANS	GUYANA	REDANS
ALKALI	LOCALE	******	ALVANS	HAVANA	REMAND
ANNALS	LOCALS	ABRAMS	ARCANA	HEXANE	REMANS
APPALL	MEDALS	ADDAMS	ARCANE	HOGANS	REPAND
APPALS	MEGALO	AFLAME	ARIANS	HUMANE	RIBAND
ARGALA	METALS	AFRAME	ARMAND	HUMANS	ROBAND
ARGALI	MORALE	BAHAMA	ARRANT	IGUANA	ROLAND
ARGALS	MORALS	BECAME	ARYANS	INBAND	ROMANS
BASALT	MURALS	BIGAMY	ASIANS	INFANT	ROMANY
BECALM	NAPALM	BREAMS	ASKANT	INLAND	ROWANS
BEFALL	NASALS	BYNAME	ASLANT	INSANE	ROXANA
BEHALF	NOBALL	CREAMS	BANANA	ISLAND	ROXANE
BUBALS	NOPALS	CREAMY	BESANT	JACANA	SATANG
BYTALK	ONFALL	DECAMP	BEZANT	JAPANS	SAVANT
CABALA	OSWALD	DEFAME	BOGANS	JOHANN	SECANT
CABALS	PEDALS	DEGAME	BORANE	JURANT	SEDANS
CANALS	PETALS	DIGAMY	BOTANY	LEVANT	SEJANT
CASALS	PHIALS	DREAMS	BRYANT	LIGAND	SHRANK
CATALO	POTALE	DREAMT	BURANS	LITANY	SKEANS

SOLAND	WATAPE	EDGARS	SENARY	CREASY	AGNATE
SOLANO	WATAPS	EDUARD	SEWARD	DAMASK	ALBATA
SOLANS	******	EDWARD	SHEARS	DEBASE	ANSATE
SONANT	---AR-	EGGARS	SIMARS	DICAST	AURATE
SPRANG	******	EMBARK	SITARS	DYNAST	AVIATE
STRAND	ABOARD	EMBARS	SIZARS	ENCASE	BALATA
SUSANS	ALTARS	ESCARP	SMEARS	ENCASH	BEMATA
TENANT	AMBARI	FEUARS	SMEARY	GREASE	BERATE
TETANY	AMBARY	FRIARS	SONARS	GREASY	BINATE
TIRANA	ANGARY	FRIARY	SOUARI	HARASS	BLEATS
TISANE	ANKARA	GEMARA	SOWARS	IMPASS	BLOATS
TITANS	APIARY	GERARD	SPEARS	INCASE	BORATE
TOMANS	ASGARD	GOCART	SQUARE	KAVASS	BOVATE
TRUANT	ATTARS	GOKART	STUART	KINASE	BREATH
TYRANT	AVIARY	HAZARD	SUDARY	LIPASE	BYPATH
UNHAND	AWEARY	HILARY	SUGARS	MEGASS	CARATE
UNMANS	AYMARA	HOBART	SUGARY	MORASS	CARATS
UPLAND	BAYARD	HOLARD	SWEARS	OBLAST	CERATE
URBANE	BEWARE	HORARY	TABARD	ORGASM	CERATO
VACANT	BICARB	HOWARD	TALARI	PHRASE	CHEATS
VOLANT	BIHARI	IMBARK	TATARS	PLEASE	CLEATS
WIGANS	BINARY	IMPARK	TELARY	POTASH	COMATE
XYLANS	BLEARS	IMPART	THWART	QUEASY	CREATE
ZANANA	BLEARY	INWARD	TOWARD	RECAST	CROATS
ZENANA	BOYARD	LAPARO	UNBARS	REHASH	CURATE
******	BOYARS	LAZARS	UNWARY	REPASS	DEBATE
---AO-	BRIARS	LIZARD	UPWARD	REPAST	DELATE
******	CANARD	MOLARS	UTGARD	SIWASH	DERATE
CACAOS	CANARY	MOZART	VAGARY	SPLASH	DILATE
******	CEDARS	NEWARK	VASARI	SQUASH	DONATE
---AP-	CESARE	NONARY	VICARS	STRASS	DUCATS
******	CIGARS	NOTARY	VISARD	THRASH	EQUATE
CANAPE	CLEARS	ONWARD	VIZARD	UNCASE	ERGATE
DOGAPE	COWARD	OSCARS	VOTARY	UNEASE	ERRATA
ENRAPT	CURARE	PETARD	WIZARD	UNEASY	ERSATZ
ESCAPE	CYMARS	RADARS	ZONARY	UNHASP	ESTATE
KAKAPO	DATARY	REGARD	******	UNLASH	FIXATE
LENAPE	DEBARK	REMARK	---AS-	UNMASK	FLOATS
PARAPH	DEBARS	RETARD	******	UPCAST	FLOATY
RECAPS	DECARE	REWARD	AGHAST	UREASE	GLOATS
SARAPE	DEKARE	RITARD	BAGASS	WABASH	GREATS
SCRAPE	DENARY	ROSARY	BREAST	******	GROATS
SCRAPS	DEPART	ROTARY	BYPASS	---AT-	GYRATE
SERAPE	DINARS	SAFARI	BYPAST	******	HECATE
SERAPH	DISARM	SAHARA	CALASH	ABWATT	HEMATO
STRAPS	DOTARD	SALARY	CAMASS	ACUATE	HEPATO
TERAPH	DREARY	SAMARA	CHIASM	ADNATE	IDEATE
UNCAPS	ECHARD	SATARA	CREASE	AERATE	INMATE

INNATE	SQUATS	******	SPLAYS	TAMBAC	BRIBES
IODATE	STOATS	---AW-	SPRAYS	TEABAG	BULBED
JUGATE	STRATA	******	STRAYS	THEBAE	BULBEL
JURATS	STRATH	BYLAWS	UNLAYS	TIMBAL	CAMBER
KARATE	STRATI	IMPAWN	UNSAYS	TOMBAC	CHEBEC
KARATS	SWEATS	INLAWS	******	TRIBAL	COBBER
KERATO	SWEATY	MACAWS	---AZ-	TURBAN	COMBED
LANATE	TERATO	MALAWI	******	VERBAL	COMBER
LEGATE	TOMATO	MOHAWK	ABLAZE	WOMBAT	CORBEL
LEGATO	TREATS	OTTAWA	SLEAZY	YERBAS	CUBBED
LIGATE	TREATY	PAPAWS	******	******	CUMBER
LOBATE	TUBATE	PSHAWS	---BA-	---BB-	CURBED
LOCATE	UBOATS	SCRAWL	******	******	DABBED
LUNATE	UNHATS	SPRAWL	AMEBAE	BLEBBY	DABBER
LUXATE	UPDATE	SQUAWK	AMEBAS	CHUBBY	DAUBED
MALATE	VACATE	SQUAWS	ANABAS	CRABBY	DAUBER
MUTATE	VALATE	STRAWS	ATABAL	FLABBY	DAYBED
NEGATE	WHEATS	STRAWY	BAOBAB	GRUBBY	DIBBED
NEMATO	WREATH	******	BILBAO	KNOBBY	DIBBER
OBLATE	ZAPATA	---AX-	BOMBAY	SCABBY	DOBBER
OLEATE	ZONATE	******	BULBAR	SHABBY	DUBBED
OPIATE	******	GALAXY	CASBAH	SNOBBY	FERBER
ORNATE	---AU-	ICEAXE	CEIBAS	STUBBS	FIBBED
PALATE	******	******	COMBAT	STUBBY	FIBBER
PEDATE	ABLAUT	---AY-	CORBAN	******	FOBBED
PEDATI	ARNAUD	******	CYMBAL	---BD-	GABBED
PILATE	BEDAUB	ALLAYS	DISBAR	******	GABBER
PIRATE	CHIAUS	ALWAYS	DUNBAR	LAMBDA	GARBED
PLEATS	DANAUS	ARRAYS	DURBAN	******	GHEBER
POTATO	HAMAUL	ASSAYS	DURBAR	---BE-	GIBBED
PUPATE	INHAUL	AYEAYE	FARBAD	******	GIBBER
REBATE	MARAUD	BELAYS	GASBAG	ADOBES	GIBBET
REBATO	UMLAUT	BYWAYS	GLOBAL	AIRBED	GLEBES
RELATE	******	DECAYS	HERBAL	ARABEL	GLOBED
ROTATE	---AV-	DELAYS	ISOBAR	BARBED	GLOBES
RUBATO	******	EMBAYS	JUBBAH	BARBEL	GOBBET
RUGATE	BEHAVE	ESSAYS	JUMBAL	BARBER	GOOBER
SAVATE	CASAVA	FORAYS	KITBAG	BARBET	GRABEN
SEBATS	CLEAVE	INLAYS	LUMBAR	BERBER	GREBES
SEDATE	GREAVE	KABAYA	MAMBAS	BIBBED	HOBBES
SENATE	MOHAVE	MALAYA	RAGBAG	BIBBER	HOTBED
SHEATH	MOJAVE	MALAYS	REDBAY	BOBBED	HUMBER
SHOATS	OCTAVE	MORAYS	RUMBAS	BOBBER	ISABEL
SOMATA	OCTAVO	NOWAYS	SABBAT	BOMBED	ISOBEL
SOMATO	OTTAVA	PAPAYA	SAMBAS	BOMBER	JABBED
SONATA	SHEAVE	RELAYS	SCUBAS	BOMBES	JABBER
SPLATS	SLEAVE	REPAYS	SHEBAT	BRIBED	JIBBED
SPRATS	ZOUAVE		SINBAD	BRIBER	JIBBER

JOBBED	******	TURBIT	NIMBLE	GUMBOS	KRUBUT
JOBBER	---BI-	TWIBIL	NIMBLY	HARBOR	LIMBUS
KERBED	******	TWOBIT	NOBBLE	HATBOX	MAHBUB
KHYBER	ALIBIS	ZAMBIA	NUBBLE	HAYBOX	MAYBUG
LAMBED	AMEBIC	ZOMBIE	NUBBLY	HOTBOX	NIMBUS
LIMBED	ANUBIS	ZOMBIS	NUMBLY	ICEBOX	REDBUD
LIMBER	ARABIA	******	PEBBLE	JERBOA	REDBUG
LOBBED	ARABIC	---BL-	PEBBLY	LESBOS	SAMBUR
LOBBER	BABBIE	******	PUEBLO	LISBOA	WILBUR
LUBBER	BARBIE	ALIBLE	RABBLE	LISBON	******
LUMBER	BOBBIE	ARABLE	RAMBLE	LOWBOY	---BW-
MEMBER	BOBBIN	BABBLE	ROUBLE	MAMBOS	******
MOBBED	BOMBIC	BAUBLE	RUBBLE	OVIBOS	OJIBWA
MOBBER	BULBIL	BOBBLE	RUMBLE	POTBOY	******
NABBED	CORBIE	BUBBLE	STABLE	RIBBON	---BY-
NIBBED	DEBBIE	BUBBLY	STABLY	SAMBOS	******
NOBBED	DOBBIN	BUMBLE	SUABLE	SUNBOW	BOBBYS
NUMBED	DUBBIN	BURBLE	TREBLE	SYMBOL	BYEBYE
NUMBER	FORBID	COBBLE	TUMBLE	TOMBOY	DEBBYS
PLEBES	GAMBIA	COBBLY	UNABLE	TURBOT	FLYBYS
PROBED	GAMBIR	DABBLE	USABLE	******	LIBBYS
PROBER	GAMBIT	DIBBLE	USABLY	---BR-	******
PROBES	GERBIL	DOABLE	VIABLE	******	---CA-
QUEBEC	GLOBIN	DOUBLE	WABBLE	BARBRA	******
RABBET	HARBIN	DOUBLY	WABBLY	CIMBRI	ABACAS
REUBEN	HENBIT	DRABLY	WAMBLE	DAUBRY	APICAL
RIBBED	IAMBIC	DUMBLY	WAMBLY	GABBRO	ARECAS
ROBBED	KRUBIS	EDIBLE	WARBLE	HOMBRE	ASHCAN
ROBBER	LAMBIE	ENABLE	WIMBLE	SOMBRE	BISCAY
RUBBED	LIEBIG	FEEBLE	WOBBLE	TIMBRE	BOBCAT
RUBBER	LIMBIC	FEEBLY	WOBBLY	******	BOXCAR
SEABEE	MORBID	FIMBLE	******	---BT-	BUCCAL
SOBBED	NIOBIC	FOIBLE	---BO-	******	CALCAR
SOMBER	NUBBIN	FUMBLE	******	DOUBTS	CANCAN
SORBET	ORIBIS	GABBLE	BALBOA	******	COCCAL
TABBED	OUTBID	GAMBLE	BAMBOO	---BU-	DECCAN
THEBES	PHOBIA	GARBLE	BONBON	******	DISCAL
TIMBER	PHOBIC	GLIBLY	BOOBOO	BEDBUG	DUNCAN
TOMBED	RABBIN	GOBBLE	BURBOT	BULBUL	EPICAL
TRIBES	RABBIS	HOBBLE	CARBON	CHABUK	FAECAL
TUBBED	RABBIT	HUMBLE	CARBOY	CHIBUK	FAUCAL
TUBBER	ROBBIA	HUMBLY	COMBOS	DORBUG	FISCAL
WEBBED	ROBBIE	JUMBLE	COWBOY	DYBBUK	FRACAS
WILBER	SERBIA	KIBBLE	DAYBOY	EREBUS	HUBCAP
WOMBED	TERBIA	LIABLE	DIOBOL	HAGBUT	ICECAP
YABBER	TIDBIT	MARBLE	FOGBOW	HUBBUB	IPECAC
	TITBIT	MUMBLE	GAMBOL	HUMBUG	LASCAR
	TURBID	NIBBLE	GIBBON	JAMBUS	MADCAP

MECCAN	CRUCES	PIECED	BEECHY	TRACHY	CRACKY
MECCAS	DANCED	PIECER	BITCHY	TRICHI	CRICKS
MESCAL	DANCER	PIECES	BOTCHY	TRICHO	CROCKS
MOBCAP	DANCES	PISCES	BRACHI	TROCHE	CROCKY
MUDCAP	DEICED	PLACED	BRACHY	******	FLACKS
MUSCAE	DEICER	PLACER	BRECHT	---CI-	FLECKS
MUSCAT	DEICES	PLACES	BROCHE	******	FLICKS
OILCAN	DEUCED	PLACET	BUNCHE	ACACIA	FLOCKS
PARCAE	DEUCES	PRICED	BUNCHY	AFLCIO	FLOCKY
PASCAL	DULCET	PRICES	CATCHY	ALICIA	FROCKS
PLICAE	DUNCES	SAUCED	CHICHI	BAUCIS	HOICKS
RASCAL	EDUCED	SAUCER	CLICHE	BOCCIE	KNACKS
REDCAP	EDUCES	SAUCES	CLOCHE	CALCIC	KNOCKS
SKYCAP	FAECES	SLICED	CONCHA	COCCID	PLACKS
SNOCAT	FARCED	SLICER	CONCHS	DULCIE	PLUCKS
SPACAE	FARCER	SLICES	CONCHY	ELICIT	PLUCKY
THECAE	FARCES	SOCCER	CRECHE	FASCIA	PRICKS
THECAL	FASCES	SPACED	DOUCHE	GLACIS	QUACKS
TINCAL	FAUCES	SPACER	DRACHM	GRACIE	SHACKO
TINCAN	FAUCET	SPACES	EPOCHS	MARCIA	SHACKS
TIPCAT	FENCED	SPICED	ERICHS	MERCIA	SHOCKS
TOECAP	FENCER	SPICER	FLECHE	NIACIN	SHUCKS
TOMCAT	FENCES	SPICES	GAUCHE	NUNCIO	SLACKS
TOUCAN	FORCED	TALCED	GAUCHO	PENCIL	SLICKS
TRICAR	FORCER	TERCEL	LEACHY	PHOCIS	SMACKS
TROCAR	FORCES	TERCET	LITCHI	PLACID	SMOCKS
TUSCAN	GLACES	TEUCER	MANCHU	PRECIS	SNACKS
VULCAN	GRACED	TRACED	ORACHS	RANCID	SNICKS
YUCCAS	GRACES	TRACER	PANCHO	SPECIE	SPECKS
******	GROCER	TRACES	PATCHY	STACIE	STACKS
---CC-	HANCES	TRICED	PEACHY	VISCID	STICKS
******	IBICES	TRICES	PITCHY	ZINCIC	STICKY
STUCCO	JOYCES	TRUCES	POACHY	******	STOCKS
******	JUICER	UNICEF	PONCHO	---CK-	STOCKY
---CE-	JUICES	VINCES	POUCHY	******	TRACKS
******	LANCED	VOICED	PSYCHE	BLACKS	TRICKS
ALICES	LANCER	VOICES	PSYCHO	BLOCKS	TRICKY
AMICES	LANCES	WINCED	PUNCHY	BLOCKY	TRUCKS
APICES	LANCET	WINCER	RANCHO	BRICKS	WHACKS
AVOCET	MARCEL	WINCES	REECHO	CHECKS	WRACKS
BRACED	MERCER	WINCEY	REICHS	CHICKS	WRECKS
BRACER	MINCED	ZINCED	ROTCHE	CHOCKS	YOICKS
BRACES	MINCER	******	ROUCHE	CHUCKS	ZINCKY
BRUCES	MINCES	---CH-	SEICHE	CLACKS	******
CALCES	NIECES	******	TETCHY	CLICKS	---CL-
CANCEL	OUNCES	AMECHE	TOUCHE	CLOCKS	******
CANCER	PARCEL	APACHE	TOUCHY	CLUCKS	BOUCLE
CARCEL	PENCEL	BEACHY	TRACHE	CRACKS	CHICLE

CIRCLE	******	******	PINDAR	BENDED	ERODED
ICICLE	---CT-	---CY-	PURDAH	BENDEE	ERODES
MUSCLE	******	******	RAGDAY	BENDER	ETUDES
ORACLE	ALECTO	COCCYX	RANDAL	BIDDEN	EVADED
SIECLE	BRACTS	NANCYS	RANDAN	BIDDER	EVADER
******	EDICTS	PERCYS	RHODAS	BINDER	EVADES
---CM-	EDUCTS	STACYS	SANDAL	BLADED	EXUDED
******	EJECTA	******	SENDAL	BLADES	EXUDES
CHACMA	EJECTS	---DA-	SERDAB	BOLDER	FEEDER
******	ELECTS	******	SIRDAR	BONDED	FENDED
---CN-	EPACTS	ABADAN	SUNDAE	BONDER	FENDER
******	ERECTS	ALIDAD	SUNDAY	BORDEL	FEUDED
PROCNE	ERUCTS	AOUDAD	THEDAS	BORDER	FINDER
******	EVICTS	APODAL	VANDAL	BRIDES	FODDER
---CO-	EXACTA	BAGDAD	VEADAR	BUDDED	FOLDED
******	EXACTS	BELDAM	WANDAS	BUDDER	FOLDER
BEACON	MULCTS	BENDAY	WHIDAH	BURDEN	FONDER
BUNCOS	PROCTO	BRIDAL	WHYDAH	CAMDEN	FORDED
CHICOS	REACTS	CAUDAD	******	CARDED	FUNDED
CISCOS	STACTE	CAUDAL	---DB-	CARDER	GADDED
CRACOW	TINCTS	CORDAY	******	CAUDEX	GADDER
DEACON	TRACTS	CREDAL	GOODBY	CHIDED	GANDER
FALCON	******	DAEDAL	******	CHIDER	GARDEN
FLACON	---CU-	DARDAN	---DD-	CHIDES	GELDED
GARCON	******	DEODAR	******	CINDER	GENDER
GASCON	ABACUS	DOODAD	CLODDY	CLYDES	GEODES
GLYCOL	AEACUS	FEUDAL	FREDDY	CODDER	GILDED
GUACOS	CAECUM	FREDAS	SHODDY	COLDER	GILDER
JUNCOS	CAUCUS	FRIDAY	THADDY	CORDED	GIRDED
MARCOS	CIRCUM	GILDAS	******	CORDER	GIRDER
MASCON	CIRCUS	GODDAM	---DE-	CRUDER	GLADES
MASCOT	COCCUS	HEYDAY	******	CURDED	GLEDES
MOSCOW	CONCUR	HILDAS	ABIDED	DANDER	GLIDED
NONCOM	CROCUS	HOWDAH	ABIDER	DAUDET	GLIDER
RANCOR	CUSCUS	IBADAN	ABIDES	DEADEN	GLIDES
ROSCOE	DISCUS	JORDAN	ABODES	DEEDED	GOADED
SEACOW	EGGCUP	KEDDAH	ALUDEL	DIADEM	GOLDEN
SUCCOR	EYECUP	KENDAL	AMIDES	DINDER	GRADED
TOMCOD	FESCUE	LANDAU	ANADEM	DIODES	GRADER
TRICOT	HICCUP	LAYDAY	ANODES	DODDER	GRADES
TURCOS	IOLCUS	LINDAS	ASIDES	DRYDEN	GRIDED
ZIRCON	MARCUS	MANDAN	BALDER	DUNDEE	GRIDES
******	MISCUE	MAYDAY	BANDED	DUODEN	GUIDED
---CR-	RESCUE	MIDDAY	BARDED	ELIDED	GUIDER
******	SULCUS	MONDAY	BARDES	ELIDES	GUIDES
DESCRY	TALCUM	OFFDAY	BEADED	ELUDED	GULDEN
FIACRE	TEACUP	PANDAS	BEDDED	ELUDES	HAMDEN
FULCRA	VISCUS	PAYDAY	BEDDER	EPODES	HANDED

HANDEL	MADDEN	SADDER	WEEDER	AMIDIN	BOODLE
HARDEN	MADDER	SANDED	WELDED	ANODIC	BRIDLE
HARDER	MAIDEN	SANDER	WELDER	AVIDIN	BUDDLE
HEADED	MAUDES	SEEDED	WENDED	BANDIT	BUNDLE
HEADER	MELDED	SEEDER	WILDER	BARDIC	CANDLE
HEEDED	MENDED	SENDER	WINDED	BIRDIE	CAUDLE
HEEDER	MENDEL	SHADED	WINDER	BRIDIE	CODDLE
HERDED	MENDER	SHADES	WOADED	BURDIE	COLDLY
HERDER	MIDDEN	SLIDER	WONDER	CADDIE	COODLE
HIDDEN	MILDEN	SLIDES	WOODED	CADDIS	CRADLE
HINDER	MILDER	SODDED	WOODEN	CANDIA	CUDDLE
HODDEN	MILDEW	SODDEN	WORDED	CANDID	CUDDLY
HOIDEN	MINDED	SOLDER	YARDED	CARDIO	CURDLE
HOLDER	MINDER	SONDER	YONDER	CREDIT	DADDLE
HOODED	MOLDED	SPADED	ZUIDER	CUDDIE	DANDLE
HORDED	MOLDER	SPADER	ZUYDER	DIKDIK	DAWDLE
HORDES	MUDDED	SPADES	******	DYADIC	DEADLY
HOYDEN	MUDDER	SPIDER	---DG-	GEODIC	DIDDLE
HYADES	MURDER	SUBDEB	******	GRADIN	DOODLE
IBIDEM	NEEDED	SUDDEN	BRIDGE	HERDIC	FIDDLE
IMIDES	NEEDER	SUEDES	DREDGE	IRIDIC	FONDLE
IRIDES	NODDED	SUNDER	DRUDGE	KIDDIE	FONDLY
KIDDED	NODDER	SUNDEW	FLEDGE	LADDIE	FUDDLE
KIDDER	OXIDES	SWEDEN	FLEDGY	LEADIN	GIRDLE
KINDER	PADDED	SWEDES	FRIDGE	MENDIP	GLADLY
LADDER	PANDER	SYNDET	GRUDGE	MISDID	GOODLY
LANDED	PENDED	TANDEM	PLEDGE	NORDIC	HANDLE
LANDER	PODDED	TEDDED	SLEDGE	OUTDID	HARDLY
LARDED	POLDER	TEDDER	SLUDGE	PUNDIT	HEDDLE
LARDER	PONDER	TENDED	SLUDGY	REEDIT	HUDDLE
LAUDED	POWDER	TENDER	SMUDGE	RHODIC	HURDLE
LAUDER	PRIDED	TILDES	SMUDGY	SORDID	KINDLE
LEADED	PRIDES	TINDER	STODGE	SPADIX	KINDLY
LEADEN	PRUDES	TRADED	STODGY	STADIA	LEWDLY
LEADER	RAIDED	TRADER	TRUDGE	STUDIO	LORDLY
LENDER	RAIDER	TRADES	******	SYNDIC	LOUDLY
LEUDES	READER	TSADES	---DH-	VERDIN	MEDDLE
LEWDER	REDDEN	VENDED	******	WIDDIE	MIDDLE
LEYDEN	REDDER	VENDEE	BUDDHA	******	MILDLY
LIDDED	REEDED	VENDER	GANDHI	---DL-	MUDDLE
LIEDER	RENDED	VOIDED	SANDHI	******	NEEDLE
LINDEN	RENDER	WADDED	******	ACIDLY	NODDLE
LOADED	RHODES	WANDER	---DI-	AGEDLY	NOODLE
LOADER	RIDDED	WARDED	******	ARIDLY	PADDLE
LORDED	RIDDEN	WARDEN	ACADIA	AVIDLY	PEDDLE
LOUDEN	RONDEL	WARDER	ACEDIA	BALDLY	PIDDLE
LOUDER	RUDDER	WEDDED	ACIDIC	BEADLE	POODLE
MADDED	SADDEN	WEEDED	AMIDIC	BOLDLY	PUDDLE

PUDDLY	VOODOO	MANDYS	LUTEAL	******	BIPEDS
RADDLE	WALDOS	PADDYS	MOREAU	---EC-.	BLEEDS
REDDLE	WINDOW	RODDYS	OCREAE	******	BREEDS
RIDDLE	WISDOM	SANDYS	ORDEAL	ABJECT	COMEDO
RUDDLE	******	TEDDYS	ORGEAT	ADJECT	COMEDY
RUNDLE	---DR-	THADYS	OSTEAL	AFFECT	CREEDS
SADDLE	******	TRUDYS	PALEAE	APIECE	EMBEDS
TODDLE	AIRDRY	WENDYS	PINEAL	ASPECT	FRIEDA
WADDLE	BAWDRY	******	POLEAX	AZTECS	GREEDS
WADDLY	DENDRI	---EA-	REHEAR	BEDECK	GREEDY
WANDLE	DENDRO	******	REHEAT	BISECT	IMBEDS
WILDLY	EXEDRA	AEGEAN	REPEAL	BREECH	IMPEDE
******	QUADRI	AENEAS	REPEAT	COPECK	LAMEDS
---DO-	SANDRA	AGLEAM	RESEAT	DEFECT	LAREDO
******	SUNDRY	ANDEAN	RESEAU	DEJECT	RECEDE
ABYDOS	TAWDRY	ANNEAL	REVEAL	DETECT	REMEDY
AMADOU	TUNDRA	APNEAL	ROSEAL	DIRECT	RESEDA
AMIDOL	******	APPEAL	SABEAN	DODECA	SECEDE
CANDOR	---DS-	APPEAR	SCREAK	EFFECT	SHREDS
CONDOM	******	ARREAR	SCREAM	EXPECT	SPEEDS
CONDOR	AMIDST	AUGEAN	SPREAD	EXSECT	SPEEDY
CORDON	WOODSY	BATEAU	SQUEAK	FLEECE	STEEDS
CREDOS	******	BEHEAD	SQUEAL	FLEECY	TELEDU
FEODOR	---DT-	BEMEAN	STREAK	GRAECO	TEREDO
FOGDOG	******	BOREAL	STREAM	GREECE	TOLEDO
GORDON	VELDTS	BOREAS	THREAD	GYNECO	TUXEDO
GUIDON	******	BUREAU	THREAT	INFECT	TWEEDS
HAGDON	---DU-	CAVEAT	UNBEAR	INJECT	******
HEADON	******	CEREAL	UNLEAD	INSECT	---EE-
HENDON	DUMDUM	COTEAU	UNREAD	KOPECK	******
HOODOO	EXODUS	CUNEAL	UNREAL	LAMECH	AGREED
ISADOR	FONDUE	DEFEAT	UNSEAL	LUBECK	AGREES
ISIDOR	FUNDUS	DEMEAN	UNSEAM	OBJECT	AILEEN
KOODOO	GRADUS	DOGEAR	UNSEAT	OBTECT	ANTEED
LAPDOG	HINDUS	ENDEAR	UPBEAT	REBECK	ARLEEN
LARDON	HOLDUP	ENNEAD	******	REBECS	ASLEEP
LONDON	MARDUK	FOVEAE	---EB-	REJECT	AWHEEL
MEADOW	PINDUS	FOVEAL	******	RESECT	AXSEED
PARDON	SIDDUR	GALEAE	AMOEBA	SELECT	BALEEN
RANDOM	SUBDUE	GATEAU	ARDEBS	SENECA	BESEEM
REDDOG	VENDUE	GILEAD	CALEBS	SPEECH	CAREEN
RONDOS	VERDUN	HABEAS	CUBEBS	XEBECS	CAREER
SEADOG	WINDUP	HEREAT	EPHEBI	ZEBECK	COOEED
SELDOM	******	JUDEAN	GAZEBO	ZEBECS	COOEES
SHADOW	---DY-	JUNEAU	HEREBY	******	DONEES
SUNDOG	CINDYS	KOREAN	PHLEBO	---ED-	DOREEN
TENDON	GLADYS	LINEAL	PHOEBE	ACCEDE	DUDEEN
VENDOR		LINEAR	SAHEBS	ALBEDO	EILEEN

EMCEED	******	ORCEIN	CREELS	MOTELS	UNBELT
EMCEES	---EF-	OSSEIN	CUPELS	MYSELF	UNWELL
ESTEEM	******	SEREIN	CUTELY	NAMELY	UPHELD
EXCEED	BEREFT	TAKEIN	CYBELE	NAVELS	VILELY
FUSEES	BRIEFS	TINEID	DIRELY	NEWELS	VOWELS
FUZEES	CASEFY	UNVEIL	DOWELS	NICELY	WEDELN
INDEED	CHIEFS	VEREIN	EASELS	NIGELS	WHEELS
JEREED	GANEFS	******	EDSELS	NOVELS	WIDELY
LATEEN	RAREFY	---EK-	ENGELS	NUDELY	WIFELY
LEVEES	TEPEFY	******	ETHELS	ORIELS	WISELY
LOREEN	TUMEFY	BREEKS	EXCELS	ORWELL	YODELS
LYCEES	******	CHEEKS	EXPELS	OUSELS	YOKELS
MELEES	---EG-	CHEEKY	FINELY	OUZELS	******
MOREEN	******	CREEKS	FREELY	PALELY	---EM-
NOREEN	ALLEGE	DEREKS	GAMELY	PAMELA	******
PAYEES	BAREGE	EUREKA	GAVELS	PANELS	ADEEMS
PEWEES	BODEGA	GREEKS	GESELL	POMELO	BIREME
POTEEN	FANEGA	KOPEKS	GIMELS	POWELL	CINEMA
PUREED	FOREGO	SLEEKS	GISELE	PURELY	ECZEMA
PUREES	MANEGE	SLEEKY	GRUELS	RARELY	HAREMS
RANEES	NONEGO	TOPEKA	HAZELS	RATELS	JEREMY
RAZEED	OSWEGO	******	HOMELY	RAVELS	OEDEMA
RAZEES	PHLEGM	---EL-	HOTELS	REBELS	OEPEMA
REDEEM	RENEGE	******	HOVELS	REPELS	PROEMS
RENEES	TELEGA	AFIELD	HUGELY	RESELL	RACEME
RUPEES	UNPEGS	ALLELE	IMPELS	RETELL	SCHEMA
SATEEN	******	ANGELA	ITSELF	REVELS	SCHEME
SCREED	---EI-	ANGELO	JEWELS	RIPELY	SEMEME
SCREEN	******	ANGELS	JURELS	ROWELS	SOLEMN
SPLEEN	AENEID	ANSELM	KEVELS	RUDELY	TAXEME
SPREES	ALBEIT	APPELS	KNEELS	SAFELY	TOTEMS
STREET	APNEIC	ARBELA	LABELS	SAGELY	XYLEMS
SYCEES	CASEIN	ARIELS	LAMELY	SANELY	******
TEHEED	CAVEIN	ARTELS	LAPELS	SEWELL	---EN-
TEHEES	CODEIA	BAGELS	LATELY	SHIELD	******
TEPEES	CODEIN	BARELY	LEVELS	SOLELY	ABSENT
THREED	COHEIR	BASELY	LIBELS	SORELS	ACAENA
THREES	DECEIT	BEFELL	LIKELY	SORELY	ACCENT
TUREEN	DEVEIN	BEHELD	LIVELY	SPIELS	ACHENE
UNMEET	FADEIN	BETELS	LONELY	STEELS	ADDEND
UNREEL	HEREIN	BEVELS	LOVELL	STEELY	ADVENT
UNSEEN	HYGEIA	BEZELS	LOVELY	SURELY	ALIENS
UPKEEP	ISSEIS	BLUELY	LOWELL	TAMELY	ALKENE
VENEER	KIBEIS	BOWELS	MABELS	TIMELY	ALLENS
VISEED	LOVEIN	CAMELS	MERELY	TOWELS	AMIENS
YOGEES	NEREID	CAVELL	MICELL	TUPELO	APPEND
	NEREIS	CICELY	MODELS	UMBELS	ARDENT
	NISEIS	COMELY	MORELS		ARGENT

ARLENE	HELENA	RESENT	RODEOS	ASTERN	DINERS
ARPENS	HELENS	RETENE	SINEON	ASTERO	DIVERS
ARPENT	HYMENO	RIDENT	VIREOS	ASTERS	DIVERT
ASCEND	HYMENS	RIPENS	WIGEON	AUGERS	DOSERS
ASCENT	IMPEND	RODENT	******	BAKERS	DOTERS
ASPENS	INDENE	ROWENA	---EP-	BAKERY	DOWERS
ASSENT	INDENT	RUBENS	******	BALERS	DOWERY
ATHENA	INTEND	SELENE	ACCEPT	BITERS	DRIERS
ATHENE	INTENT	SELENO	BICEPS	BOLERO	DRYERS
ATHENS	INVENT	SERENA	CHEEPS	BONERS	DUPERS
ATTEND	KARENS	SERENE	CREEPS	BORERS	DUPERY
AUGEND	KETENE	SEVENS	CREEPY	BOWERS	EATERS
CADENT	LAMENT	SHEENS	EXCEPT	BOWERY	EATERY
CATENA	LATENT	SHEENY	INCEPT	BOXERS	EGBERT
CEMENT	LEGEND	SILENI	JOSEPH	BRIERS	EGGERS
CLIENT	LIKENS	SILENT	JULEPS	BRIERY	ELBERT
COGENT	LIMENS	SIRENS	RECEPT	BUYERS	ELDERS
COZENS	LINENS	SOLENT	SHEEPS	CAMERA	ELMERS
CYMENE	LIVENS	SPHENE	SLEEPS	CANERS	ELVERS
CYRENE	LOMENT	SPHENO	SLEEPY	CAPERS	EMBERS
DECENT	LORENE	SPLENO	STEEPS	CARERS	EMEERS
DEFEND	LORENZ	STHENO	SWEEPS	CASERN	EMPERY
DEMENT	LUCENT	SWEENY	SWEEPY	CATERS	ENTERA
DEPEND	LUMENS	TALENT	UNWEPT	CAVERN	ENTERE
DETENT	MOMENT	TOKENS	YCLEPT	CELERY	ENTERO
DIZENS	NICENE	UNBEND	******	CHEERS	ENTERS
DOCENT	NOCENT	UNBENT	---ER-	CHEERY	ESKERS
DOYENS	NOVENA	URGENT	******	CICERO	ESTERS
DOZENS	OFFEND	VIXENS	ABNERS	CIDERS	ETHERS
ELLENS	ORIENT	WAKENS	ADDERS	COHERE	EXPERT
EOCENE	OSTEND	WERENT	ADHERE	COMERS	EXSERT
EOGENE	PARENS	WIDENS	ADVERB	COOERS	EXTERN
ESCENT	PARENT	WIZENS	ADVERT	CORERS	FACERS
ESSENE	PATENS	XYLENE	AGGERS	COVERS	FAKERS
EUGENE	PATENT	YAMENS	AIDERS	COVERT	FAKERY
EXPEND	PHRENO	YEMENI	ALBERT	COWERS	FARERS
EXTEND	PINENE	******	ALDERS	CRIERS	FEVERS
EXTENT	PONENT	---EO-	ALTERS	CURERS	FIBERS
FAGEND	POTENT	******	AMBERS	DARERS	FIFERS
FLUENT	PREENS	CAMEOS	AMBERY	DATERS	FILERS
FOMENT	PYRENE	CINEOL	AMPERE	DECERN	FINERY
FRIEND	QUEENS	COMEON	ANGERS	DEFERS	FIRERS
GALENA	RAVENS	GIDEON	ANTERO	DESERT	FIVERS
GERENT	RECENT	HEREOF	ARTERY	DETERS	FIXERS
GREENE	REGENT	HEREON	ASKERS	DICERS	FLEERS
GREENS	RELENT	MATEOS	ASPERS	DIDERO	FLIERS
HAVENS	REPENT	METEOR	ASSERT	DIMERS	FLYERS
HAVENT	RESEND	PIGEON	ASTERI	DINERO	FOYERS

FRIERS	LOVERS	PAYERS	SHOERS	VOTERS	EGRESS
FRYERS	LOWERS	PETERS	SIDERO	VOWERS	ELDEST
GAGERS	LOWERY	PIKERS	SISERA	WADERS	ENMESH
GAPERS	LUGERS	PINERY	SKIERS	WAFERS	ERNEST
GAZERS	LURERS	PIPERS	SNEERS	WAGERS	EXCESS
GEMERT	MACERS	PLIERS	SOBERS	WALERS	FEWEST
GENERA	MAKERS	POKERS	SOWERS	WATERS	FINEST
GIBERS	MASERS	POPERY	SPHERE	WATERY	FLIEST
GONERS	MAZERS	POSERS	SPHERY	WAVERS	FOREST
GOVERN	METERS	POWERS	SPIERS	WEBERS	FREEST
HALERS	MILERS	PRIERS	STEERS	WINERY	FUNEST
HATERS	MIMERS	PRYERS	SUPERB	WIPERS	GAYEST
HAZERS	MINERS	PULERS	SUPERS	WIRERS	GENESI
HETERO	MISERE	QUAERE	TAKERS	WIVERN	HERESY
HEWERS	MISERS	QUEERS	TALERS	WIVERS	HONEST
HIDERS	MISERY	RACERS	TAMERS	WOMERA	HUGEST
HIKERS	MITERS	RAKERS	TAPERS	WOOERS	ICIEST
HIRERS	MIXERS	RATERS	TAVERN	WYVERN	IDLEST
HOMERS	MODERN	RAVERS	TAWERS	YAGERS	IMMESH
HOVERS	MOPERS	REFERS	TAXERS	******	INCEST
HUBERT	MOVERS	REVERE	TEVERE	---ES-	INFEST
IDLERS	MOWERS	REVERS	TIGERS	******	INGEST
INFERO	NAMERS	REVERT	TILERS	ABBESS	INMESH
INFERS	NAPERY	RICERS	TIMERS	ABLEST	INVEST
INHERE	NOTERS	RIDERS	TONERS	ACCESS	JEWESS
INKERS	OBVERT	RIMERS	TOPERS	AFRESH	KINESI
INSERT	OCHERS	RISERS	TORERO	ARREST	LAMEST
INTERN	OCHERY	RIVERS	TOTERS	ASSESS	LATEST
INTERS	OFFERS	ROBERT	TOWERS	ATTEST	LAXEST
INVERT	OGLERS	ROGERS	TOWERY	AWLESS	LOWEST
JOKERS	OILERS	ROVERS	TOYERS	BAREST	MAYEST
LAGERS	ORDERS	ROWERS	TRIERS	BASEST	MEREST
LAKERS	ORMERS	RULERS	TUBERS	BEHEST	MODEST
LASERS	ORNERY	RUPERT	TUNERS	BLUEST	MOLEST
LATERA	ORRERY	SABERS	TUYERE	CALESA	NEWEST
LAVERS	OSBERT	SAKERS	UDDERS	CARESS	NICEST
LAYERS	OSIERS	SAVERS	ULCERS	CHEESE	OBSESS
LEGERS	OTHERS	SAWERS	UMBERS	CHEESY	OBTEST
LEPERS	OTTERS	SAYERS	UPPERS	CREESE	ODDEST
LEVERS	OUTERS	SCLERA	USHERS	CUTEST	OGRESS
LIFERS	OWNERS	SCLERO	UTTERS	DETEST	OLDEST
LINERS	PACERS	SECERN	VALERY	DEVEST	PALEST
LITERS	PAPERS	SEDERS	VENERY	DIGEST	PRIEST
LIVERS	PAPERY	SEVERE	VEXERS	DIREST	PUREST
LIVERY	PARERS	SEVERN	VINERY	DIVEST	RAREST
LONERS	PATERS	SEVERS	VIPERS	DRIEST	RAWEST
LOPERS	PAVERS	SEWERS	VOLERY	DRYEST	RECESS
LOSERS	PAWERS	SHEERS	VOMERS	DURESS	REVEST

RIPEST	EMMETS	******	STREWS	PREFAB	MIFFED
RUDEST	EMMETT	---EU-	UNHEWN	SHOFAR	MUFFED
SAFEST	FACETS	******	UNMEWS	STEFAN	PILFER
SAGEST	FILETS	ADIEUS	******	ZAFFAR	PREFER
SANEST	FLEETS	ADIEUX	---EX-	******	PUFFED
SHIEST	GAIETY	AEGEUS	******	---FE-	PUFFER
SHYEST	GAMETE	ATREUS	ANNEXE	******	REEFED
SLIEST	GAMETO	AUREUS	UNVEXT	BAFFED	REEFER
SLYEST	GAYETY	BAYEUX	URTEXT	BEEFED	ROOFED
SOREST	GENETS	CEREUS	******	BIFFED	ROOFER
STRESS	GLEETS	COLEUS	---EY-	BUFFED	RUFFED
SUREST	GLEETY	LINEUP	******	BUFFER	SUFFER
TAMEST	GREETS	LUTEUM	ABBEYS	BUFFET	SURFED
TERESA	HERETO	LYCEUM	ALLEYS	CHAFED	SURFER
THRESH	INLETS	MADEUP	BOGEYS	CHAFER	TELFER
TRUEST	INSETS	MAKEUP	BOLEYN	CHAFES	TIFFED
UNLESS	ISLETS	MUSEUM	CONEYS	COFFEE	TOFFEE
UNREST	JANETS	PAREUS	COOEYS	COFFER	TUFFET
VILEST	KINETO	PELEUS	COVEYS	COIFED	TURFED
WIDEST	LUNETS	PILEUM	CUTEYS	CONFER	TWOFER
WISEST	MOIETY	PILEUP	DAVEYS	CUFFED	WAIFED
WRIEST	MYCETE	PILEUS	HONEYS	CURFEW	WOLFED
WRYEST	NICETY	POSEUR	LIMEYS	DEAFEN	WOOFER
******	NINETY	TAKEUP	MAMEYS	DIFFER	ZAFFER
---ET-	OCTETS	TEREUS	MATEYS	DOFFED	******
******	ONSETS	TUNEUP	MONEYS	DOFFER	---FF-
AGLETS	OWLETS	URAEUS	MOSEYS	DUFFED	******
ARMETS	PESETA	VOYEUR	REDEYE	DUFFEL	BLUFFS
ASSETS	PIPETS	******	WAVEYS	DUFFER	BOUFFE
BEGETS	RESETS	---EV-	******	EIFFEL	CHAFFS
BERETS	REVETS	******	---EZ-	GAFFED	CHAFFY
BESETS	RIVETS	GENEVA	******	GAFFER	CLIFFS
BIDETS	SAFETY	GRIEVE	BREEZE	GAFFES	CLIFFY
BLUETS	SHEETS	SLEEVE	BREEZY	GOFFER	DRAFFS
CADETS	SLEETS	STEEVE	FREEZE	GOLFED	DRAFFY
CARETS	SLEETY	THIEVE	FRIEZE	GOLFER	FEOFFS
CHAETA	SURETY	******	SNEEZE	GOOFED	FLUFFS
CHAETO	SWEETS	---EW-	SNEEZY	GULFED	FLUFFY
CIVETS	TENETS	******	WHEEZE	HEIFER	GRIFFE
COMETS	TERETE	BEDEWS	WHEEZY	HOOFED	PIAFFE
COVETS	TWEETS	RENEWS	******	HOOFER	QUAFFS
CRUETS	UBIETY	SCREWS	---FA-	HUFFED	SCOFFS
CULETS	UPSETS	SCREWY	******	KNIFED	SCUFFS
DALETH	VALETS	SHREWD	CARFAX	KNIFES	SKIFFS
DELETE	ZIBETH	SHREWS	CHUFAS	LEAFED	SNIFFS
DONETS	ZIBETS	SINEWS	CONFAB	LOAFED	SNIFFY
EFFETE		SINEWY	GUFFAW	LOAFER	SNUFFS
EGRETS		STREWN	LOOFAH	LUFFED	SNUFFY

SPIFFY	RAFFLE	JARFUL	SANGAR	CONGES	GOUGER
STAFFS	RIFFLE	JOYFUL	SEGGAR	CUDGEL	GOUGES
STUFFS	RUFFLE	JUGFUL	SLOGAN	DAGGER	HAGGED
STUFFY	SAWFLY	LAPFUL	TAIGAS	DANGED	HANGED
WHIFFS	STIFLE	LAWFUL	TERGAL	DANGER	HANGER
******	TRIFLE	MANFUL	VIRGAS	DIGGED	HEDGED
---FI-	WAFFLE	RUEFUL	VULGAR	DIGGER	HEDGER
******	******	SINFUL	******	DINGED	HEDGES
BAFFIN	---FO-	SNAFUS	---GE-	DINGEY	HINGED
BIFFIN	******	SULFUR	******	DIRGES	HINGES
BOFFIN	DOGFOX	USEFUL	ADAGES	DODGED	HOGGED
BOWFIN	FYLFOT	VATFUL	APOGEE	DODGER	HUGGED
COFFIN	OUTFOX	WILFUL	BADGED	DODGES	HUNGER
COMFIT	******	WOEFUL	BADGER	DOGGED	IMAGED
DEIFIC	---FR-	******	BADGES	DOGGER	IMAGES
FULFIL	******	---GA-	BAGGED	DRAGEE	IMOGEN
KAFFIR	BELFRY	******	BANGED	DUNGED	JAEGER
MISFIT	BIAFRA	ALEGAR	BARGED	EXOGEN	JAGGED
MUFFIN	ZAFFRE	BEGGAR	BARGEE	FAGGED	JIGGED
OLEFIN	******	BELGAS	BARGES	FANGED	JIGGER
OUTFIT	---FT-	BENGAL	BEGGED	FIDGET	JOGGED
PREFIX	******	BROGAN	BEIGES	FIGGED	JOGGER
PROFIT	CLEFTS	BULGAR	BERGEN	FINGER	JORGES
PUFFIN	CRAFTS	CONGAS	BIGGER	FOGGED	JUDGED
RAFFIA	CRAFTY	COUGAR	BILGED	FORGED	JUDGER
REDFIN	CROFTS	DOUGAL	BILGES	FORGER	JUDGES
SOFFIT	DRAFTS	FANGAS	BINGES	FORGES	JUGGED
SUFFIX	DRAFTY	FRUGAL	BIOGEN	FORGET	KEDGED
TIFFIN	DRIFTS	FUNGAL	BOGGED	FUDGED	KEDGES
TRIFID	DRIFTY	GEWGAW	BONGED	FUDGES	KINGED
UNIFIC	GRAFTS	GINGAL	BRUGES	GADGET	LAAGER
ZAFFIR	SHAFTS	HANGAR	BUDGED	GAGGED	LAGGED
******	SHIFTS	JINGAL	BUDGES	GAGGER	LAGGER
---FL-	SHIFTY	LINGAM	BUDGET	GANGED	LARGER
******	SWIFTS	LINGAS	BUGGED	GANGER	LEDGER
BAFFLE	THEFTS	LONGAN	BUGGER	GANGES	LEDGES
BARFLY	******	MARGAY	BULGED	GARGET	LEGGED
BOTFLY	---FU-	MORGAN	BULGER	GAUGED	LIEGES
COFFLE	******	MUGGAR	BULGES	GAUGER	LINGER
DAYFLY	ARMFUL	NILGAI	BUNGED	GAUGES	LODGED
DEAFLY	ARTFUL	NOUGAT	BURGEE	GEIGER	LODGER
DRYFLY	CUPFUL	OMEGAS	BURGER	GIGGED	LODGES
DUFFLE	EARFUL	OREGAN	CADGED	GINGER	LOGGED
GADFLY	EYEFUL	ORIGAN	CADGER	GORGED	LOGGER
MAYFLY	FITFUL	PISGAH	CADGES	GORGER	LONGED
MUFFLE	FURFUR	PLAGAL	CODGER	GORGES	LONGER
PIFFLE	HATFUL	SAGGAR	COGGED	GORGET	LUGGED
PURFLE	IREFUL	SAIGAS	CONGER	GOUGED	LUGGER

LUNGED	RUGGER	FRIGGA	******	BOGGLE	STIGMA
LUNGEE	SAGGED	FROGGY	---GI-	BUNGLE	ZEUGMA
LUNGER	SAGGER	GROGGY	******	BURGLE	******
LUNGES	SANGER	QUAGGA	ADAGIO	DAGGLE	---GN-
MADGES	SAUGER	QUAGGY	BELGIC	DANGLE	******
MANGER	SEDGES	SHAGGY	BIGGIN	DINGLE	ALIGNS
MARGES	SIEGED	SLAGGY	BOOGIE	GAGGLE	COIGNS
MEAGER	SIEGES	SNAGGY	BORGIA	GANGLI	DEIGNS
MERGED	SINGED	STAGGY	BOUGIE	GARGLE	FEIGNE
MERGER	SINGER	TWIGGY	BRIGID	GIGGLE	FEIGNS
MERGES	SINGES	******	BUDGIE	GIGGLY	REIGNS
MIDGES	STAGED	---GH-	CORGIS	GOGGLE	SOIGNE
MIDGET	STAGER	******	DOGGIE	GOOGLY	******
MONGER	STAGES	ALIGHT	DOUGIE	GURGLE	---GO-
MORGEN	STAGEY	ARIGHT	ELEGIT	HAGGLE	******
MUGGED	STOGEY	BLIGHT	FIZGIG	HIGGLE	AMIGOS
MUGGER	SURGED	BOUGHS	FRIGID	JANGLE	ARAGON
NAGGED	SURGER	BOUGHT	FULGID	JIGGLE	BANGOR
NAGGER	SURGES	BRIGHT	HAGGIS	JINGLE	BONGOS
NIGGER	SWAGED	BURGHS	LOGGIA	JINGLY	BURGOO
NUDGED	SWAGES	CAUGHT	LUNGIS	JOGGLE	BURGOS
NUDGES	TAGGED	COUGHS	MAGGIE	JUGGLE	CARGOS
NUGGET	TAGGER	DINGHY	MARGIE	JUNGLE	CHEGOE
ONAGER	TANGED	DOUGHS	MARGIN	JUNGLY	CHIGOE
ORIGEN	TARGET	DOUGHY	NOGGIN	KINGLY	CONGOU
OXYGEN	TINGED	DWIGHT	ORIGIN	MANGLE	DRAGON
PARGET	TINGES	FLIGHT	PHAGIA	MIGGLE	FAGGOT
PEGGED	TOGGED	FOUGHT	PIDGIN	MINGLE	FLAGON
PIGGED	TONGED	FRIGHT	PIGGIE	NIGGLE	FORGOT
PINGED	TUGGED	HEIGHT	PIGGIN	SINGLE	GOOGOL
PONGEE	USAGES	KNIGHT	PLAGIO	SINGLY	GORGON
PUGGED	VERGED	LAUGHS	PLEGIA	SMUGLY	GREGOS
PURGED	VERGER	LEIGHS	PLUGIN	SNUGLY	ISOGON
PURGER	VERGES	LOUGHS	REGGIE	TANGLE	JARGON
PURGES	WAGGED	NAUGHT	TRAGIC	TANGLY	LARGOS
RAGGED	WEDGED	NEIGHS	TURGID	TINGLE	MAGGOT
RANGED	WEDGES	NOUGHT	VERGIL	TINGLY	MANGOS
RANGER	WIGGED	PLIGHT	VIRGIE	TOGGLE	MARGOS
RANGES	WINGED	ROUGHS	VIRGIL	TRIGLY	MARGOT
RIDGED	ZENGER	SLIGHT	VIRGIN	WAGGLE	MONGOL
RIDGES	ZINGED	SORGHO	WEDGIE	WAGGLY	OREGON
RIGGED	******	SOUGHS	******	WANGLE	PARGOS
RIGGER	---GG-	SOUGHT	---GK-	WIGGLE	PENGOS
RINGED	******	TAUGHT	******	WIGGLY	PINGOS
RINGER	CLOGGY	THIGHS	GINGKO	******	SAIGON
ROUGED	CRAGGY	TOUGHS	******	---GM-	SARGON
ROUGES	DREGGY	WEIGHS	---GL-	******	SORGOS
RUGGED	FLAGGY	WRIGHT	BANGLE	BREGMA	SPIGOT
		WEIGHT	BEAGLE	ENIGMA	

SUNGOD	PLAGUY	RAPHAE	DASHES	LATHED	SACHEM
TANGOS	POPGUN	SAPHAR	DISHED	LATHER	SACHET
TRIGON	PRAGUE	SASHAY	DISHES	LATHES	SASHED
TROGON	REDGUM	SUNHAT	DITHER	LECHER	SASHES
WAGGON	ROTGUT	TOPHAT	EITHER	LICHEE	SIGHED
******	SANGUI	UTAHAN	ESCHER	LICHEN	SYPHER
---GR-	SHOGUN	WITHAL	ESCHEW	LITHER	TETHER
******	TERGUM	******	ESTHER	LUSHED	TITHED
EMIGRE	TONGUE	---HE-	ETCHED	LUSHER	TITHER
GRIGRI	TRAGUS	******	ETCHER	LUSHES	TITHES
GRUGRU	TUNGUS	AACHEN	ETCHES	LUTHER	TOSHES
HUNGRY	VALGUS	AETHER	EUCHER	MASHED	TOTHER
MAIGRE		ALTHEA	FATHER	MASHER	TUSHED
MALGRE	---GY-	ANTHEA	FICHES	MASHES	TUSHES
MEAGRE	******	ANTHEM	FISHER	MAYHEM	WASHED
ONAGRI	PEGGYS	ANTHER	FISHES	MESHED	WASHER
PUGGRY	******	ARCHED	GASHED	MESHER	WASHES
******	---HA-	ARCHEO	GASHES	MESHES	WETHER
---GS-	******	ARCHER	GATHER	MICHEL	WICHES
******	AFGHAN	ARCHES	GOPHER	MOTHER	WISHED
MONGST	ALPHAS	BACHED	GORHEN	MUSHED	WISHES
******	BASHAW	BACHES	GOSHEN	MUSHER	WITHED
---GT-	BUCHAN	BASHED	GUSHED	MUSHES	WITHER
******	CASHAW	BASHES	GUSHER	NEPHEW	WITHES
LENGTH	CATHAY	BATHED	GUSHES	NETHER	ZITHER
******	CUSHAT	BATHER	HASHED	NICHED	******
---GU-	CUSHAW	BETHEL	HASHES	NICHES	---HI-
******	DACHAS	BOSHES	HIGHER	NIGHER	******
AGOGUE	DACHAU	BOTHER	HITHER	NOSHED	ARCHIE
AIRGUN	DIRHAM	BUSHED	HUGHES	PEAHEN	ARCHIL
BANGUI	DURHAM	BUSHEL	HUSHED	PISHED	COCHIN
BANGUP	ESCHAR	BUSHES	HUSHES	PISHES	ELOHIM
BROGUE	GOTHAM	BUSHEY	HYPHEN	PITHED	GOTHIC
CANGUE	GRAHAM	CACHED	INCHED	POTHER	HUGHIE
CATGUT	HAWHAW	CACHES	INCHES	PUSHED	ISCHIA
DENGUE	HEEHAW	CACHET	ISOHEL	PUSHER	JAPHIA
DINGUS	HYPHAE	CASHED	ITCHED	PUSHES	KATHIE
DROGUE	HYPHAL	CASHES	ITCHES	RACHEL	LITHIA
FUNGUS	JOTHAM	CASHEW	JAPHET	RASHER	LITHIC
GANGUE	LETHAL	CATHER	JOSHED	RASHES	LOCHIA
HANGUP	MAYHAP	CIPHER	JOSHER	RATHER	MASHIE
LANGUR	MISHAP	CITHER	JOSHES	RICHER	MENHIR
LEAGUE	NATHAN	COSHED	KOSHER	RICHES	MUZHIK
LINGUA	NUCHAE	COSHER	KUCHEN	ROCHET	MYTHIC
MIDGUT	OLDHAM	COSHES	LACHES	RUCHES	ORCHID
MORGUE	ORPHAN	CYPHER	LASHED	RUSHED	ORCHIL
MUGGUR	PASHAS	DASHED	LASHER	RUSHER	ORCHIO
PLAGUE	PATHAN	DASHER	LASHES	RUSHES	ORCHIS

ORPHIC	BATHOS	PASHTO	CURIAE	MEDIAL	******
PATHIA	BISHOP	PUSHTU	CURIAL	MEDIAN	---IB-
PYTHIA	BOOHOO	RIGHTO	DELIAN	MENIAL	******
PYTHIC	CACHOU	RIGHTS	DELIAS	MESIAL	ADLIBS
RACHIS	CARHOP	SIGHTS	DENIAL	MESIAN	CARIBE
RAPHIS	CASHOO	TIGHTS	DORIAN	MIRIAM	CARIBS
RICHIE	FATHOM	VASHTI	DURIAN	MYRIAD	IMBIBE
SOPHIA	INCHON	YACHTS	EOLIAN	NARIAL	SAHIBS
SOPHIE	METHOD	******	EONIAN	NASIAL	SCRIBE
SOTHIC	MYTHOI	---HU-	ESPIAL	NORIAS	SQUIBS
SOTHIS	MYTHOS	******	FABIAN	NUBIAN	ZARIBA
SPAHIS	NOSHOW	ARTHUR	FACIAL	NUBIAS	******
UNSHIP	OOPHOR	FICHUS	FECIAL	OOMIAK	---IC-
URCHIN	PATHOL	JOSHUA	FENIAN	OSSIAN	******
WITHIN	PATHOS	NASHUA	FERIAL	PARIAH	ADDICT
WITHIT	PYTHON	PUSHUP	FETIAL	PARIAN	ADVICE
ZECHIN	QUAHOG	SADHUS	FIJIAN	PELIAS	AFRICA
******	REDHOT	TUCHUN	FILIAL	PENIAL	ANTICS
---HL-	SIPHON	TYPHUS	FINIAL	PLEIAD	ARNICA
******	SYPHON	ZETHUS	FOLIAR	RACIAL	ASPICS
ARCHLY	TYPHON	******	GAVIAL	RADIAL	ATTICA
HIGHLY	UNSHOD	---HY-	GENIAL	RADIAN	ATTICS
POSHLY	UPSHOT	******	INDIAN	RUPIAH	BASICS
RASHLY	WARHOL	ALPHYL	IONIAN	SAMIAN	BODICE
RICHLY	YOOHOO	ARCHYS	ISAIAH	SEPIAS	CALICO
TYPHLO	ZETHOS	CATHYS	JOSIAH	SERIAL	CHOICE
******	******	KATHYS	JOSIAS	SIMIAN	CILICE
---HM-	---HR-	METHYL	JOVIAL	SOCIAL	CIVICS
******	******	TETHYS	JOVIAN	SONIAS	COMICS
ABOHMS	AMPHRS	ZEPHYR	JULIAN	STRIAE	CONICS
ASTHMA	ARTHRO	******	JULIAS	SYRIAC	CYNICS
BRAHMA	EUCHRE	---IA-	KALIAN	SYRIAN	DARICS
BRAHMS	JETHRO	******	KODIAK	TIBIAE	DELICT
******	NEPHRO	ADRIAN	LABIAL	TIBIAL	DEPICT
---HN-	TISHRI	AECIAL	LACIAL	TIBIAS	DEVICE
******	******	AERIAL	LAMIAE	TITIAN	DRYICE
DAPHNE	---HT-	ANTIAR	LAMIAS	TOBIAH	ENRICH
FOEHNS	******	APPIAN	LARIAT	TOBIAS	ENRICO
TECHNO	AUGHTS	ATRIAL	LILIAN	TYRIAN	ENTICE
VISHNU	BIGHTS	BANIAN	LIVIAS	UNCIAL	ETHICS
******	EIGHTH	BELIAL	LUCIAN	UZZIAH	EUNICE
---HO-	EIGHTS	BURIAL	LUCIAS	VEDIAC	FELICE
******	EIGHTY	CAPIAS	LYDIAS	VENIAL	FETICH
ALPHOS	FIGHTS	CAVIAR	MANIAC	VIVIAN	HELICO
ANCHOR	LIGHTS	CELIAC	MANIAS	XENIAL	INDICT
ANYHOW	MIGHTY	CELIAS	MARIAN	ZAMIAS	JANICE
ARCHON	NIGHTS	CILIAT	MARIAS	ZODIAC	LORICA
AUTHOR	NIGHTY	COBIAS	MEDIAE		LYRICS

MALICE	AVOIDS	ARMIES	DOGIES	KATIES	PYXIES
MEDICI	BESIDE	ARNIES	DOPIER	LACIER	RABIES
MEDICO	BETIDE	ARTIES	DORIES	LADIES	RACIER
MEDICS	BOLIDE	ASHIER	DOTIER	LAKIER	RAMIES
MEJICO	BORIDE	BABIED	DOXIES	LAZIER	RAPIER
MEXICO	BRAIDS	BABIES	DOZIER	LEVIED	RELIED
MIMICS	DAVIDS	BELIED	DUTIES	LEVIER	RELIEF
MONICA	DECIDE	BELIEF	EASIER	LEVIES	RELIER
MUNICH	DERIDE	BELIER	EDDIED	LILIED	RELIES
MYRICA	DIVIDE	BELIES	EDDIES	LILIES	REVIEW
NOTICE	DRUIDS	BEVIES	EDGIER	LIMIER	ROPIER
NOVICE	EXCIDE	BODIED	ELLIES	LINIER	ROSIER
OFFICE	FELIDS	BODIES	ELSIES	LIVIER	RUBIES
OPTICS	FLUIDS	BOGIES	EMMIES	LOGIER	SADIES
ORRICE	HALIDE	BONIER	ENVIED	LORIES	SAGIER
PANICE	HALIDS	BURIED	ENVIER	LUCIEN	SAMIEL
PANICS	HYOIDS	BURIES	ENVIES	MAMIES	SANIES
PLAICE	INSIDE	BUSIED	ERNIES	MARIES	SAPIEN
POLICE	IODIDE	BUSIES	ESPIED	MAZIER	SCRIED
POLICY	LEPIDO	CAGIER	ESPIES	METIER	SERIES
PUMICE	LIBIDO	CAHIER	EYRIES	MILIEU	SEXIER
RELICS	LIPIDS	CARIES	FACIES	MOLIES	SHRIEK
RELICT	ONEIDA	CAVIES	FOGIES	MONIED	SIZIER
SCHICK	OREIDE	CITIED	FOXIER	MONIES	SOVIET
SHTICK	OROIDE	CITIES	FUMIER	MOVIES	SPRIER
SILICA	OXHIDE	CIVIES	FURIES	MURIEL	SUSIES
SILICO	PLAIDS	COLIES	GAMIER	NAPIER	TAXIED
SLUICE	RAPIDS	CONIES	GENIES	NAVIES	TIDIED
SPLICE	RESIDE	COPIED	GLUIER	NIXIES	TIDIER
STOICS	SOLIDI	COPIER	GOBIES	NOSIER	TIDIES
STRICK	SOLIDS	COPIES	GOOIER	OILIER	TINIER
STRICT	SQUIDS	COZIER	GORIER	OLLIES	TOBIES
THRICE	STRIDE	COZIES	HAZIER	OOZIER	TODIES
TONICS	UNTIDY	CURIES	HOLIER	ORGIES	TONIER
TOPICS	UPSIDE	CUTIES	HOLIES	PARIES	TORIES
TUNICA	UREIDE	DANIEL	HOMIER	PINIER	UGLIER
TUNICS	ZOOIDS	DARIEN	HONIED	PINIES	UNDIES
UNPICK	******	DAVIES	HOSIER	PIPIER	UNTIED
VARICO	---IE-	DEFIED	IMMIES	PITIED	UNTIES
VENICE	******	DEFIER	INDIES	PITIES	VARIED
VESICA	ABBIES	DEFIES	INKIER	PIXIES	VARIER
VESICO	ADRIEN	DEMIES	INLIER	POGIES	VARIES
VOMICA	AERIED	DENIED	JAMIES	POKIER	VINIER
YORICK	AERIES	DENIER	JOSIEA	POKIES	VIVIEN
ZURICH	AIRIER	DENIES	JOLIET	PONIED	VIZIER
******	ALLIED	DEWIER	JULIES	PONIES	WADIES
---ID-	ALLIES	DIDIES	JULIET	POSIES	WARIER
******	ANNIES	DOBIES	JURIES	PUNIER	WAVIER
APHIDS					
AROIDS					

WAVIES	AWEIGH	ARTILY	MANILA	VERILY	ALPINE
WAXIER	BENIGN	ATTILA	MAZILY	VEXILS	ALUINO
WILIER	COSIGN	AUDILE	MEGILP	VIGILS	ALUINS
WINIER	CRAIGS	AVAILS	MOBILE	VIRILE	ALVINA
WIRIER	DESIGN	AWHILE	MOTILE	WARILY	ALVINE
XAVIER	EFFIGY	BASILS	NEVILE	WAVILY	ANGINA
ZANIER	ELOIGN	BODILY	NEVILL	WILILY	ANOINT
ZANIES	ENSIGN	BRAILS	NOSILY	WIRILY	ARCING
******	GREIGE	BROILS	NUBILE	ZORILS	ARLINE
---IF-	INDIGO	BUSILY	OILILY	******	ARMING
******	MALIGN	CAGILY	ONEILL	---IM-	ARSINE
ADRIFT	OBLIGE	CAMILA	OOZILY	******	ASKING
AERIFY	RESIGN	CAVILS	PENILE	BEDIMS	AUXINS
BASIFY	RUBIGO	CECILE	PERILS	CLAIMS	AWEING
CALIFS	SLEIGH	CECILS	PUNILY	DENIMS	AWNING
CODIFY	SPRIGS	CECILY	PUPILS	ESKIMO	BAAING
GASIFY	UNRIGS	CHEILO	QUAILS	FATIMA	BAKING
GREIFS	******	COSILY	RACILY	HAKIMS	BALING
HUMIFY	---II-	COZILY	REBILL	INTIMA	BARING
IGNIFY	******	CYRILS	REFILL	JEMIMA	BASING
MINIFY	AALIIS	DECILE	RESILE	MAXIMA	BASINS
MODIFY	TORIIS	DEFILE	REVILE	MAXIMS	BATING
MOTIFS	******	DEVILS	ROPILY	MINIMA	BAYING
NAZIFY	---IK-	DOCILE	ROSILY	MINIMS	BEGINS
NIDIFY	******	DOZILY	RUTILE	OPTIMA	BEHIND
NOTIFY	ALSIKE	EASILY	SEDILE	OPTIME	BERING
OSSIFY	AXLIKE	EERILY	SENILE	REGIME	BIDING
PACIFY	BATIKS	ENSILE	SEXILY	RHEIMS	BIKINI
PURIFY	BELIKE	FACILE	SHEILA	SCRIMP	BITING
RAMIFY	KABIKI	FAMILY	SHEILD	SHRIMP	BLAINS
RATIFY	KAMIKS	FLAILS	SHRILL	ULTIMA	BLUING
SALIFY	SHEIKH	FOXILY	SICILY	ULTIMO	BODING
SERIFS	SHEIKS	FRAILS	SIGILS	YAKIMA	BONING
SHRIFT	SHRIKE	FUSILE	SIMILE	******	BOOING
STRIFE	STRIKE	FUSILS	SNAILS	---IN-	BORING
TARIFF	TROIKA	FUTILE	SPOILS	******	BOVINE
THRIFT	TUPIKS	FUZILS	SPOILT	ACHING	BOWING
TYPIFY	UNLIKE	GAMILY	SQUILL	ACTING	BOXING
UGLIFY	UPDIKE	GORILY	SWAILS	ACTINI	BRAINS
UPLIFT	WAKIKI	HABILE	SYBILS	ACTINO	BRAINY
VERIFY	******	HAZILY	THRILL	ADDING	BRUINS
VILIFY	---IL-	HOLILY	TIDILY	AGEING	BURINS
VIVIFY	******	HOMILY	TINILY	AIDING	BUSING
******	AEDILE	ILOILO	TRAILS	AILING	BUYING
---IG-	AIRILY	LABILE	UGLILY	AIMING	BYLINE
******	ANVILS	LACILY	UNPILE	AIRING	CABINS
ASSIGN	APRILS	LAZILY	UPHILL	ALBINO	CAGING
AURIGA	AQUILA	LUCILE	VASILI	ALDINE	CAKING

CANINE	DRAINS	FIRING	HOSING	LOWING	OGLING
CANING	DRYING	FIXING	IDLING	LUMINA	OILING
CARINA	DUPING	FLYING	IMPING	LUMINI	ONLINE
CARING	DURING	FORINT	INKING	LUMINO	OOZING
CASING	DYEING	FOXING	INNING	LUPINE	OPTING
CASINO	EALING	FRYING	INWIND	LURING	ORBING
CAVING	EARING	FUMING	IODINE	LUTING	ORPINE
CAWING	EASING	FUSING	IRKING	LYSINE	ORPINS
CEDING	EATING	FUZING	IRVING	LYSING	OSCINE
CERING	EBBING	GAGING	IRVINS	LYSINS	OUTING
CHAINS	ECHINI	GAMING	IRWINS	MACING	OWNING
CITING	ECHINO	GAMINS	ISLING	MAKING	PACING
CLUING	EDGING	GAPING	JADING	MALINE	PAGING
CODING	EDWINA	GATING	JAPING	MARINA	PALING
COKING	EDWINS	GAZING	JARINA	MARINE	PARING
COLINE	EGGING	GEEING	JAWING	MATINE	PATINA
COLINS	EKEING	GEMINI	JEEING	MATING	PATINE
COMING	ELAINE	GIBING	JIBING	MATINS	PAVING
CONING	ELFINS	GIVING	JIMINY	MAXINE	PAWING
COOING	ELOINS	GLUING	JIVING	MAYING	PAYING
COPING	ENCINA	GORING	JOKING	MAZING	PEKING
CORING	ENDING	GRAINS	JOYING	MENINX	PIKING
COSINE	ENGINE	GRAINY	KEVINS	MERINO	PILING
COVING	ENWIND	GROINS	KEYING	METING	PINING
COWING	EPPING	GUYING	KININS	MEWING	PIPING
COXING	EQUINE	GYBING	KITING	MIMING	PLAINS
CRYING	ERMINE	GYVING	LACING	MINING	PLAINT
CUBING	ERRING	HADING	LADING	MIRING	PLYING
CUMINS	ERWINS	HALING	LADINO	MIXING	POKING
CURING	EYEING	HARING	LAKING	MOLINE	POLING
CUTINS	FACING	HATING	LAMINA	MOOING	PORING
DARING	FADING	HAVING	LAMING	MOPING	POSING
DATING	FAKING	HAWING	LAPINS	MOVING	PRYING
DAZING	FAMINE	HAYING	LARINE	MOWING	PUKING
DEFINE	FARINA	HAZING	LATINS	MURINE	PULING
DEKING	FARING	HEWING	LAVING	MUSING	PURINE
DICING	FATING	HEXING	LAWING	MUTING	QUAINT
DIKING	FAXING	HIDING	LAYING	MUTINY	QUOINS
DINING	FAYING	HIEING	LAZING	NADINE	RACINE
DIVINE	FAZING	HIKING	LIKING	NAMING	RACING
DIVING	FEEING	HIRING	LIMINA	NARINE	RAGING
DOLING	FELINE	HIVING	LIMING	NIDING	RAKING
DOMING	FERINE	HOEING	LINING	NIXING	RAPINE
DOMINO	FETING	HOLING	LIVING	NOSING	RAPING
DOPING	FEUING	HOMING	LOOING	NOTING	RARING
DOSING	FIFING	HOMINY	LOPING	NUMINA	RATINE
DOTING	FILING	HONING	LOSING	OARING	RATING
DOZING	FINING	HOPING	LOVING	OFFING	RAVINE

RAVING	SHRINK	TRAINS	******	SAVIOR	ENTIRE
RAYING	SHYING	TRUING	---IO-	SENIOR	EXPIRE
RAZING	SIDING	TRYING	******	SOLION	EXPIRY
REFINE	SIRING	TUBING	ACTION	TALION	FAKIRS
REGINA	SITING	TUNING	ALBION	VISION	FLAIRS
RELINE	SITINS	TYPING	AMNION	WANION	GLAIRS
REMIND	SIZING	UNBIND	BASION	******	GLAIRY
REPINE	SKEINS	UNDINE	BUNION	---IP-	HEGIRA
RESINS	SKIING	UNKIND	CAMION	******	HEJIRA
RETINA	SKYING	UNPINS	CATION	CALIPH	INFIRM
REWIND	SLUING	UNWIND	CURIOS	CERIPH	JABIRU
RICING	SOLING	UPPING	DURION	EQUIPS	NADIRS
RIDING	SOWING	URGING	ELLIOT	EURIPI	ONEIRO
RILING	SOZINE	URSINE	FANION	FELIPE	RETIRE
RIMING	SOZINS	VAGINA	FOLIOS	OXLIPS	SATIRE
RISING	SPHINX	VAGINO	FUGIOS	RECIPE	SQUIRE
RIVING	SPLINE	VEXING	FUSION	SCRIPS	SQUIRM
ROBING	SPLINT	VIKING	GABION	SCRIPT	SQUIRT
ROBINS	SPRING	VIMINA	GALIOT	STRIPE	STAIRS
ROPING	SPRINT	VISING	GONION	STRIPS	TAPIRS
ROSING	SPYING	VOLING	HELIOS	STRIPT	THEIRS
ROSINS	SQUINT	VOTING	HERIOT	STRIPY	TSHIRT
ROSINY	STAINS	VOWING	HEZION	THRIPS	UMPIRE
ROVING	STEINS	WADING	JUNIOR	TULIPS	UNGIRD
ROWING	STRING	WAGING	KATION	UNRIPE	UNGIRT
RUEING	STYING	WAHINE	LEGION	UNRIPS	VENIRE
RULING	SUPINE	WAKING	LESION	******	VIZIRS
RUMINA	SWAINS	WALING	LOGION	---IR-	******
RUNINS	SYRINX	WANING	LOTION	******	---IS-
RUSINE	TAKING	WAVING	MANIOC	ADMIRE	******
SABINA	TAMING	WAXING	MARION	AFFIRM	ADVISE
SABINE	TAPING	WILING	MINION	ALMIRA	AGUISH
SABINS	TARING	WINING	MORION	ASPIRE	AORIST
SALINE	TAWING	WIPING	MOTION	ATTIRE	ARTIST
SASINS	TAXING	WIRING	NASION	AWHIRL	ASSISI
SATING	TEEING	WISING	NATION	BEGIRD	ASSIST
SATINS	TIDING	WIVING	NOTION	BEGIRT	AURIST
SATINY	TIEINS	WOOING	OPTION	BEMIRE	AUTISM
SAVING	TILING	WOWING	PATIOS	CHAIRS	BABISM
SAVINS	TIMING	WRYING	PAVIOR	CHEIRO	BABIST
SAWING	TIRING	YAWING	PELION	CHOIRS	BANISH
SAYING	TOEING	YOGINS	PERIOD	CLAIRE	BETISE
SEEING	TONING	YOKING	PINION	DESIRE	BLAISE
SERINE	TOPING	YOKING	POTION	ELMIRA	BLUISH
SERINS	TOTING	YOWING	RADIOS	ELVIRA	BOYISH
SEWING	TOWING	ZAYINS	RATION	EMPIRE	BRAISE
SEXING	TOXINS	ZONING	RATIOS	ENGIRD	BRUISE
SHRINE	TOYING		REGION	ENGIRT	CAMISE

CERISE	LOUISE	RESIST	BINITS	LOLITA	VISITS
CHAISE	LUTIST	REVISE	BONITO	LUCITE	VOMITO
CHRISM	LYRISM	ROMISH	BRUITS	MANITO	VOMITS
CHRIST	LYRIST	SADISM	CAPITA	MANITU	WAPITI
CIVISM	MAOISM	SADIST	CAVITE	MERITS	WRAITH
CLEIST	MAOIST	SALISH	CAVITY	NIMITZ	XYLITE
COYISH	MARIST	SCHISM	CERITE	NUDITY	ZENITH
CRUISE	MODISH	SCHIST	COMITY	ODDITY	ZIZITH
CUBISM	MOMISM	SEXISM	CUBITS	OOLITE	******
CUBIST	MONISM	SEXIST	DANITE	OPHITE	---IU-
DANISH	MONIST	SHIISM	DAVITS	ORBITS	******
DEMISE	MOPISH	SPEISS	DEBITS	ORNITH	ACEIUM
DENISE	MULISH	SQUISH	DEMITS	PARITY	ACTIUM
DESIST	MUTISM	SUFISM	DEWITT	PELITE	ALLIUM
DEVISE	NANISM	TANIST	DIGITI	PETITE	ATRIUM
DOVISH	NAZISM	TAOISM	DIGITS	PEWITS	BARIUM
DRYISH	NOMISM	TAOIST	DIMITY	PINITE	CERIUM
DUDISH	NOWISE	THEISM	DIXITS	PIPITS	CESIUM
EDDISH	NUDISM	THEIST	DROITS	PLAITS	CILIUM
EGOISM	NUDIST	TOYISH	ENMITY	POLITE	CONIUM
EGOIST	OAFISH	TRUISM	ENTITY	POLITY	CORIUM
ELFISH	OBIISM	TYPIST	EOLITH	POSITS	CURIUM
ELOISE	OBOIST	UNWISE	EQUITY	PURITY	DARIUS
ELVISH	OFFISH	UNWISH	EXCITE	PYRITE	DELIUS
ENLIST	OGRISH	UPPISH	FERITY	QUOITS	ERBIUM
EONISM	OLDISH	UPRISE	FINITE	RARITY	FOLIUM
EXCISE	OWLISH	VALISE	FIXITY	RATITE	GENIUS
FAMISH	PALISH	VANISH	FRUITS	RECITE	GONIUM
FETISH	PAPIST	VERISM	FRUITY	REFITS	HELIUM
FINISH	PARISH	VERIST	GENITO	REMITS	INDIUM
FRAISE	PAVISE	******	HABITS	SAMITE	IONIUM
GARISH	PERISH	---IT-	HALITE	SANITY	JULIUS
GNEISS	POLISH	******	HAMITE	SEMITE	JUNIUS
HOLISM	POPISH	ACUITY	HIVITE	SHIITE	KALIUM
IMPISH	PRAISE	ADMITS	IGNITE	SOMITE	LABIUM
INCISE	PUNISH	ALBITE	INCITE	SPAITS	LUCIUS
INSIST	PURISM	AMBITS	INDITE	SPLITS	MEDIUM
IODISM	PURIST	AMRITA	INVITE	SPRITE	MILIUM
JADISH	RACISM	APLITE	IOLITE	SPRITS	MINIUM
JEWISH	RACIST	AUDITS	JUDITH	STAITH	MOBIUS
JURIST	RADISH	AUGITE	KENITE	SUBITO	OMNIUM
JUTISH	RAKISH	AWAITS	KIBITZ	TAHITI	OSMIUM
KUMISS	RAPIST	BABITE	KRAITS	TAXITE	PODIUM
LATISH	RAVISH	BARITE	LAXITY	TONITE	RADIUM
LAVISH	RAWISH	BEFITS	LENITY	TRAITS	RADIUS
LEGIST	RELISH	BENITA	LEVITE	UPPITY	REGIUS
LIAISE	REMISE	BENITO	LEVITY	VANITY	SIRIUS
LOUISA	REMISS	BILITY	LIMITS	VERITY	SODIUM

TEDIUM	******	AWAKEN	COOKEY	HOCKED	MICKEY
WIKIUP	---JE-	AWAKES	CORKED	HOCKEY	MILKED
******	******	AWOKEN	CORKER	HONKED	MILKER
---IV-	FANJET	BACKED	CRAKES	HONKER	MOCKED
******	GASJET	BACKER	CRIKEY	HOOKED	MOCKER
ACTIVE	KOPJES	BALKED	DANKER	HOOKER	MONKEY
ARGIVE	PROJET	BANKED	DARKEN	HOOKEY	MUCKED
ARRIVE	RAMJET	BANKER	DARKER	HULKED	MUCKER
DATIVE	******	BARKED	DECKED	HUSKED	MUSKEG
DERIVE	---JI-	BARKER	DECKEL	HUSKER	MUSKET
ENDIVE	******	BASKED	DECKER	JACKED	NARKED
GODIVA	CROJIK	BASKET	DICKER	JACKET	NECKED
MOTIVE	SHOJIS	BEAKED	DICKEY	JERKED	NICKED
NATIVE	******	BEAKER	DINKEY	JINKED	NICKEL
RELIVE	---JO-	BECKED	DIRKED	JINKER	NICKER
REVIVE	******	BECKET	DOCKED	JOCKEY	NOCKED
SALIVA	ACAJOU	BICKER	DOCKER	JUNKED	PACKED
SCRIVE	BANJOS	BILKED	DOCKET	JUNKER	PACKER
SHRIVE	DONJON	BILKER	DONKEY	JUNKET	PACKET
STRIVE	FRIJOL	BLOKES	DRAKES	KECKED	PARKED
THRIVE	ODDJOB	BOOKED	DUCKED	KICKED	PARKER
UNLIVE	******	BOSKET	DUCKER	KICKER	PAUKER
VOTIVE	---JU-	BRAKED	DUIKER	KINKED	PEAKED
******	******	BRAKES	DUNKED	KRAKEN	PECKED
---IX-	SELJUK	BROKEN	DUNKER	LACKED	PECKER
******	******	BROKER	DUSKED	LACKEY	PEEKED
ADMIXT	---JY-	BUCKED	EVOKED	LANKER	PEEKER
MAXIXE	BENJYS	BUCKER	EVOKES	LARKED	PERKED
******	******	BUCKET	FAWKES	LARKER	PICKED
---IZ-	---KA-	BULKED	FLAKED	LEAKED	PICKER
******	******	BUNKED	FLAKER	LICKED	PICKET
ASSIZE	BAIKAL	BUNKER	FLAKES	LINKED	PINKED
BELIZE	BALKAN	BURKED	FLUKED	LOCKED	POCKET
BRAIZE	HOOKAH	BURKES	FLUKES	LOCKER	PORKER
IODIZE	JACKAL	BUSKER	FLUKEY	LOCKET	PUCKER
IONIZE	MISKAL	CALKED	FORKED	LOOKED	QUAKED
SCHIZO	PARKAS	CALKER	FUNKED	LOOKER	QUAKER
******	PICKAX	CANKER	GASKET	LOWKEY	QUAKES
---JA-	POLKAS	CASKET	GAWKED	LUNKER	RACKED
******	PUNKAS	CHOKED	HACKED	LURKED	RACKER
ABIJAH	SHIKAR	CHOKER	HACKEE	LURKER	RACKET
ELIJAH	TANKAS	CHOKES	HACKER	MARKED	RANKED
JAMJAR	VODKAS	COCKED	HANKER	MARKER	RANKER
LOGJAM	******	COCKER	HARKED	MARKET	REEKED
PUNJAB	---KE-	CONKED	HARKEN	MASKED	REEKER
SANJAK	******	CONKER	HAWKED	MASKEG	RICKED
THUJAS	ARCKED	COOKED	HAWKER	MASKER	RICKEY
TROJAN	AWAKED	COOKER	HICKEY	MEEKER	RINKED

RISKED
RISKER
ROCKED
ROCKER
ROCKET
ROOKED
RUCKED
SACKED
SACKER
SECKEL
SEEKER
SHAKEN
SHAKER
SHAKES
SHEKEL
SICKED
SICKEN
SICKER
SILKEN
SINKER
SLAKED
SLAKES
SMOKED
SMOKER
SMOKES
SNAKED
SNAKES
SOAKED
SOAKER
SOCKED
SOCKET
SPIKED
SPIKES
SPOKED

---KH-

SPOKEN
******
SPOKES
STAKED
STAKES
STOKED
******
STOKER
STOKES
SUCKED
SUCKER
SULKED
SUNKEN
TACKED
TACKER
TACKEY

TALKED
TALKER
TANKED
TANKER
TASKED
TICKED
TICKER
TICKET
TINKER
TUCKED
TUCKER
TUCKET
TURKEY
TUSKED
TUSKER
WALKED
WALKER
WEAKEN
WEAKER
WICKED
WICKER
WICKET
WINKED
WINKER
WORKED
WORKER
YAKKED
YANKED
YANKEE
YONKER
YORKER
YUKKED
******

---KH-

******
GURKHA
******

---KI-

BODKIN
BOOKIE
BUMKIN
BUSKIN
CALKIN
CATKIN
COOKIE
DICKIE
FIRKIN

GASKIN
HACKIE
JACKIE
JERKIN
JUNKIE
KHAKIS
LOOKIN
MUSKIT
NAPKIN
PINKIE
PIPKIN
ROOKIE
RUSKIN
SIKKIM
SISKIN
TALKIE
TONKIN
TURKIC
TURKIS
WELKIN
******

---KK-

******
MARKKA
******

---KL-

******
BUCKLE
CACKLE
COCKLE
DANKLY
DARKLE
DARKLY
DECKLE
FICKLE
HACKLE
HECKLE
HUCKLE
KECKLE
LANKLY
MACKLE
MEEKLY
MICKLE
MUCKLE
PICKLE
RANKLE
RANKLY
SICKLE

SICKLY
SUCKLE
TACKLE
TICKLE
TINKLE
TINKLY
WEAKLY
WEEKLY
WINKLE
******

---KN-

******
ROCKNE
******

---KO-

******
ANGKOR
BECKON
CUCKOO
GECKOS
HICKOK
JOCKOS
MUSKOX
RECKON
SHAKOS
WALKON
******

---KR-

******
BUCKRA
******

---KS-

******
FOLKSY
******

---KU-

******
BUNKUM
COCKUP
DINKUM
HOOKUP
LOCKUP
MARKUP
MOCKUP
PICKUP
RUCKUS
WALKUP

******

---KY-

******
BECKYS
JACKYS
MICKYS
NICKYS
RICKYS
RYUKYU
VALKYR
VICKYS
******

---LA-

******
ALULAE
ALULAR
ASHLAR
BALLAD
BEDLAM
BELLAS
BEULAH
BEULAS
BULLAE
BURLAP
BYPLAY
CALLAO
CALLAS
CARLAS
CELLAE
CELLAR
CHELAE
CHELAS
COLLAR
CULLAY
CUTLAS
DALLAS
DELLAS
DEWLAP
DOBLAS
DOLLAR
DOWLAS
EARLAP
FALLAL
FELLAH
GULLAH
HALLAH
HARLAN
HELLAS

KIBLAH
KOALAS
MEDLAR
MILLAY
MISLAY
MOLLAH
MOOLAH
MULLAH
NULLAH
OCULAR
OUTLAW
OUTLAY
OVULAR
PALLAS
PARLAY
PAULAS
PEDLAR
PHYLAE
PILLAR
POPLAR
RAGLAN
REPLAY
SCALAR
SENLAC
SMILAX
STALAG
STELAE
STELAR
STYLAR
UNCLAD
UVULAE
UVULAR
UVULAS
VILLAS
VIOLAS
WALLAH
WALLAS
WAYLAY
ZILLAH
******

---LB-

******
SHELBY
TRILBY
******

---LC-

******
CHALCO

******	BAILER	COLLET	FALLEN	HEALED	MAULER
---LD-	BAILEY	COOLED	FALLER	HEALER	MEDLEY
******	BALLED	COOLER	FARLES	HEELED	MERLES
BUILDS	BALLET	COPLEY	FARLEY	HEELER	MEWLED
FIELDS	BARLEY	COULEE	FEELER	HELLEN	MILLED
GUILDS	BAWLED	CULLED	FELLED	HELLER	MILLER
ISOLDE	BAWLER	CULLER	FELLER	HENLEY	MILLET
MOULDS	BELLED	CULLET	FILLED	HILLED	MISLED
MOULDY	BELLES	CURLED	FILLER	HILLER	MOILED
ROALDS	BIBLES	CURLER	FILLET	HITLER	MOILER
SCALDS	BIFLEX	CURLEW	FOALED	HOLLER	MOOLEY
SCOLDS	BILLED	CUTLER	FOILED	HOWLED	MORLEY
SKALDS	BILLET	CUTLET	FOOLED	HOWLER	MOSLEM
WEALDS	BIRLED	CYCLED	FOULED	HULLED	MOSLEY
WIELDS	BIRLES	CYCLER	FOULER	HURLED	MOTLEY
WIELDY	BOGLES	CYCLES	FOWLED	HURLER	MULLED
WOALDS	BOILED	DALLES	FOWLER	HURLEY	MULLEN
WORLDS	BOILER	DEALER	FUELED	HUXLEY	MULLER
YIELDS	BOLLED	DHOLES	FUELER	INKLES	MULLET
******	BOULES	DIALED	FUGLED	JAILED	MULLEY
---LE-	BOWLED	DIALER	FUGLES	JAILER	NAILED
******	BOWLEG	DIPLEX	FULLED	JELLED	NAPLES
ABELES	BOWLER	DOLLED	FULLER	JOULES	NOBLER
ADDLED	BUGLED	DOOLEE	FURLED	KEELED	NUCLEI
ADDLES	BUGLER	DOYLEY	GABLED	KEGLER	NUTLET
AIGLET	BUGLES	DUDLEY	GABLES	KELLER	OAKLEY
AISLED	BULLET	DUELED	GALLED	KEPLER	OMELET
AISLES	BURLED	DUELER	GALLEY	KILLED	OODLES
AMBLED	BURLER	DULLED	GAOLER	KILLER	OSTLER
AMBLER	BURLEY	DULLER	GELLED	KISLEW	OUTLET
AMBLES	BUTLER	DULLES	GIBLET	LADLED	OVULES
AMOLES	CABLED	DUPLET	GIGLET	LADLER	PALLED
AMULET	CABLES	DUPLEX	GIMLET	LADLES	PALLET
ANGLED	CABLET	EAGLES	GOBLET	LALLED	PARLEY
ANGLER	CALLED	EAGLET	GOGLET	LESLEY	PEALED
ANGLES	CALLER	EARLES	GUILES	LOLLED	PEELED
ANKLES	CAMLET	ECCLES	GULLED	LOLLER	PEELER
ANKLET	CAULES	ECOLES	GULLET	LULLED	PEGLEG
ANTLER	CEILED	EDILES	HAILED	MACLES	PELLET
APPLES	CHALEH	EMBLEM	HAILER	MAHLER	PIGLET
ARMLET	CHALET	EMILES	HALLEL	MAILED	PILLED
ASHLEY	CHOLER	EXILED	HALLEY	MAILER	POLLED
ATTLEE	COALED	EXILES	HAMLET	MALLED	POLLEE
AUKLET	COALER	EYELET	HARLEM	MALLEE	POLLEN
AZALEA	COBLES	FABLED	HARLEY	MALLET	POLLER
AZOLES	COELED	FABLER	HASLET	MAPLES	POLLEX
BAILED	COILED	FABLES	HAULED	MARLED	POOLED
BAILEE	COILER	FAILED	HAULER	MAULED	PROLEG

PULLED	SPILES	VOILES	CAULIS	PHILIA	CHILLY
PULLER	STALED	VOLLEY	COLLIE	PHILIP	CHOLLA
PULLET	STALER	WAILED	COOLIE	POPLIN	COOLLY
PULLEY	STALES	WAILER	CULLIS	PRELIM	DOALLS
PURLED	STELES	WALLED	CYCLIC	PROLIX	DRILLS
PURLER	STILES	WALLET	CYMLIN	PUBLIC	DROLLS
RAILED	STOLED	WAULED	DAHLIA	PULLIN	DROLLY
REALES	STOLEN	WAWLED	DOLLIE	PURLIN	DUELLO
REELED	STOLES	WELLED	DOOLIE	RATLIN	DWELLS
REELER	STYLED	WESLEY	DUBLIN	SIALIC	EVILLY
REFLET	STYLER	WHALED	DUNLIN	SIMLIN	FAILLE
REFLEX	STYLES	WHALER	EMILIA	STALIN	FOULLY
REGLET	STYLET	WHALES	EMILIE	STELIC	FRILLS
RIFLED	SUBLET	WHILED	EMILIO	STOLID	FRILLY
RIFLER	SULLEN	WHILES	EUCLID	SUNLIT	GAULLE
RIFLES	SUTLER	WILLED	EXILIC	SUSLIK	GRILLE
RILLET	SWALES	WILLER	EYELID	THALIA	GRILLS
RIPLEY	TABLED	WILLET	FILLIN	THULIA	ICALLY
ROBLES	TABLES	WOOLEN	FILLIP	TILLIE	IDYLLS
ROILED	TABLET	YAWLED	FROLIC	TWILIT	KNELLS
ROLLED	TAILED	YELLED	GAELIC	URALIC	KNOLLS
ROLLER	TALLER	YELLER	GALLIC	VIOLIN	LUELLA
RUBLES	TATLER	YOWLED	GARLIC	WALLIE	NIELLI
RUNLET	TELLER	******	GILLIE	WALLIS	NIELLO
SABLES	THALER	---LI-	GIULIA	WILLIE	NOELLE
SAILED	THALES	******	GIULIO	WILLIS	OCELLI
SAILER	THOLES	ABULIA	GOALIE	******	ORALLY
SALLET	TILLED	AEOLIA	GOBLIN	---LK-	OVALLY
SAMLET	TILLER	AEOLIC	INULIN	******	PHYLLO
SCALED	TITLED	AEOLIS	ITALIC	CAULKS	QUELLS
SCALER	TITLES	ALALIA	JOPLIN	CHALKS	QUILLS
SCALES	TOILED	AMALIE	KAOLIN	CHALKY	REALLY
SCOLEX	TOILER	AMELIA	LESLIE	SKULKS	SCILLY
SEALED	TOILES	AMÉLIE	LUBLIN	STALKS	SCULLS
SEALER	TOILET	AMYLIC	MARLIN	STALKY	SCYLLA
SELLER	TOLLED	ANGLIA	MEALIE	WHELKS	SHELLS
SHALED	TOLLER	ANGLIC	MERLIN	WHELKY	SHELLY
SHALES	TOOLED	ANILIN	MILLIE	******	SHILLS
SIDLED	TOOLER	ANTLIA	MOLLIE	---LL-	SKILLS
SIDLER	TULLES	APULIA	MOULIN	******	SKULLS
SIDLES	UMBLES	BAALIM	MUSLIM	ABOLLA	SMALLS
SMILED	UNCLES	BAILIE	MUSLIN	APOLLO	SMELLS
SMILER	VALLEY	BERLIN	MYELIN	ATOLLS	SMELLY
SMILES	VARLET	BIBLIO	NELLIE	AXILLA	SNELLS
SOCLES	VEILED	BILLIE	OXALIC	BRILLS	SPALLS
SOILED	VEILER	BOLLIX	OXALIS	BROLLY	SPELLS
SOULED	VIALED	CAPLIN	PALLID	CHILLI	SPILLS
SPILED	VIOLET	CATLIN	PAULIN	CHILLS	STALLS

STELLA	DIPLOE	WALLOW	AMYLUM	WALLYS	FORMAL
STELLI	DOBLON	WHILOM	ASYLUM	WILLYS	FORMAT
STILLS	DOLLOP	WILLOW	CALLUP	******	FULMAR
STILLY	DUOLOG	YELLOW	CALLUS	---MA-	GAMMAS
STULLS	EMPLOY	ZEALOT	EFFLUX	******	GASMAN
SWELLS	EPILOG	******	GALLUP	ABOMAS	GEMMAE
SWILLS	FALLOW	---LP-	GALLUS	AGAMAS	GERMAN
TAILLE	FELLOE	******	HALLUX	AIDMAN	GUMMAS
TRILLS	FELLOW	ADOLPH	INFLUX	AIRMAN	GUNMAN
TROLLS	FOLLOW	SCALPS	MUKLUK	ANIMAL	HAEMAL
TUILLE	GALLON	SCULPT	OBELUS	ANIMAS	HAMMAL
TWILLS	GALLOP	WHELPS	OBOLUS	APEMAN	HERMAE
WHOLLY	GIGLOT	******	PAULUS	AROMAS	HERMAI
WOOLLY	HALLOO	---LS-	PEPLUM	ASHMAN	HERMAN
******	HALLOW	******	PEPLUS	ATAMAN	HETMAN
---LM-	HARLOT	GRILSE	PHYLUM	AXEMAN	HIEMAL
******	HARLOW	WHILST	POILUS	BADMAN	HODMAN
HAULMY	HOLLOW	******	POLLUX	BAGMAN	ICEMAN
PSALMS	INFLOW	---LT-	REFLUX	BARMAN	KARMAS
QUALMS	JAILOR	******	ROLLUP	BATMAN	LAMMAS
QUALMY	LOLLOP	ADULTS	STYLUS	BOWMAN	LAYMAN
REALMS	LUDLOW	EXALTS	TELLUS	BROMAL	LEGMAN
THELMA	MALLOW	EXULTS	UNPLUG	BRUMAL	LEMMAS
WHELMS	MARLOW	FAULTS	VALLUM	BUSMAN	LLAMAS
******	MELLON	FAULTY	VELLUM	CABMAN	MADMAN
---LO-	MELLOW	FEALTY	VILLUS	CAIMAN	MAMMAE
******	MERLON	GUILTS	******	CARMAN	MAMMAL
ANALOG	MIKLOS	GUILTY	---LV-	CAYMAN	MAMMAS
APOLOG	OCELOT	HEALTH	******	CLIMAT	MAUMAU
AVALON	PALLOR	MOULTS	EVOLVE	CLIMAX	MERMAN
BAILOR	PARLOR	POULTS	HUELVA	COMMAS	MICMAC
BALLOT	PAVLOV	QUILTS	SHELVE	CONMAN	NORMAL
BELLOC	PEPLOS	REALTY	TWELVE	COWMAN	NORMAN
BELLOW	PHILOS	RIALTO	******	DAGMAR	NORMAS
BILLON	PILLOW	SAULTS	---LY-	DAMMAR	OUTMAN
BILLOW	PUTLOG	SHELTY	******	DERMAL	PALMAR
BRULOT	SAILOR	SMALTI	BIALYS	DERMAS	PENMAN
BYBLOW	SALLOW	SMALTO	BILLYS	DERMAT	PIEMAN
CALLOW	SHILOH	SMELTS	DOLLYS	DESMAN	PITMAN
CARLOS	SLALOM	SMOLTS	EMILYS	DISMAL	POTMAN
CARLOW	STOLON	SPILTH	EVELYN	DISMAY	PRIMAL
CELLOS	TAILOR	STILTS	HOLLYS	DOGMAS	RAGMAN
CEYLON	TALLOW	SVELTE	MILLYS	DOLMAN	RODMAN
COELOM	TAYLOR	VAULTS	MOLLYS	DRAMAS	SEAMAN
COLLOP	TEFLON	WEALTH	NELLYS	ENEMAS	SHAMAN
DEPLOY	TOULON	******	POLLYS	FIRMAN	SIGMAS
DIALOG	VILLON	---LU-	SALLYS	FLYMAN	SKYMAN
DIGLOT	WALLOP	******	TILLYS	FOEMAN	SOCMAN
		AEOLUS			
		AFFLUX			

STOMAT
TARMAC
TASMAN
THOMAS
TRUMAN
ULEMAS
VANMAN
WEIMAR
WILMAS
YASMAK
YEOMAN
YESMAN
******
---MB-
******
ABOMBS
AKIMBO
CLIMBS
COOMBS
CRAMBO
CRUMBS
CRUMBY
FLAMBE
PLUMBO
PLUMBS
RHOMBI
RHUMBA
RHUMBS
THUMBS
******
---ME-
******
ACUMEN
AIDMEN
AIRMEN
ASHMEN
AXEMEN
BADMEN
BAGMEN
BARMEN
BATMEN
BEAMED
BERMES
BLAMED
BLAMES
BLIMEY
BOOMED
BOOMER

BOWMEN
BREMEN
BROMES
BRUMES
BUMMED
BUMMER
BUSMEN
CABMEN
CALMED
CALMER
CARMEL
CARMEN
CERMET
CHIMED
CHIMER
CHIMES
CLIMES
COWMEN
CREMES
CRIMEA
CRIMES
CULMED
DAMMED
DAMMER
DEEMED
DIMMED
DIMMER
DOLMEN
DOOMED
DORMER
ENAMEL
EXAMEN
FARMED
FARMER
FILMED
FIRMED
FIRMER
FLAMED
FLAMEN
FLAMES
FLUMED
FLUMES
FOAMED
FOEMEN
FORMED
FORMER
FRAMED
FRAMER

FRAMES
GAMMED
GAMMER
GASMEN
GEMMED
GERMEN
GLUMES
GNOMES
GRIMED
GRIMES
GRUMES
GUMMED
GUNMEN
HAMMED
HAMMER
HARMED
HELMED
HELMET
HEMMED
HEMMER
HERMES
HOLMES
HUMMED
HUMMER
ICEMEN
ISOMER
JAMMED
KERMES
KILMER
KISMET
KUMMEL
LAMMED
LAYMEN
LEGMEN
LOAMED
LOOMED
MADMEN
MAIMED
MAIMER
MAMMET
MERMEN
MESMER
MUMMED
MUMMER
MYRMEC
NEUMES
NUTMEG
PALMED

PALMER
PENMEN
PERMED
PIEMEN
PITMEN
PLUMED
PLUMES
POMMEL
PREMED
PRIMED
PRIMER
PRIMES
PUMMEL
RAGMEN
RAMMED
RAMMER
REAMED
REAMER
RHYMED
RHYMER
RHYMES
RIMMED
RIMMER
ROAMED
ROAMER
RODMEN
ROMMEL
ROOMED
ROOMER
RUMMER
SEAMED
SEAMEN
SEAMER
SEEMED
SEEMER
SHAMED
SHAMES
SIMMER
SKYMEN
SLIMED
SLIMES
SOCMEN
SPUMED
SPUMES
STAMEN
SUMMED
SUMMER
TEAMED

TEEMED
TEEMER
TEGMEN
TERMED
TERMER
THAMES
THEMES
THYMES
VANMEN
WARMED
WARMER
WORMED
WORMER
YAMMER
YEOMEN
ZOOMED
******
---MI-
******
AGAMIC
ALUMIN
ANEMIA
ANEMIC
ANOMIA
ANOMIC
ANOMIE
ATOMIC
BARMIE
BROMIC
CHYMIC
COMMIE
COMMIT
COMMIX
COSMIC
DAIMIO
DERMIC
DERMIS
DESMID
DORMIE
ELEMIS
FERMIS
FILMIC
FORMIC
GLAMIS
GNOMIC
HARMIN
HERMIT
HOLMIC

JIMMIE
KALMIA
KERMIS
KERMIT
NAOMIS
PERMIT
PYEMIA
PYEMIC
SALMIS
STAMIN
STYMIE
SUBMIT
SUMMIT
SUOMIC
SWAMIS
THEMIS
THYMIC
UREMIA
VERMIN
******
---ML-
******
CALMLY
FIRMLY
GLUMLY
GRIMLY
PRIMLY
SEEMLY
SLIMLY
TERMLY
TRIMLY
WARMLY
******
---MM-
******
CHAMMY
CHUMMY
CLAMMY
CRUMMY
GRAMME
PLUMMY
SCUMMY
SHAMMY
SHIMMY
SLUMMY
WHAMMY

******	CRIMPY	TALMUD	PIENAL	FRANCO	EMENDS
---MN-	CRUMPS	THYMUS	PINNAE	FRANCS	FIENDS
******	EXEMPT	WAMMUS	PINNAL	FRENCH	FOUNDS
ALUMNA	FLUMPS	WARMUP	PLANAR	GLANCE	FRONDS
ALUMNI	FRUMPS	******	PUTNAM	HAUNCH	GLANDS
******	FRUMPY	---MY-	REGNAL	JOUNCE	GRANDE
---MO-	GRUMPY	******	RHINAL	LAUNCE	GRINDS
******	GUIMPE	DAIMYO	SAUNAS	LAUNCH	GRUNDY
ALAMOS	PLUMPS	FORMYL	SENNAS	NUANCE	HOUNDS
ASIMOV	PRIMPS	JIMMYS	SIGNAL	PAUNCH	LUANDA
CLAMOR	PROMPT	SAMMYS	SPINAL	PLANCH	MAUNDS
COMMON	SCAMPI	TIMMYS	SUNNAH	PLANCK	MAUNDY
COSMOS	SCAMPS	TOMMYS	TARNAL	POUNCE	POINDS
DAEMON	SKIMPS	******	TERNAL	PRANCE	POUNDS
DAIMON	SKIMPY	---NA-	THANAT	PRINCE	ROUNDS
DROMON	SLUMPS	******	THENAL	QUENCH	RWANDA
ENAMOR	STAMPS	ADONAI	THENAR	QUINCE	SCENDS
ETYMON	STOMPS	ANANAS	TRINAL	QUINCY	SHANDY
GAMMON	STUMPS	ARENAS	URINAL	SCONCE	SHINDY
GISMOS	STUMPY	ATONAL	VERNAL	SEANCE	SOUNDS
GIZMOS	SWAMPS	CANNAE	VERNAS	STANCE	SPENDS
GNOMON	SWAMPY	CANNAS	ZOONAL	STANCH	STANDS
HAYMOW	THUMPS	CARNAL	******	STENCH	TRENDS
LUMMOX	TRAMPS	CATNAP	---NC-	THENCE	TRENDY
MAMMON	TRUMPS	COGNAC	******	TRANCE	UGANDA
MARMOT	******	DIANAS	AGENCY	TRENCH	UPENDS
MORMON	---MS-	DONNAS	BIANCA	ULENCE	VIANDS
MOTMOT	******	ELENAS	BLANCH	USANCE	WOUNDS
SALMON	AHIMSA	FAUNAE	BLENCH	WHENCE	ZOUNDS
SCHMOS	CLUMSY	FAUNAL	BOUNCE	WRENCH	******
SERMON	FLIMSY	FAUNAS	BOUNCY	******	---NE-
SKIMOS	SLIMSY	FINNAN	BRANCH	---ND-	******
SUMMON	WHIMSY	FORNAX	BRONCO	******	AGONES
TERMOR	******	GUNNAR	BRONCS	AGENDA	AKENES
THYMOL	---MT-	HANNAH	BRUNCH	AMANDA	ALINED
TREMOR	******	HANNAS	CHANCE	AMENDS	ALINES
******	WARMTH	HENNAS	CHANCY	BLENDE	ATONED
---MP-	******	HYENAS	CHINCH	BLENDS	ATONER
******	---MU-	HYMNAL	CLENCH	BLINDS	ATONES
BLIMPS	******	JAINAS	CLINCH	BLONDE	AXONES
CHAMPS	ANIMUS	KARNAK	CRUNCH	BLONDS	AZINES
CHUMPS	CADMUS	KIDNAP	DRENCH	BOUNDS	BANNED
CLAMPS	LITMUS	LEONAS	EVINCE	BRANDS	BANNER
CLUMPS	MURMUR	LIANAS	FIANCE	BRANDT	BARNEY
CLUMPY	MUUMUU	MAENAD	FLENCH	BRANDY	BEANED
COEMPT	PRIMUS	MYRNAS	FLINCH	BRENDA	BENNES
CRAMPS	SEAMUS	NOUNAL	FRANCE	DIRNDL	BENNET
CRIMPS	SHAMUS	PENNAE	FRANCK	ELANDS	BERNEY

BINNED	EARNER	LANNER	RUINED	VAINER	PLUNGE
BONNET	EUPNEA	LEANED	RUINER	VEINED	PRONGS
BORNEO	EVENED	LEANER	RUNNEL	WAGNER	SLANGY
BRINED	FANNED	LIANES	RUNNER	WANNED	SLINGS
BRINES	FANNER	LIMNED	SAWNEY	WANNER	SPONGE
BRUNEI	FAWNED	LIMNER	SCENES	WARNED	SPONGY
BRUNEL	FAWNER	LINNET	SCONES	WARNER	STINGS
BURNED	FENNEC	LIONEL	SEINED	WAYNES	STINGY
BURNER	FENNEL	LOANED	SEINER	WEANED	SWINGE
BURNET	FINNED	MAGNET	SEINES	WEANER	SWINGS
CANNED	FINNER	MANNED	SENNET	WHINED	THINGS
CANNEL	FUNNEL	MANNER	SHINED	WHINER	THONGS
CANNER	GAINED	MEANER	SHINER	WHINES	TWANGS
CANNES	GAINER	MESNES	SHINES	WIENER	TWANGY
CHINES	GANNET	MOANED	SIDNEY	WINNER	TWINGE
CLINES	GARNER	MOONED	SIGNED	WITNEY	UBANGI
CLONES	GARNET	OPENED	SIGNER	YAWNED	WHANGS
COINED	GINNED	OPENER	SIGNET	YAWNER	WRINGS
COINER	GINNER	OPINED	SIMNEL	YEANED	WRONGS
CONNED	GOONEY	OPINES	SINNED	YENNED	******
CONNER	GOWNED	ORKNEY	SINNER	******	---NI-
CORNEA	GUINEA	PAINED	SONNET	---NG-	******
CORNED	GUNNED	PANNED	SOONER	******	ADENIS
CORNEL	GUNNEL	PAWNED	SPINEL	AVENGE	ADONIC
CORNER	GUNNER	PAWNEE	SPINES	BEINGS	ADONIS
CORNET	HORNED	PAWNER	SPINET	BLUNGE	AGONIC
CRANED	HORNET	PEENED	STONED	BRINGS	AMANIA
CRANES	HYMNED	PENNED	STONER	CHANGE	ATONIC
CRENEL	IMINES	PENNER	STONES	CHANGS	AZONIC
CRONES	IRENES	PHONED	SUMNER	CLANGS	BAGNIO
CUNNER	IRONED	PHONES	SUNNED	CLINGS	BEANIE
CYGNET	IRONER	PHONEY	SWANEE	CLINGY	BERNIE
DAMNED	JENNET	PINNED	SYDNEY	CRINGE	BONNIE
DARNED	JINNEE	PINNER	TANNED	DOINGS	CANNIE
DARNEL	JITNEY	PLANED	TANNER	DRONGO	CATNIP
DARNER	JOINED	PLANER	TBONES	ERINGO	CLINIC
DAWNED	JOINER	PLANES	THANES	ERYNGO	CLONIC
DENNED	KEENED	PLANET	TINNED	FLANGE	CONNIE
DIANES	KEENER	PRUNED	TINNER	FLINGS	CRANIA
DINNED	KENNED	PRUNER	TRINED	FLONGS	CRANIO
DINNER	KENNEL	PRUNES	TRINES	FRINGE	CYANIC
DISNEY	KERNED	PUNNED	TUNNED	FRINGY	CYANID
DONNED	KERNEL	PUNNER	TUNNEL	GOINGS	CYANIN
DOWNED	KEYNES	RAINED	TURNED	GRANGE	DENNIS
DRONED	KIDNEY	REINED	TURNER	ICINGS	DONNIE
DRONES	KOINES	RENNET	TWINED	LOUNGE	EDENIC
DUNNED	KRONEN	RODNEY	TWINER	ORANGE	ETHNIC
EARNED	KRONER	ROMNEY	TWINES	ORANGS	FAFNIR

FANNIE	WINNIE	THINLY	RADNOR	FLINTY	BARNUM
FINNIC	ZINNIA	VAINLY	RHINOS	FOUNTS	CLONUS
FORNIX	******	******	SIGNOR	FRONTO	COBNUT
GDYNIA	---NK-	---NN-	STENOG	FRONTS	CORNUA
GLYNIS	******	******	TAINOS	GIANTS	CORNUS
GUANIN	ANANKE	BLENNY	VERNON	GLINTS	CRINUM
HERNIA	BLANKS	BRANNY	WINNOW	GRANTS	CRONUS
HERNIO	BLINKS	CRANNY	******	GRUNTS	CYGNUS
HORNIE	BRINKS	DUENNA	---NR-	HAUNTS	FAUNUS
HYMNIC	CHINKS	GRANNY	******	JAUNTS	FRENUM
HYPNIC	CHINKY	GWENNS	AMENRA	JAUNTY	HOGNUT
ICONIC	CHUNKS	GWYNNE	OHENRY	JOINTS	KRONUR
IRANIS	CHUNKY	JEANNE	******	LEANTO	LIGNUM
IRENIC	CLANKS	JOANNA	---NS-	MOUNTS	MAGNUM
IRONIC	CLINKS	JOANNE	******	MOUNTY	PEANUT
JONNIE	CRANKS	JOHNNY	ALONSO	ODONTO	PIGNUS
KENNIE	CRANKY	SHINNY	FLENSE	OMENTA	PIGNUT
LEONIE	DRINKS	SIENNA	GDANSK	PAINTS	PLENUM
LIGNIN	DRUNKS	SKINNY	QUINSY	PAINTY	SANNUP
MEANIE	FLANKS	SPINNY	TEENSY	PLANTS	TURNUP
MINNIE	FLUNKS	VIENNA	WEENSY	PLENTY	URANUS
NORNIR	FLUNKY	WHINNY	******	PLINTH	WALNUT
NUDNIK	FRANKS	YVONNE	---NT-	POINTE	******
ODYNIA	PLANKS	******	******	POINTS	---NW-
OZONIC	PLUNKS	---NO-	ACANTH	POINTY	******
PAYNIM	PRANKS	******	AGENTS	PRINTS	VYRNWY
PENNIA	PRINKS	BRUNOS	AMENTI	PRONTO	******
PENNIS	SHANKS	CANNON	AMENTS	QUANTA	---NY-
PHONIA	SKINKS	CANNOT	ARANTA	QUANTS	******
PHONIC	SKUNKS	CRONOS	ARUNTA	QUINTS	ANONYM
PICNIC	SLINKS	EGGNOG	BLINTZ	SAINTS	BENNYS
PYKNIC	SLINKY	ELINOR	BLUNTS	SCANTY	BONNYS
QUINIC	SPANKS	FINNOC	BOUNTY	SCENTS	DANNYS
RENNIN	SPUNKY	GUANOS	BRANTS	SHANTY	DENNYS
RONNIE	STINKS	GUENON	BRENTS	SHINTO	EPONYM
SCENIC	SWANKY	HOBNOB	BRONTE	SHUNTS	ERINYS
SENNIT	THANKS	HYPNOS	CHANTS	SLANTS	FANNYS
TAENIA	TRUNKS	KRONOR	CHANTY	STINTS	JENNYS
TANNIC	******	KRONOS	CHINTZ	STUNTS	JINNYS
TANNIN	---NL-	LEMNOS	CLINTS	TAINTS	KENNYS
TENNIS	******	LLANOS	COUNTS	TAUNTS	LENNYS
TURNIP	EVENLY	MAGNOX	COUNTY	TWENTY	PENNYS
UNKNIT	GAINLY	MIGNON	DAINTY	VAUNTS	PHENYL
URANIA	KEENLY	MINNOW	DAUNTS	******	URANYL
URANIC	LEANLY	PENNON	EVENTS	---NU-	VINNYS
VERNIX	MAINLY	PHANON	FAINTS	******	---NZ-
WEENIE	MEANLY	PHENOL	FEINTS	ACINUS	ALONZO
WIENIE	OPENLY	PIANOS	FLINTS	AVENUE	BRONZE

BRONZY	OCLOCK	ECHOES	******	INJOKE	PINOLE
FRENZY	ROCOCO	EUBOEA	---OI-	INVOKE	RESOLD
FRUNZE	SMOOCH	HALOED	******	KAPOKS	RESOLE
STANZA	UNCOCK	HALOES	ADJOIN	MOPOKE	RETOLD
******	UNLOCK	HEROES	ADROIT	REVOKE	REVOLT
---OA-	VELOCE	HOBOES	ALGOID	SNOOKS	ROMOLA
******	******	KAYOED	ARTOIS	SPOOKS	SCROLL
ABROAD	---OD-	LOCOED	BELOIT	SPOOKY	SOTOLS
AFLOAT	******	PEKOES	CEBOID	STOOKS	SPOOLS
BEMOAN	ACNODE	PHLOEM	CONOID	STROKE	STOOLS
BEZOAR	BIPODS	PHOOEY	CUBOID	UNYOKE	STROLL
BOGOAK	BLOODS	REDOES	CYMOID	******	THIOLS
BYROAD	BLOODY	SHOOED	DACOIT	---OL-	UNBOLT
COCOAS	BROODS	SILOED	DAKOIT	******	UNFOLD
EUDOAR	BROODY	SOLOED	DEVOID	ABVOLT	UNHOLY
INROAD	CORODY	THROES	DEVOIR	AGEOLD	UNROLL
MINOAN	DECODE	UNDOER	ECHOIC	ANGOLA	UNSOLD
OGDOAD	DEMODE	UNDOES	ENJOIN	AREOLA	UNTOLD
OHIOAN	DIPODY	VETOED	EOZOIC	ARNOLD	UPHOLD
RELOAD	EMBODY	VETOER	FUCOID	BEHOLD	XYLOLS
SAMOAN	ENCODE	VETOES	GADOID	BIFOLD	******
THROAT	EPHODS	WINOES	GANOID	BIKOLS	---OM-
UNLOAD	FLOODS	ZEROED	HALOID	CAJOLE	******
UPROAR	IMBODY	ZEROES	HEMOID	CAROLE	APLOMB
******	MELODY	******	HEROIC	CAROLS	ATHOME
---OB-	MONODY	---OF-	HEROIN	CIBOLS	AXIOMS
******	NOBODY	******	HESOID	CITOLA	BECOME
AEROBE	PAGODA	CUTOFF	KELOID	CREOLE	BESOMS
ARROBA	PARODY	FAROFF	LIPOID	CUPOLA	BLOOMS
CABOBS	SCRODS	LAYOFF	MEMOIR	DIPOLE	BLOOMY
CAROBS	SNOODS	ONEOFF	MUCOID	DROOLS	BOSOMS
DAGOBA	STRODE	PAYOFF	NEVOID	EIDOLA	BROOMS
DEMOBS	SYNODS	PROOFS	PATOIS	EMBOLI	BROOMY
ENROBE	TRIODE	PUTOFF	RECOIL	ENFOLD	CAEOMA
JACOBS	******	RIPOFF	REJOIN	ENROLL	CAROMS
KABOBS	---OE-	RUNOFF	RENOIR	EXTOLS	CHROMA
NABOBS	******	SETOFF	SHOOIN	GIGOLO	CHROME
STROBE	APNOEA	SHROFF	TOROID	HAROLD	CHROMO
THROBS	AUTOED	SPOOFS	UNCOIL	INFOLD	CLEOME
UNROBE	BUBOES	TIPOFF	VALOIS	INSOLE	ECTOMY
******	CANOED	******	XYLOID	KOBOLD	ENTOMB
---OC-	CANOES	---OG-	******	MOHOLE	ENTOMO
******	CHLOES	******	---OK-	NEROLI	ENWOMB
BROOCH	DADOES	BEFOGS	******	NICOLE	GLIOMA
DECOCT	DIDOES	EULOGY	BROOKE	ORIOLE	GLOOMS
IDIOCY	DODOES	LADOGA	BROOKS	ORMOLU	GLOOMY
MOHOCK	ECHOED	OOLOGY	CROOKS	PAROLE	GROOMS
MOLOCH	ECHOER	STOOGE	DECOKE	PAYOLA	IDIOMS

INCOME	DEMONO	SARONG	RACOON	******	FLOORS
INTOMB	DEMONS	SAXONS	RATOON	---OR-	FLUORO
JEROME	DEPONE	SAXONY	REFOOT	******	FLUORS
KOKOMO	DITONE	SCIONS	RETOOK	ABHORS	FURORE
LIPOMA	DUGONG	SECOND	RETOOL	ABSORB	FURORS
MYXOMA	EDMOND	SETONS	SALOON	ACCORD	GALORE
RADOME	FANONS	SIMONE	SALOOP	ACTORS	HONORE
SALOME	FELONS	SIMONS	SCHOOL	ADSORB	HONORS
SODOMY	FELONY	SIMONY	SCROOP	AFFORD	HUMORS
STROMA	FREONS	SPOONS	SIMOOM	ANGORA	IGNORE
TACOMA	GIPONS	SPOONY	TABOOS	APPORT	ILFORD
VENOMS	GYRONS	STRONG	TYCOON	ARBORI	IMPORT
ZYGOMA	HERONS	SWOONS	UNHOOK	ARBORS	INBORN
******	HEXONE	TALONS	UNMOOR	ARDORS	INCORP
---ON-	HURONS	TENONS	UNROOT	ARMORS	INFORM
******	INTONE	TETONS	UPROOT	ARMORY	JURORS
AARONS	IONONE	THRONE	WAHOOS	ASHORE	LABORS
ALFONS	JASONS	THRONG	YAHOOS	ASSORT	LAHORE
ALMOND	JUPONS	TOYONS	******	ATTORN	LENORE
ANCONA	KALONG	TYRONE	---OP-	AURORA	MAJORS
ANCONE	KETONE	UNDONE	******	BEFORE	MALORY
ANIONS	KIMONO	UNIONS	ASLOPE	BICORN	MANORS
ANNONA	LEMONS	VERONA	CANOPY	BIFORM	MASORA
ANTONS	LOMOND	WAGONS	CHEOPS	BYWORD	MAYORS
ANTONY	MASONS	YAPONS	DROOPS	BYWORK	MEMORY
ANYONE	MEKONG	YUPONS	DROOPY	CALORY	MILORD
APHONY	MELONS	ZIRONS	ESTOPS	CAVORT	MINORS
APRONS	MESONS	******	EUROPA	CHLORO	MOTORS
BACONY	MORONS	---OO-	EUROPE	COHORT	OSBORN
BARONG	NYLONS	******	GALOPS	COLORS	OXFORD
BARONS	OBLONG	ABLOOM	JALOPS	DECORS	PRIORS
BARONY	ONIONS	BABOON	JALOPY	DEFORM	PRIORY
BATONS	ONIONY	BABOOS	METOPE	DEHORN	RAZORS
BEGONE	OOLONG	BEFOOL	OCTOPI	DEPORT	REBORE
BELONG	OSMOND	BEHOOF	ORLOPS	DONORS	REBORN
BETONY	PAEONS	BETOOK	PELOPS	EFFORT	RECORD
BEYOND	PAEONY	CAHOOT	PYROPE	ENCORE	REFORM
BIGONE	PINONS	COCOON	SCOOPS	EPHORI	REMORA
BRYONY	PITONS	DAHOON	SLOOPS	EPHORS	REPORT
BYGONE	POMONA	ENROOT	SNOOPS	ERRORS	RESORB
CANONS	PUTONS	EXMOOR	SNOOPY	ESCORT	RESORT
CAPONE	PYLONS	GALOOT	STOOPS	EXHORT	RETORT
CAPONS	PYRONE	IGLOOS	STROPS	EXPORT	REWORD
CHRONO	RAMONA	INDOOR	SWOOPS	EXTORT	RIGORS
COLONS	RAYONS	KAZOOS	TROOPS	FAVORS	ROTORS
COLONY	REDONE	LAGOON	WHOOPS	FEDORA	RUMORS
CORONA	RUNONS	MAROON	WICOPY	FEMORA	SATORY
CROONS	SALONS	NOGOOD		FETORS	SAVORS

SAVORY	KIBOSH	ELIOTS	CYMOUS	SEROUS	UPBOWS
SCHORL	LANOSE	FAGOTS	DETOUR	SETOUS	UPTOWN
SENORA	MIMOSA	GAVOTS	DEVOUR	SETOUT	WIDOWS
SPOORS	MOROSE	GEMOTS	DEVOUT	SHROUD	******
SUBORN	MUCOSA	HELOTS	DIMOUT	SPROUT	---OX-
TABORS	MUCOSE	IDIOTS	DOLOUR	STROUD	******
TENORS	NODOSE	INGOTS	DUGOUT	TOROUS	BILOXI
THEORY	OPPOSE	JABOTS	ENSOUL	TRYOUT	DESOXY
TUMORS	OSMOSE	MAGOTS	EYEOUT	TUMOUR	******
TUTORS	OTIOSE	PELOTA	FAMOUS	VALOUR	---OY-
UNBORN	PILOSE	PEYOTE	FAROUT	VAPOUR	******
UNCORD	RAMOSE	PICOTS	FAVOUR	VELOUR	ALLOYS
UNCORK	REPOSE	PILOTS	FEROUS	VENOUS	ANNOYS
UNWORN	RIBOSE	PIVOTS	FUCOUS	VIGOUR	ARROYO
VAPORI	RIMOSE	REMOTE	FUMOUS	VINOUS	DECOYS
VAPORS	RIPOST	ROBOTS	GAMOUS	VOROUS	ENJOYS
VISORS	RUGOSE	SABOTS	GENOUS	WAMOUS	ENVOYS
VIZORS	SETOSE	SCOOTS	GEROUS	WAYOUT	LEROYS
******	TOROSE	SCROTA	GIAOUR	******	MCCOYS
---OS-	TRIOSE	SHOOTS	GYNOUS	---OV-	NAGOYA
******	UPMOST	SMOOTH	HONOUR	******	SEPOYS
ACCOST	UPROSE	SNOOTS	HUMOUR	ALCOVE	******
ACROSS	UTMOST	SNOOTY	INSOUL	BEHOVE	---OZ-
AFTOSA	VADOSE	TAROTS	IODOUS	GROOVE	******
ALDOSE	VAMOSE	ZYGOTE	ITIOUS	GROOVY	FLOOZY
ALMOST	VENOSE	******	JOYOUS	INWOVE	REBOZO
APPOSE	VOLOST	---OU-	LABOUR	REMOVE	SNOOZE
ARGOSY	WHOOSH	******	LAYOUT	SHROVE	******
ARIOSE	XYLOSE	ACEOUS	MAHOUT	STROVE	---PA-
ARIOSO	******	ACIOUS	MEROUS	THROVE	******
CHOOSE	---OT-	ADNOUN	MUCOUS	******	AGAPAE
CHOOSY	******	ALDOUS	ODIOUS	---OW-	BEDPAN
COHOSH	ABBOTS	ALGOUS	PILOUS	******	CALPAC
COMOSE	ALCOTT	ALLOUT	PODOUS	ALLOWS	CARPAL
CYMOSE	ALLOTS	ARBOUR	POROUS	ARROWS	CASPAR
DEPOSE	ARGOTS	ARDOUR	POYOUS	ARROWY	GASPAR
EMBOSS	ASCOTS	ARIOUS	PUTOUT	DISOWN	INSPAN
EXPOSE	BESOTS	ARMOUR	RAGOUT	ELBOWS	KALPAK
FILOSE	BIGOTS	AUROUS	RAMOUS	EMBOWS	KAPPAS
GALOSH	BOGOTA	BAYOUS	RECOUP	ENDOWS	LAMPAD
GOLOSH	CAPOTE	BEFOUL	RIGOUR	INDOWS	LAMPAS
GYROSE	COYOTE	BIJOUX	RIMOUS	OTTOWA	PAMPAS
HEXOSE	DAKOTA	CEROUS	RUFOUS	OXBOWS	PAWPAW
IMPOSE	DEMOTE	COLOUR	RUGOUS	REDOWA	PENPAL
IMPOST	DENOTE	COLOUS	RUMOUR	RENOWN	PREPAY
INMOST	DEPOTS	COMOUS	RUNOUT	SEROWS	QUAPAW
JOCOSE	DEVOTE	COPOUT	SAJOUS	THROWN	SAIPAN
KETOSE	DIVOTS	CUTOUT	SAVOUR	THROWS	SALPAS

SAMPAN	DAMPER	HIPPED	PIGPEN	SNIPER	******
SECPAR	DAPPED	HOOPED	PIMPED	SNIPES	---PH-
STEPAN	DAPPER	HOOPER	PIPPED	SOAPED	******
STUPAS	DEEPEN	HOPPED	POMPEY	SOPPED	ALEPHS
TAMPAN	DEEPER	HOPPER	POOPED	SOUPED	DELPHI
TARPAN	DIAPER	HUMPED	POPPED	STAPES	DOLPHS
TREPAN	DIPPED	JASPER	POPPER	STIPEL	GLYPHS
TROPAL	DIPPER	JUMPED	POPPET	STIPES	GRAPHO
TYMPAN	DISPEL	JUMPER	PROPEL	STOPED	GRAPHS
******	DRAPED	KASPER	PROPER	STOPES	GRAPHY
---PE-	DRAPER	KEEPER	PULPED	STUPES	LYMPHO
******	DRAPES	KIPPED	PULPER	SUPPED	MORPHO
ALIPED	DRUPEL	KIPPER	PUMPED	SUPPER	NYMPHA
AUSPEX	DRUPES	LAMPED	PUMPER	SWIPED	NYMPHO
BEEPED	DUMPED	LAPPED	PUPPED	SWIPES	NYMPHS
BOPPED	DUMPER	LAPPER	PUPPET	TAIPEI	RALPHS
BUMPED	ELOPED	LAPPET	RAMPED	TAMPED	ROLPHS
BUMPER	ELOPER	LEAPED	RAPPED	TAMPER	SAPPHO
BURPED	ELOPES	LEAPER	RAPPEE	TAPPED	SCYPHI
CAMPED	EPOPEE	LIMPED	RAPPEL	TAPPER	SCYPHO
CAMPER	ETAPES	LIMPER	RAPPER	TAPPET	SULPHA
CAPPED	GAPPED	LIMPET	RASPED	TAUPES	SULPHO
CAPPER	GASPED	LIPPED	RASPER	TEMPER	SYLPHS
CARPED	GASPER	LIPPER	REAPED	TIPPED	SYLPHY
CARPEL	GIMPED	LISPED	REAPER	TIPPER	TROPHO
CARPER	GIPPED	LISPER	REOPEN	TIPPET	TROPHY
CARPET	GOSPEL	LOOPED	RIPPED	TOPPED	******
CASPER	GRAPES	LOOPER	RIPPER	TOPPER	---PI-
CHAPEL	GRIPED	LOPPED	ROMPED	TOUPEE	******
CHAPES	GRIPER	LOUPES	ROMPER	TUPPED	ADIPIC
CLYPEI	GRIPES	LUMPED	SAPPED	UNIPED	ARMPIT
COMPEL	GROPED	LUMPEN	SAPPER	VAMPED	CARPIC
COOPED	GROPER	MAPPED	SCAPES	VESPER	CHOPIN
COOPER	GROPES	MOPPED	SCOPES	WAPPED	CUSPID
COPPED	GULPED	MOPPET	SEAPEN	WARPED	CUSPIS
COPPER	GULPER	MYOPES	SEEPED	WARPER	HATPIN
COUPES	GYPPED	NAPPED	SHAPED	WEEPER	HIPPIE
COWPEA	HAMPER	NAPPER	SHAPEN	WISPED	HISPID
COWPER	HAPPED	NAPPES	SHAPER	YAPPED	KELPIE
CRAPED	HAPPEN	NIPPED	SHAPES	YAUPED	KEWPIE
CRAPES	HARPED	NIPPER	SIMPER	YAWPED	LIMPID
CREPED	HARPER	PALPED	SIPPED	YAWPER	MAGPIE
CREPES	HASPED	PAMPER	SIPPER	YELPED	MYOPIA
CUPPED	HEAPED	PAUPER	SIPPET	YELPER	MYOPIC
CUPPER	HELPED	PEEPED	SLOPED	YIPPED	NAPPIE
CUSPED	HELPER	PEEPER	SLOPER	ZIPPED	OKAPIS
DAMPED	HEMPEN	PEPPED	SLOPES	ZIPPER	PIPPIN
DAMPEN	HERPES	PEPPER	SNIPED		POTPIE

PULPIT	SWIPLE	FRAPPE	PALPUS	******	MADRAS
SALPID	TEMPLE	GRIPPE	PAPPUS	---RA-	MITRAL
SCIPIO	TIPPLE	GRIPPY	PUTPUT	******	MOIRAS
STEPIN	TOPPLE	PHIPPS	QUIPUS	ABORAL	MURRAY
STUPID	TRIPLE	SHOPPE	RAJPUT	AFFRAY	NEURAL
TENPIN	TWOPLY	SLOPPY	RUMPUS	AGORAE	OPERAS
TIEPIN	WIMPLE	SNAPPY	SCOPUS	AGORAS	OUTRAN
TORPID	******	SNIPPY	SLAPUP	AMORAL	PARRAL
TROPIC	---PO-	STEPPE	SLIPUP	ANORAK	PLURAL
UNAPID	******	TROPPO	STEPUP	ANURAN	RIPRAP
UTOPIA	CAMPOS	WHIPPY	WAMPUM	ARARAT	SABRAS
VESPID	COMPOS	******	WRAPUP	ASTRAL	SACRAL
YIPPIE	COUPON	---PR-	******	ASTRAY	SATRAP
YUPPIE	COWPOX	******	---PY-	BASRAH	SCARAB
******	DESPOT	COPPRA	******	BETRAY	SEURAT
---PJ-	HIPPOS	SEMPRE	POPPYS	CHORAL	SHORAN
******	HOOPOE	******	PROPYL	CITRAL	SPIRAL
SKOPJE	HOTPOT	---PS-	******	CLARAS	STORAX
******	INKPOT	******	---QI-	COBRAS	SUTRAS
---PL-	ISOPOD	APEPSY	******	CONRAD	SWARAJ
******	MAYPOP	BIOPSY	IRAQIS	COPRAH	TETRAD
COMPLY	NIPPON	CORPSE	******	CORRAL	THORAC
COUPLE	POMPOM	DROPSY	---QU-	CRURAL	THORAX
DAMPLY	POMPON	ELAPSE	******	DEFRAY	TIARAS
DAPPLE	SEXPOT	******	BARQUE	DOBRAS	UMBRAE
DEEPLY	SLIPON	---PT-	BASQUE	DVORAK	UMBRAL
DIMPLE	STUPOR	******	BISQUE	ENGRAM	UMBRAS
DIMPLY	TAMPON	ADAPTS	BRAQUE	ENTRAP	UNDRAW
FIPPLE	TEAPOT	ADEPTS	CAIQUE	ENWRAP	UNWRAP
HOOPLA	TEAPOY	ADOPTS	CASQUE	ESTRAY	ZEBRAS
HOPPLE	TEMPOS	COOPTS	CHEQUE	EXTRAS	******
LIMPLY	TINPOT	CRYPTO	CINQUE	FLORAE	---RB-
NIPPLE	TORPOR	CRYPTS	CIRQUE	FLORAL	******
PEOPLE	TRIPOD	DUMPTY	CLAQUE	FLORAS	BLURBS
PIMPLE	TRIPOS	ERUPTS	CLIQUE	GIBRAN	EXURBS
PIMPLY	UROPOD	GLYPTO	CLIQUY	GOORAL	NEARBY
POPPLE	WEAPON	HUMPTY	EXEQUY	HEDRAL	******
PURPLE	YAUPON	TEMPTS	MANQUE	HOORAY	---RC-
RIMPLE	YOUPON	******	MARQUE	HURRAH	******
RIPPLE	******	---PU-	MASQUE	HURRAY	AMERCE
RIPPLY	---PP-	******	MOSQUE	HYDRAE	ARERCU
RUMPLE	******	CAMPUS	OPAQUE	HYDRAS	BIERCE
SAMPLE	ALEPPO	CARPUS	PLAQUE	INWRAP	CHURCH
SIMPLE	CHIPPY	CORPUS	PULQUE	KONRAD	COERCE
SIMPLY	CHOPPY	COYPUS	RISQUE	LAURAE	EPARCH
STAPLE	DIEPPE	HIPPUS	SESQUI	LAURAS	EXARCH
SUPPLE	DRIPPY	JAIPUR	TORQUE	LIBRAE	FIERCE
SUPPLY	FLOPPY	OUTPUT	UNIQUE	LIBRAS	INARCH

PEIRCE	BARREL	INURED	SECRET	UNBRED	CHORIC
PIERCE	BARREN	INURES	SHARED	UNDREW	CITRIC
SCARCE	BARRET	JARRED	SHARER	USURER	CLERIC
SCORCH	BEARED	JEERED	SHARES	VEERED	CLERID
SEARCH	BEARER	JEERER	SHIRES	WARRED	CORRIE
SMIRCH	BIRRED	JUAREZ	SHORED	WARREN	COWRIE
SOURCE	BLARED	LABRET	SHORES	WEARER	CUPRIC
STARCH	BLARES	LAIRED	SNARED	WHORED	CYMRIC
TIERCE	BURRED	LAUREL	SNARER	WHORES	CYPRIN
******	CADRES	LEERED	SNARES	******	DEARIE
---RD-	CARREL	LEGREE	SNORED	---RF-	DEBRIS
******	CHARED	LIVRES	SNORER	******	DERRIS
AWARDS	CHARES	LOURED	SNORES	DWARFS	EGERIA
BEARDS	CHOREA	MARRED	SOARED	SCARFS	EMERIC
BOARDS	CHOREO	MARRER	SOARER	SCURFY	EMERIE
CHARDS	CHORES	MITRED	SOCRED	WHARFS	ESPRIT
CHORDS	CLARES	MOORED	SOIREE	******	FABRIC
FIORDS	CLARET	MURRES	SORREL	---RG-	FAERIE
GOURDE	CRORES	MURREY	SOURED	******	FENRIR
GOURDS	DEARER	NEARED	SOURER	ANERGY	FERRIC
GUARDS	DECREE	NEARER	SPARED	BOURGS	FERRIS
HAIRDO	DEGREE	OSPREY	SPARER	CHARGE	FIBRIL
HOARDS	ELDRED	PADRES	SPARES	CLERGY	FIBRIN
LAIRDS	ENTREE	PAIRED	SPIREA	EMERGE	FLORID
OVERDO	EVERET	PARREL	SPIRED	ENERGY	FLORIN
SHARDS	FAIRED	PEERED	SPIRES	GEORGE	GLORIA
SHERDS	FAIRER	PETREL	SPORED	GEORGI	HARRIS
STURDY	FEARED	POORER	SPORES	SPARGE	HENRIS
SWARDS	FEARER	POURED	STARED	SPURGE	HORRID
SWORDS	FERRET	POURER	STARER	******	HOURIS
THIRDS	FLARED	PUGREE	STARES	---RH-	HUBRIS
WEIRDY	FLARES	PURRED	STEREO	******	HYBRID
******	FLORES	QUIRED	STERES	PYRRHA	HYBRIS
---RE-	FLORET	QUIRES	STORED	******	HYDRIC
******	FUHRER	REARED	STORES	---RI-	IATRIC
ADORED	FURRED	REARER	STOREY	******	IBERIA
ADORER	GARRET	REGRET	SUCRES	ACARID	INDRIS
ADORES	GEARED	ROARED	SURREY	ACERIC	INGRID
ALFRED	GENRES	ROARER	TANREC	AGARIC	ISTRIA
ANDREA	GLARED	SACRED	TARRED	ALARIC	KAURIS
ANDREI	GLARES	SAUREL	TEARED	ANTRIM	KERRIE
ANDRES	HAIRED	SCARED	TENREC	ASTRID	LATRIA
ANDREW	HATRED	SCARER	TERRET	BARRIE	LAURIE
AUBREY	HEARER	SCARES	THYREO	BARRIO	MADRID
AUDREY	HEBREW	SCORED	TIERED	BEDRID	MAORIS
AZORES	IMARET	SCORER	TOURED	CAPRIC	MATRIX
AZURES	INBRED	SCORES	TOURER	CARRIE	MEGRIM
BARRED	INGRES	SEARED	TURRET	CEDRIC	METRIC

MIDRIB	GNARLY	ETERNA	MATRON	CHERRY	FLIRTS
MORRIS	HOURLY	INURNS	METROS	CHIRRS	FLIRTY
NITRIC	KNURLS	LEARNS	MICRON	CHURRS	FOURTH
NITRID	KNURLY	LEARNT	MIRROR	FLURRY	HEARTH
NORRIS	NEARLY	LIERNE	MONROE	GHARRI	HEARTS
NUTRIA	OVERLY	MOURNS	MORROS	GHARRY	HEARTY
OSIRIS	PEARLS	QUERNS	MORROW	KNARRY	OPORTO
PEORIA	PEARLY	SCORNS	NARROW	PIERRE	QUARTE
PETRIE	POORLY	SPURNS	NATRON	QUARRY	QUARTO
PICRIC	SHORLS	STERNA	NEURON	SCURRY	QUARTS
PUTRID	SNARLS	STERNO	NIMROD	SHERRY	QUARTZ
PYURIA	SNARLY	STERNS	OBERON	SHIRRS	QUIRTS
RUBRIC	SOURLY	THORNS	OCTROI	SIERRA	SHIRTS
SCORIA	SWIRLS	THORNY	PARROT	SKERRY	SHIRTY
SEARIN	SWIRLY	UTURNS	PATROL	SKIRRS	SHORTS
SHERIF	TWIRLS	YEARNS	PATRON	SLURRY	SKIRTS
SIGRID	WHIRLS	******	PEDROS	SPARRY	SMARTS
SPIRIT	WHORLS	---RO-	PERRON	SPERRY	SNORTS
STERIC	YEARLY	******	PETROL	SPURRY	SPARTA
THORIA	******	BARROW	PHAROS	STARRY	SPIRTS
THORIC	---RM-	BORROW	POGROM	WHERRY	SPORTS
TIGRIS	******	BURROS	RAMROD	******	SPORTY
TORRID	ALARMS	BURROW	RETROD	---RS-	SPURTS
VIBRIO	CHARMS	CARROT	SHARON	******	STARTS
VITRIC	CHIRMS	CHARON	SORROW	AVERSE	SWARTH
YTTRIA	DHARMA	CHIRON	STEROL	BOURSE	SWARTY
YTTRIC	INARMS	CITRON	TERROR	COARSE	THIRTY
******	REARMS	CLAROS	THORON	COURSE	WHORTS
---RK-	SMARMY	DACRON	UNTROD	HEARSE	******
******	SPERMO	DARROW	UPHROE	HEARST	---RU-
CLERKS	STORMS	DRYROT	YARROW	HOARSE	******
QUARKS	STORMY	ESCROW	******	SPARSE	ACCRUE
QUIRKS	SWARMS	FAEROE	---RP-	THIRST	ALARUM
SHARKS	THERMO	FARROW	******	THYRSE	ANTRUM
SHIRKS	THERMS	FURROW	CHIRPS	THYRSI	ASARUM
SMIRKS	******	GENROS	CHIRPY	******	BEIRUT
SPARKS	---RN-	HARROW	SCARPS	---RT-	CHERUB
STIRKS	******	HEBRON	SHARPS	******	CHORUS
STORKS	ACORNS	HEDRON	SHERPA	ABORTS	CIRRUS
******	ADORNS	HORROR	SLURPS	ALERTS	CITRUS
---RL-	AVERNO	HOTROD	STIRPS	AVERTS	CUPRUM
******	BAIRNS	HYDROS	THORPE	BLURTS	CYPRUS
CEORLS	BOURNE	IGOROT	TWERPS	CHARTS	ELBRUS
CHURLS	BOURNS	JARROW	TWIRPS	COURTS	EMBRUE
DEARLY	CAIRNS	KARROO	USURPS	DEARTH	EPIRUS
DOURLY	CHURNS	KEDRON	******	ECARTE	ESTRUS
FAIRLY	DHARNA	MACRON	---RR-	EVERTS	FERRUM
GNARLS	DHURNA	MARROW	******	EXERTS	ICARUS
			BLURRY		
			CHARRY		

IMBRUE	CAUSAL	******	COPSES	GUISES	LOUSED
LABRUM	CORSAC	---SE-	CORSES	GUSSET	LOUSES
LARRUP	DESSAU	******	CORSET	HALSEY	MANSES
OUTRUN	DIPSAS	ABASED	COSSES	HANSEL	MASSED
PIERUS	DORSAD	ABASER	COSSET	HASSEL	MASSES
QUORUM	DORSAL	ABASES	CRISES	HAUSEN	MAUSER
SACRUM	DOSSAL	ABUSED	CRUSES	HAWSER	MENSES
SAURUS	FOSSAE	ABUSER	CRUSET	HAWSES	MERSEY
TAURUS	HUSSAR	ABUSES	CURSED	HISSED	MESSED
UNTRUE	JETSAM	AMUSED	CURSES	HISSER	MESSES
UTERUS	JIGSAW	AMUSER	CUSSED	HISSES	MISSED
WALRUS	KANSAN	AMUSES	CUSSES	HORSED	MISSEL
******	KANSAS	ANISES	DAISES	HORSES	MISSES
---RV-	MENSAL	ANUSES	DAMSEL	HORSEY	MORSEL
******	MISSAL	ARISEN	DENSER	HOUSED	MOSSES
SCURVY	NASSAU	ARISES	DIESEL	HOUSES	MOUSED
STARVE	OUTSAT	AVOSET	DIESES	IBISES	MOUSER
SWERVE	OVISAC	BASSES	DORSET	IRISED	MOUSES
WHARVE	PRESAS	BASSET	DOSSED	IRISES	MUSSED
WHERVE	PTISAN	BIASED	DOSSEL	JERSEY	MUSSEL
******	PULSAR	BIASES	DOSSER	JESSED	MUSSES
---RY-	QUASAR	BOSSED	DOUSED	JESSES	NAOSES
******	RIPSAW	BOSSES	DOUSES	JOSSES	NASSER
AVERYS	SANSAR	BOUSED	DOWSED	KAASES	NAUSEA
BARRYS	SARSAR	BOUSES	DOWSER	KAISER	NOISED
CHERYL	SEESAW	BOWSED	DOWSES	KERSEY	NOISES
EMBRYO	TARSAL	BOWSES	DRUSES	KINSEY	NOOSED
GERRYS	TUSSAH	BUNSEN	ELYSEE	KISSED	NOOSES
HARRYS	TUSSAL	BURSES	ERASED	KISSER	NURSED
HENRYS	TUSSAR	BUSSED	ERASER	KISSES	NURSER
JERRYS	VASSAL	BUSSES	ERASES	KRISES	NURSES
LARRYS	WARSAW	CAUSED	EYASES	LAPSED	OCASEY
PERRYS	******	CAUSER	FALSER	LAPSER	OFFSET
TERRYS	---SB-	CAUSES	FEASED	LAPSES	ONUSES
TETRYL	******	CEASED	FEASES	LASSEN	OUTSET
******	GEMSBO	CEASES	FESSES	LASSES	PARSEC
---SA-	THISBE	CENSED	FOSSES	LEASED	PARSED
******	******	CENSER	FRISES	LEASES	PARSEE
AIRSAC	---SC-	CENSES	FUSSED	LENSES	PARSES
BALSAM	******	CHASED	FUSSER	LESSEE	PASSED
BALSAS	BORSCH	CHASER	FUSSES	LESSEN	PASSEE
BONSAI	FIASCO	CHASES	GASSED	LESSER	PASSER
BOWSAW	FRESCO	CHISEL	GASSES	LIASED	PASSES
BURSAE	KIRSCH	CHOSEN	GEYSER	LOOSED	PAUSED
BURSAL	KITSCH	CLOSED	GOOSED	LOOSEN	PAUSER
BURSAR	PUTSCH	CLOSER	GOOSES	LOOSER	PAUSES
BURSAS	UNESCO	CLOSES	GOOSEY	LOOSES	PEASEN
CAESAR		CLOSET	GORSES	LOSSES	PEASES

PHASED	TENSES	******	PYOSIS	SEISMO	RANSOM
PHASES	TERSER	---SI-	RAISIN	SEISMS	REASON
PLUSES	THESES	******	RUSSIA	SPASMS	ROBSON
POISED	TINSEL	BEDSIT	SEISIN	******	SAMSON
POISES	TOSSED	BESSIE	SEPSIS	---SN-	SEASON
POSSES	TOSSES	BIOSIS	STASIS	******	SEISOR
POSSET	UKASES	CASSIA	TARSIA	DOESNT	SENSOR
PROSED	UNDSET	CASSIE	TESSIE	FRESNO	TELSON
PROSER	UNISEX	CASSIS	THESIS	PUISNE	TENSOR
PROSES	UNUSED	CISSIE	TOCSIN	******	TORSOS
PULSED	UPASES	COUSIN	TONSIL	---SO-	TUCSON
PULSES	VERSED	CRASIS	TUSSIS	******	UNISON
PURSED	VERSES	CRISIS	ZOYSIA	ALISON	VERSOS
PURSER	VERSET	DIESIS	******	AVISOS	VINSON
PURSES	VESSEL	DOSSIL	---SK-	BASSOS	WATSON
PUSSES	WADSET	ECESIS	******	BOLSON	WILSON
PUSSEY	WEASEL	EMESIS	ALASKA	CANSOS	******
RAISED	WESSEX	ENOSIS	BRISKS	CARSON	---SP-
RAISER	WOLSEY	FOSSIL	DROSKY	CENSOR	******
RAISES	WORSEN	GNOSIS	FLASKS	CRESOL	CLASPS
RINSED	WORSER	GOSSIP	FRISKS	CRUSOE	CRISPS
RINSER	WOWSER	GUSSIE	FRISKY	CURSOR	CRISPY
RINSES	YESSED	JESSIE	KIOSKS	CUSSOS	GRASPS
ROUSED	YESSES	KAMSIN	NEVSKI	DAMSON	KNOSPS
ROUSER	******	LASSIE	TORSKS	DAWSON	PHOSPH
ROUSES	---SH-	LEPSIA	WHISKS	DOBSON	******
RUSSET	******	MAISIE	WHISKY	EDISON	---SR-
SANSEI	AYESHA	MASSIF	******	GESSOS	******
SASSED	BRASHY	MIOSIS	---SL-	GIBSON	MESSRS
SASSES	BRUSHY	MISSIS	******	GODSON	******
SEISED	ELISHA	MYOSIN	ENISLE	HANSOM	---SS-
SENSED	FLASHY	MYOSIS	FOCSLE	HUDSON	******
SENSES	FLESHY	NOESIS	GRISLY	HYSSOP	BRASSY
SOUSED	GEISHA	OUTSIT	HASSLE	JONSON	CHASSE
SOUSES	GUNSHY	PARSIS	MEASLY	KELSON	CLASSY
STASES	HONSHU	PASSIM	PUSSLY	LASSOS	CROSSE
SUNSET	KYUSHU	PEPSIN	THUSLY	LESSON	CUISSE
SUSSED	MARSHA	PERSIA	TOUSLE	LESSOR	DRESSY
SUSSEX	MARSHY	PHASIA	TUSSLE	LISSOM	DROSSY
TASSEL	MOISHE	PHASIC	******	MAISON	FLOSSY
TASSET	PLASHY	PHASIS	---SM-	NELSON	GLASSY
TEASED	PLUSHY	PHYSIC	******	ORISON	GLOSSO
TEASEL	SAMSHU	PHYSIO	ABYSMS	PARSON	GLOSSY
TEASER	SLOSHY	PLASIA	CHASMS	PERSON	GRASSY
TEASES	SLUSHY	PLASIS	MIASMA	PODSOL	MOUSSE
TEASET	TRASHY	POTSIE	PLASMA	POISON	ODESSA
TENSED		PROSIT	PLASMO	PRISON	PRISSY
TENSER		PTOSIS	PRISMS	RAMSON	TRESSY
					WRASSE

******	ROOSTS	PATSYS	HYETAL	******	BEATER
---ST-	ROUSTS	SELSYN	INSTAR	---TC-	BELTED
******	SHASTA	******	ISHTAR	******	BESTED
AGISTS	SIESTA	---SZ-	JUNTAS	BLOTCH	BETTED
ARISTA	TOASTS	******	KAFTAN	CLUTCH	BETTER
ARISTO	TRISTE	GROSZY	LACTAM	CRATCH	BETTES
AVESTA	TRUSTS	******	LYTTAE	CROTCH	BISTER
BEASTS	TRUSTY	---TA-	MANTAS	CRUTCH	BITTED
BLASTO	TRYSTS	******	MARTAS	CULTCH	BITTEN
BLASTS	TWISTS	ACETAL	MENTAL	FLETCH	BITTER
BOASTS	TWISTY	AMYTAL	MORTAL	FLITCH	BOATED
BOOSTS	VERSTS	ANITAS	MORTAR	HOOTCH	BOATER
BURSTS	WAISTS	AORTAE	NECTAR	NAUTCH	BOLTED
CHASTE	WORSTS	AORTAL	PASTAS	QUITCH	BOLTER
CHESTS	WRESTS	AORTAS	PENTAD	SCOTCH	BOOTED
CHESTY	WRISTS	AVATAR	PLATAN	SCUTCH	BOOTEE
COASTS	YEASTS	BANTAM	PORTAL	SKETCH	BRUTES
CRESTS	YEASTY	BHUTAN	POSTAL	SMUTCH	BUNTED
CRUSTS	******	BRUTAL	QUOTAS	SNATCH	BUSTED
CRUSTY	---SU-	CAFTAN	RAGTAG	SNITCH	BUSTER
CUESTA	******	CANTAB	RATTAN	STITCH	BUTTED
DEISTS	BYSSUS	CENTAL	RECTAL	SWATCH	BUTTER
EGESTA	CATSUP	CHETAH	RENTAL	SWITCH	BUTTES
EGESTS	CENSUR	COITAL	RIATAS	THATCH	CANTED
EXISTS	CENSUS	COSTAE	RICTAL	TWITCH	CANTER
FEASTS	CONSUL	COSTAL	SEPTAL	WRETCH	CARTED
FEISTS	DORSUM	COSTAR	SEXTAN	******	CARTEL
FEISTY	GYPSUM	COTTAE	SOFTAS	---TE-	CARTER
FIESTA	LAPSUS	COTTAR	SPITAL	******	CARTES
FIRSTS	MISSUS	COTTAS	STATAL	ABATED	CASTER
FOISTS	NESSUS	CRETAN	SULTAN	ABATER	CASTES
FROSTS	OMASUM	DELTAS	SUNTAN	ABATES	CATTED
FROSTY	PASSUS	DENTAL	SURTAX	AEETES	CAUTER
FRUSTA	POSSUM	DIETAL	SYNTAX	AGATES	CENTER
GHOSTS	PURSUE	DISTAL	TAMTAM	ALATED	CERTES
GLOSTS	RHESUS	EVITAS	TARTAN	ARETES	CHUTES
GUESTS	TARSUS	FANTAN	TARTAR	AUSTEN	COATED
HEISTS	TISSUE	FESTAL	TESTAE	AUSTER	COATEE
HOISTS	TOSSUP	FOETAL	THETAS	BAITED	COLTER
HORSTE	VERSUS	FONTAL	VESTAL	BANTER	CONTES
JOISTS	******	GRETAS	VESTAS	BARTER	CORTES
JOUSTS	---SY-	GUITAR	VISTAS	BASTED	CORTEX
PIGSTY	******	GUSTAF	VITTAE	BASTES	CORTEZ
PLASTY	BESSYS	GUSTAV	WYSTAN	BATTED	COSTED
POUSTO	BETSYS	GUTTAE	******	BATTEN	COSTER
PRESTO	CISSYS	GUTTAT	---TB-	BATTER	COTTER
QUESTS	DAISYS	HARTAL	******	BAXTER	CRATED
ROASTS	PANSYS	HEPTAD	WHITBY	BEATEN	CRATER

CRATES	FOSTER	INSTEP	MATTEO	PATTER	RESTER
CUSTER	FRATER	JESTED	MATTER	PECTEN	RETTED
CUTTER	GAITED	JESTER	MATTES	PELTED	RIFTED
DARTED	GAITER	JETTED	MEETER	PELTER	RIOTED
DARTER	GARTER	JILTED	MELTED	PESTER	RIOTER
DEFTER	GENTES	JILTER	MELTER	PETTED	RITTER
DENTED	GETTER	JITTER	MESTEE	PEWTER	ROOTED
DEXTER	GIFTED	JOLTED	MILTED	PIETER	ROOTER
DIETED	GIRTED	JOLTER	MILTER	PINTER	ROSTER
DIETER	GLUTEI	JOTTED	MINTED	PITTED	ROTTED
DINTED	GLUTEN	JOTTER	MINTER	PLATED	ROTTEN
DOITED	GOATEE	JUTTED	MISTED	PLATEN	ROTTER
DOPTER	GOITER	KILTED	MISTER	PLATER	ROUTED
DOTTED	GOTTEN	KILTER	MITTEN	PLATES	ROUTER
DOTTEL	GRATED	KITTED	MOATED	PONTES	ROUTES
DOTTER	GRATER	KITTEN	MOLTED	PORTED	RUSTED
DUSTED	GRATES	LASTED	MOLTEN	PORTER	RUTTED
DUSTER	GRETEL	LASTER	MOLTER	POSTED	SALTED
EASTER	GUNTER	LASTEX	MONTES	POSTER	SALTER
EDITED	GUTTED	LATTEN	MOOTED	POTTED	SAUTES
ELATED	GUTTER	LATTER	MOOTER	POTTER	SCOTER
ELATER	HAFTED	LENTEN	MUSTEE	POUTED	SCUTES
ELATES	HALTED	LESTER	MUSTER	POUTER	SEATED
EMOTED	HALTER	LETTER	MUTTER	POWTER	SEPTET
EMOTES	HASTED	LIFTED	NANTES	PRATED	SESTET
ENATES	HASTEN	LIFTER	NATTER	PRATER	SETTEE
EXETER	HASTES	LILTED	NEATEN	PRATES	SETTER
EXITED	HATTED	LINTEL	NEATER	PRETER	SEXTET
FALTER	HATTER	LINTER	NESTED	PUNTED	SHOTES
FASTED	HEATED	LISTED	NETTED	PUNTER	SIFTED
FASTEN	HEATER	LISTEL	NEUTER	PUTTED	SIFTER
FASTER	HEFTED	LISTEN	NUTTED	PUTTEE	SILTED
FATTED	HELTER	LISTER	NUTTER	PUTTER	SINTER
FATTEN	HESTER	LITTER	OBITER	QUOTED	SISTER
FATTER	HILTED	LOFTED	ORATED	QUOTER	SITTER
FELTED	HINTED	LOFTER	ORATES	QUOTES	SIXTES
FESTER	HITTER	LOITER	OUSTED	RAFTED	SKATED
FETTER	HOOTED	LOOTED	OUSTER	RAFTER	SKATER
FILTER	HOOTER	LOOTER	OYSTER	RANTED	SKATES
FISTED	HOSTED	LUSTED	PALTER	RANTER	SLATED
FITTED	HOSTEL	LUSTER	PANTED	RASTER	SLATER
FITTER	HOTTED	MALTED	PARTED	RATTED	SLATES
FLUTED	HOTTER	MANTEL	PASTED	RATTEN	SMITER
FLUTER	HUNTED	MANTES	PASTEL	RATTER	SMITES
FLUTES	HUNTER	MARTEN	PASTER	RENTED	SOFTEN
FOOTED	HURTER	MASTED	PASTES	RENTER	SOFTER
FOOTER	HUTTED	MASTER	PATTED	RENTES	SOOTED
FORTES	HYSTER	MATTED	PATTEN	RESTED	SORTED

SORTER	VASTER	BERTHS	SPATHE	CRITIC	PANTIE
SPATES	VATTED	BIRTHS	STETHO	CUPTIE	PASTIL
SPITED	VENTED	BLITHE	STITHY	CURTIS	PECTIC
SPITES	VENTER	BOOTHS	SWATHE	CYSTIC	PECTIN
STATED	VERTEX	BROTHS	SWATHS	DENTIL	PEPTIC
STATEN	VESTED	CANTHI	TEETHE	DENTIN	PHOTIC
STATER	VESTEE	CLOTHE	TENTHS	DHOTIS	PHYTIN
STATES	VETTED	CLOTHO	TILTHS	DISTIL	PISTIL
SUBTER	VOLTED	CLOTHS	TOOTHY	EMETIC	POETIC
SUITED	VORTEX	DEATHS	TROTHS	EMETIN	PONTIC
SUITES	WAFTED	DEATHY	TRUTHS	EROTIC	PONTIL
SUTTEE	WAFTER	DEPTHS	WIDTHS	EXOTIC	PORTIA
SYSTEM	WAITED	EARTHS	WORTHY	FISTIC	RUSTIC
TARTED	WAITER	EARTHY	WRATHY	FOETID	SAITIC
TARTER	WALTER	EDITHS	WRITHE	FORTIS	SCOTIA
TASTED	WANTED	FAITHS	XANTHO	FUSTIC	SEPTIC
TASTER	WANTER	FIFTHS	YOUTHS	GERTIE	SHUTIN
TASTES	WASTED	FILTHY	******	GESTIC	SORTIE
TATTED	WASTER	FIRTHS	---TI-	GRATIN	STATIC
TATTER	WASTES	FRITHS	******	GRATIS	TACTIC
TAUTEN	WELTED	FROTHS	ABATIS	HATTIE	TESTIS
TAUTER	WELTER	FROTHY	ACETIC	HECTIC	THETIC
TEETER	WESTER	GNATHO	AORTIC	HESTIA	THETIS
TENTED	WETTED	GOETHE	ARCTIC	HOGTIE	TOMTIT
TENTER	WETTER	HEATHS	AUNTIE	INSTIL	TUTTIS
TESTED	WHITED	HEATHY	AUSTIN	IRITIC	URETIC
TESTER	WHITEN	ICHTHY	AZOTIC	IRITIS	VIATIC
TESTES	WHITER	KEITHS	BALTIC	ISATIN	VICTIM
TETTER	WHITES	LOATHE	BALTIM	JUSTIN	ZAFTIG
TILTED	WHITEY	MALTHA	BATTIK	KELTIC	******
TILTER	WILTED	MARTHA	BATTIN	KILTIE	---TK-
TINTED	WINTER	MARTHE	BERTIE	LACTIC	******
TITTER	WITTED	MONTHS	BESTIR	LENTIL	MOLTKE
TOLTEC	WONTED	MOUTHS	BIOTIC	LOTTIE	******
TOOTED	WRITER	MOUTHY	BIOTIN	LUETIC	---TL-
TOOTER	WRITES	NINTHS	BOOTIE	MANTIC	******
TOTTED	XYSTER	QUOTHA	BOWTIE	MANTIS	BATTLE
TOTTER	YESTER	RHYTHM	BUSTIC	MARTIN	BEETLE
TOUTED	ZESTED	SCATHE	CATTIE	MASTIC	BOOTLE
TOUTER	ZOSTER	SCYTHE	CELTIC	MATTIE	BOTTLE
TRITER	******	SEETHE	CHITIN	MIOTIC	BUSTLE
TUFTED	---TH-	SIXTHS	COATIS	MUFTIS	CANTLE
TUTTED	******	SLOTHS	CONTIN	MYSTIC	CASTLE
ULSTER	AGATHA	SMITHS	COOTIE	NASTIC	CATTLE
UNITED	APATHY	SMITHY	COPTIC	NETTIE	COSTLY
UNITES	APHTHA	SNATHE	CORTIN	NOETIC	CURTLY
UNSTEP	BERTHA	SNATHS	CRETIC	NOSTIC	CUTTLE
URETER	BERTHE	SOOTHE	CRETIN	OTITIS	DAFTLY

DARTLE	TURTLE	DOCTOR	SECTOR	PIETRO	CACTUS
DEFTLY	VASTLY	EASTON	SETTOS	POETRY	CANTUS
DOTTLE	WATTLE	EDITOR	SEXTON	QUATRE	CESTUS
FETTLE	******	FACTOR	STATOR	ROSTRA	COITUS
FLATLY	---TN-	FANTOM	SUITOR	SARTRE	CULTUS
FOOTLE	******	FOETOR	SUTTON	SENTRY	DICTUM
GENTLE	GRETNA	FULTON	TATTOO	SULTRY	FACTUM
GENTLY	MUSTNT	GASTON	TAUTOG	VENTRO	FLATUS
GUTTLE	******	GENTOO	TESTON	VESTRY	FOETUS
HURTLE	---TO-	HECTOR	TEUTON	WINTRY	HIATUS
HUSTLE	******	JETTON	TIPTOE	******	JUSTUS
JOSTLE	ABATOR	KOWTOW	TIPTOP	---TS-	KULTUR
JUSTLY	AMATOL	LECTOR	TOMTOM	******	MANTUA
KETTLE	BARTOK	LENTOS	TRITON	CURTSY	MEATUS
KIRTLE	BARTON	LEPTON	UNSTOP	LAOTSE	PENTUP
KITTLE	BENTON	LICTOR	VECTOR	TOOTSY	PLUTUS
LASTLY	BESTOW	MELTON	VIATOR	TSETSE	RECTUM
LITTLE	BETTOR	MENTOR	VICTOR	******	RECTUS
MANTLE	BOLTON	MILTON	WALTON	---TT-	RICTUS
MEETLY	BOSTON	MORTON	WANTON	******	SCUTUM
METTLE	BOTTOM	MOTTOS	WILTON	ANATTO	SEPTUM
MISTLE	BRETON	MOUTON	XYSTOS	CHATTY	SPUTUM
MOSTLY	BRITON	MUTTON	******	CHITTY	STATUE
MOTTLE	BURTON	NEKTON	---TR-	CLOTTY	STATUS
MYRTLE	BUTTON	NESTOR	******	FRETTY	TITTUP
NEATLY	BUXTON	NEWTON	ANITRA	GHETTO	VIRTUE
NESTLE	CANTON	ORATOR	AUSTRO	GIOTTO	XTSTUS
NETTLE	CANTOR	PASTOR	BISTRO	GLOTTO	******
PARTLY	CANTOS	PATTON	CASTRO	GRITTY	---TY-
PERTLY	CAPTOR	PEGTOP	CENTRA	GROTTO	******
PESTLE	CARTON	PHOTON	CENTRE	GROTTY	ACETYL
PINTLE	CASTOR	PHOTOS	CENTRI	KNOTTY	BETTYS
PORTLY	CAXTON	PICTOR	CENTRO	ODETTE	DACTYL
POTTLE	CENTOS	PINTOS	CONTRA	PLATTE	GERTYS
RAPTLY	CHITON	PISTOL	CONTRE	PRETTY	HATTYS
RATTLE	CONTOS	PISTON	DEXTRO	SCATTY	HETTYS
ROOTLE	COTTON	PONTON	DMITRI	SCOTTS	KITTYS
RUSTLE	CRETON	POTTOS	ELYTRA	SMUTTY	MARTYR
SETTLE	CROTON	PRETOR	GANTRY	SNOTTY	MARTYS
SOFTLY	CUSTOM	PROTON	GASTRO	SPOTTY	MONTYS
SUBTLE	CUSTOS	PUNTOS	GENTRY	******	MORTYS
SUBTLY	DALTON	RAPTOR	GOITRE	---TU-	TROTYL
TARTLY	DANTON	RECTOR	LUSTRE	******	ZLOTYS
TATTLE	DATTOS	RECTOS	MAITRE	ACETUM	******
TATTLY	DAYTON	REDTOP	PALTRY	ADYTUM	---UA-
TAUTLY	DEBTOR	RHETOR	PANTRY	BANTUS	******
TITTLE	DIATOM	SANTOL	PASTRY	BATTUE	ACTUAL
TOOTLE	DITTOS	SARTOR	PELTRY	BRUTUS	ANNUAL

CASUAL	******	REFUEL	******	LIMULI	EXHUME
JAGUAR	---UD-	REVUES	---UI-	LOBULE	FANUMS
LEHUAS	******	ROGUED	******	LUNULA	FORUMS
LOQUAR	ALLUDE	ROGUES	ACQUIT	LUNULE	HEAUME
LOQUAT	ALMUDE	ROQUET	ALCUIN	MACULA	ILLUME
MANUAL	ALMUDS	SAMUEL	BEDUIN	MACULE	INHUME
MUTUAL	CLAUDE	SEQUEL	BEGUIN	MIAULS	JORUMS
PAPUAN	CLOUDS	SPRUES	INTUIT	MODULE	LEGUME
RITUAL	CLOUDY	TENUES	JESUIT	MOGULS	MAZUMA
SEXUAL	DELUDE	TOGUES	LIQUID	MORULA	METUMP
SIOUAN	DENUDE	TOQUES	MAQUIS	MUTULE	NAHUMS
UNGUAL	ESCUDO	TUQUES	SCHUIT	NEBULA	PNEUMA
VIDUAL	FRAUDS	UNGUES	SEQUIN	NODULE	PNEUMO
VISUAL	PSEUDO	VAGUER	TENUIS	OCCULT	RESUME
******	REMUDA	VALUED	UNGUIS	OSCULE	RHEUMY
---UB-	YEHUDI	VALUER	******	PAPULA	SCRUMS
******	******	VALUES	---UK-	PAPULE	SEDUMS
DANUBE	---UE-	VENUES	******	PENULT	SERUMS
HECUBA	******	VOGUES	KABUKI	PETULA	STRUMA
INCUBI	ARGUED	******	PERUKE	PICULS	STRUMS
JUJUBE	ARGUER	---UF-	REBUKE	PILULE	THRUMS
SCRUBS	ARGUES	******	SALUKI	RADULA	TRAUMA
SHRUBS	COQUET	ARGUFY	******	RAOULS	VOLUME
YORUBA	ENDUED	REBUFF	---UL-	RESULT	******
******	ENDUES	SCRUFF	******	ROMULO	---UN-
---UC-	ENSUED	******	AMPULE	SHOULD	******
******	ENSUES	---UG-	AMPULS	TUBULE	ABOUND
ABDUCT	FIQUES	******	ANNULS	TUMULT	AMOUNT
ADDUCE	FRAUEN	AERUGO	BABULS	TWOULD	AROUND
ADDUCT	FUGUES	BELUGA	CANULA	UNDULY	ATTUNE
ALMUCE	GIGUES	CAYUGA	CEDULA	UNGULA	AVAUNT
AVOUCH	IMBUED	CHOUGH	COPULA	UNRULY	CAJUNS
BARUCH	IMBUES	CLOUGH	CUPULE	URSULA	COHUNE
CANUCK	INDUED	COLUGO	CURULE	VENULE	DEBUNK
CROUCH	INDUES	DEBUGS	ENGULF	VOGULS	EDMUND
DEDUCE	ISSUED	DELUGE	FACULA	ZONULA	EXEUNT
DEDUCT	ISSUER	ENOUGH	FECULA	ZONULE	FECUND
EUNUCH	ISSUES	IMPUGN	FERULA	******	FLAUNT
GLAUCO	LEMUEL	LANUGO	FERULE	---UM-	GERUND
GROUCH	MAGUEY	OPPUGN	FIBULA	******	GROUND
INDUCE	MANUEL	PLOUGH	GHOULS	ALBUMS	IMMUNE
INDUCT	MIGUEL	REFUGE	INDULT	ASSUME	IMMUNO
REDUCE	MINUET	SHRUGS	INGULF	AUTUMN	JEJUNE
SEDUCE	PIQUED	SLOUGH	INSULT	BEGUMS	JOCUND
SLOUCH	PIQUES	TELUGU	ISEULT	BENUMB	KORUNA
SPRUCE	PIQUET	THOUGH	LAZULI	COLUMN	KORUNY
STRUCK	QUEUED	TROUGH	LIGULA	DECUMA	LACUNA
	QUEUES		LIGULE	DEGUMS	LAGUNE

OBTUND	******	OCCURS	ILLUSE	GOMUTI	GUAVAS
OSMUND	---UR-	ORDURE	ILLUST	GROUTS	LARVAE
PODUNK	******	PARURE	INCUSE	HALUTZ	LARVAL
REFUND	ABJURE	PENURY	INFUSE	IMPUTE	OGIVAL
RERUNS	ABSURD	PLEURA	INRUSH	INPUTS	SERVAL
ROTUND	ADJURE	PLEURO	LOCUST	KNOUTS	SILVAE
SECUND	ALLURE	RECURS	MEDUSA	MINUTE	SILVAN
SHRUNK	AMOURS	RETURN	MISUSE	PAIUTE	SILVAS
SPRUNG	ARMURE	SATURN	OBTUSE	REBUTS	SLOVAK
STRUNG	ARTURO	SCOURS	ONRUSH	REFUTE	SYLVAE
TRIUNE	ASBURY	SECURE	PERUSE	REPUTE	SYLVAN
UNSUNG	ASSURE	SIEURS	PROUST	SALUTE	SYLVAS
VACUNA	AUBURN	STAURO	RECUSE	SCOUTS	VALVAL
VARUNA	AUGURS	SUBURB	REFUSE	SHOUTS	VALVAR
VICUNA	AUGURY	SUTURE	RETUSE	SLEUTH	VOLVAS
YAMUNS	CESURA	SYNURA	ROBUST	SNOUTS	VULVAE
******	COBURG	TEAURN	SCHUSS	SOLUTE	VULVAL
---UO-	COLURE	TENURE	SCOUSE	SPOUTS	VULVAR
******	DATURA	UNCURL	SPOUSE	STOUTS	******
LIQUOR	DECURY	UNFURL	THRUSH	STRUTS	---VD-
PEQUOD	DEMURE	UNHURT	THRUST	TENUTO	******
PEQUOT	DEMURS	UNSURE	UNHUSK	TROUTS	PRAVDA
TOLUOL	ENDURE	UPTURN	UNJUST	VALUTA	******
******	ENSURE	VELURE	UPRUSH	VOLUTE	---VE-
---UP-	ERFURT	YAOURT	WATUSI	******	******
******	FEMURS	YOGURT	******	---UU-	AGAVES
ABRUPT	FIGURE	******	---UT-	******	BEAVER
CROUPE	FLEURY	---US-	******	VACUUM	BEEVES
CROUPS	FLOURS	******	AGOUTI	******	BRAVED
CROUPY	FLOURY	ABLUSH	AGOUTY	---UX-	BRAVER
CUTUPS	FUTURE	ACCUSE	ALEUTS	******	BRAVES
GETUPS	IMMURE	ADJUST	ARBUTE	DELUXE	BREVES
GROUPS	IMPURE	AMBUSH	ASTUTE	******	BREVET
LETUPS	INCURS	AROUSE	BASUTO	---UY-	CALVED
MIXUPS	INJURE	AUGUST	BEAUTS	******	CALVES
OCCUPY	INJURY	BEMUSE	BEAUTY	TOLUYL	CARVED
PINUPS	INSURE	BLOUSE	CANUTE	******	CARVEL
SCAUPS	INTURN	CARUSO	CLOUTS	---UZ-	CARVEN
SETUPS	LEMURS	CAYUSE	DEBUTS	******	CARVER
SIRUPS	LIGURE	CERUSE	DEPUTE	MEZUZA	CARVES
SIRUPY	LUXURY	CLAUSE	DEPUTY	ORMUZD	CHIVES
STOUPS	MADURA	CREUSA	DILUTE	******	CLEVER
SUNUPS	MADURO	DEFUSE	DROUTH	---VA-	CLIVES
SYRUPS	MANURE	DEGUST	DULUTH	******	CLOVEN
SYRUPY	MATURE	DISUSE	EMEUTE	CANVAS	CLOVER
TIEUPS	MOHURS	EFFUSE	FLOUTS	COEVAL	CLOVES
TROUPE	NATURE	EXCUSE	GAMUTS	CRAVAT	CONVEX
	NOMURA	GROUSE	GHAUTS	CREVAS	CONVEY

CORVEE	KEEVES	SHOVES	******	******	SUBWAY
CORVES	KNAVES	SIEVED	---VI-	---VR-	TAIWAN
CRAVED	KNIVES	SIEVES	******	******	TWOWAY
CRAVEN	LEAVED	SILVER	ATAVIC	LOUVRE	WIGWAG
CRAVER	LEAVEN	SKIVED	CALVIN	OEUVRE	WIGWAM
CRAVES	LEAVER	SKIVER	CERVIX	******	******
CULVER	LEAVES	SKIVES	CLEVIS	---VU-	---WB-
CURVED	LOAVES	SLAVED	CLOVIS	******	******
CURVES	LOUVER	SLAVER	FERVID	CORVUS	BLOWBY
CURVET	MARVEL	SLAVES	FLAVIA	NAEVUS	******
DELVED	MAUVES	SLIVER	FLAVIN	PREVUE	---WD-
DELVER	NERVED	SLOVEN	FLUVIO	******	******
DELVES	NERVES	SNIVEL	GRAVID	---VV-	CROWDS
DENVER	OGIVES	SOEVER	JARVIS	******	******
DRIVEL	OLIVER	SOLVED	JERVIS	CHEVVY	---WE-
DRIVEN	OLIVES	SOLVER	KELVIN	CHIVVY	******
DRIVER	PEAVEY	SOLVES	LATVIA	SKIVVY	ANSWER
DRIVES	PEEVED	STAVED	MARVIN	******	AVOWED
DROVED	PEEVES	STAVES	MELVIN	---VY-	AVOWER
DROVER	PELVES	STEVEN	MERVIN	******	BLOWER
DROVES	PLOVER	STEVES	OLIVIA	MELVYN	BREWED
ELEVEN	PRIVET	STIVER	PARVIS	******	BREWER
FAUVES	PROVED	STOVER	PELVIC	---WA-	CHAWED
GLOVED	PROVEN	STOVES	PELVIS	******	CHEWED
GLOVER	PROVER	SURVEY	PLUVIO	AIRWAY	CHEWER
GLOVES	PROVES	SWIVEL	SALVIA	AJOWAN	CLAWED
GRAVED	PURVEY	SWIVET	SILVIA	ANYWAY	CLEWED
GRAVEL	QUAVER	TRAVEL	SLAVIC	ARAWAK	COBWEB
GRAVEN	QUIVER	TRAVES	SPAVIN	AVOWAL	CREWEL
GRAVER	REEVED	TRIVET	STEVIE	COGWAY	CROWED
GRAVES	REEVES	TROVER	SYLVIA	CONWAY	DRAWEE
GRIVET	REVVED	TROVES	TRIVIA	DEEWAN	DRAWER
GROVEL	SALVED	TURVES	WALVIS	EARWAX	FLAWED
GROVER	SALVER	UNEVEN	WEEVIL	GALWAY	FLOWED
GROVES	SALVES	VALVED	******	KEYWAY	FLOWER
HALVED	SELVES	VALVES	---VO-	LEEWAY	GLOWED
HALVES	SERVED	VARVES	******	MEDWAY	GLOWER
HARVEY	SERVER	VELVET	BRAVOS	MIDWAY	GNAWED
HEAVED	SERVES	VERVET	CONVOY	NARWAL	GNAWER
HEAVEN	SHAVED	WAIVED	ELEVON	NORWAY	GROWER
HEAVER	SHAVEN	WAIVER	FERVOR	ONEWAY	KNOWER
HEAVES	SHAVER	WAIVES	FLAVOR	PAXWAX	MEOWED
HELVES	SHAVES	WEAVED	FRIVOL	PREWAR	PEEWEE
HOOVED	SHIVER	WEAVER	REAVOW	RUNWAY	PLOWED
HOOVER	SHIVES	WEAVES	SALVOR	SCHWAS	PLOWER
HOOVES	SHOVED	WEEVER	SALVOS	SEAWAN	SHEWED
JARVEY	SHOVEL	WOLVER	SERVOS	SEAWAY	SHEWER
JAYVEE	SHOVER	WOLVES	TREVOR	SKYWAY	SHOWED
		YAHVEH	VOLVOX		

SHOWER	******	COAXED	******	SPRYER	CRAYON
SKEWED	---WN-	COAXER	---YA-	STAYED	GERYON
SKEWER	******	COAXES	******	STAYER	RUNYON
SLEWED	BRAWNY	CRUXES	BANYAN	SWAYED	******
SLOWED	BROWNS	FLAXEN	BUNYAN	THAYER	---YP-
SLOWER	CLOWNS	FLAXES	GALYAK	WHEYEY	******
SNOWED	CROWNS	FLEXED	LIBYAN	XRAYED	ECTYPE
SPEWED	DROWNS	FLEXES	MAGYAR	******	POLYPS
STEWED	FROWNS	FLUXED	PLAYAS	---YG-	******
STOWED	PRAWNS	FLUXES	SONYAS	******	---YR-
THAWED	SPAWNS	HOAXED	******	SYZYGY	******
THEWED	******	HOAXER	---YD-	******	SATYRS
TROWEL	---WO-	HOAXES	******	---YI-	******
VIEWED	******	IBEXES	FLOYDS	******	---YS-
VIEWER	BOWWOW	ILEXES	LLOYDS	BUNYIP	******
YAHWEH	POWWOW	JINXED	******	******	CHRYSO
******	******	JINXES	---YE-	---YL-	ENCYST
---WI-	---WS-	LYNXES	******	******	******
******	******	MINXES	BARYES	ALKYLS	---YT-
BIGWIG	BROWSE	ORYXES	BOWYER	ALLYLS	******
BREWIS	DROWSE	******	BRAYED	ANKYLO	BARYTA
DARWIN	DROWSY	---XI-	BRAYER	ARGYLL	OOCYTE
DIMWIT	******	******	BUOYED	BERYLS	******
EARWIG	---WT-	ALEXIA	CLAYED	ETHYLS	---YZ-
GODWIN	******	ALEXIN	CLAYEY	GRAYLY	******
GODWIT	GROWTH	ALEXIS	CLOYED	HEXYLS	CORYZA
HEDWIG	******	ANOXIA	DRAYED	JEKYLL	******
LUDWIG	---WU-	ANOXIC	FLAYED	SIBYLS	---ZA-
NITWIT	******	ATAXIA	FLAYER	SPRYLY	******
OUTWIT	BLOWUP	ATAXIC	FRAYED	VINYLS	BALZAC
PEEWIT	******	ELIXIR	GRAYED	******	BANZAI
******	---WY-	PINXIT	GRAYER	---YM-	BRAZAS
---WL-	******	PRAXIS	LAWYER	******	COLZAS
******	SELWYN	TRIXIE	LIVYER	CORYMB	ELIZAS
BRAWLS	******	******	OBEYED	ENZYME	FEZZAN
CRAWLS	---WZ-	---XO-	OBEYER	******	HAMZAS
CRAWLY	******	******	OKAYED	---YN-	HAZZAN
DRAWLS	BLOWZY	FLEXOR	OXEYED	******	PIZZAS
DRAWLY	FROWZY	KLAXON	OXEYES	ALKYNE	PLAZAS
GROWLS	******	PLEXOR	PLAYED	ELAYNE	TARZAN
PROWLS	---XA-	******	PLAYER	GROYNE	TAZZAS
SCOWLS	******	---XU-	PRAYED	LARYNG	ZIGZAG
SHAWLS	BIAXAL	******	PRAYER	LARYNX	******
SLOWLY	COAXAL	PLEXUS	PREYED	******	---ZE-
TRAWLS	******	******	PREYER	---YO-	******
******	---XE-	---XY-	SAWYER	******	AMAZED
---WM-	******	******	SLAYER	BARYON	AMAZES
******	APEXES	******	SPAYED	CANYON	AZAZEL
SHAWMS	CALXES	TRIXYS			

BLAZED	PRIZES	******	IGUANA	******	POLAND
BLAZER	RAZZED	---ZS-	IMPALA	---A-C	REGARD
BLAZES	RAZZES	******	INDABA	******	RELAID
BONZER	SEIZED	ZSASZA	ITHACA	ALCAIC	REMAND
BONZES	SEIZER	******	JACANA	ALTAIC	REPAID
BOOZED	SEIZES	---ZY-	JUDAEA	EDDAIC	REPAND
BOOZER	SMAZES	******	KABAKA	JUDAIC	RETARD
BOOZES	TETZEL	BENZYL	KABALA	MOSAIC	REWARD
BRAZED	WINZES	LIZZYS	KABAYA	ROMAIC	RIBALD
BRAZEN	******	******	KAMALA	******	RIBAND
BRAZER	---ZI-	---ZZ-	KANAKA	---A-D	RITARD
BRAZES	******	******	KERALA	******	ROBAND
BUZZED	BRAZIL	AREZZO	MALAGA	AALAND	ROLAND
BUZZER	DANZIG	FRIZZY	MALAYA	ABOARD	RONALD
BUZZES	DIAZIN	PIAZZA	MANANA	AFRAID	SEWARD
CRAZED	LIZZIE	SNAZZY	MARACA	ARMAND	SOLAND
CRAZES	RAZZIA	******	NAGANA	ARNAUD	STRAND
CROZER	RHIZIC	---A-A	NEVADA	ASGARD	TABARD
CROZES	SEIZIN	******	ORGANA	BAYARD	TOGAED
FEEZED	******	ACHAEA	OTTAVA	BOYARD	TOWARD
FEEZES	---ZL-	ACHAIA	OTTAWA	CANARD	UNHAND
FEZZES	******	AGLAIA	PAJAMA	COWARD	UNLAID
FIZZED	DAZZLE	ALBATA	PANADA	DANAID	UNSAID
FIZZER	FIZZLE	ALPACA	PANAMA	DEMAND	UPLAND
FIZZES	FOOZLE	ANKARA	PAPAYA	DONALD	UPWARD
FROZEN	GUZZLE	ARCANA	PIRANA	DOTARD	UTGARD
FURZES	MIZZLE	ARGALA	POSADA	ECHARD	VISAED
FUZZED	MUZZLE	ARMADA	PURANA	EDUARD	VISARD
FUZZES	NOZZLE	AYMARA	PYJAMA	EDWARD	VIZARD
GAUZES	NUZZLE	BAHAMA	ROXANA	ERRAND	WIZARD
GEEZER	PUZZLE	BALATA	SAHARA	EXPAND	******
GLAZED	SIZZLE	BANANA	SAMARA	GERALD	---A-E
GLAZER	ZIZZLE	BEMATA	SATARA	GERARD	******
GLAZES	******	CABALA	SOMATA	HAZARD	ABLAZE
GLOZED	---ZO-	CABANA	SONATA	HERALD	ABRADE
GLOZES	******	CANADA	SQUAMA	HOLARD	ACUATE
GRAZED	AMAZON	CASABA	STRATA	HOWARD	ADNATE
GRAZER	BENZOL	CASAVA	TIRANA	INBAND	AERATE
GRAZES	BLAZON	CICADA	ZANANA	INLAID	AFLAME
GRIZEL	BORZOI	CICALA	ZAPATA	INLAND	AFRAME
JAZZED	BRAZOS	CLOACA	ZENANA	INWARD	AGNATE
JAZZER	EPIZOA	ERRATA	******	ISLAND	AGRAFE
JAZZES	MATZOS	ESPANA	---A-B	LIGAND	ALKANE
MAIZES	MATZOT	GEMARA	******	LIZARD	ALSACE
MIZZEN	MEZZOS	GOTAMA	BEDAUB	MARAUD	AMBAGE
PANZER	PODZOL	GUIANA	BICARB	ONWARD	ANLACE
PRIZED	QUEZON	GUYANA		OSWALD	ANLAGE
PRIZER	SEIZOR	HAVANA		PETARD	ANSATE

ARCADE	DONATE	LANATE	POTAGE	UNMADE	SERAPH
ARCANE	DOSAGE	LAVAGE	POTALE	UNMAKE	SHEATH
AUBADE	DOTAGE	LEGATE	PUPATE	UNSAFE	SIWASH
AURATE	EFFACE	LENAPE	RAVAGE	UPDATE	SPLASH
AVIATE	EMPALE	LIGATE	REBATE	UPTAKE	SQUASH
AYEAYE	ENCAGE	LINAGE	REFACE	URBANE	STRATH
BECAME	ENCASE	LIPASE	REGALE	UREASE	TERAPH
BEHAVE	ENFACE	LOBATE	RELATE	VACATE	THRASH
BERATE	ENGAGE	LOCALE	REMADE	VALATE	UNLASH
BETAKE	ENLACE	LOCATE	REMAKE	VISAGE	WABASH
BEWARE	ENRAGE	LOVAGE	RESALE	VIVACE	WREATH
BINATE	EQUATE	LUNATE	RETAKE	VOYAGE	******
BORAGE	ERGATE	LUXATE	ROTATE	WATAPE	---A-I
BORANE	ESCAPE	MADAME	ROXANE	ZONATE	******
BORATE	ESTATE	MALATE	ROYALE	ZOUAVE	ALFAKI
BOVATE	ETHANE	MANAGE	RRHAGE	******	ALKALI
BUTANE	EXHALE	MENACE	RUBACE	---A-F	AMBARI
BYLANE	FACADE	MENAGE	RUGATE	******	ARGALI
BYNAME	FEMALE	METAGE	SARAPE	BEHALF	BIHARI
CANAPE	FINALE	MILAGE	SAVAGE	PILAFF	BONACI
CARAFE	FIXATE	MIRAGE	SAVATE	SCLAFF	HAWAII
CARATE	FORAGE	MOHAVE	SCRAPE	******	MALAWI
CERATE	GARAGE	MOJAVE	SEDATE	---A-G	PEDATI
CESARE	GREASE	MORALE	SENATE	******	SAFARI
CETANE	GREAVE	MUTATE	SERAPE	GOBANG	SALAMI
CLEAVE	GYRATE	NEGATE	SESAME	PARANG	SOMALI
COMATE	HECATE	NONAGE	SEWAGE	PINANG	SOUARI
COWAGE	HEXANE	OBLATE	SHEAVE	SATANG	STRATI
CREASE	HOMAGE	OCTANE	SILAGE	SPRANG	TALARI
CREATE	HORACE	OCTAVE	SLEAVE	******	TULADI
CUBAGE	HUMANE	OHMAGE	SOCAGE	---A-H	VASARI
CURARE	ICEAXE	OLEATE	SOLACE	******	WAHABI
CURATE	IDEATE	OPIATE	SPLAKE	ARMAGH	******
DAMAGE	IGNACE	ORNATE	SQUARE	ATTACH	---A-K
DEBASE	IMPALE	PALACE	STRAFE	BLEACH	******
DEBATE	INCAGE	PALATE	STRAKE	BREACH	ACKACK
DECADE	INCASE	PARADE	TAMALE	BREATH	ARRACK
DECANE	INHALE	PAVANE	TENACE	BROACH	ATTACK
DECARE	INLACE	PEDATE	TIRADE	BYPATH	BYTALK
DEFACE	INMATE	PELAGE	TISANE	CALASH	CARACK
DEFAME	INNATE	PESADE	TOWAGE	DETACH	DAMASK
DEGAGE	INSANE	PHRASE	TUBATE	ENCASH	DEBARK
DEGAME	INTAKE	PILATE	ULLAGE	PARAPH	EMBANK
DEKARE	INVADE	PIPAGE	UNCAGE	PESACH	EMBARK
DELATE	IODATE	PIRATE	UNCASE	PLEACH	HIJACK
DERATE	JUGATE	PLEASE	UNEASE	POTASH	IMBARK
DILATE	KARATE	POMACE	UNLACE	PREACH	IMPARK
DOGAPE	KINASE	POMADE	UNLADE	REHASH	MOHAWK

NEWARK	ORGASM	MIKADO	ALTARS	CORALS	GROATS
POLACK	SALAAM	MONACO	ALVANS	CRAALS	HAMALS
REMARK	******	NAVAHO	ALWAYS	CREAKS	HARASS
SHRANK	---A-N	NAVAJO	ANNALS	CREAMS	HEXADS
SQUAWK	******	NEMATO	APPALS	CROAKS	HIRAMS
THWACK	ATTAIN	OCTAVO	ARGALS	CROATS	HOGANS
UNMASK	BATAAN	ORGANO	ARIANS	CUBANS	HUMANS
UNPACK	CANAAN	PALAEO	ARRAYS	CYCADS	IBEAMS
UNTACK	COCAIN	POTATO	ARYANS	CYMARS	IDEALS
******	DERAIN	REBATO	ASIANS	DAMANS	IMPASS
---A-L	DETAIN	ROBALO	ASSAIS	DANAUS	INLAWS
******	DOMAIN	RUBATO	ASSAYS	DEBARS	INLAYS
AGNAIL	FUSAIN	SOLANO	ATTARS	DECALS	ISAACS
APPALL	GAWAIN	SOMATO	AUDADS	DECAYS	JAPANS
ASSAIL	IMPAWN	TAPALO	BAGASS	DEDANS	JIHADS
AZRAEL	JOHANN	TERATO	BAHAIS	DELAYS	JONAHS
BEFALL	LORAIN	TOBAGO	BELAYS	DEWANS	JORAMS
BEWAIL	OBTAIN	TOMATO	BLEAKS	DINAHS	JUDAHS
DERAIL	ORDAIN	VIRAGO	BLEARS	DINARS	JURATS
DETAIL	PAPAIN	******	BLEATS	DIVANS	KARATS
ENDALL	REGAIN	---A-P	BLOATS	DIWANS	KAVASS
ENTAIL	REMAIN	******	BOGANS	DREADS	KAYAKS
HAMAUL	RETAIN	DECAMP	BOYARS	DREAMS	KNEADS
INHAUL	SPRAIN	ENCAMP	BREADS	DRYADS	KODAKS
INWALL	STRAIN	ESCARP	BREAKS	DUCATS	KRAALS
ISRAEL	******	REVAMP	BREAMS	EDGARS	KULAKS
JEZAIL	---A-O	UNHASP	BRIARS	EGGARS	LANAIS
NOBALL	******	******	BROADS	EMBARS	LAZARS
ONFALL	BAMAKO	---A-R	BUBALS	EMBAYS	LILACS
OXTAIL	CATALO	******	BURANS	EPHAHS	LOCALS
RECALL	CERATO	AFFAIR	BYLAWS	EQUALS	LOTAHS
RETAIL	CYRANO	ALTAIR	BYPASS	ESSAYS	MACAWS
SCRAWL	DORADO	BAZAAR	BYWAYS	ETHANS	MADAMS
SEWALL	DYNAMO	ECLAIR	CABALS	FARADS	MALAYS
SPRAWL	GAZABO	IMPAIR	CACAOS	FEUARS	MEDALS
SQUALL	GITANO	MIDAIR	CALAIS	FINALS	MEGASS
THRALL	HEMATO	MOHAIR	CAMASS	FLEAMS	METALS
******	HEPATO	REPAIR	CANALS	FLOATS	MOLARS
---A-M	JUDAEO	UNFAIR	CARATS	FORAYS	MONADS
******	KAKAPO	UNHAIR	CASALS	FREAKS	MORALS
BALAAM	KERATO	******	CEDARS	FRIARS	MORASS
BECALM	LAPARO	---A-S	CHEATS	GLEAMS	MORAYS
CHIASM	LAVABO	******	CHIAUS	GLEANS	MURALS
COPALM	LEGATO	ABRAMS	CIGARS	GLOATS	NAIADS
DISARM	MACACO	ADDAMS	CLEANS	GONADS	NASALS
EMBALM	MALACO	ALLANS	CLEARS	GORALS	NAWABS
IMBALM	MEGALO	ALLAYS	CLEATS	GREATS	NOMADS
NAPALM	MELANO	ALMAHS	CLOAKS	GROANS	NOPALS

NOWAYS	SERAIS	TRIALS	HOBART	AWEARY	SUDARY
OCEANS	SHEARS	TWEAKS	IMPACT	BIGAMY	SUGARY
OCTADS	SHOALS	UBOATS	IMPART	BINARY	SWEATY
OREADS	SHOATS	UMIAKS	INFANT	BLEARY	TELARY
ORGANS	SIMARS	UNBARS	INTACT	BOTANY	TETANY
OSCANS	SITARS	UNCAPS	JURANT	CANARY	TREATY
OSCARS	SIZARS	UNHATS	KUWAIT	CREAKY	TWEAKY
PAEANS	SKEANS	UNLAYS	LEVANT	CREAMY	UNEASY
PAGANS	SMEARS	UNMANS	MOZART	CREASY	UNWARY
PALAIS	SNEAKS	UNSAYS	MUTANT	CROAKY	VAGARY
PAPAWS	SOLANS	VICARS	NATANT	CURACY	VOTARY
PAVANS	SONARS	VITALS	OBLAST	DATARY	ZONARY
PECANS	SOWARS	VOCALS	OCTANT	DENARY	******
PEDALS	SPEAKS	WATAPS	OPTANT	DIGAMY	---A-Z
PEKANS	SPEARS	WHEALS	PEDANT	DREAMY	******
PETALS	SPLATS	WHEATS	PLIANT	DREARY	ERSATZ
PHIALS	SPLAYS	WIGANS	RECANT	FLOATY	******
PILAFS	SPRAGS	WREAKS	RECAST	FREAKY	---B-A
PLEADS	SPRATS	XYLANS	REDACT	FRIARY	******
PLEATS	SPRAYS	******	REPAST	GALAXY	ARABIA
PSHAWS	SQUABS	---A-T	SAVANT	GLEAMY	BALBOA
PYRANS	SQUADS	******	SECANT	GREASY	BARBRA
QUEANS	SQUATS	ABLAUT	SEJANT	HILARY	GAMBIA
RADARS	SQUAWS	ABWATT	SONANT	HORARY	JERBOA
RAJABS	STEAKS	AGHAST	STRAIT	INFAMY	LAMBDA
RAJAHS	STEALS	ARRANT	STUART	LEGACY	LISBOA
RATALS	STEAMS	ASKANT	TENANT	LITANY	OJIBWA
RAYAHS	STOATS	ASLANT	THWART	LUNACY	PHOBIA
RECAPS	STRAPS	BASALT	TRUANT	MALADY	ROBBIA
REDANS	STRASS	BESANT	TYBALT	MILADY	SERBIA
RELAYS	STRAWS	BEZANT	TYRANT	NONARY	TERBIA
REMANS	STRAYS	BREAST	UMLAUT	NOTARY	ZAMBIA
REPASS	SUBAHS	BRYANT	UPCAST	PAPACY	******
REPAYS	SUGARS	BYPAST	VACANT	PIRACY	---B-B
RIVALS	SUMACS	COBALT	VOLANT	QUEASY	******
RIYALS	SURAHS	DECANT	******	ROMANY	BAOBAB
ROMANS	SUSANS	DEPART	---A-U	ROSARY	HUBBUB
ROWANS	SWEARS	DESALT	******	ROTARY	MAHBUB
ROYALS	SWEATS	DICAST	XANADU	RRHAGY	******
SALADS	TATARS	DREAMT	******	SALARY	---B-C
SARAHS	TICALS	DYNAST	---A-Y	SENARY	******
SCRAGS	TITANS	ENRAPT	******	SHOALY	AMEBIC
SCRAMS	TOMANS	ERRANT	ABBACY	SLEAZY	ARABIC
SCRAPS	TORAHS	EXTANT	ALBANY	SMEARY	BOMBIC
SEBATS	TOTALS	GALACT	AMBARY	SNEAKY	CHEBEC
SEDANS	TREADS	GIGANT	ANGARY	STEADY	IAMBIC
SEPALS	TREATS	GOCART	APIARY	STEAMY	LIMBIC
SERACS	TRIADS	GOKART	AVIARY	STRAWY	NIOBIC

PHOBIC	ROBBED	LAMBIE	******	LISBON	KHYBER
QUEBEC	RUBBED	LIABLE	---B-I	NUBBIN	LIMBER
TAMBAC	SINBAD	MARBLE	******	RABBIN	LOBBER
TOMBAC	SOBBED	MUMBLE	CIMBRI	REUBEN	LUBBER
******	TABBED	NIBBLE		RIBBON	LUMBAR
---B-D	TOMBED	NIMBLE	---B-K	TURBAN	LUMBER
******	TUBBED	NOBBLE	******	******	MEMBER
AIRBED	TURBID	NUBBLE	CHABUK	---B-O	MOBBER
BARBED	WEBBED	PEBBLE	CHIBUK	******	NUMBER
BIBBED	WOMBED	RABBLE	DYBBUK	BAMBOO	PROBER
BOBBED	******	RAMBLE	******	BILBAO	ROBBER
BOMBED	---B-E	ROBBIE	---B-L	BOOBOO	RUBBER
BRIBED	******	ROUBLE	******	GABBRO	SAMBUR
BULBED	ALIBLE	RUBBLE	ARABEL	PUEBLO	SOMBER
COMBED	AMEBAE	RUMBLE	ATABAL	******	TIMBER
CUBBED	ARABLE	SEABEE	BARBEL	---B-R	TUBBER
CURBED	BABBIE	SOMBRE	BULBEL	******	WILBER
DABBED	BABBLE	STABLE	BULBIL	BARBER	WILBUR
DAUBED	BARBIE	SUABLE	BULBUL	BERBER	YABBER
DAYBED	BAUBLE	THEBAE	CORBEL	BIBBER	******
DIBBED	BOBBIE	TIMBRE	CYMBAL	BOBBER	---B-S
DUBBED	BOBBLE	TREBLE	DIOBOL	BOMBER	******
FARBAD	BUBBLE	TUMBLE	GAMBOL	BRIBER	ADOBES
FIBBED	BUMBLE	UNABLE	GERBIL	BULBAR	ALIBIS
FOBBED	BURBLE	USABLE	GLOBAL	CAMBER	AMEBAS
FORBID	BYEBYE	VIABLE	HERBAL	COBBER	ANABAS
GABBED	COBBLE	WABBLE	ISABEL	COMBER	ANUBIS
GARBED	CORBIE	WAMBLE	ISOBEL	CUMBER	BOBBYS
GIBBED	DABBLE	WARBLE	JUMBAL	DABBER	BOMBES
GLOBED	DEBBIE	WIMBLE	SYMBOL	DAUBER	BRIBES
HOTBED	DIBBLE	WOBBLE	TIMBAL	DIBBER	CEIBAS
JABBED	DOABLE	ZOMBIE	TRIBAL	DISBAR	COMBOS
JIBBED	DOUBLE	******	TWIBIL	DOBBER	DEBBYS
JOBBED	EDIBLE	---B-G	VERBAL	DUNBAR	DOUBTS
KERBED	ENABLE	******	******	DURBAR	EREBUS
LAMBED	FEEBLE	BEDBUG	---B-N	FERBER	FLYBYS
LIMBED	FIMBLE	DORBUG	******	FIBBER	GLEBES
LOBBED	FOIBLE	GASBAG	BOBBIN	GABBER	GLOBES
MOBBED	FUMBLE	HUMBUG	BONBON	GAMBIR	GREBES
MORBID	GABBLE	KITBAG	CARBON	GHEBER	GUMBOS
NABBED	GAMBLE	LIEBIG	CORBAN	GIBBER	HOBBES
NIBBED	GARBLE	MAYBUG	DOBBIN	GOOBER	IAMBUS
NOBBED	GOBBLE	RAGBAG	DUBBIN	HARBOR	KRUBIS
NUMBED	HOBBLE	REDBUG	DURBAN	HUMBER	LESBOS
OUTBID	HOMBRE	TEABAG	GIBBON	ISOBAR	LIBBYS
PROBED	HUMBLE	******	GLOBIN	JABBER	LIMBUS
REDBUD	JUMBLE	---B-H	GRABEN	JIBBER	MAMBAS
RIBBED	KIBBLE	******	HARBIN	JOBBER	MAMBOS
		CASBAH			
		JUBBAH			

NIMBUS	HOTBOX	EJECTA	BOCCIE	LITCHI	MECCAN
ORIBIS	ICEBOX	EXACTA	BOUCLE	TRICHI	NIACIN
OVIBOS	******	FASCIA	BROCHE	******	OILCAN
PLEBES	---B-Y	FULCRA	BUNCHE	---C-L	TINCAN
PROBES	******	MARCIA	CHICLE	******	TOUCAN
RABBIS	BLEBBY	MERCIA	CIRCLE	APICAL	TUSCAN
RUMBAS	BOMBAY	******	CLICHE	BUCCAL	VULCAN
SAMBAS	BUBBLY	---C-C	CLOCHE	CANCEL	ZIRCON
SAMBOS	CARBOY	******	CRECHE	CARCEL	******
SCUBAS	CHUBBY	CALCIC	DOUCHE	COCCAL	---C-O
STUBBS	COBBLY	IPECAC	DULCIE	DISCAL	******
THEBES	COWBOY	ZINCIC	FESCUE	EPICAL	AFLCIO
TRIBES	CRABBY	******	FIACRE	FAECAL	ALECTO
YERBAS	DAUBRY	---C-D	FLECHE	FAUCAL	GAUCHO
ZOMBIS	DAYBOY	******	GAUCHE	FISCAL	NUNCIO
******	DOUBLY	BRACED	GRACIE	GLYCOL	PANCHO
---B-T	DRABLY	COCCID	ICICLE	MARCEL	PONCHO
******	DUMBLY	DANCED	MISCUE	MESCAL	PROCTO
BARBET	FEEBLY	DEICED	MUSCAE	PARCEL	PSYCHO
BURBOT	FLABBY	DEUCED	MUSCLE	PASCAL	RANCHO
COMBAT	GLIBLY	EDUCED	ORACLE	PENCEL	REECHO
GAMBIT	GRUBBY	FARCED	PARCAE	PENCIL	SHACKO
GIBBET	HUMBLY	FENCED	PLICAE	RASCAL	STUCCO
GOBBET	KNOBBY	FORCED	PROCNE	TERCEL	TRICHO
HAGBUT	LOWBOY	GRACED	PSYCHE	THECAL	******
HENBIT	NIMBLY	LANCED	RESCUE	TINCAL	---C-P
KRUBUT	NUBBLY	MINCED	ROSCOE	******	******
RABBET	NUMBLY	PIECED	ROTCHE	---C-M	EGGCUP
RABBIT	PEBBLY	PLACED	ROUCHE	******	EYECUP
SABBAT	POTBOY	PLACID	SEICHE	CAECUM	HICCUP
SHEBAT	REDBAY	PRICED	SIECLE	CIRCUM	HUBCAP
SORBET	SCABBY	RANCID	SPACAE	DRACHM	ICECAP
TIDBIT	SHABBY	SAUCED	SPECIE	NONCOM	MADCAP
TITBIT	SNOBBY	SLICED	STACIE	TALCUM	MOBCAP
TURBIT	STABLY	SPACED	STACTE	******	MUDCAP
TURBOT	STUBBY	SPICED	THECAE	---C-N	REDCAP
TWOBIT	TOMBOY	TALCED	TOUCHE	******	SKYCAP
WOMBAT	USABLY	TOMCOD	TRACHE	ASHCAN	TEACUP
******	WABBLY	TRACED	TROCHE	BEACON	TOECAP
---B-W	WAMBLY	TRICED	******	CANCAN	******
******	WOBBLY	VISCID	---C-F	DEACON	---C-R
FOGBOW	******	VOICED	******	DECCAN	******
SUNBOW	---C-A	WINCED	UNICEF	DUNCAN	BOXCAR
******	******	ZINCED	******	FALCON	BRACER
---B-X	ACACIA	******	---C-I	FLACON	CALCAR
******	ALICIA	---C-E	******	GARCON	CANCER
HATBOX	CHACMA	AMECHE	BRACHI	GASCON	CONCUR
HAYBOX	CONCHA	APACHE	CHICHI	MASCON	DANCER

DEICER	CHUCKS	GUACOS	STACYS	******	******
FARCER	CIRCUS	HANCES	STICKS	---C-X	---D-B
FENCER	CISCOS	HOICKS	STOCKS	******	******
FORCER	CLACKS	IBICES	SULCUS	COCCYX	SERDAB
GROCER	CLICKS	IOLCUS	TINCTS	******	SUBDEB
JUICER	CLOCKS	JOYCES	TRACES	---C-Y	******
LANCER	CLUCKS	JUICES	TRACKS	******	---D-C
LASCAR	COCCUS	JUNCOS	TRACTS	BEACHY	******
MERCER	CONCHS	KNACKS	TRICES	BEECHY	ACIDIC
MINCER	CRACKS	KNOCKS	TRICKS	BISCAY	AMIDIC
PIECER	CRICKS	LANCES	TRUCES	BITCHY	ANODIC
PLACER	CROCKS	MARCOS	TRUCKS	BLOCKY	BARDIC
RANCOR	CROCUS	MARCUS	TURCOS	BOTCHY	DYADIC
SAUCER	CRUCES	MECCAS	VINCES	BRACHY	GEODIC
SLICER	CUSCUS	MINCES	VISCUS	BUNCHY	HERDIC
SOCCER	DANCES	MULCTS	VOICES	CATCHY	IRIDIC
SPACER	DEICES	NANCYS	WHACKS	CONCHY	NORDIC
SPICER	DEUCES	NIECES	WINCES	CRACKY	RHODIC
SUCCOR	DISCUS	ORACHS	WRACKS	CROCKY	SYNDIC
TEUCER	DUNCES	OUNCES	WRECKS	DESCRY	******
TRACER	EDICTS	PERCYS	YOICKS	FLOCKY	---D-D
TRICAR	EDUCES	PHOCIS	YUCCAS	LEACHY	******
TROCAR	EDUCTS	PIECES	******	OUTCRY	ABIDED
WINCER	EJECTS	PISCES	---C-T	PATCHY	ALIDAD
******	ELECTS	PLACES	******	PEACHY	AOUDAD
---C-S	ENACTS	PLACKS	AVOCET	PITCHY	BAGDAD
******	EPACTS	PLUCKS	BOBCAT	PLUCKY	BANDED
ABACAS	EPOCHS	PRECIS	BRECHT	POACHY	BARDED
ABACUS	ERECTS	PRICES	DULCET	POUCHY	BEADED
AEACUS	ERICHS	PRICKS	ELICIT	PUNCHY	BEDDED
ALICES	ERUCTS	QUACKS	FAUCET	STICKY	BENDED
AMICES	EVICTS	REACTS	LANCET	STOCKY	BLADED
APICES	EXACTS	REICHS	MASCOT	TETCHY	BONDED
ARECAS	FAECES	SAUCES	MUSCAT	TOUCHY	BUDDED
BAUCIS	FARCES	SHACKS	PLACET	TRACHY	CANDID
BLACKS	FASCES	SHOCKS	SNOCAT	TRICKY	CARDED
BLOCKS	FAUCES	SHUCKS	TERCET	WINCEY	CAUDAD
BRACES	FENCES	SLACKS	TIPCAT	ZINCKY	CHIDED
BRACTS	FLACKS	SLICES	TOMCAT	******	CORDED
BRICKS	FLECKS	SLICKS	TRICOT	---D-A	CURDED
BRUCES	FLICKS	SMACKS	******	******	DEEDED
BUNCOS	FLOCKS	SMOCKS	---C-U	ACADIA	DOODAD
CALCES	FORCES	SNACKS	******	ACEDIA	ELIDED
CAUCUS	FRACAS	SNICKS	MANCHU	BUDDHA	ELUDED
CHECKS	FROCKS	SPACES	******	CANDIA	ERODED
CHICKS	GLACES	SPECKS	---C-W	EXEDRA	EVADED
CHICOS	GLACIS	SPICES	******	SANDRA	EXUDED
CHOCKS	GRACES	STACKS	CRACOW	STADIA	FENDED
			MOSCOW	TUNDRA	
			SEACOW		

FEUDED	SODDED	DUNDEE	******	******	LEYDEN
FOLDED	SORDID	FIDDLE	---D-G	---D-M	LINDEN
FORDED	SPADED	FLEDGE	******	******	LONDON
FUNDED	TEDDED	FONDLE	FOGDOG	ANADEM	LOUDEN
GADDED	TENDED	FONDUE	LAPDOG	BELDAM	MADDEN
GELDED	TRADED	FRIDGE	REDDOG	CONDOM	MAIDEN
GILDED	VENDED	FUDDLE	SEADOG	DIADEM	MANDAN
GIRDED	VOIDED	GIRDLE	SUNDOG	DUMDUM	MIDDEN
GLIDED	WADDED	GRUDGE	******	GODDAM	MILDEN
GOADED	WARDED	HANDLE	---D-H	IBIDEM	PARDON
GRADED	WEDDED	HEDDLE	******	RANDOM	RANDAN
GRIDED	WEEDED	HUDDLE	HOWDAH	SELDOM	REDDEN
GUIDED	WELDED	HURDLE	KEDDAH	TANDEM	RIDDEN
HANDED	WENDED	KIDDIE	PURDAH	WISDOM	SADDEN
HEADED	WINDED	KINDLE	WHIDAH	******	SODDEN
HEEDED	WOADED	LADDIE	WHYDAH	---D-N	SUDDEN
HERDED	WOODED	MEDDLE	******	******	SWEDEN
HOODED	WORDED	MIDDLE	---D-I	ABADAN	TENDON
HORDED	YARDED	MUDDLE	******	AMIDIN	VERDIN
KIDDED	******	NEEDLE	DENDRI	AVIDIN	VERDUN
LANDED	---D-E	NODDLE	GANDHI	BIDDEN	WARDEN
LARDED	******	NOODLE	QUADRI	BURDEN	WOODEN
LAUDED		PADDLE	SANDHI	CAMDEN	******
LEADED	BEADLE	PEDDLE	******	CORDON	---D-O
LIDDED	BENDEE	PIDDLE	---D-K	DARDAN	******
LOADED	BIRDIE	PLEDGE	******	DEADEN	CARDIO
LORDED	BOODLE	POODLE	DIKDIK	DRYDEN	DENDRO
MADDED	BRIDGE	PUDDLE	MARDUK	DUODEN	HOODOO
MELDED	BRIDIE	RADDLE	******	GARDEN	KOODOO
MENDED	BRIDLE	REDDLE	---D-L	GOLDEN	STUDIO
MINDED	BUDDLE	RIDDLE	******	GORDON	VOODOO
MISDID	BUNDLE	RUDDLE	ALUDEL	GRADIN	******
MOLDED	BURDIE	RUNDLE	AMIDOL	GUIDON	---D-P
MUDDED	CADDIE	SADDLE	APODAL	GULDEN	******
NEEDED	CANDLE	SLEDGE	BORDEL	HAGDON	HOLDUP
NODDED	CAUDLE	SLUDGE	BRIDAL	HAMDEN	MENDIP
OUTDID	CODDLE	SMUDGE	CAUDAL	HARDEN	WINDUP
PADDED	COODLE	STODGE	CREDAL	HEADON	******
PENDED	CRADLE	SUBDUE	DAEDAL	HENDON	---D-R
PODDED	CUDDIE	SUNDAE	FEUDAL	HIDDEN	******
PRIDED	CUDDLE	TODDLE	HANDEL	HODDEN	ABIDER
RAIDED	CURDLE	TRUDGE	KENDAL	HOIDEN	BALDER
REEDED	DADDLE	VENDEE	MENDEL	HOYDEN	BEDDER
RENDED	DANDLE	VENDUE	RANDAL	IBADAN	BENDER
RIDDED	DAWDLE	WADDLE	RONDEL	JORDAN	BIDDER
SANDED	DIDDLE	WANDLE	SANDAL	LARDON	BINDER
SEEDED	DOODLE	WIDDIE	SENDAL	LEADEN	BOLDER
SHADED	DREDGE		VANDAL	LEADIN	BONDER
	DRUDGE				

BORDER	LIEDER	YONDER	LINDAS	SHADOW	SLUDGY
BUDDER	LOADER	ZUIDER	MANDYS	SUNDEW	SMUDGY
CANDOR	LOUDER	ZUYDER	MAUDES	WINDOW	STODGY
CARDER	MADDER	******	OXIDES	******	SUNDAY
CHIDER	MENDER	---D-S	PADDYS	---D-X	SUNDRY
CINDER	MILDER	******	PANDAS	******	TAWDRY
CODDER	MINDER	ABIDES	PINDUS	CAUDEX	THADDY
COLDER	MOLDER	ABODES	PRIDES	SPADIX	WADDLY
CONDOR	MUDDER	ABYDOS	PRUDES	******	WILDLY
CORDER	MURDER	AMIDES	RHODAS	---D-Y	WOODSY
CRUDER	NEEDER	ANODES	RHODES	******	******
DANDER	NODDER	ASIDES	RODDYS	ACIDLY	---E-A
DEODAR	PANDER	BARDES	RONDOS	AGEDLY	******
DINDER	PINDAR	BLADES	SANDYS	AIRDRY	ACAENA
DODDER	POLDER	BRIDES	SHADES	ARIDLY	AMOEBA
EVADER	PONDER	CADDIS	SLIDES	AVIDLY	ANGELA
FEEDER	POWDER	CHIDES	SPADES	BALDLY	ARBELA
FENDER	RAIDER	CINDYS	SUEDES	BAWDRY	ATHENA
FEODOR	READER	CLYDES	SWEDES	BENDAY	BODEGA
FINDER	REDDER	CREDOS	TEDDYS	BOLDLY	CALESA
FODDER	RENDER	DIODES	THADAS	CLODDY	CAMERA
FOLDER	RUDDER	ELIDES	THEDAS	COLDLY	CATENA
FONDER	SADDER	ELUDES	TILDES	CORDAY	CHAETA
GADDER	SANDER	EPODES	TRADES	CUDDLY	CINEMA
GANDER	SEEDER	ERODES	TRUDYS	DEADLY	CODEIA
GENDER	SENDER	ETUDES	TSADES	FLEDGY	DODECA
GILDER	SIDDUR	EVADES	VELDTS	FONDLY	ECZEMA
GIRDER	SIRDAR	EXODUS	WALDOS	FREDDY	ENTERA
GLIDER	SLIDER	EXUDES	WANDAS	FRIDAY	EUREKA
GRADER	SOLDER	FREDAS	WENDYS	GLADLY	FANEGA
GUIDER	SONDER	FUNDUS	******	GOODBY	FRIEDA
HARDER	SPADER	GEODES	---D-T	GOODLY	GALENA
HEADER	SPIDER	GILDAS	******	HARDLY	GENERA
HEEDER	SUNDER	GLADES	AMIDST	HEYDAY	GENEVA
HERDER	TEDDER	GLADYS	BANDIT	KINDLY	HELENA
HINDER	TENDER	GLEDES	CREDIT	LAYDAY	HYGEIA
HOLDER	TINDER	GLIDES	DAUDET	LEWDLY	LATERA
ISADOR	TRADER	GRADES	PUNDIT	LORDLY	NOVENA
ISIDOR	VEADAR	GRADUS	REEDIT	LOUDLY	OEDEMA
KIDDER	VENDER	GRIDES	SYNDET	MAYDAY	OEPEMA
KINDER	VENDOR	GUIDES	******	MIDDAY	PAMELA
LADDER	WANDER	HILDAS	---D-U	MILDLY	PESETA
LANDER	WARDER	HINDUS	******	MONDAY	RESEDA
LARDER	WEEDER	HORDES	AMADOU	OFFDAY	ROWENA
LAUDER	WELDER	HYADES	LANDAU	PAYDAY	SCHEMA
LEADER	WILDER	IMIDES	******	PUDDLY	SCLERA
LENDER	WINDER	IRIDES	---D-W	RAGDAY	SENECA
LEWDER	WONDER	LEUDES	******	SHODDY	SERENA
			MEADOW		
			MILDEW		

SISERA	PUREED	FREEZE	******	BEFELL	******
TELEGA	RAZEED	FRIEZE	---E-F	BOREAL	---E-N
TERESA	RESEND	GALEAE	******	CAVELL	******
TOPEKA	SCREED	GAMETE	HEREOF	CEREAL	AEGEAN
WOMERA	SHIELD	GISELE	ITSELF	CINEOL	AILEEN
******	SHREWD	GREECE	MYSELF	CUNEAL	ANDEAN
---E-B	SPREAD	GREENE	******	FOVEAL	ARLEEN
******	TEHEED	GRIEVE	---E-H	GESELL	ASTERN
ADVERB	THREAD	IMPEDE	******	LINEAL	AUGEAN
SUPERB	THREED	INDENE	AFRESH	LOVELL	BALEEN
******	TINEID	INHERE	BREECH	LOWELL	BEMEAN
---E-C	UNBEND	KETENE	DALETH	LUTEAL	BOLEYN
******	UNLEAD	LORENE	ENMESH	MICELL	CAREEN
APNEIC	UNREAD	MANEGE	IMMESH	ORDEAL	CASEIN
******	UPHELD	MISERE	INMESH	ORWELL	CASERN
---E-D	VISEED	MYCETE	JOSEPH	OSTEAL	CAVEIN
******	******	NICENE	LAMECH	PINEAL	CAVERN
ADDEND	---E-E	OCREAE	SPEECH	POWELL	CODEIN
AENEID	******	PALEAE	THRESH	REPEAL	COMEON
AFIELD	ACCEDE	PHOEBE	ZIBETH	RESELL	DECERN
AGREED	ACHENE	PINENE	******	RETELL	DEMEAN
ANTEED	ADHERE	PYRENE	---E-I	REVEAL	DEVEIN
APPEND	ALKENE	QUAERE	******	ROSEAL	DOREEN
ASCEND	ALLEGE	RACEME	ASTERI	SEWELL	DUDEEN
ATTEND	ALLELE	RECEDE	EPHEBI	SQUEAL	EILEEN
AUGEND	AMPERE	REDEYE	GENESI	UNREAL	EXTERN
AXSEED	ANNEXE	RENEGE	KINESI	UNREEL	FADEIN
BEHEAD	APIECE	RETENE	SILENI	UNSEAL	GIDEON
BEHELD	ARLENE	REVERE	YEMENI	UNVEIL	GOVERN
COOEED	ATHENE	SCHEME	******	UNWELL	HEREIN
DEFEND	BAREGE	SECEDE	---E-K	******	HEREON
DEPEND	BIREME	SELENE	******	---E-M	INTERN
EMCEED	BREEZE	SEMELE	BEDECK	******	JUDEAN
ENNEAD	CHEESE	SEMEME	COPECK	AGLEAM	KOREAN
EXCEED	COHERE	SERENE	KOPECK	ANSELM	LATEEN
EXPEND	CREESE	SEVERE	LUBECK	BESEEM	LOREEN
EXTEND	CYBELE	SLEEVE	REBECK	ESTEEM	LOVEIN
FAGEND	CYMENE	SNEEZE	SCREAK	LUTEUM	MODERN
FRIEND	CYRENE	SPHENE	SQUEAK	LYCEUM	MOREEN
GILEAD	DELETE	SPHERE	STREAK	MUSEUM	NOREEN
IMPEND	EFFETE	STEEVE	ZEBECK	PHLEGM	ORCEIN
INDEED	ENTERE	TAXEME	******	PILEUM	OSSEIN
INTEND	EOCENE	TERETE	---E-L	REDEEM	PIGEON
JEREED	EOGENE	TEVERE	******	SCREAM	POTEEN
LEGEND	ESSENE	THIEVE	ANNEAL	STREAM	SABEAN
NEREID	EUGENE	TUYERE	APNEAL	UNSEAM	SATEEN
OFFEND	FLEECE	WHEEZE	APPEAL		SCREEN
OSTEND	FOVEAE	XYLENE	AWHEEL		SECERN

SEREIN	SIDERO	AGGERS	BONERS	CULETS	EXCELS
SEVERN	SPHENO	AGLETS	BOREAS	CUPELS	EXCESS
SINEON	SPLENO	AGREES	BORERS	CURERS	EXPELS
SOLEMN	STHENO	AIDERS	BOWELS	CUTEYS	FACERS
SPLEEN	TEREDO	ALDERS	BOWERS	DARERS	FACETS
STREWN	TOLEDO	ALIENS	BOXERS	DATERS	FAKERS
TAKEIN	TORERO	ALLENS	BREEDS	DAVEYS	FARERS
TAVERN	TUPELO	ALLEYS	BREEKS	DEFERS	FEVERS
TUREEN	TUXEDO	ALTERS	BRIEFS	DEREKS	FIBERS
UNHEWN	******	AMBERS	BRIERS	DETERS	FIFERS
UNSEEN	---E-P	AMIENS	BUYERS	DICERS	FILERS
VEREIN	******	ANGELS	CADETS	DIMERS	FILETS
WEDELN	ASLEEP	ANGERS	CALEBS	DINERS	FIRERS
WIGEON	LINEUP	APPELS	CAMELS	DIVERS	FIVERS
WIVERN	MADEUP	ARDEBS	CAMEOS	DIZENS	FIXERS
WYVERN	MAKEUP	ARIELS	CANERS	DONEES	FLEERS
******	PILEUP	ARMETS	CAPERS	DONETS	FLEETS
---E-O	TAKEUP	ARPENS	CARERS	DOSERS	FLIERS
******	TUNEUP	ARTELS	CARESS	DOTERS	FLYERS
ALBEDO	UPKEEP	ASKERS	CARETS	DOWELS	FOYERS
ANGELO	******	ASPENS	CATERS	DOWERS	FRIERS
ANTERO	---E-R	ASPERS	CEREUS	DOYENS	FRYERS
ASTERO	APPEAR	ASSESS	CHEEKS	DOZENS	FUSEES
BOLERO	ARREAR	ASSETS	CHEEPS	DRIERS	FUZEES
CHAETO	CAREER	ASTERS	CHEERS	DRYERS	GAGERS
CICERO	COHEIR	ATHENS	CHIEFS	DUPERS	GANEFS
COMEDO	DOGEAR	ATREUS	CIDERS	DURESS	GAPERS
DIDERO	ENDEAR	AUGERS	CIVETS	EASELS	GAVELS
DINERO	LINEAR	AUREUS	COLEUS	EATERS	GAZERS
ENTERO	METEOR	AWLESS	COMERS	EDSELS	GENETS
FOREGO	POSEUR	AZTECS	COMETS	EGGERS	GIBERS
GAMETO	REHEAR	BAGELS	CONEYS	EGRESS	GIMELS
GAZEBO	UNBEAR	BAKERS	COOEES	EGRETS	GLEETS
GRAECO	VENEER	BALERS	COOERS	ELDERS	GONERS
GYNECO	VOYEUR	BEDEWS	COOEYS	ELLENS	GREEDS
HERETO	******	BEGETS	CORERS	ELMERS	GREEKS
HETERO	---E-S	BERETS	COVERS	ELVERS	GREENS
HYMENO	******	BESETS	COVETS	EMBEDS	GREETS
INFERO	******	BETELS	COVEYS	EMBERS	GRUELS
KINETO	ABBESS	BEVELS	COWERS	EMCEES	HABEAS
LAREDO	ABBEYS	BEZELS	COZENS	EMEERS	HALERS
NONEGO	ABNERS	BICEPS	CREEDS	EMMETS	HAREMS
OSWEGO	ACCESS	BIDETS	CREEKS	ENGELS	HATERS
PHLEBO	ADDERS	BIPEDS	CREELS	ENTERS	HAVENS
PHRENO	ADEEMS	BITERS	CREEPS	ESKERS	HAVERS
POMELO	ADIEUS	BLEEDS	CRIERS	ESTERS	HAZELS
SCLERO	AEGEUS	BLUETS	CRUETS	ETHELS	HAZERS
SELENO	AENEAS	BOGEYS	CUBEBS	ETHERS	HELENS
					HEWERS

HIDERS	LINENS	OCHERS	QUEERS	SHEEPS	TOTERS
HIKERS	LINERS	OCTETS	RACERS	SHEERS	TOWELS
HIRERS	LITERS	OFFERS	RAKERS	SHEETS	TOWERS
HOMERS	LIVENS	OGLERS	RANEES	SHOERS	TOYERS
HONEYS	LIVERS	OGRESS	RATELS	SHREDS	TRIERS
HOTELS	LONERS	OILERS	RATERS	SHREWS	TUBERS
HOVELS	LOPERS	ONSETS	RAVELS	SINEWS	TUNERS
HOVERS	LOSERS	ORDERS	RAVENS	SIRENS	TWEEDS
HYMENS	LOVERS	ORIELS	RAVERS	SKIERS	TWEETS
IDLERS	LOWERS	ORMERS	RAZEES	SLEEKS	UDDERS
IMBEDS	LUGERS	OSIERS	REBECS	SLEEPS	ULCERS
IMPELS	LUMENS	OTHERS	REBELS	SLEETS	UMBELS
INFERS	LUNETS	OTTERS	RECESS	SNEERS	UMBERS
INKERS	LURERS	OUSELS	REFERS	SOBERS	UNLESS
INLETS	LYCEES	OUTERS	RENEES	SORELS	UNMEWS
INSETS	MABELS	OUZELS	RENEWS	SOWERS	UNPEGS
INTERS	MACERS	OWLETS	REPELS	SPEEDS	UPPERS
ISLETS	MAKERS	OWNERS	RESETS	SPIELS	UPSETS
ISSEIS	MAMEYS	PACERS	REVELS	SPIERS	URAEUS
JANETS	MASERS	PANELS	REVERS	SPREES	USHERS
JEWELS	MATEOS	PAPERS	REVETS	STEEDS	UTTERS
JEWESS	MATEYS	PARENS	RICERS	STEELS	VALETS
JOKERS	MAZERS	PARERS	RIDERS	STEEPS	VEXERS
JULEPS	MELEES	PAREUS	RIMERS	STEERS	VIPERS
JURELS	METERS	PATENS	RIPENS	STRESS	VIREOS
KARENS	MILERS	PATERS	RISERS	STREWS	VIXENS
KEVELS	MIMERS	PAVERS	RIVERS	SUPERS	VOMERS
KIBEIS	MINERS	PAWERS	RIVETS	SWEEPS	VOTERS
KNEELS	MISERS	PAYEES	RODEOS	SWEETS	VOWELS
KOPEKS	MITERS	PAYERS	ROGERS	SYCEES	VOWERS
LABELS	MIXERS	PELEUS	ROVERS	TAKERS	WADERS
LAGERS	MODELS	PETERS	ROWELS	TALERS	WAFERS
LAKERS	MONEYS	PEWEES	ROWERS	TAMERS	WAGERS
LAMEDS	MOPERS	PIKERS	RUBENS	TAPERS	WAKENS
LAPELS	MORELS	PILEUS	RULERS	TAWERS	WALERS
LASERS	MOSEYS	PIPERS	RUPEES	TAXERS	WATERS
LAVERS	MOTELS	PIPETS	SABERS	TEHEES	WAVERS
LAYERS	MOVERS	PLIERS	SAHEBS	TENETS	WAVEYS
LEGERS	MOWERS	POKERS	SAKERS	TEPEES	WEBERS
LEPERS	NAMERS	POSERS	SAVERS	TEREUS	WHEELS
LEVEES	NAVELS	POWERS	SAWERS	THREES	WIDENS
LEVELS	NEREIS	PREENS	SAYERS	TIGERS	WIPERS
LEVERS	NEWELS	PRIERS	SCREWS	TILERS	WIRERS
LIBELS	NIGELS	PROEMS	SEDERS	TIMERS	WIVERS
LIFERS	NISEIS	PRYERS	SEVENS	TOKENS	WIZENS
LIKENS	NOTERS	PULERS	SEVERS	TONERS	WOOERS
LIMENS	NOVELS	PUREES	SEWERS	TOPERS	XEBECS
LIMEYS	OBSESS	QUEENS	SHEENS	TOTEMS	XYLEMS

YAGERS	DEMENT	INFECT	REJECT	******	FREELY
YAMENS	DESERT	INFEST	RELENT	---E-U	GAIETY
YODELS	DETECT	INGEST	REPEAT	******	GAMELY
YOGEES	DETENT	INJECT	REPENT	BATEAU	GAYETY
YOKELS	DETEST	INSECT	RESEAT	BUREAU	GLEETY
ZEBECS	DEVEST	INSERT	RESECT	COTEAU	GREEDY
ZIBETS	DIGEST	INTENT	RESENT	GATEAU	HEREBY
******	DIRECT	INVENT	REVERT	JUNEAU	HERESY
---E-T	DIREST	INVERT	REVEST	MOREAU	HOMELY
******	DIVERT	INVEST	RIDENT	RESEAU	HUGELY
ABJECT	DIVEST	LAMENT	RIPEST	TELEDU	JEREMY
ABLEST	DOCENT	LAMEST	ROBERT	******	LAMELY
ABSENT	DRIEST	LATENT	RODENT	---E-X	LATELY
ACCENT	DRYEST	LATEST	RUDEST	******	LATELY
ACCEPT	EFFECT	LAXEST	RUPERT	ADIEUX	LIKELY
ADJECT	EGBERT	LOMENT	SAFEST	BAYEUX	LIVELY
ADVENT	ELBERT	LOWEST	SAGEST	POLEAX	LIVERY
ADVERT	ELDEST	LUCENT	SANEST	******	LONELY
AFFECT	EMMETT	MAYEST	SELECT	---E-Y	LOVELY
ALBEIT	ERNEST	MEREST	SHIEST	******	LOWERY
ALBERT	ESCENT	MODEST	SHYEST	AMBERY	MERELY
ARDENT	EXCEPT	MOLEST	SILENT	ARTERY	MISERY
ARGENT	EXPECT	MOMENT	SLIEST	BAKERY	MOIETY
ARPENT	EXPERT	NEWEST	SLYEST	BARELY	NAMELY
ARREST	EXSECT	NICEST	SOLENT	BASELY	NAPERY
ASCENT	EXSERT	NOCENT	SOREST	BLUELY	NICELY
ASPECT	EXTENT	OBJECT	STREET	BOWERY	NICETY
ASSENT	FEWEST	OBTECT	SUREST	BREEZY	NINETY
ASSERT	FINEST	OBTEST	TALENT	BRIERY	NUDELY
ATTEST	FLIEST	OBVERT	TAMEST	CASEFY	OCHERY
BAREST	FLUENT	ODDEST	THREAT	CELERY	ORNERY
BASEST	FOMENT	OLDEST	TRUEST	CHEEKY	ORRERY
BEHEST	FOREST	ORGEAT	UNBELT	CHEERY	PALELY
BEREFT	FREEST	ORIENT	UNBENT	CHEESY	PAPERY
BISECT	FUNEST	OSBERT	UNMEET	CICELY	PINERY
BLUEST	GAYEST	PALEST	UNREST	COMEDY	POPERY
CADENT	GEMERT	PARENT	UNSEAT	COMELY	PURELY
CAVEAT	GERENT	PATENT	UNVEXT	CREEPY	RAREFY
CEMENT	HAVENT	PONENT	UNWEPT	CUTELY	RARELY
CLIENT	HEREAT	POTENT	UPBEAT	DIRELY	REMEDY
COGENT	HONEST	PRIEST	URGENT	DOWERY	RIPELY
COVERT	HUBERT	PUREST	URTEXT	DUPERY	RUDELY
CUTEST	HUGEST	RAREST	VILEST	EATERY	SAFELY
DECEIT	ICIEST	RAWEST	WERENT	EMPERY	SAFETY
DECENT	IDLEST	RECENT	WIDEST	FAKERY	SAGELY
DEFEAT	INCEPT	RECEPT	WISEST	FINELY	SANELY
DEFECT	INCEST	REGENT	WRIEST	FINERY	SCREWY
DEJECT	INDENT	REHEAT	WRYEST	FLEECY	SHEENY
			YCLEPT		SINEWY

SLEEKY ******
SLEEPY ---F-D
SLEETY ******
SNEEZY BAFFED
SOLELY BEEFED
SORELY BIFFED
SPEEDY BUFFED
SPHERY CHAFED
STEELY COIFED
SURELY CUFFED
SURETY DOFFED
SWEENY DUFFED
SWEEPY GAFFED
TAMELY GOLFED
TEPEFY GOOFED
TIMELY GULFED
TOWERY HOOFED
TUMEFY HUFFED
UBIETY KNIFED
VALERY LEAFED
VENERY LOAFED
VILELY LUFFED
VINERY MIFFED
VOLERY MUFFED
WATERY PUFFED
WHEEZY REEFED
WIDELY ROOFED
WIFELY RUFFED
WINERY SURFED
WISELY TIFFED
****** TRIFID
---E-Z TURFED
****** WAIFED
LORENZ WOLFED
****** ******
---F-A ---F-E
****** ******
BIAFRA BAFFLE
RAFFIA BOUFFE
****** COFFEE
---F-B COFFLE
****** DUFFLE
CONFAB GRIFFE
PREFAB MUFFLE
****** PIAFFE
---F-C PIFFLE
****** PURFLE
DEIFIC RAFFLE
UNIFIC

RIFFLE
RUFFLE
STIFLE
TOFFEE
TRIFLE
WAFFLE
ZAFFRE
******
---F-H
******
LOOFAH
******
---F-L
******
ARMFUL
ARTFUL
CUPFUL
DUFFEL
EARFUL
EIFFEL
EYEFUL
FITFUL
FULFIL
HATFUL
IREFUL
JARFUL
JOYFUL
JUGFUL
LAPFUL
LAWFUL
MANFUL
RUEFUL
SINFUL
USEFUL
VATFUL
WILFUL
WOEFUL
******
---F-N
******
BAFFIN
BIFFIN
BOFFIN
BOWFIN
COFFIN
DEAFEN
MUFFIN
OLEFIN

PUFFIN
REDFIN
STEFAN
TIFFIN
******
---F-R
******
BUFFER
CHAFER
COFFER
CONFER
DIFFER
DOFFER
DUFFER
FURFUR
GAFFER
GOFFER
GOLFER
HEIFER
HOOFER
KAFFIR
LOAFER
PILFER
PREFER
PUFFER
REEFER
ROOFER
SHOFAR
SUFFER
SULFUR
SURFER
TELFER
TWOFER
WOOFER
ZAFFAR
ZAFFER
ZAFFIR
******
---F-S
******
BLUFFS
CHAFES
CHAFFS
CHUFAS
CLEFTS
CLIFFS
CRAFTS
CROFTS

DRAFFS
DRAFTS
DRIFTS
FEOFFS
FLUFFS
GAFFES
GRAFTS
KNIFES
QUAFFS
SCOFFS
SCUFFS
SHAFTS
SHIFTS
SKIFFS
SNAFUS
SNIFFS
SNUFFS
STAFFS
STUFFS
SWIFTS
THEFTS
WHIFFS
******
---F-T
******
******
BUFFET
COMFIT
FYLFOT
MISFIT
OUTFIT
PROFIT
SOFFIT
TUFFET
******
---F-W
******
******
CURFEW
GUFFAW
******
---F-X
******
******
CARFAX
DOGFOX
OUTFOX
PREFIX
SUFFIX

******
---F-Y
******
BARFLY
BELFRY
BOTFLY
CHAFFY
CLIFFY
CRAFTY
DAYFLY
DEAFLY
DRAFFY
DRAFTY
DRIFTY
DRYFLY
FLUFFY
GADFLY
MAYFLY
SAWFLY
SHIFTY
SNIFFY
SNUFFY
SPIFFY
STUFFY
******
---G-A
******
BORGIA
BREGMA
ENIGMA
FRIGGA
LINGUA
LOGGIA
PHAGIA
PLEGIA
QUAGGA
STIGMA
ZEUGMA
******
---G-C
******
BELGIC
TRAGIC
******
---G-D
******
BADGED
BAGGED

BANGED	LEGGED	BARGEE	NIGGLE	TERGAL	******	VERGIL
BARGED	LODGED	BEAGLE	PIGGIE	VERGIL	---G-O	VIRGIL
BEGGED	LOGGED	BOGGLE	PLAGUE	VIRGIL	******	
BILGED	LONGED	BOOGIE	PONGEE	******	ADAGIO	
BOGGED	LUGGED	BOUGIE	PRAGUE	---G-M	BURGOO	
BONGED	LUNGED	BROGUE	REGGIE	******	GINGKO	
BRIGID	MERGED	BUDGIE	SINGLE	LINGAM	PLAGIO	
BUDGED	MUGGED	BUNGLE	SOIGNE	REDGUM	SORGHO	
BUGGED	NAGGED	BURGEE	TANGLE	TERGUM	******	
BULGED	NUDGED	BURGLE	TINGLE	******	---G-P	
BUNGED	PEGGED	CANGUE	TOGGLE	---G-N	******	
CADGED	PIGGED	CHEGOE	TONGUE	******	BANGUP	
COGGED	PINGED	CHIGOE	VIRGIE	AIRGUN	HANGUP	
DANGED	PUGGED	DAGGLE	WAGGLE	ARAGON	******	
DIGGED	PURGED	DANGLE	WANGLE	BERGEN	---G-R	
DINGED	RAGGED	DENGUE	WEDGIE	BIGGIN	******	
DODGED	RANGED	DINGLE	WIGGLE	BIOGEN	ALEGAR	
DOGGED	RIDGED	DOGGIE	******	BROGAN	BADGER	
DUNGED	RIGGED	DOUGIE	---G-G	DRAGON	BANGOR	
FAGGED	RINGED	DRAGEE	******	EXOGON	BEGGAR	
FANGED	ROUGED	DROGUE	FIZGIG	FLAGON	BIGGER	
FIGGED	RUGGED	EMIGRE	******	GORGON	BUGGER	
FOGGED	SAGGED	FEIGNE	---G-H	IMOGEN	BULGAR	
FORGED	SIEGED	GAGGLE	******	ISOGON	BULGER	
FRIGID	SINGED	GANGUE	LENGTH	JARGON	BURGER	
FUDGED	STAGED	GARGLE	PISGAH	LONGAN	CADGER	
FULGID	SUNGOD	GIGGLE	******	MARGIN	CODGER	
GAGGED	SURGED	GOGGLE	---G-I	MORGAN	CONGER	
GANGED	SWAGED	GURGLE	******	MORGEN	COUGAR	
GAUGED	TAGGED	HAGGLE	BANGUI	NOGGIN	DAGGER	
GIGGED	TANGED	HIGGLE	GANGLI	OREGAN	DANGER	
GORGED	TINGED	JANGLE	GRIGRI	OREGON	DIGGER	
GOUGED	TOGGED	JIGGLE	NILGAI	ORIGAN	DODGER	
HAGGED	TONGED	JINGLE	ONAGRI	ORIGEN	DOGGER	
HANGED	TUGGED	JOGGLE	SANGUI	ORIGIN	FINGER	
HEDGED	TURGID	JUGGLE	******	OXYGEN	FORGER	
HINGED	VERGED	JUNGLE	---G-L	PIDGIN	GAGGER	
HOGGED	WAGGED	LEAGUE	******	PIGGIN	GANGER	
HUGGED	WEDGED	LUNGEE	BENGAL	PLUGIN	GAUGER	
IMAGED	WIGGED	MAGGIE	CUDGEL	POPGUN	GEIGER	
JAGGED	WINGED	MAIGRE	DOUGAL	SAIGON	GINGER	
JIGGED	ZINGED	MALGRE	FRUGAL	SARGON	GORGER	
JOGGED	******	MANGLE	FUNGAL	SHOGUN	GOUGER	
JUDGED	---G-E	MARGIE	GINGAL	SLOGAN	HANGAR	
JUGGED	******	MEAGRE	GOOGOL	TRIGON	HANGER	
KEDGED	AGOGUE	MIGGLE	JINGAL	TROGON	HEDGER	
KINGED	APOGEE	MINGLE	MONGOL	VIRGIN	HUNGER	
LAGGED	BANGLE	MORGUE	PLAGAL	WAGGON	JAEGER	

JIGGER	BADGES	LODGES	BLIGHT	******	LOCHIA
JOGGER	BARGES	LOUGHS	BOUGHT	---G-Y	NASHUA
JUDGER	BEIGES	LUNGES	BRIGHT	******	PATHIA
LAAGER	BELGAS	LUNGIS	BUDGET	CLOGGY	PYTHIA
LAGGER	BILGES	MADGES	CATGUT	CRAGGY	SOPHIA
LANGUR	BINGES	MANGOS	CAUGHT	DINGEY	******
LARGER	BONGOS	MARGES	DWIGHT	DINGHY	---H-C
LEDGER	BOUGHS	MARGOS	ELEGIT	DOUGHY	******
LINGER	BRUGES	MERGES	FAGGOT	DREGGY	GOTHIC
LODGER	BUDGES	MIDGES	FIDGET	FLAGGY	LITHIC
LOGGER	BULGES	NEIGHS	FLIGHT	FROGGY	MYTHIC
LONGER	BURGHS	NUDGES	FORGET	GIGGLY	ORPHIC
LUGGER	BURGOS	OMEGAS	FORGOT	GOOGLY	PYTHIC
LUNGER	CADGES	PARGOS	FOUGHT	GROGGY	SOTHIC
MANGER	CARGOS	PEGGYS	FRIGHT	HUNGRY	******
MEAGER	COIGNS	PENGOS	GADGET	JINGLY	---H-D
MERGER	CONGAS	PINGOS	GARGET	JUNGLY	******
MONGER	CONGES	PURGES	GORGET	KINGLY	ARCHED
MUGGAR	CORGIS	RANGES	HEIGHT	MARGAY	BACHED
MUGGER	COUGHS	REIGNS	KNIGHT	PLAGUY	BASHED
MUGGUR	DEIGNS	RIDGES	MAGGOT	PUGGRY	BATHED
NAGGER	DINGUS	ROUGES	MARGOT	QUAGGY	BUSHED
NIGGER	DIRGES	ROUGHS	MIDGET	SHAGGY	CACHED
ONAGER	DODGES	SAIGAS	MIDGUT	SINGLY	CASHED
PURGER	DOUGHS	SEDGES	MONGST	SLAGGY	COSHED
RANGER	FANGAS	SIEGES	NAUGHT	SMUGLY	DASHED
RIGGER	FEIGNS	SINGES	NOUGAT	SNAGGY	DISHED
RINGER	FORGES	SORGOS	NOUGHT	SNUGLY	ETCHED
RUGGER	FUDGES	SOUGHS	NUGGET	STAGEY	GASHED
SAGGAR	FUNGUS	STAGES	PARGET	STAGGY	GUSHED
SAGGER	GANGES	SURGES	PLIGHT	STOGEY	HASHED
SANGAR	GAUGES	SWAGES	ROTGUT	TANGLY	HUSHED
SANGER	GORGES	TAIGAS	SLIGHT	TINGLY	INCHED
SAUGER	GOUGES	TANGOS	SOUGHT	TRIGLY	ITCHED
SEGGAR	GREGOS	THIGHS	SPIGOT	TWIGGY	JOSHED
SINGER	HAGGIS	TINGES	TARGET	WAGGLY	LASHED
STAGER	HEDGES	TOUGHS	TAUGHT	WIGGLY	LATHED
SURGER	HINGES	TRAGUS	WEIGHT	******	LUSHED
TAGGER	IMAGES	TUNGUS	WRIGHT	---H-A	MASHED
VERGER	JORGES	USAGES	******	******	MESHED
VULGAR	JUDGES	VALGUS	---G-U	ALTHEA	METHOD
ZENGER	KEDGES	VERGES	******	ANTHEA	MUSHED
******	LARGOS	VIRGAS	CONGOU	ASTHMA	NICHED
---G-S	LAUGHS	WEDGES	GRUGRU	BRAHMA	NOSHED
******	LEDGES	WEIGHS	******	ISCHIA	ORCHID
ADAGES	LEIGHS	******	---G-W	JAPHIA	PISHED
ALIGNS	LIEGES	---G-T	******	JOSHUA	PITHED
AMIGOS	LINGAS	ALIGHT	GEWGAW	LITHIA	PUSHED
		ARIGHT			

RUSHED	BUSHEL	URCHIN	ESCHER	ALPHOS	PATHOS
SASHED	HYPHAL	UTAHAN	ESTHER	AMPHRS	PISHES
SIGHED	ISOHEL	WITHIN	ETCHER	ARCHES	PUSHES
TITHED	LETHAL	ZECHIN	EUCHER	ARCHYS	RACHIS
TUSHED	METHYL	******	FATHER	AUGHTS	RAPHIS
UNSHOD	MICHEL	---H-O	FISHER	BACHES	RASHES
WASHED	ORCHIL	******	GATHER	BASHES	RICHES
WISHED	PATHOL	ARCHEO	GOPHER	BATHOS	RIGHTS
WITHED	RACHEL	ARTHRO	GUSHER	BIGHTS	RUCHES
******	WARHOL	BOOHOO	HIGHER	BOSHES	RUSHES
---H-E	WITHAL	CASHOO	HITHER	BRAHMS	SADHUS
******	******	JETHRO	JOSHER	BUSHES	SASHES
ARCHIE	---H-M	NEPHRO	KOSHER	CACHES	SIGHTS
DAPHNE	******	ORCHIO	LASHER	CASHES	SOTHIS
EUCHRE	ANTHEM	PASHTO	LATHER	CATHYS	SPAHIS
HUGHIE	DIRHAM	RIGHTO	LECHER	COSHES	TETHYS
HYPHAE	DURHAM	TECHNO	LITHER	DACHAS	TIGHTS
KATHIE	ELOHIM	TYPHLO	LUSHER	DASHES	TITHES
LICHEE	FATHOM	YOOHOO	LUTHER	DISHES	TOSHES
MASHIE	GOTHAM	******	MASHER	EIGHTS	TUSHES
NUCHAE	GRAHAM	---H-P	MENHIR	ETCHES	TYPHUS
RAPHAE	JOTHAM	******	MESHER	FICHES	WASHES
RICHIE	MAYHEM	BISHOP	MOTHER	FICHUS	WICHES
SOPHIE	OLDHAM	CARHOP	MUSHER	FIGHTS	WISHES
******	SACHEM	MAYHAP	NETHER	FISHES	WITHES
---H-G	******	MISHAP	NIGHER	FOEHNS	YACHTS
******	---H-N	PUSHUP	OOPHOR	GASHES	ZETHOS
QUAHOG	******	UNSHIP	POTHER	GUSHES	ZETHUS
******	AACHEN	******	PUSHER	HASHES	******
---H-H	AFGHAN	---H-R	RASHER	HUGHES	---H-T
******	ARCHON	******	RATHER	HUSHES	******
EIGHTH	BUCHAN	AETHER	RICHER	INCHES	CACHET
******	COCHIN	ANCHOR	RUSHER	ITCHES	CUSHAT
---H-I	GORHEN	ANTHER	SAPHAR	JOSHES	JAPHET
******	GOSHEN	ARCHER	SYPHER	KATHYS	REDHOT
MYTHOI	HYPHEN	ARTHUR	TETHER	LACHES	ROCHET
TISHRI	INCHON	AUTHOR	TITHER	LASHES	SACHET
VASHTI	KUCHEN	BATHER	TOTHER	LATHES	SUNHAT
******	LICHEN	BOTHER	WASHER	LIGHTS	TOPHAT
---H-K	NATHAN	CATHER	WETHER	LUSHES	UPSHOT
******	ORPHAN	CIPHER	WITHER	MASHES	WITHIT
MUZHIK	PATHAN	CITHER	ZEPHYR	MESHES	******
******	PEAHEN	COSHER	ZITHER	MUSHES	---H-U
---H-L	PYTHON	CYPHER	******	MYTHOS	******
******	SIPHON	DASHER	---H-S	NICHES	CACHOU
ALPHYL	SYPHON	DITHER	******	NIGHTS	DACHAU
ARCHIL	TUCHUN	EITHER	ABOHMS	ORCHIS	PUSHTU
BETHEL	TYPHON	ESCHAR	ALPHAS	PASHAS	VISHNU

	FARINA	VEDIAC	******	CERITE	FRAISE
---H-W	FATIMA	ZODIAC	---I-E	CHAISE	FUSILE
******	GODIVA	******	******	CHOICE	FUTILE
ANYHOW	HEGIRA	---I-D	ACTIVE	CILICE	GREIGE
BASHAW	HEJIRA	******	ADMIRE	CLAIRE	HABILE
CASHAW	INTIMA	AERIED	ADVICE	COLINE	HALIDE
CASHEW	JARINA	ALLIED	ADVISE	COSINE	HALITE
CUSHAW	JEMIMA	BABIED	AEDILE	CRUISE	HAMITE
ESCHEW	JOSIEA	BEGIRD	ALBITE	CURIAE	HIVITE
HAWHAW	LAMINA	BEHIND	ALDINE	DANITE	IGNITE
HEEHAW	LIMINA	BELIED	ALPINE	DATIVE	IMBIBE
NEPHEW	LOLITA	BODIED	ALSIKE	DECIDE	INCISE
NOSHOW	LORICA	BURIED	ALVINE	DECILE	INCITE
******	LOUISA	BUSIED	APLITE	DEFILE	INDITE
---H-Y	LUMINA	CITIED	ARGIVE	DEFINE	INSIDE
******	MANILA	COPIED	ARLINE	DEMISE	INVITE
ARCHLY	MARINA	DEFIED	ARRIVE	DENISE	IODIDE
BUSHEY	MAXIMA	DENIED	ARSINE	DERIDE	IODINE
CATHAY	MINIMA	EDDIED	ASPIRE	DERIVE	IODIZE
EIGHTY	MONICA	ENGIRD	ASSIZE	DESIRE	IOLITE
HIGHLY	MYRICA	ENVIED	ATTIRE	DEVICE	IONIZE
MIGHTY	NUMINA	ENWIND	AUDILE	DEVISE	JANICE
NIGHTY	ONEIDA	ESPIED	AUGITE	DIVIDE	KENITE
POSHLY	OPTIMA	HONIED	AWHILE	DIVINE	LABILE
RASHLY	PATINA	INWIND	AXLIKE	DOCILE	LAMIAE
RICHLY	REGINA	LEVIED	BABITE	DRYICE	LARINE
SASHAY	RETINA	LILIED	BARITE	ELAINE	LEVITE
******	RUMINA	MONIED	BELIKE	ELOISE	LIAISE
---I-A	SABINA	MYRIAD	BELIZE	EMPIRE	LOUISE
******	SALIVA	PERIOD	BEMIRE	ENDIVE	LUCILE
AFRICA	SHEILA	PITIED	BESIDE	ENGINE	LUCITE
ALMIRA	SILICA	PLEIAD	BETIDE	ENSILE	LUPINE
ALVINA	TROIKA	PONIED	BETISE	ENTICE	LYSINE
AMRITA	TUNICA	RELIED	BLAISE	ENTIRE	MALICE
ANGINA	ULTIMA	REMIND	BODICE	EQUINE	MALINE
AQUILA	VAGINA	REWIND	BOLIDE	ERMINE	MARINE
ARNICA	VESICA	SCRIED	BORIDE	EUNICE	MATINE
ATTICA	VIMINA	SHEILD	BOVINE	EXCIDE	MAXINE
ATTILA	VOMICA	TAXIED	BRAISE	EXCISE	MAXIXE
AURIGA	YAKIMA	TIDIED	BRAIZE	EXCITE	MEDIAE
BENITA	ZARIBA	UNBIND	BRUISE	EXPIRE	MOBILE
CAMILA	******	UNGIRD	BYLINE	FACILE	MOLINE
CAPITA	---I-C	UNKIND	CAMISE	FAMINE	MOTILE
CARINA	******	UNTIED	CANINE	FELICE	MOTIVE
EDWINA	CELIAC	UNWIND	CARIBE	FELINE	MURINE
ELMIRA	MANIAC	VARIED	CAVITE	FELIPE	NADINE
ELVIRA	MANIOC		CECILE	FERINE	NARINE
ENCINA	SYRIAC		CERISE	FINITE	NATIVE

NEVILE	REVISE	UREIDE	BUSING	EBBING	HAWING
NOTICE	REVIVE	URSINE	BUYING	EDGING	HAYING
NOVICE	RUSINE	VALISE	CAGING	EGGING	HAZING
NOWISE	RUTILE	VENICE	CAKING	EKEING	HEWING
NUBILE	SABINE	VENIRE	CANING	ENDING	HEXING
OBLIGE	SALINE	VIRILE	CARING	EPPING	HIDING
OFFICE	SAMITE	VOTIVE	CASING	ERRING	HIEING
ONLINE	SATIRE	WAHINE	CAVING	EYEING	HIKING
OOLITE	SCRIBE	XYLITE	CAWING	FACING	HIRING
OPHITE	SCRIVE	******	CEDING	FADING	HIVING
OPTIME	SEDILE	---I-F	CERING	FAKING	HOEING
OREIDE	SEMITE	******	CITING	FARING	HOLING
OROIDE	SENILE	BELIEF	CLUING	FATING	HOMING
ORPINE	SERINE	RELIEF	CODING	FAXING	HONING
ORRICE	SHIITE	TARIFF	COKING	FAYING	HOPING
OSCINE	SHRIKE	******	COMING	FAZING	HOSING
OXHIDE	SHRINE	---I-G	CONING	FEEING	IDLING
PANICE	SHRIVE	******	COOING	FETING	IMPING
PATINE	SIMILE	ACHING	COPING	FEUING	INKING
PAVISE	SLUICE	ACTING	CORING	FIFING	INNING
PELITE	SOMITE	ADDING	COVING	FILING	IRKING
PENILE	SOZINE	AGEING	COWING	FINING	IRVING
PETITE	SPLICE	AIDING	COXING	FIRING	ISLING
PINITE	SPLINE	AILING	CRYING	FIXING	JADING
PLAICE	SPRITE	AIMING	CUBING	FLYING	JAPING
POLICE	SQUIRE	AIRING	CURING	FOXING	JAWING
POLITE	STRIAE	ARCING	DARING	FRYING	JEEING
PRAISE	STRIDE	ARMING	DATING	FUMING	JIBING
PUMICE	STRIFE	ASKING	DAZING	FUSING	JIVING
PURINE	STRIKE	AWEING	DEKING	FUZING	JOKING
PYRITE	STRIPE	AWNING	DICING	GAGING	JOYING
RACINE	STRIVE	BAAING	DIKING	GAMING	KEYING
RAPINE	SUPINE	BAKING	DINING	GAPING	KITING
RATINE	TAXITE	BALING	DIVING	GATING	LACING
RATITE	THRICE	BARING	DOLING	GAZING	LADING
RAVINE	THRIVE	BASING	DOMING	GEEING	LAKING
RECIPE	TIBIAE	BATING	DOPING	GIBING	LAMING
RECITE	TONITE	BAYING	DOSING	GIVING	LAVING
REFINE	UMPIRE	BERING	DOTING	GLUING	LAWING
REGIME	UNDINE	BIDING	DOZING	GORING	LAYING
RELINE	UNLIKE	BITING	DRYING	GUYING	LAZING
RELIVE	UNLIVE	BLUING	DUPING	GYBING	LIKING
REMISE	UNPILE	BODING	DURING	GYVING	LIMING
REPINE	UNRIPE	BONING	DYEING	HADING	LINING
RESIDE	UNWISE	BOOING	EALING	HALING	LIVING
RESILE	UPDIKE	BORING	EARING	HARING	LOOING
RETIRE	UPRISE	BOWING	EASING	HATING	LOPING
REVILE	UPSIDE	BOXING	EATING	HAVING	LOSING

LOVING	PLYING	SPYING	WRYING	OWLISH	******
LOWING	POKING	STRING	YAWING	PALISH	---I-K
LURING	POLING	STYING	YOKING	PARIAH	******
LUTING	PORING	TAKING	YOWING	PARISH	KODIAK
LYSING	POSING	TAMING	ZONING	PERISH	OOMIAK
MACING	PRYING	TAPING	******	POLISH	SCHICK
MAKING	PUKING	TARING	---I-H	POPISH	SHRIEK
MATING	PULING	TAWING	******	PUNISH	SHRINK
MAYING	RACING	TAXING	AGUISH	RADISH	SHTICK
MAZING	RAGING	TEEING	AWEIGH	RAKISH	STRICK
METING	RAKING	TIDING	BANISH	RAVISH	UNPICK
MEWING	RAPING	TILING	BLUISH	RAWISH	YORICK
MIMING	RARING	TIMING	BOYISH	RELISH	******
MINING	RATING	TIRING	CALIPH	ROMISH	---I-L
MIRING	RAVING	TOEING	CERIPH	RUPIAH	******
MIXING	RAYING	TONING	COYISH	SALISH	AECIAL
MOOING	RAZING	TOPING	DANISH	SHEIKH	AERIAL
MOPING	RICING	TOTING	DOVISH	SLEIGH	ATRIAL
MOVING	RIDING	TOWING	DRYISH	SQUISH	AWHIRL
MOWING	RILING	TOYING	DUDISH	STAITH	BELIAL
MUSING	RIMING	TRUING	EDDISH	TOBIAH	BURIAL
MUTING	RISING	TRYING	ELFISH	TOYISH	CURIAL
NAMING	RIVING	TUBING	ELVISH	UNWISH	DANIEL
NIDING	ROBING	TUNING	ENRICH	UPPISH	DENIAL
NIXING	ROPING	TYPING	EOLITH	UZZIAH	ESPIAL
NOSING	ROSING	UPPING	FAMISH	VANISH	FACIAL
NOTING	ROVING	URGING	FETICH	WRAITH	FECIAL
OARING	ROWING	VEXING	FETISH	ZENITH	FERIAL
OFFING	RUEING	VIKING	FINISH	ZIZITH	FETIAL
OGLING	RULING	VISING	GARISH	ZURICH	FILIAL
OILING	SATING	VOLING	IMPISH	******	FINIAL
OOZING	SAVING	VOTING	ISAIAH	---I-I	GAVIAL
OPTING	SAWING	VOWING	JADISH	******	GENIAL
ORBING	SAYING	WADING	JEWISH	ACTINI	JOVIAL
OUTING	SEEING	WAGING	JOSIAH	ASSISI	LABIAL
OWNING	SEWING	WAKING	JUDITH	BIKINI	LACIAL
PACING	SEXING	WALING	JUTISH	DIGITI	MEDIAL
PAGING	SHYING	WANING	LATISH	ECHINI	MENIAL
PALING	SIDING	WAVING	LAVISH	EURIPI	MESIAL
PARING	SIRING	WAXING	MODISH	GEMINI	MURIEL
PAVING	SITING	WILING	MOPISH	KABIKI	NARIAL
PAWING	SIZING	WINING	MULISH	LUMINI	NASIAL
PAYING	SKIING	WIPING	MUNICH	MEDICI	NEVILL
PEKING	SKYING	WIRING	OAFISH	SOLIDI	ONEILL
PIKING	SLUING	WISING	OFFISH	TAHITI	PENIAL
PILING	SOLING	WIVING	OGRISH	VASILI	RACIAL
PINING	SOWING	WOOING	OLDISH	WAKIKI	RADIAL
PIPING	SPRING	WOWING	ORNITH	WAPITI	REBILL

REFILL	MILIUM	DESIGN	RATION	SUBITO	JUNIOR
SAMIEL	MINIUM	DORIAN	REGION	ULTIMO	LACIER
SERIAL	MIRIAM	DURIAN	RESIGN	VAGINO	LAKIER
SHRILL	MOMISM	DURION	SAMIAN	VARICO	LAZIER
SOCIAL	MONISM	ELOIGN	SAPIEN	VESICO	LEVIER
SQUILL	MUTISM	ENSIGN	SIMIAN	VOMITO	LIMIER
THRILL	NANISM	EOLIAN	SOLION	******	LINIER
TIBIAL	NAZISM	EONIAN	SYRIAN	---I-P	LIVIER
UNCIAL	NOMISM	FABIAN	TALION	******	LOGIER
UPHILL	NUDISM	FANION	TITIAN	MEGILP	MAZIER
VENIAL	OBIISM	FENIAN	TYRIAN	SCRIMP	METIER
XENIAL	OMNIUM	FIJIAN	VISION	SHRIMP	NAPIER
******	OSMIUM	FUSION	VIVIAN	WIKIUP	NOSIER
---I-M	PODIUM	GABION	VIVIEN	******	OILIER
******	PURISM	GONION	WANION	---I-R	OOZIER
ACEIUM	RACISM	HEZION	******	******	PAVIOR
ACTIUM	RADIUM	INDIAN	---I-O	AIRIER	PINIER
AFFIRM	SADISM	IONIAN	******	ANTIAR	PIPIER
ALLIUM	SCHISM	JOVIAN	ACTINO	ASHIER	POKIER
ATRIUM	SEXISM	JULIAN	ALBINO	BELIER	PUNIER
AUTISM	SHIISM	KALIAN	ALUINO	BONIER	RACIER
BABISM	SODIUM	KATION	BENITO	CAGIER	RAPIER
BARIUM	SQUIRM	LEGION	BONITO	CAHIER	RELIER
CERIUM	SUFISM	LESION	CALICO	CAVIAR	ROPIER
CESIUM	TAOISM	LILIAN	CASINO	COPIER	ROSIER
CHRISM	TEDIUM	LOGION	CHEILO	COZIER	SAGIER
CILIUM	THEISM	LOTION	CHEIRO	DEFIER	SAVIOR
CIVISM	TRUISM	LUCIAN	DOMINO	DENIER	SENIOR
CONIUM	VERISM	LUCIEN	ECHINO	DEWIER	SEXIER
CORIUM	******	MALIGN	ENRICO	DOPIER	SIZIER
CUBISM	---I-N	MARIAN	ESKIMO	DOTIER	SPRIER
CURIUM	******	MARION	GENITO	DOZIER	TIDIER
EGOISM	ACTION	MEDIAN	HELICO	EASIER	TINIER
EONISM	ADRIAN	MESIAN	ILOILO	EDGIER	TONIER
ERBIUM	ADRIEN	MINION	INDIGO	ENVIER	UGLIER
FOLIUM	ALBION	MORION	LADINO	FOLIAR	VARIER
GONIUM	AMNION	MOTION	LEPIDO	FOXIER	VINIER
HELIUM	APPIAN	NASION	LIBIDO	FUMIER	VIZIER
HOLISM	ASSIGN	NATION	LUMINO	GAMIER	WARIER
INDIUM	BANIAN	NOTION	MANITO	GLUIER	WAVIER
INFIRM	BASION	NUBIAN	MEDICO	GOOIER	WAXIER
IODISM	BENIGN	OPTION	MEJICO	GORIER	WILIER
IONIUM	BUNION	OSSIAN	MERINO	HAZIER	WINIER
KALIUM	CAMION	PARIAN	MEXICO	HOLIER	WIRIER
LABIUM	CATION	PELION	ONEIRO	HOMIER	XAVIER
LYRISM	COSIGN	PINION	RUBIGO	HOSIER	ZANIER
MAOISM	DARIEN	POTION	SCHIZO	INKIER	
MEDIUM	DELIAN	RADIAN	SILICO	INLIER	

******	BURINS	DEVILS	GROINS	MINIMS	RELICS
---I-S	BUSIES	DIDIES	HABITS	MOBIUS	RELIES
******	CABINS	DIGITS	HAKIMS	MOLIES	REMISS
AALIIS	CALIFS	DIXITS	HALIDS	MONIES	REMITS
ABBIES	CAPIAS	DOBIES	HELIOS	MOTIFS	RESINS
ADLIBS	CARIBS	DOGIES	HOLIES	MOVIES	RHEIMS
ADMITS	CARIES	DORIES	HYOIDS	NADIRS	ROBINS
AERIES	CAVIES	DOXIES	IMMIES	NAVIES	ROSINS
ALLIES	CAVILS	DRAINS	INDIES	NIXIES	RUBIES
ALUINS	CECILS	DROITS	IRVINS	NORIAS	RUNINS
AMBITS	CELIAS	DRUIDS	IRWINS	NUBIAS	SABINS
ANNIES	CHAINS	DUTIES	JAMIES	OLLIES	SADIES
ANTICS	CHAIRS	EDDIES	JOSIAS	OPTICS	SAHIBS
ANVILS	CHOIRS	EDWINS	JULIAS	ORBITS	SANIES
APHIDS	CITIES	ELFINS	JULIES	ORGIES	SASINS
APRILS	CIVICS	ELLIES	JULIUS	ORPINS	SATINS
ARMIES	CIVIES	ELOINS	JUNIUS	OXLIPS	SAVINS
ARNIES	CLAIMS	ELSIES	JURIES	PANICS	SCRIPS
AROIDS	COBIAS	EMMIES	KAMIKS	PARIES	SEPIAS
ARTIES	COLIES	ENVIES	KATIES	PATIOS	SERIES
ASPICS	COLINS	EQUIPS	KEVINS	PELIAS	SERIFS
ATTICS	COMICS	ERNIES	KININS	PERILS	SERINS
AUDITS	CONICS	ERWINS	KRAITS	PEWITS	SHEIKS
AUXINS	CONIES	ESPIES	KUMISS	PINIES	SIGILS
AVAILS	COPIES	ETHICS	LADIES	PIPITS	SIRIUS
AVOIDS	COZIES	EYRIES	LAMIAS	PITIES	SITINS
AWAITS	CRAIGS	FACIES	LAPINS	PIXIES	SKEINS
BABIES	CUBITS	FAKIRS	LATINS	PLAIDS	SNAILS
BASICS	CUMINS	FELIDS	LEVIES	PLAINS	SOLIDS
BASILS	CURIES	FLAILS	LILIES	PLAITS	SONIAS
BASINS	CURIOS	FLAIRS	LIMITS	POGIES	SOZINS
BATIKS	CUTIES	FLUIDS	LIPIDS	POKIES	SPAITS
BEDIMS	CUTINS	FOGIES	LIVIAS	PONIES	SPEISS
BEFITS	CYNICS	FOLIOS	LORIES	POSIES	SPLITS
BEGINS	CYRILS	FRAILS	LUCIAS	POSITS	SPOILS
BELIES	DARICS	FRUITS	LUCIUS	PUPILS	SPRIGS
BEVIES	DARIUS	FUGIOS	LYDIAS	PYXIES	SPRITS
BINITS	DAVIDS	FURIES	LYRICS	QUAILS	SQUIBS
BLAINS	DAVIES	FUSILS	LYSINS	QUOINS	SQUIDS
BODIES	DAVITS	FUZILS	MAMIES	QUOITS	STAINS
BOGIES	DEBITS	GAMINS	MANIAS	RABIES	STAIRS
BRAIDS	DEFIES	GENIES	MARIAS	RADIOS	STEINS
BRAILS	DELIAS	GENIUS	MARIES	RADIUS	STOICS
BRAINS	DELIUS	GLAIRS	MATINS	RAMIES	STRIPS
BROILS	DEMIES	GNEISS	MAXIMS	RAPIDS	SUSIES
BRUINS	DEMITS	GOBIES	MEDICS	RATIOS	SWAILS
BRUITS	DENIES	GRAINS	MERITS	REFITS	SWAINS
BURIES	DENIMS	GREIFS	MIMICS	REGIUS	SYBILS

TAPIRS	ASSIST	SPOILT	COSILY	POLICY	******
THEIRS	AURIST	SPRINT	COZILY	POLITY	---J-K
THRIPS	BABIST	SQUINT	DIMITY	PUNILY	******
TIBIAS	BEGIRT	SQUIRT	DOZILY	PURIFY	CROJIK
TIDIES	CHRIST	STRICT	EASILY	PURITY	SANJAK
TIEINS	CILIAT	STRIPT	EERILY	RACILY	SELJUK
TOBIAS	CLEIST	TANIST	EFFIGY	RAMIFY	******
TOBIES	CUBIST	TAOIST	ENMITY	RARITY	---J-L
TODIES	DELICT	THEIST	ENTITY	RATIFY	******
TONICS	DEPICT	THRIFT	EQUITY	ROPILY	FRIJOL
TOPICS	DESIST	TSHIRT	EXPIRY	ROSILY	******
TORIES	DEWITT	TYPIST	FAMILY	ROSINY	---J-M
TORIIS	EGOIST	UNGIRT	FERITY	SALIFY	******
TOXINS	ELLIOT	UPLIFT	FIXITY	SANITY	LOGJAM
TRAILS	ENGIRT	VERIST	FOXILY	SATINY	******
TRAINS	ENLIST	******	FRUITY	SEXILY	---J-N
TRAITS	FORINT	---I-U	GAMILY	SICILY	******
TULIPS	GALIOT	******	GASIFY	STRIPY	DONJON
TUNICS	HERIOT	JABIRU	GLAIRY	TIDILY	TROJAN
TUPIKS	INDICT	MANITU	GORILY	TINILY	******
UNDIES	INSIST	MILIEU	GRAINY	TYPIFY	---J-R
UNPINS	JOLIET	******	HAZILY	UGLIFY	******
UNRIGS	JULIET	---I-W	HOLILY	UGLILY	JAMJAR
UNRIPS	JURIST	******	HOMILY	UNTIDY	******
UNTIES	LARIAT	REVIEW	HOMINY	UPPITY	---J-S
VARIES	LEGIST	******	HUMIFY	VANITY	******
VEXILS	LUTIST	---I-X	IGNIFY	VERIFY	BANJOS
VIGILS	LYRIST	******	JIMINY	VERILY	BENJYS
VISITS	MAOIST	MENINX	LACILY	VERITY	KOPJES
VIZIRS	MARIST	SPHINX	LAXITY	VILIFY	SHOJIS
VOMITS	MONIST	SYRINX	LAZILY	VIVIFY	THUJAS
WADIES	NUDIST	******	LENITY	WARILY	******
WAVIES	OBOIST	---I-Y	LEVITY	WAVILY	---J-T
YOGINS	PAPIST	******	MAZILY	WILILY	******
ZAMIAS	PLAINT	ACUITY	MINIFY	WIRILY	FANJET
ZANIES	PURIST	AERIFY	MODIFY	******	GASJET
ZAYINS	QUAINT	AIRILY	MUTINY	---I-Z	PROJET
ZOOIDS	RACIST	ARTILY	NAZIFY	******	RAMJET
ZORILS	RAPIST	BASIFY	NIDIFY	KIBITZ	******
******	RELICT	BILITY	NOSILY	NIMITZ	---J-U
---I-T	RESIST	BODILY	NOTIFY	******	******
******	SADIST	BRAINY	NUDITY	---J-B	ACAJOU
ADDICT	SCHIST	BUSILY	ODDITY	******	******
ADMIXT	SCRIPT	CAGILY	OILILY	ODDJOB	---K-A
ADRIFT	SEXIST	CAVITY	OOZILY	PUNJAB	******
ANOINT	SHRIFT	CECILY	OSSIFY	******	BUCKRA
AORIST	SOVIET	CODIFY	PACIFY	---J-H	GURKHA
ARTIST	SPLINT	COMITY	PARITY	ABIJAH	MARKKA
				ELIJAH	

******	HUSKED	SOAKED	ROCKNE	BUMKIN	BILKER
---K-C	JACKED	SOCKED	ROOKIE	BUSKIN	BROKER
******	JERKED	SPIKED	SICKLE	CALKIN	BUCKER
TURKIC	JINKED	SPOKED	SUCKLE	CATKIN	BUNKER
******	JUNKED	STAKED	TACKLE	DARKEN	BUSKER
---K-D	KECKED	STOKED	TALKIE	FIRKIN	CALKER
******	KICKED	SUCKED	TICKLE	GASKIN	CANKER
ARCKED	KINKED	SULKED	TINKLE	HARKEN	CHOKER
AWAKED	LACKED	TACKED	WINKLE	JERKIN	COCKER
BACKED	LARKED	TALKED	YANKEE	KRAKEN	CONKER
BALKED	LEAKED	TANKED	---K-G	LOOKIN	COOKER
BANKED	LICKED	TASKED	******	NAPKIN	CORKER
BARKED	LINKED	TICKED	MASKEG	PIPKIN	DANKER
BASKED	LOCKED	TUCKED	MUSKEG	RECKON	DARKER
BEAKED	LOOKED	TUSKED	******	RUSKIN	DECKER
BECKED	LURKED	WALKED	---K-H	SHAKEN	DICKER
BILKED	MARKED	WICKED	******	SICKEN	DOCKER
BOOKED	MASKED	WINKED	HOOKAH	SILKEN	DUCKER
BRAKED	MILKED	WORKED	******	SISKIN	DUIKER
BUCKED	MOCKED	YAKKED	---K-K	SPOKEN	DUNKER
BULKED	MUCKED	YANKED	******	SUNKEN	FLAKER
BUNKED	NARKED	YUKKED	HICKOK	TONKIN	HACKER
BURKED	NECKED	******	******	WALKON	HANKER
CALKED	NICKED	---K-E	---K-L	WEAKEN	HAWKER
CHOKED	NOCKED	******	******	WELKIN	HONKER
COCKED	PACKED	BOOKIE	BAIKAL	******	HOOKER
CONKED ·	PARKED	BUCKLE	DECKEL	---K-O	HUSKER
COOKED	PEAKED	CACKLE	JACKAL	******	JINKER
CORKED	PECKED	COCKLE	MISKAL	CUCKOO	JUNKER
DECKED	PEEKED	COOKIE	NICKEL	******	KICKER
DIRKED	PERKED	DARKLE	SECKEL	---K-P	LANKER
DOCKED	PICKED	DECKLE	SHEKEL	******	LARKER
DUCKED	PINKED	DICKIE	******	COCKUP	LOCKER
DUNKED	QUAKED	FICKLE	---K-M	HOOKUP	LOOKER
DUSKED	RACKED	HACKEE	******	LOCKUP	LUNKER
EVOKED	RANKED	HACKIE	BUNKUM	MARKUP	LURKER
FLAKED	REEKED	HACKLE	DINKUM	MOCKUP	MARKER
FLUKED	RICKED	HECKLE	SIKKIM	PICKUP	MASKER
FORKED	RINKED	HUCKLE	******	WALKUP	MEEKER
FUNKED	RISKED	JACKIE	---K-N	******	MILKER
GAWKED	ROCKED	JUNKIE	---K-N	---K-R	MOCKER
HACKED	ROOKED	KECKLE	******	******	MUCKER
HARKED	RUCKED	MACKLE	AWAKEN	ANGKOR	NICKER
HAWKED	SACKED	MICKLE	AWOKEN	BACKER	PACKER
HOCKED	SICKED	MUCKLE	BALKAN	BANKER	PARKER
HONKED	SLAKED	PICKLE	BECKON	BARKER	PAUKER
HOOKED	SMOKED	PINKIE	BODKIN	BEAKER	PECKER
HULKED	SNAKED	RANKLE	BROKEN	BICKER	PEEKER

PICKER	FLUKES	TICKET	ALALIA	BALLED	HILLED
PORKER	GECKOS	TUCKET	AMELIA	BAWLED	HOWLED
PUCKER	JACKYS	WICKET	ANGLIA	BELLED	HULLED
QUAKER	JOCKOS	******	ANTLIA	BILLED	HURLED
RACKER	KHAKIS	---K-U	APULIA	BIRLED	JAILED
RANKER	MICKYS	******	AXILLA	BOILED	JELLED
REEKER	NICKYS	RYUKYU	AZALEA	BOLLED	KEELED
RISKER	PARKAS	******	CHOLLA	BOWLED	KILLED
ROCKER	POLKAS	---K-X	DAHLIA	BUGLED	LADLED
SACKER	PUNKAS	******	EMILIA	BURLED	LALLED
SEEKER	QUAKES	MUSKOX	GIULIA	CABLED	LOLLED
SHAKER	RICKYS	PICKAX	HUELVA	CALLED	LULLED
SHIKAR	RUCKUS	******	LUELLA	CEILED	MAILED
SICKER	SHAKES	---K-Y	PHILIA	COALED	MALLED
SINKER	SHAKOS	******	SCYLLA	COELED	MARLED
SMOKER	SLAKES	COOKEY	STELLA	COILED	MAULED
SOAKER	SMOKES	CRIKEY	THALIA	COOLED	MEWLED
STOKER	SNAKES	DANKLY	THELMA	CULLED	MILLED
SUCKER	SPIKES	DARKLY	THULIA	CURLED	MISLED
TACKER	SPOKES	DICKEY	******	CYCLED	MOILED
TALKER	STAKES	DINKEY	---L-C	DIALED	MULLED
TANKER	STOKES	DONKEY	******	DOLLED	NAILED
TICKER	TANKAS	FLUKEY	AEOLIC	DUELED	PALLED
TINKER	TURKIS	FOLKSY	AMYLIC	DULLED	PALLID
TUCKER	VICKYS	HICKEY	ANGLIC	EUCLID	PEALED
TUSKER	VODKAS	HOCKEY	BELLOC	EXILED	PEELED
VALKYR	******	HOOKEY	CYCLIC	EYELID	PILLED
WALKER	---K-T	JOCKEY	EXILIC	FABLED	POLLED
WEAKER	******	LACKEY	FROLIC	FAILED	POOLED
WICKER	BASKET	LANKLY	GAELIC	FELLED	PULLED
WINKER	BECKET	LOWKEY	GALLIC	FILLED	PURLED
WORKER	BOSKET	MEEKLY	GARLIC	FOALED	RAILED
YONKER	BUCKET	MICKEY	ITALIC	FOILED	REELED
YORKER	CASKET	MONKEY	OXALIC	FOOLED	RIFLED
******	DOCKET	RANKLY	PUBLIC	FOULED	ROILED
---K-S	GASKET	RICKEY	SENLAC	FOWLED	ROLLED
******	JACKET	SICKLY	SIALIC	FUELED	SAILED
AWAKES	JUNKET	TACKEY	STELIC	FUGLED	SCALED
BECKYS	LOCKET	TINKLY	URALIC	FULLED	SEALED
BLOKES	MARKET	TURKEY	******	FURLED	SHALED
BRAKES	MUSKET	WEAKLY	---L-D	GABLED	SIDLED
BURKES	MUSKIT	WEEKLY	******	GALLED	SMILED
CHOKES	PACKET	******	ADDLED	GELLED	SOILED
CRAKES	PICKET	---L-A	AISLED	GULLED	SOULED
DRAKES	POCKET	******	AMBLED	HAILED	SPILED
EVOKES	RACKET	ABOLLA	ANGLED	HAULED	STALED
FAWKES	ROCKET	ABULIA	BAILED	HEALED	STOLED
FLAKES	SOCKET	AEOLIA	BALLAD	HEELED	STOLID

STYLED	GOALIE	MOLLAH	******	VIOLIN	BUTLER
TABLED	GRILLE	MOOLAH	---L-N	WOOLEN	CALLER
TAILED	GRILSE	MULLAH	******	******	CELLAR
TILLED	ISOLDE	NULLAH	ANILIN	---L-O	CHOLER
TITLED	LESLIE	SHILOH	AVALON	******	COALER
TOILED	MALLEE	SPILTH	BERLIN	APOLLO	COILER
TOLLED	MEALIE	WALLAH	BILLON	BIBLIO	COLLAR
TOOLED	MILLIE	WEALTH	CAPLIN	CALLAO	COOLER
UNCLAD	MOLLIE	ZILLAH	CATLIN	CHALCO	CULLER
VEILED	NELLIE	******	CEYLON	DUELLO	CURLER
VIALED	NOELLE	---L-I	CYMLIN	EMILIO	CUTLER
WAILED	PHYLAE	******	DOBLON	GIULIO	CYCLER
WALLED	POLLEE	CHILLI	DUBLIN	HALLOO	DEALER
WAULED	SHELVE	NIELLI	DUNLIN	NIELLO	DIALER
WAWLED	STELAE	NUCLEI	EVELYN	PHYLLO	DOLLAR
WELLED	SVELTE	OCELLI	FALLEN	RIALTO	DUELER
WHALED	TAILLE	SMALTI	FILLIN	SMALTO	DULLER
WHILED	TILLIE	STELLI	GALLON	******	FABLER
WILLED	TUILLE	******	GOBLIN	---L-P	FALLER
YAWLED	TWELVE	---L-K	HARLAN	******	FEELER
YELLED	UVULAE	******	HELLEN	BURLAP	FELLER
YOWLED	WALLIE	MUKLUK	INULIN	CALLUP	FILLER
******	WILLIE	SUSLIK	JOPLIN	COLLOP	FOULER
---L-E	******	******	KAOLIN	DEWLAP	FOWLER
******	---L-G	---L-L	LUBLIN	DOLLOP	FUELER
ALULAE	******	******	MARLIN	EARLAP	FULLER
AMALIE	ANALOG	FALLAL	MELLON	FILLIP	GAOLER
AMELIE	APOLOG	HALLEL	MERLIN	GALLOP	HAILER
ATTLEE	BOWLEG	******	MERLON	GALLUP	HAULER
BAILEE	DIALOG	---L-M	MOULIN	LOLLOP	HEALER
BAILIE	DUOLOG	******	MULLEN	PHILIP	HEELER
BILLIE	EPILOG	AMYLUM	MUSLIN	ROLLUP	HELLER
BULLAE	PEGLEG	ASYLUM	MYELIN	WALLOP	HILLER
CELLAE	PROLEG	BAALIM	PAULIN	******	HITLER
CHELAE	PUTLOG	BEDLAM	POLLEN	---L-R	HOLLER
COLLIE	STALAG	COELOM	POPLIN	******	HOWLER
COOLIE	UNPLUG	EMBLEM	PULLIN	ALULAR	HURLER
COULEE	******	HARLEM	PURLIN	AMBLER	JAILER
DIPLOE	---L-H	MOSLEM	RAGLAN	ANGLER	JAILOR
DOLLIE	******	MUSLIM	RATLIN	ANTLER	KEGLER
DOOLEE	ADOLPH	PEPLUM	SIMLIN	ASHLAR	KELLER
DOOLIE	BEULAH	PHYLUM	STALIN	BAILER	KEPLER
EMILIE	CHALEH	PRELIM	STOLEN	BAILOR	KILLER
EVOLVE	FELLAH	SLALOM	STOLON	BAWLER	LADLER
FAILLE	GULLAH	VALLUM	SULLEN	BOILER	LOLLER
FELLOE	HALLAH	VELLUM	TEFLON	BOWLER	MAHLER
GAULLE	HEALTH	WHILOM	TOULON	BUGLER	MAILER
GILLIE	KIBLAH		VILLON	BURLER	MAULER

MEDLAR	******	DOALLS	NELLYS	SOCLES	WILLIS
MILLER	---L-S	DOBLAS	OBELUS	SPALLS	WILLYS
MOILER	******	DOLLYS	OBOLUS	SPELLS	WOALDS
MULLER	ABELES	DOWLAS	OODLES	SPILES	WORLDS
NOBLER	ADDLES	DRILLS	OVULES	SPILLS	YIELDS
OCULAR	ADULTS	DROLLS	OXALIS	STALES	******
OSTLER	AEOLIS	DULLES	PALLAS	STALKS	---L-T
OVULAR	AEOLUS	DWELLS	PAULAS	STALLS	******
PALLOR	AISLES	EAGLES	PAULUS	STELES	AIGLET
PARLOR	AMBLES	EARLES	PEPLOS	STILES	AMULET
PEDLAR	AMOLES	ECCLES	PEPLUS	STILLS	ANKLET
PEELER	ANGLES	ECOLES	PHILOS	STILTS	ARMLET
PILLAR	ANKLES	EDILES	POILUS	STOLES	AUKLET
POLLER	APPLES	EMILES	POLLYS	STULLS	BALLET
POPLAR	ATOLLS	EMILYS	POULTS	STYLES	BALLOT
PULLER	AZOLES	EXALTS	PSALMS	STYLUS	BILLET
PURLER	BELLAS	EXILES	QUALMS	SWALES	BRULOT
REELER	BELLES	EXULTS	QUELLS	SWELLS	BULLET
RIFLER	BEULAS	FABLES	QUILLS	SWILLS	CABLET
ROLLER	BIALYS	FARLES	QUILTS	TABLES	CAMLET
SAILER	BIBLES	FAULTS	REALES	TELLUS	CHALET
SAILOR	BILLYS	FIELDS	REALMS	THALES	COLLET
SCALAR	BIRLES	FRILLS	RIFLES	THOLES	CULLET
SCALER	BOGLES	FUGLES	ROALDS	TILLYS	CUTLET
SEALER	BOULES	GABLES	ROBLES	TITLES	DIGLOT
SELLER	BRILLS	GALLUS	RUBLES	TOILES	DUPLET
SIDLER	BUGLES	GRILLS	SABLES	TRILLS	EAGLET
SMILER	BUILDS	GUILDS	SALLYS	TROLLS	EYELET
STALER	CABLES	GUILES	SAULTS	TULLES	FILLET
STELAR	CALLAS	GUILTS	SCALDS	TWILLS	GIBLET
STYLAR	CALLUS	HELLAS	SCALES	UMBLES	GIGLET
STYLER	CARLAS	HOLLYS	SCALPS	UNCLES	GIGLOT
SUTLER	CARLOS	IDYLLS	SCOLDS	UVULAS	GIMLET
TAILOR	CAULES	INKLES	SCULLS	VAULTS	GOBLET
TALLER	CAULIS	JOULES	SHALES	VILLAS	GOGLET
TATLER	CAULKS	KNELLS	SHELLS	VILLUS	GULLET
TAYLOR	CELLOS	KNOLLS	SHILLS	VIOLAS	HAMLET
TELLER	CHALKS	KOALAS	SIDLES	VOILES	HARLOT
THALER	CHELAS	LADLES	SKALDS	WALLAS	HASLET
TILLER	CHILLS	MACLES	SKILLS	WALLIS	MALLET
TOILER	COBLES	MAPLES	SKULKS	WALLYS	MILLET
TOLLER	CULLIS	MERLES	SKULLS	WEALDS	MULLET
TOOLER	CUTLAS	MIKLOS	SMALLS	WHALES	NUTLET
UVULAR	CYCLES	MILLYS	SMELLS	WHELKS	OCELOT
VEILER	DALLAS	MOLLYS	SMELTS	WHELMS	OMELET
WAILER	DALLES	MOULDS	SMILES	WHELPS	OUTLET
WHALER	DELLAS	MOULTS	SMOLTS	WHILES	PALLET
WILLER	DHOLES	NAPLES	SNELLS	WIELDS	PELLET
YELLER					

PIGLET	SALLOW	GALLEY	******	FARMED	******
PULLET	TALLOW	GUILTY	---M-A	FILMED	---M-E
REFLET	WALLOW	HALLEY	******	FIRMED	******
REGLET	WILLOW	HARLEY	AHIMSA	FLAMED	ANOMIE
RILLET	YELLOW	HAULMY	ALUMNA	FLUMED	BARMIE
RUNLET	******	HENLEY	ANEMIA	FOAMED	COMMIE
SALLET	---L-X	HURLEY	ANOMIA	FORMED	DORMIE
SAMLET	******	HUXLEY	CRIMEA	FRAMED	FLAMBE
SCULPT	AFFLUX	ICALLY	KALMIA	GAMMED	GEMMAE
STYLET	BIFLEX	LESLEY	PYEMIA	GEMMED	GRAMME
SUBLET	BOLLIX	MEDLEY	RHUMBA	GRIMED	GUIMPE
SUNLIT	DIPLEX	MILLAY	UREMIA	GUMMED	HERMAE
TABLET	DUPLEX	MISLAY	******	HAMMED	JIMMIE
TOILET	EFFLUX	MOOLEY	---M-C	HARMED	MAMMAE
TWILIT	HALLUX	MORLEY	******	HELMED	STYMIE
VARLET	INFLUX	MOSLEY	AGAMIC	HEMMED	******
VIOLET	POLLEX	MOTLEY	ANEMIC	HUMMED	---M-G
WALLET	POLLUX	MOULDY	ANOMIC	JAMMED	******
WHILST	PROLIX	MULLEY	ATOMIC	LAMMED	NUTMEG
WILLET	REFLEX	OAKLEY	BROMIC	LOAMED	******
ZEALOT	REFLUX	ORALLY	CHYMIC	LOOMED	---M-H
******	SCOLEX	OUTLAY	COSMIC	MAIMED	******
---L-V	SMILAX	OVALLY	DERMIC	MUMMED	WARMTH
******	******	PARLAY	FILMIC	PALMED	******
PAVLOV	---L-Y	PARLEY	FORMIC	PERMED	---M-I
******	******	PULLEY	GNOMIC	PLUMED	******
---L-W	ASHLEY	QUALMY	HOLMIC	PREMED	ALUMNI
******	BAILEY	REALLY	MICMAC	PRIMED	HERMAI
BELLOW	BARLEY	REALTY	MYRMEC	RAMMED	RHOMBI
BILLOW	BROLLY	REPLAY	PYEMIC	REAMED	SCAMPI
BYBLOW	BURLEY	RIPLEY	SUOMIC	RHYMED	******
CALLOW	BYPLAY	SCILLY	TARMAC	RIMMED	---M-K
CARLOW	CHALKY	SHELBY	THYMIC	ROAMED	******
CURLEW	CHILLY	SHELLY	******	ROOMED	YASMAK
FALLOW	COOLLY	SHELTY	---M-D	SEAMED	******
FELLOW	COPLEY	SMELLY	******	SEEMED	---M-L
FOLLOW	CULLAY	STALKY	BEAMED	SHAMED	******
HALLOW	DEPLOY	STILLY	BLAMED	SLIMED	ANIMAL
HARLOW	DOYLEY	TRILBY	BOOMED	SPUMED	BROMAL
HOLLOW	DROLLY	VALLEY	BUMMED	SUMMED	BRUMAL
INFLOW	DUDLEY	VOLLEY	CALMED	TALMUD	CARMEL
KISLEW	EMPLOY	WAYLAY	CHIMED	TEAMED	DERMAL
LUDLOW	EVILLY	WESLEY	CULMED	TEEMED	DISMAL
MALLOW	FARLEY	WHELKY	DAMMED	TERMED	ENAMEL
MARLOW	FAULTY	WHOLLY	DEEMED	WARMED	FORMAL
MELLOW	FEALTY	WIELDY	DESMID	WORMED	FORMYL
OUTLAW	FOULLY	WOOLLY	DIMMED	ZOOMED	HAEMAL
PILLOW	FRILLY		DOOMED		HAMMAL

HIEMAL	DAIMON	RODMEN	FARMER	BLAMES	LAMMAS
KUMMEL	DESMAN	SALMON	FIRMER	BLIMPS	LEMMAS
MAMMAL	DOLMAN	SEAMAN	FORMER	BROMES	LITMUS
NORMAL	DOLMEN	SEAMEN	FRAMER	BRUMES	LLAMAS
POMMEL	DROMON	SERMON	FULMAR	CADMUS	MAMMAS
PRIMAL	ETYMON	SHAMAN	GAMMER	CHAMPS	NAOMIS
PUMMEL	EXAMEN	SKYMAN	HAMMER	CHIMES	NEUMES
ROMMEL	FIRMAN	SKYMEN	HEMMER	CHUMPS	NORMAS
THYMOL	FLAMEN	SOCMAN	HUMMER	CLAMPS	PLUMBS
******	FLYMAN	SOCMEN	ISOMER	CLIMBS	PLUMES
---M-N	FOEMAN	STAMEN	KILMER	CLIMES	PLUMPS
******	FOEMEN	STAMIN	MAIMER	CLUMPS	PRIMES
ACUMEN	GAMMON	SUMMON	MESMER	COMMAS	PRIMPS
AIDMAN	GASMAN	TASMAN	MUMMER	COOMBS	PRIMUS
AIDMEN	GASMEN	TEGMEN	MURMUR	COSMOS	RHUMBS
AIRMAN	GERMAN	TRUMAN	PALMAR	CRAMPS	RHYMES
AIRMEN	GERMEN	VANMAN	PALMER	CREMES	SALMIS
ALUMIN	GNOMON	VANMEN	PRIMER	CRIMES	SAMMYS
APEMAN	GUNMAN	YEOMAN	RAMMER	CRIMPS	SCAMPS
ASHMAN	GUNMEN	YEOMEN	REAMER	CRUMBS	SCHMOS
ASHMEN	HARMIN	YESMAN	RHYMER	CRUMPS	SEAMUS
ATAMAN	HERMAN	******	RIMMER	DERMAS	SHAMES
AXEMAN	HETMAN	---M-O	ROAMER	DERMIS	SHAMUS
AXEMEN	HODMAN	******	ROOMER	DOGMAS	SIGMAS
BADMAN	ICEMAN	AKIMBO	RUMMER	DRAMAS	SKIMOS
BADMEN	ICEMEN	CRAMBO	SEAMER	ELEMIS	SKIMPS
BAGMAN	LAYMAN	DAIMIO	SEEMER	ENEMAS	SLIMES
BAGMEN	LAYMEN	DAIMYO	SIMMER	FERMIS	SLUMPS
BARMAN	LEGMAN	PLUMBO	SUMMER	FLAMES	SPUMES
BARMEN	LEGMEN	******	TEEMER	FLUMES	STAMPS
BATMAN	MADMAN	---M-P	TERMER	FLUMPS	STOMPS
BATMEN	MADMEN	******	TERMOR	FRAMES	STUMPS
BOWMAN	MAMMON	WARMUP	TREMOR	FRUMPS	SWAMIS
BOWMEN	MERMAN	******	WARMER	GAMMAS	SWAMPS
BREMEN	MERMEN	******	WEIMAR	GISMOS	THAMES
BUSMAN	MORMON	---M-R	WORMER	GIZMOS	THEMES
BUSMEN	NORMAN	******	YAMMER	GLAMIS	THEMIS
CABMAN	OUTMAN	BOOMER	******	GLUMES	THOMAS
CABMEN	PENMAN	BUMMER	---M-S	GNOMES	THUMBS
CAIMAN	PENMEN	CALMER	******	GRIMES	THUMPS
CARMAN	PIEMAN	CHIMER	ABOMAS	GRUMES	THYMES
CARMEN	PIEMEN	CLAMOR	ABOMBS	GUMMAS	THYMUS
CAYMAN	PITMAN	DAGMAR	AGAMAS	HERMES	TIMMYS
COMMON	PITMEN	DAMMAR	ALAMOS	HOLMES	TOMMYS
CONMAN	POTMAN	DAMMER	ANIMAS	JIMMYS	TRAMPS
COWMAN	RAGMAN	DIMMER	ANIMUS	KARMAS	TRUMPS
COWMEN	RAGMEN	DORMER	AROMAS	KERMES	ULEMAS
DAEMON	RODMAN	ENAMOR	BERMES	KERMIS	WAMMUS
					WILMAS

******	CLAMMY	HERNIA	******	OPENED	BRONTE
---M-T	CLUMPY	JOANNA	---N-D	OPINED	BRONZE
******	CLUMSY	LUANDA	******	PAINED	CANNAE
CERMET	CRIMPY	ODYNIA	ALINED	PANNED	CANNIE
CLIMAT	CRUMBY	OMENTA	ATONED	PAWNED	CHANCE
COEMPT	CRUMMY	PENNIA	BANNED	PEENED	CHANGE
COMMIT	DISMAY	PHONIA	BEANED	PENNED	CONNIE
DERMAT	FIRMLY	QUANTA	BINNED	PHONED	CRINGE
EXEMPT	FLIMSY	RWANDA	BRINED	PINNED	DONNIE
FORMAT	FRUMPY	SIENNA	BURNED	PLANED	EVINCE
HELMET	GLUMLY	STANZA	CANNED	PRUNED	FANNIE
HERMIT	GRIMLY	TAENIA	COINED	PUNNED	FAUNAE
KERMIT	GRUMPY	UGANDA	CONNED	RAINED	FIANCE
KISMET	PLUMMY	URANIA	CORNED	REINED	FLANGE
MAMMET	PRIMLY	VIENNA	CRANED	RUINED	FLENSE
MARMOT	SCUMMY	ZINNIA	CYANID	SEINED	FRANCE
MOTMOT	SEEMLY	******	DAMNED	SHINED	FRINGE
PERMIT	SHAMMY	---N-B	DARNED	SIGNED	FRUNZE
PROMPT	SHIMMY	******	DAWNED	SINNED	GLANCE
STOMAT	SKIMPY	HOBNOB	DENNED	STONED	GRANDE
SUBMIT	SLIMLY	******	DINNED	SUNNED	GRANGE
SUMMIT	SLIMSY	---N-C	DONNED	TANNED	GWYNNE
******	SLUMMY	******	DOWNED	TINNED	HORNIE
---M-U	STUMPY	ADONIC	DRONED	TRINED	JEANNE
******	SWAMPY	AGONIC	DUNNED	TUNNED	JINNEE
MAUMAU	TERMLY	ATONIC	EARNED	TURNED	JOANNE
MUUMUU	TRIMLY	AZONIC	EVENED	TWINED	JONNIE
******	WARMLY	CLINIC	FANNED	VEINED	JOUNCE
---M-V	WHAMMY	CLONIC	FAWNED	WANNED	KENNIE
******	WHIMSY	COGNAC	FINNED	WARNED	LAUNCE
ASIMOV	******	CYANIC	GAINED	WEANED	LEONIE
******	---N-A	EDENIC	GINNED	WHINED	LOUNGE
---M-W	******	ETHNIC	GOWNED	YAWNED	MEANIE
******	AGENDA	FENNEC	GUNNED	YEANED	MINNIE
HAYMOW	AMANDA	FINNIC	HORNED	YENNED	NUANCE
******	AMANIA	FINNOC	HYMNED	******	ORANGE
---M-X	AMENRA	HYMNIC	IRONED	---N-E	PAWNEE
******	ARANTA	HYPNIC	JOINED	******	PENNAE
CLIMAX	ARUNTA	ICONIC	KEENED	ANANKE	PINNAE
COMMIX	BIANCA	IRENIC	KENNED	AVENGE	PLUNGE
LUMMOX	BRENDA	IRONIC	KERNED	AVENUE	POINTE
******	CORNEA	OZONIC	LEANED	BEANIE	POUNCE
---M-Y	CORNUA	PHONIC	LIMNED	BERNIE	PRANCE
******	CRANIA	PICNIC	LOANED	BLENDE	PRINCE
BLIMEY	DUENNA	PYKNIC	MAENAD	BLONDE	QUINCE
CALMLY	EUPNEA	QUINIC	MANNED	BLUNGE	RONNIE
CHAMMY	GDYNIA	SCENIC	MOANED	BONNIE	SCONCE
CHUMMY	GUINEA	TANNIC	MOONED	BOUNCE	SEANCE

SPONGE	******	THENAL	FRANCO	LIMNER	AMENTS
STANCE	---N-I	TRINAL	FRONTO	MANNER	ANANAS
SWANEE	******	TUNNEL	HERNIO	MEANER	ARENAS
SWINGE	ADONAI	URANYL	LEANTO	NORNIR	ATONES
THENCE	AMENTI	URINAL	ODONTO	OPENER	AXONES
TRANCE	BRUNEI	VERNAL	PRONTO	PAWNER	AZINES
TWINGE	UBANGI	ZOONAL	SHINTO	PENNER	BEINGS
ULENCE	******	******	******	PINNER	BENNES
USANCE	---N-K	---N-M	---N-P	PLANAR	BENNYS
WEENIE	******	******	******	PLANER	BLANKS
WHENCE	FRANCK	ANONYM	CATNAP	PRUNER	BLENDS
WIENIE	GDANSK	BARNUM	CATNIP	PUNNER	BLINDS
WINNIE	KARNAK	CRINUM	KIDNAP	RADNOR	BLINKS
YVONNE	NUDNIK	EPONYM	SANNUP	RUINER	BLONDS
******	PLANCK	FRENUM	TURNIP	RUNNER	BLUNTS
---N-G	******	LIGNUM	TURNUP	SEINER	BONNYS
******	---N-L	MAGNUM	******	SHINER	BOUNDS
EGGNOG	******	PAYNIM	---N-R	SIGNER	BRANDS
STENOG	ATONAL	PLENUM	******	SIGNOR	BRANTS
******	BRUNEL	PUTNAM	ATONER	SINNER	BRENTS
---N-H	CANNEL	******	BANNER	SOONER	BRINES
******	CARNAL	---N-N	BURNER	STONER	BRINGS
ACANTH	CORNEL	******	CANNER	SUMNER	BRINKS
BLANCH	CRENEL	CANNON	COINER	TANNER	BRONCS
BLENCH	DARNEL	CYANIN	CONNER	THENAR	BRUNOS
BRANCH	DIRNDL	FINNAN	CORNER	TINNER	CANNAS
BRUNCH	FAUNAL	GUANIN	CUNNER	TURNER	CANNES
CHINCH	FENNEL	GUENON	DARNER	TWINER	CHANGS
CLENCH	FUNNEL	KRONEN	DINNER	VAINER	CHANTS
CLINCH	GUNNEL	LIGNIN	EARNER	WAGNER	CHINES
CRUNCH	HYMNAL	MIGNON	ELINOR	WANNER	CHINKS
DRENCH	KENNEL	PENNON	FAFNIR	WARNER	CHUNKS
FLENCH	KERNEL	PHANON	FANNER	WEANER	CLANGS
FLINCH	LIONEL	RENNIN	FAWNER	WHINER	CLANKS
FRENCH	NOUNAL	TANNIN	FINNER	WIENER	CLINES
HANNAH	PHENOL	VERNON	GAINER	WINNER	CLINGS
HAUNCH	PHENYL	******	GARNER	YAWNER	CLINKS
LAUNCH	PIENAL	---N-O	GINNER	******	CLINTS
PAUNCH	PINNAL	******	GUNNAR	---N-S	CLONES
PLANCH	REGNAL	ALONSO	GUNNER	******	CLONUS
PLINTH	RHINAL	ALONZO	IRONER	ACINUS	CORNUS
QUENCH	RUNNEL	BAGNIO	JOINER	ADENIS	COUNTS
STANCH	SIGNAL	BORNEO	KEENER	ADONIS	CRANES
STENCH	SIMNEL	BRONCO	KRONER	AGENTS	CRANKS
SUNNAH	SPINAL	CRANIO	KRONOR	AGONES	CRONES
TRENCH	SPINEL	DRONGO	KRONUR	AKENES	CRONOS
WRENCH	TARNAL	ERINGO	LANNER	ALINES	CRONUS
	TERNAL	ERYNGO	LEANER	AMENDS	CYGNUS

DANNYS	HYPNOS	SAINTS	WHANGS	******	QUINCY
DAUNTS	ICINGS	SAUNAS	WHINES	---N-Y	QUINSY
DENNIS	IMINES	SCENDS	WOUNDS	******	RODNEY
DENNYS	IRANIS	SCENES	WRINGS	AGENCY	ROMNEY
DIANAS	IRENES	SCENTS	WRONGS	BARNEY	SAWNEY
DIANES	JAINAS	SCONES	ZOUNDS	BERNEY	SCANTY
DOINGS	JAUNTS	SEINES	******	BLENNY	SHANDY
DONNAS	JENNYS	SENNAS	---N-T	BOUNCY	SHANTY
DRINKS	JINNYS	SHANKS	******	BOUNTY	SHINDY
DRONES	JOINTS	SHINES	BENNET	BRANDY	SHINNY
DRUNKS	KENNYS	SHUNTS	BONNET	BRANNY	SIDNEY
ELANDS	KEYNES	SKINKS	BRANDT	BRONZY	SKINNY
ELENAS	KOINES	SKUNKS	BURNET	CHANCY	SLANGY
EMENDS	KRONOS	SLANTS	CANNOT	CHANTY	SLINKY
ERINYS	LEMNOS	SLINGS	COBNUT	CHINKY	SPINNY
EVENTS	LENNYS	SLINKS	CORNET	CHUNKY	SPONGY
FAINTS	LEONAS	SOUNDS	CYGNET	CLINGY	SPUNKY
FANNYS	LIANAS	SPANKS	GANNET	COUNTY	STINGY
FAUNAS	LIANES	SPENDS	GARNET	CRANKY	SWANKY
FAUNUS	LLANOS	SPINES	HOGNUT	CRANNY	SYDNEY
FEINTS	MAUNDS	STANDS	HORNET	DAINTY	TEENSY
FIENDS	MESNES	STINGS	JENNET	DISNEY	THINLY
FLANKS	MOUNTS	STINKS	LINNET	EVENLY	TRENDY
FLINGS	MYRNAS	STINTS	MAGNET	FLINTY	TWANGY
FLINTS	OPINES	STONES	PEANUT	FLUNKY	TWENTY
FLONGS	ORANGS	STUNTS	PIGNUT	FRENZY	VAINLY
FLUNKS	PAINTS	SWINGS	PLANET	FRINGY	VYRNWY
FOUNDS	PENNIS	TAINOS	RENNET	GAINLY	WEENSY
FOUNTS	PENNYS	TAINTS	SENNET	GOONEY	WHINNY
FRANCS	PHONES	TAUNTS	SENNIT	GRANNY	WITNEY
FRANKS	PIANOS	TBONES	SIGNET	GRUNDY	******
FRONDS	PIGNUS	TENNIS	SONNET	JAUNTY	---N-Z
FRONTS	PLANES	THANES	SPINET	JITNEY	******
GIANTS	PLANKS	THANKS	THANAT	JOHNNY	BLINTZ
GLANDS	PLANTS	THINGS	UNKNIT	KEENLY	CHINTZ
GLINTS	PLUNKS	THONGS	WALNUT	KIDNEY	******
GLYNIS	POINDS	TRENDS	******	LEANLY	---O-A
GOINGS	POINTS	TRINES	---N-W	MAINLY	******
GRANTS	POUNDS	TRUNKS	******	MAUNDY	AFTOSA
GRINDS	PRANKS	TWANGS	MINNOW	MEANLY	ANCONA
GRUNTS	PRINKS	TWINES	WINNOW	MOUNTY	ANGOLA
GUANOS	PRINTS	UPENDS	******	OHENRY	ANGORA
GWENNS	PRONGS	URANUS	---N-X	OPENLY	ANNONA
HANNAS	PRUNES	VAUNTS	******	ORKNEY	APNOEA
HAUNTS	QUANTS	VERNAS	FORNAX	PAINTY	AREOLA
HENNAS	QUINTS	VIANDS	FORNIX	PHONEY	ARROBA
HOUNDS	RHINOS	VINNYS	MAGNOX	PLENTY	AURORA
HYENAS	ROUNDS	WAYNES	VERNIX	POINTY	BOGOTA

CAEOMA	******	MILORD	BYGONE	LAHORE	UNDONE
CHROMA	---O-C	MUCOID	CAJOLE	LANOSE	UNROBE
CITOLA	******	NEVOID	CAPONE	LENORE	UNYOKE
CORONA	ECHOIC	NOGOOD	CAPOTE	METOPE	UPROSE
CUPOLA	EOZOIC	OGDOAD	CAROLE	MOHOLE	VADOSE
DAGOBA	HEROIC	OSMOND	CHOOSE	MOPOKE	VAMOSE
DAKOTA	******	OXFORD	CHROME	MOROSE	VELOCE
EIDOLA	---O-D	RECORD	CLEOME	MUCOSE	VENOSE
EUBOEA	******	RELOAD	COMOSE	NICOLE	XYLOSE
EUROPA	ABROAD	RESOLD	COYOTE	NODOSE	ZYGOTE
FEDORA	ACCORD	RETOLD	CREOLE	OPPOSE	******
FEMORA	AFFORD	REWORD	CYMOSE	ORIOLE	---O-F
GLIOMA	AGEOLD	SECOND	DECODE	OSMOSE	******
LADOGA	ALGOID	SHOOED	DECOKE	OTIOSE	BEHOOF
LIPOMA	ALMOND	SHROUD	DEMODE	PAROLE	CUTOFF
MASORA	ARNOLD	SILOED	DEMOTE	PEYOTE	FAROFF
MIMOSA	AUTOED	SOLOED	DENOTE	PILOSE	LAYOFF
MUCOSA	BEHOLD	STROUD	DEPONE	PINOLE	ONEOFF
MYXOMA	BEYOND	TOROID	DEPOSE	PYRONE	PAYOFF
NAGOYA	BIFOLD	UNCORD	DEVOTE	PYROPE	PUTOFF
OTTOWA	BYROAD	UNFOLD	DIPOLE	RADOME	RIPOFF
PAGODA	BYWORD	UNLOAD	DITONE	RAMOSE	RUNOFF
PAYOLA	CANOED	UNSOLD	ENCODE	REBORE	SETOFF
PELOTA	CEBOID	UNTOLD	ENCORE	REDONE	SHROFF
POMONA	CONOID	UPHOLD	ENROBE	REMOTE	TIPOFF
RAMONA	CUBOID	VETOED	EUROPE	REMOVE	******
REDOWA	CYMOID	XYLOID	EXPOSE	REPOSE	---O-G
REMORA	DEVOID	ZEROED	FILOSE	RESOLE	******
ROMOLA	ECHOED	******	FURORE	REVOKE	BARONG
SCROTA	EDMOND	---O-E	GALORE	RIBOSE	BELONG
SENORA	ENFOLD	******	GROOVE	RIMOSE	DUGONG
STROMA	FUCOID	ACNODE	GYROSE	RUGOSE	KALONG
TACOMA	GADOID	AEROBE	HEXONE	SALOME	MEKONG
VERONA	GANOID	ALCOVE	HEXOSE	SETOSE	OBLONG
ZYGOMA	HALOED	ALDOSE	HONORE	SHROVE	OOLONG
******	HALOID	ANCONE	IGNORE	SIMONE	SARONG
---O-B	HAROLD	ANYONE	IMPOSE	SNOOZE	STRONG
******	HEMOID	APPOSE	INCOME	STOOGE	THRONG
ABSORB	HESOID	ARIOSE	INJOKE	STROBE	******
ADSORB	ILFORD	ASHORE	INSOLE	STRODE	---O-H
APLOMB	INFOLD	ASLOPE	INTONE	STROKE	******
ENTOMB	INROAD	ATHOME	INVOKE	STROVE	BROOCH
ENWOMB	KAYOED	BECOME	INWOVE	THRONE	COHOSH
INTOMB	KELOID	BEFORE	IONONE	THROVE	GALOSH
RESORB	KOBOLD	BEGONE	JEROME	TOROSE	GOLOSH
	LIPOID	BEHOVE	JOCOSE	TRIODE	KIBOSH
	LOCOED	BIGONE	KETONE	TRIOSE	MOLOCH
	LOMOND	BROOKE	KETOSE	TYRONE	SMOOCH

SMOOTH	PHLOEM	FLUORO	******	CANOES	FEROUS
WHOOSH	REFORM	GIGOLO	---O-S	CANONS	FETORS
******	SIMOOM	KIMONO	******	CAPONS	FLOODS
---O-I	******	KOKOMO	AARONS	CAROBS	FLOORS
******	---O-N	REBOZO	ABBOTS	CAROLS	FLUORS
ARBORI	******	ROCOCO	ABHORS	CAROMS	FREONS
BILOXI	ADJOIN	******	ACEOUS	CEROUS	FUCOUS
EMBOLI	ADNOUN	---O-P	ACIOUS	CHEOPS	FUMOUS
EPHORI	ATTORN	******	ACROSS	CHLOES	FURORS
NEROLI	BABOON	INCORP	ACTORS	CIBOLS	GALOPS
OCTOPI	BEMOAN	RECOUP	ALDOUS	COCOAS	GAMOUS
VAPORI	BICORN	SALOOP	ALFONS	COLONS	GAVOTS
******	COCOON	SCROOP	ALGOUS	COLORS	GEMOTS
---O-K	DAHOON	******	ALLOTS	COLOUS	GENOUS
******	DEHORN	---O-R	ALLOWS	COMOUS	GEROUS
BETOOK	DISOWN	******	ALLOYS	CROOKS	GIPONS
BOGOAK	ENJOIN	ARBOUR	ANIONS	CROONS	GLOOMS
BYWORK	HEROIN	ARDOUR	ANNOYS	CYMOUS	GROOMS
MOHOCK	INBORN	ARMOUR	ANTONS	DADOES	GYNOUS
OCLOCK	LAGOON	BEZOAR	APRONS	DECORS	GYRONS
RETOOK	MAROON	COLOUR	ARBORS	DECOYS	HALOES
UNCOCK	MINOAN	DETOUR	ARDORS	DEMOBS	HELOTS
UNCORK	OHIOAN	DEVOIR	ARGOTS	DEMONS	HEROES
UNHOOK	OSBORN	DEVOUR	ARIOUS	DEPOTS	HERONS
UNLOCK	RACOON	DOLOUR	ARMORS	DIDOES	HOBOES
******	RATOON	ECHOER	ARROWS	DIVOTS	HONORS
---O-L	REBORN	EUDOAR	ARTOIS	DODOES	HUMORS
******	REJOIN	EXMOOR	ASCOTS	DONORS	HURONS
BEFOOL	RENOWN	FAVOUR	AUROUS	DROOLS	IDIOMS
BEFOUL	SALOON	GIAOUR	AXIOMS	DROOPS	IDIOTS
ENROLL	SAMOAN	HONOUR	BABOOS	ECHOES	IGLOOS
ENSOUL	SHOOIN	HUMOUR	BARONS	ELBOWS	INDOWS
INSOUL	SUBORN	INDOOR	BATONS	ELIOTS	INGOTS
RECOIL	THROWN	LABOUR	BAYOUS	EMBOSS	IODOUS
RETOOL	TYCOON	MEMOIR	BEFOGS	EMBOWS	ITIOUS
SCHOOL	UNBORN	RENOIR	BESOMS	ENDOWS	JABOTS
SCHORL	UNWORN	RIGOUR	BESOTS	ENJOYS	JACOBS
SCROLL	UPTOWN	RUMOUR	BIGOTS	ENVOYS	JALOPS
STROLL	******	SAVOUR	BIKOLS	EPHODS	JASONS
UNCOIL	---O-O	TUMOUR	BIPODS	EPHORS	JOYOUS
UNROLL	******	UNDOER	BLOODS	ERRORS	JUPONS
******	ARIOSO	UNMOOR	BLOOMS	ESTOPS	JURORS
---O-M	ARROYO	UPROAR	BOSOMS	EXTOLS	KABOBS
******	CHLORO	VALOUR	BROODS	FAGOTS	KAPOKS
ABLOOM	CHROMO	VAPOUR	BROOKS	FAMOUS	KAZOOS
BIFORM	CHRONO	VELOUR	BROOMS	FANONS	LABORS
DEFORM	DEMONO	VETOER	BUBOES	FAVORS	LEMONS
INFORM	ENTOMO	VIGOUR	CABOBS	FELONS	LEROYS

MAGOTS	SABOTS	TUMORS	DEVOUT	ARGOSY	SPOONY
MAJORS	SAJOUS	TUTORS	DIMOUT	ARMORY	THEORY
MANORS	SALONS	UNDOES	DUGOUT	ARROWY	UNHOLY
MASONS	SAVORS	UNIONS	EFFORT	BACONY	WICOPY
MAYORS	SAXONS	UPBOWS	ENROOT	BARONY	******
MCCOYS	SCIONS	VALOIS	ESCORT	BETONY	---P-A
MELONS	SCOOPS	VAPORS	EXHORT	BLOODY	******
MEROUS	SCOOTS	VENOMS	EXPORT	BLOOMY	COPPRA
MESONS	SCRODS	VENOUS	EXTORT	BROODY	COWPEA
MINORS	SEPOYS	VETOES	EYEOUT	BROOMY	HOOPLA
MORONS	SEROUS	VINOUS	FAROUT	BRYONY	MYOPIA
MOTORS	SEROWS	VISORS	GALOOT	CALORY	NYMPHA
MUCOUS	SETONS	VIZORS	IMPORT	CANOPY	SULPHA
NABOBS	SETOUS	VOROUS	IMPOST	CHOOSY	UTOPIA
NYLONS	SHOOTS	WAGONS	INMOST	COLONY	******
ODIOUS	SIMONS	WAHOOS	LAYOUT	CORODY	---P-C
ONIONS	SLOOPS	WAMOUS	MAHOUT	DESOXY	******
ORLOPS	SNOODS	WHOOPS	PUTOUT	DIPODY	ADIPIC
OXBOWS	SNOOKS	WIDOWS	RAGOUT	DROOPY	CALPAC
PAEONS	SNOOPS	WINOES	REFOOT	ECTOMY	CARPIC
PATOIS	SNOOTS	XYLOLS	REPORT	EMBODY	MYOPIC
PEKOES	SOTOLS	YAHOOS	RESORT	EULOGY	TROPIC
PELOPS	SPOOFS	YAPONS	RETORT	FELONY	******
PICOTS	SPOOKS	YUPONS	REVOLT	FLOOZY	---P-D
PILOTS	SPOOLS	ZEROES	RIPOST	GLOOMY	******
PILOUS	SPOONS	ZIRONS	RUNOUT	GROOVY	ALIPED
PINONS	SPOORS	******	SETOUT	IDIOCY	BEEPED
PITONS	STOOKS	---O-T	SPROUT	IMBODY	BOPPED
PIVOTS	STOOLS	******	THROAT	JALOPY	BUMPED
PODOUS	STOOPS	ABVOLT	TRYOUT	MALORY	BURPED
POROUS	STROPS	ACCOST	UNBOLT	MELODY	CAMPED
POYOUS	SWOONS	ADROIT	UNROOT	MEMORY	CAPPED
PRIORS	SWOOPS	AFLOAT	UPMOST	MONODY	CARPED
PROOFS	SYNODS	ALCOTT	UPROOT	NOBODY	COOPED
PUTONS	TABOOS	ALLOUT	UTMOST	ONIONY	COPPED
PYLONS	TABORS	ALMOST	VOLOST	OOLOGY	CRAPED
RAMOUS	TALONS	APPORT	WAYOUT	PAEONY	CREPED
RAYONS	TAROTS	ASSORT	******	PARODY	CUPPED
RAZORS	TENONS	BELOIT	---O-U	PHOOEY	CUSPED
REDOES	TENORS	CAHOOT	******	PRIORY	CUSPID
RIGORS	TETONS	CAVORT	ORMOLU	SATORY	DAMPED
RIMOUS	THIOLS	COHORT	******	SAVORY	DAPPED
ROBOTS	THROBS	COPOUT	---O-X	SAXONY	DIPPED
ROTORS	THROES	CUTOUT	******	SIMONY	DRAPED
RUFOUS	THROWS	DACOIT	BIJOUX	SNOOPY	DUMPED
RUGOUS	TOROUS	DAKOIT	******	SNOOTY	ELOPED
RUMORS	TOYONS	DECOCT	---O-Y	SODOMY	GAPPED
RUNONS	TROOPS	DEPORT	******	SPOOKY	GASPED
			ANTONY		
			APHONY		

GIMPED	RIPPED	FIPPLE	******	TARPAN	DIAPER
GIPPED	ROMPED	FRAPPE	---P-L	TENPIN	DIPPER
GRIPED	SALPID	GRIPPE	******	TIEPIN	DRAPER
GROPED	SAPPED	HIPPIE	CARPAL	TREPAN	DUMPER
GULPED	SEEPED	HOOPOE	CARPEL	TYMPAN	ELOPER
GYPPED	SHAPED	HOPPLE	CHAPEL	WEAPON	GASPAR
HAPPED	SIPPED	KELPIE	COMPEL	YAUPON	GASPER
HARPED	SLOPED	KEWPIE	DISPEL	YOUPON	GRIPER
HASPED	SNIPED	MAGPIE	DRUPEL	******	GROPER
HEAPED	SOAPED	NAPPIE	GOSPEL	---P-O	GULPER
HELPED	SOPPED	NIPPLE	PENPAL	******	HAMPER
HIPPED	SOUPED	PEOPLE	PROPEL	ALEPPO	HARPER
HISPID	STOPED	PIMPLE	PROPYL	CRYPTO	HELPER
HOOPED	STUPID	POPPLE	RAPPEL	GLYPTO	HOOPER
HOPPED	SUPPED	POTPIE	STIPEL	GRAPHO	HOPPER
HUMPED	SWIPED	PURPLE	TROPAL	LYMPHO	JAIPUR
ISOPOD	TAMPED	RAPPEE	******	MORPHO	JASPER
JUMPED	TAPPED	RIMPLE	---P-M	NYMPHO	JUMPER
KIPPED	TIPPED	RIPPLE	******	SAPPHO	KASPER
LAMPAD	TOPPED	RUMPLE	POMPOM	SCIPIO	KEEPER
LAMPED	TORPID	SAMPLE	WAMPUM	SCYPHO	KIPPER
LAPPED	TRIPOD	SEMPRE	******	SULPHO	LAPPER
LEAPED	TUPPED	SHOPPE	---P-N	TROPHO	LEAPER
LIMPED	UNAPID	SIMPLE	******	TROPPO	LIMPER
LIMPID	UNIPED	SKOPJE	BEDPAN	******	LIPPER
LIPPED	UROPOD	STAPLE	CHOPIN	---P-P	LISPER
LISPED	VAMPED	STEPPE	COUPON	******	LOOPER
LOOPED	VESPID	SUPPLE	DAMPEN	MAYPOP	NAPPER
LOPPED	WAPPED	SWIPLE	DEEPEN	SLAPUP	NIPPER
LUMPED	WARPED	TEMPLE	HAPPEN	SLIPUP	PAMPER
MAPPED	WISPED	TIPPLE	HATPIN	STEPUP	PAUPER
MOPPED	YAPPED	TOPPLE	HEMPEN	WRAPUP	PEEPER
NAPPED	YAUPED	TOUPEE	INSPAN	******	PEPPER
NIPPED	YAWPED	TRIPLE	LUMPEN	---P-R	POPPER
PALPED	YELPED	WIMPLE	NIPPON	******	PROPER
PEEPED	YIPPED	YIPPIE	PIGPEN	BUMPER	PULPER
PEPPED	ZIPPED	YUPPIE	PIPPIN	CAMPER	PUMPER
PIMPED	******	******	POMPON	CAPPER	RAPPER
PIPPED	---P-E	---P-I	REOPEN	CARPER	RASPER
POOPED	******	******	SAIPAN	CASPAR	REAPER
POPPED	AGAPAE	CLYPEI	SAMPAN	CASPER	RIPPER
PULPED	CORPSE	DELPHI	SEAPEN	COOPER	ROMPER
PUMPED	COUPLE	SCYPHI	SHAPEN	COPPER	SAPPER
PUPPED	DAPPLE	TAIPEI	SLIPON	COWPER	SECPAR
RAMPED	DIEPPE	******	STEPAN	CUPPER	SHAPER
RAPPED	DIMPLE	---P-K	STEPIN	DAMPER	SIMPER
RASPED	ELAPSE	******	TAMPAN	DAPPER	SIPPER
REAPED	EPOPEE	KALPAK	TAMPON	DEEPER	SLOPER

SNIPER	HIPPUS	PULPIT	SYLPHY	DHARNA	STERIC
STUPOR	KAPPAS	PUPPET	TEAPOY	DHURNA	TANREC
SUPPER	LAMPAS	PUTPUT	TROPHY	EGERIA	TENREC
TAMPER	LOUPES	RAJPUT	TWOPLY	ETERNA	THORAC
TAPPER	MYOPES	SEXPOT	WHIPPY	GLORIA	THORIC
TEMPER	NAPPES	SIPPET	******	IBERIA	VITRIC
TIPPER	NYMPHS	TAPPET	---Q-E	ISTRIA	YTTRIC
TOPPER	OKAPIS	TEAPOT	******	LATRIA	******
TORPOR	PALPUS	TINPOT	BARQUE	NUTRIA	---R-D
VESPER	PAMPAS	TIPPET	BASQUE	PEORIA	******
WARPER	PAPPUS	******	BISQUE	PYRRHA	ACARID
WEEPER	PHIPPS	---P-W	BRAQUE	PYURIA	ADORED
YAWPER	POPPYS	******	CAIQUE	SCORIA	ALFRED
YELPER	QUIPUS	PAWPAW	CASQUE	SHERPA	ASTRID
ZIPPER	RALPHS	QUAPAW	CHEQUE	SIERRA	BARRED
******	ROLPHS	******	CINQUE	SPARTA	BEARED
---P-S	RUMPUS	---P-X	CIRQUE	SPIREA	BEDRID
******	SALPAS	******	CLAQUE	STERNA	BIRRED
ADAPTS	SCAPES	AUSPEX	CLIQUE	THORIA	BLARED
ADEPTS	SCOPES	COWPOX	MANQUE	YTTRIA	BURRED
ADOPTS	SCOPUS	******	MARQUE	******	CHARED
ALEPHS	SHAPES	---P-Y	MASQUE	---R-B	CLERID
CAMPOS	SLOPES	******	MOSQUE	******	CONRAD
CAMPUS	SNIPES	APEPSY	OPAQUE	CHERUB	ELDRED
CARPUS	STAPES	BIOPSY	PLAQUE	MIDRIB	FAIRED
CHAPES	STIPES	CHIPPY	PULQUE	SCARAB	FEARED
COMPOS	STOPES	CHOPPY	RISQUE	******	FLARED
COOPTS	STUPAS	COMPLY	TORQUE	---R-C	FLORID
CORPUS	STUPES	DAMPLY	UNIQUE	******	FURRED
COUPES	SWIPES	DEEPLY	******	ACERIC	GEARED
COYPUS	SYLPHS	DIMPLY	---Q-I	AGARIC	GLARED
CRAPES	TAUPES	DRIPPY	******	ALARIC	HAIRED
CREPES	TEMPOS	DROPSY	SESQUI	CAPRIC	HATRED
CRYPTS	TEMPTS	DUMPTY	******	CEDRIC	HORRID
CUSPIS	TRIPOS	FLOPPY	---Q-S	CHORIC	HOTROD
DOLPHS	******	GRAPHY	******	CITRIC	HYBRID
DRAPES	---P-T	GRIPPY	IRAQIS	CLERIC	INBRED
DRUPES	******	HUMPTY	******	CUPRIC	INGRID
ELOPES	ARMPIT	LIMPLY	---Q-Y	CYMRIC	INURED
ERUPTS	CARPET	PIMPLY	******	EMERIC	JARRED
ETAPES	DESPOT	POMPEY	CLIQUY	FABRIC	JEERED
GLYPHS	HOTPOT	PREPAY	EXEQUY	FERRIC	KONRAD
GRAPES	INKPOT	RIPPLY	******	HYDRIC	LAIRED
GRAPHS	LAPPET	SIMPLY	---R-A	IATRIC	LEERED
GRIPES	LIMPET	SLOPPY	******	METRIC	LOURED
GROPES	MOPPET	SNAPPY	ANDREA	NITRIC	MADRID
HERPES	OUTPUT	SNIPPY	CHOREA	PICRIC	MARRED
HIPPOS	POPPET	SUPPLY	DHARMA	RUBRIC	MITRED

MOORED	AVERSE	SPURGE
NEARED	BARRIE	STARVE
NIMROD	BIERCE	SWERVE
NITRID	BOURNE	THORPE
PAIRED	BOURSE	THYRSE
PEERED	CARRIE	TIERCE
POURED	CHARGE	UMBRAE
PURRED	COARSE	UNTRUE
PUTRID	COERCE	UPHROE
QUIRED	CORRIE	WHARVE
RAMROD	COURSE	WHERVE
REARED	COWRIE	******
RETROD	DEARIE	**---R-F**
ROARED	DECREE	******
SACRED	DEGREE	SHERIF
SCARED	ECARTE	******
SCORED	EMBRUE	**---R-H**
SEARED	EMERGE	******
SHARED	EMERIE	BASRAH
SHORED	ENTREE	CHURCH
SIGRID	FAERIE	COPRAH
SNARED	FAEROE	DEARTH
SNORED	FIERCE	EPARCH
SOARED	FLORAE	EXARCH
SOCRED	GEORGE	FOURTH
SOURED	GOURDE	HEARTH
SPARED	HEARSE	HURRAH
SPIRED	HOARSE	INARCH
SPORED	HYDRAE	SCORCH
STARED	IMBRUE	SEARCH
STORED	KERRIE	SMIRCH
TARRED	LAURAE	STARCH
TEARED	LAURIE	SWARTH
TETRAD	LEGREE	******
TIERED	LIBRAE	**---R-I**
TORRID	LIERNE	******
TOURED	MONROE	ANDREI
UNBRED	PEIRCE	GEORGI
UNTROD	PETRIE	GHARRI
VEERED	PIERCE	OCTROI
WARRED	PIERRE	THYRSI
WHORED	PUGREE	******
******	QUARTE	**---R-J**
---R-E	SCARCE	******
******	SOIREE	SWARAJ
ACCRUE	SOURCE	******
AGORAE	SPARGE	**---R-K**
AMERCE	SPARSE	******
		ANORAK
		DVORAK

******	******	******
---R-L	**---R-N**	**---R-P**
******	******	******
ABORAL	ANURAN	ENTRAP
AMORAL	BARREN	ENWRAP
ASTRAL	CHARON	INWRAP
BARREL	CHIRON	LARRUP
CARREL	CITRON	RIPRAP
CHERYL	CYPRIN	SATRAP
CHORAL	DACRON	UNWRAP
CITRAL	FIBRIN	******
CORRAL	FLORIN	**---R-R**
CRURAL	GIBRAN	******
FIBRIL	HEBRON	ADORER
FLORAL	HEDRON	BEARER
GOORAL	KEDRON	DEARER
HEDRAL	MACRON	FAIRER
LAUREL	MATRON	FEARER
MITRAL	MICRON	FENRIR
NEURAL	NATRON	FUHRER
PARRAL	NEURON	HEARER
PARREL	OBERON	HORROR
PATROL	OUTRAN	JEERER
PETREL	OUTRUN	MARRER
PETROL	PATRON	MIRROR
PLURAL	PERRON	NEARER
SACRAL	SEARIN	POORER
SAUREL	SHARON	POURER
SORREL	SHORAN	REARER
SPIRAL	THORON	ROARER
STEROL	WARREN	SCARER
TETRYL	******	SCORER
UMBRAL	**---R-O**	SHARER
******	******	SNARER
---R-M	AVERNO	SNORER
******	BARRIO	SOARER
ALARUM	CHOREO	SOURER
ANTRIM	EMBRYO	SPARER
ANTRUM	HAIRDO	STARER
ASARUM	KARROO	TERROR
CUPRUM	OPORTO	TOURER
ENGRAM	OVERDO	USURER
FERRUM	QUARTO	WEARER
LABRUM	SPERMO	******
MEGRIM	STEREO	**---R-S**
POGROM	STERNO	******
QUORUM	THERMO	ABORTS
SACRUM	THYREO	ACORNS
	VIBRIO	

ADORES	DERRIS	LIVRES	SMIRKS	YEARNS	MORROW
ADORNS	DOBRAS	MADRAS	SNARES	ZEBRAS	NARROW
AGORAS	DWARFS	MAORIS	SNARLS	******	SORROW
ALARMS	ELBRUS	METROS	SNORES	---R-T	UNDRAW
ALERTS	EPIRUS	MOIRAS	SNORTS	******	UNDREW
ANDRES	ESTRUS	MORRIS	SPARES	ARARAT	YARROW
AVERTS	EVERTS	MORROS	SPARKS	BARRET	******
AVERYS	EXERTS	MOURNS	SPIRES	BEIRUT	---R-X
AWARDS	EXTRAS	MURRES	SPIRTS	CARROT	******
AZORES	EXURBS	NORRIS	SPORES	CLARET	MATRIX
AZURES	FERRIS	OPERAS	SPORTS	DRYROT	STORAX
BAIRNS	FIORDS	OSIRIS	SPURNS	ESPRIT	THORAX
BARRYS	FLARES	PADRES	SPURTS	EVERET	******
BEARDS	FLIRTS	PEARLS	STARES	FERRET	---R-Y
BLARES	FLORAS	PEDROS	STARTS	FLORET	******
BLURBS	FLORES	PERRYS	STERES	GARRET	AFFRAY
BLURTS	GENRES	PHAROS	STERNS	HEARST	ANERGY
BOARDS	GENROS	PIERUS	STIRKS	IGOROT	ASTRAY
BOURGS	GERRYS	QUARKS	STIRPS	IMARET	AUBREY
BOURNS	GLARES	QUARTS	STORES	LABRET	AUDREY
BURROS	GNARLS	QUERNS	STORKS	LEARNT	BETRAY
CADRES	GOURDS	QUIRES	STORMS	PARROT	BLURRY
CAIRNS	GUARDS	QUIRKS	SUCRES	REGRET	CHARRY
CEORLS	HARRIS	QUIRTS	SUTRAS	SECRET	CHERRY
CHARDS	HARRYS	REARMS	SWARDS	SEURAT	CHIRPY
CHARES	HEARTS	SABRAS	SWARMS	SPIRIT	CLERGY
CHARMS	HENRIS	SAURUS	SWIRLS	TERRET	DEARLY
CHARTS	HENRYS	SCARES	SWORDS	THIRST	DEFRAY
CHIRMS	HOARDS	SCARFS	TAURUS	TURRET	DOURLY
CHIRPS	HOURIS	SCARPS	TERRYS	******	ENERGY
CHIRRS	HUBRIS	SCORES	THERMS	---R-U	ESTRAY
CHORDS	HYBRIS	SCORNS	THIRDS	******	FAIRLY
CHORES	HYDRAS	SHARDS	THORNS	ARERCU	FLIRTY
CHORUS	HYDROS	SHARES	TIARAS	******	FLURRY
CHURLS	ICARUS	SHARKS	TIGRIS	---R-W	GHARRY
CHURNS	INARMS	SHARPS	TWERPS	******	GNARLY
CHURRS	INDRIS	SHERDS	TWIRLS	ANDREW	HEARTY
CIRRUS	INGRES	SHIRES	TWIRPS	BARROW	HOORAY
CITRUS	INURES	SHIRKS	UMBRAS	BORROW	HOURLY
CLARAS	INURNS	SHIRRS	USURPS	BURROW	HURRAY
CLARES	JERRYS	SHIRTS	UTERUS	DARROW	KNARRY
CLAROS	KAURIS	SHORES	UTURNS	ESCROW	KNURLY
CLERKS	KNURLS	SHORLS	WALRUS	FARROW	MURRAY
COBRAS	LAIRDS	SHORTS	WHARFS	FURROW	MURREY
COURTS	LARRYS	SKIRRS	WHIRLS	HARROW	NEARBY
CRORES	LAURAS	SKIRTS	WHORES	HEBREW	NEARLY
CYPRUS	LEARNS	SLURPS	WHORLS	JARROW	OSPREY
DEBRIS	LIBRAS	SMARTS	WHORTS	MARROW	OVERLY

PEARLY	LEPSIA	GASSED	CASSIE	******	PASSIM
POORLY	MARSHA	GOOSED	CHASSE	---S-I	POSSUM
QUARRY	MIASMA	HISSED	CHASTE	******	RANSOM
SCURFY	NAUSEA	HORSED	CISSIE	BONSAI	******
SCURRY	ODESSA	HOUSED	CROSSE	NEVSKI	---S-N
SCURVY	PERSIA	IRISED	CRUSOE	SANSEI	******
SHERRY	PHASIA	JESSED	CUISSE	******	ALISON
SHIRTY	PLASIA	KISSED	ELYSEE	---S-L	ARISEN
SKERRY	PLASMA	LAPSED	ENISLE	******	BOLSON
SLURRY	RUSSIA	LEASED	FOCSLE	BURSAL	BUNSEN
SMARMY	SHASTA	LIASED	FOSSAE	CAUSAL	CARSON
SNARLY	SIESTA	LOOSED	GUSSIE	CHISEL	CHOSEN
SOURLY	TARSIA	LOUSED	HASSLE	CONSUL	COUSIN
SPARRY	ZOYSIA	MASSED	HORSTE	CRESOL	DAMSON
SPERRY	******	MESSED	JESSIE	DAMSEL	DAWSON
SPORTY	---S-C	MISSED	LASSIE	DIESEL	DOBSON
SPURRY	******	MOUSED	LESSEE	DORSAL	EDISON
STARRY	AIRSAC	MUSSED	MAISIE	DOSSAL	GIBSON
STOREY	CORSAC	NOISED	MOISHE	DOSSEL	GODSON
STORMY	OVISAC	NOOSED	MOUSSE	DOSSIL	HAUSEN
STURDY	PARSEC	NURSED	PARSEE	FOSSIL	HUDSON
SURREY	PHASIC	PARSED	PASSEE	HANSEL	JONSON
SWARTY	PHYSIC	PASSED	POTSIE	HASSEL	KAMSIN
SWIRLY	******	PAUSED	PUISNE	MENSAL	KANSAN
THIRTY	---S-D	PHASED	PURSUE	MISSAL	KELSON
THORNY	******	POISED	TESSIE	MISSEL	LASSEN
WEIRDY	ABASED	PROSED	THISBE	MORSEL	LESSEN
WHERRY	ABUSED	PULSED	TISSUE	MUSSEL	LESSON
YEARLY	AMUSED	PURSED	TOUSLE	PODSOL	LOOSEN
******	BIASED	RAISED	TRISTE	TARSAL	MAISON
---R-Z	BOSSED	RINSED	TUSSLE	TASSEL	MYOSIN
******	BOUSED	ROUSED	WRASSE	TEASEL	NELSON
JUAREZ	BOWSED	SASSED	******	TINSEL	ORISON
QUARTZ	BUSSED	SEISED	---S-F	TONSIL	PARSON
******	CAUSED	SENSED	******	TUSSAL	PEASEN
---S-A	CEASED	SOUSED	MASSIF	VASSAL	PEPSIN
******	CENSED	SUSSED	******	VESSEL	PERSON
ALASKA	CHASED	TEASED	---S-H	WEASEL	POISON
ARISTA	CLOSED	TENSED	******	******	PRISON
AVESTA	CURSED	TOSSED	BORSCH	---S-M	PTISAN
AYESHA	CUSSED	UNUSED	KIRSCH	******	RAISIN
CASSIA	DORSAD	VERSED	KITSCH	BALSAM	RAMSON
CUESTA	DOSSED	YESSED	PHOSPH	DORSUM	REASON
EGESTA	DOUSED	******	PUTSCH	GYPSUM	ROBSON
ELISHA	DOWSED	---S-E	TUSSAH	HANSOM	SAMSON
FIESTA	ERASED	******		JETSAM	SEASON
FRUSTA	FEASED	BESSIE		LISSOM	SEISIN
GEISHA	FUSSED	BURSAE		OMASUM	SELSYN

TELSON	DOWSER	ARISES	DAISES	JOSSES	PLUSES
TOCSIN	ERASER	AVISOS	DAISYS	JOUSTS	POISES
TUCSON	FALSER	BALSAS	DEISTS	KAASES	POSSES
UNISON	FUSSER	BASSES	DIESES	KANSAS	PRESAS
VINSON	GEYSER	BASSOS	DIESIS	KIOSKS	PRISMS
WATSON	HAWSER	BEASTS	DIPSAS	KISSES	PROSES
WILSON	HISSER	BESSYS	DOUSES	KNOSPS	PTOSIS
WORSEN	HUSSAR	BETSYS	DOWSES	KRISES	PULSES
******	KAISER	BIASES	DRUSES	LAPSES	PURSES
---S-O	KISSER	BIOSIS	ECESIS	LAPSUS	PUSSES
******	LAPSER	BLASTS	EGESTS	LASSES	PYOSIS
ARISTO	LESSER	BOASTS	EMESIS	LASSOS	QUESTS
BLASTO	LESSOR	BOOSTS	ENOSIS	LEASES	RAISES
FIASCO	LOOSER	BOSSES	ERASES	LENSES	RHESUS
FRESCO	MAUSER	BOUSES	EXISTS	LOOSES	RINSES
FRESNO	MOUSER	BOWSES	EYASES	LOSSES	ROASTS
GEMSBO	NASSER	BRISKS	FEASES	LOUSES	ROOSTS
GLOSSO	NURSER	BURSAS	FEASTS	MANSES	ROUSES
PHYSIO	PASSER	BURSES	FEISTS	MASSES	ROUSTS
PLASMO	PAUSER	BURSTS	FESSES	MENSES	SASSES
POUSTO	PROSER	BUSSES	FIRSTS	MESSES	SEISMS
PRESTO	PULSAR	BYSSUS	FLASKS	MESSRS	SENSES
SEISMO	PURSER	CANSOS	FOISTS	MIOSIS	SEPSIS
UNESCO	QUASAR	CASSIS	FOSSES	MISSES	SOUSES
******	RAISER	CAUSES	FRISES	MISSIS	SPASMS
---S-P	RINSER	CEASES	FRISKS	MISSUS	STASES
******	ROUSER	CENSES	FROSTS	MOSSES	STASIS
CATSUP	SANSAR	CENSUS	FUSSES	MOUSES	TARSUS
GOSSIP	SARSAR	CHASES	GASSES	MUSSES	TEASES
HYSSOP	SEISOR	CHASMS	GESSOS	MYOSIS	TENSES
TOSSUP	SENSOR	CHESTS	GHOSTS	NAOSES	THESES
******	TEASER	CISSYS	GLOSTS	NESSUS	THESIS
---S-R	TENSER	CLASPS	GNOSIS	NOESIS	TOASTS
******	TENSOR	CLOSES	GOOSES	NOISES	TORSKS
ABASER	TERSER	COASTS	GORSES	NOOSES	TORSOS
ABUSER	TUSSAR	COPSES	GRASPS	NURSES	TOSSES
AMUSER	WORSER	CORSES	GUESTS	ONUSES	TRUSTS
BURSAR	WOWSER	COSSES	GUISES	PANSYS	TRYSTS
CAESAR	******	CRASIS	HAWSES	PARSES	TUSSIS
CAUSER	---S-S	CRESTS	HEISTS	PARSIS	TWISTS
CENSER	******	CRISES	HISSES	PASSES	UKASES
CENSOR	ABASES	CRISIS	HOISTS	PASSUS	UPASES
CENSUR	ABUSES	CRISPS	HORSES	PATSYS	VERSES
CHASER	ABYSMS	CRUSES	HOUSES	PAUSES	VERSOS
CLOSER	AGISTS	CRUSTS	IBISES	PEASES	VERSTS
CURSOR	AMUSES	CURSES	IRISES	PHASES	VERSUS
DENSER	ANISES	CUSSES	JESSES	PHASIS	WAISTS
DOSSER	ANUSES	CUSSOS	JOISTS	PLASIS	WHISKS

WORSTS	******	SLOSHY	EMETIC	BUSTED	JILTED
WRESTS	---S-X	SLUSHY	EROTIC	BUTTED	JOLTED
WRISTS	******	THUSLY	EXOTIC	CANTED	JOTTED
YEASTS	SUSSEX	TRASHY	FISTIC	CARTED	JUTTED
YESSES	UNISEX	TRESSY	FUSTIC	CATTED	KILTED
******	WESSEX	TRUSTY	GESTIC	COATED	KITTED
---S-T	******	TWISTY	HECTIC	COSTED	LASTED
******	---S-Y	WHISKY	IRITIC	CRATED	LIFTED
AVOSET	******	YEASTY	KELTIC	DARTED	LILTED
BASSET	BRASHY	******	LACTIC	DENTED	LISTED
BEDSIT	BRASSY	---T-A	LUETIC	DIETED	LOFTED
CLOSET	BRUSHY	******	MANTIC	DINTED	LOOTED
CORSET	CHESTY	AGATHA	MASTIC	DOITED	LUSTED
COSSET	CLASSY	ANITRA	MIOTIC	DOTTED	MALTED
CRUSET	CRISPY	APHTHA	MYSTIC	DUSTED	MASTED
DOESNT	CRUSTY	BERTHA	NASTIC	EDITED	MATTED
DORSET	DRESSY	CENTRA	NOETIC	ELATED	MELTED
GUSSET	DROSKY	CONTRA	NOSTIC	EMOTED	MILTED
OFFSET	DROSSY	ELYTRA	PECTIC	EXITED	MINTED
OUTSAT	FEISTY	GRETNA	PEPTIC	FASTED	MISTED
OUTSET	FLASHY	HESTIA	PHOTIC	FATTED	MOATED
OUTSIT	FLESHY	MALTHA	POETIC	FELTED	MOLTED
POSSET	FLOSSY	MANTUA	PONTIC	FISTED	MOOTED
PROSIT	FRISKY	MARTHA	RUSTIC	FITTED	NESTED
RUSSET	FROSTY	PORTIA	SAITIC	FLUTED	NETTED
SUNSET	GLASSY	QUOTHA	SEPTIC	FOETID	NUTTED
TASSET	GLOSSY	ROSTRA	STATIC	FOOTED	ORATED
TEASET	GOOSEY	SCOTIA	TACTIC	GAITED	OUSTED
UNDSET	GRASSY	******	THETIC	GIFTED	PANTED
VERSET	GRISLY	---T-B	TOLTEC	GIRTED	PARTED
WADSET	GROSZY	******	URETIC	GRATED	PASTED
******	GUNSHY	CANTAB	VIATIC	GUTTED	PATTED
---S-U	HALSEY	******	******	HAFTED	PELTED
******	HORSEY	---T-C	---T-D	HALTED	PENTAD
DESSAU	JERSEY	******	******	HASTED	PETTED
HONSHU	KERSEY	ACETIC	ABATED	HATTED	PITTED
KYUSHU	KINSEY	AORTIC	ALATED	HEATED	PLATED
NASSAU	MARSHY	ARCTIC	BAITED	HEFTED	PORTED
SAMSHU	MEASLY	AZOTIC	BASTED	HEPTAD	POSTED
******	MERSEY	BALTIC	BATTED	HILTED	POTTED
---S-W	OCASEY	BIOTIC	BELTED	HINTED	POUTED
******	PIGSTY	BUSTIC	BESTED	HOOTED	PRATED
BOWSAW	PLASHY	CELTIC	BETTED	HOSTED	PUNTED
JIGSAW	PLASTY	COPTIC	BITTED	HOTTED	PUTTED
RIPSAW	PLUSHY	CRETIC	BOATED	HUNTED	QUOTED
SEESAW	PRISSY	CRITIC	BOLTED	HUTTED	RAFTED
WARSAW	PUSSEY	CYSTIC	BOOTED	JESTED	RANTED
	PUSSLY		BUNTED	JETTED	RATTED

RENTED	WONTED	KETTLE	SWATHE	THATCH	MORTAL
RESTED	ZESTED	KILTIE	TATTLE	TWITCH	PASTEL
RETTED	******	KIRTLE	TEETHE	WRETCH	PASTIL
RIFTED	---T-E	KITTLE	TESTAE	******	PISTIL
RIOTED	******	LAOTSE	TIPTOE	---T-I	PISTOL
ROOTED	AORTAE	LITTLE	TITTLE	******	PONTIL
ROTTED	AUNTIE	LOATHE	TOOTLE	CANTHI	PORTAL
ROUTED	BATTLE	LOTTIE	TSETSE	CENTRI	POSTAL
RUSTED	BATTUE	LUSTRE	TURTLE	DMITRI	RECTAL
RUTTED	BEETLE	LYTTAE	VESTEE	GLUTEI	RENTAL
SALTED	BERTHE	MAITRE	VIRTUE	******	RICTAL
SEATED	BERTIE	MANTLE	VITTAE	---T-K	SANTOL
SIFTED	BLITHE	MARTHE	WATTLE	******	SEPTAL
SILTED	BOOTEE	MATTIE	WRITHE	BARTOK	SPITAL
SKATED	BOOTIE	MESTEE	******	BATTIK	STATAL
SLATED	BOOTLE	METTLE	---T-F	******	TROTYL
SOOTED	BOTTLE	MISTLE	******	---T-L	VESTAL
SORTED	BOWTIE	MOLTKE	GUSTAF	******	******
SPITED	BUSTLE	MOTTLE	******	ACETAL	---T-M
STATED	CANTLE	MUSTEE	---T-G	ACETYL	******
SUITED	CASTLE	MYRTLE	******	AMATOL	ACETUM
TARTED	CATTIE	NESTLE	RAGTAG	AMYTAL	ADYTUM
TASTED	CATTLE	NETTIE	TAUTOG	AORTAL	BALTIM
TATTED	CENTRE	NETTLE	ZAFTIG	BRUTAL	BANTAM
TENTED	CLOTHE	ODETTE	******	CARTEL	BOTTOM
TESTED	COATEE	PANTIE	---T-H	CENTAL	CUSTOM
TILTED	CONTRE	PESTLE	******	COITAL	DIATOM
TINTED	COOTIE	PINTLE	BLOTCH	COSTAL	DICTUM
TOOTED	COSTAE	PLATTE	CHETAH	DACTYL	FACTUM
TOTTED	COTTAE	POTTLE	CLUTCH	DENTAL	FANTOM
TOUTED	CUPTIE	PUTTEE	CRATCH	DENTIL	LACTAM
TUFTED	CUTTLE	QUATRE	CROTCH	DIETAL	RECTUM
TUTTED	DARTLE	RATTLE	CRUTCH	DISTAL	RHYTHM
UNITED	DOTTLE	ROOTLE	CULTCH	DISTIL	SCUTUM
VATTED	FETTLE	RUSTLE	FLETCH	DOTTEL	SEPTUM
VENTED	FOOTLE	SARTRE	FLITCH	FESTAL	SPUTUM
VESTED	GENTLE	SCATHE	HOOTCH	FOETAL	SYSTEM
VETTED	GERTIE	SCYTHE	NAUTCH	FONTAL	TAMTAM
VOLTED	GOATEE	SEETHE	QUITCH	GRETEL	TOMTOM
WAFTED	GOETHE	SETTEE	SCOTCH	HARTAL	VICTIM
WAITED	GOITRE	SETTLE	SCUTCH	HOSTEL	******
WANTED	GUTTAE	SNATHE	SKETCH	HYETAL	---T-N
WASTED	GUTTLE	SOOTHE	SMUTCH	INSTIL	******
WELTED	HATTIE	SORTIE	SNATCH	LENTIL	AUSTEN
WETTED	HOGTIE	SPATHE	SNITCH	LINTEL	AUSTIN
WHITED	HURTLE	STATUE	STITCH	LISTEL	BARTON
WILTED	HUSTLE	SUBTLE	SWATCH	MANTEL	BATTEN
WITTED	JOSTLE	SUTTEE	SWITCH	MENTAL	BATTIN

BEATEN	LISTEN	BISTRO	BUSTER	GRATER	MOLTER
BENTON	MARTEN	CASTRO	BUTTER	GUITAR	MOOTER
BHUTAN	MARTIN	CENTRO	CANTER	GUNTER	MORTAR
BIOTIN	MELTON	CLOTHO	CANTOR	GUTTER	MUSTER
BITTEN	MILTON	DEXTRO	CAPTOR	HALTER	MUTTER
BOLTON	MITTEN	GASTRO	CARTER	HATTER	NATTER
BOSTON	MOLTEN	GENTOO	CASTER	HEATER	NEATER
BRETON	MORTON	GHETTO	CASTOR	HECTOR	NECTAR
BRITON	MOUTON	GIOTTO	CAUTER	HELTER	NESTOR
BURTON	MUTTON	GLOTTO	CENTER	HESTER	NEUTER
BUTTON	NEATEN	GNATHO	COLTER	HITTER	NUTTER
BUXTON	NEKTON	GROTTO	COSTAR	HOOTER	OBITER
CAFTAN	NEWTON	MATTEO	COSTER	HOTTER	ORATOR
CANTON	PATTEN	PIETRO	COTTAR	HUNTER	OUSTER
CARTON	PATTON	STETHO	COTTER	HURTER	OYSTER
CAXTON	PECTEN	TATTOO	CRATER	HYSTER	PALTER
CHITIN	PECTIN	VENTRO	CUSTER	INSTAR	PASTER
CHITON	PHOTON	XANTHO	CUTTER	ISHTAR	PASTOR
CONTIN	PHYTIN	******	DARTER	JESTER	PATTER
CORTIN	PISTON	---T-P	DEBTOR	JILTER	PELTER
COTTON	PLATAN	******	DEFTER	JITTER	PESTER
CRETAN	PLATEN	INSTEP	DEXTER	JOLTER	PEWTER
CRETIN	PONTON	PEGTOP	DIETER	JOTTER	PICTOR
CRETON	PROTON	PENTUP	DOCTOR	KILTER	PIETER
CROTON	RATTAN	REDTOP	DOPTER	KULTUR	PINTER
DALTON	RATTEN	TIPTOP	DOTTER	LASTER	PLATER
DANTON	ROTTEN	TITTUP	DUSTER	LATTER	PORTER
DAYTON	SEXTAN	UNSTEP	EASTER	LECTOR	POSTER
DENTIN	SEXTON	UNSTOP	EDITOR	LESTER	POTTER
EASTON	SHUTIN	******	ELATER	LETTER	POUTER
EMETIN	SOFTEN	---T-R	EXETER	LICTOR	POWTER
FANTAN	STATEN	******	FACTOR	LIFTER	PRATER
FASTEN	SULTAN	ABATER	FALTER	LINTER	PRETER
FATTEN	SUNTAN	ABATOR	FASTER	LISTER	PRETOR
FULTON	SUTTON	AUSTER	FATTER	LITTER	PUNTER
GASTON	TARTAN	AVATAR	FESTER	LOFTER	PUTTER
GLUTEN	TAUTEN	BANTER	FETTER	LOITER	QUOTER
GOTTEN	TESTON	BARTER	FILTER	LOOTER	RAFTER
GRATIN	TEUTON	BATTER	FITTER	LUSTER	RANTER
HASTEN	TRITON	BAXTER	FLUTER	MARTYR	RAPTOR
ISATIN	WALTON	BEATER	FOETOR	MASTER	RASTER
JETTON	WANTON	BESTIR	FOOTER	MATTER	RATTER
JUSTIN	WHITEN	BETTER	FOSTER	MEETER	RECTOR
KAFTAN	WYSTAN	BETTOR	FRATER	MELTER	RENTER
KITTEN	******	BISTER	GAITER	MENTOR	RESTER
LATTEN	---T-O	BITTER	GARTER	MILTER	RHETOR
LENTEN	******	BOATER	GETTER	MINTER	RIOTER
LEPTON	ANATTO	BOLTER	GOITER	MISTER	RITTER
	AUSTRO				

ROOTER	WASTER	CULTUS	MONTES	SWATHS	******
ROSTER	WELTER	CURTIS	MONTHS	TASTES	---T-Y
ROTTER	WESTER	CUSTOS	MONTYS	TENTHS	******
ROUTER	WETTER	DATTOS	MORTYS	TESTES	APATHY
SALTER	WHITER	DEATHS	MOTTOS	TESTIS	CHATTY
SARTOR	WINTER	DELTAS	MOUTHS	THETAS	CHITTY
SCOTER	WRITER	DEPTHS	MUFTIS	THETIS	CLOTTY
SECTOR	XYSTER	DHOTIS	NANTES	TILTHS	COSTLY
SETTER	YESTER	DITTOS	NINTHS	TROTHS	CURTLY
SIFTER	ZOSTER	EARTHS	ORATES	TRUTHS	CURTSY
SINTER	******	EDITHS	OTITIS	TUTTIS	DAFTLY
SISTER	---T-S	ELATES	PASTAS	UNITES	DEATHY
SITTER	******	EMOTES	PASTES	VESTAS	DEFTLY
SKATER	ABATES	ENATES	PHOTOS	VISTAS	EARTHY
SLATER	ABATIS	EVITAS	PINTOS	WASTES	FILTHY
SMITER	AEETES	FAITHS	PLATES	WHITES	FLATLY
SOFTER	AGATES	FIFTHS	PLUTUS	WIDTHS	FRETTY
SORTER	ANITAS	FIRTHS	PONTES	WRITES	FROTHY
STATER	AORTAS	FLATUS	POTTOS	XTSTUS	GANTRY
STATOR	ARETES	FLUTES	PRATES	XYSTOS	GENTLY
SUBTER	BANTUS	FOETUS	PUNTOS	YOUTHS	GENTRY
SUITOR	BASTES	FORTES	QUOTAS	ZLOTYS	GRITTY
TARTAR	BERTHS	FORTIS	QUOTES	******	GROTTY
TARTER	BETTES	FRITHS	RECTOS	---T-T	HEATHY
TASTER	BETTYS	FROTHS	RECTUS	******	ICHTHY
TATTER	BIRTHS	GENTES	RENTES	GUTTAT	JUSTLY
TAUTER	BOOTHS	GERTYS	RIATAS	MUSTNT	KNOTTY
TEETER	BROTHS	GRATES	RICTUS	SEPTET	LASTLY
TENTER	BRUTES	GRATIS	ROUTES	SESTET	MEETLY
TESTER	BRUTUS	GRETAS	SAUTES	SEXTET	MOSTLY
TETTER	BUTTES	HASTES	SCOTTS	TOMTIT	MOUTHY
TILTER	CACTUS	HATTYS	SCUTES	******	NEATLY
TITTER	CANTOS	HEATHS	SETTOS	---T-V	PALTRY
TOOTER	CANTUS	HETTYS	SHOTES	******	PANTRY
TOTTER	CARTES	HIATUS	SIXTES	GUSTAV	PARTLY
TOUTER	CASTES	IRITIS	SIXTHS	******	PASTRY
TRITER	CENTOS	JUNTAS	SKATES	---T-W	PELTRY
ULSTER	CERTES	JUSTUS	SLATES	******	PERTLY
URETER	CESTUS	KEITHS	SLOTHS	BESTOW	POETRY
VASTER	CHUTES	KITTYS	SMITES	KOWTOW	PORTLY
VECTOR	CLOTHS	LENTOS	SMITHS	******	PRETTY
VENTER	COATIS	MANTAS	SNATHS	---T-X	RAPTLY
VIATOR	COITUS	MANTES	SOFTAS	******	SCATTY
VICTOR	CONTES	MANTIS	SPATES	CORTEX	SENTRY
WAFTER	CONTOS	MARTAS	SPITES	LASTEX	SMITHY
WAITER	CORTES	MARTYS	STATES	SURTAX	SMUTTY
WALTER	COTTAS	MATTES	STATUS	SYNTAX	SNOTTY
WANTER	CRATES	MEATUS	SUITES	VERTEX	SOFTLY
				VORTEX	

SPOTTY	NOMURA	ROGUED	EFFUSE	PILULE	BARUCH
STITHY	PAPULA	ROTUND	EMEUTE	REBUKE	CHOUGH
SUBTLY	PETULA	SECUND	ENDURE	RECUSE	CLOUGH
SULTRY	PLEURA	SHOULD	ENSURE	REDUCE	CROUCH
TARTLY	PNEUMA	TWOULD	EXCUSE	REFUGE	DROUTH
TATTLY	RADULA	VALUED	EXHUME	REFUSE	DULUTH
TAUTLY	REMUDA	******	FERULE	REFUTE	ENOUGH
TOOTHY	STRUMA	---U-E	FIGURE	REPUTE	EUNUCH
TOOTSY	SYNURA	******	FUTURE	RESUME	GROUCH
VASTLY	TRAUMA	ABJURE	GROUSE	RETUSE	INRUSH
VESTRY	UNGULA	ACCUSE	HEAUME	SALUTE	ONRUSH
WHITBY	URSULA	ADDUCE	ILLUME	SCOUSE	PLOUGH
WHITEY	VACUNA	ADJURE	ILLUSE	SECURE	SLEUTH
WINTRY	VALUTA	ALLUDE	IMMUNE	SEDUCE	SLOUCH
WORTHY	VARUNA	ALLURE	IMMURE	SOLUTE	SLOUGH
WRATHY	VICUNA	ALMUCE	IMPURE	SPOUSE	THOUGH
******	YORUBA	ALMUDE	IMPUTE	SPRUCE	THRUSH
---T-Z	ZONULA	AMPULE	INCUSE	SUTURE	TROUGH
******	******	ARBUTE	INDUCE	TENURE	UPRUSH
CORTEZ	---U-B	ARMURE	INFUSE	TRIUNE	******
******	******	AROUSE	INHUME	TROUPE	---U-I
---U-A	BENUMB	ASSUME	INJURE	TUBULE	******
******	SUBURB	ASSURE	INSURE	UNSURE	AGOUTI
BELUGA	******	ASTUTE	JEJUNE	VELURE	GOMUTI
CANULA	---U-D	ATTUNE	JUJUBE	VENULE	INCUBI
CAYUGA	******	BEMUSE	LAGUNE	VOLUME	KABUKI
CEDULA	ABOUND	BLOUSE	LEGUME	VOLUTE	LAZULI
CESURA	ABSURD	CANUTE	LIGULE	ZONULE	LIMULI
COPULA	ARGUED	CAYUSE	LIGURE	******	SALUKI
CREUSA	AROUND	CERUSE	LOBULE	---U-F	WATUSI
DATURA	EDMUND	CLAUDE	LUNULE	******	YEHUDI
DECUMA	ENDUED	CLAUSE	MACULE	ENGULF	******
FACULA	ENSUED	COHUNE	MANURE	INGULF	---U-K
FECULA	FECUND	COLURE	MATURE	REBUFF	******
FERULA	GERUND	CROUPE	MINUTE	SCRUFF	CANUCK
FIBULA	GROUND	CUPULE	MISUSE	******	DEBUNK
HECUBA	IMBUED	CURULE	MODULE	---U-G	PODUNK
KORUNA	INDUED	DANUBE	MUTULE	******	SHRUNK
LACUNA	ISSUED	DEDUCE	NATURE	COBURG	STRUCK
LIGULA	JOCUND	DEFUSE	NODULE	SPRUNG	UNHUSK
LUNULA	LIQUID	DELUDE	OBTUSE	STRUNG	******
MACULA	OBTUND	DELUGE	ORDURE	UNSUNG	---U-L
MADURA	ORMUZD	DELUXE	OSCULE	******	******
MAZUMA	OSMUND	DEMURE	PAIUTE	---U-H	ACTUAL
MEDUSA	PEQUOD	DENUDE	PAPULE	******	ANNUAL
MEZUZA	PIQUED	DEPUTE	PARURE	ABLUSH	CASUAL
MORULA	QUEUED	DILUTE	PERUKE	AMBUSH	LEMUEL
NEBULA	REFUND	DISUSE	PERUSE	AVOUCH	MANUAL

MANUEL	GLAUCO	ENSUES	SCRUMS	EXEUNT	MAGUEY
MIGUEL	IMMUNO	FANUMS	SEDUMS	FLAUNT	OCCUPY
MUTUAL	LANUGO	FEMURS	SERUMS	ILLUST	PENURY
REFUEL	MADURO	FIQUES	SETUPS	INDUCT	RHEUMY
RITUAL	PLEURO	FLOURS	SHOUTS	INDULT	SIRUPY
SAMUEL	PNEUMO	FLOUTS	SHRUBS	INSULT	SYRUPY
SEQUEL	PSEUDO	FORUMS	SHRUGS	INTUIT	UNDULY
SEXUAL	ROMULO	FRAUDS	SIEURS	ISEULT	UNRULY
TOLUOL	STAURO	FUGUES	SIRUPS	JESUIT	******
TOLUYL	TENUTO	GAMUTS	SNOUTS	LOCUST	---U-Z
UNCURL	******	GETUPS	SPOUTS	LOQUAT	******
UNFURL	---U-P	GHAUTS	SPRUES	MINUET	HALUTZ
UNGUAL	******	GHOULS	STOUPS	OCCULT	******
VIDUAL	METUMP	GIGUES	STOUTS	PENULT	---V-A
VISUAL	******	GROUPS	STRUMS	PEQUOT	******
******	---U-R	GROUTS	STRUTS	PIQUET	FLAVIA
---U-M	******	IMBUES	SUNUPS	PROUST	LATVIA
******	ARGUER	INCURS	SYRUPS	RESULT	OLIVIA
VACUUM	ISSUER	INDUES	TENUES	ROBUST	PRAVDA
******	JAGUAR	INPUTS	TENUIS	ROQUET	SALVIA
---U-N	LIQUOR	ISSUES	THRUMS	SCHUIT	SILVIA
******	LOQUAR	JORUMS	TIEUPS	THRUST	SYLVIA
ALCUIN	VAGUER	KNOUTS	TOGUES	TUMULT	TRIVIA
AUBURN	VALUER	LEHUAS	TOQUES	UNHURT	******
AUTUMN	******	LEMURS	TROUTS	UNJUST	---V-C
BEDUIN	---U-S	LETUPS	TUQUES	YAOURT	******
BEGUIN	******	MAQUIS	UNGUES	YOGURT	ATAVIC
COLUMN	ALBUMS	MIAULS	UNGUIS	******	PELVIC
FRAUEN	ALEUTS	MIXUPS	VALUES	---U-U	SLAVIC
IMPUGN	ALMUDS	MOGULS	VENUES	******	******
INTURN	AMOURS	MOHURS	VOGUES	TELUGU	---V-D
OPPUGN	AMPULS	NAHUMS	VOGULS	******	******
PAPUAN	ANNULS	OCCURS	YAMUNS	---U-Y	BRAVED
RETURN	ARGUES	PICULS	******	******	CALVED
SATURN	AUGURS	PINUPS	---U-T	AGOUTY	CARVED
SEQUIN	BABULS	PIQUES	******	ARGUFY	CRAVED
SIOUAN	BEAUTS	QUEUES	ABDUCT	ASBURY	CURVED
TEAURN	BEGUMS	RAOULS	ABRUPT	AUGURY	DELVED
UPTURN	CAJUNS	REBUTS	ACQUIT	BEAUTY	DROVED
******	CLOUDS	RECURS	ADDUCT	CLOUDY	FERVID
---U-O	CLOUTS	RERUNS	ADJUST	CROUPY	GLOVED
******	CROUPS	REVUES	AMOUNT	DECURY	GRAVED
AERUGO	CUTUPS	ROGUES	AUGUST	DEPUTY	GRAVID
ARTURO	DEBUGS	SCAUPS	AVAUNT	FLEURY	HALVED
BASUTO	DEBUTS	SCHUSS	COQUET	FLOURY	HEAVED
CARUSO	DEGUMS	SCOURS	DEDUCT	INJURY	HOOVED
COLUGO	DEMURS	SCOUTS	DEGUST	KORUNY	LEAVED
ESCUDO	ENDUES	SCRUBS	ERFURT	LUXURY	NERVED

PEEVED	OGIVAL	CLOVER	BRAVES	SELVES	******
PROVED	SERVAL	CRAVER	BRAVOS	SERVES	---V-Y
REEVED	SHOVEL	CULVER	BREVES	SERVOS	******
REVVED	SNIVEL	DELVER	CALVES	SHAVES	CHEVVY
SALVED	SWIVEL	DENVER	CANVAS	SHIVES	CHIVVY
SERVED	TRAVEL	DRIVER	CARVES	SHOVES	CONVEY
SHAVED	VALVAL	DROVER	CHIVES	SIEVES	CONVOY
SHOVED	VULVAL	FERVOR	CLEVIS	SILVAS	HARVEY
SIEVED	WEEVIL	FLAVOR	CLIVES	SKIVES	JARVEY
SKIVED	******	GLOVER	CLOVES	SLAVES	PEAVEY
SLAVED	---V-N	GRAVER	CLOVIS	SOLVES	PURVEY
SOLVED	******	GROVER	CORVES	STAVES	SKIVVY
STAVED	CALVIN	HEAVER	CORVUS	STEVES	SURVEY
VALVED	CARVEN	HOOVER	CRAVES	STOVES	******
WAIVED	CLOVEN	LEAVER	CREVAS	SYLVAS	---W-B
WEAVED	CRAVEN	LOUVER	CURVES	TRAVES	******
******	DRIVEN	OLIVER	DELVES	TROVES	COBWEB
---V-E	ELEVEN	PLOVER	DRIVES	TURVES	******
******	ELEVON	PROVER	DROVES	VALVES	---W-D
CORVEE	FLAVIN	QUAVER	FAUVES	VARVES	******
JAYVEE	GRAVEN	QUIVER	GLOVES	VOLVAS	AVOWED
LARVAE	HEAVEN	SALVER	GRAVES	WAIVES	BREWED
LOUVRE	KELVIN	SALVOR	GROVES	WALVIS	CHAWED
OEUVRE	LEAVEN	SERVER	GUAVAS	WEAVES	CHEWED
PREVUE	MARVIN	SHAVER	HALVES	WOLVES	CLAWED
SILVAE	MELVIN	SHIVER	HEAVES	******	CLEWED
STEVIE	MELVYN	SHOVER	HELVES	---V-T	CROWED
SYLVAE	MERVIN	SILVER	HOOVES	******	FLAWED
VULVAE	PROVEN	SKIVER	JARVIS	BREVET	FLOWED
******	SHAVEN	SLAVER	JERVIS	CRAVAT	GLOWED
---V-H	SILVAN	SLIVER	KEEVES	CURVET	GNAWED
******	SLOVEN	SOEVER	KNAVES	GRIVET	MEOWED
YAHVEH	SPAVIN	SOLVER	KNIVES	PRIVET	PLOWED
******	STEVEN	STIVER	LEAVES	SWIVET	SHEWED
---V-K	SYLVAN	STOVER	LOAVES	TRIVET	SHOWED
******	UNEVEN	TREVOR	MAUVES	VELVET	SKEWED
SLOVAK	******	TROVER	NAEVUS	VERVET	SLEWED
******	---V-O	VALVAR	NERVES	******	SLOWED
---V-L	******	VULVAR	OGIVES	---V-W	SNOWED
******	FLUVIO	WAIVER	OLIVES	******	SPEWED
CARVEL	PLUVIO	WEAVER	PARVIS	REAVOW	STEWED
COEVAL	******	WEEVER	PEEVES	******	STOWED
DRIVEL	---V-R	WOLVER	PELVES	---V-X	THAWED
FRIVOL	******	******	PELVIS	******	THEWED
GRAVEL	BEAVER	---V-S	PROVES	CERVIX	VIEWED
GROVEL	BRAVER	******	REEVES	CONVEX	******
LARVAL	CARVER	AGAVES	SALVES	VOLVOX	---W-E
MARVEL	CLEVER	BEEVES	SALVOS		******
					BROWSE
					DRAWEE

DROWSE	BLOWER	******	******	ORYXES	******
PEEWEE	BREWER	---W-W	---X-D	PLEXUS	---Y-G
******	CHEWER	******	******	PRAXIS	******
---W-G	DRAWER	BOWWOW	COAXED	TRIXYS	LARYNG
******	FLOWER	POWWOW	FLEXED	******	******
BIGWIG	GLOWER	******	FLUXED	---X-T	---Y-K
EARWIG	GNAWER	---W-X	HOAXED	******	******
HEDWIG	GROWER	******	JINXED	PINXIT	GALYAK
LUDWIG	KNOWER	EARWAX	******	******	******
WIGWAG	PLOWER	PAXWAX	---X-E	---Y-A	---Y-L
******	PREWAR	******	******	******	******
---W-H	SHEWER	---W-Y	TRIXIE	BARYTA	ARGYLL
******	SHOWER	******	******	CORYZA	JEKYLL
GROWTH	SKEWER	AIRWAY	---X-L	******	******
YAHWEH	SLOWER	ANYWAY	******	---Y-B	---Y-N
******	VIEWER	BLOWBY	BIAXAL	******	******
---W-K	******	BLOWZY	COAXAL	CORYMB	BANYAN
******	---W-S	BRAWNY	******	******	BARYON
ARAWAK	******	COGWAY	---X-N	---Y-D	BUNYAN
******	BRAWLS	CONWAY	******	******	CANYON
---W-L	BREWIS	CRAWLY	ALEXIN	BRAYED	CRAYON
******	BROWNS	DRAWLY	FLAXEN	BUOYED	GERYON
AVOWAL	CLOWNS	DROWSY	KLAXON	CLAYED	LIBYAN
CREWEL	CRAWLS	FROWZY	******	CLOYED	RUNYON
NARWAL	CROWDS	GALWAY	---X-R	DRAYED	******
TROWEL	CROWNS	KEYWAY	******	FLAYED	---Y-O
******	DRAWLS	LEEWAY	COAXER	FRAYED	******
---W-M	DROWNS	MEDWAY	ELIXIR	GRAYED	ANKYLO
******	FROWNS	MIDWAY	FLEXOR	OBEYED	CHRYSO
WIGWAM	GROWLS	NORWAY	HOAXER	OKAYED	******
******	PRAWNS	ONEWAY	PLEXOR	OXEYED	---Y-P
---W-N	PROWLS	RUNWAY	******	PLAYED	******
******	SCHWAS	SEAWAY	---X-S	PRAYED	BUNYIP
AJOWAN	SCOWLS	SKYWAY	******	PREYED	******
DARWIN	SHAWLS	SLOWLY	ALEXIS	SPAYED	---Y-R
DEEWAN	SHAWMS	SUBWAY	APEXES	STAYED	******
GODWIN	SPAWNS	TWOWAY	CALXES	SWAYED	BOWYER
SEAWAN	TRAWLS	******	COAXES	XRAYED	BRAYER
SELWYN	******	---X-A	CRUXES	******	FLAYER
TAIWAN	---W-T	******	FLAXES	---Y-E	GRAYER
******	******	ALEXIA	FLEXES	******	LAWYER
---W-P	DIMWIT	ANOXIA	FLUXES	ALKYNE	LIVYER
******	GODWIT	ATAXIA	HOAXES	ECTYPE	MAGYAR
BLOWUP	NITWIT	******	IBEXES	ELAYNE	OBEYER
******	OUTWIT	---X-C	ILEXES	ENZYME	PLAYER
---W-R	PEEWIT	******	JINXES	GROYNE	PRAYER
******		ANOXIC	LYNXES	OOCYTE	PREYER
ANSWER		ATAXIC	MINXES		SAWYER
AVOWER					

SLAYER	******	BENZYL	BRAZAS	SCARAB	PLEIAD
SPRYER	---Z-D	BRAZIL	BRAZES	SERDAB	RELOAD
STAYER	******	GRIZEL	BRAZOS	******	SINBAD
THAYER	AMAZED	PODZOL	BUZZES	----AC	SPREAD
******	BLAZED	TETZEL	COLZAS	******	TETRAD
---Y-S	BOOZED	******	CRAZES	AIRSAC	THREAD
******	BRAZED	---Z-N	CROZES	BALZAC	UNCLAD
ALKYLS	BUZZED	******	ELIZAS	CALPAC	UNLEAD
ALLYLS	CRAZED	AMAZON	FEEZES	CELIAC	UNLOAD
BARYES	FEEZED	BLAZON	FEZZES	COGNAC	UNREAD
BERYLS	FIZZED	BRAZEN	FIZZES	CORSAC	******
ETHYLS	FUZZED	DIAZIN	FURZES	IPECAC	----AE
FLOYDS	GLAZED	FEZZAN	FUZZES	MANIAC	******
HEXYLS	GLOZED	FROZEN	GAUZES	MICMAC	AGAPAE
LLOYDS	GRAZED	HAZZAN	GLAZES	OVISAC	AGORAE
OXEYES	JAZZED	MIZZEN	GLOZES	SENLAC	ALULAE
PLAYAS	PRIZED	QUEZON	GRAZES	SYRIAC	AMEBAE
POLYPS	RAZZED	SEIZIN	HAMZAS	TAMBAC	AORTAE
SATYRS	SEIZED	TARZAN	JAZZES	TARMAC	BULLAE
SIBYLS	******	******	LIZZYS	THORAC	BURSAE
SONYAS	---Z-E	---Z-O	MAIZES	TOMBAC	CANNAE
VINYLS	******	******	MATZOS	VEDIAC	CELLAE
******	DAZZLE	AREZZO	MEZZOS	ZODIAC	CHELAE
---Y-T	FIZZLE	******	******	******	COSTAE
******	FOOZLE	---Z-R	PIZZAS	----AD	COTTAE
ENCYST	GUZZLE	******	PLAZAS	******	CURIAE
******	LIZZIE	BLAZER	PRIZES	ABROAD	FAUNAE
---Y-X	MIZZLE	BONZER	RAZZES	ALIDAD	FLORAE
******	MUZZLE	BOOZER	SEIZES	AOUDAD	FOSSAE
LARYNX	NOZZLE	BRAZER	SMAZES	BAGDAD	FOVEAE
******	NUZZLE	BUZZER	TAZZAS	BALLAD	GALEAE
---Y-Y	PUZZLE	CROZER	WINZES	BEHEAD	GEMMAE
******	SIZZLE	FIZZER	******	BYROAD	GUTTAE
CLAYEY	ZIZZLE	GEEZER	---Z-T	CAUDAD	HERMAE
GRAYLY	******	GLAZER	MATZOT	CONRAD	HYDRAE
SPRYLY	---Z-G	GRAZER	******	DOODAD	HYPHAE
SYZYGY	******	JAZZER	---Z-Y	DORSAD	LAMIAE
WHEYEY	DANZIG	PANZER	******	ENNEAD	LARVAE
******	ZIGZAG	PRIZER	FRIZZY	FARBAD	LAURAE
---Z-A	******	SEIZER	SNAZZY	GILEAD	LIBRAE
******	---Z-I	SEIZOR	******	HEPTAD	LYTTAE
EPIZOA	******	******	----AB	INROAD	MAMMAE
PIAZZA	BANZAI	---Z-S	******	KONRAD	MEDIAE
RAZZIA	BORZOI	******	BAOBAB	LAMPAD	MUSCAE
ZSAZSA	******	AMAZES	CANTAB	MAENAD	NUCHAE
******	---Z-L	BLAZES	CONFAB	MYRIAD	OCREAE
---Z-C	******	BONZES	PREFAB	OGDOAD	PALEAE
******	AZAZEL	BOOZES	PUNJAB	PENTAD	PARCAE
BALZAC	BENZOL				
RHIZIC					

PENNAE	HOOKAH	OOMIAK	CEREAL	GENIAL	PENIAL
PHYLAE	HOWDAH	SANJAK	CHORAL	GINGAL	PENPAL
PINNAE	HURRAH	SCREAK	CITRAL	GLOBAL	PIENAL
PLICAE	ISAIAH	SLOVAK	COAXAL	GOORAL	PINEAL
RAPHAE	JOSIAH	SQUEAK	COCCAL	HAEMAL	PINNAL
SILVAE	JUBBAH	STREAK	COEVAL	HAMMAL	PLAGAL
SPACAE	KEDDAH	YASMAK	COITAL	HARTAL	PLURAL
STELAE	KIBLAH	******	CORRAL	HEDRAL	PORTAL
STRIAE	LOOFAH	----AL	COSTAL	HERBAL	POSTAL
SUNDAE	MOLLAH	******	CREDAL	HIEMAL	PRIMAL
SYLVAE	MOOLAH	ABORAL	CRURAL	HYETAL	RACIAL
TESTAE	MULLAH	ACETAL	CUNEAL	HYMNAL	RADIAL
THEBAE	NULLAH	ACTUAL	CURIAL	HYPHAL	RANDAL
THECAE	PARIAH	AECIAL	CYMBAL	JACKAL	RASCAL
TIBIAE	PISGAH	AERIAL	DAEDAL	JINGAL	RECTAL
UMBRAE	PURDAH	AMORAL	DENIAL	JOVIAL	REGNAL
UVULAE	RUPIAH	AMYTAL	DENTAL	JUMBAL	RENTAL
VITTAE	SUNNAH	ANIMAL	DERMAL	KENDAL	REPEAL
VULVAE	TOBIAH	ANNEAL	DIETAL	LABIAL	REVEAL
******	TUSSAH	ANNUAL	DISCAL	LACIAL	RHINAL
----AF	UZZIAH	AORTAL	DISMAL	LARVAL	RICTAL
******	WALLAH	APICAL	DISTAL	LETHAL	RITUAL
GUSTAF	WHIDAH	APNEAL	DORSAL	LINEAL	ROSEAL
******	WHYDAH	APODAL	DOSSAL	LUTEAL	SACRAL
----AG	ZILLAH	APPEAL	DOUGAL	MAMMAL	SANDAL
******	******	ASTRAL	EPICAL	MANUAL	SENDAL
GASBAG	----AI	ATABAL	ESPIAL	MEDIAL	SEPTAL
KITBAG	******	ATONAL	FACIAL	MENIAL	SERIAL
RAGBAG	ADONAI	ATRIAL	FAECAL	MENSAL	SERVAL
RAGTAG	BANZAI	AVOWAL	FALLAL	MENTAL	SEXUAL
STALAG	BONSAI	BAIKAL	FAUCAL	MESCAL	SIGNAL
TEABAG	HERMAI	BELIAL	FAUNAL	MESIAL	SOCIAL
WIGWAG	NILGAI	BENGAL	FECIAL	MISKAL	SPINAL
ZIGZAG	******	BIAXAL	FERIAL	MISSAL	SPIRAL
******	----AJ	BOREAL	FESTAL	MITRAL	SPITAL
----AH	******	BRIDAL	FETIAL	MORTAL	SQUEAL
******	SWARAJ	BROMAL	FEUDAL	MUTUAL	STATAL
ABIJAH	******	BRUMAL	FILIAL	NARIAL	TARNAL
BASRAH	----AK	BRUTAL	FINIAL	NARWAL	TARSAL
BEULAH	******	BUCCAL	FISCAL	NASIAL	TERGAL
CASBAH	ANORAK	BURIAL	FLORAL	NEURAL	TERNAL
CHETAH	ARAWAK	BURSAL	FOETAL	NORMAL	THECAL
COPRAH	BOGOAK	CARNAL	FONTAL	NOUNAL	THENAL
ELIJAH	DVORAK	CARPAL	FORMAL	OGIVAL	TIBIAL
FELLAH	GALYAK	CASUAL	FOVEAL	ORDEAL	TIMBAL
GULLAH	KALPAK	CAUDAL	FRUGAL	OSTEAL	TINCAL
HALLAH	KARNAK	CAUSAL	FUNGAL	PARRAL	TRIBAL
HANNAH	KODIAK	CENTAL	GAVIAL	PASCAL	TRINAL

TROPAL	UNSEAM	CRETAN	LILIAN	SILVAN	ENWRAP
TUSSAL	WIGWAM	DARDAN	LONGAN	SIMIAN	HUBCAP
UMBRAL	******	DECCAN	LUCIAN	SIOUAN	ICECAP
UNCIAL	----AN	DEEWAN	MADMAN	SKYMAN	INWRAP
UNGUAL	******	DELIAN	MANDAN	SLOGAN	KIDNAP
UNREAL	ABADAN	DEMEAN	MARIAN	SOCMAN	MADCAP
UNSEAL	ADRIAN	DESMAN	MECCAN	STEFAN	MAYHAP
URINAL	AEGEAN	DOLMAN	MEDIAN	STEPAN	MISHAP
VALVAL	AFGHAN	DORIAN	MERMAN	SULTAN	MOBCAP
VANDAL	AIDMAN	DUNCAN	MESIAN	SUNTAN	MUDCAP
VASSAL	AIRMAN	DURBAN	MINOAN	SYLVAN	REDCAP
VENIAL	AJOWAN	DURIAN	MORGAN	SYRIAN	RIPRAP
VERBAL	ANDEAN	EOLIAN	NATHAN	TAIWAN	SATRAP
VERNAL	ANURAN	EONIAN	NORMAN	TAMPAN	SKYCAP
VESTAL	APEMAN	FABIAN	NUBIAN	TARPAN	TOECAP
VIDUAL	APPIAN	FANTAN	OHIOAN	TARTAN	UNWRAP
VISUAL	ASHCAN	FENIAN	OILCAN	TARZAN	******
VULVAL	ASHMAN	FEZZAN	OREGAN	TASMAN	----AR
WITHAL	ATAMAN	FIJIAN	ORIGAN	TINCAN	******
XENIAL	AUGEAN	FINNAN	ORPHAN	TITIAN	ALEGAR
ZOONAL	AXEMAN	FIRMAN	OSSIAN	TOUCAN	ALULAR
******	BADMAN	FLYMAN	OUTMAN	TREPAN	ANTIAR
----AM	BAGMAN	FOEMAN	OUTRAN	TROJAN	APPEAR
******	BALKAN	GASMAN	PAPUAN	TRUMAN	ARREAR
AGLEAM	BANIAN	GERMAN	PARIAN	TURBAN	ASHLAR
BALAAM	BANYAN	GIBRAN	PATHAN	TUSCAN	AVATAR
BALSAM	BARMAN	GUNMAN	PENMAN	TYMPAN	BAZAAR
BANTAM	BATAAN	HARLAN	PIEMAN	TYRIAN	BEGGAR
BEDLAM	BATMAN	HAZZAN	PITMAN	UTAHAN	BEZOAR
BELDAM	BEDPAN	HERMAN	PLATAN	VANMAN	BOXCAR
DIRHAM	BEMEAN	HETMAN	POTMAN	VIVIAN	BULBAR
DURHAM	BEMOAN	HODMAN	PTISAN	VULCAN	BULGAR
ENGRAM	BHUTAN	IBADAN	RADIAN	WYSTAN	BURSAR
GODDAM	BOWMAN	ICEMAN	RAGLAN	YEOMAN	CAESAR
GOTHAM	BROGAN	INDIAN	RAGMAN	YESMAN	CALCAR
GRAHAM	BUCHAN	INSPAN	RANDAN	******	CASPAR
JETSAM	BUNYAN	IONIAN	RATTAN	----AO	CAVIAR
JOTHAM	BUSMAN	JORDAN	RODMAN	******	CELLAR
LACTAM	CABMAN	JOVIAN	SABEAN	BILBAO	COLLAR
LINGAM	CAFTAN	JUDEAN	SAIPAN	CALLAO	COSTAR
LOGJAM	CAIMAN	JULIAN	SAMIAN	******	COTTAR
MIRIAM	CANAAN	KAFTAN	SAMOAN	----AP	COUGAR
OLDHAM	CANCAN	KALIAN	SAMPAN	******	DAGMAR
PUTNAM	CARMAN	KANSAN	SEAMAN	BURLAP	DAMMAR
SALAAM	CAYMAN	KOREAN	SEAWAN	CATNAP	DEODAR
SCREAM	CONMAN	LAYMAN	SEXTAN	DEWLAP	DISBAR
STREAM	CORBAN	LEGMAN	SHAMAN	EARLAP	DOGEAR
TAMTAM	COWMAN	LIBYAN	SHORAN	ENTRAP	DOLLAR

DUNBAR	SIRDAR	CELIAS	HYDRAS	PIZZAS	WALLAS
DURBAR	STELAR	CHELAS	HYENAS	PLAYAS	WANDAS
ENDEAR	STYLAR	CHUFAS	JAINAS	PLAZAS	WILMAS
ESCHAR	TARTAR	CLARAS	JOSIAS	POLKAS	YERBAS
EUDOAR	THENAR	COBIAS	JULIAS	PRESAS	YUCCAS
FOLIAR	TRICAR	COBRAS	JUNTAS	PUNKAS	ZAMIAS
FULMAR	TROCAR	COCOAS	KANSAS	QUOTAS	ZEBRAS
GASPAR	TUSSAR	COLZAS	KAPPAS	RHODAS	******
GUITAR	UNBEAR	COMMAS	KARMAS	RIATAS	----AT
GUNNAR	UPROAR	CONGAS	KOALAS	RUMBAS	******
HANGAR	UVULAR	COTTAS	LAMIAS	SABRAS	AFLOAT
HUSSAR	VALVAR	CREVAS	LAMMAS	SAIGAS	ARARAT
INSTAR	VEADAR	CUTLAS	LAMPAS	SALPAS	BOBCAT
ISHTAR	VULGAR	DACHAS	LAURAS	SAMBAS	CAVEAT
ISOBAR	VULVAR	DALLAS	LEHUAS	SAUNAS	CILIAT
JAGUAR	WEIMAR	DELIAS	LEMMAS	SCHWAS	CLIMAT
JAMJAR	ZAFFAR	DELLAS	LEONAS	SCUBAS	COMBAT
LASCAR	******	DELTAS	LIANAS	SENNAS	CRAVAT
LINEAR	----AS	DERMAS	LIBRAS	SEPIAS	CUSHAT
LOQUAR	******	DIANAS	LINDAS	SIGMAS	DEFEAT
LUMBAR	ABACAS	DIPSAS	LINGAS	SILVAS	DERMAT
MAGYAR	ABOMAS	DOBLAS	LIVIAS	SOFTAS	FORMAT
MEDLAR	AENEAS	DOBRAS	LLAMAS	SONIAS	GUTTAT
MORTAR	AGAMAS	DOGMAS	LUCIAS	SONYAS	HEREAT
MUGGAR	AGORAS	DONNAS	LYDIAS	STUPAS	LARIAT
NECTAR	ALPHAS	DOWLAS	MADRAS	SUTRAS	LOQUAT
OCULAR	AMEBAS	DRAMAS	MAMBAS	SYLVAS	MUSCAT
OVULAR	ANABAS	ELENAS	MAMMAS	TAIGAS	NOUGAT
PALMAR	ANANAS	ELIZAS	MANIAS	TANKAS	ORGEAT
PEDLAR	ANIMAS	ENEMAS	MANTAS	TAZZAS	OUTSAT
PILLAR	ANITAS	EVITAS	MARIAS	THEDAS	REHEAT
PINDAR	AORTAS	EXTRAS	MARTAS	THETAS	REPEAT
PLANAR	ARECAS	FANGAS	MECCAS	THOMAS	RESEAT
POPLAR	ARENAS	FAUNAS	MOIRAS	THUJAS	SABBAT
PREWAR	AROMAS	FLORAS	MYRNAS	TIARAS	SEURAT
PULSAR	BALSAS	FRACAS	NORIAS	TIBIAS	SHEBAT
QUASAR	BELGAS	FREDAS	NORMAS	TOBIAS	SNOCAT
REHEAR	BELLAS	GAMMAS	NUBIAS	ULEMAS	STOMAT
SAGGAR	BEULAS	GILDAS	OMEGAS	UMBRAS	SUNHAT
SANGAR	BOREAS	GRETAS	OPERAS	UVULAS	THANAT
SANSAR	BRAZAS	GUAVAS	PALLAS	VERNAS	THREAT
SAPHAR	BURSAS	GUMMAS	PAMPAS	VESTAS	THROAT
SARSAR	CALLAS	HABEAS	PANDAS	VILLAS	TIPCAT
SCALAR	CANNAS	HAMZAS	PARKAS	VIOLAS	TOMCAT
SECPAR	CANVAS	HANNAS	PASHAS	VIRGAS	TOPHAT
SEGGAR	CAPIAS	HELLAS	PASTAS	VISTAS	UNSEAT
SHIKAR	CARLAS	HENNAS	PAULAS	VODKAS	UPBEAT
SHOFAR	CEIBAS	HILDAS	PELIAS	VOLVAS	WOMBAT

******	SMILAX	PREPAY	******	CHUBBY	BOUNCE
----AU	STORAX	RAGDAY	----BO	CRABBY	CHANCE
******	SURTAX	REDBAY	******	CRUMBY	CHOICE
BATEAU	SYNTAX	REPLAY	AKIMBO	FLABBY	CILICE
BUREAU	THORAX	RUNWAY	CRAMBO	GOODBY	COERCE
COTEAU	******	SASHAY	GAZABO	GRUBBY	DEDUCE
DACHAU	----AY	SEAWAY	GAZEBO	HEREBY	DEFACE
DESSAU	******	SKYWAY	GEMSBO	KNOBBY	DEVICE
GATEAU	AFFRAY	SUBWAY	LAVABO	NEARBY	DRYICE
JUNEAU	AIRWAY	SUNDAY	PHLEBO	SCABBY	EFFACE
LANDAU	ANYWAY	TWOWAY	PLUMBO	SHABBY	ENFACE
MAUMAU	ASTRAY	WAYLAY	******	SHELBY	ENLACE
MOREAU	BENDAY	******	----BS	SNOBBY	ENTICE
NASSAU	BETRAY	----BA	******	STUBBY	EUNICE
RESEAU	BISCAY	******	ABOMBS	TRILBY	EVINCE
******	BOMBAY	AMOEBA	ADLIBS	WHITBY	FELICE
----AV	BYPLAY	ARROBA	ARDEBS	******	FIANCE
******	CATHAY	CASABA	BLURBS	----CA	FIERCE
GUSTAV	COGWAY	DAGOBA	CABOBS	******	FLEECE
******	CONWAY	HECUBA	CALEBS	AFRICA	FRANCE
----AW	CORDAY	INDABA	CARIBS	ALPACA	GLANCE
******	CULLAY	RHUMBA	CAROBS	ARNICA	GREECE
BASHAW	DEFRAY	YORUBA	CLIMBS	ATTICA	HORACE
BOWSAW	DISMAY	ZARIBA	COOMBS	BIANCA	IGNACE
CASHAW	ESTRAY	******	CRUMBS	CLOACA	INDUCE
CUSHAW	FRIDAY	----BE	CUBEBS	DODECA	INLACE
GEWGAW	GALWAY	******	DEMOBS	ITHACA	JANICE
GUFFAW	HEYDAY	AEROBE	EXURBS	LORICA	JOUNCE
HAWHAW	HOORAY	CARIBE	JACOBS	MARACA	LAUNCE
HEEHAW	HURRAY	DANUBE	KABOBS	MONICA	MALICE
JIGSAW	KEYWAY	ENROBE	NABOBS	MYRICA	MENACE
OUTLAW	LAYDAY	FLAMBE	NAWABS	SENECA	NOTICE
PAWPAW	LEEWAY	IMBIBE	PLUMBS	SILICA	NOVICE
QUAPAW	MARGAY	JUJUBE	RAJABS	TUNICA	NUANCE
RIPSAW	MAYDAY	PHOEBE	RHUMBS	VESICA	OFFICE
SEESAW	MEDWAY	SCRIBE	SAHEBS	VOMICA	ORRICE
UNDRAW	MIDDAY	STROBE	SAHIBS	******	PALACE
WARSAW	MIDWAY	THISBE	SCRUBS	----CE	PANICE
******	MILLAY	UNROBE	SHRUBS	******	PEIRCE
----AX	MISLAY	******	SQUABS	ADDUCE	PIERCE
******	MONDAY	----BI	SQUIBS	ADVICE	PLAICE
CARFAX	MURRAY	******	STUBBS	ALMUCE	POLICE
CLIMAX	NORWAY	EPHEBI	THROBS	ALSACE	POMACE
EARWAX	OFFDAY	INCUBI	THUMBS	AMERCE	POUNCE
FORNAX	ONEWAY	RHOMBI	******	ANLACE	PRANCE
PAXWAX	OUTLAY	WAHABI	----BY	APIECE	PRINCE
PICKAX	PARLAY		******	BLEBBY	PUMICE
POLEAX	PAYDAY		BLOWBY	BIERCE	QUINCE
				BODICE	

REDUCE	CROTCH	STANCH	******	PANICS	******
REFACE	CROUCH	STARCH	----CO	REBECS	----CU
RUBACE	CRUNCH	STENCH	******	RELICS	******
SCARCE	CRUTCH	STITCH	BRONCO	SERACS	ARERCU
SCONCE	CULTCH	SWATCH	CALICO	STOICS	******
SEANCE	DETACH	SWITCH	CHALCO	SUMACS	----CY
SEDUCE	DRENCH	THATCH	ENRICO	TONICS	******
SLUICE	ENRICH	TRENCH	FIASCO	TOPICS	ABBACY
SOLACE	EPARCH	TWITCH	FRANCO	TUNICS	AGENCY
SOURCE	EUNUCH	WRENCH	FRESCO	XEBECS	BOUNCY
SPLICE	EXARCH	WRETCH	GLAUCO	ZEBECS	CHANCY
SPRUCE	FETICH	ZURICH	GRAECO	******	CURACY
STANCE	FLENCH	******	GYNECO	----CT	FLEECY
TENACE	FLETCH	----CI	HELICO	******	IDIOCY
THENCE	FLINCH	******	MACACO	ABDUCT	LEGACY
THRICE	FLITCH	BONACI	MALACO	ABJECT	LUNACY
TIERCE	FRENCH	MEDICI	MEDICO	ADDICT	PAPACY
TRANCE	GROUCH	******	MEJICO	ADDUCT	PIRACY
ULENCE	HAUNCH	----CK	MEXICO	ADJECT	POLICY
UNLACE	HOOTCH	******	MONACO	AFFECT	QUINCY
USANCE	INARCH	ACKACK	ROCOCO	ASPECT	******
VELOCE	KIRSCH	ARRACK	SILICO	BISECT	----DA
VENICE	KITSCH	ATTACK	STUCCO	DECOCT	******
VIVACE	LAMECH	BEDECK	UNESCO	DEDUCT	AGENDA
WHENCE	LAUNCH	CANUCK	VARICO	DEFECT	AMANDA
******	MOLOCH	CARACK	VESICO	DEJECT	ARMADA
----CH	MUNICH	COPECK	******	DELICT	BRENDA
******	NAUTCH	FRANCK	----CS	DEPICT	CANADA
ATTACH	PAUNCH	HIJACK	******	DETECT	CICADA
AVOUCH	PESACH	KOPECK	ANTICS	DIRECT	FRIEDA
BARUCH	PLANCH	LUBECK	ASPICS	EFFECT	LAMBDA
BLANCH	PLEACH	MOHOCK	ATTICS	EXPECT	LUANDA
BLEACH	PREACH	OCLOCK	AZTECS	EXSECT	NEVADA
BLENCH	PUTSCH	PLANCK	BASICS	GALACT	ONEIDA
BLOTCH	QUENCH	POLACK	BRONCS	IMPACT	PAGODA
BORSCH	QUITCH	REBECK	CIVICS	INDICT	PANADA
BRANCH	SCORCH	SCHICK	COMICS	INDUCT	POSADA
BREACH	SCOTCH	SHTICK	CONICS	INFECT	PRAVDA
BREECH	SCUTCH	STRICK	CYNICS	INJECT	REMUDA
BROACH	SEARCH	STRUCK	DARICS	INSECT	RESEDA
BROOCH	SKETCH	THWACK	ETHICS	INTACT	RWANDA
BRUNCH	SLOUCH	UNCOCK	FRANCS	OBJECT	UGANDA
CHINCH	SMIRCH	UNLOCK	ISAACS	OBTECT	******
CHURCH	SMOOCH	UNPACK	LILACS	REDACT	----DE
CLENCH	SMUTCH	UNPICK	LYRICS	REJECT	******
CLINCH	SNATCH	UNTACK	MEDICS	RELICT	ABRADE
CLUTCH	SNITCH	YORICK	MIMICS	RESECT	ACCEDE
CRATCH	SPEECH	ZEBECK	OPTICS	SELECT	ACNODE
				STRICT	

ALLUDE	******	BRANDS	LIPIDS	WOUNDS	******
ALMUDE	----DI	BREADS	LLOYDS	YIELDS	----EA
ARCADE	******	BREEDS	MAUNDS	ZOOIDS	******
AUBADE	SOLIDI	BROADS	MONADS	ZOUNDS	ACHAEA
BESIDE	TULADI	BROODS	MOULDS	******	ALTHEA
BETIDE	YEHUDI	BUILDS	NAIADS	----DT	ANDREA
BLENDE	******	CHARDS	NOMADS	******	ANTHEA
BLONDE	----DL	CHORDS	OCTADS	BRANDT	APNOEA
BOLIDE	******	CLOUDS	OREADS	******	AZALEA
BORIDE	DIRNDL	CREEDS	PLAIDS	----DU	CHOREA
CLAUDE	******	CROWDS	PLEADS	******	CORNEA
DECADE	----DO	CYCADS	POINDS	TELEDU	COWPEA
DECIDE	******	DAVIDS	POUNDS	XANADU	CRIMEA
DECODE	ALBEDO	DREADS	RAPIDS	******	EUBOEA
DELUDE	COMEDO	DRUIDS	ROALDS	----DY	EUPNEA
DEMODE	DORADO	DRYADS	ROUNDS	******	GUINEA
DENUDE	ESCUDO	ELANDS	SALADS	BLOODY	JOSIEA
DERIDE	HAIRDO	EMBEDS	SCALDS	BRANDY	JUDAEA
DIVIDE	LAREDO	EMENDS	SCENDS	BROODY	NAUSEA
ENCODE	LEPIDO	EPHODS	SCOLDS	CLODDY	SPIREA
EXCIDE	LIBIDO	FARADS	SCRODS	CLOUDY	******
FACADE	MIKADO	FELIDS	SHARDS	COMEDY	----EB
GOURDE	OVERDO	FIELDS	SHERDS	CORODY	******
GRANDE	PSEUDO	FIENDS	SHREDS	DIPODY	COBWEB
HALIDE	TEREDO	FIORDS	SKALDS	EMBODY	SUBDEB
IMPEDE	TOLEDO	FLOODS	SNOODS	FREDDY	******
INSIDE	TUXEDO	FLOYDS	SOLIDS	GREEDY	----EC
INVADE	******	FLUIDS	SOUNDS	GRUNDY	******
IODIDE	----DS	FOUNDS	SPEEDS	IMBODY	CHEBEC
ISOLDE	******	FRAUDS	SPENDS	MALADY	FENNEC
OREIDE	ALMUDS	FRONDS	SQUADS	MAUNDY	MYRMEC
OROIDE	AMENDS	GLANDS	SQUIDS	MELODY	PARSEC
OXHIDE	APHIDS	GONADS	STANDS	MILADY	QUEBEC
PARADE	AROIDS	GOURDS	STEEDS	MONODY	TANREC
PESADE	AUDADS	GREEDS	SWARDS	MOULDY	TENREC
POMADE	AVOIDS	GRINDS	SWORDS	NOBODY	TOLTEC
RECEDE	AWARDS	GUARDS	SYNODS	PARODY	******
REMADE	BEARDS	GUILDS	THIRDS	REMEDY	----ED
RESIDE	BIPEDS	HALIDS	TREADS	SHANDY	******
SECEDE	BIPODS	HEXADS	TRENDS	SHINDY	ABASED
STRIDE	BLEEDS	HOARDS	TRIADS	SHODDY	ABATED
STRODE	BLENDS	HOUNDS	TWEEDS	SPEEDY	ABIDED
TIRADE	BLINDS	HYOIDS	UPENDS	STEADY	ABUSED
TRIODE	BLONDS	IMBEDS	VIANDS	STURDY	ADDLED
UNLADE	BLOODS	JIHADS	WEALDS	THADDY	ADORED
UNMADE	BOARDS	KNEADS	WIELDS	TRENDY	AERIED
UPSIDE	BOUNDS	LAIRDS	WOALDS	UNTIDY	AGREED
UREIDE	BRAIDS	LAMEDS	WORLDS	WEIRDY	AIRBED
				WIELDY	

AISLED	BEARED	BRAYED	CASHED	CREPED	DISHED
ALATED	BECKED	BRAZED	CATTED	CROWED	DOCKED
ALFRED	BEDDED	BREWED	CAUSED	CUBBED	DODGED
ALINED	BEEFED	BRIBED	CEASED	CUFFED	DOFFED
ALIPED	BEEPED	BRINED	CEILED	CULLED	DOGGED
ALLIED	BEGGED	BUCKED	CENSED	CULMED	DOITED
AMAZED	BELIED	BUDDED	CHAFED	CUPPED	DOLLED
AMBLED	BELLED	BUDGED	CHARED	CURBED	DONNED
AMUSED	BELTED	BUFFED	CHASED	CURDED	DOOMED
ANGLED	BENDED	BUGGED	CHAWED	CURLED	DOSSED
ANTEED	BESTED	BUGLED	CHEWED	CURSED	DOTTED
ARCHED	BETTED	BULBED	CHIDED	CURVED	DOUSED
ARCKED	BIASED	BULGED	CHIMED	CUSPED	DOWNED
ARGUED	BIBBED	BULKED	CHOKED	CUSSED	DOWSED
ATONED	BIFFED	BUMMED	CITIED	CYCLED	DRAPED
AUTOED	BILGED	BUMPED	CLAWED	DABBED	DRAYED
AVOWED	BILKED	BUNGED	CLAYED	DAMMED	DRONED
AWAKED	BILLED	BUNKED	CLEWED	DAMNED	DROVED
AXSEED	BINNED	BUNTED	CLOSED	DAMPED	DUBBED
BABIED	BIRLED	BUOYED	CLOYED	DANCED	DUCKED
BACHED	BIRRED	BURIED	COALED	DANGED	DUELED
BACKED	BITTED	BURKED	COATED	DAPPED	DUFFED
BADGED	BLADED	BURLED	COAXED	DARNED	DULLED
BAFFED	BLAMED	BURNED	COCKED	DARTED	DUMPED
BAGGED	BLARED	BURPED	COELED	DASHED	DUNGED
BAILED	BLAZED	BURRED	COGGED	DAUBED	DUNKED
BAITED	BOATED	BUSHED	COIFED	DAWNED	DUNNED
BALKED	BOBBED	BUSIED	COILED	DAYBED	DUSKED
BALLED	BODIED	BUSSED	COINED	DECKED	DUSTED
BANDED	BOGGED	BUSTED	COMBED	DEEDED	EARNED
BANGED	BOILED	BUTTED	CONKED	DEEMED	ECHOED
BANKED	BOLLED	BUZZED	CONNED	DEFIED	EDDIED
BANNED	BOLTED	CABLED	COOEED	DEICED	EDITED
BARBED	BOMBED	CACHED	COOKED	DELVED	EDUCED
BARDED	BONDED	CADGED	COOLED	DENIED	ELATED
BARGED	BONGED	CALKED	COOPED	DENNED	ELDRED
BARKED	BOOKED	CALLED	COPIED	DENTED	ELIDED
BARRED	BOOMED	CALMED	COPPED	DEUCED	ELOPED
BASHED	BOOTED	CALVED	CORDED	DIALED	ELUDED
BASKED	BOOZED	CAMPED	CORKED	DIBBED	EMCEED
BASTED	BOPPED	CANNED	CORNED	DIETED	EMOTED
BATHED	BOSSED	CANOED	COSHED	DIGGED	ENDUED
BATTED	BOUSED	CANTED	COSTED	DIMMED	ENSUED
BAWLED	BOWLED	CAPPED	CRANED	DINGED	ENVIED
BEADED	BOWSED	CARDED	CRAPED	DINNED	ERASED
BEAKED	BRACED	CARPED	CRATED	DINTED	ERODED
BEAMED	BRAKED	CARTED	CRAVED	DIPPED	ESPIED
BEANED	BRAVED	CARVED	CRAZED	DIRKED	ETCHED

EVADED	FOBBED	GIGGED	HALVED	HORSED	JOBBED
EVENED	FOGGED	GILDED	HAMMED	HOSTED	JOGGED
EVOKED	FOILED	GIMPED	HANDED	HOTBED	JOINED
EXCEED	FOLDED	GINNED	HANGED	HOTTED	JOLTED
EXILED	FOOLED	GIPPED	HAPPED	HOUSED	JOSHED
EXITED	FOOTED	GIRDED	HARKED	HOWLED	JOTTED
EXUDED	FORCED	GIRTED	HARMED	HUFFED	JUDGED
FABLED	FORDED	GLARED	HARPED	HUGGED	JUGGED
FAGGED	FORGED	GLAZED	HASHED	HULKED	JUMPED
FAILED	FORKED	GLIDED	HASPED	HULLED	JUNKED
FAIRED	FORMED	GLOBED	HASTED	HUMMED	JUTTED
FANGED	FOULED	GLOVED	HATRED	HUMPED	KAYOED
FANNED	FOWLED	GLOWED	HATTED	HUNTED	KECKED
FARCED	FRAMED	GLOZED	HAULED	HURLED	KEDGED
FARMED	FRAYED	GNAWED	HAWKED	HUSHED	KEELED
FASTED	FUDGED	GOADED	HEADED	HUSKED	KEENED
FATTED	FUELED	GOLFED	HEALED	HUTTED	KENNED
FAWNED	FUGLED	GOOFED	HEAPED	HYMNED	KERBED
FEARED	FULLED	GOOSED	HEATED	IMAGED	KERNED
FEASED	FUNDED	GORGED	HEAVED	IMBUED	KICKED
FEEZED	FUNKED	GOUGED	HEDGED	INBRED	KIDDED
FELLED	FURLED	GOWNED	HEEDED	INCHED	KILLED
FELTED	FURRED	GRACED	HEELED	INDEED	KILTED
FENCED	FUSSED	GRADED	HEFTED	INDUED	KINGED
FENDED	FUZZED	GRATED	HELMED	INURED	KINKED
FEUDED	GABBED	GRAVED	HELPED	IRISED	KIPPED
FIBBED	GABLED	GRAYED	HEMMED	IRONED	KISSED
FIGGED	GADDED	GRAZED	HERDED	ISSUED	KITTED
FILLED	GAFFED	GRIDED	HILLED	ITCHED	KNIFED
FILMED	GAGGED	GRIMED	HILTED	JABBED	LACKED
FINNED	GAINED	GRIPED	HINGED	JACKED	LADLED
FIRMED	GAITED	GROPED	HINTED	JAGGED	LAGGED
FISTED	GALLED	GUIDED	HIPPED	JAILED	LAIRED
FITTED	GAMMED	GULFED	HISSED	JAMMED	LALLED
FIZZED	GANGED	GULLED	HOAXED	JARRED	LAMBED
FLAKED	GAPPED	GULPED	HOCKED	JAZZED	LAMMED
FLAMED	GARBED	GUMMED	HOGGED	JEERED	LAMPED
FLARED	GASHED	GUNNED	HONIED	JELLED	LANCED
FLAWED	GASPED	GUSHED	HONKED	JEREED	LANDED
FLAYED	GASSED	GUTTED	HOODED	JERKED	LAPPED
FLEXED	GAUGED	GYPPED	HOOFED	JESSED	LAPSED
FLOWED	GAWKED	HACKED	HOOKED	JESTED	LARDED
FLUKED	GEARED	HAFTED	HOOPED	JETTED	LARKED
FLUMED	GELDED	HAGGED	HOOTED	JIBBED	LASHED
FLUTED	GELLED	HAILED	HOOVED	JIGGED	LASTED
FLUXED	GEMMED	HAIRED	HOPPED	JILTED	LATHED
FOALED	GIBBED	HALOED	HORDED	JINKED	LAUDED
FOAMED	GIFTED	HALTED	HORNED	JINXED	LEADED

LEAFED	LURKED	MOOTED	PALMED	PLAYED	RAFTED
LEAKED	LUSHED	MOPPED	PALPED	PLOWED	RAGGED
LEANED	LUSTED	MOUSED	PANNED	PLUMED	RAIDED
LEAPED	MADDED	MUCKED	PANTED	PODDED	RAILED
LEASED	MAILED	MUDDED	PARKED	POISED	RAINED
LEAVED	MAIMED	MUFFED	PARSED	POLLED	RAISED
LEERED	MALLED	MUGGED	PARTED	PONIED	RAMMED
LEGGED	MALTED	MULLED	PASSED	POOLED	RAMPED
LEVIED	MANNED	MUMMED	PASTED	POOPED	RANGED
LIASED	MAPPED	MUSHED	PATTED	POPPED	RANKED
LICKED	MARKED	MUSSED	PAUSED	PORTED	RANTED
LIDDED	MARLED	NABBED	PAWNED	POSTED	RAPPED
LIFTED	MARRED	NAGGED	PEAKED	POTTED	RASPED
LILIED	MASHED	NAILED	PEALED	POURED	RATTED
LILTED	MASKED	NAPPED	PECKED	POUTED	RAZEED
LIMBED	MASSED	NARKED	PEEKED	PRATED	RAZZED
LIMNED	MASTED	NEARED	PEELED	PRAYED	REAMED
LIMPED	MATTED	NECKED	PEENED	PREMED	REAPED
LINKED	MAULED	NEEDED	PEEPED	PREYED	REARED
LIPPED	MELDED	NERVED	PEERED	PRICED	REEDED
LISPED	MELTED	NESTED	PEEVED	PRIDED	REEFED
LISTED	MENDED	NETTED	PEGGED	PRIMED	REEKED
LOADED	MEOWED	NIBBED	PELTED	PRIZED	REELED
LOAFED	MERGED	NICHED	PENDED	PROBED	REEVED
LOAMED	MESHED	NICKED	PENNED	PROSED	REINED
LOANED	MESSED	NIPPED	PEPPED	PROVED	RELIED
LOBBED	MEWLED	NOBBED	PERKED	PRUNED	RENDED
LOCKED	MIFFED	NOCKED	PERMED	PUFFED	RENTED
LOCOED	MILKED	NODDED	PETTED	PUGGED	RESTED
LODGED	MILLED	NOISED	PHASED	PULLED	RETTED
LOFTED	MILTED	NOOSED	PHONED	PULPED	REVVED
LOGGED	MINCED	NOSHED	PICKED	PULSED	RHYMED
LOLLED	MINDED	NUDGED	PIECED	PUMPED	RIBBED
LONGED	MINTED	NUMBED	PIGGED	PUNNED	RICKED
LOOKED	MISLED	NURSED	PILLED	PUNTED	RIDDED
LOOMED	MISSED	NUTTED	PIMPED	PUPPED	RIDGED
LOOPED	MISTED	OBEYED	PINGED	PUREED	RIFLED
LOOSED	MITRED	OKAYED	PINKED	PURGED	RIFTED
LOOTED	MOANED	OPENED	PINNED	PURLED	RIGGED
LOPPED	MOATED	OPINED	PIPPED	PURRED	RIMMED
LORDED	MOBBED	ORATED	PIQUED	PURSED	RINGED
LOURED	MOCKED	OUSTED	PISHED	PUSHED	RINKED
LOUSED	MOILED	OXEYED	PITHED	PUTTED	RINSED
LUFFED	MOLDED	PACKED	PITIED	QUAKED	RIOTED
LUGGED	MOLTED	PADDED	PITTED	QUEUED	RIPPED
LULLED	MONIED	PAINED	PLACED	QUIRED	RISKED
LUMPED	MOONED	PAIRED	PLANED	QUOTED	ROAMED
LUNGED	MOORED	PALLED	PLATED	RACKED	ROARED

ROBBED	SENSED	SOCKED	SURGED	TITLED	VETOED
ROCKED	SERVED	SOCRED	SUSSED	TOGAED	VETTED
ROGUED	SHADED	SODDED	SWAGED	TOGGED	VIALED
ROILED	SHALED	SOILED	SWAYED	TOILED	VIEWED
ROLLED	SHAMED	SOLOED	SWIPED	TOLLED	VISAED
ROMPED	SHAPED	SOLVED	TABBED	TOMBED	VISEED
ROOFED	SHARED	SOOTED	TABLED	TONGED	VOICED
ROOKED	SHAVED	SOPPED	TACKED	TOOLED	VOIDED
ROOMED	SHEWED	SORTED	TAGGED	TOOTED	VOLTED
ROOTED	SHINED	SOULED	TAILED	TOPPED	WADDED
ROTTED	SHOOED	SOUPED	TALCED	TOSSED	WAFTED
ROUGED	SHORED	SOURED	TALKED	TOTTED	WAGGED
ROUSED	SHOVED	SOUSED	TAMPED	TOURED	WAIFED
ROUTED	SHOWED	SPACED	TANGED	TOUTED	WAILED
RUBBED	SICKED	SPADED	TANKED	TRACED	WAITED
RUCKED	SIDLED	SPARED	TANNED	TRADED	WAIVED
RUFFED	SIEGED	SPAYED	TAPPED	TRICED	WALKED
RUGGED	SIEVED	SPEWED	TARRED	TRINED	WALLED
RUINED	SIFTED	SPICED	TARTED	TUBBED	WANNED
RUSHED	SIGHED	SPIKED	TASKED	TUCKED	WANTED
RUSTED	SIGNED	SPILED	TASTED	TUFTED	WAPPED
RUTTED	SILOED	SPIRED	TATTED	TUGGED	WARDED
SACKED	SILTED	SPITED	TAXIED	TUNNED	WARMED
SACRED	SINGED	SPOKED	TEAMED	TUPPED	WARNED
SAGGED	SINNED	SPORED	TEARED	TURFED	WARPED
SAILED	SIPPED	SPUMED	TEASED	TURNED	WARRED
SALTED	SKATED	STAGED	TEDDED	TUSHED	WASHED
SALVED	SKEWED	STAKED	TEEMED	TUSKED	WASTED
SANDED	SKIVED	STALED	TEHEED	TUTTED	WAULED
SAPPED	SLAKED	STARED	TENDED	TWINED	WAWLED
SASHED	SLATED	STATED	TENSED	UNBRED	WEANED
SASSED	SLAVED	STAVED	TENTED	UNIPED	WEAVED
SAUCED	SLEWED	STAYED	TERMED	UNITED	WEBBED
SCALED	SLICED	STEWED	TESTED	UNTIED	WEDDED
SCARED	SLIMED	STOKED	THAWED	UNUSED	WEDGED
SCORED	SLOPED	STOLED	THEWED	VALUED	WEEDED
SCREED	SLOWED	STONED	THREED	VALVED	WELDED
SCRIED	SMILED	STOPED	TICKED	VAMPED	WELLED
SEALED	SMOKED	STORED	TIDIED	VARIED	WELTED
SEAMED	SNAKED	STOWED	TIERED	VATTED	WENDED
SEARED	SNARED	STYLED	TIFFED	VEERED	WETTED
SEATED	SNIPED	SUCKED	TILLED	VEILED	WHALED
SEEDED	SNORED	SUITED	TILTED	VEINED	WHILED
SEEMED	SNOWED	SULKED	TINGED	VENDED	WHINED
SEEPED	SOAKED	SUMMED	TINNED	VENTED	WHITED
SEINED	SOAPED	SUNNED	TINTED	VERGED	WHORED
SEISED	SOARED	SUPPED	TIPPED	VERSED	WICKED
SEIZED	SOBBED	SURFED	TITHED	VESTED	WIGGED

WILLED	BENDEE	******	BULBEL	KENNEL	TEASEL
WILTED	BOOTEE	----EF	BUSHEL	KERNEL	TERCEL
WINCED	BURGEE	******	CANCEL	KUMMEL	TETZEL
WINDED	COATEE	BELIEF	CANNEL	LAUREL	TINSEL
WINGED	COFFEE	RELIEF	CARCEL	LEMUEL	TRAVEL
WINKED	CORVEE	UNICEF	CARMEL	LINTEL	TROWEL
WISHED	COULEE	******	CARPEL	LIONEL	TUNNEL
WISPED	DECREE	----EG	CARREL	LISTEL	UNREEL
WITHED	DEGREE	******	CARTEL	MANTEL	VESSEL
WITTED	DOOLEE	BOWLEG	CARVEL	MANUEL	WEASEL
WOADED	DRAGEE	MASKEG	CHAPEL	MARCEL	******
WOLFED	DRAWEE	MUSKEG	CHISEL	MARVEL	----EM
WOMBED	DUNDEE	NUTMEG	COMPEL	MENDEL	******
WONTED	ELYSEE	PEGLEG	CORBEL	MICHEL	ANADEM
WOODED	ENTREE	PROLEG	CORNEL	MIGUEL	ANTHEM
WORDED	EPOPEE	******	CRENEL	MISSEL	BESEEM
WORKED	GOATEE	----EH	CREWEL	MORSEL	DIADEM
WORMED	HACKEE	******	CUDGEL	MURIEL	EMBLEM
XRAYED	JAYVEE	CHALEH	DAMSEL	MUSSEL	ESTEEM
YAKKED	JINNEE	YAHVEH	DANIEL	NICKEL	HARLEM
YANKED	LEGREE	YAHWEH	DARNEL	PARCEL	IBIDEM
YAPPED	LESSEE	******	DECKEL	PARREL	MAYHEM
YARDED	LICHEE	----EI	DIESEL	PASTEL	MOSLEM
YAUPED	LUNGEE	******	DISPEL	PENCEL	PHLOEM
YAWLED	MALLEE	ANDREI	DOSSEL	PETREL	REDEEM
YAWNED	MESTEE	BRUNEI	DOTTEL	POMMEL	SACHEM
YAWPED	MUSTEE	CLYPEI	DRIVEL	PROPEL	SYSTEM
YEANED	PARSEE	GLUTEI	DRUPEL	PUMMEL	TANDEM
YELLED	PASSEE	NUCLEI	DUFFEL	RACHEL	******
YELPED	PAWNEE	SANSEI	EIFFEL	RAPPEL	----EN
YENNED	PEEWEE	TAIPEI	ENAMEL	REFUEL	******
YESSED	POLLEE	******	FENNEL	ROMMEL	AACHEN
YIPPED	PONGEE	----EK	FUNNEL	RONDEL	ACUMEN
YOWLED	PUGREE	******	GOSPEL	RUNNEL	ADRIEN
YUKKED	PUTTEE	SHRIEK	GRAVEL	SAMIEL	AIDMEN
ZEROED	RAPPEE	******	GRETEL	SAMUEL	AILEEN
ZESTED	SEABEE	----EL	GRIZEL	SAUREL	AIRMEN
ZINCED	SETTEE	******	GROVEL	SECKEL	ARISEN
ZINGED	SOIREE	ALUDEL	GUNNEL	SEQUEL	ARLEEN
ZIPPED	SUTTEE	ARABEL	HALLEL	SHEKEL	ASHMEN
ZOOMED	SWANEE	AWHEEL	HANDEL	SHOVEL	AUSTEN
******	TOFFEE	AZAZEL	HANSEL	SIMNEL	AWAKEN
----EE	TOUPEE	AZRAEL	HASSEL	SNIVEL	AWOKEN
******	VENDEE	BARBEL	HOSTEL	SORREL	AXEMEN
APOGEE	VESTEE	BARREL	ISABEL	SPINEL	BADMEN
ATTLEE	YANKEE	BETHEL	ISOBEL	STIPEL	BAGMEN
BAILEE		BORDEL	ISOHEL	SWIVEL	BALEEN
BARGEE		BRUNEL	ISRAEL	TASSEL	BARMEN

BARREN	GARDEN	LUCIEN	SICKEN	UNSTEP	BICKER
BATMEN	GASMEN	LUMPEN	SILKEN	UPKEEP	BIDDER
BATTEN	GERMEN	MADDEN	SKYMEN	******	BIGGER
BEATEN	GLUTEN	MADMEN	SLOVEN	----ER	BILKER
BERGEN	GOLDEN	MAIDEN	SOCMEN	******	BINDER
BIDDEN	GORHEN	MARTEN	SODDEN	ABASER	BISTER
BIOGEN	GOSHEN	MERMEN	SOFTEN	ABATER	BITTER
BITTEN	GOTTEN	MIDDEN	SPLEEN	ABIDER	BLAZER
BOWMEN	GRABEN	MILDEN	SPOKEN	ABUSER	BLOWER
BRAZEN	GRAVEN	MITTEN	STAMEN	ADORER	BOATER
BREMEN	GULDEN	MIZZEN	STATEN	AETHER	BOBBER
BROKEN	GUNMEN	MOLTEN	STEVEN	AIRIER	BOILER
BUNSEN	HAMDEN	MOREEN	STOLEN	AMBLER	BOLDER
BURDEN	HAPPEN	MORGEN	SUDDEN	AMUSER	BOLTER
BUSMEN	HARDEN	MULLEN	SULLEN	ANGLER	BOMBER
CABMEN	HARKEN	NEATEN	SUNKEN	ANSWER	BONDER
CAMDEN	HASTEN	NOREEN	SWEDEN	ANTHER	BONIER
CAREEN	HAUSEN	ORIGEN	TAUTEN	ANTLER	BONZER
CARMEN	HEAVEN	OXYGEN	TEGMEN	ARCHER	BOOMER
CARVEN	HELLEN	PATTEN	TUREEN	ARGUER	BOOZER
CHOSEN	HEMPEN	PEAHEN	UNEVEN	ASHIER	BORDER
CLOVEN	HIDDEN	PEASEN	UNSEEN	ATONER	BOTHER
COWMEN	HOIDEN	PECTEN	VANMEN	AUSTER	BOWLER
CRAVEN	HOYDEN	PENMEN	VIVIEN	AVOWER	BOWYER
DAMPEN	HYPHEN	PIEMEN	WARDEN	BACKER	BRACER
DARIEN	ICEMEN	PIGPEN	WARREN	BADGER	BRAVER
DARKEN	IMOGEN	PITMEN	WEAKEN	BAILER	BRAYER
DEADEN	KITTEN	PLATEN	WHITEN	BALDER	BRAZER
DEAFEN	KRAKEN	POLLEN	WOODEN	BANKER	BREWER
DEEPEN	KRONEN	POTEEN	WOOLEN	BANNER	BRIBER
DOLMEN	KUCHEN	PROVEN	WORSEN	BANTER	BROKER
DOREEN	LASSEN	RAGMEN	YEOMEN	BARBER	BUCKER
DRIVEN	LATEEN	RATTEN	******	BARKER	BUDDER
DRYDEN	LATTEN	REDDEN	----EO	BARTER	BUFFER
DUDEEN	LAYMEN	REOPEN	******	BATHER	BUGGER
DUODEN	LEADEN	REUBEN	ARCHEO	BATTER	BUGLER
EILEEN	LEAVEN	RIDDEN	BORNEO	BAWLER	BULGER
ELEVEN	LEGMEN	RODMEN	CHOREO	BAXTER	BUMMER
EXAMEN	LENTEN	ROTTEN	JUDAEO	BEAKER	BUMPER
EXOGEN	LESSEN	SADDEN	MATTEO	BEARER	BUNKER
FALLEN	LEYDEN	SAPIEN	PALAEO	BEATER	BURGER
FASTEN	LICHEN	SATEEN	STEREO	BEAVER	BURLER
FATTEN	LINDEN	SCREEN	THYREO	BEDDER	BURNER
FLAMEN	LISTEN	SEAMEN	******	BELIER	BUSKER
FLAXEN	LISTEN	SEAPEN	----EP	BENDER	BUSTER
FOEMEN	LOOSEN	SHAKEN	******	BERBER	BUTLER
FRAUEN	LOREEN	SHAPEN	ASLEEP	BETTER	BUTTER
FROZEN	LOUDEN	SHAVEN	INSTEP	BIBBER	BUZZER

CADGER	COLTER	DEALER	DUMPER	FITTER	GINGER
CAGIER	COMBER	DEARER	DUNKER	FIZZER	GINNER
CAHIER	CONFER	DECKER	DUSTER	FLAKER	GIRDER
CALKER	CONGER	DEEPER	EARNER	FLAYER	GLAZER
CALLER	CONKER	DEFIER	EASIER	FLOWER	GLIDER
CALMER	CONNER	DEFTER	EASTER	FLUTER	GLOVER
CAMBER	COOKER	DEICER	ECHOER	FODDER	GLOWER
CAMPER	COOLER	DELVER	EDGIER	FOLDER	GLUIER
CANCER	COOPER	DENIER	EITHER	FONDER	GNAWER
CANKER	COPIER	DENSER	ELATER	FOOTER	GOFFER
CANNER	COPPER	DENVER	ELOPER	FORCER	GOITER
CANTER	CORDER	DEWIER	ENVIER	FORGER	GOLFER
CAPPER	CORKER	DEXTER	ERASER	FORMER	GOOBER
CARDER	CORNER	DIALER	ESCHER	FOSTER	GOOIER
CAREER	COSHER	DIAPER	ESTHER	FOULER	GOPHER
CARPER	COSTER	DIBBER	ETCHER	FOWLER	GORGER
CARTER	COTTER	DICKER	EUCHER	FOXIER	GORIER
CARVER	COWPER	DIETER	EVADER	FRAMER	GOUGER
CASPER	COZIER	DIFFER	EXETER	FRATER	GRADER
CASTER	CRATER	DIGGER	FABLER	FUELER	GRATER
CATHER	CRAVER	DIMMER	FAIRER	FUHRER	GRAVER
CAUSER	CROZER	DINDER	FALLER	FULLER	GRAYER
CAUTER	CRUDER	DINNER	FALSER	FUMIER	GRAZER
CENSER	CULLER	DIPPER	FALTER	FUSSER	GRIPER
CENTER	CULVER	DITHER	FANNER	GABBER	GROCER
CHAFER	CUMBER	DOBBER	FARCER	GADDER	GROPER
CHASER	CUNNER	DOCKER	FARMER	GAFFER	GROVER
CHEWER	CUPPER	DODDER	FASTER	GAGGER	GROWER
CHIDER	CURLER	DODGER	FATHER	GAINER	GUIDER
CHIMER	CUSTER	DOFFER	FATTER	GAITER	GULPER
CHOKER	CUTLER	DOGGER	FAWNER	GAMIER	GUNNER
CHOLER	CUTTER	DOPIER	FEARER	GAMMER	GUNTER
CINDER	CYCLER	DOPTER	FEEDER	GANDER	GUSHER
CIPHER	CYPHER	DORMER	FEELER	GANGER	GUTTER
CITHER	DABBER	DOSSER	FELLER	GAOLER	HACKER
CLEVER	DAGGER	DOTIER	FENCER	GARNER	HAILER
CLOSER	DAMMER	DOTTER	FENDER	GARTER	HALTER
CLOVER	DAMPER	DOWSER	FERBER	GASPER	HAMMER
COALER	DANCER	DOZIER	FESTER	GATHER	HAMPER
COAXER	DANDER	DRAPER	FETTER	GAUGER	HANGER
COBBER	DANGER	DRAWER	FIBBER	GEEZER	HANKER
COCKER	DANKER	DRIVER	FILLER	GEIGER	HARDER
CODDER	DAPPER	DROVER	FILTER	GENDER	HARPER
CODGER	DARKER	DUCKER	FINDER	GETTER	HATTER
COFFER	DARNER	DUELER	FINGER	GEYSER	HAULER
COILER	DARTER	DUFFER	FINNER	GHEBER	HAWKER
COINER	DASHER	DUIKER	FIRMER	GIBBER	HAWSER
COLDER	DAUBER	DULLER	FISHER	GILDER	HAZIER

HEADER	ISOMER	LAKIER	LOCKER	MESMER	OBEYER
HEALER	ISSUER	LANCER	LODGER	METIER	OBITER
HEARER	JABBER	LANDER	LOFTER	MILDER	OILIER
HEATER	JAEGER	LANKER	LOGGER	MILKER	OLIVER
HEAVER	JAILER	LANNER	LOGIER	MILLER	ONAGER
HEDGER	JASPER	LAPPER	LOITER	MILTER	OOZIER
HEEDER	JAZZER	LAPSER	LOLLER	MINCER	OPENER
HEELER	JEERER	LARDER	LONGER	MINDER	OSTLER
HEIFER	JESTER	LARGER	LOOKER	MINTER	OUSTER
HELLER	JIBBER	LARKER	LOOPER	MISTER	OYSTER
HELPER	JIGGER	LASHER	LOOSER	MOBBER	PACKER
HELTER	JILTER	LASTER	LOOTER	MOCKER	PALMER
HEMMER	JINKER	LATHER	LOUDER	MOILER	PALTER
HERDER	JITTER	LATTER	LOUVER	MOLDER	PAMPER
HESTER	JOBBER	LAUDER	LUBBER	MOLTER	PANDER
HIGHER	JOGGER	LAWYER	LUGGER	MONGER	PANZER
HILLER	JOINER	LAZIER	LUMBER	MOOTER	PARKER
HINDER	JOLTER	LEADER	LUNGER	MOTHER	PASSER
HISSER	JOSHER	LEANER	LUNKER	MOUSER	PASTER
HITHER	JOTTER	LEAPER	LURKER	MUCKER	PATTER
HITLER	JUDGER	LEAVER	LUSHER	MUDDER	PAUKER
HITTER	JUICER	LECHER	LUSTER	MUGGER	PAUPER
HOAXER	JUMPER	LEDGER	LUTHER	MULLER	PAUSER
HOLDER	JUNKER	LENDER	MADDER	MUMMER	PAWNER
HOLIER	KAISER	LESSER	MAHLER	MURDER	PECKER
HOLLER	KASPER	LESTER	MAILER	MUSHER	PEEKER
HOMIER	KEENER	LETTER	MAIMER	MUSTER	PEELER
HONKER	KEEPER	LEVIER	MANGER	MUTTER	PEEPER
HOOFER	KEGLER	LEWDER	MANNER	NAGGER	PELTER
HOOKER	KELLER	LIEDER	MARKER	NAPIER	PENNER
HOOPER	KEPLER	LIFTER	MARRER	NAPPER	PEPPER
HOOTER	KHYBER	LIMBER	MASHER	NASSER	PESTER
HOOVER	KICKER	LIMIER	MASKER	NATTER	PEWTER
HOPPER	KIDDER	LIMNER	MASTER	NEARER	PICKER
HOSIER	KILLER	LIMPER	MATTER	NEATER	PIECER
HOTTER	KILMER	LINGER	MAULER	NEEDER	PIETER
HOWLER	KILTER	LINIER	MAUSER	NETHER	PILFER
HUMBER	KINDER	LINTER	MAZIER	NEUTER	PINIER
HUMMER	KIPPER	LIPPER	MEAGER	NICKER	PINNER
HUNGER	KISSER	LISPER	MEANER	NIGGER	PINTER
HUNTER	KNOWER	LISTER	MEEKER	NIGHER	PIPIER
HURLER	KOSHER	LITHER	MEETER	NIPPER	PLACER
HURTER	KRONER	LITTER	MELTER	NOBLER	PLANER
HUSKER	LAAGER	LIVIER	MEMBER	NODDER	PLATER
HYSTER	LACIER	LIVYER	MENDER	NOSIER	PLAYER
INKIER	LADDER	LOADER	MERCER	NUMBER	PLOVER
INLIER	LADLER	LOAFER	MERGER	NURSER	PLOWER
IRONER	LAGGER	LOBBER	MESHER	NUTTER	POKIER

POLDER	RAMMER	ROUTER	SIFTER	SPRYER	TETHER
POLLER	RANGER	RUBBER	SIGNER	STAGER	TETTER
PONDER	RANKER	RUDDER	SILVER	STALER	TEUCER
POORER	RANTER	RUGGER	SIMMER	STARER	THALER
POPPER	RAPIER	RUINER	SIMPER	STATER	THAYER
PORKER	RAPPER	RUMMER	SINGER	STAYER	TICKER
PORTER	RASHER	RUNNER	SINKER	STIVER	TIDIER
POSTER	RASPER	RUSHER	SINNER	STOKER	TILLER
POTHER	RASTER	SACKER	SINTER	STONER	TILTER
POTTER	RATHER	SADDER	SIPPER	STOVER	TIMBER
POURER	RATTER	SAGGER	SISTER	STYLER	TINDER
POUTER	READER	SAGIER	SITTER	SUBTER	TINIER
POWDER	REAMER	SAILER	SIZIER	SUCKER	TINKER
POWTER	REAPER	SALTER	SKATER	SUFFER	TINNER
PRATER	REARER	SALVER	SKEWER	SUMMER	TIPPER
PRAYER	REDDER	SANDER	SKIVER	SUMNER	TITHER
PREFER	REEFER	SANGER	SLATER	SUNDER	TITTER
PRETER	REEKER	SAPPER	SLAVER	SUPPER	TOILER
PREYER	REELER	SAUCER	SLAYER	SURFER	TOLLER
PRIMER	RELIER	SAUGER	SLICER	SURGER	TONIER
PRIZER	RENDER	SAWYER	SLIDER	SUTLER	TOOLER
PROBER	RENTER	SCALER	SLIVER	SYPHER	TOOTER
PROPER	RESTER	SCARER	SLOPER	TACKER	TOPPER
PROSER	RHYMER	SCORER	SLOWER	TAGGER	TOTHER
PROVER	RICHER	SCOTER	SMILER	TALKER	TOTTER
PRUNER	RIFLER	SEALER	SMITER	TALLER	TOURER
PUCKER	RIGGER	SEAMER	SMOKER	TAMPER	TOUTER
PUFFER	RIMMER	SEEDER	SNARER	TANKER	TRACER
PULLER	RINGER	SEEKER	SNIPER	TANNER	TRADER
PULPER	RINSER	SEEMER	SNORER	TAPPER	TRITER
PUMPER	RIOTER	SEINER	SOAKER	TARTER	TROVER
PUNIER	RIPPER	SEIZER	SOARER	TASTER	TUBBER
PUNNER	RISKER	SELLER	SOCCER	TATLER	TUCKER
PUNTER	RITTER	SENDER	SOEVER	TATTER	TURNER
PURGER	ROAMER	SERVER	SOFTER	TAUTER	TUSKER
PURLER	ROARER	SETTER	SOLDER	TEASER	TWINER
PURSER	ROBBER	SEXIER	SOLVER	TEDDER	TWOFER
PUSHER	ROCKER	SHAKER	SOMBER	TEEMER	UGLIER
PUTTER	ROLLER	SHAPER	SONDER	TEETER	ULSTER
QUAKER	ROMPER	SHARER	SOONER	TELFER	UNDOER
QUAVER	ROOFER	SHAVER	SORTER	TELLER	URETER
QUIVER	ROOMER	SHEWER	SOURER	TEMPER	USURER
QUOTER	ROOTER	SHINER	SPACER	TENDER	VAGUER
RACIER	ROPIER	SHIVER	SPADER	TENSER	VAINER
RACKER	ROSIER	SHOVER	SPARER	TENTER	VALUER
RAFTER	ROSTER	SHOWER	SPICER	TERMER	VARIER
RAIDER	ROTTER	SICKER	SPIDER	TERSER	VASTER
RAISER	ROUSER	SIDLER	SPRIER	TESTER	VEILER

VENDER	WILLER	ADDLES	BARDES	BUBOES	CLINES
VENEER	WINCER	ADOBES	BARGES	BUDGES	CLIVES
VENTER	WINDER	ADORES	BARYES	BUGLES	CLONES
VERGER	WINIER	AEETES	BASHES	BULGES	CLOSES
VESPER	WINKER	AERIES	BASSES	BURIES	CLOVES
VETOER	WINNER	AGATES	BASTES	BURKES	CLYDES
VIEWER	WINTER	AGAVES	BEEVES	BURSES	COAXES
VINIER	WIRIER	AGONES	BEIGES	BUSHES	COBLES
VIZIER	WITHER	AGREES	BELIES	BUSIES	COLIES
WAFTER	WOLVER	AISLES	BELLES	BUSSES	CONGES
WAGNER	WONDER	AKENES	BENNES	BUTTES	CONIES
WAILER	WOOFER	ALICES	BERMES	BUZZES	CONTES
WAITER	WORKER	ALINES	BETTES	CABLES	COOEES
WAIVER	WORMER	ALLIES	BEVIES	CACHES	COPIES
WALKER	WORSER	AMAZES	BIASES	CADGES	COPSES
WALTER	WOWSER	AMBLES	BIBLES	CADRES	CORSES
WANDER	WRITER	AMICES	BILGES	CALCES	CORTES
WANNER	XAVIER	AMIDES	BINGES	CALVES	CORVES
WANTER	XYSTER	AMOLES	BIRLES	CALXES	COSHES
WARDER	YABBER	AMUSES	BLADES	CANNES	COSSES
WARIER	YAMMER	ANDRES	BLAMES	CANOES	COUPES
WARMER	YAWNER	ANGLES	BLARES	CARIES	COZIES
WARNER	YAWPER	ANISES	BLAZES	CARTES	CRAKES
WARPER	YELLER	ANKLES	BLOKES	CARVES	CRANES
WASHER	YELPER	ANNIES	BODIES	CASHES	CRAPES
WASTER	YESTER	ANODES	BOGIES	CASTES	CRATES
WAVIER	YONDER	ANUSES	BOGLES	CAULES	CRAVES
WAXIER	YONKER	APEXES	BOMBES	CAUSES	CRAZES
WEAKER	YORKER	APICES	BONZES	CAVIES	CREMES
WEANER	ZAFFER	APPLES	BOOZES	CEASES	CREPES
WEARER	ZANIER	ARCHES	BOSHES	CENSES	CRIMES
WEAVER	ZENGER	ARETES	BOSSES	CERTES	CRISES
WEEDER	ZIPPER	ARGUES	BOULES	CHAFES	CRONES
WEEPER	ZITHER	ARISES	BOUSES	CHAPES	CRORES
WEEVER	ZOSTER	ARMIES	BOWSES	CHARES	CROZES
WELDER	ZUIDER	ARNIES	BRACES	CHASES	CRUCES
WELTER	ZUYDER	ARTIES	BRAKES	CHIDES	CRUSES
WESTER	******	ASIDES	BRAVES	CHIMES	CRUXES
WETHER	----ES	ATONES	BRAZES	CHINES	CURIES
WETTER	******	AWAKES	BREVES	CHIVES	CURSES
WHALER	ABASES	AXONES	BRIBES	CHLOES	CURVES
WHINER	ABATES	AZINES	BRIDES	CHOKES	CUSSES
WHITER	ABBIES	AZOLES	BRINES	CHORES	CUTIES
WICKER	ABELES	AZORES	BROMES	CHUTES	CYCLES
WIENER	ABIDES	AZURES	BRUCES	CITIES	DADOES
WILBER	ABODES	BABIES	BRUGES	CIVIES	DAISES
WILDER	ABUSES	BACHES	BRUMES	CLARES	DALLES
WILIER	ADAGES	BADGES	BRUTES	CLIMES	DANCES

DASHES	ELUDES	FLUMES	GRACES	IMBUES	LATHES
DAVIES	EMCEES	FLUTES	GRADES	IMIDES	LEASES
DEFIES	EMILES	FLUXES	GRAPES	IMINES	LEAVES
DEICES	EMMIES	FOGIES	GRATES	IMMIES	LEDGES
DELVES	EMOTES	FORCES	GRAVES	INCHES	LENSES
DEMIES	ENATES	FORGES	GRAZES	INDIES	LEUDES
DENIES	ENDUES	FORTES	GREBES	INDUES	LEVEES
DEUCES	ENSUES	FOSSES	GRIDES	INGRES	LEVIES
DHOLES	ENVIES	FRAMES	GRIMES	INKLES	LIANES
DIANES	EPODES	FRISES	GRIPES	INURES	LIEGES
DIDIES	ERASES	FUDGES	GROPES	IRENES	LILIES
DIDOES	ERNIES	FUGLES	GROVES	IRIDES	LIVRES
DIESES	ERODES	FUGUES	GRUMES	IRISES	LOAVES
DIODES	ESPIES	FURIES	GUIDES	ISSUES	LODGES
DIRGES	ETAPES	FURZES	GUILES	ITCHES	LOOSES
DISHES	ETCHES	FUSEES	GUISES	JAMIES	LORIES
DOBIES	ETUDES	FUSSES	GUSHES	JAZZES	LOSSES
DODGES	EVADES	FUZEES	HALOES	JESSES	LOUPES
DODOES	EVOKES	FUZZES	HALVES	JINXES	LOUSES
DOGIES	EXILES	GABLES	HANCES	JORGES	LUNGES
DONEES	EXUDES	GAFFES	HASHES	JOSHES	LUSHES
DORIES	EYASES	GANGES	HASTES	JOSSES	LYCEES
DOUSES	EYRIES	GASHES	HAWSES	JOULES	LYNXES
DOWSES	FABLES	GASSES	HEAVES	JOYCES	MACLES
DOXIES	FACIES	GAUGES	HEDGES	JUDGES	MADGES
DRAKES	FAECES	GAUZES	HELVES	JUICES	MAIZES
DRAPES	FARCES	GENIES	HERMES	JULIES	MAMIES
DRIVES	FARLES	GENRES	HEROES	JURIES	MANSES
DRONES	FASCES	GENTES	HERPES	KAASES	MANTES
DROVES	FAUCES	GEODES	HINGES	KATIES	MAPLES
DRUPES	FAUVES	GIGUES	HISSES	KEDGES	MARGES
DRUSES	FAWKES	GLACES	HOAXES	KEEVES	MARIES
DULLES	FEASES	GLADES	HOBBES	KERMES	MASHES
DUNCES	FEEZES	GLARES	HOBOES	KEYNES	MASSES
DUTIES	FENCES	GLAZES	HOLIES	KISSES	MATTES
EAGLES	FESSES	GLEBES	HOLMES	KNAVES	MAUDES
EARLES	FEZZES	GLEDES	HOOVES	KNIFES	MAUVES
ECCLES	FICHES	GLIDES	HORDES	KNIVES	MELEES
ECHOES	FIQUES	GLOBES	HORSES	KOINES	MENSES
ECOLES	FISHES	GLOVES	HOUSES	KOPJES	MERGES
EDDIES	FIZZES	GLOZES	HUGHES	KRISES	MERLES
EDILES	FLAKES	GLUMES	HUSHES	LACHES	MESHES
EDUCES	FLAMES	GNOMES	HYADES	LADIES	MESNES
ELATES	FLARES	GOBIES	IBEXES	LADLES	MESSES
ELIDES	FLAXES	GOOSES	IBICES	LANCES	MIDGES
ELLIES	FLEXES	GORGES	IBISES	LAPSES	MINCES
ELOPES	FLORES	GORSES	ILEXES	LASHES	MINXES
ELSIES	FLUKES	GOUGES	IMAGES	LASSES	MISSES

MOLIES	PEWEES	RANGES	SERIES	SPIRES	THALES
MONIES	PHASES	RASHES	SERVES	SPITES	THAMES
MONTES	PHONES	RAZEES	SHADES	SPOKES	THANES
MOSSES	PIECES	RAZZES	SHAKES	SPORES	THEBES
MOUSES	PINIES	REALES	SHALES	SPREES	THEMES
MOVIES	PIQUES	REDOES	SHAMES	SPRUES	THESES
MURRES	PISCES	REEVES	SHAPES	SPUMES	THOLES
MUSHES	PISHES	RELIES	SHARES	STAGES	THREES
MUSSES	PITIES	RENEES	SHAVES	STAKES	THROES
MYOPES	PIXIES	RENTES	SHINES	STALES	THYMES
NANTES	PLACES	REVUES	SHIRES	STAPES	TIDIES
NAOSES	PLANES	RHODES	SHIVES	STARES	TILDES
NAPLES	PLATES	RHYMES	SHORES	STASES	TINGES
NAPPES	PLEBES	RICHES	SHOTES	STATES	TITHES
NAVIES	PLUMES	RIDGES	SHOVES	STAVES	TITLES
NERVES	PLUSES	RIFLES	SIDLES	STELES	TOBIES
NEUMES	POGIES	RINSES	SIEGES	STERES	TODIES
NICHES	POISES	ROBLES	SIEVES	STEVES	TOGUES
NIECES	POKIES	ROGUES	SINGES	STILES	TOILES
NIXIES	PONIES	ROUGES	SIXTES	STIPES	TOQUES
NOISES	PONTES	ROUSES	SKATES	STOKES	TORIES
NOOSES	POSIES	ROUTES	SKIVES	STOLES	TOSHES
NUDGES	POSSES	RUBIES	SLAKES	STONES	TOSSES
NURSES	PRATES	RUBLES	SLATES	STOPES	TRACES
OGIVES	PRICES	RUCHES	SLAVES	STORES	TRADES
OLIVES	PRIDES	RUPEES	SLICES	STOVES	TRAVES
OLLIES	PRIMES	RUSHES	SLIDES	STUPES	TRIBES
ONUSES	PRIZES	SABLES	SLIMES	STYLES	TRICES
OODLES	PROBES	SADIES	SLOPES	SUCRES	TRINES
OPINES	PROSES	SALVES	SMAZES	SUEDES	TROVES
ORATES	PROVES	SANIES	SMILES	SUITES	TRUCES
ORGIES	PRUDES	SASHES	SMITES	SURGES	TSADES
ORYXES	PRUNES	SASSES	SMOKES	SUSIES	TULLES
OUNCES	PULSES	SAUCES	SNAKES	SWAGES	TUQUES
OVULES	PUREES	SAUTES	SNARES	SWALES	TURVES
OXEYES	PURGES	SCALES	SNIPES	SWEDES	TUSHES
OXIDES	PURSES	SCAPES	SNORES	SWIPES	TWINES
PADRES	PUSHES	SCARES	SOCLES	SYCEES	UKASES
PARIES	PUSSES	SCENES	SOLVES	TABLES	UMBLES
PARSES	PYXIES	SCONES	SOUSES	TASTES	UNCLES
PASSES	QUAKES	SCOPES	SPACES	TAUPES	UNDIES
PASTES	QUEUES	SCORES	SPADES	TBONES	UNDOES
PAUSES	QUIRES	SCUTES	SPARES	TEASES	UNGUES
PAYEES	QUOTES	SEDGES	SPATES	TEHEES	UNITES
PEASES	RABIES	SEINES	SPICES	TENSES	UNTIES
PEEVES	RAISES	SEIZES	SPIKES	TENUES	UPASES
PEKOES	RAMIES	SELVES	SPILES	TEPEES	USAGES
PELVES	RANEES	SENSES	SPINES	TESTES	VALUES

VALVES	BARRET	GADGET	OFFSET	STREET	SUNDEW
VARIES	BASKET	GANNET	OMELET	STYLET	UNDREW
VARVES	BASSET	GARGET	OUTLET	SUBLET	******
VENUES	BECKET	GARNET	OUTSET	SUNSET	----EX
VERGES	BENNET	GARRET	PACKET	SWIVET	******
VERSES	BILLET	GASJET	PALLET	SYNDET	AUSPEX
VETOES	BONNET	GASKET	PARGET	TABLET	BIFLEX
VINCES	BOSKET	GIBBET	PELLET	TAPPET	CAUDEX
VOGUES	BREVET	GIBLET	PICKET	TARGET	CONVEX
VOICES	BUCKET	GIGLET	PIGLET	TASSET	CORTEX
VOILES	BUDGET	GIMLET	PIQUET	TEASET	DIPLEX
WADIES	BUFFET	GOBBET	PLACET	TERCET	DUPLEX
WAIVES	BULLET	GOBLET	PLANET	TERRET	LASTEX
WASHES	BURNET	GOGLET	POCKET	TICKET	POLLEX
WASTES	CABLET	GORGET	POPPET	TIPPET	REFLEX
WAVIES	CACHET	GRIVET	POSSET	TOILET	SCOLEX
WAYNES	CAMLET	GULLET	PRIVET	TRIVET	SUSSEX
WEAVES	CARPET	GUSSET	PROJET	TUCKET	UNISEX
WEDGES	CASKET	HAMLET	PULLET	TUFFET	VERTEX
WHALES	CERMET	HASLET	PUPPET	TURRET	VORTEX
WHILES	CHALET	HELMET	RABBET	UNDSET	WESSEX
WHINES	CLARET	HORNET	RACKET	UNMEET	******
WHITES	CLOSET	IMARET	RAMJET	VARLET	----EY
WHORES	COLLET	JACKET	REFLET	VELVET	******
WICHES	COQUET	JAPHET	REGLET	VERSET	ASHLEY
WINCES	CORNET	JENNET	REGRET	VERVET	AUBREY
WINOES	CORSET	JOLIET	RENNET	VIOLET	AUDREY
WINZES	COSSET	JULIET	RILLET	WADSET	BAILEY
WISHES	CRUSET	JUNKET	ROCHET	WALLET	BARLEY
WITHES	CULLET	KISMET	ROCKET	WICKET	BARNEY
WOLVES	CURVET	LABRET	ROQUET	WILLET	BERNEY
WRITES	CUTLET	LANCET	RUNLET	******	BLIMEY
YESSES	CYGNET	LAPPET	RUSSET	----EU	BURLEY
YOGEES	DAUDET	LIMPET	SACHET	******	BUSHEY
ZANIES	DOCKET	LINNET	SALLET	MILIEU	CLAYEY
ZEROES	DORSET	LOCKET	SAMLET	******	CONVEY
******	DULCET	MAGNET	SECRET	----EW	COOKEY
----ET	DUPLET	MALLET	SENNET	******	COPLEY
******	EAGLET	MAMMET	SEPTET	ANDREW	CRIKEY
AIGLET	EVERET	MARKET	SESTET	CASHEW	DICKEY
AMULET	EYELET	MIDGET	SEXTET	CURFEW	DINGEY
ANKLET	FANJET	MILLET	SIGNET	CURLEW	DINKEY
ARMLET	FAUCET	MINUET	SIPPET	ESCHEW	DISNEY
AUKLET	FERRET	MOPPET	SOCKET	HEBREW	DONKEY
AVOCET	FIDGET	MULLET	SONNET	KISLEW	DOYLEY
AVOSET	FILLET	MUSKET	SORBET	MILDEW	DUDLEY
BALLET	FLORET	NUGGET	SOVIET	NEPHEW	FARLEY
BARBET	FORGET	NUTLET	SPINET	REVIEW	FLUKEY

GALLEY	RIPLEY	RIPOFF	******	LADOGA	MANEGE
GOONEY	RODNEY	RUNOFF	----FY	MALAGA	MENAGE
GOOSEY	ROMNEY	SCLAFF	******	QUAGGA	METAGE
HALLEY	SAWNEY	SCRUFF	AERIFY	TELEGA	MILAGE
HALSEY	SIDNEY	SETOFF	ARGUFY	******	MIRAGE
HARLEY	STAGEY	SHROFF	BASIFY	----GE	NONAGE
HARVEY	STOGEY	TARIFF	CASEFY	******	OBLIGE
HENLEY	STOREY	TIPOFF	CHAFFY	ALLEGE	OHMAGE
HICKEY	SURREY	******	CLIFFY	AMBAGE	ORANGE
HOCKEY	SURVEY	----FS	CODIFY	ANLAGE	PELAGE
HOOKEY	SYDNEY	******	DRAFFY	AVENGE	PIPAGE
HORSEY	TACKEY	BLUFFS	FLUFFY	BAREGE	PLEDGE
HURLEY	TURKEY	BRIEFS	GASIFY	BLUNGE	PLUNGE
HUXLEY	VALLEY	CALIFS	HUMIFY	BORAGE	POTAGE
JARVEY	VOLLEY	CHAFFS	IGNIFY	BRIDGE	RAVAGE
JERSEY	WESLEY	CHIEFS	MINIFY	CHANGE	REFUGE
JITNEY	WHEYEY	CLIFFS	MODIFY	CHARGE	RENEGE
JOCKEY	WHITEY	DRAFFS	NAZIFY	COWAGE	RRHAGE
KERSEY	WINCEY	DWARFS	NIDIFY	CRINGE	SAVAGE
KIDNEY	WITNEY	FEOFFS	NOTIFY	CUBAGE	SEWAGE
KINSEY	WOLSEY	FLUFFS	OSSIFY	DAMAGE	SILAGE
LACKEY	******	GANEFS	PACIFY	DEGAGE	SLEDGE
LESLEY	----EZ	GREIFS	PURIFY	DELUGE	SLUDGE
LOWKEY	******	MOTIFS	RAMIFY	DOSAGE	SMUDGE
MAGUEY	CORTEZ	PILAFS	RAREFY	DOTAGE	SOCAGE
MEDLEY	JUAREZ	PROOFS	RATIFY	DREDGE	SPARGE
MERSEY	******	QUAFFS	SALIFY	DRUDGE	SPONGE
MICKEY	----FE	SCARFS	SCURFY	EMERGE	SPURGE
MONKEY	******	SCOFFS	SNIFFY	ENCAGE	STODGE
MOOLEY	AGRAFE	SCUFFS	SNUFFY	ENGAGE	STOOGE
MORLEY	BOUFFE	SERIFS	SPIFFY	ENRAGE	SWINGE
MOSLEY	CARAFE	SKIFFS	STUFFY	FLANGE	TOWAGE
MOTLEY	GRIFFE	SNIFFS	TEPEFY	FLEDGE	TRUDGE
MULLEY	PIAFFE	SNUFFS	TUMEFY	FORAGE	TWINGE
MURREY	STRAFE	SPOOFS	TYPIFY	FRIDGE	ULLAGE
OAKLEY	STRIFE	STAFFS	UGLIFY	FRINGE	UNCAGE
OCASEY	UNSAFE	STUFFS	VERIFY	GARAGE	VISAGE
ORKNEY	******	WHARFS	VILIFY	GEORGE	VOYAGE
OSPREY	----FF	WHIFFS	VIVIFY	GRANGE	******
PARLEY	******	******	******	GREIGE	----GH
PEAVEY	CUTOFF	----FT	----GA	GRUDGE	******
PHONEY	FAROFF	******	******	HOMAGE	ARMAGH
PHOOEY	LAYOFF	ADRIFT	AURIGA	INCAGE	AWEIGH
POMPEY	ONEOFF	BEREFT	BELUGA	LAVAGE	CHOUGH
PULLEY	PAYOFF	SHRIFT	BODEGA	LINAGE	CLOUGH
PURVEY	PILAFF	THRIFT	CAYUGA	LOUNGE	ENOUGH
PUSSEY	PUTOFF	UPLIFT	FANEGA	LOVAGE	PLOUGH
RICKEY	REBUFF		FRIGGA	MANAGE	SLEIGH

SLOUGH	CHANGS	OOLOGY	DOUCHE	MORPHO	JONAHS
THOUGH	CLANGS	QUAGGY	FLECHE	NAVAHO	JUDAHS
TROUGH	CLINGS	RRHAGY	GAUCHE	NYMPHO	KEITHS
******	CRAIGS	SHAGGY	GOETHE	PANCHO	LAUGHS
----GI	DEBUGS	SLAGGY	LOATHE	PONCHO	LEIGHS
******	DOINGS	SLANGY	MARTHE	PSYCHO	LOTAHS
GEORGI	FLINGS	SLUDGY	MOISHE	RANCHO	LOUGHS
UBANGI	FLONGS	SMUDGY	PSYCHE	REECHO	MONTHS
******	GOINGS	SNAGGY	ROTCHE	SAPPHO	MOUTHS
----GM	ICINGS	SPONGY	ROUCHE	SCYPHO	NEIGHS
******	ORANGS	STAGGY	SCATHE	SORGHO	NINTHS
PHLEGM	PRONGS	STINGY	SCYTHE	STETHO	NYMPHS
******	SCRAGS	STODGY	SEETHE	SULPHO	ORACHS
----GN	SHRUGS	SYZYGY	SEICHE	TRICHO	RAJAHS
******	SLINGS	TWANGY	SNATHE	TROPHO	RALPHS
ASSIGN	SPRAGS	TWIGGY	SOOTHE	XANTHO	RAYAHS
BENIGN	SPRIGS	******	SPATHE	******	REICHS
COSIGN	STINGS	----HA	SWATHE	----HS	ROLPHS
DESIGN	SWINGS	******	TEETHE	******	ROUGHS
ELOIGN	THINGS	AGATHA	TOUCHE	ALEPHS	SARAHS
ENSIGN	THONGS	APHTHA	TRACHE	ALMAHS	SIXTHS
IMPUGN	TWANGS	AYESHA	TROCHE	BERTHS	SLOTHS
MALIGN	UNPEGS	BERTHA	WRITHE	BIRTHS	SMITHS
OPPUGN	UNRIGS	BUDDHA	******	BOOTHS	SNATHS
RESIGN	WHANGS	CONCHA	----HI	BOUGHS	SOUGHS
******	WRINGS	ELISHA	******	BROTHS	SUBAHS
----GO	WRONGS	GEISHA	BRACHI	BURGHS	SURAHS
******	******	GURKHA	CANTHI	CLOTHS	SWATHS
AERUGO	----GU	MALTHA	CHICHI	CONCHS	SYLPHS
COLUGO	******	MARSHA	DELPHI	COUGHS	TENTHS
DRONGO	TELUGU	MARTHA	GANDHI	DEATHS	THIGHS
ERINGO	******	NYMPHA	LITCHI	DEPTHS	TILTHS
ERYNGO	----GY	PYRRHA	SANDHI	DINAHS	TORAHS
FOREGO	******	QUOTHA	SCYPHI	DOLPHS	TOUGHS
INDIGO	ANERGY	SULPHA	TRICHI	DOUGHS	TROTHS
LANUGO	CLERGY	******	******	EARTHS	TRUTHS
NONEGO	CLINGY	----HE	----HM	EDITHS	WEIGHS
OSWEGO	CLOGGY	******	******	EPHAHS	WIDTHS
RUBIGO	CRAGGY	AMECHE	DRACHM	EPOCHS	YOUTHS
TOBAGO	DREGGY	APACHE	RHYTHM	ERICHS	******
VIRAGO	EFFIGY	BERTHE	******	FAITHS	----HT
******	ENERGY	BLITHE	----HO	FIFTHS	******
----GS	EULOGY	BROCHE	******	FIRTHS	ALIGHT
******	FLAGGY	BUNCHE	CLOTHO	FRITHS	ARIGHT
BEFOGS	FLEDGY	CLICHE	GAUCHO	FROTHS	BLIGHT
BEINGS	FLEDGY	CLOCHE	GNATHO	GLYPHS	BOUGHT
BOURGS	FRINGY	CLOTHE	GRAPHO	GRAPHS	BRECHT
BRINGS	FROGGY	CRECHE	LYMPHO	HEATHS	BRIGHT
	GROGGY				

CAUGHT	LEACHY	CANDIA	RAFFIA	ANEMIC	EMERIC
DWIGHT	MARSHY	CASSIA	RAZZIA	ANGLIC	EMETIC
FLIGHT	MOUTHY	CODEIA	ROBBIA	ANODIC	EOZOIC
FOUGHT	PATCHY	CRANIA	RUSSIA	ANOMIC	EROTIC
FRIGHT	PEACHY	DAHLIA	SALVIA	ANOXIC	ETHNIC
HEIGHT	PITCHY	EGERIA	SCORIA	AORTIC	EXILIC
KNIGHT	PLASHY	EMILIA	SCOTIA	APNEIC	EXOTIC
NAUGHT	PLUSHY	FASCIA	SERBIA	ARABIC	FABRIC
NOUGHT	POACHY	FLAVIA	SILVIA	ARCTIC	FERRIC
PLIGHT	POUCHY	GAMBIA	SOPHIA	ATAVIC	FILMIC
SLIGHT	PUNCHY	GDYNIA	STADIA	ATAXIC	FINNIC
SOUGHT	SLOSHY	GIULIA	SYLVIA	ATOMIC	FISTIC
TAUGHT	SLUSHY	GLORIA	TAENIA	ATONIC	FORMIC
WEIGHT	SMITHY	HERNIA	TARSIA	AZONIC	FROLIC
WRIGHT	STITHY	HESTIA	TERBIA	AZOTIC	FUSTIC
******	SYLPHY	HYGEIA	THALIA	BALTIC	GAELIC
----HU	TETCHY	IBERIA	THORIA	BARDIC	GALLIC
******	TOOTHY	ISCHIA	THULIA	BELGIC	GARLIC
HONSHU	TOUCHY	ISTRIA	TRIVIA	BIOTIC	GEODIC
KYUSHU	TRACHY	JAPHIA	URANIA	BOMBIC	GESTIC
MANCHU	TRASHY	KALMIA	UREMIA	BROMIC	GNOMIC
SAMSHU	TROPHY	LATRIA	UTOPIA	BUSTIC	GOTHIC
******	WORTHY	LATVIA	YTTRIA	CALCIC	HECTIC
----HY	WRATHY	LEPSIA	ZAMBIA	CAPRIC	HERDIC
******	******	LITHIA	ZINNIA	CARPIC	HEROIC
APATHY	----IA	LOCHIA	ZOYSIA	CEDRIC	HOLMIC
BEACHY	******	LOGGIA	******	CELTIC	HYDRIC
BEECHY	ABULIA	MARCIA	----IB	CHORIC	HYMNIC
BITCHY	ACACIA	MERCIA	******	CHYMIC	HYPNIC
BOTCHY	ACADIA	MYOPIA	MIDRIB	CITRIC	IAMBIC
BRACHY	ACEDIA	NUTRIA	******	CLERIC	IATRIC
BRASHY	ACHAIA	ODYNIA	----IC	CLINIC	ICONIC
BRUSHY	AEOLIA	OLIVIA	******	CLONIC	IRENIC
BUNCHY	AGLAIA	PATHIA	ACERIC	COPTIC	IRIDIC
CATCHY	ALALIA	PENNIA	ACETIC	COSMIC	IRITIC
CONCHY	ALEXIA	PEORIA	ACIDIC	CRETIC	IRONIC
DEATHY	ALICIA	PERSIA	ADIPIC	CRITIC	ITALIC
DINGHY	AMANIA	PHAGIA	ADONIC	CUPRIC	JUDAIC
DOUGHY	AMELIA	PHASIA	AEOLIC	CYANIC	KELTIC
EARTHY	ANEMIA	PHILIA	AGAMIC	CYCLIC	LACTIC
FILTHY	ANGLIA	PHOBIA	AGARIC	CYMRIC	LIMBIC
FLASHY	ANOMIA	PHONIA	AGONIC	CYSTIC	LITHIC
FLESHY	ANOXIA	PLASIA	ALARIC	DEIFIC	LUETIC
FROTHY	ANTLIA	PLEGIA	ALCAIC	DERMIC	MANTIC
GRAPHY	APULIA	PORTIA	ALTAIC	DYADIC	MASTIC
GUNSHY	ARABIA	PYEMIA	AMEBIC	ECHOIC	METRIC
HEATHY	ATAXIA	PYTHIA	AMIDIC	EDDAIC	MIOTIC
ICHTHY	BORGIA	PYURIA	AMYLIC	EDENIC	MOSAIC

MYOPIC	THORIC	HEMOID	ANOMIE	DOOLIE	MINNIE
MYSTIC	THYMIC	HESOID	ARCHIE	DORMIE	MOLLIE
MYTHIC	TRAGIC	HISPID	AUNTIE	DOUGIE	NAPPIE
NASTIC	TROPIC	HORRID	BABBIE	DULCIE	NELLIE
NIOBIC	TURKIC	HYBRID	BAILIE	EMERIE	NETTIE
NITRIC	UNIFIC	INGRID	BARBIE	EMILIE	PANTIE
NOETIC	URALIC	INLAID	BARMIE	FAERIE	PETRIE
NORDIC	URANIC	KELOID	BARRIE	FANNIE	PIGGIE
NOSTIC	URETIC	LIMPID	BEANIE	GERTIE	PINKIE
ORPHIC	VIATIC	LIPOID	BERNIE	GILLIE	POTPIE
OXALIC	VITRIC	LIQUID	BERTIE	GOALIE	POTSIE
OZONIC	YTTRIC	MADRID	BESSIE	GRACIE	REGGIE
PECTIC	ZINCIC	MISDID	BILLIE	GUSSIE	RICHIE
PELVIC	******	MORBID	BIRDIE	HACKIE	ROBBIE
PEPTIC	----ID	MUCOID	BOBBIE	HATTIE	RONNIE
PHASIC	******	NEREID	BOCCIE	HIPPIE	ROOKIE
PHOBIC	ACARID	NEVOID	BONNIE	HOGTIE	SOPHIE
PHONIC	AENEID	NITRID	BOOGIE	HORNIE	SORTIE
PHOTIC	AFRAID	ORCHID	BOOKIE	HUGHIE	SPECIE
PHYSIC	ALGOID	OUTBID	BOOTIE	JACKIE	STACIE
PICNIC	ASTRID	OUTDID	BOUGIE	JESSIE	STEVIE
PICRIC	BEDRID	PALLID	BOWTIE	JIMMIE	STYMIE
POETIC	BRIGID	PLACID	BRIDIE	JONNIE	TALKIE
PONTIC	CANDID	PUTRID	BUDGIE	JUNKIE	TESSIE
PUBLIC	CEBOID	RANCID	BURDIE	KATHIE	TILLIE
PYEMIC	CLERID	RELAID	CADDIE	KELPIE	TRIXIE
PYKNIC	COCCID	REPAID	CANNIE	KENNIE	VIRGIE
PYTHIC	CONOID	SALPID	CARRIE	KERRIE	WALLIE
QUINIC	CUBOID	SIGRID	CASSIE	KEWPIE	WEDGIE
RHIZIC	CUSPID	SORDID	CATTIE	KIDDIE	WEENIE
RHODIC	CYANID	STOLID	CISSIE	KILTIE	WIDDIE
ROMAIC	CYMOID	STUPID	COLLIE	LADDIE	WIENIE
RUBRIC	DANAID	TINEID	COMMIE	LAMBIE	WILLIE
RUSTIC	DESMID	TOROID	CONNIE	LASSIE	WINNIE
SAITIC	DEVOID	TORPID	COOKIE	LAURIE	YIPPIE
SCENIC	EUCLID	TORRID	COOLIE	LEONIE	YUPPIE
SEPTIC	EYELID	TRIFID	COOTIE	LESLIE	ZOMBIE
SIALIC	FERVID	TURBID	CORBIE	LIZZIE	******
SLAVIC	FLORID	TURGID	CORRIE	LOTTIE	----IF
SOTHIC	FOETID	UNAPID	COWRIE	MAGGIE	******
STATIC	FORBID	UNLAID	CUDDIE	MAGPIE	MASSIF
STELIC	FRIGID	UNSAID	CUPTIE	MAISIE	SHERIF
STERIC	FUCOID	VESPID	DEARIE	MARGIE	******
SUOMIC	FULGID	VISCID	DEBBIE	MASHIE	----IG
SYNDIC	GADOID	XYLOID	DICKIE	MATTIE	******
TACTIC	GANOID	******	DOGGIE	MEALIE	BIGWIG
TANNIC	GRAVID	----IE	DOLLIE	MEANIE	DANZIG
THETIC	HALOID	******	DONNIE	MILLIE	EARWIG
		AMALIE			
		AMELIE			

FIZGIG	TONSIL	CALVIN	HARMIN	PIPPIN	******
HEDWIG	TWIBIL	CAPLIN	HATPIN	PLUGIN	----IO
LIEBIG	UNCOIL	CASEIN	HEREIN	POPLIN	******
LUDWIG	UNVEIL	CATKIN	HEROIN	PUFFIN	ADAGIO
ZAFTIG	VERGIL	CATLIN	INULIN	PULLIN	AFLCIO
******	VIRGIL	CAVEIN	ISATIN	PURLIN	BAGNIO
----II	WEEVIL	CHITIN	JERKIN	RABBIN	BARRIO
******	******	CHOPIN	JOPLIN	RAISIN	BIBLIO
HAWAII	----IM	COCAIN	JUSTIN	RATLIN	CARDIO
******	******	COCHIN	KAMSIN	REDFIN	CRANIO
----IK	ANTRIM	CODEIN	KAOLIN	REGAIN	DAIMIO
******	BAALIM	COFFIN	KELVIN	REJOIN	EMILIO
BATTIK	BALTIM	CONTIN	LEADIN	REMAIN	FLUVIO
CROJIK	ELOHIM	CORTIN	LIGNIN	RENNIN	GIULIO
DIKDIK	MEGRIM	COUSIN	LOOKIN	RETAIN	HERNIO
MUZHIK	MUSLIM	CRETIN	LORAIN	RUSKIN	NUNCIO
NUDNIK	PASSIM	CYANIN	LOVEIN	SEARIN	ORCHIO
SUSLIK	PAYNIM	CYMLIN	LUBLIN	SEISIN	PHYSIO
******	PRELIM	CYPRIN	MARGIN	SEIZIN	PLAGIO
----IL	SIKKIM	DARWIN	MARLIN	SEQUIN	PLUVIO
******	VICTIM	DENTIN	MARTIN	SEREIN	SCIPIO
AGNAIL	******	DERAIN	MARVIN	SHOOIN	STUDIO
ARCHIL	----IN	DETAIN	MELVIN	SHUTIN	VIBRIO
ASSAIL	******	DEVEIN	MERLIN	SIMLIN	******
BEWAIL	ADJOIN	DIAZIN	MERVIN	SISKIN	----IP
BRAZIL	ALCUIN	DOBBIN	MOULIN	SPAVIN	******
BULBIL	ALEXIN	DOMAIN	MUFFIN	SPRAIN	BUNYIP
DENTIL	ALUMIN	DUBBIN	MUSLIN	STALIN	CATNIP
DERAIL	AMIDIN	DUBLIN	MYELIN	STAMIN	FILLIP
DETAIL	ANILIN	DUNLIN	MYOSIN	STEPIN	GOSSIP
DISTIL	ATTAIN	EMETIN	NAPKIN	STRAIN	MENDIP
DOSSIL	AUSTIN	ENJOIN	NIACIN	TAKEIN	PHILIP
ENTAIL	AVIDIN	FADEIN	NOGGIN	TANNIN	TURNIP
FIBRIL	BAFFIN	FIBRIN	NUBBIN	TENPIN	UNSHIP
FOSSIL	BATTIN	FILLIN	OBTAIN	TIEPIN	******
FULFIL	BEDUIN	FIRKIN	OLEFIN	TIFFIN	----IR
GERBIL	BEGUIN	FLAVIN	ORCEIN	TOCSIN	******
INSTIL	BERLIN	FLORIN	ORDAIN	TONKIN	AFFAIR
JEZAIL	BIFFIN	FUSAIN	ORIGIN	URCHIN	ALTAIR
LENTIL	BIGGIN	GASKIN	OSSEIN	VERDIN	BESTIR
ORCHIL	BIOTIN	GAWAIN	PAPAIN	VEREIN	COHEIR
OXTAIL	BOBBIN	GLOBIN	PAULIN	VERMIN	DEVOIR
PASTIL	BODKIN	GOBLIN	PECTIN	VIOLIN	ECLAIR
PENCIL	BOFFIN	GODWIN	PEPSIN	VIRGIN	ELIXIR
PISTIL	BOWFIN	GRADIN	PHYTIN	WELKIN	FAFNIR
PONTIL	BUMKIN	GRATIN	PIDGIN	WITHIN	FENRIR
RECOIL	BUSKIN	GUANIN	PIGGIN	ZECHIN	GAMBIR
RETAIL	CALKIN	HARBIN	PIPKIN		IMPAIR

KAFFIR	ELEMIS	OTITIS	ALBEIT	TOMTIT	INTAKE
MEMOIR	EMESIS	OXALIS	ARMPIT	TURBIT	INVOKE
MENHIR	ENOSIS	PALAIS	BANDIT	TWILIT	MOLTKE
MIDAIR	FERMIS	PARSIS	BEDSIT	TWOBIT	MOPOKE
MOHAIR	FERRIS	PARVIS	BELOIT	UNKNIT	PERUKE
NORNIR	FORTIS	PATOIS	COMFIT	WITHIT	REBUKE
RENOIR	GLACIS	PELVIS	COMMIT	******	REMAKE
REPAIR	GLAMIS	PENNIS	CREDIT	----IX	RETAKE
UNFAIR	GLYNIS	PHASIS	DACOIT	******	REVOKE
UNHAIR	GNOSIS	PHOCIS	DAKOIT	BOLLIX	SHRIKE
ZAFFIR	GRATIS	PLASIS	DECEIT	CERVIX	SPLAKE
******	HAGGIS	PRAXIS	DIMWIT	COMMIX	STRAKE
----IS	HARRIS	PRECIS	ELEGIT	FORNIX	STRIKE
******	HENRIS	PTOSIS	ELICIT	MATRIX	STROKE
AALIIS	HOURIS	PYOSIS	ESPRIT	PREFIX	UNLIKE
ABATIS	HUBRIS	RABBIS	GAMBIT	PROLIX	UNMAKE
ADENIS	HYBRIS	RACHIS	GODWIT	SPADIX	UNYOKE
ADONIS	INDRIS	RAPHIS	HENBIT	SUFFIX	UPDIKE
AEOLIS	IRANIS	SALMIS	HERMIT	VERNIX	UPTAKE
ALEXIS	IRAQIS	SEPSIS	INTUIT	******	******
ALIBIS	IRITIS	SERAIS	JESUIT	----JE	----KH
ANUBIS	ISSEIS	SHOJIS	KERMIT	******	******
ARTOIS	JARVIS	SOTHIS	KUWAIT	SKOPJE	SHEIKH
ASSAIS	JERVIS	SPAHIS	MISFIT	******	******
BAHAIS	KAURIS	STASIS	MUSKIT	----JO	----KI
BAUCIS	KERMIS	SWAMIS	NITWIT	******	******
BIOSIS	KHAKIS	TENNIS	OUTFIT	NAVAJO	ALFAKI
BREWIS	KIBEIS	TENUIS	OUTSIT	******	KABIKI
CADDIS	KRUBIS	TESTIS	OUTWIT	----KA	KABUKI
CALAIS	LANAIS	THEMIS	PEEWIT	******	NEVSKI
CASSIS	LUNGIS	THESIS	PERMIT	ALASKA	SALUKI
CAULIS	MANTIS	THETIS	PINXIT	EUREKA	WAKIKI
CLEVIS	MAORIS	TIGRIS	PROFIT	KABAKA	******
CLOVIS	MAQUIS	TORIIS	PROSIT	KANAKA	----KO
COATIS	MIOSIS	TURKIS	PULPIT	MARKKA	******
CORGIS	MISSIS	TUSSIS	PUNDIT	TOPEKA	BAMAKO
CRASIS	MORRIS	TUTTIS	RABBIT	TROIKA	GINGKO
CRISIS	MUFTIS	UNGUIS	REEDIT	******	SHACKO
CULLIS	MYOSIS	VALOIS	SCHUIT	----KE	******
CURTIS	NAOMIS	WALLIS	SENNIT	******	----KS
CUSPIS	NEREIS	WALVIS	SOFFIT	ALSIKE	******
DEBRIS	NISEIS	WILLIS	SPIRIT	ANANKE	BATIKS
DENNIS	NOESIS	ZOMBIS	STRAIT	AXLIKE	BLACKS
DERMIS	NORRIS	******	SUBMIT	BELIKE	BLANKS
DERRIS	OKAPIS	----IT	SUMMIT	BETAKE	BLEAKS
DHOTIS	ORCHIS	******	SUNLIT	BROOKE	BLINKS
DIESIS	ORIBIS	ACQUIT	TIDBIT	DECOKE	BLOCKS
ECESIS	OSIRIS	ADROIT	TITBIT	INJOKE	BREAKS

BREEKS	KAYAKS	STIRKS	TRICKY	ROMOLA	BAFFLE
BRICKS	KIOSKS	STOCKS	TWEAKY	SCYLLA	BANGLE
BRINKS	KNACKS	STOOKS	WHELKY	SHEILA	BATTLE
BRISKS	KNOCKS	STORKS	WHISKY	STELLA	BAUBLE
BROOKS	KODAKS	THANKS	ZINCKY	UNGULA	BEADLE
CAULKS	KOPEKS	TORSKS	******	URSULA	BEAGLE
CHALKS	KULAKS	TRACKS	----LA	ZONULA	BEETLE
CHECKS	PLACKS	TRICKS	******	******	BOBBLE
CHEEKS	PLANKS	TRUCKS	ABOLLA	----LD	BOGGLE
CHICKS	PLUCKS	TRUNKS	ANGELA	******	BOODLE
CHINKS	PLUNKS	TUPIKS	ANGOLA	AFIELD	BOOTLE
CHOCKS	PRANKS	TWEAKS	AQUILA	AGEOLD	BOTTLE
CHUCKS	PRICKS	UMIAKS	ARBELA	ARNOLD	BOUCLE
CHUNKS	PRINKS	WHACKS	AREOLA	BEHELD	BRIDLE
CLACKS	QUACKS	WHELKS	ARGALA	BEHOLD	BUBBLE
CLANKS	QUARKS	WHISKS	ATTILA	BIFOLD	BUCKLE
CLERKS	QUIRKS	WRACKS	AXILLA	DONALD	BUDDLE
CLICKS	SHACKS	WREAKS	CABALA	ENFOLD	BUMBLE
CLINKS	SHANKS	WRECKS	CAMILA	GERALD	BUNDLE
CLOAKS	SHARKS	YOICKS	CANULA	HAROLD	BUNGLE
CLOCKS	SHEIKS	******	CEDULA	HERALD	BURBLE
CLUCKS	SHIRKS	----KY	CHOLLA	INFOLD	BURGLE
CRACKS	SHOCKS	******	CICALA	KOBOLD	BUSTLE
CRANKS	SHUCKS	BLOCKY	CITOLA	OSWALD	CACKLE
CREAKS	SKINKS	CHALKY	COPULA	RESOLD	CAJOLE
CREEKS	SKULKS	CHEEKY	CUPOLA	RETOLD	CANDLE
CRICKS	SKUNKS	CHINKY	EIDOLA	RIBALD	CANTLE
CROAKS	SLACKS	CHUNKY	FACULA	RONALD	CAROLE
CROCKS	SLEEKS	CRACKY	FECULA	SHEILD	CASTLE
CROOKS	SLICKS	CRANKY	FERULA	SHIELD	CATTLE
DEREKS	SLINKS	CREAKY	FIBULA	SHOULD	CAUDLE
DRINKS	SMACKS	CROAKY	HOOPLA	TWOULD	CECILE
DRUNKS	SMIRKS	CROCKY	IMPALA	UNFOLD	CHICLE
FLACKS	SMOCKS	DROSKY	KABALA	UNSOLD	CIRCLE
FLANKS	SNACKS	FLOCKY	KAMALA	UNTOLD	COBBLE
FLASKS	SNEAKS	FLUNKY	KERALA	UPHELD	COCKLE
FLECKS	SNICKS	FREAKY	LIGULA	UPHOLD	CODDLE
FLICKS	SNOOKS	FRISKY	LUELLA	******	COFFLE
FLOCKS	SPANKS	PLUCKY	LUNULA	----LE	COODLE
FLUNKS	SPARKS	SLEEKY	MACULA	******	COUPLE
FRANKS	SPEAKS	SLINKY	MANILA	AEDILE	CRADLE
FREAKS	SPECKS	SNEAKY	MORULA	ALIBLE	CREOLE
FRISKS	SPOOKS	SPOOKY	NEBULA	ALLELE	CUDDLE
FROCKS	STACKS	SPUNKY	PAMELA	AMPULE	CUPULE
GREEKS	STALKS	STALKY	PAPULA	ARABLE	CURDLE
HOICKS	STEAKS	STICKY	PAYOLA	AUDILE	CURULE
KAMIKS	STICKS	STOCKY	PETULA	AWHILE	CUTTLE
KAPOKS	STINKS	SWANKY	RADULA	BABBLE	CYBELE

DABBLE	FUMBLE	KETTLE	NIPPLE	RIDDLE	TOOTLE
DADDLE	FUSILE	KIBBLE	NOBBLE	RIFFLE	TOPPLE
DAGGLE	FUTILE	KINDLE	NODDLE	RIMPLE	TOUSLE
DANDLE	GABBLE	KIRTLE	NODULE	RIPPLE	TREBLE
DANGLE	GAGGLE	KITTLE	NOELLE	ROOTLE	TRIFLE
DAPPLE	GAMBLE	LABILE	NOODLE	ROUBLE	TRIPLE
DARKLE	GARBLE	LIABLE	NOZZLE	ROYALE	TUBULE
DARTLE	GARGLE	LIGULE	NUBBLE	RUBBLE	TUILLE
DAWDLE	GAULLE	LITTLE	NUBILE	RUDDLE	TUMBLE
DAZZLE	GENTLE	LOBULE	NUZZLE	RUFFLE	TURTLE
DECILE	GIGGLE	LOCALE	ORACLE	RUMBLE	TUSSLE
DECKLE	GIRDLE	LUCILE	ORIOLE	RUMPLE	UNABLE
DEFILE	GISELE	LUNULE	OSCULE	RUNDLE	UNPILE
DIBBLE	GOBBLE	MACKLE	PADDLE	RUSTLE	USABLE
DIDDLE	GOGGLE	MACULE	PAPULE	RUTILE	VENULE
DIMPLE	GRILLE	MANGLE	PAROLE	SADDLE	VIABLE
DINGLE	GURGLE	MANTLE	PEBBLE	SAMPLE	VIRILE
DIPOLE	GUTTLE	MARBLE	PEDDLE	SEDILE	WABBLE
DOABLE	GUZZLE	MEDDLE	PENILE	SEMELE	WADDLE
DOCILE	HABILE	METTLE	PEOPLE	SENILE	WAFFLE
DOODLE	HACKLE	MICKLE	PESTLE	SETTLE	WAGGLE
DOTTLE	HAGGLE	MIDDLE	PICKLE	SICKLE	WAMBLE
DOUBLE	HANDLE	MIGGLE	PIDDLE	SIECLE	WANDLE
DUFFLE	HASSLE	MINGLE	PIFFLE	SIMILE	WANGLE
EDIBLE	HECKLE	MISTLE	PILULE	SIMPLE	WARBLE
EMPALE	HEDDLE	MIZZLE	PIMPLE	SINGLE	WATTLE
ENABLE	HIGGLE	MOBILE	PINOLE	SIZZLE	WIGGLE
ENISLE	HOBBLE	MODULE	PINTLE	STABLE	WIMBLE
ENSILE	HOPPLE	MOHOLE	POODLE	STAPLE	WIMPLE
EXHALE	HUCKLE	MORALE	POPPLE	STIFLE	WINKLE
FACILE	HUDDLE	MOTILE	POTALE	SUABLE	WOBBLE
FAILLE	HUMBLE	MOTTLE	POTTLE	SUBTLE	ZIZZLE
FEEBLE	HURDLE	MUCKLE	PUDDLE	SUCKLE	ZONULE
FEMALE	HURTLE	MUDDLE	PURFLE	SUPPLE	******
FERULE	HUSTLE	MUFFLE	PURPLE	SWIPLE	----LF
FETTLE	ICICLE	MUMBLE	PUZZLE	TACKLE	******
FICKLE	IMPALE	MUSCLE	RABBLE	TAILLE	BEHALF
FIDDLE	INHALE	MUTULE	RADDLE	TAMALE	ENGULF
FIMBLE	INSOLE	MUZZLE	RAFFLE	TANGLE	INGULF
FINALE	JANGLE	MYRTLE	RAMBLE	TATTLE	ITSELF
FIPPLE	JIGGLE	NEEDLE	RANKLE	TEMPLE	MYSELF
FIZZLE	JINGLE	NESTLE	RATTLE	TICKLE	******
FOCSLE	JOGGLE	NETTLE	REDDLE	TINGLE	----LI
FOIBLE	JOSTLE	NEVILE	REGALE	TINKLE	******
FONDLE	JUGGLE	NIBBLE	RESALE	TIPPLE	ALKALI
FOOTLE	JUMBLE	NICOLE	RESILE	TITTLE	ARGALI
FOOZLE	JUNGLE	NIGGLE	RESOLE	TODDLE	CHILLI
FUDDLE	KECKLE	NIMBLE	REVILE	TOGGLE	EMBOLI

GANGLI	THRILL	ANGELS	DRILLS	MABELS	SHOALS
LAZULI	UNROLL	ANNALS	DROLLS	MEDALS	SHORLS
LIMULI	UNWELL	ANNULS	DROOLS	METALS	SIBYLS
NEROLI	UPHILL	ANVILS	DWELLS	MIAULS	SIGILS
NIELLI	******	APPALS	EASELS	MODELS	SKILLS
OCELLI	----LM	APPELS	EDSELS	MOGULS	SKULLS
SOMALI	******	APRILS	ENGELS	MORALS	SMALLS
STELLI	ANSELM	ARGALS	EQUALS	MORELS	SMELLS
VASILI	BECALM	ARIELS	ETHELS	MOTELS	SNAILS
******	COPALM	ARTELS	ETHYLS	MURALS	SNARLS
----LK	EMBALM	ATOLLS	EXCELS	NASALS	SNELLS
******	IMBALM	AVAILS	EXPELS	NAVELS	SORELS
BYTALK	NAPALM	BABULS	EXTOLS	NEWELS	SOTOLS
******	******	BAGELS	FINALS	NIGELS	SPALLS
----LL	----LN	BASILS	FLAILS	NOPALS	SPELLS
******	******	BERYLS	FRAILS	NOVELS	SPIELS
APPALL	WEDELN	BETELS	FRILLS	ORIELS	SPILLS
ARGYLL	******	BEVELS	FUSILS	OUSELS	SPOILS
BEFALL	----LO	BEZELS	FUZILS	OUZELS	SPOOLS
BEFELL	******	BIKOLS	GAVELS	PANELS	STALLS
CAVELL	ANGELO	BOWELS	GHOULS	PEARLS	STEALS
ENDALL	ANKYLO	BRAILS	GIMELS	PEDALS	STEELS
ENROLL	APOLLO	BRAWLS	GNARLS	PERILS	STILLS
GESELL	CATALO	BRILLS	GORALS	PETALS	STOOLS
INWALL	CHEILO	BROILS	GRILLS	PHIALS	STULLS
JEKYLL	DUELLO	BUBALS	GROWLS	PICULS	SWAILS
LOVELL	GIGOLO	CABALS	GRUELS	PROWLS	SWELLS
LOWELL	ILOILO	CAMELS	HAMALS	PUPILS	SWILLS
MICELL	MEGALO	CANALS	HAZELS	QUAILS	SWIRLS
NEVILL	NIELLO	CAROLS	HEXYLS	QUELLS	SYBILS
NOBALL	PHYLLO	CASALS	HOTELS	QUILLS	THIOLS
ONEILL	POMELO	CAVILS	HOVELS	RAOULS	TICALS
ONFALL	PUEBLO	CECILS	IDEALS	RATALS	TOTALS
ORWELL	ROBALO	CEORLS	IDYLLS	RATELS	TOWELS
POWELL	ROMULO	CHILLS	IMPELS	RAVELS	TRAILS
REBILL	TAPALO	CHURLS	JEWELS	REBELS	TRAWLS
RECALL	TUPELO	CIBOLS	JURELS	REPELS	TRIALS
REFILL	TYPHLO	CORALS	KEVELS	REVELS	TRILLS
RESELL	******	CRAALS	KNEELS	RIVALS	TROLLS
RETELL	----LP	CRAWLS	KNELLS	RIYALS	TWILLS
SCROLL	******	CREELS	KNOLLS	ROWELS	TWIRLS
SEWALL	MEGILP	CUPELS	KNURLS	ROYALS	UMBELS
SEWELL	******	CYRILS	KRAALS	SCOWLS	VEXILS
SHRILL	----LS	DECALS	LABELS	SCULLS	VIGILS
SQUALL	******	DEVILS	LAPELS	SEPALS	VINYLS
SQUILL	ALKYLS	DOALLS	LEVELS	SHAWLS	VITALS
STROLL	ALLYLS	DOWELS	LIBELS	SHELLS	VOCALS
THRALL	AMPULS	DRAWLS	LOCALS	SHILLS	VOGULS

VOWELS	BOLDLY	FEEBLY	LEANLY	RACILY	TERMLY
WHEALS	BOTFLY	FINELY	LEWDLY	RANKLY	THINLY
WHEELS	BROLLY	FIRMLY	LIKELY	RAPTLY	THUSLY
WHIRLS	BUBBLY	FLATLY	LIMPLY	RARELY	TIDILY
WHORLS	BUSILY	FONDLY	LIVELY	RASHLY	TIMELY
XYLOLS	CAGILY	FOULLY	LONELY	REALLY	TINGLY
YODELS	CALMLY	FOXILY	LORDLY	RICHLY	TINILY
YOKELS	CECILY	FREELY	LOUDLY	RIPELY	TINKLY
ZORILS	CHILLY	FRILLY	LOVELY	RIPPLY	TRIGLY
******	CICELY	GADFLY	MAINLY	ROPILY	TRIMLY
----LT	COBBLY	GAINLY	MAYFLY	ROSILY	TWOPLY
******	COLDLY	GAMELY	MAZILY	RUDELY	UGLILY
ABVOLT	COMELY	GAMILY	MEANLY	SAFELY	UNDULY
BASALT	COMPLY	GENTLY	MEASLY	SAGELY	UNHOLY
COBALT	COOLLY	GIGGLY	MEEKLY	SANELY	UNRULY
DESALT	COSILY	GLADLY	MEETLY	SAWFLY	USABLY
INDULT	COSTLY	GLIBLY	MERELY	SCILLY	VAINLY
INSULT	COZILY	GLUMLY	MILDLY	SEEMLY	VASTLY
ISEULT	CRAWLY	GNARLY	MOSTLY	SEXILY	VERILY
OCCULT	CUDDLY	GOODLY	NAMELY	SHELLY	VILELY
PENULT	CURTLY	GOOGLY	NEARLY	SHOALY	WABBLY
RESULT	CUTELY	GORILY	NEATLY	SICILY	WADDLY
REVOLT	DAFTLY	GRAYLY	NICELY	SICKLY	WAGGLY
SPOILT	DAMPLY	GRIMLY	NIMBLY	SIMPLY	WAMBLY
TUMULT	DANKLY	GRISLY	NOSILY	SINGLY	WARILY
TYBALT	DARKLY	HARDLY	NUBBLY	SLIMLY	WARMLY
UNBELT	DAYFLY	HAZILY	NUDELY	SLOWLY	WAVILY
UNBOLT	DEADLY	HIGHLY	NUMBLY	SMELLY	WEAKLY
******	DEAFLY	HOLILY	OILILY	SMUGLY	WEEKLY
----LU	DEARLY	HOMELY	OOZILY	SNARLY	WHOLLY
******	DEEPLY	HOMILY	OPENLY	SNUGLY	WIDELY
ORMOLU	DEFTLY	HOURLY	ORALLY	SOFTLY	WIFELY
******	DIMPLY	HUGELY	OVALLY	SOLELY	WIGGLY
----LY	DIRELY	HUMBLY	OVERLY	SORELY	WILDLY
******	DOUBLY	ICALLY	PALELY	SOURLY	WILILY
ACIDLY	DOURLY	JINGLY	PARTLY	SPRYLY	WIRILY
AGEDLY	DOZILY	JUNGLY	PEARLY	STABLY	WISELY
AIRILY	DRABLY	JUSTLY	PEBBLY	STEELY	WOBBLY
ARCHLY	DRAWLY	KEENLY	PERTLY	STILLY	WOOLLY
ARIDLY	DROLLY	KINDLY	PIMPLY	SUBTLY	YEARLY
ARTILY	DRYFLY	KINGLY	POORLY	SUPPLY	******
AVIDLY	DUMBLY	KNURLY	PORTLY	SURELY	----MA
BALDLY	EASILY	LACILY	POSHLY	SWIRLY	******
BARELY	EERILY	LAMELY	PRIMLY	TAMELY	ASTHMA
BARFLY	EVENLY	LANKLY	PUDDLY	TANGLY	BAHAMA
BASELY	EVILLY	LASTLY	PUNILY	TARTLY	BRAHMA
BLUELY	FAIRLY	LATELY	PURELY	TATTLY	BREGMA
BODILY	FAMILY	LAZILY	PUSSLY	TAUTLY	CAEOMA

CHACMA	******	******	DEGUMS	******	DHURNA
CHROMA	----ME	----MO	DENIMS	----MY	DUENNA
CINEMA	******	******	DREAMS	******	EDWINA
DECUMA	AFLAME	CHROMO	FANUMS	BIGAMY	******
DHARMA	AFRAME	DYNAMO	FLEAMS	BLOOMY	ENCINA
ECZEMA	ASSUME	ENTOMO	FORUMS	BROOMY	ESPANA
ENIGMA	ATHOME	ESKIMO	GLEAMS	CHAMMY	ETERNA
FATIMA	BECAME	KOKOMO	GLOOMS	CHUMMY	FARINA
GLIOMA	BECOME	PLASMO	GROOMS	CLAMMY	GALENA
GOTAMA	BIREME	PNEUMO	HAKIMS	CREAMY	GRETNA
INTIMA	BYNAME	SEISMO	HAREMS	CRUMMY	GUIANA
JEMIMA	CHROME	SPERMO	HIRAMS	DIGAMY	GUYANA
LIPOMA	CLEOME	THERMO	IBEAMS	DREAMY	HAVANA
MAXIMA	DEFAME	ULTIMO	IDIOMS	ECTOMY	HELENA
MAZUMA	DEGAME	******	INARMS	GLEAMY	IGUANA
MIASMA	ENZYME	----MP	JORAMS	GLOOMY	JACANA
MINIMA	EXHUME	******	JORUMS	HAULMY	JARINA
MYXOMA	GRAMME	DECAMP	MADAMS	INFAMY	JOANNA
OEDEMA	HEAUME	ENCAMP	MAXIMS	JEREMY	KORUNA
OEPEMA	ILLUME	METUMP	MINIMS	PLUMMY	LACUNA
OPTIMA	INCOME	REVAMP	NAHUMS	QUALMY	LAMINA
PAJAMA	INHUME	SCRIMP	PRISMS	RHEUMY	LIMINA
PANAMA	JEROME	SHRIMP	PROEMS	SCUMMY	LUMINA
PLASMA	LEGUME	******	PSALMS	SHAMMY	MANANA
PNEUMA	MADAME	----MS	QUALMS	SHIMMY	MARINA
PYJAMA	OPTIME	******	REALMS	SLUMMY	NAGANA
SCHEMA	RACEME	ABOHMS	REARMS	SMARMY	NOVENA
SQUAMA	RADOME	ABRAMS	RHEIMS	SODOMY	NUMINA
STIGMA	REGIME	ABYSMS	SCRAMS	STEAMY	ORGANA
STROMA	RESUME	ADDAMS	SCRUMS	STORMY	PATINA
STRUMA	SALOME	ADEEMS	SEDUMS	WHAMMY	PIRANA
TACOMA	SCHEME	ALARMS	SEISMS	******	POMONA
THELMA	SEMEME	ALBUMS	SERUMS	----NA	PURANA
TRAUMA	SESAME	AXIOMS	SHAWMS	******	RAMONA
ULTIMA	TAXEME	BEDIMS	SPASMS	ACAENA	REGINA
YAKIMA	VOLUME	BEGUMS	STEAMS	ALUMNA	RETINA
ZEUGMA	******	BESOMS	STORMS	ALVINA	ROWENA
ZYGOMA	----MI	BLOOMS	STRUMS	ANCONA	ROXANA
******	******	BOSOMS	SWARMS	ANGINA	RUMINA
----MB	SALAMI	BRAHMS	THERMS	ANNONA	SABINA
******	******	BREAMS	THRUMS	ARCANA	SERENA
APLOMB	----MN	BROOMS	TOTEMS	ATHENA	SIENNA
BENUMB	******	CAROMS	VENOMS	BANANA	STERNA
CORYMB	AUTUMN	CHARMS	WHELMS	CABANA	TIRANA
ENTOMB	COLUMN	CHASMS	XYLEMS	CARINA	VACUNA
ENWOMB	SOLEMN	CHIRMS	******	CATENA	VAGINA
INTOMB		CLAIMS	----MT	CORONA	VARUNA
		CLEAMS	******	DHARNA	VERONA
		CREAMS	DREAMT		VICUNA

VIENNA	OSTEND	BYLINE	LIERNE	SUPINE	BUYING
VIMINA	POLAND	CANINE	LORENE	THRONE	CAGING
ZANANA	REFUND	CAPONE	LUPINE	TISANE	CAKING
ZENANA	REMAND	CETANE	LYSINE	TRIUNE	CANING
******	REMIND	COHUNE	MALINE	TYRONE	CARING
----ND	REPAND	COLINE	MARINE	UNDINE	CASING
******	RESEND	COSINE	MATINE	UNDONE	CAVING
AALAND	REWIND	CYMENE	MAXINE	URBANE	CAWING
ABOUND	RIBAND	CYRENE	MOLINE	URSINE	CEDING
ADDEND	ROBAND	DAPHNE	MURINE	WAHINE	CERING
ALMOND	ROLAND	DECANE	NADINE	XYLENE	CITING
APPEND	ROTUND	DEFINE	NARINE	YVONNE	CLUING
ARMAND	SECOND	DEPONE	NICENE	******	CODING
AROUND	SECUND	DITONE	OCTANE	----NG	COKING
ASCEND	SOLAND	DIVINE	ONLINE	******	COMING
ATTEND	STRAND	ELAINE	ORPINE	ACHING	CONING
AUGEND	UNBEND	ELAYNE	OSCINE	ACTING	COOING
BEHIND	UNBIND	ENGINE	PATINE	ADDING	COPING
BEYOND	UNHAND	EOCENE	PAVANE	AGEING	CORING
DEFEND	UNKIND	EOGENE	PINENE	AIDING	COVING
DEMAND	UNWIND	EQUINE	PROCNE	AILING	COWING
DEPEND	UPLAND	ERMINE	PUISNE	AIMING	COXING
EDMOND	******	ESSENE	PURINE	AIRING	CRYING
EDMUND	----NE	ETHANE	PYRENE	ARCING	CUBING
ENWIND	******	EUGENE	PYRONE	ARMING	CURING
ERRAND	ACHENE	FAMINE	RACINE	ASKING	DARING
EXPAND	ALDINE	FEIGNE	RAPINE	AWEING	DATING
EXPEND	ALKANE	FELINE	RATINE	AWNING	DAZING
EXTEND	ALKENE	FERINE	RAVINE	BAAING	DEKING
FAGEND	ALKYNE	GREENE	REDONE	BAKING	DICING
FECUND	ALPINE	GROYNE	REFINE	BALING	DIKING
FRIEND	ALVINE	GWYNNE	RELINE	BARING	DINING
GERUND	ANCONE	HEXANE	REPINE	BARONG	DIVING
GROUND	ANYONE	HEXONE	RETENE	BASING	DOLING
IMPEND	ARCANE	HUMANE	ROCKNE	BATING	DOMING
INBAND	ARLENE	IMMUNE	ROXANE	BAYING	DOPING
INLAND	ARLINE	INDENE	RUSINE	BELONG	DOSING
INTEND	ARSINE	INSANE	SABINE	BERING	DOTING
INWIND	ATHENE	INTONE	SALINE	BIDING	DOZING
ISLAND	ATTUNE	IODINE	SELENE	BITING	DRYING
JOCUND	BEGONE	IONONE	SERENE	BLUING	DUGONG
LEGEND	BIGONE	JEANNE	SERINE	BODING	DUPING
LIGAND	BORANE	JEJUNE	SHRINE	BONING	DURING
LOMOND	BOURNE	JOANNE	SIMONE	BOOING	DYEING
OBTUND	BOVINE	KETENE	SOIGNE	BORING	EALING
OFFEND	BUTANE	KETONE	SOZINE	BOWING	EARING
OSMOND	BYGONE	LAGUNE	SPHENE	BOXING	EASING
OSMUND	BYLANE	LARINE	SPLINE	BUSING	EATING

EBBING	HAVING	LOOING	PAWING	SIDING	VOWING
EDGING	HAWING	LOPING	PAYING	SIRING	WADING
EGGING	HAYING	LOSING	PEKING	SITING	WAGING
EKEING	HAZING	LOVING	PIKING	SIZING	WAKING
ENDING	HEWING	LOWING	PILING	SKIING	WALING
EPPING	HEXING	LURING	PINANG	SKYING	WANING
ERRING	HIDING	LUTING	PINING	SLUING	WAVING
EYEING	HIEING	LYSING	PIPING	SOLING	WAXING
FACING	HIKING	MACING	PLYING	SOWING	WILING
FADING	HIRING	MAKING	POKING	SPRANG	WINING
FAKING	HIVING	MATING	POLING	SPRING	WIPING
FARING	HOEING	MAYING	PORING	SPRUNG	WIRING
FATING	HOLING	MAZING	POSING	SPYING	WISING
FAXING	HOMING	MEKONG	PRYING	STRING	WIVING
FAYING	HONING	METING	PUKING	STRONG	WOOING
FAZING	HOPING	MEWING	PULING	STRUNG	WOWING
FEEING	HOSING	MIMING	RACING	STYING	WRYING
FETING	IDLING	MINING	RAGING	TAKING	YAWING
FEUING	IMPING	MIRING	RAKING	TAMING	YOKING
FIFING	INKING	MIXING	RAPING	TAPING	YOWING
FILING	INNING	MOOING	RARING	TARING	ZONING
FINING	IRKING	MOPING	RATING	TAWING	******
FIRING	IRVING	MOVING	RAVING	TAXING	----NI
FIXING	ISLING	MOWING	RAYING	TEEING	******
FLYING	JADING	MUSING	RAZING	THRONG	ACTINI
FOXING	JAPING	MUTING	RICING	TIDING	ALUMNI
FRYING	JAWING	NAMING	RIDING	TILING	BIKINI
FUMING	JEEING	NIDING	RILING	TIMING	ECHINI
FUSING	JIBING	NIXING	RIMING	TIRING	GEMINI
FUZING	JIVING	NOSING	RISING	TOEING	LUMINI
GAGING	JOKING	NOTING	RIVING	TONING	SILENI
GAMING	JOYING	OARING	ROBING	TOPING	YEMENI
GAPING	KALONG	OBLONG	ROPING	TOTING	******
GATING	KEYING	OFFING	ROSING	TOWING	----NK
GAZING	KITING	OGLING	ROVING	TOYING	******
GEEING	LACING	OILING	ROWING	TRUING	DEBUNK
GIBING	LADING	OOLONG	RUEING	TRYING	EMBANK
GIVING	LAKING	OOZING	RULING	TUBING	PODUNK
GLUING	LAMING	OPTING	SARONG	TUNING	SHRANK
GOBANG	LARYNG	ORBING	SATANG	TYPING	SHRINK
GORING	LAVING	OUTING	SATING	UNSUNG	SHRUNK
GUYING	LAWING	OWNING	SAVING	UPPING	******
GYBING	LAYING	PACING	SAWING	URGING	----NN
GYVING	LAZING	PAGING	SAYING	VEXING	******
HADING	LIKING	PALING	SEEING	VIKING	JOHANN
HALING	LIMING	PARANG	SEWING	VISING	******
HARING	LINING	PARING	SEXING	VOLING	----NO
HATING	LIVING	PAVING	SHYING	VOTING	******
					ACTINO
					ALBINO

ALUINO	ASPENS	ELLENS	MESONS	SAVINS	YAMUNS
AVERNO	ATHENS	ELOINS	MORONS	SAXONS	YAPONS
CASINO	AUXINS	ERWINS	MOURNS	SCIONS	YEARNS
CHRONO	BAIRNS	ETHANS	NYLONS	SCORNS	YOGINS
CYRANO	BARONS	FANONS	OCEANS	SEDANS	YUPONS
DEMONO	BASINS	FEIGNS	ONIONS	SERINS	ZAYINS
DOMINO	BATONS	FELONS	ORGANS	SETONS	ZIRONS
ECHINO	BEGINS	FOEHNS	ORPINS	SEVENS	******
FRESNO	BLAINS	FREONS	OSCANS	SHEENS	----NT
GITANO	BOGANS	FROWNS	PAEANS	SIMONS	******
HYMENO	BOURNS	GAMINS	PAEONS	SIRENS	ABSENT
IMMUNO	BRAINS	GIPONS	PAGANS	SITINS	ACCENT
KIMONO	BROWNS	GLEANS	PARENS	SKEANS	ADVENT
LADINO	BRUINS	GRAINS	PATENS	SKEINS	AMOUNT
LUMINO	BURANS	GREENS	PAVANS	SOLANS	ANOINT
MELANO	BURINS	GROANS	PECANS	SOZINS	ARDENT
MERINO	CABINS	GROINS	PEKANS	SPAWNS	ARGENT
ORGANO	CAIRNS	GWENNS	PINONS	SPOONS	ARPENT
PHRENO	CAJUNS	GYRONS	PITONS	SPURNS	ARRANT
SELENO	CANONS	HAVENS	PLAINS	STAINS	ASCENT
SOLANO	CAPONS	HELENS	PRAWNS	STEINS	ASKANT
SPHENO	CHAINS	HERONS	PREENS	STERNS	ASLANT
SPLENO	CHURNS	HOGANS	PUTONS	SUSANS	ASSENT
STERNO	CLEANS	HUMANS	PYLONS	SWAINS	AVAUNT
STHENO	CLOWNS	HURONS	PYRANS	SWOONS	BESANT
TECHNO	COIGNS	HYMENS	QUEANS	TALONS	BEZANT
VAGINO	COLINS	INURNS	QUEENS	TENONS	BRYANT
******	COLONS	IRVINS	QUERNS	TETONS	CADENT
----NS	COZENS	IRWINS	QUOINS	THORNS	CEMENT
******	CROONS	JAPANS	RAVENS	TIEINS	CLIENT
AARONS	CROWNS	JASONS	RAYONS	TITANS	COGENT
ACORNS	CUBANS	JUPONS	REDANS	TOKENS	DECANT
ADORNS	CUMINS	KARENS	REIGNS	TOMANS	DECENT
ALFONS	CUTINS	KEVINS	REMANS	TOXINS	DEMENT
ALIENS	DAMANS	KININS	RERUNS	TOYONS	DETENT
ALIGNS	DEDANS	LAPINS	RESINS	TRAINS	DOCENT
ALLANS	DEIGNS	LATINS	RIPENS	UNIONS	DOESNT
ALLENS	DEMONS	LEARNS	ROBINS	UNMANS	ERRANT
ALUINS	DEWANS	LEMONS	ROMANS	UNPINS	ESCENT
ALVANS	DIVANS	LIKENS	ROSINS	UTURNS	EXEUNT
AMIENS	DIWANS	LIMENS	ROWANS	VIXENS	EXTANT
ANIONS	DIZENS	LINENS	RUBENS	WAGONS	EXTENT
ANTONS	DOYENS	LIVENS	RUNINS	WAKENS	FLAUNT
APRONS	DOZENS	LUMENS	RUNONS	WIDENS	FLUENT
ARIANS	DRAINS	LYSINS	SABINS	WIGANS	FOMENT
ARPENS	DROWNS	MASONS	SALONS	WIZENS	FORINT
ARYANS	EDWINS	MATINS	SASINS	XYLANS	GERENT
ASIANS	ELFINS	MELONS	SATINS	YAMENS	GIGANT

HAVENT	TYRANT	SAXONY	UNSHOD	******	FANTOM
INDENT	UNBENT	SHEENY	UNTROD	----OK	FATHOM
INFANT	URGENT	SHINNY	UROPOD	******	HANSOM
INTENT	VACANT	SIMONY	******	BARTOK	LISSOM
INVENT	VOLANT	SKINNY	----OE	BETOOK	NONCOM
JURANT	WERENT	SPINNY	******	HICKOK	POGROM
LAMENT	******	SPOONY	CHEGOE	RETOOK	POMPOM
LATENT	----NU	SWEENY	CHIGOE	UNHOOK	RANDOM
LEARNT	******	TETANY	CRUSOE	******	RANSOM
LEVANT	VISHNU	THORNY	DIPLOE	----OL	SELDOM
LOMENT	******	WHINNY	FAEROE	******	SIMOOM
LUCENT	----NX	******	FELLOE	AMATOL	SLALOM
MOMENT	******	----NZ	HOOPOE	AMIDOL	TOMTOM
MUSTNT	LARYNX	******	MONROE	BEFOOL	WHILOM
MUTANT	MENINX	LORENZ	ROSCOE	BENZOL	WISDOM
NATANT	SPHINX	******	TIPTOE	CINEOL	******
NOCENT	SYRINX	----OA	UPHROE	CRESOL	----ON
OCTANT	******	******	******	DIOBOL	******
OPTANT	----NY	BALBOA	----OF	FRIJOL	ACTION
ORIENT	******	EPIZOA	******	FRIVOL	ALBION
PARENT	ALBANY	JERBOA	BEHOOF	GAMBOL	AMAZON
PATENT	ANTONY	LISBOA	HEREOF	GLYCOL	AMNION
PEDANT	APHONY	******	******	GOOGOL	ARAGON
PLAINT	BACONY	----OB	----OG	MONGOL	ARCHON
PLIANT	BARONY	******	******	PATHOL	AVALON
PONENT	BETONY	HOBNOB	ANALOG	PATROL	BABOON
POTENT	BLENNY	ODDJOB	APOLOG	PETROL	BARTON
QUAINT	BOTANY	******	DIALOG	PHENOL	BARYON
RECANT	BRAINY	----OC	DUOLOG	PISTOL	BASION
RECENT	BRANNY	******	EGGNOG	PODSOL	BEACON
REGENT	BRAWNY	BELLOC	EPILOG	PODZOL	BECKON
RELENT	BRYONY	FINNOC	FOGDOG	RETOOL	BENTON
REPENT	COLONY	MANIOC	LAPDOG	SANTOL	BILLON
RESENT	CRANNY	******	PUTLOG	SCHOOL	BLAZON
RIDENT	FELONY	----OD	QUAHOG	STEROL	BOLSON
RODENT	GRAINY	******	REDDOG	SYMBOL	BOLTON
SAVANT	GRANNY	HOTROD	SEADOG	THYMOL	BONBON
SECANT	HOMINY	ISOPOD	STENOG	TOLUOL	BOSTON
SEJANT	JIMINY	METHOD	SUNDOG	WARHOL	BRETON
SILENT	JOHNNY	NIMROD	TAUTOG	******	BRITON
SOLENT	KORUNY	NOGOOD	******	----OM	BUNION
SONANT	LITANY	PEQUOD	----OH	******	BURTON
SPLINT	MUTINY	PERIOD	******	ABLOOM	BUTTON
SPRINT	ONIONY	RAMROD	******	BOTTOM	BUXTON
SQUINT	PAEONY	RETROD	SHILOH	COELOM	CAMION
TALENT	ROMANY	SUNGOD	******	CONDOM	CANNON
TENANT	ROSINY	TOMCOD	----OI	CUSTOM	CANTON
TRUANT	SATINY	TRIPOD	******	DIATOM	
			BORZOI		
			MYTHOI		
			OCTROI		

CANYON	GAMMON	MATRON	RACOON	WALKON	******
CARBON	GARCON	MELLON	RAMSON	WALTON	----OR
CARSON	GASCON	MELTON	RATION	WANION	******
CARTON	GASTON	MERLON	RATOON	WANTON	ABATOR
CATION	GERYON	MICRON	REASON	WATSON	ANCHOR
CAXTON	GIBBON	MIGNON	RECKON	WEAPON	ANGKOR
CEYLON	GIBSON	MILTON	REGION	WIGEON	AUTHOR
CHARON	GIDEON	MINION	RIBBON	WILSON	BAILOR
CHIRON	GNOMON	MORION	ROBSON	WILTON	BANGOR
CHITON	GODSON	MORMON	RUNYON	YAUPON	BETTOR
CITRON	GONION	MORTON	SAIGON	YOUPON	CANDOR
COCOON	GORDON	MOTION	SALMON	ZIRCON	CANTOR
COMEON	GORGON	MOUTON	SALOON	******	CAPTOR
COMMON	GUENON	MUTTON	SAMSON	----OO	CASTOR
CORDON	GUIDON	NASION	SARGON	******	CENSOR
COTTON	HAGDON	NATION	SEASON	BAMBOO	CLAMOR
COUPON	HEADON	NATRON	SERMON	BOOBOO	CONDOR
CRAYON	HEBRON	NEKTON	SEXTON	BOOHOO	CURSOR
CRETON	HEDRON	NELSON	SHARON	BURGOO	DEBTOR
CROTON	HENDON	NEURON	SINEON	CASHOO	DOCTOR
DACRON	HEREON	NEWTON	SIPHON	CUCKOO	EDITOR
DAEMON	HEZION	NIPPON	SLIPON	GENTOO	ELINOR
DAHOON	HUDSON	NOTION	SOLION	HALLOO	ENAMOR
DAIMON	INCHON	OBERON	STOLON	HOODOO	EXMOOR
DALTON	ISOGON	OPTION	SUMMON	KARROO	FACTOR
DAMSON	JARGON	OREGON	SUTTON	KOODOO	FEODOR
DANTON	JETTON	ORISON	SYPHON	TATTOO	FERVOR
DAWSON	JONSON	PARDON	TALION	VOODOO	FLAVOR
DAYTON	KATION	PARSON	TAMPON	YOOHOO	FLEXOR
DEACON	KEDRON	PATRON	TEFLON	******	FOETOR
DOBLON	KELSON	PATTON	TELSON	----OP	HARBOR
DOBSON	KLAXON	PELION	TENDON	******	HECTOR
DONJON	LAGOON	PENNON	TESTON	BISHOP	HORROR
DRAGON	LARDON	PERRON	TEUTON	CARHOP	INDOOR
DROMON	LEGION	PERSON	THORON	COLLOP	ISADOR
DURION	LEPTON	PHANON	TOULON	DOLLOP	ISIDOR
EASTON	LESION	PHOTON	TRIGON	GALLOP	JAILOR
EDISON	LESSON	PIGEON	TRITON	HYSSOP	JUNIOR
ELEVON	LISBON	PINION	TROGON	LOLLOP	KRONOR
ETYMON	LOGION	PISTON	TUCSON	MAYPOP	LECTOR
FALCON	LONDON	POISON	TYCOON	PEGTOP	LESSOR
FANION	LOTION	POMPON	TYPHON	REDTOP	LICTOR
FLACON	MACRON	PONTON	UNISON	SALOOP	LIQUOR
FLAGON	MAISON	POTION	VERNON	SCROOP	MENTOR
FULTON	MAMMON	PRISON	VILLON	TIPTOP	METEOR
FUSION	MARION	PROTON	VINSON	UNSTOP	MIRROR
GABION	MAROON	PYTHON	VISION	WALLOP	NESTOR
GALLON	MASCON	QUEZON	WAGGON		OOPHOR

ORATOR	BABOOS	HYPNOS	SERVOS	MATZOT	FARROW
PALLOR	BANJOS	IGLOOS	SETTOS	MOTMOT	FELLOW
PARLOR	BASSOS	JOCKOS	SHAKOS	OCELOT	FOGBOW
PASTOR	BATHOS	JUNCOS	SKIMOS	PARROT	FOLLOW
PAVIOR	BONGOS	KAZOOS	SORGOS	PEQUOT	FURROW
PICTOR	BRAVOS	KRONOS	TABOOS	REDHOT	HALLOW
PLEXOR	BRAZOS	LARGOS	TAINOS	REFOOT	HARLOW
PRETOR	BRUNOS	LASSOS	TANGOS	SEXPOT	HARROW
RADNOR	BUNCOS	LEMNOS	TEMPOS	SPIGOT	HAYMOW
RANCOR	BURGOS	LENTOS	TORSOS	TEAPOT	HOLLOW
RAPTOR	BURROS	LESBOS	TRIPOS	TINPOT	INFLOW
RECTOR	CACAOS	LLANOS	TURCOS	TRICOT	JARROW
RHETOR	CAMEOS	MAMBOS	VERSOS	TURBOT	KOWTOW
SAILOR	CAMPOS	MANGOS	VIREOS	UNROOT	LUDLOW
SALVOR	CANSOS	MARCOS	WAHOOS	UPROOT	MALLOW
SARTOR	CANTOS	MARGOS	WALDOS	UPSHOT	MARLOW
SAVIOR	CARGOS	MATEOS	XYSTOS	ZEALOT	MARROW
SECTOR	CARLOS	MATZOS	YAHOOS	******	MEADOW
SEISOR	CELLOS	METROS	ZETHOS	----OU	MELLOW
SEIZOR	CENTOS	MEZZOS	******	******	MINNOW
SENIOR	CHICOS	MIKLOS	----OT	ACAJOU	MORROW
SENSOR	CISCOS	MORROS	******	AMADOU	MOSCOW
SIGNOR	CLAROS	MOTTOS	BALLOT	CACHOU	NARROW
STATOR	COMBOS	MYTHOS	BRULOT	CONGOU	NOSHOW
STUPOR	COMPOS	OVIBOS	BURBOT	******	PILLOW
SUCCOR	CONTOS	PARGOS	CAHOOT	----OV	POWWOW
SUITOR	COSMOS	PATHOS	CANNOT	******	REAVOW
TAILOR	CREDOS	PATIOS	CARROT	ASIMOV	SALLOW
TAYLOR	CRONOS	PEDROS	DESPOT	PAVLOV	SEACOW
TENSOR	CURIOS	PENGOS	DIGLOT	******	SHADOW
TERMOR	CUSSOS	PEPLOS	DRYROT	----OW	SORROW
TERROR	CUSTOS	PHAROS	ELLIOT	******	SUNBOW
TORPOR	DATTOS	PHILOS	ENROOT	ANYHOW	TALLOW
TREMOR	DITTOS	PHOTOS	FAGGOT	BARROW	WALLOW
TREVOR	FOLIOS	PIANOS	FORGOT	BELLOW	WILLOW
UNMOOR	FUGIOS	PINGOS	FYLFOT	BESTOW	WINDOW
VECTOR	GECKOS	PINTOS	GALIOT	BILLOW	WINNOW
VENDOR	GENROS	POTTOS	GALOOT	BORROW	YARROW
VIATOR	GESSOS	PUNTOS	GIGLOT	BOWWOW	YELLOW
VICTOR	GISMOS	RADIOS	HARLOT	BURROW	******
******	GIZMOS	RATIOS	HERIOT	BYBLOW	----OX
----OS	GREGOS	RECTOS	HOTPOT	CALLOW	******
******	GUACOS	RHINOS	IGOROT	CARLOW	COWPOX
ABYDOS	GUANOS	RODEOS	INKPOT	CRACOW	DOGFOX
ALAMOS	GUMBOS	RONDOS	MAGGOT	DARROW	HATBOX
ALPHOS	HELIOS	SALVOS	MARGOT	ESCROW	HAYBOX
AMIGOS	HIPPOS	SAMBOS	MARMOT	FALLOW	HOTBOX
AVISOS	HYDROS	SCHMOS	MASCOT		

ICEBOX	STRIPE	DROOPS	STROPS	CRIMPY	EXEDRA
LUMMOX	THORPE	EQUIPS	STUMPS	CRISPY	FEDORA
MAGNOX	TROUPE	ESTOPS	SUNUPS	CROUPY	FEMORA
MUSKOX	UNRIPE	FLUMPS	SWAMPS	DRIPPY	FULCRA
OUTFOX	WATAPE	FRUMPS	SWEEPS	DROOPY	GEMARA
VOLVOX	******	GALOPS	SWOOPS	FLOPPY	GENERA
******	----PH	GETUPS	SYRUPS	FRUMPY	HEGIRA
----OY	******	GRASPS	THRIPS	GRIPPY	HEJIRA
******	ADOLPH	GROUPS	THUMPS	GRUMPY	LATERA
CARBOY	CALIPH	JALOPS	TIEUPS	JALOPY	MADURA
CONVOY	CERIPH	JULEPS	TRAMPS	OCCUPY	MASORA
COWBOY	JOSEPH	KNOSPS	TROOPS	SIRUPY	NOMURA
DAYBOY	PARAPH	LETUPS	TRUMPS	SKIMPY	PLEURA
DEPLOY	PHOSPH	MIXUPS	TULIPS	SLEEPY	REMORA
EMPLOY	SERAPH	ORLOPS	TWERPS	SLOPPY	ROSTRA
LOWBOY	TERAPH	OXLIPS	TWIRPS	SNAPPY	SAHARA
POTBOY	******	PELOPS	UNCAPS	SNIPPY	SAMARA
TEAPOY	----PI	PHIPPS	UNRIPS	SNOOPY	SANDRA
TOMBOY	******	PINUPS	USURPS	STRIPY	SATARA
******	EURIPI	PLUMPS	WATAPS	STUMPY	SCLERA
----PA	OCTOPI	POLYPS	WHELPS	SWAMPY	SENORA
******	SCAMPI	PRIMPS	WHOOPS	SWEEPY	SIERRA
EUROPA	******	RECAPS	******	SYRUPY	SISERA
SHERPA	----PO	SCALPS	----PT	WHIPPY	SYNURA
******	******	SCAMPS	******	WICOPY	TUNDRA
----PE	ALEPPO	SCARPS	ABRUPT	******	WOMERA
******	KAKAPO	SCAUPS	ACCEPT	----RA	******
ASLOPE	TROPPO	SCOOPS	COEMPT	******	----RB
CANAPE	******	SCRAPS	ENRAPT	ALMIRA	******
CROUPE	----PS	SCRIPS	EXCEPT	AMENRA	ABSORB
DIEPPE	******	SETUPS	EXEMPT	ANGORA	ADSORB
DOGAPE	BICEPS	SHARPS	INCEPT	ANITRA	ADVERB
ECTYPE	BLIMPS	SHEEPS	PROMPT	ANKARA	BICARB
ESCAPE	CHAMPS	SIRUPS	RECEPT	AURORA	RESORB
EUROPE	CHEEPS	SKIMPS	SCRIPT	AYMARA	SUBURB
FELIPE	CHEOPS	SLEEPS	SCULPT	BARBRA	SUPERB
FRAPPE	CHIRPS	SLOOPS	STRIPT	BIAFRA	******
GRIPPE	CHUMPS	SLUMPS	UNWEPT	BUCKRA	----RD
GUIMPE	CLAMPS	SLURPS	YCLEPT	CAMERA	******
LENAPE	CLASPS	SNOOPS	******	CENTRA	ABOARD
METOPE	CLUMPS	STAMPS	----PY	CESURA	ABSURD
PYROPE	CRAMPS	STEEPS	******	CONTRA	ACCORD
RECIPE	CREEPS	STIRPS	CANOPY	COPPRA	AFFORD
SARAPE	CRIMPS	STOMPS	CHIPPY	DATURA	ASGARD
SCRAPE	CRISPS	STOOPS	CHIRPY	ELMIRA	BAYARD
SERAPE	CROUPS	STOUPS	CHOPPY	ELVIRA	BEGIRD
SHOPPE	CRUMPS	STRAPS	CLUMPY	ELYTRA	BOYARD
STEPPE	CUTUPS	STRIPS	CREEPY	ENTERA	BYWORD

CANARD	BEFORE	MISERE	ONAGRI	EXTERN	NEPHRO
COWARD	BEMIRE	NATURE	QUADRI	GOVERN	ONEIRO
DOTARD	BEWARE	OEUVRE	SAFARI	INBORN	PIETRO
ECHARD	CENTRE	ORDURE	SOUARI	INTERN	PLEURO
EDUARD	CESARE	PARURE	TALARI	INTURN	SCLERO
EDWARD	CLAIRE	PIERRE	TISHRI	MODERN	SIDERO
ENGIRD	COHERE	QUAERE	VAPORI	OSBORN	STAURO
GERARD	COLURE	QUATRE	VASARI	REBORN	TORERO
HAZARD	CONTRE	REBORE	******	RETURN	VENTRO
HOLARD	CURARE	RETIRE	**----RK**	SATURN	******
HOWARD	DECARE	REVERE	******	SECERN	**----RP**
ILFORD	DEKARE	SARTRE	BYWORK	SEVERN	******
INWARD	DEMURE	SATIRE	DEBARK	SUBORN	ESCARP
LIZARD	DESIRE	SECURE	EMBARK	TAVERN	INCORP
MILORD	EMIGRE	SEMPRE	IMBARK	TEAURN	******
ONWARD	EMPIRE	SEVERE	IMPARK	UNBORN	**----RS**
OXFORD	ENCORE	SOMBRE	NEWARK	UNWORN	******
PETARD	ENDURE	SPHERE	REMARK	UPTURN	ABHORS
RECORD	ENSURE	SQUARE	UNCORK	WIVERN	ABNERS
REGARD	ENTERE	SQUIRE	******	WYVERN	ACTORS
RETARD	ENTIRE	SUTURE	**----RL**	******	ADDERS
REWARD	EUCHRE	TENURE	******	**----RO**	AGGERS
REWORD	EXPIRE	TEVERE	AWHIRL	******	AIDERS
RITARD	FIACRE	TIMBRE	SCHORL	ANTERO	ALDERS
SEWARD	FIGURE	TUYERE	UNCURL	ARTHRO	ALTARS
TABARD	FURORE	UMPIRE	UNFURL	ARTURO	ALTERS
TOWARD	FUTURE	UNSURE	******	ASTERO	AMBERS
UNCORD	GALORE	VELURE	**----RM**	AUSTRO	AMOURS
UNGIRD	GOITRE	VENIRE	******	BISTRO	AMPHRS
UPWARD	HOMBRE	ZAFFRE	AFFIRM	BOLERO	ANGERS
UTGARD	HONORE	******	BIFORM	CASTRO	ARBORS
VISARD	IGNORE	**----RG**	DEFORM	CENTRO	ARDORS
VIZARD	IMMURE	******	DISARM	CHEIRO	ARMORS
WIZARD	IMPURE	COBURG	INFIRM	CHLORO	ASKERS
******	INHERE	******	INFORM	CICERO	ASPERS
----RE	INJURE	**----RI**	REFORM	DENDRO	ASTERS
******	INSURE	******	SQUIRM	DEXTRO	ATTARS
ABJURE	LAHORE	AMBARI	******	DIDERO	AUGERS
ADHERE	LENORE	ARBORI	**----RN**	DINERO	AUGURS
ADJURE	LIGURE	ASTERI		ENTERO	BAKERS
ADMIRE	LOUVRE	BIHARI	ASTERN	FLUORO	BALERS
ALLURE	LUSTRE	CENTRI	ATTORN	GABBRO	BITERS
AMPERE	MAIGRE	CIMBRI	AUBURN	GASTRO	BLEARS
ARMURE	MAITRE	DENDRI	BICORN	HETERO	BONERS
ASHORE	MALGRE	DMITRI	CASERN	INFERO	BORERS
ASPIRE	MANURE	EPHORI	CAVERN	JETHRO	BOWERS
ASSURE	MATURE	GHARRI	DECERN	LAPARO	BOXERS
ATTIRE	MEAGRE	GRIGRI	DEHORN	MADURO	BOYARS

BRIARS	ELDERS	HEWERS	MINERS	RAKERS	SPOORS
BRIERS	ELMERS	HIDERS	MINORS	RATERS	STAIRS
BUYERS	ELVERS	HIKERS	MISERS	RAVERS	STEERS
CANERS	EMBARS	HIRERS	MITERS	RAZORS	SUGARS
CAPERS	EMBERS	HOMERS	MIXERS	RECURS	SUPERS
CARERS	EMEERS	HONORS	MOHURS	REFERS	SWEARS
CATERS	ENTERS	HOVERS	MOLARS	REVERS	TABORS
CEDARS	EPHORS	HUMORS	MOPERS	RICERS	TAKERS
CHAIRS	ERRORS	IDLERS	MOTORS	RIDERS	TALERS
CHEERS	ESKERS	INCURS	MOVERS	RIGORS	TAMERS
CHIRRS	ESTERS	INFERS	MOWERS	RIMERS	TAPERS
CHOIRS	ETHERS	INKERS	NADIRS	RISERS	TAPIRS
CHURRS	FACERS	INTERS	NAMERS	RIVERS	TATARS
CIDERS	FAKERS	JOKERS	NOTERS	ROGERS	TAWERS
CIGARS	FAKIRS	JURORS	OCCURS	ROTORS	TAXERS
CLEARS	FARERS	LABORS	OCHERS	ROVERS	TENORS
COLORS	FAVORS	LAGERS	OFFERS	ROWERS	THEIRS
COMERS	FEMURS	LAKERS	OGLERS	RULERS	TIGERS
COOERS	FETORS	LASERS	OILERS	RUMORS	TILERS
CORERS	FEUARS	LAVERS	ORDERS	SABERS	TIMERS
COVERS	FEVERS	LAYERS	ORMERS	SAKERS	TONERS
COWERS	FIBERS	LAZARS	OSCARS	SATYRS	TOPERS
CRIERS	FIFERS	LEGERS	OSIERS	SAVERS	TOTERS
CURERS	FILERS	LEMURS	OTHERS	SAVORS	TOWERS
CYMARS	FIRERS	LEPERS	OTTERS	SAWERS	TOYERS
DARERS	FIVERS	LEVERS	OUTERS	SAYERS	TRIERS
DATERS	FIXERS	LIFERS	OWNERS	SCOURS	TUBERS
DEBARS	FLAIRS	LINERS	PACERS	SEDERS	TUMORS
DECORS	FLEERS	LITERS	PAPERS	SEVERS	TUNERS
DEFERS	FLIERS	LIVERS	PARERS	SEWERS	TUTORS
DEMURS	FLOORS	LONERS	PATERS	SHEARS	UDDERS
DETERS	FLOURS	LOPERS	PAVERS	SHEERS	ULCERS
DICERS	FLUORS	LOSERS	PAWERS	SHIRRS	UMBERS
DIMERS	FLYERS	LOVERS	PAYERS	SHOERS	UNBARS
DINARS	FOYERS	LOWERS	PETERS	SIEURS	UPPERS
DINERS	FRIARS	LUGERS	PIKERS	SIMARS	USHERS
DIVERS	FRIERS	LURERS	PIPERS	SITARS	UTTERS
DONORS	FRYERS	MACERS	PLIERS	SIZARS	VAPORS
DOSERS	FURORS	MAJORS	POKERS	SKIERS	VEXERS
DOTERS	GAGERS	MAKERS	POSERS	SKIRRS	VICARS
DOWERS	GAPERS	MANORS	POWERS	SMEARS	VIPERS
DRIERS	GAZERS	MASERS	PRIERS	SNEERS	VISORS
DRYERS	GIBERS	MAYORS	PRIORS	SOBERS	VIZIRS
DUPERS	GLAIRS	MAZERS	PRYERS	SONARS	VIZORS
EATERS	GONERS	MESSRS	PULERS	SOWARS	VOMERS
EDGARS	HALERS	METERS	QUEERS	SOWERS	VOTERS
EGGARS	HATERS	MILERS	RACERS	SPEARS	VOWERS
EGGERS	HAZERS	MIMERS	RADARS	SPIERS	WADERS

WAFERS	OBVERT	CHERRY	POETRY	CALESA	DEMISE
WAGERS	OSBERT	DATARY	POPERY	CREUSA	DENISE
WALERS	REPORT	DAUBRY	PRIORY	LOUISA	DEPOSE
WATERS	RESORT	DECURY	PUGGRY	MEDUSA	DEVISE
WAVERS	RETORT	DENARY	QUARRY	MIMOSA	DISUSE
WEBERS	REVERT	DESCRY	ROSARY	MUCOSA	DROWSE
WIPERS	ROBERT	DOWERY	ROTARY	ODESSA	EFFUSE
WIRERS	RUPERT	DREARY	SALARY	TERESA	ELAPSE
WIVERS	SQUIRT	DUPERY	SATORY	ZSAZSA	ELOISE
WOOERS	STUART	EATERY	SAVORY	******	ENCASE
YAGERS	THWART	EMPERY	SCURRY	----SE	EXCISE
******	TSHIRT	EXPIRY	SENARY	******	EXCUSE
----RT	UNGIRT	FAKERY	SENTRY	ACCUSE	EXPOSE
******	UNHURT	FINERY	SHERRY	ADVISE	FILOSE
ADVERT	YAOURT	FLEURY	SKERRY	ALDOSE	FLENSE
ALBERT	YOGURT	FLOURY	SLURRY	APPOSE	FRAISE
APPORT	******	FLURRY	SMEARY	ARIOSE	GREASE
ASSERT	----RU	FRIARY	SPARRY	AROUSE	GRILSE
ASSORT	******	GANTRY	SPERRY	AVERSE	GROUSE
BEGIRT	GRUGRU	GENTRY	SPHERY	BEMUSE	GYROSE
CAVORT	JABIRU	GHARRY	SPURRY	BETISE	HEARSE
COHORT	******	GLAIRY	STARRY	BLAISE	HEXOSE
COVERT	----RY	HILARY	SUDARY	BLOUSE	HOARSE
DEPART	******	HORARY	SUGARY	BOURSE	ILLUSE
DEPORT	AIRDRY	HUNGRY	SULTRY	BRAISE	IMPOSE
DESERT	AMBARY	INJURY	SUNDRY	BROWSE	INCASE
DIVERT	AMBERY	KNARRY	TAWDRY	BRUISE	INCISE
EFFORT	ANGARY	LIVERY	TELARY	CAMISE	INCUSE
EGBERT	APIARY	LOWERY	THEORY	CAYUSE	INFUSE
ELBERT	ARMORY	LUXURY	TOWERY	CERISE	JOCOSE
ENGIRT	ARTERY	MALORY	UNWARY	CERUSE	KETOSE
ERFURT	ASBURY	MEMORY	VAGARY	CHAISE	KINASE
ESCORT	AUGURY	MISERY	VALERY	CHASSE	LANOSE
EXHORT	AVIARY	NAPERY	VENERY	CHEESE	LAOTSE
EXPERT	AWEARY	NONARY	VESTRY	CHOOSE	LIAISE
EXPORT	BAKERY	NOTARY	VINERY	CLAUSE	LIPASE
EXSERT	BAWDRY	OCHERY	VOLERY	COARSE	LOUISE
EXTORT	BELFRY	OHENRY	VOTARY	COMOSE	MISUSE
GEMERT	BINARY	ORNERY	WATERY	CORPSE	MOROSE
GOCART	BLEARY	ORRERY	WHERRY	COURSE	MOUSSE
GOKART	BLURRY	OUTCRY	WINERY	CREASE	MUCOSE
HOBART	BOWERY	PALTRY	WINTRY	CREESE	NODOSE
HUBERT	BRIERY	PANTRY	ZONARY	CROSSE	NOWISE
IMPART	CALORY	PAPERY	******	CRUISE	OBTUSE
IMPORT	CANARY	PASTRY	----SA	CUISSE	OPPOSE
INSERT	CELERY	PELTRY	******	CYMOSE	OSMOSE
INVERT	CHARRY	PENURY	AFTOSA	DEBASE	OTIOSE
MOZART	CHEERY	PINERY	AHIMSA	DEFUSE	PAVISE

PERUSE	DANISH	SALISH	MUTISM	IMPASS	DIGEST
PHRASE	DOVISH	SIWASH	NANISM	JEWESS	DIREST
PILOSE	DRYISH	SPLASH	NAZISM	KAVASS	DIVEST
PLEASE	DUDISH	SQUASH	NOMISM	KUMISS	DRIEST
PRAISE	EDDISH	SQUISH	NUDISM	MEGASS	DRYEST
RAMOSE	ELFISH	THRASH	OBIISM	MORASS	DYNAST
RECUSE	ELVISH	THRESH	ORGASM	OBSESS	EGOIST .
REFUSE	ENCASH	THRUSH	PURISM	OGRESS	ELDEST
REMISE	ENMESH	TOYISH	RACISM	RECESS	ENCYST
REPOSE	FAMISH	UNLASH	SADISM	REMISS	ENLIST
RETUSE	FETISH	UNWISH	SCHISM	REPASS	ERNEST
REVISE	FINISH	UPPISH	SEXISM	SCHUSS	FEWEST
RIBOSE	GALOSH	UPRUSH	SHIISM	SPEISS	FINEST
RIMOSE	GARISH	VANISH	SUFISM	STRASS	FLIEST
RUGOSE	GOLOSH	WABASH	TAOISM	STRESS	FOREST
SCOUSE	IMMESH	WHOOSH	THEISM	UNLESS	FREEST
SETOSE	IMPISH	******	TRUISM	******	FUNEST
SPARSE	INMESH	----SI	VERISM	----ST	GAYEST
SPOUSE	INRUSH	******	******	******	HEARST
THYRSE	JADISH	ASSISI	----SO	ABLEST	HONEST
TOROSE	JEWISH	GENESI	******	ACCOST	HUGEST
TRIOSE	JUTISH	KINESI	ALONSO	ADJUST	ICIEST
TSETSE	KIBOSH	THYRSI	ARIOSO	AGHAST	IDLEST
UNCASE	LATISH	WATUSI	CARUSO	ALMOST	ILLUST
UNEASE	LAVISH	******	CHRYSO	AMIDST	IMPOST
UNWISE	MODISH	----SK	GLOSSO	AORIST	INCEST
UPRISE -	MOPISH	******	----SP	ARREST	INFEST
UPROSE	MULISH	DAMASK	******	ARTIST	INGEST
UREASE	OAFISH	GDANSK	UNHASP	ASSIST	INMOST
VADOSE	OFFISH	UNHUSK	******	ATTEST	INSIST
VALISE	OGRISH	UNMASK	----SS	AUGUST	INVEST
VAMOSE	OLDISH	******	******	AURIST	JURIST
VENOSE	ONRUSH	----SM	******	BABIST	LAMEST
WRASSE	OWLISH	******	ABBESS	BAREST	LATEST
XYLOSE	PALISH	AUTISM	ACCESS	BASEST	LAXEST
******	PARISH	BABISM	ACROSS	BEHEST	LEGIST
----SH	PERISH	CHIASM	ASSESS	BLUEST	LOCUST
******	POLISH	CHRISM	AWLESS	BREAST	LOWEST
ABLUSH	POPISH	CIVISM	BAGASS	BYPAST	LUTIST
AFRESH	POTASH	CUBISM	BYPASS	CHRIST	LYRIST
AGUISH	PUNISH	EGOISM	CAMASS	CLEIST	MAOIST
AMBUSH	RADISH	EONISM	CARESS	CUBIST	MARIST
BANISH	RAKISH	HOLISM	DURESS	CUTEST	MAYEST
BLUISH	RAVISH	IODISM	EGRESS	DEGUST	MEREST
BOYISH	RAWISH	LYRISM	EMBOSS	DESIST	MODEST
CALASH	REHASH	MAOISM	EXCESS	DETEST	MOLEST
COHOSH	RELISH	MOMISM	GNEISS	DEVEST	MONGST
COYISH	ROMISH	MONISM	HARASS	DICAST	MONIST

NEWEST	UPCAST	******	ARBUTE	HECATE	POINTE
NICEST	UPMOST	----TA	ASTUTE	HIVITE	POLITE
NUDIST	UTMOST	******	AUGITE	HORSTE	PUPATE
OBLAST	VERIST	ALBATA	AURATE	IDEATE	PYRITE
OBOIST	VILEST	AMRITA	AVIATE	IGNITE	QUARTE
OBTEST	VOLOST	ARANTA	BABITE	IMPUTE	RATITE
ODDEST	WHILST	ARISTA	BARITE	INCITE	REBATE
OLDEST	WIDEST	ARUNTA	BERATE	INDITE	RECITE
PALEST	WISEST	AVESTA	BINATE	INMATE	REFUTE
PAPIST	WRIEST	BALATA	BORATE	INNATE	RELATE
PRIEST	WRYEST	BARYTA	BOVATE	INVITE	REMOTE
PROUST	******	BEMATA	BRONTE	IODATE	REPUTE
PUREST	----SY	BENITA	CANUTE	IOLITE	ROTATE
PURIST	******	BOGOTA	CAPOTE	JUGATE	RUGATE
RACIST	APEPSY	CAPITA	CARATE	KARATE	SALUTE
RAPIST	ARGOSY	CHAETA	CAVITE	KENITE	SAMITE
RAREST	BIOPSY	CUESTA	CERATE	LANATE	SAVATE
RAWEST	BRASSY	DAKOTA	CERITE	LEGATE	SEDATE
RECAST	CHEESY	EGESTA	CHASTE	LEVITE	SEMITE
REPAST	CHOOSY	EJECTA	COMATE	LIGATE	SENATE
RESIST	CLASSY	ERRATA	COYOTE	LOBATE	SHIITE
REVEST	CLUMSY	EXACTA	CREATE	LOCATE	SOLUTE
RIPEST	CREASY	FIESTA	CURATE	LUCITE	SOMITE
RIPOST	CURTSY	FRUSTA	DANITE	LUNATE	SPRITE
ROBUST	DRESSY	LOLITA	DEBATE	LUXATE	STACTE
RUDEST	DROPSY	OMENTA	DELATE	MALATE	SVELTE
SADIST	DROSSY	PELOTA	DELETE	MINUTE	TAXITE
SAFEST	DROWSY	PESETA	DEMOTE	MUTATE	TERETE
SAGEST	FLIMSY	QUANTA	DENOTE	MYCETE	TONITE
SANEST	FLOSSY	SCROTA	DEPUTE	NEGATE	TRISTE
SCHIST	FOLKSY	SHASTA	DERATE	OBLATE	TUBATE
SEXIST	GLASSY	SIESTA	DEVOTE	ODETTE	UPDATE
SHIEST	GLOSSY	SOMATA	DILATE	OLEATE	VACATE
SHYEST	GRASSY	SONATA	DILUTE	OOCYTE	VALATE
SLIEST	GREASY	SPARTA	DONATE	OOLITE	VOLUTE
SLYEST	HERESY	STRATA	ECARTE	OPHITE	XYLITE
SOREST	PRISSY	VALUTA	EFFETE	OPIATE	ZONATE
SUREST	QUEASY	ZAPATA	EMEUTE	ORNATE	ZYGOTE
TAMEST	QUINSY	******	EQUATE	PAIUTE	******
TANIST	SLIMSY	----TE	ERGATE	PALATE	----TH
TAOIST	TEENSY	******	ESTATE	PEDATE	******
THEIST	TOOTSY	ACUATE	EXCITE	PELITE	ACANTH
THIRST	TRESSY	ADNATE	FINITE	PETITE	BREATH
THRUST	UNEASY	AERATE	FIXATE	PEYOTE	BYPATH
TRUEST	WEENSY	AGNATE	GAMETE	PILATE	DALETH
TYPIST	WHIMSY	ALBITE	GYRATE	PINITE	DEARTH
UNJUST	WOODSY	ANSATE	HALITE	PIRATE	DROUTH
UNREST		APLITE	HAMITE	PLATTE	DULUTH

EIGHTH	CHAETO	ADOPTS	CHESTS	ERECTS	GRUNTS
EOLITH	CRYPTO	ADULTS	CIVETS	ERUCTS	GUESTS
FOURTH	FRONTO	AGENTS	CLEATS	ERUPTS	GUILTS
GROWTH	GAMETO	AGISTS	CLEFTS	EVENTS	HABITS
HEALTH	GENITO	AGLETS	CLINTS	EVERTS	HAUNTS
HEARTH	GHETTO	ALERTS	CLOUTS	EVICTS	HEARTS
JUDITH	GIOTTO	ALEUTS	COASTS	EXACTS	HEISTS
LENGTH	GLOTTO	ALLOTS	COMETS	EXALTS	HELOTS
ORNITH	GLYPTO	AMBITS	COOPTS	EXERTS	HOISTS
PLINTH	GROTTO	AMENTS	COUNTS	EXISTS	IDIOTS
SHEATH	HEMATO	ARGOTS	COURTS	EXULTS	INGOTS
SLEUTH	HEPATO	ARMETS	COVETS	FACETS	INLETS
SMOOTH	HERETO	ASCOTS	CRAFTS	FAGOTS	INPUTS
SPILTH	KERATO	ASSETS	CRESTS	FAINTS	INSETS
STAITH	KINETO	AUDITS	CROATS	FAULTS	ISLETS
STRATH	LEANTO	AUGHTS	CROFTS	FEASTS	JABOTS
SWARTH	LEGATO	AVERTS	CRUETS	FEINTS	JANETS
WARMTH	MANITO	AWAITS	CRUSTS	FEISTS	JAUNTS
WEALTH	NEMATO	BEASTS	CRYPTS	FIGHTS	JOINTS
WRAITH	ODONTO	BEAUTS	CUBITS	FILETS	JOISTS
WREATH	OPORTO	BEFITS	CULETS	FIRSTS	JOUSTS
ZENITH	PASHTO	BEGETS	DAUNTS	FLEETS	JURATS
ZIBETH	POTATO	BERETS	DAVITS	FLINTS	KARATS
ZIZITH	POUSTO	BESETS	DEBITS	FLIRTS	KNOUTS
******	PRESTO	BESOTS	DEBUTS	FLOATS	KRAITS
----TI	PROCTO	BIDETS	DEISTS	FLOUTS	LIGHTS
******	PRONTO	BIGHTS	DEMITS	FOISTS	LIMITS
AGOUTI	QUARTO	BIGOTS	DEPOTS	FOUNTS	LUNETS
AMENTI	REBATO	BINITS	DIGITS	FRONTS	MAGOTS
DIGITI	RIALTO	BLASTS	DIVOTS	FROSTS	MERITS
GOMUTI	RIGHTO	BLEATS	DIXITS	FRUITS	MOULTS
PEDATI	RUBATO	BLOATS	DONETS	GAMUTS	MOUNTS
SMALTI	SHINTO	BLUETS	DOUBTS	GAVOTS	MULCTS
STRATI	SMALTO	BLUNTS	DRAFTS	GEMOTS	NIGHTS
TAHITI	SOMATO	BLURTS	DRIFTS	GENETS	OCTETS
VASHTI	SUBITO	BOASTS	DROITS	GHAUTS	ONSETS
WAPITI	TENUTO	BOOSTS	DUCATS	GHOSTS	ORBITS
******	TERATO	BRACTS	EDICTS	GIANTS	OWLETS
----TO	TOMATO	BRANTS	EDUCTS	GLEETS	PAINTS
******	VOMITO	BRENTS	EGESTS	GLINTS	PEWITS
ALECTO	******	BRUITS	EGRETS	GLOATS	PICOTS
ANATTO	----TS	BURSTS	EIGHTS	GLOSTS	PILOTS
ARISTO	******	CADETS	EJECTS	GRAFTS	PIPETS
BASUTO	ABBOTS	CARATS	ELECTS	GRANTS	PIPITS
BENITO	ABORTS	CARETS	ELIOTS	GREATS	PIVOTS
BLASTO	ADAPTS	CHANTS	EMMETS	GREETS	PLAITS
BONITO	ADEPTS	CHARTS	ENACTS	GROATS	PLANTS
CERATO	ADMITS	CHEATS	EPACTS	GROUTS	PLEATS

POINTS	SNORTS	VOMITS	ENTITY	SCATTY	******
POSITS	SNOUTS	WAISTS	EQUITY	SHANTY	----UD
POULTS	SPAITS	WHEATS	FAULTY	SHELTY	******
PRINTS	SPIRTS	WHORTS	FEALTY	SHIFTY	ARNAUD
QUANTS	SPLATS	WORSTS	FEISTY	SHIRTY	MARAUD
QUARTS	SPLITS	WRESTS	FERITY	SLEETY	REDBUD
QUESTS	SPORTS	WRISTS	FIXITY	SMUTTY	SHROUD
QUILTS	SPOUTS	YACHTS	FLINTY	SNOOTY	STROUD
QUINTS	SPRATS	YEASTS	FLIRTY	SNOTTY	TALMUD
QUIRTS	SPRITS	ZIBETS	FLOATY	SPORTY	******
QUOITS	SPURTS	******	FRETTY	SPOTTY	----UE
REACTS	SQUATS	----TT	FROSTY	SURETY	******
REBUTS	STARTS	******	FRUITY	SWARTY	ACCRUE
REFITS	STILTS	ABWATT	GAIETY	SWEATY	AGOGUE
REMITS	STINTS	ALCOTT	GAYETY	THIRTY	AVENUE
RESETS	STOATS	DEWITT	GLEETY	TREATY	BARQUE
REVETS	STOUTS	EMMETT	GRITTY	TRUSTY	BASQUE
RIGHTS	STRUTS	******	GROTTY	TWENTY	BATTUE
RIVETS	STUNTS	----TU	GUILTY	TWISTY	BISQUE
ROASTS	SWEATS	******	HEARTY	UBIETY	BRAQUE
ROBOTS	SWEETS	MANITU	HUMPTY	UPPITY	BROGUE
ROOSTS	SWIFTS	PUSHTU	JAUNTY	VANITY	CAIQUE
ROUSTS	TAINTS	******	KNOTTY	VERITY	CANGUE
SABOTS	TAROTS	----TY	LAXITY	YEASTY	CASQUE
SAINTS	TAUNTS	******	LENITY	******	CHEQUE
SAULTS	TEMPTS	ACUITY	LEVITY	----TZ	CINQUE
SCENTS	TENETS	AGOUTY	MIGHTY	******	CIRQUE
SCOOTS	THEFTS	BEAUTY	MOIETY	BLINTZ	CLAQUE
SCOTTS	TIGHTS	BILITY	MOUNTY	CHINTZ	CLIQUE
SCOUTS	TINCTS	BOUNTY	NICETY	ERSATZ	DENGUE
SEBATS	TOASTS	CAVITY	NIGHTY	HALUTZ	DROGUE
SHAFTS	TRACTS	CHANTY	NINETY	KIBITZ	EMBRUE
SHEETS	TRAITS	CHATTY	NUDITY	NIMITZ	FESCUE
SHIFTS	TREATS	CHESTY	ODDITY	QUARTZ	FONDUE
SHIRTS	TROUTS	CHITTY	PAINTY	******	GANGUE
SHOATS	TRUSTS	CLOTTY	PARITY	----UA	IMBRUE
SHOOTS	TRYSTS	COMITY	PIGSTY	******	LEAGUE
SHORTS	TWEETS	COUNTY	PLASTY	CORNUA	MANQUE
SHOUTS	TWISTS	CRAFTY	PLENTY	JOSHUA	MARQUE
SHUNTS	UBOATS	CRUSTY	POINTY	LINGUA	MASQUE
SIGHTS	UNHATS	DAINTY	POLITY	MANTUA	MISCUE
SKIRTS	UPSETS	DEPUTY	PRETTY	NASHUA	MORGUE
SLANTS	VALETS	DIMITY	PURITY	******	MOSQUE
SLEETS	VAULTS	DRAFTY	RARITY	----UB	OPAQUE
SMARTS	VAUNTS	DRIFTY	REALTY	******	PLAGUE
SMELTS	VELDTS	DUMPTY	SAFETY	BEDAUB	PLAQUE
SMOLTS	VERSTS	EIGHTY	SANITY	CHERUB	PRAGUE
SNOOTS	VISITS	ENMITY	SCANTY	HUBBUB	PREVUE

PULQUE	ENSOUL	DICTUM	VALLUM	TITTUP	******
PURSUE	EYEFUL	DINKUM	VELLUM	TOSSUP	----US
RESCUE	FITFUL	DORSUM	WAMPUM	TUNEUP	******
RISQUE	HAMAUL	DUMDUM	******	TURNUP	ABACUS
STATUE	HATFUL	ERBIUM	----UN	WALKUP	ACEOUS
SUBDUE	INHAUL	FACTUM	******	WARMUP	ACINUS
TISSUE	INSOUL	FERRUM	ADNOUN	WIKIUP	ACIOUS
TONGUE	IREFUL	FOLIUM	AIRGUN	WINDUP	ADIEUS
TORQUE	JARFUL	FRENUM	OUTRUN	WRAPUP	AEACUS
UNIQUE	JOYFUL	GONIUM	POPGUN	******	AEGEUS
UNTRUE	JUGFUL	GYPSUM	SHOGUN	----UR	AEOLUS
VENDUE	LAPFUL	HELIUM	TUCHUN	******	ALDOUS
VIRTUE	LAWFUL	INDIUM	VERDUN	ARBOUR	ALGOUS
******	MANFUL	IONIUM	******	ARDOUR	ANIMUS
----UG	RUEFUL	KALIUM	----UP	ARMOUR	ARIOUS
******	SINFUL	LABIUM	******	ARTHUR	ATREUS
BEDBUG	USEFUL	LABRUM	BANGUP	CENSUR	AUREUS
DORBUG	VATFUL	LIGNUM	BLOWUP	COLOUR	AUROUS
HUMBUG	WILFUL	LUTEUM	CALLUP	CONCUR	BANTUS
MAYBUG	WOEFUL	LYCEUM	CATSUP	DETOUR	BAYOUS
REDBUG	******	MAGNUM	COCKUP	DEVOUR	BRUTUS
UNPLUG	----UM	MEDIUM	EGGCUP	DOLOUR	BYSSUS
******	******	MILIUM	EYECUP	FAVOUR	CACTUS
----UI	ACEIUM	MINIUM	GALLUP	FURFUR	CADMUS
******	ACETUM	MUSEUM	HANGUP	GIAOUR	CALLUS
BANGUI	ACTIUM	OMASUM	HICCUP	HONOUR	CAMPUS
SANGUI	ADYTUM	OMNIUM	HOLDUP	HUMOUR	CANTUS
SESQUI	ALARUM	OSMIUM	HOOKUP	JAIPUR	CARPUS
******	ALLIUM	PEPLUM	LARRUP	KRONUR	CAUCUS
----UK	AMYLUM	PHYLUM	LINEUP	KULTUR	CENSUS
******	ANTRUM	PILEUM	LOCKUP	LABOUR	CEREUS
CHABUK	ASARUM	PLENUM	MADEUP	LANGUR	CEROUS
CHIBUK	ASYLUM	PODIUM	MAKEUP	MUGGUR	CESTUS
DYBBUK	ATRIUM	POSSUM	MARKUP	MURMUR	CHIAUS
MARDUK	BARIUM	QUORUM	MOCKUP	POSEUR	CHORUS
MUKLUK	BARNUM	RADIUM	PENTUP	RIGOUR	CIRCUS
SELJUK	BUNKUM	RECTUM	PICKUP	RUMOUR	CIRRUS
******	CAECUM	REDGUM	PILEUP	SAMBUR	CITRUS
----UL	CERIUM	SACRUM	PUSHUP	SAVOUR	CLONUS
******	CESIUM	SCUTUM	RECOUP	SIDDUR	COCCUS
ARMFUL	CILIUM	SEPTUM	ROLLUP	SULFUR	COITUS
ARTFUL	CIRCUM	SODIUM	SANNUP	TUMOUR	COLEUS
BEFOUL	CONIUM	SPUTUM	SLAPUP	VALOUR	COLOUS
BULBUL	CORIUM	TALCUM	SLIPUP	VAPOUR	COMOUS
CONSUL	CRINUM	TEDIUM	STEPUP	VELOUR	CORNUS
CUPFUL	CUPRUM	TERGUM	TAKEUP	VIGOUR	CORPUS
EARFUL	CURIUM	VACUUM	TEACUP	VOYEUR	CORVUS
				WILBUR	

COYPUS	LAPSUS	SADHUS	COPOUT	EXEQUY	STROVE
CROCUS	LIMBUS	SAJOUS	CUTOUT	PLAGUY	SWERVE
CRONUS	LITMUS	SAURUS	DEVOUT	******	THIEVE
CULTUS	LUCIUS	SCOPUS	DIMOUT	----VA	THRIVE
CUSCUS	MARCUS	SEAMUS	DUGOUT	******	THROVE
CYGNUS	MEATUS	SEROUS	EYEOUT	CASAVA	TWELVE
CYMOUS	MEROUS	SETOUS	FAROUT	GENEVA	UNLIVE
CYPRUS	MISSUS	SHAMUS	HAGBUT	GODIVA	VOTIVE
DANAUS	MOBIUS	SIRIUS	HOGNUT	HUELVA	WHARVE
DARIUS	MUCOUS	SNAFUS	KRUBUT	OTTAVA	WHERVE
DELIUS	NAEVUS	STATUS	LAYOUT	SALIVA	ZOUAVE
DINGUS	NESSUS	STYLUS	MAHOUT	******	******
DISCUS	NIMBUS	SULCUS	MIDGUT	----VE	----VO
ELBRUS	OBELUS	TARSUS	OUTPUT	******	******
EPIRUS	OBOLUS	TAURUS	PEANUT	ACTIVE	OCTAVO
EREBUS	ODIOUS	TELLUS	PIGNUT	ALCOVE	******
ESTRUS	PALPUS	TEREUS	PUTOUT	ARGIVE	----VY
EXODUS	PAPPUS	THYMUS	PUTPUT	ARRIVE	******
FAMOUS	PAREUS	TOROUS	RAGOUT	BEHAVE	CHEVVY
FAUNUS	PASSUS	TRAGUS	RAJPUT	BEHOVE	CHIVVY
FEROUS	PAULUS	TUNGUS	ROTGUT	CLEAVE	GROOVY
FICHUS	PELEUS	TYPHUS	RUNOUT	DATIVE	SCURVY
FLATUS	PEPLUS	URAEUS	SETOUT	DERIVE	SKIVVY
FOETUS	PIERUS	URANUS	SPROUT	ENDIVE	******
FUCOUS	PIGNUS	UTERUS	TRYOUT	EVOLVE	----WA
FUMOUS	PILEUS	VALGUS	UMLAUT	GREAVE	******
FUNDUS	PILOUS	VENOUS	WALNUT	GRIEVE	OJIBWA
FUNGUS	PINDUS	VERSUS	WAYOUT	GROOVE	OTTAWA
GALLUS	PLEXUS	VILLUS	******	INWOVE	OTTOWA
GAMOUS	PLUTUS	VINOUS	----UU	MOHAVE	REDOWA
GENIUS	PODOUS	VISCUS	******	MOJAVE	******
GENOUS	POILUS	VOROUS	MUUMUU	MOTIVE	----WD
GEROUS	POROUS	WALRUS	******	NATIVE	******
GRADUS	POYOUS	WAMMUS	----UX	OCTAVE	SHREWD
GYNOUS	PRIMUS	WAMOUS	******	RELIVE	******
HIATUS	QUIPUS	XTSTUS	ADIEUX	REMOVE	----WI
HINDUS	RADIUS	ZETHUS	AFFLUX	REVIVE	******
HIPPUS	RAMOUS	******	BAYEUX	SCRIVE	MALAWI
IAMBUS	RECTUS	----UT	BIJOUX	SHEAVE	******
ICARUS	REGIUS	******	EFFLUX	SHELVE	----WK
IODOUS	RHESUS	ABLAUT	HALLUX	SHRIVE	******
IOLCUS	RICTUS	ALLOUT	INFLUX	SHROVE	MOHAWK
ITIOUS	RIMOUS	BEIRUT	POLLUX	SLEAVE	SQUAWK
JOYOUS	RUCKUS	CATGUT	REFLUX	SLEEVE	******
JULIUS	RUFOUS	COBNUT	******	STARVE	----WL
JUNIUS	RUGOUS		----UY	STEEVE	******
JUSTUS	RUMPUS		CLIQUY	STRIVE	SCRAWL
					SPRAWL

******	STRAWY	PHENYL	BENJYS	JENNYS	SEPOYS
----WN	VYRNWY	PROPYL	BENNYS	JERRYS	SPLAYS
******	******	TETRYL	BESSYS	JIMMYS	SPRAYS
DISOWN	----XE	TOLUYL	BETSYS	JINNYS	STACYS
IMPAWN	******	TROTYL	BETTYS	KATHYS	STRAYS
RENOWN	ANNEXE	URANYL	BIALYS	KENNYS	TEDDYS
STREWN	DELUXE	******	BILLYS	KITTYS	TERRYS
THROWN	ICEAXE	----YM	BOBBYS	LARRYS	TETHYS
UNHEWN	MAXIXE	******	BOGEYS	LENNYS	THADYS
UPTOWN	******	ANONYM	BONNYS	LEROYS	TILLYS
******	----XI	EPONYM	BYWAYS	LIBBYS	TIMMYS
----WS	******	******	CATHYS	LIMEYS	TOMMYS
******	BILOXI	----YN	CINDYS	LIZZYS	TRIXYS
ALLOWS	******	******	CISSYS	MALAYS	TRUDYS
ARROWS	----XT	BOLEYN	CONEYS	MAMEYS	UNLAYS
BEDEWS	******	EVELYN	COOEYS	MANDYS	UNSAYS
BYLAWS	ADMIXT	MELVYN	COVEYS	MARTYS	VICKYS
ELBOWS	UNVEXT	SELSYN	CUTEYS	MATEYS	VINNYS
EMBOWS	URTEXT	SELWYN	DAISYS	MCCOYS	WALLYS
ENDOWS	******	******	DANNYS	MICKYS	WAVEYS
INDOWS	----XY	----YO	DAVEYS	MILLYS	WENDYS
INLAWS	******	******	DEBBYS	MOLLYS	WILLYS
MACAWS	DESOXY	ARROYO	DECAYS	MONEYS	ZLOTYS
OXBOWS	GALAXY	DAIMYO	DECOYS	MONTYS	******
PAPAWS	******	EMBRYO	DELAYS	MORAYS	----YU
PSHAWS	----YA	******	DENNYS	MORTYS	******
RENEWS	******	----YR	DOLLYS	MOSEYS	RYUKYU
SCREWS	KABAYA	******	EMBAYS	NANCYS	******
SEROWS	MALAYA	MARTYR	EMILYS	NELLYS	----YX
SHREWS	NAGOYA	VALKYR	ENJOYS	NICKYS	******
SINEWS	PAPAYA	ZEPHYR	ENVOYS	NOWAYS	COCCYX
SQUAWS	******	******	ERINYS	PADDYS	******
STRAWS	----YE	----YS	ESSAYS	PANSYS	----ZA
STREWS	******	******	FANNYS	PATSYS	******
THROWS	AYEAYE	ABBEYS	FLYBYS	PEGGYS	CORYZA
UNMEWS	BYEBYE	ALLAYS	FORAYS	PENNYS	MEZUZA
UPBOWS	REDEYE	ALLEYS	GERRYS	PERCYS	PIAZZA
WIDOWS	******	ALLOYS	GERTYS	PERRYS	STANZA
******	----YL	ALWAYS	GLADYS	POLLYS	******
----WY	******	ANNOYS	HARRYS	POPPYS	----ZD
******	ACETYL	ARCHYS	HATTYS	RELAYS	******
ARROWY	ALPHYL	ARRAYS	HENRYS	REPAYS	ORMUZD
SCREWY	BENZYL	ASSAYS	HETTYS	RICKYS	******
SINEWY	CHERYL	AVERYS	HOLLYS	RODDYS	----ZE
	DACTYL	BARRYS	HONEYS	SALLYS	******
	FORMYL	BECKYS	INLAYS	SAMMYS	ABLAZE
	METHYL	BELAYS	JACKYS	SANDYS	ASSIZE

BELIZE	FRUNZE	******	SCHIZO	BRONZY	SLEAZY
BRAIZE	IODIZE	----ZO	******	FLOOZY	SNAZZY
BREEZE	IONIZE	******	----ZY	FRENZY	SNEEZY
BRONZE	SNEEZE	ALONZO	******	FRIZZY	WHEEZY
FREEZE	SNOOZE	AREZZO	BLOWZY	FROWZY	
FRIEZE	WHEEZE	REBOZO	BREEZY	GROSZY	

COMPREHENSIVE, AUTHORITATIVE REFERENCE WORKS FROM AVON TRADE BOOKS

THE OXFORD AMERICAN DICTIONARY
Edited by Stuart Berg Flexner, Eugene Ehrlich and
Gordon Carruth   51052-9/ $12.50 US/ $15.00 Can

**THE CONCISE COLUMBIA DICTIONARY
OF QUOTATIONS**
Robert Andrews   70932-5/ $9.95 US/ $11.95 Can

THE CONCISE COLUMBIA ENCYCLOPEDIA
Edited by Judith S. Levey and Agnes Greenhall
                                   63396-5/ $14.95 US

**THE NEW COMPREHENSIVE AMERICAN
RHYMING DICTIONARY**
Sue Young   71392-6/ $12.00 US/ $15.00 Can

**KIND WORDS: A THESAURUS
OF EUPHEMISMS**
Judith S. Neaman and Carole G. Silver
                                   71247-4/ $10.95 US/ $12.95 Can

**THE WORLD ALMANAC GUIDE
TO GOOD WORD USAGE**
Edited by Martin Manser with Jeffrey McQuain
                                   71449-3/ $8.95 US